P9-ARU-722

Table of Contents

Sections

Model Index

USING THIS INFORMATION

Organization

To find where a particular model section or procedure is located, look in the Table of Contents. Main topics are listed with the page number on which they may be found. Following the main topics is an alphabetical listing of all of the procedures within the section and their page numbers.

Manufacturer and Model Coverage

This product covers 2010-2011 Chrysler models that are produced in sufficient quantities to warrant coverage, and which have technical content available from the vehicle manufacturers before our publication date. Although this information is as complete as possible at the time of publication, some manufacturers may make changes which cannot be included here. While striving for total accuracy, the publisher cannot assume responsibility for any errors, changes, or omissions that may occur in the compilation of this data.

Part Numbers & Special Tools

Part numbers and special tools are recommended by the publisher and vehicle manufacturer to perform specific jobs. Before substituting any part or tool for the one recommended, you must be completely satisfied that neither your personal safety, nor the performance of the vehicle will be endangered.

ACKNOWLEDGEMENT

Portions of materials contained herein are sourced from Chrysler Group LLC.

PRECAUTIONS

Before servicing any vehicle, please be sure to read all of the following precautions, which deal with personal safety, prevention of component damage, and important points to take into consideration when servicing a motor vehicle:

- Always wear safety glasses or goggles when drilling, cutting, grinding or prying.
- Steel-toed work shoes should be worn when working with heavy parts. Pockets should not be used for carrying tools. A slip or fall can drive a screwdriver into your body.
- Work surfaces, including tools and the floor should be kept clean of grease, oil or other slippery material.
- When working around moving parts, don't wear loose clothing. Long hair should be tied back under a hat or cap, or in a hair net.
- Always use tools only for the purpose for which they were designed. Never pry with a screwdriver.
- Keep a fire extinguisher and first aid kit handy.
- Always properly support the vehicle with approved stands or lift.
- Always have adequate ventilation when working with chemicals or hazardous material.
- Carbon monoxide is colorless, odorless and dangerous. If it is necessary to operate the engine with vehicle in a closed area such as a garage, always use an exhaust collector to vent the exhaust gases outside the closed area.
- When draining coolant, keep in mind that small children and some pets are attracted by ethylene glycol antifreeze, and are quite likely to drink any left in an open container, or in puddles on the ground. This will prove fatal in sufficient quantity. Always drain the coolant into a sealable container.
- To avoid personal injury, do not remove the coolant pressure relief cap while the engine is operating or hot. The cooling system is under pressure; steam and hot liquid can come out forcefully when the cap is loosened slightly. Failure to follow these instructions may result in personal injury. The coolant must be recovered in a suitable, clean container for reuse. If the coolant is contaminated it must be recycled or disposed of correctly.
- When carrying out maintenance on the starting system be aware that heavy gauge leads are connected directly to the battery. Make sure the protective caps are in place when maintenance is completed. Failure to follow these instructions may result in personal injury.
- Do not remove any part of the engine emission control system. Operating the engine without the engine emission control system will reduce fuel economy and engine ventilation. This will weaken engine performance and shorten engine life. It is also a violation of Federal law.
- Due to environmental concerns, when the air conditioning system is drained, the refrigerant must be collected using refrigerant recovery/recycling equipment. Federal law requires that refrigerant be recovered into appropriate recovery equipment and the process be conducted by qualified technicians who have been certified by an approved organization, such as MACS, ASI, etc. Use of a recovery machine dedicated to the appropriate refrigerant is necessary to reduce the possibility of oil and refrigerant incompatibility concerns. Refer to the instructions provided by the equipment manufacturer when removing refrigerant from or charging the air conditioning system.
- Always disconnect the battery ground when working on or around the electrical system.
- Batteries contain sulfuric acid. Avoid contact with skin, eyes, or clothing. Also, shield your eyes when working near batteries to protect against possible splashing of the acid solution. In case of acid contact with skin or eyes, flush immediately with water for a minimum of 15 minutes and get prompt medical attention. If acid is swallowed, call a physician immediately. Failure to follow these instructions may result in personal injury.
- Batteries normally produce explosive gases. Therefore, do not allow flames, sparks or lighted substances to come near the battery. When charging or working near a battery, always shield your face and protect your eyes. Always provide ventilation. Failure to follow these instructions may result in personal injury.
- When lifting a battery, excessive pressure on the end walls could cause acid to spew through the vent caps, resulting in personal injury, damage to the vehicle or battery. Lift with a battery carrier or with your hands on opposite corners. Failure to follow

these instructions may result in personal injury.

• Observe all applicable safety precautions when working around fuel. Whenever servicing the fuel system, always work in a well-ventilated area. Do not allow fuel spray or vapors to come in contact with a spark, open flame, or excessive heat (a hot drop light, for example). Keep a dry chemical fire extinguisher near the work area. Always keep fuel in a container specifically designed for fuel storage; also, always properly seal fuel containers to avoid the possibility of fire or explosion. Do not smoke or carry lighted tobacco or open flame of any type when working on or near any fuel-related components.

• Fuel injection systems often remain pressurized, even after the engine has been turned OFF. The fuel system pressure must be relieved before disconnecting any fuel lines. Failure to do so may result in fire and/or personal injury.

• The evaporative emissions system contains fuel vapor and condensed fuel vapor. Although not present in large quantities, it still presents the danger of explosion or fire. Disconnect the battery ground cable from the battery to minimize the possibility of an electrical spark occurring, possibly causing a fire or explosion if fuel vapor or liquid fuel is present in the area. Failure to follow these instructions can result in personal injury.

• The EPA warns that prolonged contact with used engine oil may cause a number of skin disorders, including cancer! You should make every effort to minimize your exposure to used engine oil. Protective gloves should be worn when changing oil. Wash your hands and any other exposed skin areas as soon as possible after exposure to used engine oil. Soap and water, or waterless hand cleaner should be used.

• Some vehicles are equipped with an air bag system, often referred to as a Supplemental Restraint System (SRS) or Supplemental Inflatable Restraint (SIR) system. The system must be disabled before performing service on or around system components, steering column, instrument panel components, wiring and sensors. Failure to follow safety and disabling procedures could result in accidental air bag deployment, possible personal injury and unnecessary system repairs.

• Always wear safety goggles when working with, or around, the air bag system. When carrying a non-deployed air bag, be sure the bag and trim cover are pointed away from your body. When placing a non-deployed air bag on a work surface, always face the bag and trim cover upward, away from the surface. This will reduce the motion of the module if it is accidentally deployed.

• Electronic modules are sensitive to electrical charges. The ABS module can be damaged if exposed to these charges.

• Brake pads and shoes may contain asbestos, which has been determined to be a cancer-causing agent. Never clean brake surfaces with compressed air. Avoid inhaling brake dust. Clean all brake surfaces with a commercially available brake cleaning fluid.

• When replacing brake pads, shoes, discs or drums, replace them as complete axle sets.

• When servicing drum brakes, disassemble and assemble one side at a time, leaving the remaining side intact for reference.

• Brake fluid often contains polyglycol ethers and polyglycols. Avoid contact with the eyes and wash your hands thoroughly after handling brake fluid. If you do get brake fluid in your eyes, flush your eyes with clean, running water for 15 minutes. If eye irritation persists, or if you have taken brake fluid internally, immediately seek medical assistance.

• Clean, high quality brake fluid from a sealed container is essential to the safe and proper operation of the brake system. You should always buy the correct type of brake fluid for your vehicle. If the brake fluid becomes contaminated, completely flush the system with new fluid. Never reuse any brake fluid. Any brake fluid that is removed from the system should be discarded. Also, do not allow any brake fluid to come in contact with a painted or plastic surface; it will damage the paint.

• Never operate the engine without the proper amount and type of engine oil; doing so will result in severe engine damage.

• Timing belt maintenance is extremely important! Many models utilize an interference-type, non-freewheeling engine. If the timing belt breaks, the valves in the cylinder head may strike the pistons, causing potentially serious (also time-consuming and expensive) engine damage.

• Disconnecting the negative battery cable on some vehicles may interfere with the functions of the on-board computer system (s) and may require the computer to undergo a relearning process once the negative battery cable is reconnected.

• Steering and suspension fasteners are critical parts because they affect performance of vital components and systems and their failure can result in major service expense. They must be replaced with the same grade or part number or an equivalent part if replacement is necessary. Do not use a replacement part of lesser quality or substitute design. Torque values must be used as specified during reassembly.

DODGE

Durango

9

SPECIFICATIONS AND MAINTENANCE CHARTS

ENGINE AND VEHICLE IDENTIFICATION

Engine						
Code ①	Liters (cc)	Cu. In.	Cyl.	Fuel Sys.	Engine Type	Eng. Mfg.
G	3.6 (3597)	220	6	SEFI	DOHC	Chrysler
T	5.7 (5696)	348	8	SEFI	OHV	Chrysler

Model Year	
Code ②	Year
B	2011

① 8th position of VIN

② 10th position of VIN

SEFI Sequential Electronic Fuel Injection

25766_DURA_C0001

GENERAL ENGINE SPECIFICATIONS

All measurements are given in inches.

Year	Model	Engine Displacement Liters (cc)	Engine ID/VIN	Fuel System Type	Net Horsepower @ rpm	Net Torque @ rpm (ft. lbs.)	Bore x Stroke (in.)	Com-pression Ratio	Oil Pressure @ rpm
2011	Durango	3.6 (3597)	G	SEFI	290@6400	260@4800	3.78x3.27	10.2:1	35@1200
		5.7 (5696)	T	SEFI	360@5150	390@4250	3.92x3.58	10.5:1	25-110@3000

25766_DURA_C0002

ENGINE TUNE-UP SPECIFICATIONS

Year	Engine Displacement Liters	Engine ID/VIN	Spark Plug Gap (in.)	Ignition Timing (deg.)		Fuel Pump (psi)	Idle Speed (rpm)		Valve Clearance	
				MT	AT		MT	AT	Intake	Exhaust
2011	3.6	G	0.4	NA	①	58	NA	②	Hyd	Hyd
	5.7	T	0.4	NA	①	58	NA	②	Hyd	Hyd

NA Not Available

① Ignition timing set by Powertrain Control Module (PCM). Ignition timing is not adjustable on any of the available engines.

② Idle speed set by Powertrain Control Module (PCM). Idle speed is not adjustable on any of the available engines.

HYD Hydraulic lifters, zero lash

25766_DURA_C0003

CAPACITIES

Year	Model	Engine Displacement Liters	Engine ID/VIN	Engine Oil with Filter	Transmission (pts.) Auto.	Transmission (pts.) Manual	Drive Axle (pts.) Front	Drive Axle (pts.) Rear	Transfer Case (pts.)	Fuel Tank (gal.)	Cooling System (qts.)
2011	Durango	3.6	G	6	①	NA	2.4	2.6	04.0	24.0	11.4
		5.7	T	7	①	NA	2.4	2.6	04.0	24.0	17.1

NOTE: All capacities are approximate. Add fluid gradually and ensure a proper fluid level is obtained.

NA Not Available

① Service fill: 11.0 pts.; Overhaul: 29.6 pts.

25766_DURA_C0004

FLUID SPECIFICATIONS

Year	Model	Engine Disp. Liters	Engine Oil	Manual Trans.	Auto. Trans.	Drive Axle Front	Drive Axle Rear	Transfer Case	Power Steering Fluid	Brake Master Cylinder	Cooling System
2011	Durango	3.6	5W-30	NA	①	75W-85	75W-85	①	②	DOT-3	③
		5.7	5W-20	NA	①	75W-85	75W-85	①	②	DOT-3	③

DOT: Department Of Transpotation

NA Not Available

① MOPAR ATF+4

② MOPAR Power Steering Fluid +4

③ MOPAR Antifreeze/Coolant 5

25766_DURA_C0005

VALVE SPECIFICATIONS

Year	Engine Displacement Liters	Engine ID/VIN	Seat Angle (deg.)	Face Angle (deg.)	Spring Test Pressure (lbs. @ in.)	Spring Free-Length (in.)	Spring Installed Height (in.)	Stem-to-Guide Clearance (in.) Intake	Stem-to-Guide Clearance (in.) Exhaust	Stem Diameter (in.) Intake	Stem Diameter (in.) Exhaust
2011	3.6	G	44.50-45.00	45.00-45.50	63-69@1.57	2.067	1.575	0.0009-0.0024	0.0012-0.0027	0.2346-0.2354	0.2343-0.2351
	5.7	T	44.50-45.00	45.00-45.50	97.8@1.77	2.189	1.810	0.0008-0.0025	0.0009-0.0025	0.3120-0.3130	0.3120-0.3130

25766_DURA_C0006

CAMSHAFT SPECIFICATIONS

All measurements in inches unless noted

Year	Engine Displacement Liters	Engine Code/VIN	Journal Diameter	Brg. Oil Clearance	Shaft End-play	Runout	Journal Bore	Lobe Height Intake	Lobe Height Exhaust
2011	3.6	G	①	②	0.003-0.010	NA	③	NA	NA
	5.7	T	④	⑤	0.0031-0.0114	NA	NA	NA	NA

NA Not Available

① No. 1: 1.25889-1.2596 inches
No. 2, 3, 4: 0.9440-0.9447 inches

② No. 1: 0.0010-0.0026 inches
No. 2, 3, 4: 0.0009-0.0025 inches

③ No. 1: 1.2606-1.2615 inches
No. 2, 3, 4: 0.9457-0.9465 inches

④ No. 1: 2.29 inches
No. 2: 2.28 inches
No. 3: 2.26 inches
No. 4: 2.24 inches
No. 5: 1.72 inches

⑤ No. 1, 3, 5: 0.0015-0.003 inches
No. 2, 4: 0.0019-0.0035 inches

25766_DURA_C0007

CRANKSHAFT AND CONNECTING ROD SPECIFICATIONS

All measurements are given in inches.

Year	Engine Displacement Liters	Engine ID/VIN	Crankshaft Main Brg. Journal Dia.	Crankshaft Main Brg. Oi Clearance	Crankshaft Shaft End-play	Crankshaft Thrust on No.	Connecting Rod Journal Diameter	Connecting Rod Oil Clearance	Connecting Rod Side Clearance
2011	3.6	G	2.8310-2.8380	0.0009-0.0025	NA	NA	2.3193-2.3263	0.0009-0.0025	NA
	5.7	T	2.5585-2.5595	0.0009-0.0020	0.002-0.011	NA	NA	NA	0.0030-0.0137

NA Not Available

25766_DURA_C0008

PISTON AND RING SPECIFICATIONS

All measurements are given in inches.

	Engine			Ring Gap			Ring Side Clearance		
Year	Displacement Liters	Engine ID/VIN	Piston Clearance	Top Compression	Bottom Compression	Oil Control	Top Compression	Bottom Compression	Oil Control
2011	3.6	G	①	0.0100-0.0160	0.0120-0.0180	0.0060-0.0260	0.0010-0.0033	0.0012-0.0031	0.0003-0.0068
	5.7	T	0.0120-0.0230	0.0150-0.0210	0.0090-0.0200	0.0059-0.0259	0.0010-0.0035	0.0010-0.0031	0.0020-0.0080

① Metal to Metal: 0.0012-0.0020 inches
Metal to Coating: 0.0004-0.0012 inches

25766_DURA_C0009

TORQUE SPECIFICATIONS

All readings in ft. lbs.

Year	Engine Disp. Liters	Engine ID/VIN	Cylinder Head Bolts	Main Bearing Bolts	Rod Bearing Bolts	Crankshaft Damper Bolts	Flywheel Bolts	Manifold Intake	Manifold Exhaust	Spark Plugs	Oil Pan Drain Plug
2011	3.6	G	①	②	③	④	70	⑤	NA	13	20
	5.7	T	⑥	⑦	③	129	70	9	18	13	25

Not Available

① Step 1: 22 ft. lbs.
Step 2: 33 ft. lbs.
Step 3: Additional 75 degrees
Step 4: Additional 50 degrees
Step 5: Loosen all bolts in reverse sequence
Step 6: 22 ft. lbs.
Step 7: 33 ft. lbs.
Step 8: Additional 70 degrees
Step 9: Additional 70 degrees

② Step 1: Inner main bearing cap bolts: 15 ft. lbs.
Step 2: Additional 90 degrees
Step 3: Windage tray and main bearing cap bolts: 16 ft. lbs.
Step 4: Additional 90 degrees
Step 5: Main bearing tie bolts: 21 ft. lbs.

③ Step 1: 15 ft. lbs.
Step 2: Additional 90 degrees

④ Step 1: 30 ft. lbs.
Step 2: Additional 105 degrees

⑤ Lower intake manifold: 71 inch lbs.
Upper intake manifold: 71 inch lbs.

⑥ Step 1: Bolts 1-10: 25 ft. lbs.
Step 2: Bolts 11-15: 15 ft. lbs.
Step 3: Bolts 1-10: 40 ft. lbs.
Step 4: Bolts 11-15: 15 Ft. lbs.
Step 5: Bolts 1-10: Additional 90 degrees
Step 6: Bolts 11-15: 25 ft. lbs.

⑦ Main bearing bolts
Step 1: 10 ft. lbs.
Step 2: 20 ft. lbs.
Step 3: Additional 90 degrees
Cross bolts
Step 4: 21 ft. lbs.
Step 5: 21 ft. lbs.

25766_DURA_C0010

WHEEL ALIGNMENT

Year	Model		Caster Range (+/-Deg.)	Caster Preferred Setting (Deg.)	Camber Range (+/-Deg.)	Camber Preferred Setting (Deg.)	Toe-in (Deg.)
2011	Durango	F	0.60	5.0	0.60	①	0.20
		R	NA	NA	0.55	-0.54	0.20

F Front

R Rear

① Left: -0.12 degrees
Right: -0.62 degrees

25766_DURA_C0011

TIRE, WHEEL AND BALL JOINT SPECIFICATIONS

Year	Model	OEM Tires Standard	OEM Tires Optional	Tire Pressures (psi) Front	Tire Pressures (psi) Rear	Wheel Size	Ball Joint Inspection	Lug Nut (ft. lbs.)
2011	Durango	P245/70R17	①	②	②	NA	NA	NA

OEM: Original Equipment Manufacturer

PSI: Pounds Per Square Inch

NA: Information not available

① P245/65R18; P265/60R18; P265/50R20

② Refer to the label on the driver's door jamb for proper inflation.

25766_DURA_C0012

BRAKE SPECIFICATIONS

All measurements in inches unless noted

Year	Model		Brake Disc Original Thickness	Brake Disc Minimum Thickness	Brake Disc Max. Runout	Brake Drum Diameter Original Inside Diameter	Brake Drum Diameter Max. Wear Limit	Brake Drum Diameter Maximum Machine Diamter	Minimum Pad/Lining Thickness Front	Minimum Pad/Lining Thickness Rear	Brake Caliper Bracket Bolts (ft. lbs.)	Brake Caliper Mounting Bolts (ft. lbs.)
2011	Durango	F	NA	1.200	0.0020	NA	NA	NA	NA	NA	148	41
		R	NA	0.492	0.0020	NA	NA	NA	NA	NA	89	20

F: Front

R: Rear

NA: Information not available

25766_DURA_C0013

SCHEDULED MAINTENANCE INTERVALS

2011 Dodge Durango 3.6L Engine - Normal & Severe (as noted)

TO BE SERVICED	TYPE OF SERVICE	VEHICLE MILEAGE INTERVAL (x1000)												
		8	16	24	32	40	48	56	64	72	80	88	96	104
Engine oil & filter	Replace	✓	✓	✓	✓	✓	✓	✓	✓	✓	✓	✓	✓	✓
Rotate tires, inspect tread wear, measure tread depth and check pressure	Rotate/Inspect		✓		✓		✓		✓		✓		✓	
Brake system components - Normal	Inspect/Service						✓		✓		✓		✓	
Brake system components - Severe	Inspect/Service		✓		✓		✓		✓		✓		✓	
Exhaust system & heat shields	Inspect		✓		✓		✓		✓		✓		✓	
Inspect the front suspension, tie rod ends and boot seals for cracks or leaks and all parts for damage, wear, improper looseness or end play.	Inspect		✓		✓		✓		✓		✓		✓	
CV Joints	Inspect			✓			✓			✓			✓	
Engine air filter - Normal	Replace					✓					✓			
Engine air filter - Severe	Replace		✓		✓		✓		✓		✓		✓	
Adjust parking brake on vehicles equipped with four-wheel disc brakes	Adjust					✓					✓			
Engine coolant	Flush/Replace										✓			
Spark plugs	Replace												✓	
PCV valve	Inspect/Service												✓	
Automatic transmission fluid and filter - Normal	Inspect	Every 120,000 miles												
Automatic transmission fluid and filter - Severe	Inspect	Every 60,000 miles												
Accessory drive belt	Replace	Every 120,000 miles												
Battery	Inspect/Service	✓	✓	✓	✓	✓	✓	✓	✓	✓	✓	✓	✓	✓
Horn, exterior lamps, turn signals and hazard warning light operation	Inspect	✓	✓	✓	✓	✓	✓	✓	✓	✓	✓	✓	✓	✓
Fluid levels (all)	Inspect/Service	✓	✓	✓	✓	✓	✓	✓	✓	✓	✓	✓	✓	✓
Rear differential fluid	Inspect			✓			✓			✓			✓	
Door hinges & latches	Lubricate		✓		✓		✓		✓		✓		✓	
Passenger compartment air filter	Replace		✓		✓		✓		✓		✓		✓	

25766_DURA_C0014

SCHEDULED MAINTENANCE INTERVALS

2011 Dodge Durango 5.7L Engine - Normal & Severe (as noted)

TO BE SERVICED	TYPE OF SERVICE	VEHICLE MILEAGE INTERVAL (x1000)												
		8	16	24	32	40	48	56	64	72	80	88	96	104
Engine oil & filter	Replace	✓	✓	✓	✓	✓	✓	✓	✓	✓	✓	✓	✓	✓
Rotate tires, inspect tread wear, measure tread depth and check pressure	Rotate/Inspect	✓	✓	✓	✓	✓	✓	✓	✓	✓	✓	✓	✓	✓
Brake system components	Inspect/Service		✓		✓		✓		✓		✓		✓	
Exhaust system & heat shields	Inspect		✓		✓		✓		✓		✓		✓	
Inspect the front suspension, tie rod ends and boot seals for cracks or leaks and all parts for damage, wear, improper looseness or end play.	Inspect		✓		✓		✓		✓		✓		✓	
CV Joints	Inspect			✓			✓			✓			✓	
Engine air filter - Normal	Replace				✓				✓				✓	
Engine air filter - Severe	Replace		✓		✓		✓		✓		✓		✓	
Adjust parking brake on vehicles equipped with four-wheel disc brakes	Adjust				✓				✓				✓	
Engine coolant	Flush/Replace										✓			
Spark plugs	Replace				✓				✓				✓	
PCV valve	Inspect/Service												✓	
Automatic transmission fluid and filter - Normal	Inspect	Every 60,000 miles												
Automatic transmission fluid and filter - Severe	Inspect	Every 120,000 miles												
Accessory drive belt	Replace	Every 120,000 miles												
Battery	Inspect/Service	✓	✓	✓	✓	✓	✓	✓	✓	✓	✓	✓	✓	✓
Horn, exterior lamps, turn signals and hazard warning light operation	Inspect	✓	✓	✓	✓	✓	✓	✓	✓	✓	✓	✓	✓	✓
Fluid levels (all)	Inspect/Service	✓	✓	✓	✓	✓	✓	✓	✓	✓	✓	✓	✓	✓
Front & rear axle fluid	Inspect/Service			✓			✓			✓			✓	
Transfer case fluid -	Inspect/Service				✓				✓				✓	
Transfer case fluid -	Inspect/Service			✓			✓			✓			✓	
Door hinges & latches	Lubricate		✓		✓		✓		✓		✓		✓	
Passenger compartment air filter	Replace		✓		✓		✓		✓		✓		✓	

25766_DURA_C0015

PRECAUTIONS

Before servicing any vehicle, please be sure to read all of the following precautions, which deal with personal safety, prevention of component damage, and important points to take into consideration when servicing a motor vehicle:

- Never open, service or drain the radiator or cooling system when the engine is hot; serious burns can occur from the steam and hot coolant.
- Observe all applicable safety precautions when working around fuel. Whenever servicing the fuel system, always work in a well-ventilated area. Do not allow fuel spray or vapors to come in contact with a spark, open flame, or excessive heat (a hot drop light, for example). Keep a dry chemical fire extinguisher near the work area. Always keep fuel in a container specifically designed for fuel storage; also, always properly seal fuel containers to avoid the possibility of fire or explosion. Refer to the additional fuel system precautions later in this section.
- Fuel injection systems often remain pressurized, even after the engine has been turned **OFF**. The fuel system pressure must be relieved before disconnecting any fuel lines. Failure to do so may result in fire and/or personal injury.
- Brake fluid often contains polyglycol ethers and polyglycols. Avoid contact with the eyes and wash your hands thoroughly after handling brake fluid. If you do get brake fluid in your eyes, flush your eyes with clean, running water for 15 minutes. If eye irritation persists, or if you have taken brake fluid internally, IMMEDIATELY seek medical assistance.
- The EPA warns that prolonged contact with used engine oil may cause a number of skin disorders, including cancer. You should make every effort to minimize your exposure to used engine oil. Protective gloves should be worn when changing oil. Wash your hands and any other exposed skin areas as soon as possible after exposure to used engine oil. Soap and water, or waterless hand cleaner should be used.
- All new vehicles are now equipped with an air bag system, often referred to as a Supplemental Restraint System (SRS) or Supplemental Inflatable Restraint (SIR) system. The system must be disabled before performing service on or around system components, steering column, instrument panel components, wiring and sensors. Failure to follow safety and disabling procedures could result in accidental air bag deployment, possible personal injury and unnecessary system repairs.
- Always wear safety goggles when working with, or around, the air bag system. When carrying a non-deployed air bag, be sure the bag and trim cover are pointed away from your body. When placing a non-deployed air bag on a work surface, always face the bag and trim cover upward, away from the surface. This will reduce the motion of the module if it is accidentally deployed. Refer to the additional air bag system precautions later in this section.
- Clean, high quality brake fluid from a sealed container is essential to the safe and proper operation of the brake system. You should always buy the correct type of brake fluid for your vehicle. If the brake fluid becomes contaminated, completely flush the system with new fluid. Never reuse any brake fluid. Any brake fluid that is removed from the system should be discarded. Also, do not allow any brake fluid to come in contact with a painted surface; it will damage the paint.
- Never operate the engine without the proper amount and type of engine oil; doing so WILL result in severe engine damage.
- Timing belt maintenance is extremely important. Many models utilize an interference-type, non-freewheeling engine. If the timing belt breaks, the valves in the cylinder head may strike the pistons, causing potentially serious (also time-consuming and expensive) engine damage. Refer to the maintenance interval charts for the recommended replacement interval for the timing belt, and to the timing belt section for belt replacement and inspection.
- Disconnecting the negative battery cable on some vehicles may interfere with the functions of the on-board computer system(s) and may require the computer to undergo a relearning process once the negative battery cable is reconnected.
- When servicing drum brakes, only disassemble and assemble one side at a time, leaving the remaining side intact for reference.
- Only an MVAC-trained, EPA-certified automotive technician should service the air conditioning system or its components.

BRAKES

ANTI-LOCK BRAKE SYSTEM (ABS)

GENERAL INFORMATION

PRECAUTIONS

- Certain components within the ABS system are not intended to be serviced or repaired individually.
- Do not use rubber hoses or other parts not specifically specified for and ABS system. When using repair kits, replace all parts included in the kit. Partial or incorrect repair may lead to functional problems and require the replacement of components.
- Lubricate rubber parts with clean, fresh brake fluid to ease assembly. Do not use shop air to clean parts; damage to rubber components may result.
- Use only DOT 3 brake fluid from an unopened container.
- If any hydraulic component or line is removed or replaced, it may be necessary to bleed the entire system.
- A clean repair area is essential. Always clean the reservoir and cap thoroughly before removing the cap. The slightest amount of dirt in the fluid may plug an orifice and impair the system function. Perform repairs after components have been thoroughly cleaned; use only denatured alcohol to clean components. Do not allow ABS components to come into contact with any substance containing mineral oil; this includes used shop rags.
- The Anti-Lock control unit is a microprocessor similar to other computer units in the vehicle. Ensure that the ignition switch is **OFF** before removing or installing controller harnesses. Avoid static electricity discharge at or near the controller.
- If any arc welding is to be done on the vehicle, the control unit should be unplugged before welding operations begin.

**** CAUTION**

Chrysler LLC does not manufacture any vehicles or replacement parts that contain asbestos. Aftermarket products may or may not contain asbestos. Refer to aftermarket product packaging for product information. Whether the product contains asbestos or not, dust and dirt can accumulate on brake parts during normal use. Follow practices prescribed by appropriate regulations for the handling, processing and disposing of dust and debris.

✱✱ WARNING

Never use gasoline, kerosene, alcohol, motor oil, transmission fluid, or any fluid containing mineral oil to clean the system components. These fluids damage rubber cups and seals. Use only fresh brake fluid or Mopar brake cleaner to clean or flush brake system components. These are the only cleaning materials recommended. If system contamination is suspected, check the fluid for dirt, discoloration, or separation into distinct layers. Also check the reservoir cap seal for distortion. Drain and flush the system with new brake fluid if contamination is suspected.

✱✱ WARNING

Use Mopar brake fluid, or an equivalent quality fluid meeting SAE/DOT standards J1703 and DOT 3. Brake fluid must be clean and free of contaminants. Use fresh fluid from sealed containers only to ensure proper antilock component operation.

✱✱ WARNING

Use Mopar multi-mileage or high temperature grease to lubricate caliper slide surfaces, drum brake pivot pins, and shoe contact points on the backing plates. Use multi-mileage grease or GE 661 or Dow 111 silicone grease on caliper slide pins to ensure proper operation.

SPEED SENSORS

REMOVAL & INSTALLATION

Front

See Figures 1 and 2.

1. Raise and support the vehicle.

➡The inner wheel well can be pulled slightly out for access to electrical connector without removing wheel well retainers.

2. Disconnect the wheel speed sensor electrical connector.
3. Disconnect the wheel speed sensor wiring routing clips.
4. Remove the wheel speed sensor wiring from the brake flex hose bracket.
5. Disconnect the sensor wire routing clips from the brake hose.
6. Remove the wheel speed sensor wiring from the knuckle.
7. Remove the front wheel sensor mounting bolt and remove the sensor from the knuckle.

To install:

8. Position the wheel speed sensor in the knuckle, install the mounting bolt and tighten to 95 inch lbs. (11 Nm).
9. Attach the sensor wire routing clips to the brake hose.
10. Attach the wheel speed sensor wiring to the knuckle.
11. Connect the sensor electrical connector.
12. Attach the wheel speed sensor wiring routing clips to the body.
13. Attach the wheel speed sensor wiring to the brake flex hose bracket.
14. Remove the supports and lower vehicle.

Rear

See Figures 3 and 4.

1. Raise and support the vehicle.
2. Disconnect the wheel speed sensor wiring connector from the wiring harness connector.
3. Remove the wheel speed sensor wiring routing clip (not shown) from the top of the cradle.
4. Remove the wheel speed sensor wiring routing clips from the camber link.
5. Remove the wheel speed sensor mounting bolt, and remove the sensor from the knuckle.

To install:

6. Route the wheel speed sensor and connect the wheel speed sensor

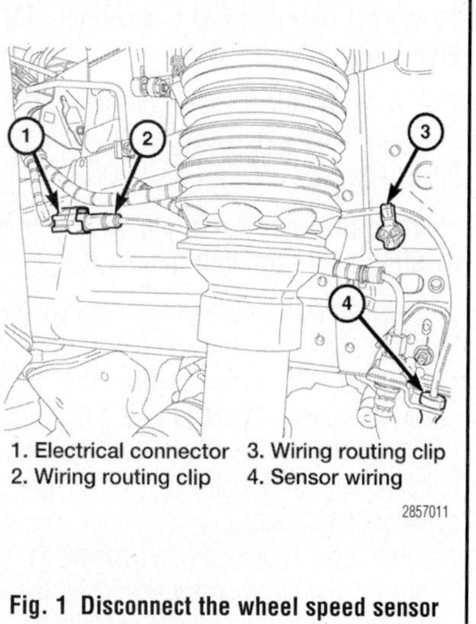

Fig. 1 Disconnect the wheel speed sensor electrical connector

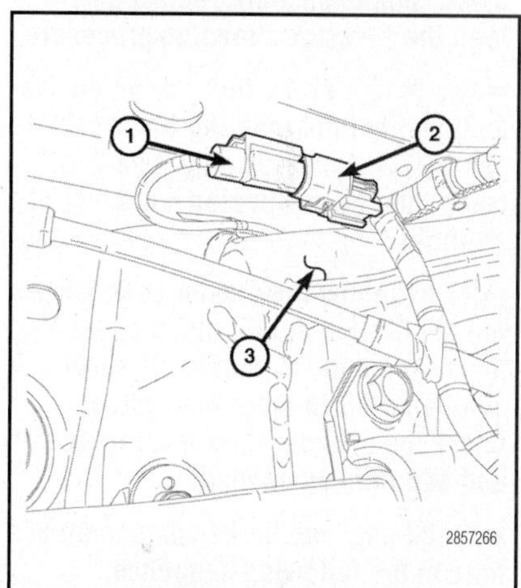

Fig. 3 Disconnect the wheel speed sensor wiring connector (1) from the wiring harness connector (2); cradle (3)

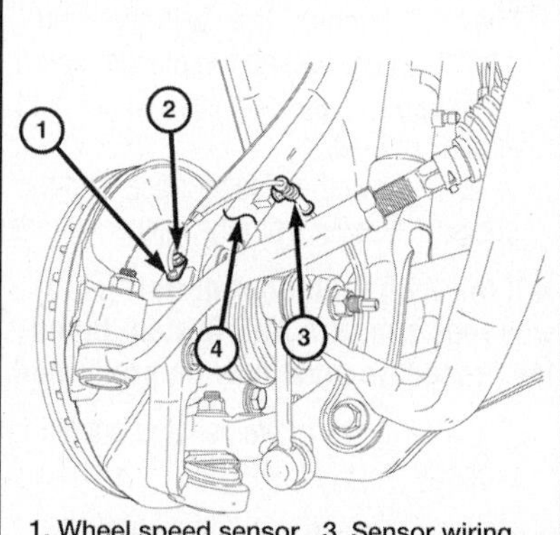

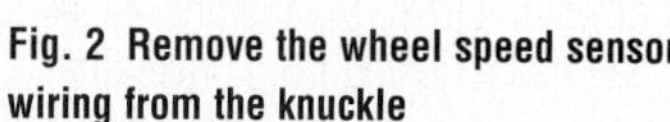

Fig. 2 Remove the wheel speed sensor wiring from the knuckle

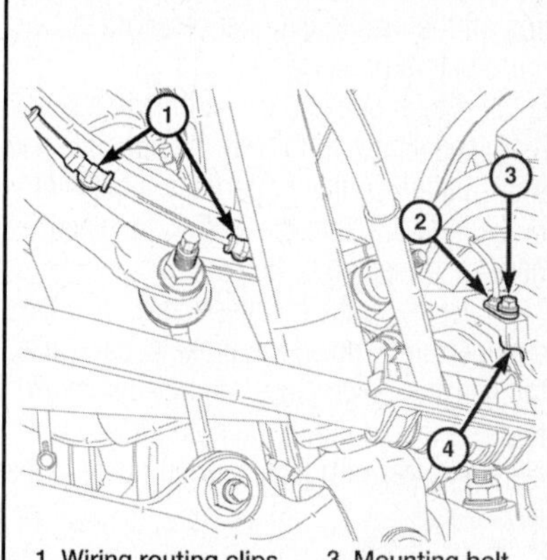

Fig. 4 Remove the wheel speed sensor wiring routing clips from the camber link

wiring connector to the wiring harness connector.

7. Attach the wheel speed sensor wiring routing clip (not shown) to the top of the cradle.

8. Route and attach the wheel speed sensor wiring routing clips to the camber link.

9. Install the wheel speed sensor and mounting bolt, and tighten to 95 inch lbs. (11 Nm).

10. Remove the supports and lower the vehicle.

BRAKES

BLEEDING THE BRAKE SYSTEM

BLEEDING PROCEDURE

BLEEDING PROCEDURE

Manual Bleeding

➡Do not use this procedure if the master cylinder, Hydraulic Control Unit (HCU), brake booster, or the lines between the master cylinder and the HCU have been replaced. If any of these components are replaced perform the Pressure Bleeding procedure.

➡Use Mopar brake fluid, or an equivalent quality fluid meeting SAE J1703-F and DOT 3 standards only. Use fresh, clean fluid from a sealed container at all times.

➡Do not allow the master cylinder to run out of fluid during bleed operations. An empty cylinder will allow additional air to enter the system. Check the cylinder fluid level frequently and add fluid as needed.

➡Bleed only one brake component at a time in the following sequence:

1. Fill the master cylinder reservoir with brake fluid.

2. If the calipers are overhauled, open the caliper bleed screws. Then close each bleed screw as fluid starts to drip from it. Top off the master cylinder reservoir once more before proceeding.

3. Attach one end of the bleed hose to the bleed screw and insert the opposite end in a suitable container partially filled with brake fluid. Be sure the end of the bleed hose is immersed in fluid.

4. Open up the bleeder screw, then have a helper press down the brake pedal. Once the pedal is down close the bleeder screw. Repeat bleeding until the fluid stream is clear and free of bubbles. Then move to the next wheel.

Pressure Bleeding

1. Use Mopar brake fluid, or an equivalent quality fluid meeting SAE J1703-F and DOT 3 standards only. Use fresh, clean fluid from a sealed container at all times.

2. Fill the master cylinder reservoir with brake fluid prior to connecting pressure bleeder.

3. Fill the bleeder tank with recommended fluid and purge air from the tank lines before bleeding.

➡Follow the manufacturer's instructions carefully when using pressure equipment. Do not exceed the tank manufacturers pressure recommendations. Generally, a tank pressure of 15–20 psi (51–67 kPa) is sufficient for bleeding.

4. Connect the pressure bleeder to the master cylinder using adapter provided with the equipment or MASTER CYLINDER CAP

➡When pressure bleeding, a helper is needed inside the vehicle.

5. Bleed only one brake component at a time beginning with the rear brake caliper furthest from the master cylinder, then the other rear caliper, followed by the furthest front caliper from the master cylinder and finishing with the closest to the master cylinder as follows:

a. Attach one end of a clear bleed hose to the bleed screw and insert the opposite end in a suitable container.

b. Open the bleeder and have the helper pump the brake pedal multiple times, until the fluid stream is clear and free of air bubbles, then with the brake pedal pushed, tighten the bleeder screw.

c. Repeat step 2 on each wheel until all are complete.

d. Remove the bleeder hose, and the pressure bleeder from the master cylinder.

➡If the Hydraulic Control Unit (HCU) was replaced, the ABS System Bleeding procedure must now be preformed.

e. Verify the brake pedal is operating properly.

MASTER CYLINDER BLEEDING

A new master cylinder should be bled before installation on the vehicle. Required bleeding tools include bleed tubes and a wood dowel to stroke the pistons. Bleed tubes can be fabricated from brake line.

1. Mount master cylinder in vise.

2. Attach bleed tubes to cylinder outlet ports. Then position each tube end into reservoir.

3. Fill reservoir with fresh brake fluid.

4. Press cylinder pistons inward with wood dowel. Then release pistons and allow them to return under spring pressure. Continue bleeding operations until air bubbles are no longer visible in fluid.

BLEEDING THE ABS SYSTEM

➡The ABS System Bleeding procedure is only necessary if the Hydraulic Control Unit (HCU) is replaced.

➡The Antilock Brake System (ABS) bleeding requires performing a base pressure brake bleeding, followed by use of the scan tool to cycle and bleed the HCU pump and solenoids.

1. Perform the Pressure Bleeding procedure.

2. After the Pressure Bleeding procedure, connect scan tool to the Data Link Connector.

3. Select ANTILOCK BRAKES, followed by MISCELLANEOUS, then ABS BLEED BRAKES and follow the instructions displayed for the procedure.

4. Remove the pressure bleeder from the master cylinder and make sure the brake fluid is properly filled and capped.

➡If the ABS module was not replaced, the ABS VERIFICATION TEST is not needed.

5. If the ABS module was replaced, perform the ABS VERIFICATION TEST.

6. Verify proper brake operation before moving vehicle

FLUID FILL PROCEDURE

1. Always clean the master cylinder reservoir and cap before checking fluid level. If not cleaned, dirt could enter the fluid.

2. The fluid fill level is indicated on the side of the master cylinder reservoir.

3. The correct fluid level is to the MAX indicator on the side of the reservoir. If necessary, add fluid to the proper level.

⁂ CAUTION

Dust and dirt accumulating on brake parts during normal use may contain asbestos fibers from production or aftermarket brake linings. Breathing excessive concentrations of asbestos fibers can cause serious bodily harm. Exercise care when servicing brake parts. Do not sand or grind brake lining unless equipment used is designed to contain the dust residue. Do not clean brake parts with compressed air or by dry brushing. Cleaning should be done by dampening the brake components with a fine mist of water, then wiping the brake components clean with a dampened cloth. Dispose of cloth and all residue containing asbestos fibers in an impermeable container with the appropriate label. Follow practices prescribed by the Occupational Safety and Health Administration (OSHA) and the Environmental Protection Agency (EPA) for the handling, processing, and disposing of dust or debris that may contain asbestos fibers.

BRAKE CALIPER

REMOVAL & INSTALLATION

See Figures 5 and 6.

1. Drain small amount of fluid from the master cylinder brake reservoir with a clean suction gun.
2. Install a prop rod on the brake pedal to keep pressure on the brake system. Holding the pedal in this position will isolate the master cylinder from the hydraulic brake system and will not allow brake fluid to drain out of the brake fluid reservoir while the brake lines are open. This will allow you to bleed out the area of repair instead of the entire system.
3. Raise and support the vehicle.
4. Remove the wheel and tire assembly.
5. Bottom the caliper pistons into the caliper.
6. Remove the brake caliper tension clip by pressing rearward on the front of the clip while pulling the clip out from the caliper.
7. Remove the brake hose banjo bolt and gasket washers. Discard the gasket washers.
8. Remove the caliper slide dust bolt shields and loosen the brake caliper slide bolts (guide pins).
9. Remove the caliper from the adapter.

To install:

➡DO NOT add grease to guide pins, pin bushings, housing shoe face or anchor bracket rails. Clean anchor bracket rails and housing shoe face with brake cleaner prior to assembly of new linings.

➡Brake caliper slide bolts (guide pins) should be free from debris.

10. Position the brake caliper/pads and tighten the brake caliper slide bolts (guide pins) to 41 ft. lbs. (55 Nm).
11. Install the caliper slide bolt dust shields.

➡Verify brake hose is not twisted or kinked before tightening banjo bolt.

12. Install brake hose to caliper with new copper washers and tighten banjo bolt to 22 ft. lbs. (30 Nm).
13. Install the brake caliper tension clip
14. Remove the prop rod from the brake pedal.
15. Bleed the area of repair for the brake system. If a proper pedal is not felt during bleeding an area of repair then a base bleed system must be performed.
16. Install wheel and tire assembly.
17. Remove supports and lower vehicle.
18. Verify brake fluid level is correct.

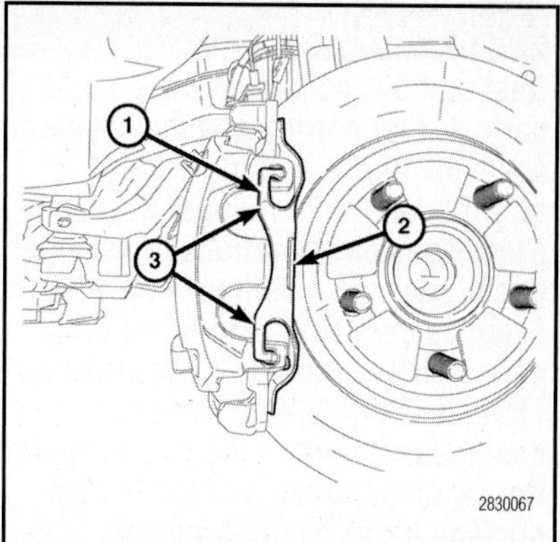

Fig. 5 Remove the brake caliper tension clip (1) by pressing rearward on the front of the clip (2) while pulling the clip out (3) from the caliper

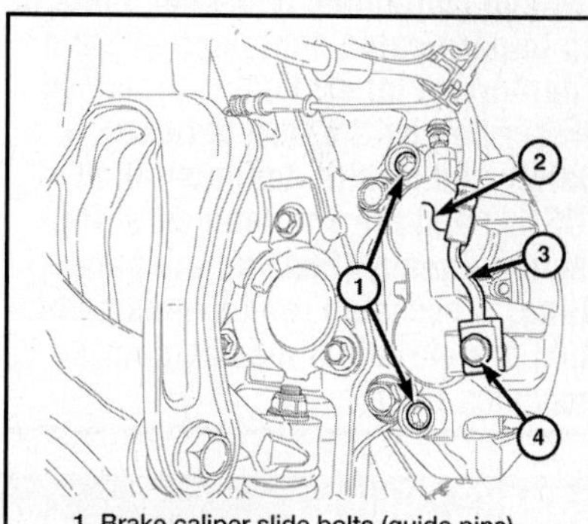

Fig. 6 Remove the brake hose banjo bolt and gasket washers

DISC BRAKE PADS

REMOVAL & INSTALLATION

1. Remove the brake calipers.
2. Remove the brake pads.
3. Installation is the reverse of removal.

CAUTION

Dust and dirt accumulating on brake parts during normal use may contain asbestos fibers from production or aftermarket brake linings. Breathing excessive concentrations of asbestos fibers can cause serious bodily harm. Exercise care when servicing brake parts. Do not sand or grind brake lining unless equipment used is designed to contain the dust residue. Do not clean brake parts with compressed air or by dry brushing. Cleaning should be done by dampening the brake components with a fine mist of water, then wiping the brake components clean with a dampened cloth. Dispose of cloth and all residue containing asbestos fibers in an impermeable container with the appropriate label. Follow practices prescribed by the Occupational Safety and Health Administration (OSHA) and the Environmental Protection Agency (EPA) for the handling, processing, and disposing of dust or debris that may contain asbestos fibers.

BRAKE CALIPER

REMOVAL & INSTALLATION

See Figures 7 and 8.

➡Front brake caliper shown, rear calipers similar.

1. Drain small amount of fluid from the master cylinder brake reservoir with a clean suction gun.
2. Install a prop rod on the brake pedal to keep pressure on the brake system. Holding the pedal in this position will isolate the master cylinder from the hydraulic brake system and will not allow brake fluid to drain out of the brake fluid reservoir while the brake lines are open. This will allow you to bleed out the area of repair instead of the entire system.
3. Raise and support the vehicle.
4. Remove the wheel and tire assembly.
5. Bottom the caliper pistons into the caliper.
6. Remove the brake caliper tension clip by pressing rearward on the front of the clip while pulling the clip out from the caliper.
7. Remove the brake hose banjo bolt and gasket washers. Discard the gasket washers.
8. Remove the caliper slide dust bolt shields and loosen the brake caliper slide bolts (guide pins).
9. Remove the caliper from the adapter.

To install:

➡DO NOT add grease to guide pins, pin bushings, housing shoe face or anchor bracket rails. Clean anchor bracket rails and housing shoe face with brake cleaner prior to assembly of new linings.

➡Brake caliper slide bolts (guide pins) should be free from debris.

10. Position the brake caliper/pads and tighten the brake caliper slide bolts (guide pins) to 20 ft. lbs. (28 Nm).
11. Install the caliper slide bolt dust shields.

➡Verify brake hose is not twisted or kinked before tightening banjo bolt.

12. Install brake hose to caliper with new copper washers and tighten banjo bolt to 22 ft. lbs. (30 Nm).
13. Install the brake caliper tension clip
14. Remove the prop rod from the brake pedal.
15. Bleed the area of repair for the brake system. If a proper pedal is not felt during bleeding an area of repair then a base bleed system must be performed.
16. Install wheel and tire assembly.

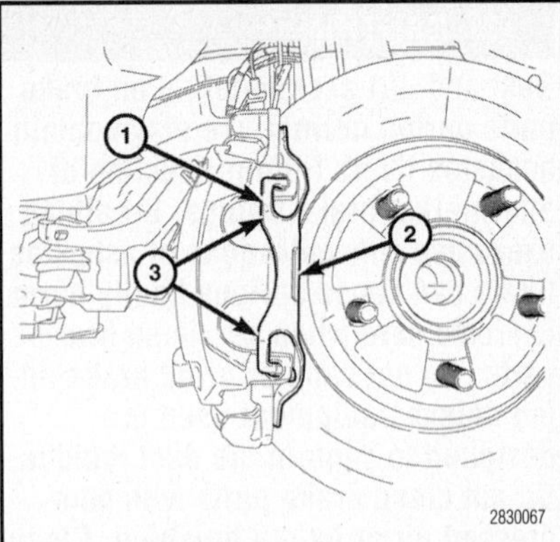

Fig. 7 Remove the brake caliper tension clip (1) by pressing rearward on the front of the clip (2) while pulling the clip out (3) from the caliper

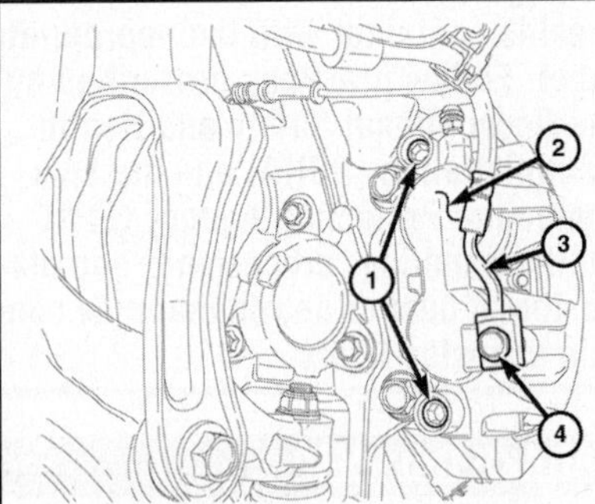

Fig. 8 Remove the brake hose banjo bolt and gasket washers

17. Remove supports and lower vehicle.
18. Verify brake fluid level is correct.

DISC BRAKE PADS

REMOVAL & INSTALLATION

1. Remove the brake calipers.
2. Remove the brake pads.
3. Installation is the reverse of removal.

PARKING BRAKE SHOES

REMOVAL & INSTALLATION

See Figures 9 and 10.

1. Raise and support the vehicle.
2. Disconnect the rear RH and LH parking brake cables from the parking brake equalizer.
3. Remove the rear wheels.
4. Remove the rotor.
5. Remove the shoe to shoe return springs.
6. Remove the adjuster.
7. Remove the shoe hold-down clips and pins.
8. Spread the shoes and remove the parking brake cable from the actuator lever, and remove the shoes.
9. Remove and transfer the parking brake actuator, and the spring behind the shoes near the parking brake actuator to the new shoes.

To install:

10. Attach the parking brake cable to the actuator and position the shoes on the support plate. Be sure shoes are properly engaged in the parking brake actuator, parking brake cable is attached, and the rear spring is still properly connected.
11. Install the hold down clips and pins.
12. Install the adjuster.
13. Install the shoe to shoe return spring.
14. Connect the rear RH and LH parking brake cables to the parking brake equalizer.
15. Install rotor and brake calipers.
16. Adjust the parking brake shoes.
17. Install wheels.
18. Remove the supports and lower the vehicle.
19. Pump brake pedal until caliper pistons and brake pads are seated and a firm brake pedal is obtained
20. Verify correct parking brake operation.

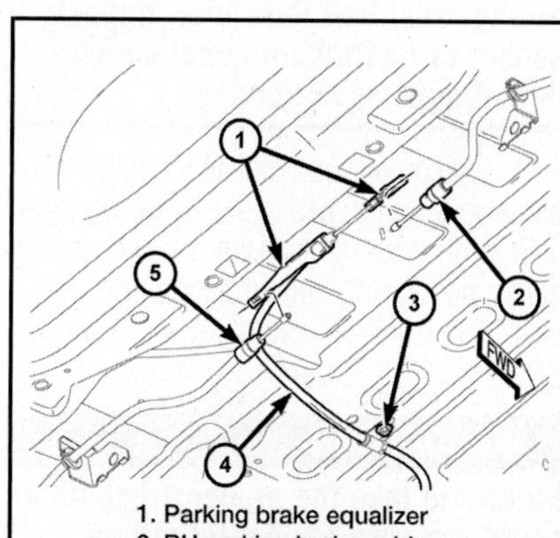

Fig. 9 Disconnect the rear RH and LH parking brake cables from the parking brake equalizer

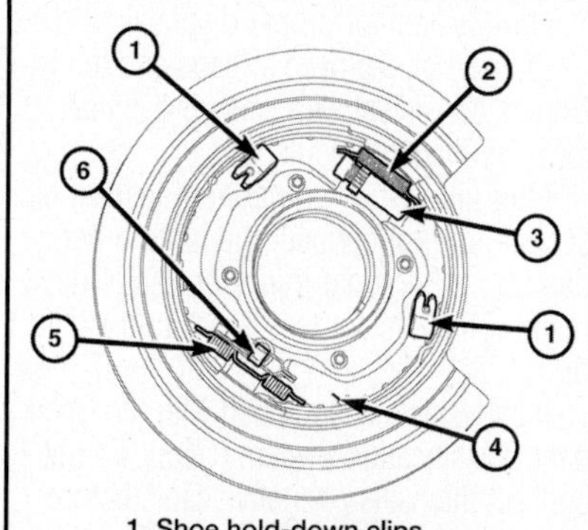

Fig. 10 Remove the shoe to shoe return springs

ADJUSTMENT

1. Be sure the parking brake lever is fully released.
2. Raise and support the vehicle.
3. Remove the rear wheels.
4. Remove the plug from each access hole in the brake support plates.
5. Insert an adjusting tool through the support plate access hole and engage the tool in the teeth of the adjusting screw star wheel.
6. Rotate the adjuster screw star wheel (move tool handle upward) until slight drag can be felt when the star wheel is rotated.
7. Back off the adjuster screw star wheel until brake drag is eliminated.
8. Repeat adjustment at the opposite wheel. Be sure adjustment is equal at both wheels.
9. Install the support plate access hole plugs.
10. Install the rear wheels.
11. Remove the supports and lower the vehicle.
12. Depress the park brake lever and make sure the park brakes hold the vehicle stationary.
13. Release the park brake lever.

GENERAL INFORMATION

** CAUTION

These vehicles are equipped with an air bag system. The system must be disarmed before performing service on, or around, system components, the steering column, instrument panel components, wiring and sensors. Failure to follow the safety precautions and the disarming procedure could result in accidental air bag deployment, possible injury and unnecessary system repairs.

SERVICE PRECAUTIONS

Disconnect and isolate the battery negative cable before beginning any airbag system component diagnosis, testing, removal, or installation procedures. Allow system capacitor to discharge for two minutes before beginning any component service. This will disable the airbag system. Failure to disable the airbag system may result in accidental airbag deployment, personal injury, or death.

Do not place an intact undeployed airbag face down on a solid surface. The airbag will propel into the air if accidentally deployed and may result in personal injury or death.

When carrying or handling an undeployed airbag, the trim side (face) of the airbag should be pointing towards the body to minimize possibility of injury if accidental deployment occurs. Failure to do this may result in personal injury or death.

Replace airbag system components with OEM replacement parts. Substitute parts may appear interchangeable, but internal differences may result in inferior occupant protection. Failure to do so may result in occupant personal injury or death.

Wear safety glasses, rubber gloves, and long sleeved clothing when cleaning powder residue from vehicle after an airbag deployment. Powder residue emitted from a deployed airbag can cause skin irritation. Flush affected area with cool water if irritation is experienced. If nasal or throat irritation is experienced, exit the vehicle for fresh air until the irritation ceases. If irritation continues, see a physician.

Do not use a replacement airbag that is not in the original packaging. This may result in improper deployment, personal injury, or death.

The factory installed fasteners, screws and bolts used to fasten airbag components have a special coating and are specifically designed for the airbag system. Do not use substitute fasteners. Use only original equipment fasteners listed in the parts catalog when fastener replacement is required.

During, and following, any child restraint anchor service, due to impact event or vehicle repair, carefully inspect all mounting hardware, tether straps, and anchors for proper installation, operation, or damage. If a child restraint anchor is found damaged in any way, the anchor must be replaced. Failure to do this may result in personal injury or death.

Deployed and non-deployed airbags may or may not have live pyrotechnic material within the airbag inflator.

Do not dispose of driver/passenger/curtain airbags or seat belt tensioners unless you are sure of complete deployment. Refer to the Hazardous Substance Control System for proper disposal.

Dispose of deployed airbags and tensioners consistent with state, provincial, local, and federal regulations.

After any airbag component testing or service, do not connect the battery negative cable. Personal injury or death may result if the system test is not performed first.

If the vehicle is equipped with the Occupant Classification System (OCS), do not connect the battery negative cable before performing the OCS Verification Test using the scan tool and the appropriate diagnostic information. Personal injury or death may result if the system test is not performed properly.

Never replace both the Occupant Restraint Controller (ORC) and the Occupant Classification Module (OCM) at the same time. If both require replacement, replace one, then perform the Airbag System test before replacing the other.

Both the ORC and the OCM store Occupant Classification System (OCS) calibration data, which they transfer to one another when one of them is replaced. If both are replaced at the same time, an irreversible fault will be set in both modules and the OCS may malfunction and cause personal injury or death.

If equipped with OCS, the Seat Weight Sensor is a sensitive, calibrated unit and must be handled carefully. Do not drop or handle roughly. If dropped or damaged, replace with another sensor. Failure to do so may result in occupant injury or death.

If equipped with OCS, the front passenger seat must be handled carefully as well. When removing the seat, be careful when setting on floor not to drop. If dropped, the sensor may be inoperative, could result in occupant injury, or possibly death.

If equipped with OCS, when the passenger front seat is on the floor, no one should sit in the front passenger seat. This uneven force may damage the sensing ability of the seat weight sensors. If sat on and damaged, the sensor may be inoperative, could result in occupant injury, or possibly death.

DISARMING THE SYSTEM

** CAUTION

To avoid serious or fatal injury on vehicles equipped with airbags, disable the Supplemental Restraint System (SRS) before attempting any steering wheel, steering column, airbag, seat belt tensioner, impact sensor or instrument panel component diagnosis or service.

1. Disconnect and isolate the battery negative (ground) cable, then wait two minutes for the system capacitor to discharge before performing further diagnosis or service. This is the only sure way to disable the SRS.

** CAUTION

Failure to take the proper precautions could result in accidental airbag deployment.

ARMING THE SYSTEM

1. Re-connect the negative battery cable.

CLOCKSPRING CENTERING

See Figure 11.

** CAUTION

To avoid serious or fatal injury on vehicles equipped with airbags, disable the Supplemental Restraint System (SRS) before attempting any steering wheel, steering column, airbag, seat belt tensioner, impact sensor or instrument panel component diagnosis or service. Disconnect and isolate the battery negative (ground) cable, then wait two minutes for the system capacitor to discharge before performing further diagnosis or service. This is the only sure way to disable the SRS. Failure to take the proper precautions could result in accidental airbag deployment.

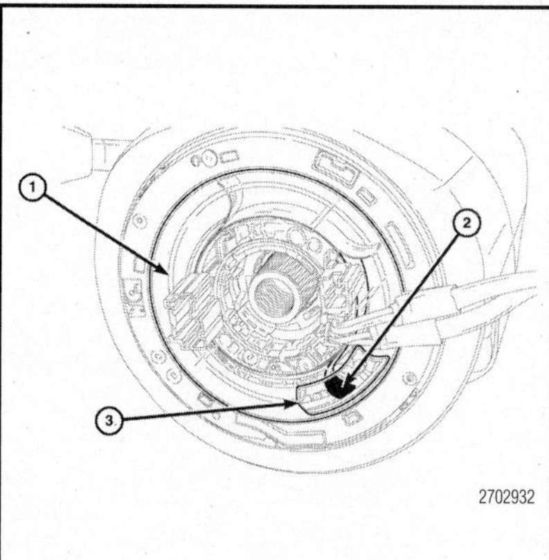

Fig. 11 Clockspring showing the clockspring rotor (1), the black squares (2), and the inspection window (3)

WARNING

Always turn the steering wheel until the front wheels are in the straight-ahead position. Then, prior to disconnecting the steering column from the steering gear, lock the steering wheel to the steering column. If clockspring centering has been compromised for ANY reason, the entire Steering Column Control Module (SCCM) and clockspring unit MUST be replaced with a new unit.

1. Like the clockspring in a timepiece, the clockspring tape has travel limits and can be damaged by being wound too tightly during full stop-to-stop steering wheel rotation. To prevent this from occurring, the clockspring is centered when it is installed on the steering column. Centering the clockspring indexes the clockspring tape to the movable steering components so that the tape can operate within its designed travel limits. However, if the steering shaft is disconnected from the steering gear, the clockspring rotor spool can change position relative to the fixed steering components.
2. Clockspring centering must always be confirmed by viewing the inspection window (3) on the clockspring rotor (1). If the black squares (2) on the clockspring tape are not visible through the inspection window, clockspring centering has been compromised and the SCCM must be replaced with a new unit.
3. The service replacement SCCM is shipped with the clockspring pre-centered and with a red plastic locking tab installed. This locking tab should not be removed until the SCCM has been properly installed on the steering column. If the locking tab is removed before the SCCM is installed on a steering column, clockspring centering must be confirmed by viewing the black squares on the clockspring tape through the inspection window on the clockspring rotor. If the black squares of the clockspring tape are not visible through the inspection window, clockspring centering has been compromised and the SCCM must be replaced with a new unit. Proper clockspring installation may also be confirmed by viewing the Steering Angle Sensor (SAS) data using a diagnostic scan tool.

➡**Service replacement clocksprings are shipped pre-centered within the SCCM and with a plastic locking tab installed. This locking tab should not be removed until the SCCM has been properly installed on the steering column. If the locking tab is removed before the SCCM is installed on a steering column, clockspring centering must be confirmed by viewing the inspection window on the clockspring rotor. If the black squares of the clockspring tape are not visible in the inspection window, the SCCM must be replaced with a new unit. Proper clockspring installation may also be confirmed by viewing the Steering Angle Sensor (SAS) data using a diagnostic scan tool.**

DRIVE TRAIN

AUTOMATIC TRANSMISSION FLUID

DRAIN AND REFILL

See Figure 12.

1. Hoist and support vehicle on safety stands.
2. Place a large diameter shallow drain pan beneath the transmission pan.
3. Remove bolts holding front and sides of pan to transmission.
4. Loosen bolts holding rear of pan to transmission.
5. Slowly separate front of pan away from transmission allowing the fluid to drain into drain pan.
6. Hold up pan and remove remaining bolts holding pan to transmission.
7. While holding pan level, lower pan away from transmission.
8. Pour remaining fluid in pan into drain pan.
9. Remove the screw holding the primary oil filter to valve body.
10. Separate filter from valve body and oil pump and pour fluid in filter into drain pan.
11. Inspect the oil filter seal in the bottom of the oil pump. If the seal is not installed completely in the oil pump, or is otherwise damaged, then remove and discard the oil filter seal from the bottom of the oil pump. If the seal is installed correctly and is in good condition, it can be reused.

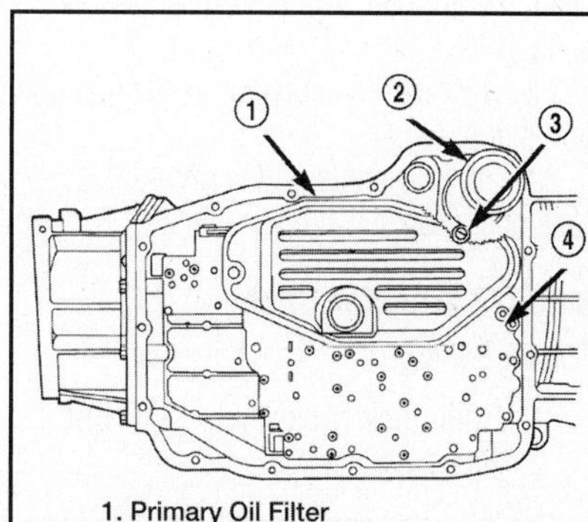

Fig. 12 Remove the screw holding the primary oil filter to valve body

12. If replacing the cooler return filter, use Oil Filter Wrench
13. to remove the filter from the transmission.
14. Dispose of used trans fluid and filter(s) properly.

To install:

WARNING

The primary oil filter seal MUST be fully installed flush against the oil pump body. DO NOT install the seal onto the filter neck and attempt to install the filter and seal as an assembly. Damage to the transmission will result.

15. If necessary, install a new primary oil filter seal in the oil pump inlet bore. Seat the seal in the bore with a suitable tool (appropriately sized drift or socket, the butt end of a hammer, or other suitable tool).
16. Place replacement filter in position on valve body and into the oil pump.
17. Install screw to hold the primary oil filter to valve body.

18. Install new cooler return filter onto the transmission, if necessary. Torque the filter to 7 ft. lbs. (9.5 Nm).
19. Place bead of Mopar RTV sealant onto the transmission case sealing surface.
20. Place pan in position on transmission.
21. Install bolts to hold pan to transmission. Tighten bolts to 106 inch lbs. (12 Nm) torque.
22. Lower vehicle and fill transmission with Mopar ATF +4.

FILTER REPLACEMENT

Refer to the above procedure.

TRANSFER CASE ASSEMBLY

REMOVAL & INSTALLATION

MP2010 Transfer Case

See Figures 13 and 14.

1. Raise vehicle.
2. Remove drain plug and drain fluid.
3. Reinstall drain plug and tighten to 16–21 ft. lbs. (22–28 Nm).

✲✲ WARNING

Do not allow propshafts to hang at attached end. Damage to joint can result.

4. Remove the front and rear propeller shafts.
5. Support transmission with jack stand.
6. Remove rear crossmember and skid plate, if equipped.
7. Support transfer case with transmission jack and secure with chains.
8. Remove all bolts attaching transfer case to transmission.
9. Pull transfer case and jack rearward to disengage transfer case.

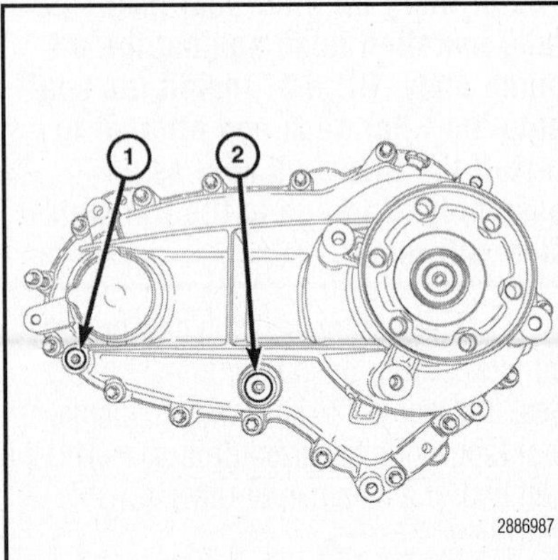

Fig. 13 Remove drain plug (1) and drain fluid; fill plug (2)

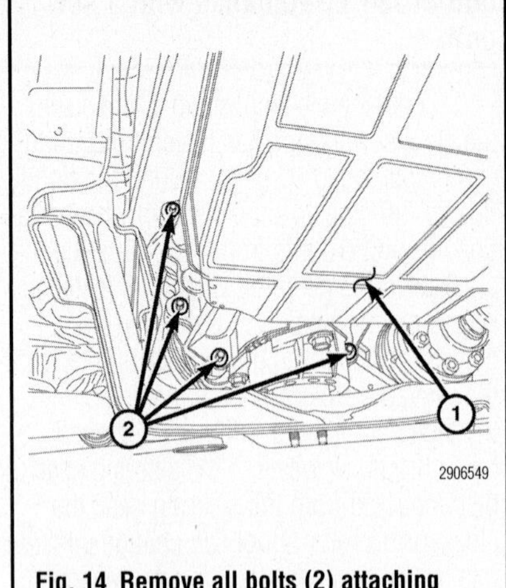

Fig. 14 Remove all bolts (2) attaching transfer case to transmission (1)

10. Remove transfer case from under vehicle.

To install:

11. Mount transfer case on a transmission jack.
12. Secure transfer case to jack with chains.
13. Position transfer case under vehicle.
14. Align transfer case and transmission shafts and install transfer case onto the transmission.
15. Install and tighten all transfer case attaching bolts to 30–36 ft. lbs. (41–49 Nm) torque.
16. Connect front propeller shaft and install rear propeller shaft.
17. Remove transfer case fill plug.
18. Fill transfer case with correct fluid. Correct as necessary.
19. Install the transfer case fill plug. Tighten the plug to 16–21 ft. lbs. (22–28 Nm).
20. Install rear crossmember and skid plate, if equipped. Tighten crossmember bolts to 30 ft. lbs. (41 Nm).
21. Remove transmission jack and support stand.
22. Lower vehicle and verify transfer case operation.

MP3023 Transfer Case

See Figure 15.

1. Shift transfer case into NEUTRAL.
2. Raise vehicle.

➡The air suspension system will auto-disable when lifted on a frame hoist, or when jacking one corner of the vehicle. The air suspension may attempt to change height slightly prior to switching to auto-disable. A manual disable is also available by pressing the "Up" and "Down" switches of the terrain select switch simultaneously for more that 5 seconds. The air suspension system will return to normal operation when the vehicle speed reaches 15 mph (25 kph).

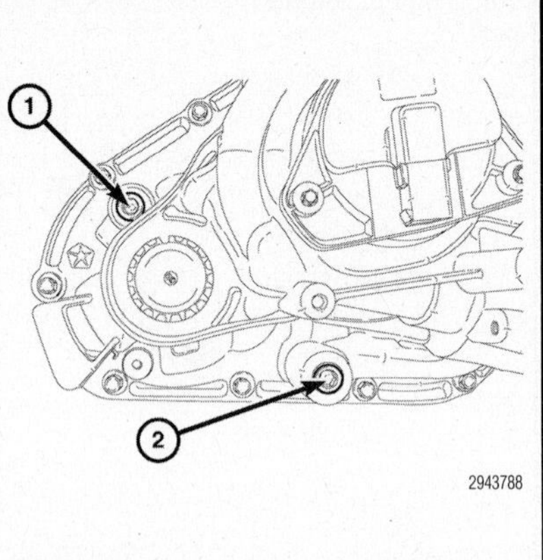

Fig. 15 Remove transfer case fill plug (1) and drain plug (2) to drain transfer case lubricant

3. Remove transfer case fill plug and drain plug to drain transfer case lubricant.
4. Support transmission with jack stand.
5. Remove rear crossmember and skid plate, if equipped.
6. Remove the rear support cushion.

✲✲ WARNING

Do not allow propeller shafts to hang at attached end. Damage to joint can result.

7. Disconnect front propeller shaft from transfer case at companion flange. Remove rear propeller shaft from vehicle.
8. Disconnect the transfer case shift motor and mode sensor electrical connector.
9. Disconnect transfer case vent hose.
10. Support transfer case with transmission jack.
11. Secure transfer case to jack with chains.
12. Remove bolts attaching transfer case to transmission.
13. Pull transfer case and jack rearward to disengage transfer case.
14. Remove transfer case from under vehicle.

To install:

15. Mount transfer case on a transmission jack.
16. Secure transfer case to jack with chains.
17. Position transfer case under vehicle.
18. Align transfer case and transmission

shafts and install transfer case onto transmission.

19. Install and tighten transfer case attaching bolts to 30–36 ft. lbs. (41–49 Nm).

20. Connect the transfer case vent hose to the transfer case.

21. Install the rear support cushion.

22. Install rear crossmember and skid plate, if equipped.

23. Remove transmission jack and support stand.

24. Connect front propeller shaft and install rear propeller shaft.

25. Install the transfer case drain plug. Tighten plug to 15–25 ft. lbs. (20–34 Nm).

26. Fill transfer case with correct fluid. Check transmission fluid level. Correct as necessary.

27. Install the transfer case fill plug. Tighten the plug to 15–25 ft. lbs. (20–34 Nm).

28. Connect the shift motor and encoder electrical connectors.

29. Lower vehicle and verify transfer case shift operation.

➡The air suspension system will auto-disable when lifted on a frame hoist, or when jacking one corner of the vehicle. The air suspension may attempt to change height slightly prior to switching to auto-disable. A manual disable is also available by pressing the "Up" and "Down" switches of the terrain select switch simultaneously for more that 5 seconds. The air suspension system will return to normal operation when the vehicle speed reaches 15 mph (25 kph).

FRONT DRIVESHAFT

REMOVAL & INSTALLATION

➡Propeller shaft is serviced as an assembly only.

1. Place vehicle on floor or drive-on hoist with full weight of vehicle on suspension.
2. Shift transmission and transfer case in to Neutral.
3. If equipped, remove skid plate.
4. Mark a line across the C/V joints to companion flanges for installation reference.
5. Raise vehicle.
6. Remove bolts from C/V joints.
7. Push propeller shaft forward to clear transfer case companion flange and remove the shaft.

To install:

➡Clean all propeller shaft bolts and apply Mopar Lock and Seal Adhesive or equivalent to the threads before installation.

8. Install propeller shaft between companion flanges.
9. Align marks on the companion flanges with the marks on the joints.
10. Install bolts to the transfer case flange and tighten bolts to 24 ft. lbs. (32 Nm).
11. Install bolts to the axle flange and tighten bolts to 24 ft. lbs. (32 Nm).
12. If equipped, install skid plates

FRONT HALFSHAFT

REMOVAL & INSTALLATION

See Figures 16 through 19.

1. With vehicle in neutral, position vehicle on hoist.
2. Remove the wheel and tire assemblies.
3. Remove half shaft hub/bearing nut.
4. Remove wheel speed sensor.
5. Remove both brake calipers and hang to the side.
6. Remove tie rod end nut.
7. Remove stabilizer bar link bolts from lower control arms.
8. Separate the outer tie rod ends from the knuckles with Ball Joint Remover.
9. Remove the upper ball joint nuts.
10. Separate the upper ball joints from the knuckles using Ball Joint Press.
11. Remove shock clevis bolt and nut from lower control arm
12. Lean the knuckle out and push half shaft out of the hub/bearing.
13. Pry half shafts from axle/axle tube with pry bar.

To install:

14. Using axle seal protector, install half shafts in the axle. Verify half shaft has engaged.

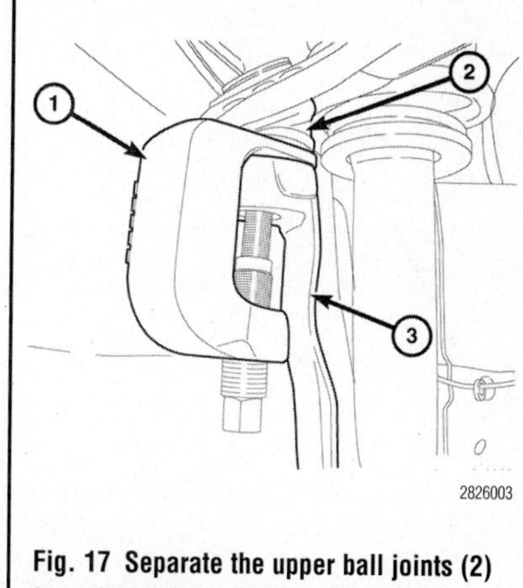

Fig. 17 Separate the upper ball joints (2) from the knuckles (3) using Ball Joint Press (1)

15. Install half shafts through the hub/bearing.
16. Install shock clevis on lower control arm and tighten nut to specifications.
17. Install upper control arm on knuckle and tighten ball joint nut to specifications.
18. Install tie rod end on knuckle and tighten to specifications.
19. Install stabilizer link on lower control arm and tighten to specifications.
20. Install caliper on caliper adapter and tighten to specifications.
21. Install wheel speed sensor on the hub/bearing.
22. Install half shaft hub/bearing nut and tighten to 229 ft. lbs. (310 Nm).
23. Install the wheel and tire assemblies.
24. Pump brake pedal until caliper pistons and brake pads are seated and a firm brake pedal is obtained.

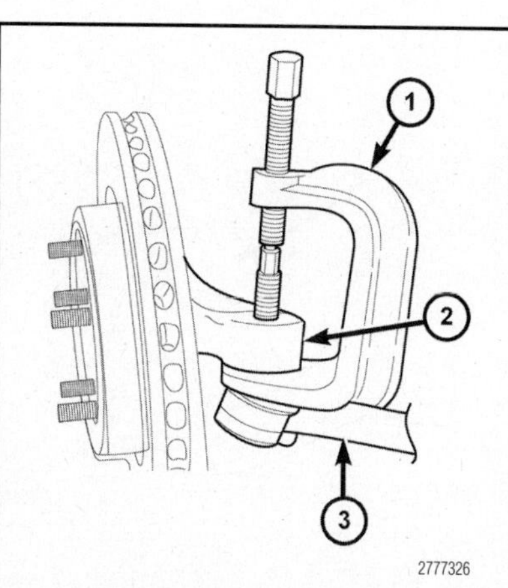

Fig. 16 Separate the outer tie rod ends (3) from the knuckles (2) with Ball Joint Remover (1)

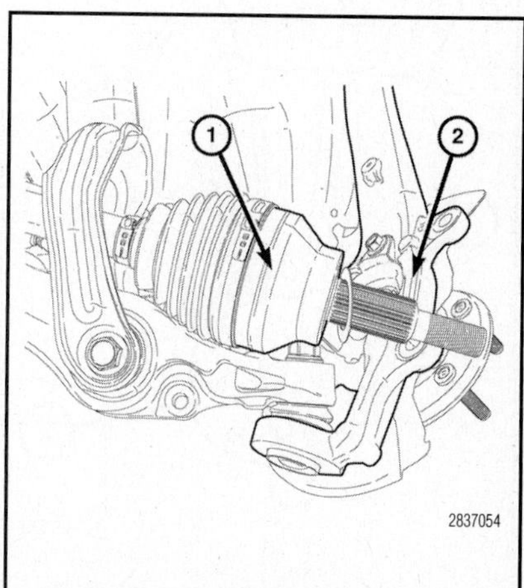

Fig. 18 Lean the knuckle (2) out and push half shaft (1) out of the hub/bearing

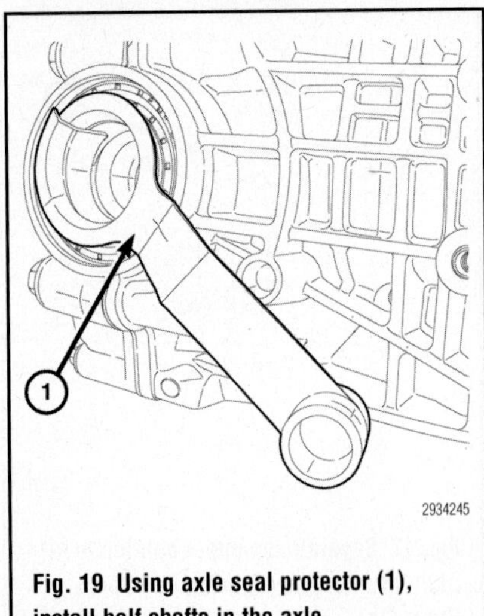

Fig. 19 Using axle seal protector (1), install half shafts in the axle

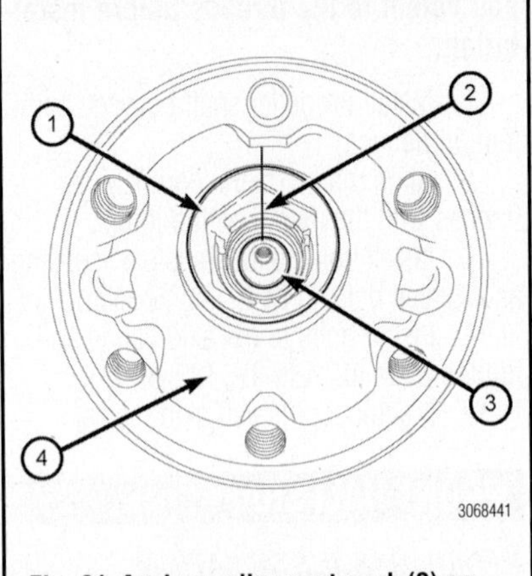

Fig. 21 Apply an alignment mark (2) on the pinion flange nut (1) to the pinion shaft (3)

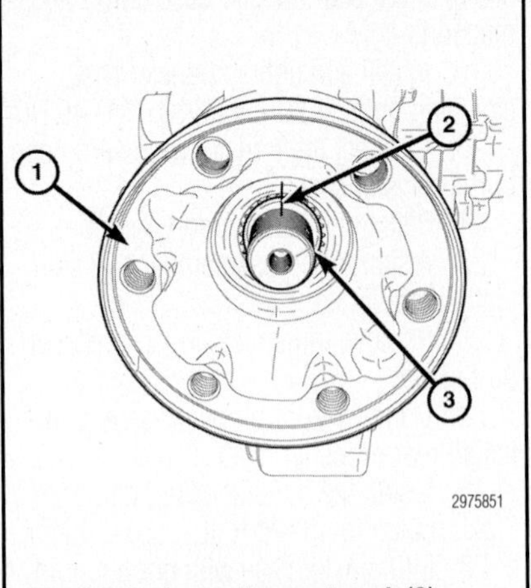

Fig. 23 Apply an alignment mark (2) on the pinion flange (1) to the pinion shaft (3)

FRONT PINION SEAL

REMOVAL & INSTALLATION

See Figures 20 through 24.

1. Remove front axle assembly from vehicle.

➡Torque reading must be taken with a constant rotational speed. Do not measure break away torque.

2. Using a torque wrench, measure and record the pinion rotational torque.

➡Due to axle imbalance concerns, it is necessary to make sure pinion nut-to-shaft orientation is maintained. If alignment marks are not visible, apply appropriate marks before removing pinion nut.

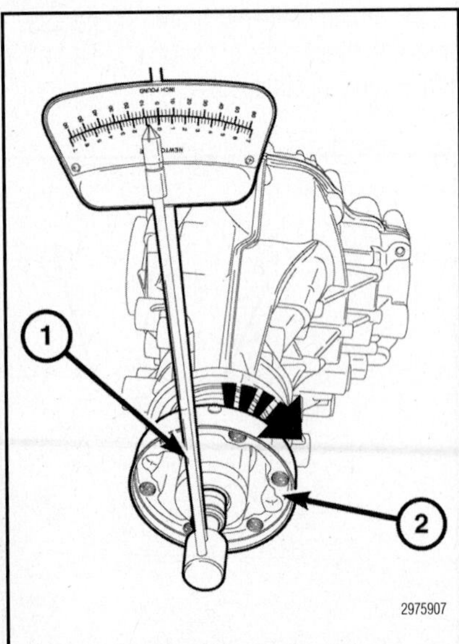

Fig. 20 Using a torque wrench (1), measure and record the pinion rotational torque

3. Apply an alignment mark on the pinion flange nut to the pinion shaft.
4. Using Flange Wrench and 32mm socket, loosen the pinion flange nut.

➡Due to axle imbalance concerns, it is necessary to make sure pinion flange-to-shaft orientation is maintained. If alignment marks are not visible, apply appropriate marks before removing pinion flange.

5. Apply an alignment mark on the pinion flange to the pinion shaft.
6. Using Puller, remove pinion flange from pinion shaft.
7. Using seal remover and slide hammer, remove pinion seal and discard.

To install:

8. Apply light coating of gear lubricant to the lip of the pinion seal.
9. Using Driver Handle and Installer, install pinion seal until tool bottoms on carrier.

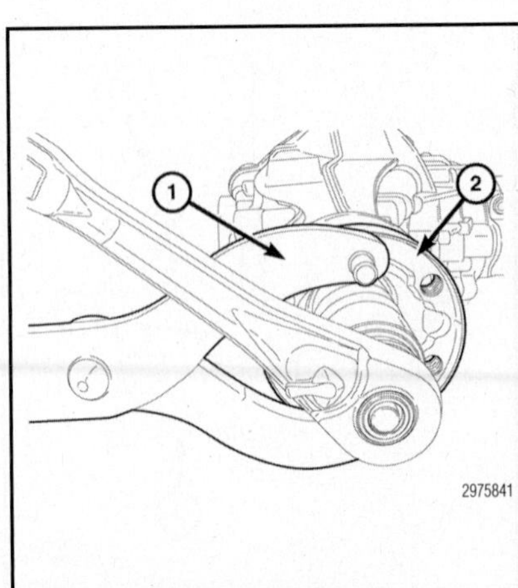

Fig. 22 Using Flange Wrench (1) and 32mm socket, loosen the pinion flange (2) nut

10. Install pinion flange into position. Align index marks between pinion flange and pinion stem to maintain assembly balance and so that bearing preload is not exceeded.
11. Using Installer, lightly tap on pinion flange until adequate pinion shaft threads are exposed.
12. Clean any thread locker from pinion flange nut and apply Mopar Lock and Seal Adhesive to the nut.
13. Install pinion flange nut. Apply 75W–85 gear oil to pinion nut washer face prior to assembly. Using Flange Wrench and 32mm socket tighten pinion flange nut in small increments until the pinion nut index mark aligns with the index marking on the pinion stem.

➡If pinion nut index mark exceeds the pinion stem index mark the unit must be discarded. If the pinion nut index mark falls short of the pinion stem

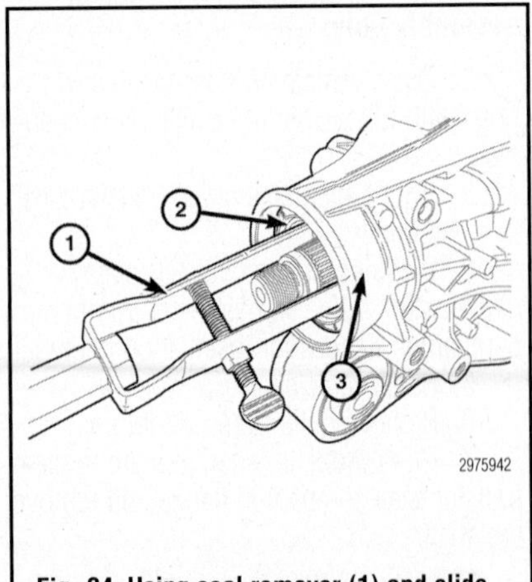

Fig. 24 Using seal remover (1) and slide hammer, remove pinion seal (2); differential (3)

index mark the unit will possibly generate an NVH concern.

➡Torque reading must be taken with a constant rotational speed. Do not measure break away torque.

14. Using a torque wrench, measure and record the pinion rotational torque.
15. After torque reading has been obtained, compare reading to the recorded reading when removing the pinion flange. The difference between the initial and final measurement will be the new seals drag torque only.
16. Install axle assembly.

REAR AXLE FLUID

DRAIN & REFILL

See Figures 25 and 26.

1. With vehicle in neutral, position and raise vehicle on hoist.
2. Using 14mm hex, remove axle drain plug and drain rear axle fluid into container suitable for fluid reuse.

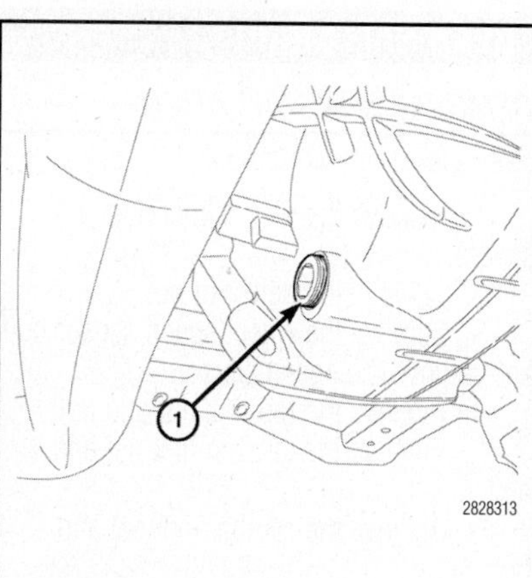

Fig. 25 Using 14mm hex, remove axle drain plug (1) and drain rear axle fluid

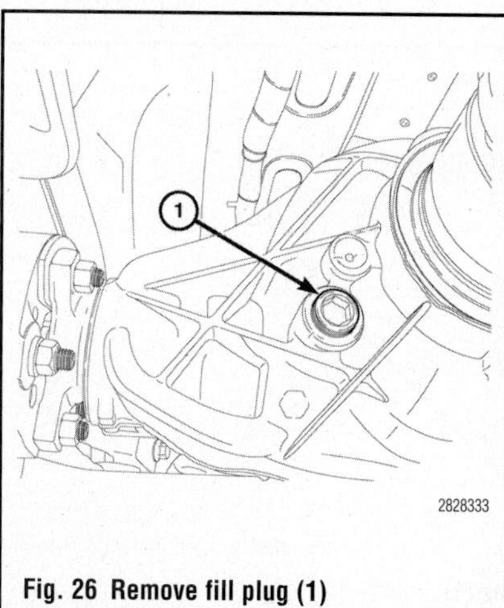

Fig. 26 Remove fill plug (1)

3. Install drain plug and torque to 26 ft. lbs. (35 Nm).
4. Remove fill plug and fill rear axle with 0.95 qts. (0.9 L) Mopar Gear and Axle Lubricant 75W–85 and insure axle is filled to the bottom of the fill hole.
5. Install fill plug and tighten to 26 ft. lbs. (35 Nm).

REAR DRIVESHAFT

REMOVAL & INSTALLATION

See Figures 25 through 33.

✲✲ WARNING

Never grasp halfshaft assembly by the inner or outer boots. Doing so may cause the boot to pucker or crease, reducing the service life of the boot and joint. Avoid over angulations or stroking the C/V joints when handling the halfshaft.

1. With vehicle in neutral, position and raise vehicle on hoist.
2. Using 14mm hex, remove axle drain plug (1) and drain rear axle fluid into container suitable for fluid reuse.
3. Install drain plug and torque to 26 ft. lbs. (35 Nm).

✲✲ WARNING

Remove axle vent tube prior to removing axle. Failure to remove vent tube will allow axle fluid to saturate the vent and cause reduced or improper axle venting resulting in axle damage.

4. Remove axle vent tube.
5. Remove rear exhaust system nuts.
6. Apply alignment index marks to the propeller shaft rubber coupler and axle flange.
7. Remove propeller shaft coupler-to-axle flange bolt/nuts.
8. Remove the rear caliper and secure.
9. Remove the halfshaft nut.
10. Remove the wheel speed sensor bolt and remove the speed sensor.
11. Remove the toe link nut and bolt
12. Remove the tension link nut and bolt.
13. Remove the camber link nut and bolt.
14. Swing rear knuckle outward as shown.
15. Remove the halfshaft from the hub.
16. Using a hammer or similar tool as a pivot point and a suitable screwdriver, or

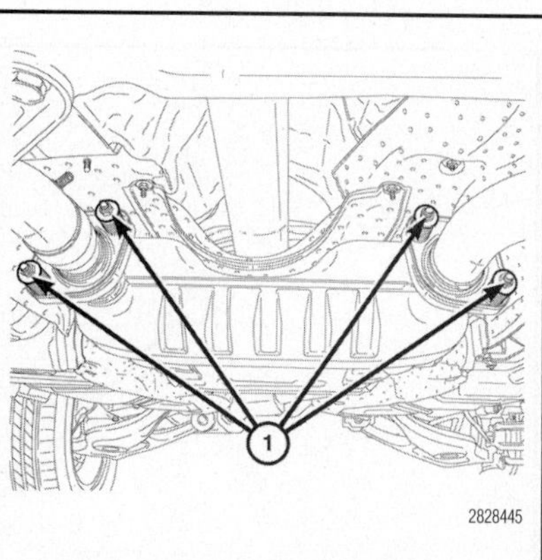

Fig. 27 Remove rear exhaust system nuts (1)

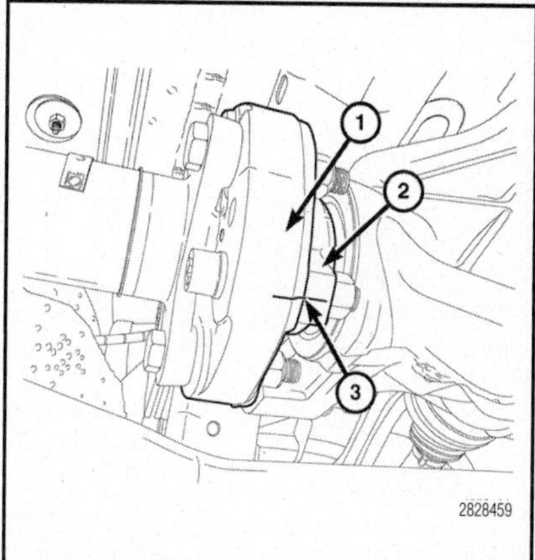

Fig. 28 Apply alignment index marks (3) to the propeller shaft rubber coupler (1) and axle flange (2)

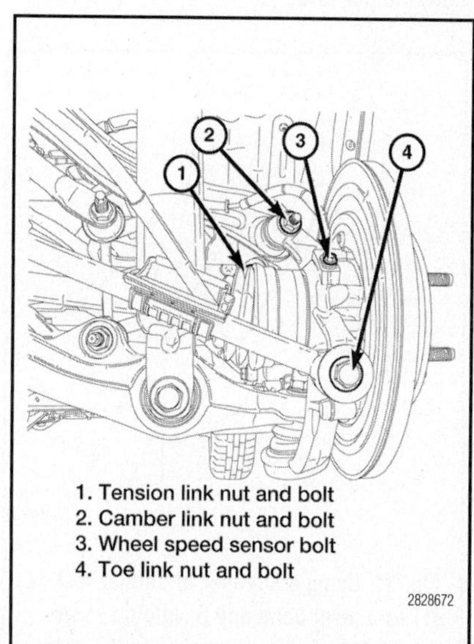

Fig. 29 Remove the wheel speed sensor bolt and remove the speed sensor

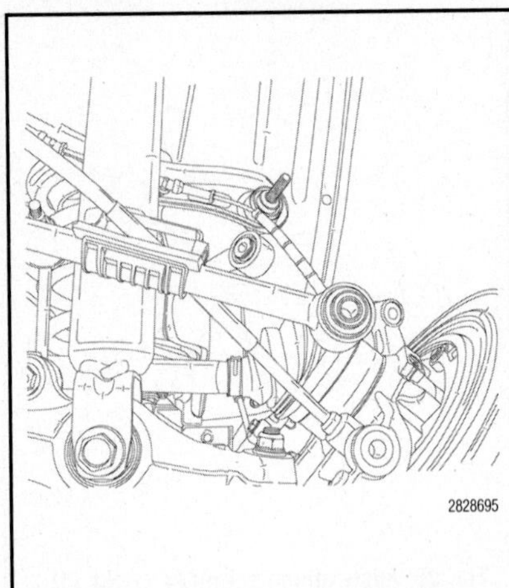

Fig. 30 Swing rear knuckle outward as shown

using the grove on the outer can of the CV joint, carefully disengage both halfshafts from axle assembly using care not to damage dust seal.

17. Carefully remove the right halfshaft from the axle assembly. Use caution to protect axle seal and journal.
18. Position transmission jack to rear axle assembly.
19. Remove rear axle forward mount isolator bolt/nut.
20. Remove two rear axle-to-crossmember bolts.
21. Carefully lower rear axle. While lowering axle, separate propeller shaft from axle and support with suitable rope or wire.
22. Lower axle just enough to remove the left halfshaft. Use caution to protect axle seal and journal.
23. Remove axle assembly from vehicle and transfer to bench.

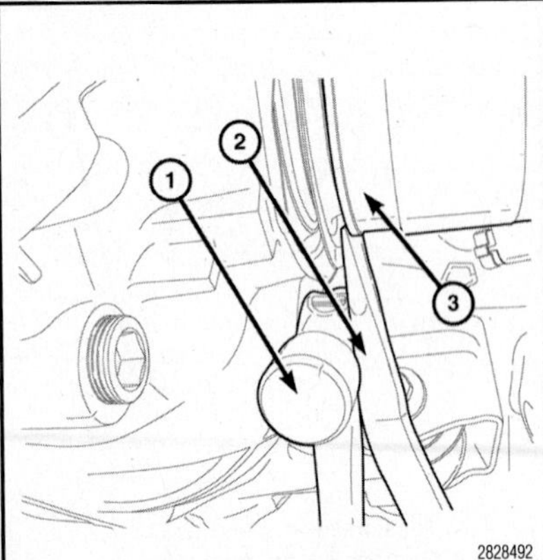

Fig. 31 Using a hammer or similar tool (1) as a pivot point and a suitable screwdriver (2), or using the grove on the outer can of the CV joint, carefully disengage both halfshafts (3) from axle assembly

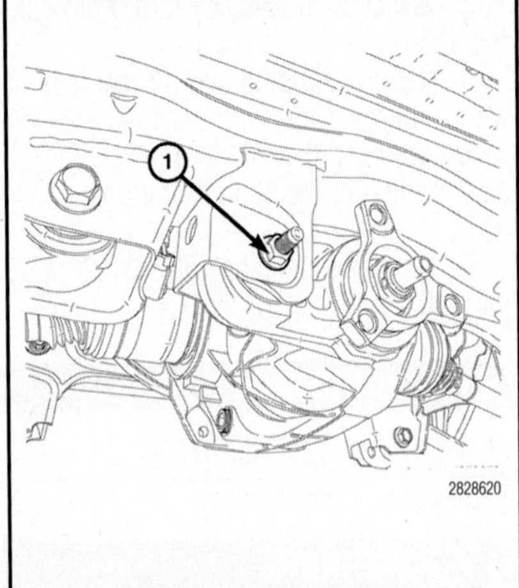

Fig. 32 Remove rear axle forward mount isolator bolt/nut (1)

To install:

24. When installing the halfshafts, use axle seal protector

➡Use care when installing halfshaft to axle assembly. The halfshaft installation angle should be minimized to avoid damage to seal upon installation.

25. Raise axle just enough to install the left halfshaft. Use caution to protect axle seal and journal. Verify proper installation by pulling outward on joint by hand.
26. Carefully raise rear axle.
27. Install two rear axle-to-crossmember bolts and torque to 100 ft. lbs. (135 Nm).
28. Install rear axle forward mount isolator bolt/nut and torque to 100 ft. lbs. (135 Nm).
29. Install axle vent tube.
30. Using axle seal protector, carefully install the right halfshaft into the axle assembly. Use caution to protect axle seal and journal.
31. Install the halfshaft into the hub.
32. Swing rear knuckle into position.
33. Install the camber link nut and bolt.
34. Install the tension link nut and bolt.
35. Install the toe link nut and bolt.
36. Install the wheel speed sensor and secure with bolt.
37. Install the halfshaft nut and torque to 229 ft. lbs. (310 Nm).
38. Install the rear caliper.
39. Align propeller shaft index marks and start propeller shaft coupler-to-axle bolt/nuts by hand. Then, torque to 43 ft. lbs. (58 Nm)..
40. Install rear exhaust system and torque nuts to specification.
41. Remove fill plug) and fill rear axle with 0.95 qts. (0.9 L) Mopar Gear and Axle Lubricant 75W–85 and insure axle is filled to the bottom of the fill hole.
42. Install fill plug and tighten to 26 ft. lbs. (35 Nm).
43. Pump brake pedal until caliper pistons and brake pads are seated and a firm brake pedal is obtained.

REAR HALFSHAFT

REMOVAL & INSTALLATION

See Figures 30, 31 and 34.

1. Remove the rear caliper and secure.
2. Remove the halfshaft nut.
3. Remove the wheel speed sensor bolt and remove the speed sensor.
4. Remove the toe link nut and bolt
5. Remove the tension link nut and bolt.
6. Remove the camber link nut and bolt.
7. Swing rear knuckle outward as shown.
8. Remove the halfshaft from the hub.

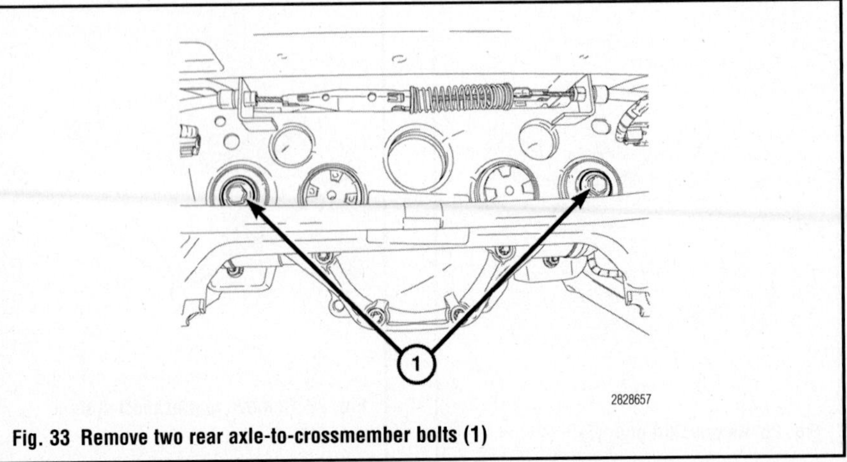

Fig. 33 Remove two rear axle-to-crossmember bolts (1)

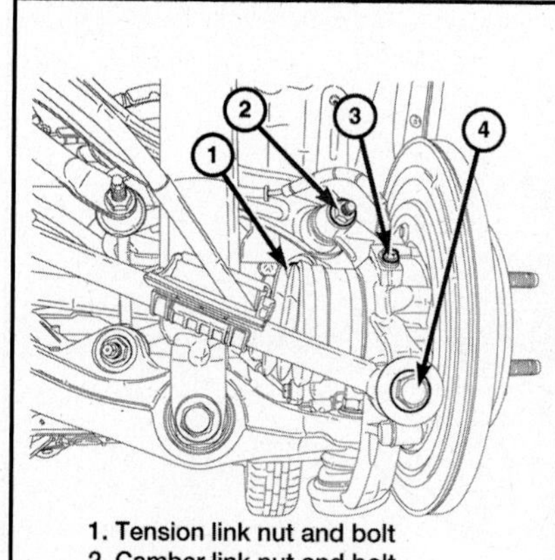

Fig. 34 Remove the wheel speed sensor bolt and remove the speed sensor

9. Using a hammer or similar tool as a pivot point and a suitable screwdriver, or using the grove on the outer can of the CV joint, carefully disengage both halfshafts from axle assembly using care not to damage dust seal.

10. Carefully remove the halfshaft from the axle assembly. Use caution to protect axle seal and journal.

To install:

11. When installing the halfshafts, use axle seal protector

➡Use care when installing halfshaft to axle assembly. The halfshaft installation angle should be minimized to avoid damage to seal upon installation.

12. Raise axle just enough to install the left halfshaft. Use caution to protect axle seal and journal. Verify proper installation by pulling outward on joint by hand.

13. Carefully raise rear axle.

14. Install two rear axle-to-crossmember bolts and torque to 100 ft. lbs. (135 Nm).

15. Install rear axle forward mount isolator bolt/nut and torque to 100 ft. lbs. (135 Nm).

16. Install axle vent tube.

17. Using axle seal protector, carefully install the right halfshaft into the axle assembly. Use caution to protect axle seal and journal.

18. Install the halfshaft into the hub.

19. Swing rear knuckle into position.

20. Install the camber link nut and bolt.

21. Install the tension link nut and bolt.

22. Install the toe link nut and bolt.

23. Install the wheel speed sensor and secure with bolt.

24. Install the halfshaft nut and torque to 229 ft. lbs. (310 Nm).

25. Install the rear caliper.

REAR PINION SEAL

REMOVAL & INSTALLATION

See Figures 35 through 39.

1. Remove rear axle assembly from vehicle.

➡Torque reading must be taken with a constant rotational speed. Do not measure break away torque.

2. Using a torque wrench, measure and record the pinion rotational torque.

➡Due to axle imbalance concerns, it is necessary to make sure pinion nut-to-shaft orientation is maintained. If alignment marks are not visible, apply appropriate marks before removing pinion nut.

3. Apply an alignment mark on the pinion flange nut to the pinion shaft.

4. Using Flange Wrench and 32mm socket, loosen the pinion flange nut.

➡Due to axle imbalance concerns, it is necessary to make sure pinion flange-to-shaft orientation is maintained. If alignment marks are not visible, apply appropriate marks before removing pinion flange.

5. Apply an alignment mark on the pinion flange to the pinion shaft.

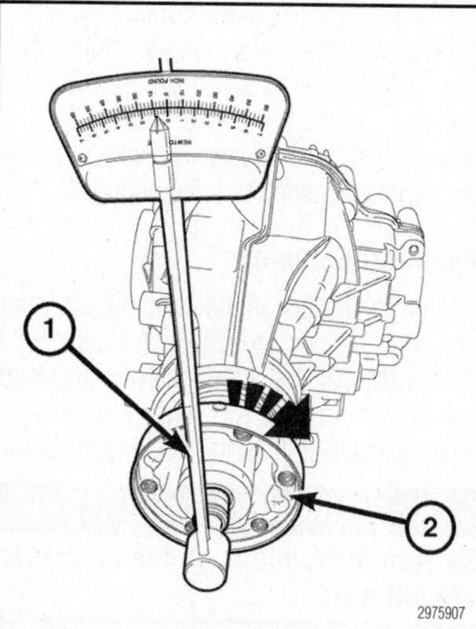

Fig. 35 Using a torque wrench (1), measure and record the pinion rotational torque

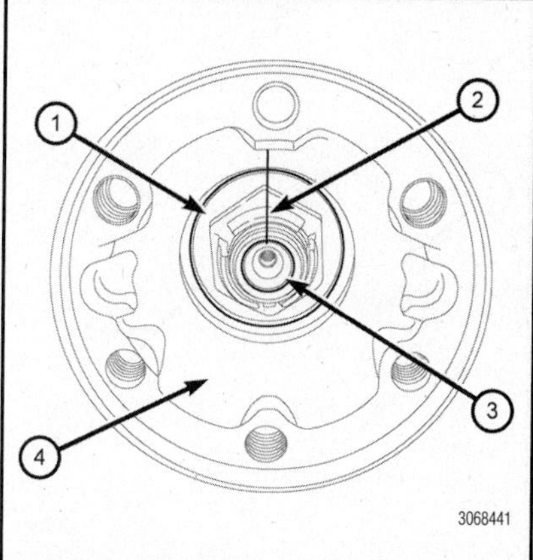

Fig. 36 Apply an alignment mark (2) on the pinion flange nut (1) to the pinion shaft (3)

6. Using Puller, remove pinion flange from pinion shaft.

7. Using seal remover and slide hammer, remove pinion seal and discard.

To install:

8. Apply light coating of gear lubricant to the lip of the pinion seal.

9. Using Driver Handle and Installer, install pinion seal until tool bottoms on carrier.

10. Install pinion flange into position. Align index marks between pinion flange and pinion stem to maintain assembly balance and so that bearing preload is not exceeded.

11. Using Installer, lightly tap on pinion flange until adequate pinion shaft threads are exposed.

12. Clean any thread locker from pinion flange nut and apply Mopar Lock and Seal Adhesive to the nut.

13. Install pinion flange nut. Apply 75W–85 gear oil to pinion nut washer face prior to assembly. Using Flange Wrench and 32mm socket tighten pinion flange nut

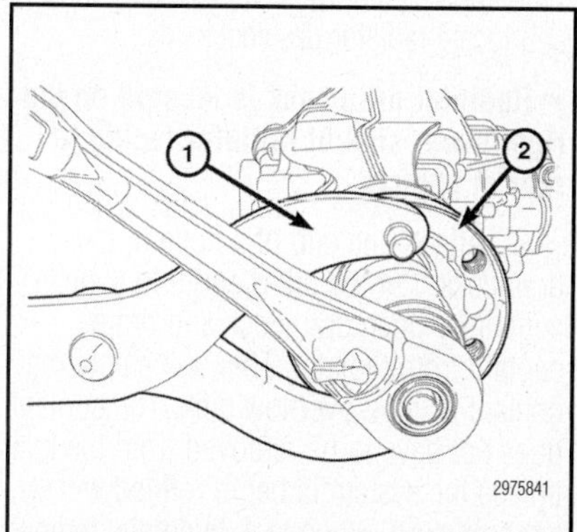

Fig. 37 Using Flange Wrench (1) and 32mm socket, loosen the pinion flange (2) nut

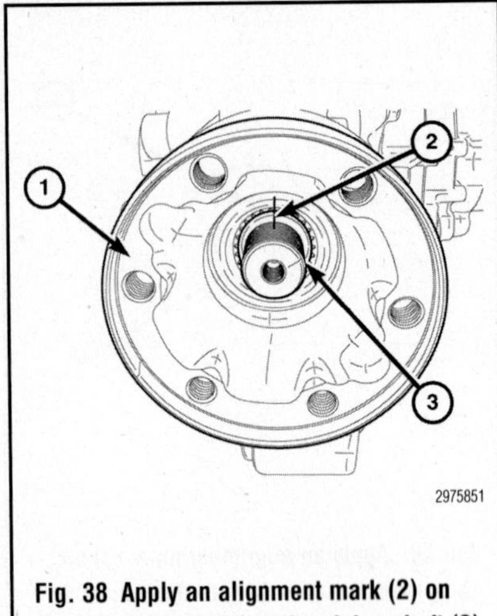

Fig. 38 Apply an alignment mark (2) on the pinion flange (1) to the pinion shaft (3)

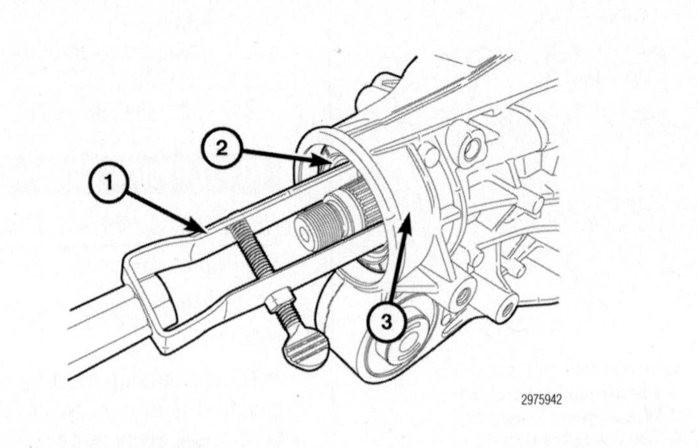

Fig. 39 Using seal remover (1) and slide hammer, remove pinion seal (2); differential (3)

in small increments until the pinion nut index mark aligns with the index marking on the pinion stem.

➡**If pinion nut index mark exceeds the pinion stem index mark the unit must be discarded. If the pinion nut index mark falls short of the pinion stem index mark the unit will possibly generate an NVH concern.**

➡**Torque reading must be taken with a constant rotational speed. Do not measure break away torque.**

14. Using a torque wrench, measure and record the pinion rotational torque.

15. After torque reading has been obtained, compare reading to the recorded reading when removing the pinion flange. The difference between the initial and final measurement will be the new seals drag torque only.

16. Install axle assembly.

ENGINE COOLING

ENGINE COOLANT

DRAIN & REFILL PROCEDURE

CAUTION

Do not remove the cylinder block drain plugs or loosen the radiator draincock with system hot and under pressure. Serious burns from coolant can occur.

1. DO NOT remove radiator cap first. With engine cold, raise vehicle on a hoist and locate radiator draincock.

➡**Radiator draincock is located on the right/lower side of radiator facing to rear of vehicle.**

2. Attach one end of a hose to the draincock. Put the other end into a clean container. Open draincock and drain coolant from radiator. This will empty the coolant reserve/overflow tank. The coolant does not have to be removed from the tank unless the system is being refilled with a fresh mixture. When tank is empty, remove radiator cap and continue draining cooling system.

FLUSHING

WARNING

The cooling system normally operates at 14–18 psi (97–124 kPa) pressure. Exceeding this pressure may damage the radiator or hoses.

Reverse flushing of the cooling system is the forcing of water through the cooling system. This is done using air pressure in the opposite direction of normal coolant flow. It is usually only necessary with very dirty systems with evidence of partial plugging.

Chemical Cleaning

If visual inspection indicates the formation of sludge or scaly deposits, use a radiator cleaner (Mopar Radiator Kleen or equivalent) before flushing. This will soften scale and other deposits and aid the flushing operation.

WARNING

Be sure instructions on the container are followed.

Reverse Flushing Radiator

1. Disconnect the radiator hoses from the radiator fittings.
2. Attach a section of radiator hose to the radiator bottom outlet fitting and insert the flushing gun.
3. Connect a water supply hose and air supply hose to the flushing gun.

WARNING

The cooling system normally operates at 14–18 psi (97–124 kPa) pressure. Exceeding this pressure may damage the radiator or hoses.

4. Allow the radiator to fill with water.
5. When radiator is filled, apply air in short blasts allowing radiator to refill between blasts.
6. Continue this reverse flushing until clean water flows out through rear of radiator cooling tube passages.
7. Have radiator cleaned more extensively by a radiator repair shop.

Reverse Flushing Engine

1. Drain the cooling system.
2. Remove the thermostat housing and thermostat.
3. Install the thermostat housing.
4. Disconnect the radiator upper hose from the radiator and attach the flushing gun to the hose.

5. Disconnect the radiator lower hose from the water pump.
6. Attach a lead away hose to the water pump inlet fitting.

**** WARNING**

Be sure that the heater control valve is closed (heat off). This is done to prevent coolant flow with scale and other deposits from entering the heater core.

7. Connect the water supply hose and air supply hose to the flushing gun.
8. Allow the engine to fill with water.
9. When the engine is filled, apply air in short blasts, allowing the system to fill between air blasts.
10. Continue until clean water flows through the lead away hose.
11. Remove the lead away hose, flushing gun, water supply hose and air supply hose.
12. Remove the thermostat housing.
13. Install the thermostat and housing with a replacement gasket.
14. Connect the radiator hoses.
15. Refill the cooling system with the correct antifreeze/water mixture.

ENGINE FAN

REMOVAL & INSTALLATION

See Figures 40 and 41.

**** WARNING**

Care must be used when trying to remove the upper and lower shroud covers. Damaging the holes in the cover may cause it to become loose and not perform properly.

1. Disconnect negative battery cable.
2. Remove the air intake assembly.
3. Raise vehicle.

➡The lower shroud cover needs to be removed in order to remove the cooling fan assembly from the mounting tabs.

4. If equipped, remove the lower engine shield.
5. Remove the lower shroud cover by using a pick to pull the cover retaining hole away from the clip along the bottom of the cooling fan assembly.
6. Lower vehicle.
7. Disconnect electric fan connector.

➡The cooling fan assembly is held in place by clips that are part of the radiator. So care must be used so the clips are not damaged during fan removal.

8. Remove shroud assembly from vehicle by pressing the locking clips inwards with a flat blade screwdriver.
9. Pull the fan/shroud assembly upwards and away from the radiator with the upper cooling fan assembly shroud cover in place.
10. Remove the cooling fan assembly from vehicle.

To install:

11. Install cooling fan assembly into vehicle.
12. Guide the fan/shroud cover assembly into position between the radiator and upper core support.
13. Position cooling fan assembly onto the mounts located on the radiator.
14. Lock in the fan assembly into place by pressing down firmly on the shroud till the locks engage.
15. Connect electric fan electrical connector.
16. Raise the vehicle.
17. Install the lower cooling shroud cover by applying upwards pressure till the cover snaps into place onto the cooling fan shroud.
18. If equipped, install the lower engine cover.
19. Lower vehicle.
20. Connect negative battery cable.
21. Install the air intake assembly.
22. Start engine and check fan operation.

RADIATOR

REMOVAL & INSTALLATION

See Figures 42 and 43.

**** CAUTION**

Do not remove the cylinder block drain plugs or loosen the radiator draincock with the system hot and under pressure. Serious burns from coolant can occur. Refer to cooling system draining.

➡Do not waste reusable coolant. If the solution is clean, drain the coolant into a clean container for reuse.

**** CAUTION**

Constant tension hose clamps are used on most cooling system hoses. When removing or installing, use only tools designed for servicing this type of clamp. Always wear safety glasses when servicing constant tension clamps.

**** WARNING**

A number or letter is stamped into the tongue of constant tension clamps. If replacement is necessary, use only an original equipment clamp with matching number or letter.

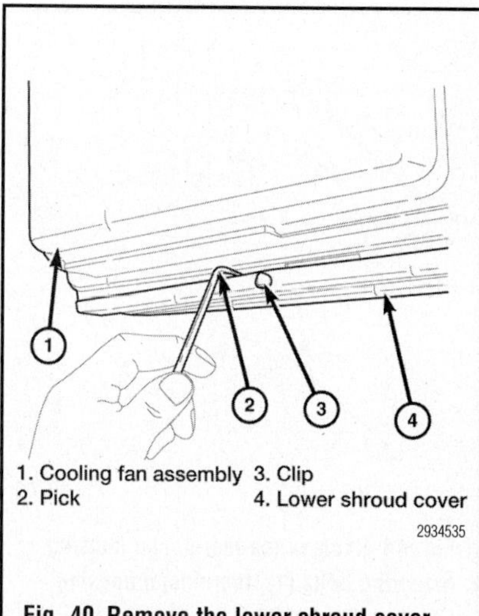

Fig. 40 Remove the lower shroud cover

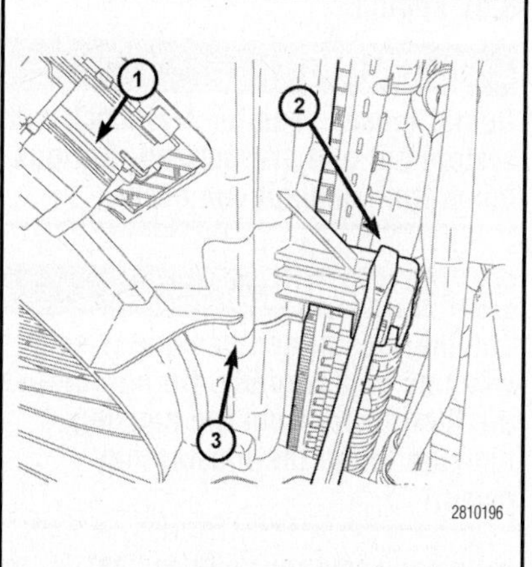

Fig. 41 Disconnect electric fan connector (1); shroud assembly (3) and clips (2)

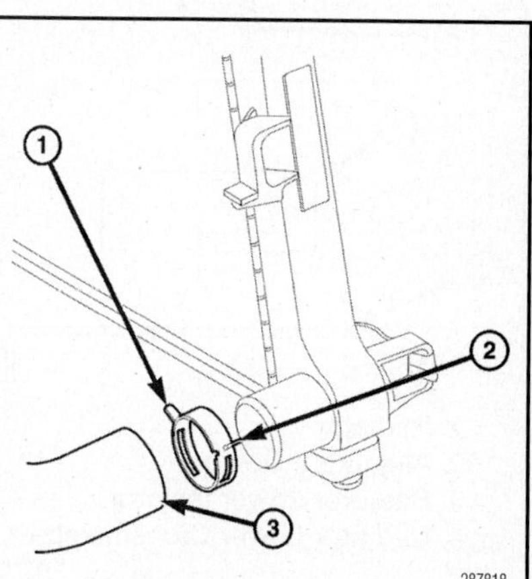

Fig. 42 A number or letter is stamped into the tongue (2) of constant tension clamps (1); radiator hose (3)

⁂ WARNING

When removing the radiator or A/C condenser for any reason, note the location of all radiator-to-body and radiator-to-A/C condenser rubber air seals. These are used at the top, bottom and sides of the radiator and A/C condenser. To prevent overheating, these seals must be installed to their original positions.

1. Disconnect the negative battery cable at battery.
2. Drain coolant from radiator.
3. Remove the A/C condenser.
4. Remove the upper radiator crossmember.
5. Disconnect the upper radiator hose.
6. Disconnect the overflow hose from radiator.
7. Remove the cooling fan assembly.
8. Remove the lower radiator hose from the water pump.
9. The lower part of the radiator is equipped with two alignment dowel pins and fit into rubber grommets. These rubber grommets are pressed onto the radiator.
10. Gently lift up and remove radiator from vehicle. Be careful not to scrape the radiator fins against any other component.
11. Remove the lower radiator hose from the radiator.

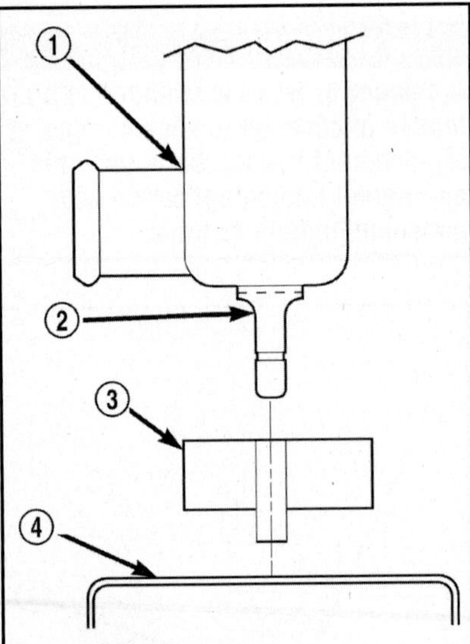

Fig. 43 Guide the two radiator rubber air seals into the lower radiator support

To install:

⁂ WARNING

Before installing the radiator or A/C condenser, be sure the radiator-to-body and radiator-to-A/C condenser rubber air seals are properly fastened to their original positions. These are used at the top, bottom and sides of the radiator and A/C condenser. To prevent overheating, these seals must be installed to their original positions.

12. Gently lower the radiator into the vehicle.
13. Guide the two radiator rubber air seals into the lower radiator support.

⁂ WARNING

The tangs on the hose clamps must be positioned straight down.

14. Install the lower radiator hose to the lower radiator outlet.
15. Install the cooling fan assembly.
16. Install coolant reserve/overflow tank hose at radiator.
17. Install the upper radiator hose.
18. Install the upper radiator crossmember. Align the upper radiator alignment dowel into the upper isolators.
19. Install the A/C condenser.
20. Refill cooling system.
21. Refill the power steering reservoir and bleed air from system.
22. Connect battery cable at battery.
23. Start and warm engine. Check for leaks.

THERMOSTAT

REMOVAL & INSTALLATION

3.6L Engine

⁂ CAUTION

Do not loosen radiator draincock with system hot and pressurized. Serious burns from coolant can occur.

⁂ WARNING

The thermostat and housing is serviced as an assembly. Do not remove the thermostat from the housing, damage to the thermostat may occur.

➡Do not waste reusable coolant. If solution is clean, drain coolant into a clean container for reuse.

➡If thermostat is being replaced, be sure that replacement is specified thermostat for vehicle model and engine type.

1. Disconnect negative battery cable at battery.
2. Remove the air intake assembly.
3. Drain cooling system.
4. Remove upper radiator hose clamp and upper radiator hose at thermostat housing.
5. Remove thermostat housing mounting bolts, thermostat housing and thermostat.

To install:

6. Clean mating areas of timing chain cover and thermostat housing.
7. Install a new gasket on to the thermostat housing.
8. Position thermostat housing on the water crossover.
9. Install two thermostat housing bolts. Tighten bolts to 106 inch lbs. (12 Nm).
10. Install upper radiator hose on thermostat housing.
11. Fill cooling system.
12. Install the air intake system.
13. Connect negative battery cable to battery.
14. Start and warm the engine. Check for leaks.

5.7L Engine

See Figure 44.

⁂ CAUTION

Do not loosen the radiator draincock with the cooling system hot and pressurized. Serious burns from the coolant can occur.

➡Do not waste reusable coolant. If the solution is clean, drain the coolant into a clean container for reuse.

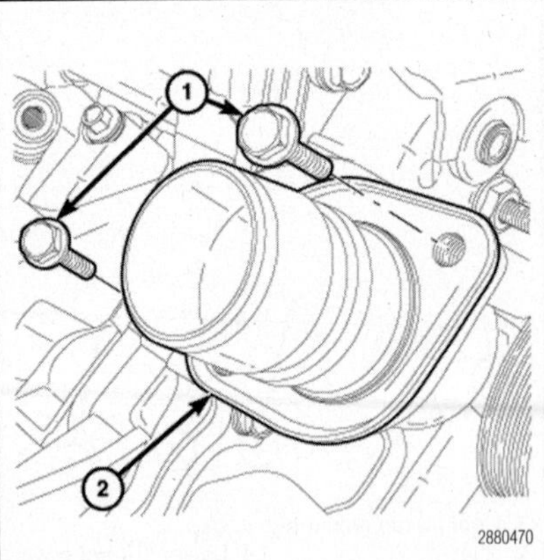

Fig. 44 Remove the thermostat housing mounting bolts (1), thermostat housing (2), and thermostat

➡**If the thermostat is being replaced, be sure that the replacement is the specified thermostat for the vehicle model and engine type.**

1. Disconnect the negative battery cable.
2. Remove the air intake system.
3. Partially drain the cooling system.
4. Remove the upper radiator hose at the thermostat housing and position aside.
5. Remove the thermostat housing mounting bolts, thermostat housing, and thermostat.

To install:

6. Position the thermostat and housing on the front cover.
7. Install thermostat housing bolts. Tighten the bolts to 10 ft. lbs. (13 Nm).
8. Install the radiator hose onto the thermostat housing.
9. Fill the cooling system.
10. Connect negative battery cable.
11. Install the air intake system.
12. Start and warm the engine. Check for leaks.

WATER PUMP

REMOVAL & INSTALLATION

3.6L Engine

See Figures 45 through 47.

➡**The water pump on 3.6L engines is bolted directly to the engine timing chain case cover.**

1. Disconnect negative battery cable from battery.
2. Disconnect the intake air temperature sensor.
3. Loosen the clamps. Remove the air intake hose and resonator assembly.
4. Drain the cooling system.
5. Remove the accessory drive belt.

**** CAUTION**

Constant tension hose clamps are used on most cooling system hoses. When removing or installing, use only tools designed for servicing this type of clamp. Always wear safety glasses when servicing constant tension clamps.

➡**A number or letter is stamped into the tongue of constant tension clamps. If replacement is necessary, use only an original equipment clamp with matching number or letter.**

6. Remove the lower heater hose at the water pump and position aside.
7. Remove the lower radiator hose from the water pump and position aside.
8. Remove idler pulley.
9. Remove the eleven water pump mounting bolts. Take notice to the four water pump bolts that bolt directly to the timing cover.

**** WARNING**

Do not pry on the water pump at the timing chain case/cover. The machined surfaces may be damaged resulting in leaks.

10. Remove water pump and seal.

To install:

11. Clean mating surfaces.

➡**Take notice the lengths of the mounting bolts. Some M6 bolts mount directly to the timing cover.**

12. Using a new gasket, position water pump and hand tighten the M6 mounting bolts.
13. Hand tighten the idler pulley bolt.
14. Hand tighten the upper M8 and M10 water pump to engine block mounting bolts.

➡**Tightening the water pump fasteners in sequential order, will insure proper sealing surface.**

15. Tighten the bolts in the sequence shown. Tighten the bolts to their respective torque:
    a. Tighten M6 mounting bolts to 9 ft. lbs. (12 Nm).
    b. Tighten M8 bolts to 18 ft. lbs. (25 Nm).
    c. Tighten M10 bolt to 41 ft. lbs. (55 Nm).
    d. Repeat the tightening sequence until the proper torque has been met.
16. Spin water pump to be sure that pump impeller does not rub against timing chain case/cover.

➡**A number or letter is stamped into the tongue of constant tension clamps. If replacement is necessary, use only an original equipment clamp with matching number or letter.**

17. Install the lower radiator hose.
18. Install the lower return heater hose.

**** WARNING**

When installing the serpentine accessory drive belt, belt must be routed correctly. If not, engine may overheat due to water pump rotating in wrong direction.

19. Install accessory drive belt.
20. Evacuate air and refill cooling system.

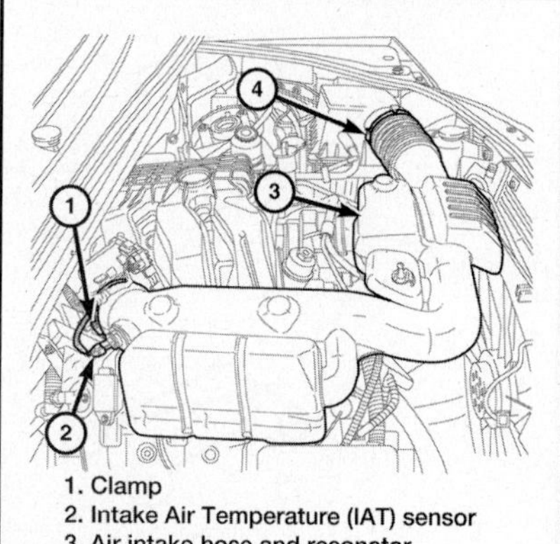

Fig. 45 Disconnect the intake air temperature sensor

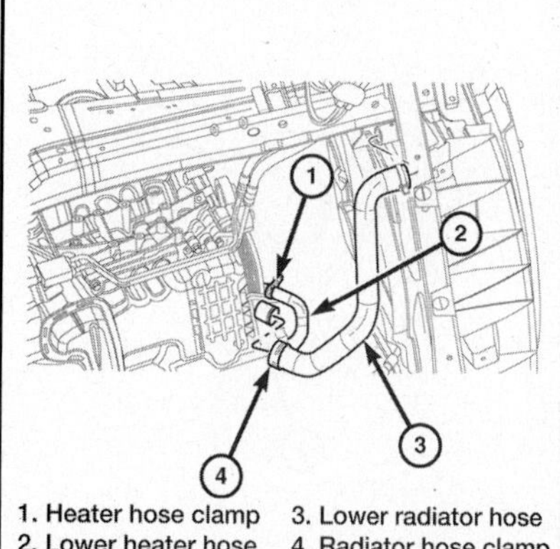

Fig. 46 Remove the lower heater hose at the water pump and position aside

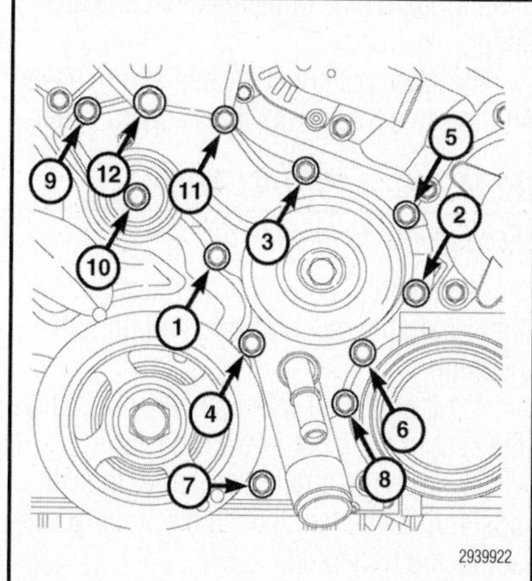

Fig. 47 Tighten the bolts in the sequence shown

21. Install the air intake hose and resonator assembly at the air filter housing.
22. Connect the intake air temperature sensor.
23. Connect negative battery cable.
24. Check the cooling system for leaks

5.7L Engine

See Figure 48.

1. Disconnect negative battery cable.
2. Remove the air intake assembly.
3. Remove the resonator mounting bracket.
4. Remove cooling fan assembly.
5. Drain coolant into a clean container.
6. Remove the upper radiator hose from the thermostat housing and position aside.
7. Remove serpentine belt.
8. Remove idler pulley.
9. Remove belt tensioner assembly.

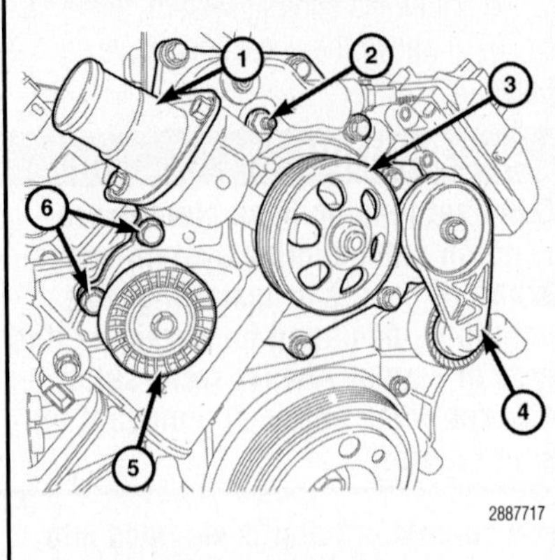

Fig. 48 Detailed view of the water pump assembly

10. Remove lower radiator hose from the water pump and position aside.
11. Remove the upper metal heater tube from the cylinder head.
12. Remove water pump mounting bolts and remove pump.

To install:

13. Clean mating surfaces and install water pump. Tighten mounting bolts to 18 ft. lbs. (24 Nm).
14. Install upper metal heater tube.
15. Install belt tensioner assembly.
16. Install idler pulley.
17. Install the lower radiator hose.
18. Install serpentine belt.
19. Install the resonator mounting bracket.
20. Install cooling fan assembly.
21. Install the upper radiator hose to the thermostat housing.
22. Install the air intake assembly.
23. Connect negative battery cable.
24. Evacuate air and refill cooling system.
25. Check cooling system for leaks

ENGINE ELECTRICAL

BATTERY SYSTEM

BATTERY

✱✱ WARNING

The Absorbent Glass Mat (AGM) battery should only be charged and tested with the Associated Battery Charger Battery Charger, Associated or Midtronics AGM Battery Tester/ Charger Station. Never test the AGM battery with a Midtronics Micro 420 battery tester.

The battery is located under the passenger seat. A breather line runs from the battery through the bottom of the recess well to the outside of the vehicle.

The battery negative cable is attached to the outboard side of the battery compartment.

The AGM battery is located and removed in the same manner as the standard batter.

REMOVAL & INSTALLATION

See Figures 49 through 52.

1. If equipped with power seats, move the seat to the most forward and upright position.
2. If equipped with manual seats, move the seat to the most forward position.
3. Turn the ignition switch to the Off position. Be certain that all electrical accessories are turned off.
4. Remove the battery cover.

➡Negative battery terminal shown, positive terminal similar.

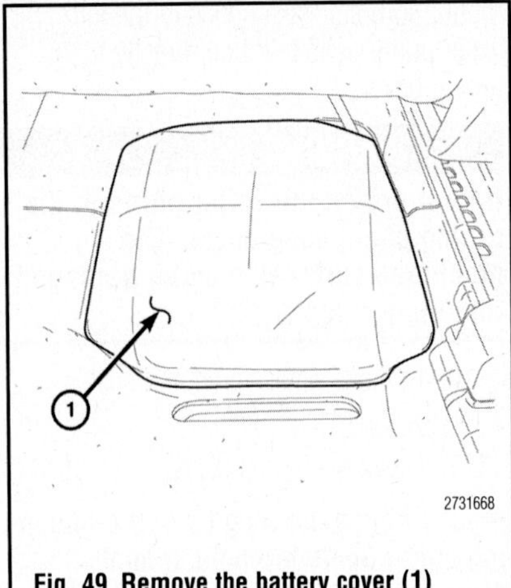

Fig. 49 Remove the battery cover (1)

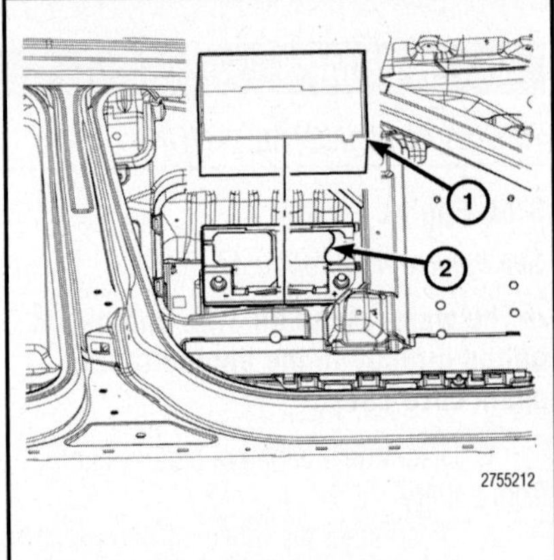

Fig. 51 Remove the battery thermal blanket (1) from the battery (2)

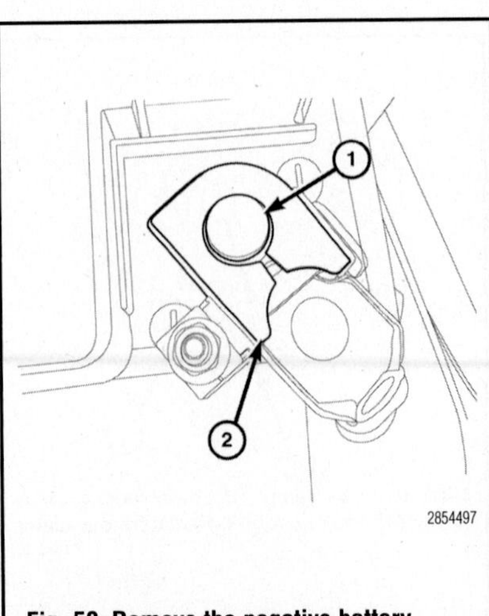

Fig. 50 Remove the negative battery cable (2) from the battery (1)

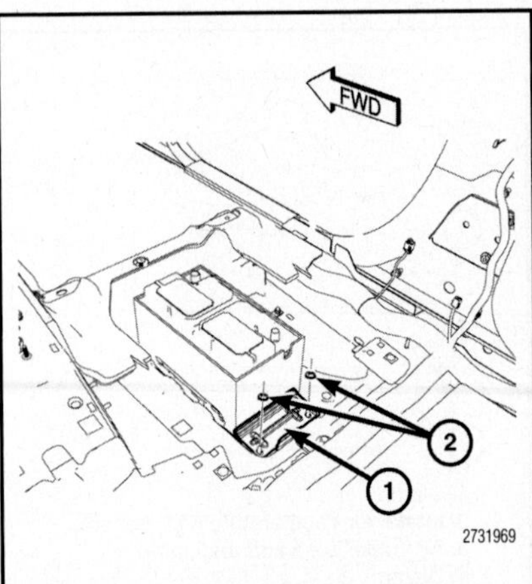

Fig. 52 Remove the battery hold down retainers (2) and remove the battery hold down (1)

5. Remove the negative battery cable from the battery.
6. Disconnect the positive battery cable and position aside.
7. Remove the battery thermal blanket.
8. Remove the battery hold down retainers and remove the battery hold down.

✲✲ CAUTION

Wear a suitable pair of rubber gloves when removing a battery by hand. Safety glasses should also be worn. If the battery is cracked or leaking, the electrolyte can burn the skin and eyes.

9. Remove the battery from the vehicle.

To install:

10. Install the battery into the vehicle.
11. Install the battery hold down into position and install the battery hold down retainers. Tighten to 15 ft. lbs. (20 Nm).
12. Install the battery thermal blanket.
13. Position back the positive battery cable and connect to the battery.
14. Position back the negative battery cable and connect to the battery.
15. Install the battery cover.
16. Move the seat back to its original position.

BATTERY RECONNECT/RELEARN PROCEDURE

✲✲ CAUTION

Never exceed 14.4 volts when charging the Absorbent Glass Mat (AGM) starter battery. Personal injury and/or battery damage may result.

Vehicles equipped with the AGM starter battery utilize a unique absorbent glass mat battery design. This battery has a maximum charging voltage that must not be exceeded in order to restore the battery to its full potential, failure to use the following AGM battery charging procedure could result in damage to the battery or personal injury.

Battery charging is the means by which the battery can be restored to its full voltage potential. A battery is fully-charged when:

- Midtronics tester indicates battery is OK.
- Open-circuit voltage of the battery is 12.65 volts or above.
- Battery passes Load Test multiple times.

✲✲ CAUTION

If the battery shows signs of freezing, leaking, loose posts or low electrolyte level, do not test, assist-boost, or charge. The battery may arc internally and explode. Personal injury and/or vehicle damage may result.

✲✲ CAUTION

Explosive hydrogen gas forms in and around the battery. Do not smoke, use flame, or create sparks near the battery. Personal injury and/or vehicle damage may result.

✲✲ CAUTION

The battery contains corrosive materials. Avoid contact with the skin, eyes, or clothing. In the event of contact, flush with water and call a physician immediately. Keep out of the reach of children.

✲✲ WARNING

Always disconnect and isolate the battery negative cable before charging a battery. Charge the battery directly at the battery terminals. Do not exceed 14.4 volts while charging a battery.

✲✲ WARNING

The battery should not be hot to the touch. If the battery feels hot to the touch, turn off the charger and let the battery cool before continuing the charging operation. Damage to the battery may result.

1. After the battery has been charged to 12.6 volts or greater, perform a load test to determine the battery cranking capacity. If the battery passes a load test, return the battery to service. If the battery fails a load test, it is faulty and must be replaced.
2. Clean and inspect the battery hold downs, well, terminals, posts, and top before completing battery service.

Charging A Completely Discharged Battery

✲✲ CAUTION

Never exceed 14.4 volts when charging the Absorbent Glass Mat (AGM) starter battery. Personal injury and/or battery damage may result. The following procedure should be used to recharge a completely discharged battery. Unless this procedure is properly followed, a good battery may be needlessly replaced.

1. Measure the voltage at the battery posts with a voltmeter, accurate to 1/10 (0.10) volt. Refer to Battery Removal and Installation for access instructions. If the reading is below ten volts, the battery charging current will be low. It could take several hours before the battery accepts a current greater than a few milliamperes. Such low current may not be detectable on the ammeters built into many battery chargers.
2. Disconnect and isolate the battery negative cable. Connect the Midtronics

➡Some battery chargers are equipped with polarity-sensing circuitry. This circuitry protects the battery charger and the battery from being damaged if they are improperly connected. If the battery state-of-charge is too low for the polarity-sensing circuitry to detect, the battery charger will not operate. This makes it appear that the battery will not accept charging current. See the instructions provided by the manufacturer of the battery charger for details on how to bypass the polarity-sensing circuitry.

3. Battery chargers vary in the amount of voltage and current they provide. The amount of time required for a battery to accept measurable charging current at various voltages is shown in the Charge Rate Table. If the charging current is still not measurable at the end of the charging time, the battery is faulty and must be replaced. If the charging current is measurable during the charging time, the battery may be good and the charging should be completed in the normal manner.

ALTERNATOR

REMOVAL & INSTALLATION

3.6L Engine

See Figures 53 and 54.

1. Disconnect and isolate the negative battery cable
2. Unplug the field circuit from alternator.
3. Remove the B+ terminal nut and wire.
4. Remove the serpentine belt.
5. Remove the lower front alternator mounting retainer.
6. Remove the three mounting retainers.
7. Remove the alternator from the vehicle.

To install:

8. Install the alternator into the vehicle.
9. Install the three mounting retainers. Tighten to 18 ft. lbs. (25 Nm).
10. Install ground wire on mounting stud.
11. Install the lower front alternator mounting retainer. Tighten to 17 ft. lbs. (23 Nm).
12. Install the serpentine belt.

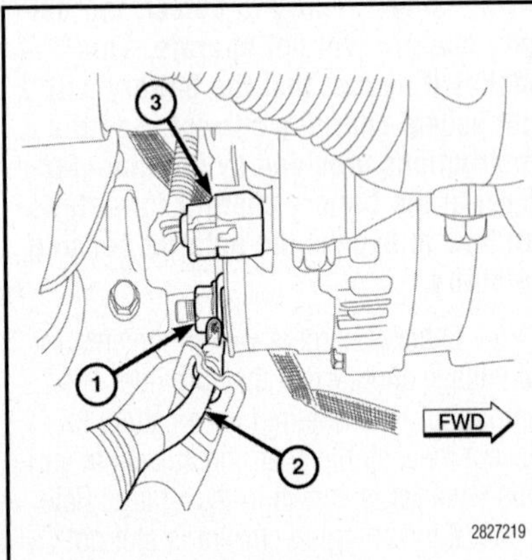

Fig. 53 Unplug the field circuit (3) from alternator; remove the B+ terminal nut (1) and wire (2)

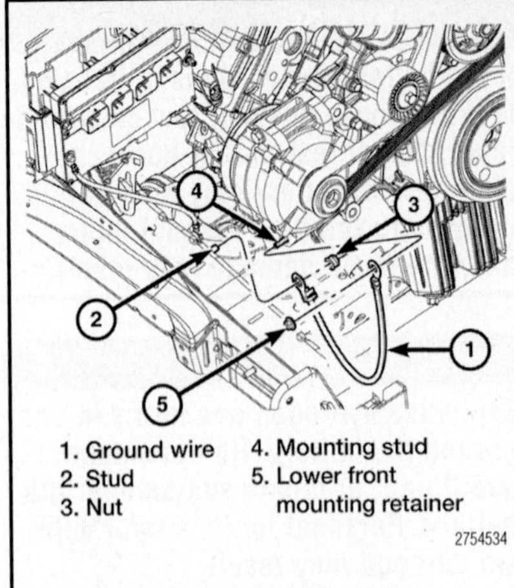

Fig. 54 Exploded view of alternator mountings

13. Install the B+ terminal to the alternator stud. Tighten to 97 inch lbs. (11 Nm).
14. Plug in the field circuit to the alternator.
15. Connect the negative battery cable.

5.7L Engine

See Figure 55.

✱✱ CAUTION

Disconnect the negative cable from the battery before removing the battery output wire (B+ wire) from the alternator. Failure to do so can result in injury or damage to the electrical system.

1. Disconnect and isolate the negative battery cable.
2. Remove the air cleaner body.
3. Remove the serpentine belt.
4. Unsnap the plastic insulator cap from the B+ output terminal.
5. Remove the B+ terminal mounting nut at the rear of the alternator. Disconnect the terminal from the alternator.
6. Disconnect the field wire connector at the rear of the alternator by pushing on the connector tab.
7. Remove two alternator mounting bolts.

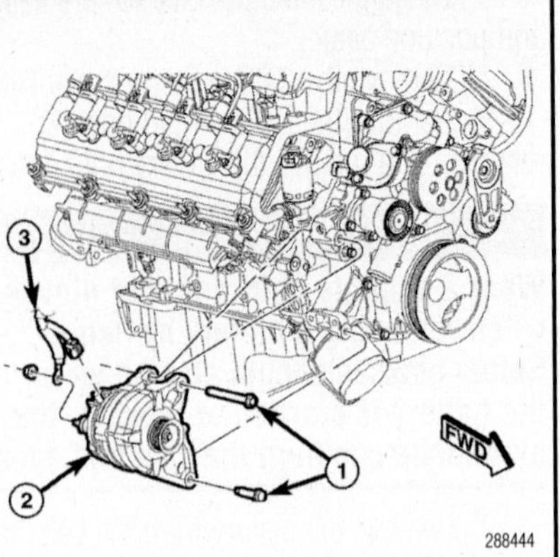

Fig. 55 Disconnect the field wire connector (3); remove two alternator mounting bolts (1) and the alternator (2)

8. Remove the alternator from vehicle.

To install:

9. Position the alternator to the engine and install the two mounting bolts. Torque the bolts to 30 ft. lbs. (41 Nm).
10. Snap the field wire connector into the rear of the alternator.
11. Install the B+ terminal eyelet to the alternator output stud. Tighten the mounting nut to 106 inch lbs. (12 Nm).

✱✱ WARNING

Never force a belt over a pulley rim using a screwdriver. The synthetic fiber of the belt can be damaged.

✱✱ WARNING

When installing a serpentine accessory drive belt, the belt must be routed correctly. The water pump may be rotating in the wrong direction if the belt is installed incorrectly, causing the engine to overheat.

12. Install the serpentine belt.
13. Install the air cleaner body.
14. Install the negative battery cable.

FIRING ORDER

The firing order for the 3.6L engine is: 1–2–3–4–5–6.

The firing order for the 5.7L engine is: 1–8–4–3–6–5–7–2.

IGNITION COIL

REMOVAL & INSTALLATION

3.6L Engine

See Figures 56 through 60.

1. Disconnect and isolate the negative battery cable.
2. If removing the ignition coils from cylinders 1 and 3 on the RH side of the engine, first remove the air inlet hose.
3. If removing the ignition coils from cylinders 2, 4, or 6 on the LH side of the engine, first remove the air inlet hose, upper intake manifold and insulator.

➡The LH ignition coils are shown, the RH ignition coils are similar.

4. Unlock and disconnect the electrical connector from the ignition coil.
5. Remove the ignition coil mounting bolt.
6. Pull the ignition coil from cylinder head cover opening with a slight twisting action.

To install:

7. Using compressed air, blow out any dirt or contaminants from around the top of spark plug.
8. Check the condition of the ignition coil rubber boot. Inspect the opening of the boot for any debris, tears or rips. Carefully remove any debris with a lint free cloth.

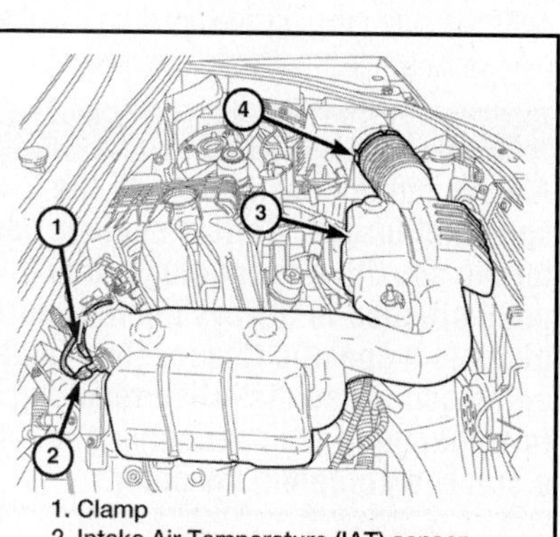

Fig. 56 If removing the ignition coils from cylinders 1 and 3 on the RH side of the engine, first remove the air inlet hose

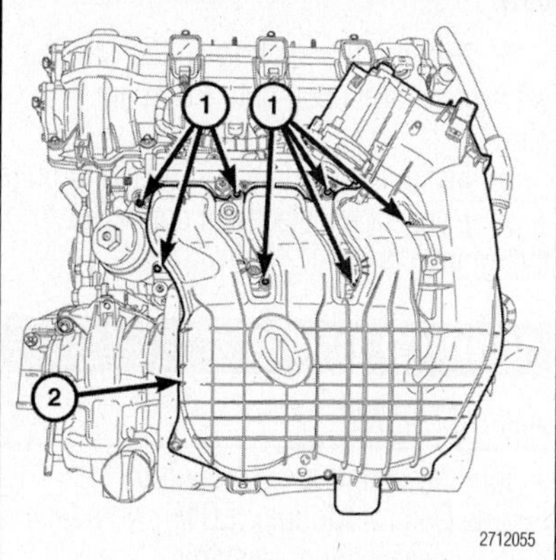

Fig. 57 If removing the ignition coils from cylinders 2, 4, or 6 on the LH side of the engine, first remove the air inlet hose, upper intake manifold (2) and insulator; retainers (1)

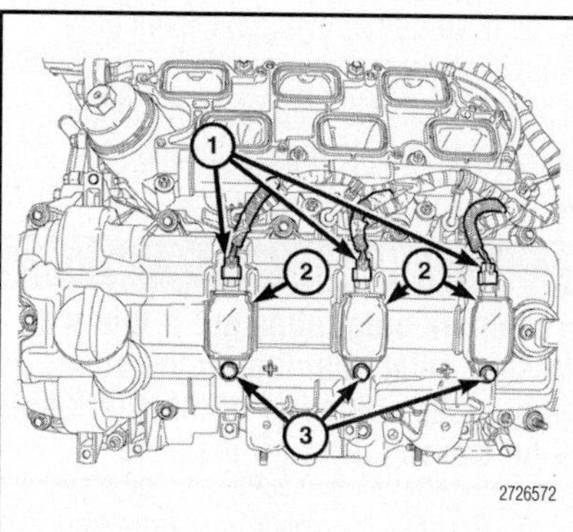

Fig. 58 Disconnect the ignition coil electrical connector (1); remove the ignition coil mounting bolt (3) and the ignition coil (2)

⁂ WARNING

Do not apply a silicone based grease such as Mopar Dielectric Grease to the ignition coil rubber boot. The silicone based grease will absorb into the boot causing it to stick and tear.

9. Place a small bead of Fluostar 2LF lubricant along the inside opening of the coil boot approximately 1 to 2 mm from the chamfer edge but not on the chamfered surface.
10. Position the ignition coil into the cylinder head cover opening. Using a twisting action, push the ignition coil onto the spark plug.

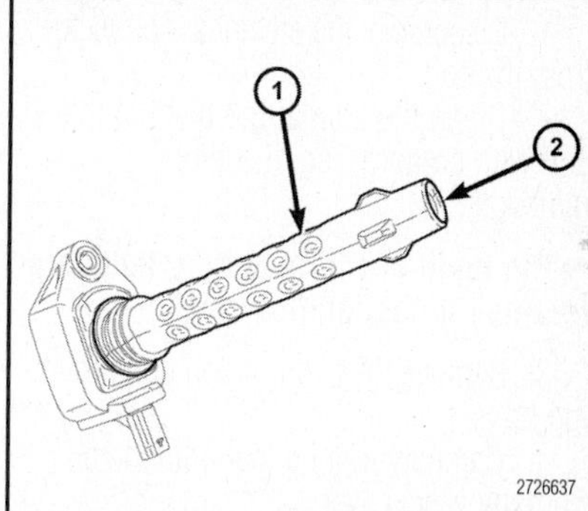

Fig. 59 Check the condition of the ignition coil rubber boot (1); inspect the opening of the boot (2) for any debris, tears or rips

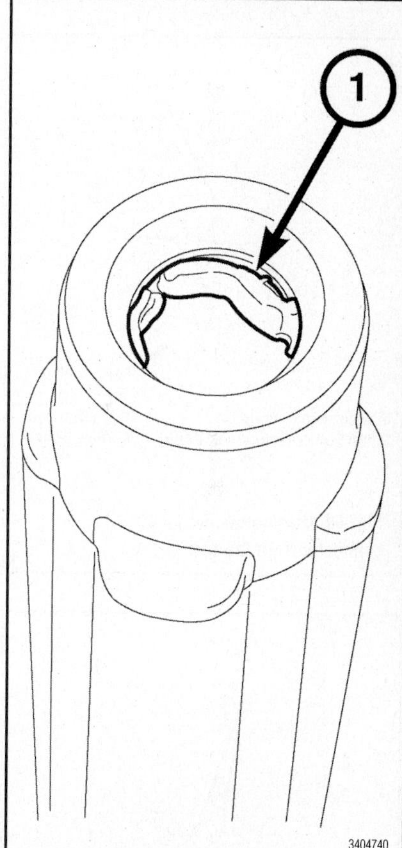

Fig. 60 Place a small bead of Fluostar 2LF lubricant (1) along the inside opening of the coil boot

11. Install the ignition coil mounting bolt.
12. Connect and lock the electrical connector to the ignition coil.
13. If removed, install the insulator, upper intake manifold and air inlet hose.
14. Connect the negative battery cable.

5.7L Engine

See Figures 61 and 62.

1. Disconnect the electrical connector from the coil.
2. Clean the area at the base of the coil with compressed air before removal.

➡The ignition coil mounting bolts are retained in the ignition coil.

3. Remove the two ignition coil mounting bolts.
4. Carefully pull up the ignition coil from the valve cover.
5. Remove ignition coil from vehicle.

To install:

6. Using compressed air, blow out any dirt or contaminants from around the top of the spark plug.

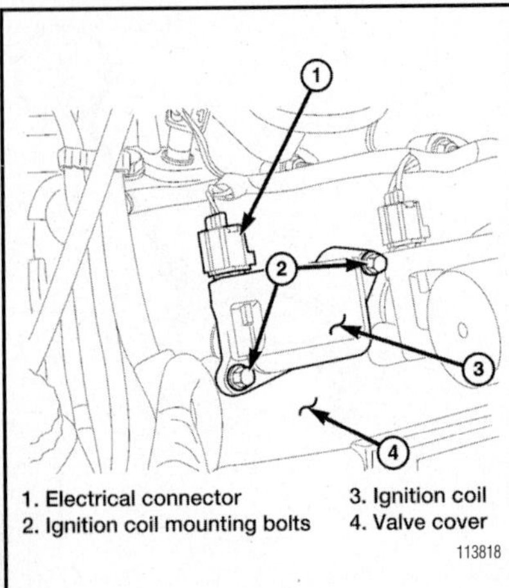

Fig. 61 Disconnect the electrical connector from the coil

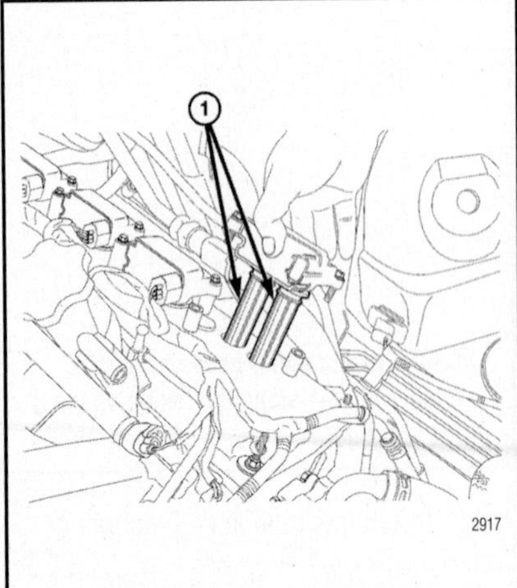

Fig. 62 Carefully pull up the ignition coil (1) from the valve cover

➡Use dielectric grease on each of the spark plug boots before installing the coil.

7. Position the ignition coil(s) into the valve cover and push onto the spark plug(s).
8. Install the ignition coil retaining bolts.
9. Connect the electrical connector to the ignition coil.

IGNITION TIMING

ADJUSTMENT

Ignition timing is controlled by the Engine Control Module (ECM). No adjustment is necessary or possible.

SPARK PLUGS

REMOVAL & INSTALLATION

3.6L Engine

1. Remove the ignition coil.
2. Prior to removing the spark plug, spray compressed air into the cylinder head opening. This will help prevent foreign material from entering combustion chamber.

**** WARNING**

The spark plug tubes are a thin wall design. Avoid damaging the spark plug tubes. Damage to the spark plug tube can result in oil leaks.

3. Remove the spark plug from the cylinder head using a quality thin wall socket with a rubber or foam insert.
4. Inspect the spark plug condition.

To install:

5. Check and adjust the spark plug gap with a gap gauging tool.

**** WARNING**

Special care should be taken when installing spark plugs into the cylinder head spark plug wells. Be sure the plugs do not drop into the plug wells as electrodes can be damaged.

**** WARNING**

The spark plug tubes are a thin wall design. Avoid damaging the spark plug tubes. Damage to the spark plug tube can result in oil leaks.

6. Start the spark plug into the cylinder head by hand to avoid cross threading.

**** WARNING**

Spark plug torque is critical and must not exceed the specified value. Overtightening stretches the spark plug shell reducing its heat transfer capability resulting in possible catastrophic engine failure.

7. Tighten the spark plugs to 13 ft. lbs. (17.5 Nm).
8. Install the ignition coil.

5.7L Engine

1. Remove the necessary air filter tubing and air intake components at the top of the engine and at the throttle body.
2. Prior to removing the ignition coil, spray compressed air around coil base at the cylinder head.
3. Remove the ignition coil.
4. Prior to removing the spark plug, spray compressed air into the cylinder head opening.
5. Remove the spark plug from the cylinder head using a quality socket with a rubber or foam insert.
6. Inspect spark plug condition.

To install:

➡Do not attempt to clean any of the spark plugs. Replace only.

7. To aid in the coil installation, apply silicone based grease such as Mopar Dielectric Grease into the spark plug end of the ignition coil rubber boots. Also apply this grease to the tops of spark plugs.
8. Check and adjust the spark plug gap with a gap gauging tool.
9. Start the spark plug into the cylinder head by hand to avoid cross threading. Special care should be taken when installing spark plugs into the cylinder head spark plug wells. Be sure the plugs do not drop into the plug wells as electrodes can be damaged.

**** WARNING**

Always tighten spark plugs to the specified torque. Certain engines use torque sensitive spark plugs. It is a good practice to always tighten spark plugs to a specific torque. Over tightening can cause distortion resulting in a change in the spark plug gap, or a cracked porcelain insulator.

10. Install the ignition coil.
11. Install necessary air filter tubing and air intake components to the top of the engine and to the throttle body.

ENGINE ELECTRICAL

STARTER

REMOVAL & INSTALLATION

3.6L Engine RWD

1. Disconnect and isolate the negative battery cable.
2. Remove the driver side engine mount and engine mount bracket.
3. Remove the battery positive cable wire harness connector eyelet from solenoid battery terminal stud.
4. Disconnect the solenoid wire from the starter motor.
5. Remove the two mounting bolts.
6. Remove the starter motor.

To install:

7. Position the starter motor to the engine.
8. Install and tighten both mounting bolts. Torque the bolts to 50 ft. lbs. (68 Nm).
9. Connect the solenoid wire to the starter motor.
10. Position the battery cable to the solenoid stud. Install and tighten battery cable eyelet nut. Torque the nut to 19 ft. lbs. (25 Nm).
11. Install the driver side engine mount.
12. Connect the negative battery cable.

3.6L Engine 4WD

1. Disconnect and isolate the negative battery cable.
2. Remove the front axle.
3. Remove the driver side engine mount and engine mount bracket.
4. Remove the battery positive cable wire harness connector eyelet from solenoid battery terminal stud.
5. Disconnect the solenoid wire from the starter motor.
6. Remove two mounting bolts.
7. Remove the starter motor.

To install:

8. Position the starter motor to the engine.
9. Install and tighten both mounting bolts. Torque the bolts to 50 ft. lbs. (68 Nm).
10. Connect the solenoid wire to starter motor.
11. Position the battery cable to the solenoid stud. Install and tighten battery cable eyelet nut. Torque the nut to 19 ft. lbs. (25 Nm).
12. Install the driver side engine mount.
13. Install the front axle.
14. Connect the negative battery cable.

5.7L Engine

1. Disconnect and isolate the negative battery cable.
2. Raise and support the vehicle.

➡If equipped with 4WD and certain transmissions, a support bracket is used between front axle and side of transmission. Remove 2 support bracket bolts at transmission. Pry support bracket slightly to gain access to lower starter mounting bolt.

3. Remove the two mounting bolts.
4. Move the starter motor towards the front of vehicle far enough for the nose of the starter pinion housing to clear the housing. Always support the starter motor during this process, do not let the starter motor hang from the wire harness.
5. Tilt the nose downwards and lower the starter motor far enough to access and remove the nut that secures the battery positive cable wire harness connector eyelet to the solenoid battery terminal stud. Do not let the starter motor hang from the wire harness.
6. Remove the battery positive cable wire harness connector eyelet from solenoid battery terminal stud.
7. Disconnect the battery positive cable wire harness connector from the solenoid terminal connector receptacle.
8. Remove the starter motor.

To install:

9. Connect the solenoid wire to the starter motor (snaps on).
10. Position the battery cable to the solenoid stud. Install and tighten the battery cable eyelet nut. Torque nut to 19 ft. lbs. (25 Nm). Do not allow the starter motor to hang from the wire harness.
11. Position the starter motor to the engine.
12. If equipped with automatic transmission, slide cooler tube bracket into position.
13. Install and tighten both mounting bolts. Torque bolts to 50 ft. lbs. (68 Nm).
14. Lower the vehicle.
15. Connect the negative battery cable.

ENGINE MECHANICAL

➡Disconnecting the negative battery cable may interfere with the functions of the on board computer systems and may require the computer to undergo a relearning process, once the negative battery cable is reconnected.

ACCESSORY DRIVE BELTS

ACCESSORY BELT ROUTING

See Figures 63 through 65.

INSPECTION

When diagnosing serpentine drive belts, small cracks that run across ribbed surface of belt from rib to rib, are considered normal. These are not a reason to replace belt.

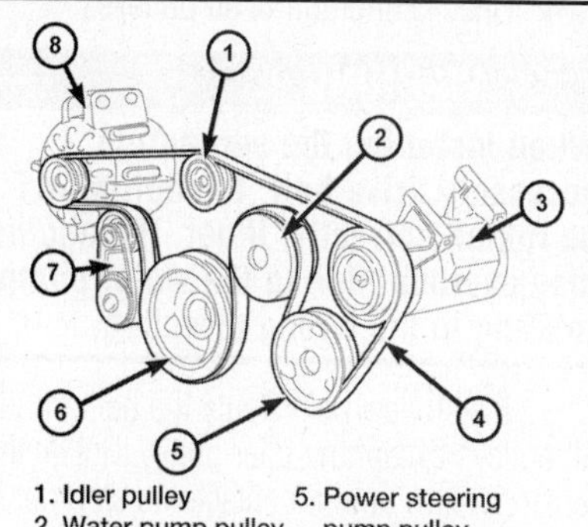

Fig. 63 3.6L engine accessory drive belt routing

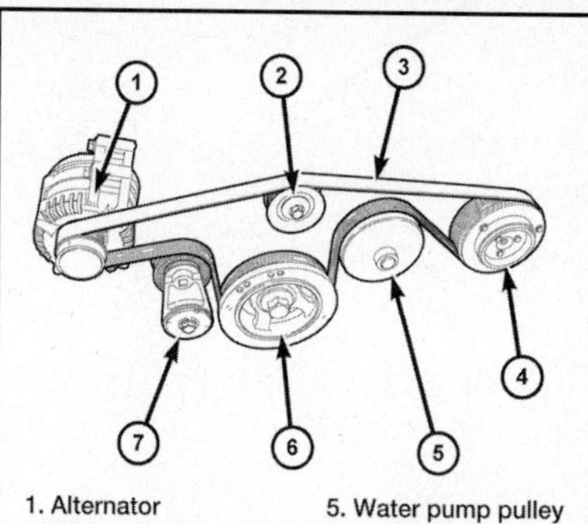

Fig. 64 3.6L engine (with electronic power steering) accessory drive belt routing

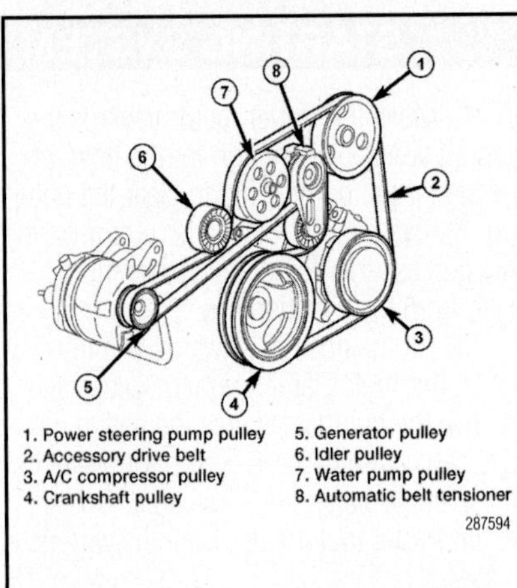

Fig. 65 5.7L engine accessory drive belt routing

However, cracks running along a rib (not across) are not normal. Any belt with cracks running along a rib must be replaced. Also replace belt if it has excessive wear, frayed cords or severe glazing.

ADJUSTMENT

Tension for the serpentine accessory drive belt is maintained by the belt tensioner. No adjustment is necessary.

REMOVAL & INSTALLATION

3.6L Engine

See Figure 66.

WARNING

Do not let tensioner arm snap back to the freearm position, severe damage may occur to the tensioner.

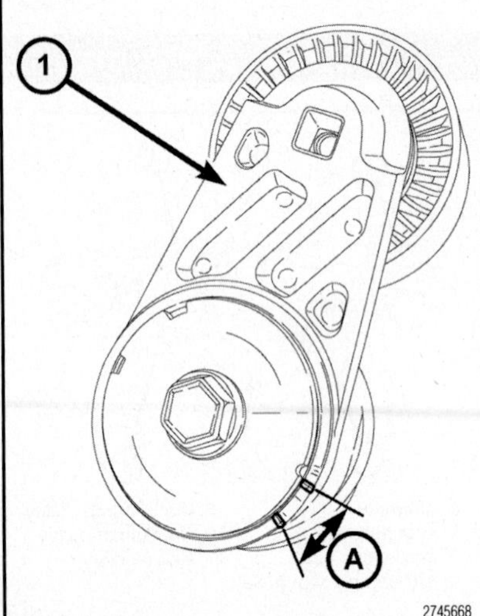

Fig. 66 The gap between the tang and the housing stop (measurement A) must not exceed 0.94 inches (24 mm)

1. Disconnect negative battery cable from battery.
2. Rotate belt tensioner until it contacts its stop. Remove belt, then slowly rotate the tensioner into the freearm position.

To install:

3. Check condition of all pulleys.

WARNING

When installing the serpentine accessory drive belt, the belt MUST be routed correctly. If not, the engine may overheat due to the water pump rotating in the wrong direction.

4. Install new belt. Route the belt around all pulleys except the idler pulley. Rotate the tensioner arm until it contacts its stop position. Route the belt around the idler and slowly let the tensioner rotate into the belt. Make sure the belt is seated onto all pulleys.
5. With the drive belt installed, inspect the belt wear indicator. The gap between the tang and the housing stop (measurement A) must not exceed 0.94 inches (24 mm).

3.6L Engine (With Electronic Power Steering)

See Figure 66.

WARNING

Do not let the tensioner arm snap back to the freearm position, severe damage may occur to the tensioner.

1. Disconnect negative battery cable from battery.
2. Remove the air cleaner intake system.
3. Rotate belt tensioner until it contacts its stop. Remove belt, then slowly rotate the tensioner into the freearm position.

To install:

4. Check condition of all pulleys.

WARNING

When installing the serpentine accessory drive belt, the belt MUST be routed correctly. If not, the engine may overheat due to the water pump rotating in the wrong direction.

5. Install new belt. Route the belt around all pulleys except the idler pulley. Rotate the tensioner arm until it contacts its stop position. Route the belt around the idler and slowly let the tensioner rotate into the belt. Make sure the belt is seated onto all pulleys.
6. With the drive belt installed, inspect the belt wear indicator. The gap between the tang and the housing stop (measurement A) must not exceed 0.94 inches (24 mm).

5.7L Engine

1. Remove the air intake tube between intake manifold and air filter assembly.
2. Using a suitable square drive tool, release the belt tension by rotating the tensioner clockwise. Rotate belt tensioner until belt can be removed from pulleys.
3. Remove belt.
4. Gently release tensioner.

To install:

➡When installing accessory drive belt onto pulleys, make sure that belt is properly routed and all V-grooves make proper contact with pulleys.

5. Position the drive belt over all pulleys except for the water pump pulley.
6. Rotate tensioner clockwise and slip the belt over the water pump pulley.
7. Gently release tensioner.
8. Install the air intake tube between intake manifold and air filter assembly.

AIR CLEANER

REMOVAL & INSTALLATION

3.6L Engine

See Figures 67 through 69.

1. Disconnect and isolate the negative battery cable.
2. Remove the engine cover.
3. Disconnect the electrical connector from the Inlet Air Temperature (IAT) sensor.
4. Loosen the clamp at the throttle body.
5. Loosen the clamp at the air cleaner body.
6. Remove the air inlet hose.
7. Disconnect the fresh air makeup hose from the air cleaner body.

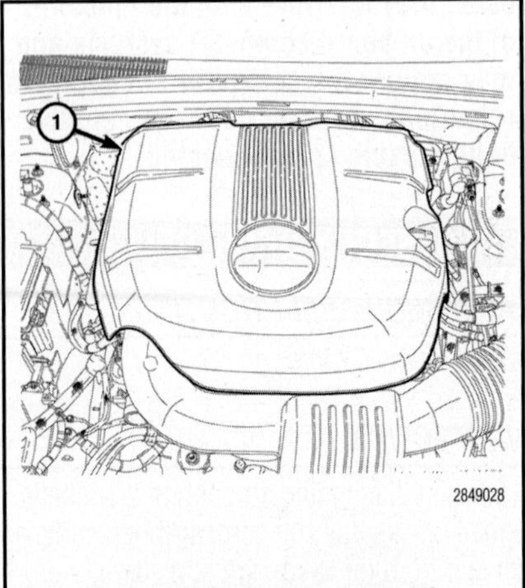

Fig. 67 Remove the engine cover (1)

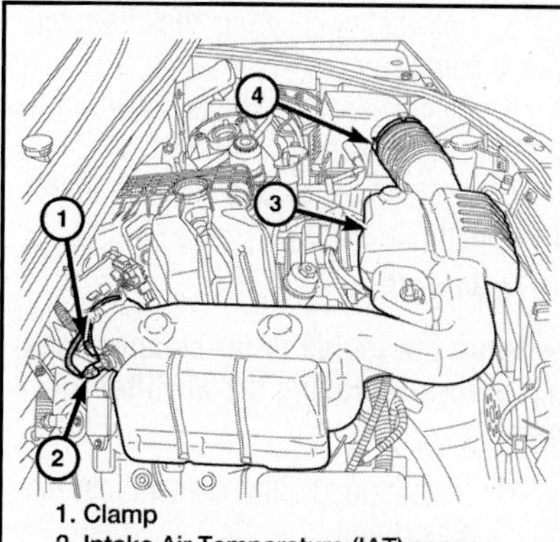

Fig. 68 Disconnect the electrical connector from the Inlet Air Temperature (IAT) sensor

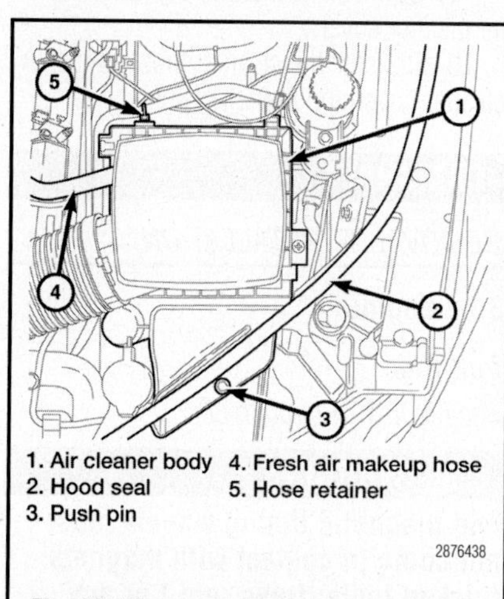

Fig. 69 Disconnect the fresh air makeup hose from the air cleaner body

8. Disengage the hose retainer from the air cleaner body.
9. Remove the push pin.
10. Reposition the hood seal and pull the air cleaner body straight up off of the locating pins.

To install:

11. Install the air cleaner body straight down on the locating pins while routing the air inlet under the hood seal.
12. Install the push pin.
13. Engage the hose retainer to the air cleaner body.
14. Install the fresh air makeup hose to the air cleaner body.
15. Install the air inlet hose to the air cleaner body and the throttle body.
16. Connect the electrical connector to the Inlet Air Temperature (IAT) sensor.
17. Install the engine cover.
18. Connect the negative battery cable and tighten.

5.7L Engine

See Figures 70 and 71.

1. Loosen the clean air hose clamp at the air cleaner cover and disconnect the clean air hose.
2. Remove the makeup air hose at the air cleaner cover.
3. Release the 2 spring clips from the air cleaner cover.
4. Remove the air cleaner cover from the housing assembly.
5. Remove the air filter element from the housing assembly.

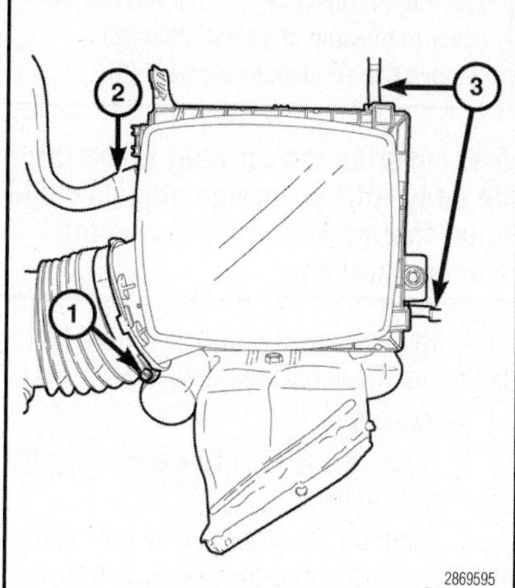

Fig. 70 Air hose clamp (1), makeup air hose (2), and spring clips (3)

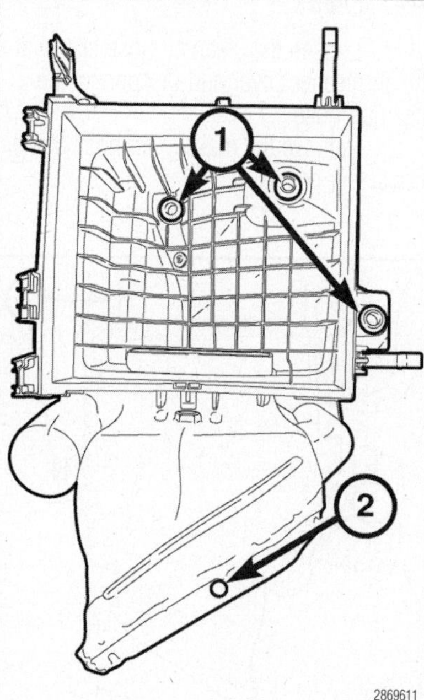

Fig. 71 Locations of air cleaner housing rubber grommets (1) and the push pin retainer (2)

6. Remove the push pin retainer at the air cleaner housing duct.
7. Lift and separate the air cleaner housing rubber grommets from the ball studs and remove the air cleaner housing.

Resonator Assembly

See Figures 72 and 73.

1. Remove the oil fill cap.
2. Lift and separate the engine cover retaining grommets from the ball studs and remove the engine cover.
3. Disconnect the electrical connector at the Intake Air Temperature (IAT) sensor.
4. Loosen the clean air hose clamp at the air cleaner housing.
5. Remove the resonator retaining bolt.
6. Loosen the resonator hose clamp at the throttle body and remove the resonator.

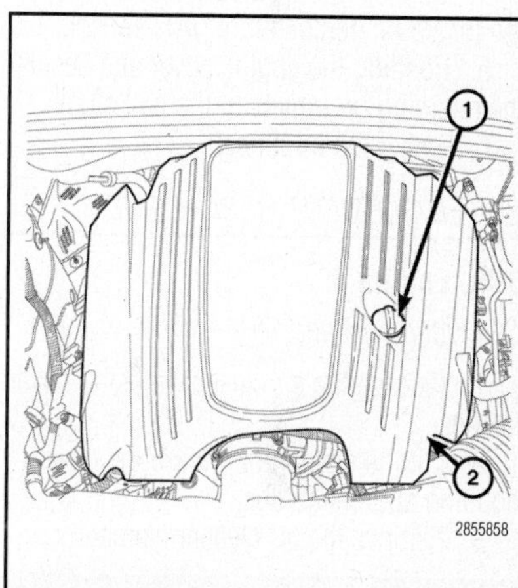

Fig. 72 Remove the oil fill cap (1) and the engine cover (2)

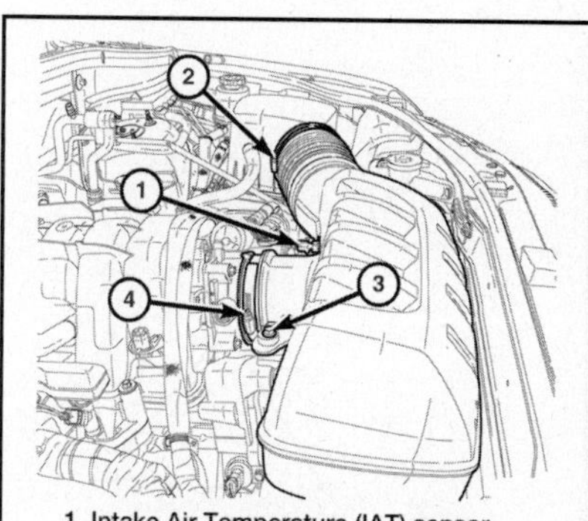

Fig. 73 Disconnect the electrical connector at the Intake Air Temperature (IAT) sensor

To install:

7. Position the air cleaner housing and secure the air cleaner housing rubber grommets to the ball studs.
8. Install the air cleaner housing duct push pin retainer.
9. Install the air filter element into the housing assembly.
10. Install the air cleaner cover onto the housing assembly locating tabs.
11. Latch the 2 spring clips and lock the air cleaner cover to the housing assembly.
12. Connect the makeup air hose to the air cleaner cover.
13. Connect the clean air hose to the air cleaner cover and tighten clamp.

Resonator Assembly

1. Connect the resonator hose at the throttle body and tighten clamp.
2. Install the resonator retaining bolt.
3. Connect the clean air hose at the air cleaner housing and tighten clamp.
4. Connect the electrical connector at the Intake Air Temperature (IAT) sensor.
5. Position the engine cover and secure the retaining grommets to the ball studs.
6. Install the oil fill cap.

FILTER/ELEMENT REPLACEMENT

3.6L Engine

See Figures 74 and 75.

1. Release the air cleaner housing cover latches.
2. Lift the cover and release the cover to housing alignment tabs.
3. Remove the air cleaner element.

⁂ WARNING

Do not use compressed air to clean out the air cleaner housing without first covering the air inlet to the throttle body. Dirt or foreign objects could enter the intake manifold causing engine damage.

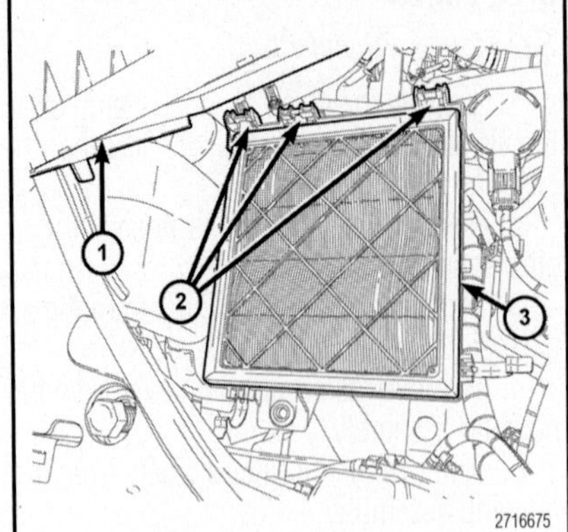

Fig. 75 Lift the cover (1) and release the cover to housing alignment tabs (2); remove the air cleaner element (3)

4. Remove any dirt or debris from the bottom of the air cleaner housing.

To install:

5. Install the air cleaner element into the air cleaner housing.
6. Position the cover so that the alignment tabs insert into the lower housing.
7. Seat the cover onto the housing and secure the housing cover latches.

5.7L Engine

See Figure 76.

1. Loosen the clean air hose clamp at the air cleaner cover and disconnect the clean air hose.
2. Remove the makeup air hose at the air cleaner cover.
3. Release the 2 spring clips from the air cleaner cover.
4. Remove the air cleaner cover from the housing assembly.
5. Remove the air filter element from the housing assembly.

To install:

➡Clean the inside of air cleaner housing before replacing the air filter element.

6. Install the air filter element into the housing assembly.
7. Install the air cleaner cover onto the housing assembly locating tabs.
8. Latch the 2 spring clips and lock the air cleaner cover to the housing assembly.
9. Connect the makeup air hose to the air cleaner cover.
10. Connect the clean air hose to the air cleaner cover and tighten clamp.

CAMSHAFT

REMOVAL & INSTALLATION

3.6L Engine

Left Side

See Figures 77 through 80.

⁂ WARNING

The magnetic timing wheels must not come in contact with magnets (pickup tools, trays, etc.) or any other strong magnetic field. This will destroy the timing wheels ability to correctly relay camshaft position to the camshaft position sensor.

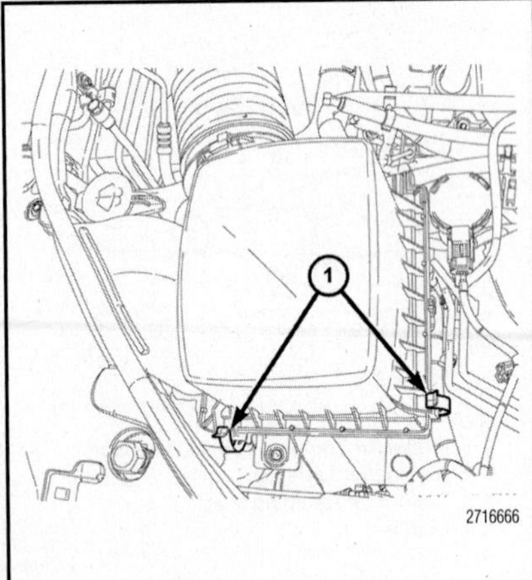

Fig. 74 Release the air cleaner housing cover latches (1)

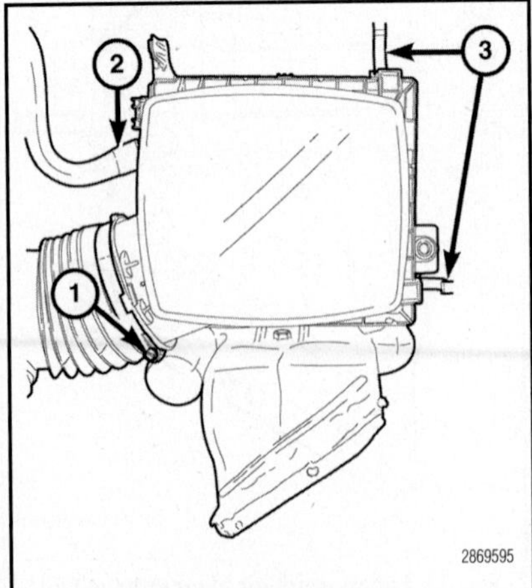

Fig. 76 Air hose clamp (1), makeup air hose (2), and spring clips (3)

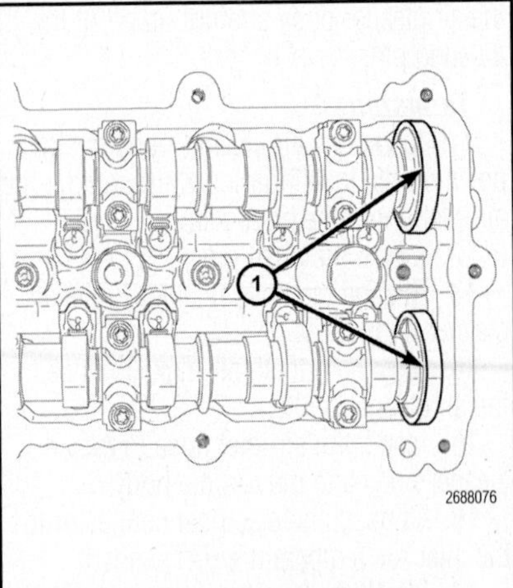

Fig. 77 The magnetic timing wheels (1) must not come in contact with magnets

⁂ WARNING

When the timing chain is removed and the cylinder heads are still installed, Do not forcefully rotate the camshafts or crankshaft independently of each other. Severe valve and/or piston damage can occur.

1. Remove the Left cylinder head cover, LH ignition coils, spark plugs and left cam phasers.
2. Gently rotate the camshafts counterclockwise approximately 30° until the camshafts are in the neutral position (no valve load).

➡Camshaft bearing caps should have been marked during engine manufacturing. For example, the number one exhaust camshaft bearing cap is marked. The caps should be installed with the notch forward.

3. Slowly loosen the camshaft bearing cap bolts in the sequence shown.

⁂ WARNING

do not stamp or strike the camshaft bearing caps. Severe damage will occur to the bearing caps.

➡When the camshaft is removed the rocker arms may slide downward, mark the rocker arms before removing the camshaft.

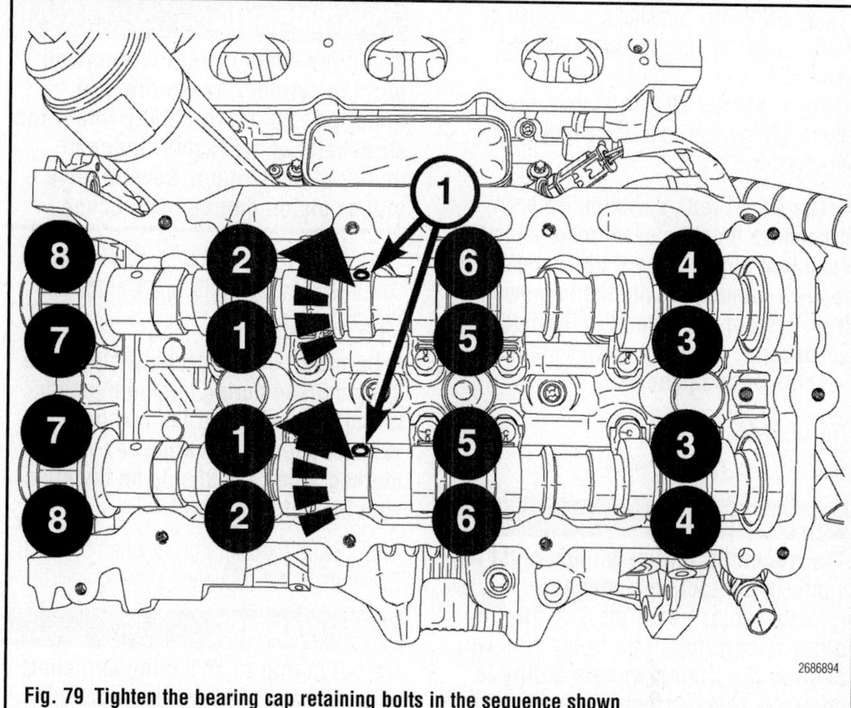

Fig. 79 Tighten the bearing cap retaining bolts in the sequence shown

4. Remove the camshaft bearing caps and the camshafts.

To install:

5. Lubricate the camshaft journals with clean engine oil.
6. Install the left side camshaft(s) approximately 30° counterclockwise from the TDC position. This will place the camshafts at the neutral position (no valve load) easing the installation of the camshaft bearing caps.
7. Install the camshaft bearing caps and hand tighten the retaining bolts.

➡Caps are identified numerically (1 through 4), intake or exhaust (I or E) and should be installed from the front to the rear of the engine. All caps should be installed with the notch forward so that the stamped arrows on the caps point toward the front of the engine.

8. Tighten the bearing cap retaining bolts in the sequence shown to 84 inch lbs. (9.5 Nm).

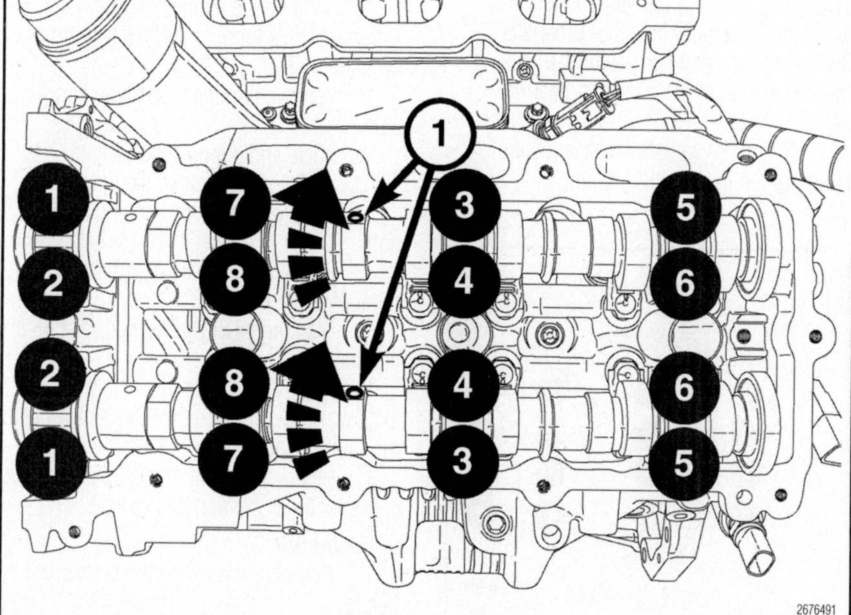

Fig. 78 Gently rotate the camshafts counterclockwise approximately 30° (1) until the camshafts are in the neutral position (no valve load)

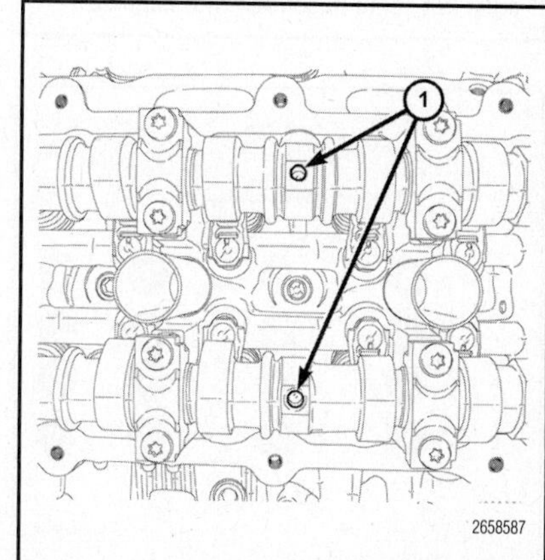

Fig. 80 Rotate the camshafts clockwise to TDC by positioning the alignment holes (1) vertically

9. Rotate the camshafts clockwise to TDC by positioning the alignment holes vertically.

10. Install the left cam phasers, spark plugs, LH ignition coils and the cylinder head cover.

➡**The Cam/Crank Variation Relearn procedure must be performed using the scan tool anytime there has been a repair/replacement made to a power-train system, for example: flywheel, valve train, camshaft and/or crankshaft sensors or components.**

Right Side

See Figures 81 through 83.

⁂ WARNING

The magnetic timing wheels must not come in contact with magnets (pickup tools, trays, etc.) or any other strong magnetic field. This will destroy the timing wheels ability to correctly relay camshaft position to the camshaft position sensor.

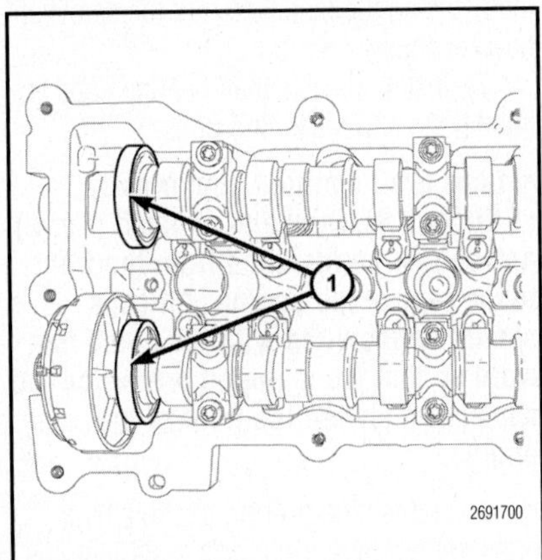

Fig. 81 The magnetic timing wheels (1) must not come in contact with magnets

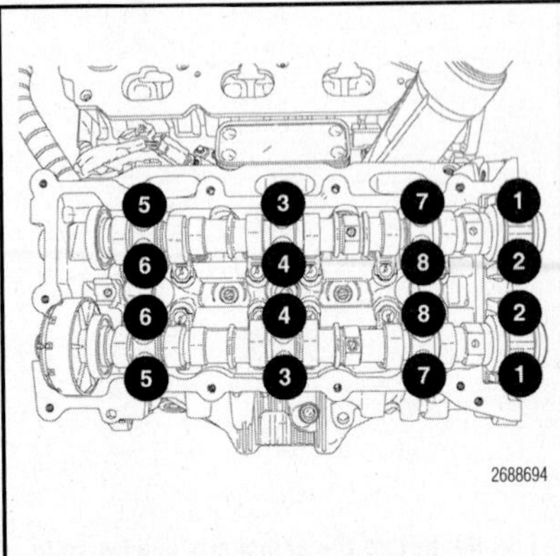

Fig. 82 Slowly loosen the camshaft bearing cap bolts in the sequence shown

⁂ WARNING

When the timing chain is removed and the cylinder heads are still installed, Do not forcefully rotate the camshafts or crankshaft independently of each other. Severe valve and/or piston damage can occur.

1. Remove the Right cylinder head cover, RH ignition coils, spark plugs and right cam phasers.

➡**Camshaft bearing caps should have been marked during engine manufacturing. For example, the number one exhaust camshaft bearing cap is marked. The caps should be installed with the notch forward.**

2. Slowly loosen the camshaft bearing cap bolts in the sequence shown.

⁂ WARNING

Do not stamp or strike the camshaft bearing caps. Severe damage will occur to the bearing caps.

➡**When the camshaft is removed the rocker arms may slide downward, mark the rocker arms before removing the camshaft.**

3. Remove the camshaft bearing caps and the camshafts.

To install:

4. Lubricate camshaft journals with clean engine oil.

5. Install the right side camshaft(s) at TDC by positioning the alignment holes vertically. This will place the camshafts at the neutral position (no valve load) easing the installation of the camshaft bearing caps.

6. Install the camshaft bearing caps, hand tighten the retaining bolts.

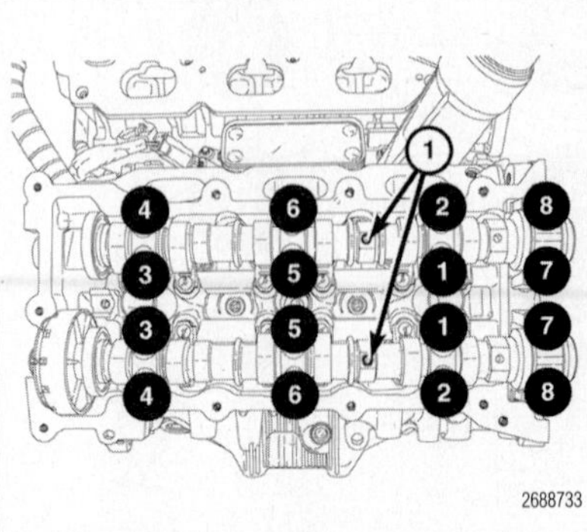

Fig. 83 Install the right side camshaft(s) at TDC by positioning the alignment holes (1) vertically

➡**Caps are identified numerically (1 through 4), intake or exhaust (I or E) and should be installed from the front to the rear of the engine. All caps should be installed with the notch forward so that the stamped arrows on the caps point toward the front of the engine.**

7. Tighten the bearing cap retaining bolts in the sequence shown to 84 inch lbs. (9.5 Nm).

8. Install the right cam phasers, spark plugs, RH ignition coils and the cylinder head cover.

➡**The Cam/Crank Variation Relearn procedure must be performed using the scan tool anytime there has been a repair/replacement made to a power-train system, for example: flywheel, valve train, camshaft and/or crankshaft sensors or components.**

CATALYTIC CONVERTER

REMOVAL & INSTALLATION

3.6L Engine

⁂ CAUTION

If torches are used when servicing the exhaust system, do not allow any flame near the fuel lines or the fuel tank. Failure to follow these instructions may result in possible serious or fatal injury.

1. Disconnect negative battery cable.
2. Remove the engine cover.
3. Saturate the exhaust flange bolts with heat valve lubricant. Allow 5 minutes for penetration.
4. Remove the upper catalytic flange bolts.
5. Raise and support the vehicle.
6. If equipped, remove skid plate.
7. Remove the lower catalytic flange bolts.
8. Remove transmission crossmember reinforcement brackets.
9. Disconnect oxygen sensor electrical connectors.
10. Remove the nuts from the front exhaust pipe/catalytic converter assembly to the muffler flange.
11. Remove the front exhaust pipe/catalytic converter assembly from the vehicle.

To install:

12. Position new exhaust gasket onto flange.
13. Position the front exhaust pipe/catalytic converter assemblies into vehicle.

14. Install the lower bolts at the front exhaust pipe/catalytic converter assembly to exhaust manifold flange. Do not tighten.
15. Lower vehicle.
16. Install the upper bolts at the front exhaust pipe/catalytic converter assemblies to exhaust manifold flanges. Tighten bolts to 17 ft. lbs. (23 Nm).
17. Raise vehicle.
18. Tighten lower flange bolts to 17 ft. lbs. (23 Nm).
19. Position the exhaust system for proper clearance with the frame and underbody parts. A minimum clearance of 1 inch (25.4 mm) is required.
20. Tighten the front exhaust pipe/catalytic converter assembly to muffler flange nuts to 35 ft. lbs. (47 Nm).
21. Connect oxygen sensor electrical connectors.
22. Install transmission crossmember reinforcement brackets. Tighten bolts to 41 ft. lbs. (55 Nm).
23. If equipped, install skid plates.
24. Lower vehicle.
25. Start the vehicle and inspect for exhaust leaks. Repair exhaust leaks as necessary.

5.7L Engine

CAUTION

If torches are used when servicing the exhaust system, do not allow any flame near the fuel lines or the fuel tank. Failure to follow these instructions may result in possible serious or fatal injury.

1. Disconnect the negative cable
2. Raise and support the vehicle.
3. If equipped, remove skid plates.
4. Saturate the bolts and nuts with heat valve lubricant. Allow 5 minutes for penetration.
5. Remove transmission crossmember reinforcement brackets.
6. If equipped, remove the lower heat shield near the front driveshaft.
7. Remove the upstream and the downstream oxygen sensors from the exhaust.
8. Remove the nuts from the front exhaust pipe/catalytic converter assembly to muffler flange.
9. Remove bolts and flanged nuts at the exhaust manifold.
10. Remove the front exhaust pipe/catalytic converter assembly from the vehicle.

To install:

11. Position the front exhaust pipe/catalytic converter assembly into vehicle.
12. Install the nuts at the front exhaust pipe/catalytic converter assembly to muffler flange at the exhaust manifold.
13. Install the bolts at the front exhaust pipe/catalytic converter assembly to exhaust manifold flange. Do not tighten.
14. Tighten the front exhaust pipe and catalytic converter assembly to muffler flange nuts to 35 ft. lbs. (47 Nm).
15. Position the exhaust pipe for proper clearance with the frame and underbody parts. A minimum clearance of 1 inch (25.4 mm) is required.
16. Tighten front exhaust pipe/catalytic converter assembly to exhaust manifold bolts to 22 ft. lbs. (30 Nm) torque.
17. Install the oxygen sensors.
18. If equipped, install the heat shield for the front drive shaft.
19. Install transmission crossmember reinforcement brackets. Tighten bolts to 41 ft. lbs. (55 Nm).
20. If equipped, install skid plates.
21. Lower vehicle.
22. Start the vehicle and inspect for exhaust leaks. Repair exhaust leaks as necessary.

CRANKSHAFT FRONT SEAL

REMOVAL & INSTALLATION

3.6L Engine

See Figures 84 through 86.

1. Remove the accessory drive belt and the crankshaft vibration damper.
2. Install the sleeve from the Seal Remover around the flywheel key and onto the nose of the crankshaft.
3. Screw the Seal Remover into the front crankshaft oil seal.
4. Install the extractor screw into the Seal Remover.

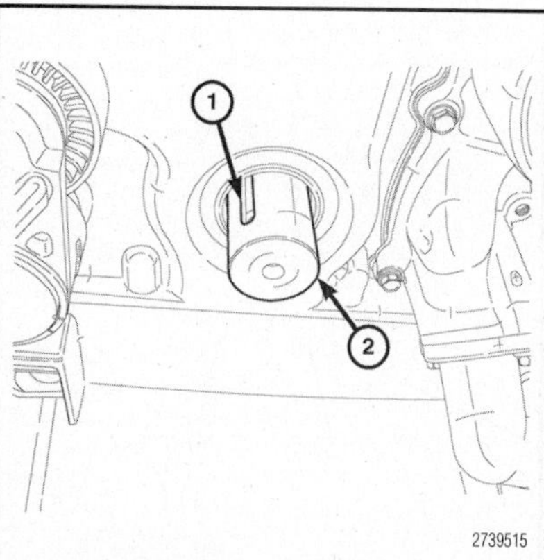

Fig. 84 Install the sleeve (2) from the Seal Remover around the flywheel key (1) and onto the nose of the crankshaft

5. Hold the seal remover stationary and tighten the extractor screw against the sleeve until the front crankshaft oil seal is removed from the engine timing cover.

To install:

6. Position the front crankshaft oil seal into place on the engine timing cover.
7. Align the Front Crankshaft Seal Installer to the flywheel key on the crankshaft and against the front crankshaft oil seal.

WARNING

Only tighten the crankshaft vibration damper bolt until the oil seal is seated in the cover. Overtightening of the bolt can crack the front timing cover.

8. Install and tighten the crankshaft vibration damper bolt until the Crankshaft oil seal is seated in the engine timing cover.
9. Install the crankshaft vibration damper and accessory drive belt.

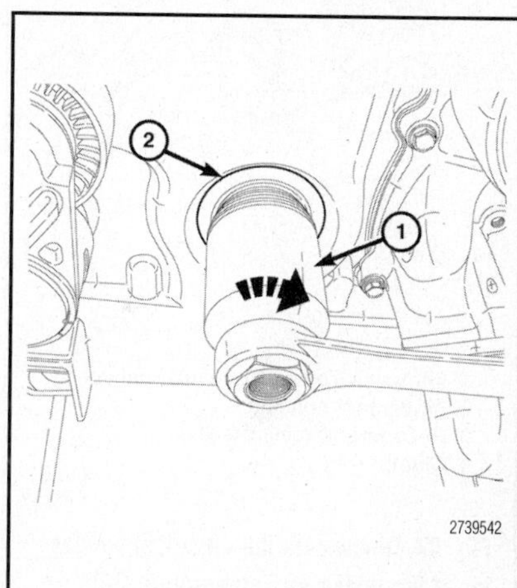

Fig. 85 Screw the Seal Remover (1) into the front crankshaft oil seal (2)

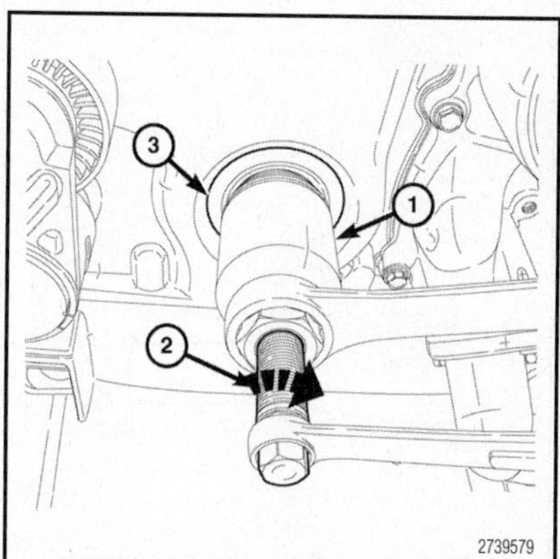

Fig. 86 Install the extractor screw (2) into the Seal Remover (1); front crankshaft oil seal (3)

5.7L Engine

See Figures 87 through 92.

1. Disconnect and isolate the negative battery cable.
2. Disconnect the electrical connector at the Intake Air Temperature (IAT) sensor.
3. Loosen the clean air hose clamp at the air cleaner housing.
4. Remove the resonator retaining bolt.
5. Loosen the resonator hose clamp at the throttle body and remove the resonator.
6. Remove the serpentine belt.
7. Drain the cooling system.
8. Remove the upper radiator hose clamp at the thermostat housing.
9. Remove the upper radiator hose retainer at the fan shroud and position the radiator hose aside.
10. Remove the cooling fan module.
11. Remove the crankshaft damper bolt.

➡**When installing the puller tool, ensure the bolts are fully threaded through the entire crankshaft damper.**

12. Install puller tool and remove the crankshaft damper.
13. Using Seal Remover, remove crankshaft front seal.

To install:

WARNING

The front crankshaft seal must be installed dry. Do not apply lubricant to the sealing lip or the outer edge.

14. Using Crankshaft Front Oil Seal Installer and Damper Installer, install the crankshaft front seal.

WARNING

To prevent severe damage to the crankshaft, damper, and damper installer, thoroughly clean the damper bore and the crankshaft nose before installing damper.

15. Position the damper onto the crankshaft.
16. Assemble the Damper Installer and the Pressing Cup from A/C Hub Installer.
17. Using the Damper Installer and A/C Hub Installer, press the damper onto the crankshaft.
18. Install the crankshaft damper bolt and tighten to 129 ft. lbs. (176 Nm).
19. Install the cooling fan module.
20. Position the upper radiator hose and secure retainer at the fan shroud.

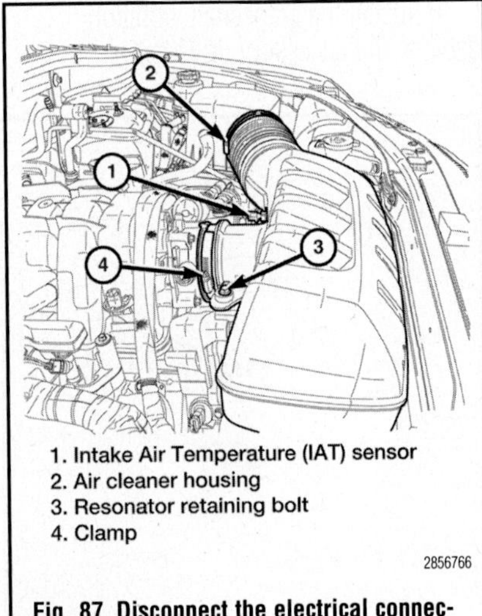

Fig. 87 Disconnect the electrical connector at the Intake Air Temperature (IAT) sensor

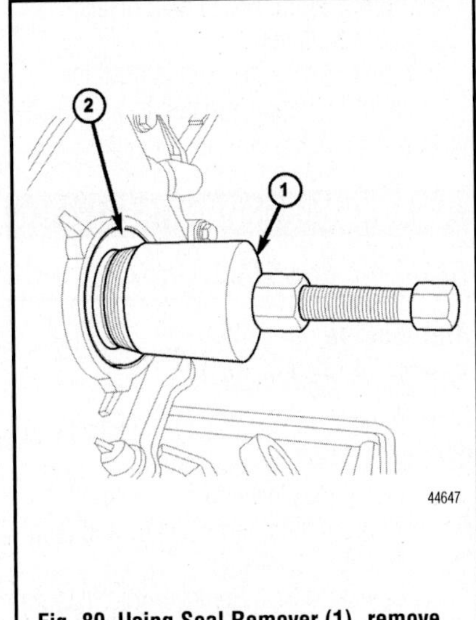

Fig. 89 Using Seal Remover (1), remove crankshaft front seal (2)

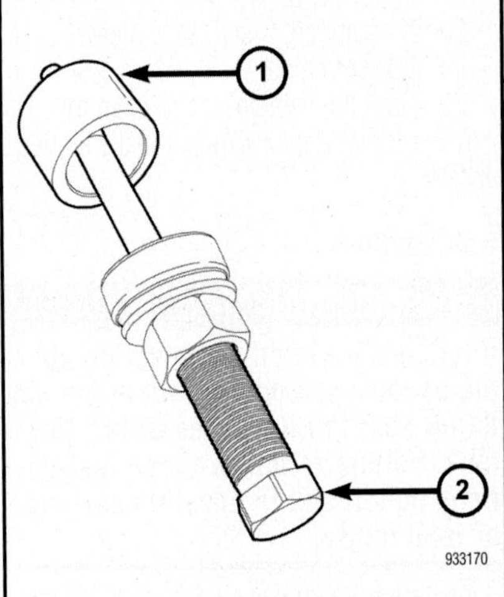

Fig. 91 Assemble the Damper Installer (2) and the Pressing Cup (1) from A/C Hub Installer

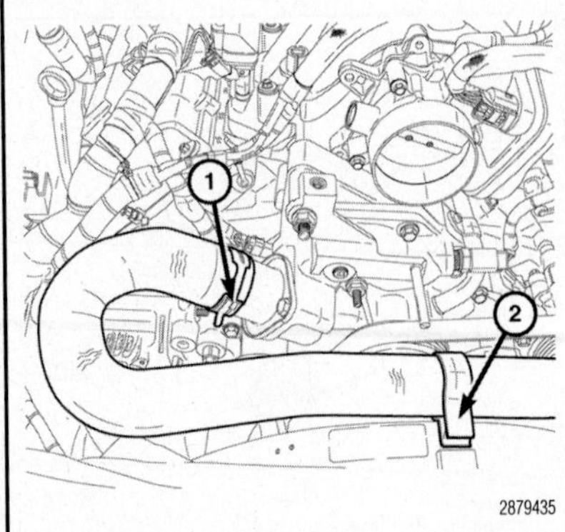

Fig. 88 Remove the upper radiator hose clamp (1) at the thermostat housing and the upper radiator hose retainer (2) at the fan shroud

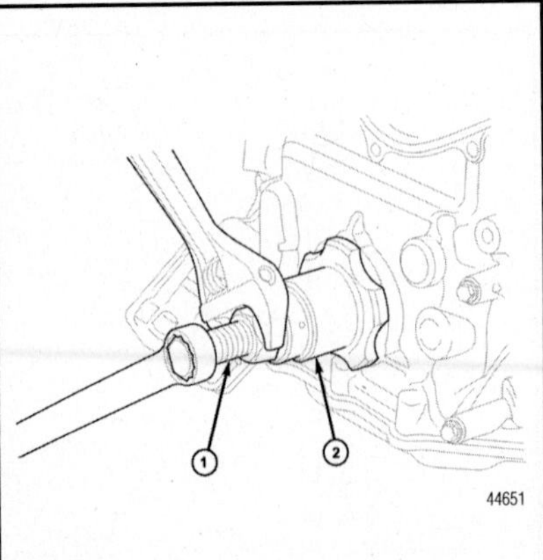

Fig. 90 Using Crankshaft Front Oil Seal Installer (2) and Damper Installer (1), install the crankshaft front seal

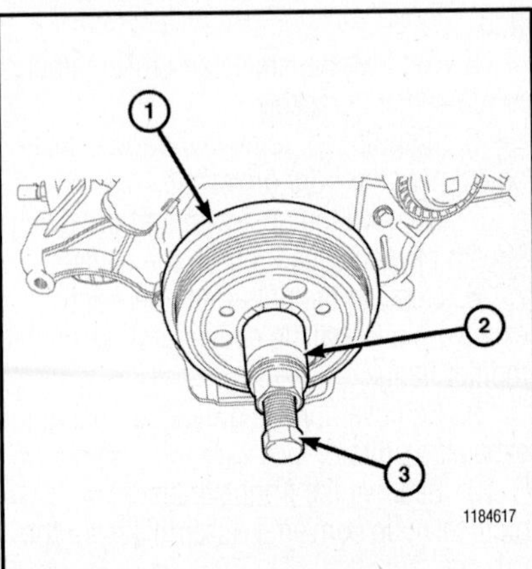

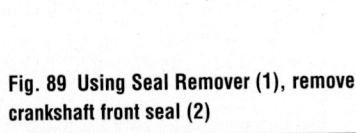

Fig. 92 Using the Damper Installer (3) and A/C Hub Installer (2), press the damper (1) onto the crankshaft

21. Install the upper radiator hose at the thermostat housing and secure hose clamp.
22. Install the air cleaner resonator support bracket at the water pump.
23. Install serpentine belt.
24. Connect the resonator hose at the throttle body and tighten clamp.
25. Install the resonator retaining bolt.
26. Connect the clean air hose at the air cleaner housing and tighten clamp.
27. Connect the electrical connector at the Intake Air Temperature (IAT) sensor.
28. Refill the cooling system.
29. Connect the negative battery cable.

CYLINDER HEAD

REMOVAL & INSTALLATION

3.6L Engine

Left Side

See Figures 93 through 114.

✱✱ WARNING

The magnetic timing wheels must not come in contact with magnets (pickup tools, trays, etc.) or any other strong magnetic field. This will destroy the timing wheels ability to correctly relay camshaft position to the camshaft position sensor.

1. Perform the fuel pressure release procedure.
2. Disconnect and isolate the negative battery cable.
3. Remove the engine cover.
4. Remove the air inlet hose and the air cleaner body.
5. Remove the electric vacuum pump and mounting bracket.

➡Power steering pump not shown.

6. Raise and support the vehicle.
7. If equipped, remove the front skid plate and front suspension skid plate.
8. Drain the cooling system.
9. Drain the engine oil.
10. Remove the nut and bolt from the support brackets of the heater core return tube.
11. Remove the A/C compressor mounting stud.
12. Lower the vehicle.
13. Remove the nut from the support bracket of the heater core return tube and reposition the tube.
14. Remove the vapor purge tube from the fuel purge solenoid.
15. Remove the upper and lower intake manifolds and insulator.
16. Disengage the clips, remove the make-up air tube from the left cylinder head cover and reposition the transmission breather hose.

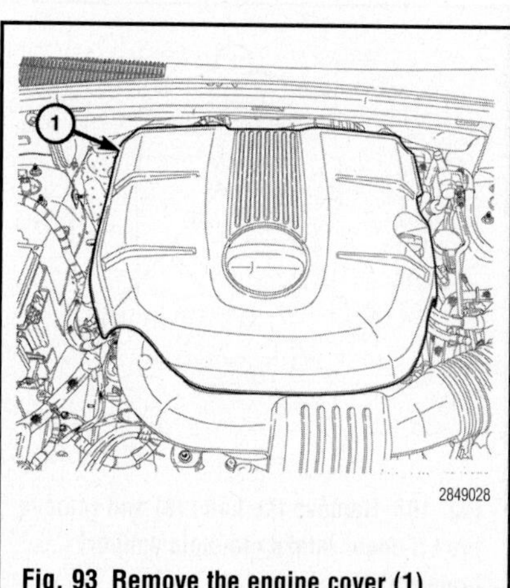

Fig. 93 Remove the engine cover (1)

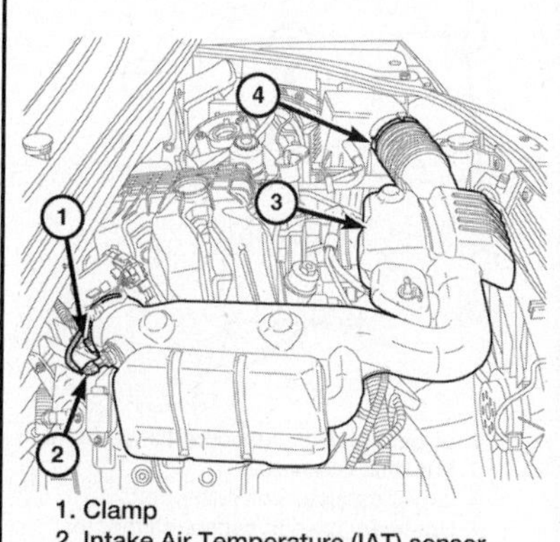

Fig. 94 Remove the air inlet hose and the air cleaner body

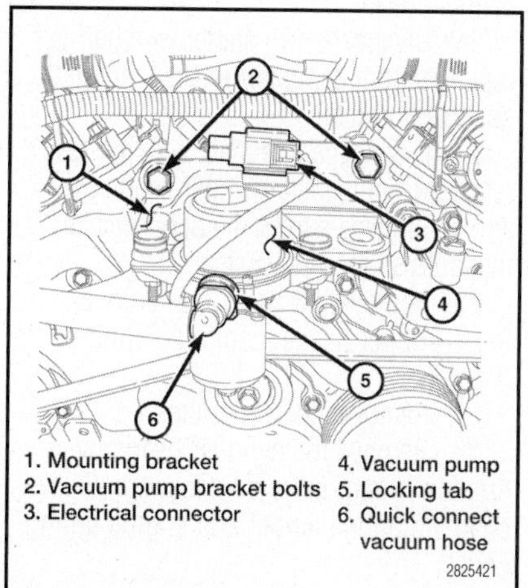

Fig. 95 Remove the electric vacuum pump and mounting bracket

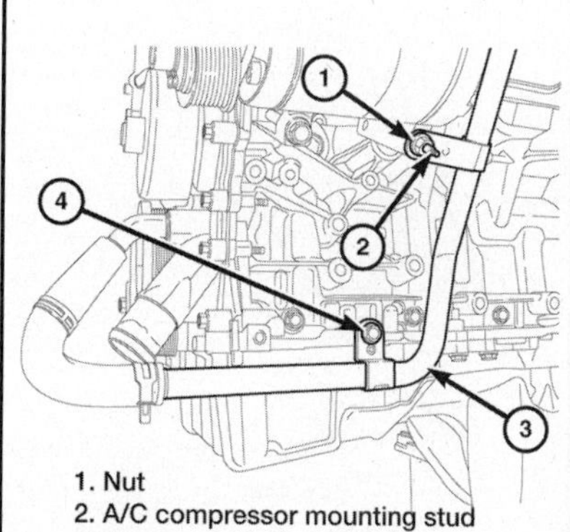

Fig. 96 Remove the nut and bolt from the support brackets of the heater core return tube

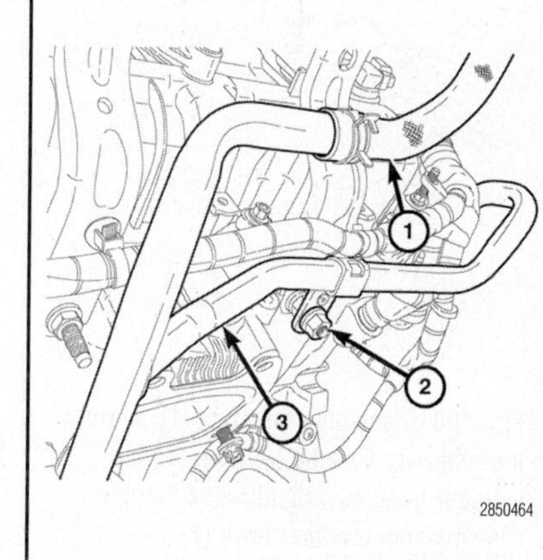

Fig. 97 Remove the nut (2) from the support bracket of the heater core return tube (3) and reposition the tube; hose (1)

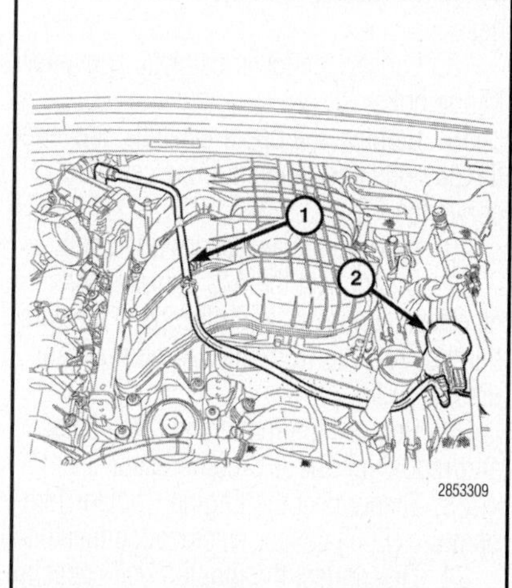

Fig. 98 Remove the vapor purge tube (1) from the fuel purge solenoid (2)

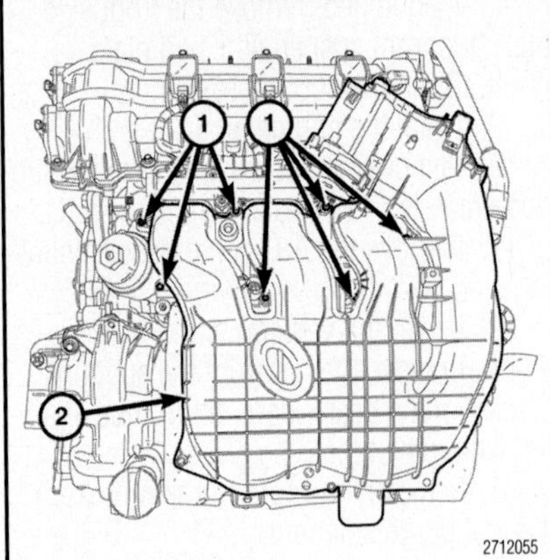

Fig. 99 Remove the upper and lower intake manifolds (2) and insulator; retainers (1)

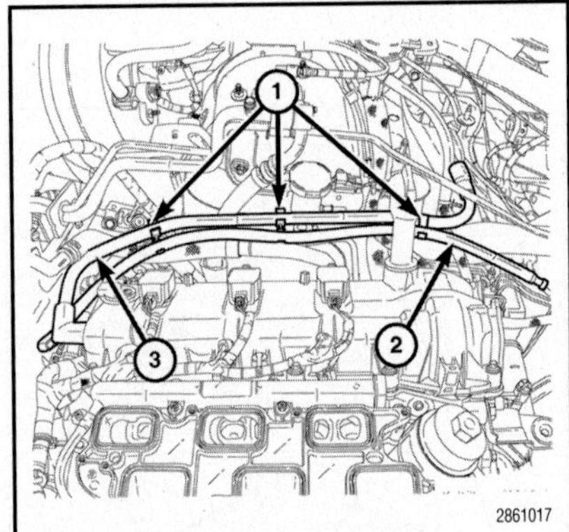

Fig. 100 Disengage the clips (1), remove the make-up air tube (3) from the left cylinder head cover and reposition the transmission breather hose (2)

➡Right catalytic converter shown, left catalytic converter similar.

17. Disconnect the left upstream oxygen sensor connector from the main wire harness.
18. Loosen the lower catalytic converter flange bolts.
19. Remove the upper catalytic converter flange bolts and reposition the catalytic converter.
20. Remove the accessory drive belt.
21. Disconnect the A/C compressor electrical connector and disengage the wire harness retainer from the A/C compressor discharge line.
22. Remove the remaining three bolts and reposition the A/C compressor.
23. Disconnect the Engine Coolant Temperature (ECT) sensor electrical connector.
24. Disconnect the ignition coil capacitor electrical connector.
25. Disengage the injection/ignition harness connector and the engine oil pressure/temperature harness connector from the retainer bracket on the rear of the left cylinder head.
26. Disengage two starter wire harness retainers from the upper intake manifold support brackets.
27. Disengage one main wire harness retainer from the left cylinder head cover and two retainers from the upper intake manifold support brackets.
28. Remove the bolts and remove the LH upper intake manifold support brackets.
29. Remove the spark plugs.
30. Remove the cylinder head covers, lower and upper oil pans, crankshaft vibration damper and engine timing cover.

➡Take this opportunity to measure timing chain wear.

31. Lower the vehicle.

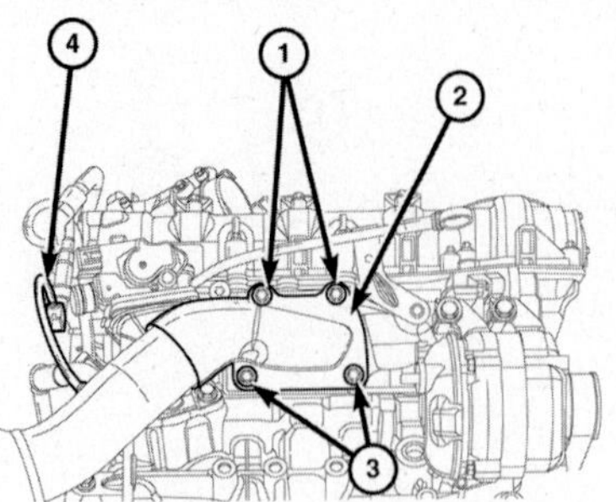

Fig. 101 Disconnect the left upstream oxygen sensor connector from the main wire harness

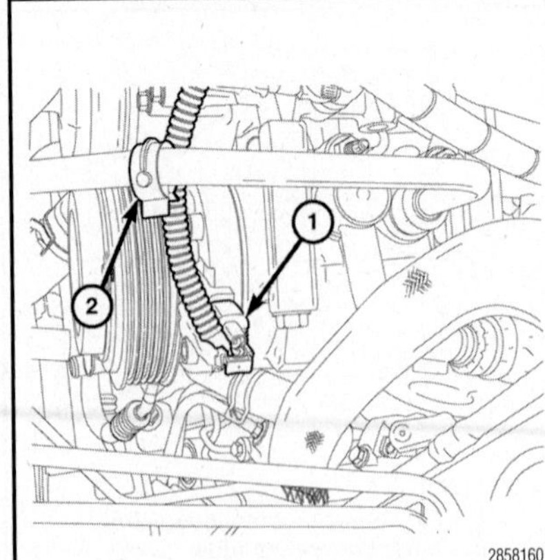

Fig. 102 Disconnect the A/C compressor electrical connector (1) and disengage the wire harness retainer (2) from the A/C compressor discharge line

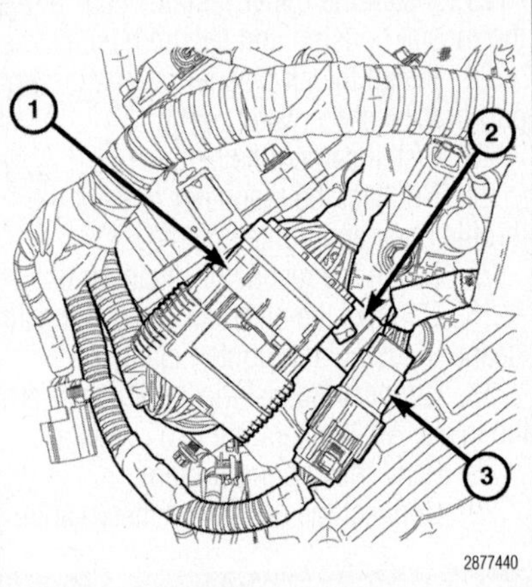

Fig. 103 Disengage the injection/ignition harness connector (1) and the engine oil pressure/temperature harness connector (3) from the retainer bracket (2) on the rear of the left cylinder head

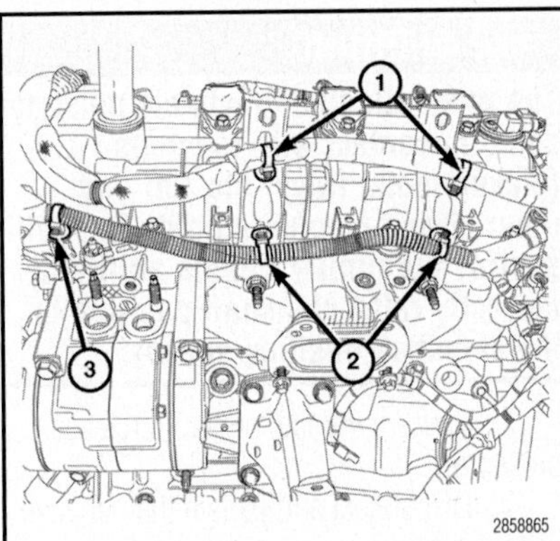

Fig. 104 Disengage two starter wire harness retainers (1) from the upper intake manifold support brackets and disengage one main wire harness retainer (3) from the left cylinder head cover and two retainers (2) from the upper intake manifold support brackets

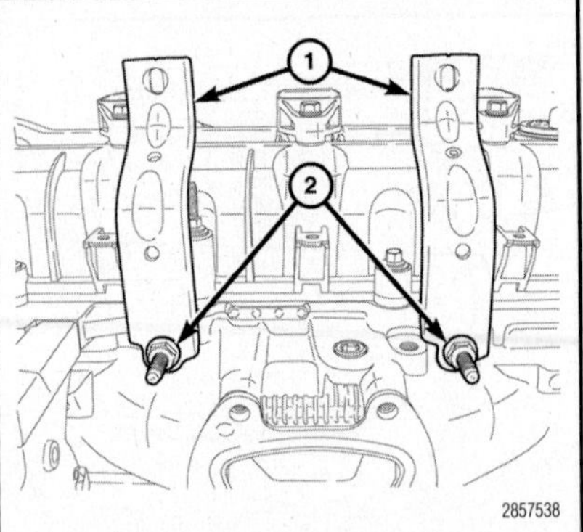

Fig. 105 Remove the bolts (2) and remove the LH upper intake manifold support brackets (1)

⁂ WARNING

When aligning timing marks, always rotate engine by turning the crankshaft. Failure to do so will result in valve and/or piston damage.

32. Rotate the crankshaft clockwise to place the number one piston at TDC on the exhaust stroke by aligning the dimple on the crankshaft with the block/bearing cap junction. The left side cam phaser arrows should point toward each other and be parallel to the valve cover sealing surface. The right side cam phaser arrows should point away from each other and the scribe lines should be parallel to the valve cover sealing surface.

⁂ WARNING

Always reinstall timing chains so that they maintain the same direction of rotation. Inverting a previously run chain on a previously run sprocket will result in excessive wear to both the chain and sprocket.

33. Mark the direction of rotation on the timing chain using a paint pen or equivalent to aid in reassembly.

⁂ WARNING

When the timing chains are removed and the cylinder heads are still installed, DO NOT rotate the camshafts or crankshaft without first locating the proper crankshaft position. Failure to do so will result in valve and/or piston damage.

34. Reset the LH cam chain tensioner by lifting the pawl, pushing back the piston and installing Tensioner Pin.

➡Minor rotation of a camshaft (a few degrees) may be required to install the camshaft phaser lock.

35. Install the LH Camshaft Phaser Lock.
36. Loosen both the intake oil control valve and exhaust oil control valve.
37. Remove the LH Camshaft Phaser Lock.
38. Remove the oil control valve from the left side exhaust cam phaser and pull the phaser off of the camshaft.
39. Remove the oil control valve from the left side intake cam phaser and pull the phaser off of the camshaft.
40. Remove the LH cam chain tensioner arm.
41. Remove two T30 bolts and the LH cam chain tensioner.
42. Remove two T30 bolts and the LH cam chain guide.
43. Remove the left camshafts.

➡If the rocker arms are to be reused, identify their positions so that they can be reassembled into their original locations.

44. Remove the rocker arms.

➡If the hydraulic lifters are to be reused, identify their positions so that they can be reassembled into their original locations.

45. If required, remove the hydraulic lifters.
46. Using the sequence shown, remove the cylinder head retaining bolts.

⁂ WARNING

The multi-layered steel head gaskets have very sharp edges that could cause personal injury if not handled carefully.

➡The head gasket crimps the locating dowels and the dowels may pull out of

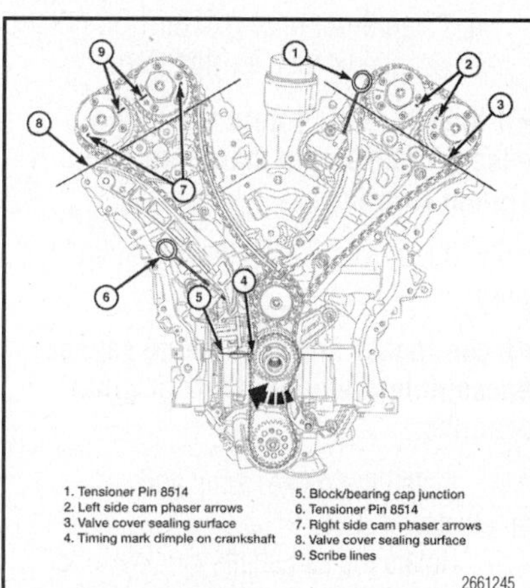

Fig. 106 When aligning timing marks, always rotate engine by turning the crankshaft

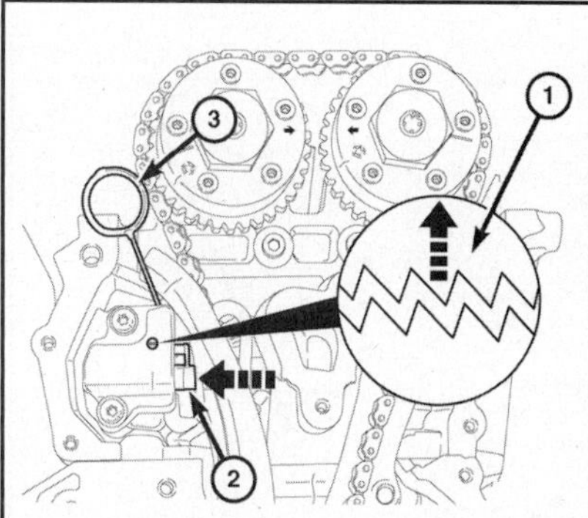

Fig. 107 Reset the LH cam chain tensioner by lifting the pawl (1), pushing back the piston (2) and installing Tensioner Pin (3)

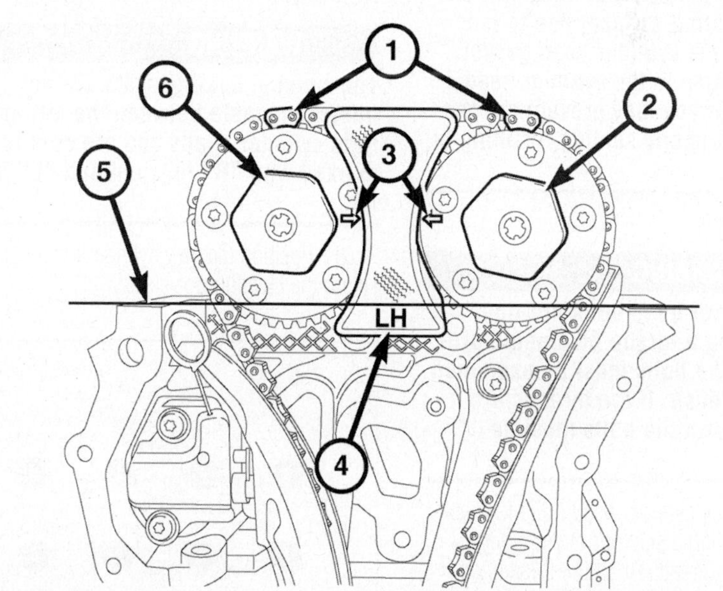

Fig. 108 Install the LH Camshaft Phaser Lock

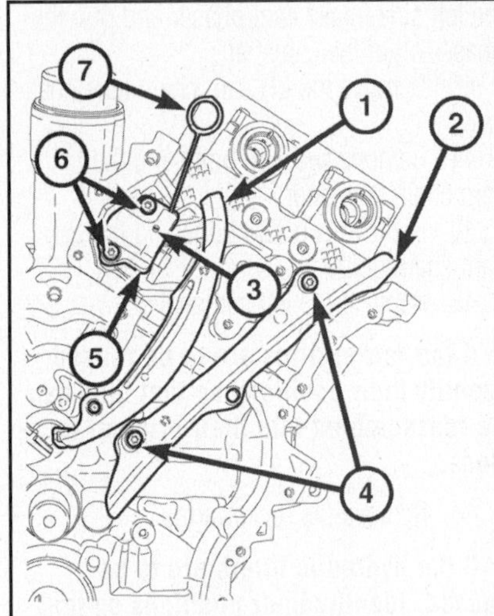

1. Left cam chain tensioner arm
2. Left cam chain guide
3. Pin
4. T30 bolts
5. Left cam chain tensioner
6. T30 bolts

2659731

Fig. 109 Remove the LH cam chain tensioner arm

the engine block when the head gasket is removed.

47. Remove the cylinder head and gasket. Discard the gasket.

✻✻ WARNING

Do not lay the cylinder head on its gasket sealing surface, due to the design of the cylinder head gasket, any distortion to the cylinder head sealing surface may prevent the gasket from properly sealing resulting in leaks.

To install:

✻✻ WARNING

The cylinder head bolts are tightened using a torque plus angle procedure. The bolts must be examined BEFORE reuse. If the threads are necked down the bolts must be replaced.

48. Check cylinder head bolts for necking by holding a scale or straight edge against the threads. If all the threads do not contact the scale the bolt must be replaced.

✻✻ WARNING

When cleaning cylinder head and cylinder block surfaces, DO NOT use a metal scraper because the surfaces could be cut or ground. Use ONLY a wooden or plastic scraper.

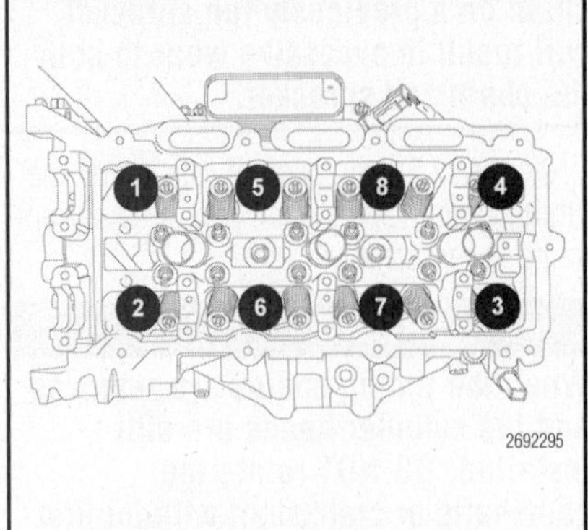

Fig. 110 Using the sequence shown, remove the cylinder head retaining bolts

49. Clean and prepare the gasket sealing surfaces of the cylinder head and block.

✻✻ WARNING

Non-compressible debris such as oil, coolant or RTV sealants that are not removed from bolt holes can cause the aluminum casting to crack when tightening the bolts.

50. Clean out the cylinder head bolt holes in the engine block.

➡The multi-layered steel head gaskets have very sharp edges that could cause personal injury if not handled carefully.

✻✻ WARNING

The cylinder head gaskets are not interchangeable between the left and right cylinder heads and are clearly marked with "R" for right and "L" for left.

51. Position the new cylinder head gasket on the locating dowels.

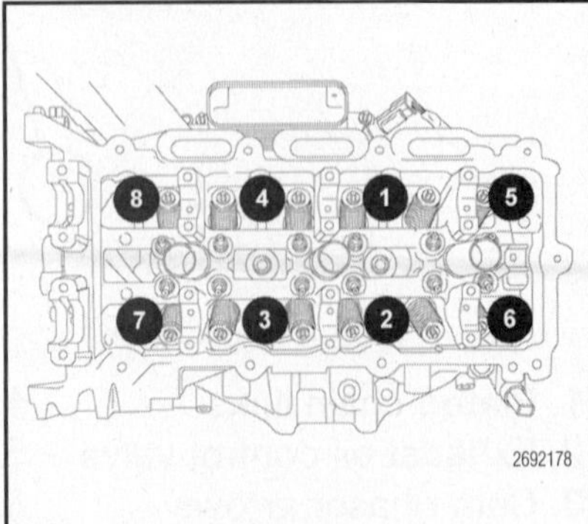

Fig. 111 Tighten the cylinder head bolts in the sequence shown

52. Position the cylinder head onto the cylinder block. Make sure the cylinder head seats fully over the locating dowels.

➡Do not apply any additional oil to the bolt threads.

53. Install the eight head bolts finger tight.

54. Tighten the cylinder head bolts in the sequence shown, following this 9 step torque plus angle method. Tighten according to the following torque values:

a. Step 1: All to 22 ft. lbs. (30 Nm)
b. Step 2: All to 33 ft. lbs. (45 Nm)
c. Step 3: All plus 75° Turn Do not use a torque wrench for this step.
d. Step 4: All plus 50° Turn Do not use a torque wrench for this step.
e. Step 5: Loosen all fasteners in reverse of sequence shown
f. Step 6: All to 22 ft. lbs. (30 Nm)
g. Step 7: All to 33 ft. lbs. (45 Nm)
h. Step 8: All plus 70° Turn Do not use a torque wrench for this step.
i. Step 9: All plus 70° Turn Do not use a torque wrench for this step.

➡If the hydraulic lifters are being reused, reassemble them into their original locations.

55. If removed, install the hydraulic lifters.

➡If the rocker arms are being reused, reassemble them into their original locations.

56. Install the rocker arms and camshafts.

57. Rotate the camshafts clockwise to TDC by positioning the alignment holes vertically.

58. Install the LH cam chain guide with

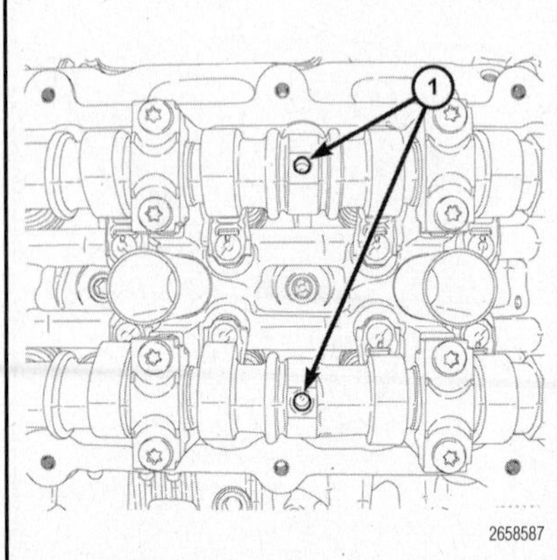

Fig. 112 Rotate the camshafts clockwise to TDC by positioning the alignment holes (1) vertically

two bolts. Tighten the T30 bolts to 106 inch lbs. (12 Nm).

59. Install the LH cam chain tensioner to the cylinder head with two bolts. Tighten the T30 bolts to 106 inch lbs. (12 Nm).

60. Reset the LH cam chain tensioner by lifting the pawl, pushing back the piston and installing Tensioner Pin.

61. Install the LH tensioner arm.

62. Press the LH intake cam phaser onto the intake camshaft. Install and hand tighten the oil control valve.

**** WARNING**

Always reinstall timing chains so that they maintain the same direction of rotation. Inverting a previously run chain on a previously run sprocket will result in excessive wear to both the chain and sprocket.

63. Drape the left side cam chain over the LH intake cam phaser and onto the idler sprocket so that the arrow is aligned with the plated link on the cam chain.

64. While maintaining this alignment, route the cam chain around the exhaust and intake cam phasers so that the plated links are aligned with the phaser timing marks. Position the left side cam phasers so that the arrows point toward each other and are parallel to the valve cover sealing surface. Press the exhaust cam phaser onto the exhaust cam, install and hand tighten the oil control valve.

➡Minor rotation of a camshaft (a few degrees) may be required to install the camshaft phaser or phaser lock.

65. Install the LH Camshaft Phaser Lock and tighten the oil control valves to 110 ft. lbs. (150 Nm).

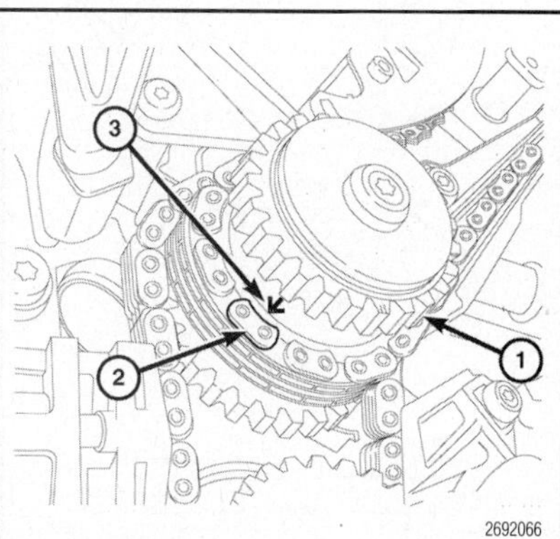

Fig. 113 Drape the left side cam chain over the LH intake cam phaser and onto the idler sprocket (1) so that the arrow (3) is aligned with the plated link (2) on the cam chain

66. Remove the LH Camshaft Phaser Lock

67. Remove the Tensioner Pin from the LH cam chain tensioner.

68. Rotate the crankshaft clockwise two complete revolutions stopping when the dimple on the crankshaft is aligned the with the block/bearing cap junction.

69. While maintaining this alignment, verify that the arrows on the left side cam phasers point toward each other and are parallel to the valve cover sealing surface and that the right side cam phaser arrows point away from each other and the scribe lines are parallel to the valve cover sealing surface.

70. There should be 12 chain pins between the exhaust cam phaser triangle marking and the intake cam phaser circle marking.

71. If the engine timing is not correct, repeat this procedure.

72. Install the engine timing cover, crankshaft vibration damper, upper and lower oil pans and cylinder head covers.

73. Install the LH upper intake manifold support brackets. Loosely install the stud bolts.

74. Engage two starter wire harness retainers to the upper intake manifold support brackets.

75. Engage one main wire harness retainer to the left cylinder head cover and two retainers to the upper intake manifold support brackets.

76. Install the spark plugs. Tighten to 13 ft. lbs. (17.5 Nm).

77. Connect the ignition coil capacitor electrical connector.

78. Engage the injection/ignition harness connector and the engine oil pressure/temperature harness connector to the retainer bracket on the rear of the left cylinder head.

79. Connect the Engine Coolant Temperature (ECT) sensor electrical connector.

80. Install the A/C compressor with three bolts tightened to 18 ft. lbs. (25 Nm).

81. Connect the A/C compressor electrical connector and Engage the wire harness retainer to the A/C compressor discharge line.

82. Install the accessory drive belt.

83. Install the left catalytic converter onto the partially installed lower catalytic converter flange bolts.

84. Install the upper catalytic converter flange bolts and tighten all M8 bolts to 17 ft. lbs. (23 Nm).

85. Connect the left upstream oxygen sensor connector to the main wire harness.

86. Install the make-up air tube to the left cylinder head cover and engage the clips to the transmission breather hose.

87. Install the upper and lower intake manifolds.

88. Install the vapor purge tube to the fuel purge solenoid.

89. Install the nut to the support bracket of the heater core return tube and tighten to 106 inch lbs. (12 Nm).

➡Power steering pump not shown.

90. Raise and support the vehicle.

91. Install the A/C compressor mounting stud and tighten to 18 ft. lbs. (25 Nm).

92. Install the nut and bolt to the support brackets of the heater core return tube. Tighten to 106 inch lbs. (12 Nm).

93. If equipped, install the front skid plate and front suspension skid plate.

94. Lower the vehicle.

95. Install the electric vacuum pump and mounting bracket.

96. Install the air inlet hose and the air cleaner body.

97. If removed, install the oil filter and fill the engine crankcase with the proper oil to the correct level.

98. Fill the cooling system.

99. Install the engine cover.

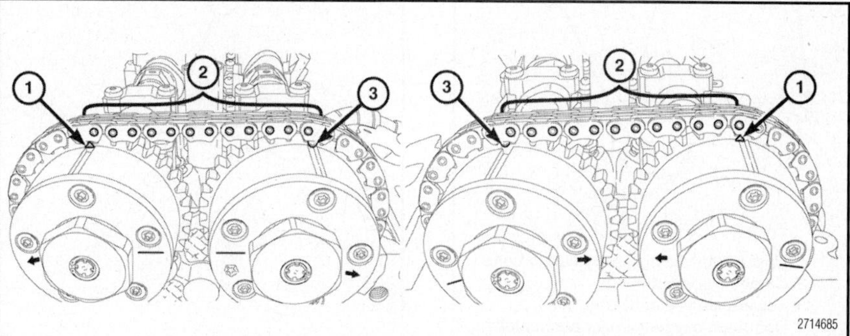

Fig. 114 There should be 12 chain pins (2) between the exhaust cam phaser triangle marking (1) and the intake cam phaser circle marking (3)

100. Connect the negative battery cable and tighten nut.

101. Run the engine until it reaches normal operating temperature. Check cooling system for correct fluid level.

➡**The Cam/Crank Variation Relearn procedure must be performed using the scan tool anytime there has been a repair/replacement made to a powertrain system, for example: flywheel, valve train, camshaft and/or crankshaft sensors or components.**

Right Side

See Figures 115 through 122.

⁂ WARNING

The magnetic timing wheels must not come in contact with magnets (pickup tools, trays, etc.) or any other strong magnetic field. This will destroy the timing wheels ability to correctly relay camshaft position to the camshaft position sensor.

1. Perform the fuel pressure release procedure.
2. Disconnect and isolate the negative battery cable.
3. Remove the engine cover.
4. Disconnect the electrical connector from the Inlet Air Temperature (IAT) sensor.
5. Loosen the clamp at the throttle body.
6. Loosen the clamp at the air cleaner body.
7. Remove the air inlet hose.
8. Remove the electric vacuum pump and mounting bracket.
9. Raise and support the vehicle.
10. If equipped, remove the front skid plate and front suspension skid plate.
11. Drain the cooling system.
12. Drain the engine oil.
13. Lower the vehicle.
14. Remove the PCV hose from the PCV valve.
15. Remove the upper and lower intake manifolds and insulator.
16. Disconnect the right upstream oxygen sensor connector from the main wire harness.
17. Loosen the lower catalytic converter flange bolts.
18. Remove the upper catalytic converter flange bolts and reposition the catalytic converter.
19. Remove the accessory drive belt.
20. Remove the alternator.
21. Remove the bolt and remove the oil level indicator.
22. Remove the bolt and the heater core supply tube.
23. Disconnect the ignition coil capacitor electrical connector.
24. Remove the stud bolt and remove the upper intake manifold support bracket.
25. Remove the spark plugs.
26. Remove the cylinder head covers, lower and upper oil pans, crankshaft vibration damper and engine timing cover.

➡**Take this opportunity to measure timing chain wear.**

27. Lower the vehicle.

⁂ WARNING

When aligning timing marks, always rotate engine by turning the crankshaft. Failure to do so will result in valve and/or piston damage.

28. Rotate the crankshaft clockwise to place the number one piston at TDC on the exhaust stroke by aligning the dimple on the crankshaft with the block/bearing cap junction. The left side cam phaser arrows should point toward each other and be parallel to the valve cover sealing surface. The right side cam phaser arrows should point away from each other and the scribe lines should be parallel to the valve cover sealing surface.

⁂ WARNING

Always reinstall timing chains so that they maintain the same direction of rotation. Inverting a previously run chain on a previously run sprocket will result in excessive wear to both the chain and sprocket.

29. Mark the direction of rotation on the timing chain using a paint pen or equivalent to aid in reassembly.

⁂ WARNING

When the timing chains are removed and the cylinder heads are still installed, DO NOT rotate the camshafts or crankshaft without first locating the proper crankshaft position. Failure to do so will result in valve and/or piston damage.

30. Reset the RH cam chain tensioner by pushing back the tensioner piston and installing Tensioner Pin.

➡**Minor rotation of a camshaft (a few degrees) may be required to install the camshaft phaser lock.**

31. Install the RH Camshaft Phaser Lock.
32. Loosen both the intake oil control valve and exhaust oil control valve.

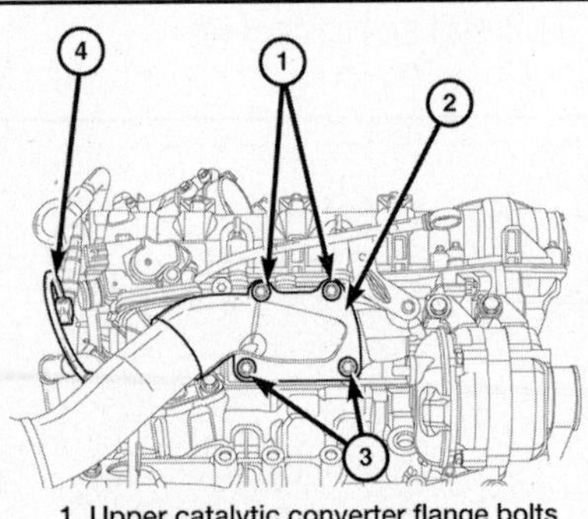

Fig. 115 Disconnect the right upstream oxygen sensor connector from the main wire harness

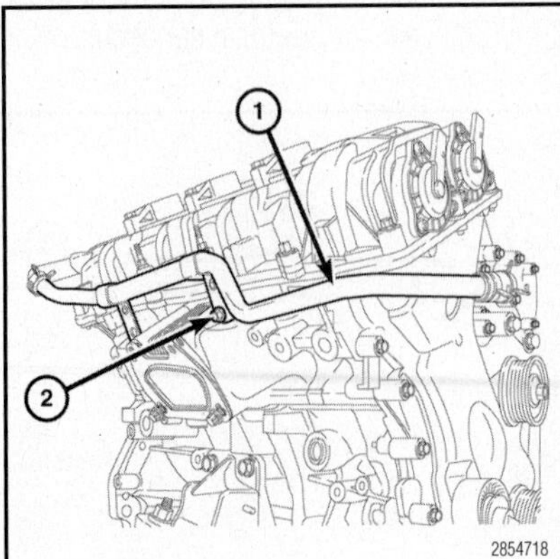

Fig. 116 Remove the bolt (2) and the heater core supply tube (1)

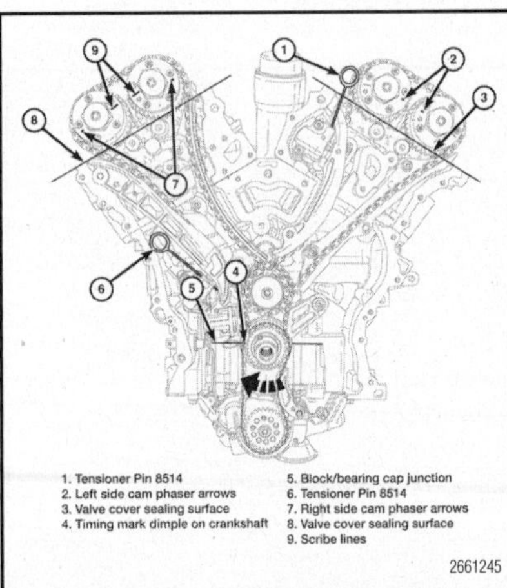

Fig. 117 Rotate the crankshaft clockwise to place the number one piston at TDC on the exhaust stroke by aligning the dimple on the crankshaft with the block/bearing cap junction

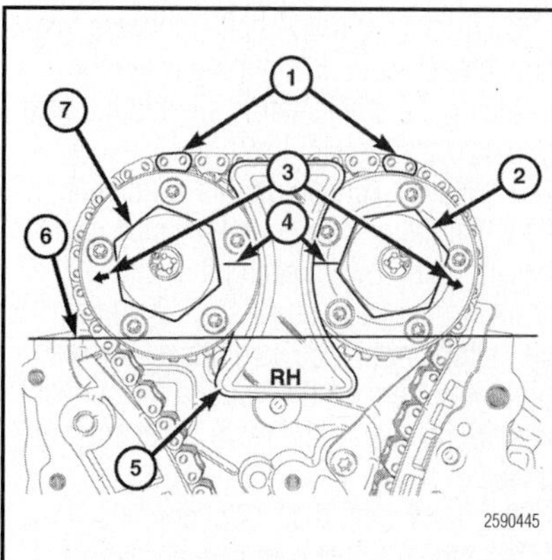

Fig. 118 Install the RH Camshaft Phaser Lock

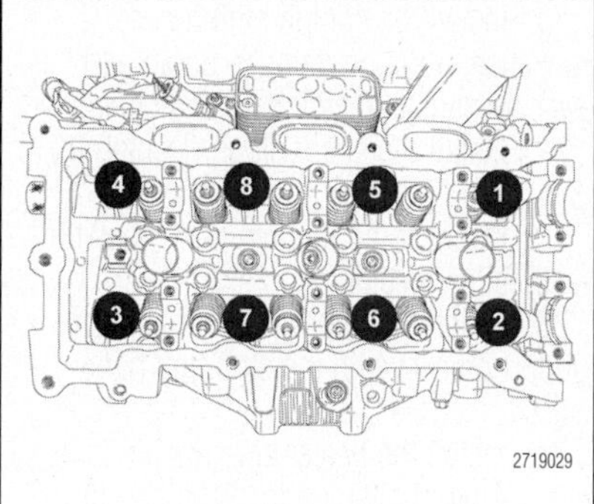

Fig. 119 Using the sequence shown, remove the cylinder head retaining bolts

33. Remove the RH Camshaft Phaser Lock.
34. Remove the oil control valve from the right side intake cam phaser and pull the phaser off of the camshaft.
35. Remove the oil control valve from the right side exhaust cam phaser and pull the phaser off of the camshaft.
36. Remove the RH cam chain tensioner arm.
37. Remove two T30 bolts and the RH cam chain tensioner.
38. Remove three T30 bolts and the RH cam chain guide.
39. Remove the right camshafts.

➡If the rocker arms are to be reused, identify their positions so that they can be reassembled into their original locations.

40. Remove the rocker arms.

➡If the hydraulic lifters are to be reused, identify their positions so that they can be reassembled into their original locations.

41. If required, remove the hydraulic lifters.
42. Using the sequence shown, remove the cylinder head retaining bolts.

✻✻ CAUTION

The multi-layered steel head gaskets have very sharp edges that could cause personal injury if not handled carefully.

➡The head gasket crimps the locating dowels and the dowels may pull out of the engine block when the head gasket is removed.

43. Remove the cylinder head and gasket. Discard the gasket.

✻✻ WARNING

Do not lay the cylinder head on its gasket sealing surface, due to the design of the cylinder head gasket, any distortion to the cylinder head sealing surface may prevent the gasket from properly sealing resulting in leaks.

44. If required, remove the bolt and the ignition coil capacitor.

To install:

✻✻ WARNING

The magnetic timing wheels must not come in contact with magnets (pickup tools, trays, etc.) or any other strong magnetic field. This will destroy the timing wheels ability to correctly relay camshaft position to the camshaft position sensor.

45. If removed, install the ignition coil capacitor with a M6 bolt tightened to 89 inch lbs. (10 Nm).

✻✻ WARNING

The cylinder head bolts are tightened using a torque plus angle procedure. The bolts must be examined BEFORE reuse. If the threads are necked down the bolts must be replaced.

46. Check cylinder head bolts for necking by holding a scale or straight edge against the threads. If all the threads do not contact the scale the bolt must be replaced.

✻✻ WARNING

When cleaning cylinder head and cylinder block surfaces, DO NOT use a metal scraper because the surfaces could be cut or ground. Use ONLY a wooden or plastic scraper.

47. Clean and prepare the gasket sealing surfaces of the cylinder head and block.

✻✻ WARNING

Non-compressible debris such as oil, coolant or RTV sealants that are not removed from bolt holes can cause the aluminum casting to crack when tightening the bolts.

48. Clean out the cylinder head bolt holes in the engine block.

✻✻ CAUTION

The multi-layered steel head gaskets have very sharp edges that could cause personal injury if not handled carefully.

✻✻ WARNING

The cylinder head gaskets are not interchangeable between the left and right cylinder heads and are clearly marked with "R" for right and "L" for left.

49. Position the new cylinder head gasket on the locating dowels.
50. Position the cylinder head onto the cylinder block. Make sure the cylinder head seats fully over the locating dowels.

➡Do not apply any additional oil to the bolt threads.

51. Install the eight head bolts finger tight.
52. Tighten the cylinder head bolts in the sequence shown, following this 9 step torque plus angle method. Tighten according to the following torque values:
    a. Step 1: All to 22 ft. lbs. (30 Nm)
    b. Step 2: All to 33 ft. lbs. (45 Nm)
    c. Step 3: All plus 75° Turn Do not use a torque wrench for this step.
    d. Step 4: All plus 50° Turn Do not use a torque wrench for this step.

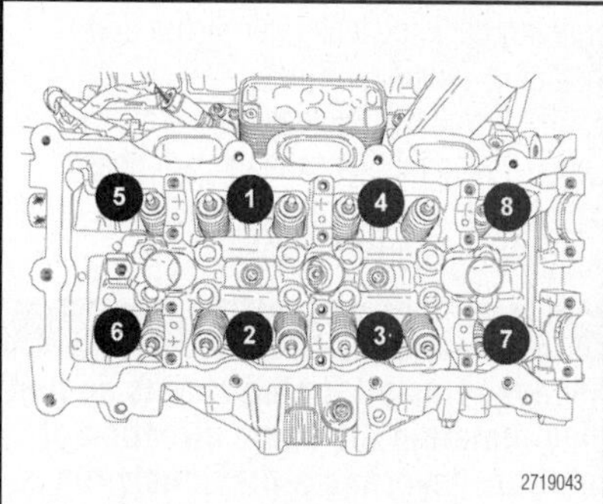

Fig. 120 Tighten the cylinder head bolts in the sequence shown

e. Step 5: Loosen all fasteners in reverse of sequence shown
f. Step 6: All to 22 ft. lbs. (30 Nm)
g. Step 7: All to 33 ft. lbs. (45 Nm)
h. Step 8: All plus 70° Turn Do not use a torque wrench for this step.
i. Step 9: All plus 70° Turn Do not use a torque wrench for this step.

➡**If the hydraulic lifters are being reused, reassemble them into their original locations.**

53. If removed, install the hydraulic lifters.

➡**If the rocker arms are being reused, reassemble them into their original locations.**

54. Install the rocker arms and camshafts.

**** WARNING**

Do not rotate the camshafts more than a few degrees independently of the crankshaft. Valve to piston contact could occur resulting in possible valve damage. If the camshafts need to be rotated more than a few degrees, first move the pistons away from the cylinder heads by rotating the crankshaft counterclockwise to a position 30° BTDC. Once the camshafts are positioned at TDC rotate the crankshaft clockwise to return the crankshaft to TDC.

55. Verify that the camshafts are set at TDC by positioning the alignment holes vertically.
56. Install the RH cam chain guide with three bolts. Tighten the T30 bolts to 106 inch lbs. (12 Nm).
57. Install the RH cam chain tensioner to the engine block with two bolts. Tighten the T30 bolts to 106 inch lbs. (12 Nm).
58. Reset the RH cam chain tensioner by pushing back the tensioner piston and installing Tensioner Pin.
59. Install the RH tensioner arm.
60. Press the RH exhaust cam phaser onto the exhaust camshaft. Install and hand tighten the oil control valve.

**** WARNING**

Always reinstall timing chains so that they maintain the same direction of rotation. Inverting a previously run chain on a previously run sprocket will result in excessive wear to both the chain and sprocket.

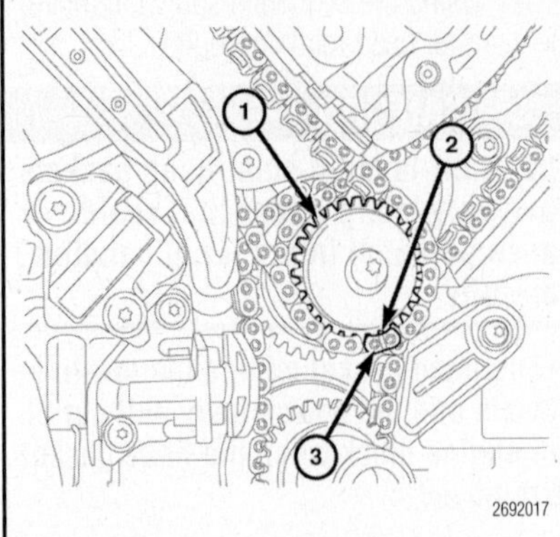

Fig. 121 Drape the right side cam chain over the RH exhaust cam phaser and onto the idler sprocket (1) so that the dimple (2) is aligned with the plated link (3) on the cam chain

61. Drape the right side cam chain over the RH exhaust cam phaser and onto the idler sprocket so that the dimple is aligned with the plated link on the cam chain.
62. While maintaining this alignment, route the cam chain around the exhaust and intake cam phasers so that the plated links are aligned with the phaser timing marks. Position the right side cam phasers so that the arrows point away from each other and the scribe lines are parallel to the valve cover sealing surface. Press the intake cam phaser onto the intake cam, install and hand tighten the oil control valve.

➡**Minor rotation of a camshaft (a few degrees) may be required to install the camshaft phaser or phaser lock.**

63. Install the RH Camshaft Phaser Lock and tighten the oil control valves to 110 ft. lbs. (150 Nm).
64. Remove the RH Camshaft Phaser Lock.
65. Remove the Tensioner Pin from the RH cam chain tensioner.
66. Rotate the crankshaft clockwise two complete revolutions stopping when the dimple on the crankshaft is aligned the with the block/bearing cap junction.
67. While maintaining this alignment, verify that the arrows on the left side cam phasers point toward each other and are parallel to the valve cover sealing surface and that the right side cam phaser arrows point away from each other and the scribe lines are parallel to the valve cover sealing surface.
68. There should be 12 chain pins between the exhaust cam phaser triangle marking and the intake cam phaser circle marking.
69. If the engine timing is not correct, repeat this procedure.
70. Install the engine timing cover, crankshaft vibration damper, upper and lower oil pans and cylinder head covers.
71. Install the spark plugs. Tighten to 13 ft. lbs. (17.5 Nm).
72. Connect the ignition coil capacitor electrical connector.
73. Install the upper intake manifold support bracket with the stud bolt hand tight.
74. Install the heater core supply tube with one bolt tightened to 106 inch lbs. (12 Nm).
75. Install the oil level indicator with bolt tightened 106 inch lbs. (12 Nm).
76. Install the alternator.
77. Install the accessory drive belt.
78. Install the right catalytic converter onto the partially installed lower catalytic converter flange bolts.
79. Install the upper catalytic converter flange bolts and tighten all M8 bolts to 17 ft. lbs. (23 Nm).
80. Connect the right upstream oxygen sensor connectors to the main wire harness.
81. Install the upper and lower intake manifolds.

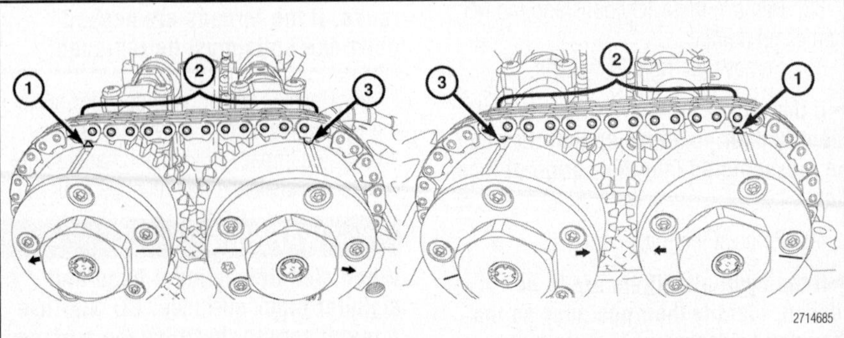

Fig. 122 There should be 12 chain pins (2) between the exhaust cam phaser triangle marking (1) and the intake cam phaser circle marking (3)

82. Install the PCV hose to the PCV valve.
83. Raise and support the vehicle.
84. If equipped, install the front skid plate and front suspension skid plate.
85. Lower the vehicle.
86. Install the electric vacuum pump and mounting bracket.
87. Install the air inlet hose to the air cleaner body and the throttle body.
88. Connect the electrical connector to the Inlet Air Temperature (IAT) sensor.
89. If removed, install the oil filter and fill the engine crankcase with the proper oil to the correct level.
90. Fill the cooling system.
91. Install the engine cover.
92. Connect the negative battery cable and tighten nut.
93. Run the engine until it reaches normal operating temperature. Check cooling system for correct fluid level.

➡The Cam/Crank Variation Relearn procedure must be performed using the scan tool anytime there has been a repair/replacement made to a powertrain system, for example: flywheel, valve train, camshaft and/or crankshaft sensors or components.

5.7L Engine

See Figures 123 through 129.

➡Sequence is the same for both the left and right side. Power steering pump left side only.

1. Remove the oil fill cap.
2. Remove the engine cover.
3. Perform the fuel pressure release procedure.
4. Disconnect and isolate the negative battery cable.
5. Remove the cowl cover panel.
6. Drain the cooling system.
7. Remove the air cleaner and resonator assembly.

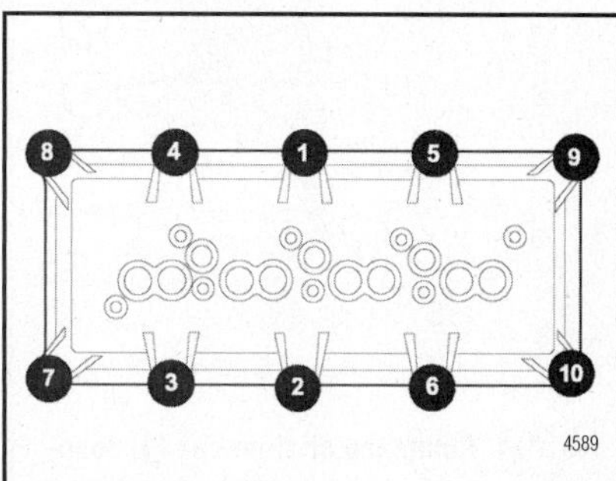

Fig. 123 Remove the cylinder head cover using sequence shown

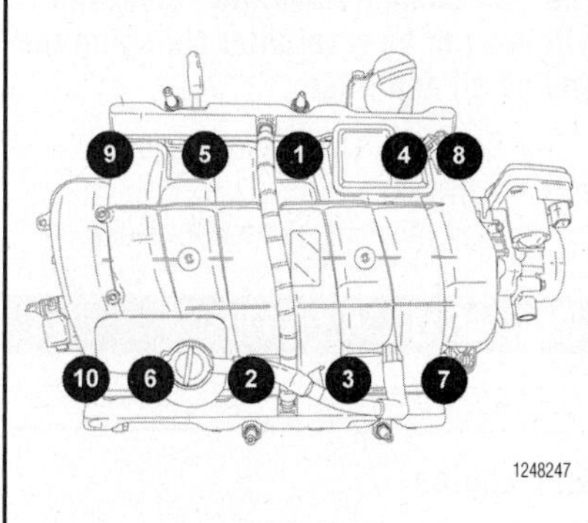

Fig. 124 Remove the intake manifold using sequence shown

8. Remove the cylinder head cover using sequence shown.
9. Remove the intake manifold using sequence shown.

➡It is not necessary to disconnect the hoses from the power steering pump, for power steering pump removal.

10. Remove the power steering pump and position aside.

➡The rocker arms and push rods must be installed in their original location as removed.

11. Remove the rocker arms and push rods using sequence shown. Note their location to ensure installation in their original locations as removed.
12. Using the sequence shown, remove the cylinder head bolts.
13. Remove the cylinder head and discard the cylinder head gasket.

To install:

14. If replacing the cylinder head, transfer the valves, valve seals and valve springs to the new cylinder head, valve refacing may be necessary.

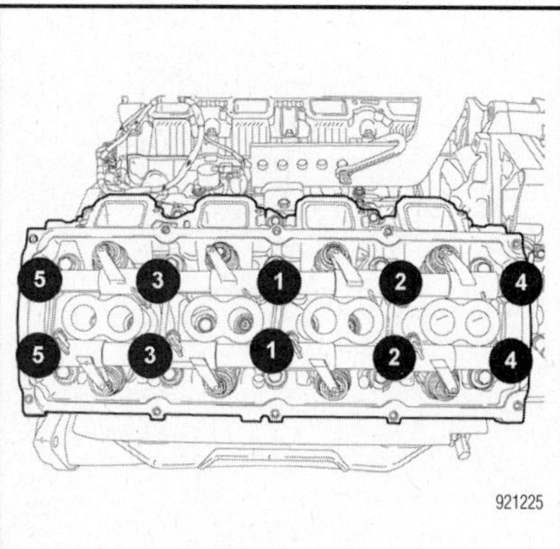

Fig. 125 Remove the rocker arms and push rods using sequence shown

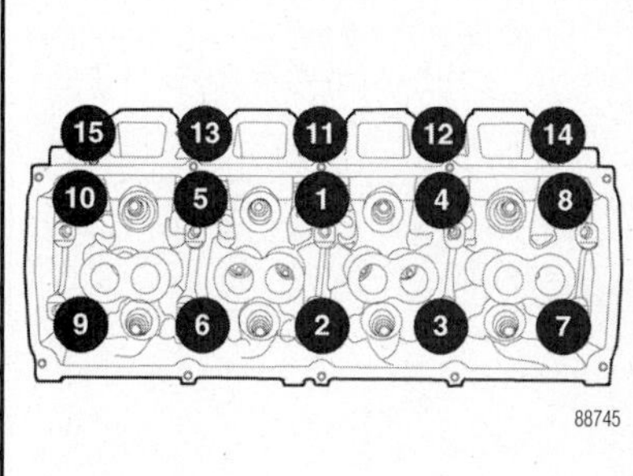

Fig. 126 Using the sequence shown, remove the cylinder head bolts

15. If replacing the cylinder head, transfer the exhaust manifold to the new cylinder head. Using the sequence shown, tighten the exhaust manifold bolts/studs to 18 ft. lbs. (25 Nm).
16. If replacing the cylinder head, transfer the spark plugs to the new cylinder head.

✲✲ WARNING

The cylinder head gaskets are not interchangeable between the left and right sides. They are marked with an "L" and "R" to indicate the left or right side and they are marked "TOP" to indicate which side goes up.

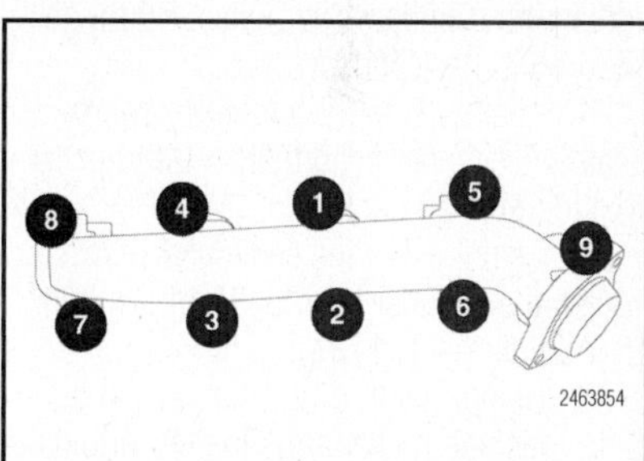

Fig. 127 Using the sequence shown, tighten the exhaust manifold bolts/studs

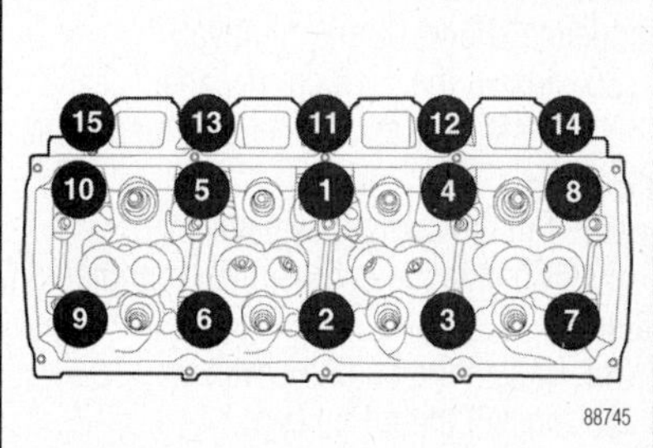

Fig. 128 Using the sequence shown, tighten the cylinder head bolts

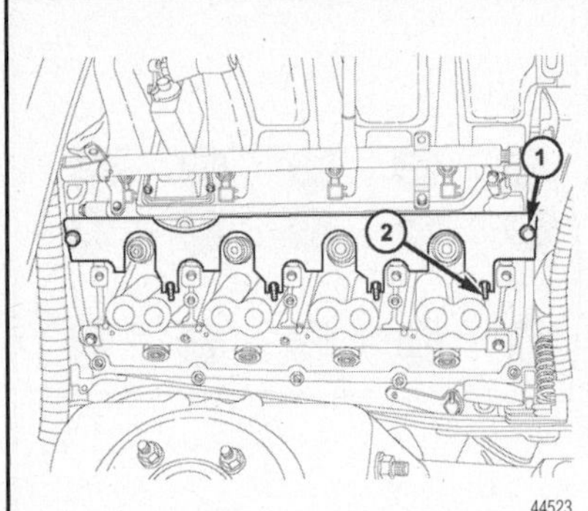

Fig. 129 Using Pushrod Retainer (1), install the push rods and rocker arms in their original location

17. Using a suitable solvent, clean all sealing surfaces of the cylinder block and cylinder heads.
18. Position the new cylinder head gasket onto the cylinder block.
19. Position the cylinder head onto the cylinder head gasket and cylinder block.
20. Using the sequence shown, tighten the cylinder head bolts 1 through 10 to 25 ft. lbs. (34 Nm).
21. Using the sequence shown, tighten the cylinder head bolts 11 through 15 to 15 ft. lbs. (20 Nm).
22. Again, using the sequence shown, tighten the cylinder head bolts 1 through 10 to 40 ft. lbs. (54 Nm).
23. Again, using the sequence shown, tighten the cylinder head bolts 11 through 15 to 15 ft. lbs. (20 Nm).
24. Again, using the sequence shown, rotate the cylinder head bolts 1 through 10 an additional 90 degrees.
25. Again, using the sequence shown, tighten the cylinder head bolts 11 through 15 to 25 ft. lbs. (34 Nm).
26. Using Pushrod Retainer, install the push rods and rocker arms in their original location as noted during removal.
27. Install the power steering pump.
28. Install the cylinder head cover using the sequence shown during removal.
29. Install the intake manifold using the sequence shown during removal.
30. Install the cowl cover panel.
31. Install the air cleaner and resonator assembly.
32. Fill the cooling system.
33. Change the engine oil and engine oil filter.
34. Install the engine cover.
35. Install the oil fill cap.
36. Connect the negative battery cable.

➡This vehicle is equipped with an engine oil change indicator system. The "Oil Change Required" message will need to be reset after changing the engine oil and filter.

37. Reset the "Oil Change Required" indicator system.
38. Start the engine check for leaks.

ENGINE OIL & FILTER

REPLACEMENT

3.6L Engine

See Figures 130 and 131.

✲✲ CAUTION

New or used engine oil can be irritating to the skin. Avoid prolonged or repeated skin contact with engine oil. Contaminants in used engine oil, caused by internal combustion, can be hazardous to your health. Thoroughly wash exposed skin with soap and water. Do not wash skin with gasoline, diesel fuel, thinner, or solvents, health problems can result. Do not pollute, dispose of used engine oil properly. Contact your dealer or government agency for location of collection center in your area.

1. Run the engine until achieving normal operating temperature.
2. Position the vehicle on a level surface and turn the engine off.
3. Remove the oil filter access cover.

➡Graphic shows engine cover removed for clarity.

✲✲ WARNING

When performing an engine oil change, the oil filter cap must be removed. Removing the oil filter cap releases oil held within the oil filter cavity and allows it to drain into the sump. Failure to remove the cap prior to reinstallation of the drain plug will not allow complete draining of the used engine oil.

4. Place an oil absorbent cloth around the oil filter housing at the base of the oil filter cap.

➡The oil filter is attached to the oil filter cap.

5. Rotate the oil filter cap counterclockwise and remove the cap and filter from the oil filter housing.
6. Raise and support the vehicle.
7. Place a suitable drain pan under the crankcase drain plug.
8. Remove the drain plug from oil pan and allow the oil to drain into the pan. Inspect the drain plug threads for stretching or other damage. Replace the drain plug and gasket if damaged.
9. Install the drain plug in the oil pan and tighten to 20 ft. lbs. (27 Nm).
10. Lower the vehicle.
11. Remove the oil filter from the oil filter cap.
12. Remove and discard the O-ring seal.

➡It is not necessary to pre-oil the oil filter or fill the oil filter housing.

13. Lightly lubricate the new O-ring seal with clean engine oil.
14. Install the O-ring seal on the filter cap.
15. Install the new oil filter into the oil filter cap.

➡Graphic shows engine cover removed for clarity.

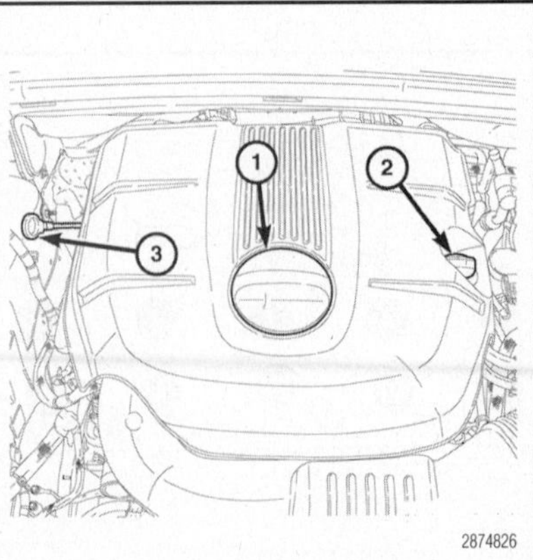

Fig. 130 Remove the oil filter access cover (1); oil fill cap (2) and oil level indicator (3)

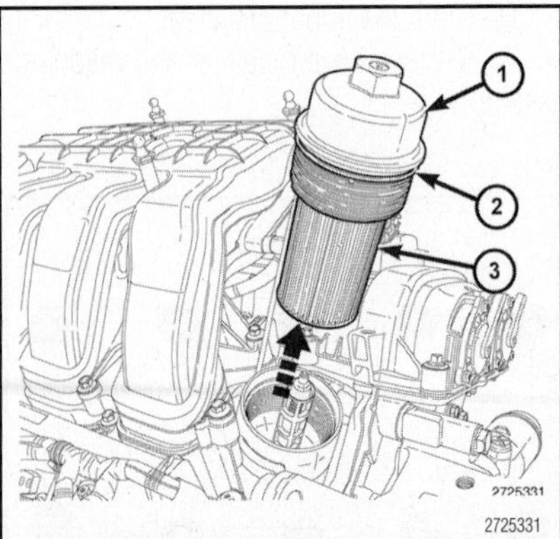

Fig. 131 Rotate the oil filter cap (1) counterclockwise and remove the cap and filter (3) from the oil filter housing; O-ring seal (2)

16. Thread the oil filter cap into the oil filter housing and tighten to 18 ft. lbs. (25 Nm).
17. Remove the oil fill cap. Fill the crankcase with the specified type and amount of engine oil.
18. Install the oil fill cap.
19. Start the engine and inspect for leaks.
20. Stop the engine and check the oil level.

5.7L Engine

WARNING

Do not overfill crankcase with engine oil, pressure loss or oil foaming can result.

1. Run engine until achieving normal operating temperature.
2. Position the vehicle on a level surface and turn engine off.
3. Hoist and support vehicle on safety stands.
4. Remove oil fill cap.
5. Place a suitable drain pan under crankcase drain.
6. Remove drain plug from crankcase and allow oil to drain into pan. Inspect drain plug threads for stretching or other damage. Replace drain plug if damaged.
7. Install drain plug in crankcase. Torque to 25 ft. lbs. (34 Nm).
8. Lower vehicle and fill crankcase with specified type and amount of engine oil described in this section.
9. Install oil fill cap.
10. Start engine and inspect for leaks.
11. Stop engine and inspect oil level.

➡Care should be exercised when disposing used engine oil after it has been drained from a vehicle engine.

EXHAUST MANIFOLD

REMOVAL & INSTALLATION

3.6L Engine

The exhaust manifolds are integrated into the cylinder heads for reduced weight.

5.7L Engine

Left Side

See Figures 132 through 134.

1. Remove the oil fill cap.
2. Remove the engine cover.
3. Perform the fuel pressure release procedure.
4. Disconnect and isolate the negative battery cable.
5. Remove the air cleaner assembly.

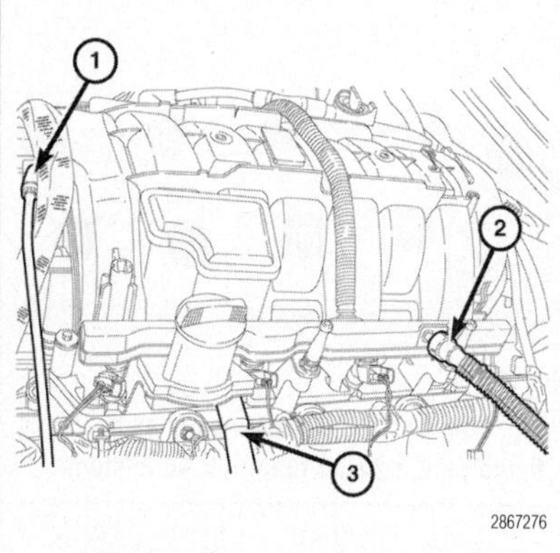

Fig. 132 Disconnect the EVAP vacuum line (1), the fuel supply line (2), and the make-up air hose (3)

6. Disconnect the EVAP vacuum line at the throttle body.
7. Disconnect the fuel supply line at the fuel rail.
8. Disconnect the make-up air hose at the intake manifold.
9. Remove the serpentine belt.

➡It is not necessary to disconnect the refrigerant lines for A/C compressor removal.

10. Remove the A/C compressor from the engine block and position aside.

WARNING

When servicing or replacing exhaust system components, disconnect the oxygen sensor connector(s). Allowing the exhaust to hang by the oxygen sensor wires will damage the harness and/or sensor.

11. Disconnect the left upstream 02 sensor electrical connector.

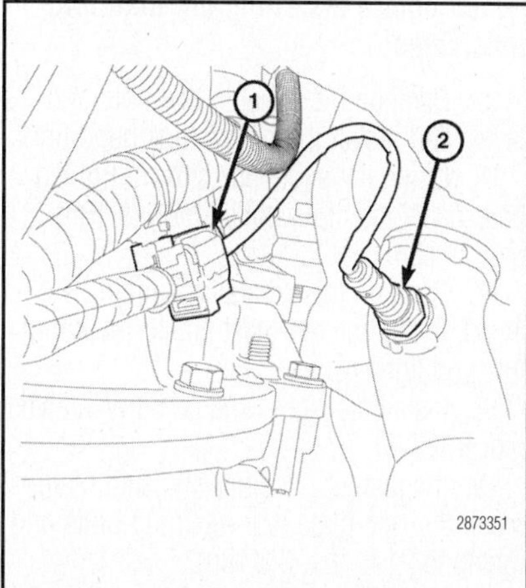

Fig. 133 Disconnect the left upstream 02 sensor (2) electrical connector (1)

12. Remove the exhaust manifold heat shield front retaining nuts.
13. Raise and support the vehicle.
14. If equipped, remove the skid plate four retaining bolts and remove the skid plate.
15. Disconnect the left exhaust pipe/catalytic converter.
16. Remove the exhaust manifold heat shield rear retaining nuts and remove the heat shield.
17. Remove the lower exhaust manifold retaining bolts.
18. Lower the vehicle.
19. Remove the upper exhaust manifold retaining bolts.

➡The left exhaust manifold is removed from below the engine and out through the front of the engine compartment.

20. Raise and support the vehicle.
21. Remove the left exhaust manifold and gasket from below the engine and out through the front of the engine compartment.
22. Inspect the exhaust manifold for any damage.
23. Clean the mating surfaces.

To install:

24. Prior to installation, make sure all gasket mating surfaces are clean and free of any debris.

➡Install the left exhaust manifold and gasket from below the engine and through the front of the engine compartment. Make sure the gasket is properly seated before installing the manifold bolts/studs.

25. Position the exhaust manifold and gasket and install the bolts/studs hand tight.
26. Using the sequence shown, tighten the exhaust manifold bolts/studs to 18 ft. lbs. (25 Nm).
27. Position the exhaust manifold heat shield, install the rear heat shield retaining nuts and tighten.
28. Install the left exhaust pipe/catalytic converter.

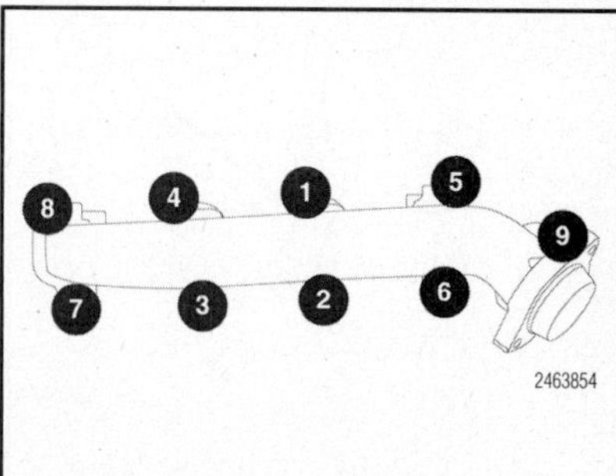

Fig. 134 Using the sequence shown, tighten the exhaust manifold bolts/studs

29. If equipped, position the skid plate, install the skid plate four retaining bolts and tighten to 21 ft. lbs. (28 Nm).
30. Lower the vehicle.
31. Install the front heat shield retaining nuts and tighten.
32. Connect the left upstream 02 sensor electrical connector.
33. Install the A/C compressor onto the engine block.
34. Install the serpentine belt.
35. Connect the make-up air hose at the intake manifold.
36. Connect the fuel supply line at the fuel rail.
37. Connect the EVAP vacuum line at the throttle body.
38. Install the air cleaner assembly.
39. Connect the negative battery cable.
40. Install the engine cover.
41. Install the oil fill cap.
Start the engine and check for leaks.

Right Side

See Figures 135 and 136.

1. Remove the oil fill cap.
2. Remove the engine cover.
3. Disconnect and isolate the negative battery cable.

➡When servicing or replacing exhaust system components, disconnect the oxygen sensor connector(s). Allowing the exhaust to hang by the oxygen sensor wires will damage the harness and/or sensor.

4. Disconnect the right upstream 02 sensor electrical connector (1).
5. Remove the exhaust manifold heat shield front retaining nuts.
6. Raise and support the vehicle.

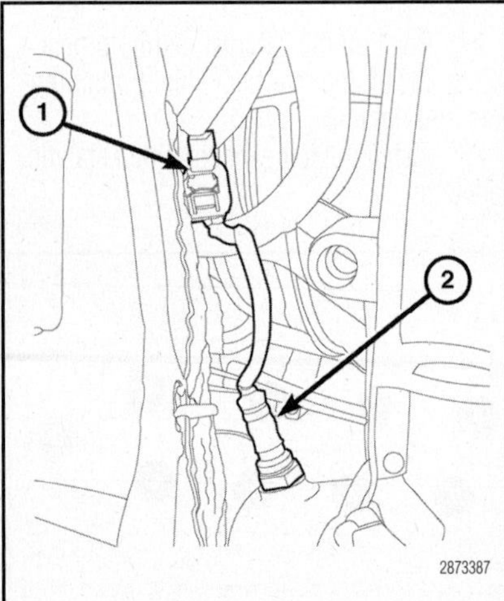

Fig. 135 Disconnect the right upstream 02 sensor (2) electrical connector (1)

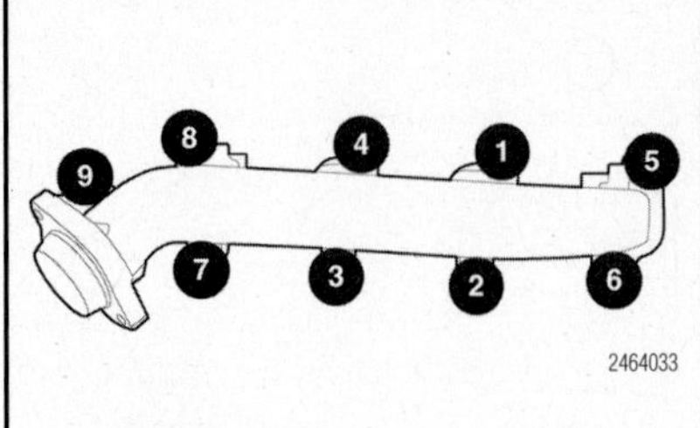

Fig. 136 Using the sequence shown, tighten the exhaust manifold bolts/studs

7. If equipped, remove the skid plate four retaining bolts and remove the skid plate.
8. Disconnect the right exhaust pipe/catalytic converter.
9. Remove the exhaust manifold heat shield rear retaining nuts and remove the heat shield.
10. Using the sequence shown, remove the exhaust manifold retaining bolts.

➡The right exhaust manifold is removed from below the engine and out through the rear of the engine compartment.

11. Remove the right exhaust manifold and gasket from below the engine and out through the rear of the engine compartment.
12. Inspect the exhaust manifold for any damage.
13. Clean the mating surfaces.

To install:

14. Prior to installation, make sure all gasket mating surfaces are clean and free of any debris.

➡Install the right exhaust manifold and gasket from below the engine and through the rear of the engine compartment. Make sure the gasket is properly seated before installing the manifold bolts/studs.

15. Position the exhaust manifold and gasket and install the bolts/studs hand tight.
16. Using the sequence shown, tighten the exhaust manifold bolts/studs to 18 ft. lbs. (25 Nm).
17. Position the exhaust manifold heat shield, install the rear heat shield retaining nuts and tighten.
18. Install the right exhaust pipe/catalytic converter.
19. If equipped, position the skid plate, install the skid plate four retaining bolts and tighten to 21 ft. lbs. (28 Nm).
20. Lower the vehicle.
21. Install the exhaust manifold heat shield front retaining nuts and tighten.
22. Connect the right upstream 02 sensor electrical connector.
23. Connect the negative battery cable.
24. Install the engine cover.
25. Install the oil fill cap.
26. Start the engine and check for leaks.

INTAKE MANIFOLD

REMOVAL & INSTALLATION

3.6L Engine

Upper Intake Manifold

See Figures 137 through 144.

1. Disconnect and isolate the negative battery cable.
2. Remove the engine cover.
3. Disconnect the electrical connector from the Inlet Air Temperature (IAT) sensor.
4. Loosen the clamp at the throttle body.
5. Loosen the clamp at the air cleaner body.
6. Remove the air inlet hose.
7. Disengage the brake booster hose retainer from the upper intake manifold.
8. Disconnect the electrical connectors from the Manifold Absolute Pressure (MAP) sensor and the Electronic Throttle Control (ETC).
9. Disengage the ETC harness from the clip on the throttle body. Disengage the wire harness retainer from the upper intake manifold near the MAP sensor and reposition the wire harness.
10. Disconnect the following hoses from the upper intake manifold:
    - Positive Crankcase Ventilation (PCV)
    - Vapor purge
    - Brake booster

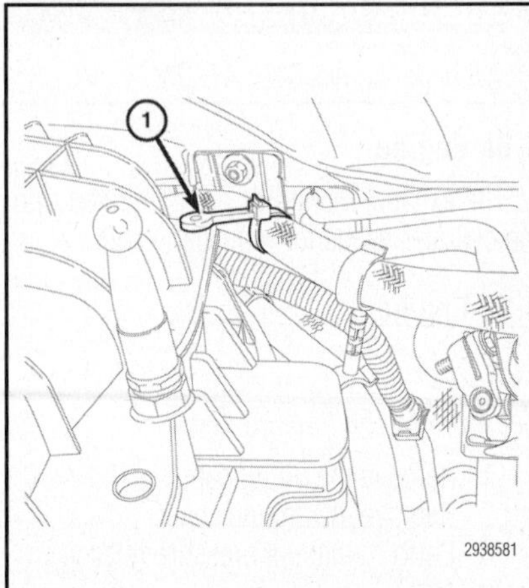

Fig. 137 Disengage the brake booster hose retainer (1) from the upper intake manifold

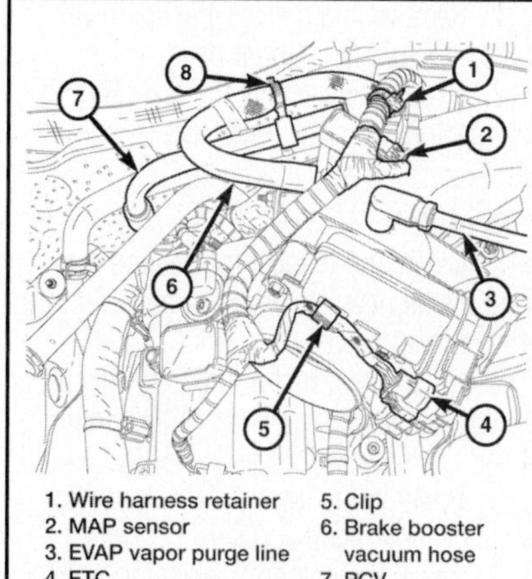

Fig. 138 Disconnect the electrical connectors from the Manifold Absolute Pressure (MAP) sensor and the Electronic Throttle Control (ETC)

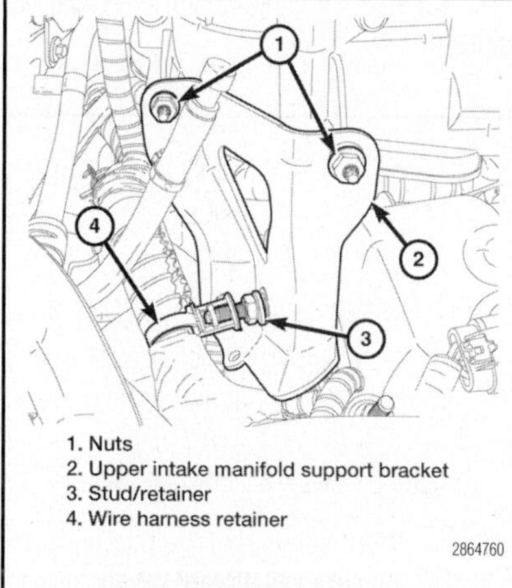

Fig. 139 Disengage the wire harness retainer from the stud bolt

11. Disengage the wire harness retainer from the stud bolt.

12. Remove two nuts, loosen the stud bolt and reposition the upper intake manifold support bracket.

13. Remove the nut from the support bracket of the heater core return tube.

14. Remove two nuts, loosen two stud bolts and reposition the two upper intake manifold support brackets.

➡The upper intake manifold attaching bolts are captured in the upper intake manifold. Once loosened, the bolts will have to be lifted out of the lower intake manifold and held while removing the upper intake manifold.

➡Exercise care not to inadvertently loosen the two fuel rail attachment bolts that are in close proximity of the upper intake manifold attaching bolts.

15. Remove seven upper intake manifold attaching bolts and remove the upper intake manifold.

16. Remove and discard the six upper to lower intake manifold seals.

17. Cover the open intake ports to prevent debris from entering the engine.

18. If required, remove the insulator from the LH cylinder head cover.

To install:

➡Prior to installing the upper intake manifold, verify that the four fuel rail bolts were not inadvertently loosened. The bolts must tightened in the sequence shown.

19. Clean and inspect the sealing surfaces. Install new upper to lower intake manifold seals.

➡Make sure the fuel injectors and wiring harnesses are in the correct position so that they don't interfere with the upper intake manifold installation.

20. If removed, install the insulator to the two alignment posts on top of the LH cylinder head cover.

21. Lift and hold the seven upper intake attaching bolts clear of the mating surface. Back the bolts out slightly or if required, use an elastic band to hold the bolts clear of the mating surface.

22. Position the upper intake manifold onto the lower intake manifold so that the two locating posts on the upper intake manifold align with corresponding holes in the lower intake manifold.

23. Install the seven upper intake manifold attaching bolts. Tighten the bolts in the sequence shown to 71 inch lbs. (8 Nm).

24. Install two nuts to the upper intake manifold support bracket. Tighten the nuts to 89 inch lbs. (10 Nm) and tighten the stud bolt to 15 ft. lbs. (20 Nm).

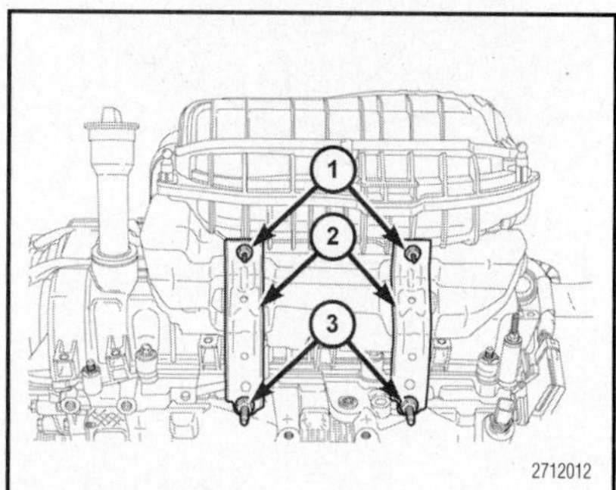

Fig. 140 Remove two nuts (1), loosen two stud bolts (3) and reposition the two upper intake manifold support brackets (2)

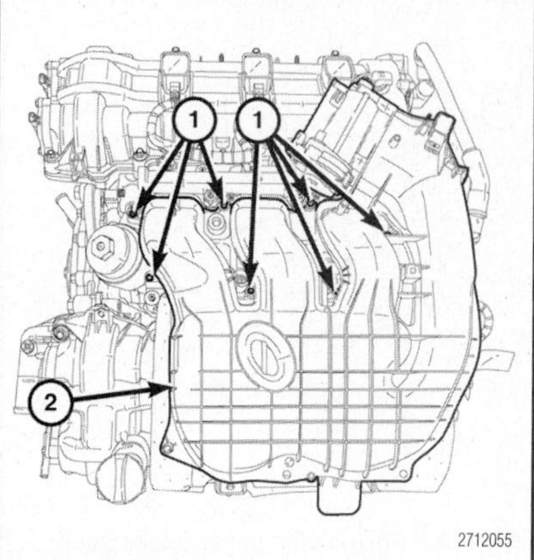

Fig. 141 Remove seven upper intake manifold attaching bolts (1) and remove the upper intake manifold (2)

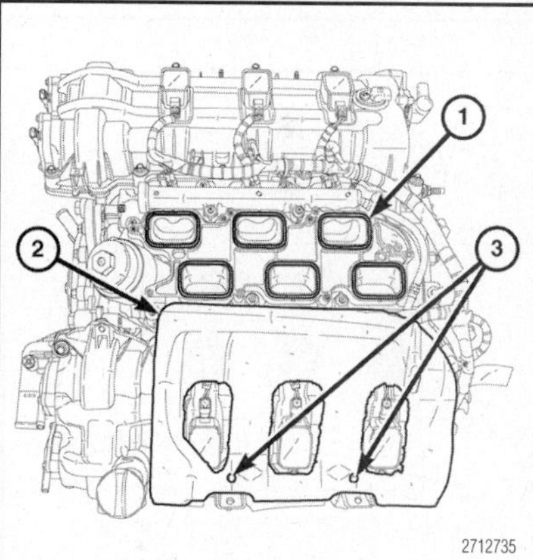

Fig. 142 Remove and discard the six upper to lower intake manifold seals (1); insulator (2) and insulator fasteners (3)

25. Engage the wire harness retainer to the stud bolt.

26. Install two upper intake manifold support brackets with two stud bolts and two nuts. Tighten the stud bolts to 15 ft. lbs. (20 Nm) and tighten the nuts to 89 inch lbs. (10 Nm).

27. Install the nut to the support bracket of the heater core return tube and tighten to 106 inch lbs. (12 Nm).

28. Connect the following hoses to the upper intake manifold:

- Positive Crankcase Ventilation (PCV)
- Vapor purge
- Brake booster

29. Connect the electrical connectors to the Manifold Absolute Pressure (MAP) sensor and the Electronic Throttle Control (ETC).

30. Secure the ETC harness to the clip on the throttle body and engage the wire

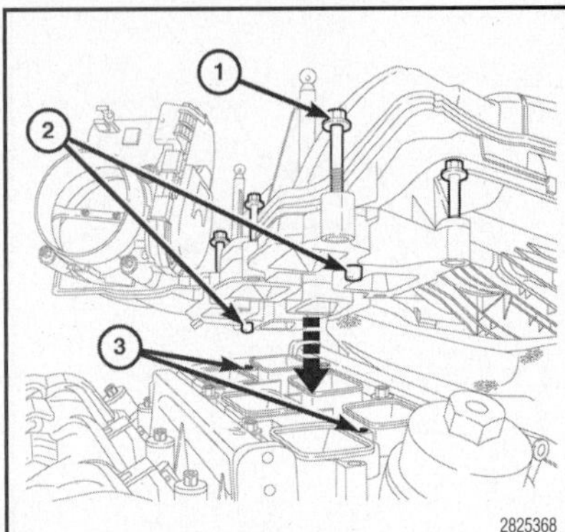

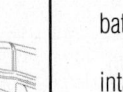

Fig. 143 Position the upper intake manifold (1) onto the lower intake manifold so that the two locating posts (2) on the upper intake manifold align with corresponding holes (3) in the lower intake manifold

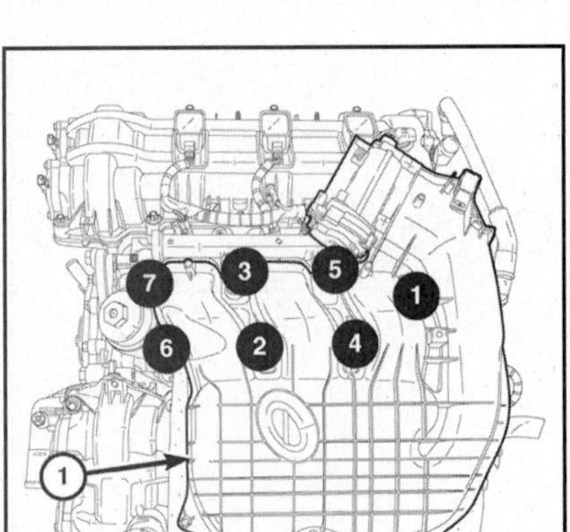

Fig. 144 Tighten the upper intake manifold attaching bolts in the sequence shown

harness retainer to the upper intake manifold near the MAP sensor.

31. Engage the brake booster hose retainer to the upper intake manifold.
32. Install the air inlet hose to the air cleaner body and the throttle body. Tighten the clamps.
33. Connect the electrical connector to the Inlet Air Temperature (IAT) sensor.
34. Install the engine cover.
35. Connect the negative battery cable.

Lower Intake Manifold

See Figures 145 through 148.

CAUTION

The fuel system is under constant pressure even with engine off. Before servicing the fuel rail, fuel system pressure must be released.

1. Release fuel system pressure.
2. Disconnect and isolate the negative battery cable.
3. Remove the air inlet hose and upper intake manifold.
4. Remove the insulator from the LH cylinder head cover.
5. Disconnect the fuel supply hose from the fuel rail.
6. Disconnect the fuel injector electrical connectors.
7. Disengage the injection/ignition harness retainer from the rear of the lower intake manifold.
8. Disengage the main wire harness retainer from the rear of the lower intake manifold.
9. Remove the eight lower intake manifold attaching bolts.
10. Remove the lower intake manifold with the fuel injectors and fuel rail.

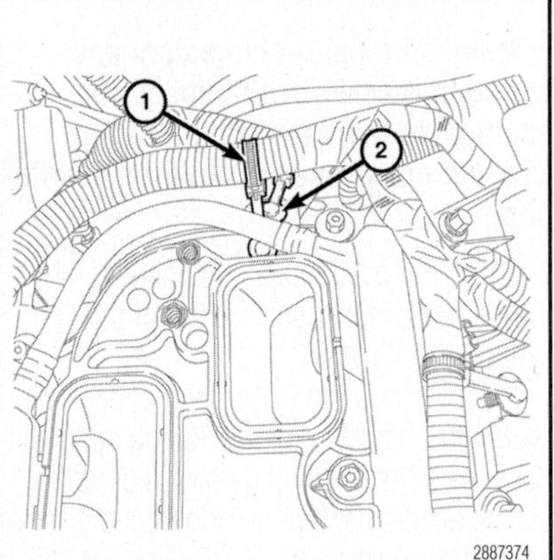

Fig. 145 Disengage the injection/ignition harness retainer (1) and the main wire harness retainer (2) from the rear of the lower intake manifold

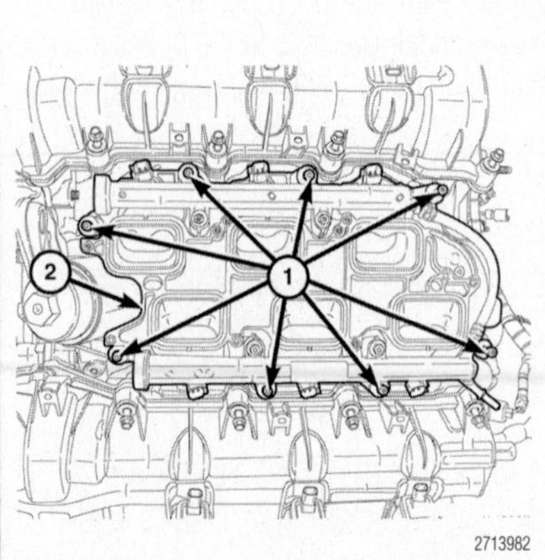

Fig. 146 Remove the eight lower intake manifold attaching bolts (1) and the lower intake manifold (2) with the fuel injectors and fuel rail

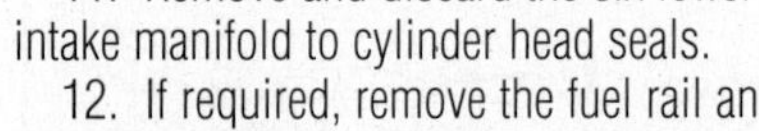

11. Remove and discard the six lower intake manifold to cylinder head seals.
12. If required, remove the fuel rail and fuel injectors from the lower intake manifold.

To install:

13. Clean and inspect the sealing surfaces. Install new lower intake manifold to cylinder head seals.
14. If removed, install the fuel injectors and the fuel rail to the lower intake manifold.
15. Position the lower intake manifold on the cylinder head surfaces.
16. Install the manifold attaching bolts and tighten in the sequence shown to 71 inch lbs. (8 Nm).
17. Engage the main wire harness retainer to the rear of the lower intake manifold.
18. Engage the injection/ignition harness retainer to the rear of the lower intake manifold.
19. Connect the fuel injector electrical connectors.

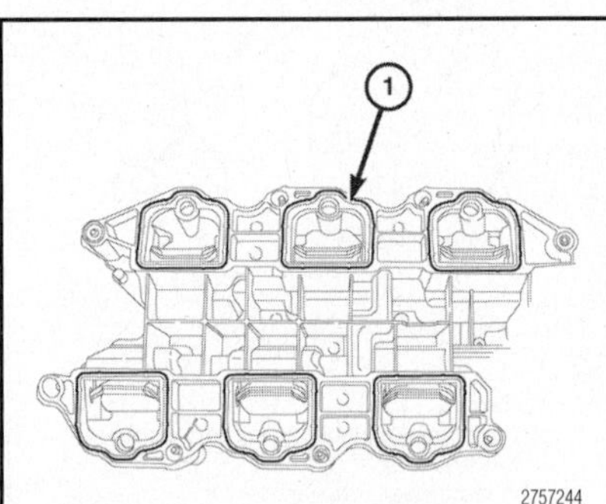

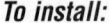

Fig. 147 Remove and discard the six lower intake manifold to cylinder head seals (1)

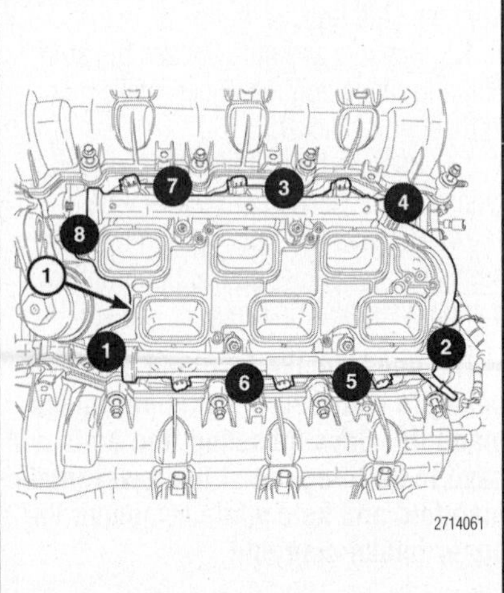

Fig. 148 Install the manifold attaching bolts and tighten in the sequence shown

20. Connect the fuel supply hose to the fuel rail.
21. Install the insulator to the two alignment posts on top of the LH cylinder head cover.
22. Install the upper intake manifold, support brackets and air inlet hose.
23. Connect the negative battery cable.
24. Start the engine and check for leaks.

5.7L Engine

See Figures 149 and 150.

1. Perform the fuel pressure release procedure.
2. Disconnect the negative battery cable.
3. Remove the oil fill cap.
4. Remove the engine cover.
5. Disconnect the electrical connector at the Intake Air Temperature (IAT) sensor.
6. Loosen the hose clamp at the air cleaner housing.
7. Remove the resonator retaining bolt.
8. Loosen the hose clamp at the throttle body and remove the resonator.
9. Disconnect the MAP sensor electrical connector at the rear of the intake manifold.
10. Disconnect the brake booster vacuum hose at the rear of the intake manifold.
11. Disconnect the fuel supply line at the fuel rail.
12. Disconnect the make-up air hose at the intake manifold.
13. Disconnect the EVAP vacuum purge hose at the throttle body.
14. Disconnect the electrical connector at the throttle body.
15. Reposition the electrical harness.

➡The factory fuel injection electrical harness is numerically tagged (INJ 1, INJ 2, etc.) for injector position identification. If the harness is not tagged, note the electrical connector's location during removal.

16. Disconnect the fuel injector electrical connectors and position aside.
17. Using the sequence shown, remove the intake manifold retaining bolts.
18. Remove the intake manifold.

To install:

➡The intake manifold seals may be used again, provided no cuts, tears, or deformation have occurred.

19. Inspect the intake manifold seals and replace as necessary.
20. Install the intake manifold seals.
21. Position the intake manifold in place.

➡If reinstalling the original manifold apply Mopar Lock Seal Adhesive to the intake manifold bolts. Not required when installing a new manifold.

22. Apply Mopar Lock Seal Adhesive to the intake manifold bolts.
23. Using the sequence shown, install the intake manifold bolts and tighten to 9 ft. lbs. (12 Nm).

➡The factory fuel injection electrical harness is numerically tagged (INJ 1, INJ 2, etc.) for injector position identification. If the harness is not tagged, use the noted electrical connector's location during removal.

24. Connect the fuel injector electrical connectors.
25. Position the electrical harness as shown.
26. Connect the electrical connector at the throttle body.
27. Connect the EVAP vacuum purge hose.
28. Connect the make-up air hose at the intake manifold.
29. Connect the fuel supply line at the fuel rail.
30. Connect the brake booster vacuum hose at the rear of the intake manifold.
31. Connect the MAP sensor electrical connector at the rear of the intake manifold.
32. Position the resonator onto the throttle body and air cleaner housing.
33. Tighten the hose clamp at the throttle body.
34. Install the resonator retaining bolt and tighten.
35. Tighten the hose clamp at the air cleaner housing.
36. Connect the electrical connector at the Intake Air Temperature (IAT) sensor.
37. Install the engine cover.
38. Install the oil fill cap.
39. Connect the negative battery cable.
40. Start the engine and check for leaks.

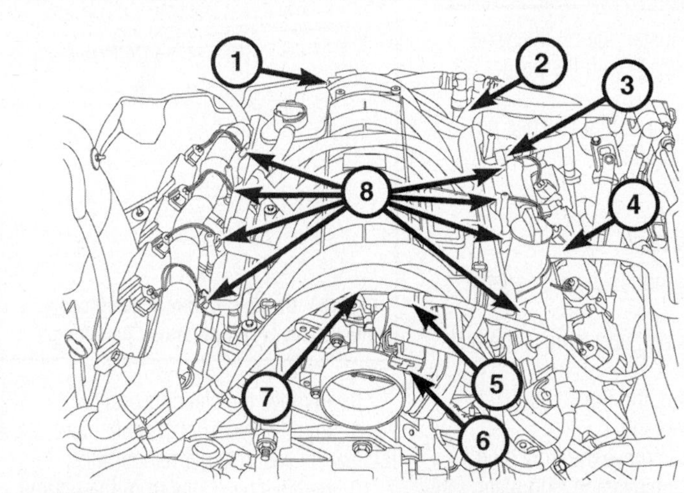

Fig. 149 Disconnect the MAP sensor electrical connector at the rear of the intake manifold

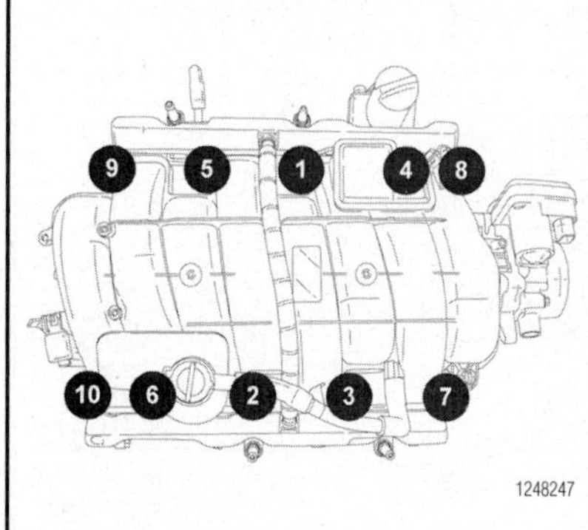

Fig. 150 Using the sequence shown, install the intake manifold bolts and tighten

OIL PAN

REMOVAL & INSTALLATION

3.6L Engine

Lower Oil Pan

See Figures 151 and 152.

1. Raise and support the vehicle.
2. Drain the engine oil.

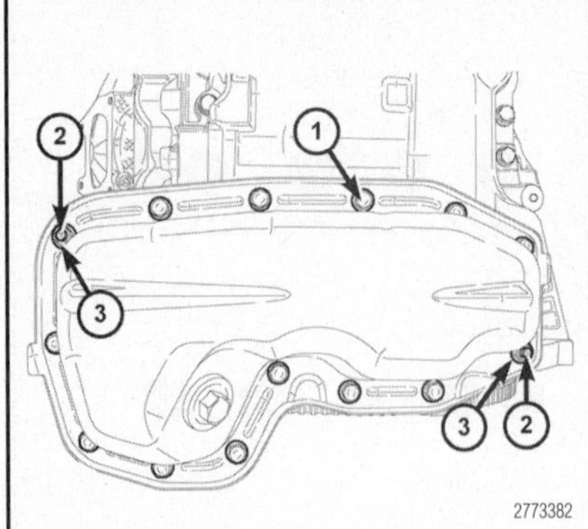

Fig. 151 Remove twelve bolts (1), two nuts (3), and two studs (2) from the flange of the lower oil pan

3. Remove the front suspension skid plate, if equipped.

➡**The lower oil pan must be removed to access all of the upper oil pan retaining bolts.**

4. Remove twelve bolts, two nuts, and two studs from the flange of the lower oil pan.

⁂ WARNING

Do not pry on the lower oil pan flange. There are no designated pry points for lower oil pan removal. Prying on only one or a few locations could bend the flange and damage the pan.

5. Using a pry bar, apply a side force to the lower oil pan in order to shear the sealant bond and remove the pan.

6. Remove all residual sealant from the upper and lower oil pans.

To install:

7. Clean the upper and lower oil pan mating surfaces with isopropyl alcohol in preparation for sealant application.

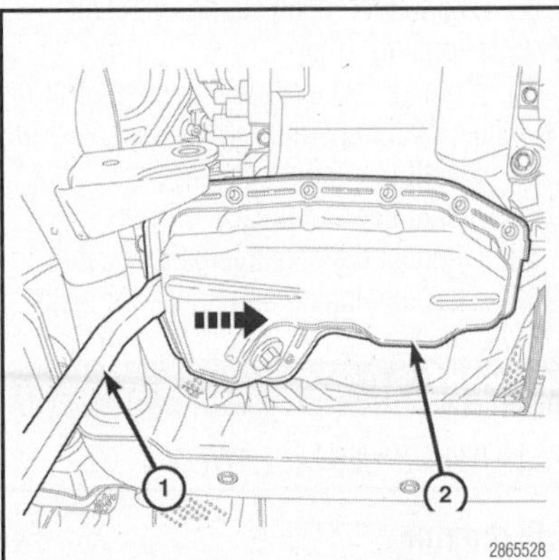

Fig. 152 Using a pry bar (1), apply a side force to the lower oil pan (2) in order to shear the sealant bond and remove the pan

⁂ WARNING

Engine assembly requires the use of a unique sealant that is compatible with engine oil. Using a sealant other than Mopar Threebond Engine RTV Sealant may result in engine fluid leakage.

⁂ WARNING

Following the application of Mopar Threebond Engine RTV Sealant to the gasket surfaces, the components must be assembled within 20 minutes and the attaching fasteners must be tightened to specification within 45 minutes. Prolonged exposure to the air prior to assembly may result in engine fluid leakage.

8. Apply a bead of Mopar Threebond Engine RTV Sealant to the lower oil pan.

9. Install two studs into the upper oil pan flange.

10. Install the lower oil pan to the upper oil pan with twelve bolts and two nuts tightened to 93 inch lbs. (10.5 Nm).

⁂ WARNING

Following assembly, the Mopar Threebond Engine RTV Sealant must be allowed to dry for 45 minutes prior to adding oil and engine operation. Premature exposure to oil prior to drying may result in engine fluid leakage.

11. If removed, install the oil filter and fill the engine crankcase with the proper oil to the correct level.

12. Run the engine until it reaches normal operating temperature.

Upper Oil Pan

See Figures 153 through 157.

1. Disconnect and isolate the negative battery cable.

2. Remove the bolt and remove the oil level indicator.

3. Raise and support the vehicle.

4. Drain the engine oil.

5. If equipped, remove the front skid plate and the front suspension skid plate.

➡**The lower oil pan must be removed to access all of the upper oil pan retaining bolts.**

6. Remove the lower oil pan.

7. If equipped with AWD, remove the front axle.

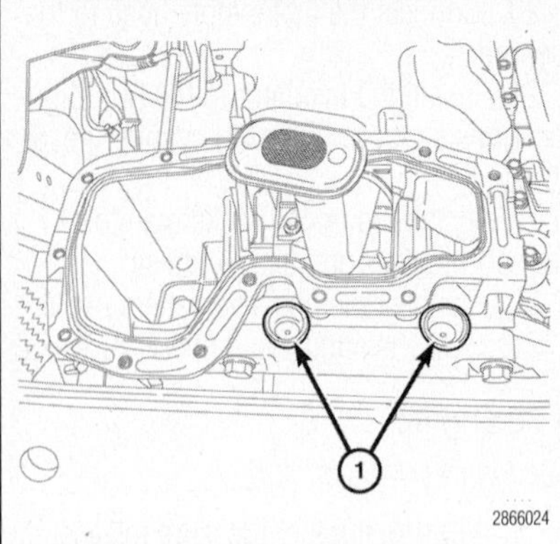

Fig. 153 Remove two rubber plugs (1) covering the rear oil seal retainer flange bolts

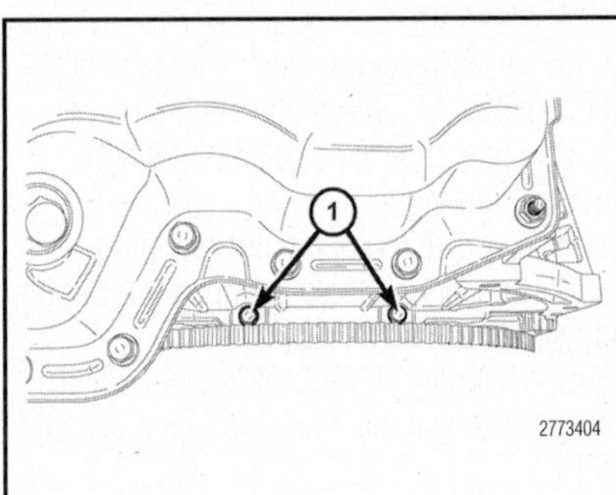

Fig. 154 Remove two bolts (1) from the rear oil seal retainer flange

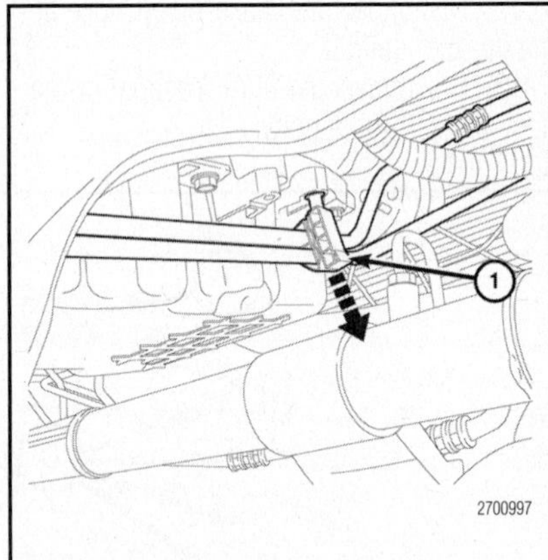

Fig. 155 Unclip the transmission cooler line retainer (1) from the oil pan flange

8. Remove the steering gear.

9. Remove two rubber plugs covering the rear oil seal retainer flange bolts.

10. Remove two bolts from the rear oil seal retainer flange.

11. Unclip the transmission cooler line retainer from the oil pan flange.

12. Remove four transmission to the engine oil pan bolts.

13. Remove nineteen oil pan mounting bolts.

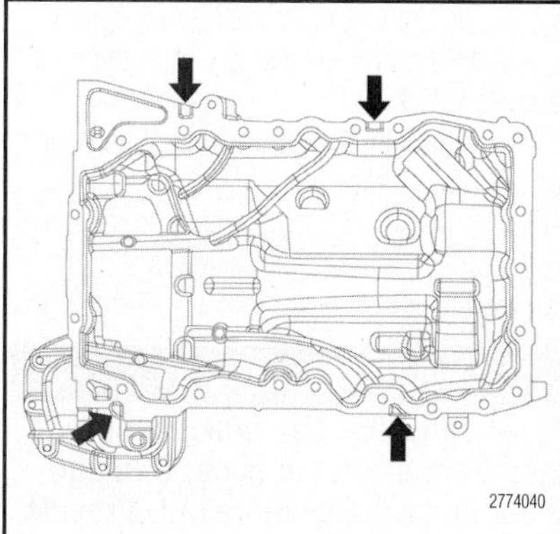

Fig. 156 Using the four indicated pry points, carefully remove the upper oil pan

14. Using the four indicated pry points, carefully remove the upper oil pan.
15. Remove all residual sealant from the upper and lower oil pans, timing chain cover, rear seal retainer and engine block mating surfaces.

To install:

16. Clean the upper and lower oil pans, timing chain cover, rear seal retainer and engine block mating surfaces with isopropyl alcohol in preparation for sealant application.

**** WARNING**

Engine assembly requires the use of a unique sealant that is compatible with engine oil. Using a sealant other than Mopar Threebond Engine RTV Sealant may result in engine fluid leakage.

**** WARNING**

Following the application of Mopar Threebond Engine RTV Sealant to the gasket surfaces, the components must be assembled within 20 minutes and the attaching fasteners must be tightened to specification within 45 minutes. Prolonged exposure to the air prior to assembly may result in engine fluid leakage.

17. Apply a bead of Mopar Threebond Engine RTV Sealant to the upper oil pan as shown in the following locations:
   - Oil pan to engine block flange
   - Two timing cover to engine block T-joints
   - Two rear seal retainer to engine block T-joints

**** WARNING**

Make sure that the rear face of the oil pan is flush to the transmission bell housing before tightening any of the oil pan mounting bolts. A gap between the oil pan and the transmission could crack the oil pan or transmission casting.

18. Install the oil pan to the engine block and flush to the transmission bell housing. Secure the oil pan to the engine block with nineteen oil pan mounting bolts finger tight.
19. Install four transmission to the engine oil pan bolts and tighten to 41 ft. lbs. (55 Nm).
20. Tighten the nineteen previously installed oil pan mounting bolts to 18 ft. lbs. (25 Nm).
21. Install two bolts to the rear oil seal retainer flange and tighten to 106 inch lbs. (12 Nm).
22. Install two rubber plugs covering the rear oil seal retainer flange bolts.
23. Clip the transmission cooler line retainer to the oil pan flange.
24. Install the steering gear.
25. If equipped with AWD, install the front axle.
26. Install the lower oil pan.
27. Install the front skid plate, if equipped.
28. Lower the vehicle.
29. Install the oil level indicator with bolt and tighten to 106 inch lbs. (12 Nm).
30. If removed, install the oil filter and fill the engine crankcase with the proper oil to the correct level.
31. Connect the negative battery cable.
32. Run the engine until it reaches normal operating temperature.

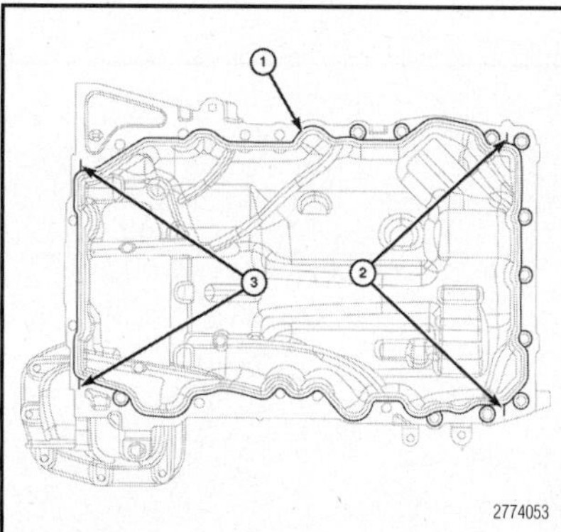

Fig. 157 Apply sealant to Oil pan to engine block flange (1), timing cover to engine block T-joints (2), and rear seal retainer to engine block T-joints (3)

5.7L Engine

See Figures 158 through 166.

1. Perform the fuel pressure release procedure.
2. Disconnect the negative battery cable.
3. Remove the oil fill cap.
4. Remove the engine cover.
5. Remove the engine oil dipstick.
6. Disconnect the electrical connector at the Intake Air Temperature (IAT) sensor.
7. Loosen the fresh air hose clamp at the air cleaner housing.
8. Remove the resonator retaining bolt.
9. Loosen the resonator hose clamp at the throttle body and remove the resonator.
10. Remove the intake manifold.

➡The engine must be at room temperature before removing the oil control valve.

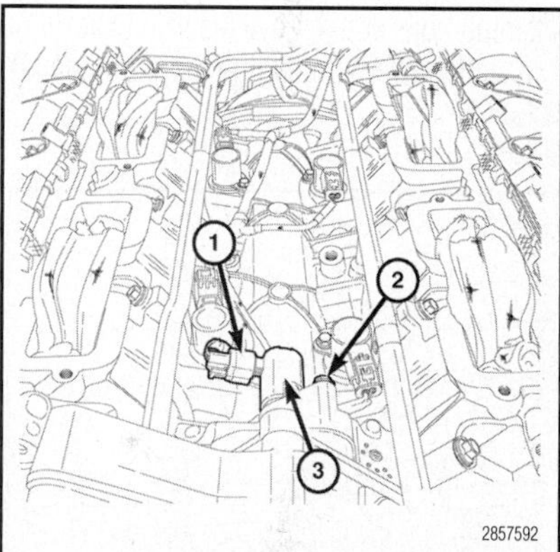

Fig. 158 Disconnect the oil control valve electrical connector (1), remove the oil control valve fastener (2), and rotate the oil control valve (3) to break the seal then pull the oil control valve straight out

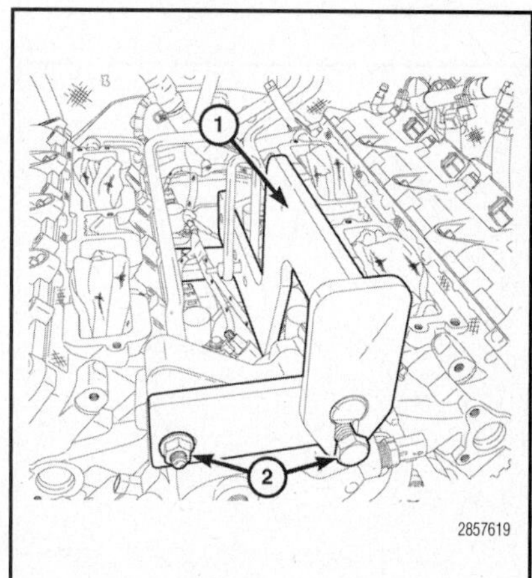

Fig. 159 Install the Engine Lift Fixture (1); tighten lifting fixture mounting bolts (2)

11. Disconnect the oil control valve electrical connector.
12. Remove the oil control valve fastener.
13. Rotate the oil control valve to break the seal then pull the oil control valve straight out.

➡**Do not use air tools to install the Engine Lift Fixture Engine Lift Fixture.**

14. Install the Engine Lift Fixture.
15. Securely tighten lifting fixture mounting bolts.
16. Position the Engine Support Fixture.
17. Connect the Engine Support Fixture to the Engine Lift Fixture and tighten to support the engine.
18. Raise and support the vehicle.
19. Drain the engine oil.
20. Remove both front wheels and tires.
21. If equipped, remove the skid plate four retaining bolts and remove the skid plate.
22. Remove both engine mount retaining nuts.

➡**Throughout this removal procedure, left side components are shown, right side similar.**

23. If equipped, mark a line across the C/V joint to companion flange for installation reference.
24. If equipped, remove the C/V joint retaining bolts and separate the C/V joint from the companion flange.
25. Remove the left catalytic converter heat shield retaining bolts and remove the heat shield.

⁂ WARNING

The steering column module is centered to the vehicles steering system. Failure to keep the system and steering column module centered and locked/inhibited from rotating can result in steering column module damage.

26. Remove the lower steering shaft coupler pinch bolt.
27. Remove the lower steering shaft coupler from the steering gear.
28. Disconnect both front wheel speed sensor wire harness retainers from the steering knuckles.
29. Remove both front wheel speed sensor retaining bolts.
30. Remove both front wheel speed sensors from the steering knuckles and position aside.

⁂ WARNING

Never allow the disc brake caliper to hang from the brake hose. Damage to the brake hose will result. Provide a suitable support to hang the caliper securely.

31. Remove both front brake caliper adapter mounting bolts and using bungee cords or bailing wire, secure the brake calipers aside.
32. Remove both upper ball joint nuts.
33. If equipped, remove both half shaft hub bearing nuts.
34. Separate both steering knuckles from the ball joints.

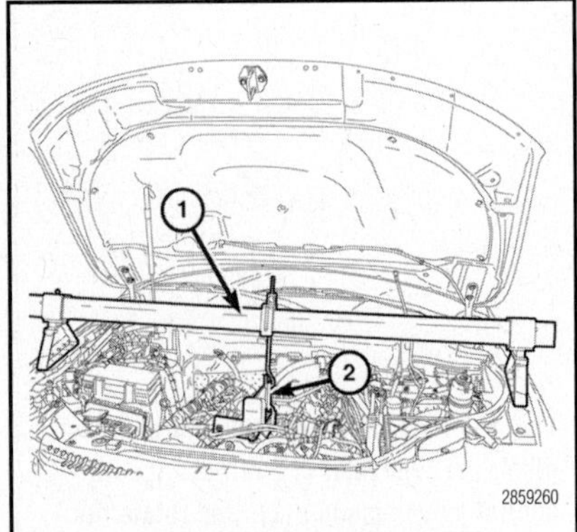

Fig. 160 Connect the Engine Support Fixture (1) to the Engine Lift Fixture (2) and tighten to support the engine

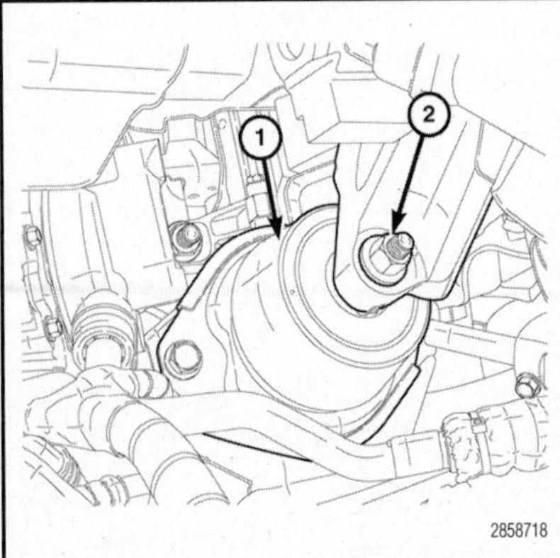

Fig. 161 Remove both engine mount (1) retaining nuts (2)

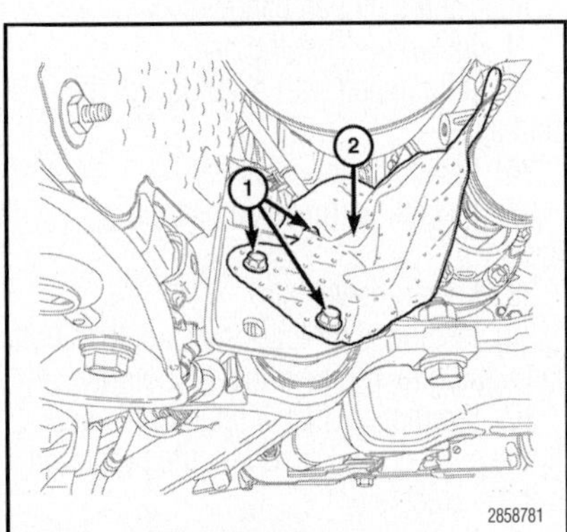

Fig. 162 Remove the left catalytic converter heat shield retaining bolts (1) and remove the heat shield (2)

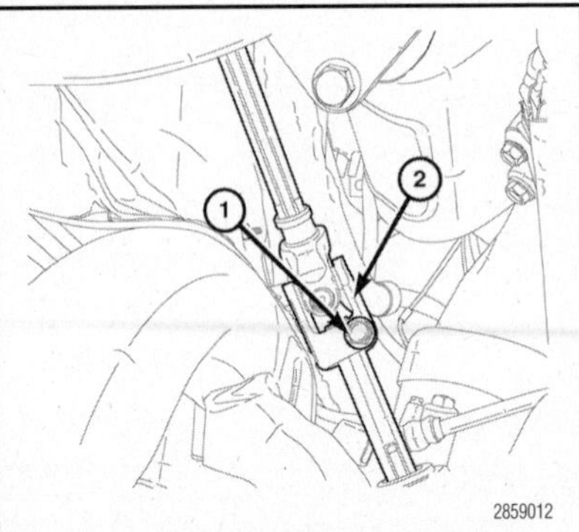

Fig. 163 Remove the lower steering shaft coupler pinch bolt (1) and remove the lower steering shaft coupler (2) from the steering gear

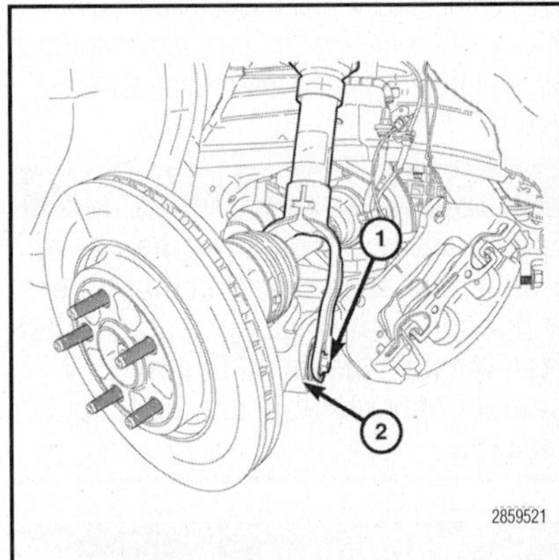

Fig. 164 Remove both lower clevis bolts (1) at the lower control arms (2)

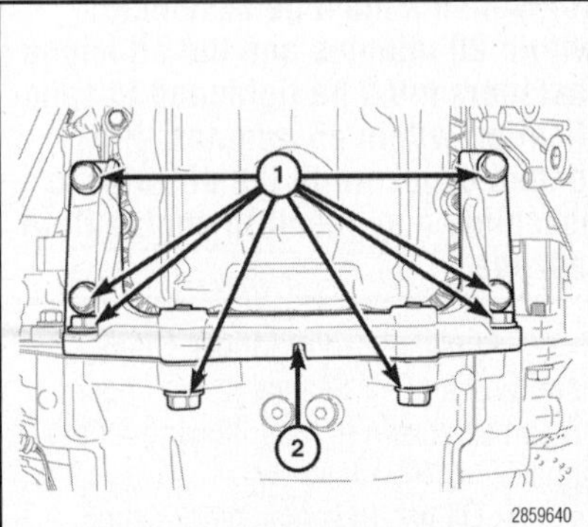

Fig. 165 Remove the structural dust cover retaining bolts (1) and the structural dust cover (2)

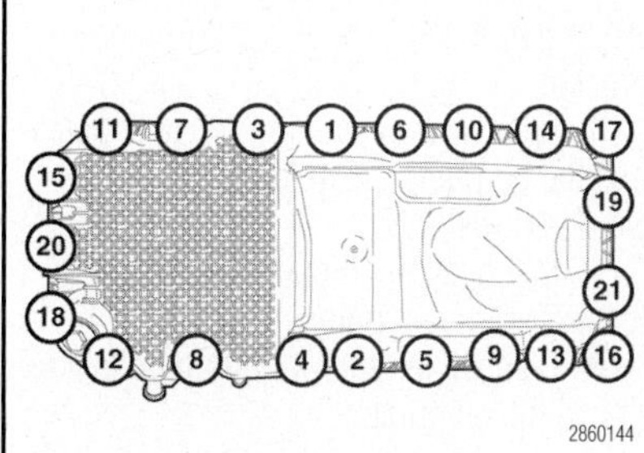

Fig. 166 Using the sequence shown, remove the oil pan retaining bolts

35. If equipped, slightly slide both axle shafts inward while tilting the hub bearing and steering knuckle assembly outward (do not remove).
36. Remove both lower clevis bolts at the lower control arms.
37. Remove the structural dust cover retaining bolts.
38. Remove the structural dust cover.
39. Remove the pressure line at the steering gear.
40. Remove the return line at the steering gear.
41. Remove the steering gear pressure line retainers at the engine cradle crossmember and position the pressure line aside.
42. Remove the engine cradle crossmember.

➡**The oil pump pickup tube, windage tray and oil pan is one assembly. When the oil pan is removed, a new oil pan gasket and pickup tube O-ring must be installed. The old gasket and O-ring cannot be reused.**

43. Remove the transmission line retaining bracket at the oil pan.
44. Using the sequence shown, remove the oil pan retaining bolts.
45. Remove the oil pan and discard the oil pan gasket and pickup tube O-ring.
46. Clean the sealing surfaces as necessary.

To install:

47. Clean the oil pan gasket mating surface of the block and oil pan.

➡**When the oil pan is removed, a new oil pan gasket and pickup tube O-ring must be installed. The old gasket and O-ring cannot be reused.**

48. Install a new oil pan gasket and pickup tube O-ring.

➡**Mopar Engine RTV must be applied to the 4 T-joints area where the front cover, rear retainer and oil pan gasket meet. The bead of RTV should cover the bottom of the gasket.**

49. Apply Mopar Engine RTV at the T- joints.
50. Position the oil pan, install the mounting bolts and using the sequence shown, tighten to 9 ft. lbs. (12 Nm).
51. Install the transmission line retaining bracket at the oil pan.
52. Install the engine cradle crossmember.
53. Position the steering gear pressure line and Install the retainers to the engine cradle crossmember.
54. Install the return line at the steering gear.
55. Install the pressure line at the steering gear.

⁂ WARNING

The structural dust cover must be held tightly against both the engine and the transmission bell housing during the tightening sequence. Failure to do so may cause severe damage to the cover.

56. Position the structural dust cover.
57. Install the structural dust cover retaining bolts hand tight.
58. Tighten the structural dust cover-to-transmission bolts to 80 inch lbs. (9 Nm).
59. Tighten the structural dust cover-to-engine bolts to 80 inch lbs. (9 Nm).
60. Retighten the structural dust cover-to-transmission bolts to 40 ft. lbs. (54 Nm).
61. Retighten the structural dust cover-to-engine bolts to 40 ft. lbs. (54 Nm).
62. Install both lower clevis bolts at the lower control arms and tighten to 125 ft. lbs. (169 Nm).
63. If equipped, slide both axle shafts into the hub bearing.
64. Position both steering knuckle assemblies onto the ball joint studs.
65. If equipped, install both half shaft hub bearing nuts and tighten to 100 ft. lbs. (135 Nm).
66. Install both upper ball joint nuts and tighten to 70 ft. lbs. (95 Nm).
67. Position the front brake calipers, install the caliper adapter mounting bolts and tighten to 125 ft. lbs. (169 Nm).
68. Position both front wheel speed sensors into the steering knuckle.
69. Install both front wheel speed sensor retaining bolts and tighten to 10 ft. lbs. (14 Nm).
70. Connect both front wheel speed sensor wire harness retainers to the steering knuckles.

⁂ WARNING

The steering gear must be centered prior to installing the coupler to prevent clockspring damage.

71. Position the lower steering shaft coupler onto the steering gear.
72. Install the a new lower steering shaft coupler pinch bolt and tighten to 36 ft. lbs. (49 Nm).
73. Position the left catalytic converter heat shield, install the retaining bolts and securely tighten bolts.
74. If equipped, position the C/V joint onto the companion flange making sure to align the reference mark made during removal.

➡**Clean all propeller shaft bolts and apply Mopar Lock and Seal Adhesive, Medium Strength Thread locker or equivalent to the threads before installation.**

75. Install the bolts to the axle flange and tighten to 24 ft. lbs. (32 Nm).

➡**For engine mount retaining nuts, apply Mopar Lock and Seal Adhesive, Medium Strength Thread locker or equivalent to the threads before installation.**

76. Install both engine mount retaining nuts and tighten to 55 ft. lbs. (75 Nm).
77. If equipped, position the front skid plate, install the four retaining bolts and tighten to 21 ft. lbs. (28 Nm).
78. Install both front wheels and tires.
79. Lower the vehicle.
80. Remove the Engine Support Fixture.
81. Remove the Engine Lift Fixture.
82. Install the oil control valve.
83. Ensure that the O-ring is fully seated into the cylinder block.
84. Securely tighten the oil control valve retaining bolt.
85. Connect the oil control valve electrical connector.
86. Install the intake manifold.
87. Position the resonator hose onto the throttle body and tighten hose clamp.
88. Install the resonator retaining bolt.
89. Install the fresh air hose to the air cleaner housing and tighten hose clamp.
90. Connect the electrical connector at the Intake Air Temperature (IAT) sensor.
91. Install the engine oil dipstick.
92. Install the engine cover.
93. Install the oil fill cap.
94. Fill the engine with clean oil.
95. Connect the negative battery cable.
96. Start the engine and check for leaks.

OIL PUMP

REMOVAL & INSTALLATION

3.6L Engine

See Figures 167 through 171.

1. Disconnect and isolate the negative battery cable.
2. Remove the upper oil pan
3. Remove the oil pump pick-up.
4. Disconnect the engine wire harness from the oil pump solenoid electrical connector.
5. Depress the connector retention lock tab to disengage the oil pump solenoid electrical connector from the engine block.
6. Push the oil pump solenoid electrical connector into the engine block, rotate the connector slightly clockwise, push it past the primary chain tensioner mounting bolt and into the engine.

Fig. 167 Disconnect the engine wire harness from the oil pump solenoid electrical connector (1)

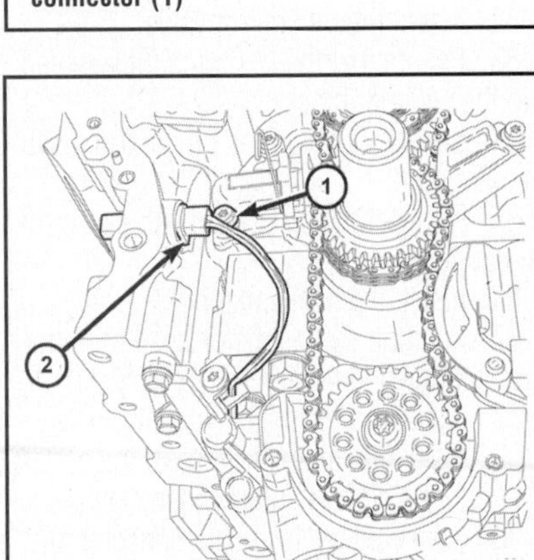

Fig. 168 Push the oil pump solenoid electrical connector (2) into the engine block, rotate the connector slightly clockwise, push it past the primary chain tensioner mounting bolt (1) and into the engine

➡**Graphic shows the engine timing cover removed for clarity.**

7. Push back the oil pump chain tensioner and insert a suitable retaining pin such as a 3 mm Allen wrench.

WARNING

Always reinstall timing chains so that they maintain the same direction of rotation. Inverting a previously run chain on a previously run sprocket will result in excessive wear to both the chain and sprocket.

8. Mark the direction of rotation on the oil pump chain and sprocket using a paint pen or equivalent to aid in reassembly.

➡**There are no timing marks on the oil pump gear or chain. Timing of the oil pump is not required.**

Fig. 169 Push back the oil pump chain tensioner (2) and insert a suitable retaining pin (1) such as a 3 mm Allen wrench

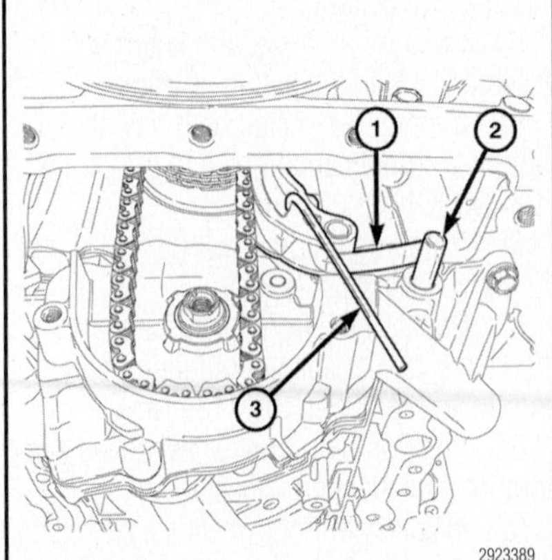

Fig. 170 Remove the retaining pin (3) and disengage the oil pump chain tensioner spring (1) from the dowel pin (2)

9. Remove the oil pump sprocket T45 retaining bolt and remove the oil pump sprocket.
10. Remove the retaining pin and disengage the oil pump chain tensioner spring from the dowel pin.
11. Remove the oil pump chain tensioner from the oil pump.
12. Remove the four oil pump bolts and remove the oil pump.

To install:

13. Align the locator pins to the engine block and install the oil pump with four bolts. Tighten the bolts to 106 inch lbs. (12 Nm).
14. Install the oil pump chain tensioner on the oil pump.
15. Position the oil pump chain tensioner spring above the dowel pin.
16. Push back the oil pump chain tensioner and insert a suitable retaining pin such as a 3 mm Allen wrench.

➡**There are no timing marks on the oil pump gear or chain. Timing of the oil pump is not required.**

WARNING

Always reinstall timing chains so that they maintain the same direction of rotation. Inverting a previously run chain on a previously run sprocket will result in excessive wear to both the chain and sprocket.

17. Place the oil pump sprocket into the oil pump chain. Align the oil pump sprocket with the oil pump shaft and install the sprocket. Install the T45 retaining bolt and tighten to 18 ft. lbs. (25 Nm).

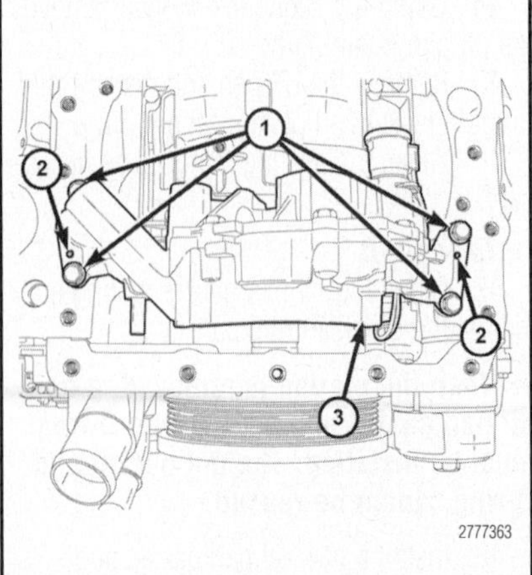

Fig. 171 Remove the four oil pump bolts (1) and remove the oil pump (3); locator pins (2)

18. Remove the retaining pin. Verify that the oil pump chain is centered on the tensioner and crankshaft sprocket.
19. Rotate the crankshaft clockwise one complete revolution to verify proper oil pump chain installation.
20. Position the oil pump solenoid electrical connector into the engine block. Rotate the connector so that it can be pushed past the primary chain tensioner mounting bolt. Then rotate the connector slightly counterclockwise and push it into the engine block until it locks in place.
21. Verify that the oil pump solenoid electrical connector retention lock tab is engaged to the engine block.
22. Connect the engine wire harness to the oil pump solenoid electrical connector.
23. Install the oil pump pick-up.
24. Install the oil pan.
25. If removed, install the oil filter and fill the engine crankcase with the proper oil to the correct level.
26. Connect the negative battery cable.

WARNING

A MIL or low oil pressure indicator that remains illuminated for more than 2 seconds may indicate low or no engine oil pressure. Stop the engine and investigate the cause of the indication.

27. Start and run the engine until it reaches normal operating temperature.

5.7L Engine

See Figures 172 and 173.

1. Remove the oil pan.
2. Remove the timing cover.
3. Remove the four bolts and the oil pump.

To install:

4. Position the oil pump on the crankshaft and install the oil pump retaining bolts finger tight.
5. Using the sequence shown, tighten the oil pump retaining bolts to 21 ft. lbs. (28 Nm).
6. Install the timing cover.
7. Install the oil pan.

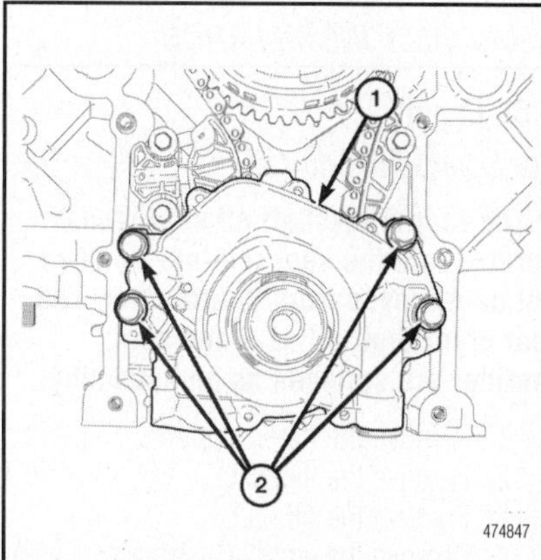

Fig. 172 Remove the four bolts (2) and the oil pump (1)

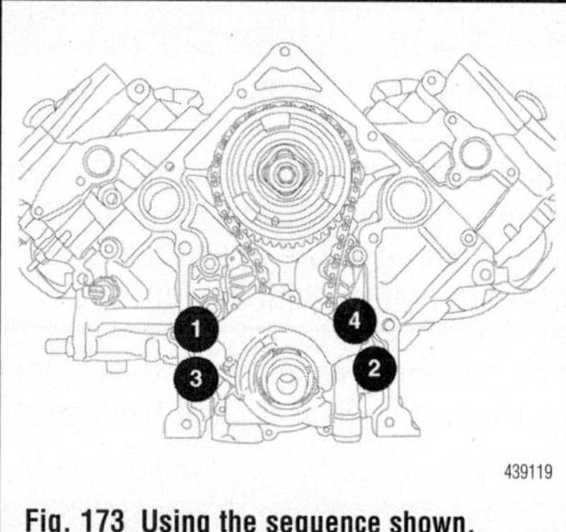

Fig. 173 Using the sequence shown, tighten the oil pump retaining bolts

PISTON AND RING

POSITIONING

3.6L Engine

See Figures 174 and 175.

5.7L Engine

See Figure 176.

ROCKER ARMS

REMOVAL & INSTALLATION

3.6L Engine

See Figure 177.

1. Disconnect and isolate the negative battery cable.
2. Remove the camshaft(s).

➡If the rocker arms are to be reused, identify their positions so that they can be reassembled into their original locations.

3. Remove the rocker arm(s).

➡The LH cylinder head rocker arms are shown, the RH cylinder head rocker arms are similar.

To install:

4. Lubricate the rocker arms with clean engine oil before installation.
5. Install the rocker arm(s).
6. Install the camshaft(s), phasers, cylinder head cover(s) and upper intake manifold.
7. Connect the negative battery cable.

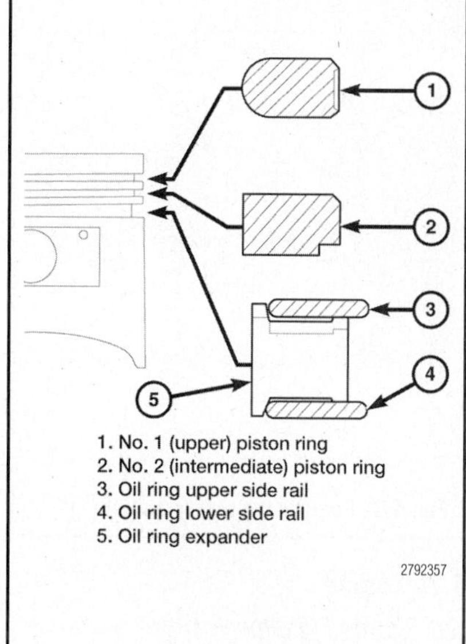

Fig. 174 Piston ring positioning

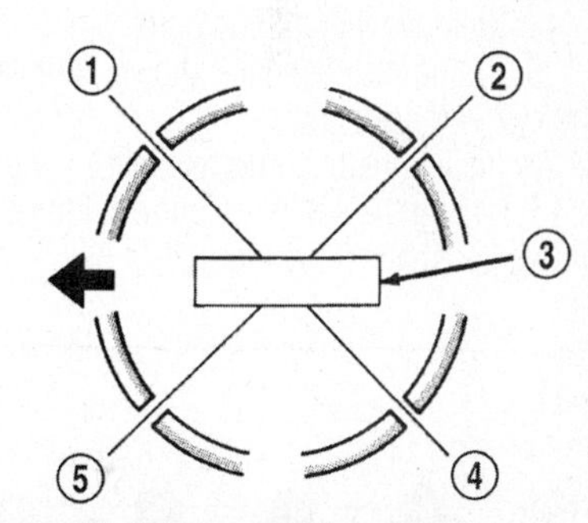

Fig. 175 Piston ring end gap positioning

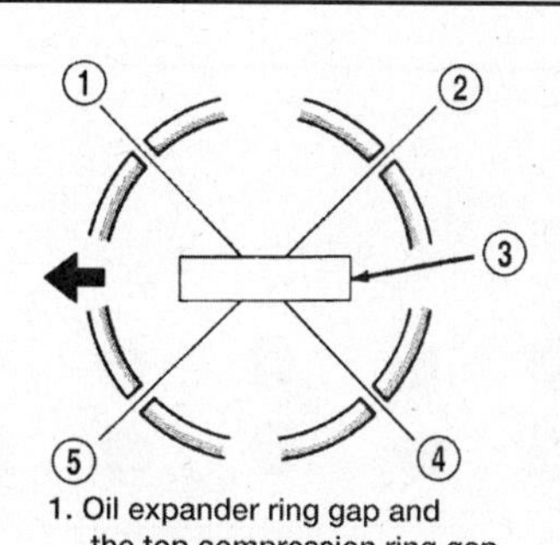

Fig. 176 Piston ring end gap positioning

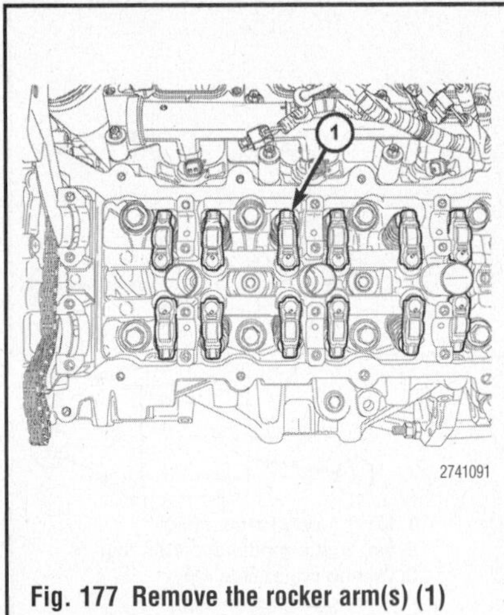

Fig. 177 Remove the rocker arm(s) (1)

5.7L Engine

See Figures 178 through 180.

1. Disconnect the negative battery cable.
2. Remove the oil fill cap.
3. Remove the engine cover.
4. Remove the ignition coils.
5. Using the sequence shown, remove the cylinder head cover.
6. Install the pushrod retainer.
7. Using the sequence shown, loosen the rocker shafts retaining bolts.

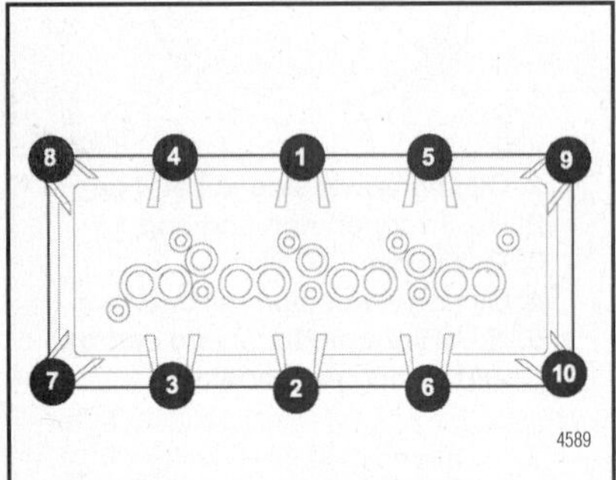

Fig. 178 Using the sequence shown, remove the cylinder head cover

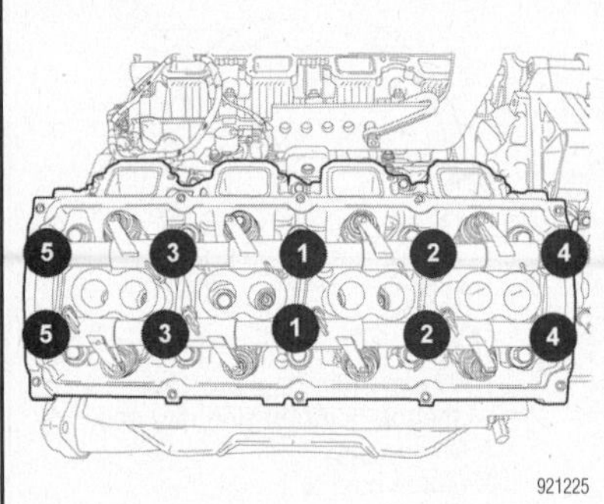

Fig. 179 Using the sequence shown, loosen the rocker shafts retaining bolts

WARNING

The rocker shaft assemblies are not interchangeable between the intake and the exhaust, failure to install them in the correct location could result in engine damage. The intake rocker arms are marked with the letter "I".

➡The rocker arms and push rods must be installed in their original location as removed.

WARNING

Do not remove the retainers from the rocker shaft.

8. Remove the rocker shaft. Note the rocker arms and rocker shafts location to ensure installation in their original locations as removed.

WARNING

The longer pushrods are for the exhaust side and the shorter pushrods are for the intake side.

9. Remove the pushrods. Note the pushrods location to ensure installation in their original locations as removed.

To install:

WARNING

The longer pushrods are for the exhaust side and the shorter pushrods are for the intake side.

10. Install the pushrods in the same order as noted during removal.
11. Install the pushrod retainer.

WARNING

Make sure that the retainers and the rocker arms are not overlapped when tightening bolts or engine damage could result.

WARNING

Verify the pushrod(s) are installed into the rocker arm(s) and the tappet(s) correctly while installing the rocker shaft assembly or engine damage could result. Recheck after the rocker shaft assembly has been tightened to specification.

WARNING

The rocker shaft assemblies are not interchangeable between the intake and the exhaust, failure to install them in the correct location could result in engine damage. The intake rocker arms are marked with the letter "I".

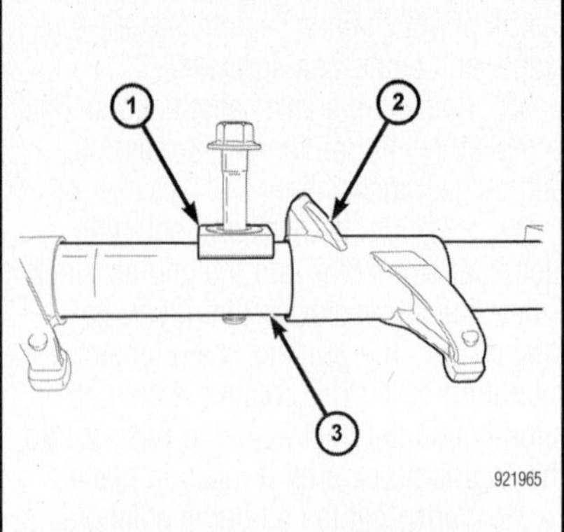

Fig. 180 Do not remove the retainers (1) from the rocker shaft (3); rocker arm (2)

12. Install the rocker shaft assemblies in the same location as noted during removal.
13. Using the sequence shown during the removal procedure, tighten the rocker shaft bolts to 16 ft. lbs. (22 Nm).

WARNING

Do Not rotate or crank the engine during or immediately after rocker arm installation. Allow the hydraulic roller tappets adequate time to bleed down (about five minutes).

14. Remove pushrod retainer.
15. Using the sequence shown during the removal procedure, install the cylinder head cover.
16. Install the ignition coils.
17. Install the engine cover.
18. Install the oil fill cap.
19. Connect the negative battery cable.

REAR MAIN SEAL

REMOVAL & INSTALLATION

3.6L Engine

See Figures 181 and 182.

➡The rear crankshaft oil seal is incorporated into the seal retainer and cannot be removed from the retainer. The rear crankshaft oil seal and seal retainer are serviced as an assembly.

1. Remove the transmission.
2. Remove the flexplate.
3. Remove the oil pan.
4. Remove the eight seal retainer attaching bolts.
5. Remove and discard the seal retainer.

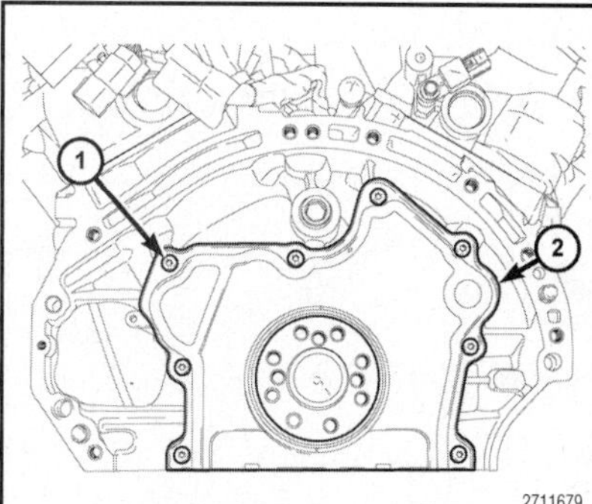

Fig. 181 Seal retainer (2) and attaching bolts (1)

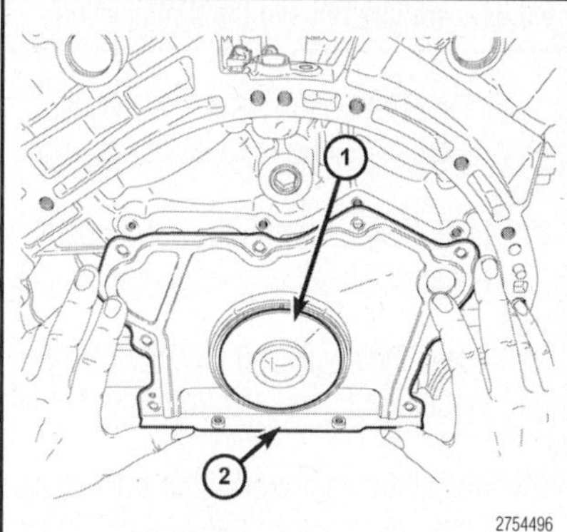

Fig. 182 Carefully position the oil seal retainer assembly (2), and seal protector (1) on the crankshaft and push firmly into place on the engine block

To install:

**** WARNING**

The rear crankshaft oil seal and retainer are an assembly. To avoid damage to the seal lip, DO NOT remove the seal protector from the rear crankshaft oil seal before installation onto the engine.

**** WARNING**

Whenever the crankshaft is replaced, the rear crankshaft oil seal must also be replaced. Failure to do so may result in engine fluid leakage.

6. Inspect the crankshaft to make sure there are no nicks or burrs on the seal surface.
7. Clean the engine block sealing surfaces thoroughly.

➡It is not necessary to lubricate the seal or the crankshaft when installing the seal retainer. Residual oil following installation can be mistaken for seal leakage.

8. Carefully position the oil seal retainer assembly, and seal protector on the crankshaft and push firmly into place on the engine block (during this step, the seal protector will be pushed from the rear oil seal assembly as a result of installing the rear oil seal).
9. Verify that the seal lip on the retainer is uniformly curled inward toward the engine on the crankshaft.
10. Install the eight seal retainer bolts and tighten to 106 inch lbs. (12 Nm).

➡Make sure that the seal retainer flange is flush with the engine block oil pan sealing surface.

11. Install the oil pan.
12. Install the flexplate.
13. Install the transmission.
14. Fill the engine crankcase with the proper oil to the correct level.

5.7L Engine

See Figure 183.

➡The crankshaft rear oil seal is integral to the crankshaft rear oil seal retainer and must be replaced as an assembly.

➡The crankshaft rear oil seal retainer cannot be reused after removal.

➡This procedure can be performed in vehicle.

1. Disconnect the negative battery cable.
2. Remove the transmission.
3. Remove the flexplate.
4. Remove the oil pan.
5. Using the sequence shown, remove the rear oil seal retainer mounting bolts.
6. Carefully remove the retainer from the engine block.

To install:

7. Thoroughly clean all gasket residue from the engine block.

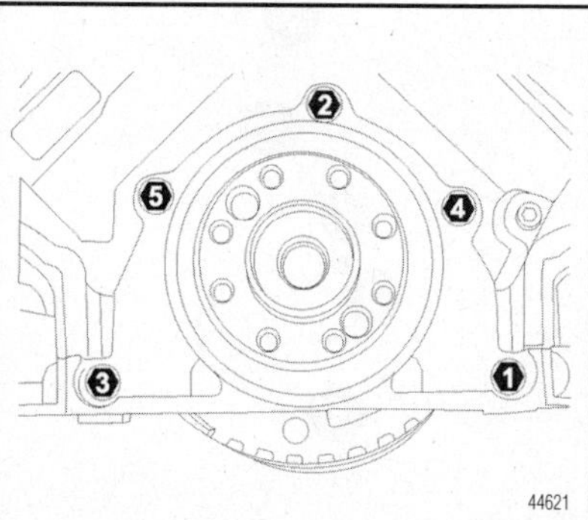

Fig. 183 Using the sequence shown, remove the rear oil seal retainer mounting bolts

8. Position the gasket onto the new crankshaft rear oil seal retainer.
9. Position the crankshaft rear oil seal retainer onto the engine block.
10. Using the sequence shown in the removal, install the crankshaft rear oil seal retainer mounting bolts and tighten to 11 ft. lbs. (15 Nm).
11. Install the oil pan.
12. Install the flexplate.
13. Install the transmission.
14. Fill the engine with oil.
15. Start the engine and check for leaks.

TIMING CHAIN FRONT COVER

REMOVAL & INSTALLATION

3.6L Engine

See Figures 184 through 188.

1. Disconnect and isolate the negative battery cable.
2. Drain the cooling system.
3. Remove the electric vacuum pump.
4. Remove the upper radiator hose and thermostat housing.
5. Remove the heater core return hose from the water pump housing.

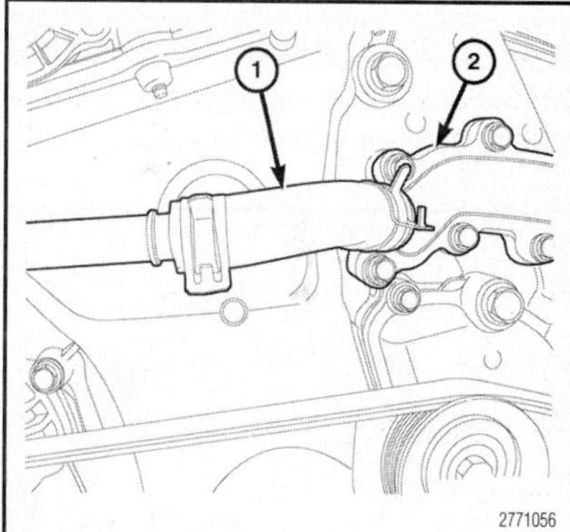

Fig. 184 Remove the heater core supply hose (1) from the coolant outlet housing (2)

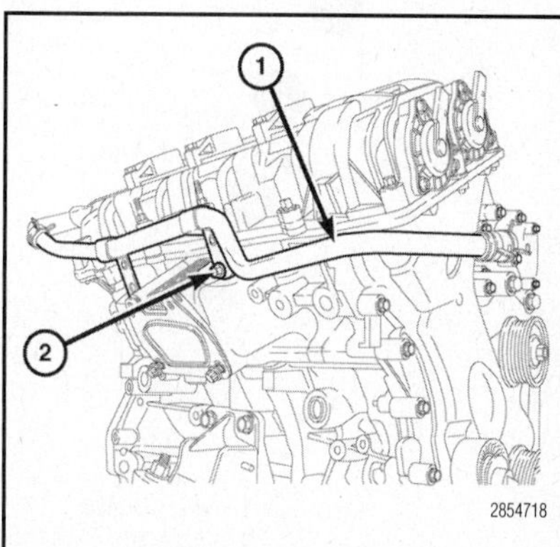

Fig. 185 Remove the bolt (2) and reposition the heater core supply tube (1)

6. Remove the lower radiator hose from the water pump housing.
7. Remove the heater core supply hose from the coolant outlet housing.
8. Remove the bolt and reposition the heater core supply tube.
9. Remove the accessory drive belt.
10. Remove the accessory drive belt tensioner.
11. Remove the accessory idler pulley.
12. Remove the power steering pump pulley.
13. Remove the crankshaft vibration damper.
14. Remove the right and left cylinder head covers.
15. Remove the upper and lower oil pans.

➡It is not necessary to remove the water pump or the coolant outlet housing for engine timing cover removal.

16. Remove the following timing cover attaching bolts:
- Three M10 bolts
- One M8 bolt
- Twenty-three M6 bolts

17. Using the seven indicated pry points, carefully remove the timing cover.

To install:

⁂ WARNING

Engine assembly requires the use of a unique sealant that is compatible with engine oil. Using a sealant other than Mopar Threebond Engine RTV Sealant may result in engine fluid leakage.

⁂ WARNING

Following the application of Mopar Threebond Engine RTV Sealant to the gasket surfaces, the components must be assembled within 20 minutes and the attaching fasteners must be tightened to specification within 45 minutes. Prolonged exposure to the air prior to assembly may result in engine fluid leakage.

18. Apply a bead of Mopar Threebond Engine RTV Sealant to the front cover as shown in the following locations:
- Three cylinder head bosses
- Right and left flanges
- Four cylinder head to engine block T-joints
- Cover to right cam chain tensioner gap

19. Align the locator pins on the engine block to the engine timing cover and install the cover.
20. Install and tighten the timing cover attaching bolts:
a. Twenty-three M6 bolts to 106 inch lbs. (12 Nm).
b. One M8 bolt to 18 ft. lbs. (25 Nm).
c. Three M10 bolts to 41 ft. lbs. (55 Nm)

21. Install the upper and lower oil pans.
22. Install the right and left cylinder head covers.
23. Install the crankshaft vibration damper.
24. Install the power steering pump pulley.
25. Install the accessory idler pulley.
26. Install accessory drive belt tensioner.
27. Install the accessory drive belt.
28. Install the heater core supply tube with one bolt tightened to 106 inch lbs. (12 Nm).
29. Install the heater core supply hose to the coolant outlet housing.
30. Install the lower radiator hose to the water pump housing.
31. Install the heater core return hose to the water pump housing.
32. Install the thermostat housing and upper radiator hose.
33. Install the electric vacuum pump.
34. If removed, install the oil filter and fill the engine crankcase with the proper oil to the correct level.
35. Connect the negative battery cable.
36. Fill the cooling system.
37. Run the engine until it reaches normal operating temperature. Check cooling system for correct fluid level.

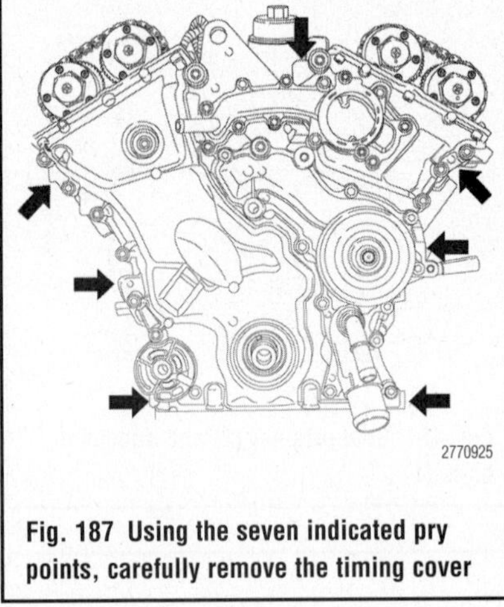

Fig. 187 Using the seven indicated pry points, carefully remove the timing cover

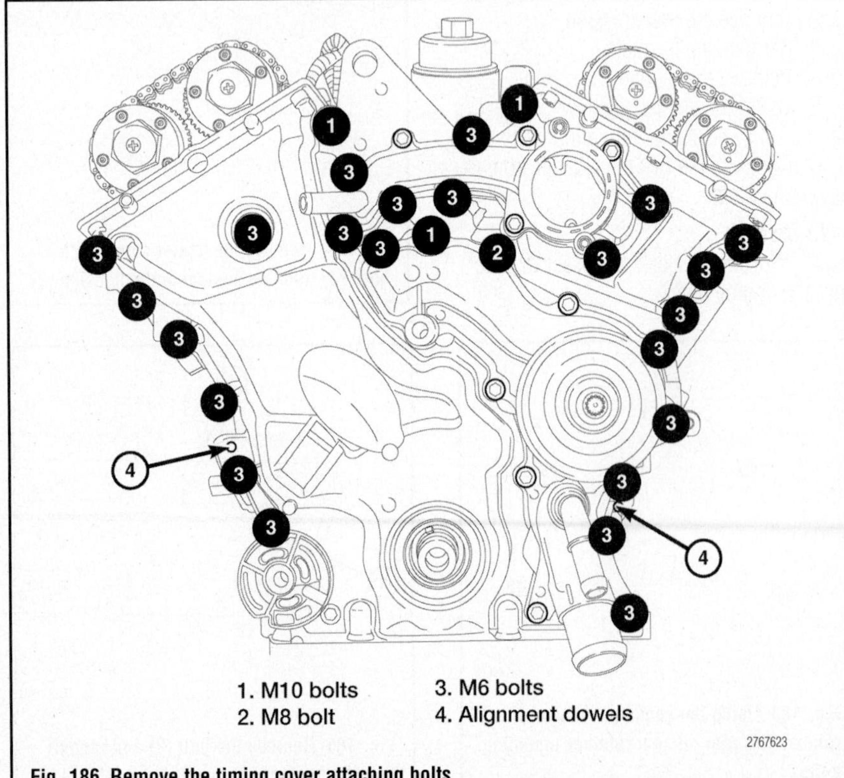

Fig. 186 Remove the timing cover attaching bolts

5.7L Engine

See Figure 189.

1. Remove the cooling fan module.
2. Remove the serpentine belt.
3. Remove the oil pan.
4. Drain the cooling system.
5. Remove the lower radiator hose clamp at the water pump.
6. Remove the lower radiator hose clamp at the radiator and remove the lower radiator hose.

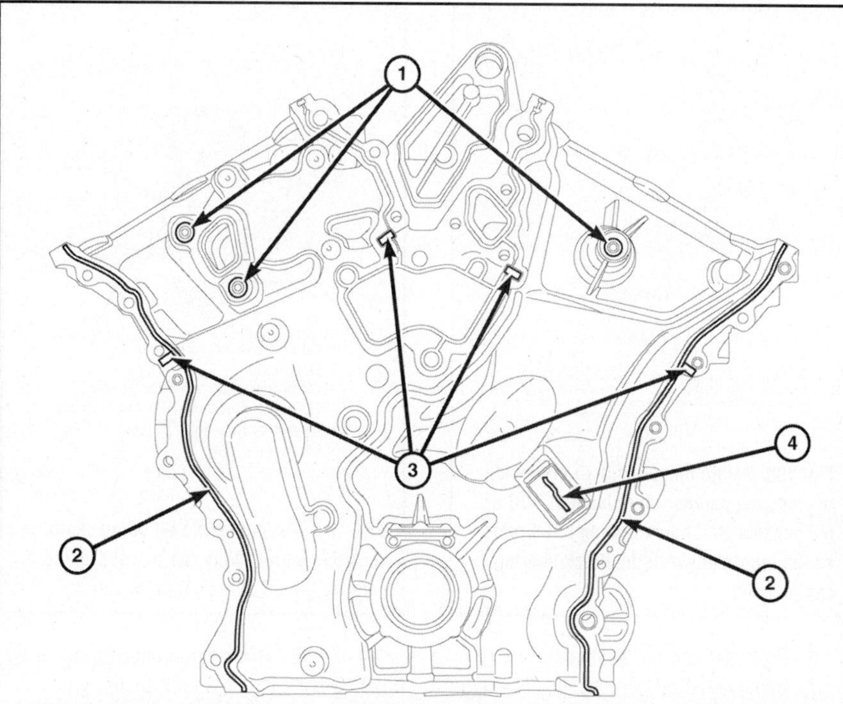

Fig. 188 Apply a bead of Mopar Threebond Engine RTV Sealant to the front cover as shown

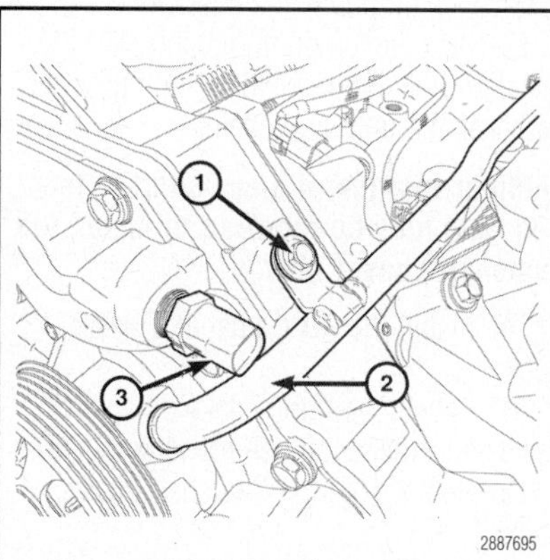

Fig. 189 Disconnect the electrical connector to the coolant temperature sensor (3), remove the heater tube retaining bolt (1), and Lift the heater tube (2) out of the water pump

➡It is not necessary to disconnect the refrigerant lines for A/C compressor removal.

7. Remove the A/C compressor from the engine block and position aside.
8. Lower the vehicle.
9. Disconnect the CMP sensor electrical connector.
10. Remove CMP sensor mounting bolt.
11. Using a slight rocking motion, carefully remove the CMP sensor from the timing cover.
12. Check the condition of the CMP sensor O-ring, replace as necessary.
13. Remove the upper radiator hose clamp at the thermostat housing.
14. Remove the upper radiator hose retainer at the fan shroud and position the radiator hose aside.
15. Remove the air cleaner resonator support bracket at the water pump.
16. Disconnect the electrical connector to the coolant temperature sensor.
17. Remove the heater tube retaining bolt.
18. Lift the heater tube out of the water pump.
19. Check condition of heater tube O-ring, replace as necessary.

➡It is not necessary to disconnect the hoses from the power steering pump, for power steering pump removal.

20. Remove the power steering pump and position aside.
21. Remove the alternator.

➡When installing the puller tool, ensure the bolts are fully threaded through the entire crankshaft damper.

22. Remove the crankshaft damper bolt.
23. Install puller tool and remove the crankshaft damper.

➡It is not necessary to remove the water pump for timing cover removal.

24. Remove the timing cover bolts and remove the timing cover.
25. Clean the sealing surfaces as necessary.

To install:

26. Clean the timing cover and engine block sealing surfaces.
27. Verify that the slide bushings are installed in the timing cover.
28. Using a new gasket, position the timing cover, install the retaining bolts and tighten to 21 ft. lbs. (28 Nm).

➡The large lifting stud is tightened to 40 ft. lbs. (55 Nm).

⁂ WARNING

To prevent severe damage to the crankshaft, damper, and damper installer, Damper, thoroughly clean the damper bore and the crankshaft nose before installing damper.

29. Position the damper onto the crankshaft.
30. Assemble the Damper Installer and the Pressing Cup from A/C Hub Installer.
31. Using the Damper Installer and Hub Install, press the damper onto the crankshaft.
32. Install the crankshaft damper bolt and tighten to 129 ft. lbs. (176 Nm).
33. Install the alternator.
34. Install the power steering pump.
35. Install the heater tube into the water pump.
36. Install the heater tube retaining bolt and tighten to 106 inch lbs. (12 Nm).
37. Connect the electrical connector to the coolant temperature sensor.
38. Position the upper radiator hose and secure retainer at the fan shroud.
39. Install the upper radiator hose at the thermostat housing and secure hose clamp.
40. Install the air cleaner resonator support bracket at the water pump.
41. Clean out the machined hole in the timing cover.
42. Install the CMP sensor into the timing cover with a slight rocking motion. Do not the twist sensor into position as damage to O-ring may result.

WARNING

Before tightening sensor retaining bolt, be sure the sensor is completely flush to the timing cover. If the sensor is not flush, damage to the sensor mounting tang may result.

43. Install the CMP sensor retaining bolt and tighten to 106 inch lbs. (12 Nm).
44. Connect the CMP sensor electrical connector.
45. Raise and support the vehicle.
46. Install the oil pan.
47. Install the A/C compressor.
48. Connect the lower radiator hose to the radiator and secure the hose clamp.
49. Connect the lower radiator hose to the water pump and secure hose clamp.
50. Lower the vehicle.
51. Install the cooling fan module.
52. Install the serpentine belt.
53. Fill the cooling system with the proper coolant.
54. Fill the engine with the proper engine oil.
55. Connect the battery negative cable.
56. Start the engine and check for leaks.

TIMING CHAIN & SPROCKETS

REMOVAL & INSTALLATION

3.6L Engine

See Figures 190 through 203.

WARNING

The magnetic timing wheels must not come in contact with magnets (pickup tools, trays, etc.) or any other strong magnetic field. This will destroy the timing wheels ability to correctly relay camshaft position to the camshaft position sensor.

WARNING

When the timing chains are removed and the cylinder heads are still installed, DO NOT rotate the camshafts or crankshaft without first locating the proper crankshaft position. Failure to do so will result in valve and/or piston damage.

1. Disconnect and isolate the negative battery cable.
2. Remove the air cleaner housing assembly and upper intake manifold.
3. Remove the cylinder head covers.
4. Remove the spark plugs.
5. Raise and support the vehicle.

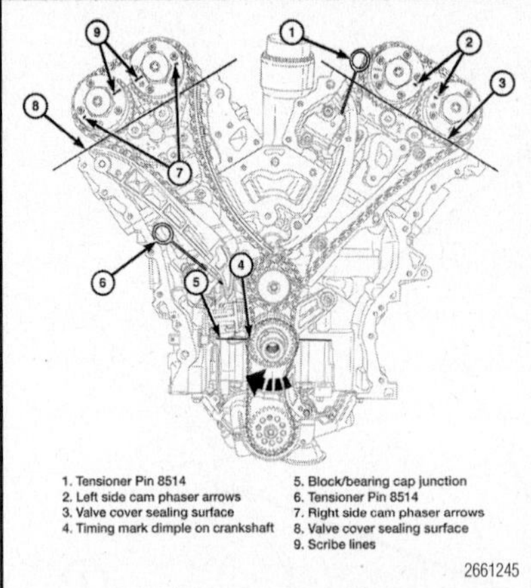

Fig. 190 Rotate the crankshaft clockwise to place the number one piston at TDC on the exhaust stroke by aligning the dimple on the crankshaft with the block/bearing cap junction

6. Drain the cooling system.
7. Remove the oil pan, accessory drive belts, crankshaft vibration damper and engine timing cover.

➡**Take this opportunity to measure timing chain wear.**

WARNING

When aligning timing marks, always rotate engine by turning the crankshaft. Failure to do so will result in valve and/or piston damage.

8. Rotate the crankshaft clockwise to place the number one piston at TDC on the exhaust stroke by aligning the dimple on the crankshaft with the block/bearing cap junction. The left side cam phaser arrows should point toward each other and be parallel to the valve cover sealing surface. The right side cam phaser arrows should point away from each other and the scribe lines should be parallel to the valve cover sealing surface.

WARNING

Always reinstall timing chains so that they maintain the same direction of rotation. Inverting a previously run chain on a previously run sprocket will result in excessive wear to both the chain and sprocket.

9. Mark the direction of rotation on the following timing chains using a paint pen or equivalent to aid in reassembly:
   - Left side cam chain
   - Right side cam chain
   - Oil pump chain
   - Primary chain

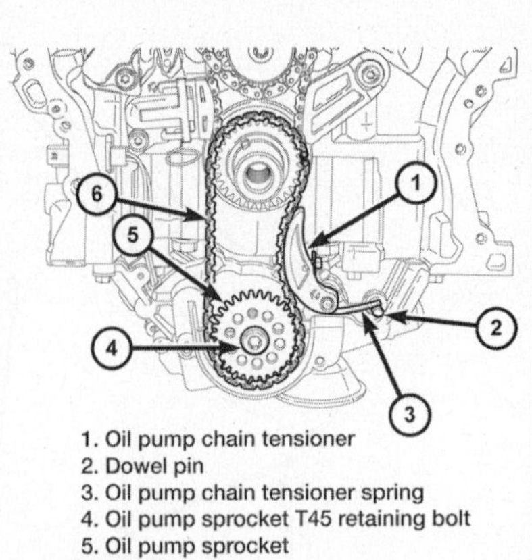

Fig. 191 Disengage the oil pump chain tensioner spring from the dowel pin and remove the oil pump chain tensioner

10. Reset the RH cam chain tensioner by pushing back the tensioner piston and installing Tensioner Pin.
11. Reset the LH cam chain tensioner by lifting the pawl, pushing back the piston and installing Tensioner Pin.
12. Disengage the oil pump chain tensioner spring from the dowel pin and remove the oil pump chain tensioner.
13. Remove the oil pump sprocket T45 retaining bolt and remove the oil pump sprocket and oil pump chain.

➡**Minor rotation of a camshaft (a few degrees) may be required to install the camshaft phaser lock.**

14. Install the RH Camshaft Phaser Lock.
15. Loosen both the intake oil control valve and exhaust oil control valve.
16. Remove the RH Camshaft Phaser Lock.

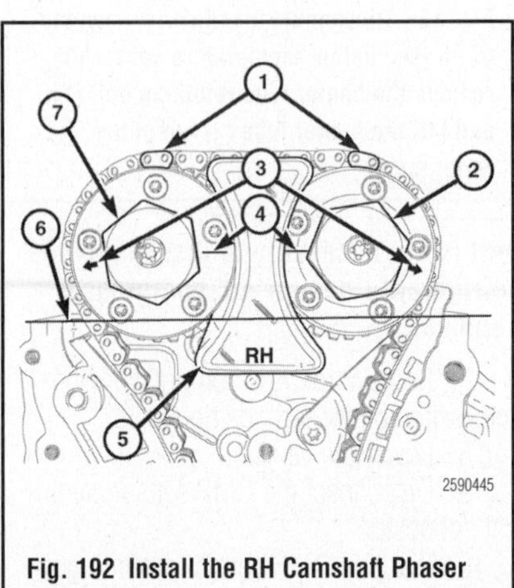

Fig. 192 Install the RH Camshaft Phaser Lock

17. Remove the oil control valve from the right side intake cam phaser.

18. Pull the right side intake cam phaser off of the camshaft and remove the right side cam chain.

19. If required, remove the oil control valve and pull the right side exhaust cam phaser off of the camshaft.

➡Minor rotation of a camshaft (a few degrees) may be required to install the camshaft phaser lock.

20. Install the LH Camshaft Phaser Lock.

21. Loosen both the intake oil control valve and exhaust oil control valve.

22. Remove the LH Camshaft Phaser Lock.

23. Remove the oil control valve from the left side exhaust cam phaser.

24. Pull the left side exhaust cam phaser off of the camshaft and remove the left side cam chain.

25. If required, remove the oil control valve and pull the left side intake cam phaser off of the camshaft.

26. Reset the primary chain tensioner by pushing back the tensioner piston and installing Tensioner Pin.

27. Remove two T30 bolts and remove the primary chain tensioner.

28. Remove the T30 bolt and the primary chain guide.

29. Remove the idler sprocket T45 retaining bolt and washer.

30. Remove the primary chain, idler sprocket and crankshaft sprocket as an assembly.

31. If required, remove two T30 bolts and the LH cam chain tensioner.

32. If required, remove two T30 bolts and the LH cam chain guide and tensioner arm.

33. If required, remove two T30 bolts and the RH cam chain tensioner.

34. If required, remove three T30 bolts and the RH cam chain guide and tensioner arm.

35. Inspect all sprockets and chain guides. Replace if damaged.

To install:

36. Inspect all sprockets and chain guides. Replace if damaged.

37. If removed, install the right side cam chain guide and tensioner arm. Tighten attaching T30 bolts to 106 inch lbs. (12 Nm).

38. If removed, install the RH cam chain tensioner to the engine block with two bolts. Tighten the T30 bolts to 106 inch lbs. (12 Nm).

39. Reset the RH cam chain tensioner by pushing back the tensioner piston and installing Tensioner Pin.

40. If removed, install the left side cam chain guide and tensioner arm. Tighten attaching T30 bolts to 106 inch lbs. (12 Nm).

41. If removed, install the LH cam chain tensioner to the cylinder head with two bolts. Tighten the T30 bolts to 106 inch lbs. (12 Nm).

42. Reset the LH cam chain tensioner by lifting the pawl, pushing back the piston and installing Tensioner Pin.

43. Verify that the key is installed in the crankshaft.

⁂ WARNING

Do not rotate the crankshaft more than a few degrees independently of the camshafts. Piston to valve contact could occur resulting in possible valve damage. If the crankshaft needs to be rotated more than a few degrees, first remove the camshafts.

44. Verify that the number one piston is positioned at TDC by aligning the dimple on

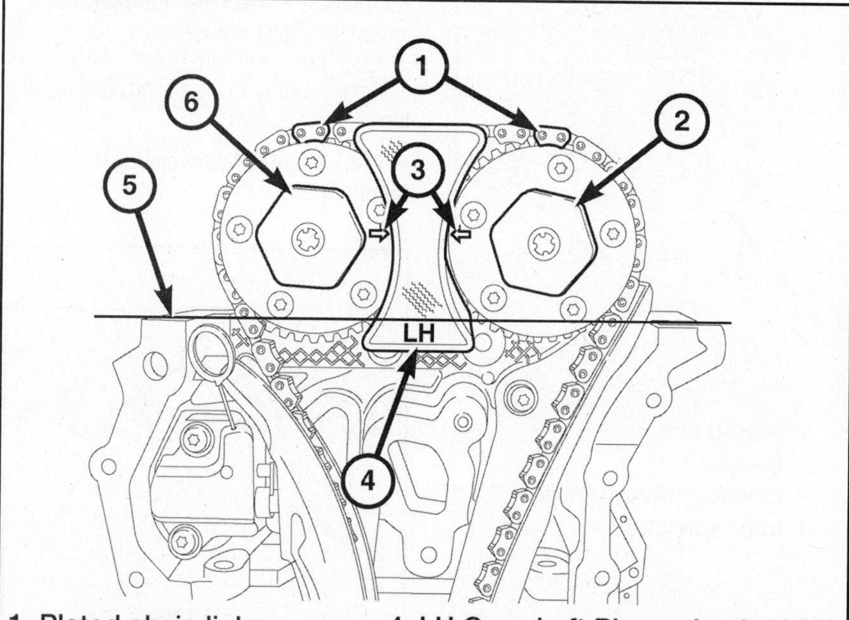

Fig. 193 Install the LH Camshaft Phaser Lock

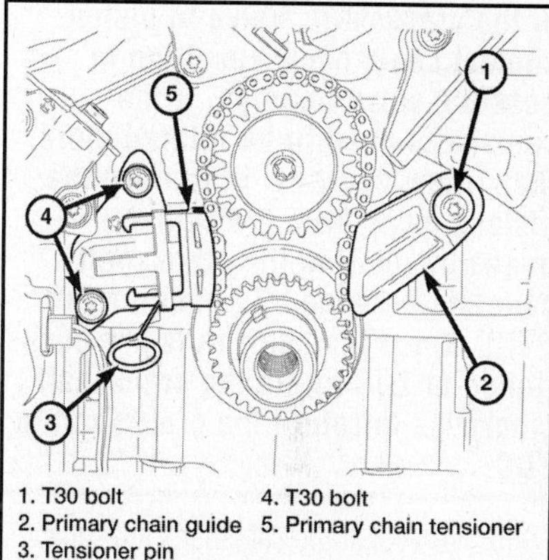

Fig. 194 Reset the primary chain tensioner by pushing back the tensioner piston and installing Tensioner Pin

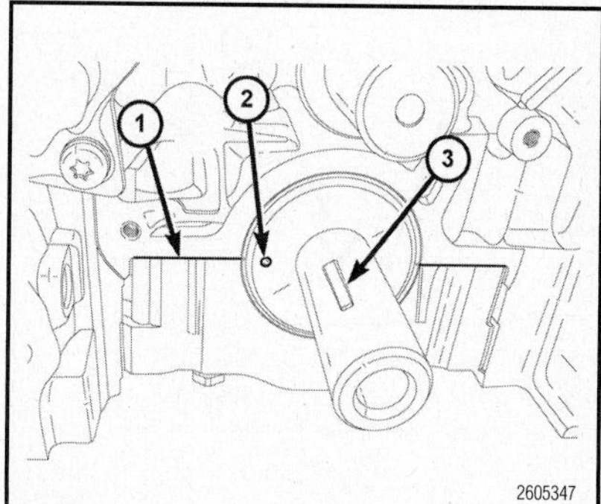

Fig. 195 Verify that the key (3) is installed in the crankshaft and that the number one piston is positioned at TDC by aligning the dimple (2) on the crankshaft with the block/bearing cap junction (1)

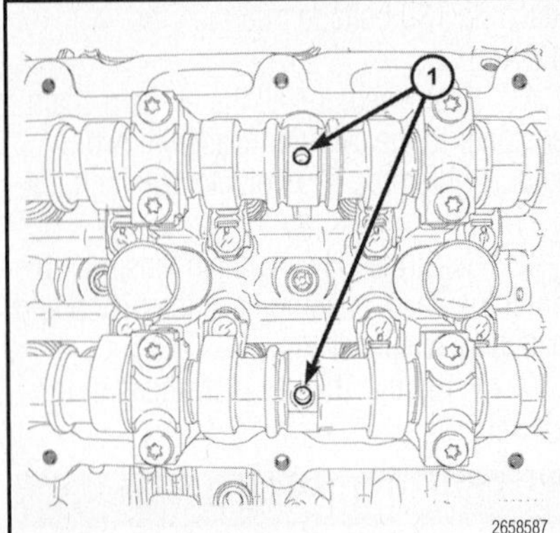

2658587

Fig. 196 Verify that the camshafts are set at TDC by positioning the alignment holes (1) vertically

the crankshaft with the block/bearing cap junction.

WARNING

Do not rotate the camshafts more than a few degrees independently of the crankshaft. Valve to piston contact could occur resulting in possible valve damage. If the camshafts need to be rotated more than a few degrees, first move the pistons away from the cylinder heads by rotating the crankshaft counterclockwise to a position 30° BTDC. Once the camshafts are positioned at TDC rotate the crankshaft clockwise to return the crankshaft to TDC.

45. Verify that the camshafts are set at TDC by positioning the alignment holes vertically.

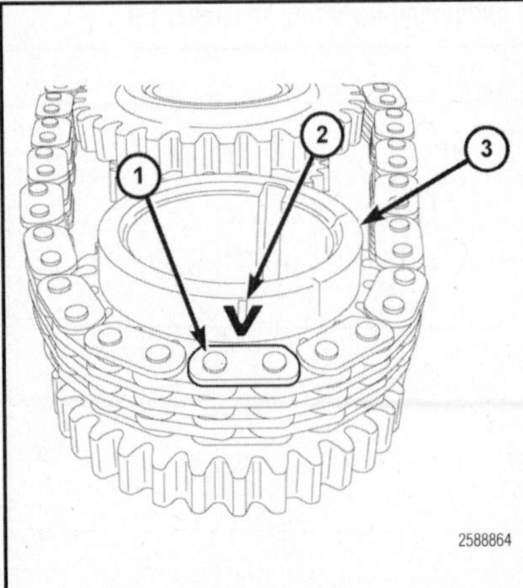

2588864

Fig. 197 Place the primary chain onto the crankshaft sprocket (3) so that the arrow (2) is aligned with the plated link (1) on the timing chain

WARNING

Always reinstall timing chains so that they maintain the same direction of rotation. Inverting a previously run chain on a previously run sprocket will result in excessive wear to both the chain and sprocket.

46. Place the primary chain onto the crankshaft sprocket so that the arrow is aligned with the plated link on the timing chain.

47. While maintaining this alignment, invert the crankshaft sprocket and timing chain and place the idler sprocket into the timing chain so that the dimple is aligned with the plated link on the timing chain.

48. While maintaining this alignment, lubricate the idler sprocket bushing with clean engine oil and install the sprockets and timing chain on the engine. To verify that the timing is still correct, the timing chain plated link should be located at 12:00 when the dimple on the crankshaft is aligned with the block/bearing cap junction.

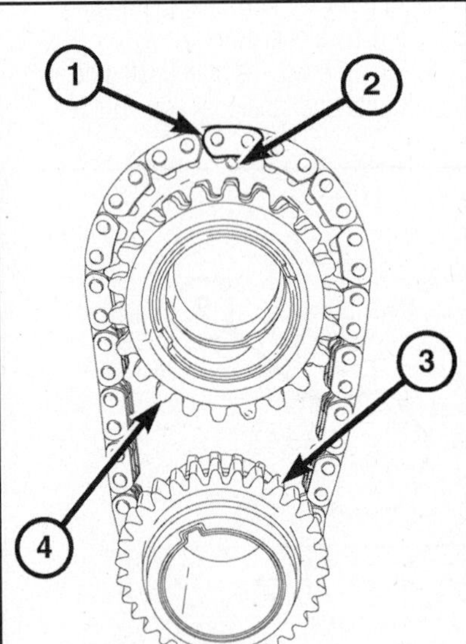

1. Plated link
2. Dimple
3. Crankshaft sprocket
4. Idler sprocket

2589142

Fig. 198 While maintaining this alignment, invert the crankshaft sprocket and timing chain and place the idler sprocket into the timing chain so that the dimple is aligned with the plated link on the timing chain

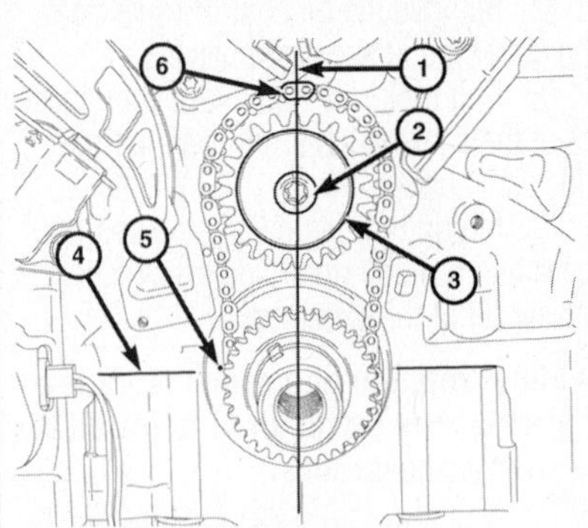

1. Perpendicular alignment line
2. Idler sprocket T45 retaining bolt
3. Washer
4. Block/bearing cap junction
5. Timing mark dimple on crankshaft sprocket
6. Plated chain link

2659817

Fig. 199 While maintaining this alignment, lubricate the idler sprocket bushing with clean engine oil and install the sprockets and timing chain on the engine

49. Install the idler sprocket retaining bolt and washer. Tighten the T45 bolt to 18 ft. lbs. (25 Nm).

50. Install the primary chain guide. Tighten attaching T30 bolt to 106 inch lbs. (12 Nm)

51. Reset the primary chain tensioner by pushing back the tensioner piston and installing Tensioner Pin.

52. Install the primary chain tensioner to the engine block with two bolts. Tighten the T30 bolts to 106 inch lbs. (12 Nm) and remove the Tensioner Pin.

53. Press the LH intake cam phaser onto the intake camshaft. Install and hand tighten the oil control valve.

➡The LH and RH cam chains are identical.

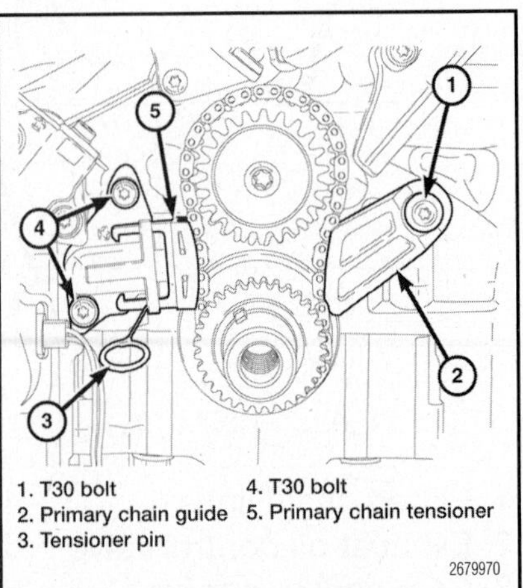

1. T30 bolt
2. Primary chain guide
3. Tensioner pin
4. T30 bolt
5. Primary chain tensioner

2679970

Fig. 200 Install the idler sprocket retaining bolt and washer

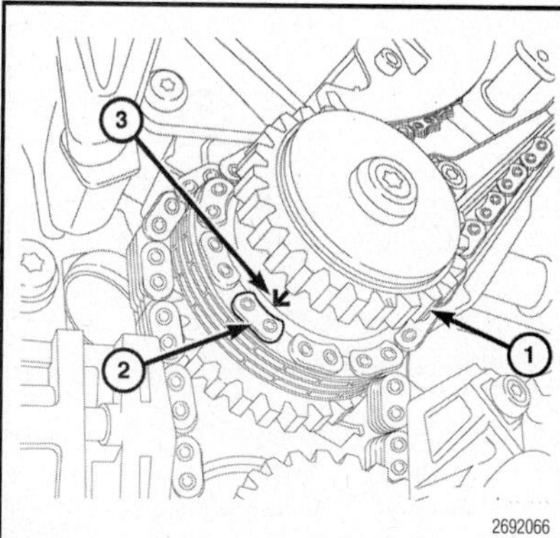

Fig. 201 Drape the left side cam chain over the LH intake cam phaser and onto the idler sprocket (1) so that the arrow (3) is aligned with the plated link (2) on the cam chain

WARNING

Always reinstall timing chains so that they maintain the same direction of rotation. Inverting a previously run chain on a previously run sprocket will result in excessive wear to both the chain and sprocket.

54. Drape the left side cam chain over the LH intake cam phaser and onto the idler sprocket so that the arrow is aligned with the plated link on the cam chain.

55. While maintaining this alignment, route the cam chain around the exhaust and intake cam phasers so that the plated links are aligned with the phaser timing marks. Position the left side cam phasers so that the arrows point toward each other and are parallel to the valve cover sealing surface. Press the exhaust cam phaser onto the exhaust cam, install and hand tighten the oil control valve.

➡Minor rotation of a camshaft (a few degrees) may be required to install the camshaft phaser or phaser lock.

56. Install the LH Camshaft Phaser Lock and tighten the oil control valves to 110 ft. lbs. (150 Nm).

57. Press the RH exhaust cam phaser onto the exhaust camshaft. Install and hand tighten the oil control valve.

WARNING

Always reinstall timing chains so that they maintain the same direction of rotation. Inverting a previously run chain on a previously run sprocket will result in excessive wear to both the chain and sprocket.

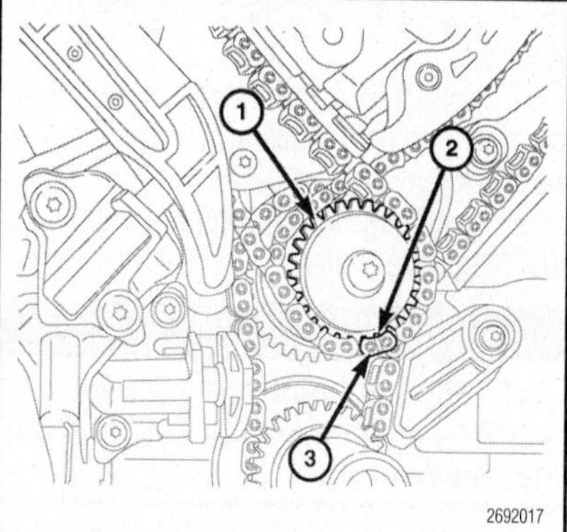

Fig. 202 Drape the right side cam chain over the RH exhaust cam phaser and onto the idler sprocket (1) so that the dimple (2) is aligned with the plated link (3) on the cam chain

58. Drape the right side cam chain over the RH exhaust cam phaser and onto the idler sprocket so that the dimple is aligned with the plated link on the cam chain.

59. While maintaining this alignment, route the cam chain around the exhaust and intake cam phasers so that the plated links are aligned with the phaser timing marks. Position the right side cam phasers so that the arrows point away from each other and the scribe lines are parallel to the valve cover sealing surface. Press the intake cam phaser onto the intake cam, install and hand tighten the oil control valve.

➡Minor rotation of a camshaft (a few degrees) may be required to install the camshaft phaser or phaser lock.

60. Install the RH Camshaft Phaser Lock and tighten the oil control valves to 110 ft. lbs. (150 Nm).

➡There are no timing marks on the oil pump gear or chain.

WARNING

Always reinstall timing chains so that they maintain the same direction of rotation. Inverting a previously run chain on a previously run sprocket will result in excessive wear to both the chain and sprocket.

61. Place the oil pump sprocket into the oil pump chain. Place the oil pump chain onto the crankshaft sprocket while aligning the oil pump sprocket with the oil pump shaft. Install the oil pump sprocket T45 retaining bolt and tighten to 18 ft. lbs. (25 Nm).

62. Install the oil pump chain tensioner. Insure that the spring is positioned above the dowel pin.

63. Remove the RH and LH Camshaft Phaser Locks.

64. Remove the Tensioner Pins and from the RH and LH cam chain tensioners.

65. Rotate the crankshaft CLOCKWISE two complete revolutions stopping when the dimple on the crankshaft is aligned the with the block/bearing cap junction.

66. While maintaining this alignment, verify that the arrows on the left side cam phasers point toward each other and are parallel to the valve cover sealing surface and that the right side cam phaser arrows point away from each other and the scribe lines are parallel to the valve cover sealing surface.

67. There should be 12 chain pins between the exhaust cam phaser triangle marking and the intake cam phaser circle marking.

68. If the engine timing is not correct, repeat this procedure.

69. Install the engine timing cover, crankshaft vibration damper, accessory drive belts and oil pan.

70. Install the spark plugs. Tighten to 13 ft. lbs. (17.5 Nm).

71. Install the cylinder head covers.

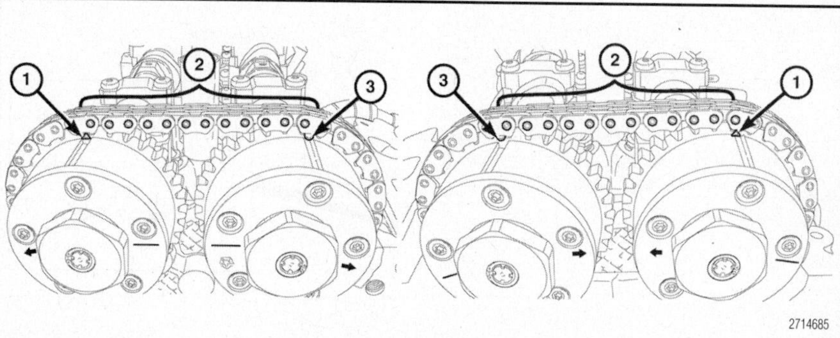

Fig. 203 There should be 12 chain pins (2) between the exhaust cam phaser triangle marking (1) and the intake cam phaser circle marking (3)

72. Install the upper intake manifold and air cleaner housing assembly.

73. Fill the engine crankcase with the proper oil to the correct level.

74. Connect the negative battery cable.

75. Fill the cooling system.

76. Operate the engine until it reaches normal operating temperature. Check cooling system for correct fluid level.

➡**The Cam/Crank Variation Relearn procedure must be performed using the scan tool anytime there has been a repair/replacement made to a powertrain system, for example: flywheel, valvetrain, camshaft and/or crankshaft sensors or components.**

5.7L Engine

See Figures 204 through 210.

1. Disconnect the negative battery cable.

2. Drain the cooling system.

➡**It is not necessary to remove water pump for timing chain cover removal.**

3. Remove the timing chain cover.

4. Verify the slide bushings remain installed in the timing chain cover during removal.

5. Remove the oil pump retaining bolts and remove the oil pump.

6. Install the vibration damper bolt finger tight. Using a suitable socket and breaker bar, rotate the crankshaft to align the timing marks with the timing chain sprockets.

7. Retract the chain tensioner arm until the hole in the arm lines up with the hole in the bracket.

8. Install the Tensioner Pin into the chain tensioner holes.

WARNING

Never attempt to disassemble the camshaft phaser, severe engine damage could result.

9. Remove the camshaft phaser retaining bolt and remove the timing chain with the camshaft phaser and crankshaft sprocket.

➡**Inspect the timing chain tensioner and timing chain guide shoes for wear and replace as necessary.**

10. If the timing chain tensioner is being replaced, remove the retaining bolts and remove the timing chain tensioner.

11. If the timing chain guide is being replaced, remove the retaining bolts and remove the timing chain guide.

To install:

12. Install the crankshaft sprocket and position halfway onto the crankshaft.

13. While holding the camshaft phaser in hand, position the timing chain on the camshaft phaser and align the timing marks as shown.

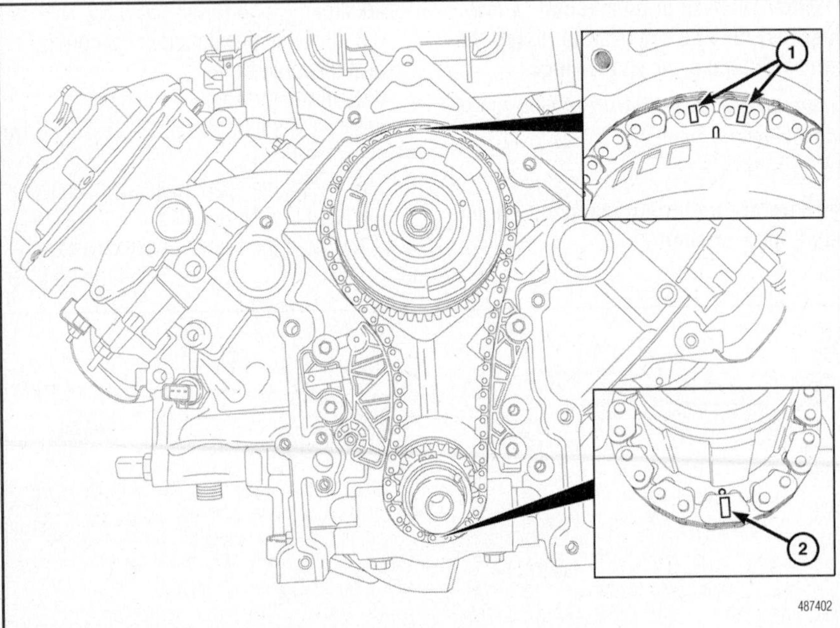

Fig. 204 Using a suitable socket and breaker bar, rotate the crankshaft to align the timing marks with the timing chain sprockets (1, 2)

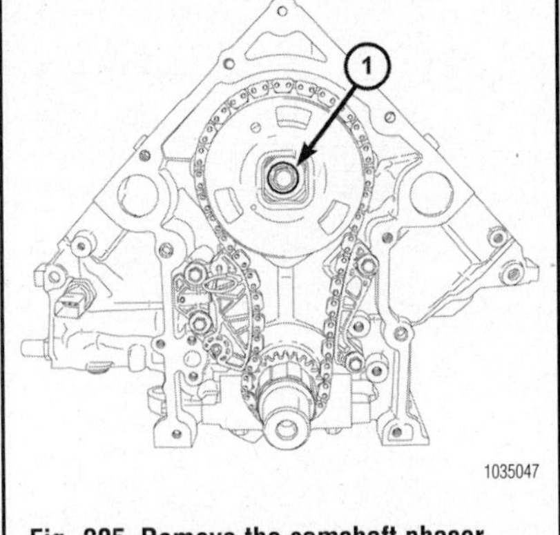

Fig. 205 Remove the camshaft phaser retaining bolt (1) and remove the timing chain with the camshaft phaser and crankshaft sprocket

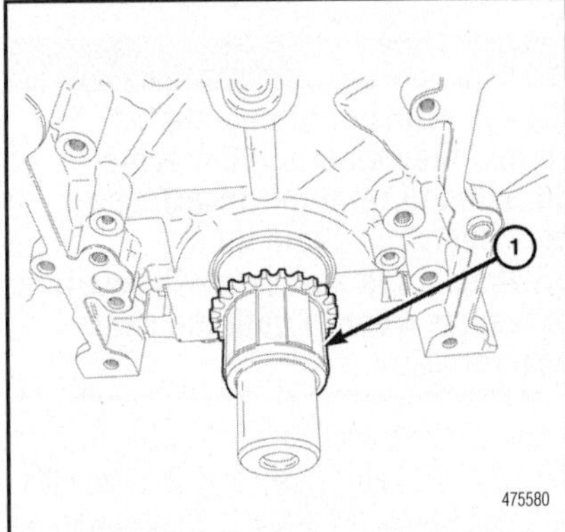

Fig. 206 Install the crankshaft sprocket (1) and position halfway onto the crankshaft

14. While holding the camshaft phaser and timing chain in hand, position the timing chain on the crankshaft sprocket and align the timing mark as shown.

15. Align the slot in the camshaft phaser with the dowel on the camshaft and position the camshaft phaser on the camshaft while sliding the crankshaft sprocket into position.

16. Install the camshaft phaser retaining bolt finger tight.

17. If removed, install the timing chain guide and tighten the bolts to 8 ft. lbs. (11 Nm).

18. If removed, install the timing chain tensioner and tighten the bolts to 8 ft. lbs. (11 Nm).

19. Remove the tensioner pin.

20. Rotate the crankshaft two revolutions and verify the alignment of the timing marks. If the timing marks do not line up, remove the camshaft sprocket and realign.

21. Tighten the camshaft phaser bolt to 63 ft. lbs. (85 Nm).

Fig. 207 While holding the camshaft phaser in hand, position the timing chain on the camshaft phaser and align the timing marks as shown

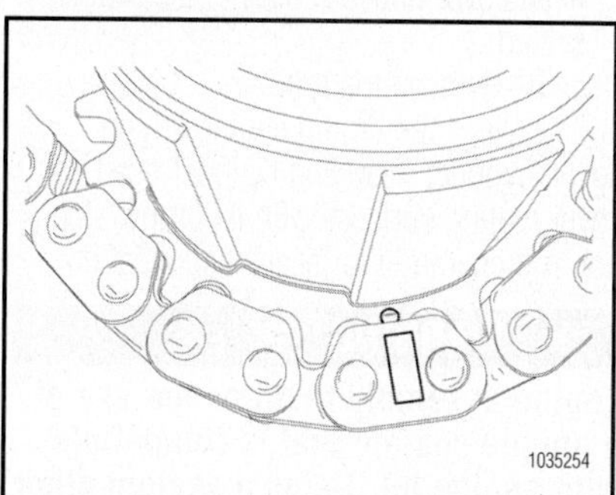

Fig. 208 While holding the camshaft phaser and timing chain in hand, position the timing chain on the crankshaft sprocket and align the timing mark as shown

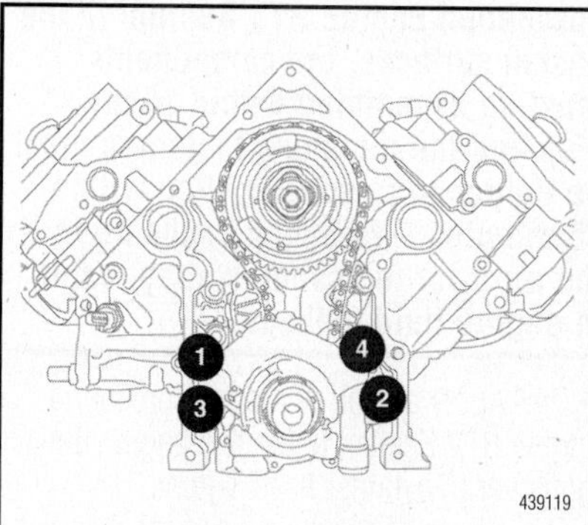

Fig. 209 Using the sequence shown, tighten the oil pump retaining bolts

22. Position the oil pump onto the crankshaft and install the oil pump retaining bolts finger tight.

23. Using the sequence shown, tighten the oil pump retaining bolts to 21 ft. lbs. (28 Nm).

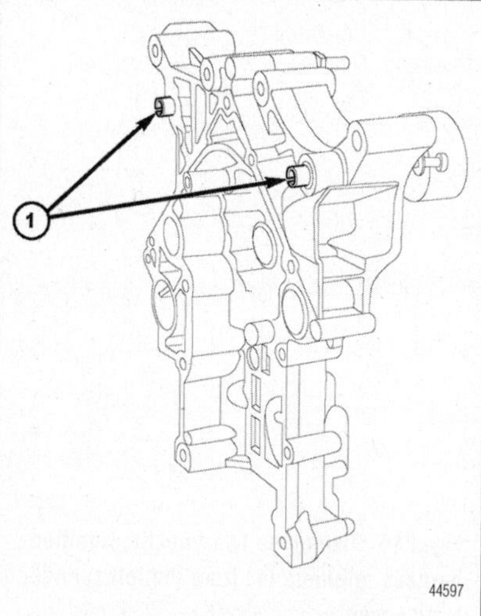

Fig. 210 Verify the slide bushings (1) are installed in the timing chain cover

24. Verify the slide bushings are installed in the timing chain cover.

25. Install the timing chain cover.

26. Fill the engine with oil.

27. Fill the cooling system.

28. Connect the negative battery cable.

29. Start the engine and check for leaks.

VALVE COVERS

REMOVAL & INSTALLATION

3.6L Engine

Left Side

See Figures 211 through 218.

**** WARNING**

The magnetic timing wheels must not come in contact with magnets (pickup tools, trays, etc.) or any other strong magnetic field. This will destroy the timing wheels ability to correctly relay camshaft position to the camshaft position sensor.

1. Disconnect and isolate the negative battery cable.

2. Remove the air inlet hose and upper intake manifold.

3. Cover the open intake ports to prevent debris from entering the engine.

4. Remove the insulator from the LH cylinder head cover.

5. Disengage the clips, remove the make-up air tube from the left cylinder head cover and reposition the transmission breather hose.

➡Mark the variable valve timing solenoid connectors with a paint pen or

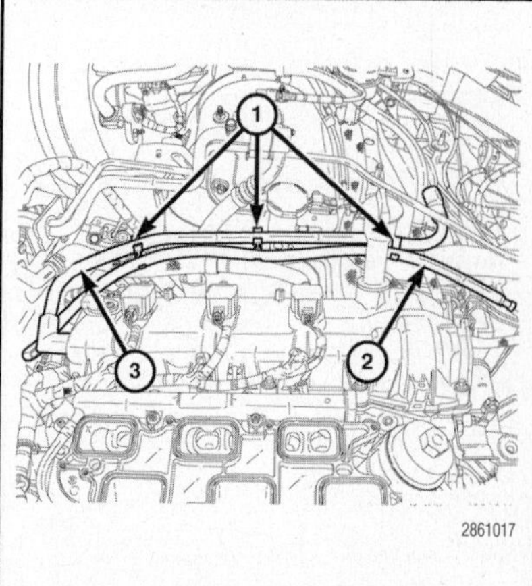

Fig. 211 Disengage the clips (1), remove the make-up air tube (3) from the left cylinder head cover and reposition the transmission breather hose (2)

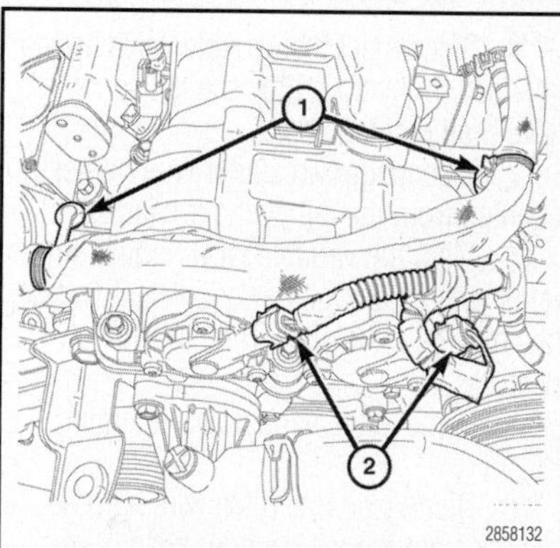

Fig. 212 Disconnect the variable valve timing solenoid connectors (2) from the left variable valve timing solenoids, and the two starter wire harness retainers (1) from the left cylinder head cover

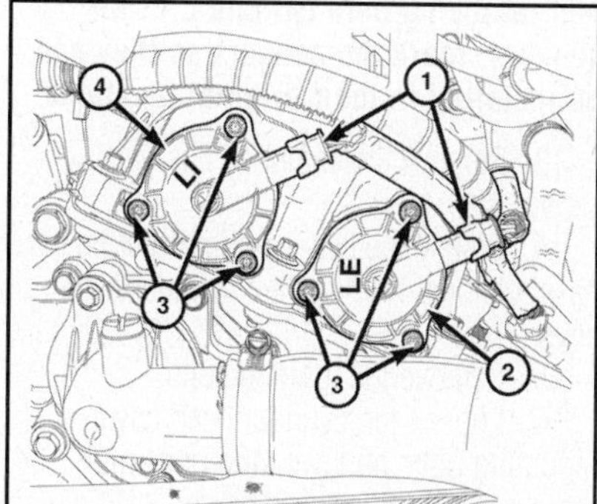

Fig. 213 Mark the variable valve timing solenoids with a paint pen or equivalent so that they may be reinstalled in their original locations

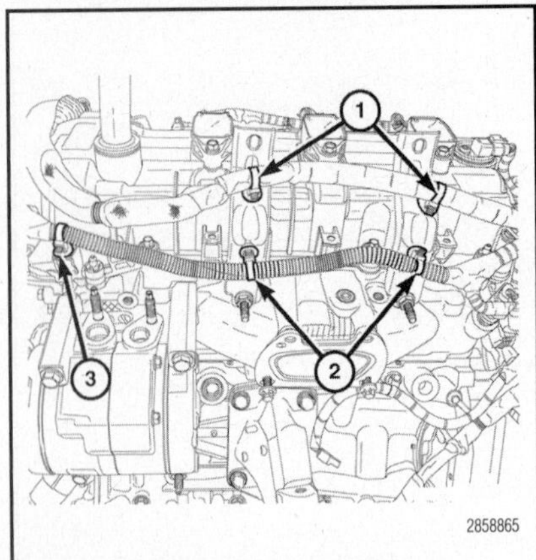

Fig. 214 Disengage one main wire harness retainer (3) from the left cylinder head cover; retainers (1, 2)

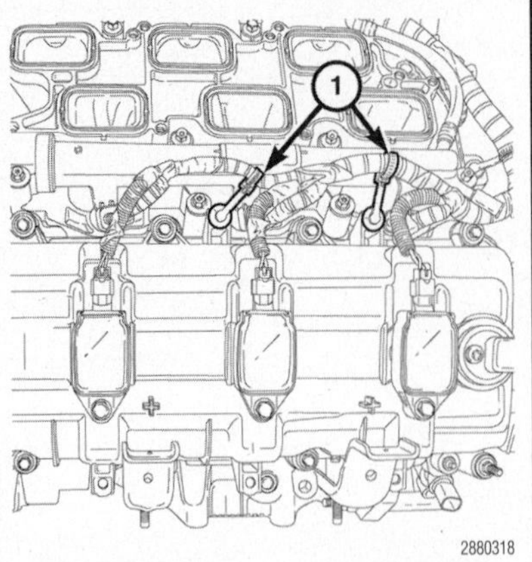

Fig. 215 Disengage two injection/ignition harness retainers (1) from the left cylinder head cover

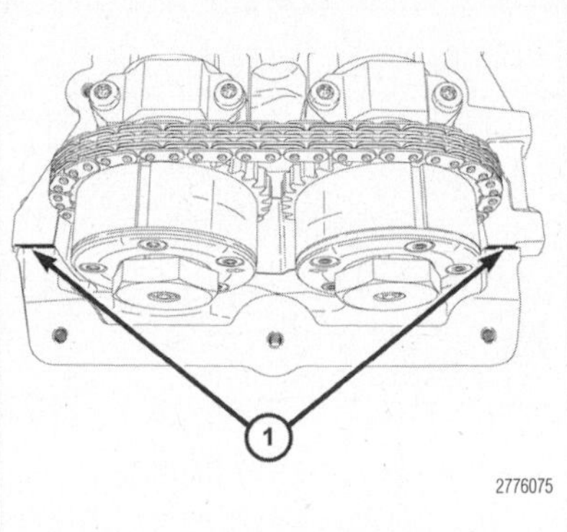

Fig. 217 Apply a bead of Mopar Threebond Engine RTV Sealant to the two engine timing cover to cylinder head T-joints (1)

equivalent so that they may be reinstalled in their original locations.

6. Disconnect the variable valve timing solenoid connectors from the left variable valve timing solenoids.
7. Disengage two starter wire harness retainers from the left cylinder head cover.
8. Mark the variable valve timing solenoids with a paint pen or equivalent so that they may be reinstalled in their original locations.
9. Remove the variable valve timing solenoids.
10. Disengage one main wire harness retainer from the left cylinder head cover.
11. Disconnect the left Camshaft Position (CMP) sensor.
12. Disengage one main wire harness retainer from the cylinder head cover and one main wire harness retainer from the cylinder head cover mounting stud.

➡If removing both RH and LH CMP sensors, mark the sensors so they can be installed in their original locations.

13. Remove the camshaft position sensor.
14. Disengage two injection/ignition harness retainers from the left cylinder head cover.
15. Remove the ignition coils.
16. Loosen ten cylinder head cover mounting bolts and two stud bolts and remove the cylinder head cover.
17. Remove and discard the cylinder head cover gasket.
18. The spark plug tube seals can be reused if not damaged.

✻✻ WARNING

Do not use oil based liquids, wire brushes, abrasive wheels or metal scrapers to clean the engine gasket surfaces. Use only isopropyl (rubbing) alcohol, along with plastic or wooden scrapers. Improper gasket surface preparation may result in engine fluid leakage.

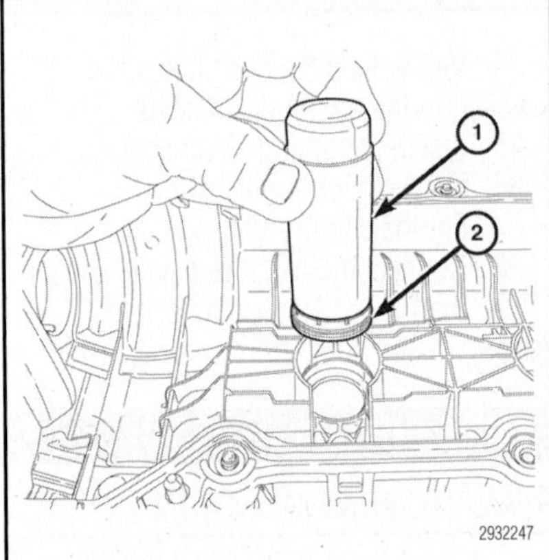

Fig. 216 Place the spark plug tube seal (2) on the Cam Sensor/Spark Plug Tube Seal Installer (1)

19. Remove all residual sealant from the cylinder head, timing chain cover and cylinder head cover mating surfaces.

To install:

20. Install the cylinder head cover gasket.
21. The spark plug tube seals can be reused if not damaged.
22. If required, install new spark plug tube seals in the cylinder head cover:
    a. Lubricate the spark plug tube seal inner and outer diameters with clean engine oil.
    b. Place the spark plug tube seal on the Cam Sensor/Spark Plug Tube Seal Installer.
    c. Push the seal into the cylinder head cover until the base of the seal is seated.
    d. Remove the tool.
23. Clean the timing engine timing cover, cylinder head and cylinder head cover mating surfaces with isopropyl alcohol in preparation for sealant application.

✻✻ WARNING

Engine assembly requires the use of a unique sealant that is compatible with engine oil. Using a sealant other than Mopar Threebond Engine RTV Sealant may result in engine fluid leakage.

✻✻ WARNING

Following the application of Mopar Threebond Engine RTV Sealant to the gasket surfaces, the components must be assembled within 20 minutes and the attaching fasteners must be tightened to specification within 45 minutes. Prolonged exposure to the air prior to assembly may result in engine fluid leakage.

24. Apply a bead of Mopar Threebond Engine RTV Sealant to the two engine timing cover to cylinder head T-joints.
25. Align the locator pins to the cylinder head and install the cylinder head cover.
26. Tighten the cylinder head cover bolts and double ended studs in the sequence shown to 106 inch lbs. (12 Nm).
27. If removed, install the spark plugs.
28. Install the ignition coils.
29. Engage two injection/ignition harness retainers to the left cylinder head cover.
30. Refer to the markings made at disas-

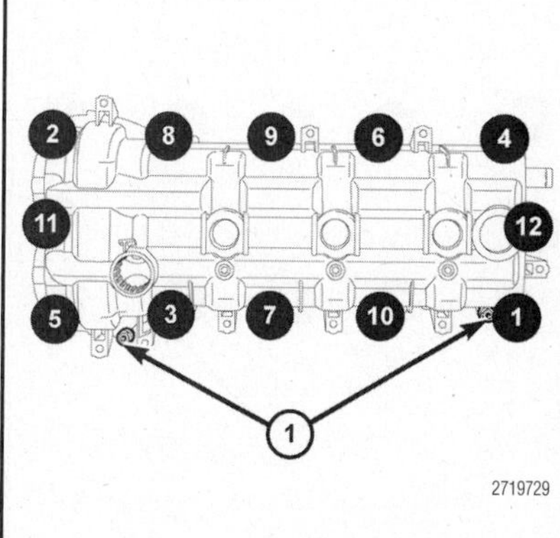

Fig. 218 Tighten the cylinder head cover bolts and double ended studs in the sequence shown; locator pins (1)

sembly and install the variable valve timing solenoids in their original locations.

31. Connect the electrical connectors to the left variable valve timing solenoids.

32. Engage two starter wire harness retainers to the left cylinder head cover.

33. Engage one main wire harness retainer to the left cylinder head cover.

➡**If both RH and LH CMP sensors where removed, install them into their original locations.**

34. Install the camshaft position sensor.

35. Connect the electrical connector to the left Camshaft Position (CMP) sensor.

36. Engage one main wire harness retainer to the cylinder head cover and one main wire harness retainer to the cylinder head cover mounting stud.

37. Install the make-up air tube to the left cylinder head cover and engage the clips to the transmission breather hose.

38. Install the insulator to the two alignment posts on top of the LH cylinder head cover.

39. Install the upper intake manifold, support brackets and air inlet hose.

40. Connect the negative battery cable.

➡**The Cam/Crank Variation Relearn procedure must be performed using the scan tool anytime there has been a repair/replacement made to a powertrain system, for example: flywheel, valvetrain, camshaft and/or crankshaft sensors or components.**

Right Side

See Figures 219 through 226.

⁂ WARNING

The magnetic timing wheels must not come in contact with magnets (pickup tools, trays, etc.) or any other strong magnetic field. This will destroy the timing wheels ability to correctly relay camshaft position to the camshaft position sensor.

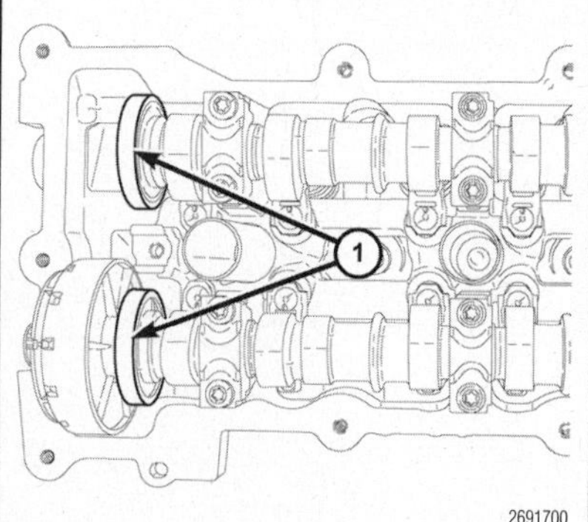

Fig. 219 The magnetic timing wheels (1) must not come in contact with magnets (pickup tools, trays, etc.) or any other strong magnetic field

1. Disconnect and isolate the negative battery cable.

2. Remove the air inlet hose and upper intake manifold.

3. Cover the open intake ports to prevent debris from entering the engine.

➡**Mark the variable valve timing solenoid connectors with a paint pen or equivalent so that they may be reinstalled in their original locations.**

4. Disconnect the electrical connectors from the variable valve timing solenoids on the right cylinder head.

5. Disengage the starter harness to main harness retainer.

6. Disengage two starter wire harness retainers from the right cylinder head cover.

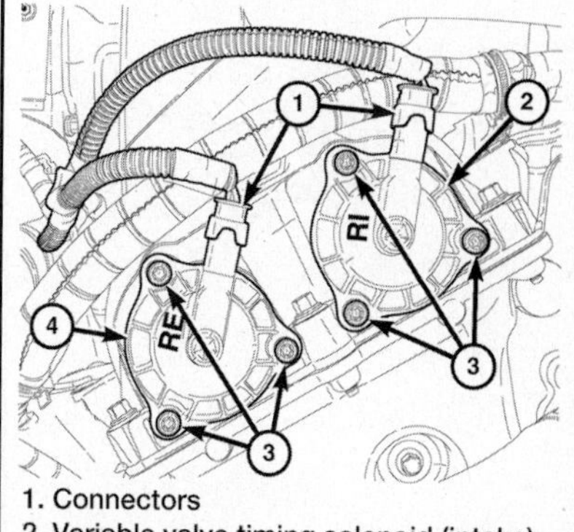

Fig. 221 Mark the variable valve timing solenoids with a paint pen or equivalent so that they may be reinstalled in their original locations

7. Mark the variable valve timing solenoids with a paint pen or equivalent so that they may be reinstalled in their original locations.

8. Remove the variable valve timing solenoids.

9. Disengage four main wire harness retainers from the right cylinder head cover.

10. Disconnect the electrical connector from the right Camshaft Position (CMP) sensor.

11. Disengage the main wire harness retainer from the right cylinder head cover mounting stud.

➡**If removing both RH and LH CMP sensors, mark the sensors so they can be installed in their original locations.**

12. Remove the camshaft position sensor.

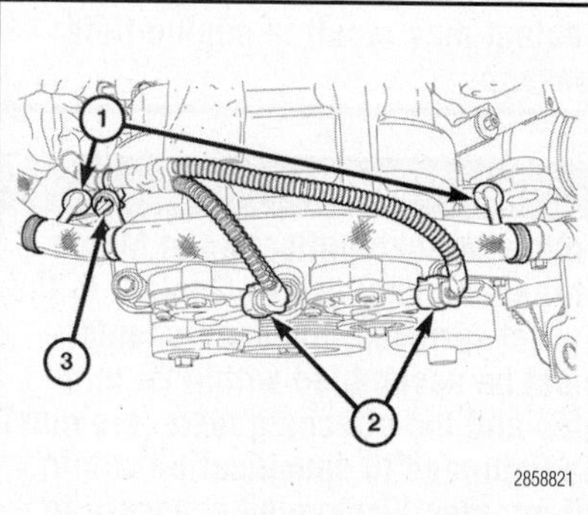

Fig. 220 Right cylinder head cover showing the electrical connectors (2), the starter harness to main harness retainer (3), and the two starter wire harness retainers (1)

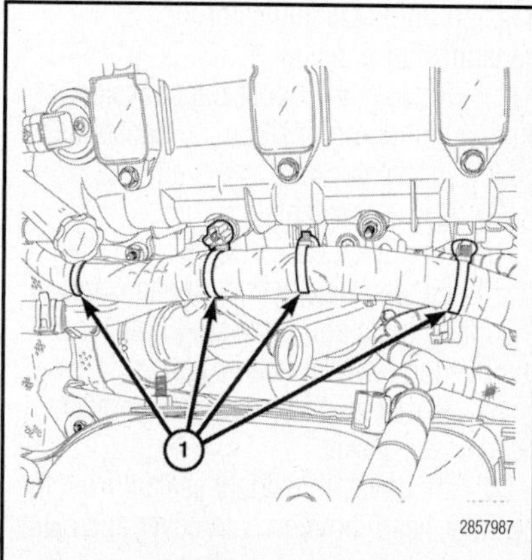

Fig. 222 Disengage four main wire harness retainers (1) from the right cylinder head cover

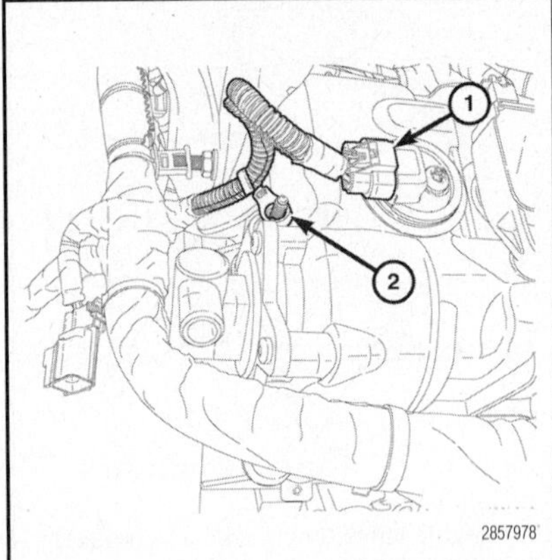

Fig. 223 Disconnect the electrical connector (1) from the right CMP sensor and disengage the main wire harness retainer (2)

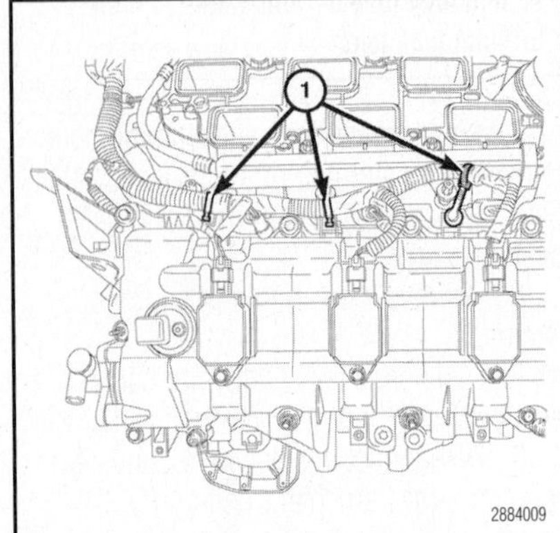

Fig. 224 Disengage three injection/ignition harness retainers (1) from the right cylinder head cover

13. Disengage three injection/ignition harness retainers from the right cylinder head cover.
14. Remove the ignition coils.
15. Raise and support the vehicle.
16. Loosen the bolt securing the transmission fluid level indicator tube to the transmission housing.
17. Remove the upper transmission to engine bolt and reposition the transmission oil level indicator tube.
18. Lower the vehicle.
19. Remove the PCV valve.
20. Loosen nine cylinder head cover mounting bolts and three stud bolts and remove the cylinder head cover.
21. Remove and discard the cylinder head cover gasket.
22. Remove all residual sealant from the cylinder head, timing chain cover and cylinder head cover mating surfaces.

To install:

23. Install the cylinder head cover gasket.

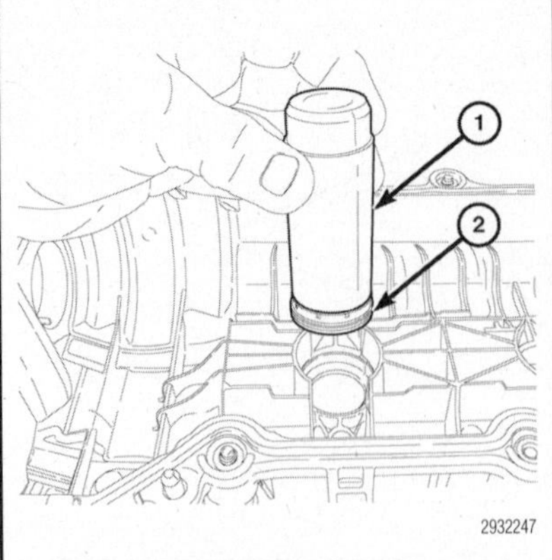

Fig. 225 Place the spark plug tube seal (2) on the Cam Sensor/Spark Plug Tube Seal Installer (1)

24. The spark plug tube seals can be reused if not damaged.
25. If required, install new spark plug tube seals in the cylinder head cover:
    a. Lubricate the spark plug tube seal inner and outer diameters with clean engine oil.
    b. Place the spark plug tube seal on the Cam Sensor/Spark Plug Tube Seal Installer.
    c. Push the seal into the cylinder head cover until the base of the seal is seated.
    d. Remove the tool.
26. Clean the timing engine timing cover, cylinder head and cylinder head cover mating surfaces with isopropyl alcohol in preparation for sealant application.

WARNING

Engine assembly requires the use of a unique sealant that is compatible with engine oil. Using a sealant other than Mopar Threebond Engine RTV Sealant may result in engine fluid leakage.

WARNING

Following the application of Mopar Threebond Engine RTV Sealant to the gasket surfaces, the components must be assembled within 20 minutes and the attaching fasteners must be tightened to specification within 45 minutes. Prolonged exposure to the air prior to assembly may result in engine fluid leakage.

27. Apply a bead of Mopar Threebond Engine RTV Sealant to the two engine timing cover to cylinder head T-joints.

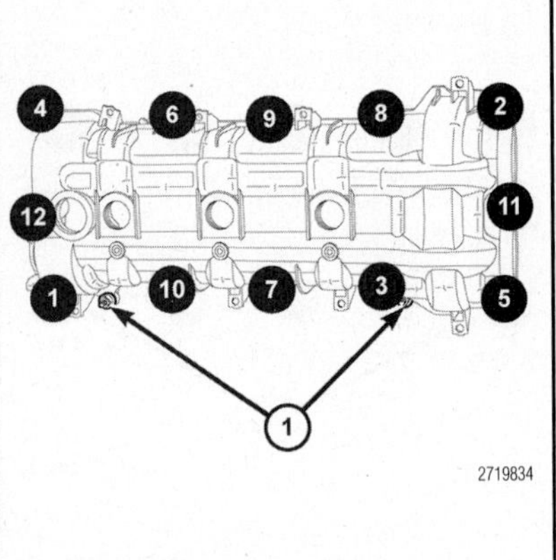

Fig. 226 Tighten the cylinder head cover bolts and double ended studs in the sequence shown

28. Align the locator pins to the cylinder head and install the cylinder head cover.
29. Tighten the cylinder head cover bolts and double ended studs in the sequence shown to 106 inch lbs. (12 Nm).
30. If removed, install the spark plugs.
31. Install the ignition coils.
32. Engage three injection/ignition harness retainers to the right cylinder head cover.
33. Refer to the markings made at disassembly and install the variable valve timing solenoids in their original locations.
34. Connect the electrical connectors to the variable valve timing solenoids on the right cylinder head.
35. Engage two starter wire harness retainers to the right cylinder head cover.
36. Engage the starter harness to main harness retainer.
37. Engage four main wire harness retainers to the right cylinder head cover.

➡If both RH and LH CMP sensors where removed, install them into their original locations.

38. Install the camshaft position sensor.
39. Connect the electrical connector to the right Camshaft Position (CMP) sensor.
40. Engage the main wire harness retainer to the right cylinder head cover mounting stud.
41. Install the PCV valve.
42. Raise and support the vehicle.
43. Install the transmission oil level indicator tube with the upper transmission to engine bolt tightened to 41 ft. lbs. (55 Nm).
44. Install the bolt securing the transmission fluid level indicator tube to the transmission housing and tighten to 106 inch lbs. (12 Nm).
45. Lower the vehicle.
46. If removed, install the insulator to

the two alignment posts on top of the LH cylinder head cover.

47. Install the upper intake manifold, support brackets and air inlet hose.
48. Connect the negative battery cable.

➡**The Cam/Crank Variation Relearn procedure must be performed using the scan tool anytime there has been a repair/replacement made to a powertrain system, for example: flywheel, valvetrain, camshaft and/or crankshaft sensors or components.**

5.7L Engine

See Figures 227 and 228.

1. Remove the oil fill cap.
2. Remove the engine cover.
3. Perform the fuel pressure release procedure.
4. Disconnect and isolate the negative battery cable.
5. Disconnect the EVAP vacuum line at the throttle body.
6. Disconnect the fuel supply line at the fuel rail.
7. Disconnect the make-up air hose at the intake manifold.
8. Disconnect the ignition coil electrical connectors.
9. Remove the ignition coil retaining bolts.
10. Remove the ignition coils.
11. Remove the wiring harness retainers at the cylinder head cover and position wiring harness aside.
12. Using the sequence shown, remove the cylinder head cover retaining bolts.
13. Remove the cylinder head cover.

➡**The cylinder head cover gasket may be used again, provided no cuts, tears, or deformation have occurred.**

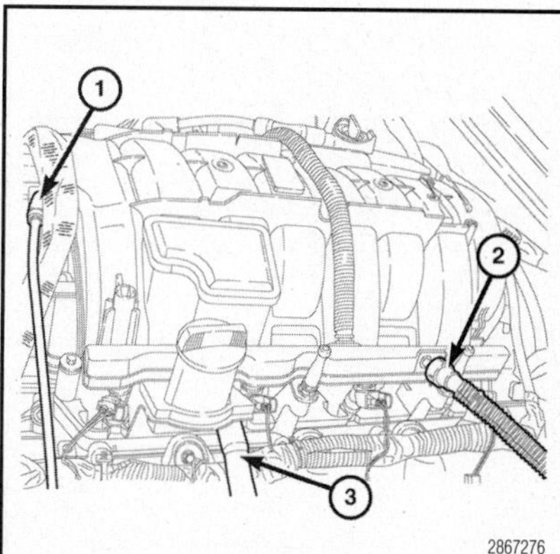

Fig. 227 Disconnect the EVAP vacuum line (1), the fuel supply line (2), and the make-up air hose (3)

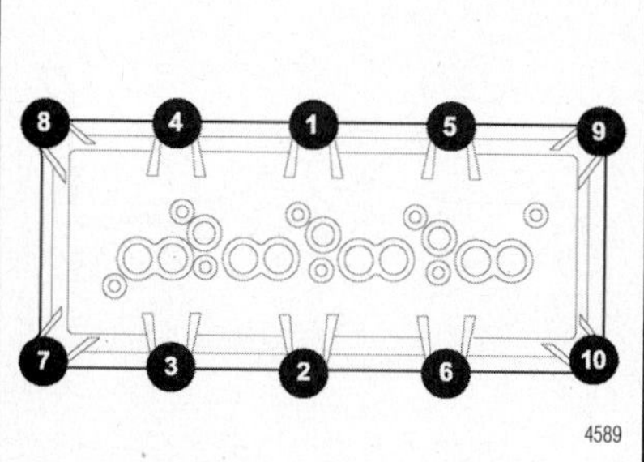

Fig. 228 Using the sequence shown, remove the cylinder head cover retaining bolts

14. Inspect the cylinder head cover gasket, replace if necessary.

To install:

⁂ WARNING

Do not use harsh cleaners to clean the cylinder head covers. Severe damage to covers may occur.

15. Clean the cylinder head cover and the cylinder head sealing surface.
16. Apply Mopar Lock Seal Adhesive to the cylinder head cover bolts.
17. Position the cylinder head cover and hand tighten the bolts.
18. Using the sequence shown in the removal section, tighten the cylinder head cover bolts to 70 inch lbs. (8 Nm).

⁂ WARNING

Do not allow other components including the wire harness to rest on or against the engine cylinder head cover. Prolonged contact with other objects may wear a hole in the cylinder head cover.

19. Position the wiring harness and attach the retainers to the cylinder head cover.
20. Before installing the ignition coils, apply dielectric grease to the inside of the spark plug boots.
21. Install the ignition coils.
22. Install the ignition coil retaining bolts.
23. Connect the ignition coil electrical connectors.
24. Connect the make-up air hose to the intake manifold.
25. Connect the fuel supply line to the fuel rail.
26. Connect the EVAP vacuum line to the throttle body.
27. Connect the negative battery cable.
28. Install the engine cover.
29. Install the oil fill cap.
30. Start the engine and check for leaks.

VALVE LIFTERS

REMOVAL & INSTALLATION

3.6L Engine

See Figure 229.

1. Disconnect and isolate the negative battery cable.
2. Remove the camshaft(s).

➡**If the rocker arms are to be reused, identify their positions so that they can be reassembled into their original locations.**

3. Remove the rocker arm(s).

➡**If the hydraulic lifters are to be reused, identify their positions so that they can be reassembled into their original locations.**

4. Remove the hydraulic lifter(s).

➡**The LH cylinder head hydraulic lifters are shown, the RH cylinder head hydraulic lifters are similar. If the hydraulic lifters are being reused, reassemble them into their original locations.**

To install:

5. Verify that the hydraulic lifters are at least partially full of oil. There should be little or no plunger travel when the hydraulic lifter is depressed.
6. Install the hydraulic lifter(s).

➡**If the rocker arms are being reused, reassemble them into their original locations.**

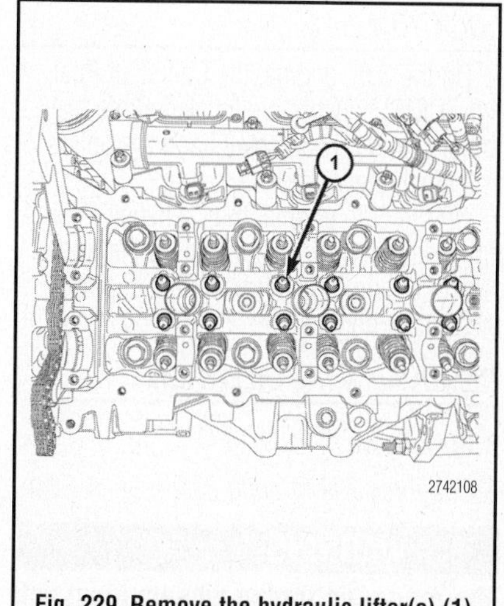

Fig. 229 Remove the hydraulic lifter(s) (1)

7. Install the rocker arm(s).
8. Install the camshaft(s), phasers, cylinder head cover(s) and upper intake manifold.
9. Connect the negative battery cable.

5.7L Engine

See Figures 230 and 231.

1. Disconnect and isolate the negative battery cable.
2. Remove the cylinder head.
3. Remove the lifter guide holder retaining bolt from the lifter guide holder assembly.

⁂ WARNING

The lifter and retainer assembly must be installed as a unit.

⁂ WARNING

If the lifter and retainer assembly are to be reused, identify lifters to ensure installation in their original location or engine damage could result.

4. Remove the lifter guide holder and lifters as an assembly.
5. Check the camshaft lobes for abnormal wear.

To install:

The Multiple Displacement System (MDS) provides cylinder deactivation during steady speed, low acceleration and shallow grade climbing conditions to increase fuel economy.

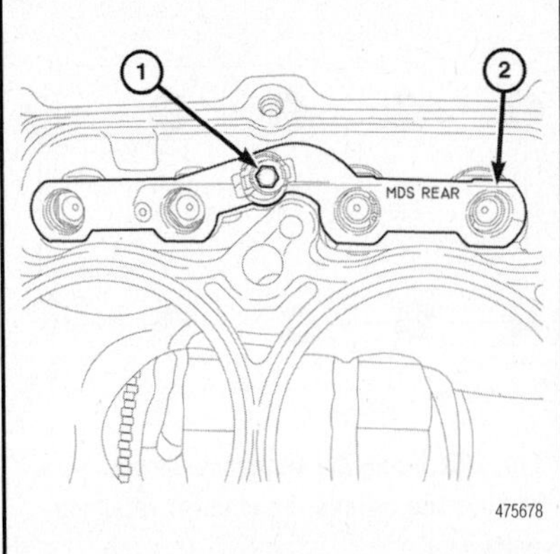

Fig. 230 Remove the lifter guide holder retaining bolt (1) from the lifter guide holder assembly (2)

⁂ WARNING

Engines equipped with MDS use both standard roller lifters and deactivating roller lifters. The deactivating roller lifters must be used in cylinders 1,4,6,7. The deactivating lifters can be identified by the two holes in the side of the lifter body, for the latching pins.

⁂ WARNING

The lifter and retainer assembly must be installed as a unit.

6. Lubricate the lifter guide holder and lifters.

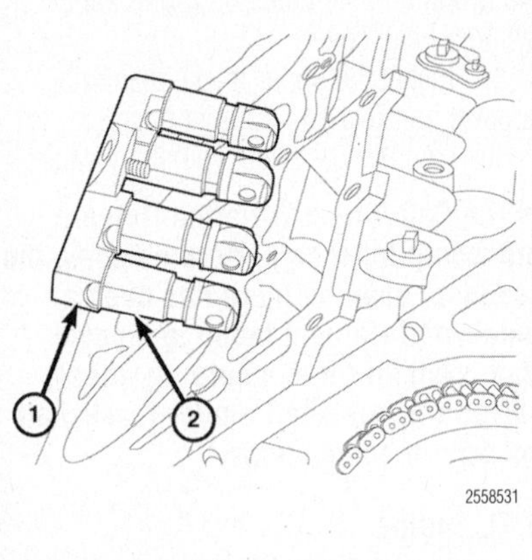

Fig. 231 Remove the lifter guide holder (1) and lifters (2) as an assembly

⁂ WARNING

If the lifters and guide holder assembly are to be reused, they must be installed in their original location.

7. Install the lifter guide holder and lifters.
8. Tighten the lifter guide holder retaining bolt to 9 ft. lbs. (12 Nm).
9. Install the cylinder head.
10. Connect the negative battery cable.

⁂ WARNING

To prevent damage to valve assemblies, do not run the engine above fast idle until all hydraulic lifters have filled with oil and have become quiet.

11. Start the engine and check for leaks.
12. Road test the vehicle.

ENGINE PERFORMANCE & EMISSION CONTROLS

CAMSHAFT POSITION (CMP) SENSOR

LOCATION

On the 3.6L engine, the Camshaft Position (CMP) sensors are located at the rear of the cylinder head covers and are bolted to the cylinder head.

On the 5.7L engine, the Camshaft Position Sensor (CMP) is located on the right side of the timing cover near the engine thermostat housing.

REMOVAL & INSTALLATION

3.6L Engine

See Figures 232 through 236.

⁂ WARNING

The magnetic timing wheels must not come in contact with magnets (pickup tools, trays, etc.) or any other strong magnetic field. This will destroy the timing wheels ability to correctly relay camshaft position to the camshaft position sensor.

➡The Camshaft Position (CMP) sensors are located at the rear of the cylinder head covers and are bolted to the cylinder head.

1. Disconnect and isolate the negative battery cable.
2. If removing the LH CMP sensor, first remove the air inlet hose and upper intake manifold (2).

➡The RH CMP sensor is shown, the LH CMP sensor is similar. If removing both RH and LH CMP sensors, mark the sensors so they can be installed in their original locations.

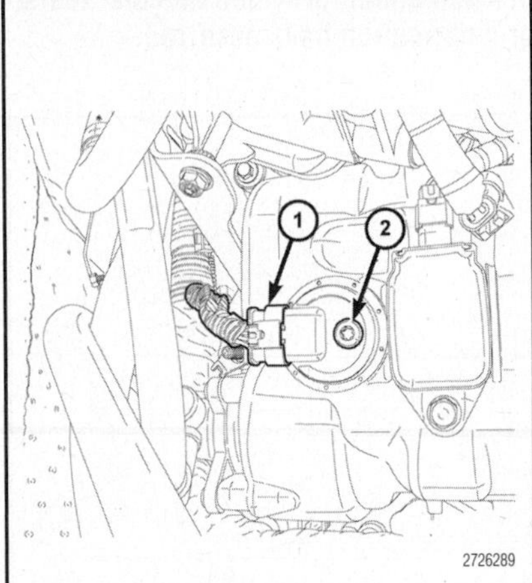

Fig. 232 Disconnect the electrical connector (1) from the CMP sensor and remove the mounting bolt (2)

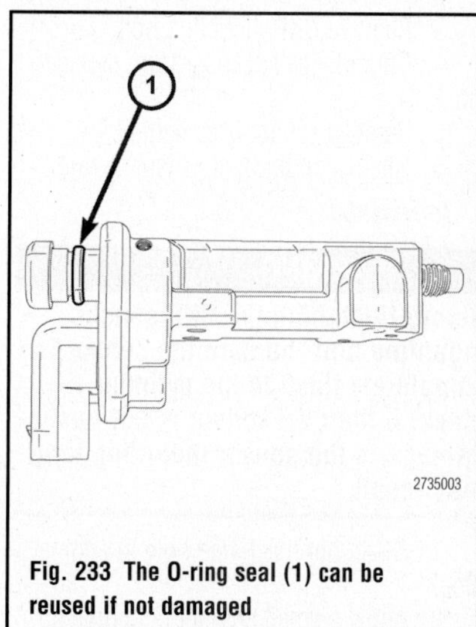

Fig. 233 The O-ring seal (1) can be reused if not damaged

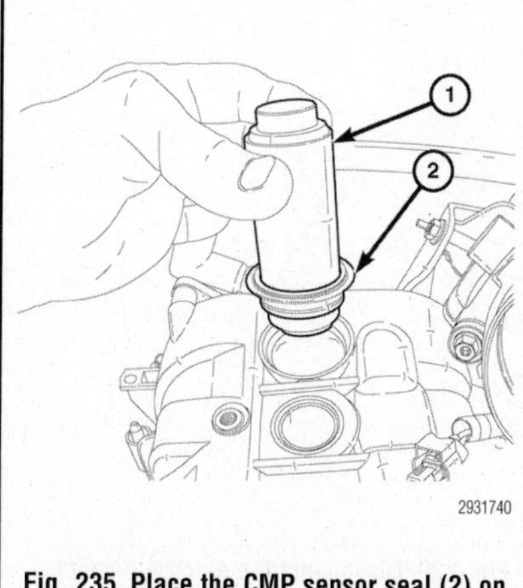

Fig. 235 Place the CMP sensor seal (2) on the Cam Sensor/Spark Plug Tube Seal Installer (1)

3. Disconnect the electrical connector from the CMP sensor.
4. Loosen the sensor mounting bolt.
5. Pull the sensor and mounting bolt from the cylinder head cover.
6. The O-ring seal can be reused if not damaged.

To install:

7. Clean out the Camshaft Position (CMP) sensor mounting bolt hole in cylinder head.
8. The CMP sensor seal can be reused if not damaged.
9. If required, install a new CMP sensor seal in the cylinder head cover:
   a. Lubricate the CMP sensor seal inner and outer diameters with clean engine oil.
   b. Place the CMP sensor seal on the Cam Sensor/Spark Plug Tube Seal Installer.
   c. Push the seal into the cylinder head cover until the base of the seal is seated.
   d. Remove the tool.

➡A properly installed CMP sensor seal will have a 0.06–0.08 inches (1.5–2.0 mm) gap between the cylinder head cover and the seal upper flange.

10. The sensor mounting bolt O-ring can be reused if not damaged.
11. Apply a small amount of engine oil to the sensor mounting bolt O-ring.
12. Install the CMP sensor to the cylinder head. Tighten the mounting bolt to 80 inch lbs. (9 Nm).
13. Connect the electrical connector to the sensor.
14. Following installation of the LH CMP sensor, install the upper intake manifold and air inlet hose.
15. Connect the negative battery cable.

➡The Cam/Crank Variation Relearn procedure must be performed using the scan tool anytime there has been a repair/replacement made to a powertrain system, for example: flywheel, valvetrain, camshaft and/or crankshaft sensors or components.

5.7L Engine

See Figure 237.

1. Disconnect the air cleaner and resonator assembly.
2. Disconnect the electrical connector at the CMP sensor.
3. Remove the CMP sensor retaining bolt.
4. Using a slight rocking motion, carefully remove the CMP sensor from the timing cover.
5. Check the condition of CMP sensor O-ring, replace as necessary.

To install:

6. Clean out the machined hole in the timing cover.
7. Install the CMP sensor into the timing cover with a slight rocking motion. Do not the twist sensor into position as damage to O-ring may result.

⁂ WARNING

Before tightening the CMP sensor retaining bolt, be sure the sensor is completely flush to the timing cover. If the sensor is not flush, damage to the sensor mounting tang may result.

8. Install the retaining bolt and tighten to 9 ft. lbs. (12 Nm).
9. Connect the electrical connector to the CMP sensor.
10. Install the air cleaner and resonator assembly.

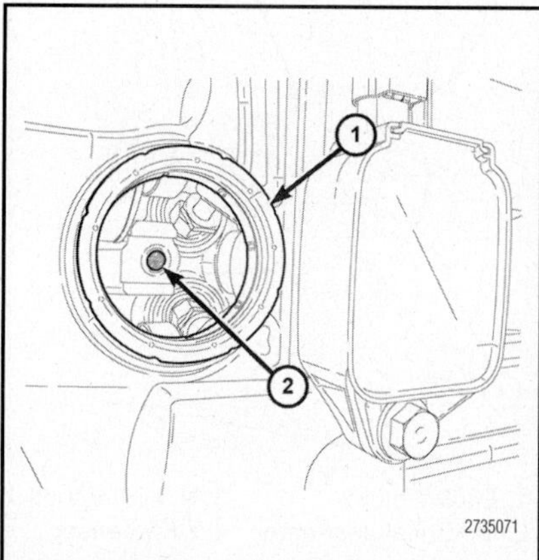

Fig. 234 CMP mounting location showing the CMP sensor seal (1) and the mounting bolt hole (2)

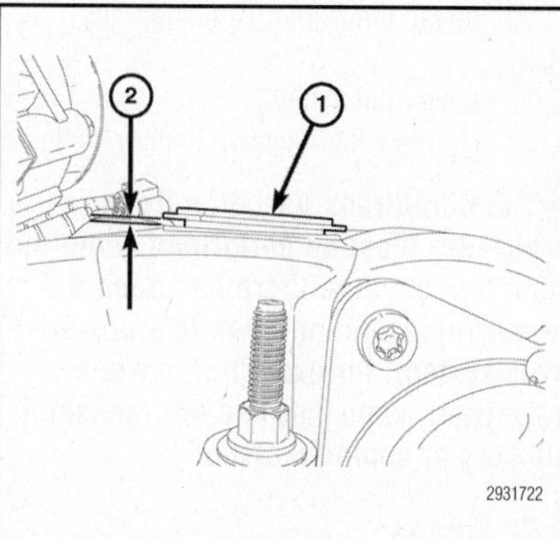

Fig. 236 A properly installed CMP sensor seal (1) will have a 0.06–0.08 inches (1.5–2.0 mm) gap (2) between the cylinder head cover and the seal upper flange

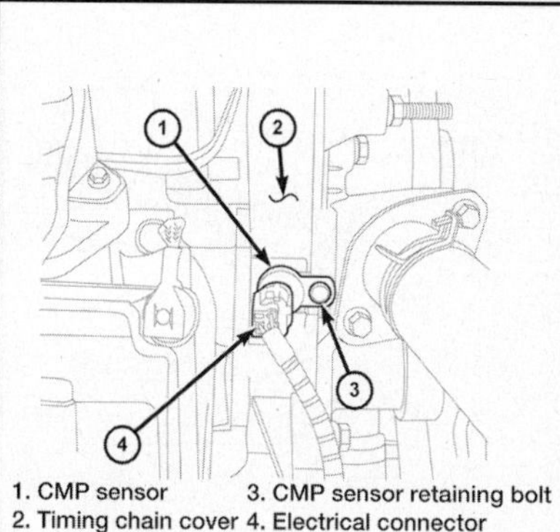

Fig. 237 Disconnect the electrical connector at the CMP sensor

CRANKSHAFT POSITION (CKP) SENSOR

LOCATION

The Crankshaft Position (CKP) sensor is mounted into the right rear side of the cylinder block.

REMOVAL & INSTALLATION

3.6L Engine

See Figures 238 through 240.

1. Disconnect and isolate the negative battery cable.
2. Raise and support the vehicle.
3. Remove the front suspension skid plate.
4. Push back the heat shield from the Crankshaft Position (CKP) sensor.
5. Disconnect the electrical connector from the CKP sensor.
6. Remove the sensor mounting bolt.
7. Carefully twist the sensor from the cylinder block.
8. The CKP sensor O-ring can be reused if not damaged.

To install:

9. The CKP sensor O-ring can be reused if not damaged.
10. Apply a small amount of engine oil to the sensor O-ring.
11. Clean out the CKP sensor mounting bolt hole in the engine block.
12. Install the sensor into the engine block with a slight rocking and twisting action.

✻✻ WARNING

Before tightening the CKP sensor mounting bolt, be sure the sensor is completely flush to the cylinder block. If the CKP sensor is not flush, damage to the sensor mounting tang may result.

13. Install the mounting bolt and tighten to 106 inch lbs. (12 Nm).
14. Connect the electrical connector to the sensor.
15. Position the heat shield over the CKP sensor.
16. Install the front suspension skid plate.
17. Lower the vehicle.
18. Connect the negative battery cable.

➡The Cam/Crank Variation Relearn procedure must be performed using the scan tool anytime there has been a repair/replacement made to a powertrain system, for example: flywheel, valvetrain, camshaft and/or crankshaft sensors or components.

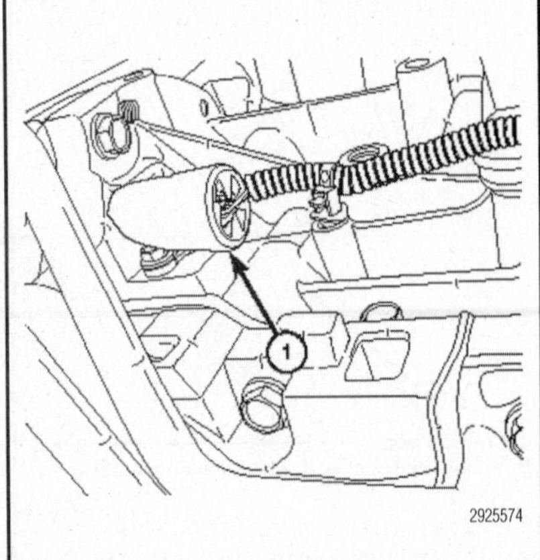

Fig. 238 Push back the heat shield (1) from the Crankshaft Position (CKP) sensor

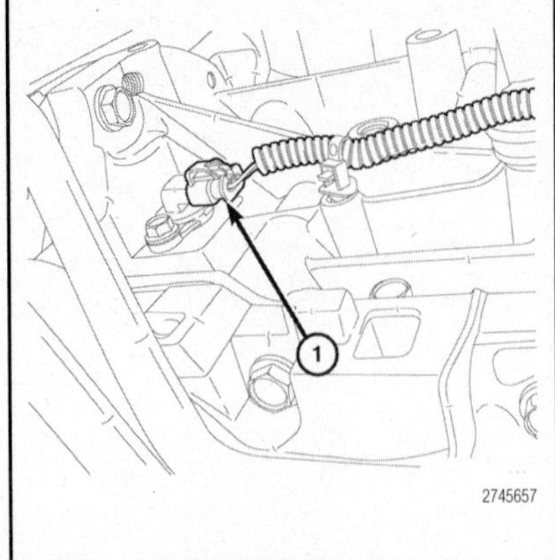

Fig. 239 Disconnect the electrical connector (1) from the CKP sensor

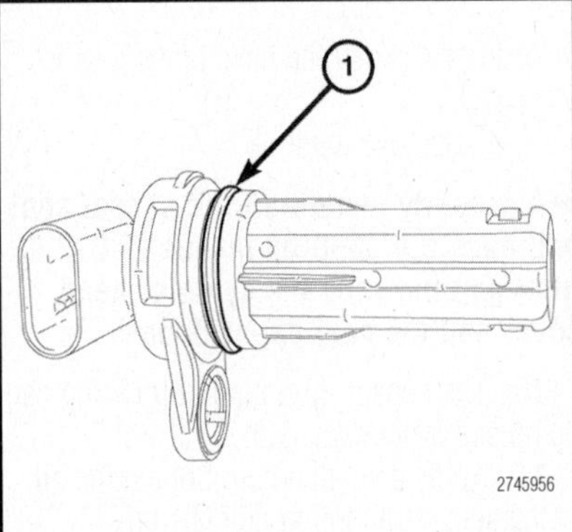

Fig. 240 The CKP sensor O-ring (1) can be reused if not damaged

5.7L Engine

See Figure 241.

1. Raise vehicle.
2. Disconnect CKP electrical connector at sensor.
3. Remove CKP mounting bolt.
4. Carefully twist sensor from cylinder block.
5. Remove sensor from vehicle.
6. Check condition of sensor O-ring.

To install:

✻✻ WARNING

Before tightening the CKP sensor mounting bolt, be sure the sensor is completely flush to the cylinder block. If the CKP sensor is not flush, damage to the sensor mounting tang may result.

7. Clean out machined hole in engine block.
8. Apply a small amount of engine oil to sensor o-ring.
9. Install sensor into engine block with a slight rocking and twisting action.
10. Install mounting bolt and tighten to 21 ft. lbs. (28 Nm).
11. Connect electrical connector to sensor.
12. Lower vehicle.

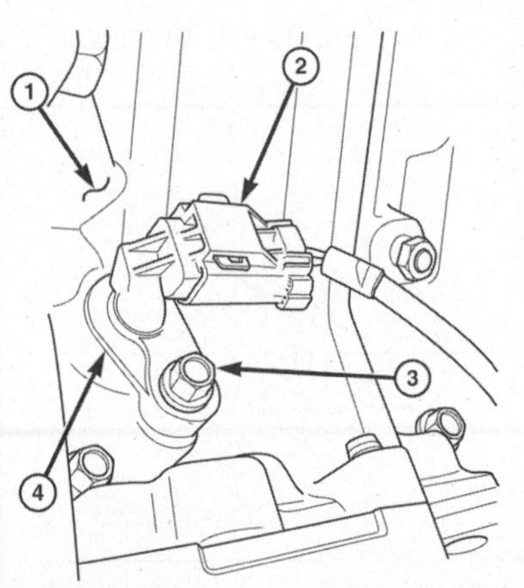

Fig. 241 Disconnect CKP electrical connector at sensor

ENGINE COOLANT TEMPERATURE (ECT) SENSOR

LOCATION

The Engine Coolant Temperature (ECT) sensor on the 3.6L engine is installed into a water jacket at rear of the cylinder head on the left side of the engine.

On the 5.7L engine, the Engine Coolant Temperature (ECT) sensor is located on the upper portion of the water pump housing. It is installed into a water jacket in line with the thermostat.

REMOVAL & INSTALLATION

3.6L Engine

⁂ CAUTION

Hot, pressurized coolant can cause injury by scalding. Cooling system must be partially drained before removing the coolant temperature sensor.

➡Do not waste reusable coolant. If solution is clean, drain coolant into a clean container for reuse.

1. Partially drain the cooling system.
2. Disconnect the electrical connector from the sensor.
3. Remove the sensor from the cylinder head.

To install:

4. Apply MOPAR thread sealant with PFTE to sensor threads.
5. Install sensor to cylinder head.
6. Tighten sensor to 8 ft. lbs. (11 Nm).
7. Connect electrical connector to sensor.
8. Replace any lost engine coolant.

5.7L Engine

⁂ CAUTION

Hot, pressurized coolant can cause injury by scalding. Cooling system must be partially drained before removing the coolant temperature sensor.

1. Remove the air intake system.

➡Do not waste reusable coolant. If solution is clean, drain coolant into a clean container for reuse.

2. Partially drain the cooling system.
3. Disconnect electrical connector from sensor.
4. Remove sensor from the water pump housing.

To install:

5. Apply MOPAR thread sealant with PFTE to the sensor threads.
6. Install the coolant temperature sensor into water pump housing.
7. Tighten the coolant temperature sensor to 8 ft. lbs. (11 Nm).
8. Connect the coolant temperature sensor electrical connector.
9. Install air intake system.
10. Replace any lost engine coolant.

HEATED OXYGEN (HO2S) SENSOR

LOCATION

3.6L Engine

See Figure 242.

5.7L Engine

See Figure 243.

REMOVAL & INSTALLATION

3.6L Engine

⁂ CAUTION

The exhaust pipes and catalytic converter become very hot during engine operation. Allow the engine to cool before removing the oxygen sensor.

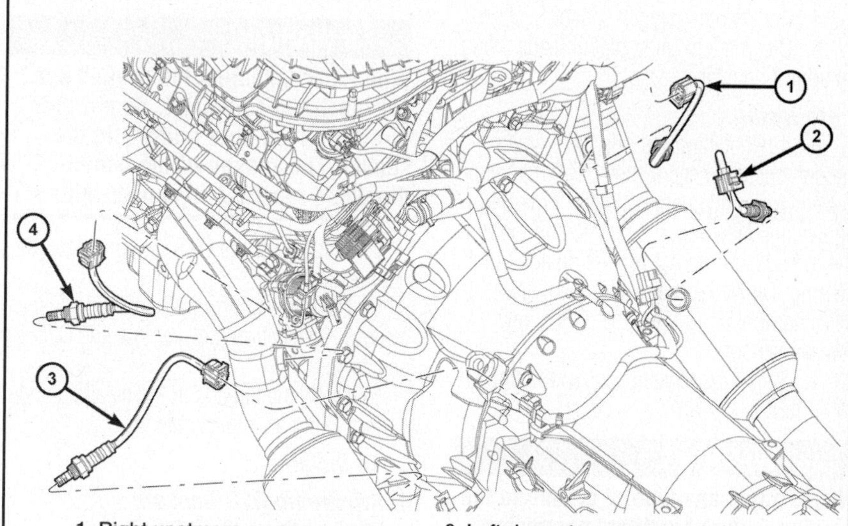

Fig. 242 Locations of the heated oxygen sensors

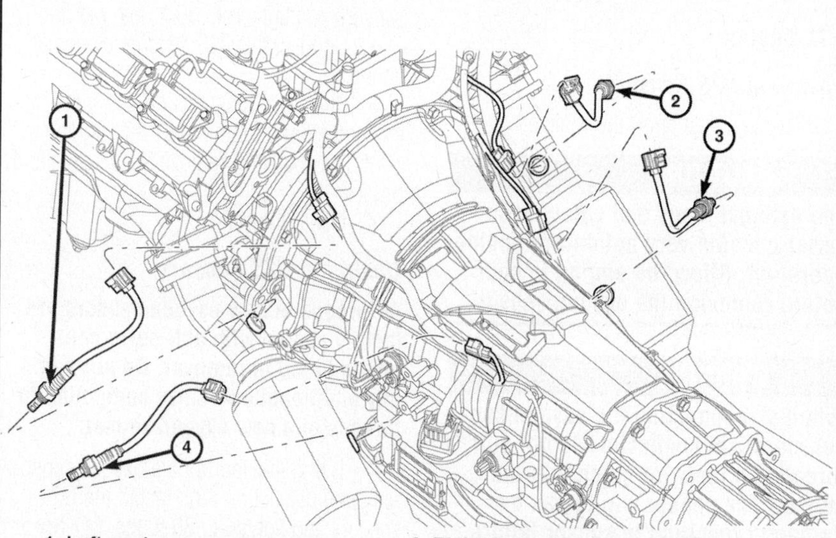

Fig. 243 Locations of the heated oxygen sensors

1. Disconnect and isolate the negative battery cable.
2. Raise and support the vehicle.

⁂ WARNING

When disconnecting the oxygen sensor electrical connector, do not pull directly on the wire going into the sensor. The sensor wiring can be damaged resulting in sensor failure.

3. Disconnect the heated oxygen sensor electrical connector.
4. Remove the oxygen sensor.
5. Clean the exhaust pipe threads using an appropriate tap.

To install:

6. If reinstalling the original oxygen sensor, coat the sensor threads with an anti-seize compound such as Loctite 771- 64 or equivalent. New sensors have compound on the threads and do not require an additional coating. Do Not add any additional anti-seize compound to the threads of a new oxygen sensor.
7. Install the oxygen sensor and tighten to 37 ft. lbs. (50 Nm).

⁂ WARNING

Never apply any type of grease to the oxygen sensor electrical connector, or attempt any repair of the sensor wiring harness.

8. Connect the heated oxygen sensor electrical connector.
9. Lower the vehicle.
10. Connect the negative battery cable.

5.7L Engine

Upstream O2S Sensors

1. Raise and support the vehicle.

⁂ CAUTION

The exhaust pipes and catalytic converter become very hot during engine operation. Allow the engine to cool before removing the oxygen sensor.

⁂ WARNING

When disconnecting the oxygen sensor electrical connector, do not pull directly on the wire going into the sensor. The sensor wiring can be damaged resulting in sensor failure.

2. Disconnect the O2S sensors electrical connectors.
3. Remove the left catalytic converter heat shield.
4. Using the appropriate oxygen sensor removal/installation tool, remove the O2S sensors.
5. Clean the threads in the exhaust pipes using an appropriate tap.

Downstream O2S Sensors

1. Raise and support the vehicle.
2. Support the transmission with a safety stand or suitable jack, remove the crossmember retaining bolts and slightly lower the transmission to gain access to the O2S sensor electrical connectors.

⁂ WARNING

When disconnecting the oxygen sensor electrical connector, do not pull directly on the wire going into the sensor. The sensor wiring can be damaged resulting in sensor failure.

3. Disconnect the O2S sensors electrical connectors.
4. Using the appropriate oxygen sensor removal/installation tool, remove the O2S sensors.
5. Clean the threads in the catalytic converters using an appropriate tap.

To install:

Downstream O2S Sensors

➡Threads of new oxygen sensors are factory coated with anti-seize compound to aid in removal. Do not add any additional anti-seize compound to threads of a new oxygen sensor.

1. Using the appropriate oxygen sensor removal/installation tool, install the O2S sensors and tighten to 30 ft. lbs. (41 Nm.).
2. Connect the O2S sensors electrical connectors.
3. Raise the transmission and install the crossmember to frame bolts and tighten to 50 ft. lbs. (68 Nm), remove the safety stand or jack.
4. Lower the vehicle.

Upstream O2S Sensors

➡Threads of new oxygen sensors are factory coated with anti-seize compound to aid in removal. Do not add any additional anti-seize compound to threads of a new oxygen sensor.

1. Using the appropriate oxygen sensor removal/installation tool, install the O2S sensors and tighten to 30 ft. lbs. (41 Nm.).
2. Install the left catalytic converter heat shield.
3. Connect the O2S sensors electrical connectors.
4. Lower the vehicle.

INTAKE AIR TEMPERATURE (IAT) SENSOR

LOCATION

On the 3.6L engine, the Intake Air Temperature (IAT) sensor is located on the air intake duct.

On the 5.7L engine, the Intake Air Temperature (IAT) sensor is installed into the air cleaner resonator.

REMOVAL & INSTALLATION

3.6L Engine

See Figures 244 and 245.

1. Disconnect and isolate the negative battery cable.
2. Remove the engine cover.
3. Disconnect the electrical connector from the Intake Air Temperature (IAT) sensor.
4. Clean dirt from the air inlet tube at the IAT sensor base.

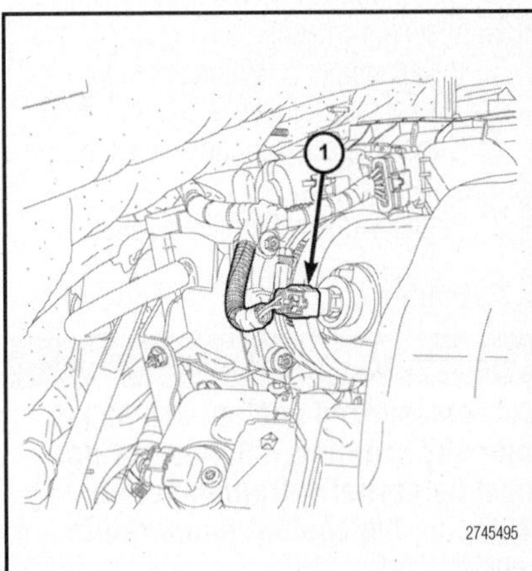

Fig. 244 Disconnect the electrical connector (1) from the Intake Air Temperature (IAT) sensor

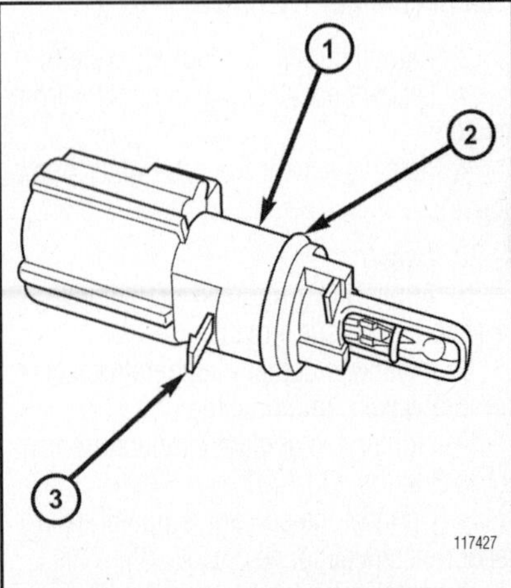

Fig. 245 IAT sensor (1), O-ring (2), and the Plastic release tab (3)

5. Gently lift the small plastic release tab, rotate the sensor about ¼ turn counterclockwise and remove the sensor from the inlet air hose.
6. The IAT sensor O-ring can be reused if not damaged.

To install:

7. The sensor mounted O-ring seal can be reused if not damaged.
8. Clean the IAT sensor mounting hole in the air inlet hose.
9. Install the IAT sensor into the air inlet hose and rotate clockwise until the release tab engages.
10. Install the electrical connector to the IAT sensor.
11. Install the engine cover.
12. Connect the negative battery cable.

5.7L Engine

See Figure 246.

1. Remove the oil fill cap.
2. Lift and separate the engine cover retaining grommets from the ball studs and remove the engine cover.
3. Disconnect the electrical connector at the IAT sensor.
4. Gently lift on the small plastic release tab and rotate the IAT sensor about ¼ turn counterclockwise and remove.
5. Check condition of sensor O-ring, replace if necessary.

To install:

6. Clean the IAT sensor mounting hole in the air cleaner resonator.
7. Position the IAT sensor into the air cleaner resonator, rotate clockwise about ¼ turn until the release tab locks into position.
8. Connect the electrical connector to the IAT sensor.
9. Position the engine cover and secure the retaining grommets to the ball studs.
10. Install the oil fill cap.

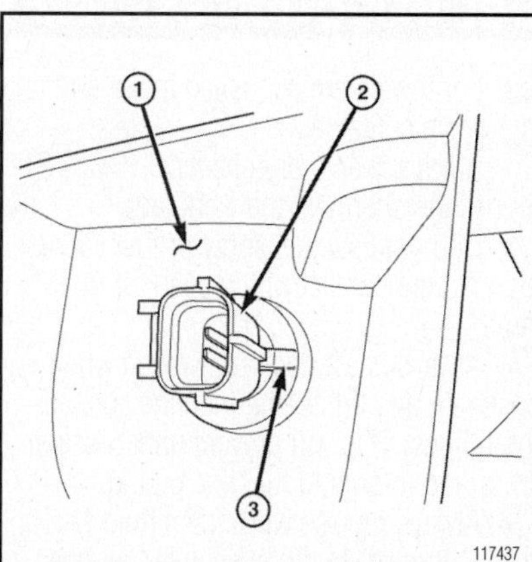

Fig. 246 Intake Air Temperature (IAT) sensor (2), the air cleaner resonator (1), and the tab (3)

KNOCK SENSOR (KS)

LOCATION

The knock sensors are located in the valley of the engine block, beneath the intake manifold.

REMOVAL & INSTALLATION

3.6L Engine

See Figure 247.

➡The forward sensor is known to the Powertrain Control Module (PCM) as knock sensor 1. The rear sensor is known to the PCM as knock sensor 2.

1. Perform the fuel pressure release procedure.
2. Disconnect and isolate the negative battery cable.
3. Drain the cooling system.
4. Remove the air cleaner housing assembly, upper and lower intake manifolds and the oil filter housing.
5. Remove the knock sensor electrical connector.

➡There may be a foam strip on the bolt threads. This foam is used only to retain the bolts to the sensors for plant assembly. It is not used as a sealant. Do not apply any adhesive, sealant or thread locking compound to these bolts.

6. Remove the mounting bolt and knock sensor 1 or knock sensor 2.

To install:

7. Thoroughly clean the knock sensor mounting holes.

1. Knock sensor 1
2. Mounting bolts
3. Knock sensor 2
4. Knock sensor electrical connectors

2726041

Fig. 247 Remove the knock sensor electrical connector

➡Over or under tightening the sensor mounting bolts will affect knock sensor performance, possibly causing improper spark control. Always use the specified torque when installing the knock sensors. The torque specification for the knock sensor bolt is less than the typical 8 mm bolt.

➡There may be a foam strip on the bolt threads. This foam is used only to retain the bolts to the sensors for plant assembly. It is not used as a sealant. Do not apply any adhesive, sealant or thread locking compound to these bolts.

8. Install knock sensor 1 and/or knock sensor 2 with mounting bolt. Tighten the mounting bolt to 16 ft. lbs. (22 Nm).
9. Connect the electrical connector.
10. Install the oil filter housing, upper and lower intake manifolds and air cleaner housing assembly.
11. If removed, install the oil filter and fill the engine crankcase with the proper oil to the correct level.
12. Connect the negative battery cable.
13. Fill the cooling system.
14. Operate the engine until it reaches normal operating temperature. Check cooling system for correct fluid level.

5.7L Engine

1. Raise and support the vehicle.
2. Disconnect the knock sensor electrical connector(s).
3. Remove the knock sensor retaining bolt(s).

➡Note the foam strip on bolt threads. This foam strip is used only to retain the bolts to the sensors for plant assembly. It is not used as a sealant. Do not apply any adhesive, sealant or thread locking compound to these bolts.

4. Remove the knock sensor(s) from the cylinder block.

To install:

5. Thoroughly clean the knock sensor(s) mounting hole.
6. Install the knock sensor(s) into the cylinder block.

➡Over or under tightening the sensor mounting bolts will affect knock sensors performance, possibly causing improper spark control. Always use the specified torque when installing the knock sensors. The torque for the knock sensor bolt is relatively light for an 8 mm bolt.

➡**Note foam strip on bolt threads. This foam is used only to retain the bolts to sensors for plant assembly. It is not used as a sealant. Do not apply any adhesive, sealant or thread locking compound to these bolts.**

7. Position the knock sensor(s), install the retaining bolt(s) and tighten to 15 ft. lbs. (20 Nm).
8. Install the electrical connector(s).

MANIFOLD AIR PRESSURE (MAP) SENSOR

LOCATION

Refer to the graphics in the Removal and Installation section for the location(s).

REMOVAL & INSTALLATION

3.6L Engine

See Figures 248 and 249.

1. Disconnect and isolate the negative battery cable.
2. Remove the engine cover.
3. Unlock and disconnect the electrical connector from the MAP sensor.
4. Rotate the MAP sensor ¼ turn counterclockwise and pull the sensor straight up and out of the upper intake manifold.
5. The MAP sensor O-ring can be reused if not damaged.

To install:

6. Apply a small amount of engine oil to the sensor O-ring.
7. Install the MAP sensor into the upper intake manifold and rotate ¼ turn clockwise.
8. Connect and lock the electrical connector to the sensor.

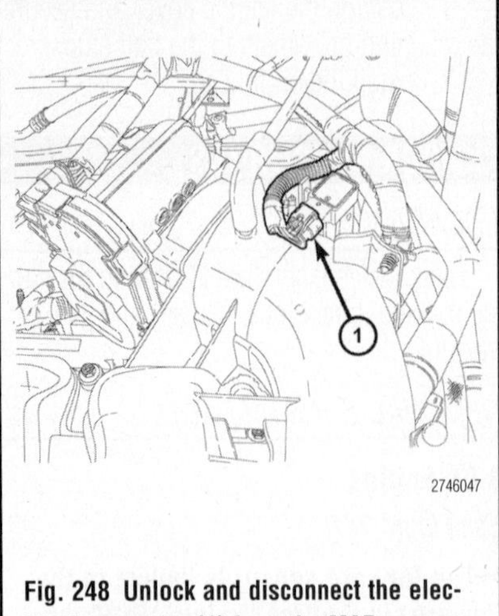

Fig. 248 Unlock and disconnect the electrical connector (1) from the MAP sensor

9. Install the engine cover.
10. Connect the negative battery cable.

5.7L Engine

See Figure 250.

1. Disconnect MAP sensor electrical connector.
2. Rotate MAP sensor counterclockwise for removal.
3. Lift MAP sensor upward.
4. Inspect O-ring for damage.

To install:

5. Clean MAP sensor mounting hole at intake manifold.
6. Check MAP sensor O-ring for cuts or tears.
7. Position MAP sensor into manifold.
8. Rotate MAP sensor clockwise for installation.
9. Connect electrical connector.

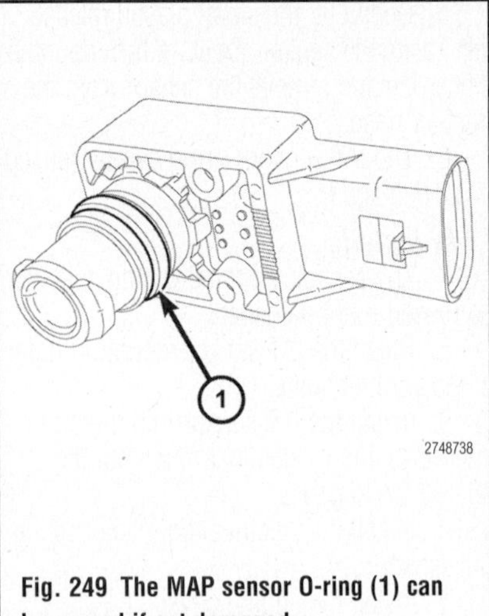

Fig. 249 The MAP sensor O-ring (1) can be reused if not damaged

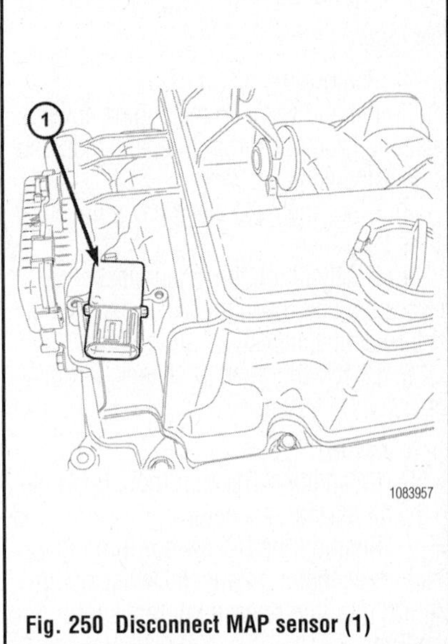

Fig. 250 Disconnect MAP sensor (1) electrical connector

FUEL — GASOLINE FUEL INJECTION SYSTEM

FUEL SYSTEM SERVICE PRECAUTIONS

Safety is the most important factor when performing not only fuel system maintenance but any type of maintenance. Failure to conduct maintenance and repairs in a safe manner may result in serious personal injury or death. Maintenance and testing of the vehicle's fuel system components can be accomplished safely and effectively by adhering to the following rules and guidelines.

- To avoid the possibility of fire and personal injury, always disconnect the negative battery cable unless the repair or test procedure requires that battery voltage be applied.
- Always relieve the fuel system pressure prior to disconnecting any fuel system component (injector, fuel rail, pressure regulator, etc.), fitting or fuel line connection. Exercise extreme caution whenever relieving fuel system pressure to avoid exposing skin, face and eyes to fuel spray. Please be advised that fuel under pressure may penetrate the skin or any part of the body that it contacts.
- Always place a shop towel or cloth around the fitting or connection prior to loosening to absorb any excess fuel due to spillage. Ensure that all fuel spillage (should it occur) is quickly removed from engine surfaces. Ensure that all fuel soaked cloths or towels are deposited into a suitable waste container.
- Always keep a dry chemical (Class B) fire extinguisher near the work area.
- Do not allow fuel spray or fuel vapors to come into contact with a spark or open flame.
- Always use a back-up wrench when loosening and tightening fuel line connection fittings. This will prevent unnecessary stress and torsion to fuel line piping.
- Always replace worn fuel fitting O-rings with new Do not substitute fuel hose or equivalent where fuel pipe is installed.

Before servicing the vehicle, make sure to also refer to the precautions in the beginning of this section as well.

RELIEVING FUEL SYSTEM PRESSURE

See Figure 251.

1. Remove the fuel fill cap.
2. Remove the fuel pump fuse from the Power Distribution Center (PDC). For location of the fuel pump fuse, refer to label on the underside of the PDC cover.
3. Start and run the engine until it stalls.
4. Attempt restarting the engine until it will no longer run.
5. Turn the ignition key to the OFF position.
6. Place a rag or towel below the fuel supply line quick-connect fitting located near the cowl.
7. Disconnect the fuel supply line quick-connect fitting at the fuel supply line.
8. Return the fuel pump fuse to the PDC.

➡One or more Diagnostic Trouble Codes (DTC) may have been stored in the PCM memory due to fuel pump fuse removal. A diagnostic scan tool must be used to erase a DTC.

FUEL FILTER

REMOVAL & INSTALLATION

Two fuel filters are integrated into the main fuel pump module. The first fuel filter is located at the bottom of the main fuel pump module and the second fuel filter is located inside the main fuel pump module. A separate frame mounted fuel filter is not used with any engine.

Both fuel filters are designed for extended service. The fuel filters are not a separate, serviceable component.

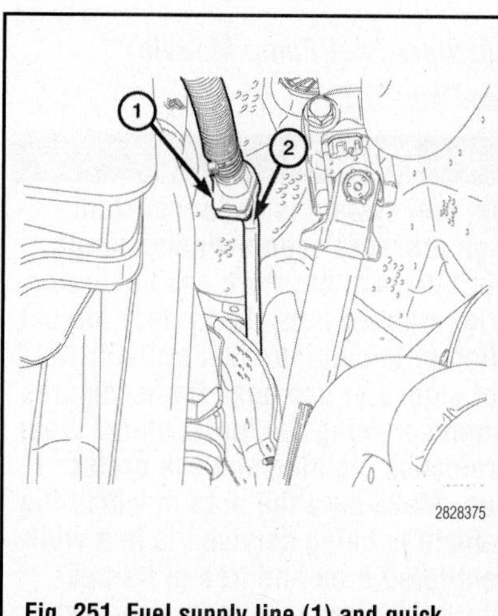

Fig. 251 Fuel supply line (1) and quick connect fitting (2)

FUEL INJECTORS

REMOVAL & INSTALLATION

3.6L Engine

See Figures 252 through 254.

✻✻ CAUTION

The fuel system is under constant pressure even with engine off. Before servicing the fuel rail, fuel system pressure must be released.

1. Release fuel system pressure.
2. Disconnect and isolate the negative battery cable.

✻✻ WARNING

When removing the fuel rail from the lower intake manifold, one or more fuel injectors may remain in the intake manifold resulting in residual fuel spilling onto the engine from the fuel rail.

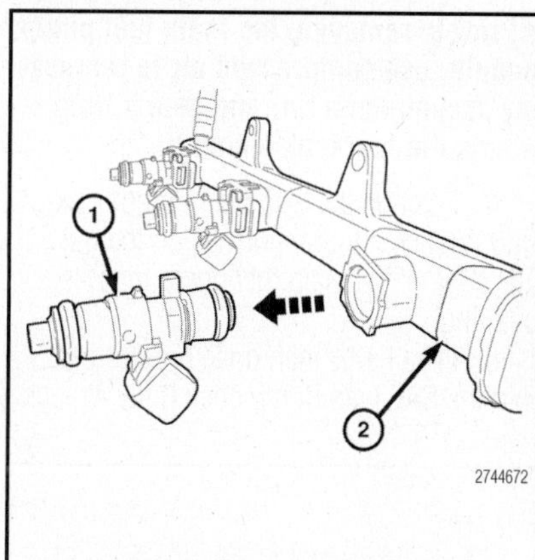

Fig. 252 Remove the fuel injectors (1) from the fuel rail (2)

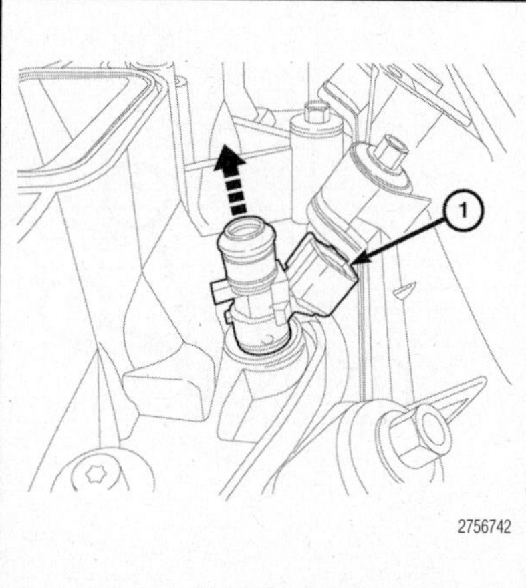

Fig. 253 Remove the fuel injectors (1) from the lower intake manifold

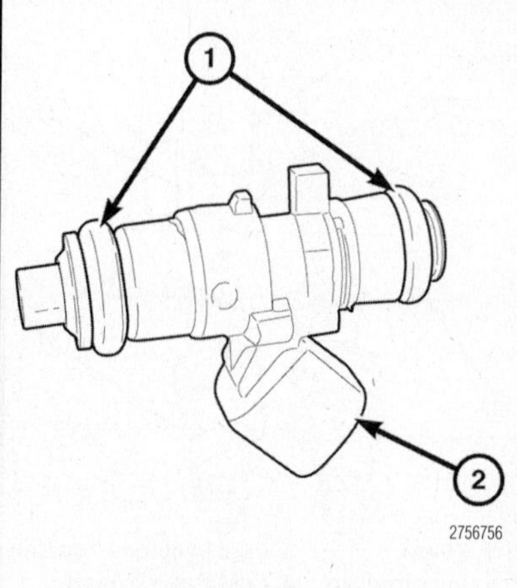

Fig. 254 Remove and discard all fuel injector (2) O-ring seals (1)

3. Remove the air inlet hose, upper intake manifold, and fuel rail.
4. Remove the fuel injectors from the fuel rail.
5. Remove the fuel injectors from the lower intake manifold.
6. Remove and discard all fuel injector O-ring seals.

To install:

7. Lightly lubricate new O-ring seals with engine oil and install on the fuel injector.
8. Install the fuel injectors to the fuel rail.
9. Install the fuel rail, upper inlet manifold and air inlet hose.
10. Connect the negative battery cable.
11. Start the engine and check for leaks.

5.7L Engine

See Figure 255.

1. Remove the fuel rail assembly.
2. Using suitable pliers, remove the fuel injector retaining clip.
3. Remove the fuel injector from the fuel rail using a side to side motion while pulling the injector out of the fuel rail assembly.

To install:

➡If the same fuel injector is to be reinstalled, install new O-rings.

➡Apply a small amount of clean engine oil to each injector O-ring. This will aid in the installation.

4. Install the fuel injector into the fuel rail using a side to side motion while pushing injector into the fuel rail assembly.
5. Using suitable pliers, install the fuel injector retaining clip.
6. Install the fuel rail assembly.

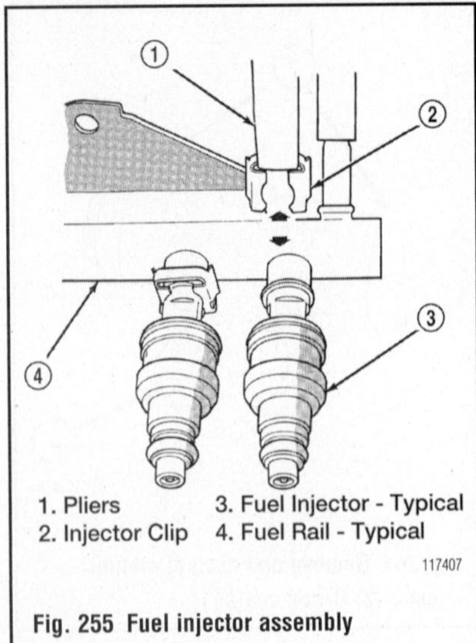

Fig. 255 Fuel injector assembly

7. Start the engine and check for fuel leaks.

FUEL PUMP MODULE

REMOVAL & INSTALLATION

See Figure 256.

This vehicle uses a saddle type tank that has a reservoir on both sides of the drive shaft. The electric fuel pump, fuel pressure regulator and fuel filters are integrated into the main fuel pump module located on the left side of the fuel tank. The auxiliary fuel pump module is on the right side of the fuel tank. The fuel supply fitting is located on top of the main fuel pump module and supplies fuel to the engine. Both modules have fuel level sending unit sensor cards. There is one hose that connect both modules together, this hose is the fuel supply line and a return or siphon hose. The lines are removed from the main fuel pump module on the left side of the fuel tank when servicing either unit. A 12 volt, permanent magnet, electric motor powers the fuel pump. The electric fuel pump is not a separate, serviceable component.

**** CAUTION**

The fuel system is under constant high pressure even with engine off. Until the fuel pressure has been properly released from the system, do not attempt to open the fuel system. Do not smoke or use open flames/sparks when servicing the fuel system. Wear protective clothing and eye protection. Make sure the area in which the vehicle is being serviced is in a well ventilated area and free of flames/sparks. Failure to comply may result in serious or fatal injury.

**** CAUTION**

No sparks, open flames or smoking. Risk of poisoning from inhaling and swallowing fuel. Pour fuel only into appropriately marked OSHA approved containers. Wear protective clothing. Risk of injury to eyes and skin from contact with fuel.

Perform the fuel system pressure release procedure.

**** WARNING**

If the fuel pump module is not operating or the fuel level sending unit is not operating and the fuel level cannot be determined, the fuel tank must be removed prior to draining.

1. Perform the fuel tank draining procedure.
2. Disconnect and isolate the negative battery cable.
3. Remove the fuel tank.

➡Prior to removing the main fuel pump module, use compressed air to remove any accumulated dirt and debris from around the fuel tank opening.

4. Position the SAE Fuel Pump Lock Ring Wrench into the notches on the outside edge of the main fuel pump module lock ring.
5. Install a ½ inch drive breaker bar onto the SAE Fuel Pump Lock Ring Wrench.

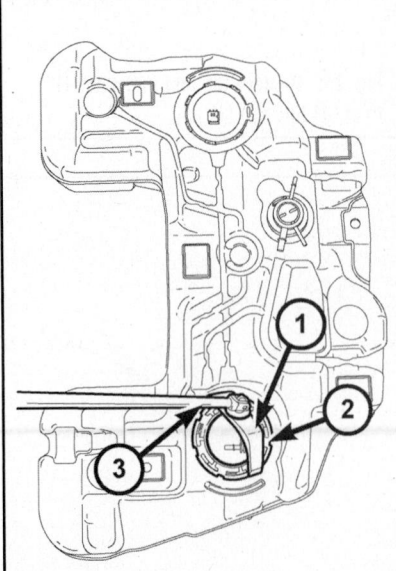

2799421

Fig. 256 Fuel Pump Lock Ring Wrench (1), fuel pump module lock ring (2), and breaker bar (3)

➡The main fuel pump module will spring up slightly when lock ring is removed.

6. Rotate the breaker bar counterclockwise and remove the lock ring.

**** WARNING**

An indexing arrow is located on top of the main fuel pump module to clock its position into the fuel tank, note its location for reassembly.

➡The main fuel pump module has to be properly located in the fuel tank for the fuel level gauge to work properly.

7. Mark the main fuel pump module orientation.

**** WARNING**

Do not allow the float arm of the main fuel pump module to come in contact with any part of the fuel tank during removal or installation, damage to the float arm and fuel level sending card may result.

8. Using caution not to bend the float arm, lift the main fuel pump module out of the fuel tank enough to gain access to the auxiliary fuel pump module supply line connection and disconnect the supply line.
9. Tip the main fuel pump module on its side to drain the remaining fuel from the reservoir and remove the main fuel pump module.

**** WARNING**

Whenever the fuel pump module is serviced, the rubber O-ring seal must be replaced.

10. Remove and discard the rubber O-ring seal.

Auxiliary Fuel Pump Module

See Figure 257.

**** CAUTION**

The fuel system is under constant high pressure even with engine off. Until the fuel pressure has been properly released from the system, do not attempt to open the fuel system. Do not smoke or use open flames/sparks when servicing the fuel system. Wear protective clothing and eye protection. Make sure the area in which the vehicle is being serviced is in a well ventilated area and free of flames/sparks. Failure to comply may result in serious or fatal injury.

⁂ CAUTION

No sparks, open flames or smoking. Risk of poisoning from inhaling and swallowing fuel. Pour fuel only into appropriately marked OSHA approved containers. Wear protective clothing. Risk of injury to eyes and skin from contact with fuel.

1. Remove the main fuel pump module.

➡Prior to removing the auxiliary fuel pump module, use compressed air to remove any accumulated dirt and debris from around fuel tank opening.

2. Position the SAE Fuel Pump Lock Ring Wrench into the notches on the outside edge of the auxiliary fuel pump module lock ring.
3. Install a ½ inch drive breaker bar onto the SAE Fuel Pump Lock Ring Wrench.

➡The auxiliary fuel pump module will spring up slightly when the lock ring is removed.

4. Rotate the breaker bar counterclockwise and remove the lock ring.

⁂ WARNING

An indexing arrow is located on top of the auxiliary fuel pump module to clock its position into the fuel tank, note its location for reassembly.

➡The auxiliary fuel pump module has to be properly located in the fuel tank for the fuel level gauge to work properly.

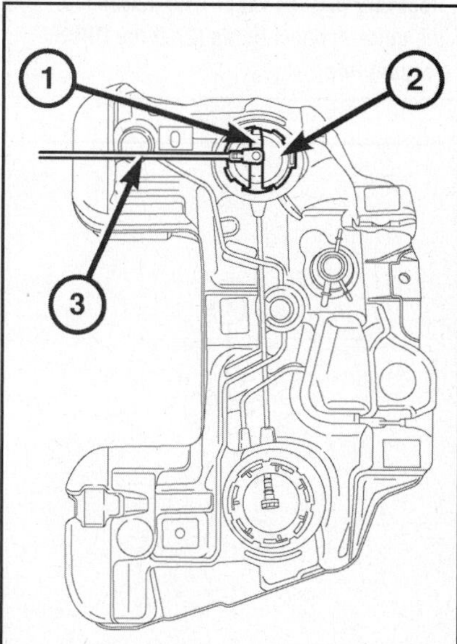

Fig. 257 Fuel Pump Lock Ring Wrench (1), fuel pump module lock ring (2), and breaker bar (3)

5. Mark the auxiliary fuel pump module orientation.

⁂ WARNING

Do not allow the float arm of the auxiliary fuel pump module to come in contact with any part of the fuel tank during removal or installation, damage to the float arm and fuel level sending card may result.

6. Using caution not to bend the float arm, lift the auxiliary fuel pump module and the auxiliary fuel pump module supply line out of the fuel tank as an assembly.

⁂ WARNING

Whenever the auxiliary fuel pump module is serviced, the rubber O-ring seal must be replaced.

7. Remove and discard the rubber O-ring seal.

To install:

⁂ WARNING

Whenever the auxiliary fuel pump module is serviced, the rubber O-ring seal must be replaced.

8. Position a new rubber O-ring seal onto the fuel tank flange.

⁂ WARNING

Do not allow the float arm of the auxiliary fuel pump module to come in contact with any part of the fuel tank during removal or installation, damage to the float arm and fuel level sending card may result.

9. Using caution not to bend the float arm, lower the auxiliary fuel pump module and the auxiliary fuel pump module supply line into the fuel tank as an assembly.

➡The auxiliary fuel pump module has to be properly located in the fuel tank for the fuel level gauge to work properly.

10. Rotate the auxiliary fuel pump module until the embossed alignment arrow points to the center alignment mark or the same position as noted during removal. This step must be performed to prevent the float from contacting the side of the fuel tank.
11. Position the lock ring over top of the auxiliary fuel pump module.
12. Install the SAE Fuel Pump Lock Ring Wrench into the notches on the outside edge of lock ring.
13. Install a breaker bar onto the SAE Fuel Pump Lock Ring Wrench.
14. Rotate the breaker bar clockwise until all seven notches have engaged.
15. Install the main fuel pump module.

Main Fuel Pump Module

⁂ WARNING

Whenever the fuel pump module is serviced, the rubber O-ring seal must be replaced.

1. Position a new rubber O-ring seal onto the fuel tank flange.

⁂ WARNING

Do not allow the float arm of the main fuel pump module to come in contact with any part of the fuel tank during removal or installation, damage to the float arm and fuel level sending card may result.

2. Using caution not to bend the float arm, lower the main fuel pump module into the fuel tank enough to gain access to the auxiliary fuel pump module supply line connection and connect the supply line.

⁂ WARNING

An indexing arrow is located on top of the main fuel pump module to clock it's position into the fuel tank. The fuel pump module must be installed in the same position as removed.

3. Rotate the main fuel pump module until the embossed alignment arrow points to the center alignment mark or the same position as noted during removal. This step must be performed to prevent the float from contacting the side of the fuel tank.
4. Position the lock ring over top of the main fuel pump module.
5. Install the SAE Fuel Pump Lock Ring Wrench into the notches on the outside edge of lock ring.
6. Install a breaker bar onto the SAE Fuel Pump Lock Ring Wrench.
7. Rotate the breaker bar clockwise until all seven notches have engaged.
8. Install the fuel tank.
9. If removed, connect the fuel line quick-connect fitting at the fuel rail.
10. Connect the negative battery cable.
11. Start the engine and check for leaks at all fuel system connections.

FUEL TANK

DRAINING

Conventional Procedure

See Figure 258.

✱✱ CAUTION

The fuel system is under constant high pressure even with engine off. Until the fuel pressure has been properly released from the system, do not attempt to open the fuel system. Do not smoke or use open flames/sparks when servicing the fuel system. Wear protective clothing and eye protection. Make sure the area in which the vehicle is being serviced is in a well ventilated area and free of flames/sparks. Failure to comply may result in serious or fatal injury.

✱✱ CAUTION

No sparks, open flames or smoking. Risk of poisoning from inhaling and swallowing fuel. Pour fuel only into appropriately marked OSHA approved containers. Wear protective clothing. Risk of injury to eyes and skin from contact with fuel.

➡Due to a one-way check valve installed into the fuel fill fitting at the tank, the tank cannot be drained at the fuel fill cap.

1. Perform the fuel system pressure release procedure.
2. Disconnect the fuel supply line at the quick-connect fitting near the cowl.

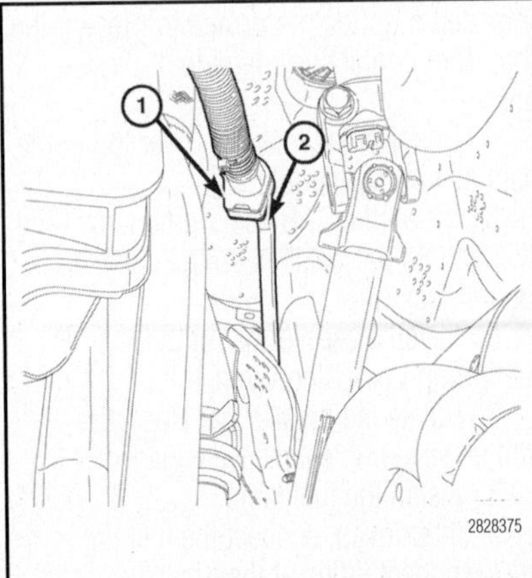

Fig. 258 Fuel supply line (1) and quick connect fitting (2)

3. Attach a 3/8 inch hose to the fuel supply line and attach the opposite end of this hose to the Fuel Chief Gas Caddy 320-FC-P30-A or an OSHA approved gas caddy.

➡Activation of the fuel pump module may time out and need to be restarted several times to completely drain the fuel tank.

4. Using a diagnostic scan tool, activate the fuel pump module until the fuel tank has been evacuated.

Alternative Procedure

➡If the electric fuel pump is not operating, the fuel tank must be removed and drained through the fuel pump module opening of the fuel tank.

1. Disconnect and isolate the negative battery cable.
2. Raise and support the vehicle.
3. Remove the fuel tank.

✱✱ WARNING

Do not allow the float arm of the fuel pump module to come in contact with any part of the fuel tank during removal or installation, damage to the float arm and fuel level sending card may result.

4. Disconnect the fuel pump module electrical connector.
5. Remove the fuel pump module.
6. Position a 3/8 inch hose into the fuel pump module opening of the fuel tank.
7. Attach the opposite end of this hose to the Fuel Chief Gas Caddy 320-FC-P30-A or an OSHA approved gas caddy.
8. Using the gas caddy, evacuate the fuel tank.

REMOVAL & INSTALLATION

See Figures 259 through 265.

1. Perform the fuel system pressure release procedure.
2. Drain the fuel tank.
3. Disconnect and isolate the negative battery cable.
4. Raise and support the vehicle.
5. Loosen the filler hose clamps and remove the filler hose from the fuel tank.
6. Disconnect the quick-connect fitting at the EVAP purge line.
7. Remove the muffler.
8. Disconnect the quick-connect fitting at the On-Board Refueling Vapor Recovery (ORVR) vapor line.
9. Disconnect the quick-connect fitting at the ORVR vacuum line.
10. Remove the propeller shaft assembly.

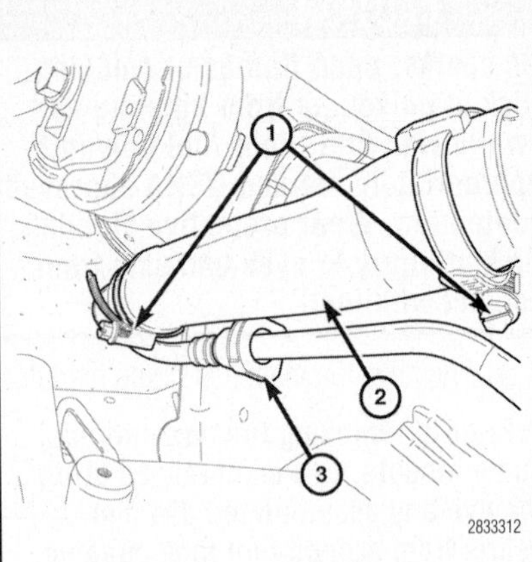

Fig. 259 Loosen the filler hose clamps (1) and remove the filler hose (2) from the fuel tank; disconnect the quick-connect fitting (3) at the EVAP purge line

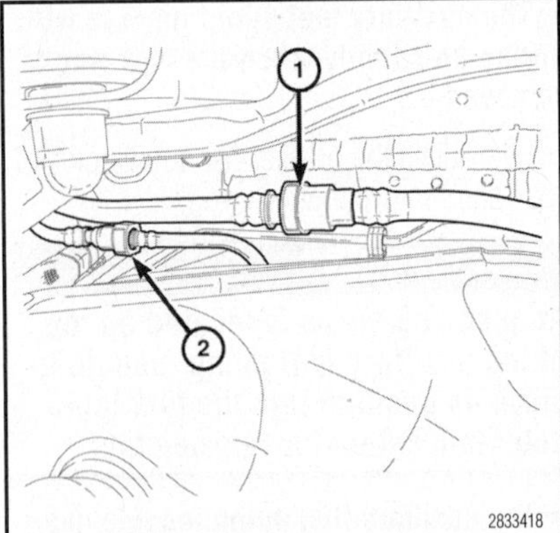

Fig. 260 Disconnect the quick-connect fitting (1) at the On-Board Refueling Vapor Recovery (ORVR) vapor line; disconnect the quick-connect fitting (2) at the ORVR vacuum line

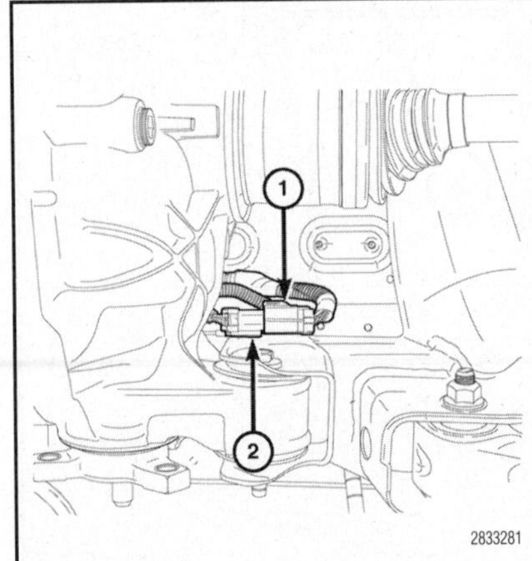

Fig. 261 Disconnect the fuel pump module electrical connector (1) and the electrical connector (2) from the retaining tab

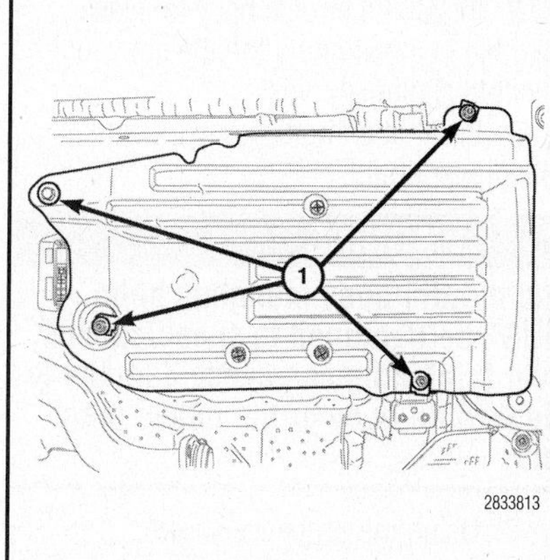

Fig. 262 If equipped, remove the left side body skid plate retainers (1) and remove the skid plate

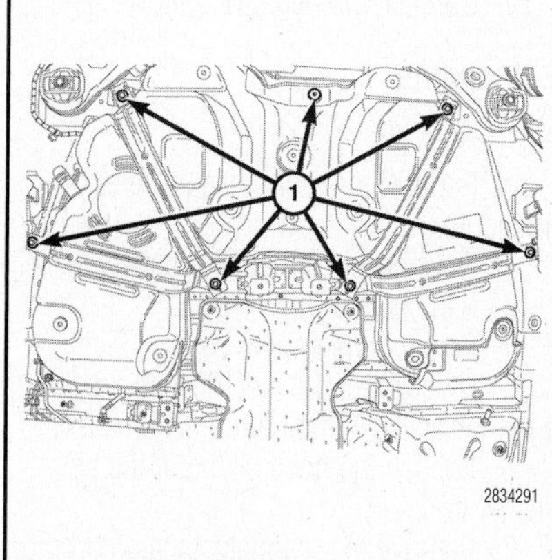

Fig. 264 Remove the fuel tank support strap retaining bolts (1)

11. Disconnect the fuel pump module electrical connector located on the rear crossmember.
12. Disconnect the electrical connector from the retaining tab on the rear crossmember and position the connector aside.
13. If equipped, remove the left side body skid plate retainers and remove the skid plate.
14. Disconnect the quick-connect fitting at the fuel supply line.
15. Using a suitable hydraulic jack and a fuel tank adapter, support the fuel tank.

➡If equipped with skid plates, remove the skid plates, fuel tank support straps and fuel tank as an assembly.

16. Remove the fuel tank support strap retaining bolts.
17. Using the hydraulic jack, lower the fuel tank, support straps and if equipped, skid plates as an assembly and remove from the vehicle.
18. If replacing the fuel tank, remove the heat shield push pin retainers and remove the heat shield.
19. If replacing the fuel tank, remove the main fuel pump module from the fuel tank.
20. If replacing the fuel tank, remove the auxiliary fuel pump module from the fuel tank.

To install:

21. If removed, position the heat shield and install the push pin retainers.
22. If removed, install the auxiliary fuel pump module.
23. If removed, install the main fuel pump module.

➡If equipped with skid plates, install the skid plates, fuel tank, and support straps as an assembly.

24. Using a suitable hydraulic jack and a fuel tank adapter, position the fuel tank, support straps and if equipped, skid plates.
25. Install the fuel tank support strap retaining bolts and tighten to 50 ft. lbs. (68 Nm).
26. Remove the hydraulic jack and the fuel tank adapter.
27. Connect the fuel supply line quick-connect fitting.
28. If equipped, position the left side body skid plate and install retainers.
29. Connect the fuel pump module electrical connector retaining tab onto the rear crossmember.
30. Connect the fuel pump module electrical connector.
31. Install the propeller shaft assembly.
32. Connect the On-Board Refueling Vapor Recovery (ORVR) vacuum line quick-connect fitting.
33. Connect the ORVR vapor line quick-connect fitting.
34. Install the muffler.
35. Connect the EVAP purge line quick-connect fitting.
36. Position the fuel filler hose and install the hose clamps.
37. Lower the vehicle.
38. Connect the negative battery cable.
39. Fill the fuel tank.
40. Start the engine and check for leaks.

IDLE SPEED

ADJUSTMENT

Idle speed is controlled by the Powertrain Control Module (PCM). No adjustment is necessary or possible.

THROTTLE BODY

REMOVAL & INSTALLATION

3.6L Engine

See Figure 266.

⁂ WARNING

Never have the ignition key in the ON position when checking the throttle body shaft for a binding condition. This may set DTC's.

1. Disconnect and isolate the negative battery cable.
2. Remove the engine cover.
3. Disconnect the electrical connector from the Inlet Air Temperature (IAT) sensor.
4. Loosen the clamp at the throttle body.
5. Loosen the clamp at the air cleaner body.
6. Remove the air inlet hose.
7. Disconnect the electrical connector from the Electronic Throttle Control (ETC)

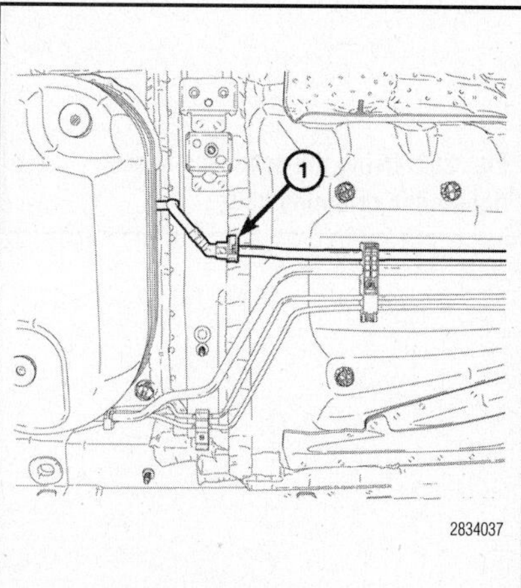

Fig. 263 Disconnect the quick-connect fitting (1) at the fuel supply line

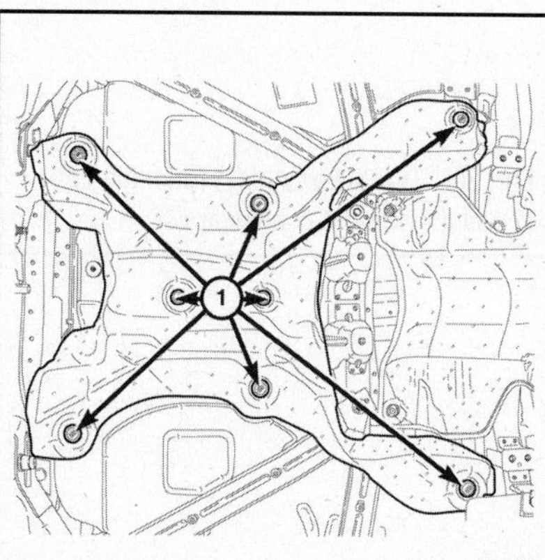

Fig. 265 If replacing the fuel tank, remove the heat shield push pin retainers (1) and remove the heat shield

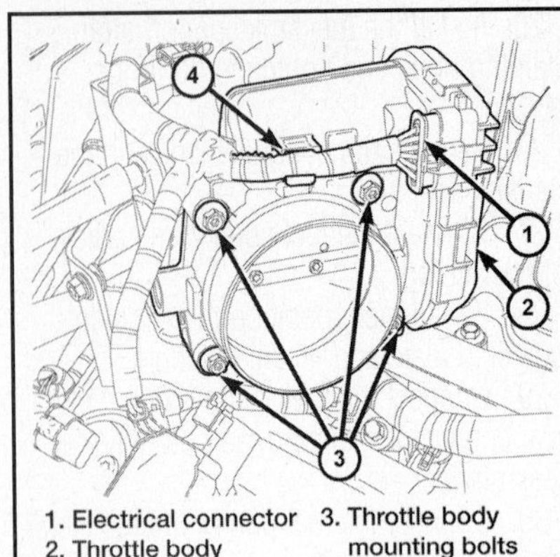

Fig. 266 Disconnect the electrical connector from the Electronic Throttle Control (ETC) and disengage the ETC harness from the clip on the throttle body

and disengage the ETC harness from the clip on the throttle body.

8. Remove four throttle body mounting bolts.
9. Remove the throttle body from the upper intake manifold.
10. Check the condition of the throttle body-to-intake manifold seal. The seal can be reused if not damaged.

To install:

11. Check the condition of the throttle body-to-intake manifold seal. The seal can be reused if not damaged.
12. Clean the mating surfaces of the throttle body and intake manifold.
13. Position the throttle body to the intake manifold.
14. Install the throttle body mounting bolts and tighten in a criss-cross pattern sequence.
15. Connect the electrical connector to the Electronic Throttle Control (ETC) and secure the ETC harness to the clip on the throttle body.
16. Install the air inlet hose to the air cleaner body and the throttle body.
17. Connect the electrical connector to the Inlet Air Temperature (IAT) sensor.
18. Install the engine cover.
19. Connect the negative battery cable.

5.7L Engine

See Figures 267 and 268.

1. Perform the fuel pressure release procedure.
2. Disconnect the negative battery cable.
3. Remove the oil fill cap.
4. Remove the engine cover.
5. Disconnect the electrical connector at the Intake Air Temperature (IAT) sensor.
6. Loosen the hose clamp at the air cleaner housing.
7. Remove the resonator retaining bolt.
8. Loosen the hose clamp at the throttle body and remove the resonator.
9. Disconnect the electrical connector at the throttle body.
10. Remove the four throttle body retaining bolts.
11. Remove the throttle body from the intake manifold.
12. Check the throttle body O-ring, replace if necessary.

To install:

13. Clean and check condition of the throttle body-to-intake manifold O-ring, replace if necessary.
14. Clean the mating surfaces of the throttle body and intake manifold.
15. Install the throttle body to intake manifold by positioning throttle body to manifold alignment pins.
16. Install the throttle body mounting bolts finger tight.

⁂ WARNING

The throttle body mounting bolts MUST be tightened to specifications. Over tightening can cause damage to the throttle body or the intake manifold.

17. Using the sequence shown, tighten the retaining bolts to 53 inch lbs. (6 Nm).
18. Connect the electrical connector.
19. Position the resonator onto the throttle body and air cleaner housing.
20. Tighten the hose clamp at the throttle body.
21. Install the resonator retaining bolt.
22. Tighten the hose clamp at the air cleaner housing.
23. Connect the electrical connector at the Intake Air Temperature (IAT) sensor.
24. Install the engine cover.
25. Install the oil fill cap.
26. Connect the negative battery cable.
27. Using the diagnostic scan tool, perform the ETC Relearn function.

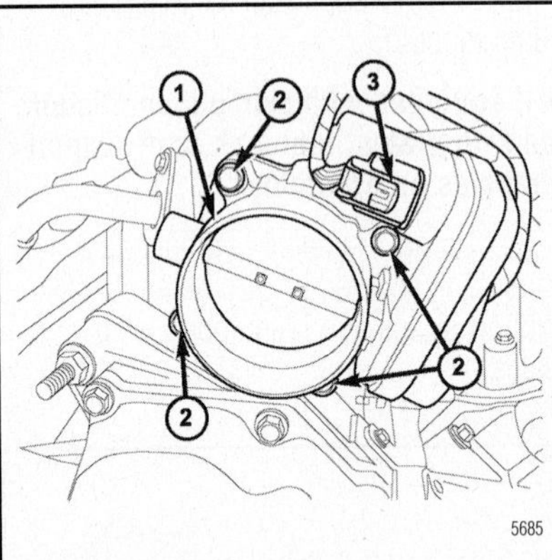

Fig. 267 Throttle body (1), retaining bolts (2), and electrical connector (3)

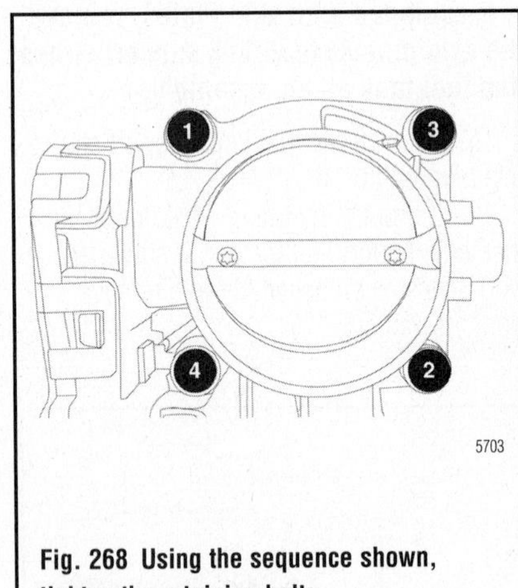

Fig. 268 Using the sequence shown, tighten the retaining bolts

HEATING & AIR CONDITIONING SYSTEM

BLOWER MOTOR

REMOVAL & INSTALLATION

See Figure 269.

**** CAUTION**

Disable the airbag system before attempting any steering wheel, steering column or instrument panel component diagnosis or service. Disconnect and isolate the negative battery (ground) cable, then wait two minutes for the airbag system capacitor to discharge before performing further diagnosis or service. This is the only sure way to disable the airbag system. Failure to follow these instructions may result in accidental airbag deployment and possible serious or fatal injury.

1. Disconnect and isolate the negative battery cable.
2. Remove the passenger side instrument panel silencer.
3. Disconnect the wire harness connector from the blower motor.
4. Remove the three screws that secure the blower motor to the HVAC housing and remove the blower motor.

To install:

5. Position the blower motor into the HVAC housing.
6. Install the three screws that secure the blower motor to the HVAC housing.
7. Connect the wire harness connector to the blower motor.
8. Install the passenger side instrument panel silencer.
9. Reconnect the negative battery cable.

HEATER CORE

REMOVAL & INSTALLATION

See Figures 270 through 273.

**** CAUTION**

Disable the airbag system before attempting any steering wheel, steering column or instrument panel component diagnosis or service. Disconnect and isolate the negative battery (ground) cable, then wait two minutes for the airbag system capacitor to discharge before performing further diagnosis or service. This is the only sure way to disable the airbag system. Failure to follow these instructions may result in accidental airbag deployment and possible serious or fatal injury.

➡Take the proper precautions to protect the front face of the instrument panel from cosmetic damage while performing this procedure.

1. Disconnect and isolate the negative battery cable.
2. Drain the engine cooling system.
3. Remove the passenger side instrument panel silencer.
4. Remove the glove box, glove box shelf and the trim panel, located behind the glove box.
5. Remove the nut that secures the passenger side end of the HVAC housing to the instrument panel support.
6. Remove the front floor console.
7. Remove the radio.
8. Remove the bin from the center of the instrument panel.

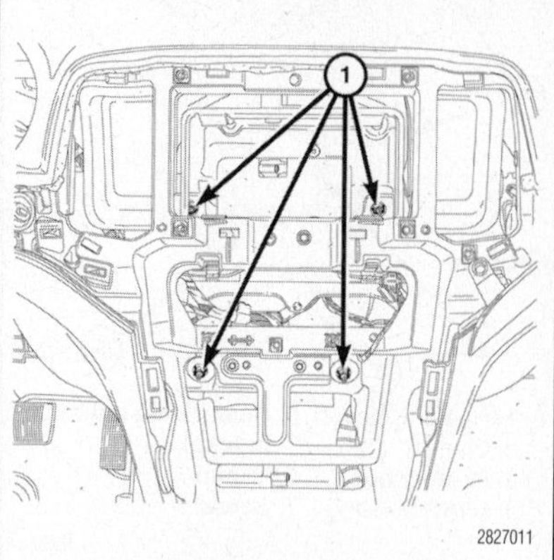

Fig. 271 Remove the four nuts (1) that secure the HVAC housing to the center of the instrument panel support

9. Remove the four nuts that secure the HVAC housing to the center of the instrument panel support.

➡Illustration shown with instrument panel removed from view for clarity.

10. Remove the driver side instrument panel silencer.
11. Remove the push pin that secures the left side floor ducts to the instrument panel.
12. Disconnect the left side floor ducts from the HVAC housing.

➡Removal of the instrument panel from the vehicle is not required to perform this procedure. It is only necessary to position the instrument panel so that removal of the heater core is possible.

13. Position the instrument panel to gain full access to the heater core located on the

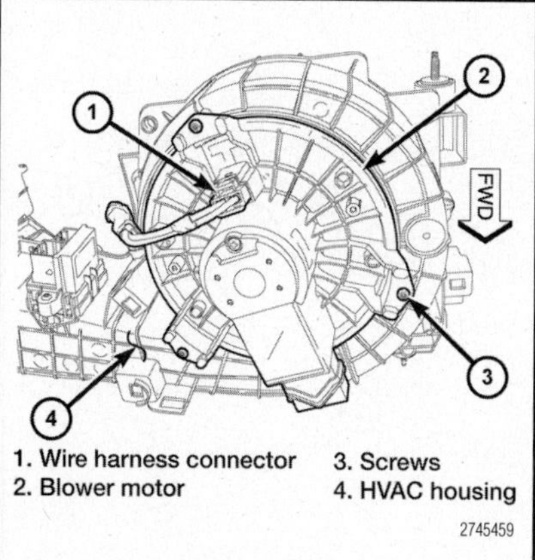

Fig. 269 Disconnect the wire harness connector from the blower motor

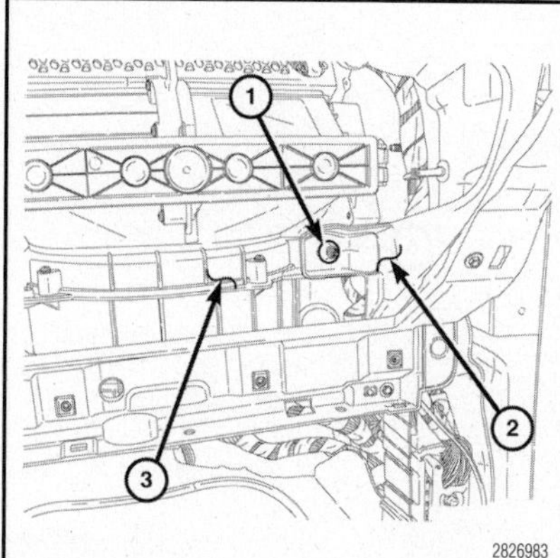

Fig. 270 Remove the nut (1) that secures the passenger side end of the HVAC housing (3) to the instrument panel support (2)

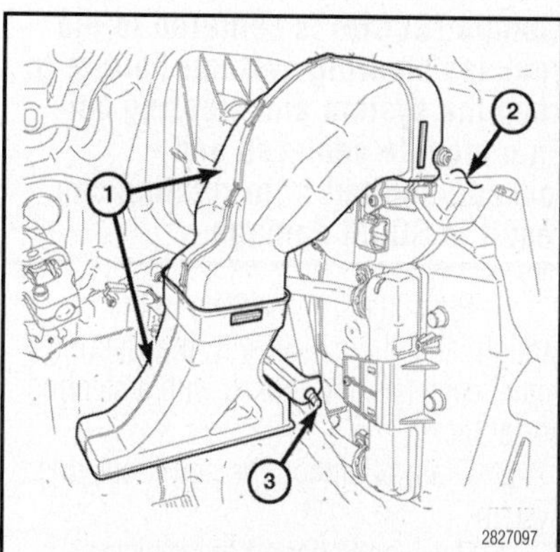

Fig. 272 Remove the push pin (3) that secures the left side floor ducts (1) to the instrument panel; disconnect the left side floor ducts from the HVAC housing (2)

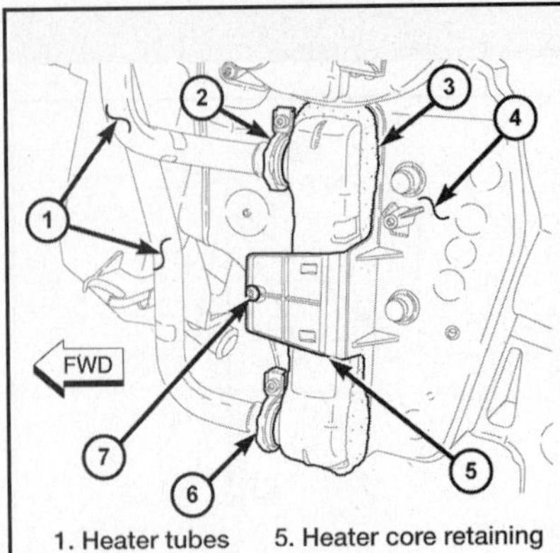

Fig. 273 Remove the two clamps that secure the heater tubes to the heater core

left side of the HVAC air distribution housing.

➡**Take proper precautions to protect the carpeting from engine coolant. Have absorbent toweling readily available to clean up any spills.**

14. Remove the two clamps that secure the heater tubes to the heater core.
15. Disconnect the heater core tubes from the heater core and remove and discard the O-ring seals.
16. Install plugs in, or tape over the opened heater core tubes and heater core ports.
17. Remove the screw that secures the heater core retaining bracket to the air distribution housing and position the bracket out of the way.

➡**If the foam seal around the heater core is deformed or damaged, it must be replaced.**

18. Carefully pull the heater core out of the air distribution housing.

To install:

19. Carefully install the heater core into the left side of the HVAC air distribution housing.
20. Reposition the heater core retaining bracket and install the screw.
21. Remove the tape or plugs from the heater core tubes and heater core ports.
22. Lubricate new rubber O-ring seals with clean engine coolant and install them onto the heater core tubes. Use only the specified O-ring as they are made of a special material for the engine cooling system.
23. Connect the heater core tubes to the heater core.
24. Install the two clamps that secure the heater core tubes to the heater core.
25. Connect the left side floor ducts to the HVAC housing.
26. Reposition and install the instrument panel as necessary.
27. Install the push pin that secures the left side floor ducts to the instrument panel.
28. Install the driver side instrument panel silencer.
29. Install the four nuts that secure the HVAC housing to the center of the instrument panel support.
30. Install the bin into the center of the instrument panel.
31. Install the radio.
32. Install the floor console.
33. Install the nut that secures the passenger side end of the HVAC housing to the instrument panel support.
34. Install the IP trim panel, glove box shelf and the glove box.
35. Install the passenger side instrument panel silencer.
36. Reconnect the negative battery cable.
37. If the heater core is being replaced, flush the cooling system.
38. Refill the engine cooling system.

STEERING

POWER STEERING GEAR

REMOVAL & INSTALLATION

3.6L Engine

See Figures 274 through 278.

⁂ WARNING

The Steering Column Control Module (SCCM) is centered to the vehicles steering system. Failure to keep the system and steering column module centered and locked/inhibited from rotating can result in SCCM damage.

1. Place the front wheels in the straight ahead position with the steering wheel centered and locked with a steering wheel lock.
2. Drain or siphon the power steering system.
3. Raise and support the vehicle.
4. Remove the front skid plate.
5. Remove the steering shaft coupler pinch bolt and disconnect the coupler from the steering shaft.
6. Disconnect the pressure line, and the return line at the gear.
7. Remove the front tires and wheels.
8. Remove the RH shock.
9. Remove the outer tie rod ends.
10. Remove the steering gear retaining nuts/bolts.
11. Lift and rotate the steering gear so that the steering shaft is forward to clear the oil pan when removing the steering gear through the RH wheel area.
12. Lift and rotate the steering gear as necessary to remove from behind the knuckle/rotor assembly of the RH wheel area.

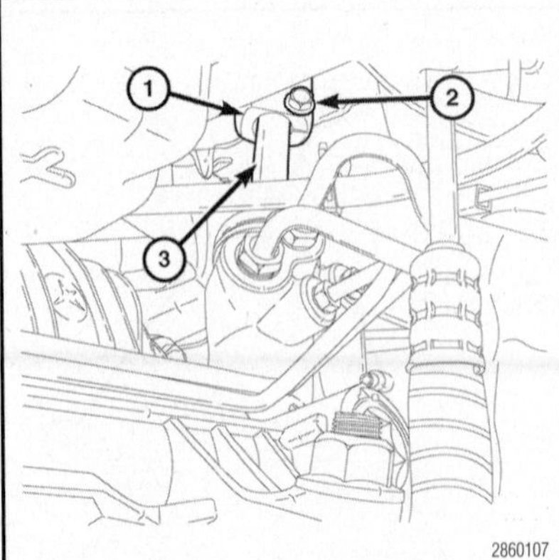

Fig. 274 Remove the steering shaft coupler pinch bolt (2) and disconnect the coupler (1) from the steering shaft (3)

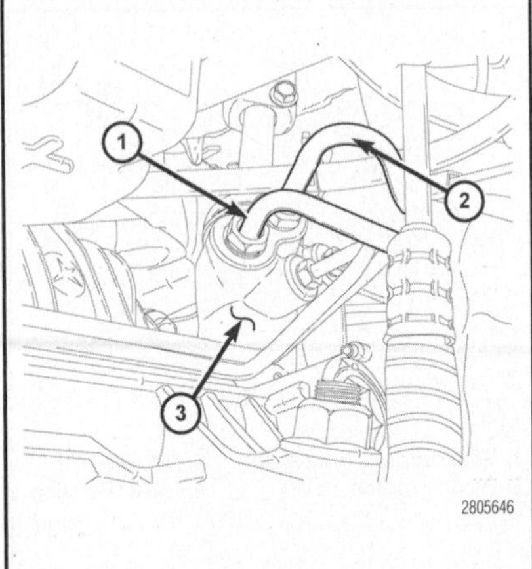

Fig. 275 Disconnect the pressure line (1), and the return line (2) at the gear (3)

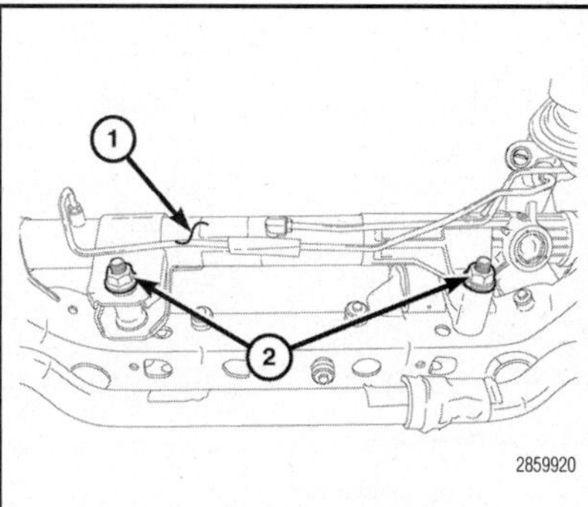

Fig. 276 Remove the steering gear (1) retaining nuts/bolts (2)

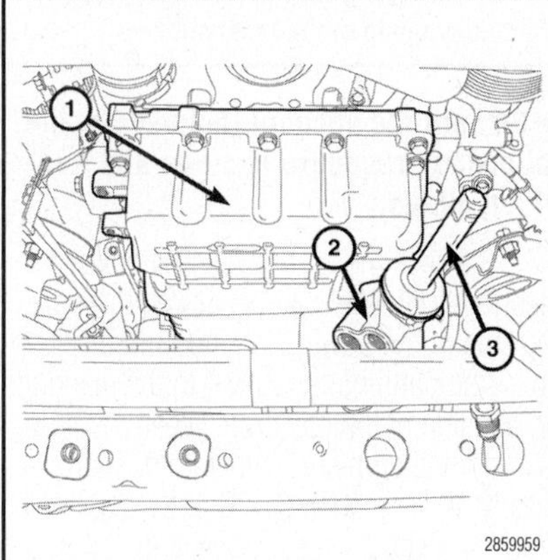

Fig. 277 Lift and rotate the steering gear (2) so that the steering shaft (3) is forward to clear the oil pan (1)

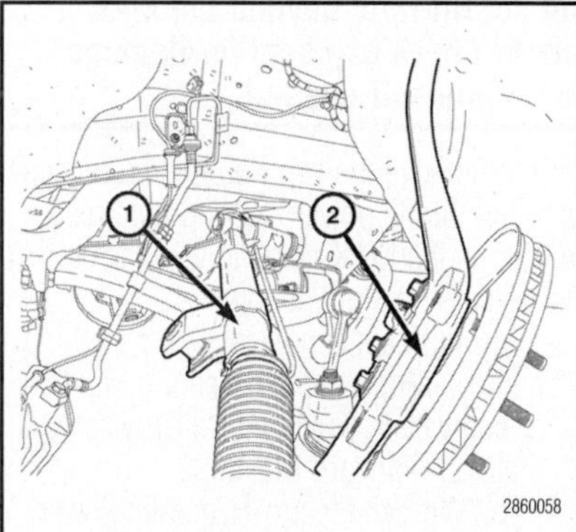

Fig. 278 Lift and rotate the steering gear (1) as necessary to remove from behind the knuckle/rotor assembly (2) of the RH wheel area

To install:

13. Lift and rotate the steering gear as necessary to install from behind the knuckle/rotor assembly of the RH wheel area.
14. Rotate the steering gear into position, install the steering gear retaining nuts/bolts and tighten to 180 ft. lbs. (244 Nm).
15. Install the outer tie rod ends.
16. Install the RH shock.
17. Connect the pressure line and the return line at the gear and tighten to 21 ft. lbs. (28 Nm).

⁂ WARNING

The steering gear must be centered prior to installing the coupler to prevent clockspring damage.

18. Connect the steering shaft coupler to the steering shaft, install a new coupler pinch bolt and tighten to 36 ft. lbs. (49 Nm).
19. Install the front skid plate.
20. Install the wheels and tires.
21. Remove the supports and lower the vehicle.
22. Remove the steering wheel lock.
23. Fill the power steering pump.
24. Set the toe.

5.7L Engine

See Figure 279.

⁂ WARNING

The Steering Column Control Module (SCCM) is centered to the vehicles steering system. Failure to keep the system and steering column module centered and locked/inhibited from rotating can result in SCCM damage.

1. If replacing the steering gear, remove the outer tie rod ends.
2. Remove the engine cradle (crossmember).
3. Remove steering gear retaining nuts/bolts.
4. Rotate and shift the steering gear to the right enough to lift the LH side of the steering gear above the engine cradle, then remove the steering gear by moving to the right above the engine cradle.

To install:

5. Position the steering gear between the RH upper and lower parts of the cradle (crossmember) as far as necessary to lower the LH side of the steering gear into position and shift to the left.
6. Install the steering gear retaining bolts/nuts and tighten to 180 ft. lbs. (244 Nm).
7. Install the engine cradle.
8. If the outer tie rods were removed, install the tie rod ends.
9. Perform a front alignment.

POWER STEERING PUMP

REMOVAL & INSTALLATION

3.6L Engine

⁂ WARNING

The 3.6L in this vehicle is equipped with an Electro-Hydraulic Power Steering (EHPS) pump requiring a different fluid. Do not mix power steering fluid types. Damage may result to the power steering pump and system if any other fluid is used. The EHPS system uses fluid which meets material specification MS-11655 or equivalent. Do not overfill.

1. Siphon the power steering reservoir.
2. Disconnect and isolate the battery negative cable.

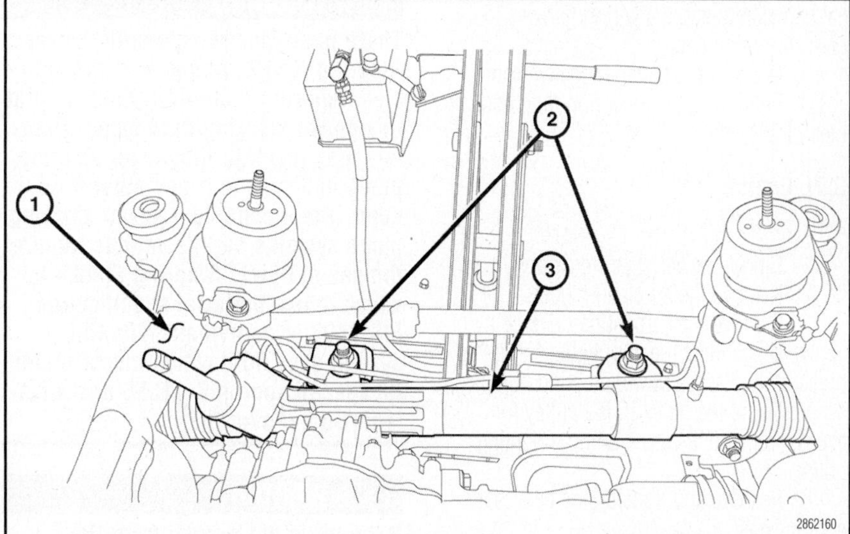

Fig. 279 Remove steering gear retaining nuts/bolts (2); showing steering gear (3), engine cradle (1)

3. Disconnect the two EHPS pump electrical connectors and the wiring harness to bracket routing clip.

4. Disconnect the supply and return lines from the EHPS pump.

5. Remove the pressure and return line routing clip bolt from the pump bracket.

6. Raise and support the vehicle.

7. If equipped, remove the front skid plate.

8. Remove the pressure line retaining bolt and line from the EHPS pump.

9. Loosen the routing clip retaining bolt and position the pressure line aside for access to remove the pump.

10. Remove the three EHPS pump retaining bolts and remove the pump from the vehicle.

11. Remove and transfer any necessary components.

To install:

12. Position the EHPS pump, install the three retaining bolts and tighten to 40 ft. lbs. (54 Nm).

➡Make sure the O-ring is clean and seats properly.

13. Position the pressure line routing clip under the bolt, install the pressure line into the pump and tighten the routing clip retaining bolt to 106 inch lbs. (12 Nm).

14. Install the pressure line routing clip to pump bracket retaining bolt and tighten to 15 ft. lbs. (20 Nm).

15. If equipped, install the front skid plate.

16. Remove the supports and lower the vehicle.

17. Connect the supply and return lines to the EHPS pump.

18. Connect the two EHPS pump electrical connectors and the wiring harness to bracket routing clip.

19. Connect the battery negative cable.

20. Refill the power steering fluid and bleed the system.

5.7L Engine

See Figure 280.

1. Siphon power steering reservoir.

2. Remove the air cleaner body.

3. Remove the serpentine drive belt.

4. Disconnect the supply hose and the pressure line at the power steering pump.

5. Using the holes in the pulley for access, remove the three pump mounting bolts.

6. Remove and transfer any necessary components.

To install:

7. Position the power steering pump and using the holes in the pulley for access, install 3 pump mounting bolts and tighten to 17 ft. lbs. (23 Nm).

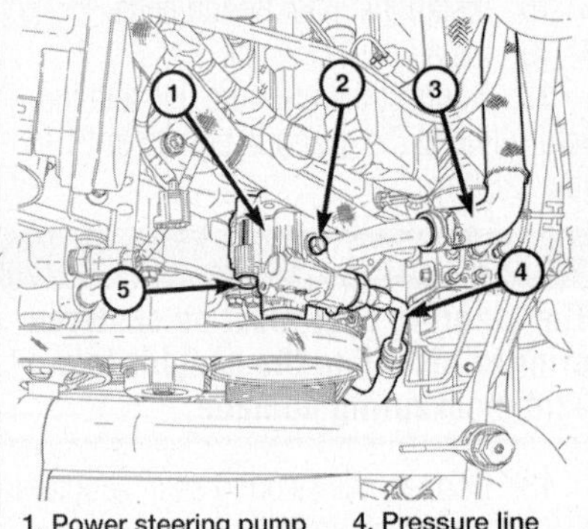

1. Power steering pump
2. Bolt
3. Supply hose
4. Pressure line
5. Mounting bolts

3065643

Fig. 280 Disconnect the supply hose and the pressure line at the power steering pump

8. Install the pressure line on the pump and tighten the nut to 21 ft. lbs. (28 Nm).

9. Install the supply hose on the pump.

10. Install the drive belt.

11. Install the air cleaner body.

12. Fill and bleed the system with power steering fluid.

BLEEDING

See Figure 281.

⁂ CAUTION

Fluid level should be checked with the engine OFF to prevent personal injury from moving parts and to assure an accurate fluid level reading.

⁂ WARNING

There is an Electro-Hydraulic Power Steering (EHPS) pump on some vehicles requiring a different fluid. Do not mix power steering fluid types. Damage may result to the power steering pump and system if any other fluid is used. The mechanical power steering pump systems on this vehicle require the use of Power Steering Fluid +4, which meets material specification MS-9602 or equivalent. The EHPS system uses fluid which meets material specification MS-11655 or equivalent. Do not overfill.

⁂ WARNING

If the air is not purged from the power steering system correctly, pump failure could result.

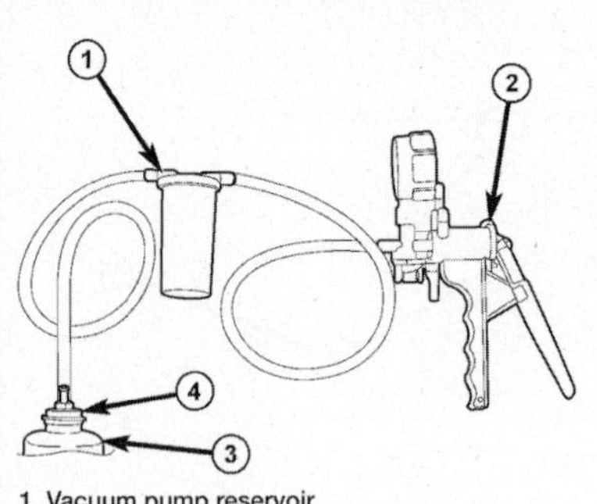

1. Vacuum pump reservoir
2. Special Tool C-4207-8, Hand Vacuum Pump
3. Mouth of the reservoir
4. Special Tool 9688A, Power Steering Cap Adapter

6153

Fig. 281 Tightly insert a P/S Cap Adaptor into the mouth of the reservoir

➡Be sure the vacuum tool used in the following procedure is clean and free of any fluids.

1. Check the fluid level. The power steering fluid level can be viewed through the side of the power steering fluid reservoir. Compare the fluid level to the markings on the side of the reservoir. When the fluid is at normal ambient temperature, approximately 70°F to 80°F (21°C to 27°C), the fluid level should read between the MAX and MIN markings. When the fluid is hot, fluid level is allowed to read up to the MAX line.

⁂ WARNING

Do not fill fluid beyond the MAX mark. Check cap seal for damage and replace if needed.

2. Remove the cap from the fluid reservoir and fill the power steering fluid reservoir up to the MAX marking with the correct power steering fluid as follows:

   a. With a mechanical power steering pump—Mopar Power Steering Fluid +4 or equivalent, which meets Chrysler Material Standard MS-9602.

   b. With an Electro-Hydraulic Power Steering (EHPS)—Mopar Hydraulic Power Steering Fluid or equivalent, which meets Chrysler Material Standard MS-11655.

3. Tightly insert a P/S Cap Adaptor into the mouth of the reservoir.

⁂ WARNING

Failure to use a vacuum pump reservoir (1) may allow power steering fluid to be sucked into the hand vacuum pump.

4. Attach Hand Vacuum Pump or equivalent, with reservoir attached, to the Power Steering Cap Adaptor.

⁂ WARNING

Do not run the vehicle while vacuum is applied to the power steering system. Damage to the power steering pump can occur.

➡When performing the following step make sure the vacuum level is maintained during the entire time period.

5. Using Hand Vacuum Pump, apply 20–25 inches HG (68–85 kPa) of vacuum to the system for a minimum of three minutes.
6. Slowly release the vacuum and remove the special tools.
7. Adjust the fluid level as necessary.
8. Repeat until the fluid no longer drops when vacuum is applied.
9. Start the engine and cycle the steering wheel lock-to-lock three times.

➡Do not hold the steering wheel at the stops.

10. Stop the engine and check for leaks at all connections.
11. Check for any signs of air in the reservoir and check the fluid level. If air is present, repeat the procedure as necessary.

FLUID FILL PROCEDURE

⁂ CAUTION

Fluid level should be checked with the engine off to prevent personal injury from moving parts.

⁂ WARNING

There is an Electro-Hydraulic Power Steering (EHPS) pump on some vehicles requiring a different fluid. Do not mix power steering fluid types. Damage may result to the power steering pump and system if any other fluid is used. The mechanical power steering pump systems on this vehicle require the use of Power Steering Fluid +4, which meets material specification MS-9602 or equivalent. The EHPS system uses fluid which meets material specification MS-11655 or equivalent. Do not overfill.

The power steering fluid level can be viewed through the reservoir with MAX and MIN level indicators on the side. Before opening power steering system, wipe the reservoir filler cap free of dirt and debris. When the fluid is at normal ambient temperature, approximately 70°F to 80°F (21°C to 27°C), the fluid level should between MAX and MIN. Use only proper fluids. Do not over fill.

SUSPENSION

FRONT SUSPENSION

CONTROL LINKS

REMOVAL & INSTALLATION

Stabilizer Bar Link

1. Raise and support the vehicle.
2. Remove the tire and wheel assembly.
3. Support the outside of the lower control arm with a suitable holding fixture, and raise to normal ride height.
4. Remove the stabilizer link lower nut.
5. Remove the stabilizer link upper nut.
6. Remove the stabilizer link.

To install:

7. Position the stabilizer link to the vehicle.
8. Install the stabilizer link upper nut and tighten to 90 ft. lbs. (122 Nm).
9. Install the stabilizer link lower nut and tighten to 90 ft. lbs. (122 Nm).
10. Install the tire and wheel assembly.
11. Remove the support and lower the vehicle

LOWER BALL JOINT

REMOVAL & INSTALLATION

See Figure 282.

1. Raise and support the vehicle.
2. Remove the knuckle.

➡Extreme pressure lubrication must be used on the threaded portions of Ball Joint Press, Ball Joint. This will increase the longevity of the tool and insure proper operation during the removal and installation process.

3. Press the ball joint (not shown, inside tool) from the knuckle using Ball Joint Press, Remover/Installer, and Ball Joint Remover/Installer.

To install:

➡Extreme pressure lubrication must be used on the threaded portions of Ball Joint Press, Ball Joint. This will increase the longevity of the tool and insure proper operation during the removal and installation process.

4. Position the ball joint into the knuckle and press in using Ball Joint Press, Remover/Installer, and Ball Joint Remover/Installer.
5. Install the steering knuckle.

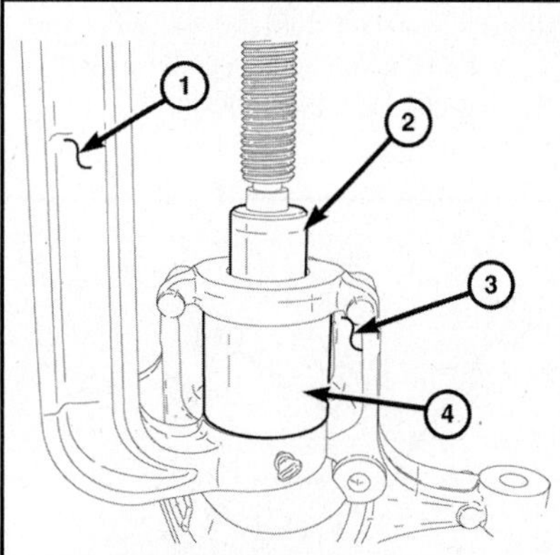

Fig. 282 Press the ball joint (not shown, inside tool) from the knuckle using Ball Joint Press, Remover/Installer, and Ball Joint Remover/Installer

LOWER CONTROL ARM

REMOVAL & INSTALLATION

See Figure 283.

1. Raise and support the vehicle.
2. Remove the tire and wheel assembly.
3. Remove the knuckle.
4. Remove the stabilizer link to lower control arm nut.

➡If equipped with four wheel drive, support the half shaft or remove with the lower control arm.

5. Remove the shock clevis bracket to lower control arm nut/bolt.
6. Remove the lower control arm front pivot nut and bolt from the lower control arm.
7. Remove the lower control arm rear pivot vertical bolt and nut and the lower control arm rear pivot horizontal bolt and nut from the lower control arm and remove from the vehicle.

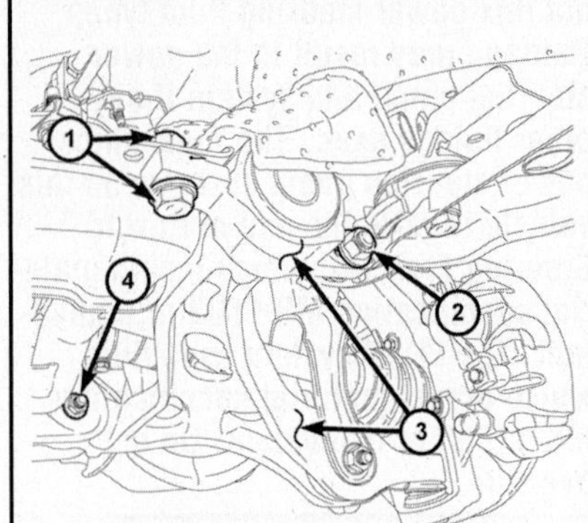

Fig. 283 Remove the lower control arm front pivot nut and bolt from the lower control arm

To install:

➡If equipped with four wheel drive, position the half shaft if removed with the lower control arm.

8. Position the lower control arm to the cradle.
9. Install the lower control arm rear pivot vertical bolt and nut. Do not tighten.
10. Install the lower control arm front pivot nut and bolt. Do not tighten.
11. Install the shock clevis bracket to lower control arm nut/bolt. Do not tighten.
12. Install the stabilizer link to lower control arm nut. Do not tighten.
13. Install the knuckle.
14. Support the outside of the lower control arm with a suitable holding fixture, and raise to normal ride height.
15. Tighten the lower control arm rear pivot vertical bolt and nut to 162 ft. lbs. (220 Nm), and tighten the lower control arm rear pivot horizontal bolt and nut to 66 ft. lbs. (90 Nm).
16. Tighten the lower control arm front pivot nut and bolt to 89 ft. lbs. (120 Nm).
17. Tighten the shock clevis bracket to lower control arm nut/bolt to 173 ft. lbs. (235 Nm).
18. Tighten the stabilizer link to lower control arm nut to 90 ft. lbs. (122 Nm).
19. Install the tire and wheel assembly.
20. Remove the supports and lower the vehicle.
21. Perform wheel alignment.

STABILIZER BAR

REMOVAL & INSTALLATION

➡A drive on hoist is recommended to keep suspension at normal ride height due to tension on the stabilizer bar.

1. Raise and support the vehicle.
2. Remove the front skid plate.
3. Remove the stabilizer bar link upper nut on both sides.
4. Remove the two stabilizer bushing clamp bolts on each side.
5. Remove the stabilizer bar.
6. Remove and transfer any necessary components.

To install:

7. Position the stabilizer bar to the vehicle.
8. Install the stabilizer bushing clamps and tighten the two bolts on each side to 90 ft. lbs. (122 Nm).
9. Position the stabilizer link to the stabilizer bar, install the nut and tighten to 90 ft. lbs. (122 Nm).
10. Install the front skid plate.
11. Remove the supports and lower the vehicle.

STEERING KNUCKLE

REMOVAL & INSTALLATION

See Figures 284 and 285.

1. Raise and support the vehicle.
2. Remove the tire and wheel assembly.
3. If equipped with four wheel drive, remove the half shaft nut.
4. Remove the speed sensor bolt, and remove the sensor from the knuckle.
5. Remove the speed sensor wiring retaining clip from the knuckle.

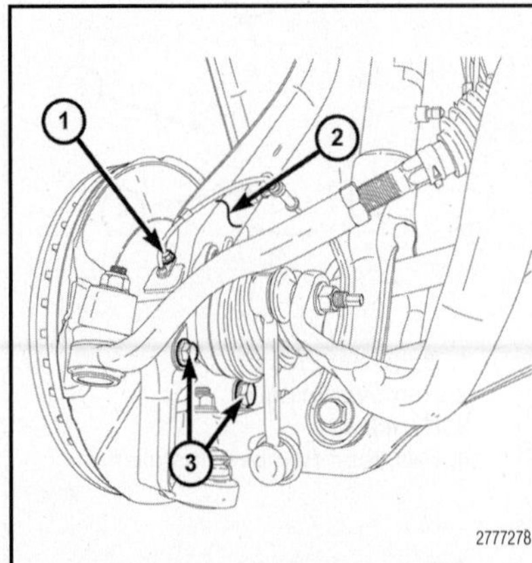

Fig. 284 Remove the speed sensor bolt (1), and remove the sensor from the knuckle (2); hub bolts (3)

✲✲ WARNING

Never allow the disc brake caliper to hang from the brake hose. Damage to the brake hose will result. Provide a suitable support to hang the caliper securely.

6. Remove the rotor.
7. Remove the outer tie rod end retaining nut.
8. Separate the outer tie rod end from the steering knuckle using Tie Rod Puller.
9. Support the outside of the lower control arm with a suitable holding fixture, and raise to normal ride height.
10. Remove the upper ball joint nut.
11. Separate the upper ball joint from the knuckle using Ball Joint Press.
12. If equipped with four wheel drive, tilt the knuckle out enough to disengage the half shaft from the hub/bearing, then pry the half shaft from the axle/axle tube with a pry bar and position aside for access to remove the lower ball joint nut.

➡Due to the taper of the lower ball joint, no special tool is needed to separate the knuckle from the control arm. When the nut is removed, the knuckle will pull away from the lower control arm.

13. While supporting the knuckle, remove the lower ball joint nut.
14. Remove the knuckle from the vehicle.
15. If necessary, remove the 3 hub bearing mounting bolts from the back of the steering knuckle and remove the hub/bearing from the steering knuckle.

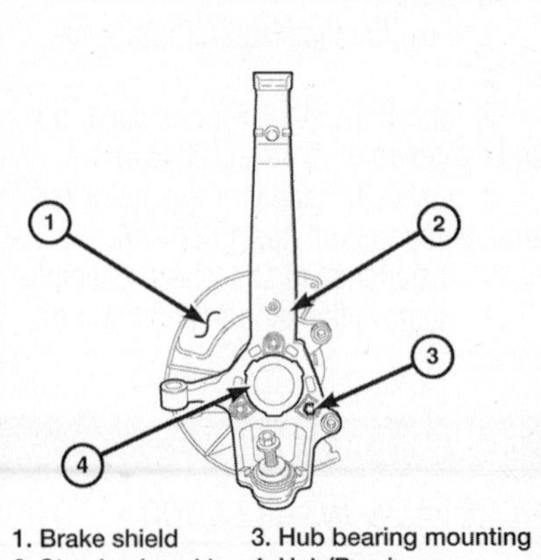

Fig. 285 If necessary, remove the 3 hub bearing mounting bolts from the back of the steering knuckle and remove the hub/bearing from the steering knuckle

16. If necessary, remove the brake shield from the knuckle.

To install:

17. Position the brake shield on the knuckle.
18. Position the hub/bearing on the knuckle, install the 3 hub bearing mounting bolts and tighten to 78 ft. lbs. (105 Nm).
19. Position the knuckle on the lower ball joint and install the lower ball joint nut and tighten to 170 ft. lbs. (230 Nm).
20. If equipped with four wheel drive, install half shaft in the axle using care not to damage the seals, and through the hub/bearing. Verify half shaft has engaged.
21. Support the outside of the lower control arm with a suitable holding fixture, and raise to position the upper ball joint into the knuckle.
22. With the holding fixture holding the suspension at normal ride height, install the upper ball joint nut and tighten to 70 ft. lbs. (95 Nm).
23. Position the outer tie rod end to the steering knuckle, install the nut and tighten to 70 ft. lbs. (95 Nm).
24. Install the brake rotor.
25. Route and attach speed sensor wiring to the knuckle.
26. Install the wheel speed sensor into the knuckle, install the mounting bolt and tighten to 95 inch lbs. (11 Nm).
27. If equipped with four wheel drive, install the half shaft nut and tighten to 229 ft. lbs. (310 Nm).
28. Install the tire and wheel assembly.
29. Remove the supports and lower the vehicle.

STRUT & SPRING ASSEMBLY

REMOVAL & INSTALLATION

RWD

See Figures 286 through 289.

1. If equipped, remove the wiring harness routing clip from the shock mounting stud.
2. Remove the three upper shock mounting nuts.
3. Turn the wheels so the front of the tire on the side being serviced is turned to the inside of the vehicle.
4. Raise and support the vehicle.
5. Remove the tire and wheel assembly.
6. Remove the speed sensor bolt, and remove the sensor from the knuckle.
7. Remove the speed sensor wiring retaining clip from the knuckle.
8. Bottom caliper pistons into the caliper.

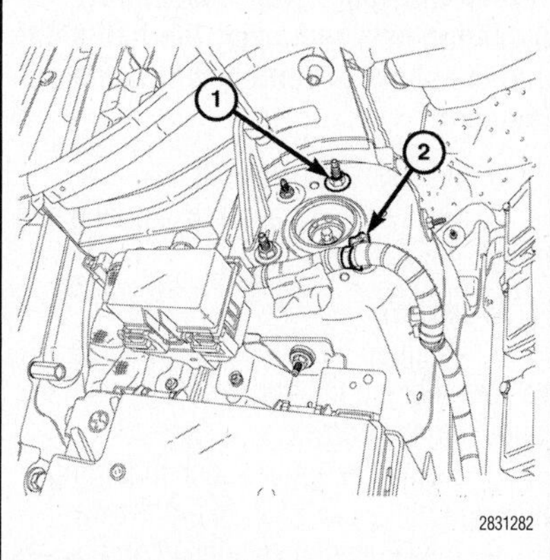

Fig. 286 If equipped, remove the wiring harness routing clip (2) from the shock mounting stud/nut (1)

9. Remove the brake caliper tension clip by pressing rearward on the front of the clip while pulling the clip out from the caliper.
10. Remove the caliper slide dust bolt shields and loosen the brake caliper slide bolts (guide pins).

WARNING

Never allow the disc brake caliper to hang from the brake hose. Damage to the brake hose will result. Provide a suitable support to hang the caliper securely.

11. Remove the brake caliper from the caliper adapter and hang the brake caliper.
12. Support the outside of the lower control arm with a suitable holding fixture, and raise to normal ride height.
13. Remove the upper ball joint nut.
14. Separate the upper ball joint from the knuckle using Ball Joint Press.

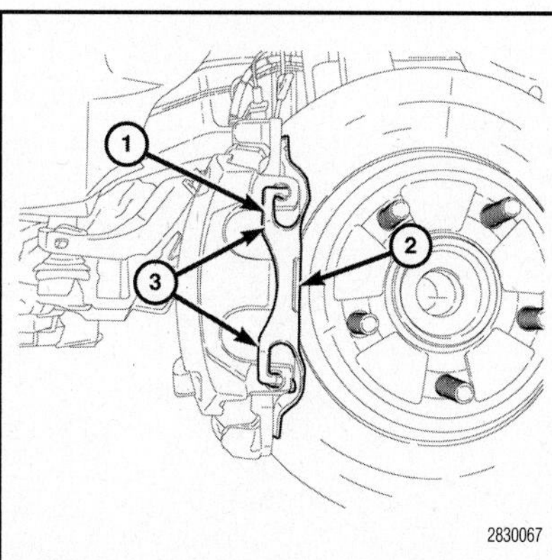

Fig. 287 Remove the brake caliper tension clip (1) by pressing rearward on the front of the clip (2) while pulling the clip out (3) from the caliper

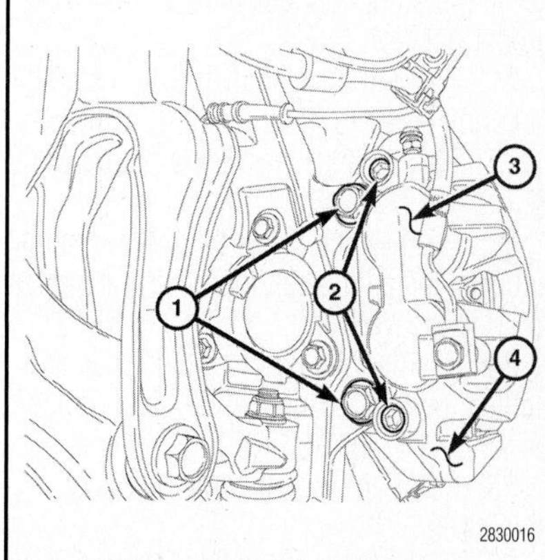

Fig. 288 Remove the caliper slide dust bolt shields and loosen the brake caliper slide bolts (guide pins)

15. Remove the lower stabilizer link nut at the lower control arm.
16. Remove the lower clevis bolt/nut at the lower control arm.

➡It may be necessary to lift on the upper control arm for clearance to remove shock.

17. With the knuckle assembly tilted out, lower the control arm support as necessary and lift the shock assembly (into the shock tower) and remove from the vehicle by tilting the bottom of the shock out and to the rear.
18. Remove and transfer the spring and mount if necessary.

To install:

19. Position the shock assembly to the vehicle and install the clevis to lower control arm bolt/nut. Do not tighten.
20. Support the outside of the lower control arm with a suitable holding fixture, and raise to normal ride height while

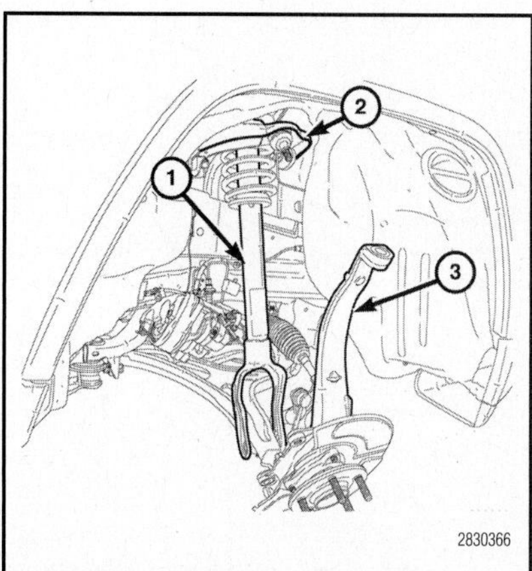

Fig. 289 Shock assembly (1), upper control arm assembly (2) and knuckle assembly (3)

guiding the upper shock mount into the proper position.

21. Position the stabilizer link, install the nut and tighten to 90 ft. lbs. (122 Nm).
22. Tighten the lower clevis bolt/nut to 173 ft. lbs. (235 Nm).
23. Position the upper ball joint into the knuckle, install the ball joint nut and tighten to 70 ft. lbs. (95 Nm).
24. Position the brake caliper/pads and tighten the brake caliper slide bolts (guide pins) to 41 ft. lbs. (55 Nm).
25. Install the caliper slide bolt dust shields.
26. Install the brake caliper tension clip.
27. Install the speed sensor and retaining bolt, and tighten to 95 inch lbs. (11 Nm).
28. Install the speed sensor wiring retaining clip to the knuckle.
29. Install the tire and wheel assembly.
30. Remove the supports and lower the vehicle.
31. Tighten the three upper shock mounting nuts to 21 ft. lbs. (28 Nm).
32. If equipped, install the wiring harness routing clip on the shock mounting stud.
33. Pump brake pedal until caliper pistons and brake pads are seated and a firm brake pedal is obtained.

4WD

See Figure 290.

1. If equipped, remove the wiring harness routing clip from the shock mounting stud.
2. Remove the three upper shock mounting nuts.
3. Turn the wheels so the front of the tire on the side being serviced is turned to the inside of the vehicle.
4. Raise and support the vehicle.

➡With the upper shock assembly mounting nuts removed, the half shaft and the shock assembly will come out together.

5. Remove the half shaft.
6. Remove and transfer the spring and mount if necessary.

To install:

7. Position the shock assembly to the vehicle aligning the upper shock mounting studs into the body.
8. Install the upper shock mounting nuts and tighten to 21 ft. lbs. (28 Nm).
9. If equipped, install the wiring harness routing clip on the shock mounting stud.
10. Install the half shaft.
11. Remove the supports and lower the vehicle.
12. Pump brake pedal until caliper pistons and brake pads are seated and a firm brake pedal is obtained.

UPPER CONTROL ARM

REMOVAL & INSTALLATION

See Figures 291 through 294.

1. Secure the steering wheel in the straight ahead position.
2. If equipped, remove the wiring harness routing clip from the shock mounting stud.

➡Loosen the shock retainer nuts only. The shock must be tilted for removal of the control arm bolts.

3. Loosen the three upper shock mounting nuts.
4. Remove the cowl panel cover, and the silencer.
5. For the left side only, remove the air cleaner housing as follows:
   a. Remove the air cleaner.
   b. Loosen the fresh air intake clamp and disconnect the hose from housing cover.
   c. Disconnecting the PCV air return hose and the power steering hose routing clip (not shown) from the air cleaner body.
   d. Disconnect the weatherstrip from the housing inlet and reposition.
   e. Remove the pushpin and lift the housing from the body grommets to remove.
6. For the left side only, remove the steering intermediate shaft pinch bolt, disconnect the coupler and position aside for clearance.
7. For the right side only, remove the two nuts that secure the HVAC air inlet duct to the engine compartment side of the dash panel and remove the duct.
8. Raise and support the vehicle.
9. Remove the tire and wheel assembly.
10. If equipped with a height sensor, disconnect the height sensor from the upper control arm ball stud.
11. Remove the speed sensor bolt, and remove the sensor from the knuckle.
12. Remove the speed sensor wiring retaining clip from the knuckle.
13. Support the outside of the lower control arm with a suitable holding fixture, and raise to normal ride height.
14. Remove the clevis to lower control arm bolt/nut.
15. Remove the upper ball joint retaining nut from the ball joint.
16. Separate the upper ball joint from the knuckle using Ball Joint Press.

➡It is necessary to pull the bottom of the shock assembly outward just enough to remove the upper control

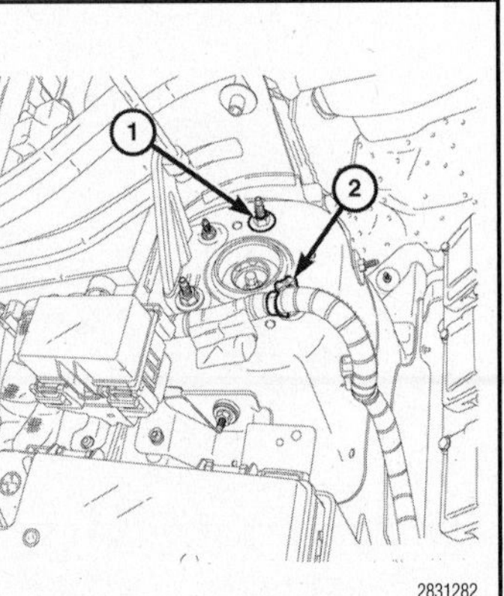

Fig. 290 If equipped, remove the wiring harness routing clip (2) from the shock mounting stud/nut (1)

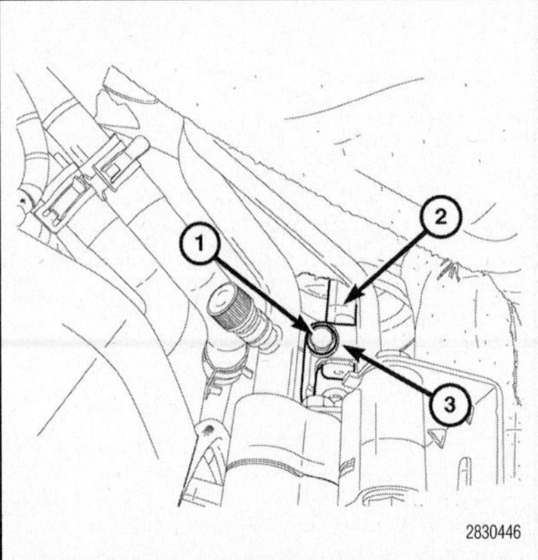

Fig. 291 For the left side only, remove the steering intermediate shaft (2) pinch bolt (1), and disconnect the coupler (3)

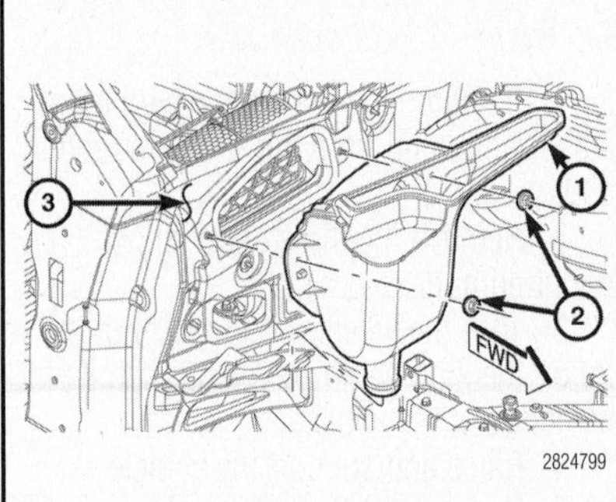

Fig. 292 For the right side only, remove the two nuts (2) that secure the HVAC air inlet duct (1) to the engine compartment side of the dash panel (3) and remove the duct

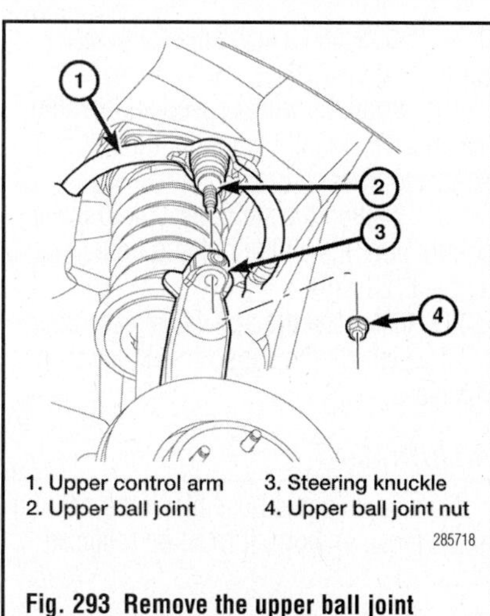

Fig. 293 Remove the upper ball joint retaining nut from the ball joint

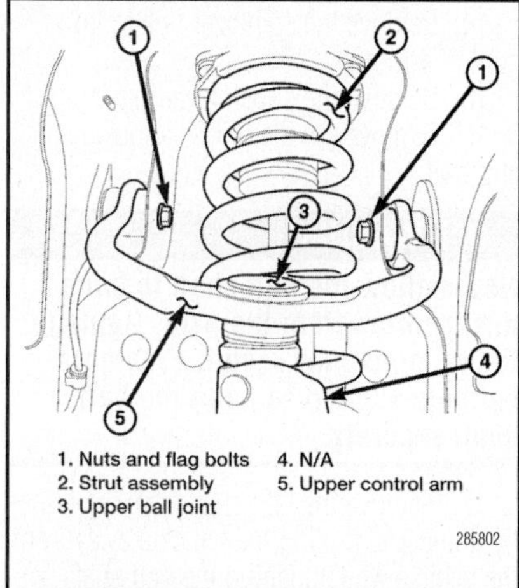

Fig. 294 Remove the nuts and flag bolts securing the upper control arm to the body

arm flag bolts without completely removing the shock assembly.

17. Remove the nuts and flag bolts securing the upper control arm to the body.
18. Remove the upper control arm from the vehicle.

To install:

19. Position the upper control arm to the vehicle.

➡It is necessary to pull the bottom of the shock assembly outward just enough to install the upper control arm flag bolts without completely removing the shock assembly.

➡Tighten the upper control arm to body bolts in the following sequence: Left side, front then rear. Right side, rear then front.

20. Install the nuts and flag bolts securing the upper control arm to the body and tighten to 44 ft. lbs. (60 Nm).
21. Install the upper ball joint into the knuckle.
22. Install the upper ball joint retaining nut and tighten to 70 ft. lbs. (95 Nm).
23. If equipped with a height sensor, connect the height sensor to the upper control arm.
24. Install the speed sensor wiring retaining clip to the knuckle.
25. Install the speed sensor, and install the speed sensor bolt and tighten to 95 inch lbs. (11 Nm).
26. Install the clevis to lower control arm bolt/nut and tighten to 173 ft. lbs. (235 Nm).
27. Install the tire and wheel.
28. Remove the supports and lower the vehicle.
29. Tighten the three upper shock mounting nuts to 21 ft. lbs. (28 Nm).
30. If equipped, attach the wiring harness routing clip to the shock mounting stud.
31. For the right side only, position the HVAC air inlet duct to the engine compartment side of the dash panel. Install the two nuts that secure the HVAC air inlet duct to the dash panel.
32. For the left side only, connect the steering intermediate shaft coupler, install the pinch bolt and tighten to 33 ft. lbs. (45 Nm).
33. For left side only, install the air cleaner housing as follows:
    a. Press the air cleaner housing onto the body grommets and install the push-pin.
    b. Route and connect the weather-strip to the housing inlet.
    c. Connect the PCV air return hose and the power steering hose routing clip (not shown) to the air cleaner body.
    d. Connect the fresh air intake hose to the housing cover and tighten the clamp.
    e. Install the air cleaner.
34. Install the silencer and the cowl panel cover.

WHEEL BEARINGS

REMOVAL & INSTALLATION

RWD

See Figure 295.

1. Raise and support the vehicle.
2. Remove the wheel and tire assembly.
3. Remove the brake rotor.
4. Remove the wheel speed sensor bolt and the wheel speed sensor from the knuckle.
5. Remove the 3 hub bearing mounting bolts from the back of the steering knuckle.

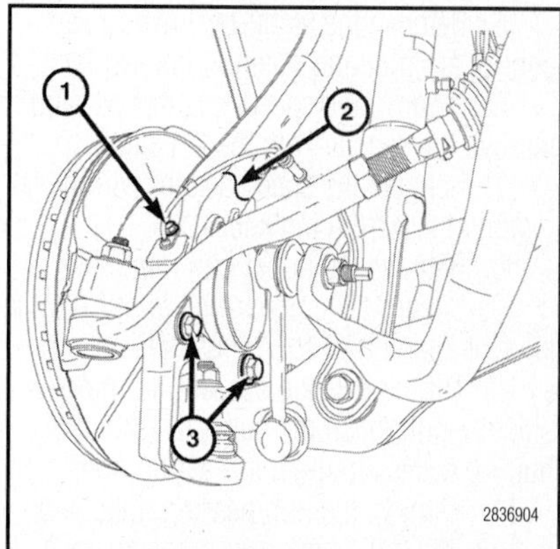

Fig. 295 Remove the wheel speed sensor bolt (1) and the wheel speed sensor from the knuckle (2); hub bearing mounting bolts (3)

Remove hub bearing from the steering knuckle.

To install:

6. Position the hub bearing into the knuckle, install the 3 bolts and tighten to 78 ft. lbs. (105 Nm).
7. Install the wheel speed sensor into the knuckle, install the sensor mounting bolt and tighten to 95 inch lbs. (11 Nm).
8. Install the brake rotor.
9. Install the wheel and tire assembly.
10. Remove the support and lower the vehicle.

4WD

See Figure 296.

1. Raise and support the vehicle.
2. Remove the wheel and tire assembly.
3. Remove the brake rotor.
4. Remove the half shaft nut.

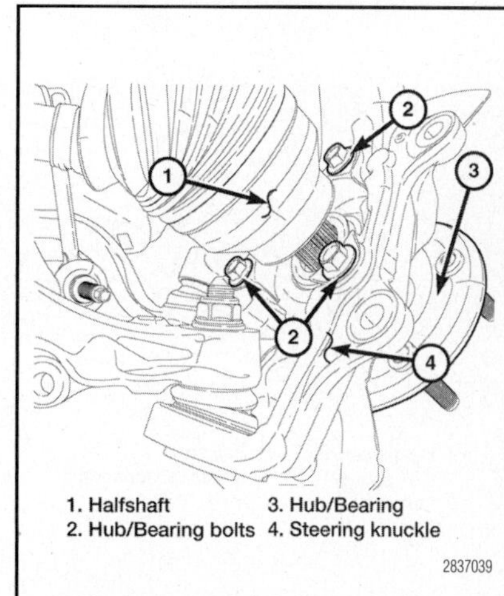

Fig. 296 Tilt the knuckle out, and from outside the hub, push the half shaft into the hub for access to the hub/bearing bolts

5. Remove the stabilizer link to lower control arm nut and position link aside.
6. Remove the speed sensor bolt, and remove the sensor from the knuckle.
7. Remove the speed sensor wiring retaining clip from the knuckle.
8. Remove the upper ball joint nut.
9. Separate the upper ball joint from the knuckle using Ball Joint Press (1).
10. Tilt the knuckle out, and from outside the hub, push the half shaft into the hub for access to the hub/bearing bolts.
11. Remove the hub/bearing bolts and remove the hub/bearing from the knuckle assembly.

To install:

12. Position the hub/bearing, install the hub/bearing bolts and tighten to 78 ft. lbs. (105 Nm).
13. Support the outside of the lower control arm with a suitable holding fixture, and raise to position the upper ball joint into the knuckle.
14. With the holding fixture holding the suspension at normal ride height, install the upper ball joint nut and tighten to 70 ft. lbs. (95 Nm).
15. Install the half shaft nut and tighten to 229 ft. lbs. (310 Nm).
16. Install the brake rotor.
17. Route and attach speed sensor wiring to the knuckle.
18. Install the wheel speed sensor into the knuckle, install the mounting bolt and tighten to 95 inch lbs. (11 Nm).
19. Position the stabilizer link to lower control arm, install the nut and tighten to 90 ft. lbs. (122 Nm).
20. Install the tire and wheel assembly.
21. Remove the supports and lower the vehicle.

ADJUSTMENT

No adjustment is possible. If the bearing is too loose or worn, it must be replaced.

SUSPENSION — REAR SUSPENSION

COIL SPRING

REMOVAL & INSTALLATION

See Figures 297 through 299.

1. Raise and support the vehicle.
2. Remove the tire and wheel.
3. If the spring is to be reused and there is no part number tag, mark the position of the spring for proper alignment on installation.
4. Remove the half shaft nut.
5. If equipped with a height sensor, disconnect the linkage from the ball stud at the lower control arm bracket by prying with a small screwdriver.
6. Bottom caliper pistons into the caliper.
7. Remove the brake caliper tension clip by pressing forward on the back of the clip while pulling out on the front of the clip.
8. Remove the caliper slide dust bolt shields and loosen the brake caliper slide bolts (guide pins).

➡Never allow the disc brake caliper to hang from the brake hose. Damage to the brake hose will result. Provide a suitable support to hang the caliper securely.

9. Remove the brake caliper from the caliper adapter and hang the brake caliper.
10. Support the outer end of the lower control arm with a suitable holding fixture.
11. Remove the tension link to knuckle nut and bolt.
12. Remove the wheel speed sensor bolt and remove the sensor.
13. Remove the camber link to knuckle bolt/nut.
14. Remove the stabilizer link to lower control arm nut.
15. Remove the shock lower nut/bolt.
16. Remove the toe link to knuckle nut and bolt.

⁂ WARNING

Never allow the half shaft to hang unsupported from the axle. Damage to the joints may result. Provide a suitable support to hang the half shaft securely.

17. Remove the half shaft from the hub by tilting and pulling the knuckle away from the vehicle while pushing the half shaft toward the axle.
18. Carefully lower control arm support until spring is loose, and remove the spring from vehicle.

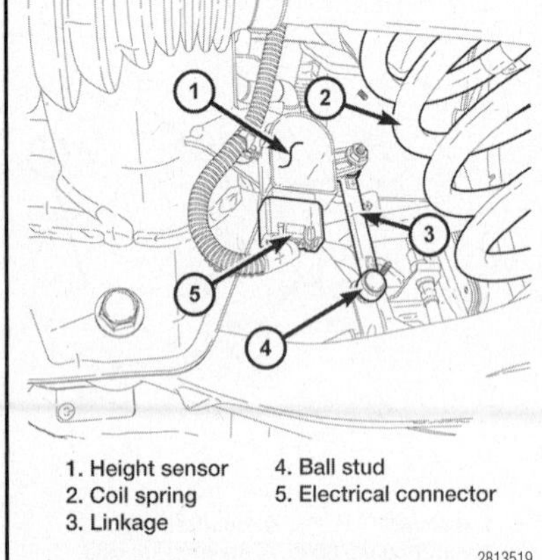

Fig. 297 If equipped with a height sensor, disconnect the linkage from the ball stud at the lower control arm bracket by prying with a small screwdriver

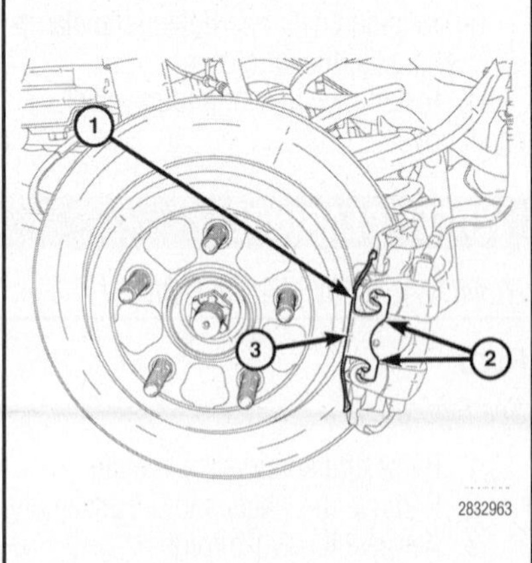

Fig. 298 Remove the brake caliper tension clip (1) by pressing forward on the back of the clip (3) while pulling out on the front of the clip (2)

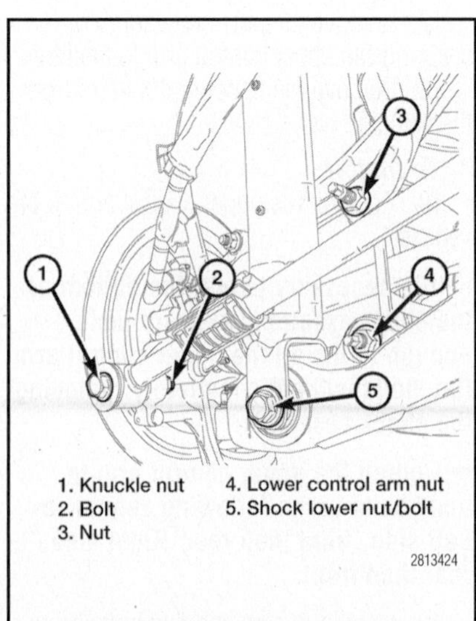

Fig. 299 Remove the stabilizer link to lower control arm nut

To install:

19. If necessary, position the spring insulators in the control arm and cradle.

➡A new spring will have a part number tag. To properly position the spring, the tag must be positioned to face straight out from the vehicle. If the existing spring is being installed (and no part number tag), align the markings made during removal.

20. Position the spring in the pocket of the lower control arm.
21. While holding the spring in position, carefully raise the lower control arm with a support fixture at the outer end of the lower control arm to normal ride height.
22. Align the knuckle to the axle shaft and install the axle through the hub/bearing. Install the half shaft nut and tighten to 229 ft. lbs. (310 Nm).
23. If equipped with a height sensor, position the height sensor linkage to its ball stud and press together to seat.
24. Position the tension link, install the nut and tighten to 79 ft. lbs. (108 Nm).
25. Position the toe link, install the nut and tighten to 79 ft. lbs. (108 Nm).
26. Install the shock lower bolt and nut and tighten to 173 ft. lbs. (235 Nm).
27. Install the stabilizer link to lower control arm nut and tighten to 81 ft. lbs. (110 Nm).
28. Install the camber link to knuckle bolt/nut and tighten to 81 ft. lbs. (110 Nm).
29. Install the wheel speed sensor and sensor retaining bolt and tighten to 95 inch lbs. (11 Nm).
30. Position the brake pads and caliper, install the brake caliper slide bolts (guide pins) and tighten to 20 ft. lbs. (28 Nm).
31. Install the caliper slide bolt dust shields.
32. Install the brake caliper tension clip.
33. Install the wheel.
34. Remove the support and lower the vehicle.
35. Pump the brake pedal until caliper pistons and brake pads are seated and a firm brake pedal is obtained.

LOWER CONTROL ARM

REMOVAL & INSTALLATION

With Electronic Limited Slip Differential (ELSD)

See Figures 300 through 303.

1. Raise and support the vehicle.
2. Remove the tire and wheel assembly.
3. Bottom caliper pistons into the caliper by prying the caliper over.
4. Remove the caliper slide pin covers and slide pins.

✱✱ WARNING

Never allow the disc brake caliper to hang from the brake hose. Damage to the brake hose will result. Provide a suitable support to hang the caliper securely.

5. Remove the disc brake caliper from the adapter and hang from a suitable support.
6. Disconnect the brake cable end from the equalizer.
7. Depress the tabs on the cable housing and pull through the cable retaining bracket.
8. Remove the parking brake cable from the retaining bracket.
9. Remove the tie straps and clips as necessary.

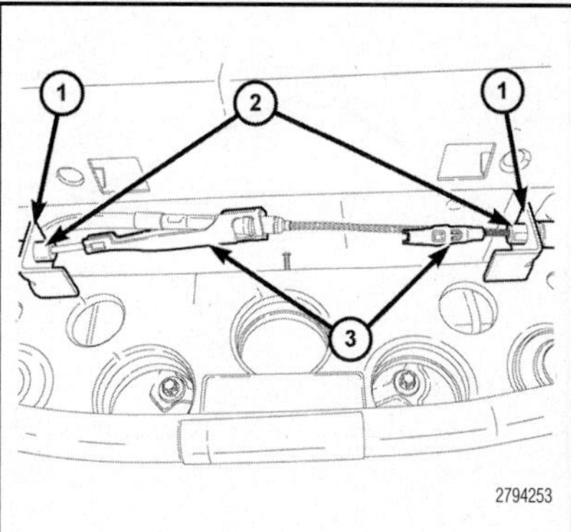

Fig. 300 Disconnect the brake cable end from the equalizer (3); depress the tabs on the cable housing (2) and pull through the cable retaining bracket (1)

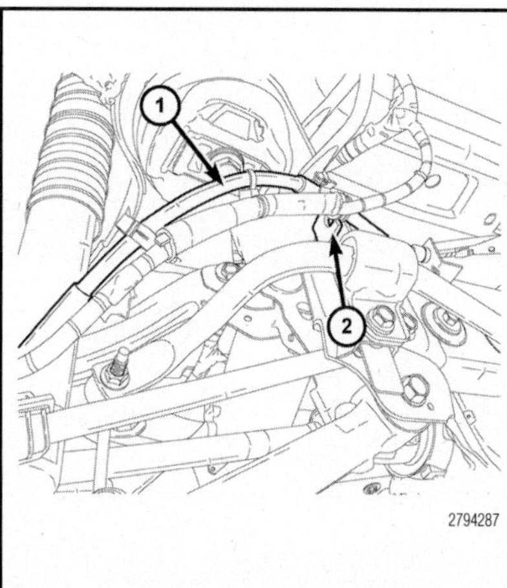

Fig. 301 Remove the parking brake cable (1) from the retaining bracket (2)

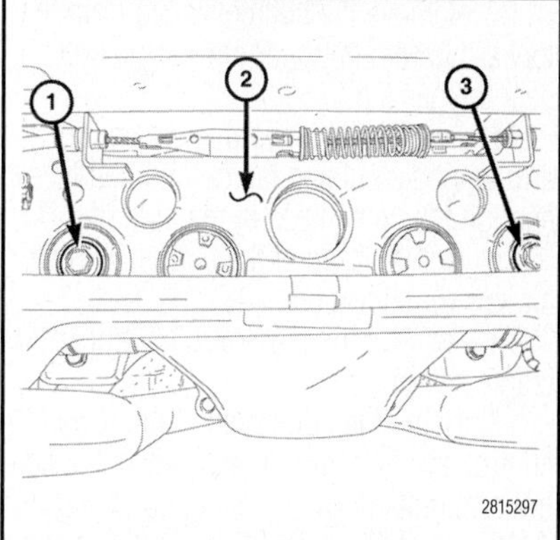

Fig. 302 Remove the left axle bolt (1); loosen the right rear axle bolt (3) and the right front axle bolt (not shown); crossmember (2)

10. Remove the rear spring.
11. Tilt the knuckle for access, remove the ball joint nut and remove the knuckle from the control arm.
12. For the left lower control arm only, loosen and tilt the axle for access to remove the forward lower control arm bolt by performing the following:
    a. Support the rear axle with a suitable holding fixture.
    b. Remove the left axle bolt.

➡Do not remove the bolts on the right side of the axle.

    c. Loosen the right rear axle bolt and the right front axle bolt (not shown).
    d. Carefully lower the axle support enough to tip the axle for clearance to remove the lower control arm bolt.

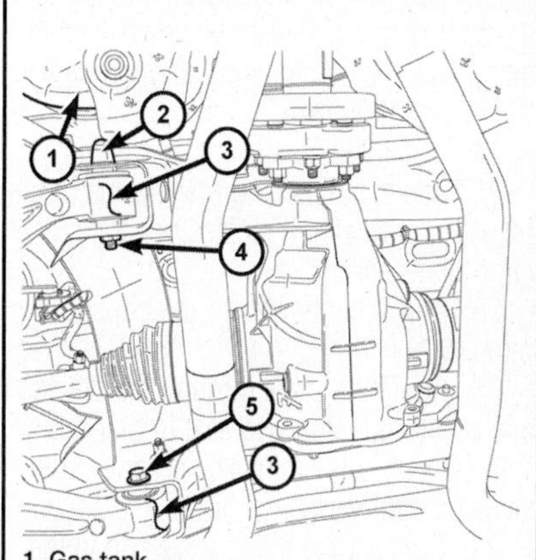

Fig. 303 Remove the bolt cover cap from the forward lower control arm to cradle bolt near the gas tank

13. Remove the bolt cover cap from the forward lower control arm to cradle bolt near the gas tank.

14. Loosen the forward lower control arm to cradle nut and tap out the bolt far enough to cut the head of the bolt off.

15. Cut the head of the bolt off with an air saw (or equivalent).

16. Remove the rear lower control arm to cradle bolts/nuts.

17. Using the nut, pry the front lower control arm bolt through the rear of the control arm mounting.

18. Carefully lower the control arm support and remove the lower control arm (3) from the vehicle.

19. Remove and transfer any necessary components.

To install:

➡Right side shown, left side similar. The axle was tilted for the left side removal and should still be tilted to install the left front control arm to cradle bolt.

➡The front control arm to cradle bolt is installed from rear to front so that the nut is installed on the fuel tank side. This is the opposite of the manufacturing installation.

20. Position the control arm on the cradle and install the bolt/nuts at the cradle. Do not tighten at this time.

21. For the left lower control arm only, raise the axle, install the left axle bolt and tighten all three axle bolts to 111 ft. lbs. (150 Nm).

22. Remove the axle support.

23. Position the knuckle/ball joint into the control arm and with the knuckle tilted out, install the ball joint nut and torque to 151 ft. lbs. (205 Nm).

24. Install the spring.

25. Attach the parking brake cable to the retaining bracket and replace tie straps or clips as necessary.

26. Attach the tie straps and clips as removed.

27. Route the cable through the bracket and pull through tight to seat in bracket. Pull back on cable to make sure the cable seated properly.

28. Connect the brake cable end to the equalizer.

Position the caliper over the rotor, install the slide pins and tighten to 20 ft. lbs. (28 Nm).

29. Install the slide pin covers.

30. Install the wheel.

31. With the vehicle weight on the tires tighten the lower control arm to cradle bolts/nuts to 142 ft. lbs. (193 Nm).

➡The bolt cover cap was removed from the bolt head but fits on the nut after the bolt direction changed from the manufacturing direction.

32. Install the bolt cover cap on the lower control arm to cradle forward nut near the gas tank.

33. Perform a rear wheel alignment.

Without ELSD

See Figures 304 through 306.

1. Raise and support the vehicle.
2. Remove the wheel.
3. Bottom caliper pistons into the caliper by prying the caliper over.
4. Remove the caliper slide pin covers and slide pins.

✲✲ WARNING

Never allow the disc brake caliper to hang from the brake hose. Damage to the brake hose will result. Provide a suitable support to hang the caliper securely.

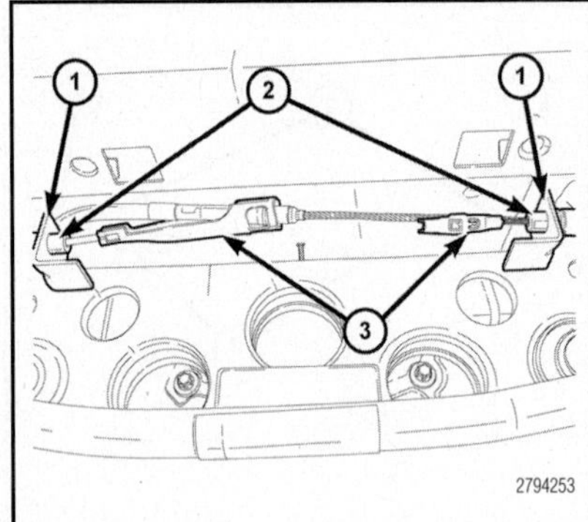

Fig. 304 Disconnect the brake cable end from the equalizer (3); depress the tabs on the cable housing (2) and pull through the cable retaining bracket (1)

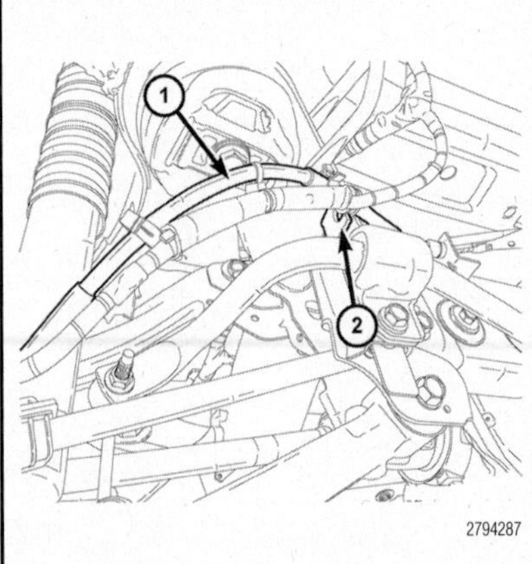

Fig. 305 Remove the parking brake cable (1) from the retaining bracket (2)

5. Remove the disc brake caliper from the adapter and hang from a suitable support.
6. Disconnect the brake cable end from the equalizer.
7. Depress the tabs on the cable housing and pull through the cable retaining bracket.
8. Remove the parking brake cable from the retaining bracket.
9. Remove the tie straps and clips as necessary.
10. Remove the rear spring.
11. Tilt the knuckle for access, remove the ball joint nut and remove the knuckle from the control arm.
12. Remove the bolt cover cap from the forward lower control arm to cradle bolt near the gas tank.
13. Loosen the forward lower control arm to cradle nut and tap out the bolt far enough to cut the head of the bolt off.
14. Cut the head of the bolt off with an air saw (or equivalent).
15. Using the nut, pry the bolt through the rear of the control arm mounting.
16. Remove the rear lower control arm to cradle bolts/nuts.
17. Carefully lower the control arm support and remove the lower control arm from the vehicle.
18. Remove and transfer any necessary components.

To install:

➡The front control arm to cradle bolt is installed from rear to front so that the nut is installed on the fuel tank side. This is the opposite of the manufacturing installation.

19. Position the control arm on the cradle and install the bolt/nuts at the cradle. Do not tighten at this time.
20. Position the knuckle/ball joint into the control arm and with the knuckle tilted out, install the ball joint nut and torque to 151 ft. lbs. (205 Nm).
21. Install the spring.
22. Attach the parking brake cable to the retaining bracket and replace tie straps or clips as necessary.
23. Attach the tie straps and clips as removed.
24. Route the cable through the bracket and pull through tight to seat in bracket. Pull back on cable to make sure the cable seated properly.
25. Connect the brake cable end to the equalizer.

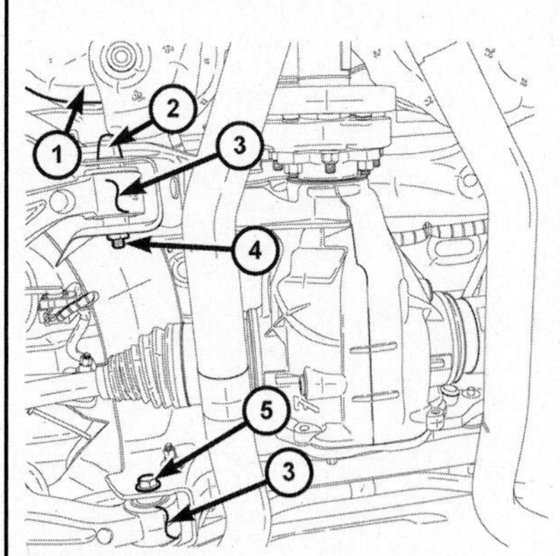

Fig. 306 Remove the bolt cover cap from the forward lower control arm to cradle bolt near the gas tank

26. Position the caliper over the rotor, install the slide pins and tighten to 20 ft. lbs. (28 Nm).
27. Install the slide pin covers.
28. Install the wheel.
29. With the vehicle weight on the tires tighten the lower control arm to cradle bolts/nuts to 142 ft. lbs. (193 Nm).

➡The bolt cover cap was removed from the bolt head but fits on the nut after the bolt direction changed from the manufacturing direction.

30. Install the bolt cover cap on the lower control arm to cradle forward nut near the gas tank.
31. Perform a rear wheel alignment.

SHOCK ABSORBER

REMOVAL & INSTALLATION

See Figures 307 and 308.

1. Raise and support the vehicle.
2. Remove the tire and wheel.
3. Remove the two push pins from the wheel well.
4. Support the outboard end of the lower control arm with a suitable holding fixture.
5. Remove the upper shock bolts.
6. Remove the lower shock bolt and nut.
7. Lower the support on the outboard end of the lower control arm just enough to tilt the shock into position for removal between the front and rear arms of the lower control arm.
8. Remove and transfer any necessary components.

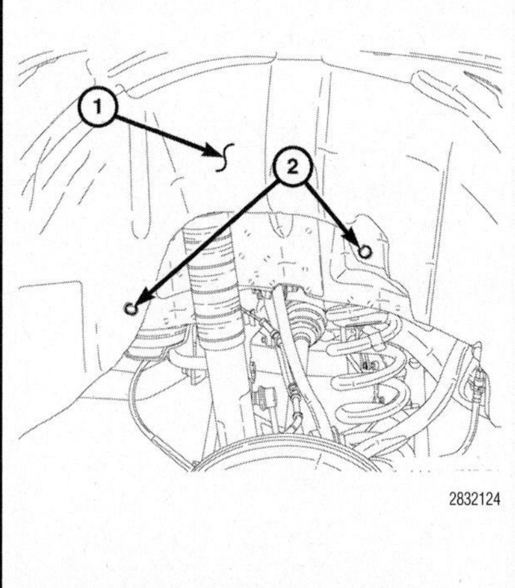

Fig. 307 Remove the two push pins (2) from the wheel well (1)

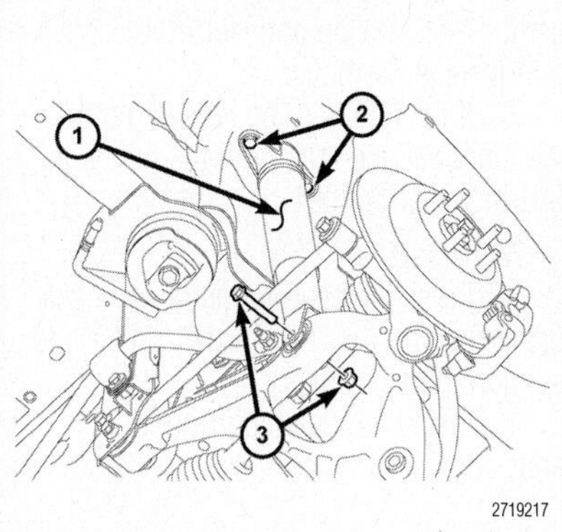

Fig. 308 Remove the upper shock bolts (2), the lower shock bolt and nut (3), and the shock (1)

To install:

9. Position the shock.
10. Install the upper shock bolts and tighten to 48 ft. lbs. (65 Nm).
11. Install the lower shock bolt/nut. Raise the support on the lower control arm to normal ride height and tighten the bolt/nut to 173 ft. lbs. (235 Nm).
12. Install the two wheel well push pins.
13. Install the tire and wheel.
14. Remove the supports and lower the vehicle.

STABILIZER BAR

REMOVAL & INSTALLATION

See Figure 309.

➡When the stabilizer bar or links are serviced it is recommended that a drive on hoist is used or the out board ends of the control arms are supported and raised to normal ride height. If the suspension is hanging, there will be tension on the stabilizer bar.

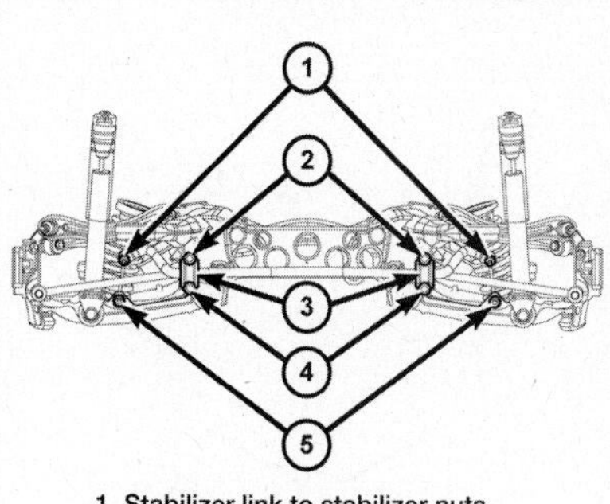

Fig. 309 Remove both stabilizer link to stabilizer nuts and position the links aside

1. Remove the parking brake cable from the retaining bracket for access to the stabilizer to cradle bolts.
2. Raise and support the vehicle.
3. Remove both stabilizer link to stabilizer nuts and position the links aside.
4. Remove both upper and lower stabilizer to cradle bolts.
5. Remove the stabilizer bar from the vehicle.

To install:

➡When the stabilizer bar or links are serviced it is recommended that a drive on hoist is used or the out board ends of the control arms are supported and raised to normal ride height. If the suspension is hanging, there will be tension on the stabilizer bar.

6. Position the stabilizer bar and install the upper and lower stabilizer bar to cradle bolts and tighten to 81 ft. lbs. (110 Nm).
7. Install both stabilizer link to stabilizer nuts and tighten to 66 ft. lbs. (90 Nm).
8. Insert and seat the parking brake cable into the open bracket.
9. Remove the supports and lower the vehicle.

WHEEL BEARINGS

REMOVAL & INSTALLATION

See Figures 310 through 312.

➡A bearing can only be removed from the knuckle one time without replacing the knuckle. If a bearing is being removed for the second time, the knuckle must be replaced.

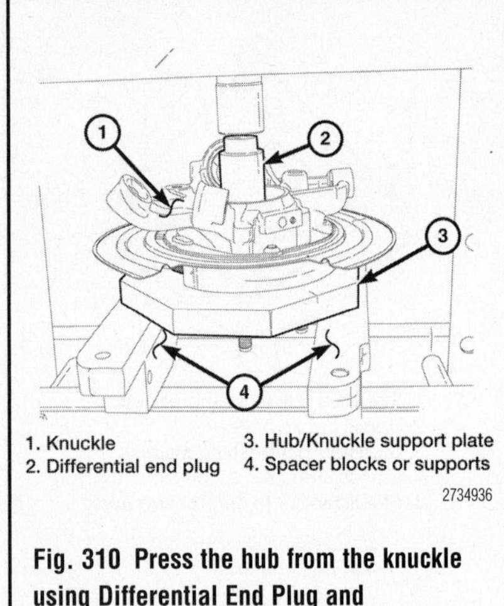

Fig. 310 Press the hub from the knuckle using Differential End Plug and Hub/Knuckle Support Plate

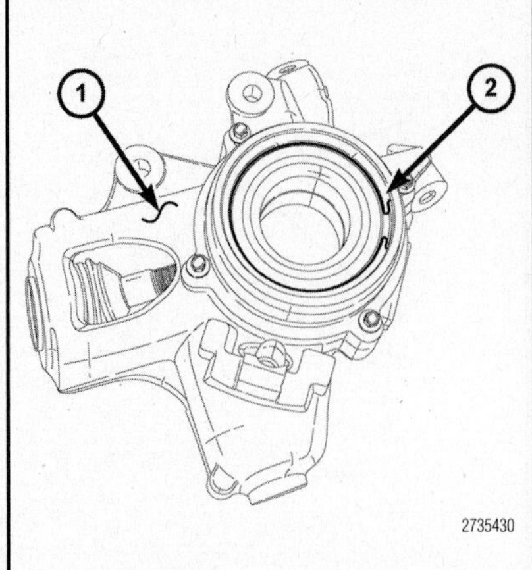

Fig. 311 Remove the retaining ring (2) from the knuckle (1)

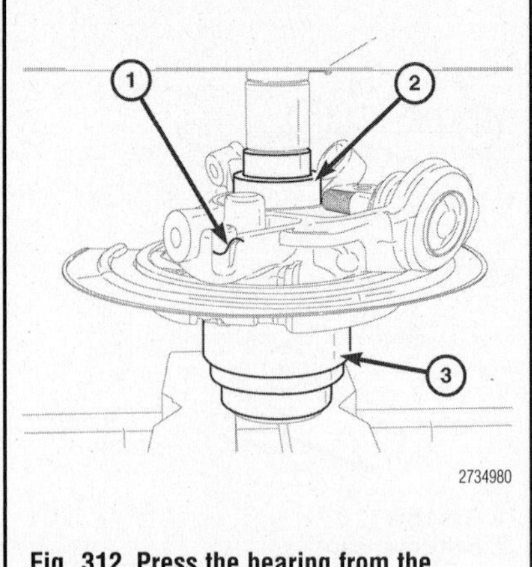

Fig. 312 Press the bearing from the knuckle (1) using Receiver Cup (2) and Hub/Knuckle Support Installer/Remover (3)

1. Raise and support the vehicle.
2. Remove the knuckle.

➡Make sure the spacer blocks or supports below the knuckle/hub raise the assembly enough for clearance to remove the hub.

3. Press the hub from the knuckle using Differential End Plug and Hub/Knuckle Support Plate.
4. Remove the retaining ring from the knuckle.
5. Press the bearing from the knuckle using Receiver Cup and Hub/Knuckle Support Installer/Remover.
6. If the hub is to be reused, remove the inner bearing race from the hub with Bearing/Gear Splitter.

To install:

7. Press the bearing into the knuckle using Bearing Cup Remover/Installer and a support plate or block.
8. Install the retaining ring in knuckle.
9. Press the hub into the bearing/knuckle using Differential End Plug and Hub/Knuckle Support Installer/Remover (3).
10. Install the knuckle to the vehicle.
11. Remove the support and lower the vehicle.

ADJUSTMENT

No adjustment is possible. If the bearing is too loose or worn, it must be replaced.

10

JEEP

Grand Cherokee

SPECIFICATIONS AND MAINTENANCE CHARTS

ENGINE AND VEHICLE IDENTIFICATION

Engine						
Code ①	Liters (cc)	Cu. In.	Cyl.	Fuel Sys.	Engine Type	Eng. Mfg.
G	3.6 (3597)	220	6	SEFI	DOHC	Chrysler
K	3.7 (3697)	226	6	SEFI	SOHC	Chrysler
T	5.7 (5696)	348	8	SEFI	OHV	Chrysler

Model Year	
Code ②	Year
A	2010
B	2011

① 8th position of VIN

② 10th position of VIN

25766_CHER_C0001

GENERAL ENGINE SPECIFICATIONS

All measurements are given in inches.

Year	Model	Engine Displacement Liters (cc)	Engine ID/VIN	Fuel System Type	Net Horsepower @ rpm	Net Torque @ rpm (ft. lbs.)	Bore x Stroke (in.)	Com-pression Ratio	Oil Pressure @ rpm
2010	Grand	3.7 (3697)	K	SEFI	211@5200	236@4000	3.66x3.40	9.6:1	25-110@3000
	Cherokee	5.7 (5696)	T	SEFI	360@5150	390@4250	3.92x3.58	10.5:1	25-110@3000
2011	Grand	3.6 (3597)	G	SEFI	290@6400	260@4800	3.78x3.27	10.2:1	35@1200
	Cherokee	5.7 (5696)	T	SEFI	360@5150	390@4250	3.92x3.58	10.5:1	25-110@3000

25766_CHER_C0002

ENGINE TUNE-UP SPECIFICATIONS

Year	Engine Displacement Liters	Engine ID/VIN	Spark Plug Gap (in.)	Ignition Timing (deg.) MT	Ignition Timing (deg.) AT	Fuel Pump (psi)	Idle Speed (rpm) MT	Idle Speed (rpm) AT	Valve Clearance Intake	Valve Clearance Exhaust
2010	3.7	K	0.43	NA	①	NA	NA	②	③	③
	5.7	T	0.40	NA	①	58	NA	②	HYD	HYD
2011	3.6	G	0.40	NA	①	58	NA	②	HYD	HYD
	5.7	T	0.40	NA	①	58	NA	②	HYD	HYD

NA Not Available

HYD Hydraulic lifters, zero lash

① Ignition timing set by Powertrain Control Module (PCM). Ignition timing is not adjustable on any of the available engines.

② Idle speed set by Powertrain Control Module (PCM). Idle speed is not adjustable on any of the available engines.

③ Stationary lash adjusters, zero lash

25766_CHER_C0003

CAPACITIES

Year	Model	Engine Displacement Liters	Engine ID/VIN	Engine Oil with Filter	Transmission (pts.) Auto.	Drive Axle (pts.) Front	Drive Axle (pts.) Rear	Transfer Case (pts.)	Fuel Tank (gal.)	Cooling System (qts.)
2010	Grand	3.7	K	5.0	①	3.6	4.4	3.8	21.0	9.0
	Cherokee	5.7	T	7.0	①	3.6	4.4	3.8	21.0	14.5
2011	Grand	3.6	G	6.0	①	2.4	2.6	4.0	24.0	11.4
	Cherokee	5.7	T	7.0	①	2.4	2.6	4.0	24.0	17.1

NOTE: All capacities are approximate. Add fluid gradually and ensure a proper fluid level is obtained.

NA Not Available

① Service fill: 11.0 pts.; Overhaul: 29.6 pts.

25766_CHER_C0004

FLUID SPECIFICATIONS

Year	Model	Engine Disp. Liters	Engine Oil	Auto. Trans.	Drive Axle Front	Drive Axle Rear	Transfer Case	Power Steering Fluid	Brake Master Cylinder	Cooling System
2010	Grand	3.7	5W-20	①	②	②	①	③	DOT-3	④
	Cherokee	5.7	5W-20	①	②	②	①	③	DOT-3	④
2011	Grand	3.6	5W-30	①	75W-85	75W-85	①	③	DOT-3	④
	Cherokee	5.7	5W-20	①	75W-85	75W-85	①	③	DOT-3	④

DOT: Department Of Transpotation

NA Not Available

① MOPAR ATF+4

② MOPAR Synthetic Gear Lubricant 75W-140

③ MOPAR Power Steering Fluid +4

④ MOPAR Antifreeze/Coolant 5

25766_CHER_C0005

VALVE SPECIFICATIONS

Year	Engine Displacement Liters	Engine ID/VIN	Seat Angle (deg.)	Face Angle (deg.)	Spring Test Pressure (lbs. @ in.)	Spring Free-Length (in.)	Spring Installed Height (in.)	Stem-to-Guide Clearance (in.) Intake	Stem-to-Guide Clearance (in.) Exhaust	Stem Diameter (in.) Intake	Stem Diameter (in.) Exhaust
2010	3.7	K	44.50-45.00	45.00-45.50	75-83@1.58	①	NA	0.0008-0.0028	0.0019-0.0039	0.2729-0.2739	0.2717-0.2728
	5.7	T	44.50-45.00	45.00-45.50	97.8@1.77	2.189	1.810	0.0008-0.0025	0.0009-0.0025	0.3120-0.3130	0.3120-0.3130
2011	3.6	G	44.50-45.00	45.00-45.50	63-69@1.57	2.067	1.575	0.0009-0.0024	0.0012-0.0027	0.2346-0.2354	0.2343-0.2351
	5.7	T	44.50-45.00	45.00-45.50	97.8@1.77	2.189	1.810	0.0008-0.0025	0.0009-0.0025	0.3120-0.3130	0.3120-0.3130

NA Not Available

① Intake: 1.896 inches

Exhaust: 1.973 inches

25766_CHER_C0006

CAMSHAFT SPECIFICATIONS

All measurements in inches unless noted

Year	Engine Displacement Liters	Engine Code/VIN	Journal Diameter	Brg. Oil Clearance	Shaft End-play	Runout	Journal Bore	Lobe Height Intake	Lobe Height Exhaust
2010	3.7	K	1.0227-1.0235	0.0010-0.0026	0.0030-0.0079	NA	1.0245-1.0252	NA	NA
	5.7	T	①	②	0.0031-0.0114	NA	NA	NA	NA
2011	3.6	G	③	④	0.0030-0.0100	NA	⑤	NA	NA
	5.7	T	①	②	0.0031-0.0114	NA	NA	NA	NA

NA Not Available

① No. 1: 2.29 inches
No. 2: 2.28 inches
No. 3: 2.26 inches
No. 4: 2.24 inches
No. 5: 1.72 inches

② No. 1, 3, 5: 0.0015-0.003 inches
No. 2, 4: 0.0019-0.0035 inches

③ No. 1: 1.25889-1.2596 inches
No. 2, 3, 4: 0.9440-0.9447 inches

④ No. 1: 0.0010-0.0026 inches
No. 2, 3, 4: 0.0009-0.0025 inches

⑤ No. 1: 1.2606-1.2615 inches
No. 2, 3, 4: 0.9457-0.9465 inches

25766_CHER_C0007

CRANKSHAFT AND CONNECTING ROD SPECIFICATIONS

All measurements are given in inches.

Year	Engine Displacement Liters	Engine ID/VIN	Crankshaft Main Brg. Journal Dia.	Crankshaft Main Brg. Oil Clearance	Crankshaft Shaft End-play	Crankshaft Thrust on No.	Connecting Rod Journal Diameter	Connecting Rod Oil Clearance	Connecting Rod Side Clearance
2010	3.7	K	2.4996-2.5005	0.00008-0.0018	0.0021-0.0112	NA	2.2798-2.2792	0.0002-0.0011	0.0002-0.0005
	5.7	T	2.5585-2.5595	0.0009-0.0020	0.002-0.011	NA	NA	NA	0.0030-0.0137
2011	3.6	G	2.8310-2.8380	0.0009-0.0025	NA	NA	2.3193-2.3263	0.0009-0.0025	NA
	5.7	T	2.5585-2.5595	0.0009-0.0020	0.002-0.011	NA	NA	NA	0.0030-0.0137

NA Not Available

25766_CHER_C0008

PISTON AND RING SPECIFICATIONS

All measurements are given in inches.

Year	Engine Displacement Liters	Engine ID/VIN	Piston Clearance	Ring Gap Top Compression	Ring Gap Bottom Compression	Ring Gap Oil Control	Ring Side Clearance Top Compression	Ring Side Clearance Bottom Compression	Ring Side Clearance Oil Control
2010	3.7	K	NA	0.0079-0.0142	0.0146-0.0249	0.0099-0.0300	0.0020-0.0037	0.0016-0.0031	0.0007-0.0091
	5.7	T	0.0120-0.0230	0.0150-0.0210	0.0090-0.0200	0.0059-0.0259	0.0010-0.0035	0.0010-0.0031	0.0020-0.0080
2011	3.6	G	①	0.0100-0.0160	0.0120-0.0180	0.0060-0.0260	0.0010-0.0033	0.0012-0.0031	0.0003-0.0068
	5.7	T	0.0120-0.0230	0.0150-0.0210	0.0090-0.0200	0.0059-0.0259	0.0010-0.0035	0.0010-0.0031	0.0020-0.0080

NA Not Available

① Metal to Metal: 0.0012-0.0020 inches

Metal to Coating: 0.0004-0.0012 inches

25766_CHER_C0009

TORQUE SPECIFICATIONS

All readings in ft. lbs.

Year	Engine Disp. Liters	Engine ID/VIN	Cylinder Head Bolts	Main Bearing Bolts	Rod Bearing Bolts	Crankshaft Damper Bolts	Flywheel Bolts	Manifold Intake	Manifold Exhaust	Spark Plugs	Oil Pan Drain Plug
2010	3.7	K	①	②	③	130	70	④	18	20	25
	5.7	T	⑤	⑥	⑦	129	70	9	18	13	25
2011	3.6	G	⑧	⑨	⑦	⑩	70	⑪	NA	13	20
	5.7	T	⑤	⑥	⑦	129	70	9	18	13	25

NA Not Available

① Step 1: Bolts 1-8: 20 ft. lbs.

Step 2: Bolts 1-8: 20 ft. lbs.

Step 3: Bolts 9-12: 10 f6t. Lbs.

Step 4: Bolts 1-8: Additional 90 degrees

Step 5: Bolts 1-8: An additional 90 degrees

Step 6: Bolts 9-12: 19 ft. lbs.

② Step 1: Bolts 1A-1J: 40 ft. lbs.

Step 2: Bolts 1-8: 62 inch lbs.

Step 3: Bolts 1-8: Additional 90 degrees

Step 4: Bolts A-E: 20 ft. lbs.

③ Step 1: 20 ft. lbs.

Step 2: Additional 90 degrees

④ 105 inch lbs.

⑤ Step 1: Bolts 1-10: 25 ft. lbs.

Step 2: Bolts 11-15: 15 ft. lbs.

Step 3: Bolts 1-10: 40 ft. lbs.

Step 4: Bolts 11-15: 15 Ft. lbs.

Step 5: Bolts 1-10: Additional 90 degrees

Step 6: Bolts 11-15: 25 ft. lbs.

⑥ Main bearing bolts

Step 1: 10 ft. lbs.

Step 2: 20 ft. lbs.

Step 3: Additional 90 degrees

Cross bolts

Step 4: 21 ft. lbs.

Step 5: 21 ft. lbs.

⑦ Step 1: 15 ft. lbs.

Step 2: Additional 90 degrees

⑧ Step 1: 22 ft. lbs.

Step 2: 33 ft. lbs.

Step 3: Additional 75 degrees

Step 4: Additional 50 degrees

Step 5: Loosen all bolts in reverse sequence

Step 6: 22 ft. lbs.

Step 7: 33 ft. lbs.

Step 8: Additional 70 degrees

Step 9: Additional 70 degrees

⑨ Step 1: Inner main bearing cap bolts: 15 ft. lbs.

Step 2: Additional 90 degrees

Step 3: Windage tray and main bearing cap bolts: 16 ft. lbs.

Step 4: Additional 90 degrees

Step 5: Main bearing tie bolts: 21 ft. lbs.

⑩ Step 1: 30 ft. lbs.

Step 2: Additional 105 degrees

⑪ Lower intake manifold: 71 inch lbs.

Upper intake manifold: 71 inch lbs.

25766_CHER_C0010

WHEEL ALIGNMENT

Year	Model		Caster Range (+/-Deg.)	Caster Preferred Setting (Deg.)	Camber Range (+/-Deg.)	Camber Preferred Setting (Deg.)	Toe-in (in.)
2010	Grand Cherokee	F	3.55 to 4.45	4.00	-0.70 to 0.20	-0.25	0.25+/-0.25
		R	NA	NA	0.25	-0.25	0.25+/-0.25
2011	Grand Cherokee	F	4.40 to 5.60	5.00	①	②	0.20+/-0.125
		R	NA	NA	-0.99 to 0.09	-0.54	0.20+/-0.25

F: Front

R: Rear

NA: Not Applicable

① Left: -0.72 to 0.48 degrees
Right: -1.22 to -0.02 degrees

② Left: -0.12 degrees
Right: -0.62 degrees

25766_CHER_C0011

TIRE, WHEEL AND BALL JOINT SPECIFICATIONS

Year	Model	OEM Tires Standard	OEM Tires Optional	Tire Pressures (psi) Front	Tire Pressures (psi) Rear	Wheel Size	Ball Joint Inspection	Lug Nut (ft. lbs.)
2010	Grand Cherokee	245/70R17	265/60R18	①	①	17x8	NA	NA
2011	Grand Cherokee	245/70R17	265/60R18	①	①	17x8	NA	NA

OEM: Original Equipment Manufacturer

PSI: Pounds Per Square Inch

NA: Information not available

① Refer to vehicle certificate label on driver's door jamb for recommended pressures.

25766_CHER_C0012

BRAKE SPECIFICATIONS

All measurements in inches unless noted

Year	Model		Brake Disc Original Thickness	Brake Disc Minimum Thickness	Brake Disc Max. Runout	Minimum Pad/Lining Thickness Front	Minimum Pad/Lining Thickness Rear	Brake Caliper Bracket Bolts (ft. lbs.)	Brake Caliper Mounting Bolts (ft. lbs.)
2010	Grand Cherokee	F	NA	1.122	0.0020	NA	NA	125	32
		R	NA	0.492	0.0008	NA	NA	85	32
2011	Grand Cherokee	F	NA	1.200	0.00035	NA	NA	148	41
		R	NA	0.492	0.0020	NA	NA	89	20

F: Front

R: Rear

NA: Information not available

25766_CHER_C0013

SCHEDULED MAINTENANCE INTERVALS

2010 Jeep Grand Cherokee

		VEHICLE MILEAGE INTERVAL (x1000)												
TO BE SERVICED	TYPE OF SERVICE	6	12	18	24	30	36	42	48	54	60	66	72	78
Engine oil & filter	R	✓	✓	✓	✓	✓	✓	✓	✓	✓	✓	✓	✓	✓
Tires	Rotate		✓		✓		✓		✓		✓		✓	
Brake linings	I/R						✓		✓		✓		✓	
Brake hoses and lines	I	✓	✓	✓	✓	✓	✓	✓	✓	✓	✓	✓	✓	✓
Manual transmission fluid level	I	✓	✓	✓	✓	✓	✓	✓	✓	✓	✓	✓	✓	✓
Drive axle fluid	R			✓			✓			✓			✓	
Parking brake	Adj					✓					✓			
CV-joints	I								✓					
Air filter	R					✓					✓			
Exhaust system	I								✓					
Transfer case fluid level	I					✓					✓			
Front suspension components	I								✓					
PCV valve	I/R										✓			
Windshield washer fluid	I/F	At every fuel stop												
Tire pressure	I/Adj	Once a month												
Brake fluid level	I/Adj	Once a month												
Power Steering fluid	I/Adj	Once a month												
Automatic transmission fluid	I/Adj	Once a month												
Engine coolant level	I/Adj	Once a month												
Transfer case fluid	R	Every 90,000 miles												
Engine coolant	R	Every 102,000 miles												
Ignition cables	I/R	Every 102,000 miles												
Spark plugs	R	Every 102,000 miles												
Automatic trans. Fluid & filter	R	Every 120,000 miles												

R: Replace S/I: Service or Inspect I/R: Inspect and replace if necessary L: Lubricate I/F Inspect and fill as needed I/Adj: Inspect and adjust

If driving in dusty or off-road conditions:

...inspect, and if necessary, replace, the air cleaner every 12,000 miles

...inspect the brake pads, replace if necessary every 12,000 miles.

...inspect the CV-joints every 12,000 miles

...inspect the exhaust system every 12,000 miles

...inspect all front suspension components every 24,000 miles

If used for police, taxi, fleet, off-road, or frequent trailer towing:

...change the front and rear axle fluid every 18,000 miles

...change the automatic transmission fluid and filter every 60,000 miles

...change the transfer case fluid every 60,000 miles

If using your vehicle for any of the following: trailer towing, snow plowing, heavy loading, taxi, police, delivery service (commercial service), off-road, desert operation or more then 50% of your driving is at sustained high speeds during hot weather, above 90°F (32°C):

...change the manual transmission fluid every 30,000 miles

25766_CHER_C0014

SCHEDULED MAINTENANCE INTERVALS

2010 Jeep Grand Cheerokee

Oil Change Indicator System

On Electronic Vehicle Information Center (EVIC) equipped vehicles, "Oil Change Require" is displayed in the EVIC and a single chime sounds indicating that an oil change is necessary.

On non-EVIC equipped vehicles, "Change Oil" flashes in the instrument cluster and a single chime sounds indicating that an oil change is necessary.

Illumination of the oil change message is based on the operating conditions of the vehicle. When the message is illuminated, the vehicle must be serviced within 500 miles.

The oil change indicator will not monitor the time since the last oil change. Change the oil if it has been more than 6 months since the last oil change, even if the oil change indicator message is not illuminated.

Under no circumstances should oil change intervals exceed 6,000 miles or 6 months, whichever comes first.

To reset the oil change indicator, refer to the following procedure:

Oil Change Indicator Reset Procedure

1. Turn the ignition switch to the ON position. Do not start the engine.
2. Fully press the accelerator pedal 3 times within 10 seconds.
3. Turn the ignition switch to the LOCK position.

If the indicator message illuminates when the vehicle is started, repeat the procedure.

25766_CHER_C0015

SCHEDULED MAINTENANCE INTERVALS

2011 Jeep Grand Cherokee 3.6L Engine - Normal & Severe (as noted)

TO BE SERVICED	TYPE OF SERVICE	VEHICLE MILEAGE INTERVAL (x1000)												
		8	16	24	32	40	48	56	64	72	80	88	96	104
Engine oil & filter	Replace	✓	✓	✓	✓	✓	✓	✓	✓	✓	✓	✓	✓	✓
Rotate tires, inspect tread wear, measure tread depth and check pressure	Rotate/Inspect		✓		✓		✓		✓		✓		✓	
Brake system components - Normal	Inspect/Service						✓		✓		✓		✓	
Brake system components - Severe	Inspect/Service		✓		✓		✓		✓		✓		✓	
Exhaust system & heat shields	Inspect		✓		✓		✓		✓		✓		✓	
Inspect the front suspension, tie rod ends and boot seals for cracks or leaks and all parts for damage, wear, improper looseness or end play.	Inspect		✓		✓		✓		✓		✓		✓	
CV Joints	Inspect			✓			✓			✓			✓	
Engine air filter - Normal	Replace					✓					✓			
Engine air filter - Severe	Replace		✓		✓		✓		✓		✓		✓	
Adjust parking brake on vehicles equipped with four-wheel disc brakes	Adjust					✓					✓			
Engine coolant	Flush/Replace										✓			
Spark plugs	Replace												✓	
PCV valve	Inspect/Service												✓	
Automatic transmission fluid and filter - Normal	Inspect	Every 120,000 miles												
Automatic transmission fluid and filter - Severe	Inspect	Every 60,000 miles												
Accessory drive belt	Replace	Every 120,000 miles												
Battery	Inspect/Service	✓	✓	✓	✓	✓	✓	✓	✓	✓	✓	✓	✓	✓
Horn, exterior lamps, turn signals and hazard warning light operation	Inspect	✓	✓	✓	✓	✓	✓	✓	✓	✓	✓	✓	✓	✓
Fluid levels (all)	Inspect/Service	✓	✓	✓	✓	✓	✓	✓	✓	✓	✓	✓	✓	✓
Rear differential fluid	Inspect			✓			✓			✓			✓	
Door hinges & latches	Lubricate		✓		✓		✓		✓		✓		✓	
Passenger compartment air filter	Replace		✓		✓		✓		✓		✓		✓	

25766_CHER_C0016

SCHEDULED MAINTENANCE INTERVALS

2011 Jeep Grand Cherokee 5.7L Engine - Normal & Severe (as noted)

		VEHICLE MILEAGE INTERVAL (x1000)												
TO BE SERVICED	**TYPE OF SERVICE**	**8**	**16**	**24**	**32**	**40**	**48**	**56**	**64**	**72**	**80**	**88**	**96**	**104**
Engine oil & filter	Replace	✓	✓	✓	✓	✓	✓	✓	✓	✓	✓	✓	✓	✓
Rotate tires, inspect tread wear, measure tread depth and check pressure	Rotate/Inspect	✓	✓	✓	✓	✓	✓	✓	✓	✓	✓	✓	✓	✓
Brake system components	Inspect/Service		✓		✓		✓		✓		✓		✓	
Exhaust system & heat shields	Inspect		✓		✓		✓		✓		✓		✓	
Inspect the front suspension, tie rod ends and boot seals for cracks or leaks and all parts for damage, wear, improper looseness or end play.	Inspect		✓		✓		✓		✓		✓		✓	
CV Joints	Inspect			✓			✓			✓			✓	
Engine air filter - Normal	Replace				✓				✓				✓	
Engine air filter - Severe	Replace		✓		✓		✓		✓		✓		✓	
Adjust parking brake on vehicles equipped with four-wheel disc brakes	Adjust				✓				✓				✓	
Engine coolant	Flush/Replace										✓			
Spark plugs	Replace				✓				✓				✓	
PCV valve	Inspect/Service												✓	
Automatic transmission fluid and filter - Normal	Inspect	**Every 60,000 miles**												
Automatic transmission fluid and filter - Severe	Inspect	**Every 120,000 miles**												
Accessory drive belt	Replace	**Every 120,000 miles**												
Battery	Inspect/Service	✓	✓	✓	✓	✓	✓	✓	✓	✓	✓	✓	✓	✓
Horn, exterior lamps, turn signals and hazard warning light operation	Inspect	✓	✓	✓	✓	✓	✓	✓	✓	✓	✓	✓	✓	✓
Fluid levels (all)	Inspect/Service	✓	✓	✓	✓	✓	✓	✓	✓	✓	✓	✓	✓	✓
Front & rear axle fluid	Inspect/Service			✓			✓			✓			✓	
Transfer case fluid - Normal	Inspect/Service				✓				✓				✓	
Transfer case fluid - Severe	Inspect/Service			✓			✓			✓			✓	
Door hinges & latches	Lubricate		✓		✓		✓		✓		✓		✓	
Passenger compartment air filter	Replace		✓		✓		✓		✓		✓		✓	

25766_CHER_C0017

PRECAUTIONS

Before servicing any vehicle, please be sure to read all of the following precautions, which deal with personal safety, prevention of component damage, and important points to take into consideration when servicing a motor vehicle:

- Never open, service or drain the radiator or cooling system when the engine is hot; serious burns can occur from the steam and hot coolant.
- Observe all applicable safety precautions when working around fuel. Whenever servicing the fuel system, always work in a well-ventilated area. Do not allow fuel spray or vapors to come in contact with a spark, open flame, or excessive heat (a hot drop light, for example). Keep a dry chemical fire extinguisher near the work area. Always keep fuel in a container specifically designed for fuel storage; also, always properly seal fuel containers to avoid the possibility of fire or explosion. Refer to the additional fuel system precautions later in this section.
- Fuel injection systems often remain pressurized, even after the engine has been turned **OFF**. The fuel system pressure must be relieved before disconnecting any fuel lines. Failure to do so may result in fire and/or personal injury.
- Brake fluid often contains polyglycol ethers and polyglycols. Avoid contact with the eyes and wash your hands thoroughly after handling brake fluid. If you do get brake fluid in your eyes, flush your eyes with clean, running water for 15 minutes. If eye irritation persists, or if you have taken brake fluid internally, IMMEDIATELY seek medical assistance.
- The EPA warns that prolonged contact with used engine oil may cause a number of skin disorders, including cancer. You should make every effort to minimize your exposure to used engine oil. Protective gloves should be worn when changing oil. Wash your hands and any other exposed skin areas as soon as possible after exposure to used engine oil. Soap and water, or waterless hand cleaner should be used.
- All new vehicles are now equipped with an air bag system, often referred to as a Supplemental Restraint System (SRS) or Supplemental Inflatable Restraint (SIR) system. The system must be disabled before performing service on or around system components, steering column, instrument panel components, wiring and sensors. Failure to follow safety and disabling procedures could result in accidental air bag deployment, possible personal injury and unnecessary system repairs.
- Always wear safety goggles when working with, or around, the air bag system. When carrying a non-deployed air bag, be sure the bag and trim cover are pointed away from your body. When placing a non-deployed air bag on a work surface, always face the bag and trim cover upward, away from the surface. This will reduce the motion of the module if it is accidentally deployed. Refer to the additional air bag system precautions later in this section.
- Clean, high quality brake fluid from a sealed container is essential to the safe and proper operation of the brake system. You should always buy the correct type of brake fluid for your vehicle. If the brake fluid becomes contaminated, completely flush the system with new fluid. Never reuse any brake fluid. Any brake fluid that is removed from the system should be discarded. Also, do not allow any brake fluid to come in contact with a painted surface; it will damage the paint.
- Never operate the engine without the proper amount and type of engine oil; doing so WILL result in severe engine damage.
- Timing belt maintenance is extremely important. Many models utilize an interference-type, non-freewheeling engine. If the timing belt breaks, the valves in the cylinder head may strike the pistons, causing potentially serious (also time-consuming and expensive) engine damage. Refer to the maintenance interval charts for the recommended replacement interval for the timing belt, and to the timing belt section for belt replacement and inspection.
- Disconnecting the negative battery cable on some vehicles may interfere with the functions of the on-board computer system(s) and may require the computer to undergo a relearning process once the negative battery cable is reconnected.
- When servicing drum brakes, only disassemble and assemble one side at a time, leaving the remaining side intact for reference.
- Only an MVAC-trained, EPA-certified automotive technician should service the air conditioning system or its components.

BRAKES — ANTI-LOCK BRAKE SYSTEM (ABS)

GENERAL INFORMATION

PRECAUTIONS

- Certain components within the ABS system are not intended to be serviced or repaired individually.
- Do not use rubber hoses or other parts not specifically specified for and ABS system. When using repair kits, replace all parts included in the kit. Partial or incorrect repair may lead to functional problems and require the replacement of components.
- Lubricate rubber parts with clean, fresh brake fluid to ease assembly. Do not use shop air to clean parts; damage to rubber components may result.
- Use only DOT 3 brake fluid from an unopened container.
- If any hydraulic component or line is removed or replaced, it may be necessary to bleed the entire system.
- A clean repair area is essential. Always clean the reservoir and cap thoroughly before removing the cap. The slightest amount of dirt in the fluid may plug an orifice and impair the system function. Perform repairs after components have been thoroughly cleaned; use only denatured alcohol to clean components. Do not allow ABS components to come into contact with any substance containing mineral oil; this includes used shop rags.
- The Anti-Lock control unit is a microprocessor similar to other computer units in the vehicle. Ensure that the ignition switch is **OFF** before removing or installing controller harnesses. Avoid static electricity discharge at or near the controller.
- If any arc welding is to be done on the vehicle, the control unit should be unplugged before welding operations begin.

SPEED SENSORS

REMOVAL & INSTALLATION

2010 Models

Front

See Figures 1 and 2.

1. Raise and support the vehicle.
2. Remove the tire and wheel assembly.
3. Remove the caliper adaptor bolts. Support the caliper and adaptor assembly Do not let assembly hang by the hose.

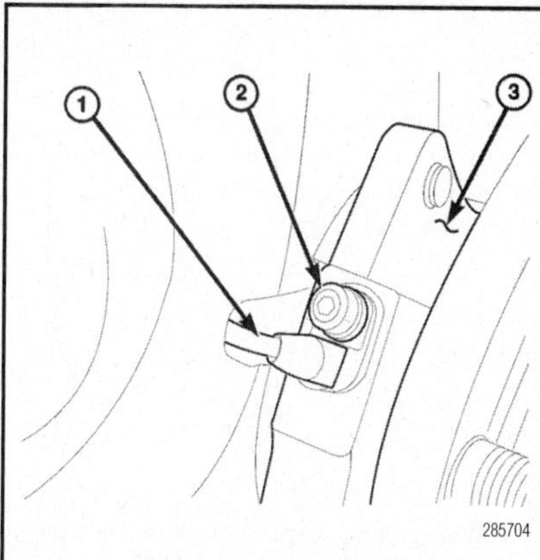

Fig. 1 Remove the front wheel sensor mounting nut (2) and the wheel speed sensor (1) from the hub (3)

4. Remove the disc brake rotor.
5. Remove the front wheel sensor mounting nut.
6. Remove the wheel speed sensor from the hub.
7. Disconnect the wire sensor routing clips.
8. Disconnect the wheel speed sensor wire connector.
9. Remove the sensor and wire.

To install:

10. Reconnect the wheel speed sensor wire connector.
11. Reroute and connect the wheel speed sensor wire to the routing clips.
12. Install the wheel speed sensor into the hub and then install the mounting bolt and tighten the nut to 106–124 inch lbs. (12–14 Nm).

➡**Check the sensor wire routing. Be sure the wire is clear of all chassis components and is not twisted or kinked at any spot.**

13. Install the disc brake rotor.
14. Install the caliper adaptor over the rotor.
15. Install the caliper adaptor bolts and tighten to 66–85 ft. lbs. (90–115 Nm).
16. Install the tire and wheel assembly.
17. Remove the support and lower vehicle.

Rear

See Figure 3.

1. Raise and support the vehicle.
2. Remove the wheel speed sensor mounting bolt from the rear support plate.
3. Remove the wheel speed sensor from the support plate.
4. Disconnect the wheel speed sensor electrical connector.

To install:

5. Insert the wheel speed sensor through the support plate.
6. Tighten the wheel speed sensor bolt to 106–124 inch lbs. (12–14 Nm).
7. Secure the wheel speed sensor wire to the routing clips.

➡**Verify that the sensor wire is secure and clear of the rotating components.**

8. Reconnect the wheel speed sensor electrical connector.
9. Lower the vehicle.

2011 Models

Front

See Figures 4 and 5.

1. Raise and support the vehicle.

➡**The inner wheel well can be pulled slightly out for access to electrical connector without removing wheel well retainers.**

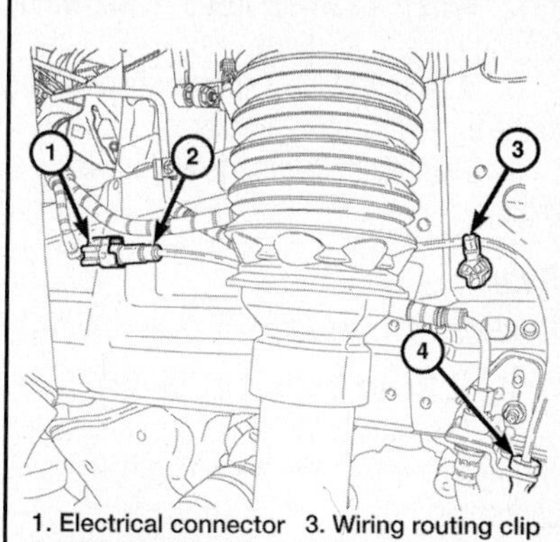

Fig. 4 Disconnect the wheel speed sensor electrical connector

2. Disconnect the wheel speed sensor electrical connector.
3. Disconnect the wheel speed sensor wiring routing clips.
4. Remove the wheel speed sensor wiring from the brake flex hose bracket.
5. Disconnect the sensor wire routing clips from the brake hose.
6. Remove the wheel speed sensor wiring from the knuckle.
7. Remove the front wheel sensor mounting bolt and remove the sensor from the knuckle.

To install:

8. Position the wheel speed sensor in the knuckle, install the mounting bolt, and tighten to 95 inch lbs. (11 Nm).
9. Attach the sensor wire routing clips to the brake hose.
10. Attach the wheel speed sensor wiring to the knuckle.
11. Connect the sensor electrical connector.

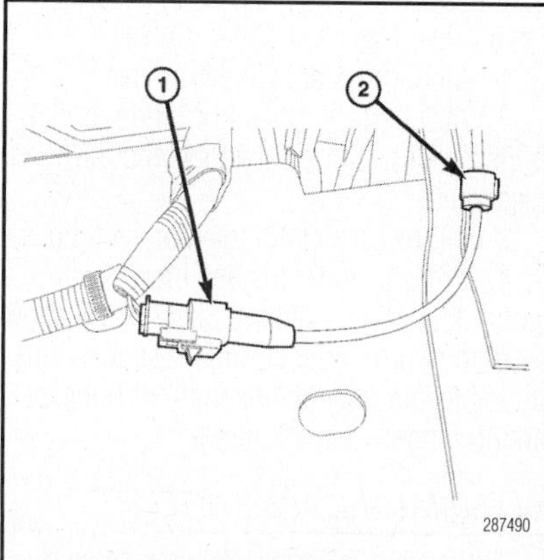

Fig. 2 Disconnect the wire sensor routing clips (2) and the wheel speed sensor wire connector (1)

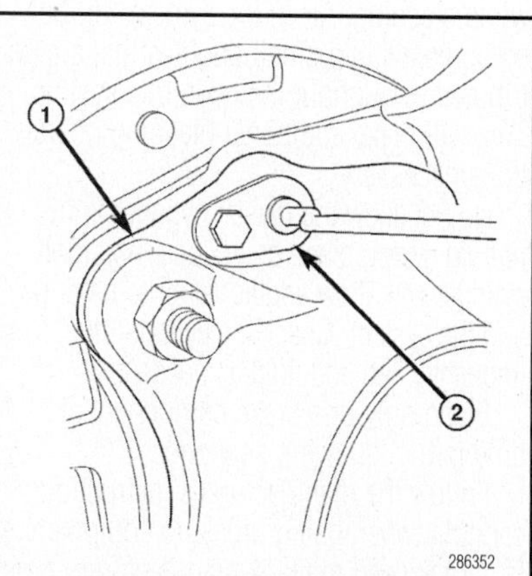

Fig. 3 Remove the wheel speed sensor mounting bolt (2) from the rear support plate (1)

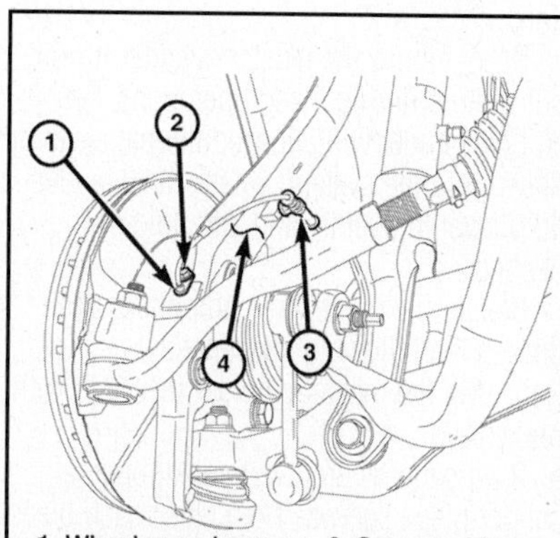

Fig. 5 Remove the wheel speed sensor wiring from the knuckle

12. Attach the wheel speed sensor wiring routing clips to the body.
13. Attach the wheel speed sensor wiring to the brake flex hose bracket.
14. Remove the supports and lower vehicle.

Rear

See Figures 6 and 7.

1. Raise and support the vehicle.
2. Disconnect the wheel speed sensor wiring connector from the wiring harness connector.
3. Remove the wheel speed sensor wiring routing clip (not shown) from the top of the cradle.
4. Remove the wheel speed sensor wiring routing clips from the camber link.
5. Remove the wheel speed sensor mounting bolt, and remove the sensor from the knuckle.

To install:

6. Route the wheel speed sensor and connect the wheel speed sensor wiring connector to the wiring harness connector.

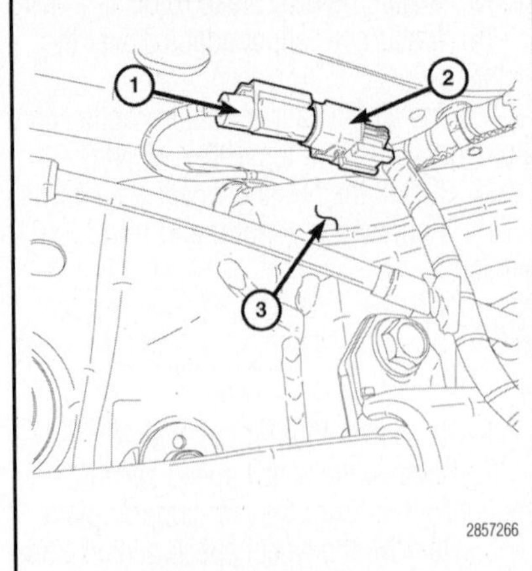

Fig. 6 Disconnect the wheel speed sensor wiring connector (1) from the wiring harness connector (2); cradle (3)

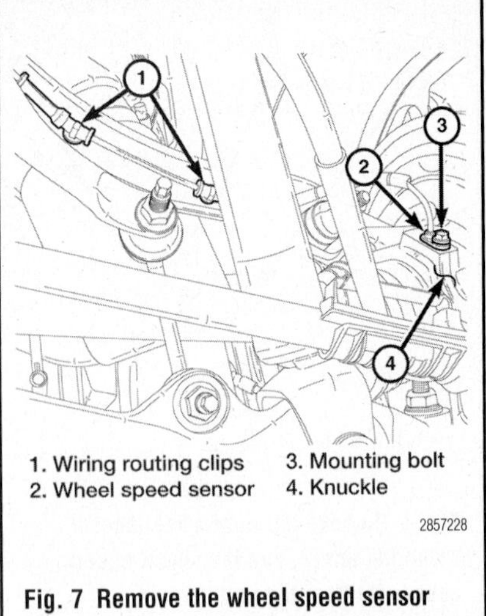

Fig. 7 Remove the wheel speed sensor wiring routing clips from the camber link

7. Attach the wheel speed sensor wiring routing clip (not shown) to the top of the cradle.
8. Route and attach the wheel speed sensor wiring routing clips to the camber link.
9. Install the wheel speed sensor, and mounting bolt, and tighten to 95 inch lbs. (11 Nm).
10. Remove the supports and lower the vehicle.

BRAKES — BLEEDING THE BRAKE SYSTEM

BLEEDING PROCEDURE

BLEEDING PROCEDURE

Manual Procedure

Use Mopar® brake fluid, or an equivalent quality fluid meeting SAE J1703-F and DOT 3 standards only. Use fresh, clean fluid from a sealed container at all times.

Do not pump the brake pedal at any time while bleeding. Air in the system will be compressed into small bubbles that are distributed throughout the hydraulic system. This will make additional bleeding operations necessary.

Do not allow the master cylinder to run out of fluid during bleed operations. An empty cylinder will allow additional air to be drawn into the system. Check the cylinder fluid level frequently and add fluid as needed.

Bleed only one brake component at a time in the following sequence:

1. Fill the master cylinder reservoir with brake fluid.
2. If calipers are overhauled, open all caliper bleed screws. Then close each bleed screw as fluid starts to drip from it. Top off master cylinder reservoir once more before proceeding.
3. Attach one end of bleed hose to bleed screw and insert opposite end in glass container partially filled with brake fluid. Be sure end of bleed hose is immersed in fluid.
4. Open up bleeder, then have a helper press down the brake pedal. Once the pedal is down close the bleeder. Repeat bleeding until fluid stream is clear and free of bubbles. Then move to the next wheel.

Pressure Procedure

Use Mopar® brake fluid, or an equivalent quality fluid meeting SAE J1703-F and DOT 3 standards only. Use fresh, clean fluid from a sealed container at all times.

Do not pump the brake pedal at any time while bleeding. Air in the system will be compressed into small bubbles that are distributed throughout the hydraulic system. This will make additional bleeding operations necessary.

Do not allow the master cylinder to run out of fluid during bleed operations. An empty cylinder will allow additional air to be drawn into the system. Check the cylinder fluid level frequently and add fluid as needed.

Bleed only one brake component at a time in the following sequence:

Follow the manufacturer's instructions carefully when using pressure equipment. Do not exceed the tank manufacturers pressure recommendations. Generally, a tank pressure of 15–20 psi (51–67 kPa) is sufficient for bleeding.

Fill the bleeder tank with recommended fluid and purge air from the tank lines before bleeding.

Do not pressure bleed without a proper master cylinder adapter. The wrong adapter can lead to leakage, or drawing air back into the system. Use adapter provided with the equipment or Adapter.

MASTER CYLINDER BLEEDING

A new master cylinder should be bled before installation on the vehicle. Required bleeding tools include bleed tubes and a wood dowel to stroke the pistons. Bleed tubes can be fabricated from brake line.

1. Mount master cylinder in vise.
2. Attach bleed tubes to cylinder outlet ports. Then position each tube end into reservoir.
3. Fill reservoir with fresh brake fluid.
4. Press cylinder pistons inward with wood dowel. Then release pistons and allow them to return under spring pressure. Continue bleeding operations until air bubbles are no longer visible in fluid.

BLEEDING THE ABS SYSTEM

ABS system bleeding requires conventional bleeding methods plus use of a scan tool. The procedure involves performing a base brake bleeding, followed by use of the scan tool to cycle and bleed the HCU pump and solenoids. A second base brake bleeding procedure is then required to remove any air remaining in the system.

1. Perform base brake bleeding.
2. Connect scan tool to the Data Link Connector.
3. Select ANTILOCK BRAKES, followed by MISCELLANEOUS, then ABS BRAKES. Follow the instructions displayed. When scan tool displays TEST COMPLETE, disconnect scan tool and proceed.
4. Perform base brake bleeding a second time.
5. Top off master cylinder fluid level and verify proper brake operation before moving vehicle.

FLUID FILL PROCEDURE

1. Always clean the master cylinder reservoir and cap before checking fluid level. If not cleaned, dirt could enter the fluid.
2. The fluid fill level is indicated on the side of the master cylinder reservoir.
3. The correct fluid level is to the MAX indicator on the side of the reservoir. If necessary, add fluid to the proper level.

BRAKES — FRONT DISC BRAKES

**** CAUTION**

Dust and dirt accumulating on brake parts during normal use may contain asbestos fibers from production or aftermarket brake linings. Breathing excessive concentrations of asbestos fibers can cause serious bodily harm. Exercise care when servicing brake parts. Do not sand or grind brake lining unless equipment used is designed to contain the dust residue. Do not clean brake parts with compressed air or by dry brushing. Cleaning should be done by dampening the brake components with a fine mist of water, then wiping the brake components clean with a dampened cloth. Dispose of cloth and all residue containing asbestos fibers in an impermeable container with the appropriate label. Follow practices prescribed by the Occupational Safety and Health Administration (OSHA) and the Environmental Protection Agency (EPA) for the handling, processing, and disposing of dust or debris that may contain asbestos fibers.

BRAKE CALIPER

REMOVAL & INSTALLATION

1. Install prop rod on the brake pedal to keep pressure on the brake system. Holding pedal in this position will isolate master cylinder from hydraulic brake system and will not allow brake fluid to drain out of brake fluid reservoir while brake lines are open. This will allow you to bleed out the area of repair instead of the entire system.
2. Raise and support vehicle.
3. Remove front wheel and tire assembly.
4. Drain small amount of fluid from master cylinder brake reservoir with clean suction gun.
5. Bottom caliper pistons into the caliper by prying the caliper over.
6. Remove brake hose banjo bolt and gasket washers. Discard gasket washers.
7. Remove the caliper slide bolts.
8. Remove the caliper from the adapter.

To install:

9. Install the caliper on the adapter.
10. Caliper slide pins should be free from debris and lightly lubricated.
11. Install the caliper slide pin bolts.
    a. On 2010 models, tighten to 32 ft. lbs. (44 Nm).
    b. On 2011 models, tighten to 41 ft. lbs. (55 Nm).
12. Gently lift one end of the slide pin boot to equalize air pressure, then release the boot and verify that the boot is fully covering the slide pin.

**** WARNING**

Verify brake hose is not twisted or kinked before tightening banjo bolt.

13. Install brake hose to caliper with new copper washers and tighten banjo bolt to 23 ft. lbs. (31 Nm).
14. Remove the prop rod from the brake pedal.
15. Bleed the area of repair for the brake system. If a proper pedal is not felt during bleeding an area of repair then a base bleed system must be performed.
16. Install wheel and tire assemblies.
17. Remove supports and lower vehicle.
18. Verify brake fluid level.

BRAKES — REAR DISC BRAKES

**** CAUTION**

Dust and dirt accumulating on brake parts during normal use may contain asbestos fibers from production or aftermarket brake linings. Breathing excessive concentrations of asbestos fibers can cause serious bodily harm. Exercise care when servicing brake parts. Do not sand or grind brake lining unless equipment used is designed to contain the dust residue. Do not clean brake parts with compressed air or by dry brushing. Cleaning should be done by dampening the brake components with a fine mist of water, then wiping the brake components clean with a dampened cloth. Dispose of cloth and all residue containing asbestos fibers in an impermeable container with the appropriate label. Follow practices prescribed by the Occupational Safety and Health Administration (OSHA) and the Environmental Protection Agency (EPA) for the handling, processing, and disposing of dust or debris that may contain asbestos fibers.

BRAKE CALIPER

REMOVAL & INSTALLATION

1. Install prop rod on the brake pedal to keep pressure on the brake system, Holding pedal in this position will isolate master cylinder from hydraulic brake system and will not allow brake fluid to drain out of brake fluid reservoir while brake lines are open. This will allow you to bleed out the area of repair instead of the entire system.
2. Raise and support vehicle.
3. Remove rear wheel and tire assembly.
4. Drain small amount of fluid from master cylinder brake reservoir with a clean suction gun.
5. Bottom caliper pistons into the caliper by prying the caliper over.
6. Remove brake hose banjo bolt and discard gasket washers.
7. Remove the caliper slide pins.
8. Remove caliper from the anchor.

To install:

9. Lubricate the slide pins and slide pin bushings with caliper slide grease or the grease provided with the caliper.
10. Install the caliper on the anchor.
11. Install the caliper slide pin bolts.
  a. On 2010 models, tighten to 18 ft. lbs. (25 Nm).
  b. On 2011 models, tighten to 20 ft. lbs. (28 Nm).

**** WARNING**

Verify that the brake hose is not twisted or kinked before tightening the fitting bolt.

12. Install brake hose to caliper with a new gasket washers and tighten banjo bolt to 23 ft. lbs. (31 Nm).
13. Remove the prop rod from the brake pedal.
14. Bleed the area of repair for the brake system, If a proper pedal is not felt during bleeding an area of repair then a base bleed system must be performed.
15. Install wheel and tire assemblies.
16. Remove supports and lower vehicle.

PARKING BRAKE SHOES

REMOVAL & INSTALLATION

2010 Models

See Figures 8 through 10.

1. Raise vehicle.
2. Remove rear wheel and tire assembly.
3. Remove the 2 caliper bolts then remove the caliper. Support the caliper, Do not let the caliper hang by the brake hose.
4. Remove rubber access plug from back of rear disc brake support plate.
5. If necessary retract parking brake shoes with brake adjuster tool. Position tool at top of star wheel and rotate wheel.
6. Remove rotor from axle hub flange.
7. Remove the four axle flange nuts.
8. Remove the axle shaft from the rear differential.
9. Remove the shoe to shoe return spring with needle nose pliers and then remove the adjuster.
10. Remove the shoe to shoe return spring with brake pliers.
11. Remove shoe hold-down clips and pins. Clip is held in place by pin which fits in clip notch. To remove clip, first push clip ends together and slide clip until head of pin clears narrow part of notch. Then remove clip and pin.
12. Remove shoes off the actuator lever for the park brake then remove the shoes.

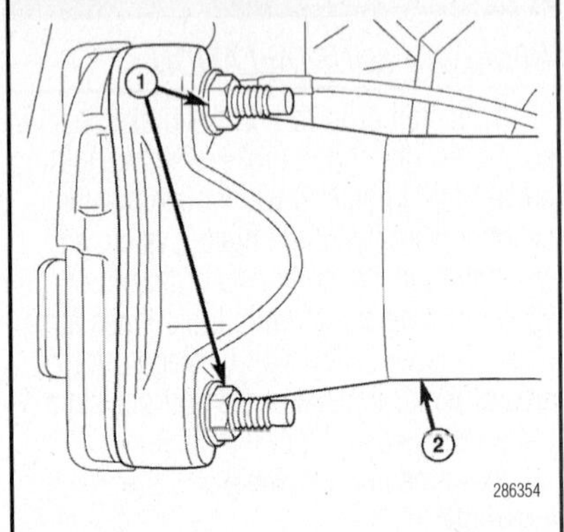

Fig. 9 Remove the four axle flange nuts (1); axle (2)

To install:

13. Install the park brake shoes onto the actuator lever.
14. Install shoes on support plate with hold down clips and pins. Be sure shoes are properly engaged in the park brake actuator lever.
15. Install the return spring.
16. Lubricate and install adjuster screw assembly. Be sure notched ends of screw assembly are properly seated on shoes and that star wheel is aligned with access hole in the support plate.
17. Install shoe to shoe adjuster spring. Needle nose pliers can be used to connect spring to each shoe.
18. Install the axle shaft to the rear differential.
19. Install and tighten the axle flange nuts.
20. Install rotor to the axle hub.
21. Install the caliper and the 2 mounting bolts to 32 ft. lbs. (44 Nm).
22. Adjust the parking brake shoes.
23. Install wheel and tire assembly.
24. Lower vehicle and verify correct parking brake operation.

2011 Models

See Figures 11 and 12.

1. Raise and support the vehicle.
2. Disconnect the rear RH and LH parking brake cables from the parking brake equalizer.
3. Remove the rear wheels.
4. Remove the rotor.
5. Remove the shoe to shoe return springs.
6. Remove the adjuster.
7. Remove the shoe hold-down clips and pins.
8. Spread the shoes and remove the parking brake cable from the actuator lever, and remove the shoes.
9. Remove and transfer the parking brake actuator, and the spring behind the shoes near the parking brake actuator to the new shoes.

To install:

10. Attach the parking brake cable to the actuator and position the shoes on the support plate. Be sure shoes are properly

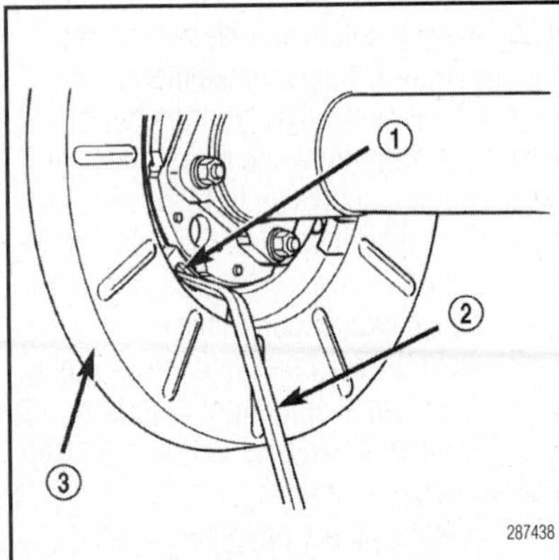

Fig. 8 Remove rubber access plug (1) from back of rear disc brake support plate (3); brake adjuster tool (2)

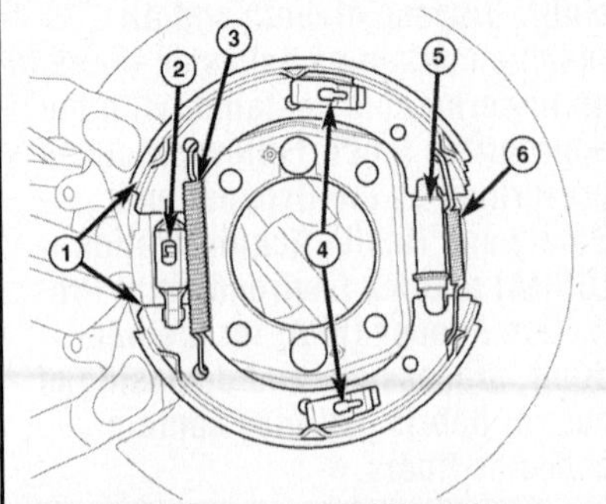

Fig. 10 Remove the shoe to shoe return spring with needle nose pliers and then remove the adjuster

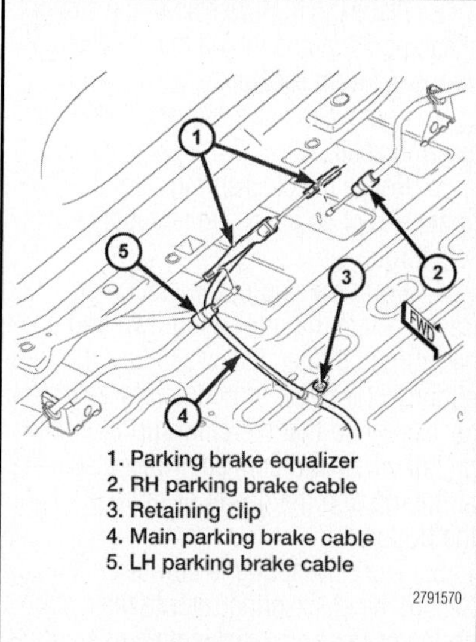

Fig. 11 Disconnect the rear RH and LH parking brake cables from the parking brake equalizer

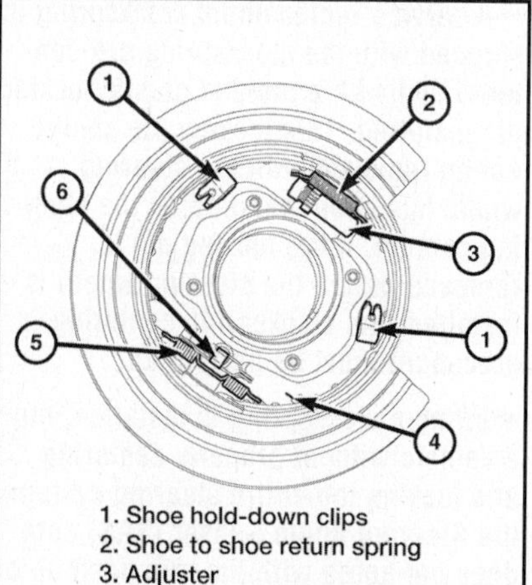

Fig. 12 Remove the shoe to shoe return springs

engaged in the parking brake actuator, parking brake cable is attached, and the rear spring is still properly connected.

11. Install the hold down clips and pins.
12. Install the adjuster.
13. Install the shoe to shoe return spring.
14. Connect the rear RH and LH parking brake cables to the parking brake equalizer.
15. Install rotor and brake calipers.
16. Adjust the parking brake shoes.
17. Install wheels.
18. Remove the supports and lower the vehicle.
19. Pump brake pedal until caliper pistons and brake pads are seated and a firm brake pedal is obtained
20. Verify correct parking brake operation.

CHASSIS ELECTRICAL

AIR BAG (SUPPLEMENTAL RESTRAINT SYSTEM)

GENERAL INFORMATION

**** CAUTION**

These vehicles are equipped with an air bag system. The system must be disarmed before performing service on, or around, system components, the steering column, instrument panel components, wiring and sensors. Failure to follow the safety precautions and the disarming procedure could result in accidental air bag deployment, possible injury and unnecessary system repairs.

SERVICE PRECAUTIONS

Disconnect and isolate the battery negative cable before beginning any airbag system component diagnosis, testing, removal, or installation procedures. Allow system capacitor to discharge for two minutes before beginning any component service. This will disable the airbag system. Failure to disable the airbag system may result in accidental airbag deployment, personal injury, or death.

Do not place an intact undeployed airbag face down on a solid surface. The airbag will propel into the air if accidentally deployed and may result in personal injury or death.

When carrying or handling an undeployed airbag, the trim side (face) of the airbag should be pointing away from the body to minimize possibility of injury if accidental deployment occurs. Failure to do this may result in personal injury or death.

Replace airbag system components with OEM replacement parts. Substitute parts may appear interchangeable, but internal differences may result in inferior occupant protection. Failure to do so may result in occupant personal injury or death.

Wear safety glasses, rubber gloves, and long sleeved clothing when cleaning powder residue from vehicle after an airbag deployment. Powder residue emitted from a deployed airbag can cause skin irritation. Flush affected area with cool water if irritation is experienced. If nasal or throat irritation is experienced, exit the vehicle for fresh air until the irritation ceases. If irritation continues, see a physician.

Do not use a replacement airbag that is not in the original packaging. This may result in improper deployment, personal injury, or death.

The factory installed fasteners, screws and bolts used to fasten airbag components have a special coating and are specifically designed for the airbag system. Do not use substitute fasteners. Use only original equipment fasteners listed in the parts catalog when fastener replacement is required.

During, and following, any child restraint anchor service, due to impact event or vehicle repair, carefully inspect all mounting hardware, tether straps, and anchors for proper installation, operation, or damage. If a child restraint anchor is found damaged in any way, the anchor must be replaced. Failure to do this may result in personal injury or death.

Deployed and non-deployed airbags may or may not have live pyrotechnic material within the airbag inflator.

Do not dispose of driver/passenger/curtain airbags or seat belt tensioners unless you are sure of complete deployment. Refer to the Hazardous Substance Control System for proper disposal.

Dispose of deployed airbags and tensioners consistent with state, provincial, local, and federal regulations.

After any airbag component testing or service, do not connect the battery negative cable. Personal injury or death may result if the system test is not performed first.

If the vehicle is equipped with the Occupant Classification System (OCS), do not connect the battery negative cable before performing the OCS Verification Test using the scan tool and the appropriate diagnostic information. Personal injury or death may result if the system test is not performed properly.

Never replace both the Occupant Restraint Controller (ORC) and the Occupant Classification Module (OCM) at the same time. If both require replacement, replace one, then perform the Airbag System test before replacing the other.

Both the ORC and the OCM store Occupant Classification System (OCS) calibration data, which they transfer to one another when one of them is replaced. If both are replaced at the same time, an irreversible fault will be set in both modules and the OCS may malfunction and cause personal injury or death.

If equipped with OCS, the Seat Weight Sensor is a sensitive, calibrated unit and must be handled carefully. Do not drop or handle roughly. If dropped or damaged, replace with another sensor. Failure to do so may result in occupant injury or death.

If equipped with OCS, the front passenger seat must be handled carefully as well. When removing the seat, be careful when setting on floor not to drop. If dropped, the sensor may be inoperative, could result in occupant injury, or possibly death.

If equipped with OCS, when the passenger front seat is on the floor, no one should sit in the front passenger seat. This uneven force may damage the sensing ability of the seat weight sensors. If sat on and damaged, the sensor may be inoperative, could result in occupant injury, or possibly death.

DISARMING THE SYSTEM

1. Disconnect and isolate the battery negative (ground) cable, then wait two minutes for the system capacitor to discharge before performing further diagnosis or service. This is the only sure way to disable the SRS. Failure to take the proper precautions could result in accidental airbag deployment.

ARMING THE SYSTEM

1. Reconnect the battery negative (ground) cable.

CLOCKSPRING CENTERING

2010 Models

See Figure 13.

⁂ CAUTION

To avoid serious or fatal injury on vehicles equipped with airbags, disable the Supplemental Restraint System (SRS) before attempting any steering wheel, steering column, airbag, seat belt tensioner, impact sensor or instrument panel component diagnosis or service. Disconnect and isolate the battery negative (ground) cable, then wait two minutes for the system capacitor to discharge before performing further diagnosis or service. This is the only sure way to disable the SRS. Failure to take the proper precautions could result in accidental airbag deployment.

➡A service replacement clockspring is shipped with the clockspring pre-centered and with a molded plastic locking pin installed. This locking pin should not be removed until the steering wheel has been installed on the steering column. If the locking pin is removed before the steering wheel is installed, the clockspring centering procedure must be performed.

➡When a clockspring is installed into a vehicle without properly centering and locking the entire steering system, the Steering Angle Sensor (SAS) data does not agree with the true position of the steering system and causes the Electronic Stability Program (ESP) system to shut down. This may also damage the clockspring without any immediate malfunction. Unlike some other Chrysler vehicles, this SAS never requires calibration. However, upon each new ignition ON cycle, the steering wheel must be rotated slightly to initialize the SAS.

➡Determining if the clockspring /SAS is centered is also possible electrically using the diagnostic scan tool. Steering wheel position is displayed as ANGLE with a range of up to 900 degrees. Refer to the appropriate menu item on the diagnostic scan tool.

➡Before starting this procedure, be certain to turn the steering wheel until the front wheels are in the straight-ahead position and that the entire steering system is locked or inhibited from rotation.

➡The clockspring may be centered and the rotor may be rotated freely once the steering wheel has been removed.

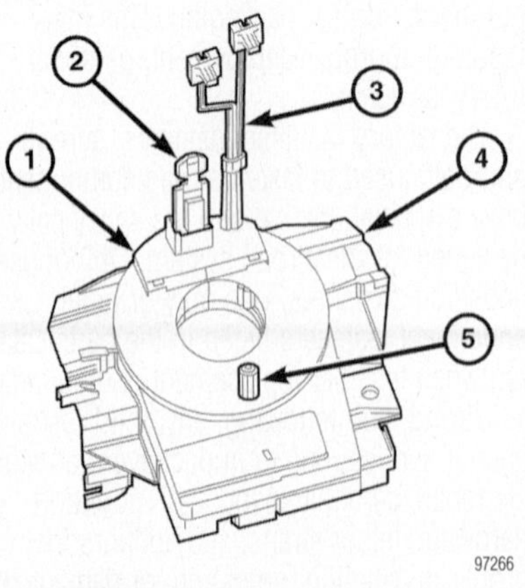

97266

Fig. 13 Rotate the clockspring rotor clockwise to the end of its travel

1. Place the front wheels in the straight-ahead position and inhibit the steering column shaft from rotation.
2. Remove the steering wheel from the steering shaft.
3. Rotate the clockspring rotor clockwise to the end of its travel. Do not apply excessive torque.
4. From the end of the clockwise travel, rotate the rotor about two and one-half turns counterclockwise. Turn the rotor slightly clockwise or counterclockwise as necessary so that the clockspring airbag pigtail wires and connector receptacle are at the top and the dowel or drive pin is at the bottom.
5. The clockspring is now centered. Secure the clockspring rotor to the clockspring case using a locking pin or some similar device to maintain clockspring centering until the steering wheel is reinstalled on the steering column.

2011 Models

See Figure 14.

⁂ CAUTION

To avoid serious or fatal injury on vehicles equipped with airbags, disable the Supplemental Restraint System (SRS) before attempting any steering wheel, steering column, airbag, seat belt tensioner, impact sensor or instrument panel component diagnosis or service. Disconnect and isolate the battery negative (ground) cable, then wait two minutes for the system capacitor to discharge before performing further diagnosis or service. This is the only sure way to disable the SRS. Failure to take the proper precautions could result in accidental airbag deployment.

⁂ WARNING

Always turn the steering wheel until the front wheels are in the straight-ahead position. Then, prior to disconnecting the steering column from the steering gear, lock the steering wheel to the steering column. If clockspring centering has been compromised for ANY reason, the entire Steering Column Control Module (SCCM) and clockspring unit MUST be replaced with a new unit.

Like the clockspring in a timepiece, the clockspring tape has travel limits and can be damaged by being wound too tightly during full stop-to-stop steering wheel rotation. To prevent this from occurring, the clockspring is centered when it is installed on the steering column. Centering the clockspring indexes the clockspring tape to the movable steering components so that the tape can operate within its designed travel limits. However, if the steering shaft is disconnected from the steering gear, the clockspring rotor spool can change position relative to the fixed steering components.

Clockspring centering must always be confirmed by viewing the inspection window on the clockspring rotor. If the black squares on the clockspring tape are not visible through the inspection window, clockspring centering has been compromised and the SCCM must be replaced with a new unit.

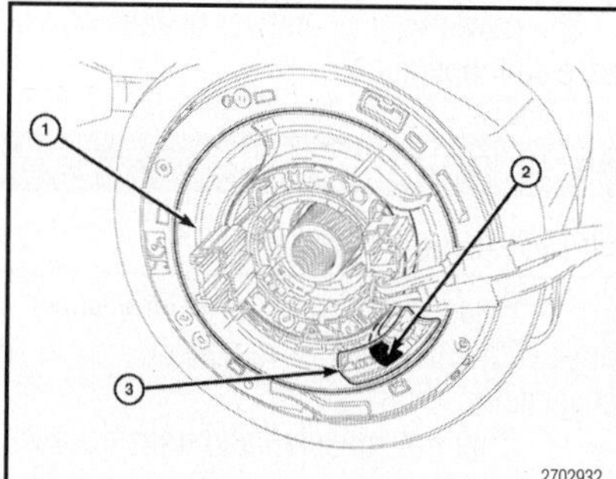

Fig. 14 Clockspring centering must always be confirmed by viewing the inspection window (3) on the clockspring rotor (1); if the black squares (2) on the clockspring tape are not visible through the inspection window, clockspring centering has been compromised and the SCCM must be replaced with a new unit

The service replacement SCCM is shipped with the clockspring pre-centered and with a red plastic locking tab installed. This locking tab should not be removed until the SCCM has been properly installed on the steering column. If the locking tab is removed before the SCCM is installed on a steering column, clockspring centering must be confirmed by viewing the black squares on the clockspring tape through the inspection window on the clockspring rotor. If the black squares of the clockspring tape are not visible through the inspection window, clockspring centering has been compromised and the SCCM must be replaced with a new unit. Proper clockspring installation may also be confirmed by viewing the Steering Angle Sensor (SAS) data using a diagnostic scan tool.

DRIVE TRAIN

AUTOMATIC TRANSMISSION FLUID

DRAIN AND REFILL

See Figure 15.

1. Hoist and support vehicle on safety stands.
2. Place a large diameter shallow drain pan beneath the transmission pan.
3. Remove bolts holding front and sides of pan to transmission.
4. Loosen bolts holding rear of pan to transmission.
5. Slowly separate front of pan away from transmission allowing the fluid to drain into drain pan.
6. Hold up pan and remove remaining bolts holding pan to transmission.
7. While holding pan level, lower pan away from transmission.
8. Pour remaining fluid in pan into drain pan.
9. Remove the screw holding the primary oil filter to valve body.
10. Separate filter from valve body and oil pump and pour fluid in filter into drain pan.
11. Inspect the oil filter seal in the bottom of the oil pump. If the seal is not installed completely in the oil pump, or is otherwise damaged, then remove and discard the oil filter seal from the bottom of the oil pump. If the seal is installed correctly and is in good condition, it can be reused.
12. If replacing the cooler return filter, use Oil Filter Wrench

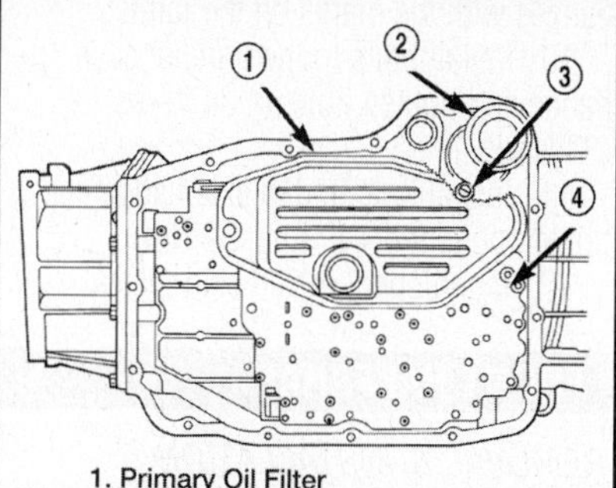

Fig. 15 Remove the screw holding the primary oil filter to valve body

13. to remove the filter from the transmission.
14. Dispose of used trans fluid and filter(s) properly.

To install:

WARNING

The primary oil filter seal MUST be fully installed flush against the oil pump body. DO NOT install the seal onto the filter neck and attempt to install the filter and seal as an assembly. Damage to the transmission will result.

15. If necessary, install a new primary oil filter seal in the oil pump inlet bore. Seat the seal in the bore with a suitable tool (appropriately sized drift or socket, the butt end of a hammer, or other suitable tool).
16. Place replacement filter in position on valve body and into the oil pump.
17. Install screw to hold the primary oil filter to valve body.
18. Install new cooler return filter onto the transmission, if necessary. Torque the filter to 7 ft. lbs. (10 Nm).
19. Place bead of Mopar® RTV sealant onto the transmission case sealing surface.
20. Place pan in position on transmission.
21. Install bolts to hold pan to transmission. Tighten bolts to 106 inch lbs. (12 Nm).
22. Lower vehicle and fill transmission with Mopar® ATF +4.
23. To avoid overfilling transmission after a fluid change or overhaul, perform the following procedure:
    a. Remove dipstick (if equipped) and insert clean funnel in transmission fill tube.
    b. Add following initial quantity of Mopar® ATF +4 to transmission:
        - If only fluid and filter were changed, add 10 pints (5 quarts) of ATF +4 to transmission.
        - If transmission was completely overhauled and the torque converter was replaced or drained, add 24 pints (12 quarts) of ATF +4 to transmission.
    c. Check the transmission fluid

FILTER REPLACEMENT

Refer to the above procedure.

TRANSFER CASE ASSEMBLY

REMOVAL & INSTALLATION

1. Shift transfer case into NEUTRAL.
2. Raise vehicle.
3. Remove transfer case drain plug and drain transfer case lubricant.
4. Support transmission with jack stand.
5. Remove rear crossmember and skid plate, if equipped.
6. Disconnect front propeller shaft from transfer case at companion flange. Remove rear propeller shaft from vehicle.

⁂ WARNING

Do not allow propshafts to hang at attached end. Damage to joint can result.

7. Disconnect the transfer case shift motor and mode sensor connector.
8. Disconnect transfer case vent hose.
9. Support transfer case with transmission jack.
10. Secure transfer case to jack with chains.
11. Remove nuts attaching transfer case to transmission.
12. Pull transfer case and jack rearward to disengage transfer case.
13. Remove transfer case from under vehicle.

To install:

14. Mount transfer case on a transmission jack.
15. Secure transfer case to jack with chains.
16. Position transfer case under vehicle.
17. Align transfer case and transmission shafts and install transfer case onto transmission.
18. Install and tighten transfer case attaching nuts to 26 ft. lbs. (35 Nm) torque.
19. Connect the transfer case vent hose to the transfer case.
20. Install rear crossmember and skid plate, if equipped.
21. Remove transmission jack and support stand.
22. Connect front propeller shaft and install rear propeller shaft.
23. Fill transfer case with correct fluid. Check transmission fluid level. Correct as necessary.
24. Install the transfer case fill plug. Tighten the plug to 15–25 ft. lbs. (20–34 Nm).
25. Connect the shift motor and mode sensor wiring connector.
26. Lower vehicle and verify transfer case shift operation.

FRONT DRIVESHAFT

REMOVAL & INSTALLATION

1. Place vehicle on floor or drive-on hoist with full weight of vehicle on suspension.
2. Shift transmission and transfer case in to Neutral.
3. If equipped, remove skid plate.
4. Mark a line across the C/V joints to companion flanges for installation reference.
5. Raise vehicle.
6. Remove bolts from C/V joints.
7. Push propeller shaft forward to clear transfer case companion flange and remove the shaft.

To install:

8. Install propeller shaft between companion flanges.
9. Align marks on the companion flanges with the marks on the joints.
10. Install bolts to the transfer case flange and tighten bolts to 24 ft. lbs. (32 Nm).
11. Install bolts to the axle flange and tighten bolts to 24 ft. lbs. (32 Nm).
12. If equipped, install skid plates.

FRONT HALFSHAFT

REMOVAL & INSTALLATION

1. Raise and safely support the vehicle.
2. Remove half shaft hub/bearing nut.
3. Remove wheel speed sensor nut from hub/bearing and remove sensor.
4. Remove brake calipers bolts and remove calipers from caliper adapters.
5. Remove lower stabilizer link bolt from control arm.
6. Remove outer tie rod end nuts and separate tie rods from knuckles with Remover
7. Remove upper ball joint nuts and separate ball joints from knuckles with Remover
8. Remove shock clevis bolt and nut from lower control arm
9. Lean the knuckle out and push half shaft out of the hub/bearing.
10. Pry half shafts from axle/axle tube with pry bar.

To install:

11. Install half shaft on the axle and through the hub/bearing. Verify half shaft has engaged.
12. Install shock clevis on lower control arm and tighten nut to specifications.
13. Install upper control arm on knuckle and tighten ball joint nut to specifications.
14. Install tie rod end on knuckle and tighten to specifications.
15. Install stabilizer link on lower control arm and tighten to specifications.
16. Install caliper on caliper adapter and tighten to specifications.
17. Install wheel speed sensor on the hub/bearing.
18. Install half shaft hub/bearing nut and tighten to 100 ft. lbs. (135 Nm).

FRONT PINION SEAL

REMOVAL & INSTALLATION

2010 Models

See Figures 16 through 19.

1. Remove wheels.
2. Push back brake pads and release hand brake.
3. Remove propeller shaft.

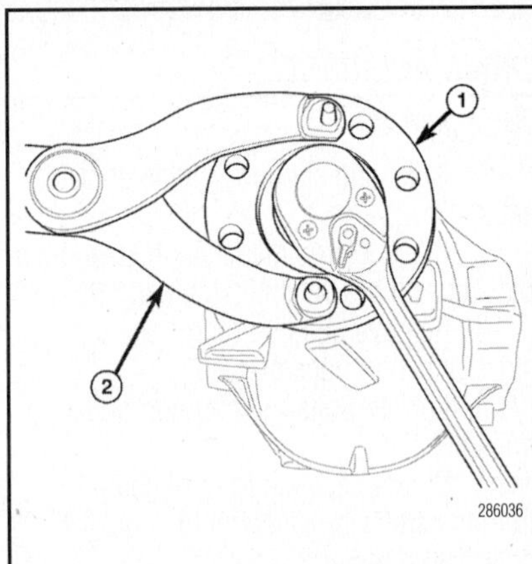

Fig. 16 Hold pinion flange (1) with flange wrench (2) and remove pinion nut

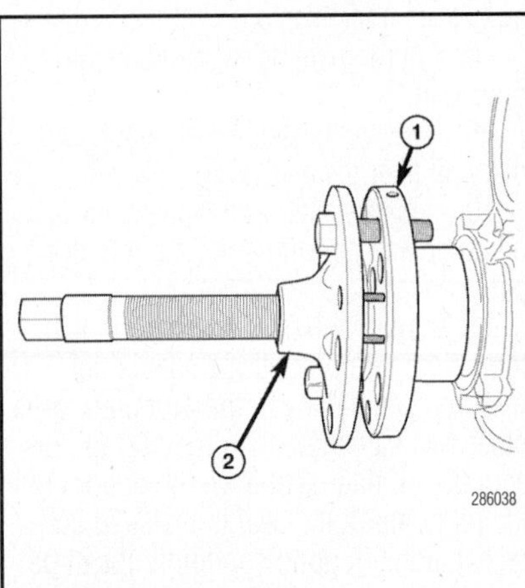

Fig. 17 Remove pinion flange (1) with puller (2)

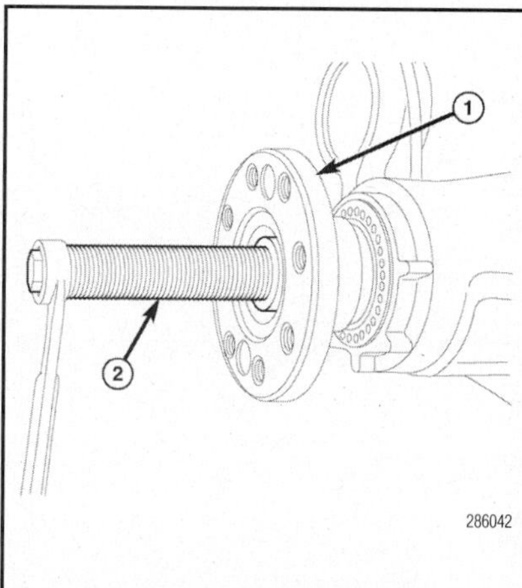

Fig. 18 Install pinion seal with seal installer and handle (2); pinion flange (1)

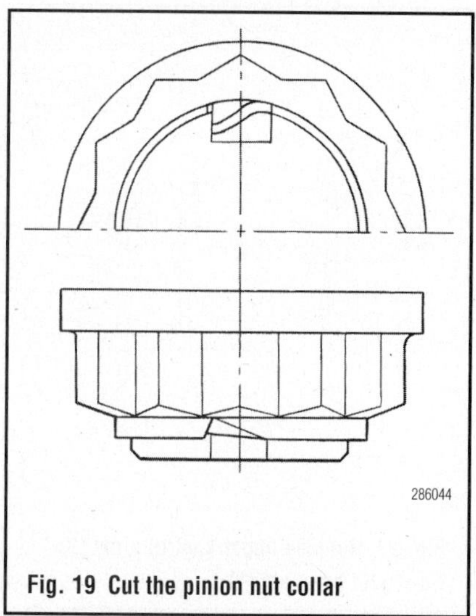

Fig. 19 Cut the pinion nut collar

4. Rotate pinion with inch pound torque and record torque to rotate.
5. Mark installation position of collared nut with respect to drive pinion.
6. Bend pinion nut lock back with a punch and hammer.
7. Hold pinion flange with flange wrench and remove pinion nut.
8. Mark a line across the pinion shaft and flange for installation reference.
9. Remove pinion flange with puller.
10. Remove pinion seal with a seal pick.

To install:

11. Install pinion seal with seal installer and handle.
12. Position pinion flange on pinion shaft with reference mark aligned.
13. Install pinion flange on pinion with flange Installer. Tap flange on pinion, then thread installer center bolt on pinion shaft and draw flange onto the pinion.
14. Install new pinion collared nut and carefully tighten nut in stages holding flange with flange wrench. Check torque to rotate after each stage, until previously value of torque to rotate is exceeded by 4.4 inch lbs. (0.5 Nm).
15. Cut the pinion nut collar.
16. Bend nut collar so it touches the wall of the slot in the pinion shaft.
17. Connect propeller shaft to pinion flange.
18. Install wheel and tires.
19. Operate brake pedal several times until brake pads contact brake discs (brake pressure built up).

2011 Models

See Figures 20 through 23.

1. Remove front axle assembly from vehicle.

➡Torque reading must be taken with a constant rotational speed. Do not measure break away torque.

2. Using a torque wrench, measure and record the pinion rotational torque.

➡Due to axle imbalance concerns, it is necessary to make sure pinion nut-to-shaft orientation is maintained. If alignment marks are not visible, apply appropriate marks before removing pinion nut.

3. Apply an alignment mark on the pinion flange nut to the pinion shaft.
4. Using Flange Wrench and 32mm socket, loosen the pinion flange nut.

➡Due to axle imbalance concerns, it is necessary to make sure pinion flange-to-shaft orientation is maintained. If alignment marks are not visible, apply appropriate marks before removing pinion flange.

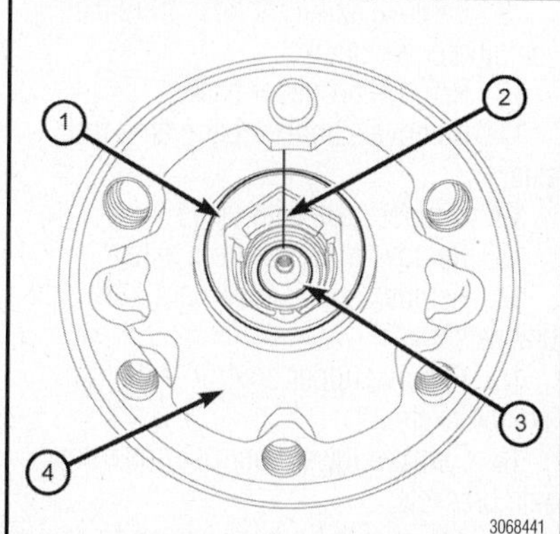

Fig. 20 Apply an alignment mark (2) on the pinion flange nut (1) to the pinion shaft (3)

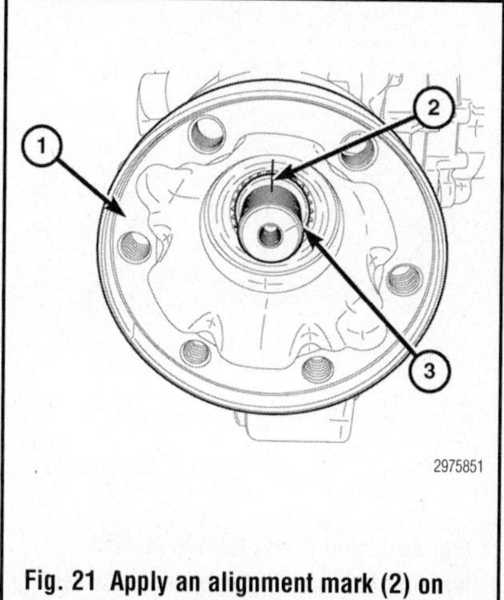

Fig. 21 Apply an alignment mark (2) on the pinion flange (1) to the pinion shaft (3)

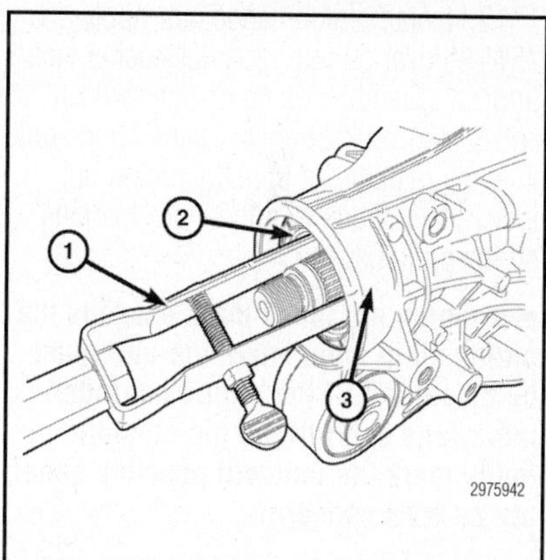

Fig. 22 Using seal remover (1) and slide hammer, remove pinion seal (2); front differential (3)

5. Apply an alignment mark on the pinion flange to the pinion shaft.
6. Using Puller, remove pinion flange from pinion shaft.
7. Using seal remover and slide hammer, remove pinion seal and discard.

To install:

8. Apply light coating of gear lubricant to the lip of the pinion seal.
9. Using Driver Handle and Installer, install pinion seal until tool bottoms on carrier.
10. Install pinion flange into position. Align index marks between pinion flange and pinion stem to maintain assembly balance and so that bearing preload is not exceeded.
11. Using Installer, lightly tap on pinion flange until adequate pinion shaft threads are exposed.
12. Clean any thread locker from pinion flange nut and apply Mopar® Lock and Seal Adhesive to the nut.

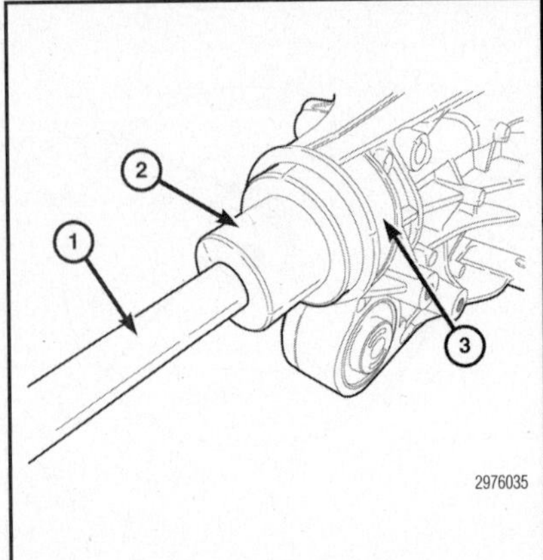

Fig. 23 Using Driver Handle (1) and Installer (2), install pinion seal until tool bottoms on carrier (3)

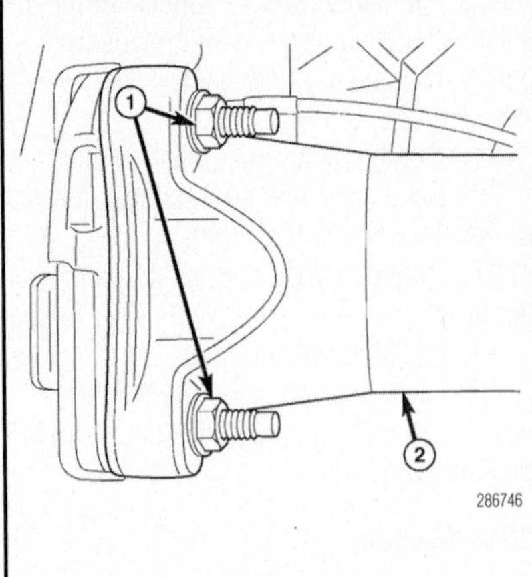

Fig. 24 Remove axle flange nuts (1) from axle (2)

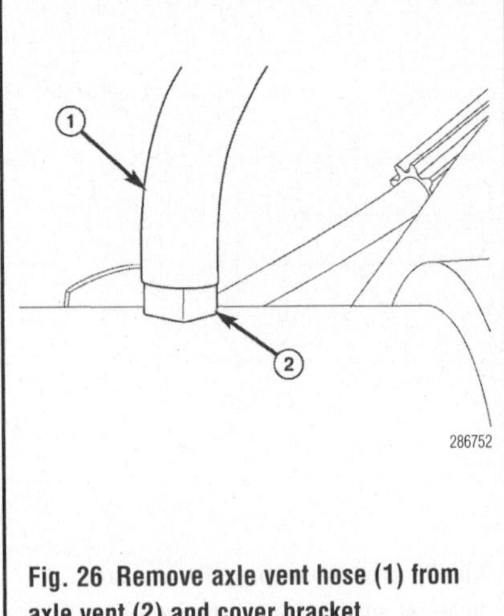

Fig. 26 Remove axle vent hose (1) from axle vent (2) and cover bracket

13. Install pinion flange nut. Apply 75W-85 gear oil to pinion nut washer face prior to assembly. Using Flange Wrench and 32mm socket tighten pinion flange nut in small increments until the pinion nut index mark aligns with the index marking on the pinion stem.

➡If pinion nut index mark exceeds the pinion stem index mark the unit must be discarded. If the pinion nut index mark falls short of the pinion stem index mark the unit will possibly generate an NVH concern.

➡Torque reading must be taken with a constant rotational speed. Do not measure break away torque.

14. Using a torque wrench, measure and record the pinion rotational torque.
15. After torque reading has been obtained, compare reading to the recorded reading when removing the pinion flange. The difference between the initial and final measurement will be the new seals drag torque only.
16. Install axle assembly.

REAR AXLE HOUSING

REMOVAL & INSTALLATION

2010 Models

See Figures 24 through 28.

1. With vehicle in neutral, position on hoist.
2. Remove differential cover and drain fluid.
3. Remove calipers and rotors.
4. Remove speed sensors from axle tube flange.
5. Remove axle flange nuts from axle.

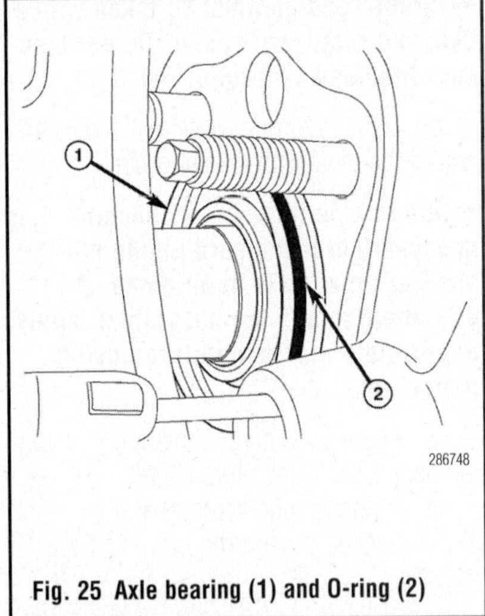

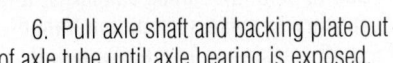

Fig. 25 Axle bearing (1) and O-ring (2)

6. Pull axle shaft and backing plate out of axle tube until axle bearing is exposed.
7. Remove O-ring from the axle bearing.
8. Remove axle shaft from axle tube and backing plate.
9. Remove axle vent hose from axle vent and cover bracket.
10. Remove propeller shaft.
11. Remove stabilizer bar clamp from axle.
12. Support axle with jack.
13. Remove track bar from axle.
14. Remove shock absorbers from axle brackets.
15. Remove upper control arms from axle brackets.
16. Remove lower control arms from axle brackets.
17. Lower axle from vehicle and remove coil springs and insulators.

To install:

18. Install coil springs and insulators. Raise axle into place.

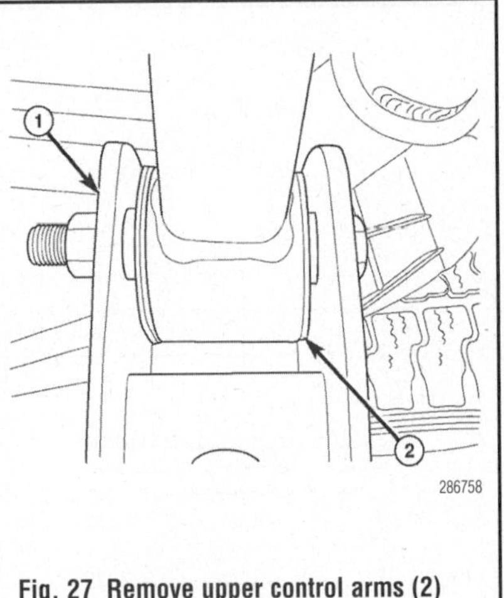

Fig. 27 Remove upper control arms (2) from axle brackets (1)

19. Install lower control arms to axle brackets.
20. Install upper control arms to axle brackets.
21. Install shock absorbers to axle brackets.
22. Install track bar to axle bracket.
23. Install stabilizer bar and clamps to axle.
24. Install propeller shaft.
25. Install axle vent hose to axle vent and cover bracket.

➡If a bearing flange stud is loose or has backed out tighten stud to 20 ft. lbs. (27 Nm).

26. Install axle shaft into axle tube and backing plate with new O-ring on axle.
27. Slip O-ring through backing plate, then push axle through backing plate until bearing is exposed.
28. Install O-ring axle bearing.
29. Push axle into axle tube.

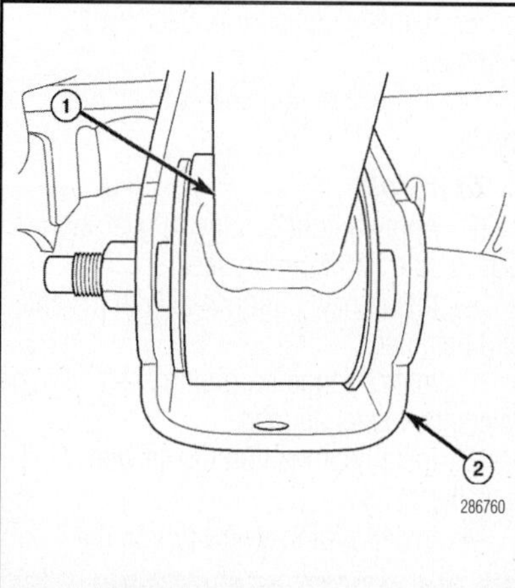
Fig. 28 Remove lower control arms (1) from axle brackets (2)

30. Install axle flange nuts and tighten to 88 ft. lbs. (119 Nm).
31. Install speed sensors in axle tube flange.
32. Install calipers and rotors.
33. Install differential cover, fill differential and install fill plug.

REAR AXLE SHAFT, BEARING & SEAL

REMOVAL & INSTALLATION

2010 Models

See Figures 24 and 25.

1. With vehicle in neutral, position on hoist.
2. Remove calipers and rotors.
3. Remove speed sensors from axle tube flange.
4. Remove axle flange nuts from axle.
5. Pull axle shaft and backing plate out of axle tube until axle bearing is exposed.
6. Remove O-ring from the axle bearing.
7. Remove axle shaft from axle tube and backing plate.
8. Tap axle shaft out of the bearing and axle flange through the plug hole with a hammer and brass drift.

To install:

9. Install axle shaft into axle bearing.
10. Install axle shaft into axle tube and backing plate with new O-ring on axle.
11. Slip O-ring through backing plate, then push axle through backing plate until bearing is exposed.
12. Install O-ring axle bearing.
13. Push axle into axle tube.
14. Install axle flange nuts and tighten to 88 ft. lbs. (119 Nm).
15. Install speed sensors in axle tube flange.
16. Install calipers and rotors.

REAR DRIVESHAFT

REMOVAL & INSTALLATION

**** WARNING**

Propeller shaft removal is a two-man operation. Never allow propeller shaft to hang from the center bearing, or while only connected to the transmission or rear axle flanges. A helper is required. If a propeller shaft section is hung unsupported, damage may occur to the shaft, coupler, and/or center bearing from over-angulation. This may result in driveline vibrations and/or component failure.

1. If equipped, remove skid plates
2. Remove the exhaust.
3. Raise and safely support the vehicle.

**** WARNING**

Failure to follow these instructions may result in a driveline vibration.

4. Mark propeller shaft to the pinion flange and transmission/transfer case flanges for installation reference.
5. Remove propeller shaft from axle pinion flange.
6. Remove the heat shield from the center bearing.
7. Remove the center support bearing.
8. With the aid of a helper, remove propeller shaft assembly.

To install:

➡Clean all propeller shaft bolts and apply Mopar® Lock and Seal Adhesive or equivalent to the threads before installation.

**** WARNING**

Failure to follow these instructions may result in a driveline vibration.

9. Install propeller shaft on transfer case or transmission with reference marks aligned. Install flange bolts and tighten to 80 ft. lbs. (108 Nm).
10. Install center bearing. Tighten to 20 ft. lbs. (27 Nm).
11. Install heat shield.
12. Install exhaust system.
13. If equipped, install skid plates.

REAR HALFSHAFT

REMOVAL & INSTALLATION

2011 Models

See Figures 29 through 32.

1. Remove the rear caliper and secure.
2. Remove the halfshaft nut.
3. Remove the wheel speed sensor bolt and remove the speed sensor.
4. Remove the toe link nut and bolt.
5. Remove the tension link nut and bolt.
6. Remove the camber link nut and bolt.
7. Swing rear knuckle outward as shown.
8. Remove the halfshaft from the hub.
9. Using a hammer or similar tool as a pivot point and a suitable screwdriver, carefully disengage both halfshafts from axle assembly using care not to damage dust seal.

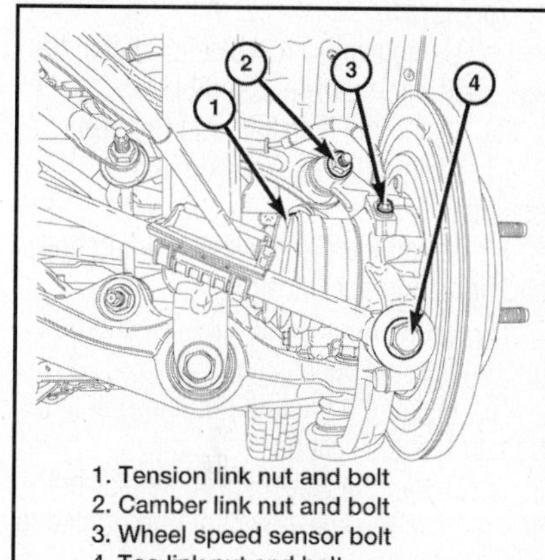

Fig. 29 Remove the wheel speed sensor bolt and remove the speed sensor

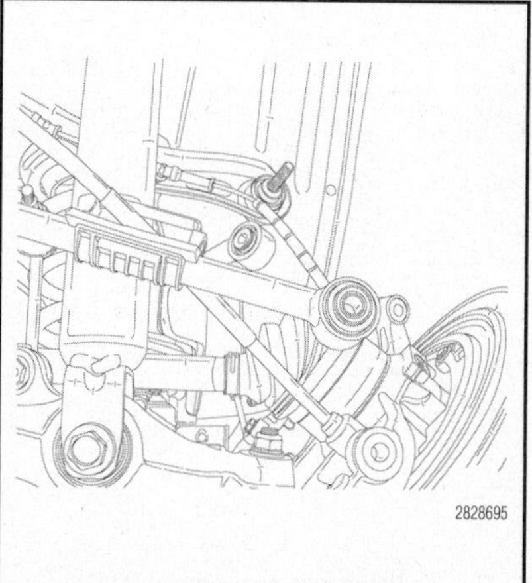

Fig. 30 Swing rear knuckle outward as shown

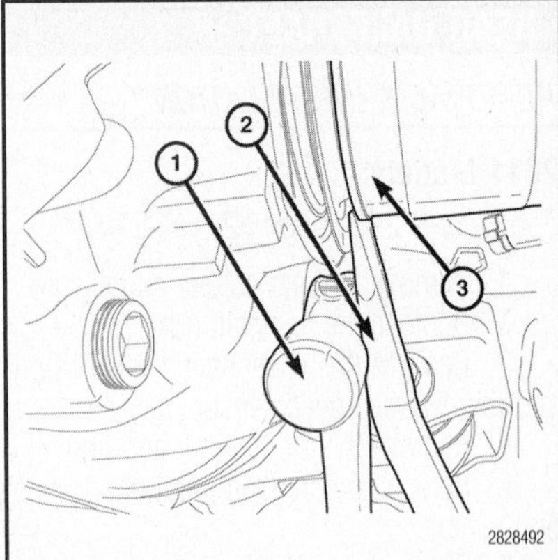

Fig. 31 Using a hammer or similar tool (1) as a pivot point and a suitable screwdriver (2), carefully disengage both halfshafts (3) from axle assembly using care not to damage dust seal

10. Carefully remove the halfshaft from the axel assembly. Use caution to protect axle seal and journal.

To install:

11. Using axle seal protector, install the half shaft into the axle assembly.
12. Install the halfshaft into the hub.
13. Swing the rear knuckle into position.
14. Install the camber link nut and bolt and tighten to specification.
15. Install the tension link nut and bolt and tighten to specification.
16. Install the toe link nut and bolt and tighten to specification.
17. Install the wheel speed sensor bolt and remove the speed sensor and tighten to specification.
18. Install the halfshaft nut and torque to 228 ft. lbs. (310 Nm).
19. Install the rear caliper.
20. Pump brake pedal until caliper pistons and brake pads are seated and a firm brake pedal is obtained.

REAR PINION SEAL

REMOVAL & INSTALLATION

2010 Models

See Figures 33 through 36.

1. Raise and safely support the vehicle.
2. Mark a reference line across the companion flange and propeller shaft flange.
3. Remove propeller shaft
4. Remove brake calipers and rotors to prevent any drag.
5. Rotate flange three or four times and verify flange rotates smoothly.
6. Measure torque to rotating pinion with a inch pound torque wrench. Record reading for installation reference.
7. Hold companion flange with wrench and remove pinion nut.
8. Remove companion flange with Remover.
9. Remove pinion seal with a seal puller.

To install:

10. Apply a light coating of gear lubricant on the lip of pinion seal.
11. Install new pinion seal with Installer and hammer.
12. Install flange on pinion shaft with the reference marks aligned.
13. Install companion flange with Installer.
14. Install pinion a new pinion nut.

**** WARNING**

Do not exceed the minimum tightening torque when installing the companion flange retaining nut at this point. Failure to follow these instructions can damage the collapsible spacer or bearings.

15. Hold companion flange with Wrench and tighten pinion nut to 220 ft. lbs. (298

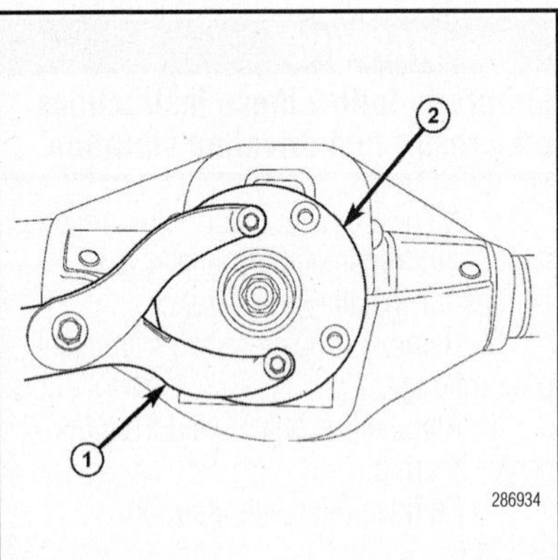

Fig. 33 Hold companion flange (2) with wrench (1) and remove pinion nut

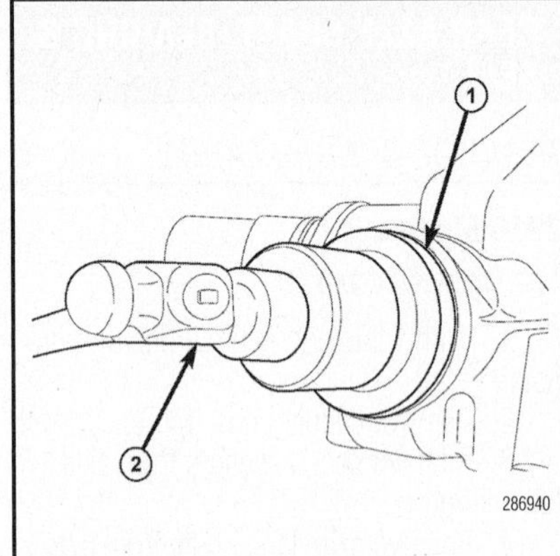

Fig. 35 Install new pinion seal with Installer (1) and hammer (2)

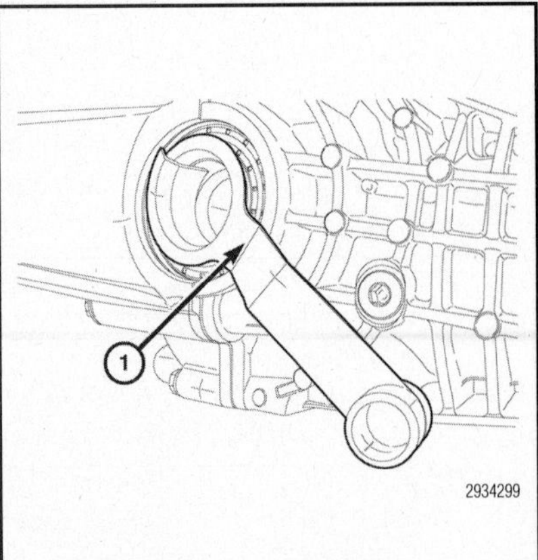

Fig. 32 Using axle seal protector (1), install the half shaft into the axle assembly

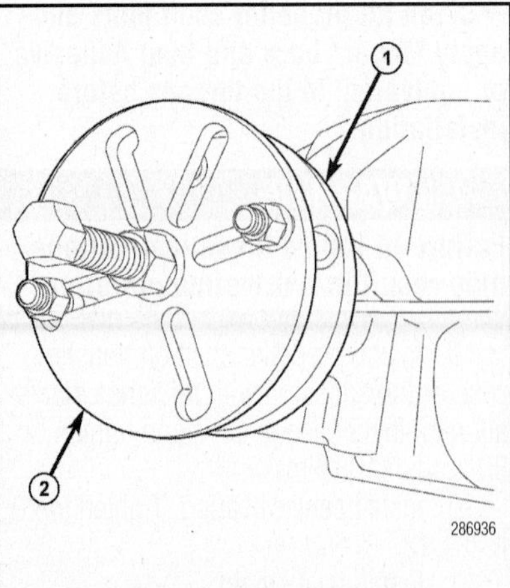

Fig. 34 Remove companion flange (1) with Remover (2)

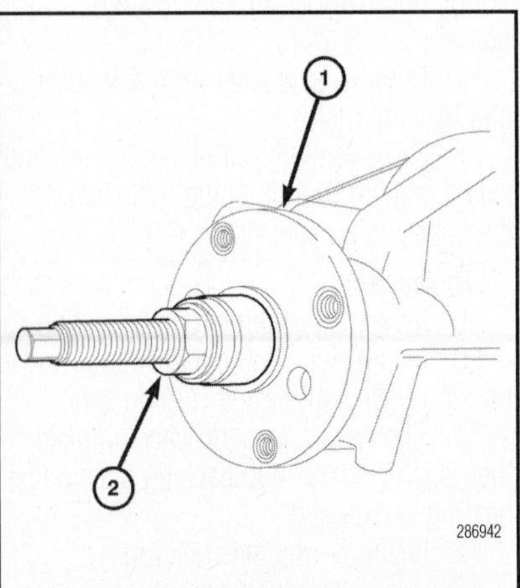

Fig. 36 Install companion flange (1) with Installer (2)

Nm). Rotate pinion several revolutions to ensure bearing rollers are seated.

16. Set torque wrench to 500 ft. lbs. (678 Nm) and tighten pinion nut in 5 ft. lbs. (6.8 Nm) increment until Pinion Torque To Rotate specification is achieved.

17. Measure pinion torque to rotate with an inch pound torque wrench. Torque To Rotating should be equal to the reading recorded during removal plus an additional 5 inch lbs. (0.56 Nm).

WARNING

Never loosen pinion nut to decrease pinion bearing rotating torque and never exceed specified preload torque. If rotating torque is exceeded, a new collapsible spacer must be installed. Failure to follow these instructions can damage the collapsible spacer or bearings.

18. If torque to rotating is low, tighten pinion nut in 5 ft. lbs. (6.8 Nm) increments until proper rotating torque is achieved.

➡**The bearing rotating torque should be constant during a complete revolution of the pinion. If the rotating torque varies, this indicates a binding condition.**

19. Install propeller shaft.

20. Install rear brake components.

2011 Models

See Figures 37 through 39.

1. Remove rear axle assembly from vehicle.

➡**Torque reading must be taken with a constant rotational speed. Do not measure break away torque.**

2. Using a torque wrench, measure and record the pinion rotational torque.

➡**Due to axle imbalance concerns and bearing preload sensitivity, it is necessary to make sure pinion nut-to-shaft orientation is maintained. If alignment marks are not visible, apply appropriate marks before removing pinion nut.**

3. Apply an alignment mark on the pinion flange nut to the pinion shaft.

➡**Due to axle imbalance concerns, it is necessary to make sure pinion nut-to-shaft orientation is maintained. If alignment marks are not visible, apply appropriate marks before removing pinion nut.**

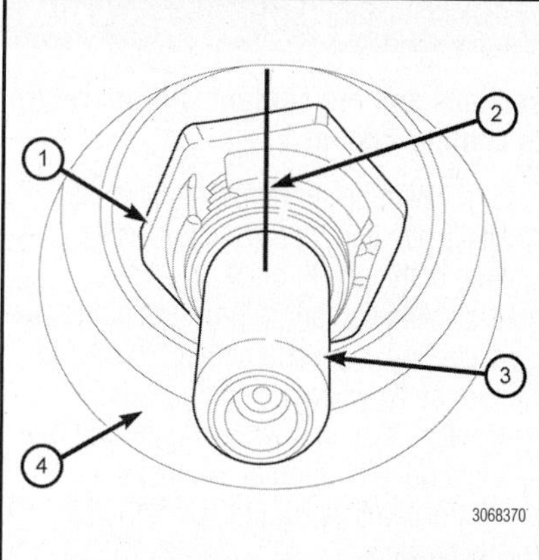

Fig. 37 Apply an alignment mark (2) on the pinion flange nut (1) to the pinion shaft (3)

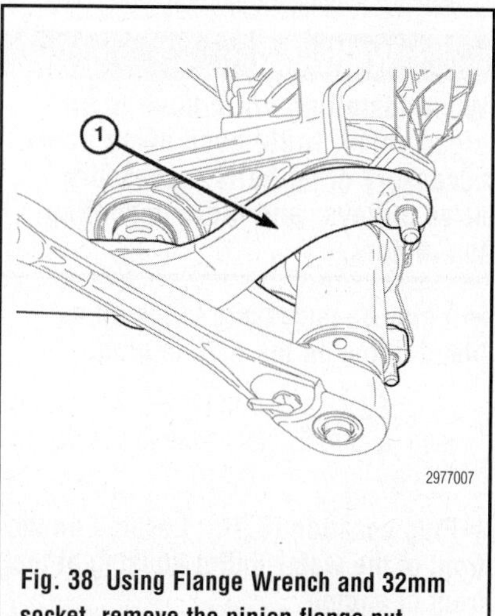

Fig. 38 Using Flange Wrench and 32mm socket, remove the pinion flange nut

4. Apply an alignment mark on the pinion flange nut to the pinion shaft.

5. Using Flange Wrench and 32mm socket, remove the pinion flange nut.

➡**Due to axle imbalance concerns, it is necessary to make sure pinion flange-to-shaft orientation is maintained. If alignment marks are not visible, apply appropriate marks before removing pinion flange.**

6. Apply an alignment mark on the pinion flange to the pinion shaft.

7. Using Puller, remove pinion flange from pinion shaft.

8. Using seal remover and slide hammer, remove pinion seal and discard.

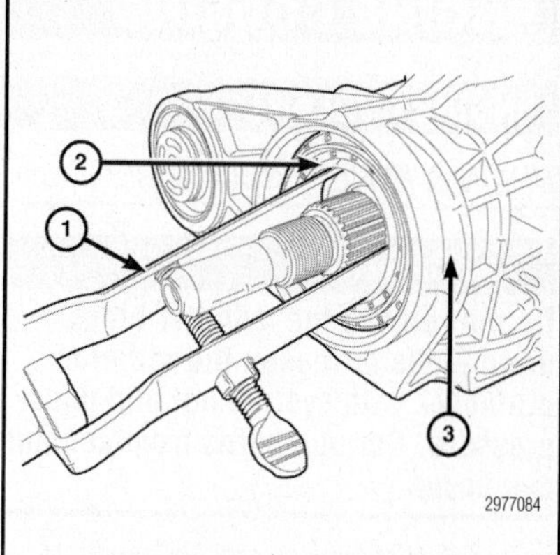

Fig. 39 Using seal remover (1) and slide hammer, remove pinion seal (2); carrier (3)

To install:

9. Apply light coating of gear lubricant to the lip of the pinion seal.

10. Using Driver Handle and Installer, install pinion seal until tool bottoms on carrier.

11. Install pinion flange into position. Align index marks to maintain assembly balance.

12. Using Installer, lightly tap on pinion flange until adequate pinion shaft threads are exposed.

13. Clean any thread locker from pinion flange nut and apply Mopar® Lock and Seal Adhesive to the nut.

14. Install pinion flange nut. Apply gear oil to pinion nut washer face prior to assembly. Using Flange Wrench and 32mm socket tighten pinion flange nut in small increments until the pinion nut index mark aligns with the index marking on the pinion stem.

➡**If pinion nut index mark exceeds the pinion stem index mark the unit must be discarded. If the pinion nut index mark falls short of the pinion stem index mark the unit will possibly generate an Noise, Vibration, or Harshness (NVH) concern.**

➡**Torque reading must be taken with a constant rotational speed. Do not measure break away torque.**

15. Using a torque wrench, measure and record the pinion rotational torque.

16. After torque reading has been obtained, compare reading to the recorded reading when removing the pinion flange. The difference between the initial and final measurement will be the new seals drag torque only.

17. Install axle assembly.

ENGINE COOLING

ENGINE COOLANT

DRAIN & REFILL PROCEDURE

CAUTION

Do not remove the cylinder block drain plugs or loosen the radiator draincock with system hot and under pressure. Serious burns from coolant can occur.

1. DO NOT remove radiator cap first. With engine cold, raise vehicle on a hoist and locate radiator draincock.

➡Radiator draincock is located on the right/lower side of radiator facing to rear of vehicle.

2. Attach one end of a hose to the draincock. Put the other end into a clean container. Open draincock and drain coolant from radiator. This will empty the coolant reserve/overflow tank. The coolant does not have to be removed from the tank unless the system is being refilled with a fresh mixture. When tank is empty, remove radiator cap and continue draining cooling system.

To install:

3. For the 3.7L Engine, perform the following steps:
   a. Tighten the radiator draincock and the cylinder block drain plug(s) (if removed).

WARNING

Failure to purge air from the cooling system can result in an overheating condition and severe engine damage.

   b. Fill cooling system with the antifreeze mixture. Fill pressure bottle to service line and install cap.

➡The engine cooling system will push any remaining air into the coolant bottle within about an hour of normal driving. As a result, a drop in coolant level in the pressure bottle may occur.

➡If the engine cooling system overheats and pushes coolant into the overflow side of the coolant bottle, this coolant will be sucked back into the cooling system ONLY IF THE PRESSURE CAP IS LEFT ON THE BOTTLE. Removing the pressure cap breaks the vacuum path between the two bottle sections and the coolant will not return to cooling system.

   c. With heater control unit in the HEAT position, operate engine with pressure bottle cap in place.
   d. Add coolant to pressure bottle as necessary. Only add coolant to the pressure bottle when the engine is cold. Coolant level in a warm engine will be higher due to thermal expansion.
4. For the 5.7L engine, perform the following steps:
   a. Close radiator draincock. Hand tighten only.
   b. Install engine block drain plugs, if removed. Coat the threads with Mopar® Thread Sealant with Teflon.

WARNING

When installing drain hose to air bleed valve, route hose away from accessory drive belts, accessory drive pulleys, and electric cooling fan motors.

➡It may be necessary to install a bleed fitting on the 5.7L engine.

   c. Attach a 4–6 ft. (1.5–2 m) long ¼ inch (6 mm) ID clear hose to bleeder fitting

➡Plug Location (5.7L): Located on the front of the water outlet housing at the front of engine.

   d. Route hose away from the accessory drive belt, drive pulleys and electric cooling fan. Place the other end of hose into a clean container. The hose will prevent coolant from contacting the accessory drive belt when bleeding the system during the refilling operation.

➡It is imperative that the cooling system air bleed valve be opened before any coolant is added to the cooling system. Failure to open the bleed valve first will result in an incomplete fill of the system.

   e. 5.7L Engine—Install a threaded and barbed fitting (¼ to 18 npt) into water pump housing.
   f. Attach Filling Aid Funnel Tool to pressure bottle filler neck.
   g. Using hose pinch-off pliers, pinch overflow hose that connects between the two chambers of the coolant bottle.
   h. Open bleed fitting.
   i. Pour the coolant into the larger section of Filling Aid Funnel (the smaller section of funnel is to allow air to escape).
   j. Slowly fill the cooling system until a steady stream of coolant flows from the hose attached to the bleed valve.
   k. Close the bleed valve and continue filling system to the top of the Filling Aid Funnel Tool.
   l. Remove pinch-off pliers from overflow hose.
   m. Allow the coolant in Filling Funnel to drain into overflow chamber of the pressure bottle.
   n. Remove Filling Aid Funnel Tool
   o. Install cap on coolant pressure bottle.
   p. Remove hose from bleed valve.
   q. Install fitting into thermostat housing. Coat the threads with Mopar® Thread Sealant with Teflon.
   r. Start engine and run at 1500–2000 RPM for 30 minutes.

➡The engine cooling system will push any remaining air into the coolant bottle within about an hour of normal driving. As a result, a drop in coolant level in the pressure bottle may occur.

➡If the engine cooling system overheats and pushes coolant into the overflow side of the coolant bottle, this coolant will be sucked back into the cooling system ONLY IF THE PRESSURE CAP IS LEFT ON THE BOTTLE. Removing the pressure cap breaks the vacuum path between the two bottle sections and the coolant will not return to cooling system.

   s. Shut off engine and allow it to cool down for 30 minutes. This permits coolant to be drawn into the pressure chamber.
   t. With engine COLD, observe coolant level in pressure chamber. Coolant level should be within MIN and MAX marks. Adjust coolant level as necessary.

FLUSHING

WARNING

The cooling system normally operates at 14–18 psi (97–124 kPa) pressure. Exceeding this pressure may damage the radiator or hoses.

1. Reverse flushing of the cooling system is the forcing of water through the cool-

ing system. This is done using air pressure in the opposite direction of normal coolant flow. It is usually only necessary with very dirty systems with evidence of partial plugging.

Chemical Cleaning

1. If visual inspection indicates the formation of sludge or scaly deposits, use a radiator cleaner (Mopar® Radiator Kleen or equivalent) before flushing. This will soften scale and other deposits and aid the flushing operation.

✻✻ WARNING

Be sure instructions on the container are followed.

Reverse Flushing Radiator

1. Disconnect the radiator hoses from the radiator fittings. Attach a section of radiator hose to the radiator bottom outlet fitting and insert the flushing gun. Connect a water supply hose and air supply hose to the flushing gun.

✻✻ WARNING

The cooling system normally operates at 14–18 psi (97–124 kPa) pressure. Exceeding this pressure may damage the radiator or hoses.

2. Allow the radiator to fill with water. When radiator is filled, apply air in short blasts allowing radiator to refill between blasts. Continue this reverse flushing until clean water flows out through rear of radiator cooling tube passages. For more information, refer to operating instructions supplied with flushing equipment. Have radiator cleaned more extensively by a radiator repair shop.

Reverse Flushing Engine

1. Drain the cooling system. Remove the thermostat housing and thermostat. Install the thermostat housing. Disconnect the radiator upper hose from the radiator and attach the flushing gun to the hose. Disconnect the radiator lower hose from the water pump. Attach a lead away hose to the water pump inlet fitting.

✻✻ WARNING

Be sure that the heater control valve is closed (heat off). This is done to prevent coolant flow with scale and other deposits from entering the heater core.

2. Connect the water supply hose and air supply hose to the flushing gun. Allow the engine to fill with water. When the engine is filled, apply air in short blasts, allowing the system to fill between air blasts. Continue until clean water flows through the lead away hose. For more information, refer to operating instructions supplied with flushing equipment.
3. Remove the lead away hose, flushing gun, water supply hose and air supply hose. Remove the thermostat housing. Install the thermostat and housing with a replacement gasket. Connect the radiator hoses. Refill the cooling system with the correct antifreeze/water mixture.

ENGINE FAN

REMOVAL & INSTALLATION

2010 Models

3.7L Engine

See Figure 40.

1. Disconnect electric fan connector.
2. Remove shroud mounting bolts.
3. Remove shroud and fan assembly from vehicle.
4. Remove fan assembly mounting bolts and remove fan from shroud.

To install:

5. Position fan assembly on shroud.
6. Install fan to fan shroud mounting nuts.
7. Position fan and shroud assembly in vehicle.
8. Install shroud mounting bolts.
9. Connect electric fan electrical connector.
10. Start engine and check fan operation.

5.7L Engine

See Figure 41.

1. Raise vehicle on hoist.
2. Drain cooling system.

➡The hydraulic fan drive is driven by the power steering pump. When removing lines or hoses from fan drive assembly use a drain pan to catch any power steering fluid that may exit the fan drive or the lines and hoses.

➡Whenever the high pressure line fittings are removed from the hydraulic fan drive the O-rings must be replaced.

3. Disconnect two high pressure lines at hydraulic fan drive. Remove and discard O-rings from line fittings.
4. Disconnect low pressure return hose at hydraulic fan drive.

➡The lower mounting bolts can only be accessed from under vehicle.

5. Remove two lower mounting bolts from the shroud.
6. Lower vehicle.
7. Disconnect the electrical connector for the fan control solenoid.
8. Disconnect the radiator upper hose at the radiator and position out of the way.
9. Disconnect the power steering gear outlet hose and fluid return hose at the cooler.
10. Remove two upper mounting bolts from the shroud.

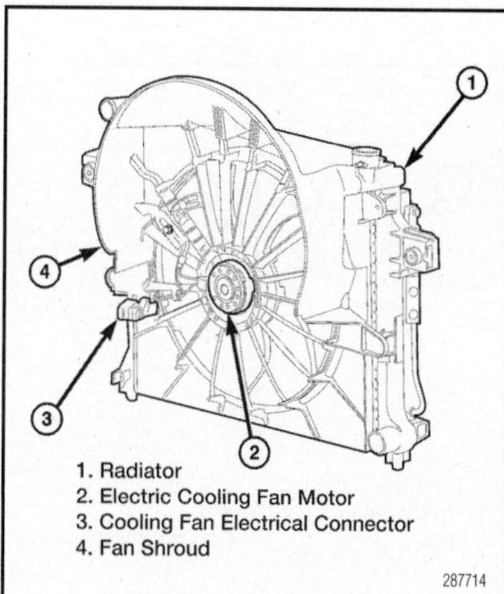

Fig. 40 Radiator cooling fan assembly

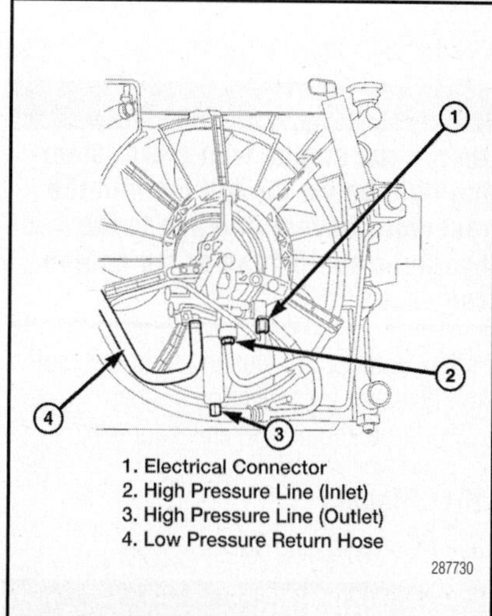

Fig. 41 Disconnect two high pressure lines at hydraulic fan drive

11. Remove the shroud and fan drive from vehicle.

To install:

⁂ WARNING

There is an external ground wire connected to the hydraulic fan drive located at the electrical connector on the fan assembly. This ground MUST remain connected at all times. Failure to ensure ground wire is connected when engine is operating can cause severe damage to the JTEC module.

12. Position fan drive and shroud in vehicle.
13. Install fan shroud upper mounting bolts. Do not tighten at this time.
14. Install radiator upper hose onto radiator.
15. Connect power steering cooler hoses.
16. Raise vehicle on hoist.
17. Install fan shroud lower mounting bolts.

➡Whenever the high pressure line fittings are removed from the hydraulic fan drive the O-rings located on the fittings must be replaced.

18. Lubricate the O-rings on the fittings with power steering fluid then connect inlet and outlet high pressure lines to fan drive. Tighten inlet line to 36 ft. lbs. (49 Nm), tighten outlet line to 22 ft. lbs. (29 Nm).
19. Connect low pressure return hose to fan drive.
20. Lower vehicle.
21. Install radiator upper hose.
22. Connect electrical connector for hydraulic fan control solenoid.
23. Tighten fan shroud upper mounting bolts.
24. Refill cooling system.

⁂ WARNING

Do not run engine with power steering fluid below the full mark in the reservoir. Severe damage to the hydraulic cooling fan or the engine can occur.

25. Refill power steering fluid reservoir and bleed air from steering system.
26. Run engine and check for leaks.

2011 Models

See Figures 42 and 43.

⁂ WARNING

Care must be used when trying to remove the upper and lower shroud covers. Damaging the holes in the cover may cause it to become loose and not perform properly.

1. Disconnect negative battery cable.
2. Remove the air intake assembly.
3. Raise vehicle.

➡The lower shroud cover needs to be removed in order to remove the cooling fan assembly from the mounting tabs.

4. If equipped, remove the lower engine shield.
5. Remove the lower shroud cover by using a pick to pull the cover retaining hole away from the clip along the bottom of the cooling fan assembly.
6. Lower vehicle.
7. Disconnect electric fan connector.

➡The cooling fan assembly is held in place by clips that are part of the radiator. So care must be used so the clips are not damaged during fan removal.

8. Remove shroud assembly from vehicle by pressing the locking clips inwards with a flat blade screwdriver.
9. Pull the fan/shroud assembly upwards and away from the radiator with the upper cooling fan assembly shroud cover in place.
10. Remove the cooling fan assembly from vehicle.
11. Remove the upper fan shroud cover by using a pick to pull the cover retaining hole away from the clip.

To install:

12. Install the upper shroud cover. Apply pressure downwards until the cover snaps into place past clips.
13. Install cooling fan assembly into vehicle.
14. Guide the fan/shroud cover assembly into position between the radiator and upper core support.
15. Position cooling fan assembly onto the mounts located on the radiator.
16. Lock in the fan assembly into place by pressing down firmly on the shroud till the locks engage.
17. Connect electric fan electrical connector.
18. Raise the vehicle.
19. Install the lower cooling shroud cover by applying upwards pressure till the cover snaps into place onto the cooling fan shroud.
20. If equipped, install the lower engine cover.
21. Lower vehicle.
22. Connect negative battery cable.
23. Install the air intake assembly.
24. Start engine and check fan operation.

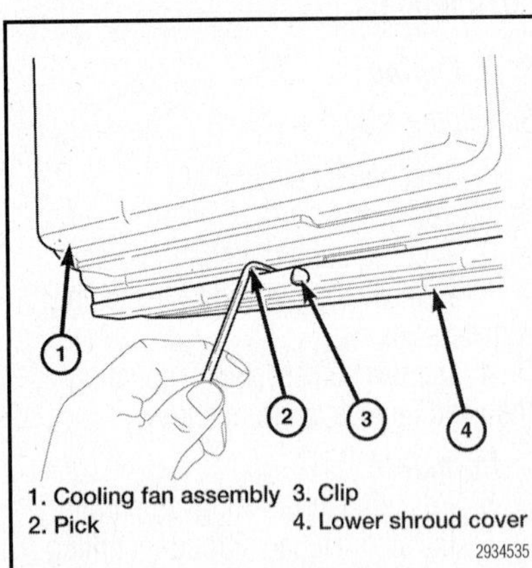

Fig. 42 Remove the lower shroud cover by using a pick to pull the cover retaining hole away from the clip along the bottom of the cooling fan assembly

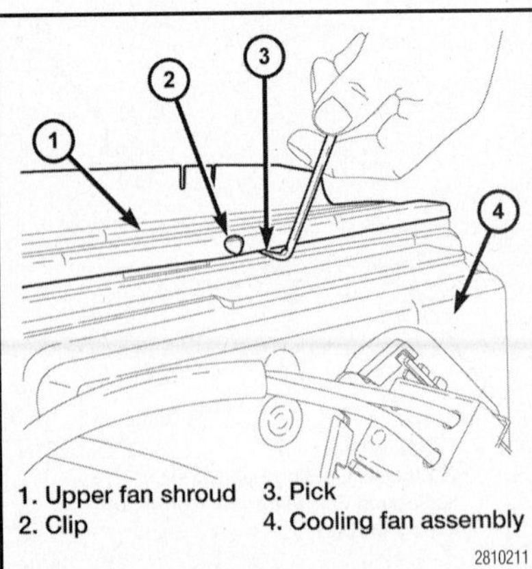

Fig. 43 Remove the upper fan shroud cover by using a pick to pull the cover retaining hole away from the clip

RADIATOR

REMOVAL & INSTALLATION

2010 Models

See Figures 44 and 45.

⁂ CAUTION

Do not remove the cylinder block drain plugs or loosen the radiator draincock with the system hot and under pressure. Serious burns from coolant can occur. Refer to cooling system draining.

➡Do not waste reusable coolant. If the solution is clean, drain the coolant into a clean container for reuse.

✱✱ CAUTION

Constant tension hose clamps are used on most cooling system hoses. When removing or installing, use only tools designed for servicing this type of clamp. Always wear safety glasses when servicing constant tension clamps.

✱✱ WARNING

A number or letter is stamped into the tongue of constant tension clamps. If replacement is necessary, use only an original equipment clamp with matching number or letter.

✱✱ WARNING

When removing the radiator or A/C condenser for any reason, note the location of all radiator-to-body and radiator-to-A/C condenser rubber air seals. These are used at the top, bottom and sides of the radiator and A/C condenser. To prevent overheating, these seals must be installed to their original positions.

1. Disconnect the negative battery cable at battery.
2. 5.7L Engine—Drain power steering fluid from reservoir.
3. Drain coolant from radiator.
4. Remove the front grille.
5. Remove two radiator mounting bolts.
6. 5.7L Engine—Disconnect the low pressure hose to the hydraulic fan drive. Re-position the spring clamp.
7. Disconnect both transmission cooler lines from radiator.

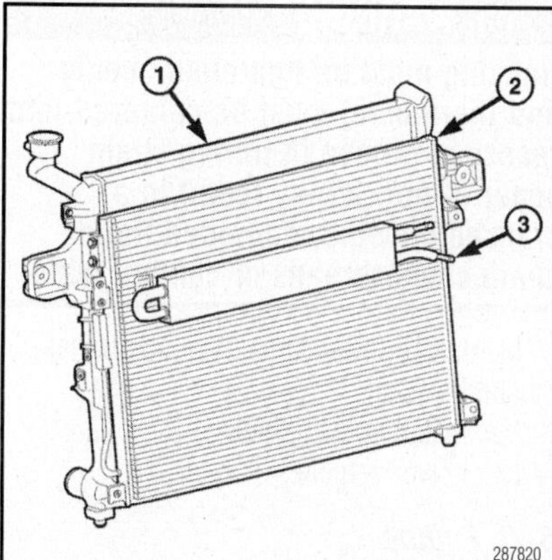

Fig. 44 Radiator (1), A/C condenser/transmission cooler assembly (2), and power steering cooler (3)

8. Disconnect the line from power steering cooler and filter.
9. Disconnect the radiator upper and lower hoses.
10. Disconnect the overflow hose from radiator.
11. 5.7L Engine—Disconnect electric connector for hydraulic fan control solenoid.
12. Remove the air inlet duct at the grille.
13. Disconnect radiator fan electrical connector.
14. The lower part of radiator is equipped with two alignment dowel pins. They are located on the bottom of radiator tank and fit into rubber grommets. These rubber grommets are pressed into the radiator lower crossmember.

✱✱ CAUTION

The air conditioning system (if equipped) is under a constant pressure even with the engine off. Refer to refrigerant warnings in, heating and air conditioning before handling any air conditioning component.

➡The radiator and radiator cooling fan can be removed as an assembly. It is not necessary to remove the cooling fan before removing or installing the radiator.

15. Gently lift up and remove radiator from vehicle. Be careful not to scrape the radiator fins against any other component. Also be careful not to disturb the air conditioning condenser (if equipped).

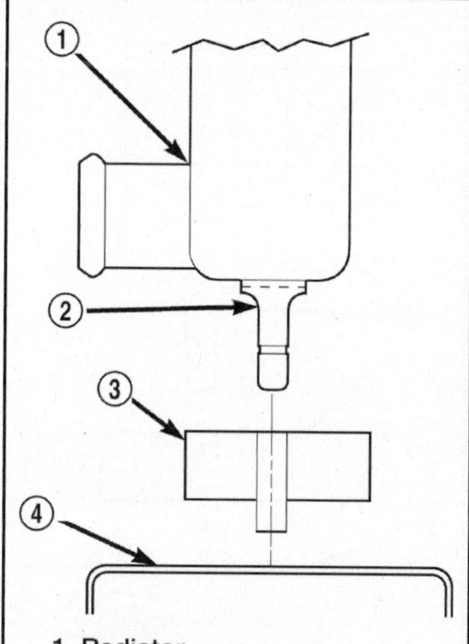

Fig. 45 The lower part of radiator is equipped with two alignment dowel pins

To install:

16. Equipped with air conditioning: Gently lower the radiator and fan shroud into the vehicle. Guide the two radiator alignment dowels through the holes in the rubber air seals first and then through the A/C support brackets. Continue to guide the alignment dowels into the rubber grommets located in lower radiator crossmember. The holes in the L-shaped brackets (located on bottom of A/C condenser) must be positioned between bottom of rubber air seals and top of rubber grommets.
17. Connect the radiator upper and lower hoses and hose clamps to radiator.

✱✱ WARNING

The tangs on the hose clamps must be positioned straight down.

18. Install coolant reserve/overflow tank hose at radiator.
19. Connect both transmission cooler lines at the radiator.
20. Install both radiator mounting bolts.
21. Install air inlet duct at grille.
22. 5.7L Engine—Attach electric connector for hydraulic fan control solenoid.
23. Install the grille.
24. Connect the two high pressure lines to the hydraulic fan drive. Tighten ½ inch pressure line fitting to 36 ft. lbs. (49 Nm). and the ⅜ inch pressure line fitting to 21 ft. lbs. (29 Nm).
25. 5.7L Engine—Connect the low pressure hose to the hydraulic fan drive. Position the spring clamp.
26. Connect the power steering filter hoses to the filter. Install new hose clamps.
27. Rotate the fan blades (by hand) and check for interference at fan shroud.
28. Refill cooling system.
29. 5.7L Engine—Refill the power steering reservoir and bleed air from system.
30. Connect battery cable at battery.
31. Start and warm engine. Check for leaks.

2011 Models

See Figure 46.

✱✱ CAUTION

Do not remove the cylinder block drain plugs or loosen the radiator draincock with the system hot and under pressure. Serious burns from coolant can occur. Refer to cooling system draining.

➡Do not waste reusable coolant. If the solution is clean, drain the coolant into a clean container for reuse.

⁂ CAUTION

Constant tension hose clamps are used on most cooling system hoses. When removing or installing, use only tools designed for servicing this type of clamp. Always wear safety glasses when servicing constant tension clamps.

⁂ WARNING

A number or letter is stamped into the tongue of constant tension clamps. If replacement is necessary, use only an original equipment clamp with matching number or letter.

⁂ WARNING

When removing the radiator or A/C condenser for any reason, note the location of all radiator-to-body and radiator-to-A/C condenser rubber air seals. These are used at the top, bottom and sides of the radiator and A/C condenser. To prevent overheating, these seals must be installed to their original positions.

1. Disconnect the negative battery cable at battery.
2. Drain coolant from radiator.
3. Remove the A/C condenser.
4. Remove the upper radiator crossmember.
5. Disconnect the upper radiator hose.
6. Disconnect the overflow hose from radiator.
7. Remove the cooling fan assembly.
8. Remove the lower radiator hose from the water pump.
9. The lower part of the radiator is equipped with two alignment dowel pins and fit into rubber grommets. These rubber grommets are pressed onto the radiator.
10. Gently lift up and remove radiator from vehicle. Be careful not to scrape the radiator fins against any other component.
11. Remove the lower radiator hose from the radiator.

To install:

⁂ WARNING

Before installing the radiator or A/C condenser, be sure the radiator-to-body and radiator-to-A/C condenser rubber air seals are properly fastened to their original positions. These are used at the top, bottom and sides of the radiator and A/C condenser. To prevent overheating, these seals must be installed to their original positions.

12. Gently lower the radiator into the vehicle. Guide the two radiator rubber air seals into the lower radiator support.

⁂ WARNING

The tangs on the hose clamps must be positioned straight down.

13. Install the lower radiator hose to the lower radiator outlet.
14. Install the cooling fan assembly.
15. Install coolant reserve/overflow tank hose at radiator.
16. Install the upper radiator hose.
17. Install the upper radiator crossmember. Align the upper radiator alignment dowel into the upper isolators.
18. Install the A/C condenser.
19. Refill cooling system.
20. Refill the power steering reservoir and bleed air from system.
21. Connect battery cable at battery.
22. Start and warm engine. Check for leaks.

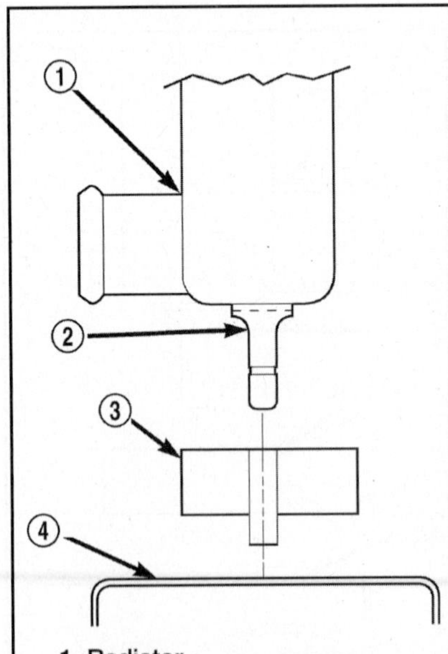

Fig. 46 The lower part of radiator is equipped with two alignment dowel pins

THERMOSTAT

REMOVAL & INSTALLATION

2010 Models

3.7L Engine

⁂ CAUTION

Do not loosen radiator draincock with system hot and pressurized. Serious burns from coolant can occur.

➡Do not waste reusable coolant. If solution is clean, drain coolant into a clean container for reuse.

➡If thermostat is being replaced, be sure that replacement is specified thermostat for vehicle model and engine type.

1. Disconnect negative battery cable at battery.
2. Drain cooling system.
3. Raise vehicle on hoist.
4. Remove splash shield.
5. Remove lower radiator hose clamp and lower radiator hose at thermostat housing.
6. Remove thermostat housing mounting bolts, thermostat housing and thermostat.

To install:

7. Clean mating areas of timing chain cover and thermostat housing.
8. Install thermostat with the spring side down into recessed machined groove on timing chain cover.
9. Position thermostat housing on timing chain cover.
10. Install two housing-to-timing chain cover bolts. Tighten bolts to 10 ft. lbs. (13 Nm).

⁂ WARNING

Housing must be tightened evenly and thermostat must be centered into recessed groove in timing chain cover. If not, it may result in a cracked housing, damaged timing chain cover threads or coolant leaks.

11. Install lower radiator hose on thermostat housing.
12. Install splash shield.
13. Lower vehicle.

5.7L Engine

⁂ CAUTION

Do not loosen the radiator draincock with the cooling system hot and pres-

surized. Serious burns from the coolant can occur.

➡**Do not waste reusable coolant. If the solution is clean, drain the coolant into a clean container for reuse.**

➡**If the thermostat is being replaced, be sure that the replacement is the specified thermostat for the vehicle model and engine type.**

1. Disconnect the negative battery cable.
2. Drain the cooling system
3. Remove the radiator hose clamp and radiator hose at the thermostat housing.
4. Remove the thermostat housing mounting bolts, thermostat housing and thermostat.

To install:

5. Position the thermostat and housing on the front cover.
6. Install thermostat housing bolts. Tighten the bolts to 10 ft. lbs. (13 Nm).
7. Install the radiator hose onto the thermostat housing.
8. Fill the cooling system.
9. Connect negative battery cable.
10. Start and warm the engine. Check for leaks.

2011 Models

3.6L Engine

⁂ CAUTION

Do not loosen radiator draincock with system hot and pressurized. Serious burns from coolant can occur.

⁂ WARNING

The Thermostat and housing is serviced as an assembly. Do not remove the thermostat from the housing, damage to the thermostat may occur.

➡**Do not waste reusable coolant. If solution is clean, drain coolant into a clean container for reuse.**

➡**If thermostat is being replaced, be sure that replacement is specified thermostat for vehicle model and engine type.**

1. Disconnect negative battery cable at battery.
2. Remove the air intake assembly.
3. Drain cooling system.
4. Remove upper radiator hose clamp and upper radiator hose at thermostat housing.
5. Remove thermostat housing mounting bolts, thermostat housing and thermostat.

To install:

6. Clean mating areas of timing chain cover and thermostat housing.
7. Install a new gasket on to the thermostat housing.
8. Position thermostat housing on the water crossover.
9. Install two thermostat housing bolts. Tighten bolts to 106 inch lbs. (12 Nm).
10. Install upper radiator hose on thermostat housing.
11. Fill cooling system.
12. Install the air intake system.
13. Connect negative battery cable to battery.
14. Start and warm the engine. Check for leaks.

5.7L Engine

⁂ CAUTION

Do not loosen the radiator draincock with the cooling system hot and pressurized. Serious burns from the coolant can occur.

➡**Do not waste reusable coolant. If the solution is clean, drain the coolant into a clean container for reuse.**

➡**If the thermostat is being replaced, be sure that the replacement is the specified thermostat for the vehicle model and engine type.**

1. Disconnect the negative battery cable.
2. Remove the air intake system.
3. Partially drain the cooling system.
4. Remove the upper radiator hose at the thermostat housing and position aside.
5. Remove the thermostat housing mounting bolts, thermostat housing and thermostat.

To install:

6. Position the thermostat and housing on the front cover.
7. Install thermostat housing bolts. Tighten the bolts to 10 ft. lbs.13 Nm).
8. Install the radiator hose onto the thermostat housing.
9. Fill the cooling system.
10. Connect negative battery cable.
11. Install the air intake system.
12. Start and warm the engine. Check for leaks.

WATER PUMP

REMOVAL & INSTALLATION

2010 Models

3.7L Engine

See Figure 47.

➡**The water pump on 3.7L engines is bolted directly to the engine timing chain case cover.**

1. Disconnect negative battery cable from battery.
2. Drain cooling system.

⁂ CAUTION

Constant tension hose clamps are used on most cooling system hoses. When removing or installing, use only tools designed for servicing this type of clamp. Always wear safety glasses when servicing constant tension clamps.

⁂ WARNING

A number or letter is stamped into the tongue of constant tension clamps. If replacement is necessary, use only an original equipment clamp with matching number or letter.

3. Remove two fan shroud-to-radiator screws.
4. Remove viscous fan (if equipped).
5. Remove accessory drive belt.
6. Remove accessory drive belt tensioner.
7. Remove seven water pump mounting bolts and one stud bolt.

⁂ WARNING

Do not pry on the water pump at the timing chain case/cover. The machined surfaces may be damaged resulting in leaks.

8. Remove water pump and gasket. Discard gasket.

To install:

9. Clean gasket mating surfaces.
10. Using a new gasket, position water pump and install mounting bolts and stud. Tighten water pump mounting bolts to 43 ft. lbs. (58 Nm) torque.
11. Spin water pump to be sure that pump impeller does not rub against timing chain case/cover.
12. Install accessory drive belt tensioner.
13. Install accessory drive belt.

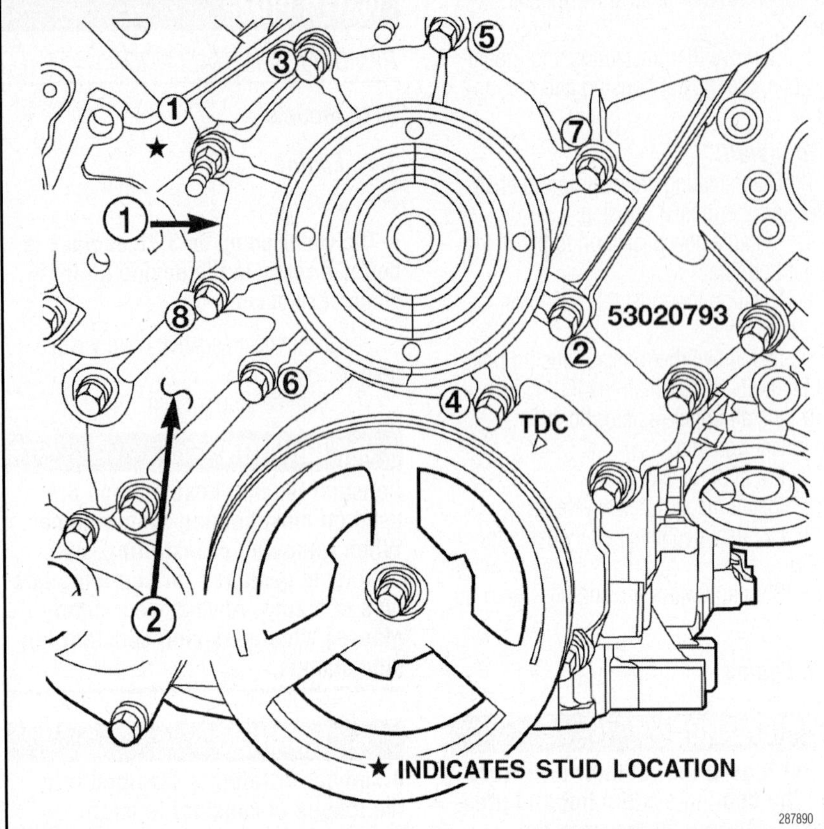

Fig. 47 The water pump (1) on 3.7L engines is bolted directly to the engine timing chain case cover (2)

⁂ WARNING

When installing the serpentine accessory drive belt, belt must be routed correctly. If not, engine may overheat due to water pump rotating in wrong direction.

14. Be sure the upper and lower portions of the fan shroud are firmly connected. All air must flow through the radiator.
15. Install two fan shroud-to-radiator screws.
16. Install viscous fan (if originally equipped).
17. Be sure of at least 1.0 inches (25 mm) between tips of fan blades and fan shroud.
18. Evacuate air and refill cooling system.
19. Connect negative battery cable.
20. Check the cooling system for leaks.

5.7L Engine

See Figure 48.

1. Disconnect negative battery cable.
2. Drain coolant.
3. Remove serpentine belt.
4. Remove fan clutch assembly.
5. Remove coolant fill bottle.
6. Disconnect washer bottle wiring and hose.
7. Remove fan shroud assembly.
8. Remove A/C compressor and alternator brace.
9. Remove idler pulleys.
10. Remove belt tensioner assembly.

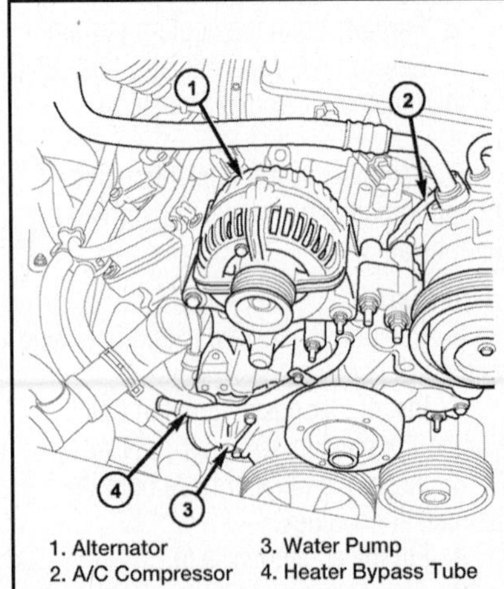

Fig. 48 Remove A/C compressor and alternator brace

11. Remove upper and lower radiator hoses.
12. Remove heater hoses.
13. Remove water pump mounting bolts and remove pump.

To install:

14. Install water pump and mounting bolts. Tighten mounting bolts to 18 ft. lbs. (24 Nm).
15. Install heater hoses.
16. Install upper and lower radiator hoses.
17. Install belt tensioner assembly.
18. Install idler pulleys.
19. Install A/C compressor and alternator brace. Tighten bolt and nuts to 21 ft. lbs. (28 Nm).
20. Install fan shroud assembly.
21. Connect washer bottle wiring and hose.
22. Install coolant fill bottle.
23. Install fan clutch assembly.
24. Install serpentine belt.
25. Connect negative battery cable.
26. Evacuate air and refill cooling system.
27. Check cooling system for leaks.

2011 Models

3.6L Engine

See Figure 49.

➡The water pump on 3.6L engines is bolted directly to the engine timing chain case cover.

1. Disconnect negative battery cable from battery.
2. Disconnect the intake air temperature sensor.
3. Loosen the clamps. Remove the air intake hose and resonator assembly.
4. Drain the cooling system.
5. Remove the accessory drive belt.

⁂ CAUTION

Constant tension hose clamps are used on most cooling system hoses. When removing or installing, use only tools designed for servicing this type of clamp. Always wear safety glasses when servicing constant tension clamps.

⁂ WARNING

A number or letter is stamped into the tongue of constant tension clamps. If replacement is necessary, use only an original equipment clamp with matching number or letter.

6. Remove the lower heater hose at the water pump and position aside.
7. Remove the lower radiator hose from the water pump and position aside.
8. Remove idler pulley.
9. Remove the eleven water pump mounting bolts. Take notice to the four water pump bolts that bolt directly to the timing cover.

⁂ WARNING

Do not pry on the water pump at the timing chain case/cover. The machined surfaces may be damaged resulting in leaks.

10. Remove water pump and seal.

To install:

11. Clean mating surfaces.

➡Take notice the lengths of the mounting bolts. Some M6 bolts mount directly to the timing cover.

12. Using a new gasket, position water pump and hand tighten the M6 mounting bolts.
13. Hand tighten the idler pulley bolt.
14. Hand tighten the upper M8 and M10 water pump to engine block mounting bolts.

➡Tightening the water pump fasteners in sequential order, will insure proper sealing surface.

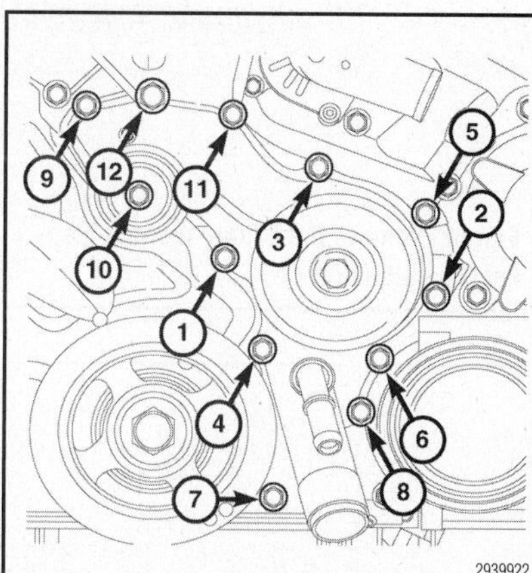

Fig. 49 Tighten the bolts in the sequence shown

15. Tighten the bolts 1–12 in the sequence shown. Tighten the bolts to their respective torque:
    a. Tighten M6 mounting bolts to 9 ft. lbs. (12 Nm).
    b. Tighten M8 bolts to 18 ft. lbs. (25 Nm).
    c. Tighten M10 bolt to 41 ft. lbs. (55 Nm).
    d. Repeat the tightening sequence until the proper torque has been met.
16. Spin water pump to be sure that pump impeller does not rub against timing chain case/cover.

⁂ WARNING

A number or letter is stamped into the tongue of constant tension clamps. If replacement is necessary, use only an original equipment clamp with matching number or letter.

17. Install the lower radiator hose.
18. Install the lower return heater hose.

⁂ WARNING

When installing the serpentine accessory drive belt, belt must be routed correctly. If not, engine may overheat due to water pump rotating in wrong direction.

19. Install accessory drive belt.
20. Evacuate air and refill cooling system.
21. Install the air intake hose and resonator assembly at the air filter housing.
22. Connect the intake air temperature sensor.
23. Connect negative battery cable. Check the cooling system for leaks.

5.7L Engine

See Figure 50.

1. Disconnect negative battery cable.
2. Remove the air intake assembly.
3. Remove the resonator mounting bracket.
4. Remove cooling fan assembly.
5. Drain coolant into a clean container.

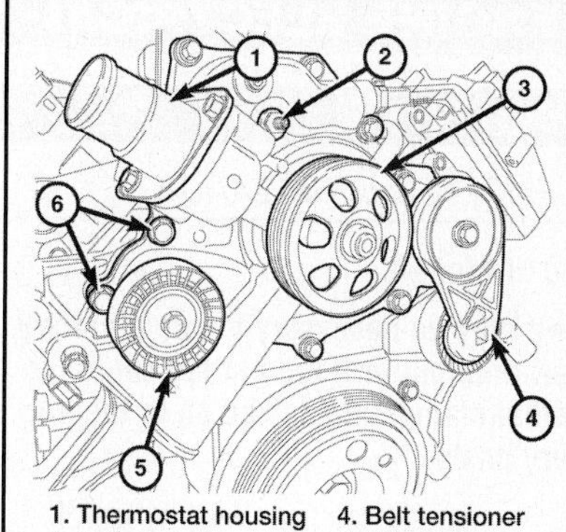

Fig. 50 Remove the upper radiator hose from the thermostat housing

6. Remove the upper radiator hose from the thermostat housing and position aside.
7. Remove serpentine belt.
8. Remove idler pulley.
9. Remove belt tensioner assembly.
10. Remove lower radiator hose from the water pump and position aside.
11. Remove the upper metal heater tube from the cylinder head.
12. Remove water pump mounting bolts and remove pump.

To install:

13. Clean mating surfaces and install water pump. Tighten mounting bolts to 18 ft. lbs. (24 Nm).
14. Install upper metal heater tube.
15. Install belt tensioner assembly.
16. Install idler pulley.
17. Install the lower radiator hose.
18. Install serpentine belt.
19. Install the resonator mounting bracket.
20. Install cooling fan assembly.
21. Install the upper radiator hose to the thermostat housing.
22. Install the air intake assembly.
23. Connect negative battery cable.
24. Evacuate air and refill cooling system.
25. Check cooling system for leaks.

BATTERY

REMOVAL & INSTALLATION

2010 Models

➡It may be necessary to use a battery terminal puller if the battery cable terminal clamps are seized on to the battery posts.

1. Turn the ignition switch to the Off position. Be certain that all electrical accessories are turned off.
2. Loosen the battery negative cable terminal clamp pinch-bolt hex nut.
3. Disconnect the battery negative cable terminal clamp from the battery negative terminal post. If necessary, use a battery terminal puller to remove the terminal clamp from the battery post.
4. Loosen the battery positive cable terminal clamp pinch-bolt hex nut.
5. Disconnect the battery positive cable terminal clamp from the battery positive terminal post. If necessary, use a battery terminal puller to remove the terminal clamp from the battery post.
6. Remove the battery hold down bolt and slide the hold down up and forward in the battery tray slots.

**** CAUTION**

Wear a suitable pair of rubber gloves when removing a battery by hand. Safety glasses should also be worn. If the battery is cracked or leaking, the electrolyte can burn the skin and eyes.

7. Remove the battery from the vehicle.

To install:

8. Clean and inspect the battery case, terminal posts and battery cable clamps.
9. Position the battery into the vehicle. Ensure that the battery positive and negative terminal posts are correctly positioned. The battery cable terminal clamps must reach the correct battery terminal post without stretching the cables.
10. Install the battery hold down by sliding it back and downward in the battery tray slots. Install the battery hold down bolt.

**** WARNING**

Be certain that the battery cable terminal clamps are connected to the correct battery terminal posts. Reverse battery polarity may damage electrical components of the vehicle.

11. Connect the battery positive cable terminal clamp to the battery positive terminal post.
12. Connect the battery negative cable terminal clamp to the battery negative terminal post.
13. Apply a thin coating of petroleum jelly or chassis grease to the exposed surfaces of the battery cable terminal clamps and the battery terminal posts.

2011 Models

See Figures 51 through 53.

**** WARNING**

The Absorbent Glass Mat (AGM) battery should only be charged and tested with the Associated Battery Charger Battery Charger, Associated or Midtronics AGM Battery Tester/Charger Station. Never test the AGM battery with a Midtronics Micro 420 battery tester.

The battery is located under the passenger seat. A breather line runs from the battery through the bottom of the recess well to the outside of the vehicle.

The battery negative cable is attached to the outboard side of the battery compartment.

1. If equipped with power seats, move the seat to the most forward and upright position.
2. If equipped with manual seats, move the seat to the most forward position.
3. Turn the ignition switch to the Off position. Be certain that all electrical accessories are turned off.
4. Remove the battery cover.

➡Negative battery terminal shown, positive terminal similar.

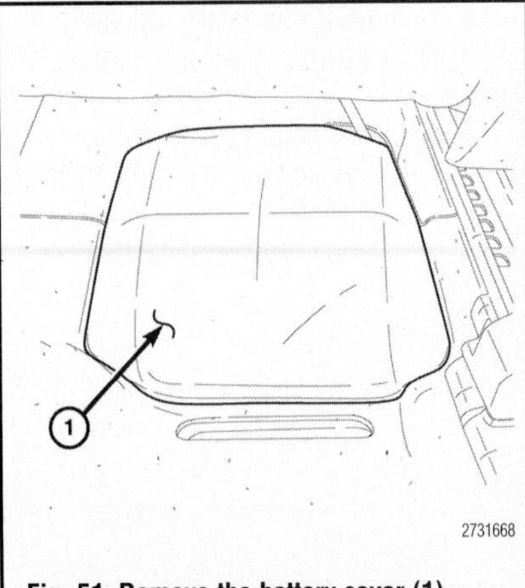

Fig. 51 Remove the battery cover (1)

5. Remove the negative battery cable from the battery.
6. Disconnect the positive battery cable and position aside.
7. Remove the battery thermal blanket.
8. Remove the battery hold down retainers and remove the battery hold down.

**** CAUTION**

Wear a suitable pair of rubber gloves when removing a battery by hand. Safety glasses should also be worn. If the battery is cracked or leaking, the electrolyte can burn the skin and eyes.

9. Remove the battery from the vehicle.

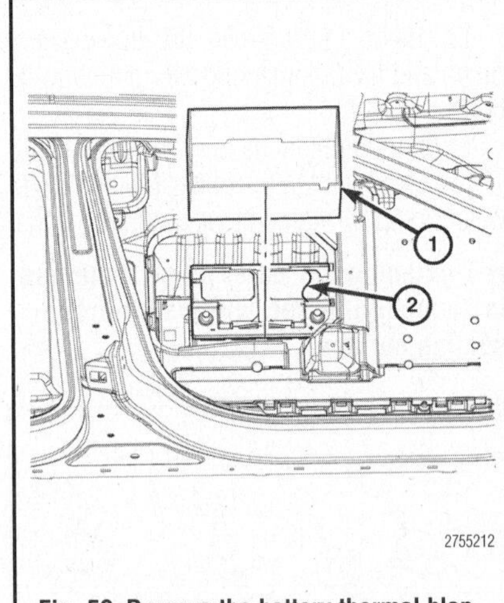

Fig. 52 Remove the battery thermal blanket (1); battery (2)

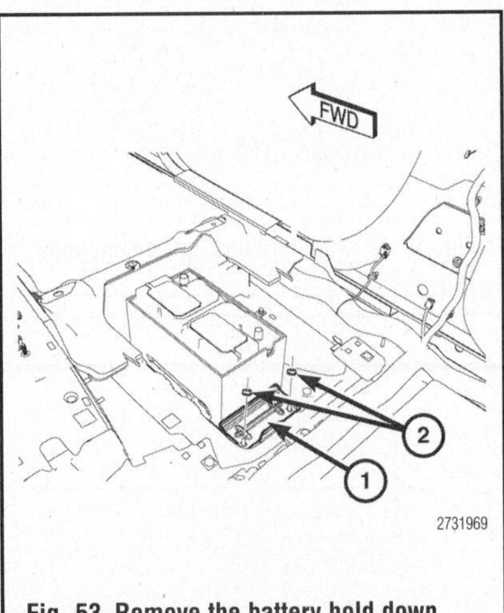

Fig. 53 Remove the battery hold down retainers (2) and remove the battery hold down (1)

To install:

⁂ CAUTION

Wear a suitable pair of rubber gloves when removing a battery by hand. Safety glasses should also be worn. If the battery is cracked or leaking, the electrolyte can burn the skin and eyes.

10. Install the battery into the vehicle.
11. Install the battery hold down into position and install the battery hold down retainers. Tighten to 15 ft. lbs. (20 Nm).
12. Install the battery thermal blanket.
13. Position back the positive battery cable and connect to the battery.
14. Position back the negative battery cable and connect to the battery.
15. Install the battery cover.
16. Move the seat back to its original position.

ENGINE ELECTRICAL

ALTERNATOR

REMOVAL & INSTALLATION

2010 Models

3.7L Engine

See Figures 54 and 55.

⁂ CAUTION

Disconnect the negative cable from the battery before removing the battery output wire (B+ wire) from the alternator. Failure to do so can result in injury or damage to the electrical system.

1. Disconnect and isolate the negative battery cable.
2. Remove the serpentine belt.
3. Unsnap the plastic insulator cap from the B+ output terminal.
4. Remove the B+ terminal mounting nut at the rear of the alternator. Disconnect the terminal from the alternator.
5. Disconnect the field wire connector at rear of the alternator by pushing on the connector tab.
6. Remove one rear vertical alternator mounting bolt.
7. Remove two front horizontal alternator mounting bolts.
8. Remove the alternator from the vehicle.

To install:

9. Position the alternator to the engine and install two horizontal bolts and one vertical bolt. Tighten all three bolts to 40 ft. lbs. (55 Nm).
10. Snap the field wire connector into the rear of alternator.
11. Install the B+ terminal eyelet to the alternator output stud. Tighten the mounting nut to 106 inch lbs. (12 Nm).

⁂ WARNING

Never force a belt over a pulley rim using a screwdriver. The synthetic fiber of the belt can be damaged.

⁂ WARNING

When installing a serpentine accessory drive belt, the belt must be routed correctly. The water pump may be rotating in the wrong direction if the belt is installed incorrectly, causing the engine to overheat. Refer to belt routing label in engine compartment, or Refer to the Belt Schematics in 7, Cooling System.

12. Install the serpentine belt.
13. Install the negative battery cable.

5.7L Engine

See Figure 56.

⁂ CAUTION

Disconnect the negative cable from the battery before removing the battery output wire (B+ wire) from the alternator. Failure to do so can result in injury or damage to the electrical system.

1. Disconnect and isolate the negative battery cable.
2. Remove the air cleaner body.
3. Remove the serpentine belt.
4. Unsnap the plastic insulator cap from the B+ output terminal.
5. Remove the B+ terminal mounting

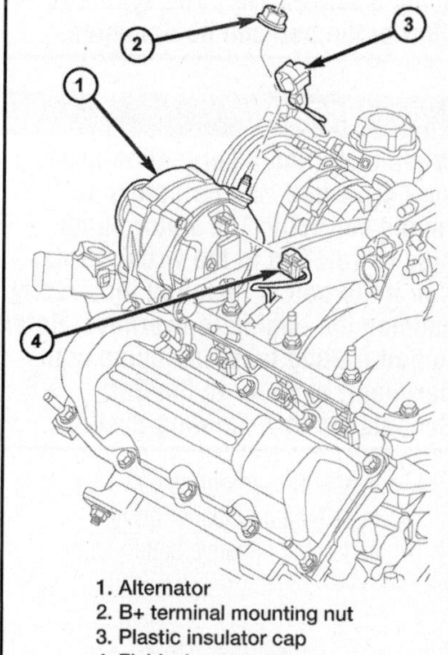

Fig. 54 Unsnap the plastic insulator cap from the B+ output terminal

Fig. 55 Remove one rear vertical alternator mounting bolt (2), two front horizontal alternator mounting bolts (1), and the alternator (3)

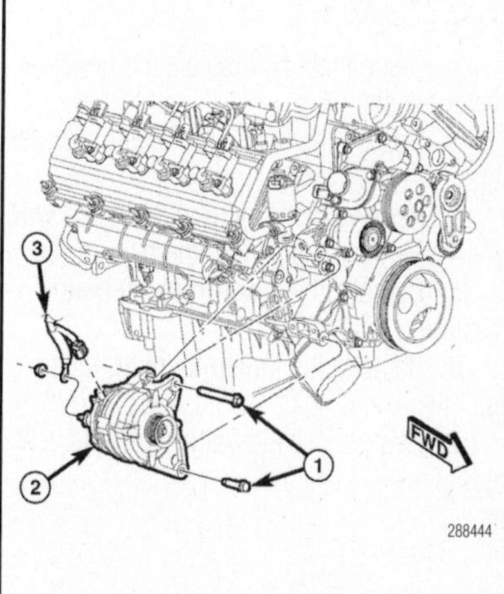

Fig. 56 Disconnect the field wire connector (3), remove the two alternator mounting bolts (1), and the alternator (2)

nut at the rear of the alternator. Disconnect the terminal from the alternator.

6. Disconnect the field wire connector at the rear of the alternator by pushing on the connector tab.
7. Remove two alternator mounting bolts.
8. Remove the alternator from vehicle.

To install:

9. Position the alternator to the engine and install the two mounting bolts. Torque the bolts to 30 ft. lbs. (41 Nm).
10. Snap the field wire connector into the rear of the alternator.
11. Install the B+ terminal eyelet to the alternator output stud. Tighten the mounting nut to 106 inch lbs. (12 Nm).

WARNING

Never force a belt over a pulley rim using a screwdriver. The synthetic fiber of the belt can be damaged.

WARNING

When installing a serpentine accessory drive belt, the belt must be routed correctly. The water pump may be rotating in the wrong direction if the belt is installed incorrectly, causing the engine to overheat. Refer to belt routing label in engine compartment, or Refer to the Belt Schematics in 7, Cooling System.

12. Install the serpentine belt.
13. Install the air cleaner body.
14. Install the negative battery cable.

2011 Models

3.6L Engine

See Figure 57.

1. Disconnect and isolate the negative battery cable
2. Unplug the field circuit from alternator.
3. Remove the B+ terminal nut and wire.
4. Remove the serpentine belt.
5. Remove the lower front alternator mounting retainer.
6. Remove the three mounting retainers.
7. Remove the alternator from the vehicle.

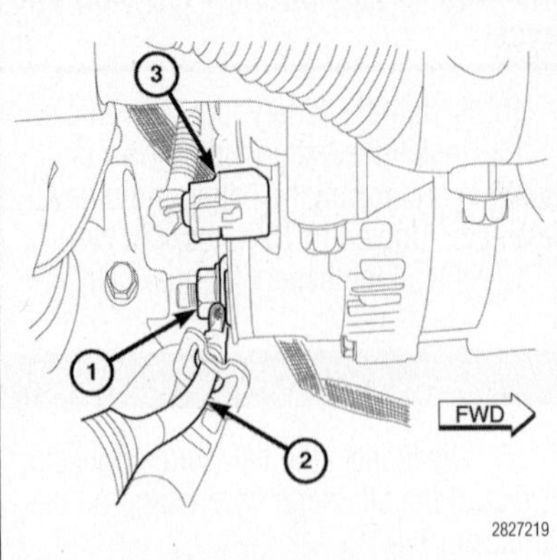

Fig. 57 Unplug the field circuit (3) from alternator; remove the B+ terminal nut (1) and wire (2)

To install:

8. Install the alternator into the vehicle.
9. Install the three mounting retainers. Tighten to 18 ft. lbs. (25 Nm).
10. Install ground wire on mounting stud.
11. Install the lower front alternator mounting retainer. Tighten to 17 ft. lbs. (23 Nm)
12. Install the serpentine belt.
13. Install the B+ terminal to the alternator stud. Tighten to 97 inch lbs. (11 Nm).
14. Plug in the field circuit to the alternator.
15. Connect the negative battery cable.

5.7L Engine

See Figure 58.

CAUTION

Disconnect the negative cable from the battery before removing the battery output wire (B+ wire) from the alternator. Failure to do so can result in injury or damage to the electrical system.

1. Disconnect and isolate the negative battery cable.
2. Remove the air cleaner body.
3. Remove the serpentine belt.
4. Unsnap the plastic insulator cap from the B+ output terminal.
5. Remove the B+ terminal mounting nut at the rear of the alternator. Disconnect the terminal from the alternator.

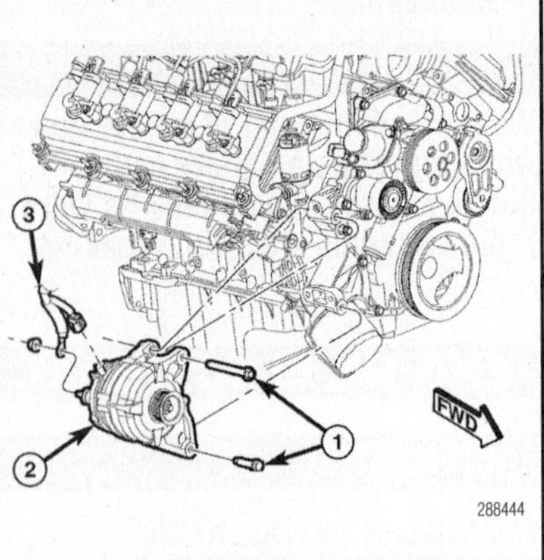

Fig. 58 Disconnect the field wire connector (3), remove the two alternator mounting bolts (1), and the alternator (2)

6. Disconnect the field wire connector at the rear of the alternator by pushing on the connector tab.
7. Remove two alternator mounting bolts.
8. Remove the alternator from vehicle.

To install:

9. Position the alternator to the engine and install the two mounting bolts. Torque the bolts to 30 ft. lbs. (41 Nm).
10. Snap the field wire connector into the rear of the alternator.
11. Install the B+ terminal eyelet to the alternator output stud. Tighten the mounting nut to 106 inch lbs. (12 Nm).

WARNING

Never force a belt over a pulley rim using a screwdriver. The synthetic fiber of the belt can be damaged.

WARNING

When installing a serpentine accessory drive belt, the belt must be routed correctly. The water pump may be rotating in the wrong direction if the belt is installed incorrectly, causing the engine to overheat. Refer to belt routing label in engine compartment, or Refer to the Belt Schematics in 7, Cooling System.

12. Install the serpentine belt.
13. Install the air cleaner body.
14. Install the negative battery cable.

FIRING ORDER

The firing order for the 3.6L engine is: 1–2–3–4–5–6.

The firing order for the 3.7L engine is: 1–6–5–4–3–2.

The firing order for the 5.7L engine is: 1–8–4–3–6–5–7–2.

IGNITION COIL

REMOVAL & INSTALLATION

3.6L Engine

See Figures 59 through 63.

1. Disconnect and isolate the negative battery cable.
2. If removing the ignition coils from cylinders 1 and 3 on the RH side of the engine, first remove the air inlet hose.
3. If removing the ignition coils from cylinders 2, 4, or 6 on the LH side of the engine, first remove the air inlet hose, upper intake manifold and insulator.

➡The LH ignition coils are shown, the RH ignition coils are similar.

4. Unlock and disconnect the electrical connector from the ignition coil.
5. Remove the ignition coil mounting bolt.
6. Pull the ignition coil from cylinder head cover opening with a slight twisting action.

To install:

7. Using compressed air, blow out any dirt or contaminants from around the top of spark plug.

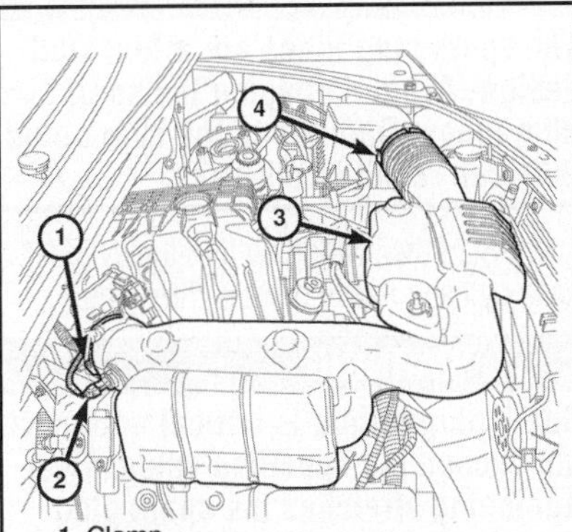

Fig. 59 If removing the ignition coils from cylinders 1 and 3 on the RH side of the engine, first remove the air inlet hose

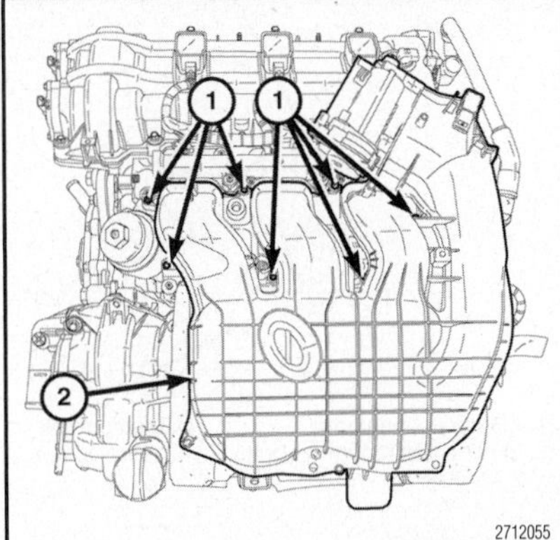

Fig. 60 If removing the ignition coils from cylinders 2, 4, or 6 on the LH side of the engine, first remove the air inlet hose, upper intake manifold (2) and insulator; retainers (1)

8. Check the condition of the ignition coil rubber boot. Inspect the opening of the boot for any debris, tears or rips. Carefully remove any debris with a lint free cloth.

⁂ WARNING

Do not apply a silicone based grease such as Mopar® Dielectric Grease to the ignition coil rubber boot. The silicone based grease will absorb into the boot causing it to stick and tear.

9. Place a small bead of Fluostar 2LF lubricant along the inside opening of the coil boot approximately 1 to 2 mm from the chamfer edge but not on the chamfered surface.
10. Position the ignition coil into the cylinder head cover opening. Using a twisting action, push the ignition coil onto the spark plug.

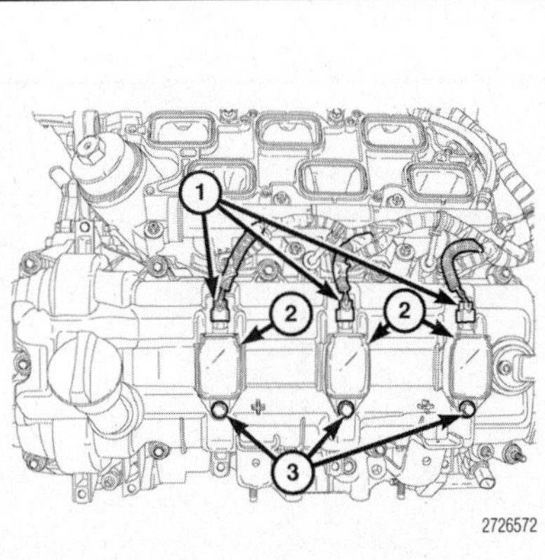

Fig. 61 Disconnect the ignition coil electrical connector (1); remove the ignition coil mounting bolt (3) and the ignition coil (2)

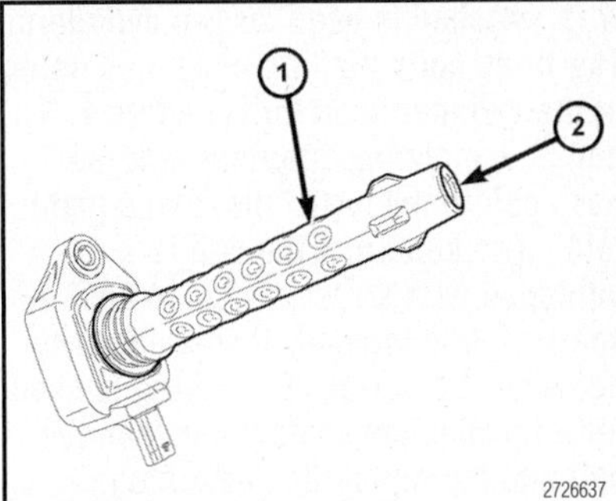

Fig. 62 Check the condition of the ignition coil rubber boot (1); inspect the opening of the boot (2) for any debris, tears or rips

11. Install the ignition coil mounting bolt.
12. Connect and lock the electrical connector to the ignition coil.
13. If removed, install the insulator, upper intake manifold and air inlet hose.
14. Connect the negative battery cable.

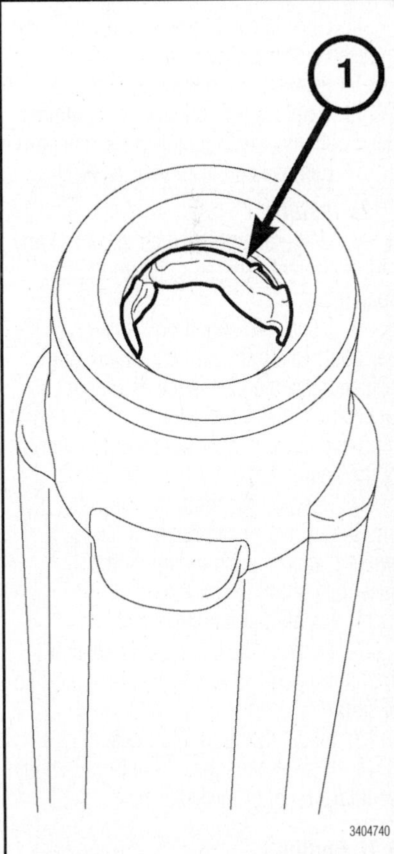

Fig. 63 Place a small bead of Fluostar 2LF lubricant (1) along the inside opening of the coil boot

3.7L Engine

➡An ignition coil with a spark plug wire attached is used for two cylinders. The three coils fits into machined holes in the cylinder head for cylinders 1, 3, and 5. A mounting stud/nut secures each coil to the top of the intake manifold . The bottom of the coil is equipped with a rubber boot to seal the spark plug to the coil. Inside each rubber boot is a spring. The spring is used for a mechanical contact between the coil and the top of the spark plug. These rubber boots and springs are a permanent part of the coil and are not serviced separately. An O-ring is used to seal the coil at the opening into the cylinder head.

1. Depending on which coil is being removed, the throttle body air intake tube or intake box may need to be removed to gain access to coil.
2. Disconnect electrical connector from coil by pushing downward on release lock on top of connector and pull connector from coil.
3. Disconnect spark plug wire from coil.
4. Clean area at base of coil with compressed air before removal.
5. Remove coil mounting bolt.
6. Carefully pull up coil from cylinder head opening with a slight twisting action.
7. Remove coil from vehicle.

To install:

8. Using compressed air, blow out any dirt or contaminants from around top of spark plug.
9. Check the condition of the coil rubber boot. To aid in coil installation, apply silicone based grease such as Mopar® Dielectric Grease # J8126688 into the spark plug end of the rubber boot and to the top of the spark plug.
10. Position the ignition coil assembly into the cylinder head opening. Using a twisting action, push the ignition coil assembly onto the spark plug.
11. Install coil mounting bolt.
12. Connect the electrical connector to the ignition coil assembly by snapping into position.
13. Install the spark plug wires.
14. If necessary, install the throttle body air intake tube, or intake air box.

5.7L Engine

See Figures 64 and 65.

1. Disconnect the electrical connector from the coil.

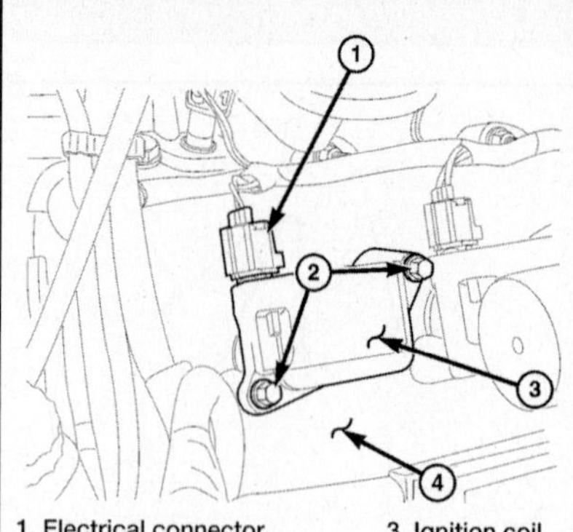

Fig. 64 Disconnect the electrical connector from the coil

2. Clean the area at the base of the coil with compressed air before removal.

➡The ignition coil mounting bolts are retained in the ignition coil.

3. Remove the two ignition coil mounting bolts.
4. Carefully pull up the ignition coil from the valve cover.
5. Remove ignition coil from vehicle.

To install:

6. Using compressed air, blow out any dirt or contaminants from around the top of the spark plug.

➡Use dielectric grease on each of the spark plug boots before installing the coil.

7. Position the ignition coil(s) into the valve cover and push onto the spark plug(s).
8. Install the ignition coil retaining bolts.
9. Connect the electrical connector to the ignition coil.

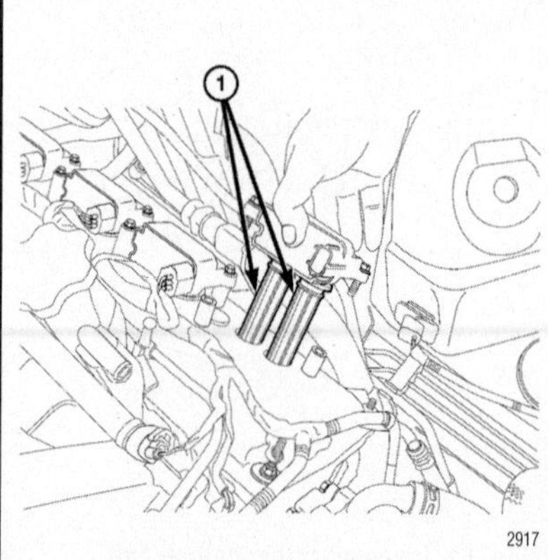

Fig. 65 Carefully pull up the ignition coil (1) from the valve cover

IGNITION TIMING

ADJUSTMENT

Ignition timing is controlled by the Engine Control Module (ECM). No adjustment is necessary or possible.

SPARK PLUGS

REMOVAL & INSTALLATION

3.6L Engine

1. Remove the ignition coil.
2. Prior to removing the spark plug, spray compressed air into the cylinder head opening. This will help prevent foreign material from entering combustion chamber.

✲✲ WARNING

The spark plug tubes are a thin wall design. Avoid damaging the spark plug tubes. Damage to the spark plug tube can result in oil leaks.

3. Remove the spark plug from the cylinder head using a quality thin wall socket with a rubber or foam insert.
4. Inspect the spark plug condition.

To install:

5. Check and adjust the spark plug gap with a gap gauging tool.

✲✲ WARNING

Special care should be taken when installing spark plugs into the cylinder head spark plug wells. Be sure the plugs do not drop into the plug wells as electrodes can be damaged.

✲✲ WARNING

The spark plug tubes are a thin wall design. Avoid damaging the spark plug tubes. Damage to the spark plug tube can result in oil leaks.

6. Start the spark plug into the cylinder head by hand to avoid cross threading.

✲✲ WARNING

Spark plug torque is critical and must not exceed the specified value. Overtightening stretches the spark plug shell reducing its heat transfer capability resulting in possible catastrophic engine failure.

7. Tighten the spark plugs to 13 ft. lbs. (17.5 Nm).
8. Install the ignition coil.

3.7L Engine

1. Remove the necessary air filter tubing and air intake components at the top of the engine at the throttle body.

➡The three spark plugs located on the left bank of the engine are under three individual ignition coils. Each individual ignition coil must be removed to gain access to each spark plug located on the left bank of the engine.

2. Prior to removing the ignition coil, spray compressed air around the coil base at the cylinder head.
3. Remove the ignition coil. Check the condition of ignition coil O-ring and replace as necessary.
4. Prior to removing the spark plug, spray compressed air into the cylinder head opening. This will help prevent foreign material from entering combustion chamber.
5. Remove the spark plug from the cylinder head using a quality thin wall socket with a rubber or foam insert.
6. Inspect the spark plug condition.

To install:

⁂ WARNING

Special care should be taken when installing spark plugs into the cylinder head spark plug wells. Be sure the plugs do not drop into the plug wells as electrodes can be damaged.

7. Start the spark plug into the cylinder head by hand to avoid cross threading.
8. Tighten the spark plugs to 20 ft. lbs. (27 Nm).
9. Before installing the ignition coil, check the condition of the coil O-ring and replace as necessary. Apply silicone based grease such as Mopar® Dielectric Grease into the spark plug end of the rubber boot, coil O-rings and to the top of spark plugs.
10. Install the ignition coil.
11. Install all the necessary air filter tubing and air intake components at the top of the engine and at the throttle body.

5.7L Engine

1. Remove the necessary air filter tubing and air intake components at the top of the engine and at the throttle body.
2. Prior to removing the ignition coil, spray compressed air around coil base at the cylinder head.
3. Remove the ignition coil.
4. Prior to removing the spark plug, spray compressed air into the cylinder head opening.
5. Remove the spark plug from the cylinder head using a quality socket with a rubber or foam insert.
6. Inspect spark plug condition.

To install:

➡Do not attempt to clean any of the spark plugs. Replace only.

7. To aid in the coil installation, apply silicone based grease such as Mopar® Dielectric Grease into the spark plug end of the ignition coil rubber boots. Also apply this grease to the tops of spark plugs.
8. Check and adjust the spark plug gap with a gap gauging tool.
9. Start the spark plug into the cylinder head by hand to avoid cross threading. Special care should be taken when installing spark plugs into the cylinder head spark plug wells. Be sure the plugs do not drop into the plug wells as electrodes can be damaged.

⁂ WARNING

Always tighten spark plugs to the specified torque. Certain engines use torque sensitive spark plugs. It is a good practice to always tighten spark plugs to a specific torque. Over tightening can cause distortion resulting in a change in the spark plug gap, or a cracked porcelain insulator.

10. Install the ignition coil.
11. Install necessary air filter tubing and air intake components to the top of the engine and to the throttle body.

ENGINE ELECTRICAL — STARTING SYSTEM

STARTER

REMOVAL & INSTALLATION

3.6L Engine

RWD Models

1. Disconnect and isolate the negative battery cable.
2. Remove the driver side engine mount and engine mount bracket.
3. Remove the battery positive cable wire harness connector eyelet from solenoid battery terminal stud.
4. Disconnect the solenoid wire from the starter motor.
5. Remove the two mounting bolts.
6. Remove the starter motor.

To install:

7. Position the starter motor to the engine.
8. Install and tighten both mounting bolts. Torque the bolts to 50 ft. lbs. (68 Nm).
9. Connect the solenoid wire to the starter motor.
10. Position the battery cable to the solenoid stud. Install and tighten battery cable eyelet nut. Torque the nut to 19 ft. lbs. (25 Nm).
11. Install the driver side engine mount.
12. Connect the negative battery cable.

4WD Models

1. Disconnect and isolate the negative battery cable.
2. Remove the front axle.
3. Remove the driver side engine mount and engine mount bracket.
4. Remove the battery positive cable wire harness connector eyelet from solenoid battery terminal stud.
5. Disconnect the solenoid wire from the starter motor.
6. Remove two mounting bolts.
7. Remove the starter motor.

To install:

8. Position the starter motor to the engine.
9. Install and tighten both mounting bolts. Torque the bolts to 50 ft. lbs. (68 Nm).
10. Connect the solenoid wire to starter motor.
11. Position the battery cable to the solenoid stud. Install and tighten battery cable eyelet nut. Torque the nut to 19 ft. lbs. (25 Nm).
12. Install the driver side engine mount.
13. Install the front axle.
14. Connect the negative battery cable.

3.7L Engine

1. Disconnect and isolate negative battery cable.
2. Raise and support vehicle.
3. If equipped with 4WD, remove front drive shaft.
4. If equipped with 4WD and certain transmissions, a support bracket is used between front axle and side of transmission. Remove 2 support bracket bolts at transmission. Pry support bracket slightly to gain access to lower starter mounting bolt.
5. Remove two bolts if equipped with an automatic transmission.

6. Move starter motor towards front of vehicle far enough for nose of starter pinion housing to clear housing. Always support starter motor during this process, do not let starter motor hang from wire harness.

7. Tilt nose downwards and lower starter motor far enough to access and remove nut that secures battery positive cable wire harness connector eyelet to solenoid battery terminal stud. Do not let starter motor hang from wire harness.

8. Remove battery positive cable wire harness connector eyelet from solenoid battery terminal stud.

9. Disconnect battery positive cable wire harness connector from solenoid terminal connector receptacle.

10. Remove starter motor.

To install:

11. Connect solenoid wire to starter motor (snaps on).

12. Position battery cable to solenoid stud. Install and tighten battery cable eyelet nut. Torque nut to 19 ft. lbs. (25 Nm). Do not allow starter motor to hang from wire harness.

13. Position starter motor to transmission.

14. If equipped with automatic transmission, slide cooler tube bracket into position.

15. Install and tighten both bolts. Torque bolts to 50 ft. lbs. (68 Nm).

16. If equipped with 4WD and certain transmissions, a support bracket is used between front axle and side of transmission. Install 2 support bracket bolts at transmission.

17. If equipped with 4WD, install front drive shaft.

18. Lower vehicle.

19. Connect negative battery cable.

5.7L Engine

1. Disconnect and isolate the negative battery cable.

2. Raise and support the vehicle.

➡If equipped with 4WD and certain transmissions, a support bracket is used between front axle and side of transmission. Remove 2 support bracket bolts at transmission. Pry support bracket slightly to gain access to lower starter mounting bolt.

3. Remove the two mounting bolts.

4. Move the starter motor towards the front of vehicle far enough for the nose of the starter pinion housing to clear the housing. Always support the starter motor during this process, do not let the starter motor hang from the wire harness.

5. Tilt the nose downwards and lower the starter motor far enough to access and remove the nut that secures the battery positive cable wire harness connector eyelet to the solenoid battery terminal stud. Do not let the starter motor hang from the wire harness.

6. Remove the battery positive cable wire harness connector eyelet from solenoid battery terminal stud.

7. Disconnect the battery positive cable wire harness connector from the solenoid terminal connector receptacle.

8. Remove the starter motor.

To install:

9. Connect the solenoid wire to the starter motor (snaps on).

10. Position the battery cable to the solenoid stud. Install and tighten the battery cable eyelet nut. Torque nut to 19 ft. lbs. (25 Nm). Do not allow the starter motor to hang from the wire harness.

11. Position the starter motor to the engine.

12. If equipped with automatic transmission, slide cooler tube bracket into position.

13. Install and tighten both mounting bolts. Torque bolts to 50 ft. lbs. (68 Nm).

14. Lower the vehicle.

15. Connect the negative battery cable.

ENGINE MECHANICAL

➡Disconnecting the negative battery cable may interfere with the functions of the on board computer systems and may require the computer to undergo a relearning process, once the negative battery cable is reconnected.

ACCESSORY DRIVE BELTS

ACCESSORY BELT ROUTING

See Figures 66 through 68.

Refer to the accompanying illustrations.

INSPECTION

When diagnosing serpentine drive belts, small cracks that run across ribbed surface of belt from rib to rib, are considered normal. These are not a reason to replace belt. However, cracks running along a rib (not across) are not normal. Any belt with cracks running along a rib must be replaced. Also replace belt if it has excessive wear, frayed cords or severe glazing.

ADJUSTMENT

Tension for the serpentine accessory drive belt is maintained by the belt tensioner. No adjustment is necessary.

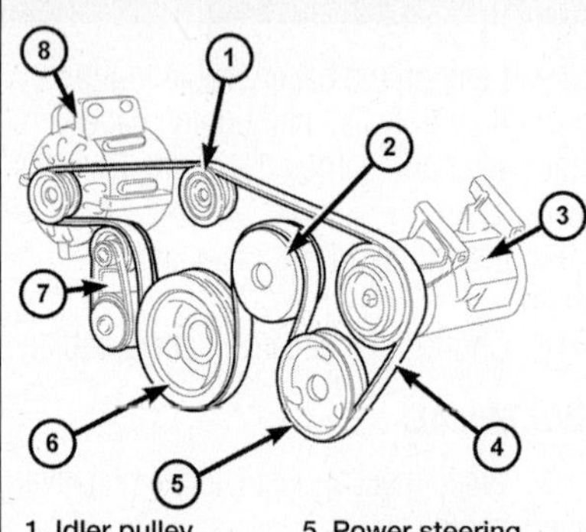

Fig. 66 Accessory drive belt routing—3.6L engine

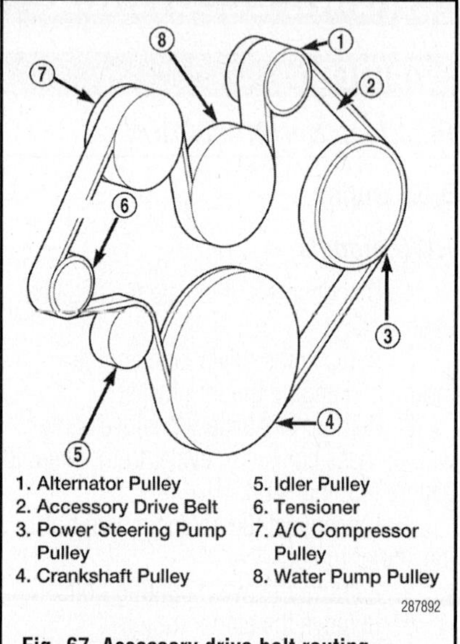

Fig. 67 Accessory drive belt routing—3.7L engine

REMOVAL & INSTALLATION

3.6L Engine

See Figure 69.

⁂ WARNING

Do not let tensioner arm snap back to the freearm position, severe damage may occur to the tensioner.

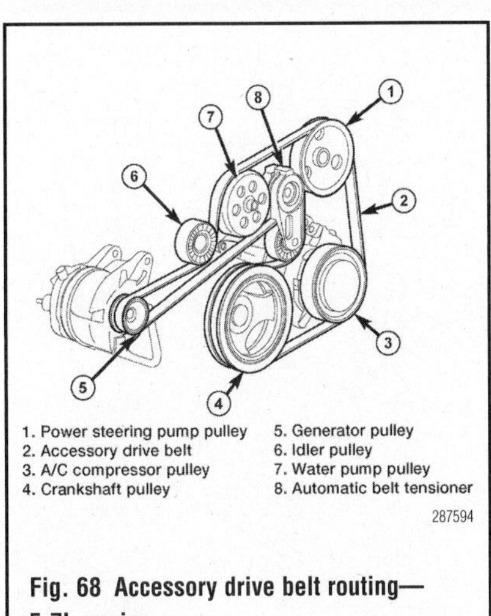

Fig. 68 Accessory drive belt routing—5.7L engine

1. Disconnect negative battery cable from battery.
2. Rotate belt tensioner until it contacts its stop. Remove belt, then slowly rotate the tensioner into the freearm position.

To install:

3. Check condition of all pulleys.

**** WARNING**

When installing the serpentine accessory drive belt, the belt MUST be routed correctly. If not, the engine may overheat due to the water pump rotating in the wrong direction.

4. Install new belt. Route the belt around all pulleys except the idler pulley. Rotate the tensioner arm until it contacts its stop position. Route the belt around the idler and slowly let the tensioner rotate into the belt. Make sure the belt is seated onto all pulleys.
5. With the drive belt installed, inspect the belt wear indicator. The gap between the tang and the housing stop (measurement A) must not exceed 0.94 inches (24 mm).

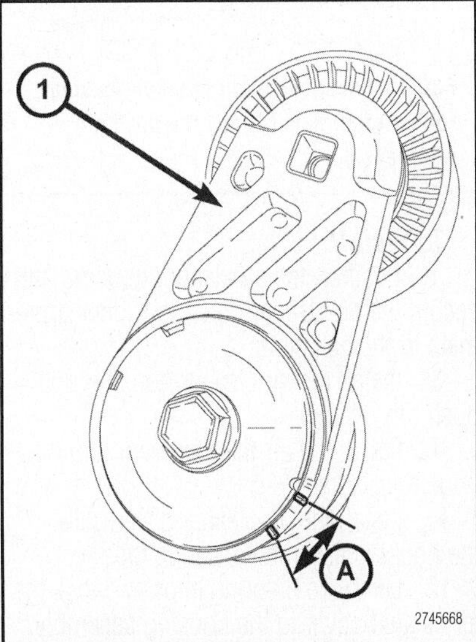

Fig. 69 The gap between the tang and the housing stop (measurement A) must not exceed 0.94 inches (24 mm)

3.7L Engine

See Figure 70.

**** WARNING**

Do not let tensioner arm snap back to the freearm position, severe damage may occur to the tensioner.

1. Disconnect negative battery cable from battery.
2. Rotate belt tensioner until it contacts its stop.
3. Remove belt, then slowly rotate the tensioner into the freearm position.

To install:

4. Check condition of all pulleys.

**** WARNING**

When installing the serpentine accessory drive belt, the belt MUST be routed correctly. If not, the engine may overheat due to the water pump rotating in the wrong direction.

5. Install new belt.
6. Route the belt around all pulleys except the idler pulley.
7. Rotate the tensioner arm until it contacts its stop position.
8. Route the belt around the idler and slowly let the tensioner rotate into the belt. Make sure the belt is seated onto all pulleys.
9. With the drive belt installed, inspect the belt wear indicator. The gap between the tang and the housing stop (measurement A) must not exceed 0.94 inches (24 mm).

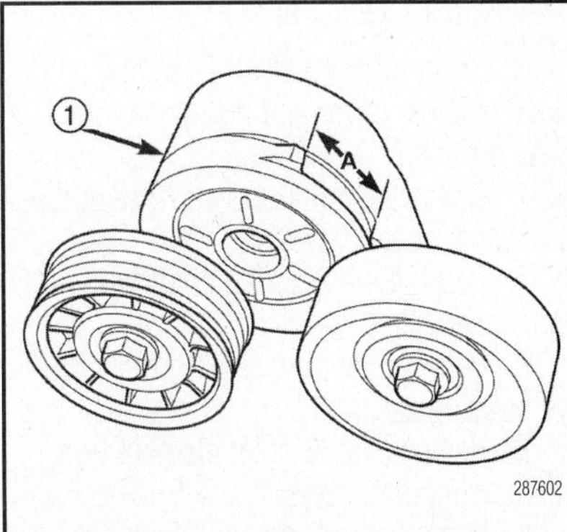

Fig. 70 The gap between the tang and the housing stop (measurement A) must not exceed 0.94 inches (24 mm); belt tensioner (1)

5.7L Engine

1. Remove the air intake tube between intake manifold and air filter assembly.
2. Using a suitable square drive tool, release the belt tension by rotating the tensioner clockwise. Rotate belt tensioner until belt can be removed from pulleys.
3. Remove belt.
4. Gently release tensioner.

To install:

➡When installing accessory drive belt onto pulleys, make sure that belt is properly routed and all V-grooves make proper contact with pulleys.

5. Position the drive belt over all pulleys except for the water pump pulley.
6. Rotate tensioner clockwise and slip the belt over the water pump pulley.
7. Gently release tensioner.
8. Install the air intake tube between intake manifold and air filter assembly.

AIR CLEANER

REMOVAL & INSTALLATION

3.6L Engine

See Figures 71 through 73.

1. Disconnect and isolate the negative battery cable.
2. Remove the engine cover.
3. Disconnect the electrical connector from the Inlet Air Temperature (IAT) sensor.
4. Loosen the clamp at the throttle body.
5. Loosen the clamp at the air cleaner body.
6. Remove the air inlet hose.

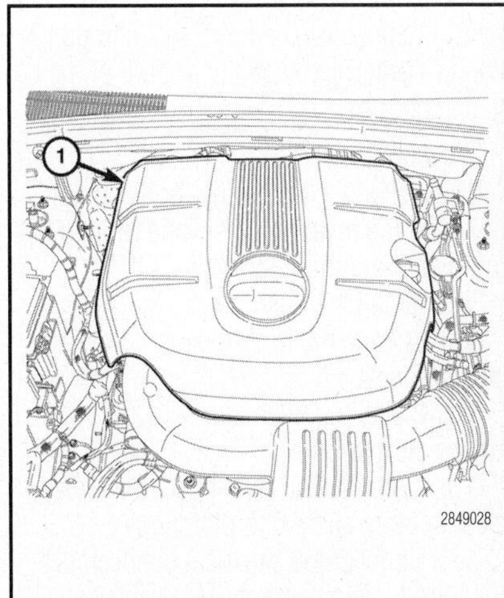

Fig. 71 Remove the engine cover (1)

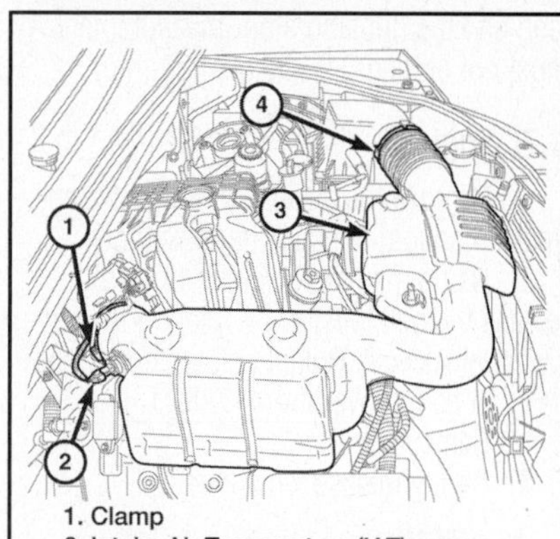

Fig. 72 Disconnect the electrical connector from the Inlet Air Temperature (IAT) sensor

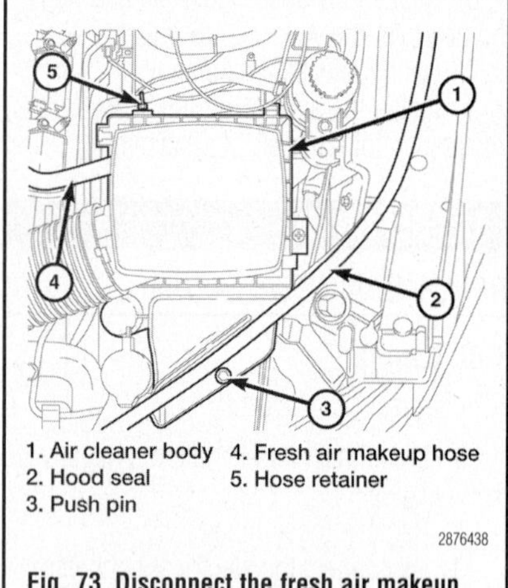

Fig. 73 Disconnect the fresh air makeup hose from the air cleaner body

7. Disconnect the fresh air makeup hose from the air cleaner body.
8. Disengage the hose retainer from the air cleaner body.
9. Remove the push pin.
10. Reposition the hood seal and pull the air cleaner body straight up off of the locating pins.

To install:

11. Install the air cleaner body straight down on the locating pins while routing the air inlet under the hood seal.
12. Install the push pin.
13. Engage the hose retainer to the air cleaner body.
14. Install the fresh air makeup hose to the air cleaner body.
15. Install the air inlet hose to the air cleaner body and the throttle body.
16. Connect the electrical connector to the Inlet Air Temperature (IAT) sensor.
17. Install the engine cover.
18. Connect the negative battery cable and tighten.

3.7L Engine

See Figure 74.

1. Loosen clamp and disconnect air duct at air cleaner cover.
2. Lift entire housing assembly from 4 locating pins.

To install:

3. Position housing cover into housing locating tabs.
4. Pry up 4 spring clips and lock cover to housing.
5. Install air duct to air cleaner cover and tighten hose clamp.
6. If any other hose clamps were removed from air intake system, tighten them.
7. If any bolts were removed from air resonator housing or air intake tubing, tighten them.

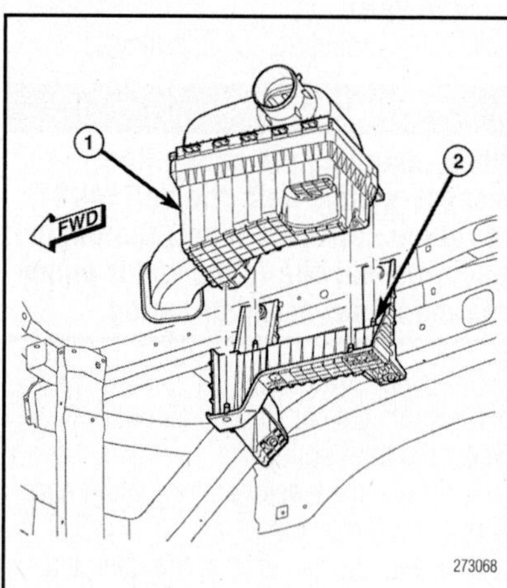

Fig. 74 Lift entire housing assembly (1) from 4 locating pins (2)

5.7L Engine

See Figures 75 and 76.

1. Loosen the clean air hose clamp at the air cleaner cover and disconnect the clean air hose.
2. Remove the makeup air hose at the air cleaner cover.
3. Release the 2 spring clips from the air cleaner cover.
4. Remove the air cleaner cover from the housing assembly.
5. Remove the air filter element from the housing assembly.
6. Remove the push pin retainer at the air cleaner housing duct.
7. Lift and separate the air cleaner housing rubber grommets from the ball studs and remove the air cleaner housing.

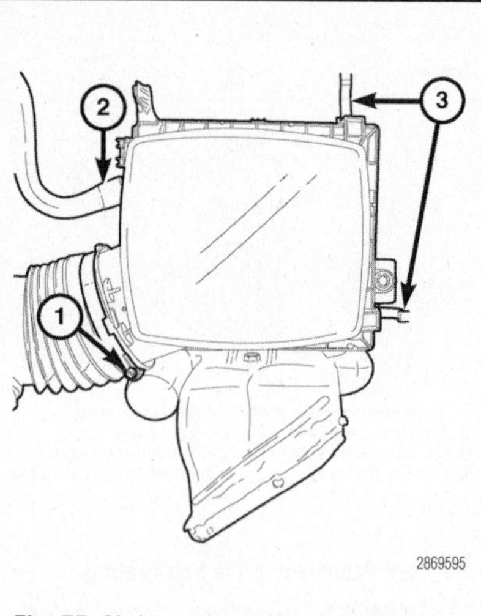

Fig. 75 Air hose clamp (1), makeup air hose (2), and spring clips (3)

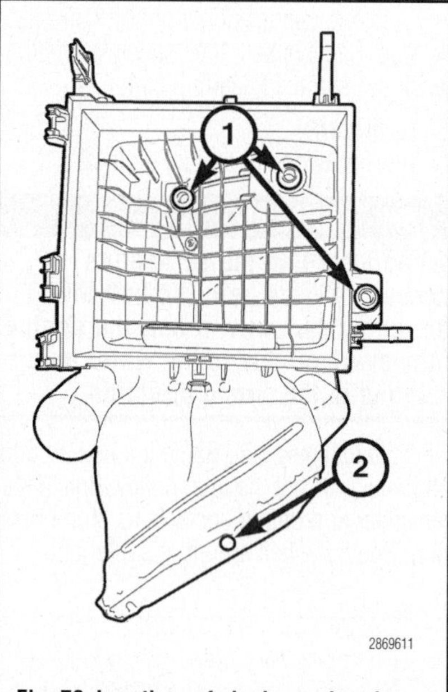

Fig. 76 Locations of air cleaner housing rubber grommets (1) and the push pin retainer (2)

To install:

8. Position the air cleaner housing and secure the air cleaner housing rubber grommets to the ball studs.
9. Install the air cleaner housing duct push pin retainer.
10. Install the air filter element into the housing assembly.
11. Install the air cleaner cover onto the housing assembly locating tabs.
12. Latch the 2 spring clips and lock the air cleaner cover to the housing assembly.
13. Connect the makeup air hose to the air cleaner cover.
14. Connect the clean air hose to the air cleaner cover and tighten clamp.

Resonator Assembly

See Figures 77 and 78.

1. Remove the oil fill cap.
2. Lift and separate the engine cover retaining grommets from the ball studs and remove the engine cover.
3. Disconnect the electrical connector at the Intake Air Temperature (IAT) sensor.
4. Loosen the clean air hose clamp at the air cleaner housing.
5. Remove the resonator retaining bolt.
6. Loosen the resonator hose clamp at the throttle body and remove the resonator.

To install:

7. Connect the resonator hose at the throttle body and tighten clamp.
8. Install the resonator retaining bolt.
9. Connect the clean air hose at the air cleaner housing and tighten clamp.

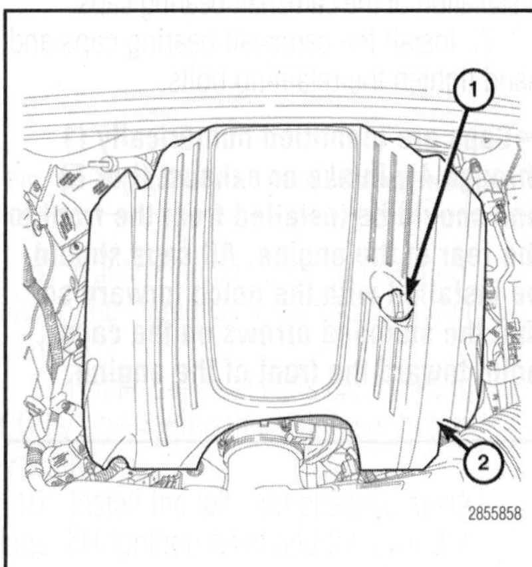

Fig. 77 Remove the oil fill cap (1) and the engine cover (2)

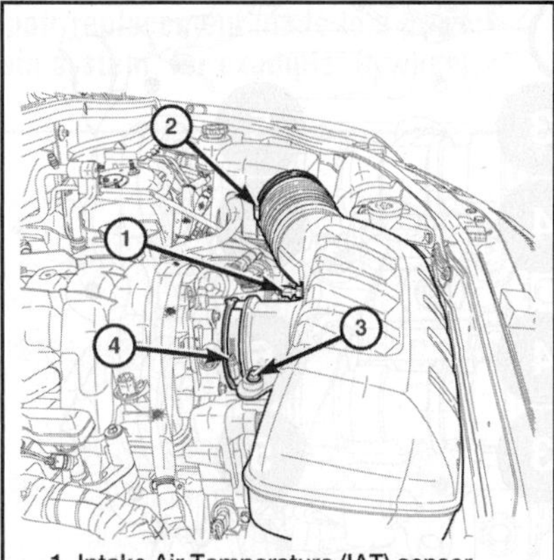

Fig. 78 Disconnect the electrical connector at the Intake Air Temperature (IAT) sensor

10. Connect the electrical connector at the Intake Air Temperature (IAT) sensor.
11. Position the engine cover and secure the retaining grommets to the ball studs.
12. Install the oil fill cap.

FILTER/ELEMENT REPLACEMENT

3.6L Engine

See Figures 79 and 80.

1. Release the air cleaner housing cover latches.
2. Lift the cover and release the cover to housing alignment tabs.
3. Remove the air cleaner element.

WARNING

Do not use compressed air to clean out the air cleaner housing without first covering the air inlet to the throttle body. Dirt or foreign objects could enter the intake manifold causing engine damage.

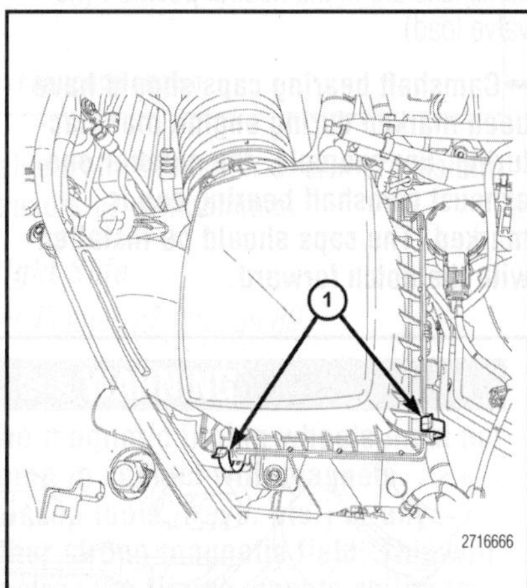

Fig. 79 Release the air cleaner housing cover latches (1)

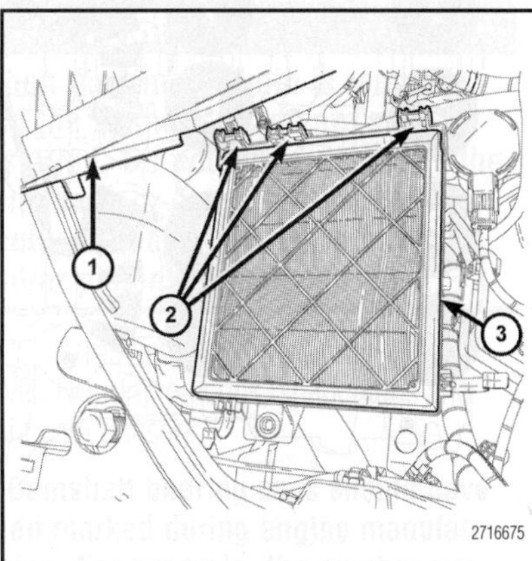

Fig. 80 Lift the cover (1) and release the cover to housing alignment tabs (2); remove the air cleaner element (3)

4. Remove any dirt or debris from the bottom of the air cleaner housing.

To install:

5. Install the air cleaner element into the air cleaner housing.
6. Position the cover so that the alignment tabs insert into the lower housing.
7. Seat the cover onto the housing and secure the housing cover latches.

3.7L Engine

See Figure 81.

➡**Housing removal is not necessary for element (filter) replacement.**

1. Loosen clamp and disconnect air duct at air cleaner cover.
2. Pry over 4 spring clips from housing cover (spring clips retain cover to housing).
3. Release housing cover from locating tabs on housing and remove cover.
4. Remove air cleaner element (filter) from housing.
5. Clean inside of housing before replacing element.
6. Installation is the reverse of removal.

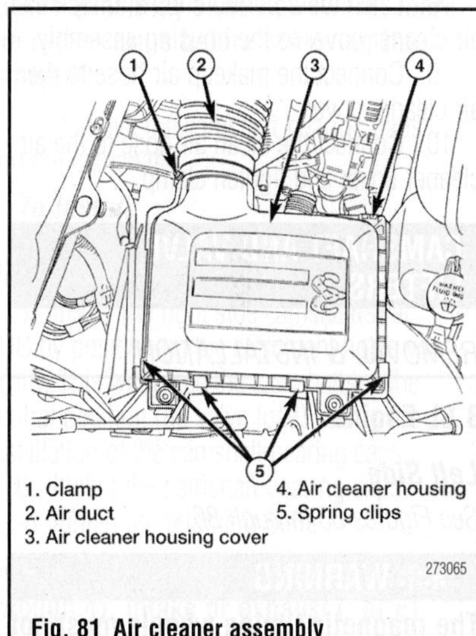

Fig. 81 Air cleaner assembly

5.7L Engine

See Figure 82.

1. Loosen the clean air hose clamp at the air cleaner cover and disconnect the clean air hose.
2. Remove the makeup air hose at the air cleaner cover.
3. Release the 2 spring clips from the air cleaner cover.
4. Remove the air cleaner cover from the housing assembly.
5. Remove the air filter element from the housing assembly.

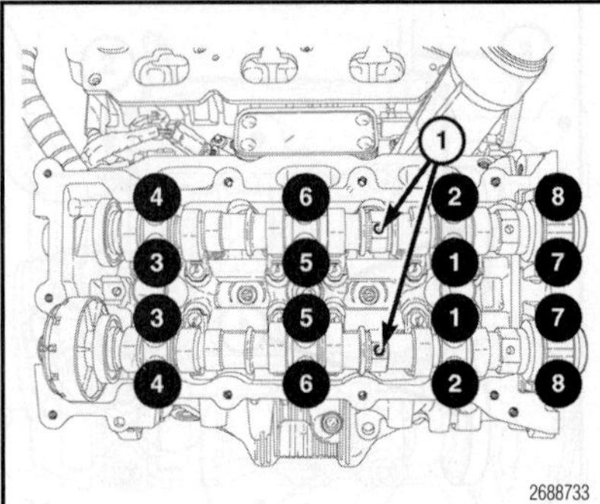

Fig. 89 Install the right side camshaft(s) at TDC by positioning the alignment holes (1) vertically

and should be installed from the front to the rear of the engine. All caps should be installed with the notch forward so that the stamped arrows on the caps point toward the front of the engine.

7. Tighten the bearing cap retaining bolts in the sequence shown to 84 inch lbs. (9.5 Nm).
8. Install the right cam phasers, spark plugs, RH ignition coils and the cylinder head cover.

➡The Cam/Crank Variation Relearn procedure must be performed using the scan tool anytime there has been a repair/replacement made to a powertrain system, for example: flywheel, valve train, camshaft and/or crankshaft sensors or components.

3.7L Engine

Left Side

See Figures 90 through 92.

⁂ WARNING

When the timing chain is removed and the cylinder heads are still installed, Do not forcefully rotate the camshafts or crankshaft independently of each other. Severe valve and/or piston damage can occur.

⁂ WARNING

When removing the cam sprocket, timing chains or camshaft, Failure to use Wedge Locking Tool Locking Tool, Wedge will result in hydraulic tensioner ratchet over extension, requiring timing chain cover removal to reset the tensioner ratchet.

1. Remove cylinder head cover.
2. Set engine to TDC cylinder No. 1, camshaft sprocket V6 marks at the 12 o'clock position.

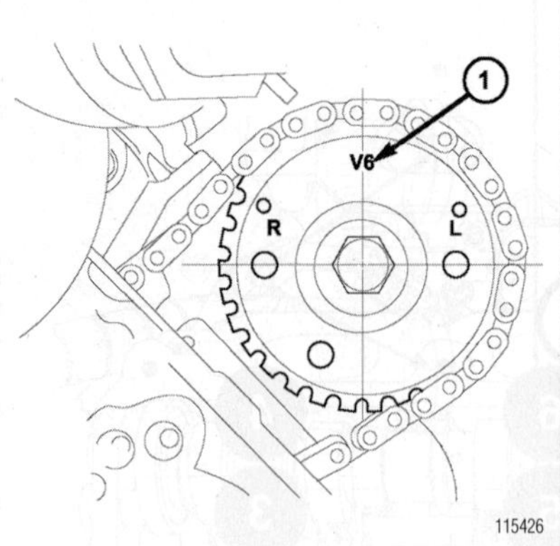

Fig. 90 Set engine to TDC cylinder No. 1, camshaft sprocket V6 marks (1) at the 12 o'clock position

3. Mark one link on the secondary timing chain on both sides of the V6 mark on the camshaft sprocket to aid in installation.

⁂ WARNING

Do not hold or pry on the camshaft target wheel (Located on the right side camshaft sprocket) for any reason, Severe damage will occur to the target wheel resulting in a vehicle no start condition.

4. Loosen but DO NOT remove the camshaft sprocket retaining bolt. Leave the bolt snug against the sprocket.

➡The timing chain tensioners must be secured prior to removing the camshaft sprockets. Failure to secure tensioners will allow the tensioners to extend, requiring timing chain cover removal in order to reset tensioners.

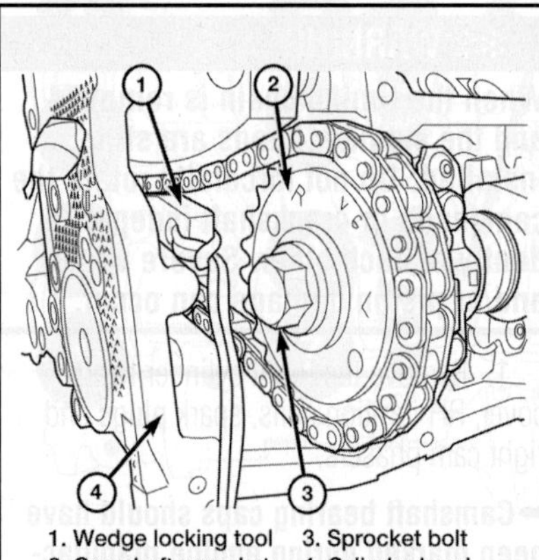

Fig. 91 Position Wedge Locking Tool between the timing chain strands

⁂ WARNING

Do not force the wedge past the narrowest point between the chain strands. Damage to the tensioners may occur.

5. Position Wedge Locking Tool between the timing chain strands, tap the tool to securely wedge the timing chain against the tensioner arm and guide.
6. Hold the camshaft with the Spanner Wrench and Adapter Pins while removing the camshaft sprocket bolt.
7. Using Camshaft Holder, remove the sprocket and gently allow the camshaft to rotate 5 degrees clockwise until the camshaft is in the neutral position (no valve load).
8. Starting at the outside working inward, loosen the camshaft bearing cap retaining bolts half turn at a time. Repeat until all load is off the bearing caps.

⁂ WARNING

Do not stamp or strike the camshaft bearing caps. Severe damage will occur to the bearing caps.

➡When the camshaft is removed the rocker arms may slide downward, mark the rocker arms before removing camshaft.

9. Remove the camshaft bearing caps and the camshaft.

To install:

10. Lubricate the camshaft journals with clean engine oil.

➡Position the left side camshaft so that the camshaft sprocket dowel is near the 1 o'clock position, This will place the camshaft at the neutral position easing the installation of the camshaft bearing caps.

11. Position the camshaft into the cylinder head.
12. Install the camshaft bearing caps, hand tighten the retaining bolts.

➡Caps should be installed so that the stamped numbers on the caps are in numerical order, (1 through 4) from the front to the rear of the engine. All caps should be installed so that the stamped arrows on the caps point toward the front of the engine.

13. Working in half turn increments, tighten the bearing cap retaining bolts starting with the middle cap working outward.
14. Tighten the camshaft bearing cap retaining bolts to 100 inch lbs. (11 Nm).

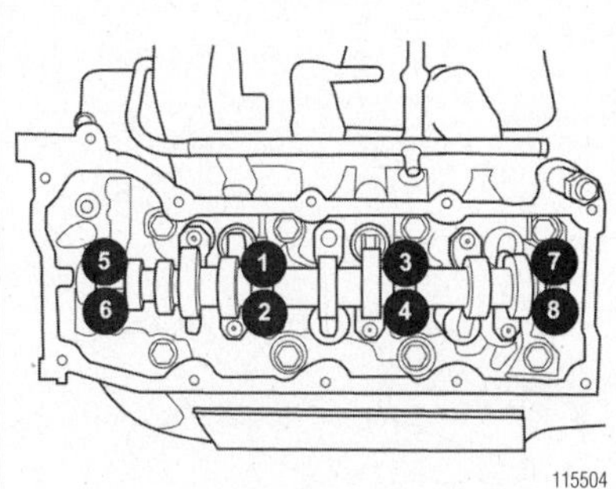

Fig. 92 Working in half turn increments, tighten the bearing cap retaining bolts starting with the middle cap working outward

15. Position the camshaft drive gear into the timing chain aligning the V6 mark between the two marked chain links (Two links marked during removal).

16. Using the Camshaft Holder, rotate the camshaft until the camshaft sprocket dowel is aligned with the slot in the camshaft sprocket. Install the sprocket onto the camshaft.

** WARNING

Remove excess oil from the camshaft sprocket retaining bolt, failure to do so can cause bolt over-torque resulting in bolt failure.

17. Remove excess oil from bolt, then install the camshaft sprocket retaining bolt and hand tighten.

18. Remove the Wedge Locking Tool.

19. Using Spanner Wrench with adapter pins, tighten the camshaft sprocket retaining bolt to 90 ft. lbs. (122 Nm).

20. Install the cylinder head cover.

Right Side

See Figures 91 through 93.

** WARNING

When the timing chain is removed and the cylinder heads are still installed, Do not forcefully rotate the camshafts or crankshaft independently of each other. Severe valve and/or piston damage can occur.

** WARNING

When removing the cam sprocket, timing chains or camshaft, Failure to use special tool Locking Tool, Wedge will result in hydraulic tensioner ratchet over extension, Requiring timing chain cover removal to re-set the tensioner ratchet.

1. Remove the cylinder head cover.

2. Set engine to TDC cylinder No. 1, camshaft sprocket V6 marks at the 12 o'clock position.

3. Mark one link on the secondary timing chain on both sides of the V6 mark on the camshaft sprocket to aid in installation.

** WARNING

Do not hold or pry on the camshaft target wheel for any reason, severe damage will occur to the target wheel resulting in a vehicle no start condition.

4. Loosen but DO NOT remove the camshaft sprocket retaining bolt. Leave bolt snug against sprocket.

➡The timing chain tensioners must be secured prior to removing the camshaft sprockets. Failure to secure tensioners will allow the tensioners to extend, requiring timing chain cover removal in order to reset tensioners.

** WARNING

Do not force the Wedge Locking Tool past the narrowest point between the chain strands. Damage to the tensioners may occur.

5. Position the Wedge Locking Tool between the timing chain strands. Tap the tool to securely wedge the timing chain against the tensioner arm and guide.

6. Remove the camshaft position sensor.

7. Hold the camshaft with Spanner Wrench, while removing the camshaft sprocket bolt and sprocket.

8. Starting at the outside working inward, loosen the camshaft bearing cap retaining bolts half turn at a time. Repeat until all load is off the bearing caps.

** WARNING

Do not stamp or strike the camshaft bearing caps. Severe damage will occur to the bearing caps.

➡When the camshaft is removed the rocker arms may slide downward, mark the rocker arms before removing camshaft.

9. Remove the camshaft bearing caps and the camshaft.

To install:

10. Lubricate camshaft journals with clean engine oil.

➡Position the right side camshaft so that the camshaft sprocket dowel is near the 10 o'clock position, This will place the camshaft at the neutral position easing the installation of the camshaft bearing caps.

11. Position the camshaft into the cylinder head.

12. Install the camshaft bearing caps, hand tighten the retaining bolts.

➡Caps should be installed so that the stamped numbers on the caps are in numerical order, (1 thru 4) from the front to the rear of the engine. All caps should be installed so that the stamped arrows on the caps point toward the front of the engine.

13. Working in half turn increments, tighten the bearing cap retaining bolts starting with the middle cap working outward.

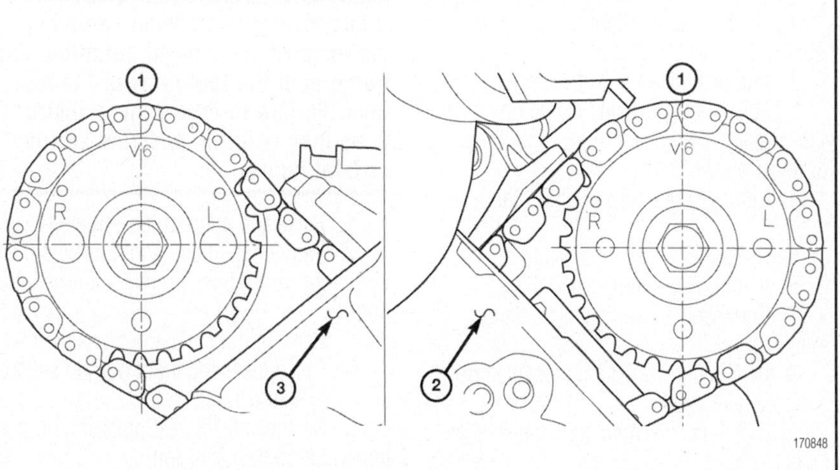

Fig. 93 Set engine to TDC cylinder No. 1, camshaft sprocket V6 marks at the 12 o'clock position (1); LH cylinder head (2), RH cylinder head (3)

14. Tighten the camshaft bearing cap retaining bolts to 100 inch lbs. (11 Nm).

15. Position the camshaft drive gear into the timing chain aligning the V6 mark between the two marked chain links (Two links marked during removal).

16. Using Camshaft Holder, rotate the camshaft until the camshaft sprocket dowel is aligned with the slot in the camshaft sprocket. Install the sprocket onto the camshaft.

✱✱ WARNING

Remove excess oil from the camshaft sprocket retaining bolt, failure to do so can cause bolt over-torque resulting in bolt failure.

17. Remove excess oil from camshaft sprocket bolt, then install the camshaft sprocket retaining bolt and hand tighten.

18. Remove the Wedge Locking Tool.

19. Using Spanner Wrench with adapter pins, tighten the camshaft sprocket retaining bolt to 90 ft. lbs. (122 Nm).

20. Install the camshaft position sensor.

21. Install the cylinder head cover.

CATALYTIC CONVERTER

REMOVAL & INSTALLATION

3.6L Engine

✱✱ CAUTION

If torches are used when servicing the exhaust system, do not allow any flame near the fuel lines or the fuel tank. Failure to follow these instructions may result in possible serious or fatal injury.

1. Disconnect negative battery cable.
2. Remove the engine cover.
3. Saturate the exhaust flange bolts with heat valve lubricant. Allow 5 minutes for penetration.
4. Remove the upper catalytic flange bolts.
5. Raise and support the vehicle.
6. If equipped, remove skid plate.
7. Remove the lower catalytic flange bolts.
8. Remove transmission crossmember reinforcement brackets.
9. Disconnect oxygen sensor electrical connectors.
10. Remove the nuts from the front exhaust pipe/catalytic converter assembly to the muffler flange.
11. Remove the front exhaust pipe/catalytic converter assembly from the vehicle.

To install:

12. Position new exhaust gasket onto flange.
13. Position the front exhaust pipe/catalytic converter assemblies into vehicle.
14. Install the lower bolts at the front exhaust pipe/catalytic converter assembly to exhaust manifold flange. Do not tighten.
15. Lower vehicle.
16. Install the upper bolts at the front exhaust pipe/catalytic converter assemblies to exhaust manifold flanges. Tighten bolts to 17 ft. lbs. (23 Nm).
17. Raise vehicle.
18. Tighten lower flange bolts to 17 ft. lbs. (23 Nm).
19. Position the exhaust system for proper clearance with the frame and underbody parts. A minimum clearance of 1 inch (25.4 mm) is required.
20. Tighten the front exhaust pipe/catalytic converter assembly to muffler flange nuts to 35 ft. lbs. (47 Nm).
21. Connect oxygen sensor electrical connectors.
22. Install transmission crossmember reinforcement brackets. Tighten bolts to 41 ft. lbs. (55 Nm).
23. If equipped, install skid plates.
24. Lower vehicle.
25. Start the vehicle and inspect for exhaust leaks. Repair exhaust leaks as necessary.

3.7L Engine

See Figure 94.

✱✱ CAUTION

If torches are used when servicing the exhaust system, do not allow any flame near the fuel lines or the fuel tank. Failure to follow these instructions may result in possible serious or fatal injury.

1. Raise and support the vehicle.
2. Saturate the bolts and nuts with heat valve lubricant. Allow 5 minutes for penetration.
3. Remove transmission crossmember.
4. Disconnect and mark oxygen sensor electrical connectors.
5. Remove steady rest bracket mounting bolt from transmission.
6. Remove the nuts from the front exhaust pipe/catalytic converter assembly to muffler flange.

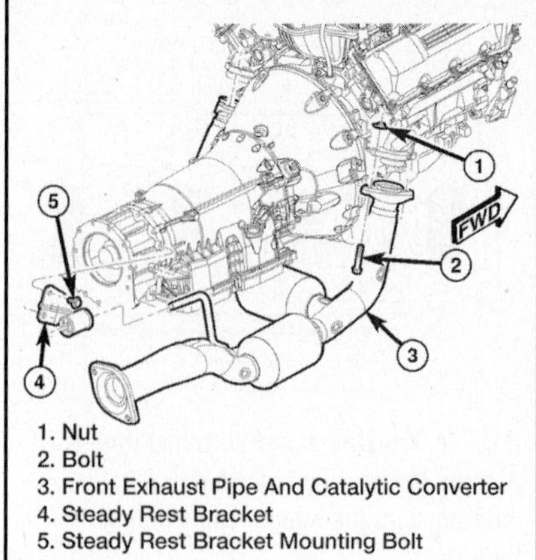

Fig. 94 Catalytic converter assembly—3.7L engine

7. Remove bolts and flanged nuts at the exhaust manifold.
8. Remove the front exhaust pipe/catalytic converter assembly from the vehicle.
9. Remove steady rest bracket from front exhaust pipe/catalytic converter assembly.

To install:

10. Position steady rest bracket onto the front exhaust pipe/catalytic converter assembly.
11. Position the front exhaust pipe/catalytic converter assembly into vehicle.
12. Install the bolts and nuts at the front exhaust pipe/catalytic converter assembly to exhaust manifold flange. Do not tighten.
13. Install the nuts at the front exhaust pipe/catalytic converter assembly to muffler flange. Do not tighten.
14. Position the exhaust pipe for proper clearance with the frame and underbody parts. A minimum clearance of 1.0 inches (25.4 mm) is required.
15. Tighten front exhaust pipe/catalytic converter assembly to exhaust manifold bolts to 19 ft. lbs. (26 Nm).
16. Tighten the front exhaust pipe and catalytic converter assembly to muffler flange nuts to 35 ft. lbs. (47 Nm).
17. Install steady rest bracket bolts. Tighten bolts to 35 ft. lbs. (47 Nm).
18. Connect oxygen sensor electrical connectors.
19. Install transmission crossmember.
20. Lower vehicle.
21. Start the vehicle and inspect for exhaust leaks. Repair exhaust leaks as necessary.

5.7L Engine

**** CAUTION**

If torches are used when servicing the exhaust system, do not allow any flame near the fuel lines or the fuel tank. Failure to follow these instructions may result in possible serious or fatal injury.

1. Disconnect the negative cable
2. Raise and support the vehicle.
3. If equipped, remove skid plates.
4. Saturate the bolts and nuts with heat valve lubricant. Allow 5 minutes for penetration.
5. Remove transmission crossmember reinforcement brackets.
6. If equipped, remove the lower heat shield near the front driveshaft.
7. Remove the upstream and the downstream oxygen sensors from the exhaust.
8. Remove the nuts from the front exhaust pipe/catalytic converter assembly to muffler flange.
9. Remove bolts and flanged nuts at the exhaust manifold.
10. Remove the front exhaust pipe/catalytic converter assembly from the vehicle.

To install:

11. Position the front exhaust pipe/catalytic converter assembly into vehicle.
12. Install the nuts at the front exhaust pipe/catalytic converter assembly to muffler flange at the exhaust manifold.
13. Install the bolts at the front exhaust pipe/catalytic converter assembly to exhaust manifold flange. Do not tighten.
14. Tighten the front exhaust pipe and catalytic converter assembly to muffler flange nuts to 35 ft. lbs. (47 Nm).
15. Position the exhaust pipe for proper clearance with the frame and underbody parts. A minimum clearance of 1 inch (25.4 mm) is required.
16. Tighten front exhaust pipe/catalytic converter assembly to exhaust manifold bolts to 22 ft. lbs. (30 Nm) torque.
17. Install the oxygen sensors.
18. If equipped, install the heat shield for the front drive shaft.
19. Install transmission crossmember reinforcement brackets. Tighten bolts to 41 ft. lbs. (55 Nm).
20. If equipped, install skid plates.
21. Lower vehicle.
22. Start the vehicle and inspect for exhaust leaks. Repair exhaust leaks as necessary.

CRANKSHAFT FRONT SEAL

REMOVAL & INSTALLATION

3.6L Engine

See Figures 95 through 97.

1. Remove the accessory drive belt and the crankshaft vibration damper.
2. Install the sleeve from the Seal Remover around the flywheel key and onto the nose of the crankshaft.
3. Screw the Seal Remover into the front crankshaft oil seal.
4. Install the extractor screw into the Seal Remover.
5. Hold the seal remover stationary and tighten the extractor screw against the sleeve until the front crankshaft oil seal is removed from the engine timing cover.

To install:

6. Position the front crankshaft oil seal into place on the engine timing cover.

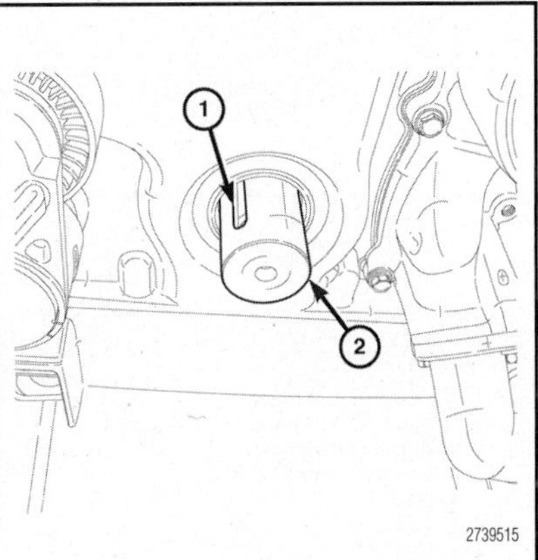

Fig. 95 Install the sleeve (2) from the Seal Remover around the flywheel key (1) and onto the nose of the crankshaft

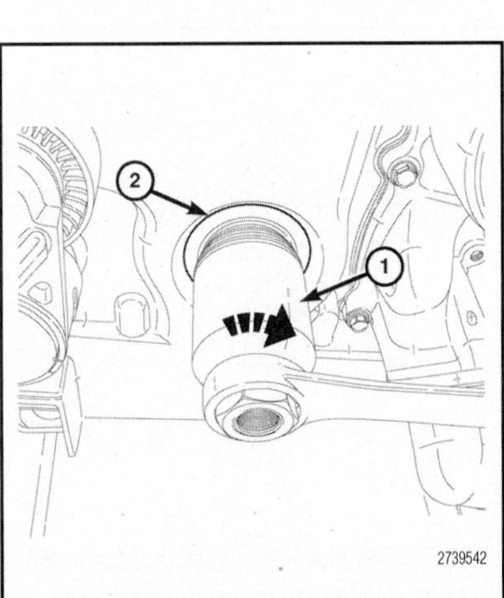

Fig. 96 Screw the Seal Remover (1) into the front crankshaft oil seal (2)

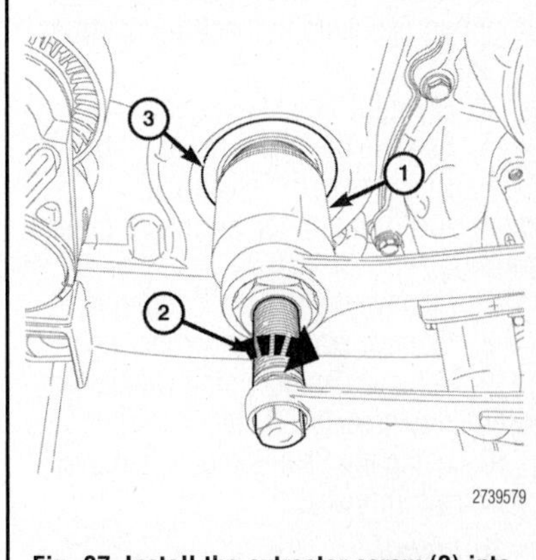

Fig. 97 Install the extractor screw (2) into the Seal Remover (1); front crankshaft oil seal (3)

7. Align the Front Crankshaft Seal Installer to the flywheel key on the crankshaft and against the front crankshaft oil seal.

**** WARNING**

Only tighten the crankshaft vibration damper bolt until the oil seal is seated in the cover. Overtightening of the bolt can crack the front timing cover.

8. Install and tighten the crankshaft vibration damper bolt until the Crankshaft oil seal is seated in the engine timing cover.
9. Install the crankshaft vibration damper and accessory drive belt.

3.7L Engine

See Figures 98 through 100.

1. Disconnect negative cable from battery.
2. Remove the accessory drive belt.

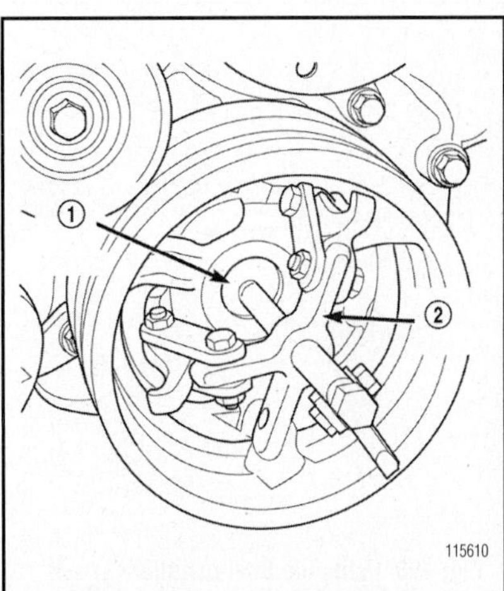

Fig. 98 Remove damper using Crankshaft Insert (1) and Three Jaw Puller (2)

3. Remove A/C compressor mounting fasteners and set the compressor aside.
4. Drain the cooling system.
5. Remove the upper radiator hose.
6. Disconnect the electrical connector for fan mounted inside radiator shroud.
7. Remove the radiator cooling fan.
8. Remove crankshaft damper bolt.
9. Remove damper using Crankshaft Insert and Three Jaw Puller.
10. Using the Seal Remover, remove crankshaft front seal.

To install:

⁂ WARNING

To prevent severe damage to the Crankshaft, Damper or Damper Installer, Damper, thoroughly clean the damper bore and the crankshaft nose before installing Damper.

11. Using the Seal Installer and Damper Installer, install the crankshaft front seal.
12. Install the vibration damper.
13. Install the radiator cooling fan and shroud.
14. Install the upper radiator hose.
15. Install A/C compressor and tighten fasteners to 40 ft. lbs. (54 Nm).
16. Install the accessory drive belt.
17. Refill the cooling system.
18. Connect the negative battery cable to battery.

5.7L Engine

See Figures 101 through 106.

1. Disconnect and isolate the negative battery cable.
2. Disconnect the electrical connector at the Intake Air Temperature (IAT) sensor.
3. Loosen the clean air hose clamp at the air cleaner housing.
4. Remove the resonator retaining bolt.
5. Loosen the resonator hose clamp at the throttle body and remove the resonator.
6. Remove the serpentine belt.
7. Drain the cooling system.
8. Remove the upper radiator hose clamp at the thermostat housing.
9. Remove the upper radiator hose retainer at the fan shroud and position the radiator hose aside.
10. Remove the cooling fan module.
11. Remove the crankshaft damper bolt.

➡When installing the puller tool, ensure the bolts are fully threaded through the entire crankshaft damper.

12. Install puller tool and remove the crankshaft damper.
13. Using Seal Remover, remove crankshaft front seal.

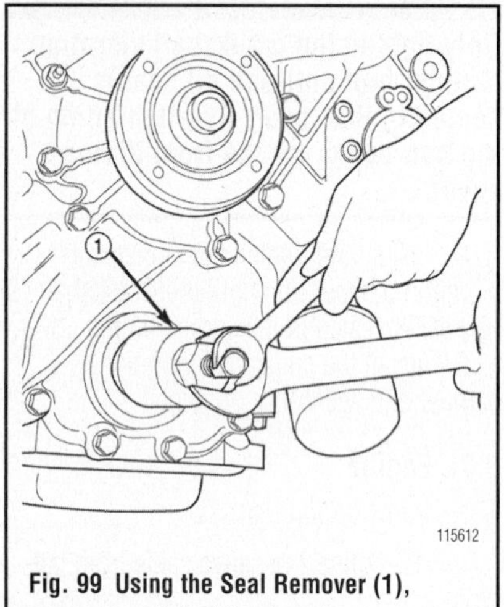

Fig. 99 Using the Seal Remover (1), remove crankshaft front seal

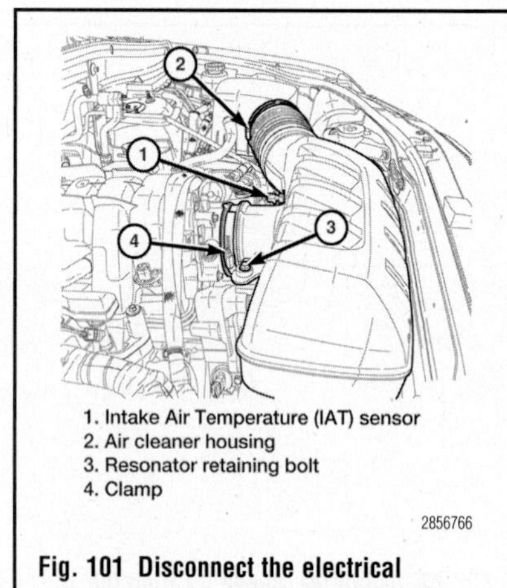

Fig. 101 Disconnect the electrical connector at the Intake Air Temperature (IAT) sensor

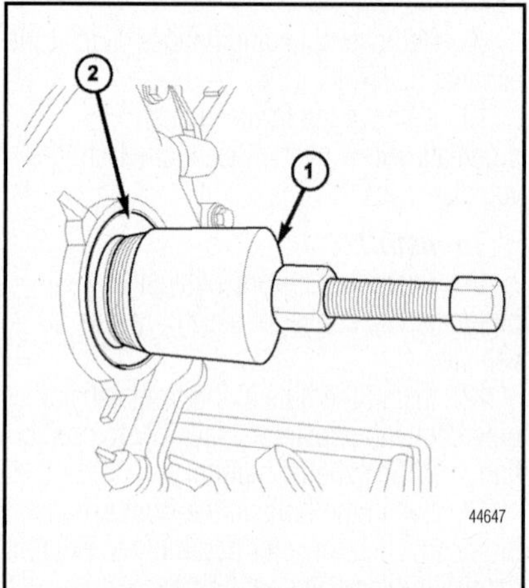

Fig. 103 Using Seal Remover (1), remove crankshaft front seal (2)

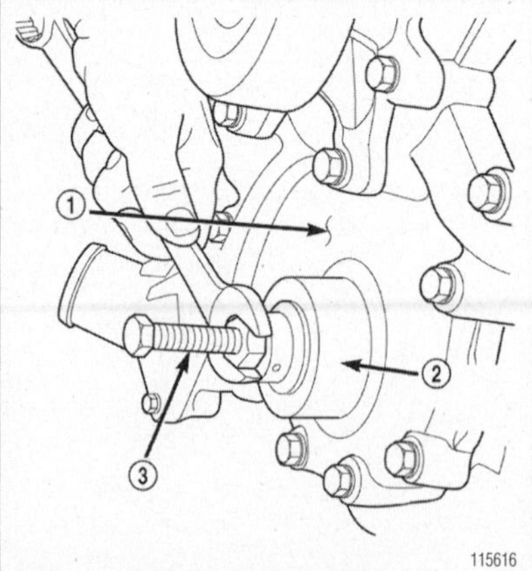

Fig. 100 Using the Seal Installer (2) and Damper Installer (3), install the crankshaft front seal; engine front cover (1)

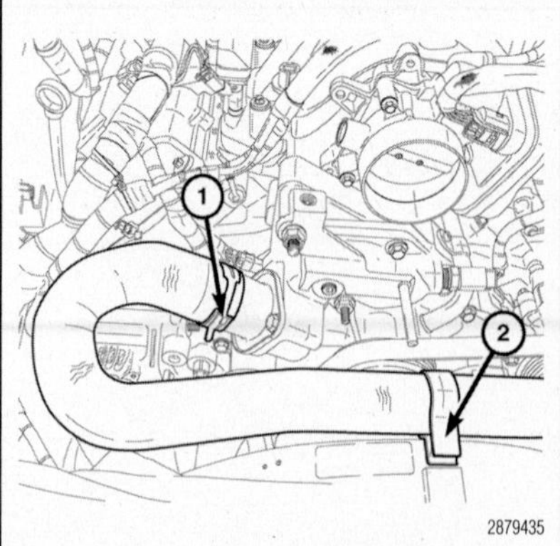

Fig. 102 Remove the upper radiator hose clamp (1) at the thermostat housing and the upper radiator hose retainer (2) at the fan shroud

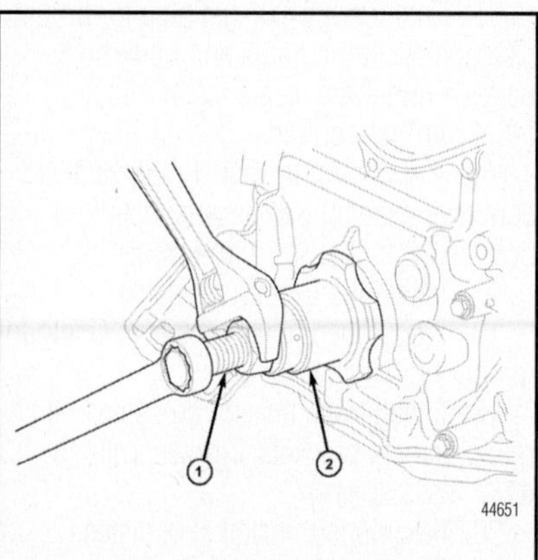

Fig. 104 Using Crankshaft Front Oil Seal Installer (2) and Damper Installer (1), install the crankshaft front seal

To install:

⁂ WARNING

The front crankshaft seal must be installed dry. Do not apply lubricant to the sealing lip or the outer edge.

14. Using Crankshaft Front Oil Seal Installer and Damper Installer, install the crankshaft front seal.

⁂ WARNING

To prevent severe damage to the crankshaft, damper, and damper installer, thoroughly clean the damper bore and the crankshaft nose before installing damper.

15. Position the damper onto the crankshaft.
16. Assemble the Damper Installer and the Pressing Cup from A/C Hub Installer.
17. Using the Damper Installer and A/C Hub Installer, press the damper onto the crankshaft.
18. Install the crankshaft damper bolt and tighten to 129 ft. lbs. (176 Nm).
19. Install the cooling fan module.
20. Position the upper radiator hose and secure retainer at the fan shroud.
21. Install the upper radiator hose at the thermostat housing and secure hose clamp.
22. Install the air cleaner resonator support bracket at the water pump.
23. Install serpentine belt.
24. Connect the resonator hose at the throttle body and tighten clamp.
25. Install the resonator retaining bolt.
26. Connect the clean air hose at the air cleaner housing and tighten clamp.
27. Connect the electrical connector at the Intake Air Temperature (IAT) sensor.
28. Refill the cooling system.
29. Connect the negative battery cable.

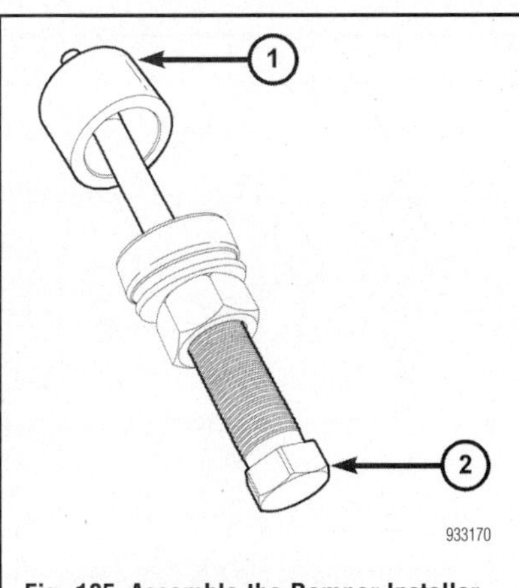

Fig. 105 Assemble the Damper Installer (2) and the Pressing Cup (1) from A/C Hub Installer

CYLINDER HEAD

REMOVAL & INSTALLATION

3.6L Engine

Left Side

See Figures 107 through 128.

⁂ WARNING

The magnetic timing wheels must not come in contact with magnets (pickup tools, trays, etc.) or any other strong magnetic field. This will destroy the timing wheels ability to correctly relay camshaft position to the camshaft position sensor.

1. Perform the fuel pressure release procedure.
2. Disconnect and isolate the negative battery cable.
3. Remove the engine cover.
4. Remove the air inlet hose and the air cleaner body.
5. Remove the electric vacuum pump and mounting bracket.

➡Power steering pump not shown.

6. Raise and support the vehicle.
7. If equipped, remove the front skid plate and front suspension skid plate.
8. Drain the cooling system.
9. Drain the engine oil.
10. Remove the nut and bolt from the support brackets of the heater core return tube.
11. Remove the A/C compressor mounting stud.
12. Lower the vehicle.
13. Remove the nut from the support bracket of the heater core return tube and reposition the tube.

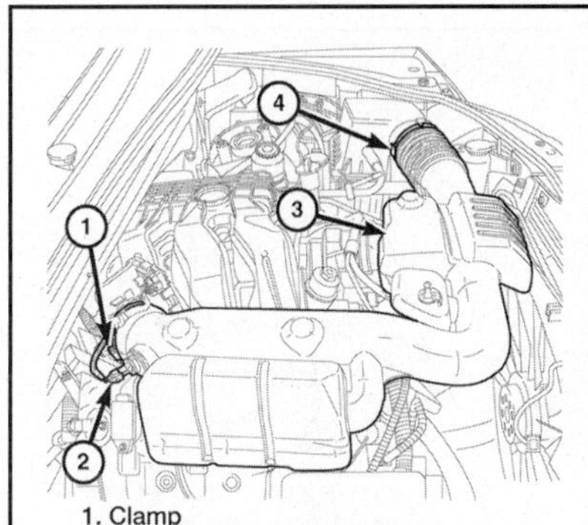

Fig. 108 Remove the air inlet hose and the air cleaner body

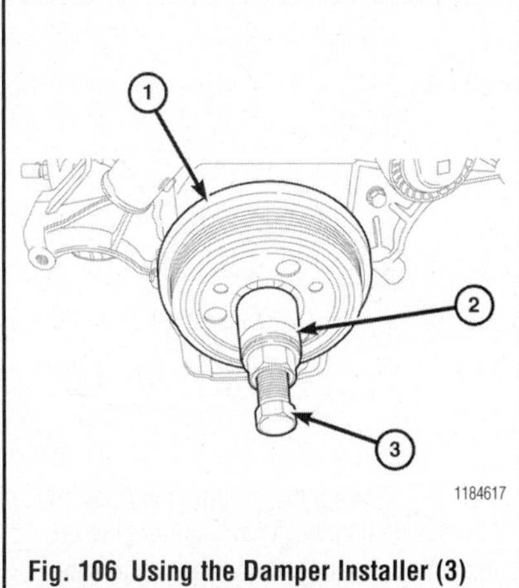

Fig. 106 Using the Damper Installer (3) and A/C Hub Installer (2), press the damper (1) onto the crankshaft

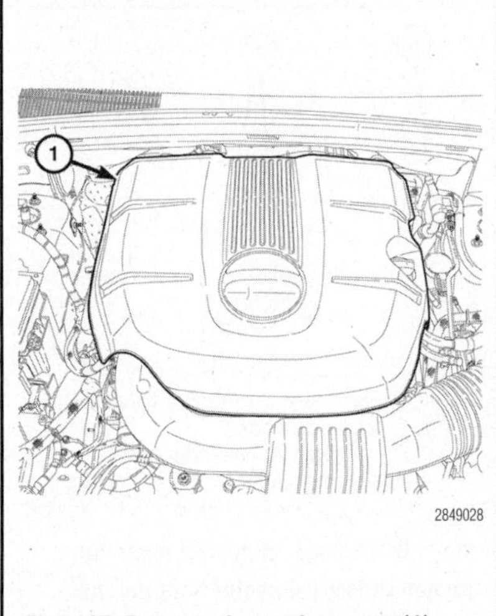

Fig. 107 Remove the engine cover (1)

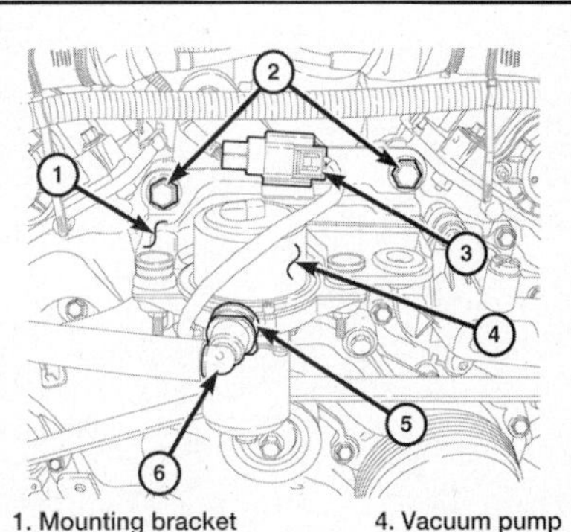

Fig. 109 Remove the electric vacuum pump and mounting bracket

14. Remove the vapor purge tube from the fuel purge solenoid.

15. Remove the upper and lower intake manifolds and insulator.

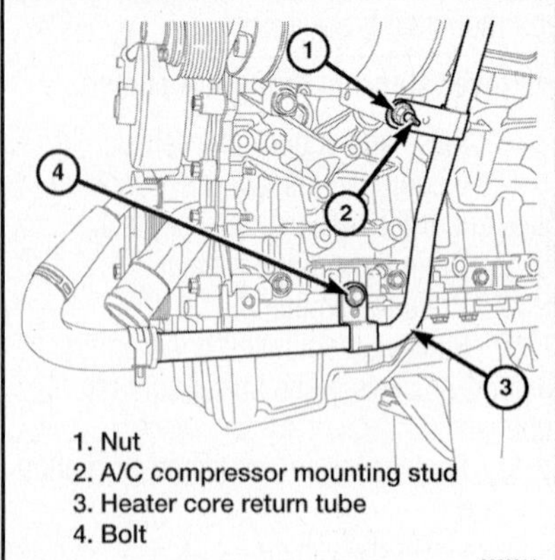

Fig. 110 Remove the nut and bolt from the support brackets of the heater core return tube

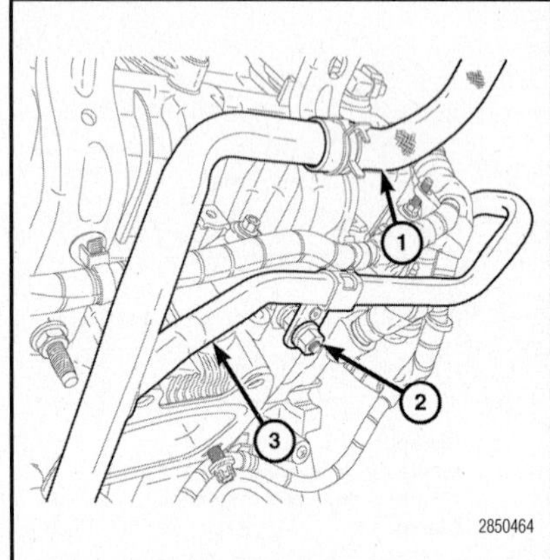

Fig. 111 Remove the nut (2) from the support bracket of the heater core return tube (3) and reposition the tube; hose (1)

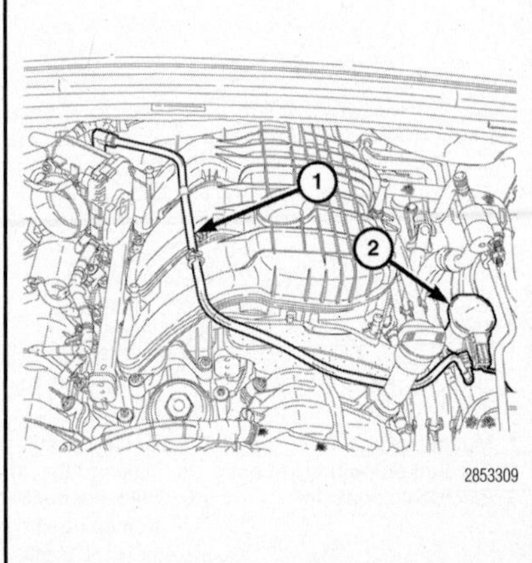

Fig. 112 Remove the vapor purge tube (1) from the fuel purge solenoid (2)

16. Disengage the clips, remove the make-up air tube from the left cylinder head cover and reposition the transmission breather hose.

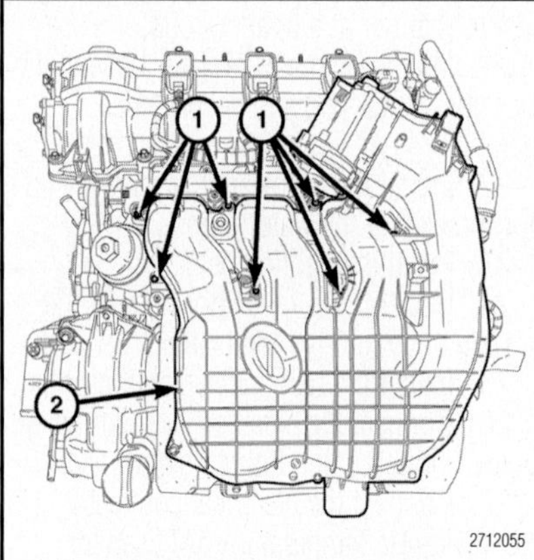

Fig. 113 Remove the upper and lower intake manifolds (2) and insulator; retainers (1)

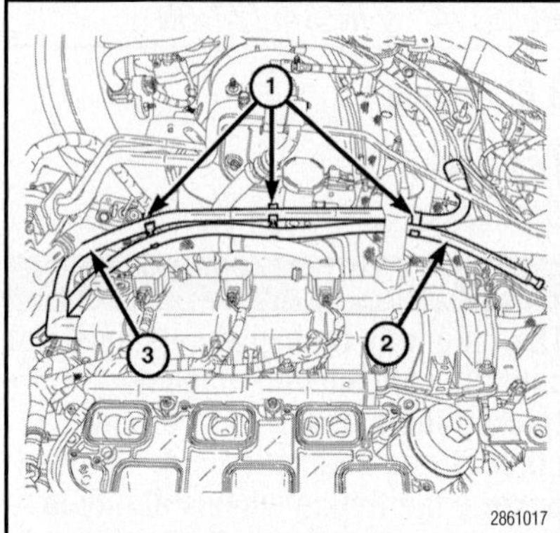

Fig. 114 Disengage the clips (1), remove the make-up air tube (3) from the left cylinder head cover and reposition the transmission breather hose (2)

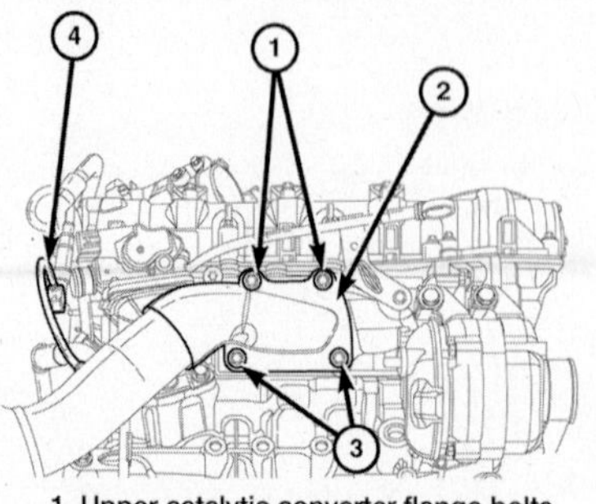

Fig. 115 Disconnect the left upstream oxygen sensor connector from the main wire harness

➡Right catalytic converter shown, left catalytic converter similar.

17. Disconnect the left upstream oxygen sensor connector from the main wire harness.

18. Loosen the lower catalytic converter flange bolts.

19. Remove the upper catalytic converter flange bolts and reposition the catalytic converter.

20. Remove the accessory drive belt.

21. Disconnect the A/C compressor electrical connector and disengage the wire harness retainer from the A/C compressor discharge line.

22. Remove the remaining three bolts and reposition the A/C compressor.

23. Disconnect the Engine Coolant Temperature (ECT) sensor electrical connector.

24. Disconnect the ignition coil capacitor electrical connector.

25. Disengage the injection/ignition harness connector and the engine oil pres-

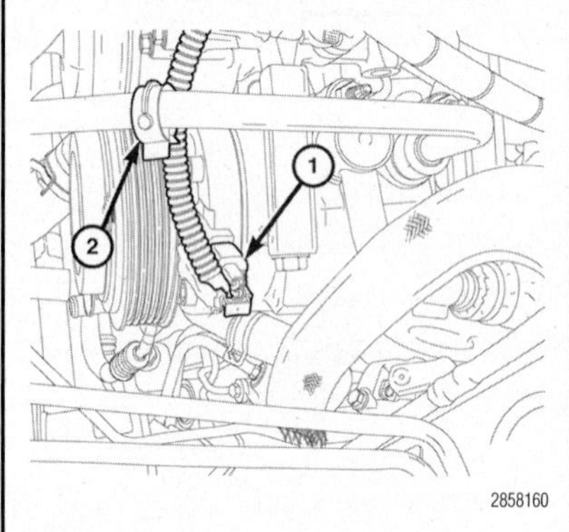

Fig. 116 Disconnect the A/C compressor electrical connector (1) and disengage the wire harness retainer (2) from the A/C compressor discharge line

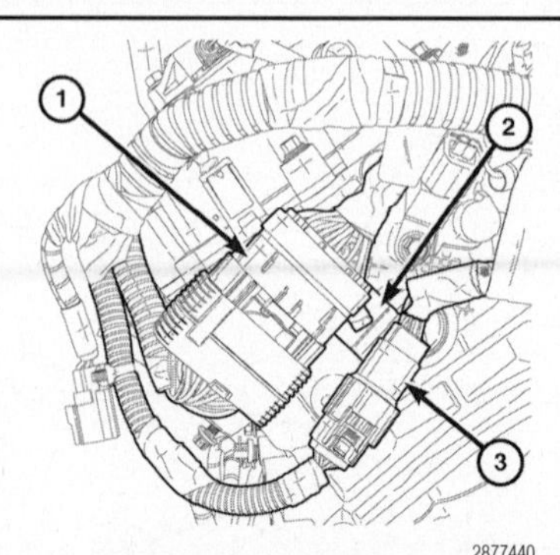

Fig. 117 Disengage the injection/ignition harness connector (1) and the engine oil pressure/temperature harness connector (3) from the retainer bracket (2) on the rear of the left cylinder head

➡**The multi-layered steel h have very sharp edges that cause personal injury if no carefully.**

⁂ WARNING

The cylinder head gasket interchangeable between right cylinder heads and marked with "R" for righ left.

51. Position the new cylin ket on the locating dowels.
52. Position the cylinder h cylinder block. Make sure th seats fully over the locating d

➡**Do not apply any additi bolt threads.**

53. Install the eight head tight.
54. Tighten the cylinder h sequence shown, following t torque plus angle method. T ing to the following torque v
 a. Step 1: All to 22 ft. (30 Nm)
 b. Step 2: All to 33 ft.
 c. Step 3: All plus 75 use a torque wrench for t
 d. Step 4: All plus 50 use a torque wrench for t
 e. Step 5: Loosen all reverse of sequence sho
 f. Step 6: All to 22 ft
 g. Step 7: All to 33 ft
 h. Step 8: All plus 70 use a torque wrench for
 i. Step 9: All plus 70 use a torque wrench for

➡**If the hydraulic lifters reused, reassemble the original locations.**

55. If removed, install t lifters.

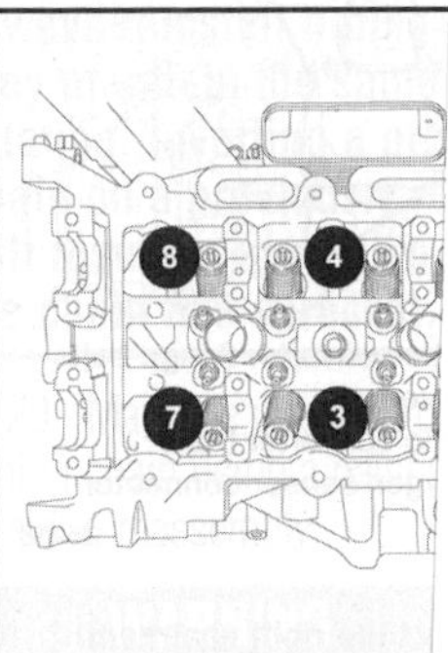

Fig. 125 Tighten the cyli in the sequence shown

sure/temperature harness connector from the retainer bracket on the rear of the left cylinder head.

26. Disengage two starter wire harness retainers from the upper intake manifold support brackets.
27. Disengage one main wire harness retainer from the left cylinder head cover and two retainers from the upper intake manifold support brackets.
28. Remove the bolts and remove the LH upper intake manifold support brackets.
29. Remove the spark plugs.
30. Remove the cylinder head covers, lower and upper oil pans, crankshaft vibration damper and engine timing cover.

➡**Take this opportunity to measure timing chain wear.**

31. Lower the vehicle.

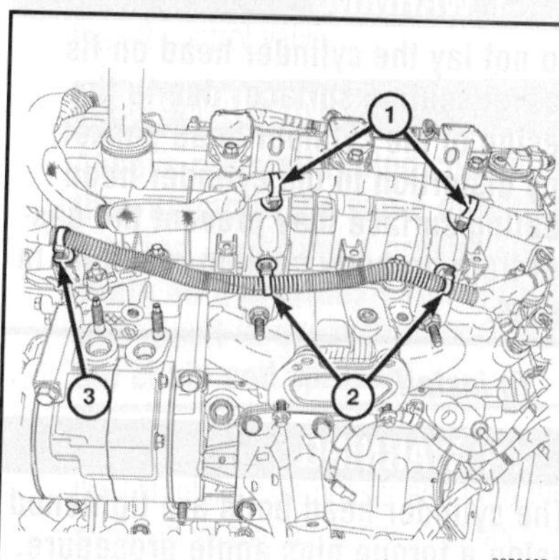

Fig. 118 Disengage two starter wire harness retainers (1) from the upper intake manifold support brackets and disengage one main wire harness retainer (3) from the left cylinder head cover and two retainers (2) from the upper intake manifold support brackets

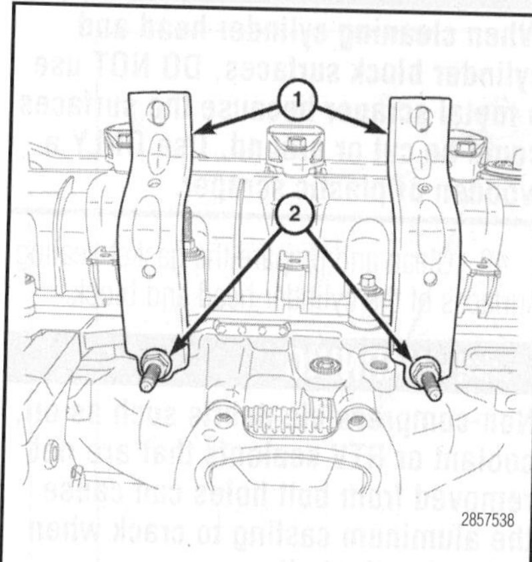

Fig. 119 Remove the bolts (2) and remove the LH upper intake manifold support brackets (1)

⁂ WARNING

When aligning timing marks, always rotate engine by turning the crankshaft. Failure to do so will result in valve and/or piston damage.

32. Rotate the crankshaft clockwise to place the number one piston at TDC on the exhaust stroke by aligning the dimple on the crankshaft with the block/bearing cap junction. The left side cam phaser arrows should point toward each other and be parallel to the valve cover sealing surface. The right side cam phaser arrows should point away from each other and the scribe lines should be parallel to the valve cover sealing surface.

⁂ WARNING

Always reinstall timing chains so that they maintain the same direction of rotation. Inverting a previously run chain on a previously run sprocket will result in excessive wear to both the chain and sprocket.

33. Mark the direction of rotation on the timing chain using a paint pen or equivalent to aid in reassembly.

⁂ WARNING

When the timing chains are removed and the cylinder heads are still installed, DO NOT rotate the camshafts or crankshaft without first locating the proper crankshaft position. Failure to do so will result in valve and/or piston damage.

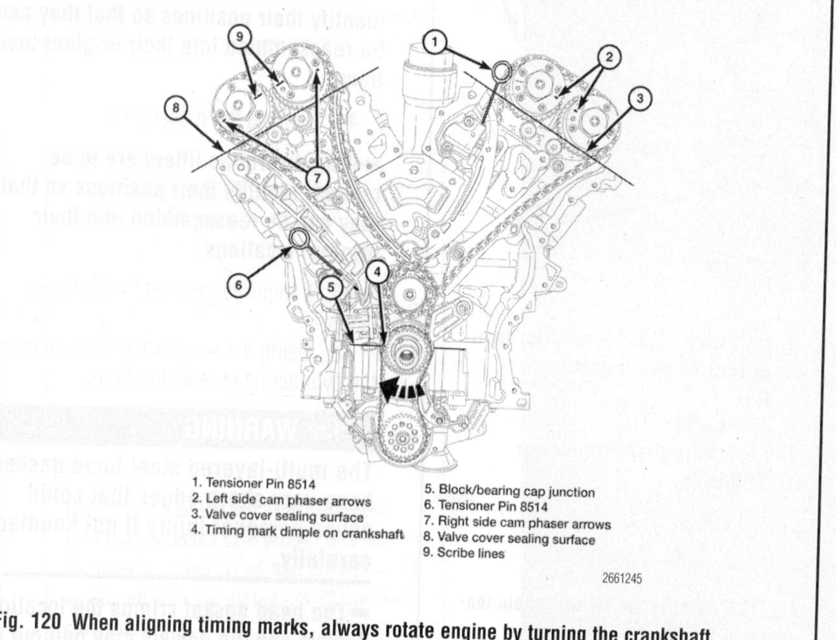

Fig. 120 When aligning timing marks, always rotate engine by turning the crankshaft

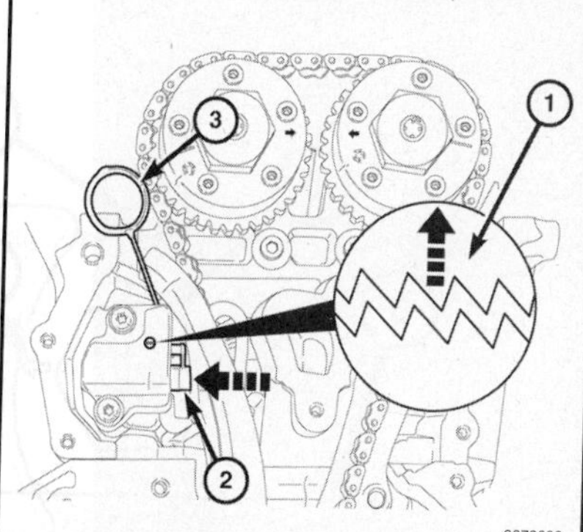

Fig. 121 Reset the LH cam chain tensioner by lifting the pawl (1), pushing back the piston (2) and installing Tensioner Pin (3)

34. Reset the LH cam chain tensioner by lifting the pawl, pushing back the piston and installing Tensioner Pin.

➡**Minor rotation of a camshaft (a few degrees) may be required to install the camshaft phaser lock.**

35. Install the LH Camshaft Phaser Lock.
36. Loosen both the intake oil control valve and exhaust oil control valve.
37. Remove the LH Camshaft Phaser Lock.
38. Remove the oil control valve from the left side exhaust cam phaser and pull the phaser off of the camshaft.
39. Remove the oil control valve from the left side intake cam phaser and pull the phaser off of the camshaft.

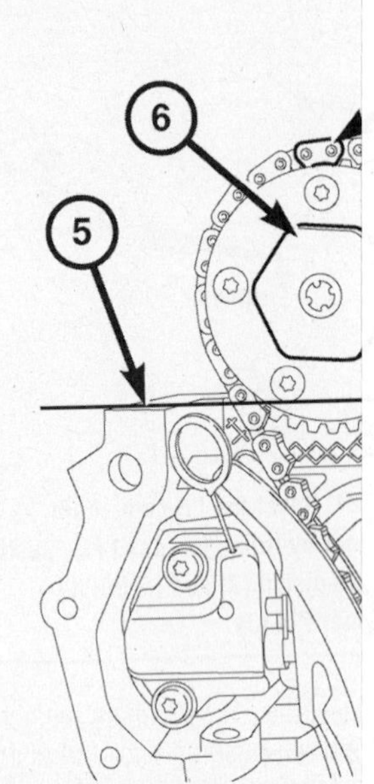

Fig. 122 Install the LH Camshaft Ph

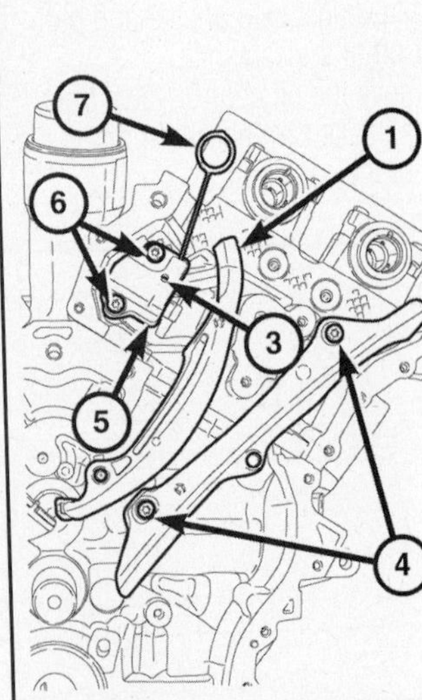

Fig. 123 Remove the LH cam ch sioner arm

87. Install the air inlet hose to the air cleaner body and the throttle body.
88. Connect the electrical connector to the Inlet Air Temperature (IAT) sensor.
89. If removed, install the oil filter and fill the engine crankcase with the proper oil to the correct level.
90. Fill the cooling system.
91. Install the engine cover.
92. Connect the negative battery cable and tighten nut.
93. Run the engine until it reaches normal operating temperature. Check cooling system for correct fluid level.

➡The Cam/Crank Variation Relearn procedure must be performed using the scan tool anytime there has been a repair/replacement made to a powertrain system, for example: flywheel, valve train, camshaft and/or crankshaft sensors or components.

3.7L Engine

Left Side

See Figures 137 through 140.

1. Disconnect the negative battery cable.
2. Raise and support the vehicle.
3. Disconnect the exhaust pipe at the left exhaust manifold.
4. Drain the engine coolant.
5. Lower the vehicle.
6. Remove the intake manifold.
7. Remove the master cylinder and booster assembly.
8. Remove the cylinder head cover.
9. Remove the fan shroud and fan blade assembly.
10. Remove the accessory drive belt.
11. Remove the power steering pump.
12. Rotate the crankshaft until the damper timing mark is aligned with TDC indicator mark.
13. Verify the V6 timing mark on the camshaft sprocket is at the 12 o'clock position, with the No. 1 cylinder at TDC on the exhaust stroke. Rotate the crankshaft one turn if necessary.
14. Remove the vibration damper.
15. Remove the timing chain cover.
16. Lock the secondary timing chains to the idler sprocket using the Secondary Camshaft Chain Holder.

➡Mark the secondary timing chain prior to removal to aid in installation.

17. Mark the secondary timing chain, one link on each side of the V6 timing mark on the camshaft drive gear.
18. Remove the left side secondary chain tensioner.
19. Remove the cylinder head access plugs.
20. Remove the left side secondary chain guide.
21. Remove the retaining bolt and the camshaft drive gear.

⁂ WARNING

Do not allow the engine to rotate. Severe damage to the valve train can occur.

⁂ WARNING

Do not overlook the four smaller bolts at the front of the cylinder head. Do not attempt to remove the cylinder head without removing these four bolts. The locations are identified with an asterisk (*).

➡The cylinder head is attached to the cylinder block with twelve bolts.

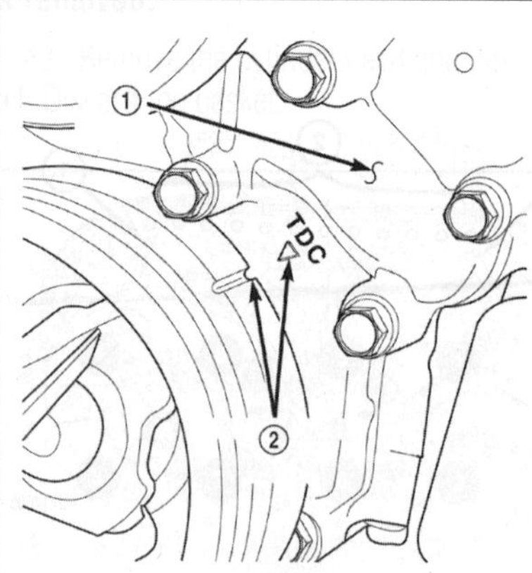

Fig. 137 Rotate the crankshaft until the damper timing mark is aligned with TDC indicator mark (2); engine front cover (1)

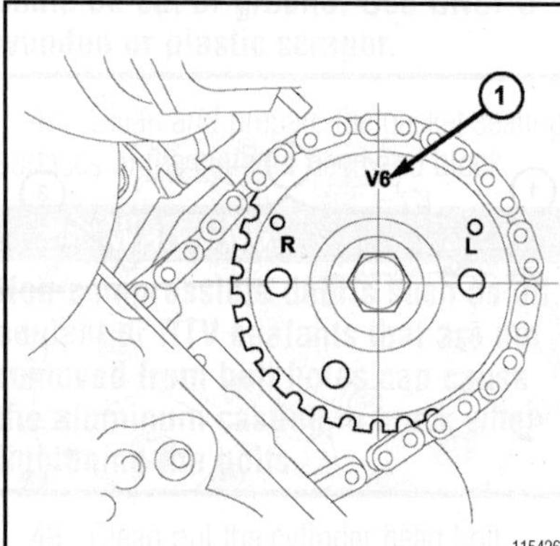

Fig. 138 Verify the V6 timing mark (1) on the camshaft sprocket is at the 12 o'clock position, with the No. 1 cylinder at TDC on the exhaust stroke

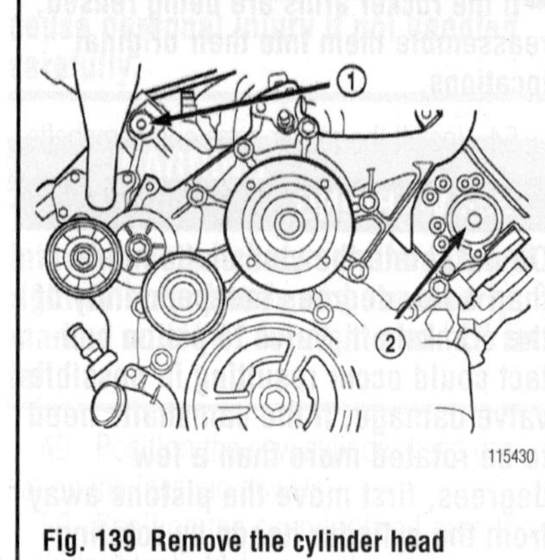

Fig. 139 Remove the cylinder head access plugs (1, 2)

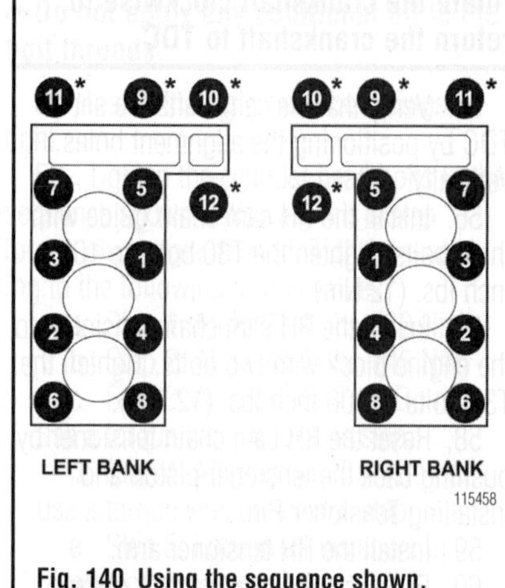

Fig. 140 Using the sequence shown, remove the cylinder head retaining bolts

22. Using the sequence shown, remove the cylinder head retaining bolts.
23. Remove the cylinder head and gasket. Discard the gasket.

⁂ WARNING

Do not lay the cylinder head on its gasket sealing surface, due to the design of the cylinder head gasket, any distortion to the cylinder head sealing surface may prevent the gasket from properly sealing resulting in leaks.

To install:

➡The cylinder head bolts are tightened using a torque plus angle procedure. The bolts must be examined BEFORE reuse. If the threads are necked down the bolts should be replaced.

➡Necking can be checked by holding a straight edge against the threads. If all the threads do not contact the scale, the bolt should be replaced.

WARNING

When cleaning cylinder head and cylinder block surfaces, DO NOT use a metal scraper, high speed Scotch Brite or rolock tool because the surfaces could be cut or ground. Use only a wooden or plastic scraper.

24. Clean the cylinder head and cylinder block mating surfaces.
25. Position the new cylinder head gasket on the locating dowels.

WARNING

When installing cylinder head, use care not damage the tensioner arm or the guide arm.

26. Position the cylinder head onto the cylinder block. Make sure the cylinder head seats fully over the locating dowels.

➡The four smaller cylinder head mounting bolts require sealant to be added to them before installing. Failure to do so may cause leaks. The locations are identified with an asterisk (*).

27. Lubricate the cylinder head bolt threads with clean engine oil and install the eight M11 bolts.
28. Coat the four M8 cylinder head bolts with Mopar® Lock and Seal Adhesive then install the bolts.

➡The cylinder head bolts are tightened using an angle torque procedure, however, the bolts are not a torque-to-yield design.

29. Tighten the bolts in sequence shown during removal using the following steps and torque values:
    a. Step 1: Tighten bolts 1–8, 20 ft. lbs. (27 Nm).
    b. Step 2: Verify that bolts 1–8, all reached 20 ft. lbs. (27 Nm), by repeating Step 1 without loosening the bolts.
    c. Step 3:Tighten bolts 9 thru 12 to 10 ft. lbs. (14 Nm).
    d. Step 4: Tighten bolts 1–8, 90 degrees.
    e. Step 5: Tighten bolts 1–8, 90 degrees, again.
    f. Step 6: Tighten bolts 9–12, 19 ft. lbs. (26 Nm).
30. Position the secondary chain onto the camshaft drive gear, making sure one marked chain link is on either side of the V6 mark on the gear then using Camshaft Holder position the gear onto the camshaft.

WARNING

Remove excess oil from camshaft sprocket retaining bolt before reinstalling bolt. Failure to do so may cause over-torquing of bolt resulting in bolt failure.

31. Install the camshaft drive gear retaining bolt.
32. Install the left side secondary chain guide.
33. Install the cylinder head access plug.
34. Re-set and install the left side secondary chain tensioner.
35. Remove Secondary Camshaft Chain Holder.
36. Install the timing chain cover.
37. Install the crankshaft damper. Tighten damper bolt 130 ft. lbs. (175 Nm).
38. Install the power steering pump.
39. Install the fan blade assembly and fan shroud.
40. Install the cylinder head cover.
41. Install the master cylinder and booster assembly.
42. Install the intake manifold.
43. Refill the cooling system.
44. Raise the vehicle.
45. Install the exhaust pipe onto the left exhaust manifold.
46. Lower the vehicle.
47. Connect the negative cable to the battery.
48. Start the engine and check for leaks.

Right Side

See Figures 137, 140 through 142.

1. Disconnect battery negative cable.
2. Raise the vehicle on a hoist.
3. Disconnect the exhaust pipe at the right side exhaust manifold.
4. Drain the engine coolant.
5. Lower the vehicle.
6. Remove the intake manifold.
7. Remove the cylinder head cover.
8. Remove the fan shroud.
9. Remove oil fill housing from cylinder head.
10. Remove accessory drive belt.
11. Rotate the crankshaft until the damper timing mark is aligned with TDC indicator mark.
12. Verify the V6 mark on the camshaft sprocket is at the 12 o'clock position. Rotate the crankshaft one turn if necessary.
13. Remove the crankshaft damper.
14. Remove the timing chain cover.
15. Lock the secondary timing chains to the idler sprocket using the Secondary Camshaft Chain Holder.

➡Mark the secondary timing chain prior to removal to aid in installation.

16. Mark the secondary timing chain, one link on each side of the V6 mark on the camshaft drive gear.
17. Remove the right side secondary chain tensioner.
18. Remove the cylinder head access plug.
19. Remove the right side secondary chain guide.

WARNING

The nut on the right side camshaft sprocket should not be removed for any reason, as the sprocket and camshaft sensor target wheel is serviced as an assembly. If the nut was removed, tighten nut to 44 inch lbs. (5 Nm).

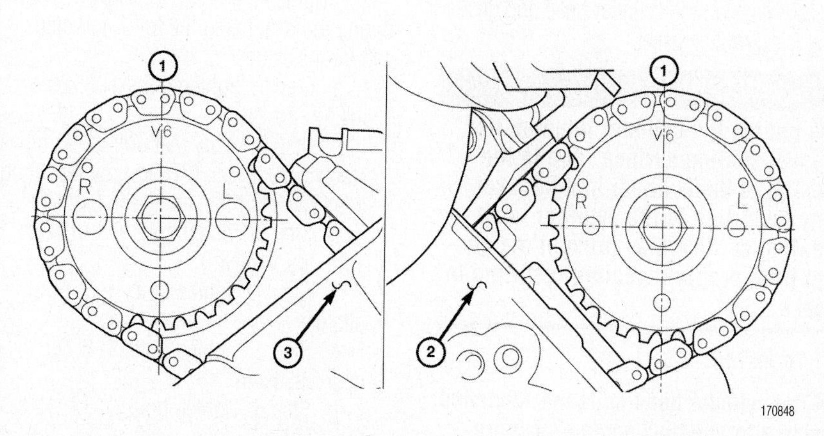

Fig. 141 Verify the V6 mark (1) on the camshaft sprocket is at the 12 o'clock position; left cylinder head (2), right cylinder head (3)

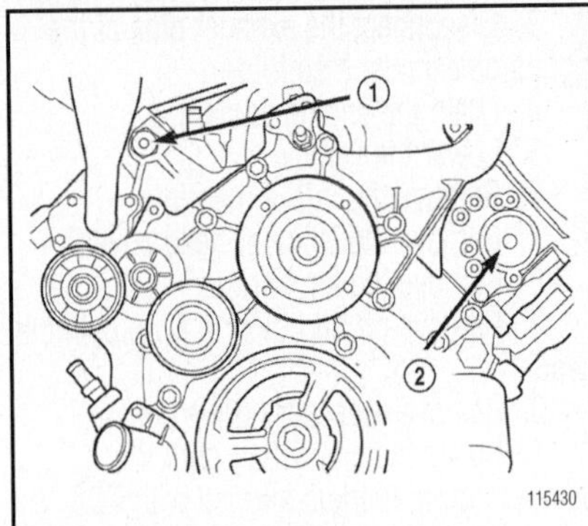

Fig. 142 Remove the cylinder head access plugs (1, 2)

20. Remove the retaining bolt and the camshaft drive gear.

✱✱ WARNING

Do not allow the engine to rotate. severe damage to the valve train can occur.

✱✱ WARNING

Do not overlook the four smaller bolts at the front of the cylinder head. Do not attempt to remove the cylinder head without removing these four bolts.

✱✱ WARNING

Do not hold or pry on the camshaft target wheel for any reason. A damaged target wheel can result in a vehicle no start condition.

➡The cylinder head is attached to the cylinder block with twelve bolts.

21. Remove the cylinder head retaining bolts.
22. Remove the cylinder head and gasket. Discard the gasket.

✱✱ WARNING

Do not lay the cylinder head on its gasket sealing surface, due to the design of the cylinder head gasket any distortion to the cylinder head sealing surface may prevent the gasket from properly sealing resulting in leaks.

To install:

➡The cylinder head bolts are tightened using a torque plus angle procedure. The bolts must be examined BEFORE reuse. If the threads are necked down (2) the bolts should be replaced.

➡Necking can be checked by holding a straight edge against the threads. If all the threads do not contact the scale, the bolt should be replaced.

✱✱ WARNING

When cleaning cylinder head and cylinder block surfaces, DO NOT use a metal scraper, high speed Scotch Brite or rolock tool because the surfaces could be cut or ground. Use only a wooden or plastic scraper.

23. Clean the cylinder head and cylinder block mating surfaces.
24. Position the new cylinder head gasket on the locating dowels.

✱✱ WARNING

When installing cylinder head, use care not damage the tensioner arm or the guide arm.

25. Position the cylinder head onto the cylinder block. Make sure the cylinder head seats fully over the locating dowels.

➡The four M8 cylinder head mounting bolts require sealant to be added to them before installing. Failure to do so may cause leaks.

26. Lubricate the cylinder head bolt threads with clean engine oil and install the eight M10 bolts.
27. Coat the four M8 cylinder head bolts with Mopar® Lock and Seal Adhesive then install the bolts.

➡The cylinder head bolts are tightened using an angle torque procedure, however, the bolts are not a torque-to-yield design.

28. Tighten the bolts in sequence shown during removal using the following steps and torque values:
    a. Step 1: Tighten bolts 1–8, 20 ft. lbs. (27 Nm).
    b. Step 2: Verify that bolts 1–8, all reached 20 ft. lbs. (27 Nm), by repeating Step 1 without loosening the bolts.
    c. Step 3:Tighten bolts 9 thru 12 to 10 ft. lbs. (14 Nm).
    d. Step 4: Tighten bolts 1–8, 90 degrees.
    e. Step 5: Tighten bolts 1–8, 90 degrees, again.
    f. Step 6: Tighten bolts 9–12, 19 ft. lbs. (26 Nm).
29. Position the secondary chain onto the camshaft drive gear, making sure one marked chain link is on either side of the V6 mark on the gear then using the Camshaft Holder, position the gear onto the camshaft.

✱✱ WARNING

Remove excess oil from camshaft sprocket retaining bolt before reinstalling bolt. Failure to do so may cause over-torquing of bolt resulting in bolt failure.

30. Install the camshaft drive gear retaining bolt.
31. Install the right side secondary chain guide.
32. Install the cylinder head access plugs.
33. Re-set and install the right side secondary chain tensioner.
34. Remove the Camshaft Holder.
35. Install the timing chain cover.
36. Install the crankshaft damper. Tighten damper bolt 130 ft. lbs. (175 Nm).
37. Install accessory drive belt.
38. Install the fan shroud.
39. Install the cylinder head cover.
40. Install the intake manifold.
41. Install oil fill housing onto cylinder head.
42. Refill the cooling system.
43. Raise the vehicle.
44. Install the exhaust pipe onto the right exhaust manifold.
45. Lower the vehicle.
46. Reconnect battery negative cable.
47. Start the engine and check for leaks.

5.7L Engine

See Figures 143 through 149.

➡Sequence is the same for both the left and right side. Power steering pump left side only.

1. Remove the oil fill cap.
2. Remove the engine cover.
3. Perform the fuel pressure release procedure.
4. Disconnect and isolate the negative battery cable.
5. Remove the cowl cover panel.
6. Drain the cooling system.
7. Remove the air cleaner and resonator assembly.
8. Remove the cylinder head cover using sequence shown.
9. Remove the intake manifold using sequence shown.

➡It is not necessary to disconnect the hoses from the power steering pump, for power steering pump removal.

10. Remove the power steering pump and position aside.

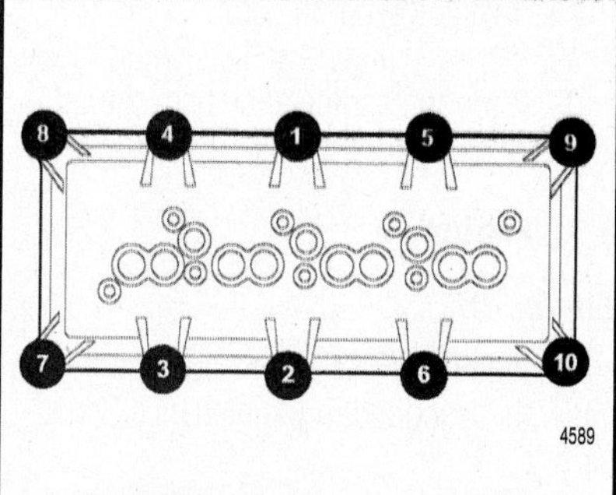

Fig. 143 Remove the cylinder head cover using sequence shown

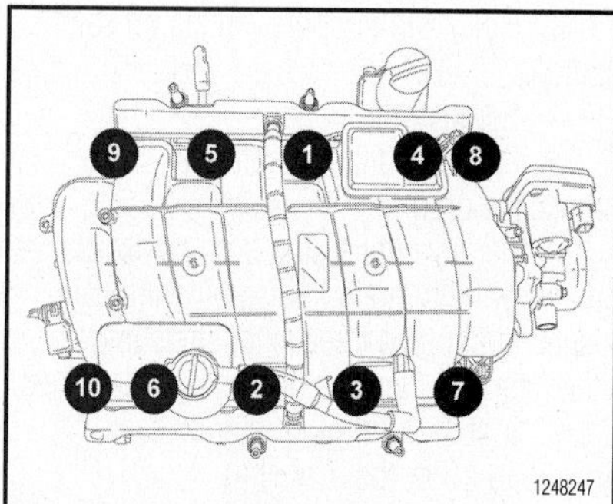

Fig. 144 Remove the intake manifold using sequence shown

➡The rocker arms and push rods must be installed in their original location as removed.

11. Remove the rocker arms and push rods using sequence shown. Note their location to ensure installation in their original locations as removed.
12. Using the sequence shown, remove the cylinder head bolts.
13. Remove the cylinder head and discard the cylinder head gasket.

To install:

14. If replacing the cylinder head, transfer the valves, valve seals and valve springs to the new cylinder head, valve refacing may be necessary.

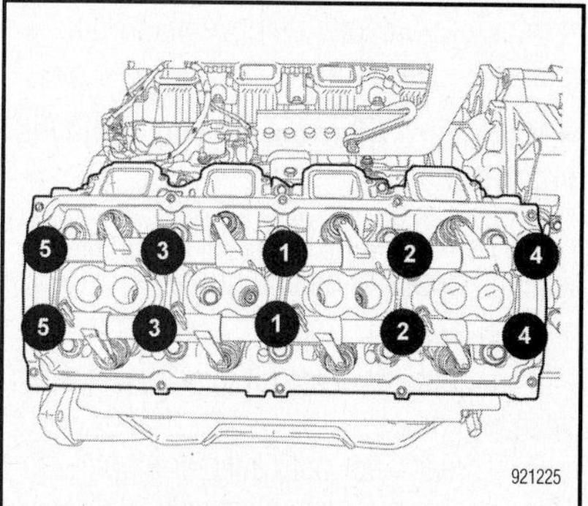

Fig. 145 Remove the rocker arms and push rods using sequence shown

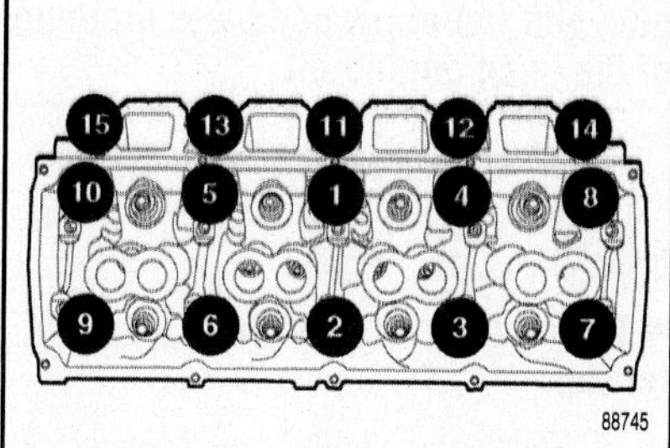

Fig. 146 Using the sequence shown, remove the cylinder head bolts

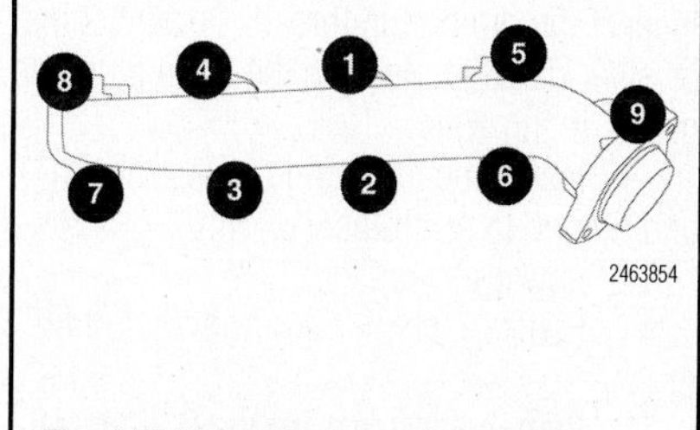

Fig. 147 Using the sequence shown, tighten the exhaust manifold bolts/studs

15. If replacing the cylinder head, transfer the exhaust manifold to the new cylinder head. Using the sequence shown, tighten the exhaust manifold bolts/studs to 18 ft. lbs. (25 Nm).
16. If replacing the cylinder head, transfer the spark plugs to the new cylinder head.

✱✱ WARNING

The cylinder head gaskets are not interchangeable between the left and right sides. They are marked with an "L" and "R" to indicate the left or right side and they are marked "TOP" to indicate which side goes up.

17. Using a suitable solvent, clean all sealing surfaces of the cylinder block and cylinder heads.
18. Position the new cylinder head gasket onto the cylinder block.
19. Position the cylinder head onto the cylinder head gasket and cylinder block.
20. Using the sequence shown, tighten the cylinder head bolts 1 through 10 to 25 ft. lbs. (34 Nm).
21. Using the sequence shown, tighten the cylinder head bolts 11 through 15 to 15 ft. lbs. (20 Nm).
22. Again, using the sequence shown, tighten the cylinder head bolts 1 through 10 to 40 ft. lbs. (54 Nm).

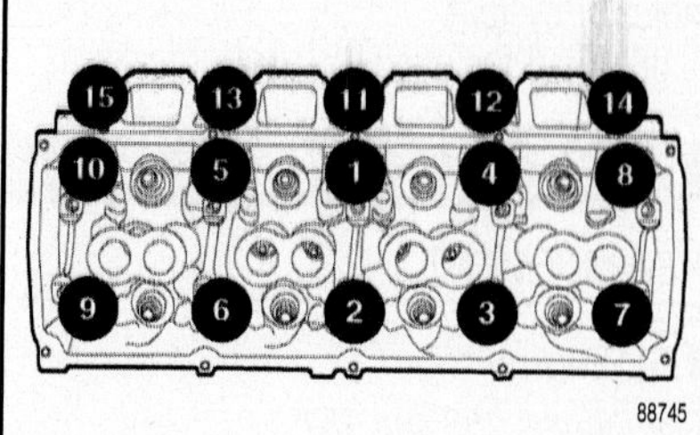

Fig. 148 Using the sequence shown, tighten the cylinder head bolts

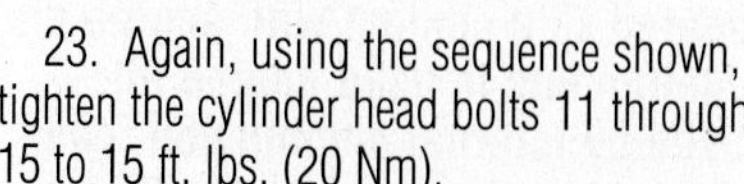

23. Again, using the sequence shown, tighten the cylinder head bolts 11 through 15 to 15 ft. lbs. (20 Nm).
24. Again, using the sequence shown, rotate the cylinder head bolts 1 through 10 an additional 90 degrees.
25. Again, using the sequence shown, tighten the cylinder head bolts 11 through 15 to 25 ft. lbs. (34 Nm).
26. Using Pushrod Retainer, install the push rods and rocker arms in their original location as noted during removal.
27. Install the power steering pump.
28. Install the cylinder head cover using the sequence shown during removal.
29. Install the intake manifold using the sequence shown during removal.
30. Install the cowl cover panel.
31. Install the air cleaner and resonator assembly.
32. Fill the cooling system.
33. Change the engine oil and engine oil filter.
34. Install the engine cover.
35. Install the oil fill cap.
36. Connect the negative battery cable.

➡This vehicle is equipped with an engine oil change indicator system. The "Oil Change Required" message will need to be reset after changing the engine oil and filter.

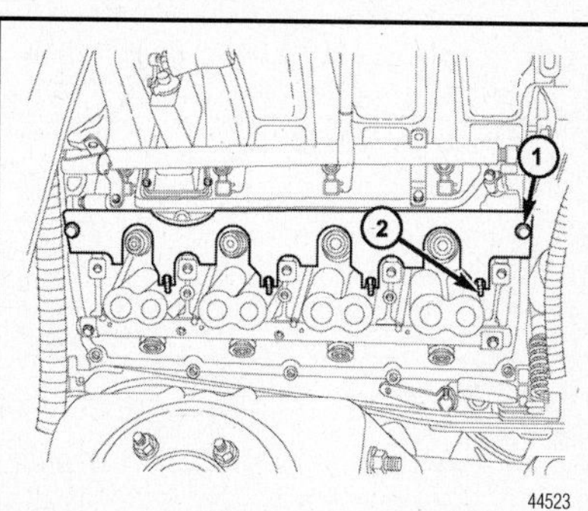

Fig. 149 Using Pushrod Retainer (1), install the push rods and rocker arms in their original location

37. Reset the "Oil Change Required" indicator system.
38. Start the engine check for leaks.

ENGINE OIL & FILTER

REPLACEMENT

3.6L Engine

See Figures 150 and 151.

✻✻ CAUTION

New or used engine oil can be irritating to the skin. Avoid prolonged or repeated skin contact with engine oil. Contaminants in used engine oil, caused by internal combustion, can be hazardous to your health. Thoroughly wash exposed skin with soap and water. Do not wash skin with gasoline, diesel fuel, thinner, or solvents, health problems can result. Do not pollute, dispose of used engine oil properly. Contact your dealer or government agency for location of collection center in your area.

1. Run the engine until achieving normal operating temperature.
2. Position the vehicle on a level surface and turn the engine off.
3. Remove the oil filter access cover.

➡Graphic shows engine cover removed for clarity.

✻✻ WARNING

When performing an engine oil change, the oil filter cap must be removed. Removing the oil filter cap releases oil held within the oil filter cavity and allows it to drain into the sump. Failure to remove the cap prior to reinstallation of the drain plug will not allow complete draining of the used engine oil.

4. Place an oil absorbent cloth around the oil filter housing at the base of the oil filter cap.

➡The oil filter is attached to the oil filter cap.

5. Rotate the oil filter cap counterclockwise and remove the cap and filter from the oil filter housing.
6. Raise and support the vehicle.
7. Place a suitable drain pan under the crankcase drain plug.
8. Remove the drain plug from oil pan and allow the oil to drain into the pan. Inspect the drain plug threads for stretching or other damage. Replace the drain plug and gasket if damaged.
9. Install the drain plug in the oil pan and tighten to 20 ft. lbs. (27 Nm).
10. Lower the vehicle.
11. Remove the oil filter from the oil filter cap.
12. Remove and discard the O-ring seal.

➡It is not necessary to pre-oil the oil filter or fill the oil filter housing.

13. Lightly lubricate the new O-ring seal with clean engine oil.
14. Install the O-ring seal on the filter cap.
15. Install the new oil filter into the oil filter cap.

➡Graphic shows engine cover removed for clarity.

16. Thread the oil filter cap into the oil filter housing and tighten to 18 ft. lbs. (25 Nm).
17. Remove the oil fill cap. Fill the crankcase with the specified type and amount of engine oil.
18. Install the oil fill cap.
19. Start the engine and inspect for leaks.
20. Stop the engine and check the oil level.

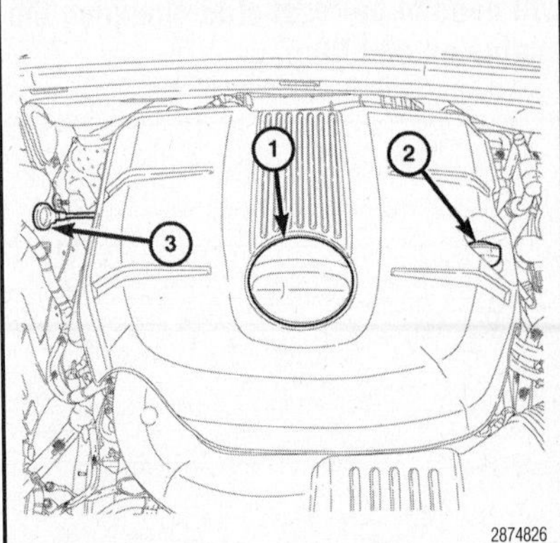

Fig. 150 Remove the oil filter access cover (1); oil fill cap (2) and oil level indicator (3)

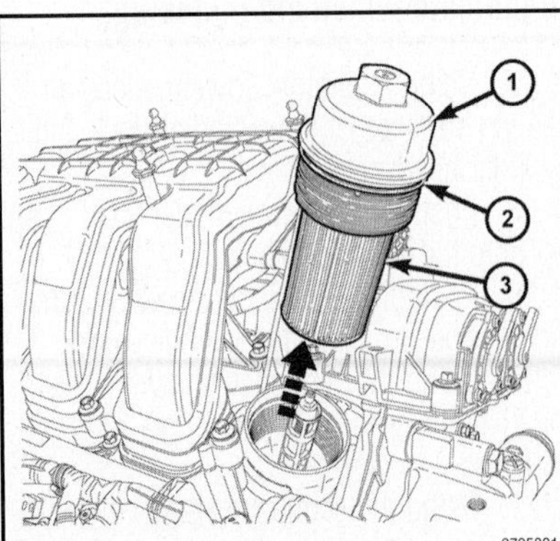

Fig. 151 Rotate the oil filter cap (1) counterclockwise and remove the cap and filter (3) from the oil filter housing; O-ring seal (2)

3.7L Engine

Engine Oil

Change engine oil at mileage and time intervals described in Maintenance Schedules.

1. Run engine until achieving normal operating temperature.
2. Position the vehicle on a level surface and turn engine off.
3. Hoist and support vehicle on safety stands.
4. Remove oil fill cap.
5. Place a suitable drain pan under crankcase drain.
6. Remove drain plug from crankcase and allow oil to drain into an oil drain pan. Inspect drain plug threads for stretching or other damage. Replace drain plug if damaged.
7. Install drain plug in crankcase. Torque to 25 ft. lbs. (34 Nm).
8. Lower vehicle and fill crankcase with specified type and amount of engine oil described in this section.
9. Install oil fill cap.
10. Start engine and inspect for leaks.
11. Stop engine and inspect oil level.

Oil Filter

➡All engines are equipped with a high quality full-flow, disposable type oil filter. Chrysler Corporation recommends a Mopar® or equivalent oil filter be used.

1. Position a drain pan under the oil filter.
2. Using a suitable oil filter wrench, loosen the filter.
3. Rotate the oil filter counterclockwise to remove it from the cylinder block oil filter boss.
4. When filter separates from cylinder block oil filter boss, tip gasket end upward to minimize oil spill. Remove filter from vehicle.

➡Make sure filter gasket was removed with filter.

5. With a wiping cloth, clean the gasket sealing surface of oil and grime.

To install:

6. Lightly lubricate oil filter gasket with clean engine oil.
7. Thread filter onto adapter nipple. When gasket makes contact with sealing surface, hand tighten filter one full turn, do not over tighten.

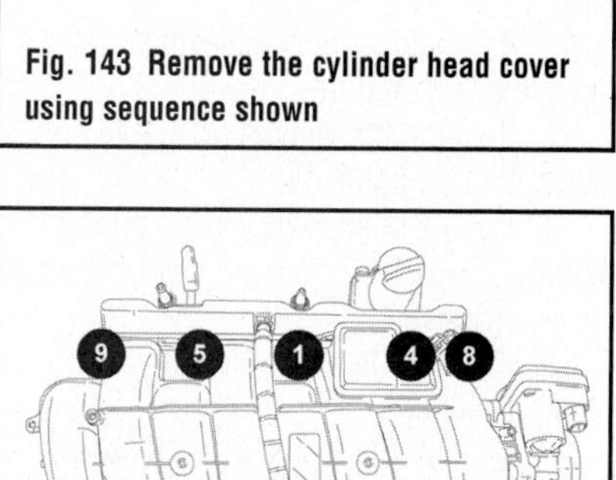

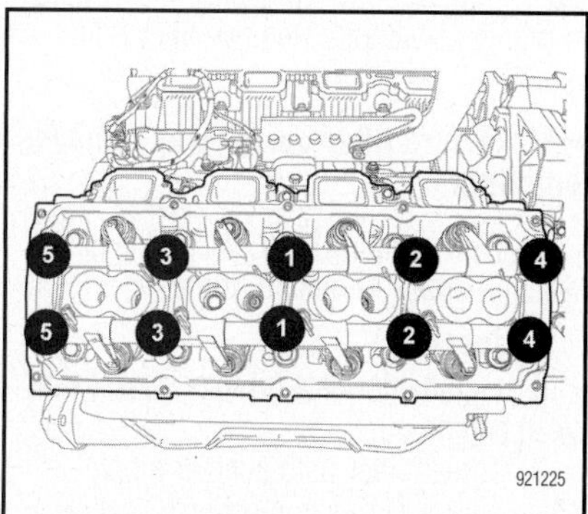

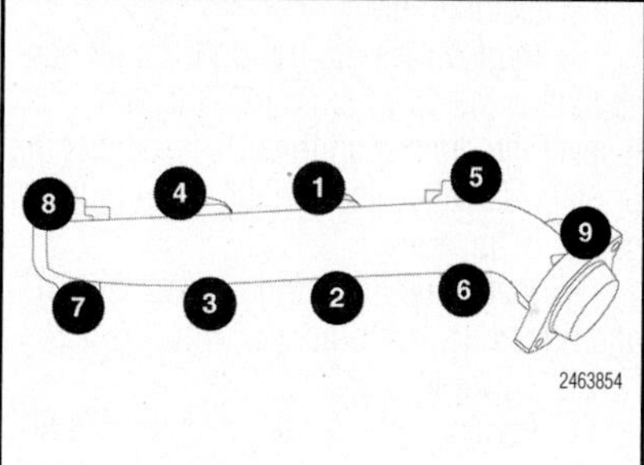

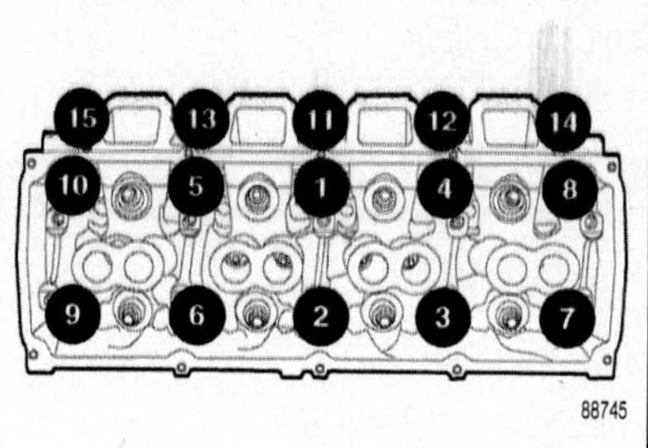

8. Add oil, verify crankcase oil level and start engine. Inspect for oil leaks.

5.7L Engine

⁂ WARNING

Do not overfill crankcase with engine oil, pressure loss or oil foaming can result.

1. Run engine until achieving normal operating temperature.
2. Position the vehicle on a level surface and turn engine off.
3. Hoist and support vehicle on safety stands.
4. Remove oil fill cap.
5. Place a suitable drain pan under crankcase drain.
6. Remove drain plug from crankcase and allow oil to drain into pan. Inspect drain plug threads for stretching or other damage. Replace drain plug if damaged.
7. Install drain plug in crankcase. Torque to 25 ft. lbs. (34 Nm).
8. Lower vehicle and fill crankcase with specified type and amount of engine oil described in this section.
9. Install oil fill cap.
10. Start engine and inspect for leaks.
11. Stop engine and inspect oil level.

➡Care should be exercised when disposing used engine oil after it has been drained from a vehicle engine.

EXHAUST MANIFOLD

REMOVAL & INSTALLATION

3.6L Engine

The exhaust manifolds are integrated into the cylinder heads for reduced weight.

3.7L Engine

Left Exhaust Manifold

See Figure 152.

1. Disconnect the negative cable from the battery.
2. Raise and support the vehicle.
3. Remove the bolts and nuts attaching the exhaust pipe to the engine exhaust manifold.
4. Lower the vehicle.
5. Remove the exhaust heat shield.
6. Remove bolts, nuts and washers attaching manifold to cylinder head.
7. Remove manifold and gasket from the cylinder head.

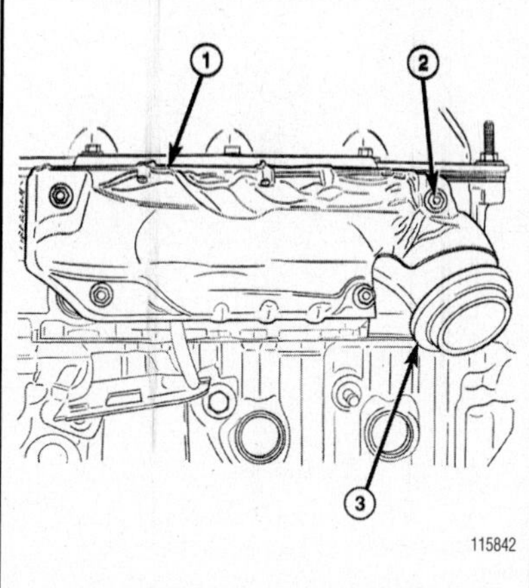

Fig. 152 Remove the exhaust heat shield (1); nuts (2)

To install:

⁂ WARNING

If the studs came out with the nuts when removing the engine exhaust manifold, install new studs. Apply sealer on the coarse thread ends. Water leaks may develop at the studs if this precaution is not taken.

8. Position the engine exhaust manifold and gasket on the two studs located on the cylinder head. Install conical washers and nuts on these studs .
9. Install remaining conical washers. Starting at the center arm and working outward, tighten the bolts and nuts to 18 ft. lbs. (25 Nm).
10. Install the exhaust heat shields.
11. Raise and support the vehicle.

⁂ WARNING

Over tightening heat shield fasteners, may cause shield to distort and/or crack.

12. Assemble exhaust pipe to manifold and secure with bolts, nuts and retainers. Tighten the bolts and nuts to 25 ft. lbs. (34 Nm).

Right Exhaust Manifold

See Figure 153.

1. Disconnect the negative cable from the battery.
2. Raise and support the vehicle.
3. Remove the bolts and nuts attaching the exhaust pipe to the engine exhaust manifold.

Lower the vehicle.

4. Remove the exhaust heat shield.
5. Remove bolts, nuts and washers attaching manifold to cylinder head.

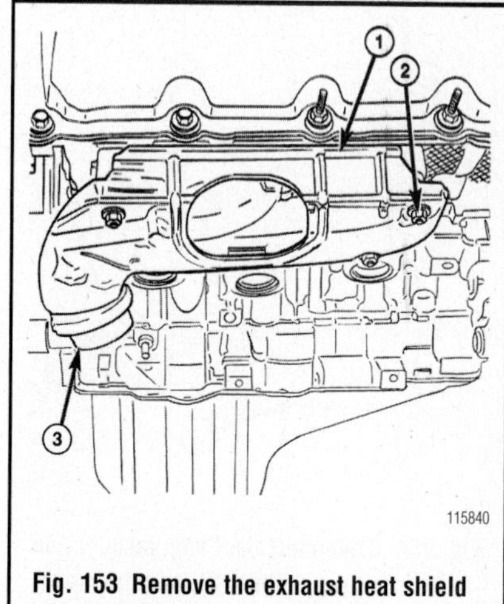

Fig. 153 Remove the exhaust heat shield (1); nuts (2)

6. Remove manifold and gasket from the cylinder head.

To install:

⁂ WARNING

If the studs came out with the nuts when removing the engine exhaust manifold, install new studs. Apply sealer on the coarse thread ends. Water leaks may develop at the studs if this precaution is not taken.

7. Position the engine exhaust manifold and gasket on the two studs located on the cylinder head. Install conical washers and nuts on these studs .
8. Install remaining conical washers. Starting at the center arm and working outward, tighten the bolts and nuts to 18 ft. lbs. (25 Nm).
9. Install the exhaust heat shields.
10. Raise and support the vehicle.

⁂ WARNING

Over tightening heat shield fasteners, may cause shield to distort and/or crack.

11. Assemble exhaust pipe to manifold and secure with bolts, nuts and retainers. Tighten the bolts and nuts to 25 ft. lbs. (34 Nm).

5.7L Engine

Left Side

See Figures 154 through 156.

1. Remove the oil fill cap.
2. Remove the engine cover.
3. Perform the fuel pressure release procedure.
4. Disconnect and isolate the negative battery cable.

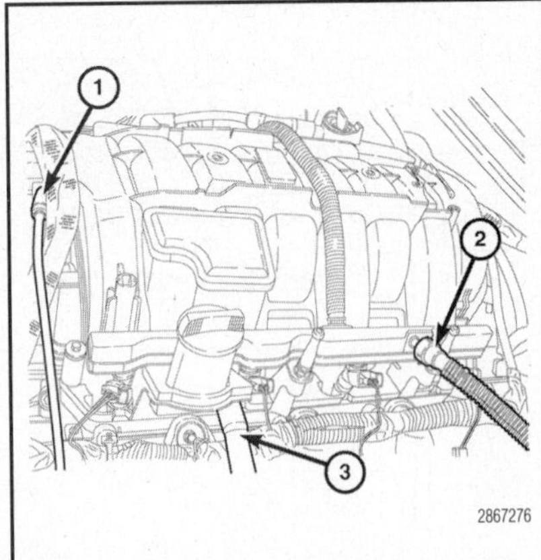

Fig. 154 Disconnect the EVAP vacuum line (1), the fuel supply line (2), and the make-up air hose (3)

5. Remove the air cleaner assembly.
6. Disconnect the EVAP vacuum line at the throttle body.
7. Disconnect the fuel supply line at the fuel rail.
8. Disconnect the make-up air hose at the intake manifold.
9. Remove the serpentine belt.

➡It is not necessary to disconnect the refrigerant lines for A/C compressor removal.

10. Remove the A/C compressor from the engine block and position aside.

WARNING

When servicing or replacing exhaust system components, disconnect the oxygen sensor connector(s). Allowing the exhaust to hang by the oxygen sensor wires will damage the harness and/or sensor.

11. Disconnect the left upstream 02 sensor electrical connector.
12. Remove the exhaust manifold heat shield front retaining nuts.
13. Raise and support the vehicle.
14. If equipped, remove the skid plate four retaining bolts and remove the skid plate.
15. Disconnect the left exhaust pipe/catalytic converter.
16. Remove the exhaust manifold heat shield rear retaining nuts and remove the heat shield.
17. Remove the lower exhaust manifold retaining bolts.
18. Lower the vehicle.
19. Remove the upper exhaust manifold retaining bolts.

➡The left exhaust manifold is removed from below the engine and out through the front of the engine compartment.

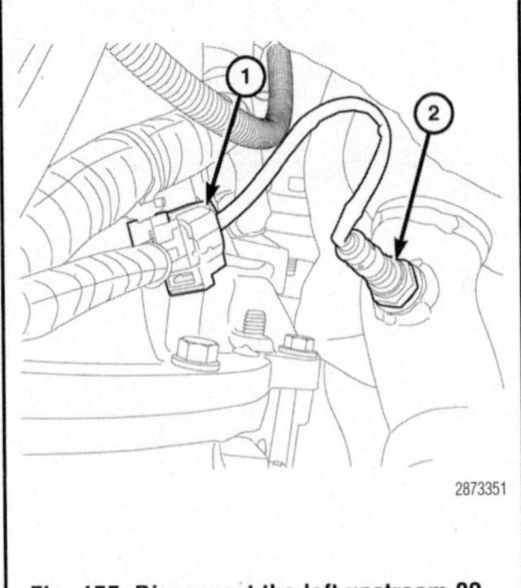

Fig. 155 Disconnect the left upstream 02 sensor (2) electrical connector (1)

20. Raise and support the vehicle.
21. Remove the left exhaust manifold and gasket from below the engine and out through the front of the engine compartment.
22. Inspect the exhaust manifold for any damage.
23. Clean the mating surfaces.

To install:

24. Prior to installation, make sure all gasket mating surfaces are clean and free of any debris.

➡Install the left exhaust manifold and gasket from below the engine and through the front of the engine compartment. Make sure the gasket is properly seated before installing the manifold bolts/studs.

25. Position the exhaust manifold and gasket and install the bolts/studs hand tight.
26. Using the sequence shown, tighten the exhaust manifold bolts/studs to 18 ft. lbs. (25 Nm).
27. Position the exhaust manifold heat shield, install the rear heat shield retaining nuts and tighten.
28. Install the left exhaust pipe/catalytic converter.
29. If equipped, position the skid plate, install the skid plate four retaining bolts and tighten to 21 ft. lbs. (28 Nm).
30. Lower the vehicle.
31. Install the front heat shield retaining nuts and tighten.
32. Connect the left upstream 02 sensor electrical connector.
33. Install the A/C compressor onto the engine block.
34. Install the serpentine belt.
35. Connect the make-up air hose at the intake manifold.
36. Connect the fuel supply line at the fuel rail.
37. Connect the EVAP vacuum line at the throttle body.
38. Install the air cleaner assembly.
39. Connect the negative battery cable.
40. Install the engine cover.
41. Install the oil fill cap.

Start the engine and check for leaks.

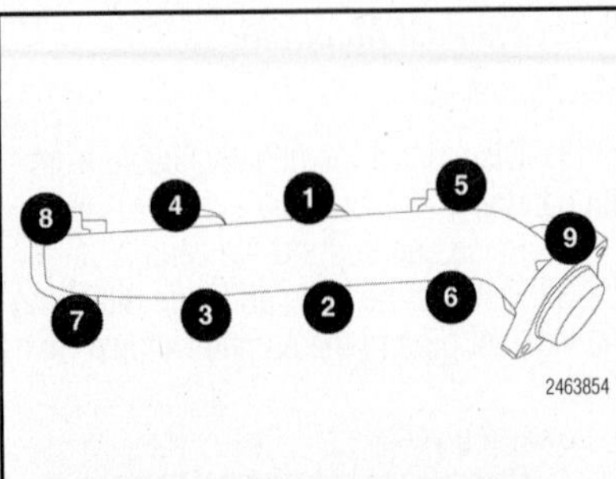

Fig. 156 Using the sequence shown, tighten the exhaust manifold bolts/studs

Right Side

See Figures 157 and 158.

1. Remove the oil fill cap.
2. Remove the engine cover.
3. Disconnect and isolate the negative battery cable.

➡When servicing or replacing exhaust system components, disconnect the oxygen sensor connector(s). Allowing the exhaust to hang by the oxygen sensor wires will damage the harness and/or sensor.

4. Disconnect the right upstream 02 sensor electrical connector (1).
5. Remove the exhaust manifold heat shield front retaining nuts.
6. Raise and support the vehicle.
7. If equipped, remove the skid plate four retaining bolts and remove the skid plate.

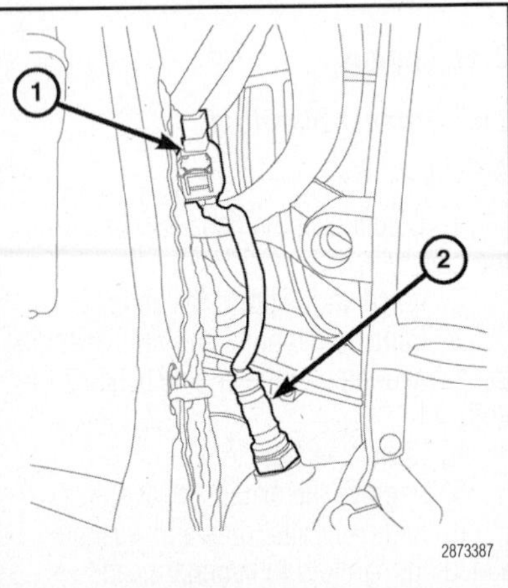

Fig. 157 Disconnect the right upstream 02 sensor (2) electrical connector (1)

8. Disconnect the right exhaust pipe/catalytic converter.

9. Remove the exhaust manifold heat shield rear retaining nuts and remove the heat shield.

10. Using the sequence shown, remove the exhaust manifold retaining bolts.

➡The right exhaust manifold is removed from below the engine and out through the rear of the engine compartment.

11. Remove the right exhaust manifold and gasket from below the engine and out through the rear of the engine compartment.

12. Inspect the exhaust manifold for any damage.

13. Clean the mating surfaces.

To install:

14. Prior to installation, make sure all gasket mating surfaces are clean and free of any debris.

➡Install the right exhaust manifold and gasket from below the engine and through the rear of the engine compartment. Make sure the gasket is properly seated before installing the manifold bolts/studs.

15. Position the exhaust manifold and gasket and install the bolts/studs hand tight.

16. Using the sequence shown, tighten the exhaust manifold bolts/studs to 18 ft. lbs. (25 Nm).

17. Position the exhaust manifold heat shield, install the rear heat shield retaining nuts and tighten.

18. Install the right exhaust pipe/catalytic converter.

19. If equipped, position the skid plate, install the skid plate four retaining bolts and tighten to 21 ft. lbs. (28 Nm).

20. Lower the vehicle.

21. Install the exhaust manifold heat shield front retaining nuts and tighten.

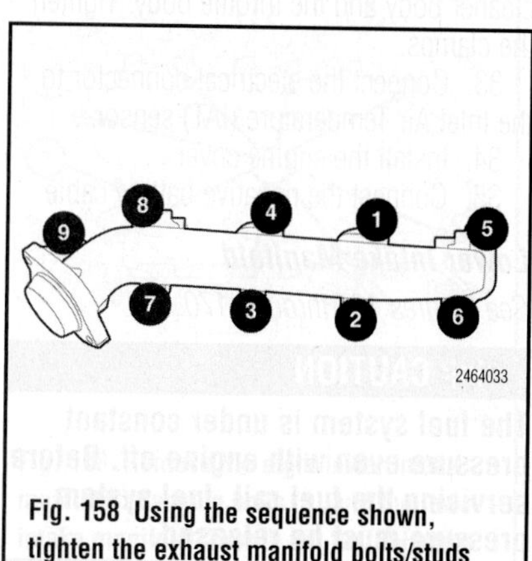

Fig. 158 Using the sequence shown, tighten the exhaust manifold bolts/studs

22. Connect the right upstream 02 sensor electrical connector.

23. Connect the negative battery cable.

24. Install the engine cover.

25. Install the oil fill cap.

26. Start the engine and check for leaks.

INTAKE MANIFOLD

REMOVAL & INSTALLATION

3.6L Engine

Upper Intake Manifold

See Figures 159 through 166.

1. Disconnect and isolate the negative battery cable.

2. Remove the engine cover.

3. Disconnect the electrical connector from the Inlet Air Temperature (IAT) sensor.

4. Loosen the clamp at the throttle body.

5. Loosen the clamp at the air cleaner body.

6. Remove the air inlet hose.

7. Disengage the brake booster hose retainer from the upper intake manifold.

8. Disconnect the electrical connectors from the Manifold Absolute Pressure (MAP) sensor and the Electronic Throttle Control (ETC).

9. Disengage the ETC harness from the clip on the throttle body. Disengage the wire harness retainer from the upper intake manifold near the MAP sensor and reposition the wire harness.

10. Disconnect the following hoses from the upper intake manifold:

- Positive Crankcase Ventilation (PCV)
- Vapor purge
- Brake booster

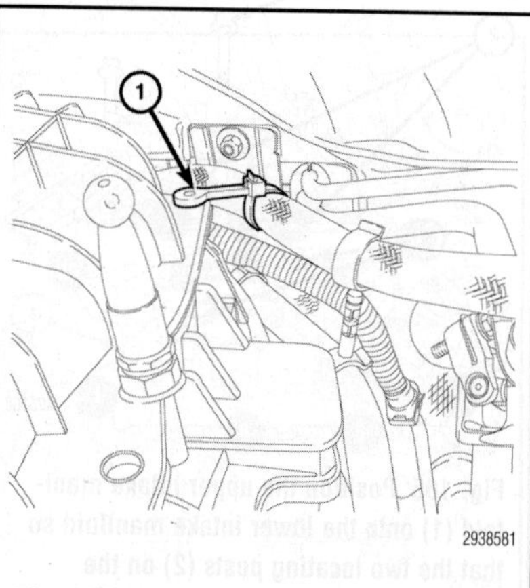

Fig. 159 Disengage the brake booster hose retainer (1) from the upper intake manifold

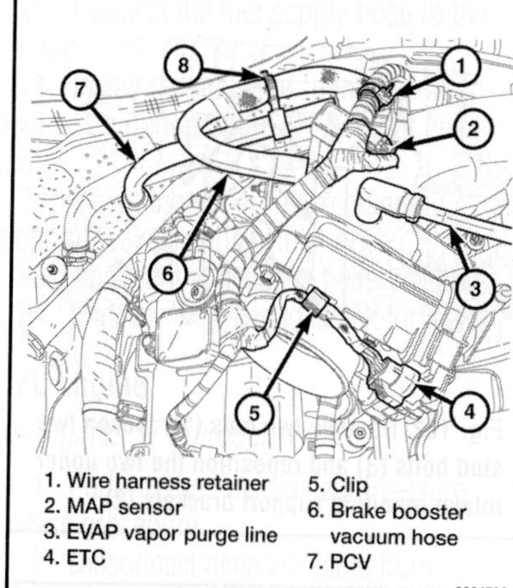

Fig. 160 Disconnect the electrical connectors from the Manifold Absolute Pressure (MAP) sensor and the Electronic Throttle Control (ETC)

11. Disengage the wire harness retainer from the stud bolt.

12. Remove two nuts, loosen the stud bolt and reposition the upper intake manifold support bracket.

13. Remove the nut from the support bracket of the heater core return tube.

14. Remove two nuts, loosen two stud bolts and reposition the two upper intake manifold support brackets.

➡The upper intake manifold attaching bolts are captured in the upper intake manifold. Once loosened, the bolts will have to be lifted out of the lower intake manifold and held while removing the upper intake manifold.

➡Exercise care not to inadvertently loosen the two fuel rail attachment

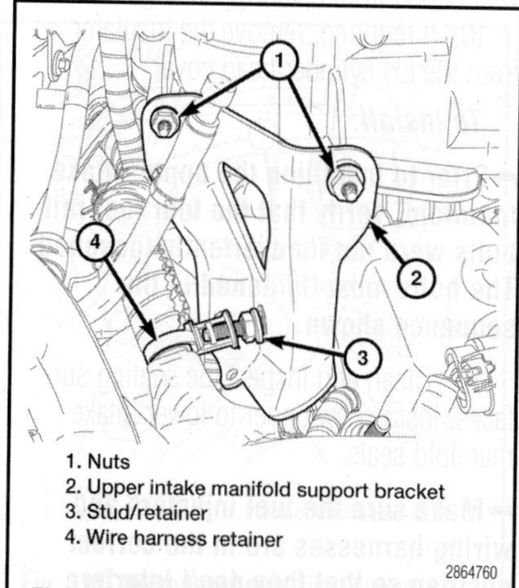

Fig. 161 Disengage the wire harness retainer from the stud bolt

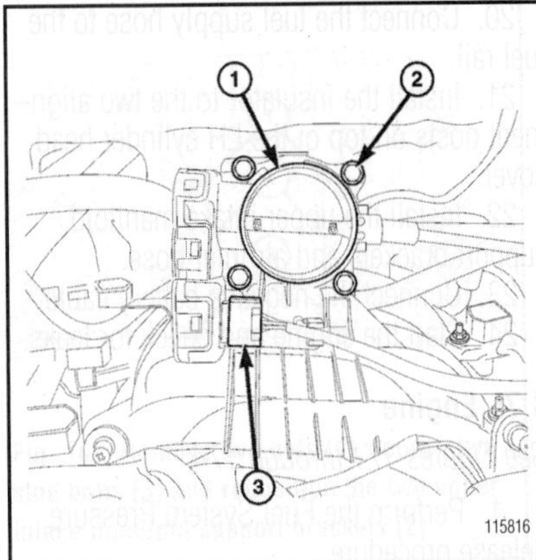

Fig. 172 Disconnect the ETC connector (3) from the throttle body (1); mounting bolts (2)

15. Support engine using engine support fixture.
16. Remove the right side engine mount to frame bolt (3).
17. With the bolt removed, lower engine until engine mount rests in frame mount.
18. Remove intake manifold retaining fasteners in reverse order of tightening sequence.
19. Remove intake manifold.

To install:

20. Install intake manifold gaskets.
21. Install intake manifold.
22. Install intake manifold retaining bolts and tighten in sequence shown to 106 inch lbs. (12 Nm).
23. Install fuel rail.
24. Install the EGR tube.
25. Install top oil dipstick tube retaining bolt.

✱✱ WARNING

Proper torque of the throttle body is critical to normal operation. If the throttle body is over-torqued, damage to the throttle body can occur resulting in throttle plate malfunction.

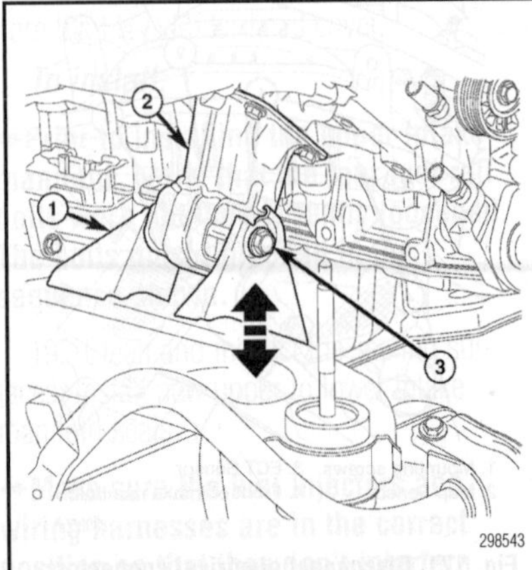

Fig. 173 Remove the right side engine mount (2) to frame bolt (3); frame (1)

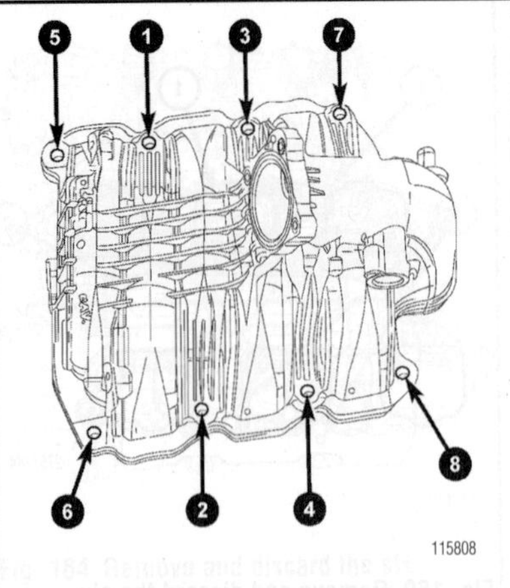

Fig. 174 Install intake manifold retaining bolts and tighten in sequence shown

26. Install throttle body-to-intake manifold O-ring.
27. Install throttle body to intake manifold.
28. Install four mounting bolts.
29. Install ignition coil towers.
30. Connect electrical connectors for the following components:
    - Manifold Absolute Pressure (MAP) Sensor
    - Coolant Temperature (CTS) Sensor
    - Ignition coil towers
31. Install alternator.
32. Install the air conditioning compressor.
33. Connect vapor purge hose, brake booster hose, Positive Crankcase Ventilation (PCV) hose.
34. Connect the ETC connector to the throttle body.
35. Fill cooling system.
36. Raise engine using engine support fixture.
37. Install the right side engine mount to frame bolt.
38. Remove engine support fixture, special tool.
39. Install resonator assembly and air inlet hose.
40. Connect negative cable to battery.
41. Using the scan tool, perform the ETC Relearn function.

5.7L Engine

See Figures 175 and 176.

1. Perform the fuel pressure release procedure.
2. Disconnect the negative battery cable.
3. Remove the oil fill cap.
4. Remove the engine cover.
5. Disconnect the electrical connector at the Intake Air Temperature (IAT) sensor.
6. Loosen the hose clamp at the air cleaner housing.
7. Remove the resonator retaining bolt.
8. Loosen the hose clamp at the throttle body and remove the resonator.
9. Disconnect the MAP sensor electrical connector at the rear of the intake manifold.
10. Disconnect the brake booster vacuum hose at the rear of the intake manifold.
11. Disconnect the fuel supply line at the fuel rail.
12. Disconnect the make-up air hose at the intake manifold.
13. Disconnect the EVAP vacuum purge hose at the throttle body.
14. Disconnect the electrical connector at the throttle body.
15. Reposition the electrical harness.

➡The factory fuel injection electrical harness is numerically tagged (INJ 1, INJ 2, etc.) for injector position identification. If the harness is not tagged, note the electrical connector's location during removal.

16. Disconnect the fuel injector electrical connectors and position aside.
17. Using the sequence shown, remove the intake manifold retaining bolts.
18. Remove the intake manifold.

To install:

➡The intake manifold seals may be used again, provided no cuts, tears, or deformation have occurred.

19. Inspect the intake manifold seals and replace as necessary.
20. Install the intake manifold seals.
21. Position the intake manifold in place.

➡If reinstalling the original manifold apply Mopar® Lock Seal Adhesive to the intake manifold bolts. Not required when installing a new manifold.

22. Apply Mopar® Lock Seal Adhesive to the intake manifold bolts.
23. Using the sequence shown, install the intake manifold bolts and tighten to 9 ft. lbs. (12 Nm).

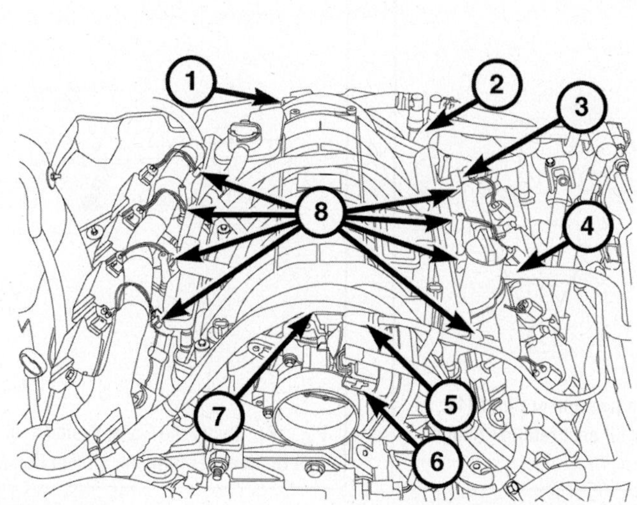

Fig. 175 Disconnect the MAP sensor electrical connector at the rear of the intake manifold

➡**The factory fuel injection electrical harness is numerically tagged (INJ 1, INJ 2, etc.) for injector position identification. If the harness is not tagged, use the noted electrical connector's location during removal.**

24. Connect the fuel injector electrical connectors.
25. Position the electrical harness as shown.
26. Connect the electrical connector at the throttle body.
27. Connect the EVAP vacuum purge hose.

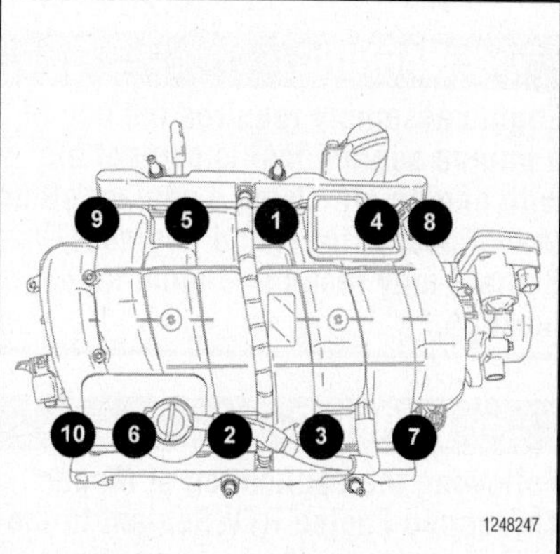

Fig. 176 Using the sequence shown, install the intake manifold bolts and tighten

28. Connect the make-up air hose at the intake manifold.
29. Connect the fuel supply line at the fuel rail.
30. Connect the brake booster vacuum hose at the rear of the intake manifold.
31. Connect the MAP sensor electrical connector at the rear of the intake manifold.
32. Position the resonator onto the throttle body and air cleaner housing.
33. Tighten the hose clamp at the throttle body.
34. Install the resonator retaining bolt and tighten.
35. Tighten the hose clamp at the air cleaner housing.
36. Connect the electrical connector at the Intake Air Temperature (IAT) sensor.
37. Install the engine cover.
38. Install the oil fill cap.
39. Connect the negative battery cable.
40. Start the engine and check for leaks.

OIL PAN

REMOVAL & INSTALLATION

3.6L Engine

Lower Oil Pan

See Figures 177 and 178.

1. Raise and support the vehicle.
2. Drain the engine oil.
3. Remove the front suspension skid plate, if equipped.

➡**The lower oil pan must be removed to access all of the upper oil pan retaining bolts.**

4. Remove twelve bolts, two nuts, and two studs from the flange of the lower oil pan.

⁂ WARNING

Do not pry on the lower oil pan flange. There are no designated pry points for lower oil pan removal. Prying on only one or a few locations could bend the flange and damage the pan.

5. Using a pry bar, apply a side force to the lower oil pan in order to shear the sealant bond and remove the pan.

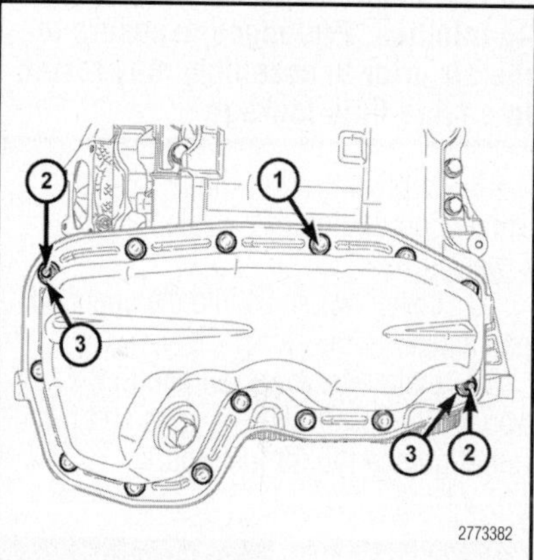

Fig. 177 Remove twelve bolts (1), two nuts (3), and two studs (2) from the flange of the lower oil pan

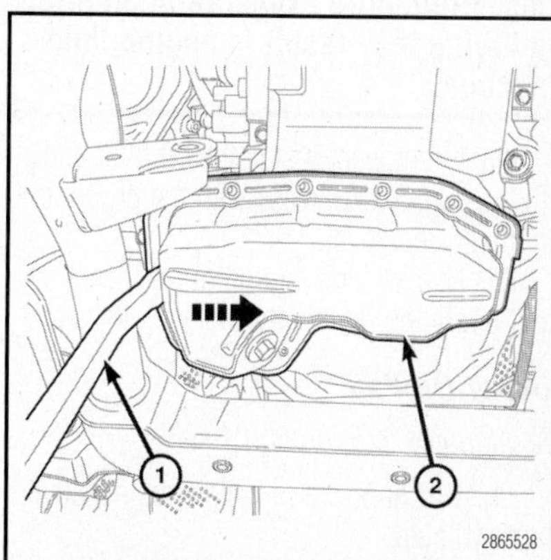

Fig. 178 Using a pry bar (1), apply a side force to the lower oil pan (2) in order to shear the sealant bond and remove the pan

6. Remove all residual sealant from the upper and lower oil pans.

To install:

7. Clean the upper and lower oil pan mating surfaces with isopropyl alcohol in preparation for sealant application.

WARNING

Engine assembly requires the use of a unique sealant that is compatible with engine oil. Using a sealant other than Mopar® Threebond Engine RTV Sealant may result in engine fluid leakage.

WARNING

Following the application of Mopar® Threebond Engine RTV Sealant to the gasket surfaces, the components must be assembled within 20 minutes and the attaching fasteners must be tightened to specification within 45 minutes. Prolonged exposure to the air prior to assembly may result in engine fluid leakage.

8. Apply a bead of Mopar® Threebond Engine RTV Sealant to the lower oil pan.
9. Install two studs into the upper oil pan flange.
10. Install the lower oil pan to the upper oil pan with twelve bolts and two nuts tightened to 93 inch lbs. (10.5 Nm).

WARNING

Following assembly, the Mopar® Threebond Engine RTV Sealant must be allowed to dry for 45 minutes prior to adding oil and engine operation. Premature exposure to oil prior to drying may result in engine fluid leakage.

11. If removed, install the oil filter and fill the engine crankcase with the proper oil to the correct level.
12. Run the engine until it reaches normal operating temperature.

Upper Oil Pan

See Figures 179 through 183.

1. Disconnect and isolate the negative battery cable.
2. Remove the bolt and remove the oil level indicator.
3. Raise and support the vehicle.
4. Drain the engine oil.

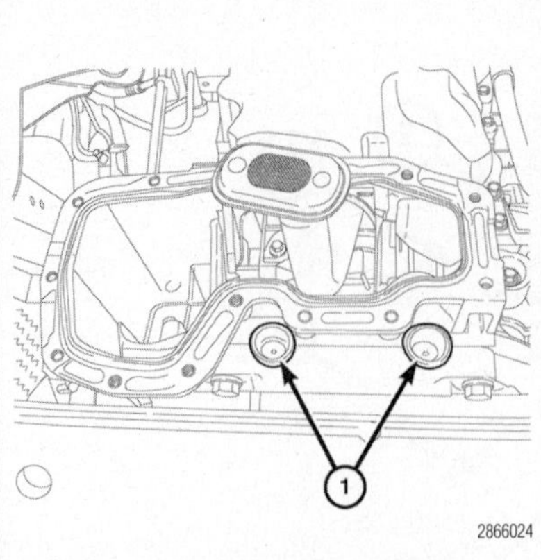

Fig. 179 Remove two rubber plugs (1) covering the rear oil seal retainer flange bolts

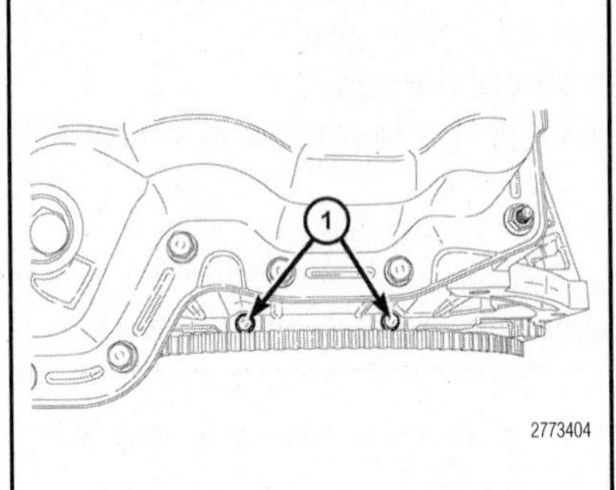

Fig. 180 Remove two bolts (1) from the rear oil seal retainer flange

5. If equipped, remove the front skid plate and the front suspension skid plate.

➡The lower oil pan must be removed to access all of the upper oil pan retaining bolts.

6. Remove the lower oil pan.
7. If equipped with AWD, remove the front axle.
8. Remove the steering gear.
9. Remove two rubber plugs covering the rear oil seal retainer flange bolts.
10. Remove two bolts from the rear oil seal retainer flange.
11. Unclip the transmission cooler line retainer from the oil pan flange.
12. Remove four transmission to the engine oil pan bolts.
13. Remove nineteen oil pan mounting bolts.
14. Using the four indicated pry points, carefully remove the upper oil pan.
15. Remove all residual sealant from the upper and lower oil pans, timing chain cover, rear seal retainer and engine block mating surfaces.

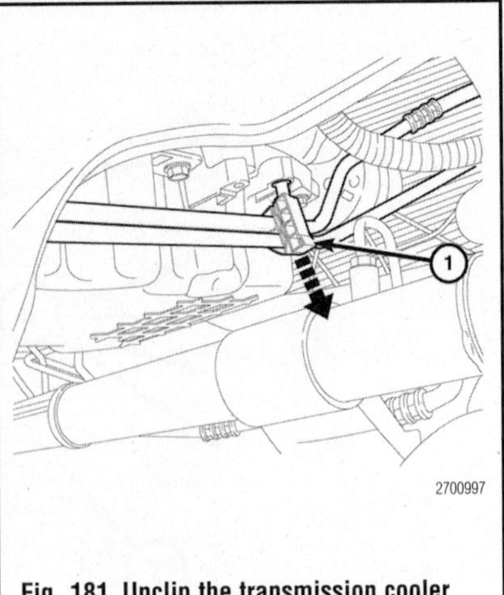

Fig. 181 Unclip the transmission cooler line retainer (1) from the oil pan flange

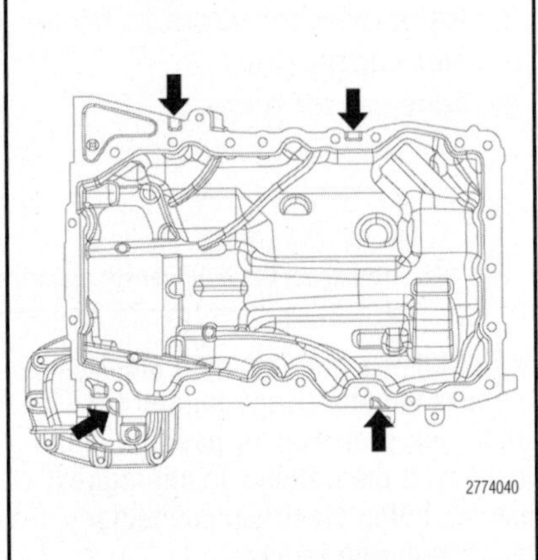

Fig. 182 Using the four indicated pry points, carefully remove the upper oil pan

To install:

16. Clean the upper and lower oil pans, timing chain cover, rear seal retainer and engine block mating surfaces with isopropyl alcohol in preparation for sealant application.

WARNING

Engine assembly requires the use of a unique sealant that is compatible with engine oil. Using a sealant other than Mopar® Threebond Engine RTV Sealant may result in engine fluid leakage.

WARNING

Following the application of Mopar® Threebond Engine RTV Sealant to the gasket surfaces, the components must be assembled within 20 minutes and the attaching fasteners must be tightened to specification within 45 minutes. Prolonged exposure to

the air prior to assembly may result in engine fluid leakage.

17. Apply a bead of Mopar® Threebond Engine RTV Sealant to the upper oil pan as shown in the following locations:
   - Oil pan to engine block flange
   - Two timing cover to engine block T-joints
   - Two rear seal retainer to engine block T-joints

⁂ WARNING

Make sure that the rear face of the oil pan is flush to the transmission bell housing before tightening any of the oil pan mounting bolts. A gap between the oil pan and the transmission could crack the oil pan or transmission casting.

18. Install the oil pan to the engine block and flush to the transmission bell housing. Secure the oil pan to the engine block with nineteen oil pan mounting bolts finger tight.
19. Install four transmission to the engine oil pan bolts and tighten to 41 ft. lbs. (55 Nm).
20. Tighten the nineteen previously installed oil pan mounting bolts to 18 ft. lbs. (25 Nm).
21. Install two bolts to the rear oil seal retainer flange and tighten to 106 inch lbs. (12 Nm).
22. Install two rubber plugs covering the rear oil seal retainer flange bolts.
23. Clip the transmission cooler line retainer to the oil pan flange.
24. Install the steering gear.
25. If equipped with AWD, install the front axle.
26. Install the lower oil pan.
27. Install the front skid plate, if equipped.
28. Lower the vehicle.
29. Install the oil level indicator with bolt and tighten to 106 inch lbs. (12 Nm).
30. If removed, install the oil filter and fill the engine crankcase with the proper oil to the correct level.
31. Connect the negative battery cable.
32. Run the engine until it reaches normal operating temperature.

3.7L Engine

See Figures 184 through 186.

1. Disconnect negative battery cable.
2. Remove the radiator fan.
3. Remove the intake manifold.
4. Install engine support tool.
5. Do not raise engine at this time.
6. Remove the structural cover using sequence shown.
7. Remove both left and right side engine mount through bolts.
8. Raise engine using Engine Support, to provide clearance to remove oil pan.
9. Drain engine oil and remove oil filter.

➡Do not pry on oil pan or oil pan gasket. Gasket is mounted to engine and does not come out with oil pan.

10. Remove the oil pan mounting bolts and oil pan.
11. Unbolt oil pump pickup tube and remove tube and oil pan gasket from engine.

To install:

12. Clean the oil pan gasket mating surface of the bedplate and oil pan.

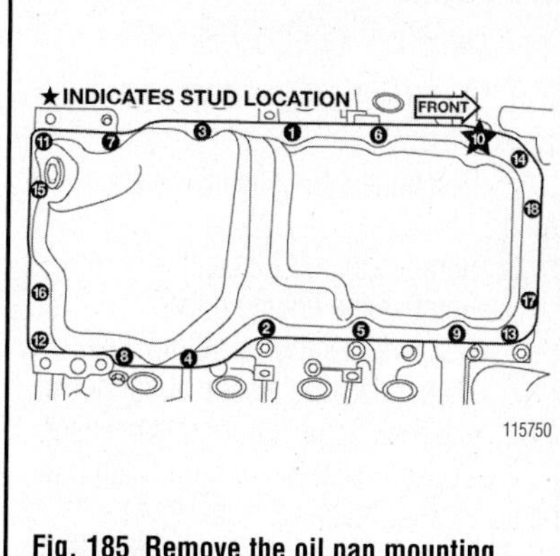

Fig. 185 Remove the oil pan mounting bolts and oil pan

13. Inspect integrated oil pan gasket, and replace as necessary.
14. Position the integrated oil pan gasket/windage tray assembly.
15. Install the oil pickup tube
16. If removed, install stud at position No. 9.
17. Install the mounting bolt and nuts. Tighten nuts to 20 ft. lbs. (28 Nm).
18. Position the oil pan and install the mounting bolts. Tighten the mounting bolts to 12 ft. lbs. (16 Nm) in the sequence shown.
19. Install structural dust cover.
20. Lower the engine into mounts using Engine Support.
21. Remove Engine Support.
22. Install both the left and right side engine mount through bolts. Tighten the nuts to 50 ft. lbs. (68 Nm).
23. Install the intake manifold.
24. Fill engine oil.
25. Reconnect the negative battery cable.
26. Start engine and check for leaks.

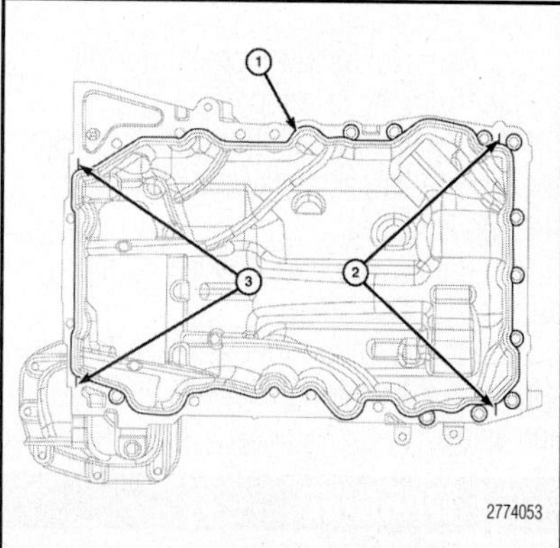

Fig. 183 Apply sealant to Oil pan to engine block flange (1), timing cover to engine block T-joints (2), and rear seal retainer to engine block T-joints (3)

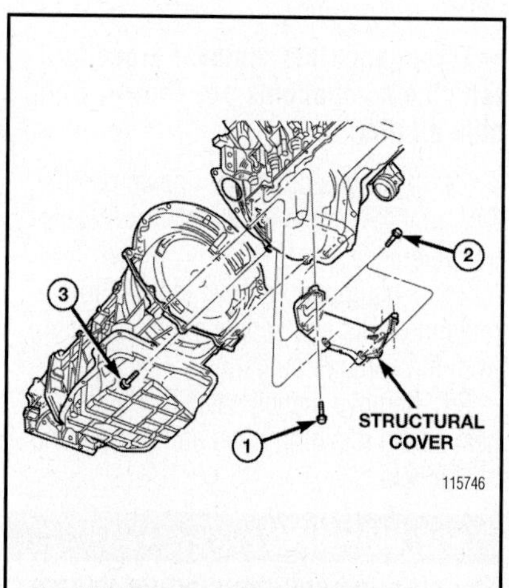

Fig. 184 Remove the structural cover using sequence shown

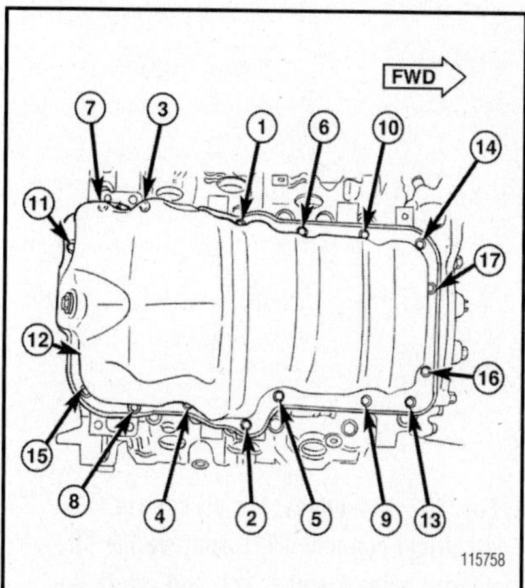

Fig. 186 Tighten the mounting bolts in the sequence shown

5.7L Engine

See Figures 187 through 195.

1. Perform the fuel pressure release procedure.
2. Disconnect the negative battery cable.
3. Remove the oil fill cap.
4. Remove the engine cover.
5. Remove the engine oil dipstick.
6. Disconnect the electrical connector at the Intake Air Temperature (IAT) sensor.
7. Loosen the fresh air hose clamp at the air cleaner housing.
8. Remove the resonator retaining bolt.
9. Loosen the resonator hose clamp at the throttle body and remove the resonator.
10. Remove the intake manifold.

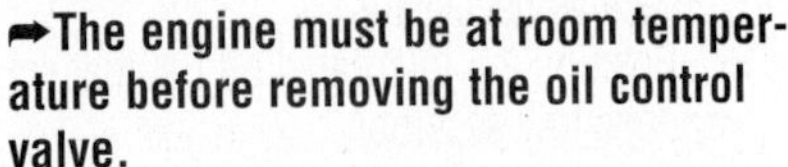

➡The engine must be at room temperature before removing the oil control valve.

11. Disconnect the oil control valve electrical connector.
12. Remove the oil control valve fastener.
13. Rotate the oil control valve to break the seal then pull the oil control valve straight out.

➡Do not use air tools to install the Engine Lift Fixture Engine Lift Fixture.

14. Install the Engine Lift Fixture.
15. Securely tighten lifting fixture mounting bolts.
16. Position the Engine Support Fixture.
17. Connect the Engine Support Fixture to the Engine Lift Fixture and tighten to support the engine.
18. Raise and support the vehicle.
19. Drain the engine oil.

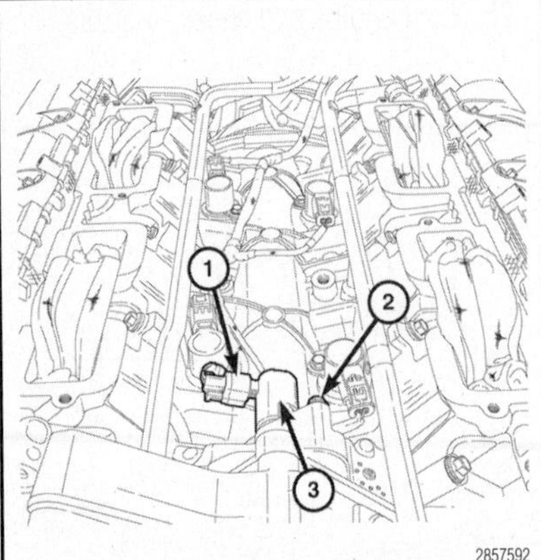

Fig. 187 Disconnect the oil control valve electrical connector (1), remove the oil control valve fastener (2), and rotate the oil control valve (3) to break the seal then pull the oil control valve straight out

Fig. 188 Install the Engine Lift Fixture (1); tighten lifting fixture mounting bolts (2)

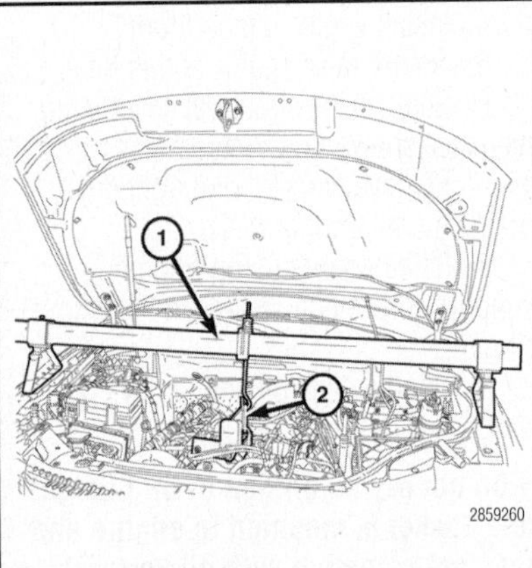

Fig. 189 Connect the Engine Support Fixture (1) to the Engine Lift Fixture (2) and tighten to support the engine

20. Remove both front wheels and tires.
21. If equipped, remove the skid plate four retaining bolts and remove the skid plate.
22. Remove both engine mount retaining nuts.

➡Throughout this removal procedure, left side components are shown, right side similar.

23. If equipped, mark a line across the C/V joint to companion flange for installation reference.
24. If equipped, remove the C/V joint retaining bolts and separate the C/V joint from the companion flange.
25. Remove the left catalytic converter heat shield retaining bolts and remove the heat shield.

⁂ WARNING

The steering column module is centered to the vehicles steering system. Failure to keep the system and steering column module centered and locked/inhibited from rotating can result in steering column module damage.

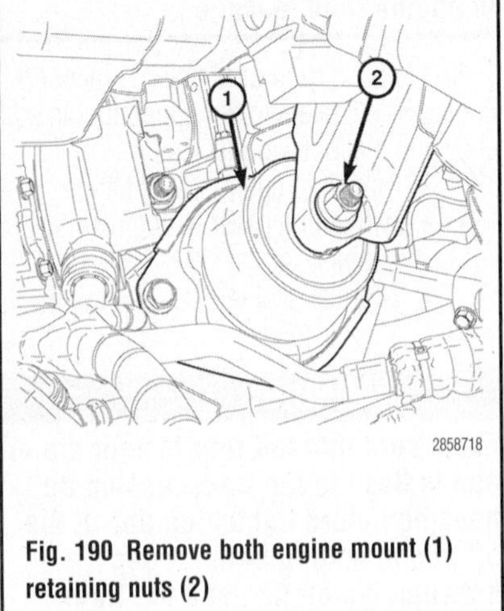

Fig. 190 Remove both engine mount (1) retaining nuts (2)

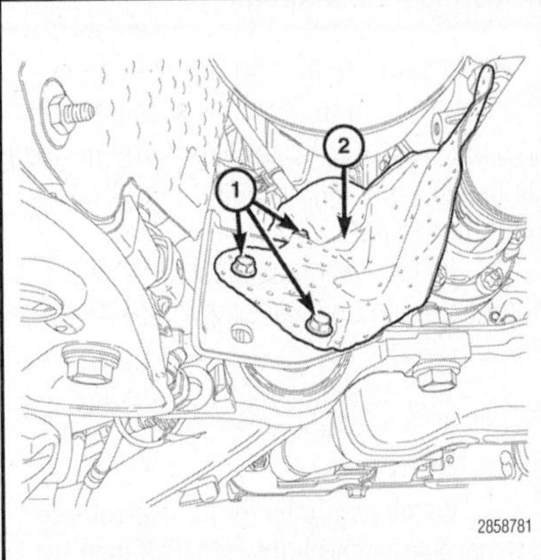

Fig. 191 Remove the left catalytic converter heat shield retaining bolts (1) and remove the heat shield (2)

26. Remove the lower steering shaft coupler pinch bolt.
27. Remove the lower steering shaft coupler from the steering gear.
28. Disconnect both front wheel speed sensor wire harness retainers from the steering knuckles.
29. Remove both front wheel speed sensor retaining bolts.
30. Remove both front wheel speed sensors from the steering knuckles and position aside.

⁂ WARNING

Never allow the disc brake caliper to hang from the brake hose. Damage to the brake hose will result. Provide a suitable support to hang the caliper securely.

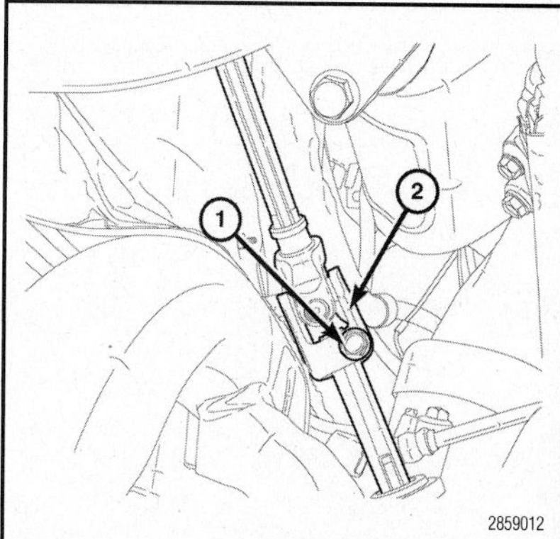

Fig. 192 Remove the lower steering shaft coupler pinch bolt (1) and remove the lower steering shaft coupler (2) from the steering gear

31. Remove both front brake caliper adapter mounting bolts and using bungee cords or bailing wire, secure the brake calipers aside.
32. Remove both upper ball joint nuts.
33. If equipped, remove both half shaft hub bearing nuts.
34. Separate both steering knuckles from the ball joints.
35. If equipped, slightly slide both axle shafts inward while tilting the hub bearing and steering knuckle assembly outward (do not remove).
36. Remove both lower clevis bolts at the lower control arms.
37. Remove the structural dust cover retaining bolts.
38. Remove the structural dust cover.
39. Remove the pressure line at the steering gear.
40. Remove the return line at the steering gear.
41. Remove the steering gear pressure line retainers at the engine cradle crossmember and position the pressure line aside.

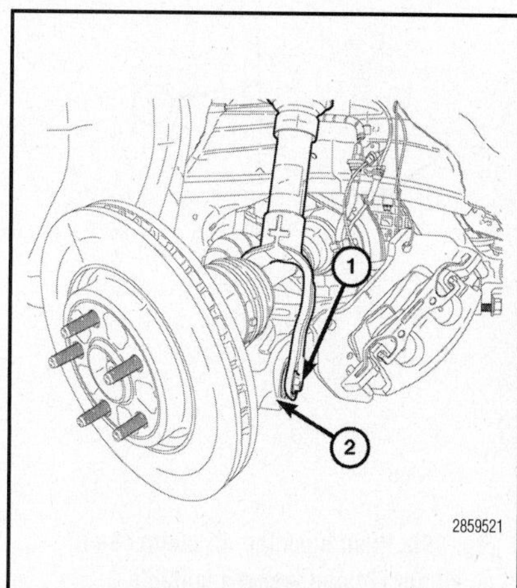

Fig. 193 Remove both lower clevis bolts (1) at the lower control arms (2)

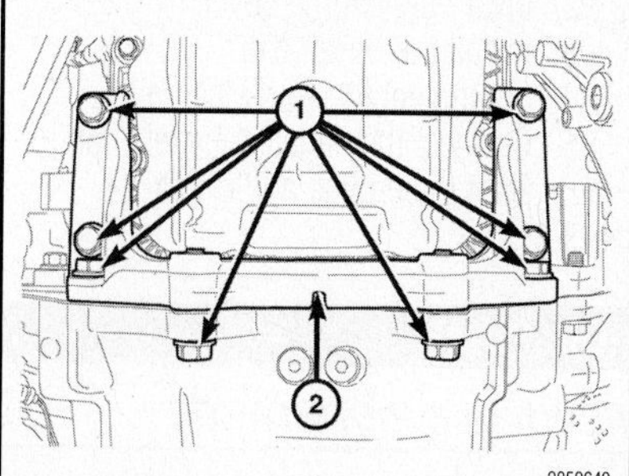

Fig. 194 Remove the structural dust cover retaining bolts (1) and the structural dust cover (2)

42. Remove the engine cradle crossmember.

➡The oil pump pickup tube, windage tray and oil pan is one assembly. When the oil pan is removed, a new oil pan gasket and pickup tube O-ring must be installed. The old gasket and O-ring cannot be reused.

43. Remove the transmission line retaining bracket at the oil pan.
44. Using the sequence shown, remove the oil pan retaining bolts.
45. Remove the oil pan and discard the oil pan gasket and pickup tube O-ring.
46. Clean the sealing surfaces as necessary.

To install:

47. Clean the oil pan gasket mating surface of the block and oil pan.

➡When the oil pan is removed, a new oil pan gasket and pickup tube O-ring must be installed. The old gasket and O-ring cannot be reused.

48. Install a new oil pan gasket and pickup tube O-ring.

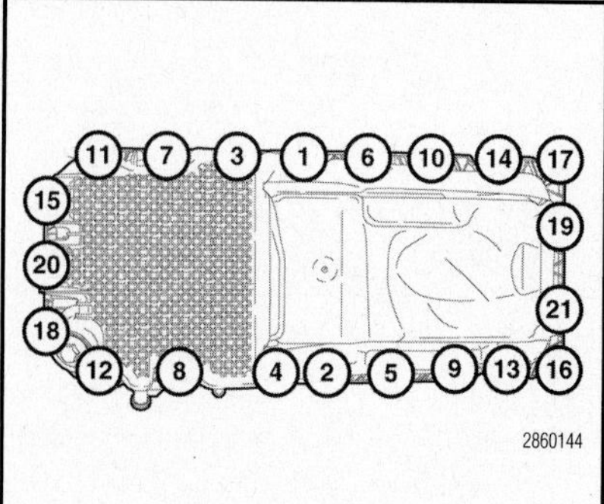

Fig. 195 Using the sequence shown, remove the oil pan retaining bolts

➡Mopar® Engine RTV must be applied to the 4 T-joints area where the front cover, rear retainer and oil pan gasket meet. The bead of RTV should cover the bottom of the gasket.

49. Apply Mopar® Engine RTV at the T- joints.
50. Position the oil pan, install the mounting bolts and using the sequence shown, tighten to 9 ft. lbs. (12 Nm).
51. Install the transmission line retaining bracket at the oil pan.
52. Install the engine cradle crossmember.
53. Position the steering gear pressure line and Install the retainers to the engine cradle crossmember.
54. Install the return line at the steering gear.
55. Install the pressure line at the steering gear.

WARNING

The structural dust cover must be held tightly against both the engine and the transmission bell housing during the tightening sequence. Failure to do so may cause severe damage to the cover.

56. Position the structural dust cover.
57. Install the structural dust cover retaining bolts hand tight.
58. Tighten the structural dust cover-to-transmission bolts to 80 inch lbs. (9 Nm).
59. Tighten the structural dust cover-to-engine bolts to 80 inch lbs. (9 Nm).
60. Retighten the structural dust cover-to-transmission bolts to 40 ft. lbs. (54 Nm).
61. Retighten the structural dust cover-to-engine bolts to 40 ft. lbs. (54 Nm).
62. Install both lower clevis bolts at the lower control arms and tighten to 125 ft. lbs. (169 Nm).
63. If equipped, slide both axle shafts into the hub bearing.
64. Position both steering knuckle assemblies onto the ball joint studs.
65. If equipped, install both half shaft hub bearing nuts and tighten to 100 ft. lbs. (135 Nm).
66. Install both upper ball joint nuts and tighten to 70 ft. lbs. (95 Nm).
67. Position the front brake calipers, install the caliper adapter mounting bolts and tighten to 125 ft. lbs. (169 Nm).
68. Position both front wheel speed sensors into the steering knuckle.
69. Install both front wheel speed sensor retaining bolts and tighten to 10 ft. lbs. (14 Nm).

70. Connect both front wheel speed sensor wire harness retainers to the steering knuckles.

⁂ WARNING

The steering gear must be centered prior to installing the coupler to prevent clockspring damage.

71. Position the lower steering shaft coupler onto the steering gear.
72. Install the a new lower steering shaft coupler pinch bolt and tighten to 36 ft. lbs. (49 Nm).
73. Position the left catalytic converter heat shield, install the retaining bolts and securely tighten bolts.
74. If equipped, position the C/V joint onto the companion flange making sure to align the reference mark made during removal.

➡Clean all propeller shaft bolts and apply Mopar® Lock and Seal Adhesive, Medium Strength Thread locker or equivalent to the threads before installation.

75. Install the bolts to the axle flange and tighten to 24 ft. lbs. (32 Nm).

➡For engine mount retaining nuts, apply Mopar® Lock and Seal Adhesive, Medium Strength Thread locker or equivalent to the threads before installation.

76. Install both engine mount retaining nuts and tighten to 55 ft. lbs. (75 Nm).
77. If equipped, position the front skid plate, install the four retaining bolts and tighten to 21 ft. lbs. (28 Nm).
78. Install both front wheels and tires.
79. Lower the vehicle.
80. Remove the Engine Support Fixture.
81. Remove the Engine Lift Fixture.
82. Install the oil control valve.
83. Ensure that the O-ring is fully seated into the cylinder block.
84. Securely tighten the oil control valve retaining bolt.
85. Connect the oil control valve electrical connector.
86. Install the intake manifold.
87. Position the resonator hose onto the throttle body and tighten hose clamp.
88. Install the resonator retaining bolt.
89. Install the fresh air hose to the air cleaner housing and tighten hose clamp.
90. Connect the electrical connector at the Intake Air Temperature (IAT) sensor.
91. Install the engine oil dipstick.
92. Install the engine cover.
93. Install the oil fill cap.
94. Fill the engine with clean oil.
95. Connect the negative battery cable.
96. Start the engine and check for leaks.

OIL PUMP

REMOVAL & INSTALLATION

3.6L Engine

See Figures 196 through 200.

1. Disconnect and isolate the negative battery cable.
2. Remove the upper oil pan
3. Remove the oil pump pick-up.
4. Disconnect the engine wire harness from the oil pump solenoid electrical connector.
5. Depress the connector retention lock tab to disengage the oil pump solenoid electrical connector from the engine block.
6. Push the oil pump solenoid electrical connector into the engine block, rotate the connector slightly clockwise, push it past the primary chain tensioner mounting bolt and into the engine.

➡Graphic shows the engine timing cover removed for clarity.

7. Push back the oil pump chain tensioner and insert a suitable retaining pin such as a 3 mm Allen wrench.

⁂ WARNING

Always reinstall timing chains so that they maintain the same direction of rotation. Inverting a previously run chain on a previously run sprocket will result in excessive wear to both the chain and sprocket.

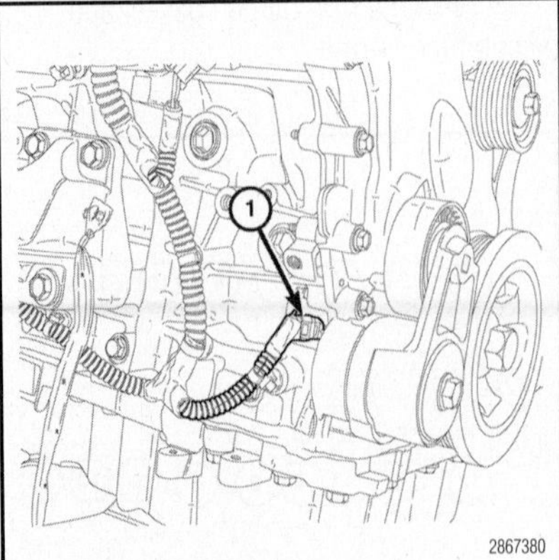

Fig. 196 Disconnect the engine wire harness from the oil pump solenoid electrical connector (1)

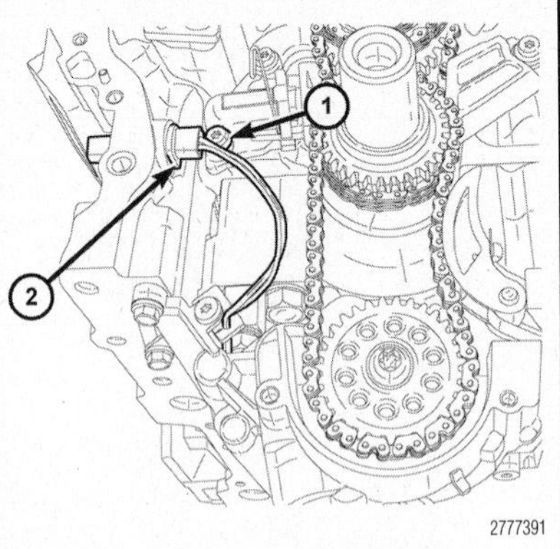

Fig. 197 Push the oil pump solenoid electrical connector (2) into the engine block, rotate the connector slightly clockwise, push it past the primary chain tensioner mounting bolt (1) and into the engine

8. Mark the direction of rotation on the oil pump chain and sprocket using a paint pen or equivalent to aid in reassembly.

➡There are no timing marks on the oil pump gear or chain. Timing of the oil pump is not required.

9. Remove the oil pump sprocket T45 retaining bolt and remove the oil pump sprocket.
10. Remove the retaining pin and disengage the oil pump chain tensioner spring from the dowel pin.
11. Remove the oil pump chain tensioner from the oil pump.
12. Remove the four oil pump bolts and remove the oil pump.

To install:

13. Align the locator pins to the engine block and install the oil pump with four bolts. Tighten the bolts to 106 inch lbs. (12 Nm).

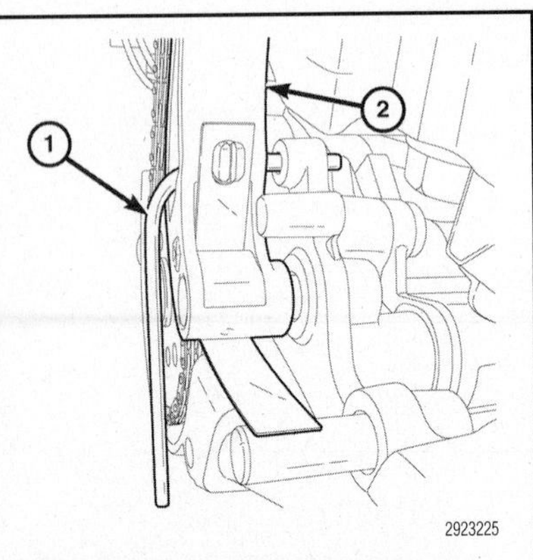

Fig. 198 Push back the oil pump chain tensioner (2) and insert a suitable retaining pin (1) such as a 3 mm Allen wrench

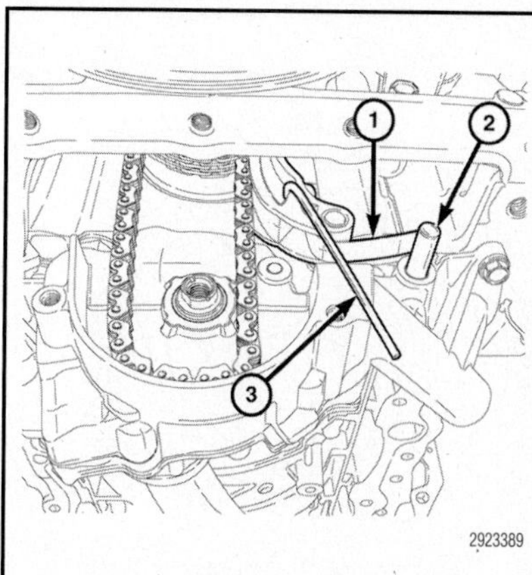

Fig. 199 Remove the retaining pin (3) and disengage the oil pump chain tensioner spring (1) from the dowel pin (2)

14. Install the oil pump chain tensioner on the oil pump.
15. Position the oil pump chain tensioner spring above the dowel pin.
16. Push back the oil pump chain tensioner and insert a suitable retaining pin such as a 3 mm Allen wrench.

➡There are no timing marks on the oil pump gear or chain. Timing of the oil pump is not required.

⁂ WARNING

Always reinstall timing chains so that they maintain the same direction of rotation. Inverting a previously run chain on a previously run sprocket will result in excessive wear to both the chain and sprocket.

17. Place the oil pump sprocket into the oil pump chain. Align the oil pump sprocket with the oil pump shaft and install the sprocket. Install the T45 retaining bolt and tighten to 18 ft. lbs. (25 Nm).
18. Remove the retaining pin. Verify that the oil pump chain is centered on the tensioner and crankshaft sprocket.
19. Rotate the crankshaft clockwise one complete revolution to verify proper oil pump chain installation.
20. Position the oil pump solenoid electrical connector into the engine block. Rotate the connector so that it can be pushed past the primary chain tensioner mounting bolt. Then rotate the connector slightly counterclockwise and push it into the engine block until it locks in place.
21. Verify that the oil pump solenoid electrical connector retention lock tab is engaged to the engine block.
22. Connect the engine wire harness to the oil pump solenoid electrical connector.
23. Install the oil pump pick-up.
24. Install the oil pan.
25. If removed, install the oil filter and fill the engine crankcase with the proper oil to the correct level.
26. Connect the negative battery cable.

⁂ WARNING

A MIL or low oil pressure indicator that remains illuminated for more than 2 seconds may indicate low or no engine oil pressure. Stop the engine and investigate the cause of the indication.

27. Start and run the engine until it reaches normal operating temperature.

3.7L Engine

See Figure 201.

1. Remove the oil pan and pick-up tube.
2. Remove the timing chain cover.
3. Remove the timing chains and tensioners.
4. Remove the four bolts, primary timing chain tensioner and the oil pump.

To install:

5. Position the oil pump onto the crankshaft and install one oil pump retaining bolt.
6. Position the primary timing chain tensioner and install three retaining bolts.
7. Tighten the oil pump and primary timing chain tensioner retaining bolts to 21 ft. lbs. (28 Nm) in the sequence shown.
8. Install the secondary timing chain tensioners and timing chains.
9. Install the timing chain cover.
10. Install the pick-up tube and oil pan.

5.7L Engine

See Figures 202 and 203.

1. Remove the oil pan.
2. Remove the timing cover.

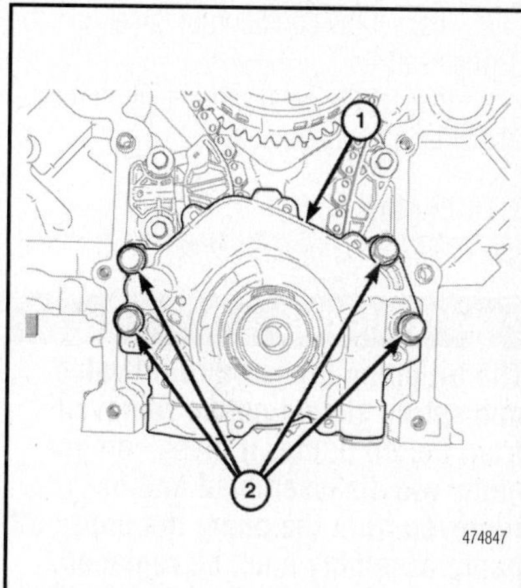

Fig. 202 Remove the four bolts (2) and the oil pump (1)

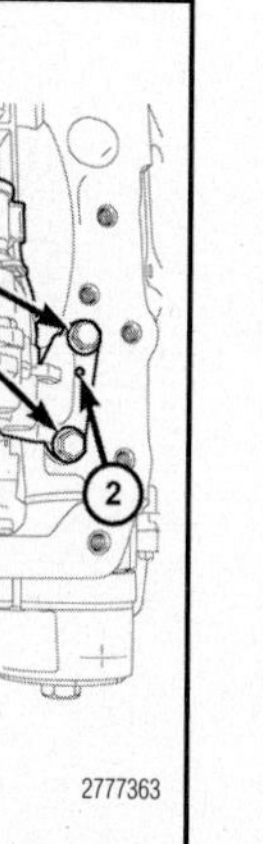

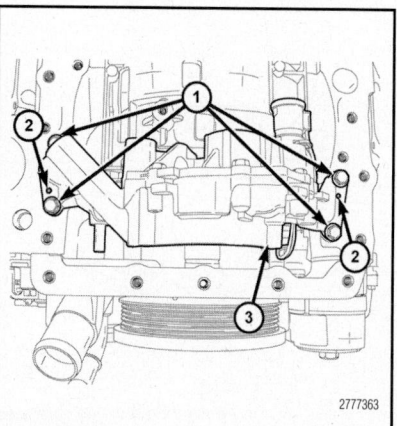

Fig. 200 Remove the four oil pump bolts (1) and remove the oil pump (3); locator pins (2)

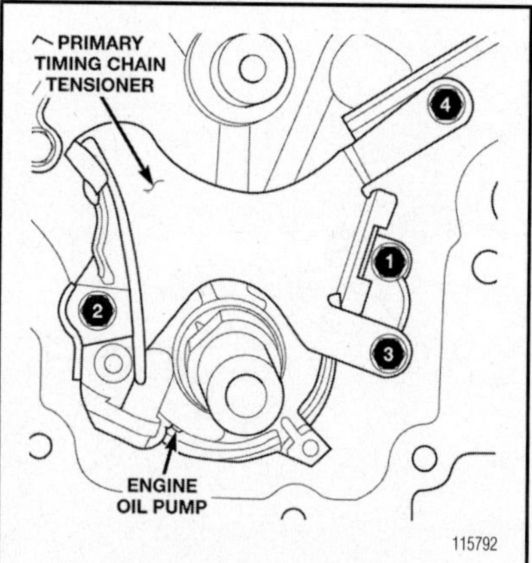

Fig. 201 Tighten the oil pump and primary timing chain tensioner retaining bolts in the sequence shown

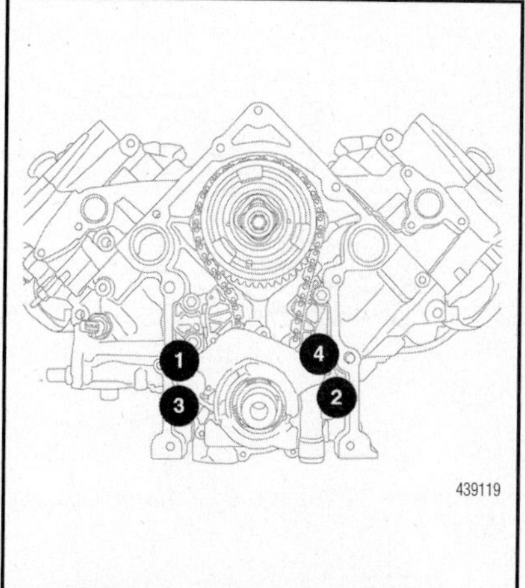

Fig. 203 Using the sequence shown, tighten the oil pump retaining bolts

3. Remove the four bolts and the oil pump.

To install:

4. Position the oil pump on the crankshaft and install the oil pump retaining bolts finger tight.
5. Using the sequence shown, tighten the oil pump retaining bolts to 21 ft. lbs. (28 Nm).
6. Install the timing cover.
7. Install the oil pan.

INSPECTION

3.6L Engine

➡The 3.6L Oil pump is released as an assembly. The assembly includes both the pump and the solenoid. There are no serviceable sub-assembly components. In the event the oil pump or solenoid are not functioning or out of specification they must be replaced as an assembly.

1. Inspect the solenoid wires for cuts or chaffing.
2. Inspect the condition of the connector O-ring seal.
3. Inspect the connector retention lock tab for fatigue or damage.

3.7L Engine

See Figures 204 through 209.

⁂ WARNING

The oil pump pressure relief valve and spring should not be removed from the oil pump. If these components are disassembled and or removed from the pump the entire oil pump assembly must be replaced.

1. Clean all parts thoroughly. Mating surface of the oil pump housing should be smooth. If the pump cover is scratched or grooved, the oil pump assembly should be replaced.
2. Lay a straight edge across the pump cover surface. If a 0.001 inches (0.025 mm) feeler gauge can be inserted between the cover and the straight edge, the oil pump assembly should be replaced.
3. Measure the thickness of the outer rotor. If the outer rotor thickness measures at 0.472 inches (12.005 mm) or less the oil pump assembly must be replaced.
4. Measure the diameter of the outer rotor. If the outer rotor diameter measures at 3.382 inches (85.925 mm) or less the oil pump assembly must be replaced.
5. Measure the thickness of the inner rotor. If the inner rotor thickness measures at 0.472 inches (12.005 mm) or less then the oil pump assembly must be replaced.
6. Slide outer rotor into the body of the oil pump. Press the outer rotor to one side of the oil pump body and measure clearance between the outer rotor and the body. If the measurement is 0.009 inches (0.235 mm) or more the oil pump assembly must be replaced.
7. Install the inner rotor in the into the oil pump body. Measure the clearance between the inner and outer rotors. If the clearance between the rotors is 0.006 inches (0.150 mm) or more the oil pump assembly must be replaced.
8. Place a straight edge across the body of the oil pump (between the bolt holes), if a feeler gauge of 0.0038 inches (0.095 mm) or greater can be inserted between the straightedge and the rotors, the pump must be replaced.

➡The 3.7 Oil pump is released as an assembly. There are no Chrysler part numbers for Sub-Assembly components. In the event the oil pump is not functioning or out of specification it must be replaced as an assembly.

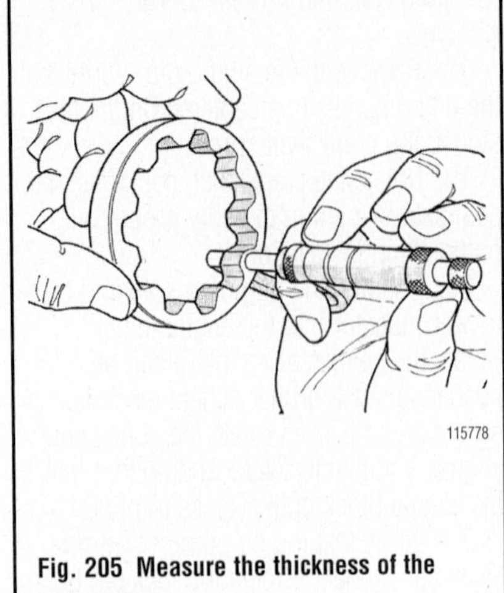

Fig. 205 Measure the thickness of the outer rotor

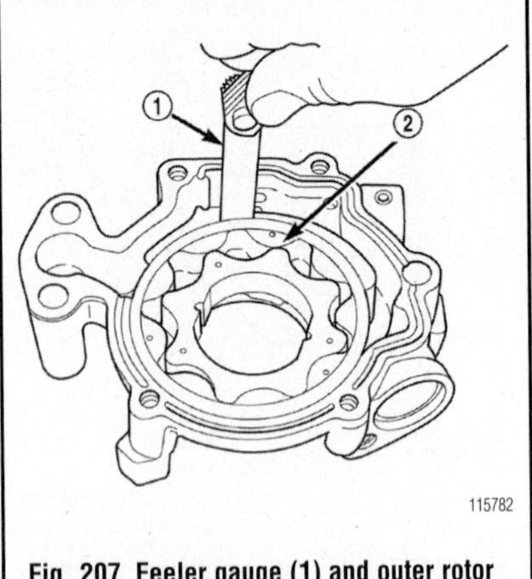

Fig. 207 Feeler gauge (1) and outer rotor (2); measure clearance between the outer rotor and the body

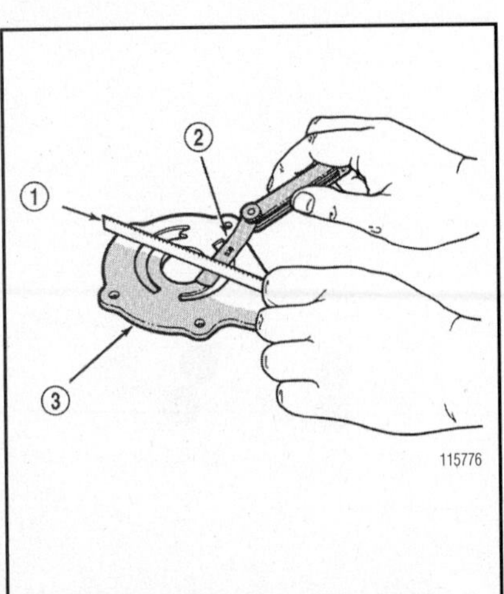

Fig. 204 Straight edge (1), feeler gauge (2), and pump cover surface (3)

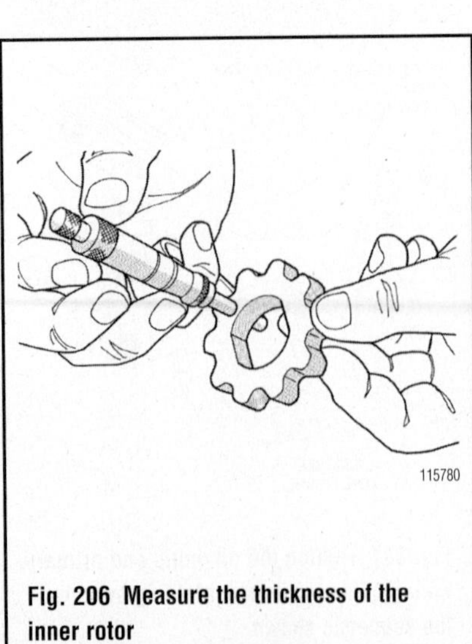

Fig. 206 Measure the thickness of the inner rotor

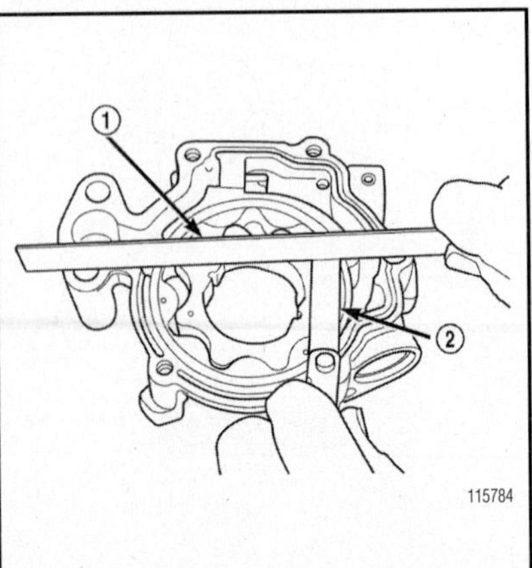

Fig. 208 Straight edge (1) and feeler gauge (2); measure the clearance between the inner and outer rotors

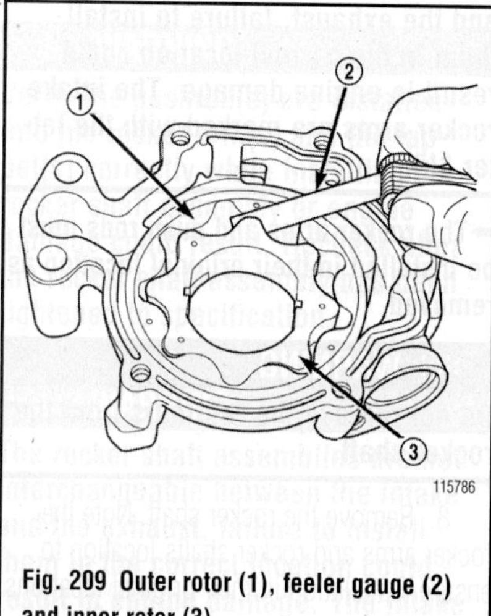

Fig. 209 Outer rotor (1), feeler gauge (2) and inner rotor (3)

5.7L Engine

See Figures 210 through 212.

WARNING

The oil pump pressure relief valve and spring should not be removed from the oil pump. If these components are disassembled and or removed from the pump the entire oil pump assembly must be replaced.

1. Remove the pump cover.
2. Clean all parts thoroughly. Mating surface of the oil pump housing should be smooth. If the pump cover is scratched or grooved the oil pump assembly should be replaced.
3. Slide outer rotor into the body of the oil pump. Press the outer rotor to one side of the oil pump body and measure clearance between the outer rotor and the body. If the measurement is 0.009 inches (0.235mm) or more the oil pump assembly must be replaced.

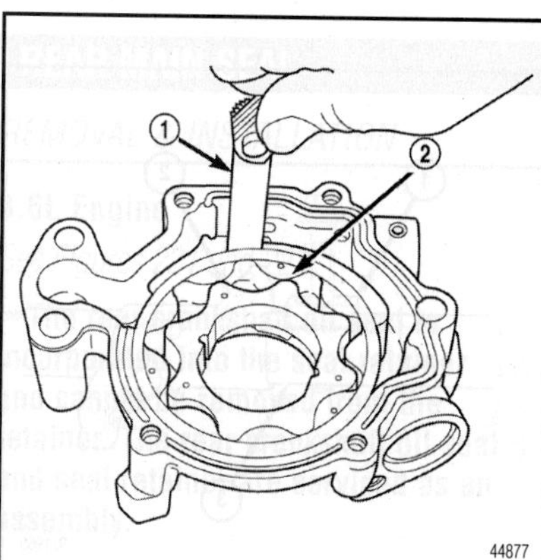

Fig. 210 Feeler gauge (1); measure clearance between the outer rotor (2) and the body

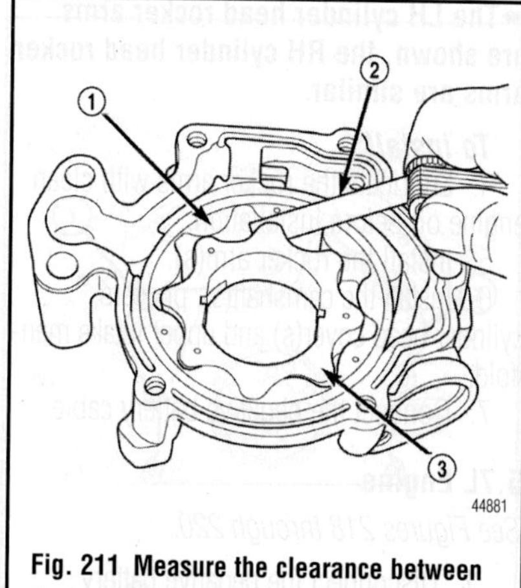

Fig. 211 Measure the clearance between the inner (3) and outer rotors (1); feeler gauge (2)

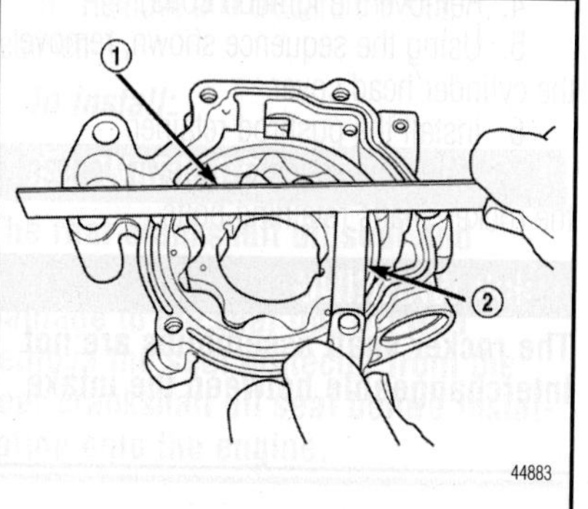

Fig. 212 Insert a feeler gauge (2) between the straight edge (1) and rotors

4. Install the inner rotor into the oil pump body. Measure the clearance between the inner and outer rotors. If the clearance between the rotors is 0.006 inches (0.150 mm) or more the oil pump assembly must be replaced.
5. Place a straight edge (1) across the body of the oil pump (between the bolt holes), if a feeler gauge (2) of 0.0038 inches (0.095 mm) or greater can be inserted between the straightedge and the rotors, the pump must be replaced.
6. Reinstall the pump cover. Tighten fasteners to 11 ft. lbs. (15 Nm).

➡The 5.7 Oil pump is serviced as an assembly. In the event the oil pump is not functioning or out of specification, it must be replaced as an assembly.

PISTON AND RING

POSITIONING

3.6L Engine

See Figures 213 and 214.

Refer to the accompanying illustrations.

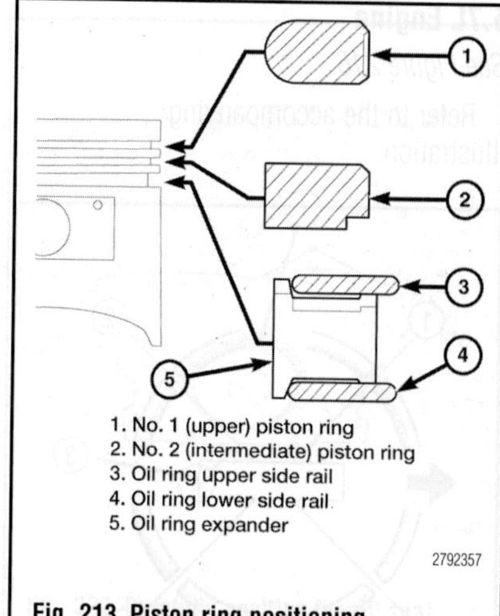

Fig. 213 Piston ring positioning

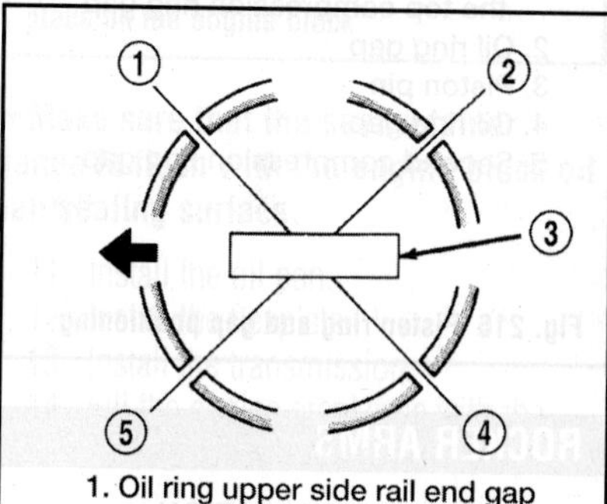

Fig. 214 Piston ring end gap positioning

3.7L Engine

See Figure 215.

Refer to the accompanying illustration.

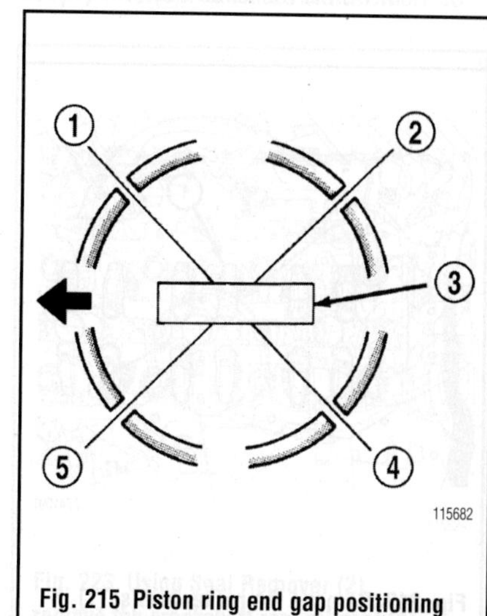

Fig. 215 Piston ring end gap positioning

21. Install the upper and lower oil pans.
22. Install the right and left cylinder head covers.
23. Install the crankshaft vibration damper.
24. Install the power steering pump pulley.
25. Install the accessory idler pulley.
26. Install accessory drive belt tensioner.
27. Install the accessory drive belt.
28. Install the heater core supply tube with one bolt tightened to 106 inch lbs. (12 Nm).
29. Install the heater core supply hose to the coolant outlet housing.
30. Install the lower radiator hose to the water pump housing.
31. Install the heater core return hose to the water pump housing.
32. Install the thermostat housing and upper radiator hose.
33. Install the electric vacuum pump.
34. If removed, install the oil filter and fill the engine crankcase with the proper oil to the correct level.
35. Connect the negative battery cable.
36. Fill the cooling system.
37. Run the engine until it reaches normal operating temperature. Check cooling system for correct fluid level.

3.7L Engine

See Figure 231.

1. Disconnect the battery negative cable.
2. Drain the cooling system.
3. Remove electric cooling fan and fan shroud assembly.
4. Remove the radiator fan.
5. Disconnect both heater hoses at timing cover.
6. Disconnect lower radiator hose at engine.
7. Remove accessory drive belt tensioner assembly.
8. Remove crankshaft damper.
9. Remove the alternator.
10. Remove the A/C compressor.

⁂ WARNING

The 3.7L engine uses an anaerobic sealer instead of a gasket to seal the front cover to the engine block, from the factory. For service, Mopar® Grey Engine RTV sealant must be substituted.

➡It is not necessary to remove the water pump for timing cover removal.

11. Remove the bolts holding the timing cover to engine block.
12. Remove the timing cover.

To install:

⁂ WARNING

Do not use oil based liquids to clean timing cover or block surfaces. Use only rubbing alcohol, along with plastic or wooden scrapers. Use no wire brushes or abrasive wheels or metal scrapers, or damage to surfaces could result.

13. Clean timing chain cover and block surface using rubbing alcohol.

⁂ WARNING

The 3.7L uses a special anaerobic sealer instead of a gasket to seal the timing cover to the engine block, from the factory. For service repairs, Mopar® Engine RTV must be used as a substitute.

14. Inspect the water passage O-rings for any damage, and replace as necessary.
15. Apply Mopar® Engine RTV sealer to front cover using a 3 to 4 mm thick bead.
16. Install cover.
17. Tighten fasteners in sequence as shown in to 43 ft. lbs. (58 Nm).
18. Install crankshaft damper.
19. Install the A/C compressor.
20. Install the alternator.
21. Install accessory drive belt tensioner.
22. Install radiator upper and lower hoses.
23. Install both heater hoses.
24. Install the radiator fan.
25. Fill the cooling system.
26. Connect the battery negative cable.

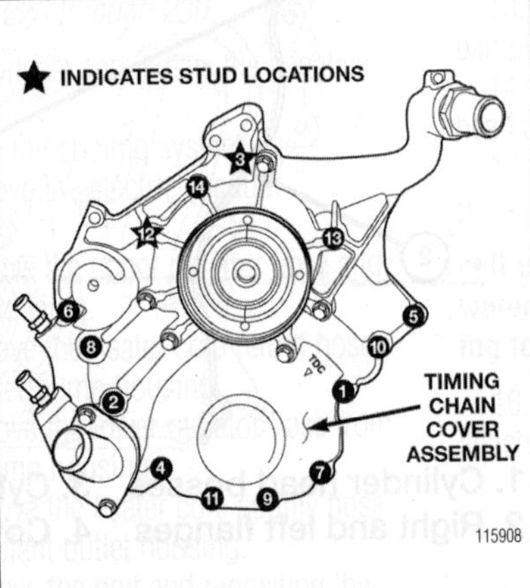

Fig. 231 Tighten fasteners in sequence as shown

5.7L Engine

See Figure 232.

1. Remove the cooling fan module.
2. Remove the serpentine belt.
3. Remove the oil pan.
4. Drain the cooling system.
5. Remove the lower radiator hose clamp at the water pump.
6. Remove the lower radiator hose clamp at the radiator and remove the lower radiator hose.

➡It is not necessary to disconnect the refrigerant lines for A/C compressor removal.

7. Remove the A/C compressor from the engine block and position aside.
8. Lower the vehicle.
9. Disconnect the CMP sensor electrical connector.
10. Remove CMP sensor mounting bolt.
11. Using a slight rocking motion, carefully remove the CMP sensor from the timing cover.
12. Check the condition of the CMP sensor O-ring, replace as necessary.
13. Remove the upper radiator hose clamp at the thermostat housing.
14. Remove the upper radiator hose retainer at the fan shroud and position the radiator hose aside.
15. Remove the air cleaner resonator support bracket at the water pump.
16. Disconnect the electrical connector to the coolant temperature sensor.
17. Remove the heater tube retaining bolt.
18. Lift the heater tube out of the water pump.

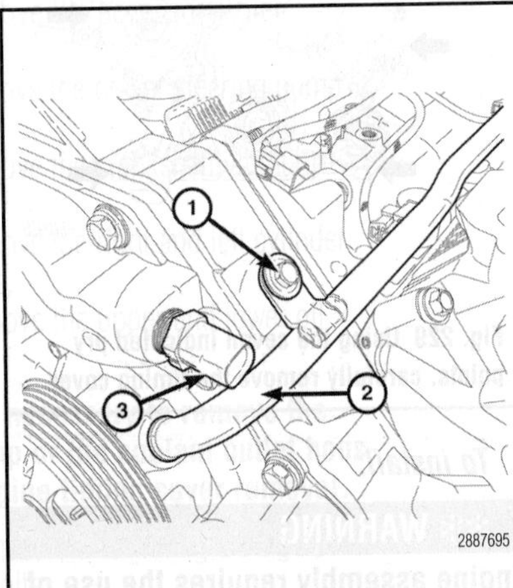

Fig. 232 Disconnect the electrical connector to the coolant temperature sensor (3), remove the heater tube retaining bolt (1), and Lift the heater tube (2) out of the water pump

19. Check condition of heater tube O-ring, replace as necessary.

➡**It is not necessary to disconnect the hoses from the power steering pump, for power steering pump removal.**

20. Remove the power steering pump and position aside.
21. Remove the alternator.

➡**When installing the puller tool, ensure the bolts are fully threaded through the entire crankshaft damper.**

22. Remove the crankshaft damper bolt.
23. Install puller tool and remove the crankshaft damper.

➡**It is not necessary to remove the water pump for timing cover removal.**

24. Remove the timing cover bolts and remove the timing cover.
25. Clean the sealing surfaces as necessary.

To install:

26. Clean the timing cover and engine block sealing surfaces.
27. Verify that the slide bushings are installed in the timing cover.
28. Using a new gasket, position the timing cover, install the retaining bolts and tighten to 21 ft. lbs. (28 Nm).

➡**The large lifting stud is tightened to 40 ft. lbs. (55 Nm).**

WARNING

To prevent severe damage to the crankshaft, damper, and damper installer, Damper, thoroughly clean the damper bore and the crankshaft nose before installing damper.

29. Position the damper onto the crankshaft.
30. Assemble the Damper Installer and the Pressing Cup from A/C Hub Installer.
31. Using the Damper Installer and Hub Install, press the damper onto the crankshaft.
32. Install the crankshaft damper bolt and tighten to 129 ft. lbs. (176 Nm).
33. Install the alternator.
34. Install the power steering pump.
35. Install the heater tube into the water pump.
36. Install the heater tube retaining bolt and tighten to 106 inch lbs. (12 Nm).
37. Connect the electrical connector to the coolant temperature sensor.
38. Position the upper radiator hose and secure retainer at the fan shroud.
39. Install the upper radiator hose at the thermostat housing and secure hose clamp.
40. Install the air cleaner resonator support bracket at the water pump.
41. Clean out the machined hole in the timing cover.
42. Install the CMP sensor into the timing cover with a slight rocking motion. Do not the twist sensor into position as damage to O-ring may result.

WARNING

Before tightening sensor retaining bolt, be sure the sensor is completely flush to the timing cover. If the sensor is not flush, damage to the sensor mounting tang may result.

43. Install the CMP sensor retaining bolt and tighten to 106 inch lbs. (12 Nm).
44. Connect the CMP sensor electrical connector.
45. Raise and support the vehicle.
46. Install the oil pan.
47. Install the A/C compressor.
48. Connect the lower radiator hose to the radiator and secure the hose clamp.
49. Connect the lower radiator hose to the water pump and secure hose clamp.
50. Lower the vehicle.
51. Install the cooling fan module.
52. Install the serpentine belt.
53. Fill the cooling system with the proper coolant.
54. Fill the engine with the proper engine oil.
55. Connect the battery negative cable.
56. Start the engine and check for leaks.

TIMING CHAIN & SPROCKETS

REMOVAL & INSTALLATION

3.6L Engine

See Figures 233 through 246.

WARNING

The magnetic timing wheels must not come in contact with magnets (pickup tools, trays, etc.) or any other strong magnetic field. This will destroy the timing wheels ability to correctly relay camshaft position to the camshaft position sensor.

WARNING

When the timing chains are removed and the cylinder heads are still installed, DO NOT rotate the camshafts or crankshaft without first locating the proper crankshaft position. Failure to do so will result in valve and/or piston damage.

1. Disconnect and isolate the negative battery cable.
2. Remove the air cleaner housing assembly and upper intake manifold.
3. Remove the cylinder head covers.
4. Remove the spark plugs.
5. Raise and support the vehicle.
6. Drain the cooling system.
7. Remove the oil pan, accessory drive belts, crankshaft vibration damper and engine timing cover.

➡**Take this opportunity to measure timing chain wear.**

WARNING

When aligning timing marks, always rotate engine by turning the crankshaft. Failure to do so will result in valve and/or piston damage.

8. Rotate the crankshaft clockwise to place the number one piston at TDC on the exhaust stroke by aligning the dimple on the crankshaft with the block/bearing cap junction. The left side cam phaser arrows should point toward each other and be parallel to the valve cover sealing surface. The right side cam phaser arrows should point away from each other and the scribe lines should be parallel to the valve cover sealing surface.

WARNING

Always reinstall timing chains so that they maintain the same direction of rotation. Inverting a previously run chain on a previously run sprocket will result in excessive wear to both the chain and sprocket.

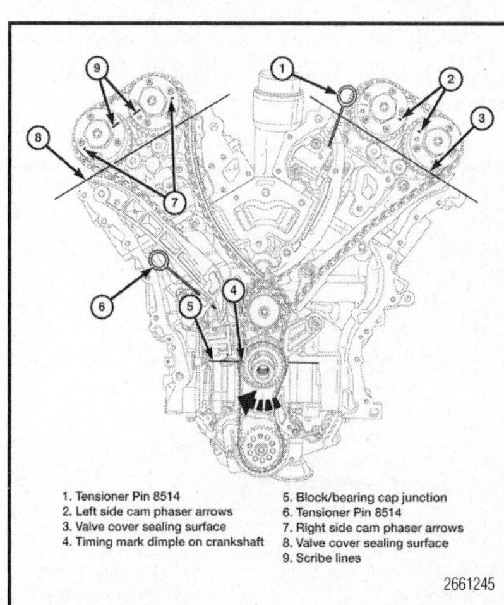

Fig. 233 Rotate the crankshaft clockwise to place the number one piston at TDC on the exhaust stroke by aligning the dimple on the crankshaft with the block/bearing cap junction

9. Mark the direction of rotation on the following timing chains using a paint pen or equivalent to aid in reassembly:

- Left side cam chain
- Right side cam chain
- Oil pump chain
- Primary chain

10. Reset the RH cam chain tensioner by pushing back the tensioner piston and installing Tensioner Pin.
11. Reset the LH cam chain tensioner by lifting the pawl, pushing back the piston and installing Tensioner Pin.
12. Disengage the oil pump chain tensioner spring from the dowel pin and remove the oil pump chain tensioner.
13. Remove the oil pump sprocket T45 retaining bolt and remove the oil pump sprocket and oil pump chain.

➡Minor rotation of a camshaft (a few degrees) may be required to install the camshaft phaser lock.

14. Install the RH Camshaft Phaser Lock.
15. Loosen both the intake oil control valve and exhaust oil control valve.
16. Remove the RH Camshaft Phaser Lock.
17. Remove the oil control valve from the right side intake cam phaser.
18. Pull the right side intake cam phaser off of the camshaft and remove the right side cam chain.
19. If required, remove the oil control valve and pull the right side exhaust cam phaser off of the camshaft.

➡Minor rotation of a camshaft (a few degrees) may be required to install the camshaft phaser lock.

20. Install the LH Camshaft Phaser Lock.
21. Loosen both the intake oil control valve and exhaust oil control valve.

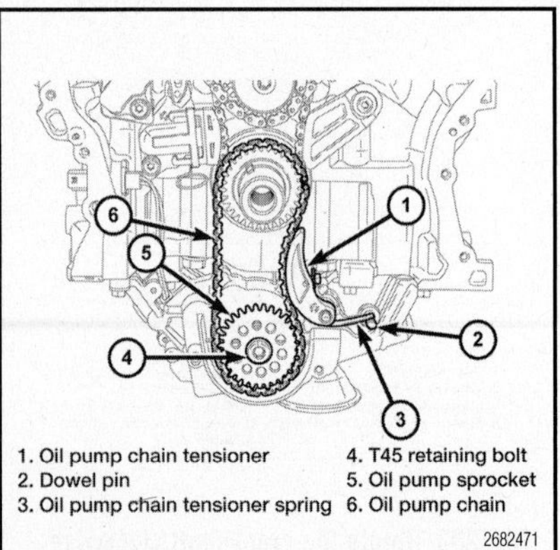

Fig. 234 Disengage the oil pump chain tensioner spring from the dowel pin and remove the oil pump chain tensioner

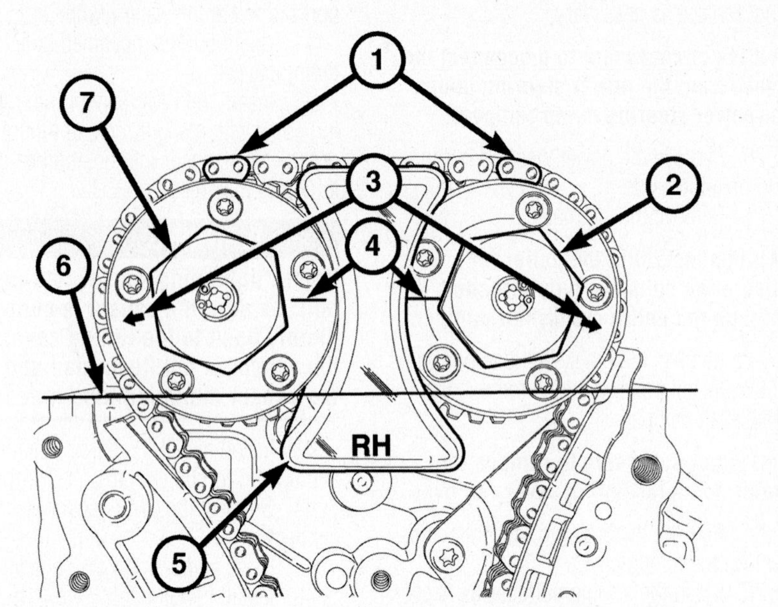

Fig. 235 Install the RH Camshaft Phaser Lock

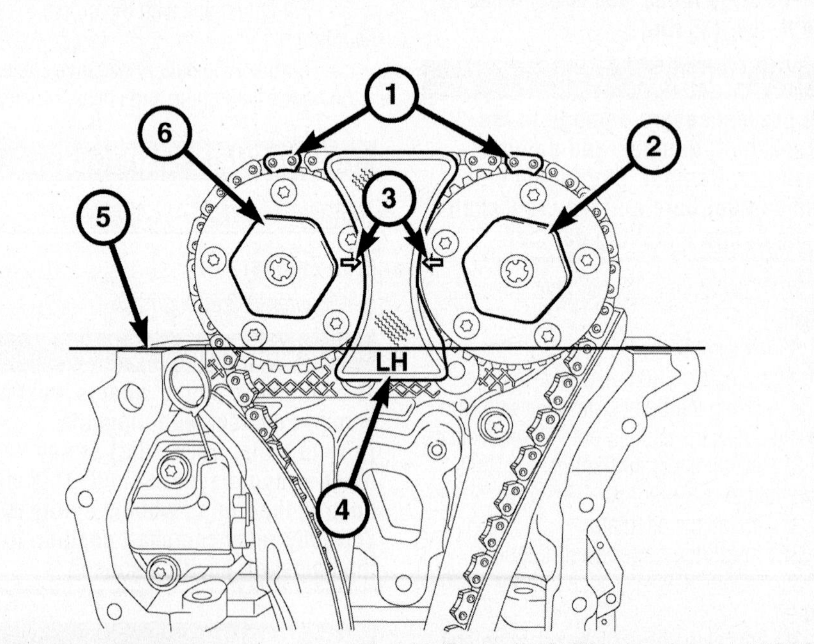

Fig. 236 Install the LH Camshaft Phaser Lock

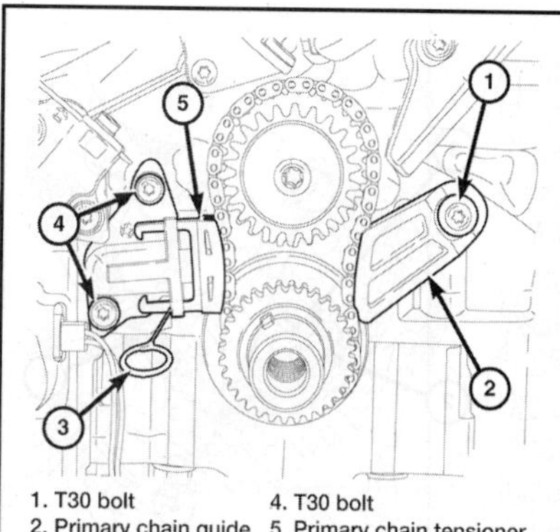

Fig. 237 Reset the primary chain tensioner by pushing back the tensioner piston and installing Tensioner Pin

22. Remove the LH Camshaft Phaser Lock.
23. Remove the oil control valve from the left side exhaust cam phaser.
24. Pull the left side exhaust cam phaser off of the camshaft and remove the left side cam chain.
25. If required, remove the oil control valve and pull the left side intake cam phaser off of the camshaft.
26. Reset the primary chain tensioner by pushing back the tensioner piston and installing Tensioner Pin.
27. Remove two T30 bolts and remove the primary chain tensioner.
28. Remove the T30 bolt and the primary chain guide.
29. Remove the idler sprocket T45 retaining bolt and washer.
30. Remove the primary chain, idler sprocket and crankshaft sprocket as an assembly.
31. If required, remove two T30 bolts and the LH cam chain tensioner.
32. If required, remove two T30 bolts and the LH cam chain guide and tensioner arm.
33. If required, remove two T30 bolts and the RH cam chain tensioner.
34. If required, remove three T30 bolts and the RH cam chain guide and tensioner arm.
35. Inspect all sprockets and chain guides. Replace if damaged.

To install:

36. Inspect all sprockets and chain guides. Replace if damaged.
37. If removed, install the right side cam chain guide and tensioner arm. Tighten attaching T30 bolts to 106 inch lbs. (12 Nm).
38. If removed, install the RH cam chain tensioner to the engine block with two bolts. Tighten the T30 bolts to 106 inch lbs. (12 Nm).
39. Reset the RH cam chain tensioner by pushing back the tensioner piston and installing Tensioner Pin.
40. If removed, install the left side cam chain guide and tensioner arm. Tighten attaching T30 bolts to 106 inch lbs. (12 Nm).
41. If removed, install the LH cam chain tensioner to the cylinder head with two bolts. Tighten the T30 bolts to 106 inch lbs. (12 Nm).
42. Reset the LH cam chain tensioner by lifting the pawl, pushing back the piston and installing Tensioner Pin.
43. Verify that the key is installed in the crankshaft.

**** WARNING**

Do not rotate the crankshaft more than a few degrees independently of the camshafts. Piston to valve contact could occur resulting in possible valve damage. If the crankshaft needs to be rotated more than a few degrees, first remove the camshafts.

44. Verify that the number one piston is positioned at TDC by aligning the dimple on the crankshaft with the block/bearing cap junction.

**** WARNING**

Do not rotate the camshafts more than a few degrees independently of the crankshaft. Valve to piston contact could occur resulting in possible valve damage. If the camshafts need to be rotated more than a few degrees, first move the pistons away from the cylinder heads by rotating the crankshaft counterclockwise to a position 30° BTDC. Once the camshafts are positioned at TDC rotate the crankshaft clockwise to return the crankshaft to TDC.

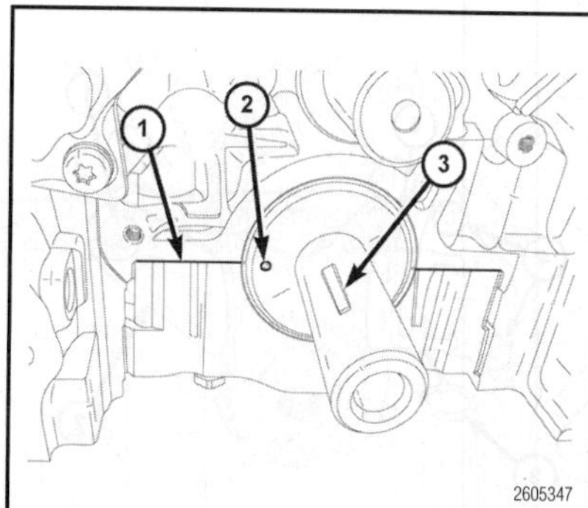

Fig. 238 Verify that the key (3) is installed in the crankshaft and that the number one piston is positioned at TDC by aligning the dimple (2) on the crankshaft with the block/bearing cap junction (1)

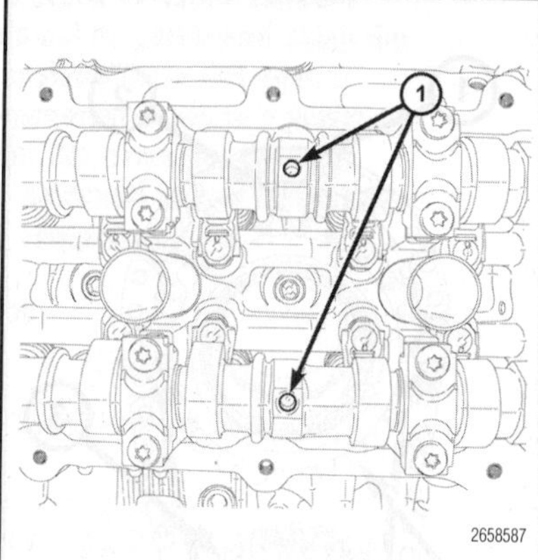

Fig. 239 Verify that the camshafts are set at TDC by positioning the alignment holes (1) vertically

45. Verify that the camshafts are set at TDC by positioning the alignment holes vertically.

**** WARNING**

Always reinstall timing chains so that they maintain the same direction of rotation. Inverting a previously run chain on a previously run sprocket will result in excessive wear to both the chain and sprocket.

46. Place the primary chain onto the crankshaft sprocket so that the arrow is aligned with the plated link on the timing chain.
47. While maintaining this alignment, invert the crankshaft sprocket and timing

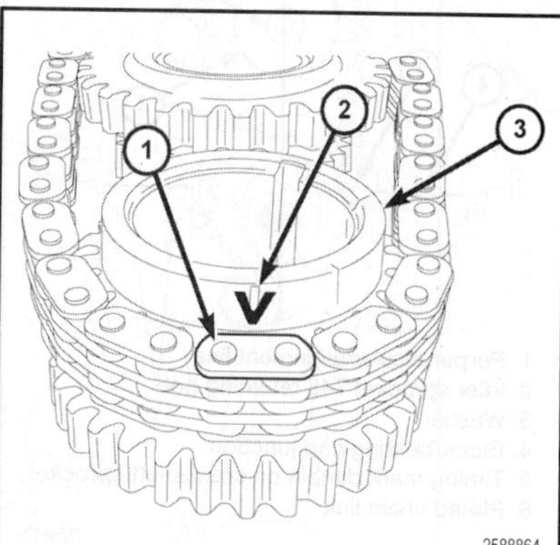

Fig. 240 Place the primary chain onto the crankshaft sprocket (3) so that the arrow (2) is aligned with the plated link (1) on the timing chain

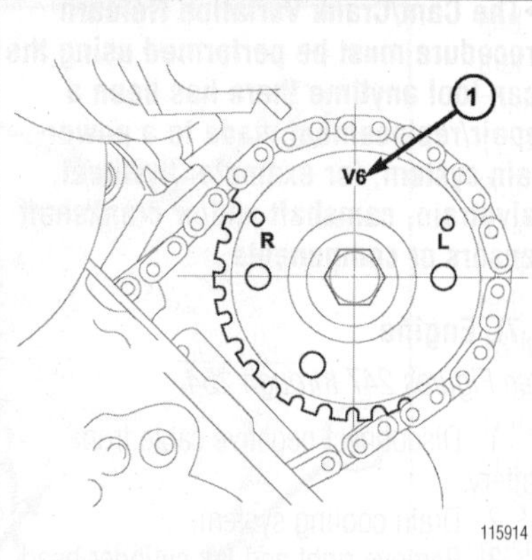

Fig. 248 Make sure the camshaft sprocket "V6" marks (1) are at the 12 o'clock position (No. 1 TDC exhaust stroke)

✻✻ WARNING

Care should be taken not to damage the camshaft target wheel. Do not hold the target wheel while loosening or tightening the camshaft sprocket. Do not place the target wheel near a magnetic source of any kind. A damaged or magnetized target wheel could cause a vehicle no start condition.

✻✻ WARNING

Do not forcefully rotate the camshafts or crankshaft independently of each other. Damaging intake valve to piston contact will occur. Ensure the negative battery cable is disconnected and isolated to guard against accidental starter engagement.

14. Remove left and right camshaft sprocket bolts.

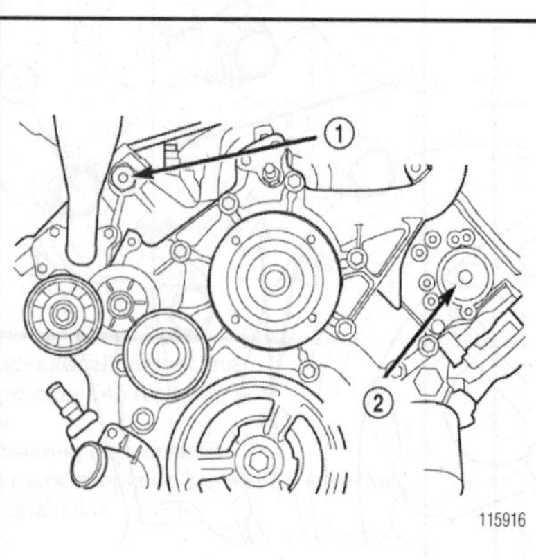

Fig. 249 Remove access plugs (1, 2) from left and right cylinder heads for access to chain guide fasteners

15. While holding the left camshaft steel tube Camshaft Holder (2), remove the left camshaft sprocket. Slowly rotate the camshaft approximately 5 degrees clockwise to a neutral position.

16. While holding the right camshaft steel tube with Camshaft Holder (2), remove the right camshaft sprocket.

17. Remove idler sprocket assembly bolt.

18. Slide the idler sprocket assembly and crank sprocket forward simultaneously to remove the primary and secondary chains.

19. Remove both pivoting tensioner arms and chain guides.

20. Remove primary chain tensioner.

To install:

21. Using a vise, lightly compress the secondary chain tensioner piston until the piston step is flush with the tensioner body. Using a pin or suitable tool, release ratchet pawl by pulling pawl back against spring force through access hole on side of tensioner. While continuing to hold pawl back, Push ratchet device to approximately 2 mm from the tensioner body. Install Tensioner Pins into hole on front of tensioner. Slowly open vise to transfer piston spring force to lock pin.

22. Position primary chain tensioner over oil pump and insert bolts into lower two holes on tensioner bracket. Tighten bolts to 21 ft. lbs. (28 Nm).

23. Install right side chain tensioner arm. Install Torx bolt. Tighten Torx bolt to 21 ft. lbs. (28 Nm).

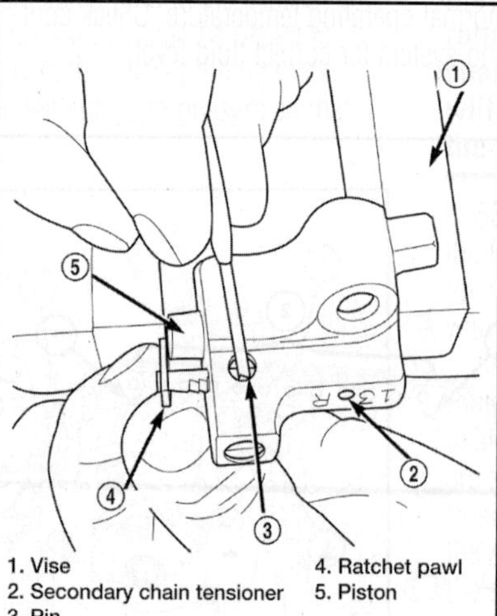

Fig. 250 Using a vise, lightly compress the secondary chain tensioner piston until the piston step is flush with the tensioner body

✻✻ WARNING

The silver bolts retain the guides to the cylinder heads and the black bolts retain the guides to the engine block.

24. Install the left side chain guide. Tighten the bolts to 21 ft. lbs. (28 Nm).

25. Install left side chain tensioner arm, and Torx bolt. Tighten Torx bolt to 21 ft. lbs. (28 Nm).

26. Install the right side chain guide. Tighten the bolts to 21 ft. lbs. (28 Nm).

27. Install both secondary chains onto the idler sprocket. Align two plated links on the secondary chains to be visible through the two lower openings on the idler sprocket (4 o'clock and 8 o'clock). Once the secondary timing chains are installed, Secondary Camshaft Chain Holder to hold chains in place for installation.

28. Align primary chain double plated links with the timing mark at 12 o'clock on the idler sprocket. Align the primary chain single plated link with the timing mark at 6 o'clock on the crankshaft sprocket.

29. Lubricate idler shaft and bushings with clean engine oil.

➡The idler sprocket must be timed to the counterbalance shaft drive gear before the idler sprocket is fully seated.

30. Install all chains, crankshaft sprocket, and idler sprocket as an assembly. After guiding both secondary chains through the block and cylinder head openings, affix chains with a elastic strap or equivalent. This will maintain tension on chains to aid in installation. Align the timing mark (2) on the idler sprocket gear (3) to the timing mark on the counterbalance shaft drive gear (1), then seat idler sprocket fully. Before installing idler sprocket bolt, lubricate washer with oil, and tighten idler sprocket assembly retaining bolt to 25 ft. lbs. (34 Nm).

➡It will be necessary to slightly rotate camshafts for sprocket installation.

31. Align left camshaft sprocket "L" dot to plated link on chain.

32. Align right camshaft sprocket "R" dot to plated link on chain.

✻✻ WARNING

Remove excess oil from the camshaft sprocket bolt. Failure to do so can result in over-torque of bolt resulting in bolt failure.

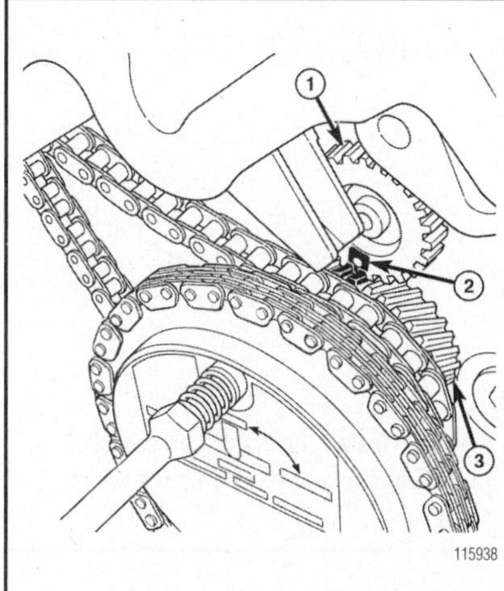

Fig. 251 Counterbalance shaft drive gear (1), timing mark (2), and idler sprocket gear (3)

33. Remove Secondary Camshaft Chain Holder, then attach both sprockets to camshafts. Remove excess oil from bolts, then Install sprocket bolts, but do not tighten at this time.

34. Verify that all plated links are aligned with the marks on all sprockets and the "V6" marks on camshaft sprockets are at the 12 o'clock position.

WARNING

Ensure the plate between the left secondary chain tensioner and block is correctly installed.

35. Install both secondary chain tensioners. Tighten bolts to 21 ft. lbs. (28 Nm).

➡Left and right secondary chain tensioners are not common.

36. Remove all locking pins from tensioners.

WARNING

After pulling locking pins out of each tensioner, DO NOT manually extend the tensioner(s) ratchet. Doing so will over tension the chains, resulting in noise and/or high timing chain loads.

37. Using Spanner Wrench, with Adaptor Pins, tighten left camshaft sprocket bolts to 90 ft. lbs. (122 Nm).

38. Using Spanner Wrench, with Adaptor Pins, tighten right camshaft sprocket bolts to 90 ft. lbs. (122 Nm).

39. Rotate engine two full revolutions. Verify timing marks are at the follow locations:

- Primary chain idler sprocket dot is at 12 o'clock

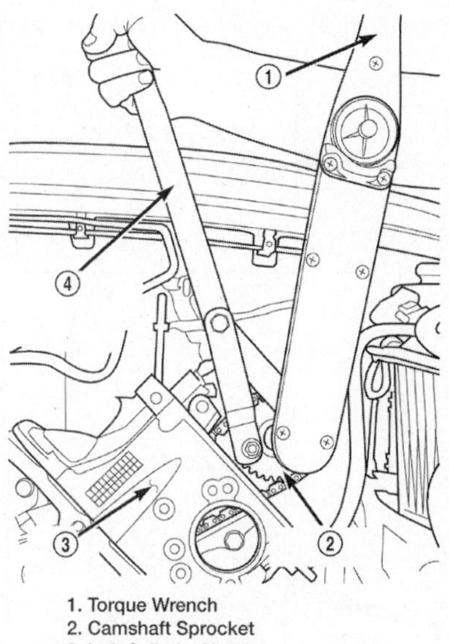

Fig. 252 Using Spanner Wrench, with Adaptor Pins, tighten left camshaft sprocket bolts

- Primary chain crankshaft sprocket dot is at 6 o'clock
- Secondary chain camshaft sprockets "V6" marks are at 12 o'clock
- Balance shaft drive gear dot is aligned to the idler sprocket gear dot

40. Lubricate all three chains with engine oil.

41. After installing all chains, it is recommended that the idler gear end play be checked. The end play must be within

Fig. 253 Using Spanner Wrench, with Adaptor Pins, tighten right camshaft sprocket bolts

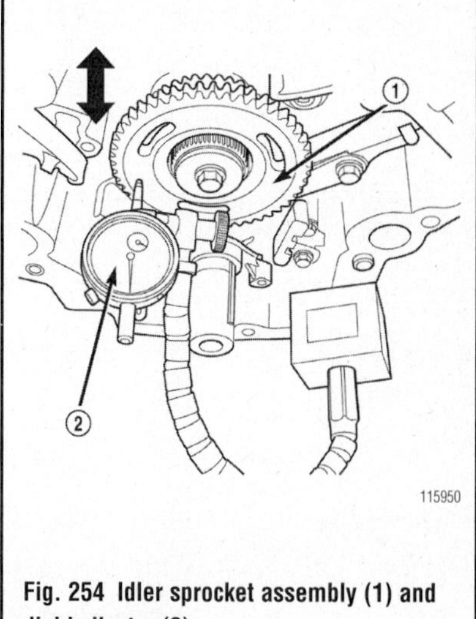

Fig. 254 Idler sprocket assembly (1) and dial indicator (2)

0.004–0.010 inches (0.10–0.25 mm). If not within specification, the idler gear (1) must be replaced.

42. Install timing chain cover and crankshaft damper.

43. Install cylinder head covers.

➡Before installing threaded plug in right cylinder head, the plug must be coated with sealant to prevent leaks.

44. Coat the large threaded access plug with Mopar® Thread Sealant with Teflon, then install into the right cylinder head and tighten to 60 ft. lbs. (81 Nm).

45. Install the oil fill housing.

46. Install access plug in left cylinder head.

47. Install power steering pump.

48. Fill cooling system.

49. Connect negative cable to battery.

5.7L Engine

See Figures 255 through 261.

1. Disconnect the negative battery cable.
2. Drain the cooling system.

➡It is not necessary to remove water pump for timing chain cover removal.

3. Remove the timing chain cover.
4. Verify the slide bushings remain installed in the timing chain cover during removal.
5. Remove the oil pump retaining bolts and remove the oil pump.
6. Install the vibration damper bolt finger tight. Using a suitable socket and breaker bar, rotate the crankshaft to align the timing marks with the timing chain sprockets.

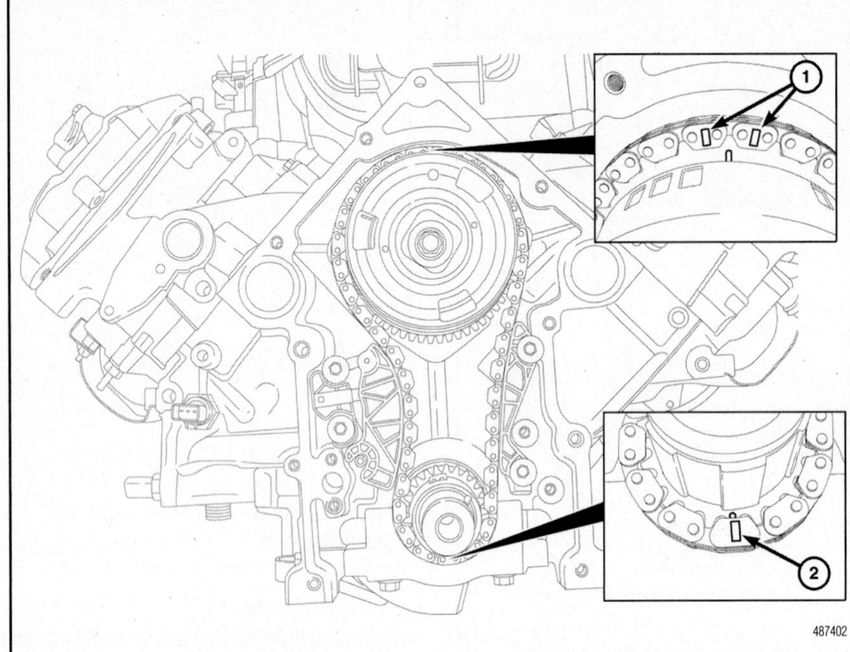

Fig. 255 Using a suitable socket and breaker bar, rotate the crankshaft to align the timing marks with the timing chain sprockets (1, 2)

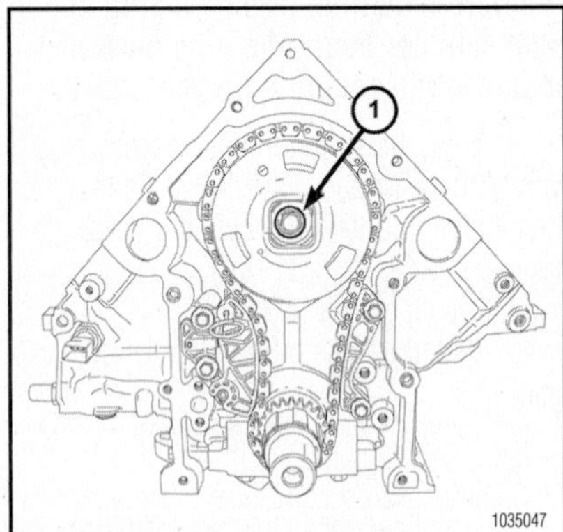

Fig. 256 Remove the camshaft phaser retaining bolt (1) and remove the timing chain with the camshaft phaser and crankshaft sprocket

7. Retract the chain tensioner arm until the hole in the arm lines up with the hole in the bracket.

8. Install the Tensioner Pin into the chain tensioner holes.

WARNING

Never attempt to disassemble the camshaft phaser, severe engine damage could result.

9. Remove the camshaft phaser retaining bolt and remove the timing chain with the camshaft phaser and crankshaft sprocket.

➡Inspect the timing chain tensioner and timing chain guide shoes for wear and replace as necessary.

10. If the timing chain tensioner is being replaced, remove the retaining bolts and remove the timing chain tensioner.

11. If the timing chain guide is being replaced, remove the retaining bolts and remove the timing chain guide.

To install:

12. Install the crankshaft sprocket and position halfway onto the crankshaft.

13. While holding the camshaft phaser in hand, position the timing chain on the camshaft phaser and align the timing marks as shown.

14. While holding the camshaft phaser and timing chain in hand, position the timing chain on the crankshaft sprocket and align the timing mark as shown.

15. Align the slot in the camshaft phaser with the dowel on the camshaft and position the camshaft phaser on the camshaft while sliding the crankshaft sprocket into position.

16. Install the camshaft phaser retaining bolt finger tight.

17. If removed, install the timing chain guide and tighten the bolts to 8 ft. lbs. (11 Nm).

18. If removed, install the timing chain tensioner and tighten the bolts to 8 ft. lbs. (11 Nm).

19. Remove the tensioner pin.

20. Rotate the crankshaft two revolutions and verify the alignment of the timing marks. If the timing marks do not line up, remove the camshaft sprocket and realign.

21. Tighten the camshaft phaser bolt to 63 ft. lbs. (85 Nm).

22. Position the oil pump onto the crankshaft and install the oil pump retaining bolts finger tight.

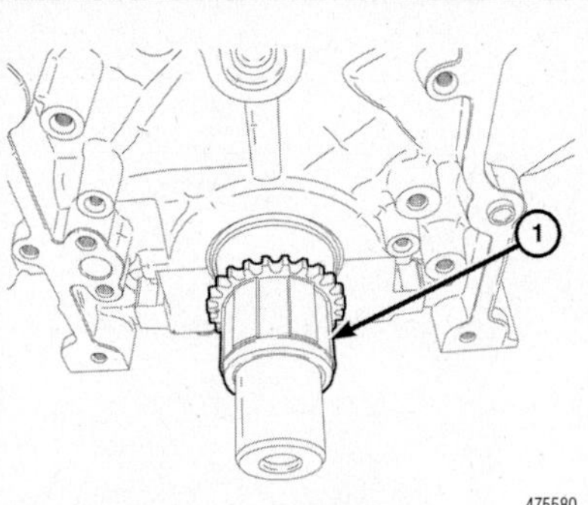

Fig. 257 Install the crankshaft sprocket (1) and position halfway onto the crankshaft

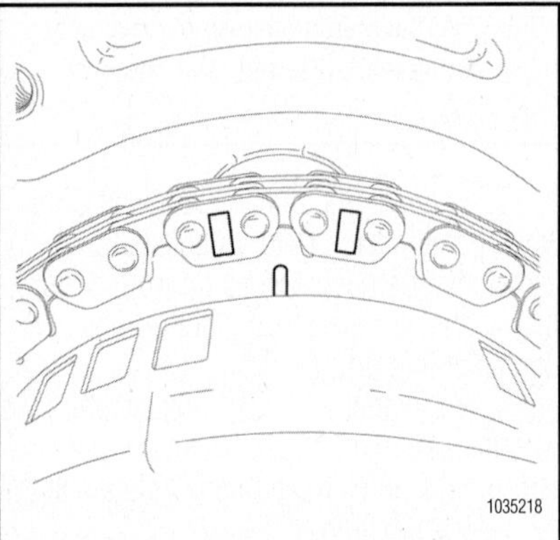

Fig. 258 While holding the camshaft phaser in hand, position the timing chain on the camshaft phaser and align the timing marks as shown

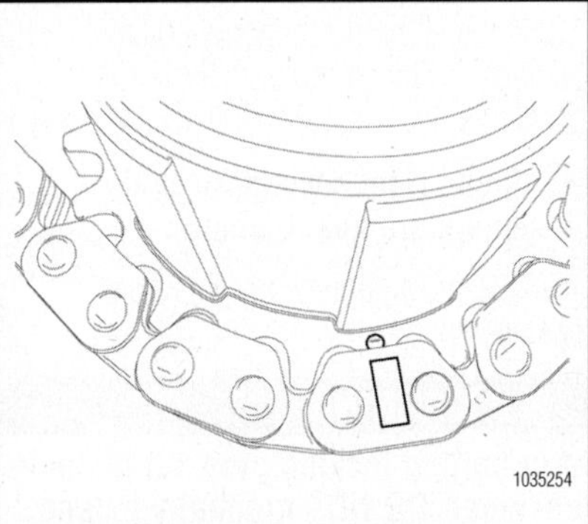

Fig. 259 While holding the camshaft phaser and timing chain in hand, position the timing chain on the crankshaft sprocket and align the timing mark as shown

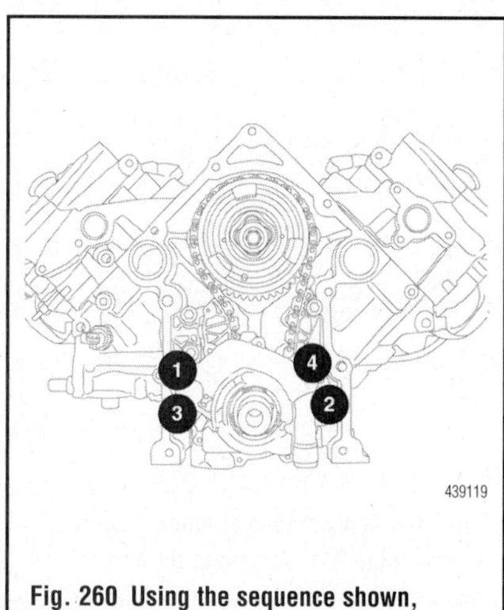

Fig. 260 Using the sequence shown, tighten the oil pump retaining bolts

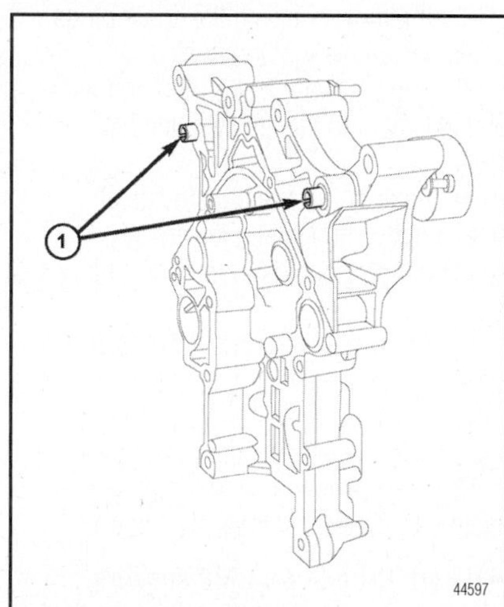

Fig. 261 Verify the slide bushings (1) are installed in the timing chain cover

23. Using the sequence shown, tighten the oil pump retaining bolts to 21 ft. lbs. (28 Nm).
24. Verify the slide bushings are installed in the timing chain cover.
25. Install the timing chain cover.
26. Fill the engine with oil.
27. Fill the cooling system.
28. Connect the negative battery cable.
29. Start the engine and check for leaks.

VALVE COVERS

REMOVAL & INSTALLATION

3.6L Engine

Left Side

See Figures 262 through 269.

**** WARNING**

The magnetic timing wheels must not come in contact with magnets (pickup tools, trays, etc.) or any other strong magnetic field. This will destroy the timing wheels ability to correctly relay camshaft position to the camshaft position sensor.

1. Disconnect and isolate the negative battery cable.
2. Remove the air inlet hose and upper intake manifold.
3. Cover the open intake ports to prevent debris from entering the engine.
4. Remove the insulator from the LH cylinder head cover.
5. Disengage the clips, remove the make-up air tube from the left cylinder head cover and reposition the transmission breather hose.

➡Mark the variable valve timing solenoid connectors with a paint pen or equivalent so that they may be reinstalled in their original locations.

6. Disconnect the variable valve timing solenoid connectors from the left variable valve timing solenoids.
7. Disengage two starter wire harness retainers from the left cylinder head cover.
8. Mark the variable valve timing solenoids with a paint pen or equivalent so that they may be reinstalled in their original locations.
9. Remove the variable valve timing solenoids.
10. Disengage one main wire harness retainer from the left cylinder head cover.
11. Disconnect the left Camshaft Position (CMP) sensor.
12. Disengage one main wire harness retainer from the cylinder head cover and

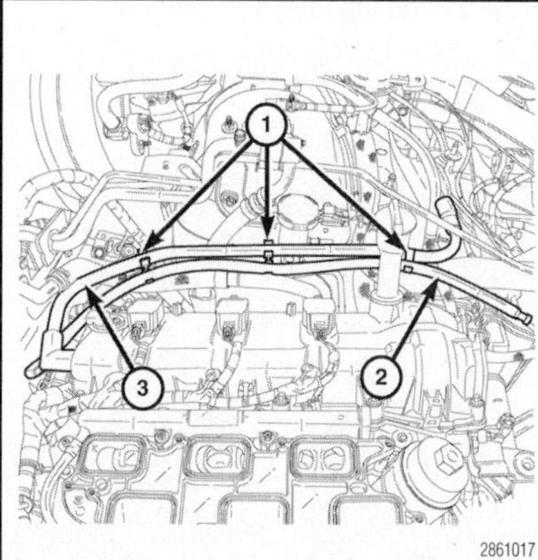

Fig. 262 Disengage the clips (1), remove the make-up air tube (3) from the left cylinder head cover and reposition the transmission breather hose (2)

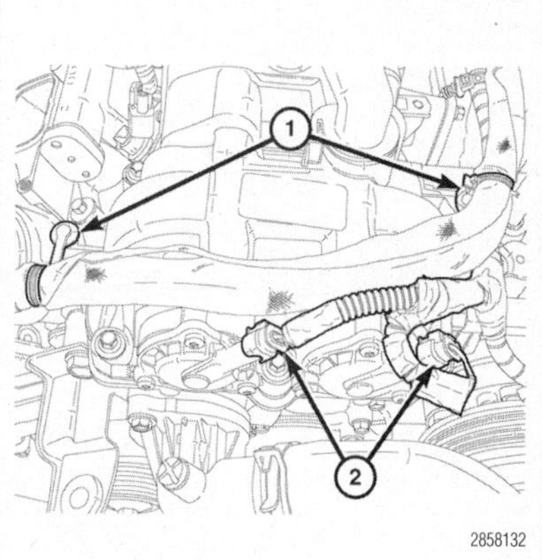

Fig. 263 Disconnect the variable valve timing solenoid connectors (2) from the left variable valve timing solenoids, and the two starter wire harness retainers (1) from the left cylinder head cover

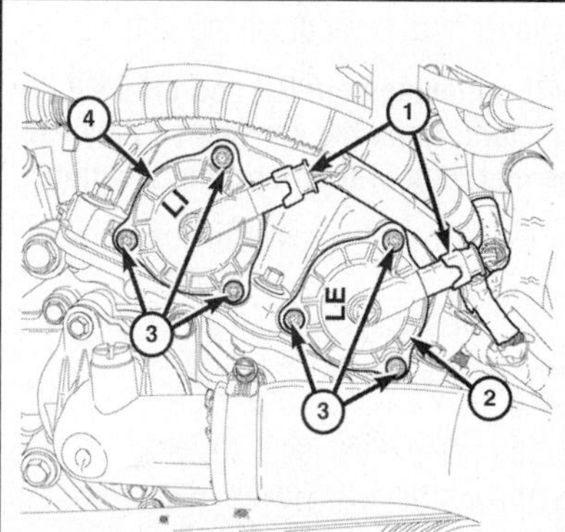

Fig. 264 Mark the variable valve timing solenoids with a paint pen or equivalent so that they may be reinstalled in their original locations

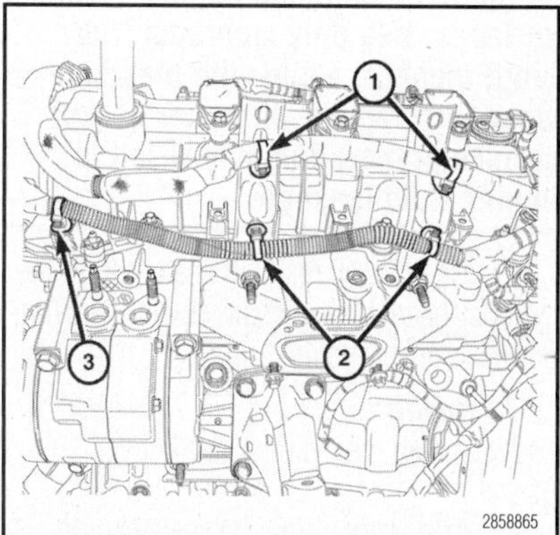

Fig. 265 Disengage one main wire harness retainer (3) from the left cylinder head cover; retainers (1, 2)

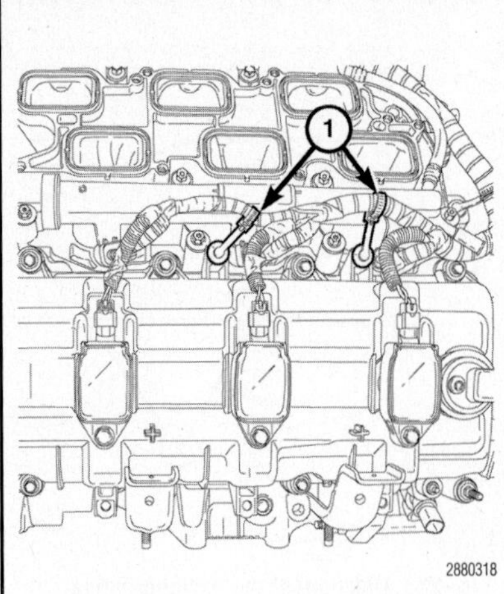

Fig. 266 Disengage two injection/ignition harness retainers (1) from the left cylinder head cover

one main wire harness retainer from the cylinder head cover mounting stud.

➡If removing both RH and LH CMP sensors, mark the sensors so they can be installed in their original locations.

13. Remove the camshaft position sensor.
14. Disengage two injection/ignition harness retainers from the left cylinder head cover.
15. Remove the ignition coils.
16. Loosen ten cylinder head cover mounting bolts and two stud bolts and remove the cylinder head cover.
17. Remove and discard the cylinder head cover gasket.
18. The spark plug tube seals can be reused if not damaged.

WARNING

Do not use oil based liquids, wire brushes, abrasive wheels or metal scrapers to clean the engine gasket surfaces. Use only isopropyl (rubbing) alcohol, along with plastic or wooden scrapers. Improper gasket surface preparation may result in engine fluid leakage.

19. Remove all residual sealant from the cylinder head, timing chain cover and cylinder head cover mating surfaces.

To install:

20. Install the cylinder head cover gasket.
21. The spark plug tube seals can be reused if not damaged.
22. If required, install new spark plug tube seals in the cylinder head cover:
    a. Lubricate the spark plug tube seal inner and outer diameters with clean engine oil.
    b. Place the spark plug tube seal on the Cam Sensor/Spark Plug Tube Seal Installer.
    c. Push the seal into the cylinder head cover until the base of the seal is seated.
    d. Remove the tool.
23. Clean the timing engine timing cover, cylinder head and cylinder head cover mating surfaces with isopropyl alcohol in preparation for sealant application.

WARNING

Engine assembly requires the use of a unique sealant that is compatible with engine oil. Using a sealant other than Mopar® Threebond Engine RTV Sealant may result in engine fluid leakage.

WARNING

Following the application of Mopar® Threebond Engine RTV Sealant to the gasket surfaces, the components must be assembled within 20 minutes and the attaching fasteners must be tightened to specification within 45 minutes. Prolonged exposure to the air prior to assembly may result in engine fluid leakage.

24. Apply a bead of Mopar® Threebond Engine RTV Sealant to the two engine timing cover to cylinder head T-joints.
25. Align the locator pins to the cylinder head and install the cylinder head cover.
26. Tighten the cylinder head cover bolts and double ended studs in the sequence shown to 106 inch lbs. (12 Nm).

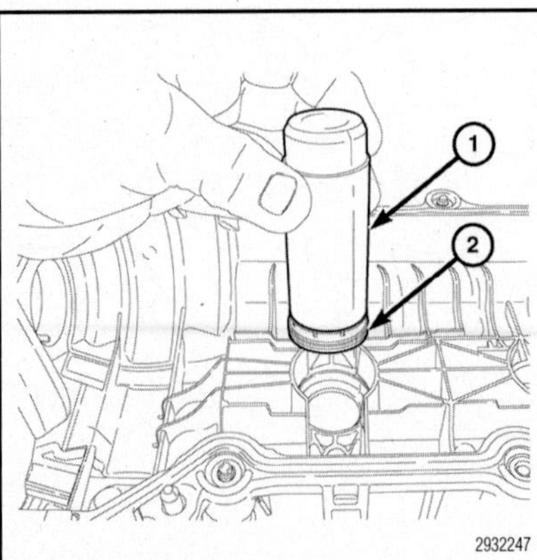

Fig. 267 Place the spark plug tube seal (2) on the Cam Sensor/Spark Plug Tube Seal Installer (1)

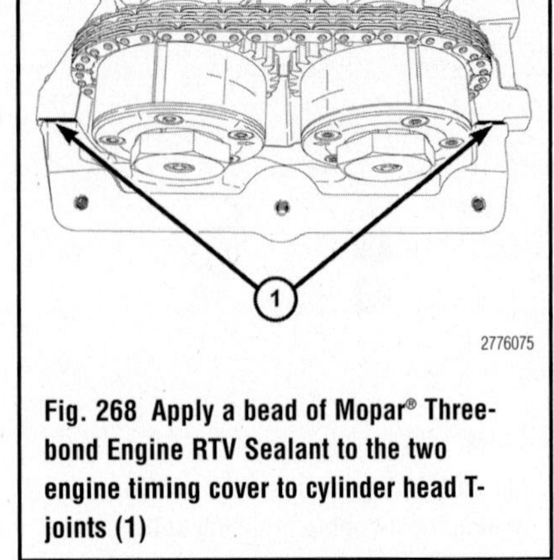

Fig. 268 Apply a bead of Mopar® Threebond Engine RTV Sealant to the two engine timing cover to cylinder head T-joints (1)

27. If removed, install the spark plugs.
28. Install the ignition coils.
29. Engage two injection/ignition harness retainers to the left cylinder head cover.
30. Refer to the markings made at disassembly and install the variable valve timing solenoids in their original locations.
31. Connect the electrical connectors to the left variable valve timing solenoids.
32. Engage two starter wire harness retainers to the left cylinder head cover.
33. Engage one main wire harness retainer to the left cylinder head cover.

➡If both RH and LH CMP sensors where removed, install them into their original locations.

34. Install the camshaft position sensor.
35. Connect the electrical connector to the left Camshaft Position (CMP) sensor.
36. Engage one main wire harness retainer to the cylinder head cover and one

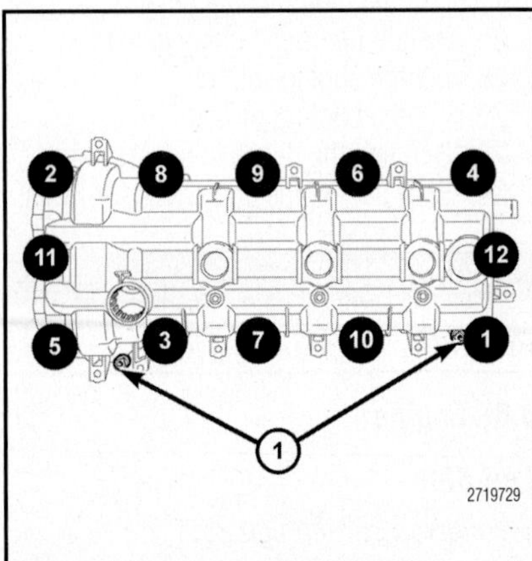

Fig. 269 Tighten the cylinder head cover bolts and double ended studs in the sequence shown; locator pins (1)

main wire harness retainer to the cylinder head cover mounting stud.

37. Install the make-up air tube to the left cylinder head cover and engage the clips to the transmission breather hose.

38. Install the insulator to the two alignment posts on top of the LH cylinder head cover.

39. Install the upper intake manifold, support brackets and air inlet hose.

40. Connect the negative battery cable.

➡The Cam/Crank Variation Relearn procedure must be performed using the scan tool anytime there has been a repair/replacement made to a powertrain system, for example: flywheel, valvetrain, camshaft and/or crankshaft sensors or components.

Right Side

See Figures 270 through 277.

⁂ WARNING

The magnetic timing wheels must not come in contact with magnets (pickup tools, trays, etc.) or any other strong magnetic field. This will destroy the timing wheels ability to correctly relay camshaft position to the camshaft position sensor.

1. Disconnect and isolate the negative battery cable.

2. Remove the air inlet hose and upper intake manifold.

3. Cover the open intake ports to prevent debris from entering the engine.

➡Mark the variable valve timing solenoid connectors with a paint pen or equivalent so that they may be reinstalled in their original locations.

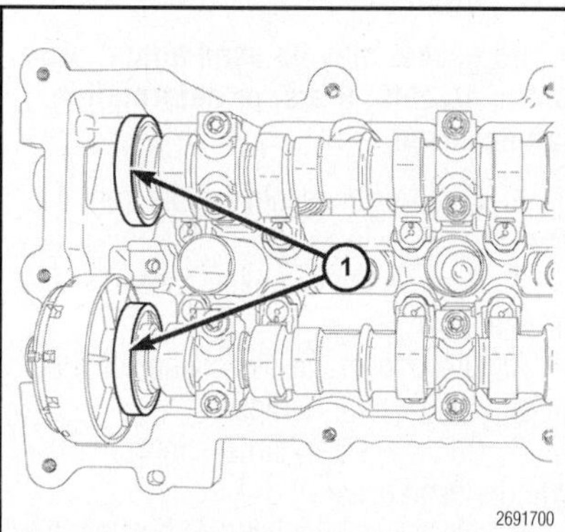

Fig. 270 The magnetic timing wheels (1) must not come in contact with magnets (pickup tools, trays, etc.) or any other strong magnetic field

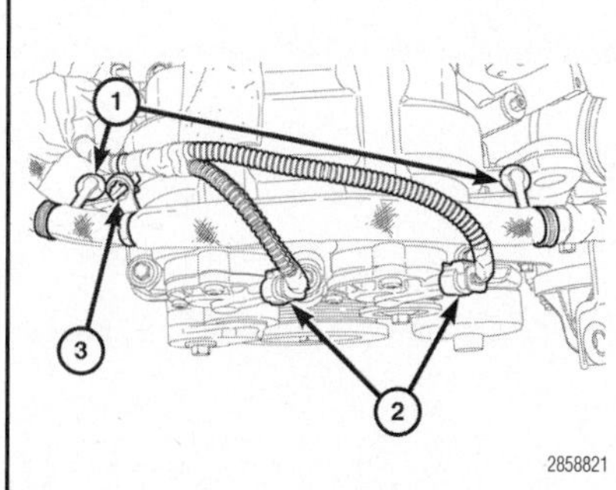

Fig. 271 Right cylinder head cover showing the electrical connectors (2), the starter harness to main harness retainer (3), and the two starter wire harness retainers (1)

4. Disconnect the electrical connectors from the variable valve timing solenoids on the right cylinder head.

5. Disengage the starter harness to main harness retainer.

6. Disengage two starter wire harness retainers from the right cylinder head cover.

7. Mark the variable valve timing solenoids with a paint pen or equivalent so that they may be reinstalled in their original locations.

8. Remove the variable valve timing solenoids.

9. Disengage four main wire harness retainers from the right cylinder head cover.

10. Disconnect the electrical connector from the right Camshaft Position (CMP) sensor.

11. Disengage the main wire harness

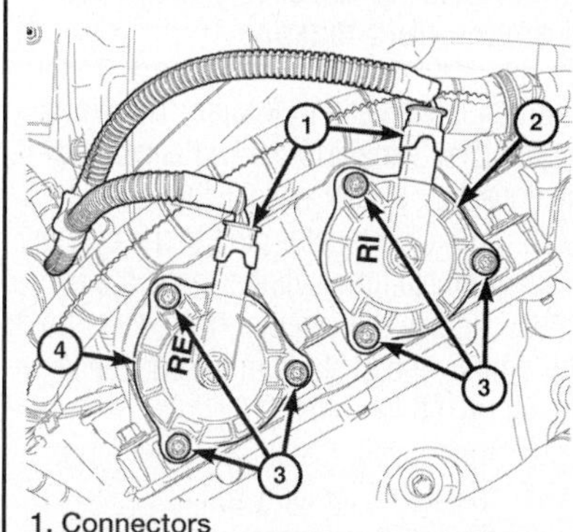

Fig. 272 Mark the variable valve timing solenoids with a paint pen or equivalent so that they may be reinstalled in their original locations

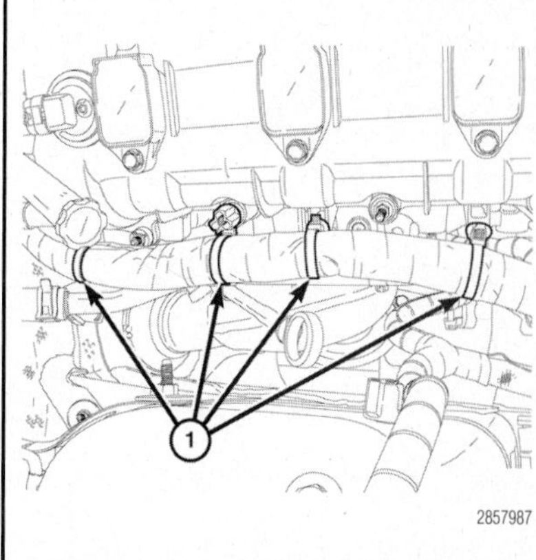

Fig. 273 Disengage four main wire harness retainers (1) from the right cylinder head cover

retainer from the right cylinder head cover mounting stud.

➡If removing both RH and LH CMP sensors, mark the sensors so they can be installed in their original locations.

12. Remove the camshaft position sensor.

13. Disengage three injection/ignition harness retainers from the right cylinder head cover.

14. Remove the ignition coils.

15. Raise and support the vehicle.

16. Loosen the bolt securing the transmission fluid level indicator tube to the transmission housing.

17. Remove the upper transmission to engine bolt and reposition the transmission oil level indicator tube.

18. Lower the vehicle.

19. Remove the PCV valve.

20. Loosen nine cylinder head cover mounting bolts and three stud bolts and remove the cylinder head cover.

21. Remove and discard the cylinder head cover gasket.

22. Remove all residual sealant from the cylinder head, timing chain cover and cylinder head cover mating surfaces.

To install:

23. Install the cylinder head cover gasket.

24. The spark plug tube seals can be reused if not damaged.

25. If required, install new spark plug tube seals in the cylinder head cover:

   a. Lubricate the spark plug tube seal inner and outer diameters with clean engine oil.

   b. Place the spark plug tube seal on the Cam Sensor/Spark Plug Tube Seal Installer.

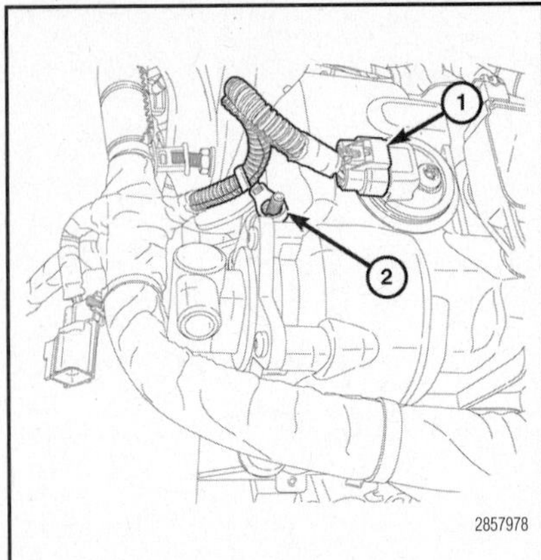

Fig. 274 Disconnect the electrical connector (1) from the right CMP sensor and disengage the main wire harness retainer (2)

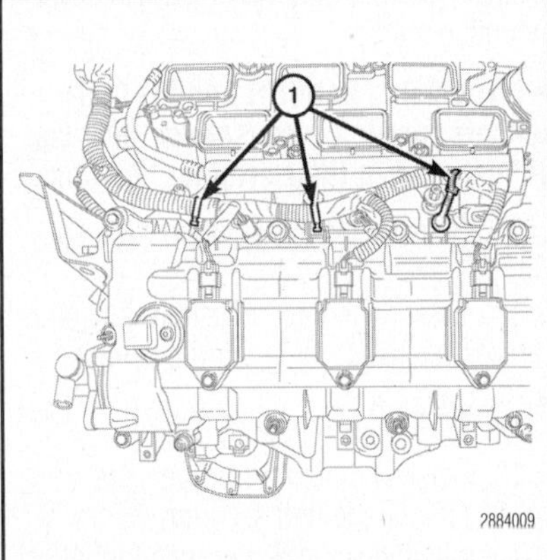

Fig. 275 Disengage three injection/ignition harness retainers (1) from the right cylinder head cover

c. Push the seal into the cylinder head cover until the base of the seal is seated.

d. Remove the tool.

26. Clean the timing engine timing cover, cylinder head and cylinder head cover mating surfaces with isopropyl alcohol in preparation for sealant application.

⁂ WARNING

Engine assembly requires the use of a unique sealant that is compatible with engine oil. Using a sealant other than Mopar® Threebond Engine RTV Sealant may result in engine fluid leakage.

⁂ WARNING

Following the application of Mopar® Threebond Engine RTV Sealant to the gasket surfaces, the components must be assembled within 20 minutes and the attaching fasteners must be tightened to specification within 45 minutes. Prolonged exposure to the air prior to assembly may result in engine fluid leakage.

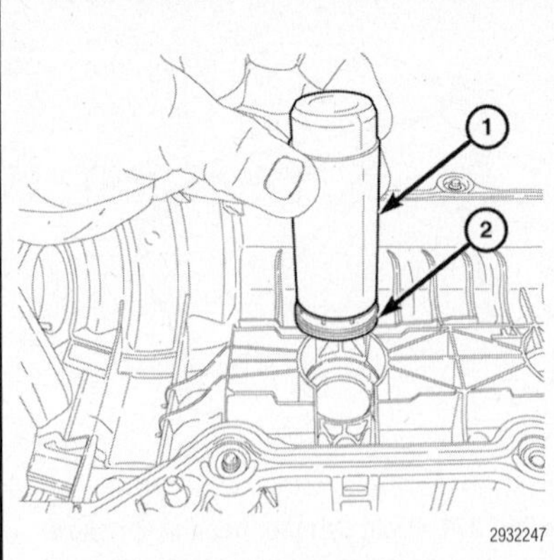

Fig. 276 Place the spark plug tube seal (2) on the Cam Sensor/Spark Plug Tube Seal Installer (1)

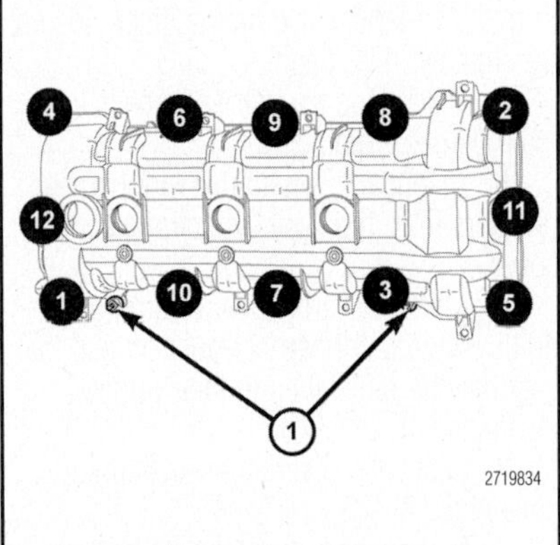

Fig. 277 Tighten the cylinder head cover bolts and double ended studs in the sequence shown

27. Apply a bead of Mopar® Threebond Engine RTV Sealant to the two engine timing cover to cylinder head T-joints.

28. Align the locator pins to the cylinder head and install the cylinder head cover.

29. Tighten the cylinder head cover bolts and double ended studs in the sequence shown to 106 inch lbs. (12 Nm).

30. If removed, install the spark plugs.

31. Install the ignition coils.

32. Engage three injection/ignition harness retainers to the right cylinder head cover.

33. Refer to the markings made at disassembly and install the variable valve timing solenoids in their original locations.

34. Connect the electrical connectors to the variable valve timing solenoids on the right cylinder head.

35. Engage two starter wire harness retainers to the right cylinder head cover.

36. Engage the starter harness to main harness retainer.

37. Engage four main wire harness retainers to the right cylinder head cover.

➡If both RH and LH CMP sensors where removed, install them into their original locations.

38. Install the camshaft position sensor.

39. Connect the electrical connector to the right Camshaft Position (CMP) sensor.

40. Engage the main wire harness retainer to the right cylinder head cover mounting stud.

41. Install the PCV valve.

42. Raise and support the vehicle.

43. Install the transmission oil level indicator tube with the upper transmission to engine bolt tightened to 41 ft. lbs. (55 Nm).

44. Install the bolt securing the transmission fluid level indicator tube to the transmission housing and tighten to 106 inch lbs. (12 Nm).

45. Lower the vehicle.

46. If removed, install the insulator to the two alignment posts on top of the LH cylinder head cover.

47. Install the upper intake manifold, support brackets and air inlet hose.

48. Connect the negative battery cable.

➡The Cam/Crank Variation Relearn procedure must be performed using the scan tool anytime there has been a repair/replacement made to a powertrain system, for example: flywheel, valvetrain, camshaft and/or crankshaft sensors or components.

3.7L Engine

➡The gasket may be used again, providing no cuts, tears, or deformation has occurred.

1. Disconnect negative cable from battery.

2. Remove the resonator assemble and air inlet hose.

3. Disconnect injector connectors and un-clip the injector harness.

4. Route injector harness in front of cylinder head cover.

5. Disconnect the left side breather tube and remove the breather tube.

6. Remove the cylinder head cover mounting bolts.

7. Remove cylinder head cover and gasket.

To install:

⁂ WARNING

Do not use harsh cleaners to clean the cylinder head covers. Severe damage to covers may occur.

➡The gasket may be used again, provided no cuts, tears, or deformation has occurred.

8. Clean the cylinder head cover and both sealing surfaces. Inspect and replace gasket as necessary.
9. Install the cylinder cover.
10. Tighten the cylinder head cover bolts and double ended studs to 9 ft. lbs. (12 Nm).
11. Install the left side breather and connect breather tube.
12. Connect the fuel injector electrical connectors and injector harness retaining clips.
13. Install the resonator and air inlet hose.
14. Connect negative battery cable.

5.7L Engine

See Figures 278 and 279.

1. Remove the oil fill cap.
2. Remove the engine cover.
3. Perform the fuel pressure release procedure.
4. Disconnect and isolate the negative battery cable.
5. Disconnect the EVAP vacuum line at the throttle body.
6. Disconnect the fuel supply line at the fuel rail.
7. Disconnect the make-up air hose at the intake manifold.
8. Disconnect the ignition coil electrical connectors.

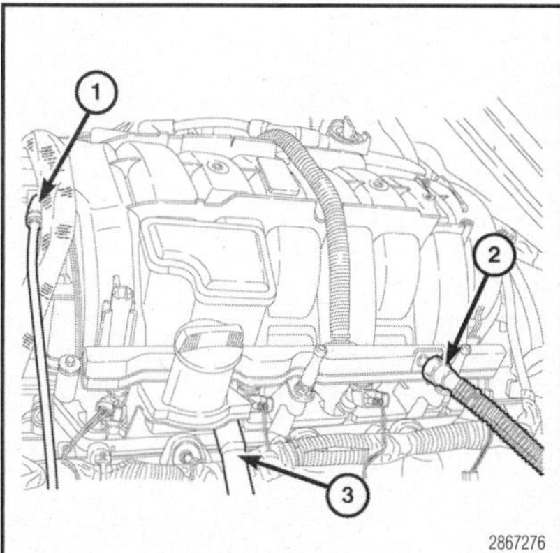

Fig. 278 Disconnect the EVAP vacuum line (1), the fuel supply line (2), and the make-up air hose (3)

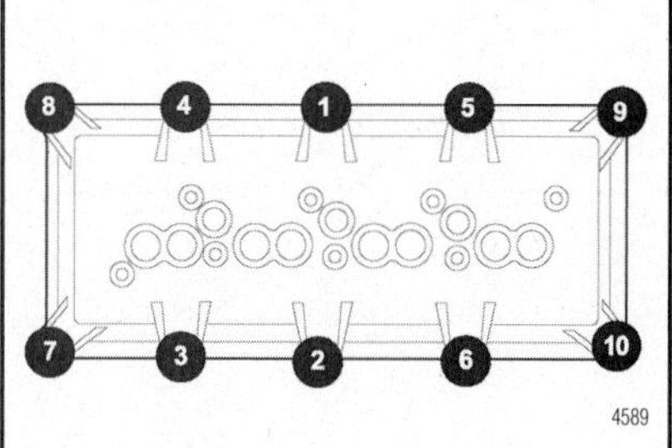

Fig. 279 Using the sequence shown, remove the cylinder head cover retaining bolts

9. Remove the ignition coil retaining bolts.
10. Remove the ignition coils.
11. Remove the wiring harness retainers at the cylinder head cover and position wiring harness aside.
12. Using the sequence shown, remove the cylinder head cover retaining bolts.
13. Remove the cylinder head cover.

➡The cylinder head cover gasket may be used again, provided no cuts, tears, or deformation have occurred.

14. Inspect the cylinder head cover gasket, replace if necessary.

To install:

⁂ WARNING

Do not use harsh cleaners to clean the cylinder head covers. Severe damage to covers may occur.

15. Clean the cylinder head cover and the cylinder head sealing surface.
16. Apply Mopar® Lock Seal Adhesive to the cylinder head cover bolts.
17. Position the cylinder head cover and hand tighten the bolts.
18. Using the sequence shown in the removal section, tighten the cylinder head cover bolts to 70 inch lbs. (8 Nm).

⁂ WARNING

Do not allow other components including the wire harness to rest on or against the engine cylinder head cover. Prolonged contact with other objects may wear a hole in the cylinder head cover.

19. Position the wiring harness and attach the retainers to the cylinder head cover.
20. Before installing the ignition coils, apply dielectric grease to the inside of the spark plug boots.
21. Install the ignition coils.
22. Install the ignition coil retaining bolts.
23. Connect the ignition coil electrical connectors.
24. Connect the make-up air hose to the intake manifold.
25. Connect the fuel supply line to the fuel rail.
26. Connect the EVAP vacuum line to the throttle body.
27. Connect the negative battery cable.
28. Install the engine cover.
29. Install the oil fill cap.
30. Start the engine and check for leaks.

VALVE LIFTERS

REMOVAL & INSTALLATION

3.6L Engine

See Figure 280.

1. Disconnect and isolate the negative battery cable.
2. Remove the camshaft(s).

➡If the rocker arms are to be reused, identify their positions so that they can be reassembled into their original locations.

3. Remove the rocker arm(s).

➡If the hydraulic lifters are to be reused, identify their positions so that they can be reassembled into their original locations.

4. Remove the hydraulic lifter(s).

➡The LH cylinder head hydraulic lifters are shown, the RH cylinder head hydraulic lifters are similar. If the hydraulic lifters are being reused,

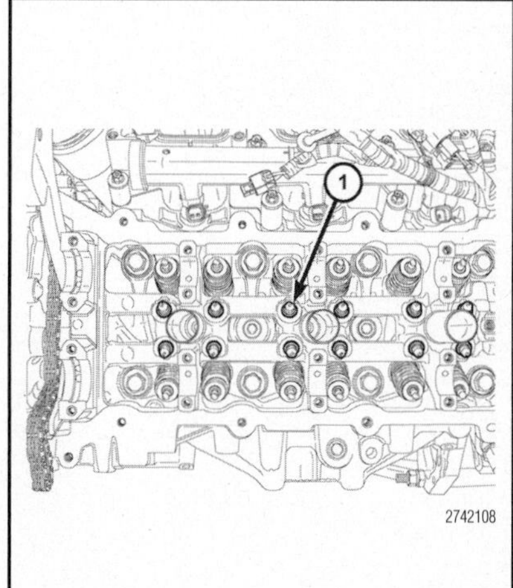

Fig. 280 Remove the hydraulic lifter(s) (1)

reassemble them into their original locations.

To install:

5. Verify that the hydraulic lifters are at least partially full of oil. There should be little or no plunger travel when the hydraulic lifter is depressed.
6. Install the hydraulic lifter(s).

➡If the rocker arms are being reused, reassemble them into their original locations.

7. Install the rocker arm(s).
8. Install the camshaft(s), phasers, cylinder head cover(s) and upper intake manifold.
9. Connect the negative battery cable.

5.7L Engine

See Figures 281 and 282.

1. Disconnect and isolate the negative battery cable.
2. Remove the cylinder head.
3. Remove the lifter guide holder retaining bolt from the lifter guide holder assembly.

⁂ WARNING

The lifter and retainer assembly must be installed as a unit.

⁂ WARNING

If the lifter and retainer assembly are to be reused, identify lifters to ensure installation in their original location or engine damage could result.

4. Remove the lifter guide holder and lifters as an assembly.
5. Check the camshaft lobes for abnormal wear.

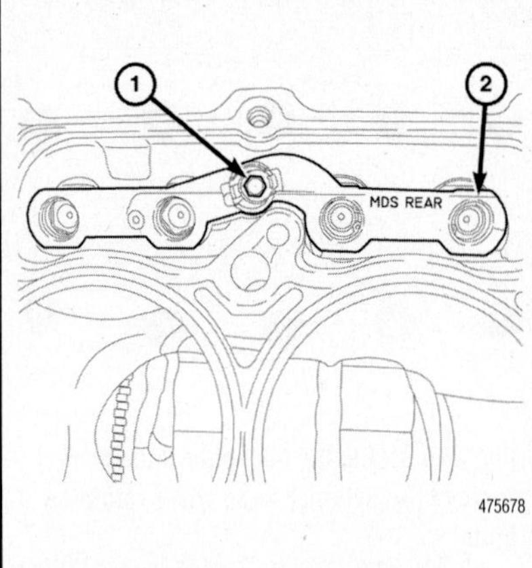

Fig. 281 Remove the lifter guide holder retaining bolt (1) from the lifter guide holder assembly (2)

To install:

The Multiple Displacement System (MDS) provides cylinder deactivation during steady speed, low acceleration and shallow grade climbing conditions to increase fuel economy.

⁂ WARNING

Engines equipped with MDS use both standard roller lifters and deactivating roller lifters. The deactivating roller lifters must be used in cylinders 1,4,6,7. The deactivating lifters can be identified by the two holes in the side of the lifter body, for the latching pins.

⁂ WARNING

The lifter and retainer assembly must be installed as a unit.

6. Lubricate the lifter guide holder and lifters.

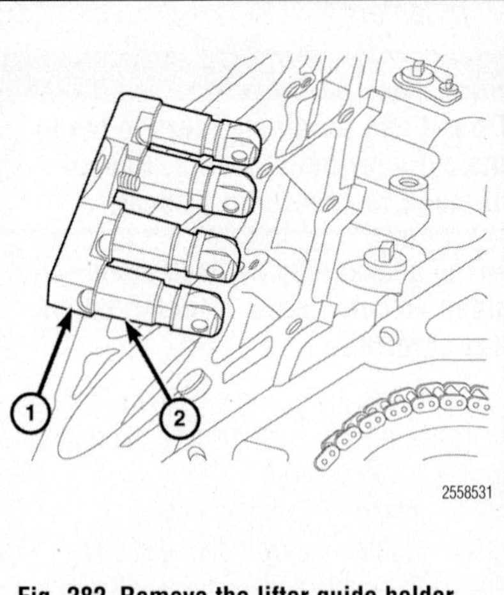

Fig. 282 Remove the lifter guide holder (1) and lifters (2) as an assembly

⁂ WARNING

If the lifters and guide holder assembly are to be reused, they must be installed in their original location.

7. Install the lifter guide holder and lifters.
8. Tighten the lifter guide holder retaining bolt to 9 ft. lbs. (12 Nm).
9. Install the cylinder head.
10. Connect the negative battery cable.

⁂ WARNING

To prevent damage to valve assemblies, do not run the engine above fast idle until all hydraulic lifters have filled with oil and have become quiet.

11. Start the engine and check for leaks.
12. Road test the vehicle.

ENGINE PERFORMANCE & EMISSION CONTROLS

CAMSHAFT POSITION (CMP) SENSOR

LOCATION

On the 3.6L engine, the Camshaft Position (CMP) sensors are located at the rear of the cylinder head covers and are bolted to the cylinder head.

On the 3.7L engine, the Camshaft Position Sensor (CMP) is bolted to the front/top of the right cylinder head.

On the 5.7L engine, the Camshaft Position Sensor (CMP) is located on the right side of the timing cover near the engine thermostat housing.

REMOVAL & INSTALLATION

3.6L Engine

See Figures 283 through 287.

**** WARNING**

The magnetic timing wheels must not come in contact with magnets (pickup tools, trays, etc.) or any other strong magnetic field. This will destroy the timing wheels ability to correctly relay camshaft position to the camshaft position sensor.

➡The Camshaft Position (CMP) sensors are located at the rear of the cylinder head covers and are bolted to the cylinder head.

1. Disconnect and isolate the negative battery cable.
2. If removing the LH CMP sensor, first remove the air inlet hose and upper intake manifold (2).

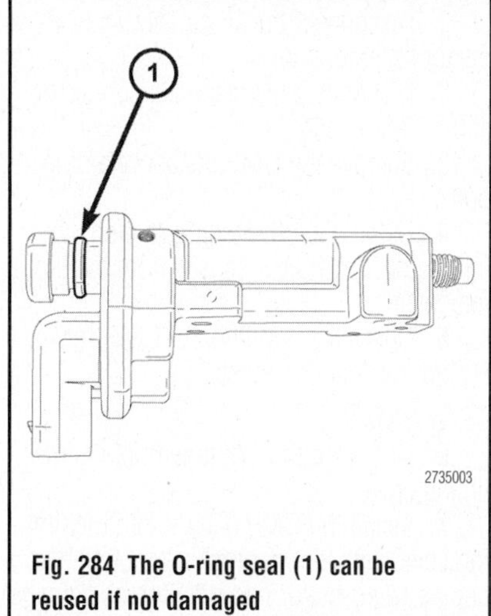

Fig. 284 The O-ring seal (1) can be reused if not damaged

➡The RH CMP sensor is shown, the LH CMP sensor is similar. If removing both RH and LH CMP sensors, mark the sensors so they can be installed in their original locations.

3. Disconnect the electrical connector from the CMP sensor.
4. Loosen the sensor mounting bolt.
5. Pull the sensor and mounting bolt from the cylinder head cover.
6. The O-ring seal can be reused if not damaged.

To install:

7. Clean out the Camshaft Position (CMP) sensor mounting bolt hole in cylinder head.
8. The CMP sensor seal can be reused if not damaged.
9. If required, install a new CMP sensor seal in the cylinder head cover:

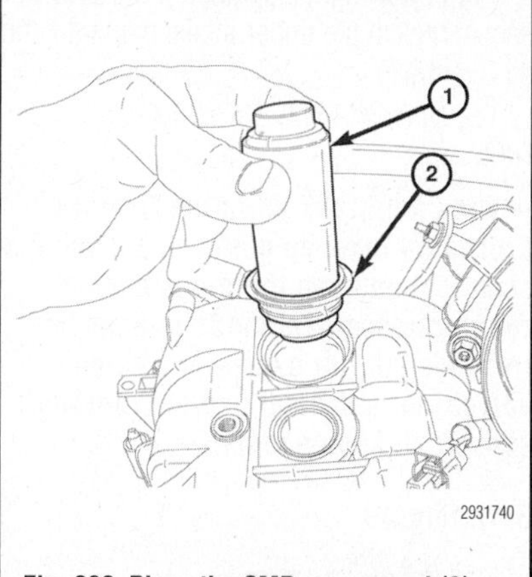

Fig. 286 Place the CMP sensor seal (2) on the Cam Sensor/Spark Plug Tube Seal Installer (1)

a. Lubricate the CMP sensor seal inner and outer diameters with clean engine oil.
b. Place the CMP sensor seal on the Cam Sensor/Spark Plug Tube Seal Installer.
c. Push the seal into the cylinder head cover until the base of the seal is seated.
d. Remove the tool.

➡A properly installed CMP sensor seal will have a 0.06–0.08 inches (1.5–2.0 mm) gap between the cylinder head cover and the seal upper flange.

10. The sensor mounting bolt O-ring can be reused if not damaged.
11. Apply a small amount of engine oil to the sensor mounting bolt O-ring.
12. Install the CMP sensor to the cylinder head. Tighten the mounting bolt to 80 inch lbs. (9 Nm).

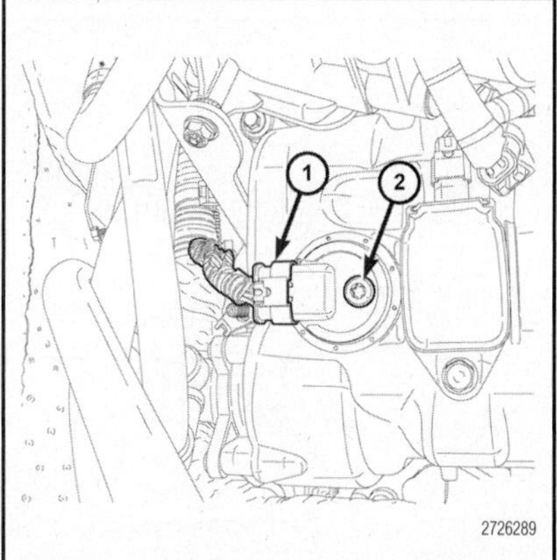

Fig. 283 Disconnect the electrical connector (1) from the CMP sensor and remove the mounting bolt (2)

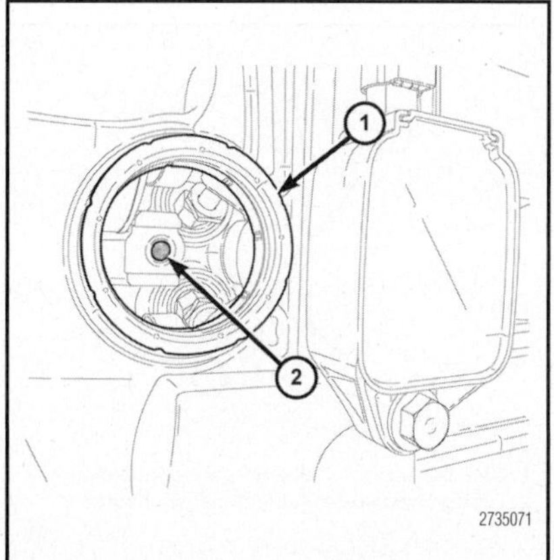

Fig. 285 CMP mounting location showing the CMP sensor seal (1) and the mounting bolt hole (2)

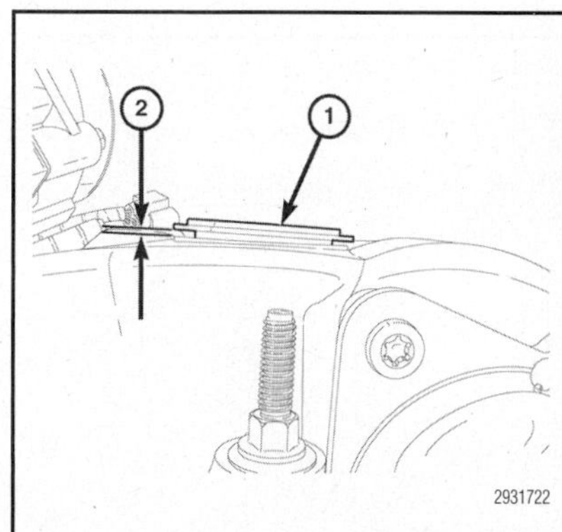

Fig. 287 A properly installed CMP sensor seal (1) will have a 0.06–0.08 inches (1.5–2.0 mm) gap (2) between the cylinder head cover and the seal upper flange

13. Connect the electrical connector to the sensor.

14. Following installation of the LH CMP sensor, install the upper intake manifold and air inlet hose.

15. Connect the negative battery cable.

➡The Cam/Crank Variation Relearn procedure must be performed using the scan tool anytime there has been a repair/replacement made to a powertrain system, for example: flywheel, valvetrain, camshaft and/or crankshaft sensors or components.

3.7L Engine

See Figure 288.

1. Disconnect electrical connector at Camshaft Position (CMP) sensor.
2. Remove sensor mounting bolt.
3. Carefully twist sensor from cylinder head.
4. Check condition of sensor O-ring.

To install:

5. Clean out machined hole in cylinder head.
6. Apply a small amount of engine oil to sensor O-ring.
7. Install sensor into cylinder head with a slight rocking and twisting action.

**** WARNING**

Before tightening sensor mounting bolt, be sure sensor is completely flush to cylinder head. If sensor is not flush, damage to sensor mounting tang may result.

8. Install mounting bolt and tighten to 106 inch lbs. (12 Nm).
9. Connect electrical connector to sensor.

5.7L Engine

See Figure 289.

1. Disconnect the air cleaner and resonator assembly.
2. Disconnect the electrical connector at the CMP sensor.
3. Remove the CMP sensor retaining bolt.
4. Using a slight rocking motion, carefully remove the CMP sensor from the timing cover.
5. Check the condition of CMP sensor O-ring, replace as necessary.

To install:

6. Clean out the machined hole in the timing cover.
7. Install the CMP sensor into the timing cover with a slight rocking motion. Do not the twist sensor into position as damage to O-ring may result.

**** WARNING**

Before tightening the CMP sensor retaining bolt, be sure the sensor is completely flush to the timing cover. If the sensor is not flush, damage to the sensor mounting tang may result.

8. Install the retaining bolt and tighten to 9 ft. lbs. (12 Nm).
9. Connect the electrical connector to the CMP sensor.
10. Install the air cleaner and resonator assembly.

CRANKSHAFT POSITION (CKP) SENSOR

LOCATION

The Crankshaft Position (CKP) sensor is mounted into the right rear side of the cylinder block.

REMOVAL & INSTALLATION

3.6L Engine

See Figures 290 through 292.

1. Disconnect and isolate the negative battery cable.
2. Raise and support the vehicle.
3. Remove the front suspension skid plate.
4. Push back the heat shield from the Crankshaft Position (CKP) sensor.
5. Disconnect the electrical connector from the CKP sensor.
6. Remove the sensor mounting bolt.
7. Carefully twist the sensor from the cylinder block.
8. The CKP sensor O-ring can be reused if not damaged.

To install:

9. The CKP sensor O-ring can be reused if not damaged.
10. Apply a small amount of engine oil to the sensor O-ring.
11. Clean out the CKP sensor mounting bolt hole in the engine block.
12. Install the sensor into the engine block with a slight rocking and twisting action.

**** WARNING**

Before tightening the CKP sensor mounting bolt, be sure the sensor is completely flush to the cylinder block. If the CKP sensor is not flush, damage to the sensor mounting tang may result.

13. Install the mounting bolt and tighten to 106 inch lbs. (12 Nm).
14. Connect the electrical connector to the sensor.
15. Position the heat shield over the CKP sensor.

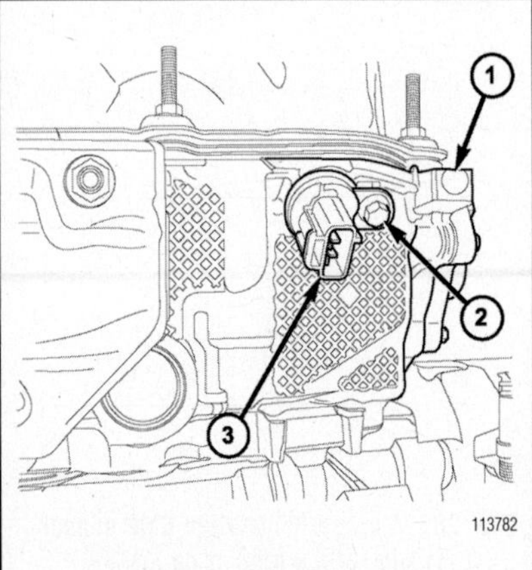

Fig. 288 RH cylinder head (1), sensor mounting bolt (2), and the CMP sensor (3)

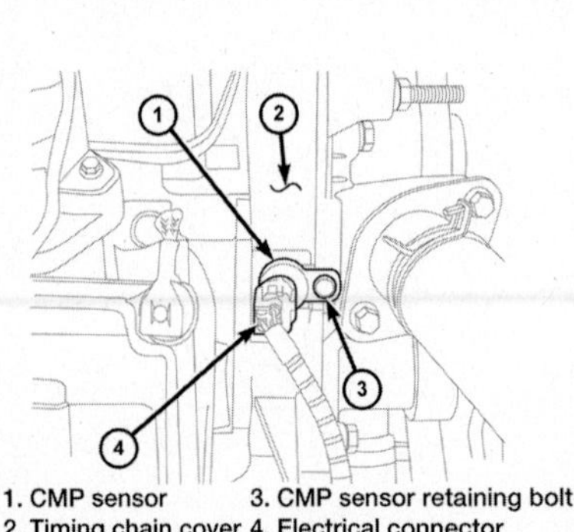

Fig. 289 Disconnect the electrical connector at the CMP sensor

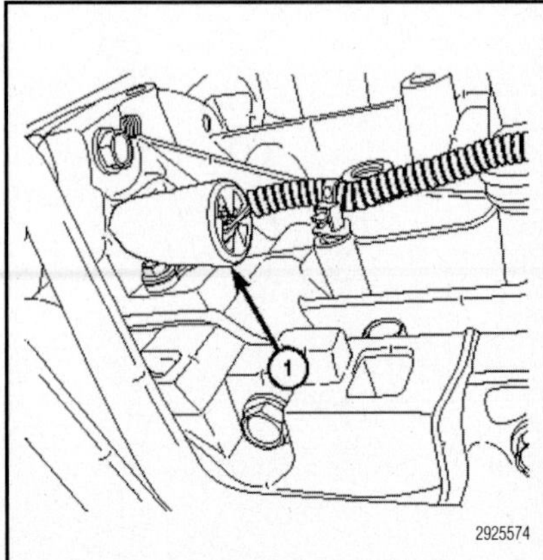

Fig. 290 Push back the heat shield (1) from the Crankshaft Position (CKP) sensor

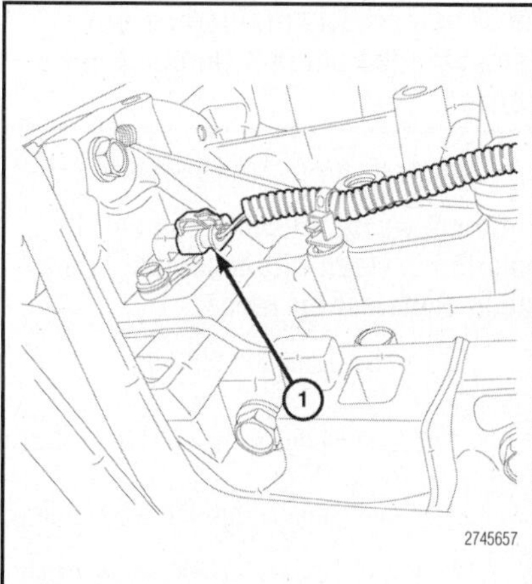

Fig. 291 Disconnect the electrical connector (1) from the CKP sensor

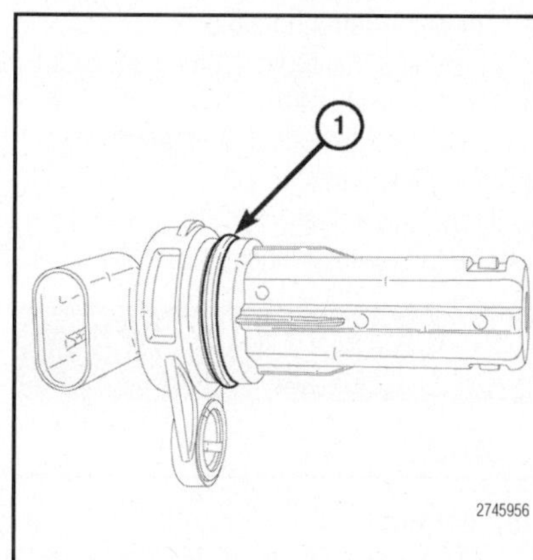

Fig. 292 The CKP sensor O-ring (1) can be reused if not damaged

16. Install the front suspension skid plate.
17. Lower the vehicle.
18. Connect the negative battery cable.

➡The Cam/Crank Variation Relearn procedure must be performed using the scan tool anytime there has been a repair/replacement made to a power-train system, for example: flywheel, valvetrain, camshaft and/or crankshaft sensors or components.

3.7L Engine

See Figure 293.

1. Raise vehicle.
2. Disconnect sensor electrical connector.
3. Remove sensor mounting bolt.
4. Carefully twist sensor from cylinder block.
5. Check condition of sensor O-ring.
6. Installation is the reverse of removal.

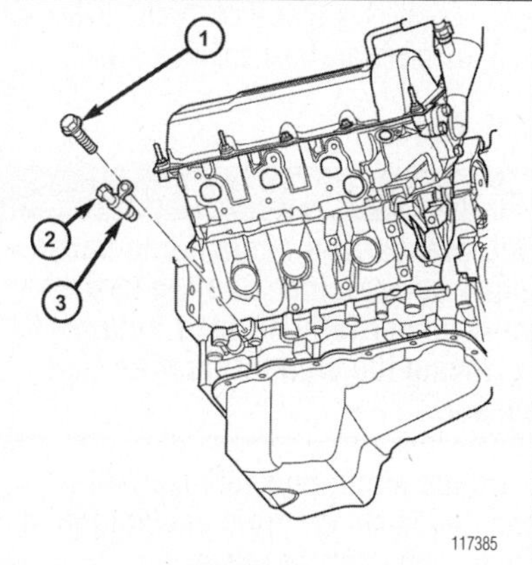

Fig. 293 Exploded view showing the crankshaft sensor mounting bolt (1), the sensor (2) and the O-ring (3)

5.7L Engine

See Figure 294.

1. Raise vehicle.
2. Disconnect CKP electrical connector at sensor.
3. Remove CKP mounting bolt.
4. Carefully twist sensor from cylinder block.
5. Remove sensor from vehicle.
6. Check condition of sensor O-ring.

To install:

✻✻ WARNING

Before tightening the CKP sensor mounting bolt, be sure the sensor is completely flush to the cylinder block. If the CKP sensor is not flush, damage to the sensor mounting tang may result.

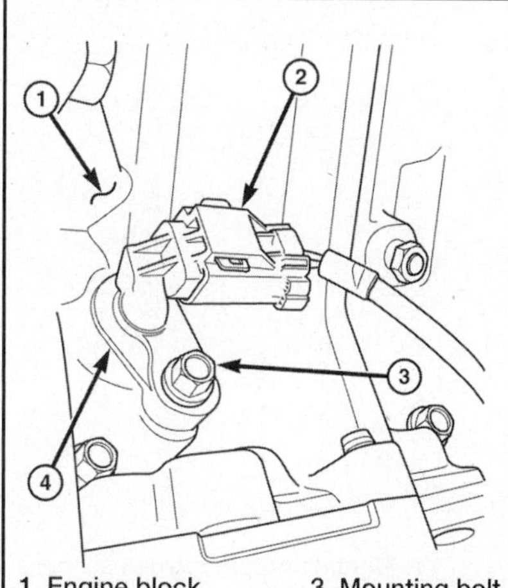

Fig. 294 Disconnect CKP electrical connector at sensor

7. Clean out machined hole in engine block.
8. Apply a small amount of engine oil to sensor O-ring.
9. Install sensor into engine block with a slight rocking and twisting action.
10. Install mounting bolt and tighten to 21 ft. lbs. (28 Nm).
11. Connect electrical connector to sensor.
12. Lower vehicle.

ENGINE CONTROL MODULE (ECM)

LOCATION

Refer to the graphics in the Removal and Installation section for the location(s).

REMOVAL & INSTALLATION

See Figures 295 and 296.

1. Remove the battery.
2. Remove the battery tray.
3. Disconnect Engine Control Module (ECM) electrical connectors.
4. Remove the two ECM hold down bolts.
5. Pull the ECM from the bracket.
6. Remove the ECM from the vehicle.

To install:

7. Install Engine Control Module (ECM) into the bracket.
8. Position ECM into bracket and align bolt holes.
9. Tight two hold down bolts
10. Connect two ECM electrical connectors.
11. Install the battery tray.
12. Install the battery.

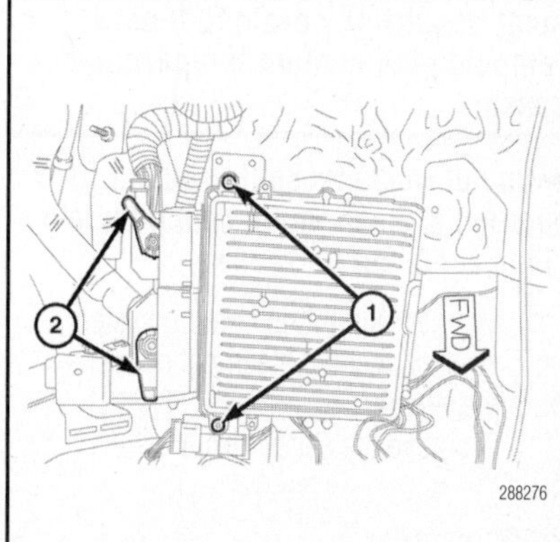

Fig. 295 Disconnect Engine Control Module (ECM) electrical connectors (2); remove the two ECM hold down bolts (1)

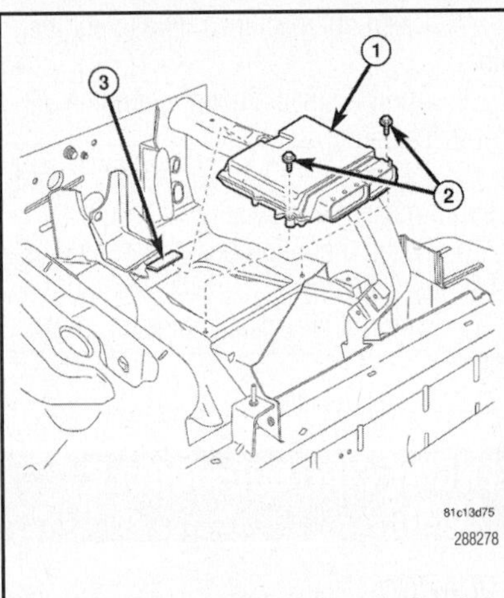

Fig. 296 Pull the ECM (1) from the bracket (3); mounting bolts (2)

ENGINE COOLANT TEMPERATURE (ECT) SENSOR

LOCATION

The Engine Coolant Temperature (ECT) sensor on the 3.6L engine is installed into a water jacket at rear of the cylinder head on the left side of the engine.

The Engine Coolant Temperature (ECT) sensor on the 3.7L engine is installed into a water jacket at front of intake manifold near rear of alternator.

On the 5.7L engine, the Engine Coolant Temperature (ECT) sensor is located on the upper portion of the water pump housing. It is installed into a water jacket in line with the thermostat.

REMOVAL & INSTALLATION

3.6L Engine

**** CAUTION**

Hot, pressurized coolant can cause injury by scalding. Cooling system must be partially drained before removing the coolant temperature sensor.

➡Do not waste reusable coolant. If solution is clean, drain coolant into a clean container for reuse.

1. Partially drain the cooling system.
2. Disconnect the electrical connector from the sensor.
3. Remove the sensor from the cylinder head.

To install:

4. Apply MOPAR® thread sealant with PFTE to sensor threads.
5. Install sensor to cylinder head.
6. Tighten sensor to 8 ft. lbs. (11 Nm).
7. Connect electrical connector to sensor.
8. Replace any lost engine coolant.

3.7L Engine

**** CAUTION**

Hot, pressurized coolant can cause injury by scalding. Cooling system must be partially drained before removing the coolant temperature sensor.

➡Do not waste reusable coolant. If solution is clean, drain coolant into a clean container for reuse.

1. Partially drain the cooling system.
2. Disconnect the electrical connector from the sensor.
3. Remove the sensor from the intake manifold.

To install:

4. Apply MOPAR® thread sealant with PFTE to sensor threads.
5. Install sensor to the engine.
6. Tighten sensor to 8 ft. lbs. (11 Nm).
7. Connect electrical connector to sensor.
8. Replace any lost engine coolant.

5.7L Engine

**** CAUTION**

Hot, pressurized coolant can cause injury by scalding. Cooling system must be partially drained before removing the coolant temperature sensor.

1. Remove the air intake system.

➡Do not waste reusable coolant. If solution is clean, drain coolant into a clean container for reuse.

2. Partially drain the cooling system.
3. Disconnect electrical connector from sensor.
4. Remove sensor from the water pump housing.

To install:

5. Apply MOPAR® thread sealant with PFTE to the sensor threads.
6. Install the coolant temperature sensor into water pump housing.
7. Tighten the coolant temperature sensor to 8 ft. lbs. (11 Nm).
8. Connect the coolant temperature sensor electrical connector.
9. Install air intake system.
10. Replace any lost engine coolant.

HEATED OXYGEN (HO2S) SENSOR

LOCATION

3.6L Engine

See Figure 297.

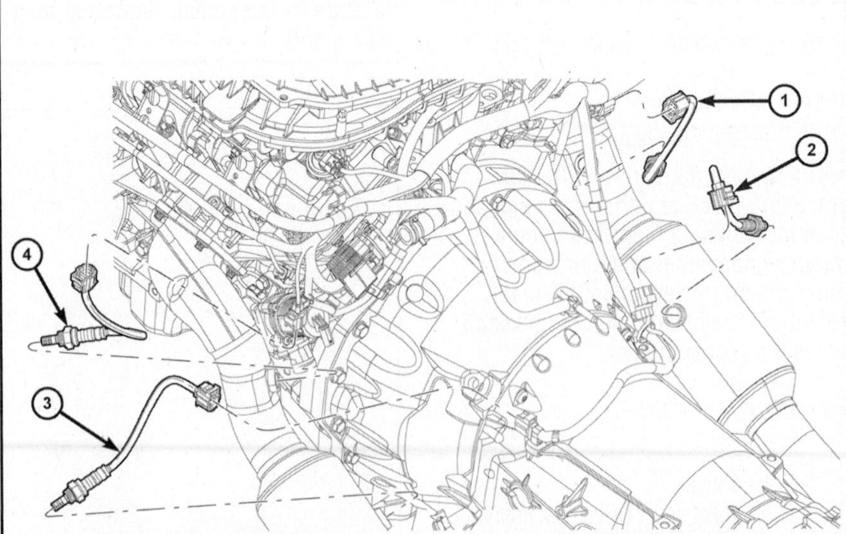

Fig. 297 Locations of the heated oxygen sensors

5.7L Engine

See Figure 298.

REMOVAL & INSTALLATION

3.6L Engine

✲✲ CAUTION

The exhaust pipes and catalytic converter become very hot during engine operation. Allow the engine to cool before removing the oxygen sensor.

1. Disconnect and isolate the negative battery cable.
2. Raise and support the vehicle.

✲✲ WARNING

When disconnecting the oxygen sensor electrical connector, do not pull directly on the wire going into the sensor. The sensor wiring can be damaged resulting in sensor failure.

3. Disconnect the heated oxygen sensor electrical connector.
4. Remove the oxygen sensor.
5. Clean the exhaust pipe threads using an appropriate tap.

To install:

6. If reinstalling the original oxygen sensor, coat the sensor threads with an anti-seize compound such as Loctite® 771- 64 or equivalent. New sensors have compound on the threads and do not require an additional coating. Do Not add any additional anti-seize compound to the threads of a new oxygen sensor.
7. Install the oxygen sensor and tighten to 37 ft. lbs. (50 Nm).

✲✲ WARNING

Never apply any type of grease to the oxygen sensor electrical connector, or attempt any repair of the sensor wiring harness.

8. Connect the heated oxygen sensor electrical connector.
9. Lower the vehicle.
10. Connect the negative battery cable.

5.7L Engine

Upstream O2 Sensors

1. Raise and support the vehicle.

✲✲ CAUTION

The exhaust pipes and catalytic converter become very hot during engine operation. Allow the engine to cool before removing the oxygen sensor.

✲✲ WARNING

When disconnecting the oxygen sensor electrical connector, do not pull directly on the wire going into the sensor. The sensor wiring can be damaged resulting in sensor failure.

2. Disconnect the O2S sensors electrical connectors.
3. Remove the left catalytic converter heat shield.
4. Using the appropriate oxygen sensor removal/installation tool, remove the O2S sensors.
5. Clean the threads in the exhaust pipes using an appropriate tap.

To install:

➡Threads of new oxygen sensors are factory coated with anti-seize compound to aid in removal. Do not add any additional anti-seize compound to threads of a new oxygen sensor.

6. Using the appropriate oxygen sensor removal/installation tool, install the O2S sensors and tighten to 30 ft. lbs. (41 Nm.).
7. Install the left catalytic converter heat shield.
8. Connect the O2S sensors electrical connectors.
9. Lower the vehicle.

Downstream O2 Sensors

1. Raise and support the vehicle.
2. Support the transmission with a safety stand or suitable jack, remove the crossmember retaining bolts and slightly lower the transmission to gain access to the O2S sensor electrical connectors.

✲✲ WARNING

When disconnecting the oxygen sensor electrical connector, do not pull directly on the wire going into the sensor. The sensor wiring can be damaged resulting in sensor failure.

3. Disconnect the O2S sensors electrical connectors.
4. Using the appropriate oxygen sensor removal/installation tool, remove the O2S sensors.
5. Clean the threads in the catalytic converters using an appropriate tap.

To install:

➡Threads of new oxygen sensors are factory coated with anti-seize compound to aid in removal. Do not add any additional anti-seize compound to threads of a new oxygen sensor.

6. Using the appropriate oxygen sensor removal/installation tool, install the O2S sensors and tighten to 30 ft. lbs. (41 Nm.).
7. Connect the O2S sensors electrical connectors.

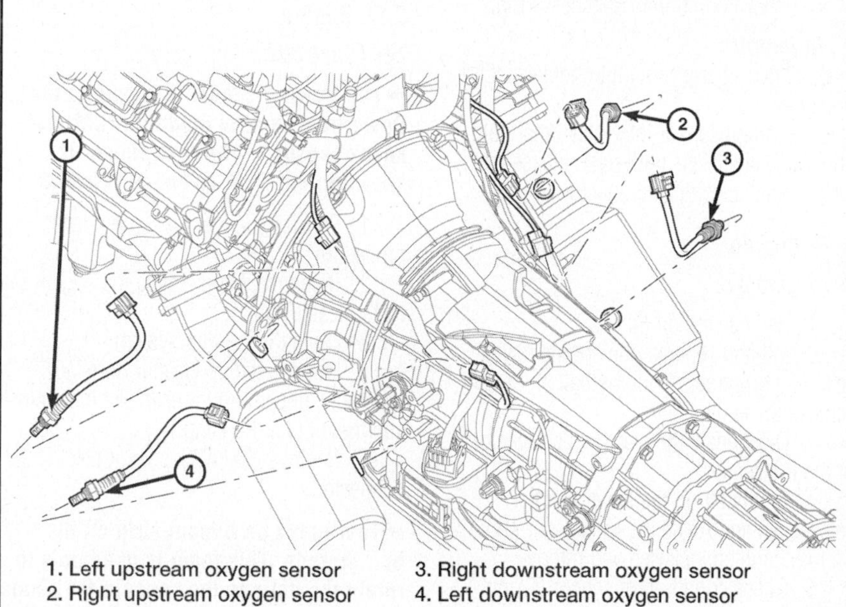

Fig. 298 Locations of the heated oxygen sensors

8. Raise the transmission and install the crossmember to frame bolts and tighten to 50 ft. lbs. (68 Nm), remove the safety stand or jack.
9. Lower the vehicle.

INTAKE AIR TEMPERATURE (IAT) SENSOR

LOCATION

On the 3.6L engine, the Intake Air Temperature (IAT) sensor is located on the air intake duct.

On the 3.7L engine, the intake manifold air temperature (IAT) sensor is installed into the air inlet tube.

On the 5.7L engine, the Intake Air Temperature (IAT) sensor is installed into the air cleaner resonator.

REMOVAL & INSTALLATION

3.6L Engine

See Figures 299 and 300.

1. Disconnect and isolate the negative battery cable.
2. Remove the engine cover.
3. Disconnect the electrical connector from the Intake Air Temperature (IAT) sensor.
4. Clean dirt from the air inlet tube at the IAT sensor base.
5. Gently lift the small plastic release tab, rotate the sensor about ¼ turn counter-clockwise and remove the sensor from the inlet air hose.
6. The IAT sensor O-ring can be reused if not damaged.

To install:

7. The sensor mounted O-ring seal can be reused if not damaged.
8. Clean the IAT sensor mounting hole in the air inlet hose.

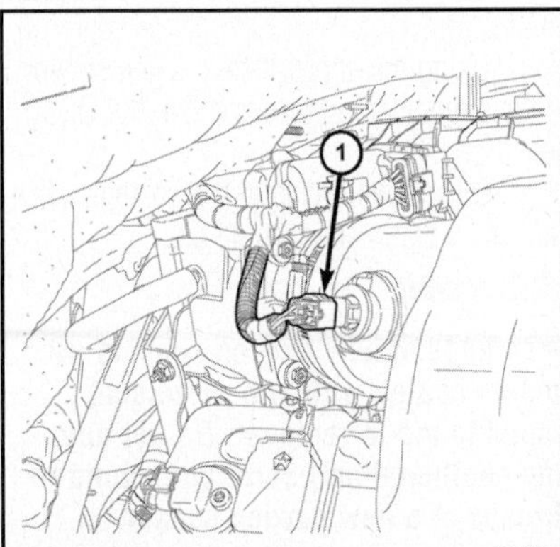

Fig. 299 Disconnect the electrical connector (1) from the Intake Air Temperature (IAT) sensor

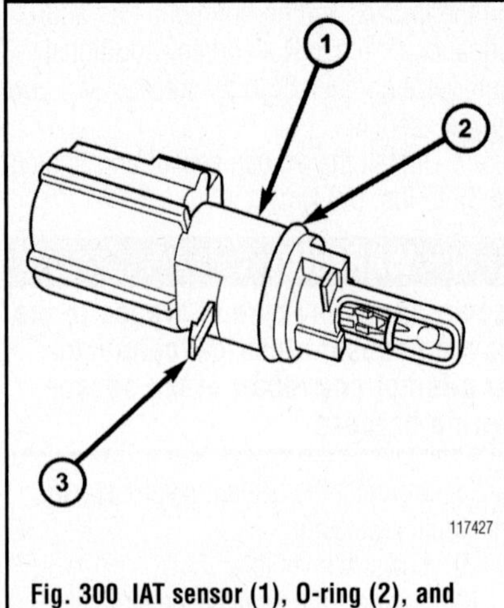

Fig. 300 IAT sensor (1), O-ring (2), and the Plastic release tab (3)

9. Install the IAT sensor into the air inlet hose and rotate clockwise until the release tab engages.
10. Install the electrical connector to the IAT sensor.
11. Install the engine cover.
12. Connect the negative battery cable.

3.7L Engine

See Figure 300.

1. Disconnect electrical connector from IAT sensor.
2. Clean dirt from air inlet tube at sensor base.
3. Gently lift on small plastic release tab and rotate sensor about a quarter turn counter-clockwise for removal.
4. Check condition of sensor O-ring.

To install:

5. Clean sensor mounting hole in intake manifold.
6. Position sensor into intake manifold and rotate clockwise until past release tab.
7. Install electrical connector.

5.7L Engine

See Figure 301.

1. Remove the oil fill cap.
2. Lift and separate the engine cover retaining grommets from the ball studs and remove the engine cover.
3. Disconnect the electrical connector at the IAT sensor.
4. Gently lift on the small plastic release tab and rotate the IAT sensor about ¼ turn counterclockwise and remove.
5. Check condition of sensor O-ring, replace if necessary.

To install:

6. Clean the IAT sensor mounting hole in the air cleaner resonator.

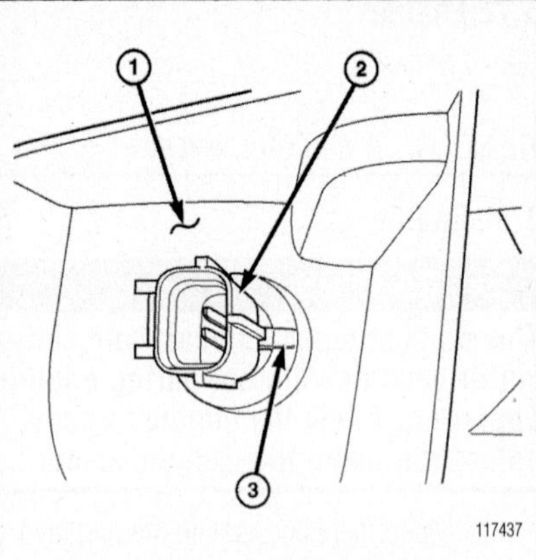

Fig. 301 Intake Air Temperature (IAT) sensor (2), the air cleaner resonator (1), and the tab (3)

7. Position the IAT sensor into the air cleaner resonator, rotate clockwise about ¼ turn until the release tab locks into position.
8. Connect the electrical connector to the IAT sensor.
9. Position the engine cover and secure the retaining grommets to the ball studs.
10. Install the oil fill cap.

KNOCK SENSOR (KS)

LOCATION

The Knock Sensors (KS) are located in the valley of the engine block, beneath the intake manifold.

REMOVAL & INSTALLATION

3.6L Engine

See Figure 302.

➡The forward sensor is known to the Powertrain Control Module (PCM) as knock sensor 1. The rear sensor is known to the PCM as knock sensor 2.

1. Perform the fuel pressure release procedure.
2. Disconnect and isolate the negative battery cable.
3. Drain the cooling system.
4. Remove the air cleaner housing assembly, upper and lower intake manifolds and the oil filter housing.
5. Remove the knock sensor electrical connector.

➡There may be a foam strip on the bolt threads. This foam is used only to retain the bolts to the sensors for plant assembly. It is not used as a sealant. Do not apply any adhesive, sealant or thread locking compound to these bolts.

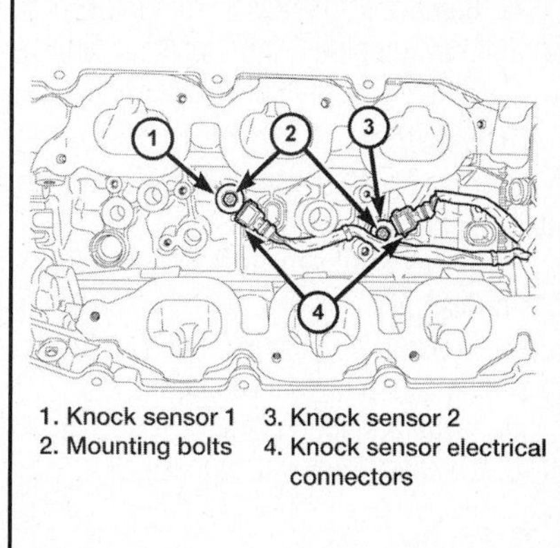

Fig. 302 Remove the knock sensor electrical connector

6. Remove the mounting bolt and knock sensor 1 or knock sensor 2.

To install:

7. Thoroughly clean the knock sensor mounting holes.

➡Over or under tightening the sensor mounting bolts will affect knock sensor performance, possibly causing improper spark control. Always use the specified torque when installing the knock sensors. The torque specification for the knock sensor bolt is less than the typical 8 mm bolt.

➡There may be a foam strip on the bolt threads. This foam is used only to retain the bolts to the sensors for plant assembly. It is not used as a sealant. Do not apply any adhesive, sealant or thread locking compound to these bolts.

8. Install knock sensor 1 and/or knock sensor 2 with mounting bolt. Tighten the mounting bolt to 16 ft. lbs. (22 Nm).
9. Connect the electrical connector.
10. Install the oil filter housing, upper and lower intake manifolds and air cleaner housing assembly.
11. If removed, install the oil filter and fill the engine crankcase with the proper oil to the correct level.
12. Connect the negative battery cable.
13. Fill the cooling system.
14. Operate the engine until it reaches normal operating temperature. Check cooling system for correct fluid level.

3.7L Engine

See Figure 303.

➡The two sensors share a common wiring harness using one electrical connector. Because of this, they must be replaced as a pair.

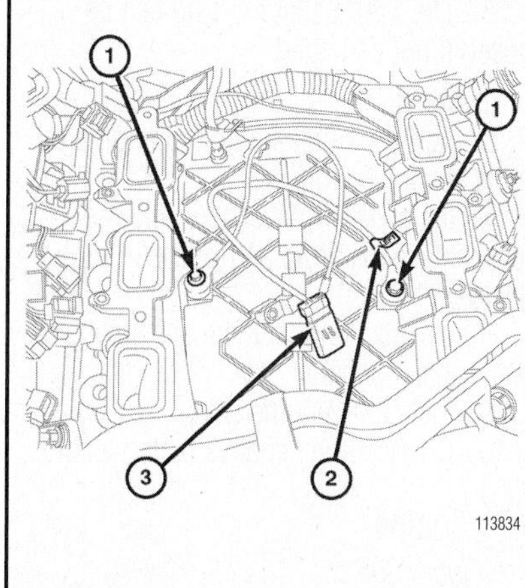

Fig. 303 Knock sensors (1), LEFT tag (2), and electrical connector (3)

➡The left sensor is identified by an identification tag (LEFT). It is also identified by a larger bolt head. The Powertrain Control Module (PCM) must have and know the correct sensor left/right positions. Do not mix the sensor locations.

1. Remove intake manifold.
2. Disconnect knock sensor dual pigtail harness from engine wiring harness. This connection is made near rear of engine.
3. Remove both sensor mounting bolts.

➡Note foam strip on bolt threads. This foam is used only to retain the bolts to sensors for plant assembly. It is not used as a sealant. Do not apply any adhesive, sealant or thread locking compound to these bolts.

4. Remove sensors from engine.

To install:

➡The left sensor is identified by an identification tag (LEFT). It is also identified by a larger bolt head. The Powertrain Control Module (PCM) must have and know the correct sensor left/right positions. Do not mix the sensor locations.

5. Thoroughly clean knock sensor mounting holes.
6. Install sensors into cylinder block.

➡Over or under tightening the sensor mounting bolts will affect knock sensor performance, possibly causing improper spark control. Always use the specified torque when installing the knock sensors. The torque for the knock senor bolt is relatively light for an 8 mm bolt.

➡Note foam strip on bolt threads. This foam is used only to retain the bolts to sensors for plant assembly. It is not used as a sealant. Do not apply any adhesive, sealant or thread locking compound to these bolts.

7. Install and tighten mounting bolts. Tighten to 15 2 ft. lbs. (20 Nm).
8. Connect knock sensor wiring harness to engine harness at rear of intake manifold.
9. Install intake manifold.

5.7L Engine

1. Raise and support the vehicle.
2. Disconnect the knock sensor electrical connector(s).
3. Remove the knock sensor retaining bolt(s).

➡Note the foam strip on bolt threads. This foam strip is used only to retain the bolts to the sensors for plant assembly. It is not used as a sealant. Do not apply any adhesive, sealant or thread locking compound to these bolts.

4. Remove the knock sensor(s) from the cylinder block.

To install:

5. Thoroughly clean the knock sensor(s) mounting hole.
6. Install the knock sensor(s) into the cylinder block.

➡Over or under tightening the sensor mounting bolts will affect knock sensors performance, possibly causing improper spark control. Always use the specified torque when installing the knock sensors. The torque for the knock sensor bolt is relatively light for an 8 mm bolt.

➡Note foam strip on bolt threads. This foam is used only to retain the bolts to sensors for plant assembly. It is not used as a sealant. Do not apply any adhesive, sealant or thread locking compound to these bolts.

7. Position the knock sensor(s), install the retaining bolt(s) and tighten to 15 ft. lbs. (20 Nm).
8. Install the electrical connector(s).

MANIFOLD AIR PRESSURE (MAP) SENSOR

LOCATION

Refer to the graphics in the Removal and Installation section for the location(s).

REMOVAL & INSTALLATION

3.6L Engine

See Figures 304 and 305.

1. Disconnect and isolate the negative battery cable.
2. Remove the engine cover.
3. Unlock and disconnect the electrical connector from the MAP sensor.
4. Rotate the MAP sensor ¼ turn counterclockwise and pull the sensor straight up and out of the upper intake manifold.

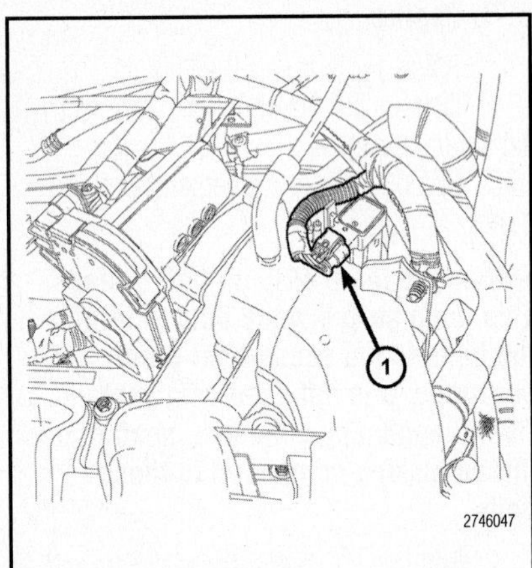

Fig. 304 Unlock and disconnect the electrical connector (1) from the MAP sensor

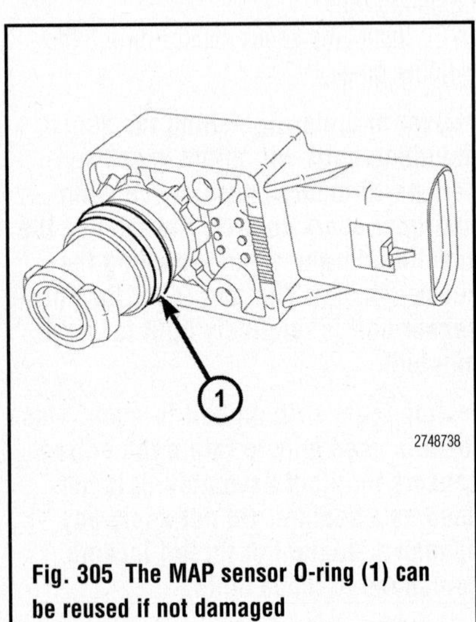

Fig. 305 The MAP sensor O-ring (1) can be reused if not damaged

5. The MAP sensor O-ring can be reused if not damaged.

To install:

6. Apply a small amount of engine oil to the sensor O-ring.
7. Install the MAP sensor into the upper intake manifold and rotate ¼ turn clockwise.
8. Connect and lock the electrical connector to the sensor.
9. Install the engine cover.
10. Connect the negative battery cable.

3.7L Engine

See Figure 306.

➡The Manifold Absolute Pressure (MAP) sensor is mounted into the front of the intake manifold.

1. Disconnect electrical connector at sensor.
2. Clean area around MAP sensor.
3. Remove one sensor mounting screw.

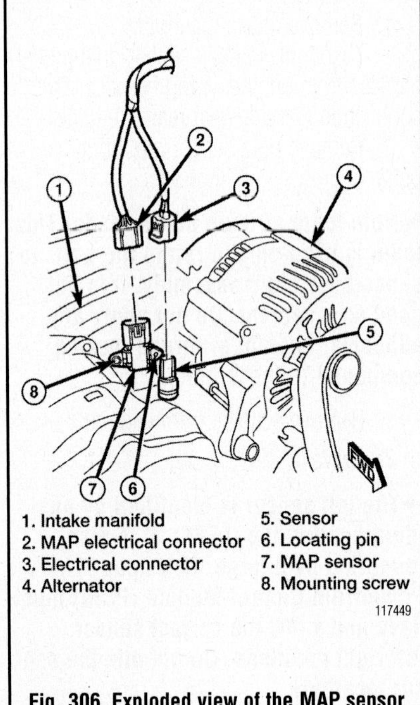

Fig. 306 Exploded view of the MAP sensor assembly

4. Remove MAP sensor from intake manifold by slipping it from locating pin.
5. Check condition of sensor O-ring.

To install:

6. Clean MAP sensor mounting hole at intake manifold.
7. Check MAP sensor O-ring seal for cuts or tears.
8. Position MAP sensor into manifold by sliding sensor over locating pin.
9. Install mounting bolt.
10. Connect electrical connector.

5.7L Engine

See Figure 307.

1. Disconnect MAP sensor electrical connector.
2. Rotate MAP sensor counterclockwise for removal.
3. Lift MAP sensor upward.
4. Inspect O-ring for damage.

To install:

5. Clean MAP sensor mounting hole at intake manifold.
6. Check MAP sensor O-ring for cuts or tears.
7. Position MAP sensor into manifold.
8. Rotate MAP sensor clockwise for installation.
9. Connect electrical connector.

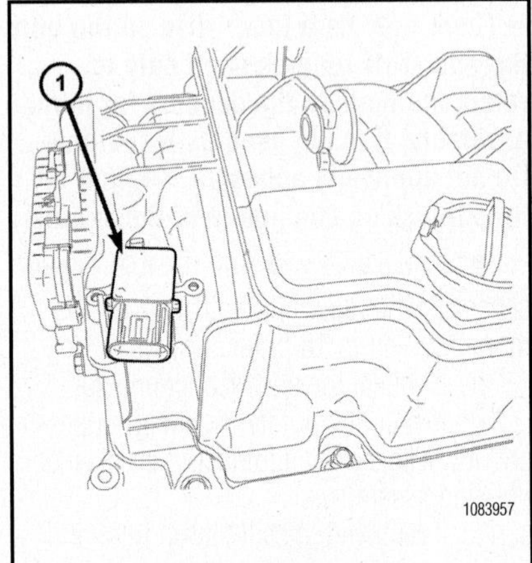

Fig. 307 Disconnect MAP sensor (1) electrical connector

FUEL SYSTEM SERVICE PRECAUTIONS

Safety is the most important factor when performing not only fuel system maintenance but any type of maintenance. Failure to conduct maintenance and repairs in a safe manner may result in serious personal injury or death. Maintenance and testing of the vehicle's fuel system components can be accomplished safely and effectively by adhering to the following rules and guidelines.

- To avoid the possibility of fire and personal injury, always disconnect the negative battery cable unless the repair or test procedure requires that battery voltage be applied.
- Always relieve the fuel system pressure prior to disconnecting any fuel system component (injector, fuel rail, pressure regulator, etc.), fitting or fuel line connection. Exercise extreme caution whenever relieving fuel system pressure to avoid exposing skin, face and eyes to fuel spray. Please be advised that fuel under pressure may penetrate the skin or any part of the body that it contacts.
- Always place a shop towel or cloth around the fitting or connection prior to loosening to absorb any excess fuel due to spillage. Ensure that all fuel spillage (should it occur) is quickly removed from engine surfaces. Ensure that all fuel soaked cloths or towels are deposited into a suitable waste container.
- Always keep a dry chemical (Class B) fire extinguisher near the work area.
- Do not allow fuel spray or fuel vapors to come into contact with a spark or open flame.
- Always use a back-up wrench when loosening and tightening fuel line connection fittings. This will prevent unnecessary stress and torsion to fuel line piping.
- Always replace worn fuel fitting O-rings with new Do not substitute fuel hose or equivalent where fuel pipe is installed.

Before servicing the vehicle, make sure to also refer to the precautions in the beginning of this section as well.

RELIEVING FUEL SYSTEM PRESSURE

1. Remove the fuel fill cap.
2. Remove the fuel pump fuse from the Power Distribution Center (PDC). For location of the fuel pump fuse, refer to label on the underside of the PDC cover.
3. Start and run the engine until it stalls.
4. Attempt restarting the engine until it will no longer run.
5. Turn the ignition key to the OFF position.
6. Place a rag or towel below the fuel supply line quick-connect fitting located near the cowl.
7. Disconnect the fuel supply line quick-connect fitting at the fuel supply line.
8. Return the fuel pump fuse to the PDC.

➡One or more Diagnostic Trouble Codes (DTC) may have been stored in the PCM memory due to fuel pump fuse removal. A diagnostic scan tool must be used to erase a DTC.

FUEL FILTER

REMOVAL & INSTALLATION

Two fuel filters are used. One is located at the bottom of the fuel pump module. The other is located inside the module. A separate frame mounted fuel filter is not used with any engine.

Both fuel filters are designed for extended service. They do not require normal scheduled maintenance. Filters should only be replaced if a diagnostic procedure indicates to do so.

FUEL INJECTORS

REMOVAL & INSTALLATION

3.6L Engine

See Figures 308 through 310.

⁂ CAUTION

The fuel system is under constant pressure even with engine off. Before servicing the fuel rail, fuel system pressure must be released.

1. Release fuel system pressure.
2. Disconnect and isolate the negative battery cable.

⁂ WARNING

When removing the fuel rail from the lower intake manifold, one or more fuel injectors may remain in the intake manifold resulting in residual fuel spilling onto the engine from the fuel rail.

3. Remove the air inlet hose, upper intake manifold, and fuel rail.
4. Remove the fuel injectors from the fuel rail.
5. Remove the fuel injectors from the lower intake manifold.
6. Remove and discard all fuel injector O-ring seals.

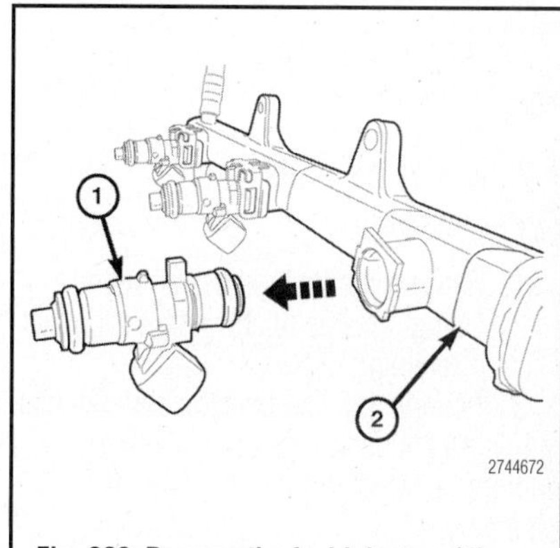

Fig. 308 Remove the fuel injectors (1) from the fuel rail (2)

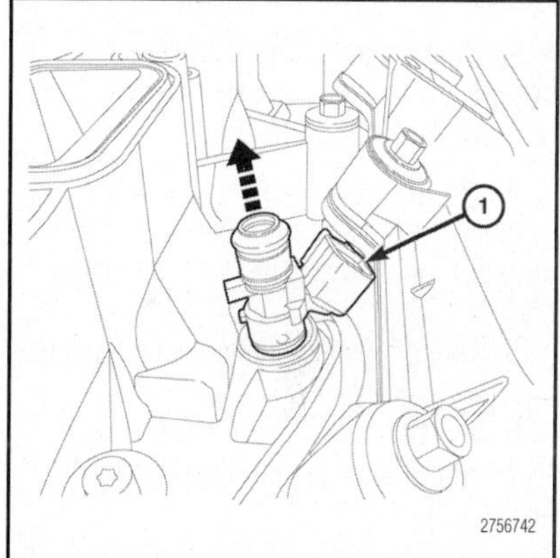

Fig. 309 Remove the fuel injectors (1) from the lower intake manifold

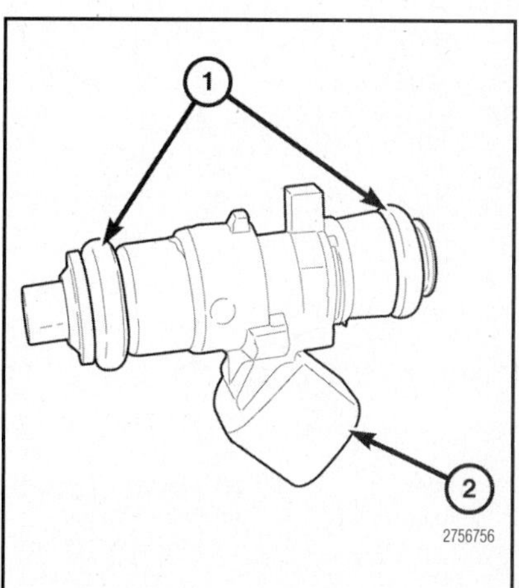

Fig. 310 Remove and discard all fuel injector (2) O-ring seals (1)

To install:

7. Lightly lubricate new O-ring seals with engine oil and install on the fuel injector.
8. Install the fuel injectors to the fuel rail.
9. Install the fuel rail, upper inlet manifold and air inlet hose.
10. Connect the negative battery cable.
11. Start the engine and check for leaks.

3.7L & 5.7L Engines

See Figure 311.

1. Remove the fuel rail assembly.
2. Using suitable pliers, remove the fuel injector retaining clip.
3. Remove the fuel injector from the fuel rail using a side to side motion while pulling the injector out of the fuel rail assembly.

To install:

➡If the same fuel injector is to be reinstalled, install new O-rings.

➡Apply a small amount of clean engine oil to each injector O-ring. This will aid in the installation.

4. Install the fuel injector into the fuel rail using a side to side motion while pushing injector into the fuel rail assembly.
5. Using suitable pliers, install the fuel injector retaining clip.
6. Install the fuel rail assembly.
7. Start the engine and check for fuel leaks.

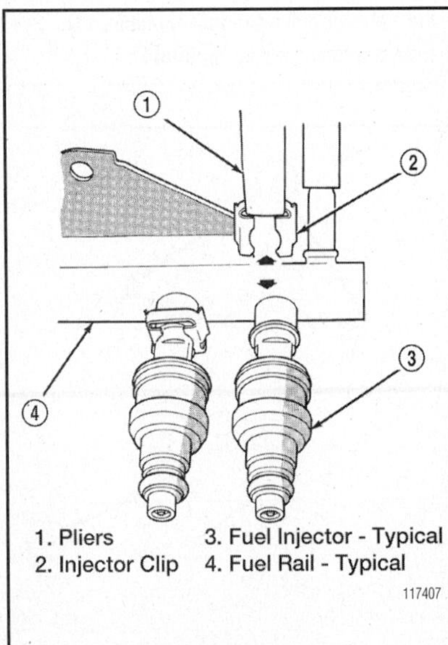

Fig. 311 Fuel injector assembly

FUEL PUMP MODULE

REMOVAL & INSTALLATION

2010 Models

⁑ CAUTION

The fuel system is under a constant pressure, even with the engine off. Before servicing the fuel system, the fuel pressure must be released.

1. Perform the fuel pressure release procedure.
2. Disconnect the negative battery cable.
3. Drain and remove fuel tank.
4. Note rotational position of module before attempting removal. An indexing arrow is located on top of module for this purpose.
5. Position SAE Fuel Pump Lock Ring Wrench into notches on outside edge of lockring.
6. Install ½ inch drive breaker bar to SAE Fuel Pump Lock Ring Wrench.
7. Rotate breaker bar counter-clockwise to remove lockring.
8. Remove lockring. The module will spring up slightly when lockring is removed.
9. Remove module from fuel tank. Be careful not to bend float arm while removing.

To install:

➡Whenever the fuel pump module is serviced, the module seal must be replaced.

10. Using a new seal, position fuel pump module into opening in fuel tank.
11. Position lockring over top of fuel pump module.
12. Rotate module until embossed alignment arrow points to center alignment mark. This step must be performed to prevent float from contacting side of fuel tank. Also be sure fuel fitting on top of pump module is pointed to drivers side of vehicle.
13. Install SAE Fuel Pump Lock Ring Wrench to lockring.
14. Tighten lockring until all seven notches have engaged.
15. Install fuel tank.

2011 Models

See Figure 312.

This vehicle uses a saddle type tank that has a reservoir on both sides of the drive shaft. The electric fuel pump, fuel pressure regulator and fuel filters are integrated into the main fuel pump module located on the left side of the fuel tank. The auxiliary fuel pump module is on the right side of the fuel tank. The fuel supply fitting is located on top of the main fuel pump module and supplies fuel to the engine. Both modules have fuel level sending unit sensor cards. There is one hose that connect both modules together, this hose is the fuel supply line and a return or siphon hose. The lines are removed from the main fuel pump module on the left side of the fuel tank when servicing either unit. A 12 volt, permanent magnet, electric motor powers the fuel pump. The electric fuel pump is not a separate, serviceable component.

⁑ CAUTION

The fuel system is under constant high pressure even with engine off. Until the fuel pressure has been properly released from the system, do not attempt to open the fuel system. Do not smoke or use open flames/sparks when servicing the fuel system. Wear protective clothing and eye protection. Make sure the area in which the vehicle is being serviced is in a well ventilated area and free of flames/sparks. Failure to comply may result in serious or fatal injury.

⁑ CAUTION

No sparks, open flames or smoking. Risk of poisoning from inhaling and swallowing fuel. Pour fuel only into appropriately marked OSHA approved containers. Wear protective clothing. Risk of injury to eyes and skin from contact with fuel.

1. Perform the fuel system pressure release procedure.

⁑ WARNING

If the fuel pump module is not operating or the fuel level sending unit is not operating and the fuel level cannot be determined, the fuel tank must be removed prior to draining.

2. Perform the fuel tank draining procedure.
3. Disconnect and isolate the negative battery cable.
4. Remove the fuel tank.

➡Prior to removing the main fuel pump module, use compressed air to remove any accumulated dirt and debris from around the fuel tank opening.

5. Position the SAE Fuel Pump Lock Ring Wrench into the notches on the outside edge of the main fuel pump module lock ring.

6. Install a ½ inch drive breaker bar onto the SAE Fuel Pump Lock Ring Wrench.

➡**The main fuel pump module will spring up slightly when lock ring is removed.**

7. Rotate the breaker bar counterclockwise and remove the lock ring.

⁂ WARNING

An indexing arrow is located on top of the main fuel pump module to clock its position into the fuel tank, note its location for reassembly.

➡**The main fuel pump module has to be properly located in the fuel tank for the fuel level gauge to work properly.**

8. Mark the main fuel pump module orientation.

⁂ WARNING

Do not allow the float arm of the main fuel pump module to come in contact with any part of the fuel tank during removal or installation, damage to the float arm and fuel level sending card may result.

9. Using caution not to bend the float arm, lift the main fuel pump module out of the fuel tank enough to gain access to the auxiliary fuel pump module supply line connection and disconnect the supply line.

10. Tip the main fuel pump module on its side to drain the remaining fuel from the reservoir and remove the main fuel pump module.

⁂ WARNING

Whenever the fuel pump module is serviced, the rubber O-ring seal must be replaced.

11. Remove and discard the rubber O-ring seal.

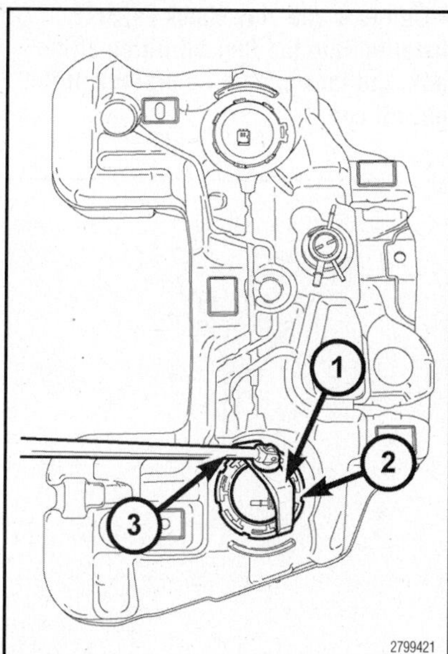

Fig. 312 Fuel Pump Lock Ring Wrench (1), fuel pump module lock ring (2), and breaker bar (3)

Auxiliary Fuel Pump Module

See Figure 313.

⁂ CAUTION

The fuel system is under constant high pressure even with engine off. Until the fuel pressure has been properly released from the system, do not attempt to open the fuel system. Do not smoke or use open flames/sparks when servicing the fuel system. Wear protective clothing and eye protection. Make sure the area in which the vehicle is being serviced is in a well ventilated area and free of flames/sparks. Failure to comply may result in serious or fatal injury.

⁂ CAUTION

No sparks, open flames or smoking. Risk of poisoning from inhaling and swallowing fuel. Pour fuel only into appropriately marked OSHA approved containers. Wear protective clothing. Risk of injury to eyes and skin from contact with fuel.

1. Remove the main fuel pump module.

➡**Prior to removing the auxiliary fuel pump module, use compressed air to remove any accumulated dirt and debris from around fuel tank opening.**

2. Position the SAE Fuel Pump Lock Ring Wrench into the notches on the outside edge of the auxiliary fuel pump module lock ring.

3. Install a ½ inch drive breaker bar onto the SAE Fuel Pump Lock Ring Wrench.

➡**The auxiliary fuel pump module will spring up slightly when the lock ring is removed.**

4. Rotate the breaker bar counterclockwise and remove the lock ring.

⁂ WARNING

An indexing arrow is located on top of the auxiliary fuel pump module to clock its position into the fuel tank, note its location for reassembly.

➡**The auxiliary fuel pump module has to be properly located in the fuel tank for the fuel level gauge to work properly.**

5. Mark the auxiliary fuel pump module orientation.

⁂ WARNING

Do not allow the float arm of the auxiliary fuel pump module to come in contact with any part of the fuel tank during removal or installation, damage to the float arm and fuel level sending card may result.

6. Using caution not to bend the float arm, lift the auxiliary fuel pump module and the auxiliary fuel pump module supply line out of the fuel tank as an assembly.

⁂ WARNING

Whenever the auxiliary fuel pump module is serviced, the rubber O-ring seal must be replaced.

7. Remove and discard the rubber O-ring seal.

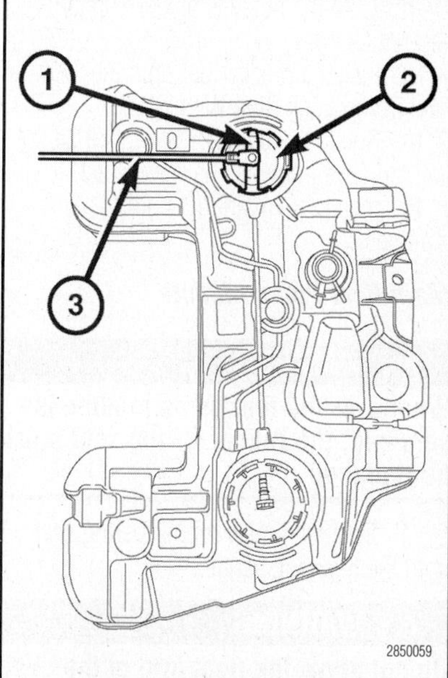

Fig. 313 Fuel Pump Lock Ring Wrench (1), fuel pump module lock ring (2), and breaker bar (3)

To install:

⁂ WARNING

Whenever the auxiliary fuel pump module is serviced, the rubber O-ring seal must be replaced.

8. Position a new rubber O-ring seal onto the fuel tank flange.

⁂ WARNING

Do not allow the float arm of the auxiliary fuel pump module to come in contact with any part of the fuel tank during removal or installation, damage to the float arm and fuel level sending card may result.

9. Using caution not to bend the float arm, lower the auxiliary fuel pump module and the auxiliary fuel pump module supply line into the fuel tank as an assembly.

➡The auxiliary fuel pump module has to be properly located in the fuel tank for the fuel level gauge to work properly.

10. Rotate the auxiliary fuel pump module until the embossed alignment arrow points to the center alignment mark or the same position as noted during removal. This step must be performed to prevent the float from contacting the side of the fuel tank.
11. Position the lock ring over top of the auxiliary fuel pump module.
12. Install the SAE Fuel Pump Lock Ring Wrench into the notches on the outside edge of lock ring.
13. Install a breaker bar onto the SAE Fuel Pump Lock Ring Wrench.
14. Rotate the breaker bar clockwise until all seven notches have engaged.
15. Install the main fuel pump module.

Main Fuel Pump Module

⁂ WARNING

Whenever the fuel pump module is serviced, the rubber O-ring seal must be replaced.

1. Position a new rubber O-ring seal onto the fuel tank flange.

⁂ WARNING

Do not allow the float arm of the main fuel pump module to come in contact with any part of the fuel tank during removal or installation, damage to the float arm and fuel level sending card may result.

2. Using caution not to bend the float arm, lower the main fuel pump module into the fuel tank enough to gain access to the auxiliary fuel pump module supply line connection and connect the supply line.

⁂ WARNING

An indexing arrow is located on top of the main fuel pump module to clock it's position into the fuel tank. The fuel pump module must be installed in the same position as removed.

3. Rotate the main fuel pump module until the embossed alignment arrow points to the center alignment mark or the same position as noted during removal. This step must be performed to prevent the float from contacting the side of the fuel tank.
4. Position the lock ring over top of the main fuel pump module.
5. Install the SAE Fuel Pump Lock Ring Wrench into the notches on the outside edge of lock ring.
6. Install a breaker bar onto the SAE Fuel Pump Lock Ring Wrench.
7. Rotate the breaker bar clockwise until all seven notches have engaged.
8. Install the fuel tank.
9. If removed, connect the fuel line quick-connect fitting at the fuel rail.
10. Connect the negative battery cable.
11. Start the engine and check for leaks at all fuel system connections.

FUEL TANK

DRAINING

2010 Models

⁂ CAUTION

The fuel system may be under constant fuel pressure even with the engine off. This pressure must be released before servicing fuel tank.

Two different procedures may be used to drain fuel tank: through the fuel fill fitting on tank, or using a diagnostic scan tool.

1. Release fuel system pressure.
2. Raise vehicle.
3. Thoroughly clean area around fuel fill fitting and rubber fuel fill hose at rear of fuel tank.
4. Loosen clamp at tank fitting and disconnect rubber fuel fill hose at fuel tank fitting.
5. Position a drain hose into fitting. Using an approved gasoline draining station, drain fuel from tank.

2011 Models

Conventional Procedure

See Figure 314.

⁂ CAUTION

The fuel system is under constant high pressure even with engine off. Until the fuel pressure has been properly released from the system, do not attempt to open the fuel system. Do not smoke or use open flames/sparks when servicing the fuel system. Wear protective clothing and eye protection. Make sure the area in which the vehicle is being serviced is in a well ventilated area and free of flames/sparks. Failure to comply may result in serious or fatal injury.

⁂ CAUTION

No sparks, open flames or smoking. Risk of poisoning from inhaling and swallowing fuel. Pour fuel only into appropriately marked OSHA approved containers. Wear protective clothing. Risk of injury to eyes and skin from contact with fuel.

➡Due to a one-way check valve installed into the fuel fill fitting at the tank, the tank cannot be drained at the fuel fill cap.

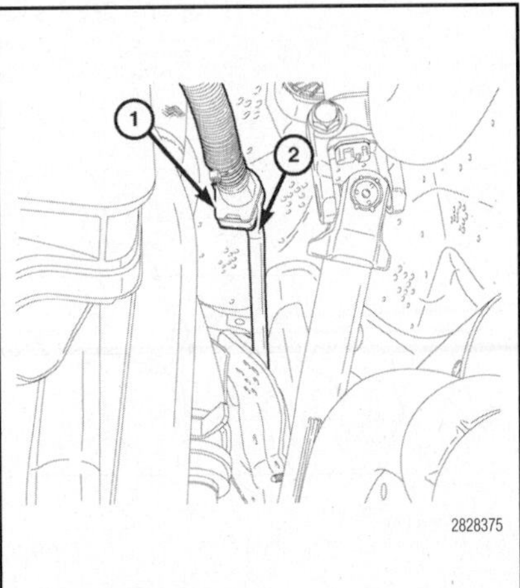

Fig. 314 Fuel supply line (1) and quick connect fitting (2)

1. Perform the fuel system pressure release procedure.
2. Disconnect the fuel supply line at the quick-connect fitting near the cowl.
3. Attach a ⅜ inch hose to the fuel supply line and attach the opposite end of this hose to the Fuel Chief Gas Caddy 320-FC-P30-A or an OSHA approved gas caddy.

➡Activation of the fuel pump module may time out and need to be restarted several times to completely drain the fuel tank.

4. Using a diagnostic scan tool, activate the fuel pump module until the fuel tank has been evacuated.

Alternative Procedure

➡If the electric fuel pump is not operating, the fuel tank must be removed and drained through the fuel pump module opening of the fuel tank.

1. Disconnect and isolate the negative battery cable.
2. Raise and support the vehicle.
3. Remove the fuel tank.

WARNING

Do not allow the float arm of the fuel pump module to come in contact with any part of the fuel tank during removal or installation, damage to the float arm and fuel level sending card may result.

4. Disconnect the fuel pump module electrical connector.
5. Remove the fuel pump module.
6. Position a ⅜ inch hose into the fuel pump module opening of the fuel tank.
7. Attach the opposite end of this hose to the Fuel Chief Gas Caddy 320-FC-P30-A or an OSHA approved gas caddy.
8. Using the gas caddy, evacuate the fuel tank.

REMOVAL & INSTALLATION

2010 Models

See Figure 315.

1. Release fuel system pressure.
2. Drain fuel tank.
3. Loosen clamp and disconnect rubber fill hose at tank fitting.
4. At rear of tank, disconnect fuel pump module electrical jumper connector from body connector.
5. At rear of tank, disconnect EVAP lines.
6. At front of tank, disconnect fuel and EVAP lines.

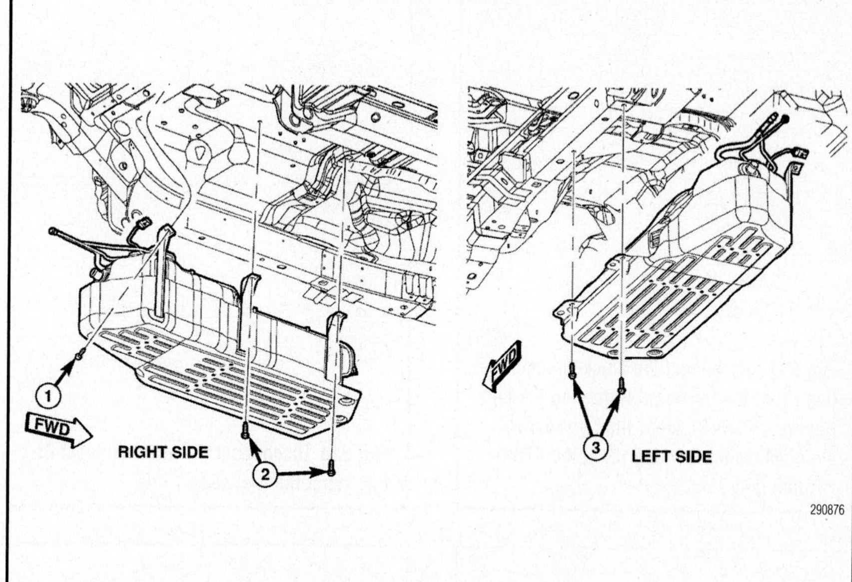

Fig. 315 Remove bolts (1, 2) at right side of fuel tank, and bolts (3) at left side of fuel tank

7. Support tank with a hydraulic jack.
8. Remove bolts at right side of fuel tank.
9. Remove bolts at left side of fuel tank.
10. Lower tank for removal.
11. If fuel tank is to be replaced, remove fuel pump module from tank.

To install:

12. If fuel tank is to be replaced, install fuel pump module into tank.
13. Position fuel tank to hydraulic jack.
14. Raise tank until positioned to body.
15. Install and tighten bolts.
16. Remove hydraulic jack.
17. Connect EVAP, ORVR, fuel and NVLD lines at front and rear of tank.
18. Connect fuel pump module electrical jumper connector to body connector.
19. Connect rubber fill hose to tank fitting and tighten clamp.
20. Lower vehicle.
21. Fill fuel tank with fuel.
22. Start engine and check for fuel leaks near top of module.

2011 Models

See Figures 316 through 322.

1. Perform the fuel system pressure release procedure.
2. Drain the fuel tank.
3. Disconnect and isolate the negative battery cable.
4. Raise and support the vehicle.
5. Loosen the filler hose clamps and remove the filler hose from the fuel tank.
6. Disconnect the quick-connect fitting at the EVAP purge line.
7. Remove the muffler.
8. Disconnect the quick-connect fitting at the On-Board Refueling Vapor Recovery (ORVR) vapor line.
9. Disconnect the quick-connect fitting at the ORVR vacuum line.
10. Remove the propeller shaft assembly.
11. Disconnect the fuel pump module electrical connector located on the rear crossmember.
12. Disconnect the electrical connector from the retaining tab on the rear crossmember and position the connector aside.
13. If equipped, remove the left side body skid plate retainers and remove the skid plate.
14. Disconnect the quick-connect fitting at the fuel supply line.
15. Using a suitable hydraulic jack and a fuel tank adapter, support the fuel tank.

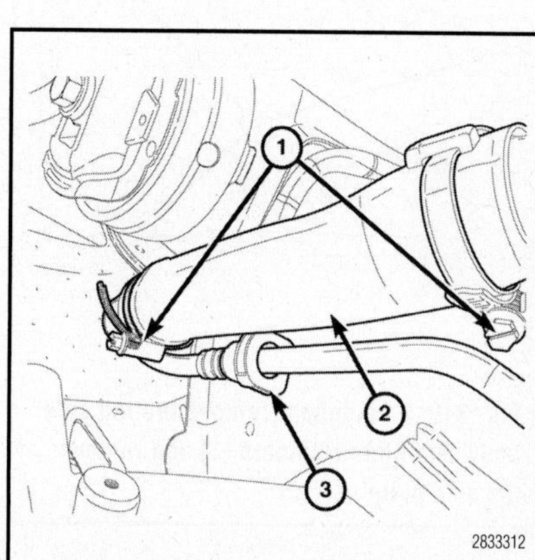

Fig. 316 Loosen the filler hose clamps (1) and remove the filler hose (2) from the fuel tank; disconnect the quick-connect fitting (3) at the EVAP purge line

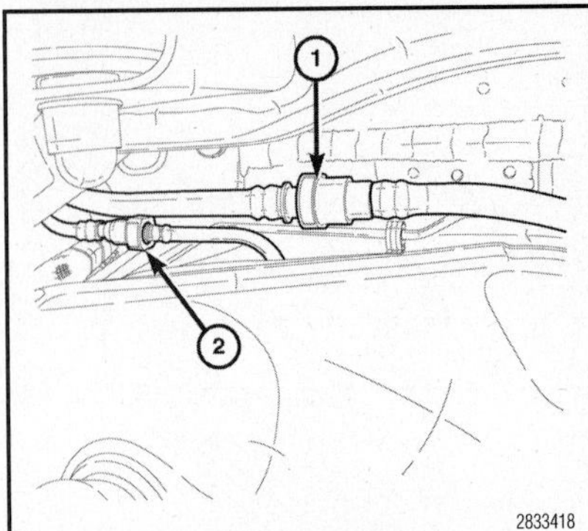

Fig. 317 Disconnect the quick-connect fitting (1) at the On-Board Refueling Vapor Recovery (ORVR) vapor line; disconnect the quick-connect fitting (2) at the ORVR vacuum line

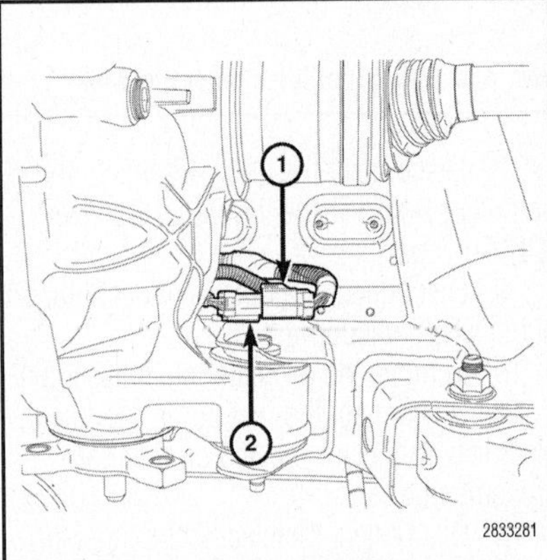

Fig. 318 Disconnect the fuel pump module electrical connector (1) and the electrical connector (2) from the retaining tab

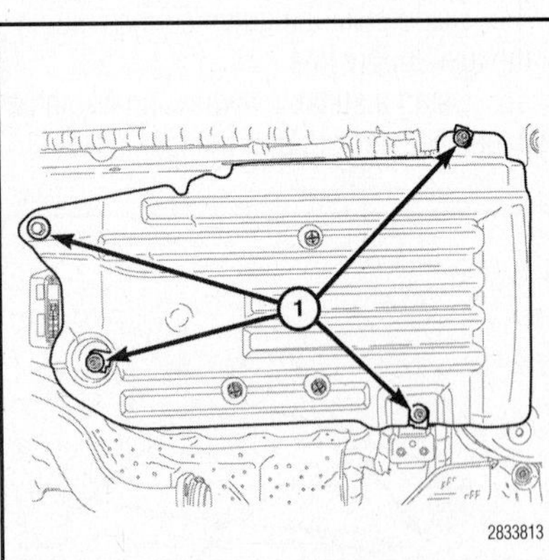

Fig. 319 If equipped, remove the left side body skid plate retainers (1) and remove the skid plate

➡If equipped with skid plates, remove the skid plates, fuel tank support straps and fuel tank as an assembly.

16. Remove the fuel tank support strap retaining bolts.

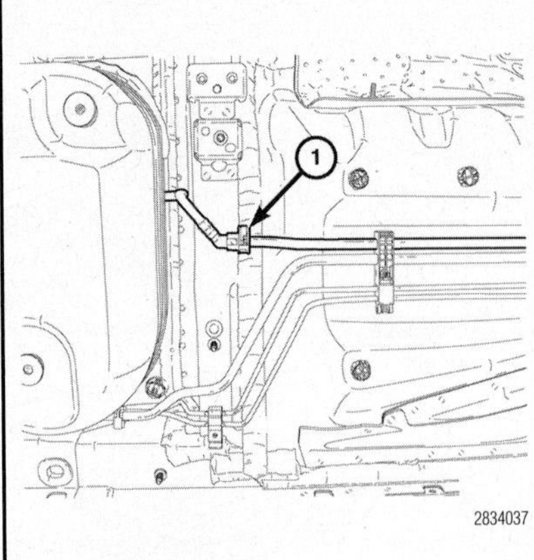

Fig. 320 Disconnect the quick-connect fitting (1) at the fuel supply line

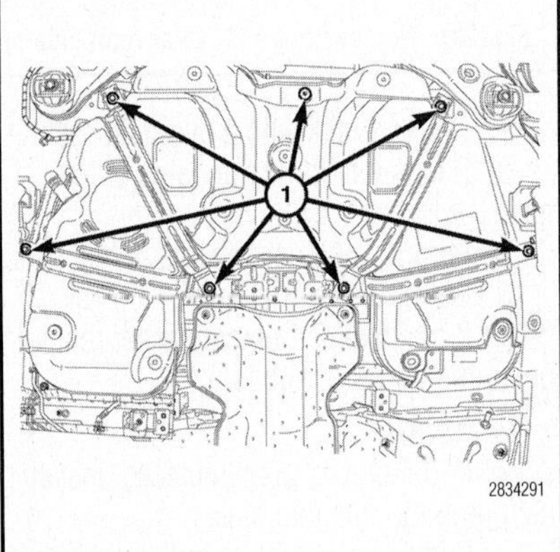

Fig. 321 Remove the fuel tank support strap retaining bolts (1)

17. Using the hydraulic jack, lower the fuel tank, support straps and if equipped, skid plates as an assembly and remove from the vehicle.
18. If replacing the fuel tank, remove the heat shield push pin retainers and remove the heat shield.
19. If replacing the fuel tank, remove the main fuel pump module from the fuel tank.
20. If replacing the fuel tank, remove the auxiliary fuel pump module from the fuel tank.

To install:

21. If removed, position the heat shield and install the push pin retainers.
22. If removed, install the auxiliary fuel pump module.
23. If removed, install the main fuel pump module.

➡If equipped with skid plates, install the skid plates, fuel tank, and support straps as an assembly.

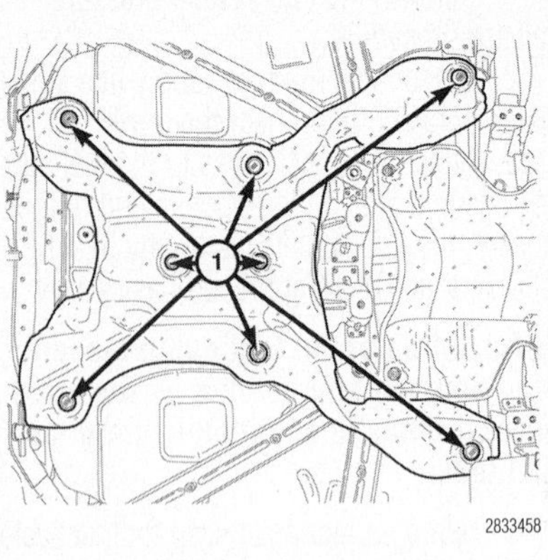

Fig. 322 If replacing the fuel tank, remove the heat shield push pin retainers (1) and remove the heat shield

24. Using a suitable hydraulic jack and a fuel tank adapter, position the fuel tank, support straps and if equipped, skid plates.
25. Install the fuel tank support strap retaining bolts and tighten to 50 ft. lbs. (68 Nm).
26. Remove the hydraulic jack and the fuel tank adapter.
27. Connect the fuel supply line quick-connect fitting.
28. If equipped, position the left side body skid plate and install retainers.
29. Connect the fuel pump module electrical connector retaining tab onto the rear crossmember.
30. Connect the fuel pump module electrical connector.
31. Install the propeller shaft assembly.
32. Connect the On-Board Refueling Vapor Recovery (ORVR) vacuum line quick-connect fitting.
33. Connect the ORVR vapor line quick-connect fitting.
34. Install the muffler.
35. Connect the EVAP purge line quick-connect fitting.
36. Position the fuel filler hose and install the hose clamps.
37. Lower the vehicle.
38. Connect the negative battery cable.
39. Fill the fuel tank.
40. Start the engine and check for leaks.

IDLE SPEED

ADJUSTMENT

Idle speed is controlled by the Powertrain Control Module (PCM). No adjustment is necessary or possible.

THROTTLE BODY

REMOVAL & INSTALLATION

3.6L Engine

See Figure 323.

**** WARNING**

Never have the ignition key in the ON position when checking the throttle body shaft for a binding condition. This may set DTC's.

1. Disconnect and isolate the negative battery cable.
2. Remove the engine cover.
3. Disconnect the electrical connector from the Inlet Air Temperature (IAT) sensor.
4. Loosen the clamp at the throttle body.
5. Loosen the clamp at the air cleaner body.
6. Remove the air inlet hose.
7. Disconnect the electrical connector from the Electronic Throttle Control (ETC) and disengage the ETC harness from the clip on the throttle body.
8. Remove four throttle body mounting bolts.
9. Remove the throttle body from the upper intake manifold.
10. Check the condition of the throttle body-to-intake manifold seal. The seal can be reused if not damaged.

To install:

11. Check the condition of the throttle body-to-intake manifold seal. The seal can be reused if not damaged.
12. Clean the mating surfaces of the throttle body and intake manifold.

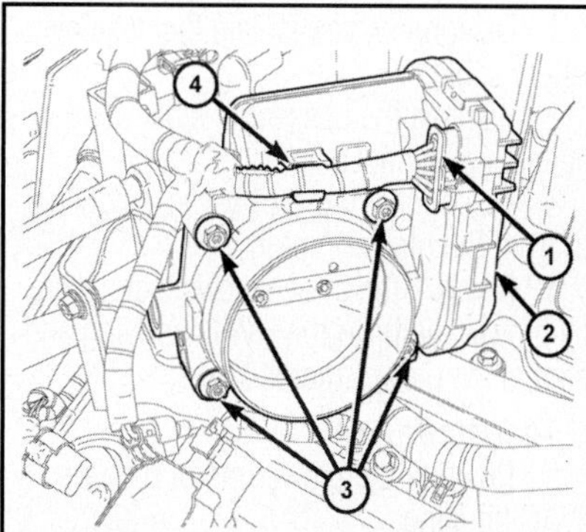

Fig. 323 Disconnect the electrical connector from the Electronic Throttle Control (ETC) and disengage the ETC harness from the clip on the throttle body

13. Position the throttle body to the intake manifold.
14. Install the throttle body mounting bolts and tighten in a criss-cross pattern sequence.
15. Connect the electrical connector to the Electronic Throttle Control (ETC) and secure the ETC harness to the clip on the throttle body.
16. Install the air inlet hose to the air cleaner body and the throttle body.
17. Connect the electrical connector to the Inlet Air Temperature (IAT) sensor.
18. Install the engine cover.
19. Connect the negative battery cable.

3.7L Engine

**** WARNING**

Using a diagnostic scan tool, record any previous DTC's (Diagnostic Trouble Codes).

**** WARNING**

Never have the ignition key in the ON position when checking the throttle body shaft for a binding condition. This may set DTC's.

➡A (factory adjusted) set screw is used to mechanically limit the position of the throttle body throttle plate. Never attempt to adjust the engine idle speed using this screw. All idle speed functions are controlled by the Powertrain Control Module (PCM).

1. Disconnect and isolate negative battery cable at battery.
2. Remove air intake tube at throttle body flange.
3. Disconnect throttle body electrical connector.
4. Disconnect necessary vacuum lines at throttle body.
5. Remove four throttle body mounting bolts.
6. Remove throttle body from intake manifold.
7. Check condition of old throttle body-to-intake manifold O-ring.

To install:

8. Check condition of throttle body-to-intake manifold O-ring. Replace as necessary.
9. Clean mating surfaces of throttle body and intake manifold.
10. Install O-ring between throttle body and intake manifold.
11. Position throttle body to intake manifold.
12. Install all throttle body mounting bolts finger tight.

**** WARNING**

The throttle body mounting bolts MUST be tightened to specifications. Over tightening can cause damage to the throttle body or the intake manifold.

13. Tighten mounting bolts to 65 inch lbs. (8 Nm) in a criss-cross pattern sequence.
14. Install electrical connector.
15. Install necessary vacuum lines.
16. Install air cleaner duct at throttle body.
17. Connect negative battery cable.
18. Using the diagnostic scan tool, erase all previous DTC's and perform the ETC Relearn function.

5.7L Engine

See Figures 324 and 325.

1. Perform the fuel pressure release procedure.
2. Disconnect the negative battery cable.
3. Remove the oil fill cap.
4. Remove the engine cover.
5. Disconnect the electrical connector at the Intake Air Temperature (IAT) sensor.
6. Loosen the hose clamp at the air cleaner housing.
7. Remove the resonator retaining bolt.
8. Loosen the hose clamp at the throttle body and remove the resonator.
9. Disconnect the electrical connector at the throttle body.
10. Remove the four throttle body retaining bolts.

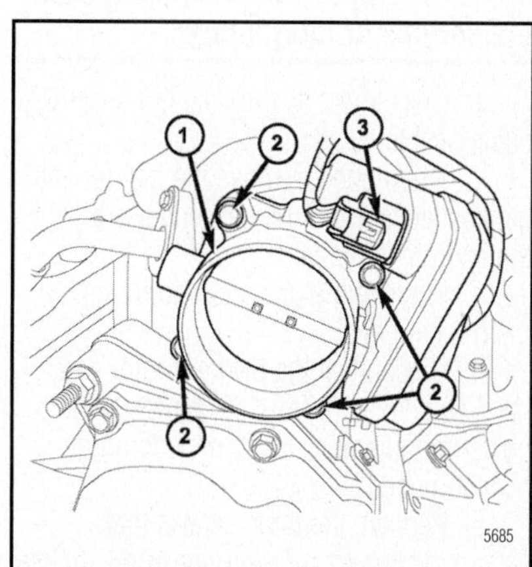

Fig. 324 Throttle body (1), retaining bolts (2), and electrical connector (3)

11. Remove the throttle body from the intake manifold.
12. Check the throttle body O-ring, replace if necessary.

To install:

13. Clean and check condition of the throttle body-to-intake manifold O-ring, replace if necessary.
14. Clean the mating surfaces of the throttle body and intake manifold.
15. Install the throttle body to intake manifold by positioning throttle body to manifold alignment pins.
16. Install the throttle body mounting bolts finger tight.

WARNING

The throttle body mounting bolts MUST be tightened to specifications.

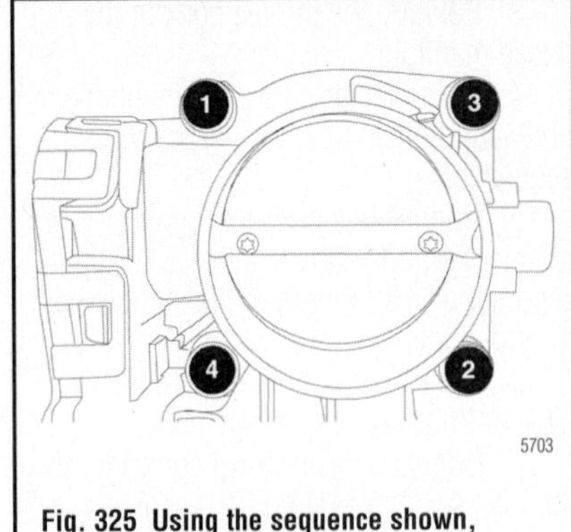

Fig. 325 Using the sequence shown, tighten the retaining bolts

Over tightening can cause damage to the throttle body or the intake manifold.

17. Using the sequence shown, tighten the retaining bolts to 53 inch lbs. (6 Nm).
18. Connect the electrical connector.
19. Position the resonator onto the throttle body and air cleaner housing.
20. Tighten the hose clamp at the throttle body.
21. Install the resonator retaining bolt.
22. Tighten the hose clamp at the air cleaner housing.
23. Connect the electrical connector at the Intake Air Temperature (IAT) sensor.
24. Install the engine cover.
25. Install the oil fill cap.
26. Connect the negative battery cable.
27. Using the diagnostic scan tool, perform the ETC Relearn function.

HEATING & AIR CONDITIONING SYSTEM

BLOWER MOTOR

REMOVAL & INSTALLATION

2010 Models

See Figure 326.

CAUTION

Disable the airbag system before attempting any steering wheel, steering column or instrument panel component diagnosis or service. Disconnect and isolate the negative battery (ground) cable, then wait two minutes for the airbag system capacitor to discharge before performing further diagnosis or service. This is the only sure way to disable the airbag system. Failure to follow these instructions may result in accidental airbag deployment and possible serious or fatal injury.

1. Disconnect and isolate the negative battery cable.
2. If equipped, remove the instrument panel silencer from the passenger side of the instrument panel.
3. Remove the glove box from the instrument panel.
4. Disconnect the blower motor wire harness connector from the blower motor power module or resistor, depending on how equipped.
5. Remove the three screws that secure the blower motor to the HVAC housing.
6. Remove the blower motor from the HVAC housing.

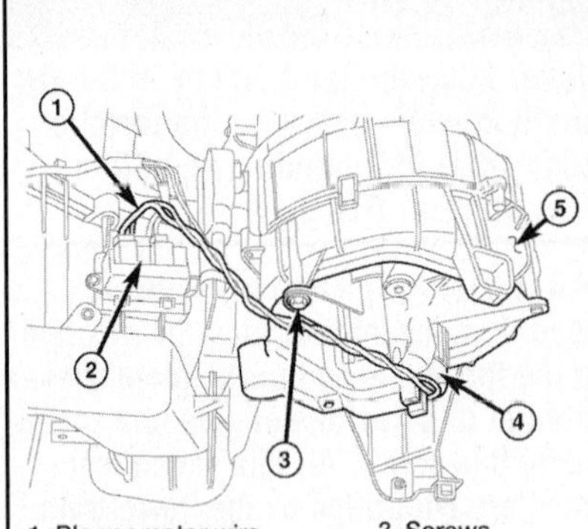

Fig. 326 Disconnect the blower motor wire harness connector from the blower motor power module or resistor

To install:

7. Position the blower motor into the HVAC housing.
8. Install the three screws that secure the blower motor to the HVAC housing.
9. Connect the wire harness connector to the blower motor power module or resistor, depending on how equipped.
10. Install the glove box into the instrument panel.
11. If equipped, install the instrument panel silencer onto the passenger side of the instrument panel.
12. Reconnect the negative battery cable.

2011 Models

See Figure 327.

CAUTION

Disable the airbag system before attempting any steering wheel, steering column or instrument panel component diagnosis or service. Disconnect and isolate the negative battery (ground) cable, then wait two minutes for the airbag system capacitor to discharge before performing further diagnosis or service. This is the only sure way to disable the airbag system. Failure to follow these instructions may result in accidental airbag deployment and possible serious or fatal injury.

1. Disconnect and isolate the negative battery cable.
2. Remove the passenger side instrument panel silencer.
3. Disconnect the wire harness connector from the blower motor.
4. Remove the three screws that secure the blower motor to the HVAC housing and remove the blower motor.

To install:

5. Position the blower motor into the HVAC housing.
6. Install the three screws that secure the blower motor to the HVAC housing.
7. Connect the wire harness connector to the blower motor.
8. Install the passenger side instrument panel silencer.
9. Reconnect the negative battery cable.

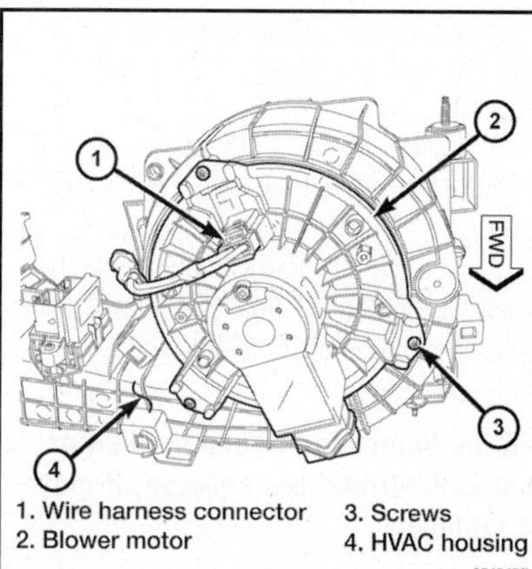

Fig. 327 Disconnect the wire harness connector from the blower motor

HEATER CORE

REMOVAL & INSTALLATION

2010 Models

See Figures 328 and 329.

⁂ CAUTION

Disable the airbag system before attempting any steering wheel, steering column or instrument panel component diagnosis or service. Disconnect and isolate the negative battery (ground) cable, then wait two minutes for the airbag system capacitor to discharge before performing further diagnosis or service. This is the only sure way to disable the airbag system. Failure to follow these instructions may result in accidental airbag deployment and possible serious or fatal injury.

➡Take the proper precautions to protect the front face of the instrument panel from cosmetic damage while performing this procedure.

1. Drain the engine cooling system.
2. Disconnect and isolate the negative battery cable.
3. If required, disconnect the heater hoses from the heater core tubes in the engine compartment.
4. Remove the instrument panel.
5. Remove the five screws that secure the heater core and tube cover to the HVAC housing.
6. Remove the heater core and tube cover from the HVAC housing.
7. If equipped with dual zone heating-A/C, remove the blend door actuator from the passenger side of the HVAC air distribution housing.
8. Remove the screw that secure the heater core tubes and retaining bracket to the HVAC housing.

➡Take proper precautions to protect the carpeting from engine coolant. Have absorbent toweling readily available to clean up any spills.

9. Remove the bolt that secures the heater tubes to the heater core.
10. Disconnect the heater core tubes from the heater core and remove and discard the O-ring seals.
11. Install plugs in, or tape over the opened heater core ports.
12. Carefully pull the heater core out of the HVAC air distribution housing.
13. If required, remove the heater core tubes from the vehicle.

To install:

14. Carefully install the heater core into the passenger side of the HVAC air distribution housing.
15. Remove the tape or plugs from the heater core ports.
16. If removed, position the heater core tubes into the vehicle.
17. Lubricate new rubber O-ring seals with clean engine coolant and install them onto the heater core tubes. Use only the specified O-ring as they are made of a special material for the engine cooling system.
18. Connect the heater core tubes to the heater core.
19. Install the bolt that secures the heater core tubes to the heater core. Tighten the bolt securely.
20. Install the screw that secures the heater core tube retaining bracket to the HVAC housing.
21. If equipped with dual zone heating-A/C, install the blend door actuator onto the passenger side of the HVAC air distribution housing.
22. Install the heater core and tube cover onto the HVAC housing.
23. Install the five screws that secure the heater core and tube cover to the HVAC housing.
24. Install the instrument panel.
25. If disconnected, connect the heater hoses to the heater core tubes in the engine compartment.
26. Connect the negative battery cable.
27. If the heater core is being replaced, flush the cooling system.
28. Refill the engine cooling system.

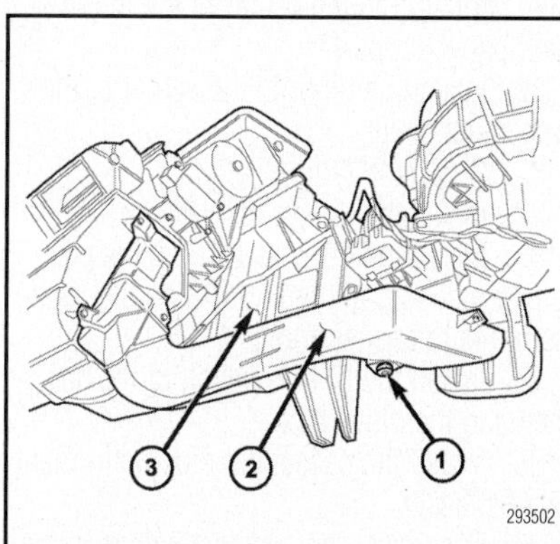

Fig. 328 Remove the five screws (1) that secure the heater core and tube cover (2) to the HVAC housing (3)

1. Blend door actuator
2. HVAC air distribution housing
3. Screw
4. Heater core tubes
5. Retaining bracket
6. HVAC housing
7. Bolt
8. Heater core

293666

Fig. 329 If equipped with dual zone heating-A/C, remove the blend door actuator from the passenger side of the HVAC air distribution housing

2011 Models

See Figures 330 through 333.

⁂ CAUTION

Disable the airbag system before attempting any steering wheel, steering column or instrument panel component diagnosis or service. Disconnect and isolate the negative battery (ground) cable, then wait two minutes for the airbag system capacitor to discharge before performing further diagnosis or service. This is the only sure way to disable the airbag system. Failure to follow these instructions may result in accidental airbag deployment and possible serious or fatal injury.

➡Take the proper precautions to protect the front face of the instrument panel from cosmetic damage while performing this procedure.

1. Disconnect and isolate the negative battery cable.
2. Drain the engine cooling system.
3. Remove the passenger side instrument panel silencer.
4. Remove the glove box, glove box shelf and the trim panel, located behind the glove box.
5. Remove the nut that secures the passenger side end of the HVAC housing to the instrument panel support.
6. Remove the front floor console.
7. Remove the radio.
8. Remove the bin from the center of the instrument panel.
9. Remove the four nuts that secure the HVAC housing to the center of the instrument panel support.

➡Illustration shown with instrument panel removed from view for clarity.

10. Remove the driver side instrument panel silencer.

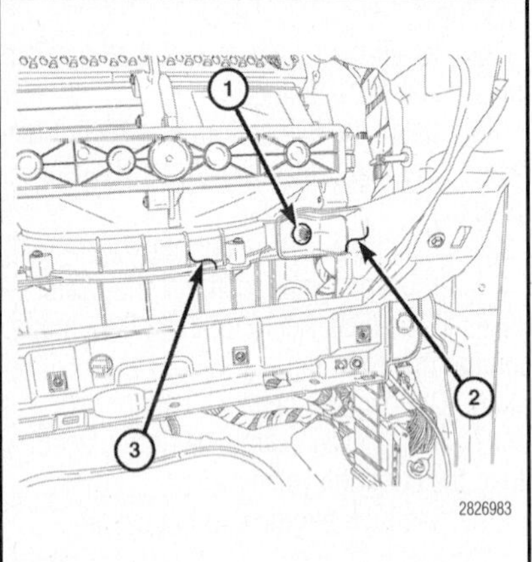

Fig. 330 Remove the nut (1) that secures the passenger side end of the HVAC housing (3) to the instrument panel support (2)

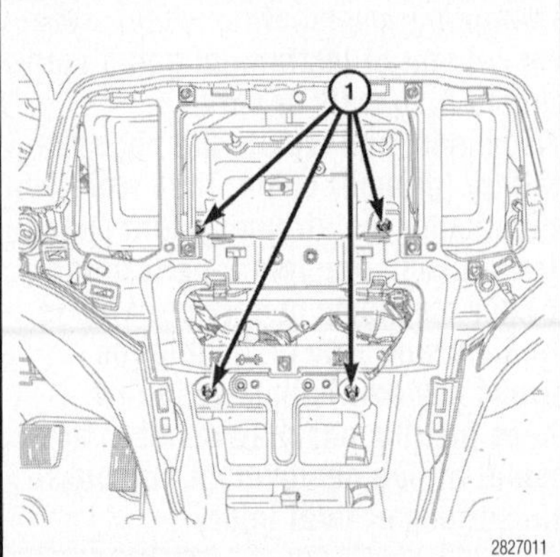

Fig. 331 Remove the four nuts (1) that secure the HVAC housing to the center of the instrument panel support

11. Remove the push pin that secures the left side floor ducts to the instrument panel.
12. Disconnect the left side floor ducts from the HVAC housing.

➡Removal of the instrument panel from the vehicle is not required to perform this procedure. It is only necessary to position the instrument panel so that removal of the heater core is possible.

13. Position the instrument panel to gain full access to the heater core located on the left side of the HVAC air distribution housing.

➡Take proper precautions to protect the carpeting from engine coolant. Have absorbent toweling readily available to clean up any spills.

14. Remove the two clamps that secure the heater tubes to the heater core.

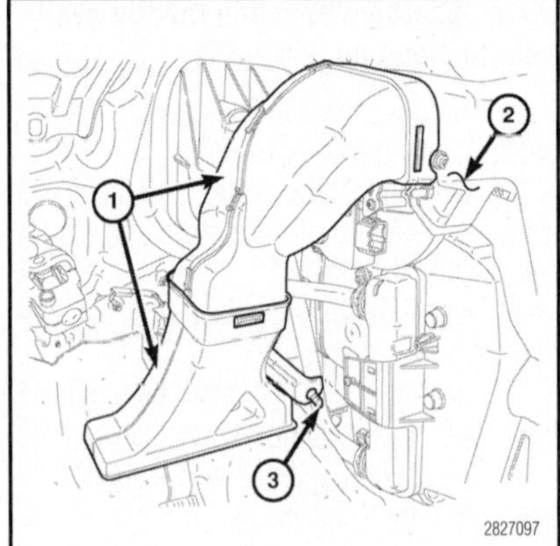

Fig. 332 Remove the push pin (3) that secures the left side floor ducts (1) to the instrument panel; disconnect the left side floor ducts from the HVAC housing (2)

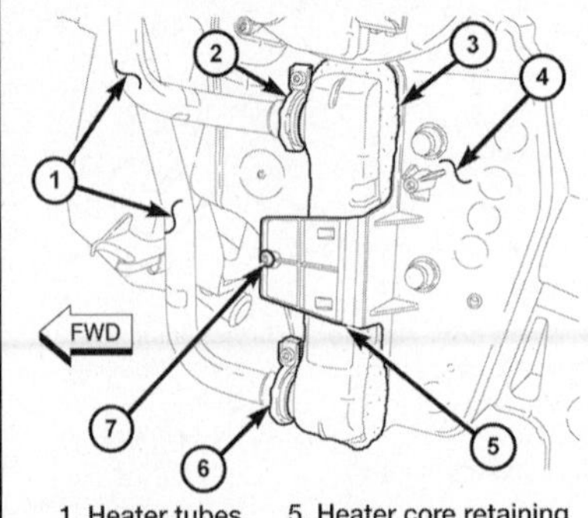

Fig. 333 Remove the two clamps that secure the heater tubes to the heater core

15. Disconnect the heater core tubes from the heater core and remove and discard the O-ring seals.
16. Install plugs in, or tape over the opened heater core tubes and heater core ports.
17. Remove the screw that secures the heater core retaining bracket to the air distribution housing and position the bracket out of the way.

➡If the foam seal around the heater core is deformed or damaged, it must be replaced.

18. Carefully pull the heater core out of the air distribution housing.

To install:

19. Carefully install the heater core into the left side of the HVAC air distribution housing.
20. Reposition the heater core retaining bracket and install the screw.
21. Remove the tape or plugs from the heater core tubes and heater core ports.
22. Lubricate new rubber O-ring seals with clean engine coolant and install them onto the heater core tubes. Use only the specified O-ring as they are made of a special material for the engine cooling system.
23. Connect the heater core tubes to the heater core.
24. Install the two clamps that secure the heater core tubes to the heater core.
25. Connect the left side floor ducts to the HVAC housing.
26. Reposition and install the instrument panel as necessary.
27. Install the push pin that secures the left side floor ducts to the instrument panel.
28. Install the driver side instrument panel silencer.
29. Install the four nuts that secure the HVAC housing to the center of the instrument panel support.
30. Install the bin into the center of the instrument panel.
31. Install the radio.
32. Install the floor console.
33. Install the nut that secures the passenger side end of the HVAC housing to the instrument panel support.
34. Install the IP trim panel, glove box shelf and the glove box.
35. Install the passenger side instrument panel silencer.
36. Reconnect the negative battery cable.
37. If the heater core is being replaced, flush the cooling system.
38. Refill the engine cooling system.

STEERING

POWER STEERING GEAR

REMOVAL & INSTALLATION

3.6L Engine

See Figures 334 through 338.

⁂ WARNING

The Steering Column Control Module (SCCM) is centered to the vehicles steering system. Failure to keep the system and steering column module centered and locked/inhibited from rotating can result in SCCM damage.

1. Place the front wheels in the straight ahead position with the steering wheel centered and locked with a steering wheel lock.
2. Drain or siphon the power steering system.

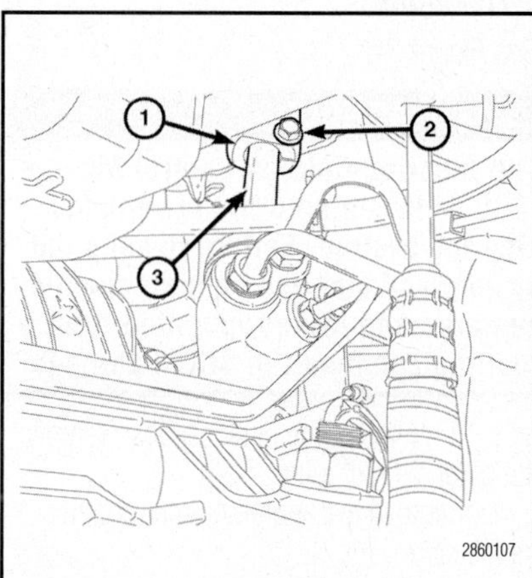

Fig. 334 Remove the steering shaft coupler pinch bolt (2) and disconnect the coupler (1) from the steering shaft (3)

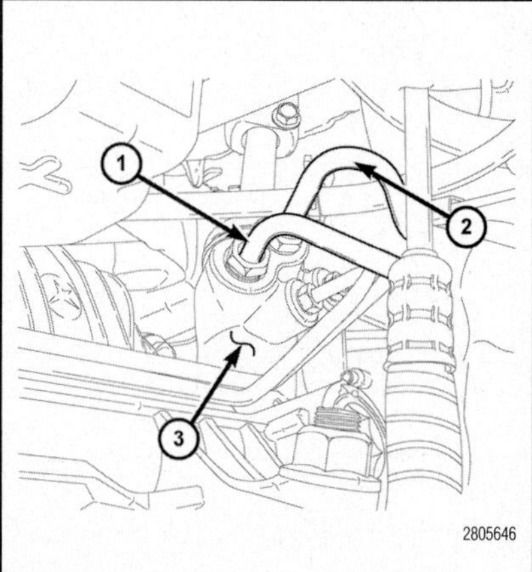

Fig. 335 Disconnect the pressure line (1), and the return line (2) at the gear (3)

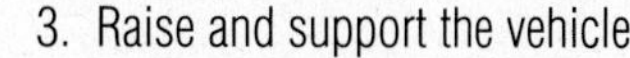

3. Raise and support the vehicle.
4. Remove the front skid plate.
5. Remove the steering shaft coupler pinch bolt and disconnect the coupler from the steering shaft.
6. Disconnect the pressure line, and the return line at the gear.
7. Remove the front tires and wheels.
8. Remove the RH shock.
9. Remove the outer tie rod ends.
10. Remove the steering gear retaining nuts/bolts.
11. Lift and rotate the steering gear so that the steering shaft is forward to clear the oil pan when removing the steering gear through the RH wheel area.
12. Lift and rotate the steering gear as necessary to remove from behind the knuckle/rotor assembly of the RH wheel area.

To install:

13. Lift and rotate the steering gear as necessary to install from behind the knuckle/rotor assembly of the RH wheel area.

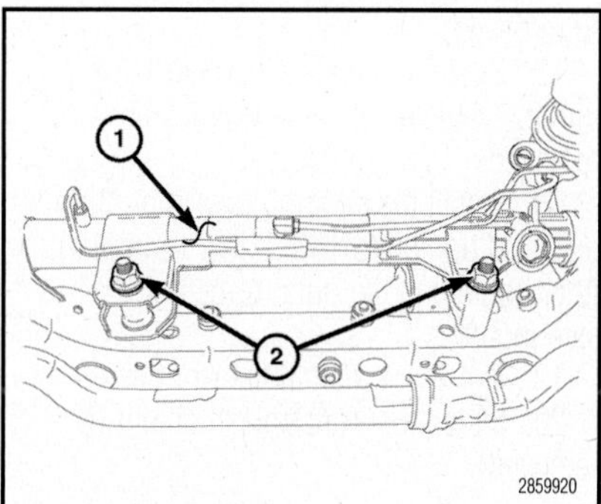

Fig. 336 Remove the steering gear (1) retaining nuts/bolts (2)

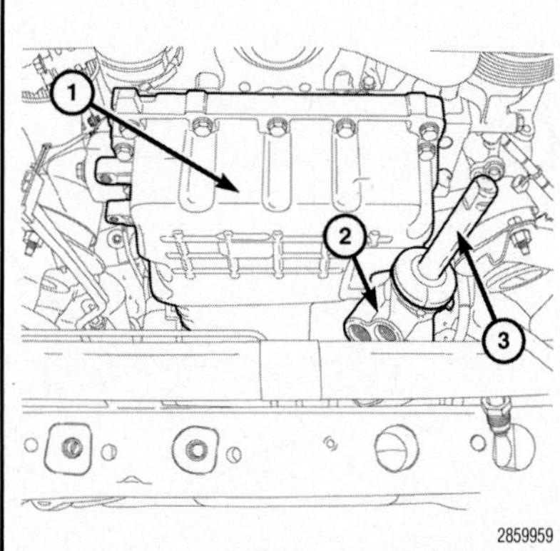

Fig. 337 Lift and rotate the steering gear (2) so that the steering shaft (3) is forward to clear the oil pan (1)

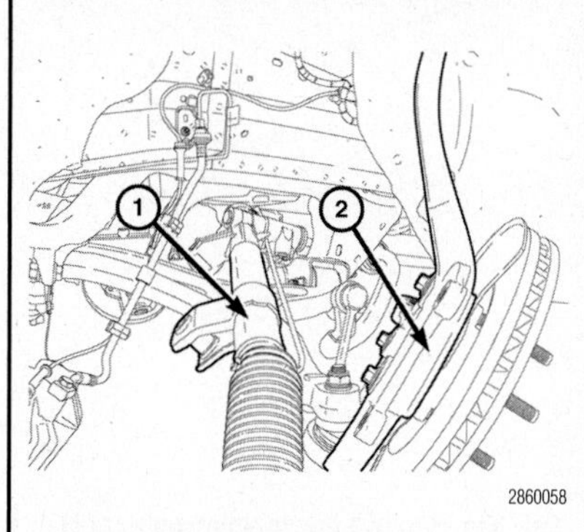

Fig. 338 Lift and rotate the steering gear (1) as necessary to remove from behind the knuckle/rotor assembly (2) of the RH wheel area

14. Rotate the steering gear into position, install the steering gear retaining nuts/bolts and tighten to 180 ft. lbs. (244 Nm).
15. Install the outer tie rod ends.
16. Install the RH shock.
17. Connect the pressure line and the return line at the gear and tighten to 21 ft. lbs. (28 Nm).

⁂ WARNING

The steering gear must be centered prior to installing the coupler to prevent clockspring damage.

18. Connect the steering shaft coupler to the steering shaft, install a new coupler pinch bolt and tighten to 36 ft. lbs. (49 Nm).
19. Install the front skid plate.
20. Install the wheels and tires.
21. Remove the supports and lower the vehicle.
22. Remove the steering wheel lock.
23. Fill the power steering pump.
24. Set the toe-in.

3.7L Engine

See Figures 339 through 341.

⁂ WARNING

Steering column module is centered to the vehicles steering system. Failure to keep the system and steering column module centered and locked/inhibited from rotating can result in steering column module damage.

1. Place the front wheels in the straight ahead position with the steering wheel centered and locked with a steering wheel lock.

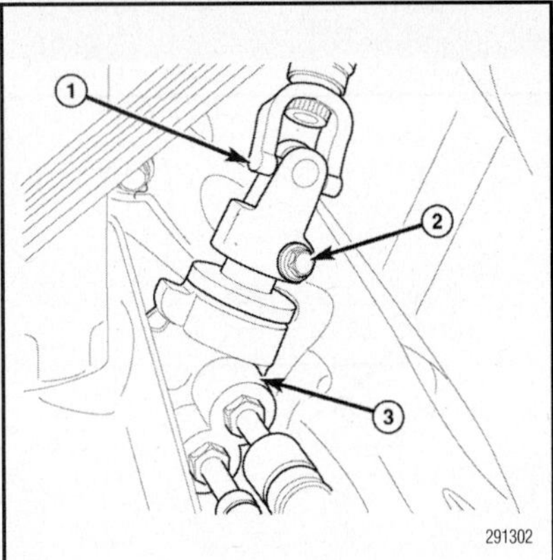

Fig. 339 Remove the column coupler (1) shaft bolt (2) and remove the shaft from the gear (3)

2. Drain or siphon the power steering system.
3. Remove the column coupler shaft bolt and remove the shaft from the gear.
4. Remove the pressure line, and the return line at the gear.
5. Raise and support the vehicle.
6. Remove the front tires.
7. Loosen the tie rod end jam nuts.
8. Remove the oil drip tray, if equipped.
9. Remove the outer tie rod end nut and separate the tie rod from the knuckle using Ball Joint Remover.
10. If equipped, remove the front skid plate.
11. Remove the front splash shield (if equipped).
12. 4x4 ONLY, remove the front axle.
13. Remove the two steering gear mounting bolts.

➡The tie rods would move to the right when turning the steering gear to the left.

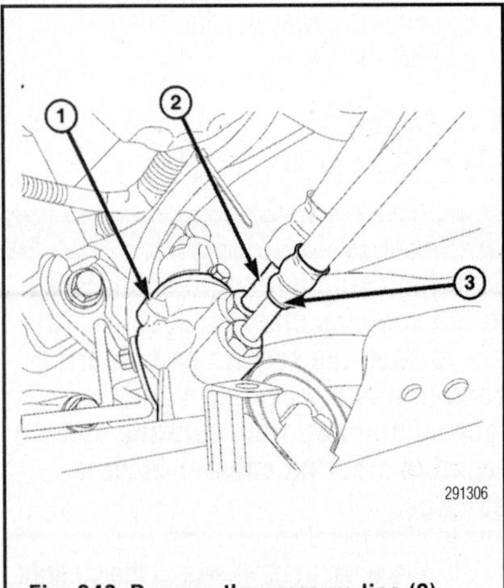

Fig. 340 Remove the pressure line (2), and the return line (3) at the gear (1)

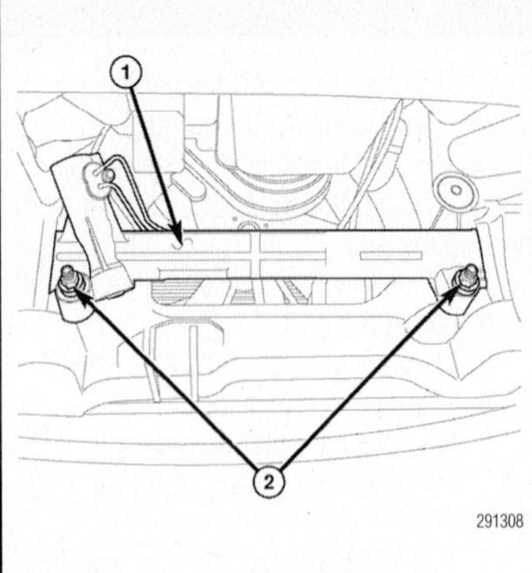

Fig. 341 Remove the two steering gear (1) mounting bolts (2)

14. Move the steering gear to the right side of the vehicle, then turn the steering gear to the full left position to allow clearance from the control arms and remove the gear by lowering the left side first.
15. Remove the outer tie rod ends from the steering gear (if needed).

To install:

16. Install the outer tie rod ends. (if removed).
17. Position the steering gear back into the vehicle the same way it was removed.
18. Install the steering gear mounting nuts and tighten to 180 ft. lbs. (244 Nm). After tightening the nuts, re-center the steering gear.
19. 4x4 ONLY, install the front axle.
20. Install the front splash shield (if removed).
21. If equipped, install the front skid plate.
22. Install the oil filter drip tray.
23. Install the outer tie rod ends to the knuckles and tighten the tie rod end nuts to 70 ft. lbs. (95 Nm).
24. Install the wheel and tire assembly.
25. Remove the support and lower the vehicle.
26. Install the pressure and return hoses to the steering gear and tighten to 21 ft. lbs. (28 Nm).

✻✻ WARNING

The steering gear must be centered prior to installing the coupler to prevent clockspring damage.

27. Install the column coupler shaft into the lower coupling, install a new bolt, and tighten to 36 ft. lbs. (49 Nm).
28. Remove the steering wheel lock.
29. Fill the power steering pump.
30. Set the toe-in.

5.7L Engine

See Figure 342.

✻✻ WARNING

The Steering Column Control Module (SCCM) is centered to the vehicles steering system. Failure to keep the system and steering column module centered and locked/inhibited from rotating can result in SCCM damage.

1. If replacing the steering gear, remove the outer tie rod ends.
2. Remove the engine cradle (crossmember).

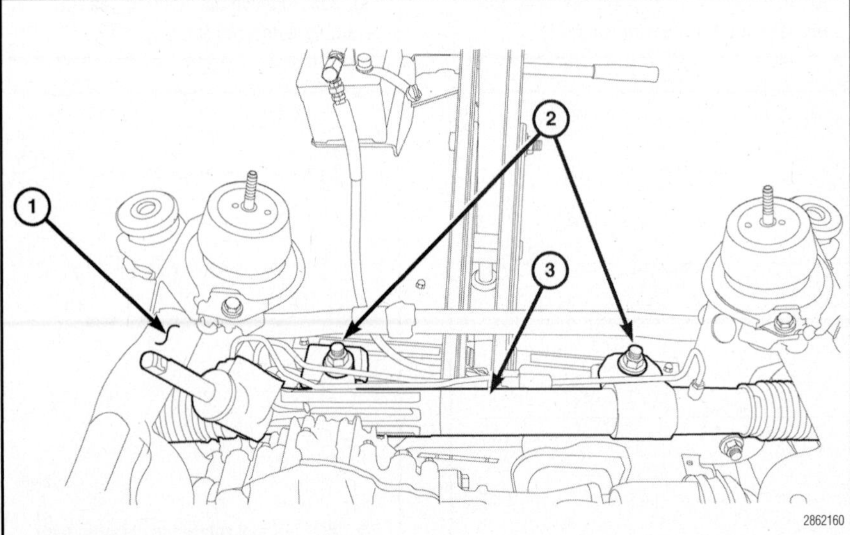

Fig. 342 Remove steering gear retaining nuts/bolts (2); showing steering gear (3), engine cradle (1)

3. Remove steering gear retaining nuts/bolts.

4. Rotate and shift the steering gear to the right enough to lift the LH side of the steering gear above the engine cradle, then remove the steering gear by moving to the right above the engine cradle.

To install:

5. Position the steering gear between the RH upper and lower parts of the cradle (crossmember) as far as necessary to lower the LH side of the steering gear into position and shift to the left.

6. Install the steering gear retaining bolts/nuts and tighten to 180 ft. lbs. (244 Nm).

7. Install the engine cradle.

8. If the outer tie rods were removed, install the tie rod ends.

9. Perform a front alignment.

POWER STEERING PUMP

REMOVAL & INSTALLATION

3.6L Engine

⁂ WARNING

The 3.6L in this vehicle is equipped with an Electro-Hydraulic Power Steering (EHPS) pump requiring a different fluid. Do not mix power steering fluid types. Damage may result to the power steering pump and system if any other fluid is used. The EHPS system uses fluid which meets material specification MS-11655 or equivalent. Do not overfill.

1. Siphon the power steering reservoir.

2. Disconnect and isolate the battery negative cable.

3. Disconnect the two EHPS pump electrical connectors and the wiring harness to bracket routing clip.

4. Disconnect the supply and return lines from the EHPS pump.

5. Remove the pressure and return line routing clip bolt from the pump bracket.

6. Raise and support the vehicle.

7. If equipped, remove the front skid plate.

8. Remove the pressure line retaining bolt and line from the EHPS pump.

9. Loosen the routing clip retaining bolt and position the pressure line aside for access to remove the pump.

10. Remove the three EHPS pump retaining bolts and remove the pump from the vehicle.

11. Remove and transfer any necessary components.

To install:

12. Position the EHPS pump, install the three retaining bolts and tighten to 40 ft. lbs. (54 Nm).

➡Make sure the O-ring is clean and seats properly.

13. Position the pressure line routing clip under the bolt, install the pressure line into the pump and tighten the routing clip retaining bolt to 106 inch lbs. (12 Nm).

14. Install the pressure line routing clip to pump bracket retaining bolt and tighten to 15 ft. lbs. (20 Nm).

15. If equipped, install the front skid plate.

16. Remove the supports and lower the vehicle.

17. Connect the supply and return lines to the EHPS pump.

18. Connect the two EHPS pump electrical connectors and the wiring harness to bracket routing clip.

19. Connect the battery negative cable.

20. Refill the power steering fluid and bleed the system.

3.7L Engine

1. Siphon power steering reservoir.

2. Remove the cooler return hose at the reservoir.

3. Disconnect the pressure hose nut at the pump.

4. Remove the pressure hose at the pump.

5. Remove the serpentine drive belt.

6. Remove the three pump mounting bolts.

7. Remove the pulley from the pump if necessary.

To install:

8. Install the pulley on the pump if removed.

9. Install the three pump mounting bolts and tighten to 21 ft. lbs. (28 Nm).

10. Install the drive belt.

11. Install the pressure hose on the pump and tighten the nut to 21 ft. lbs. (28 Nm).

12. Install the cooler return hose at the reservoir.

13. Add power steering fluid.

5.7L Engine

See Figure 343.

1. Siphon power steering reservoir.

2. Remove the air cleaner body.

3. Remove the serpentine drive belt.

4. Disconnect the supply hose and the pressure line at the power steering pump.

5. Using the holes in the pulley for access, remove the three pump mounting bolts.

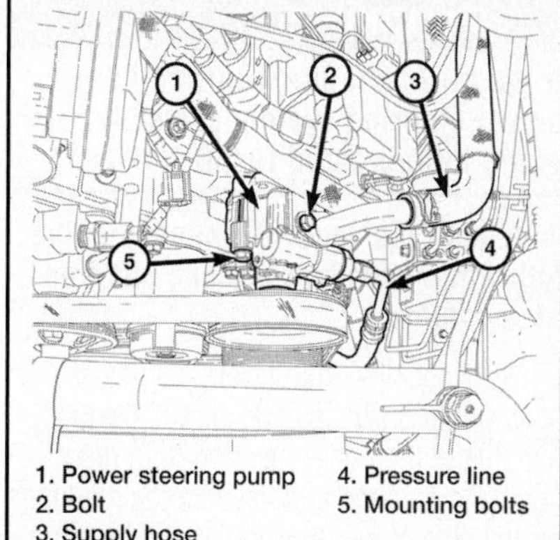

Fig. 343 Disconnect the supply hose and the pressure line at the power steering pump

6. Remove and transfer any necessary components.

To install:

7. Position the power steering pump and using the holes in the pulley for access, install 3 pump mounting bolts and tighten to 17 ft. lbs. (23 Nm).

8. Install the pressure line on the pump and tighten the nut to 21 ft. lbs. (28 Nm).

9. Install the supply hose on the pump.

10. Install the drive belt.

11. Install the air cleaner body, refer to section 9 - Engine/Air Intake System.

12. Fill and bleed the system with power steering fluid.

BLEEDING

2010 Models

⁂ CAUTION

Fluid level should be checked with the engine OFF to prevent personal injury from moving parts and to assure an accurate fluid level reading.

⁂ WARNING

This system requires the use of Mopar® Hydraulic System Power Steering Fluid (P/N 05142893AA) or equivalent, which meets Chrysler Material Standard MS-10838. Do NOT use Transmission Fluid (ATF+4) to fill or top-off the power steering system. MS-10838 is a special heavy-duty fluid and is required for this system. Damage may result to the power steering pump and system if another fluid is used. Do not over-fill the system.

WARNING

If the air is not purged from the power steering system correctly, pump failure could result.

➡Be sure the vacuum tool used in the following procedure is clean and free of any fluids.

1. Check the fluid level. The power steering fluid level can be viewed through the side of the power steering fluid reservoir. Compare the fluid level to the markings on the side of the reservoir. When the fluid is at normal ambient temperature, approximately 70°F to 80°F (21°C to 27°C), the fluid level should read between the MAX and MIN markings. When the fluid is hot, fluid level is allowed to read up to the MAX line.

WARNING

Do not fill fluid beyond the MAX mark. Check cap seal for damage and replace if needed.

2. Remove the cap from the fluid reservoir and fill the power steering fluid reservoir up to the MAX marking with Mopar® Hydraulic System Power Steering Fluid (P/N 05142893AA) or equivalent, which meets Chrysler Material Standard MS-10838.
3. Tightly insert Power Steering Cap Adapter into the mouth of the reservoir.

WARNING

Failure to use a vacuum pump reservoir may allow power steering fluid to be sucked into the hand vacuum pump.

Attach Hand Vacuum Pump, Special Tool or equivalent, with reservoir attached, to the Power Steering Cap Adapter.

WARNING

Do not run the vehicle while vacuum is applied to the power steering system. Damage to the power steering pump can occur.

➡When performing the following step make sure the vacuum level is maintained during the entire time period.

4. Using Hand Vacuum Pump, apply 20–25 inches HG (68–85 kPa) of vacuum to the system for a minimum of three minutes.
5. Slowly release the vacuum and remove the special tools.
6. Adjust the fluid level as necessary.
7. Repeat steps until the fluid no longer drops when vacuum is applied.
8. Start the engine and cycle the steering wheel lock-to-lock three times.

➡Do not hold the steering wheel at the stops.

9. Stop the engine and check for leaks at all connections.
10. Check for any signs of air in the reservoir and check the fluid level. If air is present, repeat the procedure as necessary.

2011 Models

See Figure 344.

CAUTION

Fluid level should be checked with the engine OFF to prevent personal injury from moving parts and to assure an accurate fluid level reading.

WARNING

There is an Electro-Hydraulic Power Steering (EHPS) pump on some vehicles requiring a different fluid. Do not mix power steering fluid types. Damage may result to the power steering pump and system if any other fluid is used. The mechanical power steering pump systems on this vehicle require the use of Power Steering Fluid +4, which meets material specification MS-9602 or equivalent. The EHPS system uses fluid which meets material specification MS-11655 or equivalent. Do not overfill.

WARNING

If the air is not purged from the power steering system correctly, pump failure could result.

➡Be sure the vacuum tool used in the following procedure is clean and free of any fluids.

1. Check the fluid level. The power steering fluid level can be viewed through the side of the power steering fluid reservoir. Compare the fluid level to the markings on the side of the reservoir. When the fluid is at normal ambient temperature, approximately 70°F to 80°F (21°C to 27°C), the fluid level should read between the MAX and MIN markings. When the fluid is hot, fluid level is allowed to read up to the MAX line.

WARNING

Do not fill fluid beyond the MAX mark. Check cap seal for damage and replace if needed.

2. Remove the cap from the fluid reservoir and fill the power steering fluid reservoir up to the MAX marking with the correct power steering fluid as follows:
   a. With a mechanical power steering pump—Mopar® Power Steering Fluid +4 or equivalent, which meets Chrysler Material Standard MS-9602.
   b. With an Electro-Hydraulic Power Steering (EHPS)—Mopar® Hydraulic Power Steering Fluid or equivalent, which meets Chrysler Material Standard MS-11655.
3. Tightly insert a P/S Cap Adaptor into the mouth of the reservoir.

WARNING

Failure to use a vacuum pump reservoir may allow power steering fluid to be sucked into the hand vacuum pump.

4. Attach Hand Vacuum Pump or equivalent, with reservoir attached, to the Power Steering Cap Adaptor.

WARNING

Do not run the vehicle while vacuum is applied to the power steering system. Damage to the power steering pump can occur.

➡When performing the following step make sure the vacuum level is maintained during the entire time period.

5. Using Hand Vacuum Pump, apply 20–25 inches HG (68–85 kPa) of vacuum

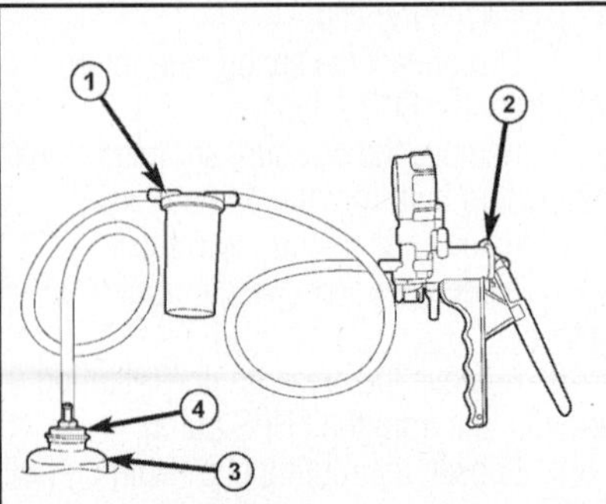

Fig. 344 Tightly insert a P/S Cap Adaptor into the mouth of the reservoir

to the system for a minimum of three minutes.

6. Slowly release the vacuum and remove the special tools.
7. Adjust the fluid level as necessary.
8. Repeat until the fluid no longer drops when vacuum is applied.
9. Start the engine and cycle the steering wheel lock-to-lock three times.

➡Do not hold the steering wheel at the stops.

10. Stop the engine and check for leaks at all connections.
11. Check for any signs of air in the reservoir and check the fluid level. If air is present, repeat the procedure as necessary.

FLUID FILL PROCEDURE

**** CAUTION**

Fluid level should be checked with the engine off to prevent personal injury from moving parts.

**** WARNING**

There is an Electro-Hydraulic Power Steering (EHPS) pump on some vehicles requiring a different fluid. Do not mix power steering fluid types. Damage may result to the power steering pump and system if any other fluid is used. The mechanical power steering pump systems on this vehicle require the use of Power Steering Fluid +4, which meets material specification MS-9602 or equivalent. The EHPS system uses fluid which meets material specification MS-11655 or equivalent. Do not overfill.

The power steering fluid level can be viewed through the reservoir with MAX and MIN level indicators on the side. Before opening power steering system, wipe the reservoir filler cap free of dirt and debris. When the fluid is at normal ambient temperature, approximately 70°F to 80°F (21°C to 27°C), the fluid level should between MAX and MIN. Use only proper fluids. Do not over fill.

SUSPENSION

FRONT SUSPENSION

Some models are equipped with air suspension.

**** CAUTION**

All pressurized air suspension components contain high pressure air (up to 220 psi). Use extreme caution when inspecting for leaks. Wear safety goggles and adequate protective clothing when inspecting or servicing the air suspension system. A sudden release of air under this amount of pressure can cause personal injury or death.

**** CAUTION**

Support the vehicle by supplemental means before performing any work on the air suspension system to prevent the vehicle from changing height. Before any given component is to be serviced it must be deflated. Servicing the air suspension system without supplemental support, or with pressure in the specific component, can cause personal injury or death.

The air suspension system automatically or manually (operator control) lowers and lifts the vehicle using rear air suspension springs (air bag) and front air suspension spring and shock assemblies which replace the standard springs in the rear, and standard spring/shock in the front. The air suspension system uses multiple integrated components in various areas of the vehicle to accomplish this.

CONTROL LINKS

REMOVAL & INSTALLATION

Stabilizer Bar Link

2010 Models

See Figure 345.

1. Raise and support the vehicle.
2. Remove the tire and wheel assembly.
3. Remove the upper link bolt/nut.
4. Remove the lower link bolt.
5. Remove the stabilizer link.

To install:

6. Install the stabilizer link to the vehicle.
7. Install the lower link bolt and tighten to 85 ft. lbs. (115 Nm)
8. Install the upper link bolt/nut and tighten to 80 ft. lbs. (108 Nm).

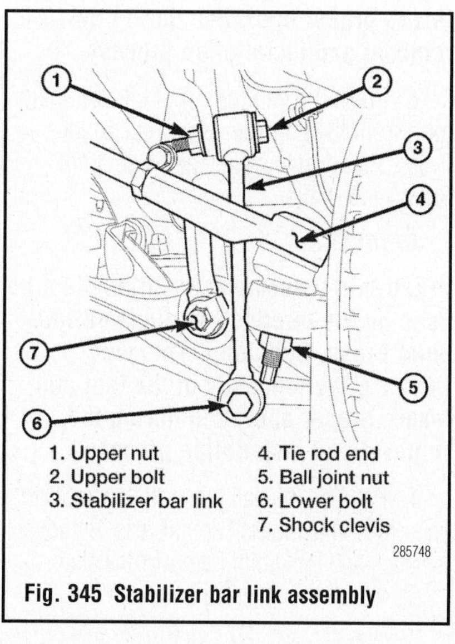

Fig. 345 Stabilizer bar link assembly

9. Install the tire and wheel assembly.
10. lower the vehicle

2011 Models

See Figure 346.

1. Raise and support the vehicle.
2. Remove the tire and wheel assembly.
3. Support the outside of the lower control arm with a suitable holding fixture, and raise to normal ride height.
4. Remove the stabilizer link lower nut.
5. Remove the stabilizer link upper nut.
6. Remove the stabilizer link.

To install:

7. Position the stabilizer link to the vehicle.
8. Install the stabilizer link upper nut and tighten to 90 ft. lbs. (122 Nm).
9. Install the stabilizer link lower nut and tighten to 90 ft. lbs. (122 Nm).

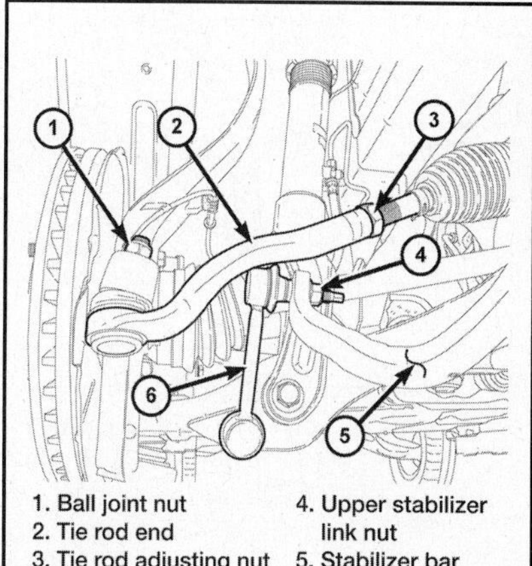

Fig. 346 Stabilizer bar link assembly

10. Install the tire and wheel assembly.
11. Remove the support and lower the vehicle.

LOWER BALL JOINT

REMOVAL & INSTALLATION

2010 Models

See Figures 347 and 348.

1. Remove the tire and wheel assembly.
2. Remove the brake caliper and rotor.
3. Disconnect the tie rod from the steering knuckle.
4. Separate the upper ball joint from the knuckle using special tool.
5. Separate the lower ball joint from the steering knuckle using special tool.
6. Remove the steering knuckle.
7. Remove the clevis bracket and move the halfshaft to the side and support the halfshaft out of the way—4X4 only.

➡Extreme pressure lubrication must be used on the threaded portions of the tool. This will increase the longevity of the tool and insure proper operation during the removal and installation process .

8. Press the ball joint from the lower control arm using special tools (PRESS), (Driver) and (Receiver).

To install:

9. Install the ball joint into the control arm and press in using special tools (press), (driver) and (receiver).
10. Stake the ball joint flange in four evenly spaced places around the ball joint flange, using a chisel and hammer.
11. Remove the support for the halfshaft and install into position, then install the clevis bracket. (4X4 only).
12. Install the steering knuckle.
13. Install the tie rod end into the steering knuckle.
14. Install and tighten the halfshaft nut to 185 ft. lbs. (251 Nm). (If Equipped).
15. Install the brake caliper and rotor.
16. Install the tire and wheel assembly.
17. Check the vehicle ride height.
18. Perform a wheel alignment.

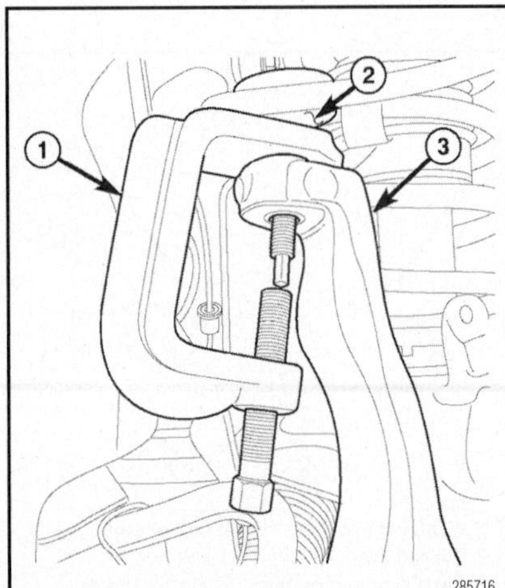

Fig. 347 Separate the lower ball joint (3) from the steering knuckle (1) using special tool (2)

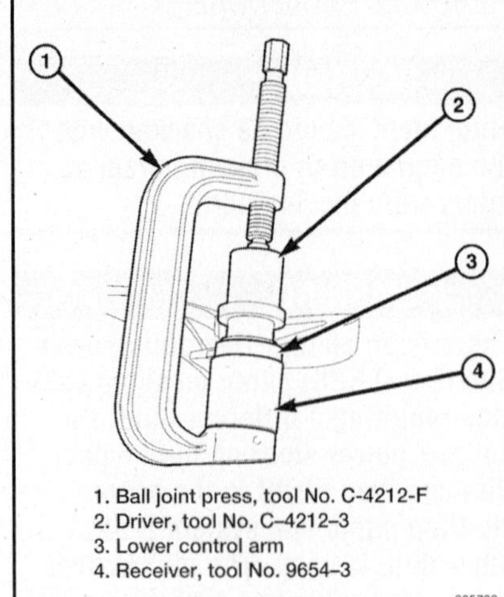

Fig. 348 Press the ball joint from the lower control arm using special tools (PRESS), (Driver) and (Receiver)

2011 Models

See Figure 349.

1. Raise and support the vehicle.
2. Remove the knuckle.

➡Extreme pressure lubrication must be used on the threaded portions of Ball Joint Press, Ball Joint. This will increase the longevity of the tool and insure proper operation during the removal and installation process.

3. Press the ball joint (not shown, inside tool) from the knuckle using Ball Joint Press, Remover/Installer, and Ball Joint Remover/Installer.

To install:

➡Extreme pressure lubrication must be used on the threaded portions of Ball Joint Press, Ball Joint. This will increase the longevity of the tool and insure proper operation during the removal and installation process.

4. Position the ball joint into the knuckle and press in using Ball Joint Press, Remover/Installer, and Ball Joint Remover/Installer.
5. Install the steering knuckle.

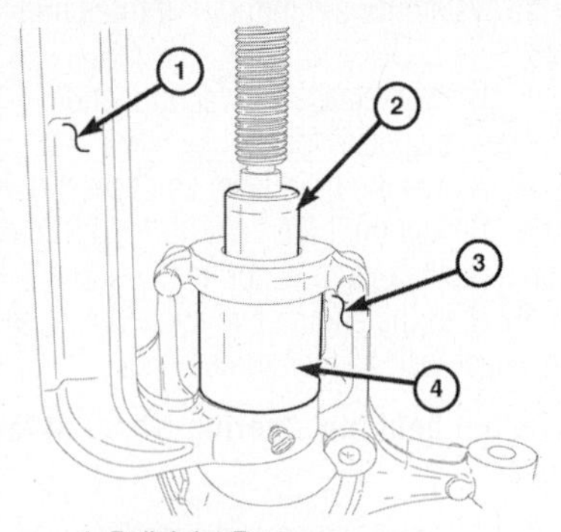

Fig. 349 Press the ball joint (not shown, inside tool) from the knuckle using Ball Joint Press, Remover/Installer, and Ball Joint Remover/Installer

LOWER CONTROL ARM

REMOVAL & INSTALLATION

2010 Models

See Figure 350.

1. Raise and support the vehicle.
2. Remove the tire and wheel assembly.
3. Remove the steering knuckle.
4. Remove the shock clevis bracket from the lower control arm.
5. Remove the stabilizer link at the lower control arm.
6. Remove the nut and bolt from the front of the lower control arm.
7. Remove the rear bolts and flag nuts from the lower control arm.
8. Remove the lower control arm from the vehicle.

To install:

9. Position the lower suspension arm into the cradle.
10. Install the rear bolts and flag nuts to secure the lower control arm to the frame. Tighten the bolts to 65 ft. lbs. (88 Nm).
11. Install the nut and bolt for the front of the lower control arm. Tighten to 125 ft. lbs. (169 Nm).

➡Orientation of the flag bolt is critical Flag and head of the bolt must be installed on the forward side of the lower control arm.

12. Install the lower clevis bolt at the lower control arm and tighten to 125 ft. lbs. (169 Nm).
13. Install the stabilizer link at the lower control arm and tighten to 85 ft. lbs. (115 Nm).

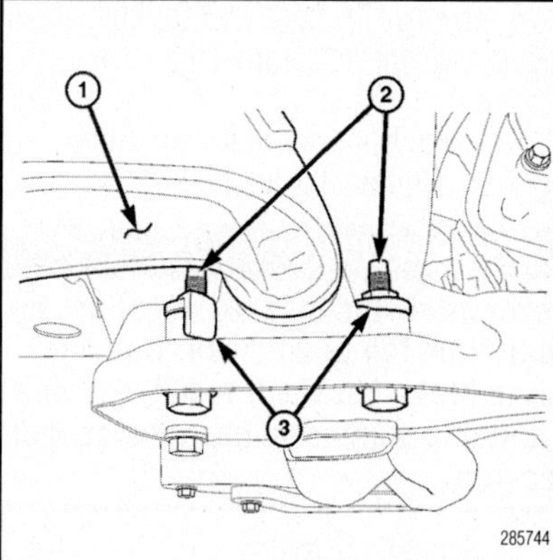

Fig. 350 Remove the rear bolts (2) and flag nuts (3) from the lower control arm (1)

14. Install the steering knuckle to the upper ball joint and tighten the nut to 70 ft. lbs. (95 Nm).
15. Install the tire and wheel assembly.
16. Lower the vehicle.
17. Perform wheel alignment.

2011 Models

See Figure 351.

⁂ CAUTION

All pressurized air suspension components contain high pressure air (up to 220 psi). Use extreme caution when inspecting for leaks. Wear safety goggles and adequate protective clothing when inspecting or servicing the air suspension system. A sudden release of air under this amount of pressure can cause personal injury or death.

⁂ CAUTION

Support the vehicle by supplemental means before performing any work on the air suspension system to prevent the vehicle from changing height. Before any given component is to be serviced it must be deflated. Servicing the air suspension system without supplemental support, or with pressure in the specific component, can cause personal injury or death.

1. Raise and support the vehicle.
2. Remove the tire and wheel assembly.
3. Remove the knuckle.
4. Remove the stabilizer link to lower control arm nut.

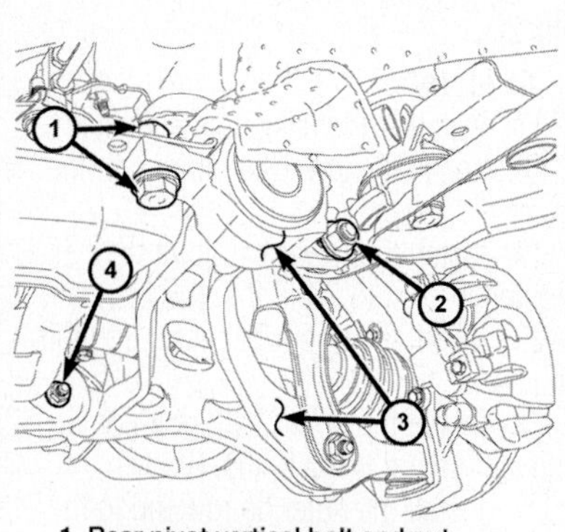

1. Rear pivot vertical bolt and nut
2. Rear pivot horizontal bolt and nut
3. Lower control arm
4. Front pivot bolt and nut

2772206

Fig. 351 Remove the lower control arm front pivot nut and bolt from the lower control arm

➡If equipped with four wheel drive, support the half shaft or remove with the lower control arm.

5. Remove the shock clevis bracket to lower control arm nut/bolt.
6. Remove the lower control arm front pivot nut and bolt from the lower control arm.
7. Remove the lower control arm rear pivot vertical bolt and nut and the lower control arm rear pivot horizontal bolt and nut from the lower control arm and remove from the vehicle.

To install:

➡If equipped with four wheel drive, position the half shaft if removed with the lower control arm.

8. Position the lower control arm to the cradle.
9. Install the lower control arm rear pivot vertical bolt and nut. Do not tighten.
10. Install the lower control arm front pivot nut and bolt. Do not tighten.
11. Install the shock clevis bracket to lower control arm nut/bolt. Do not tighten.
12. Install the stabilizer link to lower control arm nut. Do not tighten.
13. Install the knuckle.
14. Support the outside of the lower control arm with a suitable holding fixture, and raise to normal ride height.
15. Tighten the lower control arm rear pivot vertical bolt and nut to 162 ft. lbs. (220 Nm), and tighten the lower control arm rear pivot horizontal bolt and nut to 66 ft. lbs. (90 Nm).
16. Tighten the lower control arm front pivot nut and bolt to 89 ft. lbs. (120 Nm).
17. Tighten the shock clevis bracket to lower control arm nut/bolt to 173 ft. lbs. (235 Nm).
18. Tighten the stabilizer link to lower control arm nut to 90 ft. lbs. (122 Nm).
19. Install the tire and wheel assembly.
20. Remove the supports and lower the vehicle.
21. Perform wheel alignment.

STABILIZER BAR

REMOVAL & INSTALLATION

2010 Models

1. Raise and support the vehicle.
2. Remove the front splash shield.
3. Remove the stabilizer bar link upper nut and bolt.
4. Remove the two stabilizer bushing clamp bolts.
5. Remove the stabilizer bar.

To install:

6. Install the stabilizer bar to the vehicle.
7. Install the stabilizer bushing clamp and tighten the bolts to 95 ft. lbs. (129Nm).
8. Install the upper stabilizer link and tighten nut and bolt to 80 ft. lbs. (108 Nm).
9. Install the front splash shield.
10. Lower the vehicle.

2011 Models

➡A drive on hoist is recommended to keep suspension at normal ride height due to tension on the stabilizer bar.

1. Raise and support the vehicle.
2. Remove the front skid plate.
3. Remove the stabilizer bar link upper nut on both sides.
4. Remove the two stabilizer bushing clamp bolts on each side.
5. Remove the stabilizer bar.
6. Remove and transfer any necessary components.

To install:

7. Position the stabilizer bar to the vehicle.
8. Install the stabilizer bushing clamps and tighten the two bolts on each side to 90 ft. lbs. (122 Nm).
9. Position the stabilizer link to the stabilizer bar, install the nut and tighten to 90 ft. lbs. (122 Nm).

10. Install the front skid plate.
11. Remove the supports and lower the vehicle.

STEERING KNUCKLE

REMOVAL & INSTALLATION

2010 Models

See Figure 352.

1. Raise and support the vehicle.
2. Remove the tire and wheel assembly.

WARNING

Never allow the disc brake caliper to hang from the brake hose. Damage to the brake hose will result. Provide a suitable support to hang the caliper securely.

3. Remove the brake caliper.
4. Remove the caliper adapter.
5. Remove the O-ring and discard.
6. Remove disc brake rotor.
7. Remove the wheel speed sensor bolt and disconnect the wire from the retaining clips from the knuckle.
8. Remove the axle shaft nut. (if equipped with four wheel drive)
9. Remove the hub/bearing.
10. Remove the outer tie rod end retaining nut.
11. Separate the outer tie rod end from the steering knuckle.
12. Remove the lower ball joint nut.
13. Separate the lower ball joint from the knuckle.
14. Remove the upper ball joint nut.
15. Separate the upper ball joint from the knuckle.

1. Upper control arm
2. Upper ball joint
3. Steering knuckle
4. Upper ball joint nut

285718

Fig. 352 Separate the upper ball joint from the knuckle

16. Remove the knuckle from the vehicle.

To install:

17. Install the knuckle to the vehicle.
18. Install the lower ball joint into the knuckle.
19. Install the lower ball joint nut. Tighten the nut to 70 ft. lbs. (95 Nm).
20. Install the upper ball joint into the knuckle.
21. Install the upper ball joint nut. Tighten the nut to 70 ft. lbs. (95 Nm).
22. Install the outer tie rod end to the steering knuckle.
23. Install the hub/bearing. Tighten to 85 ft. lbs. (115 Nm).
24. Install the axle shaft nut. Tighten the nut to 96 ft. lbs. (135 Nm).(if equipped with four wheel drive).

➡Check the sensor wire routing (1). Be sure the wire is clear of all chassis components and is not twisted or kinked at any spot.

25. Install the wheel speed sensor into the hub and then install the mounting bolt and tighten to 106–124 inch lbs. (12–14 Nm).
26. Install the disc brake rotor.
27. Install the caliper adapter.
28. Install the tire and wheel assembly.
29. Perform wheel alignment.

2011 Models

See Figures 353 and 354.

1. Raise and support the vehicle.
2. Remove the tire and wheel assembly.
3. If equipped with four wheel drive, remove the half shaft nut.

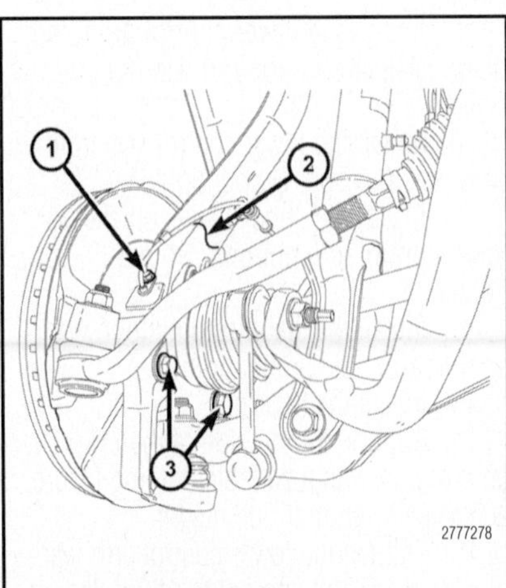

Fig. 353 Remove the speed sensor bolt (1), and remove the sensor from the knuckle (2); hub bolts (3)

4. Remove the speed sensor bolt, and remove the sensor from the knuckle.
5. Remove the speed sensor wiring retaining clip from the knuckle.

WARNING

Never allow the disc brake caliper to hang from the brake hose. Damage to the brake hose will result. Provide a suitable support to hang the caliper securely.

6. Remove the rotor.
7. Remove the outer tie rod end retaining nut.
8. Separate the outer tie rod end from the steering knuckle using Tie Rod Puller.
9. Support the outside of the lower control arm with a suitable holding fixture, and raise to normal ride height.
10. Remove the upper ball joint nut.
11. Separate the upper ball joint from the knuckle using Ball Joint Press.
12. If equipped with four wheel drive, tilt the knuckle out enough to disengage the half shaft from the hub/bearing, then pry the half shaft from the axle/axle tube with a pry bar and position aside for access to remove the lower ball joint nut.

➡Due to the taper of the lower ball joint, no special tool is needed to separate the knuckle from the control arm. When the nut is removed, the knuckle will pull away from the lower control arm.

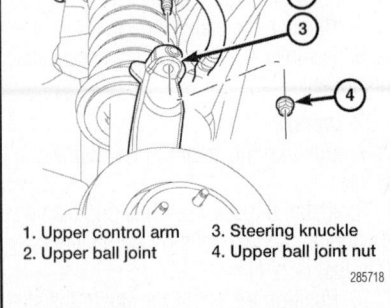

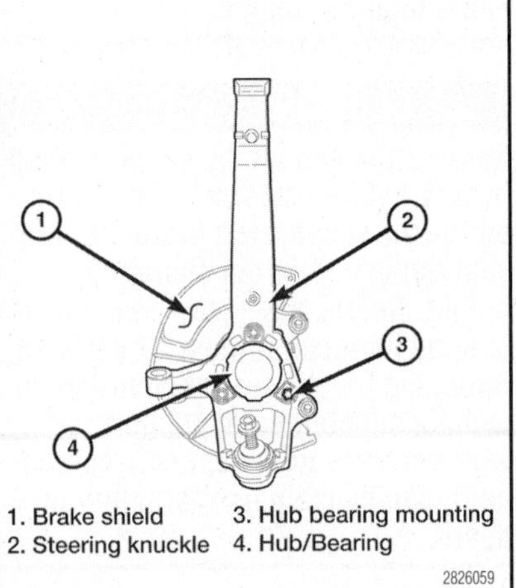

Fig. 354 If necessary, remove the 3 hub bearing mounting bolts from the back of the steering knuckle and remove the hub/bearing from the steering knuckle

13. While supporting the knuckle, remove the lower ball joint nut.

14. Remove the knuckle from the vehicle.

15. If necessary, remove the 3 hub bearing mounting bolts from the back of the steering knuckle and remove the hub/bearing from the steering knuckle.

16. If necessary, remove the brake shield from the knuckle.

To install:

17. Position the brake shield on the knuckle.

18. Position the hub/bearing on the knuckle, install the 3 hub bearing mounting bolts and tighten to 78 ft. lbs. (105 Nm).

19. Position the knuckle on the lower ball joint and install the lower ball joint nut and tighten to 170 ft. lbs. (230 Nm).

20. If equipped with four wheel drive, install half shaft in the axle using care not to damage the seals, and through the hub/bearing. Verify half shaft has engaged.

21. Support the outside of the lower control arm with a suitable holding fixture, and raise to position the upper ball joint into the knuckle.

22. With the holding fixture holding the suspension at normal ride height, install the upper ball joint nut and tighten to 70 ft. lbs. (95 Nm).

23. Position the outer tie rod end to the steering knuckle, install the nut and tighten to 70 ft. lbs. (95 Nm).

24. Install the brake rotor.

25. Route and attach speed sensor wiring to the knuckle.

26. Install the wheel speed sensor into the knuckle, install the mounting bolt and tighten to 95 inch lbs. (11 Nm).

27. If equipped with four wheel drive, install the half shaft nut and tighten to 229 ft. lbs. (310 Nm).

28. Install the tire and wheel assembly.

29. Remove the supports and lower the vehicle.

STRUT & SPRING ASSEMBLY

REMOVAL & INSTALLATION

2010 Models

Left Front

See Figures 355 and 356.

1. Remove the air box cover and air intake hose.

2. Remove the Power Distribution Center (PDC) bracket nuts.

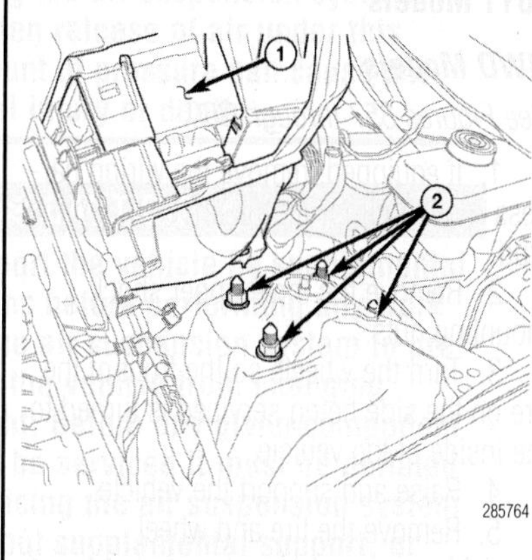

Fig. 355 Move the PDC (1) off to the side to access the four upper shock mount nuts (2)

3. Move the PDC off to the side to access the four upper shock mount nuts.

4. Remove the four upper shock mount nuts.

5. Raise and support the vehicle.

6. Remove the tire and wheel.

7. Remove the two brake caliper adapter bolts.

8. Support the brake caliper adaptor and caliper. Do not allow the caliper to hang by the brake hose.

9. Remove the disc brake rotor.

10. Remove the upper ball joint nut.

11. Separate the upper ball joint from the knuckle.

12. Remove the lower clevis bolt at the lower control arm.

13. Remove the lower stabilizer bolt at the lower control arm.

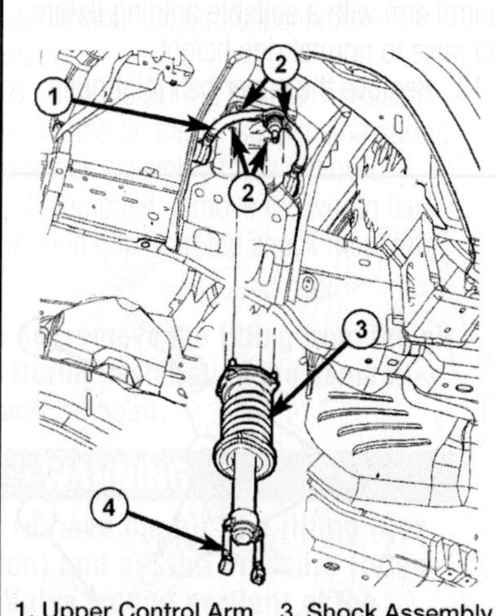

Fig. 356 Remove the shock from the vehicle

14. Remove the shock from the vehicle.

15. Remove the spring if necessary.

To install:

16. Install the clevis bracket to the shock and tighten to 90 ft. lbs. (122 Nm).

17. Install the shock assembly to the vehicle.

18. Install the four upper shock nuts. Tighten to 70 ft. lbs. (95 Nm).

19. Install the 3 PDC bracket nuts.

20. Raise the vehicle.

21. Install the lower stabilizer bolt at the lower control arm and tighten to 85 ft. lbs. (115 Nm).

22. Install the lower clevis bolt at the lower control arm and tighten to 125 ft. lbs. (169 Nm).

23. Install the upper ball joint into the knuckle and tighten the nut to 55 ft. lbs. (75 Nm).

24. Install the disc brake rotor.

25. Install the caliper adaptor mounting bolts to 130 ft. lbs. (176 Nm).

26. Install the tire and wheel assembly.

27. Lower the vehicle.

Right Front

1. Remove the air box cover and air intake hose.

2. Disconnect the cruise control servo electrical connector.

3. Remove the coolant reservoir mounting bolt and move the coolant reservoir off to the side.

4. Remove the four upper shock mounting nuts.

5. Raise and support the vehicle.

6. Remove the tire and wheel.

7. Remove the two brake caliper adapter bolts.

8. Support the brake caliper adaptor and caliper. Do not allow the caliper to hang by the brake hose.

9. Remove the disc brake rotor.

10. Remove the upper ball joint nut.

11. Separate the upper ball joint from the knuckle.

12. Remove the lower clevis bolt at the lower control arm.

13. Remove the lower stabilizer bolt at the lower control arm.

14. Remove the shock from the vehicle.

15. Remove the spring if necessary.

To install:

16. Install the clevis bracket to the shock and tighten to 90 ft. lbs. (122 Nm).

17. Install the shock assembly to the vehicle.

✻✻ WARNING

When removing an air line from a component and the air line is to be reused, do not remove the 90° fitting or the brass fitting from the air line. If either is removed, the air line must be replaced. New components have air line fittings attached; however if the original air line is used the original fitting must also be used. Do not remove protective caps or plugs from air lines or components until ready to install the air line to prevent moisture or dirt intrusion. All air line fittings must be hand started to avoid cross threading.

8. Position the half shaft and air suspension spring and shock assembly to the vehicle aligning the upper shock mounting studs into the body, and the halfshaft to the axle.
9. Install the half shaft.
10. Install the upper shock mounting nuts and tighten to 21 ft. lbs. (28 Nm).
11. If a new air suspension spring and shock assembly is used, remove the cap/fitting from the air line connection of the assembly.
12. Using the original fitting connect the air line to the air suspension spring and shock assembly.
13. If equipped, install the wiring harness routing clip on the shock mounting stud.
14. Install the tire and wheel.
15. Remove the support and lower the vehicle.
16. With a scan tool, using the routines under the Air Suspension Control Module (ASCM), perform the following:

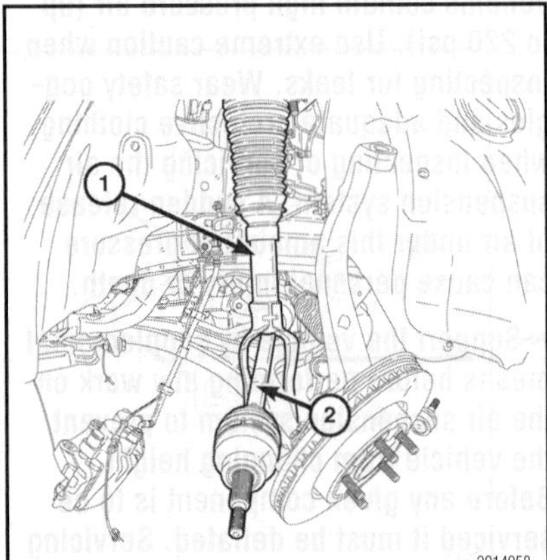

Fig. 362 Position the half shaft (2) and air suspension spring and shock assembly (1) to the vehicle

a. Fill Spring From Reservoir/Complete Fill (on the spring/shock replaced).
b. Run the Air Mass Calculation routine on the air suspension system.
c. If necessary, add to the system or deflate to atmosphere using the ASCM routines, then repeat the Air Mass Calculation routine again until system responds with Air Mass OK (188–216 bar-liters).
d. Enable the air suspension system.

17. Perform the ASCM Verification Test.

ASCM VERIFICATION TEST

1. Disconnect all jumper wires and reconnect all previously disconnected components and connectors.
2. With the scan tool, erase DTCs.
3. Make sure that all accessories are turned off and that the battery is fully charged.
4. Test drive the vehicle and verify proper operation.
5. With the scan tool, read DTCs in the ASCM.
6. If there aren't any DTCs present in the Air Suspension Control Module (ASCM), the repair is complete.

UPPER BALL JOINT

REMOVAL & INSTALLATION

2010 Models

1. Raise vehicle and support the axle.
2. Remove the tire and wheel.
3. Remove the upper ball joint retaining nut.
4. Separate the upper ball joint from the knuckle.
5. Move the knuckle out of the way to allow ball joint removal tool access.

➡When installing a new ball joint, Do not remove the rubber grease boot on the new ball joint during installation.

6. Remove the rubber grease boot from the ball joint in the control arm. This will allow better fit of the ball joint tool when removing.

➡Extreme pressure lubrication must be used on the threaded portions of the tool. This will increase the longevity of the tool and insure proper operation during the removal and installation process .

7. Press the ball joint from the upper control arm.

To install:

➡Do not remove the grease boot from the new ball joint. When installing the new ball joint the grease boot should not be removed.

➡Extreme pressure lubrication must be used on the threaded portions of the tool. This will increase the longevity of the tool and insure proper operation during the removal and installation process .

8. Install the ball joint into the upper control arm and press in using special tools press, driver and receiver.
9. Install the upper ball joint into the knuckle.
10. Install the upper ball joint retaining nut and tighten to 70 ft. lbs. (95 Nm).
11. Install the tire and wheel.
12. Remove the supports and lower the vehicle.
13. Perform a wheel alignment.

UPPER CONTROL ARM

REMOVAL & INSTALLATION

2011 Models

See Figures 363 through 367.

✻✻ CAUTION

All pressurized air suspension components contain high pressure air (up to 220 psi). Use extreme caution when inspecting for leaks. Wear safety goggles and adequate protective clothing when inspecting or servicing the air suspension system. A sudden release of air under this amount of pressure can cause personal injury or death.

✻✻ CAUTION

Support the vehicle by supplemental means before performing any work on the air suspension system to prevent the vehicle from changing height. Before any given component is to be serviced it must be deflated. Servicing the air suspension system without supplemental support, or with pressure in the specific component, can cause personal injury or death.

1. If equipped with air suspension (SER), with a scan tool, using the routines under the ASCM, perform the following:
a. Disable the air suspension system.

b. Run the Spring Deflate To Reservoir routine on the air suspension spring on the side where the upper control arm is to be removed.

2. Secure the steering wheel in the straight ahead position.

3. If equipped, remove the wiring harness routing clip from the shock mounting stud.

➡Loosen the shock retainer nuts only. The shock must be tilted for removal of the control arm bolts.

4. Loosen the three upper shock mounting nuts.

5. Remove the cowl panel cover, and the silencer.

6. For the left side only, remove the air cleaner housing as follows:

a. Remove the air cleaner.

b. Loosen the fresh air intake clamp and disconnect the hose from housing cover.

c. Disconnecting the PCV air return hose and the power steering hose routing clip (not shown) from the air cleaner body.

d. Disconnect the weatherstrip from the housing inlet and reposition.

e. Remove the pushpin and lift the housing from the body grommets to remove.

7. For the left side only, remove the steering intermediate shaft pinch bolt, disconnect the coupler and position aside for clearance.

8. For the right side only, remove the two nuts that secure the HVAC air inlet duct to the engine compartment side of the dash panel and remove the duct.

9. Raise and support the vehicle.

10. Remove the tire and wheel assembly.

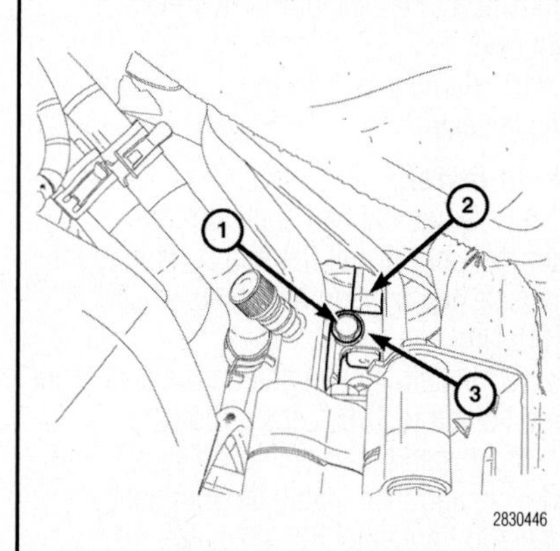

Fig. 364 For the left side only, remove the steering intermediate shaft (2) pinch bolt (1), and disconnect the coupler (3)

11. If equipped with a height sensor, disconnect the height sensor from the upper control arm ball stud.

12. Remove the speed sensor bolt, and remove the sensor from the knuckle.

13. Remove the speed sensor wiring retaining clip from the knuckle.

14. Support the outside of the lower control arm with a suitable holding fixture, and raise to normal ride height.

15. Remove the clevis to lower control arm bolt/nut.

16. Remove the upper ball joint retaining nut from the ball joint.

17. Separate the upper ball joint from the knuckle using Ball Joint Press.

➡It is necessary to pull the bottom of the shock assembly outward just enough to remove the upper control arm flag bolts without completely removing the shock assembly.

18. Remove the nuts and flag bolts securing the upper control arm to the body.

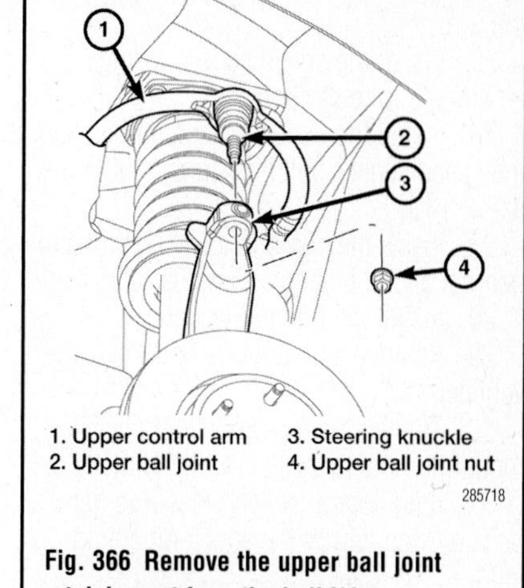

Fig. 366 Remove the upper ball joint retaining nut from the ball joint

19. Remove the upper control arm from the vehicle.

To install:

20. Position the upper control arm to the vehicle.

➡It is necessary to pull the bottom of the shock assembly outward just enough to install the upper control arm flag bolts without completely removing the shock assembly.

➡Tighten the upper control arm to body bolts in the following sequence: Left side, front then rear. Right side, rear then front.

21. Install the nuts and flag bolts securing the upper control arm to the body and tighten to 44 ft. lbs. (60 Nm).

22. Install the upper ball joint into the knuckle.

23. Install the upper ball joint retaining nut and tighten to 70 ft. lbs. (95 Nm).

24. If equipped with a height sensor,

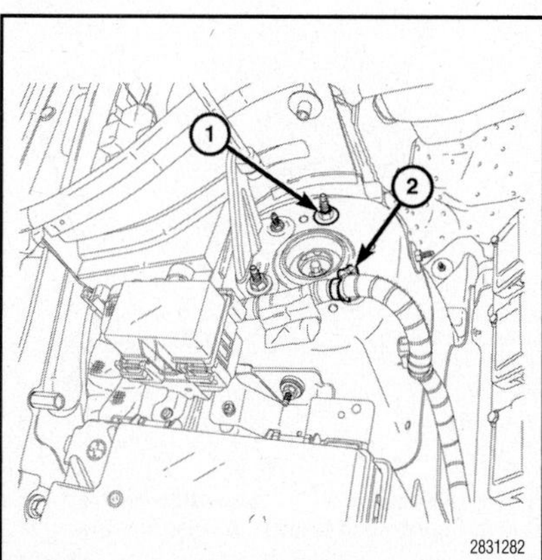

Fig. 363 If equipped, remove the wiring harness routing clip (2) from the shock mounting stud/nut (1)

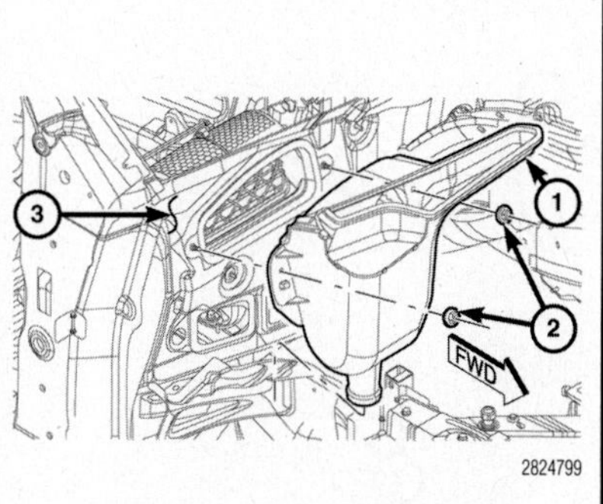

Fig. 365 For the right side only, remove the two nuts (2) that secure the HVAC air inlet duct (1) to the engine compartment side of the dash panel (3) and remove the duct

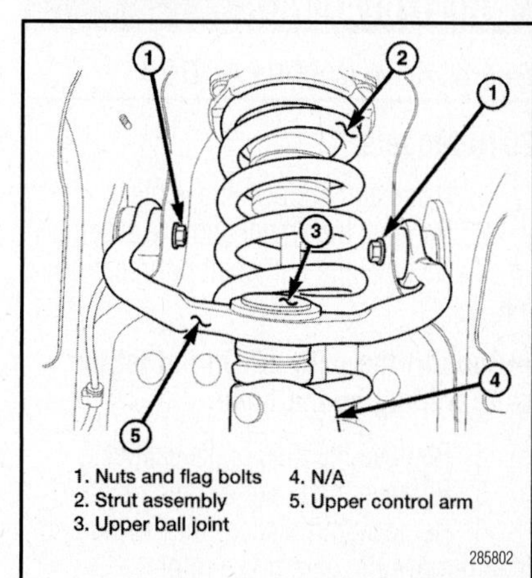

Fig. 367 Remove the nuts and flag bolts securing the upper control arm to the body

connect the height sensor to the upper control arm.

25. Install the speed sensor wiring retaining clip to the knuckle.

26. Install the speed sensor, and install the speed sensor bolt and tighten to 95 inch lbs. (11 Nm).

27. Install the clevis to lower control arm bolt/nut and tighten to 173 ft. lbs. (235 Nm).

28. Install the tire and wheel.

29. Remove the supports and lower the vehicle.

30. Tighten the three upper shock mounting nuts to 21 ft. lbs. (28 Nm).

31. If equipped, attach the wiring harness routing clip to the shock mounting stud.

32. For the right side only, position the HVAC air inlet duct to the engine compartment side of the dash panel. Install the two nuts that secure the HVAC air inlet duct to the dash panel.

33. For the left side only, connect the steering intermediate shaft coupler, install the pinch bolt and tighten to 33 ft. lbs. (45 Nm).

34. For left side only, install the air cleaner housing as follows:

a. Press the air cleaner housing onto the body grommets and install the push-pin.

b. Route and connect the weatherstrip to the housing inlet.

c. Connect the PCV air return hose and the power steering hose routing clip (not shown) to the air cleaner body.

d. Connect the fresh air intake hose to the housing cover and tighten the clamp.

e. Install the air cleaner.

35. Install the silencer and the cowl panel cover.

WHEEL BEARINGS

REMOVAL & INSTALLATION

2010 Models

1. Raise and support the vehicle.
2. Remove the wheel and tire assembly.
3. Remove the half shaft hub/bearing nut.

➡Support the caliper. Do not let the caliper hang by the hose.

4. Remove the disc brake caliper.
5. Remove the brake caliper adaptor.
6. Remove and discard the O-ring and then remove the disc brake rotor.
7. Remove the wheel speed sensor nut.
8. Remove the wheel speed sensor.
9. Remove the 3 hub bearing mounting bolts from the back of the steering knuckle.
10. Remove hub bearing from the steering knuckle.

To install:

11. Guide the half shaft into the hub/bearing, install the hub bearing to the knuckle and tighten the 3 bolts to 85 ft. lbs. (115 Nm).
12. Install the half shaft hub/bearing nut and tighten to 100 ft. lbs. (135 Nm).
13. Install the wheel speed sensor into the hub and then install the mounting bolt and tighten to 106–124 inch lbs. (12–14 Nm).
14. Install the brake rotor.
15. Install the brake caliper adaptor.
16. Install the caliper.
17. Install the wheel and tire assembly.
18. Remove the support and lower the vehicle.

2011 Models

RWD Models

See Figure 368.

1. Raise and support the vehicle.
2. Remove the wheel and tire assembly.
3. Remove the brake rotor.
4. Remove the wheel speed sensor bolt and the wheel speed sensor from the knuckle.
5. Remove the 3 hub bearing mounting bolts from the back of the steering knuckle. Remove hub bearing from the steering knuckle.

To install:

6. Position the hub bearing into the knuckle, install the 3 bolts and tighten to 78 ft. lbs. (105 Nm).
7. Install the wheel speed sensor into the knuckle, install the sensor mounting bolt and tighten to 95 inch lbs. (11 Nm).
8. Install the brake rotor.
9. Install the wheel and tire assembly.
10. Remove the support and lower the vehicle.

4WD Models

See Figure 369.

1. Raise and support the vehicle.
2. Remove the wheel and tire assembly.
3. Remove the brake rotor.
4. Remove the half shaft nut.
5. Remove the stabilizer link to lower control arm nut and position link aside.
6. Remove the speed sensor bolt, and remove the sensor from the knuckle.
7. Remove the speed sensor wiring retaining clip from the knuckle.
8. Remove the upper ball joint nut.
9. Separate the upper ball joint from the knuckle using Ball Joint Press (1).
10. Tilt the knuckle out, and from outside the hub, push the half shaft into the hub for access to the hub/bearing bolts.
11. Remove the hub/bearing bolts and remove the hub/bearing from the knuckle assembly.

To install:

12. Position the hub/bearing, install the hub/bearing bolts and tighten to 78 ft. lbs. (105 Nm).
13. Support the outside of the lower control arm with a suitable holding fixture, and raise to position the upper ball joint into the knuckle.
14. With the holding fixture holding the suspension at normal ride height, install the upper ball joint nut and tighten to 70 ft. lbs. (95 Nm).
15. Install the half shaft nut and tighten to 229 ft. lbs. (310 Nm).

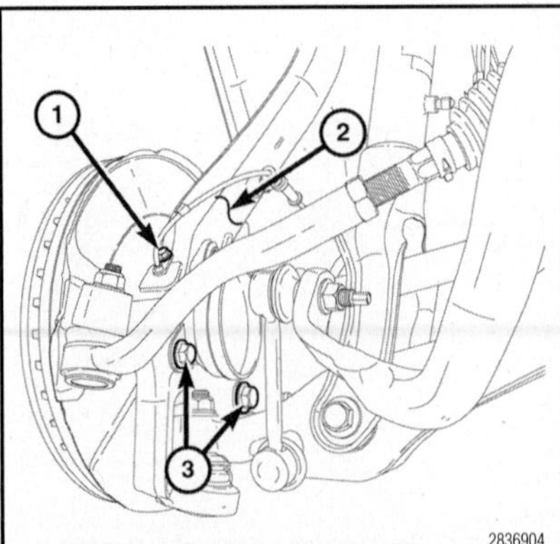

Fig. 368 Remove the wheel speed sensor bolt (1) and the wheel speed sensor from the knuckle (2); hub bearing mounting bolts (3)

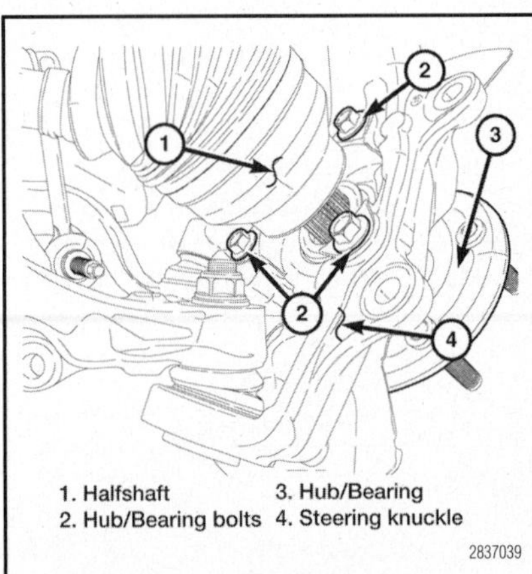

Fig. 369 Tilt the knuckle out, and from outside the hub, push the half shaft into the hub for access to the hub/bearing bolts

16. Install the brake rotor.
17. Route and attach speed sensor wiring to the knuckle.
18. Install the wheel speed sensor into the knuckle, install the mounting bolt and tighten to 95 inch lbs. (11 Nm).
19. Position the stabilizer link to lower control arm, install the nut and tighten to 90 ft. lbs. (122 Nm).
20. Install the tire and wheel assembly.
21. Remove the supports and lower the vehicle.

ADJUSTMENT

No adjustment is possible. If the bearing is too loose or worn, it must be replaced.

SUSPENSION

REAR SUSPENSION

Some models are equipped with air suspension.

CAUTION

All pressurized air suspension components contain high pressure air (up to 220 psi). Use extreme caution when inspecting for leaks. Wear safety goggles and adequate protective clothing when inspecting or servicing the air suspension system. A sudden release of air under this amount of pressure can cause personal injury or death.

CAUTION

Support the vehicle by supplemental means before performing any work on the air suspension system to prevent the vehicle from changing height. Before any given component is to be serviced it must be deflated. Servicing the air suspension system without supplemental support, or with pressure in the specific component, can cause personal injury or death.

The air suspension system automatically or manually (operator control) lowers and lifts the vehicle using rear air suspension springs (air bag) and front air suspension spring and shock assemblies which replace the standard springs in the rear, and standard spring/shock in the front. The air suspension system uses multiple integrated components in various areas of the vehicle to accomplish this.

COIL SPRING

REMOVAL & INSTALLATION

2010 Models

See Figure 370.

1. Raise and support the vehicle. Position a hydraulic jack under the axle to support the axle.
2. Remove the wheel and tire assembly on the side of the repair.
3. Remove the lower shock bolt from the axle bracket.

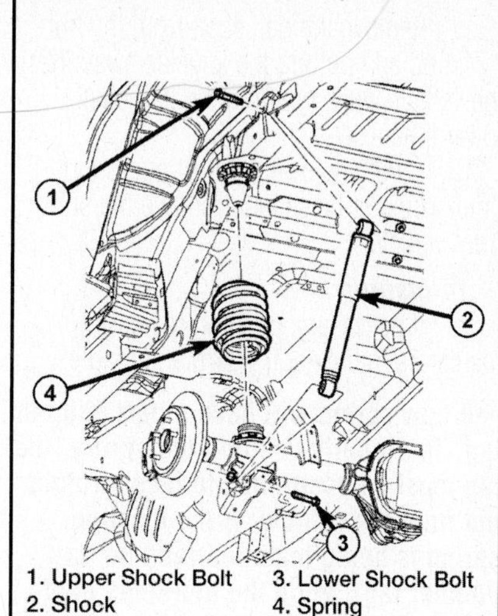

Fig. 370 Exploded view of coil spring assembly

4. If the left spring is being serviced, remove the left rear bolt securing the fuel tank skid plate in place. This will allow clearance for the suspension when the spring is removed.
5. Remove the stabilizer bar link from the body rail.
6. Lower the hydraulic jack and tilt the axle.
7. Pull down on the axle as necessary and remove the coil spring by lifting it up and off the lower perch first.
8. Remove and inspect the spring isolators.

To install:

9. Install the upper isolator on the spring seat on body.
10. Install the lower isolator on the axle bracket.
11. Pull down on the axle and position the coil spring, ID tag end up, over the upper perch, then lower it onto the lower perch.
12. Raise the axle with the hydraulic jack.
13. Install the shock absorber to the axle bracket and tighten the bolt to 85 ft. lbs. (115 Nm.).
14. If the left spring is being serviced, install the previously removed fuel tank skid plate bolt and tighten to 50 ft. lbs. (68 Nm).
15. Install the stabilizer bar link to the body rail and tighten the bolt to 75 ft. lbs. (102 Nm).
16. Install the wheel and tire assembly.
17. Remove the supports and lower the vehicle.

2011 Models

Without Air Suspension

See Figures 371 through 373.

1. Raise and support the vehicle.
2. Remove the tire and wheel.
3. If the spring is to be reused and there is no part number tag, mark the position of the spring for proper alignment on installation.
4. Remove the half shaft nut.
5. If equipped with a height sensor, disconnect the linkage from the ball stud at the lower control arm bracket by prying with a small screwdriver.
6. Bottom caliper pistons into the caliper.
7. Remove the brake caliper tension clip by pressing forward on the back of the

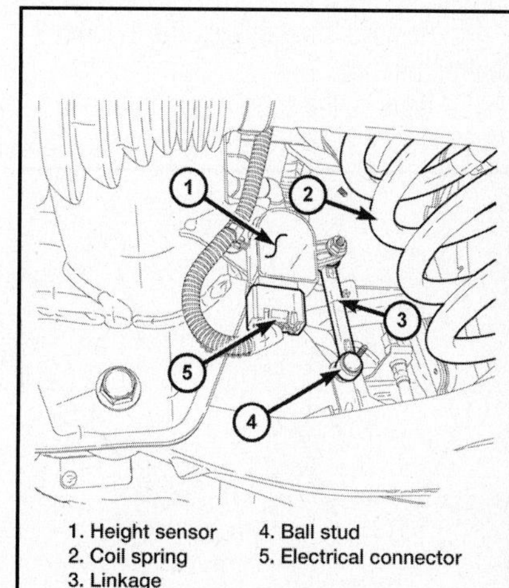

Fig. 371 If equipped with a height sensor, disconnect the linkage from the ball stud at the lower control arm bracket by prying with a small screwdriver

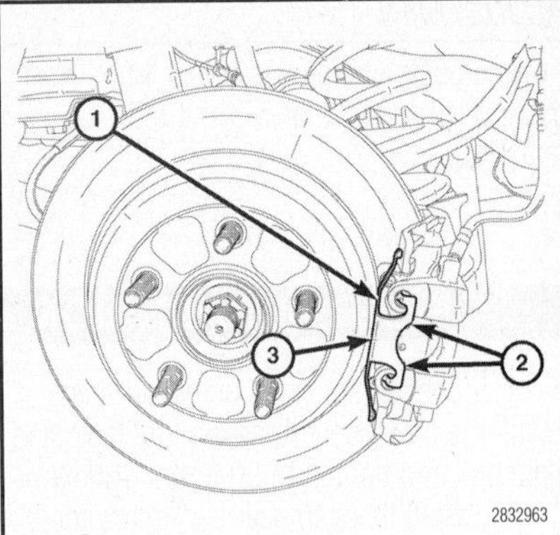

Fig. 372 Remove the brake caliper tension clip (1) by pressing forward on the back of the clip (3) while pulling out on the front of the clip (2)

clip while pulling out on the front of the clip.

8. Remove the caliper slide dust bolt shields and loosen the brake caliper slide bolts (guide pins).

➡Never allow the disc brake caliper to hang from the brake hose. Damage to the brake hose will result. Provide a suitable support to hang the caliper securely.

9. Remove the brake caliper from the caliper adapter and hang the brake caliper.
10. Support the outer end of the lower control arm with a suitable holding fixture.
11. Remove the tension link to knuckle nut and bolt.
12. Remove the wheel speed sensor bolt and remove the sensor.
13. Remove the camber link to knuckle bolt/nut.
14. Remove the stabilizer link to lower control arm nut.
15. Remove the shock lower nut/bolt.

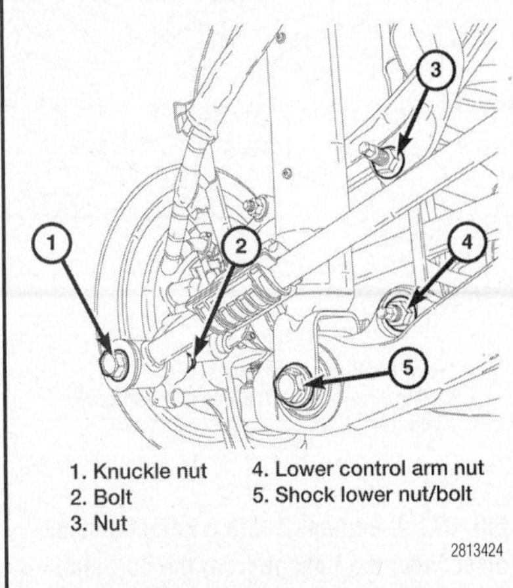

Fig. 373 Remove the stabilizer link to lower control arm nut

16. Remove the toe link to knuckle nut and bolt.

WARNING

Never allow the half shaft to hang unsupported from the axle. Damage to the joints may result. Provide a suitable support to hang the half shaft securely.

17. Remove the half shaft from the hub by tilting and pulling the knuckle away from the vehicle while pushing the half shaft toward the axle.
18. Carefully lower control arm support until spring is loose, and remove the spring from vehicle.

To install:

19. If necessary, position the spring insulators in the control arm and cradle.

➡A new spring will have a part number tag. To properly position the spring, the tag must be positioned to face straight out from the vehicle. If the existing spring is being installed (and no part number tag), align the markings made during removal.

20. Position the spring in the pocket of the lower control arm.
21. While holding the spring in position, carefully raise the lower control arm with a support fixture at the outer end of the lower control arm to normal ride height.
22. Align the knuckle to the axle shaft and install the axle through the hub/bearing. Install the half shaft nut and tighten to 229 ft. lbs. (310 Nm).
23. If equipped with a height sensor, position the height sensor linkage to its ball stud and press together to seat.
24. Position the tension link, install the nut and tighten to 79 ft. lbs. (108 Nm).
25. Position the toe link, install the nut and tighten to 79 ft. lbs. (108 Nm).
26. Install the shock lower bolt and nut and tighten to 173 ft. lbs. (235 Nm).
27. Install the stabilizer link to lower control arm nut and tighten to 81 ft. lbs. (110 Nm).
28. Install the camber link to knuckle bolt/nut and tighten to 81 ft. lbs. (110 Nm).
29. Install the wheel speed sensor and sensor retaining bolt and tighten to 95 inch lbs. (11 Nm).
30. Position the brake pads and caliper, install the brake caliper slide bolts (guide pins) and tighten to 20 ft. lbs. (28 Nm).
31. Install the caliper slide bolt dust shields.
32. Install the brake caliper tension clip.
33. Install the wheel.
34. Remove the support and lower the vehicle.
35. Pump the brake pedal until caliper pistons and brake pads are seated and a firm brake pedal is obtained.

With Air Suspension

See Figures 374 and 375.

CAUTION

All pressurized air suspension components contain high pressure air (up to 220 psi). Use extreme caution when inspecting for leaks. Wear safety goggles and adequate protective clothing when inspecting or servicing the air suspension system. A sudden release of air under this amount of pressure can cause personal injury or death.

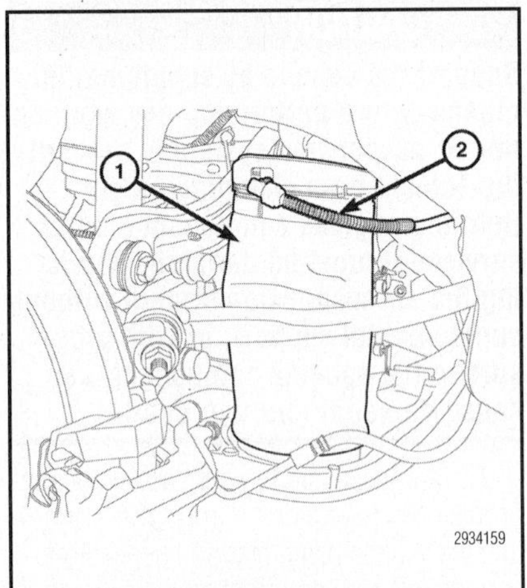

Fig. 374 Remove air line fitting and air line (2) from the air spring (1)

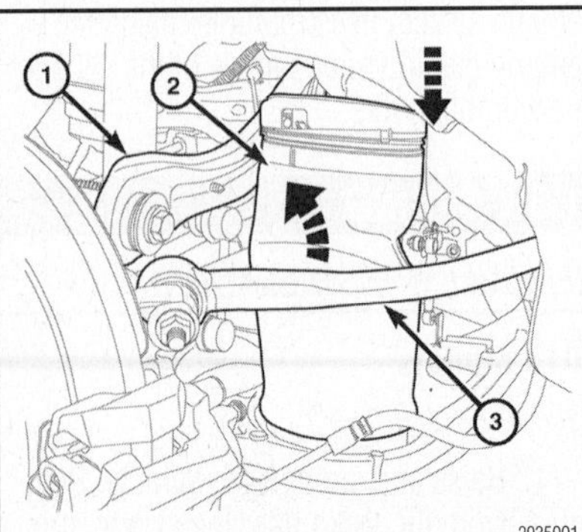

Fig. 375 To remove the air spring (2), push down on the air spring to compress, tilt the top out and lift the air spring from the lower control arm between the tension link (3) and camber link (1)

✲✲ CAUTION

Support the vehicle by supplemental means before performing any work on the air suspension system to prevent the vehicle from changing height. Before any given component is to be serviced it must be deflated. Servicing the air suspension system without supplemental support, or with pressure in the specific component, can cause personal injury or death.

✲✲ WARNING

When removing an air line from a component and the air line is to be reused, do not remove the 90° fitting or the brass fitting from the air line. If either is removed, the air line must be replaced. New components have air line fittings attached; however if the original air line is used the original fitting must also be used. Do not remove protective caps or plugs from air lines or components until ready to install the air line to prevent moisture or dirt intrusion. All air line fittings must be hand started to avoid cross threading.

1. Raise and support the vehicle.
2. With a scan tool, using the routines under the ASCM, perform the following:
   a. Disable the air suspension system.
   b. Run the Spring Deflate To Reservoir routine on the air suspension spring to be removed.
3. Remove the tire and wheel.

➡Do not remove the fitting from the air line. During installation the same fitting will be used. If the fitting is removed from the air line, the air line must be replaced.

4. Remove air line fitting and air line from the air spring.
5. To remove the air spring, push down on the air spring to compress, tilt the top out and lift the air spring from the lower control arm between the tension link and camber link.

To install:

✲✲ CAUTION

All pressurized air suspension components contain high pressure air (up to 220 psi). Use extreme caution when inspecting for leaks. Wear safety goggles and adequate protective clothing when inspecting or servicing the air suspension system. A sudden release of air under this amount of pressure can cause personal injury or death.

✲✲ CAUTION

Support the vehicle by supplemental means before performing any work on the air suspension system to prevent the vehicle from changing height. Before any given component is to be serviced it must be deflated. Servicing the air suspension system without supplemental support, or with pressure in the specific component, can cause personal injury or death.

✲✲ WARNING

When removing an air line from a component and the air line is to be reused, do not remove the 90° fitting or the brass fitting from the air line. If either is removed, the air line must be replaced. New components have air line fittings attached; however if the original air line is used the original fitting must also be used. Do not remove protective caps or plugs from air lines or components until ready to install the air line to prevent moisture or dirt intrusion. All air line fittings must be hand started to avoid cross threading.

6. Position the rear air spring with the lower alignment tab into the slot in the lower control arm and align the upper portion of the rear air spring into the upper pocket as when removed.
7. If a new rear air spring is used, remove the cap/fitting from the air line connection of the rear air spring.
8. Using the original fitting, connect the air line to the rear air spring.
9. With a scan tool, using the routines under the Air Suspension Control Module (ASCM), perform the following:
   a. Run the Fill Spring From Reservoir routine on the spring that was installed. Choose the Short Time Fill option from the menu selections and the spring will inflate for approximately one second, then verify the air spring is properly seated into its mounting sockets, and any wrinkles in the air bag have unfolded properly.
   b. Run the Fill Spring From Reservoir routine on the spring that was installed. Choose the Complete Fill option from the menu selections.
10. Install the tire and wheel.
11. Remove the support and lower the vehicle.
12. With a scan tool, using the routines under the Air Suspension Control Module (ASCM), perform the following:
   a. Command the vehicle to Normal Ride Height.
   b. Run the Air Mass Calculation routine on the air suspension system.
   c. If necessary, add to the system or deflate to atmosphere using the ASCM routines, then repeat the Air Mass Calculation routine again until system responds with Air Mass OK (188–216 bar-liters).
   d. Enable the air suspension system.
13. Perform the ASCM Verification Test.

ASCM VERIFICATION TEST

1. Disconnect all jumper wires and reconnect all previously disconnected components and connectors.
2. With the scan tool, erase DTCs.
3. Make sure that all accessories are turned off and that the battery is fully charged.
4. Test drive the vehicle and verify proper operation.
5. With the scan tool, read DTCs in the ASCM.
6. If there aren't any DTCs present in the Air Suspension Control Module (ASCM), the repair is complete.

LOWER CONTROL ARM

REMOVAL & INSTALLATION

2010 Models

Left Side

See Figures 376 and 377.

1. Raise the vehicle and support the rear axle.
2. Remove the fuel tank.
3. Remove the lower suspension arm nut and bolt from the axle bracket.
4. Remove the nut and bolt from the frame rail and remove the lower suspension arm.

To install:

➡All torques should be done with vehicle on the ground with full vehicle weight.

5. Position the lower suspension arm in the frame rail.
6. Install the frame rail bracket bolt and nut tighten to 130 ft. lbs. (176 Nm).
7. Position the lower suspension arm in the axle bracket.

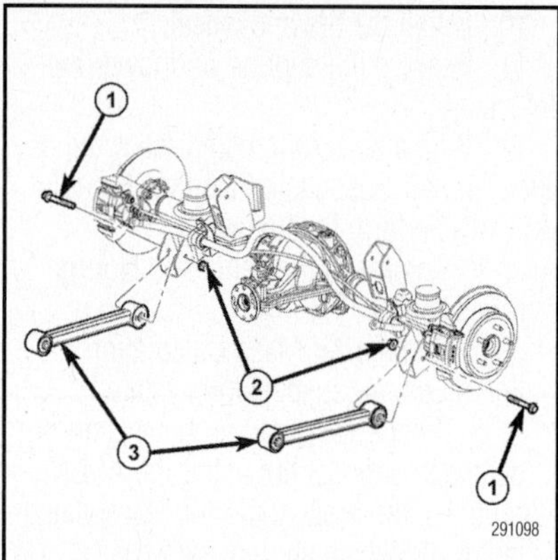

Fig. 376 Remove the lower suspension arm (3) nut (2) and bolt (1) from the axle bracket

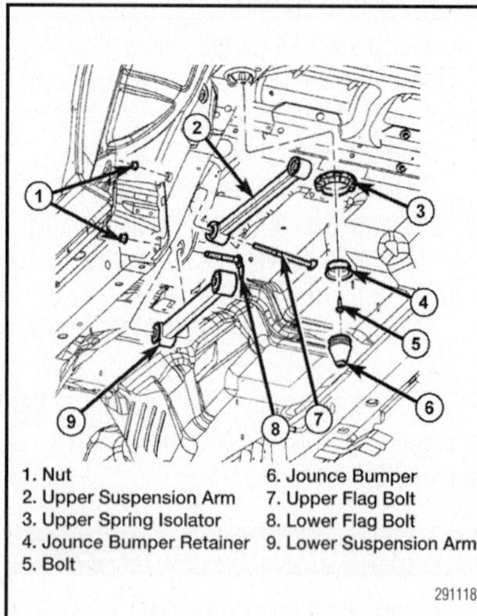

Fig. 377 Remove the nut and bolt from the frame rail and remove the lower suspension arm

8. Install the axle bracket bolt and nut Tighten to 155 ft. lbs. (210 Nm).
9. Install the fuel tank.
10. Remove the supports and lower the vehicle.

Right Side

See Figures 376 and 377.

1. Raise the vehicle and support the rear axle.
2. Remove the lower suspension arm nut and bolt from the axle bracket.
3. Remove the nut and bolt from the frame rail and remove the lower suspension arm.

To install:

➡All torques should be done with vehicle on the ground with full vehicle weight.

4. Position the lower suspension arm in the frame rail.
5. Install the frame rail bracket bolt and nut. Tighten to 130 ft. lbs. (176 Nm).
6. Position the lower suspension arm in the axle bracket.
7. Install the axle bracket bolt and nut. Tighten to 155 ft. lbs. (210 Nm).
8. Remove the supports and lower the vehicle.

2011 Models

With Electronic Limited Slip Differential (ELSD)

See Figures 378 through 381.

1. Raise and support the vehicle.
2. Remove the tire and wheel assembly.
3. Bottom caliper pistons into the caliper by prying the caliper over.
4. Remove the caliper slide pin covers and slide pins.

**** WARNING**

Never allow the disc brake caliper to hang from the brake hose. Damage to the brake hose will result. Provide a suitable support to hang the caliper securely.

5. Remove the disc brake caliper from the adapter and hang from a suitable support.
6. Disconnect the brake cable end from the equalizer.
7. Depress the tabs on the cable housing and pull through the cable retaining bracket.
8. Remove the parking brake cable from the retaining bracket.
9. Remove the tie straps and clips as necessary.

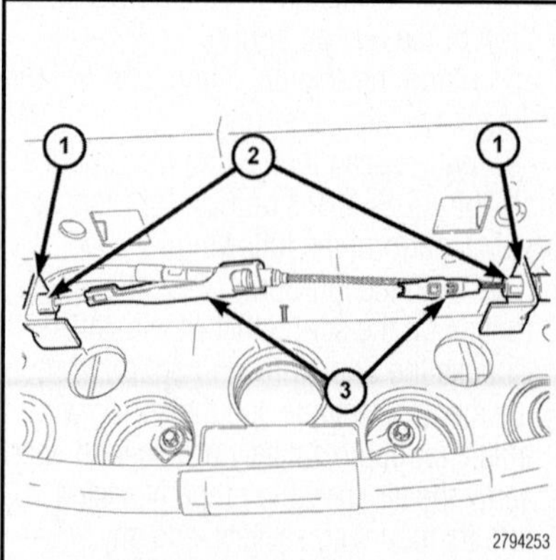

Fig. 378 Disconnect the brake cable end from the equalizer (3); depress the tabs on the cable housing (2) and pull through the cable retaining bracket (1)

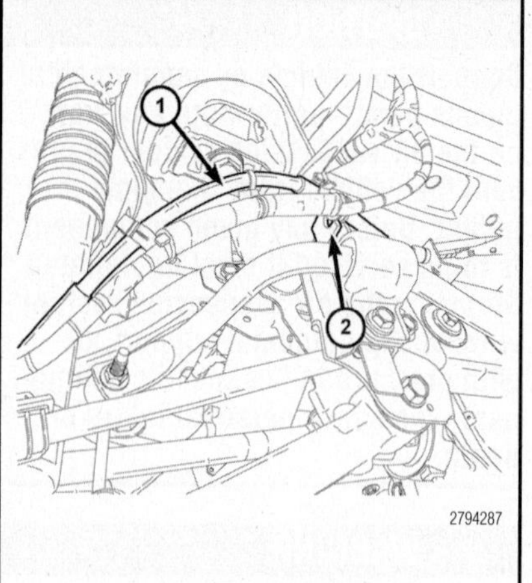

Fig. 379 Remove the parking brake cable (1) from the retaining bracket (2)

10. Remove the rear spring.
11. Tilt the knuckle for access, remove the ball joint nut and remove the knuckle from the control arm.
12. For the left lower control arm only, loosen and tilt the axle for access to remove the forward lower control arm bolt by performing the following:
    a. Support the rear axle with a suitable holding fixture.
    b. Remove the left axle bolt.

➡Do not remove the bolts on the right side of the axle.

    c. Loosen the right rear axle bolt and the right front axle bolt (not shown).
    d. Carefully lower the axle support enough to tip the axle for clearance to remove the lower control arm bolt.
13. Remove the bolt cover cap from the forward lower control arm to cradle bolt near the gas tank.
14. Loosen the forward lower control

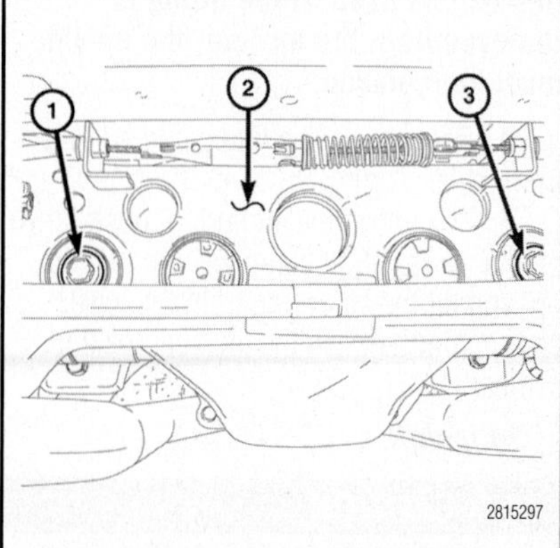

Fig. 380 Remove the left axle bolt (1); loosen the right rear axle bolt (3) and the right front axle bolt (not shown); cross-member (2)

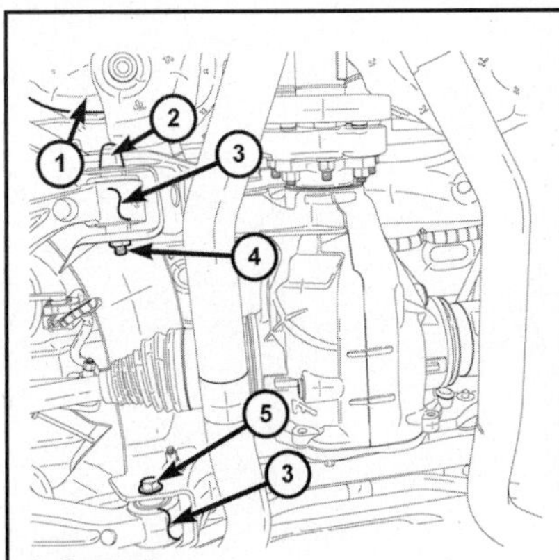

1. Gas tank
2. Bolt cover cap
3. Lower control arm
4. Lower control arm to cradle nut
5. Rear lower control arm to cradle bolts/nuts

2814659

Fig. 381 Remove the bolt cover cap from the forward lower control arm to cradle bolt near the gas tank

arm to cradle nut and tap out the bolt far enough to cut the head of the bolt off.

15. Cut the head of the bolt off with an air saw (or equivalent).
16. Remove the rear lower control arm to cradle bolts/nuts.
17. Using the nut, pry the front lower control arm bolt through the rear of the control arm mounting.
18. Carefully lower the control arm support and remove the lower control arm (3) from the vehicle.
19. Remove and transfer any necessary components.

To install:

➡Right side shown, left side similar. The axle was tilted for the left side removal and should still be tilted to install the left front control arm to cradle bolt.

➡The front control arm to cradle bolt is installed from rear to front so that the nut is installed on the fuel tank side. This is the opposite of the manufacturing installation.

20. Position the control arm on the cradle and install the bolt/nuts at the cradle. Do not tighten at this time.
21. For the left lower control arm only, raise the axle, install the left axle bolt and tighten all three axle bolts to 111 ft. lbs. (150 Nm).
22. Remove the axle support.
23. Position the knuckle/ball joint into the control arm and with the knuckle tilted out, install the ball joint nut and torque to 151 ft. lbs. (205 Nm).
24. Install the spring.
25. Attach the parking brake cable to the retaining bracket and replace tie straps or clips as necessary.
26. Attach the tie straps and clips as removed.
27. Route the cable through the bracket and pull through tight to seat in bracket. Pull back on cable to make sure the cable seated properly.
28. Connect the brake cable end to the equalizer.

Position the caliper over the rotor, install the slide pins and tighten to 20 ft. lbs. (28 Nm).

29. Install the slide pin covers.
30. Install the wheel.
31. With the vehicle weight on the tires tighten the lower control arm to cradle bolts/nuts to 142 ft. lbs. (193 Nm).

➡The bolt cover cap was removed from the bolt head but fits on the nut after the bolt direction changed from the manufacturing direction.

32. Install the bolt cover cap on the lower control arm to cradle forward nut near the gas tank.
33. Perform a rear wheel alignment.

Without ELSD

See Figures 378, 379 and 381.

1. Raise and support the vehicle.
2. Remove the wheel.
3. Bottom caliper pistons into the caliper by prying the caliper over.
4. Remove the caliper slide pin covers and slide pins.

⁂ WARNING

Never allow the disc brake caliper to hang from the brake hose. Damage to the brake hose will result. Provide a suitable support to hang the caliper securely.

5. Remove the disc brake caliper from the adapter and hang from a suitable support.
6. Disconnect the brake cable end from the equalizer.
7. Depress the tabs on the cable housing and pull through the cable retaining bracket.
8. Remove the parking brake cable from the retaining bracket.
9. Remove the tie straps and clips as necessary.
10. Remove the rear spring.
11. Tilt the knuckle for access, remove the ball joint nut and remove the knuckle from the control arm.
12. Remove the bolt cover cap from the forward lower control arm to cradle bolt near the gas tank.
13. Loosen the forward lower control arm to cradle nut and tap out the bolt far enough to cut the head of the bolt off.
14. Cut the head of the bolt off with an air saw (or equivalent).
15. Using the nut, pry the bolt through the rear of the control arm mounting.
16. Remove the rear lower control arm to cradle bolts/nuts.
17. Carefully lower the control arm support and remove the lower control arm from the vehicle.
18. Remove and transfer any necessary components.

To install:

➡The front control arm to cradle bolt is installed from rear to front so that the nut is installed on the fuel tank side. This is the opposite of the manufacturing installation.

19. Position the control arm on the cradle and install the bolt/nuts at the cradle. Do not tighten at this time.
20. Position the knuckle/ball joint into the control arm and with the knuckle tilted out, install the ball joint nut and torque to 151 ft. lbs. (205 Nm).
21. Install the spring.
22. Attach the parking brake cable to the retaining bracket and replace tie straps or clips as necessary.
23. Attach the tie straps and clips as removed.
24. Route the cable through the bracket and pull through tight to seat in bracket. Pull back on cable to make sure the cable seated properly.
25. Connect the brake cable end to the equalizer.
26. Position the caliper over the rotor, install the slide pins and tighten to 20 ft. lbs. (28 Nm).
27. Install the slide pin covers.
28. Install the wheel.
29. With the vehicle weight on the tires tighten the lower control arm to cradle bolts/nuts to 142 ft. lbs. (193 Nm).

➡The bolt cover cap was removed from the bolt head but fits on the nut after the bolt direction changed from the manufacturing direction.

30. Install the bolt cover cap on the lower control arm to cradle forward nut near the gas tank.
31. Perform a rear wheel alignment.

SHOCK ABSORBER

REMOVAL & INSTALLATION

2010 Models

1. Raise and support the vehicle.
2. Position a hydraulic jack under the axle to support the axle.
3. Remove the upper bolt from the frame bracket.
4. Remove the lower bolt from the axle bracket.
5. Remove the shock absorber.

To install:

6. Install the shock absorber in the frame bracket and install the bolt.
7. Install the shock absorber in the axle bracket and install the bolt.
8. Tighten the upper mounting bolt/nut to 70 ft. lbs. (95 Nm).
9. Tighten the lower mounting bolt/nut to 85 ft. lbs. (115 Nm).
10. Remove the supports and lower the vehicle.

2011 Models

See Figures 382 and 383.

1. Raise and support the vehicle.
2. Remove the tire and wheel.
3. Remove the two push pins from the wheel well.
4. Support the outboard end of the lower control arm with a suitable holding fixture.
5. Remove the upper shock bolts.
6. Remove the lower shock bolt and nut.
7. Lower the support on the outboard end of the lower control arm just enough to tilt the shock into position for removal between the front and rear arms of the lower control arm.

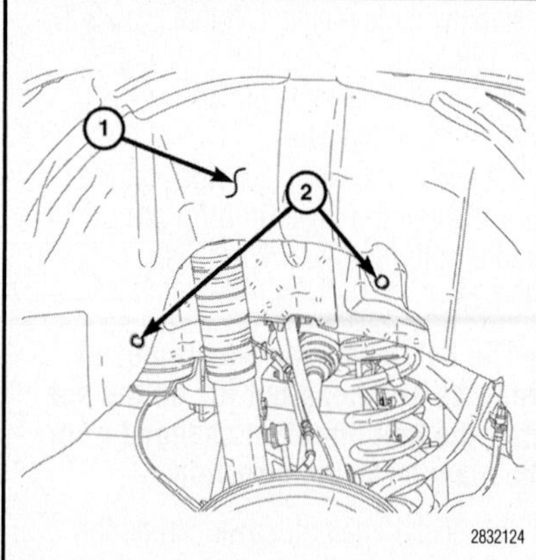

Fig. 382 Remove the two push pins (2) from the wheel well (1)

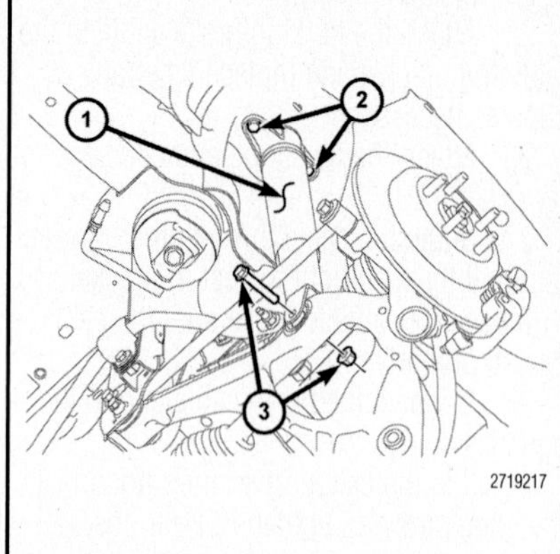

Fig. 383 Remove the upper shock bolts (2), the lower shock bolt and nut (3), and the shock (1)

8. Remove and transfer any necessary components.

To install:

9. Position the shock.
10. Install the upper shock bolts and tighten to 48 ft. lbs. (65 Nm).
11. Install the lower shock bolt/nut. Raise the support on the lower control arm to normal ride height and tighten the bolt/nut to 173 ft. lbs. (235 Nm).
12. Install the two wheel well push pins.
13. Install the tire and wheel.
14. Remove the supports and lower the vehicle.

STABILIZER BAR

REMOVAL & INSTALLATION

2010 Models

See Figure 384.

1. Raise and support the vehicle.
2. Remove both rear tire assemblies.
3. Remove the stabilizer bar links from stabilizer bar.
4. Remove the stabilizer bar retainer bolts from the retainer.
5. Remove the stabilizer bar by twisting it out and around the rotor and caliper from the right rear side of the vehicle.

To install:

6. Twist and rotate to position the stabilizer bar on the axle from the right rear side of the vehicle.
7. Install the retainers) and bolts. Ensure the bar is centered with equal spacing on both sides. Tighten the bolts to 31 ft. lbs. (42 Nm).
8. Install the links to the stabilizer bar.
9. Tighten the nuts at the stabilizer bar to 90 ft. lbs. (122 Nm).
10. Install the tire and wheel assemblies.

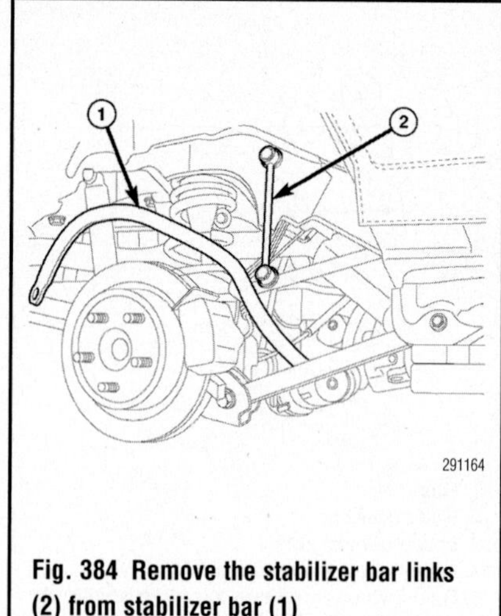

Fig. 384 Remove the stabilizer bar links (2) from stabilizer bar (1)

11. Remove support and lower the vehicle.

2011 Models

See Figures 385 and 386.

➡When the stabilizer bar or links are serviced it is recommended that a drive on hoist is used or the out board ends of the control arms are supported and raised to normal ride height. If the suspension is hanging, there will be tension on the stabilizer bar.

1. Remove the parking brake cable from the retaining bracket for access to the stabilizer to cradle bolts.
2. Raise and support the vehicle.
3. Remove both stabilizer link to stabilizer nuts and position the links aside.
4. Remove both upper and lower stabilizer to cradle bolts.
5. Remove the stabilizer bar from the vehicle.

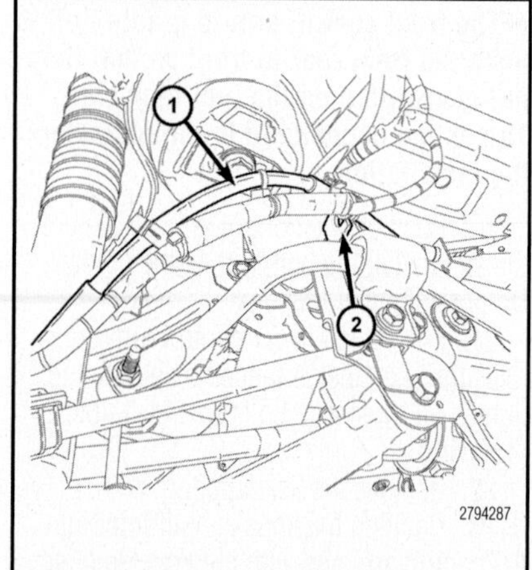

Fig. 385 Remove the parking brake cable (1) from the retaining bracket (2)

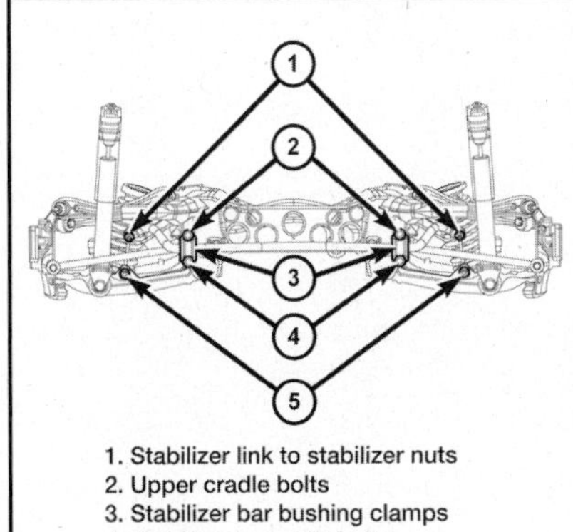

Fig. 386 Remove both stabilizer link to stabilizer nuts and position the links aside

To install:

➡When the stabilizer bar or links are serviced it is recommended that a drive on hoist is used or the out board ends of the control arms are supported and raised to normal ride height. If the suspension is hanging, there will be tension on the stabilizer bar.

6. Position the stabilizer bar and install the upper and lower stabilizer bar to cradle bolts and tighten to 81 ft. lbs. (110 Nm).
7. Install both stabilizer link to stabilizer nuts and tighten to 66 ft. lbs. (90 Nm).
8. Insert and seat the parking brake cable into the open bracket.
9. Remove the supports and lower the vehicle.

TRACK BAR

REMOVAL & INSTALLATION

2010 Models

See Figures 387 and 388.

1. Raise and support the vehicle. Position a hydraulic jack under the axle to support the axle.
2. Remove the track bar bolt and nut from the frame bracket.
3. Remove the left lower shock bolt at the axle.
4. Pry in between the coil springs to remove track bar bolt.
5. Remove the track bar bolt and nut from the axle bracket.

To install:

6. Install the track bar to the vehicle.
7. Pry in between the coil springs to install track bar bolt.
8. Install the track bar bolt and nut in the frame bracket.

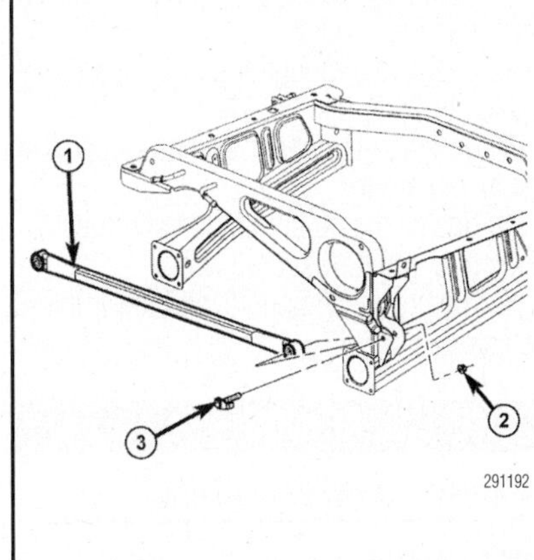

Fig. 387 Remove the track bar (1) bolt (3) and nut (2) from the frame bracket

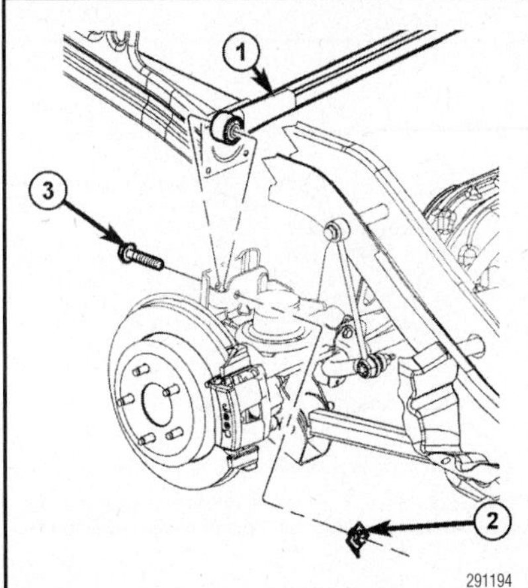

Fig. 388 Remove the track bar (1) bolt (3) and nut (2) from the axle bracket

9. Install the track bar into the axle bracket.
10. Install the track bar bolt and nut in the axle bracket.
11. Install the left lower shock bolt to the axle Tighten to 85 ft. lbs. (115 Nm).
12. Remove the supports and lower the vehicle.
13. Tighten the upper mounting bolt/nut to 140 ft. lbs. (190 Nm).
14. Tighten the lower mounting bolt/nut to 140 ft. lbs. (190 Nm) with full vehicle weight.

UPPER CONTROL ARM

REMOVAL & INSTALLATION

2010 Models

Left Side

See Figures 389 and 390.

1. Raise and support the vehicle.

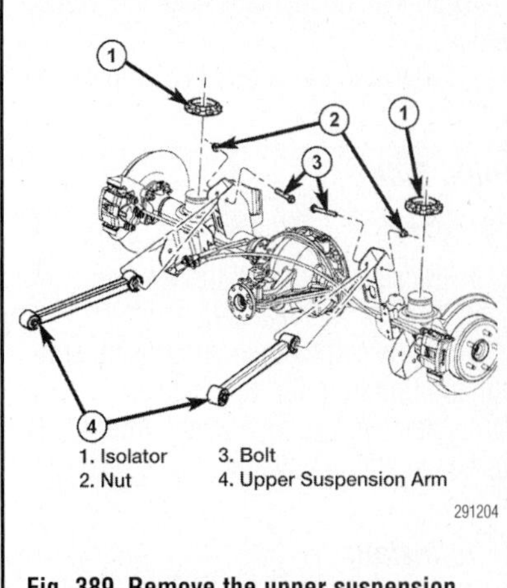

Fig. 389 Remove the upper suspension arm nut and bolt from the axle bracket

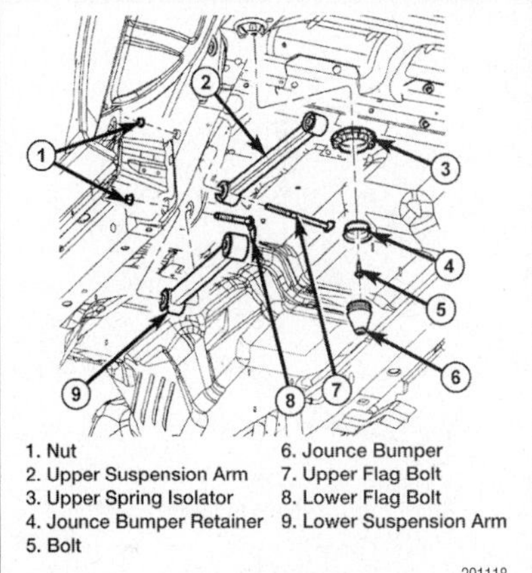

Fig. 390 Remove the nut and bolt from the frame rail and remove the upper suspension arm

2. Support the rear axle.
3. Lower the fuel tank in order to gain access to the bolt.
4. Remove the upper suspension arm nut and bolt from the axle bracket.
5. Remove the nut and bolt from the frame rail and remove the upper suspension arm.

To install:

➡All torques should be done with vehicle on the ground with full vehicle weight.

6. Position the upper suspension arm in the frame rail bracket.
7. Install the mounting bolt and nut tighten to 95 ft. lbs. (129 Nm).
8. Position the upper suspension arm in the axle bracket.
9. Install the mounting bolt and nut tighten to 100 ft. lbs. (136 Nm).

10. Raise the fuel tank back into place and secure.
11. Remove the supports and lower the vehicle.

Right Side

See Figures 391 and 392.

1. Raise and support the vehicle.
2. Support the rear axle.
3. Remove the upper suspension arm nut and bolt from the axle bracket.
4. Remove the nut and bolt from the frame rail and remove the upper suspension arm.

To install:

➡All torques should be done with vehicle on the ground with full vehicle weight.

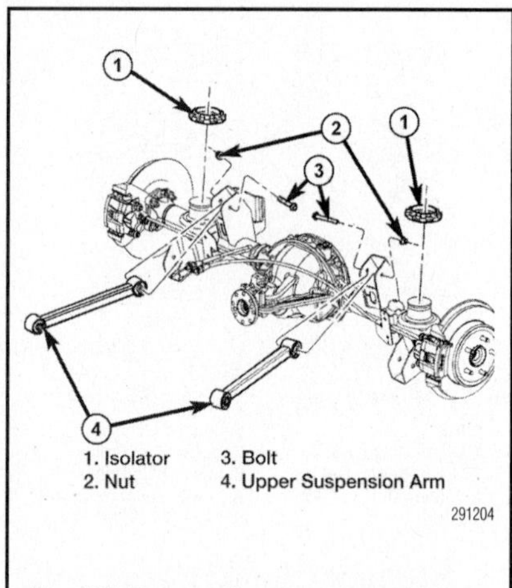

Fig. 391 Remove the upper suspension arm nut and bolt from the axle bracket

1. Nut
2. Upper Suspension Arm
3. Upper Spring Isolator
4. Jounce Bumper Retainer
5. Bolt
6. Jounce Bumper
7. Upper Flag Bolt
8. Lower Flag Bolt
9. Lower Suspension Arm

291118

Fig. 392 Remove the nut and bolt from the frame rail and remove the upper suspension arm

5. Position the upper suspension arm in the frame rail bracket.
6. Install the mounting bolt and nut tighten to 95 ft. lbs. (129 Nm).
7. Position the upper suspension arm in the axle bracket.
8. Install the mounting bolt and nut tighten to 100 ft. lbs. (136 Nm).
9. Remove the supports and lower the vehicle.

WHEEL BEARINGS

REMOVAL & INSTALLATION

2011 Models

See Figures 393 through 395.

➡A bearing can only be removed from the knuckle one time without replacing the knuckle. If a bearing is being removed for the second time, the knuckle must be replaced.

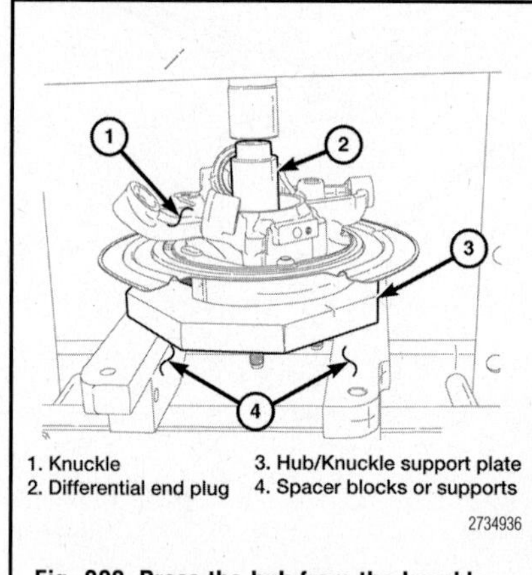

Fig. 393 Press the hub from the knuckle using Differential End Plug and Hub/Knuckle Support Plate

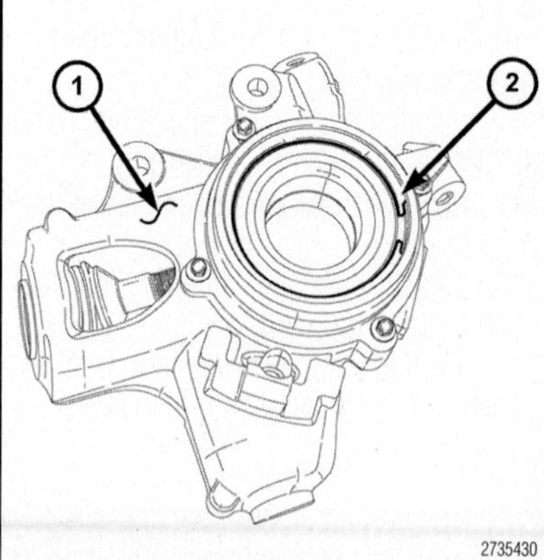

Fig. 394 Remove the retaining ring (2) from the knuckle (1)

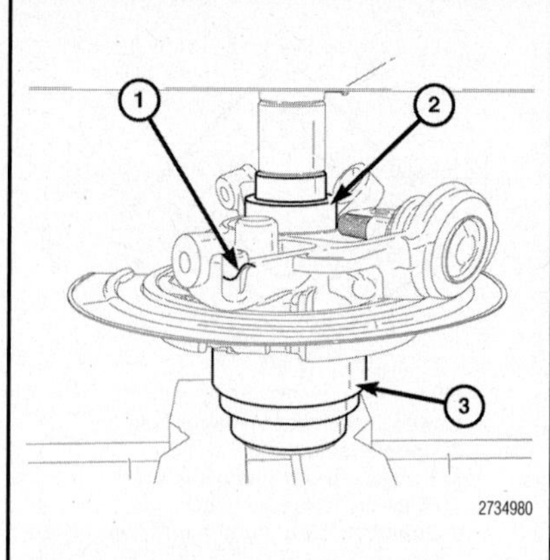

Fig. 395 Press the bearing from the knuckle (1) using Receiver Cup (2) and Hub/Knuckle Support Installer/Remover (3)

1. Raise and support the vehicle.
2. Remove the knuckle.

➡Make sure the spacer blocks or supports below the knuckle/hub raise the assembly enough for clearance to remove the hub.

3. Press the hub from the knuckle using Differential End Plug and Hub/Knuckle Support Plate.
4. Remove the retaining ring from the knuckle.
5. Press the bearing from the knuckle using Receiver Cup and Hub/Knuckle Support Installer/Remover.
6. If the hub is to be reused, remove the inner bearing race from the hub with Bearing/Gear Splitter.

To install:

7. Press the bearing into the knuckle using Bearing Cup Remover/Installer and a support plate or block.
8. Install the retaining ring in knuckle.
9. Press the hub into the bearing/knuckle using Differential End Plug and Hub/Knuckle Support Installer/Remover.
10. Install the knuckle to the vehicle.
11. Remove the support and lower the vehicle.

ADJUSTMENT

No adjustment is possible. If the bearing is too loose or worn, it must be replaced.

DODGE

Journey

11

SPECIFICATIONS AND MAINTENANCE CHARTS

ENGINE AND VEHICLE IDENTIFICATION

Engine						
Code ①	Liters	Cu. In.	Cyl.	Fuel Sys.	Engine Type	Eng. Mfg.
B	2.4	146.5	4	MFI	DOHC	Chrysler
V	3.5	214.7	6	MFI	SOHC	Chrysler
G	3.6	219.7	6	MFI	DOHC	Chrysler

Model Year	
Code ②	Year
A	2010
B	2011

MFI: Multiport Fuel Injection

DOHC: Double Overhead Camshafts

① 8th position of VIN

② 10th position of VIN

25766_JOUR_C0001

GENERAL ENGINE SPECIFICATIONS

All measurements are given in inches.

Year	Model	Engine Displacement Liters (VIN)	Fuel System Type	Net Horsepower @ rpm	Net Torque @ rpm (ft. lbs.)	Bore x Stroke (in.)	Com-pression Ratio	Oil Pressure @ rpm
2010	Journey SE	2.4 (B)	MFI	173@6,000	166@4,400	3.47 x 3.82	10.5:1	25-80 psi @3,000
	Journey SXT-Crew-R/T	3.5 (V)	MFI	235@6,400	232@4,000	3.78 x 3.19	10.1:1	45-105 psi @3,000
2011	Journey Express	2.4 (B)	MFI	173@6,000	166@4,400	3.47 x 3.82	10.5:1	25-80 psi @3,000
	Journey Mainstreet-R/T-Crew-LUX	3.6 (G)	MFI	283@6,400	260@4,400	3.78 x 3.27	10.2:1	30 psi @1,201-3,500

25766_JOUR_C0002

ENGINE TUNE-UP SPECIFICATIONS

Year	Engine Displacement Liters	Engine ID/VIN	Spark Plug Gap (in.)	Ignition Timing (deg.) MT	Ignition Timing (deg.) AT	Fuel Pump (psi)	Idle Speed (rpm) MT	Idle Speed (rpm) AT	Valve Clearance Intake	Valve Clearance Exhaust
2010	2.4	B	①	N/A	②	53-63	N/A	③	0.006-0.009	0.010-0.012
	3.5	V	0.050	N/A	②	53-63	N/A	③	HYD	HYD
2011	2.4	B	①	N/A	②	53-63	N/A	③	0.006-0.009	0.010-0.012
	3.6	G	0.040	N/A	②	53-63	N/A	③	HYD	HYD

NOTE: The Vehicle Emission Control Information label often reflects specification changes made during production. The label figures must be used if they differ from those in this chart.

HYD: Hydraulic

① Partial Zero Emission Vehicle (PZEV): 0.031 inch
Without PZEV: 0.043 inch

N/A: Not Applicable

② Ignition timing is controlled by the PCM and is not adjustable

③ Idle speed is controlled by the PCM and is not adjustable

25766_JOUR_C0003

CAPACITIES

Year	Model	Engine Displacement Liters (VIN)	Engine Oil with Filter (qts.)	Transaxle (pts.) Auto.	Drive Axle (pts.) Front	Drive Axle (pts.) Rear ①	Transfer Case (pts.) ①	Fuel Tank (gal.)	Cooling System (qts.)
2010	Journey SE	2.4 (B)	4.5	②	N/A	N/A	N/A	③	④
	Journey SXT	3.5 (V)	5.5	⑤	N/A	1.3	1.7	⑥	⑦
	Journey Crew	3.5 (V)	5.5	⑤	N/A	1.3	1.7	⑥	⑦
	Journey R/T	3.5 (V)	5.5	⑤	N/A	1.3	1.7	⑥	⑦
2011	Journey Express	2.4 (B)	4.5	②	N/A	N/A	N/A	③	④
	Journey Mainstreet	3.6 (G)	6.0	⑤	N/A	1.3	1.7	⑥	7.7
	Journey R/T	3.6 (G)	6.0	⑤	N/A	1.3	1.7	⑥	7.7
	Journey Crew	3.6 (G)	6.0	⑤	N/A	1.3	1.7	⑥	7.7
	Journey LUX	3.6 (G)	6.0	⑤	N/A	1.3	1.7	⑥	7.7

NOTE: All capacities are approximate. Add fluid gradually and ensure a proper fluid level is obtained.

N/A: Not Applicable

① AWD vehicles only

② Drain and refill capacity: 8 pints. Total capacity: 18.4 pints.

③ Partial Zero Emission Vehicle (PZEV): 18.5 gallons; Without PZEV: 20.5 gallons

④ Single or dual-zone climate control: 7.9 qts.; Three-zone climate control system: 9.8 qts.

⑤ Drain and refill capacity: 11 pints. Total capacity: 18.0 pints.

⑥ FWD vehicles: 20.5 gallons; AWD vehicles: 21.1 gallons

⑦ Single or dual-zone climate control: 9.8 qts.; Three-zone climate control system: 12.0 qts.

25766_JOUR_C0004

FLUID SPECIFICATIONS

Year	Model	Engine Disp. Liters	Engine Oil	Auto. Trans.	Drive Axle Front	Drive Axle Rear ①	Transfer Case ①	Power Steering Fluid	Brake Master Cylinder	Cooling System
2010	Journey SE	2.4	5W-20	②	N/A	N/A	N/A	③	DOT 3	④
	Journey SXT	3.5	10W-30	②	N/A	⑤	⑥	③	DOT 3	④
	Journey Crew	3.5	10W-30	②	N/A	⑤	⑥	③	DOT 3	④
	Journey R/T	3.5	10W-30	②	N/A	⑤	⑥	③	DOT 3	④
2011	Journey Express	2.4	5W-20	②	N/A	N/A	N/A	③	DOT 3	④
	Journey Mainstreet	3.6	5W-30	②	N/A	⑤	⑥	③	DOT 3	④
	Journey R/T	3.6	5W-30	②	N/A	⑤	⑥	③	DOT 3	④
	Journey Crew	3.6	5W-30	②	N/A	⑤	⑥	③	DOT 3	④
	Journey LUX	3.6	5W-30	②	N/A	⑤	⑥	③	DOT 3	④

DOT: Department Of Transportation

① AWD vehicles only

② MOPAR® ATF+4 Automatic Transmission Fluid

③ MOPAR® Power Steering Fluid +4

N/A: Not Applicable

④ MOPAR® Antifreeze/Coolant 5 Year/100,000 Mile Formula HOAT (Hybrid Organic Additive Technolo

⑤ MOPAR® Gear & Axle Lubricant SAE 80W-90

⑥ MOPAR® Synthetic Gear & Axle Lubricant SAE 75W-90

25766_JOUR_C0005

VALVE SPECIFICATIONS

Year	Engine Displacement Liters	Engine ID/VIN	Seat Angle (deg.)	Face Angle (deg.)	Spring Test Pressure (lbs. @ in.)	Spring Free-Length (in.)	Spring Installed Height (in.)	Stem-to-Guide Clearance (in.)		Stem Diameter (in.)	
								Intake	Exhaust	Intake	Exhaust
2010	2.4	B	44.75-45.10	45.25-45.75	78.19-85.83 @1.152	1.850	1.378	0.0008-0.0021	0.0012-0.0024	0.2151-0.2157	0.2148-0.2153
	3.5	V	45.00-45.50	44.50-45.00	①	②	1.496	0.0009-0.0026	0.0020-0.0037	0.2730-0.2737	0.2719-0.2726
2011	2.4	B	44.75-45.10	45.25-45.75	78.19-85.83 @1.152	1.850	1.378	0.0008-0.0021	0.0012-0.0024	0.2151-0.2157	0.2148-0.2153
	3.6	G	44.50-45.00	45.00-45.50	63-69 @1.57	2.067	1.575	0.0009-0.0024	0.0012-0.0027	0.2346-0.2354	0.2343-0.2351

① Intake: 69.5-80.5 lbs. @ 1.496 inches
Exhaust (Yellow): 70.5-79.5 lbs. @ 1.496 inches
Exhaust (White): 80-90 lbs. @ 1.496 inches

② Intake: 1.7195 inches
Exhaust (Yellow): 1.8543 inches
Exhaust (White): 1.9015 inches

25766_JOUR_C0006

CAMSHAFT SPECIFICATIONS

All measurements in inches unless noted

Year	Engine Displacement Liters	Engine Code/VIN	Journal Diameter	Brg. Oil Clearance	Shaft End-play	Runout	Journal Bore	Lobe Height	
								Intake	Exhaust
2010	2.4	B	①	②	0.0043-0.0098	NS	③	④	⑤
	3.5	V	1.6905-1.6913	0.0031-0.0047	0.0012-0.0014	NS	1.6944-1.6953	0.3367	0.2571
2011	2.4	B	①	②	0.0043-0.0098	NS	③	④	⑤
	3.6	G	⑥	⑦	0.0030-0.0099	NS	⑧	0.4055	0.3937

NS: Not Specified

① Front Intake Cam: 1.1797-1.1803 inches (29.964-29.980 mm)
Front Exhaust Cam: 1.4166-1.4173 inches (35.984-36.000 mm)
Cam Journal Diameter No. 1-4: 0.943-0.944 inch (23.954-23.970 mm)

② Front Intake Journal: 0.0008-0.0022 inch (0.020-0.057 mm)
Front Exhaust Journal: 0.0007-0.0020 inch (0.019-0.051 mm)
All Others: 0.0008-0.0026 inch (0.020-0.067 mm)

③ Front Intake: 1.1810-1.1819 inches (30.000-30.021 mm)
Front Exhaust: 1.5747-1.5756 inches (40.000-40.024 mm)
Cam Bearing Bore No. 1-4: 0.9448-0.9457 inches (24.000-24.021 mm)

④ Max Lift @ 0.007 inch (0.2 mm) lash: 0.362 inch (9.2 mm)

⑤ Max Lift @ 0.011 inch (0.28 mm) lash: 0.331 inch (8.42 mm)

⑥ No. 1: 1.2589-1.2596 inches (31.976-31.995 mm)
No. 2, 3, 4: 0.9440-0.9447 inch (23.977-23.996 mm)

⑦ No. 1: 0.00010-0.0026 inch (0.025-0.065 mm)
No. 2, 3, 4: 0.0009-0.0025 inch (0.024-0.064 mm)

⑧ No. 1 Cam Towers: 1.2606-1.2615 inches (32.020-32.041 mm)
No. 2, 3, 4 Cam Towers: 0.9457-0.9465 inch (24.020-24.041 mm)

25766_JOUR_C0007

CRANKSHAFT AND CONNECTING ROD SPECIFICATIONS

All measurements are given in inches.

Year	Engine Displacement Liters	Engine ID/VIN	Crankshaft: Main Brg. Journal Dia.	Crankshaft: Main Brg. Oil Clearance	Crankshaft: Shaft End-play	Crankshaft: Thrust on No.	Connecting Rod: Journal Diameter	Connecting Rod: Oil Clearance	Connecting Rod: Side Clearance
2010	2.4	B	①	0.0011-0.0019	0.0019-0.0098	3	②	0.0012-0.0023	0.0039-0.0098
	3.5	V	2.5192-2.5202	0.0013-0.0024	0.0019-0.0102	3	2.2828-2.2835	0.0009-0.0021	0.0051-0.0153
2011	2.4	B	①	0.0011-0.0019	0.0019-0.0098	3	②	0.0012-0.0023	0.0039-0.0098
	3.6	G	2.8310-2.8380	0.0009-0.0020	0.0020-0.0114	3	2.3193-2.3263	0.0009-0.0025	0.0028-0.0146

① Journal grade

0: 2.0466-2.0467 inches (51.985-51.988 mm)

1: 2.0465-2.0466 inches (51.982-51.985 mm)

2: 2.0464-2.0465 inches (51.979-51.982 mm)

3: 2.0462-2.0464 inches (51.976-51.979 mm)

4: 2.0461-2.0462 inches (51.973-51.976 mm)

② Journal grade

1: 1.8884-1.8887 inches (47.966-47.972 mm)

2: 1.8882-1.8884 inches (47.960-47.966 mm)

3: 1.8880-1.8882 inches (47.954-47.960 mm)

25766_JOUR_C0008

PISTON AND RING SPECIFICATIONS

All measurements are given in inches.

Year	Engine Displacement Liters	Engine ID/VIN	Piston Clearance	Ring Gap: Top Compression	Ring Gap: Bottom Compression	Ring Gap: Oil Control	Ring Side Clearance: Top Compression	Ring Side Clearance: Bottom Compression	Ring Side Clearance: Oil Control
2010	2.4	B	(-0.0006)-0.0006	0.0059-0.0118	0.0118-0.0177	0.0079-0.0276	0.0012-0.0028	0.0012-0.0028	0.0024-0.0059
	3.5	V	(-0.0003)-0.0018	0.0079-0.0142	0.0079-0.0157	0.0098-0.0299	0.0016-0.0031	0.0016-0.0031	0.0015-0.0072
2011	2.4	B	(-0.0006)-0.0006	0.0059-0.0118	0.0118-0.0177	0.0079-0.0276	0.0012-0.0028	0.0012-0.0028	0.0024-0.0059
	3.6	G	0.0012-0.0020	0.0098-0.0157	0.0118-0.0177	0.0059-0.0260	0.0010-0.0033	0.0012-0.0031	0.0003-0.0068

25766_JOUR_C0009

TORQUE SPECIFICATIONS

All readings in ft. lbs.

Year	Engine Disp. Liters	Engine ID/VIN	Cylinder Head Bolts	Main Bearing Bolts	Rod Bearing Bolts	Crankshaft Damper Bolts	Flywheel Bolts	Manifold: Intake	Manifold: Exhaust	Spark Plugs	Oil Pan Drain Plug
2010	2.4	B	①	②	③	155	④	18	25	20	30
	3.5	V	⑤	⑥	⑦	70	70	⑧	17	20	20
2011	2.4	B	①	②	③	155	④	18	25	20	30
	3.6	G	⑨	⑩	③	⑪	70	6	17	13	20

① Short head bolts:

Step 1: 25 ft. lbs.

Step 2: 45 ft. lbs.

Step 3: 45 ft. lbs.

Step 4: Plus 90 degrees

Long head bolts:

Step 1: 25 ft. lbs.

Step 2: 54 ft. lbs.

Step 3: 54 ft. lbs.

Step 4: Plus 90 degrees

② Step 1: 11 ft. lbs.

Step 2: 20 ft. lbs.

Step 3: Plus 45 degrees

③ Step 1: 15 ft. lbs.

Step 2: Plus 90 degrees

④ Step 1: 22 ft. lbs.

Step 2: Plus 51 degrees

⑤ Step 1: 45 ft. lbs.

Step 2: 65 ft. lbs.

Step 3: 65 ft. lbs.

Step 4: Plus 90 degrees

⑥ Tie Bolts: 21 ft. lbs.

Outer Cap Bolts: 20 ft. lbs., plus 90 degrees

Inner Cap Bolts: 15 ft. lbs., plus 90 degrees

⑦ Step 1: 20 ft. lbs.

Step 2: Plus 90 degrees

⑧ Intake Manifold (Lower): 21 ft. lbs.

Intake Manifold (Upper): 9 ft. lbs.

⑨ Step 1: 22 ft. lbs.

Step 2: 33 ft. lbs.

Step 3: Plus 75 degrees

Step 4: Plus 50 degrees

Step 5: Loosen all bolts

Step 6: 22 ft. lbs.

Step 7: 33 ft. lbs.

Step 8: Plus 70 degrees

Step 9: Plus 70 degrees

⑩ Outer Cap and Windage Tray (M8 Bolts):

Step 1: 16 ft. lbs.

Step 2: Plus 90 degrees

Inner Cap (M11 Bolts):

Step 1: 15 ft. lbs.

Step 2: Plus 90 degrees

Side Cap-Tie Bolt (M8 Bolts): 21 ft. lbs.

⑪ Step 1: 30 ft. lbs.

Step 2: Plus 105 degrees

25766_JOUR_C0010

WHEEL ALIGNMENT

Year	Model		Caster Range (+/-Deg.)	Caster Preferred Setting (Deg.)	Camber Range (+/-Deg.)	Camber Preferred Setting (Deg.)	Toe-in (in.)
2010	All Models	F	1.00	+3.00	0.55	-0.10	0.10 +/- 0.35
		R	N/A	N/A	0.65	-0.60	0.00 +/- 0.30
2011	FWD Models	F	0.60	+3.00	0.50	-0.10	0.10 +/- 0.25
		R	N/A	N/A	0.55	-0.50	0.10 +/- 0.15
	AWD Models	F	0.60	+3.00	0.50	-0.05	0.10 +/- 0.25
		R	N/A	N/A	0.55	-0.36	0.10 +/- 0.15

N/A: Not Applicable

25766_JOUR_C0011

TIRE, WHEEL AND BALL JOINT SPECIFICATIONS

Year	Model	OEM Tires Standard	OEM Tires Optional	Tire Pressures (psi) Front	Tire Pressures (psi) Rear	Wheel Size Standard	Wheel Size Optional	Ball Joint Inspection	Lug Nut (ft. lbs.)
2010	Journey SE	P225/70R16	NA	①	①	16 x 6.5	NA	②	100
	Journey SXT (FWD)	P225/65R17	P225/55R19	①	①	17 x 6.5	19 x 7.0	②	100
	Journey SXT (AWD)	P225/55R19	NA	①	①	19 x 7.0	NA	②	100
	Journey Crew (FWD)	P225/65R17	P225/55R19	①	①	17 x 6.5	19 x 7.0	②	100
	Journey Crew (AWD)	P225/55R19	NA	①	①	19 x 7.0	NA	②	100
	Journey R/T	P225/55R19	NA	①	①	19 x 7.0	NA	②	100
2011	Journey Express	P225/70R16	NA	①	①	16 x 6.5	NA	②	100
	Journey Mainstreet	P225/65R17	NA	①	①	17 x 6.5	NA	②	100
	Journey R/T-Crew-LUX	P225/55R19	NA	①	①	19 x 7.0	NA	②	100

OEM: Original Equipment Manufacturer

PSI: Pounds Per Square Inch

NA: Information not available

FWD: Front Wheel Drive model

AWD: All Wheel Drive model

① Always refer to the owner's manual and/or vehicle label

② End play is acceptable if no more than 0.039 inch (1.0 mm) of movement is achieved

25766_JOUR_C0012

BRAKE SPECIFICATIONS

All measurements in inches unless noted

Year	Model		Brake Disc Original Thickness	Brake Disc Minimum Thickness	Brake Disc Max. Runout	Brake Drum Diameter Original Inside Diameter	Brake Drum Diameter Max. Wear Limit	Brake Drum Diameter Maximum Machine Diameter	Minimum Pad/Lining Thickness Front	Minimum Pad/Lining Thickness Rear	Brake Caliper Bracket Bolts (ft. lbs.)	Brake Caliper Guide Pin Bolts (ft. lbs.)
2010	All Models	F	1.097-1.107	1.040	0.002	N/A	N/A	N/A	0.039	0.039	125	26
		R	0.163-0.482	0.409	0.002	N/A	N/A	N/A	0.039	0.039	74	26
2011	All Models	F	1.097-1.107	1.040	0.002	N/A	N/A	N/A	0.039	0.039	125	26
		R	0.163-0.482	0.409	0.002	N/A	N/A	N/A	0.039	0.039	74	26

F: Front

R: Rear

N/A: Not Applicable

25766_JOUR_C0013

to install a NEW brake hose washer on each side of the hose fitting as the banjo bolt is guided through the fitting. Thread the banjo bolt into the caliper and tighten it to 19 ft. lbs. (26 Nm).

16. Access the interior of the vehicle, remove the brake pedal holder, then slowly pump the brake pedal until the rear caliper fingers touch the outboard surface of the brake rotor where the brake pad was removed. Release the pedal.

17. Remove the 2 caliper guide pin bolts.

18. Slide the disc brake caliper from the disc brake adapter bracket.

19. Reinstall the outboard pad in the adapter bracket.

20. Open the caliper bleeder screw at least 1 full turn.

21. Seat (bottom) the caliper piston in the bore as follows:

a. Assemble a 3⁄8 inch drive ratchet handle and an extension.

b. Insert the extension through Special Tool 8807-1.

c. Place Special Tool 8807-2 on the end of the extension.

d. Insert the lugs on Special Tool 8807-2 into the notches in the face of the caliper piston.

e. Thread the screw drive on 8807-1 down until it contacts the top of 8807-2 which is against the caliper piston. Do not over tighten the screw-drive. Damage to the piston can occur.

f. Turn 8807-2 with the ratchet, rotating the piston in a clockwise direction until fully seated (bottomed) in the bore. It may be necessary to turn 8807-1 with 8807-2 to start the process of piston retraction.

22. Close the bleeder screw.

1. Special Tool 8807-2
2. Special Tool 8807-1
3. Drive ratchet handle and an extension
4. Lugs on Special Tool 8807-2
5. Notches in the face of the caliper piston

57811

Fig. 7 Using special tools to retract the rear caliper piston

23. Return the brake caliper back down over the adapter bracket into the mounted position and install the guide pin bolts. Tighten both guide pin bolts to 26 ft. lbs. (35 Nm).

➡While bleeding air from the brake caliper in the following steps, be sure to monitor the fluid level in the master cylinder reservoir making sure it does not go dry.

24. Have a helper pump the brake pedal 3–4 times and hold it in the down position.

25. With the pedal in the down position, open the bleeder screw at least 1 full turn and let out fluid and air, if any.

26. Once the brake pedal has dropped, close the bleeder screw. Once the bleeder screw is closed, release the brake pedal.

27. Repeat the previous 3 steps as necessary until all trapped air is removed.

28. If necessary, bleed the remaining wheel circuits using the normal bleeding procedure. Refer to Bleeding The Brake System, Bleeding Procedure.

29. Pull the parking brake cable strand outward from the cable housing and hook it onto the caliper lever.

30. Push the excess cable strand back into the cable housing, then insert the cable housing into the mounting bracket until the retainer fingers lock into place. Make sure both fingers are engaged preventing removal of the cable from the bracket.

31. Install the wheel and tire assembly. Tighten the wheel nuts in a star pattern until all nuts are torqued to half the required specification. Then repeat the tightening sequence to the full specified torque of 100 ft. lbs. (135 Nm).

32. Reconnect the parking brake cable equalizer and reset the cable tension.

33. Lower the vehicle.

34. Connect the battery negative (-) cable to the battery post. Refer to Battery, removal & installation.

35. Road test the vehicle making several stops to wear off any foreign material on the brakes and to seat the brake pads.

DISC BRAKE PADS

REMOVAL & INSTALLATION

See Figures 7 and 8.

➡Perform steps 3–9 on each side of vehicle to complete the pad set removal.

1. Before servicing the vehicle, refer to the Precautions Section.

2. Raise and safely support the vehicle.

3. Remove the wheel mounting nuts, then the tire and wheel assembly.

WARNING

When removing or installing a caliper guide pin bolt, it is necessary to hold the guide pin stationary while turning the bolt. Hold the guide pin stationary using a wrench placed upon the pin's hex-shaped head.

4. Remove the 2 caliper guide pin bolts.

5. Remove the disc brake caliper from the disc brake adapter bracket and hang it out of the way using wire or a bungee cord. Use care not to overextend the brake hose or parking brake cable when doing this.

6. Prior to pad removal, inspect for freedom of the pads to slide on the caliper adapter.

7. Remove the brake pads from the caliper adapter bracket.

8. If the pads show signs of very uneven wear, and/or pads did not slide easily on the adapter, replace the adapter bracket. Remove the 2 mounting bolts and remove the caliper bracket.

9. If the pads did not show signs of very uneven wear, remove and discard the old pad shims, and clean the abutments (area behind the shims) of any debris or corrosion.

To install:

➡Perform steps 1–7 of the installation on each side of the vehicle to complete the pad set installation, then proceed to step 8.

WARNING

Anytime the brake rotor or brake pads are being replaced, the rear

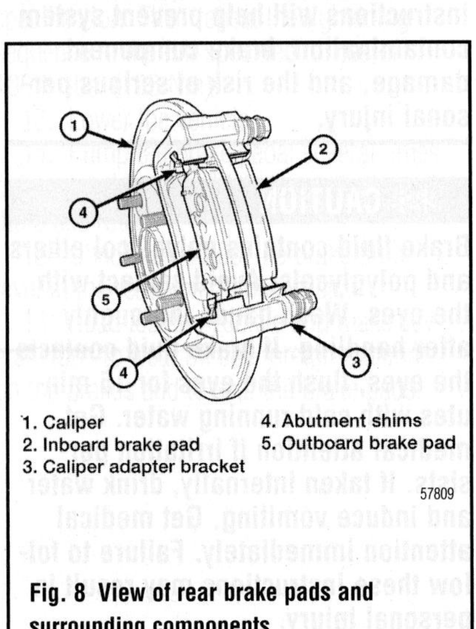

Fig. 8 View of rear brake pads and surrounding components

✲✲ WARNING

Internal radiator pressure must not exceed 20 psi (138 kPa) as damage to the radiator may result.

5. Allow the radiator to fill with water. When the radiator is filled, apply air in short blasts.
6. Allow the radiator to refill between blasts.
7. Continue this reverse flushing until clean water flows out through the rear of the radiator cooling tube passages.

Reverse Flushing Engine

1. Before servicing the vehicle, refer to the Precautions Section.
2. Drain the cooling system.
3. Remove the thermostat housing and thermostat.
4. Install the thermostat housing.
5. Disconnect the radiator upper hose from the radiator and attach the flushing gun to the hose.
6. Disconnect the radiator lower hose from the water pump and attach a lead-away hose to the water pump inlet fitting.
7. Connect the water supply hose and air supply hose to the flushing gun.
8. Allow the engine to fill with water.
9. When the engine is filled, apply air in short blasts, allowing the system to fill between air blasts.
10. Continue until clean water flows through the lead away hose.
11. Remove the lead away hose, flushing gun, water supply hose and air supply hose.
12. Remove the thermostat housing and install the thermostat.
13. Install the thermostat housing with a replacement gasket. Refer to Thermostat, removal & installation.
14. Connect the radiator hoses.
15. Refill the cooling system with the correct antifreeze/water mixture. Refer to Engine Coolant, Drain & Refill Procedure.

Chemical Cleaning

1. Before servicing the vehicle, refer to the Precautions Section.
2. In some instances, use a radiator cleaner (MOPAR® Radiator Kleen, or equivalent) before flushing. This will soften scale and other deposits and aid the flushing operation.

✲✲ WARNING

Follow the manufacturer's instructions when using these products.

ENGINE FAN

REMOVAL & INSTALLATION

See Figure 33.

➡The cooling fan is integrated into the front radiator closure panel and can be removed separately.

1. Before servicing the vehicle, refer to the Precautions Section.
2. Disconnect and isolate the negative battery cable. Refer to Battery, removal & installation.
3. Remove the air filter box assembly. Refer to Air Cleaner, removal & installation.
4. Remove the windshield washer reservoir.
5. Disconnect the radiator fan electrical connectors.
6. Remove the wiring harness from the lower fan.
7. Remove the 4 mounting bolts from the radiator fan assembly.
8. Remove the radiator fan assembly from the core shroud.

To install:

9. Position the radiator fan into the core support frame.
10. Install the mounting bolts. Tighten the bolts to 25 ft. lbs. (35 Nm).
11. Install the wiring harness to the lower area of the fan frame.
12. Connect the radiator fan electrical connector.
13. Install the windshield washer reservoir.
14. Install the air intake assembly.
15. Connect the negative battery cable. Refer to Battery, removal & installation.

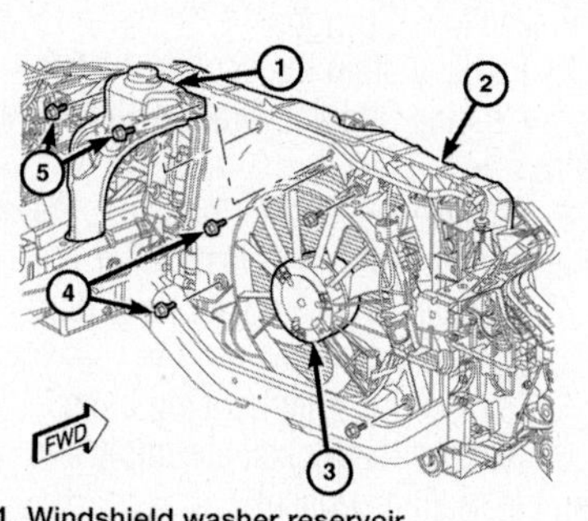

Fig. 33 Radiator fan assembly components shown

RADIATOR

REMOVAL & INSTALLATION

See Figure 34.

1. Before servicing the vehicle, refer to the Precautions Section.
2. Disconnect the negative battery cable. Refer to Battery, removal & installation.
3. Remove the engine cover.
4. Remove the air intake assembly. Refer to Air Cleaner, removal & installation.
5. Evacuate the A/C system.

✲✲ CAUTION

Do not remove the pressure cap or any hose with the system hot and under pressure as serious burns from coolant can occur.

6. Drain the cooling system. Refer to Engine Coolant, Drain & Refill Procedure.
7. Remove the front bumper fascia:
    a. Remove the pushpins for the fascia at the radiator support.
    b. Raise and safely support vehicle.
    c. Remove the pop rivets at the wheel well opening.
    d. Remove the Torx® screw at the wheel well housing.
    e. Separate the fascia tabs at the bracket.
    f. Remove the pushpins for the fascia at the lower closeout panel.
    g. Slide the fascia out from the mounting tab under the headlamp.
    h. Disengage the fog lamp wire connector and the side marker connector from the body harness, if equipped.
    i. Disengage the ambient temperature sensor wire connector, if equipped.

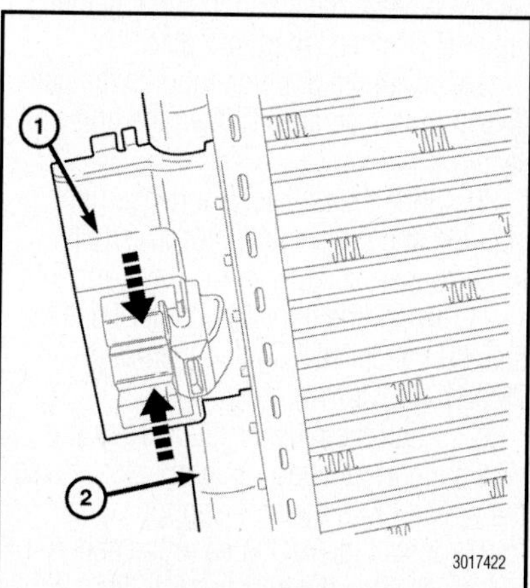

Fig. 34 Compress the tabs (1) that hold the radiator (2) to the core support frame located at the upper ends of the radiator

j. Remove the front bumper fascia from the vehicle.

8. Disconnect the horn connectors.

9. Remove the bolt holding the horn assembly to the upper core support.

10. Remove the upper and lower radiator hoses.

11. Remove the A/C line nuts at the A/C condenser.

➡**The radiator is held in place by plastic tabs. The tabs need to be compressed in order to remove the radiator.**

12. Compress the tabs that hold the radiator to the core support frame located at the upper ends of the radiator.

13. Tilt the radiator/condenser assembly away from the core support frame.

14. Remove the transaxle cooler lines from the condenser and position them aside.

15. Carefully lift the radiator/condenser assembly out of the vehicle between the engine and the front bumper support.

16. Remove the bolt that supports the condenser to the radiator.

17. Separate the A/C condenser from the radiator by compressing the tabs at the sides.

To install:

**** WARNING**

Use care when using force to merge the condenser to the radiator. Damage may occur to the clips on the radiator and the mounting tabs on the condenser.

18. Position the A/C condenser onto the radiator. Carefully align the slots on the condenser to the retainers on the radiator. Gently squeeze the components together until the retainers snap into place.

19. Install the bolt that mounts the condenser to the radiator. Tighten the bolt securely.

20. Slide the radiator/condenser into position and seat the radiator assembly lower rubber isolators in the lower mounts.

21. Install the transaxle cooler lines to the A/C condenser. Tighten the nut to 70 inch lbs. (8 Nm).

22. Align the radiator retainers to the core support radiator mounting tabs. Press the radiator into the core support.

23. Install the A/C lines to the condenser. Tighten the nuts to 15 ft. lbs. (20 Nm).

24. Install the lower radiator hose at the radiator.

25. Install the upper radiator hose.

26. Fill the cooling system. Refer to Engine Coolant, Drain & Refill Procedure.

27. Charge the A/C system.

28. Install the air filter housing. Refer to Air Cleaner, removal & installation.

29. Install the engine cover.

30. Install the horn assembly. Tighten the bolt to 70 inch lbs. (8 Nm).

31. Install the front bumper fascia.

a. Install the fascia to the vehicle:

b. Connect the ambient temperature sensor wire connector, if equipped.

c. Connect the fog lamp wire connector and side marker connector to the body harness, if equipped.

d. Slide the fascia into the mounting tab under the headlamp.

e. Install the pushpins for the fascia at the lower closeout panel.

f. Insert and snap into place the fascia tabs at the bracket.

g. Install the Torx® screw at the wheel well housing.

h. Install the pop rivets at the wheel well opening.

i. Lower the vehicle.

j. Install the pushpins for the fascia at the radiator support.

k. Close the hood and check for proper fit.

32. Connect the negative battery cable. Refer to Battery, removal & installation.

THERMOSTAT

REMOVAL & INSTALLATION

2.4L Engine

Primary Thermostat

See Figure 35.

1. Before servicing the vehicle, refer to the Precautions Section.

2. Partially drain the cooling system. Refer to Engine Coolant, Drain & Refill Procedure.

3. Remove the air filter housing. Refer to Air Cleaner, removal & installation.

4. Disconnect the coolant hose from the inlet housing.

5. Remove the inlet housing bolts.

6. Remove thermostat assembly and clean the sealing surfaces.

To install:

7. Position the thermostat into the water plenum, aligning the air bleed with the location notch on the inlet housing.

8. Install the inlet housing onto the coolant adapter. Tighten the bolts to 79 inch lbs. (9 Nm).

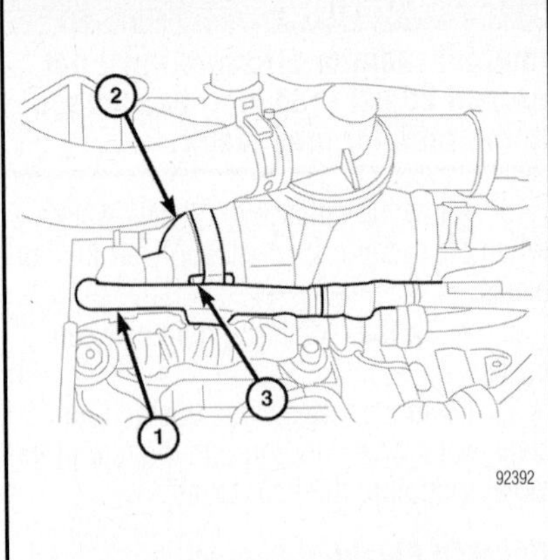

Fig. 35 Disconnect the coolant hose (1) from the inlet housing (2) and remove the inlet housing bolts (3)—2.4L engine

9. Connect the coolant hose.

10. Install the air filter housing. Refer to Air Cleaner, removal & installation.

11. Fill the cooling system. Refer to Engine Coolant, Drain & Refill Procedure.

Secondary Thermostat

See Figure 36.

1. Before servicing the vehicle, refer to the Precautions Section.

2. Partially the drain cooling system.

3. Remove air filter housing. Refer to Air Cleaner, removal & installation.

4. Disconnect the coolant hoses from the rear of the coolant adapter.

5. Remove the radiator hose.

6. Remove the radiator hose from the front of the coolant adapter.

7. Remove the coolant adapter mounting bolts.

8. Carefully slide the coolant adapter off the water pump inlet tube and remove the coolant adapter and secondary thermostat.

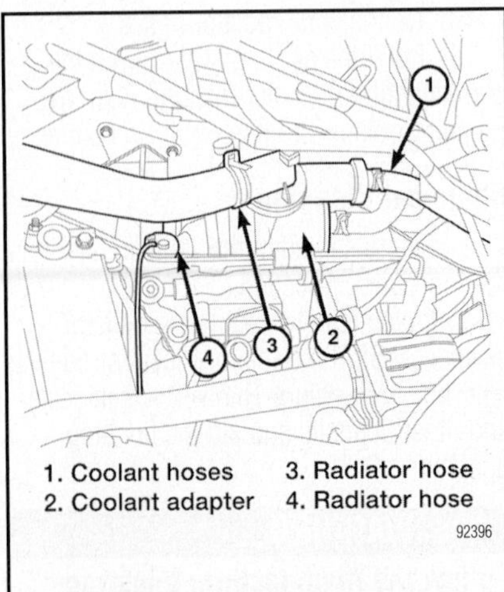

Fig. 36 Secondary thermostat removal—2.4L engine

To install:

9. Position the thermostat into the cylinder head.

10. Inspect the water pump inlet tube O-rings for damage before installing the tube in the coolant adapter. Replace the O-ring as necessary.

11. Lubricate the O-rings with soapy water.

12. Position the coolant adapter on the water pump inlet tube and the cylinder head.

13. Install the coolant adapter mounting bolts. Tighten the bolts to 159 inch lbs. (18 Nm).

14. Connect the front coolant hose.

15. Connect the 2 rear coolant hoses.

16. Connect the radiator hose.

17. Install the air filter housing. Refer to Air Cleaner, removal & installation.

18. Fill the cooling system. Refer to Engine Coolant, Drain & Refill Procedure.

3.5L Engine

See Figure 37.

**** CAUTION**

Do not remove the pressure cap with the system hot and under pressure as serious burns from coolant can occur.

1. Before servicing the vehicle, refer to the Precautions Section.
2. Disconnect the negative battery cable.
3. Drain the cooling system.
4. Disconnect the radiator upper hose from the thermostat housing.
5. Remove the thermostat housing bolts.
6. Remove the housing, thermostat, and gasket.

To install:

7. Clean the gasket sealing surfaces.

8. Install the thermostat and gasket into the thermostat housing. For ease of installation, install the bolts in the housing for thermostat and gasket retention.

9. Install the thermostat and housing to the intake manifold. Tighten the bolts to 106 inch lbs. (12 Nm).

10. Connect the radiator hoses and install the hose clamp.

11. Fill the cooling system. Refer to Engine Coolant, Drain & Refill Procedure.

12. Connect the negative battery cable. Refer to Battery, removal & installation.

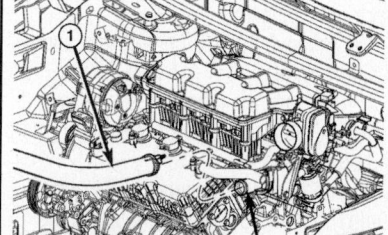

Fig. 37 Disconnect the radiator upper hose from the thermostat housing (1) and remove the thermostat housing bolts (2)—3.5L engine

3.6L Engine

Thermostat Housing

See Figure 38.

**** CAUTION**

Do not loosen the radiator draincock with the system hot and pressurized. Serious burns from coolant can occur.

**** WARNING**

The thermostat and housing is serviced as an assembly. Do not remove the thermostat from the housing, damage to the thermostat may occur.

➡**Do not waste reusable coolant. If the solution is clean, drain the coolant into a clean container for reuse.**

➡**If the thermostat is being replaced, be sure that the replacement is a specified thermostat for the vehicle model and engine type.**

1. Before servicing the vehicle, refer to the Precautions Section.
2. Disconnect the negative battery cable at the battery.
3. Drain the cooling system.
4. Remove the coolant recovery bottle and position aside.
5. Remove the upper radiator hose clamp and upper radiator hose at the thermostat housing.
6. Remove the thermostat housing mounting bolts.
7. Remove the thermostat housing from the vehicle and discard the gasket seal.

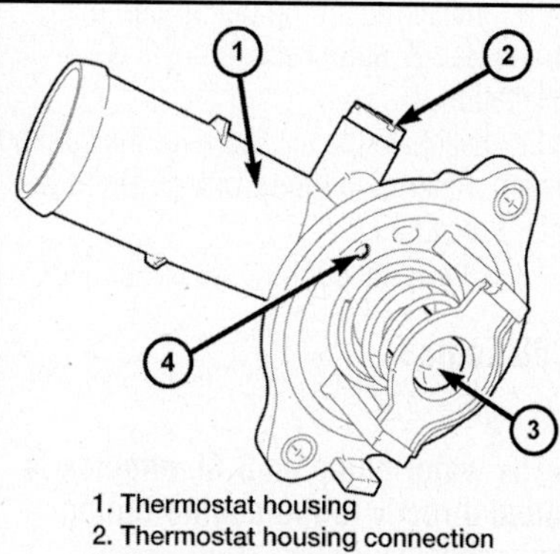

Fig. 38 View of thermostat housing—3.6L engine

To install:

8. Clean the mating areas of the timing chain cover and thermostat housing.

9. Install a new gasket seal to the thermostat housing.

10. Position the thermostat housing on the water crossover.

11. Install the 2 thermostat housing bolts. Tighten the bolts to 106 inch lbs. (12 Nm).

12. Install the upper radiator hose on the thermostat housing.

13. Install the coolant recovery bottle. Tighten the bolts to 70 inch lbs. (8 Nm).

14. Fill the cooling system. Refer to Engine Coolant, Drain & Refill Procedure.

15. Connect the negative battery cable to the battery. Refer to Battery, removal & installation.

16. Start and warm the engine. Check for leaks.

Coolant Crossover

1. Before servicing the vehicle, refer to the Precautions Section.
2. Remove the thermostat housing assembly. Refer to Thermostat Housing, removal & installation.
3. Remove the heater supply hose from the coolant crossover.
4. Remove the coolant crossover mounting bolts. Take notice to the 4 bolts that bolt directly to the timing cover.
5. Remove the coolant crossover and discard the gaskets.

To install:

6. Clean the gasket sealing surfaces.

7. Install the new gasket onto the coolant crossover.

➡**The shorter M6 mounting bolts, bolt directly to the engine timing cover.**

8. Hand tighten the M6 mounting bolts. Tighten the bolts in a crisscross pattern to 106 inch lbs. (12 Nm).

9. Install the heater supply hose to the coolant crossover.

10. Install the thermostat housing. Refer to Thermostat Housing, removal & installation.

WATER PUMP

REMOVAL & INSTALLATION

2.4L Engine

1. Before servicing the vehicle, refer to the Precautions Section.
2. Remove the accessory drive belt. Refer to Accessory Drive Belts, removal & installation.
3. Drain the engine coolant.
4. Raise and safely support the vehicle.
5. Remove the accessory drive belt splash shield.
6. Remove the screws attaching the water pump pulley. Remove the pulley.
7. Remove the water pump mounting bolts.
8. Remove the water pump.

To install:

9. Position the water pump assembly into the water pump housing.
10. Install the mounting bolts. Tighten the bolts to 18 ft. lbs. (24 Nm).
11. Install the water pump pulley. Tighten the bolts to 80 inch lbs. (9 Nm).
12. Install the drive belt splash shield.
13. Lower the vehicle.
14. Install the accessory drive belt. Refer to Accessory Drive Belts, removal & installation.
15. Connect the negative battery terminal. Refer to Battery, removal & installation.
16. Evacuate the air and refill the cooling system. Refer to Engine Coolant, Drain & Refill Procedure.
17. Check the cooling system for leaks.

3.5L Engine

See Figure 39.

➡The water pump can be replaced without discharging the air conditioning system.

⁂ CAUTION

Do not remove the pressure cap with the system hot and under pressure as serious burns from the coolant can occur.

➡It is normal for the water pump to weep a small amount of coolant from the weep hole (black stain on the water pump body). Do not replace the water pump if this condition exists. Replace the water pump if a heavy deposit or a steady flow of engine coolant is evident on the water pump body from the weep hole (shaft seal failure). Be sure to perform a thorough analysis before replacing water pump.

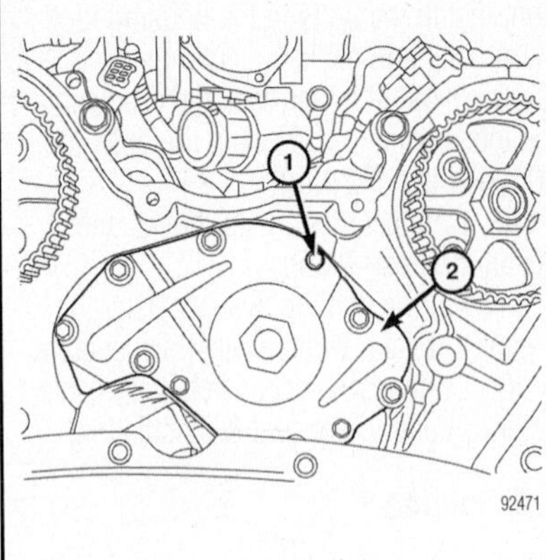

Fig. 39 View of the water pump (2) and bolts (1)—3.5L engine

1. Before servicing the vehicle, refer to the Precautions Section.
2. Drain the cooling system.

➡The water pump is driven by the timing belt.

3. Remove the engine timing belt. Refer to Timing Belt & Sprockets, removal & installation.
4. Remove the water pump mounting bolts. Note the position of the longer bolt for proper installation.
5. Remove the water pump body from the engine.

To install:

6. Clean all O-ring surfaces on the pump and cover.
7. Apply MOPAR® Dielectric Grease or the equivalent silicone grease to the O-ring to facilitate assembly. Install a new O-ring on the water pump.
8. Position the water pump to the engine.
9. Install the mounting bolts and tighten to 106 inch lbs. (12 Nm).
10. Install the timing belt. Refer to Timing Belt & Sprockets, removal & installation.
11. Evacuate the air and refill the cooling system. Refer to Engine Coolant, Drain & Refill Procedure.
12. Check the cooling system for leaks.

3.6L Engine

See Figure 40.

➡The water pump on 3.6L engines is bolted directly to the engine timing chain case cover.

1. Before servicing the vehicle, refer to the Precautions Section.
2. Disconnect the negative battery cable from the battery.

⁂ CAUTION

Constant tension hose clamps are used on most of the cooling system hoses. When removing or installing, use only tools designed for servicing this type of clamp. Always wear safety glasses when servicing constant tension clamps.

⁂ CAUTION

A number or letter is stamped into the tongue of the constant tension clamps. If replacement is necessary, use only an original equipment clamp with the matching number or letter.

3. Remove the coolant bottle assembly and position aside.
4. Using a suitable jack, support the engine.
5. Remove the right side engine mount assembly.
6. Remove the engine mounting block from the water pump.
7. Raise and safely support the vehicle.

⁂ WARNING

Do not pry on the water pump at the timing chain case/cover. The machined surfaces may be damaged resulting in leakage.

8. Remove the lower engine cover.
9. Drain the coolant into a clean container for reuse.
10. Remove the right front wheel.
11. Remove the inner splash shield.
12. Remove the accessory drive belt. Refer to Accessory Drive Belts, removal & installation.
13. Remove the accessory drive belt idler pulley.
14. Disconnect the A/C compressor electrical connector.
15. Remove the A/C compressor and position aside.
16. Remove the lower bypass hose and the lower radiator hose from the water pump and position aside.
17. Remove the remaining 10 water pump mounting bolts. Take notice to the 4 water pump bolts that mount directly to the timing chain cover.
18. Remove the water pump and discard the seal.

To install:

19. Clean the mating surfaces.
20. Using a new seal, position the water pump and install the mounting bolts. Note

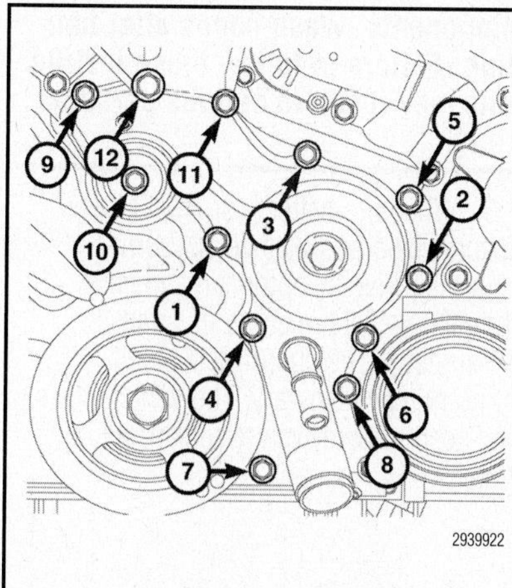

Fig. 40 View of water pump bolt tightening sequence—3.6L engine

the shorter bolts fasten directly to the timing cover. Loosely tighten the M6 water pump mounting bolts.

21. Spin the water pump to be sure that the pump impeller does not rub against the timing chain case/cover.
22. Install the idler pulley bolt. Tighten the mounting bolt to 18 ft. lbs. (25 Nm).
23. Tighten the M6 water pump mounting bolts to 106 inch lbs. (12 Nm) in sequential order.

**** WARNING**

When installing the serpentine accessory drive belt, the belt must be routed correctly. If not, the engine may overheat due to the water pump rotating in the wrong direction.

24. Install the accessory drive belt. Refer to Accessory Drive Belts, removal & installation.
25. Install the lower radiator hose and the bypass hose.
26. Install the right inner splash shield.
27. Install the right front wheel.
28. Lower the vehicle.
29. Position a jack under the engine.
30. Install the engine mounting block onto the front of the water pump. Tighten the M8 mounting bolt to 18 ft. lbs. (25 Nm). Tighten the M10 mounting bolt to 41 ft. lbs. (55 Nm).
31. Install the engine mount. Tighten the mounting bolt to the engine block to 45 ft. lbs. (61 Nm).
32. Install the coolant bottle.
33. Install the air intake assembly.
34. Evacuate the air and refill the cooling system. Refer to Engine Coolant, Drain & Refill Procedure.
35. Connect the negative battery cable. Refer to Battery, removal & installation.
36. Check the cooling system for leaks.

ENGINE ELECTRICAL

BATTERY SYSTEM

BATTERY

REMOVAL & INSTALLATION

See Figures 41 and 42.

**** CAUTION**

To protect the hands from battery acid, a suitable pair of heavy duty rubber gloves should be worn when removing or servicing a battery. Safety glasses also should be worn.

**** CAUTION**

Remove metallic jewelry to avoid injury by accidental arcing of battery current.

➡The negative battery cable remote terminal must be disconnected and isolated from the remote battery post prior to service of the vehicle electrical systems. The negative battery cable remote terminal can be isolated by using the supplied isolation hole in the terminal casing.

1. Before servicing the vehicle, refer to the Precautions Section.
2. Disconnect and isolate the negative battery cable remote terminal from the remote battery post.
3. Remove the left front wheel and tire assembly.
4. Remove the push pins and remove the left front wheelhouse splash shield.

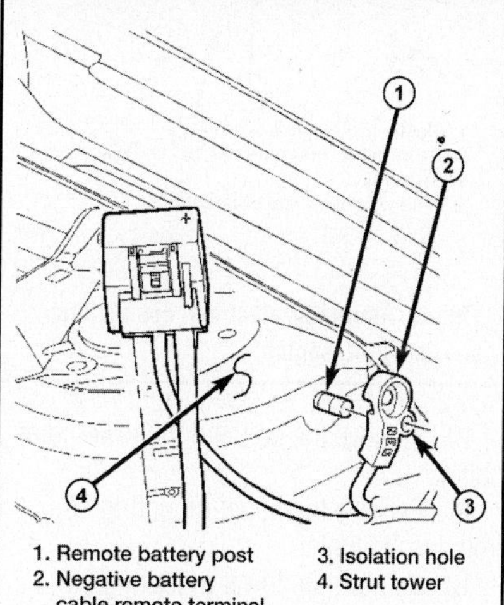

Fig. 41 Location of the negative battery cable remote terminal

5. Loosen the nut and position the battery hold down bracket out of the way.
6. Loosen the pinch clamp bolts and position aside the battery cable clamps from the battery.
7. Remove the battery from the battery tray.

To install:

8. Install the battery into the battery tray.
9. Install the battery terminal pinch clamps onto the battery posts. Tighten the pinch clamp nuts to 13 inch lbs. (18 Nm).

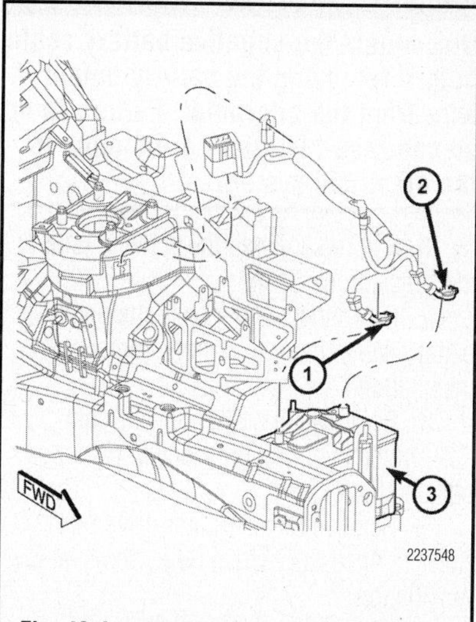

Fig. 42 Loosen the pinch clamp bolts and position aside the battery cable clamps (1, 2) from the battery (3)

10. Position the battery hold down bracket and install the bracket nut. Tighten the pinch clamp nut to 40 ft. lbs. (55 Nm).
11. Install the left front wheelhouse splash shield and push pins.
12. Install the left front wheel and tire assembly. Tighten the wheel nuts in a star pattern until all nuts are torqued to half the required specification. Then repeat the tightening sequence to the full specified torque of 100 ft. lbs. (135 Nm).
13. Install the negative battery cable remote terminal onto the remote battery post. Tighten the nut to 21 ft. lbs. (28 Nm).

BATTERY RECONNECT/RELEARN PROCEDURE

⁂ CAUTION

Always deplete the backup power supply before repairing or installing any new front or side air bag Supplemental Restraint System (SRS) component and before servicing, removing, installing, adjusting, or striking components near the front or side impact sensors. Nearby components include doors, instrument panel, console, door latches, strikers, seats, and hood latches.

1. Before servicing the vehicle, refer to the Precautions Section.
2. To deplete the backup power supply energy, disconnect the battery ground cable and wait at least 1 minute. Be sure to disconnect auxiliary batteries and power supplies (if equipped).

⁂ CAUTION

Battery posts, terminals and related accessories contain lead and lead components. Wash hands after handling. Failure to follow these instructions may result in serious personal injury.

3. When the battery (or PCM) is disconnected and connected, some abnormal drive symptoms may occur while the vehicle relearns its adaptive strategy. The charging system set point may also vary. The vehicle may need to be driven to relearn its strategy.

ENGINE ELECTRICAL

ALTERNATOR

REMOVAL & INSTALLATION

2.4L Engine

See Figures 43 and 44.

⁂ WARNING

Disconnect the negative battery cable before removing the battery output wire from the alternator. Failure to do so can result in injury or damage to the electrical system.

1. Before servicing the vehicle, refer to the Precautions Section.
2. Disconnect and isolate the negative battery cable. Refer to Battery, removal & installation.
3. Remove the underbody air dam.
4. Remove the right front wheelhouse splash shield.
5. Remove the alternator drive belt. Refer to Accessory Drive Belts, removal & installation.

➡Do not disconnect the A/C lines when relocating the A/C compressor.

⁂ WARNING

Support the A/C compressor when relocating. Failure to properly support the A/C compressor can cause damage to the lines and seals. This can cause a leak in the A/C system.

6. Relocate the A/C compressor.
7. Unsnap the plastic protective cover from the B+ mounting stud.
8. Remove the B+ terminal mounting nut and the B+ terminal from the alternator.
9. Disconnect the field wire electrical connector by pushing on the connector tab.

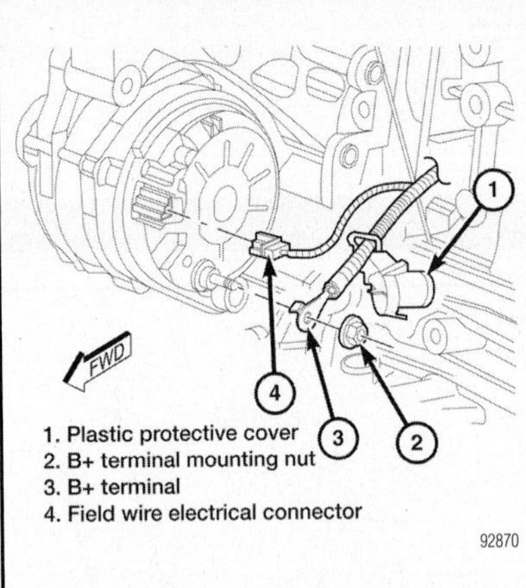

Fig. 43 Alternator electrical connections shown—2.4L engine

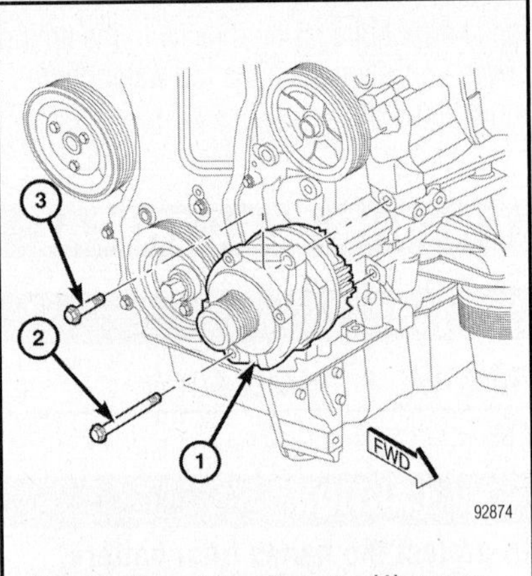

Fig. 44 View of the alternator (1), upper mounting bolt (3), and lower mounting bolt (2)—2.4L engine

10. Remove the bolt and the lower idler pulley.
11. Remove the upper mounting bolt from the alternator.
12. Remove the lower mounting bolt from the alternator.
13. Remove the alternator from the engine mounting bracket.
14. Rotate the alternator so that the pulley faces down.
15. Position the alternator in order to move past the A/C compressor and out of the vehicle.

To install:

16. Position the alternator in order to move it past the A/C compressor and up toward the alternator mounting bracket.
17. Continue moving the alternator up towards the alternator mounting bracket.
18. Install the alternator to the engine mounting bracket.
19. Install the lower mounting bolt and upper mounting bolt to the alternator. Tighten the bolts to 45 ft. lbs. (61 Nm).
20. Install the lower idler pulley and bolt. Tighten the bolt to 37 ft. lbs. (50 Nm).
21. Connect the field wire connector into the alternator.
22. Install the B+ terminal and nut to the alternator mounting stud. Tighten the nut to 89 inch lbs. (10 Nm).
23. Snap the plastic protective cover to the B+ terminal.
24. Install the A/C compressor.

⁂ WARNING

Never force a belt over a pulley rim using a screwdriver. The synthetic fiber of the belt can be damaged.

⁂ WARNING

When installing a serpentine accessory drive belt, the belt MUST be routed correctly. The water pump will be rotating in the wrong direction if the belt is installed incorrectly, causing the engine to overheat.

25. Install the drive belt. Refer to Accessory Drive Belts, removal & installation.
26. Install the right front wheelhouse splash shield.
27. Install the underbody air dam.
28. Connect the negative battery cable, tighten the nut to 40 inch lbs. (5 Nm). Refer to Battery, removal & installation.

3.5L Engine

See Figures 45 and 46.

**** WARNING**

Never force a belt over a pulley rim using a screwdriver. The synthetic fiber of the belt can be damaged.

1. Before servicing the vehicle, refer to the Precautions Section.
2. Disconnect and isolate the negative battery cable.
3. Remove the alternator drive belt. Refer to Accessory Drive Belts, removal & installation.
4. Unsnap the plastic protective cover from the B+ mounting stud.
5. Remove the B+ terminal mounting nut and the B+ terminal at the top of the alternator.
6. Disconnect the field wire electrical connector by pushing on the connector tab.
7. Remove the short mounting bolt from the alternator.
8. Remove the long mounting bolt from the alternator.
9. Remove the alternator from the engine mounting bracket.

To install:

10. Install the alternator to the vehicle.
11. Install the mounting bolts and tighten to 19 ft. lbs. (26 Nm).
12. Install the B+ terminal wire. Tighten the nut to 89 inch lbs. (10 Nm).

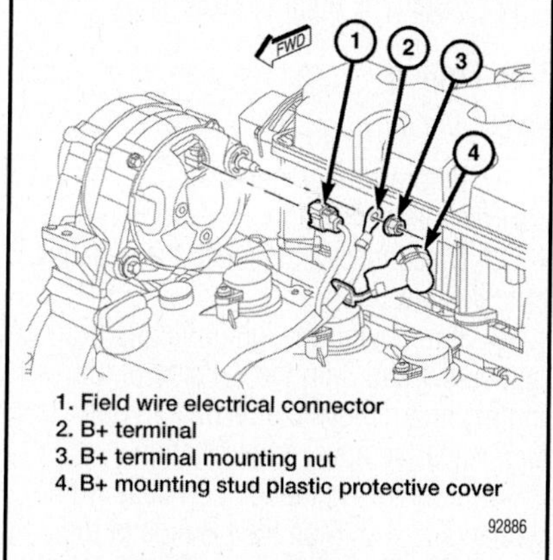

Fig. 45 Removing the alternator electrical connections—3.5L engine

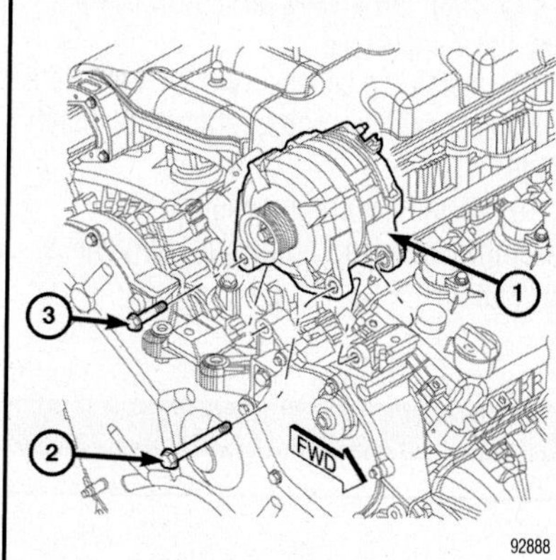

Fig. 46 Removing the alternator (1), long mounting bolt (2), and short mounting bolt (3)—3.5L engine

13. Connect the electrical connector to the alternator.
14. Install the alternator drive belt. Refer to Accessory Drive Belts, removal & installation.
15. Install the negative battery cable remote terminal onto the remote battery post. Tighten the nut to 12 ft. lbs. (17 Nm).

3.6L Engine

See Figures 47 and 48.

➡The negative battery cable remote terminal must be disconnected and isolated from the remote battery post prior to service of the vehicle electrical systems. The negative battery cable remote terminal can be isolated by using the supplied isolation hole in the terminal casing.

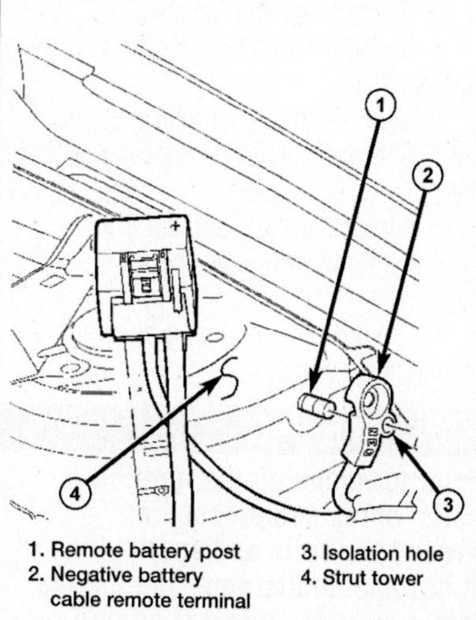

Fig. 47 Location of the negative battery cable remote terminal

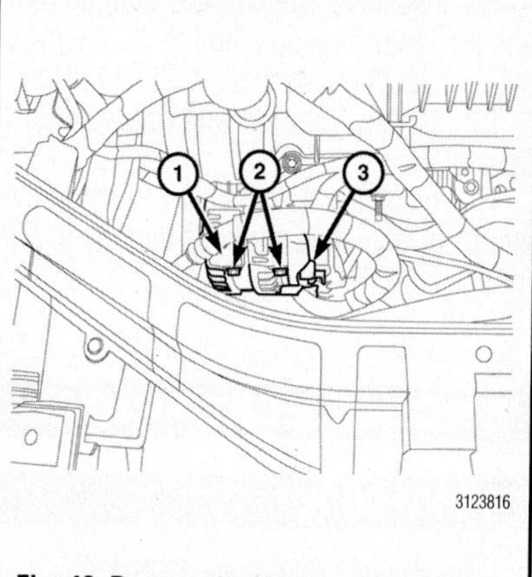

Fig. 48 Remove the electrical connector (3) from the alternator (1) and the upper mounting bolts (2)

1. Disconnect and isolate the negative battery cable remote terminal from the remote battery post.
2. Before servicing the vehicle, refer to the Precautions Section.
3. Remove the air cleaner assembly. Refer to Air Cleaner, removal & installation.
4. Remove the engine oil dipstick tube.
5. Remove the cooling fan. Refer to Engine Fan, removal & installation.

**** WARNING**

Never force a belt over a pulley rim using a screwdriver. The synthetic fiber of the belt can be damaged.

**** WARNING**

Do not let tensioner arm snap back to the free-arm position, severe damage may occur to the tensioner.

6. Rotate the belt tensioner counterclockwise until it contacts the stop, remove the accessory drive belt and then slowly rotate the tensioner into the free-arm position.
7. Unsnap the plastic insulator cover from the B+ terminal.
8. Remove the B+ terminal retaining nut and remove the B+ terminal.
9. Depress the field wire electrical connector tab and remove the electrical connector from the alternator.
10. Remove the 2 upper mounting bolts from the alternator.
11. Remove the lower mounting bolt from the alternator.
12. Remove the alternator from the engine mounting bracket without damaging the radiator.

To install:

13. Position the alternator onto the engine mounting bracket.

14. Install the 2 upper mounting bolts and the lower mounting bolt to the alternator. Tighten the bolts to 31 ft. lbs. (42 Nm).
15. Connect the field wire connector to the alternator.
16. Install the B+ terminal and nut to the alternator mounting stud. Tighten nut to 89 inch lbs. (10 Nm).
17. Snap the plastic protective cover over the B+ terminal.
18. Install the accessory drive belt. Refer to Accessory Drive Belts, removal & installation.
19. Install the engine cooling fan assembly. Refer to Engine Fan, removal & installation.
20. Install the engine oil dipstick tube.
21. Install the air cleaner body. Refer to Air Cleaner, removal & installation.
22. Connect the negative battery cable. Tighten the nut to 40 inch lbs. (5 Nm).
23. Start the engine and verify the alternator is functioning properly.

ENGINE ELECTRICAL

IGNITION SYSTEM

FIRING ORDER

2.4L engine firing order: 1–3–4–2
3.5L and 3.6L engine firing order: 1–2–3–4–5–6

IGNITION COIL

REMOVAL & INSTALLATION

2.4L Engine

See Figures 49 and 50.

➡Prior to removing the coil, spray compressed air around the coil top to make sure no dirt drops into the spark plug tube.

➡The electronic ignition coil attaches directly to the valve cover.

1. Before servicing the vehicle, refer to the Precautions Section.
2. Remove the negative battery cable.
3. Disconnect the electrical connector from the ignition coil.
4. Remove the ignition coil mounting bolts.
5. Remove the ignition coil.

To install:

6. Install the ignition coil. Tighten the bolt to 80 inch lbs. (9 Nm).

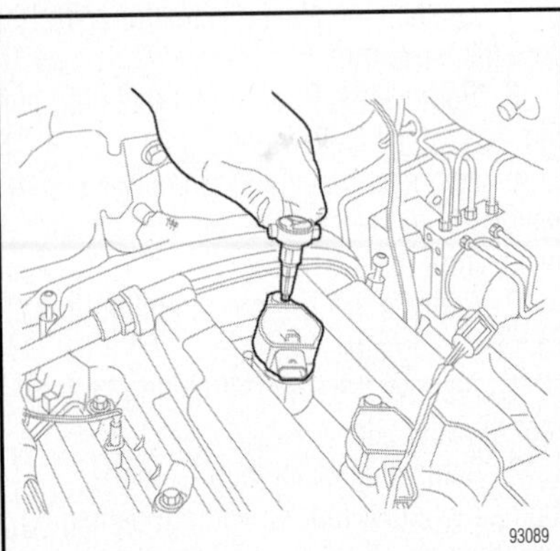

Fig. 49 Removing the ignition coil mounting bolts—2.4L engine

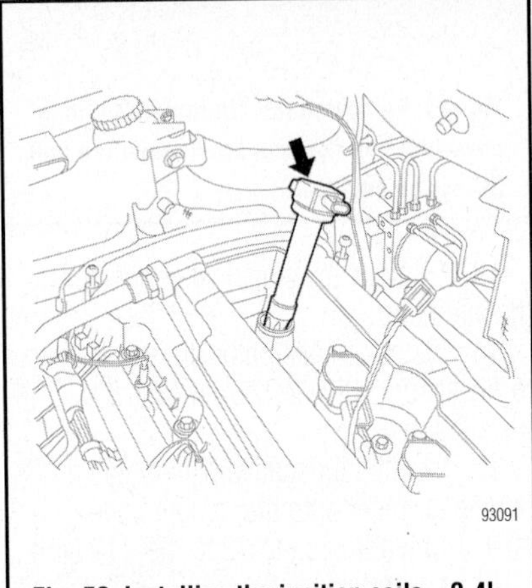

Fig. 50 Installing the ignition coils—2.4L engine

7. Connect the electrical connectors and lock.
8. Install the negative battery cable. Refer to Battery, removal & installation.

3.5L Engine

See Figure 51.

1. Before servicing the vehicle, refer to the Precautions Section.
2. Remove the engine cover.
3. Disconnect and isolate the negative battery cable.
4. Remove the upper intake manifold. Refer to Intake Manifold, removal & installation.
5. Unlock and disconnect the electrical connector from the ignition coils.
6. Remove the mounting bolts and the engine cover studs.

⁂ WARNING

Prior to removing the ignition coils, spray compressed air around the coils and spark plugs. If dirt and debris enter the engine, this may cause internal engine damage.

7. Twist, lift, and remove the ignition coils from the engine.

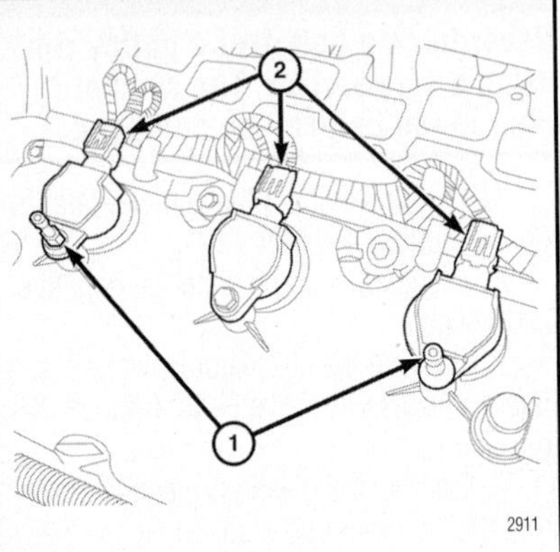

Fig. 51 Removing the ignition coil mounting bolts/studs (1) and electrical connectors (2)—3.5L engine

To install:

8. Install the ignition coils.
9. Install the engine cover studs in the 2 outside ignition coils on the front of the engine. Install bolts on the other ignition coils. Tighten the studs and bolts to 71 inch lbs. (8 Nm).
10. Connect the electrical connector and lock.
11. Install the intake manifold. Refer to Intake Manifold, removal & installation.
12. Connect the negative battery cable and tighten the nut to 45 inch lbs. (5 Nm).
13. Install the engine cover.

3.6L Engine

See Figure 52.

1. Before servicing the vehicle, refer to the Precautions Section.
2. Disconnect and isolate the negative battery cable.
3. If removing the ignition coils from cylinders 1 and 3 on the RH side of the engine, first remove the resonator. Refer to Air Cleaner, removal & installation.
4. If removing the ignition coils from cylinders 2, 4 or 6 on the LH side of the engine, first remove the upper intake manifold and insulator. Refer to Intake Manifold, removal & installation.

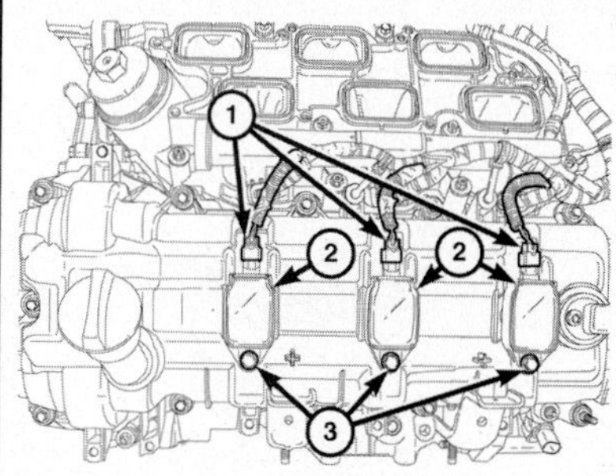

Fig. 52 Unlock and disconnect the electrical connector (1), remove the mounting bolt (3), and pull the ignition coil (2) from the cylinder head cover opening (LH shown, RH ignition coils are similar)—3.6L engine

5. Unlock and disconnect the electrical connector from the ignition coil.

6. Remove the ignition coil mounting bolt.

7. Pull the ignition coil from the cylinder head cover opening with a slight twisting action.

To install:

8. Using compressed air, blow out any dirt or contaminants from around the top of the spark plug.

9. Check the condition of the ignition coil rubber boot. Inspect the opening of the boot for any debris, tears, or rips. Carefully remove any debris with a lint free cloth.

✲✲ WARNING

Do not apply silicone based grease such as MOPAR® Dielectric Grease to the ignition coil rubber boot. The silicone based grease will absorb into the boot causing it to stick and tear.

10. Place a small, 360° bead of Fluostar® 2LF lubricant along the inside opening of the coil boot approximately 0.039–0.079 inch (1–2mm) from the chamfer edge, but not on the chamfered surface.

11. Position the ignition coil into the cylinder head cover opening. Using a twisting action, push the ignition coil onto the spark plug.

12. Install the ignition coil mounting bolt and tighten to 71 inch lbs. (8 Nm).

13. Connect and lock the electrical connector to the ignition coil.

14. If removed, install the insulator, upper intake manifold, and air inlet hose. Refer to Intake Manifold, removal & installation.

15. Connect the negative battery cable and tighten the nut to 45 inch lbs. (5 Nm). Refer to Battery, removal & installation.

IGNITION TIMING

ADJUSTMENT

The ignition timing is controlled by the Powertrain Control Module (PCM). No adjustment is necessary.

SPARK PLUGS

REMOVAL & INSTALLATION

2.4L Engine

See Figure 53.

1. Before servicing the vehicle, refer to the Precautions Section.

2. Disconnect the negative battery cable.

3. Remove the ignition coils. Refer to Ignition Coil, removal & installation.

✲✲ WARNING

Prior to loosening the spark plug, use compressed air to blow out any debris that might be in the spark plug tube.

4. Remove the spark plug using a quality socket with a rubber or foam insert.

5. Inspect the spark plug condition.

To install:

✲✲ WARNING

Handle the spark plugs with care. Do not drop or force the spark plugs into the wells, damage to the electrodes and/or porcelain body may occur. Always start each spark plug by hand in order to avoid cross-threading the spark plug in the cylinder head. Always tighten spark plugs to the specified torque. Too much or not enough torque will cause damage to the cylinder head and/or spark plug and may lead to poor engine performance.

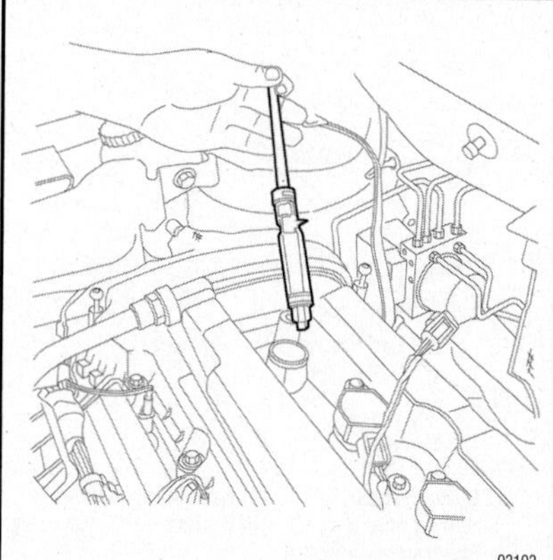

Fig. 53 Using a spark plug socket, remove the spark plugs from the engine—2.4L engine

6. Install each spark plug to the cylinder head. Tighten the spark plugs to 20 ft. lbs. (27 Nm).

7. Install the ignition coil onto spark plug. Refer to Ignition Coil, removal & installation.

8. Connect the negative battery cable. Refer to Battery, removal & installation.

3.5L Engine

1. Before servicing the vehicle, refer to the Precautions Section.

2. Remove the engine cover.

3. Disconnect and isolate the negative battery cable.

4. Remove the ignition coils. Refer to Ignition Coil, removal & installation.

✲✲ WARNING

Prior to removing the spark plugs, use compressed air to remove any accumulated dirt and debris. If dirt and debris enter the engine, this may cause internal engine damage.

5. Remove the spark plugs using a quality socket with a rubber or foam insert.

To install:

✲✲ WARNING

Handle the spark plugs with care. Do not drop or force the spark plugs into the wells, damage to the electrodes and/or porcelain body may occur. Always start each spark plug by hand in order to avoid cross-threading the spark plug in the cylinder head. Always tighten spark plugs to the specified torque. Too much or not enough torque will cause damage to the cylinder head and/or spark plug and may lead to poor engine performance.

6. To avoid cross threading, start the spark plug into the cylinder head by hand.

7. Tighten the spark plugs to 20 ft. lbs. (27 Nm).

8. Install the ignition coils. Refer to Ignition Coils, removal & installation.

9. Reconnect the negative battery cable. Refer to Battery, removal & installation.

10. Install the engine cover.

3.6L Engine

See Figure 54.

1. Before servicing the vehicle, refer to the Precautions Section.

2. Remove the ignition coils. Refer to Ignition Coil, removal & installation.

WARNING

Prior to removing the spark plug, spray compressed air into the cylinder head opening. This will help prevent foreign material from entering the combustion chamber.

WARNING

The spark plug tubes are a thin wall design. Avoid damaging the spark plug tubes. Damage to the spark plug tube can result in oil leaks.

3. Remove the spark plug from the cylinder head using a quality thin wall socket with a rubber or foam insert.
4. Inspect the spark plug condition.

To install:

5. Check and adjust the spark plug gap with a gap gauging tool.

WARNING

Special care should be taken when installing spark plugs into the cylinder head spark plug wells. Be sure the plugs do not drop into the plug wells as electrodes can be damaged.

6. Start the spark plug into the cylinder head by hand to avoid cross threading.

WARNING

Spark plug torque is critical and must not exceed the specified value. Overtightening stretches the spark plug shell reducing its heat transfer capability resulting in possible catastrophic engine failure.

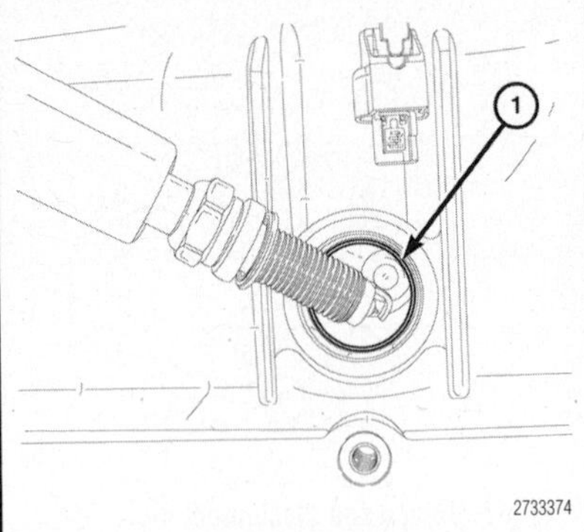

Fig. 54 The spark plug tubes (1) are a thin wall design. Avoid damaging the spark plug tubes

7. Tighten the spark plugs to 13 ft. lbs. (18 Nm).
8. Install the ignition coils. Refer to Ignition Coil, removal & installation.

ENGINE ELECTRICAL

STARTING SYSTEM

STARTER

REMOVAL & INSTALLATION

2.4L Engine

See Figures 55 and 56.

1. Before servicing the vehicle, refer to the Precautions Section.
2. Disconnect and isolate the negative battery cable. Refer to Battery, removal & installation.
3. Remove the throttle body. Refer to Throttle Body, removal & installation.
4. Remove the starter mounting bolts and the negative battery cable from the transaxle housing.
5. Remove the starter motor from the transaxle housing.
6. Position the starter to move it past the intake manifold.
7. Remove the battery cable nut, ignition sense wire, and battery cable from the solenoid stud.
8. Disconnect the electrical connector from the starter solenoid.
9. Remove the starter from the vehicle.

To install:

10. Install the starter to the vehicle.
11. Connect the electrical connector to the starter solenoid.
12. Install the battery cable, ignition sense wire, and battery cable nut to the solenoid stud. Tighten the nut to 89 inch lbs. (10 Nm).
13. Position the starter motor past the intake manifold.
14. Install the starter motor to the transaxle housing.
15. Install the negative battery cable and the starter mounting bolts to the transaxle housing. Tighten the bolts to 40 ft. lbs. (54 Nm).
16. Install the throttle body. Refer to Throttle Body, removal & installation.
17. Connect the negative battery cable and tighten the nut to 40 inch lbs. (5 Nm).

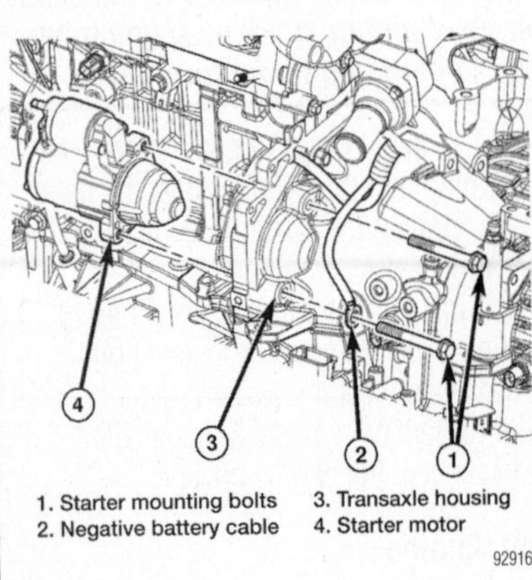

Fig. 55 Starter motor removal—2.4L engine

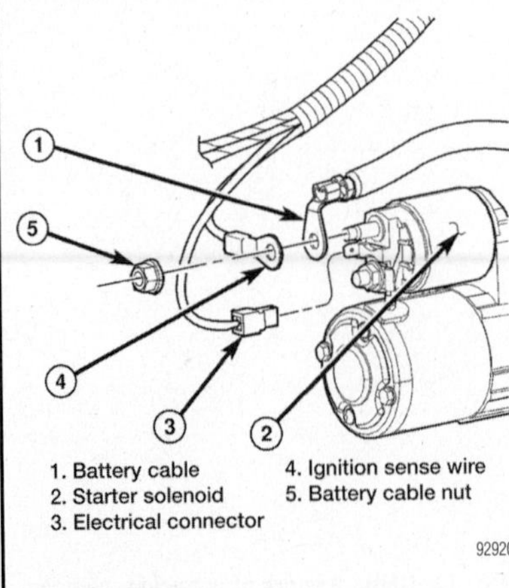

Fig. 56 Starter motor electrical connections shown—2.4L engine

3.5L Engine

See Figures 57 through 60.

1. Before servicing the vehicle, refer to the Precautions Section.
2. Disconnect and isolate the negative battery cable at the battery.
3. Remove the heat shield nuts, and position the heat shield aside.
4. Remove the belly pan, if equipped.
5. Remove the front mount through bolt from the transaxle bracket and mount.
6. Remove the rear bolts from the transaxle crossmember.
7. Remove the front bolts from the transaxle crossmember.
8. Remove the transaxle crossmember.
9. Remove the heat shield bolts and remove the heat shield.
10. Remove the oxygen sensor and position aside.

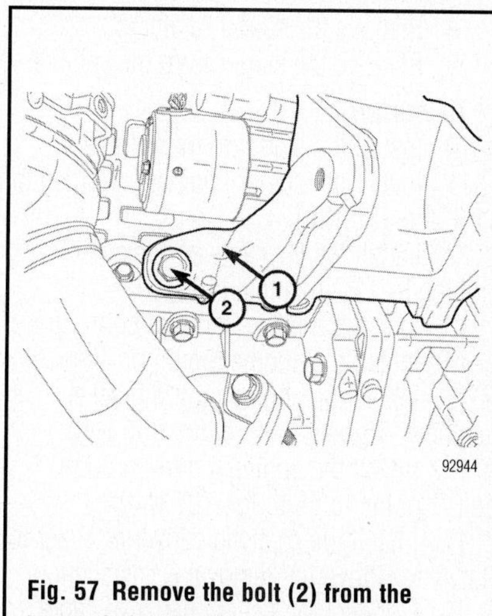

Fig. 57 Remove the bolt (2) from the transaxle bracket (1)—3.5L engine

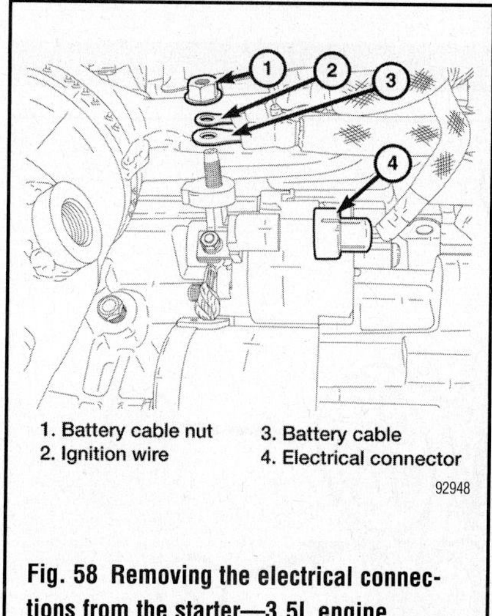

Fig. 58 Removing the electrical connections from the starter—3.5L engine

11. Remove the bolt from the transaxle bracket.
12. Remove the bolts, and the transaxle bracket from the transaxle housing.
13. Remove the battery cable nut, ignition wire, and battery cable from the starter solenoid stud.
14. Disconnect the electrical connector from the starter solenoid.
15. Remove the starter mounting bolts and ground wire and remove the starter from the transaxle housing.
16. Remove the starter motor dust shield from the starter.

➡If the flywheel is damaged, the flywheel will require replacement.

17. Rotate and fully inspect the flywheel gears and wields for damage.

To install:

18. Install the starter motor dust shield to the starter.

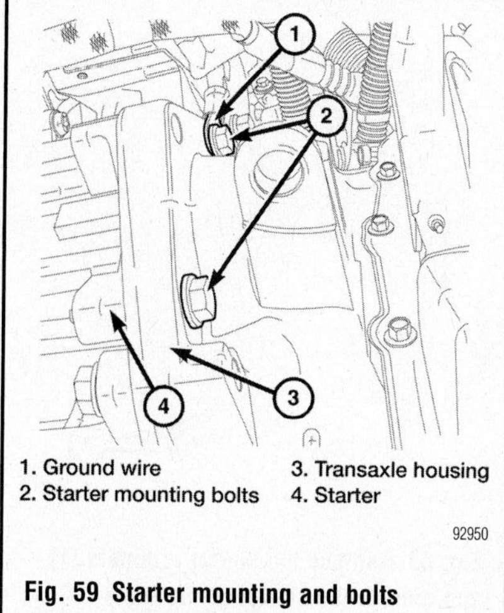

Fig. 59 Starter mounting and bolts shown—3.5L engine

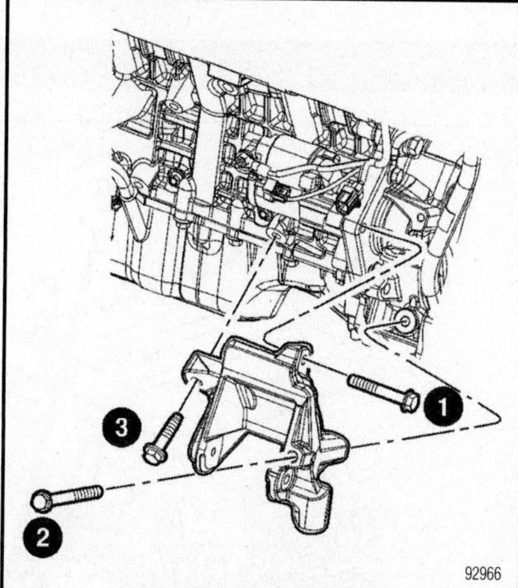

Fig. 60 Torque reaction bracket mandatory torque sequence shown—3.5L engine

19. Position the starter into the transaxle housing, install the ground wire and starter mounting bolts. Tighten the bolts to 40 ft. lbs. (54 Nm).
20. Install the battery cable, ignition wire, and battery cable nut to the starter solenoid stud. Tighten the nut to 89 inch lbs. (10 Nm).
21. Connect the electrical connector to the starter solenoid.
22. Install the transaxle bracket and the bolts, to the transaxle housing. Hand tighten the bolts.
23. Install the bolt to the transaxle bracket. Hand tighten the bolt.

WARNING

The torque reaction bracket bolts need to be tightened using a mandatory torque sequence. Failure to tighten the bolts using the mandatory torque sequence provided may result in damage to the fasteners, bracket, and threaded bolt holes for the engine and transaxle.

24. Tighten the bolts in a mandatory torque sequence to 37 ft. lbs. (50 Nm).
25. Install the oxygen sensor and tighten to 30 ft. lbs. (41 Nm).
26. Install the heat shield and bolts. Tighten the bolts to 106 inch lbs. (12 Nm).
27. Install the bolts to the transaxle crossmember. Tighten the 2 bolts to 41 ft. lbs. (55 Nm) and the 4 bolts to 37 ft. lbs. (50 Nm).
28. Install the front mount through bolt to the transaxle bracket and mount. Tighten the bolt to 35 ft. lbs. (47 Nm).
29. If equipped, install the belly pan.

➡Make sure the lower heat shield is installed to the lower stud before the upper heat shield is installed. The upper heat shield stacks on top of the lower heat shield, and both shields are held together by the lower nut.

30. Position the heat shield over the studs and install the heat shield nuts,. Tighten the nuts to 106 inch lbs. (12 Nm).
31. Connect the negative battery cable and tighten the nut to 45 inch lbs. (5 Nm). Refer to Battery, removal & installation.

3.6L Engine

See Figures 61 through 63.

1. Before servicing the vehicle, refer to the Precautions Section.
2. Disconnect and isolate the negative battery cable.
3. Remove the catalytic converter. Refer to Catalytic Converter, removal & installation.
4. Remove the front engine mount through bolt.
5. Remove the retainers from the front engine mount bracket and remove the bracket.

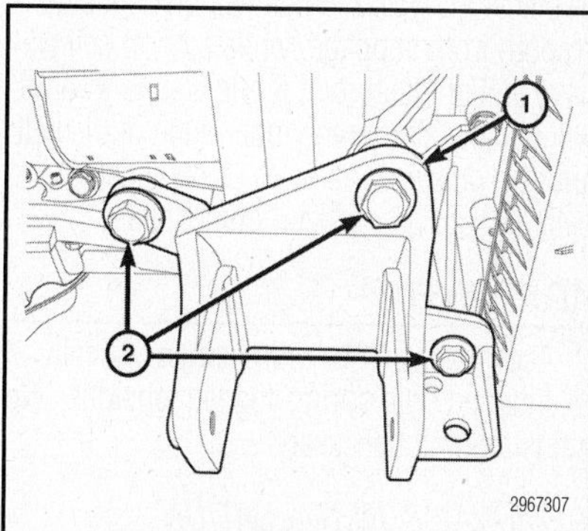

Fig. 61 Remove the retainers (2) and the front engine mount bracket (1)—3.6L engine

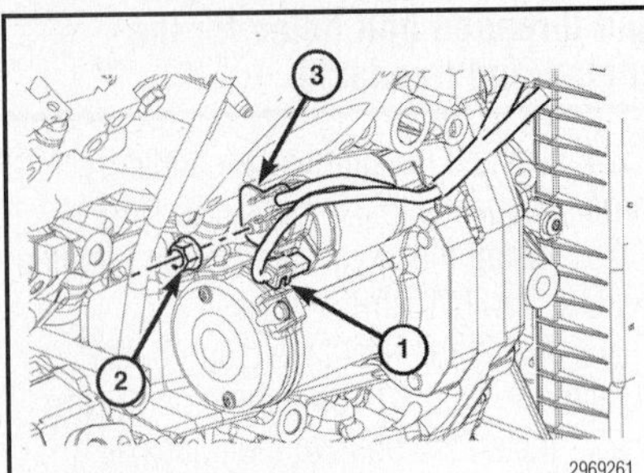

Fig. 62 View of starter field alternator connector (1), B+ retainer (2), and B+ cable (3)—3.6L engine

6. Remove the field alternator connector.
7. Remove the B+ retainer and B+ cable.

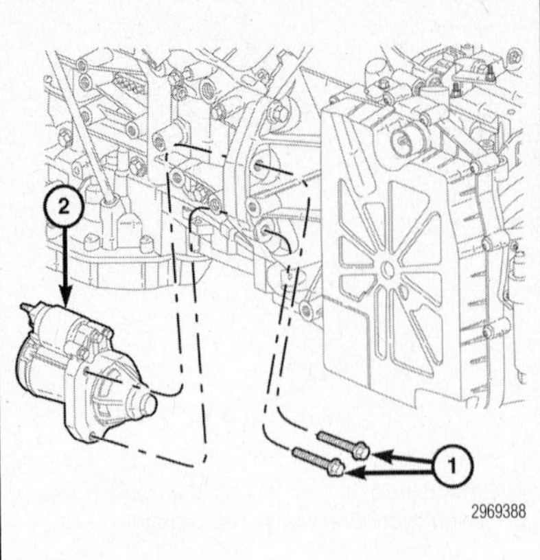

Fig. 63 Remove the starter retainers (1) and remove the starter (2) from the vehicle—3.6L engine

8. Remove the starter retainers.
9. Remove the starter from the vehicle.

To install:

10. Install the starter to the vehicle.
11. Install the starter retainers. Tighten to 41 ft. lbs. (55 Nm).
12. Install the B+ cable and retainer. Tighten to 115 inch lbs. (13 Nm).
13. Install the field alternator connector.
14. Install the engine mount bracket.
15. Install the engine mount bracket retainers. Tighten to 41 ft. lbs. (55 Nm).
16. Install the engine mount through bolt. Tighten to 45 ft. lbs. (61 Nm).
17. Install the catalytic converter. Refer to Catalytic Converter, removal & installation.
18. Connect the battery negative cable. Refer to Battery, removal & installation.

ENGINE MECHANICAL

➡Disconnecting the negative battery cable may interfere with the functions of the on board computer systems and may require the computer to undergo a relearning process, once the negative battery cable is reconnected.

ACCESSORY DRIVE BELTS

ACCESSORY BELT ROUTING

2.4L Engine

See Figure 64.

3.5L Engine

See Figure 65.

3.6L Engine

See Figure 66.

INSPECTION

Inspect the drive belt for signs of glazing or cracking. A glazed belt will be perfectly smooth from slippage, while a good belt will have a slight texture of fabric visible. Cracks will usually start at the inner edge of the belt and run outward. All worn or damaged drive belts should be replaced immediately.

ADJUSTMENT

Accessory belt tension is automatically maintained by a spring-loaded tensioner. No adjustment is necessary.

REMOVAL & INSTALLATION

2.4L Engine

1. Before servicing the vehicle, refer to the Precautions Section.

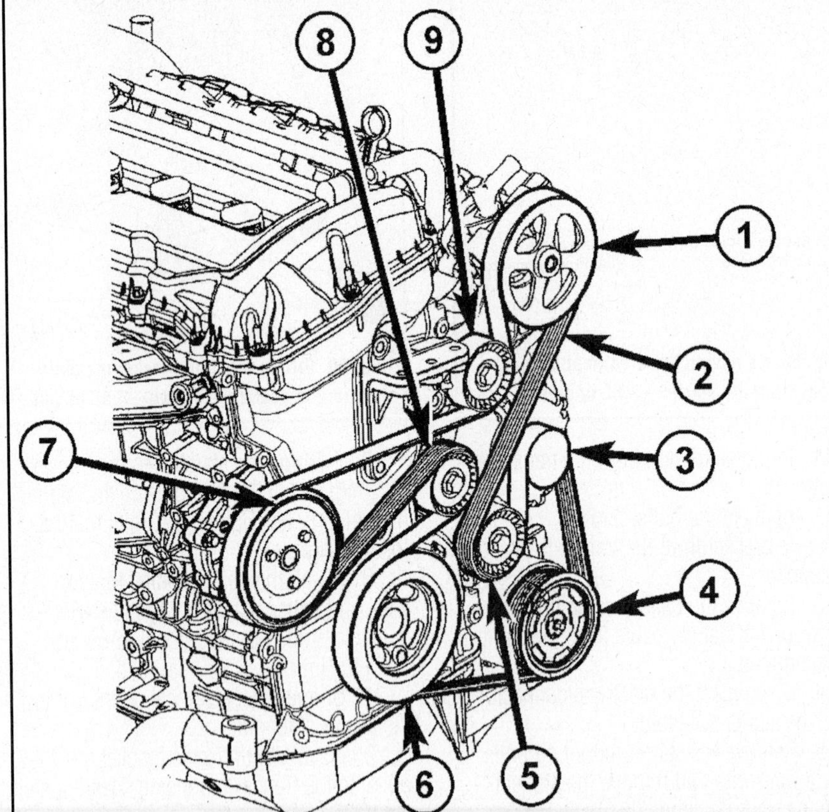

Fig. 64 Accessory drive belt routing—2.4L engine

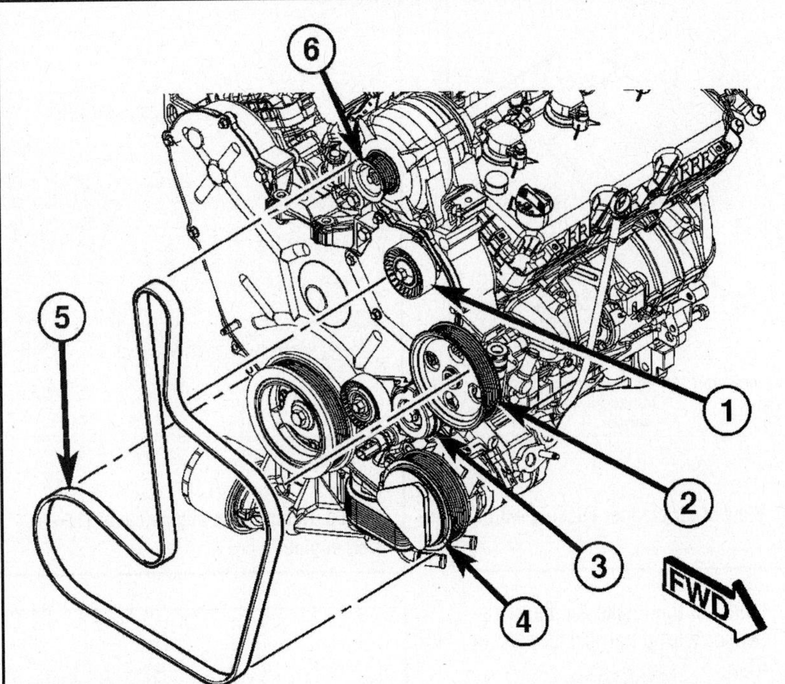

Fig. 65 Accessory drive belt routing—3.5L engine

1. Idler pulley
2. Water pump pulley
3. A/C pulley
4. Accessory drive belt
5. Power steering pulley
6. Crankshaft pulley
7. Tensioner arm
8. Alternator pulley

2743106

Fig. 66 Accessory drive belt routing—3.6L engine

2. Using a wrench, rotate the accessory drive belt tensioner counterclockwise until the accessory drive belt can be removed from the lower and upper idler pulleys.
3. Remove the accessory drive belt from the vehicle.

To install:

➡When installing the drive belt on the pulleys, make sure that belt is properly routed and that all V-grooves make proper contact with the pulley grooves.

4. Install the accessory drive belt around all the pulleys except for the alternator pulley.
5. Using a wrench, rotate the accessory drive belt tensioner counterclockwise until the accessory drive belt can be installed on the alternator pulley. Release the spring tension onto the accessory drive belt.

3.5L Engine

✲✲ WARNING

Do not let the tensioner arm snap back to the free-arm position, severe damage may occur to the tensioner.

➡Belt tension is not adjustable. The belt adjustment is maintained by an automatic, spring loaded belt tensioner.

1. Before servicing the vehicle, refer to the Precautions Section.
2. Disconnect the negative battery cable from the battery.
3. Rotate the belt tensioner clockwise until it contacts the stop. Remove the belt, then slowly rotate the tensioner into the free-arm position.

To install:

4. Check the condition of all pulleys.

✲✲ WARNING

When installing the accessory drive belt, the belt MUST be routed correctly. If not, the engine may overheat due to the water pump rotating in the wrong direction.

5. Install a new belt. Route the belt around all the pulleys except the idler pulley. Rotate the tensioner arm until it contacts its stop position. Route the belt around the idler and slowly let the tensioner rotate into the belt. Make sure the belt is seated onto all the pulleys.

➡The tensioner is equipped with an indexing tang on the back of the tensioner and an indexing stop on the tensioner housing. If a new belt is being installed, the tang must be within approximately 0.24–0.32 inch (6–8mm) of the indexing stop (i.e. the tang is approximately between the two indexing stops). The belt is considered new if it has been used 15 minutes or less.

6. With the drive belt installed, inspect the belt wear indicator.
7. Connect the negative battery cable. Refer to Battery, removal & installation.

3.6L Engine

✲✲ WARNING

Do not let tensioner the arm snap back to the free-arm position, severe damage may occur to the tensioner.

1. Before servicing the vehicle, refer to the Precautions Section.
2. Disconnect the negative battery cable from the battery.
3. Raise and safely support the vehicle.
4. Remove the right front wheel.
5. Remove the inner splash shield.
6. Rotate the belt tensioner until it contacts its stop.
7. Remove the belt, then slowly rotate the tensioner into the free-arm position.

To install:

8. Check the condition of all pulleys.

✲✲ WARNING

When installing the serpentine accessory drive belt, the belt MUST be routed correctly. If not, the engine may overheat due to the water pump rotating in the wrong direction.

9. Install a new belt. Route the belt around all the pulleys except the idler pulley. Rotate the tensioner arm until it contacts its stop position. Route the belt around the idler and slowly let the tensioner rotate into the belt. Make sure the belt is seated onto all the pulleys.

10. With the drive belt installed, inspect the belt wear indicator. The gap between the tang and the housing stop must not exceed 0.94 inch (24mm).

11. Install the inner splash shield.

12. Install the wheel.

13. Lower the vehicle.

14. Connect the negative battery cable. Refer to Battery, removal & installation.

AIR CLEANER

REMOVAL & INSTALLATION

2.4L Engine

See Figure 67.

1. Before servicing the vehicle, refer to the Precautions Section.
2. Remove the air cleaner housing retaining bolt.
3. Remove the clean air hose from the air cleaner housing.
4. Lift the air cleaner housing upwards and remove.

To install:

5. Position the air cleaner housing in place.
6. Install the retaining bolt.
7. Install the clean air hose.

3.5L Engine

See Figure 68.

1. Before servicing the vehicle, refer to the Precautions Section.

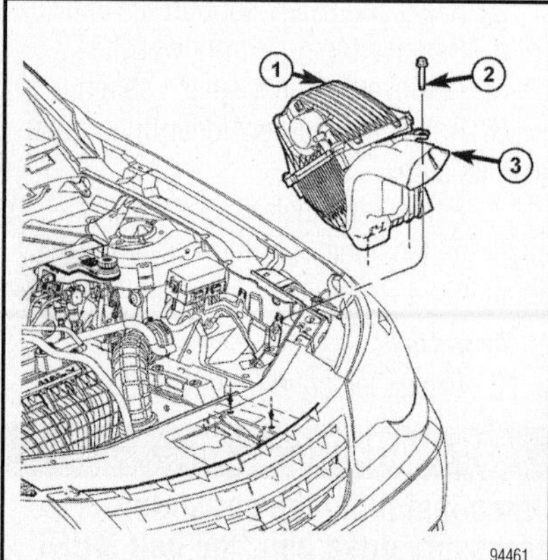

Fig. 67 View of air cleaner housing (1), retaining bolt (2), and clean air hose connection—2.4L engine

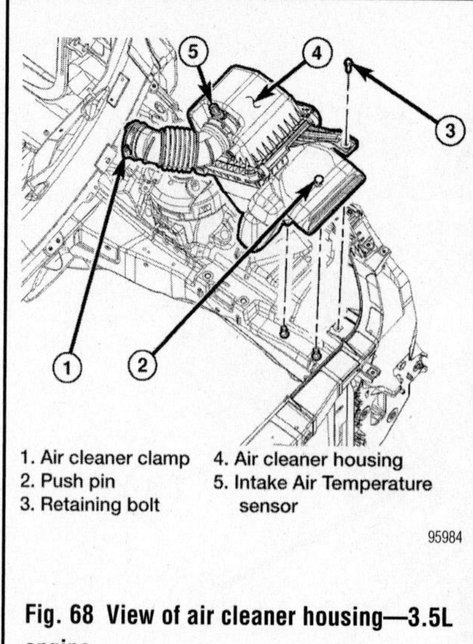

Fig. 68 View of air cleaner housing—3.5L engine

2. Disconnect the Intake Air Temperature (IAT) sensor wiring harness connector from the IAT.
3. Loosen the clamp and disconnect the air inlet hose from the throttle body.
4. Disconnect the makeup air hose from the top half of the air filter housing.
5. Remove the air filter housing retaining bolt and the push pin that secures the air scoop to the top of the radiator core support.
6. Pull the air filter housing up and off of the locating pins.

To install:

7. Push the air filter housing onto the locating pins.
8. Install the air filter housing straight down on the locating pins.
9. Reposition the bracket and install the retainer. Tighten the retainer to 44 inch lbs. (5 Nm).
10. Install the push pin that secures the air scoop to the top of the radiator core support.
11. Connect the inlet air temperature sensor harness connector.
12. Reconnect the air inlet hose to the throttle body, and tighten the clamp.
13. Connect the negative battery cable. Refer to Battery, removal & installation.

3.6L Engine

See Figures 69 and 70.

1. Before servicing the vehicle, refer to the Precautions Section.
2. Disconnect and isolate the negative battery cable. Refer to Battery, removal & installation.
3. Remove the engine cover.
4. Disconnect the fresh air makeup hose from the air cleaner body.

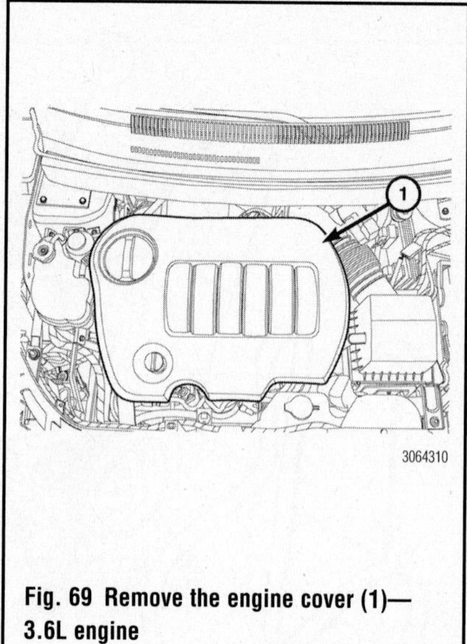

Fig. 69 Remove the engine cover (1)—3.6L engine

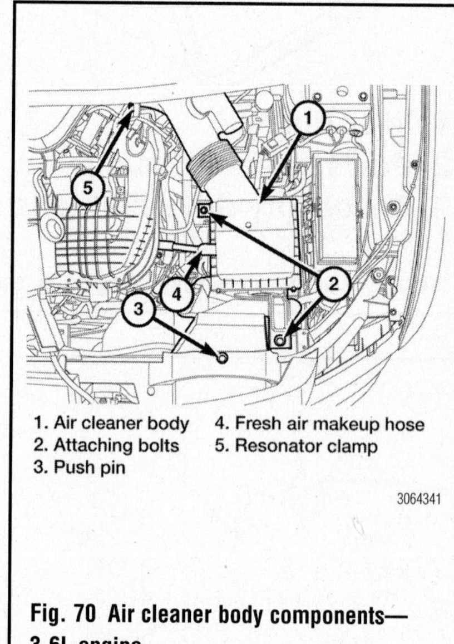

Fig. 70 Air cleaner body components—3.6L engine

5. Remove the push pin.
6. Remove the 2 bolts from the air cleaner body.
7. Loosen the clamp at the resonator and remove the air cleaner body.

To install:

8. Engage the air inlet hose to the resonator and install the air cleaner body with the 2 bolts tightened to 80 inch lbs. (9 Nm).
9. Tighten the air inlet hose to the resonator clamp to 35 inch lbs. (4 Nm).
10. Install the push pin.
11. Install the fresh air makeup hose to the air cleaner body.
12. Install the engine cover.
13. Connect the negative battery cable and tighten the nut to 45 inch lbs. (5 Nm).

FILTER/ELEMENT REPLACEMENT

2.4L Engine

See Figures 71 and 72.

**** WARNING**

Do not use an assist tool or excessive force when unlocking the air box lid tabs. Excessive force may break the tabs off of the lid.

1. Before servicing the vehicle, refer to the Precautions Section.
2. Unlock the air box lid tabs and lift the air cleaner housing cover.
3. Pull the cover forward to disengage the rear tabs.
4. Remove the air filter element.

To install:

5. Install the air filter element into the air cleaner housing.
6. Install the cover so that the rear tabs insert into the lower air box.

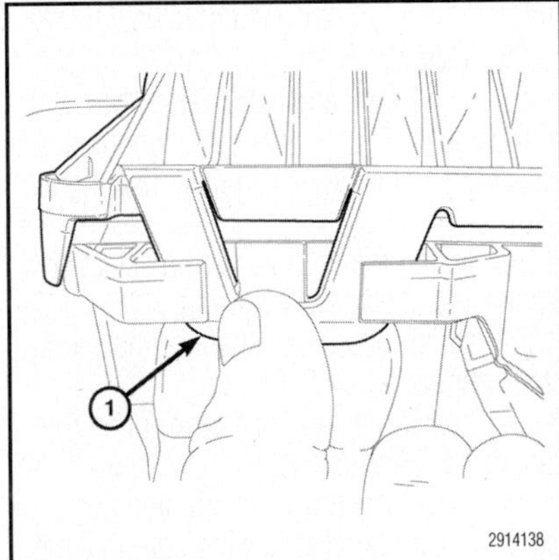

Fig. 71 Unlock the air box lid tabs and lift the air cleaner housing cover (1)—2.4L engine

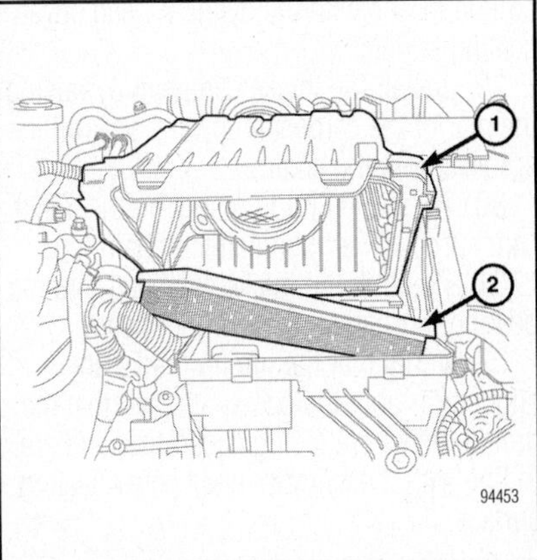

Fig. 72 Pull the cover (1) forward to disengage the rear tabs and remove the air filter element (2)—2.4L engine

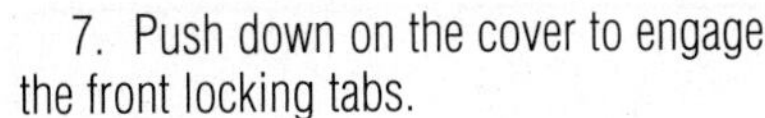

7. Push down on the cover to engage the front locking tabs.

3.5L Engine

See Figure 73.

1. Before servicing the vehicle, refer to the Precautions Section.
2. Disengage the air filter housing clips.
3. Slide the air filter housing cover forward slightly to disengage the tabs from the bottom of the air filter housing.
4. Remove the air cleaner element from the air cleaner housing.

To install:

5. Install the air filter element into the bottom half of the air filter housing.
6. Slide the air filter housing cover rearward to engage the tabs into the bottom half of the air filter housing.
7. Engage the air filter housing clips.

3.6L Engine

See Figure 74.

1. Before servicing the vehicle, refer to the Precautions Section.
2. Disconnect the fresh air makeup hose from the air cleaner housing cover.
3. Loosen the 4 screws securing the air cleaner housing cover.
4. Lift the cover and remove the air cleaner element.

**** WARNING**

Do not use compressed air to clean out the air cleaner housing without first covering the air inlet to the throttle body. Dirt or foreign objects could enter the intake manifold causing engine damage.

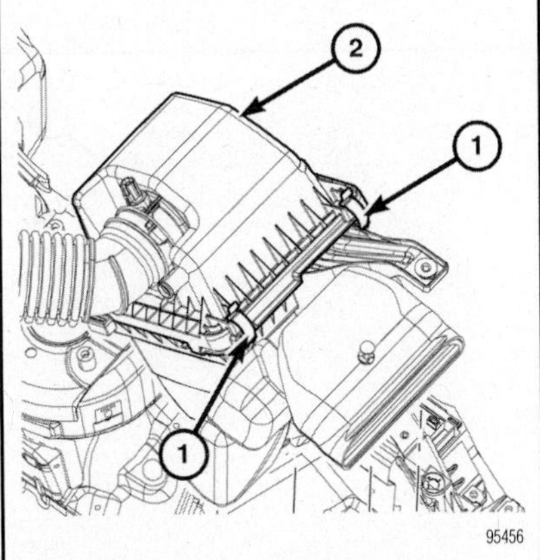

Fig. 73 View of air filter housing cover (2) and air filter housing clips (1)—3.5L engine

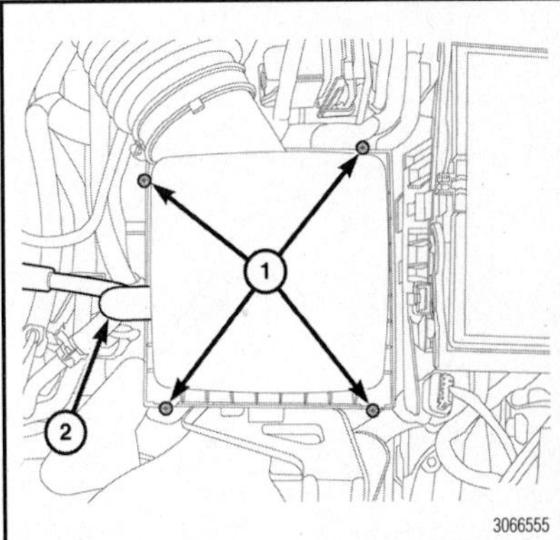

Fig. 74 Disconnect the fresh air makeup hose (2) and loosen the screws (1) securing the air cleaner housing cover—3.6L engine

5. Remove any dirt or debris from the bottom of the air cleaner housing.

To install:

6. Install the air cleaner element into the air cleaner housing.
7. Seat the cover onto the housing and tighten the 4 housing cover screws.
8. Connect the fresh air makeup hose to the air cleaner housing cover.

CAMSHAFT AND VALVE LIFTERS

INSPECTION

1. Before servicing the vehicle, refer to the Precautions Section.
2. Inspect the camshaft bearing journals for damage and binding. If the journals are binding, check the cylinder head for damage. Also check the cylinder head oil holes for clogging.
3. Check the surface of the cam lobes for abnormal wear. Measure and compare the unworn area to the worn area. Replace camshafts that are not within specification.

REMOVAL & INSTALLATION

2.4L Engine

See Figures 75 through 81.

Special Tools

- Locking Wedge 9701

1. Before servicing the vehicle, refer to the Precautions Section.
2. Remove the engine cover by pulling upward.
3. Disconnect and isolate the negative battery cable.
4. Remove the cylinder head cover. Refer to Valve Covers, removal & installation.

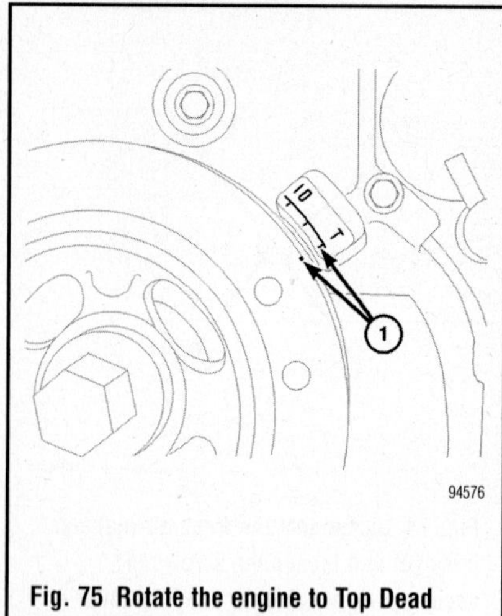

Fig. 75 Rotate the engine to Top Dead Center (TDC) (1)—2.4L engine

5. Raise and safely support the vehicle.
6. Remove the frame cover portion of the right splash shield.
7. Rotate the engine to Top Dead Center (TDC).
8. Make sure the camshaft timing marks are in line with the cylinder head cover sealing surface.
9. Mark the chain link corresponding to the timing marks with a paint marker.
10. Remove the timing tensioner plug from the front cover.
11. Insert a small Allen® wrench through the timing tensioner plug hole and lift the ratchet upward to release the tensioner and push the Allen® wrench inward. Leave the Allen® wrench installed during the remainder of this procedure.
12. Insert Locking Wedge 9701 between the camshaft phasers.

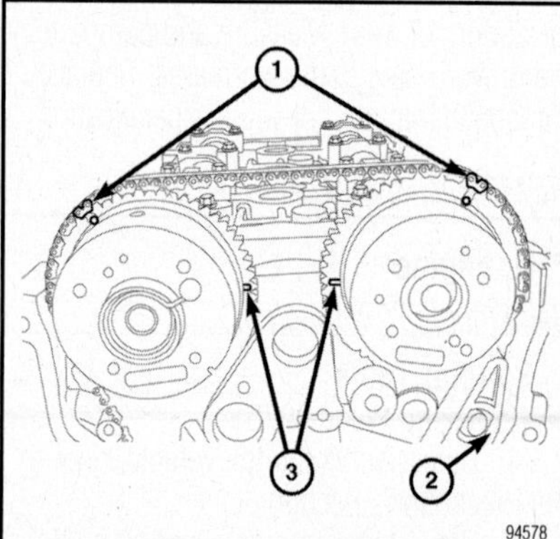

Fig. 76 Make sure the camshaft timing marks (3) are in line with the cylinder head cover sealing surface and mark the chain link corresponding to the timing marks (1). Cylinder head (2) shown—2.4L engine

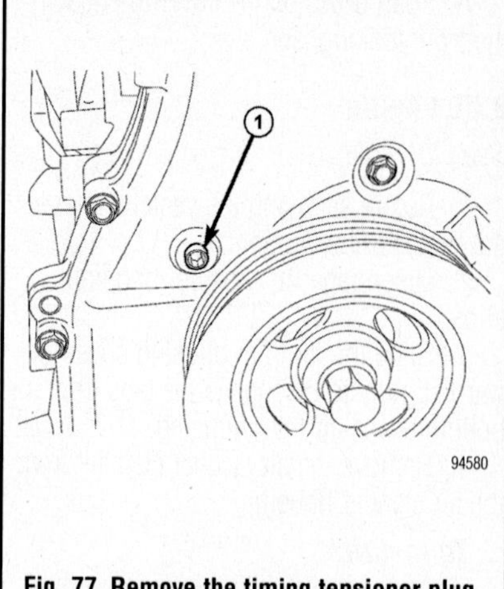

Fig. 77 Remove the timing tensioner plug (1) from the front cover

13. Lightly tap Locking Wedge 9701 into place until it will no longer sink down.

➡The camshaft bearing caps should have been marked during engine manufacturing. For example, number one exhaust camshaft bearing is marked E1.

WARNING

DO NOT use a number stamp or a punch to mark the camshaft bearing caps. Damage to the bearing caps could occur.

14. Using a permanent ink or paint marker, identify the location and position on each camshaft bearing cap.
15. Remove the front camshaft bearing cap.
16. Slowly remove the remaining intake and exhaust camshaft bearing cap bolts one turn at a time.
17. Remove the intake camshaft by lifting the rear of the camshaft upward.

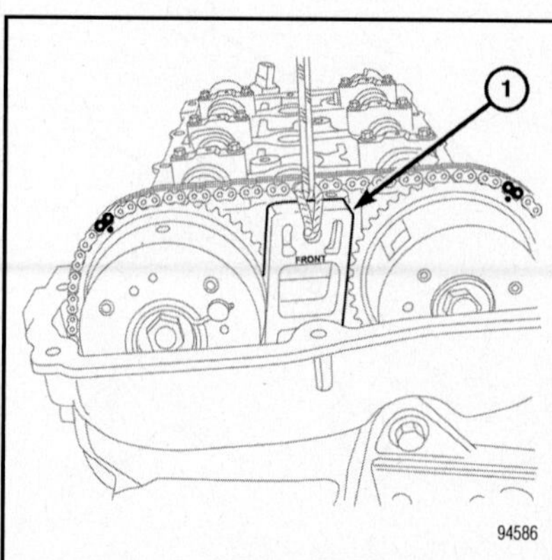

Fig. 78 Insert Locking Wedge 9701 (1) between the camshaft phasers

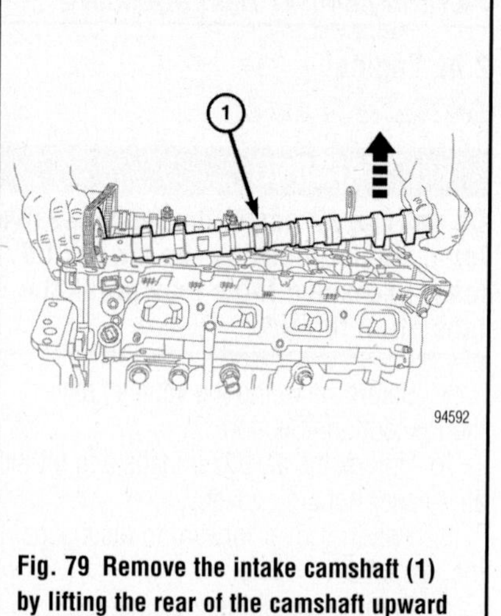

Fig. 79 Remove the intake camshaft (1) by lifting the rear of the camshaft upward

18. Rotate the camshaft while lifting out of the front bearing cradle.
19. Lift the timing chain off the sprocket.
20. Remove the exhaust camshaft.
21. Secure the timing chain with wire so that it does fall into the timing chain cover.

To install:

22. The front camshaft bearing cap is numbered 1, 2, or 3, this corresponds to the select fit front exhaust camshaft bearing to use.
23. Install the corresponding select fit front exhaust camshaft bearing.
24. Oil all of the camshaft journals with clean engine oil.
25. Install the camshaft phasers on the camshafts, if removed.
26. Install the timing chain onto the exhaust cam sprocket making sure that the timing marks on the sprocket and the painted chain link are aligned.
27. Position the exhaust camshaft on the bearing journals in the cylinder head.
28. Align the exhaust cam timing mark so it is in line with the cylinder head cover sealing surface.
29. Install the intake camshaft by raising the rear of the camshaft upward and roll the sprocket into the chain.
30. Align the timing marks on the intake cam sprocket with the painted chain link.
31. Position the intake camshaft into the bearing journals in the cylinder head.
32. Verify that the timing marks are aligned on both the camshafts and that the timing marks are facing each other and are in line with the cylinder head cover sealing surface.

WARNING

Install the front intake and exhaust camshaft bearing cap last. Ensure

that the dowels are seated and follow the torque sequence or damage to the engine could result.

⁂ WARNING

If the front camshaft bearing cap is broken, the cylinder head MUST be replaced.

33. Install the intake and exhaust camshaft bearing caps and slowly tighten the bolts to 85 inch lbs. (10 Nm) in the proper sequence.

⁂ WARNING

Verify that the exhaust bearing shells are correctly installed, and the dowels are seated in the head, prior to torqueing the bolts.

34. Install the front intake and exhaust bearing cap and tighten the bolts to 18 ft. lbs. (25 Nm) in the proper sequence.
35. Verify that all the timing marks are aligned.
36. Remove the Allen® wrench from the timing chain tensioner.
37. Remove Locking Wedge 9701 by pulling it straight upward on the pull rope.

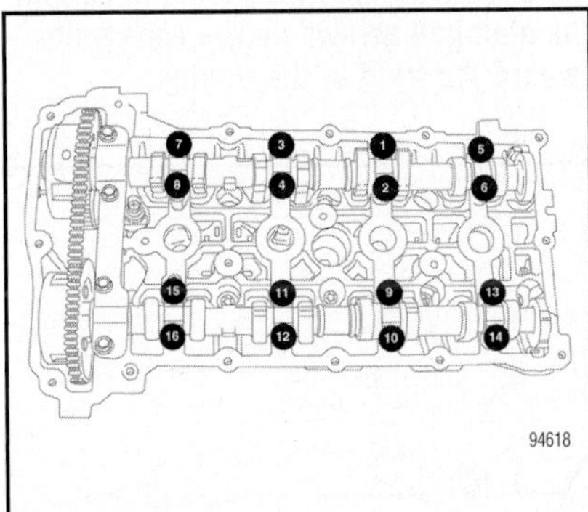

Fig. 80 Camshaft bearing cap bolt tightening sequence—2.4L engine

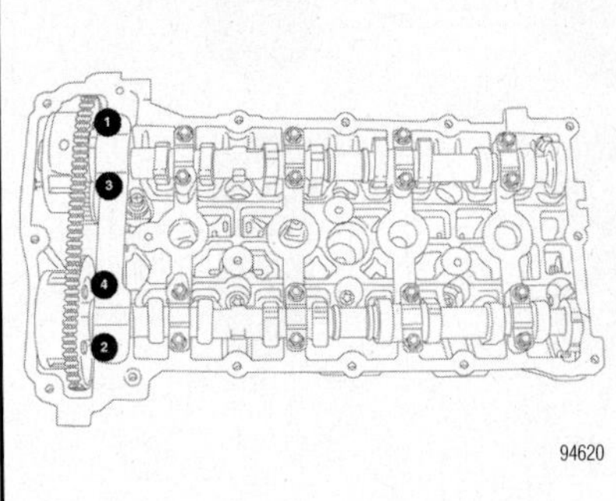

Fig. 81 Front intake and exhaust bearing cap tightening sequence—2.4L engine

38. Apply MOPAR® thread sealant to the timing tensioner plug and install.
39. Rotate the crankshaft CLOCKWISE 2 complete revolutions until the crankshaft is repositioned at the TDC position.
40. Verify that the camshaft timing marks are in the proper position and in line with the cylinder head cover sealing surface. If the marks do not line up, the timing chain is not correctly installed.
41. Install the right splash shield.
42. Remove any RTV from the gasket.
43. Inspect the cylinder head cover gaskets for damage. If no damage is present, the gaskets can be re-installed.
44. Install the cylinder head cover. Refer to Valve Covers, removal & installation.
45. Connect the negative battery cable. Refer to Battery, removal & installation.
46. Fill the cooling system. Refer to Engine Coolant, Drain & Refill Procedure.
47. Fill the engine with the proper type and amount of oil.
48. Operate the engine until it reaches the normal operating temperature. Check the oil and cooling systems for correct fluid levels.
49. Install the engine cover.

3.5L Engine

See Figure 82.

➡The camshafts are removed from the rear of the cylinder heads.

⁂ WARNING

Care must be taken not to nick or scratch the journals when removing the camshaft.

1. Before servicing the vehicle, refer to the Precautions Section.

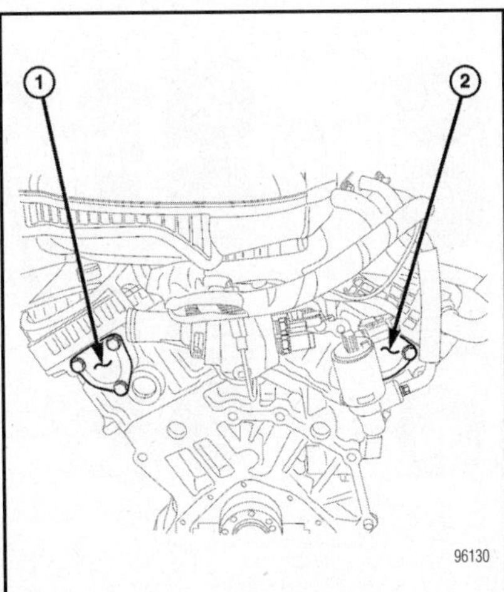

Fig. 82 Remove the camshaft thrust plate (1) or (2)—3.5L engine

2. Remove the camshaft sprocket. Refer to Timing Belt & Sprockets, removal & installation.
3. Remove the rocker arm shaft assembly.
4. To remove the right camshaft, remove the EGR Valve assembly.
5. Remove the camshaft thrust plate(s).
6. Carefully remove the camshaft from the rear of the cylinder head.

➡It may be necessary to remove the Powertrain Control Module (PCM) in order to remove the camshaft from the right cylinder head.

To install:

⁂ WARNING

Care must be taken not to scrape or nick the camshaft journals when installing the camshaft into position.

7. Lubricate the camshaft bearing journals, camshaft lobes, and camshaft seal with clean engine oil and install the camshaft into the cylinder head.
8. Install the camshaft sprocket. Refer to Timing Belt & Sprockets, removal & installation.
9. Install the camshaft thrust plate(s). Clean the mating surfaces and apply the appropriate sealer as necessary. Torque the fasteners to 21 ft. lbs. (28 Nm).
10. If necessary, install the EGR Valve assembly and PCM.
11. Install the rocker arm assembly.

3.6L Engine

Left Bank

See Figures 83 through 86.

⁂ WARNING

The magnetic timing wheels must not come in contact with magnets (pickup tools, trays, etc.) or any other strong magnetic field. This will destroy the timing wheels ability to correctly relay camshaft position to the camshaft position sensor.

⁂ WARNING

When the timing chain is removed and the cylinder heads are still installed, DO NOT forcefully rotate the camshafts or crankshaft independently of each other. Severe valve and/or piston damage can occur.

1. Before servicing the vehicle, refer to the Precautions Section.

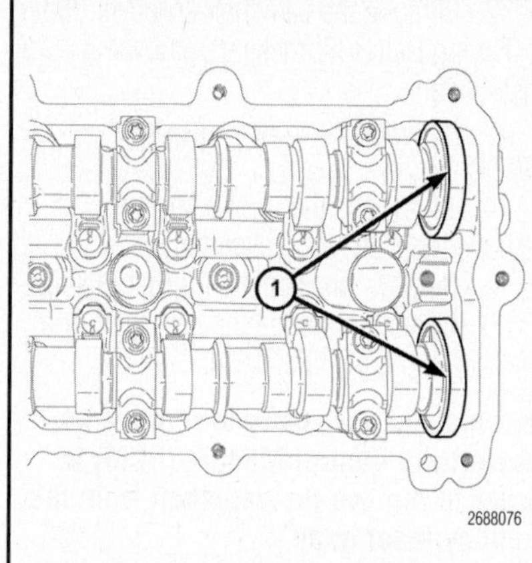

Fig. 83 The magnetic timing wheels (1) must not come in contact with and other magnetic objects (left bank)—3.6L engine

2. Remove the left cylinder head cover. Refer to Valve Covers, removal & installation.

3. Remove the ignition coils. Refer to Ignition Coil, removal & installation.

4. Remove the spark plugs. Refer to Spark Plugs, removal & installation.

5. Remove the cam phasers.

6. Gently rotate the camshafts counterclockwise approximately 30° until the camshafts are in the neutral position (no valve load).

➡The camshaft bearing caps should have been marked during engine manufacturing. For example, the number 1 exhaust camshaft bearing cap is marked 1E->. The caps should be installed with the notch forward.

7. Slowly loosen the camshaft bearing cap bolts in proper sequence.

⁂ WARNING

Do not stamp or strike the camshaft bearing caps. Severe damage may occur to the bearing caps.

➡When the camshaft is removed, the rocker arms may slide downward, mark the rocker arms before removing the camshaft.

8. Remove the camshaft bearing caps and the camshafts.

To install:

9. Lubricate the camshaft journals with clean engine oil.

10. Install the left side camshaft(s) approximately 30° counterclockwise from the Top Dead Center (TDC) position. This will place the camshafts at the neutral position (no valve load) easing the installation of the camshaft bearing caps.

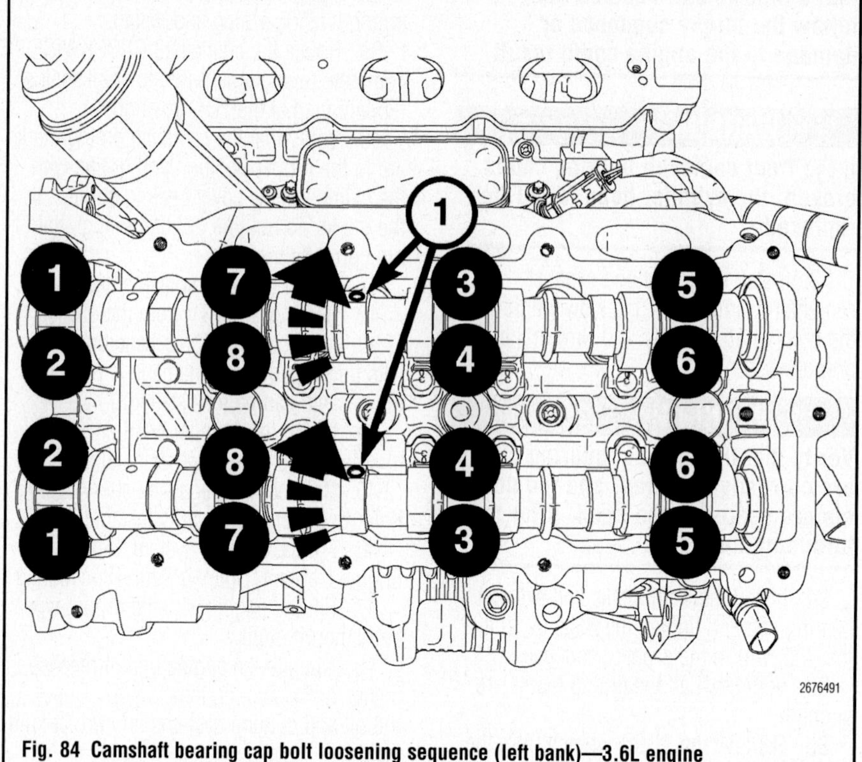

Fig. 84 Camshaft bearing cap bolt loosening sequence (left bank)—3.6L engine

11. Install the camshaft bearing caps and hand tighten the retaining bolts to 18 inch lbs. (2 Nm).

➡The caps are identified numerically (1–4), Intake or Exhaust (I or E) and should be installed from the front to the rear of the engine. All caps should be installed with the notch forward so that the stamped arrows on the caps point toward the front of the engine.

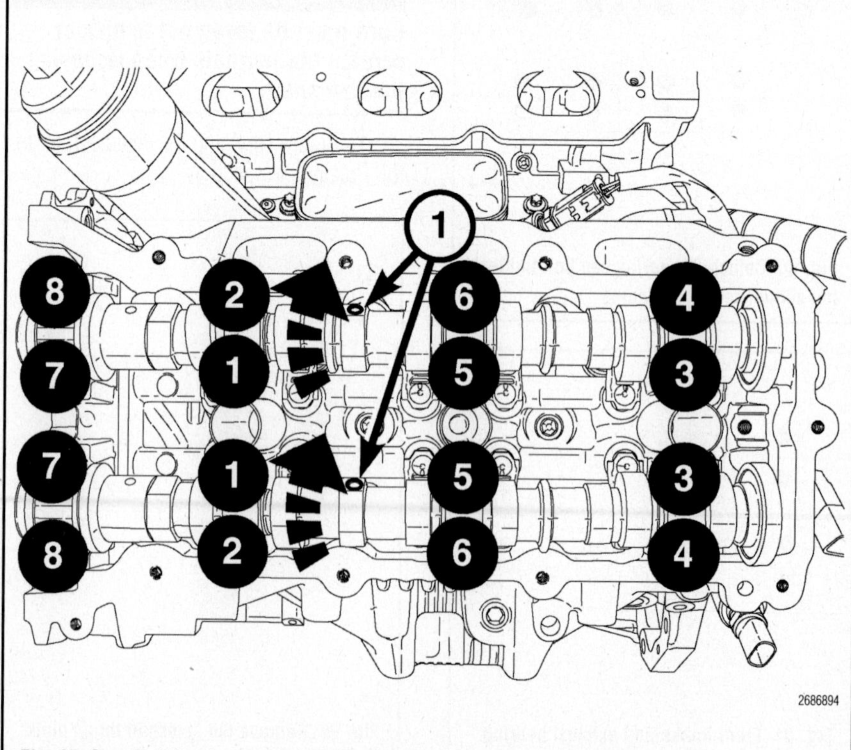

Fig. 85 Camshaft bearing cap bolt tightening sequence (left bank)—3.6L engine

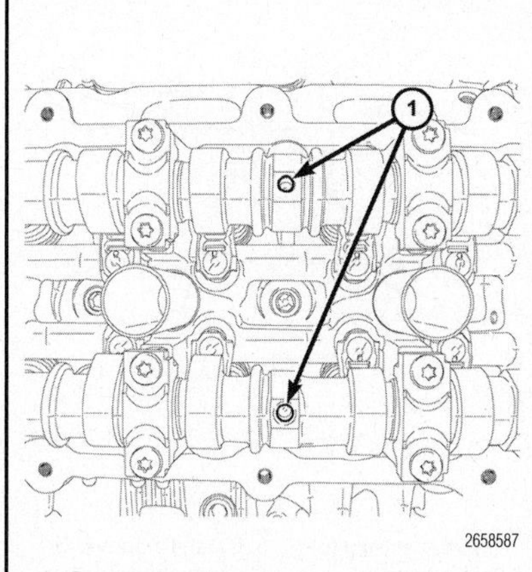

Fig. 86 Rotate the camshafts clockwise to TDC by positioning the alignment holes (1) vertically (left bank)—3.6L engine

12. Tighten the bearing cap retaining bolts, in sequence, to 84 inch lbs. (10 Nm).
13. Rotate the camshafts clockwise to TDC by positioning the alignment holes vertically.
14. Install the left cam phasers.
15. Install the spark plugs. Refer to Spark Plugs, removal & installation.
16. Install the ignition coils. Refer to Ignition Coil, removal & installation.
17. Install the cylinder head cover. Refer to Valve Covers, removal & installation.

➡The Cam/Crank Variation Relearn procedure must be performed using the scan tool anytime there has been a repair/replacement made to a powertrain system, for example: flywheel, valvetrain, camshaft and/or crankshaft sensors or components. Refer to Powertrain Control Module (PCM), Powertrain Verification Test.

Right Bank

See Figures 87 through 89.

⁂ WARNING

The magnetic timing wheels (1) must not come in contact with magnets (pickup tools, trays, etc.) or any other strong magnetic field. This will destroy the timing wheels ability to correctly relay the camshaft position to the camshaft position sensor.

⁂ WARNING

When the timing chain is removed and the cylinder heads are still installed, DO NOT forcefully rotate the camshafts or crankshaft independently of each other. Severe valve and/or piston damage can occur.

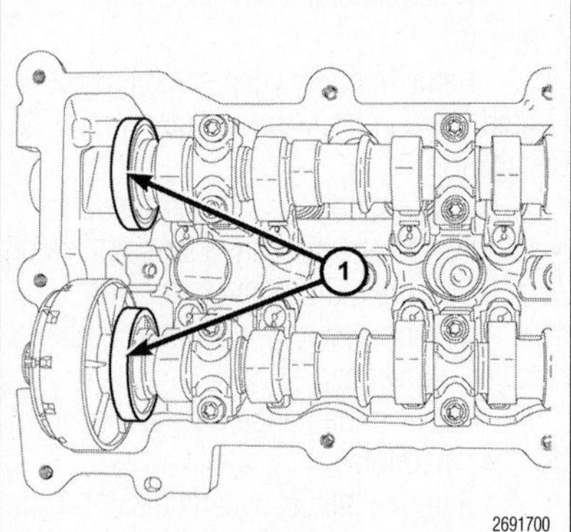

Fig. 87 The magnetic timing wheels (1) must not come in contact with and other magnetic objects (right bank)—3.6L engine

1. Before servicing the vehicle, refer to the Precautions Section.
2. Remove the right cylinder head cover. Refer to Valve Covers, removal & installation.
3. Remove the ignition coils. Refer to Ignition Coil, removal & installation.
4. Remove the spark plugs. Refer to Spark Plugs, removal & installation.
5. Remove the cam phasers.

➡The camshaft bearing caps should have been marked during engine manufacturing. For example, the number 1 exhaust camshaft bearing cap is marked 1E->. The caps should be installed with the notch forward.

6. Slowly loosen the camshaft bearing cap bolts in the proper sequence.

⁂ WARNING

Do not stamp or strike the camshaft bearing caps. Severe damage may occur to the bearing caps.

➡When the camshaft is removed, the rocker arms may slide downward. Mark the rocker arms before removing the camshaft.

7. Remove the camshaft bearing caps and the camshafts.

To install:

8. Lubricate camshaft journals with clean engine oil.
9. Install the right side camshaft(s) at Top Dead Center (TDC) by positioning the alignment holes vertically. This will place the camshafts at the neutral position (no valve load) easing the installation of the camshaft bearing caps.
10. Install the camshaft bearing caps, hand tighten the retaining bolts to 18 inch lbs. (2 Nm).

➡The caps are identified numerically (1–4), Intake or Exhaust (I or E) and should be installed from the front to the rear of the engine. All caps should be installed with the notch forward so that the stamped arrows on the caps point toward the front of the engine.

11. Tighten the bearing cap retaining bolts, in sequence, to 84 inch lbs. (10 Nm).
12. Install the right cam phasers.
13. Install the spark plugs. Refer to Spark Plugs, removal & installation.
14. Install the ignition coils. Refer to Ignition Coil, removal & installation.

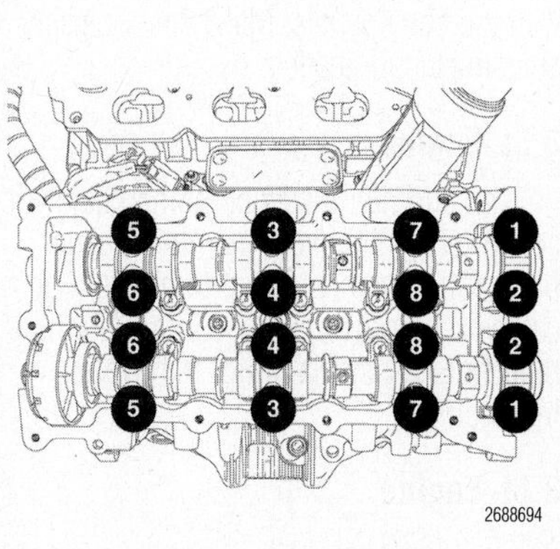

Fig. 88 Camshaft bearing cap bolt loosening sequence (right bank)—3.6L engine

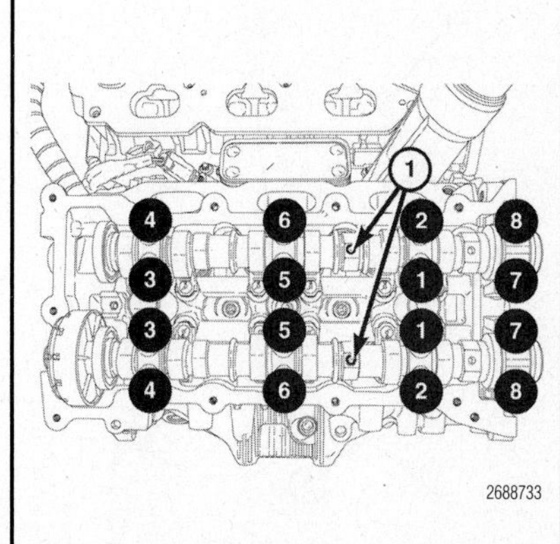

Fig. 89 Camshaft bearing cap bolt tightening sequence showing the vertical alignment holes (1) (right bank)—3.6L engine

15. Install the cylinder head cover. Refer to Valve Covers, removal & installation.

➡The Cam/Crank Variation Relearn procedure must be performed using the scan tool anytime there has been a repair/replacement made to a powertrain system, for example: flywheel, valvetrain, camshaft and/or crankshaft sensors or components. Refer to Powertrain Control Module (PCM), Powertrain Verification Test.

CATALYTIC CONVERTER

REMOVAL & INSTALLATION

2.4L Engine

See Figure 90.

CAUTION

The normal operating temperature of the exhaust system is very high. Therefore, never work around or attempt to service any part of the exhaust system until it is cooled. Special care should be taken when working near the catalytic converter. The temperature of the converter rises to a high level after a short period of engine operation time.

➡When replacement is required on any component of the exhaust system, use original equipment parts (or their equivalent).

1. Before servicing the vehicle, refer to the Precautions Section.
2. Raise and safely support the vehicle.
3. Apply penetrating oil to the band clamp nut and bolt.

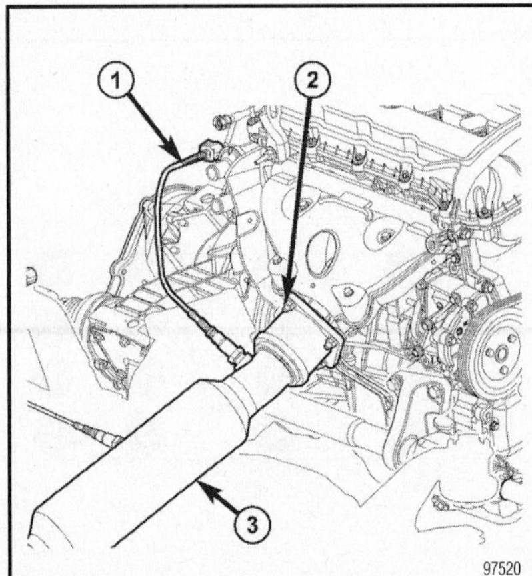

Fig. 90 View of catalytic converter (3), oxygen sensor connector (1), and exhaust fasteners (2)—2.4L engine

4. Disconnect the oxygen sensor connector.
5. Remove the oxygen sensor. Refer to Heated Oxygen (HO2S) Sensor, removal & installation.
6. Loosen the resonator and muffler assembly-to-catalytic converter band clamp.
7. Pull the muffler and resonator assembly rearward to remove it from the catalytic converter.
8. Remove the flange nuts at the exhaust manifold.
9. Remove the catalytic converter from the vehicle.
10. Remove and discard the gasket.

To install:

➡Always work from the front to the rear of the exhaust system when aligning and tightening the exhaust system components.

11. Clean the manifold-to-converter sealing surfaces.
12. Using a new gasket, position the catalytic converter to the exhaust manifold.
13. Install the catalytic converter mounting bolts. Tighten the bolts to 21 ft. lbs. (28 Nm).
14. Position a new band clamp onto the resonator and muffler assembly.
15. Install the resonator and muffler assembly onto the catalytic converter.
16. Align the exhaust system to maintain the position and proper clearance with the underbody parts. All support isolators should have equal load on them.
17. Tighten the resonator and muffler assembly band clamp to 40 ft. lbs. (54 Nm).
18. Lower the vehicle.
19. Start the engine and inspect for exhaust leaks. Repair exhaust leaks as necessary.
20. Check the exhaust system for contact with the body panels. Make the necessary adjustments, if needed.

3.5L Engine

This engine utilizes combined catalytic converter and exhaust manifold assemblies called maniverter assemblies. For catalytic converter service information, refer to Exhaust Manifold, removal & installation.

3.6L Engine

See Figure 91.

1. Before servicing the vehicle, refer to the Precautions Section.
2. Remove the cross under pipe from the vehicle.

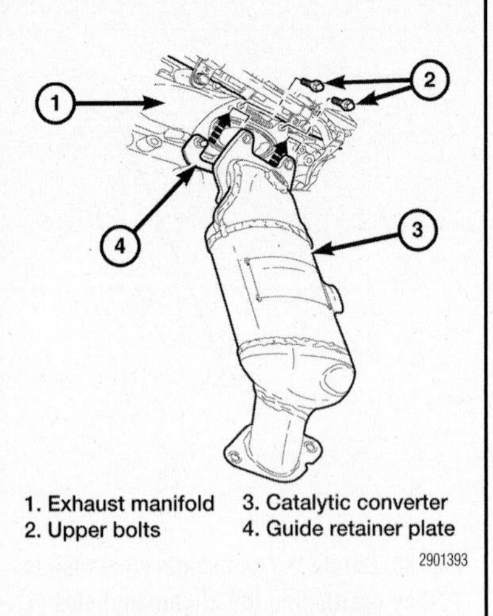

Fig. 91 View of catalytic converter removal—3.6L engine

➡The lower bolts for the converter flange are used to hold a guide retainer plate. The retainer does not need to be removed. The catalytic converter is held in by the plate and the upper bolts.

3. Disconnect the temperature and oxygen sensor electrical connectors.
4. Remove the catalytic converter-to-exhaust manifold upper bolts.
5. Remove the catalytic converter by lifting and sliding the flange up and away from the exhaust manifold.
6. Remove the temperature and oxygen sensors.

To install:

7. If gaskets need replacing, position a new gasket onto the manifold flange and install the lower retainer plate. Loosely install all 4 bolts to align the gasket. Tighten the lower retainer bolts to 27 ft. lbs. (37 Nm).
8. Position the catalytic converter against the exhaust manifold. Position the converter flange to the retainer.
9. Install the upper flange bolts. Tighten the upper bolts to 27 ft. lbs. (37 Nm).

WARNING

Be careful not to twist or kink the oxygen sensor wires.

10. Install the temperature and oxygen sensors. Connect the electrical connectors.
11. Install the cross under pipe.
12. Start the engine and inspect for exhaust leaks. Repair exhaust leaks as necessary.

13. Check the exhaust system for contact with the body panels. Make the necessary adjustments, if needed.

CRANKSHAFT FRONT SEAL

REMOVAL & INSTALLATION

2.4L Engine

See Figures 92 through 94.

1. Before servicing the vehicle, refer to the Precautions Section.
2. Remove the accessory drive belt. Refer to Accessory Drive Belts, removal & installation.
3. Install the damper holder 9707 and remove the damper retaining bolt.
4. Pull the damper off the crankshaft.
5. Remove the front crankshaft oil seal by prying out with a screw driver. Be careful not to damage the cover seal surface.

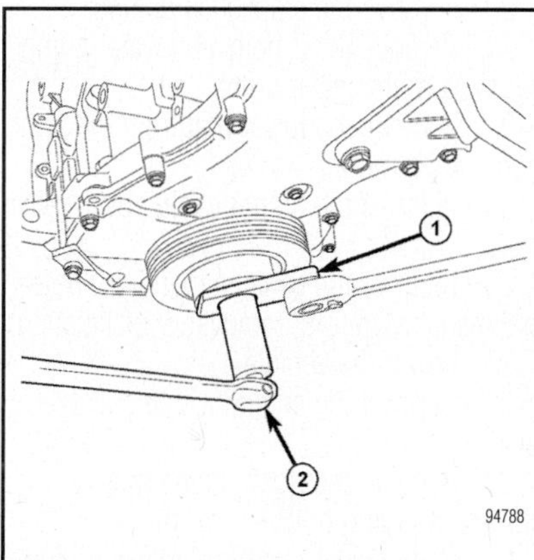

Fig. 92 Using the damper holder 9707 (1) to remove the damper retaining bolt (2)—2.4L engine

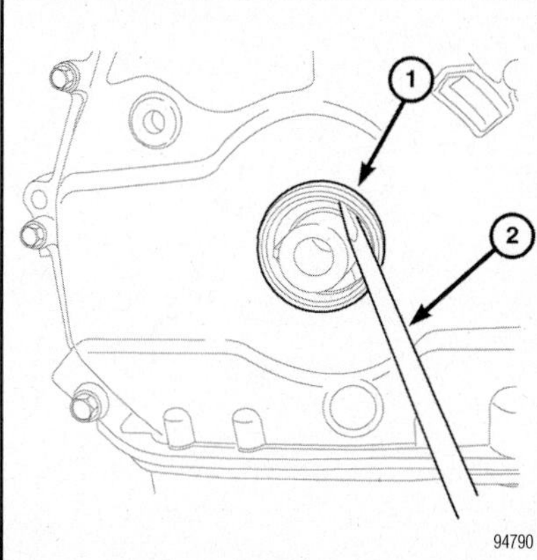

Fig. 93 Removing the front crankshaft oil seal (1) using a screw driver (2)—2.4L engine

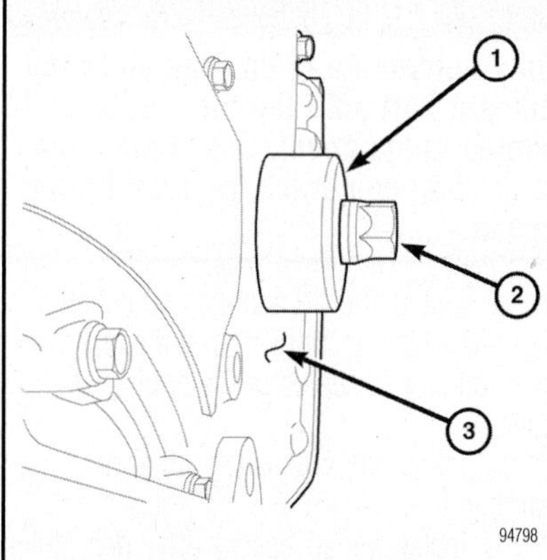

Fig. 94 Using the Seal installer 9506 (1) and the crankshaft damper bolt (2), press the seal until the seal installer seats against the timing chain cover (3)—2.4L engine

To install:

6. Place the seal onto the Seal installer 9506 with the seal spring towards the inside of the engine.
7. Install a new seal by using the Seal installer 9506 and the crankshaft damper bolt.
8. Press the seal into the front cover until the Seal Installer 9506 seats against the timing chain cover.
9. Remove the seal installer 9506.
10. Install the crankshaft vibration damper.
11. Oil the bolt threads and between the bolt head and washer.
12. Install the damper retaining bolt and damper holder 9707. Tighten the bolt to 155 ft. lbs. (210 Nm).

3.5L Engine

See Figures 95 through 97.

1. Before servicing the vehicle, refer to the Precautions Section.
2. Remove the crankshaft sprocket. Refer to Timing Belt & Sprockets, removal & installation.
3. Tap the dowel pin out of the crankshaft.
4. Remove the crankshaft seal using Special Tool 6341A.

✻✻ WARNING

Do not nick the shaft seal surface or seal bore.

To install:

5. The shaft seal lip surface must be free of varnish, dirt or nicks. Polish with 400 grit paper if necessary.
6. Install the crankshaft seal using Special Tool 6342.

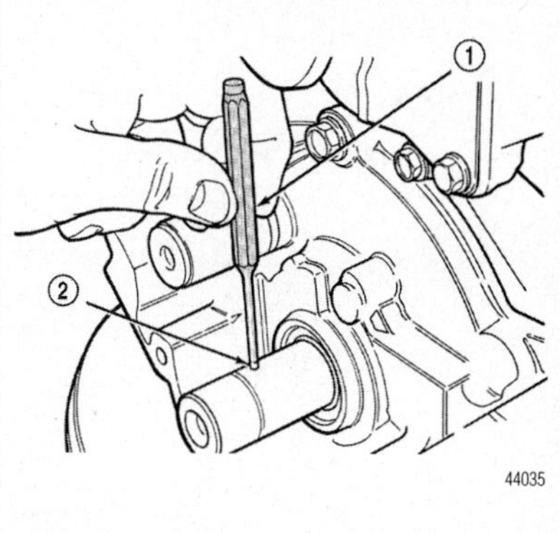

Fig. 95 Tap the dowel pin (2) out of the crankshaft using a punch (1)—3.5L engine

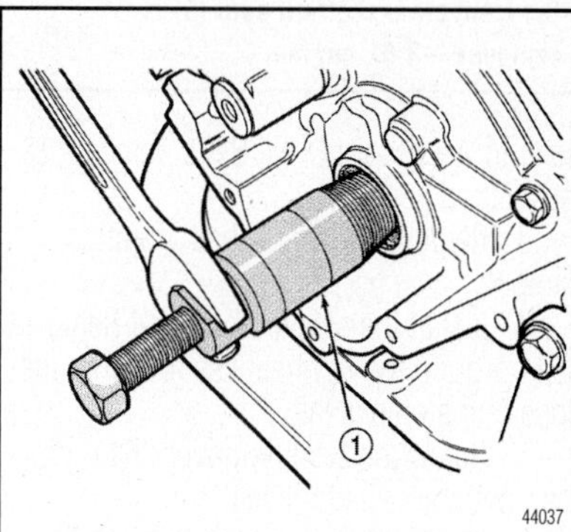

Fig. 96 Using Special Tool 6341A (1) to remove the front crankshaft seal—3.5L engine

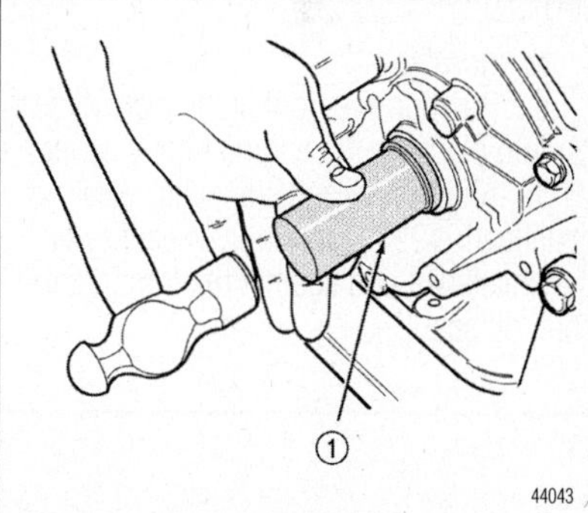

Fig. 97 Using Special Tool 6342 (1) to install the front crankshaft seal—3.5L engine

7. Install the dowel pin into the crankshaft to 0.047 inch (1.2mm) protrusion.
8. Install the crankshaft sprocket. Refer to Timing Belt & Sprockets, removal & installation.

3.6L Engine

See Figures 98 and 99.

1. Before servicing the vehicle, refer to the Precautions Section.
2. Remove the accessory drive belt.

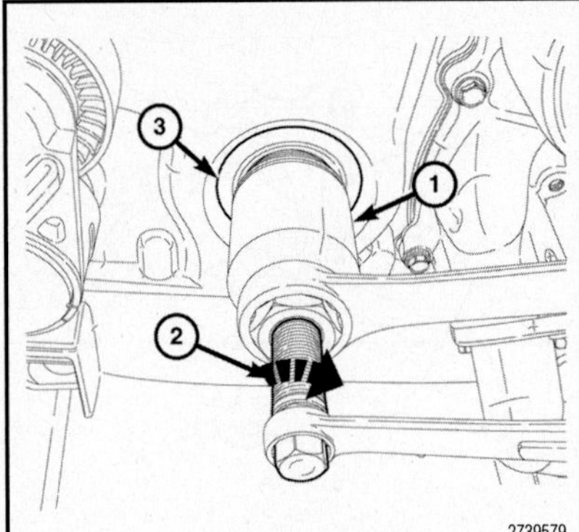

Fig. 98 Install the extractor screw (2) into the Seal Remover 8511 (1) and tighten the extractor screw against the sleeve until the front crankshaft oil seal (3) is removed—3.6L engine

Refer to Accessory Drive Belts, removal & installation.

3. Remove the crankshaft vibration damper.
4. Install the sleeve from Seal Remover 8511 around the flywheel key and onto the nose of the crankshaft.
5. Screw the Seal Remover 8511 into the front crankshaft oil seal.
6. Install the extractor screw into the Seal Remover 8511. Hold the seal remover stationary and tighten the extractor screw against the sleeve until the front crankshaft oil seal is removed from the engine timing cover.

To install:

7. Position the front crankshaft oil seal (3) into place on the engine timing cover.
8. Align the Front Crankshaft Seal Installer 10199 (1) to the flywheel key on the crankshaft and against the front crankshaft oil seal (3).

✲✲ WARNING

Only tighten the crankshaft vibration damper bolt until the oil seal is seated in the cover. Over-tightening of the bolt can crack the front timing cover.

9. Install and tighten the crankshaft vibration damper bolt (2) until the crankshaft oil seal is seated in the engine timing cover.
10. Install the crankshaft vibration damper.
11. Install the accessory drive belt. Refer to Accessory Drive Belts, removal & installation.

CYLINDER HEAD

REMOVAL & INSTALLATION

2.4L Engine

See Figures 100 through 111.

1. Before servicing the vehicle, refer to the Precautions Section.
2. Remove the engine cover by pulling upward.
3. Release the fuel system pressure. Refer to Relieving Fuel System Pressure.
4. Disconnect and isolate the negative battery cable.
5. Drain the cooling system. Refer to Engine Cooling, Engine Coolant, Drain & Refill Procedure.
6. Remove the clean air hose and air cleaner housing. Refer to Air Cleaner, removal & installation.
7. Remove the coolant recovery bottle.
8. Remove and reposition the power steering reservoir.
9. Remove the accessory drive belt. Refer to Accessory Drive Belts, removal & installation.
10. Remove the power steering hose hold down.
11. Remove the 3 power steering pump mounting bolts through the openings in the pulley and reposition the pump.
12. Remove the cylinder head cover. Refer to Valve Covers, removal & installation.
13. Remove the ignition coils from the cylinder head cover. Refer to Ignition Coil, removal & installation.
14. Raise and safely support the vehicle.
15. Remove the frame cover portion of the right splash shield.
16. Set the engine to Top Dead Center (TDC).
17. Remove the lower A/C compressor bolts, if equipped.
18. Remove the lower A/C compressor mount, if equipped.
19. Remove the accessory drive belt lower idler pulley.
20. Remove the crankshaft damper.
21. Remove the 3 bolts and water pump pulley from the water pump.
22. Remove the lower bolt from the right side engine mount bracket.
23. Remove the timing chain cover lower bolts.
24. Remove the exhaust manifold. Refer to Exhaust Manifold, removal & installation.
25. Lower the vehicle.
26. Support the engine with a suitable jack.
27. Remove the right engine mount bracket retaining bolts.
28. Remove the retaining nuts and reposition the mount bracket.
29. Remove the accessory drive upper idler pulley.

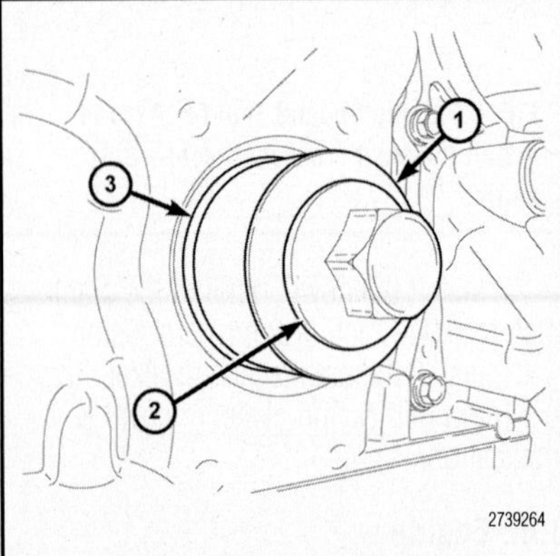

Fig. 99 Using the Front Crankshaft Seal Installer 10199 (1) and crankshaft vibration damper bolt (2) to install the front crankshaft oil seal (3)—3.6L engine

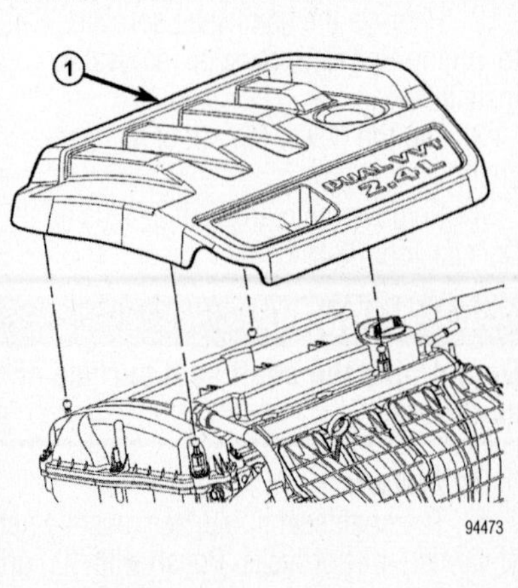

Fig. 100 Remove the engine cover (1) by pulling upward—2.4L engine

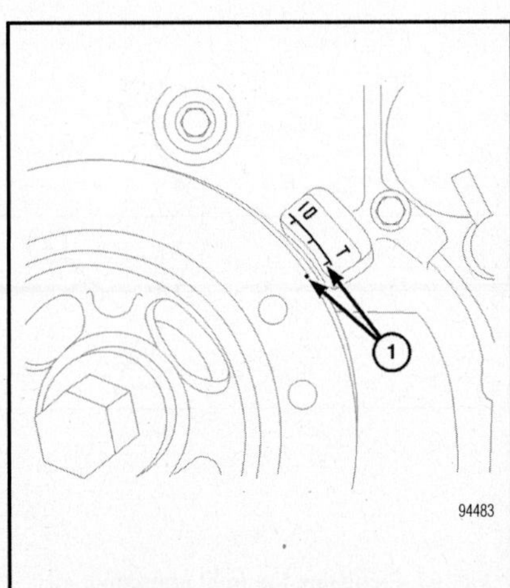

Fig. 101 Engine shown set to Top Dead Center (TDC) (1)—2.4L engine

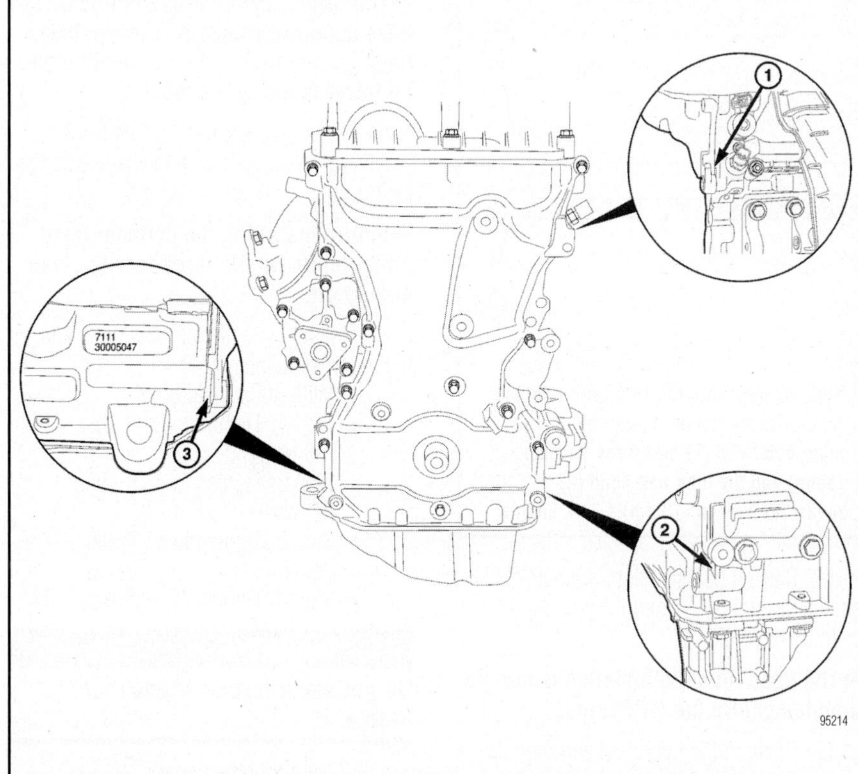

Fig. 102 Remove the timing chain cover using the pry points (1, 2, 3)—2.4L engine

30. Remove the right upper engine mount bracket.
31. Remove the accessory drive belt tensioner.
32. Remove the upper timing chain cover retaining bolts.
33. Remove the timing chain cover using the pry points.
34. Remove the tensioner and the timing chain. Refer to Timing Chain & Sprockets, removal & installation.
35. Remove the timing chain guide and the timing chain pivot guide.
36. Disconnect the fuel line from the fuel rail.
37. Unlock and disconnect the electrical connectors from the fuel injectors.
38. Remove the 2 fuel rail retaining bolts and remove the fuel rail.
39. Disconnect the electrical connectors from the coolant temperature sensor, oil temperature sensor, variable valve timing solenoids, camshaft position sensors, MAP sensor, manifold tuning valve, ignition interference suppressor, and electronic throttle control.
40. Remove the wiring harness retainer from the intake manifold and reposition the harness.
41. Remove the throttle body support bracket.
42. Disconnect the vacuum lines at the intake.
43. Remove the intake manifold retaining bolts and remove the intake manifold. Refer to Intake Manifold, removal & installation.
44. Remove the 4 bolts and reposition the coolant adapter.
45. Remove the ground strap at the right rear of the cylinder head, if equipped.

➡The camshaft bearing caps should have been marked during engine manufacturing. For example, number 1 exhaust camshaft bearing is marked E1.

⁂ WARNING

DO NOT use a number stamp or a punch to mark the camshaft bearing caps. Damage to the bearing caps could occur.

46. Using a permanent ink or paint marker, identify the location and position on each camshaft bearing cap.
47. Remove the front camshaft bearing cap.
48. Slowly remove the remaining intake and exhaust camshaft bearing cap bolts one turn at a time.
49. Remove the camshafts.

➡All of the cylinder head bolts have captured washers EXCEPT the front two.

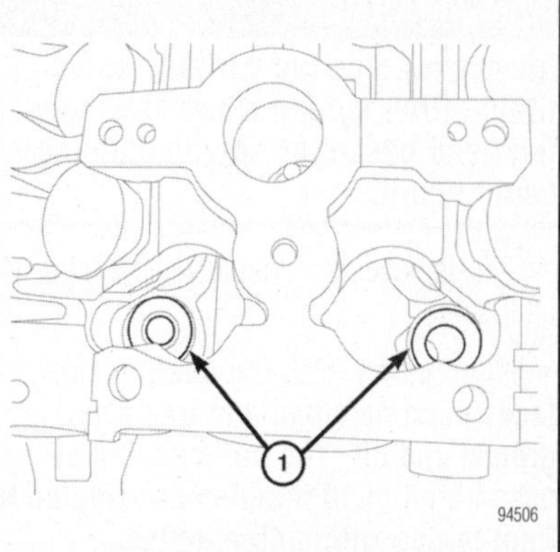

Fig. 103 All of the cylinder head bolts have captured washers EXCEPT the front two (1) shown—2.4L engine

50. Remove the cylinder head bolts and the 2 uncaptured washers.
51. Remove the cylinder head from the engine block.
52. Inspect and clean the cylinder head and block sealing surfaces.

➡Ensure the cylinder head bolt holes in the block are clean, dry (free of residual oil or coolant), and the threads are not damaged.

To install:

⁂ WARNING

The cylinder head bolts are tightened using a torque plus angle procedure. The bolts must be examined BEFORE reuse. If the threads are necked down, the bolts must be replaced.

53. Check the cylinder head bolts for necking by holding a scale or straight edge against the threads. If all the threads do not contact the scale, the bolt must be replaced.

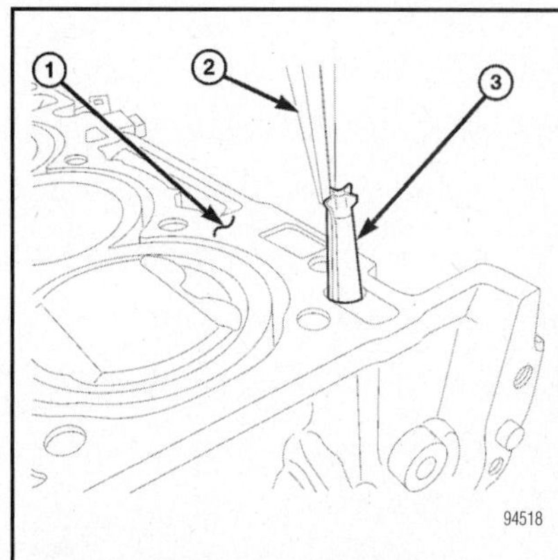

Fig. 104 Replace the variable valve timing filter screen (3) from the block (1) using a needle-nosed pliers (2)–2.4L engine

✲✲ WARNING

Always replace the variable valve timing filter screen when servicing the head gasket or engine damage could result.

54. Replace the variable valve timing filter screen.

➡When using RTV, the sealing surfaces must be clean and free from grease and oil. The parts should be assembled in 10 minutes and tighten to final torque within 45 minutes.

55. Place 2 pea size dots of MOPAR® engine sealant RTV, or equivalent, on the cylinder block.

56. Position the new cylinder head gasket on the engine block with the part number facing up. Ensure the gasket is seated over the locating dowels in the block.

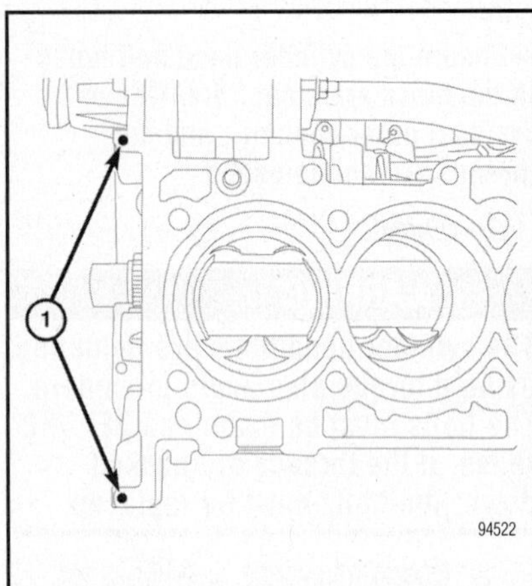

Fig. 105 Place 2 pea size dots of engine sealant RTV (1) on the cylinder block—2.4L engine

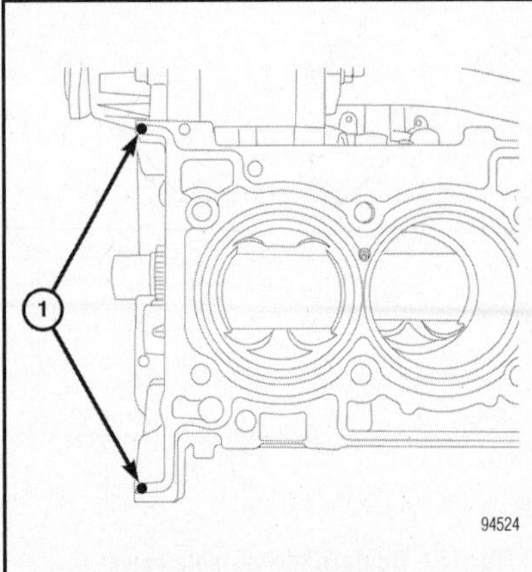

Fig. 106 Place 2 pea size dots of engine sealant RTV (1) on the cylinder head gasket—2.4L engine

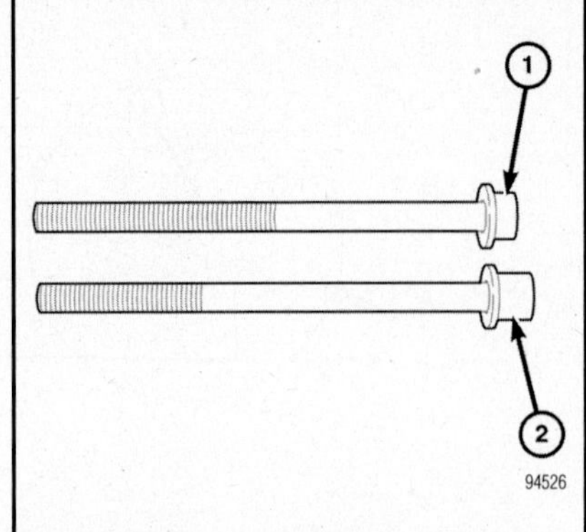

Fig. 107 Measure the bolt head from the washer to the top of the bolt head. The short bolt head (1) measures 5⁄16 inch (8mm) and the long bolt head (2) measures ½ inch (13mm)—2.4L engine

57. Place 2 pea size dots of MOPAR® engine sealant RTV, or equivalent, on the cylinder head gasket.

➡The head must be installed within 15 minutes before the RTV skins.

58. Position the cylinder head onto the engine block.

➡This engine was built with 2 different style cylinder head bolts. Each style bolt requires a different torque value. The bolts can be identified by the short bolt head and the long bolt head.

59. Measure the bolt head from the washer to the top of the bolt head. The short bolt head measures 5⁄16 inch (8mm) and the long bolt head measures ½ inch (13mm).

60. Identify whether the engine has the short head design or the long head design.

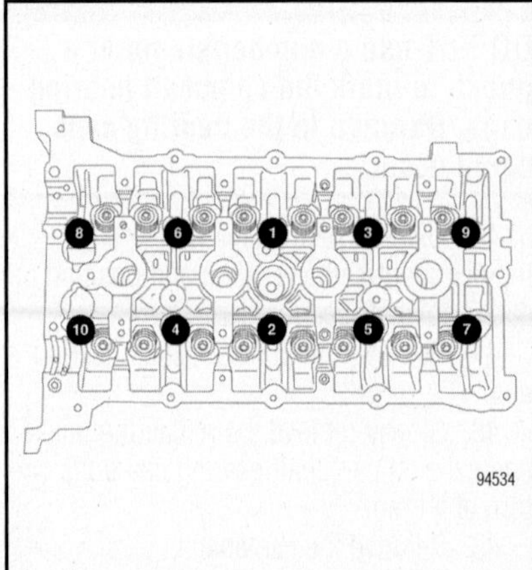

Fig. 108 Cylinder head bolt tightening sequence—2.4L engine

➡The front 2 cylinder head bolts do not have captured washers. The washers must be installed with the bevel edge up towards the bolt head.

61. Install the washers for the front 2 cylinder head bolts with the beveled edge facing up.

➡Before installing the cylinder head bolts, lubricate the threads with clean engine oil.

62. Install the cylinder head bolts and tighten in sequence.

a. With short head bolts:
- Step 1: Tighten to 25 ft. lbs. (30 Nm)
- Step 2: Tighten to 45 ft. lbs. (61 Nm)
- Step 3: Tighten to 45 ft. lbs. (61 Nm)
- Step 4: Tighten an additional 90°

✲✲ WARNING

Do not use a torque wrench for Step 4.

b. With long head bolts:
- Step 1: Tighten to 25 ft. lbs. (30 Nm)
- Step 2: Tighten to 54 ft. lbs. (73 Nm)
- Step 3: Tighten to 54 ft. lbs. (73 Nm)
- Step 4: Tighten an additional 90°

✲✲ WARNING

Do not use a torque wrench for Step 4.

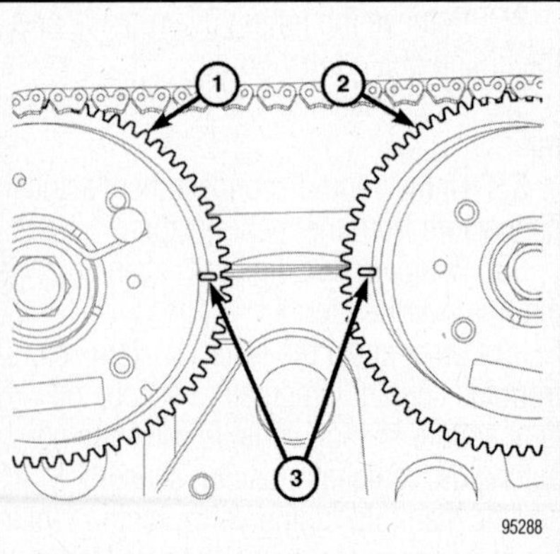

Fig. 109 Position the exhaust camshaft (1) and intake camshaft (2) on the bearing journals in the cylinder head. Align the camshaft timing marks (3) so that they are facing each other and are in line with the cylinder head cover sealing surface—2.4L engine

63. Clean the excess RTV from the timing chain cover sealing surface.

64. Install the coolant adapter with new seals. Tighten the bolts to 13 ft. lbs. (18 Nm).

65. The front camshaft bearing cap is numbered 1, 2, or 3. This corresponds to the select fit front exhaust camshaft bearing to use.

66. Install the corresponding select fit front exhaust camshaft bearing.

67. Oil all of the camshaft journals with clean engine oil.

68. Position the exhaust camshaft and intake camshaft on the bearing journals in the cylinder head.

69. Align the camshaft timing marks so that they are facing each other and are in line with the cylinder head cover sealing surface.

**** WARNING**

Install the front intake and exhaust camshaft bearing cap last. Ensure that the dowels are seated and follow the torque sequence or damage to the engine could result.

➡If the front camshaft bearing cap is broken, the cylinder head MUST be replaced.

70. Install the intake and exhaust camshaft bearing caps and slowly tighten the bolts to 85 inch lbs. (10 Nm) in sequence.

**** WARNING**

Verify that the exhaust bearing shells are correctly installed, and the dowels are seated in the head, prior to torqueing the bolts.

71. Install the front intake and exhaust bearing cap and tighten the bolts to 18 ft. lbs. (25 Nm) in sequence.

72. Install the timing chain guide and tighten the bolts to 106 inch lbs. (12 Nm).

73. Install the moveable timing chain pivot guide and tighten the bolt to 106 inch lbs. (12 Nm).

74. Install the timing chain and tensioner. Refer to Timing Chain & Sprockets, removal & installation.

75. Install timing chain cover, engine mount, pulleys and accessory drive belt. Refer to Timing Chain Front Cover, removal & installation.

76. Install the cylinder head cover. Refer to Valve Covers, removal & installation.

77. Install the ignition coils. Refer to Ignition Coil, removal & installation.

78. Install the exhaust manifold. Refer to Exhaust Manifold, removal & installation.

79. Install the ground strap at the right rear of the cylinder head, if equipped.

80. Install the intake manifold, vacuum lines and fuel rail. Refer to Intake Manifold, removal & installation.

81. Connect the coil and injector electrical connectors.

82. Connect the electrical connectors to the coolant temperature sensor, camshaft position sensors, oil temperature sensor, variable valve timing solenoids, MAP sensor, manifold tuning valve, ignition interference suppressor, and electronic throttle control.

83. Install the power steering pump reservoir. Tighten the mounting screw to 106 inch lbs. (12 Nm).

84. Install the coolant recovery reservoir. Tighten the mounting bolts to 89 inch lbs. (10 Nm).

85. Install the clean air hose and air cleaner housing. Refer to Air Cleaner, removal & installation.

86. Fill the cooling system. Refer to Engine Coolant, Drain & Refill Procedure.

87. Install a new oil filter and fill the engine with the proper type and amount of oil.

88. Connect the negative battery cable to the battery. Refer to Battery, removal & installation.

89. Operate the engine until it reaches the normal operating temperature. Check the oil and cooling systems for leaks and correct fluid levels.

90. Install the engine cover.

3.5L Engine

Left Side

See Figure 112.

1. Before servicing the vehicle, refer to the Precautions Section.
2. Remove the engine cover.
3. Release the fuel system pressure. Refer to Relieving Fuel System Pressure.
4. Disconnect the negative battery cable.
5. Drain the cooling system. Refer to Engine Coolant, Drain & Refill Procedure.
6. Remove the air cleaner element housing. Refer to Air Cleaner, removal & installation.
7. Remove the radiator fan assembly. Refer to Engine Fan, removal & installation.
8. Remove the coolant recovery container.
9. Remove the alternator. Refer to Alternator, removal & installation.
10. Disconnect the fuel line at the fuel rail.
11. Remove the upper intake manifold. Refer to Intake Manifold, removal & installation.
12. Remove the fuel rail.
13. Remove the lower intake manifold. Refer to Intake Manifold, removal & installation.
14. Raise and safely support the vehicle.
15. Remove the left exhaust manifold. Refer to Exhaust Manifold, removal & installation.
16. Remove the right front tire.
17. Remove the right inner splash shield.
18. Remove the crankshaft vibration damper.
19. Remove the lower accessory drive belt idler pulley.
20. Remove the power steering mounting bolts and set the pump aside.

94618

Fig. 110 Camshaft bearing cap bolt tightening sequence—2.4L engine

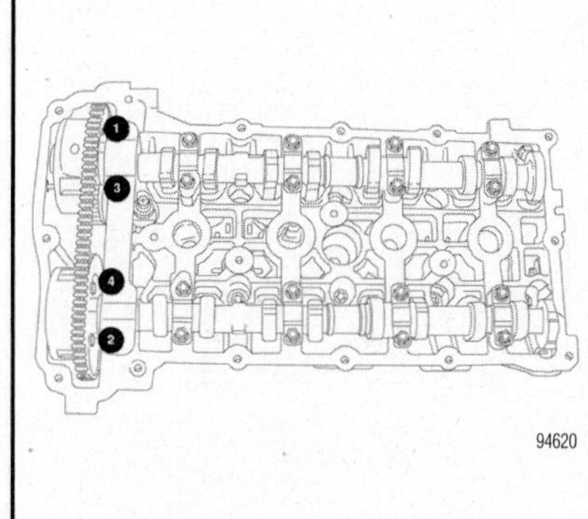

94620

Fig. 111 Front camshaft bearing cap bolt tightening sequence—2.4L engine

21. Remove the lower outer timing belt cover bolts.
22. Remove the support and lower the vehicle.
23. Remove the upper accessory drive belt idler pulley.
24. Remove the accessory belt tensioner.
25. Support the engine with a block of wood and a floor jack.
26. Remove the upper engine mount.
27. Remove the power steering reservoir bolts and set the reservoir aside.
28. Remove the remaining outer timing belt cover bolts and remove cover.
29. Remove the timing belt. Refer to Timing Belt & Sprockets, removal & installation.
30. Remove the left cylinder head cover-to-cylinder head ground strap.
31. Remove the left cylinder head cover. Refer to Valve Covers, removal & installation.
32. Remove the left rocker arm assembly.
33. Hold the left cam gear and loosen the cam gear retaining bolt.
34. Remove the front timing belt housing-to-cylinder head bolts.
35. Remove the left camshaft thrust plate.
36. Carefully push the camshaft out of the back of the cylinder head approximately 3.5 inches (88.9mm). Remove the camshaft sprocket and bolt.

➡It may be necessary to raise the engine slightly in order to remove the camshaft sprocket bolt.

37. Remove the cylinder head bolts in REVERSE of the tightening sequence.
38. Remove the cylinder head.
39. Clean and inspect all the mating surfaces.

To install:

⁂ WARNING

When cleaning the cylinder head and cylinder block surfaces, DO NOT use a metal scraper as the surfaces could be damaged. Use ONLY a wooden or plastic scraper.

40. Clean the sealing surfaces of the cylinder head and block.

➡The cylinder head gaskets are not interchangeable between cylinder heads and are clearly marked right or left.

41. Install the head gasket over the locating dowels. Ensure the gasket is installed on the correct side of the engine.

⁂ WARNING

The cylinder head bolts are tightened using a torque plus angle procedure. The bolts must be examined BEFORE reuse. If the threads are necked down, the bolts must be replaced. Failure to replace a damaged bolt may lead to possible engine damage.

42. Inspect the cylinder head bolts for straightness, head damage, thread damage, and necking. Necking can be checked by holding a scale or straight edge against the threads. If all the threads do not contact the scale evenly the bolt must be replaced.
43. Install the cylinder head over the locating dowels.

➡Lightly lubricate the threads of the cylinder head bolts with clean engine oil prior to installation.

44. Install the cylinder head bolts finger tight.
45. Tighten the cylinder head bolts in sequence using the following steps:
   a. Step 1: Tighten to 45 ft. lbs. (61 Nm).
   b. Step 2: Tighten to 65 ft. lbs. (88 Nm).
   c. Step 3: Tighten again to 65 ft. lbs. (88 Nm).
   d. Step 4: Tighten 90°. (Do not use a torque wrench for this step).

➡The bolt torque after a 90° turn should be over 90 ft. lbs. (122 Nm) in the tightening direction. If not, replace the bolt.

46. Install the inner timing cover-to-cylinder head bolts. Tighten the bolts to 40 ft. lbs. (54 Nm).

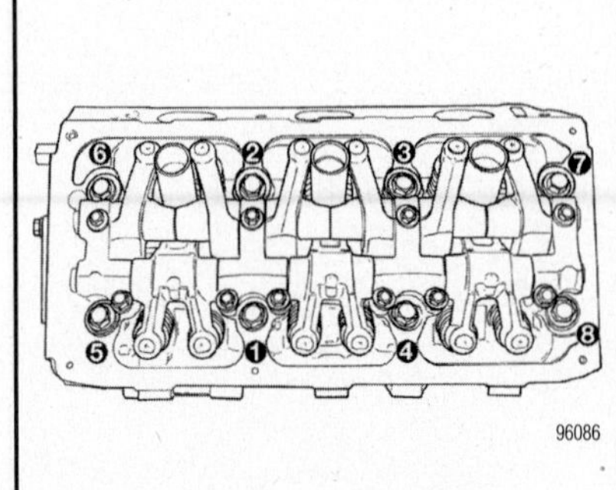

Fig. 112 Cylinder head bolt tightening sequence—3.5L engine

47. Apply a light coat of clean engine oil to the lip of the camshaft oil seal and Seal Protector Sleeve 6788.

➡When installing the camshaft into the cylinder head, first insert the seal protector through the camshaft seal until the camshaft seats, then remove the Seal Protector Sleeve 6788 from the camshaft.

48. Install the oil seal onto the camshaft using the Seal Protector Sleeve 6788 and install the camshaft into the cylinder head.
49. Install the camshaft sprocket. Hold the camshaft sprocket gear and tighten the camshaft sprocket bolt to 85 ft. lbs. (115 Nm), plus 90°. Refer to Timing Belt & Sprockets, removal & installation.
50. Install the rear camshaft thrust plate.
51. Rotate the left camshaft gear to the alignment mark on the rear timing belt cover. Check the right camshaft gear and crankshaft gear timing alignment marks.
52. Install the timing belt. Refer to Timing Belt & Sprockets, removal & installation.
53. Install the tensioner.
54. Install the timing belt front covers. Refer to Timing Belt Front Cover, removal & installation.
55. Install the power steering reservoir.
56. Install the crankshaft vibration damper.
57. Install the upper engine mount.
58. Install the accessory drive belt tensioner.
59. Install the lower accessory drive belt idler pulley.
60. Install the left exhaust manifold. Refer to Exhaust Manifold, removal & installation.
61. Install the exhaust cross over pipe.
62. Install the left rocker arm assembly.
63. Install the left cylinder head cover and ground strap. Refer to Valve Covers, removal & installation.
64. Install the lower intake manifold and gasket. Refer to Intake Manifold, removal & installation.
65. Install the fuel rail.
66. Install the upper intake manifold. Refer to Intake Manifold, removal & installation.
67. Connect the fuel line to the fuel rail.
68. Install the radiator cooling fan assembly. Refer to Engine Fan, removal & installation.
69. Install the radiator core support.
70. Install the radiator close out panel.

71. Install the air cleaner housing. Refer to Air Cleaner, removal & installation.

72. Install the engine cover.

73. Fill the cooling system. Refer to Engine Coolant, Drain & Refill Procedure.

74. Connect the negative battery cable. Refer to Battery, removal & installation.

Right Side

See Figure 113.

1. Before servicing the vehicle, refer to the Precautions Section.
2. Remove the engine cover.
3. Release the fuel system pressure. Refer to Relieving Fuel System Pressure.
4. Disconnect the negative battery cable.
5. Drain the cooling system. Refer to Engine Coolant, Drain & Refill Procedure.
6. Remove air cleaner element housing. Refer to Air Cleaner, removal & installation.
7. Remove the coolant recovery container.
8. Remove the alternator. Refer to Alternator, removal & installation.
9. Disconnect the fuel line at the fuel rail.
10. Remove the upper intake manifold. Refer to Intake Manifold, removal & installation.
11. Remove the fuel rail.
12. Remove the lower intake manifold. Refer to Intake Manifold, removal & installation.
13. Raise and safely support the vehicle.
14. Remove the right exhaust manifold. Refer to Exhaust Manifold, removal & installation.
15. Remove the right front tire.
16. Remove the right inner splash shield.
17. Remove the crankshaft vibration damper.
18. Remove the lower accessory drive belt idler pulley.
19. Remove the lower outer timing belt cover bolts.
20. Remove the supports and lower the vehicle.
21. Remove the upper accessory drive belt idler pulley.
22. Remove the belt tensioner.
23. Support the engine with a block of wood and a floor jack.
24. Remove the upper engine mount.
25. Remove the power steering reservoir bolts and set the reservoir aside.
26. Remove the remaining outer timing belt cover bolts and cover.
27. Remove the timing belt. Refer to Timing Belt & Sprockets, removal & installation.
28. Remove the right valve cover-to-cylinder head ground strap.
29. Remove the EGR valve and tube assembly.
30. Remove the right cylinder head cover. Refer to Valve Covers, removal & installation.
31. Remove the right rocker arm and shaft assembly.
32. Hold the cam gear and loosen the right cam gear retaining bolt.
33. Remove the inner timing cover-to-right cylinder head retaining bolts.
34. Remove the right rear camshaft thrust plate.
35. Carefully push the camshaft out of the back of the cylinder head approximately 3.5 inches (88.9mm). Remove the camshaft sprocket and bolt.

➡It may be necessary to raise the engine slightly in order to remove the camshaft sprocket bolt.

36. Remove the cylinder head bolts in the REVERSE of the tightening sequence.

➡Because of clearance restrictions when removing the right cylinder head, the front four cylinder head bolts must be loosened, raised, and supported with rubber bands before the cylinder head can be removed.

37. Remove the cylinder head.
38. Clean and inspect all mating surfaces.

To install:

⁂ WARNING

When cleaning the cylinder head and cylinder block surfaces, DO NOT use a metal scraper as the surfaces could be damaged. Use ONLY a wooden or plastic scraper.

39. Clean the sealing surfaces of the cylinder head and block.

➡The cylinder head gaskets are not interchangeable between the cylinder heads and are clearly marked right or left.

40. Install the head gasket over the locating dowels. Ensure the gasket is installed on the correct side of the engine.

⁂ WARNING

The cylinder head bolts are tightened using a torque plus angle procedure. The bolts must be examined BEFORE reuse. If the threads are necked down, the bolts must be replaced. Failure to replace a damaged bolt may lead to possible engine damage.

41. Inspect the cylinder head bolts for straightness, head damage, thread damage, and necking. Necking can be checked by holding a scale or straight edge against the threads. If all the threads do not contact the scale evenly the bolt must be replaced.

➡Before installing the cylinder head bolts, lubricate the threads with engine oil.

42. Insert the front 4 cylinder head bolts into the cylinder head. Pull the bolts up to the top of their travel and retain with rubber bands.
43. Install the cylinder head over the locating dowels and finger tighten the head bolts.
44. Tighten the cylinder head bolts in sequence using the following steps:
    a. Step 1: Tighten to 45 ft. lbs. (61 Nm).
    b. Step 2: Tighten to 65 ft. lbs. (88 Nm).
    c. Step 3: Tighten again to 65 ft. lbs. (88 Nm).
    d. Step 4: Tighten 90°. (Do not use a torque wrench for this step).
45. The bolt torque after the 90° turn should be over 90 ft. lbs. (122 Nm) in the tightening direction. If not, replace the bolt.
46. Install the inner timing cover-to-cylinder head bolts. Tighten the bolts to 40 ft. lbs. (54 Nm).
47. Apply a light coat of clean engine oil to the lip of the camshaft oil seal and the Seal Protector Sleeve 6788.

➡When installing the camshaft into the cylinder head, first insert the Seal Protector Sleeve 6788 through the camshaft seal until the camshaft seats, then remove the Seal Protector Sleeve 6788 from the camshaft.

48. Install the camshaft using the Seal Protector Sleeve 6788 into the cylinder head.
49. Install the camshaft sprocket. Hold the camshaft sprocket gear and tighten the camshaft sprocket bolt to 75 ft. lbs. (102 Nm), plus 90°. Refer to Timing Belt & Sprockets, removal & installation.
50. Install the rear camshaft thrust plate.
51. Rotate the camshaft gear to the timing mark and verify the left camshaft gear and crankshaft gear timing marks are aligned.

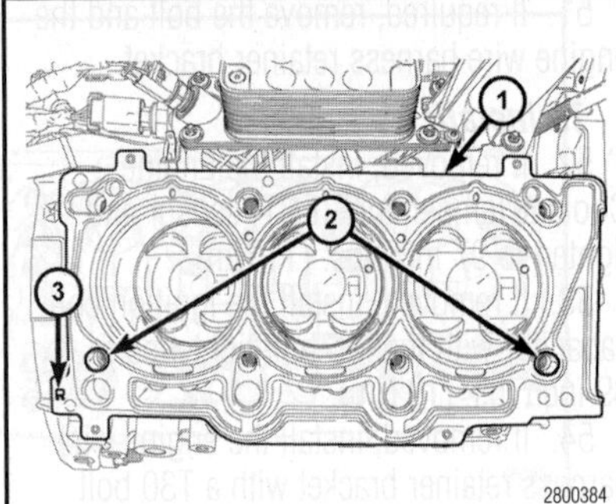

Fig. 116 The cylinder head gaskets are clearly marked with R for Right and L for Left (3). Position the cylinder head gasket (1) on the locating dowels (2)—3.6L engine

61. Tighten the cylinder head bolts in sequence, using the following steps:
   a. Step 1: Tighten to 22 ft. lbs. (30 Nm).
   b. Step 2: Tighten to 33 ft. lbs. (45 Nm).
   c. Step 3: Tighten 75°. (Do not use a torque wrench for this step).
   d. Step 4: Tighten 50°. (Do not use a torque wrench for this step).
   e. Step 5: Loosen all the fasteners in reverse of the tightening sequence.
   f. Step 6: Tighten to 22 ft. lbs. (30 Nm).
   g. Step 7: Tighten to 33 ft. lbs. (45 Nm).
   h. Step 8: Tighten 70°. (Do not use a torque wrench for this step).
   i. Step 9: Tighten 70°. (Do not use a torque wrench for this step).

➡If the hydraulic lifters are being reused, reassemble them into their original locations.

62. If removed, install the hydraulic lifters.

➡If the rocker arms are being reused, reassemble them into their original locations.

63. Install the rocker arms and camshafts. Refer to Camshaft and Lifters, removal & installation.
64. Rotate the camshafts clockwise to TDC by positioning the alignment holes vertically.
65. Install the LH cam chain guide with two bolts. Tighten the T30 bolts to 106 inch lbs. (12 Nm).
66. Install the LH cam chain tensioner to the cylinder head with two bolts. Tighten the T30 bolts to 106 inch lbs. (12 Nm).
67. Reset the LH cam chain tensioner by

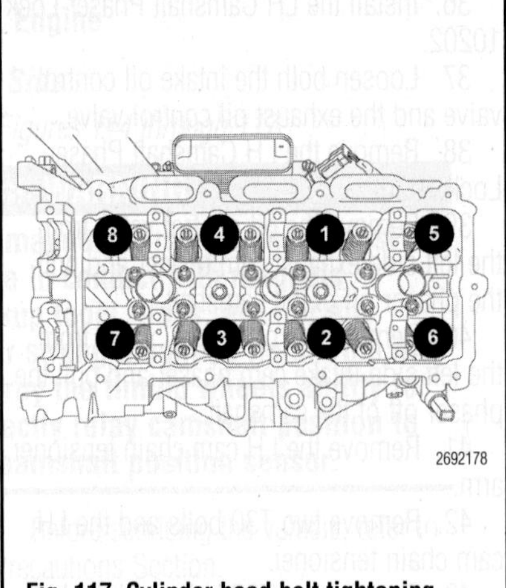

Fig. 117 Cylinder head bolt tightening sequence—3.6L engine

lifting the pawl, pushing back the piston, and installing Tensioner Pin 8514.
68. Install the LH tensioner arm.
69. Press the LH intake cam phaser onto the intake camshaft. Install and hand tighten the oil control valve.

WARNING

Always reinstall the timing chains so that they maintain the same direction of rotation. Inverting a previously run chain on a previously run sprocket will result in excessive wear to both the chain and sprocket.

70. Drape the left side cam chain over the LH intake cam phaser and onto the idler sprocket so that the arrow is aligned with the plated link on the cam chain.
71. While maintaining alignment, route the cam chain around the exhaust and intake cam phasers so that the plated links are aligned with the phaser timing marks. Position the left side cam phasers so that the arrows point toward each other and are parallel to the valve cover sealing surface. Press the exhaust cam phaser onto the exhaust cam, install and hand tighten the oil control valve.

➡Minor rotation of a camshaft (a few degrees) may be required to install the camshaft phaser or phaser lock.

72. Install the LH Camshaft Phaser Lock 10202 and tighten the oil control valves to 110 ft. lbs. (150 Nm).
73. Remove the LH Camshaft Phaser Lock 10202.
74. Remove the Tensioner Pin 8514 from the LH cam chain tensioner.
75. Rotate the crankshaft clockwise 2 complete revolutions stopping when the dimple on the crankshaft is aligned with the block/bearing cap junction.
76. While maintaining this alignment, verify that the arrows on the left side cam phasers point toward each other and are parallel to the valve cover sealing surface and that the right side cam phaser arrows point away from each other and the scribe lines are parallel to the valve cover sealing surface.
77. There should be 12 chain pins between the exhaust cam phaser triangle marking and the intake cam phaser circle marking.
78. If the engine timing is not correct, repeat this procedure.
79. Install the engine timing cover. Refer to Timing Chain Front Cover, removal & installation.
80. Install the crankshaft vibration damper.
81. Install the upper and lower oil pans.
82. Install the cylinder head covers. Refer to Valve Covers, removal & installation.
83. Install the spark plugs. Refer to Spark Plugs, removal & installation.
84. Connect the main harness to the engine oil pressure/temperature harness at the rear of the left cylinder head.
85. Connect the main harness to the engine injection/ignition harness at the rear of the left cylinder head.
86. Connect the Engine Coolant Temperature (ECT) sensor connector.
87. Connect the ignition coil capacitor electrical connector.
88. Install the A/C compressor to the engine compartment.
89. Install the alternator. Refer to Alternator, removal & installation.
90. Install the accessory drive belt. Refer to Accessory Drive Belts, removal & installation.
91. Install the LH upper intake manifold support brackets. Loosely install the studbolts.
92. Install the lower and upper intake manifolds and insulator. Refer to Intake Manifold, removal & installation.
93. Install the oil level indicator tube and the bolt. Tighten the bolt to 106 inch lbs. (12 Nm).
94. Install the heater core return tube, the nut, and bolt. Tighten the nut and bolt to 106 inch lbs. (12 Nm).
95. Engage the 2 lower and 2 upper wire harness retainers to the intake manifold support brackets.
96. Connect the left upstream oxygen sensor connector to the main wire harness.
97. Connect the heater core return hose.
98. Install the resonator and air cleaner

body. Refer to Air Cleaner, removal & installation.

99. Evacuate and charge the refrigerant system.

100. Install the engine cover.

101. If removed, install the oil filter and fill the engine crankcase with the proper type and amount of oil.

102. Fill the cooling system. Refer to Engine Coolant, Drain & Refill Procedure.

103. Raise and safely support the vehicle.

104. Install the belly pan.

105. Lower the vehicle.

106. Connect the negative battery cable and tighten the nut to 45 inch lbs. (5 Nm).

107. Run the engine until it reaches the normal operating temperature. Check the cooling system for correct fluid level.

➡The Cam/Crank Variation Relearn procedure must be performed using the scan tool anytime there has been a repair/replacement made to a powertrain system, for example: flywheel, valvetrain, camshaft and/or crankshaft sensors or components. Refer to Powertrain Control Module (PCM), Powertrain Verification Test.

Right Side

See Figures 118 through 120.

⁂ WARNING

The magnetic timing wheels must not come in contact with magnets (pickup tools, trays, etc.) or any other strong magnetic field. This may destroy the timing wheels ability to correctly relay camshaft position to the camshaft position sensor.

1. Before servicing the vehicle, refer to the Precautions Section.
2. Release the fuel system pressure. Refer to Relieving Fuel System Pressure.
3. Disconnect and isolate the negative battery cable.
4. Raise and safely support the vehicle.
5. Remove the belly pan.
6. Drain the cooling system. Refer to Engine Coolant, Drain & Refill Procedure.
7. Drain the engine oil.
8. Lower the vehicle.
9. Remove the engine cover.
10. Recover the refrigerant from the refrigerant system.
11. Remove the air cleaner body. Refer to Air Cleaner, removal & installation.
12. Remove the resonator.
13. Remove the upper and lower intake manifolds and insulator. Refer to Intake Manifold, removal & installation.
14. Remove the accessory drive belt. Refer to Accessory Drive Belts, removal & installation.
15. Remove the 3 bolts and the power steering pump heat shield.
16. Disengage the wire harness retainer from the power steering pump.
17. Remove the 3 bolts and reposition the power steering pump and bracket as an assembly. Do not disconnect the power steering lines from the pump.
18. Remove the 2 bolts and the heater core supply tube.
19. Disconnect the ignition coil capacitor electrical connector.
20. Disengage the wire harness retainer from the intake manifold support bracket.
21. Remove the studbolt and remove the upper intake manifold support bracket.
22. Remove the spark plugs. Refer to Spark Plugs, removal & installation.
23. Remove the cylinder head covers. Refer to Valve Covers, removal & installation.
24. Remove the lower and upper oil pans.
25. Remove the crankshaft vibration damper.
26. Remove the engine timing cover. Refer to Timing Chain Front Cover, removal & installation.

⁂ WARNING

When aligning the timing marks, always rotate the engine by turning the crankshaft. Failure to do so may result in valve and/or piston damage.

27. Rotate the crankshaft clockwise to place the number 1 piston at Top Dead Center (TDC) on the exhaust stroke by aligning the dimple on the crankshaft with the block/bearing cap junction. The left side cam phaser arrows should point toward each other and be parallel to the valve cover sealing surface. The right side cam phaser arrows should point away from each other and the scribe lines should be parallel to the valve cover sealing surface.

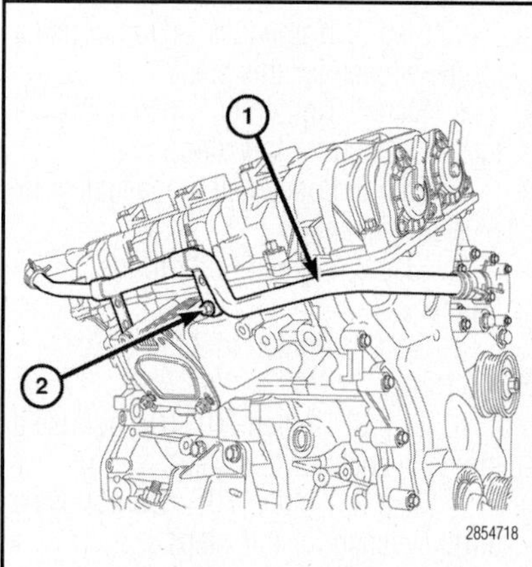

Fig. 118 Remove the 2 bolts (2) and the heater core supply tube (1)—3.6L engine

⁂ WARNING

Always reinstall timing chains so that they maintain the same direction of rotation. Inverting a previously run chain on a previously run sprocket will result in excessive wear to both the chain and sprocket.

28. Mark the direction of rotation on the timing chain using a paint pen or equivalent to aid in reassembly.

⁂ WARNING

When the timing chains are removed and the cylinder heads are still installed, DO NOT rotate the camshafts or crankshaft without first locating the proper crankshaft position. Failure to do so will result in valve and/or piston damage.

29. Reset the RH cam chain tensioner by pushing back the tensioner piston and installing Tensioner Pin 8514.

➡Minor rotation of a camshaft (a few degrees) may be required to install the camshaft phaser lock.

30. Install the RH Camshaft Phaser Lock 10202.
31. Loosen both the intake oil control valve and exhaust oil control valve.
32. Remove the RH Camshaft Phaser Lock 10202.
33. Remove the oil control valve from the right side intake cam phaser and pull the phaser off of the camshaft.
34. Remove the oil control valve from the right side exhaust cam phaser and pull the phaser off of the camshaft.
35. Remove the RH cam chain tensioner arm.
36. Remove the 2 T30 bolts and the RH cam chain tensioner.
37. Remove the 3 T30 bolts and the RH cam chain guide.
38. Remove the right camshafts. Refer to Camshaft and Lifters, removal & installation.

➡If the rocker arms are to be reused, identify their positions so that they can be reassembled into their original locations.

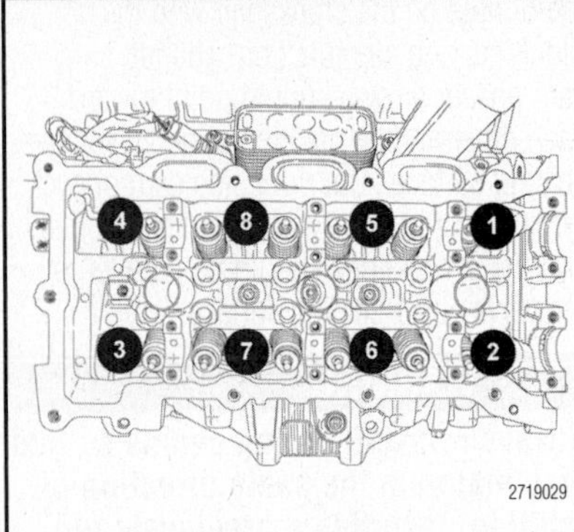

Fig. 119 Cylinder head bolt removal sequence (right side)—3.6L engine

39. Remove the rocker arms.

➡**If the hydraulic lifters are to be reused, identify their positions so that they can be reassembled into their original locations.**

40. If required, remove the hydraulic lifters.

41. Using the proper sequence, remove the cylinder head retaining bolts.

⁂ CAUTION

The multi-layered steel head gaskets have very sharp edges that could cause personal injury if not handled carefully.

➡**The head gasket crimps the locating dowels and the dowels may pull out of the engine block when the head gasket is removed.**

42. Remove the cylinder head and gasket. Discard the gasket.

⁂ WARNING

Do not lay the cylinder head on its gasket sealing surface, due to the design of the cylinder head gasket, any distortion to the cylinder head sealing surface may prevent the gasket from properly sealing resulting in leaks.

43. If required, remove the bolt and the ignition coil capacitor.

To install:

44. If removed, install the ignition coil capacitor with the M6 bolt tightened to 89 inch lbs. (10 Nm).

➡**The cylinder head bolts are tightened using a torque plus angle procedure. The bolts must be examined BEFORE reuse. If the threads are necked down the bolts must be replaced.**

45. Check the cylinder head bolts for necking by holding a scale or straight edge against the threads. If all the threads do not contact the scale, the bolt must be replaced.

⁂ WARNING

When cleaning the cylinder head and cylinder block surfaces, DO NOT use a metal scraper as the surfaces could be damaged. Use ONLY a wooden or plastic scraper.

46. Clean and prepare the gasket sealing surfaces of the cylinder head and block.

⁂ WARNING

Non-compressible debris such as oil, coolant or RTV sealants that are not removed from bolt holes can cause the aluminum casting to crack when tightening the bolts.

47. Clean out the cylinder head bolt holes in the engine block.

➡**The cylinder head gaskets are not interchangeable between the left and right cylinder heads and are clearly marked with R for Right and L for Left.**

48. Position the new cylinder head gasket on the locating dowels.

49. Position the cylinder head onto the cylinder block. Make sure the cylinder head seats fully over the locating dowels.

➡**Do not apply any additional oil to the bolt threads.**

50. Install the 8 head bolts finger tight.

51. Tighten the cylinder head bolts in sequence according to the following steps:

a. Step 1: Tighten to 22 ft. lbs. (30 Nm).

b. Step 2: Tighten to 33 ft. lbs. (45 Nm).

c. Step 3: Tighten 75°. (Do not use a torque wrench for this step).

d. Step 4: Tighten 50°. (Do not use a torque wrench for this step).

e. Step 5: Loosen all the fasteners in reverse sequence.

f. Step 6: Tighten to 22 ft. lbs. (30 Nm).

g. Step 7: Tighten to 33 ft. lbs. (45 Nm).

h. Step 8: Tighten 70°. (Do not use a torque wrench for this step).

i. Step 9: Tighten 70°. (Do not use a torque wrench for this step).

➡**If the hydraulic lifters are being reused, reassemble them into their original locations.**

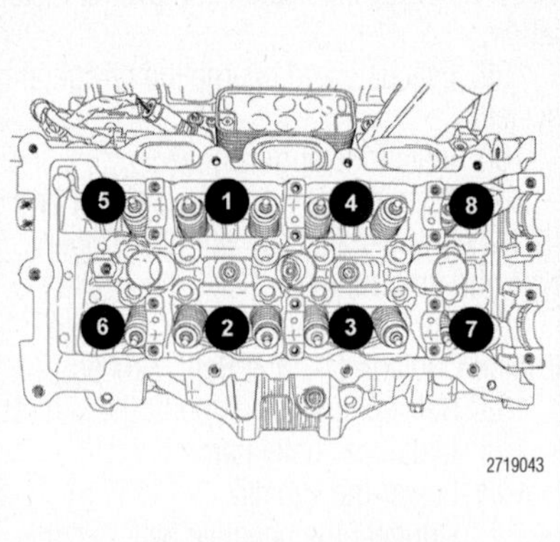

Fig. 120 Cylinder head bolt tightening sequence (right side)—3.6L engine

52. If removed, install the hydraulic lifters.

➡**If the rocker arms are being reused, reassemble them into their original locations.**

53. Install the rocker arms and camshafts. Refer to Camshaft and Lifters, removal & installation.

⁂ WARNING

Do not rotate the camshafts more than a few degrees independently of the crankshaft. Valve to piston contact could occur resulting in possible valve damage. If the camshafts need to be rotated more than a few degrees, first move the pistons away from the cylinder heads by rotating the crankshaft counterclockwise to a position 30° BTDC. Once the camshafts are positioned at TDC, rotate the crankshaft clockwise to return the crankshaft to TDC.

54. Verify that the camshafts are set at TDC by positioning the alignment holes vertically.

55. Install the RH cam chain guide with the 3 bolts. Tighten the T30 bolts to 106 inch lbs. (12 Nm).

56. Install the RH cam chain tensioner to the engine block with the 2 bolts. Tighten the T30 bolts to 106 inch lbs. (12 Nm).

57. Reset the RH cam chain tensioner by pushing back the tensioner piston and installing Tensioner Pin 8514.

58. Install the RH tensioner arm.

59. Press the RH exhaust cam phaser onto the exhaust camshaft. Install and hand tighten the oil control valve.

⁂ WARNING

Always reinstall timing chains so that they maintain the same direction of

rotation. Inverting a previously run chain on a previously run sprocket will result in excessive wear to both the chain and sprocket.

60. Drape the right side cam chain over the RH exhaust cam phaser and onto the idler sprocket so that the dimple is aligned with the plated link on the cam chain.

61. While maintaining this alignment, route the cam chain around the exhaust and intake cam phasers so that the plated links are aligned with the phaser timing marks. Position the right side cam phasers so that the arrows point away from each other and the scribe lines are parallel to the valve cover sealing surface. Press the intake cam phaser onto the intake cam, install and hand tighten the oil control valve.

➡Minor rotation of a camshaft (a few degrees) may be required to install the camshaft phaser or phaser lock.

62. Install the RH Camshaft Phaser Lock 10202 and tighten the oil control valves to 110 ft. lbs. (150 Nm).

63. Remove the RH Camshaft Phaser Lock 10202.

64. Remove the Tensioner Pin 8514 from the RH cam chain tensioner.

65. Rotate the crankshaft clockwise 2 complete revolutions stopping when the dimple on the crankshaft is aligned the with the block/bearing cap junction.

66. While maintaining this alignment, verify that the arrows on the left side cam phasers point toward each other and are parallel to the valve cover sealing surface and that the right side cam phaser arrows point away from each other and the scribe lines are parallel to the valve cover sealing surface.

67. There should be 12 chain pins between the exhaust cam phaser triangle marking and the intake cam phaser circle marking.

68. If the engine timing is not correct, repeat this procedure.

69. Install the engine timing cover, crankshaft vibration damper, upper and lower oil pans and cylinder head covers.

70. Install the spark plugs. Refer to Spark Plugs, removal & installation.

71. Install the upper intake manifold support bracket with the studbolt hand tight.

72. Engage the wire harness retainer from the intake manifold support bracket.

73. Connect the ignition coil capacitor electrical connector.

74. Install the heater core supply tube with 1 bolt tightened to 106 inch lbs. (12 Nm).

75. Reposition the power steering pump and bracket as an assembly and install the 3 bolts. Tighten the bolts to 18 ft. lbs. (25 Nm).

76. Disengage the wire harness retainer from the power steering pump.

77. Install the power steering pump heat shield and the 3 bolts. Tighten the bolts to 18 ft. lbs. (25 Nm).

78. Install the accessory drive belt. Refer to Accessory Drive Belts, removal & installation.

79. Install the upper and lower intake manifolds and insulator. Refer to Intake Manifold, removal & installation.

80. Install the resonator and air cleaner body. Refer to Air Cleaner, removal & installation.

81. Evacuate and charge the refrigerant system.

82. Install the engine cover.

83. If removed, install the oil filter and fill the engine crankcase with the proper type and amount of oil.

84. Fill the cooling system. Refer to Engine Coolant, Drain & Refill Procedure.

85. Raise and safely support the vehicle.

86. Install the belly pan.

87. Lower the vehicle.

88. Connect the negative battery cable and tighten the nut to 45 inch lbs. (5 Nm). Refer to Battery, removal & installation.

89. Run the engine until it reaches the normal operating temperature. Check the cooling system for correct fluid level.

➡The Cam/Crank Variation Relearn procedure must be performed using the scan tool anytime there has been a repair/replacement made to a powertrain system, for example: flywheel, valvetrain, camshaft and/or crankshaft sensors or components. Refer to Powertrain Control Module (PCM), Powertrain Verification Test.

ENGINE OIL & FILTER

REPLACEMENT

2.4L Engine

See Figures 121 and 122.

⁂ CAUTION

New or used engine oil can be irritating to the skin. Avoid prolonged or repeated skin contact with engine oil. Contaminants in used engine oil, caused by internal combustion, can be hazardous to health. Thoroughly wash exposed skin with soap and water. Do not wash skin with gasoline, diesel fuel, thinner, or solvents as health problems can result. Dispose of used engine oil properly. Contact your dealer or government agency for location of collection center in your area.

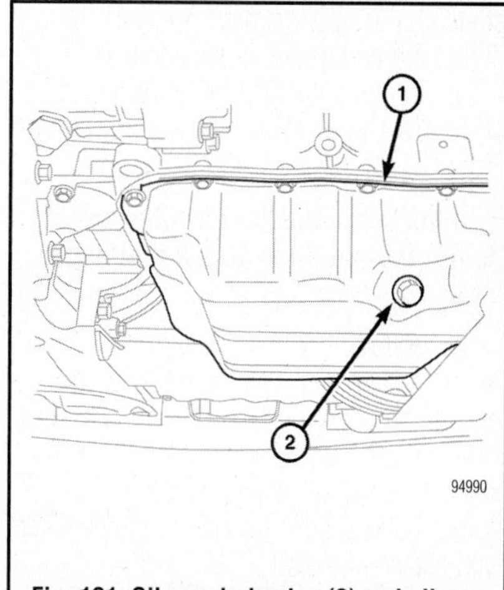

Fig. 121 Oil pan drain plug (2) and oil pan (1) shown—2.4L engine

➡Change the engine oil at mileage and time intervals described in the Maintenance Schedule.

1. Before servicing the vehicle, refer to the Precautions Section.

2. Run the engine until achieving the normal operating temperature.

3. Position the vehicle on a level surface and turn the engine off.

4. Remove the oil fill cap.

5. Raise and safely support the vehicle.

6. Place a suitable oil collecting container under the oil pan drain plug.

7. Remove the oil pan drain plug and allow oil to drain into the collecting container. Inspect the drain plug threads for

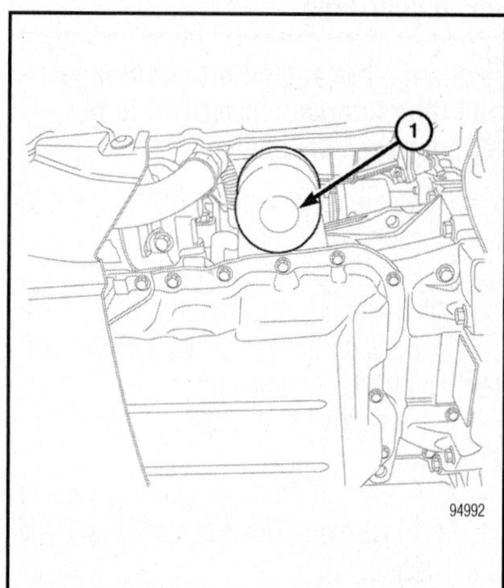

Fig. 122 Oil filter location (1)—2.4L engine

stretching or other damage. Replace the drain plug and gasket if damaged.

8. Remove the oil filter allowing the oil to drain when loosening before removing.

➡When servicing the oil filter, avoid deforming the filter. Use a tool band strap.

To install:

9. Install the oil pan drain plug and tighten the drain plug to 30 ft. lbs. (40 Nm).

10. Wipe the filter base clean, then inspect the gasket sealing surface.

11. Lubricate the gasket of the new filter with clean engine oil.

12. Install a new oil filter and tighten to 10 ft. lbs. (14 Nm) after the gasket contacts the base. Use a filter wrench if necessary.

13. Lower the vehicle and fill the crankcase with the specified type and amount of engine oil.

14. Install the oil fill cap.

15. Start the engine and inspect for leaks.

16. Stop the engine and inspect oil level.

3.5L Engine

See Figures 123 and 124.

CAUTION

New or used engine oil can be irritating to the skin. Avoid prolonged or repeated skin contact with engine oil. Contaminants in used engine oil, caused by internal combustion, can be hazardous to health. Thoroughly wash exposed skin with soap and water. Do not wash skin with gasoline, diesel fuel, thinner, or solvents as health problems can result. Dispose of used engine oil properly. Contact your dealer or government agency for location of collection center in your area.

➡Change the engine oil at mileage and time intervals described in the Maintenance Schedule.

1. Before servicing the vehicle, refer to the Precautions Section.

2. Run the engine until achieving the normal operating temperature.

3. Position the vehicle on a level surface and turn the engine off.

4. Open the hood, remove the engine oil fill cap.

5. Raise and safely support the vehicle.

6. Place a suitable drain pan under the crankcase drain.

7. Remove the oil pan drain plug from the crankcase and allow the oil to drain into

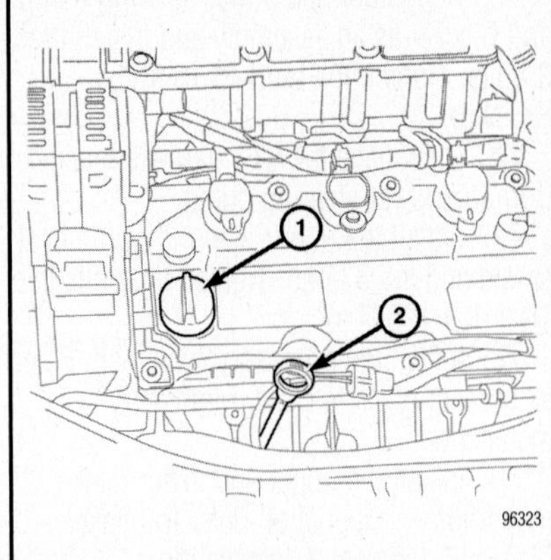

Fig. 123 Location of the engine oil fill cap (1) and engine oil dip stick (2)—3.5L engine

the pan. Inspect the drain plug threads for stretching or other damage. Replace the drain plug and gasket if damaged.

8. Remove the oil filter.

To install:

9. Install the drain plug in the crankcase. Tighten the oil pan drain plug to 20 ft. lbs. (27 Nm).

10. Install a new oil filter.

a. Wipe the base clean, then inspect the gasket contact surface.

b. Lubricate the gasket of the new filter with clean engine oil.

c. Install and tighten the oil filter to 12 ft. lbs. (16 Nm) of torque after the gasket contacts the base. Use a filter wrench if necessary.

11. Lower the vehicle.

12. Fill the crankcase with the specified type and amount of engine oil.

13. Install the oil fill cap.

14. Start the engine and inspect for leaks.

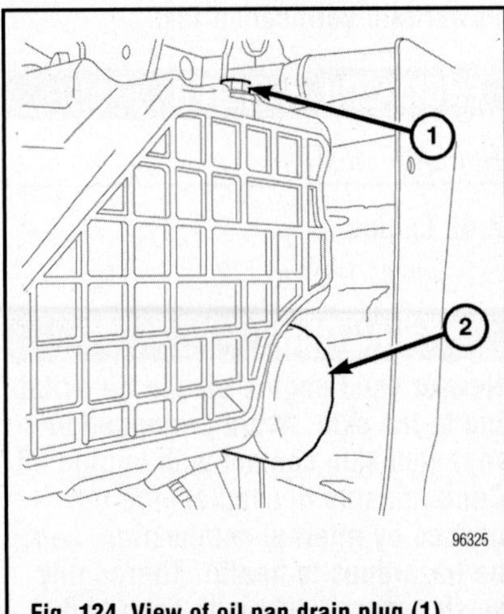

Fig. 124 View of oil pan drain plug (1) and oil filter (2)—3.5L engine

15. Turn the engine off and inspect the oil level.

3.6L Engine

See Figures 125 and 126.

CAUTION

New or used engine oil can be irritating to the skin. Avoid prolonged or repeated skin contact with engine oil. Contaminants in used engine oil, caused by internal combustion, can be hazardous to health. Thoroughly wash exposed skin with soap and water. Do not wash skin with gasoline, diesel fuel, thinner, or solvents as health problems can result. Dispose of used engine oil properly. Contact your dealer or government agency for location of collection center in your area.

➡Change the engine oil at mileage and time intervals described in the Maintenance Schedule.

1. Before servicing the vehicle, refer to the Precautions Section.

2. Run the engine until achieving the normal operating temperature.

3. Position the vehicle on a level surface and turn the engine off.

4. Remove the engine cover.

➡When performing an engine oil change, the oil filter cap must be removed. Removing the oil filter cap releases oil held within the oil filter cavity and allows it to drain into the sump. Failure to remove the cap prior to reinstallation of the drain plug will not allow complete draining of the used engine oil.

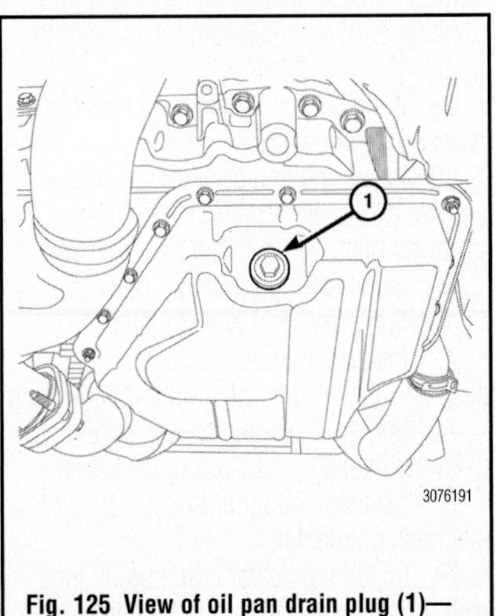

Fig. 125 View of oil pan drain plug (1)—3.6L engine

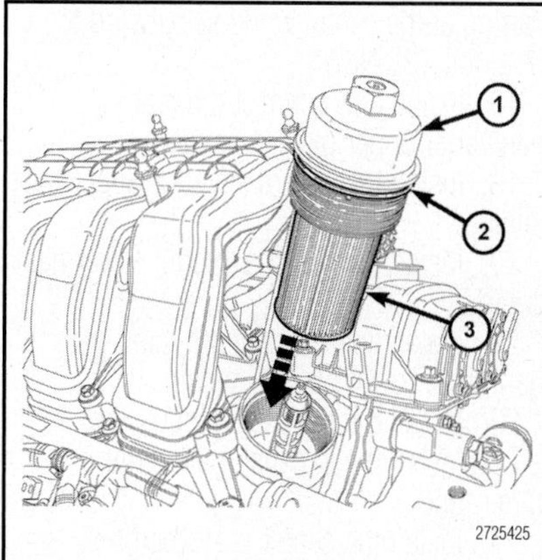

Fig. 126 Oil filter O-ring seal (1), filter cap (2), and oil filter (3) installation—3.6L engine

5. Place an oil absorbent cloth around the oil filter housing at the base of the oil filter cap.

➡The oil filter is attached to the oil filter cap.

6. Rotate the oil filter cap counterclockwise and remove the cap and filter from the oil filter housing.
7. Raise and safely support the vehicle.
8. Place a suitable drain pan under the crankcase drain plug.
9. Remove the drain plug from the oil pan and allow the oil to drain into the pan. Inspect the drain plug threads for stretching or other damage. Replace the drain plug and gasket if damaged.
10. Install the drain plug in the oil pan and tighten to 20 ft. lbs. (27 Nm).
11. Lower the vehicle.
12. Remove the oil filter from the oil filter cap.
13. Remove and discard the O-ring seal.

To install:

➡It is not necessary to pre-oil the oil filter or fill the oil filter housing.

14. Lightly lubricate the new O-ring seal with clean engine oil.
15. Install the O-ring seal on the filter cap.
16. Install the new oil filter into the oil filter cap.
17. Thread the oil filter cap into the oil filter housing and tighten to 18 ft. lbs. (25 Nm).
18. Remove the oil fill cap. Fill the crankcase with the specified type and amount of engine oil.
19. Install the oil fill cap.
20. Start the engine and inspect for leaks.
21. Stop the engine and check the oil level.
22. Install the engine cover.

EXHAUST MANIFOLD

REMOVAL & INSTALLATION

2.4L Engine

See Figures 127 and 128.

✻✻ CAUTION

In order to avoid being burned, do not service the exhaust system while it is still hot. Service the system when it is cool.

✻✻ CAUTION

Always wear protective goggles and gloves when removing exhaust parts as falling rust and sharp edges from worn exhaust components could result in serious personal injury.

1. Before servicing the vehicle, refer to the Precautions Section.
2. Remove the engine cover.
3. Disconnect the negative cable from the battery.
4. Remove the bolts attaching the upper heat shield.
5. Remove the upper heat shield.
6. Disconnect the exhaust pipe from the manifold.
7. Disconnect the oxygen sensor electrical connector.
8. Remove the manifold support bracket.
9. Remove the lower exhaust manifold heat shield.
10. Remove the exhaust manifold retaining fasteners.

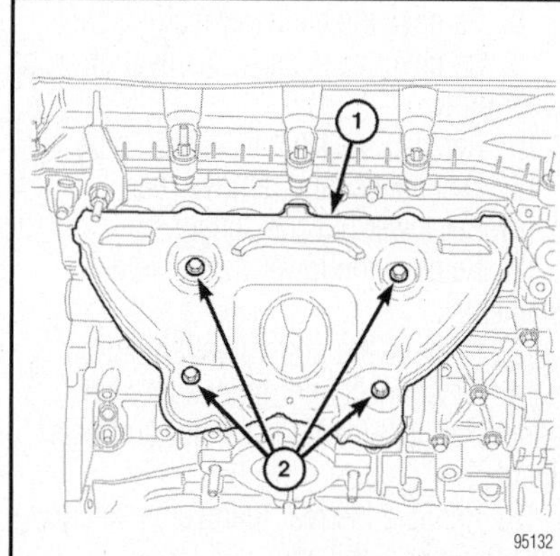

Fig. 127 Remove the bolts (2) attaching the exhaust manifold upper heat shield (1)—2.4L engine

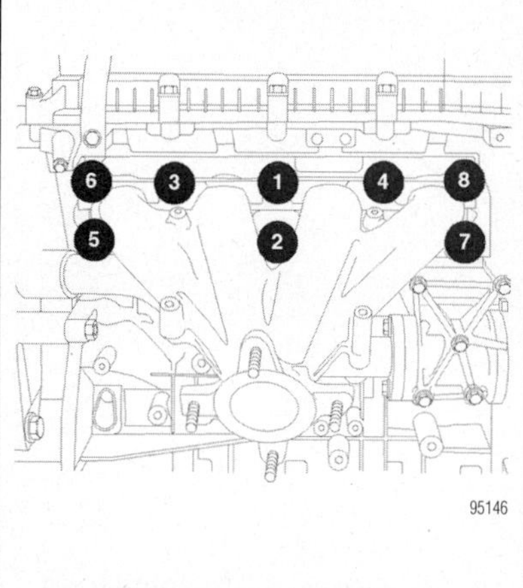

Fig. 128 Exhaust manifold tightening sequence—2.4L engine

11. Remove and discard the manifold gasket.

To install:

12. Install a new exhaust manifold gasket. Do not apply sealer.
13. Position the exhaust manifold in place.
14. Tighten the exhaust manifold bolts to 25 ft. lbs. (34 Nm).
15. Install the exhaust manifold heat shield. Tighten the bolts to 106 inch lbs. (12 Nm).
16. Install the exhaust manifold support bracket.
17. Install a new catalytic converter gasket.
18. Install the exhaust pipe to the manifold. Tighten the fasteners to 21 ft. lbs. (28 Nm).
19. Connect the oxygen sensor electrical connector.
20. Connect the negative battery cable.
21. Install the engine cover.

3.5L Engine

Front Manifold/Converter

See Figures 129 and 130.

✻✻ CAUTION

In order to avoid being burned, do not service the exhaust system while it is still hot. Service the system when it is cool.

✻✻ CAUTION

Always wear protective goggles and gloves when removing exhaust parts as falling rust and sharp edges from worn exhaust components could result in serious personal injury.

1. Before servicing the vehicle, refer to the Precautions Section.

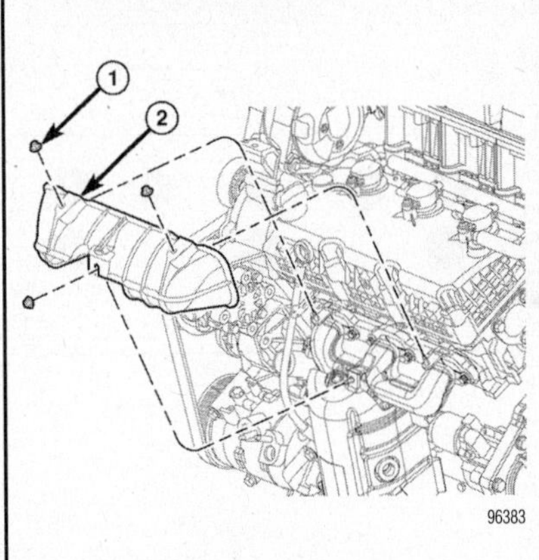

Fig. 129 Remove the 3 fasteners (1) and remove the upper heat shield (2) (front maniverter)—3.5L engine

2. Disconnect and isolate the negative battery cable.
3. Remove the 3 fasteners, and remove the upper heat shield.
4. Remove the 12 belly pan fasteners and remove the belly pan.
5. Remove the front cross under pipe bolts.
6. Disconnect and remove the front lower maniverter oxygen sensor.
7. Loosen the oil level indicator tube retaining bolt and position the dipstick out of the way.
8. Disconnect and remove the front upper maniverter oxygen sensor.
9. Remove the maniverter retaining bolts and maniverter.

To install:

10. Position the maniverter and gasket. Install the retaining bolts. Tighten the bolts starting at the center working outward to 17 ft. lbs. (23 Nm).
11. Install the upper heat shield, and torque the nuts to 106 inch lbs. (12 Nm).

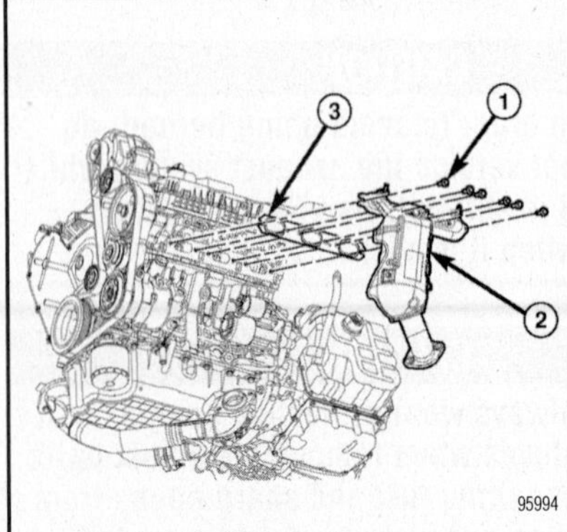

Fig. 130 View of maniverter (front) (2), gasket (3), and retaining bolts (1)—3.5L engine

12. Install and connect the front upper maniverter oxygen sensor.
13. Position the oil level indicator tube and install the retaining bolt.
14. Install and connect the front lower maniverter oxygen sensor.
15. Install the maniverter cross under pipe retaining bolts. Tighten the bolts to 23 ft. lbs. (31 Nm).
16. Install the belly pan and the 12 belly pan fasteners.
17. Connect the negative battery cable. Refer to Battery, removal & installation.

Rear Manifold/Converter

⁂ CAUTION

In order to avoid being burned, do not service the exhaust system while it is still hot. Service the system when it is cool.

⁂ CAUTION

Always wear protective goggles and gloves when removing exhaust parts as falling rust and sharp edges from worn exhaust components could result in serious personal injury.

1. Before servicing the vehicle, refer to the Precautions Section.
2. Disconnect the negative battery cable.
3. Raise and safely support the vehicle.
4. Remove the 12 belly pan fasteners and remove the belly pan.
5. Remove the right front halfshaft. Refer to Front Halfshaft, removal & installation.
6. Remove the retainer nuts at the extension pipe.
7. Remove the retainer from the bracket-to-bell housing.
8. Remove the center crossmember.
9. Remove the exhaust maniverter cross under pipe.
10. Remove the front extension pipe.
11. Disconnect and remove rear maniverter lower oxygen sensor.
12. Remove the lower heat shield retainers.
13. Remove the upper heat shield nuts.
14. Disconnect and remove the rear maniverter upper oxygen sensor and heat shields.
15. Remove the rear maniverter retaining bolts the rear maniverter.

To install:

16. Clean the gasket surfaces.
17. Position the maniverter and gasket. Install the retaining bolts. Tighten the bolts starting at the center working outward to 17 ft. lbs. (23 Nm).
18. Install and connect the rear maniverter upper oxygen sensor.
19. Install the rear maniverter upper heat shield.
20. Install the rear maniverter lower heat shield.
21. Install and connect the rear maniverter lower oxygen sensor.
22. Install the front extension pipe.
23. Install the exhaust maniverter cross under pipe.
24. Install the center crossmember.
25. Install the bracket-to-bell housing retainer.
26. Position the extension pipe and install the retainer nuts.
27. Install the right front halfshaft. Refer to Front Halfshaft, removal & installation.
28. Install the belly pan and the 12 belly pan fasteners.
29. Lower the vehicle.
30. Connect the negative battery cable. Refer to Battery, removal & installation.

3.6L Engine

The 3.6L aluminum cylinder heads are a unique design with left and right castings. The exhaust manifolds are integrated into the cylinder heads. If any damage is found to the exhaust manifold portion, the cylinder head must be removed for repair or replacement. Refer to Cylinder Head, removal & installation.

INTAKE MANIFOLD

REMOVAL & INSTALLATION

2.4L Engine

See Figures 131 and 132.

⁂ CAUTION

Release the fuel system pressure before servicing system components. Service vehicles in well ventilated areas and avoid ignition sources. Never smoke while servicing the vehicle.

1. Before servicing the vehicle, refer to the Precautions Section.
2. Remove the engine cover.
3. Release the fuel system pressure. Refer to Relieving Fuel System Pressure.
4. Remove the air cleaner housing. Refer to Air Cleaner, removal & installation.
5. Disconnect the negative battery cable. Refer to Battery, removal & installation.
6. Disconnect the fuel line at the rail.

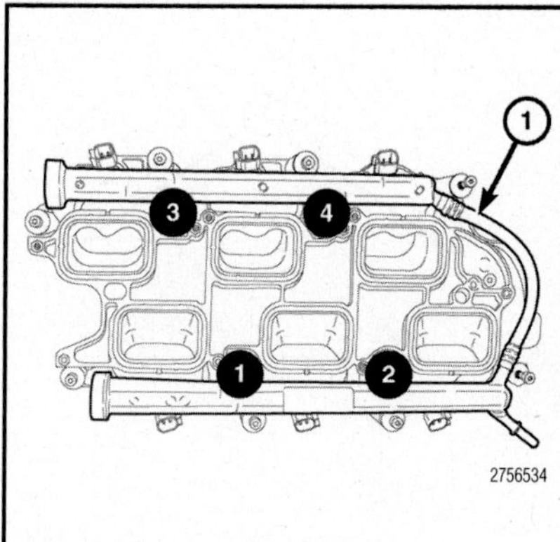

Fig. 139 Fuel rail bolt tightening sequence—3.6L engine

12. Remove and discard the 6 lower intake manifold-to-cylinder head seals.

13. If required, remove the fuel rail and fuel injectors from the lower intake manifold.

To install:

14. Clean and inspect the sealing surfaces. Install new lower intake manifold-to-cylinder head seals.

15. If removed, install the fuel injectors and the fuel rail to the lower intake manifold. Tighten the 4 bolts, in sequence, to 62 inch lbs. (7 Nm).

16. Position the lower intake manifold on the cylinder head surfaces.

17. Install the manifold attaching bolts and tighten in sequence to 71 inch lbs. (8 Nm).

18. Engage the main wire harness retainer to the rear of the lower intake manifold.

19. Engage the injection/ignition harness retainer to the rear of the lower intake manifold.

20. Connect the fuel injector electrical connectors.

21. Connect the fuel supply hose to the fuel rail inlet.

22. Install the insulator to the 2 alignment posts on top of the LH cylinder head cover.

23. Install the upper intake manifold, support brackets, and resonator. Refer to Upper Manifold, removal & installation.

24. Connect the negative battery cable and tighten the nut to 45 inch lbs. (5 Nm). Refer to Battery, removal & installation.

25. Start the engine and check for leaks.

Upper Manifold

See Figures 141 through 145.

1. Before servicing the vehicle, refer to the Precautions Section.

2. Disconnect and isolate the negative battery cable. Refer to Battery, removal & installation.

3. Remove the engine cover.

4. Remove the resonator. Refer to Air Cleaner, removal & installation.

5. Disconnect the electrical connectors from the Manifold Absolute Pressure (MAP) sensor and the Electronic Throttle Control (ETC).

6. Disengage the ETC harness from the clip on the throttle body. Disengage the wire harness retainers from the upper intake manifold near the MAP sensor and reposition the wire harness.

7. Disconnect the following hoses from the upper intake manifold:
   - The Positive Crankcase Ventilation (PCV)
   - The vapor purge
   - The brake booster

8. Disengage the wire harness retainer from the upper intake manifold support bracket.

9. Disengage the wire harness retainer from the studbolt.

10. Remove 2 nuts, loosen the studbolt, and reposition the upper intake manifold support bracket.

11. Remove the nut from the support bracket of the heater core return tube.

12. Remove the 2 nuts, loosen the 2 studbolts, and reposition the 2 upper intake manifold support brackets.

➡The upper intake manifold attaching bolts are captured in the upper intake manifold. Once loosened, the bolts will have to be lifted out of the lower intake manifold and held while removing the upper intake manifold.

➡Exercise care to avoid inadvertently loosening the 2 fuel rail attachment bolts that are in close proximity of the upper intake manifold attaching bolts.

13. Remove the 7 manifold attaching bolts and remove the upper intake manifold.

14. Remove and discard the 6 upper-to-lower intake manifold seals.

15. Cover the open intake ports to prevent debris from entering the engine.

16. If required, remove the insulator from the LH cylinder head cover.

To install:

➡Prior to installing the upper intake manifold, verify that the 4 fuel rail bolts were not inadvertently loosened. The bolts must tightened in sequence to 62 inch lbs. (7 Nm).

17. Clean and inspect the sealing surfaces. Install new upper-to-lower intake manifold seals.

➡Make sure the fuel injectors and wiring harnesses are in the correct

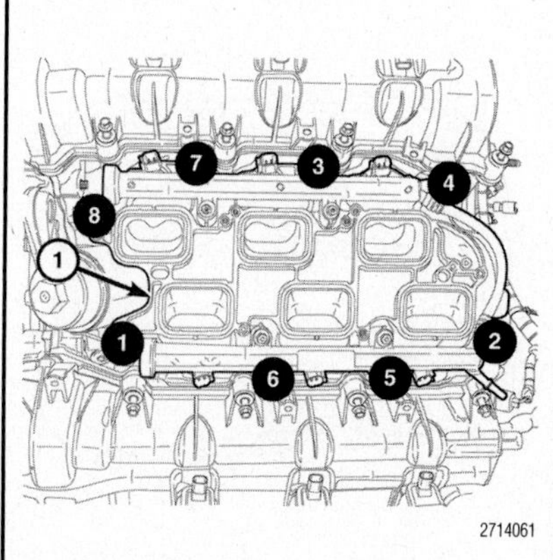

Fig. 140 Lower intake manifold (1) bolt tightening sequence—3.6L engine

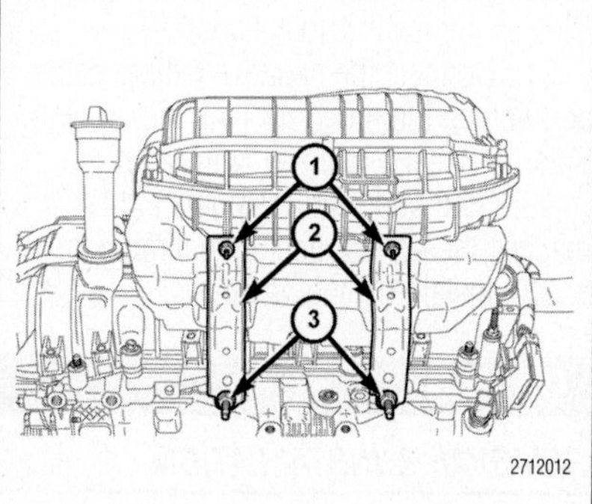

Fig. 141 Remove the nuts (1), loosen the studbolts (3), and reposition the upper intake manifold support brackets (2)—3.6L engine

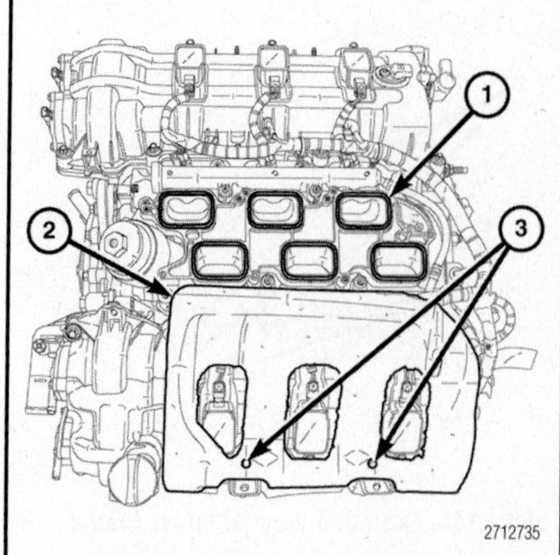

Fig. 142 View of the upper-to-lower intake manifold seals (1) and LH cylinder head cover insulator (2)—3.6L engine

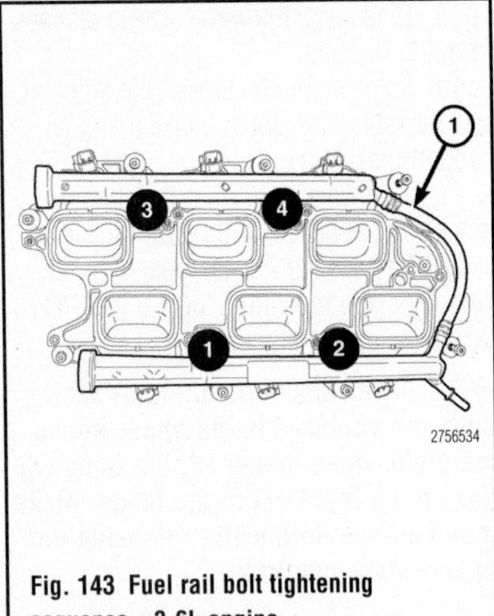

Fig. 143 Fuel rail bolt tightening sequence—3.6L engine

position so that they don't interfere with the upper intake manifold installation.

18. If removed, install the insulator to the 2 alignment posts on top of the LH cylinder head cover.
19. Lift and hold the 7 upper intake attaching bolts clear of the mating surface. Back the bolts out slightly or if required, use an elastic band to hold the bolts clear of the mating surface.
20. Position the upper intake manifold onto the lower intake manifold so that the 2 locating posts on the upper intake manifold align with the corresponding holes in the lower intake manifold.
21. Install the 7 upper intake manifold attaching bolts. Tighten the bolts in sequence to 71 inch lbs. (8 Nm).
22. Install the 2 nuts to the upper intake manifold support bracket. Tighten the nuts to 89 inch lbs. (10 Nm) and tighten the studbolt to 15 ft. lbs. (20 Nm).

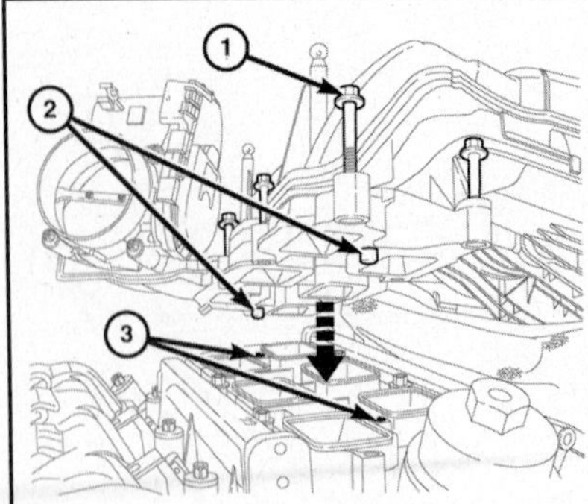

Fig. 144 Exploded view of upper intake attaching bolts (1), locating posts (2) on the upper intake manifold, and alignment holes (3) in the lower intake manifold—3.6L engine

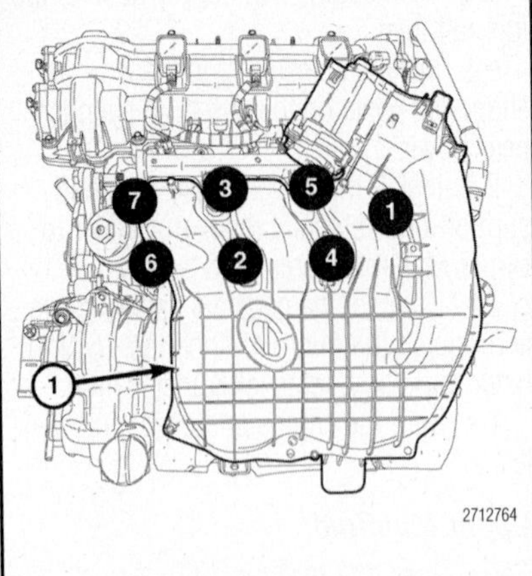

Fig. 145 View of upper intake manifold (1) bolt tightening sequence—3.6L engine

23. Engage the wire harness retainer to the studbolt.
24. Engage the wire harness retainer to the upper intake manifold support bracket.
25. Install the 2 upper intake manifold support brackets with the 2 studbolts and 2 nuts. Tighten the studbolts to 15 ft. lbs. (20 Nm) and tighten the nuts to 89 inch lbs. (10 Nm).
26. Install the nut to the support bracket of the heater core return tube and tighten to 106 inch lbs. (12 Nm).
27. Connect the following hoses to the upper intake manifold:
- The PCV
- The vapor purge
- The brake booster

28. Connect the electrical connectors to the MAP sensor and the ETC.
29. Secure the ETC harness to the clip on the throttle body and engage the wire harness retainers to the upper intake manifold near the MAP sensor.
30. Install the resonator. Refer to Air Cleaner, removal & installation.
31. Connect the negative battery cable and tighten the nut to 45 inch lbs. (5 Nm). Refer to Battery, removal & installation.
32. Start and run the engine until it reaches the normal operating temperature.
33. Install the engine cover.

OIL PAN

REMOVAL & INSTALLATION

2.4L Engine

See Figures 146 and 147.

1. Before servicing the vehicle, refer to the Precautions Section.
2. Raise and safely support the vehicle.

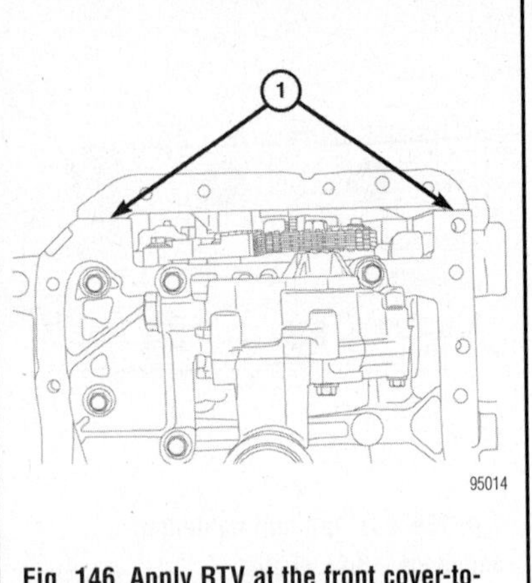

Fig. 146 Apply RTV at the front cover-to-engine block parting lines (1)—2.4L engine

3. Remove the oil drain plug and drain the engine oil.
4. Remove the accessory drive belt splash shield.
5. Remove the lower A/C compressor mounting bolt (if equipped).
6. Remove the A/C mounting bracket.

➡Do not use pry points in the block to remove the oil pan.

7. Remove the oil pan retaining bolts.
8. Using a putty knife, loosen the seal around the oil pan.
9. Remove the oil pan.

To install:

➡The oil pan sealing surfaces must be free of grease or oil.

➡Parts must be assembled within 10 minutes of applying RTV.

10. Apply MOPAR® Engine RTV GEN II at the front cover-to-engine block parting lines.

Fig. 147 Apply a bead of RTV sealant around the oil pan as shown—2.4L engine

11. Apply a 0.079 inch (2mm) bead of MOPAR® Engine RTV GEN II around the oil pan.

12. Position the oil pan and install the bolts. Tighten the bolts to 106 inch lbs. (12 Nm).

➡The 2 long bolts must be tightened to 16 ft. lbs. (22 Nm).

13. Install the oil drain plug.

14. Lower the vehicle and fill the engine crankcase with the proper oil to the correct level.

15. Start the engine and check for leaks.

3.5L Engine

See Figures 148 through 150.

1. Before servicing the vehicle, refer to the Precautions Section.
2. Disconnect the negative battery cable. Refer to Battery, removal & installation.
3. Remove the engine oil indicator.
4. Remove the engine oil indicator tube bolt.
5. Remove the engine oil indicator tube.
6. Raise and safely support the vehicle.
7. Remove the front crossmember.
8. Remove the crossover pipe.
9. Loosen the front exhaust manifold. Refer to Exhaust Manifold, removal & installation.
10. Remove the oil pan bell housing bolts.
11. Drain the engine oil. Refer to Engine Oil & Filter, Replacement procedure.
12. Remove the engine oil filter.
13. Remove the oil pan fasteners. Remove the oil pan.

CAUTION

A small amount of oil will remain in the oil pan. Use care when removing the oil pan from the engine.

14. Remove the oil pan gasket.

To install:

15. Clean the oil pan and all gasket surfaces.

16. Apply a ⅛ inch (3.2mm) bead of MOPAR® Engine RTV GEN II at the parting line of the oil pump housing and the rear seal retainer.

17. Install the oil pan gasket to the engine block.

18. Install the oil pan and tighten the oil pan bolts to 21 ft. lbs. (28 Nm).

19. Tighten the oil pan bell housing bolts to 40 ft. lbs. (55 Nm).

20. All engines are equipped with a high quality full-flow, disposable type oil filter. When replacing oil filter, use a MOPAR® filter or equivalent.

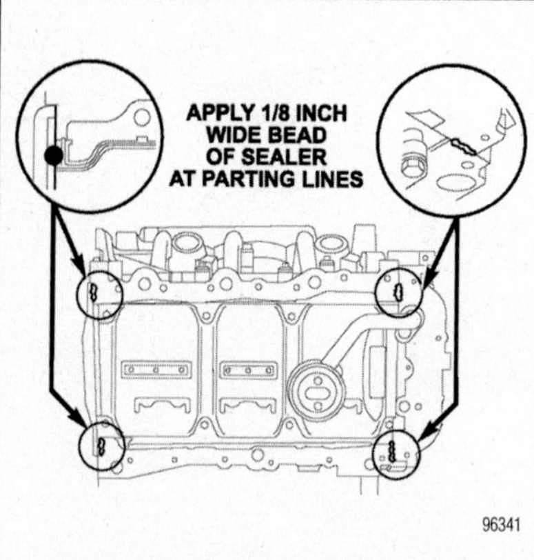

Fig. 148 Apply a bead of RTV sealant at the parting line of the oil pump housing and the rear seal retainer—3.5L engine

21. Wipe the oil filter base clean, then inspect the gasket contact surface.

22. Lubricate the gasket of a new oil filter with clean engine oil.

23. Install and tighten the oil filter to 12 ft. lbs. (16 Nm) of torque after the gasket contacts the base. Use a filter wrench if necessary.

24. Lower the vehicle.

25. Install and tighten the oil pan drain bolt to 20 ft. lbs. (27 Nm).

26. Tighten the front maniverter bolts. Refer to Exhaust Manifold, removal & installation.

27. Install the crossover pipe.

28. Install the front crossmember.

29. Lower the vehicle.

30. Install the oil level indicator tube.

31. Tighten the oil level indicator tube bolt.

32. Install the oil indicator.

33. Fill the engine crankcase with the proper oil to the correct level. Refer to Engine Oil & Filter, Replacement procedure.

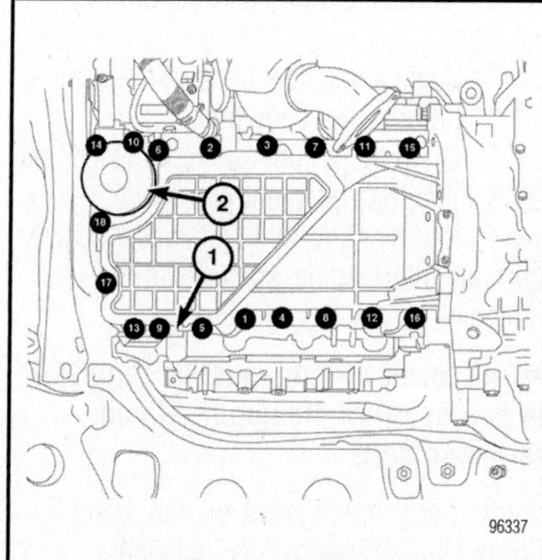

Fig. 149 Oil pan (1) bolt tightening sequence shown along with the engine oil filter (2) location—3.5L engine

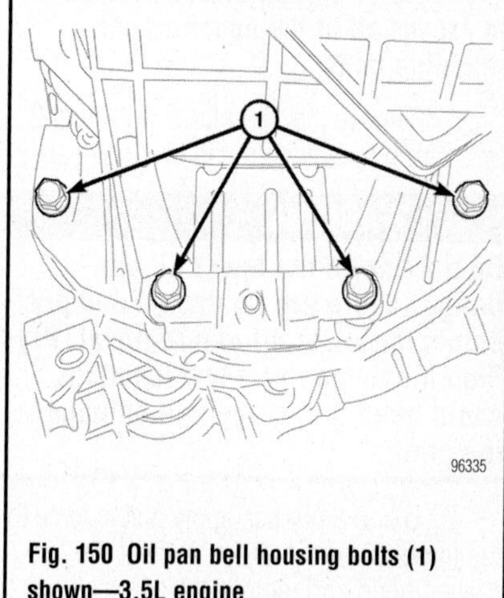

Fig. 150 Oil pan bell housing bolts (1) shown—3.5L engine

34. Connect the negative battery cable. Refer to Battery, removal & installation.

3.6L Engine

On 3.6L engines, there is an upper and lower oil pan. The upper oil pan is cast aluminum and also serves as the lower end structural support. The lower pan is a stamped steel design. Both upper and lower oil pans are sealed using MOPAR® Three-bond Engine RTV Sealant. The lower oil pan must be removed in order to access the upper oil pan attaching bolts.

Lower Oil Pan

See Figures 151 through 153.

1. Before servicing the vehicle, refer to the Precautions Section.
2. Raise and safely support the vehicle.
3. Drain the engine oil. Refer to Engine Oil & Filter, Replacement procedure.
4. Remove the belly pan.
5. Remove the inner splash shield.

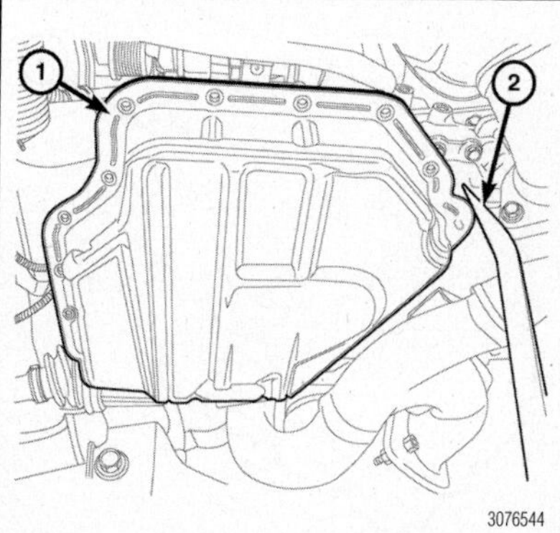

Fig. 151 Using a pry bar (2), apply a side force to the lower oil pan (1) in order to shear the sealant bond and remove the pan—3.6L engine

➡The lower oil pan must be removed to access all of the upper oil pan retaining bolts.

6. Remove the 15 bolts, 2 nuts, and 2 studs from the flange of the lower oil pan.

WARNING

Do not pry on the lower oil pan flange. There are no designated pry points for lower oil pan removal. Prying on only one or a few locations could bend the flange and damage the pan.

7. Using a pry bar, apply a side force to the lower oil pan in order to shear the sealant bond and remove the pan.

To install:

8. Clean the upper and lower oil pan mating surfaces with isopropyl alcohol in preparation for sealant application.

➡Engine assembly requires the use of a unique sealant that is compatible with engine oil. Using a sealant other than MOPAR® Threebond Engine RTV Sealant may result in engine fluid leakage.

➡Following the application of MOPAR® Threebond Engine RTV Sealant to the gasket surfaces, the components must be assembled within 20 minutes and the attaching fasteners must be tightened to specification within 45 minutes. Prolonged exposure to the air, prior to assembly, may result in engine fluid leakage.

9. Apply a 0.08–0.12 inch (2–3mm) wide bead of MOPAR® Threebond Engine RTV Sealant (1) to the lower oil pan.

10. Install 2 studs into the upper oil pan flange.

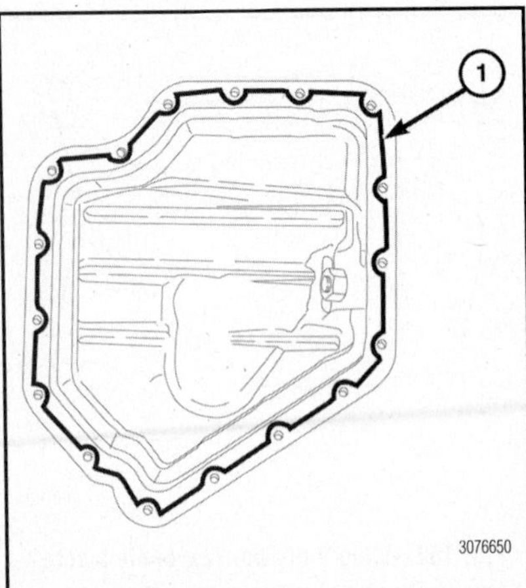

Fig. 152 Apply a bead of RTV sealant (1) to the lower oil pan—3.6L engine

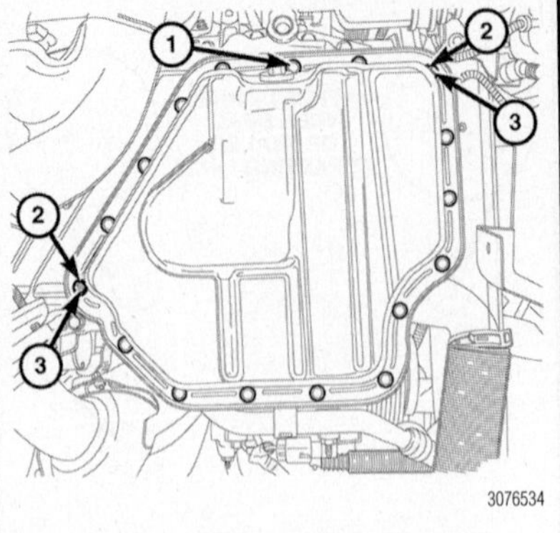

Fig. 153 Install the 2 studs (3) into the upper oil pan flange. Install the lower oil pan to the upper oil pan with 15 bolts (1) and 2 nuts (2)—3.6L engine

11. Install the lower oil pan to the upper oil pan with 15 bolts and 2 nuts tightened to 97 inch lbs. (11 Nm).

➡Following assembly, the MOPAR® Threebond Engine RTV Sealant must be allowed to dry for 45 minutes prior to adding oil and engine operation. Premature exposure to oil prior to drying may result in engine fluid leakage.

12. If removed, install the oil filter and fill the engine crankcase with the proper oil to the correct level. Refer to Engine Oil & Filter, Replacement procedure.

13. Run the engine until it reaches the normal operating temperature.

Upper Oil Pan

See Figures 154 through 159.

1. Before servicing the vehicle, refer to the Precautions Section.
2. Disconnect and isolate the negative battery cable. Refer to Battery, removal & installation.
3. Remove the bolt and the oil level indicator.
4. Raise and safely support the vehicle.
5. Remove the belly pan.
6. Drain the engine oil. Refer to Engine Oil & Filter, Replacement procedure.
7. Remove the right halfshaft assembly from the intermediate shaft. Refer to Front Halfshaft, removal & installation.

➡The lower oil pan must be removed to access all of the upper oil pan retaining bolts.

8. Remove the lower oil pan. Refer to Lower Oil Pan, removal & installation.
9. Remove the cross under pipe.
10. Remove the front fore-aft crossmember.

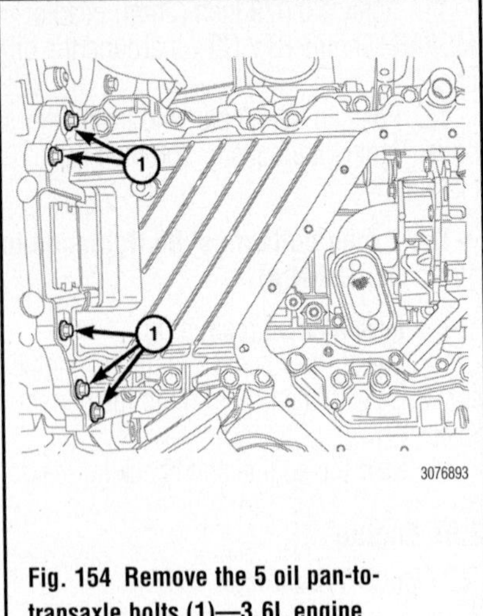

Fig. 154 Remove the 5 oil pan-to-transaxle bolts (1)—3.6L engine

11. Remove the bolt securing the coolant tube to the oil pan.
12. Remove the 5 oil pan-to-transaxle bolts.
13. Remove the torque converter bolt access cover.
14. Remove 2 rubber plugs covering the rear oil seal retainer flange bolts.

WARNING

There are 2 hidden M6 bolts that must be removed from the rear of the upper oil pan flange. If these bolts are not removed, the rear oil seal retainer flange will be severely damaged.

15. Remove the 2 M6 bolts from the rear oil seal retainer flange.
16. Remove the 19 M8 oil pan mounting bolts.
17. Using the 4 indicated pry points, carefully remove the upper oil pan.

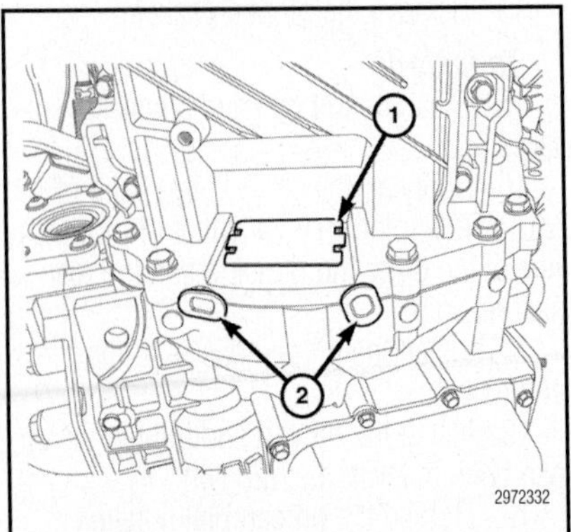

Fig. 155 Remove the torque converter bolt access cover (1) and the rubber plugs (2) covering the rear oil seal retainer flange bolts—3.6L engine

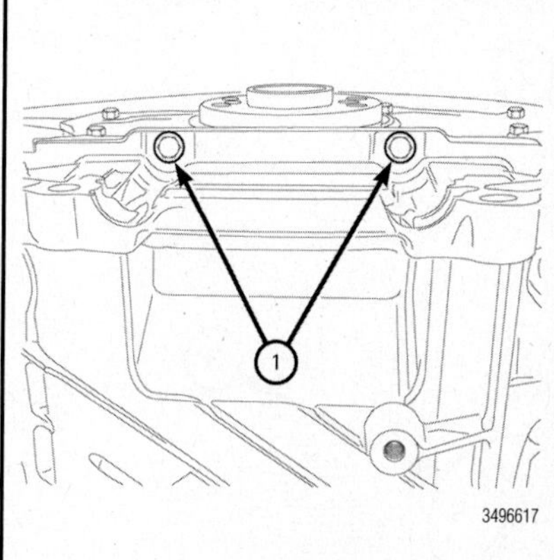

Fig. 156 Remove the 2 M6 bolts (1) from the rear oil seal retainer flange—3.6L engine

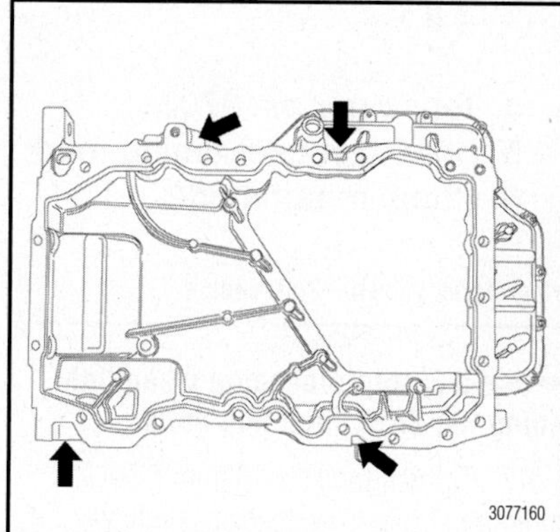

Fig. 157 Using the 4 indicated pry points, carefully remove the upper oil pan—3.6L engine

To install:

18. Clean the upper and lower oil pans, timing chain cover, rear seal retainer, and engine block mating surfaces with isopropyl alcohol in preparation for sealant application.

➡Engine assembly requires the use of a unique sealant that is compatible with engine oil. Using a sealant other than MOPAR® Threebond Engine RTV Sealant may result in engine fluid leakage.

➡Following the application of MOPAR® Threebond Engine RTV Sealant to the gasket surfaces, the components must be assembled within 20 minutes and the attaching fasteners must be tightened to specification within 45 minutes. Prolonged exposure to the air, prior to assembly, may result in engine fluid leakage.

19. Apply a 0.08–0.12 inch (2–3mm) wide bead of MOPAR® Threebond Engine RTV Sealant to the upper oil pan at the oil pan-to-engine block flange, the 2 timing cover-to-engine block T-joints, and the 2 rear seal retainer to engine block T-joints.

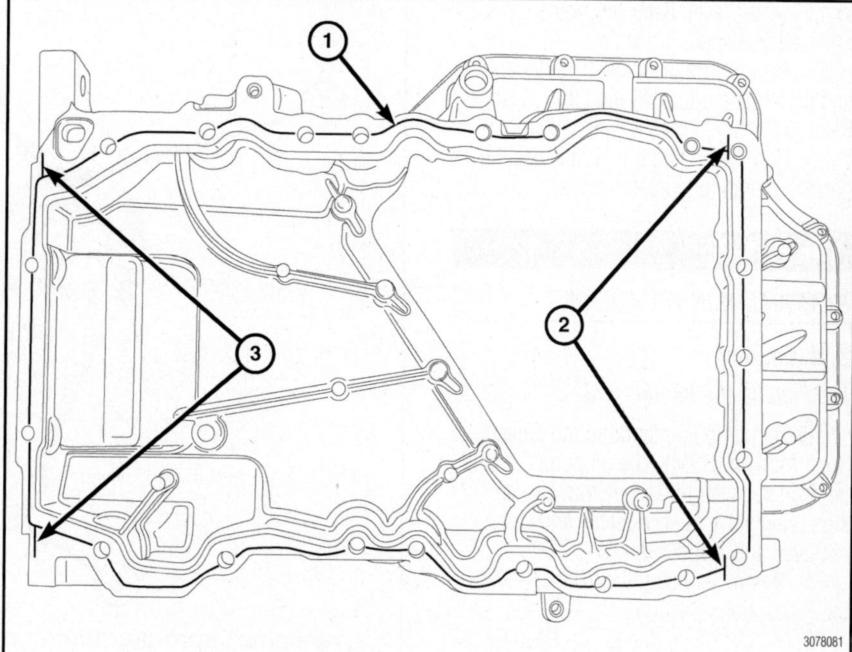

Fig. 158 Apply a bead of RTV sealant to the upper oil pan at the oil pan-to-engine block flange (1), the 2 timing cover-to-engine block T-joints (2), and the 2 rear seal retainer to engine block T-joints (3)

✻✻ WARNING

Make sure that the rear face of the oil pan is flush to the transaxle bell housing before tightening any of the oil pan mounting bolts. A gap between the oil pan and the transaxle could crack the oil pan or transaxle casting.

20. Install the oil pan to the engine block so that it is flush to the transaxle bell housing. Secure the oil pan to the engine block with 19 M8 oil pan mounting bolts finger tight.
21. Install the 5 oil pan-to-transaxle bolts and tighten to 41 ft. lbs. (55 Nm).
22. Tighten the 19 previously installed M8 oil pan mounting bolts to 18 ft. lbs. (25 Nm).
23. Install the 2 M6 bolts to the rear oil seal retainer flange and tighten to 106 inch lbs. (12 Nm).
24. Install the torque converter bolt access cover.
25. Install the 2 rubber plugs covering the rear oil seal retainer flange bolts.
26. Install the bolt securing the coolant tube to the oil pan and tighten to 106 inch lbs. (12 Nm).
27. Install the lower oil pan. Refer to Lower Oil Pan, removal & installation.
28. Install the front fore-aft cross-member.
29. Install the cross under pipe.
30. Install the right halfshaft assembly, steering knuckle, wheel and tire. Refer to Front Halfshaft, removal & installation.
31. Install the belly pan.
32. Lower the vehicle.
33. Install the oil level indicator with the bolt and tightened to 106 inch lbs. (12 Nm).
34. If removed, install the oil filter and fill the engine crankcase with the proper oil

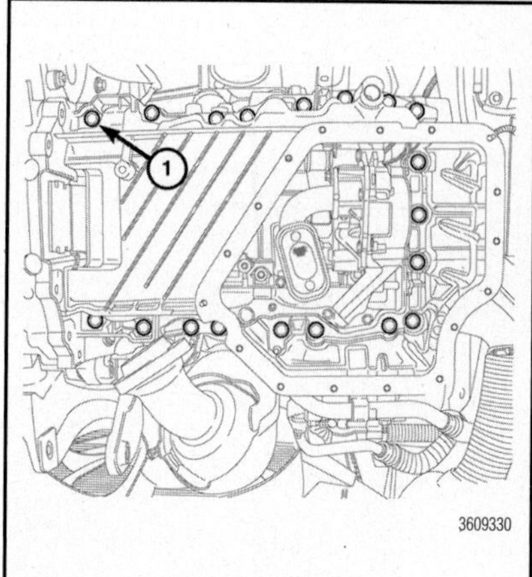

Fig. 159 Tighten the 19 M8 oil pan mounting bolts (1)—3.6L engine

to the correct level. Refer to Engine Oil & Filter, Replacement procedure.

35. Connect the negative battery cable and tighten the nut to 45 inch lbs. (5 Nm). Refer to Battery, removal & installation.

36. Run the engine until it reaches the normal operating temperature.

OIL PUMP

REMOVAL & INSTALLATION

2.4L Engine

See Figures 160 through 162.

The oil pump is integral to the Balance Shaft Module (BSM). The oil pump cannot be disassembled for inspection. The pressure relief valve is serviceable and can be removed and inspected.

1. Before servicing the vehicle, refer to the Precautions Section.
2. Rotate the engine to Top Dead Center (TDC) on the number 1 compression stroke.
3. Remove the oil pan. Refer to Oil Pan, removal & installation.
4. Mark the chain and the sprocket for reassembly.
5. Push the tensioner piston back into the tensioner body.
6. With the piston held back, insert the tensioner pin 9703 into the tensioner body to hold the piston in the retracted position.

➡Do not remove sprocket from the BSM.

7. Remove the BSM mounting bolts. Discard the 180mm bolts, the 185mm bolts can be reused.
8. Lower the back of the BSM and remove the chain from the sprocket.
9. Remove the BSM from the engine.

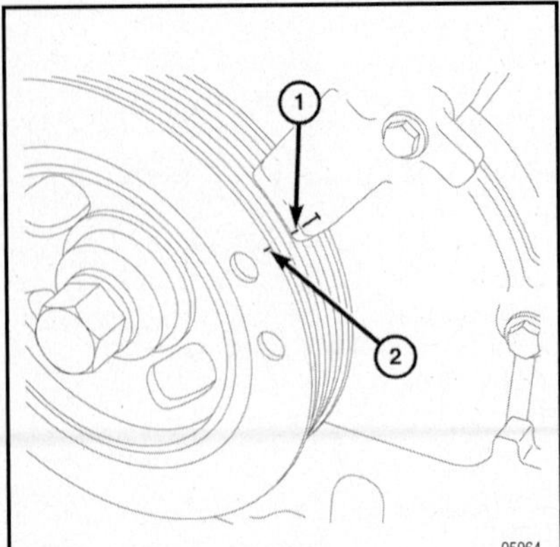

Fig. 160 Rotate the engine to Top Dead Center (TDC) markings (1, 2) on the number 1 compression stroke—2.4L engine

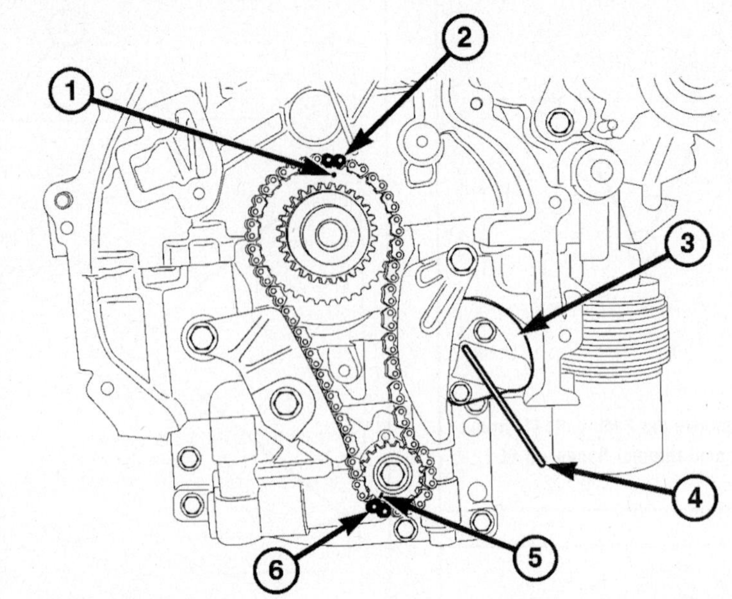

Fig. 161 Balance Shaft Module (BSM)/oil pump timing marks shown—2.4L engine

To install:

⁂ WARNING

There are 2 different BSM-to-engine block bolts used: 180mm bolts with a lock-patch on the threads or 185mm bolts without lock-patch. Do NOT reuse the 180mm bolts. Always discard the 180mm bolts after removing. Failure to replace these bolts can result in engine damage. The 185mm bolts are reusable. Install the same length bolts that were removed and use either 4 new 180mm bolts or 4 185mm bolts.

10. The 7.3 inch (185mm) length bolts must be checked for stretching. Check the bolts with a straight edge for necking. If the bolts are necked down, they must be replaced.
11. Clean the BSM mounting holes with MOPAR® brake parts cleaner.
12. If the chain was removed, align the marks on the crankshaft sprocket and the chain.
13. Align the marks on the oil pump sprocket and the chain.
14. Install the chain on the sprocket.
15. Pivot the BSM assembly upwards and position it on the ladder frame.
16. Start the BSM mounting bolts by hand.

➡Use a 3-step procedure when tightening the BSM mounting bolts.

17. Tighten the new 180mm BSM mounting bolts in sequence as follows:
    a. Step 1: Tighten to 11 ft. lbs. (15 Nm).
    b. Step 2: Tighten to 24 ft. lbs. (33 Nm).
    c. Step 3: Tighten an additional 90°.
18. Tighten the 185mm BSM mounting bolts in sequence as follows:
    a. Step 1: Tighten to 11 ft. lbs. (15 Nm).

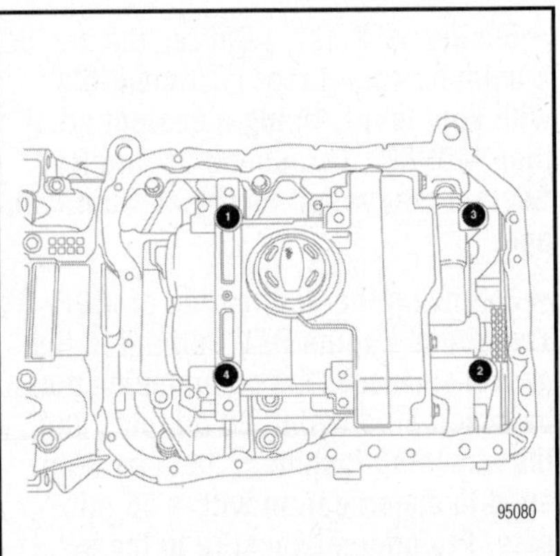

Fig. 162 Balance Shaft Module (BSM)/oil pump bolt tightening sequence—2.4L engine

b. Step 2: Tighten to 22 ft. lbs. (29 Nm).
c. Step 3: Tighten an additional 90°.
19. Remove the tensioner pin 9703.
20. Install the oil pan. Refer to Oil Pan, removal & installation.
21. Fill the engine with the proper type and amount of oil. Refer to Engine Oil & Filter, Replacement procedure.
22. Start the engine and check for leaks.

3.5L Engine

See Figure 163.

➡It is necessary to remove the oil pump body to service the oil pump rotors. The oil pump pressure relief valve can be serviced by removing the oil pan.

1. Before servicing the vehicle, refer to the Precautions Section.
2. Drain the cooling system. Refer to Engine Coolant, Drain & Refill Procedure.
3. Remove the timing belt and crankshaft sprocket. Refer to Timing Belt & Sprockets, removal & installation.
4. Remove the oil pan. Refer to Oil Pan, removal & installation.
5. Remove the oil pickup tube.
6. Remove the oil pump fasteners. Remove the pump and gasket from the engine.

To install:

➡Thoroughly clean all bolt threads and threaded areas in the engine, removing all oil residue, before assembly.

7. Prime the oil pump before installation by filling the rotor cavity with clean engine oil.
8. Install the oil pump and gasket carefully over the crankshaft and position the pump onto the block.

➡DO NOT apply the thread sealant to the underside of the bolt head.

9. Apply MOPAR® Thread Sealant as directed on the package to the oil pump cover bolts where indicated. The sealant must be applied from the tip to approximately 0.39 inch (10mm) of the thread length. Tighten the oil pump cover bolts to 106 inch lbs. (12 Nm). Tighten the oil pump-to-block bolts to 21 ft. lbs. (28 Nm).
10. Install a new O-ring on the oil pickup tube.
11. Install the oil pickup tube.
12. Install the oil pan. Refer to Oil Pan, removal & installation.
13. Install the crankshaft sprocket and the timing belt. Refer to Timing Belt & Sprockets, removal & installation.
14. Install the timing belt covers. Refer to Timing Belt Front Cover/Timing Belt Rear Cover, removal & installation.
15. Install the crankshaft vibration damper.
16. Install the accessory drive belts. Refer to Accessory Drive Belts, removal & installation.
17. Fill the cooling system. Refer to Engine Coolant, Drain & Refill Procedure.
18. Fill the engine crankcase with proper type and amount of oil.
19. Check for fluid leakage.

3.6L Engine

See Figures 164 through 168.

1. Before servicing the vehicle, refer to the Precautions Section.
2. Disconnect and isolate the negative battery cable. Refer to Battery, removal & installation.
3. Remove the upper oil pan. Refer to Oil Pan, removal & installation.

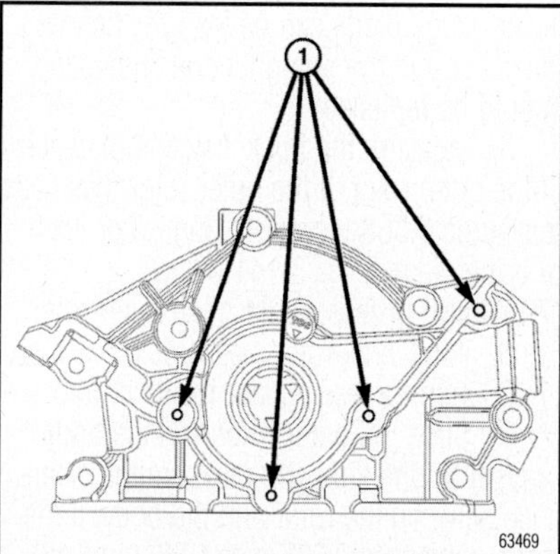

Fig. 163 Apply MOPAR® Thread Sealant as directed on the package to the oil pump cover bolts where indicated (1)—3.5L engine

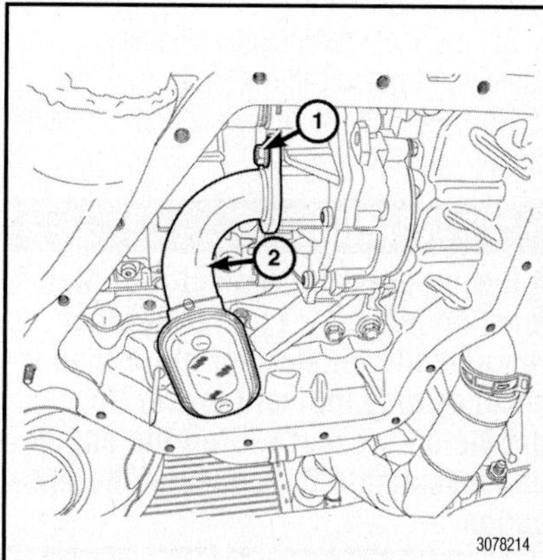

Fig. 164 Remove the oil pump pick-up bolt (1) and oil pump pick-up (2)—3.6L engine

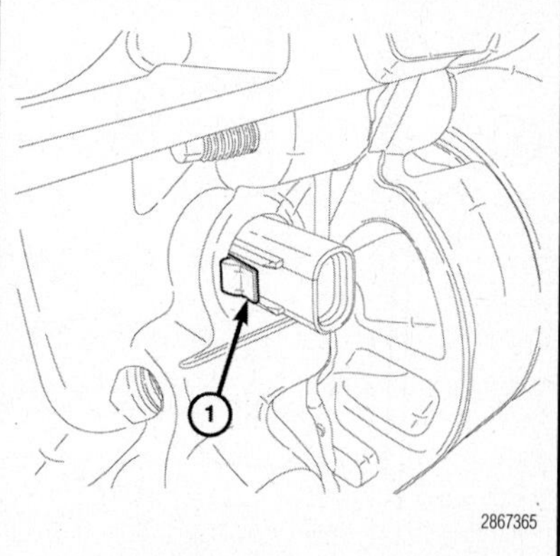

Fig. 165 Depress the connector retention lock tab (1) to disengage the oil pump solenoid electrical connector from the engine block—3.6L engine

4. Remove the oil pump pick-up.
5. Disconnect the engine wire harness from the oil pump solenoid electrical connector.
6. Depress the connector retention lock tab to disengage the oil pump solenoid electrical connector from the engine block.
7. Remove the bolts and the timing gear splash shield.
8. Push the oil pump solenoid electrical connector into the engine block, rotate the connector slightly clockwise, push it past the primary chain tensioner mounting bolt and into the engine.
9. Push back the oil pump chain tensioner and insert a suitable retaining pin such as a 3mm Allen® wrench.

⁂ WARNING

Always reinstall timing chains so that they maintain the same direction of rotation. Inverting a previously run chain on a previously run sprocket will result in excessive wear to both the chain and sprocket.

10. Mark the direction of rotation on the oil pump chain and sprocket using a paint pen or equivalent to aid in reassembly.

➡There are no timing marks on the oil pump gear or chain. Timing of the oil pump is not required.

11. Remove the oil pump sprocket T45 retaining bolt and remove the oil pump sprocket.
12. Remove the retaining pin and disengage the oil pump chain tensioner spring from the dowel pin.
13. Remove the oil pump chain tensioner from the oil pump.
14. Remove the 4 oil pump bolts and remove the oil pump.

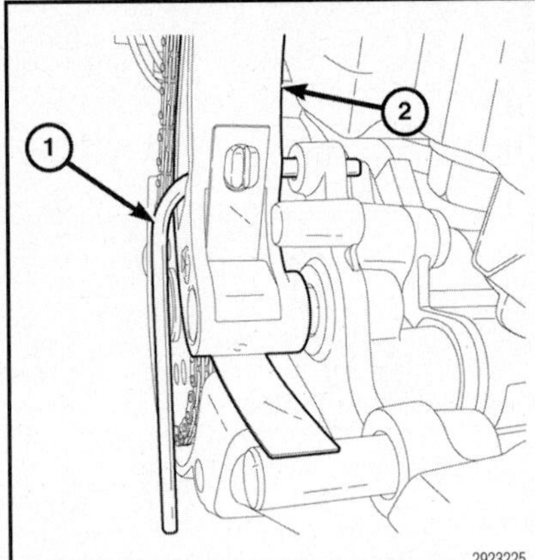

Fig. 166 Push back the oil pump chain tensioner (2) and insert a suitable retaining pin (1)—3.6L engine

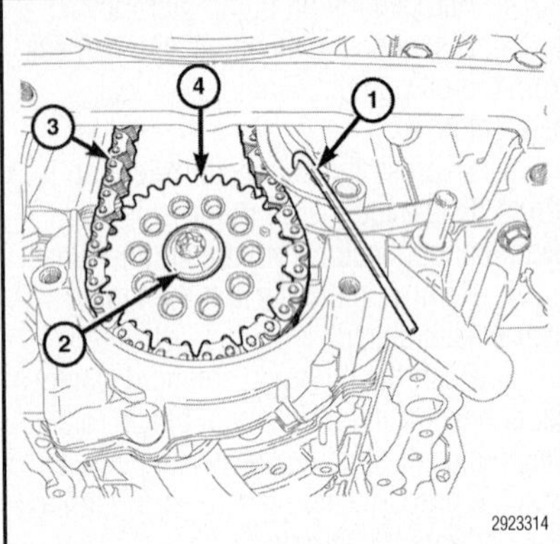

Fig. 167 View of the oil pump sprocket T45 retaining bolt (2), oil pump sprocket (4), tensioner retaining pin (1), and oil pump chain (3)—3.6L engine

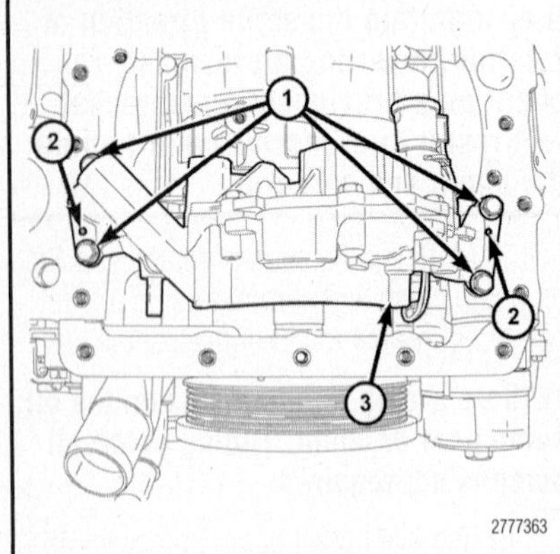

Fig. 168 View of oil pump bolts (1), oil pump (3), and locator pins (2)—3.6L engine

To install:

15. Align the locator pins to the engine block and install the oil pump with 4 bolts. Tighten the bolts to 106 inch lbs. (12 Nm).
16. Install the oil pump chain tensioner on the oil pump.
17. Position the oil pump chain tensioner spring above the dowel pin.
18. Push back the oil pump chain tensioner and insert a suitable retaining pin such as a 3mm Allen® wrench.
19. Place the oil pump sprocket into the oil pump chain. Align the oil pump sprocket with the oil pump shaft and install the sprocket. Install the T45 retaining bolt and tighten to 18 ft. lbs. (25 Nm).
20. Remove the retaining pin. Verify that the oil pump chain is centered on the tensioner and crankshaft sprocket.
21. Rotate the crankshaft clockwise 1 complete revolution to verify proper oil pump chain installation.
22. Position the oil pump solenoid electrical connector into the engine block. Rotate the connector so that it can be pushed past the primary chain tensioner mounting bolt. Then rotate the connector slightly counter clockwise and push it into the engine block until it locks in place.
23. Install the timing gear splash shield. Tighten the bolts to 35 inch lbs. (5 Nm).
24. Verify that the oil pump solenoid electrical connector retention lock tab is engaged to the engine block.
25. Connect the engine wire harness to the oil pump solenoid electrical connector.
26. Install the oil pump pick-up.
27. Install the oil pan. Refer to Oil Pan, removal & installation.
28. If removed, install the oil filter and fill the engine crankcase with the proper oil to the correct level. Refer to Engine Oil & Filter, Replacement.
29. Connect the negative battery cable and tighten the nut to 45 inch lbs. (5 Nm). Refer to Battery, removal & installation.

⁂ WARNING

A low oil pressure indicator or Malfunction Indicator Light (MIL) that remains illuminated for more than 2 seconds may indicate low or no engine oil pressure. Stop the engine and investigate the cause of the indication.

30. Start and run the engine until it reaches the normal operating temperature.
31. Check for fluid leakage.

INSPECTION

2.4L Engine

See Figure 169.

1. Before servicing the vehicle, refer to the Precautions Section.
2. Remove the timing chain cover. Refer to Timing Chain Front Cover, removal & installation.
3. Remove the oil pan. Refer to Oil Pan, removal & installation.
4. Measure the distance between the tensioner body and the guide shoe.
5. If the distance is 0.397 inch (10.1mm) or greater, replace the chain.

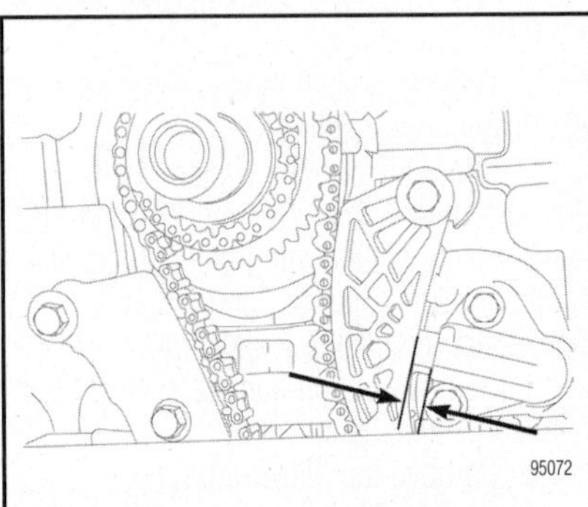

Fig. 169 Measuring the distance between the tensioner body and the guide shoe—2.4L engine

3.5L Engine

1. Before servicing the vehicle, refer to the Precautions Section.
2. Disassemble the oil pump.
3. Clean all the parts thoroughly. The mating surface of the oil pump housing should be smooth. Replace the pump cover if scratched or grooved.
4. Lay a straightedge across the pump cover surface. If a 0.001 inch (0.025mm) feeler gauge blade can be inserted between the cover and the straight edge, the cover should be replaced.
5. Measure the thickness and diameter of the outer rotor. If the outer rotor thickness measures 0.563 inch (14.299mm) or less, or if the diameter is 3.141 inches (79.78mm) or less, replace the outer rotor.
6. If the inner rotor measures 0.563 inch (14.299mm) or less replace the inner rotor.
7. Slide the outer rotor into the body, press it to one side and measure the clearance between the rotor and the body. If the measurement is 0.015 inch (0.39mm) or more, replace the body only if the outer rotor is within specifications.
8. Install the inner rotor into the body. If the clearance between the inner and the

outer rotors is 0.008 inch (0.20mm) or more, replace both rotors.

9. Place a straightedge across the face of the body, between the bolt holes. If a feeler gauge of 0.003 inch (0.077mm) or more can be inserted between the rotors and the straightedge, replace the pump assembly ONLY if the rotors are within specifications.

10. Inspect the oil pressure relief valve plunger for scoring and free operation in its bore. Small marks may be removed with 400-grit wet or dry sandpaper.

11. The relief valve spring has a free length of approximately 1.95 inches (49.5mm). It should test between 23–25 lbs. (101–110 N) when compressed to 1 1⁄32 inches (34mm). Replace the spring that fails to meet specifications.

12. Assemble the oil pump.

3.6L Engine

See Figure 170.

➡The 3.6L Oil pump is released as an assembly. The assembly includes both the pump and the solenoid. There are no serviceable sub-assembly components. In the event the oil pump or solenoid are not functioning or out of specification, they must be replaced as an assembly.

1. Before servicing the vehicle, refer to the Precautions Section.
2. Inspect the solenoid wires for cuts or chaffing.
3. Inspect the condition of the connector O-ring seal.
4. Inspect the connector retention lock tab for fatigue or damage.

PISTON AND RING

POSITIONING

2.4L Engine

See Figures 171 and 172.

3.5L and 3.6L Engines

See Figure 173.

REAR MAIN SEAL

REMOVAL & INSTALLATION

2.4L Engine

See Figures 174 and 175.

1. Before servicing the vehicle, refer to the Precautions Section.
2. Remove the transaxle and flexplate.
3. Insert a 3⁄16 inch flat-bladed screwdriver between the dust lip and the metal case of the crankshaft seal. Angle the screwdriver through the dust lip against the metal case of the seal. Pry out the seal.

⁂ WARNING

Do not permit the screwdriver blade to contact the crankshaft seal surface. Contact of the screwdriver blade against the crankshaft edge (chamfer) is permitted.

4. Check to make sure the seals garter spring is not on the crankshaft.

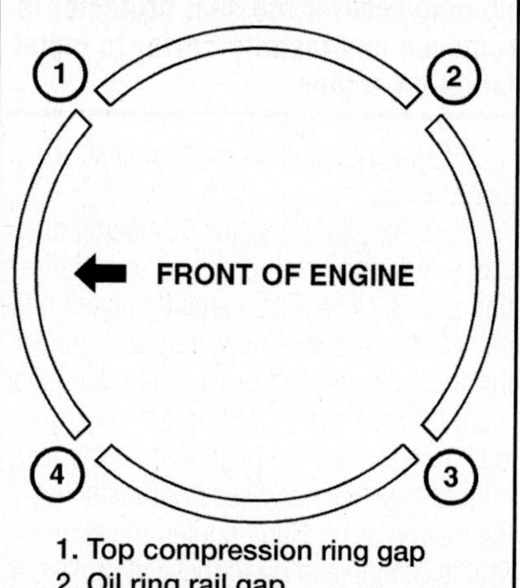

Fig. 171 Piston ring positioning—2.4L engine

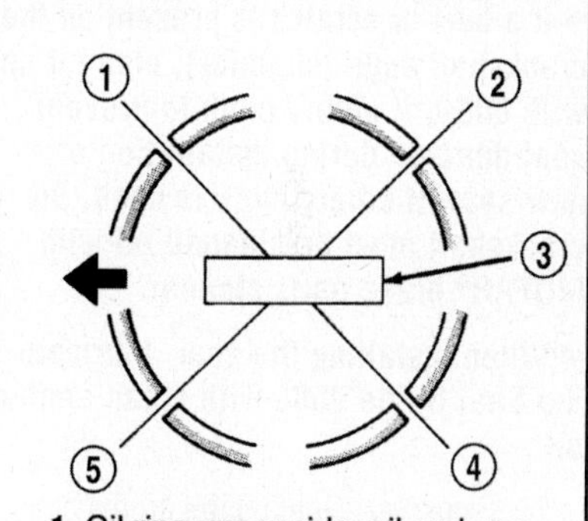

Fig. 173 Piston ring positioning with arrow pointing toward the front of the engine—3.5L and 3.6L engines

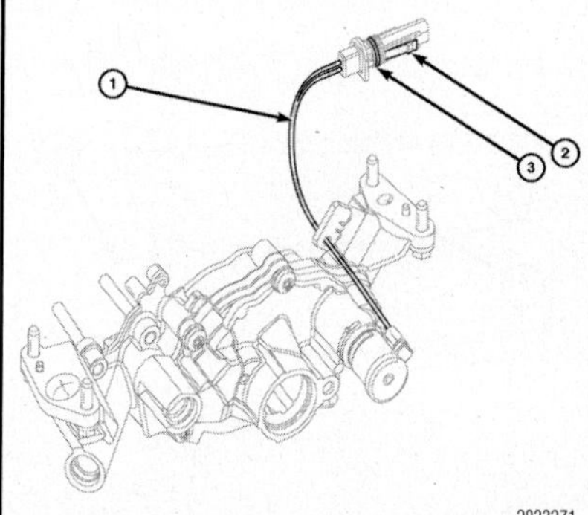

Fig. 170 Inspect the solenoid wires (1) for cuts or chaffing, the condition of the connector O-ring seal (3), and the connector retention lock tab (2) for fatigue or damage—3.6L engine

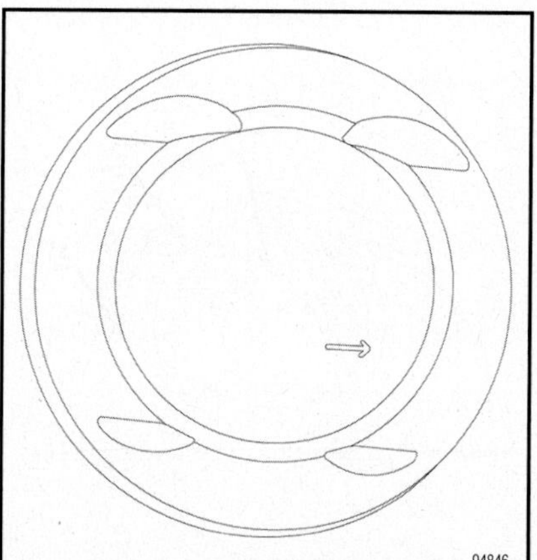

Fig. 172 The directional arrow stamped on the piston should face toward the front of the engine—2.4L engine

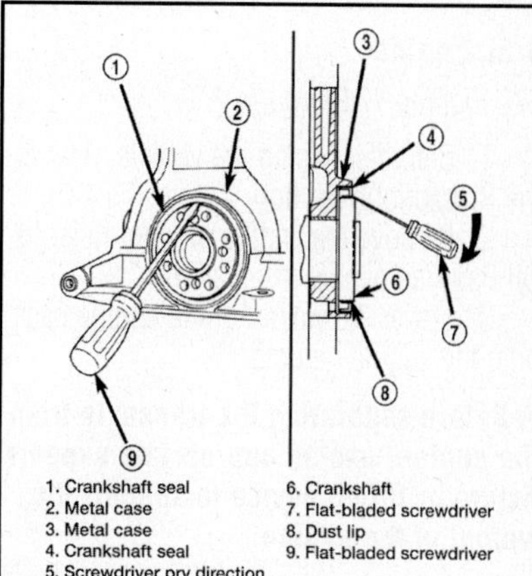

Fig. 174 Rear crankshaft seal removal—2.4L engine

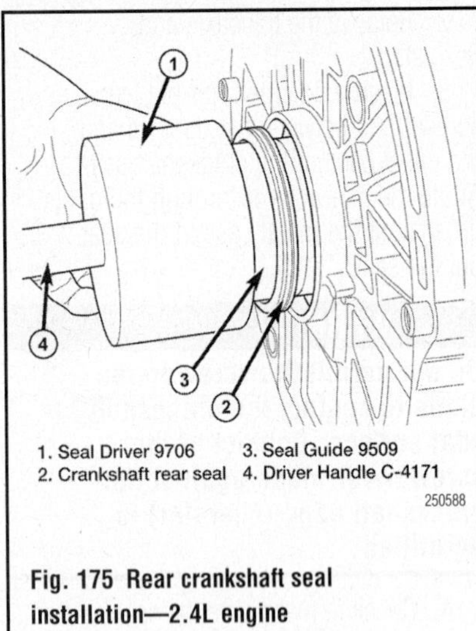

Fig. 175 Rear crankshaft seal installation—2.4L engine

To install:

➡If a burr or scratch is present on the crankshaft edge (chamfer), clean it up with 800-grit emery cloth to prevent seal damage during installation of a new seal. If emery cloth is used, the crankshaft must be cleaned off with MOPAR® brake parts cleaner.

➡When installing the seal, lubricate the Seal Guide 9509 with clean engine oil.

5. Place Seal Guide 9509 on the crankshaft.
6. Position the seal over the guide tool. The guide tool should remain on the crankshaft during the installation of the seal. Ensure that the lip of the seal is facing towards the crankcase during installation.
7. Drive the seal into the block using Seal Driver 9706 and Driver Handle C-4171 until the Seal Driver 9706 bottoms out against the block.
8. Install the flexplate and transaxle.

3.5L Engine

See Figures 176 through 179.

1. Before servicing the vehicle, refer to the Precautions Section.
2. Remove the engine oil pan. Refer to Oil Pan, removal & installation.
3. Lower the weight of the engine back onto the engine mounts.

➡Before separating the transaxle from the engine, use an appropriate support fixture or lifting device to support the weight of the engine.

4. Remove the transaxle from the vehicle.
5. Remove the flexplate.
6. Remove the rear crankshaft oil seal retainer bolts.
7. Remove the crankshaft oil seal and clean all mating surfaces.

To install:

WARNING

If a burr or scratch is present on the crankshaft edge (chamfer), clean the surface using 400-grit sand paper to prevent seal damage during installation. Make sure the rear crankshaft oil seal surface is clean and free of any abrasive materials.

WARNING

The rear crankshaft oil seal and retainer are an assembly. DO NOT separate the seal protector from the rear crankshaft oil seal before installation on engine. Damage to the seal lip may occur if the seal protector is removed and installed prior to installation on engine.

8. Apply engine oil to the crankshaft seal surface.
9. If the seal protector is missing or was accidentally dislodged, go to installation step 3. Otherwise, carefully position the oil seal retainer assembly, and seal protector on crankshaft and push firmly into place on the engine block (during this step, the seal protector will be pushed from the rear oil seal assembly as a result of installing the rear oil seal). Hand tighten the rear oil seal fasteners, and go to installation step 4.

➡The seal lip must always uniformly curl inward toward the engine on the crankshaft.

➡If for any reason the installation sleeve is missing or dislodged from the rear crankshaft oil seal prior to installation, the following procedure must be performed.

10. Using the chamfered seal guide from Special Tool 6926, insert the tapered end into the transaxle side of the rear crankshaft oil seal assembly, and push the seal guide through the seal assembly. This will ensure the seal lip is positioned toward the engine when the seal assembly is installed. When the seal lip is correctly positioned, go to installation step 2.

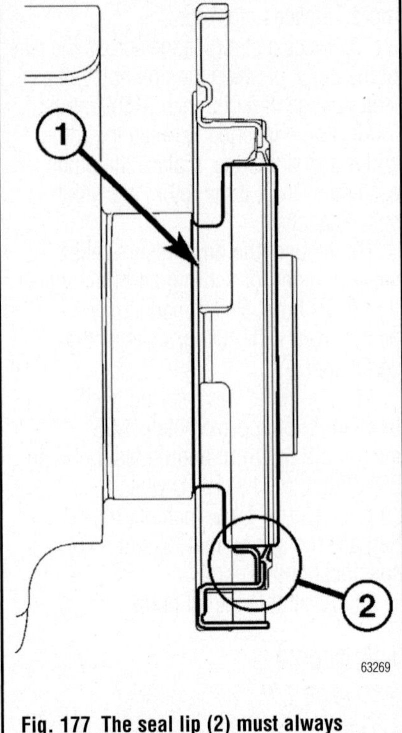

Fig. 177 The seal lip (2) must always uniformly curl inward toward the engine on the crankshaft (1)—3.5L engine

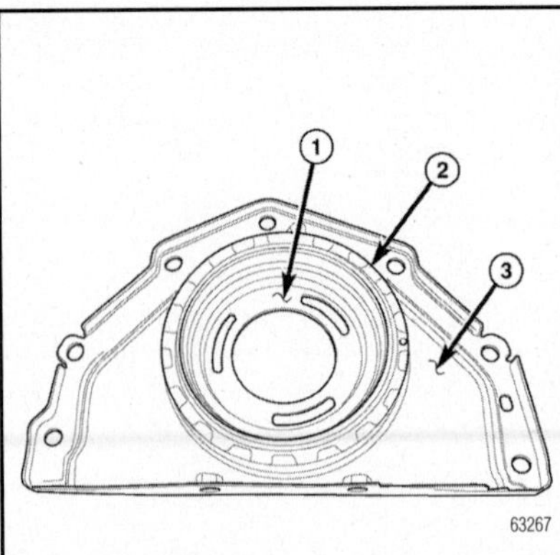

Fig. 176 View of the seal protector (1), oil seal retainer assembly (3), and seal protector (1)—3.5L engine

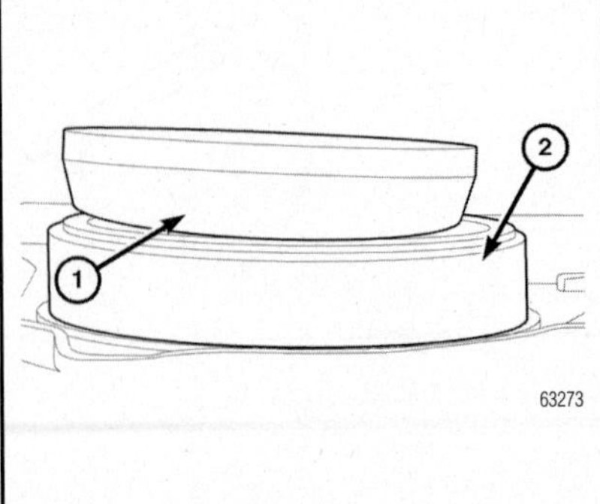

Fig. 178 Using the chamfered seal guide from Special Tool 6926, insert the tapered end (1) into the transaxle side of the rear crankshaft oil seal assembly (2)—3.5L engine

seals. Tighten the
(28 Nm).

19. Install the t
the crankshaft spro
sprockets in a cou

20. Install the l
sprocket. Maintair
is positioned arou
The camshaft spro
crankshaft sprocke
be aligned with the

**➡It is necessary
plunger into the
install a locking
the tensioner. Se
cedure for tensio
instructions.**

21. Hold the ter
belt and install the
tensioner into the l
attaching bolts to 2

22. Remove the
to allow the tensior
bracket.

23. Hold the rig
with a 1 7⁄16 inch (3
tighten the right ca
(102 Nm), plus 90°

24. Hold the left
with a 1 7⁄16 inch (3
tighten the left cam
(102 Nm), plus 90°

25. Install the ro

26. Install the cy
Refer to Valve Cove
tion.

27. Install the fro
Refer to Timing Belt
installation.

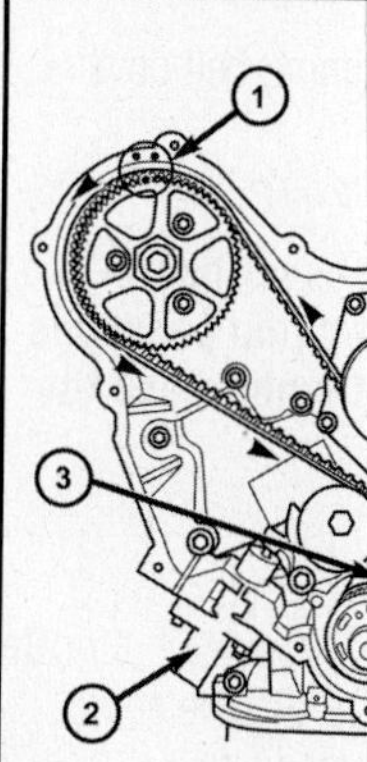

**Fig. 184 View of ca
marks (1), cranksha
mark (3), and timing
3.5L engine**

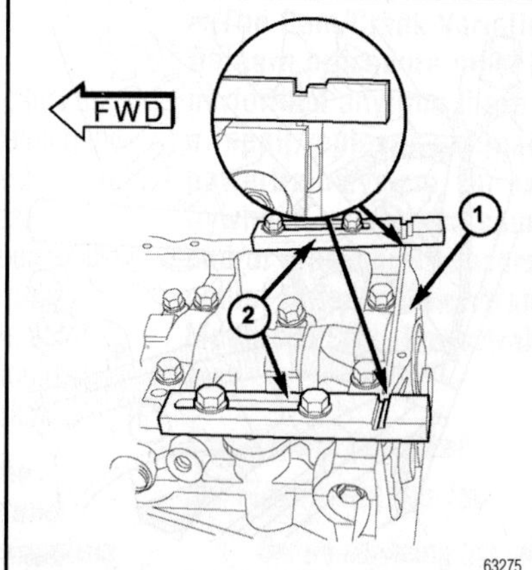

Fig. 179 Attach Special Tools 8225 (1) to the pan rail using the oil pan fasteners (2)—3.5L engine

➡The following steps must be performed to prevent oil leaks at sealing joints.

11. Attach Special Tools 8225 to the pan rail using the oil pan fasteners.

➡Special Tools 8225, are used to assist with the fit of the flush mount rear main seal retainer. The notch on the tool should be located away from the seal retainer.

12. While applying firm pressure to the seal retainer against Special Tools 8225, tighten the seal retainer screws to 106 inch lbs. (12 Nm).

13. Remove Special Tools 8225.

➡Make sure that the seal flange is flush with the block oil pan sealing surface.

14. Install the oil pan. Tighten the 6mm fasteners to 106 inch lbs. (12 Nm) and the 8mm fasteners to 21 ft. lbs. (28 Nm). Refer to Oil Pan, removal & installation.

15. Install the flexplate and transaxle.

3.6L Engine

See Figures 180 and 181.

1. Before servicing the vehicle, refer to the Precautions Section.

2. Remove the upper and lower oil pans. Refer to Oil Pan, removal & installation.

⁂ WARNING

Do not attempt to support the weight of the engine on the windage tray. The windage tray is a thin cast aluminum construction and can be easily damaged.

3. Support the rear of the engine with a screw-jack when removing the transaxle. Position the support on the engine oil pan flange and not the windage tray.

4. Remove the transaxle.

5. Remove the flexplate.

➡The rear crankshaft oil seal is incorporated into the seal retainer and cannot be removed from the retainer. The rear crankshaft oil seal and seal retainer are serviced as an assembly.

6. Remove the 8 seal retainer attaching screws.

7. Remove and discard the seal retainer.

To install:

⁂ WARNING

The rear crankshaft oil seal and retainer are an assembly. To avoid damage to the seal lip, DO NOT remove the seal protector from the rear crankshaft oil seal before installation onto the engine.

➡Whenever the crankshaft is replaced, the rear crankshaft oil seal must also be replaced. Failure to do so may result in engine fluid leakage.

8. Inspect the crankshaft to make sure there are no nicks or burrs on the seal surface.

9. Clean the engine block sealing surfaces thoroughly.

➡It is not necessary to lubricate the seal or the crankshaft when installing the seal retainer. Residual oil following installation can be mistaken for seal leakage.

10. Carefully position the oil seal retainer assembly, and seal protector on the crankshaft and push it firmly into place on the engine block (during this step, the seal protector will be pushed from the rear oil seal assembly as a result of installing the rear oil seal).

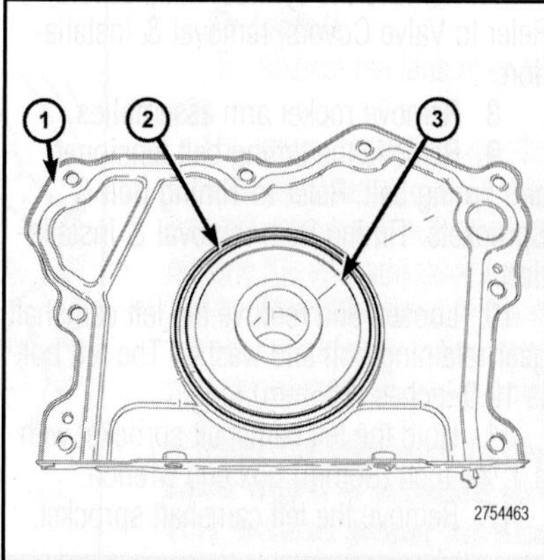

Fig. 180 View of the rear crankshaft oil seal (2), retainer (1), and seal protector (3)—3.6L engine

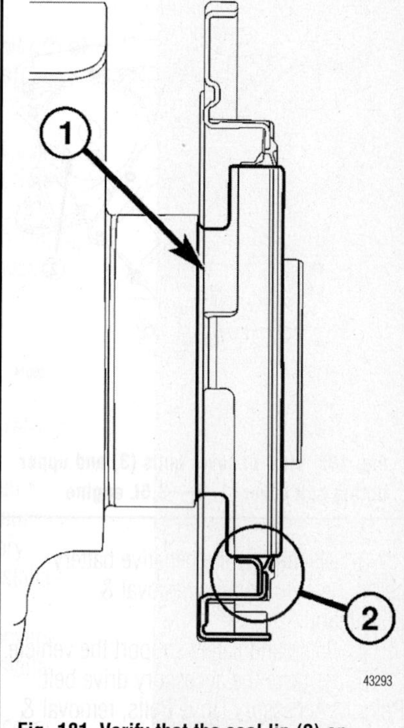

Fig. 181 Verify that the seal lip (2) on the retainer is uniformly curled inward toward the engine on the crankshaft (1)—3.6L engine

11. Verify that the seal lip on the retainer is uniformly curled inward toward the engine on the crankshaft.

➡Make sure that the seal retainer flange is flush with the engine block oil pan sealing surface.

12. Install the 8 seal retainer bolts and tighten to 106 inch lbs. (12 Nm).

13. Install the flexplate.

14. Install the transaxle.

15. Install the upper and lower oil pans. Refer to Oil Pan, removal & installation.

16. Fill the engine crankcase with the proper oil to the correct level. Refer to Engine Oil & Filter, Replacement.

TIMING BELT FRONT COVER

REMOVAL & INSTALLATION

3.5L Engine

See Figure 182.

1. Before servicing the vehicle, refer to the Precautions Section.

2. Release the fuel system pressure. Refer to Relieving Fuel System Pressure.

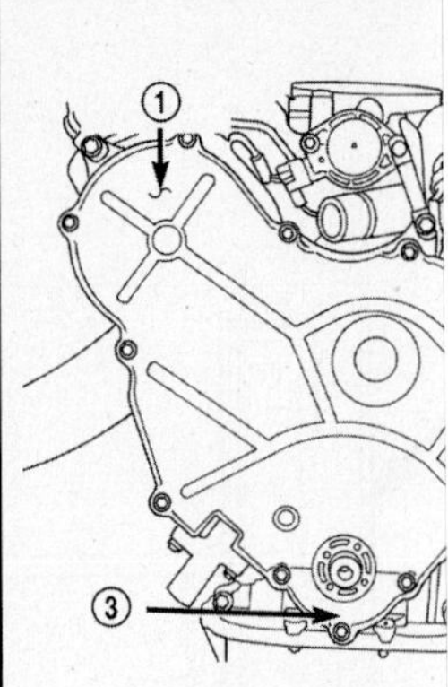

Fig. 182 View of cover bolt timing belt cover (1, 2)—3.

3. Disconnect the nega cable. Refer to Battery, remo installation.

4. Raise and safely sup

5. Remove the accesso Refer to Accessory Drive Be installation.

6. Remove the accesso tensioner.

7. Remove the bolts for steering pump. Reposition t ing pump aside.

8. Remove the cranksh

9. Remove the lower fr cover fasteners.

10. Lower the vehicle.

11. Support the engine v

12. Remove the front en

13. Disconnect the fuel s fuel rail.

14. Remove the upper ti bolts and remove the front t

To install:

➡The timing cover bolts to the engine block must cleaned and free of oil re assembly. IN ADDITION, sealant to the timing cov mount to the oil pump.

15. Install the front timin

16. Install the upper eng

17. Connect the fuel sup fuel rail.

18. Raise and safely sup

19. Install the power ste teners. Tighten the bolts to (23 Nm).

20. Install the crankshaft

21. Install the accessory sioner. Torque the fastener t (28 Nm).

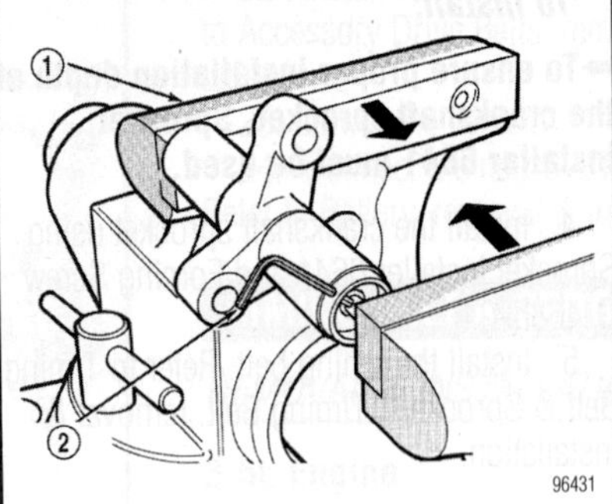

Fig. 187 Timing belt tensioner shown installed to a vise (1). When the plunger is compressed into the tensioner body, install a pin (2) through the body and the plunger to retain the plunger in place—3.5L engine

down of the tensioner should take about 5 minutes.

13. When the plunger is compressed into the tensioner body, install a pin through the body and the plunger to retain the plunger in place until the tensioner is installed.

⁂ WARNING

The 3.5L is NOT a freewheeling engine. Therefore, the valve train rocker assemblies must be removed before attempting to rotate either the crankshaft or camshafts independently of each other.

⁂ WARNING

If the camshafts have moved from the timing marks, always rotate the camshaft towards the direction nearest to the timing marks. DO NOT TURN THE CAMSHAFTS A FULL REVOLUTION OR DAMAGE to the valves and/or pistons could result.

14. Align the crankshaft sprocket with the TDC mark on the oil pump cover.

15. Align the camshaft sprockets timing reference marks with the marks on the rear cover.

16. Install the timing belt starting at the crankshaft sprocket going in a counterclockwise direction. Install the belt around the last sprocket and maintain tension on the belt as it is positioned around the tensioner pulley.

➡It is necessary to compress the plunger into the tensioner body and install a locking pin prior to reinstalling the tensioner.

17. Hold the tensioner pulley against the belt and install the reset (pinned) timing belt tensioner into the housing. Tighten the attaching bolts to 21 ft. lbs. (28 Nm).

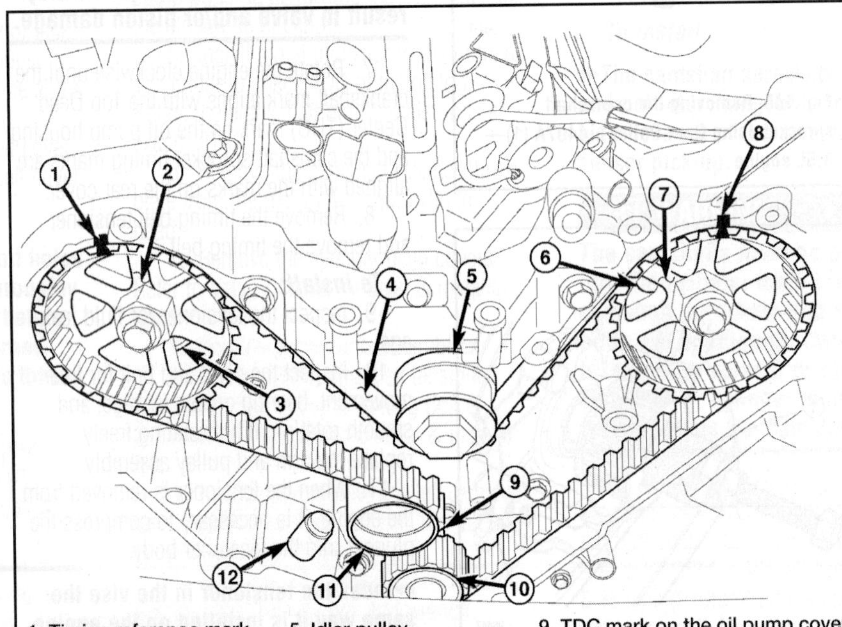

Fig. 188 Timing belt and sprocket alignment—3.5L engine

18. When the tensioner is in place, pull the retaining pin to allow the tensioner to extend to the pulley bracket.

19. Rotate the crankshaft sprocket 2 revolutions and check the timing marks on the camshafts and crankshaft. The marks should line up within their respective locations. If the marks do not line up, repeat the procedure.

20. Install the front timing belt cover. Refer to Timing Belt Front Cover, removal & installation.

21. Connect the negative battery cable and tighten the nut to 45 inch lbs. (5 Nm). Refer to Battery, removal & installation.

➡The Cam/Crank Variation Relearn procedure must be performed anytime there has been a repair/replacement made to a powertrain system, for example: flywheel, valvetrain, camshaft and/or crankshaft sensors or components. Refer to Powertrain Control Module (PCM), Powertrain Verification Test.

TIMING BELT REAR COVER

REMOVAL & INSTALLATION

3.5L Engine

See Figure 189.

1. Before servicing the vehicle, refer to the Precautions Section.

2. Release the fuel system pressure. Refer to Relieving Fuel System Pressure.

3. Disconnect the negative battery cable. Refer to Battery, removal & installation.

4. Remove the timing belt and camshaft sprockets. Refer to Timing Belt & Sprockets, removal & installation.

5. Remove the rear timing belt cover bolts.

6. Remove the rear cover.

➡The rear timing belt cover has O-rings to seal the water pump passages to the cylinder block. Do not reuse the O-rings.

To install:

7. Clean the rear timing belt cover O-ring sealing surfaces and grooves. Lubricate the new O-rings with MOPAR® Dielectric Grease, or equivalent, to facilitate assembly.

8. Position the NEW O-rings on the cover.

9. Install the rear timing belt cover. Tighten the bolts to the following specified torque:

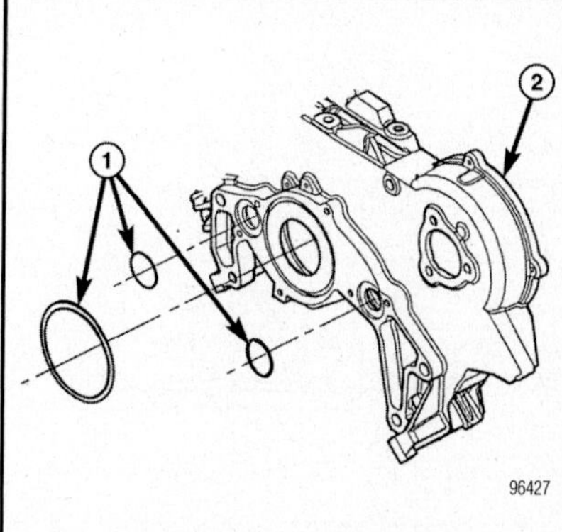

Fig. 189 Position NEW O-rings (1) on the timing belt rear cover (2)—3.5L engine

a. Tighten the M10 bolts to 40 ft. lbs. (54 Nm).

b. Tighten the M8 bolts to 20 ft. lbs. (28 Nm).

c. Tighten the M6 bolts to 106 inch lbs. (12 Nm).

10. Install the camshaft sprockets and the timing belt. Refer to Timing Belt & Sprockets, removal & installation.

TIMING CHAIN FRONT COVER

REMOVAL & INSTALLATION

2.4L Engine

See Figures 190 through 196.

1. Before servicing the vehicle, refer to the Precautions Section.
2. Remove the engine cover by pulling upward.
3. Release the fuel system pressure. Refer to Relieving Fuel System Pressure.
4. Disconnect the negative battery cable. Refer to Battery, removal & installation.
5. Remove the coolant recovery bottle.
6. Remove and reposition the power steering reservoir.
7. Remove the accessory drive belt. Refer to Accessory Drive Belts, removal & installation.
8. Remove the power steering hose hold down.
9. Remove the 3 power steering pump mounting bolts through the openings in the pulley and reposition the pump.
10. Remove the cylinder head cover. Refer to Valve Covers, removal & installation.
11. Remove the ignition coils from the cylinder head cover. Refer to Ignition Coil, removal & installation.
12. Raise and safely support the vehicle.

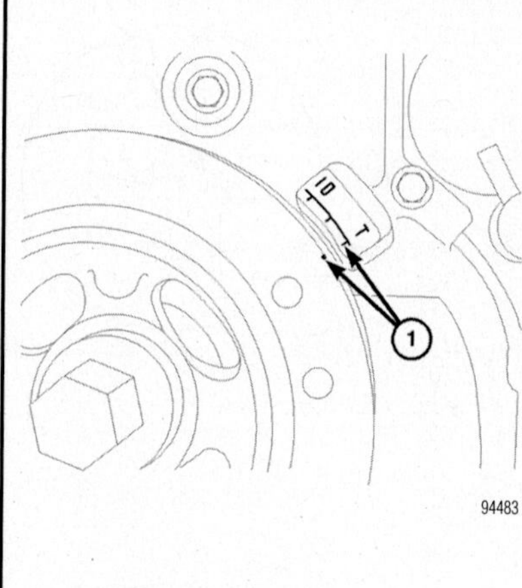

Fig. 190 Set the engine to Top Dead Center (TDC) (1)—2.4L engine

13. Remove the frame cover portion of the right splash shield.
14. Set the engine to Top Dead Center (TDC).
15. Remove the lower A/C compressor bolts if equipped.
16. Remove the lower A/C compressor mount if equipped.
17. Remove the accessory drive belt lower idler pulley.
18. Remove the crankshaft damper.
19. Remove the 3 bolts and the water pump pulley from the water pump.
20. Remove the lower bolt from the right side engine mount bracket.
21. Remove the timing chain cover lower bolts.
22. Lower the vehicle.
23. Support the engine with a suitable jack.
24. Remove the right engine mount bracket retaining bolts.
25. Remove the retaining nuts and reposition the mount bracket.

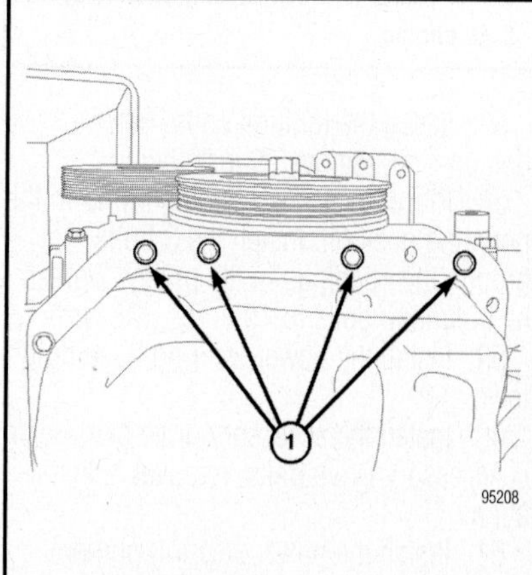

Fig. 191 Remove the timing chain cover lower bolts (1)–2.4L engine

26. Remove the accessory drive upper idler pulley.
27. Remove the right upper engine mount bracket.
28. Remove the accessory drive belt tensioner.
29. Remove the upper timing chain cover retaining bolts.
30. Remove the timing chain cover using the pry points.
31. Remove the timing chain cover out through the bottom of the vehicle.

To install:

➡When using RTV, the sealing surfaces must be clean and free from grease and oil. The parts should be assembled in 10 minutes and tighten to final torque within 45 minutes.

32. Clean all sealing surfaces.
33. Apply MOPAR® engine sealant RTV (or equivalent) at the cylinder head-to-block parting line.
34. Apply MOPAR® engine sealant RTV (or equivalent) at the ladder frame-to-block parting line.
35. Apply MOPAR® engine sealant RTV (or equivalent) in the corner of the oil pan and block.
36. Apply a 0.08 inch (2mm) bead of MOPAR® engine sealant RTV (or equivalent) to the oil pan.
37. Apply a 0.08 inch (2mm) bead of MOPAR® engine sealant RTV (or equivalent) to the engine block.
38. Install the timing chain cover upwards from under the vehicle.
39. Install the timing chain cover upper retaining bolts and tighten the M6 bolts to 80 inch lbs. (9 Nm) and the M8 bolts to 19 ft. lbs. (26 Nm).
40. Install the accessory drive belt tensioner. Tighten the bolt to 18 ft. lbs. (24 Nm).
41. Install the right engine mount bracket. Tighten the bolts to 37 ft. lbs. (50 Nm).
42. Install the accessory drive belt upper idler pulley. Tighten the bolt to 35 ft. lbs. (48 Nm).
43. Position the engine mount adapter and install the bolts.
44. Install the retaining nuts and tighten the nuts to 22 ft. lbs. (30 Nm).
45. Tighten the bolts to 37 ft. lbs. (50 Nm).
46. Remove the jack from under the engine.
47. Raise and safely support the vehicle.
48. Install the oil pan-to-timing chain cover lower retaining bolts and tighten the M6 bolts to 80 inch lbs. (9 Nm).

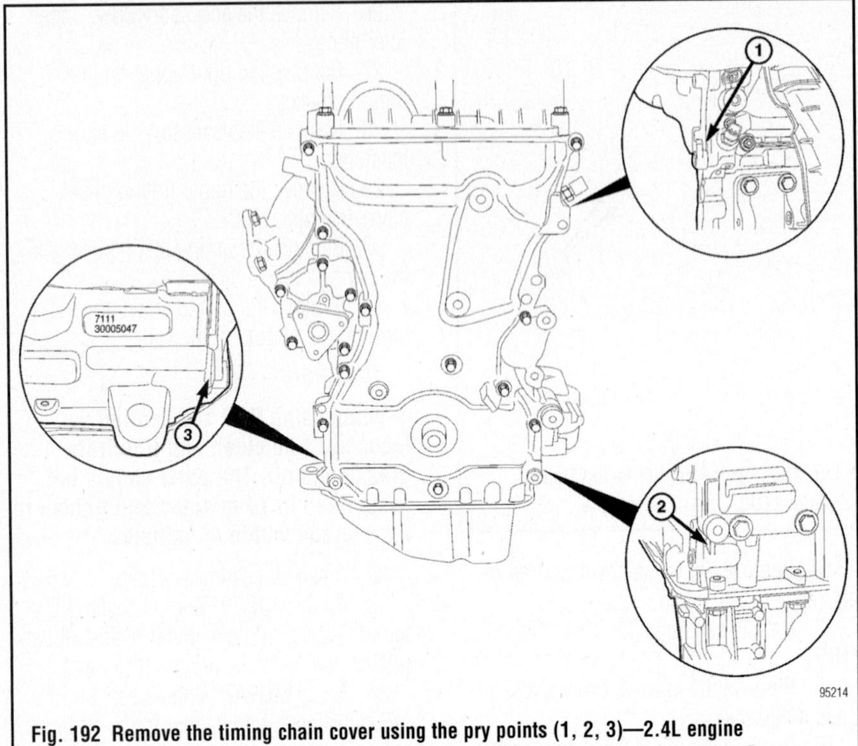

Fig. 192 Remove the timing chain cover using the pry points (1, 2, 3)—2.4L engine

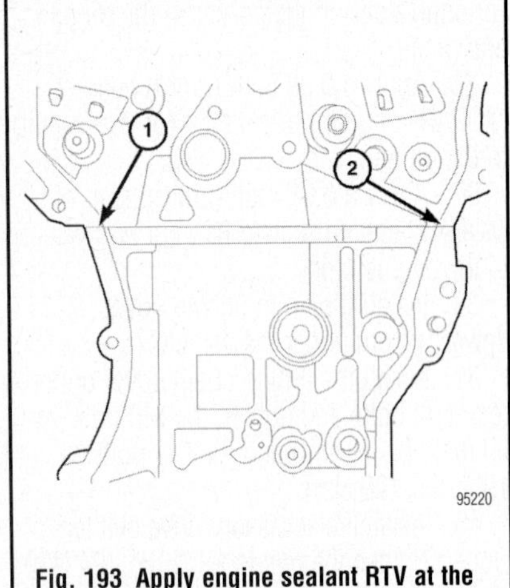

Fig. 193 Apply engine sealant RTV at the cylinder head-to-block parting line (1, 2)—2.4L engine

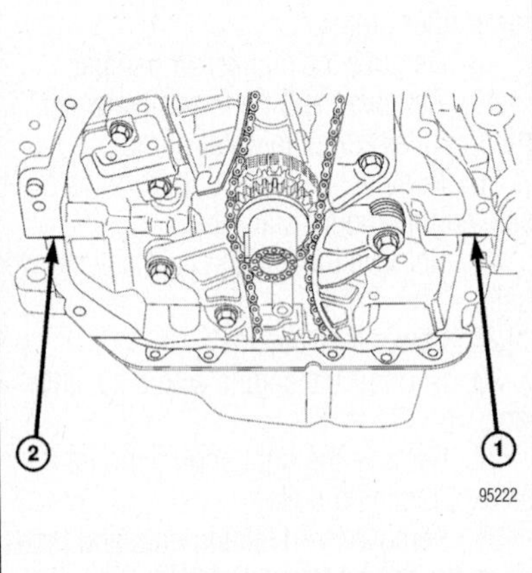

Fig. 194 Apply engine sealant RTV at the ladder frame-to-block parting line (1, 2)—2.4L engine

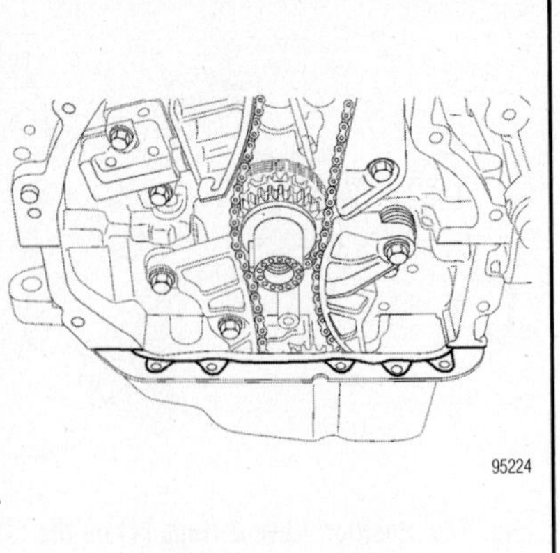

Fig. 195 Apply engine sealant RTV in the corner of the oil pan and block and a bead to the oil pan as shown—2.4L engine

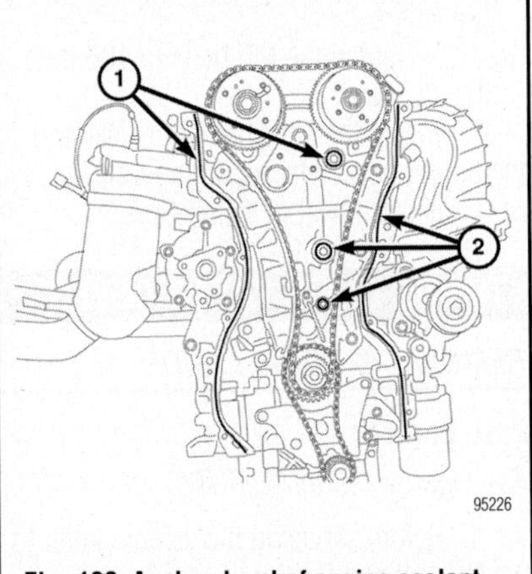

Fig. 196 Apply a bead of engine sealant RTV to the engine block (1, 2) as shown—2.4L engine

49. Install the water pump pulley and tighten the 3 bolts to 80 inch lbs. (9 Nm).
50. Install the crankshaft damper.
51. Install the accessory drive belt lower idler pulley. Tighten the bolt to 35 ft. lbs. (48 Nm).
52. Install the lower A/C compressor mounting bracket. Tighten the bolts to 18 ft. lbs. (24 Nm).
53. Install the A/C compressor. Tighten the bolts to 18 ft. lbs. (25 Nm).
54. Install the right lower splash shield.
55. Lower the vehicle.
56. Install the cylinder head cover. Refer to Valve Covers, removal & installation.
57. Install the ignition coils. Refer to Ignition Coil, removal & installation.
58. Place the power steering pump in the mounting position. Install the 3 bolts through the openings in the pulley. Tighten the mounting bolts to 19 ft. lbs. (26 Nm).
59. Install the power steering hose hold down.
60. Install the accessory drive belt. Refer to Accessory Drive Belts, removal & installation.
61. Install the power steering pump reservoir. Tighten the mounting screw to 106 inch lbs. (12 Nm).
62. Install the coolant recovery reservoir. Tighten the mounting bolts to 89 inch lbs. (10 Nm).
63. Install the clean air hose and the air cleaner housing. Refer to Air Cleaner, removal & installation.
64. Connect the negative battery cable. Refer to Battery, removal & installation.
65. Operate the engine until it reaches the normal operating temperature. Check the oil system for leaks and the correct fluid level.
66. Install the engine cover.

3.6L Engine

See Figures 197 through 200.

1. Before servicing the vehicle, refer to the Precautions Section.
2. Disconnect and isolate the negative battery cable. Refer to Battery, removal & installation.
3. Drain the cooling system. Refer to Engine Coolant, Drain & Refill Procedure.
4. Remove the upper radiator hose and

thermostat housing. Refer to Thermostat, removal & installation.

5. Remove the heater core return hose from the water pump housing.

6. Remove the lower radiator hose from the water pump housing.

7. Remove the heater core supply hose from the coolant outlet housing.

8. Remove the bolt and reposition the heater core supply tube.

9. Remove the accessory drive belt. Refer to Accessory Drive Belts, removal & installation.

10. Remove the accessory drive belt tensioner.

11. Remove the accessory idler pulley.

12. Remove the power steering pump pulley.

13. Remove the crankshaft vibration damper.

14. Remove the right and left cylinder head covers. Refer to Valve Covers, removal & installation.

15. Remove the upper and lower oil pans. Refer to Oil Pan, removal & installation.

16. Temporarily reinstall the front fore and aft crossmember.

17. Remove the right engine mount isolator and bracket.

➡It is not necessary to remove the water pump or the coolant outlet housing for engine timing cover removal.

➡One of the timing cover bolts could be an M6 (early production) or an M8 (late production).

18. Remove the following timing cover attaching bolts:

a. The 22 M6 bolts.

b. The 1 M6 (early production) or 1 M8 (late production) bolt.

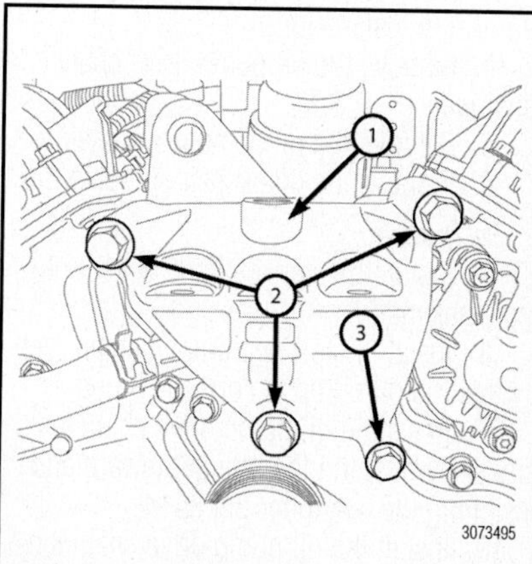

Fig. 197 Remove the right engine mount isolator bolts (2, 3) and bracket (1)—3.6L engine

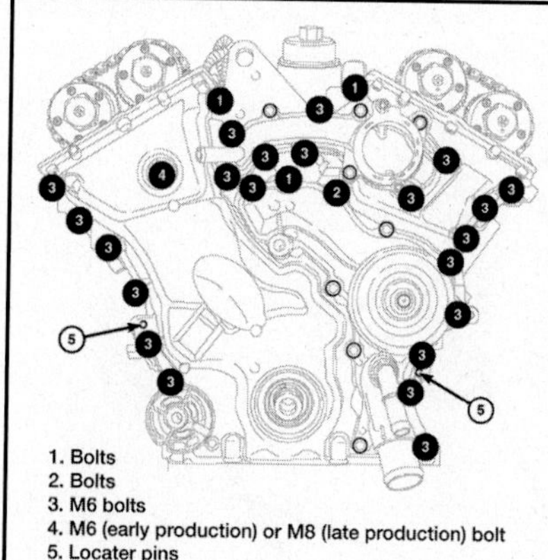

Fig. 198 Timing chain front cover bolt identifications—3.6L engine

19. Using the 7 indicated pry points, carefully remove the timing cover.

20. If required, remove the remaining 4 M6 bolts and the coolant outlet housing from the engine timing cover.

21. If required, remove the remaining 4 M6 bolts and the water pump from the engine timing cover.

⁂ WARNING

Do not use oil based liquids, wire brushes, abrasive wheels, or metal scrapers to clean the engine gasket surfaces. Use only isopropyl (rubbing) alcohol, along with plastic or wooden scrapers. Improper gasket surface preparation may result in engine fluid leakage.

22. Remove all residual sealant from the timing chain cover, cylinder head, and engine block mating surfaces.

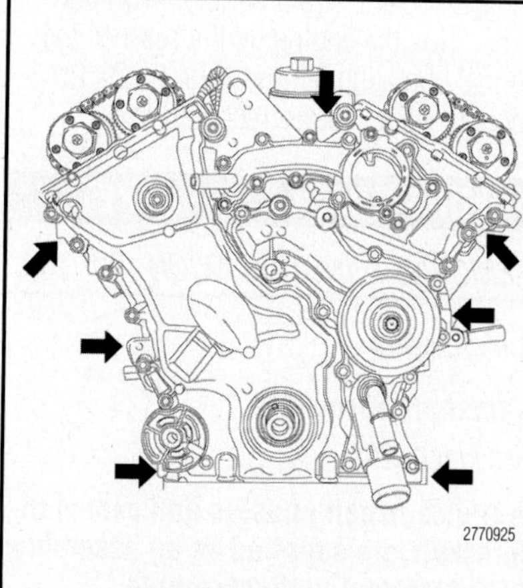

Fig. 199 Remove the timing cover using the 7 indicated pry points—3.6L engine

23. Remove and discard the coolant outlet housing gasket and the water pump gasket.

To install:

24. If removed, install the coolant outlet housing to the timing cover with a new gasket using only 4 bolts tightened to 106 inch lbs. (12 Nm).

25. If removed, install the water pump to the timing cover using only 4 bolts tightened to 106 inch lbs. (12 Nm).

26. Install the coolant outlet housing gasket and the water pump gasket.

27. Clean the engine timing cover, cylinder head, and block mating surfaces with isopropyl alcohol in preparation for sealant application.

➡Engine assembly requires the use of a unique sealant that is compatible with engine oil. Using a sealant other than MOPAR® Threebond Engine RTV Sealant may result in engine fluid leakage.

➡Following the application of MOPAR® Threebond Engine RTV Sealant to the gasket surfaces, the components must be assembled within 20 minutes and the attaching fasteners must be tightened to specification within 45 minutes. Prolonged exposure to the air, prior to assembly, may result in engine fluid leakage.

28. Apply a 0.08–0.12 inch (2–3mm) wide bead of MOPAR® Threebond Engine RTV Sealant to the front cover in the following locations:

a. The 3 cylinder head bosses.

b. The right and left flanges.

c. The 4 cylinder head-to-engine block T-joints.

d. The cover-to-right cam chain tensioner gap.

29. Align the locator pins on the engine block to the engine timing cover and install the cover.

30. Install and tighten the timing cover attaching bolts:

a. Tighten the 22 M6 bolts to 106 inch lbs. (12 Nm).

b. Tighten the 1 M6 (early production) or 1 M8 (late production) bolt. Tighten the M6 bolt to 106 inch lbs. (12 Nm) or tighten the M8 bolt to 18 ft. lbs. (25 Nm).

31. Install the right engine mount bracket and isolator.

32. Remove the temporarily installed front fore and aft crossmember.

33. Install the upper and lower oil pans. Refer to Oil Pan, removal & installation.

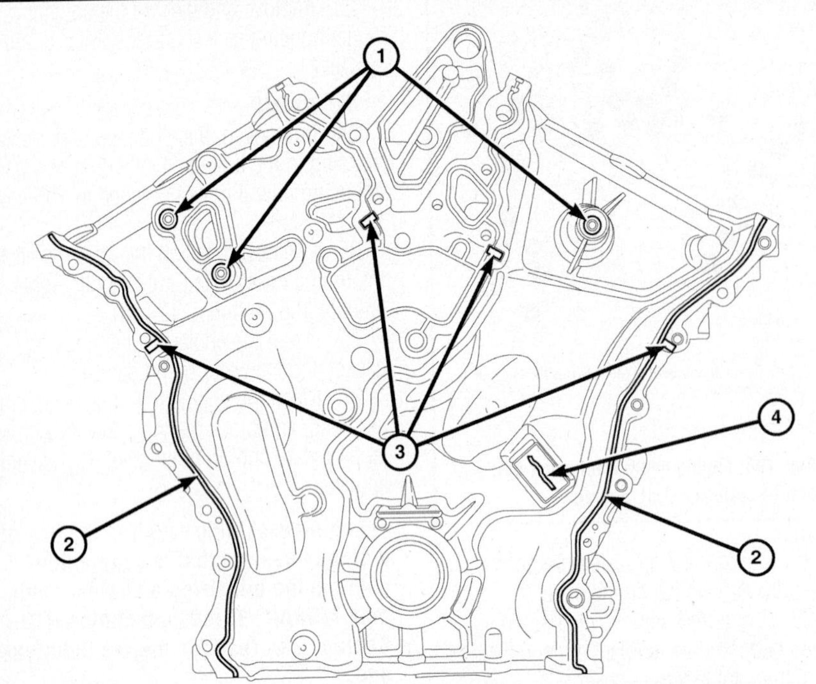

Fig. 200 Apply a wide bead of engine RTV sealant to the front cover at the indicated locations—3.6L engine

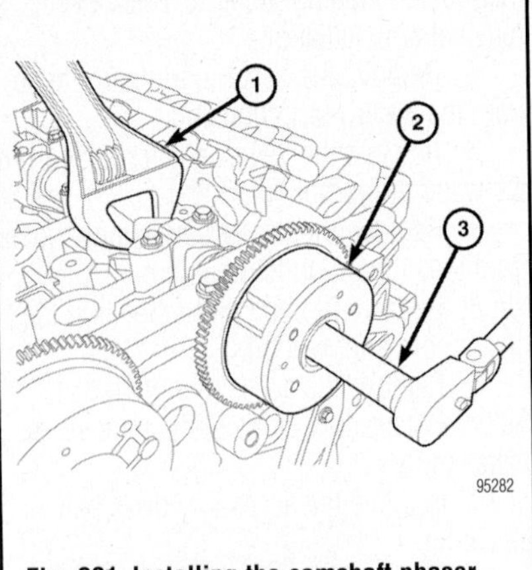

Fig. 201 Installing the camshaft phaser (2) with an adjustable wrench (1) and socket wrench (3)—2.4L engine

34. Install the front fore-aft crossmember and cross under pipe.
35. Install the right halfshaft assembly. Refer to Front Halfshaft, removal & installation.
36. Install the right and left cylinder head covers. Refer to Valve Covers, removal & installation.
37. Install the upper intake manifold. Refer to Intake Manifold, removal & installation.
38. Install the crankshaft vibration damper.
39. Install the power steering pump pulley. Refer to Power Steering Pump, removal & installation.
40. Install the accessory idler pulley.
41. Install the accessory drive belt tensioner.
42. Install the accessory drive belt. Refer to Accessory Drive Belts, removal & installation.
43. Install the heater core supply tube with 1 bolt tightened to 106 inch lbs. (12 Nm).
44. Install the heater core supply hose to the coolant outlet housing.
45. Install the lower radiator hose to the water pump housing.
46. Install the heater core return hose to the water pump housing.
47. Install the thermostat housing and upper radiator hose. Refer to Thermostat, removal & installation.
48. Install the electric vacuum pump.
49. If removed, install the oil filter and fill the engine crankcase with the proper oil to the correct level. Refer to Engine Oil & Filter, Replacement.
50. Connect the negative battery cable and tighten the nut to 45 inch lbs. (5 Nm). Refer to Battery, removal & installation.
51. Fill the cooling system. Refer to Engine Coolant, Drain & Refill Procedure.
52. Run the engine until it reaches the normal operating temperature. Check the cooling system for correct fluid level.

TIMING CHAIN & SPROCKETS

REMOVAL & INSTALLATION

2.4L Engine

Camshaft Sprockets

See Figure 201.

➡The camshaft phasers and camshaft sprockets are supplied as an assembly, do not attempt to disassemble.

1. Before servicing the vehicle, refer to the Precautions Section.
2. Remove the camshaft phasers. Refer to Camshaft and Valve Lifters, removal & installation.

To install:

⁂ WARNING

Do not use an impact wrench to tighten the camshaft sprocket bolts. Damage to the camshaft-to-sprocket locating dowel pin and camshaft phaser may occur.

3. Install the camshaft phasers. Refer to Camshaft and Valve Lifters, removal & installation.

Crankshaft Sprocket

See Figure 202.

1. Before servicing the vehicle, refer to the Precautions Section.
2. Remove the timing chain. Refer to Timing Chain & Sprockets, Timing Chain, removal & installation.
3. Remove the oil pan. Refer to Oil Pan, removal & installation.
4. Remove the oil pump drive chain tensioner.
5. Remove the oil pump drive chain.
6. Remove the crankshaft sprocket.

To install:

7. Install the crankshaft sprocket onto the crankshaft.
8. Install the oil pump drive chain. Verify that the oil pump is correctly timed.
9. Reset the oil pump drive chain tensioner by pushing the plunger inward and installing the tensioner pin 8514.
10. Install the oil pump drive chain tensioner and remove the Tensioner Pin 8514.
11. Install the timing chain. Refer to Timing Chain & Sprockets, Timing Chain, removal & installation.

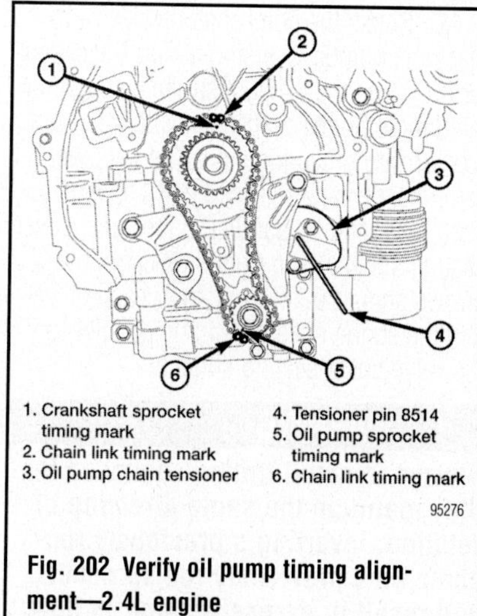

Fig. 202 Verify oil pump timing alignment—2.4L engine

12. Install the oil pan. Refer to Oil Pan, removal & installation.

13. Fill the engine with the proper type and amount of oil.

14. Start the engine and check for leaks.

Timing Chain

See Figures 203 and 204.

1. Before servicing the vehicle, refer to the Precautions Section.

2. Remove timing chain cover. Refer to Timing Chain Front Cover, removal & installation.

➡The crankshaft timing mark can be in 1 of 2 locations depending on whether the engine is early production, late production, or assembled with service parts. In all cases, the keyway will always be in the 9 o'clock position, in line with the ladder frame mounting surface when the engine is at Top Dead Center (TDC).

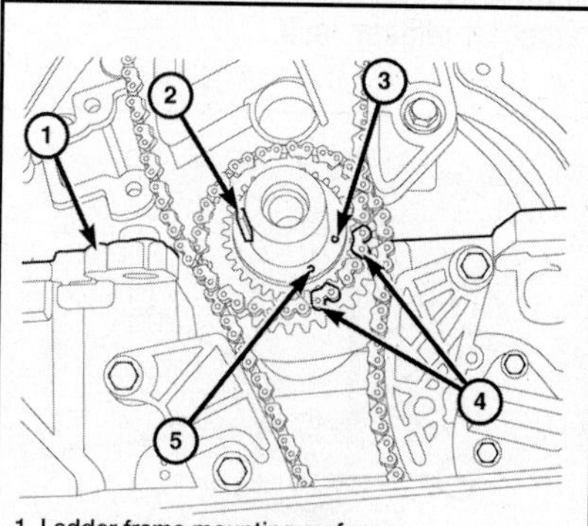

1. Ladder frame mounting surface
2. Keyway
3. Crankshaft timing mark (late production or assembled with service parts)
4. Marked chain links
5. Crankshaft timing mark (early production)

2189748

Fig. 203 Crankshaft timing mark alignment based on production—2.4L engine

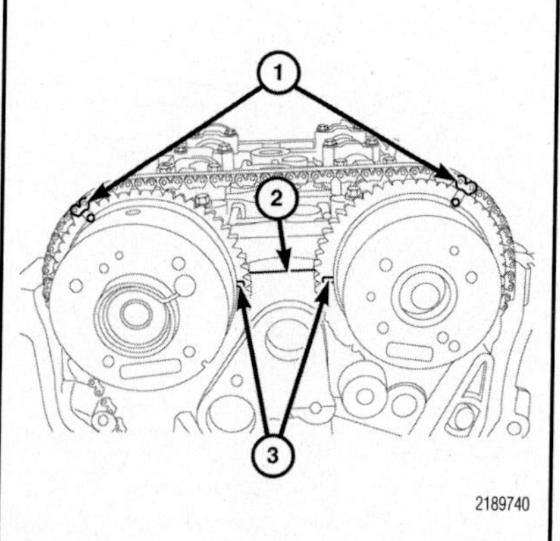

Fig. 204 View of camshaft timing marks: camshaft sprockets (2) in line with cylinder head cover sealing surface (3) and marked chain link corresponding to the camshaft timing mark (1)—2.4L engine

3. Verify that the engine is still set to TDC.

➡If the timing chain plated links can no longer be seen, the timing chain links corresponding to the timing marks must be marked prior to removal if the chain is to be reused.

4. Mark the chain link corresponding to the crankshaft timing mark.

5. With the engine still set to TDC, verify that the marks on the camshaft sprockets are in line with the cylinder head cover sealing surface. If the marks do not line up, the timing chain is not correctly installed.

6. Mark the chain link corresponding to the camshaft timing mark.

7. Remove the timing chain tensioner.

8. Remove the timing chain.

To install:

9. Verify that the engine is still set to TDC.

10. Align the camshaft timing marks so they are facing each other and in line with the cylinder head cover sealing surface.

11. Install the timing chain so the plated (or marked) links on the chain align with the timing marks on the camshaft sprockets.

12. Align the timing mark on the crankshaft sprocket with the plated (or marked) link on the timing chain. Position the chain so slack will be on the tensioner side.

➡Keep the slack in the timing chain on the tensioner side.

13. Install the timing chain tensioner.

14. Rotate the crankshaft CLOCKWISE 2 complete revolutions until the crankshaft is repositioned at the TDC position with the key way at the 9 o'clock position.

15. Verify that the camshafts timing marks are in the proper position and in line with the cylinder head cover sealing surface. If the marks do not line up, the timing chain is not correctly installed.

16. Install front timing chain cover. Refer to Timing Chain Front Cover, removal & installation.

17. Connect the negative battery cable. Refer to Battery, removal & installation.

18. Operate the engine until it reaches the normal operating temperature. Check the oil and cooling systems for correct fluid levels. Adjust as needed.

3.6L Engine

See Figures 205 through 215.

⁂ WARNING

The magnetic timing wheels must not come in contact with magnets (pickup tools, trays, etc.) or any other strong magnetic field. This may destroy the timing wheels ability to correctly relay the camshaft position to the camshaft position sensor.

⁂ WARNING

When the timing chains are removed and the cylinder heads are still installed, DO NOT rotate the camshafts or crankshaft without first locating the proper crankshaft position. Failure to do so may result in valve and/or piston damage.

➡The Variable Valve Timing (VVT) assemblies (Phasers) and Oil Control Valves (OCVs) can be serviced without removing the engine timing cover.

1. Before servicing the vehicle, refer to the Precautions Section.

2. Disconnect and isolate the negative battery cable. Refer to Battery, removal & installation.

3. Remove the air cleaner housing assembly. Refer to Air Cleaner, removal & installation.

4. Remove the upper intake manifold. Refer to Intake Manifold, removal & installation.

5. Remove the cylinder head covers. Refer to Valve Covers, removal & installation.

6. Remove the spark plugs. Refer to Spark Plugs, removal & installation.

7. Raise and safely support the vehicle.

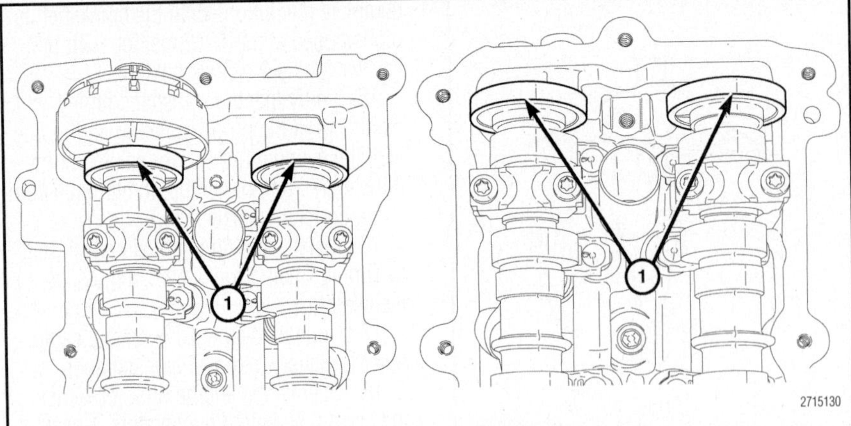

Fig. 205 The magnetic timing wheels (1) must not come in contact with any other magnetic device—3.6L engine

8. Drain the cooling system. Refer to Engine Coolant, Drain & Refill Procedure.
9. Remove the oil pan. Refer to Oil Pan, removal & installation.
10. Remove the accessory drive belts. Refer to Accessory Drive Belts, removal & installation.
11. Remove the crankshaft vibration damper.
12. Remove the engine timing cover. Refer to Timing Chain Front Cover, removal & installation.

⁂ WARNING

When aligning the timing marks, always rotate the engine by turning the crankshaft. Failure to do so may result in valve and/or piston damage.

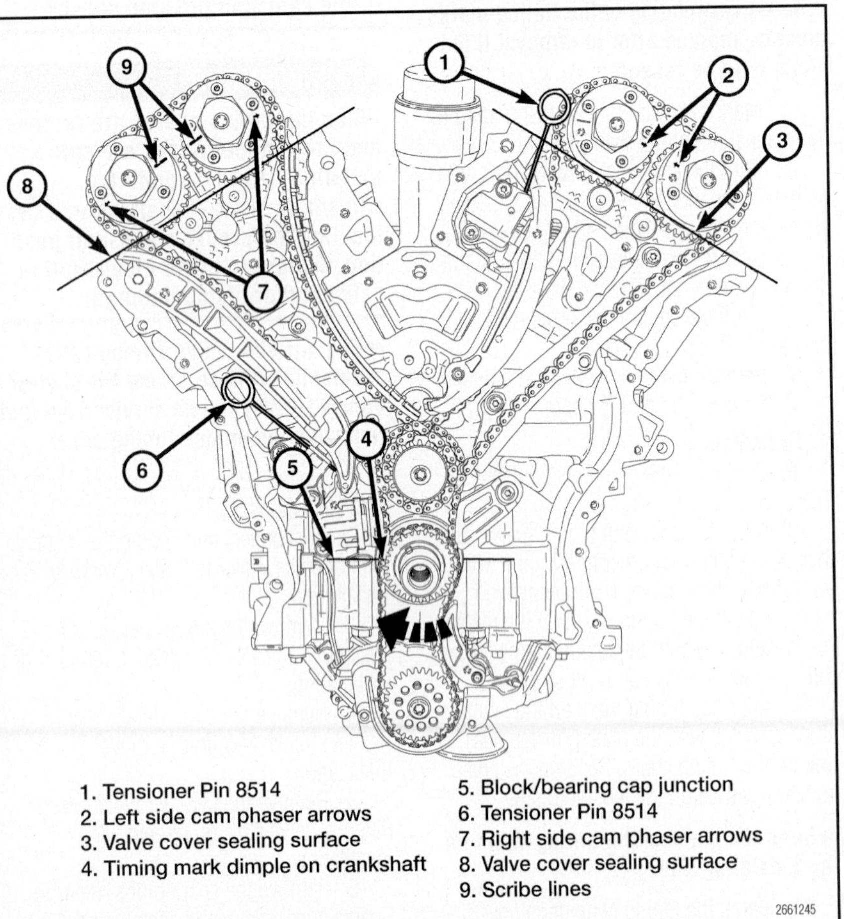

1. Tensioner Pin 8514
2. Left side cam phaser arrows
3. Valve cover sealing surface
4. Timing mark dimple on crankshaft
5. Block/bearing cap junction
6. Tensioner Pin 8514
7. Right side cam phaser arrows
8. Valve cover sealing surface
9. Scribe lines

2661245

Fig. 206 Alignment of timing marks shown at TDC—3.6L engine

13. Rotate the crankshaft clockwise to place the number 1 piston at Top Dead Center (TDC) on the exhaust stroke by aligning the dimple on the crankshaft with the block/bearing cap junction. The left side cam phaser arrows should point toward each other and be parallel to the valve cover sealing surface. The right side cam phaser arrows should point away from each other and the scribe lines should be parallel to the valve cover sealing surface.

⁂ WARNING

Always reinstall timing chains so that they maintain the same direction of rotation. Inverting a previously run chain on a previously run sprocket will result in excessive wear to both the chain and sprocket.

14. Mark the direction of rotation on the left side cam chain, right side cam chain, oil pump chain, and the primary chain using a paint pen, or equivalent, to aid in reassembly.
15. Reset the RH cam chain tensioner by pushing back the tensioner piston and installing Tensioner Pin 8514.
16. Reset the LH cam chain tensioner by lifting the pawl, pushing back the piston and installing Tensioner Pin 8514.
17. Remove the bolts and the timing gear splash shield.
18. Disengage the oil pump chain tensioner spring from the dowel pin and remove the oil pump chain tensioner.
19. Remove the oil pump sprocket T45 retaining bolt and remove the oil pump sprocket and oil pump chain.

➡Minor rotation of a camshaft (a few degrees) may be required to install the camshaft phaser lock.

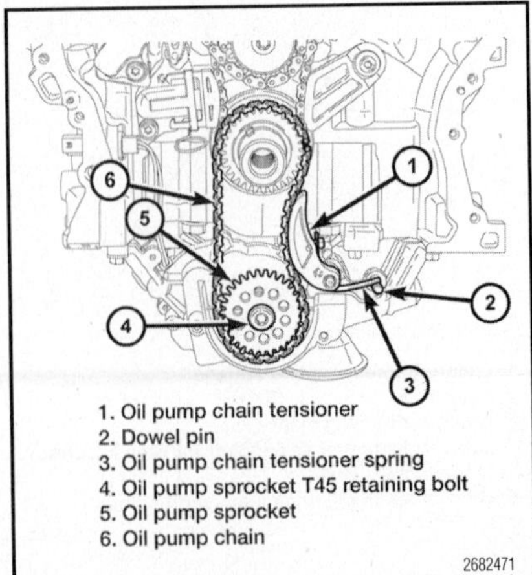

Fig. 207 Removing the oil pump sprocket and chain—3.6L engine

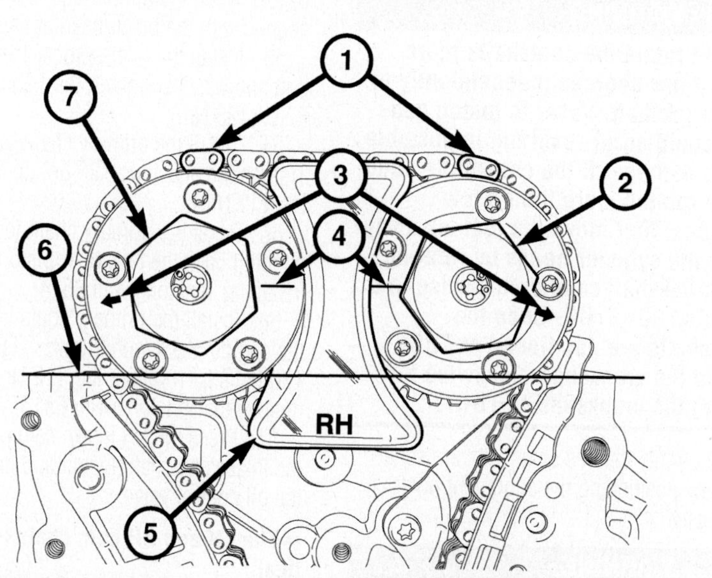

1. Plated chain links
2. Intake oil control valve
3. Cam phaser arrows
4. Scribe lines
5. RH Camshaft Phaser Lock 10202
6. Valve cover sealing surface
7. Exhaust oil control valve

2590445

Fig. 208 Aligning the RH Camshaft Phaser—3.6L engine

20. Install the RH Camshaft Phaser Lock 10202.
21. Loosen both the intake oil control valve and exhaust oil control valve.
22. Remove the RH Camshaft Phaser Lock 10202.
23. Remove the oil control valve from the right side intake cam phaser.
24. Pull the right side intake cam phaser off of the camshaft and remove the right side cam chain.
25. If required, remove the oil control valve and pull the right side exhaust cam phaser off of the camshaft.
26. Install the LH Camshaft Phaser Lock 10202.
27. Loosen both the intake oil control valve and exhaust oil control valve.
28. Remove the LH Camshaft Phaser Lock 10202.
29. Remove the oil control valve from the left side exhaust cam phaser.
30. Pull the left side exhaust cam phaser off of the camshaft and remove the left side cam chain.
31. If required, remove the oil control valve and pull the left side intake cam phaser off of the camshaft.
32. Reset the primary chain tensioner by pushing back the tensioner piston and installing Tensioner Pin 8514. Remove the 2 T30 bolts and remove the primary chain tensioner.
33. Remove the T30 bolt and the primary chain guide.
34. Remove the idler sprocket T45 retaining bolt and washer.
35. Remove the primary chain, idler sprocket, and crankshaft sprocket as an assembly.
36. If required, remove the 2 T30 bolts and the LH cam chain tensioner.
37. If required, remove the 2 T30 bolts and the LH cam chain guide and tensioner arm.
38. If required, remove the 2 T30 bolts and the RH cam chain tensioner.
39. If required, remove the 3 T30 bolts and the RH cam chain guide and tensioner arm.

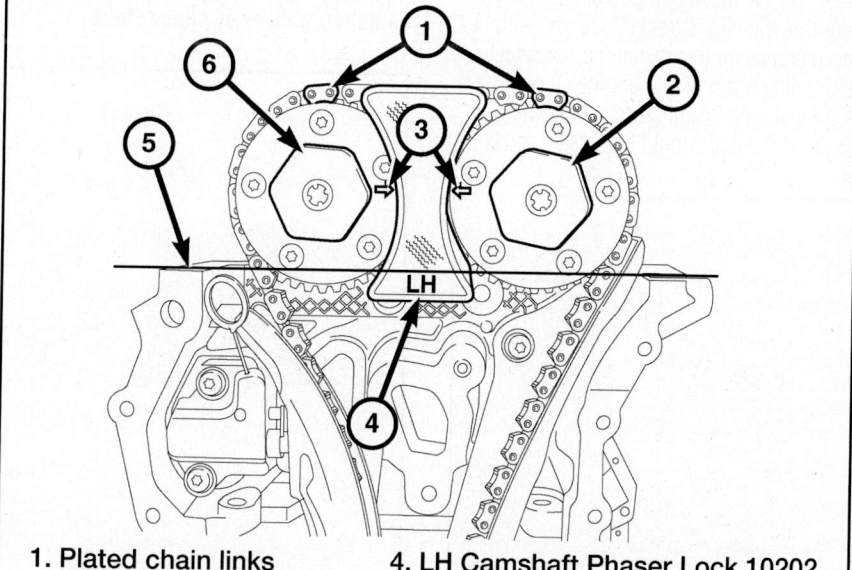

1. Plated chain links
2. Exhaust oil control valve
3. Cam phaser arrows
4. LH Camshaft Phaser Lock 10202
5. Valve cover sealing surface
6. Intake oil control valve

2692045

Fig. 209 Aligning the LH Camshaft Phaser—3.6L engine

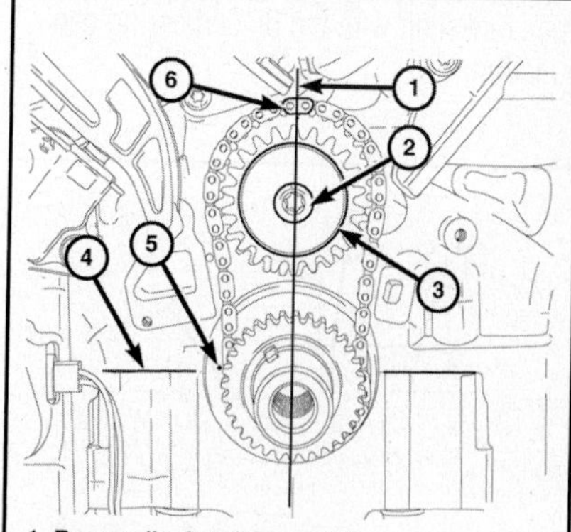

1. Perpendicular alignment line
2. Idler sprocket T45 retaining bolt
3. Washer
4. Block/bearing cap junction
5. Timing mark dimple on crankshaft sprocket
6. Plated chain link

2659817

Fig. 210 View of idler sprocket and components—3.6L engine

To install:

40. Inspect all sprockets and chain guides. Replace if damaged.

41. If removed, install the right side cam chain guide and tensioner arm. Tighten the attaching T30 bolts to 106 inch lbs. (12 Nm).

42. If removed, install the RH cam chain tensioner to the engine block with the 2 bolts. Tighten the T30 bolts to 106 inch lbs. (12 Nm).

43. Reset the RH cam chain tensioner by pushing back the tensioner piston and installing the Tensioner Pin 8514.

44. If removed, install the left side cam chain guide and tensioner arm. Tighten the attaching T30 bolts to 106 inch lbs. (12 Nm).

45. If removed, install the LH cam chain tensioner to the cylinder head with 2 bolts. Tighten the T30 bolts to 106 inch lbs. (12 Nm).

46. Reset the LH cam chain tensioner by lifting the pawl, pushing back the piston and installing Tensioner Pin 8514.

47. Verify that the key is installed in the crankshaft.

**** WARNING**

Do not rotate the crankshaft more than a few degrees independently of the camshafts. Piston to valve contact could occur resulting in possible valve damage. If the crankshaft needs to be rotated more than a few degrees, first remove the camshafts. Refer to Camshaft and Valve Lifters, removal & installation.

48. Verify that the number 1 piston is positioned at TDC by aligning the dimple on the crankshaft with the block/bearing cap junction.

**** WARNING**

Do not rotate the camshafts more than a few degrees independently of the crankshaft. Valve to piston contact could occur resulting in possible valve damage. If the camshafts need to be rotated more than a few degrees, first move the pistons away from the cylinder heads by rotating the crankshaft counterclockwise to a position 30° BTDC. Once the camshafts are positioned at TDC rotate the crankshaft clockwise to return the crankshaft to TDC.

49. Verify that the camshafts are set at TDC by positioning the alignment holes vertically.

**** WARNING**

Always reinstall timing chains so that they maintain the same direction of rotation. Inverting a previously run chain on a previously run sprocket will result in excessive wear to both the chain and sprocket.

50. Place the primary chain onto the crankshaft sprocket so that the arrow is aligned with the plated link on the timing chain.

51. While maintaining this alignment, invert the crankshaft sprocket and timing chain and place the idler sprocket into the timing chain so that the dimple is aligned with the plated link on the timing chain.

52. While maintaining this alignment, lubricate the idler sprocket bushing with clean engine oil and install the sprockets and timing chain on the engine. To verify that the timing is still correct, the timing chain plated link should be located at 12 o'clock when the dimple on the crankshaft is aligned with the block/bearing cap junction.

53. Install the idler sprocket retaining bolt and washer. Tighten the T45 bolt to 18 ft. lbs. (25 Nm).

54. Install the primary chain guide. Tighten the attaching T30 bolt to 106 inch lbs. (12 Nm).

55. Reset the primary chain tensioner by pushing back the tensioner piston and installing Tensioner Pin 8514.

56. Install the primary chain tensioner to the engine block with 2 bolts. Tighten the T30 bolts to 106 inch lbs. (12 Nm) and remove the Tensioner Pin 8514.

57. Press the LH intake cam phaser onto the intake camshaft. Install and hand tighten the oil control valve.

➡The LH and RH cam chains are identical.

58. Drape the left side cam chain over the LH intake cam phaser and onto the idler sprocket so that the arrow is aligned with the plated link on the cam chain.

59. While maintaining this alignment, route the cam chain around the exhaust and intake cam phasers so that the plated links are aligned with the phaser timing marks. Position the left side cam phasers so that the arrows point toward each other and are parallel to the valve cover sealing surface. Press the exhaust cam phaser onto the exhaust cam, install and hand tighten the oil control valve.

➡Minor rotation of a camshaft (a few degrees) may be required to install the camshaft phaser or phaser lock.

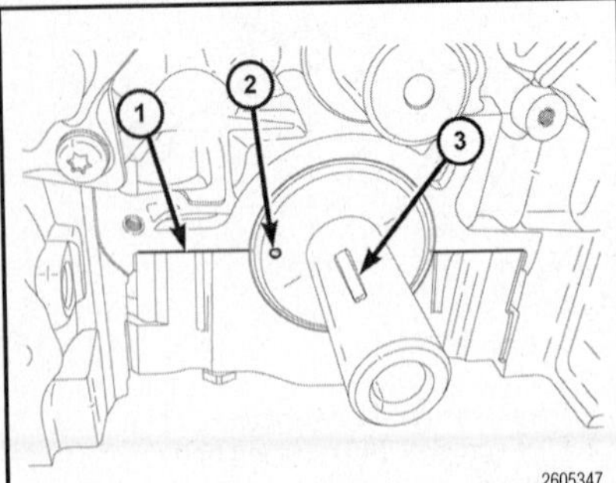

Fig. 211 Verify that the key (3) is installed in the crankshaft and that the number 1 piston is positioned at TDC by aligning the dimple (2) on the crankshaft with the block/bearing cap junction (1)—3.6L engine

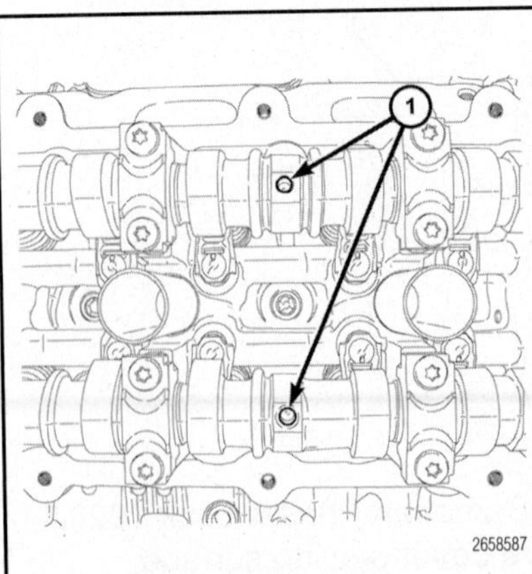

Fig. 212 Verify that the camshafts are set at TDC by positioning the alignment holes (1) vertically—3.6L engine

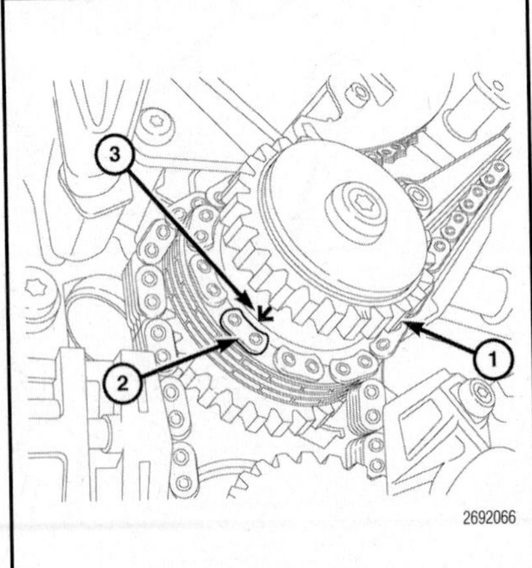

Fig. 213 Drape the left side cam chain over the LH intake cam phaser and onto the idler sprocket (1) so that the arrow (3) is aligned with the plated link (2) on the cam chain—3.6L engine

60. Install the LH Camshaft Phaser Lock 10202 and tighten the oil control valves to 110 ft. lbs. (150 Nm).

61. Press the RH exhaust cam phaser onto the exhaust camshaft. Install and hand tighten the oil control valve.

62. Drape the right side cam chain over the RH exhaust cam phaser and onto the idler sprocket so that the dimple is aligned with the plated link on the cam chain.

63. While maintaining this alignment, route the cam chain around the exhaust and intake cam phasers so that the plated links are aligned with the phaser timing marks. Position the right side cam phasers so that the arrows point away from each other and the scribe lines are parallel to the valve cover sealing surface. Press the intake cam phaser onto the intake cam, install and hand tighten the oil control valve.

64. Install the RH Camshaft Phaser Lock 10202 and tighten the oil control valves to 110 ft. lbs. (150 Nm).

➡**There are no timing marks on the oil pump gear or chain.**

65. Place the oil pump sprocket into the oil pump chain. Place the oil pump chain onto the crankshaft sprocket while aligning the oil pump sprocket with the oil pump shaft. Install the oil pump sprocket T45 retaining bolt and tighten to 18 ft. lbs. (25 Nm).

66. Install the oil pump chain tensioner. Insure that the spring is positioned above the dowel pin.

67. Install the timing gear splash shield. Tighten the bolts to 35 inch lbs. (5 Nm).

68. Remove the RH and LH Camshaft Phaser Locks 10202.

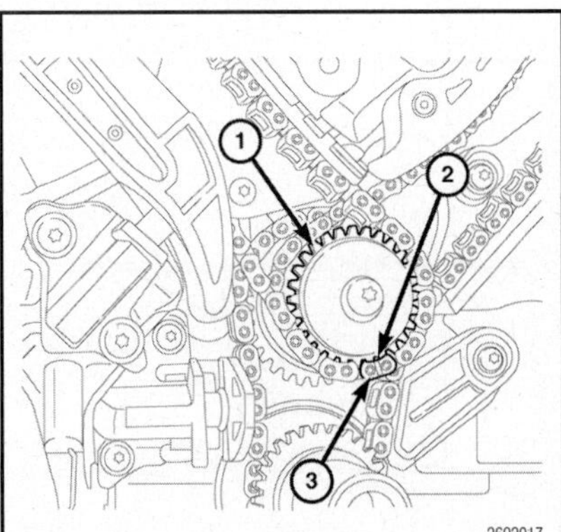

Fig. 214 Drape the right side cam chain over the RH exhaust cam phaser and onto the idler sprocket (1) so that the dimple (2) is aligned with the plated link (3) on the cam chain—3.6L engine

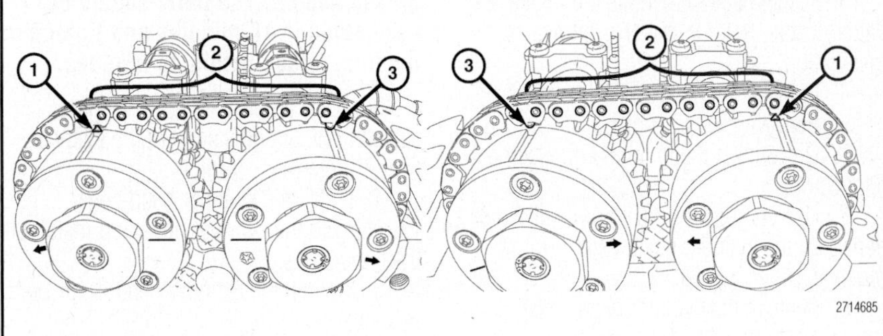

Fig. 215 When properly aligned, there should be 12 chain pins (2) between the exhaust cam phaser triangle marking (1) and the intake cam phaser circle marking (3)—3.6L engine

69. Remove the Tensioner Pins 8514 from the RH and LH cam chain tensioners.

70. Rotate the crankshaft clockwise 2 complete revolutions stopping when the dimple on the crankshaft is aligned the with the block/bearing cap junction.

71. While maintaining this alignment, verify that the arrows on the left side cam phasers point toward each other and are parallel to the valve cover sealing surface and that the right side cam phaser arrows point away from each other and the scribe lines are parallel to the valve cover sealing surface.

72. There should be 12 chain pins between the exhaust cam phaser triangle marking and the intake cam phaser circle marking.

73. If the engine timing is not correct, repeat this procedure.

74. Install the engine timing cover. Refer to Timing Chain Front Cover, removal & installation.

75. Install the crankshaft vibration damper.

76. Install the accessory drive belts. Refer to Accessory Drive Belts, removal & installation.

77. Install the and oil pan. Refer to Oil Pan, removal & installation.

78. Install the spark plugs. Tighten to 13 ft. lbs. (18 Nm). Refer to Spark Plug, removal & installation.

79. Install the cylinder head covers. Refer to Valve Covers, removal & installation.

80. Install the upper intake manifold. Refer to Intake Manifold, removal & installation.

81. Install the air cleaner housing assembly. Refer to Air Cleaner, removal & installation.

82. Fill the engine crankcase with the proper oil to the correct level. Refer to Engine Oil & Filter, Replacement.

83. Connect the negative battery cable and tighten the nut to 45 inch lbs. (5 Nm). Refer to Battery, removal & installation.

84. Fill the cooling system. Refer to Engine Coolant, Drain & Refill Procedure.

85. Operate the engine until it reaches the normal operating temperature. Check the cooling system for correct fluid level.

➡**The Cam/Crank Variation Relearn procedure must be performed using the scan tool anytime there has been a repair/replacement made to a powertrain system, for example: flywheel, valvetrain, camshaft and/or crankshaft sensors or components. Refer to Powertrain Control Module (PCM), Powertrain Verification Test.**

VALVE COVERS

REMOVAL & INSTALLATION

2.4L Engine

See Figures 216 through 220.

1. Before servicing the vehicle, refer to the Precautions Section.

2. Remove the engine cover by pulling upward.

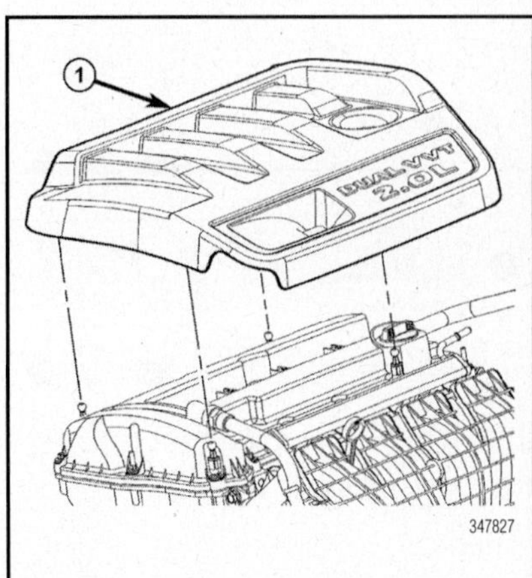

Fig. 216 Engine cover (1) shown—2.4L engine

3. Disconnect and isolate the negative battery cable. Refer to Battery, removal & installation.
4. Remove the makeup air hose.
5. Remove the PCV hose.
6. Disconnect the ignition coil electrical connectors.
7. Use compressed air to blow dirt and debris off the cylinder head cover prior to removal.
8. Remove the cylinder head cover (valve cover) bolts.
9. Remove the cylinder head cover from the cylinder head.

To install:

10. Install new cylinder head cover gaskets.
11. Install the studs in the cover.
12. Clean all RTV from the cylinder head.

➡When using RTV, the sealing surfaces must be clean and free from grease and oil. The parts should be assembled in 10 minutes and tighten to the final torque within 45 minutes.

13. Apply a dot of MOPAR® engine sealant RTV, or equivalent, to the cylinder head/front cover T-joint.
14. Install the cylinder head cover assembly to the cylinder head and install all the bolts/studs.
15. Tighten the cylinder head cover bolts in sequence:
    a. Step 1: Tighten all bolts to 44 inch lbs. (5 Nm).
    b. Step 2: Tighten all bolts to 89 inch lb. (10 Nm).
16. Install ignition coils. Tighten the fasteners to 70 inch lbs. (8 Nm). Refer to Ignition Coil, removal & installation.
17. If the PCV valve was removed, tighten the PCV valve to 44 inch lbs. (5 Nm).
18. Connect the coil electrical connectors.
19. Connect the PCV hose to the PCV valve.
20. Connect the makeup air hose.
21. Connect the negative battery cable. Refer to Battery, removal & installation.
22. Install the engine cover by pressing the rear of the cover down first.

3.5L Engine

Left Side

See Figure 221.

⁂ CAUTION

Do not start or run the engine with the cylinder head cover (valve cover) removed. Damage or personal injury may occur.

1. Before servicing the vehicle, refer to the Precautions Section.
2. Disconnect and isolate the negative battery cable. Refer to Battery, removal & installation.
3. Disconnect and remove the ignition coils. Refer to Ignition Coil, removal & installation.
4. Disconnect the engine harness retaining clips from the cylinder head cover studs. Position the engine harness aside.
5. Disconnect the PCV hose from the cylinder head cover (valve cover) assembly (if required).
6. Completely loosen the 8 cylinder head cover retaining bolts and remove the cylinder head cover.

To install:

7. Clean the cylinder head and all the gasket sealing surfaces. Inspect and replace the gasket and seals as necessary.
8. Using a suitable pry tool, carefully remove the spark plug tube seals.

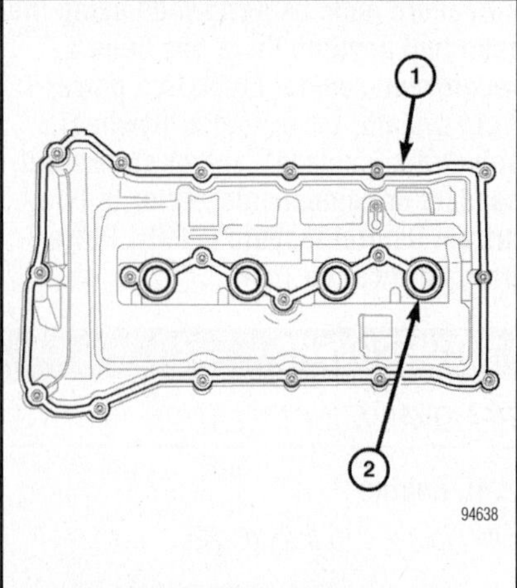

Fig. 217 Install new cylinder head cover gaskets (1, 2)—2.4L engine

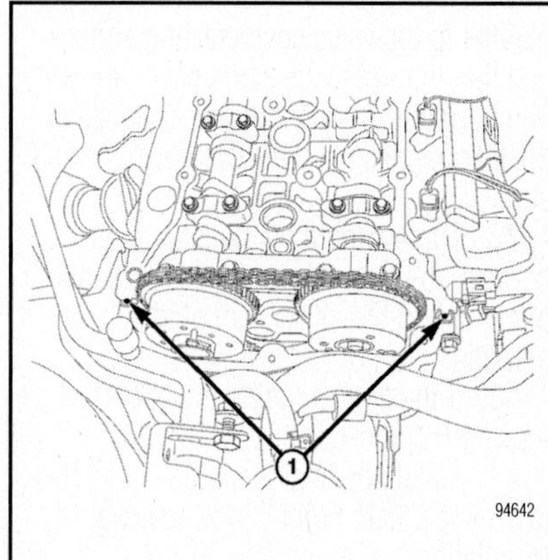

Fig. 219 Apply a dot of engine sealant RTV to the cylinder head/front cover T-joint (1)—2.4L engine

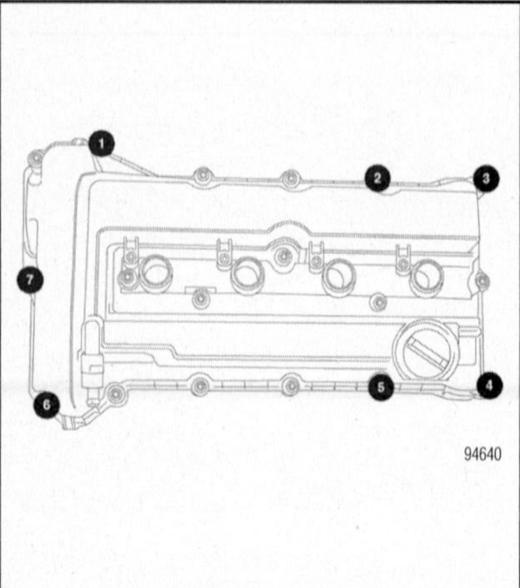

Fig. 218 Cylinder head cover stud locations—2.4L engine

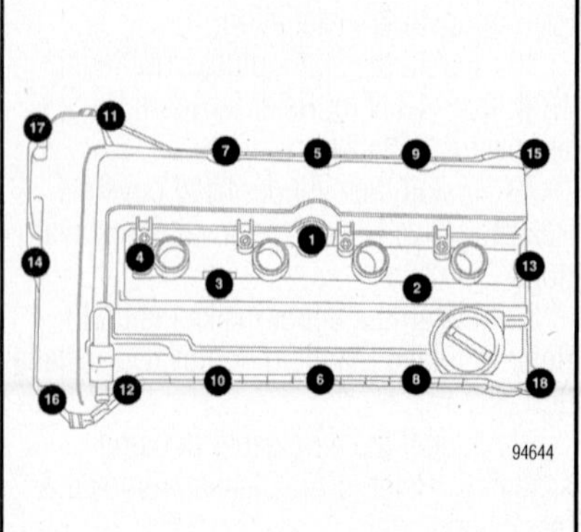

Fig. 220 Cylinder head cover bolt tightening sequence—2.4L engine

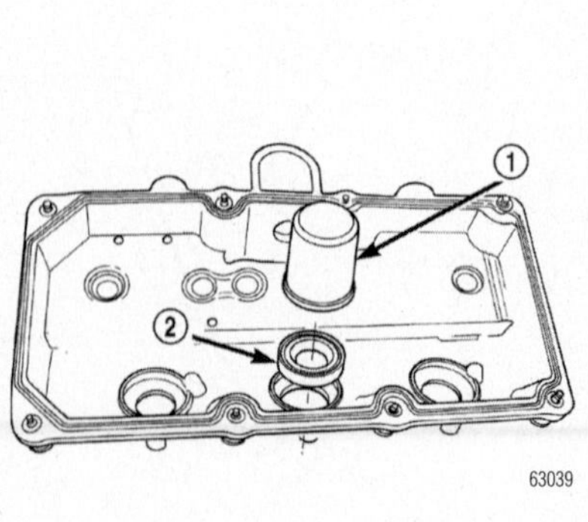

Fig. 221 Using Camshaft Installer MD-998306 (1) to install the cylinder head cover seals (2)—3.5L engine

9. Position the new seal with the part number on the seal facing the cylinder head cover.

10. Install the seals using Camshaft Installer MD-998306.

11. Install the cylinder head cover and bolts. Tighten the bolts to 89 inch lbs. (10 Nm).

12. Install the PCV hose (if required).

13. Position the wiring harness on the cylinder head cover.

14. Reinstall the wire harness retainers around the perimeter of the valve cover.

15. Install the ignition coils. Refer to Ignition Coil, removal & installation.

16. Connect the ignition coil electrical connectors.

17. Connect the negative battery cable. Refer to Battery, removal & installation.

Right Side

See Figure 222.

⁂ CAUTION

Do not start or run the engine with the cylinder head cover (valve cover) removed. Damage or personal injury may occur.

1. Before servicing the vehicle, refer to the Precautions Section.

2. Disconnect and isolate the negative battery cable. Refer to Battery, removal & installation.

3. Remove the upper intake manifold from the engine. Refer to Intake Manifold, removal & installation.

4. Cover the lower intake manifold intake ports with a clean cover to prevent dirt or debris from entering the ports during service.

5. Disconnect the ignition coil harness connectors.

6. Remove the ignition coils. Refer to Ignition Coil, removal & installation.

7. Disconnect the engine wiring harness retainers from the cylinder head cover (valve cover).

8. Disconnect the makeup air hose.

9. Completely loosen the cylinder head cover retaining bolts and remove the cylinder head cover.

To install:

10. Clean the cylinder head and cover mating surfaces. Inspect and replace the gasket and seals as necessary.

11. Using a suitable pry tool, carefully remove tube seals.

12. Position the new seal with the part number on the seal facing the cylinder head cover.

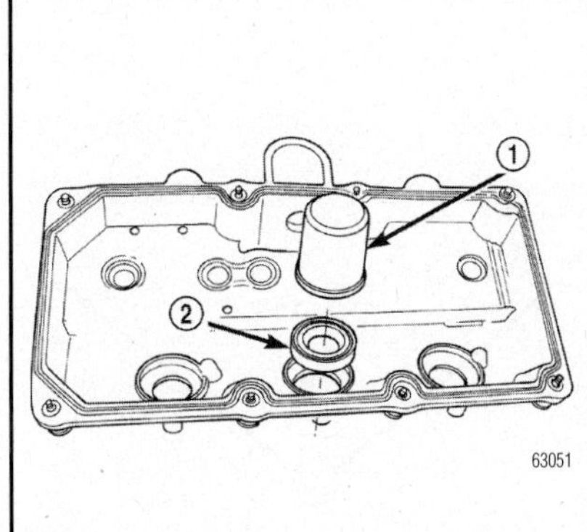

Fig. 222 Using Camshaft Installer MD-998306 (1) to install the cylinder head cover seals (2)—3.5L engine

13. Install the seals using Camshaft Installer MD-998306.

14. Install the cylinder head cover bolts and tighten to 89 inch lbs. (10 Nm).

15. Reconnect the wire harness retainers to the cylinder head cover.

16. Install the ignition coils. Refer to Ignition Coil, removal & installation.

17. Connect the ignition coil electrical connectors.

18. Reconnect the makeup air hose.

19. Install the upper intake manifold. Refer to Intake Manifold, removal & installation.

20. Connect the negative battery cable. Refer to Battery, removal & installation.

3.6L Engine

Left Side

See Figures 223 through 226.

⁂ WARNING

The magnetic timing wheels must not come in contact with magnets (pickup tools, trays, etc.) or any other strong magnetic field. This may destroy the timing wheels ability to correctly relay the camshaft position to the camshaft position sensor.

1. Before servicing the vehicle, refer to the Precautions Section.

2. Disconnect and isolate the negative battery cable. Refer to Battery, removal & installation.

3. Remove the air cleaner body, resonator, and upper intake manifold. Refer to Intake Manifold, removal & installation.

4. Cover the open intake ports to prevent debris from entering the engine.

5. Remove the insulator from the LH cylinder head cover (valve cover).

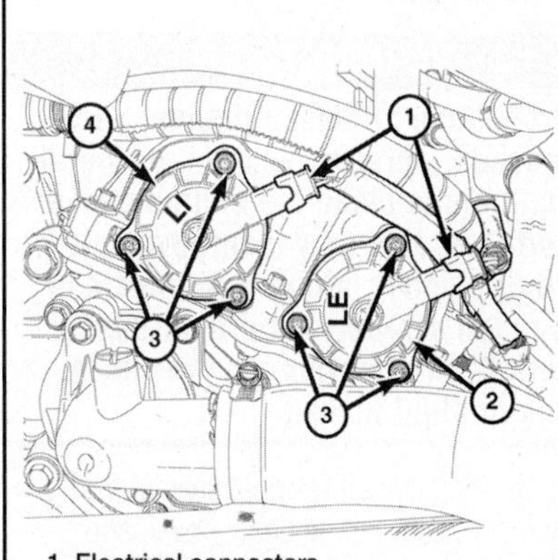

Fig. 223 Variable valve timing solenoids shown marked for reinstallation in original locations—3.6L engine

6. Disconnect the electrical connectors from the variable valve timing solenoids on the left cylinder head cover.

7. Disengage the 3 wire harness retainers from the left cylinder head cover.

8. Mark the variable valve timing solenoids with a paint pen or equivalent so that they may be reinstalled in their original locations.

9. Remove the variable valve timing solenoids.

10. Disconnect the left Camshaft Position (CMP) sensor.

11. Disengage one main wire harness retainer from the cylinder head cover and one main wire harness retainer from the cylinder head cover mounting stud.

➡If removing both RH and LH CMP sensors, mark the sensors so they can be installed in their original locations.

12. Remove the camshaft position sensor. Refer to Camshaft Position (CMP) Sensor, removal & installation.

13. Disengage the 2 injection/ignition harness retainers from the left cylinder head cover.

14. Remove the ignition coils. Refer to Ignition Coil, removal & installation.

15. Loosen the 10 cylinder head cover mounting bolts and the 2 studbolts and remove the cylinder head cover.

16. Remove and discard the cylinder head cover gasket.

17. The spark plug tube seals can be reused if not damaged.

To install:

WARNING

Do not use oil based liquids, wire brushes, abrasive wheels, or metal scrapers to clean the engine gasket surfaces. Use only isopropyl (rubbing) alcohol, along with plastic or wooden scrapers. Improper gasket surface preparation may result in engine fluid leakage.

18. Remove all residual sealant from the cylinder head, timing chain cover, and cylinder head cover mating surfaces.
19. Install the cylinder head cover gasket. The spark plug tube seals can be reused if not damaged.
20. If required, install new spark plug tube seals in the cylinder head cover:
    a. Lubricate the spark plug tube seal inner and outer diameters with clean engine oil.
    b. Place the spark plug tube seal on the Cam Sensor/Spark Plug Tube Seal Installer 10256.
    c. Push the seal into the cylinder head cover until the base of the seal is seated.
    d. Remove the tool.
21. Clean the engine timing cover, cylinder head, and cylinder head cover mating surfaces with isopropyl alcohol in preparation for sealant application.

➡Engine assembly requires the use of a unique sealant that is compatible with engine oil. Using a sealant other than MOPAR® Threebond Engine RTV Sealant may result in engine fluid leakage.

➡Following the application of MOPAR® Threebond Engine RTV Sealant to the gasket surfaces, the components must be assembled within 20 minutes and the attaching fasteners must be tightened to specification within 45 minutes. Prolonged exposure to the air, prior to assembly, may result in engine fluid leakage.

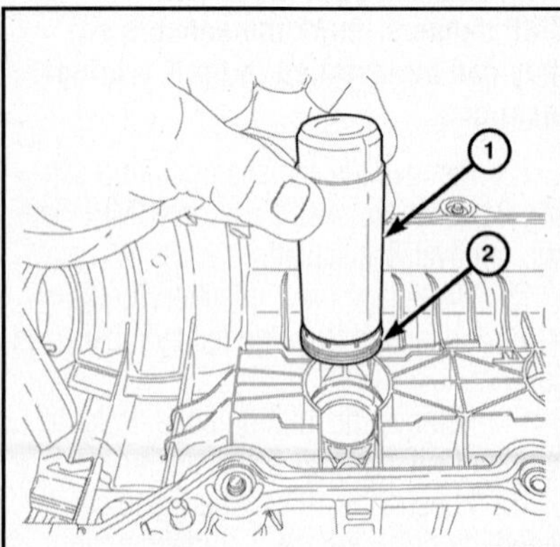

Fig. 224 Using the Cam Sensor/Spark Plug Tube Seal Installer 10256 (1) to install a new spark plug tube seal (2) into the cylinder head cover—3.6L engine

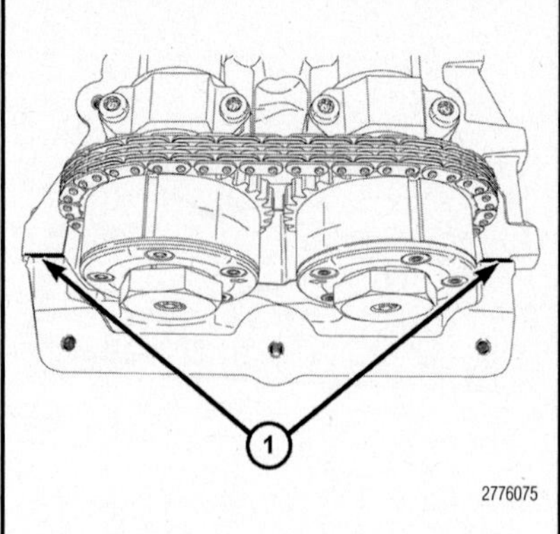

Fig. 225 Apply a wide bead of engine RTV sealant (1) to the 2 engine timing cover-to-cylinder head T-joints—3.6L engine

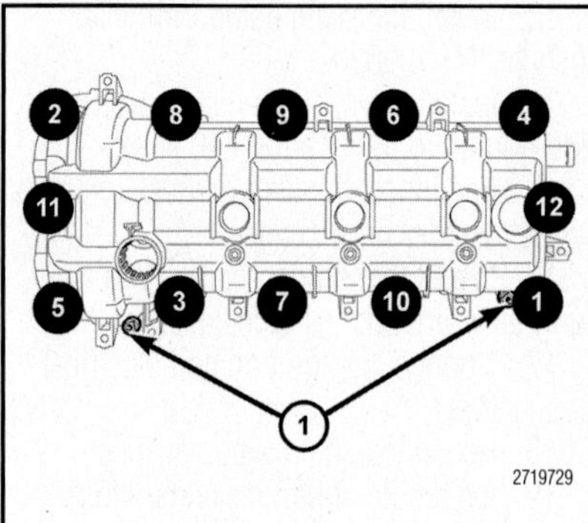

Fig. 226 Cylinder head cover (left side) bolt tightening sequence shown along with the alignment locator pins (1)—3.6L engine

22. Apply a 0.08–0.12 inch (2–3mm) wide bead of MOPAR® Threebond Engine RTV Sealant to the 2 engine timing cover-to-cylinder head T-joints.
23. Align the locator pins to the cylinder head and install the cylinder head cover.
24. Tighten the cylinder head cover bolts and double-ended studs in sequence to 106 inch lbs. (12 Nm).
25. If removed, install the spark plugs. Refer to Spark Plugs, removal & installation.
26. Install the ignition coils. Refer to Ignition Coil, removal & installation.
27. Engage the 2 injection/ignition harness retainers to the left cylinder head cover.

➡If both RH and LH CMP sensors were removed, install them into their original locations.

28. Install the camshaft position sensor. Refer to Camshaft Position (CMP) Sensor, removal & installation.
29. Connect the electrical connector to the left CMP sensor.
30. Engage the 1 main wire harness retainer to the cylinder head cover and the 1 main wire harness retainer to the cylinder head cover mounting stud.
31. Refer to the markings made at disassembly and install the variable valve timing solenoids in their original locations.
32. Engage the 3 wire harness retainers to the left cylinder head cover.
33. Connect the electrical connectors to the left variable valve timing solenoids.
34. Install the insulator to the 2 alignment posts on top of the LH cylinder head cover.
35. Install the upper intake manifold, support brackets, resonator and air cleaner body. Refer to Intake Manifold, removal & installation.
36. Connect the negative battery cable and tighten the nut to 45 inch lbs. (5 Nm). Refer to Battery, removal & installation.

➡The Cam/Crank Variation Relearn procedure must be performed using the scan tool anytime there has been a repair/replacement made to a powertrain system, for example: flywheel, valvetrain, camshaft and/or crankshaft sensors or components. Refer to Powertrain Control Module (PCM), Powertrain Verification Test.

Right Side

See Figures 225 and 227.

WARNING

The magnetic timing wheels must not come in contact with magnets (pickup tools, trays, etc.) or any other strong magnetic field. This may destroy the timing wheels ability to correctly relay the camshaft position to the camshaft position sensor.

1. Before servicing the vehicle, refer to the Precautions Section.
2. Disconnect and isolate the negative battery cable. Refer to Battery, removal & installation.
3. Remove the air cleaner body, resonator, and upper intake manifold. Refer to Intake Manifold, removal & installation.
4. Cover the open intake ports to prevent debris from entering the engine.
5. Disconnect the electrical connectors from the variable valve timing solenoids on the right cylinder head.

6. Disengage the 2 wire harness retainers from the right cylinder head cover.

7. Mark the variable valve timing solenoids with a paint pen or equivalent so that they may be reinstalled in their original locations.

8. Remove the variable valve timing solenoids.

9. Disengage the 3 main wire harness retainers from the right cylinder head cover.

10. Disconnect the electrical connector from the right Camshaft Position (CMP) sensor.

➡**If removing both RH and LH CMP sensors, mark the sensors so they can be installed in their original locations.**

11. Remove the camshaft position sensor. Refer to Camshaft Position (CMP) Sensor, removal & installation.

12. Disengage the 3 injection/ignition harness retainers from the right cylinder head cover.

13. Remove the ignition coils. Refer to Ignition Coil, removal & installation.

14. Remove the PCV valve.

15. Remove the 2 resonator mounts from the studbolts.

16. Loosen the 9 cylinder head cover mounting bolts and 3 studbolts and remove the cylinder head cover.

17. Remove and discard the cylinder head cover gasket.

18. The spark plug tube seals can be reused if not damaged.

To install:

⁂ WARNING

Do not use oil based liquids, wire brushes, abrasive wheels or metal scrapers to clean the engine gasket surfaces. Use only isopropyl (rubbing) alcohol, along with plastic or wooden scrapers. Improper gasket surface preparation may result in engine fluid leakage.

19. Remove all residual sealant from the cylinder head, timing chain cover, and cylinder head cover mating surfaces.

20. Install the cylinder head cover gasket.

21. The spark plug tube seals can be reused if not damaged.

22. If required, install new spark plug tube seals in the cylinder head cover:

a. Lubricate the spark plug tube seal inner and outer diameters with clean engine oil.

b. Place the spark plug tube seal on the Cam Sensor/Spark Plug Tube Seal Installer 10256.

c. Push the seal into the cylinder head cover until the base of the seal is seated.

d. Remove the tool.

23. Clean the engine timing cover, cylinder head, and cylinder head cover mating surfaces with isopropyl alcohol in preparation for sealant application.

➡**Engine assembly requires the use of a unique sealant that is compatible with engine oil. Using a sealant other than MOPAR® Threebond Engine RTV Sealant may result in engine fluid leakage.**

➡**Following the application of MOPAR® Threebond Engine RTV Sealant to the gasket surfaces, the components must be assembled within 20 minutes and the attaching fasteners must be tightened to specification within 45 minutes. Prolonged exposure to the air, prior to assembly, may result in engine fluid leakage.**

24. Apply a 0.08–0.12 inch (2–3mm) wide bead of MOPAR® Threebond Engine RTV Sealant to the 2 engine timing cover-to-cylinder head T-joints.

25. Align the locator pins to the cylinder head and install the cylinder head cover.

26. Tighten the cylinder head cover bolts and double-ended studs in sequence to 106 inch lbs. (12 Nm).

27. Install the 2 resonator mounts to the studbolts.

28. Install the PCV valve.

29. If removed, install the spark plugs. Refer to Spark Plugs, removal & installation.

30. Install the ignition coils. Refer to Ignition Coil, removal & installation.

31. Engage the 3 injection/ignition harness retainers to the right cylinder head cover.

➡**If both RH and LH CMP sensors were removed, install them into their original locations.**

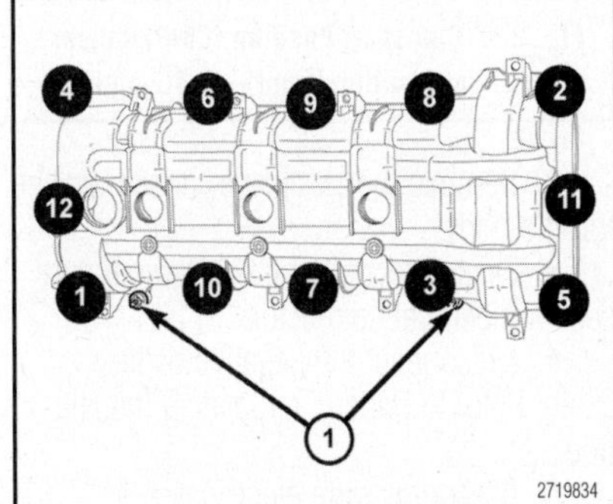

Fig. 227 Cylinder head cover (right side) bolt tightening sequence shown along with the alignment locator pins (1)—3.6L engine

32. Install the camshaft position sensor. Refer to Camshaft Position (CMP) Sensor, removal & installation.

33. Connect the electrical connector to the right Camshaft Position (CMP) sensor.

34. Engage the 3 main wire harness retainers to the right cylinder head cover.

35. Refer to the markings made at disassembly and install the variable valve timing solenoids in their original locations.

36. Connect the electrical connectors to the variable valve timing solenoids on the right cylinder head.

37. Engage the 2 wire harness retainers to the right cylinder head cover.

38. If removed, install the insulator to the 2 alignment posts on top of the LH cylinder head cover.

39. Install the upper intake manifold, support brackets, resonator, and air cleaner body. Refer to Intake Manifold, removal & installation.

40. Connect the negative battery cable and tighten the nut to 45 inch lbs. (5 Nm). Refer to Battery, removal & installation.

➡**The Cam/Crank Variation Relearn procedure must be performed using the scan tool anytime there has been a repair/replacement made to a powertrain system, for example: flywheel, valvetrain, camshaft and/or crankshaft sensors or components. Refer to Powertrain Control Module (PCM), Powertrain Verification Test.**

VALVE LASH

ADJUSTMENT

2.4L Engine

See Figures 228 and 229.

➡**The engine must be cold to measure valve lash.**

1. Before servicing the vehicle, refer to the Precautions Section.

2. Remove the engine cover.

3. Remove the cylinder head cover. Refer to Valve Covers, removal & installation.

4. Rotate the camshaft so the lobes are vertical.

5. Check the clearance using feeler gauges.

6. Repeat for all the tappets and record the readings.

7. If the clearance is too small:

a. Remove the camshafts. Refer to Camshaft and Valve Lifters, removal & installation.

b. Decrease the tappet thickness to match specifications.

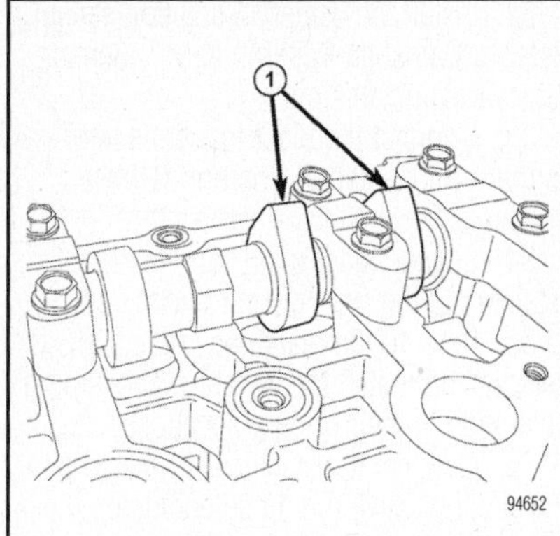

Fig. 228 Rotate the camshaft so the lobes are vertical (1) before measuring the valve lash—2.4L engine

c. Install the camshafts. Refer to Camshaft and Valve Lifters, removal & installation.

d. Verify that the valve lash is correct.

8. If clearance is too large:

a. Remove the camshafts. Refer to Camshaft and Valve Lifters, removal & installation.

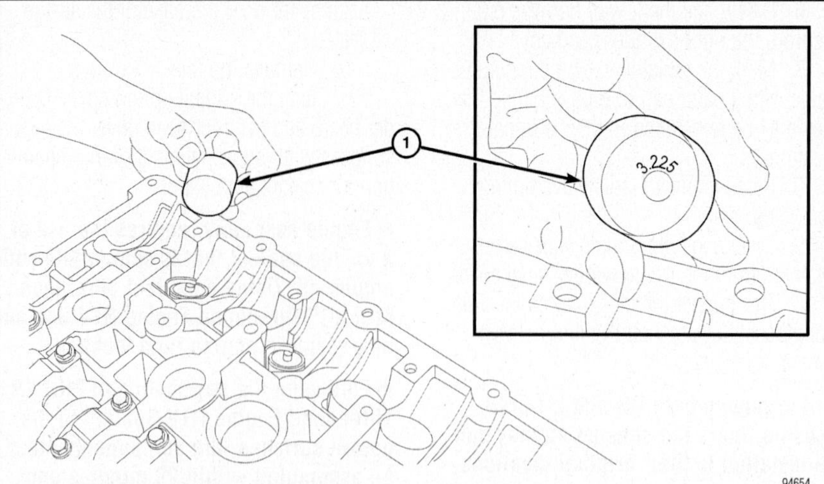

Fig. 229 Increase or decrease the thickness until specifications are met. Tappet thickness is marked on the tappet (1)—2.4L engine

b. Increase the tappet thickness to match specifications.

c. Install the camshafts. Refer to Camshaft and Valve Lifters, removal & installation.

d. Verify that the valve lash is correct.

3.5L and 3.6L Engines

These engines utilize hydraulic lash adjusters; no adjustment is necessary.

ENGINE PERFORMANCE & EMISSION CONTROLS

CAMSHAFT POSITION (CMP) SENSOR

LOCATION

2.4L Engine

See Figures 230 and 231.

The Camshaft Position (CMP) sensor is located in the cylinder head near the camshaft, is retained by a single fastener and has an O-ring seal.

3.5L Engine

See Figure 232.

The Camshaft Position (CMP) sensor is mounted in the front of the head.

3.6L Engine

See Figure 233.

The Camshaft Position (CMP) sensors are located at the rear of the cylinder head covers and are bolted to the cylinder head.

REMOVAL & INSTALLATION

2.4L Engine

Front

See Figure 230.

1. Before servicing the vehicle, refer to the Precautions Section.

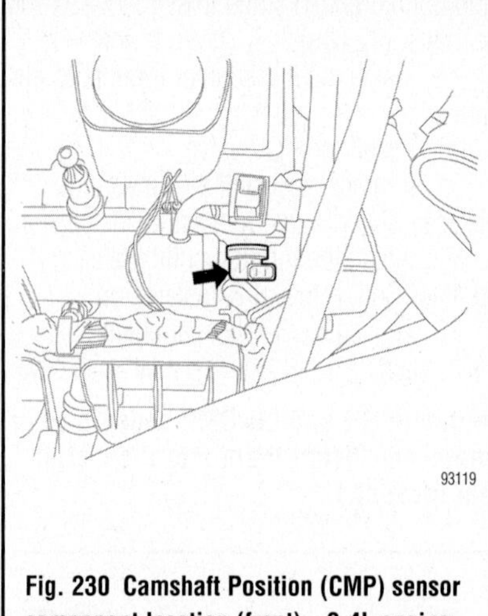

Fig. 230 Camshaft Position (CMP) sensor component location (front)—2.4L engine

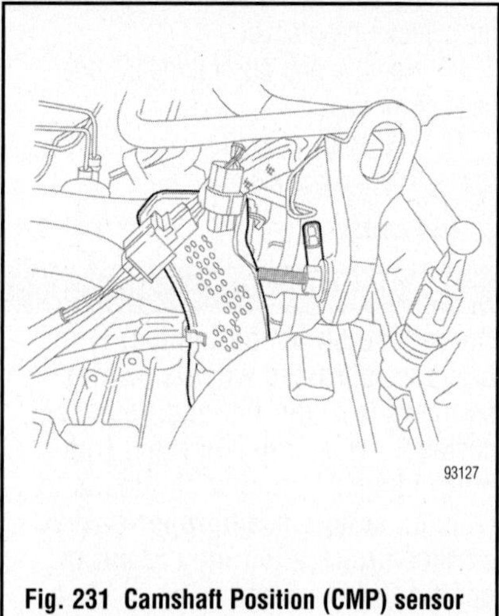

Fig. 231 Camshaft Position (CMP) sensor component location (rear)—2.4L engine

2. Remove the air cleaner hose from the throttle body.

3. Disconnect the inlet air temperature sensor electrical connector.

4. Disconnect the negative battery cable. Refer to Battery, removal & installation.

5. Disconnect the electrical connector from the camshaft position sensor.

6. Remove the camshaft position sensor mounting screws.

7. Remove the sensor.

To install:

WARNING

Install the Camshaft Position (CMP) sensor utilizing a twisting motion. Make sure the CMP sensor is fully seated. Do not drive the CMP sensor into the bore with the mounting screw. This may cause the CMP sensor to be incorrectly seated causing a faulty signal or no signal at all.

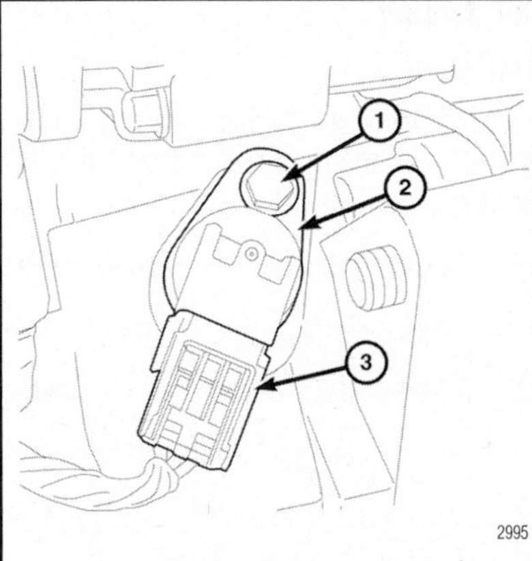

Fig. 232 Camshaft Position (CMP) sensor component location (2), attaching bolt (1), and electrical connector (3)—3.5L engine

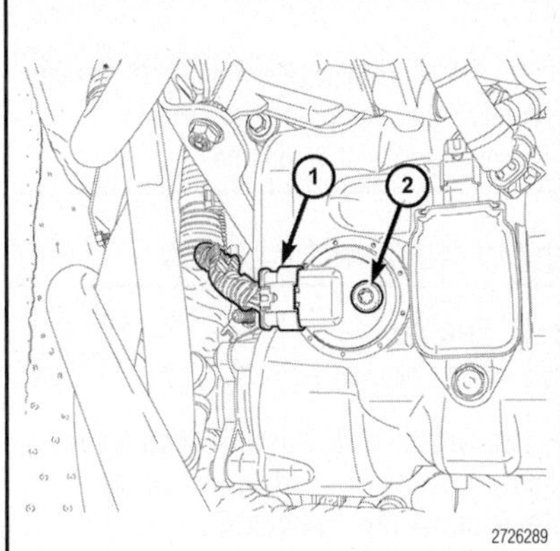

Fig. 233 Camshaft Position (CMP) sensor component location, attaching bolt (2), and electrical connector (1)—3.6L engine

8. Lubricate the sensor O-ring.
9. Install the CMP sensor and mounting bolt and tighten to 80 inch lbs. (9 Nm).
10. Connect the electrical connector to the camshaft position sensor.
11. Install the negative battery cable. Refer to Battery, removal & installation.
12. Install the air cleaner to the throttle body hose.
13. Connect the inlet air temperature sensor electrical connector.

Rear

See Figure 231.

1. Before servicing the vehicle, refer to the Precautions Section.
2. Disconnect the negative battery cable. Refer to Battery, removal & installation.
3. Disconnect the electrical connector at the sensor.
4. Remove the nut retaining the heat shield.
5. Pull the heat shield out to uncover the sensor.
6. Remove the mounting bolt.
7. Remove the sensor.

To install:

⁂ WARNING

Install the Camshaft Position (CMP) sensor utilizing a twisting motion. Make sure the CMP sensor is fully seated. Do not drive the CMP sensor into the bore with the mounting screw. This may cause the CMP sensor to be incorrectly seated causing a faulty signal or no signal at all.

8. Lubricate the sensor O-ring.
9. Install the CMP sensor and mounting bolt and tighten to 80 inch lbs. (9 Nm).
10. Connect the electrical connector to the camshaft position sensor.
11. Install the heat shield onto the mounting stud.
12. Install the heat shield retaining nut and tighten.
13. Connect the electrical connector.
14. Connect the negative battery cable. Refer to Battery, removal & installation.

3.5L Engine

See Figure 232.

1. Before servicing the vehicle, refer to the Precautions Section.
2. Disconnect and isolate the negative battery cable at the battery. Refer to Battery, removal & installation.
3. Disconnect the electrical connector from the Camshaft Position (CMP) sensor.
4. Remove the bolt and the CMP sensor.

To install:

⁂ WARNING

Install the Camshaft Position (CMP) sensor utilizing a twisting motion. Make sure the CMP sensor is fully seated. Do not drive the CMP sensor into the bore with the mounting screw. This may cause the CMP sensor to be incorrectly seated causing a faulty signal or no signal at all.

➡If reinstalling the sensor, check the sensor O-ring for damage and replace if necessary. Lubricate the O-ring with clean engine oil before installing the sensor.

5. Push the CMP sensor into the timing belt cover with a twisting motion until fully seated.
6. While holding the sensor in this position, install and tighten the retaining bolt to 106 inch lbs. (12 Nm).
7. Connect and lock the electrical connector to the CMP sensor.
8. Connect the negative battery cable and tighten the nut to 45 inch lbs. (5 Nm). Refer to Battery, removal & installation.

➡The Cam/Crank Variation Relearn procedure must be performed anytime there has been a repair/replacement made to a powertrain system, for example: flywheel, valvetrain, camshaft and/or crankshaft sensors or components. Refer to Powertrain Control Module (PCM), Powertrain Verification Test.

3.6L Engine

See Figures 233 and 234.

➡The Camshaft Position (CMP) sensors are located at the rear of the cylinder head covers and are bolted to the cylinder head.

⁂ WARNING

The magnetic timing wheels must not come in contact with magnets (pickup tools, trays, etc.) or any other strong magnetic field. This may destroy the timing wheels ability to correctly relay the camshaft position to the camshaft position sensor.

1. Before servicing the vehicle, refer to the Precautions Section.
2. Disconnect and isolate the negative battery cable. Refer to Battery, removal & installation.

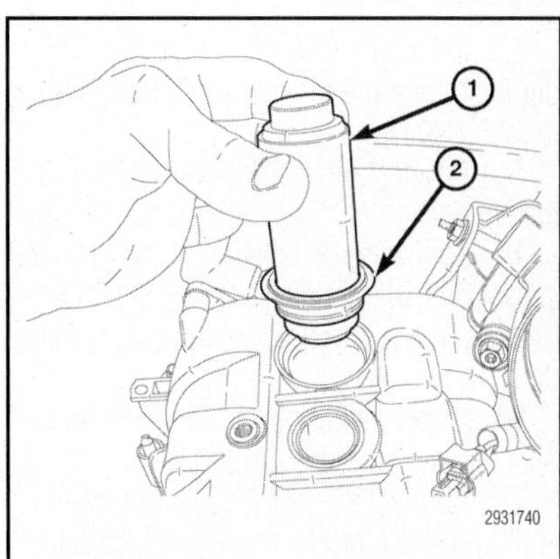

Fig. 234 Using the Cam Sensor/Spark Plug Tube Seal Installer 10256 (1) to install the CMP sensor seal (2) to the cylinder head cover—3.6L engine

3. Remove the air cleaner body. Refer to Air Cleaner, removal & installation.

4. If removing the LH CMP sensor, first remove the upper intake manifold. Refer to Intake Manifold, removal & installation.

➡If removing both RH and LH CMP sensors, mark the sensors so they can be installed in their original locations.

5. Disconnect the electrical connector from the CMP sensor.

6. Loosen the sensor mounting bolt.

7. Pull the sensor and mounting bolt from the cylinder head cover.

To install:

8. Clean out the CMP sensor mounting bolt hole in the cylinder head.

9. The CMP sensor seal can be reused if not damaged.

10. If required, install a new CMP sensor seal in the cylinder head cover:

   a. Lubricate the CMP sensor seal inner and outer diameters with clean engine oil.

   b. Place the CMP sensor seal on the Cam Sensor/Spark Plug Tube Seal Installer 10256.

   c. Push the seal into the cylinder head cover until the base of the seal is seated.

   d. Remove the tool.

➡A properly installed CMP sensor seal will have a 0.06–0.08 inch (1.5–2.0mm) gap between the cylinder head cover and the seal upper flange.

11. The sensor mounting bolt O-ring can be reused if not damaged.

12. Apply a small amount of engine oil to the sensor mounting bolt O-ring.

➡If both RH and LH CMP sensors where removed, install them into their original locations.

13. Install the CMP sensor to the cylinder head. Tighten the mounting bolt to 80 inch lbs. (9 Nm).

14. Connect the electrical connector to the sensor.

15. Following installation of the LH CMP sensor, install the upper intake manifold. Refer to Intake Manifold, removal & installation.

16. Install the air cleaner body. Refer to Air Cleaner, removal & installation.

17. Connect the negative battery cable and tighten the nut to 45 inch lbs. (5 Nm). Refer to Battery, removal & installation.

➡The Cam/Crank Variation Relearn procedure must be performed using the scan tool anytime there has been a repair/replacement made to a powertrain system, for example: flywheel, valvetrain, camshaft and/or crankshaft sensors or components. Refer to Powertrain Control Module (PCM), Powertrain Verification Test.

CRANKSHAFT POSITION (CKP) SENSOR

LOCATION

2.4L Engine

See Figure 235.

The Crankshaft Position (CKP) sensor is located at the rear of the cylinder block, near the transaxle.

3.5L Engine

See Figure 236.

The Crankshaft Position (CKP) sensor is located on the driver side of the vehicle, above the differential housing. The bottom of the sensor sits above the driveplate.

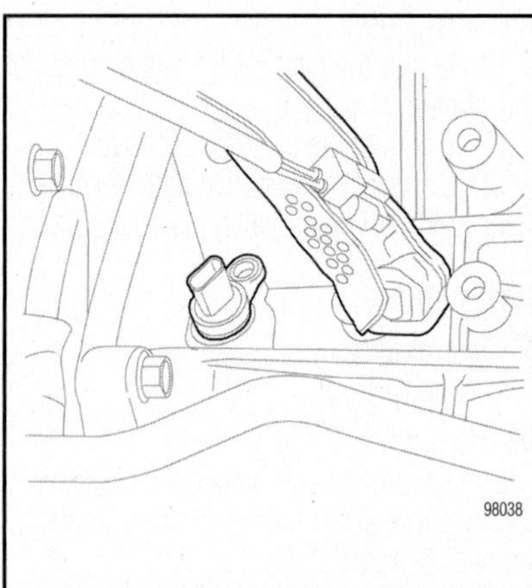

Fig. 235 Crankshaft Position (CKP) sensor component location—2.4L engine

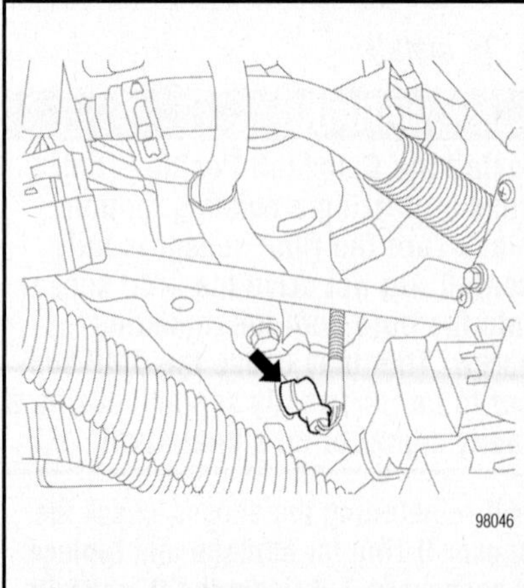

Fig. 236 Crankshaft Position (CKP) sensor component location—3.5L engine

3.6L Engine

See Figure 237.

The Crankshaft Position (CKP) sensor is mounted into the right rear side of the cylinder block.

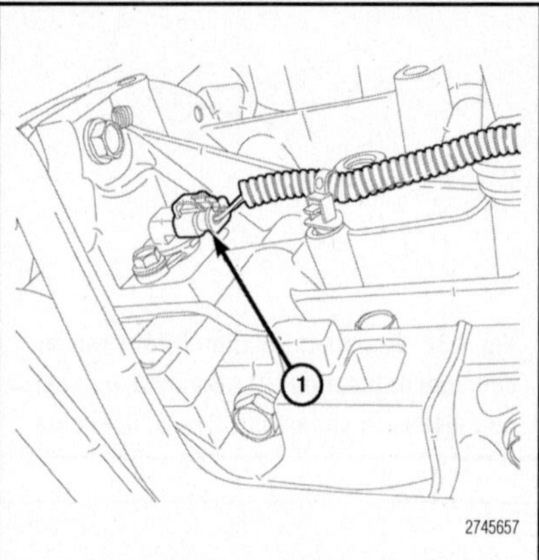

Fig. 237 Crankshaft Position (CKP) sensor component location and electrical connector (1)—3.6L engine

REMOVAL & INSTALLATION

2.4L Engine

See Figure 235.

➡The Crankshaft Position Sensor is located at the rear of the cylinder block, near the transaxle.

1. Before servicing the vehicle, refer to the Precautions Section.

2. Disconnect and isolate the negative battery cable. Refer to Battery, removal & installation.

3. Raise and safely support the vehicle.

4. Remove the heat shield retaining bolt.

5. Remove the heat shield.

6. Unlock and disconnect the electrical connector from the crankshaft position sensor.

7. Remove the crankshaft position sensor bolt.

8. Remove the sensor.

To install:

9. Check the O-ring for damage and lubricate the O-ring with engine oil before installing the sensor.

10. Use a twisting motion when installing the sensor.

11. Install and tighten the crankshaft position sensor bolt to 80 inch lbs. (9 Nm).

12. Connect and lock the electrical connector to the crankshaft position sensor.

13. Install the heat shield and retaining bolt.

14. Lower the vehicle.

15. Connect the negative battery cable and tighten the nut to 45 inch lbs. (5 Nm). Refer to Battery, removal & installation.

3.5L Engine

See Figure 236.

➡The Crankshaft Position (CKP) sensor is located on the driver side of the vehicle, above the differential housing. The bottom of the sensor sits above the driveplate.

1. Before servicing the vehicle, refer to the Precautions Section.
2. Disconnect and isolate the negative battery cable.
3. Unlock and disconnect the electrical connector from the CKP.
4. Remove the CKP sensor mounting screw and the CKP sensor.

To install:

➡If reinstalling the sensor, check the sensor O-ring for damage and replace if necessary. Lubricate the O-ring with clean engine oil before installing the sensor.

5. Push the CKP sensor into the transaxle case with a twisting motion until fully seated.

⁂ WARNING

Before tightening the sensor mounting bolt, be sure the sensor is completely flush to the mounting surface. If the sensor is not flush, damage to the sensor mounting tang may result.

6. While holding the sensor in this position, install and tighten the retaining bolt to 106 inch lbs. (12 Nm).
7. Connect and lock the electrical connector to the CKP sensor.
8. Connect the negative battery cable and tighten the nut to 45 inch lbs. (5 Nm).

➡The Cam/Crank Variation Relearn procedure must be performed anytime there has been a repair/replacement made to a powertrain system, for example: flywheel, valvetrain, camshaft and/or crankshaft sensors or components. Refer to Powertrain Control Module (PCM), Powertrain Verification Test.

3.6L Engine

See Figure 237.

➡The Crankshaft Position (CKP) sensor is mounted into the right rear side of the cylinder block.

1. Before servicing the vehicle, refer to the Precautions Section.
2. Disconnect and isolate the negative battery cable.
3. Raise and safely support the vehicle.
4. Push back the heat shield from the CKP sensor.
5. Disconnect the electrical connector from the CKP sensor.
6. Remove the sensor mounting bolt.
7. Carefully twist the sensor from the cylinder block.

To install:

8. The CKP sensor O-ring can be reused if not damaged.
9. Apply a small amount of engine oil to the sensor O-ring.
10. Clean out the CKP sensor mounting bolt hole in the engine block.
11. Install the sensor into the engine block with a slight rocking and twisting action.

⁂ WARNING

Before tightening the CKP sensor mounting bolt, be sure the sensor is completely flush to the cylinder block. If the CKP sensor is not flush, damage to the sensor mounting tang may result.

12. Install the mounting bolt and tighten to 106 inch lbs. (12 Nm).
13. Connect the electrical connector to the sensor.
14. Position the heat shield over the CKP sensor.
15. Lower the vehicle.
16. Connect the negative battery cable and tighten the nut to 45 inch lbs. (5 Nm).

➡The Cam/Crank Variation Relearn procedure must be performed using the scan tool anytime there has been a repair/replacement made to a powertrain system, for example: flywheel, valvetrain, camshaft and/or crankshaft sensors or components. Refer to Powertrain Control Module (PCM), Powertrain Verification Test.

ENGINE COOLANT TEMPERATURE (ECT) SENSOR

LOCATION

2.4L Engine

See Figures 238 and 239.

The Engine Coolant Temperature (ECT) sensor is mounted to the coolant adapter or to the engine block.

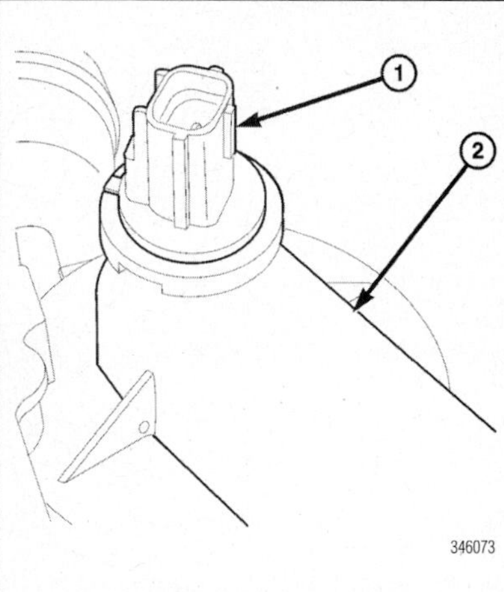

Fig. 238 Engine Coolant Temperature (ECT) sensor component location (1) and coolant adapter (2) shown (coolant adapter mounted)—2.4L engine

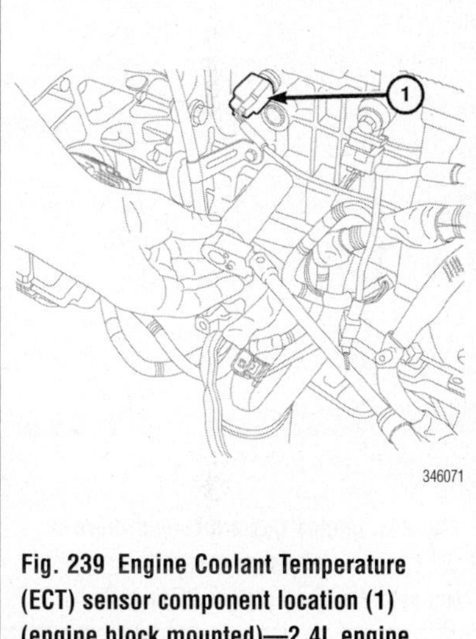

Fig. 239 Engine Coolant Temperature (ECT) sensor component location (1) (engine block mounted)—2.4L engine

3.5L Engine

See Figure 240.

3.6L Engine

See Figure 241.

➡The Engine Coolant Temperature (ECT) sensor on the 3.6L engine is installed into a water jacket at the rear of the cylinder head on the left side of the engine.

REMOVAL & INSTALLATION

2.4L Engine

Coolant Adapter Mounted

See Figure 242.

1. Before servicing the vehicle, refer to the Precautions Section.

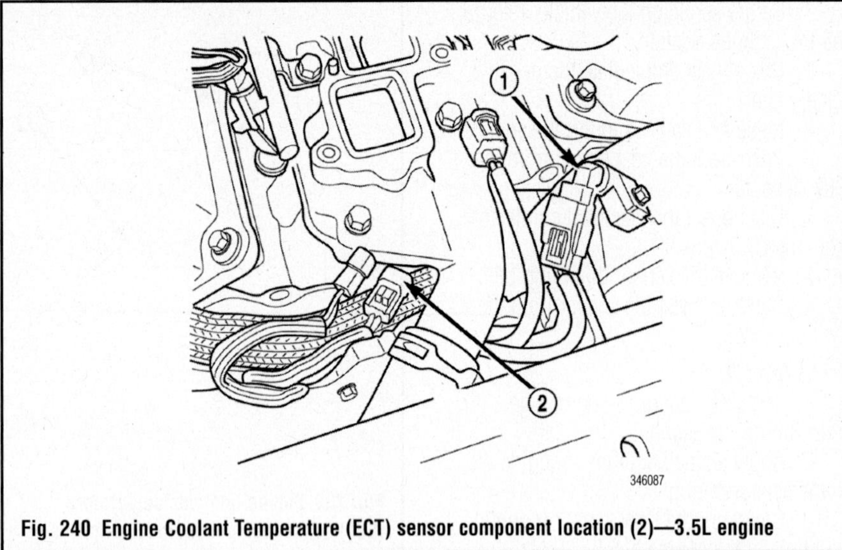

Fig. 240 Engine Coolant Temperature (ECT) sensor component location (2)—3.5L engine

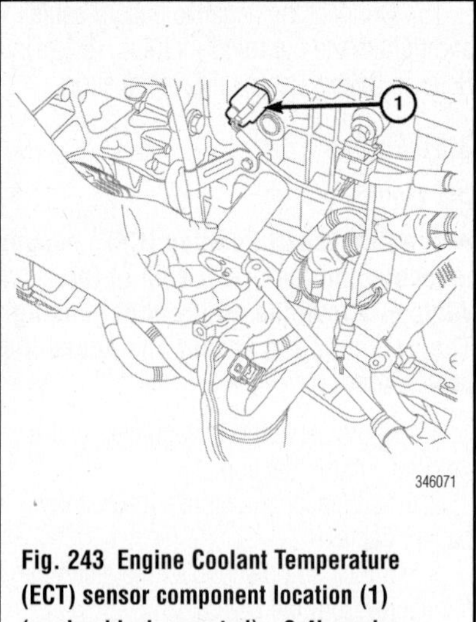

Fig. 243 Engine Coolant Temperature (ECT) sensor component location (1) (engine block mounted)—2.4L engine

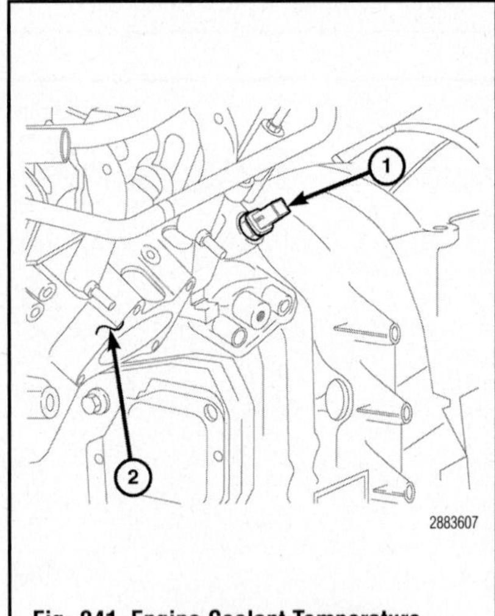

Fig. 241 Engine Coolant Temperature (ECT) sensor component location (1) on left cylinder head (2)—3.6L engine

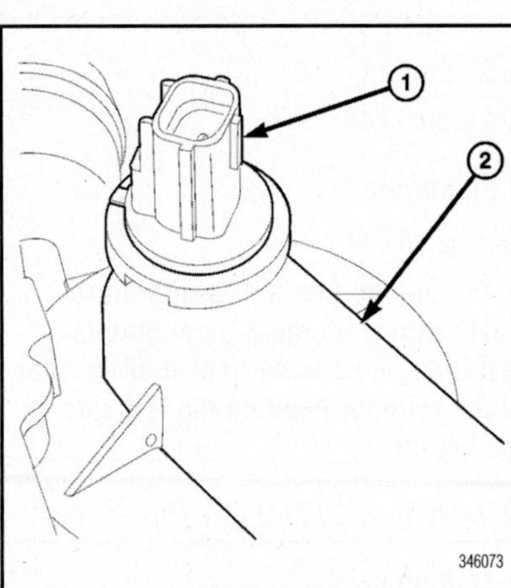

Fig. 242 Engine Coolant Temperature (ECT) sensor component location (1) and coolant adapter (2) shown (coolant adapter mounted)—2.4L engine

2. Disconnect the negative battery cable. Refer to Battery, removal & installation.
3. Partially drain the cooling system below the level of the Engine Coolant Temperature (ECT) sensor.
4. Disconnect the ECT sensor electrical connector.
5. Remove the ECT sensor by pressing the locking tab and twisting the sensor counter clockwise.

To install:

6. Install the ECT sensor. Make sure the coolant sensor is locked in place.
7. Connect the ECT sensor electrical connector.
8. Fill the cooling system. Refer to Engine Coolant, Drain & Refill Procedure.
9. Connect the negative battery cable. Refer to Battery, removal & installation.

Engine Block Mounted

See Figure 243.

1. Before servicing the vehicle, refer to the Precautions Section.
2. Disconnect the negative battery cable. Refer to Battery, removal & installation.
3. Partially drain the cooling system below the level of the Engine Coolant Temperature (ECT) sensor.
4. Disconnect the ECT sensor electrical connector.
5. Remove the ECT sensor.

To install:

6. Install the ECT sensor. Tighten the sensor to 14 ft. lbs. (19 Nm).
7. Connect the ECT sensor electrical connector.
8. Fill the cooling system. Refer to Engine Coolant, Drain & Refill Procedure.
9. Connect the negative battery cable. Refer to Battery, removal & installation.

3.5L Engine

See Figure 240.

1. Before servicing the vehicle, refer to the Precautions Section.
2. Disconnect the negative battery cable. Refer to Battery, removal & installation.
3. Partially drain the cooling system.
4. With the engine cold, disconnect the Engine Coolant Temperature (ECT) sensor electrical connector.
5. Remove the ECT sensor.

To install:

6. Install the ECT sensor and tighten to 20 ft. lbs. (28 Nm).
7. Attach the electrical connector to the ECT sensor.
8. Connect the negative battery cable. Refer to Battery, removal & installation.
9. Fill the cooling system. Refer to Engine Coolant, Drain & Refill Procedure.

3.6L Engine

See Figure 241.

➡The Engine Coolant Temperature (ECT) sensor on the 3.6L engine is installed into a water jacket at the rear of the cylinder head on the left side of the engine.

⁂ CAUTION

Hot, pressurized coolant can cause injury by scalding.

➡Do not waste reusable coolant. If the solution is clean, drain the coolant into a clean container for reuse.

1. Before servicing the vehicle, refer to the Precautions Section.
2. Partially drain the cooling system.
3. Disconnect the electrical connector from the ECT sensor.
4. Remove the ECT sensor from the cylinder head.

To install:

5. Apply MOPAR® thread sealant with PFTE to the ECT sensor threads.
6. Install the ECT sensor to the cylinder head.
7. Tighten the ECT sensor to 97 inch lbs. (11 Nm).
8. Connect the electrical connector to the ECT sensor.
9. Fill the cooling system. Refer to Engine Coolant, Drain & Refill Procedure.

HEATED OXYGEN SENSOR (HO2S)

LOCATION

2.4L Engine

See Figure 244.

3.5L Engine

See Figures 245 and 246.

3.6L Engine

See Figure 247.

REMOVAL & INSTALLATION

2.4L Engine

Upstream Oxygen Sensor (1/1)

See Figure 248.

CAUTION

The exhaust manifold, exhaust pipes, and catalytic converter(s) become very hot during engine operation. Allow the engine to cool before removing the oxygen sensor(s). Failure to allow the engine to cool before removal may result in personal injury.

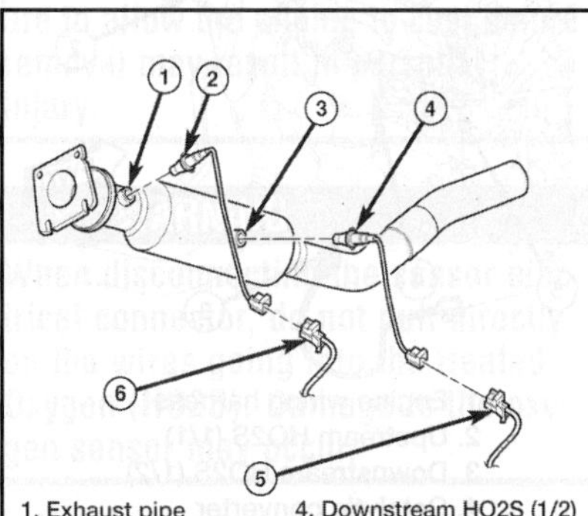

Fig. 244 Heated Oxygen (HO2S) sensor and related component locations—2.4L engine

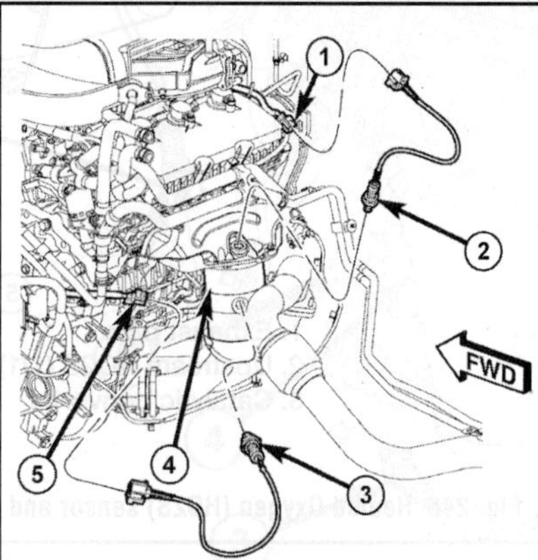

Fig. 245 Heated Oxygen (HO2S) sensors and related component locations (bank 1)—3.5L engine

WARNING

When disconnecting the sensor electrical connector, do not pull directly on the wires going into the Heated Oxygen Sensor (HO2S). Damage to the oxygen sensor may occur.

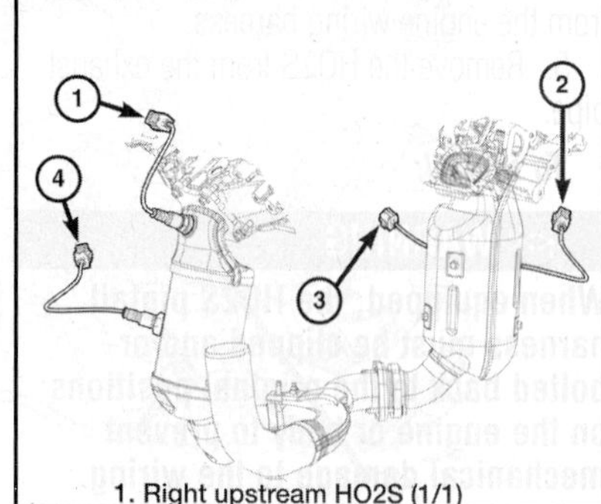

Fig. 247 Heated Oxygen (HO2S) sensors and related component locations—3.6L engine

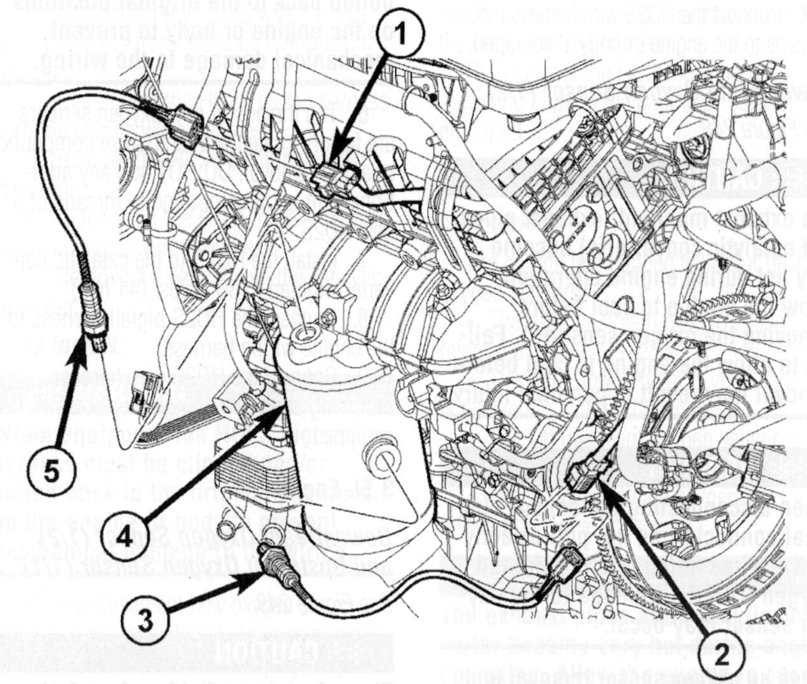

Fig. 246 Heated Oxygen (HO2S) sensors and related component locations (bank 2)—3.5L engine

3.5L Engine

See Figure 257.

3.6L Engine

See Figure 258.

REMOVAL & INSTALLATION

2.4L Engine

See Figure 259.

1. Before servicing the vehicle, refer to the Precautions Section.
2. Disconnect and isolate the negative battery cable. Refer to Battery, removal & installation.
3. Disconnect the electrical connector from the Manifold Absolute Pressure (MAP) sensor.
4. Remove the screw from the MAP sensor.
5. Remove the MAP sensor.

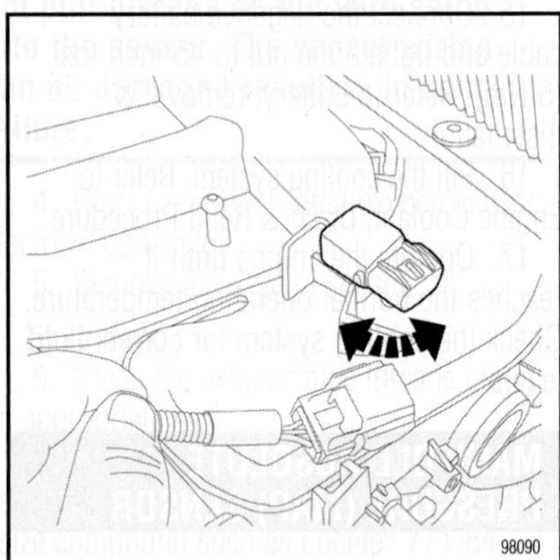

Fig. 257 Manifold Absolute Pressure (MAP) sensor component location—3.5L engine

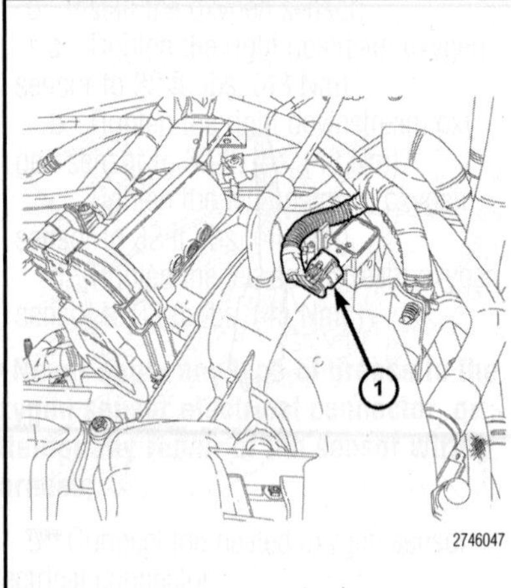

Fig. 258 Manifold Absolute Pressure (MAP) sensor component location and electrical connection (1)—3.6L engine

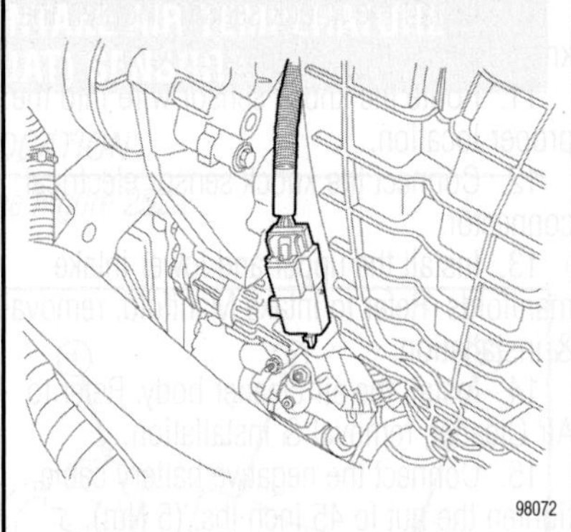

Fig. 259 Manifold Absolute Pressure (MAP) sensor wire and component location—2.4L engine

To install:

6. Install the MAP sensor to the intake manifold. Tighten the screw to 40 inch lbs. (5 Nm).
7. Connect the electrical connector to the MAP sensor.
8. Install the negative battery cable and tighten the nut to 45 inch lbs. (5 Nm). Refer to Battery, removal & installation.

3.5L Engine

See Figure 257.

1. Before servicing the vehicle, refer to the Precautions Section.
2. Disconnect and isolate the negative battery cable. Refer to Battery, removal & installation.
3. Disconnect the electrical connector from the MAP sensor.
4. Rotate the MAP sensor and lift to remove.

To install:

5. Install the MAP sensor.
6. Rotate the MAP sensor into position.
7. Attach the electrical connector to the MAP sensor.
8. Connect the negative battery cable, tighten the nut to 45 inch lbs. (5 Nm). Refer to Battery, removal & installation.

3.6L Engine

See Figure 258.

1. Before servicing the vehicle, refer to the Precautions Section.
2. Disconnect and isolate the negative battery cable. Refer to Battery, removal & installation.
3. Remove the engine cover.
4. Unlock and disconnect the electrical connector from the MAP sensor.
5. Rotate the MAP sensor ¼ turn counterclockwise and pull the sensor straight up and out of the upper intake manifold.
6. The MAP sensor O-ring can be reused if not damaged.

To install:

7. Apply a small amount of engine oil to the MAP sensor O-ring.
8. Install the MAP sensor into the upper intake manifold and rotate ¼ turn clockwise.
9. Connect and lock the electrical connector to the sensor.
10. Install the engine cover.
11. Connect the negative battery cable and tighten the nut to 45 inch lbs. (5 Nm). Refer to Battery, removal & installation.

MASS AIR FLOW (MAF) SENSOR

LOCATION

See Figure 260.

REMOVAL & INSTALLATION

See Figure 260.

1. Before servicing the vehicle, refer to the Precautions Section.
2. Disconnect the Mass Air Flow (MAF) sensor electrical connector.
3. Remove the constant tension clamps, securing the MAF sensor.
4. Remove the MAF sensor from the hoses.

To install:

5. Note the arrow direction on the sensor and correctly position the sensor to the hoses.
6. Install the constant tension clamps, to secure the MAF sensor to the hoses.
7. Connect the MAF sensor electrical connector.

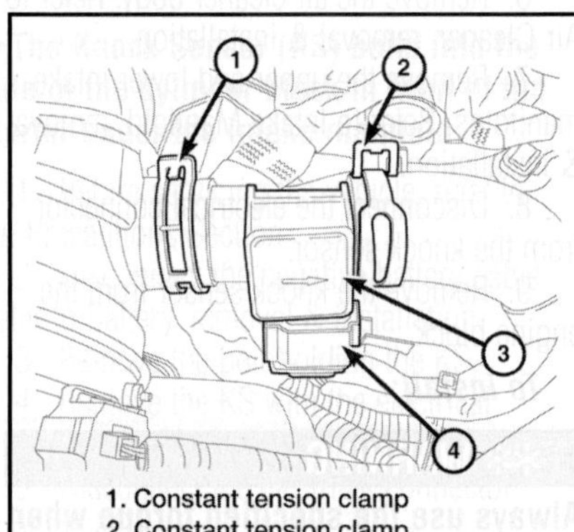

1. Constant tension clamp
2. Constant tension clamp
3. Mass Air Flow (MAF) sensor
4. MAF sensor electrical connector

Fig. 260 Mass Air Flow (MAF) sensor component location

POWERTRAIN CONTROL MODULE (PCM)

LOCATION

See Figure 261.

REMOVAL & INSTALLATION

See Figure 261.

⁂ WARNING

To avoid possible voltage spike damage to the Powertrain Control Module (PCM), the ignition key must be OFF and the negative battery cable disconnected before unplugging the PCM connectors.

➡Use the scan tool to reprogram the new PCM with the original Vehicle Identification Number (VIN) and the original vehicle mileage. If this step is not done, a Diagnostic Trouble Code (DTC) may be set.

1. Before servicing the vehicle, refer to the Precautions Section.
2. Disconnect and isolate the negative battery cable at the battery. Refer to Battery, removal & installation.
3. Unlock and disconnect the 2 electrical connectors at the PCM.
4. Remove the 4 bolts holding the PCM to the bracket and remove the PCM from the vehicle.

To install:

5. Install the PCM to the bracket with the 4 bolts.
6. Install and lock the 2 electrical connectors to the PCM.
7. Connect the negative battery cable and tighten the nut to 45 inch lbs. (5 Nm).

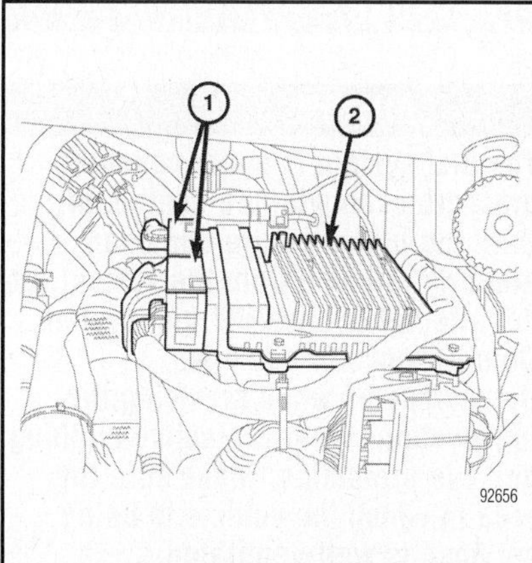

Fig. 261 View of the Powertrain Control Module (PCM) (2) and electrical connectors (1) component location

8. Use the scan tool to reprogram new PCM with the original VIN and original vehicle mileage.

PCM Programming

The secret key is an ID code that is unique to each WIN. This code is programmed and stored in the WIN, the PCM, and each ignition key transponder chip. When the PCM or WIN is replaced, it is necessary to program the Secret Key Code into the new module using a diagnostic scan tool. Follow the programming steps outlined in the diagnostic scan tool for PCM REPLACED, WIN REPLACED, or TIPM REPLACED under MISCELLANEOUS FUNCTIONS for the WIRELESS CONTROL MODULE menu item as appropriate.

Programming the PCM or WIN is done using a diagnostic scan tool and a PIN to enter secure access mode. If three attempts are made to enter secure access mode using an incorrect PIN, secure access mode will be locked out for one hour. To exit this lockout mode, turn the ignition to the RUN position for one hour and then enter the correct PIN. Be certain that all accessories are turned OFF. Also, monitor the battery state and connect a battery charger if necessary.

Read all notes and cautions for programming procedures.

1. Before servicing the vehicle, refer to the Precautions Section.
2. Connect a battery charger to the vehicle.
3. Connect the scan tool.
4. Have a unique vehicle PIN readily available before running the routine.
5. The ignition key should be in the RUN position.
6. Select "ECU View".
7. Select "WIN Wireless Control".
8. Select "Miscellaneous Functions".
9. Select "PCM Replaced".
10. Enter the PIN when prompted.
11. Verify the correct information.
12. Cycle the ignition key after a successful routine completion.

POWERTRAIN VERIFICATION TEST

The Cam/Crank Variation Relearn must be performed any time there has been a repair or replacement made to a powertrain system. For example: flywheel, valvetrain, camshaft sensors and components, or crankshaft sensors and components.

If the PCM has been replaced and the correct VIN and mileage have not been programmed, a DTC will set in the ABS Module, Airbag Module and the Wireless Control Module (WCM) or Wireless Ignition Node (WIN).

If the vehicle is equipped with a Sentry Key Remote Entry, Secret Key data must be updated. Using the scan tool, program the Secret Key information into the PCM using the PCM replaced function under the WCM menu.

If this vehicle is equipped with an Electronic Throttle Control system and the APP Sensors, PCM or Throttle Body Assembly have been replaced, use the scan tool to perform the ETC RELEARN function.

When replacing an O2 Sensor, the PCM RAM memory must be cleared, either by disconnecting the PCM C1 connector or momentarily disconnecting the Battery negative terminal.

After completing the Powertrain Verification Test, the Transmission Verification Test must be performed.

1. Before servicing the vehicle, refer to the Precautions Section.
2. The PCM learns the characteristics of each O2 heater element and these learned values should be cleared when installing a new O2 sensor. The vehicle may experience drive-ability issues if this is not performed.
3. Inspect the vehicle to make sure that all engine components are properly installed and connected. Reassemble and reconnect components as necessary.
4. Connect the scan tool to the data link connector.
5. Make sure the fuel tank has at least ¼ tank of fuel. Turn off all accessories.
6. If the Catalyst was replaced, with the scan tool select "Catalyst Replaced" under the Miscellaneous Menu Option.
7. If a repair/replacement was made to a powertrain system, with the scan tool select the "Cam Crank Relearn" procedure under PCM Miscellaneous Menu Option.
8. If a Comprehensive Component DTC was repaired, perform steps 10–12. If a Major OBDII Monitor DTC was repaired, skip those steps and continue verification.
9. After the ignition has been off for at least 10 seconds, restart the vehicle and run 2 minutes.
10. Using the scan tool, monitor the appropriate pre-test enabling conditions until all conditions have been met. Once the conditions have been met, switch screen to the appropriate OBDII monitor, (there will be audible beeps when the monitor is running).
11. If the repaired OBDII DTC has reset or was seen in the monitor while on the road test, the repair is not complete. Check for any related technical service bulletins or flash updates and perform the appropriate diagnostic procedure.
12. If the conditions cannot be duplicated, erase all DTCs with the scan tool.
13. If another DTC has set, follow the path specified for that DTC.

THROTTLE POSITION SENSOR (TPS)

LOCATION

The Throttle Position (TP) sensor is located on the throttle body.

REMOVAL & INSTALLATION

The Throttle Position Sensor (TPS) is integral to the electronic throttle body. Refer to Throttle Body, removal & installation.

VEHICLE SPEED SENSOR (VSS)

LOCATION

40TE Transaxle

See Figure 262.

62TE Transaxle

See Figure 263.

REMOVAL & INSTALLATION

40TE Transaxle

See Figure 262.

1. Before servicing the vehicle, refer to the Precautions Section.
2. Disconnect the battery negative cable. Refer to Battery, removal & installation.
3. Raise and safely support the vehicle.
4. Disconnect the output speed sensor connector.

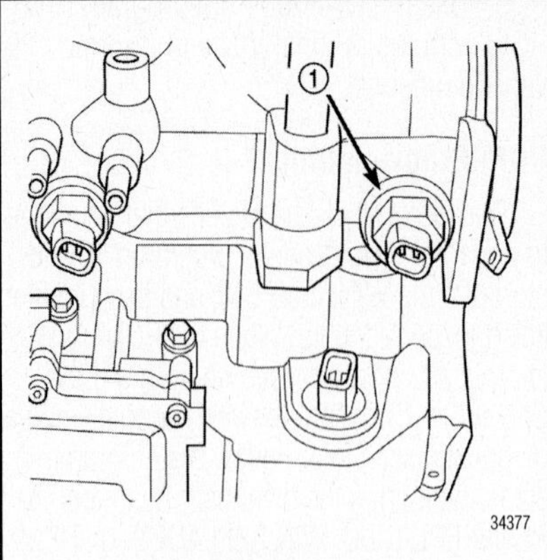

Fig. 262 Output speed sensor component location (1)—40TE transaxle

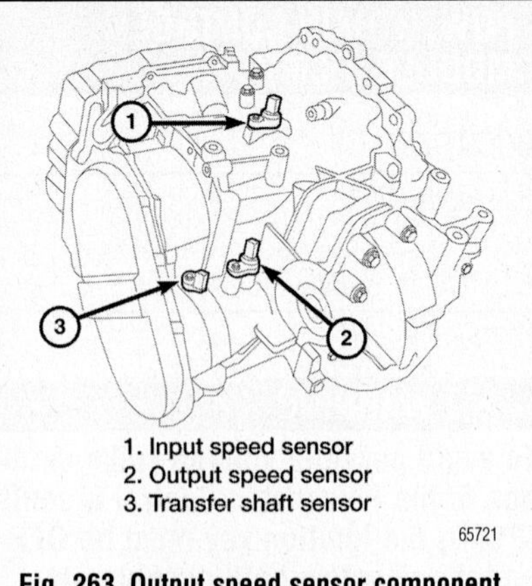

Fig. 263 Output speed sensor component location—62TE transaxle

5. Unscrew and remove the output speed sensor.
6. Inspect the speed sensor O-ring and replace if necessary.

To install:

7. Verify the O-ring is installed into position.
8. Install and tighten the output speed sensor to 20 ft. lbs. (27 Nm).
9. Connect the output speed sensor connector.
10. Connect the battery negative cable. Refer to Battery, removal & installation.

62TE Transaxle

See Figure 263.

1. Before servicing the vehicle, refer to the Precautions Section.
2. Unplug the electrical connector at the output speed sensor.
3. Remove the bolt at the output speed sensor.
4. Pull up on the output speed sensor to remove.

To install:

5. Install a new O-ring on the output speed sensor.
6. Install the output speed sensor into the case.
7. Install the bolt at the output speed sensor and tighten to 106 inch lbs. (12 Nm).
8. Engage the electrical connector to the output speed sensor.

FUEL — GASOLINE FUEL INJECTION SYSTEM

FUEL SYSTEM SERVICE PRECAUTIONS

Safety is the most important factor when performing not only fuel system maintenance but any type of maintenance. Failure to conduct maintenance and repairs in a safe manner may result in serious personal injury or death. Maintenance and testing of the vehicle's fuel system components can be accomplished safely and effectively by adhering to the following rules and guidelines.

- To avoid the possibility of fire and personal injury, always disconnect the negative battery cable unless the repair or test procedure requires that battery voltage be applied.
- Always relieve the fuel system pressure prior to disconnecting any fuel system component (injector, fuel rail, pressure regulator, etc.), fitting or fuel line connection. Exercise extreme caution whenever relieving fuel system pressure to avoid exposing skin, face and eyes to fuel spray. Please be advised that fuel under pressure may penetrate the skin or any part of the body that it contacts.
- Always place a shop towel or cloth around the fitting or connection prior to loosening to absorb any excess fuel due to spillage. Ensure that all fuel spillage (should it occur) is quickly removed from engine surfaces. Ensure that all fuel soaked cloths or towels are deposited into a suitable waste container.
- Always keep a dry chemical (Class B) fire extinguisher near the work area.
- Do not allow fuel spray or fuel vapors to come into contact with a spark or open flame.
- Always use a back-up wrench when loosening and tightening fuel line connection fittings. This will prevent unnecessary stress and torsion to fuel line piping.
- Always replace worn fuel fitting O-rings with new Do not substitute fuel hose or equivalent where fuel pipe is installed.

Before servicing the vehicle, make sure to also refer to the precautions in the beginning of this section as well.

RELIEVING FUEL SYSTEM PRESSURE

**** CAUTION**

The fuel system is under constant pressure even with the engine off. Until the fuel pressure has been properly relieved from the system, do not attempt to open the fuel system. Do not smoke or use open flames/sparks when servicing the fuel system. Wear protective clothing and eye protection. Make sure the area in which the vehicle is being serviced is well-ventilated.

1. Before servicing the vehicle, refer to the Precautions Section.
2. Remove the fuel fill cap.

3. Remove the fuel pump fuse from the Totally Integrated Power Module (TIPM). For location of the fuse, refer to the label on the underside of the TIPM cover.

4. Start and run the engine until it stalls.

5. Attempt restarting the engine until it will no longer run.

6. Turn the ignition key to the OFF position.

7. Place a rag or towel below the fuel line quick-connect fitting at the fuel rail.

8. Disconnect the quick-connect fitting at the fuel rail.

9. When the repair is complete, reconnect the fuel fittings and return the fuel pump fuse to the TIPM.

10. One or more Diagnostic Trouble Codes (DTCs) may have been stored in the PCM memory due to fuel pump fuse removal. A diagnostic scan tool must be used to erase a DTC.

FUEL FILTER

REMOVAL & INSTALLATION

A lifetime fuel filter is serviced as part of the fuel pump module. Refer to Fuel Pump, removal & installation.

FUEL INJECTORS

REMOVAL & INSTALLATION

2.4L Engine

See Figures 264 and 265.

⁂ CAUTION

There is a risk of injury to eyes and skin from contact with fuel. Wear protective clothing and eye protection. There is also a risk of poisoning from inhaling and swallowing fuel. Pour fuel only into appropriately marked and approved containers. Failure to follow these instructions may result in possible serious or fatal injury.

1. Before servicing the vehicle, refer to the Precautions Section.

2. Release the fuel system pressure. Refer to Relieving Fuel System Pressure.

3. Disconnect and isolate the negative battery cable. Refer to Battery, removal & installation.

4. Disconnect the electrical connectors from the fuel injectors.

5. Disconnect the fuel line connection at the fuel rail.

6. Remove the fuel line from the fuel rail.

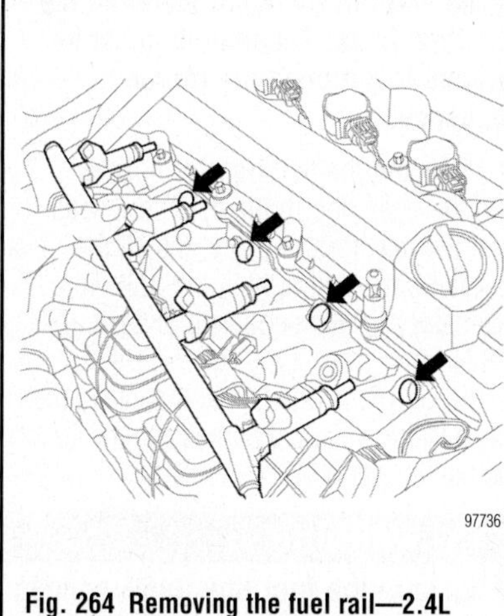

Fig. 264 Removing the fuel rail—2.4L engine

7. Remove the wire harness from the fuel rail mounting studs.

8. Remove the 2 bolts from the fuel rail at the lower manifold.

9. Remove the fuel rail.

10. Remove the clip holding the fuel injector to the fuel rail.

11. Remove the fuel injector clip and the fuel injector from the fuel rail.

To install:

12. Apply a light coating of clean engine oil to the upper O-ring of the fuel injector.

13. Install the injector into the cup on the fuel rail.

14. Install the retaining clip.

15. Apply a light coating of clean engine oil to the O-ring on the nozzle end of each injector.

16. Insert the fuel injector nozzles into the openings in the lower intake manifold. Seat the injectors in place.

17. Tighten the fuel rail mounting screws to 20 ft. lbs. (27 Nm).

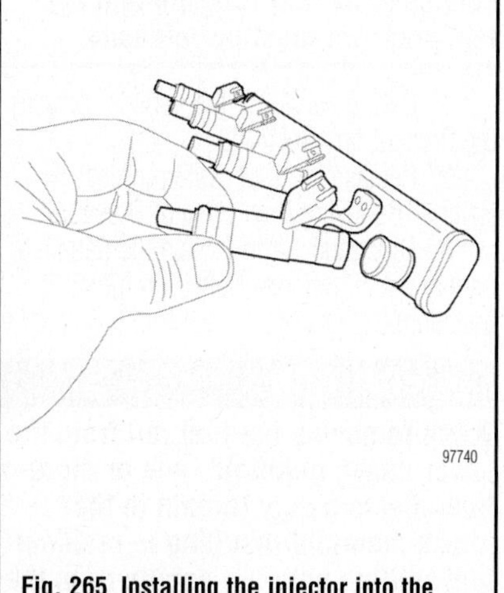

Fig. 265 Installing the injector into the cup on the fuel rail

18. Install the wiring harness clips to the fuel rail mounting studs.

19. Connect the electrical connectors to the fuel injectors.

20. Connect the fuel supply tube to the fuel rail.

21. Connect the negative battery cable and tighten the nut to 45 inch lbs. (5 Nm).

22. Use the scan tool to pressurize the fuel system. Check for leaks.

3.5L Engine

See Figures 266 and 267.

⁂ CAUTION

The fuel system is under constant pressure (even with the engine OFF). Before servicing any part on the fuel system, the fuel system pressure must be released.

1. Before servicing the vehicle, refer to the Precautions Section.

2. Release the fuel system pressure. Refer to Relieving Fuel System Pressure.

3. Disconnect and isolate the negative battery cable. Refer to Battery, removal & installation.

4. Remove the upper intake manifold. Refer to Intake Manifold, removal & installation.

5. Disconnect the quick connect fuel line from the fuel rail.

➡Mark the fuel injector electrical harness connectors with the correct corresponding cylinder numbers.

6. Disconnect all the fuel injector electrical connectors from the fuel injectors.

7. Remove the fuel rail mounting bolts from the fuel rail and the lower intake manifold.

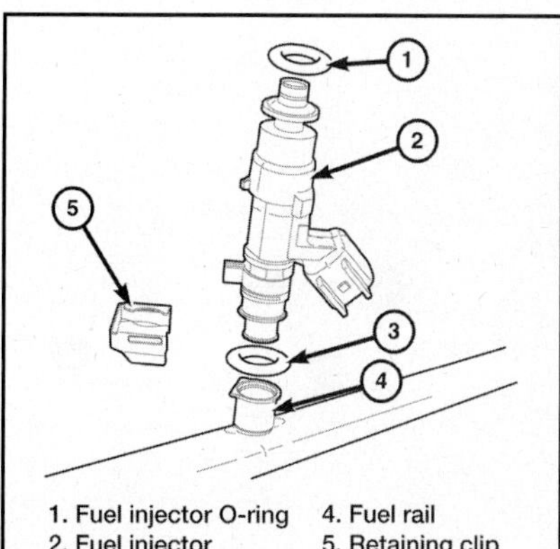

Fig. 266 Exploded view of fuel injector—3.5L engine

➡**Gently rock the fuel rail and injectors back and forth to loosen the seals on the fuel injectors from the cylinder heads.**

⁂ WARNING

Do Not use excessive force or prying tools to remove the fuel rail and injectors. Damage to the fuel rail and injectors may result.

8. Lift the fuel rail straight up off of the cylinder heads.
9. Drain any excess fuel from the fuel rail into an approved fuel storage container.

➡**When replacing individual fuel injectors, each fuel injector must be installed to its original position. Mark or tag each fuel injector to identify the correct cylinder.**

10. Remove the retaining clips from the fuel injectors at the fuel rail.

To install:

➡**Inspect each O-ring seal on all the fuel injectors, replace O-ring seals if any damage is noted. Note the fuel injector O-rings are color coded. The Blue colored O-ring is for the fuel rail side and the Green colored O-ring is for the cylinder head side.**

11. Install and lubricate each of the fuel injector O-rings, with a light drop of clean engine oil.
12. Install all of the fuel injectors to the fuel rail, then install the retaining clip to the fuel rail.
13. Inspect each fuel injector for proper installation. Note how the retaining clip secures the fuel injector to the fuel rail.

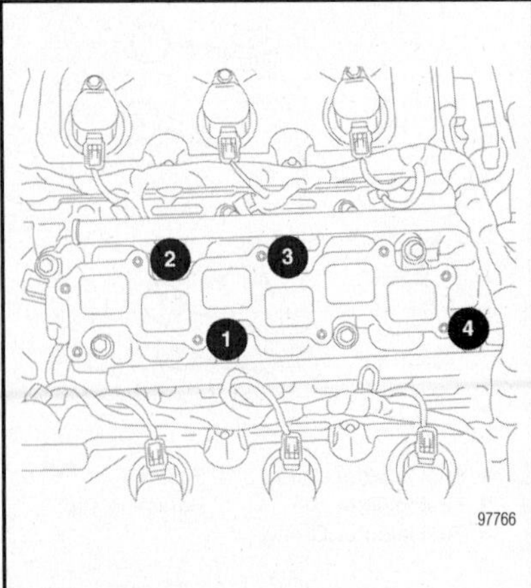

Fig. 267 Fuel rail bolt tightening sequence—3.5L engine

➡**The fuel rail bolts are lower intake manifold bolts. These bolts must be torqued in a mandatory torque sequence.**

14. Insert the fuel injector nozzles into the openings in the cylinder heads. Seat the injectors in place. Install the fuel rail bolts and tighten the bolts in a mandatory torque sequence to 21 ft. lbs. (28 Nm).
15. Correctly position and connect the fuel injector electrical harness connectors to the fuel injectors.

⁂ WARNING

Make sure the fuel line quick connector is connected properly. Failure to connect the fuel line correctly may result in a fuel leak at the rail assembly. Fuel leaked onto a hot engine may ignite resulting in damage to the vehicle.

16. Connect the quick connect fuel line to the fuel rail.
17. Connect all of the fuel injector electrical connectors to the fuel injectors.
18. Install the upper intake manifold. Refer to Intake Manifold, removal & installation.
19. Connect the negative battery cable, tighten the nut to 45 inch lbs. (5 Nm). Refer to Battery, removal & installation.
20. Use the scan tool ASD Fuel System Test to pressurize the fuel system. Check for leaks.

3.6L Engine

See Figures 268 and 269.

⁂ CAUTION

The fuel system is under constant pressure even with engine off. Before servicing the fuel rail, the fuel system pressure must be released.

1. Before servicing the vehicle, refer to the Precautions Section.
2. Release the fuel system pressure. Refer to Relieving Fuel System Pressure.
3. Disconnect and isolate the negative battery cable. Refer to Battery, removal & installation.

⁂ CAUTION

When removing the fuel rail from the lower intake manifold, one or more fuel injectors may remain in the intake manifold resulting in residual fuel spilling onto the engine from the fuel rail.

4. Remove the air inlet hose.
5. Remove the upper intake manifold. Refer to Intake Manifold, removal & installation.
6. Remove the bolts securing the fuel rail and remove the fuel rail with the fuel injectors.
7. Remove the fuel injectors from the fuel rail.
8. Remove the fuel injectors from the lower intake manifold.
9. Remove and discard all of the fuel injector O-ring seals.

To install:

10. Clean out the fuel injector bores in the lower intake manifold.
11. Lightly lubricate the new O-ring seals with engine oil and install them on the fuel injector.
12. Install the fuel injectors to the fuel rail.
13. Install the fuel rail to the lower intake manifold with the 4 bolts tightened in sequence to 62 inch lbs. (7 Nm).

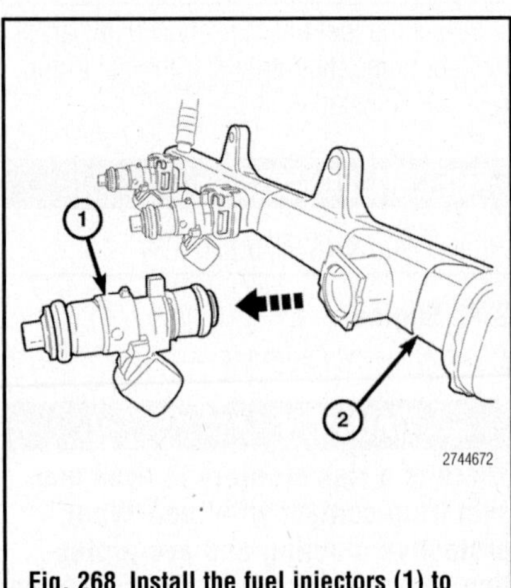

Fig. 268 Install the fuel injectors (1) to the fuel rail (2)—3.6L engine

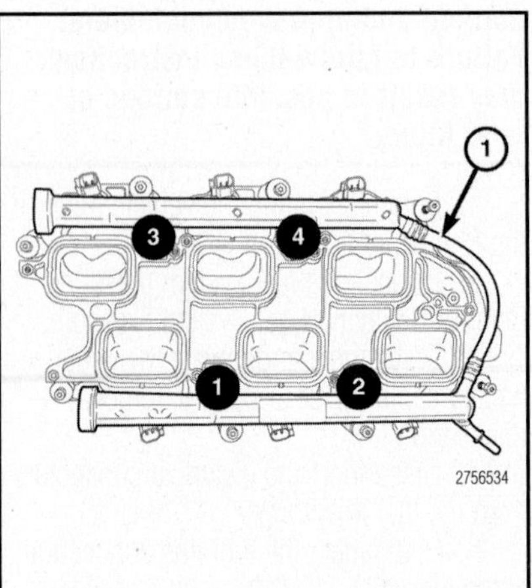

Fig. 269 Fuel rail (1) bolt tightening sequence—3.6L engine

14. Connect the fuel injector electrical connectors.

15. Connect the fuel supply hose to the fuel rail.

16. Install the insulator to the 2 alignment posts on the top of the LH cylinder head cover.

17. Install the upper intake manifold. Refer to Intake Manifold, removal & installation.

18. Install the air inlet hose.

19. Connect the negative battery cable and tighten the nut to 45 inch lbs. (5 Nm). Refer to Battery, removal & installation.

20. Start the engine and check for leaks.

FUEL PUMP

REMOVAL & INSTALLATION

Main Fuel Pump Module

See Figures 270 and 271.

**** CAUTION**

There is a risk of injury to eyes and skin from contact with fuel. Wear protective clothing and eye protection. There is also a risk of poisoning from inhaling and swallowing fuel. Pour fuel only into appropriately marked and approved containers. Failure to follow these instructions may result in possible serious or fatal injury.

**** CAUTION**

The fuel system is under constant high pressure even with engine OFF. Until the fuel pressure has been properly released from the system, do not attempt to open the fuel system. Do not smoke or use open flames/sparks when servicing the fuel system. Make sure the area in which the vehicle is being serviced is well-ventilated. Failure to comply may result in serious or fatal injury.

1. Before servicing the vehicle, refer to the Precautions Section.

2. Drain and remove the fuel tank. Refer to Fuel Tank, removal & installation.

➡Prior to removing the main fuel pump module, use compressed air to remove any accumulated dirt and debris from around the fuel tank opening.

3. Position the lock-ring remover/installer 9340 into the notches on the outside edge of the fuel pump lock-ring.

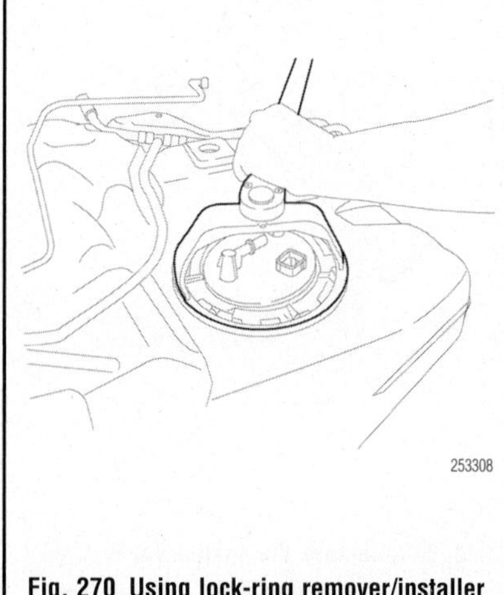

Fig. 270 Using lock-ring remover/installer 9340 on the fuel pump lock-ring

4. Install a ½ inch drive breaker bar into the lock-ring remover/installer 9340.

5. Rotate the breaker bar counterclockwise and remove the lock-ring.

6. Mark the main fuel pump module orientation.

**** WARNING**

The fuel pump module reservoir does not empty out when the tank is drained. The fuel in the reservoir will spill out when the module is removed. Do not spill fuel into the interior of the vehicle.

7. Raise the main fuel pump module out of the fuel tank using caution not to spill fuel inside the vehicle.

8. Tip the main fuel pump module and drain enough fuel from the main fuel pump module reservoir to gain access to the internal fuel line without spilling fuel into the interior of the vehicle.

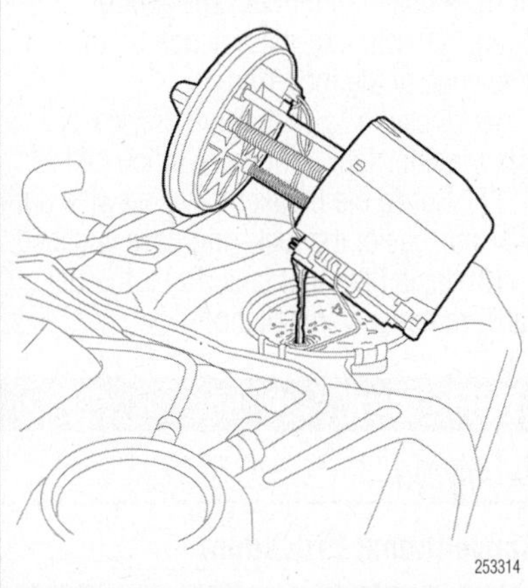

Fig. 271 Tip the main fuel pump module and drain the fuel from the module reservoir

9. If equipped with AWD, disconnect the internal fuel line from the main fuel pump module.

10. Remove the main fuel pump module from the fuel tank using caution not to bend the float arm.

11. Remove and discard the rubber O-ring seal.

To install:

➡Whenever the fuel pump module is serviced, the rubber O-ring seal must be replaced.

12. Clean the rubber O-ring seal area of the fuel tank and install a new rubber O-ring seal.

13. If equipped with AWD, connect the internal fuel line to the main fuel pump module.

14. Lower the main fuel pump module into the fuel tank using caution not to bend the float arm.

➡The main fuel pump module must be properly located in the fuel tank for the fuel level gauge to work properly.

15. Align the rubber O-ring seal and rotate the main fuel pump module to the orientation marks noted during removal. This step must be performed for the fuel level gauge to work properly.

16. Position the lock-ring over the top of the main fuel pump module.

17. Position the lock-ring remover/installer 9340 into the notches on the outside edge of the lock-ring.

18. Install a ½ inch drive breaker bar into the lock-ring remover/installer 9340.

19. Rotate the breaker bar clockwise until all 7 notches of the lock-ring have engaged.

20. Install the fuel tank. Refer to Fuel Tank, removal & installation.

Auxiliary Fuel Pump Module (AWD Models)

See Figures 272 and 273.

**** CAUTION**

There is a risk of injury to eyes and skin from contact with fuel. Wear protective clothing and eye protection. There is also a risk of poisoning from inhaling and swallowing fuel. Pour fuel only into appropriately marked and approved containers. Failure to follow these instructions may result in possible serious or fatal injury.

CAUTION

The fuel system is under constant high pressure even with engine OFF. Until the fuel pressure has been properly released from the system, do not attempt to open the fuel system. Do not smoke or use open flames/sparks when servicing the fuel system. Make sure the area in which the vehicle is being serviced is well-ventilated. Failure to comply may result in serious or fatal injury.

1. Before servicing the vehicle, refer to the Precautions Section.
2. Drain and remove the fuel tank. Refer to Fuel Tank, removal & installation.
3. Mark the auxiliary fuel pump module orientation.

➡Prior to removing the auxiliary fuel pump module, use compressed air to remove any accumulated dirt and debris from around the fuel tank opening.

4. Position the Fuel Tank Module Wrench 10189 into the notches on the outside edge of the lock-ring.
5. Install a ½ inch drive breaker bar into the Fuel Tank Module Wrench 10189.
6. Rotate the breaker bar counterclockwise and remove the lock-ring.
7. Raise the auxiliary fuel pump module and disconnect the internal fuel line.
8. Remove the auxiliary fuel pump module from the fuel tank using caution not to bend the float arm.
9. Remove and discard the rubber O-ring seal.

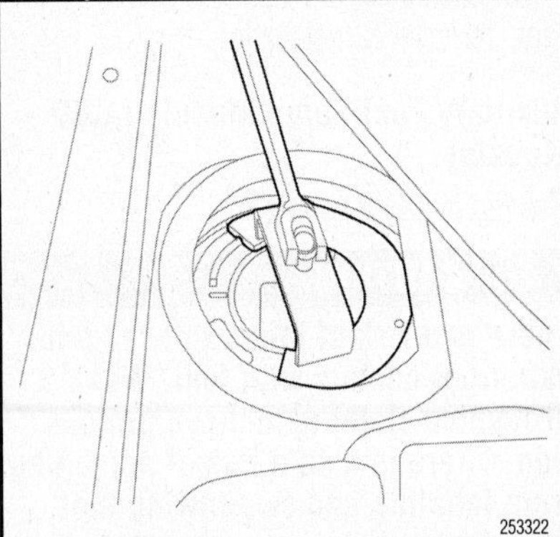

Fig. 272 Position the Fuel Tank Module Wrench 10189 into the notches on the outside edge of the fuel pump module lock-ring

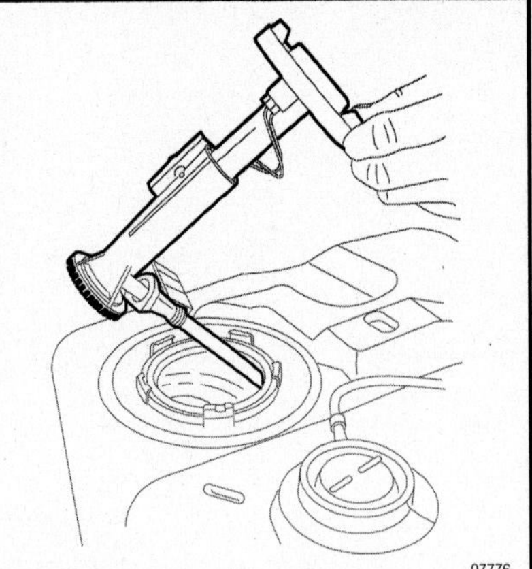

Fig. 273 Remove the auxiliary fuel pump module and disconnect the internal fuel line

To install:

➡Whenever the fuel pump module is serviced, the rubber O-ring seal must be replaced.

10. Clean the rubber O-ring seal area of the fuel tank and install a new rubber O-ring seal.
11. Connect the internal fuel line to the auxiliary fuel pump module.
12. Lower the auxiliary fuel pump module into the fuel tank using caution not to bend the float arm.

➡The auxiliary fuel pump module must be properly located in the fuel tank for the fuel level gauge to work properly.

13. Align the rubber O-ring seal and rotate the auxiliary fuel pump module to the orientation marks noted during removal. This step must be performed for the fuel gauge to work properly.
14. Position the lock-ring over the top of the auxiliary fuel pump module.
15. Position the Fuel Tank Module Wrench 10189 into the notches on the outside edge of the lock-ring.
16. Install a ½ inch drive breaker bar into the Fuel Tank Module Wrench 10189.
17. Rotate the breaker bar clockwise until all 7 notches of the lock-ring have engaged.
18. Install the fuel tank. Refer to Fuel Tank, removal & installation.

FUEL TANK

DRAINING

Conventional Procedure

CAUTION

The fuel system is under constant high pressure even with engine OFF. Until the fuel pressure has been properly released from the system, do not attempt to open the fuel system. Do not smoke or use open flames/sparks when servicing the fuel system. Wear protective clothing and eye protection. Make sure the area in which the vehicle is being serviced is well-ventilated and free of flames/sparks. Failure to comply may result in serious or fatal injury.

CAUTION

There is a risk of poisoning from inhaling and swallowing fuel. Pour fuel only into appropriately marked OSHA approved containers. Wear protective clothing. There is also a risk of injury to eyes and skin from contact with fuel.

➡Due to a one-way check valve installed into the fuel fill fitting at the tank, the tank cannot be drained at the fuel fill cap.

1. Before servicing the vehicle, refer to the Precautions Section.
2. Release the fuel system pressure. Refer to Relieving Fuel System Pressure.
3. Disconnect the fuel supply line from the fuel rail.
4. Install the appropriate fuel line adapter fitting from the Decay Tool, Fuel 8978A to the fuel supply line. Route the opposite end of this hose to an OSHA approved fuel storage tank such as the JohnDow Gas Caddy® 320-FC-P30-A, or equivalent.

➡The activation of the fuel pump module may time out and need to be restarted several times to completely drain the fuel tank.

5. Using a diagnostic scan tool, activate the fuel pump module until the fuel tank has been evacuated.

Alternative Procedure

CAUTION

The fuel system is under constant high pressure even with engine OFF. Until the fuel pressure has been properly released from the system, do not attempt to open the fuel system. Do not smoke or use open flames/sparks when servicing the fuel system. Wear protective clothing and eye protection. Make sure the area in which the vehicle is being serviced is well-ventilated and free

of flames/sparks. Failure to comply may result in serious or fatal injury.

⁂ CAUTION

There is a risk of poisoning from inhaling and swallowing fuel. Pour fuel only into appropriately marked OSHA approved containers. Wear protective clothing. There is also a risk of injury to eyes and skin from contact with fuel.

➡Due to a one-way check valve installed into the fuel fill fitting at the tank, the tank cannot be drained at the fuel fill cap.

1. Before servicing the vehicle, refer to the Precautions Section.
2. Release the fuel system pressure. Refer to Relieving Fuel System Pressure.

➡If the electric fuel pump is not operating, the fuel tank must be drained through the fuel pump module opening of the fuel tank.

3. Disconnect and isolate the negative battery cable. Refer to Battery, removal & installation.
4. Remove the fuel pump module. Refer to Fuel Pump, removal & installation.
5. Position a ⅜ inch hose into the fuel pump module opening of the fuel tank.
6. Attach the opposite end of this hose to an OSHA approved fuel storage tank such as the JohnDow Gas Caddy® 320-FC-P30-A, or equivalent.
7. Using the gas caddy, evacuate the fuel tank.

REMOVAL & INSTALLATION

AWD Models

See Figure 274.

⁂ CAUTION

The fuel system is under constant pressure even with engine OFF. Until the fuel pressure has been properly relieved from the system, do not attempt to open the fuel system. Do not smoke or use open flames/sparks when servicing the fuel system. Wear protective clothing and eye protection. Make sure the area in which the vehicle is being serviced is well-ventilated.

⁂ CAUTION

There is a risk of poisoning from inhaling and swallowing fuel. Pour fuel only into appropriately marked and approved containers. Failure to follow these instructions may result in possible serious or fatal injury.

1. Before servicing the vehicle, refer to the Precautions Section.
2. Release the fuel system pressure. Refer to Relieving Fuel System Pressure.
3. Drain the fuel tank. Refer to Fuel Tank, Draining.
4. Remove the exhaust system muffler.
5. Remove the rear propeller shaft. Refer to Rear Driveshaft, removal & installation.
6. Remove the bolt, 2 nuts, and the splash shield.
7. Disconnect the fuel pump module quick connect fitting from the body mounted fuel line bundle.
8. Disconnect the purge line quick connect fitting from the body mounted fuel line bundle.
9. Disconnect the purge line quick connect fitting from the fuel tank connection.

➡The fuel fill tube vent line quick connect fitting is located at the rear of the fuel tank near the parking brake cable.

10. Disconnect the fuel fill tube vent line and remove it from the fuel tank quick connect fitting.

⁂ CAUTION

Support the fuel tank with a transmission jack or equivalent. Use straps to secure the fuel tank to the jack. Failure to properly support and secure the fuel tank during removal may cause fuel to spill or the fuel tank to fall from the jack.

11. Use a transmission jack to support the fuel tank.
12. Remove the fuel tank strap bolts and straps.
13. Partially lower the tank to gain access to the pump module and fuel level sensor electrical connectors.
14. Disconnect the electrical connector at the fuel pump module.
15. Continue lowering the tank for removal.
16. If the fuel tank is to be replaced, remove the fuel pump module from the tank. Refer to Fuel Pump, removal & installation.
17. If the fuel tank is to be replaced, remove the 3 fasteners and the fuel tank shield from the fuel tank.

To install:

18. Install the fuel tank shield to the fuel tank.
19. Install the fuel pump module to the fuel tank. Refer to Fuel Pump, removal & installation.
20. Position the fuel tank onto a transmission jack or equivalent and raise the fuel tank into vehicle position.
21. Connect the electrical connector to the fuel pump module and fuel level sensor.
22. Install the fuel tank straps and bolts. Tighten the bolts to 35 ft. lbs. (48 Nm).
23. Install the fuel tube vent line to the fuel tank quick connect fitting.
24. Install the purge line quick connect fitting to the fuel tank connection.
25. Install the fuel filler tube to the fuel tank. Tighten the hose clamp to 27 inch lbs. (3 Nm).

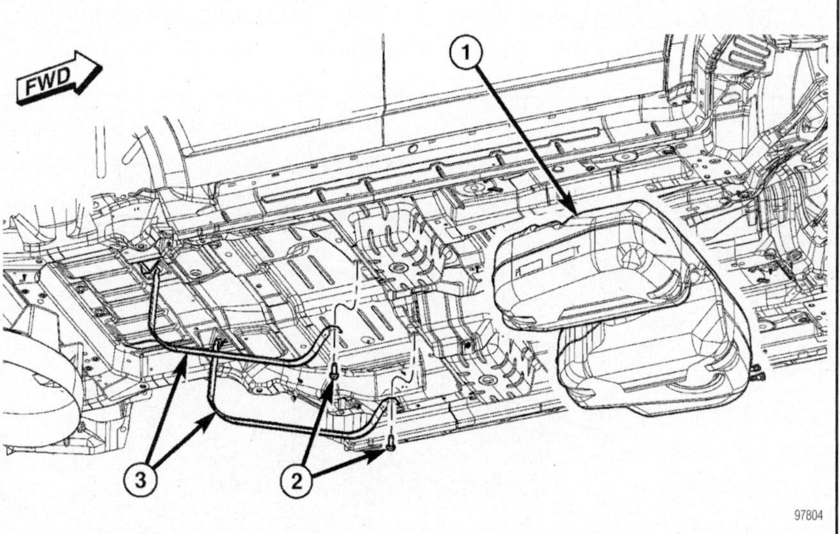

Fig. 274 View of the fuel tank (1), fuel tank straps (3), and strap bolts (2)—AWD models

26. Connect the purge line quick connect fitting to the body mounted fuel line bundle.

27. Connect the fuel pump module quick connect fitting to the body mounted fuel line bundle.

28. Install the splash shield with 1 bolt and 2 nuts.

29. Install the rear propeller shaft. Refer to Rear Driveshaft, removal & installation.

30. Install the exhaust muffler.

31. Connect the negative battery cable and tighten the nut to 45 inch lbs. (5 Nm).

32. Fill the fuel tank. Use the scan tool to pressurize the fuel system. Check for leaks.

FWD Models

See Figure 275.

⁂ CAUTION

The fuel system is under constant pressure even with engine OFF. Until the fuel pressure has been properly relieved from the system, do not attempt to open the fuel system. Do not smoke or use open flames/sparks when servicing the fuel system. Wear protective clothing and eye protection. Make sure the area in which the vehicle is being serviced is well-ventilated.

⁂ CAUTION

There is a risk of poisoning from inhaling and swallowing fuel. Pour fuel only into appropriately marked and approved containers. Failure to follow these instructions may result in possible serious or fatal injury.

1. Before servicing the vehicle, refer to the Precautions Section.

2. Release the fuel system pressure. Refer to Relieving Fuel System Pressure.

3. Drain the fuel tank. Refer to Fuel Tank, Draining.

4. Remove the exhaust muffler.

5. Remove the bolt, 2 nuts, and the splash shield.

6. Disconnect the fuel pump module quick connect fitting from the body mounted fuel line bundle.

7. Disconnect the purge line quick connect fitting from the body mounted fuel line bundle.

8. Disconnect the fuel purge line quick connect fitting from the fuel tank connection.

➡The fuel fill tube vent line quick connect fitting is located at the rear of the fuel tank near the parking brake cable.

9. Disconnect the fuel fill tube vent line and remove from the fuel tank quick connect fitting.

⁂ CAUTION

Support the fuel tank with a transmission jack or equivalent. Use straps to secure the fuel tank to the jack. Failure to properly support and secure the fuel tank during removal may cause fuel to spill or the fuel tank to fall from the jack.

10. Use a transmission jack to support the fuel tank.

11. Remove the fuel tank strap bolts and straps.

12. Partially lower the tank to gain access to the pump module electrical connector.

13. Disconnect the electrical connector at the fuel pump module.

14. Continue lowering the tank for removal.

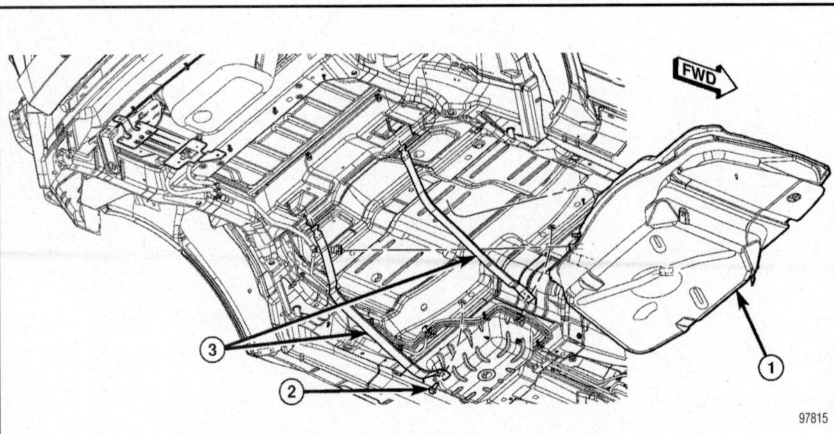

Fig. 275 View of the fuel tank (1), fuel tank straps (3), and strap bolts (2)—FWD models

15. If the fuel tank is to be replaced, remove the fuel pump module from the tank. Refer to Fuel Pump, removal & installation.

16. If the fuel tank is to be replaced, remove the 4 four fasteners and the fuel tank shield from the fuel tank.

To install:

17. Install the fuel tank shield to the fuel tank.

18. Install the fuel pump module to the fuel tank and connect the fuel line. Refer to Fuel Pump, removal & installation.

19. Position the fuel tank onto a transmission jack or equivalent and raise the fuel tank into vehicle position.

20. Connect the electrical connector to the fuel pump module.

21. Install the fuel tank straps and bolts. Tighten the bolts to 35 ft. lbs. (48 Nm).

22. Install the fuel fill tube vent line to the fuel tank quick connect fitting.

23. Install the purge line quick connect fitting to the fuel tank connection.

24. Install the fuel filler tube to the fuel tank. Tighten the hose clamp to 27 inch lbs. (3 Nm).

25. Connect the purge line quick connect fitting to the body mounted fuel line bundle.

26. Connect the fuel pump module quick connect fitting to the body mounted fuel line bundle.

27. Install the splash shield with 1 bolt and 2 nuts.

28. Install the exhaust muffler.

29. Connect the negative battery cable and tighten the nut to 45 inch lbs. (5 Nm).

30. Fill the fuel tank. Use the scan tool to pressurize the fuel system. Check for leaks.

IDLE SPEED

ADJUSTMENT

The idle speed is controlled by the Powertrain Control Module (PCM). No adjustment is necessary.

THROTTLE BODY

REMOVAL & INSTALLATION

2.4L Engine

See Figure 276.

⁂ CAUTION

DO NOT place fingers in or around the throttle body plate. If the throttle body is energized, the throttle plate could move causing personal injury. Always

disconnect the negative battery cable prior to servicing the throttle body.

➡DO NOT move the throttle plate while power is connected to the throttle body. This may cause fault codes to set.

1. Before servicing the vehicle, refer to the Precautions Section.
2. Disconnect and isolate the negative battery cable. Refer to Battery, removal & installation.
3. Remove the throttle body air intake hose.
4. Disconnect the throttle body electrical connector from the throttle body.
5. Remove the throttle body support bracket bolt.
6. Remove the 4 bolts, throttle body bracket, and throttle body from the intake manifold.
7. Inspect the 4 j-nuts for damage or excessive wear, remove if necessary.
8. Inspect the intake manifold-to-throttle body gasket for damage, remove if necessary.

To install:

9. Install a new intake manifold-to-throttle body gasket, if replacement was necessary.
10. Install the 4 new j-nuts, if replacement was necessary.

⁂ WARNING

DO NOT OVER TORQUE. Over tightening can cause damage to the throttle body, gaskets, bolts and/or the intake manifold.

11. Install the throttle body to the intake manifold.
12. Install the throttle body support bracket and bolt and hand tighten.
13. Install the 4 throttle body bolts and hand tighten.

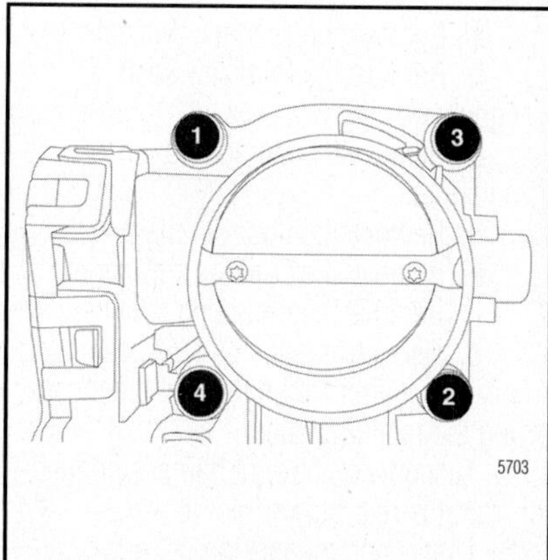

Fig. 276 Throttle body bolt tightening sequence—2.4L engine

⁂ WARNING

The throttle body must be torqued in a mandatory torque sequence.

14. Tighten the bolts in a mandatory torque crisscross pattern sequence to 65 inch lbs. (8 Nm).
15. Tighten the bracket bolt to 18 ft. lbs. (25 Nm).
16. Connect the electrical connector to the throttle body.
17. Install the clean air hose and tighten the clamps to 35 inch lbs. (4 Nm).
18. Install the negative battery cable and tighten the nut to 45 inch lbs. (5 Nm). Refer to Battery, removal & installation.
19. Use a scan tool and clear all fault codes, then perform the ETC RELEARN function.

3.5L Engine

See Figure 277.

⁂ CAUTION

DO NOT place fingers in or around the throttle body plate. If the throttle body is energized, the throttle plate could move causing personal injury. Always disconnect the negative battery cable prior to servicing the throttle body.

➡DO NOT move the throttle plate while power is connected to the throttle body. This may cause fault codes to set.

1. Before servicing the vehicle, refer to the Precautions Section.
2. Disconnect and isolate the negative battery cable at the battery. Refer to Battery, removal & installation.
3. Remove the engine cover.
4. Remove the clean air hose from the throttle body.
5. Disconnect the electrical connector from the throttle body.
6. Remove the nut from the throttle body bracket.
7. Remove the bolt and the throttle body bracket.
8. Remove the bolts, stud, and throttle body from the intake manifold.

To install:

➡Make sure the intake gasket is clean and free of debris. Inspect the intake gasket for damage. Replace as necessary.

⁂ WARNING

DO NOT OVER TORQUE. Over tightening can cause damage to the throttle body, gaskets, bolts and/or the intake manifold.

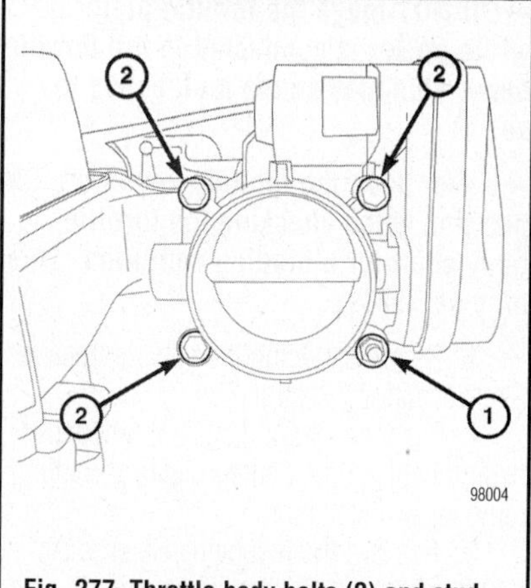

Fig. 277 Throttle body bolts (2) and stud (1) location shown—3.5L engine

9. Install the throttle body, gasket, and bolts to the intake manifold.
10. Install the throttle body and the 3 throttle body bolts, and stud hand tight.

⁂ WARNING

The throttle body must be torqued in a mandatory torque sequence. Tighten in a crisscross pattern to specification.

11. Tighten the 3 bolts and 1 stud in a mandatory torque crisscross pattern sequence to 50 inch lbs. (6 Nm).
12. Install the throttle body bracket, nut, and bolt. Tighten the nut to 106 inch lbs. (12 Nm). Tighten the bolt to 21 ft. lbs. (28 Nm).
13. Connect the electrical connector to the throttle body.
14. Install the clean air hose to the throttle body.
15. Install the engine cover.
16. Connect the negative battery cable, tighten the nut to 45 inch lbs. (5 Nm). Refer to Battery, removal & installation.
17. Use a scan tool and perform the ETC RELEARN function.

3.6L Engine

See Figure 278.

⁂ CAUTION

DO NOT place fingers in or around the throttle body plate. If the throttle body is energized, the throttle plate could move causing personal injury. Always disconnect the negative battery cable prior to servicing the throttle body.

➡DO NOT move the throttle plate while power is connected to the throttle body. This may cause fault codes to set.

➡Never have the ignition key in the ON position when checking the throttle body shaft for a binding condition. This may set DTCs.

1. Before servicing the vehicle, refer to the Precautions Section.
2. Disconnect and isolate the negative battery cable at the battery. Refer to Battery, removal & installation.
3. Remove the resonator. Refer to Air Cleaner, removal & installation.
4. Disconnect the electrical connector from the Electronic Throttle Control (ETC) and disengage the ETC harness from the clip on the throttle body.
5. Remove the 4 throttle body mounting bolts.
6. Remove the throttle body from the upper intake manifold.

To install:

7. Check the condition of the throttle body-to-intake manifold seal. The seal can be reused if not damaged.
8. Clean the mating surfaces of the throttle body and intake manifold.
9. Position the throttle body to the intake manifold.
10. Install the throttle body mounting bolts and tighten in a crisscross pattern sequence to 62 inch lbs. (7 Nm).
11. Connect the electrical connector to the ETC and secure the ETC harness to the clip on the throttle body.
12. Install the resonator. Refer to Air Cleaner, removal & installation.
13. Connect the negative battery cable and tighten the nut to 45 inch lbs. (5 Nm). Refer to Battery, removal & installation.

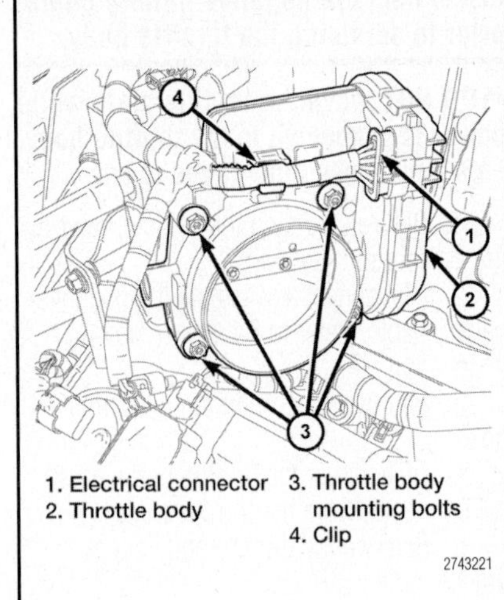

Fig. 278 View of the throttle body—3.6L engine

HEATING & AIR CONDITIONING SYSTEM

BLOWER MOTOR

REMOVAL & INSTALLATION

Front Blower Motor

See Figure 279.

⁂ CAUTION

Disable the airbag system before attempting any steering wheel, steering column, or instrument panel component diagnosis or service. Disconnect and isolate the negative battery (ground) cable, then wait 2 minutes for the airbag system capacitor to discharge before performing further diagnosis or service. This is the only sure way to disable the airbag system. Failure to follow these instructions may result in accidental airbag deployment and possible serious or fatal injury.

➡The blower motor is located on the bottom of the passenger side of the HVAC housing. The blower motor can be removed from the vehicle without having to remove the HVAC housing.

1. Before servicing the vehicle, refer to the Precautions Section.
2. Disconnect and isolate the negative battery cable. Refer to Battery, removal & installation.
3. If equipped, remove the silencer from below the passenger side of the instrument panel.
4. From underneath the instrument panel, disengage the connector lock and disconnect the instrument panel wire harness connector from the blower motor.
5. Remove the 3 screws that secure the blower motor and the wire lead bracket (if equipped) to the bottom of the HVAC housing.
6. Remove the blower motor.

To install:

7. Position the blower motor into the bottom of the HVAC housing.
8. Install the 3 screws that secure the blower motor and the wire lead bracket (if equipped) to the HVAC housing. Tighten the screws to 10 inch lbs. (1 Nm).

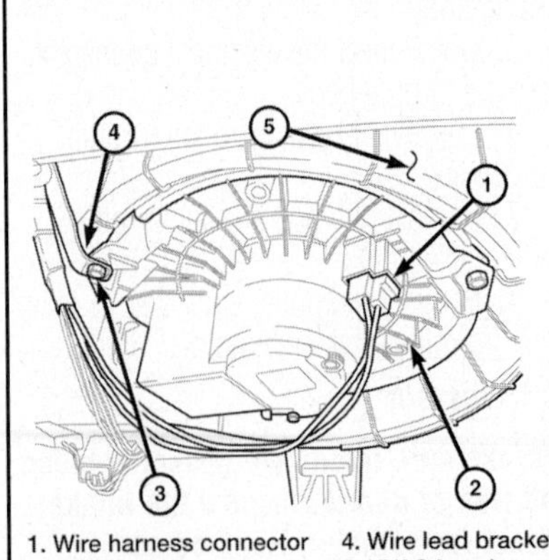

Fig. 279 View of the front blower motor

9. Connect the instrument panel wire harness connector to the blower motor and engage the connector lock.
10. If equipped, install the silencer below the passenger side of the instrument panel.
11. Connect the negative battery cable. Refer to Battery, removal & installation.

Rear Blower Motor

See Figures 280 and 281.

1. Before servicing the vehicle, refer to the Precautions Section.
2. Disconnect and isolate the negative battery cable. Refer to Battery, removal & installation.
3. Remove the right rear quarter trim panel.
   a. Remove the second row seats.
   b. Remove the third row seats, if equipped.
   c. Remove the storage box, if equipped.
   d. Remove the door sill plate.
   e. Remove the D-pillar trim panel.
   f. Remove the mounting fasteners.
   g. Using trim stick C-4755, carefully pry the quarter trim panel out disengaging the retaining clips.
4. Disconnect the wire harness connector from the rear blower motor.
5. Disengage the locking tab and remove the rear blower motor from the rear heater-A/C housing by turning the blower motor counterclockwise.

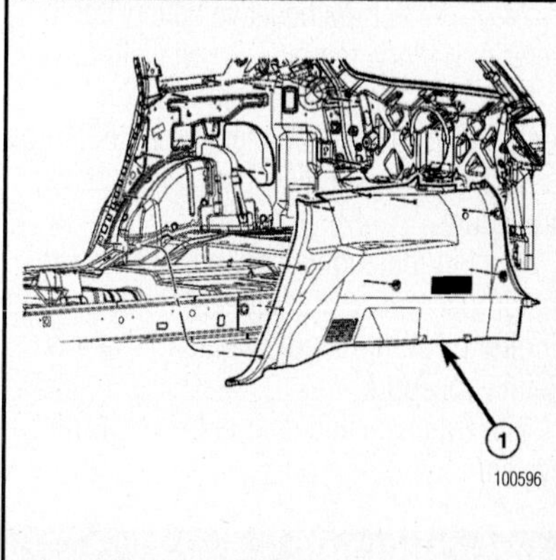

Fig. 280 Right rear quarter trim panel (1) removal

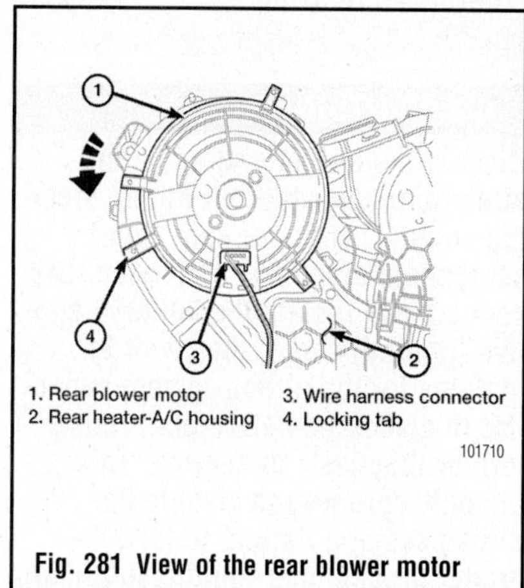

Fig. 281 View of the rear blower motor

To install:

6. Position the rear blower motor into the rear heater-A/C housing and rotate the blower motor clockwise until the blower motor is fully engaged to the housing and the retaining tab is in the locked position.
7. Connect the wire harness connector to the rear blower motor.
8. Install the right rear quarter trim panel.
   a. Install the quarter trim panel.
   b. Install the mounting fasteners.
   c. Install the door sill plate.
   d. Install the D-pillar trim panel.
   e. Install the storage box, if equipped.
   f. Install the third row seats, if equipped.
   g. Install the second row seats.
9. Connect the negative battery cable. Refer to Battery, removal & installation.

HEATER CORE

REMOVAL & INSTALLATION

Front Heater Core

See Figures 282 and 283.

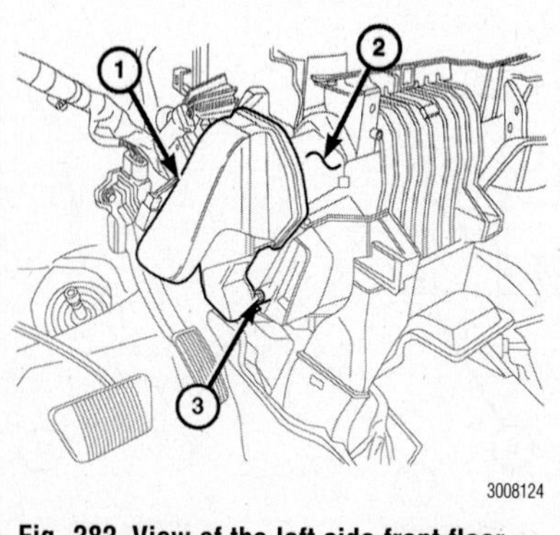

Fig. 282 View of the left side front floor duct (1), HVAC housing (2), and attaching screw (3)

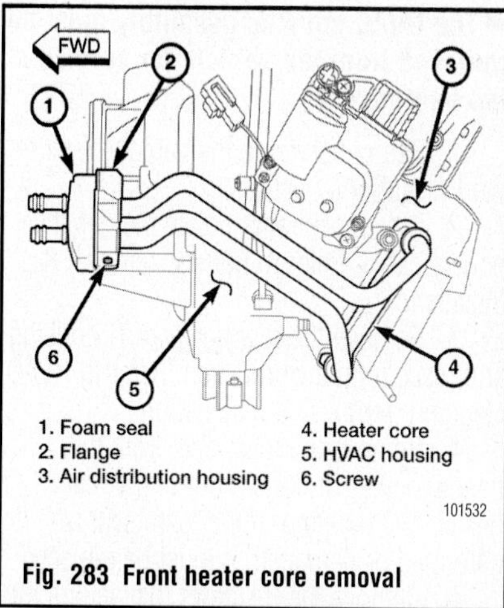

Fig. 283 Front heater core removal

CAUTION

The engine cooling system is designed to develop internal pressures up to 21 psi (145 kPa). Do not remove or loosen the coolant pressure cap, cylinder block drain plugs, radiator drain, radiator hoses, heater hoses, or hose clamps while the engine cooling system is hot and under pressure. Allow the vehicle to cool for a minimum of 15 minutes before opening the cooling system for service. Failure to observe this warning can result in serious burns from the heated engine coolant.

➡The HVAC housing assembly must be removed from the vehicle for service of the heater core.

1. Before servicing the vehicle, refer to the Precautions Section.
2. Remove the HVAC housing assembly and place it on a workbench. Refer to HVAC Housing, removal & installation.
3. Remove the left side front floor duct:
4. Remove the screw that secures the left floor duct to the left side of the HVAC housing.
5. Disconnect the left floor duct from the HVAC housing and remove the duct.
6. Remove the foam seal from the flange located on the front of the HVAC housing.
7. Remove the screw that secures the flange to the front of the HVAC housing and remove the flange.
8. Carefully pull the heater core out of the driver's side of the air distribution housing.

To install:

9. Carefully install the heater core into the side of the air distribution housing.
10. Install the flange that secures the heater core tubes to the front of the HVAC housing.
11. Install the screw that secures the flange to the HVAC housing. Tighten the screw to 10 inch lbs. (1 Nm).

➡If the foam seal for the flange is deformed or damaged, it must be replaced.

12. Install the foam seal onto the flange.
13. Install the left side front floor duct:
    a. Connect the left floor duct to the left side of the HVAC housing. Make sure the duct is fully engaged to the housing.
    b. Install the screw that secures the left floor duct to the HVAC housing. Tighten the screw to 17 inch lbs. (2 Nm).

➡If the heater core is being replaced, flush the cooling system. Refer to Engine Cooling, Engine Coolant, Flushing procedure.

14. Install the HVAC housing assembly. Refer to HVAC Housing, removal & installation.

Rear Heater Core

See Figure 284.

CAUTION

The engine cooling system is designed to develop internal pressures up to 21 psi (145 kPa). Do not remove or loosen the coolant pressure cap, cylinder block drain plugs, radiator drain, radiator hoses, heater hoses, or hose clamps while the engine cooling system is hot and under pressure. Allow the vehicle to cool for a minimum of 15 minutes before opening the cooling system for service. Failure to observe this warning can result in serious burns from the heated engine coolant.

➡The HVAC housing assembly must be removed from the vehicle for service of the heater core.

1. Before servicing the vehicle, refer to the Precautions Section.
2. Disconnect and isolate the negative battery cable. Refer to Battery, removal & installation.
3. Remove the rear heater-A/C housing and place it on a workbench. Refer to HVAC Housing, removal & installation.
4. Remove the foam seal from the flange located at the bottom of the rear heater-A/C housing. If the foam seal is deformed or damaged, it must be replaced.
5. Remove the 3 screws that secure the flange to the bottom of the rear heater-A/C housing and remove the flange.
6. Disconnect the wire harness connector from the rear blend door actuator located on the outboard side of the rear heater-A/C housing.
7. Remove the 2 screws that secure the rear blend door actuator to the rear heater-A/C housing and remove the actuator.
8. Disconnect the wire harness connector from the rear mode door actuator located on the outboard side of the rear heater-A/C distribution housing.
9. Remove the 3 metal retaining clips that secure the rear distribution housing to the rear heater-A/C housing.
10. Release the 5 plastic retaining tabs that secure the rear distribution housing and rear heater-A/C housing together and separate the housings.
11. Remove the screw that secures the rear heater core tubes to the outboard side of the rear heater-A/C housing.

⁂ WARNING

To prevent damage to the plastic evaporator tube bracket, carefully guide the heater core tubes past the bracket during removal of the heater core.

12. Carefully pull the rear heater core out of the top of the rear heater-A/C housing. Guide the heater core tubes past the plastic evaporator tube bracket. If the foam seals on the heater core are deformed or damaged, they must be replaced.

To install:

⁂ WARNING

To prevent damage to the plastic evaporator tube bracket, carefully guide the heater core tubes past the bracket during installation of the heater core.

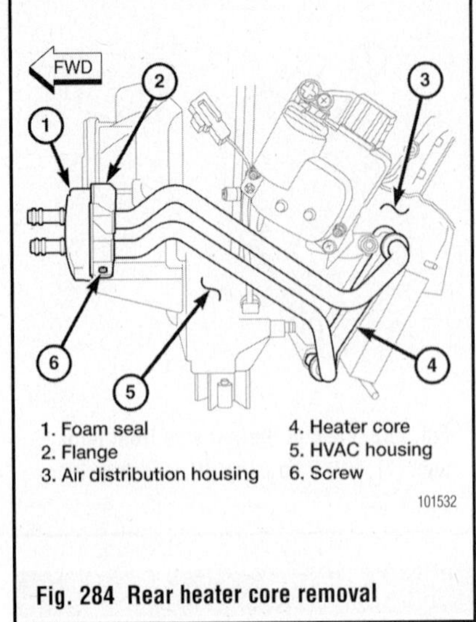

Fig. 284 Rear heater core removal

13. Carefully install the rear heater core into the rear heater-A/C housing. Guide the heater core tubes past the plastic evaporator tube bracket. Make sure that the foam seals are properly installed.
14. Install the screw that secures the rear heater core tubes to the outboard side of the rear heater-A/C housing. Tighten the screw to 10 inch lbs. (1 Nm).
15. Position the rear heater-A/C distribution housing to the rear heater-A/C housing and engage the 5 plastic retaining tabs. Make sure the retaining tabs are fully engaged.
16. Install the 3 metal retaining clips that secure the rear distribution housing to the rear heater-A/C housing.
17. Connect the wire harness connector to the rear mode door actuator.
18. Position the rear blend door actuator onto the rear heater-A/C housing. If necessary, rotate the actuator slightly to align the splines on the actuator output shaft with those on the rear blend-air door pivot shaft.
19. Install the 2 screws that secure the rear blend door actuator to the rear heater-A/C housing. Tighten the screws to 10 inch lbs. (1 Nm).
20. Connect the wire harness connector to the rear blend door actuator.
21. Position the flange to the bottom of the rear heater-A/C housing and install the 3 retaining screws. Tighten the screws to 10 inch lbs. (1 Nm).
22. Install the foam seal onto the flange at the bottom of the rear heater-A/C housing. Make sure that the foam seal is properly installed.
23. Install the rear heater-A/C housing. Refer to HVAC Housing, removal & installation.
24. Connect the negative battery cable. Refer to Battery, removal & installation.
25. If the rear heater core is being replaced, flush the cooling system. Refer to Engine Cooling, Engine Coolant, Flushing procedure.
26. Fill the engine cooling system with the proper type and amount of fluid. Refer to Engine Cooling, Engine Coolant, Drain & Refill Procedure.
27. Evacuate and charge the refrigerant system.

HVAC HOUSING

REMOVAL & INSTALLATION

Front HVAC Housing

See Figures 285 through 288.

⁂ CAUTION

Disable the airbag system before attempting any steering wheel, steering column, or instrument panel component diagnosis or service. Disconnect and isolate the battery negative (ground) cable, then wait 2 minutes for the airbag system capacitor to discharge before performing further diagnosis or service. This is the only sure way to disable the airbag system. Failure to take the proper precautions could result in an accidental airbag deployment and possible serious or fatal injury.

➡The HVAC housing must be removed from the vehicle and disassembled for service of the heater core, A/C evaporator, air intake housing, and the mode-air and blend-air doors.

1. Before servicing the vehicle, refer to the Precautions Section.
2. Disconnect and isolate the negative battery cable. Refer to Battery, removal & installation.
3. Recover the refrigerant from the refrigerant system.
4. Partially drain the engine cooling system. Refer to Engine Cooling, Engine Coolant, Drain & Refill Procedure.
5. If equipped with a heat shield, remove the top nut that secures the heat shield to the stud located on the dash panel.

➡Two slots are provided at the bottom of the heat shield to aid in heat shield removal, if equipped. Complete removal of the 2 bottom heat shield retaining nuts is not required.

6. If equipped, reach behind the engine

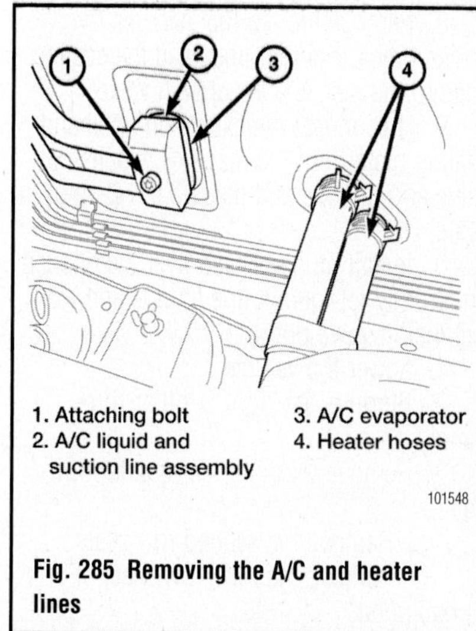

Fig. 285 Removing the A/C and heater lines

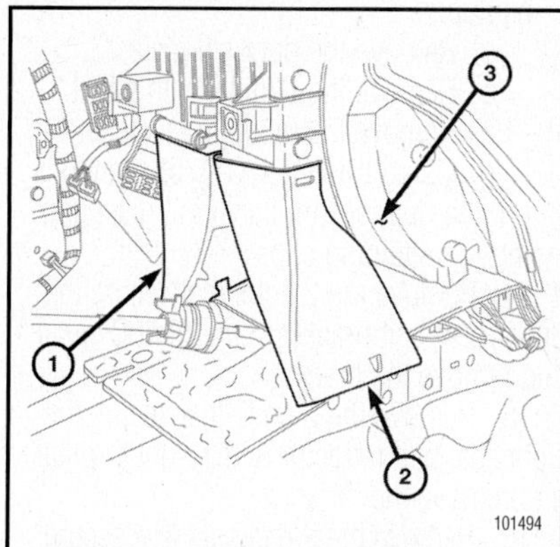

Fig. 286 Disconnect the left rear floor distribution duct (1) and the right rear floor distribution duct (2) from the HVAC housing (3)

and remove the 2 bottom nuts the that secure the heat shield to the studs located on the dash panel and remove the heat shield. Rotate and tilt the heat shield as required.

7. Remove the nut that secures the A/C liquid and suction line assembly to the A/C expansion valve.

8. Disconnect the A/C liquid and suction line assembly from the A/C evaporator and remove and discard the dual-plane seals.

9. Install plugs or tape over the opened refrigerant line fittings and the evaporator ports.

10. Disconnect the heater hoses from the heater core tubes. Install plugs or tape over the opened heater core tubes to prevent coolant spillage during housing removal.

➡Make sure to remove the 5 bolts that secure the HVAC housing to the instrument panel support prior to removing the instrument panel from the vehicle.

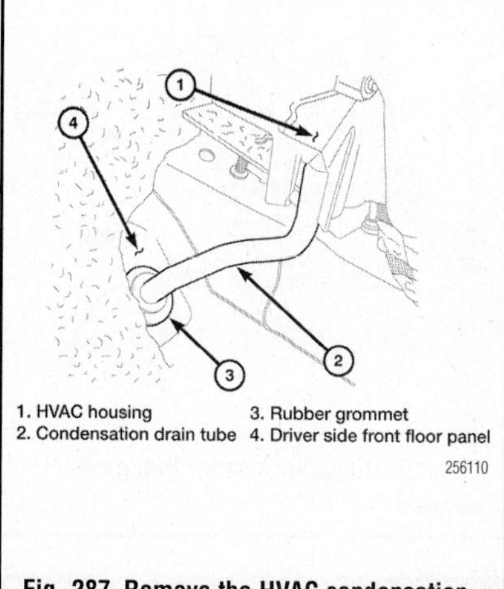

Fig. 287 Remove the HVAC condensation drain tube

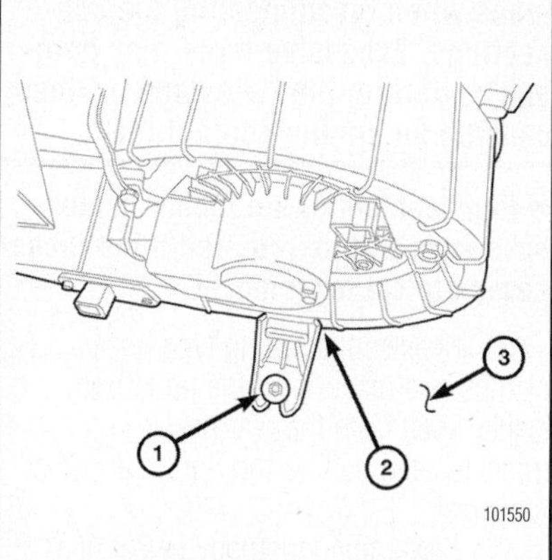

Fig. 288 Remove the nut (1) that secures the passenger side of the HVAC housing (2) to the dash panel (3)

11. Remove the instrument panel.

12. Remove the rear floor ducts.

13. Remove the condensation drain tube.

14. Remove the nut that secures the passenger side of the HVAC housing to the dash panel.

⁂ WARNING

Use care to ensure that the interior is covered in case of loss of residual fluids from the heater and evaporator cores.

15. Pull the HVAC housing rearward and remove the HVAC housing assembly from the passenger compartment.

16. If required, remove the HVAC housing air inlet duct from the passenger compartment side of the dash panel.

To install:

17. If removed, install the HVAC housing air inlet duct onto the passenger compartment side of the dash panel. Make sure the foam seal is not missing or damaged and that the retaining tabs are fully engage to the dash panel.

18. Position the HVAC housing assembly to the dash panel. Be certain that the passenger side of the HVAC housing is correctly located over the dash panel mounting stud.

19. Install the nut that secures the HVAC housing to the passenger compartment side of dash panel. Tighten the nut to 40 inch lbs. (5 Nm).

20. Install the condensation drain tube.

21. Install the rear floor ducts.

22. Install the instrument panel.

23. Remove the previously installed plugs or caps and connect the heater hoses to the heater core tubes.

24. Remove the tape or plugs from the refrigerant line fittings and the expansion valve ports.

25. Lubricate the rubber O-ring seals with clean refrigerant oil and install them onto the liquid and suction line fittings. Use only the specified O-ring seals as they are made of special materials compatible to the R-134a system. Use only refrigerant oil of the type recommended for the A/C compressor in the vehicle.

26. Connect the A/C liquid and suction line assembly to the A/C expansion valve.

27. Install the nut that secures the A/C liquid and suction line assembly to the A/C expansion valve. Tighten the nut to 15 ft. lbs. (20 Nm).

28. If equipped, position the heat shield onto the studs located on the dash panel in the engine compartment and install the retaining nuts. Tighten the nuts to 10 inch lbs. (1 Nm).

29. Reconnect the negative battery cable. Refer to Battery, removal & installation.

30. If the heater core is being replaced, flush the cooling system. Refer to Engine Cooling, Engine Coolant, Flushing procedure.

31. Fill the engine cooling system with the proper type and amount of fluid. Refer to Engine Cooling, Engine Coolant, Drain & Refill Procedure.

⁂ WARNING

Do NOT run the engine with a vacuum pump in operation or with a vacuum present within the A/C system when equipped with a variable displacement compressor. Failure to follow these instructions will result in serious A/C compressor damage.

32. Evacuate and charge the refrigerant system.

33. Initiate the Actuator Calibration function using a scan tool.

Rear HVAC Housing

See Figures 289 through 292.

⁂ CAUTION

Disable the airbag system before attempting any steering wheel, steering column, or instrument panel component diagnosis or service. Disconnect and isolate the battery negative (ground) cable, then wait 2 minutes for the airbag system capacitor to discharge before performing further diagnosis or service. This is the only sure way to disable the airbag system. Failure to take the proper precautions could result in an accidental airbag deployment and possible serious or fatal injury.

➡The rear heater-A/C housing must be removed from the vehicle for service of the mode door actuator and blend door actuator and it must be disassembled for service of the A/C evaporator and the heater core.

1. Before servicing the vehicle, refer to the Precautions Section.
2. Disconnect and isolate the negative battery cable. Refer to Battery, removal & installation.
3. Recover the refrigerant from the refrigerant system.
4. Drain the engine cooling system. Refer to Engine Cooling, Engine Coolant, Drain & Refill Procedure.
5. Raise and safely support the vehicle.

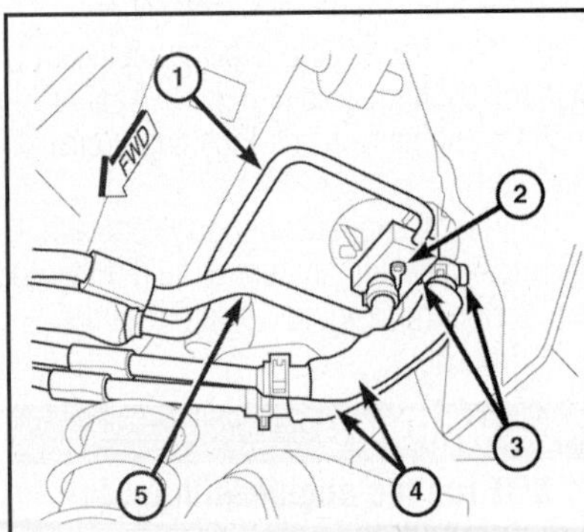

Fig. 289 Removing the rear A/C and heater lines

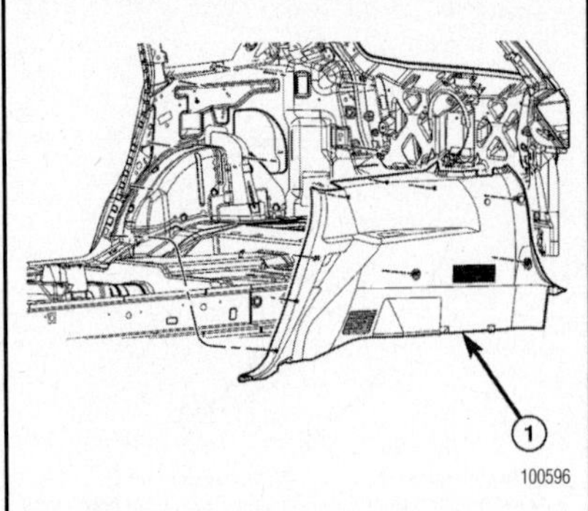

Fig. 290 Right rear quarter trim panel (1) removal

⁂ WARNING

DO NOT apply excessive force on underbody heater lines or rear heater tubes when disconnecting the connections. Excessive force may damage or deform the tubes and or lines, causing an engine coolant leak.

➡Replacement of the rubber heater hose ends will be required if the rubber hoses are cut for removal.

6. Release the spring type hose clamps and disconnect the underbody heater lines from the rear heater core tubes located behind the right rear wheel housing.
7. Lower the underbody heater lines and drain any residual coolant from the lines into a suitable container.
8. Remove the nut that secures the underbody refrigerant lines and the sealing plate to the rear A/C expansion valve.
9. Disconnect the extension lines and sealing plate from the rear A/C expansion valve and remove and discard the O-ring seals.
10. Install plugs or tape over the opened underbody refrigerant line fittings and rear expansion valve ports.
11. Lower the vehicle.
12. Remove the right D-pillar trim panel.
13. Remove the right rear quarter trim panel.
    a. Remove the second row seats.
    b. Remove the third row seats, if equipped.
    c. Remove the storage box, if equipped.
    d. Remove the door sill plate.
    e. Remove the D-pillar trim panel.
    f. Remove the mounting fasteners.
    g. Using trim stick C-4755, carefully pry the quarter trim panel out disengaging the retaining clips.
14. Remove the 2 bolts that secure the upper seat belt bracket to the right D-pillar and remove the bracket.
15. Remove the 2 bolts that secure the right seat belt retractor to the right D-pillar and remove the retractor.
16. Remove the 2 retainers that secure the rear ceiling distribution duct to the right D-pillar.
17. Lift the rear ceiling distribution duct

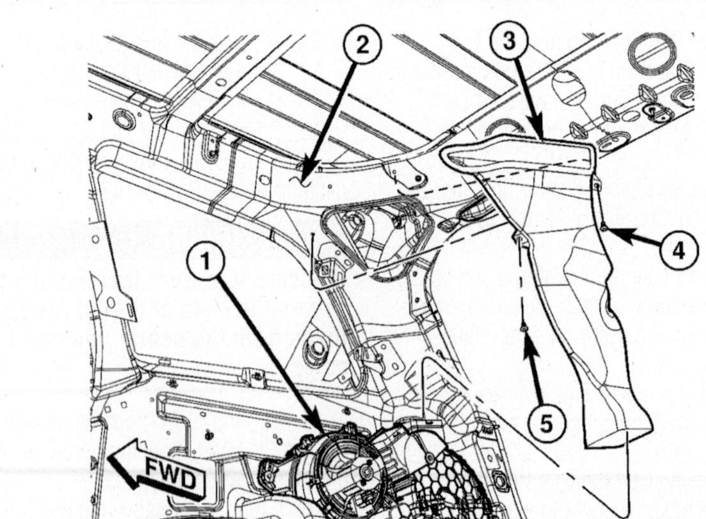

Fig. 291 Removing the rear ceiling distribution duct

upward and disengage it from the rear heater-A/C housing.

WARNING

Use care when removing the rear ceiling distribution duct from the heater-A/C housing to prevent damage to the molded plastic support brace located on the top of the housing outlet. Failure to follow this caution could result in part, or all, of the support brace falling into the rear housing, which may interfere with rear mode door operation.

18. Pull the bottom end of the rear ceiling distribution duct away from the rear heater-A/C housing and remove the duct.
19. Remove the push-pin retainer that secures the rear floor distribution duct to the right inner quarter panel.
20. Disengage the rear floor distribution duct from the stud located on the right inner quarter panel.
21. Disengage the rear floor distribution duct from the rear heater-A/C housing and remove the duct.
22. Disconnect the body wire harness connectors from the rear blower motor and the rear blower motor power module.
23. Disconnect the body wire harness connector from the rear heater-A/C wire harness connector.
24. Remove the 2 bolts that secure the rear heater-A/C housing to the right inner quarter panel and remove the housing.

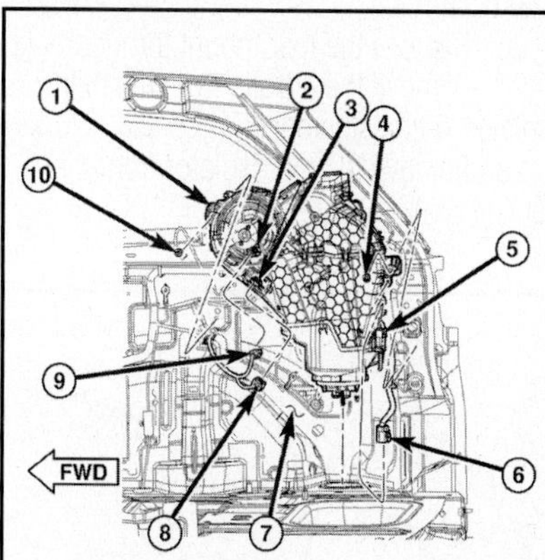

Fig. 292 Removing the rear HVAC housing assembly

To install:

25. Position the rear heater-A/C housing into the vehicle and align the guide pins on the housing to the holes in the right inner quarter panel.
26. Install the 2 bolts that secure the rear heater-A/C housing to the right inner quarter panel. Tighten the bolts to 27 inch lbs. (3 Nm).
27. Connect the body wire harness connector to the rear heater-A/C wire harness connector.
28. Connect the body wire harness connectors to the rear blower motor and the rear blower motor power module.
29. Install the rear floor distribution duct onto the rear heater-A/C housing. Make sure the duct is fully engaged to the housing.
30. Engage the rear floor distribution duct to the stud located on the right inner quarter panel.
31. Install the push-pin retainer that secures the rear floor distribution duct to the right inner quarter panel.
32. Position the rear ceiling distribution duct to the right D-pillar.

WARNING

Use care when installing the rear ceiling distribution duct onto the heater-A/C housing to prevent damage to the molded plastic support brace located on the top of the housing outlet. Failure to follow this caution could result in part, or all, of the support brace falling into the rear housing, which may interfere with rear mode door operation.

33. Install the rear ceiling distribution duct onto the top of the rear heater-A/C housing. Make sure the duct is fully engaged to the housing.
34. Install the 2 retainers that secure the rear ceiling distribution duct to the right D-pillar.
35. Position the upper seat belt bracket onto the D-pillar and install the 2 retaining bolts. Tighten the bolts to 39 ft. lbs. (52 Nm).
36. Install the right seat belt retractor and retaining bolts onto the D-pillar. Tighten the bolts to 39 ft. lbs. (52 Nm).
37. Install the right rear quarter trim panel:
    a. Install the quarter trim panel.
    b. Install the mounting fasteners.
    c. Install the door sill plate.
    d. Install the D-pillar trim panel.
    e. Install the storage box, if equipped.
    f. Install the third row seats, if equipped.
    g. Install the second row seats.
38. Install the right D-pillar trim panel.
39. Raise and safely support the vehicle.

WARNING

DO NOT apply excessive force on the underbody heater lines or rear heater tubes fittings when connecting the connections. Excessive force may damage or deform the tubes and or lines, causing an engine coolant leak.

➡Replacement of the rubber heater hose ends will be required if the rubber hoses were cut for removal.

40. Remove the tape or plugs from all the opened refrigerant line fittings and the rear expansion valve ports.
41. Lubricate new rubber O-ring seals with clean refrigerant oil and install them onto the underbody refrigerant line fittings. Use only the specified O-rings as they are made of a special material for the R-134a refrigerant system. Use only refrigerant oil of the type recommended for the A/C compressor in the vehicle.
42. Connect the underbody refrigerant lines and the sealing plate to the rear A/C expansion valve.
43. Install the nut that secures the underbody refrigerant lines and sealing plate to the rear A/C expansion valve. Tighten the nut to 97 inch lbs. (11 Nm).
44. Connect the underbody heater lines to the rear heater core tubes located behind the right rear wheel housing and engage the spring type hose clamps.
45. Lower the vehicle.
46. Connect the negative battery cable. Refer to Battery, removal & installation.
47. If the heater core is being replaced, flush the cooling system. Refer to Engine Cooling, Engine Coolant, Flushing procedure.
48. Fill the engine cooling system with the proper type and amount of fluid. Refer to Engine Cooling, Engine Coolant, Drain & Refill Procedure.

WARNING

DO NOT run the engine with a vacuum pump in operation or with a vacuum present within the A/C system when equipped with a variable displacement compressor. Failure to follow these instructions may result in serious A/C compressor damage.

49. Evacuate and charge the refrigerant system.
50. Initiate the Actuator Calibration function using a scan tool.

STEERING

POWER STEERING GEAR

REMOVAL & INSTALLATION

AWD Models

See Figures 293 through 295.

⁂ WARNING

Power steering fluid, engine parts and exhaust system may be extremely hot if engine has been running. Do not start engine with any loose or disconnected hoses. Do not allow hoses to touch hot exhaust manifold or catalyst.

⁂ CAUTION

Fluid level should be checked with the engine off to prevent personal injury from moving parts.

⁂ WARNING

When the system is open, cap all open ends of the hoses, power steering pump fittings, or power steering gear ports to prevent entry of foreign material into the components.

1. Before servicing the vehicle, refer to the Precautions Section.
2. Siphon out as much power steering fluid as possible from the reservoir.
3. Place the front wheels of vehicle (and steering wheel) in the STRAIGHT-AHEAD position.
4. Using a steering wheel holder, lock the steering wheel in place to keep it from rotating. This keeps the clockspring in the proper orientation while the intermediate shaft is disconnected.
5. Reposition the floor carpeting and sound deadening insulation to access the intermediate shaft coupling at the base of the column.
6. Remove the intermediate shaft coupling bolt.
7. Separate the intermediate shaft coupling from the steering gear pinion shaft.
8. Release the clips securing the dash seal to the dash panel and push the seal away from the dash panel.
9. Raise and safely support the vehicle.
10. On each side of the vehicle, remove the wheel mounting nuts, then the tire and wheel assembly.
11. On each side of the gear, remove the nut from the outer tie rod end at the knuckle.
12. On each side of the gear, separate the outer tie rod end from the knuckle using Remover, Special Tool 9360, or equivalent.
13. If equipped, remove the engine belly pan.
14. Remove the front engine mount through-bolt.
15. Remove the fore-aft crossmember forward mounting bolts at the radiator support.
16. Remove the fore-aft crossmember rearward mounting bolts at the crossmember.
17. Remove the fore-aft crossmember.
18. Remove the screws securing the power steering hose routing clamps to the rear of the crossmember.
19. Remove the tube nut, then remove the return hose at the steering gear.
20. Remove the tube nut, then remove the pressure hose at the steering gear.

➡Before lowering the front suspension crossmember, the location of the crossmember must be marked on the body of the vehicle. Do this so the crossmember can be relocated, upon reinstallation, against the body of vehicle in the same location as before removal. If the front suspension crossmember is not reinstalled in exactly the same location as before removal, the preset front wheel alignment settings (caster and camber) may be lost.

21. Using a crayon or marker that will not break the paint surface, mark the location of the front crossmember on the body near each mounting bolt. Do not use any type of sharp instrument that will damage the underbody of the vehicle.
22. Support the crossmember with a transmission jack.
23. Remove the 4 mounting bolts securing the front crossmember to the body.
24. Remove the mounting screws securing the front crossmember reinforcement brackets (one each side of vehicle) to the body. Remove the brackets.
25. Using the jack, slowly lower the crossmember approximately 3 inches (76mm) (as measured at the rear crossmember mounts). Do not lower the crossmember more than necessary as damage may occur.
26. Remove the rear mount through bolt.
27. Remove the 4 bolts from the rear isolator to crossmember.
28. Remove the rear isolator from the vehicle.

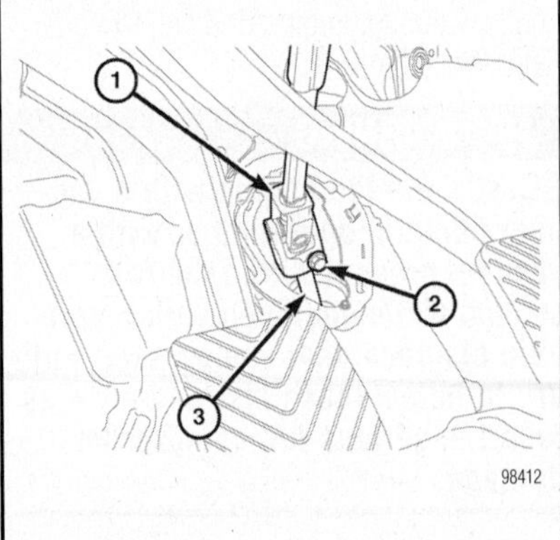

Fig. 293 View of the intermediate shaft coupling bolt (2), intermediate shaft coupling (1), and steering gear pinion shaft (3)

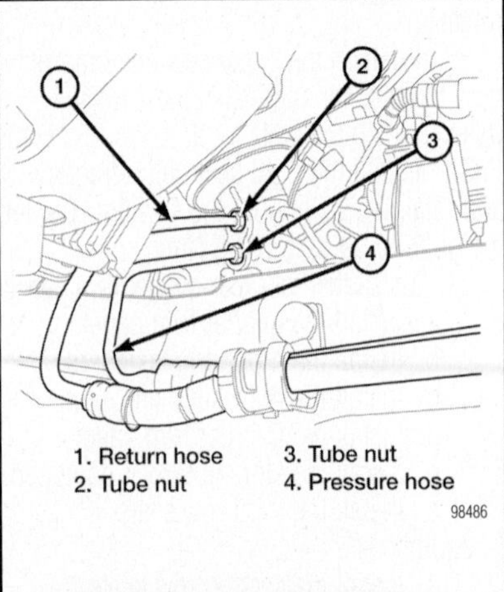

Fig. 294 Remove the power steering hoses at the steering gear

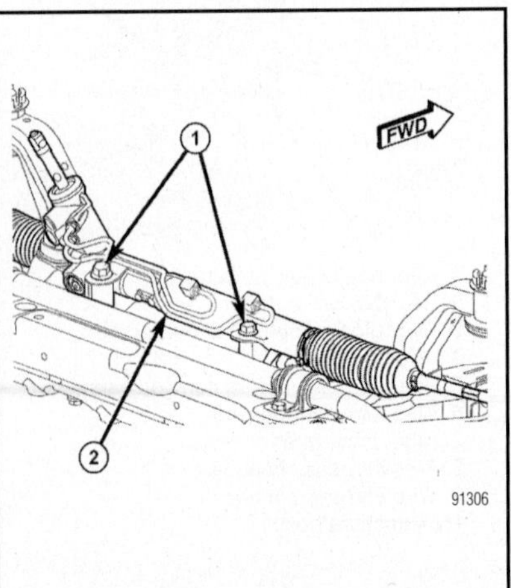

Fig. 295 Remove the 2 bolts (1) securing the steering gear (2) to the crossmember

29. Remove the screws and push-pins securing the heat shield over the right side of the steering gear. Remove the shield.

30. Remove the 2 bolts securing the steering gear to the crossmember.

31. Tip the steering gear pinion shaft straight up and remove the dash seal from the steering gear.

32. Slide the steering gear across the crossmember and out through the left wheel opening.

33. If necessary, remove the outer tie rods from the inner tie rod threads. Count how many rotations it takes to remove each the outer tie rod for installation reference.

To install:

34. If necessary, install the outer tie rods onto the inner tie rod threads. As the outer tie rods are installed, count out the same number of rotations as were counted on tie rod removal. This will get the toe setting somewhat close to the specification before the vehicle is aligned at the end of this procedure. Snug the tie rod jam nuts on both ends of the gear. Tighten the tie rod jam nuts to specification while performing the wheel alignment at the end of this procedure.

35. Carefully install the steering gear through the left wheel opening using the reverse of how it was removed. Move it across the crossmember until centered.

36. Tip the steering gear pinion shaft straight up and install the dash seal matching it to the contour of the steering gear housing.

37. Position the steering gear in mounted position on the crossmember.

38. Install the 2 bolts securing the steering gear to the crossmember. Tighten the gear mounting bolts to 74 ft. lbs. (100 Nm).

39. Install the heat shield over the steering gear. Install the mounting screws and push-pins. Tighten the screws to 53 inch lbs. (6 Nm).

40. Install the rear engine mount isolator.

41. Install the 4 mounting bolts and tighten to 37 ft. lbs. (50 Nm).

42. Install the rear mount bracket through bolt. Tighten to 55 ft. lbs. (75 Nm).

43. Center the power steering gear rack in its travel as necessary.

➡When installing the front suspension crossmember it is very important that the crossmember be attached to the body in exactly the same spot as when it was removed. Otherwise, the vehicle's wheel alignment settings (caster and camber) will be lost making wheel alignment more difficult.

44. Slowly raise the crossmember into mounted position using the transmission jack matching the crossmember to the marked locations on the body made during removal.

45. Position the front crossmember reinforcement brackets (one each side of vehicle) over the crossmember rear mounting bushings and install the mounting screws, but do not tighten at this time.

46. Install the 4 mounting bolts securing the front crossmember to the body. Tighten the crossmember mounting bolts to 100 ft. lbs. (135 Nm).

47. Tighten the crossmember reinforcement bracket mounting screws to 37 ft. lbs. (50 Nm).

48. Remove the transmission jack.

49. Install the pressure hose tube at the gear. Tighten the tube nut to 24 ft. lbs. (32 Nm).

50. Install the return hose tube at the gear. Tighten the tube nut to 24 ft. lbs. (32 Nm).

51. Position the power steering hose routing clamps on the crossmember. Install and tighten the screws to 71 inch lbs. (8 Nm).

52. Position the fore-aft crossmember in the engine compartment and install the mounting bolts. Tighten the forward mounting bolts at the radiator support to 41 ft. lbs. (55 Nm). Tighten the rearward mounting bolts at the suspension crossmember to 41 ft. lbs. (55 Nm).

53. Install the front engine mount through-bolt and tighten to 44 ft. lbs. (60 Nm).

54. If equipped, install the engine belly pan.

➡Prior to attaching the outer tie rod end to the knuckle, inspect the tie rod seal boot. If the seal boot is damaged, replace the outer tie rod end.

55. On each side of the gear, install the outer tie rod end into the hole in the knuckle arm. Start a NEW tie rod mounting nut onto the stud. While holding the tie rod end stud with a wrench, tighten the nut with a wrench or crowfoot wrench. Tighten the nut to 63 ft. lbs. (85 Nm).

56. Install the wheel and tire assembly. Tighten the wheel nuts in a star pattern until all nuts are torqued to half the required specification. Then repeat the tightening sequence to the full specified torque of 100 ft. lbs. (135 Nm).

57. Lower the vehicle.

58. Lift the dash seal into position and engage the retaining clips securing the dash seal to the dash panel.

59. Remove the steering wheel holder using care not to rotate the steering wheel.

60. Verify the front wheels of vehicle are in the STRAIGHT-AHEAD position.

61. Center the intermediate shaft coupling over the steering gear pinion shaft, then slide the intermediate shaft onto the steering gear pinion shaft.

62. Install the intermediate shaft coupling bolt. Tighten the bolt to 31 ft. lbs. (42 Nm).

63. Position the sound deadening insulation and floor carpet back into place.

64. Fill and bleed the power steering system. Refer to Power Steering Pump, Bleeding procedure.

65. Check for fluid leaks.

66. Perform a wheel alignment as necessary.

FWD Models

See Figures 296 through 298.

⁂ WARNING

Power steering fluid, engine parts and exhaust system may be extremely hot if engine has been running. Do not start engine with any loose or disconnected hoses. Do not allow hoses to touch hot exhaust manifold or catalyst.

⁂ CAUTION

Fluid level should be checked with the engine off to prevent personal injury from moving parts.

⁂ WARNING

When the system is open, cap all open ends of the hoses, power steering pump fittings, or power steering gear ports to prevent entry of foreign material into the components.

1. Before servicing the vehicle, refer to the Precautions Section.

2. Siphon out as much power steering fluid as possible from the reservoir.

3. Reposition the floor carpeting to access the intermediate shaft coupling at the base of the column.

4. Position the front wheels of vehicle in the STRAIGHT-AHEAD position, then turn the steering wheel to the right until the intermediate shaft coupling bolt at the base of the column can be accessed.

5. Remove the intermediate shaft coupling bolt. Do not separate the intermediate shaft from the steering gear pinion shaft at this time.

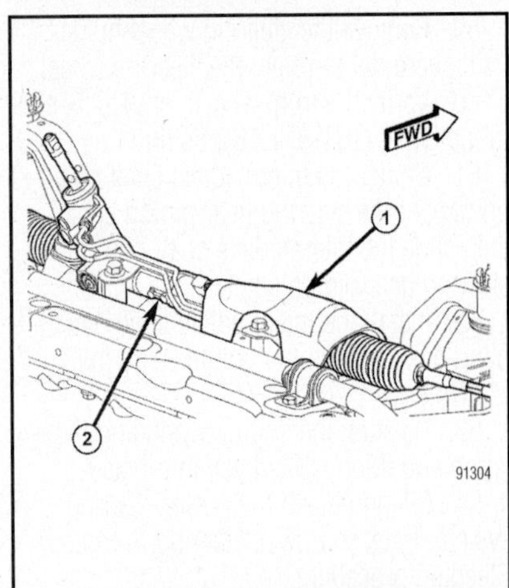

Fig. 296 Remove the heat shield (1) over the right side of the steering gear (2)

6. Return the front wheels of vehicle (and steering wheel) to the STRAIGHT-AHEAD position. Using a steering wheel holder, lock the steering wheel in place to keep it from rotating. This keeps the clockspring in the proper orientation.
7. Raise and safely support the vehicle.
8. Remove the front wheel and tire assemblies.
9. On each side of the gear, remove the nut from the out tie rod end at the knuckle.
10. On each side of the gear, separate the outer tie rod end from the knuckle using Remover 9360, or equivalent.
11. If equipped, remove the engine belly pan.
12. Remove the rear engine mount.
13. Remove the front engine mount through-bolt.
14. Remove the 2 bolts fastening the fore/aft crossmember to the lower radiator support.
15. Remove the 4 bolts fastening the fore/aft crossmember to the front crossmember. Remove the fore/aft crossmember.
16. Remove the screws securing the power steering hose routing clamps to the rear of the crossmember.
17. Unscrew the tube nut, then remove the return hose at the steering gear.
18. Unscrew the tube nut, then remove the pressure hose at the steering gear.
19. Remove the screws and push-pins securing the heat shield over the right side of the steering gear. Remove the shield.

➡Before removing the front suspension crossmember from the vehicle, the location of the crossmember must be marked on the body of the vehicle. Do this so the crossmember can be relocated, upon reinstallation, against the body of vehicle in the same location as before removal. If the front suspension crossmember is not reinstalled in exactly the same location as before removal, the preset front wheel alignment settings (caster and camber) may be lost.

20. Mark the location of the front crossmember on the body near each mounting bolt.
21. Support the crossmember with a transmission jack.
22. Remove the 4 mounting bolts securing the front crossmember to the body.
23. If equipped, remove the mounting screws securing the front crossmember reinforcement brackets (one each side of vehicle) to the body. Remove the brackets.
24. If equipped, remove the mounting screws securing the front cross brace/reinforcement bracket to the body. Remove the bracket.
25. Using the jack, slowly lower the crossmember enough to access the intermediate shaft coupling at the steering gear pinion shaft. Slide the coupling off the pinion shaft.
26. Remove the dash seals as necessary.
27. Remove the 2 bolts securing the steering gear to the crossmember.
28. Remove the steering gear from the crossmember.

To install:

29. Install the steering gear on the crossmember.
30. Install the 2 bolts securing the steering gear to the crossmember. Tighten the gear mounting bolts to 74 ft. lbs. (100 Nm).
31. Install the dash seals as necessary.
32. Center the power steering gear rack in its travel as necessary.

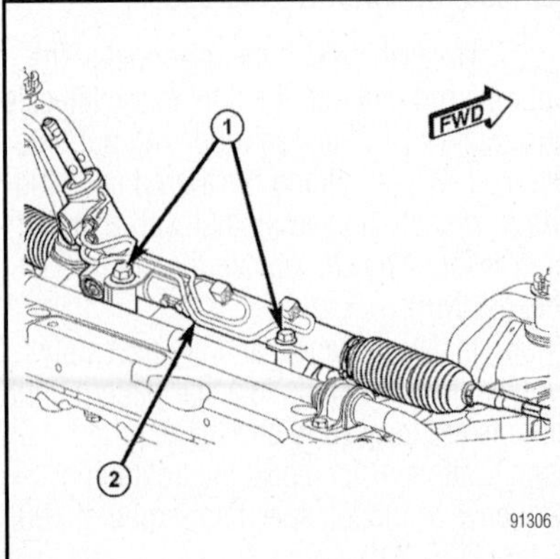

Fig. 297 Remove the bolts (1) securing the steering gear (2) to the crossmember

➡When installing the front suspension crossmember back in the vehicle, it is very important that the crossmember be attached to the body in exactly the same spot as when it was removed. Otherwise, the vehicle wheel alignment settings (caster and camber) will be lost making wheel alignment more difficult.

➡While raising the steering gear into place, it is not necessary to install the intermediate shaft coupling on the steering gear pinion shaft at this time. It can be installed once the vehicle is lowered. Make sure the coupling does not interfere with steering gear/dash seals at this time.

33. Slowly raise the crossmember into mounted position using the transmission jack matching the crossmember to the marked locations on the body made during removal.
34. Check the positioning of the seals at the dash panel and adjust as necessary.
35. If equipped, position the front crossmember reinforcement brackets (one each side of vehicle) over the crossmember rear mounting bushings and install the mounting screws, but do not tighten at this time.
36. If equipped, position the front cross brace/reinforcement bracket over the crossmember rear mounting bushings and body, then install the mounting screws. Do not tighten screws at this time.
37. Install the 4 mounting bolts securing the front crossmember to the body. Tighten the crossmember mounting bolts to 100 ft. lbs. (135 Nm).
38. If equipped, tighten the crossmember reinforcement bracket mounting screws to 37 ft. lbs. (50 Nm).
39. If equipped, tighten the cross brace/reinforcement bracket mounting screws to 37 ft. lbs. (50 Nm).
40. Remove the transmission jack.
41. Install the heat shield over the steering gear. Install the mounting screws and push-pins. Tighten the screws to 53 inch lbs. (6 Nm).
42. Install the pressure hose tube at the gear. Tighten the tube nut to 24 ft. lbs. (32 Nm).
43. Install the return hose tube at the gear. Tighten the tube nut to 24 ft. lbs. (32 Nm).
44. Position the power steering hose routing clamps on the crossmember. Install and tighten the screws to 71 inch lbs. (8 Nm).
45. Install the fore/aft crossmember and front engine mount through-bolt.
46. Install the rear engine mount.

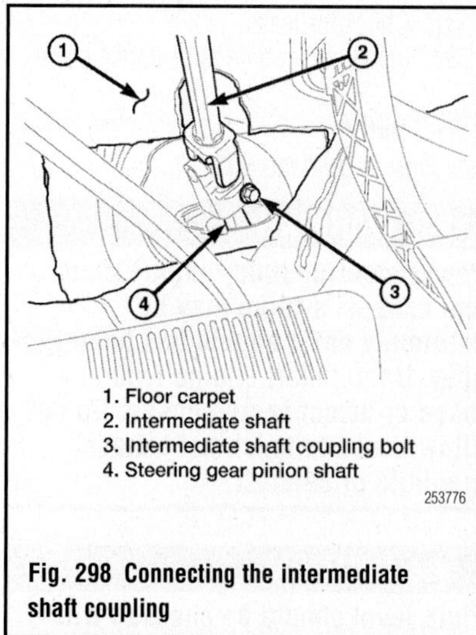

Fig. 298 Connecting the intermediate shaft coupling

47. If equipped, install the engine belly pan.

➡Prior to attaching the outer tie rod end to the knuckle, inspect the tie rod seal boot. If the seal boot is damaged, replace the outer tie rod end.

48. On each side of the gear, install the outer tie rod end into the hole in the knuckle arm. Start a NEW tie rod mounting nut onto the stud. While holding the tie rod end stud with a wrench, tighten the nut with a wrench or crowfoot wrench. Tighten the nut to 63 ft. lbs. (85 Nm).
49. Install the wheel and tire assemblies. Tighten the wheel nuts in a star pattern until all nuts are torqued to half the required specification. Then repeat the tightening sequence to the full specified torque of 100 ft. lbs. (135 Nm).
50. Lower the vehicle.
51. Remove the steering wheel holder.
52. Verify the front wheels of vehicle are in the STRAIGHT-AHEAD position.
53. Center the intermediate shaft over the steering gear pinion shaft, lining up the ends, then slide the intermediate shaft onto the steering gear pinion shaft.
54. From center, rotate the steering wheel to the right until the intermediate shaft coupling bolt can be easily installed.
55. Install the intermediate shaft coupling bolt. Tighten the bolt to 31 ft. lbs. (42 Nm).
56. Reposition the floor carpet in place.
57. Fill and bleed the power steering system. Refer to Power Steering Pump, Bleeding procedure.
58. Check for fluid leaks.
59. Perform a wheel alignment as necessary.

POWER STEERING PUMP

REMOVAL & INSTALLATION

2.4L Engine

See Figure 299.

⁂ WARNING

Power steering fluid, engine parts and exhaust system may be extremely hot if engine has been running. Do not start engine with any loose or disconnected hoses. Do not allow hoses to touch hot exhaust manifold or catalyst.

⁂ CAUTION

Fluid level should be checked with the engine off to prevent personal injury from moving parts.

⁂ WARNING

When the system is open, cap all open ends of the hoses, power steering pump fittings, or power steering gear ports to prevent entry of foreign material into the components.

1. Before servicing the vehicle, refer to the Precautions Section.
2. Siphon out as much fluid as possible from the power steering fluid reservoir.
3. Remove the engine appearance cover.
4. Remove the pressure hose routing bracket bolt at the upper mount.
5. Remove the pressure hose at the pump pressure port.
6. Remove the hose clamp securing the supply hose at the pump.

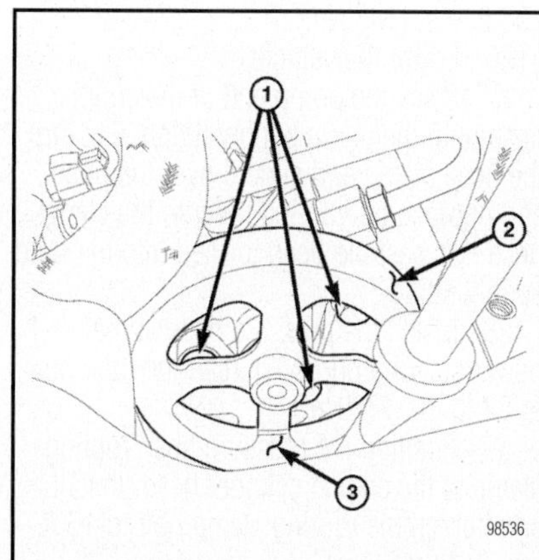

Fig. 299 View of power steering pump mounting bolts (1), pulley (3), and drive belt (2)—2.4L engine

7. Remove the supply hose from the pump.
8. Remove the drive belt. Refer to Accessory Drive Belts, removal & installation.
9. Remove the 3 pump mounting bolts through the pulley openings.
10. Remove the power steering pump from the vehicle.

To install:

11. Using a lint free towel, wipe clean the open power steering pressure hose end and the power steering pump port. Replace any used O-rings with new. Lubricate the O-ring with clean power steering fluid.
12. Place the pump in the mounting position. Install the 3 bolts through the pulley openings. Tighten the mounting bolts to 19 ft. lbs. (26 Nm).
13. Install the drive belt. Refer to Accessory Drive Belts, removal & installation.
14. Install the supply hose at the pump.
15. Clamp the hose clamp securing the supply hose to the pump.
16. Install the pressure hose at the pump pressure port. Tighten the tube nut to 24 ft. lbs. (32 Nm).
17. Install the pressure hose routing bracket bolt to the engine mount. Tighten the bolt to 18 ft. lbs. (24 Nm).
18. Fill and bleed the power steering system. Refer to Power Steering Pump, Bleeding procedure.
19. Check for leaks.
20. Install the engine appearance cover.

3.5L Engine

See Figures 300 and 301.

⁂ WARNING

Power steering fluid, engine parts and exhaust system may be extremely hot if engine has been running. Do not start engine with any loose or disconnected hoses. Do not allow hoses to touch hot exhaust manifold or catalyst.

⁂ CAUTION

Fluid level should be checked with the engine off to prevent personal injury from moving parts.

⁂ WARNING

When the system is open, cap all open ends of the hoses, power steering pump fittings, or power steering gear ports to prevent entry of foreign material into the components.

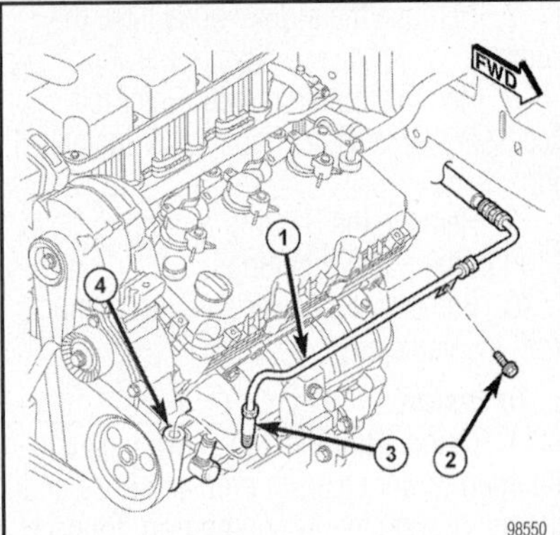

Fig. 300 Unscrew the tube nut (3), remove the pressure hose (1) at the pump (4), and remove the pressure hose routing clamp bolt (2) at the engine cylinder head—3.5L engine

1. Before servicing the vehicle, refer to the Precautions Section.
2. Siphon as much fluid as possible from the power steering fluid reservoir.
3. Remove the engine appearance cover.
4. Unscrew the tube nut, then remove the pressure hose at the pump.
5. Remove the pressure hose routing clamp bolt at the engine cylinder head.
6. Remove the clamp securing the supply hose to the power steering pump supply fitting, then remove the hose from the supply fitting.
7. Raise and safely support the vehicle.
8. Remove the right front tire and wheel assembly.
9. Remove the drive belt splash shield.
10. Remove the drive belt. Refer to Accessory Drive Belts, removal & installation.
11. Lower the vehicle.

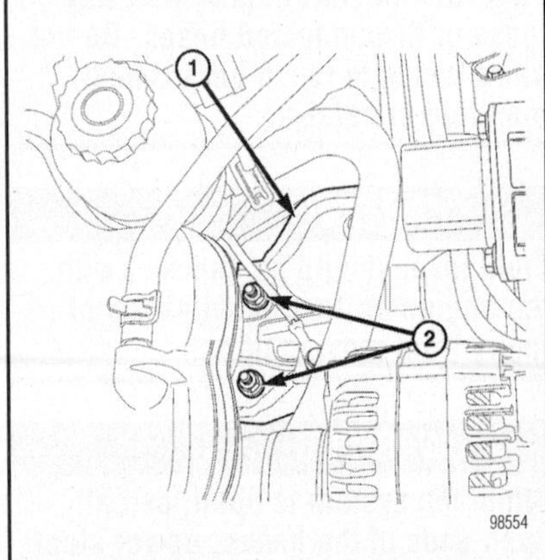

Fig. 301 Remove the nuts (2) securing the right engine mount bracket (1) to the mount—3.5L engine

12. Remove the 2 nuts securing the right engine mount bracket to the mount.
13. Position a floor jack with an appropriate size block of wood below the engine oil pan. Raise the jack until the block of wood just comes into contact with the bottom of the oil pan, but no further.
14. Slowly raise the right side of the engine using the floor jack while viewing the pump drive pulley. Raise the engine until all 3 power steering pump mounting bolts can be accessed through the openings in the drive pulley.
15. Remove the 3 pump mounting bolts through the pulley openings.
16. Remove the power steering pump.

To install:

17. Using a lint free towel, wipe clean the open power steering pressure hose end and the power steering pump port. Replace any used O-rings with new. Lubricate the O-ring with clean power steering fluid.
18. Place the pump in the mounted position. Install the 3 bolts through the pulley openings. Tighten the mounting bolts to 22 ft. lbs. (30 Nm).
19. Slowly lower the right side of the engine using the floor jack, guiding the right engine mount bracket mounting holes over the mounting studs of the right engine mount.
20. Remove the floor jack and block of wood from below the engine.
21. Install the 2 nuts securing the right engine mount bracket to the mount.
22. Raise and safely support the vehicle.
23. Install the drive belt. Refer to Accessory Drive Belts, removal & installation.
24. Install the drive belt splash shield.
25. Install the wheel and tire assembly. Tighten the wheel nuts in a star pattern until all nuts are torqued to half the required specification. Then repeat the tightening sequence to the full specified torque of 100 ft. lbs. (135 Nm).
26. Lower the vehicle.
27. Place the pump end of the supply hose onto the pump supply fitting. Expand the hose clamp and slide it over the hose and pump supply fitting. Secure the clamp once it is past the bead formed into the fluid supply fitting.
28. Install the pressure hose at the power steering pump. Tighten the tube nut to 24 ft. lbs. (32 Nm).
29. Position the pressure hose routing clamp at the engine cylinder head. Install and tighten the routing clamp bolt to 16 ft. lbs. (22 Nm).
30. Fill and bleed the power steering system. Refer to Power Steering Pump, Bleeding procedure.
31. Check for leaks.
32. Install the engine appearance cover.

3.6L Engine

See Figures 302 and 303.

✲✲ WARNING

Power steering fluid, engine parts and exhaust system may be extremely hot if engine has been running. Do not start engine with any loose or disconnected hoses. Do not allow hoses to touch hot exhaust manifold or catalyst.

✲✲ CAUTION

Fluid level should be checked with the engine off to prevent personal injury from moving parts.

✲✲ WARNING

When the system is open, cap all open ends of the hoses, power steering pump fittings, or power steering gear ports to prevent entry of foreign material into the components.

1. Before servicing the vehicle, refer to the Precautions Section.
2. Remove the negative (-) battery cable from the battery and isolate the cable. Refer to Battery, removal & installation.
3. Remove the cap from the power steering fluid reservoir.
4. Using a siphon pump, remove as much power steering fluid as possible from the power steering fluid reservoir.
5. Remove the accessory drive belt. Refer to Accessory Drive Belts, removal & installation.

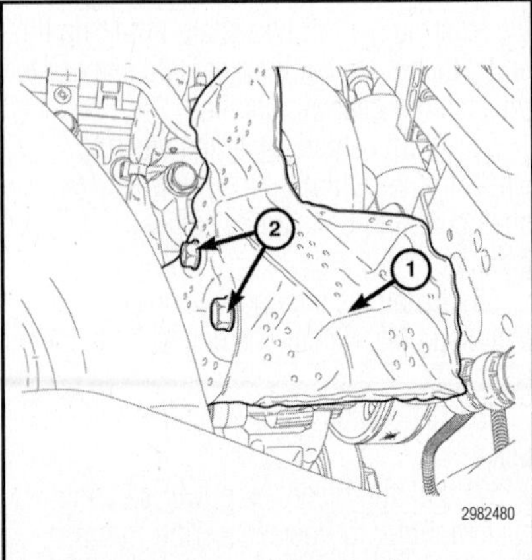

Fig. 302 Remove the heat shield mounting bolts (2) and heat shield (1)—3.6L engine

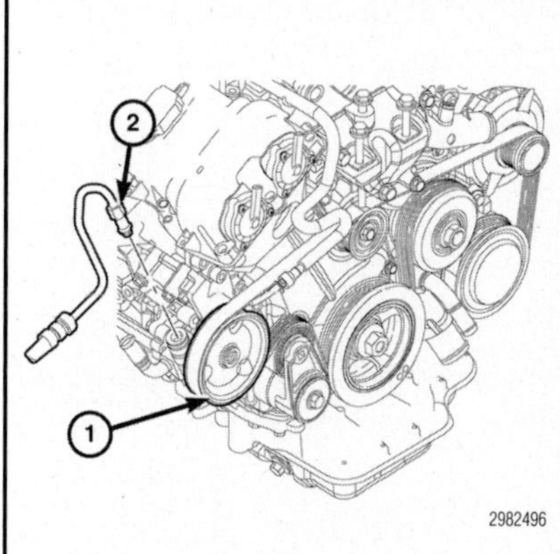

Fig. 303 View of the pressure hose fitting (2) and power steering pump with pulley (1)—3.6L engine

6. Raise and safely support the vehicle.
7. Remove the heat shield mounting bolts and remove the heat shield from the vehicle.
8. Remove the supply hose clamp and remove the supply hose from the power steering pump fitting.
9. Remove the power steering pump pressure hose fitting.
10. Remove the 3 pump mounting bolts through the pump pulley.
11. Remove the pump (with the pulley) from below.

To install:

➡Before installing the power steering pressure hose on the power steering pump, replace the O-ring on the end of the power steering pressure hose. Lubricate the O-ring using clean power steering fluid.

12. Install the power steering pump onto its mounting bracket.
13. Install the 3 power steering pump mounting bolts through the pulley. Tighten the pump mounting bolts to 22 ft. lbs. (30 Nm).
14. Install the power steering pump pressure fitting and tighten it to 14 ft. lbs. (32 Nm).
15. Slide the fluid supply hose onto the pump fitting and install the clamp securing it in place.
16. Install the heat shield and secure it with the 3 mounting bolts. Tighten the bolts to 18 ft. lbs. (25 Nm).
17. Lower the vehicle.
18. Install the accessory drive belt. Refer to Accessory Drive Belts, removal & installation.
19. Connect the negative (-) battery cable on the negative battery post. Refer to Battery, removal & installation.
20. Fill and bleed the power steering system. Refer to Power Steering Pump, Bleeding procedure.
21. Check for leaks.

BLEEDING

See Figure 304.

✱✱ WARNING

Power steering fluid, engine parts and exhaust system may be extremely hot if engine has been running. Do not start engine with any loose or disconnected hoses. Do not allow hoses to touch hot exhaust manifold or catalyst.

✱✱ CAUTION

Fluid level should be checked with the engine off to prevent personal injury from moving parts.

✱✱ WARNING

When the system is open, cap all open ends of the hoses, power steering pump fittings, or power steering gear ports to prevent entry of foreign material into the components.

✱✱ WARNING

MOPAR® Power Steering Fluid+4 or MOPAR® ATF+4 Automatic Transmission Fluid is to be used in the power steering system. Both Fluids have the same material standard specifications. No other power steering or automatic transaxle fluid is to be used in the system. Damage may result to the power steering pump and system if another fluid is used. Do not overfill the system.

✱✱ WARNING

If the air is not purged from the power steering system correctly, pump failure could result.

➡Be sure the vacuum tool used in the following procedure is clean and free of any fluids.

1. Before servicing the vehicle, refer to the Precautions Section.
2. Check the fluid level. As measured on the side of the reservoir, the level should indicate between MAX and MIN when the fluid is at normal ambient temperature. Adjust the fluid level as necessary.
3. Tightly insert the Power Steering Cap Adapter, Special Tool 9688A, into the mouth of the reservoir.

➡Failure to use a vacuum pump reservoir may allow power steering fluid to be sucked into the hand vacuum pump.

4. Attach Hand Vacuum Pump, Special Tool C-4207-8, or equivalent, with reservoir attached, to the Power Steering Cap Adapter.

✱✱ WARNING

Do not run the vehicle while vacuum is applied to the power steering system. Damage to the power steering pump can occur.

➡When performing the following step make sure the vacuum level is maintained during the entire time period.

5. Using the Hand Vacuum Pump, apply 20–25 inches Hg (68–85 kPa) of vacuum to the system for a minimum of 3 minutes.
6. Slowly release the vacuum and remove the special tools.
7. Adjust the fluid level as necessary.
8. Repeat the steps until the fluid no longer drops when vacuum is applied.
9. Start the engine and cycle the steering wheel lock-to-lock 3 times.

➡Do not hold the steering wheel at the stops.

10. Stop the engine and check for leaks at all connections.
11. Check for any signs of air in the reservoir and check the fluid level. If air is present, repeat the procedure as necessary.

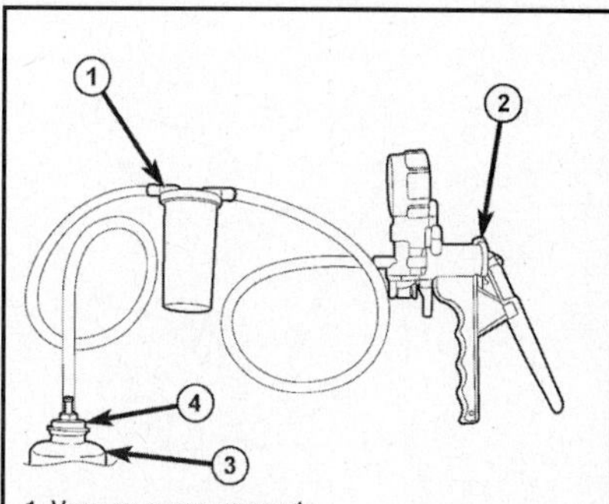

1. Vacuum pump reservoir
2. Special Tool C-4207-8, Hand Vacuum Pump
3. Mouth of the reservoir
4. Special Tool 9688A, Power Steering Cap Adapter

6153

Fig. 304 Special tools for bleeding the power steering system shown

FLUID FILL PROCEDURE

See Figure 305.

CAUTION

The fluid level should be checked with the engine OFF to prevent personal injury from moving parts and to assure an accurate fluid level reading.

WARNING

MOPAR® Power Steering Fluid+4 or MOPAR® ATF+4 Automatic Transmission Fluid is to be used in the power steering system. Both fluids have the same material standard specifications (MS-9602). No other power steering or automatic transaxle fluid is to be used in the system. Damage may result to the power steering pump and system if another fluid is used. Do not overfill the system.

➡Although not required at specific intervals, the fluid level may be checked periodically. Check the fluid level anytime there is a system noise or fluid leak suspected.

1. Before servicing the vehicle, refer to the Precautions Section.
2. The power steering fluid level can be viewed through the side of the power steering fluid reservoir.
3. Compare the fluid level to the markings on the side of the reservoir. When the fluid is at normal ambient temperature, approximately 70–80° F (21–27° C), the fluid level should read between the MAX and MIN markings. When the fluid is hot, the fluid level is allowed to read up to the MAX line.
4. To add fluid, clean the reservoir cap of any dirt or debris.
5. Remove the power steering reservoir cap.
6. Add specified fluid from a sealed container to the reservoir so that the level is between the MAX and MIN levels marked on the power steering reservoir.
7. Install the power steering reservoir cap.

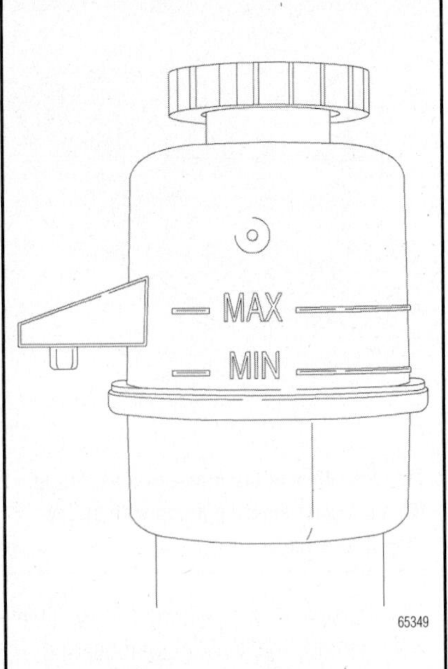

Fig. 305 The fluid level should be maintained between the MIN and MAX markings—power steering reservoir shown

SUSPENSION

FRONT SUSPENSION

CONTROL LINKS

REMOVAL & INSTALLATION

See Figure 306.

1. Before servicing the vehicle, refer to the Precautions Section.
2. Raise and safely support the vehicle.
3. Remove the front tire and wheel assemblies.
4. While holding the stabilizer bar link stud stationary, remove the nut securing the link to the strut.
5. While holding the stabilizer bar link lower stud stationary, remove the nut securing the link to the stabilizer bar.
6. Remove the stabilizer bar link.

To install:

7. Attach the stabilizer bar link to the stabilizer bar. Install and tighten the nut while holding the stabilizer bar link lower stud stationary. Tighten the nut to 35 ft. lbs. (48 Nm).
8. Attach the stabilizer bar link to the strut. Install and tighten the nut while holding the stabilizer bar link stud stationary. Tighten the nut to 35 ft. lbs. (48 Nm).
9. Install the wheel and tire assemblies. Tighten the wheel nuts in a star pattern until all nuts are torqued to half the required specification. Then repeat the tightening sequence to the full specified torque of 100 ft. lbs. (135 Nm).
10. Lower the vehicle.

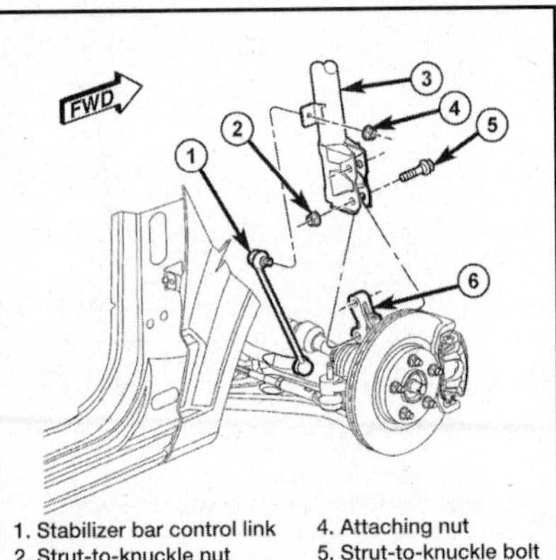

Fig. 306 Exploded view of front suspension components

LOWER BALL JOINT

REMOVAL & INSTALLATION

See Figures 307 through 309.

1. Before servicing the vehicle, refer to the Precautions Section.
2. Raise and safely support the vehicle.
3. Remove the front tire and wheel assemblies.
4. While a helper applies the brakes to keep the hub from rotating, remove the hub nut from the axle halfshaft.
5. Access and remove the front brake rotor.
6. Remove the routing clip securing the wheel speed sensor cable to the knuckle.
7. Remove the screw fastening the wheel speed sensor head to the knuckle. Pull the sensor head out of the knuckle.
8. Remove the nut attaching the lower ball joint to the lower control arm.
9. Release the lower ball joint from the

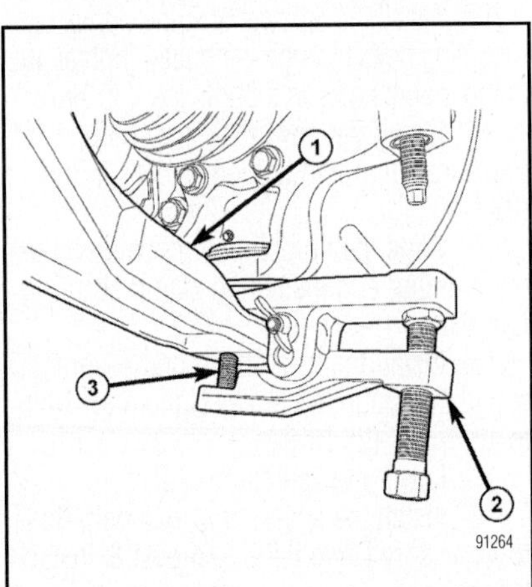

Fig. 307 Using Remover, Special Tool 9360 (2) to release the lower ball joint (3) from the lower control arm (1)

lower control arm using Remover, Special Tool 9360, or equivalent.

10. Lift the knuckle out of the lower control arm.

WARNING

Do not allow the halfshaft to hang by the inner CV-joint; it must be supported to keep the joint from separating during this operation.

11. Pull the knuckle off the axle halfshaft outer CV-joint splines and support the halfshaft.

12. Through the access hole in the knuckle, tap the ends of the snap-ring with a drift punch and remove it from the ball joint.

13. Install Remover, Special Tool 9964-3, and Remover, Special Tool 9964-4 on Remover/Installer, Special Tool 8441-1. Place the tools over the ball joint, then hand tighten the screw-drive.

14. Using hand-tools, tighten the screw-drive forcing the ball joint out of the knuckle.

15. Loosen the screw-drive and remove the tools and the ball joint.

To install:

16. Install Installer, Special Tool 9964-1, and Installer, Special Tool 9964-2 on Remover/Installer, Special Tool 8441-1. Place a new ball joint (stem down) into Installer 9964-2.

17. Position the assembly onto the knuckle, then hand tighten the screw-drive.

18. Using hand-tools, tighten the screw-drive forcing the ball joint into the knuckle. Continue to install the ball joint until the flange on the ball joint comes to a stop against the bottom of the knuckle.

19. Loosen the screw-drive and remove the tools.

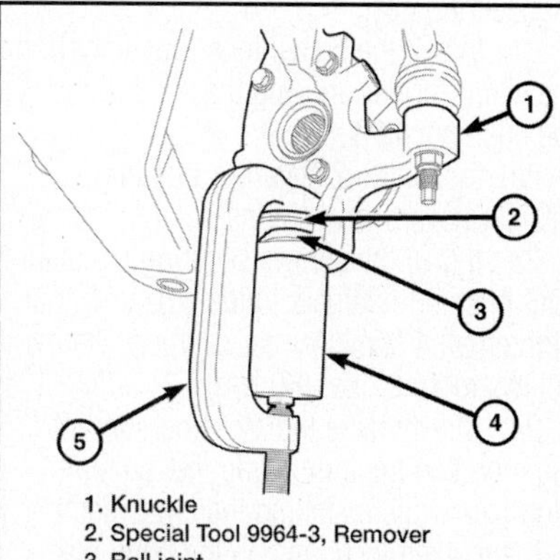

Fig. 308 Using Special Tools to remove the lower ball joint from the steering knuckle

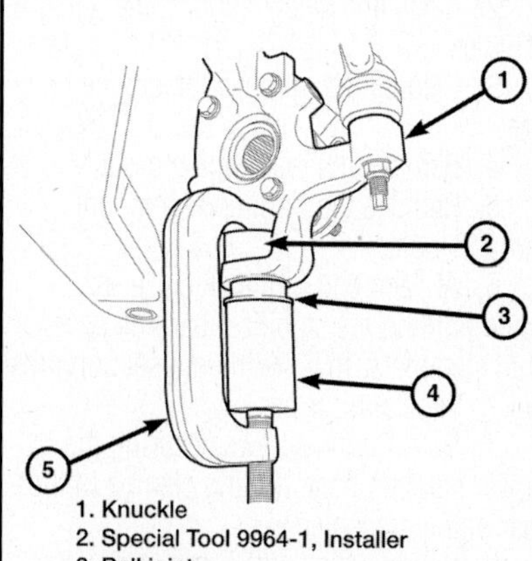

Fig. 309 Using Special Tools to install the lower ball joint to the steering knuckle

20. Install a NEW snap-ring into the groove in the ball joint using a drift punch.

21. Slide the hub and bearing in the knuckle onto the splines of the halfshaft outer CV-joint.

22. Insert the lower ball joint stud into the mounting hole in the lower control arm.

23. Install a NEW ball joint stud nut. Tighten the nut to 70 ft. lbs. (95 Nm).

24. Install the wheel speed sensor head into the knuckle. Install the mounting screw and tighten it to 106 inch lbs. (12 Nm).

25. Install the routing clip securing the wheel speed sensor cable to the knuckle.

26. Install the brake rotor, disc brake caliper, and adapter.

27. Clean all foreign matter from the threads of the halfshaft outer CV-joint.

28. Install the hub nut on the end of the halfshaft and snug it.

29. While a helper applies the brakes to keep the hub from rotating, tighten the hub nut to 97 ft. lbs. (132 Nm).

30. Install the wheel and tire assemblies. Tighten the wheel nuts in a star pattern until all nuts are torqued to half the required specification. Then repeat the tightening sequence to the full specified torque of 100 ft. lbs. (135 Nm).

31. Lower the vehicle.

32. Perform a wheel alignment as necessary.

LOWER CONTROL ARM

REMOVAL & INSTALLATION

See Figure 310.

1. Before servicing the vehicle, refer to the Precautions Section.

2. Raise and safely support the vehicle.

3. Remove the front tire and wheel assemblies.

4. Remove the nut attaching the lower ball joint to the lower control arm.

5. Release the lower ball joint from the lower control arm using Remover 9360. Do not lift the knuckle out of the lower control arm at this time.

WARNING

Upon removing the knuckle from the ball joint stud, do not pull outward on the knuckle. Pulling the knuckle outward at this point can separate the inner CV-joint on the halfshaft thus damaging it.

6. At each end of the stabilizer bar, while holding the stabilizer bar link lower stud stationary, remove the nut securing the link to the stabilizer bar.

7. Rotate the ends of the stabilizer bar upward away from the lower control arm.

8. Remove the front bolt attaching the lower control arm to the front suspension crossmember.

9. Remove the nut on the rear bolt attaching the lower control arm to the front suspension crossmember. Remove the bolt.

10. Remove the lower control arm from the crossmember.

To install:

11. Place the lower control arm into the front suspension crossmember.

12. Insert the rear bolt up through the crossmember and lower control arm. Install the nut on the top-end of the bolt, but do not tighten it at this time.

13. Install, but do not fully tighten, the front bolt attaching the lower control arm to the crossmember.

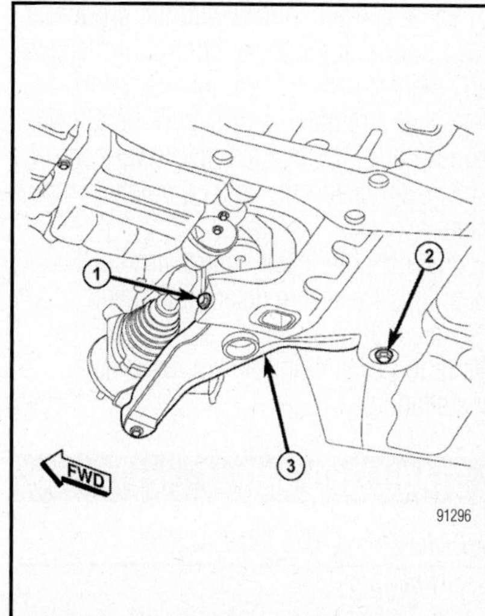

Fig. 310 View of lower control arm (3), control arm front bolt (1), and rear bolt (2)

14. With no weight or obstruction on the lower control arm, tighten the lower control arm front mounting bolt to 129 ft. lbs. (175 Nm).

15. With no weight or obstruction on the lower control arm, tighten the lower control arm rear mounting bolt nut to 107 ft. lbs. (145 Nm).

16. Attach the stabilizer bar link at each end of the stabilizer bar. At each link, install and tighten the nut while holding the stabilizer bar link lower stud stationary. Tighten the nuts to 35 ft. lbs. (48 Nm).

➡If a new or cleaned lower control arm is being installed, it is important to have a film of general purpose grease around the ball joint mounting hole on the lower control arm to avoid any future corrosion issues. Make sure the grease does not get inside the ball joint mounting hole or on the ball joint stud during installation.

17. Insert the lower ball joint stud into the mounting hole in the lower control arm.

18. Install a NEW ball joint stud nut. Tighten the nut to 70 ft. lbs. (95 Nm).

19. Install the wheel and tire assembly. Tighten the wheel nuts in a star pattern until all nuts are torqued to half the required specification. Then repeat the tightening sequence to the full specified torque of 100 ft. lbs. (135 Nm).

20. Lower the vehicle.

21. Perform a wheel alignment as necessary.

CONTROL ARM BUSHING REPLACEMENT

Inspect the lower control arm for signs of damage from contact with the ground or road debris. If the lower control arm shows any sign of damage, do not attempt to repair or straighten a broken or bent lower control arm. If damaged, the lower control arm is serviced only as a complete component.

Inspect both lower control arm isolator bushings for severe deterioration and replace the lower control arm as required. Refer to Lower Control Arm, removal & installation.

STABILIZER BAR

REMOVAL & INSTALLATION

See Figure 311.

1. Before servicing the vehicle, refer to the Precautions Section.

2. Raise and safely support the vehicle.

3. If equipped, remove the engine belly pan.

4. Remove the rear engine mount.

5. Remove the front engine mount through-bolt.

6. At each end of the stabilizer bar, while holding the stabilizer bar link lower stud stationary, remove the nut securing the link to the stabilizer bar.

7. Remove the screws securing the power steering hose routing clamps to the rear of the crossmember.

8. Remove the screws and push-pins securing the heat shield over the right side of the steering gear.

9. Remove the 2 bolts securing the steering gear to the crossmember.

10. Support the steering gear using a bungee cord, or equivalent, to keep the steering gear from lowering when the crossmember is lowered.

➡Before removing the front suspension crossmember from the vehicle, the location of the crossmember must be marked on the body of the vehicle. Do this so the crossmember can be relocated, upon reinstallation, against the body of vehicle in the same location as before removal. If the front suspension crossmember is not reinstalled in exactly the same location as before removal, the preset front wheel alignment settings (caster and camber) may be lost.

11. Mark the location of the front crossmember on the body near each mounting bolt.

12. Support the crossmember with a transmission jack.

13. Remove the 4 mounting bolts securing the front crossmember to the body.

14. Remove the mounting screws securing the front crossmember reinforcement brackets (one each side of vehicle) to the body. Remove the brackets.

15. Slowly lower the crossmember using the jack until there is enough space present to remove the stabilizer bar between the rear of the crossmember and the body. Due to the fact that the fore-and-aft crossmember is still attached, do not lower the crossmember any more than necessary to remove the stabilizer bar.

16. Remove the screws securing the stabilizer bushing retainers to the crossmember.

17. Remove the 2 stabilizer bushing retainers.

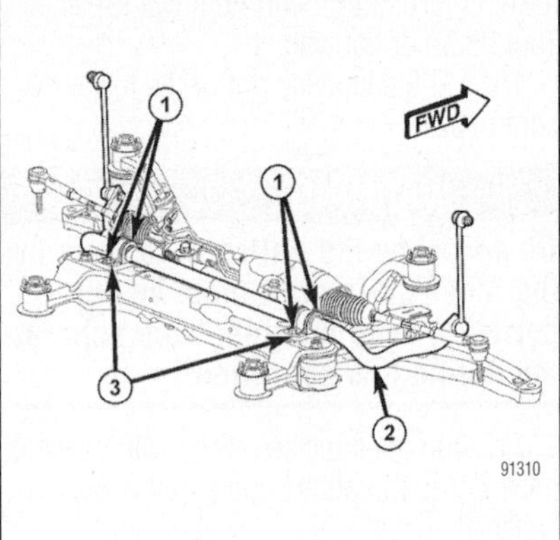

Fig. 311 Remove the screws (1) securing the stabilizer bushing retainers (3) to the crossmember and remove the stabilizer bar (2)

18. Utilizing the slit cut into the cushions (bushings), remove the two cushions from the stabilizer bar.

19. Remove the stabilizer bar from the vehicle.

To install:

➡Before stabilizer bar installation, inspect the cushions and links for excessive wear, cracks, damage, and distortion. Replace any pieces failing inspection.

➡Before installing the stabilizer bar, make sure the bar is not upside down. The stabilizer bar must be installed so that when it is in the mounted position, the ends of the bar curve under the steering gear tie rods, up to the links.

20. Install the stabilizer bar, link ends first, from the rear over top of the crossmember. Curve the ends of the bar under the steering gear.

21. Install the 2 cushions (bushings) on the stabilizer bar utilizing the slit cut into the cushion sides.

22. Install the 2 stabilizer bushing retainers over the cushions.

23. Install the screws securing the stabilizer bushing retainers to the crossmember. Tighten all 4 stabilizer bar cushion retainer screws to 44 ft. lbs. (60 Nm).

24. Slowly raise the crossmember into the mounted position using the transmission jack while matching the crossmember to the marked locations on the body made during removal.

25. Position the front crossmember reinforcement brackets (one each side of vehicle) over the crossmember rear mounting bushings and install the mounting screws, but do not tighten at this time.

26. Install the 4 mounting bolts securing the front crossmember to the body. Tighten the crossmember mounting bolts to 100 ft. lbs. (135 Nm).

27. Tighten the crossmember reinforcement bracket mounting screws to 37 ft. lbs. (50 Nm).

28. Remove the transmission jack.

29. Remove the bungee cord, or equivalent, supporting the steering gear.

30. Install the 2 bolts securing the steering gear to the crossmember. Tighten the steering gear mounting bolts to 74 ft. lbs. (100 Nm).

31. Position the heat shield over the steering gear. Install the mounting screws and push-pins. Tighten the screws to 53 inch lbs. (6 Nm).

32. Position the power steering hose routing clamps on the crossmember. Install and tighten the screws to 71 inch lbs. (8 Nm).

33. Attach the stabilizer bar link at each end of the stabilizer bar. At each link, install and tighten the nut while holding the stabilizer bar link lower stud stationary. Tighten the nuts to 35 ft. lbs. (48 Nm).

34. Install the rear engine mount.

35. Install the front engine mount through-bolt.

36. If equipped, install the engine belly pan.

37. Lower the vehicle.

STEERING KNUCKLE

REMOVAL & INSTALLATION

See Figure 312.

1. Before servicing the vehicle, refer to the Precautions Section.

2. Raise and safely support the vehicle.

3. Remove the front tire and wheel assemblies.

➡The hub nut is a single use type. A new nut is required for reassembly. Do not reuse the hub nut.

4. While a helper applies the brakes to keep the hub from rotating, remove the hub nut from the axle halfshaft.

5. Access and remove the front brake rotor.

6. Remove the routing clip securing the wheel speed sensor cable to the knuckle.

7. Remove the screw fastening the wheel speed sensor head to the knuckle. Pull the sensor head out of the knuckle.

8. Remove the nut attaching the outer tie rod to the knuckle. To do this, it might be necessary to hold the tie rod end stud with a wrench while loosening and removing the nut with a standard wrench or crowfoot wrench.

9. Release the outer tie rod end from the knuckle using Remover, Special Tool 9360.

10. Remove the outer tie rod from the knuckle.

11. Remove the nut attaching the lower ball joint to the lower control arm.

12. Release the lower ball joint from the lower control arm using Remover, Special Tool 9360. Do not lift the knuckle out of the lower control arm at this time.

✻✻ WARNING

The strut assembly-to-knuckle attaching bolts are serrated and must not be turned during removal. Proper removal is required. Refer to the following steps for the correct method.

13. While holding the bolt heads stationary, remove the 2 nuts from the bolts attaching the strut to the knuckle.

14. Remove the 2 bolts attaching the strut to the knuckle using a pin punch.

✻✻ WARNING

Do not allow the halfshaft to hang by the inner CV-joint; it must be supported to keep the joint from separating during this operation.

15. Pull the knuckle off the halfshaft outer CV-joint splines and remove the knuckle from the vehicle.

16. If required, remove the 3 screws fastening the shield to the knuckle. Remove the shield.

17. If required, remove the 4 bolts fastening the hub and bearing to the knuckle.

18. If required, slide the hub and bearing out of the knuckle.

To install:

19. If required, install the hub and bearing by sliding it into the knuckle.

20. If installing the hub and bearing, install the 4 bolts fastening the hub and bearing to the knuckle. Tighten the 4 bolts to 60 ft. lbs. (82 Nm).

21. If required, install the shield on the knuckle. Install and tighten the 3 mounting screws to 89 inch lbs. (10 Nm).

22. Slide the hub and bearing in the knuckle onto the splines of the halfshaft outer CV-joint.

23. Insert the lower ball joint stud into the mounting hole in the lower control arm.

24. Install a NEW ball joint stud nut. Tighten the nut to 70 ft. lbs. (95 Nm).

✻✻ WARNING

The strut clevis-to-knuckle bolts are serrated and must not be turned during installation. Install the nuts while holding the bolts stationary in the steering knuckle. Refer to the following step.

25. Position the lower end of the strut assembly in line with the upper end of the knuckle, aligning the mounting holes. Install the 2 mounting bolts.

26. Install the nuts on the 2 bolts. While holding the bolts in place, tighten the nuts to 103 ft. lbs. (140 Nm).

➡If a new tie rod end is to be installed, make sure the boot is properly lubricated.

27. Clean all old grease and debris from the boot with a clean cloth.

28. Apply outer tie rod grease to the tie rod end boot.

29. Install the outer tie rod ball stud into the hole in the knuckle arm. Start the tie rod end-to-knuckle nut onto the stud. While holding the tie rod end stud with a wrench, tighten the nut with a wrench or crowfoot wrench to 63 ft. lbs. (85 Nm).

30. Install the wheel speed sensor head into the knuckle. Install the mounting screw and tighten it to 106 inch lbs. (12 Nm).

31. Install the routing clip securing the wheel speed sensor cable to the knuckle.

32. Install the brake rotor, disc brake caliper, and adapter.

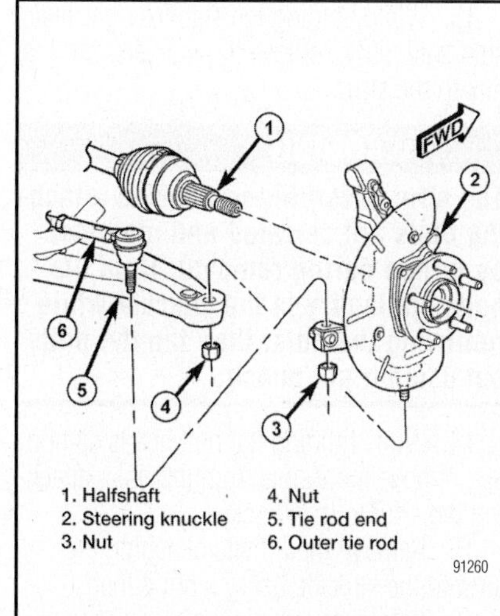

Fig. 312 Removing the steering knuckle

33. Clean all foreign matter from the threads of the halfshaft outer CV-joint.

➡**The hub nut is a single use type. A new nut is required for reassembly. Do not reuse the hub nut.**

34. Install the hub nut on the end of the halfshaft and snug it.
35. While a helper applies the brakes to keep the hub from rotating, tighten the hub nut to 97 ft. lbs. (132 Nm).
36. Install the wheel and tire assemblies. Tighten the wheel nuts in a star pattern until all nuts are torqued to half the required specification. Then repeat the tightening sequence to the full specified torque of 100 ft. lbs. (135 Nm).
37. Lower the vehicle.
38. Perform a wheel alignment as necessary.

STRUT & SPRING ASSEMBLY

REMOVAL & INSTALLATION

See Figures 313 through 315.

⁂ WARNING

Do not remove the strut rod nut while the strut assembly is installed in the vehicle, or before the coil spring is compressed with a compression tool. The spring is held under high pressure.

⁂ WARNING

At no time when servicing a vehicle can a sheet metal screw, bolt, or other metal fastener be installed in the shock tower to take the place of an original plastic clip. It may come into contact with the strut or coil spring.

1. Before servicing the vehicle, refer to the Precautions Section.
2. Remove the engine appearance cover.
3. Remove the 2 push-pins securing the cowl top screen at the ends. Remove the remaining push-pins. Remove the cowl top screen.
4. Lift the front wiper arm to its over-center position to hold the wiper blade off of the glass and relieve the spring tension on the wiper arm to pivot shaft connection.
5. Carefully pry the plastic nut cap off of the pivot end of the wiper arm.
6. Remove the nut that secures the wiper arm to the wiper pivot shaft.
7. If necessary, use a suitable battery terminal puller to disengage the wiper arm from the pivot shaft.

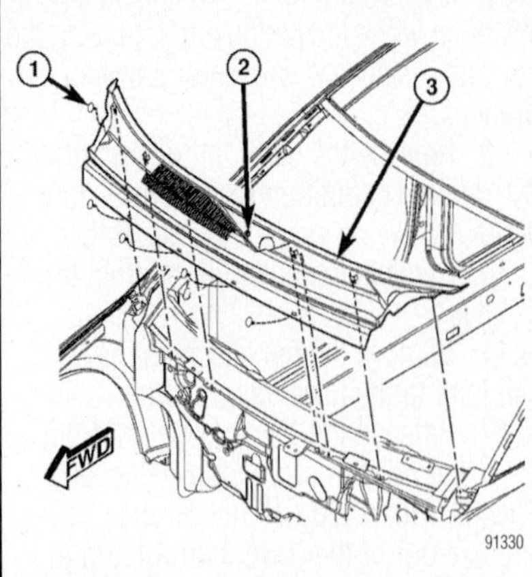

Fig. 313 Remove the push-pins (1) securing the cowl screen. Rotate the screw (2) in the center of the cowl screen 90° clockwise to release and remove the cowl screen (3)

8. Remove the front wiper arm pivot end from the pivot shaft.
9. Remove the push-pins securing the cowl screen to the wheelhouse brace and cowl. Rotate the screw in the center of the cowl screen 90° clockwise to release the screen. Remove the cowl screen.
10. Raise and safely support the vehicle.
11. Remove the wheel mounting nuts, then the tire and wheel assembly.

➡**If both strut assemblies are to be removed, mark the strut assemblies right or left and keep the parts separated to avoid mix-up. Not all parts of the strut assembly are interchangeable side-to-side.**

12. Remove the screw securing the hydraulic brake flex hose routing bracket to the strut.
13. While holding the stabilizer bar link stud stationary, remove the nut securing the link to the strut.

⁂ WARNING

The strut assembly-to-knuckle attaching bolts are serrated and must not be turned during removal. Hold the bolts stationary in the knuckle while removing the nuts, then tap the bolts out using a pin punch.

14. While holding the bolt heads stationary, remove the 2 nuts from the bolts attaching the strut to the knuckle.
15. Remove the 2 bolts attaching the strut to the knuckle using a pin punch.
16. Lower the vehicle just enough to open the hood without allowing the tires to touch the floor.

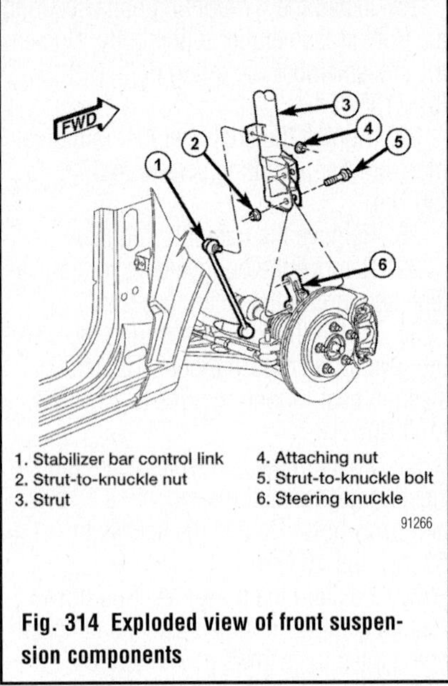

Fig. 314 Exploded view of front suspension components

17. Remove the 3 nuts attaching the strut assembly upper mount to the strut tower.
18. Remove the strut assembly from the vehicle.

To install:

19. Raise the strut assembly into the strut tower, aligning the 3 studs on the strut assembly upper mount with the holes in strut tower. Install the 3 mounting nuts on the studs. Tighten the 3 nuts to 41 ft. lbs. (55 Nm).

➡**The strut clevis-to-knuckle bolts are serrated and must not be turned during installation. Install the nuts while holding the bolts stationary in the knuckle.**

20. Position the lower end of the strut assembly in line with the upper end of the knuckle, aligning the mounting holes. Install the 2 attaching bolts. Install the nuts.

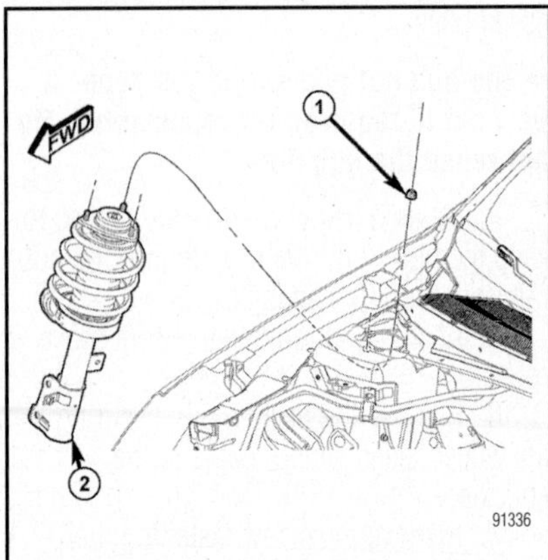

Fig. 315 Remove the nuts (1) attaching the strut assembly (2) upper mount to the strut tower

While holding the bolts in place, tighten the nuts to 103 ft. lbs. (140 Nm).

21. Attach the stabilizer bar link to the strut. Install and tighten the nut while holding the stabilizer bar link stud stationary. Tighten the nut to 74 ft. lbs. (100 Nm).

22. Secure the flex hose routing bracket to the strut with the mounting screw. Tighten the mounting screw to 115 inch lbs. (13 Nm).

23. Install the wheel and tire assembly. Tighten the wheel nuts in a star pattern until all nuts are torqued to half the required specification. Then repeat the tightening sequence to the full specified torque of 100 ft. lbs. (135 Nm).

24. Lower the vehicle.

25. Install the cowl screen. Install the push-pins securing the cowl screen to the wheelhouse brace and cowl. Rotate the screw in the center of the cowl screen 90° counterclockwise to lock the screen in place.

➡Be certain that the wiper motor is in the park position before attempting to install the front wiper arms. Turn the ignition switch to the ON position and move the multi-function switch control knob to its OFF position. If the wiper pivots move, wait until they stop moving, then turn the ignition switch back to the OFF position. The front wiper motor is now in its park position.

26. The front wiper arms must be indexed to the pivot shafts with the front wiper motor in the park position to be properly installed. Position the wiper arm pivot ends onto the wiper pivot shafts so that the tip of the wiper blade is aligned with the wiper alignment lines located within the lower margin (blackout area) of the windshield glass.

27. Once the wiper blade is aligned, lift the wiper arm away from the windshield slightly to relieve the spring tension on the pivot end and push the pivot end of the wiper arm down firmly and evenly over the pivot shaft.

28. Install and tighten the nut that secures the wiper arm to the pivot shaft. Tighten the nut to 18 ft. lbs. (24 Nm).

29. Wet the windshield glass, then operate the front wipers. Turn the front wipers OFF, then check for the correct wiper arm position and readjust as required.

30. Reinstall the plastic nut cap onto the wiper arm pivot nut.

31. Install the cowl top screen. Install the 2 push-pins securing the cowl top screen at the ends. Install the remaining push-pins.

32. Install the engine appearance cover.

OVERHAUL

See Figures 316 and 317.

➡The strut assembly must be removed from the vehicle for overhaul.

➡For disassembly and assembly of the strut, use a strut spring compressor to compress the coil spring. Follow the manufacturer's instructions closely.

⁂ CAUTION

Do not remove the strut rod nut before the coil spring is properly compressed. The coil spring is held under pressure. The coil spring must be compressed, removing spring tension from the upper mount and bearing, before the strut rod nut is removed.

1. Before servicing the vehicle, refer to the Precautions Section.

2. If both struts are being serviced at the same time, mark both the coil spring and strut assembly according to the side of the vehicle from which the strut is being removed.

3. Position the strut assembly in the strut coil spring compressor following the manufacturer's instructions and set the lower and upper hooks of the compressor on the coil spring. Position the strut clevis bracket straight outward, away from the compressor.

4. Compress the coil spring until all coil spring tension is removed from the upper mount and bearing.

⁂ WARNING

Never use impact or high speed tools to remove the strut rod nut. Damage to the strut internal bearings can occur.

5. Once the spring is sufficiently compressed, install Strut Nut Wrench, Special Tool 9362, on the strut rod nut. Next, install a deep socket on the end of the strut rod. While holding the strut rod from turning, remove the nut using the strut nut wrench.

6. Remove the clamp (if installed) from the bottom of the coil spring and remove the strut (damper) out through the bottom of the coil spring.

7. Remove the lower spring isolator from the strut seat.

8. Remove the dust shield and jounce bumper.

9. Remove the upper strut mount from the top of the bearing and upper spring seat.

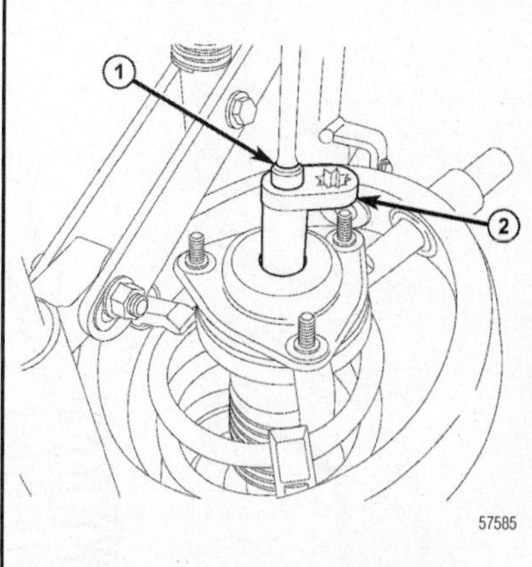

Fig. 316 Install Special Tool 9362, Strut Nut Wrench (2), on the strut rod nut and a deep socket (1) on the end of the strut rod

10. Remove the upper spring seat and isolator from the top of the coil spring.

11. Release the tension from the coil spring by backing off the compressor drive completely. Push back the compressor hooks and remove the coil spring.

12. Inspect the strut assembly components for the following and replace as necessary:

a. Inspect the strut (damper) for shaft binding over the full stroke of the shaft.

b. Inspect the jounce bumper for cracks and signs of deterioration.

c. Inspect the dust shield for cracks and tears.

d. Check the upper mount for cracks and distortion and its retaining studs for any sign of damage.

e. Check the bearing and upper spring seat for any binding.

f. Inspect the upper and lower spring isolators (4, 8) for material deterioration and distortion.

g. Inspect the coil spring for any sign of damage to the coating.

To assemble:

➡To determine the flat coil end of the coil spring for the following step, attempt to stand the coil spring on-end on a flat, level surface. If the coil spring stands on end, the end on the flat surface is the flat coil end. If the coil spring falls over, the end on the flat surface is not the flat coil end. Stand the coil spring on the opposite end to verify.

13. Place the coil spring flat coil end upward (see above note) in the spring compressor following the manufacturer's instructions. Before compressing the spring, rotate the spring so the end of the

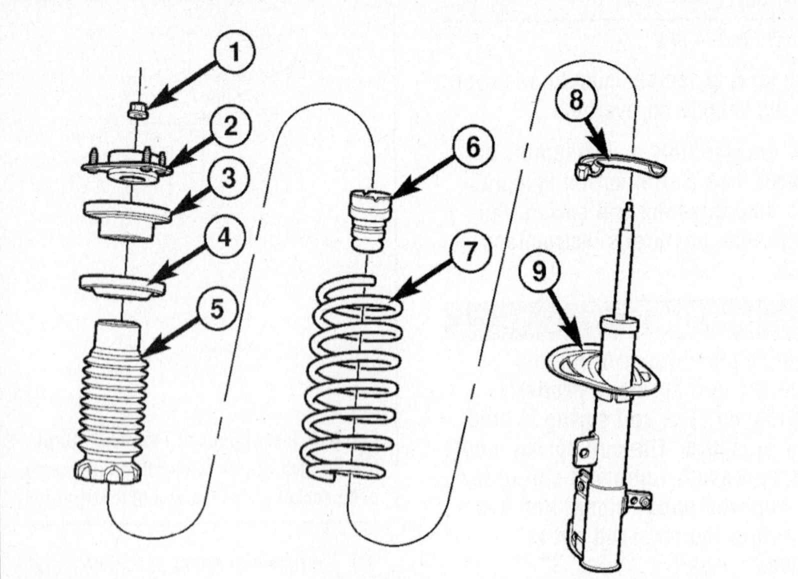

Fig. 317 Exploded view of front strut assembly

bottom coil is at approximately the 9 o'clock position as viewed above (or to where the spring was when removed from the compressor). This action will allow the strut (damper) clevis bracket to be positioned outward, away from the compressor once installed.

14. Slowly compress the coil spring until enough room is available for strut assembly reassembly.
15. Install the bearing and upper spring seat, and isolator on top of the coil spring.
16. Install the upper mount on top of the bearing and upper spring seat.
17. Install the lower spring isolator on the spring seat on the strut (damper).
18. Slide the jounce bumper and dust shield onto the strut rod.
19. Install the strut up through the bottom of the coil spring and upper spring seat, mount, and bearing until the lower spring seat contacts the lower end of the coil spring. Rotate the strut as necessary until the end of the bottom coil comes in contact with the stop built into the lower spring isolator.
20. While holding the strut in position, install the nut on the end of the strut rod.
21. Install Strut Nut Wrench, Special Tool 9362, on the strut rod nut. Next, install a deep socket on the end of the strut rod. While holding the strut rod from turning, tighten the strut rod nut to 44 ft. lbs. (60 Nm) using a torque wrench on the end of Special Tool 9362.
22. Slowly release the tension from the coil spring by backing off the compressor drive completely. As the tension is relieved, make sure the upper mount and bearing align properly. Verify the upper mount does not bind when rotated.
23. Remove the strut assembly from the spring compressor.
24. Install the strut assembly on the vehicle.

WHEEL BEARINGS

REMOVAL & INSTALLATION

See Figure 318.

WARNING

Wheel bearing damage will result if after loosening the axle hub nut, the vehicle is rolled on the ground or the weight of the vehicle is allowed to be supported by the tires for any length of time.

1. Before servicing the vehicle, refer to the Precautions Section.
2. Raise and safely support the vehicle.
3. Remove the front tire and wheel assemblies.
4. While a helper applies the brakes to

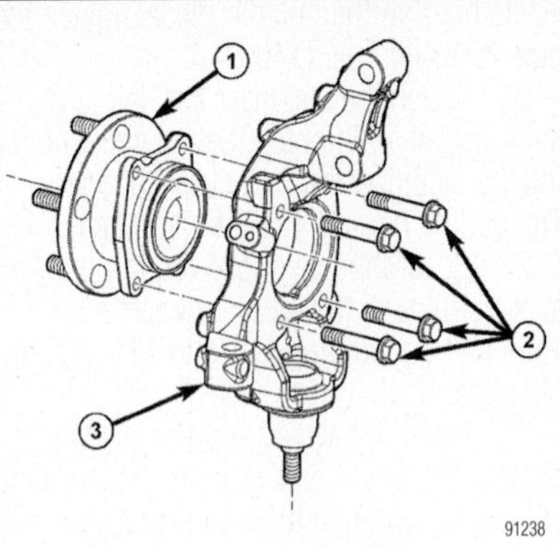

Fig. 318 Remove the bolts (2) fastening the hub and bearing to the knuckle (3) and slide the hub and bearing (1) off the halfshaft and out of the knuckle

keep the hub from rotating, remove the hub nut from the axle halfshaft.

5. Access and remove the front brake rotor.
6. Remove the 4 bolts fastening the hub and bearing to the knuckle.
7. Slide the hub and bearing off the halfshaft and out of the knuckle.

To install:

8. Install the hub and bearing by sliding it over the halfshaft and into the knuckle.
9. Install the 4 bolts fastening the hub and bearing to the knuckle. Tighten the 4 bolts to 60 ft. lbs. (82 Nm).
10. Install the brake rotor, disc brake caliper, and adapter.

➡Always install a new hub nut. The original hub nut is one-time use only and should be discarded when removed.

11. Clean all foreign matter from the threads of the halfshaft outer CV-joint.
12. Install the hub nut on the end of the halfshaft and lightly tighten it.
13. While a helper applies the brakes to keep the hub from rotating, tighten the hub nut to 97 ft. lbs. (132 Nm).
14. Install the wheel and tire assembly. Tighten the wheel nuts in a star pattern until all nuts are torqued to half the required specification. Then repeat the tightening sequence to the full specified torque of 100 ft. lbs. (135 Nm).
15. Lower the vehicle.

ADJUSTMENT

The wheel bearings are sealed at the factory and do not require any adjustment or maintenance.

LOWER CONTROL ARM

REMOVAL & INSTALLATION

See Figure 319.

1. Before servicing the vehicle, refer to the Precautions Section.
2. Raise and safely support the vehicle.
3. Remove the rear tire and wheel assemblies.
4. If equipped, while holding the stabilizer bar link lower stud stationary, remove the nut securing the link to the lower control arm.
5. If equipped with load-leveling shocks, support the lower shock with a jack using just enough force to allow easy removal of the lower shock mounting bolt in the following step. Lower the jack following bolt removal.
6. Remove the lower shock mounting nut and bolt.
7. Remove the nut and bolt securing the lower control arm to the knuckle.
8. Remove the nut and bolt securing the lower control arm to the rear crossmember.
9. Remove the lower control arm.

To install:

10. Position the lower control arm and install the bolt and nut securing the lower control arm to the crossmember. Do not tighten at this time.
11. Install the bolt and nut securing the lower control arm to the knuckle. Do not tighten at this time.
12. If equipped with load-leveling shocks, place a jack against the lower shock eye and support the lower end of the shock assembly. Lift the shock assembly using the jack until the hole in the lower shock eye lines up with that in the lower control arm.
13. Install the mounting bolt and nut fastening the shock assembly to the lower control arm. Do not tighten at this time.

➡When attaching a stabilizer bar link to the lower control arm it is important that the lower mounting stud be positioned properly. The lower mounting stud on the right side link needs to point toward the front of the vehicle when inserted through the lower control arm mounting flange. The left side link lower stud needs to point toward the rear of the vehicle. Otherwise the suspension geometry will not function properly.

14. If equipped, attach the stabilizer bar link to the lower control arm. Install the nut and while holding the stabilizer bar link lower stud stationary, tighten the nut to 35 ft. lbs. (48 Nm).
15. Install the wheel and tire assembly. Tighten the wheel nuts in a star pattern until all nuts are torqued to half the required specification. Then repeat the tightening sequence to the full specified torque of 100 ft. lbs. (135 Nm).
16. Lower the vehicle.
17. Position the vehicle on an alignment rack/drive-on lift. Raise the vehicle as necessary to access mounting bolts and nuts.
18. Tighten the lower control arm mounting bolt nut at the crossmember to 77 ft. lbs. (105 Nm).
19. Tighten the lower control arm mounting bolt nut at the knuckle to 77 ft. lbs. (105 Nm).
20. Tighten the shock assembly lower mounting bolt nut to 73 ft. lbs. (99 Nm).
21. Perform a wheel alignment as necessary.

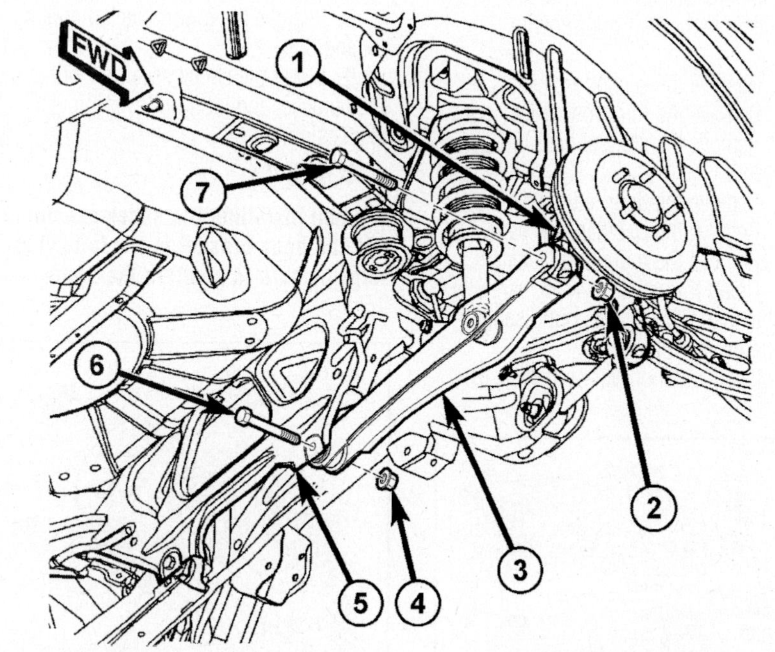

Fig. 319 View of lower control arm and related components

STABILIZER BAR

REMOVAL & INSTALLATION

See Figure 320.

⁂ WARNING

Only frame contact or wheel lift hoisting equipment can be used on this vehicle. It cannot be hoisted using equipment designed to lift a vehicle by the rear axle. If this type of hoisting equipment is used, damage to rear suspension components may occur.

➡If a rear suspension component becomes bent, damaged, or fails, no attempt should be made to straighten or repair it. Always replace it with a new component.

1. Before servicing the vehicle, refer to the Precautions Section.
2. Raise and safely support the vehicle.
3. On each side of the vehicle, while holding the stabilizer bar link upper stud stationary, remove the nut securing the link to the stabilizer bar.
4. If equipped with AWD, remove the rear driveline module. Refer to Rear Axle Housing, removal & installation.

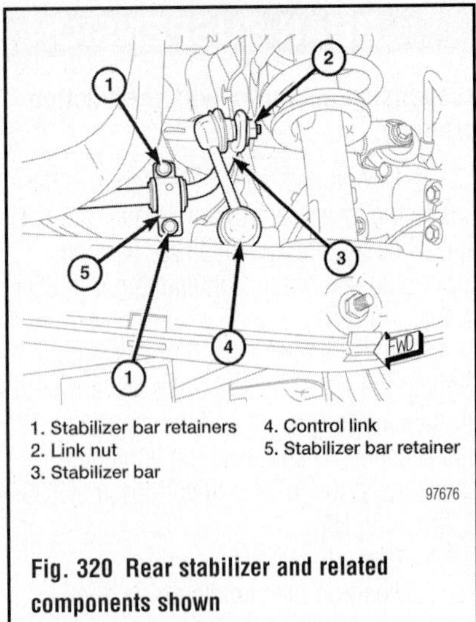

Fig. 320 Rear stabilizer and related components shown

5. On each side of the vehicle, remove the screws securing the stabilizer bar retainer to the crossmember.
6. Remove the 2 stabilizer bar retainers.
7. Remove the stabilizer bar from the vehicle.
8. If required, remove the 2 cushions (bushings) from the stabilizer bar utilizing the slit cut into the cushions.

To install:

9. If required, install the 2 cushions (bushings) on the stabilizer bar (one on each side) utilizing the slit cut into the cushions.

➡When installing the stabilizer bar on a vehicle with AWD, position the bar so that the bar loops over the axle half-shafts once installed, not under the axle halfshafts.

10. Position the stabilizer bar on the rear crossmember.

➡Before installing the screws in the following step, it is especially important to clean the threads and apply MOPAR® Lock AND Seal Adhesive or equivalent.

11. Install the 2 retainers over the cushions at the mounting holes and install the retainer screws. Do not tighten the screws at this time.
12. If equipped with AWD, install the rear driveline module. Refer to Rear Axle Housing, removal & installation.

➡Before installing the nut in the following step, it is especially important to clean the threads and apply MOPAR® Lock AND Seal Adhesive or equivalent.

13. On each side of the vehicle, install the stabilizer link upper stud in the end of the stabilizer bar. Install the nut on the upper stud and while holding the stabilizer link stud stationary, tighten the nut to 74 ft. lbs. (100 Nm).
14. On each side of the vehicle, tighten the stabilizer bar retainer screws to 18 ft. lbs. (25 Nm).
15. Lower the vehicle.

STRUT & SPRING ASSEMBLY

REMOVAL & INSTALLATION

With Third Row Seating

See Figures 321 through 324.

⁂ WARNING

Only frame contact or wheel lift hoisting equipment can be used on this vehicle. It cannot be hoisted using equipment designed to lift a vehicle by the rear axle. If this type of hoisting equipment is used, damage to rear suspension components may occur.

➡If a rear suspension component becomes bent, damaged, or fails, no attempt should be made to straighten or repair it. Always replace it with a new component.

1. Before servicing the vehicle, refer to the Precautions Section.
2. Remove the rear quarter trim panel:
   a. Remove the second row seats.
   b. Remove the third row seats.
   c. Remove the storage box, if equipped.
   d. Remove the door sill plate.
   e. Remove the D-pillar trim panel.
   f. Remove the mounting fasteners.
   g. Using trim stick C-4755, carefully pry the quarter trim panel out disengaging the retaining clips.
3. Move insulation out of the way to access the shock assembly upper mounting nuts.

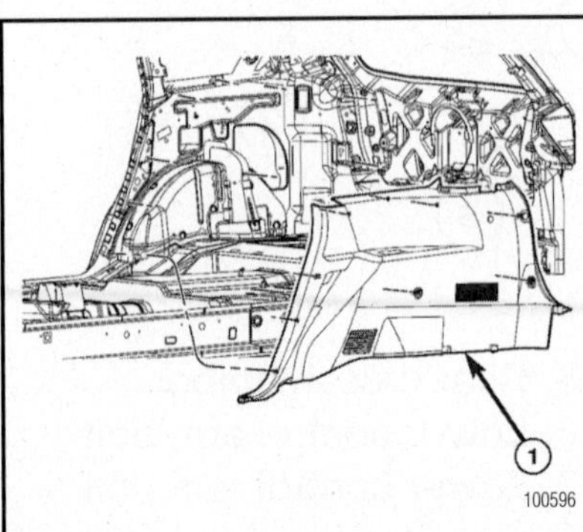

Fig. 321 Right rear quarter trim panel (1) removal

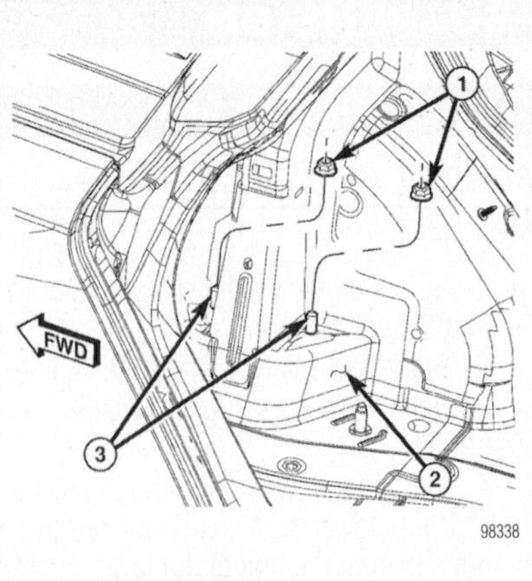

Fig. 322 Remove the 2 nuts (1) securing the shock assembly (3) to the body bracket (2)

4. Remove the 2 nuts securing the shock assembly to the body bracket.
5. Raise and safely support the vehicle.
6. Remove the wheel mounting nuts, then the rear tire and wheel assembly.
7. If equipped with load-leveling shocks, support the lower shock with a jack using just enough force to allow easy removal of the lower shock mounting bolt in the following step. Lower the jack following bolt removal.
8. Remove the lower shock mounting nut and bolt.
9. Lower the shock assembly out of the body bracket and lift it out over the rear suspension.

To install:

➡When installing the shock assembly into the body bracket in the following step, be sure to position the upper

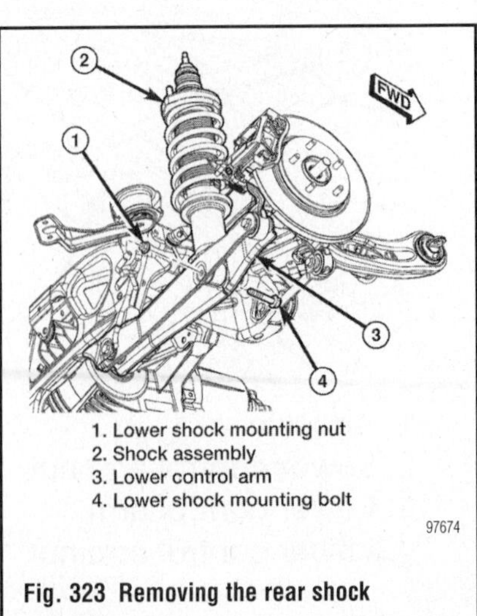

Fig. 323 Removing the rear shock assembly

mounting bracket so that the angular formed side (as viewed from above) of the mounting bracket flange is facing outboard of the vehicle (the opposite side of the bracket is rounded).

10. Insert the lower end of the shock assembly down through the lower control arm from above just enough to clear the body with the upper mount, then lift it up, inserting the upper mounting studs through the body bracket.
11. If equipped with load-leveling shocks, place a jack against the lower shock eye and support the lower end of the shock assembly. Lift the shock assembly using the jack until the hole in the lower shock eye lines up with that in the lower control arm.
12. Install the mounting bolt and nut fastening the shock assembly to the lower control arm. Do not tighten at this time.
13. Install the wheel and tire assembly. Tighten the wheel nuts in a star pattern until all nuts are torqued to half the required specification. Then repeat the tightening sequence to the full specified torque of 100 ft. lbs. (135 Nm).
14. Lower the vehicle.
15. Install the 2 nuts on the studs securing the shock assembly to the body bracket. Tighten the mounting nuts to 41 ft. lbs. (55 Nm).
16. Install the rear quarter trim panel:
    a. Install the quarter trim panel.
    b. Install the mounting fasteners.
    c. Install the door sill plate.
    d. Install the D-pillar trim panel.
    e. Install the storage box, if equipped.
    f. Install the third row seats.
    g. Install the second row seats.

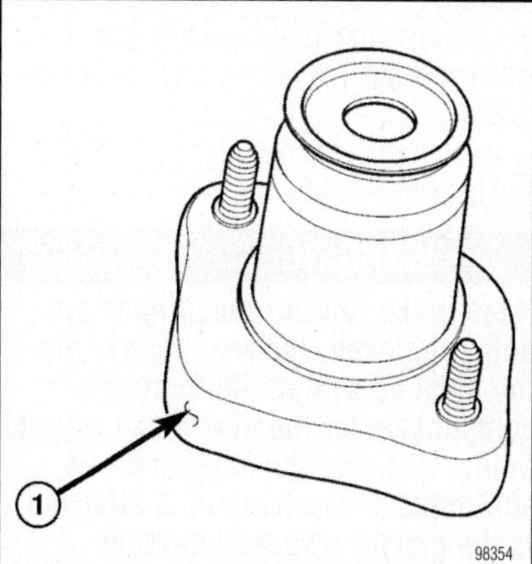

Fig. 324 Position the upper mounting bracket so that the angular formed side (as viewed from above) of the mounting bracket flange (1) is facing outboard of the vehicle

17. Position the vehicle on an alignment rack or drive-on lift. Raise the lift as necessary to access the shock mounting bolt and nut.
18. Tighten the shock assembly lower mounting bolt nut to 73 ft. lbs. (99 Nm).

Without Third Row Seating

See Figures 322 through 324.

⁂ WARNING

Only frame contact or wheel lift hoisting equipment can be used on this vehicle. It cannot be hoisted using equipment designed to lift a vehicle by the rear axle. If this type of hoisting equipment is used, damage to rear suspension components may occur.

➡If a rear suspension component becomes bent, damaged, or fails, no attempt should be made to straighten or repair it. Always replace it with a new component.

1. Before servicing the vehicle, refer to the Precautions Section.
2. Remove the 4 nuts and remove the load floor.
3. Open the access panel by breaking the perforations along the panel, then folding the panel upward.
4. Move the insulation out of the way to access the shock assembly upper mounting nuts.
5. Remove the 2 nuts securing the shock assembly to the body bracket.
6. Raise and safely support the vehicle.
7. Remove the wheel mounting nuts, then the rear tire and wheel assembly.
8. If equipped with load-leveling shocks, support the lower shock with a jack using just enough force to allow easy removal of the lower shock mounting bolt in the following step. Lower the jack following bolt removal.
9. Remove the lower shock mounting nut and bolt.
10. Lower the shock assembly out of the body bracket and lift it out over the rear suspension.

To install:

➡When installing the shock assembly into the body bracket in the following step, be sure to position the upper mounting bracket so that the angular formed side (as viewed from above) of the mounting bracket flange is facing outboard of the vehicle (the opposite side of the bracket is rounded).

11. Insert the lower end of the shock assembly down through the lower control arm from above just enough to clear the body with the upper mount, then lift it up, inserting the upper mounting studs through the body bracket.
12. If equipped with load-leveling shocks, place a jack against the lower shock eye and support the lower end of the shock assembly. Lift the shock assembly using the jack until the hole in the lower shock eye lines up with that in the lower control arm.
13. Install the mounting bolt and nut fastening the shock assembly to the lower control arm. Do not tighten at this time.
14. Install the wheel and tire assembly. Tighten the wheel nuts in a star pattern until all nuts are torqued to half the required specification. Then repeat the tightening sequence to the full specified torque of 100 ft. lbs. (135 Nm).
15. Lower the vehicle.
16. Install the 2 nuts on the studs securing the shock assembly to the body bracket. Tighten the mounting nuts to 41 ft. lbs. (55 Nm).
17. Fold the access panel back into place.
18. Install the load floor.
19. Position the vehicle on an alignment rack or drive-on lift. Raise the lift as necessary to access the shock mounting bolt and nut.
20. Tighten the shock assembly lower mounting bolt nut to 73 ft. lbs. (99 Nm).

UPPER CONTROL ARM

REMOVAL & INSTALLATION

See Figure 325.

1. Before servicing the vehicle, refer to the Precautions Section.

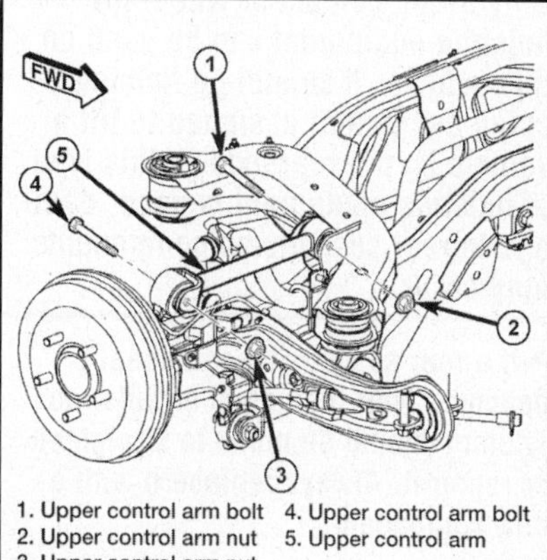

Fig. 325 Exploded view of upper control arm—rear suspension

2. Raise and safely support the vehicle.
3. Remove the tire and wheel assemblies.
4. Remove the nut and bolt securing the upper control arm to the knuckle.
5. Remove the nut and bolt securing the upper control arm to the crossmember.
6. Remove the upper control arm.

To install:

7. Position the upper control arm and install the bolt and nut securing the arm to the crossmember. Do not tighten at this time.
8. Install the bolt and nut securing the upper control arm to the knuckle. Do not tighten at this time.
9. Install the wheel and tire assembly. Tighten the wheel nuts in a star pattern until all nuts are torqued to half the required specification. Then repeat the tightening sequence to the full specified torque of 100 ft. lbs. (135 Nm).
10. Lower the vehicle.
11. Position the vehicle on an alignment rack/drive-on lift. Raise the vehicle as necessary to access mounting bolts and nuts.
12. Tighten the upper control arm mounting bolt nut at the crossmember to 77 ft. lbs. (105 Nm).
13. Tighten the upper control arm mounting bolt nut at the knuckle to 77 ft. lbs. (105 Nm).
14. Perform a wheel alignment as necessary.

WHEEL BEARINGS

REMOVAL & INSTALLATION

AWD Models

See Figures 326 through 328.

**** WARNING**

Only frame contact or wheel lift hoisting equipment can be used on this vehicle. It cannot be hoisted using equipment designed to lift a vehicle by the rear axle. If this type of hoisting equipment is used, damage to rear suspension components may occur.

➡If a rear suspension component becomes bent, damaged or fails, no attempt should be made to straighten or repair it. Always replace it with a new component.

1. Before servicing the vehicle, refer to the Precautions Section.
2. Raise and safely support the vehicle.
3. Remove the tire and wheel assemblies.

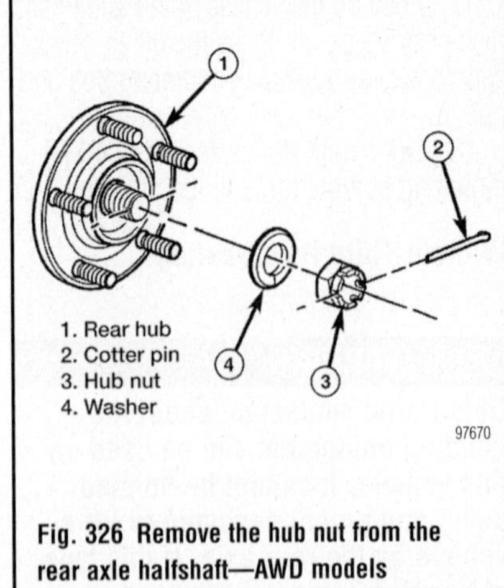

Fig. 326 Remove the hub nut from the rear axle halfshaft—AWD models

4. Remove the cotter pin from the hub nut on the end of the axle halfshaft.
5. While a helper applies the brakes to keep the hub from rotating, remove the hub nut and washer from the axle halfshaft.
6. Tap the end of the halfshaft inward, loosening it from the hub and bearing. This will also allow more room to access the hub and bearing mounting bolts in a later step.

➡In some cases, it may be necessary to retract the caliper piston in its bore a small amount in order to provide sufficient clearance between the pads and the rotor to easily remove the caliper from the knuckle. This can usually be accomplished before removal by grasping the inboard side of the caliper and pulling outward working with the guide pins, thus retracting the piston. Never push on the piston directly as it may get damaged.

7. Remove the 2 bolts securing the disc brake caliper and adapter bracket to the knuckle.
8. Remove the disc brake caliper and adapter bracket as an assembly from the knuckle and rotor. Hang the assembly out of the way using wire or a bungee cord. Use care not to overextend the brake hose when doing this.
9. Remove any retaining clips, then slide the brake rotor off the hub and bearing.

➡Prior to removal, clean the area around sensor head to help prevent contaminants from entering the bearing when the sensor head is removed.

10. Remove the screw fastening the speed sensor head to the hub and bearing.
11. Remove the wheel speed sensor head from the hub and bearing, then pass it through the brake shield.

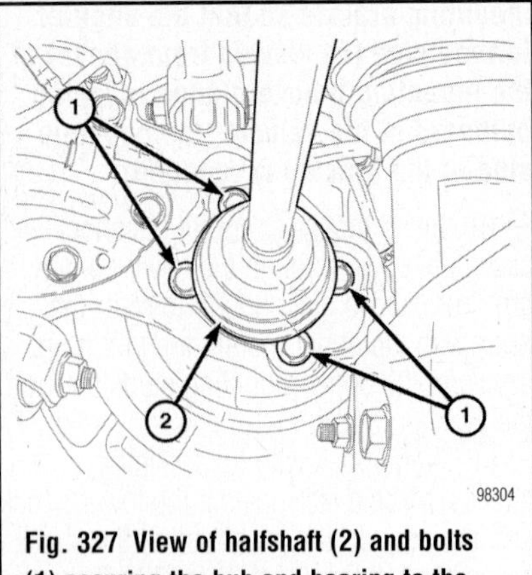

Fig. 327 View of halfshaft (2) and bolts (1) securing the hub and bearing to the knuckle—AWD models

12. Remove the 4 bolts securing the hub and bearing to the knuckle.
13. Remove the hub and bearing from the knuckle and halfshaft.

To install:

14. With the brake shield in place on the knuckle, slide the hub and bearing over the axle halfshaft and position it on the knuckle.
15. Install the 4 bolts securing the hub and bearing to the knuckle. Tighten the bolts to 44 ft. lbs. (60 Nm).

➡Ensure that the sensor mounting surface on the bearing is clean before sensor installation.

16. Pass the wheel speed sensor head through the hole in the brake shield, then push it into the mounting hole in the hub and bearing and align the mounting screw hole.
17. Install a NEW mounting screw. Tighten the mounting screw to 55 inch lbs. (6 Nm).
18. Clean the rotor mounting face of the hub and bearing to remove any dirt or corrosion.
19. Install the brake rotor over the hub and bearing.

**** WARNING**

If the brake rotor or brake pads are being replaced, the rear caliper piston must be seated (bottomed) to compensate for the new brake rotor or lining. Because the parking brake self-adjuster mechanism is attached to the piston, a special seating method is required. The only acceptable method is by rotating the piston back into the bore using Retractor, Special Tool 8807, as described below. Any other seating method will damage the self-adjuster mechanism.

20. If necessary, seat (bottom) the caliper piston in the bore as follows:

a. Assemble a 3/8 inch drive ratchet handle and an extension.

b. Insert the extension through Special Tool 8807-1.

c. Place Special Tool 8807-2 on the end of the extension.

d. Insert the lugs on Special Tool 8807-2 into the notches in the face of the caliper piston.

e. Thread the screw drive on 8807-1 down until it contacts the top of 8807-2 which is against the caliper piston. Do not over tighten the screw-drive. Damage to the piston can occur.

f. Turn 8807-2 with the ratchet, rotating the piston in a clockwise direction until fully seated (bottomed) in the bore. It may be necessary to turn 8807-1 with 8807-2 to start the process of piston retraction.

21. Install the disc brake caliper and adapter bracket over the knuckle and rotor as an assembly.

22. Install the 2 bolts securing the disc brake caliper and adapter bracket to the knuckle. Tighten the mounting bolts to 74 ft. lbs. (100 Nm).

➡Always install a new hub nut. The original hub nut is for one-time use only and should be discarded when removed.

23. Clean all foreign matter from the threads of the halfshaft outer CV-joint.

24. Install the washer and hub nut on the end of the halfshaft and snug it.

25. While a helper applies the brakes to keep the hub from rotating, tighten the hub nut to 181 ft. lbs. (245 Nm).

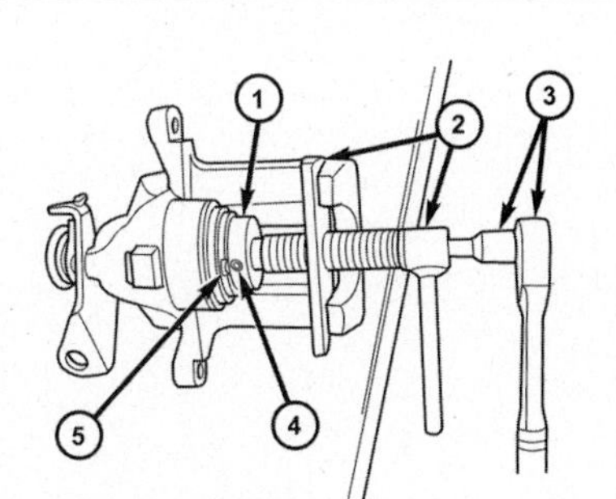

Fig. 328 Using special tools to retract the rear caliper piston

26. Insert the cotter pin through the notches in the nut and the hole in halfshaft. If the notches in the nut do not line up with the hole in the halfshaft, continue to tighten the nut until they do. Do not loosen the nut.

27. Wrap the cotter pin ends tightly around the lock nut.

28. Install the wheel and tire assembly. Tighten the wheel nuts in a star pattern until all nuts are torqued to half the required specification. Then repeat the tightening sequence to the full specified torque of 100 ft. lbs. (135 Nm).

29. Lower the vehicle.

30. Pump the brake pedal several times to ensure the vehicle has a firm brake pedal before moving it.

31. Check the brake fluid level.

FWD Models

See Figures 329 and 330.

**** WARNING**

Only frame contact or wheel lift hoisting equipment can be used on this vehicle. It cannot be hoisted using equipment designed to lift a vehicle by the rear axle. If this type of hoisting equipment is used, damage to rear suspension components may occur.

➡If a rear suspension component becomes bent, damaged or fails, no attempt should be made to straighten or repair it. Always replace it with a new component.

1. Before servicing the vehicle, refer to the Precautions Section.

2. Raise and safely support the vehicle.

3. Remove the tire and wheel assemblies.

➡In some cases, it may be necessary to retract the caliper piston in its bore a small amount in order to provide sufficient clearance between the pads and the rotor to easily remove the caliper from the knuckle. This can usually be accomplished before removal by grasping the inboard side of the caliper and pulling outward working with the guide pins, thus retracting the piston. Never push on the piston directly as it may get damaged.

4. Remove the 2 bolts securing the disc brake caliper and adapter bracket to the knuckle.

5. Remove the disc brake caliper and adapter bracket as an assembly from the knuckle and rotor. Hang the assembly out of the way using wire or a bungee cord. Use care not to overextend the brake hose when doing this.

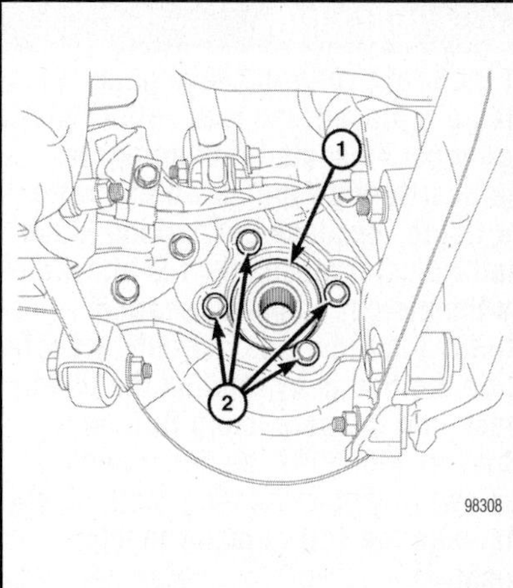

Fig. 329 Remove the bolts (2) securing the hub and bearing (1) to the knuckle

6. Remove any retaining clips, then slide the brake rotor off the hub and bearing.

➡Prior to removal, clean the area around the sensor head to help prevent contaminants from entering the bearing when the sensor head is removed.

7. Remove the screw fastening the speed sensor head to the hub and bearing.

8. Remove the wheel speed sensor head from the hub and bearing, then pass it through the brake shield.

9. Remove the 4 bolts securing the hub and bearing to the knuckle.

10. Remove the hub and bearing.

To install:

11. With the brake shield in place on the knuckle, slide and position the hub and bearing into the knuckle.

12. Install the 4 bolts securing the hub and bearing to the knuckle. Tighten the bolts to 44 ft. lbs. (60 Nm).

➡Ensure that the sensor mounting surface on the bearing is clean before sensor installation.

13. Pass the wheel speed sensor head through the hole in the brake shield, then push it into the mounting hole in hub and bearing and align the mounting screw hole.

14. Install a NEW mounting screw. Tighten the mounting screw to 55 inch lbs. (6 Nm).

15. Clean the rotor mounting face of the hub and bearing to remove any dirt or corrosion.

16. Install the brake rotor over the hub and bearing.

**** WARNING**

If the brake rotor or brake pads are being replaced, the rear caliper piston must be seated (bottomed) to compensate for the new brake rotor or lining. Because the parking brake self-adjuster mechanism is attached to the piston, a special seating method is required. The only acceptable method is by rotating the piston back into the bore using Retractor, Special Tool 8807, as described below. Any other seating method will damage the self-adjuster mechanism.

17. If necessary, seat (bottom) the caliper piston in the bore as follows:
   a. Assemble a ⅜ inch drive ratchet handle and an extension.
   b. Insert the extension through Special Tool 8807-1.
   c. Place Special Tool 8807-2 on the end of the extension.
   d. Insert the lugs on Special Tool 8807-2 into the notches in the face of the caliper piston.
   e. Thread the screw drive on 8807-1 down until it contacts the top of 8807-2 which is against the caliper piston. Do not over tighten the screw-drive. Damage to the piston can occur.
   f. Turn 8807-2 with the ratchet, rotating the piston in a clockwise direction until fully seated (bottomed) in the bore. It may be necessary to turn 8807-1 with 8807-2 to start the process of piston retraction.
18. Install the disc brake caliper and adapter bracket over the knuckle and rotor as an assembly.
19. Install the 2 bolts securing the disc brake caliper and adapter bracket to the knuckle. Tighten the mounting bolts to 74 ft. lbs. (100 Nm).
20. Install the wheel and tire assembly. Tighten the wheel nuts in a star pattern until all nuts are torqued to half the required specification. Then repeat the tightening sequence to the full specified torque of 100 ft. lbs. (135 Nm).
21. Lower the vehicle.
22. Pump the brake pedal several times to ensure the vehicle has a firm brake pedal before moving it.

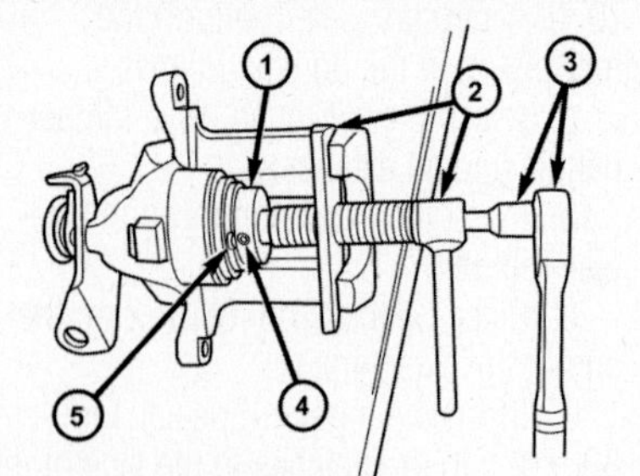

Fig. 330 Using special tools to retract the rear caliper piston

23. Check the brake fluid level.

ADJUSTMENT

The rear hub/bearing assembly is a sealed assembly, which requires no periodic maintenance and cannot be serviced. If the hub/bearing assembly becomes worn or damaged, the entire unit must be replaced.

JEEP

Liberty

12

CAPACITIES

Year	Model	Engine Displ. Liters	Engine VIN	Engine Oil with Filter	Transmission (pts.) Man.	Transmission (pts.) Auto.	Transfer Case (pts.)	Drive Axle Front (pts.)	Drive Axle Rear (pts.)	Fuel Tank (gal.)	Cooling System (qts.)
2010	Liberty	3.7	K	5.0	3.17	①	②	2.6	4.4	19.5	14.0
2011	Liberty	3.7	K	5.0	3.17	①	②	2.6	4.4	19.5	14.0

NOTE: All capacities are approximate. Add fluid gradually and check to be sure a proper fluid level is obtained.

For rear axles, when equipped with Trac Lok, add 4 oz. of limited slip additive.

Capacities for automatic trnasmissions is for service.

① NAG1: 10.6

42RLE: 8.0

② MP1522: 3.8 pts.

MP3022: 4.0 pts.

25766_LIBE_C0004

FLUID SPECIFICATIONS

Year	Model	Engine Displacement Liters (cc)	Engine ID/VIN	Engine Oil	Auto. Trans.	Transfer Case	Drive Axle	Power Steering Fluid	Brake Master Cylinder
2010	Liberty	3.7	K	5W-20	Mopar ATF+4	Mopar ATF+4	①	Mopar ATF+4	DOT-3
2011	Liberty	3.7	K	5W-20	Mopar ATF+4	Mopar ATF+4	①	Mopar ATF+4	DOT-3

DOT: Department Of Transpotation

① Front axle: GL5 80W-90

Rear axle: 75W-140 Synthetic

25766_LIBE_C0005

VALVE SPECIFICATIONS

Year	Engine Displ. Liters	Engine VIN	Seat Angle (deg.)	Face Angle (deg.)	Spring Test Pressure (lbs. @ in.)	Spring Installed Height (in.)	Stem-to-Guide Clearance (in.) Intake	Stem-to-Guide Clearance (in.) Exhaust	Stem Diameter (in.) Intake	Stem Diameter (in.) Exhaust
2010	3.7	K	44.5-45	44.5-45	221-242@ 1.107	1.619	0.0008-0.0028	0.0019-0.0039	0.2729-0.2739	0.2717-0.2728
2011	3.7	K	44.5-45	44.5-45	221-242@ 1.107	1.619	0.0008-0.0028	0.0019-0.0039	0.2729-0.2739	0.2717-0.2728

NA: Information not available

① Intake Valve Closed: 69.5-80.5 lbs. @ 1.496 in.

Exhaust Valve Closed: 79.9-90.1 @ 1.496 in

Inake Valve Open: 145.3-160.7 @ 122 in.

Exhaust Valve Closed: 195.8-212.2 @ 1.22 in.

25766_LIBE_C0006

CAMSHAFT AND BEARING SPECIFICATIONS CHART

All measurements are given in inches.

Year	Engine Displacement Liters (cc)	Engine VIN	Journal Diameter	Brg. Oil Clearance	Shaft End-play	Runout	Journal Bore	Lobe Lift Intake	Lobe Lift Exhaust
2010	3.7	K	1.0227-1.0235	0.0010-0.0026	0.0030-0.0079	N/S	N/S	N/S	N/S
2011	3.7	K	1.0227-1.0235	0.0010-0.0026	0.0030-0.0079	N/S	N/S	N/S	N/S

N/S: Information not Supplied

25766_LIBE_C0007

CRANKSHAFT AND CONNECTING ROD SPECIFICATIONS

All measurements are given in inches.

	Engine		Crankshaft				Connecting Rod		
Year	Displ. Liters	Engine VIN	Main Brg. Journal Dia.	Main Brg. Oil Clearance	Shaft End-play	Thrust on No.	Journal Diameter	Oil Clearance	Side Clearance
2010	3.7	K	2.4996-2.5005	0.0008-0.0018	0.0021-0.0112	2	2.2792-2.2798	0.0002-0.0017	0.0040-0.0138
2011	3.7	K	2.4996-2.5005	0.0008-0.0018	0.0021-0.0112	2	2.2792-2.2798	0.0002-0.0017	0.0040-0.0138

25766_LIBE_C0008

PISTON AND RING SPECIFICATIONS

All measurements are given in inches.

	Engine			Ring Gap			Ring Side Clearance		
Year	Displ. Liters	Engine VIN	Piston Clearance	Top Compression	Bottom Compression	Oil Control	Top Compression	Bottom Compression	Oil Control
2010	3.7	K	NS	0.0079-0.0142	0.0146-0.0249	0.0100-0.0300	0.0020-0.0037	0.0016-0.0031	0.0007-0.0091
2011	3.7	K	NS	0.0079-0.0142	0.0146-0.0249	0.0100-0.0300	0.0020-0.0037	0.0016-0.0031	0.0007-0.0091

NS: Information not Supplied

25766_LIBE_C0009

TORQUE SPECIFICATIONS

All readings in ft. lbs.

Year	Engine Displ. Liters	Engine VIN	Cylinder Head Bolts	Main Bearing Bolts	Rod Bearing Bolts	Crankshaft Damper Bolts	Flywheel Bolts	Manifold Intake	Manifold Exhaust	Spark Plugs	Oil Pan Drain Plug
2010	3.7	K	①	②	③	130	70	9	18	20	25
2011	3.7	K	①	②	③	130	70	9	18	20	25

① Step 1: Bolts 1-8 to 20 ft. lbs.
Step 2: Bolts 1-10, verify torque
Step 3: Bolts 9-12 to 10 ft. lbs.
Step 4: Bolts 1-8, plus 90 degrees
Step 5: Bolts 1-8, plus 90 degrees again
Step 6: Bolts 9-12 to 19 ft. lbs.

② Bed plate bolt sequence. Refer to illustration
Step 1: Hand tighten bolts 1D,1G, 1F until bedplate contacts block.
Step 2: Tighten bolts 1A - 1J to 40 ft. lbs.
Step 3: Tighten bolts 1 - 8 to 5 ft. lbs.
Step 4: Turn bolts 1 - 8 an additional 90 degrees
Step 5: Tighten bolts A - E to 20 ft. lbs.

③ 20 ft. lbs. plus 90 degrees

25766_LIBE_C0010

WHEEL ALIGNMENT

Year	Model		Caster Range (+/-Deg.)	Caster Preferred Setting (Deg.)	Camber Range (+/-Deg.)	Camber Preferred Setting (Deg.)	Toe-in (deg.)
2010	Liberty	F	.50	3.300	-0.375	-0.20	0.075-0.325
		R	N/A	N/S	-0.625-+0.125	-0.25	-0.16-+0.66
2011	Liberty	F	.50	3.300	-0.375	-0.20	0.075-0.325
		R	N/A	N/S	-0.625-+0.125	-0.25	-0.16-+0.66

N/S: Information not Supplied

25766_LIBE_C0011

TIRE, WHEEL AND BALL JOINT SPECIFICATIONS

Year	Model	OEM Tires		Tire Pressures (psi)		Wheel Size	Ball Joint Inspection	Lug Nut Torque (ft. lbs.)
		Standard	Optional	Front	Rear			
2010	Liberty	P225/75R16	P235/65R17 P235/60R18	①	①	N/S	②	85-115
2011	Liberty	P225/75R16	P235/65R17 P235/60R18	①	①	N/S	②	85-115

N/S: Information not supplied

OEM: Original Equipment Manufacturer

STD: Standard

OPT: Optional

① See placard on vehicle

② Replace if any measurable movement is found.

25766_LIBE_C0012

BRAKE SPECIFICATIONS

All measurements in inches unless noted

Year	Model		Brake Disc			Minimum Lining Thickness	Caliper Mounting Bolts (ft. lbs.)
			Original Thickness	Minimum Thickness	Maximum Run-out		
2010	Liberty	F	1.100	1.049	0.0008	0.04	28
		R	0.472	0.409	0.0008	0.04	28
2011	Liberty	F	1.100	1.049	0.0008	0.04	28
		R	0.472	0.409	0.0008	0.04	28

F- Front

R - Rear

N/A Not applicable

25766_LIBE_C0013

SCHEDULED MAINTENANCE INTERVALS

2010-2011 Jeep LIberty 3.7L Engine - Normal & Severe (as noted)

TO BE SERVICED	TYPE OF SERVICE	VEHICLE MILEAGE INTERVAL (x1000)												
		8	16	24	32	40	48	56	64	72	80	88	96	104
Engine oil & filter	Replace	✓	✓	✓	✓	✓	✓	✓	✓	✓	✓	✓	✓	✓
Rotate tires, inspect tread wear, measure tread depth and check pressure - Normal	Rotate/Inspect		✓		✓		✓		✓		✓		✓	
Rotate tires, inspect tread wear, measure tread depth and check pressure - Severe	Rotate/Inspect	✓	✓	✓	✓	✓	✓	✓	✓	✓	✓	✓	✓	✓
Brake system components	Inspect/Servic		✓		✓		✓		✓		✓		✓	
Exhaust system & heat shields	Inspect		✓		✓		✓		✓		✓		✓	
Inspect the front suspension, tie rod ends and boot seals for cracks or leaks and all parts for damage, wear, improper looseness or end play.	Inspect		✓		✓		✓		✓		✓		✓	
CV Joints	Inspect			✓			✓			✓			✓	
Engine air filter - Normal	Replace				✓				✓				✓	
Engine air filter - Severe	Replace		✓		✓		✓		✓		✓		✓	
Adjust parking brake on vehicles equipped with four-wheel disc brakes.	Adjust				✓				✓				✓	
Engine coolant	Flush/Replace										✓			
Spark plugs	Replace				✓				✓				✓	
PCV valve	Inspect/Servic	At 96,000 miles then every 32,000 miles												
Automatic transmission fluid and filter - Normal	Inspect	Every 128,000 miles												
Automatic transmission fluid and filter - Severe	Inspect	Every 64,000 miles												
Accessory drive belt	Replace	Every 120,000 miles												
Battery	Inspect/Servic	✓	✓	✓	✓	✓	✓	✓	✓	✓	✓	✓	✓	✓
Horn, exterior lamps, turn signals and hazard warning light operation	Inspect	✓	✓	✓	✓	✓	✓	✓	✓	✓	✓	✓	✓	✓
Fluid levels (all)	Inspect/Servic	✓	✓	✓	✓	✓	✓	✓	✓	✓	✓	✓	✓	✓
Passenger compartment air filter	Replace		✓		✓		✓		✓		✓		✓	
Front & rear axle fuild	Inspect			✓			✓			✓			✓	
Transfer case fluid	Inspect				✓				✓				✓	
Ignition cables - Normal	Replace										✓			
Ignition cables - Severe	Replace	Every 64,000 miles												

25766_LIBE_C0014

PRECAUTIONS

Before servicing any vehicle, please be sure to read all of the following precautions, which deal with personal safety, prevention of component damage, and important points to take into consideration when servicing a motor vehicle:

- Never open, service or drain the radiator or cooling system when the engine is hot; serious burns can occur from the steam and hot coolant.
- Observe all applicable safety precautions when working around fuel. Whenever servicing the fuel system, always work in a well-ventilated area. Do not allow fuel spray or vapors to come in contact with a spark, open flame, or excessive heat (a hot drop light, for example). Keep a dry chemical fire extinguisher near the work area. Always keep fuel in a container specifically designed for fuel storage; also, always properly seal fuel containers to avoid the possibility of fire or explosion. Refer to the additional fuel system precautions later in this section.
- Fuel injection systems often remain pressurized, even after the engine has been turned **OFF**. The fuel system pressure must be relieved before disconnecting any fuel lines. Failure to do so may result in fire and/or personal injury.
- Brake fluid often contains polyglycol ethers and polyglycols. Avoid contact with the eyes and wash your hands thoroughly after handling brake fluid. If you do get brake fluid in your eyes, flush your eyes with clean, running water for 15 minutes. If eye irritation persists, or if you have taken brake fluid internally, IMMEDIATELY seek medical assistance.
- The EPA warns that prolonged contact with used engine oil may cause a number of skin disorders, including cancer. You should make every effort to minimize your exposure to used engine oil. Protective gloves should be worn when changing oil. Wash your hands and any other exposed skin areas as soon as possible after exposure to used engine oil. Soap and water, or waterless hand cleaner should be used.
- All new vehicles are now equipped with an air bag system, often referred to as a Supplemental Restraint System (SRS) or Supplemental Inflatable Restraint (SIR) system. The system must be disabled before performing service on or around system components, steering column, instrument panel components, wiring and sensors. Failure to follow safety and disabling procedures could result in accidental air bag deployment, possible personal injury and unnecessary system repairs.
- Always wear safety goggles when working with, or around, the air bag system. When carrying a non-deployed air bag, be sure the bag and trim cover are pointed away from your body. When placing a non-deployed air bag on a work surface, always face the bag and trim cover upward, away from the surface. This will reduce the motion of the module if it is accidentally deployed. Refer to the additional air bag system precautions later in this section.
- Clean, high quality brake fluid from a sealed container is essential to the safe and proper operation of the brake system. You should always buy the correct type of brake fluid for your vehicle. If the brake fluid becomes contaminated, completely flush the system with new fluid. Never reuse any brake fluid. Any brake fluid that is removed from the system should be discarded. Also, do not allow any brake fluid to come in contact with a painted surface; it will damage the paint.
- Never operate the engine without the proper amount and type of engine oil; doing so WILL result in severe engine damage.
- Timing belt maintenance is extremely important. Many models utilize an interference-type, non-freewheeling engine. If the timing belt breaks, the valves in the cylinder head may strike the pistons, causing potentially serious (also time-consuming and expensive) engine damage. Refer to the maintenance interval charts for the recommended replacement interval for the timing belt, and to the timing belt section for belt replacement and inspection.
- Disconnecting the negative battery cable on some vehicles may interfere with the functions of the on-board computer system(s) and may require the computer to undergo a relearning process once the negative battery cable is reconnected.
- When servicing drum brakes, only disassemble and assemble one side at a time, leaving the remaining side intact for reference.
- Only an MVAC-trained, EPA-certified automotive technician should service the air conditioning system or its components.

BRAKES

ANTI-LOCK BRAKE SYSTEM (ABS)

GENERAL INFORMATION

PRECAUTIONS

- Certain components within the ABS system are not intended to be serviced or repaired individually.
- Do not use rubber hoses or other parts not specifically specified for and ABS system. When using repair kits, replace all parts included in the kit. Partial or incorrect repair may lead to functional problems and require the replacement of components.
- Lubricate rubber parts with clean, fresh brake fluid to ease assembly. Do not use shop air to clean parts; damage to rubber components may result.
- Use only DOT 3 brake fluid from an unopened container.
- If any hydraulic component or line is removed or replaced, it may be necessary to bleed the entire system.
- A clean repair area is essential. Always clean the reservoir and cap thoroughly before removing the cap. The slightest amount of dirt in the fluid may plug an orifice and impair the system function. Perform repairs after components have been thoroughly cleaned; use only denatured alcohol to clean components. Do not allow ABS components to come into contact with any substance containing mineral oil; this includes used shop rags.
- The Anti-Lock control unit is a microprocessor similar to other computer units in the vehicle. Ensure that the ignition switch is **OFF** before removing or installing controller harnesses. Avoid static electricity discharge at or near the controller.
- If any arc welding is to be done on the vehicle, the control unit should be unplugged before welding operations begin.

SPEED SENSORS

REMOVAL & INSTALLATION

Front

1. Before servicing the vehicle, refer to the Precautions Section.

2. Raise and support the vehicle.
3. Remove the tire and wheel assembly.
4. Remove the caliper adapter.

WARNING

Never allow the disc brake caliper to hang from the brake hose. Damage to the brake hose will result. Provide a suitable support to hang the caliper securely.

5. Remove the disc brake rotor.
6. Remove the bolt mounting the wheel speed sensor to the hub.
7. Remove the wheel speed sensor wire from the hub/bearing and through the brake shield.
8. Remove the wheel speed sensor wire hold down clips.
9. Remove the locking connector at the wheel liner from the sensor connector.
10. Remove the wheel speed sensor from the vehicle.

To install:

WARNING

When installing, do not rotate sensor, as this may cause the sensor to rub on the tone ring and be damaged.

11. Install the wheel speed sensor to the vehicle.
12. Install the wheel speed sensor through the brake shield and to the hub/bearing.
13. Install the wheel speed sensor wire hold down routing clips.
14. Install the wheel speed sensor mounting bolt to the hub. Tighten the mounting bolt to 71 inch lbs. (8 Nm).
15. Install the disc brake rotor.
16. Install the disc brake caliper adapter.
17. Install the tire and wheel assembly.

Rear

1. Before servicing the vehicle, refer to the Precautions Section.
2. Raise and support the vehicle.
3. Disengage the locking tab connector.
4. Disconnect the wheel speed sensor electrical connector.
5. Remove the wheel speed sensor mounting bolt from the rear support plate.
6. Remove the wheel speed sensor from the support plate.

To install:

7. Insert the wheel speed sensor through the support plate.
8. Tighten the wheel speed sensor bolt to 80 inch lbs. (9 Nm).
9. Secure the wheel speed sensor wire to the routing clips. Verify that the sensor wire is secure and clear of the rotating components.
10. Reconnect the wheel speed sensor electrical connector. Make sure the connector locking tab is fully engaged and locked in position.
11. Lower the vehicle.

BRAKES

BLEEDING THE BRAKE SYSTEM

BLEEDING PROCEDURE

BLEEDING THE ABS SYSTEM

1. Before servicing the vehicle, refer to the Precautions Section.
2. See all applicable precautions before beginning service procedures.
3. Perform conventional base brake bleeding (Manual or Pressure).
4. Connect scan tool to the Data Link Connector.
5. Select ANTILOCK BRAKES, followed by MISCELLANEOUS, then ABS BRAKES. Follow the instructions displayed. When scan tool displays TEST COMPLETE, disconnect scan tool and proceed.
6. Perform base brake bleeding a second time.
7. Top off master cylinder fluid level and verify proper brake operation before moving vehicle.

HYDRAULIC BRAKE SYSTEM BLEEDING

Manual Bleeding

➡Before servicing the vehicle, refer to the Precautions Section.

WARNING

Use Mopar® brake fluid, or an equivalent quality fluid meeting SAE J1703-F and DOT 3 standards only. Use fresh, clean fluid from a sealed container at all times.

➡Do not pump the brake pedal at any time while bleeding. Air in the system will be compressed into small bubbles that are distributed throughout the hydraulic system. This will make additional bleeding operations necessary.

➡Do not allow the master cylinder to run out of fluid during bleed operations. An empty cylinder will allow additional air to be drawn into the system. Check the cylinder fluid level frequently and add fluid as needed.

1. Bleed only one brake component at a time in the following sequence:
   a. Master Cylinder
   b. Junction Block
   c. Right Rear Wheel
   d. Left Rear Wheel
   e. Right Front Wheel
   f. Left Front Wheel
2. Remove reservoir filler caps and fill the reservoir.
3. If calipers were overhauled, open all caliper bleed screws. Close each bleed screw as fluid starts to drip from it. Top off master cylinder reservoir once more before proceeding.
4. Attach one end of bleed hose to bleed screw and insert opposite end in glass container partially filled with brake fluid. Be sure end of bleed hose is immersed in fluid.
5. Open up bleeder and have a helper press down the brake pedal. Once the pedal is down close the bleeder. Repeat bleeding until fluid stream is clear and free of bubbles. Move to the next wheel.

Pressure Bleeding

➡Before servicing the vehicle, refer to the Precautions Section.

WARNING

Use Mopar® brake fluid, or an equivalent quality fluid meeting SAE J1703-F and DOT 3 standards only. Use fresh, clean fluid from a sealed container at all times.

➡Do not pump the brake pedal at any time while bleeding. Air in the system will be compressed into small bubbles that are distributed throughout the hydraulic system. This will make additional bleeding operations necessary.

➡Do not allow the master cylinder to run out of fluid during bleed operations. An empty cylinder will allow additional air to be drawn into the system. Check the cylinder fluid level frequently and add fluid as needed.

WARNING

Follow the manufacturer's instructions carefully when using pressure equipment. Do not exceed the tank manufacturer's pressure recommendations. Generally, a tank pressure of 15–20 psi (103–139 kPa) is sufficient for bleeding.

➡Fill the bleeder tank with recommended fluid and purge air from the tank lines before bleeding.

WARNING

Do not pressure bleed without a proper master cylinder adapter. The wrong adapter can lead to leakage, or drawing air back into the system. Use adapter provided with the equipment or Adapter 6921.

1. Bleed only one brake component at a time in the following sequence:
   a. Master Cylinder
   b. Right Rear Wheel
   c. Left Rear Wheel
   d. Right Front Wheel
   e. Left Front Wheel

FLUID FILL PROCEDURE

1. Always clean the master cylinder reservoir and caps before checking fluid level. If not cleaned, dirt could enter the fluid.
2. The fluid fill level is indicated on the side of the master cylinder reservoir.
3. The correct fluid level is to the MAX indicator on the side of the reservoir. If necessary, add fluid to the proper level.

BRAKES

FRONT DISC BRAKES

CAUTION

Dust and dirt accumulating on brake parts during normal use may contain asbestos fibers from production or aftermarket brake linings. Breathing excessive concentrations of asbestos fibers can cause serious bodily harm. Exercise care when servicing brake parts. Do not sand or grind brake lining unless equipment used is designed to contain the dust residue. Do not clean brake parts with compressed air or by dry brushing. Cleaning should be done by dampening the brake components with a fine mist of water and wiping the brake components clean with a dampened cloth. Dispose of cloth and all residue containing asbestos fibers in an impermeable container with the appropriate label. Follow practices prescribed by the Occupational Safety and Health Administration (OSHA) and the Environmental Protection Agency (EPA) for the handling, processing, and disposing of dust or debris that may contain asbestos fibers.

BRAKE CALIPER

REMOVAL & INSTALLATION

See Figure 1.

1. Before servicing the vehicle, refer to the Precautions Section.
2. Install prop rod on the brake pedal to keep pressure on the brake system. Holding the pedal in this position will isolate the master cylinder from the hydraulic brake system and will not allow brake fluid to drain out of the brake fluid reservoir while brake lines are open. This will allow you to bleed out the area of repair instead of the entire system.
3. Raise and support vehicle.
4. Remove front wheel and tire assembly.
5. Remove the brake hose banjo bolt.
6. Remove the caliper mounting bolts.
7. Remove the caliper from vehicle.

To install:

8. Install caliper to the caliper adapter.
9. Coat the caliper mounting bolts with silicone grease. Beginning with the bolt closest to the bleeder screws (top), install and tighten the bolts to 28 ft. lbs. (37 Nm).
10. Install the brake hose banjo bolt and brake hose to the caliper with **NEW** seal washers and tighten fitting bolt to 23 ft. lbs. (31 Nm). Verify that the brake hose is not twisted or kinked before tightening the fitting bolt.
11. Remove the prop rod from the vehicle.
12. Bleed the area of repair for brake system. If a proper pedal is not felt during bleeding the area of repair, a base bleed system must be performed.
13. Install the wheel and tire assemblies.
14. Remove the supports and lower the vehicle.
15. Verify a firm pedal before moving the vehicle.

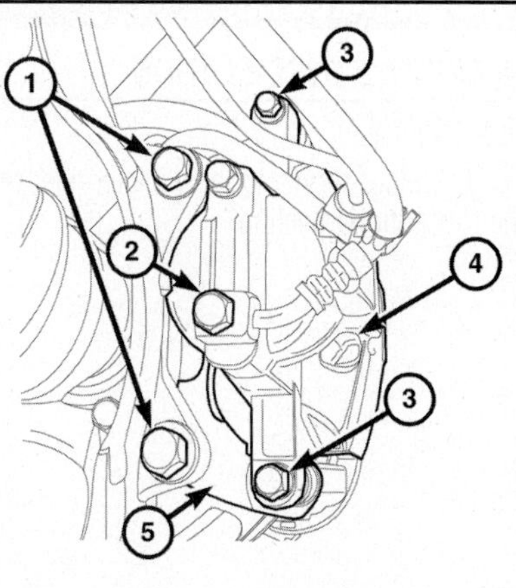

Fig. 1 Brake hose banjo bolt (2), caliper mounting bolts (3), caliper (4), and adapter (5)

DISC BRAKE PADS

REMOVAL & INSTALLATION

See Figure 2.

1. Before servicing the vehicle, refer to the Precautions Section.
2. Raise and support the vehicle.
3. Remove the front wheel and tire assembly.
4. Drain a small amount of fluid from the master cylinder brake reservoir with a clean suction gun.
5. Bottom the caliper pistons into the caliper by prying the caliper over.
6. Remove the caliper mounting bolts.
7. Remove the disc brake caliper from the adapter.
8. Remove the inboard and outboard pads.

To install:

9. Install the inboard and outboard pads.
10. Install the caliper.
11. Install the tire and wheel assembly.

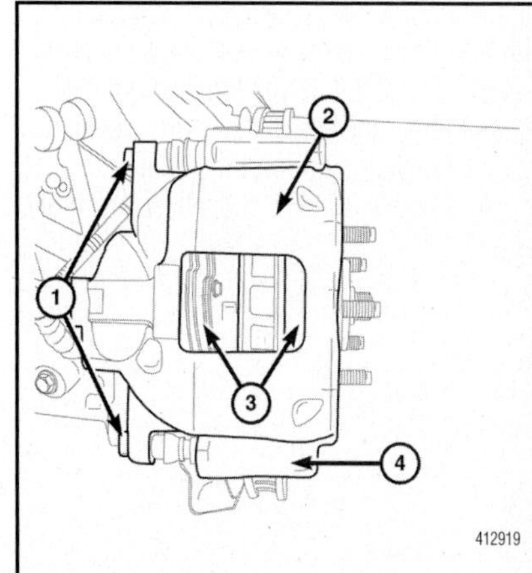

Fig. 2 Front brake caliper (2) and mounting bolts (1); adapter (4), and inboard and outboard pads (3)

**** CAUTION**

Dust and dirt accumulating on brake parts during normal use may contain asbestos fibers from production or aftermarket brake linings. Breathing excessive concentrations of asbestos fibers can cause serious bodily harm. Exercise care when servicing brake parts. Do not sand or grind brake lining unless equipment used is designed to contain the dust residue. Do not clean brake parts with compressed air or by dry brushing. Cleaning should be done by dampening the brake components with a fine mist of water and wiping the brake components clean with a dampened cloth. Dispose of cloth and all residue containing asbestos fibers in an impermeable container with the appropriate label. Follow practices prescribed by the Occupational Safety and Health Administration (OSHA) and the Environmental Protection Agency (EPA) for the handling, processing, and disposing of dust or debris that may contain asbestos fibers.

BRAKE CALIPER

REMOVAL & INSTALLATION

See Figure 3.

1. Before servicing the vehicle, refer to the Precautions Section.
2. Install prop rod on the brake pedal to keep pressure on the brake system, Holding the pedal in this position will isolate the master cylinder from the hydraulic brake system and will not allow brake fluid to drain out of the brake fluid reservoir while brake lines are open. This will allow you to bleed out the area of repair instead of the entire system.
3. Raise and support the vehicle.
4. Remove the tire and wheel assembly.

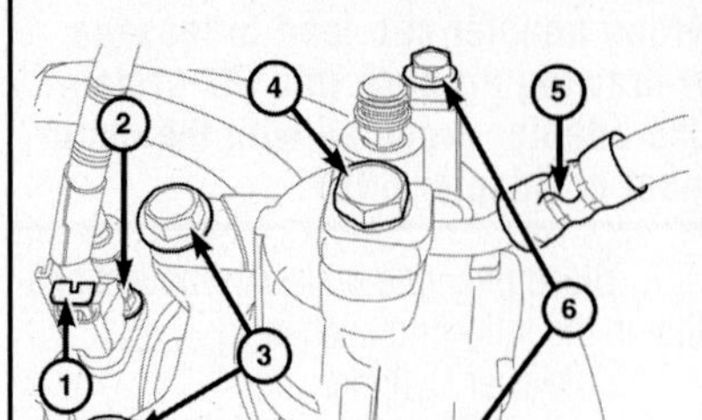

Fig. 3 Bake hose (5), banjo bolt (4), and caliper mounting bolts (6)

5. Remove the brake hose banjo bolt.
6. Remove the caliper mounting bolts.
7. Remove the caliper from vehicle.

To install:

8. Install the brake caliper and tighten the mounting bolts to 28 ft. lbs. (37 Nm).
9. Install the brake hose to the caliper with new seal washers, install the banjo bolt, tighten fitting bolt to 23 ft. lbs. (31 Nm).
10. Remove the prop rod from the vehicle.
11. Bleed the area of repair for the brake system. If a proper pedal is not felt during bleeding an area of repair, a base bleed system must be performed.
12. Install the tire and wheel assembly.
13. Remove the supports and lower the vehicle.
14. Verify a firm pedal before moving the vehicle.

DISC BRAKE PADS

REMOVAL & INSTALLATION

See Figure 4.

1. Before servicing the vehicle, refer to the Precautions Section.

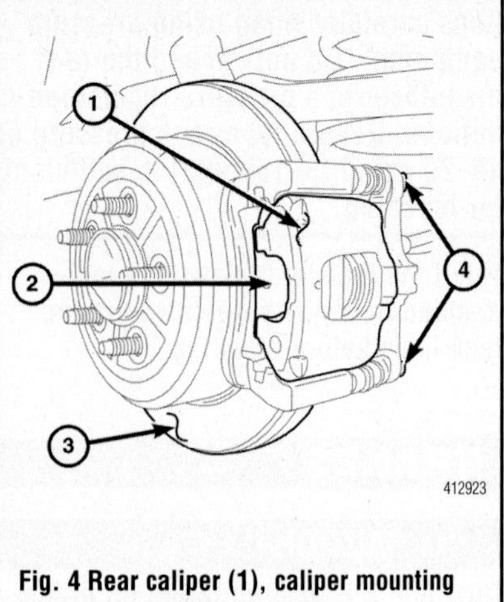

Fig. 4 Rear caliper (1), caliper mounting bolts (4), and brake pads (2)

2. Raise and support vehicle.
3. Remove the wheel and tire assemblies.
4. Compress the caliper.
5. Remove the rear caliper mounting bolts.
6. Remove the caliper by tilting the top up and off the caliper adapter.
7. Support and hang the caliper with heavy mechanic wire or equivalent. Do not allow brake hose to support caliper assembly.
8. Remove the brake pads from the caliper.

To install:

9. Install the brake pads to the caliper adapter.
10. Install caliper to the rotor and install the caliper mounting bolts.
11. Install wheel and tire assemblies and lower vehicle.
12. Apply brakes several times to seat caliper pistons and brake shoes and obtain firm pedal.
13. Top off master cylinder fluid level.

PARKING BRAKE CABLES

ADJUSTMENT

No adjustment is needed, as the parking brake cables are self-adjusting. If the cables have been replaced, follow the parking shoe replacement procedure to set the shoes correctly.

LOCK OUT

See Figure 5.

➡**The parking brake is self-adjusting, it cannot be adjusted.**

1. Before servicing the vehicle, refer to the Precautions Section.
2. Remove the center floor console.
3. With lever in DOWN position, pull up on the core cable rotating the drum until the drum cut-out aligns with hole on lever tab and install a punch in this hole and drum cut-out. Release grasp on core cable.
4. The park brake system is now locked out to perform necessary repairs

PARKING BRAKE SHOES

REMOVAL & INSTALLATION

1. Before servicing the vehicle, refer to the Precautions Section.
2. Raise and support the vehicle.
3. Remove the tire and wheel assembly.
4. Remove the disc brake caliper.
5. Remove the disc brake rotor.
6. Remove the axle shaft.
7. Disassemble the rear parking brake shoes.

To install:

8. Reassemble the rear parking brake shoes.
9. Adjust the rear parking brake shoes.

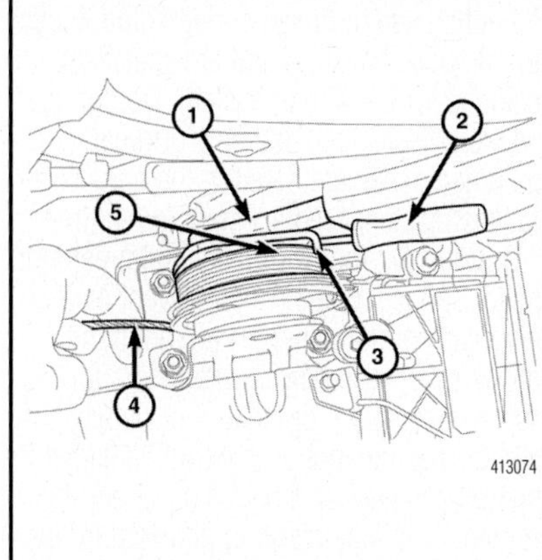

Fig. 5 Core cable (4), drum (5), lever tab (3), punch (2)

10. Install axle shaft.
11. Install the disc brake rotor.
12. Install the disc brake caliper.
13. Install the tire and wheel assembly.
14. Lower the vehicle.

➡**On a new vehicle or after parking brake lining replacement, it is recommended that the parking brake system be conditioned prior to use. This is done by making one stop from 25 mph on dry pavement or concrete using light to moderate force on the parking brake foot pedal.**

ADJUSTMENT

See Figure 6.

Adjustment can be made with a standard brake gauge or with adjusting tool. Adjustment is performed with the complete brake assembly installed on the backing plate.

1. Be sure the parking brake lever is fully released.
2. Raise the vehicle so rear wheels can be rotated freely.

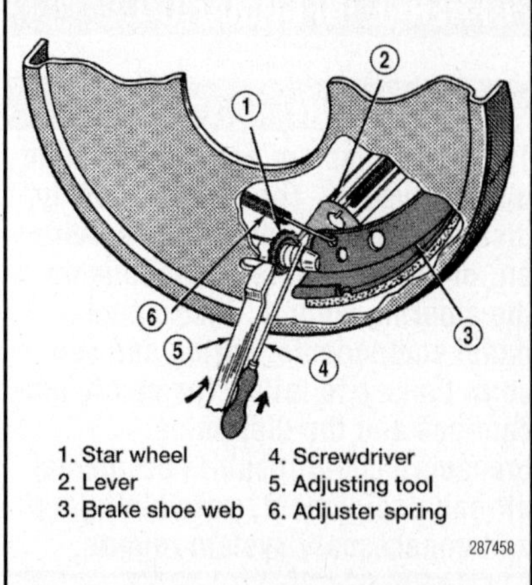

Fig. 6 Rear parking brake shoe adjustment

3. Remove the plug from each access hole in brake support plates.
4. Insert the adjusting tool through the support plate access hole and engage the tool in the teeth of adjusting screw star wheel.
5. Rotate the adjuster screw star wheel (move tool handle upward) until slight drag can be felt when the wheel is rotated.
6. Push and hold the adjuster lever away from the star wheel with thin screwdriver.
7. Back off the adjuster screw star wheel until brake drag is eliminated.
8. Repeat the adjustment at opposite wheel. Be sure the adjustment is equal at both wheels.
9. Install support plate access hole plugs.
10. Lower the vehicle.
11. Apply the parking brake hand lever and make sure the parking brakes hold the vehicle stationary.
12. Release the parking brake hand lever.

GENERAL INFORMATION

CAUTION

These vehicles are equipped with an air bag system. The system must be disarmed before performing service on, or around, system components, the steering column, instrument panel components, wiring and sensors. Failure to follow the safety precautions and the disarming procedure could result in accidental air bag deployment, possible injury and unnecessary system repairs.

SERVICE PRECAUTIONS

Disconnect and isolate the battery negative cable before beginning any airbag system component diagnosis, testing, removal, or installation procedures. Allow system capacitor to discharge for two minutes before beginning any component service. This will disable the airbag system. Failure to disable the airbag system may result in accidental airbag deployment, personal injury, or death.

Do not place an intact undeployed airbag face down on a solid surface. The airbag will propel into the air if accidentally deployed and may result in personal injury or death.

When carrying or handling an undeployed airbag, the trim side (face) of the airbag should be pointing away from the body to minimize possibility of injury if accidental deployment occurs. Failure to do this may result in personal injury or death.

Replace airbag system components with OEM replacement parts. Substitute parts may appear interchangeable, but internal differences may result in inferior occupant protection. Failure to do so may result in occupant personal injury or death.

Wear safety glasses, rubber gloves, and long sleeved clothing when cleaning powder residue from vehicle after an airbag deployment. Powder residue emitted from a deployed airbag can cause skin irritation. Flush affected area with cool water if irritation is experienced. If nasal or throat irritation is experienced, exit the vehicle for fresh air until the irritation ceases. If irritation continues, see a physician.

Do not use a replacement airbag that is not in the original packaging. This may result in improper deployment, personal injury, or death.

The factory installed fasteners, screws and bolts used to fasten airbag components have a special coating and are specifically designed for the airbag system. Do not use substitute fasteners. Use only original equipment fasteners listed in the parts catalog when fastener replacement is required.

During, and following, any child restraint anchor service, due to impact event or vehicle repair, carefully inspect all mounting hardware, tether straps, and anchors for proper installation, operation, or damage. If a child restraint anchor is found damaged in any way, the anchor must be replaced. Failure to do this may result in personal injury or death.

Deployed and non-deployed airbags may or may not have live pyrotechnic material within the airbag inflator.

Do not dispose of driver/passenger/curtain airbags or seat belt tensioners unless you are sure of complete deployment. Refer to the Hazardous Substance Control System for proper disposal.

Dispose of deployed airbags and tensioners consistent with state, provincial, local, and federal regulations.

After any airbag component testing or service, do not connect the battery negative cable. Personal injury or death may result if the system test is not performed first.

If the vehicle is equipped with the Occupant Classification System (OCS), do not connect the battery negative cable before performing the OCS Verification Test using the scan tool and the appropriate diagnostic information. Personal injury or death may result if the system test is not performed properly.

Never replace both the Occupant Restraint Controller (ORC) and the Occupant Classification Module (OCM) at the same time. If both require replacement, replace one, and perform the Airbag System test before replacing the other.

Both the ORC and the OCM store Occupant Classification System (OCS) calibration data, which they transfer to one another when one of them is replaced. If both are replaced at the same time, an irreversible fault will be set in both modules and the OCS may malfunction and cause personal injury or death.

If equipped with OCS, the Seat Weight Sensor is a sensitive, calibrated unit and must be handled carefully. Do not drop or handle roughly. If dropped or damaged, replace with another sensor. Failure to do so may result in occupant injury or death.

If equipped with OCS, the front passenger seat must be handled carefully as well. When removing the seat, be careful when setting on floor not to drop. If dropped, the sensor may be inoperative, could result in occupant injury, or possibly death.

If equipped with OCS, when the passenger front seat is on the floor, no one should sit in the front passenger seat. This uneven force may damage the sensing ability of the seat weight sensors. If sat on and damaged, the sensor may be inoperative, could result in occupant injury, or possibly death.

DISARMING THE SYSTEM

Disconnect and isolate the negative battery cable. Wait 2 minutes for the system capacitor to discharge before performing any service.

ARMING THE SYSTEM

To arm the system, connect the negative battery cable.

CLOCKSPRING CENTERING

CAUTION

To avoid serious or fatal injury on vehicles equipped with airbags, disable the Supplemental Restraint System (SRS) before attempting any steering wheel, steering column, airbag, Occupant Classification System (OCS), seat belt tensioner, impact sensor, or instrument panel component diagnosis or service. Disconnect and isolate the battery negative (ground) cable, then wait two minutes for the system capacitor to discharge before performing further diagnosis or service. This is the only sure way to disable the SRS. Failure to take the proper precautions could result in accidental airbag deployment.

WARNING

When a clockspring is installed into a vehicle without properly centering and locking the entire steering system, the Steering Angle Sensor (SAS) data does not agree with the true position of the steering system and causes the Electronic Stability Program (ESP) system to shut down. This may also damage the clockspring without any immediate malfunction. Unlike some other Chrysler vehicles, this SAS never requires cal-

ibration. However, upon each new ignition ON cycle, the steering wheel must be rotated slightly to initialize the SAS.

➡A service replacement clockspring is shipped with the clockspring pre-centered and with a molded plastic locking pin installed. This locking pin should not be removed until the steering wheel has been installed on the steering column. If the locking pin is removed before the steering wheel is installed, the clockspring centering procedure must be performed.

➡Determining if the clockspring/SAS is centered is also possible electrically using the diagnostic scan tool. Steering wheel position is displayed as ANGLE with a range of up to 900 degrees. Refer to the appropriate menu item on the diagnostic scan tool.

1. Place the front wheels in the straight-ahead position and prevent the steering column shaft from rotation.
2. Remove the steering wheel from the steering shaft.
3. Rotate the clockspring rotor clockwise to the end of its travel. Do not apply excessive torque.
4. From the end of the clockwise travel, rotate the rotor about two and one-half turns counterclockwise. Turn the rotor slightly clockwise or counterclockwise as necessary so that the clockspring airbag pigtail wires and connector receptacle are at the top and the dowel or drive pin is at the bottom.
5. The clockspring is now centered. Secure the clockspring rotor to the clockspring case using a locking pin or some similar device to maintain clockspring centering until the steering wheel is reinstalled on the steering column.

DRIVE TRAIN

AUTOMATIC TRANSMISSION FLUID

CHECKING FLUID

See Figure 7.

CAUTION

There is a risk of accident from vehicle starting off by itself when engine running. There is a risk of injury from contusions and burns if you insert your hands into the engine when it is started or when it is running. Secure vehicle to prevent it from moving off by itself. Wear properly fastened and close-fitting work clothes. Do not touch hot or rotating parts.

1. Before servicing the vehicle, refer to the Precautions Section.
2. Verify that the vehicle is parked on a level surface.
3. Remove the dipstick tube cap.
4. Actuate the service brake. Start engine and let it run at idle speed in selector lever position "P".
5. Shift through the transmission modes several times with the vehicle stationary and the engine idling
6. Warm up the transmission, wait at least 2 minutes and check the oil level with the engine running. Push the oil dipstick into transmission fill tube until the dipstick tip contacts the oil pan and pull out again, read off oil level, repeat if necessary.

➡The dipstick protrudes from the fill tube when installed.

7. Check transmission oil temperature using the appropriate scan tool.

➡The true transmission oil temperature can only be read by a scan tool in Reverse or any forward gear position.

8. The transmission oil dipstick has indicator marks every 10mm. Determine the height of the oil level on the dipstick and using the height, the transmission temperature, and the Transmission Fluid Graph, determine if the transmission oil level is correct.
9. Add or remove oil as necessary and recheck the oil level.
10. Once the oil level is correct, install the dipstick tube cap.

FLUID REFILL

1. Before servicing the vehicle, refer to the Precautions Section.
2. Remove the plug or dipstick and insert a clean funnel in transmission fill tube.
3. Add Automatic Transmission Fluid (Mopar® ATF +4) to the transmission:

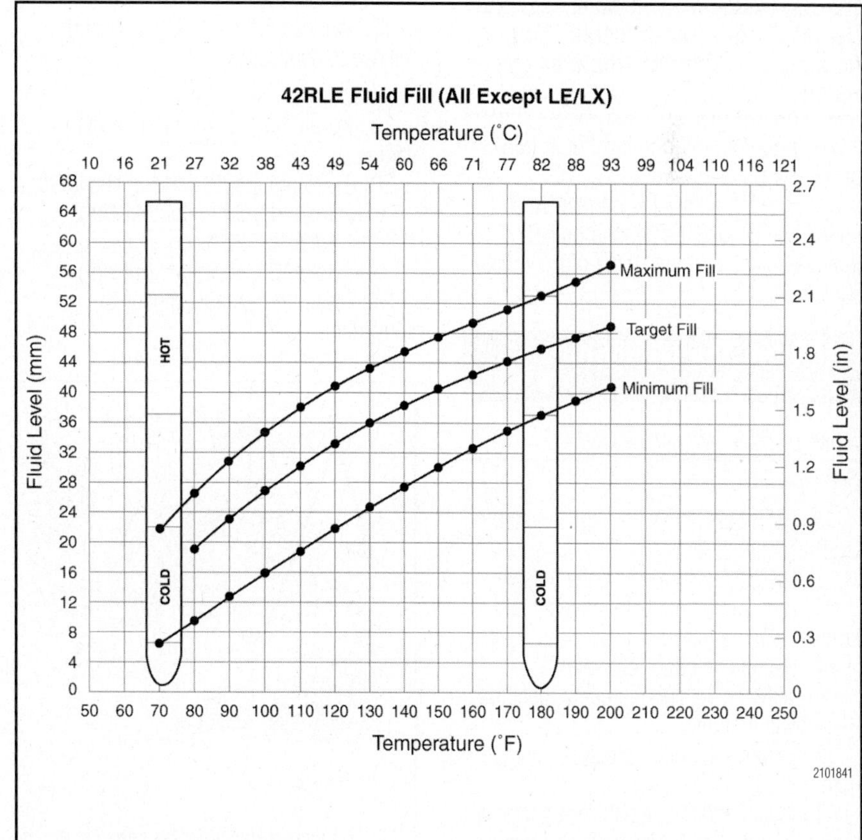

Fig. 7 Transmission Fluid Graph

a. If only fluid and filter were changed, add 6 pints (3 quarts) of ATF +4 to transmission.

b. If the transmission was completely overhauled, or torque converter was replaced or drained, add 10 pints (5 quarts) of ATF +4 to transmission.

4. Apply the parking brakes.
5. Start and run the engine at normal curb idle speed.
6. Apply service brakes, shift transmission through all gear ranges then back to NEUTRAL, set the parking brake, and leave the engine running at curb idle speed.
7. Remove funnel, insert dipstick and check fluid level. If level is low, add fluid to bring level to MIN mark on dipstick. Check to see if the oil level is equal on both sides of the dipstick. If one side is noticeably higher than the other, the dipstick has picked up some oil from the dipstick tube. Allow the oil to drain down the dipstick tube and re-check.
8. Drive the vehicle until the transmission fluid is at normal operating temperature.
9. With the engine running at curb idle speed, the gear selector in NEUTRAL, and the parking brake applied, check the transmission fluid level.

**** WARNING**

Do not overfill transmission, fluid foaming and shifting problems can result.

10. Add fluid to bring level up to MAX arrow mark.
11. When fluid level is correct, shut engine off, release the parking brake, remove funnel, and install the plug or dipstick in fill tube.

MANUAL TRANSMISSION ASSEMBLY

REMOVAL & INSTALLATION

See Figure 8.

1. Before servicing the vehicle, refer to the Precautions Section.
2. Disconnect negative battery cable.
3. Remove the console manual shift bezel.
4. Remove the floor console.
5. With the vehicle in neutral, position the vehicle on hoist.
6. Remove the drain plug and drain the fluid.
7. Matchmark the installation reference marks on propeller shaft/shafts and remove the shafts.
8. Remove the transfer case shift cable, wiring connector and vent hose, if equipped.
9. Remove the transfer case from the transmission, if equipped.
10. Support the transmission with a jack.
11. Remove the transmission mount bolts and the crossmember bolts. Remove the transmission mount with crossmember.
12. Remove the exhaust pipe with converters.
13. Pull hydraulic line clip from the slave cylinder.
14. Remove the line from the bracket and the cylinder.
15. Remove the clutch slave cylinder nuts and remove the cylinder by pulling straight back.

**** WARNING**

Do not allow release lever plunger to pivot more than 2° in either direction in the slave cylinder bore. Allowing the plunger to pivot more than 2° in the bore will cause fluid to bypass the seal and result in fluid leakage.

16. Remove the backup lamp switch wiring connector.
17. Remove the starter.
18. Remove transmission bolts and remove transmission.

To install:

19. Install the transmission on the engine.
20. Tighten the bolts (shown above) to:
    - Bolts "1": 30 ft. lbs. (41 Nm)
    - Bolts "2": 50 ft. lbs. (67 Nm)
    - Bolts "3": 40 ft. lbs. (54 Nm)
21. Install the exhaust pipe with converters.

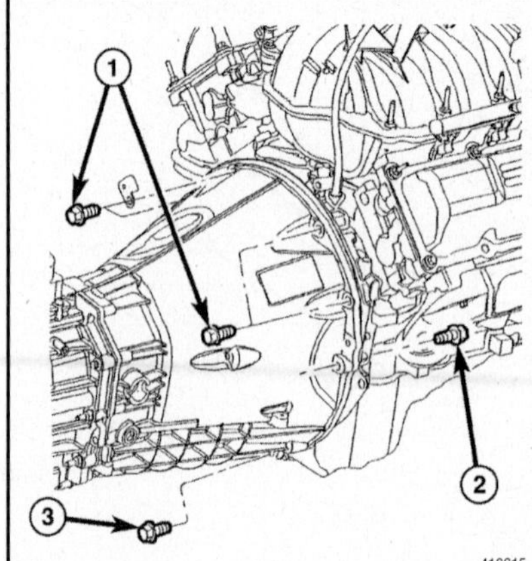

Fig. 8 Remove transmission bolts (1, 2, 3)

22. Install the transmission crossmember and tighten the bolts to 35 ft. lbs. (47 Nm). Install the transmission mount bolts and tighten to 35 ft. lbs. (47 Nm).
23. Install the back-up lamp wiring connector.

**** WARNING**

Do not allow release lever plunger to pivot more than 2° in either direction in the slave cylinder bore.

24. Install the slave cylinder in the transmission. Pull the clutch release lever toward the slave cylinder opening to insure proper seating of the slave cylinder plunger to the release lever pocket.
25. Install the hydraulic line and bracket to slave cylinder. Verify the O-ring is on the hydraulic line.
26. Install clutch slave cylinder and tighten mounting nuts to 17 ft. lbs. (23 Nm).
27. Bleed the hydraulic system.
28. Install the transfer case on the transmission, if equipped.
29. Install the propeller shaft/shafts with the matchmarks aligned.
30. Remove the fill plug and fill the transmission to specifications.
31. Install the inner shift boot, shift lever and lever screw.
32. Install the shift boot, shift knob and console.
33. Connect the battery.

MANUAL TRANSMISSION FLUID

DRAIN AND REFILL

1. Before servicing the vehicle, refer to the Precautions Section.
2. With vehicle in neutral, position vehicle on hoist.
3. Remove drain plug and drain fluid.
4. Install drain plug and remove fill plug.
5. Fill transmission with 3.17 pts. (1.5L) of Mopar® Manual Transmission Lubricant MS-9224, or equivalent, to the bottom of the fill plug hole.

CLUTCH

REMOVAL & INSTALLATION

See Figure 9.

1. Before servicing the vehicle, refer to the Precautions Section.
2. Remove the transmission.
3. Mark position of the pressure plate on the flywheel with paint or a scriber for

assembly reference, if clutch is not being replaced.

4. Loosen the pressure plate bolts evenly and in rotation to relieve spring tension and avoid warping the plate.

5. Remove the pressure plate bolts and the pressure plate and disc.

To install:

6. Lightly scuff sand the flywheel face with 180 grit emery cloth, and clean with a wax and grease remover.

7. Lubricate the pilot bearing with Mopar®high temperature bearing grease, or equivalent.

8. Check runout and operation of new clutch disc. Disc must slide freely on transmission input shaft splines.

9. With the disc on the input shaft, check face runout with dial indicator. Check runout at disc hub ¼ in. (6mm) from outer edge of facing. Obtain another clutch disc if runout exceeds 0.020 in. (0.5mm).

10. Position the clutch disc on the flywheel with the side marked flywheel against the flywheel. If not marked, the flat side of disc hub goes towards the flywheel.

11. Insert a clutch alignment tool through the clutch disc and into the pilot bearing.

12. Position the clutch pressure plate over the disc and on the flywheel.

13. Install the pressure plate bolts finger tight.

**** WARNING**

Use only the factory bolts to mount the pressure plate.

14. Tighten the pressure plate bolts evenly and in rotation a few threads at a time. The bolts must be tightened evenly and to specified torque. Failure to follow these instructions will distort the pressure plate.

15. Tighten the pressure plate bolts to 24 ft. lbs. (33 Nm).

**** WARNING**

Failure to tighten the bolts evenly and to the specified torque will distort the pressure plate.

16. Apply a light coat of Mopar®high temperature bearing grease, or equivalent, to the clutch disc hub and splines of the transmission input shaft. Do not over lubricate the shaft splines. This will result in grease contamination of the disc.

17. Install the transmission.

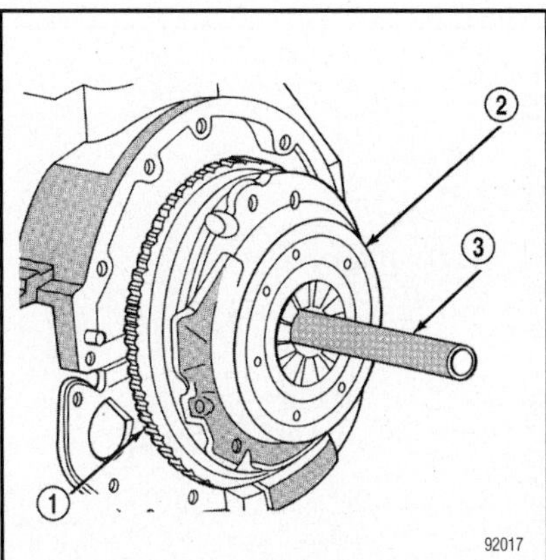

Fig. 9 Clutch wheel alignment, showing the flywheel (1), pressure plate (2), and alignment tool (3)

BLEEDING

Bleeding Clutch Hydraulic Circuit

1. Use Mopar® brake fluid, or an equivalent quality fluid meeting SAE J1703-F and DOT 3 standards only. Use fresh, clean fluid from a sealed container at all times.

2. Do not allow the master cylinder to run out of fluid during bleed operations. An empty cylinder will allow additional air to be drawn into the system. Check the cylinder fluid level frequently and add fluid as needed.

3. Verify the fluid level in the brake master cylinder; top off brake fluid as necessary.

➡Pre filling a new slave cylinder will reduce bleeding time required.

4. Install a length of clear hose to divert the fluid into a suitable container.

5. Push and hold the clutch pedal down, open the bleeder on the slave cylinder, allow fluid to bleed out, then close the bleeder. Repeat this step several times until no air is observed coming out of the bleeder.

6. Remove the drain hose and replace the dust cap on the bleeder and install the slave cylinder on the transmission.

7. Actuate the clutch pedal 25 times, then start the engine and verify clutch operation and pedal feel. If pedal feels spongy or clutch does not fully disengage, air is still trapped in the hydraulic circuit and must be bled again.

Pressure Bleeding Clutch Hydraulic Circuit

1. Follow manufacturer's instructions carefully when using pressure equipment. Do not exceed the tank manufacturer's pressure recommendations. Generally, a tank pressure of 15–20 psi is sufficient for bleeding.

2. Fill bleeder tank with recommended DOT 3 fluid and purge air from the tank lines before bleeding.

3. Do not pressure bleed without a proper master cylinder adapter. The wrong adapter can lead to leakage, or drawing air back into the system.

TRANSFER CASE ASSEMBLY

REMOVAL & INSTALLATION

See Figures 10 and 11.

1. Before servicing the vehicle, refer to the Precautions Section.

2. Shift the transfer case into NEUTRAL.

3. Raise the vehicle.

4. Remove the transfer case drain plug and drain the transfer case lubricant.

5. Support the transmission with a jack stand.

6. Remove the rear crossmember and skid plate, if equipped.

7. Remove the rear support cushion.

8. Disconnect the front propeller shaft from the transfer case at the companion flange. Remove the rear propeller shaft from the vehicle.

**** WARNING**

Do not allow the prop shafts to hang at attached end. Damage to the joint can result.

9. Disconnect the transfer case shift motor and mode sensor electrical harness connector.

10. Disconnect the transfer case vent hose.

11. Support the transfer case with a transmission jack.

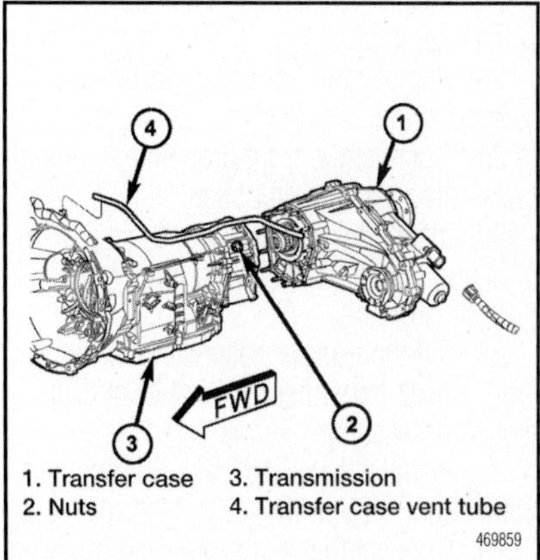

Fig. 10 Transfer case—MP1522 Transfer Case

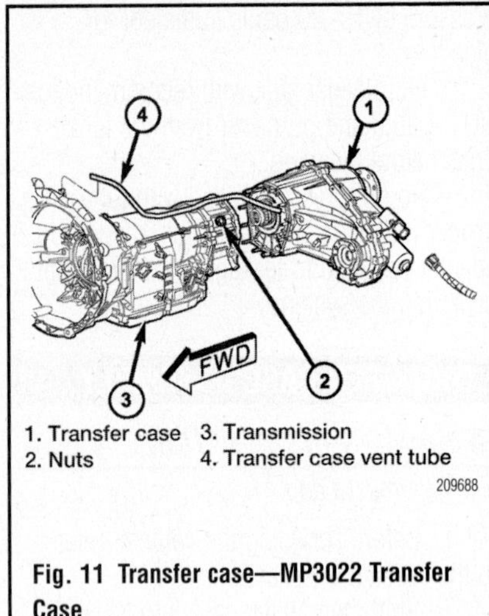

Fig. 11 Transfer case—MP3022 Transfer Case

12. Secure the transfer case to jack with chains.
13. Remove the nuts attaching the transfer case to the transmission.
14. Pull the transfer case and jack rearward to disengage the transfer case.
15. Remove the transfer case from under the vehicle.

To install:

16. Mount the transfer case on a transmission jack.
17. Secure the transfer case to the jack with chains.
18. Position the transfer case under the vehicle.
19. Align the transfer case and transmission shafts and install the transfer case onto the transmission.
20. Install and tighten the transfer case mounting nuts to 26 ft. lbs. (35 Nm).
21. Connect the transfer case vent hose to the transfer case.
22. Install the rear support cushion.
23. Install the rear crossmember and skid plate, if equipped.
24. Remove the transmission jack and support stand.
25. Connect the front propeller shaft and install the rear propeller shaft.
26. Install the transfer case drain plug and tighten to 15–25 ft. lbs. (20–34 Nm).
27. Fill the transfer case with correct fluid. Check transmission fluid level. Correct as necessary.
28. Install the transfer case fill plug and tighten to 15–25 ft. lbs. (20–34 Nm).
29. Connect the shift motor and mode sensor wiring connector.
30. Lower the vehicle and verify transfer case shift operation.

FRONT AXLE BEARING

REMOVAL & INSTALLATION

See Figures 12 and 13.

1. Before servicing the vehicle, refer to the Precautions Section.
2. Remove the front halfshafts.
3. On the right side, remove the axle shaft using a remover and a slide hammer.
4. Remove the shaft seal using a seal puller and a slide hammer.
5. Remove shaft bearing/bushing using a bearing puller and a slide hammer.

To install:

6. Position the bearing/bushing in the housing bore.
7. Install the shaft bearing/bushing using the large diameter end of a bearing installer and handle.
8. Drive the bearing/bushing in flush with housing bore.
9. Apply a light coat of lubricant on the lip of the shaft seal.
10. Install a new shaft seal in the axle using a seal installer.

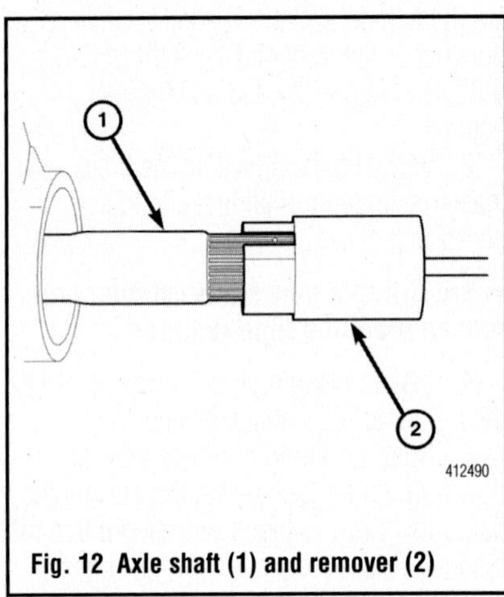

Fig. 12 Axle shaft (1) and remover (2)

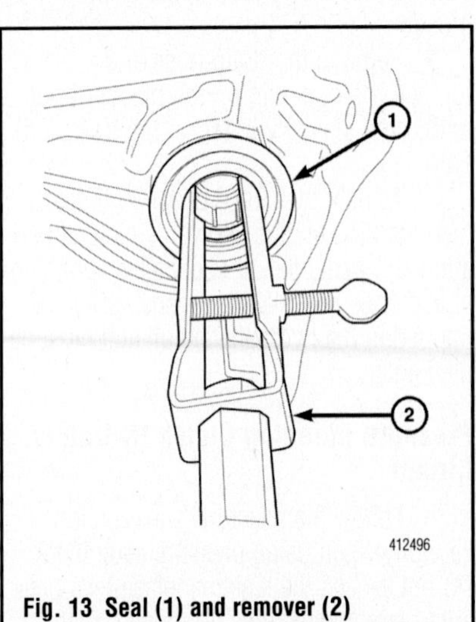

Fig. 13 Seal (1) and remover (2)

11. Install the right axle shaft and the halfshafts.

FRONT DRIVESHAFT/ PROPELLER SHAFT

REMOVAL & INSTALLATION

See Figure 14.

1. Before servicing the vehicle, refer to the Precautions Section.
2. With vehicle in neutral, position vehicle on hoist.
3. Mark an installation reference line across the front propeller shaft CV joint and transfer case flange.
4. Mark an installation reference line across the front propeller shaft flange and the axle flange.
5. Remove the axle flange bolts.
6. Remove the CV joint bolts and retainers.
7. Compress the propeller shaft enough to remove the shaft from the flanges.

To install:

8. Clean all propeller shaft bolts and apply Mopar® Lock and Seal Adhesive or equivalent to the threads before installation.
9. Compress the propeller shaft enough to install the shaft into the axle and transfer case flanges.
10. Align installation reference marks on the transfer case flange front shaft CV joint.
11. Install CV joint retainers and bolts. Tighten bolts to 22 ft. lbs. (30 Nm).
12. Align installation reference marks on the front propeller shaft flange and axle flange.
13. Install the axle flange bolts and tighten to 80 ft. lbs. (108 Nm).

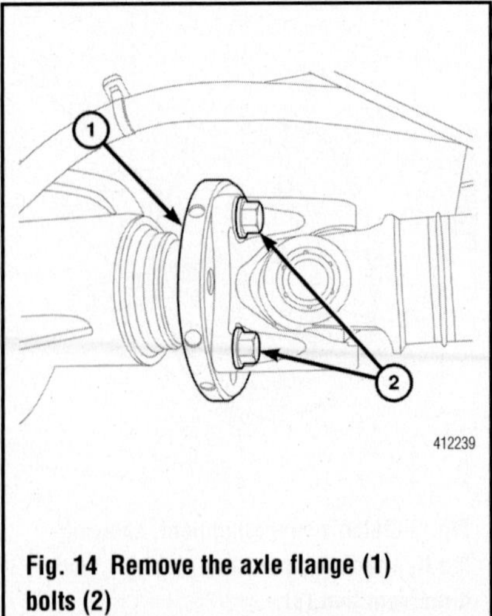

Fig. 14 Remove the axle flange (1) bolts (2)

FRONT HALFSHAFT

REMOVAL & INSTALLATION

See Figures 15 and 16.

1. Before servicing the vehicle, refer to the Precautions Section.
2. With the vehicle in neutral, position the vehicle on a hoist.
3. Remove the brake caliper and rotor.
4. Remove the nut from halfshaft.
5. Remove the sensor from the hub bearing.
6. Remove the stabilizer link from the stabilizer bar.
7. Remove the tie rod end nut and the tie rod from steering knuckle.
8. Remove the clevis bracket lower nut and bolt.
9. Remove the upper ball joint nut and separate the upper control arm from the steering knuckle.

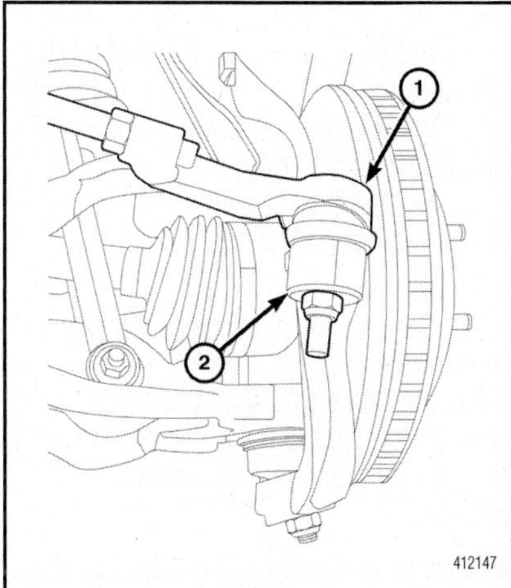

Fig. 15 Remove the tie rod end (1) nut and the tie rod from steering knuckle (2)

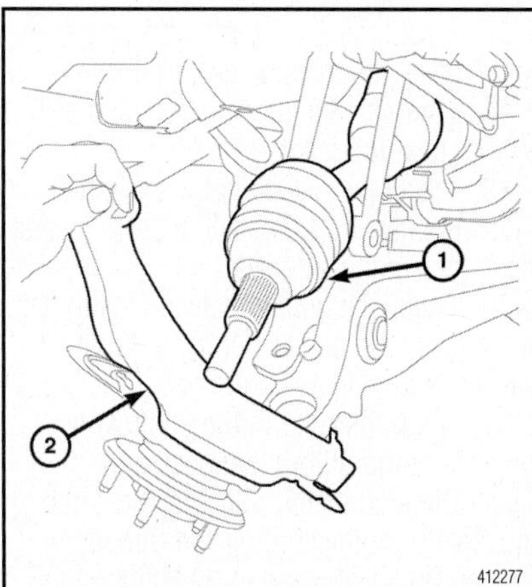

Fig. 16 Push the halfshaft (1) out of the hub bearing and knuckle (2)

10. Pull out on the steering knuckle and push the halfshaft out of the hub bearing and knuckle.
11. Using a pry bar, remove the half shaft from the axle.

To install:

12. Apply a light coat of wheel bearing grease on the female splines of the inner C/V joint.
13. Clean the hub bearing bore and apply a light coat of wheel bearing grease.
14. Install the halfshaft in the axle and push firmly to engage the snap ring.
15. Pull out on the steering knuckle and push the halfshaft through the knuckle and hub bearing.
16. Install the upper control arm on the steering knuckle and tighten the ball joint nut to 30 ft. lbs. (41 Nm) plus an additional 90 degrees.
17. Align the clevis with the lower control arm. Install the lower clevis and tighten the nut to 110 ft. lbs. (150 Nm) with full vehicle weight.
18. Install the tie rod end in the steering knuckle and tighten the nut to 30 ft. lbs. (41 Nm) plus an additional 90 degrees.
19. Install the stabilizer bar link and tie rod end.
20. Install the halfshaft hub nut and tighten to 100 ft. lbs. (136 Nm).

FRONT PINION SEAL

REMOVAL & INSTALLATION

See Figure 17.

1. Before servicing the vehicle, refer to the Precautions Section.
2. With the vehicle in neutral, position the vehicle on hoist.
3. Remove the brake calipers and rotors.
4. Remove the driveshaft/propeller shaft.
5. Rotate the pinion gear several times and verify the pinion rotates smoothly.
6. Record the torque to rotate the pinion gear with an inch pound torque wrench.
7. Using a short piece of pipe and a wrench, hold the pinion flange and remove the pinion nut.
8. Mark a line on the pinion shaft and flange for installation reference.
9. Remove the pinion flange using a puller and a flange holder.
10. Remove the pinion seal with a seal puller.

To install:

11. Apply a light coating of gear lubricant on the lip of the pinion seal. Install the pinion seal with a seal installer and handle.
12. Position the flange on the pinion shaft with the reference marks aligned.

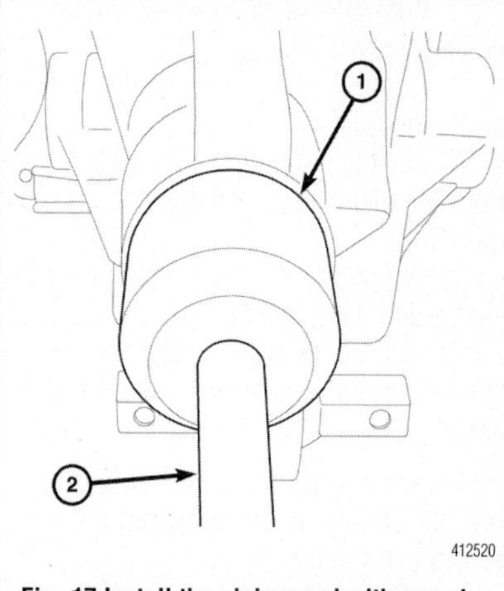

Fig. 17 Install the pinion seal with a seal installer (1) and handle (2)

13. Install the pinion flange with a flange installer and screw.
14. Install a NEW nut on the pinion gear. Hold the pinion flange with a flange holder and tighten the nut to 160 ft. lbs. (217 Nm).

**** WARNING**

Do not exceed the minimum tightening torque.

15. Rotate the pinion several times and verify the pinion rotates smoothly.
16. Measure the torque to rotate the pinion gear with an inch pound torque wrench. Rotating torque should be equal to the reading recorded during removal plus 5 inch lbs. (0.56 Nm). If rotating torque is low, tighten the pinion nut in 5 ft. lb. (7 Nm) increments until proper rotating torque is achieved.

**** WARNING**

If maximum tightening torque is reached [260 ft. lbs. (352 Nm)] prior to reaching required rotating torque, the collapsible spacer may have been damaged. Never loosen the pinion nut to decrease pinion rotating torque and never exceed specified preload torque. Failure to follow these instructions will result in damage.

17. Install the brake rotors, calipers and driveshaft/propeller shaft.
18. Fill the differential with gear lubricant.

REAR AXLE HOUSING

REMOVAL & INSTALLATION

1. Before servicing the vehicle, refer to the Precautions Section.

2. With the vehicle in neutral, position the vehicle on a hoist.

3. Position a lift/jack under the axle and secure the axle.

4. Mark the axle pinion flange and the propeller shaft flange for installation reference.

5. Remove the propeller shaft and suspend it under the vehicle.

6. Remove the brake sensor from the axle and remove the calipers, rotors and cables.

➡The parking brake is self-adjusting, and the cables must be locked out before removal.

7. Remove the track bar bolt from the axle bracket.

8. Remove the vent hose from the axle shaft tube.

9. Remove the stabilizer bar axle bracket.

10. Remove the shock absorbers from the axle brackets.

11. Remove the upper control arm nuts and bolts from the axle brackets.

12. Lower the axle enough to remove the coil springs and spring insulators.

13. Remove the lower control arm mounting bolts from the axle brackets.

14. Lower and remove the axle.

To install:

⁂ WARNING

The weight of the vehicle must be supported by the springs before the control arms and track bar are tightened. Failure to follow these instructions will cause premature bushing failure.

15. Raise the axle under the vehicle.

16. Install the lower control arms onto the axle brackets. Loosely install the mounting bolts and nuts.

17. Install the coil spring isolators and springs.

18. Raise the axle up until the springs are seated.

19. Install the upper control arms into the axle brackets. Loosely install the mounting bolts and nuts.

20. Install the shock absorbers to the axle brackets. Install the shock nuts/bolts and tighten to 85 ft. lbs. (115 Nm).

21. Install the stabilizer bar and clamps on the axle. Tighten the clamp bolts to 35 ft. lbs. (47 Nm).

22. Install the vent hose to the axle shaft tube.

23. Install the track bar to the axle bracket. Loosely install the track bar bolt.

24. Install the brake rotors, calipers and brake sensor on the axle.

25. Install the parking brake cables.

26. Align the reference marks and install the propeller shaft with pinion flange.

27. Clean all propeller shaft bolts and apply Mopar Lock and Seal Adhesive or equivalent to the threads.

28. Install the propeller shaft bolts and tighten to 80 ft. lbs. (108 Nm).

29. Install the wheels and tires.

30. Remove the lifting device from the axle and lower the vehicle.

31. Tighten the upper control arm-to-axle bracket bolts and nuts to 85 ft. lbs. (115 Nm), the lower control arm-to-axle bracket bolts and nuts to 150 ft. lbs. (203 Nm), and the track bar bolts to 130 ft. lbs. (176 Nm).

REAR AXLE SHAFT, BEARING & SEAL

REMOVAL & INSTALLATION

See Figures 18 and 19.

1. Before servicing the vehicle, refer to the Precautions Section.

2. With the vehicle in neutral, position the vehicle on hoist.

3. Remove the rear brake components.

4. Remove the wheel speed sensor.

5. Remove the differential housing cover and drain the lubricant.

6. Rotate the differential case so the pinion mate shaft lock screw is accessible. Remove the pinion mate shaft lock screw from the differential case.

7. Remove the pinion mate shaft from the differential case.

8. Push the axle shaft inward and remove the axle shaft C-lock from the axle shaft.

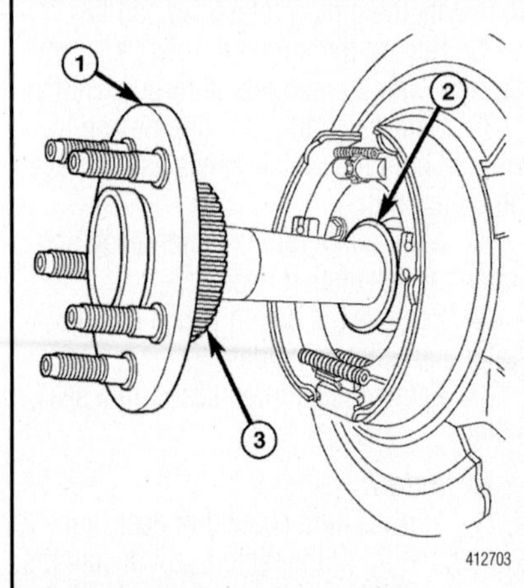

Fig. 18 Remove the axle shaft (1) from the axle tube (2)

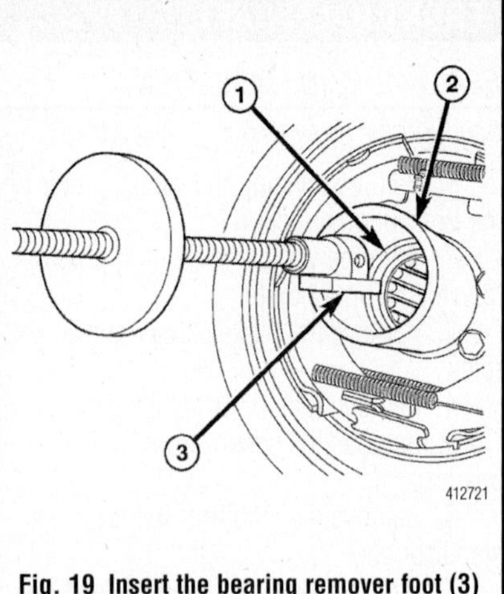

Fig. 19 Insert the bearing remover foot (3) through the receiver (2) and bearing (1)

9. Remove the axle shaft from the axle tube.

10. Remove the axle shaft seal from axle tube using a seal puller.

11. Position the bearing receiver on the axle tube.

12. Insert bearing remover foot through the receiver and bearing.

13. Tighten the nut on the shaft to pull the bearing into the receiver.

To install:

14. Remove any old sealer/burrs from the axle tube.

15. Install the axle shaft bearing with the bearing installer and driver handle. Drive the bearing in until the tool contacts the axle tube.

➡Bearing is installed with the bearing part number against installer.

16. Coat the new axle seal lip with axle lubricant. Install the seal with the seal installer and driver handle.

17. Install the axle shaft in the axle tube and engage into the side gear splines.

18. Lubricate the bearing bore and seal lip with gear lubricant.

19. Install the C-lock in the axle shaft end, and push the axle shaft outward to seat the C-lock in the side gear.

20. Install the pinion mate shaft into the differential case and through the thrust washers and differential pinions.

21. Align the hole in the shaft with the hole in the differential case and install the lock screw with Mopar® Lock and Seal or equivalent on the threads. Tighten the lock screw to 19 ft. lbs. (26 Nm).

22. Install the differential cover.

23. Install the rear brake components.

REAR DRIVESHAFT/ PROPELLER SHAFT

REMOVAL & INSTALLATION

1. Before servicing the vehicle, refer to the Precautions Section.
2. With vehicle in neutral, position the vehicle on a hoist.
3. Mark a reference line across the axle flange and propeller shaft flange for installation.
4. Mark a reference line across the transmission/transfer case flange and propeller shaft flange for installation.
5. Remove the propeller shaft flange bolts from the axle flange.
6. Remove the propeller shaft flange bolts from the transmission/transfer case flange.
7. Remove the propeller shaft.

To install:

8. Clean all propeller shaft bolts and apply Mopar® Lock and Seal Adhesive or equivalent to the threads before installation.
9. Install the propeller shaft.
10. Align the reference mark on the axle flange with the propeller shaft flange.
11. Align the reference mark on the transmission/transfer case flange with the propeller shaft flange.
12. Install the propeller shaft bolts in the axle flange and tighten to 80 ft. lbs. (108 Nm).
13. Install the propeller shaft bolts in the transmission/transfer case flange and tighten to 80 ft. lbs. (108 Nm).

REAR PINION SEAL

REMOVAL & INSTALLATION

See Figure 20.

1. Before servicing the vehicle, refer to the Precautions Section.
2. With the vehicle in neutral, position the vehicle on a hoist.
3. Remove wheel and tire assemblies.
4. Mark a reference line across the axle flange and propeller shaft flange.
5. Remove the companion flange bolts and remove the propeller shaft.
6. Remove the brake calipers and rotors to prevent any drag.
7. Rotate the companion flange three or four times and verify flange rotates smoothly.
8. Rotate the pinion gear with an inch pound torque wrench, and record the torque for installation reference.
9. Hold the pinion flange with a holding tool and remove the pinion nut.
10. Mark a line across the pinion shaft and flange for installation reference.
11. Remove the pinion flange with flange puller.
12. Remove pinion seal with a seal puller.

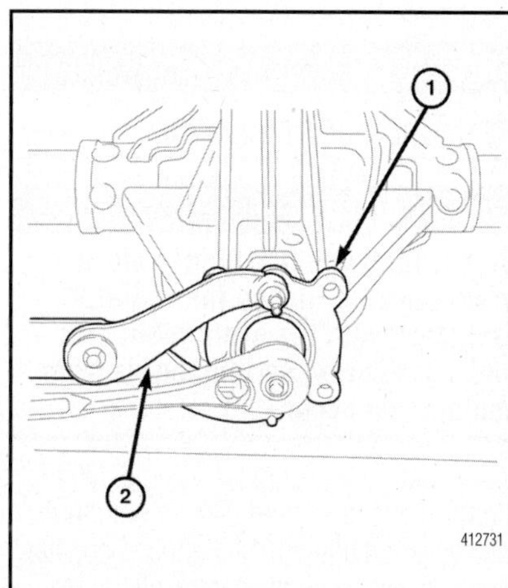

Fig. 20 Hold the pinion flange (1) with a holding tool (2)

To install:

13. Apply a light coating of gear lubricant on the lip of pinion seal.
14. Install a new pinion seal with a seal driver and handle.
15. Align the reference marks and install the flange on the pinion shaft.
16. Install the flange with flange installer.
17. Install a new pinion nut. Hold the flange with a holding tool, and tighten the pinion nut to 210 ft. lbs. (285 Nm). Rotate the pinion several revolutions to ensure the bearing rollers are seated.

**** WARNING**

Do not exceed the minimum tightening torque of 210 ft. lbs. (285 Nm) while installing pinion nut at this point.

18. Rotate the pinion with an inch pound torque wrench, and measure the torque. Rotating torque should be equal to the reading recorded during removal plus 5 inch lbs. (0.56 Nm). If rotating torque is low, tighten the pinion nut in 5 ft. lbs. (6.8 Nm) increments until proper rotating torque is achieved.

**** WARNING**

Never loosen the pinion nut to decrease pinion bearing rotating torque. If rotating torque is exceeded, a new collapsible spacer must be installed. Failure to follow these instructions will result in damage to the axle.

19. Align the reference marks and install the propeller shaft with axle flange.
20. Install the rear brake components.
21. Install the wheel and tire assemblies.

ENGINE COOLING

ENGINE FAN

REMOVAL & INSTALLATION

See Figure 21.

✻✻ CAUTION

If the fan blade is bent, warped, cracked or damaged in any way, it must be replaced only with a replacement fan blade. Do not attempt to repair a damaged fan blade.

➡For 3.7L Heavy Duty/Max Cool/Trailer Tow cooling package, the viscous fan cannot be removed separate from the shroud. Both fan and shroud must be removed together.

1. Before servicing the vehicle, refer to the Precautions Section.
2. Disconnect the negative battery cable.
3. Remove the combination coolant recovery/washer fluid bottle.
4. Remove the viscous fan from the water pump (if equipped).
5. Disengage the radiator hose retainer from the electric fan shroud.
6. Remove the transmission cooling line retainer bolt from the electric fan shroud.
7. Disconnect the electric fan connector from the electric fan shroud.
8. Remove the two bolts and lift the electric fan shroud from the vehicle.
9. Remove the cooling fan from the shroud.

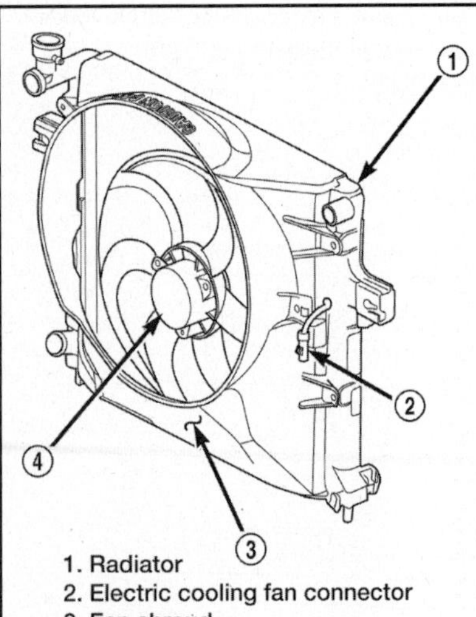

Fig. 21 Engine fan

To install:

10. Install the cooling fan to the shroud. Tighten the fan shroud-to-radiator bolts to 80 inch lbs. (9 Nm).
11. Install the fan shroud assembly into the vehicle.
12. Install the fan shroud-to-radiator mounting bolts. Tighten the bolts to 80 inch lbs. (9 Nm).
13. Connect the fan motor wire connector to harness connector and attach connector to shroud.
14. Install the radiator hose retainer to the electric fan shroud.
15. Install the transmission cooling line retainer bolt to the electric fan shroud.
16. Install the viscous fan drive (if equipped).
17. Install the combination coolant recovery/washer fluid bottle.
18. Connect the battery negative cable.
19. Start the engine and check fan operation.

RADIATOR

REMOVAL & INSTALLATION

✻✻ CAUTION

Do not remove the cylinder block drain plugs or loosen the radiator draincock with the system hot and under pressure. Serious burns from coolant can occur.

1. Before servicing the vehicle, refer to the Precautions Section. The air conditioning system (if equipped) is under a constant pressure, even with the engine off.
2. Disconnect the negative battery cable.
3. When removing the radiator or A/C condenser, note the location of all radiator-to-body and radiator-to-A/C condenser rubber air seals. These are used at the top, bottom and sides of the radiator and A/C condenser. To prevent overheating, these seals must be installed to their original positions.
4. Drain the coolant from the radiator.
5. Remove the combination coolant recovery/washer fluid reservoir assembly, if applicable.
6. Remove the front grill.
7. Remove the viscous cooling fan from the engine (if equipped).
8. Remove the two radiator mounting bolts.
9. Disconnect the electric cooling fan connector.
10. Disconnect the power steering cooler line from the cooler.
11. Disconnect the radiator upper and lower hoses.
12. Disconnect the overflow hose from the radiator.
13. The lower part of the radiator is equipped with two alignment dowel pins. They are located on the bottom of the radiator tank and fit into rubber grommets. These rubber grommets are pressed into the radiator lower crossmember.
14. Gently lift up and remove the radiator from the vehicle. The radiator and radiator cooling fan can be removed as an assembly. It is not necessary to remove the cooling fan before removing or installing the radiator. Be careful not to scrape the radiator fins against any other component. Also be careful not to disturb the air conditioning condenser (if equipped).

To install:

15. Before installing the radiator or A/C condenser, be sure the radiator-to-body and radiator-to-A/C condenser rubber air seals are properly fastened to their original positions. To prevent overheating, these seals must be installed to their original positions
16. Gently lower the radiator and fan shroud into the vehicle. Guide the two radiator alignment dowels into the rubber grommets located in lower radiator crossmember.
17. Connect the radiator upper and lower hoses and hose clamps to radiator. The tangs on the hose clamps MUST be positioned straight down.
18. Install both radiator mounting bolts.
19. Reconnect the electric cooling fan connector.
20. Install the grill.
21. Reinstall the viscous cooling fan to the engine (if equipped).
22. Rotate the fan blades (by hand) and check for interference at the fan shroud.
23. Install the combination coolant recovery/washer fluid reservoir assembly, if applicable.
24. Install the coolant reserve/overflow tank hose at the radiator.
25. Refill the cooling system.
26. Connect the negative battery cable.
27. Start the engine and check for leaks.

THERMOSTAT

REMOVAL & INSTALLATION

See Figure 22.

CAUTION

Do not loosen the radiator draincock with the system hot and pressurized. Serious burns from coolant can occur.

1. Before servicing the vehicle, refer to the Precautions Section.
2. Disconnect the negative battery cable.
3. Drain the cooling system.
4. Raise the vehicle on hoist.
5. Remove the splash shield.
6. Remove the lower radiator hose clamp and the lower radiator hose at thermostat housing.
7. Remove the mounting bolts, thermostat housing and thermostat.

To install:

8. Clean the mating areas of the timing chain cover and thermostat housing.
9. Install the thermostat (spring side down) into the recessed machined groove on the housing assembly. Make sure the rubber seal locating tab is positioned in the corresponding notch in the housing.
10. Position the thermostat housing on the timing chain cover.
11. Install the two housing-to-timing chain cover bolts and tighten to 105 inch lbs. (12 Nm).
12. Install the lower radiator hose on the thermostat housing.
13. Install the splash shield.
14. Lower the vehicle.
15. Fill the cooling system.
16. Connect the negative battery cable to battery.
17. Start the engine and check for leaks.

WATER PUMP

REMOVAL & INSTALLATION

See Figure 23.

1. Before servicing the vehicle, refer to the Precautions Section.
2. Drain the cooling system.
3. Disconnect the negative battery cable.
4. If the water pump is being replaced, do not unbolt the fan blade assembly from the thermal viscous fan drive.
5. Remove the two fan shroud-to-radiator screws. Disconnect the coolant overflow hose.
6. Remove the upper fan shroud and fan blade/viscous fan drive assembly from the vehicle. After removing the fan blade/viscous fan drive assembly, do NOT place the fan drive in a horizontal position.

WARNING

If stored horizontally, silicone fluid in viscous fan drive could drain into its bearing assembly and contaminate lubricant.

7. Remove the accessory drive belt.
8. Remove the lower radiator hose clamp and remove the lower hose at the water pump.
9. Remove the seven water pump mounting bolts and one stud bolt.

WARNING

Do not pry on the water pump at the timing chain case/cover. The machined surfaces may be damaged, resulting in leaks.

10. Remove the water pump and gasket. Discard the gasket.

To install:

11. Clean the gasket mating surfaces.
12. Using a new gasket, position the water pump onto the engine timing chain cover. Tighten the water pump mounting bolts in the sequence shown to 40 ft. lbs. (54 Nm).
13. Spin the water pump to be sure that the pump impeller does not rub against the timing chain cover.
14. Connect the radiator lower hose to the water pump.
15. Install the accessory drive belt.
16. Position the upper fan shroud and fan blade/viscous fan drive assembly.
17. Be sure the upper and lower portions of the fan shroud are firmly connected. All air must flow through the radiator.
18. Install the two fan shroud-to-radiator screws.
19. Be sure of at least 1.0 inch (25 mm) between the tips of fan blades and the fan shroud.
20. Evacuate the air and refill the cooling system.
21. Connect the negative battery cable.
22. Check the cooling system for leaks.

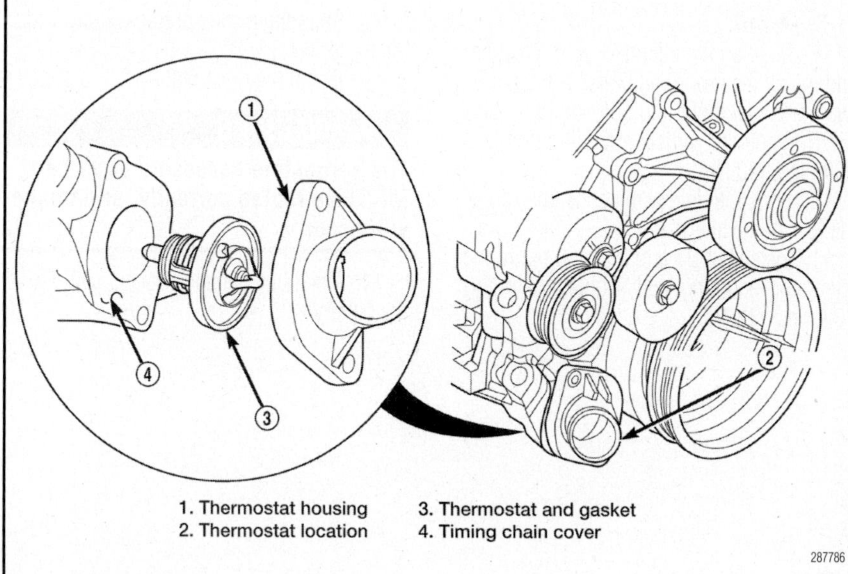

Fig. 22 Thermostat

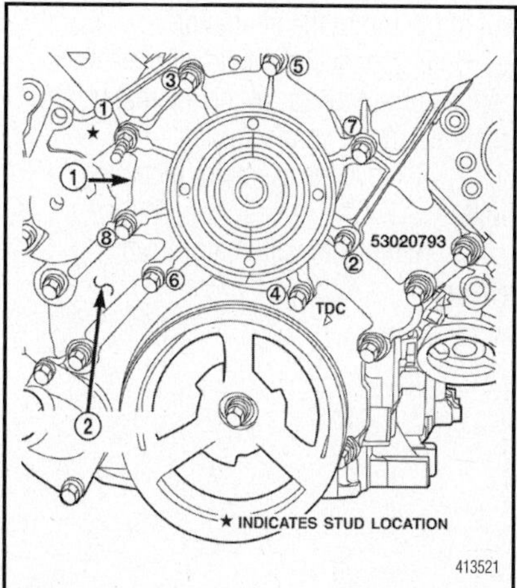

Fig. 23 Water pump (1) positioned on the timing chain cover (2), bolt tightening sequence

BATTERY

REMOVAL & INSTALLATION

1. Before servicing the vehicle, refer to the Precautions Section.
2. Loosen the pinch clamp bolt and disconnect and isolate the battery negative cable.
3. Loosen the pinch clamp bolt and disconnect the battery positive cable.
4. Loosen bolt and remove the retainer that holds the battery to the battery tray.
5. Remove the battery from the vehicle.
6. Remove the thermal guard from the battery.

To install:

7. Carefully install the thermal guard onto the battery.
8. Install battery into the vehicle making sure that the thermal guard is present and battery is properly positioned on battery tray.
9. Install the battery hold down retainer and bolt making sure that it is properly positioned. Tighten the hold down bolt to 62 inch lbs. (7 Nm).
10. Connect the battery positive cable and tighten the pinch clamp nut to 45 inch lbs. (5 Nm).
11. Connect the battery negative cable and tighten the pinch clamp nut to 45 inch lbs. (5 Nm).
12. Verify proper vehicle operation.

ALTERNATOR

REMOVAL & INSTALLATION

See Figure 24.

1. Before servicing the vehicle, refer to the Precautions Section.

✲✲ CAUTION

Failure to disconnect the negative cable from the battery before removing battery output wire from the alternator can result in injury.

✲✲ WARNING

Never force a belt over a pulley rim using a screwdriver. The synthetic fiber of the belt can be damaged.

2. Disconnect and isolate the negative battery cable at the battery.
3. Remove the alternator drive belt.
4. Unsnap the plastic protective cover from the B+ mounting stud.
5. Remove the B+ terminal mounting nut at the top of the alternator.
6. Disconnect the field wire electrical connector at the rear of the alternator by pushing on the connector tab.
7. Remove the alternator mounting bolts.
8. Remove the alternator from vehicle.

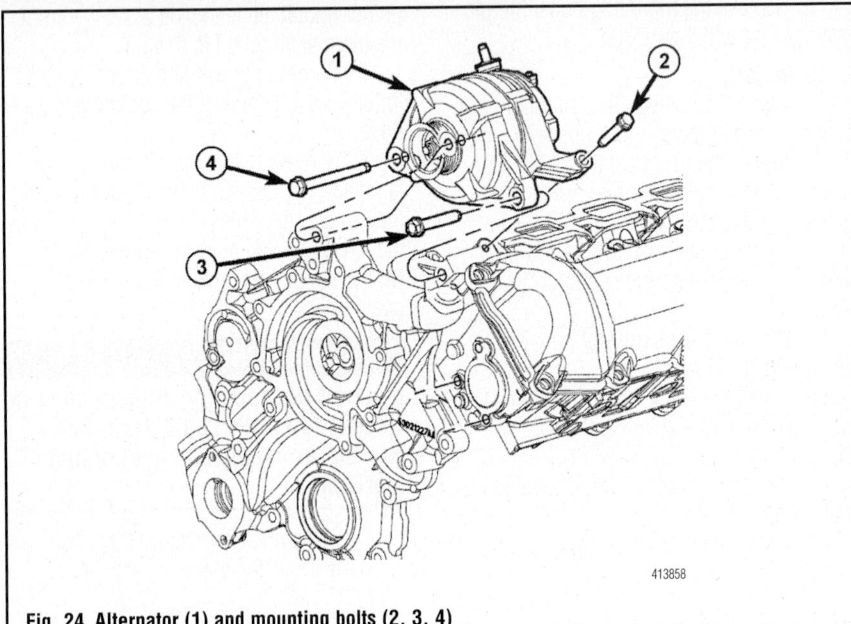

Fig. 24 Alternator (1) and mounting bolts (2, 3, 4)

To install:

9. Position the alternator to the engine and install the mounting bolts. Tighten the two horizontal mounting bolts to 42 ft. lbs. (57 Nm) and the vertical mounting bolt to 29 ft. lbs. (40 Nm).
10. Snap the field wire connector into the rear of the alternator.
11. Install the B+ terminal and nut to the alternator mounting stud. Tighten the nut to 10 ft. lbs. (13 Nm).
12. Snap the plastic protective cover to the B+ terminal.
13. Install the drive belt.

✲✲ WARNING

The serpentine accessory drive belt MUST be routed correctly, or damage will occur.

14. Install the negative battery cable to the battery.

FIRING ORDER

3.7L Engine Firing order: 1–6–5–4–3–2

IGNITION COIL

REMOVAL & INSTALLATION

1. Before servicing the vehicle, refer to the Precautions Section.

➡An ignition coil with a spark plug wire attached is used for two cylinders. The three coils fits into machined holes in the cylinder head for cylinders 1, 3, and 5. A mounting stud/nut secures each coil to the top of the intake manifold . The bottom of the coil is equipped with a rubber boot to seal the spark plug to the coil. Inside each rubber boot is a spring. The spring is used for a mechanical contact between the coil and the top of the spark plug. These rubber boots and springs are a permanent part of the coil and are not serviced separately. An O-ring is used to seal the coil at the opening into the cylinder head.

2. Depending on which coil is being removed, the throttle body air intake tube or intake box may need to be removed to gain access to the coil.
3. Disconnect the electrical connector from the coil by pushing downward on the release lock on top of connector and pull the connector from coil.
4. Disconnect spark plug wire from coil.
5. Clean the area at the base of the coil with compressed air before removal.
6. Remove the coil mounting bolt.
7. Carefully pull up the coil from the cylinder head opening with a slight twisting action.
8. Remove the coil from the vehicle.

To install:

9. Using compressed air, blow out any dirt or contaminants from around the top of the spark plug.
10. Check the condition of the coil rubber boot. To aid in coil installation, apply silicone based grease (such as Mopar® Dielectric Grease No. J8126688) into the spark plug end of the rubber boot and to the top of the spark plug.
11. Position the ignition coil assembly into the cylinder head opening. Using a twisting action, push the ignition coil assembly onto the spark plug.
12. Install the coil mounting bolt. Tighten to 70 inch lbs. (8 Nm).
13. Connect the electrical connector to the ignition coil assembly by snapping into position.
14. Install the spark plug wires.
15. If necessary, install the throttle body air intake tube, or intake air box.

IGNITION TIMING

ADJUSTMENT

The ignition timing is controlled by the Engine Control Module (ECM). No adjustment is necessary or possible.

SPARK PLUGS

REMOVAL & INSTALLATION

1. Before servicing the vehicle, refer to the Precautions Section.

➡Each individual spark plug is located under each ignition coil. Each individual ignition coil must be removed to gain access to each spark plug.

2. Remove the necessary air filter tubing at the throttle body.
3. Prior to removing the ignition coil, spray compressed air around the coil base at the cylinder head.
4. Prior to removing the spark plug, spray compressed air into the cylinder head opening. This will help prevent foreign material from entering the combustion chamber.
5. Remove the spark plug from the cylinder head using a quality socket with a rubber or foam insert. Also check condition of the ignition coil O-ring and replace as necessary.
6. Inspect the spark plug condition.

To install:

⁂ WARNING

When installing the spark plugs into the cylinder head spark plug wells, be sure the plugs do not drop into the plug wells as electrodes can be damaged. Do not over tighten the spark plugs.

7. Start the spark plug into the cylinder head by hand to avoid cross threading.
8. Tighten the spark plugs to 20 ft. lbs. (37 Nm).
9. Before installing the coil(s), check the condition of the coil O-ring and replace as necessary. To aid in coil installation, apply silicone to coil O-ring.
10. Install the ignition coil(s).

ENGINE ELECTRICAL

STARTER

REMOVAL & INSTALLATION

See Figure 25.

1. Before servicing the vehicle, refer to the Precautions Section.
2. Disconnect and isolate negative battery cable.
3. Raise and support vehicle.
4. For 4WD vehicles, remove the front driveshaft/propeller shaft.
5. Remove the two heat shield bolts and remove the starter heat shield.
6. Remove the solenoid nut from the mounting stud.
7. After the nut has been removed, pull the battery cable from the mounting stud while removing the electrical connector from the solenoid terminal.

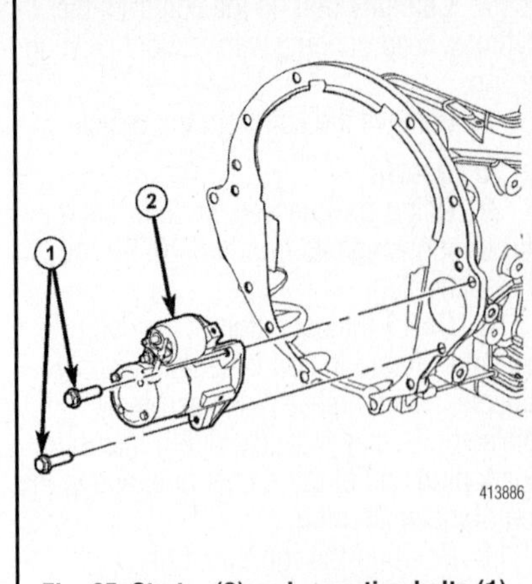

Fig. 25 Starter (2) and mounting bolts (1)

8. Remove the two starter mounting bolts.
9. Remove the starter assembly from the transmission.
10. Rotate the starter assembly to allow removal from the vehicle.

To install:

11. Rotate the starter assembly to allow positioning into the transmission.
12. Install the two starter mounting bolts and tighten to 40 ft. lbs. (54 Nm).
13. Position the battery cable assembly onto the stud while pushing the solenoid connector onto the solenoid terminal. Install the nut and tighten to 97 inch lbs. (11 Nm).
14. Position the starter heat shield and tighten the two bolts to 53 inch lbs. (6 Nm).
15. Install the front driveshaft/propeller shaft, if applicable.
16. Lower the vehicle.
17. Connect the negative battery cable.

ENGINE MECHANICAL

➡Disconnecting the negative battery cable may interfere with the functions of the on board computer systems and may require the computer to undergo a relearning process, once the negative battery cable is reconnected.

ACCESSORY DRIVE BELTS

ACCESSORY BELT ROUTING

See Figure 26.

1. Alternator pulley
2. Accessory drive belt
3. Power steering pump pulley
4. Crankshaft pulley
5. Idler pulley
6. Tensioner
7. A/C compressor pulley
8. Water pump pulley

413290

Fig. 26 Drive belt routing

INSPECTION

When inspecting serpentine drive belts, small cracks that run across the ribbed surface of the belt from rib to rib are considered normal. These are not a reason to replace the belt. However, cracks running along a rib (not across) are not normal. Any belt with cracks running along a rib must be replaced. Also replace belt if it has excessive wear, frayed cords or severe glazing.

ADJUSTMENT

Tension is automatically adjusted by the belt tensioner.

REMOVAL & INSTALLATION

1. Before servicing the vehicle, refer to the Precautions Section.
2. Disconnect the negative battery cable.
3. Remove the combination washer reservoir/coolant recovery container.
4. Rotate the belt tensioner until it contacts its stop.
5. Remove the belt, then slowly rotate the tensioner into the free arm position.

To install:

6. Check the condition of all pulleys.

⁂ WARNING

When installing the serpentine accessory drive belt, the belt MUST be routed correctly. If not, the engine may overheat due to the water pump rotating in the wrong direction.

7. Install the new belt. Route the belt around all the pulleys except the idler pulley. Rotate the tensioner arm until it contacts its stop position. Route the belt around the idler and slowly let the tensioner rotate into the belt. Make sure the belt is seated onto all pulleys.
8. With the drive belt installed, inspect the belt wear indicator. On 3.7L engines, the gap between the tang and the housing stop must not exceed .94 in. (24 mm).
9. Install the combination washer reservoir/coolant recovery container.
10. Connect negative battery cable.

AIR CLEANER

FILTER/ELEMENT REPLACEMENT

➡Housing removal is not necessary for filter (element) replacement.

1. Before servicing the vehicle, refer to the Precautions Section.
2. Disconnect the negative battery cable.
3. Pry up the spring clips from the front of the housing cover (spring clips retain cover to housing).
4. Release the housing cover from the 4 tabs located on the rear of the housing, and remove the cover.
5. Remove the air cleaner filter (element) from the housing.
6. Clean the inside of the housing before replacing the filter.

To install:

7. Install the filter into housing.
8. Position the housing cover into the housing locating tabs.
9. Pry up the spring clips and lock the cover to the housing.

10. If any air filter, air resonator, air intake tubes or air filter housing clamps have been loosened or removed, tighten them to 40 inch lbs. (5 Nm).

11. Connect the negative battery cable.

CAMSHAFT AND VALVE LIFTERS

INSPECTION

1. Inspect the camshaft bearing journals for wear or damage.
2. Inspect the cylinder head and check oil return holes.
3. Check both camshaft surfaces for wear or damage.
4. Check camshaft lobe height and replace if out of limit.

REMOVAL & INSTALLATION

See Figures 27 and 28.

1. Before servicing the vehicle, refer to the Precautions Section.
2. Disconnect the negative battery cable.

⁂ WARNING

When the timing chain is removed and the cylinder heads are still installed, do not forcefully rotate the camshafts or crankshaft independently of each other. Severe valve and/or piston damage can occur.

⁂ WARNING

When removing the cam sprocket, timing chains or camshaft, failure to use the Wedge Locking Tool will result in hydraulic tensioner ratchet over extension, requiring timing chain cover removal to reset the tensioner ratchet.

3. Remove the cylinder head cover.
4. Set No. 1 engine cylinder to TDC, camshaft sprocket V6 marks at the 12 o'clock position.
5. Matchmark one link on the secondary timing chain on both sides of the V6 mark on the camshaft sprocket to aid in installation.

⁂ WARNING

Do not hold or pry on the camshaft target wheel for any reason. Severe damage will occur to the target wheel, resulting in a vehicle no start condition.

6. Loosen but DO NOT remove the camshaft sprocket retaining bolt. Leave the bolt snug against the sprocket.
7. The timing chain tensioners must be secured prior to removing the camshaft sprockets. Failure to secure tensioners will allow the tensioners to extend, requiring timing chain cover removal in order to reset tensioners.
8. Position the Wedge Locking Tool between the timing chain strands, tap the tool to securely wedge the timing chain against the tensioner arm and guide.

⁂ WARNING

Do not force Locking Wedge past the narrowest point between the chain strands. Damage to the tensioners may occur.

9. Remove the camshaft position sensor.
10. Hold the camshaft with the camshaft holder (Special Tool 8428A or equivalent), while removing the camshaft sprocket bolt and sprocket.
11. Using the camshaft holder, gently allow the camshaft to rotate 5° until the camshaft is in the neutral position (no valve load).
12. Starting at the outside working inward, loosen the camshaft bearing cap retaining bolts ½ turn at a time. Repeat until all load is off the bearing caps.

⁂ WARNING

Do not stamp or strike the camshaft bearing caps. Severe damage will occur to the bearing caps.

13. When the camshaft is removed, the rocker arms may slide downward. Matchmark the rocker arms before removing the camshaft.
14. Remove the camshaft bearing caps and the camshaft.

Fig. 27 Hold the camshaft (1) with the camshaft holder (2)

To install:

15. Lubricate camshaft journals with clean engine oil.
16. Position the camshaft into the cylinder head. Position the left side camshaft so that the camshaft sprocket dowel is near the 1 o'clock position, This will place the camshaft at the neutral position, easing the installation of the camshaft bearing caps.
17. Install the camshaft bearing caps. Hand tighten the retaining bolts.
18. Caps should be installed so that the stamped numbers on the caps are in numerical order, (1 through 4) from the front to the rear of the engine. All caps should be installed so that the stamped arrows on the caps point toward the front of the engine.
19. Working in ½ turn increments, tighten the bearing cap retaining bolts in the sequence shown to 100 inch lbs. (11 Nm).
20. Position the camshaft drive gear into the timing chain, aligning the V6 mark between the two marked chain links (marked during removal).
21. Using the camshaft holding tool, rotate the camshaft until the camshaft sprocket dowel is aligned with the slot in the camshaft sprocket. Install the sprocket onto the camshaft.
22. Remove excess oil from the camshaft sprocket retaining bolt. Failure remove excess oil can cause bolt over-torque, resulting in bolt failure.
23. Install the camshaft sprocket retaining bolt and hand tighten.
24. Remove the tensioner wedge locking tool.
25. Using the wrench with adapter pins, tighten the camshaft sprocket retaining bolt to 90 ft. lbs. (122 Nm).
26. Install the cylinder head cover.
27. Connect the negative battery cable.

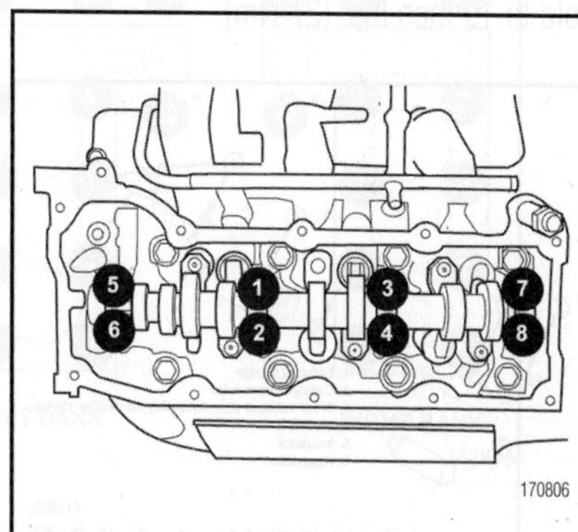

Fig. 28 Camshaft bearing cap bolt tightening sequence

Tighten the damper bolt to 130 ft. lbs. (175 Nm).

41. Install the power steering pump.
42. Install the fan blade assembly and fan shroud.
43. Install the cylinder head covers.
44. Install the intake manifold.
45. Install the oil fill housing onto cylinder head.
46. Refill the cooling system.
47. Raise the vehicle.
48. Install the exhaust pipe onto the left exhaust manifold.
49. Install the exhaust pipe onto the right exhaust manifold.
50. Lower the vehicle.
51. Connect the negative battery cable.
52. Start the engine and check for leaks.

ENGINE OIL & FILTER

REPLACEMENT

1. Before servicing the vehicle, refer to the Precautions Section.
2. Remove the oil fill cap.
3. Raise and support the vehicle.
4. Place a suitable drain pan under crankcase drain.
5. Remove the drain plug from crankcase and allow oil to drain into pan. Inspect drain plug threads for stretching or other damage. Replace drain plug if damaged.
6. Using a suitable oil filter wrench, remove the filter.
7. Install the drain plug in crankcase.
8. Clean the gasket sealing surface of oil and grime.

To install:

9. Lightly lubricate the oil filter gasket with engine oil.
10. Install the filter. Hand tighten.
11. Lower the vehicle and fill crankcase with specified type and amount of engine oil.
12. Install the oil fill cap.
13. Start the engine and inspect for leaks.

EXHAUST MANIFOLD

REMOVAL & INSTALLATION

See Figures 34 and 35.

1. Before servicing the vehicle, refer to the Precautions Section.
2. Disconnect the negative battery cable.
3. Raise and support the vehicle.
4. Remove the bolts and nuts attaching the exhaust pipe to the engine exhaust manifold.

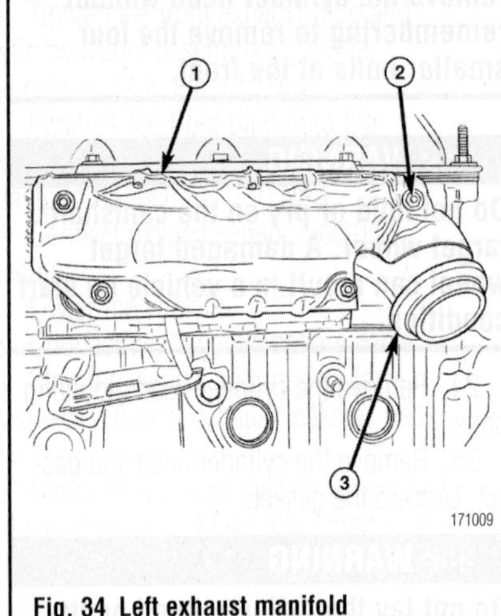

Fig. 34 Left exhaust manifold

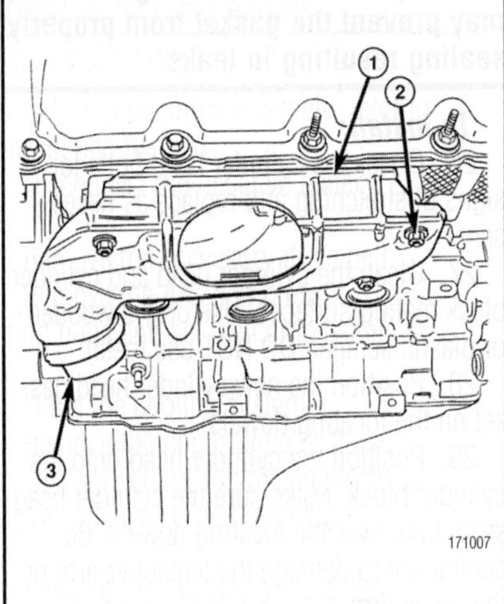

Fig. 35 Right exhaust manifold

5. Lower the vehicle.
6. Remove the exhaust heat shield.
7. Remove bolts, nuts and washers attaching manifold to cylinder head.
8. Remove manifold and gasket from the cylinder head.

To install:

WARNING

If the studs came out with the nuts when removing the engine exhaust manifold, install new studs. Apply sealer on the coarse thread ends. Water leaks may develop at the studs if this precaution is not taken.

9. Position the engine exhaust manifold and gasket on the two studs located on the cylinder head.
10. Install conical washers and nuts on these studs.
11. Install remaining conical washers. Starting at the center arm and working outward, tighten the bolts and nuts to 18 ft. lbs. (25 Nm).
12. Install the exhaust heat shields.
13. Raise and support the vehicle.

WARNING

Over-tightening heat shield fasteners may cause shield to distort and/or crack.

14. Assemble exhaust pipe to manifold and secure with bolts, nuts and retainers. Tighten the bolts and nuts to 25 ft. lbs. (34 Nm).

INTAKE MANIFOLD

REMOVAL & INSTALLATION

See Figure 36.

1. Before servicing the vehicle, refer to the Precautions Section.
2. Properly relieve the fuel system pressure.
3. Disconnect the negative cable from battery.
4. Remove the resonator assembly and air inlet hose.
5. Drain the cooling system below the coolant temperature sensor level.
6. Disconnect the electronic throttle control (ETC) connector.
7. Disconnect the electrical connectors for the following components:
   - Coolant Temperature Sensor
   - Manifold Absolute Pressure (MAP) Sensor
8. Disconnect the vapor purge hose, brake booster hose, and Positive Crankcase Ventilation (PCV) hose.
9. Disconnect and remove the ignition coil towers.
10. Remove the top oil dipstick tube retaining bolt.
11. Remove the EGR tube.
12. Remove fuel rail.
13. Remove the throttle body assembly.
14. Remove the intake manifold retaining fasteners in reverse order of tightening sequence.
15. Remove the intake manifold.

To install:

16. Install the intake manifold seals.
17. Install the intake manifold.
18. Install the intake manifold retaining bolts and tighten in sequence shown to 105 inch lbs. (12 Nm).

WARNING

Proper torque of the throttle body is critical to normal operation. If the throttle body is over-torqued, damage

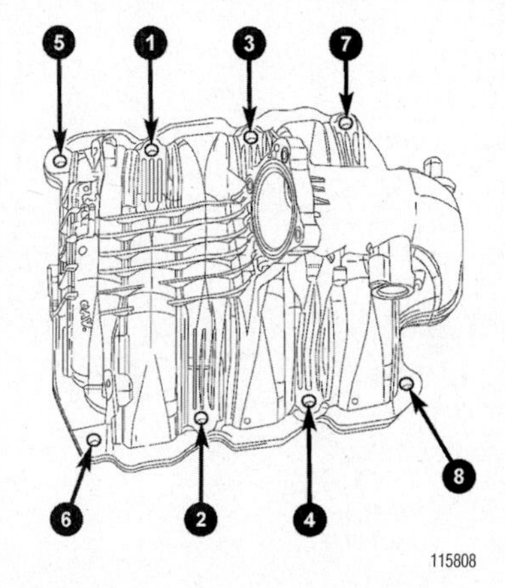

Fig. 36 Intake manifold bolt tightening sequence

to the throttle body can occur resulting in throttle plate malfunction.

19. Install the throttle body-to-intake manifold O-ring.
20. Install the throttle body to intake manifold.
21. Install the four mounting bolts. Tighten bolts to 60 inch lbs. (7 Nm).
22. Install the electrical connector.
23. Install the fuel rail.
24. Install the EGR tube.
25. Install the ignition coil towers.
26. Connect the electrical connectors for the following components:
    - MAP Sensor
    - Coolant temperature sensor
    - Ignition coil towers
27. Install the top oil dipstick tube retaining bolt.
28. Connect the vapor purge hose, brake booster hose, and PCV hose.
29. Fill the cooling system.
30. Install the resonator assembly and the air inlet hose.
31. Connect the negative cable to battery.
32. Using the scan tool, perform the ETC relearn function.

OIL PAN

REMOVAL & INSTALLATION

2WD Models

See Figure 37.

1. Before servicing the vehicle, refer to the Precautions Section.
2. Disconnect the negative battery cable.
3. Install engine support fixture.
4. Raise and support vehicle.
5. Remove the front wheel assemblies.
6. Remove the skid plate (if equipped).
7. Drain engine oil.
8. Mark adjustment cam position of front lower control arm bolts.
9. Remove the front lower control arm bolts.
10. Disconnect the left-hand tie rod.
11. Disconnect the left-hand lower ball joint.
12. Disconnect the left-hand strut clevis.
13. Remove the left-hand front axle.
14. Remove the front axle brace bolts.
15. Remove the front prop shaft.
16. Drain front axle.
17. Using a transmission jack, support the front axle.
18. Remove the axle bracket bolts.
19. With the right-hand axle still in place, remove front differential.
20. Remove the transmission oil cooler line bracket.
21. Remove the engine to transmission stiffening bracket.
22. Position the Engine Support Tool 8534 on the fender lip and align the slots in the brackets with the fender mounting holes.
23. Secure brackets to the fender using four M6 X 1.0 X 25 MM flanged cap screws.
24. Tighten the thumbscrews to secure the sleeves to the support tube.
25. Secure the support tube in an upright position.
26. Assemble the flat washer, thrust bearing, hook and T handle.
27. Using the M10 X 1.75 mm flanged nut supplied with the support fixture, secure the chain to the front engine lifting stud.
28. Loosen the engine mounts.
29. Remove the oil pan bolts.
30. Separate the oil pan from the engine.
31. Move the oil pan to one side, remove oils sump bolt and windage tray bolts.

➡Do not pry on oil pan or oil pan gasket. Gasket is integral to engine windage tray and does not come out with oil pan.

32. Move the oil pan and windage tray toward the front of vehicle and remove from vehicle.

To install:

33. Clean the oil pan gasket mating surface of the bedplate and oil pan.
34. Clean the oil pan and block gasket mating surfaces.
35. Inspect integrated oil pan gasket, and replace as necessary.
36. Drop the oil pump pick-up tube into the oil pan, and install the oil pan, pick-up tube, and the windage tray, as an assembly, from the front of the vehicle.

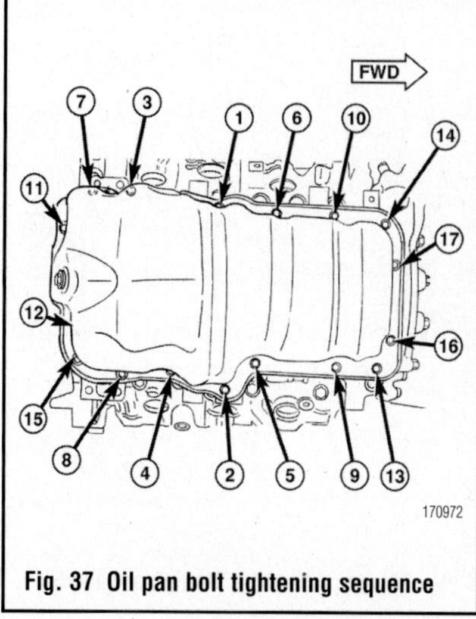

Fig. 37 Oil pan bolt tightening sequence

37. Install the windage tray, then the oil pump pick-up tube, and the nuts and bolt holding the oil pump pick-up tube in place.

➡It will be necessary to move the oil pan from side to side to gain access to these fasteners.

38. Tighten the pick-up tube fasteners.
39. Install the oil pan.
40. Install and tighten the oil pan bolts.
41. Install the engine to transmission structural cover, (if equipped).
42. Lower engine, and remove Engine Support Fixture 8534.
43. Lower the vehicle.
44. Lower the engine using Engine Support Fixture.
45. Remove the Engine Support Fixture.
46. Raise the vehicle.
47. Tighten both engine mount through bolts.
48. Install the transmission oil cooler line bracket.
49. Install the skid plate (if equipped).
50. Install the front wheel and tire assemblies.
51. Lower the vehicle.
52. Refill engine oil.
53. Reconnect battery.
54. Start engine and check for leaks.

4WD Models

See Figure 38.

1. Before servicing the vehicle, refer to the Precautions Section.
2. Disconnect the battery.
3. Install Engine Support Fixture 8534.
4. Raise and support vehicle.
5. Remove front wheel and tire assemblies.

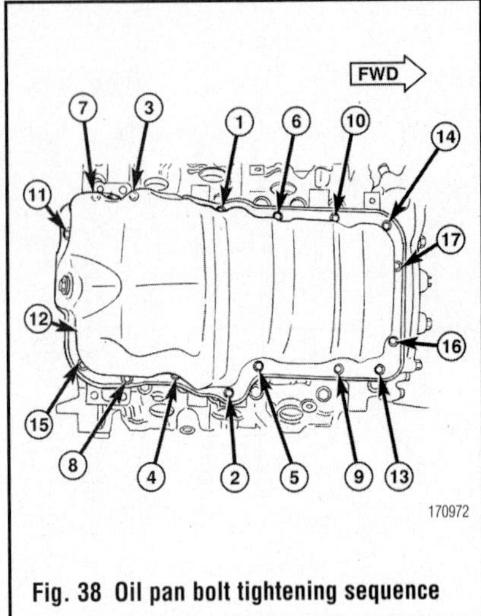

Fig. 38 Oil pan bolt tightening sequence

6. Remove skid plate (if equipped).
7. Drain engine oil.
8. Remove engine to transmission structural cover (if equipped).
9. Remove transmission oil cooler line bracket.
10. Remove the front axle assembly from the vehicle.
11. Loosen both engine mount through bolts.
12. Lower the vehicle.

➡It is not necessary to remove the viscous fan , or fan shroud, for oil pan removal.

13. Raise the engine using support fixture special tool 8534, until the viscous fan almost touches the fan shroud.
14. Raise the vehicle.
15. Remove the oil pan bolts.
16. Separate the oil pan from the engine.
17. Remove the nuts and bolt holding the oil pump pick-up tube and windage tray in place.

➡It will be necessary to move the oil pan from side to side to gain access to these fasteners.

18. Drop the oil pump pick-up tube into the oil pan, and remove the oil pan, pick-up tube, and the windage tray as an assembly from the front of the vehicle.

To install:

19. Inspect oil pan gasket for defects, and replace if necessary.
20. Clean the oil pan and block gasket mating surfaces.
21. Drop the oil pump pick-up tube into the oil pan and install the oil pan, pick-up tube, and the windage tray as an assembly from the front of the vehicle.
22. Install the windage tray, then the oil pump pick-up tube, and the nuts and bolt holding the oil pump pick-up tube in place.

➡It will be necessary to move the oil pan from side to side to gain access to these fasteners.

23. Torque the pick-up tube fasteners.
24. Install the oil pan.
25. Install and tighten the oil pan bolts.
26. Install the engine to transmission structural cover, (if equipped).
27. Lower the vehicle.
28. Lower the engine using Engine Support Fixture 8534.
29. Remove the Engine Support Fixture 8534.
30. Raise the vehicle.
31. Tighten both engine mount through bolts.
32. Install the transmission oil cooler line bracket.
33. Install the front axle assembly to the vehicle.
34. Install the skid plate (if equipped).
35. Install the front wheel and tire assemblies.
36. Lower the vehicle.
37. Refill engine oil.
38. Reconnect battery.
39. Start engine, and check for leaks.

OIL PUMP

REMOVAL & INSTALLATION

See Figure 39.

1. Before servicing the vehicle, refer to the Precautions Section.
2. Remove the oil pan.
3. Remove the timing chain cover.
4. Remove the timing chains and tensioners.
5. Remove the four bolts, primary timing chain tensioner and the oil pump.

To install:

6. Position the oil pump onto the crankshaft and install two oil pump retaining bolts.
7. Position the primary timing chain tensioner and install the two retaining bolts.
8. Tighten the oil pump and primary timing chain tensioner retaining bolts to 21 ft. lbs. (28 Nm) in the sequence shown.
9. Install the secondary timing chain tensioners and timing chains.
10. Install the timing chain cover.
11. Install the pick-up tube and oil pan.

INSPECTION

The oil pump is replaced as an assembly; there are no subassembly components.

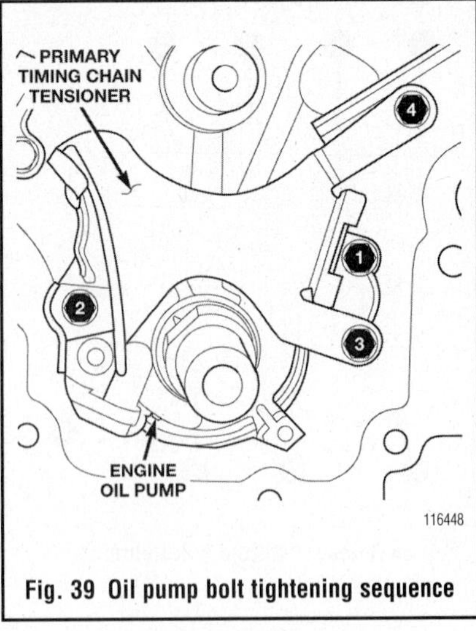

Fig. 39 Oil pump bolt tightening sequence

In the event the oil pump is not functioning it must be replaced as an assembly.

➡DO NOT inspect the oil relief valve assembly. If the oil relief valve is suspect, replace the oil pump.

1. Disassemble oil pump.
2. Clean all parts thoroughly. Mating surface of the oil pump housing should be smooth. Replace pump cover if scratched or grooved.
3. Lay a straightedge across the pump cover surface. If a 0.001 in. (0.025 mm) feeler gauge can be inserted between cover and straight edge, the oil pump assembly should be replaced.
4. Measure thickness and diameter of outer rotor. If outer rotor thickness measures 0.472 in. (12.005 mm) or less, or if the diameter is 3.382 in. (85.925 mm) or less, the oil pump assembly must be replaced.
5. Measure thickness of the inner rotor. If inner rotor measures 0.472 in. (12.005 mm) or less, the oil pump assembly must be replaced.
6. Slide the outer rotor into oil pump body. Press the outer rotor to one side of the oil pump body and measure clearance between rotor and body. If measurement is 0.009 in. (0.235 mm) or more, the oil pump assembly must be replaced.
7. Install inner rotor into body. If clearance between inner and outer rotors is 0.006 in. (0.150 mm) or more, the oil pump assembly must be replaced.
8. Place a straightedge across the face of the body, between bolt holes. If a feeler gauge of 0.0038 in. (0.095 mm) or more can be inserted between rotors and the straightedge, the oil pump assembly must be replaced.
9. Assemble the oil pump.

PISTON AND RING

POSITIONING

See Figure 40.

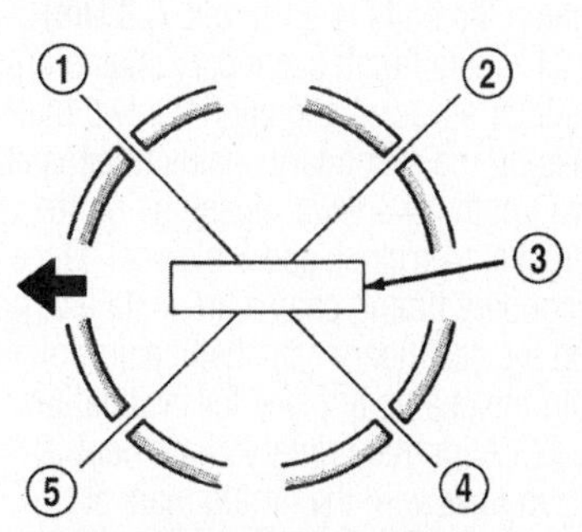

Fig. 40 Piston ring end-gap position; expander ring gap must be at least 45° from the side rail gaps, but not on the piston pin center or on the thrust direction

REAR MAIN SEAL

REMOVAL & INSTALLATION

See Figure 41.

1. Before servicing the vehicle, refer to the Precautions Section.
2. Remove the transmission.
3. Remove the flexplate.
4. Using the oil seal removal tool, remove the rear main seal. The crankshaft rear oil seal remover must be installed deeply into the seal. Continue to tighten the removal tool into the seal until the tool cannot be turned farther. Failure to install tool correctly the first time will cause tool to pull free of seal without removing seal from engine.

To install:

5. Lubricate the crankshaft flange with engine oil.
6. Position the magnetic seal guide onto the crankshaft rear face. Position the crankshaft rear oil seal onto the guide.
7. Using the crankshaft rear oil seal installer and driver handle with a hammer, tap the seal into place. Continue to tap on the driver handle until the seal installer seats against the cylinder block crankshaft bore.
8. Install the flexplate.
9. Install the transmission.

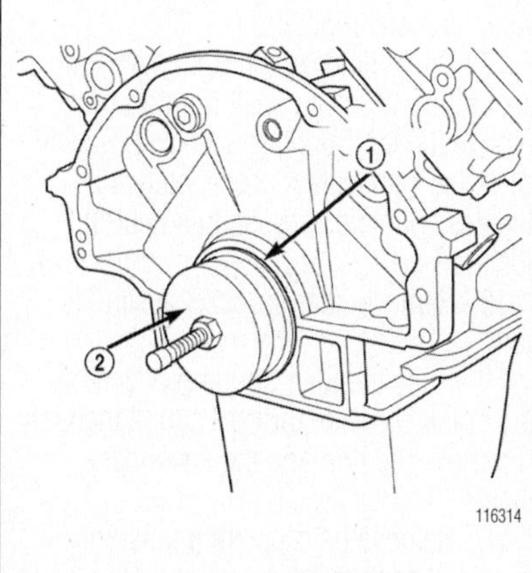

Fig. 41 Using the oil seal removal tool (2), remove the rear main seal (1)

10. Start the engine, check for leaks and repair if necessary.

TIMING CHAIN FRONT COVER

REMOVAL & INSTALLATION

See Figure 42.

1. Before servicing the vehicle, refer to the Precautions Section.
2. Disconnect the battery negative cable.
3. Drain the cooling system.
4. Remove electric cooling fan and fan shroud assembly.
5. Remove radiator fan.
6. Disconnect both heater hoses at timing cover.
7. Disconnect lower radiator hose at engine.
8. Remove accessory drive belt tensioner assembly.
9. Remove crankshaft damper.
10. Remove the alternator.
11. Remove A/C compressor.

➡The 3.7L engine uses an anaerobic sealer instead of a gasket to seal the front cover to the engine block, from the factory. For service, Mopar® Grey Engine RTV sealant must be substituted.

➡It is not necessary to remove the water pump for timing cover removal.

12. Remove the bolts holding the timing cover to engine block.
13. Remove the timing cover.

To install:

14. Clean timing chain cover and block surface using rubbing alcohol. Do not use oil based liquids to clean timing cover or block surfaces.

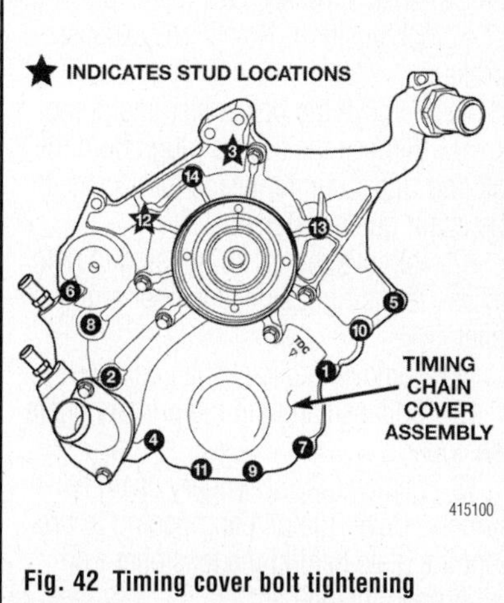

Fig. 42 Timing cover bolt tightening sequence

✱✱ WARNING

Use only rubbing alcohol, along with plastic or wooden scrapers. Use no wire brushes or abrasive wheels or metal scrapers, or damage to surfaces could result.

15. Inspect the water passage o-rings for any damage, and replace as necessary.
16. Apply Mopar® Engine RTV sealer to front cover using a 3 to 4mm thick bead.
17. Install the cover. Tighten fasteners in sequence as shown in to 43 ft. lbs. (58 Nm).
18. Install crankshaft damper.
19. Install the A/C compressor.
20. Install the generator.
21. Install accessory drive belt tensioner.
22. Install radiator upper and lower hoses.
23. Install both heater hoses.
24. Install the electric fan shroud and viscous fan drive assembly.
25. Fill cooling system.
26. Connect negative battery cable.

TIMING CHAIN & SPROCKETS

REMOVAL & INSTALLATION

See Figures 43 through 46.

1. Before servicing the vehicle, refer to the Precautions Section.
2. Disconnect the battery negative cable.
3. Drain the cooling system.
4. Remove the cylinder head covers.
5. Remove the electric cooling fan and fan shroud assembly.
6. Remove the timing chain front cover.
7. Rotate the engine until the timing mark on the crankshaft damper aligns with the TDC mark on the timing chain cover and

the camshaft sprocket "V6" marks are at the 12 o'clock position (No. 1 TDC exhaust stroke).

8. Remove the power steering pump.

9. Remove the access plugs from the left and right cylinder heads for access to the chain guide fasteners.

10. Remove the oil fill housing to gain access to the right side tensioner arm fastener.

11. Remove the crankshaft damper.

12. Collapse and pin the primary chain tensioner.

13. Remove the secondary chain tensioners. Cover the oil pan opening to prevent the plate behind the tensioner from falling into the oil pan.

14. Remove the camshaft position sensor.

15. Remove left and right camshaft sprocket bolts.

⁂ WARNING

Care should be taken not to damage the camshaft target wheel. Do not hold the target wheel while loosening or tightening the camshaft sprocket. Do not place the target wheel near a magnetic source of any kind. A damaged or magnetized target wheel could cause a vehicle no start condition. Do not forcefully rotate the camshafts or crankshaft independently of each other. Damaging intake valve to piston contact will occur. Ensure the negative battery cable is disconnected and isolated to guard against accidental starter engagement

16. While holding the left camshaft steel tube with a camshaft holding tool, remove the left camshaft sprocket. Slowly rotate the camshaft approximately 15 degrees clockwise to a neutral position.

17. While holding the right camshaft steel tube with a camshaft holding tool, remove the left camshaft sprocket. Slowly rotate the camshaft approximately 45 degrees counterclockwise to a neutral position.

18. Remove idler sprocket assembly bolt.

19. Slide the idler sprocket assembly and crank sprocket forward simultaneously to remove the primary and secondary chains.

20. Remove both pivoting tensioner arms and chain guides.

21. Remove the primary chain tensioner.

To install:

22. Using a vise, lightly compress the secondary chain tensioner piston until the piston step is flush with the tensioner body.

23. Using a pin or suitable tool, release the ratchet pawl by pulling the pawl back against spring force through the access hole on the side of the tensioner.

24. While continuing to hold the pawl back, push the ratchet device to approximately 2 mm from the tensioner body.

25. Install the tensioner pin into the hole on the front of the tensioner. Slowly open the vise to transfer the piston spring force to lock pin.

26. Position the primary chain tensioner over the oil pump and insert the bolts into the lower two holes on the tensioner bracket and tighten the bolts to 21 ft. lbs. (28 Nm).

27. Install the right side chain tensioner arm. Install the Torx® bolt and tighten Torx® bolt to 21 ft. lbs. (28 Nm).

➡The silver bolts retain the guides to the cylinder heads and the black bolts retain the guides to the engine block.

28. Install the left side chain guide and tighten the bolts to 21 ft. lbs. (28 Nm).

29. Install the left side chain tensioner arm and the Torx® bolt and tighten Torx® bolt to 21 ft. lbs. (28 Nm).

30. Install the right side chain guide and tighten the bolts to 21 ft. lbs. (28 Nm).

31. Install both secondary chains onto the idler sprocket and align the two plated links on the secondary chains to be visible through the two lower openings on the idler sprocket (4 o'clock and 8 o'clock). Once the secondary timing chains are installed, position the secondary camshaft chain holder to hold the chains in place for installation.

32. Align the primary chain double plated links with the timing mark at 12 o'clock on the idler sprocket and align the primary chain single plated link with the timing mark at 6 o'clock on the crankshaft sprocket.

33. Lubricate the idler shaft and bushings with clean engine oil.

34. The idler sprocket must be timed to the counterbalance shaft drive gear before the idler sprocket is fully seated.

35. Install all chains, crankshaft sprocket, and idler sprocket as an assembly.

36. Guide both secondary chains through the block and cylinder head openings.

37. Affix the chains with an elastic strap or equivalent. This will maintain tension on chains to aid in the installation.

38. Align the timing mark on the idler sprocket gear to the timing mark on the counterbalance shaft drive gear , and seat idler sprocket fully.

39. Lubricate the idler sprocket bolt washer with oil, install the idler sprocket assembly and tighten the retaining bolt to 25 ft. lbs. (34 Nm).

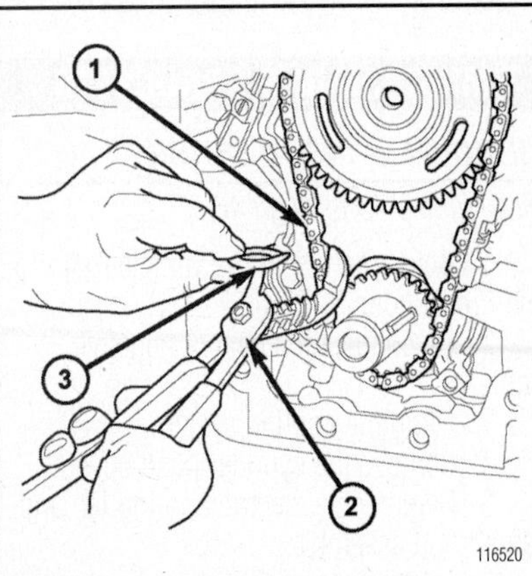

Fig. 43 Primary chain tensioner (1), adjustable pliers (2), and special tool 8514 (3)

Fig. 44 Camshaft hole (1) and special tool 8428A (2)

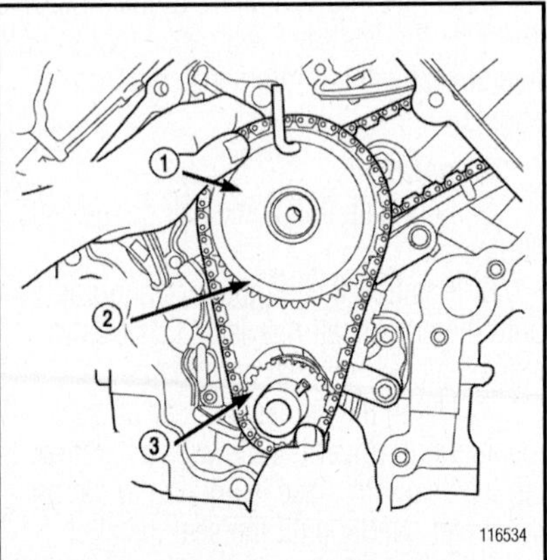

Fig. 45 Secondary camshaft holding tool No. 8429 (1), primary chain idler sprocket (2), and crankshaft sprocket (3)

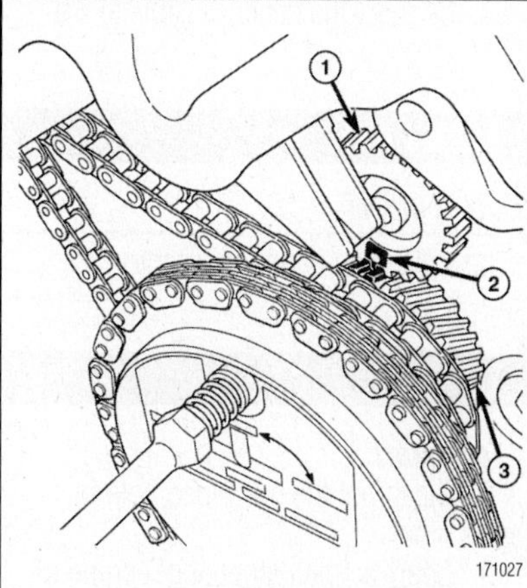

Fig. 46 Counterbalance shaft gear (1), timing mark (2), and idler sprocket gear

40. It will be necessary to slightly rotate the camshafts for sprocket installation.
41. Align the left camshaft sprocket "L" dot to the plated link on the chain.
42. Align the right camshaft sprocket "R" dot to the plated link on the chain.

⁂ WARNING

Remove excess oil from the camshaft sprocket bolt. Failure to do so can result in over-torque of bolt resulting in bolt failure.

43. Remove the secondary camshaft chain holder, and attach both sprockets to the camshafts. Remove excess oil from the bolts, and install sprocket bolts, but do not tighten at this time.
44. Verify that all plated links are aligned with the marks on all the sprockets and the "V6" marks on the camshaft sprockets are at the 12 o'clock position.
45. Install both secondary chain tensioners and tighten the bolts to 21 ft. lbs. (28 Nm). Ensure the plate between the left secondary chain tensioner and block is correctly installed.

➡Left and right secondary chain tensioners are not common.

46. Remove all 3 locking pins from the tensioners.

⁂ WARNING

After pulling locking pins out of each tensioner, DO NOT manually extend the tensioner(s) ratchet. Doing so will over tension the chains, resulting in noise and/or high timing chain loads.

47. Using the Special tool 6958 with adapter pins 8346 and a torque wrench, tighten the left camshaft sprocket bolt to 90 ft. lbs. (122 Nm). Tighten the
48. Using the Special tool 6958 with adapter pins 8346, tighten the right camshaft sprocket bolt to 90 ft. lbs. (122 Nm).
49. Rotate the engine two full revolutions and verify the timing marks are at the follow locations:
   - Primary chain idler sprocket dot is at 12 o'clock
   - Primary chain crankshaft sprocket dot is at 6 o'clock
   - Secondary chain camshaft sprockets "V6" marks are at 12 o'clock
   - Counter-balancer shaft drive gear dot is aligned to the idler sprocket gear dot
50. Lubricate all three chains with engine oil.
51. After installing all the chains, it is recommended that the idler gear end play be checked. The end play must be within 0.004–0.010 in. (0.10–0.25 mm). If not within specification, the idler gear must be replaced.
52. Install the timing chain cover and the crankshaft damper.
53. Install the cylinder head covers.
54. Coat the large threaded cylinder head access plug with Mopar® Thread Sealant with Teflon and then install into the right cylinder head and tighten to 60 ft. lbs. (81 Nm).
55. Install the oil fill housing.
56. Install access plug in the left cylinder head.
57. Install the power steering pump.
58. Fill the cooling system.
59. Connect the negative battery cable.

VALVE COVERS

REMOVAL & INSTALLATION

See Figure 47.

1. Before servicing the vehicle, refer to the Precautions Section.
2. Disconnect the negative cable from battery.
3. Remove the air cleaner assembly, resonator assembly and air inlet hose.
4. To prepare for removal of the left valve cover (cylinder head cover):
   a. Disconnect the injector connectors and unclip the injector harness.
   b. Route the injector harness in front of the valve cover (cylinder head cover).
   c. Disconnect the left side breather tube and remove the breather tube.
5. To prepare for removal of the right valve cover (cylinder head cover):
   a. Drain the cooling system, below the level of the heater hoses.
   b. Remove the accessory drive belt.
   c. Remove the air conditioning compressor retaining bolts and move the compressor to the left.
   d. Remove the heater hoses.
   e. Disconnect the injector and the ignition coil connectors.
   f. Disconnect and remove the Positive Crankcase Ventilation (PCV) hose.
   g. Remove the oil fill tube.
   h. Unclip the injector and ignition coil harness and move away from the valve cover.
   i. Remove right rear breather tube and filter assembly.
6. Remove the valve cover mounting bolts.
7. Remove the valve covers and gaskets.

➡The gasket may be used again, providing no cuts, tears, or deformations have occurred.

To install:

⁂ WARNING

Do not use harsh cleaners to clean the valve covers. Severe damage to covers may occur.

8. Clean the valve cover and both sealing surfaces. Inspect and replace gasket as necessary.
9. Install the valve cover. Tighten the valve cover bolts and the double ended studs to 105 in. lbs (12 Nm).
10. To complete the installation of the left cylinder head cover:
   a. Install the left side breather and connect the breather tube.
   b. Connect the injector electrical connectors and the injector harness retaining clips.

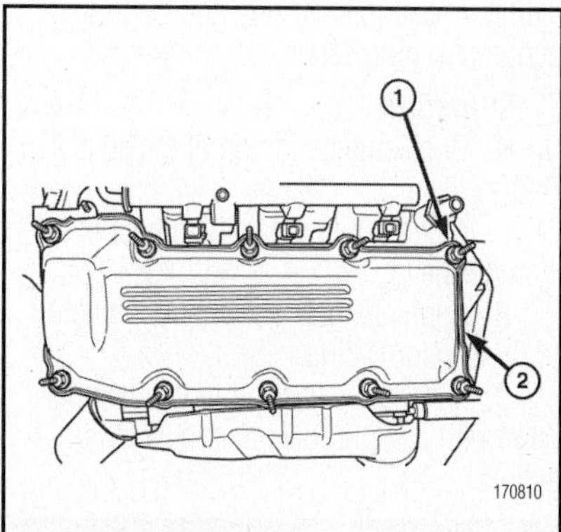

Fig. 47 Typical valve cover (2) and mounting bolts (1)

11. To complete the installation of the right cylinder head cover:
   a. Install the right rear breather tube and filter assembly.
   b. Connect the injector, ignition coil electrical connectors and harness retaining clips.
   c. Install the oil fill tube.
   d. Install the PCV hose.
   e. Install the heater hoses.
   f. Install the air conditioning compressor retaining bolts.
   g. Install the accessory drive belt.
   h. Fill the cooling system.
12. Install the air cleaner assembly, resonator assembly and air inlet hose.
13. Connect the negative cable to battery.

VALVE LASH

ADJUSTMENT

The valve lash is not adjustable.

ENGINE PERFORMANCE & EMISSION CONTROLS

CAMSHAFT POSITION (CMP) SENSOR

LOCATION

See Figure 48.

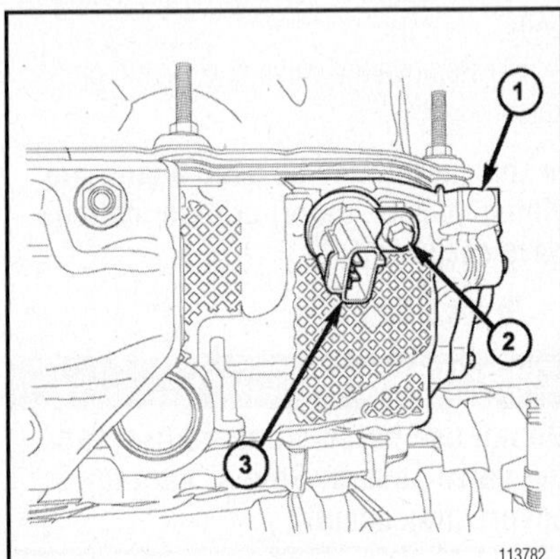

Fig. 48 The Camshaft Position (CMP) Sensor (3) is bolted (2) to the front/top of the right cylinder head (1)

REMOVAL & INSTALLATION

1. Before servicing the vehicle, refer to the Precautions Section.
2. Disconnect the negative battery cable.
3. Disconnect the electrical connector at the Camshaft Position (CMP) sensor.
4. Remove the sensor mounting bolt.
5. Carefully remove the sensor from the cylinder head in a rocking and twisting action. Twisting sensor eases removal.

To install:

6. Check the condition of the sensor O-ring.
7. Clean out the machined hole in cylinder head.
8. Apply a small amount of engine oil to the sensor O-ring.
9. Install the sensor into the cylinder head with a slight rocking and twisting action.

**** WARNING**

Before tightening the sensor mounting bolt, be sure the sensor is completely flush to the cylinder head. If sensor is not flush, damage to sensor mounting tang may result.

10. Install the mounting bolt and tighten to 105 in. lbs (12 Nm).
11. Connect the electrical connector to the sensor.
12. Connect the negative cable to battery.

CRANKSHAFT POSITION (CKP) SENSOR

LOCATION

See Figure 49.

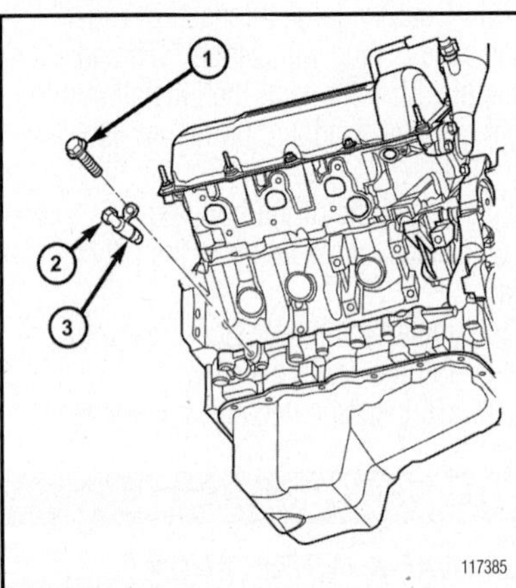

Fig. 49 Crankshaft Position (CKP) Sensor (2), mounting bolt (1), and O-ring (3)—3.7L engine

REMOVAL & INSTALLATION

1. Before servicing the vehicle, refer to the Precautions Section.
2. Disconnect the negative battery cable.
3. Raise the vehicle.
4. Disconnect the sensor electrical connector.
5. Remove the sensor mounting bolt.
6. Carefully twist the sensor from the cylinder block.
7. Check the condition of the sensor O-ring.

To install:

8. Clean out the machined hole in engine block.
9. Apply a small amount of engine oil to the sensor O-ring.
10. Install the sensor into the engine block with a slight rocking and twisting action.

**** WARNING**

Before tightening the sensor mounting bolt, be sure sensor is completely flush to cylinder block. If sensor is not flush, damage to sensor mounting tang may result.

11. Install the mounting bolt and tighten to 21 ft. lbs. (28 Nm).
12. Connect electrical connector to sensor.
13. Lower the vehicle.
14. Connect the negative cable to battery.

ELECTRONIC CONTROL MODULE (ECM)

LOCATION

See Figure 50.

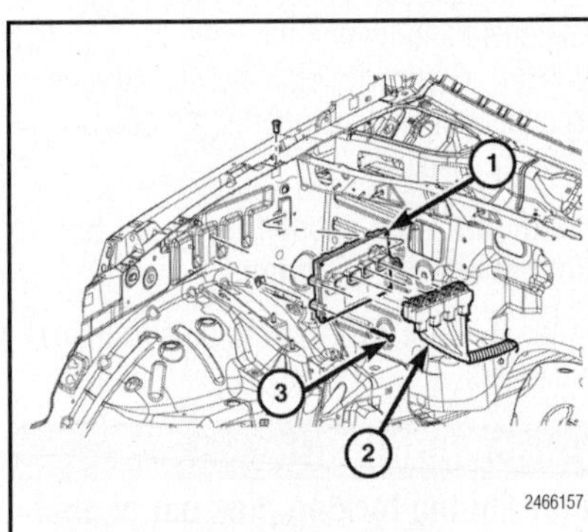

Fig. 50 Electronic Control Module (ECM/PCM) (1), electrical connectors (2), and mounting bolts (3)

REMOVAL & INSTALLATION

1. Before servicing the vehicle, refer to the Precautions Section.

2. Disconnect the negative battery cable.
3. Disconnect the electrical connectors.
4. Remove the mounting bolts.
5. Remove the ECM from the vehicle.

To install:

6. Position the ECM into the vehicle.
7. Tighten the mounting bolts to 71 inch lbs. (8 Nm).
8. Connect the electrical connectors.
9. Connect the negative battery cable.

ENGINE COOLANT TEMPERATURE (ECT) SENSOR

LOCATION

See Figure 51.

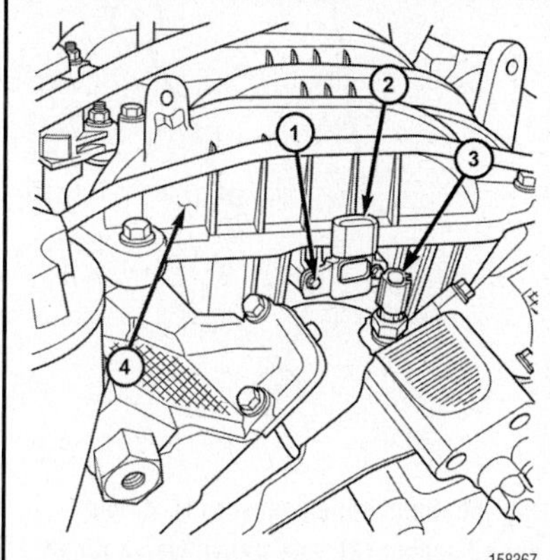

Fig. 51 Engine Coolant Temperature (ECT) Sensor (3) and mounting bolts (1); and MAP Sensor (2)—3.7L engines

REMOVAL & INSTALLATION

⁂ CAUTION

Hot, pressurized coolant can cause injury by scalding. Cooling system must be partially drained before removing the coolant temperature sensor.

➡The ECT sensor is installed into a water jacket at front of intake manifold near rear of alternator.

1. Before servicing the vehicle, refer to the Precautions Section.
2. Disconnect the negative battery cable.
3. Partially drain the cooling system.
4. Disconnect the sensor electrical connector.
5. Remove the ECT sensor from the intake manifold.

To install:

6. Apply thread sealant to the sensor threads.
7. Install the ECT sensor to the engine and tighten the mounting bolts to 8 ft. lbs. (11 Nm).
8. Connect the electrical connector.
9. Refill the cooling system to the correct level.
10. Connect the negative battery cable.

HEATED OXYGEN (HO2S) SENSOR

LOCATION

See Figure 52.

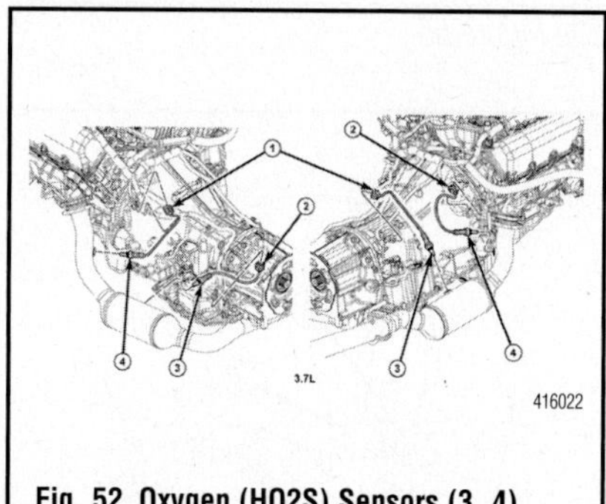

Fig. 52 Oxygen (HO2S) Sensors (3, 4)

REMOVAL & INSTALLATION

⁂ WARNING

Never apply any type of grease to the oxygen sensor electrical connector, or attempt any repair of the sensor wiring harness.

1. Before servicing the vehicle, refer to the Precautions Section.
2. Disconnect the negative battery cable.
3. Raise and safely support the vehicle.
4. Disconnect the wire connector from oxygen sensor.

⁂ WARNING

When disconnecting sensor electrical connector, do not pull directly on wire going into sensor.

5. Remove the sensor with an oxygen sensor removal and installation tool.
6. Clean the threads in exhaust pipe using appropriate tap.

To install:

⁂ WARNING

Threads of new oxygen sensors are factory coated with anti-seize compound. Do not add any additional anti-seize compound to the threads of a new oxygen sensor.

7. Install the oxygen sensor and tighten to 30 ft. lbs. (41 Nm).
8. Connect the electrical connector.
9. Lower the vehicle.
10. Connect the negative battery cable.

INTAKE AIR TEMPERATURE (IAT) SENSOR

LOCATION

See Figure 53.

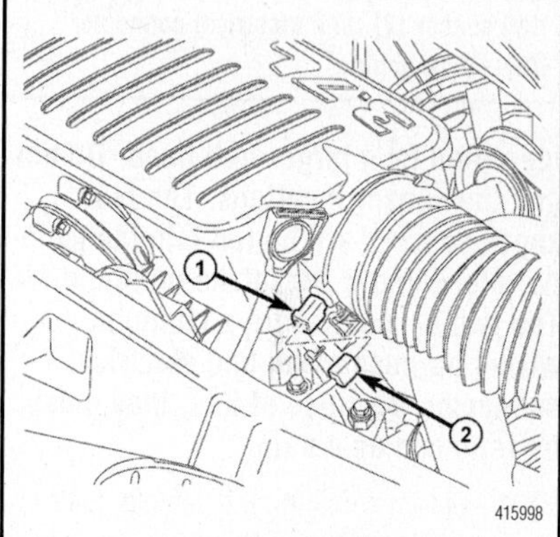

Fig. 53 The Intake Air Temperature (IAT) Sensor (1) with the electrical connector (2) is installed into the rubber air intake tube near the throttle body

REMOVAL & INSTALLATION

1. Before servicing the vehicle, refer to the Precautions Section.
2. Disconnect the negative battery cable.
3. Disconnect electrical connector from the IAT sensor. Clean dirt from the IAT at the sensor base.
4. Pull out on the IAT sensor while rotating for removal.
5. Check the condition of sensor O-ring.

To install:

6. Clean the sensor mounting hole.
7. To install, push the IAT sensor into the rubber intake tube while rotating.
8. Connect the electrical connector to the IAT sensor.
9. Connect the negative battery cable.

KNOCK SENSOR (KS)

LOCATION

See Figure 54.

REMOVAL & INSTALLATION

➡The left sensor is identified by an identification tag (LEFT). It is also

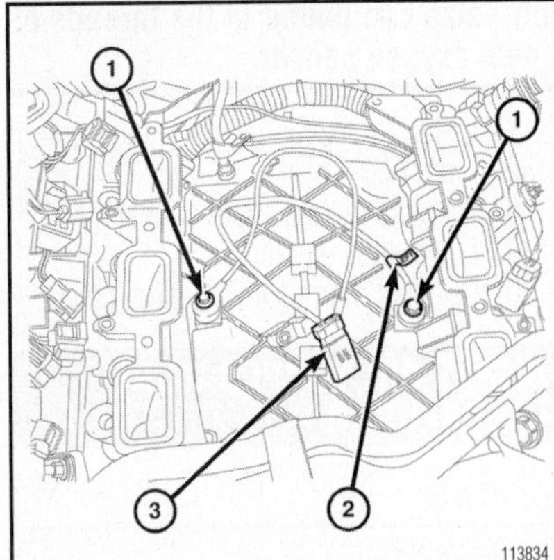

Fig. 54 Knock Sensors (KS) (1), label for left sensor (2), and electrical connector (3)—3.7L engine

identified by a larger bolt head. Do not mix the sensor locations. The two knock sensors are bolted into the cylinder block under the intake manifold. The two sensors share a common wiring harness using one electrical connector. Because of this, they must be replaced as a pair.

1. Before servicing the vehicle, refer to the Precautions Section.
2. Disconnect the negative battery cable.
3. Remove the intake manifold.
4. Disconnect the knock sensor dual pigtail harness from the engine wiring harness. This connection is made near the rear of the engine.
5. Remove both sensor mounting bolts.

➡Note the foam strip on bolt threads. This foam is used only to retain the bolts to sensors for plant assembly. It is not used as a sealant. Do not apply any adhesive, sealant or thread locking compound to these bolts.

6. Remove the sensors from the engine.

To install:

⁂ WARNING

Over or under tightening the sensor mounting bolts will affect knock sensor performance, possibly causing improper spark control. Always use the specified torque when installing the knock sensors. The torque for the knock sensor bolt is relatively light for an 8mm bolt.

7. Thoroughly clean the knock sensor mounting holes.
8. Install the sensors into the cylinder block. Tighten the mounting bolts to 15 ft. lbs. (20 Nm).
9. Connect the knock sensor wiring harness to the engine harness at the rear of the intake manifold.
10. Install the intake manifold.
11. Connect the negative battery cable.

MANIFOLD ABSOLUTE PRESSURE (MAP) SENSOR

LOCATION

See Figure 55.

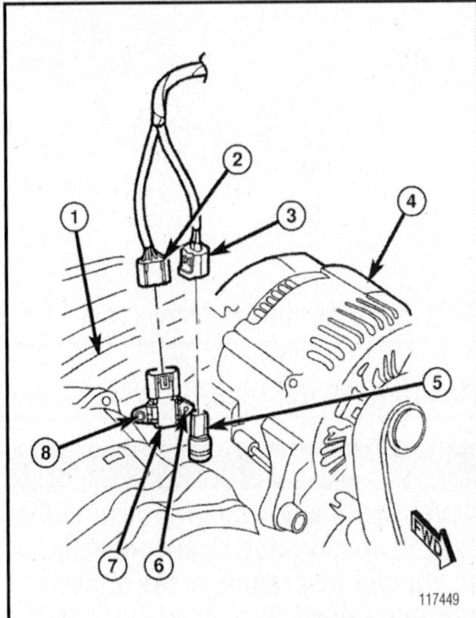

Fig. 55 The Manifold Absolute Pressure (MAP) Sensor (7) is mounted into the front of the intake manifold (1)

REMOVAL & INSTALLATION

1. Before servicing the vehicle, refer to the Precautions Section.
2. Disconnect the negative battery cable.
3. Disconnect the electrical connector at the sensor.
4. Clean the area around the MAP sensor.
5. Remove one sensor mounting screw.
6. Remove the MAP sensor from the intake manifold.

To install:

7. Check the condition of the sensor O-ring.
8. Clean the MAP sensor mounting hole at the intake manifold.
9. Check the MAP sensor O-ring seal for cuts or tears.
10. Position the sensor into the manifold by sliding the sensor over the locating pin.
11. Tighten the mounting bolt to 25 inch lbs. (3 Nm).
12. Connect the electrical connector.
13. Reconnect the negative battery cable at battery.

VEHICLE SPEED SENSOR (VSS)

LOCATION

See Figure 56.

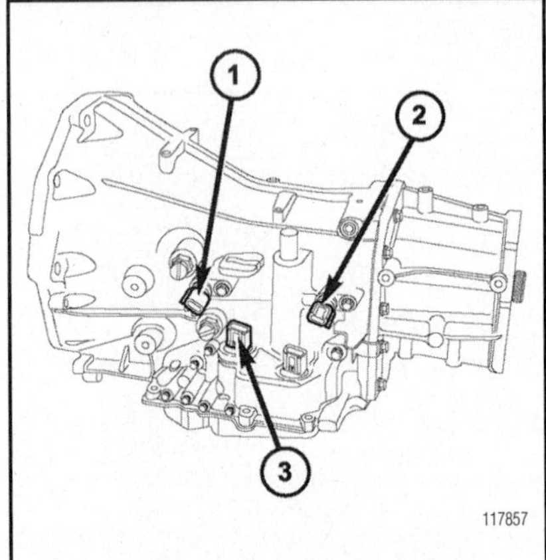

Fig. 56 Input speed sensor (1), output speed sensor (2), and transmission range sensor (3)

REMOVAL & INSTALLATION

1. Before servicing the vehicle, refer to the Precautions Section.
2. Raise and safely support the vehicle.
3. Place a suitable catch pan under the transmission for any fluid.
4. Remove the wiring connector from the speed sensor.
5. Remove the mounting bolt and remove the speed sensor from the transmission case.

To install:

6. Install the speed sensor into the transmission case and tighten the bolt to 80 inch lbs. (9 Nm).
7. Install the wiring connector to the speed sensor.
8. Verify the proper transmission fluid level and refill as necessary.
9. Lower the vehicle.

FUEL SYSTEM SERVICE PRECAUTIONS

Safety is the most important factor when performing not only fuel system maintenance but any type of maintenance. Failure to conduct maintenance and repairs in a safe manner may result in serious personal injury or death. Maintenance and testing of the vehicle's fuel system components can be accomplished safely and effectively by adhering to the following rules and guidelines.

- To avoid the possibility of fire and personal injury, always disconnect the negative battery cable unless the repair or test procedure requires that battery voltage be applied.
- Always relieve the fuel system pressure prior to disconnecting any fuel system component (injector, fuel rail, pressure regulator, etc.), fitting or fuel line connection. Exercise extreme caution whenever relieving fuel system pressure to avoid exposing skin, face and eyes to fuel spray. Please be advised that fuel under pressure may penetrate the skin or any part of the body that it contacts.
- Always place a shop towel or cloth around the fitting or connection prior to loosening to absorb any excess fuel due to spillage. Ensure that all fuel spillage (should it occur) is quickly removed from engine surfaces. Ensure that all fuel soaked cloths or towels are deposited into a suitable waste container.
- Always keep a dry chemical (Class B) fire extinguisher near the work area.
- Do not allow fuel spray or fuel vapors to come into contact with a spark or open flame.
- Always use a back-up wrench when loosening and tightening fuel line connection fittings. This will prevent unnecessary stress and torsion to fuel line piping.
- Always replace worn fuel fitting O-rings with new Do not substitute fuel hose or equivalent where fuel pipe is installed.

Before servicing the vehicle, make sure to also refer to the precautions in the beginning of this section as well.

RELIEVING FUEL SYSTEM PRESSURE

1. Remove the fuel fill cap.
2. Remove the fuel pump fuse from Totally Integrated Power Module (TIPM). For location of the fuse, refer to the label on underside of TIPM cover.
3. Start and run the engine until it stalls.
4. Attempt restarting engine until it will no longer run.
5. Turn the ignition key to OFF position.
6. Place a rag or towel below the fuel line quick-connect fitting at fuel rail.
7. Disconnect the quick-connect fitting at fuel rail.
8. When the repair is complete, return the fuel pump fuse to TIPM.
9. One or more Diagnostic Trouble Codes (DTC's) may have been stored in PCM memory due to the fuel pump fuse removal. A diagnostic scan tool must be used to erase a DTC.

FUEL FILTER

REMOVAL & INSTALLATION

The fuel filter and fuel pressure regulator are combined within the fuel pump module assembly. They are not serviceable.

FUEL INJECTORS

REMOVAL & INSTALLATION

See Figure 57.

✱✱ CAUTION

The fuel system is under constant pressure even with engine off. Before servicing fuel rail, fuel system pressure must be released.

✱✱ WARNING

The left and right fuel rails are replaced as an assembly. Do not attempt to separate rail halves at connector tube. Due to design of tube, it does not use any clamps. Never attempt to install a clamping device of any kind to tube. When removing fuel rail assembly for any reason, be careful not to bend or kink tube.

1. Before servicing the vehicle, refer to the Precautions Section.
2. Remove the fuel tank filler tube cap.
3. Perform the fuel system pressure release procedure.
4. Remove the negative battery cable at battery.
5. Remove the air duct at the throttle body air box.
6. Remove the air box at the throttle body.
7. Disconnect the fuel line latch clip and the fuel line at the fuel rail. A special tool will be necessary for fuel line disconnection.
8. Remove the necessary vacuum/vapor lines at the throttle body.
9. Disconnect the electrical connectors at all 6 fuel injectors. Push the red colored slider away from the injector. While pushing the slider, depress the tab and remove the connector from the injector. The factory fuel injection wiring harness is numerically tagged (INJ 1, INJ 2, etc.) for injector position identification. If the harness is not tagged, note wiring location before removal.
10. Disconnect the electrical connectors at the throttle body sensors.
11. Remove the 6 ignition coils.
12. Remove the 4 fuel rail mounting bolts.
13. Gently rock and pull the left side of the fuel rail until the fuel injectors just start to clear the machined holes in the cylinder head. Gently rock and pull the right side of rail until the injectors just start to clear the cylinder head holes. Repeat this procedure (left/right) until all injectors have cleared cylinder head holes.
14. Remove the fuel rail (with injectors attached) from the engine.
15. Disconnect the injector clips; and remove the injectors from the rail.

To install:

16. Install the fuel injectors into the fuel rail assembly and install the retaining clips.
17. If the same injectors are being reinstalled, install new O-rings. Two different

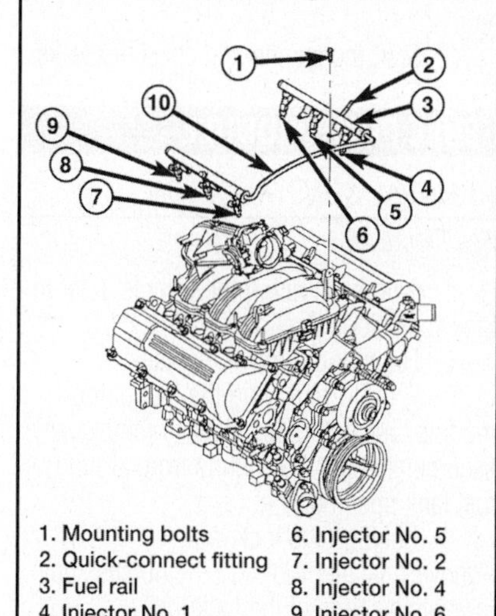

Fig. 57 Fuel rail and injectors

O-rings are being used. These can be easily identified by color. Install the black O-ring at intake manifold end of injector. Install the red/rust colored O-ring at the fuel rail end of injector.

18. Clean out the fuel injector machined bores in the intake manifold.
19. Apply a small amount of engine oil to each fuel injector O-ring. This will help in fuel rail installation.
20. Position the fuel rail/fuel injector assembly to the machined injector openings in the cylinder head.
21. Guide each injector into the cylinder head. Be careful not to tear the injector O-rings.
22. Push the right side of the fuel rail down until the fuel injectors have bottomed on the cylinder head shoulder.
23. Push the left fuel rail down until the injectors have bottomed on the cylinder head shoulder.
24. Install the 4 fuel rail mounting bolts and tighten to 100 inch lbs. (11 Nm).
25. Install the 6 ignition coils.
26. Connect the electrical connectors to the throttle body.
27. Connect the electrical connectors at all fuel injectors. Push the connector onto the injector and then push and lock the red colored slider. Verify the connector is locked to the injector by lightly tugging on the connector.
28. Connect the necessary vacuum lines to the throttle body.
29. Connect the fuel line latch clip and the fuel line to the fuel rail.
30. Install the air box to the throttle body.
31. Install the air duct to the air box.
32. Connect the battery cable to the battery.
33. Start the engine and check for leaks.

FUEL PUMP MODULE

REMOVAL & INSTALLATION

See Figure 58.

1. Before servicing the vehicle, refer to the Precautions Section.
2. Drain and remove fuel tank.
3. Prior to removing the fuel pump module, use compressed air to remove any accumulated dirt and debris from around fuel tank opening.
4. Position the lockring remover/installer tool into the notches on the outside edge of the lockring.
5. Install a ½ inch drive breaker bar into the lockring remover/installer tool.
6. Rotate the breaker bar counterclockwise and remove the lockring.
7. Mark the fuel pump module orientation.

⁂ WARNING

The fuel pump module reservoir does not empty out when the tank is drained. The fuel in the reservoir will spill out when the module is removed.

8. Raise the fuel pump module out of the fuel tank using caution not spill fuel inside the vehicle.
9. Tip the fuel pump module on its side and drain all fuel from the reservoir.
10. Remove the fuel pump module from the fuel tank using caution not to bend the float arm.
11. Remove and discard the rubber O-ring seal.

To install:

➡Whenever the fuel pump module is serviced, the rubber O-ring seal must be replaced.

12. Clean the rubber O-ring seal area of the fuel tank and install a new rubber O-ring seal.
13. Lower the fuel pump module into the fuel tank using caution not to bend the float arm.

➡The fuel pump module must be properly located in the fuel tank for the fuel level gauge to work properly.

14. Align the rubber O-ring seal and rotate the fuel pump module to the orientation marks noted during removal. This step must be performed for the fuel level gauge to work properly.
15. Position the lockring over top of the fuel pump module.
16. Position the lockring remover/installer into the notches on the outside edge of the lockring.

253312

Fig. 58 Fuel pump module removal

17. Install a ½ inch drive breaker bar into the lockring remover/installer.
18. Rotate the breaker bar clockwise until all seven notches of the lockring have engaged.
19. Install the fuel tank.

FUEL TANK

DRAINING

1. Before servicing the vehicle, refer to the Precautions Section.
2. Disconnect the negative battery cable.
3. Remove the fuel fill cap.
4. Raise and support the vehicle.
5. Remove the fuel fill hose clamp at the rear of tank.
6. Remove the fuel fill hose from the fuel tank fitting.
7. Position a drain hose into the fuel fill hose opening. Note that a small flapper valve is installed into the opening.
8. Drain the fuel tank using an approved gasoline draining station.

REMOVAL & INSTALLATION

1. Before servicing the vehicle, refer to the Precautions Section.
2. Remove the fuel tank filler tube cap.
3. Perform the fuel system pressure release procedure.
4. Raise and support the vehicle.
5. Disconnect the fuel line quick connect fittings and at the front of the fuel tank.
6. Remove the fuel fill hose and clamp at the rear of the tank.
7. Position a drain hose into the fuel fill hose opening. Note that a small flapper valve is installed into the opening.
8. Disconnect the vapor lines and at the rear of the tank.
9. Remove the rear propshaft.
10. Support the tank with a hydraulic jack.
11. Loosen the two nuts at the tank support bracket.
12. Remove the bolt from the tank support bracket.
13. Remove the tank mounting bolts at both sides of the tank.
14. Partially lower the tank to gain access to the pump module electrical connector.
15. Disconnect the electrical connector at the fuel pump module.
16. Continue lowering the tank for removal.
17. If the fuel tank is to be replaced, remove the fuel pump module from the tank.

To install:

18. Place the tank to a hydraulic jack and raise it just enough to connect the fuel pump module electrical connector.

19. Continue raising the tank until it's snug to the vehicle body.

20. Install the tank mounting bolts at both sides of the tank. Tighten to 45 ft. lbs. (61 Nm).

21. Tighten the two nuts at the tank support bracket to 45 ft. lbs. (61 Nm). Install the bolt and tighten to 45 ft. lbs. (61 Nm).

22. Install the rear propshaft.

23. Connect the vapor lines and at the rear of the tank.

24. Connect the fuel fill hose and clamp at the rear of the tank.

25. Connect the fuel line quick connect fittings at the front of the fuel tank.

26. Lower the vehicle, fill the tank with fuel and install the fuel fill cap.

27. Check for fuel leaks.

IDLE SPEED

ADJUSTMENT

Idle speed is maintained by the Engine Control Module (ECM). No adjustment is necessary or possible.

THROTTLE BODY

REMOVAL & INSTALLATION

See Figure 59.

✻✻ WARNING

A (factory adjusted) set screw is used to mechanically limit the position of the throttle body throttle plate. Never attempt to adjust the engine idle speed using this screw. All idle speed functions are controlled by the ECM. Never have the ignition key in the ON position when checking the throttle body shaft for a binding condition. This may set DTC's.

1. Before servicing the vehicle, refer to the Precautions Section.
2. Using a diagnostic scan tool, record any previous DTC's (Diagnostic Trouble Codes).
3. Disconnect and isolate the negative battery cable.
4. Remove the air intake tube at the throttle body flange.
5. Disconnect the throttle body electrical connector.
6. Disconnect the necessary vacuum lines at the throttle body.
7. Remove the four throttle body mounting bolts.
8. Remove the throttle body from the intake manifold.

To install:

9. Check the condition of throttle body-to-intake manifold O-ring. Replace as necessary.
10. Clean the mating surfaces of throttle body and intake manifold.
11. Install the O-ring between throttle body and intake manifold.
12. Position the throttle body to intake manifold.
13. Install all throttle body mounting bolts finger tight.

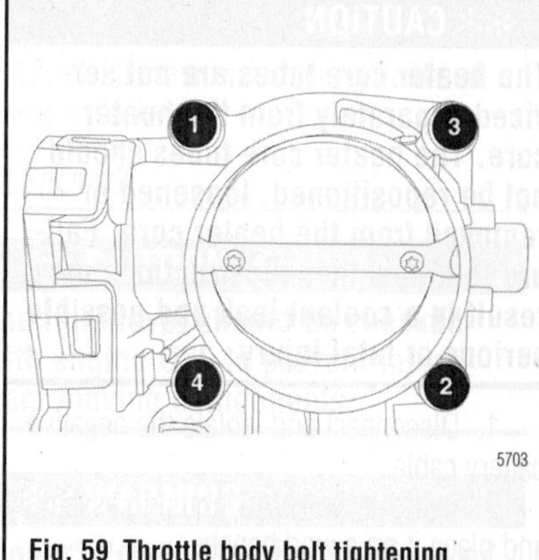

Fig. 59 Throttle body bolt tightening sequence

✻✻ WARNING

The throttle body mounting bolts MUST be tightened to specifications. Over tightening can cause damage to the throttle body or the intake manifold.

14. Obtain a torque wrench. Tighten the mounting bolts (as shown) in a mandatory torque criss-cross pattern sequence to 65 inch lbs. (8 Nm).
15. Install the electrical connector.
16. Install the necessary vacuum lines.
17. Install the air cleaner duct at throttle body.
18. Connect the negative battery cable.
19. Using the diagnostic scan tool, erase all previous DTC's and perform the ETC Relearn function.

HEATING & AIR CONDITIONING SYSTEM

BLOWER MOTOR

REMOVAL & INSTALLATION

✻✻ CAUTION

Before servicing components near or affected by the SRS (air bag) system, read and observe all SRS Service Precautions and disable the SIR system. Refer to Supplemental Restraint System (SRS), in the Chassis Electrical section. Failure to observe all precautions may result in accidental airbag deployment, personal injury, or death.

➡The blower motor is located on the passenger side of the vehicle under the instrument panel. The blower motor can be removed without having to remove the instrument panel or the HVAC housing.

1. Disconnect and isolate the negative battery cable.
2. If equipped, remove the silencer from below the passenger side of the instrument panel.
3. From underneath the instrument panel, disconnect the instrument panel wire harness connector from the blower motor.
4. Remove the three screws that secure the blower motor to the bottom of the HVAC housing and remove the blower motor.

To install:

5. Position the blower motor into the bottom of the HVAC housing.
6. Install the three screws that secure the blower motor to the HVAC housing. Tighten the screws to 10 inch lbs. (1 Nm).
7. Connect the instrument panel wire harness connector to the blower motor.
8. If equipped, install the silencer below the passenger side of the instrument panel.
9. Reconnect the negative battery cable.

HEATER CORE

REMOVAL & INSTALLATION

✻✻ CAUTION

Before servicing components near or affected by the SRS (air bag) system, read and observe all SRS Service Precautions and disable the SIR system. Refer to Supplemental Restraint System (SRS), in the Chassis Electrical section. Failure to observe all precautions may result in accidental airbag deployment, personal injury, or death.

➡**When performing the following step make sure the vacuum level is maintained during the entire time period.**

5. Using Hand Vacuum Pump, apply 68-85 kPa (20-25 in. Hg) of vacuum to the system for a minimum of three minutes.
6. Slowly release the vacuum and remove the special tools.
7. Adjust the fluid level as necessary.
8. Repeat until the fluid no longer drops when vacuum is applied.
9. Start the engine and cycle the steering wheel lock-to-lock three times.

➡**Do not hold the steering wheel at the stops.**

10. Stop the engine and check for leaks at all connections.
11. Check for any signs of air in the reservoir and check the fluid level. If air is present, repeat the procedure as necessary.

FLUID FILL PROCEDURE

1. Run the engine until the power steering fluid reaches about 170°F (80°C).
2. Turn the engine OFF.
3. Clean the power steering fluid reservoir and the reservoir cap.
4. Remove the reservoir cap.

➡**Inspect the power steering pump fluid level at regular intervals.**

5. Inspect the power steering fluid level on the cap stick. Ensure that the fluid level is at the MAX mark on the cap stick.

**** WARNING**

When adding fluid or making a complete fluid change, always use the proper power steering fluid. Failure to use the proper fluid will cause hose and seal damage and fluid leaks.

➡**Mopar® Power Steering Fluid + 4 or Mopar® ATF+4 Automatic Transmission Fluid is to be used in the power steering system. Both fluids have the same material standard specifications (MS-9602).**

6. Add the proper fluid to the reservoir, if necessary.
7. Install the reservoir cap.

SUSPENSION

CONTROL LINKS

REMOVAL & INSTALLATION

1. Before servicing the vehicle, refer to the Precautions Section.
2. Raise and support the vehicle.
3. Remove the tire and wheel assembly.
4. Remove the stabilizer link bolt at the lower control arm.
5. Remove the stabilizer link bolt at the stabilizer bar.
6. Remove the stabilizer link.

To install:

7. Install the stabilizer link.
8. Install the stabilizer link bolt at the stabilizer bar. Tighten the bolt to 85 ft. lbs. (115 Nm) with full vehicle weight.
9. Install the stabilizer link bolt at the lower control arm. Tighten the bolt to 75 ft. lbs. (102 Nm) with full vehicle weight.
10. Install the tire and wheel assembly.

LOWER BALL JOINT

REMOVAL & INSTALLATION

See Figure 62.

1. Before servicing the vehicle, refer to the Precautions Section.
2. Remove the steering knuckle.

➡**Extreme pressure lubrication must be used on the threaded portions of the tool. This will increase the longevity of the tool and insure proper operation during the removal and installation process.**

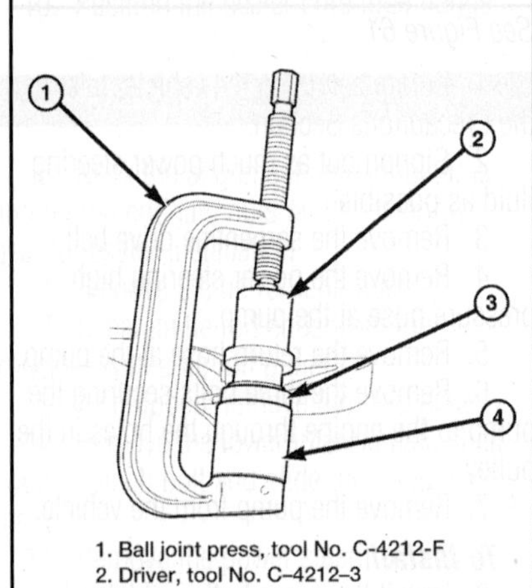

Fig. 62 Press the ball joint from the lower control arm

3. Press the ball joint from the lower control arm using special tools.

To install:

4. Install the ball joint into the lower control arm using the special tools.
5. Stake the ball joint flange in four evenly spaced places around the ball joint flange, using a chisel and hammer.
6. Install steering knuckle.

LOWER CONTROL ARM

REMOVAL AND & INSTALLATION

See Figure 63.

1. Before servicing the vehicle, refer to the Precautions Section.

FRONT SUSPENSION

2. Remove the front wheel.
3. Remove the lower clevis bracket bolt from the control arm.
4. Remove the stabilizer link at the control arm.
5. Remove the lower ball joint nut.
6. Remove the control arm from lower ball joint with tool C4150A.

➡**Matchmark the front and rear control arm pivot bolts.**

7. Remove the front pivot bolt.
8. Remove the rear pivot bolt.
9. Remove the control arm.

To install:

10. Install the lower control arm.
11. Install the rear pivot bolt.
12. Install the front pivot bolt.
13. Install the ball joint nut and tighten to 40 ft. lbs. (54 Nm) plus 90° turn.
14. Align the matchmarks and tighten the pivot bolts to 125 ft. lbs. (170 Nm).

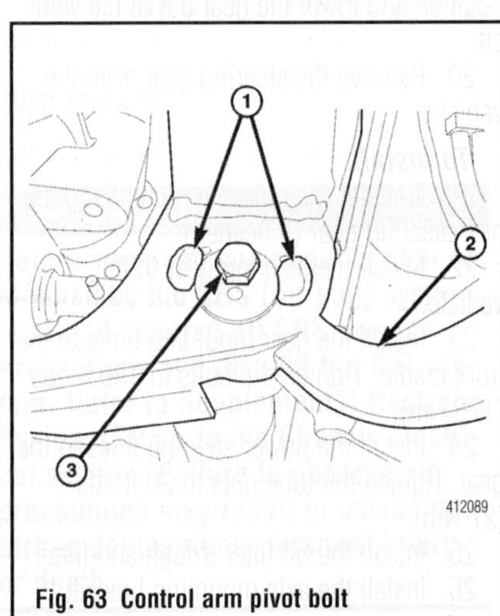

Fig. 63 Control arm pivot bolt

15. Install the stabilizer link and tighten the bolt to 75 ft. lbs. (102 Nm).
16. Install the lower clevis bracket bolt and tighten to 110 ft. lbs. (150 Nm).
17. Install the front wheel.
18. Perform a wheel alignment

STABILIZER BAR

REMOVAL & INSTALLATION

1. Before servicing the vehicle, refer to the Precautions Section.
2. Raise and support the vehicle.
3. Remove the tire and wheel assembly.
4. Remove the upper stabilizer link bolts at the stabilizer bar.
5. Remove the stabilizer bar bushing clamps from the frame.
6. Remove the stabilizer bar from the vehicle.

To install:

7. Install the stabilizer bar to the vehicle.
8. Install the stabilizer bar bushing clamps. Tighten the nuts to 110 ft. lbs. (149 Nm).
9. Install the upper stabilizer link bolts and washer at the stabilizer bar. Tighten the bolt to 85 ft. lbs. (115 Nm).
10. Install the tire and wheel assembly.
11. Lower the vehicle.

STEERING KNUCKLE

REMOVAL & INSTALLATION

See Figure 64.

1. Before servicing the vehicle, refer to the Precautions Section.
2. Raise and support the vehicle.
3. Remove the tire and wheel assembly.
4. Remove the caliper adapter.

WARNING

Never allow the disc brake caliper to hang from the brake hose. Damage to the brake hose will result. Provide a suitable support to hang the caliper securely.

5. Remove the disc brake rotor.
6. Remove the wheel speed sensor.
7. Remove the axle shaft nut (if equipped with 4WD).
8. Remove the outer tie rod nut.
9. Separate the outer tie rod end from the steering knuckle using tool 9360.
10. Remove the lower ball joint nut.
11. Separate the lower ball joint from the suspension arm using tool C-4150A.

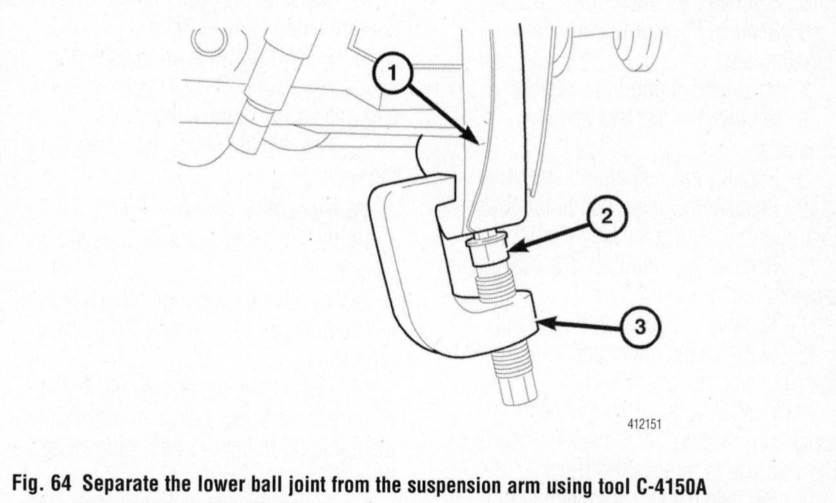

Fig. 64 Separate the lower ball joint from the suspension arm using tool C-4150A

12. Remove the upper ball joint nut.
13. Separate the upper ball joint from the knuckle using tool 9360.
14. Inspect the seal side surface of the upper ball joint, lower ball joint AND outer tie rod knuckle bosses. If any significant grooves or gouges are present (or heavily scratched) replace the steering knuckle.
15. Remove the knuckle from the vehicle.
16. Remove the hub/bearing, if necessary.

To install:

17. Install the hub/bearing, if removed.
18. Install the knuckle to the vehicle.
19. Install the upper ball joint nut. Tighten the nut to 30 ft. lbs. (41 Nm) plus 90° turn.
20. Install the lower ball joint nut. Tighten the nut to 40 ft. lbs. (54 Nm) plus 90° turn.
21. Install the outer tie rod end to the steering knuckle Tighten the nut to 30 ft. lbs. (41 Nm) plus 90° turn.
22. Install the axle shaft nut (if equipped with 4WD). Tighten the nut to 100 ft. lbs. (136 Nm).
23. Install the wheel speed sensor.
24. Install the disc brake rotor.
25. Install the caliper adapter.
26. Install the tire and wheel assembly.
27. Perform the set toe procedure.

STEERING LINKAGE OUTER TIE ROD

REMOVAL & INSTALLATION

1. Before servicing the vehicle, refer to the Precautions Section.
2. Raise and safely support the vehicle.
3. Remove the tire and wheel.
4. Remove the steering linkage outer tie rod nut.

WARNING

Do not free the ball stud by using a pickle fork or a wedge-type tool. Damage to the seal or bushing may result.

5. Separate the outer tie rod end from the steering knuckle using tool 9360.
6. Loosen the steering linkage outer tie rod lock nut.
7. Remove the steering linkage outer tie rod.
8. Clean the tapered surface of the steering knuckle.

To install:

9. Installation is the reverse of removal, noting the following:
    a. Do not tighten the inner tie rod lock nut during installation. Tighten after adjusting the front toe.
    b. Tighten the nut to 30 ft. lbs. (41 Nm) plus 90° turn.
    c. After the installation is complete, measure and adjust the front toe. Tighten the inner tie rod lock nut.

STRUT & SPRING ASSEMBLY

REMOVAL & INSTALLATION

Left Side

1. Before servicing the vehicle, refer to the Precautions Section.
2. Disconnect the battery.
3. Remove the battery.
4. Unclip the power center and move it to the side out of the way to access the battery tray.

5. Remove the battery tray.
6. Remove the four upper shock mounting nuts.
7. Raise and support the vehicle.
8. Remove the tire and wheel assembly.
9. Remove the caliper and support.
10. Remove the lower bolt at the lower control arm securing the clevis bracket.
11. Remove the stabilizer link bolt at the lower control arm.
12. Remove the upper ball joint nut.
13. Separate the upper ball joint from the knuckle using remover 9360.
14. Push downward on the steering knuckle and support the knuckle this will allow access to remove the shock.
15. Remove the shock assembly from the vehicle.

To install:

16. Install the shock assembly to the vehicle.
17. Install the four upper shock mounting nuts. Tighten the nuts to 80 ft. lbs. (108 Nm).
18. Raise the knuckle into place and reconnect the upper ball joint nut. Tighten the nut to 30 ft. lbs (41 Nm) plus an additional 90° turn.
19. Install the clevis bracket bolt at the lower control arm. Tighten the bolt to 110 ft. lbs. (150 Nm) with full vehicle weight.
20. Install the caliper.
21. Install the lower stabilizer link at the lower control arm. Tighten the bolt to 75 ft. lbs. (102 Nm) with full vehicle weight.
22. Install the tire and wheel assembly.
23. Lower the vehicle.
24. Install the battery tray.
25. Install the battery.
26. Reinstall the power center back into place.
27. Reconnect the battery cables.

Right Side

1. Before servicing the vehicle, refer to the Precautions Section.
2. Remove the air box.
3. Remove the four upper shock mounting nuts.
4. Raise and support the vehicle.
5. Remove the tire and wheel assembly.
6. Remove the caliper and support.
7. Remove the lower bolt at the lower control arm securing the clevis bracket.
8. Remove the stabilizer link bolt at the lower control arm.
9. Remove the upper ball joint nut.
10. Separate the upper ball joint from the knuckle using remover 9360.
11. Push downward on the steering knuckle and support the knuckle this will allow access to remove the shock.
12. Remove the shock assembly from the vehicle.

To install:

13. Install the shock assembly to the vehicle.
14. Install the four upper shock mounting nuts. Tighten the nuts to 80 ft. lbs. (108 Nm).
15. Raise the knuckle into place and reconnect the upper ball joint nut. Tighten the nut to 30 ft. lbs (41 Nm) plus an additional 90° turn.
16. Install the clevis bracket bolt at the lower control arm. Tighten the bolt to 110 ft. lbs. (150 Nm) with full vehicle weight.
17. Install the caliper.
18. Install the lower stabilizer link at the lower control arm. Tighten the bolt to 75 ft. lbs. (102 Nm) with full vehicle weight.
19. Install the tire and wheel assembly.
20. Lower the vehicle.
21. Install the air box.

OVERHAUL

See Figure 65.

1. Before servicing the vehicle, refer to the Precautions Section.
2. Secure the shock assembly into a Pentastar® Service Equipment W-7200 Spring compressor.
3. Compress the spring.
4. Remove the shock mount nut.
5. Remove the shock from the spring compressor.
6. Transfer the necessary parts to the type of repair being done.

To install:

7. Install the shock to the spring and spring compressor, after the transfer of the necessary parts to the type of repair being done (Insulator, Spring, shock and mount).
8. Install the shock mounting nut. Tighten the bolt to 30 ft. lbs. (41 Nm).
9. Loosen the compressed spring.
10. Remove the shock assembly from the spring compressor.

UPPER BALL JOINT

REMOVAL & INSTALLATION

The upper ball joint is serviced as an assembly with the control arm.

UPPER CONTROL ARM

REMOVAL & INSTALLATION

Left

1. Before servicing the vehicle, refer to the Precautions Section.
2. Raise and support the vehicle.
3. Remove the left side tire and wheel assembly.
4. Remove the upper ball joint nut.
5. Separate the upper ball joint from the steering knuckle using remover 9360.
6. Lower the vehicle.
7. Remove the battery.
8. Unclip the power center and move it to the side out of the way.
9. Remove the battery tray.

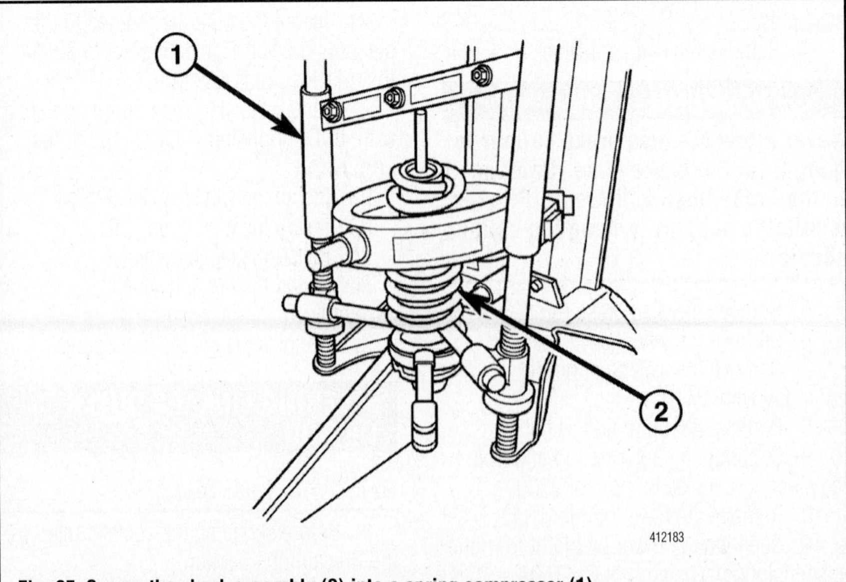

Fig. 65 Secure the shock assembly (2) into a spring compressor (1)

10. Remove the upper control arm rear nut by using a ratchet and extension under the steering shaft.

11. Remove the upper control arm front bolt.

12. Remove the upper control arm from the vehicle.

To install:

13. Install the upper control arm to the vehicle.

14. Install the upper control arm front flag bolt. Tighten the nut to 90 ft. lbs. (122 Nm) with full vehicle weight.

15. Install the upper control arm rear flag bolt. Tighten the nut to 90 ft. lbs. (122 Nm) with full vehicle weight.

16. Install the battery tray.

17. Install the battery.

18. Re-clip and mount the power center.

19. Install the upper ball joint nut. Tighten the nut to 30 ft. lbs. (41 Nm) plus an additional 90° turn.

20. Install the left side tire and wheel assembly.

21. Lower the vehicle.

22. Set the steering toe.

Right

1. Before servicing the vehicle, refer to the Precautions Section.

2. Raise and support the vehicle.

3. Remove the right side tire and wheel assembly.

4. Remove the upper ball joint nut.

5. Separate the upper ball joint from the steering knuckle using remover 9360.

6. Lower the vehicle.

7. Remove the air box assembly.

8. Remove the upper control arm rear bolt/nut.

9. Remove the upper control arm front bolt/nut.

10. Remove the upper control arm from the vehicle.

To install:

11. Install the upper control arm to the vehicle.

12. Install the upper control arm front flag bolt. Tighten the nut to 90 ft. lbs (122 Nm). with full vehicle weight.

13. Install the upper control arm rear flag bolt. Tighten the nut to 90 ft. lbs (122 Nm). with full vehicle weight.

14. Install the air box.

15. Install the upper ball joint nut. Tighten the nut to 30 ft. lbs. (41 Nm) plus an additional 90° turn.

16. Install the right side tire and wheel assembly.

17. Lower the vehicle.

18. Set the steering toe.

WHEEL BEARINGS

REMOVAL & INSTALLATION

See Figure 66.

1. Before servicing the vehicle, refer to the Precautions Section.

2. Raise and support the vehicle.

3. Remove the tire and wheel assembly.

4. Remove the caliper adapter.

WARNING

Never allow the disc brake caliper to hang from the brake hose. Damage to the brake hose will result. Provide a suitable support to hang the caliper securely.

5. Remove the disc brake rotor.

6. Remove the wheel speed sensor.

7. Remove the bracket securing the wheel speed sensor wire.

8. Remove the axle shaft nut, if equipped with 4WD.

9. Remove the three mounting bolts for the hub/bearing assembly.

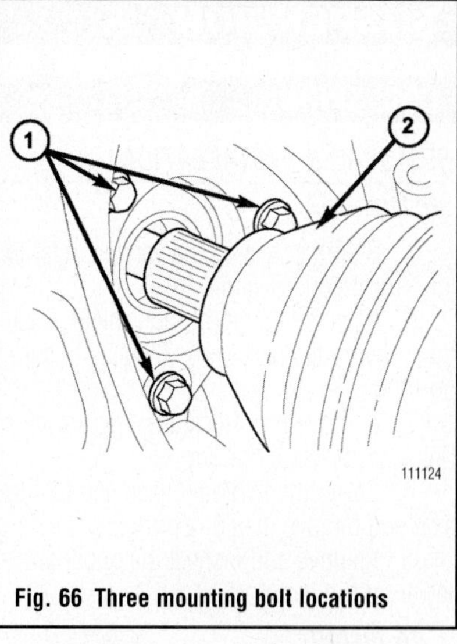

Fig. 66 Three mounting bolt locations

10. Remove the hub/bearing.

To install:

11. Install the hub/bearing assembly to the vehicle.

12. Install the three mounting bolts for the hub/bearing. Tighten the bolt to 96 ft. lbs. (130 Nm).

13. Install the axle shaft nut. Tighten the nut to 100 ft. lbs. (135 Nm), if equipped with 4WD.

14. Install the bracket to the wheel speed sensor wire.

15. Install the wheel speed sensor to the hub. Tighten the bolt to 10 ft. lbs. (14 Nm).

16. Install the disc brake rotor.

17. Install the disc brake caliper adapter. Tighten the nut to 100 ft. lbs. (135 Nm).

18. Install the tire and wheel assembly.

ADJUSTMENT

The wheel bearings are not adjustable.

COIL SPRING

REMOVAL & INSTALLATION

See Figure 67.

1. Before servicing the vehicle, refer to the Precautions Section.
2. Raise and support the vehicle. Position a hydraulic jack under the axle to support the axle.
3. Remove the shock absorber lower bolt from the axle bracket.
4. Lower the hydraulic jack and tilt the axle and remove the coil spring.
5. Remove and inspect the upper and lower spring isolators.

To install:

6. Install the upper isolator.
7. Install the lower isolator.
8. Pull down on the axle and position the coil spring in the lower isolator.

WARNING

Ensure the spring is positioned on the lower isolator.

9. Raise the axle with the hydraulic jack.
10. Install the shock absorber to the axle bracket and tighten to 85 ft. lbs. (115 Nm).
11. Remove the supports and lower the vehicle.

CONTROL LINKS

REMOVAL & INSTALLATION

1. Before servicing the vehicle, refer to the Precautions Section.

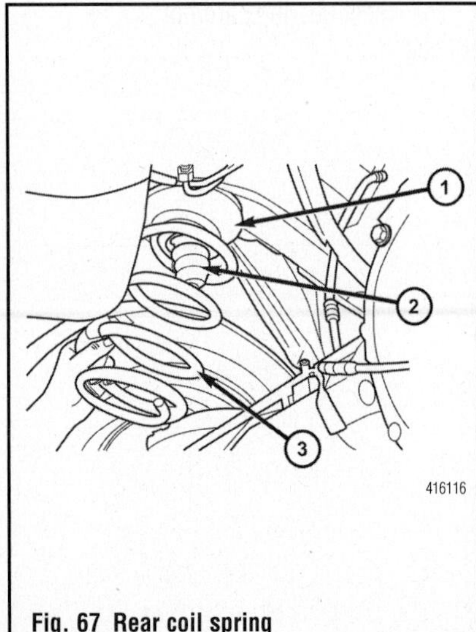

Fig. 67 Rear coil spring

2. Raise and support the vehicle.
3. Support the rear axle with a jack.
4. Remove the rear tire, right side only.
5. Remove the upper link bolt at the frame.
6. Remove the lower link nut at the stabilizer bar.
7. Remove stabilizer link.

To install:

8. Install the upper bolt for the stabilizer link to the frame and tighten to 75 ft. lbs. (102 Nm).
9. Install the stabilizer link to the stabilizer bar.
10. Install the nut and tighten to 85 ft. lbs. (115 Nm) with full vehicle weight.
11. Install the spare tire right side only.
12. Remove the jack and lower the vehicle.

LOWER CONTROL ARM

REMOVAL & INSTALLATION

Left Side

1. Before servicing the vehicle, refer to the Precautions Section.
2. Raise the vehicle and support the rear axle.
3. Remove the fuel tank.
4. Remove the lower suspension arm nut and bolt from the axle bracket.
5. Remove the nut and bolt from the frame rail and remove the lower suspension arm.

To install:

➡All torques should be done with vehicle on the ground with full vehicle weight.

6. Position the lower suspension arm in the frame rail.
7. Install the frame rail bracket bolt and nut. Tighten to 120 ft. lbs. (163 Nm) with full vehicle weight.
8. Position the lower suspension arm in the axle bracket.
9. Install the axle bracket bolt and nut. Tighten to 150 ft. lbs. (203 Nm) with full vehicle weight.
10. Install the fuel tank.
11. Remove the supports and lower the vehicle.

Right Side

1. Before servicing the vehicle, refer to the Precautions Section.
2. Raise the vehicle and support the rear axle.
3. Remove the lower suspension arm nut and bolt from the axle bracket.
4. Remove the exhaust from the mid and rear hanger rubber isolators to allow the exhaust system to lower enough to remove the bolt at the frame rail.
5. Remove the nut and bolt from the frame rail and remove the lower suspension arm.

To install:

➡All torques should be done with vehicle on the ground with full vehicle weight.

6. Position the lower suspension arm in the frame rail.
7. Install the frame rail bracket bolt and nut. Tighten to 120 ft. lbs. (163 Nm). with full vehicle weight.
8. Install the exhaust back in the mid and rear hanger rubber isolators.
9. Position the lower suspension arm in the axle bracket.
10. Install the axle bracket bolt and nut. Tighten to 150 ft. lbs. (203 Nm). with full vehicle weight.
11. Remove the supports and lower the vehicle.

SHOCK ABSORBER

REMOVAL & INSTALLATION

1. Before servicing the vehicle, refer to the Precautions Section.
2. Raise and support the vehicle. Position a hydraulic jack under the axle to support the axle.

WARNING

Do not allow the axle to hang from the upper suspension arm ball joint.

3. Remove the upper nut and bolt from the frame bracket.
4. Remove the lower nut and bolt from the axle bracket. Remove the shock absorber.

To install:

5. Install the shock absorber in the frame bracket and install the bolt and nut.
6. Install the shock absorber in the axle bracket and install the bolt and nut.
7. Remove the supports and lower the vehicle.
8. Tighten the upper mounting nuts to 80 ft. lbs. (108 Nm). Tighten the lower mounting nuts to 85 ft. lbs. (115 Nm).

STABILIZER BAR

REMOVAL & INSTALLATION

1. Before servicing the vehicle, refer to the Precautions Section.
2. Raise and support the vehicle.
3. Remove the stabilizer nut at the bar.
4. Remove the stabilizer links from the stabilizer bar.
5. Remove the stabilizer bar bolts from the axle.
6. Remove the stabilizer bar.

To install:

7. Position the stabilizer bar on the axle. Ensure the bar is centered with equal spacing on both sides. Tighten the bolts to 35 ft. lbs. (47 Nm).
8. Install the stabilizer links to the bar. Tighten the nuts to 65 ft. lbs. (88 Nm) with full vehicle weight.
9. Remove the support and lower the vehicle.

TRACK BAR

REMOVAL & INSTALLATION

1. Before servicing the vehicle, refer to the Precautions Section.
2. Raise and support the vehicle. Position a hydraulic jack under the axle to support the axle.
3. Remove the track bar flag bolt and nut from the frame bracket.
4. Remove the track bar bolt and nut from the axle bracket.
5. Remove the track bar.

To install:

6. Install the track bar to the vehicle.
7. Install the track bar bolt and nut in the frame bracket.
8. Install the track bar into the axle bracket.
9. Install the track bar bolt and nut in the axle bracket.
10. Remove the supports and lower the vehicle.
11. Tighten the body side mounting bolt/nut to 135 ft. lbs. (183 Nm).
12. Tighten the axle side mounting bolt/nut to 130 ft. lbs. (176 Nm).

UPPER CONTROL ARM

REMOVAL & INSTALLATION

Left Side

1. Before servicing the vehicle, refer to the Precautions Section.
2. Raise and support the vehicle.
3. Support the rear axle.
4. Lower the fuel tank in order to gain access to the bolt.
5. Remove the upper suspension arm nut and bolt from the axle bracket.
6. Remove the nut and bolt from the frame rail and remove the upper suspension arm.

To install:

➡All torques should be done with vehicle on the ground with full vehicle weight.

7. Position the upper suspension arm in the frame rail bracket.
8. Install the mounting bolt and nut. Tighten to 70 ft. lbs. (95 Nm) with full vehicle weight.
9. Position the upper suspension arm in the axle bracket.
10. Install the mounting bolt and nut. Tighten to 85 ft. lbs. (115 Nm) with full vehicle weight.
11. Raise the fuel tank back into place and secure.
12. Remove the supports and lower the vehicle.

Right Side

See Figure 68.

1. Before servicing the vehicle, refer to the Precautions Section.
2. Raise and support the vehicle.
3. Support the rear axle.
4. Remove the upper suspension arm nut and bolt from the axle bracket.
5. Remove the nut and flag bolt from the frame rail and remove the upper suspension arm.

To install:

➡All torques should be done with vehicle on the ground with full vehicle weight.

6. Position the upper suspension arm in the frame rail bracket.
7. Install the mounting flag bolt and nut. Tighten to 70 ft. lbs. (95 Nm) with full vehicle weight.
8. Position the upper suspension arm in the axle bracket.
9. Install the mounting bolt and nut. Tighten to 85 ft. lbs. (115 Nm) with full vehicle weight.
10. Remove the supports and lower the vehicle.

WHEEL BEARINGS

REMOVAL & INSTALLATION

See Figure 69.

1. Before servicing the vehicle, refer to the Precautions Section.

➡Remove bearing with Bearing Remover 6310 and Foot 6310-9.

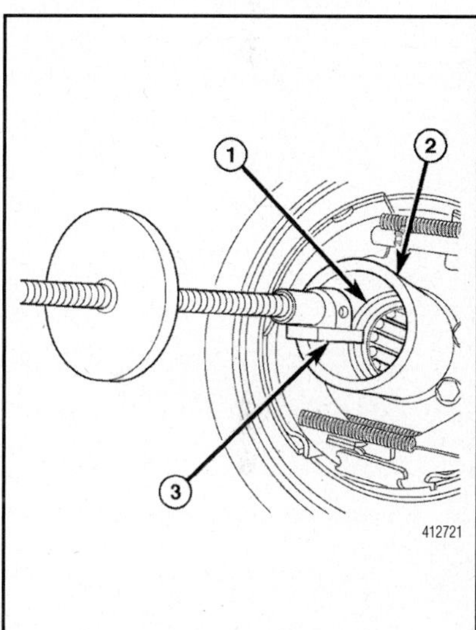

Fig. 69 Insert bearing remover foot (3) through receiver (2) and bearing (1)

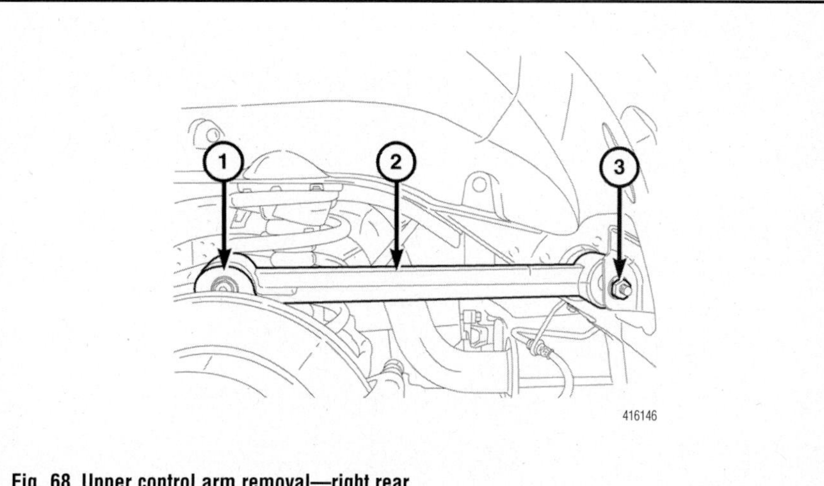

Fig. 68 Upper control arm removal—right rear

2. Remove the axle shaft.
3. Remove the axle seal with seal pick.
4. Position the bearing receiver on axle tube.
5. Insert the bearing remover foot 6310-9 through the receiver and bearing.
6. Tighten remove nut on the shaft to pull bearing into the receiver.

To install:

7. Remove any old sealer/burrs from axle tube.

➡Bearing is installed with the bearing part number against installer.

8. Install axle shaft bearing with Installer C-4198 and Handle C-4171.
9. Drive bearing in until tool contacts the axle tube.
10. Coat new axle seal lip with axle lubricant. Install seal with Installer 8493 and Handle C-4171.
11. Install axle shaft in axle tube.

ADJUSTMENT

The wheel bearings are not adjustable.

DODGE

13

Nitro

SPECIFICATIONS AND MAINTENANCE CHARTS

ENGINE AND VEHICLE IDENTIFICATION

Engine						
Code	Liters (cc)	Cu. In.	Cyl.	Fuel Sys.	Engine Type	Eng. Mfg.
K	3.7 (3701)	226	6	MFI	SOHC	Chrysler
X	4.0 (3966)	244	6	MFI	SOHC	Chrysler

Model Year	
Code	Year
A	2010
B	2011

MFI: Multi-port Fuel Injection

SOHC: Single Overhead Camshaft

25766_NITR_C0001

GENERAL ENGINE SPECIFICATIONS

Year	Model	Engine Displ. Liters	Engine VIN	Net Horsepower @ rpm	Net Torque @ rpm (ft. lbs.)	Bore x Stroke (in.)	Comp. Ratio	Oil Pressure @ rpm
2010	Nitro	3.7	K	210@5200	235@4000	3.66x3.40	9.1:1	25-110@3000
	Nitro	4.0	X	255@5800	265@4200	3.78x3.58	10.3:1	45-105@3000
2011	Nitro	3.7	K	210@5200	235@4000	3.66x3.40	9.1:1	25-110@3000
	Nitro	4.0	X	255@5800	265@4200	3.78x3.58	10.3:1	45-105@3000

25766_NITR_C0002

GASOLINE ENGINE TUNE-UP SPECIFICATIONS

Year	Engine Displ. Liters	Engine VIN	Spark Plug Gap (in.)	Ignition Timing (deg.)	Fuel Pump (psi)	Idle Speed (rpm)	Valve Clearance Intake	Valve Clearance Exhaust
2010	3.7	K	0.042	①	53-63	①	HYD	HYD
	4.0	X	0.050	①	53-63	①	HYD	HYD
2011	3.7	K	0.042	①	53-63	①	HYD	HYD
	4.0	X	0.050	①	53-63	①	HYD	HYD

Note: The information on the Vehicle Emission Control label must be used, if different from the figures in this chart.

HYD: Hydraulic

① Ignition timing and idle speed are controlled by the PCM. No adjustment is necessary.

25766_NITR_C0003

TORQUE SPECIFICATIONS

All readings in ft. lbs.

Year	Engine Displ. Liters	Engine VIN	Cylinder Head Bolts	Main Bearing Bolts	Rod Bearing Bolts	Crankshaft Damper Bolts	Flywheel Bolts	Manifold Intake	Manifold Exhaust	Spark Plugs	Oil Pan Drain Plug
2010	3.7	K	①	②	③	130	70	9	18	20	25
	4.0	X	④	⑤	⑥	70	70	⑦	⑧	20	20
2011	3.7	K	①	②	③	130	70	9	18	20	25
	4.0	X	④	⑤	⑥	70	70	⑦	⑧	20	20

① Step 1: Bolts 1-8 to 20 ft. lbs.
Step 2: Bolts 1-10, verify torque
Step 3: Bolts 9-12 to 10 ft. lbs.
Step 4: Bolts 1-8, plus 90 degrees
Step 5: Bolts 9-12 to 19 ft. lbs.

② Bed plate bolt sequence. Refer to illustration
Step 1: Hand tighten bolts 1D,1G, 1F until bedplate contacts block.
Step 2: Tighten bolts 1A - 1J to 40 ft. lbs.
Step 3: Tighten bolts 1 - 8 to 5 ft. lbs.
Step 4: Turn bolts 1 - 8 an additional 90 degrees
Step 5: Tighten bolts A - E to 20 ft. lbs.

③ 20 ft. lbs. plus 90 degrees

④ Step 1: 45 ft. lbs.
Step 2: 65 ft. lbs.
Step 3: 65 ft. lbs.
Step 4: Plus 90 degrees

⑤ Refer to the procedure.
Step 1: Inner 15 ft. lbs. plus 90 degrees
Step 2: Outer 20 ft. lbs. plus 90 degrees
Step 3: Lateral bolts 250 inch lbs.

⑥ Step 1: 20 ft. lbs.
Step 2: plus 90 degrees

⑦ Lower manifold:
Step 1: 250 inch lbs.
Upper manifold: 105 inch lbs.
Step 1: 105 inch lbs.

⑧ 250 inch. lbs.

25766_NITR_C0010

WHEEL ALIGNMENT

Year	Model		Caster Range (+/-Deg.)	Caster Preferred Setting (Deg.)	Camber Range (+/-Deg.)	Camber Preferred Setting (Deg.)	Toe-in (deg.)
2010	Nitro	F	0.50	3.300	-0.375	-0.20	0.075-0.325
		R	N/A	N/S	-0.625-+0.125	-0.25	-0.16-+0.66
2011	Nitro	F	0.50	3.300	-0.375	-0.20	0.075-0.325
		R	N/A	N/S	-0.625-+0.125	-0.25	-0.16-+0.66

N/S: Information not supplied

25766_NITR_C0011

SPECIFICATIONS AND MAINTENANCE CHARTS

ENGINE AND VEHICLE IDENTIFICATION

Engine							Model Year	
Code	Liters (cc)	Cu. In.	Cyl.	Fuel Sys.	Engine Type	Eng. Mfg.	Code	Year
K	3.7 (3701)	226	6	MFI	SOHC	Chrysler	A	2010
X	4.0 (3966)	244	6	MFI	SOHC	Chrysler	B	2011

MFI: Multi-port Fuel Injection

SOHC: Single Overhead Camshaft

25766_NITR_C0001

GENERAL ENGINE SPECIFICATIONS

Year	Model	Engine Displ. Liters	Engine VIN	Net Horsepower @ rpm	Net Torque @ rpm (ft. lbs.)	Bore x Stroke (in.)	Comp. Ratio	Oil Pressure @ rpm
2010	Nitro	3.7	K	210@5200	235@4000	3.66x3.40	9.1:1	25-110@3000
	Nitro	4.0	X	255@5800	265@4200	3.78x3.58	10.3:1	45-105@3000
2011	Nitro	3.7	K	210@5200	235@4000	3.66x3.40	9.1:1	25-110@3000
	Nitro	4.0	X	255@5800	265@4200	3.78x3.58	10.3:1	45-105@3000

25766_NITR_C0002

GASOLINE ENGINE TUNE-UP SPECIFICATIONS

Year	Engine Displ. Liters	Engine VIN	Spark Plug Gap (in.)	Ignition Timing (deg.)	Fuel Pump (psi)	Idle Speed (rpm)	Valve Clearance	
							Intake	Exhaust
2010	3.7	K	0.042	①	53-63	①	HYD	HYD
	4.0	X	0.050	①	53-63	①	HYD	HYD
2011	3.7	K	0.042	①	53-63	①	HYD	HYD
	4.0	X	0.050	①	53-63	①	HYD	HYD

Note: The information on the Vehicle Emission Control label must be used, if different from the figures in this chart.

HYD: Hydraulic

① Ignition timing and idle speed are controlled by the PCM. No adjustment is necessary.

25766_NITR_C0003

CAPACITIES

Year	Model	Engine Displ. Liters	Engine VIN	Engine Oil with Filter	Transmission (pts.) Man.	Transmission (pts.) Auto.	Transfer Case (pts.)	Drive Axle Front (pts.)	Drive Axle Rear (pts.)	Fuel Tank (gal.)	Cooling System (qts.)
2010	Nitro	3.7	K	5.0	3.17	①	②	2.6	4.4	19.5	14.0
	Nitro	4.0	X	5.5	3.17	①	②	2.6	4.4	19.5	14.0
2011	Nitro	3.7	K	5.0	3.17	①	②	2.6	4.4	19.5	14.0
	Nitro	4.0	X	5.5	3.17	①	②	2.6	4.4	19.5	14.0

NOTE: All capacities are approximate. Add fluid gradually and check to be sure a proper fluid level is obtained.

For rear axles, when equipped with Trac Lok, add 4 oz. of limited slip additive.

Capacities for automatic trnasmissions is for service.

① NAG1: 10.6
42RLE: 8.0

② MP1522: 3.8 pts.
MP3022: 4.0 pts.

25766_NITR_C0004

FLUID SPECIFICATIONS

Year	Model	Engine Displacement Liters (cc)	Engine ID/VIN	Engine Oil	Auto. Trans.	Transfer Case	Drive Axle	Power Steering Fluid	Brake Master Cylinder
2010	Nitro	3.7	K	5W-20	Mopar ATF+4	Mopar ATF+4	①	Mopar ATF+4	DOT-3
	Nitro	4.0	X	10W-30	Mopar ATF+4	Mopar ATF+4	①	Mopar ATF+4	DOT-3
2011	Nitro	3.7	K	5W-20	Mopar ATF+4	Mopar ATF+4	①	Mopar ATF+4	DOT-3
	Nitro	4.0	X	10W-30	Mopar ATF+4	Mopar ATF+4	①	Mopar ATF+4	DOT-3

DOT: Department Of Transpotation

① Front axle: GL5 80W-90
Rear axle: 75W-140 Synthetic

25766_NITR_C0005

VALVE SPECIFICATIONS

Year	Engine Displ. Liters	Engine VIN	Seat Angle (deg.)	Face Angle (deg.)	Spring Test Pressure (lbs. @ in.)	Spring Installed Height (in.)	Stem-to-Guide Clearance (in.) Intake	Stem-to-Guide Clearance (in.) Exhaust	Stem Diameter (in.) Intake	Stem Diameter (in.) Exhaust
2010	3.7	K	44.5-45	44.5-45	221-242@ 1.107	1.619	0.0008-0.0028	0.0019-0.0039	0.2729-0.2739	0.2717-0.2728
	4.0	X	44.5-45	44.5-45	①	1.496	0.0009-0.0026	0.0020-0.0037	0.2730-0.2737	0.2719-0.2726
2011	3.7	K	44.5-45	44.5-45	221-242@ 1.107	1.619	0.0008-0.0028	0.0019-0.0039	0.2729-0.2739	0.2717-0.2728
	4.0	X	44.5-45	44.5-45	①	1.496	0.0009-0.0026	0.0020-0.0037	0.2730-0.2737	0.2719-0.2726

NA: Information not available

① Intake Valve Closed: 69.5-80.5 lbs. @ 1.496 in.
Exhaust Valve Closed: 79.9-90.1 @ 1.496 in
Inake Valve Open: 145.3-160.7 @ 122 in.
Exhaust Valve Closed: 195.8-212.2 @ 1.22 in.

25766_NITR_C0006

CAMSHAFT AND BEARING SPECIFICATIONS CHART

All measurements are given in inches.

Year	Engine Displacement Liters (cc)	Engine VIN	Journal Diameter	Brg. Oil Clearance	Shaft End-play	Runout	Journal Bore	Lobe Lift Intake	Lobe Lift Exhaust
2010	3.7	K	1.0227-1.0235	0.0010-0.0026	0.0030-0.0079	N/S	N/S	N/S	N/S
	4.0	X	1.6905-1.6913	0.0010-0.0040	0.002-0.0020	N/S	N/S	N/S	N/S
2011	3.7	K	1.0227-1.0235	0.0010-0.0026	0.0030-0.0079	N/S	N/S	N/S	N/S
	4.0	X	1.6905-1.6913	0.0010-0.0040	0.002-0.0020	N/S	N/S	N/S	N/S

N/S: Information not Supplied

25766_NITR_C0007

CRANKSHAFT AND CONNECTING ROD SPECIFICATIONS

All measurements are given in inches.

	Engine		Crankshaft				Connecting Rod		
Year	Displ. Liters	Engine VIN	Main Brg. Journal Dia.	Main Brg. Oil Clearance	Shaft End-play	Thrust on No.	Journal Diameter	Oil Clearance	Side Clearance
2010	3.7	K	2.4996-2.5005	0.0008-0.0018	0.0021-0.0112	2	2.2792-2.2798	0.0002-0.0017	0.0040-0.0138
	4.0	X	2.7170-2.7160	0.0013-0.0024	0.002-0.010	2	2.2828-2.2835	0.0009-0.0021	0.0153
2011	3.7	K	2.4996-2.5005	0.0008-0.0018	0.0021-0.0112	2	2.2792-2.2798	0.0002-0.0017	0.0040-0.0138
	4.0	X	2.7170-2.7160	0.0013-0.0024	0.002-0.010	2	2.2828-2.2835	0.0009-0.0021	0.0153

25766_NITR_C0008

PISTON AND RING SPECIFICATIONS

All measurements are given in inches.

	Engine			Ring Gap			Ring Side Clearance		
Year	Displ. Liters	Engine VIN	Piston Clearance	Top Compression	Bottom Compression	Oil Control	Top Compression	Bottom Compression	Oil Control
2010	3.7	K	N/S	0.0079-0.0142	0.0146-0.0249	0.0100-0.0300	0.0020-0.0037	0.0016-0.0031	0.0007-0.0091
	4.0	X	0.003-0.0018	0.008-0.014	0.008-0.016	0.010-0.030	0.0016-0.0031	0.0016-0.0031	0.0015-0.0073
2011	3.7	K	N/S	0.0079-0.0142	0.0146-0.0249	0.0100-0.0300	0.0020-0.0037	0.0016-0.0031	0.0007-0.0091
	4.0	X	0.003-0.0018	0.008-0.014	0.008-0.016	0.010-0.030	0.0016-0.0031	0.0016-0.0031	0.0015-0.0073

N/S: Information not supplied

25766_NITR_C0009

TORQUE SPECIFICATIONS

All readings in ft. lbs.

Year	Engine Displ. Liters	Engine VIN	Cylinder Head Bolts	Main Bearing Bolts	Rod Bearing Bolts	Crankshaft Damper Bolts	Flywheel Bolts	Manifold Intake	Manifold Exhaust	Spark Plugs	Oil Pan Drain Plug
2010	3.7	K	①	②	③	130	70	9	18	20	25
	4.0	X	④	⑤	⑥	70	70	⑦	⑧	20	20
2011	3.7	K	①	②	③	130	70	9	18	20	25
	4.0	X	④	⑤	⑥	70	70	⑦	⑧	20	20

① Step 1: Bolts 1-8 to 20 ft. lbs.
Step 2: Bolts 1-10, verify torque
Step 3: Bolts 9-12 to 10 ft. lbs.
Step 4: Bolts 1-8, plus 90 degrees
Step 5: Bolts 9-12 to 19 ft. lbs.

② Bed plate bolt sequence. Refer to illustration
Step 1: Hand tighten bolts 1D,1G, 1F until bedplate contacts block.
Step 2: Tighten bolts 1A - 1J to 40 ft. lbs.
Step 3: Tighten bolts 1 - 8 to 5 ft. lbs.
Step 4: Turn bolts 1 - 8 an additional 90 degrees
Step 5: Tighten bolts A - E to 20 ft. lbs.

③ 20 ft. lbs. plus 90 degrees

④ Step 1: 45 ft. lbs.
Step 2: 65 ft. lbs.
Step 3: 65 ft. lbs.
Step 4: Plus 90 degrees

⑤ Refer to the procedure.
Step 1: Inner 15 ft. lbs. plus 90 degrees
Step 2: Outer 20 ft. lbs. plus 90 degrees
Step 3: Lateral bolts 250 inch lbs.

⑥ Step 1: 20 ft. lbs.
Step 2: plus 90 degrees

⑦ Lower manifold:
Step 1: 250 inch lbs.
Upper manifold: 105 inch lbs.
Step 1: 105 inch lbs.

⑧ 250 inch. lbs.

25766_NITR_C0010

WHEEL ALIGNMENT

Year	Model		Caster Range (+/-Deg.)	Caster Preferred Setting (Deg.)	Camber Range (+/-Deg.)	Camber Preferred Setting (Deg.)	Toe-in (deg.)
2010	Nitro	F	0.50	3.300	-0.375	-0.20	0.075-0.325
		R	N/A	N/S	-0.625-+0.125	-0.25	-0.16-+0.66
2011	Nitro	F	0.50	3.300	-0.375	-0.20	0.075-0.325
		R	N/A	N/S	-0.625-+0.125	-0.25	-0.16-+0.66

N/S: Information not supplied

25766_NITR_C0011

TIRE, WHEEL AND BALL JOINT SPECIFICATIONS

Year	Model	OEM Tires		Tire Pressures (psi)		Wheel	Ball Joint	Lug Nut Torque
		Standard	Optional	Front	Rear	Size	Inspection	(ft. lbs.)
2010	Nitro	P225/75R16	P235/65R17 P245/50R20	①	①	N/S	②	85-115
2011	Nitro	P225/75R16	P235/65R17 P245/50R20	①	①	N/S	②	85-115

N/S: Information not supplied

OEM: Original Equipment Manufacturer

STD: Standard

OPT: Optional

① See placard on vehicle

② Replace if any measurable movement is found.

25766_NITR_C0012

BRAKE SPECIFICATIONS

All measurements in inches unless noted

Year	Model		Brake Disc			Minimum Lining Thickness	Caliper Mounting Bolts (ft. lbs.)
			Original Thickness	Minimum Thickness	Maximum Run-out		
2010	Nitro	F	1.100	1.049	0.0008	0.04	28
		R	0.472	0.409	0.0008	0.04	28
2011	Nitro	F	1.100	1.049	0.0008	0.04	28
		R	0.472	0.409	0.0008	0.04	28

F- Front

R - Rear

N/A Not applicable

25766_NITR_C0013

SCHEDULED MAINTENANCE INTERVALS

2010-2011 Dodge Nitro 3.7L Engine - Normal & Severe (as noted)

TO BE SERVICED	TYPE OF SERVICE	VEHICLE MILEAGE INTERVAL (x1000)												
		6	12	18	24	30	36	42	48	54	60	66	72	78
Engine oil & filter	Replace	✓	✓	✓	✓	✓	✓	✓	✓	✓	✓	✓	✓	✓
Rotate tires, inspect tread wear, measure tread depth and check pressure	Rotate/Inspect	✓	✓	✓	✓	✓	✓	✓	✓	✓	✓	✓	✓	✓
Brake system components - Normal	Inspect/Servic e						✓		✓		✓		✓	
Brake system components - Severe	Inspect/Servic e		✓		✓		✓		✓		✓		✓	
Exhaust system & heat shields	Inspect		✓		✓		✓		✓		✓		✓	
Inspect the front suspension, tie rod ends and boot seals for cracks or leaks and all parts for damage, wear, improper looseness or end play.	Inspect		✓		✓		✓		✓		✓		✓	
CV Joints	Inspect		✓		✓		✓		✓		✓		✓	
Rear axle fluid	Replace			✓			✓			✓			✓	
Engine air filter - Normal	Replace					✓					✓			
Engine air filter - Severe	Replace		✓		✓					✓				
Adjust parking brake on vehicles equipped with four-wheel disc brakes.	Adjust					✓					✓			
Engine coolant	Flush/Replace										✓			
Spark plugs	Replace					✓					✓			
PCV valve	Inspect/Servic	Every 90,000 miles												
Automatic transmission fluid and filter - Normal	Inspect	Every 120,000 miles												
Automatic transmission fluid and filter - Severe	Inspect	Every 60,000 miles												
Accessory drive belt	Replace	Every 120,000 miles												
Battery	Inspect/Servic	✓	✓	✓	✓	✓	✓	✓	✓	✓	✓	✓	✓	✓
Horn, exterior lamps, turn signals and hazard warning light operation	Inspect	✓	✓	✓	✓	✓	✓	✓	✓	✓	✓	✓	✓	✓
Fluid levels (all)	Inspect/Servic	✓	✓	✓	✓	✓	✓	✓	✓	✓	✓	✓	✓	✓
Ignition cables	Replace										✓			

25766_NITR_C0014

SCHEDULED MAINTENANCE INTERVALS

2010-2011 Dodge Nitro 4.0L Engine - Normal & Severe (as noted)

TO BE SERVICED	TYPE OF SERVICE	VEHICLE MILEAGE INTERVAL (x1000)												
		6	12	18	24	30	36	42	48	54	60	66	72	78
Engine oil & filter	Replace	✓	✓	✓	✓	✓	✓	✓	✓	✓	✓	✓	✓	✓
Rotate tires, inspect tread wear, measure tread depth and check pressure	Rotate/Inspect	✓	✓	✓	✓	✓	✓	✓	✓	✓	✓	✓	✓	✓
Brake system components - Normal	Inspect/Service						✓		✓		✓		✓	
Brake system components - Severe	Inspect/Service		✓		✓		✓		✓		✓		✓	
Exhaust system & heat shields	Inspect		✓		✓		✓		✓		✓		✓	
Inspect the front suspension, tie rod ends and boot seals for cracks or leaks and all parts for damage, wear, improper looseness or end play.	Inspect		✓		✓		✓		✓		✓		✓	
CV Joints	Inspect		✓		✓		✓		✓		✓		✓	
Rear axle fluid	Replace			✓			✓			✓			✓	
Engine air filter - Normal	Replace					✓					✓			
Engine air filter - Severe	Replace		✓		✓					✓				
Adjust parking brake on vehicles equipped with four-wheel disc brakes.	Adjust					✓					✓			
Engine coolant	Flush/Replace										✓			
Spark plugs	Replace					✓					✓			
PCV valve	Inspect/Servic	Every 90,000 miles												
Automatic transmission fluid and filter - Normal	Inspect	Every 120,000 miles												
Automatic transmission fluid and filter - Severe	Inspect	Every 60,000 miles												
Accessory drive belt	Replace	Every 120,000 miles												
Battery	Inspect/Servic	✓	✓	✓	✓	✓	✓	✓	✓	✓	✓	✓	✓	✓
Horn, exterior lamps, turn signals and hazard warning light operation	Inspect	✓	✓	✓	✓	✓	✓	✓	✓	✓	✓	✓	✓	✓
Fluid levels (all)	Inspect/Servic	✓	✓	✓	✓	✓	✓	✓	✓	✓	✓	✓	✓	✓
Ignition cables	Replace										✓			
Timing belt	Replace	Every 102,000 miles												

25766_NITR_C0015

PRECAUTIONS

Before servicing any vehicle, please be sure to read all of the following precautions, which deal with personal safety, prevention of component damage, and important points to take into consideration when servicing a motor vehicle:

- Never open, service or drain the radiator or cooling system when the engine is hot; serious burns can occur from the steam and hot coolant.
- Observe all applicable safety precautions when working around fuel. Whenever servicing the fuel system, always work in a well-ventilated area. Do not allow fuel spray or vapors to come in contact with a spark, open flame, or excessive heat (a hot drop light, for example). Keep a dry chemical fire extinguisher near the work area. Always keep fuel in a container specifically designed for fuel storage; also, always properly seal fuel containers to avoid the possibility of fire or explosion. Refer to the additional fuel system precautions later in this section.
- Fuel injection systems often remain pressurized, even after the engine has been turned **OFF**. The fuel system pressure must be relieved before disconnecting any fuel lines. Failure to do so may result in fire and/or personal injury.
- Brake fluid often contains polyglycol ethers and polyglycols. Avoid contact with the eyes and wash your hands thoroughly after handling brake fluid. If you do get brake fluid in your eyes, flush your eyes with clean, running water for 15 minutes. If eye irritation persists, or if you have taken brake fluid internally, IMMEDIATELY seek medical assistance.
- The EPA warns that prolonged contact with used engine oil may cause a number of skin disorders, including cancer. You should make every effort to minimize your exposure to used engine oil. Protective gloves should be worn when changing oil. Wash your hands and any other exposed skin areas as soon as possible after exposure to used engine oil. Soap and water, or waterless hand cleaner should be used.
- All new vehicles are now equipped with an air bag system, often referred to as a Supplemental Restraint System (SRS) or Supplemental Inflatable Restraint (SIR) system. The system must be disabled before performing service on or around system components, steering column, instrument panel components, wiring and sensors. Failure to follow safety and disabling procedures could result in accidental air bag deployment, possible personal injury and unnecessary system repairs.
- Always wear safety goggles when working with, or around, the air bag system. When carrying a non-deployed air bag, be sure the bag and trim cover are pointed away from your body. When placing a non-deployed air bag on a work surface, always face the bag and trim cover upward, away from the surface. This will reduce the motion of the module if it is accidentally deployed. Refer to the additional air bag system precautions later in this section.
- Clean, high quality brake fluid from a sealed container is essential to the safe and proper operation of the brake system. You should always buy the correct type of brake fluid for your vehicle. If the brake fluid becomes contaminated, completely flush the system with new fluid. Never reuse any brake fluid. Any brake fluid that is removed from the system should be discarded. Also, do not allow any brake fluid to come in contact with a painted surface; it will damage the paint.
- Never operate the engine without the proper amount and type of engine oil; doing so WILL result in severe engine damage.
- Timing belt maintenance is extremely important. Many models utilize an interference-type, non-freewheeling engine. If the timing belt breaks, the valves in the cylinder head may strike the pistons, causing potentially serious (also time-consuming and expensive) engine damage. Refer to the maintenance interval charts for the recommended replacement interval for the timing belt, and to the timing belt section for belt replacement and inspection.
- Disconnecting the negative battery cable on some vehicles may interfere with the functions of the on-board computer system(s) and may require the computer to undergo a relearning process once the negative battery cable is reconnected.
- When servicing drum brakes, only disassemble and assemble one side at a time, leaving the remaining side intact for reference.
- Only an MVAC-trained, EPA-certified automotive technician should service the air conditioning system or its components.

BRAKES — ANTI-LOCK BRAKE SYSTEM (ABS)

GENERAL INFORMATION

PRECAUTIONS

- Certain components within the ABS system are not intended to be serviced or repaired individually.
- Do not use rubber hoses or other parts not specifically specified for and ABS system. When using repair kits, replace all parts included in the kit. Partial or incorrect repair may lead to functional problems and require the replacement of components.
- Lubricate rubber parts with clean, fresh brake fluid to ease assembly. Do not use shop air to clean parts; damage to rubber components may result.
- Use only DOT 3 brake fluid from an unopened container.
- If any hydraulic component or line is removed or replaced, it may be necessary to bleed the entire system.
- A clean repair area is essential. Always clean the reservoir and cap thoroughly before removing the cap. The slightest amount of dirt in the fluid may plug an orifice and impair the system function. Perform repairs after components have been thoroughly cleaned; use only denatured alcohol to clean components. Do not allow ABS components to come into contact with any substance containing mineral oil; this includes used shop rags.
- The Anti-Lock control unit is a microprocessor similar to other computer units in the vehicle. Ensure that the ignition switch is **OFF** before removing or installing controller harnesses. Avoid static electricity discharge at or near the controller.
- If any arc welding is to be done on the vehicle, the control unit should be unplugged before welding operations begin.

SPEED SENSORS

REMOVAL & INSTALLATION

Front

1. Before servicing the vehicle, refer to the Precautions Section.
2. Raise and support the vehicle.
3. Remove the tire and wheel assembly.
4. Remove the caliper adapter.

⁂ WARNING

Never allow the disc brake caliper to hang from the brake hose. Damage to the brake hose will result. Provide

a suitable support to hang the caliper securely.

5. Remove the disc brake rotor.
6. Remove the bolt mounting the wheel speed sensor to the hub.
7. Remove the wheel speed sensor wire from the hub/bearing and through the brake shield.
8. Remove the wheel speed sensor wire hold down clips.
9. Remove the locking connector at the wheel liner from the sensor connector.
10. Remove the wheel speed sensor from the vehicle.

To install:

WARNING

When installing, do not rotate sensor, as this may cause the sensor to rub on the tone ring and be damaged.

11. Install the wheel speed sensor to the vehicle.
12. Install the wheel speed sensor through the brake shield and to the hub/bearing.
13. Install the wheel speed sensor wire hold down routing clips.
14. Install the wheel speed sensor mounting bolt to the hub. Tighten the mounting bolt to 71 inch lbs. (8 Nm).
15. Install the disc brake rotor.
16. Install the disc brake caliper adapter.
17. Install the tire and wheel assembly.

Rear

1. Before servicing the vehicle, refer to the Precautions Section.
2. Raise and support the vehicle.
3. Disengage the locking tab connector.
4. Disconnect the wheel speed sensor electrical connector.
5. Remove the wheel speed sensor mounting bolt from the rear support plate.
6. Remove the wheel speed sensor from the support plate.

To install:

7. Insert the wheel speed sensor through the support plate.
8. Tighten the wheel speed sensor bolt to 80 inch lbs. (9 Nm).
9. Secure the wheel speed sensor wire to the routing clips. Verify that the sensor wire is secure and clear of the rotating components.
10. Reconnect the wheel speed sensor electrical connector. Make sure the connector locking tab is fully engaged and locked in position.
11. Lower the vehicle.

BRAKES — BLEEDING THE BRAKE SYSTEM

BLEEDING PROCEDURE

BLEEDING THE ABS SYSTEM

1. Before servicing the vehicle, refer to the Precautions Section.
2. See all applicable precautions before beginning service procedures.
3. Perform conventional base brake bleeding (Manual or Pressure).
4. Connect scan tool to the Data Link Connector.
5. Select ANTILOCK BRAKES, followed by MISCELLANEOUS, then ABS BRAKES. Follow the instructions displayed. When scan tool displays TEST COMPLETE, disconnect scan tool and proceed.
6. Perform base brake bleeding a second time.
7. Top off master cylinder fluid level and verify proper brake operation before moving vehicle.

HYDRAULIC BRAKE SYSTEM BLEEDING

Manual Bleeding

➡Before servicing the vehicle, refer to the Precautions Section.

WARNING

Use Mopar® brake fluid, or an equivalent quality fluid meeting SAE J1703-F and DOT 3 standards only. Use fresh, clean fluid from a sealed container at all times.

➡Do not pump the brake pedal at any time while bleeding. Air in the system will be compressed into small bubbles that are distributed throughout the hydraulic system. This will make additional bleeding operations necessary.

➡Do not allow the master cylinder to run out of fluid during bleed operations. An empty cylinder will allow additional air to be drawn into the system. Check the cylinder fluid level frequently and add fluid as needed.

1. Bleed only one brake component at a time in the following sequence:
    a. Master Cylinder
    b. Junction Block
    c. Right Rear Wheel
    d. Left Rear Wheel
    e. Right Front Wheel
    f. Left Front Wheel
2. Remove reservoir filler caps and fill the reservoir.
3. If calipers were overhauled, open all caliper bleed screws. Close each bleed screw as fluid starts to drip from it. Top off master cylinder reservoir once more before proceeding.
4. Attach one end of bleed hose to bleed screw and insert opposite end in glass container partially filled with brake fluid. Be sure end of bleed hose is immersed in fluid.
5. Open up bleeder and have a helper press down the brake pedal. Once the pedal is down close the bleeder. Repeat bleeding until fluid stream is clear and free of bubbles. Move to the next wheel.

Pressure Bleeding

➡Before servicing the vehicle, refer to the Precautions Section.

WARNING

Use Mopar® brake fluid, or an equivalent quality fluid meeting SAE J1703-F and DOT 3 standards only. Use fresh, clean fluid from a sealed container at all times.

➡Do not pump the brake pedal at any time while bleeding. Air in the system will be compressed into small bubbles that are distributed throughout the hydraulic system. This will make additional bleeding operations necessary.

➡Do not allow the master cylinder to run out of fluid during bleed operations. An empty cylinder will allow additional air to be drawn into the system. Check the cylinder fluid level frequently and add fluid as needed.

WARNING

Follow the manufacturer's instructions carefully when using pressure equipment. Do not exceed the tank manufacturer's pressure recommendations. Generally, a tank pressure of 15–20 psi (103–139 kPa) is sufficient for bleeding.

➡Fill the bleeder tank with recommended fluid and purge air from the tank lines before bleeding.

✲✲ WARNING

Do not pressure bleed without a proper master cylinder adapter. The wrong adapter can lead to leakage, or drawing air back into the system.

Use adapter provided with the equipment or Adapter 6921.

1. Bleed only one brake component at a time in the following sequence:
   a. Master Cylinder
   b. Right Rear Wheel
   c. Left Rear Wheel
   d. Right Front Wheel
   e. Left Front Wheel

FLUID FILL PROCEDURE

1. Always clean the master cylinder reservoir and caps before checking fluid level. If not cleaned, dirt could enter the fluid.
2. The fluid fill level is indicated on the side of the master cylinder reservoir.
3. The correct fluid level is to the MAX indicator on the side of the reservoir. If necessary, add fluid to the proper level.

BRAKES

FRONT DISC BRAKES

✲✲ CAUTION

Dust and dirt accumulating on brake parts during normal use may contain asbestos fibers from production or aftermarket brake linings. Breathing excessive concentrations of asbestos fibers can cause serious bodily harm. Exercise care when servicing brake parts. Do not sand or grind brake lining unless equipment used is designed to contain the dust residue. Do not clean brake parts with compressed air or by dry brushing. Cleaning should be done by dampening the brake components with a fine mist of water and wiping the brake components clean with a dampened cloth. Dispose of cloth and all residue containing asbestos fibers in an impermeable container with the appropriate label. Follow practices prescribed by the Occupational Safety and Health Administration (OSHA) and the Environmental Protection Agency (EPA) for the handling, processing, and disposing of dust or debris that may contain asbestos fibers.

BRAKE CALIPER

REMOVAL & INSTALLATION

See Figure 1.

1. Before servicing the vehicle, refer to the Precautions Section.
2. Install prop rod on the brake pedal to keep pressure on the brake system. Holding the pedal in this position will isolate the master cylinder from the hydraulic brake system and will not allow brake fluid to drain out of the brake fluid reservoir while brake lines are open. This will allow you to bleed out the area of repair instead of the entire system.
3. Raise and support vehicle.
4. Remove front wheel and tire assembly.
5. Remove the brake hose banjo bolt.
6. Remove the caliper mounting bolts.
7. Remove the caliper from vehicle.

To install:

8. Install caliper to the caliper adapter.
9. Coat the caliper mounting bolts with silicone grease. Beginning with the bolt closest to the bleeder screws (top), install and tighten the bolts to 28 ft. lbs. (37 Nm).
10. Install the brake hose banjo bolt and brake hose to the caliper with **NEW** seal washers and tighten fitting bolt to 23 ft. lbs. (31 Nm). Verify that the brake hose is not twisted or kinked before tightening the fitting bolt.
11. Remove the prop rod from the vehicle.
12. Bleed the area of repair for brake system. If a proper pedal is not felt during bleeding the area of repair, a base bleed system must be performed.
13. Install the wheel and tire assemblies.
14. Remove the supports and lower the vehicle.
15. Verify a firm pedal before moving the vehicle.

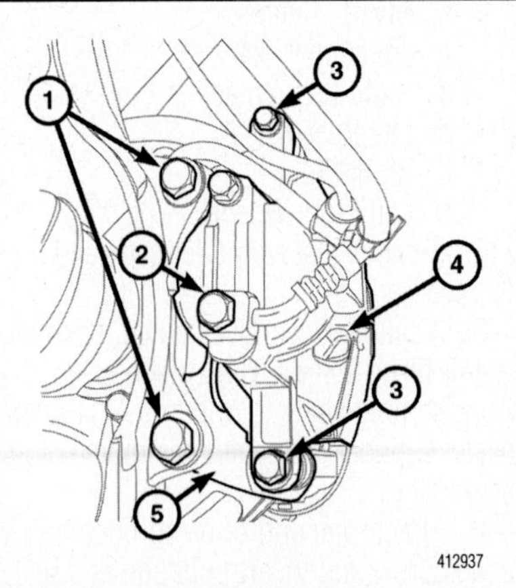

Fig. 1 Brake hose banjo bolt (2), caliper mounting bolts (3), caliper (4), and adapter (5)

DISC BRAKE PADS

REMOVAL & INSTALLATION

See Figure 2.

1. Before servicing the vehicle, refer to the Precautions Section.
2. Raise and support the vehicle.
3. Remove the front wheel and tire assembly.
4. Drain a small amount of fluid from the master cylinder brake reservoir with a clean suction gun.
5. Bottom the caliper pistons into the caliper by prying the caliper over.
6. Remove the caliper mounting bolts.
7. Remove the disc brake caliper from the adapter.
8. Remove the inboard and outboard pads.

To install:

9. Install the inboard and outboard pads.
10. Install the caliper.
11. Install the tire and wheel assembly.

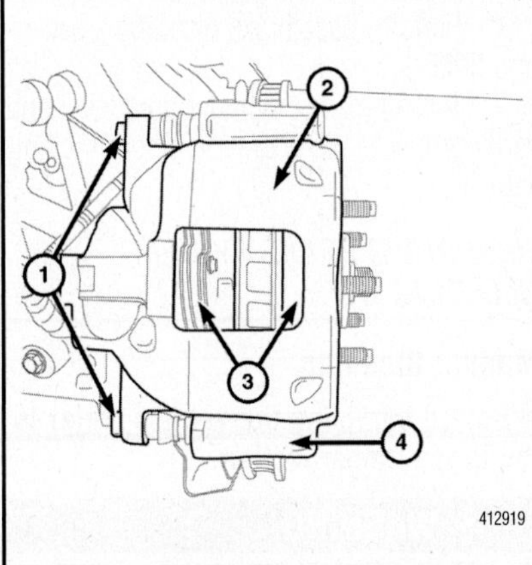

Fig. 2 Front brake caliper (2) and mounting bolts (1); adapter (4), and inboard and outboard pads (3)

※※ CAUTION

Dust and dirt accumulating on brake parts during normal use may contain asbestos fibers from production or aftermarket brake linings. Breathing excessive concentrations of asbestos fibers can cause serious bodily harm. Exercise care when servicing brake parts. Do not sand or grind brake lining unless equipment used is designed to contain the dust residue. Do not clean brake parts with compressed air or by dry brushing. Cleaning should be done by dampening the brake components with a fine mist of water and wiping the brake components clean with a dampened cloth. Dispose of cloth and all residue containing asbestos fibers in an impermeable container with the appropriate label. Follow practices prescribed by the Occupational Safety and Health Administration (OSHA) and the Environmental Protection Agency (EPA) for the handling, processing, and disposing of dust or debris that may contain asbestos fibers.

BRAKE CALIPER

REMOVAL & INSTALLATION

See Figure 3.

1. Before servicing the vehicle, refer to the Precautions Section.
2. Install prop rod on the brake pedal to keep pressure on the brake system, Holding the pedal in this position will isolate the master cylinder from the hydraulic brake system and will not allow brake fluid to drain out of the brake fluid reservoir while brake lines are open. This will allow you to bleed out the area of repair instead of the entire system.
3. Raise and support the vehicle.

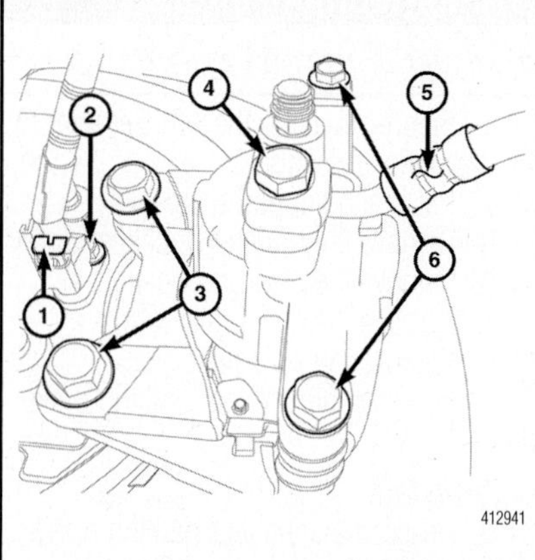

Fig. 3 Bake hose (5), banjo bolt (4), and caliper mounting bolts (6)

4. Remove the tire and wheel assembly.
5. Remove the brake hose banjo bolt.
6. Remove the caliper mounting bolts.
7. Remove the caliper from vehicle.

To install:

8. Install the brake caliper and tighten the mounting bolts to 28 ft. lbs. (37 Nm).
9. Install the brake hose to the caliper with new seal washers, install the banjo bolt, tighten fitting bolt to 23 ft. lbs. (31 Nm).
10. Remove the prop rod from thc vehicle.
11. Bleed the area of repair for the brake system. If a proper pedal is not felt during bleeding an area of repair, a base bleed system must be performed.
12. Install the tire and wheel assembly.
13. Remove the supports and lower the vehicle.
14. Verify a firm pedal before moving the vehicle.

DISC BRAKE PADS

REMOVAL & INSTALLATION

See Figure 4.

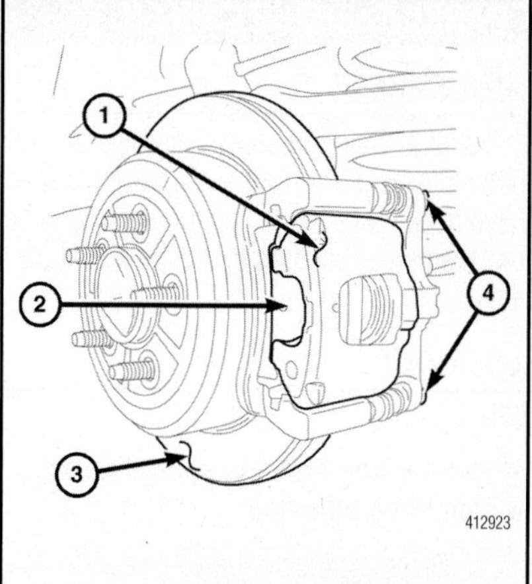

Fig. 4 Rear caliper (1), caliper mounting bolts (4), and brake pads (2)

1. Before servicing the vehicle, refer to the Precautions Section.
2. Raise and support vehicle.
3. Remove the wheel and tire assemblies.
4. Compress the caliper.
5. Remove the rear caliper mounting bolts.
6. Remove the caliper by tilting the top up and off the caliper adapter.
7. Support and hang the caliper with heavy mechanic wire or equivalent. Do not allow brake hose to support caliper assembly.
8. Remove the brake pads from the caliper.

To install:

9. Install the brake pads to the caliper adapter.
10. Install caliper to the rotor and install the caliper mounting bolts.
11. Install wheel and tire assemblies and lower vehicle.
12. Apply brakes several times to seat caliper pistons and brake shoes and obtain firm pedal.
13. Top off master cylinder fluid level.

PARKING BRAKE CABLES

ADJUSTMENT

No adjustment is needed, as the parking brake cables are self-adjusting. If the cables have been replaced, follow the parking shoe replacement procedure to set the shoes correctly.

LOCK OUT

See Figure 5.

➡The parking brake is self-adjusting, it cannot be adjusted.

1. Before servicing the vehicle, refer to the Precautions Section.
2. Remove the center floor console.
3. With lever in DOWN position, pull up on the core cable rotating the drum until the drum cut-out aligns with hole on lever tab and install a punch in this hole and drum cut-out. Release grasp on core cable.
4. The park brake system is now locked out to perform necessary repairs

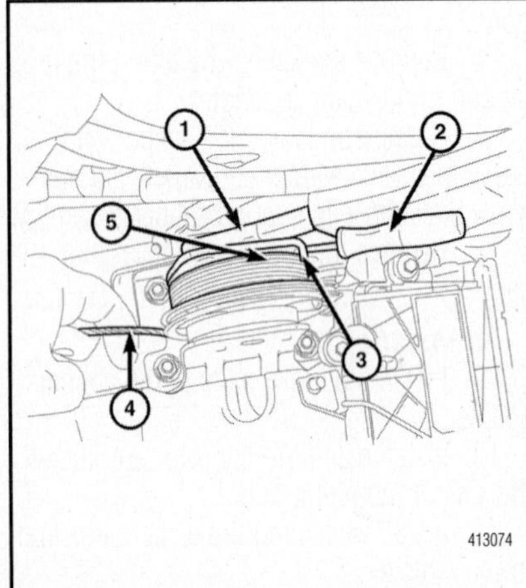

Fig. 5 Core cable (4), drum (5), lever tab (3), punch (2)

PARKING BRAKE SHOES

REMOVAL & INSTALLATION

1. Before servicing the vehicle, refer to the Precautions Section.
2. Raise and support the vehicle.
3. Remove the tire and wheel assembly.
4. Remove the disc brake caliper.
5. Remove the disc brake rotor.
6. Remove the axle shaft.
7. Disassemble the rear parking brake shoes.

To install:

8. Reassemble the rear parking brake shoes.
9. Adjust the rear parking brake shoes.
10. Install axle shaft.
11. Install the disc brake rotor.
12. Install the disc brake caliper.
13. Install the tire and wheel assembly.
14. Lower the vehicle.

➡On a new vehicle or after parking brake lining replacement, it is recommended that the parking brake system be conditioned prior to use. This is done by making one stop from 25 mph on dry pavement or concrete using light to moderate force on the parking brake foot pedal.

ADJUSTMENT

See Figure 6.

Adjustment can be made with a standard brake gauge or with adjusting tool. Adjustment is performed with the complete brake assembly installed on the backing plate.

1. Be sure the parking brake lever is fully released.
2. Raise the vehicle so rear wheels can be rotated freely.

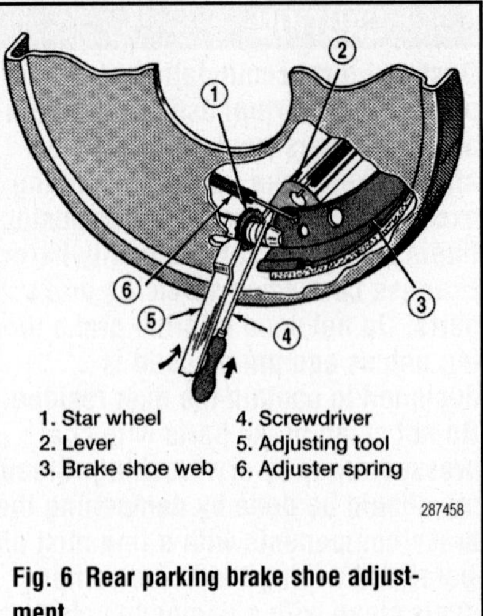

Fig. 6 Rear parking brake shoe adjustment

3. Remove the plug from each access hole in brake support plates.
4. Insert the adjusting tool through the support plate access hole and engage the tool in the teeth of adjusting screw star wheel.
5. Rotate the adjuster screw star wheel (move tool handle upward) until slight drag can be felt when the wheel is rotated.
6. Push and hold the adjuster lever away from the star wheel with thin screwdriver.
7. Back off the adjuster screw star wheel until brake drag is eliminated.
8. Repeat the adjustment at opposite wheel. Be sure the adjustment is equal at both wheels.
9. Install support plate access hole plugs.
10. Lower the vehicle.
11. Apply the parking brake hand lever and make sure the parking brakes hold the vehicle stationary.
12. Release the parking brake hand lever.

GENERAL INFORMATION

⁂ CAUTION

These vehicles are equipped with an air bag system. The system must be disarmed before performing service on, or around, system components, the steering column, instrument panel components, wiring and sensors. Failure to follow the safety precautions and the disarming procedure could result in accidental air bag deployment, possible injury and unnecessary system repairs.

SERVICE PRECAUTIONS

Disconnect and isolate the battery negative cable before beginning any airbag system component diagnosis, testing, removal, or installation procedures. Allow system capacitor to discharge for two minutes before beginning any component service. This will disable the airbag system. Failure to disable the airbag system may result in accidental airbag deployment, personal injury, or death.

Do not place an intact undeployed airbag face down on a solid surface. The airbag will propel into the air if accidentally deployed and may result in personal injury or death.

When carrying or handling an undeployed airbag, the trim side (face) of the airbag should be pointing away from the body to minimize possibility of injury if accidental deployment occurs. Failure to do this may result in personal injury or death.

Replace airbag system components with OEM replacement parts. Substitute parts may appear interchangeable, but internal differences may result in inferior occupant protection. Failure to do so may result in occupant personal injury or death.

Wear safety glasses, rubber gloves, and long sleeved clothing when cleaning powder residue from vehicle after an airbag deployment. Powder residue emitted from a deployed airbag can cause skin irritation. Flush affected area with cool water if irritation is experienced. If nasal or throat irritation is experienced, exit the vehicle for fresh air until the irritation ceases. If irritation continues, see a physician.

Do not use a replacement airbag that is not in the original packaging. This may result in improper deployment, personal injury, or death.

The factory installed fasteners, screws and bolts used to fasten airbag components have a special coating and are specifically designed for the airbag system. Do not use substitute fasteners. Use only original equipment fasteners listed in the parts catalog when fastener replacement is required.

During, and following, any child restraint anchor service, due to impact event or vehicle repair, carefully inspect all mounting hardware, tether straps, and anchors for proper installation, operation, or damage. If a child restraint anchor is found damaged in any way, the anchor must be replaced. Failure to do this may result in personal injury or death.

Deployed and non-deployed airbags may or may not have live pyrotechnic material within the airbag inflator.

Do not dispose of driver/passenger/curtain airbags or seat belt tensioners unless you are sure of complete deployment. Refer to the Hazardous Substance Control System for proper disposal.

Dispose of deployed airbags and tensioners consistent with state, provincial, local, and federal regulations.

After any airbag component testing or service, do not connect the battery negative cable. Personal injury or death may result if the system test is not performed first.

If the vehicle is equipped with the Occupant Classification System (OCS), do not connect the battery negative cable before performing the OCS Verification Test using the scan tool and the appropriate diagnostic information. Personal injury or death may result if the system test is not performed properly.

Never replace both the Occupant Restraint Controller (ORC) and the Occupant Classification Module (OCM) at the same time. If both require replacement, replace one, and perform the Airbag System test before replacing the other.

Both the ORC and the OCM store Occupant Classification System (OCS) calibration data, which they transfer to one another when one of them is replaced. If both are replaced at the same time, an irreversible fault will be set in both modules and the OCS may malfunction and cause personal injury or death.

If equipped with OCS, the Seat Weight Sensor is a sensitive, calibrated unit and must be handled carefully. Do not drop or handle roughly. If dropped or damaged, replace with another sensor. Failure to do so may result in occupant injury or death.

If equipped with OCS, the front passenger seat must be handled carefully as well. When removing the seat, be careful when setting on floor not to drop. If dropped, the sensor may be inoperative, could result in occupant injury, or possibly death.

If equipped with OCS, when the passenger front seat is on the floor, no one should sit in the front passenger seat. This uneven force may damage the sensing ability of the seat weight sensors. If sat on and damaged, the sensor may be inoperative, could result in occupant injury, or possibly death.

DISARMING THE SYSTEM

Disconnect and isolate the negative battery cable. Wait 2 minutes for the system capacitor to discharge before performing any service.

ARMING THE SYSTEM

To arm the system, connect the negative battery cable.

CLOCKSPRING CENTERING

⁂ CAUTION

To avoid serious or fatal injury on vehicles equipped with airbags, disable the Supplemental Restraint System (SRS) before attempting any steering wheel, steering column, airbag, Occupant Classification System (OCS), seat belt tensioner, impact sensor, or instrument panel component diagnosis or service. Disconnect and isolate the battery negative (ground) cable, then wait two minutes for the system capacitor to discharge before performing further diagnosis or service. This is the only sure way to disable the SRS. Failure to take the proper precautions could result in accidental airbag deployment.

⁂ WARNING

When a clockspring is installed into a vehicle without properly centering and locking the entire steering system, the Steering Angle Sensor (SAS) data does not agree with the true position of the steering system and causes the Electronic Stability Program (ESP) system to shut down. This may also damage the clockspring without any immediate malfunction. Unlike some other Chrysler vehicles, this SAS never requires calibration. However, upon each new ignition ON cycle, the steering wheel must be rotated slightly to initialize the SAS.

➡A service replacement clockspring is shipped with the clockspring pre-centered and with a molded plastic locking pin installed. This locking pin should not be removed until the steering wheel has been installed on the steering column. If the locking pin is removed before the steering wheel is installed, the clockspring centering procedure must be performed.

➡Determining if the clockspring/SAS is centered is also possible electrically using the diagnostic scan tool. Steering wheel position is displayed as ANGLE with a range of up to 900 degrees. Refer to the appropriate menu item on the diagnostic scan tool.

1. Place the front wheels in the straight-ahead position and prevent the steering column shaft from rotation.
2. Remove the steering wheel from the steering shaft.
3. Rotate the clockspring rotor clockwise to the end of its travel. Do not apply excessive torque.
4. From the end of the clockwise travel, rotate the rotor about two and one-half turns counterclockwise. Turn the rotor slightly clockwise or counterclockwise as necessary so that the clockspring airbag pigtail wires and connector receptacle are at the top and the dowel or drive pin is at the bottom.
5. The clockspring is now centered. Secure the clockspring rotor to the clockspring case using a locking pin or some similar device to maintain clockspring centering until the steering wheel is reinstalled on the steering column.

DRIVE TRAIN

AUTOMATIC TRANSMISSION FLUID

CHECKING FLUID LEVEL

See Figures 7 and 8.

1. Before servicing the vehicle, refer to the Precautions Section.
2. Verify the vehicle is parked on a level surface.
3. Remove the dipstick tube cap.
4. Actuate the service brake. Start engine and let it run at idle speed in selector lever position "P".
5. Shift through the transmission modes several times with the vehicle stationary and the engine idling
6. Warm up the transmission, wait at least 2 minutes and check the oil level with the engine running. Push the oil dipstick into transmission fill tube until the dipstick tip contacts the oil pan and pull out again, and the read oil level; repeat if necessary.
7. Using the appropriate scan tool, check the transmission oil temperature. The true transmission oil temperature can only be read by a scan tool in reverse or any forward gear position.
8. The transmission oil dipstick has indicator marks every 10mm. Determine the height of the oil level on the dipstick and using the height, the transmission temperature, and the Transmission Fluid Graph, determine if the transmission oil level is correct.
9. Add or remove oil as necessary and recheck the oil level.
10. Once the oil level is correct, install the dipstick tube cap.

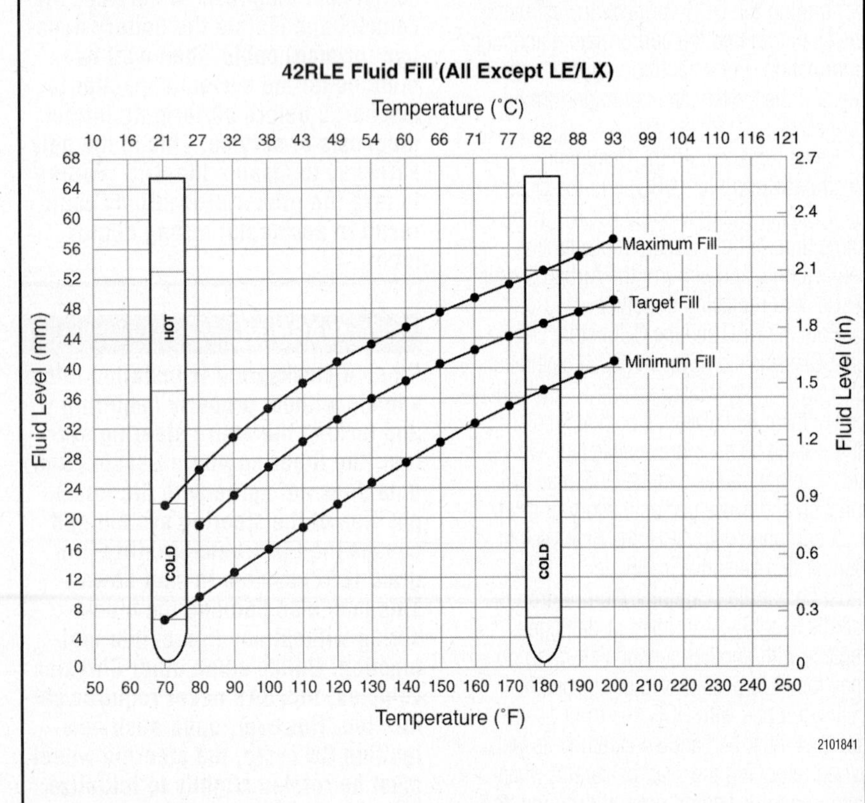

Fig. 7 Transmission Fluid Graph—4-speed transmission

FLUID FILL

4-Speed Transmission

1. Before servicing the vehicle, refer to the Precautions Section.
2. Remove the plug or dipstick and insert a clean funnel in transmission fill tube.
3. Add Mopar® ATF +4 (or equivalent) to the transmission:
   a. If only fluid and filter were changed, add 3 quarts (6 pints) of ATF +4 to transmission.
   b. If the transmission was completely overhauled, or torque converter was replaced or drained, add 5 quarts (10 pints) of ATF +4 to transmission.
4. Apply the parking brakes.
5. Start and run the engine at normal curb idle speed.
6. Apply service brakes, shift transmission through all gear ranges then back to NEUTRAL, set the parking brake, and leave the engine running at curb idle speed.
7. Remove funnel, insert dipstick and check fluid level. If level is low, add fluid to bring level to MIN mark on dipstick. Check to see if the oil level is equal on both sides of the dipstick. If one side is noticeably higher than the other, the dipstick has picked up some oil from the dipstick tube. Allow the oil to drain down the dipstick tube and re-check.

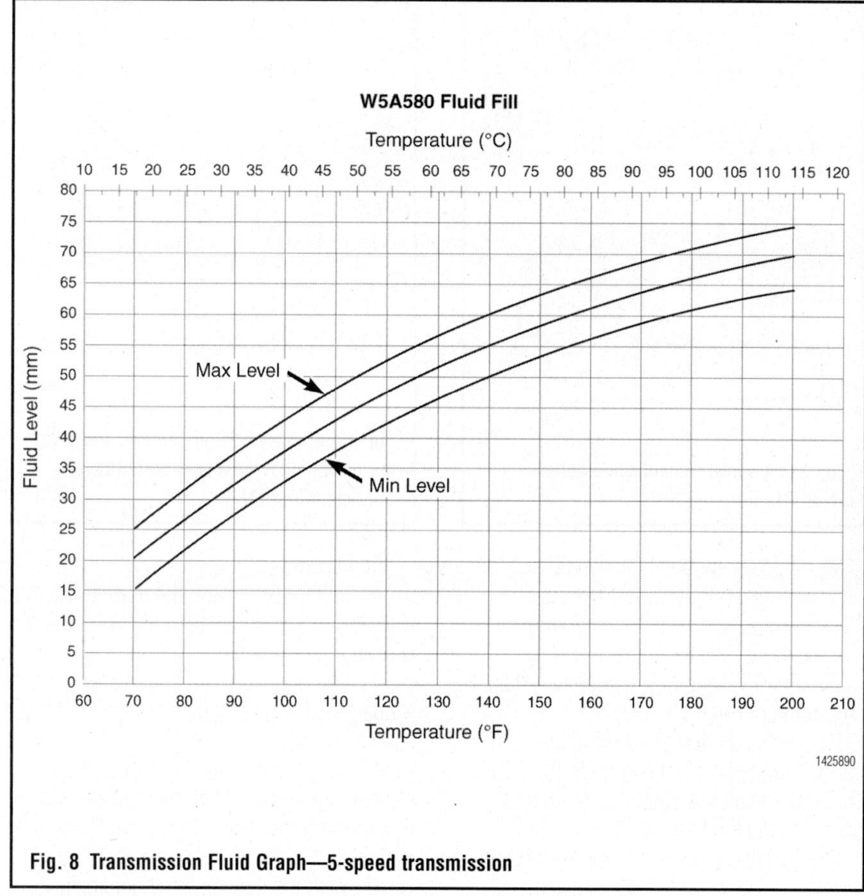

Fig. 8 Transmission Fluid Graph—5-speed transmission

8. Drive the vehicle until the transmission fluid is at normal operating temperature.

9. With the engine running at curb idle speed, the gear selector in NEUTRAL, and the parking brake applied, check the transmission fluid level.

10. Add fluid and bring the level up to MAX arrow mark. Do not overfill transmission; fluid foaming and shifting problems can result.

11. When fluid level is correct, shut engine off, release the parking brake, remove funnel, and install the plug or dipstick in fill tube.

5-Speed Transmission

1. Verify that the vehicle is parked on a level surface.
2. Remove the dipstick tube cap.
3. Add Mopar® ATF +4 (or equivalent) to the transmission:
   a. If only fluid and filter were changed, add 10.6 pts. (5.0L) of transmission fluid to the transmission.
   b. If the transmission was completely overhauled or the torque converter was replaced or drained, add 16.3 pts. (7.7L) of transmission fluid to transmission.
4. Check the transmission fluid and adjust as needed.

FLUID & FILTER REPLACEMENT

4-Speed Transmission

See Figure 9.

If the transmission is disassembled for any reason, the fluid and filter should be changed.

1. Raise the vehicle on a hoist. Place a drain container with a large opening, under transmission oil pan.

2. One of the oil pan bolts has a sealing patch applied from the factory. Separate this bolt for reuse.

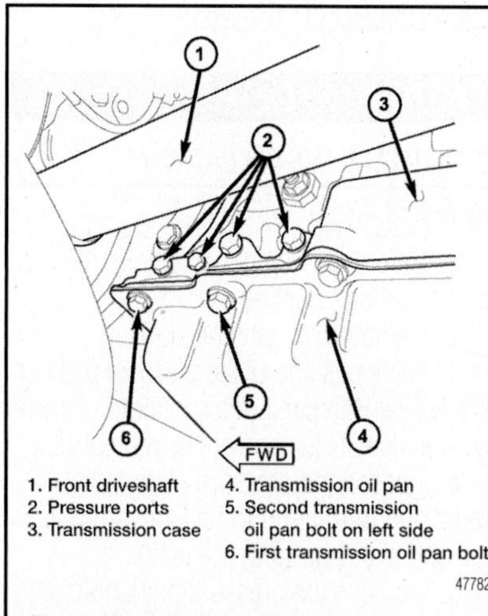

Fig. 9 Transmission oil pan

3. Loosen pan bolts and tap the pan at one corner to break it loose allowing fluid to drain, then remove the oil pan.

4. Install a new filter and O-ring on bottom of the valve body and tighten retaining screws to 45 inch lbs. (5 Nm).

Before installing the oil pan bolt in the bolt hole located between the torque converter clutch on and U/D clutch pressure tap circuits, it will be necessary to replenish the sealing patch on the bolt using Mopar® Lock and Seal Adhesive, or equivalent.

5. Clean the oil pan and magnet. Reinstall pan using new silicone adhesive sealant. Tighten the bolts to 15 ft. lbs. (20 Nm).

6. Pour four quarts of Mopar® ATF+4 (or equivalent), through the dipstick opening.

7. Start engine and allow to idle for at least one minute. Then, with parking and service brakes applied, move selector lever momentarily to each position, ending in the park or neutral position.

8. Check the transmission fluid level and add an appropriate amount to bring the transmission fluid level to ⅛ in. (3mm) below the lowest mark on the dipstick.

9. Recheck the fluid level after the transmission has reached normal operating temperature, 180°F (82° C).

10. To prevent dirt from entering transmission, make certain that dipstick is fully seated into the dipstick opening.

5-Speed Transmission

See Figure 10.

1. Run the engine until the transmission oil reaches operating temperature.
2. Raise and support vehicle.
3. Remove the bolts and retainers holding the oil pan to the transmission.
4. Remove the transmission oil pan and gasket from the transmission.
5. Remove the transmission oil filter and O-ring from the electro hydraulic control unit.
6. Clean the inside of the oil pan of any debris. Inspect the oil pan gasket and replace if necessary.
7. Install a new oil filter and O-ring into the electro hydraulic control unit.
8. Install the oil pan and gasket onto the transmission.
9. Install the oil pan bolts and retainers. Tighten the bolts to 70 inch lbs. (8 Nm).
10. Lower the vehicle and add 10.6 pts. (5.0L) of transmission fluid to the transmission.
11. Check the oil level.

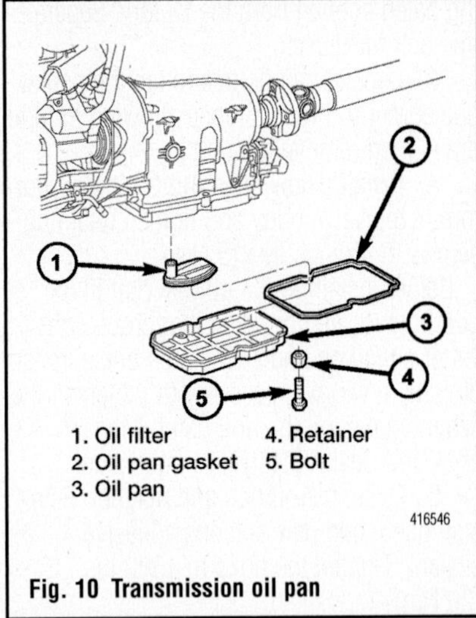

Fig. 10 Transmission oil pan

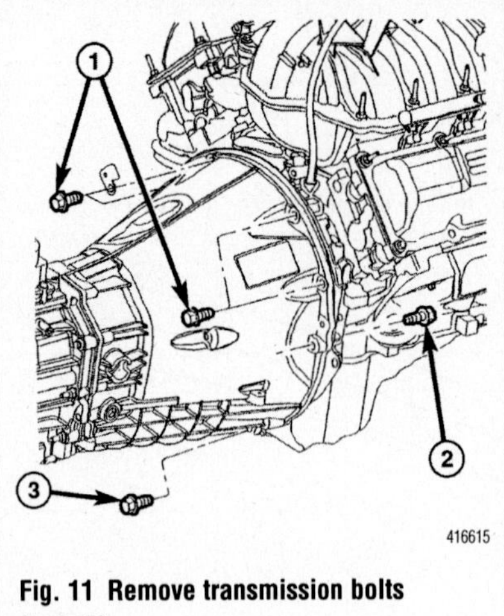

Fig. 11 Remove transmission bolts (1, 2, 3)

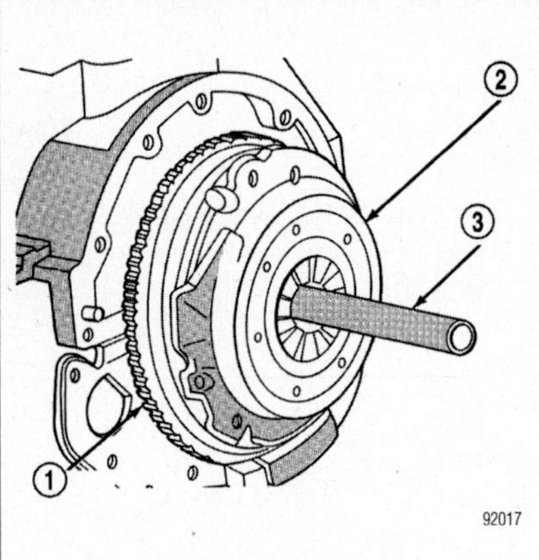

Fig. 12 Clutch wheel alignment, showing the flywheel (1), pressure plate (2), and alignment tool (3)

MANUAL TRANSMISSION ASSEMBLY

REMOVAL & INSTALLATION

See Figure 11.

1. Before servicing the vehicle, refer to the Precautions Section.
2. Disconnect negative battery cable.
3. Remove the console manual shift bezel.
4. Remove the floor console.
5. With the vehicle in neutral, position the vehicle on a hoist.
6. Remove the drain plug and drain the fluid.
7. Matchmark the installation reference marks on the propeller shaft/shafts and remove the shafts.
8. Remove the transfer case shift cable, wiring connector and vent hose, if equipped.
9. Remove the transfer case from the transmission, if equipped.
10. Support the transmission with a jack.
11. Remove the transmission mount bolts and the crossmember bolts. Remove the transmission mount with crossmember.
12. For 3.7L engines, remove the exhaust pipe with converters.
13. Pull hydraulic line clip from the slave cylinder.
14. Remove the clutch slave cylinder nuts and remove the cylinder.
15. Remove the backup lamp switch wiring connector.
16. Remove the mounting bolts and remove the starter.
17. Remove the transmission bolts and remove the transmission.

To install:

18. Install the transmission on the engine.
19. Tighten the bolts (shown above) to:
    - Bolts "1": 30 ft. lbs. (41 Nm)
    - Bolts "2": 50 ft. lbs. (67 Nm)
    - Bolts "3": 40 ft. lbs. (54 Nm)
20. For 3.7L engines, install the exhaust pipe with converters.
21. Install the transmission crossmember and tighten the bolts to 35 ft. lbs. (47 Nm). Install the transmission mount bolts and tighten to 35 ft. lbs. (47 Nm).
22. Install the back-up lamp wiring connector.
23. Install clutch slave cylinder and tighten the mounting nuts to 17 ft. lbs. (23 Nm).
24. Install the transfer case on the transmission, if equipped.
25. Align the reference marks and install the propeller shaft/shafts.
26. Remove the fill plug and fill the transmission to specifications.
27. Install the inner shift boot, shift lever, and lever screw.
28. Install the shift boot, shift knob, and console.
29. Connect the battery.

CLUTCH

REMOVAL & INSTALLATION

See Figure 12.

1. Before servicing the vehicle, refer to the Precautions Section.
2. Remove the transmission.
3. Mark position of the pressure plate on the flywheel with paint or a scriber for assembly reference, if clutch is not being replaced.
4. Loosen the pressure plate bolts evenly and in rotation to relieve spring tension and avoid warping the plate.
5. Remove the pressure plate bolts and the pressure plate and disc.

To install:

6. Lightly scuff sand the flywheel face with 180 grit emery cloth, and clean with a wax and grease remover.
7. Lubricate the pilot bearing with Mopar® high temperature bearing grease, or equivalent.
8. Check the runout and operation of new clutch disc. Disc must slide freely on transmission input shaft splines.
9. With the disc on the input shaft, check the face runout with a dial indicator. Check runout at disc hub ¼ in. (6mm) from the outer edge of the facing. Obtain another clutch disc if runout exceeds 0.020 in. (0.5mm).
10. Position the clutch disc on the flywheel with the side marked "flywheel" against the flywheel. If not marked, the flat side of the disc hub goes towards the flywheel.
11. Insert a clutch alignment tool through the clutch disc and into the pilot bearing.
12. Position the clutch pressure plate over the disc and on the flywheel.
13. Install the pressure plate bolts finger tight.

WARNING

Use only the factory bolts to mount the pressure plate. The bolts must be the correct size. If bolts are too short, there isn't enough thread engagement. If too long, bolts interfere with the Dual Mass Flywheel.

14. Tighten the pressure plate bolts evenly and in rotation a few threads at a time.
15. Tighten the pressure plate bolts to 24 ft. lbs. (33 Nm).

⁂ WARNING

Failure to tighten the bolts evenly and to the specified torque will distort the pressure plate.

16. Apply a light coat of Mopar® high temperature bearing grease, or equivalent, to the clutch disc hub and splines of the transmission input shaft. Do not over lubricate the shaft splines. This will result in grease contamination of the disc.
17. Install the transmission.

BLEEDING

Bleeding Clutch Hydraulic Circuit

1. Use Mopar® brake fluid, or an equivalent quality fluid meeting SAE J1703-F and DOT 3 standards only. Use fresh, clean fluid from a sealed container at all times.
2. Do not allow the master cylinder to run out of fluid during bleed operations. An empty cylinder will allow additional air to be drawn into the system. Check the cylinder fluid level frequently and add fluid as needed.
3. Verify the fluid level in the brake master cylinder; top off brake fluid as necessary.

➡Pre filling a new slave cylinder will reduce bleeding time required.

4. Install a length of clear hose to divert the fluid into a suitable container.
5. Push and hold the clutch pedal down, open the bleeder on the slave cylinder, allow fluid to bleed out, then close the bleeder. Repeat this step several times until no air is observed coming out of the bleeder.
6. Remove the drain hose and replace the dust cap on the bleeder and install the slave cylinder on the transmission.
7. Actuate the clutch pedal 25 times, then start the engine and verify clutch operation and pedal feel. If pedal feels spongy or clutch does not fully disengage, air is still trapped in the hydraulic circuit and must be bled again.

Pressure Bleeding Clutch Hydraulic Circuit

1. Follow manufacturer's instructions carefully when using pressure equipment. Do not exceed the tank manufacturer's pressure recommendations. Generally, a tank pressure of 15–20 psi is sufficient for bleeding.
2. Fill bleeder tank with recommended DOT 3 fluid and purge air from the tank lines before bleeding.
3. Do not pressure bleed without a proper master cylinder adapter. The wrong adapter can lead to leakage, or drawing air back into the system.

TRANSFER CASE ASSEMBLY

REMOVAL & INSTALLATION

See Figures 13 and 14.

1. Before servicing the vehicle, refer to the Precautions Section.
2. Raise the vehicle.
3. Remove the front and rear driveshafts/propeller shafts.

⁂ WARNING

Do not allow the prop shafts to hang at attached end. Damage to the joint can result.

4. Support the transmission with a jack stand.
5. Remove the rear crossmember and skid plate, if equipped.
6. Disconnect the transfer case vent hose.
7. Disconnect the wiring connector from the shift motor, if necessary.
8. Support the transfer case with a transmission jack and secure with chains.
9. Remove the nuts attaching the transfer case to the transmission.
10. Pull the transfer case and jack rearward to disengage the transfer case from the transmission case.
11. Remove the transfer case from under the vehicle.

To install:

12. Mount the transfer case on a transmission jack.
13. Secure the transfer case to the jack with chains.
14. Position the transfer case under the vehicle.

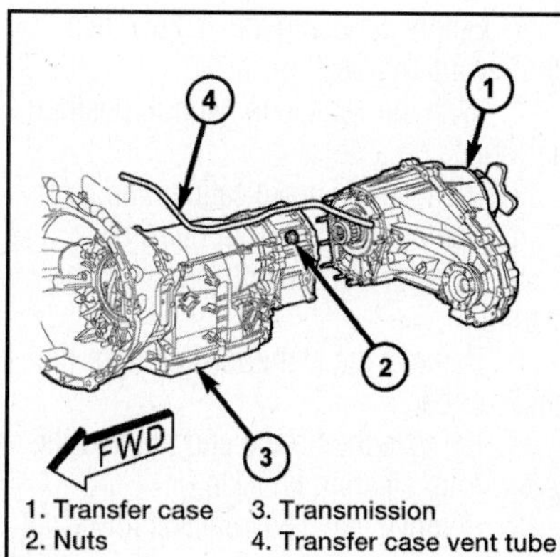

Fig. 13 Transfer case—MP140 Transfer Case, for Full-Time 4WD System

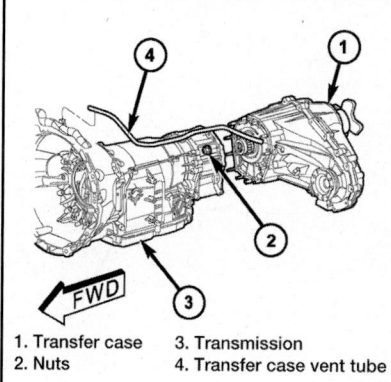

1. Transfer case
2. Nuts
3. Transmission
4. Transfer case vent tube

416691

Fig. 14 Transfer case—MP143 Transfer Case, for Part-Time 4WD System

15. Align the transfer case and transmission shafts and install the transfer case onto the transmission.
16. Install and tighten the transfer case mounting nuts to 26 ft. lbs. (35 Nm).
17. Connect the transfer case shift motor electrical connector.
18. Connect the transfer case vent hose.
19. Connect the front driveshaft/propeller shaft and install the rear driveshaft/propeller shaft.
20. Fill the transfer case with MOPAR® ATF +4, or equivalent.
21. Install the transfer case fill plug and tighten to 9–11 ft. lbs. (12–15 Nm).
22. Install the rear crossmember and skid plate, if equipped. Tighten crossmember bolts to 30 ft. lbs. (41 Nm).
23. Remove the transmission jack and support stand.
24. Lower the vehicle and verify transfer case shift operation.

FRONT AXLE BEARING

REMOVAL & INSTALLATION

See Figures 15 and 16.

1. Before servicing the vehicle, refer to the Precautions Section.
2. Remove the front halfshafts.
3. On the right side, remove the axle shaft using a remover and a slide hammer.
4. Remove the shaft seal using a seal puller and a slide hammer.
5. Remove shaft bearing/bushing using a bearing puller and a slide hammer.

To install:

6. Position the bearing/bushing in the housing bore.
7. Install the shaft bearing/bushing using the large diameter end of a bearing installer and handle.

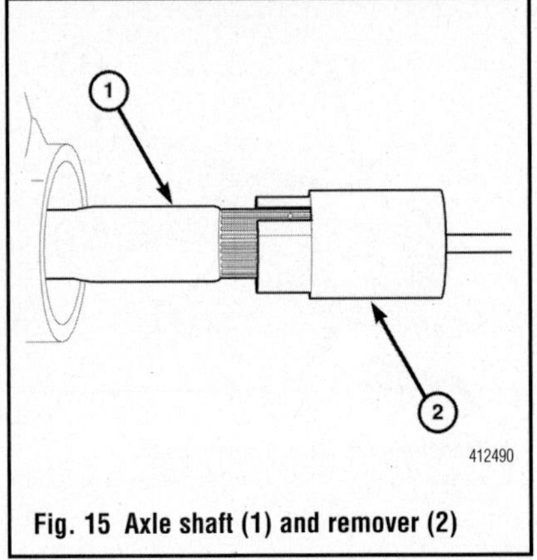

Fig. 15 Axle shaft (1) and remover (2)

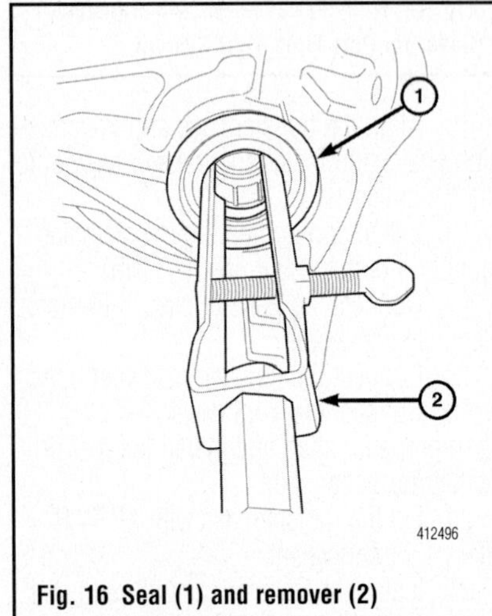

Fig. 16 Seal (1) and remover (2)

8. Drive the bearing/bushing in flush with housing bore.
9. Apply a light coat of lubricant on the lip of the shaft seal.
10. Install a new shaft seal in the axle using a seal installer.
11. Install the right axle shaft and the halfshafts.

FRONT DRIVESHAFT/ PROPELLER SHAFT

REMOVAL & INSTALLATION

See Figure 17.

1. Before servicing the vehicle, refer to the Precautions Section.
2. With vehicle in neutral, position vehicle on hoist.
3. Mark an installation reference line across the front propeller shaft CV joint and transfer case flange.
4. Mark an installation reference line across the front propeller shaft flange and the axle flange.
5. Remove the axle flange bolts.
6. Remove the CV joint bolts and retainers.

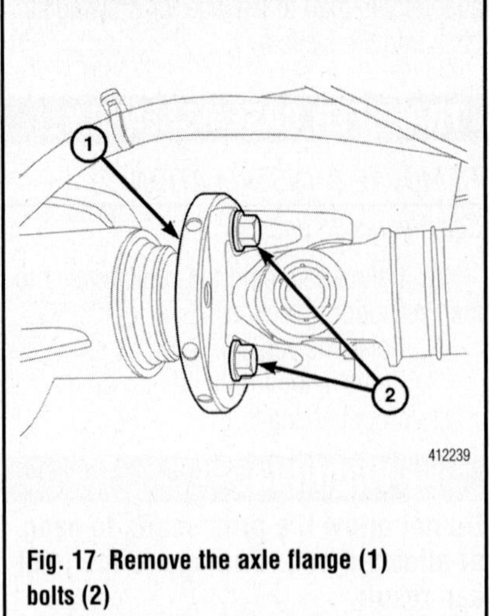

Fig. 17 Remove the axle flange (1) bolts (2)

7. Compress the propeller shaft enough to remove the shaft from the flanges.

To install:

8. Clean all propeller shaft bolts and apply Mopar® Lock and Seal Adhesive, or equivalent, to the threads before installation.
9. Compress the propeller shaft enough to install the shaft into the axle and transfer case flanges.
10. Align the reference marks on the transfer case flange front shaft CV joint.
11. Install the CV joint retainers and bolts. Tighten bolts to 22 ft. lbs. (30 Nm).
12. Align the reference marks on the front propeller shaft flange and axle flange.
13. Install the axle flange bolts and tighten to 80 ft. lbs. (108 Nm).

FRONT HALFSHAFT

REMOVAL & INSTALLATION

See Figure 18.

1. Before servicing the vehicle, refer to the Precautions Section.
2. With the vehicle in neutral, position the vehicle on a hoist.
3. Remove the brake caliper and rotor.
4. Remove the nut from halfshaft.
5. Remove the sensor from the hub bearing.
6. Remove the stabilizer link from the stabilizer bar.
7. Remove the tie rod end nut and the tie rod from steering knuckle.
8. Remove the clevis bracket lower nut and bolt.
9. Remove the upper ball joint nut and separate the upper control arm from the steering knuckle.
10. Pull out on the steering knuckle and push the halfshaft out of the hub bearing and knuckle.

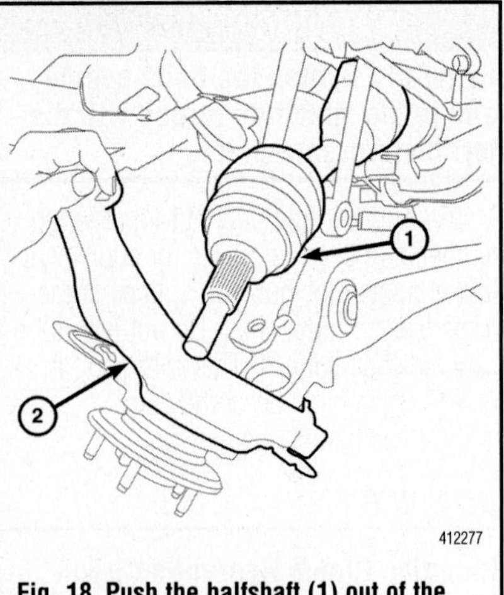

Fig. 18 Push the halfshaft (1) out of the hub bearing and knuckle (2)

11. Using a pry bar, remove the half shaft from the axle.

To install:

12. Apply a light coat of wheel bearing grease on the female splines of the inner C/V joint.
13. Clean the hub bearing bore and apply a light coat of wheel bearing grease.
14. Install the halfshaft in the axle and push firmly to engage the snap ring.
15. Pull out on the steering knuckle and push the halfshaft through the knuckle and hub bearing.
16. Install the upper control arm on the steering knuckle and tighten the ball joint nut to 30 ft. lbs. (41 Nm) plus an additional 90 degrees.
17. Align the clevis with the lower control arm. Install the lower clevis and tighten the nut to 110 ft. lbs. (150 Nm) with full vehicle weight.
18. Install the tie rod end in the steering knuckle and tighten the nut to 30 ft. lbs. (41 Nm) plus an additional 90 degrees.
19. Install the stabilizer bar link and tie rod end.
20. Install the halfshaft hub nut and tighten to 100 ft. lbs. (136 Nm).

FRONT PINION SEAL

REMOVAL & INSTALLATION

See Figure 19.

1. Before servicing the vehicle, refer to the Precautions Section.
2. With the vehicle in neutral, position the vehicle on hoist.
3. Remove the brake calipers and rotors.

4. Remove the driveshaft/propeller shaft.

5. Rotate the pinion gear several times and verify the pinion rotates smoothly.

6. Record the torque to rotate the pinion gear with an inch pound torque wrench.

7. Using a short piece of pipe and a wrench, hold the pinion flange and remove the pinion nut.

8. Mark a line on the pinion shaft and flange for installation reference.

9. Remove the pinion flange using a puller and a flange holder.

10. Remove the pinion seal with a seal puller.

To install:

11. Apply a light coating of gear lubricant on the lip of the pinion seal. Install the pinion seal with a seal installer and handle.

12. Position the flange on the pinion shaft with the reference marks aligned.

13. Install the pinion flange with a flange installer and screw.

14. Install a NEW nut on the pinion gear. Hold the pinion flange with a flange holder and tighten the nut to 160 ft. lbs. (217 Nm).

**** WARNING**

Do not exceed the minimum tightening torque.

15. Rotate the pinion several times and verify the pinion rotates smoothly.

16. Measure the torque to rotate the pinion gear with an inch pound torque wrench. Rotating torque should be equal to the reading recorded during removal plus 5 inch lbs. (0.56 Nm). If rotating torque is low, tighten the pinion nut in 5 ft. lb. (7 Nm) increments until proper rotating torque is achieved.

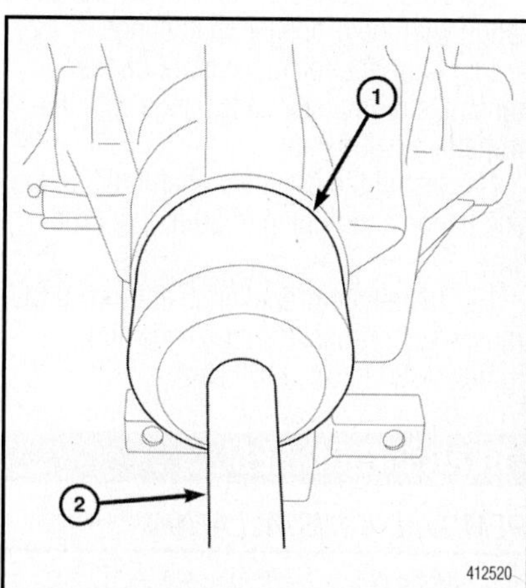

Fig. 19 Install the pinion seal with a seal installer (1) and handle (2)

**** WARNING**

If maximum tightening torque is reached [260 ft. lbs. (352 Nm)] prior to reaching required rotating torque, the collapsible spacer may have been damaged. Never loosen the pinion nut to decrease pinion rotating torque and never exceed specified preload torque. Failure to follow these instructions will result in damage.

17. Install the brake rotors, calipers and driveshaft/propeller shaft.

18. Fill the differential with gear lubricant.

REAR AXLE HOUSING

REMOVAL & INSTALLATION

See Figure 20.

1. Before servicing the vehicle, refer to the Precautions Section.

2. With the vehicle in neutral, position the vehicle on a hoist.

3. Position a lift/jack under the axle and secure the axle.

4. Mark the axle pinion flange and the propeller shaft flange for installation reference.

5. Remove the propeller shaft and suspend it under the vehicle.

6. Remove the brake sensor from the axle and remove the calipers, rotors and cables.

➡The parking brake is self-adjusting, and the cables must be locked out before removal.

7. Remove the track bar bolt from the axle bracket.

8. Remove the vent hose from the axle shaft tube.

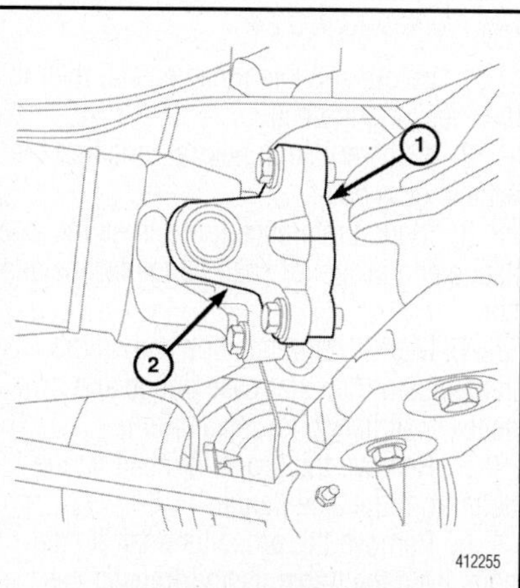

Fig. 20 Matchmark the axle pinion flange (1) and propeller shaft flange (2)

9. Remove the stabilizer bar axle bracket.

10. Remove the shock absorbers from the axle brackets.

11. Remove the upper control arm nuts and bolts from the axle brackets.

12. Lower the axle enough to remove the coil springs and spring insulators.

13. Remove the lower control arm mounting bolts from the axle brackets.

14. Lower and remove the axle.

To install:

**** WARNING**

The weight of the vehicle must be supported by the springs before the control arms and track bar are tightened. Failure to follow these instructions will cause premature bushing failure.

15. Raise the axle under the vehicle.

16. Install the lower control arms onto the axle brackets. Loosely install the mounting bolts and nuts.

17. Install the coil spring isolators and springs.

18. Raise the axle up until the springs are seated.

19. Install the upper control arms into the axle brackets. Loosely install the mounting bolts and nuts.

20. Install the shock absorbers to the axle brackets. Install the shock nuts/bolts and tighten to 85 ft. lbs. (115 Nm).

21. Install the stabilizer bar and clamps on the axle. Tighten the clamp bolts to 35 ft. lbs. (47 Nm).

22. Install the vent hose to the axle shaft tube.

23. Install the track bar to the axle bracket. Loosely install the track bar bolt.

24. Install the brake rotors, calipers and brake sensor on the axle.

25. Install the parking brake cables.

26. Align the reference marks and install the propeller shaft with pinion flange.

27. Clean all propeller shaft bolts and apply Mopar Lock and Seal Adhesive or equivalent to the threads.

28. Install the propeller shaft bolts and tighten to 80 ft. lbs. (108 Nm).

29. Install the wheels and tires.

30. Remove the lifting device from the axle and lower the vehicle.

31. Tighten the upper control arm nuts to 70 ft. lbs. (95 Nm), the lower control arm nuts to 150 ft. lbs. (203 Nm), and the track bar bolts to 130 ft. lbs. (176 Nm).

REAR AXLE SHAFT, BEARING & SEAL

REMOVAL & INSTALLATION

See Figures 21 and 22.

1. Before servicing the vehicle, refer to the Precautions Section.
2. With the vehicle in neutral, position the vehicle on hoist.
3. Remove the rear brake components.
4. Remove the wheel speed sensor.
5. Remove the differential housing cover and drain the lubricant.
6. Rotate the differential case so the pinion mate shaft lock screw is accessible. Remove the pinion mate shaft lock screw from the differential case.
7. Remove the pinion mate shaft from the differential case.
8. Push the axle shaft inward and remove the axle shaft C-lock from the axle shaft.
9. Remove the axle shaft from the side gear and axle tube.
10. Remove the axle shaft seal from axle tube using a seal puller.
11. Position the bearing receiver on the axle tube.
12. Insert the bearing remover foot through the receiver and bearing.
13. Tighten the nut on the shaft to pull the bearing into the receiver.

To install:

14. Remove any old sealer/burrs from the axle tube.
15. Install the axle shaft bearing with the bearing installer and driver handle. Drive the bearing in until the tool contacts the axle tube.

➡Bearing is installed with the bearing part number against installer.

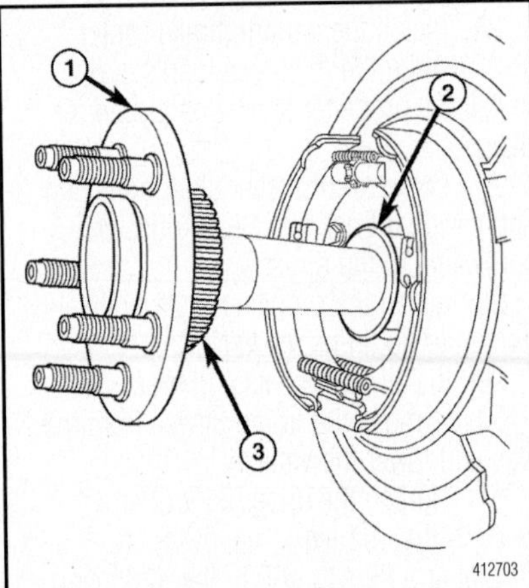

Fig. 21 Remove the axle shaft (1) from the side gear and axle tube (2)

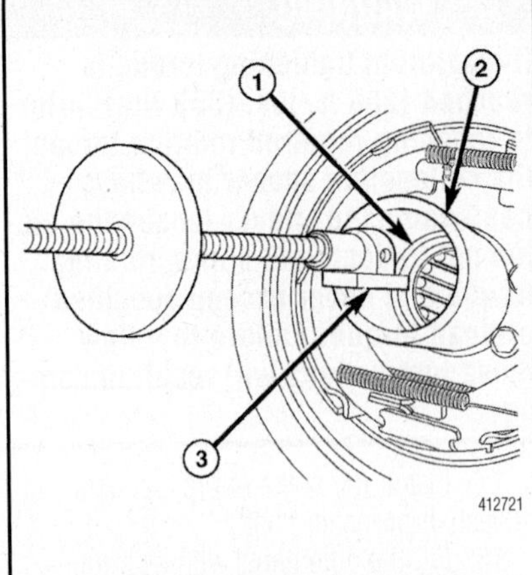

Fig. 22 Insert the bearing remover foot (3) through the receiver (2) and bearing (1)

16. Coat the new axle seal lip with axle lubricant. Install the seal with the seal installer and driver handle.
17. Install the axle shaft in the axle tube and engage into the side gear splines.
18. Lubricate the bearing bore and seal lip with gear lubricant.
19. Install the C-lock in the axle shaft end, and push the axle shaft outward to seat the C-lock in the side gear.
20. Install the pinion mate shaft into the differential case and through the thrust washers and differential pinions.
21. Align the hole in the shaft with the hole in the differential case and install the lock screw with Mopar® Lock and Seal or equivalent on the threads. Tighten the lock screw to 19 ft. lbs. (26 Nm).
22. Install the differential cover.
23. Install the rear brake components.

REAR DRIVESHAFT/ PROPELLER SHAFT

REMOVAL & INSTALLATION

See Figures 23 and 24.

1. Before servicing the vehicle, refer to the Precautions Section.
2. With vehicle in neutral, position the vehicle on a hoist.
3. Mark a reference line across the axle flange and propeller shaft flange for installation.
4. Mark a reference line across the transmission/transfer case flange and propeller shaft flange for installation.
5. Remove the propeller shaft flange bolts from the axle flange.
6. Remove the propeller shaft flange bolts from the transmission/transfer case flange.
7. Remove the propeller shaft.

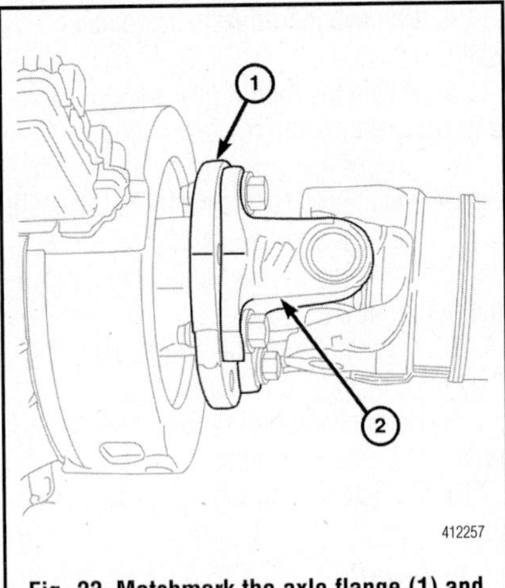

Fig. 23 Matchmark the axle flange (1) and propeller shaft flange (2)

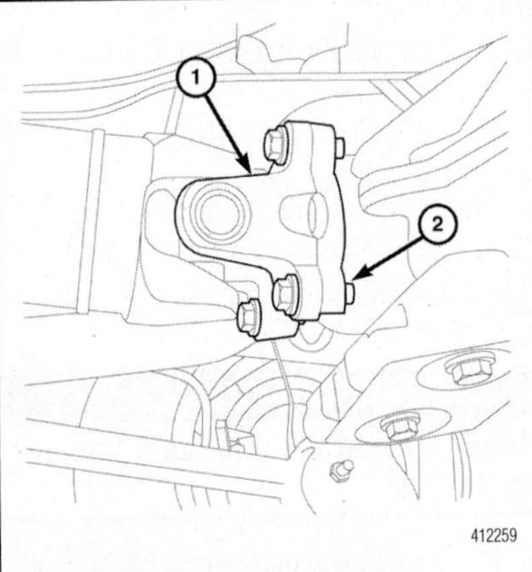

Fig. 24 Matchmark the transmission/transfer case flange (1) and propeller shaft flange (2)

To install:

8. Clean all the propeller shaft bolts and apply Mopar® Lock and Seal Adhesive or equivalent to the threads before installation.
9. Install the propeller shaft.
10. Align the reference mark on the axle flange with the propeller shaft flange.
11. Align the reference mark on the transmission/transfer case flange with the propeller shaft flange.
12. Install the propeller shaft bolts in the axle flange and tighten to 80 ft. lbs. (108 Nm).
13. Install the propeller shaft bolts in the transmission/transfer case flange and tighten to 80 ft. lbs. (108 Nm).

REAR PINION SEAL

REMOVAL & INSTALLATION

See Figure 25.

1. Before servicing the vehicle, refer to the Precautions Section.

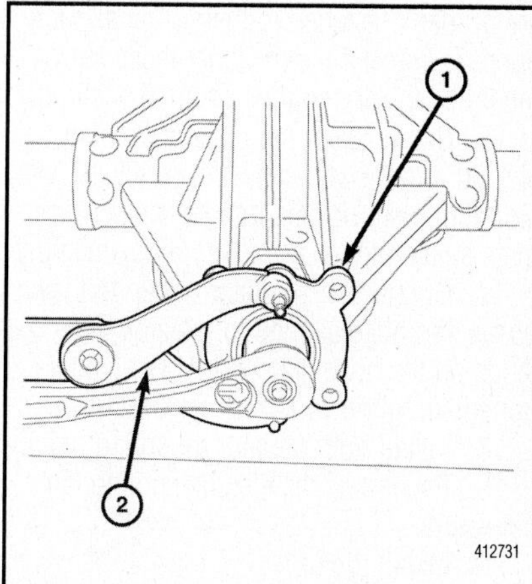

Fig. 25 Hold the pinion flange (1) with a holding tool (2)

2. With the vehicle in neutral, position the vehicle on a hoist.
3. Remove wheel and tire assemblies.
4. Mark a reference line across the axle flange and propeller shaft flange.
5. Remove the companion flange bolts and remove the propeller shaft.
6. Remove the brake calipers and rotors to prevent any drag.
7. Rotate the companion flange three or four times and verify flange rotates smoothly.
8. Rotate the pinion gear with an inch pound torque wrench, and record the torque for installation reference.
9. Hold the pinion flange with a holding tool and remove the pinion nut.
10. Mark a line across the pinion shaft and flange for installation reference.
11. Remove the pinion flange with flange puller.
12. Remove pinion seal with a seal puller.

To install:

13. Apply a light coating of gear lubricant on the lip of pinion seal.
14. Install a new pinion seal with a seal driver and handle.
15. Align the reference marks and install the flange on the pinion shaft.
16. Install the flange with flange installer.
17. Install a new pinion nut. Hold the flange with a holding tool, and tighten the pinion nut to 210 ft. lbs. (285 Nm). Rotate the pinion several revolutions to ensure the bearing rollers are seated.

⁂ WARNING

Do not exceed the minimum tightening torque of 210 ft. lbs. (285 Nm) while installing pinion nut at this point.

18. Rotate the pinion with an inch pound torque wrench, and measure the torque. Rotating torque should be equal to the reading recorded during removal plus 5 inch lbs. (0.56 Nm). If rotating torque is low, tighten the pinion nut in 5 ft. lbs. (6.8 Nm) increments until proper rotating torque is achieved.

⁂ WARNING

Never loosen the pinion nut to decrease pinion bearing rotating torque. If rotating torque is exceeded, a new collapsible spacer must be installed. Failure to follow these instructions will result in damage to the axle.

19. Align the reference marks and install the propeller shaft with axle flange.
20. Install the rear brake components.
21. Install the wheel and tire assemblies.

ENGINE COOLING

ENGINE FAN

REMOVAL & INSTALLATION

Electric Fan

See Figure 26.

⁂ CAUTION

If the fan blade is bent, warped, cracked or damaged in any way, it must be replaced only with a replacement fan blade. Do not attempt to repair a damaged fan blade.

➡For 3.7L Heavy Duty/Max Cool/Trailer Tow cooling package, the viscous fan cannot be removed separate from the shroud. Both fan and shroud must be removed together.

1. Before servicing the vehicle, refer to the Precautions Section.
2. Disconnect the negative battery cable.
3. Remove the combination coolant recovery/washer fluid bottle.
4. Remove the viscous fan from the water pump (if equipped).
5. Disengage the radiator hose retainer from the electric fan shroud.
6. Remove the transmission cooling line retainer bolt from the electric fan shroud.
7. Disconnect the electric fan connector from the electric fan shroud.
8. Remove the two bolts and lift the electric fan shroud from the vehicle.

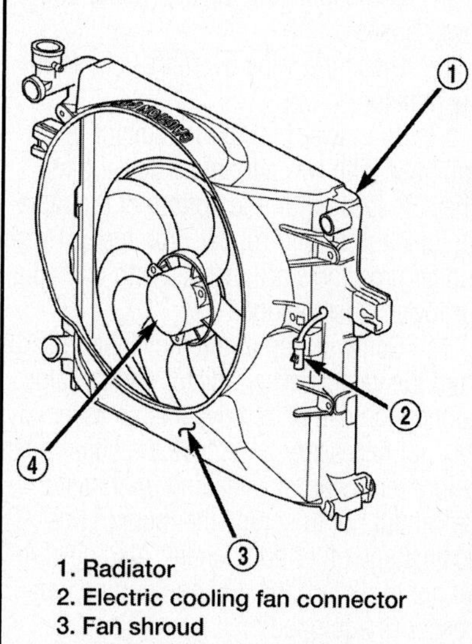

Fig. 26 Engine fan

9. Remove the cooling fan from the shroud.

To install:

10. Install the cooling fan to the shroud. Tighten the fan shroud-to-radiator bolts to 80 inch lbs. (9 Nm).
11. Install the fan shroud assembly into the vehicle.
12. Install the fan shroud-to-radiator mounting bolts. Tighten the bolts to 80 inch lbs. (9 Nm).
13. Connect the fan motor wire connector to harness connector and attach connector to shroud.
14. Install the radiator hose retainer to the electric fan shroud.
15. Install the transmission cooling line retainer bolt to the electric fan shroud.
16. Install the viscous fan drive (if equipped).
17. Install the combination coolant recovery/washer fluid bottle.
18. Connect the battery negative cable.
19. Start the engine and check fan operation.

Viscous Fan

See Figure 27.

1. Before servicing the vehicle, refer to the Precautions Section.

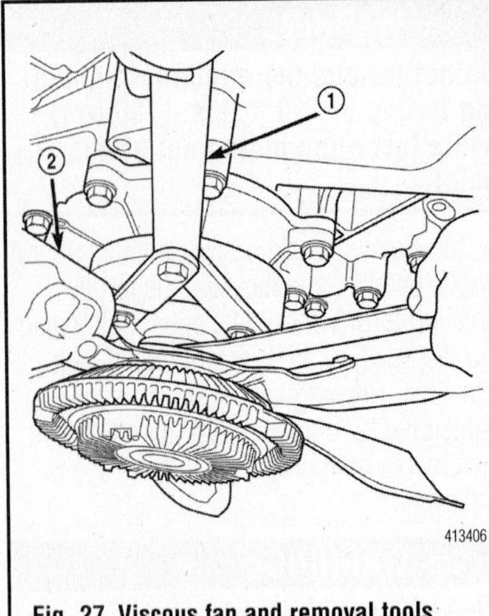

Fig. 27 Viscous fan and removal tools

2. Disconnect the negative battery cable.
3. Partially drain the cooling system.
4. Remove the upper radiator hose.
5. Remove the air filter housing.
6. Using a Tool 6958 and adapter pins 8346, remove the fan/viscous fan drive assembly from the water pump. Do not attempt to the remove fan/viscous fan drive assembly from the vehicle at this time.
7. Position the fan/fan drive assembly in the radiator shroud.
8. Remove the two shroud mounting screws.
9. Remove the radiator shroud and fan drive assembly.
10. After removing the fan blade/viscous fan drive assembly, do not place the viscous fan drive in the horizontal position. If stored horizontally, silicone fluid in the viscous fan drive could drain into its bearing assembly and contaminate lubricant.
11. Remove the four bolts securing fan blade assembly to viscous fan drive.

To install:

12. Install the fan blade assembly to the viscous fan drive. Tighten the bolts to 17 ft. lbs. (23 Nm).
13. Position the fan blade/viscous fan drive assembly into the radiator shroud.
14. Install the radiator shroud and fan drive assembly into the vehicle.
15. Install the fan shroud retaining screws. Tighten the screws to 50 inch lbs. (6 Nm).
16. Using an installation tool, install the fan blade/viscous fan drive assembly to the water pump shaft. Tighten the mounting nut to 37 ft. lbs. (50 Nm).
17. Install the upper radiator hose.
18. Fill the cooling system.
19. Connect the battery negative cable.

RADIATOR

REMOVAL & INSTALLATION

⁂ CAUTION

Do not remove the cylinder block drain plugs or loosen the radiator draincock with the system hot and under pressure. Serious burns from coolant can occur.

1. Before servicing the vehicle, refer to the Precautions Section. The air conditioning system (if equipped) is under a constant pressure, even with the engine off.
2. Disconnect the negative battery cable.
3. When removing the radiator or A/C condenser, note the location of all radiator-to-body and radiator-to-A/C condenser rubber air seals. These are used at the top, bottom and sides of the radiator and A/C condenser. To prevent overheating, these seals must be installed to their original positions.
4. Drain the coolant from the radiator.
5. Remove the combination coolant recovery/washer fluid reservoir assembly, if applicable.
6. Remove the front grill.
7. Remove the viscous cooling fan from the engine (if equipped).
8. Remove the two radiator mounting bolts.
9. Disconnect the electric cooling fan connector.
10. Disconnect the power steering cooler line from the cooler.
11. Disconnect the radiator upper and lower hoses.
12. Disconnect the overflow hose from the radiator.
13. The lower part of the radiator is equipped with two alignment dowel pins. They are located on the bottom of the radiator tank and fit into rubber grommets. These rubber grommets are pressed into the radiator lower crossmember.
14. Gently lift up and remove the radiator from the vehicle. The radiator and radiator cooling fan can be removed as an assembly. It is not necessary to remove the cooling fan before removing or installing the radiator. Be careful not to scrape the radiator fins against any other component. Also be careful not to disturb the air conditioning condenser (if equipped).

To install:

15. Before installing the radiator or A/C condenser, be sure the radiator-to-body and radiator-to-A/C condenser rubber air seals are properly fastened to their original positions. To prevent overheating, these seals must be installed to their original positions
16. Gently lower the radiator and fan shroud into the vehicle. Guide the two radiator alignment dowels into the rubber grommets located in lower radiator crossmember.
17. Connect the radiator upper and lower hoses and hose clamps to radiator. The tangs on the hose clamps MUST be positioned straight down.
18. Install both radiator mounting bolts.
19. Reconnect the electric cooling fan connector.
20. Install the grill.
21. Reinstall the viscous cooling fan to the engine (if equipped).
22. Rotate the fan blades (by hand) and check for interference at the fan shroud.
23. Install the combination coolant recovery/washer fluid reservoir assembly, if applicable.
24. Install the coolant reserve/overflow tank hose at the radiator.
25. Refill the cooling system.
26. Connect the negative battery cable.
27. Start the engine and check for leaks.

THERMOSTAT

REMOVAL & INSTALLATION

3.7L Engines

See Figure 28.

1. Before servicing the vehicle, refer to the Precautions Section.
2. Disconnect the negative battery cable.
3. Drain the cooling system.
4. Raise the vehicle on hoist.
5. Remove the splash shield.
6. Remove the lower radiator hose clamp and the lower radiator hose at thermostat housing.
7. Remove the mounting bolts, thermostat housing and thermostat.

To install:

8. Clean the mating areas of the timing chain cover and thermostat housing.
9. Install the thermostat (spring side down) into the recessed machined groove on the housing assembly. Make sure the rubber seal locating tab is positioned in the corresponding notch in the housing.
10. Position the thermostat housing on the timing chain cover.
11. Install the two housing-to-timing chain cover bolts and tighten to 105 inch lbs. (12 Nm).
12. Install the lower radiator hose on the thermostat housing.

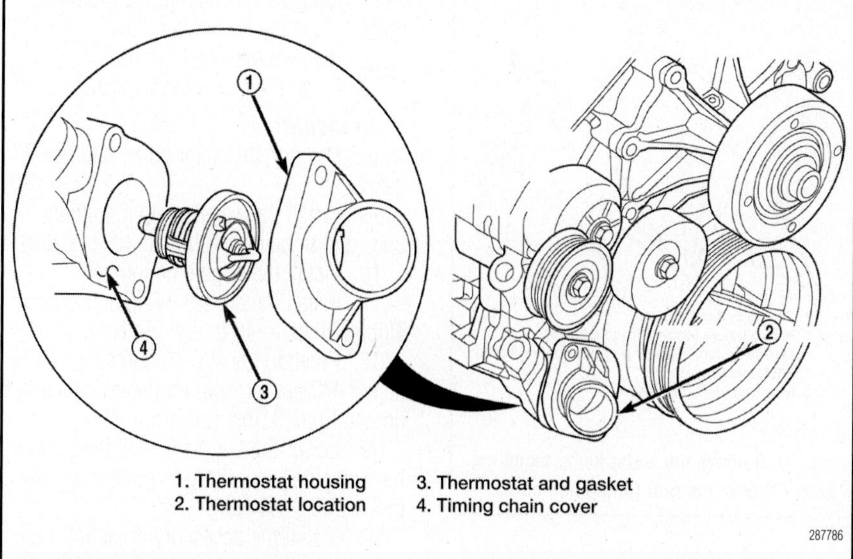

Fig. 28 Thermostat—3.7L engine

13. Install the splash shield.
14. Lower the vehicle.
15. Fill the cooling system.
16. Connect the negative battery cable to battery.
17. Start the engine and check for leaks.

4.0L Engines

See Figure 29.

1. Before servicing the vehicle, refer to the Precautions Section.
2. Disconnect the negative battery cable.
3. Drain the cooling system.
4. Remove the air filter housing.
5. Remove the upper intake manifold .
6. Remove the radiator tube mounting nuts.
7. Remove the radiator hose at the thermostat housing.
8. Remove thermostat housing bolts, thermostat housing and thermostat.
9. Clean the thermostat housing mating surface on the lower intake manifold.

To install:

10. Make sure the jiggle pin is at the 12 O'clock position. Position the thermostat and thermostat housing onto the lower intake manifold.
11. Install the thermostat housing bolts and tighten to 25 ft. lbs. (35 Nm).
12. Install the upper radiator hose onto the thermostat housing.
13. Position the upper radiator hose tube, install the mounting nuts and tighten to 85 inch lbs. (9 Nm).
14. Install the upper intake manifold.
15. Install the air cleaner housing.
16. Fill the cooling system.

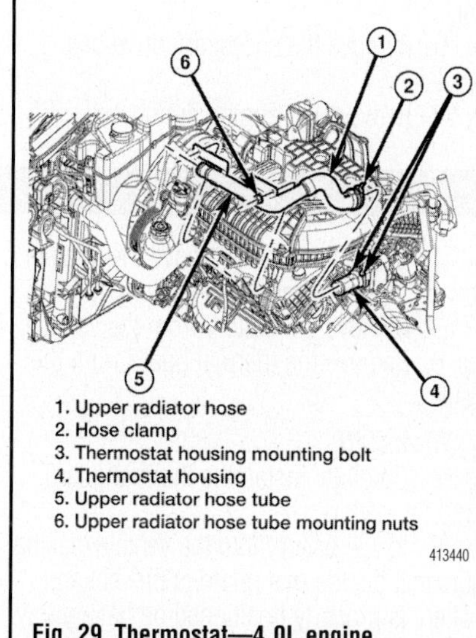

Fig. 29 Thermostat—4.0L engine

WATER PUMP

REMOVAL & INSTALLATION

3.7L Engines

See Figure 30.

1. Before servicing the vehicle, refer to the Precautions Section.
2. Drain the cooling system.
3. Disconnect the negative battery cable.
4. If the water pump is being replaced, do not unbolt the fan blade assembly from the thermal viscous fan drive.
5. Remove the two fan shroud-to-radiator screws. Disconnect the coolant overflow hose.
6. Remove the upper fan shroud and fan blade/viscous fan drive assembly from the vehicle. After removing the fan blade/viscous fan drive assembly, do NOT place the fan drive in a horizontal position.

WARNING

If stored horizontally, silicone fluid in viscous fan drive could drain into its bearing assembly and contaminate lubricant.

7. Remove the accessory drive belt.
8. Remove the lower radiator hose clamp and remove the lower hose at the water pump.
9. Remove the seven water pump mounting bolts and one stud bolt.

WARNING

Do not pry on the water pump at the timing chain case/cover. The machined surfaces may be damaged, resulting in leaks.

10. Remove the water pump and gasket. Discard the gasket.

To install:

11. Clean the gasket mating surfaces.
12. Using a new gasket, position the water pump onto the engine timing chain cover. Tighten the water pump mounting bolts in the sequence shown to 40 ft. lbs. (54 Nm).
13. Spin the water pump to be sure that the pump impeller does not rub against the timing chain cover.
14. Connect the radiator lower hose to the water pump.
15. Install the accessory drive belt.
16. Position the upper fan shroud and fan blade/viscous fan drive assembly.

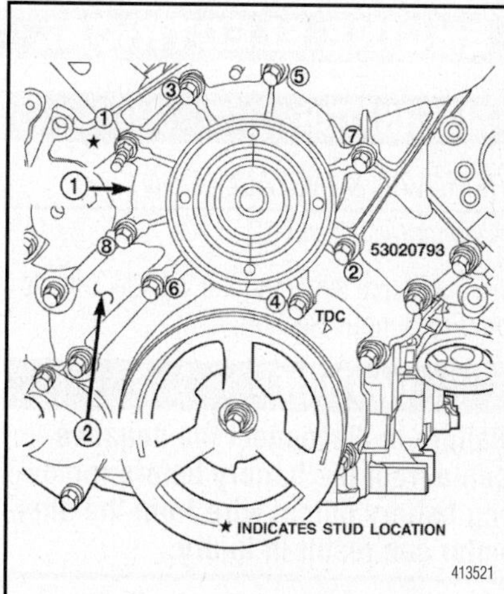

Fig. 30 Water pump (1) positioned on the timing chain cover (2), bolt tightening sequence

17. Be sure the upper and lower portions of the fan shroud are firmly connected. All air must flow through the radiator.
18. Install the two fan shroud-to-radiator screws.
19. Be sure of at least 1.0 inch (25 mm) between the tips of fan blades and the fan shroud.
20. Evacuate the air and refill the cooling system.
21. Connect the negative battery cable.
22. Check the cooling system for leaks

4.0L Engines

See Figure 31.

1. Before servicing the vehicle, refer to the Precautions Section.
2. Drain the cooling system.
3. Disconnect the negative battery cable.
4. Remove the coolant recovery container.
5. Remove the viscous radiator fan.
6. Remove the right-hand engine mount through bolt.
7. Raise the engine assembly.

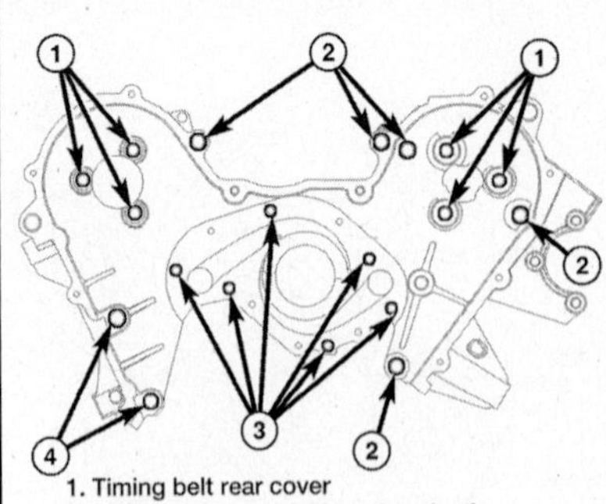

Fig. 31 Remove the water pump mounting bolts (3) from the rear timing belt cover

8. Carefully unbolt the air conditioning compressor from the front of engine. Do not disconnect any A/C hoses from the compressor. Temporarily support the compressor.
9. Remove the accessory drive belt bracket.
10. Remove the engine timing belt.
11. Remove the water pump mounting bolts.
12. Remove the water pump.
13. Clean the mounting surface.

To install:

14. Position the water pump and new gasket.
15. Install the water pump mounting bolts and tighten to 105 inch lbs. (12 Nm).
16. Install the engine timing belt.
17. Install the accessory drive bracket. Tighten bolts to 40 ft. lbs. (54 Nm).
18. Position the A/C compressor and install A/C compressor mounting nuts and tighten to 21 ft. lbs. (28 Nm).
19. Lower the engine. Install the right-hand engine mount through bolt and tighten to 40 ft. lbs. (54 Nm).
20. Install the accessory drive belt.
21. Install the viscous radiator fan.
22. Install the coolant recover container.
23. Install the air filter assembly.
24. Connect the negative battery cable.
25. Evacuate the air and refill the cooling system.
26. Check the cooling system for leaks.

ENGINE ELECTRICAL — BATTERY SYSTEM

BATTERY

REMOVAL & INSTALLATION

1. Before servicing the vehicle, refer to the Precautions Section.
2. Loosen the pinch clamp bolt and disconnect and isolate the battery negative cable.
3. Loosen the pinch clamp bolt and disconnect the battery positive cable.
4. Loosen bolt and remove the retainer that holds the battery to the battery tray.
5. Remove the battery from the vehicle.
6. Remove the thermal guard from the battery.

To install:

7. Carefully install the thermal guard onto the battery.
8. Install battery into the vehicle making sure that the thermal guard is present and battery is properly positioned on battery tray.
9. Install the battery hold down retainer and bolt making sure that it is properly positioned. Tighten the hold down bolt to 62 inch lbs. (7 Nm).
10. Connect the battery positive cable and tighten the pinch clamp nut to 45 inch lbs. (5 Nm).
11. Connect the battery negative cable and tighten the pinch clamp nut to 45 inch lbs. (5 Nm).
12. Verify proper vehicle operation.

ENGINE ELECTRICAL — CHARGING SYSTEM

ALTERNATOR

REMOVAL & INSTALLATION

See Figures 32 and 33.

1. Before servicing the vehicle, refer to the Precautions Section.

⁂ CAUTION

Failure to disconnect the negative cable from the battery before removing battery output wire from the alternator can result in injury.

⁂ WARNING

Never force a belt over a pulley rim using a screwdriver. The synthetic fiber of the belt can be damaged.

2. Disconnect and isolate the negative battery cable at the battery.
3. Remove the alternator drive belt.
4. Unsnap the plastic protective cover from the B+ mounting stud.
5. Remove the B+ terminal mounting nut at the top of the alternator.
6. Disconnect the field wire electrical connector at the rear of the alternator by pushing on the connector tab.
7. Remove the alternator mounting bolts.
8. Remove the alternator from vehicle.

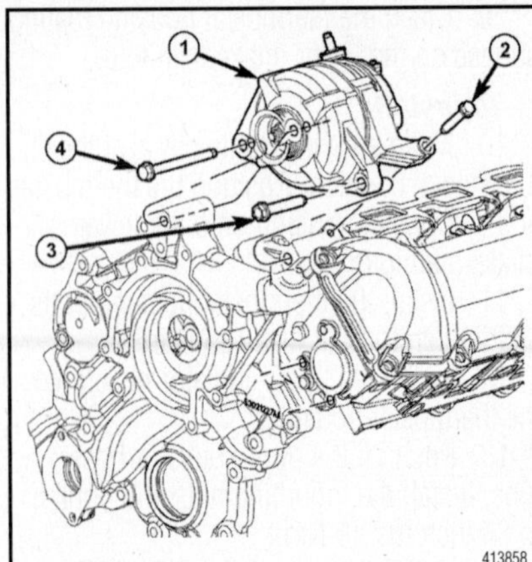

Fig. 32 Alternator (1) and mounting bolts (2, 3, 4)—3.7L engine

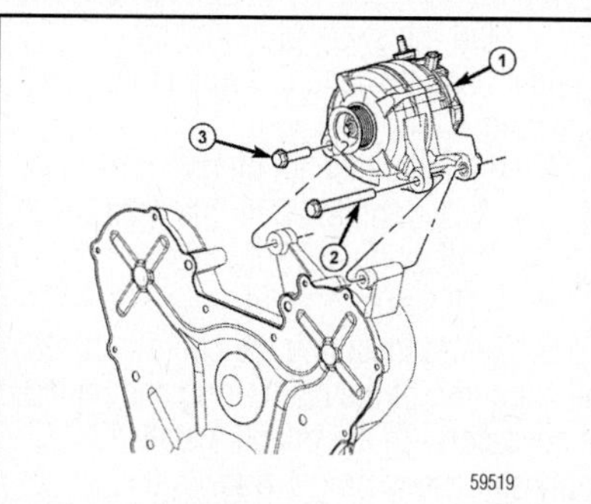

Fig. 33 Alternator (1) and mounting bolts (2, 3)—4.0L engine

To install:

9. Position the alternator to the engine and install the mounting bolts. Tighten:
- 3.7L engine: 2 horizontal mounting bolts: 42 ft. lbs. (57 Nm), vertical mounting bolt: 29 ft. lbs. (40 Nm)
- 4.0L engine: 2 mounting bolts: 42 ft. lbs. (57 Nm)

10. Snap the field wire connector into the rear of the alternator.
11. Install the B+ terminal and nut to the alternator mounting stud. Tighten the nut to 10 ft. lbs. (13 Nm).
12. Snap the plastic protective cover to the B+ terminal.
13. Install the drive belt.

**** WARNING**

The serpentine accessory drive belt MUST be routed correctly, or damage will occur.

14. Install the negative battery cable to the battery.

ENGINE ELECTRICAL

IGNITION SYSTEM

FIRING ORDER

3.7L Engine Firing Order: 1–6–5–4–3–2
4.0L Engine Firing Order: 1–2–3–4–5–6

IGNITION COIL

REMOVAL & INSTALLATION

3.7L Engines

1. Before servicing the vehicle, refer to the Precautions Section.

➡An ignition coil with a spark plug wire attached is used for two cylinders. The three coils fit into machined holes in the cylinder head for cylinders 1, 3, and 5. A mounting stud/nut secures each coil to the top of the intake manifold . The bottom of the coil is equipped with a rubber boot to seal the spark plug to the coil. Inside each rubber boot is a spring. The spring is used for a mechanical contact between the coil and the top of the spark plug. These rubber boots and springs are a permanent part of the coil and are not serviced separately. An O-ring is used to seal the coil at the opening into the cylinder head.

2. Depending on which coil is being removed, the throttle body air intake tube or intake box may need to be removed to gain access to the coil.
3. Disconnect the electrical connector from the coil by pushing downward on the release lock on top of connector and pull the connector from coil.
4. Disconnect spark plug wire from coil.
5. Clean the area at the base of the coil with compressed air before removal.
6. Remove the coil mounting bolt.
7. Carefully pull up the coil from the cylinder head opening with a slight twisting action.
8. Remove the coil from the vehicle.

To install:

9. Using compressed air, blow out any dirt or contaminants from around the top of the spark plug.
10. Check the condition of the coil rubber boot. To aid in coil installation, apply silicone based grease (such as Mopar® Dielectric Grease No. J8126688) into the spark plug end of the rubber boot and to the top of the spark plug.
11. Position the ignition coil assembly into the cylinder head opening. Using a twisting action, push the ignition coil assembly onto the spark plug.
12. Install the coil mounting bolt. Tighten to 70 inch lbs. (8 Nm).
13. Connect the electrical connector to the ignition coil assembly by snapping into position.
14. Install the spark plug wires.
15. If necessary, install the throttle body air intake tube, or intake air box.

4.0L Engines

See Figure 34.

1. Before servicing the vehicle, refer to the Precautions Section.
2. Remove the upper intake manifold including EGR tube, PCV, purge and power brake booster vacuum hoses.
3. Unlock and disconnect the electrical connector from the ignition coil.
4. Clean the area at the base of the coil with compressed air before removal.
5. Remove the coil mounting bolt.
6. Carefully pull up the coil from the cylinder head opening with a slight twisting action.
7. Remove the coil from the engine.

To install:

8. Install the ignition coil into the cylinder head.

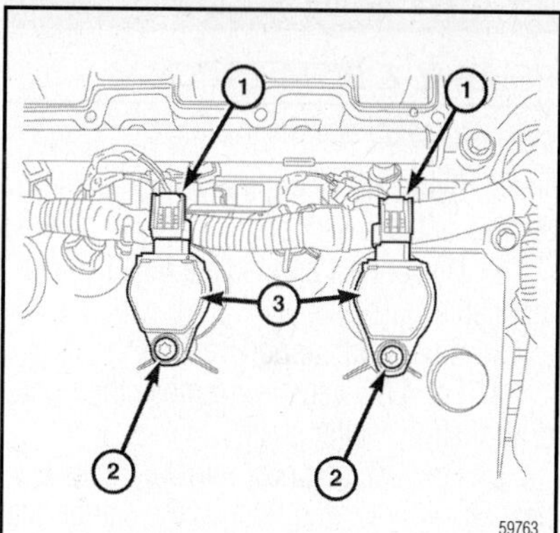

Fig. 34 Ignition coil electrical connector (1), ignition coil (3), and coil mounting bolt (2)—4.0L engine

9. Install and tighten the coil mounting bolt to 60 inch lbs. (7 Nm).
10. Connect and lock the electrical connector.
11. Install the upper intake manifold, EGR tube, PCV, purge and power brake booster vacuum hoses.
12. Connect the negative battery cable. Tighten the nut to 40 inch lbs. (5 Nm).

IGNITION TIMING

ADJUSTMENT

The ignition timing is controlled by the Engine Control Module (ECM). No adjustment is necessary or possible.

SPARK PLUGS

REMOVAL & INSTALLATION

1. Before servicing the vehicle, refer to the Precautions Section.

➡Each individual spark plug is located under each ignition coil. Each individual ignition coil must be removed to gain access to each spark plug.

2. Remove the necessary air filter tubing at the throttle body.

3. Prior to removing the ignition coil, spray compressed air around the coil base at the cylinder head.

4. Prior to removing the spark plug, spray compressed air into the cylinder head opening. This will help prevent foreign material from entering the combustion chamber.

5. Remove the spark plug from the cylinder head using a quality socket with a rubber or foam insert. Also check condition of the ignition coil O-ring and replace as necessary.

6. Inspect the spark plug condition.

To install:

✻✻ WARNING

When installing the spark plugs into the cylinder head spark plug wells, be sure the plugs do not drop into the plug wells as electrodes can be damaged. Do not over tighten the spark plugs.

7. Start the spark plug into the cylinder head by hand to avoid cross threading.

8. Tighten the spark plugs:

- 3.7L engine: 20 ft. lbs. (27 Nm)
- 4.0L engine: 13 ft. lbs. (18 Nm)

9. Before installing the coil(s), check the condition of the coil O-ring and replace as necessary. To aid in coil installation, apply silicone to coil O-ring.

10. Install the ignition coil(s).

ENGINE ELECTRICAL

STARTING SYSTEM

STARTER

REMOVAL & INSTALLATION

See Figures 35 and 36.

1. Before servicing the vehicle, refer to the Precautions Section.

2. Disconnect and isolate negative battery cable.

3. Raise and support vehicle.

4. For 4WD vehicles, remove the front driveshaft/propeller shaft.

5. For 3.7L engines, remove the two heat shield bolts and remove the starter heat shield.

6. Remove the solenoid nut from the mounting stud.

7. After the nut has been removed, pull the battery cable from the mounting stud while removing the electrical connector from the solenoid terminal.

8. Remove the two starter mounting bolts.

9. Remove the starter assembly from the transmission.

10. For 4.0L engines, remove the plate from the transmission.

11. Rotate the starter assembly to allow removal from the vehicle.

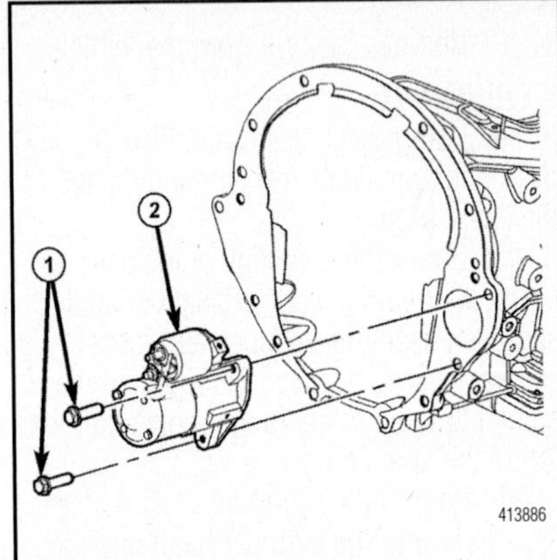

Fig. 35 Starter (2) and mounting bolts (1)—3.7L engine

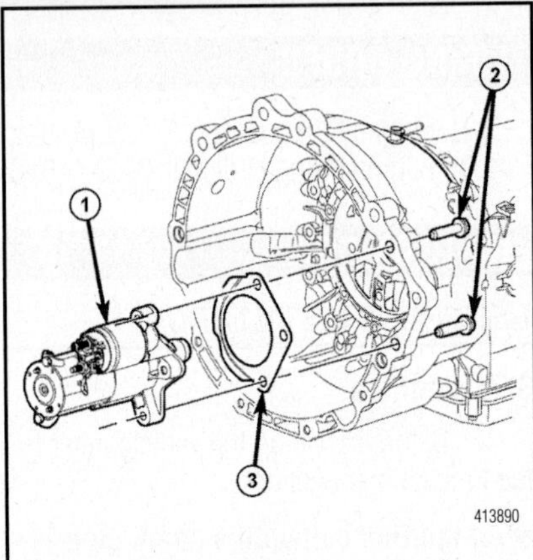

Fig. 36 Starter (1), plate (3), and mounting bolts (2)—4.0L engine

To install:

12. For 4.0L engines, install the plate to the transmission.

13. Rotate the starter assembly to allow positioning into the transmission.

14. Install the two starter mounting bolts and tighten to 40 ft. lbs. (54 Nm).

15. Position the battery cable assembly onto the stud while pushing the solenoid connector onto the solenoid terminal. Install the nut and tighten to 97 inch lbs. (11 Nm).

16. For 3.7L engines, install the starter heat shield and tighten the bolts to 53 inch lbs. (6 Nm).

17. Install the front driveshaft/propeller shaft, if applicable.

18. Lower the vehicle.

19. Connect the negative battery cable.

ENGINE MECHANICAL

➡**Disconnecting the negative battery cable may interfere with the functions of the on board computer systems and may require the computer to undergo a relearning process, once the negative battery cable is reconnected.**

ACCESSORY DRIVE BELTS

ACCESSORY BELT ROUTING

See Figures 37 and 38.

INSPECTION

Inspect the drive belt for signs of glazing or cracking. A glazed belt will be perfectly smooth from slippage, while a good belt will have a slight texture of fabric visible. Cracks will usually start at the inner edge of the belt and run outward. All worn or damaged drive belts should be replaced immediately.

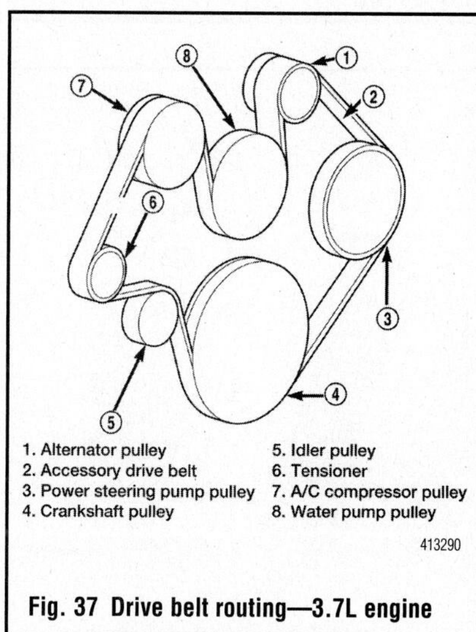

Fig. 37 Drive belt routing—3.7L engine

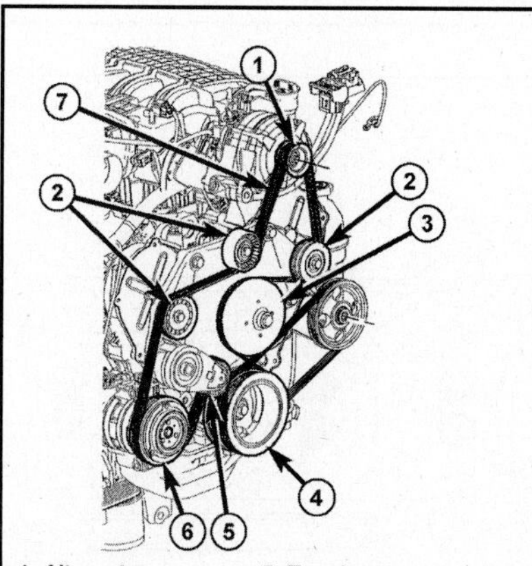

Fig. 38 Drive belt routing—4.0L engine

ADJUSTMENT

Tension is automatically adjusted by the belt tensioner.

REMOVAL & INSTALLATION

3.7L Engine

1. Before servicing the vehicle, refer to the Precautions Section.
2. Disconnect the negative battery cable.
3. Remove the combination washer reservoir/coolant recovery container.
4. Rotate the belt tensioner until it contacts its stop.
5. Remove the belt, then slowly rotate the tensioner into the free arm position.

To install:

6. Check the condition of all pulleys.

⁂ WARNING

When installing the serpentine accessory drive belt, the belt MUST be routed correctly. If not, the engine may overheat due to the water pump rotating in the wrong direction.

7. Install the new belt. Route the belt around all the pulleys except the idler pulley. Rotate the tensioner arm until it contacts its stop position. Route the belt around the idler and slowly let the tensioner rotate into the belt. Make sure the belt is seated onto all pulleys.
8. With the drive belt installed, inspect the belt wear indicator. On 3.7L engines, the gap between the tang and the housing stop must not exceed .94 in. (24 mm).
9. Install the combination washer reservoir/coolant recovery container.
10. Connect negative battery cable.

4.0L Engine

1. Before servicing the vehicle, refer to the Precautions Section.
2. Disconnect the negative battery cable.
3. Remove the combination coolant recovery/washer reservoir.
4. Insert a suitable square drive ratchet into the square hole on the belt tensioner arm.
5. Rotate the accessory drive belt tensioner clockwise to release the belt tension.
6. Remove the accessory drive belt.

To install:

➡**When installing the accessory drive belt onto the pulleys, make sure that the belt is properly routed and all V-grooves make proper contact with the pulleys.**

7. Rotate the tensioner clockwise and position the accessory drive belt over all pulleys.
8. Gently release the tensioner.
9. Install the combination coolant recovery/washer reservoir.
10. Connect negative battery cable.

AIR CLEANER

REMOVAL & INSTALLATION

4.0L Engine

1. Before servicing the vehicle, refer to the Precautions Section.
2. Disconnect the negative battery cable.
3. Disconnect the CCV hose at the element housing.
4. Loosen the two clamps; disengage and reposition the air inlet hose.
5. Pull the housing up and off of the three locating grommets.
6. Disengage the air inlet duct and remove the housing from the vehicle.

To install:

7. Align the housing with the air inlet duct and the locating grommets in the wheel housing.
8. Properly position the housing while engaging the air inlet duct. Lift up on the air inlet duct to engage the lock tabs.
9. Install the air inlet hose to the housing and throttle body. Tighten the clamps.
10. Connect the CCV hose to the housing.
11. Connect the negative battery cable.

FILTER/ELEMENT REPLACEMENT

3.7L Engine

➡**Housing removal is not necessary for filter (element) replacement.**

1. Before servicing the vehicle, refer to the Precautions Section.
2. Disconnect the negative battery cable.
3. Pry up the spring clips from the front of the housing cover (spring clips retain cover to housing).
4. Release the housing cover from the 4 tabs located on the rear of the housing, and remove the cover.

5. Remove the air cleaner filter (element) from the housing.

6. Clean the inside of the housing before replacing the filter.

To install:

7. Install the filter into housing.

8. Position the housing cover into the housing locating tabs.

9. Pry up the spring clips and lock the cover to the housing.

10. If any air filter, air resonator, air intake tubes or air filter housing clamps have been loosened or removed, tighten them to 40 inch lbs. (5 Nm).

11. Connect the negative battery cable.

4.0L Engine

1. Before servicing the vehicle, refer to the Precautions Section.

2. Disconnect the negative battery cable.

3. Release the housing cover latches.

4. Lift the cover and remove the air filter element.

To install:

5. Install the air filter element into the air box.

6. Position the cover onto the element housing and lock the front latches.

7. Connect the negative battery cable.

CAMSHAFT AND VALVE LIFTERS

INSPECTION

3.7L Engine

1. Inspect the camshaft bearing journals for wear or damage.

2. Inspect the cylinder head and check oil return holes.

3. Check both camshaft surfaces for wear or damage.

4. Check camshaft lobe height and replace if out of limit.

4.0L Engine

See Figure 39.

1. Inspect camshaft bearing journals (4) for damage and binding. If journals are binding, check the cylinder head for damage. Also check cylinder head oil holes for clogging.

2. Check the cam lobe (5) and bearing surfaces for abnormal wear and damage. Replace camshaft if defective.

3. Measure the lobe (5) actual wear and replace camshaft if out of limit. Standard value is 0.001 in. (0.0254 mm), wear limit is 0.010 in. (0.254 mm).

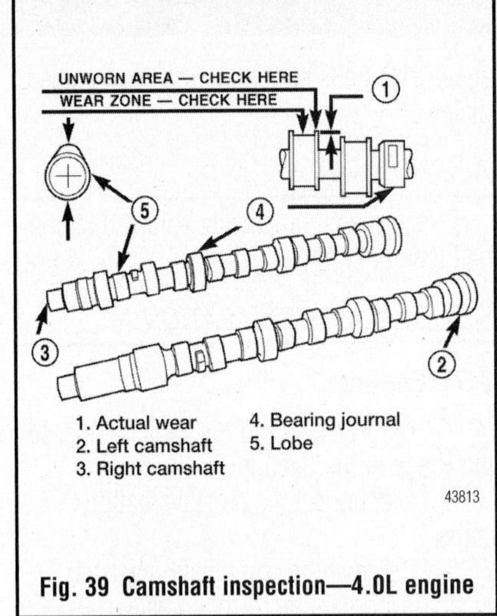

Fig. 39 Camshaft inspection—4.0L engine

➡If camshaft is replaced due to lobe wear or damage, always replace the rocker arms.

REMOVAL & INSTALLATION

3.7L Engine

See Figures 40 and 41.

1. Before servicing the vehicle, refer to the Precautions Section.

2. Disconnect the negative battery cable.

**** WARNING**

When the timing chain is removed and the cylinder heads are still installed, do not forcefully rotate the camshafts or crankshaft independently of each other. Severe valve and/or piston damage can occur.

**** WARNING**

When removing the cam sprocket, timing chains or camshaft, failure to use the Wedge Locking Tool will result in hydraulic tensioner ratchet over extension, requiring timing chain cover removal to reset the tensioner ratchet.

3. Remove the cylinder head cover.

4. Set No. 1 engine cylinder to TDC, camshaft sprocket V6 marks at the 12 o'clock position.

5. Matchmark one link on the secondary timing chain on both sides of the V6 mark on the camshaft sprocket to aid in installation.

**** WARNING**

Do not hold or pry on the camshaft target wheel for any reason. Severe damage will occur to the target wheel, resulting in a vehicle no start condition.

6. Loosen but DO NOT remove the camshaft sprocket retaining bolt. Leave the bolt snug against the sprocket.

7. The timing chain tensioners must be secured prior to removing the camshaft sprockets. Failure to secure tensioners will allow the tensioners to extend, requiring timing chain cover removal in order to reset tensioners.

8. Position the Wedge Locking Tool between the timing chain strands, tap the tool to securely wedge the timing chain against the tensioner arm and guide.

**** WARNING**

Do not force Locking Wedge past the narrowest point between the chain strands. Damage to the tensioners may occur.

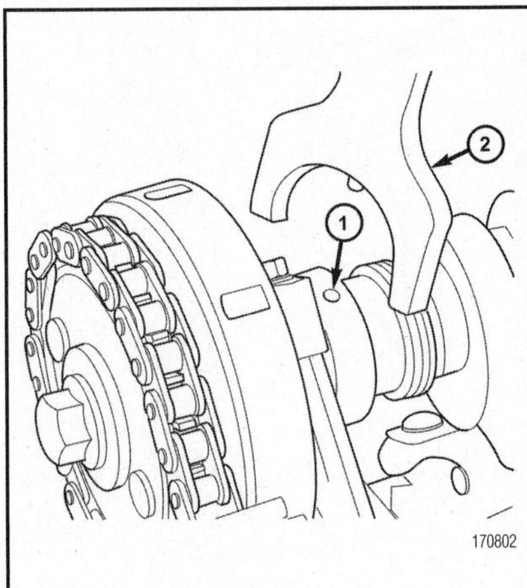

Fig. 40 Hold the camshaft (1) with the camshaft holder (2)

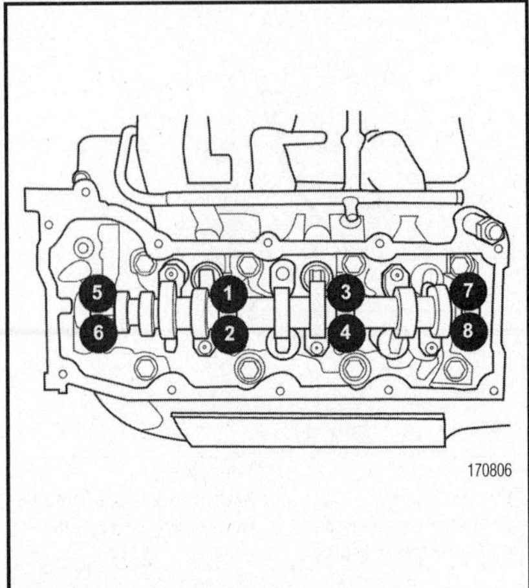

Fig. 41 Camshaft bearing cap bolt tightening sequence

9. Remove the camshaft position sensor.

10. Hold the camshaft with the camshaft holder (Special Tool 8428A or equivalent), while removing the camshaft sprocket bolt and sprocket.

11. Using the camshaft holder, gently allow the camshaft to rotate 5° until the camshaft is in the neutral position (no valve load).

12. Starting at the outside working inward, loosen the camshaft bearing cap retaining bolts ½ turn at a time. Repeat until all load is off the bearing caps.

⁂ WARNING

Do not stamp or strike the camshaft bearing caps. Severe damage will occur to the bearing caps.

13. When the camshaft is removed, the rocker arms may slide downward. Matchmark the rocker arms before removing the camshaft.

14. Remove the camshaft bearing caps and the camshaft.

To install:

15. Lubricate camshaft journals with clean engine oil.

16. Position the camshaft into the cylinder head. Position the left side camshaft so that the camshaft sprocket dowel is near the 1 o'clock position, This will place the camshaft at the neutral position, easing the installation of the camshaft bearing caps.

17. Install the camshaft bearing caps. Hand tighten the retaining bolts.

18. Caps should be installed so that the stamped numbers on the caps are in numerical order, (1 through 4) from the front to the rear of the engine. All caps should be installed so that the stamped arrows on the caps point toward the front of the engine.

19. Working in ½ turn increments, tighten the bearing cap retaining bolts in the sequence shown to 100 inch lbs. (11 Nm).

20. Position the camshaft drive gear into the timing chain, aligning the V6 mark between the two marked chain links (marked during removal).

21. Using the camshaft holding tool, rotate the camshaft until the camshaft sprocket dowel is aligned with the slot in the camshaft sprocket. Install the sprocket onto the camshaft.

22. Remove excess oil from the camshaft sprocket retaining bolt. Failure remove excess oil can cause bolt over-torque, resulting in bolt failure.

23. Install the camshaft sprocket retaining bolt and hand tighten.

24. Remove the tensioner wedge locking tool.

25. Using the wrench with adapter pins, tighten the camshaft sprocket retaining bolt to 90 ft. lbs. (122 Nm).

26. Install the cylinder head cover.

27. Connect the negative battery cable.

4.0L Engine

See Figure 42.

1. Before servicing the vehicle, refer to the Precautions Section.

➡**Camshafts are removed from the rear of each cylinder head.**

2. Remove the cylinder head.

⁂ WARNING

Care must be taken not to nick or scratch the journals when removing the camshaft.

3. Carefully remove the camshaft from the rear of the cylinder head.

To install:

4. Lubricate camshaft bearing journals, camshaft lobes and camshaft seal with clean engine oil and install camshaft into cylinder head.

5. Install the cylinder head.

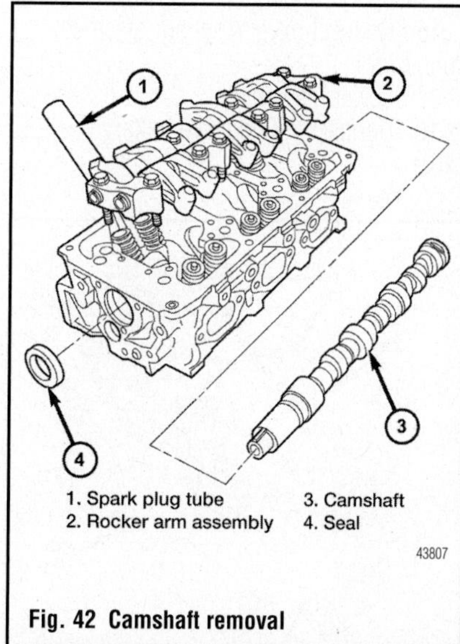

Fig. 42 Camshaft removal

CATALYTIC CONVERTER

REMOVAL & INSTALLATION

3.7L Engine

See Figure 43.

⁂ CAUTION

If torches are used when working on the exhaust system, do not allow the flame near the fuel lines or fuel tank.

1. Before servicing the vehicle, refer to the Precautions Section.

2. Disconnect the negative battery cable.

3. Raise and support the vehicle.

4. Saturate the bolts and nuts with heat valve lubricant. Allow 5 minutes for penetration.

5. Disconnect the oxygen sensor electrical connectors.

6. Remove the nuts from the front exhaust pipe and catalytic converter assembly to muffler flange.

7. Remove the bolts and flanged nuts at the manifold.

8. Lower the front exhaust pipe/catalytic converter assembly and slide out of the mount at the transmission (if equipped).

9. Remove the front exhaust pipe/catalytic converter assembly from the vehicle.

To install:

10. Position the front exhaust pipe and catalytic converter assembly into the mount at the transmission (if equipped) and onto the exhaust manifold flange connection.

11. Install the nuts at the front exhaust pipe and catalytic converter assembly to muffler flange. Do not tighten.

12. Position the exhaust pipe for proper clearance with the frame and underbody parts. A minimum clearance of 1.0 in. (25mm) is required.

13. Tighten the bolt at the exhaust manifold to 19 inch lbs. (27 Nm).

14. Tighten the front exhaust pipe and catalytic converter assembly to muffler flange nuts to 19 ft. lbs. (27 Nm).

15. Position the front pipe onto the exhaust manifold flange connection. Tighten the clamp to 95 inch lbs. (10 Nm).

16. Connect oxygen sensor electrical connectors.

17. Lower the vehicle.

18. Connect the negative battery cable.

19. Start the vehicle and inspect for exhaust leaks. Repair exhaust leaks as necessary.

20. Check the exhaust system for contact with the body panels. Make adjustments, if necessary.

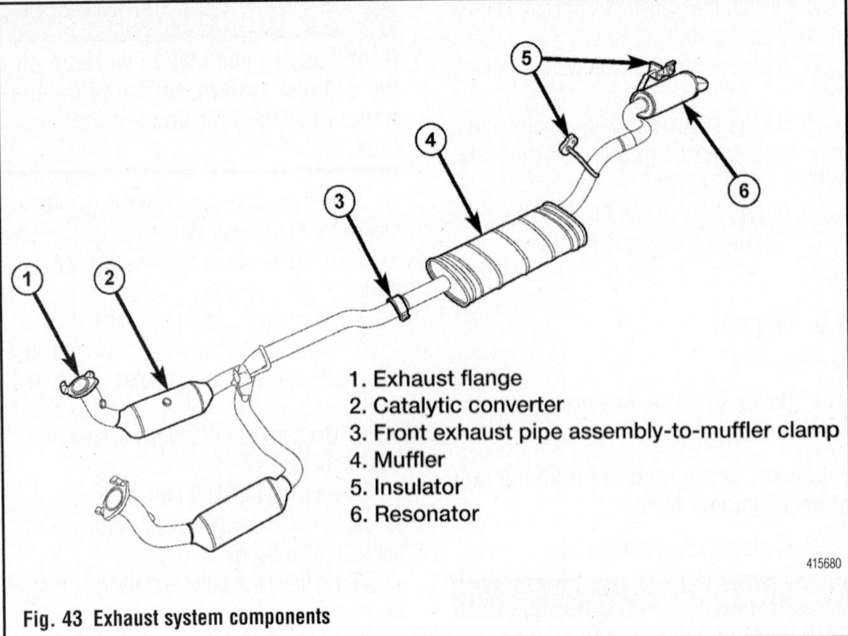

Fig. 43 Exhaust system components

4.0L Engine

See Figure 44.

CAUTION

If torches are used when working on the exhaust system, do not allow the flame near the fuel lines or fuel tank.

1. Before servicing the vehicle, refer to the Precautions Section.
2. Disconnect and isolate the negative battery cable.
3. Raise and support the vehicle.
4. Remove the nuts from the front exhaust pipe and catalytic converter assembly to muffler flange.
5. Saturate the bolts and nuts with heat valve lubricant. Allow 5 minutes for penetration.
6. Disconnect oxygen sensor electrical connectors.
7. Separate the front exhaust pipe to manifold flange connection.
8. Lower the front exhaust pipe/catalytic converter assembly and slide the isolator out of the mount at the transmission (if equipped).
9. Remove the front exhaust pipe/catalytic converter assembly from the vehicle.

To install:

10. Position the front exhaust pipe and catalytic converter assembly isolator into the mount at the transmission (if equipped) and onto the exhaust manifold flange connection.
11. Install the nuts at the front exhaust pipe and catalytic converter assembly to muffler flange. Do not tighten.
12. Position the exhaust pipe for proper clearance with the frame and underbody parts. A minimum clearance of 1.0 in. (25.4 mm) is required.
13. Tighten the bolt at exhaust manifold to 28 ft. lbs. (36 Nm).
14. Tighten the front exhaust pipe and catalytic converter assembly to muffler flange nuts to 28 ft. lbs (36 Nm).
15. Position the front pipe onto the exhaust manifold flange connection. Tighten the clamp to 95 inch lbs. (10 Nm).
16. Connect oxygen sensor electrical connectors.
17. Lower the vehicle.
18. Connect the negative battery cable.

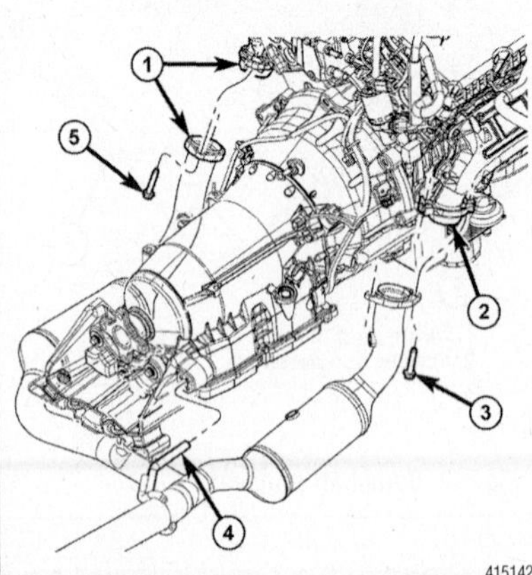

Fig. 44 Saturate the bolts and nuts (3, 5) with heat valve lubricant, separate the front exhaust pipe to manifold flange connection (2), slide the isolator (4) out of the mount

19. Start the vehicle and inspect for exhaust leaks. Repair exhaust leaks as necessary.
20. Check the exhaust system for any contact with the body panels. Make adjustments, if necessary.

CRANKSHAFT FRONT SEAL

REMOVAL & INSTALLATION

3.7L Engine

See Figures 45 and 46.

1. Before servicing the vehicle, refer to the Precautions Section.
2. Disconnect the negative battery cable.
3. Remove the accessory drive belt.
4. Remove the A/C compressor mounting bolts and set the compressor aside.
5. Drain the cooling system.
6. Remove the upper radiator hose.
7. Disconnect the engine fan electrical connector, located inside the radiator shroud.
8. Remove the radiator shroud and engine fan.
9. Remove the crankshaft damper (balancer) bolt.
10. Using the crankshaft insert tool (Special Tool 8513) and three-jaw puller (Special Tool 1026), remove the crankshaft damper.
11. Using the seal removal tool (Special Tool 8511), remove the crankshaft front seal.

To install:

12. Using the seal installer (Special Tool 8348) and damper installer (Special Tool 8512-A), install the crankshaft front seal.

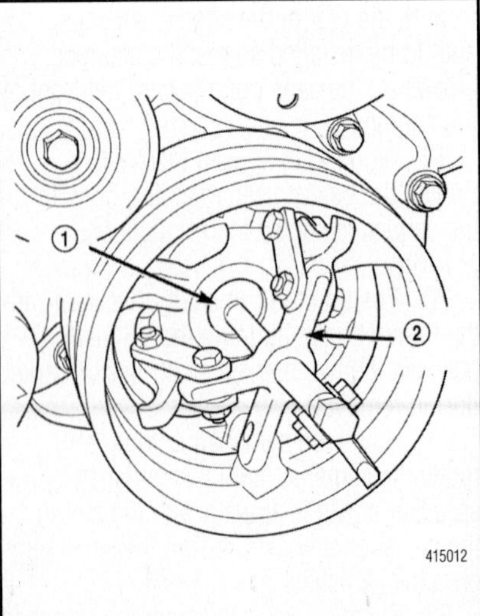

Fig. 45 Crankshaft damper, insert tool (1), and puller (2)

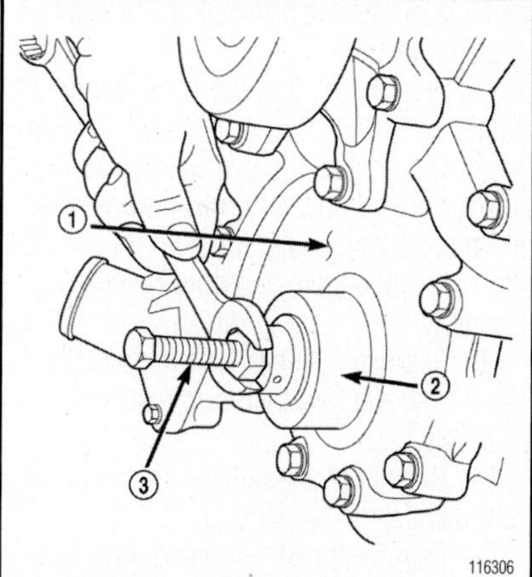

Fig. 46 Timing chain cover (1), seal installer (2), and damper installer (3)

13. Install the crankshaft damper.
14. Install the engine fan and shroud.
15. Install the upper radiator hose.
16. Install the A/C compressor and tighten the mounting bolts to 40 ft. lbs. (54 Nm).
17. Install the accessory drive belt.
18. Refill the cooling system to the correct level.
19. Connect the negative battery cable.
20. Start the engine and check for leaks.

4.0L Engine

See Figure 47.

1. Before servicing the vehicle, refer to the Precautions Section.
2. Disconnect the negative battery cable.
3. Remove the crankshaft sprocket.
4. Tap the dowel pin out of the crankshaft.
5. Using the seal removal tool (Special Tool 6341A), remove the crankshaft front seal.
6. Shaft seal lip surface must be free of varnish, dirt or nicks. Polish with 400 grit paper if necessary.

To install:

7. Using the seal installer (Special Tool 6342), install the crankshaft front seal.
8. Install the dowel pin into the crankshaft to 0.047 in. (1.2mm) protrusion.
9. Install the crankshaft sprocket.
10. Connect the negative battery cable.

CYLINDER HEAD

REMOVAL & INSTALLATION

3.7L Engine

See Figures 48 and 49.

1. Before servicing the vehicle, refer to the Precautions Section.
2. Disconnect the negative cable from the battery.
3. Raise the vehicle on a hoist.
4. Disconnect the exhaust pipe at the left side exhaust manifold.
5. Disconnect the exhaust pipe at the right side exhaust manifold.
6. Drain the engine coolant.
7. Lower the vehicle.
8. Remove the intake manifold.
9. Remove the cylinder head covers.
10. Remove the fan shroud and fan blade assembly.
11. Remove the oil fill housing from the cylinder head.
12. Remove the accessory drive belt.
13. Remove the power steering pump and set aside.
14. Rotate the crankshaft until the damper timing mark is aligned with TDC indicator mark.
15. Verify the V6 mark on the camshaft sprocket is at the 12 o'clock position. Rotate the crankshaft one turn if necessary.
16. Remove the crankshaft damper.
17. Remove the timing chain cover.
18. Lock the secondary timing chains to the idler sprocket using a Secondary Camshaft Chain Holder (Special Tool 8429).
19. Mark the secondary timing chain prior to removal, one link on each side of the V6 mark on the camshaft drive gear.
20. Remove the secondary chain tensioners.
21. Remove the cylinder head access plugs.
22. Remove the secondary chain guides.
23. Remove the retaining bolt and the camshaft drive gear.

WARNING

The nut on the right side camshaft sprocket should not be removed. The sprocket and camshaft sensor target wheel is serviced as an assembly. If the nut was removed, tighten it to 44 inch lbs. (5 Nm).

WARNING

Do not allow the engine to rotate. Severe damage to the valve train can occur.

WARNING

The cylinder had is attached with twelve bolts. Do not attempt to remove the cylinder head without remembering to remove the four smaller bolts at the front.

WARNING

Do not hold or pry on the camshaft target wheel. A damaged target wheel can result in a vehicle no start condition.

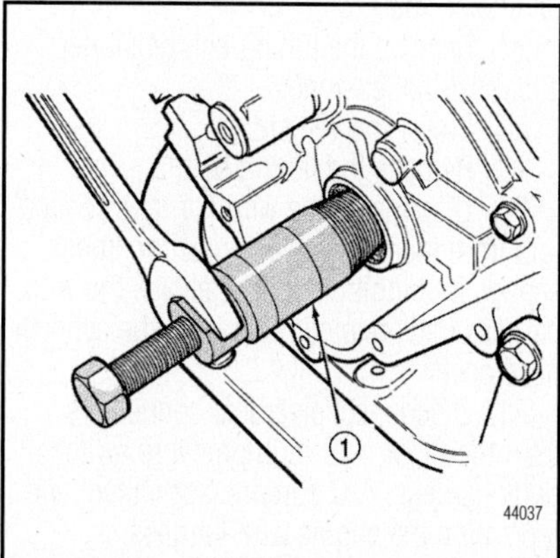

Fig. 47 Crankshaft front seal and seal removal tool (1)

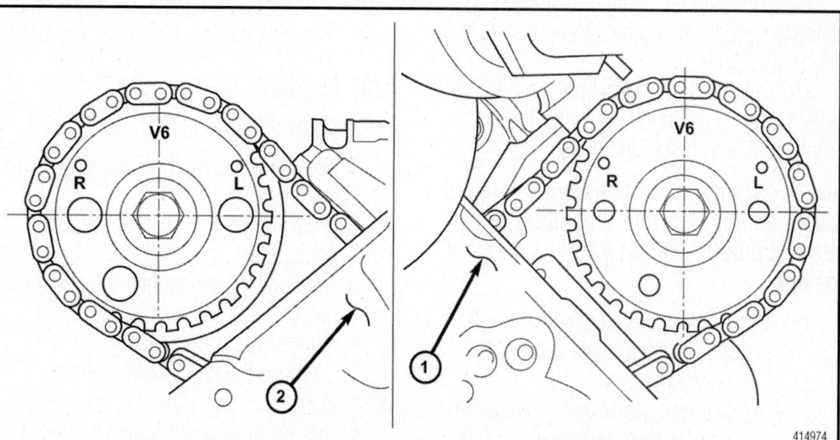

Fig. 48 Camshaft sprocket V6 marks: left cylinder head (1), and right cylinder head (2)

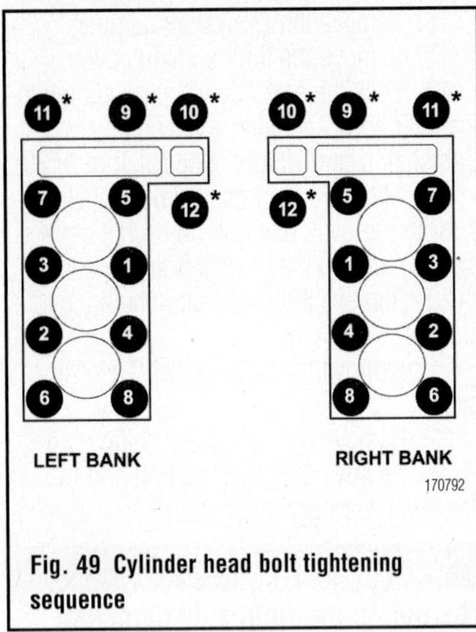

Fig. 49 Cylinder head bolt tightening sequence

24. Remove the cylinder head mounting bolts.

25. Remove the cylinder head and gasket. Discard the gasket.

WARNING

Do not lay the cylinder head on its gasket sealing surface, any distortion to the cylinder head sealing surface may prevent the gasket from properly sealing resulting in leaks.

To install:

26. Check the cylinder head bolts for signs of stretching and replace as necessary.

27. Clean the cylinder head and cylinder block mating surfaces. Use only a wooden or plastic scraper. DO NOT use metal.

28. Position the new cylinder head gasket on the locating dowels.

29. Position the cylinder head onto the cylinder block. Make sure the cylinder head seats fully over the locating dowels. Be careful not to damage the tensioner arm or the guide arm.

30. Lubricate the cylinder head bolt threads with clean engine oil and install the eight M11 bolts.

31. Coat the four M8 cylinder head bolts with Mopar® Lock and Seal Adhesive or equivalent, and install the bolts.

➡The cylinder head bolts are tightened using an angle torque procedure, however, the bolts are not a torque-to-yield design.

32. Tighten the bolts in sequence:
- Step 1: Tighten bolts 1–8 to 20 ft. lbs. (27 Nm)
- Step 2: Verify that bolts 1–8 are 20 ft. lbs. (27 Nm), by repeating Step 1 without loosening the bolts. Tighten bolts 9–12 to 10 ft. lbs. (14 Nm)
- Step 3: Tighten bolts 1–8 another 90 degrees
- Step 4: Tighten bolts 1–8 an additional 90 degrees. Tighten bolts 9–12 to 19 ft. lbs. (26 Nm)

33. Position the secondary chain onto the camshaft drive gear, making sure one marked chain link is on either side of the V6 mark on the gear. Using the camshaft holder, position the gear onto the camshaft.

WARNING

Remove excess oil from camshaft sprocket retaining bolt before reinstalling bolt. Failure to do so may result in bolt failure.

34. Install the camshaft drive gear retaining bolt.

35. Install the secondary chain guides.

36. Install the cylinder head access plugs.

37. Reset and install the secondary chain tensioners.

38. Remove the camshaft chain holder.

39. Install the timing chain cover.

40. Install the crankshaft damper. Tighten the damper bolt to 130 ft. lbs. (175 Nm).

41. Install the power steering pump.

42. Install the fan blade assembly and fan shroud.

43. Install the cylinder head covers.

44. Install the intake manifold.

45. Install the oil fill housing onto cylinder head.

46. Refill the cooling system.

47. Raise the vehicle.

48. Install the exhaust pipe onto the left exhaust manifold.

49. Install the exhaust pipe onto the right exhaust manifold.

50. Lower the vehicle.

51. Connect the negative battery cable.

52. Start the engine and check for leaks.

4.0L Engine

See Figures 50 through 54.

1. Before servicing the vehicle, refer to the Precautions Section.

2. Perform the fuel system pressure relief procedure.

3. Disconnect and isolate the negative battery cable.

4. Drain the cooling system.

5. Remove the air cleaner element housing.

6. Remove the upper intake manifold including support brackets, EGR tube, and the PCV, purge and power brake booster vacuum hoses.

7. Remove the fuel rail and lower intake manifold.

8. Disconnect the two washer pump hoses, coolant recovery hose and washer pump electrical connector from the coolant recovery/washer fluid reservoir assembly.

9. Remove 5 screws and remove the coolant recovery/washer fluid reservoir assembly.

10. Disengage the radiator hose retainer from the electric fan shroud.

11. Remove transmission cooling line retainer bolt from the electric fan shroud.

12. Disconnect the electric fan connector from the electric fan shroud. Remove two bolts and lift the electric fan shroud from the vehicle.

13. Using the adapter pins and wrench, hold the pulley and remove the fan/viscous fan drive assembly.

14. Remove the accessory drive belt.

15. Remove the power steering belt.

16. Remove the alternator.

17. Remove nuts securing the front of the A/C compressor.

18. Back out the A/C compressor mounting bolt and stud from the accessory drive bracket.

19. Remove the four bolts, nut, and the accessory drive bracket.

20. Remove the crankshaft damper bolt.

21. Using the puller and crankshaft insert, remove the crankshaft damper.

22. Remove the fourteen bolts and the front timing belt cover.

23. Rotate the engine to TDC and align the timing belt marks.

24. Raise and support the vehicle.

25. Remove the front exhaust pipe-to-exhaust manifold mounting bolts.

26. Remove the bolt and reposition the oil cooler hose.

27. Remove the timing belt tensioner and reset the tensioner.

28. Lower the vehicle.

29. Remove the timing belt.

30. Disconnect the wire harness connectors from the EGR valve, capacitor, knock sensor, and ignition coils. Release the wire harness track retainer tabs from the cylinder head cover.

31. Disconnect electrical connectors from the PCM, A/C high pressure switch, body harness, A/C compressor clutch, and reposition the engine wire harness.

32. Remove the EGR valve and gasket.

33. Remove the ignition coils.

34. Remove the spark plugs.

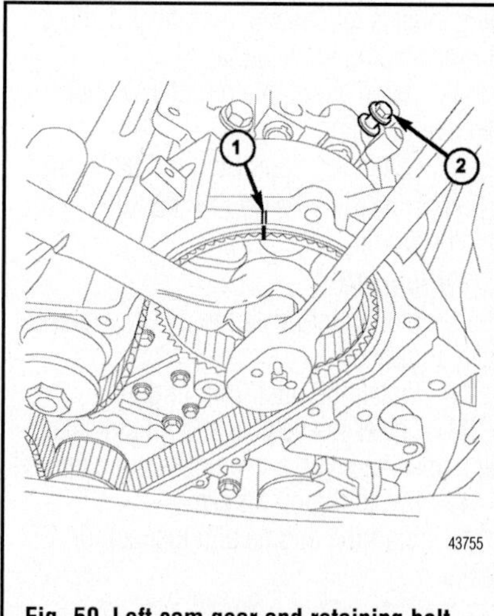

Fig. 50 Left cam gear and retaining bolt

35. Remove the dipstick retaining bolt and the dipstick tube.

36. Remove the bolts and the left and right cylinder head covers.

37. Remove the bolts and the left and right rocker arm assemblies.

38. Remove the three bolts and the left camshaft thrust plate.

39. Counter-hold the left cam gear and remove the cam gear retaining bolt.

40. Remove the left cam gear.

41. Counter-hold the right cam gear and remove the cam gear retaining bolt.

42. Remove the right cam gear.

43. Remove the rear timing belt cover-to-cylinder head retaining bolts.

44. Remove the cylinder head bolts in reverse of tightening sequence.

45. Push the camshafts out of the back of the cylinder heads approximately 3.5 inches and remove the left and right cylinder heads.

46. Clean and inspect all mating surfaces. If replacing the cylinder heads, transfer the capacitor and exhaust manifold.

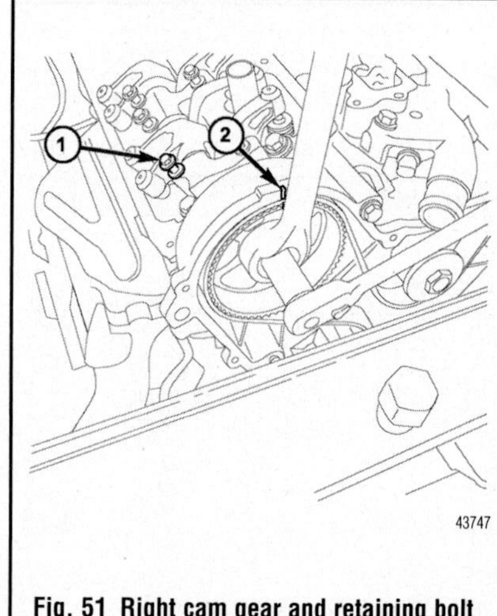

Fig. 51 Right cam gear and retaining bolt

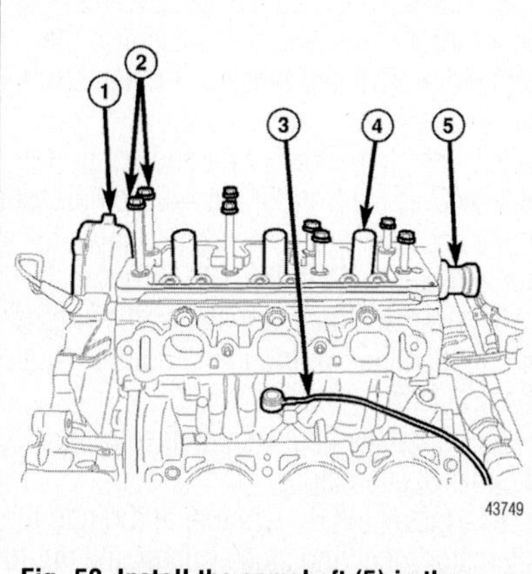

Fig. 52 Install the camshaft (5) in the cylinder head, and finger-tighten the head bolts (2)

To install:

47. Check the cylinder head bolts for signs of stretching and replace as necessary.

48. Clean the sealing surfaces of the cylinder head and cylinder head block. Use only a wooden or plastic scraper. DO NOT use metal.

49. Install the camshafts in the cylinder heads.

50. Push the camshafts out of the back of the cylinder heads approximately 3.5 inches. Install the head gaskets and cylinder heads over the locating dowels. The cylinder head gaskets are not interchangeable between cylinder heads and are clearly marked right or left. Ensure the correct gaskets are used and are correctly positioned.

51. Install and finger-tighten the head bolts.

52. Tighten the cylinder head bolts in the following sequence, using the 4 step torque-turn method. Tighten according to the following torque values:

a. Step 1: All to 45 ft. lbs. (61 Nm)

b. Step 2: All to 65 ft. lbs. (88 Nm)

c. Step 3: All (again) to 65 ft. lbs. (88 Nm)

d. Step 4: Plus 90° turn. Do not use a torque wrench for this step.

53. Bolt torque after 90° turn should be over 90 ft. lbs. (122 Nm) in the tightening direction. If not, replace the bolt.

54. Install the rear timing belt cover-to-cylinder head bolts and tighten to 40 ft. lbs. (54 Nm).

55. Push the camshaft back into the cylinder head and install the camshaft sprocket. The camshaft sprockets are keyed and not interchangeable from side to side because of the camshaft position sensor pick-up.

56. Install a NEW sprocket attaching bolt into place. The 10 in. (255 mm) bolt is to be installed in the left camshaft and the 8 3/8 in. (213 mm) bolt is to be installed into the right camshaft. Counter-hold the camshaft sprocket and tighten the camshaft sprocket bolt to 75 ft. lbs. (102 Nm) plus a 90° turn.

57. Install the camshaft thrust plate and gasket. Tighten the bolts to 21 ft. lbs. (28 Nm).

58. Install a new gasket between the EGR solenoid/valve and the rear of cylinder head.

59. Position the EGR solenoid/valve assembly to rear of the cylinder head. Install and tighten the two mounting bolts to 80 inch lbs. (8 Nm).

60. Rotate the right camshaft gear to align its timing mark. Verify that the left camshaft gear timing mark and crankshaft gear timing mark are still aligned.

61. Install the timing belt, starting at the crankshaft sprocket and going in a counterclockwise direction. Install the belt around the last sprocket. Maintain tension on the belt as it is positioned around the tensioner pulley.

62. Holding the tensioner pulley against the belt, install the tensioner into the housing and tighten the two bolts to 21 ft. lbs. (28 Nm). Each camshaft sprocket mark should remain aligned with the cover marks.

63. When the tensioner is in place, pull

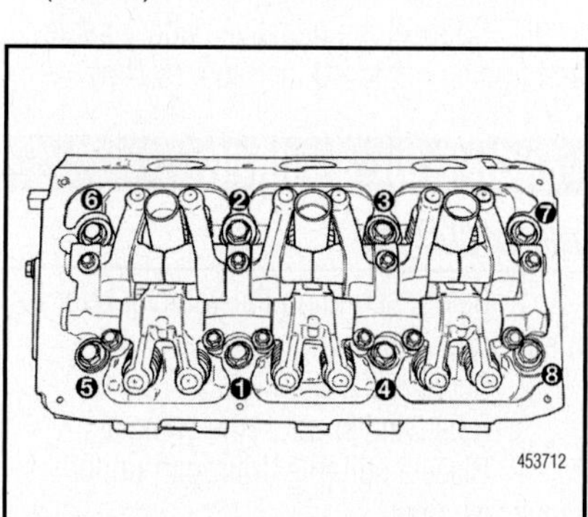

Fig. 53 Cylinder head bolt tightening sequence

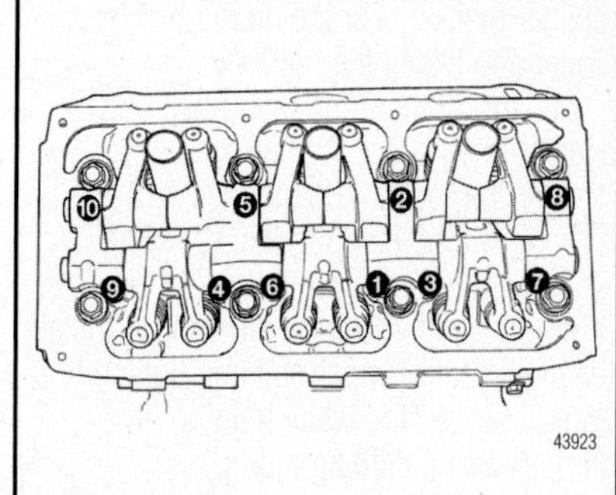

Fig. 54 Rocker arm/shaft assembly bolt tightening sequence

the retaining pin to allow the tensioner to extend to the tensioner pulley bracket.

64. Rotate crankshaft sprocket two revolutions and check the timing marks on the camshafts and crankshaft. The marks should line up within their respective locations. If the marks do not line up, repeat the procedure.

➡With the camshaft gears in these positions, the lobes are in a neutral position (no load to the valve). This will allow the rocker arm shaft assembly to be tightened into position with little or no valve spring load on it.

65. Install the rocker arm and shaft assembly and ten bolts, making sure that the identification marks face toward the front of engine for the left head and toward the rear of the engine for the right head.

66. Tighten the ten rocker arm/shaft assembly bolts in sequence to 23 ft. lbs. (31 Nm).

67. Clean the sealing surfaces of the cylinder heads and covers. Inspect and replace gaskets and seals as necessary.

68. Install the cylinder head covers and tighten the bolts to 105 inch lbs. (12 Nm).

69. Install the spark plugs. Tighten to 20 ft. lbs. (28 Nm).

70. Install ignition coils into cylinder head.

71. Install and tighten coil mounting bolts to 60 inch lbs. (7 Nm).

72. Reposition the engine wire harness and install the retainers to the cylinder head covers. Connect and lock the electrical connectors to the ignition coils, knock sensor, capacitor, and EGR valve.

73. Reposition the engine wire harness; connect and lock the electrical connectors to the PCM, body harness, A/C high pressure switch and A/C compressor clutch.

74. Install dipstick tube and bolt.

75. Connect the front exhaust pipe to the exhaust manifold. Tighten the bolts to 25 ft. lbs. (34 Nm).

76. Reposition the oil cooler hose retainer bracket near the timing belt tensioner and install the bolt.

77. Install the front timing belt outer cover and 14 bolts. Tighten the bolts:

- M6 bolts: 105 inch lbs. (12 Nm)
- M8 bolts: 20 ft. lbs. (28 Nm)
- M10 bolts: 40 ft. lbs. (54 Nm)

78. Install the crankshaft damper. Install the crankshaft damper bolt and tighten to 70 ft. lbs. (95 Nm) while holding the damper with a holding tool.

79. Install the accessory drive bracket and tighten bolts and nut to 40 ft. lbs. (54 Nm).

80. Install the stud that secures the upper front of the A/C compressor to the accessory drive belt bracket. Tighten studs the securely.

81. Install the lower bolt and upper nut that secures the front of the A/C compressor to the accessory drive bracket. Tighten the nut and bolt to 21 ft. lbs. (28 Nm).

82. Position the alternator to the engine and tighten the two mounting bolts to 42 ft. lbs. (57 Nm).

83. Snap the field wire connector into the rear of alternator.

84. Install the B+ terminal and nut to the alternator mounting stud. Tighten the nut to 10 ft. lbs. (13 Nm).

85. Snap the plastic protective cover to the B+ terminal.

86. Install the power steering belt.

87. Install the accessory drive belt.

88. Using the appropriate tools and procedure, install the fan blade/viscous fan drive assembly. Tighten the mounting nut to 37 ft. lbs. (50 Nm).

89. Install the electric fan shroud and tighten the two screws to 50 inch lbs. (6 Nm).

90. Connect and lock the electric fan connector.

91. Install the transmission cooler line retainer to the electric fan shroud with one screw.

92. Install the radiator hose retainer to the electric fan shroud.

93. Install the coolant recovery/washer fluid reservoir assembly with five screws. Connect the two washer pump hoses, coolant recovery hose, and the washer pump electrical connector.

94. Install the lower intake manifold and fuel rail.

95. Install the upper intake manifold, EGR tube, and the PCV, purge and power brake booster vacuum hoses.

96. Install and connect the air cleaner element housing.

97. Fill the coolant system.

98. Connect the negative battery cable and tighten nut to 40 inch lbs. (5 Nm).

ENGINE OIL & FILTER

REPLACEMENT

1. Before servicing the vehicle, refer to the Precautions Section.
2. Remove the oil fill cap.
3. Raise and support the vehicle.
4. Place a suitable drain pan under crankcase drain.
5. Remove the drain plug from crankcase and allow oil to drain into pan. Inspect drain plug threads for stretching or other damage. Replace drain plug if damaged.
6. Using a suitable oil filter wrench, remove the filter.
7. Install the drain plug in crankcase.
8. Clean the gasket sealing surface of oil and grime.

To install:

9. Lightly lubricate the oil filter gasket with engine oil.
10. Install the filter. Hand tighten.
11. Lower the vehicle and fill crankcase with specified type and amount of engine oil.
12. Install the oil fill cap.
13. Start the engine and inspect for leaks.

EXHAUST MANIFOLD

REMOVAL & INSTALLATION

3.7L Engines

See Figures 55 and 56.

1. Before servicing the vehicle, refer to the Precautions Section.
2. Disconnect the negative battery cable.
3. Raise and support the vehicle.
4. Remove the bolts and nuts attaching the exhaust pipe to the engine exhaust manifold.
5. Lower the vehicle.
6. Remove the exhaust heat shield.
7. Remove the bolts, nuts and washers attaching manifold to cylinder head.
8. Remove the manifold and gasket from the cylinder head.

To install:

⁂ WARNING

If the studs came out with the nuts when removing the engine exhaust

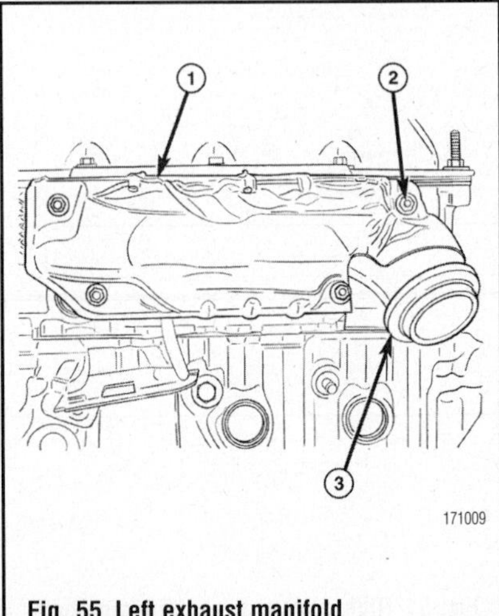

Fig. 55 Left exhaust manifold

Fig. 56 Right exhaust manifold

manifold, install new studs. Apply sealer on the coarse thread ends. Water leaks may develop at the studs if this precaution is not taken.

9. Position the engine exhaust manifold and gasket on the two studs located on the cylinder head.
10. Install the conical washers and nuts on these studs.
11. Install the remaining conical washers. Starting at the center arm and working outward, tighten the bolts and nuts to 18 ft. lbs. (25 Nm).
12. Install the exhaust heat shields.
13. Raise and support the vehicle.

**** WARNING**

Over-tightening heat shield fasteners may cause shield to distort and/or crack.

14. Assemble the exhaust pipe to manifold and secure with bolts, nuts and retainers. Tighten the bolts and nuts to 25 ft. lbs. (34 Nm).

4.0L Engine

See Figures 57 and 58.

1. Before servicing the vehicle, refer to the Precautions Section.
2. Disconnect and isolate the negative battery cable.
3. Disconnect the upstream oxygen sensor electrical connector, if necessary.
4. Raise and support the vehicle.
5. Separate the front exhaust pipe to from the exhaust manifold.
6. Lower the vehicle.
7. Disconnect and remove the oxygen sensor from the exhaust manifold.

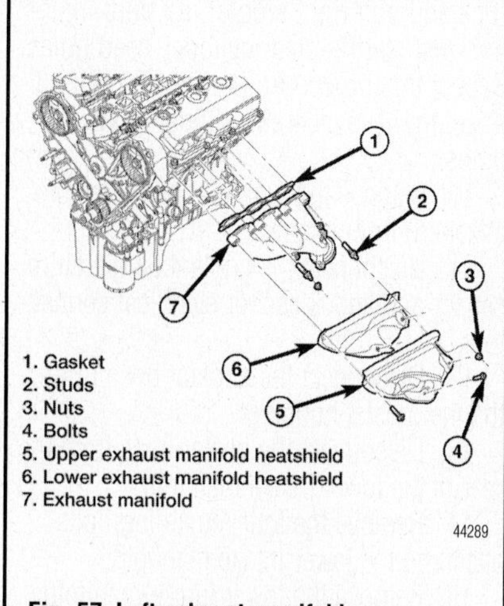

Fig. 57 Left exhaust manifold

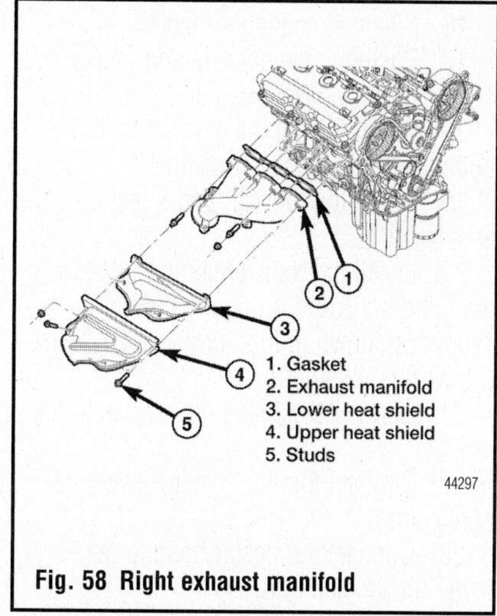

Fig. 58 Right exhaust manifold

8. Remove the manifold heat shield.
9. Remove the exhaust manifold. Discard the gasket.

To install:

10. Clean the gasket surfaces.

➡If replacing the exhaust manifold, tighten the exhaust outlet studs to 29 ft. lbs. (39 Nm).

11. Position the exhaust manifold and gasket. Install the retaining bolts. Tighten 4 bolts starting at the center working outward to 17 ft. lbs. (23 Nm).
12. Install the heat shields. Tighten the bolts to 105 inch lbs. (12 Nm).
13. Tighten the 2 out most nuts to 73 inch lbs. (8 Nm).
14. Connect the oxygen sensor.
15. Raise and support the vehicle.
16. Connect the front exhaust pipe to exhaust manifold. Tighten the fasteners to 25 ft. lbs. (34 Nm).
17. Connect the negative battery cable.

INTAKE MANIFOLD

REMOVAL & INSTALLATION

3.7L Engine

See Figure 59.

1. Before servicing the vehicle, refer to the Precautions Section.
2. Properly relieve the fuel system pressure.
3. Disconnect the negative cable from battery.
4. Remove the resonator assembly and air inlet hose.
5. Drain the cooling system below the coolant temperature sensor level.
6. Disconnect the electronic throttle control (ETC) connector.
7. Disconnect the electrical connectors for the following components:
    - Coolant Temperature Sensor
    - Manifold Absolute Pressure (MAP) Sensor
8. Disconnect the vapor purge hose, brake booster hose, and Positive Crankcase Ventilation (PCV) hose.
9. Disconnect and remove the ignition coil towers.
10. Remove the top oil dipstick tube retaining bolt.
11. Remove the EGR tube.
12. Remove fuel rail.
13. Remove the throttle body assembly.
14. Remove the intake manifold retaining fasteners in reverse order of tightening sequence.
15. Remove the intake manifold.

To install:

16. Install the intake manifold seals.
17. Install the intake manifold.
18. Install the intake manifold retaining bolts and tighten in sequence shown to 105 inch lbs. (12 Nm).

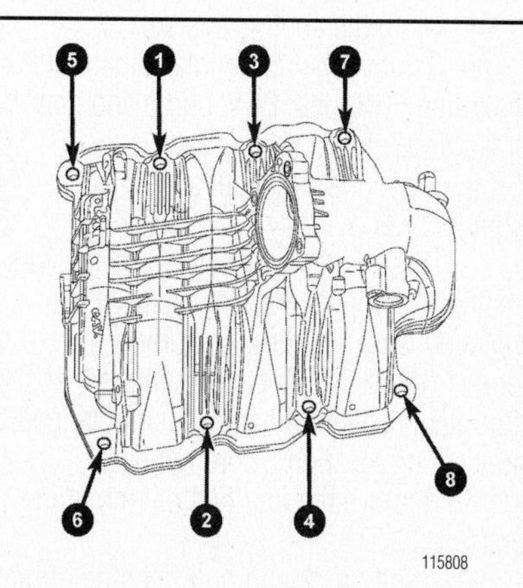

Fig. 59 Intake manifold bolt tightening sequence

⁂ WARNING

Proper torque of the throttle body is critical to normal operation. If the throttle body is over-torqued, damage to the throttle body can occur resulting in throttle plate malfunction.

19. Install the throttle body-to-intake manifold O-ring.
20. Install the throttle body to intake manifold.
21. Install the four mounting bolts. Tighten bolts to 60 inch lbs. (7 Nm).
22. Install the electrical connector.
23. Install the fuel rail.
24. Install the EGR tube.
25. Install the ignition coil towers.
26. Connect the electrical connectors for the following components:
    - MAP Sensor
    - Coolant temperature sensor
    - Ignition coil towers
27. Install the top oil dipstick tube retaining bolt.
28. Connect the vapor purge hose, brake booster hose, and PCV hose.
29. Fill the cooling system.
30. Install the resonator assembly and the air inlet hose.
31. Connect the negative cable to battery.
32. Using the scan tool, perform the ETC relearn function.

4.0L Engine

Lower

See Figure 60.

1. Before servicing the vehicle, refer to the Precautions Section.
2. Perform the fuel pressure release procedure.
3. Remove and isolate negative battery cable at battery.
4. Drain the cooling system.
5. Remove the upper intake manifold including EGR tube, PCV, purge and power brake booster vacuum hoses.
6. Disconnect the fuel supply hose from fuel rail.
7. Disconnect the electrical connectors at all six fuel injectors. The factory fuel injection wiring harness is numerically tagged (INJ 1, INJ 2, etc.) for injector position identification. If harness is not tagged, note wiring location before removal.
8. Remove the four fuel rail mounting bolts.
9. Gently rock and pull left side of fuel rail until fuel injectors just start to clear machined holes in cylinder head. Gently rock and pull right side of rail until injectors just start to clear cylinder head holes. Repeat this procedure (left/right) until all injectors have cleared cylinder head holes.
10. Remove the fuel rail (with injectors attached) from engine.
11. Disconnect the coolant temperature sensor and knock sensor electrical connectors.
12. Disconnect the coolant hose from the thermostat housing.
13. Disconnect the heater hose from the rear of the lower intake manifold.
14. Remove the four remaining bolts attaching the lower intake manifold.
15. Remove the lower intake manifold and gaskets.

To install:

16. Clean all sealing surfaces.
17. Position new gaskets and intake manifold on cylinder head surfaces.
18. Install four of the eight manifold bolts. Do not tighten at this time.
19. Install the fuel rail and injectors as an assembly.
20. Install the four remaining intake manifold bolts and gradually tighten in sequence shown until a torque of 21 ft. lbs. (28 Nm) is obtained.
21. Connect the fuel supply hose to fuel rail.
22. Connect the fuel injector electrical connectors.
23. Connect the heater hose to rear lower intake manifold.
24. Connect the coolant hose to thermostat housing.
25. Connect the coolant temperature sensor and knock sensor electrical connectors.
26. Install the upper intake manifold, EGR tube, PVC, purge and power brake booster vacuum hoses.
27. Fill the cooling system.
28. Connect the negative battery cable. Tighten nut to 40 inch lbs. (5 Nm).

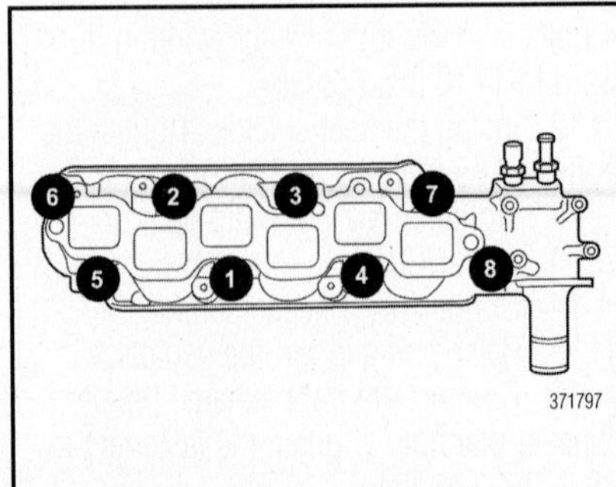

Fig. 60 Lower intake manifold bolt tightening sequence

Upper

See Figure 61.

1. Before servicing the vehicle, refer to the Precautions Section.
2. Disconnect and isolate the negative battery cable.
3. Disconnect the Intake Air Temperature (IAT) sensor, Manifold Absolute Pressure (MAP) sensor, electronic throttle control and manifold tuning valve electrical connectors.
4. Loosen the clamps and remove the air inlet hose from the throttle body.
5. Disconnect the PCV, purge and power brake booster vacuum hoses from the upper intake manifold.
6. Remove the two EGR tube mounting flange bolts at the intake manifold.
7. Remove the two EGR tube mounting flange bolts at the EGR solenoid/valve.
8. Separate the EGR tube and gasket from the EGR solenoid/valve. Slip the opposite end of tube from the intake manifold.
9. Remove the two nuts from the studs on the left intake manifold support brackets.
10. Remove the upper intake manifold retaining bolts and the manifold. Clean all gasket sealing surfaces.

To install:

11. Clean and inspect gasket sealing surfaces.
12. Position new upper intake manifold gasket.
13. Install the upper intake manifold. Tighten the bolts to 105 inch lbs. (12 Nm), starting in the center working outward in a cross sequence pattern.
14. Install the two nuts to the left manifold support brackets. Tighten the nuts to 105 inch lbs. (12 Nm).

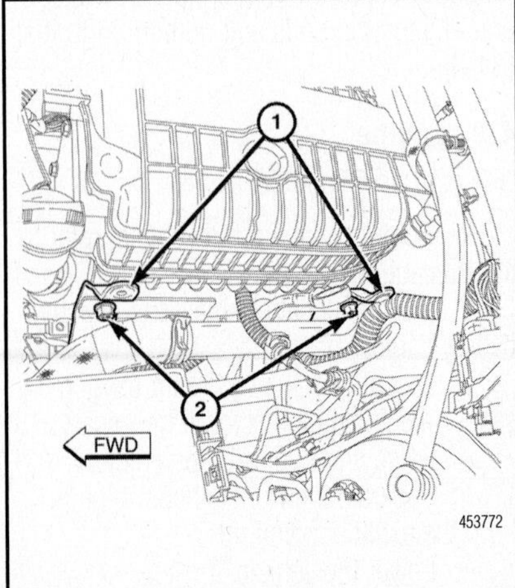

Fig. 61 Left intake manifold support brackets

⁂ WARNING

Do Not use metal scrapers when cleaning the mounting surface of the EGR valve. Damage from scratching the surface may cause an improper seal. Do not allow debris to enter the EGR valve when cleaning the mounting surface. Debris can lodge between the pintle and the seat causing valve leakage.

15. Install the new silicone rubber seal on the intake manifold end of the EGR tube. Position the seal 0.67 in. (17 mm) from the tube flange.
16. Lubricate the EGR mounting tube hole in the intake manifold with Mopar® Rubber Bushing Installation Lube. Do not lubricate the EGR tube or seal.
17. Install the EGR tube into the intake manifold, being careful not to damage the silicone rubber seals. Verify that the seals are correctly positioned in the intake manifold.
18. Install new gasket between the EGR valve and tube and tighten the bolts to 80 inch lbs. (8 Nm).

⁂ WARNING

DO NOT use air tools to install bolts to intake manifold. Install bolts using hand tools only. Torque all fasteners to specification. The use of air tools can cause the threads of the intake manifold to become stripped.

19. Install the EGR tube flange mounting bolts to intake manifold and tighten to 35 inch lbs. (4 Nm). The EGR tube flange does not need to be flush with the intake manifold to be sealed. The EGR tube flange can be up to 0.08 in. (2 mm) from intake manifold and still be sealed.
20. Connect the PVC, purge and power brake booster vacuum hoses to the intake manifold.
21. Connect the manifold tuning valve, electronic throttle control, MAP sensor and IAT sensor electrical connectors.
22. Install the inlet hose and tighten clamps.
23. Connect the negative battery cable. Tighten nut to 45 inch lbs. (5 Nm).

OIL PAN

REMOVAL & INSTALLATION

3.7L Engine

2WD Vehicles

See Figure 62.

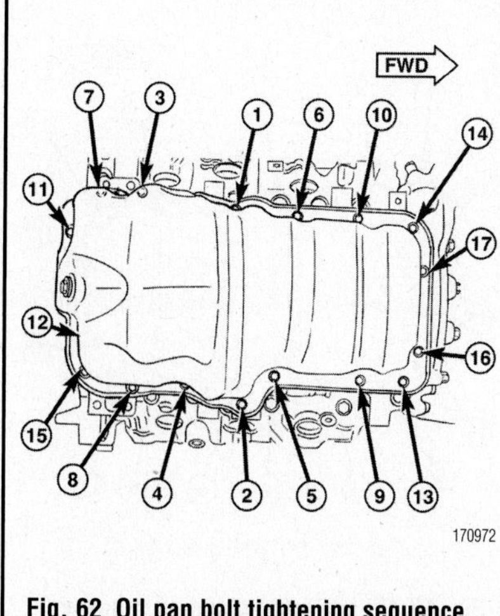

Fig. 62 Oil pan bolt tightening sequence

1. Before servicing the vehicle, refer to the Precautions Section.
2. Disconnect the negative battery cable.
3. Install engine support fixture.
4. Raise and support vehicle.
5. Remove the front wheel assemblies.
6. Remove the skid plate (if equipped).
7. Drain engine oil.
8. Mark adjustment cam position of front lower control arm bolts.
9. Remove the front lower control arm bolts.
10. Disconnect the left-hand tie rod.
11. Disconnect the left-hand lower ball joint.
12. Disconnect the left-hand strut clevis.
13. Remove the left-hand front axle.
14. Remove the front axle brace bolts.
15. Remove the front prop shaft.
16. Drain front axle.
17. Using a transmission jack, support the front axle.
18. Remove the axle bracket bolts.
19. With the right-hand axle still in place, remove front differential.
20. Remove the transmission oil cooler line bracket.
21. Remove the engine to transmission stiffening bracket.
22. Position the Engine Support Tool 8534 on the fender lip and align the slots in the brackets with the fender mounting holes.
23. Secure brackets to the fender using four M6 X 1.0 X 25 MM flanged cap screws.
24. Tighten the thumbscrews to secure the sleeves to the support tube.
25. Secure the support tube in an upright position.
26. Assemble the flat washer, thrust bearing, hook and T handle.
27. Using the M10 X 1.75 mm flanged nut supplied with the support fixture, secure the chain to the front engine lifting stud.
28. Loosen the engine mounts.
29. Remove the oil pan bolts.
30. Separate the oil pan from the engine.
31. Move the oil pan to one side, remove oils sump bolt and windage tray bolts.

➡Do not pry on oil pan or oil pan gasket. Gasket is integral to engine windage tray and does not come out with oil pan.

32. Move the oil pan and windage tray toward the front of vehicle and remove from vehicle.

To install:

33. Clean the oil pan gasket mating surface of the bedplate and oil pan.
34. Clean the oil pan and block gasket mating surfaces.
35. Inspect integrated oil pan gasket, and replace as necessary.
36. Drop the oil pump pick-up tube into the oil pan, and install the oil pan, pick-up tube, and the windage tray, as an assembly, from the front of the vehicle.
37. Install the windage tray, then the oil pump pick-up tube, and the nuts and bolt holding the oil pump pick-up tube in place.

➡It will be necessary to move the oil pan from side to side to gain access to these fasteners.

38. Tighten the pick-up tube fasteners.
39. Install the oil pan.
40. Install and tighten the oil pan bolts.
41. Install the engine to transmission structural cover, (if equipped).
42. Lower engine, and remove Engine Support Fixture 8534.
43. Lower the vehicle.
44. Lower the engine using Engine Support Fixture.
45. Remove the Engine Support Fixture.
46. Raise the vehicle.
47. Tighten both engine mount through bolts.
48. Install the transmission oil cooler line bracket.
49. Install the skid plate (if equipped).
50. Install the front wheel and tire assemblies.
51. Lower the vehicle.
52. Refill engine oil.
53. Reconnect battery.
54. Start engine and check for leaks.

4WD Vehicles

See Figure 63.

1. Before servicing the vehicle, refer to the Precautions Section.
2. Disconnect the battery.
3. Install Engine Support Fixture 8534.
4. Raise and support vehicle.
5. Remove front wheel and tire assemblies.
6. Remove skid plate (if equipped).
7. Drain engine oil.
8. Remove engine to transmission structural cover (if equipped).
9. Remove transmission oil cooler line bracket.
10. Remove the front axle assembly from the vehicle.
11. Loosen both engine mount through bolts.
12. Lower the vehicle.

➡It is not necessary to remove the viscous fan, or fan shroud, for oil pan removal.

13. Raise the engine using support fixture special tool 8534, until the viscous fan almost touches the fan shroud.
14. Raise the vehicle.
15. Remove the oil pan bolts.
16. Separate the oil pan from the engine.
17. Remove the nuts and bolt holding the oil pump pick-up tube and windage tray in place.

➡It will be necessary to move the oil pan from side to side to gain access to these fasteners.

18. Drop the oil pump pick-up tube into the oil pan, and remove the oil pan, pick-up tube, and the windage tray as an assembly from the front of the vehicle.

To install:

19. Inspect oil pan gasket for defects, and replace if necessary.
20. Clean the oil pan and block gasket mating surfaces.
21. Drop the oil pump pick-up tube into the oil pan and install the oil pan, pick-up tube, and the windage tray as an assembly from the front of the vehicle.
22. Install the windage tray, then the oil pump pick-up tube, and the nuts and bolt holding the oil pump pick-up tube in place.

➡It will be necessary to move the oil pan from side to side to gain access to these fasteners.

23. Torque the pick-up tube fasteners.
24. Install the oil pan.
25. Install and tighten the oil pan bolts.

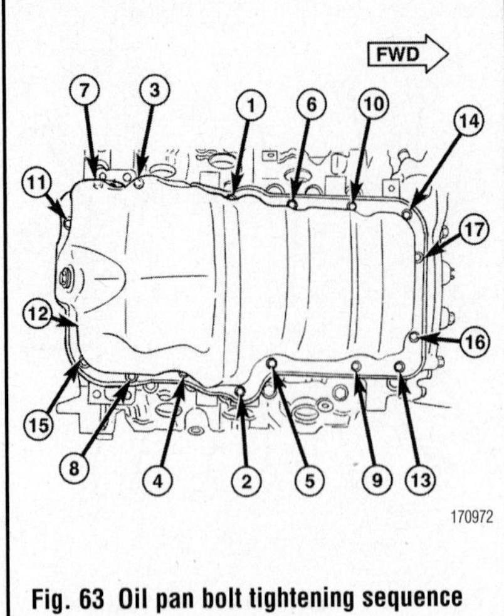

Fig. 63 Oil pan bolt tightening sequence

26. Install the engine to transmission structural cover, (if equipped).
27. Lower the vehicle.
28. Lower the engine using Engine Support Fixture 8534.
29. Remove the Engine Support Fixture 8534.
30. Raise the vehicle.
31. Tighten both engine mount through bolts.
32. Install the transmission oil cooler line bracket.
33. Install the front axle assembly to the vehicle.
34. Install the skid plate (if equipped).
35. Install the front wheel and tire assemblies.
36. Lower the vehicle.
37. Refill engine oil.
38. Reconnect battery.
39. Start engine, and check for leaks.

4.0L Engine

See Figures 64 through 66.

1. Before servicing the vehicle, refer to the Precautions Section.
2. Disconnect negative battery cable.
3. Lock the steering wheel with the tires in the straight ahead position.

➡The steering column on vehicles with an automatic transmission may not be equipped with an internal locking shaft that allows the ignition key cylinder to be locked with the key. Alternative methods of locking the steering wheel for service will have to be used.

4. Remove two nuts and reposition the upper radiator hose.
5. Remove the engine oil level indicator tube retaining bolt and remove the indicator tube.
6. Install an engine support fixture.
7. Raise and support the vehicle.
8. Drain engine oil and remove the oil filter.
9. Remove the oil cooler attaching fastener from the center of oil cooler and reposition the oil cooler.
10. Remove the stabilizer bar.
11. Remove both steering knuckles.
12. Remove both shock absorber lower clevis bolts.
13. Mark an installation reference line across the front propeller shaft flange and the axle flange.
14. Remove the axle flange bolts and reposition the front propeller shaft.
15. Remove the lower coupler pinch bolt at the steering gear.
16. Remove the coupler from the steering gear and reposition the intermediate shaft.
17. Remove the power steering pressure hose mounting bolts from the frame.
18. Remove the vent hose from the front differential case.
19. Loosen the engine mount through bolts.
20. Support the engine cradle with jackstands. Mark the location of the engine support cradle.
21. Remove the engine cradle support bolts and lower the engine cradle approximately 5 inches.
22. Remove the flex plate access cover.
23. Remove the two rear oil pan bolts.
24. Disengage the transmission oil cooling line retainer from the oil pan mounting

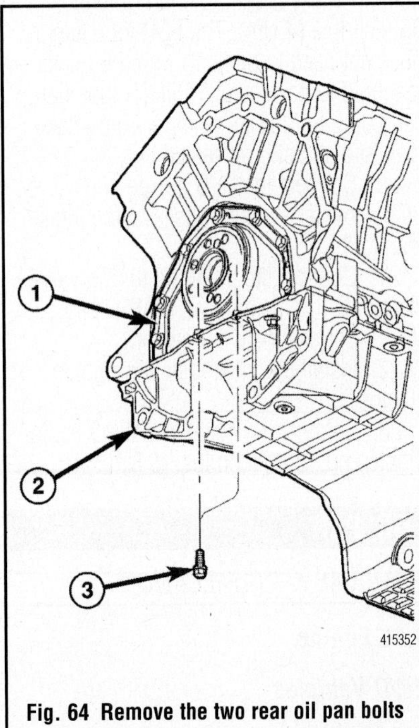

Fig. 64 Remove the two rear oil pan bolts

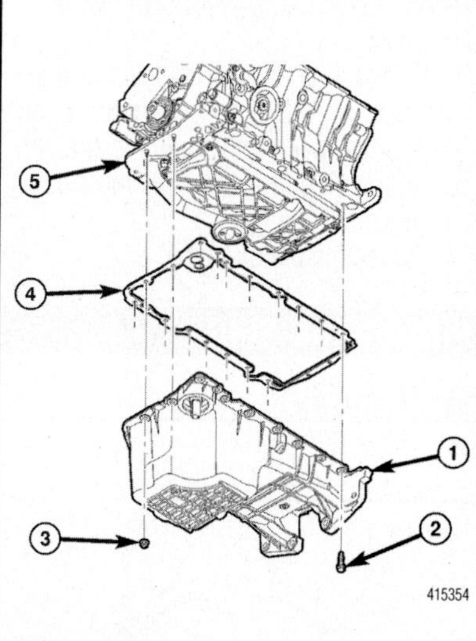

Fig. 65 Remove the remaining oil pan bolts (2) and nuts (3)

stud and discard the retainer. The transmission oil cooling line retainer is intended for one-time use only.

25. Remove the remaining oil pan bolts and nuts.

26. Remove the oil pan.

➡**A small amount of oil will remain in the oil pan. Use care when removing the oil pan from the engine.**

27. Clean all mating surfaces.

To install:

28. Clean oil pan and all gasket surfaces.

29. Apply a ⅛ inch bead of Mopar® Engine RTV GEN II at the parting line of the oil pump housing and the rear seal retainer.

30. Install oil pan gasket to the engine block.

31. Install the oil pan while aligning the oil level indicator tube and attach fasteners finger tight.

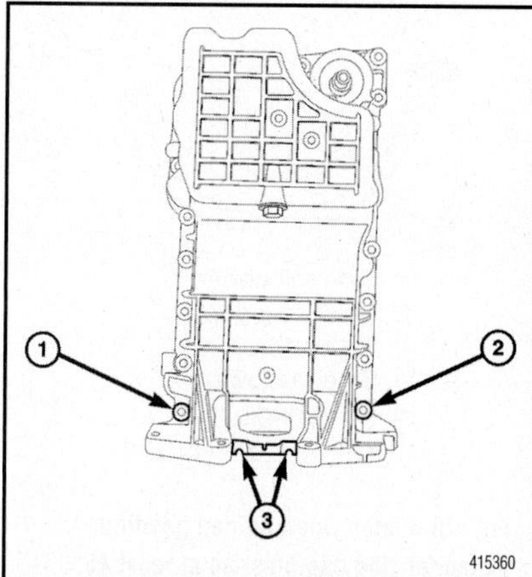

Fig. 66 First tighten the M8 oil pan alignment bolt (1) and then tighten the other bolt (2)

32. Be sure that the rear face of the oil pan is flush to the transmission bell housing when installing the oil pan.

33. Pre-tighten the horizontal rear oil pan to transmission bolts to 12 inch lbs. (1 Nm).

34. First tighten the M8 oil pan alignment bolt to 21 ft. lbs. (28 Nm), then tighten the other bolt to 21 ft. lbs. (28 Nm).

35. Tighten the remaining M8 bolts and M8 nuts to 21 ft. lbs. (28 Nm), and the M6 bolts to 105 inch lbs. (12 Nm).

36. Tighten the four M10 oil pan to transmission bolts to 40 ft. lbs. (55 Nm).

37. Lower the engine and remove the lifting fixture. Tighten the engine mount to cradle fasteners to 55 lbs. ft. (75 Nm).

38. Install the flex plate inspection cover and tighten the fastener to 97 inch lbs. (1 Nm).

39. Install the retainer to the transmission oil cooling lines and engage the retainer to the oil pan mounting stud.

40. Raise the engine cradle into the vehicle while lining up the engine mount through bolts.

41. Refer to the reference marks made during disassembly and align the cradle to those marks.

42. Install the cradle mounting bolts and tighten the front bolts to 90 ft. lbs. (122 Nm) and tighten the rear bolts to 85 ft. lbs. (115 Nm).

43. Tighten the engine mount through bolts to 65 ft. lbs. (88 Nm).

44. Connect the vent hose to the front differential case.

45. Install the power steering pressure hose mounting bolts to the frame. Tighten to 105 inch lbs. (12 Nm).

46. Install the coupler to the steering gear and tighten the lower coupler pinch bolt to 39 ft. lbs. (53 Nm).

47. Clean all propeller shaft bolts and apply Mopar® Lock and Seal Adhesive or equivalent to the threads before installation.

48. Align the installation reference marks on the front propeller shaft flange and axle flange.

49. Install the axle flange bolts and tighten to 80 ft. lbs. (108 Nm).

50. Install both shock absorber lower clevis bolt/nut. Tighten the nut to 110 ft. lbs. (150 Nm) with full vehicle weight.

51. Install the steering knuckles and tire/wheel assemblies.

52. Install the stabilizer bar.

53. Position the oil cooler to the fitting on the oil pan.

⁂ WARNING

Remove all oil and debris from the seal retainer surface. The cut out section of the oil cooler seal retainer flange (top), must be aligned with the tab on the oil pan. The oil cooler must be prevented from turning during the tightening sequence.

54. Install the oil cooler attaching fastener to the center of the oil cooler and tighten to 45 ft. lbs. (61 Nm).

55. Install the oil filter.

56. Lower the vehicle and remove the engine support tool.

57. Install the engine oil level indicator tube and tighten the retaining bolt to 105 inch lbs. (12 Nm).

58. Install two nuts to the left manifold support brackets and upper radiator hose. Tighten the nuts to 105 inch lbs. (12 Nm).

59. Fill engine crankcase with proper oil to correct level.

60. Unlock the steering wheel.

61. Connect negative battery cable.

OIL PUMP

REMOVAL & INSTALLATION

3.7L Engine

See Figure 67.

1. Before servicing the vehicle, refer to the Precautions Section.
2. Remove the oil pan.
3. Remove the timing chain cover.
4. Remove the timing chains and tensioners.
5. Remove the four bolts, primary timing chain tensioner and the oil pump.

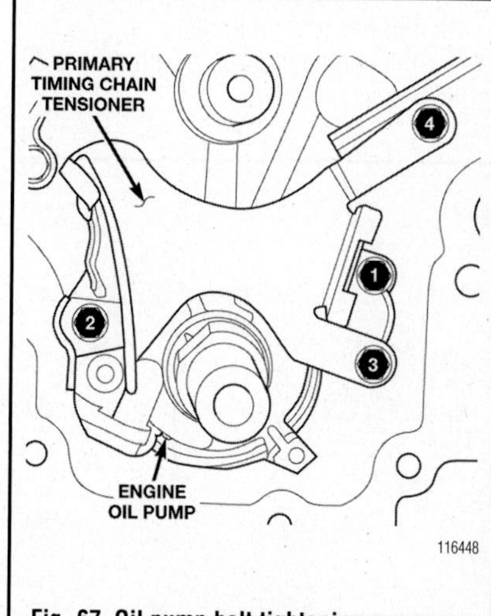

Fig. 67 Oil pump bolt tightening sequence

To install:

6. Position the oil pump onto the crankshaft and install two oil pump retaining bolts.
7. Position the primary timing chain tensioner and install the two retaining bolts.
8. Tighten the oil pump and primary timing chain tensioner retaining bolts to 21 ft. lbs. (28 Nm) in the sequence shown.
9. Install the secondary timing chain tensioners and timing chains.
10. Install the timing chain cover.
11. Install the pick-up tube and oil pan.

4.0L Engine

See Figure 68.

1. Before servicing the vehicle, refer to the Precautions Section.
2. Drain the cooling system.
3. Remove the timing belt.
4. Remove the crankshaft sprocket.
5. Remove the oil pan.
6. Remove the oil pickup tube.
7. Remove the oil pump fasteners.
8. Remove the oil pump and gasket from engine.

To install:

9. Prime oil pump before installation by filling rotor cavity with clean engine oil.
10. Install oil pump and gasket carefully over the crankshaft. Position pump onto block and tighten bolts to 21 ft. lbs. (28 Nm).
11. Install new O-ring on oil pickup tube.
12. Install oil pickup tube.
13. Install oil pan.
14. Install crankshaft sprocket.
15. Install timing belt.
16. Install the timing belt covers.
17. Install the crankshaft vibration damper.
18. Install the accessory drive belt.
19. Fill the cooling system.
20. Fill engine crankcase with proper oil to the correct level.

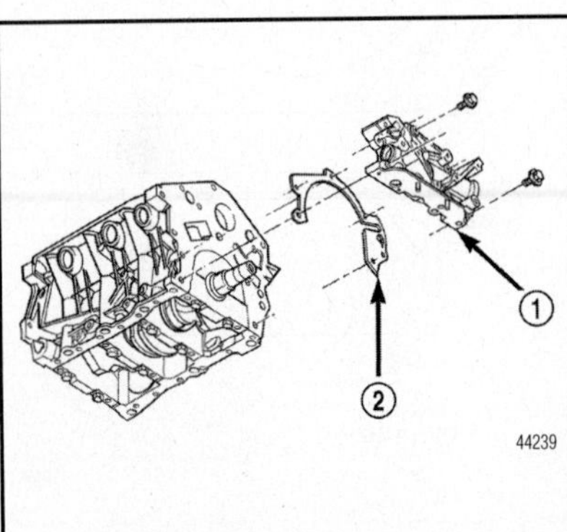

Fig. 68 Oil pump and (1) gasket (2)

INSPECTION

The oil pump is replaced as an assembly; there are no subassembly components. In the event the oil pump is not functioning it must be replaced as an assembly.

➡DO NOT inspect the oil relief valve assembly. If the oil relief valve is suspect, replace the oil pump.

1. Disassemble oil pump.
2. Clean all parts thoroughly. Mating surface of the oil pump housing should be smooth. Replace pump cover if scratched or grooved.
3. Lay a straightedge across the pump cover surface. If a 0.001 in. (0.025 mm) feeler gauge can be inserted between cover and straight edge, the oil pump assembly should be replaced.
4. Measure thickness and diameter of the outer and inner rotors:
   a. For 3.7L engine, if outer rotor thickness measures 0.472 in. (12.005 mm) or less, or if the diameter is 3.382 in. (85.925 mm) or less, the oil pump assembly must be replaced.
   b. For 4.0L engine, if outer rotor thickness measures 0.563 in. (14.299 mm) or less, or if the diameter is 3.141 in. (79.78 mm) or less, the oil pump assembly must be replaced.
   c. For 3.7L engine, if inner rotor measures 0.472 in. (12.005 mm) or less, the oil pump assembly must be replaced.
   d. For 4.0L engine, if inner rotor measures 0.563 in. (14.299 mm) or less, the oil pump assembly must be replaced.
5. Slide the outer rotor into oil pump body. Press the outer rotor to one side of the oil pump body and measure clearance between rotor and body:
   a. For 3.7L engine, if measurement is 0.009 in. (0.235 mm) or more, the oil pump assembly must be replaced.
   b. For 4.0L engine, if measurement is 0.015 in. (0.39 mm) or more, the oil pump assembly must be replaced.
6. Install inner rotor into body:
   a. For 3.7L engine, if clearance between inner and outer rotors is 0.006 in. (0.150 mm) or more, the oil pump assembly must be replaced.
   b. For 4.0L engine, if clearance between inner and outer rotors is 0.008 in. (0.20 mm) or more, the oil pump assembly must be replaced.
7. Place a straightedge across the face of the body, between bolt holes:
   a. For 3.7L engine, if a feeler gauge of 0.0038 in. (0.095 mm) or more can be inserted between rotors and the straightedge, the oil pump assembly must be replaced.
   b. For 4.0L engine, if a feeler gauge of 0.003 in. (0.077 mm) or more can be inserted between rotors and the straightedge, the oil pump assembly must be replaced.
8. Assemble the oil pump.

PISTON AND RING

POSITIONING

See Figures 69 and 70.

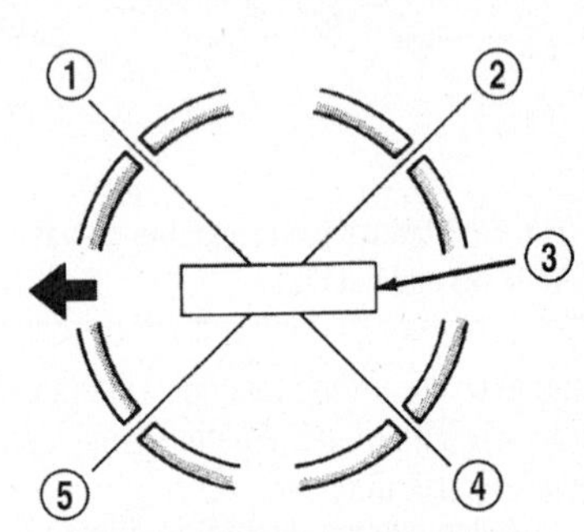

Fig. 69 Piston ring end-gap position; expander ring gap must be at least 45° from the side rail gaps, but not on the piston pin center or on the thrust direction—3.7L engine

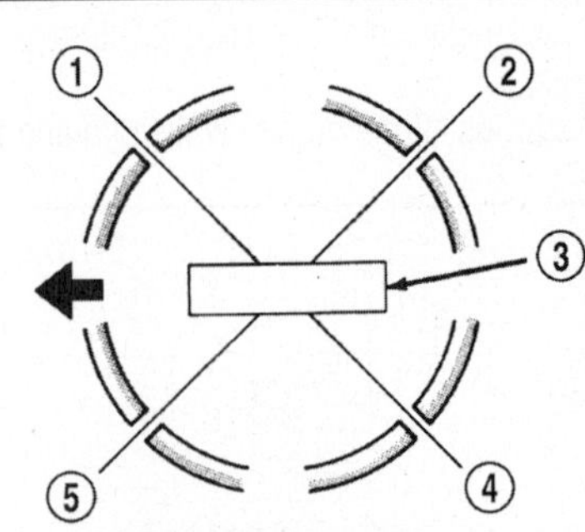

Fig. 70 Piston ring end-gap position; expander ring gap must be at least 45° from the side rail gaps, but not on the piston pin center or on the thrust direction—4.0L engine

REAR MAIN SEAL

REMOVAL & INSTALLATION

3.7L Engine

See Figure 71.

1. Before servicing the vehicle, refer to the Precautions Section.
2. Remove the transmission.
3. Remove the flexplate.
4. Using the oil seal removal tool, remove the rear main seal. The crankshaft rear oil seal remover must be installed deeply into the seal. Continue to tighten the removal tool into the seal until the tool cannot be turned farther. Failure to install tool correctly the first time will cause tool to pull free of seal without removing seal from engine.

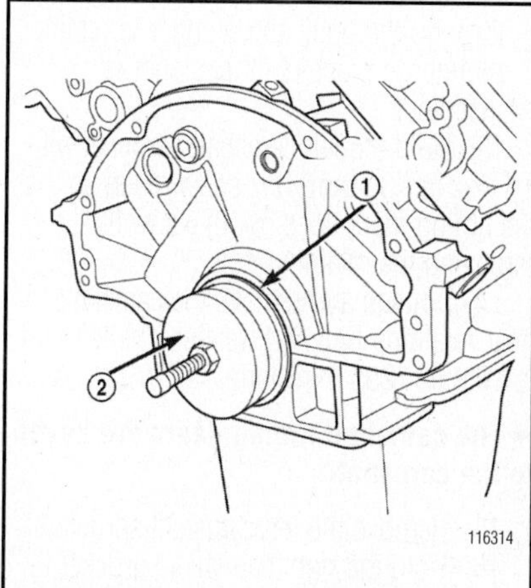

Fig. 71 Using the oil seal removal tool (2), remove the rear main seal (1)

To install:

5. Lubricate the crankshaft flange with engine oil.
6. Position the magnetic seal guide onto the crankshaft rear face. Position the crankshaft rear oil seal onto the guide.
7. Using the crankshaft rear oil seal installer and driver handle with a hammer, tap the seal into place. Continue to tap on the driver handle until the seal installer seats against the cylinder block crankshaft bore.
8. Install the flexplate.
9. Install the transmission.
10. Start the engine, check for leaks and repair if necessary.

4.0L Engine

See Figure 72.

1. Before servicing the vehicle, refer to the Precautions Section.

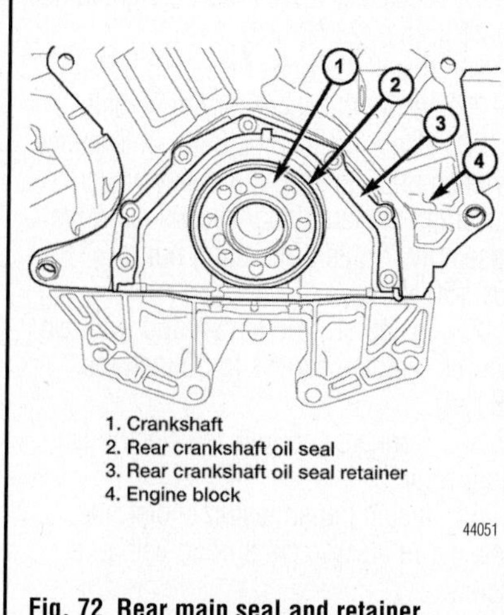

Fig. 72 Rear main seal and retainer

2. Remove the engine oil pan.
3. Lower the weight of the engine back onto the engine mounts.
4. Remove transmission from vehicle.
5. Remove the flexplate.
6. Remove the rear crankshaft oil seal retainer bolts.
7. Remove the crankshaft oil seal and clean all mating surfaces.

To install:

⁂ WARNING

Make sure the rear crankshaft oil seal surface is clean and free of any abrasive materials. The rear crankshaft oil seal and retainer are an assembly. DO NOT separate the seal protector from the rear crankshaft oil seal before installation on engine. Damage to the seal lip will occur if the seal protector is removed and installed prior to installation on engine.

8. Apply engine oil to crankshaft seal surface.
9. If the seal protector is missing or was accidentally dislodged, go to Step No. 3. Otherwise, carefully position the oil seal retainer assembly, and seal protector on crankshaft and push firmly into place on engine block (during this step, the seal protector will be pushed from the rear oil seal assembly as a result of installing the rear oil seal). Hand tighten the rear oil seal fasteners, and go to Step No. 4.

➡The seal lip must always uniformly curl inward toward the engine on the crankshaft. If for any reason the installation sleeve is missing or dislodged from rear crankshaft oil seal prior to installation, the following procedure must be performed:

10. Using the chamfered seal guide from Special Tool 6926, insert the tapered end into the transmission side of the rear crankshaft oil seal assembly, and push the seal guide through the seal assembly. This will ensure the seal lip is positioned toward the engine when the seal assembly is installed. When the seal lip is correctly positioned, go to Step No. 2.

➡The following steps must be performed to prevent oil leaks at sealing joints:

11. Attach Special Tools 8225 to pan rail using the oil pan fasteners.

➡Special Tools 8225, are used to assist with the fit of the flush mount rear main seal retainer. The notch on tool should be located away the seal retainer.

12. While applying firm pressure to the seal retainer against Special Tools 8225, tighten seal retainer screws to 105 inch lbs. (12 Nm).
13. Remove special tool No. 8225.
14. Install oil pan. Tighten the 6mm fasteners to 105 inch lbs. (12 Nm) and the 8mm fasteners to 21 ft. lbs. (28 Nm).
15. Install the flexplate and transmission.

TIMING BELT FRONT COVER

REMOVAL & INSTALLATION

4.0L Engine

See Figure 73.

1. Before servicing the vehicle, refer to the Precautions Section.
2. Disconnect and isolate the negative battery cable.
3. Remove the air cleaner element housing.
4. Disconnect two washer pump hoses, coolant recovery hose and washer pump electrical connector from the coolant recovery/washer fluid reservoir assembly.
5. Remove 5 screws and remove the coolant recovery/washer fluid reservoir assembly.
6. Disengage the radiator hose retainer from the electric fan shroud.
7. Remove transmission cooling line retainer bolt from the electric fan shroud.
8. Disconnect the electric fan connector from the electric fan shroud.
9. Remove two bolts and lift the electric fan shroud from vehicle.

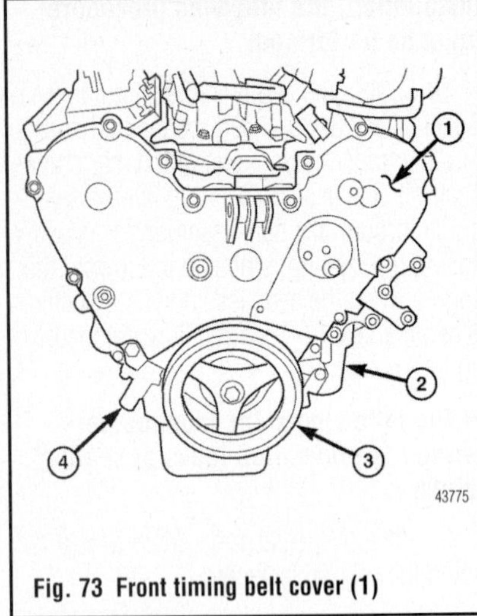

Fig. 73 Front timing belt cover (1)

10. Use Adapter Pins 8346 in Spanner Wrench 6958 to hold the pulley and remove fan/viscous fan drive assembly.
11. Remove the accessory drive belt.
12. Remove the power steering belt.
13. Remove the two nuts that secure the front of the A/C compressor.
14. Back out the two A/C compressor mounting studs from the accessory drive bracket.
15. Remove the four bolts and the nut and remove the accessory drive bracket.
16. Remove crankshaft damper bolt.
17. Using Puller 1023 and Crankshaft Insert 9020, remove crankshaft damper.
18. Remove the fourteen outer timing belt cover bolts and cover.

To install:

19. Install the front timing belt outer cover and 14 bolts.
20. Tighten the timing cover bolts as follows:
- M6 bolts: 105 inch lbs. (12 Nm)
- M8 bolts: 21 ft. lbs. (28 Nm)
- M10 bolts: 40 ft. lbs. (54 Nm)

21. Install crankshaft damper using Forcing Screw C-4685-C1, with Nut and Thrust Bearing from 6792, and 6792-1 Installer.
22. Install crankshaft damper bolt. Tighten bolt to 70 ft. lbs. (95 Nm) while holding damper with Damper Holding Fixture 9365.
23. Install the accessory drive bracket. Tighten four bolts and nut to 40 ft. lbs. (54 Nm).
24. Install the lower stud and upper stud that secures the front of the A/C compressor to the accessory drive bracket. Tighten studs securely.
25. Install the lower nut and upper nut that secures the front of the A/C compressor to the accessory drive bracket. Tighten nuts to 21 ft. lbs. (28 Nm).
26. Install the power steering belt.
27. Install the accessory drive belt.
28. Use Adapter Pins 8346 in Spanner Wrench 6958 to hold the pulley while installing the fan blade/viscous fan drive assembly. Tighten mounting nut to 37 ft. lbs. (50 Nm).
29. Install electric fan shroud with two screws. Tighten screws to 50 inch lbs. (6 Nm).
30. Connect and lock the electric fan connector.
31. Install transmission cooler line retainer to electric fan shroud with one screw.
32. Install radiator hose retainer to electric fan shroud.
33. Install the coolant recovery/washer fluid reservoir assembly with five screws. Connect two washer pump hoses, coolant recovery hose, and washer pump electrical connector.
34. Install and connect the air cleaner element housing.
35. Fill the coolant system.
36. Connect the negative battery cable. Tighten nut to 40 inch lbs. (4.5 Nm).

TIMING BELT & SPROCKETS

REMOVAL & INSTALLATION

4.0L Engine

See Figures 74 and 75.

1. Before servicing the vehicle, refer to the Precautions Section.
2. Disconnect the negative battery cable.
3. Remove the front timing belt cover. Mark belt running direction, if timing belt is to be reused.

**** WARNING**

When aligning the timing marks, always rotate engine by turning the crankshaft. Failure to do so will result in valve and/or piston damage.

4. Rotate the engine clockwise until crankshaft mark aligns with the TDC mark on oil pump housing and the camshaft sprocket timing marks are aligned with the marks on the rear cover.
5. Raise and support the vehicle.
6. Remove the bolt and reposition the oil cooler hose.
7. Remove the timing belt tensioner.
8. Lower the vehicle.
9. Remove the timing belt.
10. Inspect the tensioner for fluid leakage.
11. Inspect the pivot and bolt for free movement, bearing grease leakage, and smooth rotation. If not rotating freely, replace the arm and pulley assembly.

➡When tensioner is removed from the engine it is necessary to compress the plunger into the tensioner body.

12. Index the tensioner in the vise the same way it is installed on the engine. This ensures proper pin orientation when tensioner is installed on the engine.
    a. Place the tensioner into a vise and SLOWLY compress the plunger. Total bleed down of tensioner should take approximately two minutes.
    b. When the plunger is compressed into the tensioner body install a pin through the body and plunger to retain plunger in place until tensioner is installed.
13. Hold the left camshaft sprocket with a 1 7/16 in. (36 mm) box end wrench so that the timing mark does not move while removing the retaining bolt.
14. Loosen and remove the camshaft gear retaining bolt and washer. The left bolt is 10.0 in. (255 mm) long.

➡The camshaft timing gears are keyed to the camshaft.

15. Remove the left camshaft sprocket.
16. Hold the right camshaft sprocket with a 1 7/16 in. (36 mm) box end wrench so that the timing mark does not move while removing the retaining bolt.
17. Loosen and remove the camshaft gear retaining bolt and washer. The right bolt is 8 3/8 in. (213 mm) long.
18. Remove the right camshaft sprocket.
19. Using a gear puller, remove the crankshaft sprocket.

To install:

20. Install crankshaft sprocket using Forcing Screw C-4685-C1, with Nut and Thrust Bearing from 6792, and Sprocket Installer 6641.

➡The camshaft sprockets are keyed and not interchangeable from side to side because of the camshaft position sensor pick-up.

21. Install the left camshaft sprocket onto the camshaft.
22. Install a NEW sprocket attaching bolt into place. The 10 in. (255 mm) bolt is to be installed in the left camshaft.
23. Hold the left camshaft sprocket 1 7/16 in. (36 mm) box end wrench so that the tim-

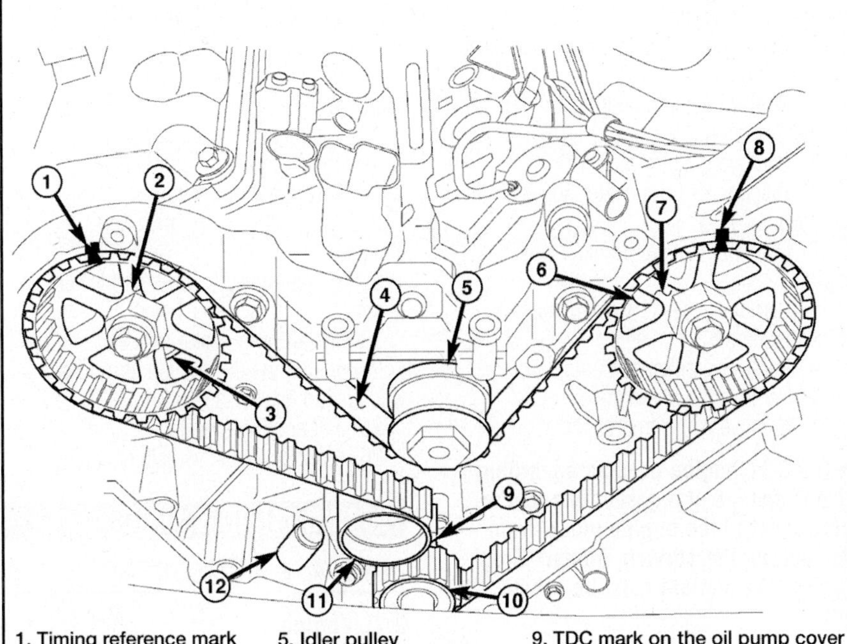

Fig. 74 Timing gear alignment—4.0L engine

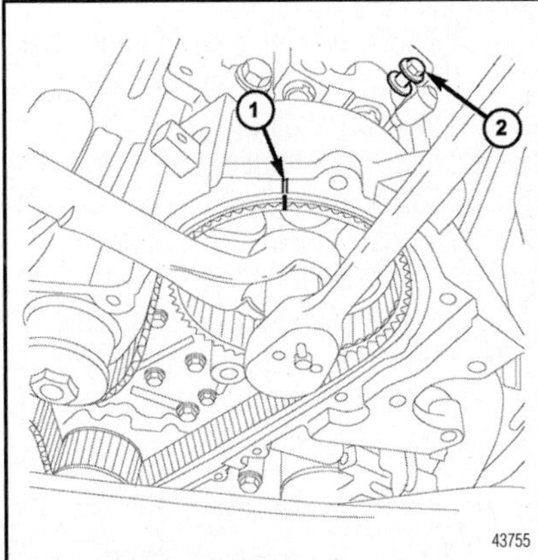

Fig. 75 Left camshaft sprocket, bolt (2), and timing mark (1)—right camshaft sprocket similar

ing mark does not move while tightening the retaining bolt. Tighten bolt to 75 ft. lbs. (102 Nm) plus a 90° turn.

24. Install the right camshaft sprocket onto the camshaft.

25. Install a NEW sprocket attaching bolt into place. The 8 3/8 in. (213 mm) bolt is to be installed into the right camshaft.

26. Hold the right camshaft sprocket 1 7/16 in. (36 mm) box end wrench so that the timing mark does not move while tightening the retaining bolt. Tighten bolt to 75 ft. lbs. (102 Nm) plus a 90° turn.

**** WARNING**

If camshafts have moved from the timing marks, always rotate camshaft towards the direction nearest to the timing marks (DO NOT TURN CAMSHAFTS A FULL REVOLUTION OR DAMAGE to valves and/or pistons could result).

27. Align the crankshaft sprocket with the TDC mark on the oil pump cover.

28. Align the camshaft sprockets timing reference marks with the marks on the rear cover.

29. Install the timing belt starting at the crankshaft sprocket going in a counter-clockwise direction. Install the belt around the last sprocket and maintain tension on the belt as it is positioned around the tensioner pulley.

➡It is necessary to compress the plunger into the tensioner body and install a locking pin prior to reinstalling the tensioner.

30. Holding the tensioner pulley against the belt, install the tensioner into the housing and tighten two bolts to 21 ft. lbs. (28 Nm).

31. When tensioner is in place, pull retaining pin to allow the tensioner to extend to the pulley bracket.

32. Rotate crankshaft sprocket two revolutions and check the timing marks on the camshafts and crankshaft. The marks should line up within their respective locations. If marks do not line up, repeat procedure.

33. Reposition the oil cooler hose retainer bracket near the timing belt tensioner and install the bolt.

34. Install the front timing belt cover.

35. Connect negative battery cable. Tighten nut to 40 inch lbs. (4.5 Nm).

TIMING BELT REAR COVER

REMOVAL & INSTALLATION

4.0L Engine

See Figures 76 and 77.

➡The rear timing belt cover has O-rings to seal the water pump passages to cylinder block. Do not reuse the O-rings.

1. Before servicing the vehicle, refer to the Precautions Section.
2. Perform fuel pressure release procedure.
3. Disconnect and isolate the negative battery cable.
4. Drain the cooling system.
5. Remove the timing belt.
6. Remove the camshaft sprockets.
7. Remove the alternator.
8. Remove the three pump mounting bolts through the pump pulley and reposition the power steering pump.
9. Remove the rear timing belt cover bolts.
10. Remove the rear cover.

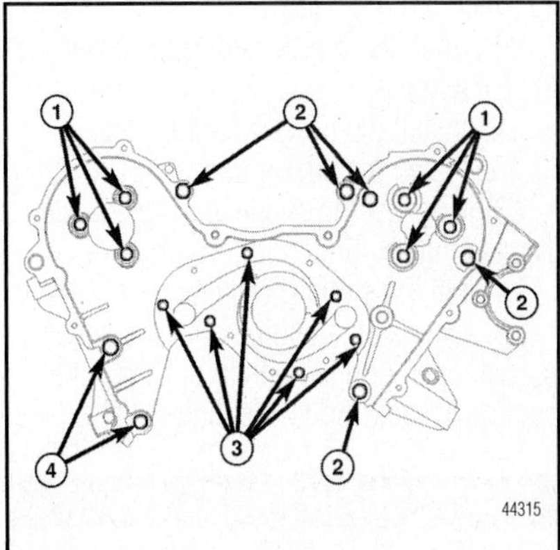

Fig. 76 Rear timing belt cover M10 (2, 4) and M8 (1) bolts, and water pump bolts (3)

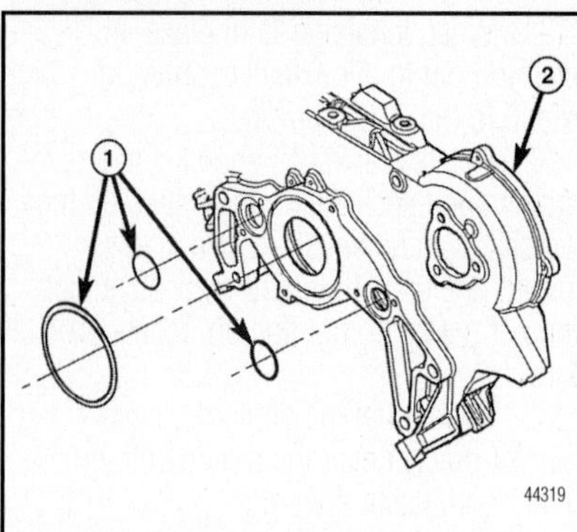

Fig. 77 Position NEW O-rings (1) on the cover (2)

To install:

11. Clean the rear timing belt cover O-ring sealing surfaces and grooves. Lubricate the new O-rings with Mopar® Dielectric Grease or equivalent to facilitate assembly.
12. Position NEW O-rings on the cover.
13. Install the rear timing belt cover. Tighten nuts and bolts to the following specified torque:
    - M10: 40 ft. lbs. (54 Nm)
    - M8: 20 ft. lbs. (28 Nm)
14. Position the water pump and new gasket.
15. Install the water pump mounting bolts. Tighten to 105 inch lbs. (12 Nm).
16. Install the three power steering pump mounting bolts through the pulley. Tighten the bolts to 21 ft. lbs. (28 Nm).
17. Position the alternator to the engine and install the two mounting bolts and tighten both bolts to 42 ft. lbs. (57 Nm).
18. Snap the field wire connector into the rear of the alternator.
19. Install the B+ terminal and nut to the alternator mounting stud. Tighten the nut to 115 inch lbs. (13 Nm).
20. Snap the plastic protective cover to the B+ terminal.
21. Install the camshaft sprockets.
22. Install the timing belt.
23. Connect the negative battery cable. Tighten nut to 45 inch lbs. (5 Nm).
24. Fill the cooling system.
25. Operate the engine until it reaches normal operating temperature. Check the cooling system for correct fluid level.

TIMING CHAIN FRONT COVER

REMOVAL & INSTALLATION

3.7L Engine

See Figure 78.

1. Before servicing the vehicle, refer to the Precautions Section.
2. Disconnect the battery negative cable.
3. Drain the cooling system.
4. Remove electric cooling fan and fan shroud assembly.
5. Remove radiator fan.
6. Disconnect both heater hoses at timing cover.
7. Disconnect lower radiator hose at engine.
8. Remove accessory drive belt tensioner assembly.
9. Remove crankshaft damper.
10. Remove the alternator.
11. Remove A/C compressor.

➡The 3.7L engine uses an anaerobic sealer instead of a gasket to seal the front cover to the engine block, from the factory. For service, Mopar® Grey Engine RTV sealant must be substituted.

➡It is not necessary to remove the water pump for timing cover removal.

12. Remove the bolts holding the timing cover to engine block.
13. Remove the timing cover.

To install:

14. Clean timing chain cover and block surface using rubbing alcohol. Do not use oil based liquids to clean timing cover or block surfaces.

⁂ WARNING

Use only rubbing alcohol, along with plastic or wooden scrapers. Use no wire brushes or abrasive wheels or metal scrapers, or damage to surfaces could result.

15. Inspect the water passage o-rings for any damage, and replace as necessary.

★ INDICATES STUD LOCATIONS

TIMING CHAIN COVER ASSEMBLY

415100

Fig. 78 Timing cover bolt tightening sequence

16. Apply Mopar® Engine RTV sealer to front cover using a 3 to 4mm thick bead.
17. Install the cover. Tighten fasteners in sequence as shown in to 43 ft. lbs. (58 Nm).
18. Install crankshaft damper.
19. Install the A/C compressor.
20. Install the generator.
21. Install accessory drive belt tensioner.
22. Install radiator upper and lower hoses.
23. Install both heater hoses.
24. Install the electric fan shroud and viscous fan drive assembly.
25. Fill cooling system.
26. Connect negative battery cable.

TIMING CHAIN & SPROCKETS

REMOVAL & INSTALLATION

3.7L Engine

See Figures 79 through 82.

1. Before servicing the vehicle, refer to the Precautions Section.
2. Disconnect the battery negative cable.
3. Drain the cooling system.
4. Remove the cylinder head covers.
5. Remove the electric cooling fan and fan shroud assembly.
6. Remove the timing chain front cover.
7. Rotate the engine until the timing mark on the crankshaft damper aligns with the TDC mark on the timing chain cover and the camshaft sprocket "V6" marks are at the 12 o'clock position (No. 1 TDC exhaust stroke).
8. Remove the power steering pump.
9. Remove the access plugs from the left and right cylinder heads for access to the chain guide fasteners.

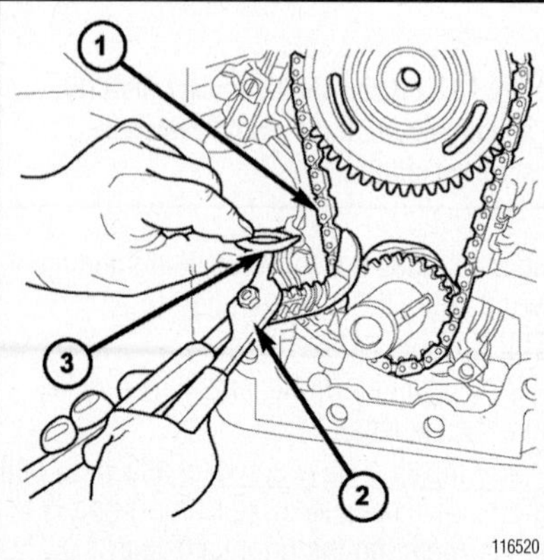

Fig. 79 Primary chain tensioner (1), adjustable pliers (2), and special tool 8514 (3)

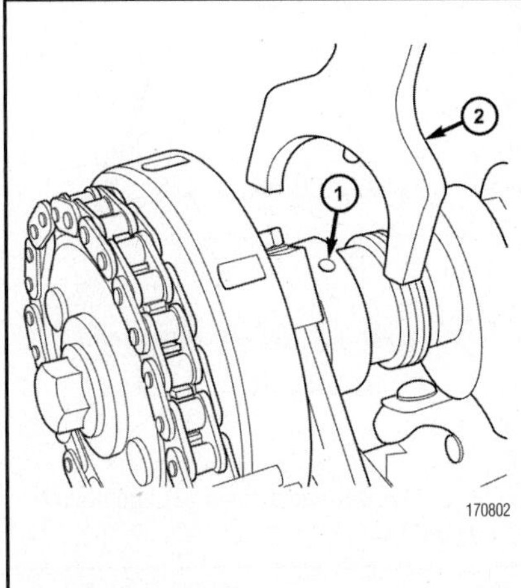

Fig. 80 Camshaft hole (1) and special tool 8428A (2)

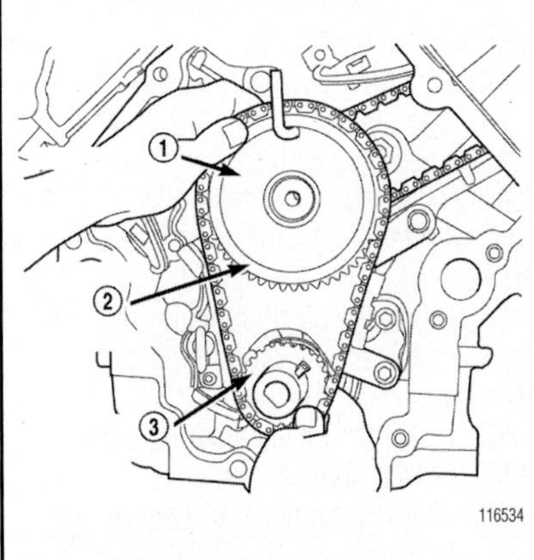

Fig. 81 Secondary camshaft holding tool No. 8429 (1), primary chain idler sprocket (2), and crankshaft sprocket (3)

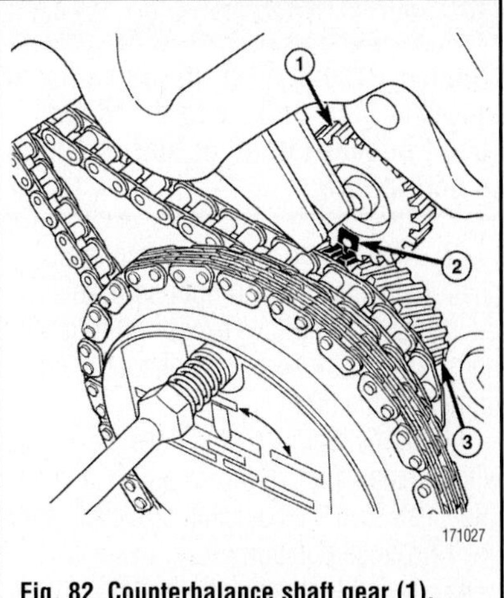

Fig. 82 Counterbalance shaft gear (1), timing mark (2), and idler sprocket gear

10. Remove the oil fill housing to gain access to the right side tensioner arm fastener.
11. Remove the crankshaft damper.
12. Collapse and pin the primary chain tensioner.
13. Remove the secondary chain tensioners. Cover the oil pan opening to prevent the plate behind the tensioner from falling into the oil pan.
14. Remove the camshaft position sensor.
15. Remove left and right camshaft sprocket bolts.

⁂ WARNING

Care should be taken not to damage the camshaft target wheel. Do not hold the target wheel while loosening or tightening the camshaft sprocket. Do not place the target wheel near a magnetic source of any kind. A damaged or magnetized target wheel could cause a vehicle no start condition. Do not forcefully rotate the camshafts or crankshaft independently of each other. Damaging intake valve to piston contact will occur. Ensure the negative battery cable is disconnected and isolated to guard against accidental starter engagement

16. While holding the left camshaft steel tube with a camshaft holding tool, remove the left camshaft sprocket. Slowly rotate the camshaft approximately 15 degrees clockwise to a neutral position.
17. While holding the right camshaft steel tube with a camshaft holding tool, remove the left camshaft sprocket. Slowly rotate the camshaft approximately 45 degrees counterclockwise to a neutral position.
18. Remove idler sprocket assembly bolt.
19. Slide the idler sprocket assembly and crank sprocket forward simultaneously to remove the primary and secondary chains.
20. Remove both pivoting tensioner arms and chain guides.
21. Remove the primary chain tensioner.

To install:

22. Using a vise, lightly compress the secondary chain tensioner piston until the piston step is flush with the tensioner body.
23. Using a pin or suitable tool, release the ratchet pawl by pulling the pawl back against spring force through the access hole on the side of the tensioner.
24. While continuing to hold the pawl back, push the ratchet device to approximately 2 mm from the tensioner body.
25. Install the tensioner pin into the hole on the front of the tensioner. Slowly open the vise to transfer the piston spring force to lock pin.
26. Position the primary chain tensioner over the oil pump and insert the bolts into the lower two holes on the tensioner bracket and tighten the bolts to 21 ft. lbs. (28 Nm).
27. Install the right side chain tensioner arm. Install the Torx® bolt and tighten Torx® bolt to 21 ft. lbs. (28 Nm).

➡The silver bolts retain the guides to the cylinder heads and the black bolts retain the guides to the engine block.

28. Install the left side chain guide and tighten the bolts to 21 ft. lbs. (28 Nm).
29. Install the left side chain tensioner arm and the Torx® bolt and tighten Torx® bolt to 21 ft. lbs. (28 Nm).
30. Install the right side chain guide and tighten the bolts to 21 ft. lbs. (28 Nm).
31. Install both secondary chains onto the idler sprocket and align the two plated links on the secondary chains to be visible through the two lower openings on the idler sprocket (4 o'clock and 8 o'clock). Once the secondary timing chains are installed, position the secondary camshaft chain holder to hold the chains in place for installation.
32. Align the primary chain double plated links with the timing mark at 12 o'clock on the idler sprocket and align the primary chain single plated link with the timing mark at 6 o'clock on the crankshaft sprocket.
33. Lubricate the idler shaft and bushings with clean engine oil.
34. The idler sprocket must be timed to the counterbalance shaft drive gear before the idler sprocket is fully seated.
35. Install all chains, crankshaft sprocket, and idler sprocket as an assembly.
36. Guide both secondary chains through the block and cylinder head openings.
37. Affix the chains with an elastic strap or equivalent. This will maintain tension on chains to aid in the installation.
38. Align the timing mark on the idler sprocket gear to the timing mark on the counterbalance shaft drive gear , and seat idler sprocket fully.
39. Lubricate the idler sprocket bolt washer with oil, install the idler sprocket assembly and tighten the retaining bolt to 25 ft. lbs. (34 Nm).
40. It will be necessary to slightly rotate the camshafts for sprocket installation.
41. Align the left camshaft sprocket "L" dot to the plated link on the chain.
42. Align the right camshaft sprocket "R" dot to the plated link on the chain.

✻✻ WARNING

Remove excess oil from the camshaft sprocket bolt. Failure to do so can result in over-torque of bolt resulting in bolt failure.

43. Remove the secondary camshaft chain holder, and attach both sprockets to the camshafts. Remove excess oil from the bolts, and install sprocket bolts, but do not tighten at this time.
44. Verify that all plated links are aligned with the marks on all the sprockets and the "V6" marks on the camshaft sprockets are at the 12 o'clock position.
45. Install both secondary chain tensioners and tighten the bolts to 21 ft. lbs. (28 Nm). Ensure the plate between the left secondary chain tensioner and block is correctly installed.

➡Left and right secondary chain tensioners are not common.

46. Remove all 3 locking pins from the tensioners.

✻✻ WARNING

After pulling locking pins out of each tensioner, DO NOT manually extend the tensioner(s) ratchet. Doing so will over tension the chains, resulting in noise and/or high timing chain loads.

47. Using the Special tool 6958 with adapter pins 8346 and a torque wrench, tighten the left camshaft sprocket bolt to 90 ft. lbs. (122 Nm). Tighten the
48. Using the Special tool 6958 with adapter pins 8346, tighten the right camshaft sprocket bolt to 90 ft. lbs. (122 Nm).
49. Rotate the engine two full revolutions and verify the timing marks are at the follow locations:
    - Primary chain idler sprocket dot is at 12 o'clock
    - Primary chain crankshaft sprocket dot is at 6 o'clock
    - Secondary chain camshaft sprockets "V6" marks are at 12 o'clock
    - Counter-balancer shaft drive gear dot is aligned to the idler sprocket gear dot
50. Lubricate all three chains with engine oil.
51. After installing all the chains, it is recommended that the idler gear end play be checked. The end play must be within 0.004–0.010 in. (0.10–0.25 mm). If not within specification, the idler gear must be replaced.
52. Install the timing chain cover and the crankshaft damper.
53. Install the cylinder head covers.
54. Coat the large threaded cylinder head access plug with Mopar® Thread Sealant with Teflon and then install into the right cylinder head and tighten to 60 ft. lbs. (81 Nm).
55. Install the oil fill housing.
56. Install access plug in the left cylinder head.
57. Install the power steering pump.
58. Fill the cooling system.
59. Connect the negative battery cable.

VALVE COVERS

REMOVAL & INSTALLATION

3.7L Engine

See Figure 83.

1. Before servicing the vehicle, refer to the Precautions Section.
2. Disconnect the negative cable from battery.
3. Remove the air cleaner assembly, resonator assembly and air inlet hose.
4. To prepare for removal of the left valve cover (cylinder head cover):
    a. Disconnect the injector connectors and unclip the injector harness.
    b. Route the injector harness in front of the valve cover (cylinder head cover).
    c. Disconnect the left side breather tube and remove the breather tube.
5. To prepare for removal of the right valve cover (cylinder head cover):
    a. Drain the cooling system, below the level of the heater hoses.
    b. Remove the accessory drive belt.
    c. Remove the air conditioning compressor retaining bolts and move the compressor to the left.
    d. Remove the heater hoses.
    e. Disconnect the injector and the ignition coil connectors.
    f. Disconnect and remove the Positive Crankcase Ventilation (PCV) hose.
    g. Remove the oil fill tube.
    h. Unclip the injector and ignition coil harness and move away from the valve cover.
    i. Remove right rear breather tube and filter assembly.
6. Remove the valve cover mounting bolts.
7. Remove the valve covers and gaskets.

➡The gasket may be used again, providing no cuts, tears, or deformations have occurred.

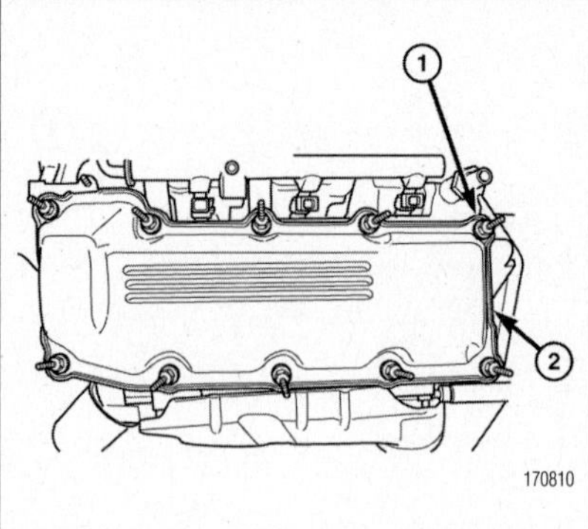

Fig. 83 Typical valve cover (2) and mounting bolts (1)

To install:

✻✻ WARNING

Do not use harsh cleaners to clean the valve covers. Severe damage to covers may occur.

8. Clean the valve cover and both sealing surfaces. Inspect and replace gasket as necessary.
9. Install the valve cover. Tighten the valve cover bolts and the double ended studs to 105 in. lbs (12 Nm).
10. To complete the installation of the left cylinder head cover:
    a. Install the left side breather and connect the breather tube.
    b. Connect the injector electrical connectors and the injector harness retaining clips.
11. To complete the installation of the right cylinder head cover:
    a. Install the right rear breather tube and filter assembly.
    b. Connect the injector, ignition coil electrical connectors and harness retaining clips.
    c. Install the oil fill tube.
    d. Install the PCV hose.
    e. Install the heater hoses.
    f. Install the air conditioning compressor retaining bolts.
    g. Install the accessory drive belt.
    h. Fill the cooling system.
12. Install the air cleaner assembly, resonator assembly and air inlet hose.
13. Connect the negative cable to battery.

4.0L Engine

See Figure 84.

1. Before servicing the vehicle, refer to the Precautions Section.
2. Disconnect and isolate the negative battery cable.

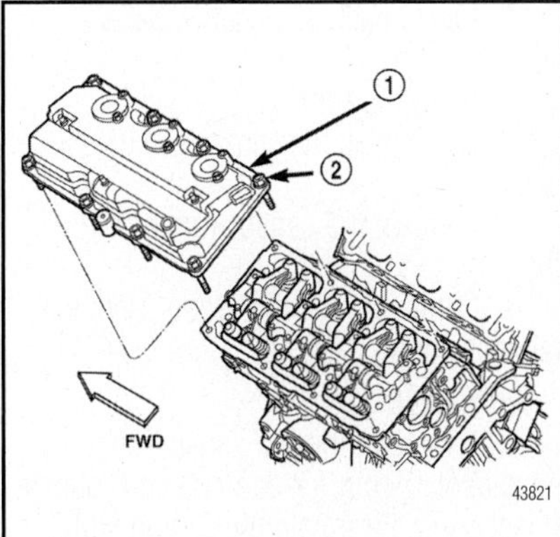

Fig. 84 Typical valve cover (1) and mounting bolts (2)

3. Remove the upper intake manifold from the engine.
4. Cover the lower intake manifold openings.
5. Disconnect and remove the three ignition coils.
6. Lift up on the wire harness track retaining tabs and reposition the wire harness.
7. Completely loosen the cylinder head cover (valve cover) retaining bolts and remove the cylinder head covers.

**** CAUTION**

Do not start or run engine with cylinder head cover removed from the engine. Damage or personal injury may occur.

To install:

8. Clean the cylinder head and cover mating surfaces. Inspect and replace the gasket and seals as necessary.
9. To replace spark plug tube seals:
   a. Using a suitable pry tool, carefully remove tube seals.
   b. Position new seal with the part number on seal facing the cylinder head cover.
   c. Install the seals using a camshaft installer tool.
10. Install the cylinder head covers and tighten the bolts to 105 inch lbs. (12 Nm).
11. Position the wiring harness on the cylinder head covers.
12. Reinstall the wire harness track retaining tabs into the covers.
13. Install the ignition coils. Tighten mounting screws to 60 inch lbs. (7 Nm).
14. Connect the ignition coil electrical connectors.
15. Install the upper intake manifold.
16. Connect the negative battery cable.

VALVE LASH

ADJUSTMENT

The valve lash is not adjustable.

ENGINE PERFORMANCE & EMISSION CONTROLS

CAMSHAFT POSITION (CMP) SENSOR

LOCATION

See Figures 85 and 86.

REMOVAL & INSTALLATION

3.7L Engine

1. Before servicing the vehicle, refer to the Precautions Section.
2. Disconnect the negative battery cable.
3. Disconnect the electrical connector at the Camshaft Position (CMP) sensor.
4. Remove the sensor mounting bolt.
5. Carefully remove the sensor from the cylinder head in a rocking and twisting action. Twisting sensor eases removal.

To install:

6. Check the condition of the sensor O-ring.
7. Clean out the machined hole in cylinder head.
8. Apply a small amount of engine oil to the sensor O-ring.
9. Install the sensor into the cylinder head with a slight rocking and twisting action.

**** WARNING**

Before tightening the sensor mounting bolt, be sure the sensor is completely flush to the cylinder head. If sensor is not flush, damage to sensor mounting tang may result.

10. Install the mounting bolt and tighten to 105 in. lbs (12 Nm).
11. Connect the electrical connector to the sensor.
12. Connect the negative cable to battery.

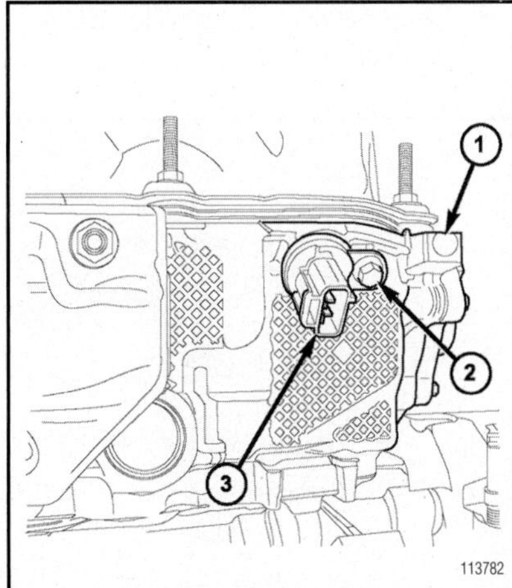

Fig. 85 The Camshaft Position (CMP) Sensor (3) is bolted (2) to the front/top of the right cylinder head (1)—3.7L engine

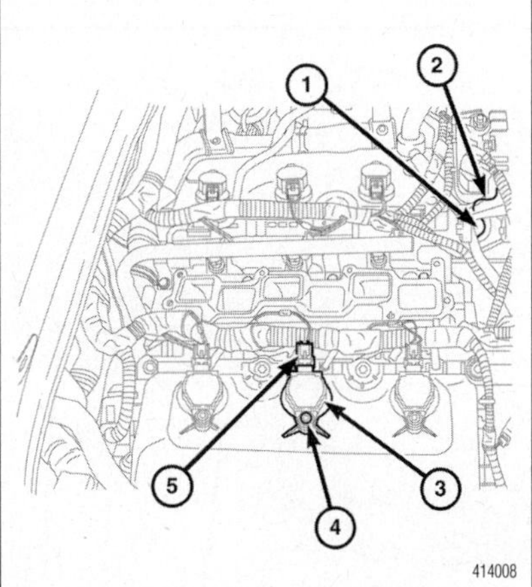

Fig. 86 Camshaft Position (CMP) Sensor (1) is located at the front/top of the timing gear cover below the alternator (2)—4.0L engine

4.0L Engine

1. Before servicing the vehicle, refer to the Precautions Section.
2. Disconnect the negative battery cable.
3. Remove the alternator.
4. Disconnect the electrical connector at the Camshaft Position (CMP) sensor.
5. Remove the sensor mounting bolt.
6. Carefully twist the sensor from the timing gear cover.
7. Check the condition of the sensor O-ring.

To install:

8. Push the CMP sensor into the timing belt cover with a twisting motion until fully seated.

✲✲ WARNING

Make sure the CMP sensor is fully seated. Do not drive the CMP sensor into the bore with mounting screw. This may cause a faulty signal or no signal at all.

9. While holding the sensor in this position, install the mounting bolt and tighten to 105 in. lbs (12 Nm).
10. Connect and lock the electrical connector to the CMP sensor.
11. Install the alternator.
12. Connect the negative cable to battery.

CRANKSHAFT POSITION (CKP) SENSOR

LOCATION

See Figures 87 and 88.

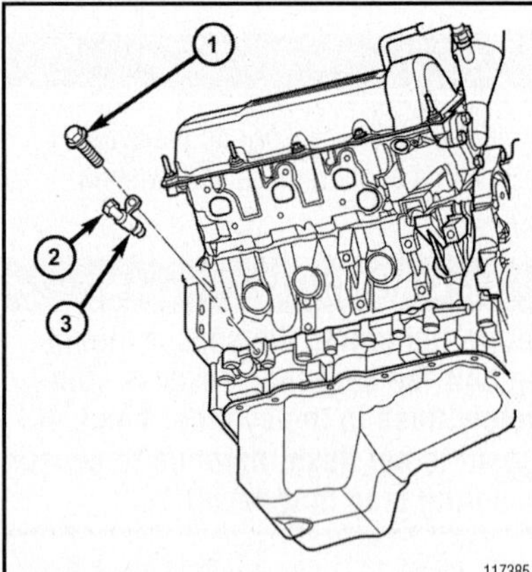

Fig. 87 Crankshaft Position (CKP) Sensor (2), mounting bolt (1), and O-ring (3)—3.7L engine

REMOVAL & INSTALLATION

3.7L Engine

1. Before servicing the vehicle, refer to the Precautions Section.
2. Disconnect the negative battery cable.
3. Raise the vehicle.
4. Disconnect the sensor electrical connector.
5. Remove the sensor mounting bolt.
6. Carefully twist the sensor from the cylinder block.
7. Check the condition of the sensor O-ring.

To install:

8. Clean out the machined hole in engine block.
9. Apply a small amount of engine oil to the sensor O-ring.
10. Install the sensor into the engine block with a slight rocking and twisting action.

✲✲ WARNING

Before tightening the sensor mounting bolt, be sure sensor is completely flush to cylinder block. If sensor is not flush, damage to sensor mounting tang may result.

11. Install the mounting bolt and tighten to 21 ft. lbs. (28 Nm).
12. Connect electrical connector to sensor.
13. Lower the vehicle.
14. Connect the negative cable to battery.

4.0L Engine

1. Before servicing the vehicle, refer to the Precautions Section.
2. Disconnect the negative battery cable.
3. Raise the vehicle.
4. Disconnect the sensor electrical connector.
5. Remove the sensor mounting bolt.
6. Carefully twist the sensor from the transmission.

To install:

7. If reinstalling the sensor, check the sensor O-ring for damage and replace if necessary. Lubricate the O-ring with clean engine oil before installing the sensor.
8. Push the CKP sensor into the transmission case with a twisting motion until fully seated.

➡Before tightening sensor mounting bolt, be sure sensor is completely flush to transmission. If sensor is not flush, damage to sensor mounting tang may result.

9. While holding the sensor in this position, install the mounting bolt and tighten to 105 in. lbs (12 Nm).
10. Connect and lock the electrical connector to the CKP sensor.
11. Install the alternator.
12. Connect the negative cable to battery.

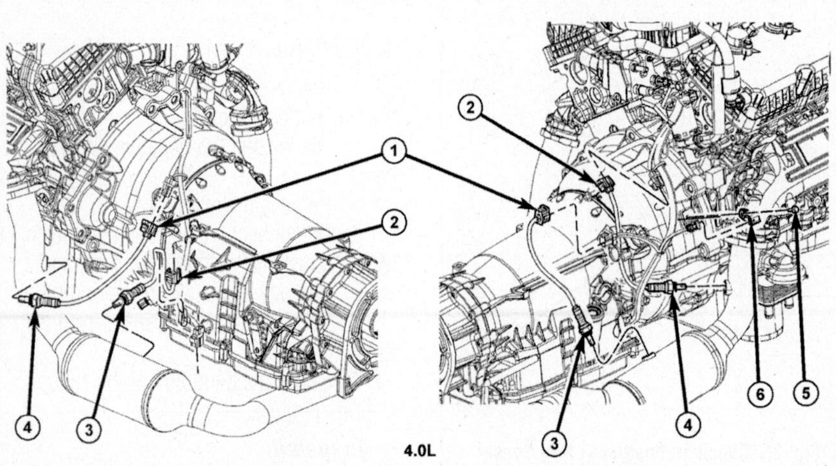

Fig. 88 The Crankshaft Position (CKP) Sensor (6) is mounted into the right side of the transmission bellhousing—4.0L engine

ELECTRONIC CONTROL MODULE (ECM)

LOCATION

See Figure 89.

REMOVAL & INSTALLATION

1. Before servicing the vehicle, refer to the Precautions Section.

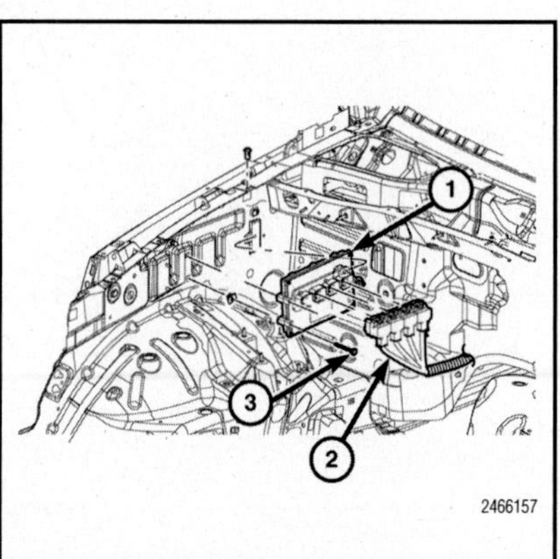

Fig. 89 Electronic Control Module (ECM/PCM) (1), electrical connectors (2), and mounting bolts (3)

2. Disconnect the negative battery cable.
3. Disconnect the electrical connectors.
4. Remove the mounting bolts.
5. Remove the ECM from the vehicle.

To install:

6. Position the ECM into the vehicle.
7. Tighten the mounting bolts to 71 inch lbs. (8 Nm).
8. Connect the electrical connectors.
9. Connect the negative battery cable.

ENGINE COOLANT TEMPERATURE (ECT) SENSOR

LOCATION

See Figure 90.

REMOVAL & INSTALLATION

3.7L Engine

⁂ CAUTION

Hot, pressurized coolant can cause injury by scalding. Cooling system must be partially drained before removing the coolant temperature sensor.

➡The ECT sensor is installed into a water jacket at front of intake manifold near rear of alternator.

1. Before servicing the vehicle, refer to the Precautions Section.
2. Disconnect the negative battery cable.
3. Partially drain the cooling system.
4. Disconnect the sensor electrical connector.
5. Remove the ECT sensor from the intake manifold.

To install:

6. Apply thread sealant to the sensor threads.
7. Install the ECT sensor to the engine and tighten the mounting bolts to 8 ft. lbs. (11 Nm).
8. Connect the electrical connector.
9. Refill the cooling system to the correct level.
10. Connect the negative battery cable.

HEATED OXYGEN (HO2S) SENSOR

LOCATION

See Figures 91 and 92.

REMOVAL & INSTALLATION

⁂ WARNING

Never apply any type of grease to the oxygen sensor electrical connector, or attempt any repair of the sensor wiring harness.

1. Before servicing the vehicle, refer to the Precautions Section.
2. Disconnect the negative battery cable.
3. Raise and safely support the vehicle.
4. Disconnect the wire connector from oxygen sensor.

⁂ WARNING

When disconnecting sensor electrical connector, do not pull directly on wire going into sensor.

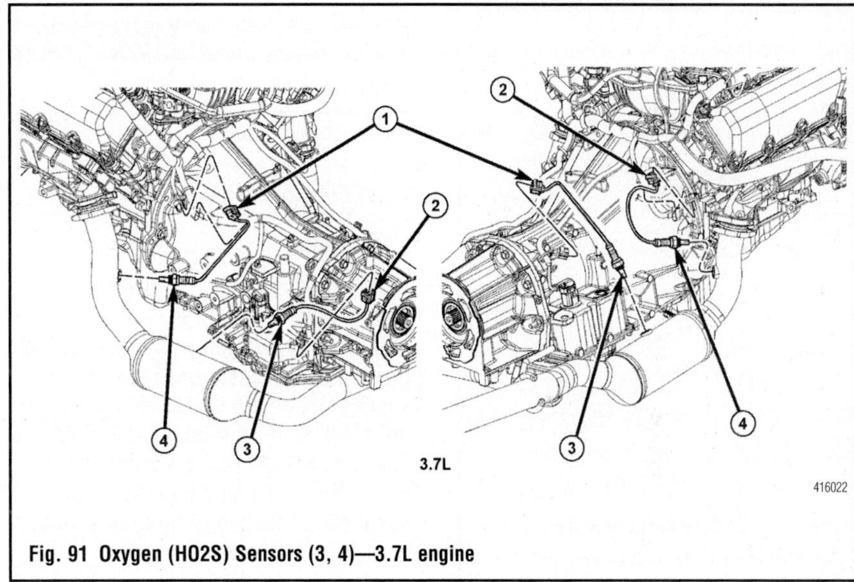

Fig. 91 Oxygen (HO2S) Sensors (3, 4)—3.7L engine

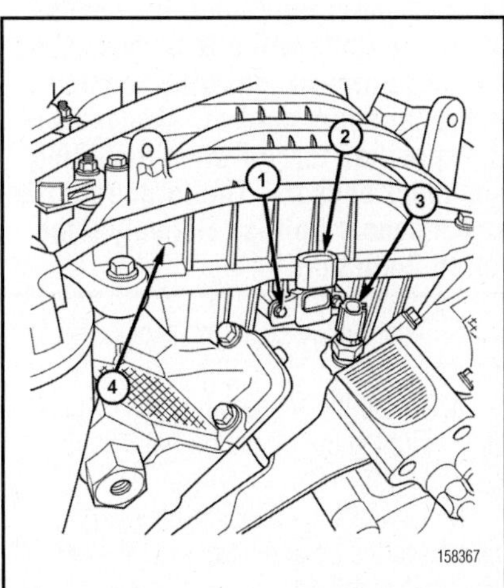

Fig. 90 Engine Coolant Temperature (ECT) Sensor (3) and mounting bolts (1); and MAP Sensor (2)—3.7L engines

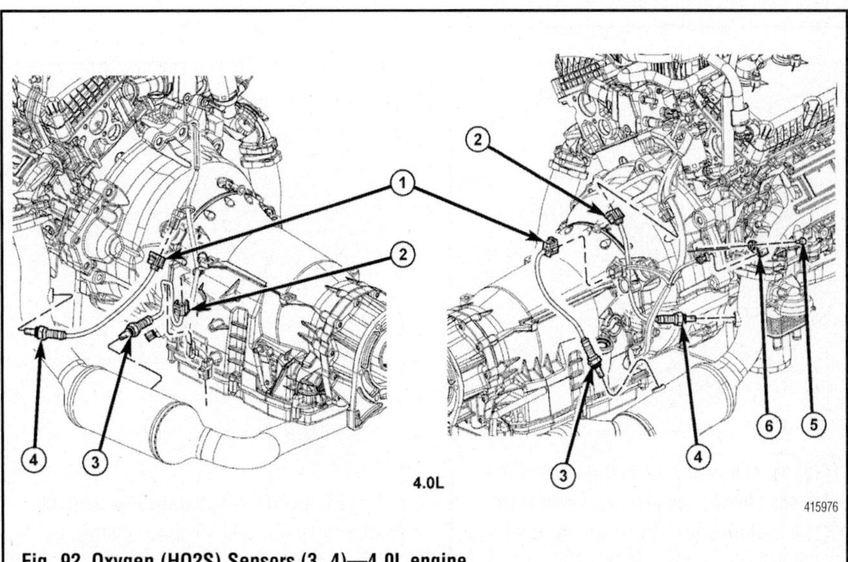

Fig. 92 Oxygen (HO2S) Sensors (3, 4)—4.0L engine

5. Remove the sensor with an oxygen sensor removal and installation tool.
6. Clean the threads in exhaust pipe using appropriate tap.

To install:

⁂ WARNING

Threads of new oxygen sensors are factory coated with anti-seize compound. Do not add any additional anti-seize compound to the threads of a new oxygen sensor.

7. Install the oxygen sensor and tighten to 30 ft. lbs. (41 Nm).
8. Connect the electrical connector.
9. Lower the vehicle.
10. Connect the negative battery cable.

INTAKE AIR TEMPERATURE (IAT) SENSOR

LOCATION

See Figures 93 and 94.

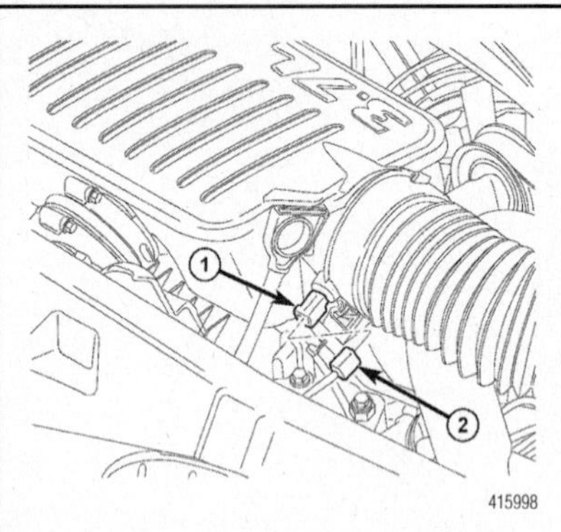

Fig. 93 The Intake Air Temperature (IAT) Sensor (1) with the electrical connector (2) is installed into the rubber air intake tube near the throttle body—3.7L engine

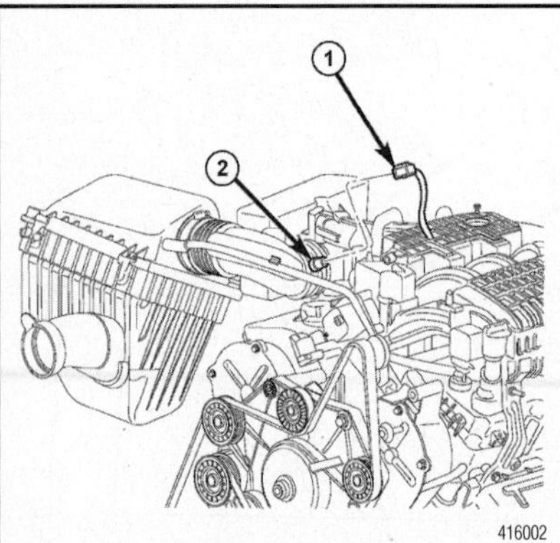

Fig. 94 The Intake Air Temperature (IAT) Sensor 21) with the electrical connector (1) is installed into the rubber air intake tube near the throttle body—4.0L engine

REMOVAL & INSTALLATION

1. Before servicing the vehicle, refer to the Precautions Section.
2. Disconnect the negative battery cable.
3. Disconnect electrical connector from the IAT sensor. Clean dirt from the IAT at the sensor base.
4. Pull out on the IAT sensor while rotating for removal.
5. Check the condition of sensor O-ring.

To install:

6. Clean the sensor mounting hole.
7. To install, push the IAT sensor into the rubber intake tube while rotating.
8. Connect the electrical connector to the IAT sensor.
9. Connect the negative battery cable.

KNOCK SENSOR (KS)

LOCATION

See Figures 95 and 96.

REMOVAL & INSTALLATION

3.7L Engine

➡The left sensor is identified by an identification tag (LEFT). It is also identified by a larger bolt head. Do not mix the sensor locations. The two knock sensors are bolted into the cylinder block under the intake manifold. The two sensors share a common wiring harness using one electrical connector. Because of this, they must be replaced as a pair.

1. Before servicing the vehicle, refer to the Precautions Section.

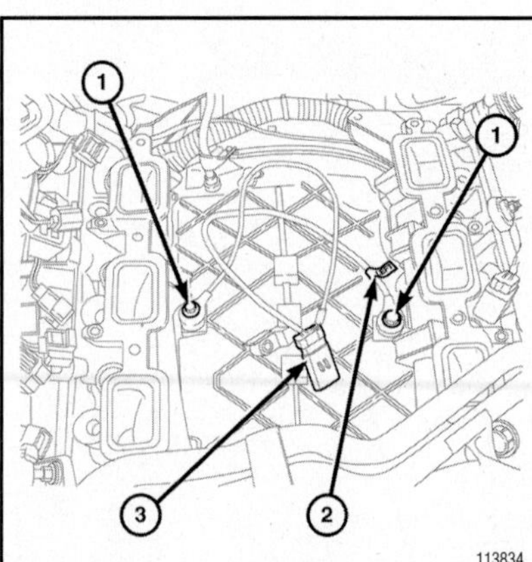

Fig. 95 Knock Sensors (KS) (1), label for left sensor (2), and electrical connector (3)—3.7L engine

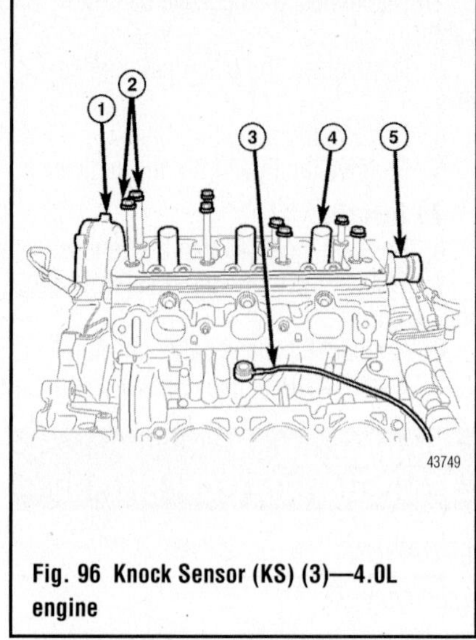

Fig. 96 Knock Sensor (KS) (3)—4.0L engine

2. Disconnect the negative battery cable.
3. Remove the intake manifold.
4. Disconnect the knock sensor dual pigtail harness from the engine wiring harness. This connection is made near the rear of the engine.
5. Remove both sensor mounting bolts.

➡Note the foam strip on bolt threads. This foam is used only to retain the bolts to sensors for plant assembly. It is not used as a sealant. Do not apply any adhesive, sealant or thread locking compound to these bolts.

6. Remove the sensors from the engine.

To install:

⁂ WARNING

Over or under tightening the sensor mounting bolts will affect knock sensor performance, possibly causing improper spark control. Always use the specified torque when installing the knock sensors. The torque for the knock sensor bolt is relatively light for an 8mm bolt.

7. Thoroughly clean the knock sensor mounting holes.
8. Install the sensors into the cylinder block. Tighten the mounting bolts to 15 ft. lbs. (20 Nm).
9. Connect the knock sensor wiring harness to the engine harness at the rear of the intake manifold.
10. Install the intake manifold.
11. Connect the negative battery cable.

4.0L Engine

1. Before servicing the vehicle, refer to the Precautions Section.
2. Perform the fuel system pressure relief procedure.
3. Disconnect the negative battery cable.
4. Drain the cooling system.
5. Remove the upper intake manifold including EGR tube, PCV, purge and power brake booster vacuum hoses.
6. Remove the fuel rail and the lower intake manifold.
7. Remove the sensor mounting bolt.

➡Note foam strip on bolt threads. This foam is used only to retain the bolt to sensor for plant assembly. It is not used as a sealant. Do not apply any adhesive, sealant or thread locking compound to this bolt.

8. Remove the knock sensor from engine.

To install:

9. Position the sensor to the engine. Install and tighten the mounting bolt to 7 ft. lbs. (10 Nm).
10. Install the lower intake manifold and the fuel rail.
11. Install the upper intake manifold, EGR tube, PCV, purge and power brake booster vacuum hoses.
12. Fill the coolant system.
13. Connect the negative battery cable.

MANIFOLD ABSOLUTE PRESSURE (MAP) SENSOR

LOCATION

See Figures 97 and 98.

REMOVAL & INSTALLATION

3.7L Engine

1. Before servicing the vehicle, refer to the Precautions Section.
2. Disconnect the negative battery cable.
3. Disconnect the electrical connector at the sensor.
4. Clean the area around the MAP sensor.
5. Remove one sensor mounting screw.
6. Remove the MAP sensor from the intake manifold.

To install:

7. Check the condition of the sensor O-ring.
8. Clean the MAP sensor mounting hole at the intake manifold.
9. Check the MAP sensor O-ring seal for cuts or tears.
10. Position the sensor into the manifold by sliding the sensor over the locating pin.
11. Tighten the mounting bolt to 25 inch lbs. (3 Nm).
12. Connect the electrical connector.
13. Reconnect the negative battery cable at battery.

4.0L Engine

➡An O-ring is used to seal the sensor to the intake manifold.

1. Before servicing the vehicle, refer to the Precautions Section.
2. Disconnect the negative battery cable.
3. Disconnect the electrical connector at sensor.
4. Clean the area around the MAP sensor.
5. Rotate sensor ¼ turn counter-clockwise until tangs align.
6. Pull the MAP sensor from the intake manifold.
7. Check the condition of the sensor O-ring.

To install:

8. Position the MAP sensor into the intake manifold. Note locating tangs.
9. Rotate the sensor ¼ turn clockwise.
10. Connect the electrical connector at the sensor.
11. Connect the negative battery cable.

VEHICLE SPEED SENSOR (VSS)

LOCATION

See Figure 99.

REMOVAL & INSTALLATION

1. Before servicing the vehicle, refer to the Precautions Section.
2. Raise and safely support the vehicle.
3. Place a suitable catch pan under the transmission for any fluid.
4. Remove the wiring connector from the speed sensor.
5. Remove the mounting bolt and remove the speed sensor from the transmission case.

To install:

6. Install the speed sensor into the transmission case and tighten the bolt to 80 inch lbs. (9 Nm).
7. Install the wiring connector to the speed sensor.
8. Verify the proper transmission fluid level and refill as necessary.
9. Lower the vehicle.

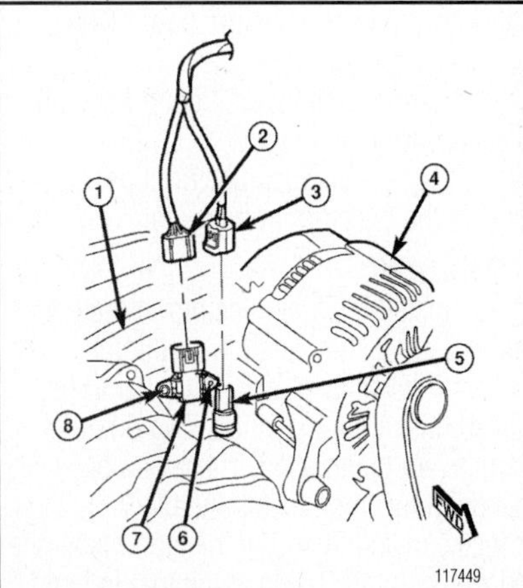

Fig. 97 The Manifold Absolute Pressure (MAP) Sensor (7) is mounted into the front of the intake manifold (1)—3.7L engines

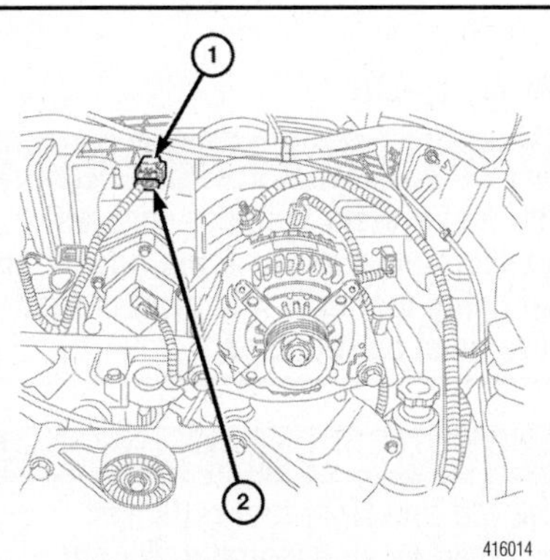

Fig. 98 The Manifold Absolute Pressure (MAP) Sensor (2) and electrical connector (1) is mounted into the top/front of the upper half of the intake manifold—4.0L engines

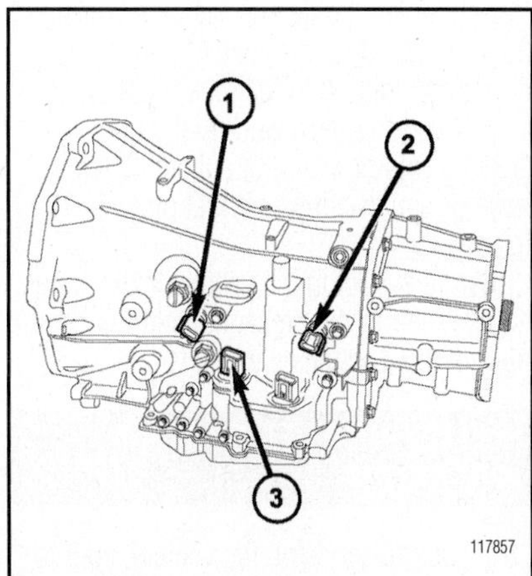

Fig. 99 Input speed sensor (1), output speed sensor (2), and transmission range sensor (3)

FUEL SYSTEM SERVICE PRECAUTIONS

Safety is the most important factor when performing not only fuel system maintenance but any type of maintenance. Failure to conduct maintenance and repairs in a safe manner may result in serious personal injury or death. Maintenance and testing of the vehicle's fuel system components can be accomplished safely and effectively by adhering to the following rules and guidelines.

- To avoid the possibility of fire and personal injury, always disconnect the negative battery cable unless the repair or test procedure requires that battery voltage be applied.
- Always relieve the fuel system pressure prior to disconnecting any fuel system component (injector, fuel rail, pressure regulator, etc.), fitting or fuel line connection. Exercise extreme caution whenever relieving fuel system pressure to avoid exposing skin, face and eyes to fuel spray. Please be advised that fuel under pressure may penetrate the skin or any part of the body that it contacts.
- Always place a shop towel or cloth around the fitting or connection prior to loosening to absorb any excess fuel due to spillage. Ensure that all fuel spillage (should it occur) is quickly removed from engine surfaces. Ensure that all fuel soaked cloths or towels are deposited into a suitable waste container.
- Always keep a dry chemical (Class B) fire extinguisher near the work area.
- Do not allow fuel spray or fuel vapors to come into contact with a spark or open flame.
- Always use a back-up wrench when loosening and tightening fuel line connection fittings. This will prevent unnecessary stress and torsion to fuel line piping.
- Always replace worn fuel fitting O-rings with new Do not substitute fuel hose or equivalent where fuel pipe is installed.

Before servicing the vehicle, make sure to also refer to the precautions in the beginning of this section as well.

RELIEVING FUEL SYSTEM PRESSURE

1. Before servicing the vehicle, refer to the Precautions Section.
2. Disconnect the negative battery cable.
3. Remove the fuel tank filler cap to release any fuel tank pressure.
4. Remove the fuel pump relay from the PDC.
5. Start and run the engine until it stops.
6. Unplug the connector from any injector and connect a jumper wire from either injector terminal to the positive battery terminal. Connect another jumper wire to the other terminal and momentarily touch the other end to the negative battery terminal.

⁂ WARNING

Just touch the jumper to the battery. Powering the injector for more than a few seconds will permanently damage it.

7. Place a rag below the quick-disconnect coupling at the fuel rail and disconnect it.

FUEL FILTER

REMOVAL & INSTALLATION

See Fuel Pump for Removal and Installation instructions.

These vehicles incorporate the use of a fuel pump module which comprises:

- An internal fuel filter
- A separate fuel pick-up, or inlet filter
- A fuel pressure regulator
- An electric fuel pump
- A fuel gauge sending unit (fuel level sensor)

If the filter(s), regulator, pump or sending unit requires service, the fuel pump module must be replaced.

FUEL INJECTORS

REMOVAL & INSTALLATION

3.7L Engine

See Figure 100.

⁂ CAUTION

The fuel system is under constant pressure even with engine off. Before servicing fuel rail, fuel system pressure must be released.

⁂ WARNING

The left and right fuel rails are replaced as an assembly. Do not attempt to separate rail halves at connector tube. Due to design of tube, it does not use any clamps. Never attempt to install a clamping device of any kind to tube. When removing fuel rail assembly for any reason, be careful not to bend or kink tube.

1. Before servicing the vehicle, refer to the Precautions Section.
2. Remove the fuel tank filler tube cap.
3. Perform the fuel system pressure release procedure.
4. Remove the negative battery cable at battery.
5. Remove the air duct at the throttle body air box.
6. Remove the air box at the throttle body.
7. Disconnect the fuel line latch clip and the fuel line at the fuel rail. A special tool will be necessary for fuel line disconnection.
8. Remove the necessary vacuum/vapor lines at the throttle body.
9. Disconnect the electrical connectors at all 6 fuel injectors. Push the red colored slider away from the injector. While pushing the slider, depress the tab and remove the connector from the injector. The factory fuel injection wiring harness is numerically tagged (INJ 1, INJ 2, etc.) for injector position identification. If the harness is not tagged, note wiring location before removal.
10. Disconnect the electrical connectors at the throttle body sensors.
11. Remove the 6 ignition coils.
12. Remove the 4 fuel rail mounting bolts.
13. Gently rock and pull the left side of the fuel rail until the fuel injectors just start to clear the machined holes in the cylinder head. Gently rock and pull the right side of rail until the injectors just start to clear the cylinder head holes. Repeat this procedure (left/right) until all injectors have cleared cylinder head holes.
14. Remove the fuel rail (with injectors attached) from the engine.
15. Disconnect the injector clips; and remove the injectors from the rail.

To install:

16. Install the fuel injectors into the fuel rail assembly and install the retaining clips.
17. If the same injectors are being reinstalled, install new O-rings. Two different O-rings are being used. These can be easily identified by color. Install the black O-ring at intake manifold end of injector. Install the red/rust colored O-ring at the fuel rail end of injector.
18. Clean out the fuel injector machined bores in the intake manifold.

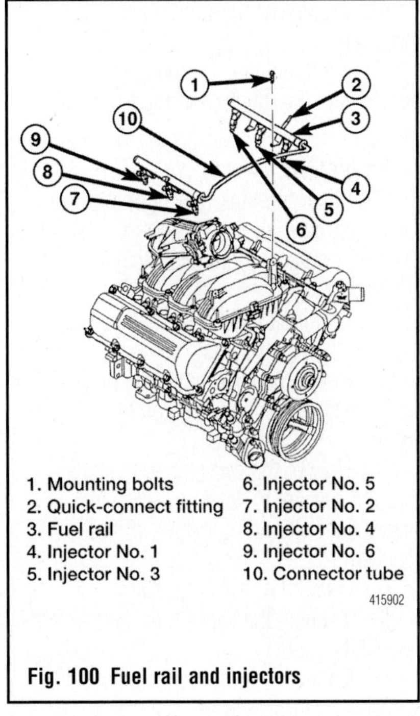

Fig. 100 Fuel rail and injectors

19. Apply a small amount of engine oil to each fuel injector O-ring. This will help in fuel rail installation.

20. Position the fuel rail/fuel injector assembly to the machined injector openings in the cylinder head.

21. Guide each injector into the cylinder head. Be careful not to tear the injector O-rings.

22. Push the right side of the fuel rail down until the fuel injectors have bottomed on the cylinder head shoulder.

23. Push the left fuel rail down until the injectors have bottomed on the cylinder head shoulder.

24. Install the 4 fuel rail mounting bolts and tighten to 100 inch lbs. (11 Nm).

25. Install the 6 ignition coils.

26. Connect the electrical connectors to the throttle body.

27. Connect the electrical connectors at all fuel injectors. Push the connector onto the injector and then push and lock the red colored slider. Verify the connector is locked to the injector by lightly tugging on the connector.

28. Connect the necessary vacuum lines to the throttle body.

29. Connect the fuel line latch clip and the fuel line to the fuel rail.

30. Install the air box to the throttle body.

31. Install the air duct to the air box.

32. Connect the battery cable to the battery.

33. Start the engine and check for leaks.

4.0L Engine

See Figure 101.

⁂ CAUTION

The fuel system is under constant pressure even with engine off. Before servicing fuel rail, fuel system pressure must be released.

1. Before servicing the vehicle, refer to the Precautions Section.

2. Perform the fuel system pressure release procedure.

3. Remove and isolate the negative battery cable at the battery.

4. Remove the upper intake manifold including EGR tube, PVC, purge and power brake booster vacuum.

5. Disconnect the fuel supply hose from the fuel rail.

6. Disconnect the electrical connectors at all six fuel injectors. The factory fuel injection wiring harness is numerically tagged (INJ 1, INJ 2, etc.) for injector position identification. If harness is not tagged, note wiring location before removal.

7. Remove the four fuel rail mounting bolts.

8. Gently rock and pull the left side of fuel rail until the fuel injectors just start to clear the machined holes in cylinder head. Gently rock and pull the right side of rail until the injectors just start to clear the cylinder head holes. Repeat this procedure (left/right) until all injectors have cleared cylinder head holes.

9. Remove the fuel rail (with injectors attached) from the engine.

10. Disconnect the injector clips; and remove the injectors from the rail.

To install:

11. Install the fuel injectors into the fuel rail assembly and install the retaining clips.

12. If the same injectors are being reinstalled, install new O-rings. Two different O-rings are being used. These can be easily identified by color. Install the black O-ring at intake manifold end of injector. Install the red/rust colored O-ring at the fuel rail end of injector.

13. Clean out the fuel injector machined bores in the intake manifold.

14. Apply a small amount of engine oil to each fuel injector O-ring. This will help in fuel rail installation.

15. Position the fuel rail/fuel injector assembly to the machined injector openings in the cylinder head.

16. Guide each injector into the cylinder head. Be careful not to tear the injector O-rings.

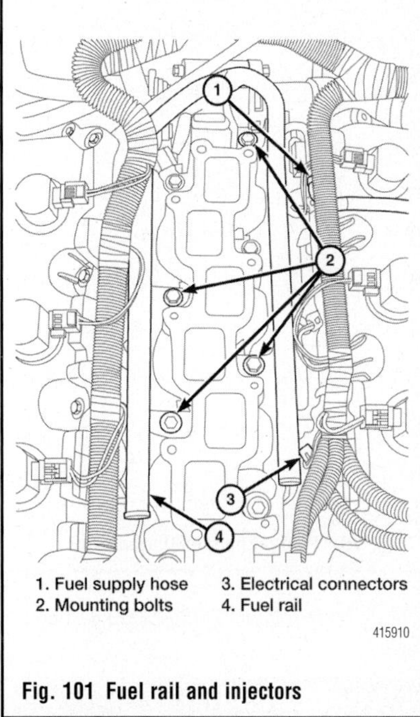

Fig. 101 Fuel rail and injectors

17. Push the right side of the fuel rail down until the fuel injectors have bottomed on the cylinder head shoulder. Push the left fuel rail down until the injectors have bottomed on the cylinder head shoulder.

18. Install the 4 fuel rail mounting bolts and tighten to 21 ft. lbs. (28 Nm).

19. Connect the fuel supply hose to the fuel rail.

20. Connect the fuel injector electrical connectors.

21. Install the upper intake manifold, EGR tube, PVC, purge and power brake booster vacuum hoses.

22. Connect the battery cable to battery.

23. Start engine and check for leaks.

FUEL PUMP

REMOVAL & INSTALLATION

See Figure 102.

1. Before servicing the vehicle, refer to the Precautions Section.

2. Drain and remove fuel tank.

3. Prior to removing the fuel pump module, use compressed air to remove any accumulated dirt and debris from around fuel tank opening.

4. Position the lockring remover/installer tool into the notches on the outside edge of the lockring.

5. Install a ½ inch drive breaker bar into the lockring remover/installer tool.

6. Rotate the breaker bar counterclockwise and remove the lockring.

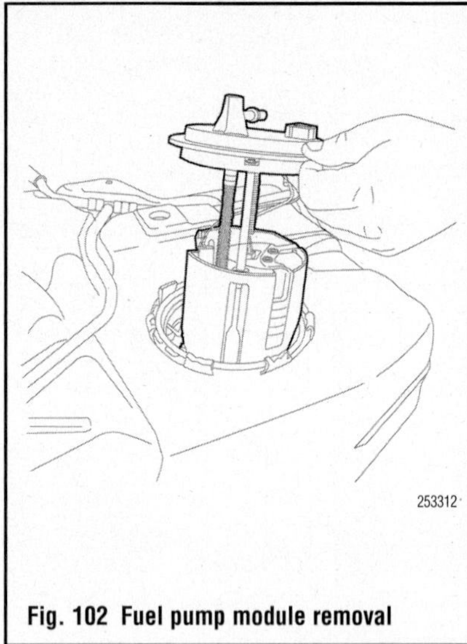

Fig. 102 Fuel pump module removal

7. Mark the fuel pump module orientation.

⁂ WARNING

The fuel pump module reservoir does not empty out when the tank is drained. The fuel in the reservoir will spill out when the module is removed.

8. Raise the fuel pump module out of the fuel tank using caution not spill fuel inside the vehicle.
9. Tip the fuel pump module on its side and drain all fuel from the reservoir.
10. Remove the fuel pump module from the fuel tank using caution not to bend the float arm.
11. Remove and discard the rubber O-ring seal.

To install:

➡Whenever the fuel pump module is serviced, the rubber O-ring seal must be replaced.

12. Clean the rubber O-ring seal area of the fuel tank and install a new rubber O-ring seal.
13. Lower the fuel pump module into the fuel tank using caution not to bend the float arm.

➡The fuel pump module must be properly located in the fuel tank for the fuel level gauge to work properly.

14. Align the rubber O-ring seal and rotate the fuel pump module to the orientation marks noted during removal. This step must be performed for the fuel level gauge to work properly.
15. Position the lockring over top of the fuel pump module.
16. Position the lockring remover/installer into the notches on the outside edge of the lockring.
17. Install a ½ inch drive breaker bar into the lockring remover/installer.
18. Rotate the breaker bar clockwise until all seven notches of the lockring have engaged.
19. Install the fuel tank.

FUEL TANK

DRAINING

1. Before servicing the vehicle, refer to the Precautions Section.
2. Disconnect the negative battery cable.
3. Remove the fuel fill cap.
4. Raise and support the vehicle.
5. Remove the fuel fill hose clamp at the rear of tank.
6. Remove the fuel fill hose from the fuel tank fitting.
7. Position a drain hose into the fuel fill hose opening. Note that a small flapper valve is installed into the opening.
8. Drain the fuel tank using an approved gasoline draining station.

REMOVAL & INSTALLATION

1. Before servicing the vehicle, refer to the Precautions Section.
2. Remove the fuel tank filler tube cap.
3. Perform the fuel system pressure release procedure.
4. Raise and support the vehicle.
5. Disconnect the fuel line quick connect fittings and at the front of the fuel tank.
6. Remove the fuel fill hose and clamp at the rear of the tank.
7. Position a drain hose into the fuel fill hose opening. Note that a small flapper valve is installed into the opening.
8. Disconnect the vapor lines and at the rear of the tank.
9. Remove the rear propshaft.
10. Support the tank with a hydraulic jack.
11. Loosen the two nuts at the tank support bracket.
12. Remove the bolt from the tank support bracket.
13. Remove the tank mounting bolts at both sides of the tank.
14. Partially lower the tank to gain access to the pump module electrical connector.
15. Disconnect the electrical connector at the fuel pump module.
16. Continue lowering the tank for removal.
17. If the fuel tank is to be replaced, remove the fuel pump module from the tank.

To install:

18. Place the tank to a hydraulic jack and raise it just enough to connect the fuel pump module electrical connector.
19. Continue raising the tank until it's snug to the vehicle body.
20. Install the tank mounting bolts at both sides of the tank. Tighten to 45 ft. lbs. (61 Nm).
21. Tighten the two nuts at the tank support bracket to 45 ft. lbs. (61 Nm). Install the bolt and tighten to 45 ft. lbs. (61 Nm).
22. Install the rear propshaft.
23. Connect the vapor lines and at the rear of the tank.
24. Connect the fuel fill hose and clamp at the rear of the tank.
25. Connect the fuel line quick connect fittings at the front of the fuel tank.
26. Lower the vehicle, fill the tank with fuel and install the fuel fill cap.
27. Check for fuel leaks.

IDLE SPEED

ADJUSTMENT

Idle speed is maintained by the Engine Control Module (ECM). No adjustment is necessary or possible.

THROTTLE BODY

REMOVAL & INSTALLATION

3.7L Engine

See Figure 103.

⁂ WARNING

A (factory adjusted) set screw is used to mechanically limit the position of the throttle body throttle plate. Never attempt to adjust the engine idle speed using this screw. All idle speed functions are controlled by the ECM. Never have the ignition key in the ON position when checking the throttle body shaft for a binding condition. This may set DTC's.

1. Before servicing the vehicle, refer to the Precautions Section.
2. Using a diagnostic scan tool, record any previous DTC's (Diagnostic Trouble Codes).

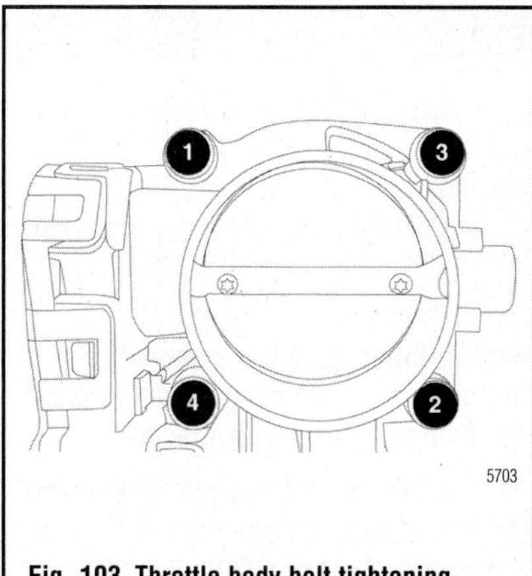

Fig. 103 Throttle body bolt tightening sequence

3. Disconnect and isolate the negative battery cable.
4. Remove the air intake tube at the throttle body flange.
5. Disconnect the throttle body electrical connector.
6. Disconnect the necessary vacuum lines at the throttle body.
7. Remove the four throttle body mounting bolts.
8. Remove the throttle body from the intake manifold.

To install:

9. Check the condition of throttle body-to-intake manifold O-ring. Replace as necessary.
10. Clean the mating surfaces of throttle body and intake manifold.
11. Install the O-ring between throttle body and intake manifold.
12. Position the throttle body to intake manifold.
13. Install all throttle body mounting bolts finger tight.

⁂ WARNING

The throttle body mounting bolts MUST be tightened to specifications. Over tightening can cause damage to the throttle body or the intake manifold.

14. Obtain a torque wrench. Tighten the mounting bolts (as shown) in a mandatory torque criss-cross pattern sequence to 65 inch lbs. (8 Nm).
15. Install the electrical connector.
16. Install the necessary vacuum lines.
17. Install the air cleaner duct at throttle body.
18. Connect the negative battery cable.
19. Using the diagnostic scan tool, erase all previous DTC's and perform the ETC Relearn function.

4.0L Engine

See Figure 103.

⁂ WARNING

A (factory adjusted) set screw is used to mechanically limit the position of the throttle body throttle plate. Never attempt to adjust the engine idle speed using this screw. All idle speed functions are controlled by the ECM. Never have the ignition key in the ON position when checking the throttle body shaft for a binding condition. This may set DTC's.

1. Before servicing the vehicle, refer to the Precautions Section.
2. Using a diagnostic scan tool, record any previous DTC's (Diagnostic Trouble Codes).
3. Disconnect and isolate the negative battery cable.
4. Loosen the clamps and reposition the air inlet hose.
5. Disconnect the throttle body electrical connector.
6. Remove the four throttle body mounting bolts.
7. Remove the throttle body from the intake manifold.

To install:

8. Check condition of throttle body-to-intake manifold O-ring. Replace as necessary.
9. Clean mating surfaces of the throttle body and intake manifold.
10. Install the O-ring between throttle body and intake manifold.
11. Position the throttle body to the intake manifold.
12. Install all throttle body mounting bolts finger tight.

⁂ WARNING

The throttle body mounting bolts MUST be tightened to specifications. Over tightening can cause damage to the throttle body or the intake manifold.

13. Obtain a torque wrench. Tighten mounting bolts in a mandatory torque crisscross pattern sequence to 65 inch lbs. (8 Nm).
14. Connect the electronic throttle control, MAP sensor, and IAT sensor electrical connectors.
15. Install the inlet hose and tighten the clamps.
16. Connect the negative battery cable.
17. Using the diagnostic scan tool, erase all previous DTC's.

HEATING & AIR CONDITIONING SYSTEM

BLOWER MOTOR

REMOVAL & INSTALLATION

⁂ CAUTION

Before servicing components near or affected by the SRS (air bag) system, read and observe all SRS Service Precautions and disable the SIR system. Refer to Supplemental Restraint System (SRS), in the Chassis Electrical section. Failure to observe all precautions may result in accidental airbag deployment, personal injury, or death.

➡The blower motor is located on the passenger side of the vehicle under the instrument panel. The blower motor can be removed without having to remove the instrument panel or the HVAC housing.

1. Disconnect and isolate the negative battery cable.
2. If equipped, remove the silencer from below the passenger side of the instrument panel.
3. From underneath the instrument panel, disconnect the instrument panel wire harness connector from the blower motor.
4. Remove the three screws that secure the blower motor to the bottom of the HVAC housing and remove the blower motor.

To install:

5. Position the blower motor into the bottom of the HVAC housing.
6. Install the three screws that secure the blower motor to the HVAC housing. Tighten the screws to 10 in. lbs. (1 Nm).
7. Connect the instrument panel wire harness connector to the blower motor.
8. If equipped, install the silencer below the passenger side of the instrument panel.
9. Reconnect the negative battery cable.

HEATER CORE

REMOVAL & INSTALLATION

⁂ CAUTION

Before servicing components near or affected by the SRS (air bag) system, read and observe all SRS Service Precautions and disable the SIR system. Refer to Supplemental Restraint System (SRS), in the Chassis Electrical section. Failure to observe all precautions may result in accidental airbag deployment, personal injury, or death.

⁂ CAUTION

The heater core tubes are not serviced separately from the heater core. The heater core tubes should not be repositioned, loosened or removed from the heater core. Failure to follow these instructions may result in a coolant leak and possible serious or fatal injury.

1. Disconnect and isolate the negative battery cable.
2. Remove the HVAC housing assembly and place it on a workbench.
3. Remove the air distribution housing from the HVAC housing.
4. Remove the two screws that secure the upper front passenger side floor duct to the passenger side of the air distribution housing and remove the duct.
5. Carefully remove the foam seal from the heater core tube flange. If the seal is deformed or damaged, it must be replaced.
6. Remove the screw that secures the heater core tube flange to the air distribution housing.
7. Disengage the plastic retainer from around the heater core tubes and remove the flange.

➡If the foam insulator around the heater core is deformed or damaged, the insulator must be replaced.

8. Disengage the four plastic retaining tabs that secure the heater core to the passenger side of the air distribution housing and carefully remove the heater core from the housing.

To install:

9. Carefully install the heater core into the passenger side of the air distribution housing and engage the four plastic retainer tabs that secure the heater core to the housing. Make sure the retaining tabs are fully engaged.
10. Position the heater core tube flange over the heater core tubes and onto the to the passenger side of the air distribution housing.
11. Engage the plastic retainer around the heater core tubes. Make sure the retainer is fully engaged around the tubes.
12. Install the screw that secures the heater core tube flange to the air distribution housing. Tighten the screws to 10 inch lbs. (1 Nm).
13. Install the upper front passenger side floor duct onto the air distribution housing and install the two retaining screws. Tighten the screws to 10 inch lbs. (1 Nm).
14. Install the foam seal onto the heater core tube flange.
15. Install the air distribution housing onto the HVAC housing.
16. If the heater core is being replaced, flush the cooling system.
17. Install the HVAC housing assembly.
18. Reconnect the negative battery cable.

STEERING

POWER STEERING GEAR

REMOVAL & INSTALLATION

2WD Models

See Figure 104.

⁂ CAUTION

Before servicing components near or affected by the SRS (air bag) system, read and observe all SRS Service Precautions and disable the SIR system. Refer to Supplemental Restraint System (SRS), in the Chassis Electrical section. Failure to observe all precautions may result in accidental airbag deployment, personal injury, or death.

1. Before servicing the vehicle, refer to the Precautions Section.
2. Siphon the power steering fluid from the power steering reservoir.
3. Lock the steering wheel to prevent spinning of the clockspring.

➡The steering column on vehicles with an automatic transmission may not be equipped with an internal locking shaft that allows the ignition key cylinder to be locked with the key. Alternative methods of locking the steering wheel for service will have to be used.

4. Raise and support the vehicle.
5. Remove the tire and wheel assembly.
6. Mark the alignment adjusting cams and tie rod end jam nuts on the steering gear for easier installation.
7. Remove the tie rod end nuts.
8. Separate tie rod ends from the knuckles with a tie rod puller.
9. If equipped, remove the skid plate.
10. Remove the lower intermediate shaft coupler pinch bolt and slide the coupler off the gear.
11. Remove the power steering lines from the gear.
12. Remove the mounting bolts from the gear to the front cradle.
13. Remove the steering gear from the vehicle.

To install:

14. Transfer the outer tie rod ends to the new steering gear (if needed).
15. Install the steering gear to the vehicle.
16. Install the gear mounting bolts to the front cradle. Tighten the bolts to 130 ft. lbs. (176 Nm).

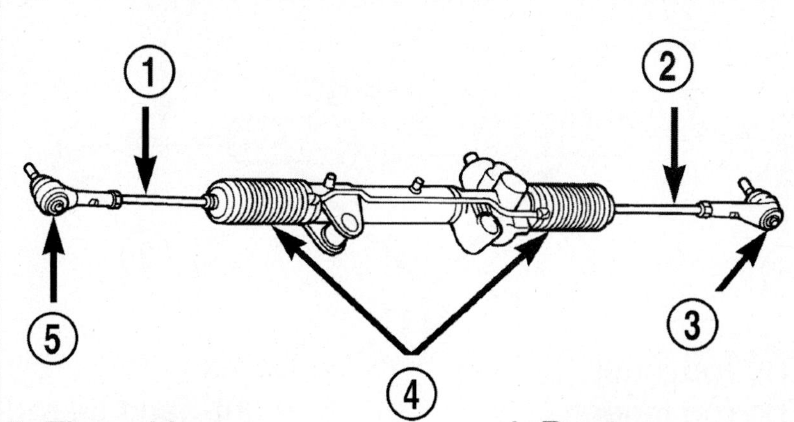

Fig. 104 Power steering gear

17. Install the power steering lines to the gear. Tighten the tube nuts to 20 ft. lbs. (27 Nm).
18. Install the lower coupler pinch bolt and slide the coupler onto the gear.
19. Install the tie rod end to the knuckle and tighten the nuts to 30 ft. lbs (41 Nm) plus an additional 90° turn.
20. Install the tire and wheel assembly.
21. Install the skid plate.
22. Lower the vehicle.
23. Unlock the steering wheel.
24. Fill the power steering fluid.
25. Reset the toe and center the steering wheel.

4WD Models

3.7L Engine

See Figure 105.

⁂ CAUTION

Before servicing components near or affected by the SRS (air bag) system, read and observe all SRS Service Precautions and disable the SIR system. Refer to Supplemental Restraint System (SRS), in the Chassis Electrical section. Failure to observe all precautions may result in accidental airbag deployment, personal injury, or death.

1. Before servicing the vehicle, refer to the Precautions Section.
2. Siphon the power steering fluid from the power steering reservoir.
3. Lock the steering wheel to prevent spinning of the clockspring.

➡The steering column on vehicles with an automatic transmission may not be equipped with an internal locking shaft that allows the ignition key cylinder to be locked with the key. Alternative methods of locking the steering wheel for service will have to be used.

4. Disconnect the battery cables ends from the battery.
5. Remove the battery.
6. Disengage the retaining clips of the power center and move it to the side out of the way to access the battery tray.
7. Remove the battery tray.
8. Remove the lower intermediate shaft coupler pinch bolt and slide the coupler off the gear.
9. Raise and support the vehicle.
10. Remove the tire and wheel assembly.
11. Mark the alignment adjusting cams and tie rod end jam nuts on the steering gear for easier installation.
12. Remove the tie rod end nuts.
13. Separate tie rod ends from the knuckles with a tie rod puller.
14. Remove the power steering lines from the gear.
15. Remove the mounting bolts from the gear to the front cradle.
16. Remove the left front lower suspension arm cam/bolt and lower the control

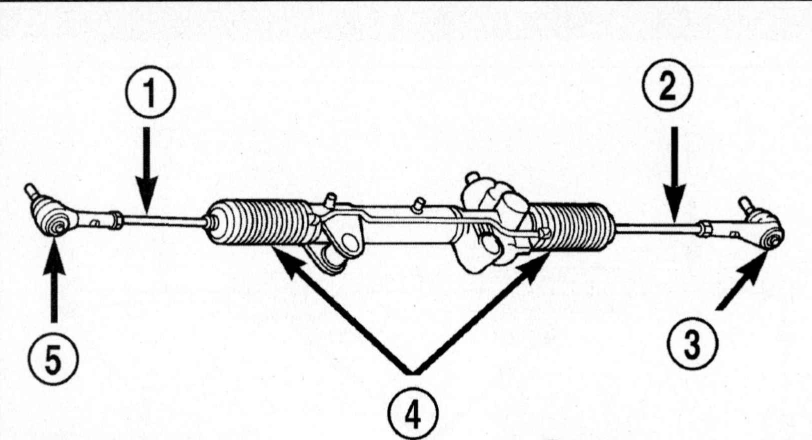

Fig. 105 Power steering gear

arm enough to get the axle mounting bracket bolt out. This must be done to remove the axle mounting bracket.

17. Remove the axle mounting bracket.
18. Remove the oil filter and trough.
19. Put the steering gear in the full right position and lower the gear out of the vehicle.
20. Remove the steering gear from the vehicle.

To install:

21. Transfer the outer tie rod ends to the new steering gear (if needed).
22. Install the steering gear to the vehicle.
23. Install the gear mounting bolts to the front cradle. Tighten the bolts to 130 ft. lbs. (176 Nm).
24. Install the power steering lines to the gear. Tighten the tube nuts to 20 ft. lbs. (27 Nm).
25. Install the oil filter trough and filter.
26. Install the axle mounting bracket.
27. Install the left lower control arm into position and install the cam/bolt.
28. Install the tie rod end to the knuckle and tighten the nuts to 30 ft. lbs (41 Nm) plus an additional 90° turn.
29. Install the tire and wheel assembly.
30. Lower the vehicle.
31. Install the lower coupler pinch bolt and slide the coupler onto the gear. Tighten the pinch bolt to 39 ft. lbs. (53).
32. Install the battery tray and the battery.
33. Reinstall the power center back into place.
34. Reconnect the battery cables.
35. Unlock the steering wheel.
36. Fill the power steering fluid.
37. Perform a wheel alignment.

4.0L Engine

See Figure 105.

**** CAUTION**

Before servicing components near or affected by the SRS (air bag) system, read and observe all SRS Service Precautions and disable the SIR system. Refer to Supplemental Restraint System (SRS), in the Chassis Electrical section. Failure to observe all precautions may result in accidental airbag deployment, personal injury, or death.

1. Before servicing the vehicle, refer to the Precautions Section.
2. Siphon the power steering fluid from the power steering reservoir.
3. Lock the steering wheel to prevent spinning of the clockspring.

➡The steering column on vehicles with an automatic transmission may not be equipped with an internal locking shaft that allows the ignition key cylinder to be locked with the key. Alternative methods of locking the steering wheel for service will have to be used.

4. Raise and support the vehicle.
5. Remove the air cleaner housing.
6. Remove the washer/coolant reservoir assembly .
7. Remove the fan shroud.
8. Remove the pressure and return lines at the gear.
9. Remove the front tire and wheel assemblies.
10. Remove the front axle.
11. Remove the tie rod end nuts.
12. Separate tie rod ends from the knuckles with a tie rod puller.
13. Remove the intermediate shaft lower coupler pinch bolt and slide the coupler off the gear.
14. Remove the power steering lines from the gear.
15. Remove the mounting bolts from the gear to the front cradle.
16. Remove the steering gear from the vehicle.

To install:

17. Transfer the tie rod ends to the new steering gear (if needed).
18. Install the steering gear to the vehicle.
19. Install the gear mounting bolts to the front cradle. Tighten the gear mounting bolts to 130 ft. lbs. (176 Nm).
20. Install the power steering lines to the gear and tighten to 20 ft. lbs. (27 Nm).
21. Install the lower coupler bolt and slide the coupler onto the gear. Tighten the bolt to 39 ft. lbs. (53 Nm).
22. Install the tie rod end to the knuckle and tighten the nuts to 30 ft. lbs (41 Nm) plus an additional 90° turn.
23. Install the front axle.
24. Install the tire and wheel assembly.
25. Lower the vehicle.
26. Unlock the steering wheel.
27. Fill the power steering fluid.
28. Reset the toe and center the steering wheel.

POWER STEERING PUMP

REMOVAL & INSTALLATION

3.7L Engine

See Figure 106.

1. Before servicing the vehicle, refer to the Precautions Section.
2. Siphon out as much power steering fluid as possible.
3. Remove the serpentine drive belt.
4. Remove the power steering high pressure hose at the pump.
5. Remove the return hose at the pump.
6. Remove the three bolts securing the pump to the engine through the holes in the pulley.
7. Remove the pump from the vehicle.

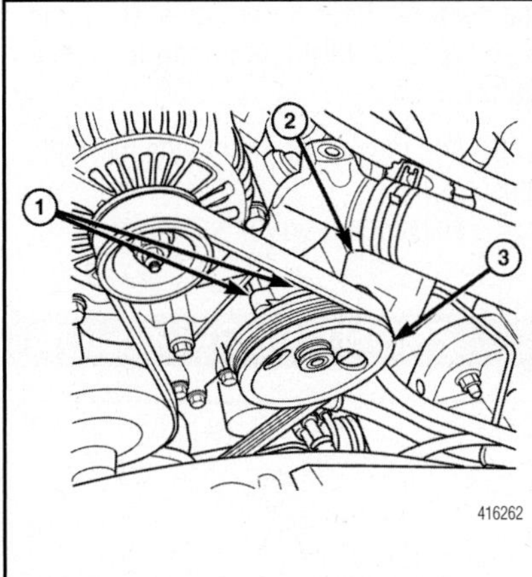

Fig. 106 Power steering pump mounting bolts (1), reservoir (2), pulley (3)

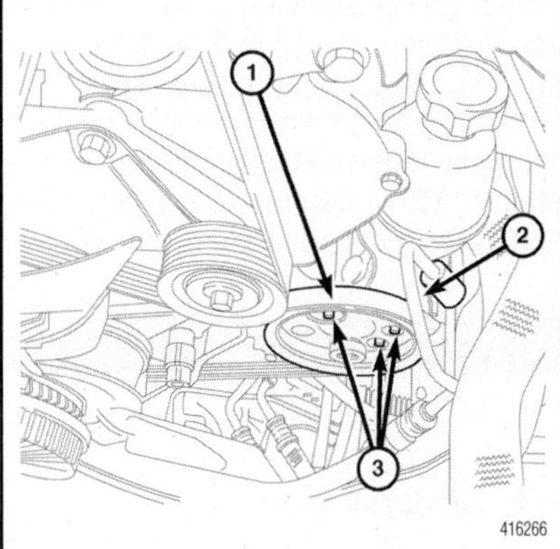

Fig. 107 Remove the power steering belt (1), pressure line (2), and mounting bolts (3)

To install:

8. Install the pump to the vehicle.
9. Install the three bolts securing the pump to the engine. Tighten the bolts to 21 ft. lbs. (28 Nm).
10. Install the power steering hoses. Tighten to 20 ft. lbs. (27 Nm).
11. Install the serpentine belt.
12. Refill the power steering fluid and check for leaks.

4.0L Engine

See Figure 107.

1. Before servicing the vehicle, refer to the Precautions Section.
2. Siphon out as much power steering fluid as possible.
3. Remove the air cleaner housing.
4. Remove the washer/coolant reservoir assembly .
5. Remove the fan shroud.
6. Remove the power steering belt.
7. Remove the pressure line at the pump.
8. Remove the return line at the reservoir.
9. Remove the three pump mounting bolts through the pump pulley.
10. Remove the pump from the vehicle.

To install:

11. Install the power steering pump back in the engine compartment using the reverse order of its removal.
12. Install the three power steering pump mounting bolts through the pulley. Tighten the bolts to 21 ft. lbs. (28 Nm).
13. Before installing the power steering pressure hose on the power steering pump, replace the O-ring on the end of power the steering pressure hose. Lubricate the O-ring using clean power steering fluid.
14. Install the pressure line into the pump. Thread the pressure line tube nut into the pump and tighten to 20 ft. lbs (27 Nm).
15. Install the return line into the reservoir.
16. Install the power steering belt.
17. Install the fan shroud.
18. Install the washer/coolant reservoir assembly.
19. Install the air cleaner housing.
20. Fill and bleed the power steering system.
21. Inspect for leaks.

BLEEDING

**** CAUTION**

The fluid level should be checked with engine OFF to prevent injury from moving components.

**** WARNING**

Mopar® Power Steering Fluid + 4 or Mopar® ATF+4 Automatic Transmission Fluid is to be used in the power steering system. Both fluids have the same material standard specifications (MS-9602). No other power steering or automatic transmission fluid is to be used in the system. Damage may result to the power steering pump and system if another fluid is used. Do not overfill the system.

**** WARNING**

If the air is not purged from the power steering system correctly, pump failure could result.

1. Before servicing the vehicle, refer to the Precautions Section.
2. Check the fluid level. The power steering fluid level can be viewed through the side of the power steering fluid reservoir. Compare the fluid level to the markings on the side of the reservoir. When the fluid is at normal ambient temperature, approximately 70°–80° F (21°–27° C), the fluid level should read between the MAX and MIN markings. When the fluid is hot, fluid level is allowed to read up to the MAX line.
3. Tightly insert Power Steering Cap Adapter into the mouth of the reservoir.

**** CAUTION**

Failure to use a vacuum pump reservoir may allow power steering fluid to be sucked into the hand vacuum pump.

4. Attach Hand Vacuum Pump or equivalent to the Power Steering Cap Adapter.

**** CAUTION**

Do not run the vehicle while vacuum is applied to the power steering system. Damage to the power steering pump can occur.

➡When performing the following step make sure the vacuum level is maintained during the entire time period.

5. Using Hand Vacuum Pump, apply 68-85 kPa (20-25 in. Hg) of vacuum to the system for a minimum of three minutes.
6. Slowly release the vacuum and remove the special tools.
7. Adjust the fluid level as necessary.
8. Repeat until the fluid no longer drops when vacuum is applied.
9. Start the engine and cycle the steering wheel lock-to-lock three times.

➡Do not hold the steering wheel at the stops.

10. Stop the engine and check for leaks at all connections.
11. Check for any signs of air in the reservoir and check the fluid level. If air is present, repeat the procedure as necessary.

FLUID FILL PROCEDURE

1. Run the engine until the power steering fluid reaches about 170°F (80°C).
2. Turn the engine OFF.
3. Clean the power steering fluid reservoir and the reservoir cap.
4. Remove the reservoir cap.

➡Inspect the power steering pump fluid level at regular intervals.

5. Inspect the power steering fluid level on the cap stick. Ensure that the fluid level is at the MAX mark on the cap stick.

⁂ WARNING

When adding fluid or making a complete fluid change, always use the proper power steering fluid. Failure to use the proper fluid will cause hose and seal damage and fluid leaks.

➡Mopar® Power Steering Fluid + 4 or Mopar® ATF+4 Automatic Transmission Fluid is to be used in the power steering system. Both fluids have the same material standard specifications (MS-9602).

6. Add the proper fluid to the reservoir, if necessary.

7. Install the reservoir cap.

SUSPENSION

FRONT SUSPENSION

CONTROL LINKS

REMOVAL & INSTALLATION

1. Before servicing the vehicle, refer to the Precautions Section.
2. Raise and support the vehicle.
3. Remove the tire and wheel assembly.
4. Remove the stabilizer link bolt at the lower control arm.
5. Remove the stabilizer link bolt at the stabilizer bar.
6. Remove the stabilizer link.

To install:

7. Install the stabilizer link.
8. Install the stabilizer link bolt at the stabilizer bar. Tighten the bolt to 85 ft. lbs. (115 Nm) with full vehicle weight.
9. Install the stabilizer link bolt at the lower control arm. Tighten the bolt to 75 ft. lbs. (102 Nm) with full vehicle weight.
10. Install the tire and wheel assembly.

LOWER BALL JOINT

REMOVAL & INSTALLATION

See Figure 108.

1. Ball joint press, tool No. C-4212-F
2. Driver, tool No. C-4212-3
3. Lower control arm
4. Receiver, tool No. 9654-3

285732

Fig. 108 Press the ball joint from the lower control arm

1. Before servicing the vehicle, refer to the Precautions Section.
2. Remove the steering knuckle.

➡Extreme pressure lubrication must be used on the threaded portions of the tool. This will increase the longevity of the tool and insure proper operation during the removal and installation process.

3. Press the ball joint from the lower control arm using special tools.

To install:

4. Install the ball joint into the lower control arm using the special tools.
5. Stake the ball joint flange in four evenly spaced places around the ball joint flange, using a chisel and hammer.
6. Install steering knuckle.

LOWER CONTROL ARM

REMOVAL & INSTALLATION

See Figure 109.

1. Before servicing the vehicle, refer to the Precautions Section.
2. Remove the front wheel.
3. Remove the lower clevis bracket bolt from the control arm.
4. Remove the stabilizer link at the control arm.
5. Remove the lower ball joint nut.
6. Remove the control arm from lower ball joint with tool C4150A.

➡Matchmark the front and rear control arm pivot bolts.

7. Remove the front pivot bolt.
8. Remove the rear pivot bolt.
9. Remove the control arm.

To install:

10. Install the lower control arm.
11. Install the rear pivot bolt.
12. Install the front pivot bolt.
13. Install the ball joint nut and tighten to 40 ft. lbs. (54 Nm) plus 90° turn.
14. Align the matchmarks and tighten the pivot bolts to 125 ft. lbs. (170 Nm).
15. Install the stabilizer link and tighten the bolt to 75 ft. lbs. (102 Nm).

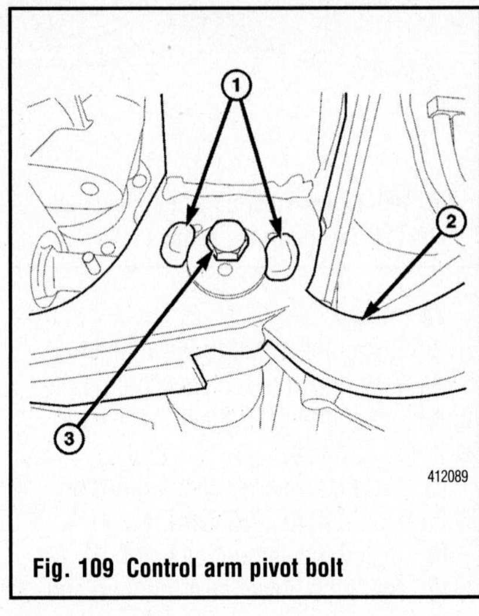

Fig. 109 Control arm pivot bolt

16. Install the lower clevis bracket bolt and tighten to 110 ft. lbs. (150 Nm).
17. Install the front wheel.
18. Perform a wheel alignment

STABILIZER BAR

REMOVAL & INSTALLATION

1. Before servicing the vehicle, refer to the Precautions Section.
2. Raise and support the vehicle.
3. Remove the tire and wheel assembly.
4. Remove the upper stabilizer link bolts at the stabilizer bar.
5. Remove the stabilizer bar bushing clamps from the frame.
6. Remove the stabilizer bar from the vehicle.

To install:

7. Install the stabilizer bar to the vehicle.
8. Install the stabilizer bar bushing clamps. Tighten the nuts to 110 ft. lbs. (149 Nm).
9. Install the upper stabilizer link bolts and washer at the stabilizer bar. Tighten the bolt to 85 ft. lbs. (115 Nm).
10. Install the tire and wheel assembly.
11. Lower the vehicle.

STEERING KNUCKLE

REMOVAL & INSTALLATION

See Figure 110.

1. Before servicing the vehicle, refer to the Precautions Section.
2. Raise and support the vehicle.
3. Remove the tire and wheel assembly.
4. Remove the caliper adapter.

WARNING

Never allow the disc brake caliper to hang from the brake hose. Damage to the brake hose will result. Provide a suitable support to hang the caliper securely.

5. Remove the disc brake rotor.
6. Remove the wheel speed sensor.
7. Remove the axle shaft nut (if equipped with 4WD).
8. Remove the outer tie rod nut.
9. Separate the outer tie rod end from the steering knuckle using tool 9360.
10. Remove the lower ball joint nut.
11. Separate the lower ball joint from the suspension arm using tool C-4150A.
12. Remove the upper ball joint nut.
13. Separate the upper ball joint from the knuckle using tool 9360.
14. Inspect the seal side surface of the upper ball joint, lower ball joint AND outer tie rod knuckle bosses. If any significant grooves or gouges are present (or heavily scratched) replace the steering knuckle.
15. Remove the knuckle from the vehicle.
16. Remove the hub/bearing, if necessary.

To install:

17. Install the hub/bearing, if removed.
18. Install the knuckle to the vehicle.
19. Install the upper ball joint nut. Tighten the nut to 30 ft. lbs. (41 Nm) plus 90° turn.
20. Install the lower ball joint nut. Tighten the nut to 40 ft. lbs. (54 Nm) plus 90° turn.
21. Install the outer tie rod end to the steering knuckle Tighten the nut to 30 ft. lbs. (41 Nm) plus 90° turn.
22. Install the axle shaft nut (if equipped with 4WD). Tighten the nut to 100 ft. lbs. (136 Nm).
23. Install the wheel speed sensor.
24. Install the disc brake rotor.
25. Install the caliper adapter.
26. Install the tire and wheel assembly.
27. Perform the set toe procedure.

STEERING LINKAGE OUTER TIE ROD

REMOVAL & INSTALLATION

1. Before servicing the vehicle, refer to the Precautions Section.
2. Raise and safely support the vehicle.
3. Remove the tire and wheel.
4. Remove the steering linkage outer tie rod nut.

WARNING

Do not free the ball stud by using a pickle fork or a wedge-type tool. Damage to the seal or bushing may result.

5. Separate the outer tie rod end from the steering knuckle using tool 9360.
6. Loosen the steering linkage outer tie rod lock nut.
7. Remove the steering linkage outer tie rod.
8. Clean the tapered surface of the steering knuckle.

To install:

9. Installation is the reverse of removal, noting the following:
   a. Do not tighten the inner tie rod lock nut during installation. Tighten after adjusting the front toe.
   b. Tighten the nut to 30 ft. lbs. (41 Nm) plus 90° turn.
   c. After the installation is complete, measure and adjust the front toe. Tighten the inner tie rod lock nut.

STRUT & SPRING ASSEMBLY

REMOVAL & INSTALLATION

Left Side

1. Before servicing the vehicle, refer to the Precautions Section.
2. Disconnect the battery.
3. Remove the battery.
4. Unclip the power center and move it to the side out of the way to access the battery tray.
5. Remove the battery tray.
6. Remove the four upper shock mounting nuts.
7. Raise and support the vehicle.
8. Remove the tire and wheel assembly.
9. Remove the caliper and support.
10. Remove the lower bolt at the lower control arm securing the clevis bracket.
11. Remove the stabilizer link bolt at the lower control arm.
12. Remove the upper ball joint nut.
13. Separate the upper ball joint from the knuckle using remover 9360.
14. Push downward on the steering knuckle and support the knuckle this will allow access to remove the shock.
15. Remove the shock assembly from the vehicle.

To install:

16. Install the shock assembly to the vehicle.
17. Install the four upper shock mounting nuts. Tighten the nuts to 80 ft. lbs. (108 Nm).
18. Raise the knuckle into place and reconnect the upper ball joint nut. Tighten

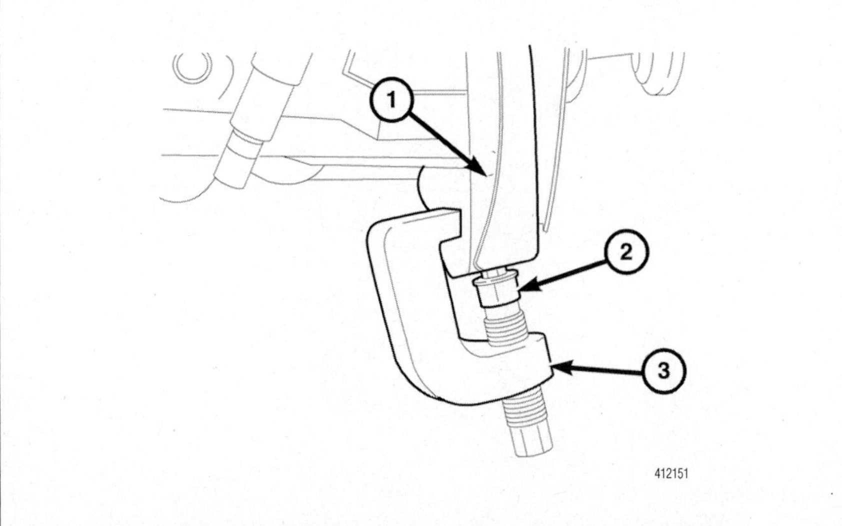

Fig. 110 Separate the lower ball joint from the suspension arm using tool C-4150A

the nut to 30 ft. lbs (41 Nm) plus an additional 90° turn.

19. Install the clevis bracket bolt at the lower control arm. Tighten the bolt to 110 ft. lbs. (150 Nm) with full vehicle weight.
20. Install the caliper.
21. Install the lower stabilizer link at the lower control arm. Tighten the bolt to 75 ft. lbs. (102 Nm) with full vehicle weight.
22. Install the tire and wheel assembly.
23. Lower the vehicle.
24. Install the battery tray.
25. Install the battery.
26. Reinstall the power center back into place.
27. Reconnect the battery cables.

Right Side

1. Before servicing the vehicle, refer to the Precautions Section.
2. Remove the air box.
3. Remove the four upper shock mounting nuts.
4. Raise and support the vehicle.
5. Remove the tire and wheel assembly.
6. Remove the caliper and support.
7. Remove the lower bolt at the lower control arm securing the clevis bracket.
8. Remove the stabilizer link bolt at the lower control arm.
9. Remove the upper ball joint nut.
10. Separate the upper ball joint from the knuckle using remover 9360.
11. Push downward on the steering knuckle and support the knuckle this will allow access to remove the shock.
12. Remove the shock assembly from the vehicle.

To install:

13. Install the shock assembly to the vehicle.
14. Install the four upper shock mounting nuts. Tighten the nuts to 80 ft. lbs. (108 Nm).
15. Raise the knuckle into place and reconnect the upper ball joint nut. Tighten the nut to 30 ft. lbs (41 Nm) plus an additional 90° turn.
16. Install the clevis bracket bolt at the lower control arm. Tighten the bolt to 110 ft. lbs. (150 Nm) with full vehicle weight.
17. Install the caliper.
18. Install the lower stabilizer link at the lower control arm. Tighten the bolt to 75 ft. lbs. (102 Nm) with full vehicle weight.
19. Install the tire and wheel assembly.
20. Lower the vehicle.
21. Install the air box.

OVERHAUL

See Figure 111.

1. Before servicing the vehicle, refer to the Precautions Section.
2. Secure the shock assembly into a Pentastar® Service Equipment W-7200 Spring compressor.
3. Compress the spring.
4. Remove the shock mount nut.
5. Remove the shock from the spring compressor.
6. Transfer the necessary parts to the type of repair being done.

To install:

7. Install the shock to the spring and spring compressor, after the transfer of the necessary parts to the type of repair being done (Insulator, Spring, shock and mount).
8. Install the shock mounting nut. Tighten the bolt to 30 ft. lbs. (41 Nm).
9. Loosen the compressed spring.
10. Remove the shock assembly from the spring compressor.

UPPER BALL JOINT

REMOVAL & INSTALLATION

The upper ball joint is serviced as an assembly with the control arm.

UPPER CONTROL ARM

REMOVAL & INSTALLATION

Left

1. Before servicing the vehicle, refer to the Precautions Section.
2. Raise and support the vehicle.
3. Remove the left side tire and wheel assembly.
4. Remove the upper ball joint nut.
5. Separate the upper ball joint from the steering knuckle using remover 9360.
6. Lower the vehicle.
7. Remove the battery.
8. Unclip the power center and move it to the side out of the way.
9. Remove the battery tray.
10. Remove the upper control arm rear nut by using a ratchet and extension under the steering shaft.
11. Remove the upper control arm front bolt.
12. Remove the upper control arm from the vehicle.

To install:

13. Install the upper control arm to the vehicle.
14. Install the upper control arm front flag bolt. Tighten the nut to 90 ft. lbs. (122 Nm) with full vehicle weight.
15. Install the upper control arm rear flag bolt. Tighten the nut to 90 ft. lbs. (122 Nm) with full vehicle weight.
16. Install the battery tray.
17. Install the battery.
18. Re-clip and mount the power center.
19. Install the upper ball joint nut. Tighten the nut to 30 ft. lbs. (41 Nm) plus an additional 90° turn.
20. Install the left side tire and wheel assembly.
21. Lower the vehicle.
22. Set the steering toe.

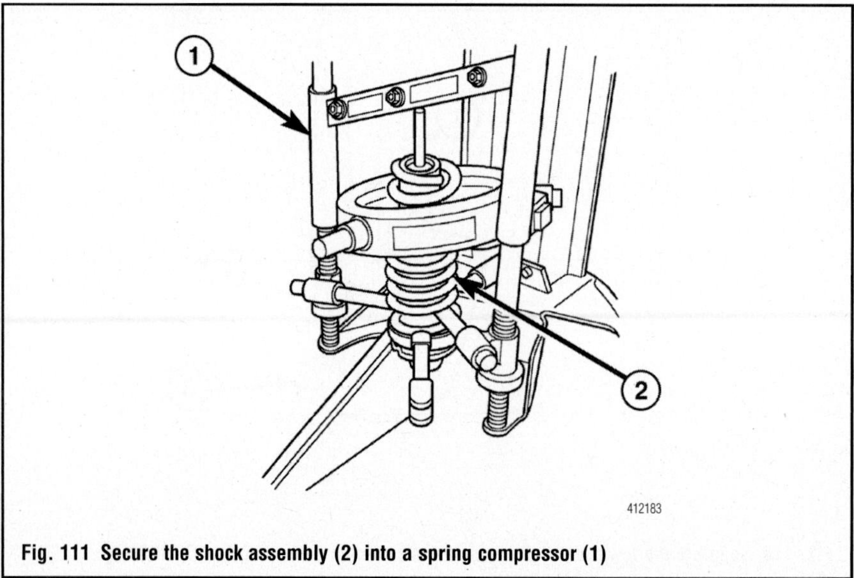

Fig. 111 Secure the shock assembly (2) into a spring compressor (1)

Right

1. Before servicing the vehicle, refer to the Precautions Section.
2. Raise and support the vehicle.
3. Remove the right side tire and wheel assembly.
4. Remove the upper ball joint nut.
5. Separate the upper ball joint from the steering knuckle using remover 9360.
6. Lower the vehicle.
7. Remove the air box assembly.
8. Remove the upper control arm rear bolt/nut.
9. Remove the upper control arm front bolt/nut.
10. Remove the upper control arm from the vehicle.

To install:

11. Install the upper control arm to the vehicle.
12. Install the upper control arm front flag bolt. Tighten the nut to 90 ft. lbs (122 Nm). with full vehicle weight.
13. Install the upper control arm rear flag bolt. Tighten the nut to 90 ft. lbs (122 Nm). with full vehicle weight.
14. Install the air box.
15. Install the upper ball joint nut. Tighten the nut to 30 ft. lbs. (41 Nm) plus an additional 90° turn.
16. Install the right side tire and wheel assembly.
17. Lower the vehicle.
18. Set the steering toe.

WHEEL BEARINGS

REMOVAL & INSTALLATION

See Figure 112.

1. Before servicing the vehicle, refer to the Precautions Section.

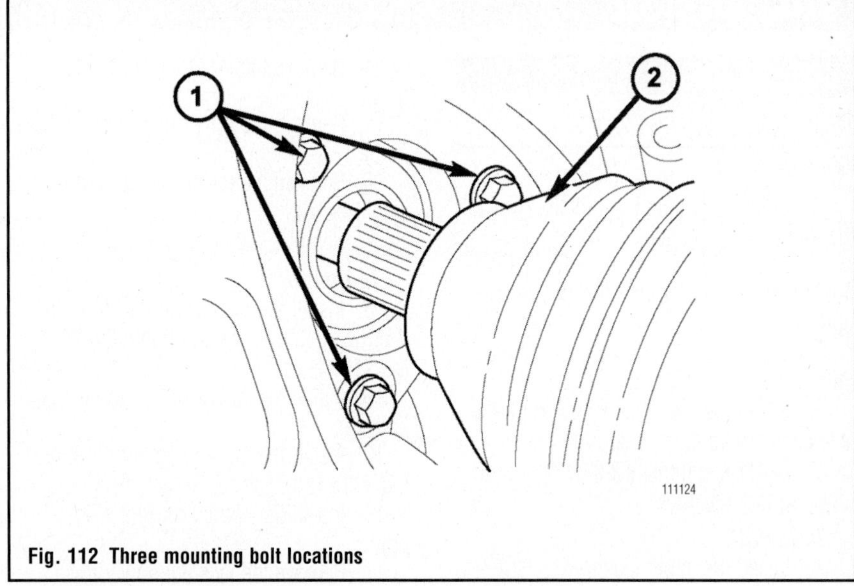

Fig. 112 Three mounting bolt locations

2. Raise and support the vehicle.
3. Remove the tire and wheel assembly.
4. Remove the caliper adapter.

WARNING

Never allow the disc brake caliper to hang from the brake hose. Damage to the brake hose will result. Provide a suitable support to hang the caliper securely.

5. Remove the disc brake rotor.
6. Remove the wheel speed sensor.
7. Remove the bracket securing the wheel speed sensor wire.
8. Remove the axle shaft nut, if equipped with 4WD.
9. Remove the three mounting bolts for the hub/bearing assembly.
10. Remove the hub/bearing.

To install:

11. Install the hub/bearing assembly to the vehicle.
12. Install the three mounting bolts for the hub/bearing. Tighten the bolt to 96 ft. lbs. (130 Nm).
13. Install the axle shaft nut. Tighten the nut to 100 ft. lbs. (135 Nm), if equipped with 4WD.
14. Install the bracket to the wheel speed sensor wire.
15. Install the wheel speed sensor to the hub. Tighten the bolt to 10 ft. lbs. (14 Nm).
16. Install the disc brake rotor.
17. Install the disc brake caliper adapter. Tighten the nut to 100 ft. lbs. (135 Nm).
18. Install the tire and wheel assembly.

ADJUSTMENT

The wheel bearings are not adjustable.

COIL SPRING

REMOVAL & INSTALLATION

See Figure 113.

1. Before servicing the vehicle, refer to the Precautions Section.
2. Raise and support the vehicle. Position a hydraulic jack under the axle to support the axle.
3. Remove the shock absorber lower bolt from the axle bracket.
4. Lower the hydraulic jack and tilt the axle and remove the coil spring.
5. Remove and inspect the upper and lower spring isolators.

To install:

6. Install the upper isolator.
7. Install the lower isolator.
8. Pull down on the axle and position the coil spring in the lower isolator.

⁑ WARNING

Ensure the spring is positioned on the lower isolator.

9. Raise the axle with the hydraulic jack.
10. Install the shock absorber to the axle bracket and tighten to 85 ft. lbs. (115 Nm).
11. Remove the supports and lower the vehicle.

CONTROL LINKS

REMOVAL & INSTALLATION

1. Before servicing the vehicle, refer to the Precautions Section.
2. Raise and support the vehicle.
3. Support the rear axle with a jack.

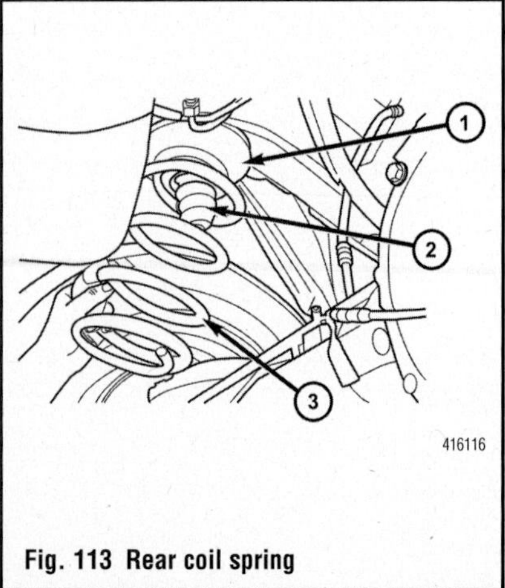

Fig. 113 Rear coil spring

4. Remove the rear tire, right side only.
5. Remove the upper link bolt at the frame.
6. Remove the lower link nut at the stabilizer bar.
7. Remove stabilizer link.

To install:

8. Install the upper bolt for the stabilizer link to the frame and tighten to 75 ft. lbs. (102 Nm).
9. Install the stabilizer link to the stabilizer bar.
10. Install the nut and tighten to 85 ft. lbs. (115 Nm) with full vehicle weight.
11. Install the spare tire right side only.
12. Remove the jack and lower the vehicle.

LOWER CONTROL ARM

REMOVAL & INSTALLATION

Left Side

1. Before servicing the vehicle, refer to the Precautions Section.
2. Raise the vehicle and support the rear axle.
3. Remove the fuel tank.
4. Remove the lower suspension arm nut and bolt from the axle bracket.
5. Remove the nut and bolt from the frame rail and remove the lower suspension arm.

To install:

➡All torques should be done with vehicle on the ground with full vehicle weight.

6. Position the lower suspension arm in the frame rail.
7. Install the frame rail bracket bolt and nut. Tighten to 120 ft. lbs. (163 Nm) with full vehicle weight.
8. Position the lower suspension arm in the axle bracket.
9. Install the axle bracket bolt and nut. Tighten to 150 ft. lbs. (203 Nm) with full vehicle weight.
10. Install the fuel tank.
11. Remove the supports and lower the vehicle.

Right Side

1. Before servicing the vehicle, refer to the Precautions Section.
2. Raise the vehicle and support the rear axle.
3. Remove the lower suspension arm nut and bolt from the axle bracket.
4. Remove the exhaust from the mid and rear hanger rubber isolators to allow the exhaust system to lower enough to remove the bolt at the frame rail.
5. Remove the nut and bolt from the frame rail and remove the lower suspension arm.

To install:

➡All torques should be done with vehicle on the ground with full vehicle weight.

6. Position the lower suspension arm in the frame rail.
7. Install the frame rail bracket bolt and nut. Tighten to 120 ft. lbs. (163 Nm). with full vehicle weight.
8. Install the exhaust back in the mid and rear hanger rubber isolators.
9. Position the lower suspension arm in the axle bracket.
10. Install the axle bracket bolt and nut. Tighten to 150 ft. lbs. (203 Nm). with full vehicle weight.
11. Remove the supports and lower the vehicle.

SHOCK ABSORBER

REMOVAL & INSTALLATION

1. Before servicing the vehicle, refer to the Precautions Section.
2. Raise and support the vehicle. Position a hydraulic jack under the axle to support the axle.

⁑ WARNING

Do not allow the axle to hang from the upper suspension arm ball joint.

3. Remove the upper nut and bolt from the frame bracket.
4. Remove the lower nut and bolt from the axle bracket. Remove the shock absorber.

To install:

5. Install the shock absorber in the frame bracket and install the bolt and nut.
6. Install the shock absorber in the axle bracket and install the bolt and nut.
7. Remove the supports and lower the vehicle.
8. Tighten the upper mounting nuts to 80 ft. lbs. (108 Nm). Tighten the lower mounting nuts to 85 ft. lbs. (115 Nm).

STABILIZER BAR

REMOVAL & INSTALLATION

1. Before servicing the vehicle, refer to the Precautions Section.
2. Raise and support the vehicle.
3. Remove the stabilizer nut at the bar.
4. Remove the stabilizer links from the stabilizer bar.
5. Remove the stabilizer bar bolts from the axle.
6. Remove the stabilizer bar.

To install:

7. Position the stabilizer bar on the axle. Ensure the bar is centered with equal spacing on both sides. Tighten the bolts to 35 ft. lbs. (47 Nm).
8. Install the stabilizer links to the bar. Tighten the nuts to 65 ft. lbs. (88 Nm) with full vehicle weight.
9. Remove the support and lower the vehicle.

TRACK BAR

REMOVAL & INSTALLATION

1. Before servicing the vehicle, refer to the Precautions Section.
2. Raise and support the vehicle. Position a hydraulic jack under the axle to support the axle.
3. Remove the track bar flag bolt and nut from the frame bracket.
4. Remove the track bar bolt and nut from the axle bracket.
5. Remove the track bar.

To install:

6. Install the track bar to the vehicle.
7. Install the track bar bolt and nut in the frame bracket.
8. Install the track bar into the axle bracket.
9. Install the track bar bolt and nut in the axle bracket.
10. Remove the supports and lower the vehicle.
11. Tighten the body side mounting bolt/nut to 135 ft. lbs. (183 Nm).
12. Tighten the axle side mounting bolt/nut to 130 ft. lbs. (176 Nm).

UPPER CONTROL ARM

REMOVAL & INSTALLATION

Left Side

1. Before servicing the vehicle, refer to the Precautions Section.
2. Raise and support the vehicle.
3. Support the rear axle.
4. Lower the fuel tank in order to gain access to the bolt.
5. Remove the upper suspension arm nut and bolt from the axle bracket.
6. Remove the nut and bolt from the frame rail and remove the upper suspension arm.

To install:

➡All torques should be done with vehicle on the ground with full vehicle weight.

7. Position the upper suspension arm in the frame rail bracket.
8. Install the mounting bolt and nut. Tighten to 70 ft. lbs. (95 Nm) with full vehicle weight.
9. Position the upper suspension arm in the axle bracket.
10. Install the mounting bolt and nut. Tighten to 85 ft. lbs. (115 Nm) with full vehicle weight.
11. Raise the fuel tank back into place and secure.
12. Remove the supports and lower the vehicle.

Right Side

See Figure 114.

1. Before servicing the vehicle, refer to the Precautions Section.
2. Raise and support the vehicle.
3. Support the rear axle.
4. Remove the upper suspension arm nut and bolt from the axle bracket.
5. Remove the nut and flag bolt from the frame rail and remove the upper suspension arm.

To install:

➡All torques should be done with vehicle on the ground with full vehicle weight.

6. Position the upper suspension arm in the frame rail bracket.
7. Install the mounting flag bolt and nut. Tighten to 70 ft. lbs. (95 Nm) with full vehicle weight.
8. Position the upper suspension arm in the axle bracket.
9. Install the mounting bolt and nut. Tighten to 85 ft. lbs. (115 Nm) with full vehicle weight.
10. Remove the supports and lower the vehicle.

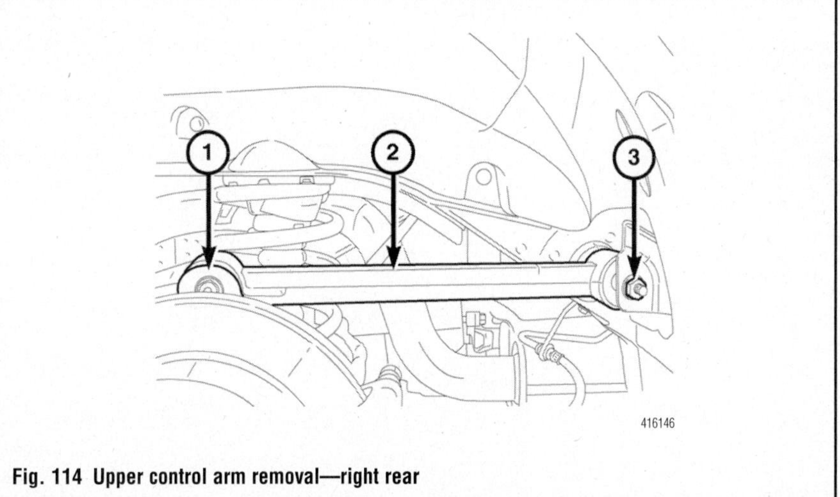

Fig. 114 Upper control arm removal—right rear

WHEEL BEARINGS

REMOVAL & INSTALLATION

See Figure 115.

1. Before servicing the vehicle, refer to the Precautions Section.

➡Remove bearing with Bearing Remover 6310 and Foot 6310-9.

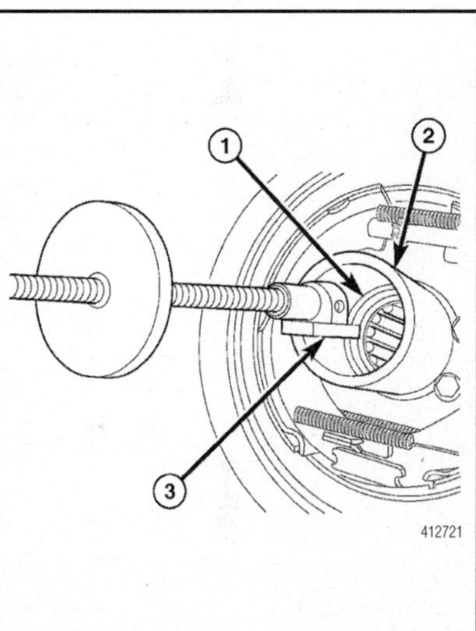

Fig. 115 Insert bearing remover foot (3) through receiver (2) and bearing (1)

2. Remove the axle shaft.
3. Remove the axle seal with seal pick.
4. Position the bearing receiver on axle tube.
5. Insert the bearing remover foot 6310-9 through the receiver and bearing.
6. Tighten remove nut on the shaft to pull bearing into the receiver.

To install:

7. Remove any old sealer/burrs from axle tube.

➡Bearing is installed with the bearing part number against installer.

8. Install axle shaft bearing with Installer C-4198 and Handle C-4171.
9. Drive bearing in until tool contacts the axle tube.
10. Coat new axle seal lip with axle lubricant. Install seal with Installer 8493 and Handle C-4171.
11. Install axle shaft in axle tube.

ADJUSTMENT

The wheel bearings are not adjustable.

14

CHRYSLER

PT Cruiser

SPECIFICATIONS AND MAINTENANCE CHARTS

ENGINE AND VEHICLE IDENTIFICATION

Engine							Model Year	
Code ①	Liters	Cu. In.	Cyl.	Fuel Sys. ②	Engine Type	Eng. Mfg.	Code ③	Year
9	2.4	146	4	MPI	DOHC I4	NS	A	2010

① 8th position of VIN

② Multi-Port Electronic Fuel Injection

③ 10th position of VIN

NS: Not Specified.

25766_PTCR_C0001

GENERAL ENGINE SPECIFICATIONS

All measurements are given in inches.

Year	Model	Engine Displacement Liters	Engine ID/VIN	Fuel System Type	Net Horsepower @ rpm	Net Torque @ rpm (ft. lbs.)	Bore x Stroke (in.)	Com-pression Ratio	Oil Pressure @ rpm
2010	PT Cruiser	2.4	9	MPI	150 @ 5100	165 @ 4000	3.445 x 3.976	9.5:1	①

① 4 psi @ curb idle speed
25-80 psi @ 3000 rpm

25766_PTCR_C0002

ENGINE TUNE-UP SPECIFICATIONS

Year	Engine Displacement Liters	Engine ID/VIN	Spark Plug Gap (in.)	Ignition Timing (deg.)		Fuel Pump (psi)	Idle Speed (rpm)		Valve Clearance	
				MT	AT		MT	AT	Intake	Exhaust
2010	2.4	9	0.040	NA	①	53-63	NA	①	N/A	N/A

NA: Not available

① Adjusted by powertrain control module (PCM).

25766_PTCR_C0003

CAPACITIES

Year	Model	Engine Displacement Liters	Engine ID/VIN	Engine Oil (qts.)	Transaxle (pts.) Auto.	Transaxle (pts.) Manual	Drive Axle (pts.) Front	Drive Axle (pts.) Rear	Transfer Case (pts.)	Fuel Tank (gals.)	Cooling System (qts.)
2010	PT Cruiser	2.4	9	5.0	①	NA	NA	NA	NA	15	6.5 ②

NOTE: All capacities are approximate. Add fluid gradually and ensure a proper fluid level is obtained.

NA: Not Applicable.

① Drain and Refill: 4.0 Quarts.
Dry Fill: 8.6 Quarts. (May vary depending on type and size of internal cooler, length and inside diameter of cooler lines, or use of an auxiliary cooler).

② System fill capacity includes heater and coolant recovery bottle filled to MAX level.

25766_PTCR_C0004

FLUID SPECIFICATIONS

Year	Model	Engine Disp. Liters	Engine Oil	Auto. Trans.	Drive Axle Front	Drive Axle Rear	Transfer Case	Power Steering Fluid	Brake Master Cylinder	Cooling System
2010	PT Cruiser	2.4	5W-30	MOPAR® ATF+4	N/A	N/A	N/A	①	②	③

N/A: Not Applicable

① MOPAR® Power Steering Fluid +4. If unavailable, then MOPAR® ATF +4 Automatic Transmission Fluid (P/N 05166226AA) is acceptable.

② MOPAR® Brake Fluid DOT 3, SAE J1703. If unavailable, then MOPAR® Brake and Clutch Fluid DOT 4 (P/N 04549625AC) is acceptable.

③ MOPAR® Antifreeze/Coolant 5 Year/100,000 Mile Formula HOAT (Hybrid Organic Additive Technology)

25766_PTCR_C0005

VALVE SPECIFICATIONS

Year	Engine Displacement Liters	Engine ID/VIN	Seat Angle (deg.)	Face Angle (deg.)	Spring Test Pressure (lbs. @ in.)	Spring Free-Length (in.)	Spring Installed Height (in.)	Stem-to-Guide Clearance (in.) Intake	Stem-to-Guide Clearance (in.) Exhaust	Stem Diameter (in.) Intake	Stem Diameter (in.) Exhaust
2010	2.4	9	44.5-45	44.5-45	①	1.943	1.496	.0018-.0030	.0029-.0040	.2337-.2344	.2326-.2333

① Nominal force - valve closed: 70 lbs. @ 1.496 in.
Nominal force - valve open: 134 lbs. @ 1.152 in.

25766_PTCR_C0006

CAMSHAFT SPECIFICATIONS

All measurements in inches unless noted

Year	Engine Displacement Liters	Engine ID/VIN	Camshaft	Journal Diameter	Brg. Oil Clearance	Shaft End-play	Runout	Journal Bore	Lobe Height
2010	2.4	9	Intake	1.022-1.023	0.0009-0.0025	0.0019-0.0066	NS	1.024-1.025	0.324
			Exhaust	1.022-1.023	0.0009-0.0025	0.0019-0.0066	NS	1.024-1.025	0.259

NS: Not specified

25766_PTCR_C0007

CRANKSHAFT AND CONNECTING ROD SPECIFICATIONS

All measurements are given in inches.

Year	Engine Displacement Liters	Engine ID/VIN	Crankshaft				Connecting Rod		
			Main Brg. Journal Dia.	Main Brg. Oil Clearance	Shaft End-play	Thrust on No.	Journal Diameter	Oil Clearance	Side Clearance
2010	2.4	9	2.3620-2.3625	.0007-.0024	.0035-.0094	3	1.968-1.9685	.0009-.0027	.005-.015

25766_PTCR_C0008

PISTON AND RING SPECIFICATIONS

All measurements are given in inches.

Year	Engine Displacement Liters	Engine ID/VIN	Piston Clearance	Ring Gap			Ring Side Clearance		
				Top Compression	Bottom Compression	Oil Control	Top Compression	Bottom Compression	Oil Control
2010	2.4	9	0.0007-0.002	0.0098-0.020	0.009-0.018	0.009-0.025	0.0011-0.0031	0.0011-0.0031	0.0004-0.007

25766_PTCR_C0009

TORQUE SPECIFICATIONS

All readings in ft. lbs.

Year	Engine Disp. Liters	Engine ID/VIN	Cylinder Head Bolts	Main Bearing Bolts	Rod Bearing Bolts	Crankshaft Damper Bolts	Flexplate Bolts	Manifold Intake	Manifold Exhaust	Spark Plugs	Oil Pan Drain Plug
2010	2.4	9	①	②	③	100	70	9	17	13	20

① Step 1: 25 ft. lbs.
Step 2: 60 ft. lbs.
Step 3: Confirm all bolts torqued to 60 ft. lbs.
Step 4: Plus 90 degrees (do not use torque wrench)

② M8 Bolts: 21 ft. lbs.
M11 Bolts: 55 ft. lbs.

③ Step 1: 20 ft. lbs.
Step 2: Plus 90 degrees

25766_PTCR_C0010

WHEEL ALIGNMENT

Year	Model		Caster Range (+/-Deg.)	Caster Preferred Setting (Deg.)	Camber Range (+/-Deg.)	Camber Preferred Setting (Deg.)	Toe (Deg.)
2010	PT Cruiser	Front	1.00	+2.45	0.40	0.00	+0.10 +/- 0.10
		Rear	NA	NA	0.25	0.00	+0.30 +/- 0.20

NA: Not Applicable

Note: Positive toe (+) is toe-in and negative toe (–) is toe-out.

25766_PTCR_C0011

TIRE, WHEEL AND BALL JOINT SPECIFICATIONS

Year	Model	OEM Tires		Tire Pressures (psi)		Wheel	Ball Joint	Lug Nut
		Standard	Optional	Front	Rear	Size	Inspection	(ft. lbs.)
2010	PT Cruiser	P205/55R16	NA	①	①	16	②	100

OEM: Original Equipment Manufacturer

PSI: Pounds Per Square Inch

① Always refer to the owner's manual and/or vehicle label

② Replace if any measurable movement is found

NA: Not Available

25766_PTCR_C0012

BRAKE SPECIFICATIONS

All measurements in inches unless noted

Year	Model		Brake Disc			Brake Drum Diameter			Minimum Pad/Lining Thickness		Brake Caliper	
			Original Thickness	Minimum Thickness	Max. Runout	Original Inside Diameter	Max. Wear Limit	Maximum Machine Diameter	Front	Rear	Guide Pin Bolts (ft. lbs.)	Mounting Bolts (ft. lbs.)
2010	PT Cruiser	F	0.902-0.909	0.843	0.005 ①	NA	NA	NA	0.04	0.04	26	100
		R	0.344-0.364	0.285	0.005 ①	NA	NA	NA	0.04	0.04	16	100

F: Front

R: Rear

NA: Not available.

25766_PTCR_C0013

SCHEDULED MAINTENANCE INTERVALS

2010 Chrysler PT Cruiser 2.4L Engine - Normal

TO BE SERVICED	TYPE OF SERVICE	VEHICLE MILEAGE INTERVAL (x1000)												
		6	12	18	24	30	36	42	48	54	60	66	72	78
Engine oil & filter	Replace	✓	✓	✓	✓	✓	✓	✓	✓	✓	✓	✓	✓	✓
Rotate tires, inspect tread wear, measure tread depth and check pressure	Rotate/Inspect	✓	✓	✓	✓	✓	✓	✓	✓	✓	✓	✓	✓	✓
Air conditioner filter	Replace					✓					✓			
Brake system components	Inspect/Service			✓			✓			✓			✓	
Exhaust system & heat shields	Inspect	✓	✓	✓	✓	✓	✓	✓	✓	✓	✓	✓	✓	✓
Inspect the front suspension, tie rod ends and boot seals for cracks or leaks and all parts for damage, wear, improper looseness or end play.	Inspect	✓	✓	✓	✓	✓	✓	✓	✓	✓	✓	✓	✓	✓
CV Joints	Inspect	✓	✓	✓	✓	✓	✓	✓	✓	✓	✓	✓	✓	✓
Adjust parking brake on vehicles equipped with four-wheel disc brakes.	Adjust					✓					✓			
Engine air filter	Replace					✓					✓			
Engine coolant	Flush/Replace										✓			
Spark plugs	Replace					✓					✓			
PCV valve	Inspect/Service					✓					✓			
Automatic transmission fluid	Inspect	Every 120,000 miles												
Accessory drive belt	Replace	Every 120,000 miles												
Battery	Inspect/Service	✓	✓	✓	✓	✓	✓	✓	✓	✓	✓	✓	✓	✓
Horn, exterior lamps, turn signals and hazard warning light operation	Inspect	✓	✓	✓	✓	✓	✓	✓	✓	✓	✓	✓	✓	✓
Fluid levels (all)	Inspect/Service	✓	✓	✓	✓	✓	✓	✓	✓	✓	✓	✓	✓	✓
Make-up air filter	Inspect/Service	Every 120,000 miles												
Generator belt	Adjust					✓					✓			

25766_PTCR_C0014

SCHEDULED MAINTENANCE INTERVALS

2010 Chrysler PT Cruiser 2.4L Engine - Severe

TO BE SERVICED	TYPE OF SERVICE	VEHICLE MILEAGE INTERVAL (x1000)												
		3	6	9	12	15	18	21	24	27	30	33	36	39
Engine oil & filter	Replace	✓	✓	✓	✓	✓	✓	✓	✓	✓	✓	✓	✓	✓
Rotate tires, inspect tread wear, measure tread depth and check pressure	Rotate/Inspect		✓		✓		✓		✓		✓		✓	
Air conditioner filter	Replace					✓					✓			
Brake system components	Inspect/Service				✓				✓				✓	
Exhaust system & heat shields	Inspect	✓	✓	✓	✓	✓	✓	✓	✓	✓	✓	✓	✓	✓
Inspect the front suspension, tie rod ends and boot seals for cracks or leaks and all parts for damage, wear, improper looseness or end play.	Inspect	✓	✓	✓	✓	✓	✓	✓	✓	✓	✓	✓	✓	✓
CV Joints	Inspect	✓	✓	✓	✓	✓	✓	✓	✓	✓	✓	✓	✓	✓
Adjust parking brake on vehicles equipped with four-wheel disc brakes.	Adjust					✓					✓			
Engine air filter	Replace					✓					✓			
Engine coolant	Flush/Replace	Every 60,000 miles												
Spark plugs	Replace										✓			
PCV valve	Inspect/Service										✓			
Automatic transmission fluid	Inspect	Every 120,000 miles												
Accessory drive belt	Replace	Every 120,000 miles												
Battery	Inspect/Service	✓	✓	✓	✓	✓	✓	✓	✓	✓	✓	✓	✓	✓
Horn, exterior lamps, turn signals and hazard warning light operation	Inspect	✓	✓	✓	✓	✓	✓	✓	✓	✓	✓	✓	✓	✓
Fluid levels (all)	Inspect/Service	✓	✓	✓	✓	✓	✓	✓	✓	✓	✓	✓	✓	✓
Make-up air filter	Inspect/Service					✓					✓			
Ignition cables	Replace	Every 60,000 miles												
Generator belt	Adjust										✓			

25766_PTCR_C0015

PRECAUTIONS

- Certain components within the ABS system are not intended to be serviced or repaired individually.
- Do not use rubber hoses or other parts not specifically specified for an ABS system. When using repair kits, replace all parts included in the kit. Partial or incorrect repair may lead to functional problems and require the replacement of components.
- Lubricate rubber parts with clean, fresh brake fluid to ease assembly. Do not use shop air to clean parts; damage to rubber components may result.
- Use only DOT 3 brake fluid from an unopened container.
- If any hydraulic component or line is removed or replaced, it may be necessary to bleed the entire system.
- A clean repair area is essential. Always clean the reservoir and cap thoroughly before removing the cap. The slightest amount of dirt in the fluid may plug an orifice and impair the system function. Perform repairs after components have been thoroughly cleaned; use only denatured alcohol to clean components. Do not allow ABS components to come into contact with any substance containing mineral oil; this includes used shop rags.
- The Anti-Lock control unit is a microprocessor similar to other computer units in the vehicle. Ensure that the ignition switch is **OFF** before removing or installing controller harnesses. Avoid static electricity discharge at or near the controller.
- If any arc welding is to be done on the vehicle, the control unit should be unplugged before welding operations begin.

BRAKES — ANTI-LOCK BRAKE SYSTEM (ABS)

GENERAL INFORMATION

PRECAUTIONS

- Certain components within the ABS system are not intended to be serviced or repaired individually.
- Do not use rubber hoses or other parts not specifically specified for and ABS system. When using repair kits, replace all parts included in the kit. Partial or incorrect repair may lead to functional problems and require the replacement of components.
- Lubricate rubber parts with clean, fresh brake fluid to ease assembly. Do not use shop air to clean parts; damage to rubber components may result.
- Use only DOT 3 brake fluid from an unopened container.
- If any hydraulic component or line is removed or replaced, it may be necessary to bleed the entire system.
- A clean repair area is essential. Always clean the reservoir and cap thoroughly before removing the cap. The slightest amount of dirt in the fluid may plug an orifice and impair the system function. Perform repairs after components have been thoroughly cleaned; use only denatured alcohol to clean components. Do not allow ABS components to come into contact with any substance containing mineral oil; this includes used shop rags.
- The Anti-Lock control unit is a microprocessor similar to other computer units in the vehicle. Ensure that the ignition switch is **OFF** before removing or installing controller harnesses. Avoid static electricity discharge at or near the controller.
- If any arc welding is to be done on the vehicle, the control unit should be unplugged before welding operations begin.
- In testing for open or short circuits, do not ground or apply voltage to any of the circuits unless instructed to do so for a diagnostic procedure.
- These circuits should only be tested using a high impedance multi-meter or the designated scan tool as described in this section. Power should never be removed or applied to any control module with the ignition in the **ON** position. Before removing or connecting battery cables, fuses, or connectors, always turn the ignition to the **OFF** position.
- The ABM 47-way connector should never be connected or disconnected with the ignition switch in the **ON** position.
- This vehicle utilizes active wheel speed sensors. Do not apply voltage to wheel speed sensors at any time.
- Use only factory wiring harnesses. Do not cut or splice wiring to the brake circuits. The addition of aftermarket electrical equipment (car phone, radar detector, citizen band radio, trailer lighting, trailer brakes, etc.) on a vehicle equipped with antilock brakes may affect the function of the antilock brake system.
- When performing any service procedure on a vehicle equipped with ABS, do not apply a 12-volt power source to the ground circuit of the pump motor in the HCU. Doing this will damage the pump motor and will require replacement of the entire HCU.
- Many components of the ABS are not serviceable and must be replaced as an assembly. Do not disassemble any component which is not designed to be serviced.
- Brake fluid will damage painted surfaces. If brake fluid is spilled on any painted surface, wash off with water immediately.

SPEED SENSORS

REMOVAL & INSTALLATION

Front Speed Sensor

See Figures 1 through 4

1. Before servicing the vehicle, refer to the Precautions Section.
2. Raise and support the vehicle.
3. Disconnect the wheel speed sensor cable connector from the wiring harness on the inside of the frame rail above the front suspension crossmember.

➡The connector has a locking tab which must be pulled back before the connector release tab can be depressed, releasing the connection.

4. For the left side sensor, remove the speed sensor cable routing clips from the brake tube on the inside of and under the frame rail.

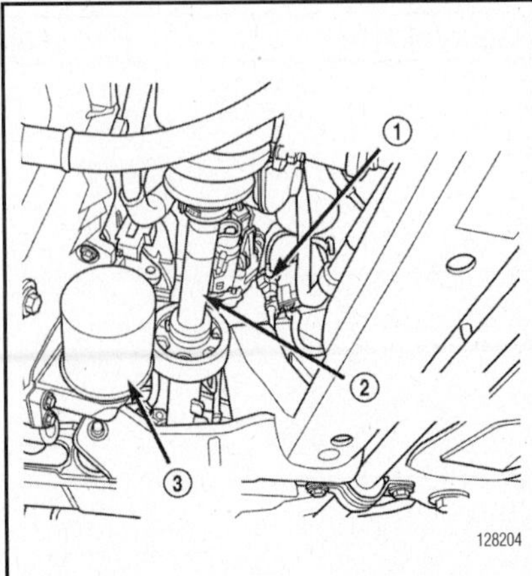

Fig. 1 View of right front wheel speed sensor cable connector (1) near axle shaft (2) and oil filter (3)

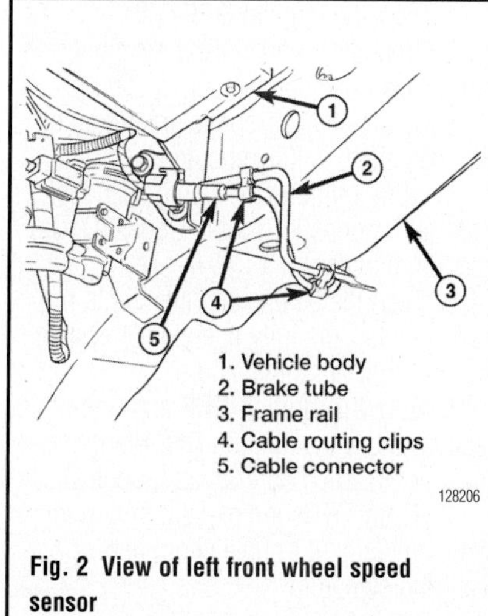

Fig. 2 View of left front wheel speed sensor

5. Remove the speed sensor cable from the retainer on the brake hose bracket mounted to the frame rail.

6. Remove the screw fastening the wheel speed sensor head to the knuckle.

⁂ WARNING

When removing a wheel speed sensor from the knuckle, do not use pliers on the sensor head. This may damage the sensor head. If the sensor has seized, use a hammer and a punch to tap the edge of the sensor head ear, rocking the sensor side-to-side until free.

7. Carefully pull the sensor head with heat shield out of the knuckle. Separate the shield from the sensor head.

8. Remove the screw securing the wheel speed sensor routing bracket to the rear of the strut. Remove the wheel speed sensor from the vehicle.

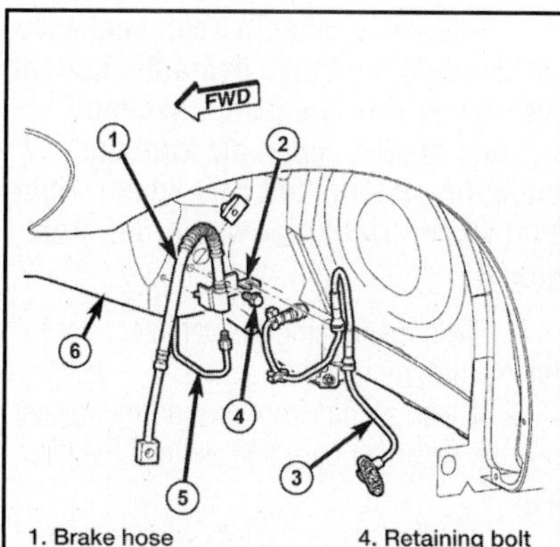

Fig. 3 View of front wheel speed sensor cable at brake flex hose bracket

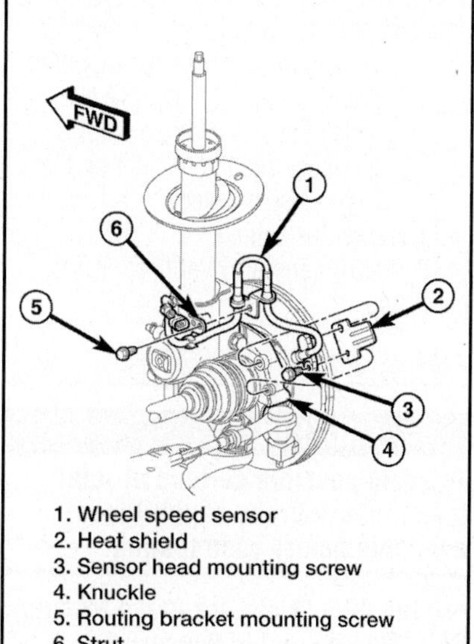

Fig. 4 Front wheel speed sensor mounting

To install:

⁂ WARNING

Failure to install speed sensor cables properly may result in contact with moving parts or an over extension of cables causing an open circuit. Be sure that cables are installed, routed, and clipped properly.

9. To install, reverse the removal procedure and note the following:
   - Place the routing bracket of the wheel speed sensor against the mounting flange (rearward ear) on the rear of the strut.
   - Tighten the wheel speed sensor screw to 105 inch lbs. (12 Nm).
   - Tighten the wheel speed sensor-to-knuckle mounting screw to 105 inch lbs. (12 Nm).

10. From the sensor bracket on the strut, loop the harness end of the sensor cable upward, then downward at the outside of the frame rail. Install the speed sensor cable grommet into the retainer on the brake hose bracket on the frame rail.
   - Remember to push in the locking tab on the connector.

11. Lower the vehicle.

12. Perform the ABS Verification Test procedure.

Rear Speed Sensor

See Figures 5 through 7

1. Before servicing the vehicle, refer to the Precautions Section.

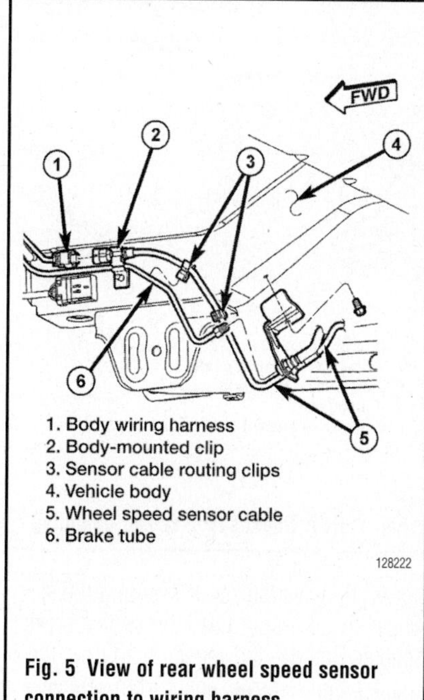

Fig. 5 View of rear wheel speed sensor connection to wiring harness

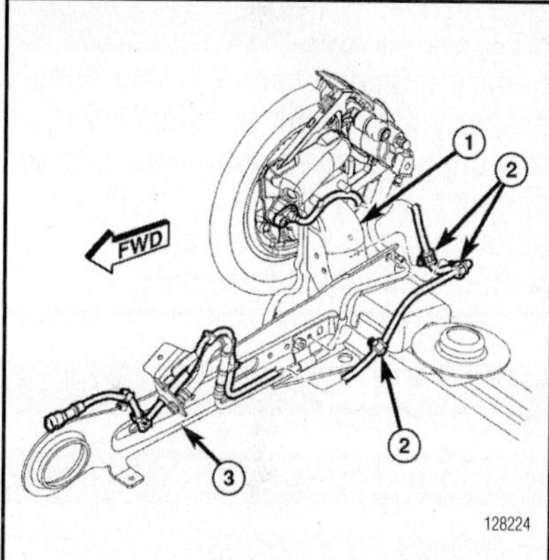

Fig. 6 Remove the rear wheel speed sensor routing clips (2) from the axle (1) and trailing arm (3)

2. Raise and support the vehicle.

3. Disconnect the wheel speed sensor cable connector at the body wiring harness. The connector has a locking tab which must be pulled back before the connector release tab can be depressed, releasing the connection.

4. Remove the wheel speed sensor cable connector from the body-mounted clip.

5. Remove the speed sensor cable routing clips from the brake tube.

6. Remove the rear wheel speed sensor routing clips from the axle and trailing arm.

7. Remove the wheel speed sensor cable from the retainer on the brake hose bracket.

8. Remove the cable from the routing clips running along the brake hose.

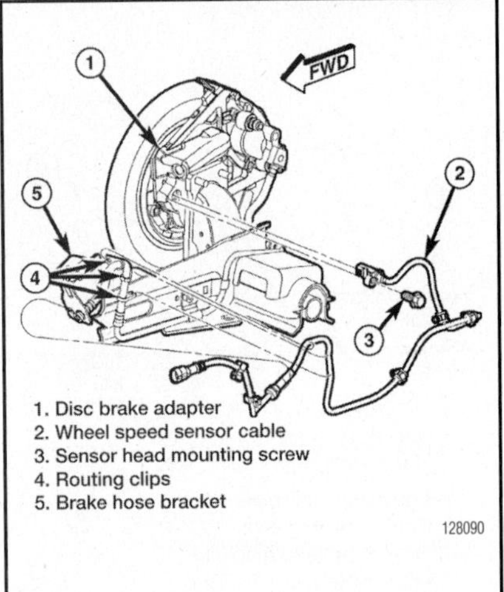

Fig. 7 Rear wheel speed sensor mounting

9. Remove the screw securing the wheel speed sensor head to the disc brake adapter. Remove the sensor head from the adapter, and remove sensor from vehicle.

To install:

⁂ WARNING

Failure to install speed sensor cables properly may result in contact with moving parts or an over extension of cables causing an open circuit. Be sure that cables are installed, routed, and clipped properly.

10. To install, reverse the removal procedure and note the following:
    - Tighten the sensor head mounting screw to 105 inch lbs. (12 Nm).
    - Install the speed sensor cable grommet into the retainer on the brake hose bracket.
11. Lower the vehicle.
12. Perform the ABS Verification Test procedure.

ABS VERIFICATION TEST

⁂ CAUTION

To avoid possible serious or fatal injury, check brake capability is available before road testing.

➡If the ABM (Anti-Lock Brake Module), SAS (Steering Angle Sensor), or dynamics sensor was replaced, it must be initialized using the scan tool. If not initialized, the ABS indicator will flash continuously with no DTCs. To initialize the ABM and clear offsets have wheels pointing straight ahead and follow the directions on the scan tool. The drive test requires a 90 ° turn. If the Dynamics Sensor was replaced, test drive the vehicle by turning the vehicle left or right in a curving manner at a velocity between 10 – 25 KM/H (6 – 15 MPH).

1. Turn the ignition **OFF**.
2. Connect all previously disconnected components and connectors.
3. Verify all accessories are turned off and the battery is fully charged.
4. Turn ignition **ON**. Using scan tool, erase all Diagnostic Trouble Codes (DTCs) from all modules.
5. Start the engine and allow it to run for 2 minutes and fully operate the system that was indicating the failure.
6. Turn the ignition **OFF** and wait 5 seconds. Turn the ignition **ON**. Using the scan tool, read DTCs from all modules.
7. If any DTCs are present, return to symptom list and trouble shoot new or recurring symptom.

➡For sensor signal and pump motor faults, the ABM must sense all 4 wheels at 12 KM/H (7.5 MPH) before it will extinguish the ABS indicator.

8. If there are no DTCs present after turning ignition **ON**, road test the vehicle for at least 5 minutes. Perform several anti-lock braking stops.
9. Again, with the scan tool read DTCs. If any DTCs are present, repair as necessary.
10. If there are no DTCs present, and the customer's concern can no longer be duplicated, the repair is complete.

BRAKES — BLEEDING THE BRAKE SYSTEM

BLEEDING PROCEDURE

BLEEDING PROCEDURE

Manual Bleeding

⁂ WARNING

Use only Mopar ® brake fluid or an equivalent from a fresh, tightly sealed container. Brake fluid must conform to DOT 3 specifications. Do not use petroleum-based fluid, as seal damage in the brake system will result.

⁂ WARNING

Before removing the master cylinder cap, wipe it clean to prevent dirt and other foreign matter from dropping into the master cylinder reservoir.

⁂ WARNING

Do not allow the master cylinder reservoir to run out of brake fluid while bleeding the system. An empty reservoir will allow additional air into the brake system. Check the fluid level frequently and add fluid as needed.

⁂ CAUTION

Brake fluid contains polyglycol ethers and polyglycols. Avoid contact with the eyes and wash your hands thoroughly after handling brake fluid. If you do get brake fluid in your eyes, flush your eyes with clean, running water for 15 minutes. If eye irritation persists, or if you have taken brake fluid internally, IMMEDIATELY seek medical assistance.

⁂ WARNING

When bleeding the brake system, wear safety glasses. A clear bleed tube must be attached to the bleeder screws and submerged in a clear container filled part way with clean brake fluid. Direct the flow of brake fluid away from yourself and the painted surfaces of the vehicle. Brake fluid at high pressure may come out of the bleeder screws when opened.

➡The following wheel circuit sequence for bleeding the brake hydraulic system should be used to ensure adequate removal of all trapped air from the hydraulic system: Left rear wheel, right front wheel, right rear wheel, left front wheel.

1. Before servicing the vehicle, refer to the Precautions Section.
2. Clean all dirt from around the master cylinder reservoir cap, and remove the filler cap.
3. Fill the brake master cylinder reservoir with clean, specified brake fluid.
4. Attach a clear plastic hose to the left rear wheel bleeder screw and feed the hose into a clear jar containing enough fresh brake fluid to submerge the end of the hose.

5. Have an assistant pump the brake pedal 3 – 4 times and hold it in the down position.

6. With the pedal in the down position, open the bleeder screw at least one full turn.

➡Do not pump the brake pedal at any time while having a bleeder screw open during the bleeding process. This will only increase the amount of air in the system and make additional bleeding necessary.

7. Once the brake pedal has dropped, close the bleeder screw. After the bleeder screw is closed, release the brake pedal.

8. Repeat the above steps until all trapped air is removed from that wheel circuit (usually 4 – 5 times).

9. Bleed the right front, right rear and left front wheel circuits in the same manner until all air is removed from the brake system. Monitor the fluid level in the master cylinder reservoir to make sure it does not go dry.

10. Check the brake pedal travel. If pedal travel is excessive or has not been improved, some air may still be trapped in the system. Repeat the bleed procedure as necessary.

11. Test drive the vehicle to verify the brakes are operating properly and pedal feel is correct.

Pressure Bleeding

**** WARNING**

Use only Mopar ® brake fluid or an equivalent from a fresh, tightly sealed container. Brake fluid must conform to DOT 3 specifications. Do not use petroleum-based fluid, as seal damage in the brake system will result.

**** WARNING**

Before removing the master cylinder cap, wipe it clean to prevent dirt and other foreign matter from dropping into the master cylinder reservoir.

**** WARNING**

Do not allow the master cylinder reservoir to run out of brake fluid while bleeding the system. An empty reservoir will allow additional air into the brake system. Check the fluid level frequently and add fluid as needed.

**** CAUTION**

Brake fluid contains polyglycol ethers and polyglycols. Avoid contact with the eyes and wash your hands thoroughly after handling brake fluid. If you do get brake fluid in your eyes, flush your eyes with clean, running water for 15 minutes. If eye irritation persists, or if you have taken brake fluid internally, IMMEDIATELY seek medical assistance.

**** WARNING**

When bleeding the brake system, wear safety glasses. A clear bleed tube must be attached to the bleeder screws and submerged in a clear container filled part way with clean brake fluid. Direct the flow of brake fluid away from yourself and the painted surfaces of the vehicle. Brake fluid at high pressure may come out of the bleeder screws when opened.

➡Do not pump the brake pedal at any time while having a bleeder screw open during the bleeding process. This will only increase the amount of air in the system and make additional bleeding necessary.

1. Before servicing the vehicle, refer to the Precautions Section.

2. Clean all dirt from around the master cylinder reservoir cap, and remove the filler cap.

3. Fill the brake master cylinder reservoir with clean, specified brake fluid.

➡Master cylinder pressure bleeder adapter tools are available from various manufacturers of pressure bleeding equipment. Follow pressure bleeder manufacturer's instructions when installing the adapter.

4. Install the bleeder adapter in place of the filler cap on the master cylinder reservoir, and attach the bleeder tank hose to the fitting on the adapter.

➡The following wheel circuit sequence for bleeding the brake hydraulic system should be used to ensure adequate removal of all trapped air from the hydraulic system: Left rear wheel, right front wheel, right rear wheel, left front wheel.

5. Attach a clear plastic hose to the left rear wheel bleeder screw and feed the hose into a clear jar containing enough fresh brake fluid to submerge the end of the hose.

6. Open the bleeder screw at least one full turn or more to obtain a steady stream of brake fluid.

7. After approximately 4 – 8 ounces of fluid have been bled through the brake circuit and an air-free flow is maintained in the clear plastic hose and jar, close the bleeder screw.

8. Repeat this procedure at all the remaining bleeder screws.

9. Check the brake pedal travel. If pedal travel is excessive or has not been improved, some air may still be trapped in the system. Repeat the bleed procedure as necessary.

10. Test drive the vehicle to verify the brakes are operating properly and pedal feel is correct.

MASTER CYLINDER BLEEDING

Refer to Bleeding Procedure, Manual Bleeding or Pressure Bleeding.

BRAKE LINE BLEEDING

Refer to Bleeding Procedure, Manual Bleeding or Pressure Bleeding.

BLEEDING THE ABS SYSTEM

➡When bleeding the ABS system, the following bleeding sequence must be followed to ensure complete and adequate bleeding.

1. Before servicing the vehicle, refer to the Precautions Section.

2. Make sure all hydraulic fluid lines are installed and properly tightened.

3. Connect the scan tool to the diagnostic connector. The diagnostic connector is located under the lower steering column cover to the left of the steering column.

4. Using the scan tool, check to make sure the Anti-lock Brake Module (ABM) does not have any fault codes stored. If it does, clear them.

5. Bleed the base brake system. Refer to Bleeding Procedure, Manual Bleeding or Pressure Bleeding.

**** WARNING**

When bleeding the brake system, wear safety glasses. A clear bleed tube must be attached to the bleeder screws and submerged in a clear container filled part way with clean brake fluid. Direct the flow of brake fluid away from yourself and the painted surfaces of the vehicle. Brake fluid at high pressure may come out of the bleeder screws when opened.

6. Using the scan tool, select ECU VIEW, followed by ABS MISCELLANEOUS FUNCTIONS to access bleeding. Follow the instructions displayed. When finished, disconnect the scan tool and proceed.

7. Bleed the base brake system a second time. Check brake fluid level in the reservoir periodically to prevent emptying, causing air to enter the hydraulic system.

8. Fill the master cylinder fluid reservoir to the FULL level.

9. Test drive the vehicle to be sure the brakes are operating correctly and that the brake pedal does not feel spongy.

FLUID FILL PROCEDURE

See Figure 8.

➡**Brake fluid level should be checked a minimum of twice a year.**

⁂ WARNING

Use only Mopar ® brake fluid or an equivalent from a fresh, tightly sealed container. Brake fluid must conform to DOT 3 specifications. Do not use petroleum-based fluid, as seal damage in the brake system will result.

Master cylinder reservoirs are marked (FULL and ADD), indicating the allowable brake fluid level range in the master cylinder fluid reservoir.

Although there is a range, the preferred level is FULL. As necessary, adjust the brake fluid level to the FULL mark listed on the side of the master cylinder fluid reservoir. Do not overfill the system.

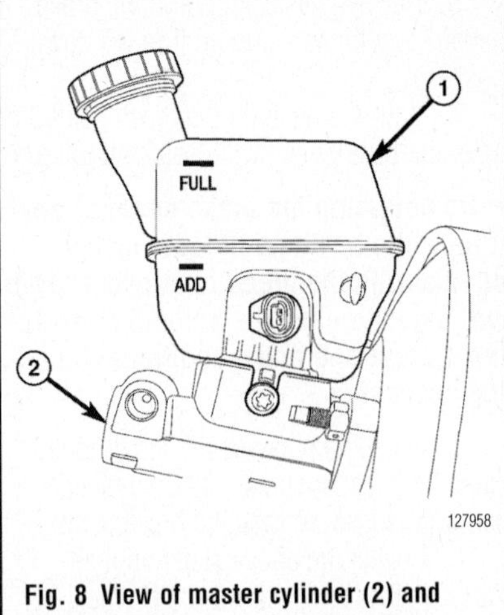

Fig. 8 View of master cylinder (2) and fluid reservoir (1), showing fluid level markings

BRAKES

FRONT DISC BRAKES

⁂ CAUTION

Dust and dirt accumulating on brake parts during normal use may contain asbestos fibers from production or aftermarket brake linings. Breathing excessive concentrations of asbestos fibers can cause serious bodily harm. Exercise care when servicing brake parts. Do not sand or grind brake lining unless equipment used is designed to contain the dust residue. Do not clean brake parts with compressed air or by dry brushing. Cleaning should be done by dampening the brake components with a fine mist of water, then wiping the brake components clean with a dampened cloth. Dispose of cloth and all residue containing asbestos fibers in an impermeable container with the appropriate label. Follow practices prescribed by the Occupational Safety and Health Administration (OSHA) and the Environmental Protection Agency (EPA) for the handling, processing, and disposing of dust or debris that may contain asbestos fibers.

BRAKE CALIPER

REMOVAL & INSTALLATION

See Figure 9.

1. Before servicing the vehicle, refer to the Precautions Section.

2. Using a brake pedal holding tool, depress the brake pedal past its first one inch of travel and hold it in this position. This will isolate the master cylinder from the brake hydraulic system, and will not allow the brake fluid to drain out of the master cylinder reservoir when the lines are opened.

3. Raise and support the vehicle.

4. Remove the tire and wheel assembly.

5. Remove the banjo bolt connecting the brake hose to the brake caliper. There are 2 washers (one on each side of the flex hose fitting) that will come off with the banjo bolt. Discard the washers.

6. Remove the 2 brake caliper guide pin bolts.

7. Slide the disc brake caliper off the disc brake adapter and pads.

To install:

⁂ WARNING

When installing new brake components, be sure to use the correct parts. Parts designed for BR4 Performance Brake System must not be mixed with other brake systems.

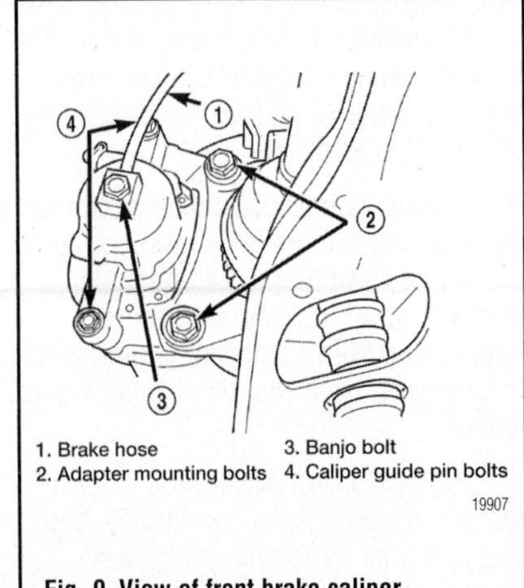

Fig. 9 View of front brake caliper

8. Completely retract the caliper piston back into the bore of the caliper. Use a C-clamp to retract the piston. Place a wood block over the piston before installing the C-clamp to avoid damaging the piston.

⁂ WARNING

Use care when installing the caliper onto the disc brake adapter to avoid damaging the boots on the caliper guide pins.

9. Install the disc brake caliper over the brake pads on the brake caliper adapter. Make sure the springs on the pads do not get caught in the hole formed into the center of the caliper housing.

10. Align the caliper guide pin bolt holes with the guide pins. Install the caliper guide pin bolts, and tighten them to 26 ft. lbs. (35 Nm).

11. Install the banjo bolt connecting the brake hose to the brake caliper. Install NEW washers on each side of the hose fitting as the banjo bolt is guided through the fitting. Thread the banjo bolt into the caliper, and tighten it to 18 ft. lbs. (24 Nm).

12. Install the tire and wheel assembly. Install and tighten the wheel mounting nuts to 100 ft. lbs. (135 Nm).

13. Lower the vehicle.

14. Remove the brake pedal holding tool.

15. Bleed the caliper as necessary. Refer to Bleeding Procedure.

16. Road test the vehicle and make several stops to wear off any foreign material on the brakes and to seat the brake shoes.

DISC BRAKE PADS

REMOVAL & INSTALLATION

See Figures 9 and 10.

1. Before servicing the vehicle, refer to the Precautions Section.
2. Raise and support the vehicle.
3. Remove the tire and wheel assembly.
4. Remove the 2 brake caliper guide pin bolts.
5. Remove the disc brake caliper from the disc brake adapter, and hang it out of the way using wire or a bungee cord. Use care not to overextend the brake hose when doing this.
6. Remove the brake pads from the disc brake caliper adapter.
7. Repeat the procedure to remove brake pads from the other front wheel and tire assembly.

To install:

➡Inboard brake pads are not identical side-to-side. This is due to placement of the audible wear indicator on the end of each inboard pad. Make sure that the audible wear indicators are placed toward the top when the inboard pads are installed on each side of the vehicle.

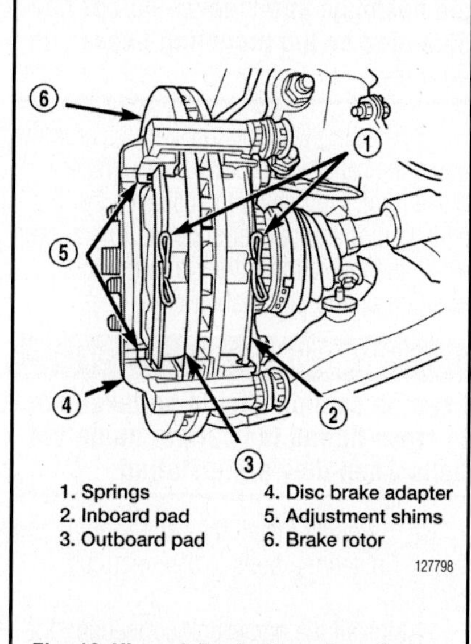

Fig. 10 View of disc brake pads — front

8. Place the brake pads in the abutment shims clipped into the disc brake caliper adapter as shown. Place the pad with the wear indicator attached on the inboard side.
9. Completely retract the caliper piston back into the bore of the caliper.

⁂ WARNING

Use care when installing the caliper onto the disc brake adapter to avoid damaging the boots on the caliper guide pins.

10. Install the disc brake caliper over the brake pads on the brake caliper adapter. Make sure the springs on the pads do not get caught in the hole formed into the center of the caliper housing.
11. Align the caliper guide pin bolt holes with the guide pins. Install the caliper guide pin bolts and tighten to 312 inch lbs. (35 Nm).
12. Install tire and wheel assembly. Install and tighten the wheel mounting nuts to 100 ft. lbs. (135 Nm).
13. Repeat the procedure to install brake pads into other front wheel and tire assembly.
14. Lower the vehicle.
15. Pump the brake pedal several times before moving the vehicle to set the pads to the brake rotor.
16. Check and adjust the brake fluid level as necessary.
17. Road test the vehicle and make several stops to wear off any foreign material on the brakes and to seat the brake pads.

BRAKES

REAR DISC BRAKES

⁂ CAUTION

Dust and dirt accumulating on brake parts during normal use may contain asbestos fibers from production or aftermarket brake linings. Breathing excessive concentrations of asbestos fibers can cause serious bodily harm. Exercise care when servicing brake parts. Do not sand or grind brake lining unless equipment used is designed to contain the dust residue. Do not clean brake parts with compressed air or by dry brushing. Cleaning should be done by dampening the brake components with a fine mist of water, then wiping the brake components clean with a dampened cloth. Dispose of cloth and all residue containing asbestos fibers in an impermeable container with the appropriate label. Follow practices prescribed by the Occupational Safety and Health Administration (OSHA) and the Environmental Protection Agency (EPA) for the handling, processing, and disposing of dust or debris that may contain asbestos fibers.

BRAKE CALIPER

REMOVAL & INSTALLATION

See Figures 11 and 12.

1. Before servicing the vehicle, refer to the Precautions Section.
2. Using a brake pedal holding tool, depress the brake pedal past its first one inch of travel and hold it in this position. This will isolate the master cylinder from the brake hydraulic system and will not allow the brake fluid to drain out of the master cylinder reservoir when the lines are opened.
3. Raise and support the vehicle.
4. Remove the tire and wheel assembly.
5. Remove the banjo bolt connecting the brake hose to the brake caliper. There are 2 washers (one on each side of the flex hose fitting) that will come off with the banjo bolt. Discard the washers.

➡In some cases, it may be necessary to retract the caliper piston in its bore a small amount in order to provide sufficient clearance between the shoes and the rotor to easily remove the caliper from the knuckle. This can usually be accomplished before the guide pin bolts are removed by grasping the

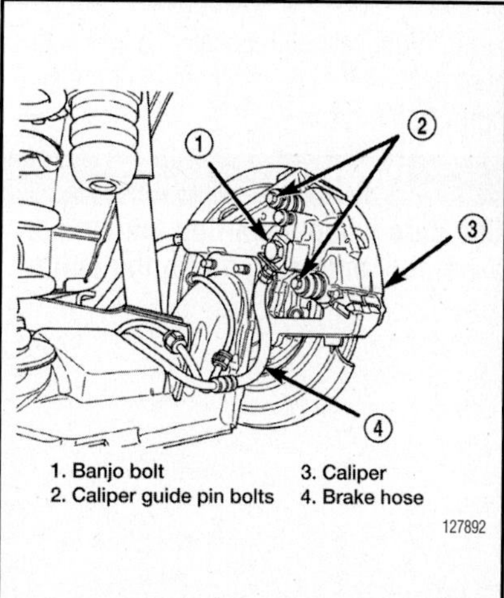

Fig. 11 View of rear brake hose mounting

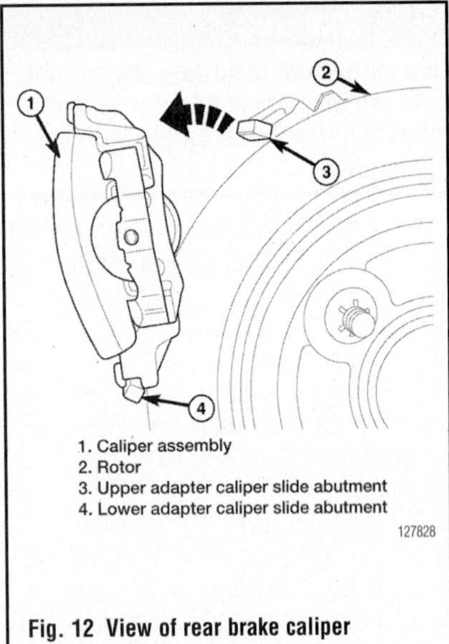

Fig. 12 View of rear brake caliper

rear of the caliper and pulling outward working with the guide pins, thus retracting the piston.

WARNING

Never push on the piston directly, as it may get damaged.

6. Remove the 2 brake caliper guide pin bolts.
7. Remove the caliper assembly from the brake adapter by first rotating the top of the caliper away from the rotor, and then lifting the caliper assembly off the lower machined abutment on the adapter.

To install:

WARNING

When installing new brake components, be sure to use the correct parts. Parts designed for BR4 Performance Brake System must not be mixed with other brake systems.

8. Lubricate both adapter caliper slide abutments with a liberal amount of multipurpose lubricant.

WARNING

Use care when installing the caliper assembly onto adapter so the guide pin bushings and sleeves do not get damaged by the mounting bosses on adapter.

9. Starting with the lower end, carefully guide the caliper and brake pads over the brake rotor. First catch the caliper's bottom edge behind the caliper slide abutment, then rotate the top of the caliper into mounted position on the upper abutment.

WARNING

Extreme caution should be taken not to cross-thread the caliper guide pin bolts when they are installed.

10. Carefully install the caliper guide pin bolts. Tighten the bolts to 192 inch lbs. (22 Nm).
11. Install the banjo bolt connecting the brake hose to the brake caliper. Install NEW washers on each side of the hose fitting as the banjo bolt is guided through the fitting. Thread the banjo bolt into the caliper, and tighten it to 18 ft. lbs. (24 Nm).
12. Install the tire and wheel assembly. Install and tighten the wheel mounting nuts to 100 ft. lbs. (135 Nm).
13. Lower the vehicle.
14. Remove the brake pedal holding tool.
15. Bleed the caliper as necessary. Refer to Bleeding Procedure.
16. Road test the vehicle and make several stops to wear off any foreign material on the brakes and to seat the brake shoes.

DISC BRAKE PADS

REMOVAL & INSTALLATION

See Figure 13.

1. Before servicing the vehicle, refer to the Precautions Section.
2. Remove the brake caliper. Refer to Brake Caliper, removal & installation.
3. Remove the outboard brake pad from the caliper by prying the brake pad retaining clip over the raised area on the caliper. Slide the brake pad off of the brake caliper.
4. Pull the inboard brake pad away from the caliper piston until the retaining clip is free from the cavity in the piston. Remove the pad.

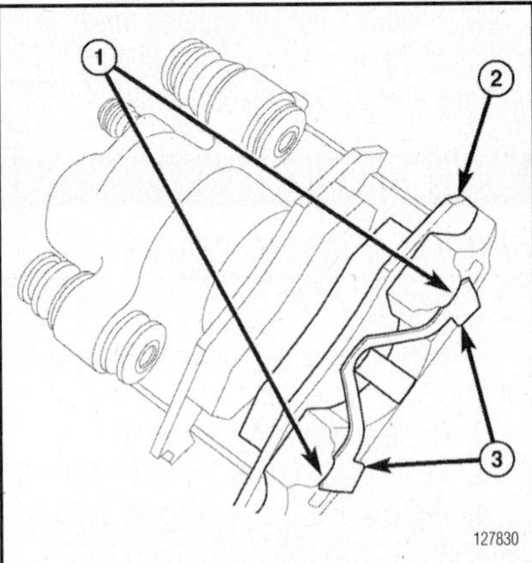

Fig. 13 Remove the outboard brake pad from the caliper by prying the brake pad retaining clip (3) over the raised area (1) on the caliper. Slide the brake pad (2) off of the brake caliper

To install:

WARNING

When installing new brake components, be sure to use the correct parts. Parts designed for BR4 Performance Brake System must not be mixed with other brake systems.

5. Completely retract the caliper piston back into the bore of the caliper. Use a C-clamp to retract the piston. Place a wood block over the piston before installing the C-clamp to avoid damaging the piston.
6. Install the inboard brake pad into the caliper piston by firmly pressing the pad in with the thumbs. Be sure the inboard brake pad is positioned squarely against the face of the caliper piston once installed.
7. Slide the outboard brake pad onto the caliper. Be sure the retaining clip is squarely seated in the depressed areas on the caliper beyond the raised retaining bead.
8. Install the brake caliper. Refer to Brake Caliper, removal & installation.

CAUTION

Dust and dirt accumulating on brake parts during normal use may contain asbestos fibers from production or aftermarket brake linings. Breathing excessive concentrations of asbestos fibers can cause serious bodily harm. Exercise care when servicing brake parts. Do not sand or grind brake lining unless equipment used is designed to contain the dust residue. Do not clean brake parts with compressed air or by dry brushing. Cleaning should be done by dampening the brake components with a fine mist of water, then wiping the brake components clean with a dampened cloth. Dispose of cloth and all residue containing asbestos fibers in an impermeable container with the appropriate label. Follow practices prescribed by the Occupational Safety and Health Administration (OSHA) and the Environmental Protection Agency (EPA) for the handling, processing, and disposing of dust or debris that may contain asbestos fibers.

PARKING BRAKE CABLES

ADJUSTMENT

See Figure 14.

CAUTION

The automatic adjusting feature of this parking brake lever contains a clockspring loaded to approximately 19 pounds. Do not release the automatic adjuster lockout device unless the rear parking brake cables and equalizer are connected to the lever output cable. Keep hands out of automatic adjuster sector and pawl area. Failure to observe caution in handling this mechanism could lead to serious injury.

CAUTION

When repairs to the parking brake lever or cables are required, the automatic adjuster must be loaded and locked out to avoid possible injury.

To lock automatic adjuster out:

1. Block the tire and wheels so the vehicle does not move once the vehicle parking brake lever is released.
2. Remove the transmission shift knob as necessary.
3. Place parking brake lever in released (full OFF position.
4. Remove the screws attaching the center console.
5. Remove the rear window switch panel from the console.
6. Working through switch opening, grasp a parking brake cable or equalizer, and pull back about 1 inch (25.4 mm).
7. While holding the cable or equalizer, pull the parking brake handle to its full upright position.
8. Remove the center console.
9. Grasp the parking brake lever output cable by hand and pull upward. Continue pulling the parking brake lever output cable until an appropriate pin punch (drill bit or locking pin) can be inserted sufficiently through the hole in the left side of the lever mounting bracket. This will lock the parking brake automatic adjustment mechanism in place and take tension off the parking brake cables. Slowly release the output cable. There should now be slack in the cables.

To unlock automatic adjuster (unloading):

10. Be sure the rear parking brake cables are both properly installed in the equalizer.
11. Raise the parking brake lever to the full upright position.
12. Keeping your hands clear of the automatic adjuster sector and pawl area, firmly grasp the parking brake lever pin punch (drill bit or locking pin if a new mechanism has been installed), then quickly remove it from the parking brake lever mechanism. This will allow the parking brake lever mechanism to automatically adjust the parking brake cables.
13. Install the center console and its mounting screws.
14. Cycle the parking brake lever once to position the parking brake cables, then return the parking brake lever to its released (full OFF) position.
15. Check the rear wheels of the vehicle. They should rotate freely without dragging with the lever in its released (full OFF) position.
16. Install rear window switch panel.
17. Remove the blocks from the tire and wheels.

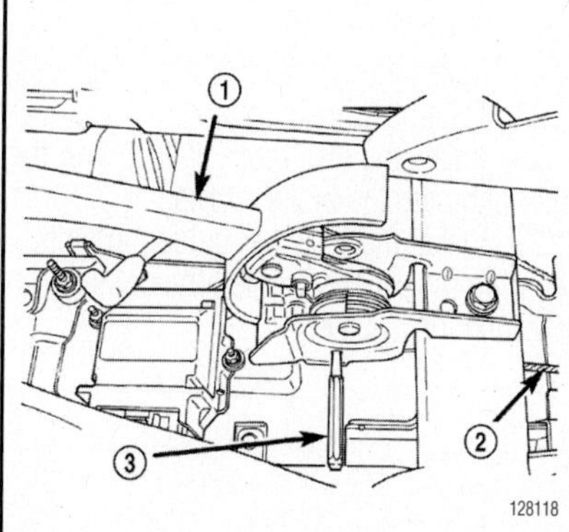

Fig. 14 Pull the parking brake lever output cable (2) until an appropriate pin punch (3) can be inserted sufficiently through the hole in the left side of the lever (1) mounting bracket

PARKING BRAKE SHOES

REMOVAL & INSTALLATION

See Figures 15 through 19.

1. Before servicing the vehicle, refer to the Precautions Section.
2. Raise and support the vehicle.
3. Remove the tire and wheel assembly.
4. Remove the rear brake caliper. Refer to Brake Caliper, removal & installation.
5. Hang the brake caliper from rear strut using wire or cord to prevent the weight of the caliper from damaging the brake hose.
6. Remove any clips retaining the brake rotor to the wheel studs.
7. Slide the brake rotor off the hub and bearing.
8. Remove the dust cap from the rear hub and bearing.
9. Remove the rear hub and bearing retaining nut.

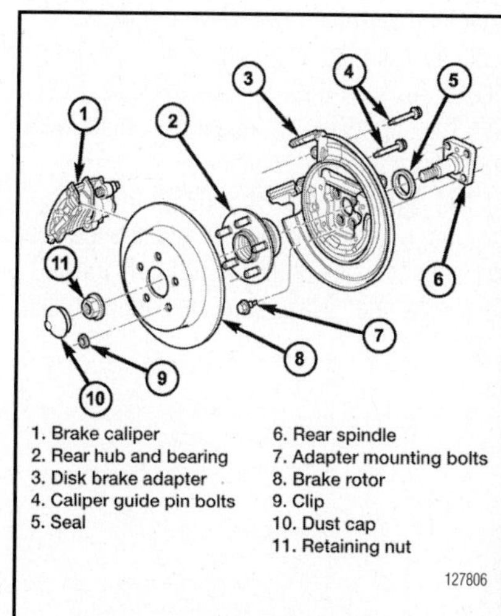

Fig. 15 Removing the rear hub and bearing

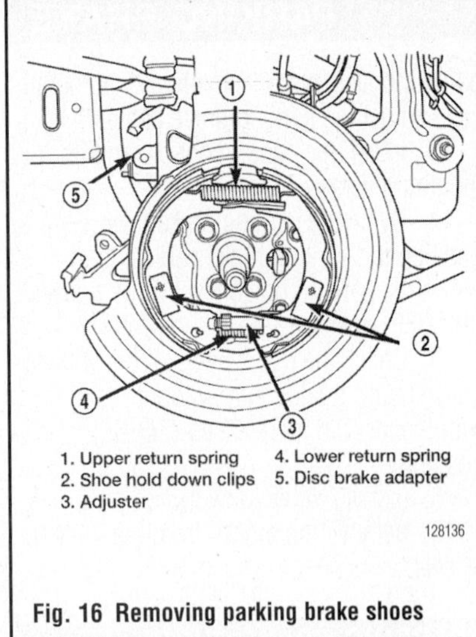

Fig. 16 Removing parking brake shoes

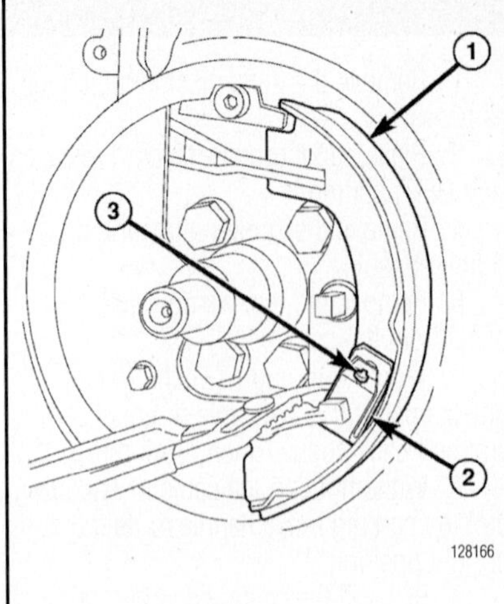

Fig. 17 Install the front brake shoe (1) on the adapter. Insert the hold-down pin (3) (from the rear) through the shoe, and install the hold-down clip (2) securing the shoe in place. Position the clip as shown

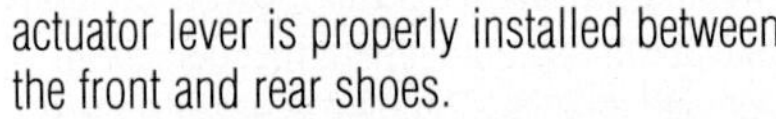

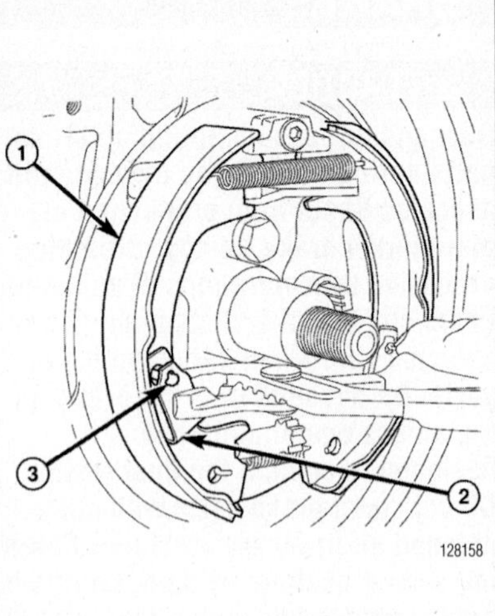

Fig. 18 Insert the hold-down pin (3) (from the rear) through the rear shoe (1), and install the hold-down clip (2) securing the shoe in place. Position the clip as shown

10. Remove the rear hub and bearing from the rear spindle.
11. Remove the rear brake shoe hold-down clip from the hold-down pin.
12. Turn the brake shoe adjuster wheel until the adjuster is at its shortest length.
13. Remove the adjuster from the parking brake shoes.
14. Remove the lower return spring.
15. Pull the rear brake shoe away from the anchor, and disconnect the upper return spring. Remove both from the vehicle.
16. Remove the front brake shoe hold-down clip from the hold-down pin.
17. Remove the front brake shoe.

➡If removing parking brake shoes on both sides of the vehicle, repeat procedure on other side of the vehicle.

To install:

18. Install the front brake shoe on the adapter. Insert the hold-down pin (from the rear) through the shoe, and install the hold-down clip securing the shoe in place. Position the clip as shown to avoid contact with other components.
19. Attach the upper shoe return spring on both shoes. Pull the rear brake shoe over the anchor block until it is properly located on the adapter. Make sure the parking brake actuator lever is properly installed between the front and rear shoes.
20. Install the lower return spring on the shoes.
21. Install the brake shoe adjuster between the front and rear shoes. The star wheel mounts toward the rear of the vehicle.
22. Insert the hold-down pin (from the rear) through the rear shoe, and install the hold-down clip securing the shoe in place. Position the clip as shown to avoid contact with other components.
23. Using a brake shoe gauge, adjust the parking brake shoes to a diameter of 6.75 inches (171 mm).
24. Slide the hub and bearing onto the rear spindle.
25. Install a NEW hub and bearing retaining nut. Tighten the hub nut to 160 ft. lbs. (217 Nm).
26. Install the hub and bearing dust cap.
27. Install the brake rotor.
28. Install the disc brake caliper over the rotor and onto the brake adapter.
29. Install the 2 caliper guide pin bolts securing the caliper. Tighten the bolts to 192 inch lbs. (22 Nm).

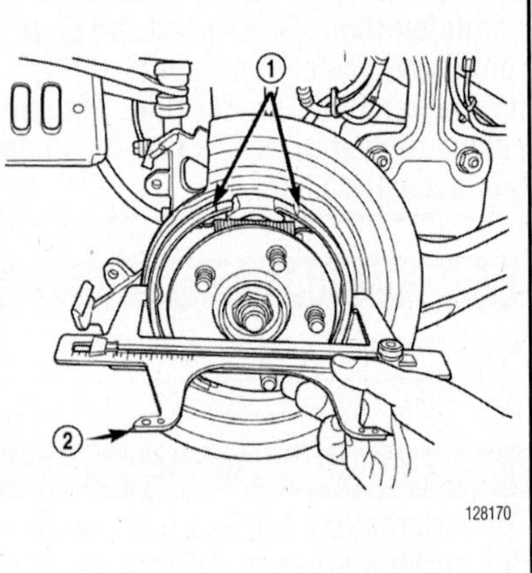

Fig. 19 Using a brake shoe gauge (2), adjust the parking brake shoes (1)

30. Install tire and wheel assembly. Install and tighten wheel mounting nuts to 100 ft. lbs. (135 Nm).
31. Adjust the parking brake shoes as necessary. Refer to Parking Brake Cables, adjustment.
32. Lower the vehicle.

GENERAL INFORMATION

CAUTION

These vehicles are equipped with an air bag system. The system must be disarmed before performing service on, or around, system components, the steering column, instrument panel components, wiring and sensors. Failure to follow the safety precautions and the disarming procedure could result in accidental air bag deployment, possible injury and unnecessary system repairs.

SERVICE PRECAUTIONS

Disconnect and isolate the battery negative cable before beginning any airbag system component diagnosis, testing, removal, or installation procedures. Allow system capacitor to discharge for two minutes before beginning any component service. This will disable the airbag system. Failure to disable the airbag system may result in accidental airbag deployment, personal injury, or death.

Do not place an intact undeployed airbag face down on a solid surface. The airbag will propel into the air if accidentally deployed and may result in personal injury or death.

When carrying or handling an undeployed airbag, the trim side (face) of the airbag should be pointing towards the body to minimize possibility of injury if accidental deployment occurs. Failure to do this may result in personal injury or death.

Replace airbag system components with OEM replacement parts. Substitute parts may appear interchangeable, but internal differences may result in inferior occupant protection. Failure to do so may result in occupant personal injury or death.

Wear safety glasses, rubber gloves, and long sleeved clothing when cleaning powder residue from vehicle after an airbag deployment. Powder residue emitted from a deployed airbag can cause skin irritation. Flush affected area with cool water if irritation is experienced. If nasal or throat irritation is experienced, exit the vehicle for fresh air until the irritation ceases. If irritation continues, see a physician.

Do not use a replacement airbag that is not in the original packaging. This may result in improper deployment, personal injury, or death.

The factory installed fasteners, screws and bolts used to fasten airbag components have a special coating and are specifically designed for the airbag system. Do not use substitute fasteners. Use only original equipment fasteners listed in the parts catalog when fastener replacement is required.

During, and following, any child restraint anchor service, due to impact event or vehicle repair, carefully inspect all mounting hardware, tether straps, and anchors for proper installation, operation, or damage. If a child restraint anchor is found damaged in any way, the anchor must be replaced. Failure to do this may result in personal injury or death.

Deployed and non-deployed airbags may or may not have live pyrotechnic material within the airbag inflator.

Do not dispose of driver/passenger/curtain airbags or seat belt tensioners unless you are sure of complete deployment. Refer to the Hazardous Substance Control System for proper disposal.

Dispose of deployed airbags and tensioners consistent with state, provincial, local, and federal regulations.

After any airbag component testing or service, do not connect the battery negative cable. Personal injury or death may result if the system test is not performed first.

If the vehicle is equipped with the Occupant Classification System (OCS), do not connect the battery negative cable before performing the OCS Verification Test using the scan tool and the appropriate diagnostic information. Personal injury or death may result if the system test is not performed properly.

Never replace both the Occupant Restraint Controller (ORC) and the Occupant Classification Module (OCM) at the same time. If both require replacement, replace one, then perform the Airbag System test before replacing the other.

Both the ORC and the OCM store Occupant Classification System (OCS) calibration data, which they transfer to one another when one of them is replaced. If both are replaced at the same time, an irreversible fault will be set in both modules and the OCS may malfunction and cause personal injury or death.

If equipped with OCS, the Seat Weight Sensor is a sensitive, calibrated unit and must be handled carefully. Do not drop or handle roughly. If dropped or damaged, replace with another sensor. Failure to do so may result in occupant injury or death.

If equipped with OCS, the front passenger seat must be handled carefully as well. When removing the seat, be careful when setting on floor not to drop. If dropped, the sensor may be inoperative, could result in occupant injury, or possibly death.

If equipped with OCS, when the passenger front seat is on the floor, no one should sit in the front passenger seat. This uneven force may damage the sensing ability of the seat weight sensors. If sat on and damaged, the sensor may be inoperative, could result in occupant injury, or possibly death.

CLOCKSPRING CENTERING

See Figure 20.

CAUTION

To avoid serious or fatal injury on vehicles equipped with air bags, disable the Supplemental Restraint System (SRS) before attempting any steering wheel, steering column, air bag, seat belt tensioner, impact sensor or instrument panel component diagnosis or service. Disconnect and isolate the battery negative (ground) cable, then wait 2 minutes for the system capacitor to discharge before performing further diagnosis or service. This is the only sure way to disable the SRS. Failure to take the proper precautions could result in accidental air bag deployment.

➡**A service replacement clockspring is shipped with the clockspring pre-centered and with a molded plastic locking**

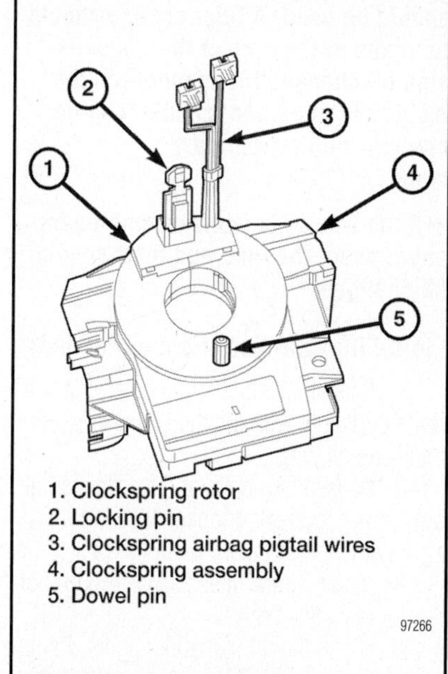

Fig. 20 Centering clockspring

pin installed. This locking pin should not be removed until the steering wheel has been installed on the steering column. If the locking pin is removed before the steering wheel is installed, the clockspring centering procedure must be performed.

⁂ CAUTION

When a clockspring is installed into a vehicle without properly centering and locking the entire steering system, the Steering Angle Sensor (SAS) data does not agree with the true position of the steering system, which will cause the Electronic Stability Program (ESP) system to shut down. This may also damage the clockspring without any immediate malfunction. Unlike some other Chrysler vehicles, this SAS never requires calibration. However, upon each new ignition ON cycle, the steering wheel must be rotated slightly to initialize the SAS.

➡Determining if the clockspring/SAS is centered is also possible electrically using the diagnostic scan tool. Steering wheel position is displayed as ANGLE with a range of up to 900 degrees. Refer to the appropriate menu item on the diagnostic scan tool.

➡Before starting this procedure, be certain to turn the steering wheel until the front wheels are in the straight-ahead position and that the entire steering system is locked or inhibited from rotation.

➡The clockspring may be centered and the rotor may be rotated freely once the steering wheel has been removed.

1. Place the front wheels in the straight-ahead position and inhibit the steering column shaft from rotation.
2. Remove the steering wheel from the steering shaft.
3. Rotate the clockspring rotor clockwise to the end of its travel. Do not apply excessive torque.
4. From the end of the clockwise travel, rotate the rotor about 2-1/2 turns counterclockwise. Turn the rotor slightly clockwise or counterclockwise as necessary so that the clockspring air bag pigtail wires and connector receptacle are at the top and the dowel or drive pin is at the bottom.
5. The clockspring is now centered. Secure the clockspring rotor to the clockspring case using a locking pin or some similar device to maintain clockspring centering until the steering wheel is reinstalled on the steering column.

DRIVE TRAIN

AUTOMATIC TRANSAXLE FLUID

DRAIN AND REFILL

Refer to Filter Replacement procedure.

FILTER REPLACEMENT

See Figure 21.

➡Refer to the maintenance schedules in the vehicle owner's manual for the recommended maintenance (fluid/filter change) intervals for this transaxle.

➡Only fluids of the type labeled Mopar ® ATF+4 (Automatic Transmission Fluid) should be used. A filter change should be made at the time of the transmission oil change. The magnet (on the inside of the oil pan) should also be cleaned with a clean, dry cloth.

➡If the transaxle is disassembled for any reason, the fluid and filter should be changed.

Fluid/Filter Service (Recommended)

1. Raise the vehicle on a hoist. Place a drain container with a large opening under transaxle oil pan.
2. Loosen pan bolts and tap the pan at one corner to break it loose, allowing fluid to drain, Remove the oil pan.
3. Install a new filter and O-ring on bottom of the valve body.
4. Clean the oil pan and magnet. Reinstall pan using new Mopar ® Silicone Adhesive sealant. Tighten oil pan bolts to 165 inch lbs. (19 Nm).
5. Pour 4 quarts of Mopar ® ATF+4 through the dipstick opening.
6. Start engine and allow it to idle for at least one minute. Then, with parking and service brakes applied, move selector lever momentarily to each position, ending in the Park or Neutral position.
7. Check the transaxle fluid level and add an appropriate amount to bring the transaxle fluid level to 1/8 inch (3 mm) below the lowest mark on the dipstick.
8. Recheck the fluid level after the transaxle has reached normal operating temperature 180 ° F (82 ° C). Refer to Fluid Level and Condition Check for the proper fluid fill procedure.
9. To prevent dirt from entering transaxle, make certain that dipstick is fully seated into the dipstick opening.

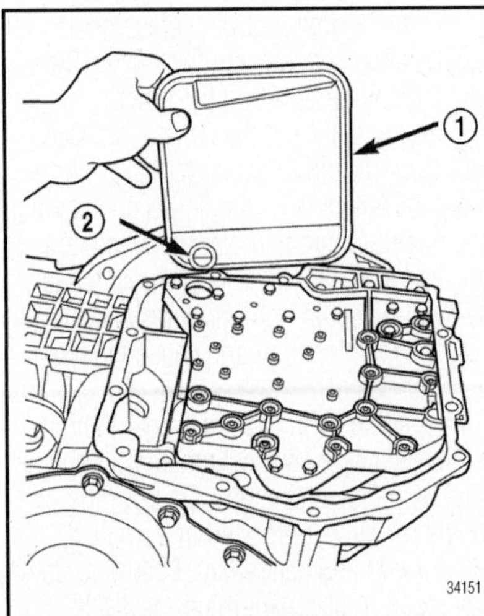

Fig. 21 Install a new filter (1) and O-ring (2) on bottom of the valve body

Dipstick tube fluid suction method (alternative)

10. When performing the fluid suction method, make sure the transaxle is at full operating temperature.
11. To perform the dipstick tube fluid suction method, use a suitable fluid suction device (Vacula(tm) or equivalent).
12. Insert the fluid suction line into the dipstick tube.

➡Verify that the suction line is inserted to the lowest point of the transaxle oil pan. This will ensure complete evacuation of the fluid in the pan.

13. Following the manufacturer's recommended procedure, evacuate the fluid from the transaxle.
14. Remove the suction line from the dipstick tube.
15. Pour 4 quarts of Mopar® ATF+4 through the dipstick opening.
16. Start engine and allow it to idle for at least one minute. Then, with parking and service brakes applied, move selector lever momentarily to each position, ending in the Park or Neutral position.
17. Check the transaxle fluid level and add an appropriate amount to bring the transaxle fluid level to 3 mm (1/8 in.) below the lowest mark on the dipstick.

18. Recheck the fluid level after the transaxle has reached normal operating temperature (180 ° F.).

19. To prevent dirt from entering transaxle, make certain that dipstick is fully seated into the dipstick opening.

FRONT HALFSHAFT

REMOVAL & INSTALLATION

See Figures 22 through 30.

**** WARNING**

Boot sealing is vital to retain special lubricants and to prevent foreign contaminants from entering the CV-joint. Mishandling, such as allowing the assemblies to dangle unsupported, or pulling/pushing the ends can cut boots or damage CV-joints. During removal and installation procedures, always support both ends of the halfshaft to prevent damage.

**** WARNING**

The halfshaft, when installed, acts as a bolt and secures the front hub/bearing assembly. If vehicle is to be supported or moved on its wheels with a halfshaft removed, install a PROPER-SIZED BOLT AND NUT through front hub. Tighten bolt and nut to 180 ft. lbs. (244 Nm). This will ensure that the hub bearing cannot loosen.

1. Disconnect the battery negative cable.
2. Place the transaxle in gated park.
3. Raise the vehicle on a hoist.
4. Remove the wheel and tire assembly.
5. Remove the cotter pin, nut lock, spring washer, and hub nut from the end of the outer CV-joint stub axle.
6. Disconnect the front wheel speed sensor, and secure harness out of the way.
7. Remove nut and bolt retaining the ball joint stud into the steering knuckle.

**** WARNING**

Use caution when separating ball joint stud from the steering knuckle, so ball joint seal does not get damaged.

8. Separate ball joint stud from steering knuckle by prying down on lower control arm.

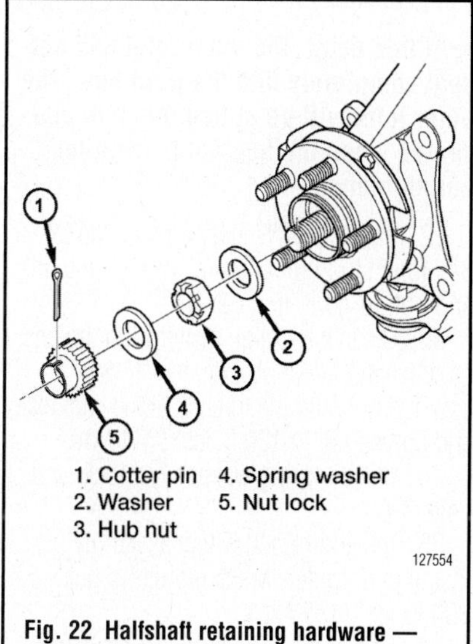

Fig. 22 Halfshaft retaining hardware — exploded view

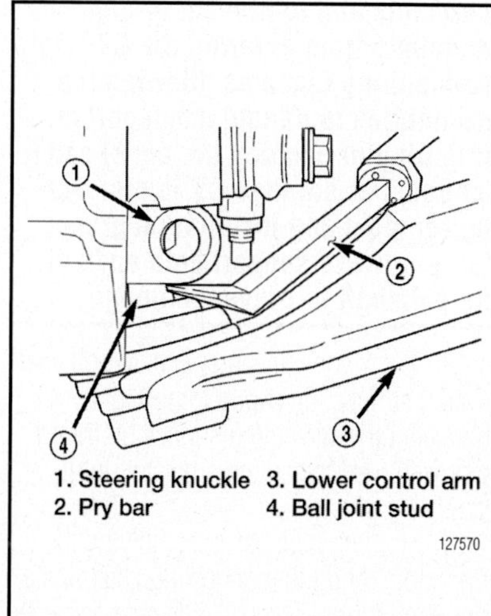

Fig. 24 Separating lower control arm from steering knuckle

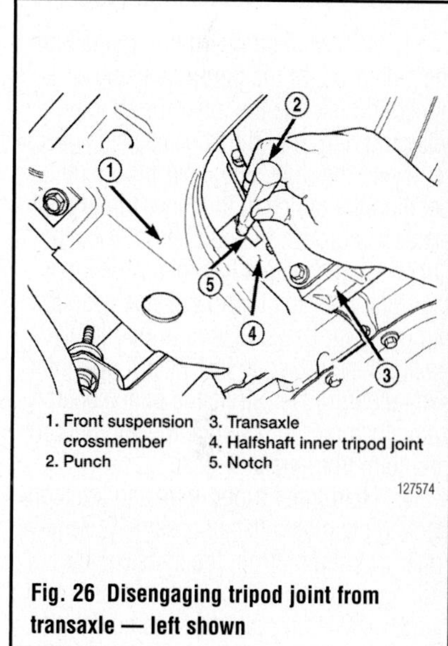

Fig. 26 Disengaging tripod joint from transaxle — left shown

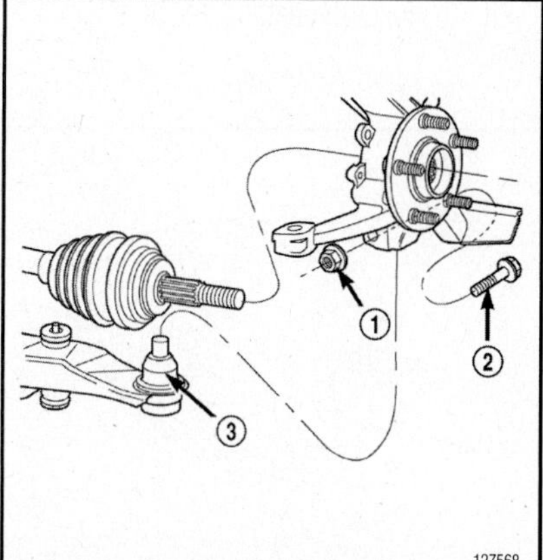

Fig. 23 Remove nut (1) and bolt (2) retaining the ball joint stud (3) into steering knuckle

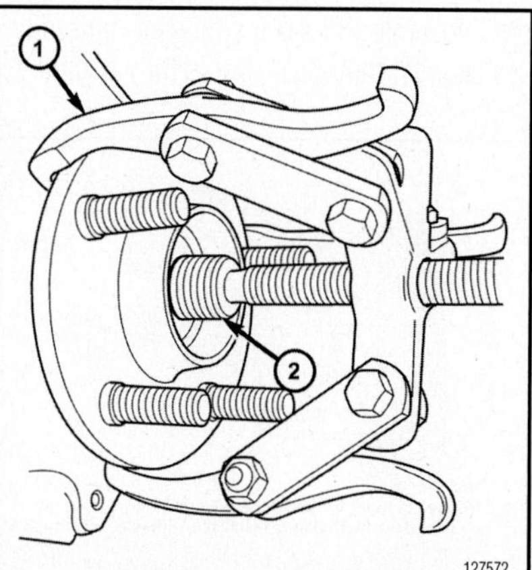

Fig. 25 If difficulty in separating halfshaft (2) from hub is encountered, use puller (1) to separate

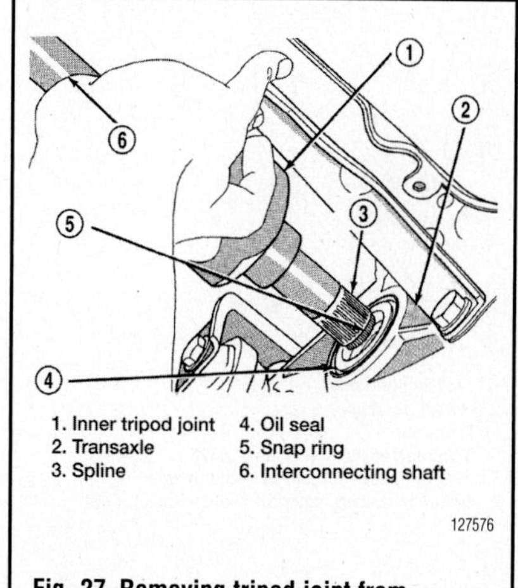

Fig. 27 Removing tripod joint from transaxle

✱✱ WARNING

Care must be taken not to separate the inner CV-joint during this operation. Do not allow the halfshaft to hang by inner CV-joint. Halfshaft must be supported.

9. Remove the halfshaft from the steering knuckle by pulling outward on knuckle while pressing in on halfshaft. Support the outer end of halfshaft assembly. If difficulty in separating halfshaft from hub is encountered, do not strike shaft with hammer; instead, use puller (1026) to separate.
10. Support the outer end of the halfshaft assembly.

➡Removal of the inner tripod joints is made easier if you apply outward pressure on the joint as you strike the punch with a hammer. Do not pull on interconnecting shaft to remove, as the inner joint will become separated.

11. Remove the inner tripod joints from the side gears of the transaxle using a punch to dislodge the inner tripod joint retaining ring from the transaxle side gear. If removing the right side inner tripod joint, position the punch to the inner tripod joint extraction groove (if equipped). Strike the punch sharply with a hammer to dislodge the right inner joint from the side gear. If removing the left side inner tripod joint, position the punch to the inner tripod joint extraction groove. Strike the punch sharply with a hammer to dislodge the left inner tripod joint from the side gear.
12. Hold inner tripod joint and interconnecting shaft of halfshaft assembly. Remove inner tripod joint from the transaxle by pulling it straight out of transaxle side gear and transaxle oil seal. When removing the tripod joint, do not let spline or snap ring drag across sealing lip of the transaxle to tripod joint oil seal. When tripod joint is removed from transaxle, some fluid will leak out.

✱✱ WARNING

The halfshaft, when installed, acts as a bolt and secures the front hub/bearing assembly. If vehicle is to be supported or moved on its wheels with a halfshaft removed, install a PROPER-SIZED BOLT AND NUT through front hub. Tighten bolt and nut to 180 ft. lbs. (244 Nm). This will ensure that the hub bearing cannot loosen.

To install:

✱✱ WARNING

Boot sealing is vital to retain special lubricants and to prevent foreign contaminants from entering the CV-joint. Mishandling (such as allowing the assemblies to dangle unsupported, or pulling or pushing the ends) can cut boots or damage CV-joints. During removal and installation procedures, always support both ends of the halfshaft to prevent damage.

13. Thoroughly clean spline and oil seal sealing surface, on tripod joint. Lightly lubricate oil seal sealing surface on tripod joint with fresh clean transmission lubricant.
14. Holding halfshaft assembly by the tripod joint and interconnecting shaft, install tripod joint into transaxle side gear as far as possible by hand.
15. Carefully align the tripod joint with the transaxle side gears. Then grasp the halfshaft interconnecting shaft, and push tripod joint into transaxle side gear until fully seated. Test that snap ring is fully engaged with side gear by attempting to remove tripod joint from transaxle by hand. If snap ring is fully engaged with side gear, tripod joint will not be removable by hand.
16. Clean all debris and moisture out of steering knuckle.
17. Ensure that the front of the outer CV-joint which fits into steering knuckle is free of debris and moisture before assembling into steering knuckle.
18. Apply a light coating of multi-purpose wheel bearing grease around the circumference of the flat surface. Do not apply too much grease, which could spill on to the non-mating surfaces and adversely affect the function of the halfshaft.
19. Wipe the rear of the hub and bearing in the knuckle clean where they contact the CV-joint.
20. Install the halfshaft back into front hub.
21. Install the steering knuckle onto the ball joint stud.

➡At this point, the outer joint will not seat completely into the front hub. The outer joint will be pulled into hub and seated when the hub nut is installed and tightened.

22. Install a NEW steering knuckle to ball joint stud bolt and nut. Tighten the nut and bolt to 70 ft. lbs. (95 Nm).
23. Clean all foreign matter from threads of halfshaft outer stub axle. Install washer and hub nut onto the threads of the stub axle, and tighten nut to 180 ft. lbs. (244 Nm).
24. Install spring washer, nut lock, and cotter pin.
25. Install tire and wheel assembly. Install and tighten wheel mounting nuts to 100 ft. lbs. (135 Nm).
26. Check for correct fluid level in the transaxle assembly.
27. Lower the vehicle.
28. Connect the battery negative cable.

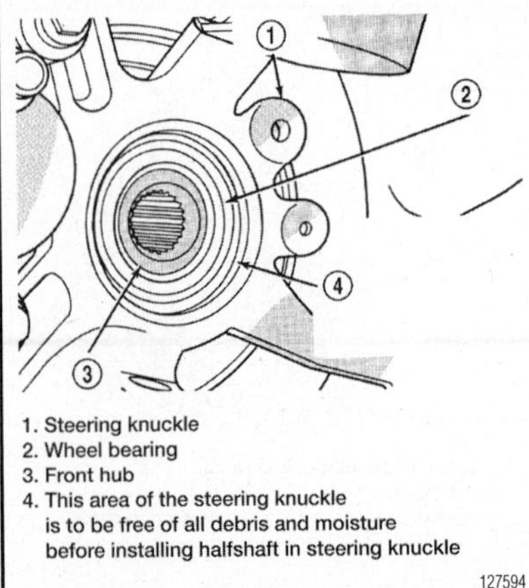

Fig. 28 Clean all debris and moisture out of steering knuckle

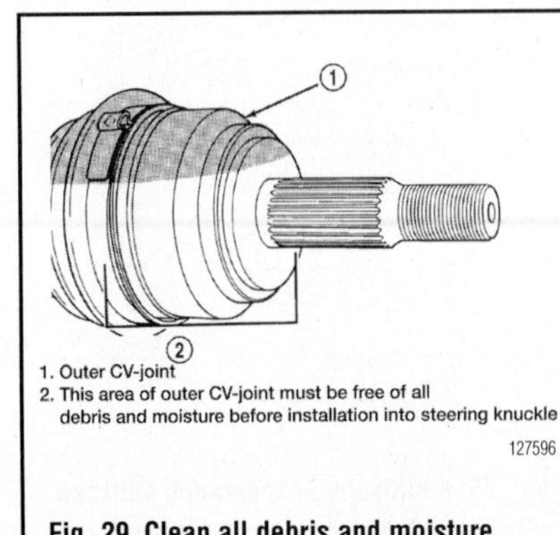

Fig. 29 Clean all debris and moisture from the front of the outer CV-joint

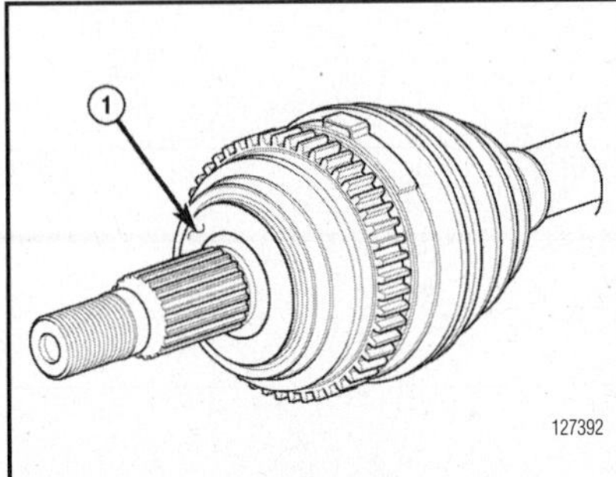

Fig. 30 Apply a light coating of multi-purpose wheel bearing grease around the circumference of the flat surface (1)

ENGINE COOLING

ENGINE COOLANT

PRECAUTIONS

✻✻ CAUTION

Antifreeze is an ethylene glycol based coolant, and is harmful if swallowed or inhaled. If swallowed, drink 2 glasses of water and induce vomiting. If inhaled, move to fresh air area. Seek medical attention immediately. Do not store in opened or unmarked containers. Wash skin and clothing thoroughly after coming in contact with ethylene glycol. Keep out of reach of children and pets. Dispose of glycol based coolant properly; contact your dealer or government agency for location of collection center in your area. Do not open a cooling system when the engine is at operating temperature or hot under pressure, or personal injury can result. Avoid radiator cooling fan when engine compartment related service is performed, as personal injury can result.

DRAIN & REFILL

See Figures 31 and 32.

✻✻ CAUTION

Do not open the radiator draincock with the system hot and under pressure. Serious burns from coolant can occur.

1. Position a clean collecting container under draincock location.
2. Without removing the pressure cap and with system not under pressure, turn the draincock counterclockwise to open.
3. The coolant reserve bottle should empty first. If not:
   - Check condition of the pressure cap and cap seals.
   - Check for kinked/torn overflow hose from filler neck to reserve bottle.
4. Remove the pressure cap.
5. Allow the cooling system to drain completely.

To refill:

6. Close the radiator draincock. Hand tighten only.
7. Open, but do not remove, cooling system bleed valve.
8. Attach a 0.250 inch (6.35 mm) inside diameter clear hose that is 48 inches (120.0 cm) long to the bleed valve.

➡The hose will prevent coolant from contacting the accessory drive belts, A/C compressor, and other components.

9. Route the hose away from the accessory drive belts and radiator fan.
10. Position the other end of the hose into a clean collecting container.

➡Be careful not to spill coolant on the drive belts or the alternator.

➡While filling the cooling system, pour coolant into the larger section of the filling aid funnel.

11. Remove the cooling system pressure cap.
12. Install the filling aid funnel (8195).
13. Use the supplied clip to pinch overflow hose.
14. Slowly fill the cooling system until a steady stream of coolant flows from the attached hose on the bleed valve.
15. Close the bleed valve and remove the hose.
16. Remove the clip from the overflow hose, and allow the filling aid funnel to drain through the overflow hose.
17. Remove the filling aid funnel.
18. Fill coolant to the top of the pressure cap neck.
19. Install the cooling system pressure cap.

✻✻ WARNING

Coolant may leak out of the bottle overflow tube if filling too rapidly.

20. Slowly fill coolant recovery container to at least the FULL HOT mark with the recommended coolant.

➡It may be necessary to add additional coolant to the reserve/recovery bottle after 3 – 4 warm-up/cool down cycles to maintain coolant level between the FULL HOT and ADD marks. This is due to the removal of trapped air from the system.

BLEEDING

See Figures 33 through 36.

➡Evacuating or purging air from the cooling system involves the use of a pressurized air operated vacuum generator. The vacuum created allows for a quick and complete coolant refilling while removing any airlocks present in the system components.

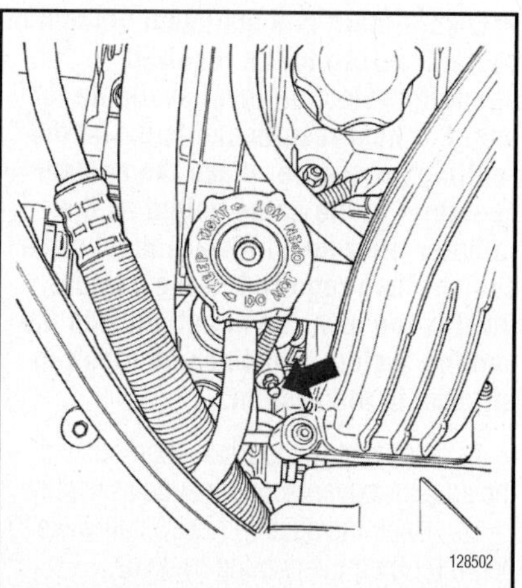

Fig. 31 Open, but do not remove, cooling system bleed valve

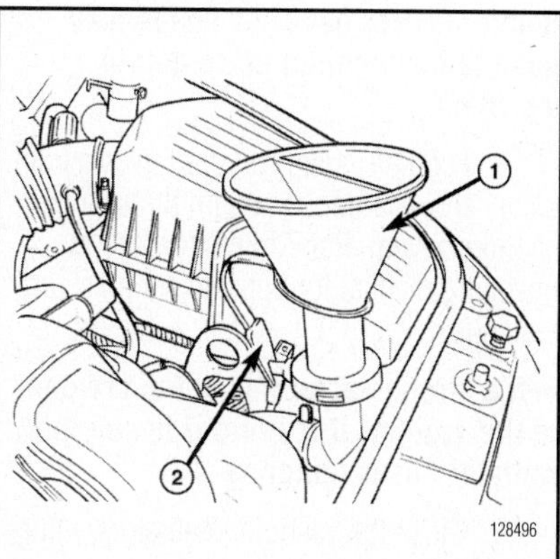

Fig. 32 Install filling aid funnel (1). Use the supplied clip (2) to pinch overflow hose

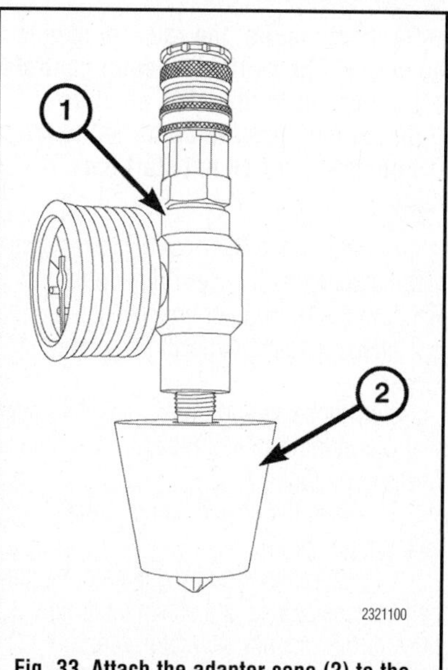

Fig. 33 Attach the adapter cone (2) to the vacuum gauge (1)

➡To avoid damage to the cooling system, ensure that no component would be susceptible to damage when a vacuum is drawn on the system.

⁂ CAUTION

Antifreeze is an ethylene glycol base coolant and is harmful if swallowed or inhaled. If swallowed, drink 2 glasses of water and induce vomiting. If inhaled, move to fresh air area. Seek medical attention immediately. Do not store in open or unmarked containers. Wash skin and clothing thoroughly after coming in contact with ethylene glycol. Keep out of reach of children. Dispose of glycol based coolant properly. Contact your dealer or government agency for location of collection center in your area. Do not open a cooling system when the engine is at operating temperature or hot under pressure, or personal injury can result. Avoid radiator cooling fan when engine compartment related service is performed, or personal injury can result.

⁂ CAUTION

Wear appropriate eye and hand protection when performing this procedure.

➡**The service area where this procedure is performed should have a minimum shop air requirement of 80 psi (5.5 bar) and should be equipped with an air dryer system.**

➡**For best results, the radiator should be empty. The vehicle's heater control should be set to the HEAT position (ignition may need to be turned to the ON position, but do not start the motor).**

1. Refer to the Chrysler Pentastar Service Equipment (Chrysler PSE) Coolant Refiller #85-15-0650 or equivalent tool's operating manual for specific assembly steps.
2. Choose an appropriate adapter cone that will fit the vehicle's radiator filler neck or reservoir tank.
3. Attach the adapter cone to the vacuum gauge.
4. Ensure the vacuum generator/venturi ball valve is closed and attach an airline hose to the vacuum generator/venturi.
5. Position the adaptor cone/vacuum gauge assembly into the radiator filler neck or reservoir tank. Ensure that the adapter cone is sealed properly.
6. Connect the vacuum generator/venturi to the positioned adaptor cone/vacuum gauge assembly.
7. Open the vacuum generator/venturi ball valve.

➡**Do not bump or move the assembly, as it may result in loss of vacuum. Some radiator overflow hoses may need to be clamped off to obtain vacuum.**

8. Let the system run until the vacuum gauge shows a good vacuum through the cooling system. Refer to the tool's operating manual for appropriate pressure readings.

➡**If a strong vacuum is being created in the system, it is normal to see the radiator hoses collapse.**

9. Close the vacuum generator/venturi ball valve.
10. Disconnect the vacuum generator/venturi and airline from the adaptor cone/vacuum gauge assembly.

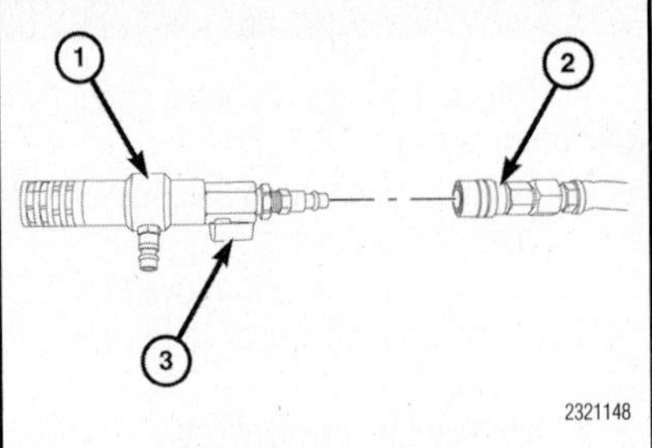

Fig. 34 Ensure the vacuum generator/venturi ball valve (3) is closed and attach an airline hose (2) to the vacuum generator/venturi (1)

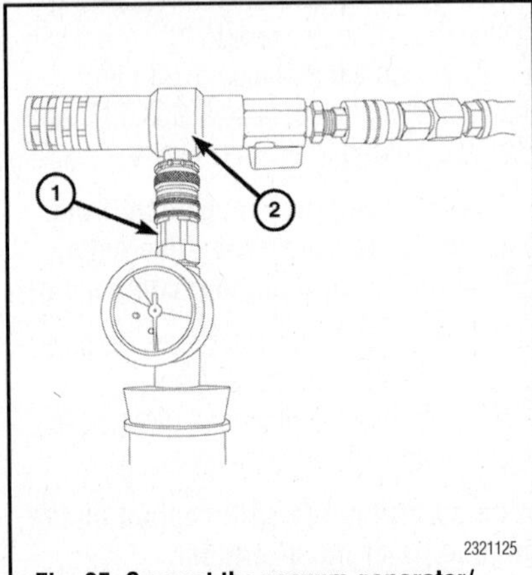

Fig. 35 Connect the vacuum generator/venturi (2) to the positioned adaptor cone/vacuum gauge assembly (1).

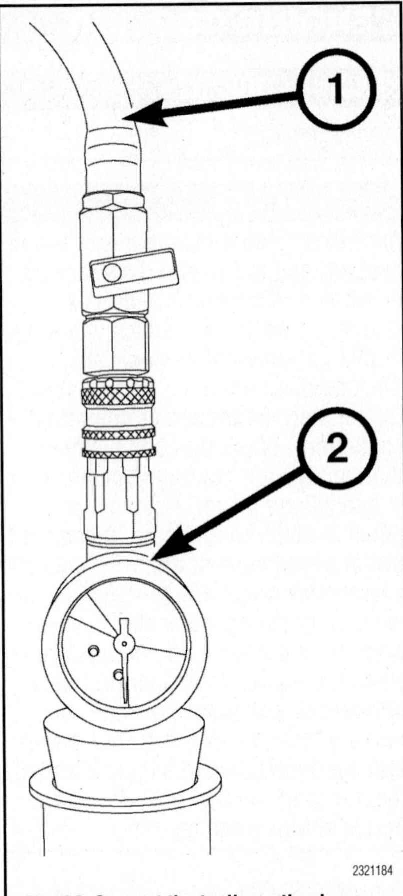

Fig. 36 Connect the tool's suction hose (1) to the adaptor cone/vacuum gauge assembly (2)

11. Wait approximately 20 seconds. If the pressure readings do not move, the system has no leaks. If the pressure readings move, a leak could be present in the system and the cooling system should be checked for leaks and the procedure should be repeated.
12. Place the tool's suction hose into the coolant's container.

➡**Ensure there is a sufficient amount of coolant, mixed to the required strength/protection level available for use. For best results and to assist the refilling procedure, place the coolant container at the same height as the radiator filler neck. Always draw more coolant than required. If the coolant level is too low, it will pull air into the cooling system, which could result in airlocks in the system.**

13. Connect the tool's suction hose to the adaptor cone/vacuum gauge assembly.
14. Open the suction hose's ball valve to begin refilling the cooling system.
15. When the vacuum gauge reads zero, the system is filled.

➡On some remote pressurized tanks, it is recommended to stop filling when the proper level is reached.

16. Close the suction hose's ball valve, and remove the suction hose from the adaptor cone/vacuum gauge assembly.
17. Remove the adaptor cone/vacuum gauge assembly from the radiator filler neck or reservoir tank.
18. With heater control unit in the HEAT position, operate engine with container cap in place.
19. After engine has reached normal operating temperature, shut engine off and allow it to cool. When engine is cooling down, coolant will be drawn into the radiator from the pressure container.

➡Only add coolant to the container when the engine is cold. Coolant level in a warm engine will be higher due to thermal expansion. Add necessary coolant to raise container level to the COLD MINIMUM mark after each cool down period.

20. Add coolant to the recovery bottle/container as necessary.
21. Once the appropriate coolant level is achieved, attach the radiator cap or reservoir tank cap.

NORMAL FLUSHING

➡In some instances, use a radiator cleaner (Mopar ® Radiator Kleen or equivalent) before flushing. This will soften scale and other deposits and aid flushing operation.

**** WARNING**

Follow the manufacturer's instructions when using radiator cleaner products.

1. Drain the cooling system and refill with water.
2. Run the engine with the radiator cap installed until the upper radiator hose is hot.
3. Stop the engine and drain the water from system. If the water is dirty, fill the system with water, run the engine and drain the system. Repeat this procedure until the water drains clean.

REVERSE FLUSHING

➡Reverse flushing of the cooling system is the forcing of water through the cooling system. This is done using air pressure in the opposite direction of normal coolant flow. It is usually only necessary with very dirty systems with evidence of partial plugging.

Radiator

1. Disconnect the radiator hoses from the radiator inlet and outlet.
2. Attach a section of the radiator hose to the radiator bottom outlet fitting and insert the flushing gun.
3. Connect a water supply hose and air supply hose to the flushing gun.

**** WARNING**

Internal radiator pressure must not exceed 20 psi (138 kPa), as damage to radiator may result.

4. Allow the radiator to fill with water.
5. When the radiator is filled, apply air in short blasts. Allow the radiator to refill between blasts.
6. Continue this reverse flushing until clean water flows out through the rear of the radiator cooling tube passages.

Engine

1. Drain the cooling system. Refer to Drain & Refill procedure.
2. Remove the thermostat housing and thermostat. Refer to Thermostat, removal & installation.
3. Install the thermostat housing.
4. Disconnect the radiator upper hose from the radiator, and attach the flushing gun to the hose.
5. Disconnect the radiator lower hose from the water pump, and attach a lead-away hose to the water pump inlet fitting.

**** WARNING**

On vehicles equipped with a heater water control valve, be sure the heater control valve is closed (heat off). This will prevent coolant flow with scale and other deposits from entering the heater core.

6. Connect the water supply hose and air supply hose to flushing gun.
7. Allow the engine to fill with water.
8. When the engine is filled, apply air in short blasts, allowing the system to fill between air blasts. Continue until clean water flows through the lead-away hose.
9. Remove the lead-away hose, flushing gun, water supply hose and air supply hose.
10. Remove the thermostat housing and install the thermostat. Refer to Thermostat, removal & installation.
11. Install the thermostat housing with a replacement gasket.
12. Connect the radiator hoses.
13. Refill the cooling system with the correct antifreeze/water mixture. Refer to Drain & Refill procedure.

ENGINE FAN

REMOVAL & INSTALLATION

See Figure 37.

**** CAUTION**

Do not open the radiator draincock with the system hot and under pressure, because serious burns from coolant can occur.

➡The fan motor, fan, and the shroud are serviced as an assembly.

1. Disconnect negative cable from battery.
2. Remove the battery and battery tray.
3. Drain the cooling system below upper radiator hose level.
4. Remove the grille.
5. Remove the upper radiator closure panel and center brace.
6. Disconnect the upper radiator hose from the radiator.
7. Hoist the vehicle.
8. Disconnect the radiator fan electrical connector.
9. Remove the 2 lower and left side radiator fan screws from the radiator.
10. Lower the vehicle, and remove the remaining radiator fan attaching screws.

**** WARNING**

Care should be taken not to damage the radiator cooling fins and tubes during fan removal.

11. Remove the radiator fan by lifting up from the engine compartment.

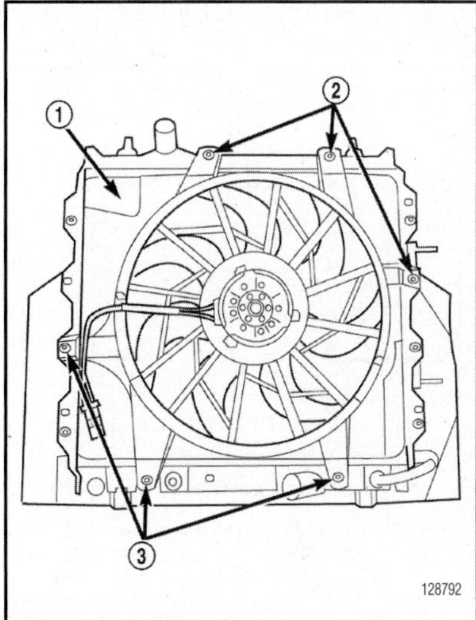

Fig. 37 Remove the 2 lower and left side radiator fan screws (2, 3) from the radiator (1)

To install:

12. Install the radiator fan into position on the radiator.
13. Hand start all radiator fan fasteners.
14. Tighten all radiator fan retaining screws to 55 inch lbs. (6 Nm).
15. Connect the radiator fan electrical connector.
16. Lower the vehicle.
17. Connect the upper radiator hose to radiator. Align hose and position clamp so it will not interfere with the engine or the hood.
18. Install the upper radiator closure panel and center brace.
19. Install the grille.
20. Install the battery tray and battery.
21. Connect cables to battery.
22. Fill the cooling system. Refer to Drain & Refill procedure.

RADIATOR

REMOVAL & INSTALLATION

See Figure 38.

CAUTION

Do not open the radiator draincock with the system hot and under pressure, because serious burns from coolant can occur.

➡It is not necessary to discharge the air conditioning system to remove the radiator.

1. Drain the cooling system. Refer to Drain & Refill procedure.
2. Remove the radiator fan. Refer to Radiator Fan, removal & installation.
3. Disconnect the lower radiator hose.

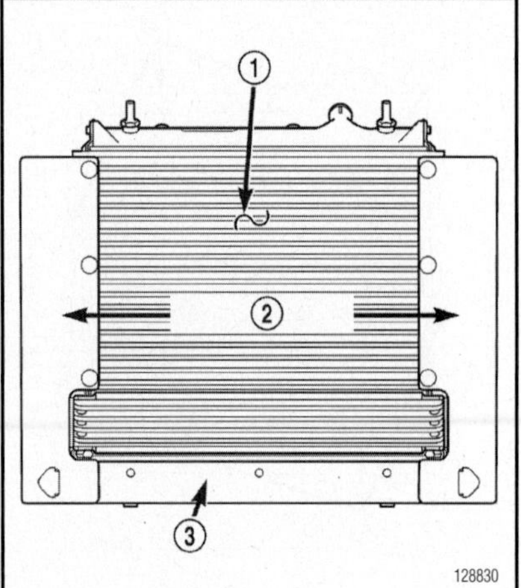

Fig. 38 Remove the lower radiator air seal from the side radiator air seals (2, 3) on the A/C condenser (1)

4. Remove the 2 fasteners attaching the transmission oil cooler to the radiator.
5. Remove the lower radiator air seal from the side radiator air seals on the A/C condenser.
6. Remove the fasteners attaching the A/C condenser to the radiator. Reposition the A/C condenser.
7. Remove the radiator assembly by lifting it up from the engine compartment. Care should be taken not to damage the cooling fins and tubes during removal.
8. Remove the lower air seal from radiator.

To install:

9. Install the lower air seal to radiator.
10. Position the radiator into mounting position.
11. Position the A/C condenser against the radiator. Hand start the fasteners.
12. Install the radiator fan/shroud assembly. Hand start the fasteners.
13. Tighten all condenser fasteners to 70 inch lbs. (8 Nm).
14. Tighten all radiator fan fasteners to 55 inch lbs. (6 Nm).
15. Install the fasteners attaching the transmission oil cooler to the radiator. Tighten the fasteners to 70 inch lbs. (8 Nm).
16. Raise the vehicle on a hoist.
17. Connect the lower air seal to the side air seals.
18. Connect the lower radiator hose. Align the hose and position the clamp so it will not interfere with engine components.
19. Connect the radiator fan electrical connector.
20. Close radiator draincock.
21. Lower the vehicle.
22. Connect the upper radiator hose. Align the hose and position the clamp to prevent interference with the engine or hood.
23. Install the upper radiator closure panel and center brace.
24. Install the grille.
25. Install the battery tray and battery.
26. Connect the positive battery cable. Connect negative battery cable.
27. Install the air cleaner housing assembly.
28. Fill the cooling system with coolant. Refer to Drain & Refill procedure.
29. Operate engine until it reaches normal operating temperature. Check cooling system for correct fluid level.

THERMOSTAT

REMOVAL & INSTALLATION

See Figures 39 and 40.

1. Remove upper intake manifold. Refer to Intake Manifold, removal & installation.
2. Partially drain the cooling system below the thermostat level.
3. Disconnect the upper radiator hose from outlet connector.
4. Disconnect the coolant recovery system hose from outlet connector.
5. Remove coolant outlet connector bolts.

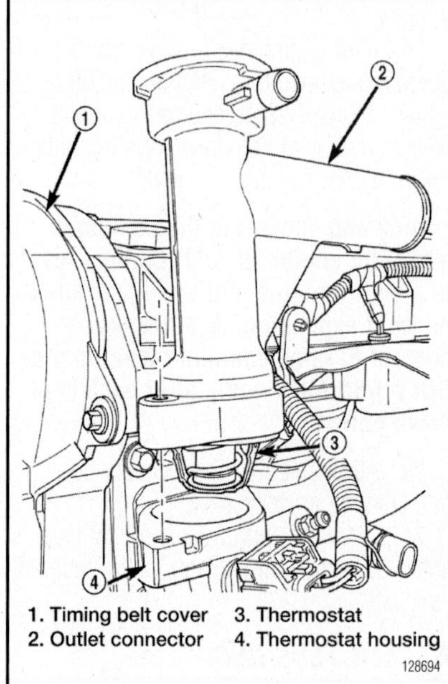

Fig. 39 View of thermostat and coolant outlet connector

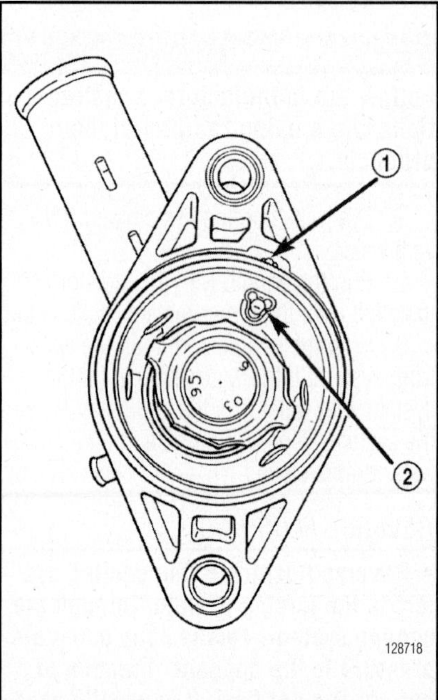

Fig. 40 Aligning air bleed (2) with the location notch (1) on outlet connector

6. Remove thermostat assembly, and clean sealing surfaces.

To install:

7. Place the new thermostat assembly into the coolant outlet connector, aligning air bleed with the location notch on outlet connector.
8. Install the coolant outlet connector with thermostat in position onto thermostat housing. Tighten bolts to 110 inch lbs. (12.5 Nm).
9. Connect the upper radiator hose.
10. Connect the coolant recovery system hose.
11. Install the upper intake manifold. Refer to Intake Manifold, removal & installation.
12. Fill the cooling system. Refer to Drain & Refill procedure.

WATER PUMP

REMOVAL & INSTALLATION

See Figures 41 and 42.

1. Drain the cooling system. Refer to Drain & Refill procedure.
2. Remove the timing belt. Refer to Timing Belt & Sprockets, removal & installation.
3. Remove the camshaft sprockets and the rear timing belt cover. Refer to Camshaft, removal & installation.
4. Remove screws attaching the water pump to the engine. Remove the water pump.

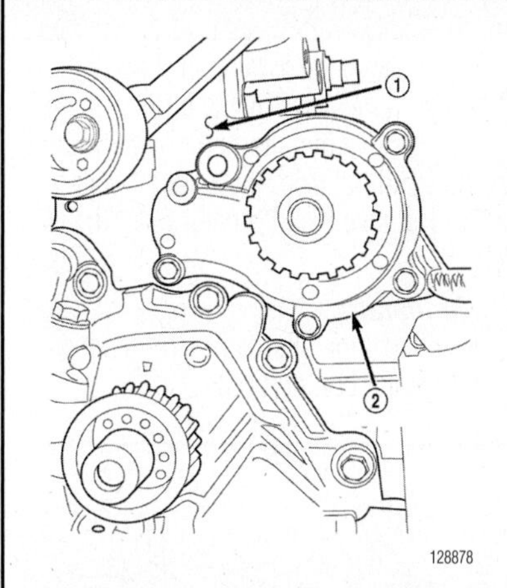

Fig. 41 Remove screws attaching the water pump to the engine (1). Remove the water pump (2)

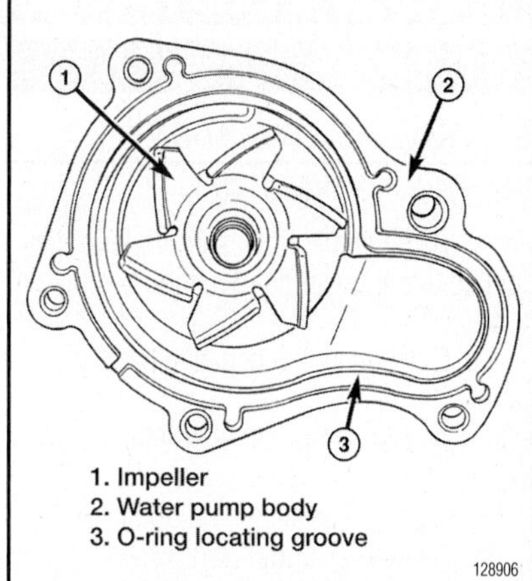

Fig. 42 Installing O-ring gasket in water pump body groove

To install:

5. Apply MOPAR ® Dielectric Grease to new O-ring before installation.
6. Install the O-ring gasket in water pump body groove.

⁂ WARNING

Make sure O-ring gasket is properly seated in water pump groove before tightening screws. An improperly located O-ring may cause damage to the O-ring, resulting in a coolant leak.

7. Assemble the pump body to the block and tighten screws to 105 inch lbs. (12 Nm).
8. Rotate pump by hand to check for freedom of movement.
9. Evacuate air and refill cooling system. Refer to Drain & Refill procedure.
10. Pressurize the cooling system to 15 psi (103 kPa) with pressure tester, and check water pump shaft seal and O-ring for leaks.
11. Install the rear timing belt cover and the camshaft sprockets. Refer to Camshaft, removal & installation.
12. Install the timing belt. Refer to Timing Belt & Sprockets, removal & installation.

ENGINE ELECTRICAL

BATTERY SYSTEM

BATTERY

REMOVAL & INSTALLATION

⁂ CAUTION

To protect the hands from battery acid, a suitable pair of heavy duty rubber gloves should be worn when removing or servicing a battery. Safety glasses also should be worn.

⁂ CAUTION

Remove metallic jewelry to avoid injury by accidental arcing of battery current.

1. Make sure ignition switch is in **OFF** position and all accessories are off.
2. Open the hood.
3. Remove the air cleaner housing. Refer to Air Cleaner, removal & installation.
4. Disconnect and isolate the negative battery cable, then the positive cable.
5. Loosen the bolt and retainer that holds the battery down to the tray.
6. Lift battery out of battery tray and remove from vehicle.
7. Remove the thermal guard (if equipped) from battery.

To install:

➡When replacing battery, the thermal guard MUST be transferred to the new battery (if equipped).

8. Install battery in vehicle making sure that the thermal guard (if equipped) is present and battery is properly positioned on battery tray.
9. Install the bolt and retainer that hold the battery down to the tray making sure that they are properly positioned on battery. Tighten retaining bolt to 110 inch lbs. (12.5 Nm).
10. Install battery cables on battery posts. Install positive battery cable first.
11. Tighten clamp nuts to 110 inch lbs. (12.5 Nm).
12. Install air cleaner housing. Refer to Air Cleaner, removal & installation.
13. Close the hood.
14. Verify proper vehicle operation.

ALTERNATOR

REMOVAL & INSTALLATION

See Figures 43 through 46.

1. Remove the air cleaner lid, and disconnect the inlet air sensor and makeup air hose.
2. Disconnect the negative battery cable.
3. Loosen the upper alternator T-bolt locknut.
4. Raise the vehicle on a hoist.
5. Remove the right front wheel.
6. Remove the accessory drive splash shield.
7. Remove the pencil strut.
8. Loosen the lower pivot bolt.
9. Loosen the accessory drive belt T-bolt.
10. Unplug the field circuit connector from alternator.
11. Remove the B+ terminal nut and B+ terminal.
12. Remove the accessory drive belt. Refer to Accessory Drive Belts, removal & installation.
13. Remove the axle shaft. Refer to Halfshaft, removal & installation.
14. Remove the alternator lower mounting bolt and nut from the upper T-bolt.
15. Remove the alternator from the vehicle.

To install:

16. Install the alternator, and loosely assemble the bolt and nut.

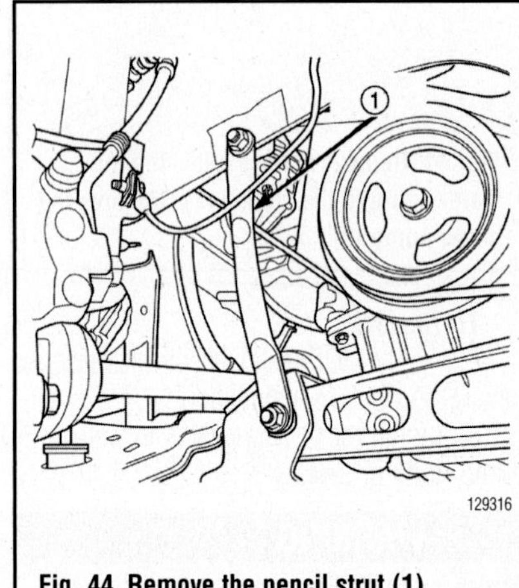

Fig. 44 Remove the pencil strut (1)

17. Install and tension the accessory drive belt. Refer to Accessory Drive Belts, removal & installation.
18. Tighten the lower pivot bolt to 40 ft. lbs. (54 Nm).
19. Install the axle shaft. Refer to Halfshaft, removal & installation.
20. Install the pencil strut, and tighten nut to 38 ft. lbs. (52 Nm).
21. Install the B+ terminal nut and B+ terminal. Tighten nut to 100 inch lbs. (11.3 Nm).
22. Plug in the field circuit connector to the alternator.
23. Install the accessory drive splash shield.
24. Install the right front wheel.
25. Lower the vehicle.
26. Tighten the T-bolt locknut to 40 ft. lbs. (54 Nm).
27. Connect the negative battery cable.
28. Install the air cleaner lid, and connect the inlet air temperature sensor and makeup hose.
29. Check the transmission fluid.

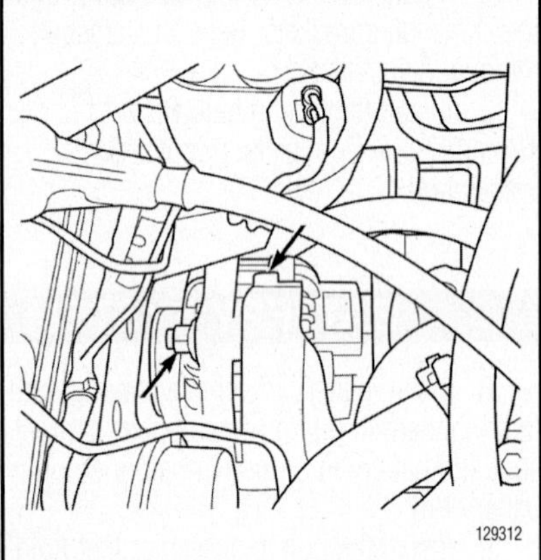

Fig. 43 Loosen the upper alternator T-bolt locknut

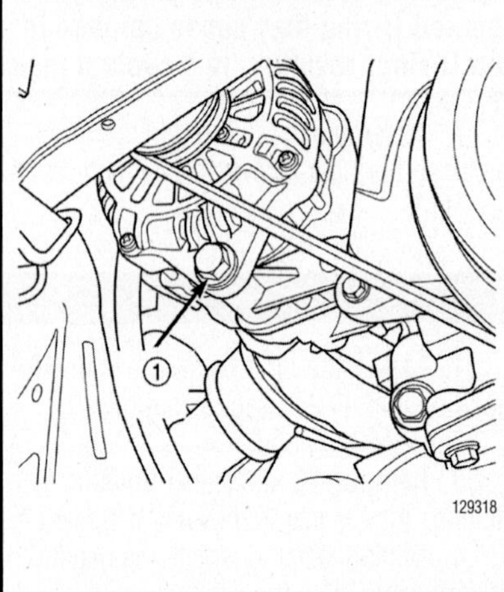

Fig. 45 Loosen the lower pivot bolt (1)

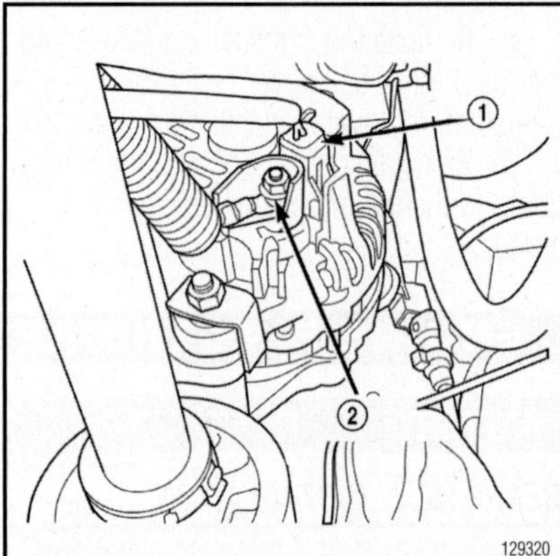

Fig. 46 Unplug field circuit connector (1) from alternator. Remove the B+ terminal nut (2) and B+ terminal

FIRING ORDER

See Figure 47.

2.4L engine firing order is 1 – 3 – 4 – 2.

IGNITION COIL

REMOVAL & INSTALLATION

1. Remove the negative battery cable.
2. Disconnect the electrical connector from the coil pack.
3. Remove the spark plug cables from the coil pack.
4. Remove coil pack mounting bolts.
5. Remove the coil pack.

To install:

➡**The electronic ignition coil pack attaches directly to the valve cover.**

6. Install the coil pack on valve cover. Tighten the bolts to 105 inch lbs. (12 Nm).
7. Transfer the spark plug cables to new coil pack. The coil pack towers are numbered with the cylinder identification. Be sure the ignition cables snap onto the towers.
8. Install the negative battery cable.

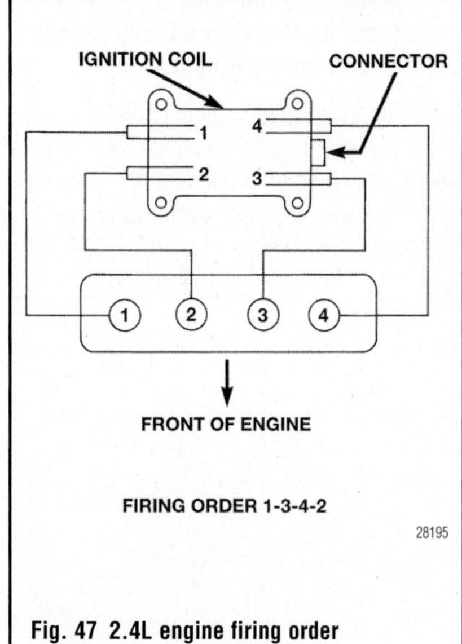

Fig. 47 2.4L engine firing order

IGNITION TIMING

ADJUSTMENT

The ignition timing is controlled by the Powertrain Control Module. No adjustment is necessary.

SPARK PLUGS

REMOVAL & INSTALLATION

✲✲ WARNING

Special care should be used when installing spark plugs in the cylinder head spark plug wells. Be sure the plugs do not drop into the wells, or damage to the electrodes can occur.

✲✲ WARNING

Always tighten spark plugs to the specified torque. Over-tightening can cause distortion, resulting in a change in the spark plug gap. Over-tightening can also damage the cylinder head.

1. Remove the air cleaner lid. Disconnect the inlet air sensor and makeup air hose.
2. Disconnect the negative battery cable.
3. Remove the upper intake manifold. Refer to Intake Manifold, removal & installation.
4. Disconnect the cable from the ignition coil first.

➡**Always remove cables by grasping at the boot, rotating the boot 1/2 turn, and pulling straight back in a steady motion.**

5. Prior to removing the spark plug, spray compressed air around the spark plug hole and the area around the spark plug.
6. Remove the spark plug using a quality socket with a rubber or foam insert.
7. Inspect the spark plug condition.

To install:

✲✲ WARNING

The tapered seat plugs for this application are torque-critical! It is imperative that 13 ft. lbs. (17.5 Nm) is NOT exceeded!

✲✲ WARNING

When replacing the spark plugs and spark plug cables, route the cables correctly and secure them in the appropriate retainers. Failure to route the cables properly can cause the radio to reproduce ignition noise, cross ignition of the spark plugs or short circuit the cables to ground.

✲✲ WARNING

Do not over apply anti-seize compound. Only use enough to lightly coat threads on the spark plug.

8. Apply a small amount of anti-seize to threads of each spark plug.
9. Check and adjust spark plug gap to .040 inch (1 mm).

✲✲ WARNING

To avoid cross threading and plug damage, use a quality socket with a rubber insert and start each spark plug into the cylinder head by hand.

10. Install spark plug and tighten to 13 ft. lbs. (17.5 Nm).
11. Install ignition cables over spark plugs. An audible click noise can be heard and felt when the ignition cable is properly attached to spark plug.
12. Install the upper intake manifold. Refer to Intake Manifold, removal & installation.
13. Connect the negative battery cable.
14. Install the air cleaner lid, and connect the inlet air temperature sensor and makeup hose.

ENGINE ELECTRICAL

STARTER

REMOVAL & INSTALLATION

See Figure 48.

1. Open the hood.
2. Remove the air cleaner box cover. Refer to Air Cleaner, removal & installation.
3. Disconnect and isolate the negative battery cable.
4. Raise the vehicle on a hoist.
5. Remove the structural collar. Refer to Structural Collar, removal & installation.
6. Disconnect the starter motor wiring.
7. Remove the starter motor mounting bolts.
8. Remove the starter motor from vehicle.

To install:

9. Reinstall the starter motor into vehicle lower engine compartment.

1. Bolt
2. Ground
3. Starter
4. Bolt

129350

Fig. 48 View of starter motor and components

10. Install the starter motor mounting bolts and torque to 40 ft. lbs. (54 Nm).
11. Connect the starter motor wiring. Tighten the solenoid battery cable nut to 90 inch lbs. (10 Nm).
12. Install the structural collar. Refer to Structural Collar, removal & installation.
13. Lower the vehicle from the hoist.
14. Reconnect the negative battery cable.
15. Remove the air cleaner box cover. Refer to Air Cleaner, removal & installation.
16. Verify the operation of the vehicle and its systems.
17. Close the hood, and remove vehicle from hoist.

ENGINE MECHANICAL

➡Disconnecting the negative battery cable may interfere with the functions of the onboard computer systems and may require the computer to undergo a relearning process once the negative battery cable is reconnected.

ACCESSORY DRIVE BELTS

ACCESSORY BELT ROUTING

See Figure 49.

The accessory drive consist of 2 Poly-V type drive belts. One belt drives the power steering pump and air conditioning compressor, the other drives the generator.

1. Belt tensioner
2. Power steering pump/AC compressor belt
3. Alternator belt

128532

Fig. 49 Accessory drive belt routing

- The power steering/air conditioning belt is tensioned by an automatically-controlled belt tensioner.
- The alternator belt is manually tensioned using an adjusting bolt and a locking nut.

INSPECTION

1. When diagnosing serpentine accessory drive belts, small cracks that run across the ribbed surface of the belt from rib to rib, are considered normal. These are not a reason to replace the belt. However, cracks running along a rib (not across) are not normal. Any belt with cracks running along a rib must be replaced. Also replace the belt if it has excessive wear, frayed cords or severe glazing.

ADJUSTMENT

The automatic belt tensioner maintains proper tension on the power steering and air conditioning belt. The tensioner pulley can be serviced separately.

Bottom of Form

REMOVAL & INSTALLATION

➡The power steering pump/AC compressor belt must be removed in order to remove and install the alternator belt.

Power Steering Pump/Air Conditioning Compressor Belt

See Figures 50 and 51.

CAUTION

Do not check belt tension with the engine running.

➡When installing drive belt onto pulleys, make sure that belt is properly routed and all V-grooves make proper contact with pulley grooves.

1. Remove the belt splash shield.
2. Using a wrench, rotate the belt tensioner clockwise until belt can be removed from the power steering pump pulley. Gently, release spring tension on the tensioner.

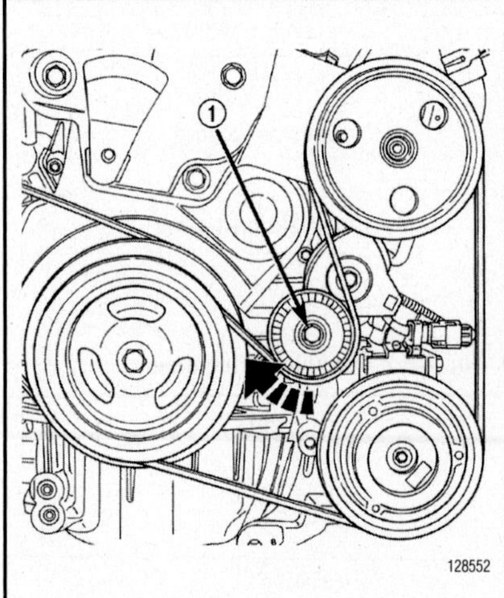

Fig. 50 Rotate belt tensioner (1) clockwise until belt can be removed from power steering pump pulley

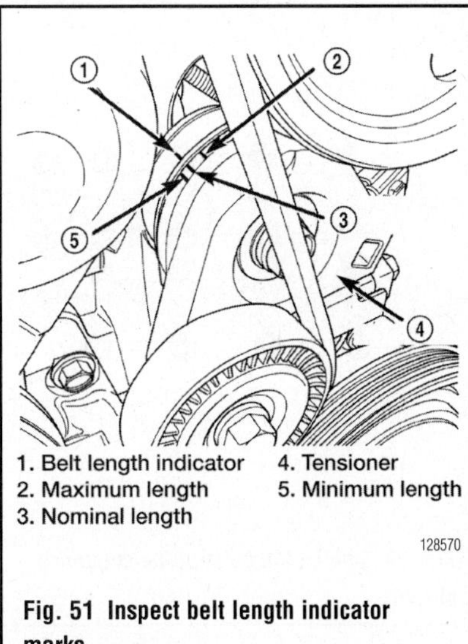

Fig. 51 Inspect belt length indicator marks

3. Remove the belt, and inspect. Refer to Inspection procedure. Replace belt if necessary.

To install:

⁂ CAUTION

Do not check belt tension with the engine running.

➡When installing drive belt onto pulleys, make sure that belt is properly routed and all V-grooves make proper contact with pulley grooves.

4. Install the belt over all of the pulleys except for the power steering pump pulley.
5. Using a wrench, rotate the belt tensioner clockwise until the belt can be installed onto the power steering pump pulley. Release spring tension onto belt.
6. After the belt is installed, inspect the 3 belt length indicator marks. The indicator mark should be within the minimum belt length and maximum belt length marks. On a new belt, the indicator mark should align approximately with the nominal belt length mark.
7. Install the belt splash shield.

Alternator Belt

See Figures 52 and 53.

1. Remove the power steering pump/air conditioning compressor drive belt.
2. Loosen the pivot bolt, then the locking nut and adjusting bolt.
3. Remove the alternator belt.

To install:

⁂ CAUTION

Do not check belt tension with engine running.

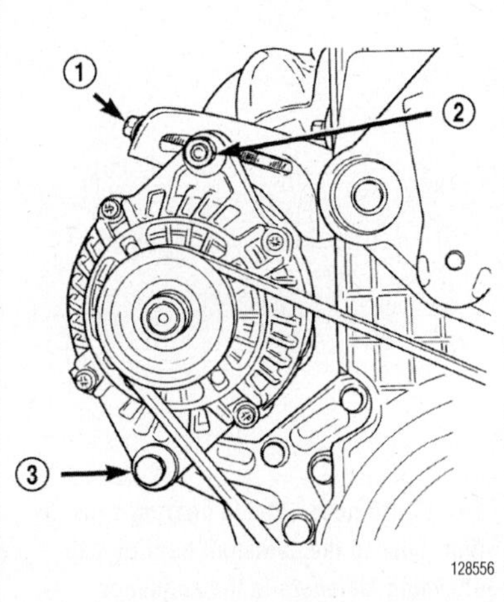

Fig. 52 Loosen the pivot bolt (3), then the locking nut (2) and adjusting bolt (1)

➡When installing drive belt onto pulleys, make sure that belt is properly routed and all V-grooves make proper contact with pulley grooves.

4. Install belt and/or adjust belt tension by tightening adjusting bolt. Adjust belt to specification:
   - New belt: tighten to 135 lbs.
   - Used belt: tighten to 100 lbs.
5. Check alternator belt tension using tension gauge adapter (8371) and a scan tool using the following procedures:
   a. Connect the scan tool following the manufacturer's instructions.
   b. Place end of microphone probe approximately 1 inch (2.54 cm) from the belt at one of the belt center span locations.
   c. Pluck the belt a minimum of 3 times. (Use your finger or other suitable object)
   d. The frequency of the belt in hertz (Hz) will display on the scan tool screen.

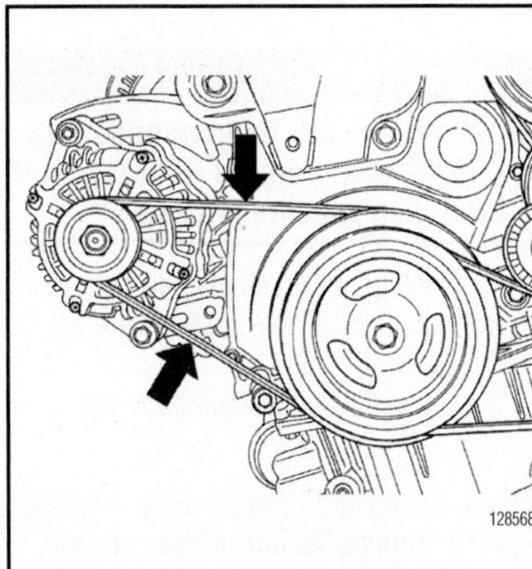

Fig. 53 Belt center span locations

   e. Adjust belt to obtain proper frequency (tension).
      - New belt: 235 – 247 Hz.
      - Used belt: 207 – 217 Hz.
6. Tighten pivot bolt and locking nut to 40 ft. lbs. (54 Nm).

AIR CLEANER

REMOVAL & INSTALLATION

See Figure 54.

1. Disconnect the throttle body air inlet hose/clean air hose from the air cleaner housing.
2. Pull air cleaner housing straight up to remove.
3. Remove the fresh air inlet duct from the air cleaner housing.

To install:

4. Install the inlet duct to the air cleaner housing.
5. Make sure the rubber grommets (for the air cleaner housing lower pins) are in place when reinstalling the air cleaner housing. The rubber grommets mount to the Totally Integrated Power Module (TIPM) bracket.
6. Push the air cleaner housing down while aligning pins into the grommets.
7. Connect the throttle body air inlet hose/clean air hose to the air cleaner housing.

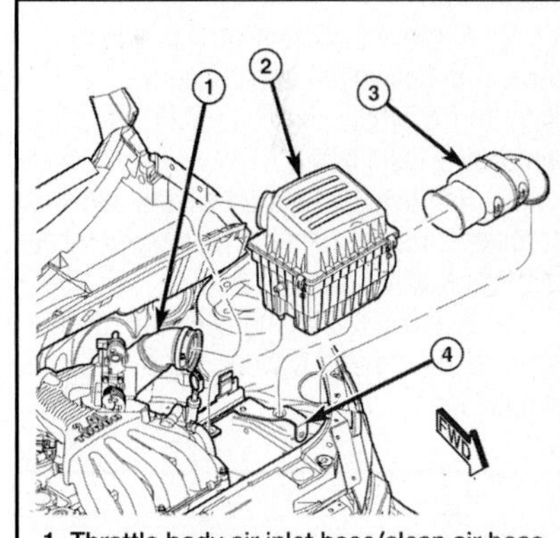

Fig. 54 View of air cleaner assembly — typical

FILTER/ELEMENT REPLACEMENT

See Figure 55.

1. Unfasten the clasps on the sides of the air cleaner housing cover. Lift the cover off the air cleaner housing.
2. Remove the filter element.

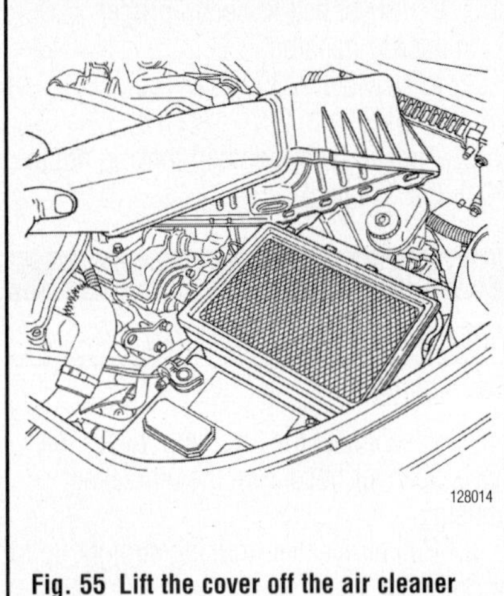

Fig. 55 Lift the cover off the air cleaner housing

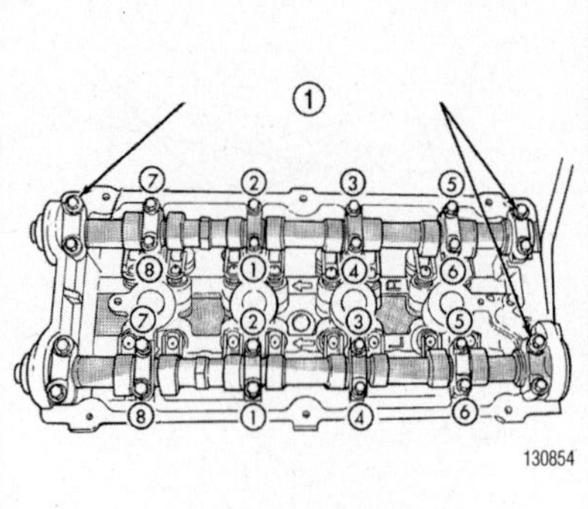

Fig. 57 Remove outside bearing caps (1) first. Loosen the camshaft bearing cap attaching fasteners in the sequence shown, one camshaft at a time

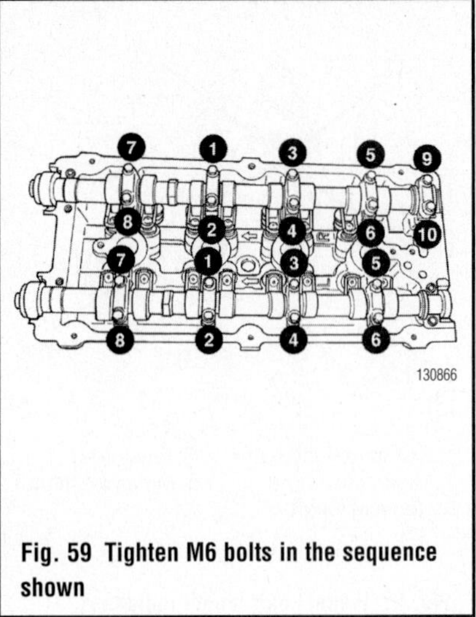

Fig. 59 Tighten M6 bolts in the sequence shown

3. If necessary, clean the inside of the air cleaner housing.

To install:

4. Install a new filter element.
5. Place the cover over the air cleaner housing. Snap clasps in place.

CAMSHAFTS

REMOVAL & INSTALLATION

See Figures 56 through 61.

1. Remove the cylinder head cover. Refer to Cylinder Head Cover, removal & installation.
2. Remove the camshaft position sensor and camshaft target magnet. Refer to Camshaft Position (CMP) Sensor, removal & installation.
3. Remove the timing belt and camshaft sprockets. Refer to Timing Belt & Sprockets, removal & installation.
4. Remove the timing belt rear cover. Refer to Timing Belt Covers, removal & installation.

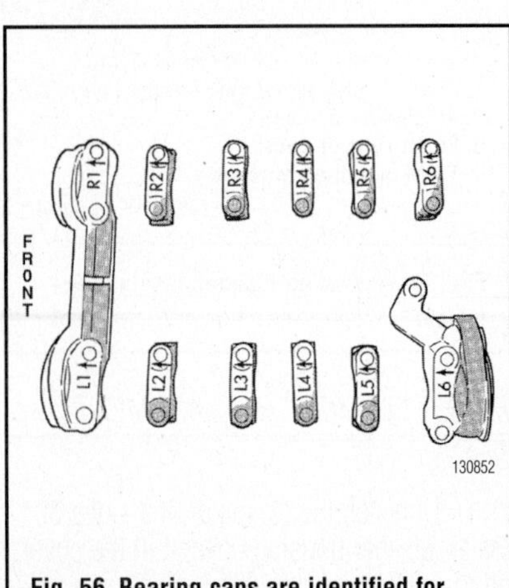

Fig. 56 Bearing caps are identified for location

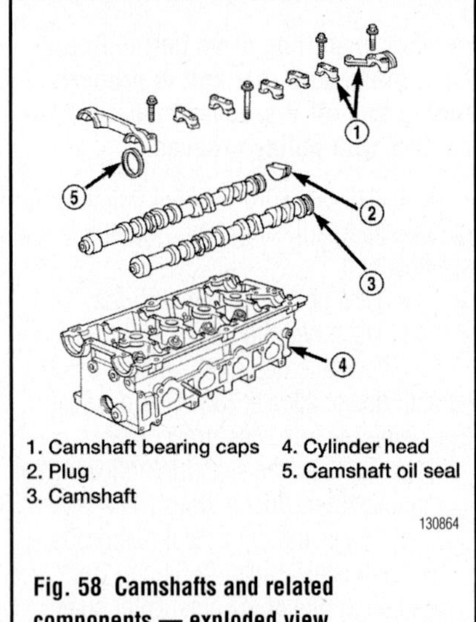

Fig. 58 Camshafts and related components — exploded view

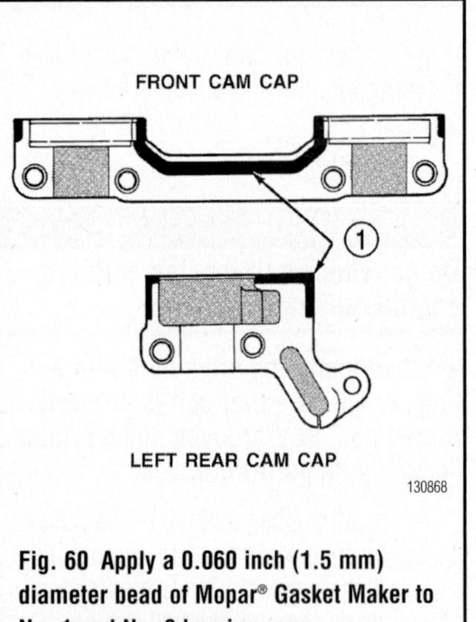

Fig. 60 Apply a 0.060 inch (1.5 mm) diameter bead of Mopar® Gasket Maker to No. 1 and No. 6 bearing caps

5. Bearing caps are identified for location. Remove the outside bearing caps first.
6. Loosen the camshaft bearing cap attaching fasteners in the sequence shown, one camshaft at a time.

WARNING

Camshafts are not interchangeable. The intake cam number 6 thrust bearing face spacing is wider.

7. Identify the camshafts before removing from the head. The camshafts are not interchangeable.
8. Remove the camshafts from the cylinder head.

➡If removing the rocker arms, identify them for reinstallation in the original position.

To install:

WARNING

Ensure that NONE of the pistons are at top dead center when installing the camshafts.

9. Lubricate all camshaft bearing journals, rocker arms and camshaft lobes.
10. Install all rocker arms in original positions, if reused.
11. Position the camshafts on the cylinder head bearing journals. Install right and left camshaft bearing caps No. 2 – 5 and right No. 6. Tighten M6 bolts to 105 inch lbs. (12 Nm) in the sequence shown.
12. Apply a 0.060 inch (1.5 mm) diameter bead of Mopar ® Gasket Maker to No. 1 and No. 6 bearing caps. Install bearing caps, and tighten M8 bolts to 250 inch lbs. (28 Nm).

➡Bearing end caps must be installed before seals can be installed.

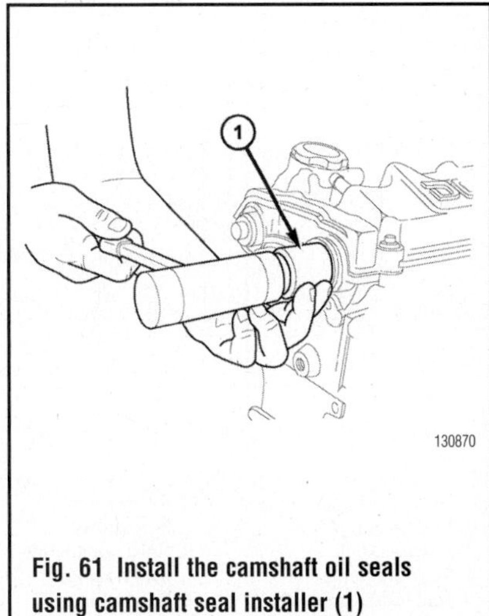

Fig. 61 Install the camshaft oil seals using camshaft seal installer (1)

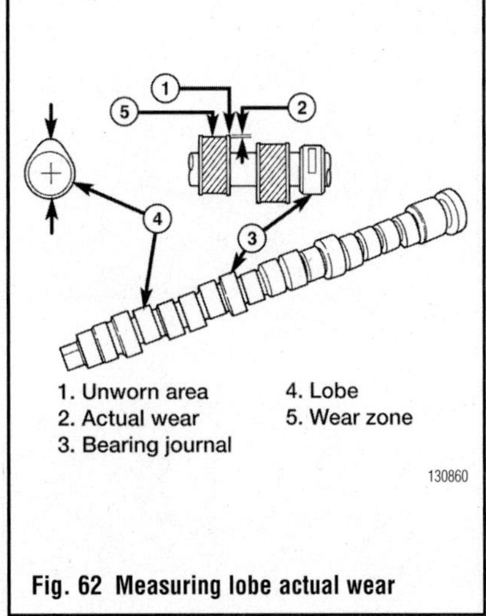

Fig. 62 Measuring lobe actual wear

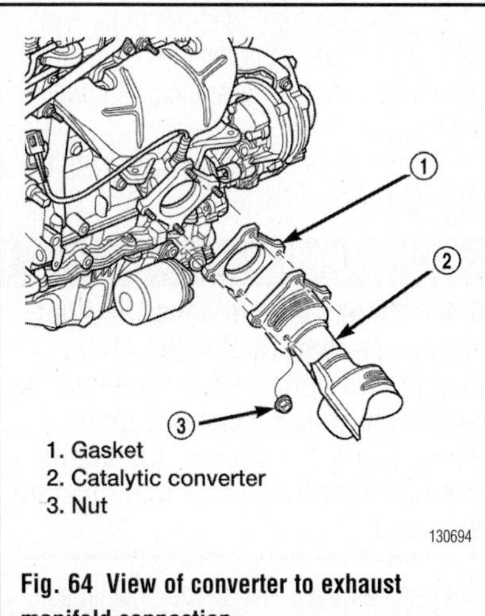

Fig. 64 View of converter to exhaust manifold connection

13. Install the camshaft oil seals using camshaft seal installer (MD-998306).
14. Install the camshaft position sensor and camshaft target magnet. Refer to Camshaft Position (CMP) Sensor, removal & installation.
15. Install the cylinder head cover. Refer to Cylinder Head Cover, removal & installation.
16. Install the timing belt rear cover and timing belt tensioner. Refer to Timing Belt Covers, removal & installation.
17. Install the timing belt and camshaft sprockets. Refer to Timing Belt & Sprockets, removal & installation.

INSPECTION

See Figures 62 and 63.

1. Inspect the camshaft bearing journals for damage and binding. If journals are binding, check the cylinder head for damage. Also check cylinder head oil holes for clogging.
2. Check the cam lobe and bearing surfaces for abnormal wear and damage. Replace camshaft if defective.

➡If the camshaft is replaced due to lobe wear or damage, always replace the rocker arms.

3. Measure the lobe actual wear (unworn area - wear zone = actual wear), and replace camshaft if out of limit. Standard value is 0.001 inch (0.0254 mm), and wear limit is 0.010 inch (0.254 mm).
4. Oil the camshaft journals, and install the camshaft WITHOUT the rocker arms. Install the rear cam caps, and tighten the screws to 105 inch lbs. (12 Nm).
5. Using a suitable tool, move the camshaft as far rearward as it will go.
6. Zero the dial indicator.

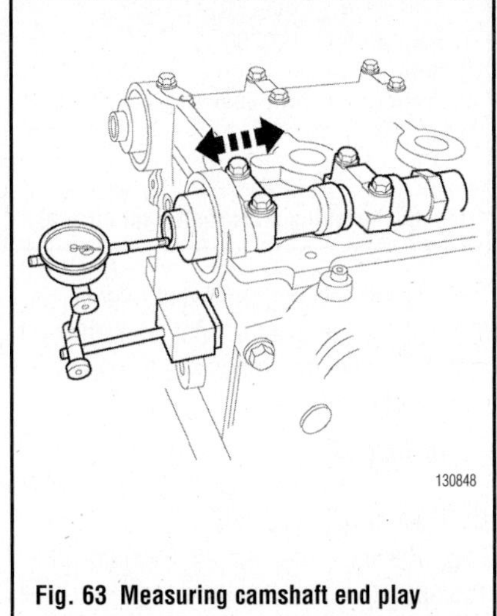

Fig. 63 Measuring camshaft end play

7. Move the camshaft as far forward as it will go.
8. Record the reading on the dial indicator. For end play specification, refer to Camshaft Specifications chart.
9. If the end play is excessive, check cylinder head and camshaft for wear. Replace as necessary.

CATALYTIC CONVERTER

REMOVAL & INSTALLATION

See Figure 64.

CAUTION

The normal operating temperature of the exhaust system is very high. Therefore, never attempt to service any part of the exhaust system until it is cooled. Special care should be taken when working near the catalytic converter. The temperature of the converter rises to a high level after a short period of engine operation time.

1. Loosen the intermediate pipe-to-catalytic converter clamp.

WARNING

Do not use petroleum-based lubricants when removing/installing muffler or exhaust pipe isolators, as it may compromise the life of the part. A suitable substitute is a mixture of liquid dish soap and water.

2. Disconnect the 2 oxygen sensor electrical connectors.
3. Remove the muffler/intermediate pipe isolators as necessary to slide the muffler/intermediate pipe assembly out of the catalytic converter.
4. Remove the catalytic converter-to-exhaust manifold attaching fasteners, and remove the converter from the vehicle.
5. Remove and discard the flange gasket.

To install:

➡When replacement is required on any component of the exhaust system, original equipment parts (or equivalent) must be used.

➡When assembling the exhaust system, do not tighten clamps until all components are aligned and clearances are checked.

6. Assemble the catalytic converter to exhaust manifold connection. Use a new flange gasket.
7. Tighten the catalytic converter to exhaust manifold fasteners to 250 inch lbs. (28 Nm).
8. Install intermediate pipe and muffler.

9. Working from the front of the system, align each component to maintain position and proper clearance with underbody parts.

10. Tighten the band clamps to 35 ft. lbs. (47 Nm).

⁂ WARNING

Band clamps should never be tightened such that the 2 sides of the clamps are bottomed out against the center hourglass-shaped center block. Once this occurs, the clamp has lost clamping force and must be replaced.

11. If removed, install the downstream oxygen sensor.

12. Connect the downstream oxygen sensor electrical connector.

13. Start the engine and inspect for exhaust leaks. Repair exhaust leaks as necessary.

14. Check the exhaust system for contact with the body panels. Make the necessary adjustments, if needed.

CRANKSHAFT FRONT SEAL

REMOVAL & INSTALLATION

See Figures 65 and 66.

1. Remove the crankshaft vibration damper. Refer to Crankshaft Vibration Damper, removal & installation.
2. Remove the timing belt. Refer to Timing Belt, removal & installation.
3. Remove the crankshaft sprocket. Refer to Crankshaft Sprocket, removal & installation.

⁂ WARNING

Do not nick shaft seal surface or seal bore.

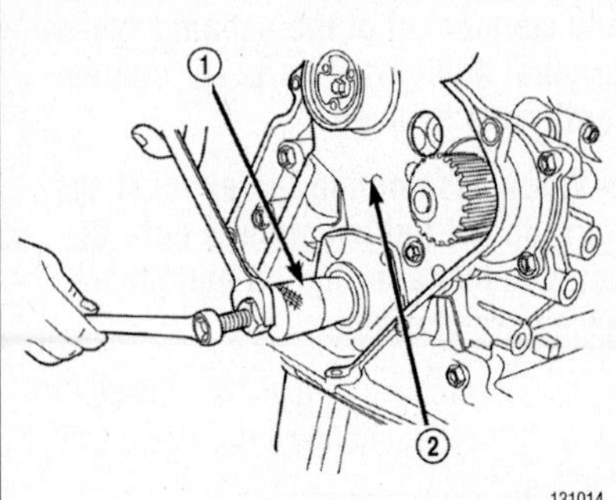

Fig. 65 Use crankshaft front seal remover (1) to remove front crankshaft oil seal. Be careful not to damage the seal surface of cover (2)

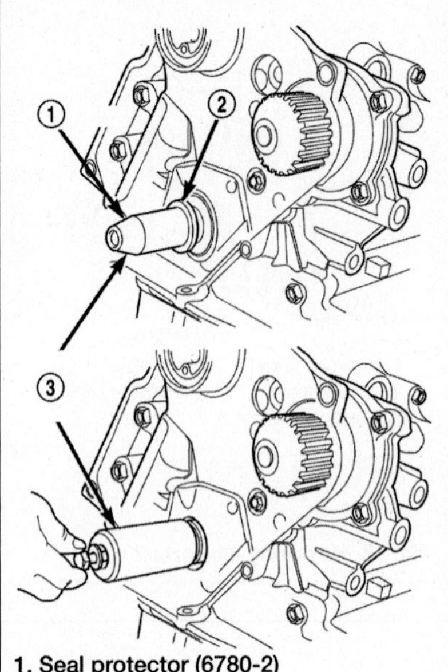

Fig. 66 Installing crankshaft front oil seal

4. Use crankshaft front seal remover (6771SG) to remove the front crankshaft oil seal. Be careful not to damage the seal surface of cover.

To install:

5. Install new seal by using front crankshaft seal installer (6780).
6. Place the seal into the opening with seal spring towards the inside of the engine. Install seal until flush with cover.
7. Install the crankshaft sprocket. Refer to Crankshaft Sprocket, removal & installation.
8. Install the timing belt. Refer to Timing Belt, removal & installation.
9. Install the crankshaft vibration damper. Refer to Crankshaft Vibration Damper, removal & installation.

CRANKSHAFT REAR SEAL

REMOVAL & INSTALLATION

See Figures 67 through 69.

1. Remove the transaxle.
2. Remove the flexplate.
3. Insert a 3/16 flat-bladed screwdriver between the dust lip and the metal case of the crankshaft seal. Angle the screwdriver through the dust lip against metal case of the seal. Pry out seal.

⁂ WARNING

Do not permit the screwdriver blade to contact crankshaft seal surface.

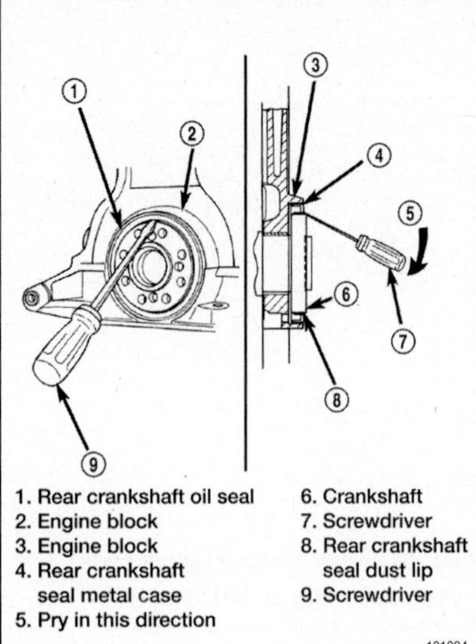

Fig. 67 Removing rear crankshaft oil seal

Contact of the screwdriver blade against crankshaft edge (chamfer) is permitted.

To install:

⁂ WARNING

If a burr or scratch is present on the crankshaft edge (chamfer), cleanup with 400 grit sand paper to prevent seal damage during installation of new seal.

➡When installing seal, no lube on seal is needed.

4. Place rear crankshaft seal guide (6926) on the crankshaft.

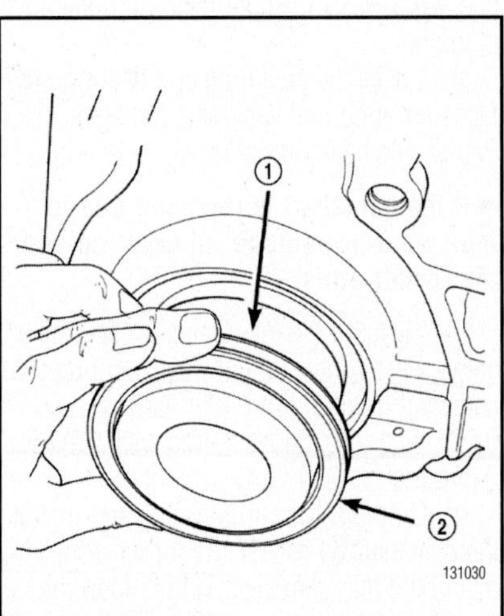

Fig. 68 Place rear crankshaft seal guide (1) on the crankshaft. Position the seal (2) over the guide tool

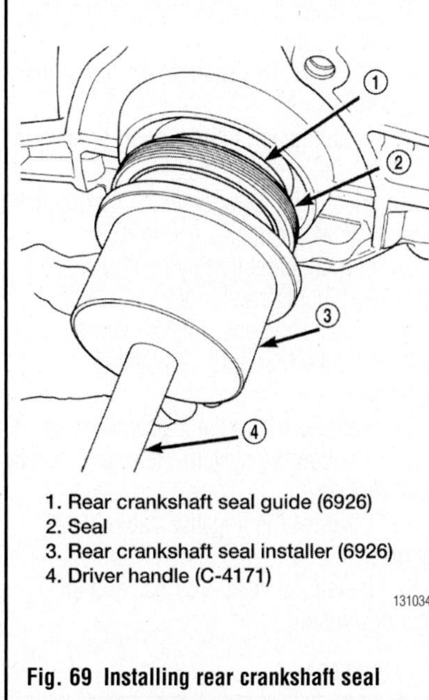

Fig. 69 Installing rear crankshaft seal

5. Position the seal over the guide tool. Rear crankshaft seal guide should remain on crankshaft during installation of seal. Ensure that the lip of the seal is facing towards the crankcase during installation.

WARNING

If the seal is driven into the block past flush, this may cause an oil leak.

6. Drive the seal into the block using rear crankshaft seal installer and driver handle until the tool bottoms out against the block.
7. Install the flexplate. Apply Mopar ® Lock and Seal Adhesive to bolt threads, and tighten bolts to 70 ft. lbs. (95 Nm).
8. Install the transaxle.

CRANKSHAFT VIBRATION DAMPER

REMOVAL & INSTALLATION

See Figures 70 and 71.

1. Remove the accessory drive belts. Refer to Accessory Drive Belts, removal & installation.
2. Remove the lower splash shield.
3. Remove the crankshaft damper bolt.
4. Remove the damper by using puller (1026) and crankshaft damper removal insert (6827A).

To install:

5. Install crankshaft damper using crankshaft damper/sprocket installer (6792) (composed of M12 1.75 x 150-mm bolt, washer, thrust bearing and nut).

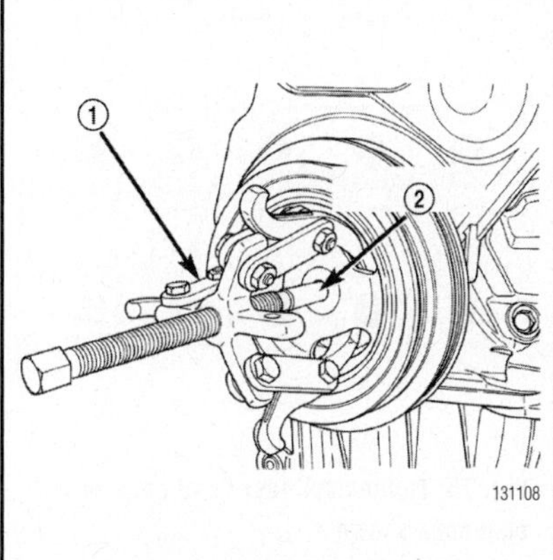

Fig. 70 Remove the damper by using puller (1) and crankshaft damper removal insert (2)

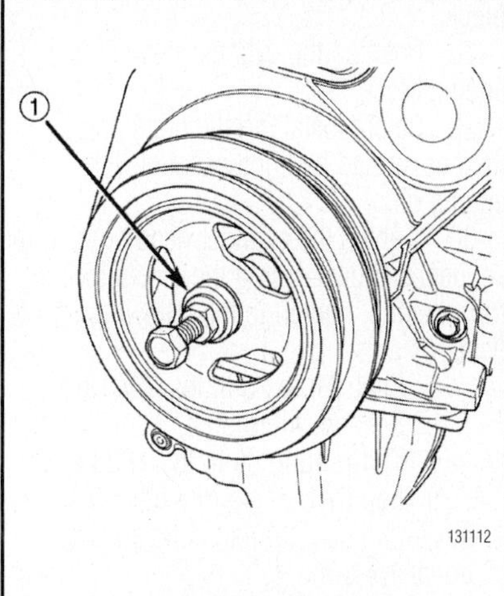

Fig. 71 Install crankshaft damper using crankshaft damper/sprocket installer (1)

➡Lubricate the threads of the M12 1.75 x 150-mm bolt using Mopar ® Nickel Anti-seize Compound or equivalent, before beginning to press the damper on.

6. Remove the crankshaft damper/sprocket installer.
7. Apply Mopar ® Lock and Seal Adhesive (Medium Strength Threadlocker) to crankshaft damper bolt, and tighten to 100 ft. lbs. (136 Nm).
8. Install the accessory drive belts. Refer to Accessory Drive Belts, removal & installation.

CYLINDER HEAD

REMOVAL & INSTALLATION

See Figures 72 through 75.

1. Perform fuel system pressure release procedure before attempting any repairs. Refer to Relieving Fuel Pressure Procedure.

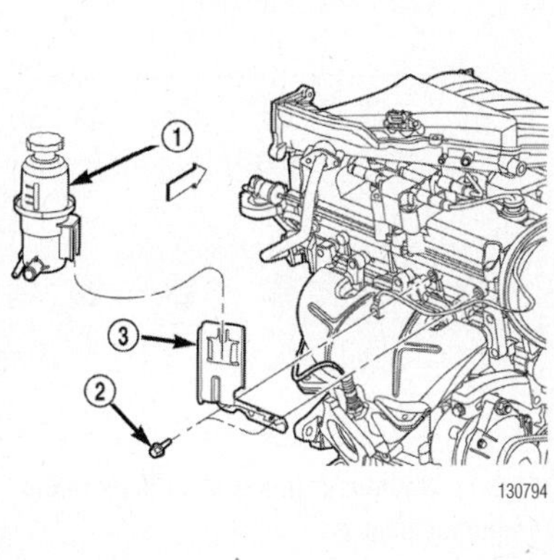

Fig. 72 Remove the fasteners (2) securing power steering pump fluid reservoir (1) and bracket (3) to cylinder head

2. Remove the clean air hose and air cleaner housing.
3. Disconnect the negative cable from battery.
4. Open the draincock and drain cooling system into a clean container.
5. Remove the upper intake manifold. Refer to Intake Manifold, removal & installation.
6. Remove the fastener attaching the dipstick tube to the lower intake manifold.
7. Disconnect the fuel supply line quick-connect at the fuel rail assembly.
8. Remove the heater tube support bracket from the cylinder head.
9. Remove the upper radiator hose.
10. Disconnect the heater hoses from the thermostat housing.
11. Disconnect the engine coolant temperature sensor connector.
12. Remove the accessory drive belts. Refer to Accessory Drive Belts, removal & installation.
13. Raise the vehicle on a suitable hoist.
14. Disconnect the exhaust pipe from the manifold.
15. Disconnect the ignition coil wiring connector. Remove ignition coil and plug wires from engine.
16. Disconnect the camshaft position sensor wiring connector.
17. Remove the timing belt and camshaft sprockets. Refer to Timing Belt & Sprockets, removal & installation.
18. Remove timing belt idler pulley and rear timing belt cover. Refer to Timing Belt Covers, removal & installation.
19. Remove the fasteners securing power steering pump fluid reservoir and bracket to cylinder head.
20. Remove the cylinder head cover. Refer to Cylinder Head Cover, removal & installation.

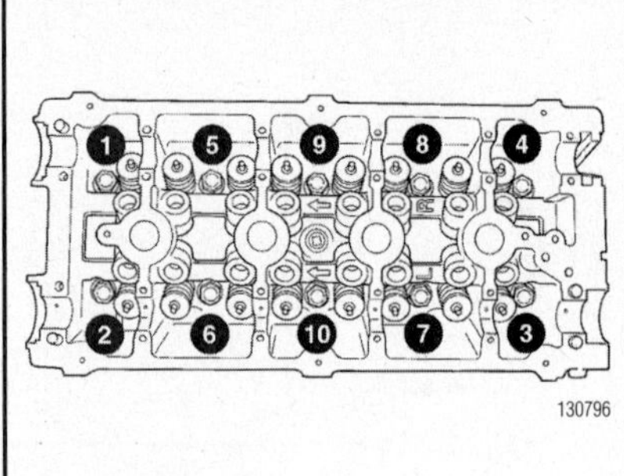

Fig. 73 Remove cylinder head bolts in the sequence shown

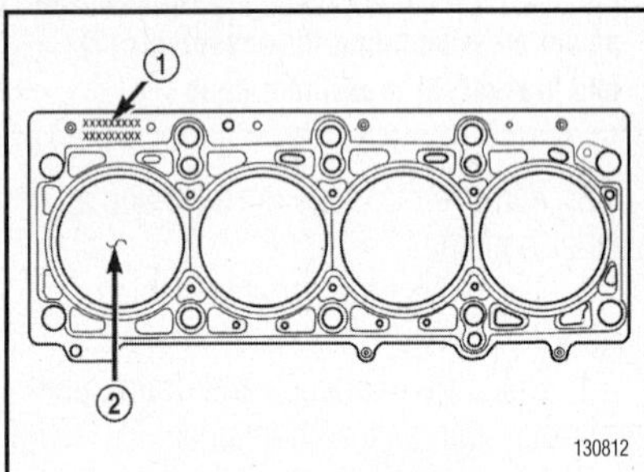

Fig. 74 Position the new cylinder head gasket on engine block with the part number (1) facing up on No. 1 cylinder (2)

21. Remove the camshafts. Refer to Camshaft, removal & installation.

➡Identify rocker arm location for reassembly prior to removal.

22. Remove the rocker arms.
23. Remove cylinder head bolts in the sequence shown.
24. Remove cylinder head from engine block.
25. Inspect and clean cylinder head and block sealing surfaces. Refer to Inspection procedure.

➡Ensure cylinder head bolt holes in the block are clean, dry (free of residual oil or coolant), and threads are not damaged.

To install:

➡The cylinder head bolts should be examined BEFORE reuse. If the threads are necked down, the bolts should be replaced

26. Necking can be checked by holding a scale or straightedge against the threads. If all the threads do not contact the scale, the bolt should be replaced.

➡Cylinder head should be cleaned and inspected prior to replacement.

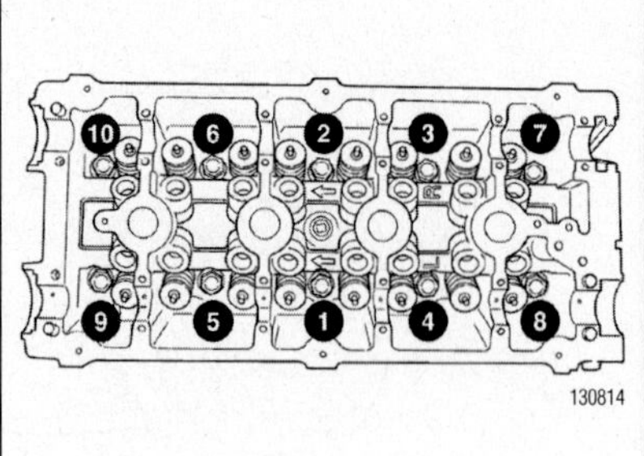

Fig. 75 Tighten cylinder head bolts in the sequence shown

27. Position the new cylinder head gasket on engine block with the part number facing up on No. 1 cylinder. Ensure gasket is seated over the locating dowels in block.
28. Position the cylinder head onto engine block.
29. Before installing the bolts, the threads should be lightly coated with engine oil.
30. Tighten the cylinder head bolts in the sequence shown. Using the 4 step torque-turn method, tighten to the following specifications:
    a. First: All to 25 ft. lbs. (34 Nm).
    b. Second: All to 60 ft. lbs. (82 Nm).
    c. Third: All to 60 ft. lbs. (82 Nm).
    d. Fourth: Using a tool other than a torque wrench, turn all bolts an additional 1/4 turn.
31. Install rocker arms.
32. Install the camshafts. Refer to Camshafts, removal & installation.
33. Install the cylinder head cover. Refer to Cylinder Head Cover, removal & installation.
34. Install the rear timing belt cover and tighten fasteners. Refer to Timing Belt Covers, removal & installation.
35. Install the timing belt tensioner.
36. Install camshaft sprockets and timing belt. Refer to Timing Belt & Sprockets, removal & installation.
37. Connect the camshaft position sensor wiring connector.
38. Install ignition coil and plug wires. Connect ignition coil wiring connector.
39. Install power steering pump bracket and reservoir to cylinder head.
40. Install exhaust pipe to manifold. Tighten fasteners to 20 ft. lbs. (28 Nm).
41. Install the accessory drive belts. Refer to Accessory Drive Belts, removal & installation.
42. Connect the engine coolant temperature sensor connector.
43. Connect the upper radiator hose to the coolant outlet.
44. Connect the heater hoses to the thermostat housing.
45. Install heater tube support bracket to cylinder head.
46. Install the fastener attaching dipstick tube to the lower intake manifold.
47. Connect fuel supply line quick-connect at the fuel rail assembly.
48. Install the upper intake manifold. Refer to Intake Manifold, removal & installation.
49. Remove the radiator pressure cap, and fill the cooling system. Refer to Drain & Refill procedure.
50. Connect the negative cable to battery.
51. Install the clean air hose and air cleaner housing.

INSPECTION

See Figures 76 through 78.

➡To ensure engine gasket sealing, proper surface preparation must be performed, especially with the use of aluminum engine components and multi-layer steel cylinder head gaskets.

➡Multi-Layer Steel (MLS) head gaskets require a scratch-free sealing surface.

1. Remove all gasket material from cylinder head and block. Be careful not to gouge or scratch the aluminum head sealing surface.
2. Clean all engine oil passages.

To inspect:

3. Using a feeler gauge and straightedge, check cylinder head for flatness. Cylinder head must be flat within 0.004 inch (0.1 mm).

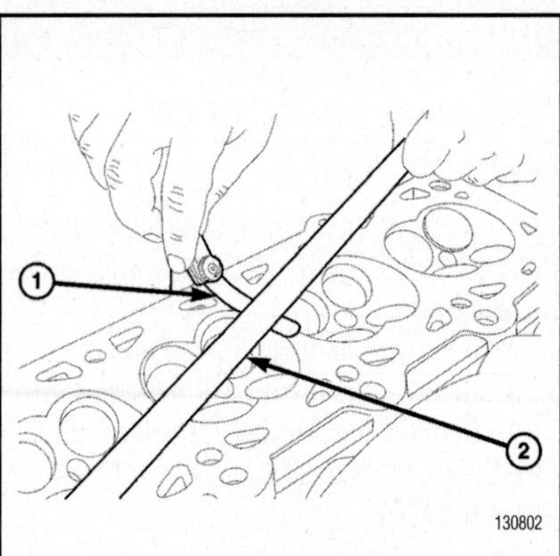

Fig. 76 Using a feeler gauge (2) and straightedge (1), check cylinder head for flatness

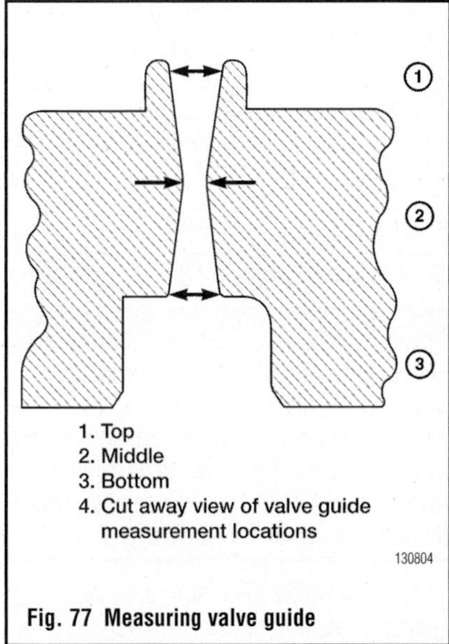

Fig. 77 Measuring valve guide

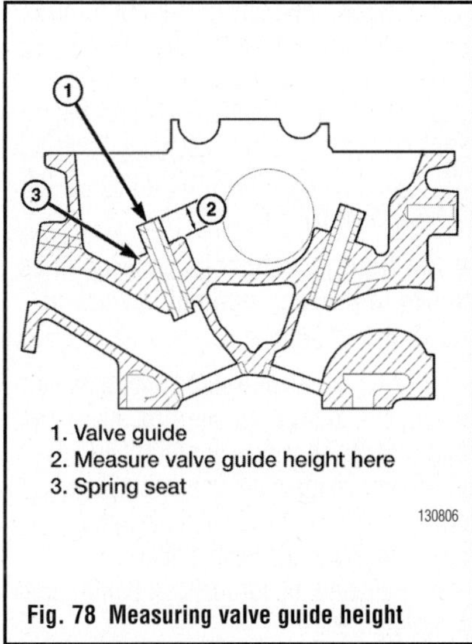

Fig. 78 Measuring valve guide height

4. Inspect the camshaft bearing journals for scoring.
5. Remove carbon and varnish deposits from inside of valve guides with a reliable guide cleaner.
6. Using a small hole gauge and a micrometer, measure valve guides in the 3 places shown (top, middle and bottom). Replace guides if they are not within specification. Refer to Valve Specifications Chart.
7. Ensure valve guide height is 0.521 – 0.541 inch (13.25 – 13.75 mm).

CYLINDER HEAD COVER

REMOVAL & INSTALLATION

See Figures 79 through 83.

1. Remove the intake manifold cover.
2. Remove the upper intake manifold. Refer to Intake Manifold, removal & installation.
3. Remove the ignition coil and spark plug wires.
4. Disconnect the PCV and make-up air hoses from the cylinder head cover.
5. Remove cylinder head cover bolts by reversing the order shown.

**** WARNING**

When removing the cylinder head cover bolts, be careful not to interchange the 2 center bolts with the 7 perimeter bolts. The 2 center bolts contain an aluminum washer between the bolt head and torque limiter for sealing purposes.

6. Remove the cylinder head cover from the cylinder head.

To install:

➡Replace spark plug well seals and bolt seals when installing a new cylinder head cover gasket.

7. Install new cylinder head cover gaskets and spark plug well seals.
8. Replace cylinder head cover bolt seals.

**** WARNING**

Do not allow oil or solvents to contact the timing belt, as they can deteriorate the rubber and cause tooth skipping.

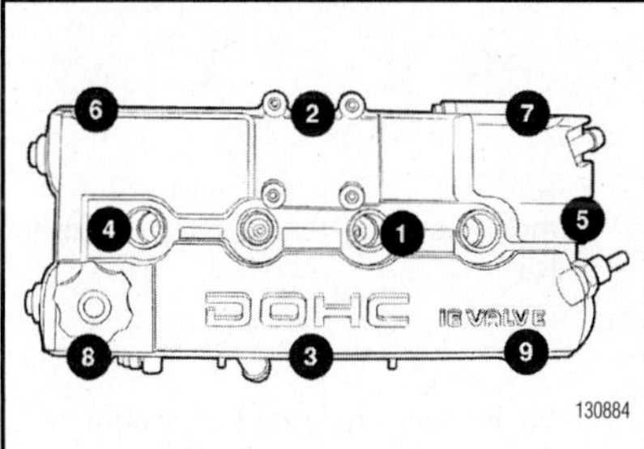

Fig. 79 Remove cylinder head cover bolts by reversing the order shown

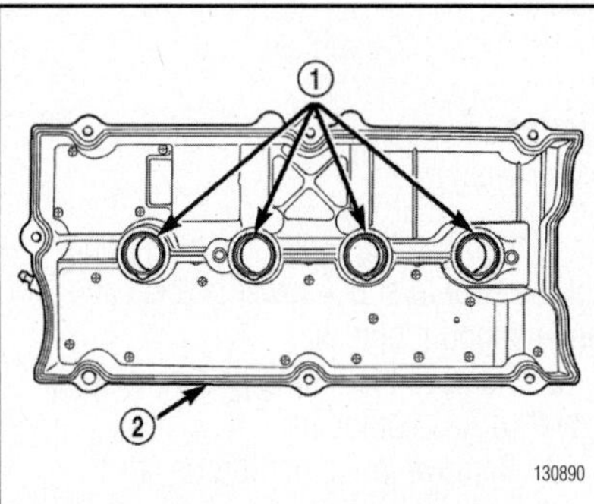

Fig. 80 Install new cylinder head cover gaskets (2) and spark plug well seals (1)

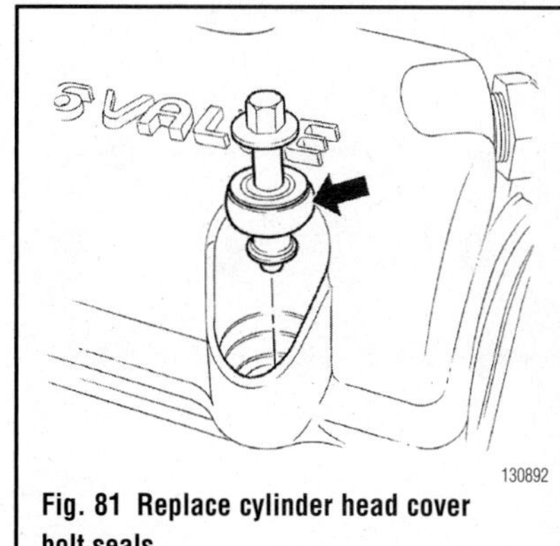

Fig. 81 Replace cylinder head cover bolt seals

9. Apply Mopar ® Engine RTV GEN II at the camshaft cap corners and at the top edges of the 1/2 round seal.

**** WARNING**

When installing the cylinder head cover bolts, be careful not to interchange the 2 center bolts with the 7 perimeter bolts. The 2 center bolts contain an aluminum washer between the bolt head and torque limiter for sealing purposes.

10. Install the cylinder head cover assembly to the cylinder head. Install all bolts, ensuring the 2 bolts containing the

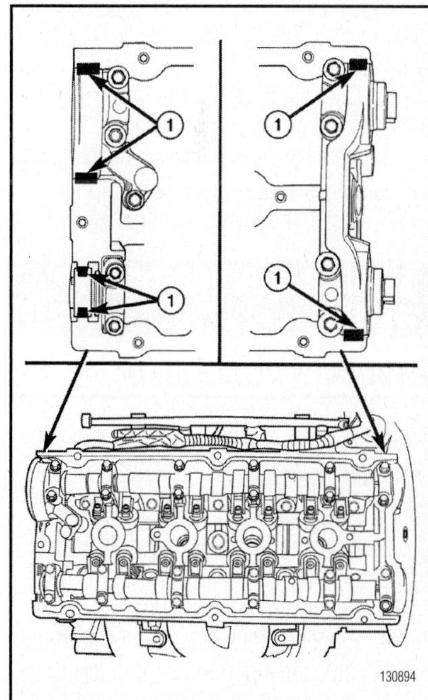

Fig. 82 Apply Mopar® Engine RTV GEN II at the camshaft cap corners and at the top edges of the 1/2 round seal (1)Fig. 83 Apply Mopar® Engine RTV GEN II at the camshaft cap corners and at the top edges of the 1/2 round seal (1)

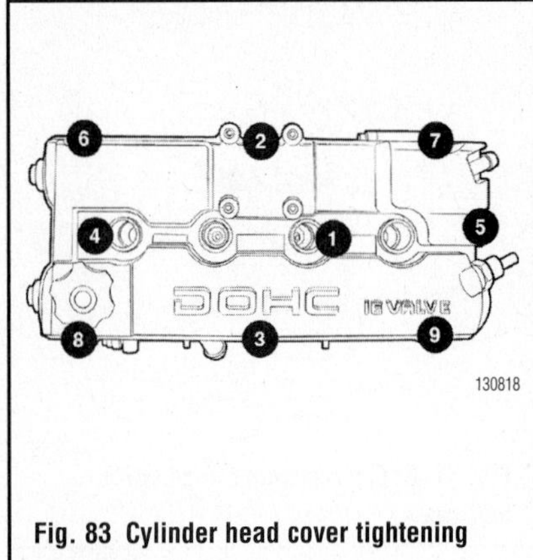

Fig. 83 Cylinder head cover tightening sequence

sealing washer are located in the center locations of cover. Tighten bolts in the indicated sequence, using a 3-step tightening method as follows:

a. Tighten all bolts to 40 inch lbs. (4.5 Nm).
b. Tighten all bolts to 80 inch lbs. (9.0 Nm).
c. Tighten all bolts to 105 inch lbs. (12 Nm).

11. Install the ignition coil and spark plug wires. Tighten fasteners to 105 inch lbs. (12 Nm).
12. If the PCV valve was removed, apply Mopar ® Thread Sealant with Teflon to threads and install the valve to the cylinder head cover. Tighten PCV valve to 70 inch lbs. (8 Nm).
13. Connect the PCV and make-up air hoses to the cylinder head cover.
14. Install the upper intake manifold. Refer to Intake Manifold, removal & installation.
15. Install the intake manifold cover.

ENGINE MOUNTING TORQUE STRUT

REMOVAL & INSTALLATION

Lower

See Figures 84 and 85.

1. Raise the vehicle on a hoist.
2. Remove the accessory drive belt splash shield.
3. Remove the pencil strut.
4. Remove bolts attaching lower torque strut to crossmember and strut bracket.
5. Remove the lower torque strut.

To install:

6. Position lower torque strut into mounting locations.
7. Install the torque strut mounting bolts, and adjust components. Refer to Adjustment procedure.

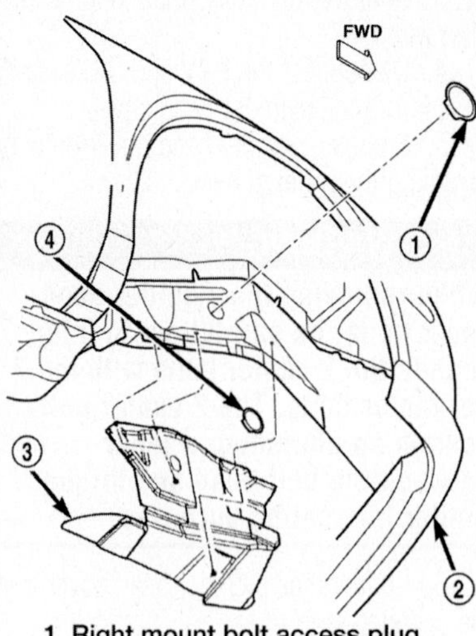

Fig. 84 Remove the accessory drive belt splash shield

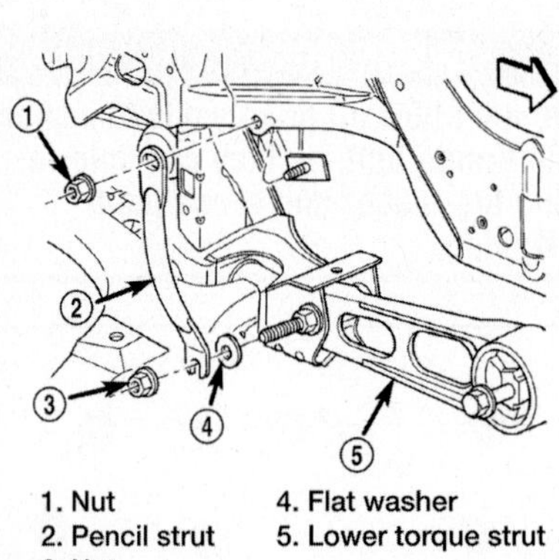

Fig. 85 Remove the lower torque strut

8. Install the pencil strut, and tighten nuts to 43 ft lbs. (58 Nm).
9. Install the accessory belt splash shield.
10. Lower the vehicle.

Upper

See Figure 86.

1. Remove the bolts attaching upper torque strut to shock tower bracket and engine mount bracket.
2. Remove the timing belt front upper cover (if A/C equipped).
3. Remove the upper torque strut.

To install:

4. Position the upper torque strut into mounting location.
5. Move torque strut aside (towards right fender) and install timing belt front upper cover.
6. Install the torque strut mounting bolts, and adjust components. Refer to Adjustment procedure.

ADJUSTMENT

See Figures 86 through 88.

⁂ WARNING

The upper and lower torque struts need to be adjusted together to assure proper engine positioning and engine mount loading. Whenever a torque strut bolt(s) is loosened, this procedure must be performed.

1. Remove the accessory drive belt splash shield and pencil strut. Refer to Removal & Installation procedure.
2. Loosen the upper and lower torque strut attaching bolts at the suspension crossmember and shock tower bracket.
3. The engine position may now be adjusted by positioning a suitable floor jack and wood block on the forward edge of the transmission bell housing.

➡The floor jack must be positioned as shown to prevent minimal upward lifting of the engine.

4. With the engine supported, remove the upper and lower torque strut attachment bolt(s) at the shock tower bracket and suspension crossmember. Verify that the torque struts are free to move within the shock tower bracket and crossmember.
5. Reinstall the torque strut bolt(s), but do not tighten.
6. Carefully apply upward force, allowing the upper engine to rotate rearward until the distance between the center of the rearmost attaching bolt on the engine mount bracket (point "A") and the center of the hole on the shock tower bracket (point "B") is 14.70 inches (19 mm).

⁂ WARNING

The engine must be held in position with jack until both the upper and lower torque strut bolts are tightened.

7. With the engine held at the proper position, tighten both the upper strut and lower torque strut bolts to 85 ft. lbs. (115 Nm).
8. Remove the floor jack.
9. Install the pencil strut and accessory drive belt splash shield. Refer to Removal & Installation procedure.

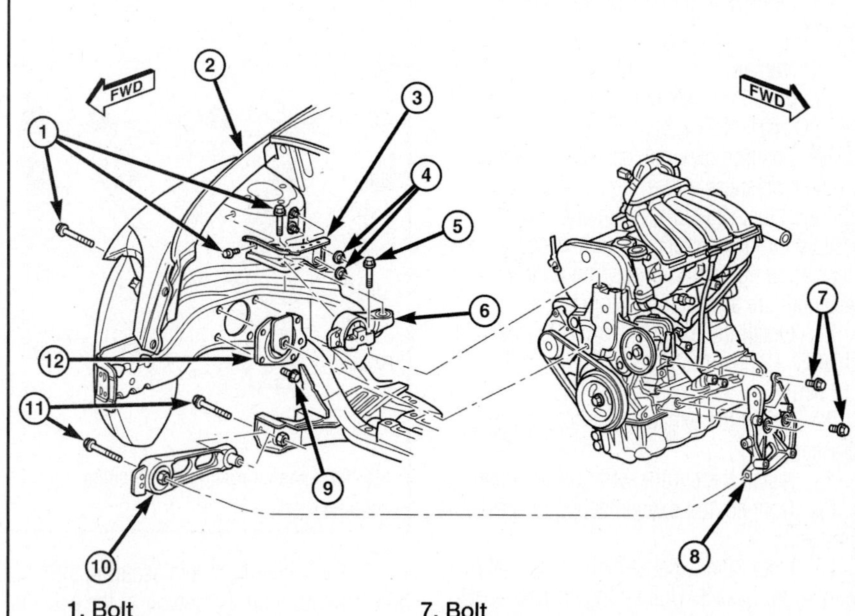

Fig. 86 Right engine mounting components — exploded view

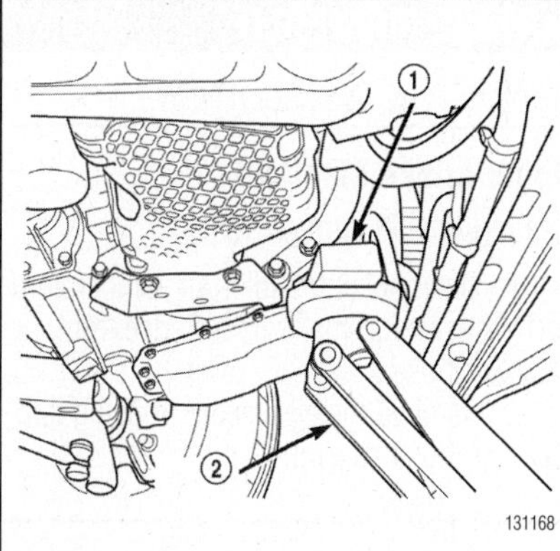

Fig. 87 The engine position may now be adjusted by positioning a suitable floor jack (2) and wood block (1) on the forward edge of the transmission bell housing

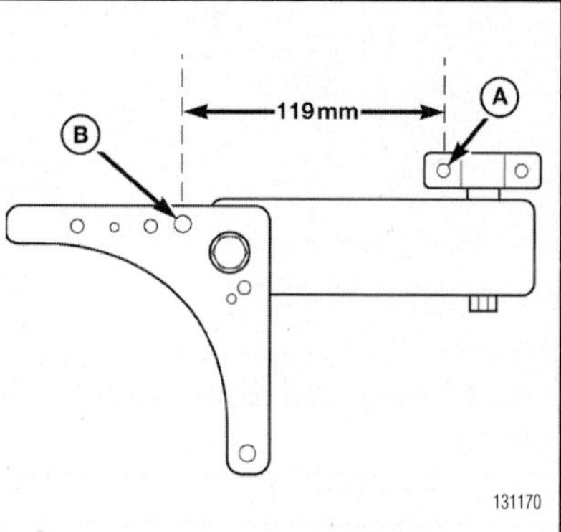

Fig. 88 Check distance between the center of the rearmost attaching bolt on the engine mount bracket (point "A") and the center of the hole on the shock tower bracket (point "B")

ENGINE OIL & FILTER

REPLACEMENT

See Figure 89.

CAUTION

New or used engine oil can be irritating to the skin. Avoid prolonged or repeated skin contact with engine oil. Contaminants in used engine oil, caused by internal combustion, can be hazardous to your health. Thoroughly wash exposed skin with soap and water. Do not wash skin with gasoline, diesel fuel, thinner, or solvents, health problems can result. Do not pollute, dispose of used engine oil properly. Contact your dealer or government agency for location of collection center in your area.

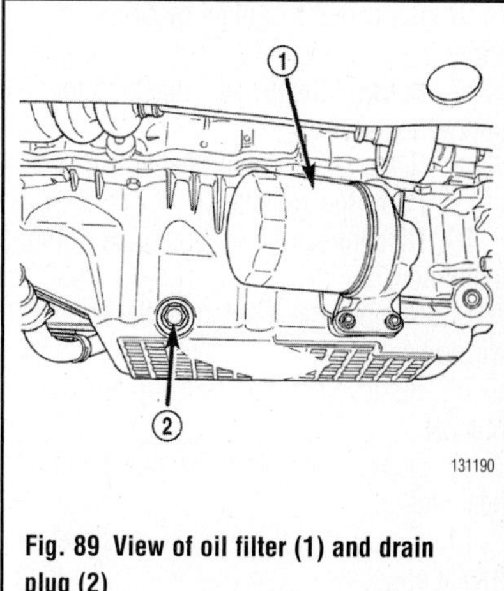

Fig. 89 View of oil filter (1) and drain plug (2)

1. Run engine until it reaches normal operating temperature.
2. Position the vehicle on a level surface, and turn the engine off.
3. Remove the oil fill cap.
4. Raise the vehicle on a hoist.
5. Place a suitable oil collecting container under the oil pan drain plug.
6. Remove the oil pan drain plug, and allow oil to drain into collecting container. Inspect the drain plug threads for stretching or other damage. Replace the drain plug and gasket if damaged.
7. Remove the oil filter.

To install:

8. Install the oil pan drain plug. Tighten drain plug to 20 ft. lbs. (28 Nm).
9. Install a new oil filter.
10. Lower the vehicle.
11. Fill crankcase with the specified type and amount of engine oil.
12. Install the oil fill cap.
13. Start the engine and inspect for leaks.
14. Stop the engine and inspect the oil level.

EXHAUST MANIFOLD

REMOVAL & INSTALLATION

See Figures 90 through 94.

1. Remove the clean air hose and air cleaner housing.
2. Disconnect the negative cable from battery.
3. Disconnect the throttle and speed control cables from the throttle lever and bracket.
4. Disconnect the Manifold Air Pressure (MAP) sensor electrical connector.
5. Remove the fasteners securing the power steering fluid reservoir to the cylinder head.

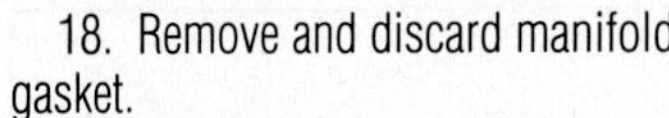

6. Remove the coolant recovery container.
7. Remove the 4 bolts attaching the upper heat shield.
8. Remove the upper heat shield.
9. Raise the vehicle.
10. Disconnect the exhaust pipe from the manifold.
11. Remove the 3 nuts and the engine wiring heat shield.
12. Remove the manifold support bracket.
13. Remove the lower exhaust manifold heat shield.
14. Disconnect the oxygen sensor electrical connector.
15. Remove the exhaust manifold lower retaining fasteners.
16. Lower the vehicle, and remove the upper exhaust manifold retaining fasteners.
17. Remove the exhaust manifold from above/between the engine and cowl panel.
18. Remove and discard manifold gasket.

To install:

19. Install a new exhaust manifold gasket. DO NOT APPLY SEALER.
20. Position exhaust manifold in place. Tighten fasteners in the sequence shown to 200 inch lbs. (23 Nm). Raise and lower vehicle for fastener access as necessary. Repeat the tightening procedure until all fasteners are at specified torque.
21. Install the exhaust manifold heat shields. Tighten the bolts to 105 inch lbs. (12 Nm).
22. Install the exhaust manifold support bracket.
23. Install the engine wiring heat shield.
24. Connect the oxygen sensor electrical connector.
25. Install the exhaust pipe to manifold with a new gasket. Tighten the fasteners to 250 inch lbs. (28 Nm).
26. Install the coolant recovery container.

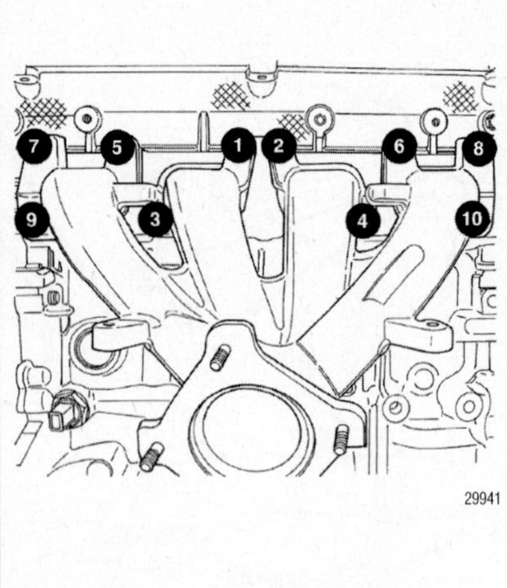

Fig. 94 Exhaust manifold tightening sequence

27. Install the fasteners securing the power steering fluid reservoir to the cylinder head.
28. Connect the MAP sensor electrical connector.
29. Connect the throttle and speed control cables to the throttle lever and bracket.
30. Connect the negative cable to battery.
31. Install the clean air hose and air cleaner housing.

Fig. 90 Disconnect the Manifold Air Pressure (MAP) sensor (1) electrical connector

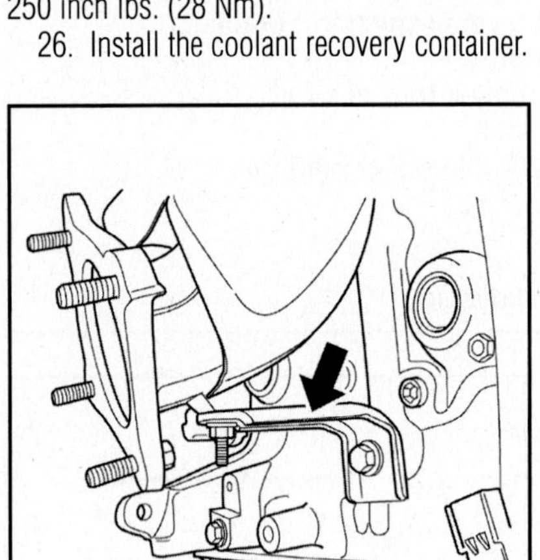

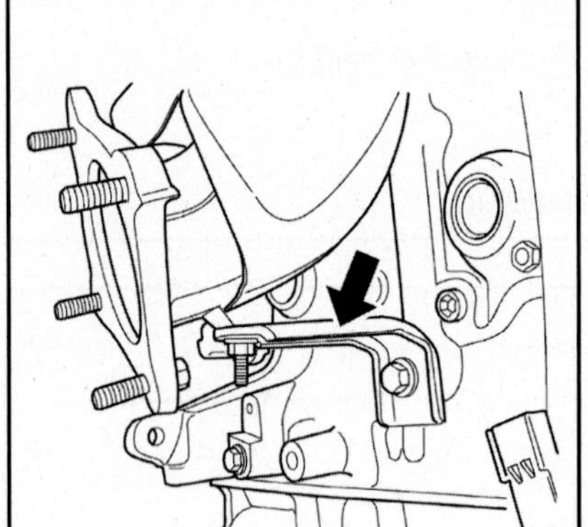

Fig. 92 Remove the manifold support bracket

INTAKE MANIFOLD

REMOVAL & INSTALLATION

Upper Intake Manifold

See Figures 95 through 101.

1. Disconnect the Inlet Air Temperature (IAT) sensor and make-up air hose from clean air hose.
2. Remove the air cleaner housing and clean air hose assembly.

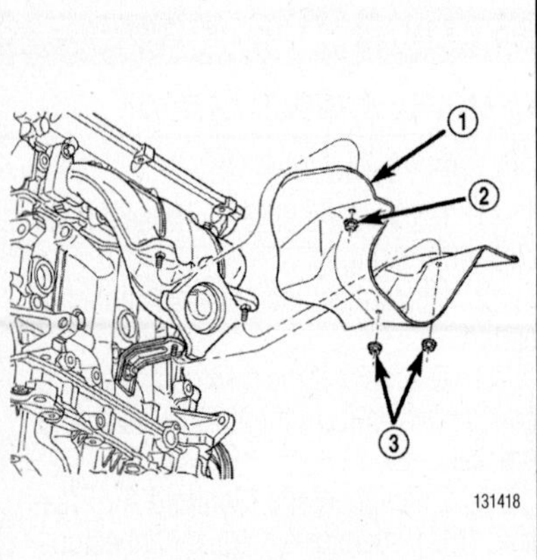

Fig. 91 Remove the 3 nuts (2, 3) and the engine wiring heat shield (1)

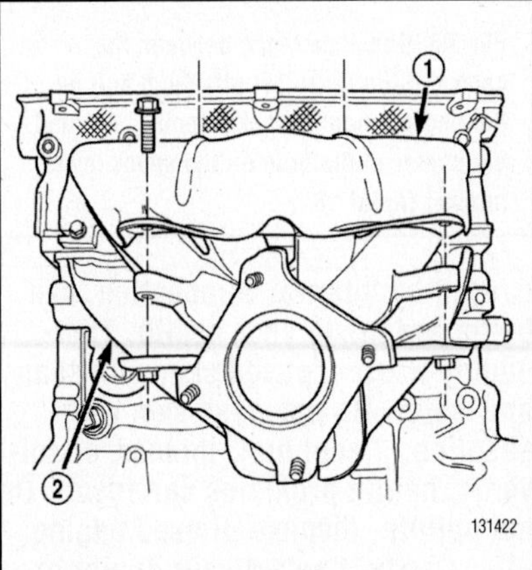

Fig. 93 View of upper and lower exhaust manifold heat shields (1, 2)

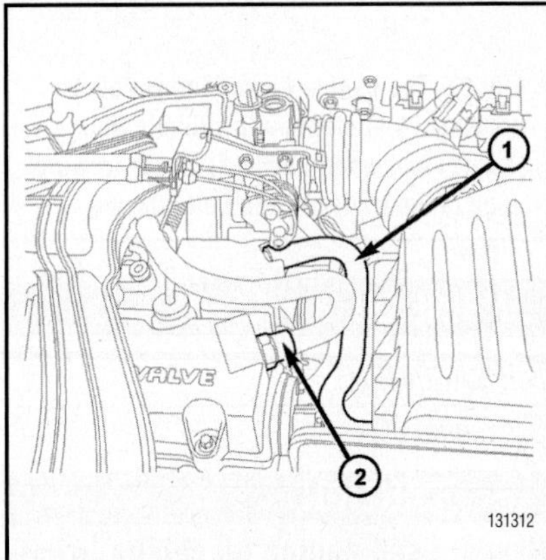

Fig. 95 Disconnect the Inlet Air Temperature (IAT) (2) and make-up air hose (1) from clean air hose

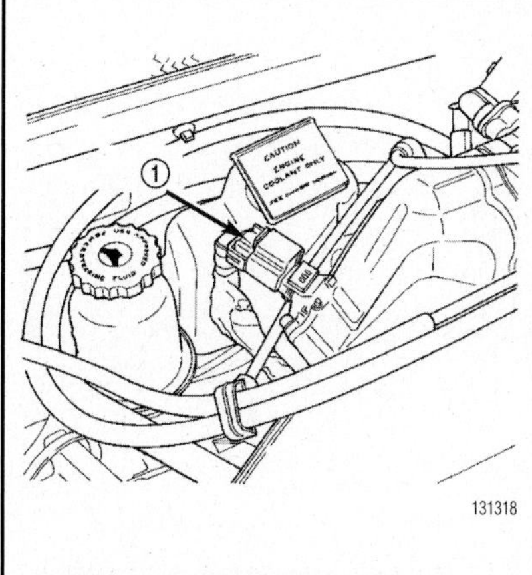

Fig. 96 Disconnect the Manifold Absolute Pressure (MAP) sensor (1)

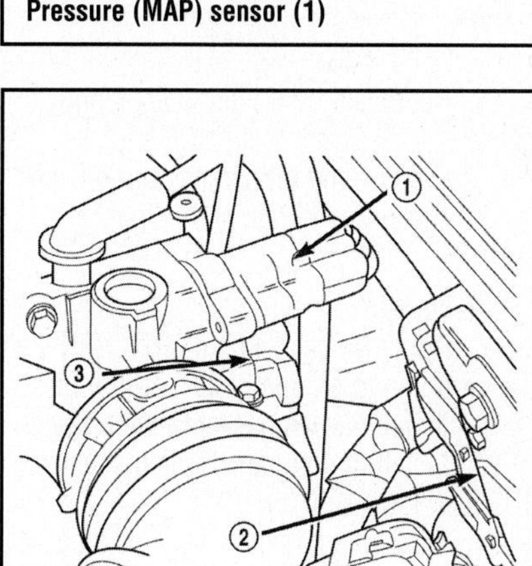

Fig. 97 Disconnect Idle Air Control (IAC) motor (1) and Throttle Position Sensor (TPS) (3) wiring connectors

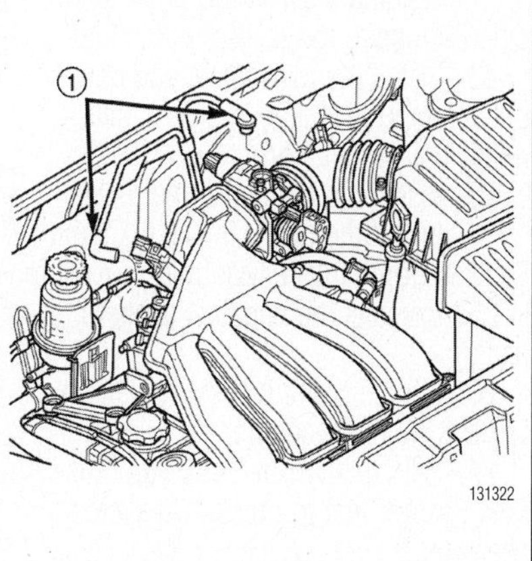

Fig. 98 Disconnect the proportional purge hoses (1)

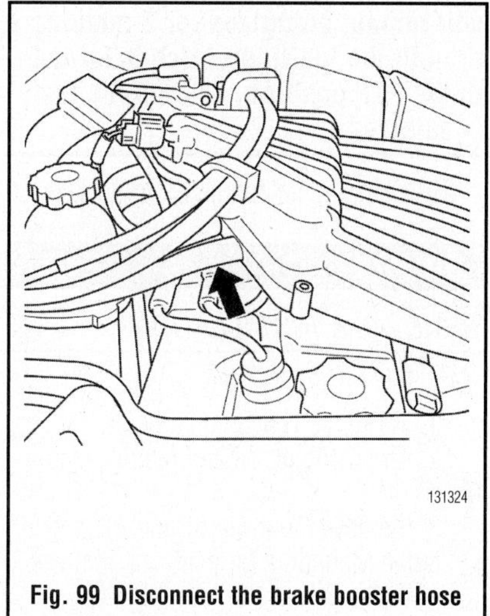

Fig. 99 Disconnect the brake booster hose

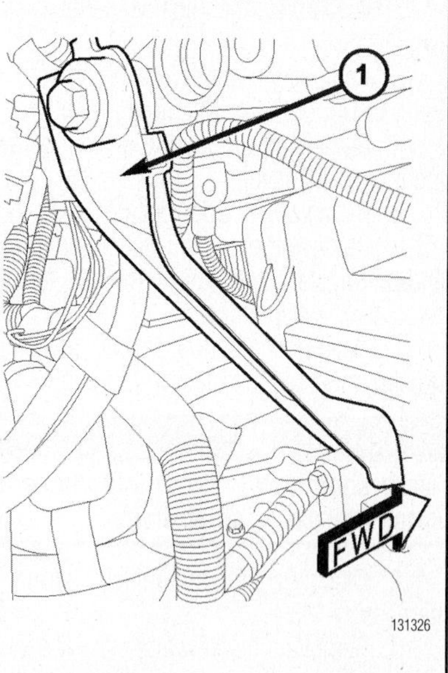

Fig. 100 Remove the rear intake manifold support bracket (1)

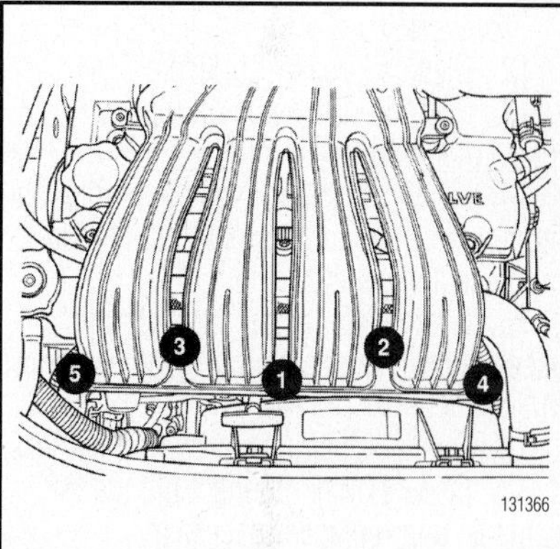

Fig. 101 Tighten upper intake manifold fasteners in the sequence shown

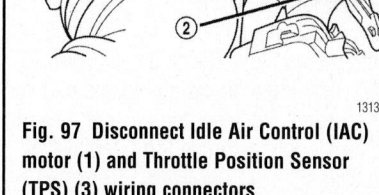

3. Disconnect the negative cable from battery.
4. Remove throttle and speed control cables from throttle lever and bracket.
5. Disconnect the Manifold Absolute Pressure (MAP) sensor.
6. Disconnect the Idle Air Control (IAC) motor and Throttle Position Sensor (TPS) wiring connectors.
7. Disconnect the proportional purge hoses.
8. Disconnect the brake booster hose.
9. Disconnect the PCV hose from the intake manifold.
10. Remove the rear intake manifold support bracket.
11. Remove the upper intake manifold fasteners.
12. Remove the upper intake manifold.
13. If further service is required, cover the lower intake manifold openings to prevent foreign materials from entering the engine.

To install:

14. If the lower intake manifold was covered during service, remove cover.
15. Clean all sealing surfaces. Replace seals as necessary.
16. Position the new seals on manifold.
17. Position the upper intake manifold on lower intake manifold. Tighten upper intake manifold fasteners to 105 inch lbs. (12 Nm) in the sequence shown.
18. Connect the PCV hose to the intake manifold.
19. Connect the MAP electrical connector.
20. Connect the proportional purge hoses.
21. Connect the brake booster hose.
22. Connect the IAC motor and TPS wiring connectors.
23. Install throttle and speed control cables to bracket. Connect the cables to the throttle lever.
24. Connect the negative cable to battery.
25. Install the air cleaner housing and clean air hose. Tighten the clean air hose clamp to 15 inch lbs. (1.7 Nm).
26. Connect the make-up air hose and IAT sensor.

Lower Intake Manifold

See Figure 102.

CAUTION

Release the fuel system pressure before servicing system components. Service vehicles in well ventilated areas and avoid ignition sources. Never smoke while servicing the vehicle.

1. Perform fuel system pressure release procedure before attempting any repairs. Refer to Relieving Fuel System Procedure.

2. Disconnect the negative battery cable.
3. Remove the upper intake manifold. Refer to Upper Intake Manifold procedure.
4. Partially drain cooling system below the thermostat level.
5. Remove the upper radiator hose.
6. Remove the coolant outlet connector and thermostat. Refer to Thermostat, removal & installation.
7. Disconnect the fuel supply line quick-connect at the fuel rail assembly.

✲✲ CAUTION

Wrap shop towels around the hose to catch any gasoline spillage.

8. Disconnect the fuel injector wiring harness.
9. Remove the screw attaching the oil dipstick tube to the lower intake manifold.
10. Remove the lower intake manifold support bracket fasteners.
11. Remove the lower intake manifold.

To install:

12. Clean all gasket surfaces.
13. Position new seals on the lower intake manifold.
14. Install the lower intake manifold, and tighten fasteners to 105 inch lbs. (12 Nm) in the sequence shown.
15. If removed, install the fuel rail assembly to intake manifold. Tighten screws to 200 inch lbs. (23 Nm).
16. Connect fuel injector wiring harness.
17. Inspect quick-connect fittings for damage, and replace if necessary.
18. Lubricate tube with clean engine oil.
19. Connect the fuel supply hose to fuel rail assembly.
20. Check the connection by pulling on connector to ensure it is locked into position.

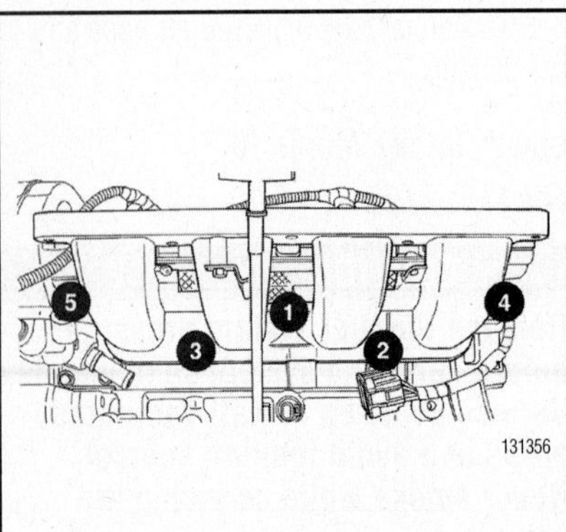

Fig. 102 Install the lower intake manifold, and tighten fasteners in the sequence shown

21. Install the screw attaching the oil dipstick tube to lower intake manifold.
22. Install the thermostat and coolant outlet connector. Refer to Thermostat, removal & installation.
23. Install the radiator upper hose.
24. Install the upper intake manifold. Refer to Upper Intake Manifold procedure.
25. Connect the negative cable to battery.
26. Fill the cooling system. Refer to Drain & Refill procedure.
27. With the DRBIII ® scan tool, use ASD Fuel System Test to pressurize system to check for leaks.

✲✲ WARNING

When using the ASD Fuel System Test, the Auto Shutdown (ASD) relay will remain energized for 7 minutes or until the ignition switch is turned to the OFF position, or Stop All Test is selected.

28. Start engine and check for leaks.

OIL PAN

REMOVAL & INSTALLATION

See Figures 103 and 104.

1. Raise the vehicle on a hoist.
2. Drain engine oil and remove the oil filter.
3. Remove the lower torque strut. Refer to Engine Mounting Torque Strut, removal & installation.
4. Remove the structural collar. Refer to Structural Collar, removal & installation.

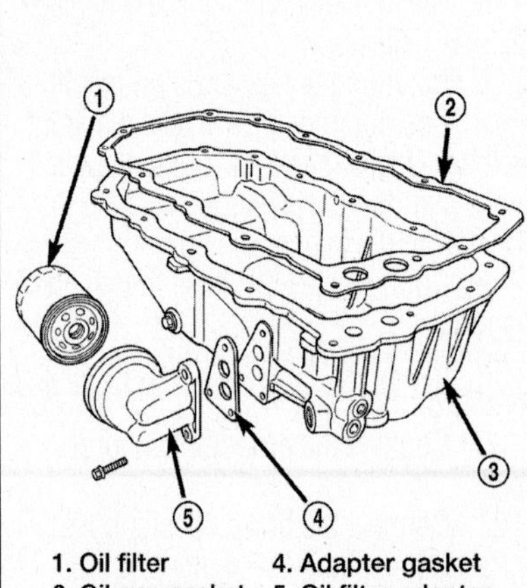

Fig. 103 Oil pan and components — exploded view

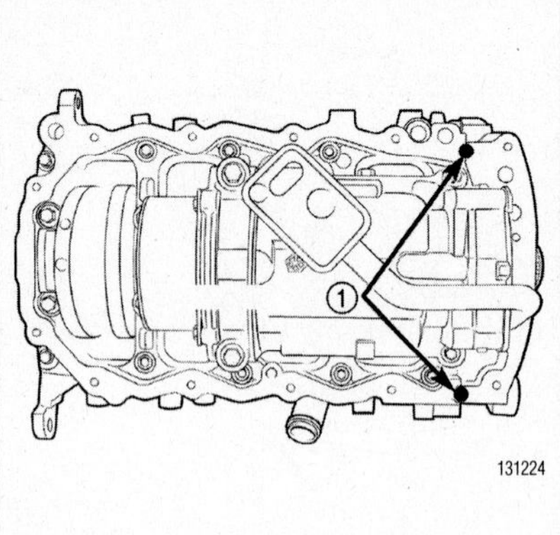

Fig. 104 Apply Mopar® Engine RTV GEN II at the oil pump to engine block parting lines

5. Remove the oil filter adapter and gasket.
6. Remove the oil pan and gasket.
7. Clean the oil pan and all gasket surfaces.

To install:

8. Apply Mopar ® Engine RTV GEN II at the oil pump to engine block parting lines.
9. Install oil pan gasket to the block.
10. Install the oil pan. Tighten screws to 105 inch lbs. (12 Nm).
11. Install the oil filter adapter and gasket. Tighten screws to 105 inch lbs. (12 Nm).
12. Install the oil drain plug and oil filter.
13. Install the lower torque strut. Refer to Engine Mounting Torque Strut, removal & installation.
14. Install the structural collar. Refer to Structural Collar, removal & installation.
15. Lower the vehicle. Fill engine crankcase with proper oil to correct level.
16. Start engine and check for leaks.

OIL PUMP

REMOVAL & INSTALLATION

See Figures 105 through 108.

1. Disconnect the negative cable from battery.
2. Remove the timing belt. Refer to Timing Belt, removal & installation.
3. Remove the timing belt rear cover. Refer to Rear Cover, removal & installation.
4. Remove the oil pan. Refer to Oil Pan, removal & installation.
5. Remove the crankshaft sprocket. Refer to Crankshaft Sprocket, removal & installation.
6. Remove the crankshaft key.
7. Remove the oil pick-up tube.
8. Remove the 5 bolts, oil pump and front crankshaft seal.

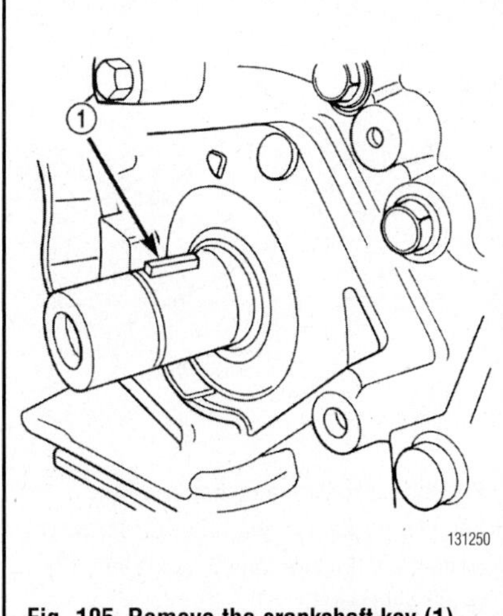

Fig. 105 Remove the crankshaft key (1)

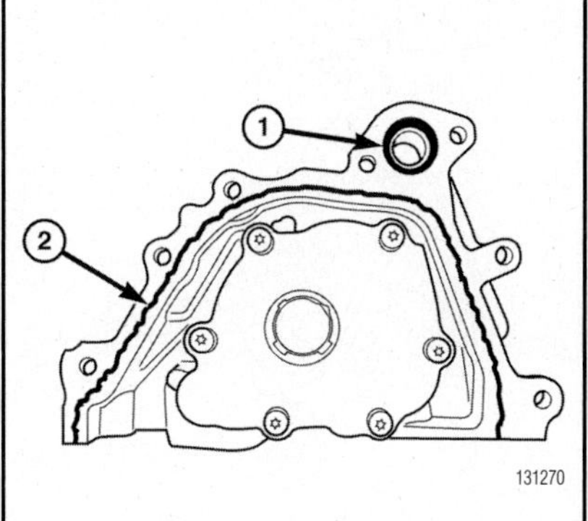

Fig. 107 Apply Mopar® Gasket Maker (2) to oil pump as shown. Install O-ring (1) into oil pump body discharge passage

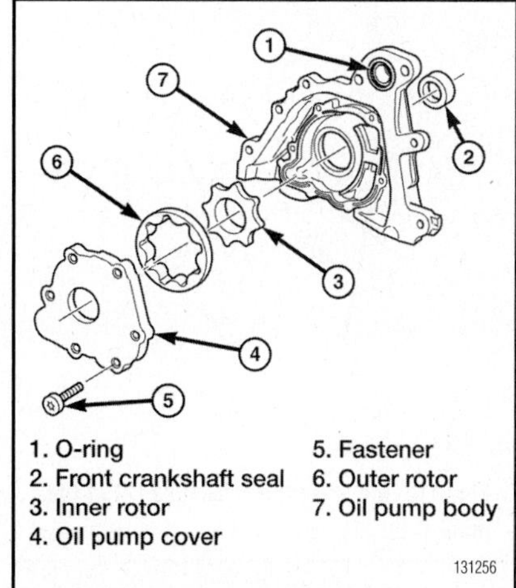

Fig. 109 Oil pump — exploded view

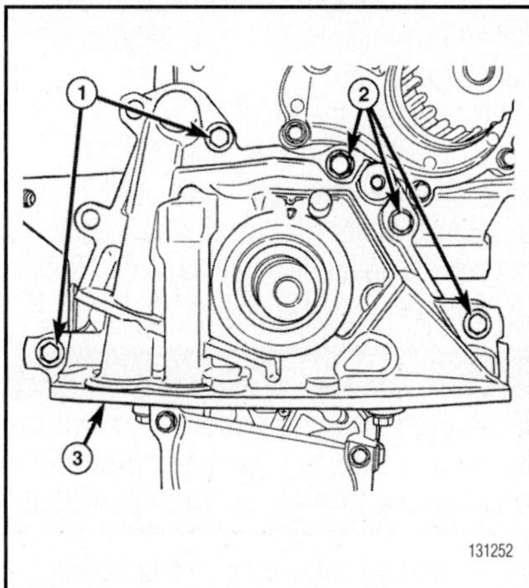

Fig. 106 Remove the 5 bolts (1, 2), oil pump (3) and front crankshaft seal

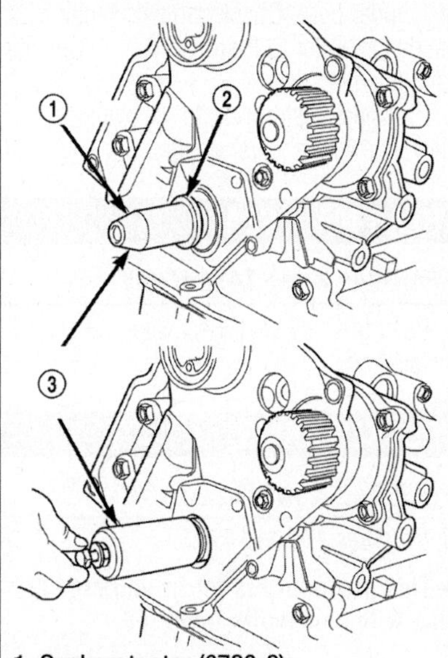

Fig. 108 Installing new front crankshaft seal

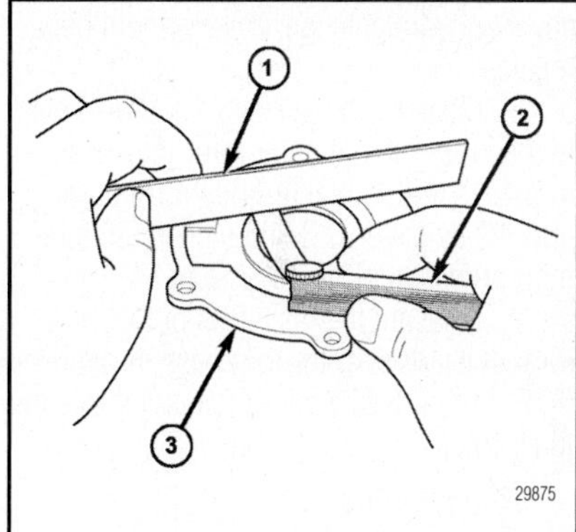

Fig. 110 Lay a straightedge (1) across the pump cover (3) surface. If a feeler gauge (2) can be inserted between cover and straightedge, cover should be replaced

To install:

9. Ensure all surfaces are clean and free of oil and dirt.
10. Apply Mopar ® Gasket Maker (2) to oil pump as shown
11. Install O-ring into oil pump body discharge passage.
12. Prime oil pump with engine oil before installation.
13. Align the oil pump rotor flats with flats on crankshaft.
14. Install the oil pump to the block.

⁂ WARNING

To align, the front crankshaft seal MUST be out of the pump, or damage may result.

15. Install a new front crankshaft seal using front crankshaft oil seal installer.
16. Install the crankshaft key.
17. Install the crankshaft sprocket. Refer to Crankshaft Sprocket, removal & installation.
18. Install the oil pump pick-up tube.
19. Install the oil pan. Refer to Oil Pan, removal & installation.
20. Install the timing belt rear cover. Refer to Rear Cover, removal & installation.
21. Install the timing belt. Refer to Timing Belt, removal & installation.

INSPECTION

See Figures 109 through 112.

To disassemble:

1. Remove the oil pump cover fasteners, and lift off cover.
2. Remove the inner and outer pump rotors.

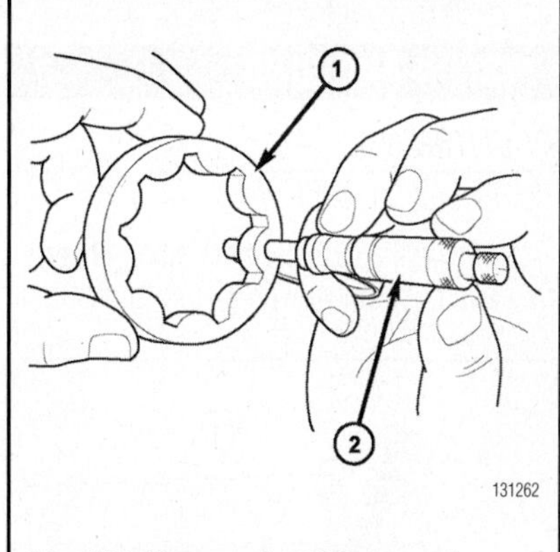

Fig. 111 Measure the thickness and diameter of the outer rotor (1)

To inspect:

3. Wash all parts in a suitable solvent, and inspect carefully for damage or wear.
4. Inspect the mating surface of the oil pump. Surface should be smooth. Replace pump cover if scratched or grooved.

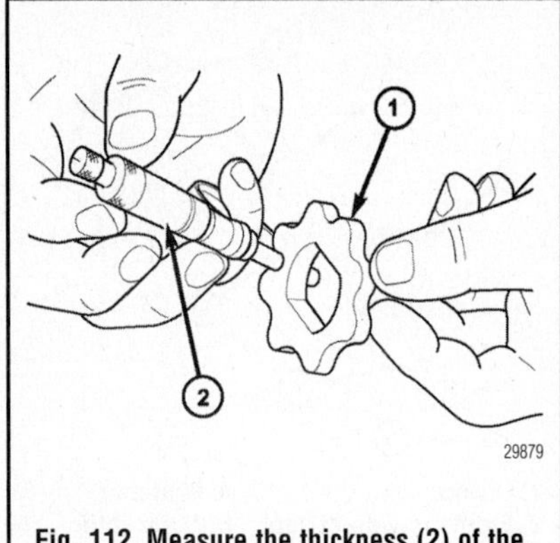

Fig. 112 Measure the thickness (2) of the inner rotor (1)

5. Lay a straightedge across the pump cover surface. If a 0.001 inch (0.025 mm) feeler gauge can be inserted between the cover and straightedge, cover should be replaced.

6. Measure the thickness and diameter of the outer rotor. If outer rotor thickness measures 0.421 inch (10.699 mm) or less, or if the diameter is 3.383 inches (85.924 mm) or less, replace outer rotor.

7. Measure the thickness of the inner rotor. If the inner rotor thickness measures 0.421 inch (10.699 mm) or less, replace the inner rotor.

To assemble:

8. Assemble pump, using new parts as required. Install the inner rotor with chamfer facing the cast iron oil pump cover.

9. Prime the oil pump before installation by filling rotor cavity with engine oil.

10. Install the cover, and tighten fasteners to 118 ft. lbs. (13 Nm).

PISTON AND RING

POSITIONING

See Figures 113 and 114.

1. Wipe the cylinder bore clean. Insert ring and push down with piston to ensure it is square in bore. The ring gap measurement must be made with the ring positioning at least 0.50 inch (12 mm) from bottom of cylinder bore. Check gap with feeler gauge (1). Refer to Piston and Ring Specifications chart.

2. Check piston ring to groove side clearance with a feeler gauge.

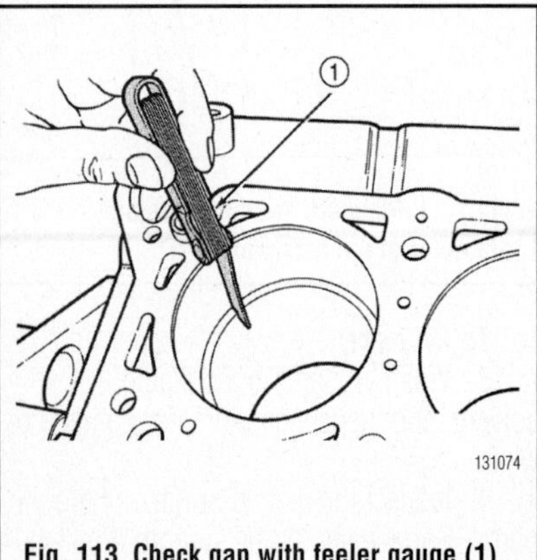

Fig. 113 Check gap with feeler gauge (1)

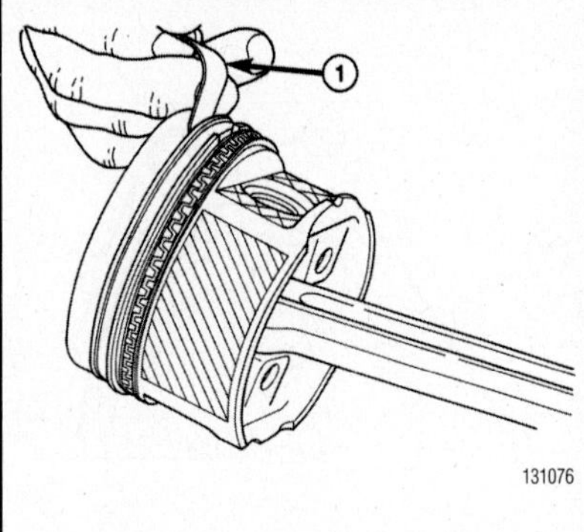

Fig. 114 Check piston ring to groove side clearance with a feeler gauge (1)

REAR MAIN SEAL

REMOVAL & INSTALLATION

Refer to Crankshaft Rear Seal, removal & installation.

ROCKER ARMS

REMOVAL & INSTALLATION

See Figures 115 and 116.

➡**This procedure is for in-vehicle service with camshafts installed.**

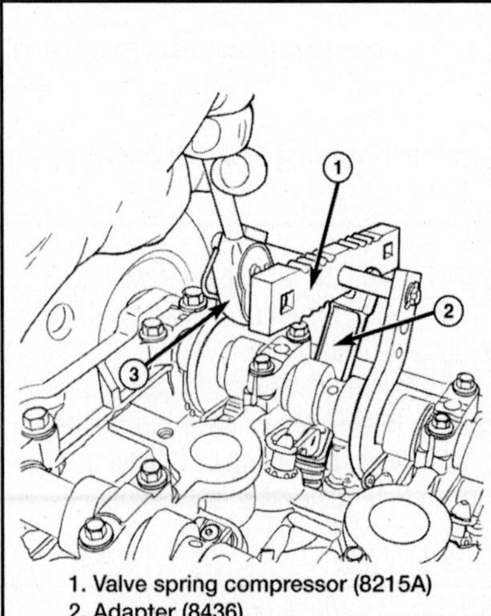

Fig. 115 Removing rocker arm

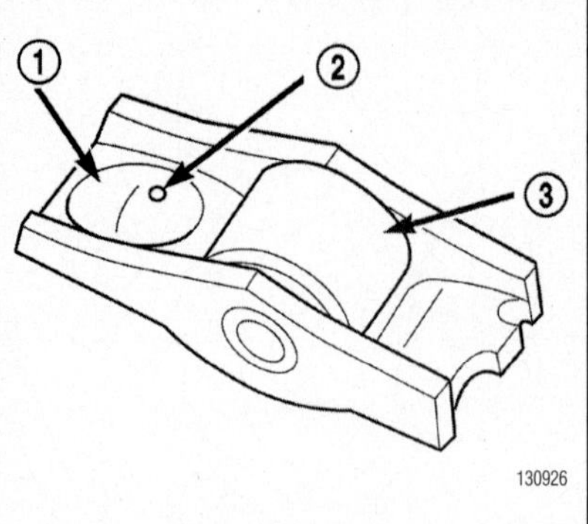

Fig. 116 Inspect the rocker arm lash adjuster pocket (1) and roller (3) for wear or damage. Ensure the oil squirt hole (2) is not plugged

1. Remove the cylinder head cover. Refer to Cylinder Head Cover, removal & installation.

2. Remove the spark plugs.

3. Rotate engine until the camshaft lobe, on the follower being removed, is positioned on its base circle (heel). Also, the piston should be a minimum of 6.3 mm (0.25 in) below TDC position.

⁂ WARNING

If the cam follower assemblies are to be reused, always mark position for reassembly in their original positions.

4. Using a valve spring compressor (8215A) with adapter (8436), slowly depress valve assembly until rocker arm can be removed.

5. Repeat removal procedure for each rocker arm.

To inspect:

6. Inspect the rocker arm lash adjuster pocket and roller for wear or damage. Ensure the oil squirt hole (2) is not plugged. Replace as necessary.

To install:

7. Lubricate the rocker arm with clean engine oil.

8. Using the valve spring compressor (8215A) and adapter (8436), slowly depress valve assembly until the rocker arm can be installed on the hydraulic lifter and valve stem.

9. Install spark plugs.

10. Install the cylinder head cover. Refer to Cylinder Head Cover, removal & installation.

STRUCTURAL COLLAR

REMOVAL & INSTALLATION

See Figures 117 through 119.

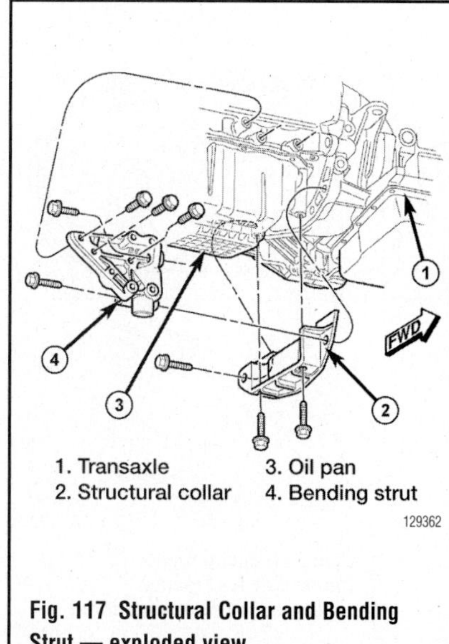

Fig. 117 Structural Collar and Bending Strut — exploded view

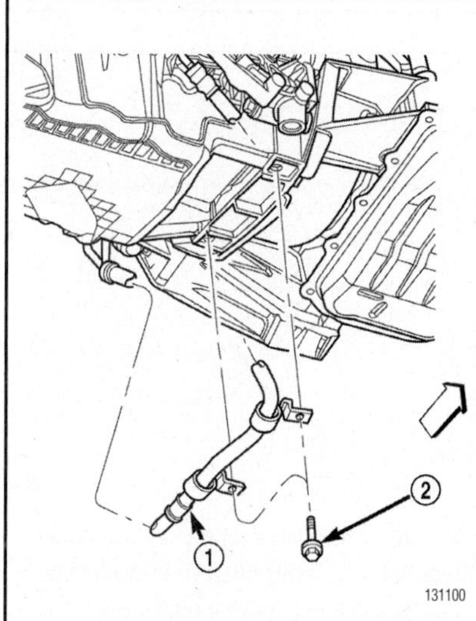

Fig. 118 View of power steering hose (1) and bolts (2)

1. Raise the vehicle on a hoist.
2. Remove bolts attaching the bending strut to engine and transaxle.
3. Disconnect the power steering hose support brackets from the structural collar.
4. Remove bolts attaching the structural collar to the engine, oil pan, and transaxle.
5. Remove the strut and collar.

To install:

WARNING

Torque procedure for the structural collar and bending strut must be followed, or damage could occur to oil pan, collar, and/or bending strut.

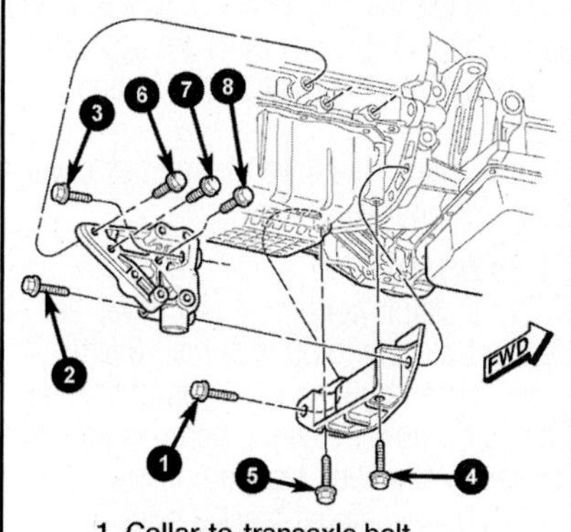

Fig. 119 Structural collar tightening sequence

6. Place the collar into position between transaxle and oil pan. Install collar-to-transaxle bolt (hand start only).
7. Position power steering hose support bracket, and install collar-to-oil pan bolt (hand tight only).
8. Position bending strut in place and loosely install bolt into the upper transaxle hole (hand start only).
9. Install bolt through strut and collar (hand start only).
10. Install strut-to-cylinder block bolt no. 6 (hand tight only).
11. Position power steering hose support bracket, and install the remaining collar-to-oil pan bolt (hand tight only).
12. Final torque bolts no. 1 – 3 to 75 ft. lbs. (101 Nm).
13. Install bolts no. 7 and 8 through strut and into cylinder block.
14. Final torque bolts no. 4 – 8 to 45 ft. lbs. (61 Nm).
15. Lower the vehicle.

TIMING BELT FRONT COVERS

REMOVAL & INSTALLATION

See Figures 120 through 122.

1. Remove the upper torque strut. Refer to Engine Mounting Torque Strut, removal & installation.
2. Remove upper timing belt cover fasteners and remove cover.
3. Disconnect the negative battery cable.
4. Raise vehicle on a hoist and remove the right front wheel.
5. Remove the right splash shield.
6. Remove the accessory drive belts. Refer to Accessory Drive Belts, removal & installation.
7. Remove the crankshaft vibration damper. Refer to Crankshaft Vibration Damper, removal & installation.
8. Remove the lower torque strut. Refer to Engine Mounting Torque Strut, removal & installation.
9. Disconnect the catalytic converter from the manifold.

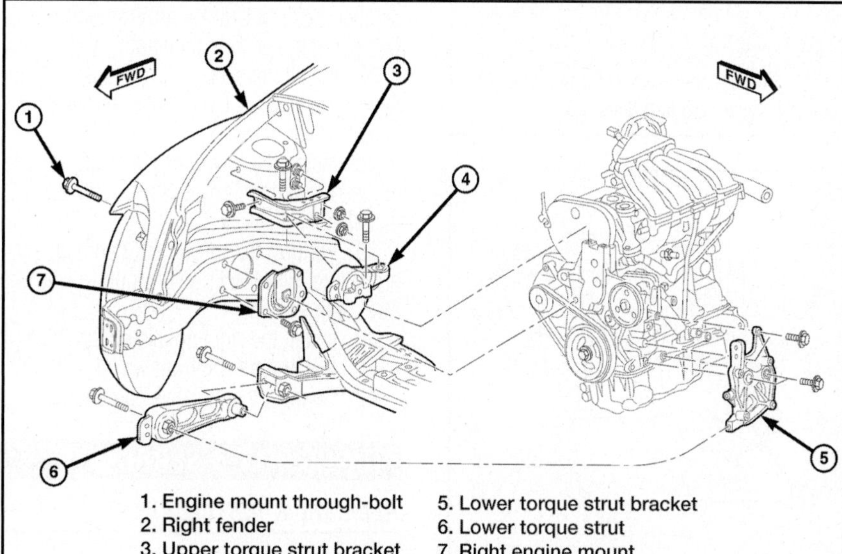

Fig. 120 Remove the right engine mount through-bolt

10. Disconnect the A/C pressure switch at rear of compressor housing.
11. Lower the vehicle, and support engine with a jack.
12. Discharge A/C system and disconnect the A/C lines at the coupling block.
13. Remove the screw attaching the ground strap to strut bracket.
14. Remove the upper torque strut bracket from the strut tower.
15. Remove the upper radiator closure panel.
16. Remove the power steering pump and bracket. Set pump aside. Do not disconnect the lines from the pump.
17. With the engine properly supported, remove the right engine mount through-bolt.

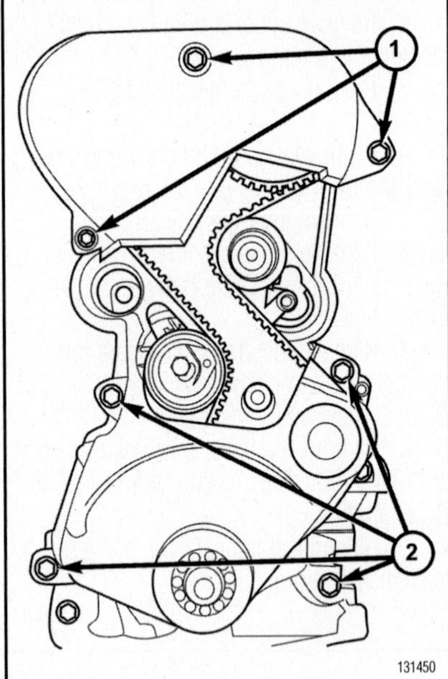

Fig. 121 Locating upper (1) and lower (2) front cover timing belt fasteners

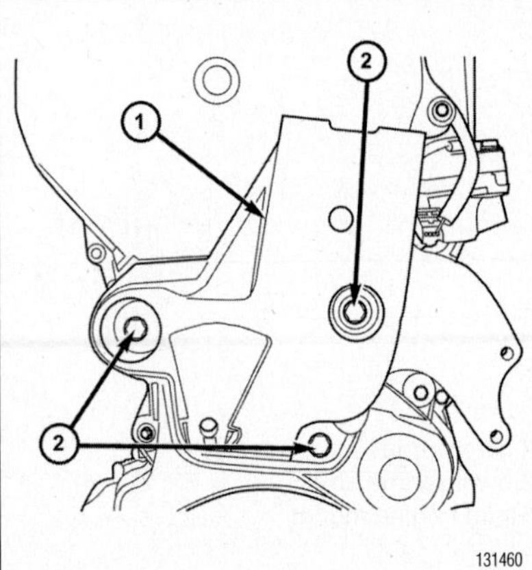

Fig. 122 View of right engine support bracket (1) and bolts (2)

18. Raise the engine with a jack until the engine support bracket bolts are accessible.
19. Remove the right engine support bracket.
20. Remove the lower timing belt cover fasteners, and remove cover.

To install:

21. Install lower timing belt cover, and tighten fasteners to 50 inch lbs. (6 Nm).
22. Install right engine support bracket. Ensure the power steering pump is properly located in mounting location on bracket.
23. Tighten mount bracket bolts to 45 ft. lbs. (61 Nm).
24. Lower engine into mounting position, and install the right engine mount through-bolt.
25. Tighten the bolt to 87 ft. lbs. (118 Nm).
26. Install the power steering pump and bracket.
27. Install the upper radiator closure panel.
28. Install the upper torque strut bracket to the strut tower.
29. Connect ground strap to bracket.
30. Install the upper torque strut. Refer to Engine Mounting Torque Strut, removal & installation.
31. Install upper timing belt cover, and tighten fasteners to 50 inch lbs. (6 Nm).
32. Connect A/C lines, and charge the A/C system.
33. Raise the vehicle.
34. Connect the catalytic converter to manifold.
35. Connect the A/C pressure switch connector.
36. Install the crankshaft vibration damper. Refer to Crankshaft Vibration Damper, removal & installation.
37. Install the accessory drive belts. Refer to Accessory Drive Belts, removal & installation.
38. Install the lower torque strut. Refer to Engine Mounting Torque Strut, removal & installation.
39. Perform the torque strut adjustment procedure. Refer to Engine Mounting Torque Strut, adjustment.
40. Install the right splash shield.
41. Install the right front wheel.
42. Connect the negative cable to battery.

TIMING BELT & SPROCKETS

REMOVAL & INSTALLATION

Timing Belt

See Figures 123 through 128.

1. Disconnect the negative battery cable.

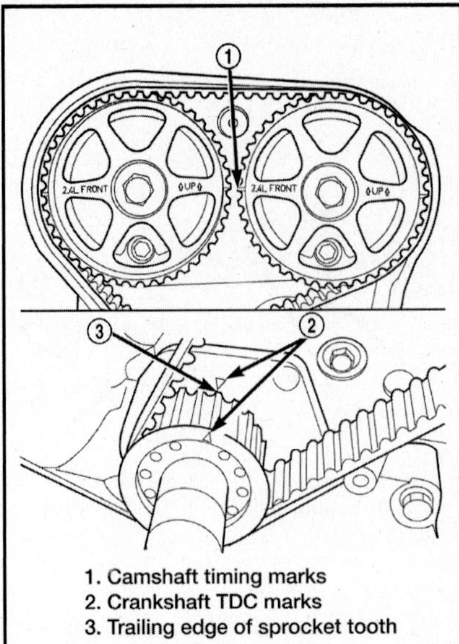

Fig. 123 Crankshaft and camshaft timing

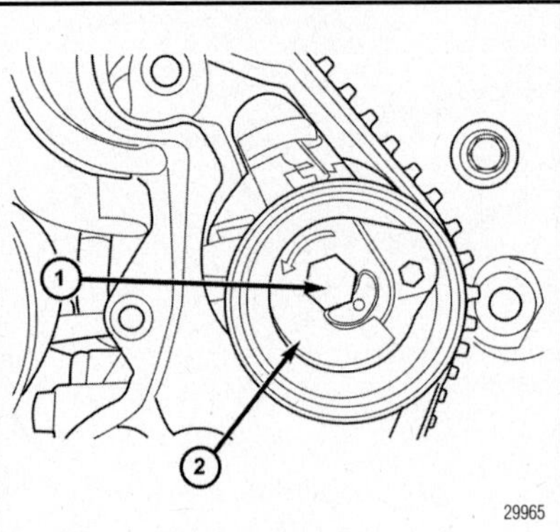

Fig. 124 Loosen the timing belt tensioner lock bolt (1). Insert Allen wrench into the hexagon opening located on the top plate (2) of the belt tensioner pulley

2. Remove the upper and lower front timing belt covers. Refer to Timing Belt Front Covers, removal & installation.

WARNING

When aligning the crankshaft and camshaft timing marks, always rotate engine from crankshaft. Camshaft should not be rotated after timing belt is removed. Damage to valve components may occur. Always align timing marks before removing the timing belt.

3. Before removal of the timing belt, rotate crankshaft until the Top Dead Center (TDC) mark on the oil pump housing aligns with the TDC mark on the crankshaft sprocket (trailing edge of sprocket tooth).

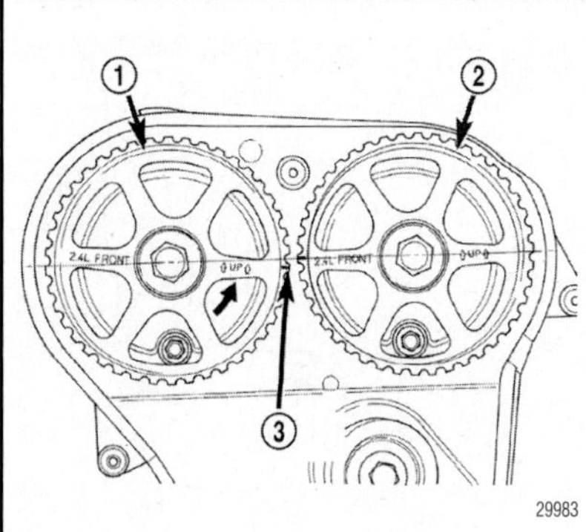

Fig. 125 Set camshafts timing marks so that the exhaust camshaft sprocket (1) is a 1/2 notch (3) below the intake camshaft sprocket (2)

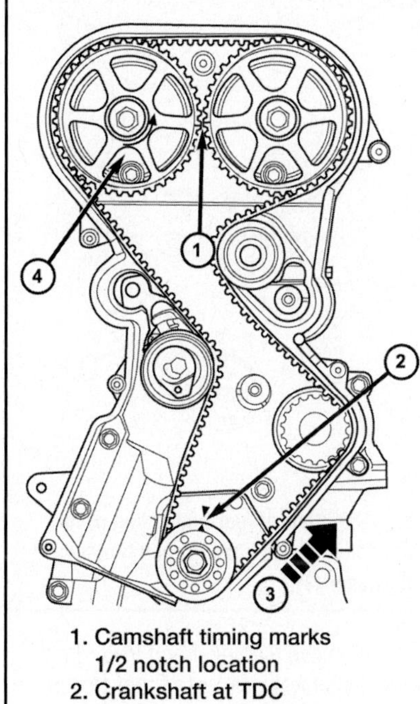

Fig. 126 Installing timing belt

➡The crankshaft sprocket TDC mark is located on the trailing edge of the sprocket tooth. Failure to align the trailing edge of the sprocket tooth to TDC mark on oil pump housing will cause the camshaft timing marks to be misaligned.

4. Loosen the timing belt tensioner lock bolt.
5. Insert an Allen wrench into the hexagon opening located on the top plate of the belt tensioner pulley.
6. Rotate the top plate CLOCKWISE until there is enough slack in the timing belt to allow for removal.
7. Remove the timing belt.

**** WARNING**

If timing belt was damaged due to incorrect tracking (alignment), the belt tensioner pulley and bracket must be replaced as an assembly. Refer to Timing Belt Tensioner, removal & installation.

To install:

8. Set crankshaft sprocket to TDC by aligning the sprocket with the arrow on the oil pump housing.
9. Set camshafts timing marks so that the exhaust camshaft sprocket is a 1/2 notch below the intake camshaft sprocket.

**** WARNING**

Ensure that the arrows on both camshaft sprockets are facing up.

10. Install the timing belt. Starting at the crankshaft, go around the water pump sprocket, idler pulley, camshaft sprockets and then around the tensioner.
11. Move the exhaust camshaft sprocket counterclockwise to align marks and take up belt slack.
12. Insert an Allen wrench into the hexagon opening located on the top plate of the belt tensioner pulley.
13. Rotate the top plate COUNTER-CLOCKWISE. The tensioner pulley will move against the belt and the tensioner setting notch will eventually start to move clockwise.
14. Watching the movement of the setting notch, continue rotating the top plate counterclockwise until the setting notch is aligned with the spring tang.
15. Using the Allen wrench to prevent the top plate from moving, tighten the tensioner lock bolt to 220 inch lbs. (25 Nm). Setting notch and spring tang should remain aligned after the lock bolt is tightened.
16. Remove the Allen wrench and torque wrench.

➡Repositioning the crankshaft to the TDC position must be done only during the CLOCKWISE rotation movement. If TDC is missed, rotate a further 2 revolutions until TDC is achieved. DO NOT rotate crankshaft counterclockwise, as this will make verification of proper tensioner setting impossible.

17. Rotate the crankshaft CLOCKWISE 2 complete revolutions manually for seating of the belt, until the crankshaft is repositioned at the TDC position.
18. Verify that the camshaft and crankshaft timing marks are in the proper positions.
19. Ensure the spring tang is within the tolerance window.
   - If the spring tang is within the tolerance window, the installation process is complete and nothing further is required.
   - If the spring tang is not within the tolerance window, repeat procedure as necessary.
20. Install the upper and lower front timing belt covers. Refer to Timing Belt Front Covers, removal & installation.
21. Connect the negative cable to battery.

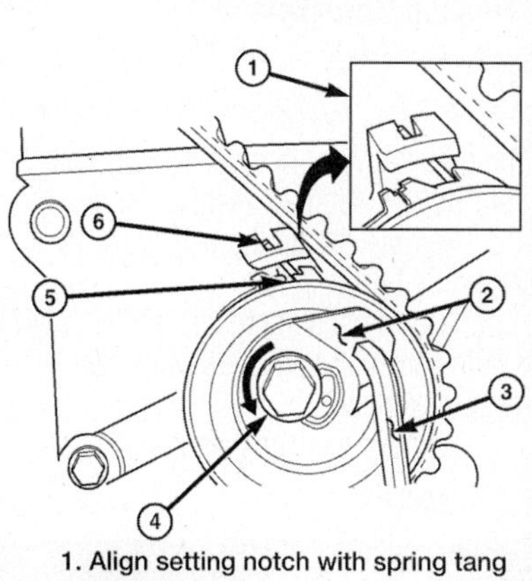

Fig. 127 Adjusting timing belt tension

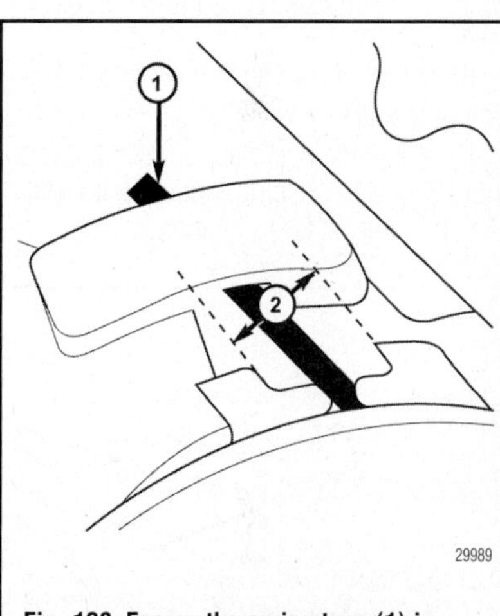

Fig. 128 Ensure the spring tang (1) is within the tolerance window (2)

Camshaft Sprockets

See Figure 129.

1. Remove the upper and lower front timing belt covers. Refer to Timing Belt Front Covers, removal & installation.
2. Remove the timing belt. Refer to Timing Belt procedure.
3. Use camshaft sprocket holder (6847) to hold camshaft sprockets while removing the sprocket bolts.
4. Remove the camshaft sprocket(s).

To install:

WARNING

Do not use an impact wrench to tighten the camshaft sprocket bolts. Damage to the camshaft-to-sprocket locating dowel pin may occur.

5. Install the camshaft sprockets. Hold sprockets with camshaft sprocket holder while tightening center bolt to 85 ft. lbs. (115 Nm).
6. Install the timing belt. Refer to Timing Belt procedure.
7. Install the upper and lower front timing belt covers. Refer to Timing Belt Front Covers, removal & installation.

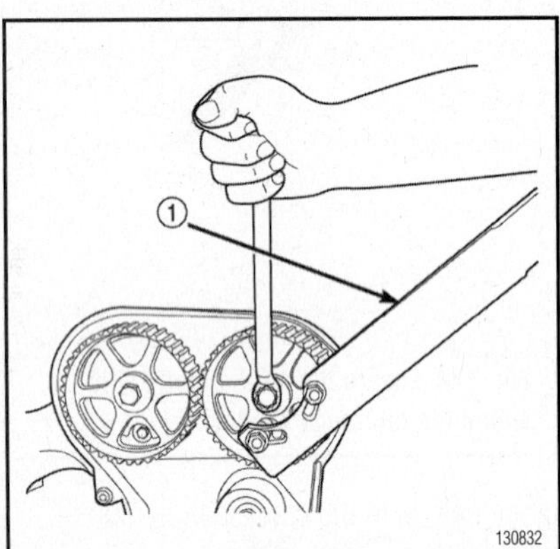

Fig. 129 Use camshaft sprocket holder (1) to hold camshaft sprockets while removing the sprocket bolts

Crankshaft Sprocket

See Figures 130 and 131.

1. Remove the upper and lower front timing belt covers. Refer to Timing Belt Front Covers, removal & installation.
2. Remove the timing belt. Refer to Timing Belt procedure.
3. Remove crankshaft sprocket using crankshaft sprocket remover (6793) and crankshaft sprocket remover insert (C-4685-C2).

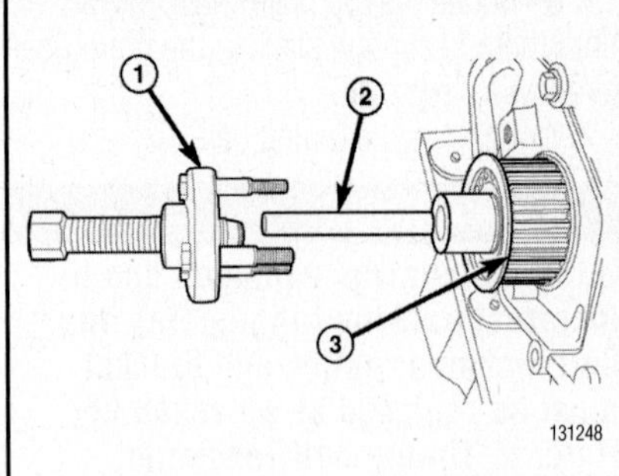

Fig. 130 Remove crankshaft sprocket (3) using crankshaft sprocket remover (1) and crankshaft sprocket remover insert (2)

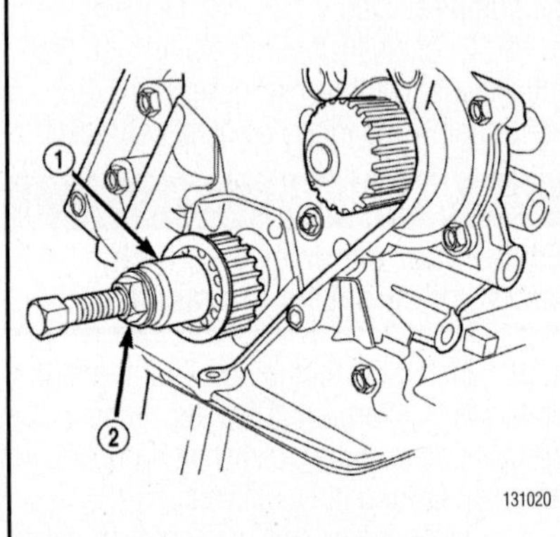

Fig. 131 Install crankshaft sprocket using crankshaft damper/sprocket installer (1), and tighten nut (2)

To install:

WARNING

The crankshaft sprocket is set to a predetermined depth from the factory for correct timing belt tracking. If removed, use of a crankshaft damper/sprocket installer is required to set the sprocket to original installation depth. An incorrectly installed sprocket will result in timing belt and engine damage.

4. Install the crankshaft sprocket using crankshaft damper/sprocket installer (6792), and tighten nut.
5. Install the timing belt. Refer to Timing Belt procedure.
6. Install the upper and lower front timing belt covers. Refer to Timing Belt Front Covers, removal & installation.

TIMING BELT REAR COVER

REMOVAL & INSTALLATION

See Figures 129, 132 and 133.

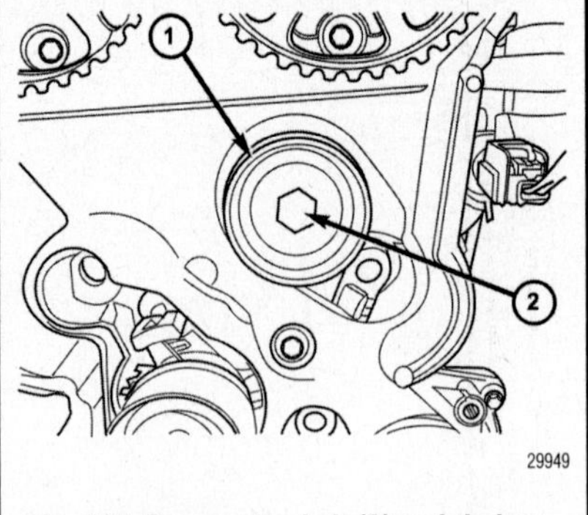

Fig. 132 Remove the bolt (2) and timing belt idler pulley (1)

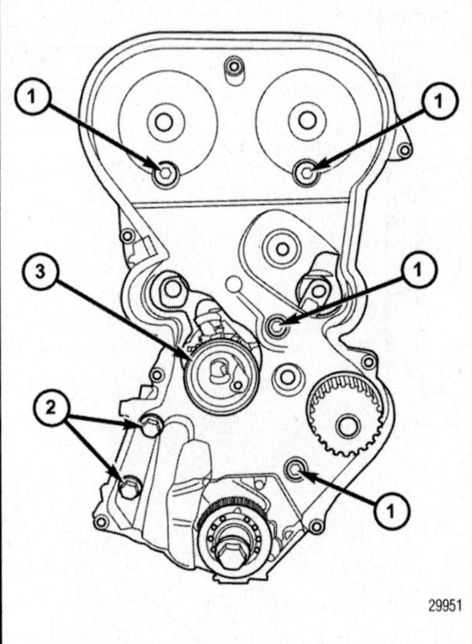

Fig. 133 View of rear timing belt cover M6 bolts (1), M8 bolts (2) and timing belt tensioner (3)

1. Remove the upper and lower front timing belt covers. Refer to Front Covers procedure.
2. Remove the timing belt. Refer to Timing Belt and Sprockets, removal & installation.
3. Remove the bolt and timing belt idler pulley.
4. Remove the camshaft sprockets. Use camshaft sprocket holder (6847) to hold camshaft sprockets while removing the sprocket bolts.
5. Remove the rear timing belt cover fasteners, and remove cover from the engine.

To install:

6. Install the rear timing belt cover, and tighten:
    - The M6 bolts to 105 inch lbs. (12 Nm).
    - The M8 bolts to 250 inch lbs. (28 Nm).

7. Install the timing belt idler pulley.

8. Tighten the timing belt idler pulley fastener to 45 ft. lbs. (61 Nm).

WARNING

Do not use an impact wrench to tighten camshaft sprocket bolts. Damage to the camshaft-to-sprocket locating dowel pin may occur.

9. Install the camshaft sprockets. Hold sprockets with the camshaft sprocket holder while tightening the center bolt to 85 ft. lbs. (115 Nm).

10. Install the timing belt. Refer to Timing Belt & Sprockets, removal & installation.

11. Install the upper and lower front timing belt covers. Refer to Front Covers procedure.

TIMING BELT TENSIONER

REMOVAL & INSTALLATION

See Figure 134.

1. Remove the timing belt and camshaft sprockets. Refer to Timing Belt & Camshaft Sprockets, removal & installation.

2. Remove the timing belt rear cover. Refer to Timing Belt Rear Cover, removal & installation.

3. Remove lower bolt attaching timing belt tensioner assembly to engine, and remove tensioner as an assembly.

To install:

4. Align timing belt tensioner assembly to engine and install lower mounting bolt, but do not tighten.

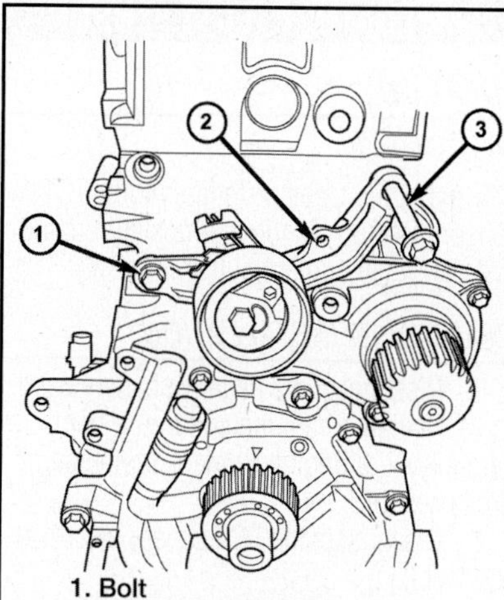

Fig. 134 Removing tensioner assembly

5. To properly align tensioner assembly to engine; temporarily install one of the engine bracket mounting bolts (M10) 5 – 7 turns into the tensioner assembly upper mounting location.

6. Torque the tensioner's lower mounting bolt to 45 ft. lbs. (61 Nm). Remove the upper bolt used for tensioner alignment.

7. Install the timing belt rear cover. Refer to Timing Belt Rear Cover, removal & installation.

VALVE COVERS

REMOVAL & INSTALLATION

Refer to Cylinder Head Cover, removal & installation.

VALVE LASH ADJUSTERS

HYDRAULIC LASH ADJUSTER NOISE DIAGNOSIS

A tappet-like noise may result from any of the following conditions:

- Engine oil level too high or too low. This may cause aerated oil to enter the adjusters and cause them to be spongy.
- Insufficient running time after rebuilding the cylinder head. Low speed running up to 1 hour may be required. During this time, turn engine off and let set for a few minutes before restarting. Repeat this several times after engine has reached normal operating temperature.
- Low oil pressure.
- The oil restrictor (integral to the cylinder head gasket) in the vertical oil passage to the cylinder head is plugged with debris.
- Air ingested into oil due to broken or cracked oil pump pick up.
- Worn valve guides.
- Rocker arm ears contacting valve spring retainer.
- Rocker arm loose, adjuster stuck or at maximum extension and still leaves lash in the system.
- Faulty lash adjuster.

ADJUSTMENT

1. Check the lash adjusters for sponginess while installed in cylinder head. Depress part of rocker arm over adjuster. Normal adjusters should feel very firm. Spongy adjusters can be bottomed out easily.

2. Remove suspected lash adjusters, and replace as necessary.

REMOVAL & INSTALLATION

See Figure 135.

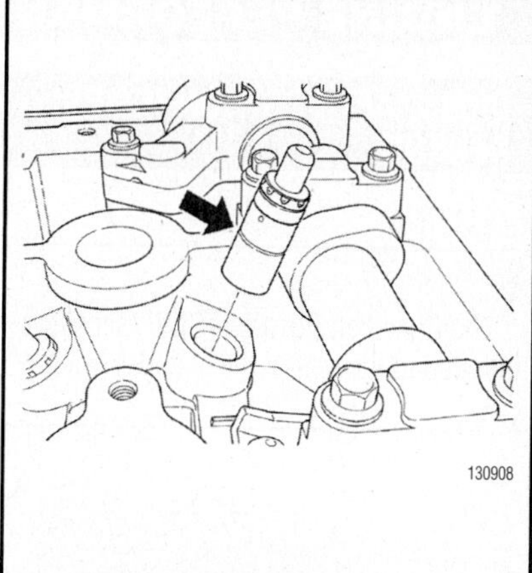

Fig. 135 Remove the hydraulic lash adjuster

1. Remove the intake manifold cover.

2. Remove the upper intake manifold. Refer to Intake Manifold, removal & installation.

➡This procedure is for in-vehicle service with camshafts installed.

3. Remove the cylinder head cover. Refer to Cylinder Head Cover, removal & installation.

➡If reusing, mark each rocker arm and each hydraulic lash adjuster for reassembly in original position. Lash adjusters are serviced as an assembly.

4. Remove the rocker arm.

5. Remove the hydraulic lash adjuster.

6. Repeat removal procedure for each hydraulic lash adjuster.

To install:

7. Install the hydraulic lash adjuster. Ensure the lash adjusters are at least partially full of engine oil. This is indicated by little or no plunger travel when the lifter is depressed.

8. Install the rocker arm.

9. Repeat installation procedure for each hydraulic lash adjuster.

10. Install the cylinder head cover. Refer to Cylinder Head Cover, removal & installation.

11. Install the upper intake manifold. Refer to Intake Manifold, removal & installation.

12. Install the intake manifold cover.

VALVE LIFTERS

Refer to Valve Lash Adjusters.

ENGINE PERFORMANCE & EMISSION CONTROLS

CAMSHAFT POSITION (CMP) SENSOR

LOCATION

See Figure 136.

The Camshaft Position (CMP) sensor is mounted to the rear of the cylinder head.

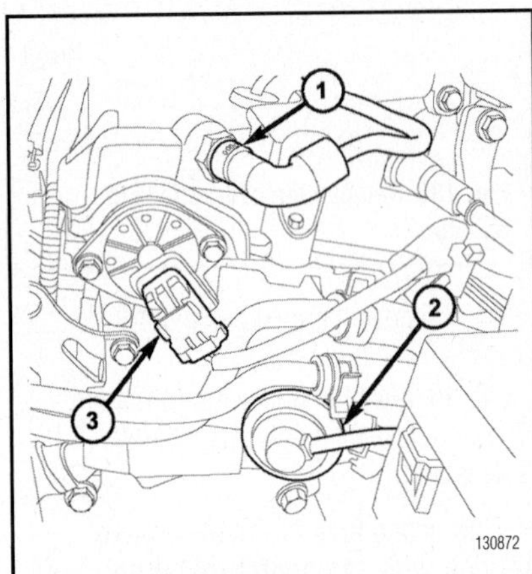

Fig. 136 PCV valve (1), EGR valve (2) and Camshaft Position (CMP) sensor (3) location

REMOVAL & INSTALLATION

See Figures 137 and 138.

1. Remove the air cleaner lid. Disconnect the inlet air temperature sensor and makeup air hose.
2. Remove the negative battery cable.
3. Disconnect the electrical connector from the camshaft position sensor.
4. Remove the Camshaft Position (CMP) sensor mounting screws. Remove sensor.

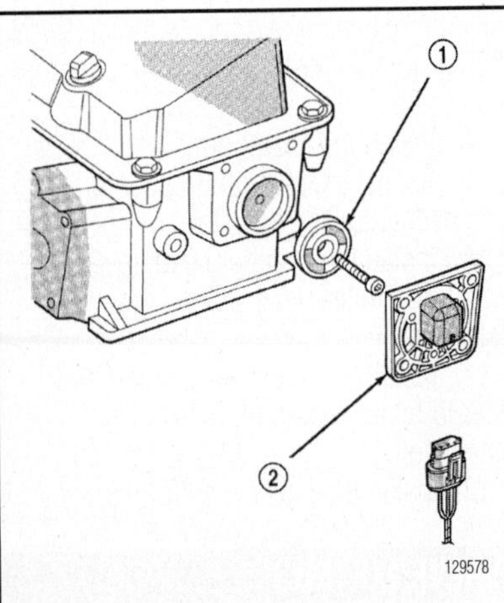

Fig. 137 View of target magnet (1) and CMP sensor (2)

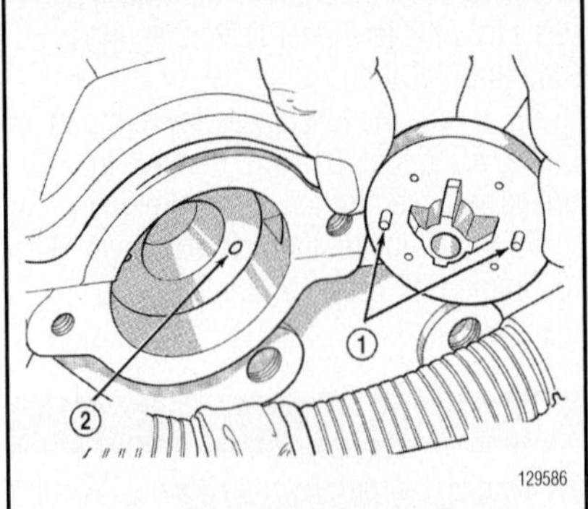

Fig. 138 The target magnet has locating dowels (1) that fit into machined locating holes (2) in the end of the camshaft

5. Loosen the screw attaching the target magnet to rear of camshaft.

To install:

➡The target magnet has locating dowels that fit into machined locating holes in the end of the camshaft.

6. Install the target magnet in end of camshaft. Tighten mounting screw to 32 inch lbs. (3.5 Nm). Over-tightening could cause cracks in magnet. If the magnet cracks, replace it.
7. Install the CMP sensor. Tighten sensor mounting screws to 80 inch lbs. (9 Nm).

⁂ WARNING

Use care when attaching the electrical connector to the CMP sensor. Installation at an angle may damage the sensor pins.

8. Carefully attach the electrical connector to the CMP sensor.
9. Install the negative battery cable.
10. Install the air cleaner lid. Connect the inlet air temperature sensor and makeup air hose.

CRANKSHAFT POSITION (CKP) SENSOR

LOCATION

See Figure 139.

The Crankshaft Position (CKP) sensor is in the front of the engine block, just under the starter motor.

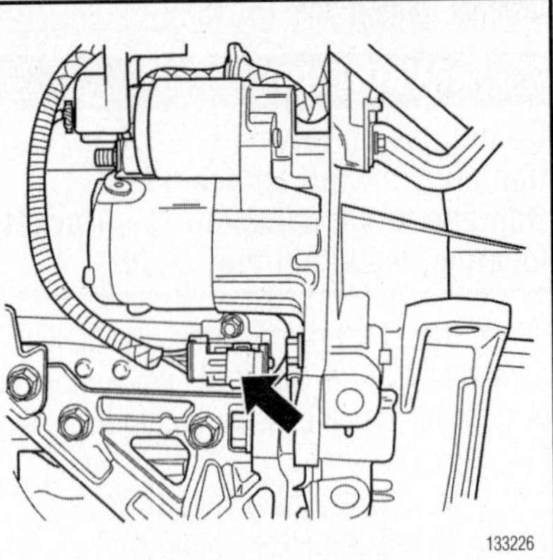

Fig. 139 Crankshaft Position (CKP) sensor location

REMOVAL & INSTALLATION

1. Disconnect the negative battery cable.
2. Raise the vehicle and support.
3. Unlock and disconnect the electrical connector to the Crankshaft Position (CKP) sensor.
4. Remove the CKP sensor bolt.
5. Remove the sensor.

To install:

6. Check O-ring for damage. Lubricate the O-ring with engine oil before installing sensor.
7. Use a twisting motion when installing the sensor.
8. Install and tighten the CKP sensor bolt to 65 – 95 inch lbs. (8 – 10 Nm).
9. Connect and lock the electrical connector to the crankshaft position sensor.
10. Lower the vehicle.
11. Connect the negative battery cable.

ENGINE COOLANT TEMPERATURE (ECT) SENSOR

LOCATION

See Figure 140.

The Engine Coolant Temperature (ECT) sensor threads into the thermostat housing just below the coolant outlet connector.

REMOVAL & INSTALLATION

1. Disconnect the negative battery cable.
2. Partially drain the cooling system below level of Engine Coolant Temperature (ECT) sensor.
3. Disconnect the ECT sensor electrical connector.
4. Remove the ECT sensor.

To install:

5. Install the ECT sensor. Tighten sensor to 168 inch lbs. (19 Nm).
6. Reconnect the ECT sensor electrical connector.

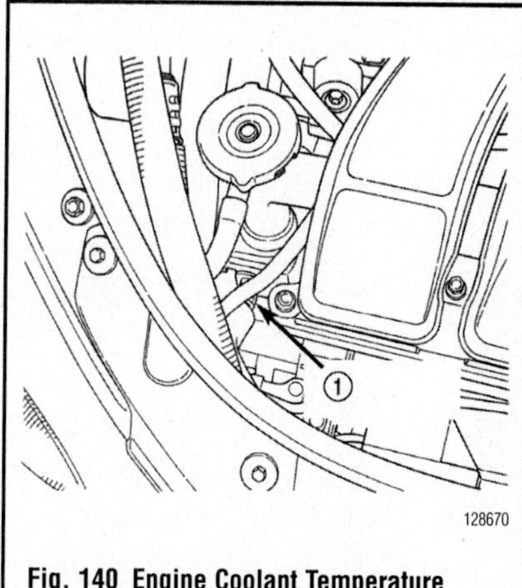

Fig. 140 Engine Coolant Temperature (ECT) sensor location

7. Fill the cooling system. Refer to Drain & Refill procedure.
8. Connect the negative battery cable.

HEATED OXYGEN (HO2S) SENSOR

LOCATION

Upstream HO2S Sensor

See Figure 141.

The upstream oxygen sensor threads into the outlet flange of the exhaust manifold.

Downstream HO2S Sensor

See Figures 142 and 143.

The downstream heated oxygen sensor threads into the catalytic convertor or into the exhaust pipe behind the catalytic convertor (depending on emission package).

REMOVAL & INSTALLATION

1. Remove the air cleaner lid and makeup air hose.

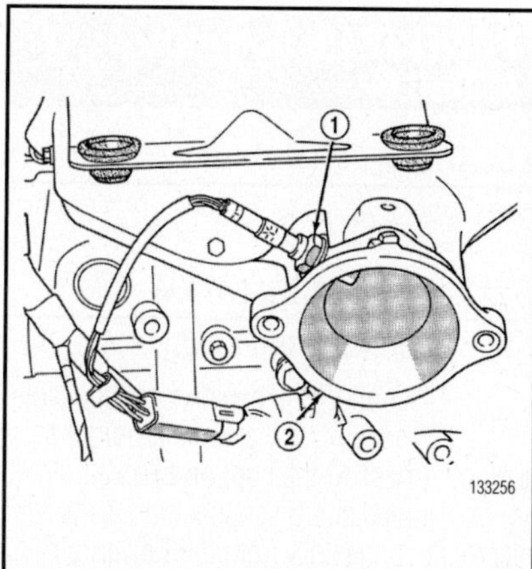

Fig. 141 Upstream Heated Oxygen (HO2S) Sensor (1) located on exhaust manifold (2)

Fig. 142 Downstream Heated Oxygen Sensor location — into catalytic convertor

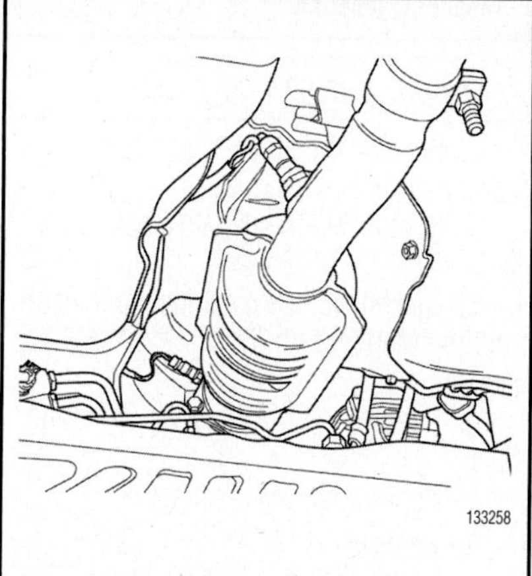

Fig. 143 Downstream Heated Oxygen Sensor location — into exhaust pipe

2. Disconnect the negative battery cable.
3. If removing downstream oxygen sensor, raise vehicle and support.
4. Disconnect the sensor harness at connector.
5. Disconnect the sensor electrical harness from retaining clips.
6. Remove the sensor using an oxygen sensor crow's foot wrench or socket.

To install:

7. Before installing the sensor, clean the exhaust component threads using an 18 mm X 1.5 + 6E tap.

➡If reusing the original sensor, coat the sensor threads with an anti-seize compound (such as Loctite ® 771-64 or equivalent). New sensors have compound on the threads and do not require an additional coating.

8. Install the oxygen sensor.
9. Tighten the sensor to 30 ft. lbs. (41 Nm).
10. Connect the sensor electrical harness to retaining clips.
11. Connect the sensor harness at the connector.
12. If installing downstream sensor, lower the vehicle.
13. Reconnect the negative battery cable.
14. Install the air cleaner lid and makeup air hose.

INTAKE AIR TEMPERATURE (IAT) SENSOR

LOCATION

See Figure 144.

The Intake Air Temperature (IAT) sensor is located on the air inlet tube.

REMOVAL & INSTALLATION

1. Unlatch or unbolt the air cleaner lid.
2. Lift air cleaner lid, and reposition aside.
3. Disconnect the negative battery cable.
4. Disconnect the electrical connector from the Intake Air Temperature (IAT) sensor.
5. Remove the IAT sensor.

To install:

6. Install the inlet air temperature sensor.
7. Attach electrical connector to the IAT sensor.
8. Connect the negative battery cable.
9. Install the air cleaner lid.

Fig. 144 Intake Air Temperature (IAT) sensor (1) location

KNOCK SENSOR (KS)

LOCATION

See Figure 145.

The knock sensor bolts into the side of the cylinder block in front of the starter, under the intake manifold.

REMOVAL & INSTALLATION

1. Disconnect the negative battery cable.
2. Remove the bolt holding the knock sensor.
3. Remove the knock sensor with electrical connector attached.
4. Disconnect electrical connector from the knock sensor.
5. Remove the knock sensor.

To install:

6. Attach electrical connector to the knock sensor.
7. Install the knock sensor.
8. Tighten the knock sensor bolt to 195 inch lbs. (22 Nm).

**** WARNING**

Over- or under-tightening effects knock sensor performance, possibly causing improper spark control.

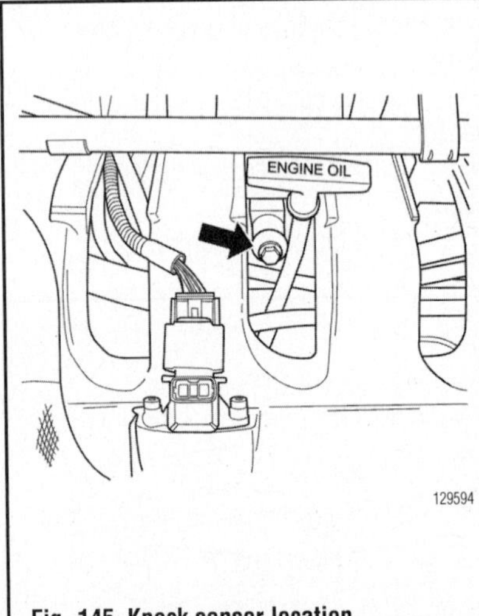

Fig. 145 Knock sensor location

9. Connect the negative battery cable.

MANIFOLD ABSOLUTE PRESSURE (MAP) SENSOR

LOCATION

See Figure 146.

The Manifold Air Pressure (MAP) sensor is located on the intake manifold.

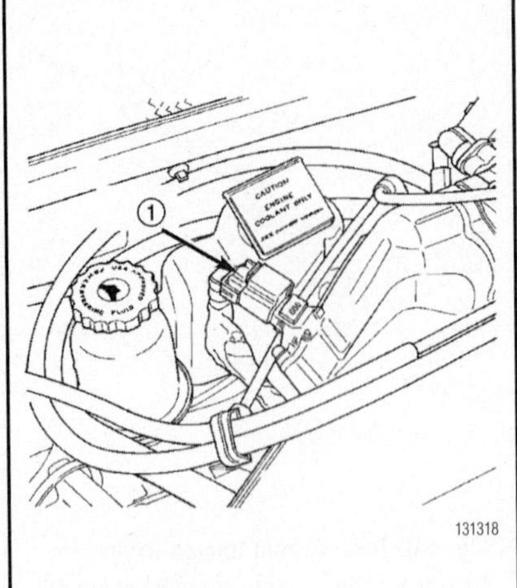

Fig. 146 Manifold Air Pressure (MAP) sensor (1) location

REMOVAL & INSTALLATION

1. Remove the air cleaner lid and makeup air hose.
2. Disconnect the negative battery cable.
3. Disconnect the electrical connector from the Manifold Air Pressure (MAP) sensor.
4. Remove the MAP sensor mounting screws.
5. Remove the MAP sensor.

To install:

**** WARNING**

Exercise caution to prevent damage to the O-ring seal.

6. Insert the MAP sensor into the intake manifold.
7. Tighten the mounting screws to 20 inch lbs. (2 Nm).
8. Attach electrical connector to the MAP sensor.
9. Reconnect the negative battery cable.
10. Install the air cleaner lid and makeup air hose.

OUTPUT SPEED SENSOR (OSS)

LOCATION

See Figure 147.

REMOVAL & INSTALLATION

See Figure 147.

**** WARNING**

When disconnecting the speed sensor connector, be sure that the connector weather seal does not fall off or remain in the old sensor.

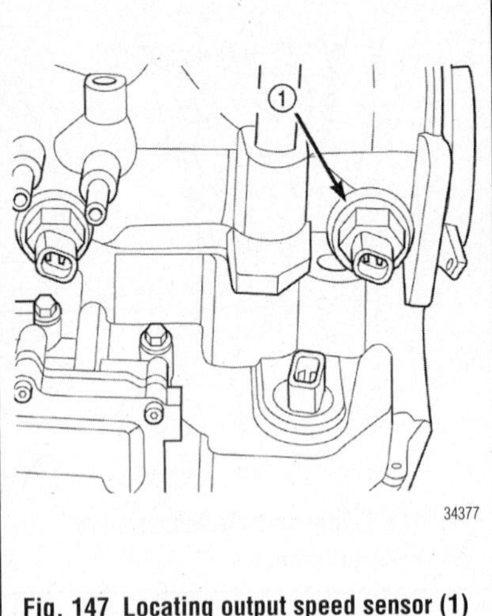

Fig. 147 Locating output speed sensor (1) on the transaxle case

1. Disconnect the battery cables.
2. Remove the air cleaner assembly. Refer to Air Cleaner, removal & installation.
3. Remove the battery hold down clamp, and remove the battery.
4. Remove the battery tray.
5. Disconnect the output speed sensor connector.
6. Unscrew and remove the output speed sensor.
7. Inspect speed sensor O-ring and replace if necessary.

To install:

8. Verify O-ring is installed into position.
9. Install and tighten output speed sensor to 20 ft. lbs. (27 Nm).
10. Connect the speed sensor connector.
11. Install the battery tray.
12. Install the battery and hold-down clamp.
13. Install the air cleaner assembly. Refer to Air Cleaner, removal & installation.

POWERTRAIN CONTROL MODULE

LOCATION

See Figure 148.

REMOVAL & INSTALLATION

See Figures 149 through 152.

1. Disconnect the negative battery cable.
2. Remove plastic clips that hold the wiring harness to the support bracket.
3. Unlock and disconnect the 3 – 4 electrical connectors from the Powertrain Control Module (PCM).
4. Remove the clutch reservoir and relocate out of way.

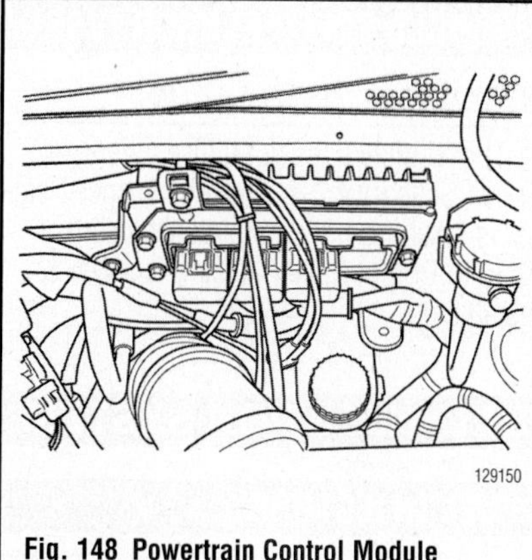

Fig. 148 Powertrain Control Module (PCM) location

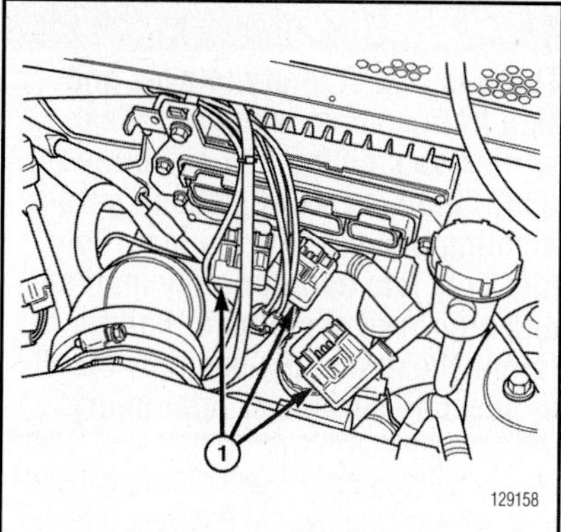

Fig. 149 Unlock and disconnect the 3 – 4 electrical connectors (1) from the Powertrain Control Module (PCM)

5. Remove the 4 mounting bolts from the PCM mounting bracket.

6. Remove the PCM and mounting bracket.

7. Remove the 3 bolts mounting the PCM to the PCM bracket.

To install:

8. Install the PCM bracket and 3 mounting bolts to the PCM, and tighten to 105 inch lbs. (11.8 Nm).

9. Tip the PCM and bracket assembly into the bracket.

10. Locate the PCM and bracket assembly bracket on the tab.

11. Install the 4 mounting bolts to the PCM mounting bracket, and tighten to 95 inch lbs. (10.7 Nm).

12. Relocate and install the clutch reservoir.

➡The electrical connectors for the PCM are color-coded.

13. Connect and lock the 3 – 4 electrical connectors to the Powertrain Control Module (PCM).

14. Install plastic clips that hold the wiring harness to the support bracket.

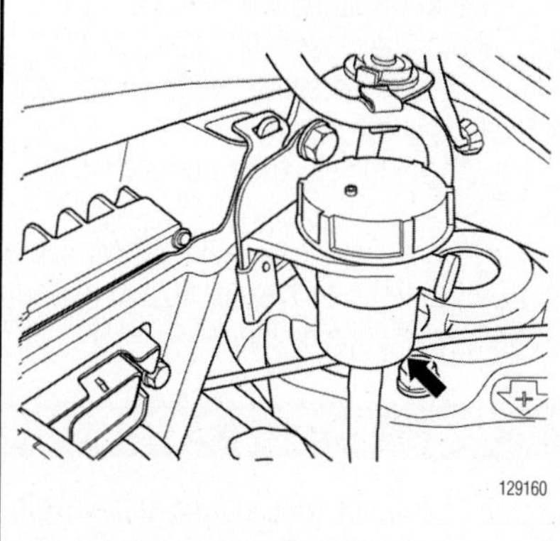

Fig. 150 Remove the clutch reservoir and relocate out of way

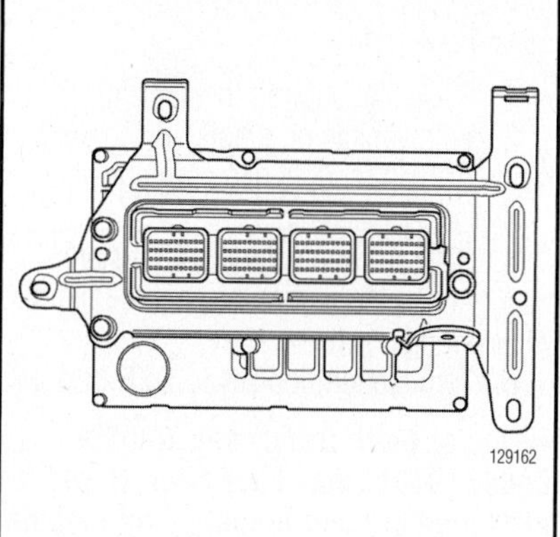

Fig. 151 View of PCM and mounting bracket

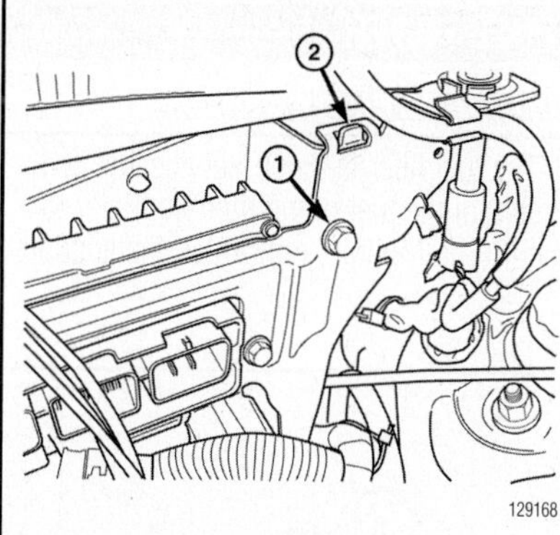

Fig. 152 Locate the PCM and bracket assembly bracket on the tab (2). Install the 4 mounting bolts to the PCM mounting bracket (1)

15. Reconnect the negative battery cable.

THROTTLE POSITION SENSOR (TPS)

LOCATION

See Figure 153.

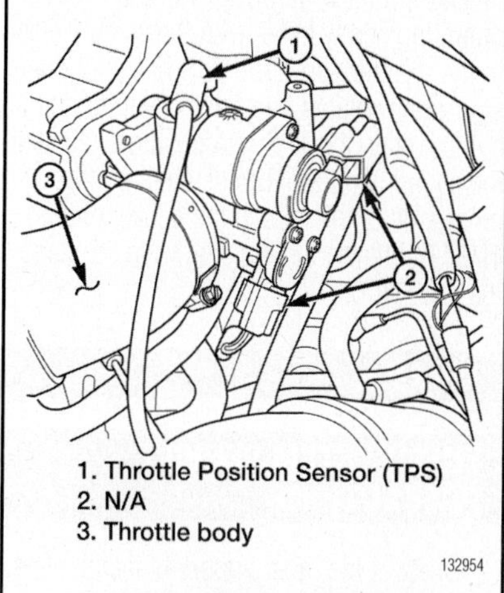

Fig. 153 Throttle Position Sensor (TPS) location

The Throttle Position Sensor (TPS) is located on the side of the throttle body.

REMOVAL & INSTALLATION

See Figure 154.

1. Remove the air cleaner lid and makeup air hose.

2. Loosen the clamp and relocate assembly.

3. Disconnect the negative battery cable.

4. Disconnect electrical connector from the Throttle Position Sensor (TPS).

5. Remove the TPS mounting screws.

6. Remove the TPS.

To install:

7. The throttle shaft end of the throttle body slides into a socket in the TPS.

8. Ensure the rubber O-ring is in place and seated around the TPS rotor housing surface. The socket has 2 tabs inside it. The throttle shaft rests against the tabs. When indexed correctly, the TPS can rotate

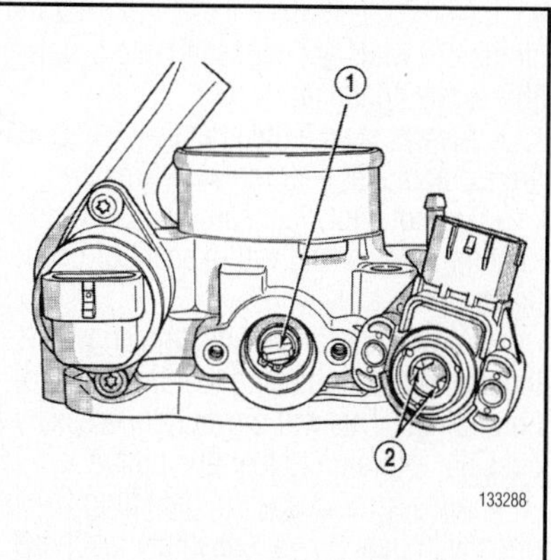

Fig. 154 Locating throttle shaft (1) and tabs (2)

clockwise a few degrees to line up the mounting screw holes with the screw holes in the throttle body. The TPS has slight tension when rotated into position. If it is difficult to rotate the TPS into position, reinstall the sensor with the throttle shaft on the other side of the tabs in the socket of the TPS. Tighten mounting screws to 55 inch lbs. (6.2 Nm).

9. After installing the TPS, the throttle plate should be closed. If the throttle plate is open, install the sensor on the other side of the tabs in the socket.

10. Attach the electrical connectors to the TPS.

11. Reconnect the negative battery cable.

12. Install the air cleaner lid and makeup air hose, and tighten clamp.

VEHICLE SPEED SENSOR (VSS)

REMOVAL & INSTALLATION

This vehicle does not utilize a Vehicle Speed Sensor (VSS). The vehicle speed signal is taken from the output speed sensor. Refer to Output Speed Sensor, removal & installation.

FUEL

GASOLINE FUEL INJECTION SYSTEM

FUEL SYSTEM SERVICE PRECAUTIONS

Safety is the most important factor when performing not only fuel system maintenance but any type of maintenance. Failure to conduct maintenance and repairs in a safe manner may result in serious personal injury or death. Maintenance and testing of the vehicle's fuel system components can be accomplished safely and effectively by adhering to the following rules and guidelines.

- To avoid the possibility of fire and personal injury, always disconnect the negative battery cable unless the repair or test procedure requires that battery voltage be applied.
- Always relieve the fuel system pressure prior to disconnecting any fuel system component (injector, fuel rail, pressure regulator, etc.), fitting or fuel line connection. Exercise extreme caution whenever relieving fuel system pressure to avoid exposing skin, face and eyes to fuel spray. Please be advised that fuel under pressure may penetrate the skin or any part of the body that it contacts.
- Always place a shop towel or cloth around the fitting or connection prior to loosening to absorb any excess fuel due to spillage. Ensure that all fuel spillage (should it occur) is quickly removed from engine surfaces. Ensure that all fuel soaked cloths or towels are deposited into a suitable waste container.
- Always keep a dry chemical (Class B) fire extinguisher near the work area.
- Do not allow fuel spray or fuel vapors to come into contact with a spark or open flame.
- Always use a back-up wrench when loosening and tightening fuel line connection fittings. This will prevent unnecessary stress and torsion to fuel line piping.
- Always replace worn fuel fitting O-rings with new Do not substitute fuel hose or equivalent where fuel pipe is installed.

Before servicing the vehicle, make sure to also refer to the precautions in the beginning of this section as well.

RELIEVING FUEL SYSTEM PRESSURE

See Figure 155.

1. Raise and support the vehicle.
2. With vehicle on a hoist, disconnect the fuel pump module harness connector.
3. Lower the vehicle.
4. Start and run engine until it stalls.
5. Attempt to restart the engine until it will no longer run.
6. Turn the ignition key to **OFF** position.

➡One or more Diagnostic Trouble Codes (DTCs) may have been stored in PCM memory due to fuel pump module being removed.

7. When the repair is complete, use the scan tool to erase the DTC(s).

FUEL FILTER

REMOVAL & INSTALLATION

The fuel filter is a non-serviceable component of the fuel pump module. Refer to Fuel Pump Module, removal & installation.

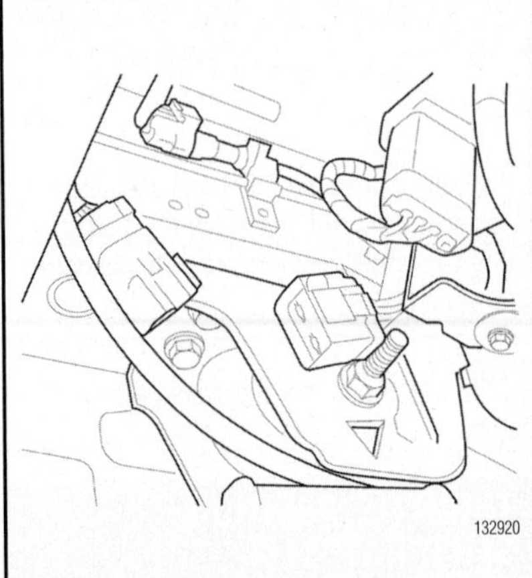

Fig. 155 Fuel pump module harness connector location

FUEL INJECTORS

REMOVAL & INSTALLATION

See Figure 156.

⁂ CAUTION

There is risk of injury to eyes and skin from contact with fuel. Wear protective clothing and eye protection. There is risk of poisoning from inhaling and swallowing fuel. Pour fuel only into appropriately marked and approved containers. Failure to follow these instructions may result in possible serious or fatal injury.

1. Release fuel system pressure. Refer to Relieving Fuel System Pressure procedure.
2. Remove the air cleaner lid. Disconnect the inlet air temperature sensor and makeup air hose.
3. Disconnect the negative battery cable.
4. Remove the engine cover or throttle control shield (if equipped).

➡Wrap shop towels around hose to catch any gasoline spillage.

5. Disconnect fuel supply tube from the fuel rail.
6. Remove the intake manifold. Refer to Intake Manifold, removal & installation.
7. Disconnect the electrical connectors from fuel injectors.
8. Remove the bolts holding the fuel rail.
9. Remove the fuel rail and injectors.
10. Remove the fuel injectors from the fuel rail.

To install:

11. Install the fuel injectors to the fuel rail.
12. Apply a light coating of clean engine oil to the O-ring on the nozzle end of each injector.
13. Insert fuel injector nozzles into openings in the intake manifold. Seat the injectors in place.

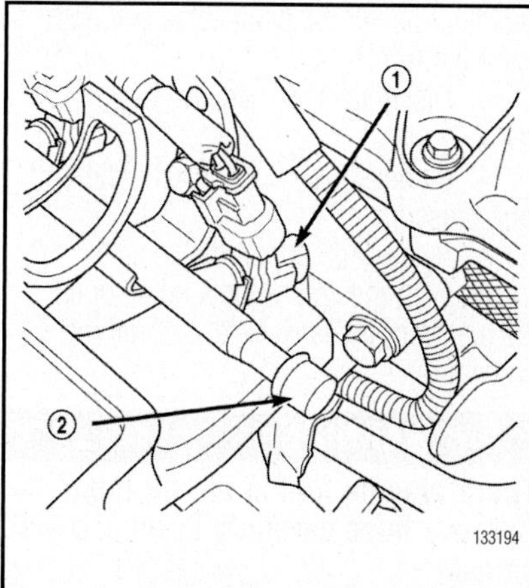

Fig. 156 Fuel injector (1) and fuel rail test port (2) location

14. Tighten the fuel rail bolts to 16.5 ft. lbs. (22.5 Nm).
15. Attach the electrical connectors to fuel injectors.
16. Connect fuel supply tube to the fuel rail.
17. Install the intake manifold. Refer to Intake Manifold, removal & installation.
18. Install the engine cover or throttle control shield (if equipped).
19. Reconnect the negative battery cable.
20. Install the air cleaner lid. Connect the inlet air temperature sensor and makeup air hose.
21. Tighten the air inlet tube clamps to 25 inch lbs. (3 Nm).

FUEL PUMP MODULE

REMOVAL & INSTALLATION

See Figures 157 through 159.

**** CAUTION**

There is risk of injury to eyes and skin from contact with fuel. Wear protective clothing and eye protection. There is risk of poisoning from inhaling and swallowing fuel. Pour fuel only into appropriately marked and approved containers. Failure to follow these instructions may result in possible serious or fatal injury.

1. Remove fuel filler cap and relieve fuel pressure. Refer to Relieving Fuel System Pressure procedure.
2. Remove the air cleaner lid. Disconnect the inlet air temperature sensor and makeup air hose.
3. Remove the negative battery cable.
4. Raise the vehicle and support.

Fig. 157 Using Fuel Pump Lock Ring Wrench (9340), remove lock ring to release pump module.

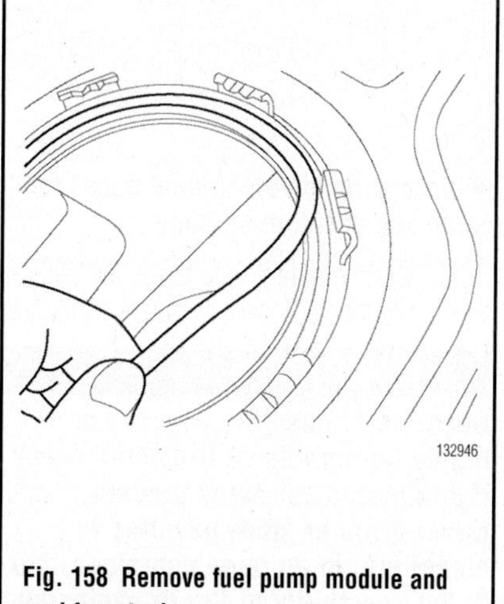

Fig. 158 Remove fuel pump module and seal from tank

5. Remove the fuel tank. Refer to Fuel Tank, removal & installation.

**** WARNING**

Clean top of fuel tank around the fuel pump module to remove loose dirt and debris. Failure to clean the fuel tank properly can cause dirt and debris to enter the fuel system, causing damage to the fuel system and/or engine components.

6. Disconnect fuel filter lines from fuel pump module.

**** WARNING**

Mark the position of the fuel pump module on the top of the fuel tank prior to removal. The pump has to be properly aligned in the tank for the fuel gauge to work properly.

7. Using Fuel Pump Lock Ring Wrench (9340), remove lock ring to release pump module.

**** CAUTION**

The fuel reservoir of the fuel pump module does not empty out when the tank is drained. The fuel in the reservoir may spill out when the module is removed. Use caution to avoid personal injury.

8. Remove fuel pump module and seal from tank. Discard seal.

To install:

9. Wipe seal area of tank clean. Place a new seal between the tank threads and the pump module opening.

➡The pump has to properly positioned to the tank for the fuel gauge to work properly.

10. Position fuel pump module in tank. Make sure the alignment tab lines up on the fuel tank and pump module for Gas or Diesel fuel tanks.
11. While holding the pump module in position, install lock ring and use fuel pump lock ring wrench to tighten the lock ring.
12. Install fuel tank. Refer to Fuel Tank, removal & installation.
13. Lower the vehicle.
14. Install the negative battery cable.
15. Install the air cleaner lid. Connect the inlet air temperature sensor and makeup air hose.
16. Fill fuel tank with clean fuel. Use a scan tool to pressurize the system and check for leaks.

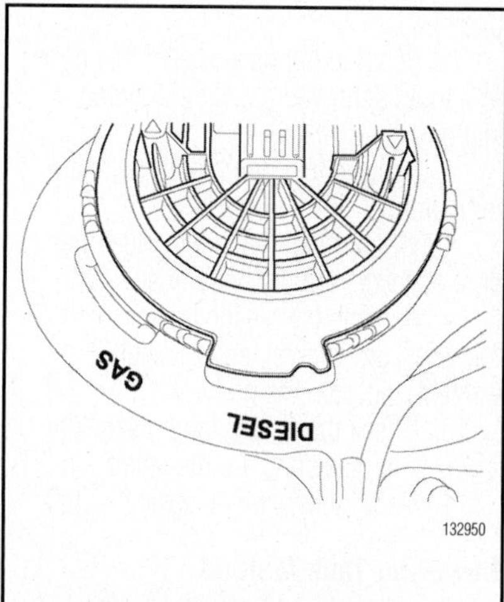

Fig. 159 Make sure the alignment tab lines up on the fuel tank and pump module for Gas or Diesel fuel tanks

FUEL TANK

DRAINING

⁂ CAUTION

There is risk of injury to eyes and skin from contact with fuel. Wear protective clothing and eye protection. There is risk of poisoning from inhaling and swallowing fuel. Pour fuel only into appropriately marked and approved containers. Failure to follow these instructions may result in possible serious or fatal injury.

Two different procedures may be used to drain fuel tank:

- Using a scan tool.
- Lowering the fuel tank.

➡The quickest draining procedure involves lowering the fuel tank. As an alternative procedure, the electric fuel pump may be activated, allowing tank to be drained at fuel rail connection (refer to scan tool for fuel pump activation procedures).

Scan Tool Method

1. Before disconnecting fuel line at fuel rail, release the fuel system pressure. Refer to Relieving Fuel System Pressure procedure.
2. Disconnect the fuel line at the fuel rail, and remove the plastic retainer from the fuel rail.
3. Reinstall the plastic retainer back into the fuel line from the body.
4. Check the O-ring, and make sure that it is in place and not damaged.
5. Attach end of fuel pressure adapter (6539SG) at fuel line connection from the body line.
6. Position opposite end of this hose tool to an approved gasoline draining station.
7. Activate fuel pump and drain tank until empty.
8. When done, remove the fuel pressure adapter from the body line.
9. Remove the plastic retainer from the fuel pressure adapter, and reinstall it into the fuel line from the body.
10. Check the O-ring, and make sure that it is in place and not damaged.
11. Install the fuel line to the fuel rail.

Lowering Tank Method

➡If electric fuel pump is not operating, tank must be lowered for fuel draining.

1. Remove fuel filler cap.
2. Release the fuel system pressure. Refer to Relieving Fuel System Pressure procedure.
3. Disconnect negative cable from battery.
4. Raise the vehicle and support.
5. Certain models are equipped with a separate grounding wire (strap) connecting the fuel fill tube assembly to the body. Disconnect wire by removing screw.
6. Open fuel fill door, and remove screws mounting fuel filler tube assembly to body. Do not disconnect rubber fuel fill or vent hoses from tank at this time.
7. Place a transmission jack under center of fuel tank. Apply a slight amount of pressure to fuel tank with transmission jack.
8. Remove fuel tank mounting straps.
9. Lower the tank just enough so that the filler tube fitting is the highest point of the fuel tank.
10. Remove the filler tube from the fuel tank. Tank will be drained through this fitting.

➡Wrap shop towels around hoses to catch any gasoline spillage.

11. Drain fuel tank into a holding tank or a properly labeled gasoline safety container.

⁂ CAUTION

Gasoline or gasoline vapors are highly flammable. A fire could occur if an ignition source is present. Never drain or store gasoline or diesel fuel in an open container, due to the possibility of fire or explosion. This may result in personal injury or death.

12. If fuel pump module removal is necessary, refer to Fuel Pump Module, removal & installation.

REMOVAL & INSTALLATION

See Figure 160.

⁂ CAUTION

There is risk of injury to eyes and skin from contact with fuel. Wear protective clothing and eye protection. There is risk of poisoning from inhaling and swallowing fuel. Pour fuel only into appropriately marked and approved containers. Failure to follow these instructions may result in possible serious or fatal injury.

1. Release the fuel system pressure. Refer to Relieving Fuel System Pressure procedure.
2. Remove the air cleaner lid. Disconnect the inlet air temperature sensor and makeup air hose.
3. Disconnect the negative battery cable.
4. Remove fuel cap slowly to release tank pressure.
5. Raise and support the vehicle.
6. With the vehicle on a hoist, drain the fuel from the tank. Refer to Draining procedure.

⁂ WARNING

There may be fuel in the fill tube. Remove hose carefully to reduce fuel splash.

7. Disconnect fuel tank from rubber fill hose.

➡Wrap shop towels around hoses to catch any gasoline spillage.

8. Remove the bolts from the fuel tank straps.
9. Disconnect fuel line, in the front of the fuel tank at the quick-connect fitting.
10. Lower the fuel tank, and remove the EVAP line and recirculation line.
11. Remove vacuum line from Leak Detection Pump.
12. Unlock the electrical connector, then disconnect the electrical connector.
13. Remove hoses from EVAP canister.
14. Remove fuel tank from vehicle.

To install:

15. Position the fuel tank on the transmission jack.
16. Raise fuel tank into position.
17. Connect the vacuum line to Leak Detection Pump.
18. Install the EVAP line and recirculation line.

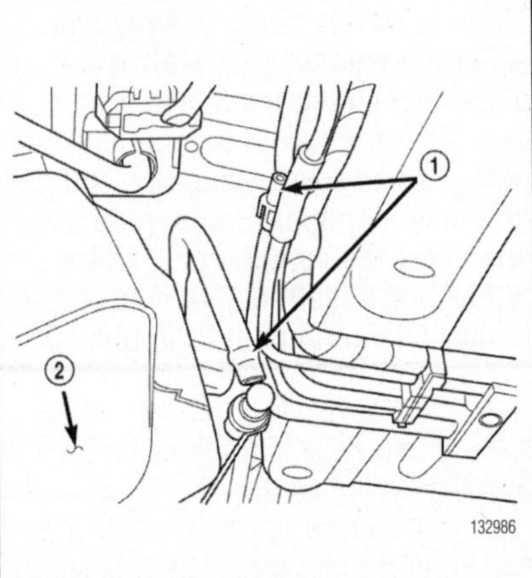

Fig. 160 Disconnect fuel line (1), in the front of the fuel tank (2) at the quick-connect fitting

19. Connect electrical connector and lock the connector.
20. Connect the fuel line.
21. Connect fuel fill tube to tank inlet.
22. Tighten the hose clamp to 38 inch lbs. (4.1 Nm).
23. Position fuel tank straps. Ensure straps are not twisted or bent.
24. Tighten the fuel tank strap bolts to 200 inch lbs. (22.5 Nm).
25. Remove the transmission jack.
26. Lower the vehicle.
27. Fill the fuel tank and install filler cap.
28. Reconnect the negative battery cable.
29. Install the air cleaner lid. Connect the inlet air temperature sensor and makeup air hose.
30. Use the scan tool ASD FUEL SYSTEM TEST to pressurize the fuel system.
31. Check system for leaks.

IDLE SPEED

ADJUSTMENT

Idle speed is not manually adjustable. All idle speed functions are controlled by the Powertrain Control Module (PCM).

THROTTLE BODY

REMOVAL & INSTALLATION

See Figures 161 through 163.

1. Remove the air cleaner lid. Disconnect the inlet air temperature sensor and makeup air hose.
2. Disconnect the negative battery cable.
3. Remove the engine cover or throttle control shield (if equipped).
4. Remove the throttle cable from the throttle body cam.
5. Lift the retaining tabs on the cable, and slide cable out of bracket.
6. Remove the speed control cable from throttle lever by sliding clasp out of hole used for throttle cable.
7. Remove the EVAP purge hose from the nipple on throttle body.

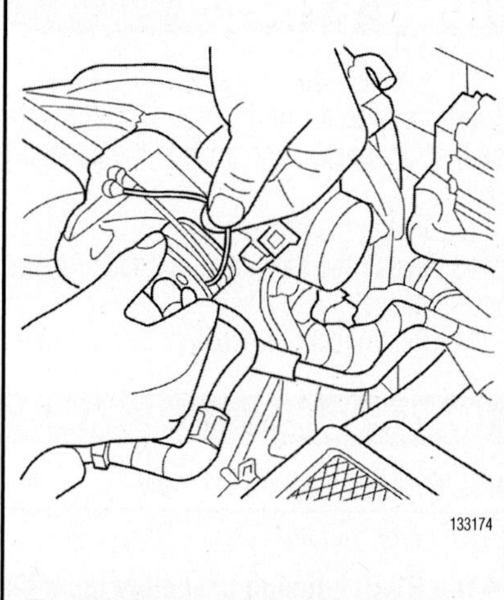

Fig. 161 Remove the throttle cable from the throttle body cam

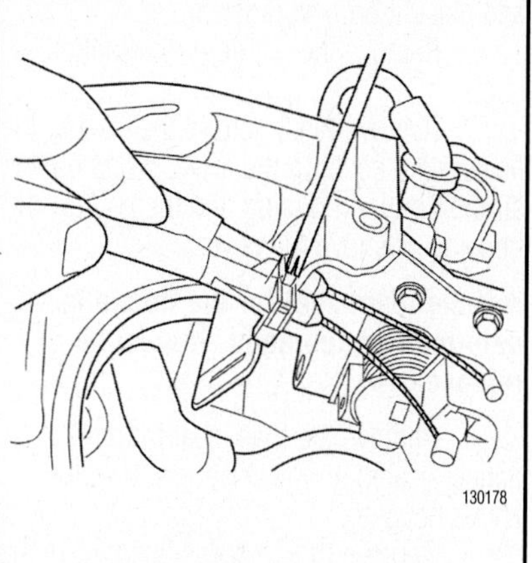

Fig. 162 Lift the retaining tabs on the cable, and slide cable out of bracket

8. Remove the electrical connectors from the throttle position sensor and idle air control motor.
9. Remove the 2 screws holding the cable mounting bracket and support bracket.
10. Remove the 3 throttle body mounting bolts.
11. Lift the throttle body straight up and away to remove the throttle body.

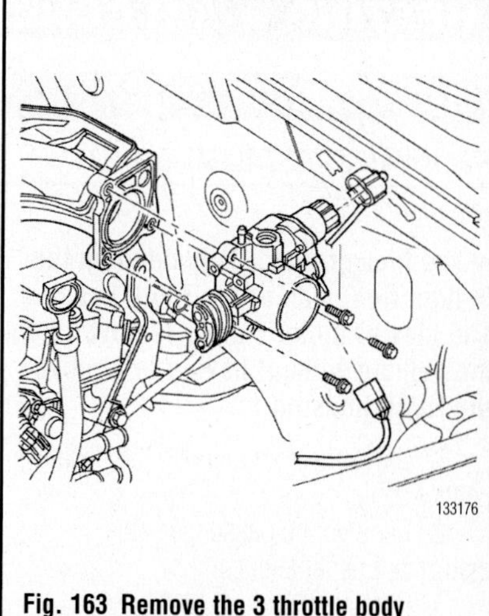

Fig. 163 Remove the 3 throttle body mounting bolts

To install:

12. Attach electrical connectors to the idle air control motor and throttle position sensor.
13. Make sure that the throttle body gasket is in place in the manifold.
14. Position the throttle body on intake and install mounting bolts. Do not tighten bolts at this time.
15. Install the throttle cable bracket. Do not tighten bolts at this time.
16. Tighten the throttle body bolts to 85 – 125 inch lbs. (10 – 14 Nm).
17. Tighten throttle cable bracket bolts to 85 – 125 inch lbs. (10 – 14 Nm).
18. Install the EVAP purge hose to the throttle body nipple.
19. Install cable housing(s) retainer tabs into the bracket.
20. Install the throttle body cables by rotating the throttle cam forward to the wide-open position.
21. Install the engine cover or throttle control shield (if equipped).
22. Reconnect the negative battery cable.
23. Install the air cleaner lid. Connect the inlet air temperature sensor and makeup air hose.

HEATING & AIR CONDITIONING SYSTEM

BLOWER MOTOR

REMOVAL & INSTALLATION

See Figure 164.

➡The blower motor is located on the bottom right side of the HVAC housing. The blower motor can be removed from the vehicle without having to remove the HVAC housing.

1. Disconnect and isolate the negative battery cable.
2. Remove the passenger-side instrument panel silencer.
3. Remove the glove box.
4. Reach through the glove box opening, and disengage the connector lock. Disconnect the instrument panel wire harness connector from the connector of the blower motor wire harness.
5. Disengage the blower motor connector from the retainer located on the HVAC housing.
6. From underneath the instrument panel, remove the 3 screws that secure the blower motor to the bottom of the HVAC housing. Remove the blower motor.

To install:

7. Position the blower motor into the bottom of the HVAC housing.
8. Install the 3 screws that secure the blower motor to the HVAC housing.
9. Tighten the screws to 17 inch lbs. (2 Nm).
10. Reach through the glove box opening, and engage the connector for the blower motor wire harness leads to the retainer located on the HVAC housing.
11. Connect the instrument panel wire harness connector to the blower motor wire harness connector, and engage the connector lock.
12. Install the glove box.
13. Install the passenger-side instrument panel silencer.
14. Reconnect the negative battery cable.

HEATER CORE

REMOVAL & INSTALLATION

See Figures 165 and 166.

➡The HVAC housing assembly must be removed from vehicle for service of the heater core.

1. Remove the HVAC housing assembly and place it on a workbench.
2. Remove the left floor distribution duct.
3. Remove the 3 screws that secure the heater core cover to the driver's side of the air distribution housing and the HVAC housing. Remove the cover.

➡If the foam seal for the flange is deformed or damaged, it must be replaced.

4. Remove the foam seal from the flange located on the driver's side of the HVAC housing.
5. Remove the 2 screws that secure the heater core to the driver's side of the air distribution housing.
6. Carefully pull the heater core out of the driver side of the air distribution housing.
7. If required, remove the retaining clips that secure the heater core tubes to the heater core; disconnect the tubes from the heater core; and remove and discard the O-ring seals.

To install:

8. If removed, lubricate new O-rings with clean engine coolant and install them onto the heater core tubes. Connect the tubes to the heater core, and install the retaining clips.
9. Carefully install the heater core into the driver's side of the air distribution housing.
10. Install the 2 screws that secure the heater core to the air distribution housing, and tighten to 17 inch lbs. (2 Nm).

➡If the foam seal for the flange is deformed or damaged, it must be replaced.

11. Install the foam seal onto the flange located on the driver's side of the HVAC housing.
12. Position the heater core cover onto the driver's side of the air distribution housing and HVAC housing.
13. Install the 3 screws that secure the heater core cover to the air distribution housing and HVAC housing, and tighten to 17 inch lbs. (2 Nm).
14. Install the left floor distribution duct.

➡If the heater core is being replaced, flush the cooling system Refer to Normal Flushing procedure.

15. Install the HVAC housing assembly.

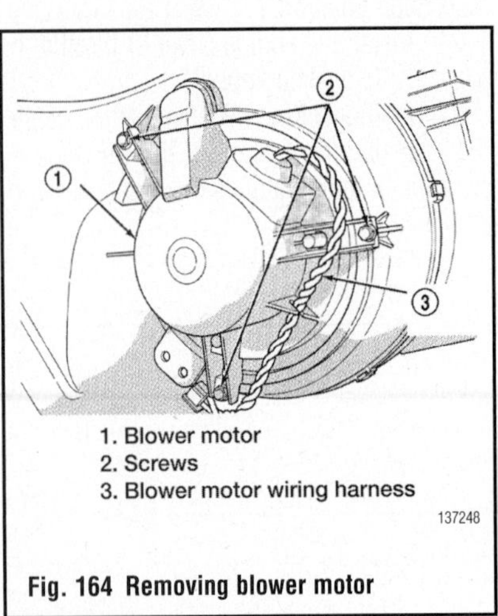

1. Blower motor
2. Screws
3. Blower motor wiring harness

137248

Fig. 164 Removing blower motor

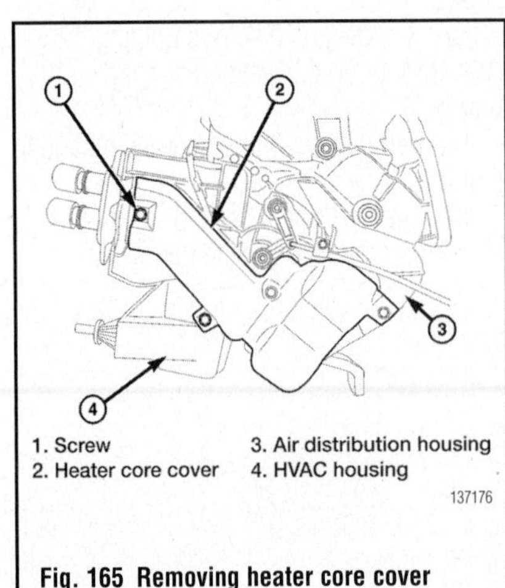

1. Screw
2. Heater core cover
3. Air distribution housing
4. HVAC housing

137176

Fig. 165 Removing heater core cover

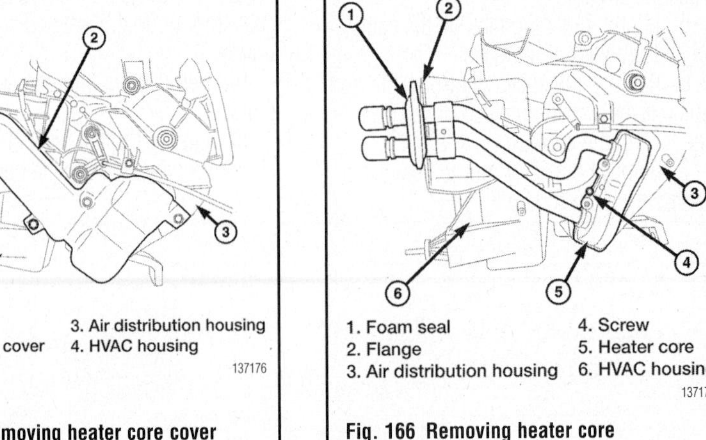

1. Foam seal
2. Flange
3. Air distribution housing
4. Screw
5. Heater core
6. HVAC housing

137178

Fig. 166 Removing heater core

STEERING

PRECAUTIONS

⁂ CAUTION

Power steering fluid, engine parts and exhaust system may be extremely hot if engine has been running. Do not start engine with any loose or disconnected hoses. Do not allow hoses to touch hot exhaust manifold or catalyst.

⁂ CAUTION

Fluid level should be checked with the engine off to prevent personal injury from moving parts.

⁂ WARNING

When the system is open, cap all open ends of the hoses, power steering pump fittings or power steering gear ports to prevent entry of foreign material into the components.

POWER STEERING GEAR

REMOVAL & INSTALLATION

See Figures 167 through 178.

➡Before proceeding, refer to Steering - Precautions.

1. Place the steering wheel in the straight-ahead position. Using a steering wheel holder, lock the steering wheel in place to keep it from rotating. This keeps the clockspring in the proper orientation.
2. At the base of the steering column, remove the coupling retainer clip, back off the pinch bolt nut, and remove the steering column coupling pinch bolt (the pinch bolt nut is caged to the coupling and is not removable). Separate the upper from the lower steering column coupling.
3. Raise and support the vehicle.
4. Remove both front tire and wheel assemblies.
5. On each side of the vehicle, remove the nut attaching the outer tie rod to the knuckle. To do this, hold the tie rod end stud with a wrench while loosening and removing the nut with a standard wrench or crowfoot wrench.
6. On each side of the vehicle, release the tie rod end from the knuckle using remover (MB991113).
7. On each side of the vehicle, remove the outer tie rod and heat shield from the knuckle.
8. If equipped with a power steering fluid pressure switch, release the locking tab on the wiring harness connector at the pressure switch, then disconnect the wiring harness connector.
9. Back out the tube nut, and remove the power steering fluid pressure hose at the gear.
10. Remove the hose clamp, then remove the cooler hose at the power steering gear outlet port fitting.
11. On vehicles equipped with crossmember-mounted power steering fluid coolers:
    a. Remove the cooler tube from the right routing clip on the gear.

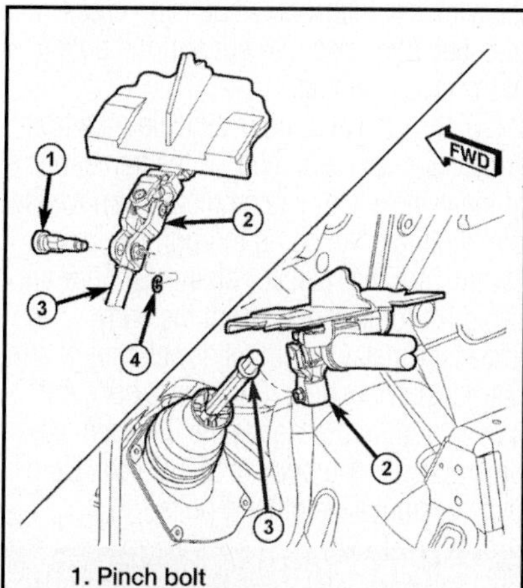

Fig. 167 Separating upper and lower steering column couplings

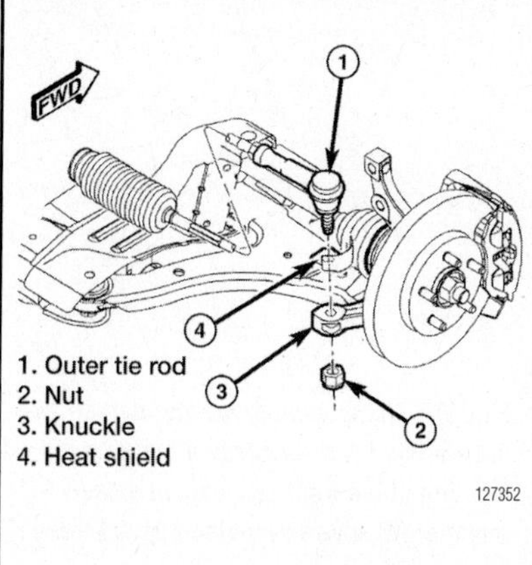

Fig. 168 View of tie rod attachment at knuckle

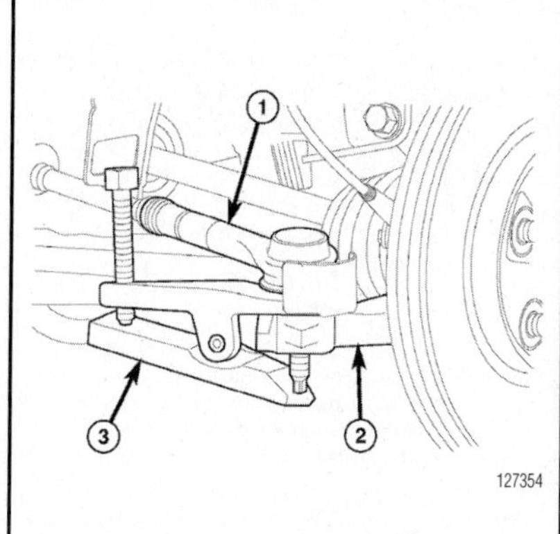

Fig. 169 Release the tie rod end (1) from the knuckle (2) using remover (3)

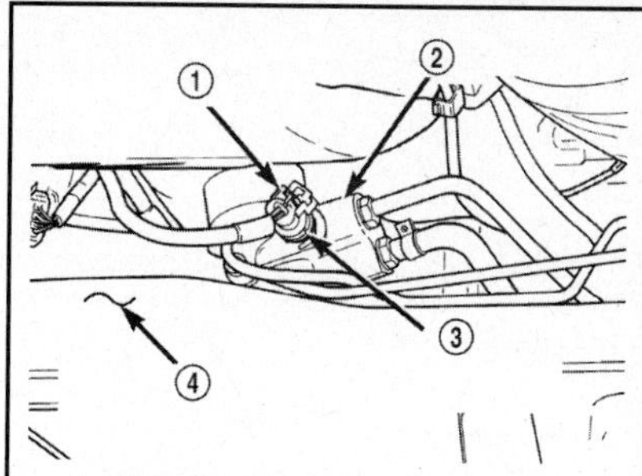

Fig. 170 Disconnecting power steering fluid pressure switch wiring harness connector

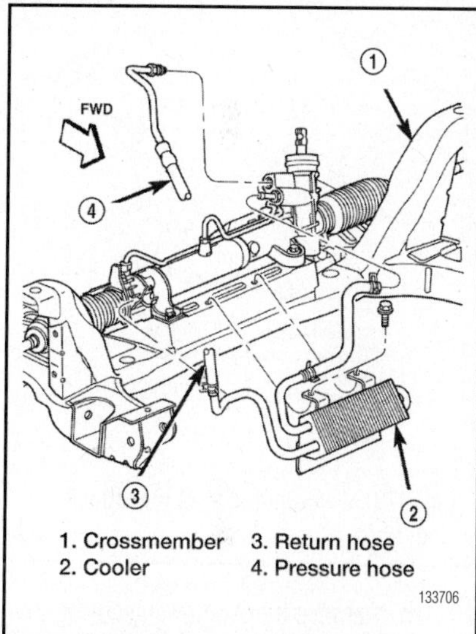

Fig. 171 Crossmember-mounted power steering fluid cooler — exploded view

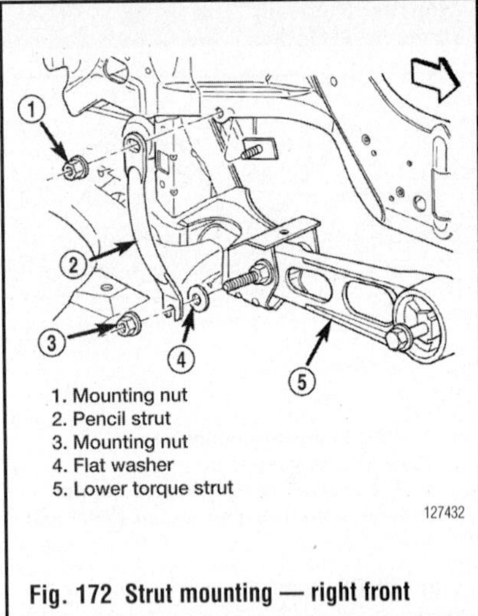

Fig. 172 Strut mounting — right front

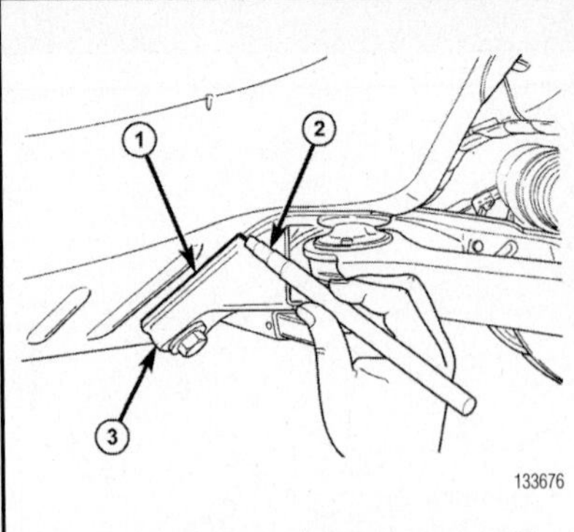

Fig. 174 Using an appropriate marker (2), draw a line (1) as necessary marking the location of the front suspension crossmember (3) where mounted against the body of the vehicle

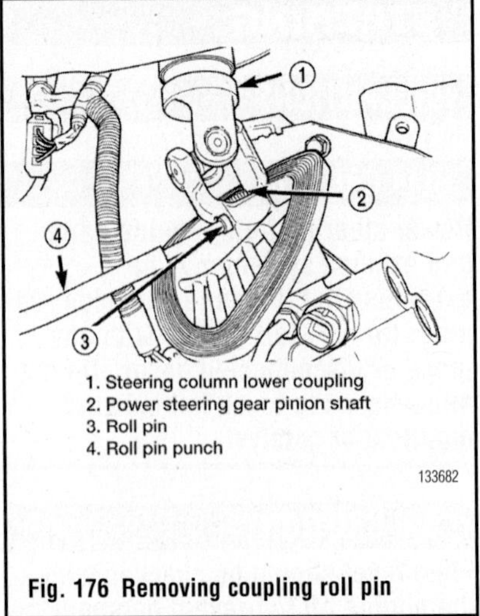

Fig. 176 Removing coupling roll pin

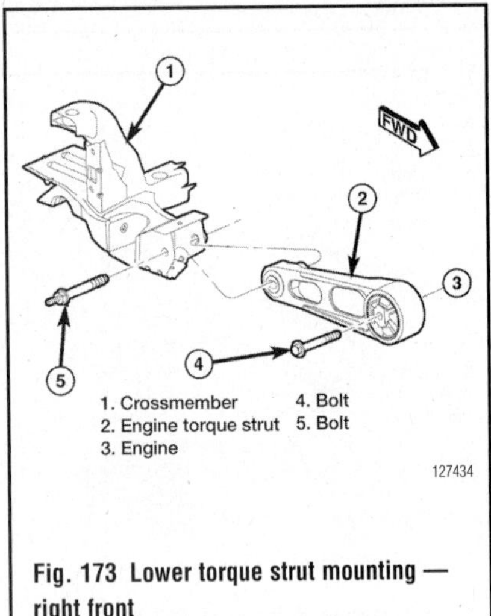

Fig. 173 Lower torque strut mounting — right front

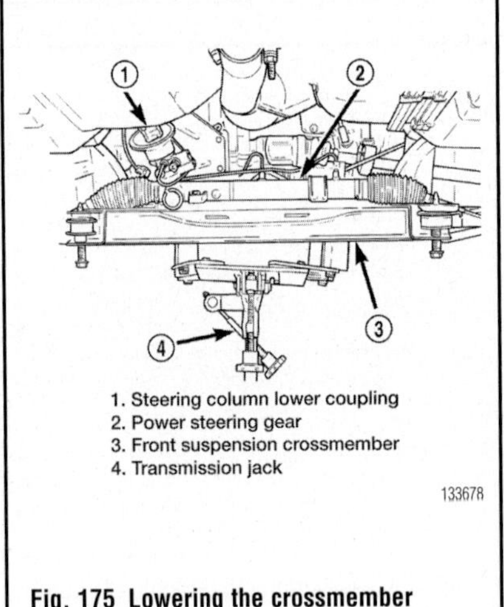

Fig. 175 Lowering the crossmember

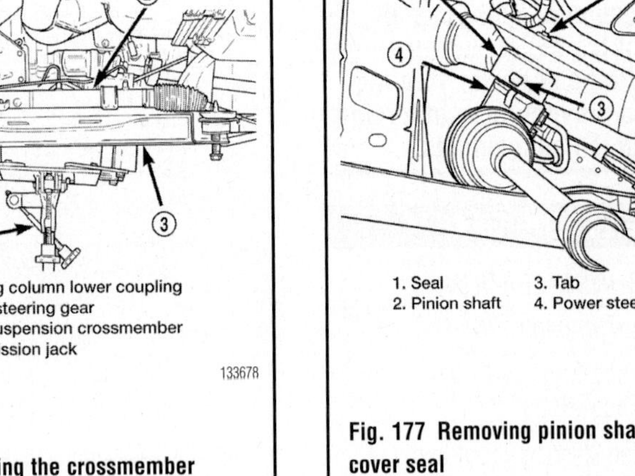

Fig. 177 Removing pinion shaft dash cover seal

b. Remove the 2 screws securing the cooler to the front suspension crossmember. Allow the cooler to hang out of the way.

12. Remove the 2 mounting nuts, then the pencil strut from the right front corner of the crossmember and body of the vehicle. Remove the washer behind the strut from the torque strut bolt.

13. Remove the one fastener securing the wheel house splash shield to the drive belt splash shield.

➡Depending on application, it may be necessary to remove some fasteners securing the front fascia to the body lower reinforcement in order to access the drive belt splash shield forward fastener.

14. Remove the fastener securing the drive belt splash shield to the front suspension crossmember.

15. Remove the fasteners securing the splash shield to the body.

16. Remove the drive belt splash shield.

17. Remove the bolt mounting the engine torque strut to the crossmember.

➡Before removing the front suspension crossmember from the vehicle, the location of the crossmember must be scribed on the body of the vehicle. Do this so the crossmember can be relocated, upon reinstallation, against the body of vehicle in the same location as before removal. If the front suspension crossmember is not reinstalled in exactly the same location as before removal, the preset front wheel alignment settings (caster and camber) will be lost.

18. Using an appropriate marker, draw a line as necessary marking the location of the front suspension crossmember where mounted against the body of the vehicle.

19. Position a transmission jack under the center of the front suspension crossmember, and raise it to support the bottom of the crossmember.

20. Loosen all 6 bolts attaching the front suspension crossmember to the frame rails of the vehicle. Do not completely remove the 2 mounting bolts going through the lower control arm rear isolator bushings. They are designed to disengage from the body threads, yet stay within the lower control arm rear isolator bushing. Back the 2 bolts out just enough to disengage the threaded tapping plates in the body of the vehicle. Completely remove the other 4 bolts.

WARNING

Lower the steering gear slowly, paying special attention to the power steering fluid hoses. Do not strain or overextend the hoses, because damage to the hoses or connecting hardware may occur.

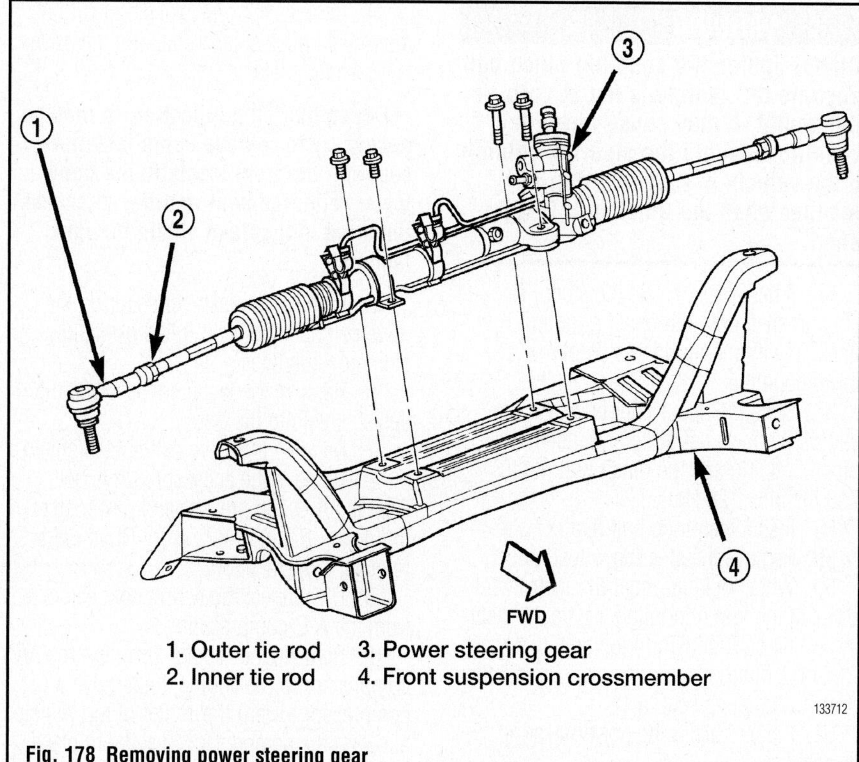

Fig. 178 Removing power steering gear

21. Lower the front suspension crossmember using the transmission jack just enough to allow access to the steering column lower coupling. When lowering front suspension crossmember, do not let the crossmember hang from the lower control arms. The weight should be supported by the transmission jack.

22. Remove the roll pin securing the steering column coupling to the power steering gear pinion shaft using a roll pin punch. Push the steering column lower coupling up and off of the power steering gear pinion shaft.

23. Release the pinion shaft dash cover seal from the tabs cast into the power steering gear housing, and remove the seal from the gear.

24. Remove the 4 bolts attaching the power steering gear to the front suspension crossmember.

25. Remove the gear from the crossmember.

To install:

26. Install the steering gear on the front suspension crossmember. Install the four gear mounting bolts. Tighten the mounting bolts to 45 ft. lbs. (61 Nm).

27. Center the power steering gear rack in its travel.

28. Install the pinion shaft dash cover seal over the power steering pinion shaft and onto the power steering gear housing. Align the holes on each side of the seal with the tabs cast into the power steering gear housing.

29. Push the column end of the steering column lower coupling partway up through the hole in the dash panel, then match the flat on the inside of the coupling to the flat on the power steering gear pinion shaft and slide the coupling onto the shaft.

30. Align the roll pin hole in the coupling to the notch in the gear pinion shaft, and install the roll pin through the coupling until it is centered.

31. Re-center the power steering gear rack in its travel as necessary.

32. Using the transmission jack, raise the front suspension crossmember and power steering gear until the crossmember contacts its mounting spot against the body and frame rails of the vehicle. As the crossmember is raised, carefully guide the steering column lower coupling up through its hole in the dash panel.

33. Start the 2 crossmember mounting bolts through the lower control arm rear isolator bushings into the tapping plates mounted in the body. Next, install the 2 front and the 2 rear mounting bolts attaching the front suspension crossmember to the frame rails of the vehicle. Lightly tighten all 6 mounting bolts to approximately 20 inch lbs. (2 Nm) to hold the front suspension crossmember in position at this time.

➡When installing the front suspension crossmember back in the vehicle, it is very important that the crossmember be attached to the body in exactly the same spot as when it was removed. Otherwise, the vehicle's wheel alignment settings (caster and camber) will be lost.

34. Using a soft-face hammer, tap the front suspension crossmember back-and-forth or side-to-side until it is aligned with the previously made positioning marks on the body of the vehicle.

35. Once the front suspension crossmember is correctly positioned:

a. Tighten the 2 crossmember mounting bolts through the lower control arm rear isolator bushings to 185 ft. lbs. (250 Nm).

b. Tighten the 4 remaining crossmember mounting bolts to 113 ft. lbs. (153 Nm).

36. Install the engine torque strut to the crossmember. To properly align and tighten the torque strut, refer to Engine Mounting Torque Struts, adjustment procedure.

37. Position the drive-belt splash shield, and install the fasteners securing it to the body.

38. Install the fastener securing the drive belt splash shield to the front suspension crossmember.

39. If previously removed, install the fasteners securing the front fascia to the body lower reinforcement.

40. Install the one fastener securing the wheel house splash shield to the drive belt splash shield.

41. Install the washer on the end of the stud extending from the torque strut bolt at the crossmember.

42. Position the pencil strut on the right front corner of the crossmember and body of the vehicle, and install the 2 mounting nuts. Tighten the nuts to 38 ft. lbs. (52 Nm).

43. Using a lint free towel, wipe clean the open power steering hose ends and the power steering gear ports.

44. Replace the pressure hose O-ring. Lubricate the new O-ring with power steering fluid.

45. On vehicles equipped with crossmember-mounted power steering fluid coolers:

a. Place the cooler in mounting position, and snap the cooler tube going to the pump into the right routing clip on the front of the gear. Close the routing clip.

b. Install the 2 screws securing the cooler to the front suspension crossmember. Tighten the screws to 90 inch lbs. (10 Nm).

46. Slide the cooler hose onto the gear outlet port fitting. Secure the clamp on the hose past the bead on the steel fitting.

WARNING

On vehicles equipped with crossmember mounted power steering fluid coolers, forward of the steering gear, the power steering fluid pressure hose routes between the front suspension crossmember and the driveshaft. When tightening the pressure hose tube nut to the steering gear, the pressure hose must be positioned (clocked) such that its final routing (after tightened) offers 4 – 10 mm clearance to the front suspension crossmember (measured at the pressure hose steel-to-rubber coupling). There should be a clocking donut on the hose to preset this distance.

47. Insert the pressure hose into its port on the power steering gear.
48. Thread the pressure hose tube nut into the gear. While making sure the pressure hose is not in contact with any vehicle components, tighten the tube nut to 23 ft. lbs. (31 Nm).
49. If equipped with a power steering fluid pressure switch, connect the wiring harness connector to the power steering fluid pressure switch. Be sure the locking tab on the wiring harness connector is securely latched following installation.
50. On each side of the vehicle, place the tie rod heat shield on the knuckle arm so that the shield is positioned straight away from the steering gear and tie rod end once installed. Align the hole in the shield with the tie rod end mounting hole.
51. On each side of the vehicle, install the outer tie rod ball stud into the hole in the knuckle arm. Start the tie rod mounting nut onto the stud. While holding the tie rod end stud with a wrench, tighten the nut with a wrench or crowfoot wrench. Tighten the nut to 40 ft. lbs. (55 Nm).
52. On both sides of vehicle, install the tire and wheel assembly. Install and tighten wheel mounting nuts to 100 ft. lbs. (135 Nm).
53. Lower the vehicle.
54. Position the dash-to-lower coupling seal in place over the lower coupling's plastic collar.

➡Verify that grease is present on the lip of the dash-to-coupling seal where it contacts the coupling's plastic collar.

55. Verify the front wheels of the vehicle are in the straight-ahead position.

WARNING

Do not tighten the coupling pinch bolt anytime the vehicle is not at curb riding height. It may cause unwanted conditions within the steering column if the vehicle is suspended in any manner when the pinch bolt is tightened.

56. If necessary, rotate the steering column shaft until the upper coupling lines up with the rounded side of the lower coupling.
57. Slide the upper coupling over the end of the lower coupling and install the pinch bolt. Tighten the pinch bolt nut to 250 inch lbs. (28 Nm).
58. Install the pinch bolt retainer clip.
59. Remove the steering wheel holder.
60. While looking under the instrument panel at the lower coupling, rotate the steering wheel back-and-forth to verify that the lower coupling does not squeak against the dash-to-coupling seal.
61. Fill and bleed the power steering system.
62. Check for fluid leaks.
63. Adjust the front wheel toe setting.

POWER STEERING PUMP

REMOVAL & INSTALLATION

See Figures 179 through 184.

➡Before proceeding, refer to Steering - Precautions.

1. Siphon as much fluid as possible from the power steering fluid reservoir.
2. Raise and support the vehicle.
3. Remove the right front tire and wheel assembly.
4. Remove the one fastener securing the wheel house splash shield to the drive belt splash shield.

➡Depending on application, it may be necessary to remove some fasteners securing the front fascia to the body lower reinforcement in order to access the drive belt splash shield forward fastener.

5. Remove the fastener securing the drive belt splash shield to the front suspension crossmember.
6. Remove the fasteners securing the splash shield to the body.
7. Remove the drive belt splash shield.
8. Remove the accessory drive belt from the A/C compressor and power steering pump. Refer to Accessory Drive Belts, removal & installation.
9. Disconnect the wiring connectors from the A/C compressor.
10. Remove the 4 bolts fastening the A/C compressor to the engine, then move the compressor toward the center of the vehicle, allowing the compressor to settle in place.
11. From below, place a crowfoot wrench on a long extension onto the pressure hose tube nut at the pump.
12. Place a shop towel between the crowfoot and the pump pulley to avoid slipping and possibly damaging the pulley.
13. Unthread the tube nut, and lower the pressure hose out of the pump.
14. Lower the vehicle.
15. Remove the grille from the front of the vehicle.
16. Remove the hood-opening weatherstrip from across the radiator closure panel.
17. Remove the fastener, then the ambient temperature sensor from the radiator closure panel.

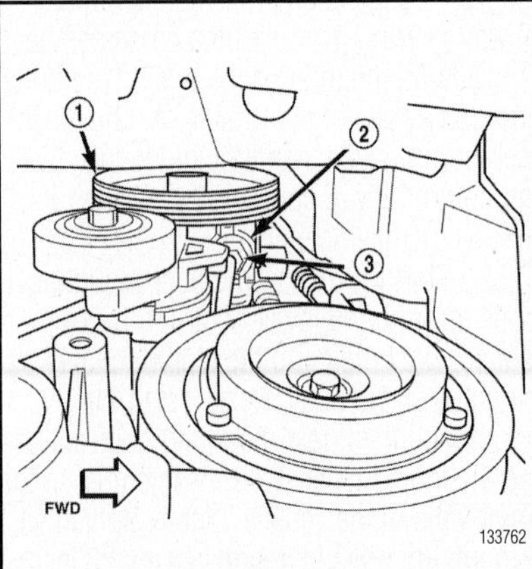

Fig. 179 View of pump pulley (1), power steering pump (2) and pressure hose tube nut (3)

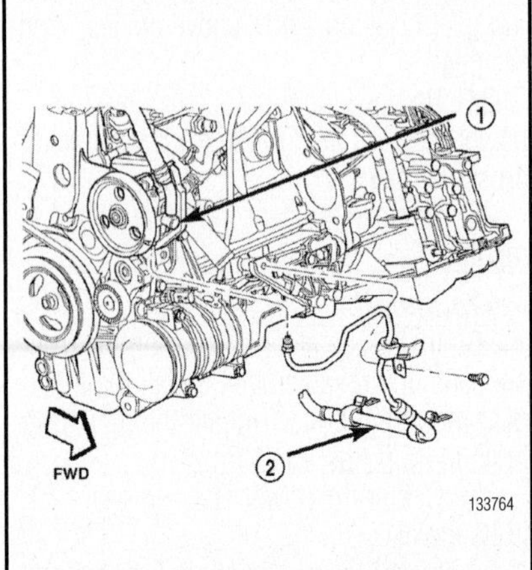

Fig. 180 Unthread the tube nut, and lower the pressure hose (2) out of the pump (1)

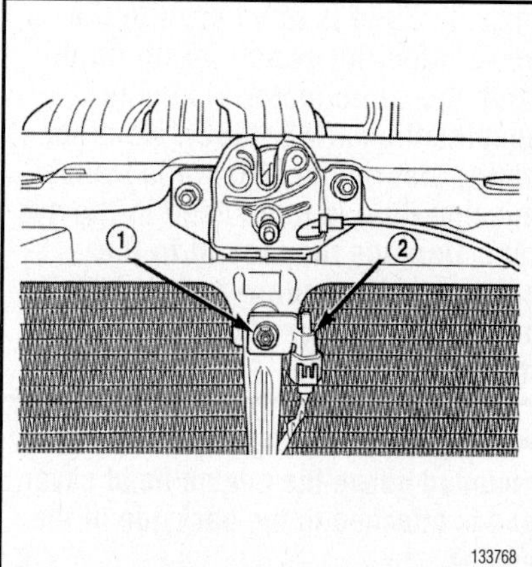

Fig. 181 Remove the fastener (1), then the ambient temperature sensor (2) from the radiator closure panel

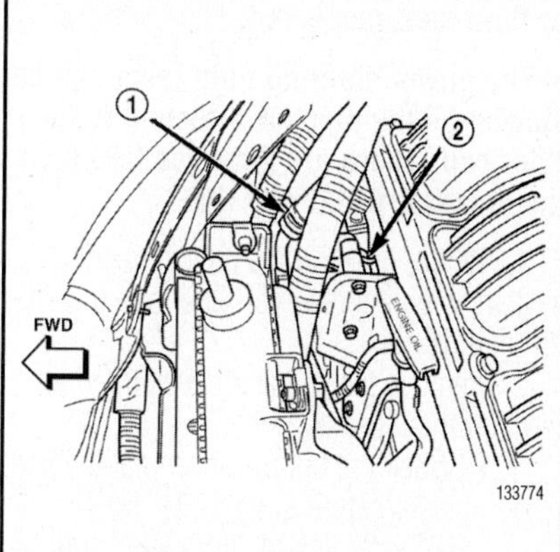

Fig. 182 Remove the clamp (1) securing the supply hose to the power steering pump (2) supply fitting

18. Remove the 7 fasteners securing the upper radiator closure panel in place, then remove the panel.

19. Lift the cooling module out of its lower mounts, and carefully move it toward the left side of the vehicle. It will move only a limited amount with the hoses still connected. Do not force it.

➡For additional room, the right side bolts securing the lower radiator closure panel in front of the cooling module can be removed.

20. Using a bungee cord, tie the cooling module forward as shown. Be sure to attach the cord in a location that will not damage the vehicle. Do not over-tighten the bungee cord. It just needs to hold the module forward.

21. Remove the clamp securing the supply hose to the power steering pump supply fitting, then remove the hose from the supply fitting.

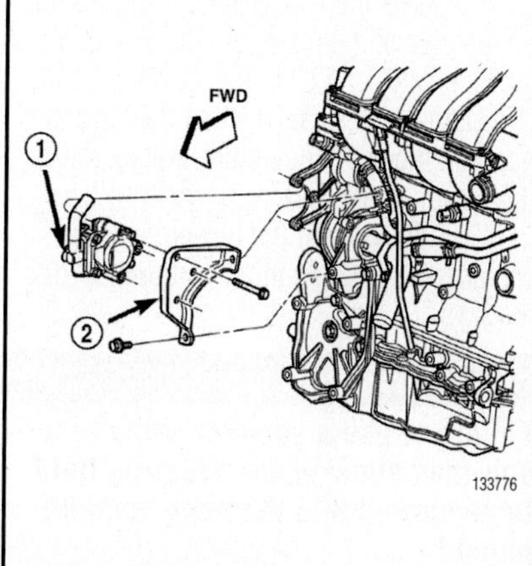

Fig. 183 View of power steering pump (1) and support bracket (2)

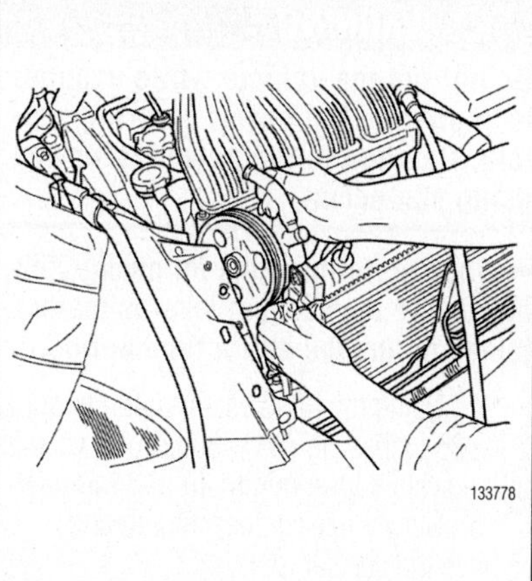

Fig. 184 Removing the power steering pump with pulley

22. Remove the 3 bolts securing the pump in place.

23. Remove the 2 bolts securing the stamped steel support bracket to the engine block. Remove the bracket.

24. Ease the cooling module forward (don't force it), and remove the power steering pump with pulley where shown.

To install:

25. Using a lint free towel, wipe clean the open power steering pressure hose end and the power steering pump port.

26. Replace any used O-rings. Lubricate the new O-rings with power steering fluid.

27. Ease the cooling module forward, don't force it, and install the power steering pump with pulley into its mounting area.

28. Place the pump in mounting position with the stamped steel support bracket behind it. Install the 3 bolts through the bracket and pump, into the threaded engine cover. Do not tighten the bolts at this time.

29. Install the 2 bolts fastening the bracket to the engine block, and tighten to 40 ft. lbs. (54 Nm).

30. Tighten the 3 pump mounting bolts previously installed to 250 inch lbs. (28 Nm).

✲✲ WARNING

Make sure the supply hose is routed above the engine timing chain cover. The power steering fluid supply hose must remain clear of any unfriendly surface that can cause possible damage to it.

31. Push the fluid supply hose onto the pump supply fitting. Expand the hose clamp and slide it over the hose and pump supply fitting. Secure the clamp once it is past the bead formed into the fluid reservoir fitting.

32. Raise and support the vehicle.

33. Insert the end of the pressure hose into the pump. Thread the fluid pressure hose tube nut into the pump.

34. Using a crowfoot wrench on a long extension with a torque wrench, tighten the pressure hose tube nut (from below) at the power steering pump to 23 ft. lbs. (31 Nm).

35. Install the 4 bolts fastening the A/C compressor to the engine.

36. Tighten the mounting bolts to 250 inch lbs. (28 Nm).

37. Install the A/C compressor wiring connectors.

38. Install the A/C drive belt. Refer to Accessory Drive Belts, removal & installation.

39. Position the drive-belt splash shield and install the fasteners securing it to the body.

40. Install the fastener securing the drive belt splash shield to the front suspension crossmember.

41. If previously removed, install the fasteners securing the front fascia to the body lower reinforcement.

42. Install the one fastener securing the wheel house splash shield to the drive belt splash shield.

43. Install the tire and wheel assembly. Install and tighten wheel mounting nuts to 100 ft. lbs. (135 Nm).

44. Lower the vehicle.

45. Remove the bungee cord and move the cooling module back into is lower mounts.

46. If previously removed, install the right side bolts securing the lower radiator closure panel in front of the cooling module.

47. Install the radiator closure panel and fasten it in place.

48. Install the ambient temperature sensor on the radiator closure panel using the fastener.

49. Install the hood-opening weather-strip across the radiator closure panel.

50. Install the grille on the front of the vehicle.

51. Fill and bleed the power steering system.

52. Check for leaks.

BLEEDING

See Figure 185.

✽✽ CAUTION

The fluid level should be checked with engine off to prevent injury from moving components.

✽✽ WARNING

Mopar ® Power Steering Fluid + 4 or Mopar ® ATF+4 Automatic Transmission Fluid is to be used in the power steering system. Both fluids have the same material standard specifications (MS-9602). No other power steering or automatic transmission fluid is to be used in the system. Damage may result to the power steering pump and system if another fluid is used. Do not overfill the system.

✽✽ WARNING

If the air is not purged from the power steering system correctly, pump failure could result.

➡Be sure the vacuum tool used in the following procedure is clean and free of any fluids.

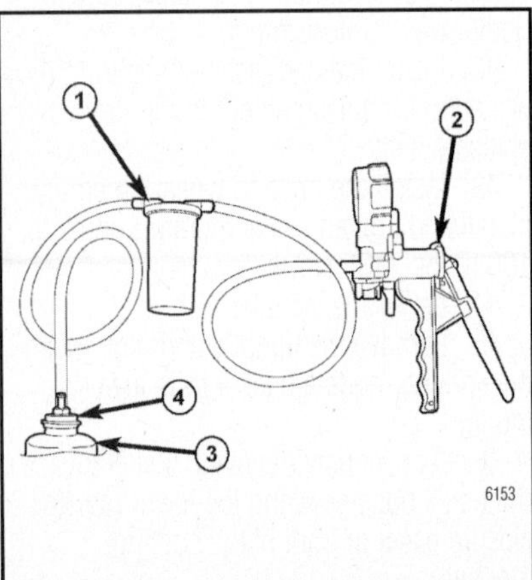

Fig. 185 Bleeding power steering system

1. Check the fluid level. As measured on the side of the reservoir, the level should indicate between FULL and ADD (or MAX. COLD and MIN. COLD) when the fluid is at normal ambient temperature. Adjust the fluid level as necessary.

2. Tightly insert the power steering cap adapter (9688A) into the mouth of the reservoir.

✽✽ WARNING

Failure to use a vacuum pump reservoir may allow power steering fluid to be sucked into the hand vacuum pump.

3. Attach hand vacuum pump (C-4207-A), with vacuum pump reservoir attached, to the power steering cap adapter.

✽✽ WARNING

Do not run the vehicle while vacuum is applied to the power steering system. Damage to the power steering pump can occur.

➡When performing the following step, make sure the vacuum level is maintained during the entire time period.

4. Using the hand vacuum pump, apply 20 – 25 inches Hg (68 – 85 kPa) of vacuum to the system for a minimum of 3 minutes.

5. Slowly release the vacuum and remove the special tools.

6. Adjust the fluid level as necessary.

7. Repeat the procedure until the fluid no longer drops when vacuum is applied.

8. Start the engine and cycle the steering wheel lock-to-lock 3 times.

➡Do not hold the steering wheel at the stops.

9. Stop the engine and check for leaks at all connections.

10. Check for any signs of air in the reservoir, and check the fluid level.

11. If air is present, repeat the procedure as necessary.

FLUID FILL PROCEDURE

See Figure 186.

✽✽ CAUTION

Fluid level should be checked with the engine OFF to prevent personal injury from moving parts and to assure an accurate fluid level reading.

✽✽ WARNING

Only Mopar ® Power Steering Fluid + 4 or Mopar ® ATF+4 Automatic Transmission Fluid is to be used in the power steering system. Both fluids have the same material standard specifications (MS-9602). No other power steering or automatic transmission fluid is to be used in the system. Damage may result to the power steering pump and system if another fluid is used. Do not overfill the system.

➡The power steering fluid reservoir is mounted above the engine head cover, and is attached to the backside of the engine.

➡Although not required at specific intervals, the fluid level may be checked periodically. Check the fluid level any time there is a system noise or fluid leak suspected.

➡The power steering fluid level can be viewed on the dipstick attached to the filler cap. There are 2 ranges listed on the dipstick: COLD and HOT.

1. Before opening the power steering system, wipe the reservoir filler cap free of dirt and debris.

2. Remove the cap and check the fluid level on the dipstick.

- When the fluid is at normal ambient temperature (about 70 – 80°F (21 – 27°C), the fluid level should read between the minimum and maximum area of the COLD range.
- When the fluid is hot, fluid level is allowed to read up to the highest end of the HOT range.

3. If fluid level is below recommended range, add fluid until fluid level is within appropriate range.

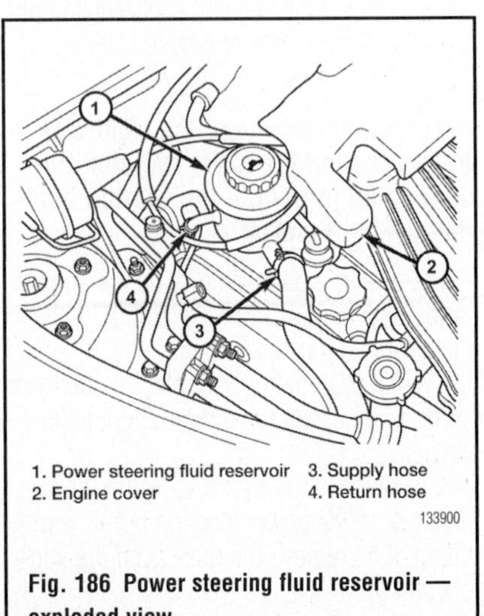

Fig. 186 Power steering fluid reservoir — exploded view

PRECAUTIONS

**** CAUTION**

Chrysler LLC does not manufacture any vehicles or replacement parts that contain asbestos. Aftermarket products may or may not contain asbestos. Refer to aftermarket product packaging for product information.

**** CAUTION**

Whether the product contains asbestos or not, dust and dirt can accumulate on brake parts during normal use. Follow practices prescribed by appropriate regulations for the handling, processing and disposing of dust and debris.

**** WARNING**

Only frame contact or wheel lift hoisting equipment can be used on this vehicle. It cannot be hoisted using equipment designed to lift a vehicle by the rear axle. If this type of hoisting equipment is used, damage to rear suspension components will occur.

➡If a suspension component becomes bent, damaged or fails, no attempt should be made to straighten or repair it. Always replace it with a new component.

LOWER BALL JOINT

REMOVAL & INSTALLATION

See Figures 187 through 190.

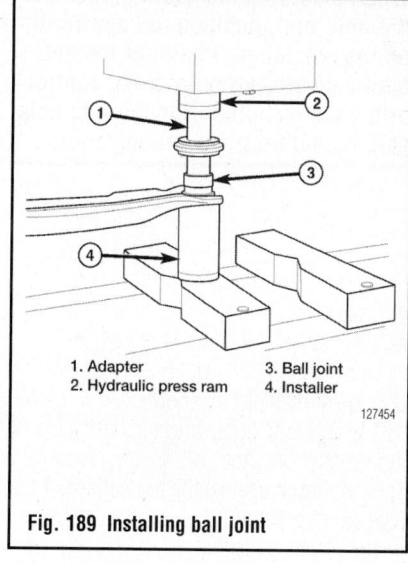

1. Before servicing the vehicle, refer to the Precautions section.
2. Remove the lower control arm from the vehicle. Refer to Lower Control Arm, removal & installation.
3. Using a screwdriver or other suitable tool, pry the seal boot off of the ball joint.
4. Position the receiver cup on a hydraulic press open end up.
5. Position the control arm on top of the receiver cup so that the bottom of the ball joint sets inside.
6. Place the larger diameter end of the adapter on top of the ball joint as shown.
7. Lower the hydraulic press ram, pressing the ball joint completely out of the lower control arm, into the receiver cup.

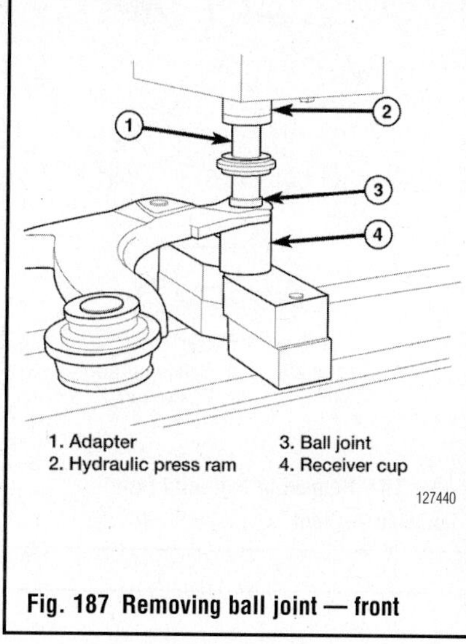

Fig. 187 Removing ball joint — front

8. Remove the tools, ball joint and arm from the hydraulic press.

To install:

9. By hand, position the ball joint into its bore on the lower control arm from the bottom side. To avoid binding upon installation, be sure the ball joint is not cocked in the bore.

**** WARNING**

When installing a ball joint in its mounting hole in the lower control arm, position the ball joint so the notch in the ball joint stud is facing the lower control arm front isolator bushing. This will ease pinch bolt installation once the ball joint is installed to the knuckle.

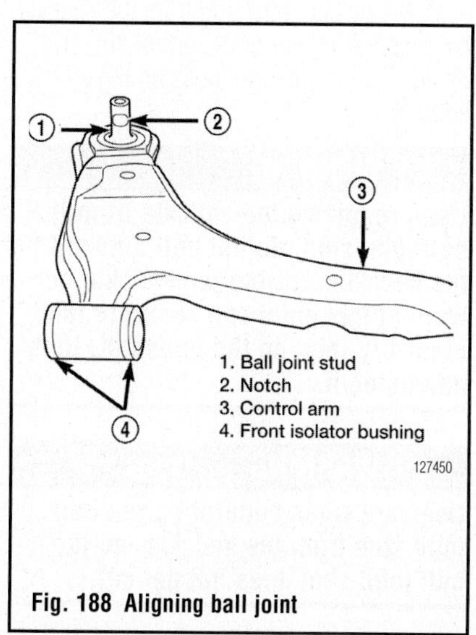

Fig. 188 Aligning ball joint

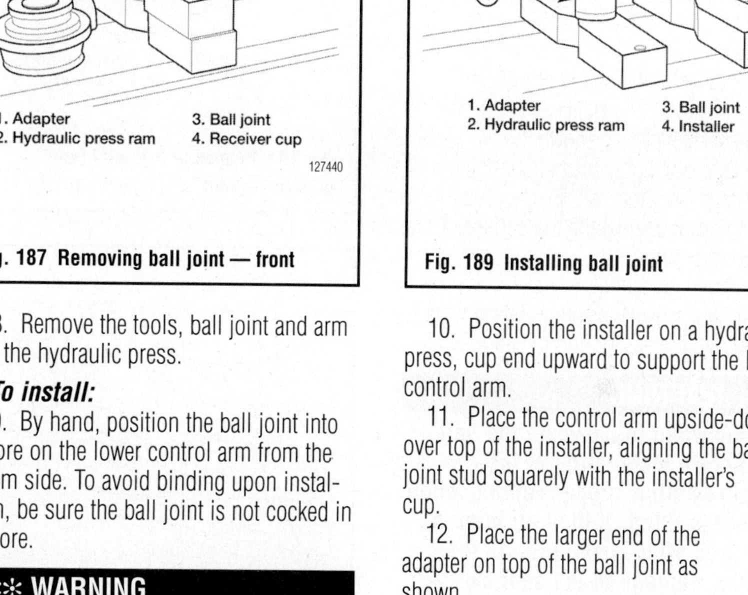

Fig. 189 Installing ball joint

10. Position the installer on a hydraulic press, cup end upward to support the lower control arm.
11. Place the control arm upside-down over top of the installer, aligning the ball joint stud squarely with the installer's cup.
12. Place the larger end of the adapter on top of the ball joint as shown.
13. Lower the hydraulic press ram, pressing the ball joint into the lower control arm until the shoulder on the ball joint bottoms against the lower control arm ball joint bore. Do not apply excessive pressure against ball joint and lower control arm once the ball joint bottoms.
14. Remove the tools and arm from the hydraulic press.

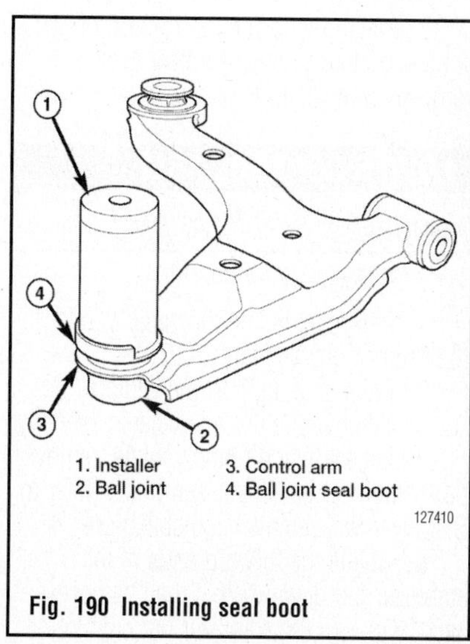

Fig. 190 Installing seal boot

✱✱ WARNING

When installing the sealing boot on the ball joint, position the upward lip on the outside perimeter of the seal boot outward, away from the control arm once installed. It is there to help shield heat from the sealing boot.

15. Place a NEW ball joint seal boot over the ball joint stud. The upward lip located on the outside perimeter of the seal boot must point outward away from the control arm once installed. Start the sealing boot over the sides of the ball joint by hand.
16. Position the installer over the sealing boot outer diameter as shown.
17. By hand, apply pressure to the top of the installer until the seal boot is pressed squarely down against the top surface of the lower control arm.
18. Remove the tool.
19. If not already installed, install a standard zirc-type grease fitting in ball joint.

✱✱ WARNING

It is important to lubricate the ball joint before installation of the knuckle to allow proper venting when the seal is filled. If the ball joint is lubricated after installation to the knuckle, damage to the seal can occur.

20. Using a hand-operated pump grease gun, fill the ball joint seal boot with multi-mileage lube until grease pushes out past the ball joint stem. Wipe off any overfill.
21. Remove the standard zirc-type grease fitting and reinstall the headless grease fitting from the original ball joint to prevent future lubricating. Be sure to properly clean headless grease fitting prior to installation.
22. Install the lower control arm on the vehicle. Refer to Lower Control Arm, removal & installation.

LOWER CONTROL ARM

REMOVAL & INSTALLATION

See Figures 191 through 195.

1. Before servicing the vehicle, refer to the Precautions section.
2. Raise and support the vehicle.
3. Remove the tire and wheel assembly.
4. On each side of the vehicle, remove both stabilizer bar link assemblies. Refer to Stabilizer Bar, removal & installation.
5. Rotate the forward ends of the stabilizer bar downward. It may be necessary to loosen the stabilizer bar cushion retainer bolts a little to ease any turning resistance.
6. Remove the nut and pinch bolt clamping the ball joint stud to the knuckle.
7. Using an appropriate prying tool, separate the ball joint stud from the knuckle by prying down on lower control arm and up against the ball joint boss on the knuckle.

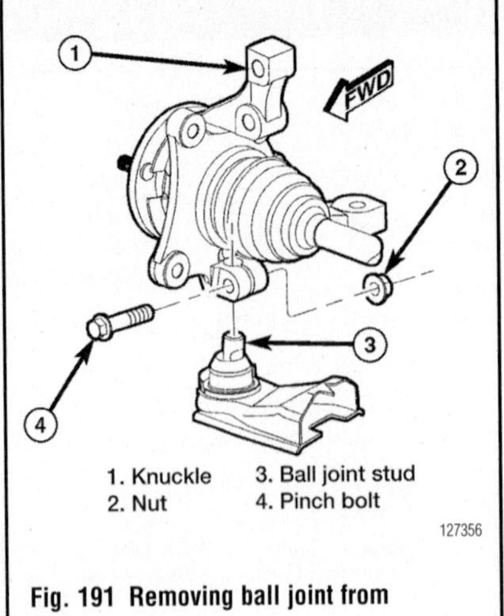

Fig. 191 Removing ball joint from knuckle — front

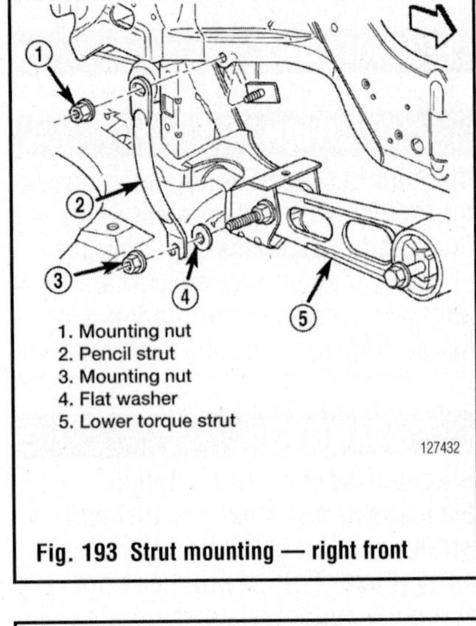

Fig. 193 Strut mounting — right front

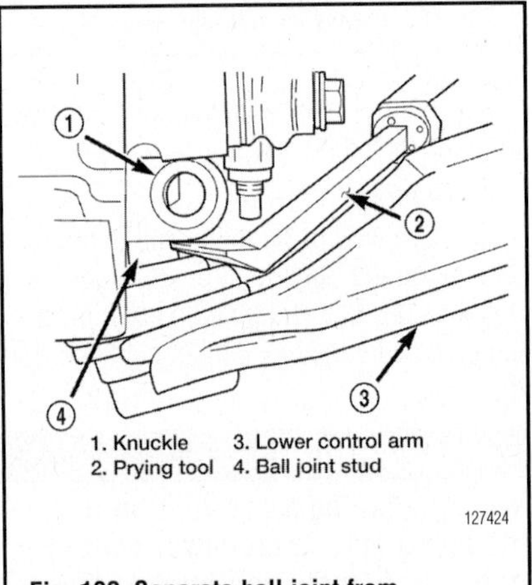

Fig. 192 Separate ball joint from knuckle — front

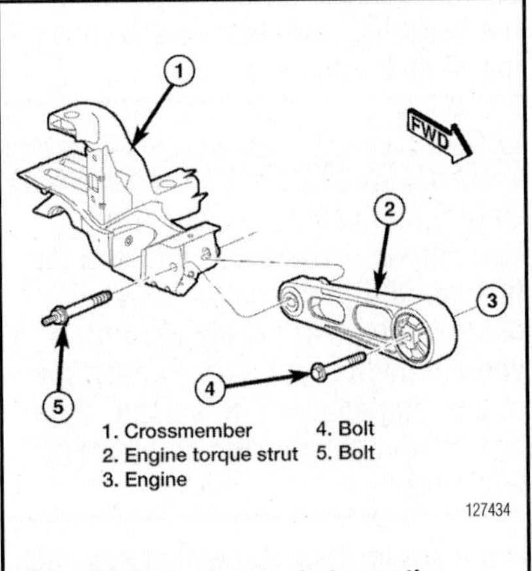

Fig. 194 Lower torque strut mounting — right front

✱✱ WARNING

Upon removing the knuckle from the ball joint stud, do not pull outward on the knuckle. Pulling the knuckle outward at this point can separate the inner C/V joint on the halfshaft, thus damaging it.

✱✱ WARNING

Use care when separating the ball joint stud from the knuckle, so the ball joint seal does not get cut.

8. If the right lower control arm is being serviced:
   a. Remove the one fastener securing the wheel house splash shield to the drive belt splash shield.
   b. Remove the fastener securing the drive belt splash shield to the front suspension crossmember.
   c. Remove the 3 fasteners securing the splash shield to the body.
   d. Remove the drive belt splash shield.

➡Depending on application, it may be necessary to remove some fasteners securing the front fascia to the body lower reinforcement in order to access drive belt splash shield forward fastener.

9. If the right lower control arm is being serviced:
   a. Remove the mounting nuts, then the pencil strut from the right front corner of the crossmember and body of the vehicle.

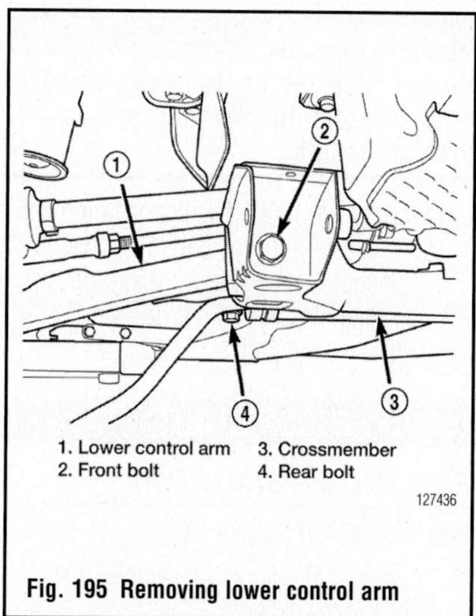

Fig. 195 Removing lower control arm

b. Remove the washer behind the strut from the torque strut bolt.

10. If the right lower control arm is being serviced:

a. Remove the bolt mounting the engine torque strut to the engine.

b. Remove the bolt mounting the engine torque strut to the crossmember.

c. Remove the engine torque strut.

11. Remove the front bolt attaching the lower control arm to the front suspension crossmember.

12. Remove the rear bolt attaching the lower control arm to the front suspension crossmember and frame rail.

13. Remove the lower control arm from the crossmember.

To inspect:

➡Do not attempt to repair or straighten a broken or bent lower control arm. If damaged, the lower control arm stamping is serviced only as a complete component.

➡The serviceable components of the lower control arm are: the ball joint, the ball joint grease seal and the lower control arm rear isolator bushing. The front isolator bushing is not replaceable. If the front isolator bushing needs to be replaced, the entire lower control arm must be replaced.

14. Inspect the lower control arm for signs of damage from contact with the ground or road debris. If the lower control arm shows any sign of damage, look for distortion.

15. Inspect both lower control arm isolator bushings for severe deterioration, and replace lower control arm or rear bushing as required.

To install:

16. Place the lower control arm into the front suspension crossmember.

17. Install, but do not fully tighten, the rear bolt attaching the lower control arm to the crossmember and frame rail.

18. Install, but do not fully tighten, the front bolt attaching the lower control arm to the crossmember.

19. With no weight on the lower control arm, tighten the lower control arm rear (and suspension crossmember) bolt to 185 ft. lbs. (250 Nm).

20. With no weight on the lower control arm, tighten the lower control arm front bolt to 125 ft. lbs. (170 Nm).

21. Install the ball joint stud into the knuckle, aligning the bolt hole in the knuckle boss with the notch formed in the side of the ball joint stud.

22. Install a NEW ball joint stud pinch bolt and nut. Tighten the nut to 70 ft. lbs. (95 Nm).

23. If the right lower control arm is being serviced, install the engine torque strut. To properly align and tighten the torque strut, refer to Engine Mounting Torque Strut, adjustment procedure.

24. If the right lower control arm is being serviced, install the pencil strut as follows:

a. Install the washer on the end of the stud extending from the torque strut bolt at the crossmember.

b. Position the pencil strut on the right front corner of the crossmember and body of the vehicle, and install the mounting nuts. Tighten the nuts to 38 ft. lbs. (52 Nm).

25. If the right lower control arm is being serviced:

a. Position the drive-belt splash shield and install the fasteners securing it to the body.

b. Install the fastener securing the drive belt splash shield to the front suspension crossmember.

c. If previously removed, install the fasteners securing the front fascia to the body lower reinforcement.

d. Install the one fastener securing the wheel house splash shield to the drive belt splash shield.

26. Rotate the forward ends of the stabilizer bar into mounted position.

27. Clean the threads of the stabilizer bar link bolts, then apply Mopar ® Lock And Seal or equivalent to the threads.

28. On both sides of the vehicle, install both stabilizer bar link assemblies. Start each stabilizer bar link bolt with the lower bushing from the bottom, through the stabilizer bar, inner link bushing, lower control arm, and into the upper retainer/nut and bushing. Do not fully tighten the link assemblies at this time.

29. Install tire and wheel assembly. Install and tighten wheel mounting nuts to 100 ft. lbs. (135 Nm).

30. Lower the vehicle.

➡It may be necessary to put the vehicle on a platform hoist or alignment rack to gain access to the stabilizer bar mounting bolts with the vehicle at curb height.

31. With the vehicle at curb height, tighten each stabilizer bar link by holding the upper retainer/nut with a wrench while turning the link bolt. Tighten each link bolt to 22 ft. lbs. (29 Nm).

32. If previously loosened, tighten the stabilizer bar cushion retainer bolts to 18 ft. lbs. (25 Nm).

33. Perform wheel alignment as necessary.

CONTROL ARM BUSHING REPLACEMENT

See Figures 196 through 199.

➡The removal and installation of the rear isolator bushing from the lower control arm is only to be done with the lower control arm removed from the vehicle. The front isolator bushing is not serviceable

➡To maintain better control when removing the rear isolator bushing, it works best to mount the bushing removal tools in a vise.

1. Install the receiver cup into the cup of the ball joint press, and tighten the set screw.

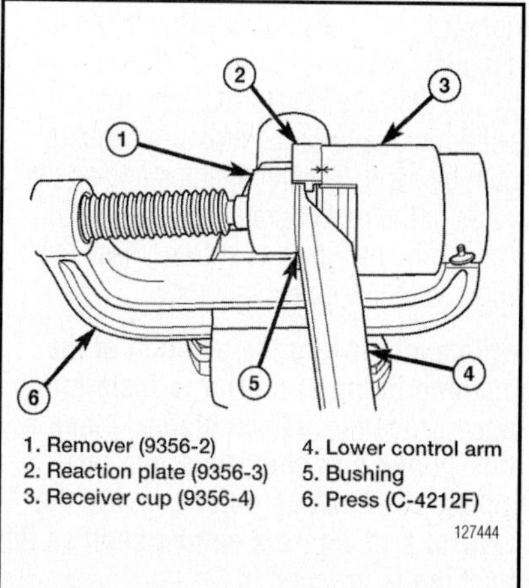

Fig. 196 Positioning tools for bushing removal — front

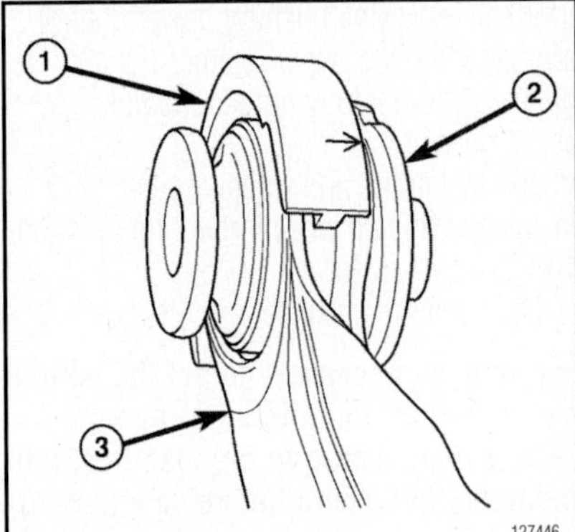

Fig. 197 Install the reaction plate (1) over the end of the lower control arm (3) so that the arrows on the reaction plate point toward the bushing flange (2) on the bottom of the arm

2. Install the remover on the tip of the ball joint press screw-drive.
3. Install the reaction plate over the end of the control arm so that the arrows on the reaction plate point toward the bushing flange on the bottom of the arm as shown.
4. Place the reaction plate (on the lower control arm) against the outer flange of the receiver cup as shown. Line up the arrows on the reaction plate with that on the receiver cup, and tighten the press screw-drive until the remover contacts the outer circumference of the bushing. Make sure the remover contacts the bushing circumference evenly all the way around.
5. Continue to tighten the screw-drive until the bushing is pressed completely out of the lower control arm.
6. Back off the screw-drive, and remove the lower control arm and isolator bushing. Remove the reaction plate from the arm.

To install:

7. Back the ball joint press set screw outward so it does not extend out into the cup area.
8. Start the isolator bushing into the bottom of the lower control arm bushing bore by hand. Position the bushing so the voids in the rubber are aligned in relationship to the ball joint as shown. Place the wider void toward the ball joint.

➡To avoid losing the position of the bushing in the arm prior to installation, once procedure is completed, place a line (using an appropriate marker) across the bushing outer can and the control arm where it can be seen as the bushing is pressed in.

9. Install the installer on the tip of the ball joint press screw-drive.

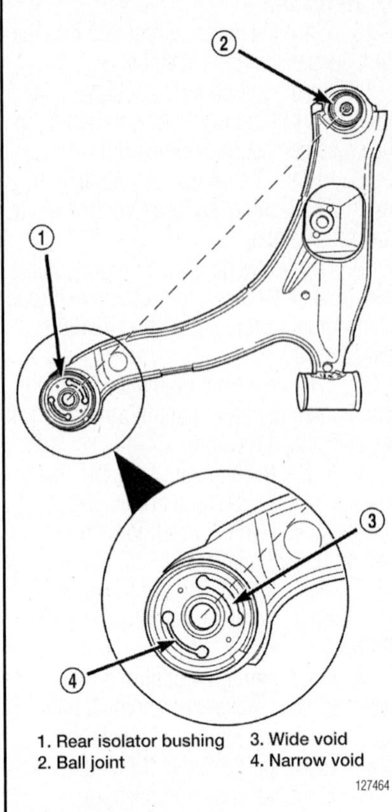

Fig. 198 Aligning bushing with ball joint — front

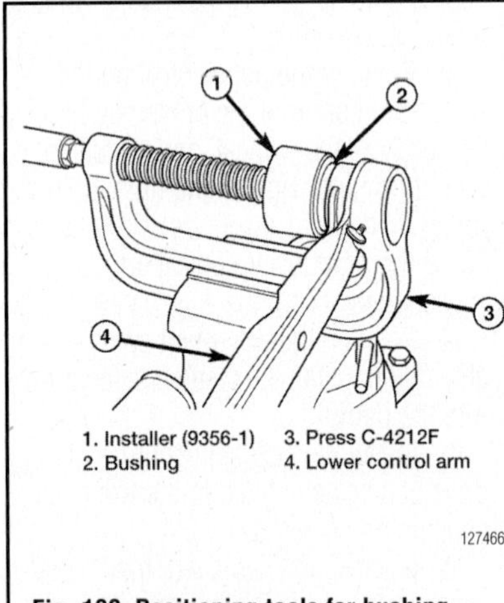

Fig. 199 Positioning tools for bushing installation — front

10. Place the lower control arm upper flange against the cup area of the ball joint press, and turn the screw-drive until the installer contacts the outer circumference of the bushing. Make sure the bushing flange sits squarely in the step built into the installer.
11. Using hand tools, slowly tighten the screw-drive until the bushing bottoms in the lower control arm bushing bore.

**** WARNING**

Do not over-tighten the screw-drive, or damage to the bushing, arm or tool can result.

12. Back off the screw-drive and remove the control arm from the ball joint press.
13. Install the lower control arm on the vehicle. Refer to Lower Control Arm, removal & installation.

MACPHERSON STRUT

REMOVAL & INSTALLATION

See Figures 200 through 202.

1. Before servicing the vehicle, refer to the Precautions section.
2. Raise and support the vehicle.
3. Remove the tire and wheel assembly.

➡If both strut assemblies are to be removed, mark the strut assemblies right or left and keep the parts separated to avoid mix-up. Not all parts of the strut assembly are interchangeable side-to-side.

➡The ground strap attached to the rear of the strut mounts to the ear extending toward the front of the vehicle.

4. Remove the screw securing the ground strap to the rear of the strut.
5. If the vehicle is equipped with Anti-lock Brakes (ABS), remove the screw securing the wheel speed sensor routing bracket to the rear of the strut.

**** WARNING**

The strut assembly-to-knuckle attaching bolts are serrated and must not be turned during removal. Hold the bolts stationary in the knuckle while removing the nuts, and then tap the bolts out using a pin punch.

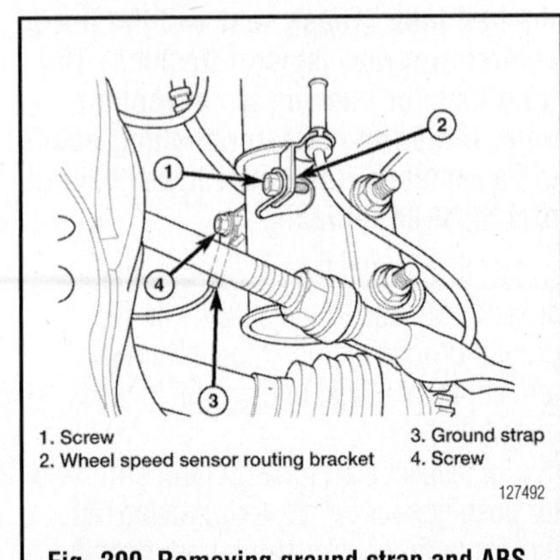

Fig. 200 Removing ground strap and ABS sensor at strut

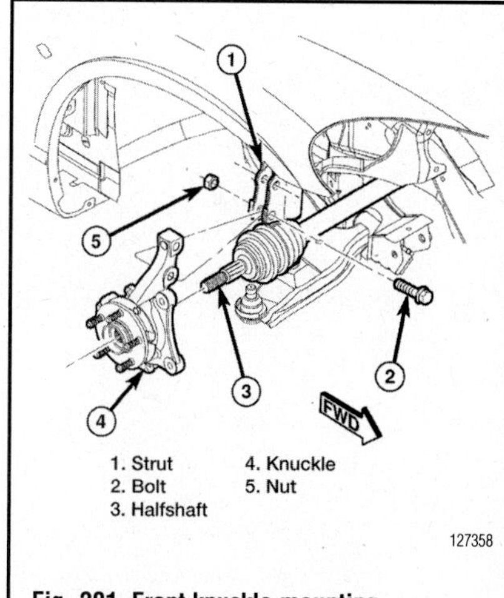

Fig. 201 Front knuckle mounting — exploded view

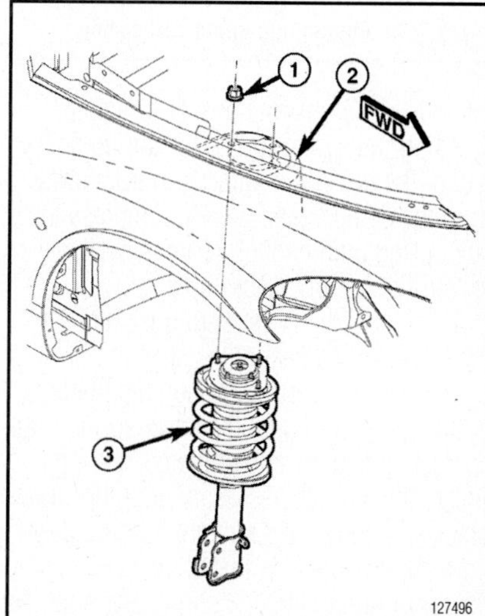

Fig. 202 Remove the 3 nuts (1) attaching the strut assembly upper mount to the strut tower (2). Remove the strut assembly (3) from the vehicle

6. While holding the bolt heads stationary, remove the 2 nuts from the bolts attaching the strut to the knuckle.

7. Remove the 2 bolts attaching the strut to the knuckle using a pin punch.

8. Lower the vehicle just enough to open the hood, but without letting the tires touch the ground.

9. Remove the 3 nuts attaching the strut assembly upper mount to the strut tower.

10. Remove the strut assembly from the vehicle.

11. For disassembly, refer to Overhaul procedure.

To install:

12. Raise the strut assembly into the strut tower, aligning the 3 studs on the strut assembly upper mount with the holes in strut tower. Install the 3 mounting nuts on the studs. Tighten the 3 nuts to 19 ft. lbs. (26 Nm).

**** WARNING**

The strut assembly-to-knuckle attaching bolts are serrated and must not be turned during installation. Install the nuts while holding the bolts stationary in the knuckle.

13. Position the lower end of the strut assembly in line with the upper end of the knuckle, aligning the mounting holes. Install the 2 attaching bolts from the front of the vehicle. Install the nuts. While holding the bolts in place, tighten the nuts to 120 ft. lbs. (163 Nm).

14. If equipped with ABS, attach the wheel speed sensor routing bracket to the rear of the strut (rearward ear) using its mounting screw. Tighten the mounting screw to 120 inch lbs. (13 Nm).

15. Attach the ground strap to the rear of the strut (forward ear) using its mounting screw. Tighten the mounting screw to 120 inch lbs. (13 Nm).

16. Install tire and wheel assembly. Install and tighten wheel mounting nuts to 100 ft. lbs. (135 Nm).

17. Lower the vehicle.

OVERHAUL

See Figures 203 through 206.

➡The strut assembly must be removed from the vehicle for it to be disassembled and assembled.

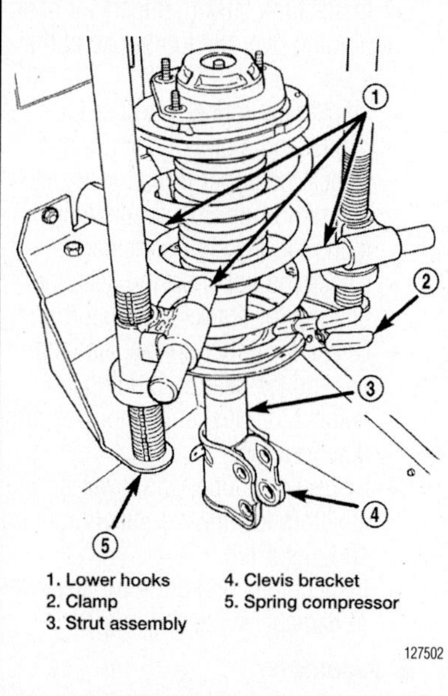

Fig. 203 View of strut assembly in compressor — lower

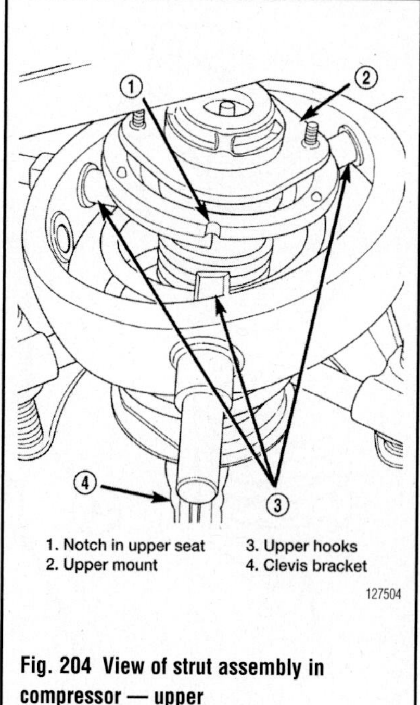

Fig. 204 View of strut assembly in compressor — upper

➡For the disassembly and assembly of the strut assembly, use strut spring compressor to compress the coil spring. Follow the manufacturer's instructions closely.

**** CAUTION**

Do not remove the strut shaft nut before the coil spring is compressed. The coil spring is held under pressure and must be compressed, removing spring tension from the upper mount and pivot bearing, before the shaft nut is removed.

1. Remove strut assembly. Refer to MacPherson Strut, removal & installation.

2. If both struts are being serviced at the same time, mark both the coil spring and strut assembly according to which side of the vehicle the strut is being removed from.

3. Position the strut assembly in the strut coil spring compressor following the manufacturer's instructions. Set the lower hooks. Position the strut clevis bracket straight outward, away from the compressor. Place a clamp on the lower end of the coil spring, so the strut is held in place once the strut shaft nut is removed.

4. Lower the upper hooks and set them on the coil spring following the manufacturer's instructions.

5. Compress the coil spring until all coil spring tension is removed from the upper mount.

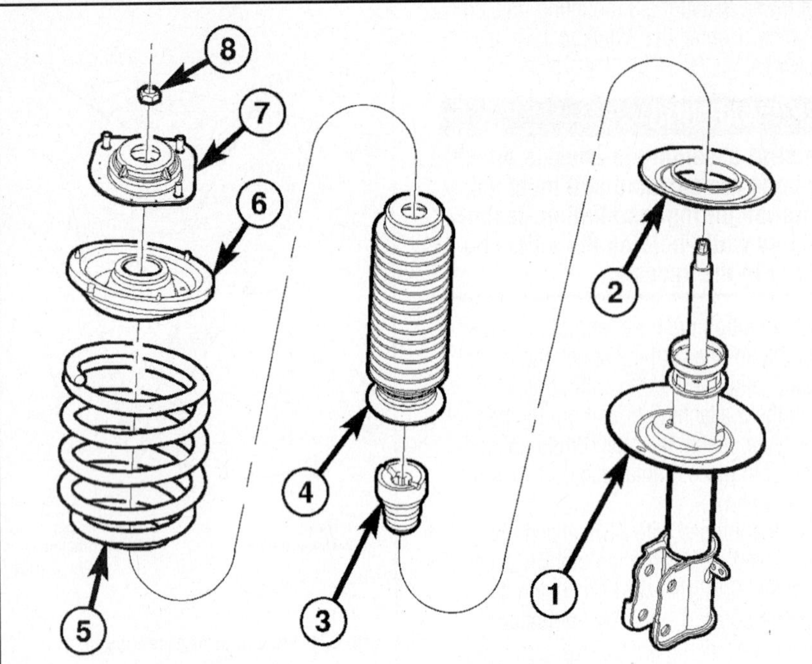

Fig. 205 MacPherson strut — exploded view

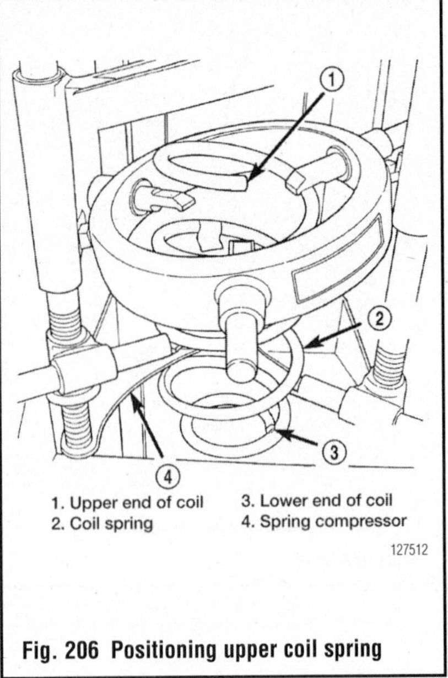

Fig. 206 Positioning upper coil spring

WARNING

Never use impact or high speed tools to remove the strut shaft nut. Damage to the strut internal bearings may occur.

6. Once the spring is sufficiently compressed, install a strut nut wrench on the strut shaft retaining nut. Next, install a socket on the hex on the end of the strut shaft. While holding the strut shaft from turning, remove the nut from the strut shaft.
7. Remove the upper mount from the strut shaft.
8. Remove the upper spring seat and bearing, along with the upper spring isolator as an assembly from the top of the coil spring by pulling them straight up. The upper spring isolator can be separated from the spring seat and bearing once removed from the strut.
9. Slide the dust shield, then the jounce bumper from the strut shaft.
10. Remove the clamp from the bottom of the coil spring and remove the strut out through the bottom of the coil spring.
11. Remove the lower spring isolator from the lower spring seat on the strut.

➡If the coil spring needs to be serviced, perform the following steps.

12. Release the tension from the coil spring by backing off the compressor drive completely. Push back the compressor hooks, and remove the coil spring.
13. Inspect the strut assembly components for the following and replace as necessary:
   - Inspect the strut (damper) for shaft binding over the full stroke of the shaft.
   - Inspect the jounce bumper for cracks and signs of deterioration.
   - Check the upper mount for cracks and distortion and its retaining studs for any sign of damage.
   - Check the upper spring seat and bearing for cracks and distortion.
   - Check for upper spring seat and bearing for bearing binding.
   - Inspect the dust shield for rips and deterioration.
   - Inspect the upper and lower spring isolators for material deterioration and distortion.
   - Inspect the coil spring for any sign of damage to the coating.

To assemble:

14. If the coil spring has been removed from the spring compressor, place the spring in the compressor following the manufacturer's instructions. Before compressing the spring, rotate the spring so the end of the top coil is directly in front away from the compressor. Slowly compress the coil spring until enough room is available for strut assembly reassembly.
15. Install the lower spring isolator on the lower spring seat of the strut.
16. Install the strut through the bottom of the coil spring until the lower spring seat contacts the lower end of the coil spring. Rotate the strut as necessary until the clevis bracket is positioned straight outward away from the compressor. Install the clamp on the lower end of the coil spring and strut, so the strut is temporarily held in place.
17. Slide the jounce bumper onto the strut shaft. The jounce bumper is to be installed with the smaller end pointing downward toward the lower seat.
18. Install the dust shield over the jounce bumper. Snap the bottom of the dust shield onto the retainer on top of the strut housing.
19. If disassembled, reinstall the upper spring isolator on the upper spring seat and bearing.
20. Install the upper spring seat and bearing on top of the coil spring.
21. Position the notch formed into the edge of the upper seat straight out away from the compressor. It should line up with the very end of the coil spring coil.
22. Install the strut upper mount over the strut shaft, onto the top of the upper spring seat and bearing. Position the mount so that the third mounting stud on the mount top is inward toward the compressor, opposite the clevis bracket.

⁂ WARNING

Never use impact or high speed tools to install the strut shaft nut. Damage to the strut internal bearings may occur.

23. Loosely install the retaining nut on the strut shaft.
24. Position strut nut wrench on the strut shaft retaining nut. Next, install a socket on the hex on the end of the strut shaft. While holding the strut shaft from turning, tighten the strut shaft retaining nut to 55 ft. lbs. (75 Nm).
25. Slowly release the tension from the coil spring by backing off the compressor drive completely. As the tension is relieved, make sure the upper mount and the seat and bearing align properly. Verify the upper mount does not bind when rotated.
26. Remove the clamp from the lower end of the coil spring and strut. Push back the spring compressor upper and lower hooks, and then remove the strut assembly from the spring compressor.
27. Install the strut assembly on the vehicle. Refer to MacPherson Strut, removal & installation.

STABILIZER BAR

REMOVAL & INSTALLATION

See Figures 207 and 208.

1. Before servicing the vehicle, refer to the Precautions section.
2. Raise and support the vehicle.
3. On both sides of the vehicle, remove the stabilizer bar link assembly (3, 4, 6, 7) from the vehicle. Remove each link by holding the upper retainer/nut with a wrench and turning the link bolt.
4. On both sides of the vehicle, remove the stabilizer bar cushion retainer bolts and retainers., then remove the stabilizer bar with cushions attached from the vehicle.
5. Remove the stabilizer bar with cushions from the vehicle.
6. To remove the cushions from the stabilizer bar, peel back each cushion at the slit and roll it off the bar.

To install:

➡Before stabilizer bar installation, inspect the cushions and link assemblies (3, 4, 6, 7) for excessive wear, cracks, damage and distortion. Replace any pieces failing inspection.

7. If removed, install the stabilizer bar cushions on the stabilizer bar utilizing the slit in each cushion. Position the cushions at each end of the bar's straight beam, just before it begins to curve forward.

➡Before installing the stabilizer bar, make sure the bar is not upside-down. The stabilizer bar must be installed with the curve on the outboard ends of the bar bowing downward to clear the control arms once fully installed.

8. First, place the stabilizer bar in position on the front suspension crossmember. The slits in each cushion must point toward the front of the vehicle and sit directly on top of the raised beads formed into the stamping on the crossmember. Next, install the cushion retainer on each side, matching the raised beads formed into the cushion retainers to the grooves formed into the cushions. Install the cushion retainer bolts, but do not completely tighten them at this time.

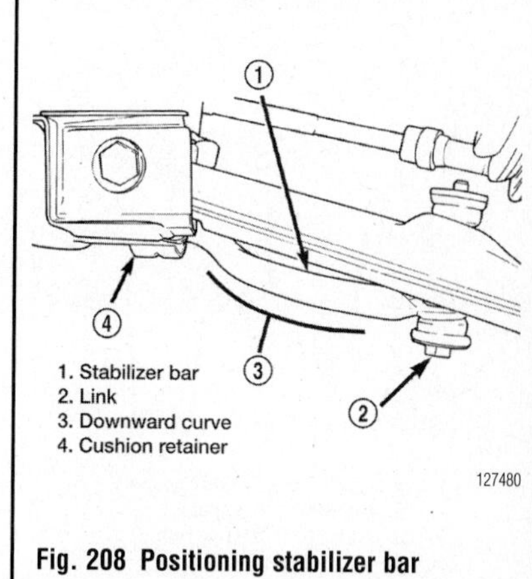

Fig. 208 Positioning stabilizer bar

9. Clean the threads of both stabilizer bar link bolts, then apply Mopar ® Lock And Seal or equivalent to the threads.
10. On each side of the vehicle, install each stabilizer bar link assembly on the vehicle. Start each stabilizer bar link bolt with bushing from the bottom, through the stabilizer bar, inner link bushing, lower control arm, and into the upper retainer/nut and bushing. Do not fully tighten the link assemblies at this time.
11. Lower the vehicle.

➡It may be necessary to put the vehicle on a platform hoist or alignment rack to gain access to the stabilizer bar mounting bolts with the vehicle at curb height.

12. Tighten each stabilizer bar link by holding the upper retainer/nut with a wrench while turning the link bolt. Tighten each link bolt to 22 ft. lbs. (29 Nm).
13. Tighten the stabilizer bar cushion retainer bolts to 18 ft. lbs. (25 Nm).

STEERING KNUCKLE

REMOVAL & INSTALLATION

See Figures 209 through 214.

1. Before servicing the vehicle, refer to the Precautions section.
2. Raise and support the vehicle.
3. Remove wheel and tire assembly.
4. Remove the cotter pin, lock nut and spring washer from the hub nut.

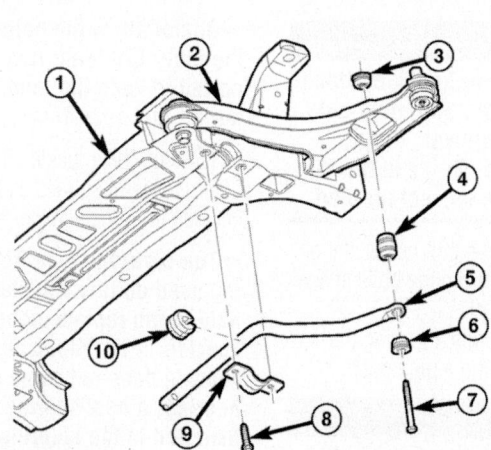

1. Crossmember
2. Lower control arm
3. Link assembly upper retainer/nut
4. Link assembly inner link bushing
5. Stabilizer bar
6. Link assembly bushing
7. Link assembly bolt
8. Cushion retainer bolt
9. Retainer
10. Cushion

127422

Fig. 207 Stabilizer bar and link — exploded view

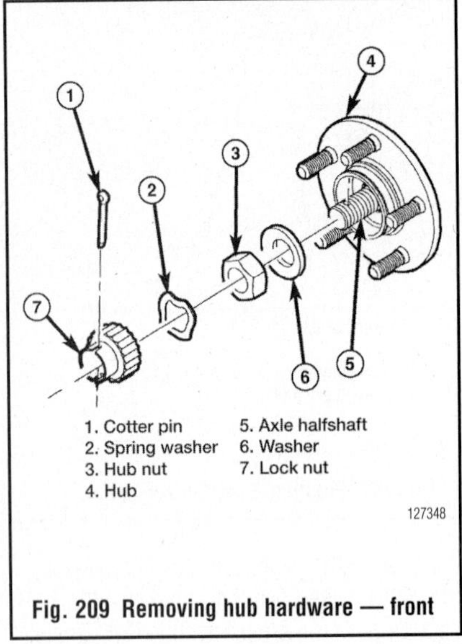

Fig. 209 Removing hub hardware — front

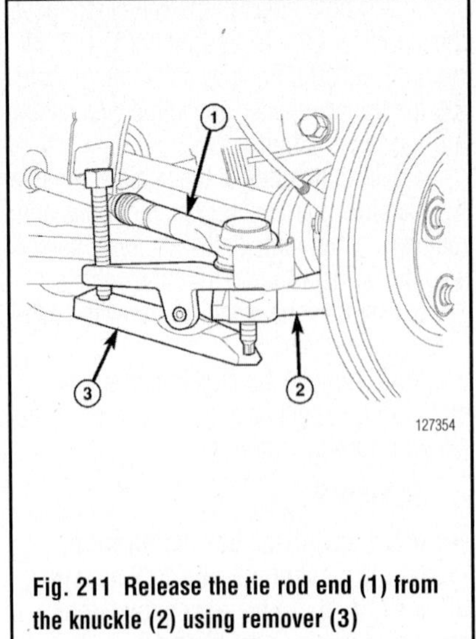

Fig. 211 Release the tie rod end (1) from the knuckle (2) using remover (3)

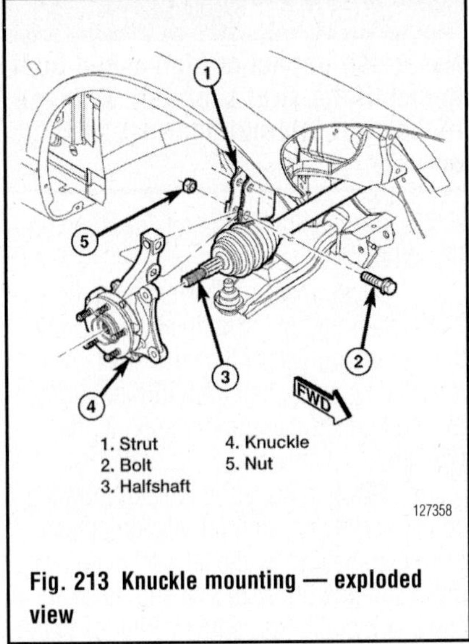

Fig. 213 Knuckle mounting — exploded view

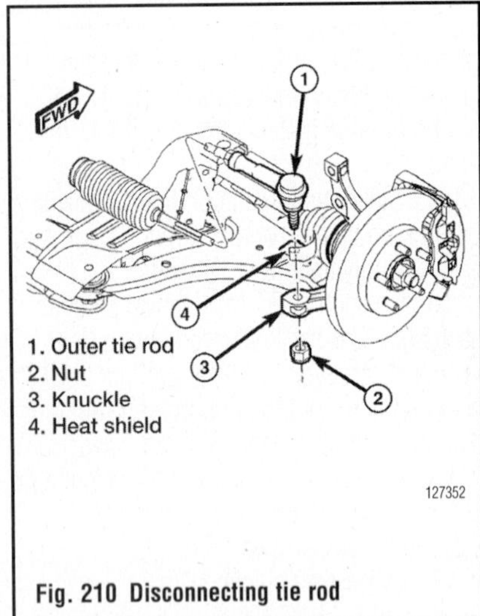

Fig. 210 Disconnecting tie rod

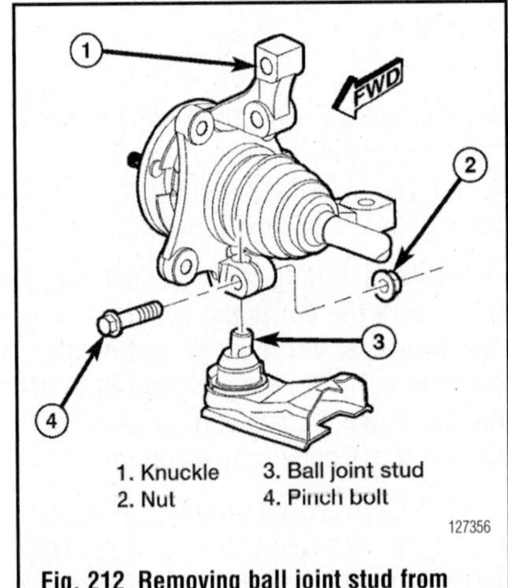

Fig. 212 Removing ball joint stud from knuckle

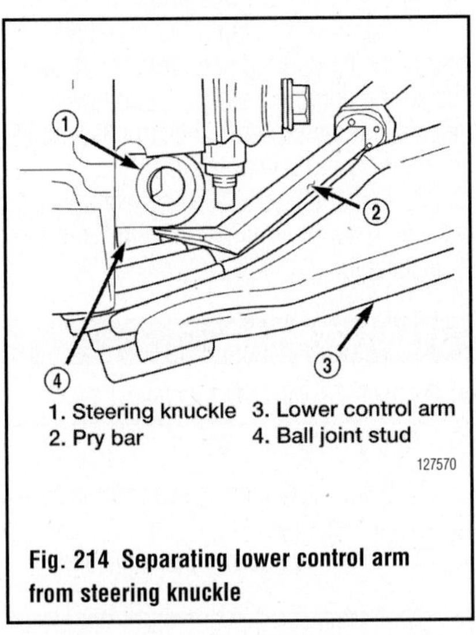

Fig. 214 Separating lower control arm from steering knuckle

5. While a helper applies the brakes to keep the hub from rotating, remove the hub nut and washer from the axle halfshaft.

6. Access and remove the front brake rotor.

7. Remove the screw fastening the wheel speed sensor to the knuckle. Pull the sensor head with heat shield out of the knuckle.

8. Remove the nut attaching the outer tie rod to the knuckle. To do this, hold the tie rod end stud with a wrench while loosening and removing the nut with a standard wrench or crowfoot wrench.

9. Release the tie rod end from the knuckle using remover.

10. Remove the outer tie rod and heat shield from the knuckle.

11. Remove the nut and pinch bolt clamping the ball joint stud to the knuckle.

WARNING

The strut assembly-to-knuckle attaching bolts are serrated and must not be turned during removal. Proper removal is required. Refer to the following steps for the correct method.

12. While holding the bolt heads stationary, remove the 2 nuts from the bolts attaching the strut to the knuckle.

13. Remove the 2 bolts attaching the strut to the knuckle using a pin punch.

WARNING

Use care when separating the ball joint stud from the knuckle, so the ball joint seal does not get cut.

14. Using an appropriate prying tool, separate the ball joint stud from the knuckle by prying down on lower control arm and up against the ball joint boss on the knuckle.

➡Do not allow the halfshaft to hang by the inner C/V joint; it must be supported to keep the joint from separating during this operation.

15. Pull the knuckle off the halfshaft outer C/V joint splines and remove the knuckle from the vehicle.

➡The cartridge type front wheel bearing used on this vehicle is not transferable to the replacement steering knuckle. If the replacement steering knuckle does not come with a wheel bearing, a new bearing must be installed in the steering knuckle. Installation of the new wheel bearing and hub must be done before installing the steering knuckle on the vehicle.

16. If the wheel bearing and hub require removal, refer to Hub & Bearing, removal & installation. Do not reuse the wheel bearing.

To install:

17. Wipe the halfshaft outer C/V joint-to-knuckle mating surface clean and apply a light coating of wheel bearing or multi-purpose grease around the circumference of that flat surface. Do not apply too much grease or allow it to come in contact with the ABS tone wheel.
18. Wipe the rear of the hub and bearing in the knuckle clean where they contact the C/V joint.
19. Slide the hub of the knuckle onto the splines of the halfshaft outer C/V joint.
20. Install the knuckle onto the ball joint stud aligning the bolt hole in the knuckle boss with the notch formed into the side of the ball joint stud.
21. Install a new ball joint stud pinch bolt and nut. Tighten the nut to 70 ft. lbs. (95 Nm).

WARNING

The strut assembly-to-knuckle attaching bolts are serrated and must not be turned during installation. Install the nuts while holding the bolts stationary in the steering knuckle.

22. Position the lower end of the strut assembly in line with the upper end of the knuckle, aligning the mounting holes. Install the 2 attaching bolts from the front of the vehicle.
23. Install the nuts. While holding the bolts in place, tighten the nuts to 120 ft. lbs. (163 Nm).
24. Place the tie rod heat shield on the knuckle arm so that the shield is positioned straight away from the steering gear and tie rod end once installed. Align the hole in the shield with the tie rod end mounting hole.
25. Install the outer tie rod ball stud into the hole in the knuckle arm. Start the tie rod mounting nut onto the stud. While holding the tie rod end stud with a wrench, tighten the nut with a wrench or crowfoot wrench. Tighten the nut to 40 ft. lbs. (54 Nm).
26. Install the wheel speed sensor with heat shield on the knuckle. Install the mounting screw and tighten it to 105 inch lbs. (12 Nm).
27. Install the brake rotor, disc brake caliper and adapter.
28. Clean all foreign matter from the threads of the halfshaft outer C/V joint.
29. Install the washer and hub nut on the end of the halfshaft and snug it.
30. While a helper applies the brakes to keep the hub from rotating, tighten the hub nut to 180 ft. lbs. (244 Nm).
31. Install the spring washer, and lock nut over the hub nut. Insert the cotter pin through the notches in the lock nut and hole in halfshaft.
32. Wrap the cotter pin ends tightly around the lock nut.
33. Install tire and wheel assembly. Install and tighten wheel mounting nuts to 100 ft. lbs. (135 Nm).
34. Lower the vehicle.
35. Perform wheel alignment as necessary.

DISASSEMBLY & ASSEMBLY

See Figures 215 through 224.

➡**The removal and installation of the wheel bearing and hub from the steering knuckle is only to be done with the knuckle removed from the vehicle.**

1. Remove knuckle. Refer to Steering Knuckle, removal & installation.

➡**Three wheel mounting studs across from one another require removal from the hub flange.**

2. Using press (C-4150A), one at a time, press one of the 3 wheel mounting studs (across from one another) out of the hub flange. Repeat this procedure until all studs are removed.
3. Rotate the hub to align the loosened wheel mounting stud(s) with the notch in the bearing retainer plate. Remove the stud through the open notch.
4. Rotate the hub so that the empty stud mounting holes in the hub are facing in the direction shown in the figure in relationship to the knuckle. Absence of the 3 wheel mounting studs and positioning the hub in this direction allows the bearing splitter to be installed behind the flange in the next step.
5. Install the bearing splitter (1130) between the hub and the bearing retainer plate as shown. Hand tighten the nuts to hold bearing splitter in place on knuckle.
6. Place the steering knuckle face down in an arbor press supported by the bearing splitter as shown. The press support blocks must not obstruct the wheel hub while it is being pressed out of the knuckle.

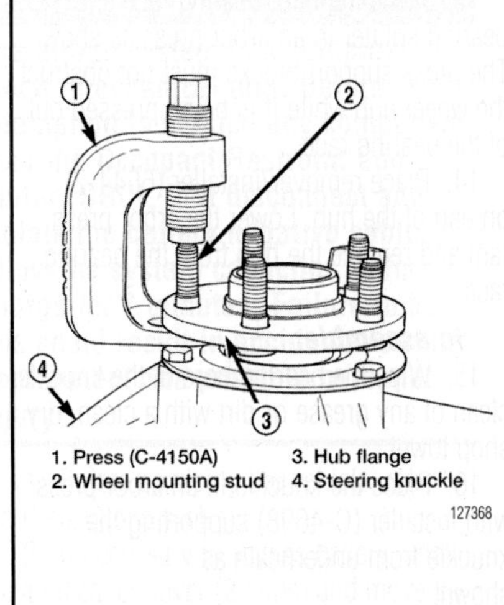

Fig. 215 Removing wheel mounting studs

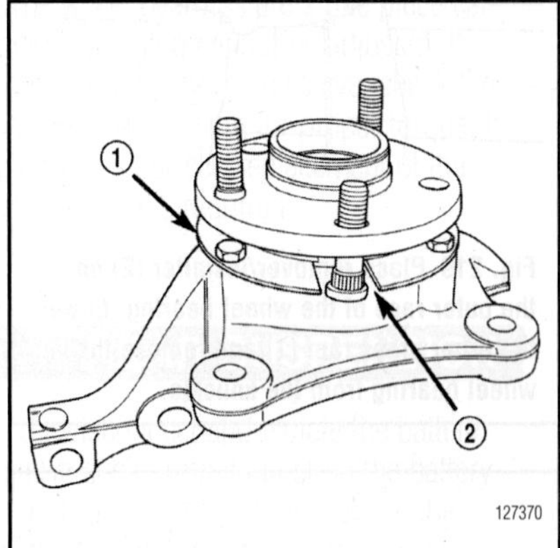

Fig. 216 Rotate the hub to align the loosened wheel mounting stud(s) with the notch (2) in the bearing retainer plate (1)

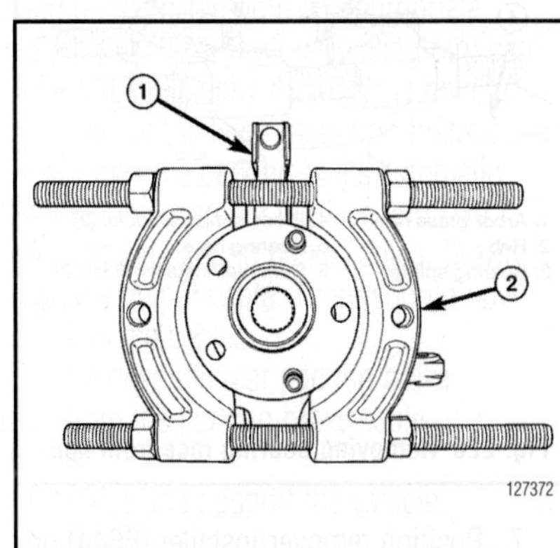

Fig. 217 View of bearing splitter (2) installed on knuckle (1)

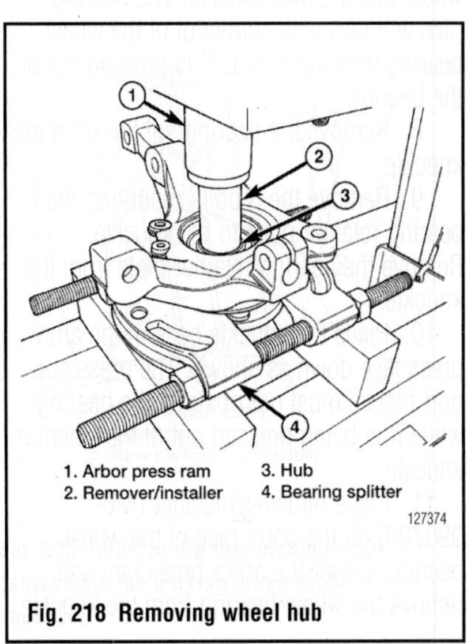

Fig. 218 Removing wheel hub

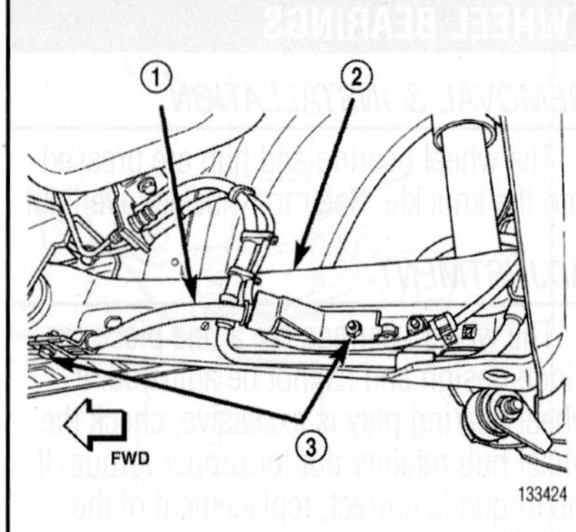

Fig. 226 Remove the 2 bolts (3) on the axle trailing arm securing the parking brake cable (1) and routing brackets to the axle trailing arm (2)

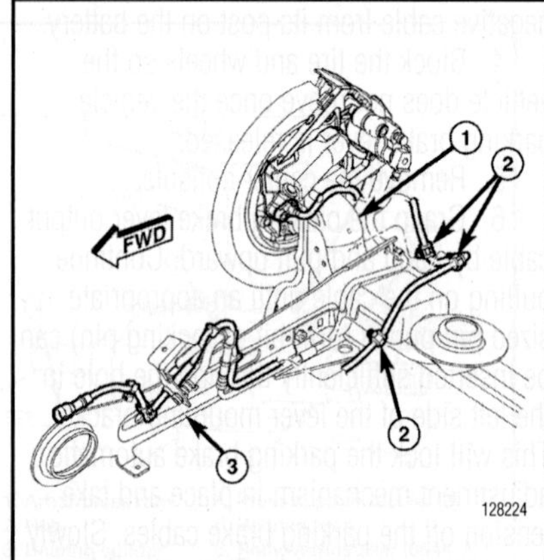

Fig. 227 Remove the anti-lock wheel speed sensor routing clips (2) from the axle (1) and trailing arm (3)

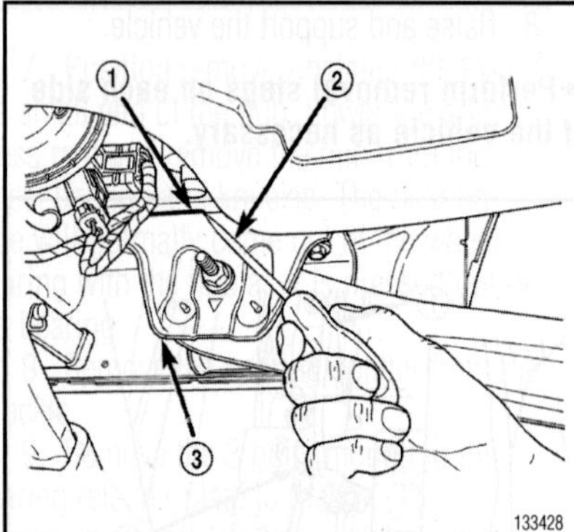

Fig. 228 Using an awl (2), scribe a line (1) marking the location of the axle trailing arm bracket (3), side-to-side and front-to-rear, on the body of the vehicle

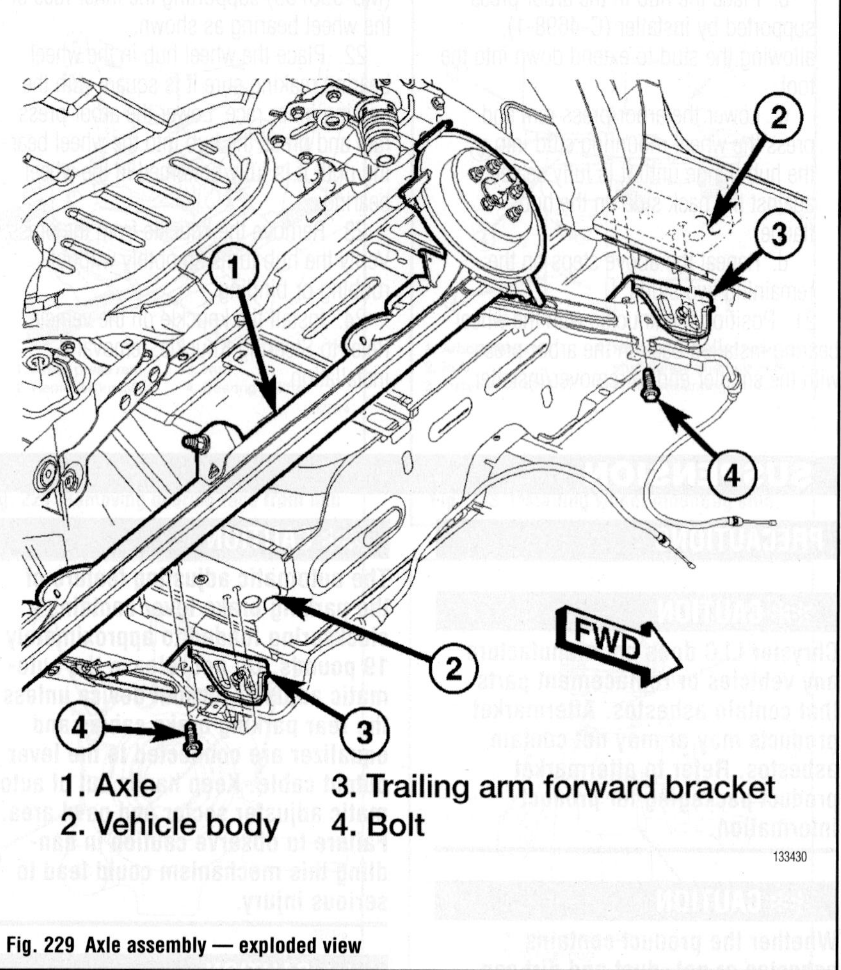

Fig. 229 Axle assembly — exploded view

9. Remove the rear tire and wheel assembly.

10. Remove the bolt securing the disc brake flex hose to the axle trailing arm.

11. Remove the hub and bearing. Refer to Hub and Bearing, removal & installation.

12. Remove the parking brake shoes as an assembly from the disc brake adapter. Refer to Parking Brake Shoes, removal & installation.

13. Using a 1/2-inch offset box wrench, compress the locking fingers on the cable retainer, then slide the parking brake cable from the rear disc brake adapter.

14. Remove the 2 bolts on the axle trailing arm securing the parking brake cable and routing brackets to the axle trailing arm.

15. Pull the cable through the hole in the trailing arm.

16. Remove the anti-lock wheel speed sensor routing clips from the axle and trailing arm.

17. Remove the spindle. Refer to Spindle, removal & installation.

18. Remove the coil springs. Refer to Coil Spring, removal & installation.

19. Using an awl, scribe a line marking the location of the axle trailing arm bracket, side-to-side and front-to-rear, on the body of the vehicle. Perform this for the axle trailing arm bracket on the opposite side bracket as well.

20. Remove the bolts securing both trailing arm forward brackets to the body of the vehicle.

21. Remove the axle from the vehicle.

22. If necessary, remove the nuts and through-bolts fastening the trailing arm forward brackets to the axle.

23. Remove the brackets.

To install:

24. If removed, install the trailing arm forward brackets on each side of the axle in the following way:

a. From above the axle, place the bracket down over the axle trailing arm bushing aligning the hole in the bracket with the center hole in the bushing.

b. From the outboard side of the axle and bracket, push the through-bolt through the bracket and bushing. The trailing arm bracket through -bolts must be installed from the outside, in toward the center of the axle assembly, otherwise the bolt threaded ends will come in contact with the body of the vehicle upon axle installation on vehicle.

c. Install the nut on the inboard end of the bolt. Tighten the nut until the bracket has resistance when turned, but still moves independently of the axle bushing. Do not tighten at this time; it must be fully tightened with the vehicle at curb height.

25. Center the axle beam on a transmission jack standing at axle removal height.

26. Swing the axle trailing arms up aligning the brackets with the scribed marks made upon removal.

27. Install all eight (four per side) axle bracket-to-body mounting bolts. Thread the bolts in, but do not fully tighten at this time.

28. Tap the brackets as necessary to align the brackets with the scribed marks, then tighten all the bolts to 40 ft. lbs. (54 Nm).

29. Install the coil springs. Refer to Coil Spring, removal & installation.

➡Perform installation steps on each side of the vehicle as necessary.

30. Install the spindle. Refer to Spindle, removal & installation.

31. Guide the end of each parking brake cable through hole in the trailing arm towards the wheel brake.

32. Align the cable routing brackets with their mounts on the trailing arm. Install the two bolts securing the cable and routing brackets to the trailing arm. Tighten the mounting bolts to 100 inch lbs. (11 Nm).

33. Install the parking brake cable into the disc brake adapter. Be sure the locking fingers on the cable retainer are expanded once the cable is pushed all the way into the brake adapter hole to ensure the cable is securely held in place.

34. Install the parking brake shoe actuator lever on the parking brake cable.

35. Install the parking brake shoe assembly. Refer to Parking Brake Shoes, removal & installation.

36. Install the screw securing the brake flex hose bracket and wheel speed sensor cable to the vehicle body above the leading end of the axle trailing arm.

37. Install tire and wheel assembly. Install and tighten wheel mounting nuts to 100 ft. lbs. (135 Nm).

38. Lower the vehicle to a point where the rear wheels just clear the floor.

39. Install the hub and bearing. Refer to Hub and Bearing, removal & installation.

40. Install the rear parking brake cables into the equalizer on the parking brake lever output cable.

⁂ CAUTION

The automatic adjusting feature of this parking brake lever contains a clockspring loaded to approximately 19 pounds. Do not release the automatic adjuster lockout device unless the rear parking brake cables and equalizer are connected to the lever output cable. Keep hands out of automatic adjuster sector and pawl area. Failure to observe caution in handling this mechanism could lead to serious injury.

➡The parking brake lever can only be in the released position when releasing the automatic adjuster.

41. Ensure that the parking brake cables are correctly installed on the equalizer and aligned with the cable track on the parking brake lever.

42. Keeping hands clear of the automatic adjuster sector and pawl area, firmly grasp the pin punch (drill bit or locking pin) installed in the parking brake lever, then quickly remove it from the lever mechanism. This will allow the parking brake lever mechanism to automatically adjust the parking brake cables.

43. Cycle the parking brake lever once to position the parking brake cables, then return the parking brake lever its released position.

44. Check the rear wheels of the vehicle. They should rotate freely without excessive dragging with the lever in the released position.

45. Lower the vehicle.

46. Install the center console.

47. Apply the parking brake.

48. Remove the blocks from the tires and wheels.

49. Connect the battery negative cable to its post on the battery.

50. Install the air cleaner cover.

51. Pump the brake pedal several times to ensure the vehicle has a firm brake pedal before moving the vehicle.

52. Place the vehicle on an alignment rack or drive-on hoist.

53. With the vehicle at curb height, tighten both trailing arm to mounting bracket pivot through-bolts to 90 ft. lbs. (122 Nm).

54. Perform a rear wheel alignment. If necessary, thrust angle may be adjusted by loosening the axle trailing arm bracket bolts and shifting the axle forward or rearward, then retightening the bolts to 40 ft. lbs. (54 Nm).

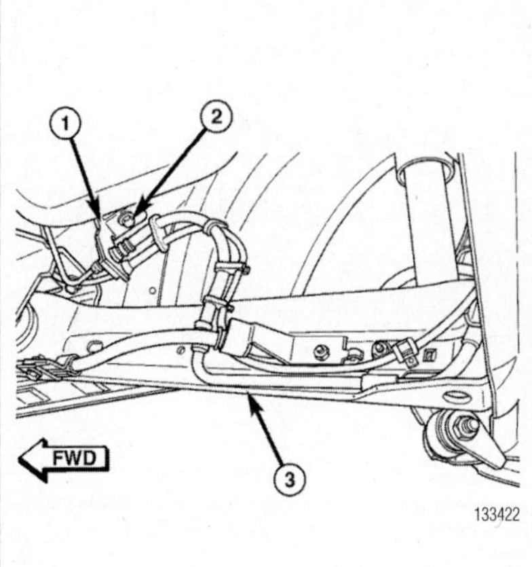

Fig. 230 Remove the screw (2) securing the rear brake flex hose and wheel speed sensor cable routing bracket (1) to the vehicle body above the leading end of the axle trailing arm (3)

TRAILING ARM BUSHING REPLACEMENT

See Figures 226, 229 through 232.

1. Raise and support the vehicle.

➡Perform removal steps on each side of the vehicle as necessary.

2. Remove the rear tire and wheel assembly.

3. Remove the screw securing the rear brake flex hose and wheel speed sensor cable routing bracket to the vehicle body above the leading end of the axle trailing arm.

4. Remove the 2 bolts on the axle trailing arm securing the parking brake cable and routing brackets to the axle trailing arm.

5. Move the parking brake cable from its mounted position away from the bottom of the trailing arm bushing and the forward bracket.

6. Remove the bolt, nut and washer securing the watts link bell crank to the center of the axle.

7. Position a transmission jack or equivalent under the center of the axle raising it just enough to support the axle.

8. Using an awl, scribe a line marking the location of one axle trailing arm bracket, side-to-side and front-to-rear, on the body of the vehicle. Perform this for the bracket on the opposite side of the vehicle as well.

9. Remove the bolts securing both trailing arm forward brackets to the body of the vehicle.

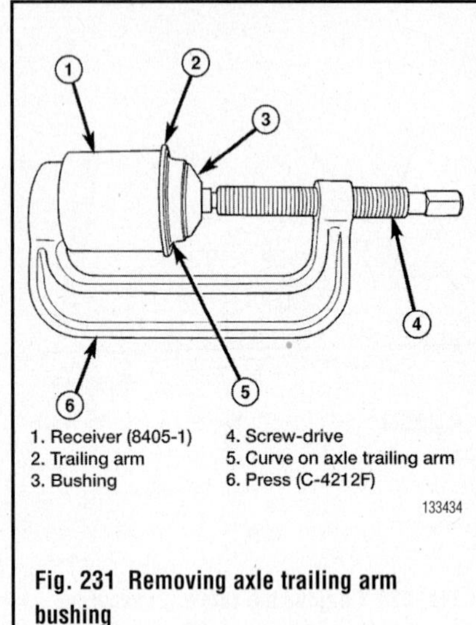

Fig. 231 Removing axle trailing arm bushing

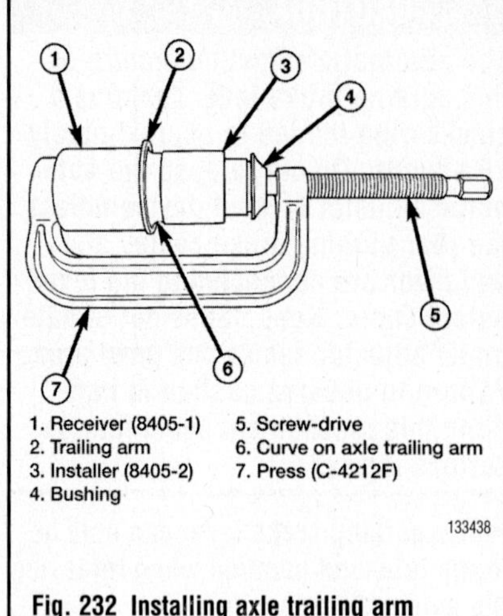

Fig. 232 Installing axle trailing arm bushing

10. Using the lower shock mounts as a pivot point, pry down on the forward end of the trailing arms and place a block of wood between the top of the arms and the body of the vehicle just to the rear of the forward mounting bracket. Be careful not to pinch any hoses or cables.
11. Remove the nut and through-bolt fastening the trailing arm forward bracket to the axle trailing arm bushing requiring service.
12. Place receiver (8405-1) on press (C-4212F), and tighten the set-screw.
13. Place the special tool assembly over the bushing as shown. When properly installed, the press screw-drive will be toward the center of the vehicle. Note the curve on the axle trailing arm. This curve prevents the tool from being properly installed in the opposite direction.
14. Tighten the press screw-drive, pressing the bushing out of the trailing arm into the receiver.
15. Remove the tool and the bushing from the trailing arm. Discard the used bushing.
16. If the opposite side bushing needs to be removed, repeat necessary steps on that side of the vehicle.

To install:

17. Apply rubber bushing installation lube to the outside edges of the NEW bushing. Also, lubricate the inside of installer (8405-2) with the special lube.
18. Place the stepped end of installer (8405-2) on the end of the trailing arm bushing sleeve that has the curved flange at the arm.
19. Place the lubricated bushing inside the large opening in the installer.
20. Place the press with receiver installed, over the arm, installer and bushing as shown. When properly installed, the press screw-drive will be toward the center of the vehicle. Note the curve on the axle trailing arm. This curve prevents the tool from being properly installed in the opposite direction.
21. Using hand tools, slowly tighten the press screw-drive, pressing the bushing into the trailing arm sleeve. Do not over-install the bushing; the bushing can be pushed out the other side if care is not used. Push the bushing in until freed from the installer and centered in the trailing arm sleeve. The outer lips of the bushing must hang out past the end of the sleeve on each side of the trailing arm.
22. Remove the tools from the trailing arm.
23. If the opposite side bushing needs to be installed, repeat necessary steps on that side of the vehicle.
24. Install the trailing arm forward bracket(s) on the axle in the following way:
    a. From above the axle, place the bracket down over the axle trailing arm bushing aligning the hole in the bracket with the center hole in the bushing.
    b. From the outboard side of the axle and bracket, push the through-bolt through the bracket and bushing. The trailing arm bracket through-bolts must be installed from the outside, in toward the center of the axle assembly, otherwise the bolt threaded ends will come in contact with the body of the vehicle upon axle installation on vehicle.
    c. Install the nut on the inboard end of the bolt. Tighten the nut until the bracket has resistance when turned, but still moves independent of the axle bushing. Do not tighten at this time; it must be fully tightened with the vehicle at curb height.
25. Remove the wood block between the arm and body of the vehicle.
26. Swing the axle trailing arms up aligning the brackets with the scribed marks made upon removal.
27. Install all 8 (4 per side) axle bracket-to-body mounting bolts. Thread the bolts in, but do not fully tighten at this time.
28. Tap the brackets as necessary to align the brackets with the scribed marks, then tighten all the bolts to 40 ft. lbs. (54 Nm).
29. Remove the jack.

WARNING

When installing the watts links and bell crank to the axle, make sure the bell crank is right-side-up. When mounted properly, the words "BACK UP" should be able to be read from the rear over the top of the axle.

30. Install the bolt from the front securing the watts link bell crank to the center of the axle. Place the washer and nut on the end of the mounting bolt and tighten it to 110 ft. lbs. (149 Nm).

➡Perform installation steps on each side of the vehicle as necessary.

31. Move the parking brake cable to its original mounting position below the axle pivot bushing on the inboard side of the trailing arm.
32. Align the cable routing brackets with their mounts on the trailing arm. Install the two bolts securing the cable and routing brackets to the trailing arm. Tighten the mounting bolts to 100 inch lbs. (11 Nm).
33. Make sure the parking brake cable and grommet is still in the proper position at the body access hole.
34. Install the screw securing the brake flex hose bracket and wheel speed sensor cable to the vehicle body above the leading end of the axle trailing arm.
35. Install tire and wheel assembly. Install and tighten wheel mounting nuts to 100 ft. lbs. (135 Nm).
36. Lower the vehicle.
37. Place the vehicle on an alignment rack or drive-on hoist.
38. With the vehicle at curb height, tighten both trailing arm to mounting bracket pivot through-bolts to 90 ft. lbs. (122 Nm).

COIL SPRING

REMOVAL & INSTALLATION

See Figures 233 through 236.

1. Before servicing the vehicle, refer to the Precautions section.
2. Raise and support the vehicle.
3. Remove the tire and wheel assembly.
4. Remove the bolt, nut and washer securing the watts link bell crank to the center of the axle.
5. Position a transmission jack or equivalent under the center of the axle raising it enough to support the axle.
6. On each side, remove the lower mounting bolt, nut and washer securing the shock absorber to the axle.
7. Lower the transmission jack until the coil springs can be removed from the axle.
8. Remove the coil springs and rubber isolators.

To install:

9. Install a rubber isolator on each end of the coil springs wrapping the rubber fingers around the coil. Turn each isolator until the rubber abutment butts up against the flat end of the spring coil.

➡Both ends of the coil spring are identical. Either end of the spring can be the top or bottom.

10. Place the coil springs on top of the axle spring perches.

➡The coil springs require proper orientation to the body when installed.

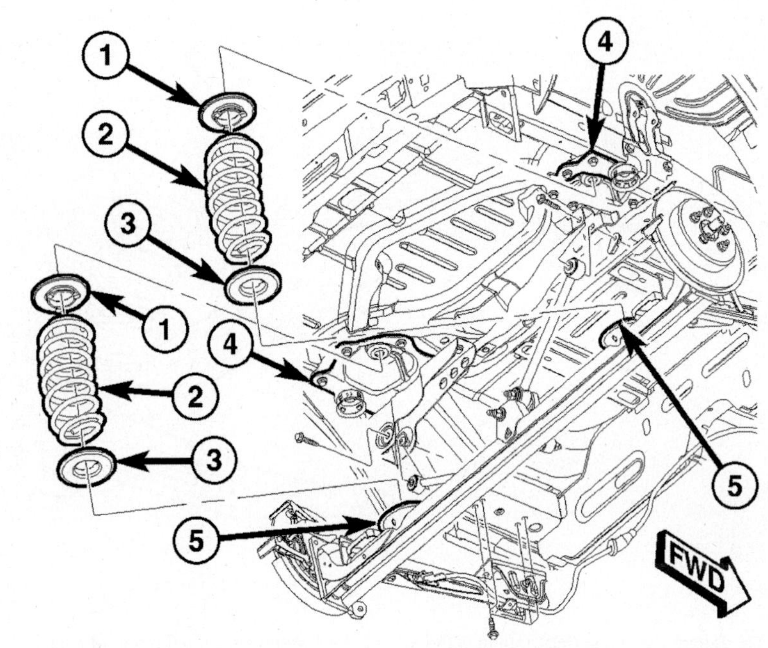

Fig. 234 Coil springs — exploded view

11. Rotate the coil springs (along with the rubber isolators) until the flat end of each upper spring coil lines up with an imaginary line running parallel with the axle beam as shown. Also, make sure that each upper coil ends near the outboard sides of the vehicle (as shown) and not 180 ° of that location.
12. Raise the transmission jack guiding the coil springs into the spring mounting brackets on the body of the vehicle.
13. Continue to raise the jack until the shock absorber lower mounting

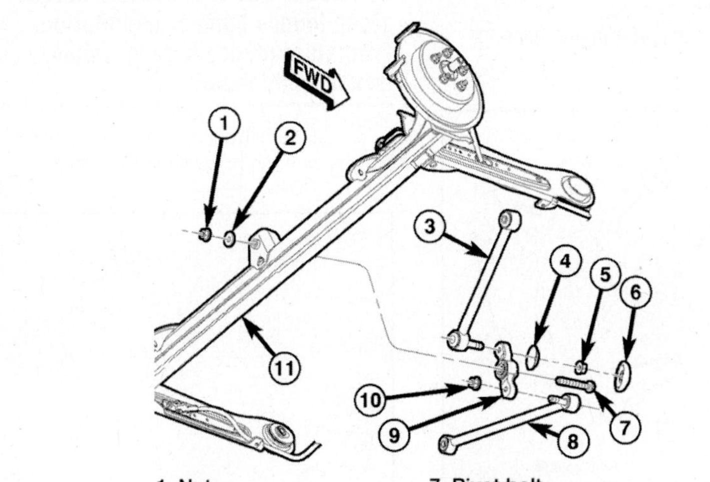

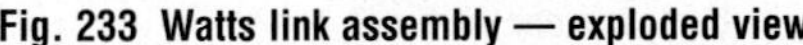

Fig. 233 Watts link assembly — exploded view

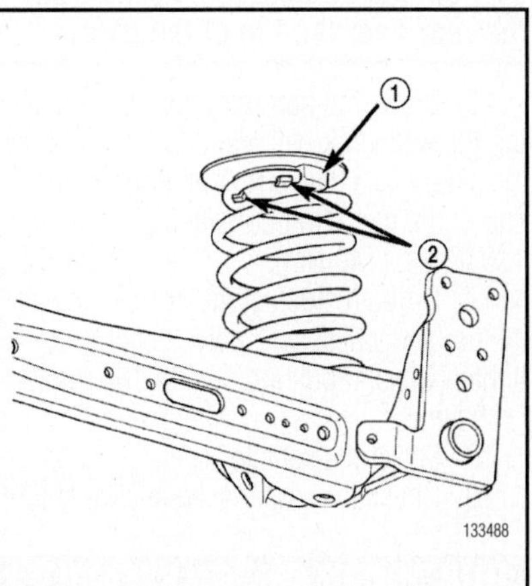

Fig. 235 Install a rubber isolator on each end of the coil springs wrapping the rubber fingers around the coil (2). Turn each isolator until the rubber abutment (1) butts up against the flat end of the spring coil

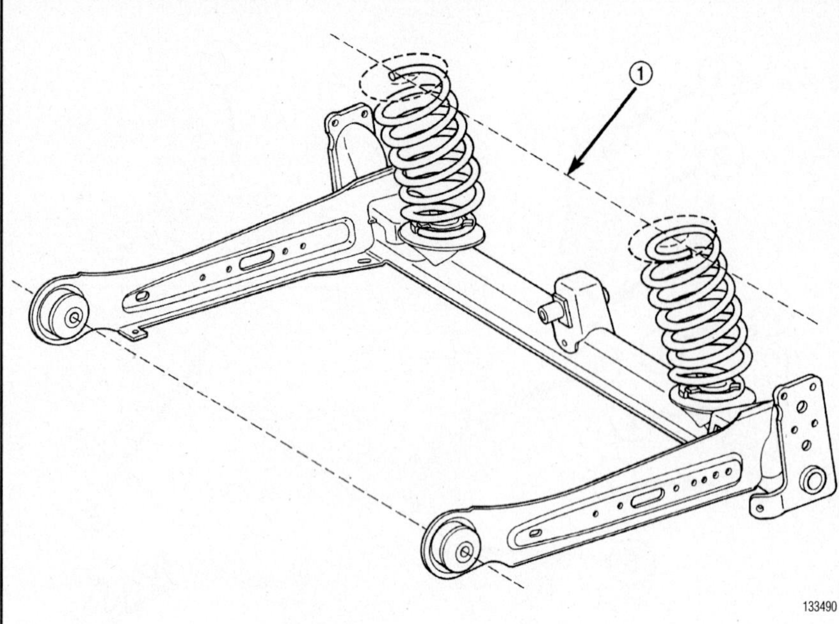

Fig. 236 Rotate the coil springs (along with the rubber isolators) until the flat end of each upper spring coil lines up with an imaginary line (1) running parallel with the axle beam

bolts can be inserted though the axle brackets and shock absorber lower mounting eyes.

14. Install the washer and nut on the end of each shock absorber lower mounting bolt. Tighten the mounting bolts to 65 ft. lbs. (88 Nm).

15. Remove the jack.

**** WARNING**

When installing the watts links and bell crank to the axle, make sure the bell crank is right-side-up. When mounted properly, the words "BACK UP" should be able to be read from the rear over the top of the axle.

16. Install the bolt from the front securing the watts link bell crank to the center of the axle. Place the washer and nut on the end of the mounting bolt and tighten it to 110 ft. lbs. (149 Nm).

17. On both sides of the vehicle, install the tire and wheel assembly. Install and tighten wheel mounting nuts to 100 ft. lbs. (135 Nm).

18. Lower the vehicle.

19. Check for proper vehicle curb height.

HUB AND BEARING ASSEMBLY

REMOVAL & INSTALLATION

See Figure 237.

1. Before servicing the vehicle, refer to the Precautions section.

2. Raise and support the vehicle.

3. Remove the tire and wheel assembly.

4. Remove rear brake caliper. Refer to Brake Caliper, removal & installation.

5. Hang the brake caliper from rear strut using wire or cord to prevent the weight of the caliper from damaging the brake hose.

6. Remove any clips retaining the brake rotor to the wheel studs.

7. Slide the brake rotor off the hub and bearing.

8. Remove the dust cap from the rear hub and bearing.

9. Remove the rear hub and bearing retaining nut.

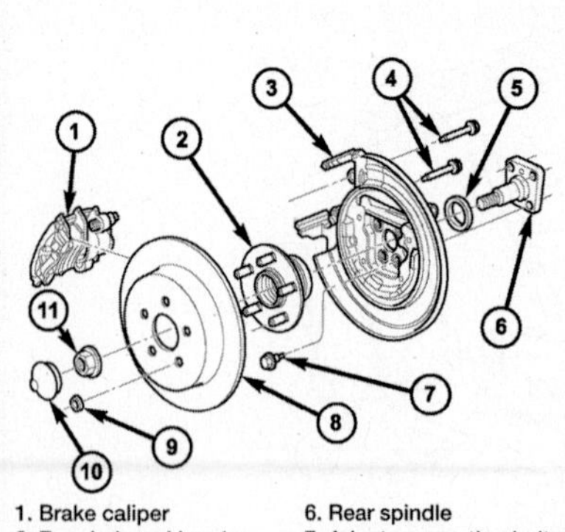

Fig. 237 Removing the rear hub and bearing

10. Remove the rear hub and bearing from the rear spindle.

To install:

11. Slide the hub and bearing onto the rear spindle.

12. Install a NEW hub and bearing retaining nut. Tighten the hub nut to 160 ft. lbs. (217 Nm).

13. Install the hub and bearing dust cap.

14. Install the brake rotor.

15. Install the disc brake caliper over the rotor and onto the brake adapter.

16. Install the 2 caliper guide pin bolts securing the caliper. Tighten the bolts to 192 inch lbs. (22 Nm).

17. Install the bolt securing the disc brake flex hose to the axle.

18. Install tire and wheel assembly. Install and tighten wheel mounting nuts to 100 ft. lbs. (135 Nm).

19. Lower the vehicle.

20. Pump the brake pedal several times to ensure the vehicle has a firm brake pedal before moving the vehicle.

JOUNCE BUMPER

REMOVAL & INSTALLATION

See Figure 238.

1. Raise and support the vehicle.

2. Grasp the jounce bumper and with a twisting motion, remove the jounce bumper from the bracket mounted to the body.

To install:

**** WARNING**

Do not use any type of lubricant to aid in jounce bumper installation. Premature jounce bumper failure issues could result.

3. Carefully twist and push the jounce bumper into the bracket mounted to the

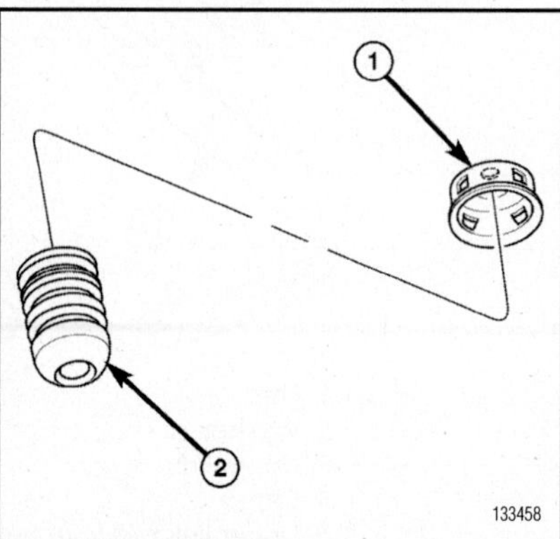

Fig. 238 Grasp the jounce bumper (2) and with a twisting motion, remove the jounce bumper from the bracket (1)

body of the vehicle until it bottoms in the bracket.

4. Lower the vehicle.

SHOCK ABSORBER

REMOVAL & INSTALLATION

See Figure 239.

1. Before servicing the vehicle, refer to the Precautions section.
2. Raise and support the vehicle.
3. Remove the tire and wheel assembly.
4. Position a transmission jack or equivalent under the center of the axle, raising it enough to support the axle.
5. Remove the shock absorber lower mounting bolt, nut and washer at the axle.
6. Remove the shock absorber upper mounting bolt at the body bracket, then remove the shock absorber from the vehicle.

To install:

7. Install the shock absorber by first attaching the top shock absorber eye to the body bracket using the upper mounting bolt. Do not fully tighten the bolt at this time.
8. Raise or lower the jack as necessary until the shock absorber lower mounting bolt can be inserted through the axle flange and the shock absorber lower mounting eye.
9. Install the washer and nut on the lower mounting bolt. Tighten the lower mounting bolt to 65 ft. lbs. (88 Nm).
10. Tighten the upper shock absorber mounting bolt to 73 ft. lbs. (99 Nm).
11. Remove the jack.
12. Install tire and wheel assembly. Install and tighten wheel mounting nuts to 100 ft. lbs. (135 Nm).
13. Lower the vehicle.

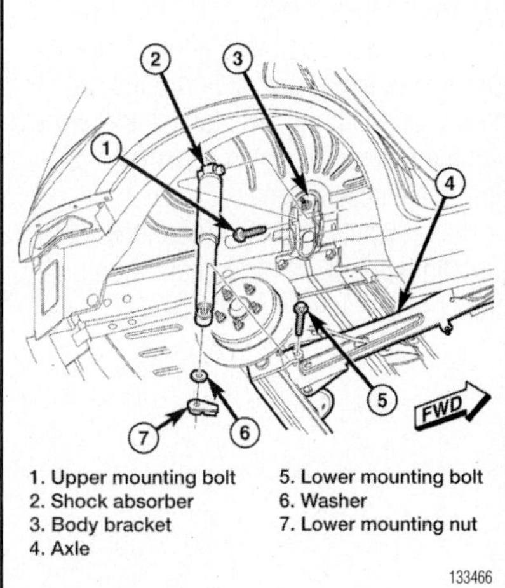

Fig. 239 Shock absorber and related components — exploded view

SPINDLE

REMOVAL & INSTALLATION

See Figures 240 and 241.

1. Before servicing the vehicle, refer to the Precautions section.
2. Raise and support the vehicle.
3. Remove the tire and wheel assembly.
4. Remove the hub and bearing assembly. Refer to Hub and Bearing Assembly, removal & installation.
5. Remove the 2 bolts on the axle trailing arm securing the parking brake cable and routing brackets to the axle trailing arm.
6. Remove the screw securing the anti-lock wheel speed sensor to the disc brake adapter. Remove the sensor head from the adapter.
7. Remove the 4 bolts securing the disc brake adapter and spindle to the axle.
8. Move the disc brake adapter outward, away from the axle. At the same time, loosen the spindle from the axle and remove it from the back of the disc brake adapter.

To install:

9. Place a NEW seal on the spindle.
10. Insert the spindle (with seal) from the back into the disc brake adapter, then position the spindle and disc brake adapter on the end of the axle.
11. If not using new mounting bolts, clean the threads of the old bolts used to mount the disc brake adapter and spindle to the axle, then apply stud and bearing mount adhesive to the bolt threads.
12. Install the 4 bolts securing the disc brake adapter and spindle to the axle. Tighten the mounting bolts to 70 ft. lbs. (95 Nm).

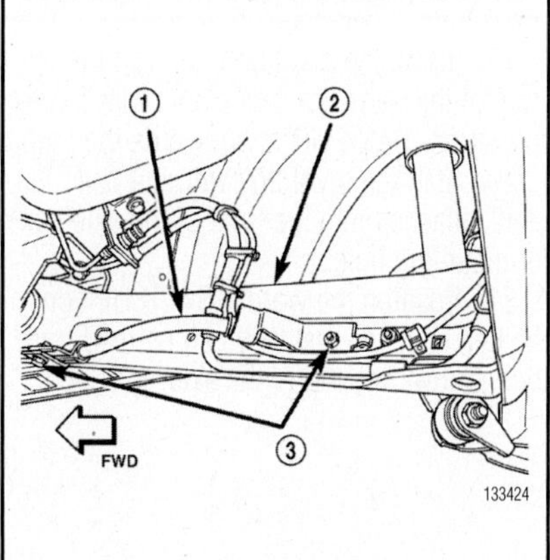

Fig. 240 Remove the 2 bolts (3) on the axle trailing arm securing the parking brake cable (1) and routing brackets to the axle trailing arm (2)

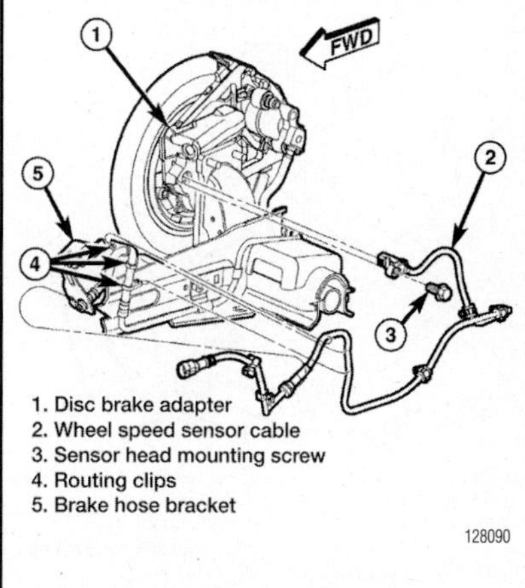

Fig. 241 Rear wheel speed sensor mounting

13. On vehicles equipped with ABS, install the wheel speed sensor head in the disc brake adapter. Install and tighten the mounting screw to 105 inch lbs. (12 Nm).
14. Align the cable routing brackets with their mounts on the trailing arm. Install the 2 bolts securing the cable and routing brackets to the trailing arm. Tighten the mounting bolts to 100 inch lbs. (11 Nm).
15. Install the hub and bearing assembly. Refer to Hub and Bearing Assembly, removal & installation.
16. Install tire and wheel assembly. Install and tighten wheel mounting nuts to 100 ft. lbs. (135 Nm).
17. Lower the vehicle.
18. Pump the brake pedal several times to ensure the vehicle has a firm brake pedal before moving the vehicle.

WATTS LINK ASSEMBLY

REMOVAL & INSTALLATION

See Figures 242 and 243.

1. Before servicing the vehicle, refer to the Precautions section.
2. Raise and support the vehicle.
3. Remove the cap from the upper link ball joint nut.
4. Remove the nut securing the upper link ball joint to the bell crank.
5. Install remover on the upper link ball joint at the bell crank, and release the ball joint from the bell crank.
6. Remove the bolt and nut securing the upper link to the body bracket.
7. Remove the upper link.
8. Remove the nut securing the bell crank pivot bolt in the center of the axle.
9. With the bolt still installed, slide the bell crank away from the axle just enough to

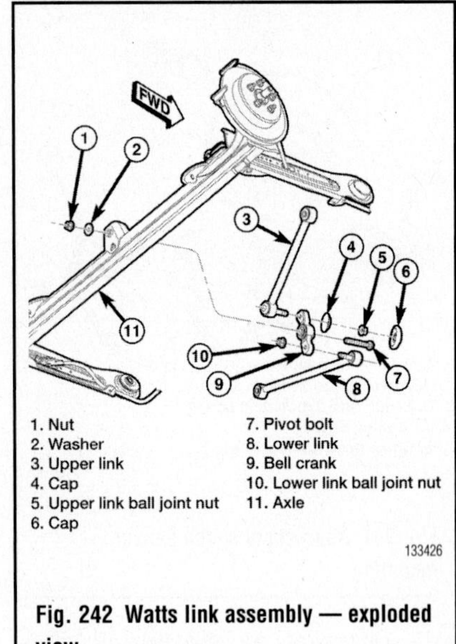

Fig. 242 Watts link assembly — exploded view

allow removal of the nut securing the lower link to the bell crank.

10. Remove the nut securing the lower link ball joint to the bell crank.
11. Install remover on the lower link ball joint at the bell crank, and release the ball joint from the bell crank.
12. Remove the pivot bolt and bell crank.
13. Remove the bolt securing the link to the body bracket.
14. Remove the lower link.

To install:

WARNING

When installing the upper and lower links, DO NOT attempt to turn the ball joint end of the link independently.

15. Install the upper link into the body bracket. Make sure the ball joint end is positioned properly for mounting to the bell crank.
16. Install the bolt securing the link to the bracket. Do not fully tighten at this time.
17. Install the lower link into the body bracket. Make sure the ball joint end is positioned properly for mounting to the bell crank.
18. Install the bolt securing the link to the bracket. Do not fully tighten at this time.

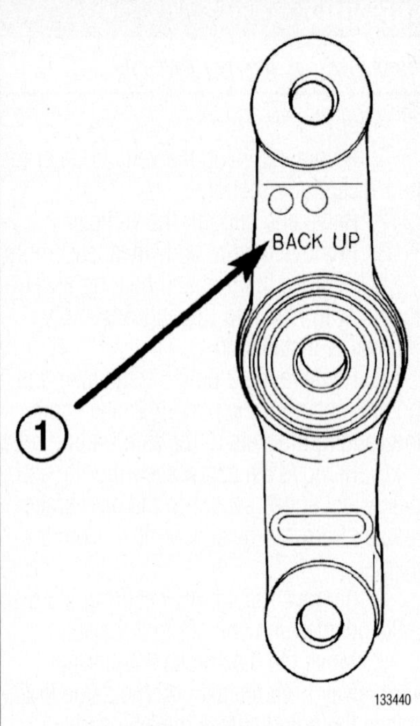

Fig. 243 Position the words "BACK UP" (1) on the bell crank so that they can be read from the rear over the top of the axle

WARNING

Although both ends of the bell crank appear to be the same, they are not. When installing the watts links or bell crank, make sure the bell crank is properly positioned. When mounted properly, the words "BACK UP" should be able to be read from the rear over the top of the axle. If the words cannot be read at this position, the bell crank must be removed and reinstalled so that the words "BACK UP" can be read on the upper rear of the bell crank once installed.

19. Install the pivot bolt through the front of the watts link bell crank. Make sure the words "BACK UP" are towards the rear.
20. Start the pivot bolt with the bell crank attached into the front of the axle center mounting hole.
21. Position the words "BACK UP" on the bell crank so that they can be read from the rear over the top of the axle.

WARNING

When installing and tightening the watts link ball joint nuts, DO NOT allow the stud to rotate. If the stud spins in its socket, damage to the joint can occur.

22. Attach the lower link to the bell crank. Install the nut on the ball joint stud. While holding the ball joint stud from turning, tighten the nut to 10 ft. lbs. (14 Nm) plus an additional 180 ° turn after torque is met.
23. Slide the bell crank pivot bolt all the way through the axle.
24. Place the washer and nut on the end of the pivot bolt, and tighten it to 110 ft. lbs. (149 Nm).
25. Attach the upper link to the bell crank. Install the cap, and nut on the ball joint stud. While holding the ball joint stud from turning, tighten the nut to 10 ft. lbs. (14 Nm) plus an additional 180 ° turn after torque is met.
26. Install the cap on the ball joint nut.
27. Place the vehicle on an alignment rack or drive-on hoist.
28. With the suspension at curb height, tighten the link mounting bolt at the body bracket to 68 ft. lbs. (92 Nm).

WHEEL BEARINGS

REMOVAL & INSTALLATION

The rear wheel bearing and wheel mounting hub used on this vehicle are a one-piece sealed unit or hub and bearing assembly. It is permanently lubricated when assembled and is sealed for life. There is no periodic lubrication or maintenance recommended for these units.

Vehicles equipped with antilock brakes have a tone wheel pressed onto the rear of the hub and bearing. The tone wheel works with the rear wheel speed sensors to provide wheel speed signal.

The only serviceable components of the hub and bearing are the wheel mounting studs pressed into the hub.

DODGE

Ram 1500

15

SPECIFICATIONS AND MAINTENANCE CHARTS

ENGINE AND VEHICLE IDENTIFICATION

Engine							Model Year	
Code ①	Liters (cc)	Cu. In.	Cyl.	Fuel Sys.	Engine Type	Eng. Mfg.	Code ②	Year
K	3.7 (3703)	226	6	Fuel Inj.	SOHC	Chrysler	A	2010
P	4.7 (4700)	287	8	Fuel Inj.	SOHC	Chrysler	B	2011
T	5.7 (5700)	348	8	Fuel Inj.	SOHC	Chrysler		

① 8th position of VIN

② 10th position of VIN

25766_RAM1_C0001

GENERAL ENGINE SPECIFICATIONS

All measurements are given in inches.

Year	Model	Engine Displacement Liters	Engine ID/VIN	Fuel System Type	Net Horsepower @ rpm	Net Torque @ rpm (ft. lbs.)	Bore x Stroke (in.)	Com-pression Ratio	Oil Pressure @ rpm
2010	1500	3.7	K	Fuel Inj.	211@5200	236@4000	3.66x3.40	9.6:1	25-110@3000
	1500	4.7	P	Fuel Inj.	310@5650	330@3950	3.66x3.40	9.6:1	30-105@3000
	1500	5.7	T	Fuel Inj.	390@5600	407@4000	3.92x3.58	10.5:1	25-110@3000
2011	1500	3.7	K	Fuel Inj.	211@5200	236@4000	3.66x3.40	9.6:1	25-110@3000
	1500	4.7	P	Fuel Inj.	310@5650	330@3950	3.66x3.40	9.6:1	30-105@3000
	1500	5.7	T	Fuel Inj.	390@5600	407@4000	3.92x3.58	10.5:1	25-110@3000

25766_RAM1_C0002

ENGINE TUNE-UP SPECIFICATIONS

Year	Engine Displacement Liters	Engine ID/VIN	Spark Plug Gap (in.)	Ignition Timing (deg.)		Fuel Pump (psi)	Idle Speed (rpm)		Valve Clearance	
				MT	AT		MT	AT	Intake	Exhaust
2010	3.7	K	0.043	---	①	58 +/- 2	---	①	②	②
	4.7	P	③	---	①	58 +/- 2	---	①	②	②
	5.7	T	0.04	---	①	58 +/- 2	---	①	②	②
2011	3.7	K	0.043	---	①	58 +/- 2	---	①	②	②
	4.7	P	③	---	①	58 +/- 2	---	①	②	②
	5.7	T	0.04	---	①	58 +/- 2	---	①	②	②

N/A: Information not available.

① Not adjustable on any engine; computer controlled.

② Valve clearance is maintained by hydraulic lash adjusters.

③ Intake plugs (upper row): 0.040 in.
Exhaust plugs (lower row): 0.050 in.

25766_RAM1_C0003

CAPACITIES

Year	Model	Engine Displacement Liters	Engine ID/VIN	Engine Oil with Filter (qts.)	Transmission (pts.) Auto.	Drive Axle (pts.) Front	Drive Axle (pts.) Rear	Transfer Case (pts.)	Fuel Tank (gal.)	Cooling System (qts.)
2010	Ram 1500	3.7	K	5.0	①	②	③	④	⑤	14.0
		4.7	P	6.0	①	②	③	④	⑤	14.0
		5.7	T	7.0	①	②	③	④	⑤	16.0
2011	Ram 1500	3.7	K	5.0	①	②	③	④	⑤	14.0
		4.7	P	6.0	①	②	③	④	⑤	14.0
		5.7	T	7.0	①	②	③	④	⑤	16.0

NOTE: All capacities are approximate. Add fluid gradually and ensure a proper fluid level is obtained.

① Service fill: 8.8 pts.
Overhaul/fill: 17.6 pts.

② Corporate Axles:
C200F axle: 3.5 pts.
C205F axle: 3.4 pts.
Dana Axles:
Dana 186 FBI axle: 2.11 pts.
Dana 186 FIA axle: 2.26 pts.
Dana 216 FBI axle: 2.74 pts.
American Axles:
9.25 axle: 4.64 pts.
9.25 axle w/anti-spin: 4.22 pts.

③ Corporate Axles:
8.25 axle: 4.39 pts
8.25 w/anti-spin: 4.43 pts.
9.25 axle: 4.64 pts.
9.25 w/anti-spin: 4.43 pts.
Dana Axles:
226 RBI axle: 4.75 pts
226 RIA w/anti-spin: 2.85 pts.
American Axles:
10.5 axle: 5.28 pts.
10.5 axle w/anti-spin: 5.28 pts.

④ NV243: 3.4 pts.
NV271: 4.0 pts.
NV273: 4.0 pts.
BW 44-44: 3.0 pts.

⑤ Standard: 26 gal.
Optional: 32 gal.

25766_RAM1_C0004

FLUID SPECIFICATIONS

Year	Model	Engine Disp. Liters	Engine Oil	Auto. Trans.	Drive Axle Front	Drive Axle Rear	Transfer Case	Power Steering Fluid	Brake Master Cylinder	Cooling System
2010	Ram 1500	3.7	5W-20	Mopar ATF+4	75W-140 ①	75W-140 ①	Mopar ATF+4	Mopar ATF+4	DOT 3	Mopar Coolant
		4.7	5W-20	Mopar ATF+4	75W-140 ①	75W-140 ①	Mopar ATF+4	Mopar ATF+4	DOT 3	Mopar Coolant
		5.7	5W-20	Mopar ATF+4	75W-140 ①	75W-140 ①	Mopar ATF+4	Mopar ATF+4	DOT 3	Mopar Coolant
2011	Ram 1500	3.7	5W-20	Mopar ATF+4	75W-140 ①	75W-140 ①	Mopar ATF+4	Mopar ATF+4	DOT 3	Mopar Coolant
		4.7	5W-20	Mopar ATF+4	75W-140 ①	75W-140 ①	Mopar ATF+4	Mopar ATF+4	DOT 3	Mopar Coolant
		5.7	5W-20	Mopar ATF+4	75W-140 ①	75W-140 ①	Mopar ATF+4	Mopar ATF+4	DOT 3	Mopar Coolant

DOT: Department Of Transpotation
① Synthetic gear lubricant for all axles, except C205F which uses 75W-90 synthetic gear oil.

25766_RAM1_C0005

VALVE SPECIFICATIONS

Year	Engine Displacement Liters	Engine ID/VIN	Seat Angle (deg.)	Face Angle (deg.)	Spring Test Pressure (lbs. @ in.)	Spring Free-Length (in.)	Spring Installed Height (in.)	Stem-to-Guide Clearance (in.)		Stem Diameter (in.)	
								Intake	Exhaust	Intake	Exhaust
2010	3.7	K	44.5-45.0	44.5-45.0	①	②	N/A	0.0008-0.0028	0.0019-0.0039	0.2729-0.2739	0.2717-0.2728
	4.7	P	45.0-45.5	45.0-45.5	③	1.929	1.579	0.0008-0.0028	0.0019-0.0039	0.2729-0.2739	0.2717-0.2728
	5.7	T	44.5-45.0	44.5-45.0	④	2.189	1.810	0.0008-0.0025	0.0009-0.0025	0.312-0.313	0.312-0.313
2011	3.7	K	44.5-45.0	44.5-45.0	①	②	N/A	0.0008-0.0028	0.0019-0.0039	0.2729-0.2739	0.2717-0.2728
	4.7	P	45.0-45.5	45.0-45.5	③	1.929	1.579	0.0008-0.0028	0.0019-0.0039	0.2729-0.2739	0.2717-0.2728
	5.7	T	44.5-45.0	44.5-45.0	④	2.189	1.810	0.0008-0.0025	0.0009-0.0025	0.312-0.313	0.312-0.313

N/A: Information not available.

① Intake (valve closed): 74.63-82.72 lbs. @ 1.5795 in.
Exhaust (valve closed): 80.031-88.57 lbs. @ 1.54 in.
Intake (valve open): 213.2-233.8 lbs. @ 1.107 in.
Exhaust (valve open): 196.5-214.9 lbs. @ 1.067 in.

② Intake: 1.896 in.
Exhaust: 1.973 in.

③ Intake (valve closed): 70.365-79.582 lbs. @ 1.5795 in.
Exhaust (valve closed): 70.365-79.582 lbs. @ 1.5795 in.
Intake (valve open): 174.45-195.58 lbs. @ 1.137 in.
Exhaust (valve open): 174.45-195.58 lbs. @ 1.137 in.

④ Intake & exhaust (valve closed): 92.8-102.8 lbs. @ 1.771 in.
Intake & exhaust (valve open): 231.0-253.0 lbs. @ 1.283 in.

25766_RAM1_C0006

WHEEL ALIGNMENT

Year	Model		Caster Range (+/-Deg.)	Caster Preferred Setting (Deg.)	Camber Range (+/-Deg.)	Camber Preferred Setting (Deg.)	Toe-in (in.)
2010	1500	LF	3.00 to 4.00 ①	3.50 ①	-0.40 to 0.60	0.10	0.10
		RF	3.25 to 4.25 ①	3.75 ①	-0.60 to 0.40	-0.10	0.10
		R	---	---	-0.60 to 0.40	-0.10	0.30
2011	1500	LF	3.00 to 4.00 ①	3.50 ①	-0.40 to 0.60	0.10	0.10
		RF	3.25 to 4.25 ①	3.75 ①	-0.60 to 0.40	-0.10	0.10
		R	---	---	-0.60 to 0.40	-0.10	0.30

① With 17 in. tires.

With 20 in. tires:

Range for LF is 3.00 to 4.00 degrees.

Preferred setting for LF is 3.50 degrees.

Range for RF is 3.40 to 4.40 degrees.

Preferred setting for RF is 3.90 degrees.

25766_RAM1_C0011

TIRE, WHEEL AND BALL JOINT SPECIFICATIONS

Year	Model	OEM Tires Standard	OEM Tires Optional	Tire Pressures (psi) Front	Tire Pressures (psi) Rear	Wheel Size	Ball Joint Inspection	Lug Nut (ft. lbs.)
2010	1500	P245/70R17	①	②	②	③	0.20 in.	130
2011	1500	P265/70R17	①	②	②	③	0.20 in.	130

OEM: Original Equipment Manufacturer

PSI: Pounds Per Square Inch

NA: Information not available

① These vehicles use a wide variety of optional tire sizes. Contact dealer or local tire supplier for sizes and applications.

② See label on front door jamb or consult Owner's Manual for tire pressures.

③ Wheel sizes vary according to tire applications.

25766_RAM1_C0012

BRAKE SPECIFICATIONS

All measurements in inches unless noted

Year	Model		Brake Disc Original Thickness	Brake Disc Minimum Thickness	Brake Disc Max. Runout	Brake Drum Original Inside Diameter	Brake Drum Max. Wear Limit	Brake Drum Maximum Machine Diamter	Minimum Pad/Lining Thickness Front	Minimum Pad/Lining Thickness Rear	Brake Caliper Bracket Bolts (ft. lbs.)	Brake Caliper Mounting Bolts (ft. lbs.)
2010	1500	F	1.100	1.039	0.0020	---	---	---	N/A	N/A	130	24
		R	0.860	0.803	0.0020	---	---	---	N/A	N/A	120	22
2011	1500	F	1.100	1.039	0.0020	---	---	---	N/A	N/A	130	24
		R	0.860	0.803	0.0020	---	---	---	N/A	N/A	120	22

F: Front

R: Rear

N/A: Information not available

25766_RAM1_C0013

SCHEDULED MAINTENANCE INTERVALS

2010-2011 Ram 1500 3.7L Engine - Normal & Severe (as noted)

TO BE SERVICED	TYPE OF SERVICE	VEHICLE MILEAGE INTERVAL (x1000)												
		6	12	18	24	30	36	42	48	54	60	66	72	78
Engine oil & filter	Replace	✓	✓	✓	✓	✓	✓	✓	✓	✓	✓	✓	✓	✓
Rotate tires, inspect tread wear, measure tread depth and check pressure	Rotate/Inspect	✓	✓	✓	✓	✓	✓	✓	✓	✓	✓	✓	✓	✓
Brake system components	Inspect/Service		✓		✓		✓		✓		✓		✓	
Exhaust system & heat shields	Inspect		✓		✓		✓		✓		✓		✓	
Inspect the front suspension, tie rod ends and boot seals for cracks or leaks and all parts for damage, wear, improper looseness or end play.	Inspect		✓		✓		✓		✓		✓		✓	
Engine air filter - Normal	Replace					✓					✓			
Engine air filter - Severe	Replace		✓		✓		✓		✓		✓		✓	
Engine coolant	Flush/Replace										✓			
Spark plugs	Replace					✓					✓			
PCV valve	Inspect/Service	Every 90,000 miles												
Automatic transmission fluid and filter - Normal	Inspect	Every 120,000 miles												
Automatic transmission fluid and filter - Severe	Inspect	Every 60,000 miles												
Accessory drive belt	Replace	Every 120,000 miles												
Battery	Inspect/Service	✓	✓	✓	✓	✓	✓	✓	✓	✓	✓	✓	✓	✓
Horn, exterior lamps, turn signals and hazard warning light operation	Inspect	✓	✓	✓	✓	✓	✓	✓	✓	✓	✓	✓	✓	✓
Fluid levels (all)	Inspect/Service	✓	✓	✓	✓	✓	✓	✓	✓	✓	✓	✓	✓	✓
Rear axle fluid - Severe	Replace			✓			✓			✓			✓	
Ignition cables	Replace										✓			

25766_RAM1_C0014

SCHEDULED MAINTENANCE INTERVALS

2010-2011 Ram 1500 4.7L Engine - Normal & Severe (as noted)

TO BE SERVICED	TYPE OF SERVICE	VEHICLE MILEAGE INTERVAL (x1000)												
		6	12	18	24	30	36	42	48	54	60	66	72	78
Engine oil & filter	Replace	✓	✓	✓	✓	✓	✓	✓	✓	✓	✓	✓	✓	✓
Rotate tires, inspect tread wear, measure tread depth and check pressure	Rotate/Inspect	✓	✓	✓	✓	✓	✓	✓	✓	✓	✓	✓	✓	✓
Brake system components - Normal	Inspect/Service						✓		✓		✓		✓	
Brake system components - Severe	Inspect/Service		✓		✓		✓		✓		✓		✓	
Exhaust system & heat shields	Inspect		✓		✓		✓		✓		✓		✓	
Inspect the front suspension, tie rod ends and boot seals for cracks or leaks and all parts for damage, wear, improper looseness or end play.	Inspect		✓		✓		✓		✓		✓		✓	
CV Joints - Severe	Inspect		✓		✓		✓		✓		✓		✓	
Engine air filter - Normal	Replace					✓					✓			
Engine air filter - Severe	Replace		✓		✓		✓		✓		✓		✓	
Adjust parking brake on vehicles equipped with four-wheel disc brakes	Adjust					✓					✓			
Engine coolant	Flush/Replace										✓			
Spark plugs - (top row only) - Normal	Replace								✓					
Spark plugs - (side row only) - Normal	Replace	Every 96,000 miles												
PCV valve	Inspect/Service	Every 90,000 miles												
Automatic transmission fluid and filter - Normal	Inspect	Every 120,000 miles												
Automatic transmission fluid and filter - Severe	Inspect	Every 60,000 miles												
Accessory drive belt	Replace	Every 120,000 miles												
Battery	Inspect/Service	✓	✓	✓	✓	✓	✓	✓	✓	✓	✓	✓	✓	✓
Horn, exterior lamps, turn signals and hazard warning light operation	Inspect	✓	✓	✓	✓	✓	✓	✓	✓	✓	✓	✓	✓	✓
Fluid levels (all)	Inspect/Service	✓	✓	✓	✓	✓	✓	✓	✓	✓	✓	✓	✓	✓
Passenger compartment air filter	Replace				✓				✓				✓	
Ignition cables	Replace	Every 96,000 miles												

25766_RAM1_C0015

SCHEDULED MAINTENANCE INTERVALS

2010-2011 Ram 1500 5.7L Engine - Normal & Severe (as noted)

TO BE SERVICED	TYPE OF SERVICE	VEHICLE MILEAGE INTERVAL (x1000)												
		6	12	18	24	30	36	42	48	54	60	66	72	84
Engine oil & filter	Replace	✓	✓	✓	✓	✓	✓	✓	✓	✓	✓	✓	✓	✓
Rotate tires, inspect tread wear, measure tread depth and check pressure	Rotate/Inspect	✓	✓	✓	✓	✓	✓	✓	✓	✓	✓	✓	✓	✓
Brake system components	Inspect/Service		✓		✓		✓		✓		✓		✓	
Exhaust system & heat shields	Inspect		✓		✓		✓		✓		✓		✓	
Inspect the front suspension, tie rod ends and boot seals for cracks or leaks and all parts for damage, wear, improper looseness or end play.	Inspect		✓		✓		✓		✓		✓		✓	
CV Joints	Inspect			✓			✓			✓			✓	
Engine air filter - Normal	Replace				✓				✓				✓	
Engine air filter - Severe	Replace		✓		✓		✓		✓		✓		✓	
Adjust parking brake on vehicles equipped with four-wheel disc brakes	Adjust				✓				✓				✓	
Engine coolant	Flush/Replace										✓			
Spark plugs	Replace				✓				✓				✓	
PCV valve	Inspect/Service												✓	
Automatic transmission fluid and filter - Normal	Inspect	Every 60,000 miles												
Automatic transmission fluid and filter - Severe	Inspect	Every 120,000 miles												
Accessory drive belt	Replace	Every 120,000 miles												
Battery	Inspect/Service	✓	✓	✓	✓	✓	✓	✓	✓	✓	✓	✓	✓	✓
Horn, exterior lamps, turn signals and hazard warning light operation	Inspect	✓	✓	✓	✓	✓	✓	✓	✓	✓	✓	✓	✓	✓
Fluid levels (all)	Inspect/Service	✓	✓	✓	✓	✓	✓	✓	✓	✓	✓	✓	✓	✓
Rear axle fluid	Inspect/Service			✓			✓			✓			✓	
Passenger compartment air filter	Replace		✓		✓		✓		✓		✓		✓	

25766_RAM1_C0016

PRECAUTIONS

Before servicing any vehicle, please be sure to read all of the following precautions, which deal with personal safety, prevention of component damage, and important points to take into consideration when servicing a motor vehicle:

- Never open, service or drain the radiator or cooling system when the engine is hot; serious burns can occur from the steam and hot coolant.
- Observe all applicable safety precautions when working around fuel. Whenever servicing the fuel system, always work in a well-ventilated area. Do not allow fuel spray or vapors to come in contact with a spark, open flame, or excessive heat (a hot drop light, for example). Keep a dry chemical fire extinguisher near the work area. Always keep fuel in a container specifically designed for fuel storage; also, always properly seal fuel containers to avoid the possibility of fire or explosion. Refer to the additional fuel system precautions later in this section.
- Fuel injection systems often remain pressurized, even after the engine has been turned **OFF**. The fuel system pressure must be relieved before disconnecting any fuel lines. Failure to do so may result in fire and/or personal injury.
- Brake fluid often contains polyglycol ethers and polyglycols. Avoid contact with the eyes and wash your hands thoroughly after handling brake fluid. If you do get brake fluid in your eyes, flush your eyes with clean, running water for 15 minutes. If eye irritation persists, or if you have taken brake fluid internally, IMMEDIATELY seek medical assistance.
- The EPA warns that prolonged contact with used engine oil may cause a number of skin disorders, including cancer. You should make every effort to minimize your exposure to used engine oil. Protective gloves should be worn when changing oil. Wash your hands and any other exposed skin areas as soon as possible after exposure to used engine oil. Soap and water, or waterless hand cleaner should be used.
- All new vehicles are now equipped with an air bag system, often referred to as a Supplemental Restraint System (SRS) or Supplemental Inflatable Restraint (SIR) system. The system must be disabled before performing service on or around system components, steering column, instrument panel components, wiring and sensors. Failure to follow safety and disabling procedures could result in accidental air bag deployment, possible personal injury and unnecessary system repairs.
- Always wear safety goggles when working with, or around, the air bag system. When carrying a non-deployed air bag, be sure the bag and trim cover are pointed away from your body. When placing a non-deployed air bag on a work surface, always face the bag and trim cover upward, away from the surface. This will reduce the motion of the module if it is accidentally deployed. Refer to the additional air bag system precautions later in this section.
- Clean, high quality brake fluid from a sealed container is essential to the safe and proper operation of the brake system. You should always buy the correct type of brake fluid for your vehicle. If the brake fluid becomes contaminated, completely flush the system with new fluid. Never reuse any brake fluid. Any brake fluid that is removed from the system should be discarded. Also, do not allow any brake fluid to come in contact with a painted surface; it will damage the paint.
- Never operate the engine without the proper amount and type of engine oil; doing so WILL result in severe engine damage.
- Timing belt maintenance is extremely important. Many models utilize an interference-type, non-freewheeling engine. If the timing belt breaks, the valves in the cylinder head may strike the pistons, causing potentially serious (also time-consuming and expensive) engine damage. Refer to the maintenance interval charts for the recommended replacement interval for the timing belt, and to the timing belt section for belt replacement and inspection.
- Disconnecting the negative battery cable on some vehicles may interfere with the functions of the on-board computer system(s) and may require the computer to undergo a relearning process once the negative battery cable is reconnected.
- When servicing drum brakes, only disassemble and assemble one side at a time, leaving the remaining side intact for reference.
- Only an MVAC-trained, EPA-certified automotive technician should service the air conditioning system or its components.

BRAKES

ANTI-LOCK BRAKE SYSTEM (ABS)

GENERAL INFORMATION

PRECAUTIONS

- Certain components within the ABS system are not intended to be serviced or repaired individually.
- Do not use rubber hoses or other parts not specifically specified for and ABS system. When using repair kits, replace all parts included in the kit. Partial or incorrect repair may lead to functional problems and require the replacement of components.
- Lubricate rubber parts with clean, fresh brake fluid to ease assembly. Do not use shop air to clean parts; damage to rubber components may result.
- Use only DOT 3 brake fluid from an unopened container.
- If any hydraulic component or line is removed or replaced, it may be necessary to bleed the entire system.
- A clean repair area is essential. Always clean the reservoir and cap thoroughly before removing the cap. The slightest amount of dirt in the fluid may plug an orifice and impair the system function. Perform repairs after components have been thoroughly cleaned; use only denatured alcohol to clean components. Do not allow ABS components to come into contact with any substance containing mineral oil; this includes used shop rags.
- The Anti-Lock control unit is a microprocessor similar to other computer units in the vehicle. Ensure that the ignition switch is **OFF** before removing or installing controller harnesses. Avoid static electricity discharge at or near the controller.
- If any arc welding is to be done on the vehicle, the control unit should be unplugged before welding operations begin.

ABS CONTROL MODULE

The Antilock Brake Module (ABM) (2) is mounted to the Hydraulic Control Unit (HCU) (3) and operates the ABS system.

REMOVAL & INSTALLATION

See Figure 1.

1. Remove the negative battery cable from the battery.
2. Pull up on the ABM harness connector release and remove connector.
3. Remove the ABM mounting bolts.
4. Remove the pump connector from the ABM.
5. Remove the ABM from the HCU.

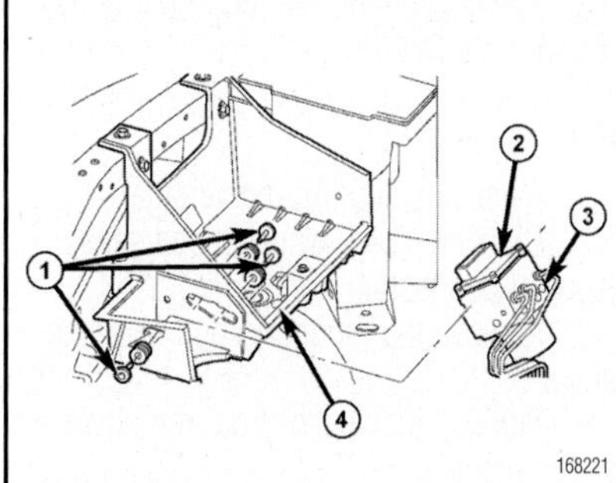

Fig. 1 The Antilock Brake Module (ABM) (2) is mounted to the Hydraulic Control Unit (HCU) (3) and operates the ABS system. Remove the retaining bolts (1) from the bracket (4)

CAUTION

When removing ABM from HCU, be sure to completely separate the two components (approximately 38 mm (1.5 in.) before removing ABM. Otherwise, damage to the pressure sensor or Pump Motor connection may result requiring HCU replacement. Do not to touch the sensor terminals on the HCU side or the contact pads on the ABM side as this may result in contamination and issues in the future.

To install:

➡If the ABM is being replaced with a new ABM is must be reprogrammed with the use of a scan tool.

6. Install ABM to the HCU.
7. Install the pump connector to the ABM.
8. Install mounting bolts and tighten.
9. Install the wiring harness connector to the ABM and push down on the release to secure the connector.
10. Install negative battery cable to the battery.
11. Connect the scan tool and initialize the ABM by performing the ABS Verification Test as follows:
    a. Turn the ignition off.
    b. Connect all previously disconnected components and connectors.
    c. Verify all accessories are turned off and the battery is fully charged.
    d. Verify that the ignition is on, with the scan tool, erase all Diagnostic Trouble Codes (DTCs) from all modules. Start the engine and allow it to run for two minutes and fully operate the system that was indicating the failure.
    e. Turn the ignition off and wait five seconds. Turn the ignition on and using the scan tool, read DTCs from all modules.
    f. If any Diagnostic Trouble Codes are present perform the appropriate diagnostic procedure.

➡For Sensor Signal and Pump Motor faults, the ABS Module must sense all 4 wheels at 7.5 mph before it will extinguish the ABS indicator.

    g. If there are no DTCs present after turning ignition on, road test the vehicle for at least five minutes. Perform several anti-lock braking stops.
    h. Again, with the scan tool read DTCs. If any DTCs are present, perform the diagnostic procedure and troubleshoot the new or recurring DTC.
    i. If there are no Diagnostic Trouble Codes (DTCs) present, and the customer's concern can no longer be duplicated, the repair is complete.
    j. If any DTCs are present or if the original concern is still present, repair is not complete, perform the appropriate diagnostic procedure.
    k. If no DTCs are present and the original concern is resolved, repair is complete.

DYNAMICS SENSOR (YAW RATE & LATERAL ACCELERATION SENSORS)

DESCRIPTION & OPERATION

See Figure 2.

The yaw rate, lateral acceleration and longitudinal acceleration sensors are housed into one unit known as the dynamics sensor. The sensor is used to measure vehicle rotational sensing (how fast the vehicle is turning - yaw), side-to-side (lateral) motion and longitudinal acceleration (forward). The dynamics sensor is located on the floor panel transmission tunnel under the center floor console (or if equipped with a bench seat, under the front center seat section) next to the Occupant Restraint Controller (ORC).

➡If the dynamics sensor is replaced, it must be initialized using the scan tool.

The yaw rate and lateral acceleration sensors cannot be serviced separately. The entire dynamics sensor must be replaced when necessary.

REMOVAL & INSTALLATION

1. Disconnect and isolate the battery negative cable.
2. If equipped with a center floor console, remove the console.

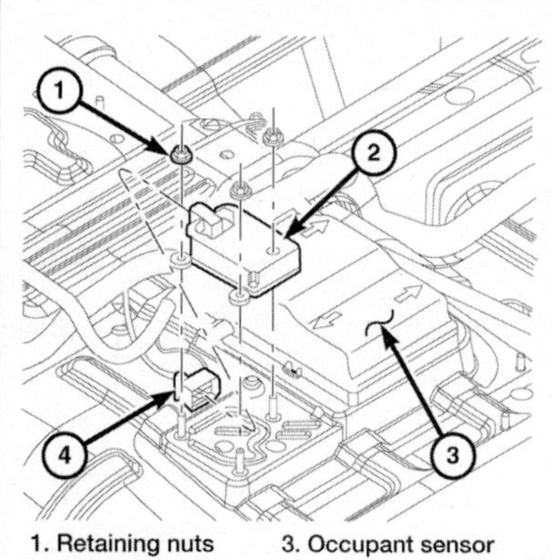

Fig. 2 Showing the location of the dynamics sensor

3. If equipped with a 40/20/40 bench seat, remove the passenger seat.
4. Disconnect the electrical connector for the dynamics sensor.
5. Remove the three mounting nuts for the sensor.
6. Remove the sensor from the vehicle.
7. Installation is the reverse of the removal procedure.

ELECTRONIC STABILITY CONTROL (ESC) SWITCH

REMOVAL & INSTALLATION

1. Remove the instrument panel center bezel.
2. Disconnect the Electronic Stability Control (ESC) electrical connector from the radio trim panel.
3. Remove the ESC switch from the switch bank.
4. Installation is the reverse of the removal procedure.

SPEED SENSORS

REMOVAL & INSTALLATION

Front

See Figure 3.

1. Remove the front rotor. See "Brake Rotor" in this section.
2. Remove the wheel speed sensor mounting bolt from the hub.
3. Remove the wheel speed sensor from the hub.
4. Remove the wiring from the clips and disconnect the electrical connector.

To install:

5. Installation is the reverse of the removal procedure.

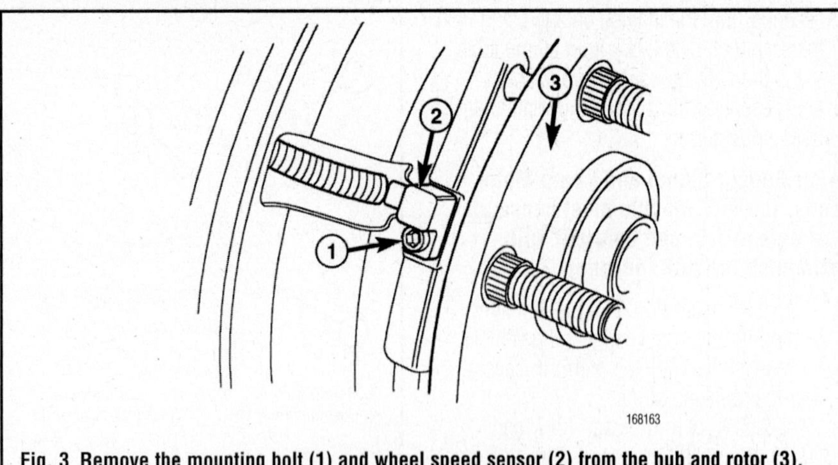

Fig. 3 Remove the mounting bolt (1) and wheel speed sensor (2) from the hub and rotor (3).

6. Tighten sensor retaining bolt to 190 inch lbs. (21 Nm).

Rear

1. Raise and support the vehicle.
2. Disconnect the wheel speed sensor electrical connector.
3. Remove the mounting bolt from the sensor.
4. Remove the sensor from the brake caliper adapter.

To install:

5. Installation is the reverse of the removal procedure.
6. Tighten sensor retaining bolt to 200 inch lbs. (24 Nm).

BRAKES — BLEEDING THE BRAKE SYSTEM

BLEEDING PROCEDURE

BLEEDING PROCEDURE

➡Use Mopar brake fluid, or an equivalent quality fluid meeting SAE J1703-F and DOT 3 standards only. Use fresh, clean fluid from a sealed container at all times.

1. Remove reservoir filler caps and fill reservoir.
2. If calipers were overhauled, open all caliper bleed screws. Then close each bleed screw as fluid starts to drip from it. Top off master cylinder reservoir once more before proceeding.
3. Attach one end of bleed hose to bleed screw and insert opposite end in glass container partially filled with brake fluid. Be sure end of bleed hose is immersed in fluid.

➡Bleed procedure should be in this order: Right rear, Left rear, Right front, Left front.

4. Open up bleeder, then have a helper press down the brake pedal. Once the pedal is down, hold the pedal down while closing the bleeder. Repeat bleeding until fluid stream is clear and free of bubbles. Then move to the next wheel.
5. Before moving the vehicle verify the pedal is firm and not mushy.
6. Top off the brake fluid and install the reservoir cap.

BRAKES — FRONT DISC BRAKES

⁂ CAUTION

Dust and dirt accumulating on brake parts during normal use may contain asbestos fibers from production or aftermarket brake linings. Breathing excessive concentrations of asbestos fibers can cause serious bodily harm. Exercise care when servicing brake parts. Do not sand or grind brake lining unless equipment used is designed to contain the dust residue. Do not clean brake parts with compressed air or by dry brushing. Cleaning should be done by dampening the brake components with a fine mist of water, then wiping the brake components clean with a dampened cloth. Dispose of cloth and all residue containing asbestos fibers in an impermeable container with the appropriate label. Follow practices prescribed by the Occupational Safety and Health Administration (OSHA) and the Environmental Protection Agency (EPA) for the handling, processing, and disposing of dust or debris that may contain asbestos fibers.

BRAKE CALIPER

REMOVAL & INSTALLATION

⁂ CAUTION

Never allow the disc brake caliper to hang from the brake hose. Damage to the brake hose will result. Provide a suitable support to hang the caliper securely.

1. Install prop rod on the brake pedal to keep pressure on the brake system, Holding pedal in this position will isolate master cylinder from hydraulic brake system and will not allow brake fluid to drain out of brake fluid reservoir while brake lines are open. This will allow you to bleed out the area of repair instead of the entire system.
2. Raise and support the vehicle.
3. Remove the tire and wheel assembly.
4. Compress the disc brake caliper.
5. Remove the banjo bolt and discard the copper washers.
6. Remove the caliper slide pin bolts.
7. Remove the disc brake caliper from the caliper adapter.

To install:

➡Petroleum based grease should not be used on any of the rubber components of the caliper, Use only Non-Petroleum based grease.

8. Install the disc brake caliper to the brake caliper adapter.
9. Install a new copper washers on the banjo bolt when installing the banjo bolt to the caliper. Tighten to 21 ft. lbs. (28 Nm).
10. Install the caliper slide pin bolts. Tighten to 24 ft. lbs. (32 Nm).
11. Remove the prop rod from the brake pedal.
12. Bleed the area of repair for the brake system. If a proper pedal is not felt during bleeding an area of repair then a base bleed system must be performed.
13. Install the tire and wheel assembly.
14. Remove the supports and lower the vehicle.

DISC BRAKE PADS

REMOVAL & INSTALLATION

1. Raise and support vehicle.
2. Remove the wheel and tire assemblies.
3. Compress the caliper.
4. Remove the caliper slide pin bolts.
5. Remove the caliper from the caliper adapter.

CAUTION

Do not allow brake hose to support caliper assembly.

6. Support and hang the caliper.
7. Remove the inboard brake pad from the caliper adapter.
8. Remove the outboard brake pad from the caliper adapter.
9. Remove the anti-rattle clips from the pad.

To install:

10. Bottom pistons in caliper bore with C-clamp. Place an old brake shoe between a C-clamp and caliper piston.
11. Clean caliper mounting adapter.
12. Install new anti-rattle clips to the brake pads.
13. Install inboard brake pad in adapter.
14. Install outboard brake pad in adapter.
15. Install the caliper over rotor, Then push the caliper onto the adapter.
16. Install caliper slide pin bolts.
17. Install wheel and tire assemblies and lower vehicle.
18. Apply brakes several times to seat caliper pistons and brake shoes and obtain firm pedal.
19. Top off master cylinder fluid level.

BRAKES

REAR DISC BRAKES

CAUTION

Dust and dirt accumulating on brake parts during normal use may contain asbestos fibers from production or aftermarket brake linings. Breathing excessive concentrations of asbestos fibers can cause serious bodily harm. Exercise care when servicing brake parts. Do not sand or grind brake lining unless equipment used is designed to contain the dust residue. Do not clean brake parts with compressed air or by dry brushing. Cleaning should be done by dampening the brake components with a fine mist of water, then wiping the brake components clean with a dampened cloth. Dispose of cloth and all residue containing asbestos fibers in an impermeable container with the appropriate label. Follow practices prescribed by the Occupational Safety and Health Administration (OSHA) and the Environmental Protection Agency (EPA) for the handling, processing, and disposing of dust or debris that may contain asbestos fibers.

BRAKE CALIPER

REMOVAL & INSTALLATION

CAUTION

Never allow the disc brake caliper to hang from the brake hose. Damage to the brake hose will result. Provide a suitable support to hang the caliper securely.

1. Install prop rod on the brake pedal to keep pressure on the brake system, Holding pedal in this position will isolate master cylinder from hydraulic brake system and will not allow brake fluid to drain out of brake fluid reservoir while brake lines are open. This will allow you to bleed out the area of repair instead of the entire system.
2. Raise and support vehicle.
3. Remove the wheel and tire assembly.
4. Drain small amount of fluid from master cylinder brake reservoir with suction gun.
5. Remove the brake hose banjo bolt and discard the copper washers if replacing caliper.
6. Remove the caliper slide bolts.
7. Remove the caliper from vehicle.

To install:

8. Install caliper to the caliper adapter.
9. Coat the caliper mounting slide pin bolts with silicone grease. Then, install and tighten the bolts to 22 ft. lbs. (30 Nm).
10. Verify that the brake hose is not twisted or kinked before tightening the fitting bolt.
11. Install the brake hose to the caliper with new copper washers and tighten fitting bolt to 21 ft. lbs. (28 Nm).
12. Remove the prop rod from the brake pedal.
13. Bleed the area of repair for the brake system. If a proper pedal is not felt during bleeding an area of repair then a base bleed system must be performed.
14. Install the wheel and tire assemblies.
15. Remove the supports and lower the vehicle.
16. Verify a firm pedal before moving the vehicle.

DISC BRAKE PADS

REMOVAL & INSTALLATION

1. Raise and support the vehicle.
2. Remove the rear wheel and tire assemblies.
3. Compress the caliper.
4. Remove caliper slide bolts.

CAUTION

Do not allow brake hose to support caliper assembly.

5. Remove the caliper by tilting the top out and off the caliper adapter.
6. Remove inboard brake shoe from the caliper adapter.
7. Remove outboard brake shoe from caliper adapter.

CAUTION

Anti-rattle springs are not interchangeable.

8. Remove the top anti-rattle spring from the caliper adapter.
9. Remove the bottom anti-rattle spring from the caliper adapter

To install:

10. Clean caliper mounting adapter and anti-rattle springs.

Lubricate anti-rattle springs with Mopar brake grease.

CAUTION

Anti-rattle springs are not interchangeable.

11. Install new top anti-rattle spring.
12. Install new bottom anti-rattle spring.
13. Install inboard brake shoe in adapter.
14. Install outboard brake shoe in adapter.
15. Tilt the bottom of the caliper over rotor and under adapter. Then push the top of the caliper down onto the adapter.
16. Install caliper.
17. Install wheel and tire assemblies.
18. Remove the supports and lower the vehicle.
19. Apply brakes several times to seat caliper pistons and brake shoes and obtain firm pedal.
20. Top off master cylinder fluid level.

PARKING BRAKE CABLES

ADJUSTMENT

See Figure 4.

➡Tensioner adjustment is only necessary when the tensioner, or a cable has been replaced or disconnected for service. When adjustment is necessary, perform adjustment only as described in the following procedure. This is necessary to avoid faulty park brake operation.

1. Raise the vehicle.
2. Back off the cable tensioner adjusting nut to create slack in the cables.
3. Remove the rear wheel/tire assemblies. Then remove the brake rotors.
4. Verify the brakes are in good condition and operating properly.
5. Verify the park brake cables operate freely and are not binding, or seized.
6. Check the rear brake shoe adjustment with standard brake gauge.
7. Install the rotors and verify that the rotors rotate freely without drag.
8. Install the wheel/tire assemblies.
9. Lower the vehicle enough for access to the park brake foot pedal. Then fully apply the park brakes.

➡Leave park brakes applied until adjustment is complete.

10. Raise the vehicle again.
11. Mark the tensioner rod 1/4 in. (6.35 mm) from edge of the tensioner.
12. Tighten the adjusting nut on the tensioner rod until the mark is no longer visible.

➡Do not loosen, or tighten the tensioner adjusting nut for any reason after completing adjustment.

13. Lower the vehicle until the rear wheels are 6–8 in. (15–20 cm) off the shop floor.
14. Release the park brake foot pedal and verify that rear wheels rotate freely without drag. Then lower the vehicle.

PARKING BRAKE SHOES

REMOVAL & INSTALLATION

See Figures 5 through 7.

1. Raise and support the vehicle.
2. Remove the tire and wheel assembly.
3. Remove the disc brake caliper and rotor, as described in this section.
4. Lockout the parking brake cable.
5. Disengage the park brake cable from behind the rotor assembly to allow easier disassembly of the park brake shoes.
6. Remove the rear axle shaft. See "DRIVE TRAIN" section.
7. Disassemble the rear park brake shoes

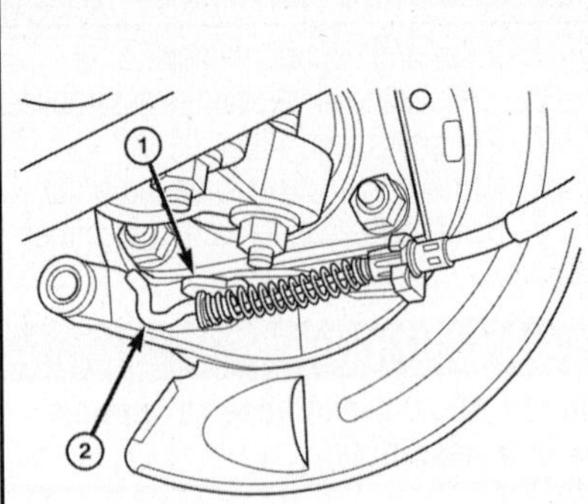

Fig. 6 Disengage the park brake cable (2) from behind the rotor assembly (1) to allow easier disassembly of the park brake shoes.

To install:

8. Reassemble the rear park brake shoes.
9. Install the axle shaft. See "DRIVE TRAIN" section.
10. Install the park brake cable to the lever behind the support plate.
11. Unlock the park brake cable.
12. Install the disc brake rotor.
13. Install the disc brake caliper.
14. Adjust the rear brake shoes.
15. Install the tire and wheel assembly.
16. Remove the support and lower the vehicle.

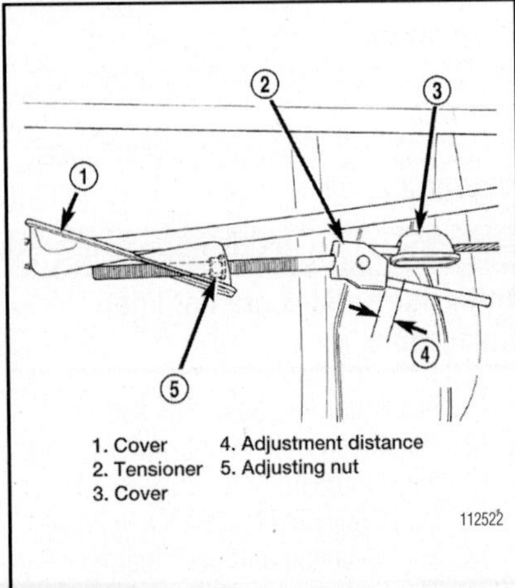

Fig. 4 Showing the parking brake adjustment points

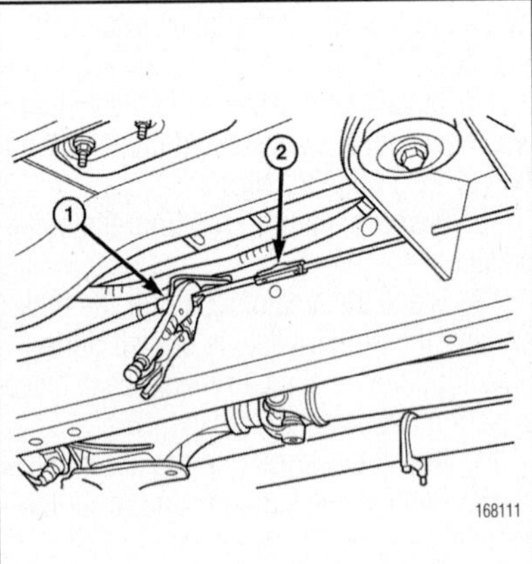

Fig. 5 Lockout the parking brake cable (2), using vice grip pliers (1).

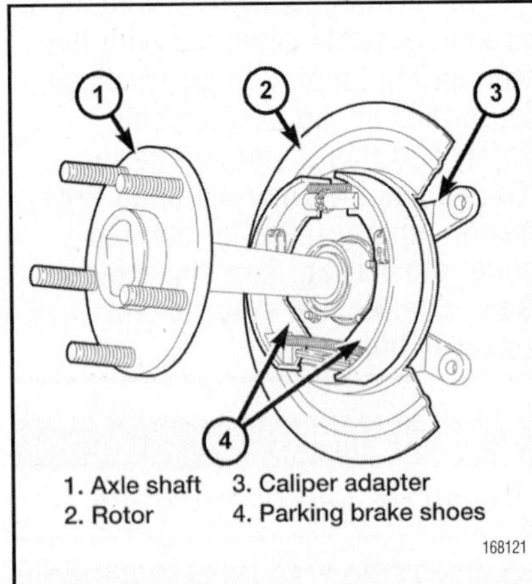

Fig. 7 Showing parking brake shoes and components

GENERAL INFORMATION

** CAUTION

These vehicles are equipped with an air bag system. The system must be disarmed before performing service on, or around, system components, the steering column, instrument panel components, wiring and sensors. Failure to follow the safety precautions and the disarming procedure could result in accidental air bag deployment, possible injury and unnecessary system repairs.

SERVICE PRECAUTIONS

Disconnect and isolate the battery negative cable before beginning any airbag system component diagnosis, testing, removal, or installation procedures. Allow system capacitor to discharge for two minutes before beginning any component service. This will disable the airbag system. Failure to disable the airbag system may result in accidental airbag deployment, personal injury, or death.

Do not place an intact undeployed airbag face down on a solid surface. The airbag will propel into the air if accidentally deployed and may result in personal injury or death.

When carrying or handling an undeployed airbag, the trim side (face) of the airbag should be pointing away from the body to minimize possibility of injury if accidental deployment occurs. Failure to do this may result in personal injury or death.

Replace airbag system components with OEM replacement parts. Substitute parts may appear interchangeable, but internal differences may result in inferior occupant protection. Failure to do so may result in occupant personal injury or death.

Wear safety glasses, rubber gloves, and long sleeved clothing when cleaning powder residue from vehicle after an airbag deployment. Powder residue emitted from a deployed airbag can cause skin irritation. Flush affected area with cool water if irritation is experienced. If nasal or throat irritation is experienced, exit the vehicle for fresh air until the irritation ceases. If irritation continues, see a physician.

Do not use a replacement airbag that is not in the original packaging. This may result in improper deployment, personal injury, or death.

The factory installed fasteners, screws and bolts used to fasten airbag components have a special coating and are specifically designed for the airbag system. Do not use substitute fasteners. Use only original equipment fasteners listed in the parts catalog when fastener replacement is required.

During, and following, any child restraint anchor service, due to impact event or vehicle repair, carefully inspect all mounting hardware, tether straps, and anchors for proper installation, operation, or damage. If a child restraint anchor is found damaged in any way, the anchor must be replaced. Failure to do this may result in personal injury or death.

Deployed and non-deployed airbags may or may not have live pyrotechnic material within the airbag inflator.

Do not dispose of driver/passenger/curtain airbags or seat belt tensioners unless you are sure of complete deployment. Refer to the Hazardous Substance Control System for proper disposal.

Dispose of deployed airbags and tensioners consistent with state, provincial, local, and federal regulations.

After any airbag component testing or service, do not connect the battery negative cable. Personal injury or death may result if the system test is not performed first.

If the vehicle is equipped with the Occupant Classification System (OCS), do not connect the battery negative cable before performing the OCS Verification Test using the scan tool and the appropriate diagnostic information. Personal injury or death may result if the system test is not performed properly.

Never replace both the Occupant Restraint Controller (ORC) and the Occupant Classification Module (OCM) at the same time. If both require replacement, replace one, then perform the Airbag System test before replacing the other.

Both the ORC and the OCM store Occupant Classification System (OCS) calibration data, which they transfer to one another when one of them is replaced. If both are replaced at the same time, an irreversible fault will be set in both modules and the OCS may malfunction and cause personal injury or death.

If equipped with OCS, the Seat Weight Sensor is a sensitive, calibrated unit and must be handled carefully. Do not drop or handle roughly. If dropped or damaged, replace with another sensor. Failure to do so may result in occupant injury or death.

If equipped with OCS, the front passenger seat must be handled carefully as well. When removing the seat, be careful when setting on floor not to drop. If dropped, the sensor may be inoperative, could result in occupant injury, or possibly death.

If equipped with OCS, when the passenger front seat is on the floor, no one should sit in the front passenger seat. This uneven force may damage the sensing ability of the seat weight sensors. If sat on and damaged, the sensor may be inoperative, could result in occupant injury, or possibly death.

DISARMING THE SYSTEM

1. Disconnect and isolate the battery negative cable.
2. Wait two minutes for the system capacitor to discharge before further service.

ARMING THE SYSTEM

1. Reconnect battery negative cable.

CLOCKSPRING CENTERING

Like the clockspring in a timepiece, the clockspring tape has travel limits and can be damaged by being wound too tightly during full stop-to-stop steering wheel rotation. To prevent this from occurring, the clockspring is centered when it is installed on the steering column. Centering the clockspring indexes the clockspring tape and the SAS integral to the clockspring to the movable steering components so that the tape can operate within its designed travel limits and the SAS can accurately monitor and communicate steering wheel inputs.

However, if the clockspring is removed from the steering column or if the steering shaft is disconnected from the steering gear, the clockspring spool and the SAS can change position relative to the movable steering components and relative to each other. The clockspring must be replaced if proper centering has been compromised or the tape may be damaged and Diagnostic Trouble Codes (DTC) or faults may be set within the SAS.

Service replacement clocksprings are shipped pre-centered and with a plastic locking pin installed. This locking pin should not be removed until the clockspring has been installed on the steering column. If the locking pin is removed before the clockspring is installed on a steering column, the clockspring must be replaced with a new unit. Proper clockspring installation must also be confirmed by viewing the SAS Menu Item, Data Display function using a diagnostic scan tool.

DRIVE TRAIN

AUTOMATIC TRANSMISSION FLUID

DRAIN & REFILL

➡To avoid overfilling transmission after a fluid change or overhaul, perform the following procedure:

1. Remove dipstick and insert clean funnel in transmission fill tube.
2. Add following initial quantity of Mopar ATF+4 to transmission:
   a. If only fluid and filter were changed, add 3 pints (1-1/2 quarts) of ATF+4 to transmission.
   b. If transmission was completely overhauled, torque converter was replaced or drained, and cooler was flushed, add 12 pints (6 quarts) of ATF+4 to transmission.
3. Apply parking brakes.
4. Start and run engine at normal curb idle speed.
5. Apply service brakes, shift transmission through all gear ranges then back to NEUTRAL, set parking brake, and leave engine running at curb idle speed.
6. Remove funnel, insert dipstick and check fluid level. If level is low, add fluid to bring level to MIN mark on dipstick. Check to see if the oil level is equal on both sides of the dipstick. If one side is noticeably higher than the other, the dipstick has picked up some oil from the dipstick tube. Allow the oil to drain down the dipstick tube and re-check.
7. Drive vehicle until transmission fluid is at normal operating temperature.
8. With the engine running at curb idle speed, the gear selector in NEUTRAL, and the parking brake applied, check the transmission fluid level.

CAUTION

Do not overfill transmission, fluid foaming and shifting problems can result.

9. Add fluid to bring level up to MAX arrow mark.
10. When fluid level is correct, shut engine off, release park brake, remove funnel, and install dipstick in fill tube.

FLUID & FILTER REPLACEMENT

➡Only fluids of the type labeled Mopar® ATF+4, Automatic Transmission Fluid, should be used in the transmission sump. A filter change should be made at the time of the transmission oil change. The magnet (on the inside of the oil pan) should also be cleaned with a clean, dry cloth.

➡If the transmission is disassembled for any reason, the fluid and filter should be changed.

1. Raise vehicle on a hoist. Place a drain container with a large opening, under transmission oil pan.

➡One of the oil pan bolts has a sealing patch applied from the factory. Separate this bolt for reuse.

2. Loosen pan bolts and tap the pan at one corner to break it loose allowing fluid to drain, then remove the oil pan.
3. Install a new filter and o-ring on bottom of the valve body and tighten retaining screws to 45 INCH LBS. (5 Nm).

➡Before installing the oil pan bolt in the bolt hole located between the torque converter clutch on and U/D clutch pressure tap circuits, it will be necessary to replenish the sealing patch on the bolt using Mopar Lock & Seal Adhesive or equivalent.

4. Clean the oil pan and magnet. Reinstall pan using new Mopar® Silicone Adhesive sealant. Tighten oil pan bolts to 15 ft. lbs. (20 Nm).
5. Pour 4 quarts of Mopar ATF+4 ATF through the dipstick opening.
6. Start engine and allow to idle for at least one minute. Then, with parking and service brakes applied, move selector lever momentarily to each position, ending in the park or neutral position.
7. Check the transmission fluid level and add an appropriate amount to bring the transmission fluid level to 1/8 in. (3mm) below the lowest mark on the dipstick.
8. Recheck the fluid level after the transmission has reached normal operating temperature of 180°F (82°C).
9. To prevent dirt from entering transmission, make certain that dipstick is fully seated into the dipstick opening.

FRONT AXLE ASSEMBLY

REMOVAL & INSTALLATION

See Figures 8 through 11.

1. With vehicle in neutral, position vehicle on hoist.
2. Remove axle half shafts.
3. Mark front propeller shaft and companion flange for installation reference. Remove front propeller shaft.
4. Remove skid plate bolts and remove skid plate.
5. Remove suspension crossmember nuts and bolts. Remove crossmember.
6. Remove disconnect actuator wiring connector.
7. Remove vent hose from differential cove tube.
8. Support axle with hydraulic jack.
9. Remove axle housing pinion mounting bolts.
10. Remove axle shaft tube mounting nuts and bolts.
11. Remove differential housing to engine mounting nuts. Leave bolts in differential housing.
12. Slide axle over with engine mount bolts to clear engine mount. Lower axle from the vehicle.

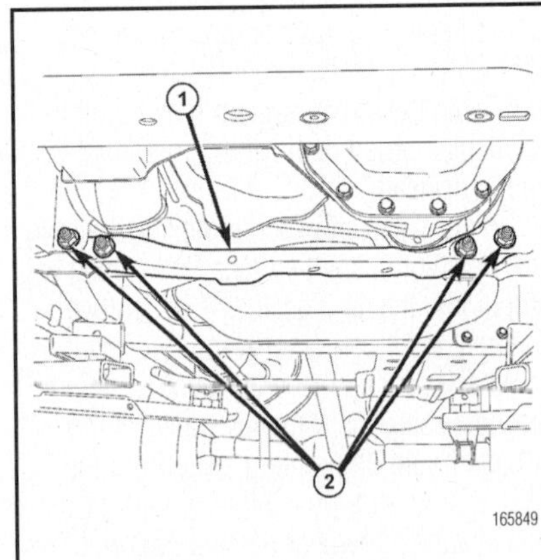

Fig. 8 Remove suspension crossmember (1) nuts (2) and bolts. Remove crossmember.

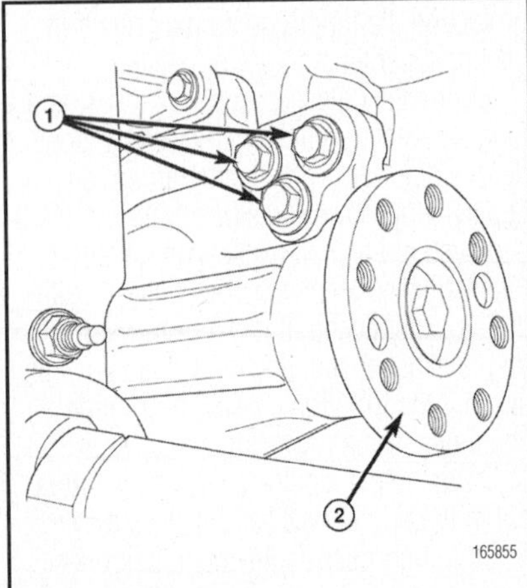

Fig. 9 Remove axle housing pinion mounting bolts (1).

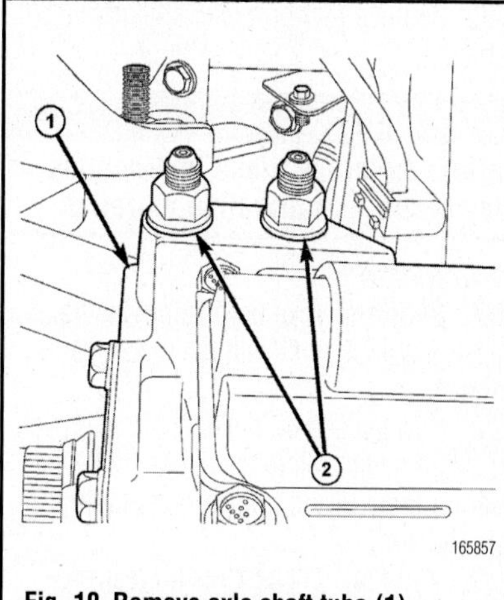

Fig. 10 Remove axle shaft tube (1) mounting nuts (2) and bolts.

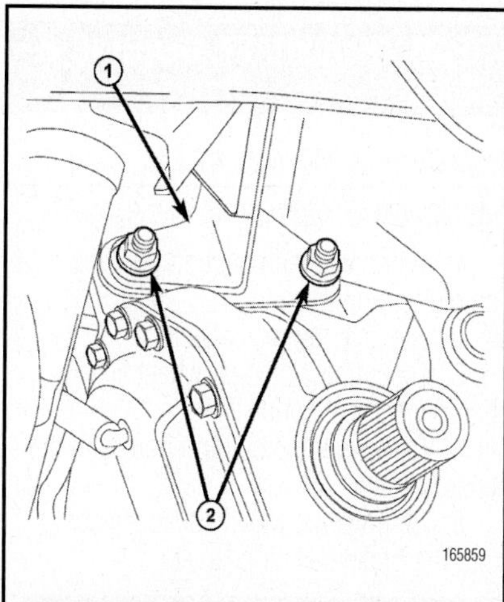

Fig. 11 Remove differential housing to engine mounting (1) nuts (2). Leave bolts in differential housing.

To install:

13. Raise axle and slide axle with engine mounting bolts into engine mount. Install engine mount nuts and tighten to 70 ft. lbs. (95 Nm).
14. Install axle shaft tube mounting bolts and nuts. Tighten nuts to 70 ft. lbs. (95 Nm).
15. Install axle housing pinion nose mounting bolts and tighten to 70 ft. lbs. (95 Nm).
16. Install vent hose on differential cover tube.
17. Install actuator wiring connector.
18. Install suspension crossmember, bolts and nuts. Tighten nuts to 90 ft. lbs. (122 Nm).
19. Install skid plate and bolts.
20. Install front propeller shaft with reference marks aligned and tighten bolts to 85 ft. lbs. (115 Nm).
21. Install axle half shafts.

FRONT INTERMEDIATE AXLE SHAFT

REMOVAL & INSTALLATION

See Figures 12 through 18.

1. Remove half shaft from disconnect side of the axle.
2. Remove disconnect actuator wiring connector. Remove disconnect actuator bolts and remove actuator.
3. Remove O-ring and snap ring from output shaft.
4. Remove disconnect seal housing bolts at end of shaft. Remove output shaft and disconnect seal with a proper remover (8402B or equivalent) and a slide hammer.
5. Slide disconnect collar from intermediate shaft and remove through disconnect pocket.
6. Remove differential cover.
7. Drive intermediate shaft out of side gear with a hammer and brass punch.
8. Remove intermediate shaft from axle tube.

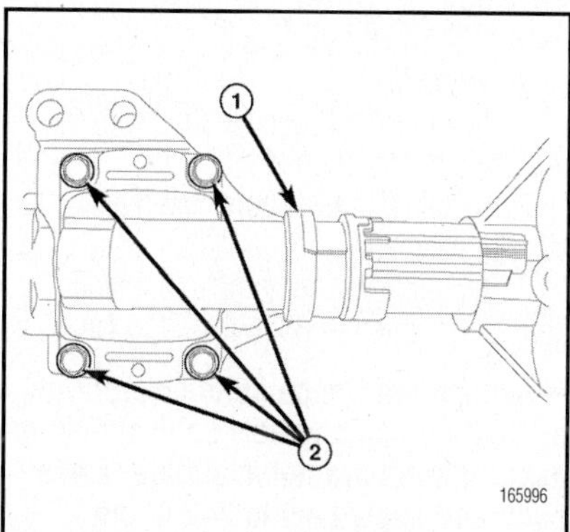

Fig. 12 Remove disconnect actuator (1) bolts (2) and remove actuator.

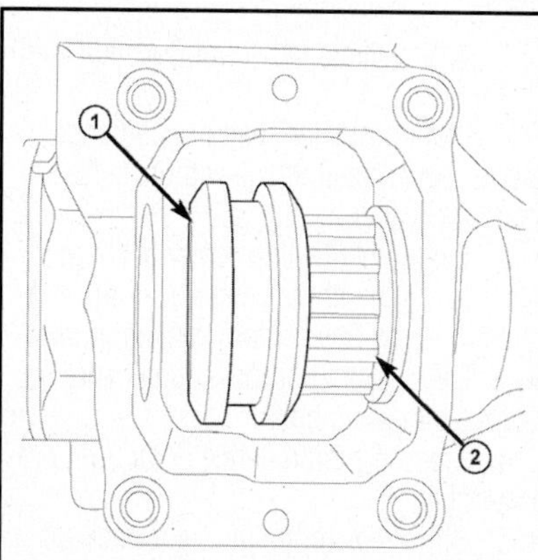

Fig. 13 Slide disconnect collar (1) from intermediate shaft (2) and remove through disconnect pocket.

To install:

9. Install **new** intermediate shaft snap ring.
10. Install shaft into axle tube and side gear. Verify intermediate shaft snap ring is seated in side gear.
11. Install disconnect collar through disconnect pocket onto intermediate shaft. Position disconnect collar on intermediate shaft, so collar is in 2WD position.
12. Verify output shaft bearing cup is seated in the disconnect pocket.
13. Install output shaft with bearing into disconnect pocket.
14. Install disconnect seal on output shaft.
15. Align disconnect seal with bolt holes in disconnect pocket with locator pins (MD998412 or equivalent).
16. Install disconnect seal in disconnect pocket using installer tool (6761) and a hammer.
17. Install disconnect seal bolts and tighten to 21 ft. lbs. (28 Nm).

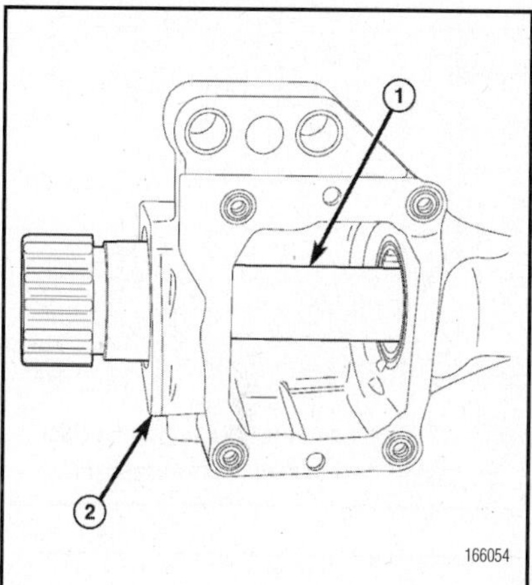

Fig. 14 Remove intermediate shaft (1) from axle tube (2).

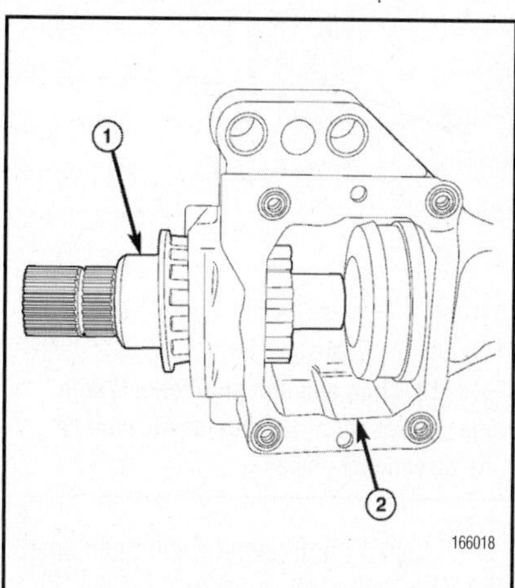

Fig. 15 Install output shaft (1) with bearing into disconnect pocket (2).

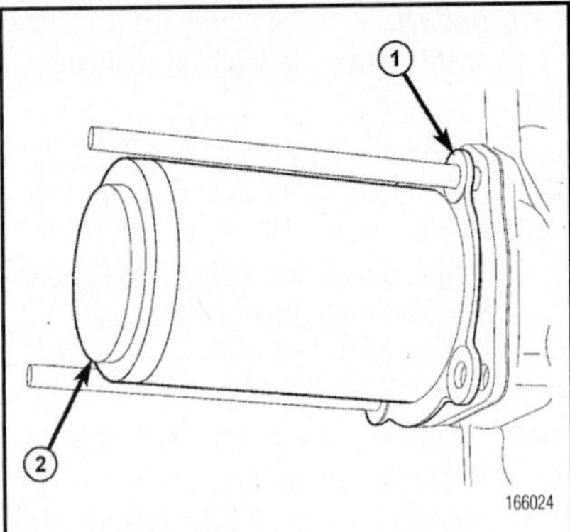

Fig. 16 Install disconnect seal (1) in disconnect pocket using installer tool (6761) (2) and a hammer (locator pins shown installed)

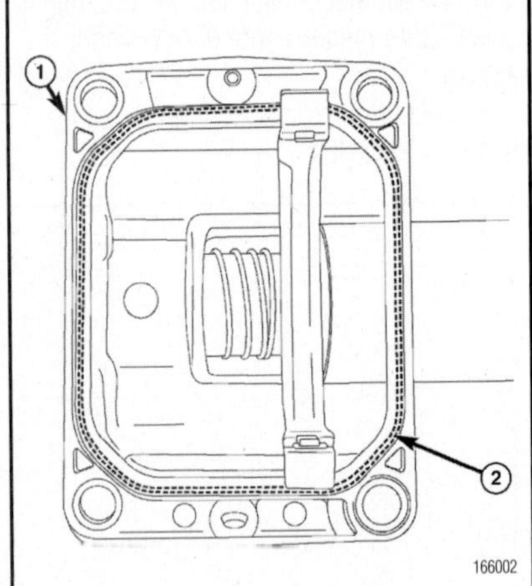

Fig. 17 Clean actuator (1) sealing surface and install new gasket (2) if necessary.

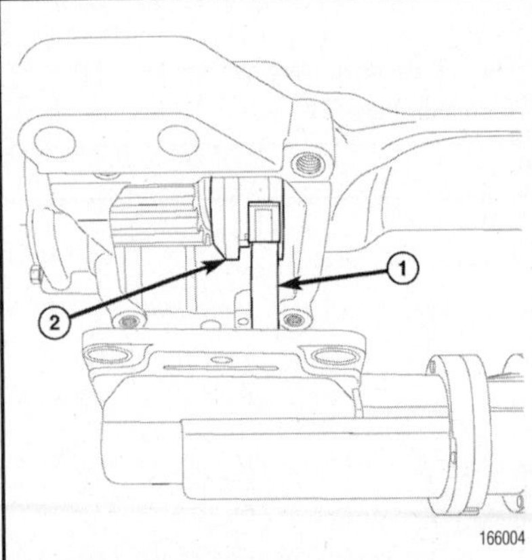

Fig. 18 Align actuator shift fork (1) with disconnect collar (2) and install actuator on disconnect pocket.

18. Install output shaft O-ring and snap ring.
19. Clean actuator sealing surface and install new gasket if necessary.
20. Align actuator shift fork with disconnect collar and install actuator on disconnect pocket.
21. Install disconnect actuator bolts and tighten to 20 ft. lbs. (27 Nm).
22. Install disconnect actuator wiring connector.
23. Install differential cover and fill differential to specification.
24. Install half shaft.

PROPELLER SHAFT

REMOVAL & INSTALLATION

Front

1. With vehicle in neutral, position vehicle on hoist.
2. Remove exhaust crossover pipe.
3. Mark a line across the axle companion flange, propeller shaft, flange yoke and transfer case for installation reference.
4. Remove axle/transfer case companion flange bolts. Remove dust boot clamp from the CV joint end of the shaft if equipped.
5. Remove propeller shaft.

To install:

6. Install front propeller shaft with all reference marks aligned.
7. Install with dust boot clamp at transfer case end.
8. Install new axle companion flange bolts and tighten to 85 ft. lbs. (115 Nm).

➡Companion flange bolts incorporate a Loctite patch and new bolts should be used. If bolts are not available, clean bolts and apply Loctite 242 to the threads.

9. Install skid plate, if equipped.

Rear

1. With vehicle in neutral, position vehicle on hoist.
2. Mark propeller shaft pinion flange and propeller shaft flange with installation reference marks.
3. If equipped with a center bearing, mark an outline of the center bearing on the center bearing bracket for installation reference. Then support propeller shaft and remove mounting bolts.
4. Remove pinion flange bolts from propeller shaft.
5. Slide rear propeller shaft back off automatic transmission output shaft, then mark propeller shaft and transmission output shaft for installation reference.
6. Remove rear propeller shaft from vehicle.

✻✻ CAUTION

Failure to follow these instructions may result in a driveline vibration.

To install:

7. Slide slip yoke onto automatic transmission output shaft with reference marks aligned.
8. If two-piece propeller shaft, align center bearing with reference marks on center bearing bracket and tighten bolts to 40 ft. lbs. (50 Nm).
9. Align reference marks on rear propeller shaft and pinion flange. Install new companion flange bolts and tighten to 85 ft. lbs. (115 Nm).

REAR AXLE SHAFT, BEARING & SEAL

REMOVAL & INSTALLATION

See Figures 19 through 22.

1. With vehicle in neutral, position vehicle on hoist.
2. Remove the rear wheels.
3. Disconnect the rear wheel speed sensor electrical connector.
4. Remove the mounting bolt from the sensor.
5. Remove the wheel speed sensor from the brake caliper adapter.

✻✻ CAUTION

Do not allow brake hose to support caliper assembly. Mechanics wire can be used to support the caliper and adapter plate assemblies.

6. Remove the rear caliper adapter plate bolts from both sides and position the calipers aside.
7. Disconnect the axle vent hose from the axle.

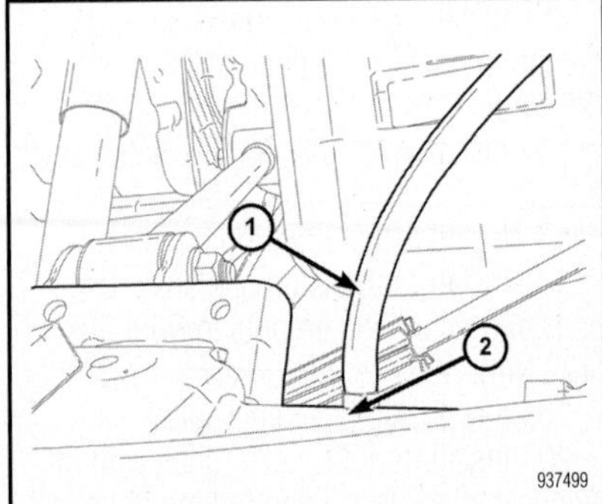

Fig. 19 Disconnect the axle vent hose (1) from the axle (2).

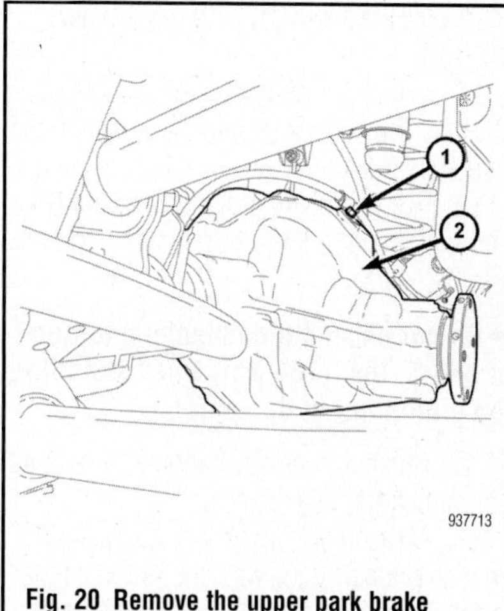

Fig. 20 Remove the upper park brake cable bolt (1) from the rear axle (2).

8. Remove the rear propeller shaft, as described in this section.
9. Pull the park brake cable spring back.

➡A 13mm line wrench can be used to compress the cable tabs. Insert while spring is pulled back and rotate the wrench to compress the tabs.

10. Compress the cable tabs on each cable end fitting at the brake cable support plate.
11. Remove the park brake cable from the brake cable support plate.
12. Remove the upper park brake cable bolt from the rear axle.
13. Remove the park brake bolt from the upper control arm bracket.
14. Position the park brake cable away from the rear axle.

➡For suspension components referenced in the following steps, refer to "REAR SUSPENSION" section.

15. Remove the stabilizer bar bolts and position the stabilizer bar aside.

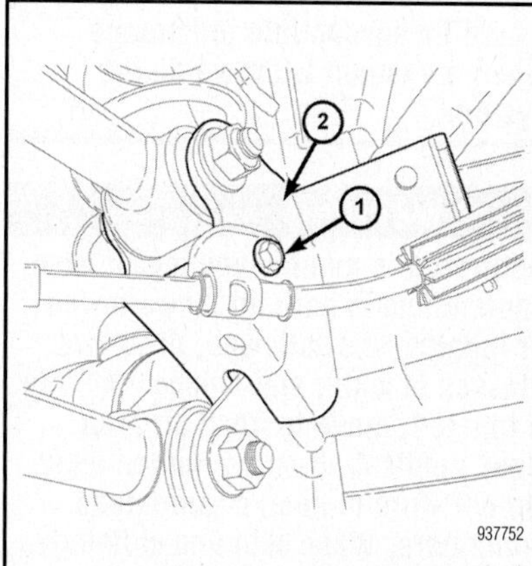

Fig. 21 Remove the park brake bolt (1) from the upper control arm bracket (2).

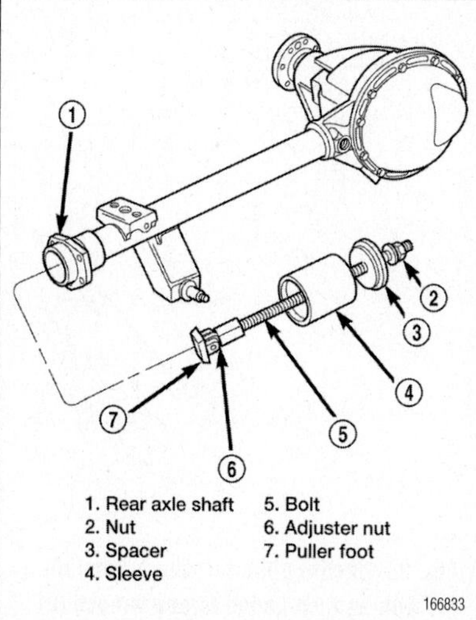

Fig. 22 Removing rear axle shaft bearing and seal

16. Position a lift under the axle and secure the axle to the lift.
17. Remove both lower shock absorber bolts and position the shock absorbers away from the axle.
18. Remove the track bar bolt and position the track bar away from the rear axle.
19. Remove both the upper control arm to rear axle bolts, discard nut, and position the upper control arms away from the axle.
20. Remove both the lower control arm to rear axle bolts, discard nut, and position the lower control arms away from the axle.
21. Slightly lower the rear axle assembly and remove the rear springs.
22. Remove the rear axle from the vehicle.
23. Remove axle shaft seal from axle tube with a small pry bar.

➡The seal and bearing can be removed at the same time with the bearing removal tool.

24. Remove axle shaft bearing with Bearing Remover and Foot (6310 and 6310-9, or equivalent).

To install:

25. Wipe axle tube bore clean and remove any old sealer or burrs from the tube.
26. Install axle shaft bearing with Installer and Handle (C-4198 and C-4171, or equivalent). Drive bearing in until tool contacts the axle tube.

➡Bearing is installed with the bearing part number against the installer.

27. Coat lip of the new axle seal with axle lubricant and install with Installer and Handle (C-4076-B and C-4735 or equivalent).

➡All suspension torques should be made with the full vehicle weight on the ground being supported by the tires.

28. Position the spring and isolator on the axle and align into the spring upper pocket.
29. Carefully raise the rear axle into place.
30. Position both the lower control arms into the rear axle brackets and loosely install the bolts with new nuts.
31. Position both the upper control arms into the rear axle brackets and loosely install the bolts with new nuts.
32. Position the rear track bar to the rear axle bracket and loosely install the bolt.
33. Position both the rear shock absorbers to the axle brackets and loosely install the rear shock absorber bolts.
34. Remove the axle lift.

➡The stabilizer bar must be centered with equal spacing on both sides.

35. Position the stabilizer bar to the rear axle and install and tighten the bolts to 48 ft. lbs. (65 Nm).
36. Position the park brake cable back to the rear axle.
37. Install the park brake cable bolt on the upper control arm bracket and tighten to 16 ft. lbs. (22 Nm).
38. Install the upper park brake cable bolt to the rear axle and tighten to 16 ft. lbs. (22 Nm).
39. Install the rear cable into the tensioner rods behind the rear of the brake assemblies.
40. Pull the park brake cable springs back until the cable end fitting tabs lock into place.

➡Pull on the cable to ensure that it is locked into place.

41. Install the rear propeller shaft.
42. Connect the axle vent hose to the axle.
43. Position the calipers back onto the brake rotors and install and tighten the adapter plate bolts to 100 ft. lbs. (135 Nm).
44. Position the rear wheel speed sensors to the brake caliper adapters.
45. Install the mounting bolts to the wheel speed sensor and tighten to 18 ft. lbs. (24 Nm).
46. Connect the rear wheel speed sensor electrical connectors.
47. Install the rear wheels.
48. Lower the vehicle.

49. Tighten the upper and lower control arm retainers to 221 ft. lbs. (300 Nm).
50. Tighten the track bar mounting bolt to 115 ft. lbs. (155 Nm).
51. Tighten shock bolt to 101 ft. lbs. (136 Nm).

REAR PINION SEAL

REMOVAL & INSTALLATION

See Figure 23.

1. Mark universal joint, companion flange and pinion shaft for installation reference.
2. Remove propeller shaft from the companion flange.
3. Remove the brake rotors to prevent any drag.
4. Rotate companion flange three or four times.
5. Record pinion torque to rotating with an inch pound torque wrench.
6. Install two bolts into the companion flange threaded holes, 180 degrees apart. Position a holding tool against the companion flange and install and tighten two bolts and washers into the remaining holes.
7. Counterhold the companion flange and remove pinion nut and washer.
8. Mark a line across the pinion shaft and flange for installation reference.
9. Remove companion flange with a suitable puller (C-452 or equivalent).
10. Remove pinion seal with seal puller or slide-hammer mounted screw.

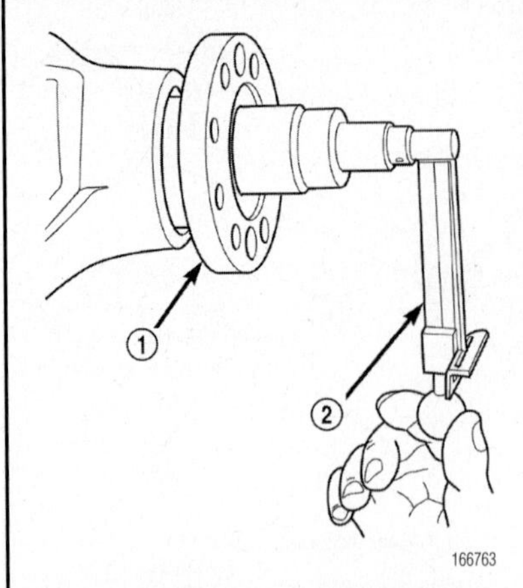

Fig. 23 Record pinion torque to rotating (1) with an inch pound torque wrench (2).

To install:

11. Apply a light coating of gear lubricant on the lip of pinion seal.
12. Install new pinion seal with Handle (C-4735) and Installer (C-4076-B).
13. Install flange on the pinion shaft with the reference marks aligned.
14. Install two bolts into the threaded holes in the companion flange, 180 degrees apart.
15. Position Holder (6719A) against the companion flange and install a bolt and washer into one of the remaining threaded holes. Tighten the bolts so holder is held to the flange.
16. Install companion flange on pinion shaft with Installer (C-3718) and Holder (6719A).
17. Install pinion washer and a new pinion nut. The convex side of the washer must face outward.
18. Hold companion flange and tighten pinion nut with a torque wrench to 210 ft. lbs. (285 Nm).

➡Do not exceed the maximum torque of 210 ft. lbs. (285 Nm) when installing the pinion nut at this point.

19. Rotate pinion several times to ensure pinion bearings are seated.
20. Measure pinion torque to rotate with an inch pound torque wrench. Pinion torque to rotate should be equal to recorded reading plus an additional 5 inch lbs. (0.56 Nm).
21. If pinion torque to rotate is low, tighten pinion nut in 5 ft. lbs. (6.8 Nm) increments until pinion torque to rotating is achieved.

**** CAUTION**

Never loosen pinion nut to decrease pinion bearing rotating torque. If pinion torque to rotating is exceeded, a new collapsible spacer must be installed. Failure to follow these instructions will result in damage to the axle.

22. Install propeller shaft.
23. Install rear brake rotors components. See "BRAKES" section.

ENGINE COOLING

ENGINE COOLANT

DRAINING PROCEDURE

See Figure 24.

**** CAUTION**

Do not remove cylinder block drain plugs or loosen radiator draincock with system hot and under pressure. Serious burns from coolant can occur.

1. Attach one end of a hose to the draincock. Put the other end into a clean container.
2. do not remove the radiator cap when draining the coolant from the reservoir/overflow tank. Open radiator draincock and when the tank is empty, remove the radiator cap and continue draining the cooling system.
3. If draining the entire engine, remove the cylinder block drain plugs.

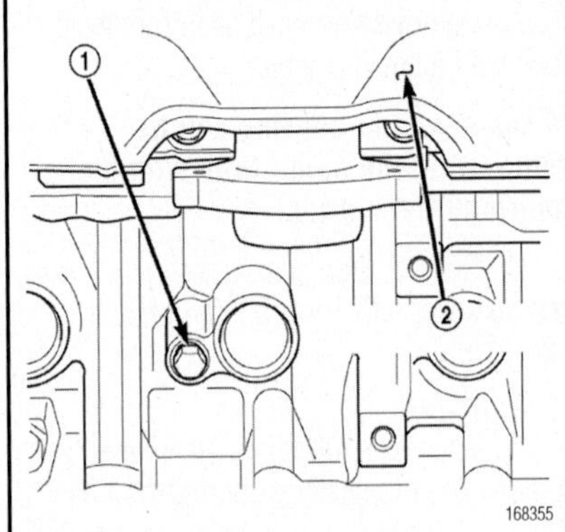

Fig. 24 If draining the entire engine, remove the cylinder block drain plugs (1)—intake manifold noted (2).

BLEEDING

Evacuating or purging air from the cooling system involves the use of a pressurized air operated vacuum generator. The vacuum created allows for a quick and complete coolant refilling while removing any airlocks present in the system components.

**** CAUTION**

To avoid damage to the cooling system, ensure that no component would be susceptible to damage when a vacuum is drawn on the system.

**** WARNING**

Antifreeze is an ethylene glycol base coolant and is harmful if swallowed or inhaled. If swallowed, drink two glasses of water and induce vomiting. If inhaled, move to fresh air area. Seek medical attention immediately. Do not store in open or unmarked containers. Wash skin and clothing thoroughly after coming in contact with ethylene glycol. Keep out of reach of children. Dispose of glycol

based coolant properly. Contact your dealer or government agency for location of collection center in your area. Do not open a cooling system when the engine is at operating temperature or hot under pressure; personal injury can result. Avoid radiator cooling fan when engine compartment related service is performed; personal injury can result.

⁂ CAUTION

Wear appropriate eye and hand protection when performing this procedure.

➡The service area where this procedure is performed should have a minimum shop air requirement of 80 PSI (5.5 bar) and should be equipped with an air dryer system.

➡For best results, the radiator should be empty. The vehicle's heater control should be set to the heat position (ignition may need to be turned to the on position but do not start the motor).

➡Refer to the Chrysler Pentastar Service Equipment (Chrysler PSE) Coolant Refiller #85-15-0650 or equivalent tool's operating manual for specific assembly steps.

1. Choose an appropriate adapter cone that will fit the vehicle's radiator filler neck or reservoir tank.
2. Attach the adapter cone to the vacuum gauge.
3. Make sure the vacuum generator/venturi ball valve is closed and attach an airline hose (minimum shop air requirement of 80 PSI/5.5 bar) to the vacuum generator/venturi.
4. Position the adaptor cone/vacuum gauge assembly into the radiator filler neck or reservoir tank. Ensure that the adapter cone is sealed properly.
5. Connect the vacuum generator/venturi to the positioned adaptor cone/vacuum gauge assembly.
6. Open the vacuum generator/venturi ball valve.

➡Do not bump or move the assembly as it may result in loss of vacuum. Some radiator overflow hoses may need to be clamped off to obtain vacuum.

7. Let the system run until the vacuum gauge shows a good vacuum through the cooling system. Refer to the tool's operating manual for appropriate pressure readings.

➡If a strong vacuum is being created in the system, it is normal to see the radiator hoses to collapse.

8. Close the vacuum generator/venturi ball valve.
9. Disconnect the vacuum generator/venturi and airline from the adaptor cone/vacuum gauge assembly.
10. Wait approximately 20 seconds, if the pressure readings do not move, the system has no leaks. If the pressure readings move, a leak could be present in the system and the cooling system should be checked for leaks and the procedure should be repeated.
11. Place the tool's suction hose into the coolant's container.

➡Ensure there is a sufficient amount of coolant, mixed to the required strength/protection level available for use. For best results and to assist the refilling procedure, place the coolant container at the same height as the radiator filler neck. Always draw more coolant than required. If the coolant level is too low, it will pull air into the cooling system which could result in airlocks in the system.

12. Connect the tool's suction hose to the adaptor cone/vacuum gauge assembly.
13. Open the suction hose's ball valve to begin refilling the cooling system.
14. When the vacuum gauge reads zero, the system is filled.

➡On some remote pressurized tanks, it is recommended to stop filling when the proper level is reached.

15. Close the suction hose's ball valve and remove the suction hose from the adaptor cone/vacuum gauge assembly.
16. Remove the adaptor cone/vacuum gauge assembly from the radiator filler neck or reservoir tank.
17. With heater control unit in the HEAT position, operate engine with container cap in place.
18. After engine has reached normal operating temperature, shut engine off and allow it to cool. When engine is cooling down, coolant will be drawn into the radiator from the pressure container.
19. Add coolant to the recovery bottle/container as necessary.

➡Only add coolant to the container when the engine is cold. Coolant level in a warm engine will be higher due to thermal expansion.

20. Add necessary coolant to raise container level to the COLD MINIMUM mark after each cool down period.
21. Once the appropriate coolant level is achieved, attach the radiator cap or reservoir tank cap.

ENGINE FAN

REMOVAL & INSTALLATION

Electric Fan

1. Disconnect and isolate the negative battery cable.
2. Remove the upper radiator seal push pins and plastic rivets. Remove the upper radiator seal.
3. If equipped, remove the viscous fan assembly from the water pump hub shaft.(
4. Disconnect the radiator fan electrical connector.
5. Remove the fan shroud to radiator mounting bolts.
6. Disengage the fan shroud's lower retaining clips and position the fan shroud towards the rear of vehicle.
7. Disengage the electric cooling fan to radiator upper retaining clips.
8. Disengage the electric fan to radiator lower retaining clips.
9. Pulling upward remove the viscous fan, radiator fan shroud and the electric cooling fan as an assembly.

➡The lower fan shroud can be removed from the upper fan shroud if needed.

10. If damaged, remove radiator fan resistor from shroud.

To install:

11. If removed, install the electric cooling fan resistor. Tighten the mounting screw securely.
12. If removed, install the lower fan shroud to the upper fan shroud.
13. Position the viscous fan (if equipped), radiator fan shroud and electric cooling fan into the vehicle as an assembly.
14. Install the electric cooling fan by engaging the upper and lower retaining clips to the radiator.
15. Install the fan shroud by engaging the lower retaining clips to the radiator/electric cooling fan.

➡Make sure all retaining clips lock into place.

16. Install the fan shroud mounting bolts. Tighten to 89 inch lbs. (10 Nm).
17. Connect the electric cooling fan electrical connector.

18. Position the upper radiator seal. Install the upper radiator seal plastic rivets. Install the upper radiator push pins.

19. Connect the negative battery cable.

Viscous Fan

See Figure 25.

➡Do not attempt to remove the fan/viscous fan drive assembly from the vehicle at this time.

➡If the viscous fan drive is replaced because of mechanical damage, the cooling fan blades should also be inspected. Inspect for fatigue cracks, loose blades, or loose rivets that could have resulted from excessive vibration. Replace fan blade assembly if any of these conditions are found. Also inspect water pump bearing and shaft assembly for any related damage due to a viscous fan drive malfunction.

1. Disconnect negative battery cable from battery.

2. The thermal viscous fan drive/fan blade assembly is attached (threaded) to the water pump hub shaft. Remove the fan blade/viscous fan drive assembly from the water pump by turning the mounting nut clockwise as viewed from the front. Threads on the viscous fan drive are LEFT-HAND. A 36 mm fan wrench should be used to prevent pulley from rotating.

3. Do not unbolt the fan blade assembly from viscous fan drive at this time.

4. Remove the fan shroud-to-radiator mounting bolts. Pull the lower shroud mounts out of the radiator tank clips.

5. Remove the fan shroud, electric cooling fan, and fan blade/viscous fan drive assembly as a complete unit from vehicle.

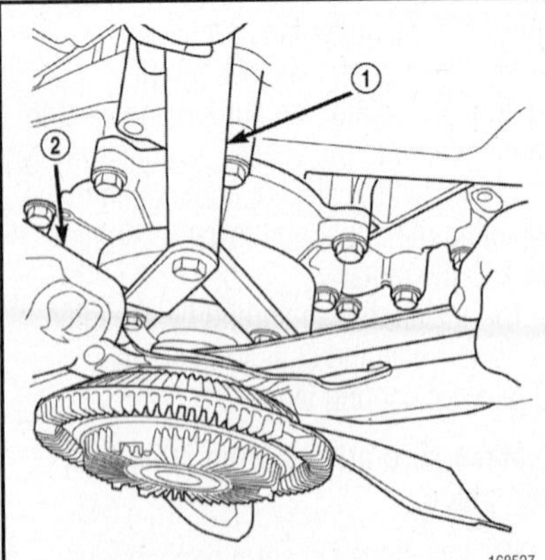

Fig. 25 Showing the fan drive assembly (2) and the fan wrench (1) used to prevent pulley rotation.

6. After removing the fan blade/viscous fan drive assembly, do not place the viscous fan drive in a horizontal position. If stored horizontally, silicone fluid in the viscous fan drive could drain into its bearing assembly and contaminate lubricant.

✲✲ CAUTION

Do not remove water pump pulley-to-water pump bolts. This pulley is under spring tension.

7. Remove four bolts securing fan blade assembly to viscous fan drive.

✲✲ CAUTION

Some engines equipped with serpentine drive belts have reverse rotating fans and viscous fan drives. They are marked with the word REVERSE to designate their usage. Installation of the wrong fan or viscous fan drive can result in engine overheating.

To install:

➡If the viscous fan drive is replaced because of mechanical damage, the cooling fan blades should also be inspected. Inspect for fatigue cracks, loose blades, or loose rivets that could have resulted from excessive vibration. Replace fan blade assembly if any of these conditions are found. Also inspect water pump bearing and shaft assembly for any related damage due to a viscous fan drive malfunction.

➡Viscous Fan Drive Fluid Pump Out Requirement: After installing a new viscous fan drive, bring the engine speed up to approximately 2000 rpm and hold for approximately two minutes. This will ensure proper fluid distribution within the drive.

8. Install fan blade assembly to the viscous fan drive. Tighten the bolts to 18 ft. lbs. (24 Nm) torque.

9. Position the fan shroud, electric cooling fan and the fan blade/viscous fan drive assembly to the vehicle as a complete unit.

10. Install the fan shroud.

➡The thermal viscous fan drive/fan blade assembly is attached (threaded) to the water pump hub shaft.

11. Install the fan blade/viscous fan drive assembly to the water pump by turning the mounting nut counterclockwise as viewed from the front. Threads on the viscous fan drive are LEFT-HAND. A 36 mm fan wrench should be used to prevent pulley from rotating. Tighten mounting nut to 37 ft. lbs. (50 Nm).

12. Connect the negative battery cable.

RADIATOR

REMOVAL & INSTALLATION

1. Disconnect and isolate the negative battery cable.

2. Raise and secure the vehicle.

3. Drain the cooling system.

✲✲ WARNING

Do not remove the cylinder block drain plugs or loosen the radiator draincock with the system hot and under pressure. Serious burns from the coolant can occur.

4. Remove the lower radiator clamp and hose.

5. Remove the lower radiator seal.

6. Remove the lower center electric fan to radiator retaining clip.

7. Lower the vehicle.

8. Remove the upper radiator clamp and hose.

9. Remove the upper radiator seal push pins and plastic rivets. Remove the upper radiator seal.

10. Remove the grille as follows:

   a. Remove the four push pins, remove the two plastic rivets, and remove the upper radiator seal.

   b. Remove the four upper grille support bolts.

   c. Using a trim stick, separate the two lower spring clips.

   d. Release the two lower hooks and remove the grille.

11. Remove the bolt from the transmission cooler line to radiator bracket.

12. Remove the washer reserve tank.

13. Remove the coolant overflow/recovery bottle.

14. Remove the front bolts from the A/C compressor/transmission combination cooler.

15. Remove the upper center electric fan to radiator retaining clip.

16. Disconnect the transmission cooler lines from the transmission cooler, then plug the transmission lines and cooler to prevent leakage.

17. Disengage the two A/C compressor/transmission combination cooler mounting brackets from the left side of the radiator. Do not disconnect the A/C lines.

18. After the A/C compressor/transmission combination cooler is disengaged, secure it to the upper radiator support with a strap, cord or equivalent.

19. Remove the fan shroud mounting bolts and pull up and out of the radiator tank clips. Position the shroud rearward over the fan blades towards engine.
20. Disengage the electric cooling fan to radiator upper retaining clips.
21. Disengage the electric fan tó radiator lower retaining clips.
22. Remove the viscous fan, fan shroud and electric cooling fan as an assembly.
23. Remove the two radiator upper mounting bolts.
24. Lift the radiator straight up and out of the engine compartment. Take care not to damage cooling fins or tubes on the radiator and oil coolers when removing.

To install:

25. Position the radiator into the engine compartment. Take care not to damage cooling fins or tubes on the radiator and oil coolers when installing.
26. Install the rubber insulators to the lower radiator mounting features (alignment dowel and support bracket at the lower part of the radiator).
27. Install and tighten the two radiator upper mounting bolts.
28. Install the electric cooling fan.
29. Install the fan shroud by engaging the fan shroud lower retaining clips to the radiator/electric cooling fan.
30. Install the fan shroud to radiator lower center retaining clip.
31. Install the fan shroud mounting bolts. Tighten to 89 inch lbs. (10 Nm).
32. Install the fan shroud to radiator upper center retaining clip.

➡Make sure all retaining clips lock into place.

33. Connect the electric cooling fan electrical connector.
34. Engage the two A/C compressor/transmission combination cooler mounting brackets to the left side of the radiator.
35. Connect the transmission cooler lines to the transmission cooler.
36. Install and tighten the two bolts that secure the A/C condenser to the right side of the radiator.
37. Install the bolt securing the transmission cooler line to radiator bracket. Tighten the bolt securely.
38. Install the coolant overflow/recovery bottle.
39. Install the windshield washer reserve tank.
40. Install the front grille in reverse of the removal sequence.
41. Connect the upper radiator hose and install the clamp in it's proper position.
42. Install the upper radiator seal plastic rivets and push pins.
43. Raise and secure the vehicle.
44. Install the lower center electric fan to radiator retaining clip.
45. Install the lower radiator clamp and hose.
46. Install the lower radiator seal.
47. Install battery negative cable.
48. Fill cooling system.
49. Check the system for any leaks.
50. Operate the engine until it reaches normal operating temperature. Check cooling system fluid levels.

THERMOSTAT

REMOVAL & INSTALLATION

3.7L & 4.7L

See Figure 26.

1. Disconnect the negative battery cable.
2. Drain the cooling system.
3. Raise and support the vehicle.
4. Remove the splash shield.
5. Remove the lower radiator hose clamp and the lower radiator hose at the thermostat housing.
6. Remove the thermostat housing mounting bolts, thermostat housing and thermostat.

To install:

7. Clean the mating areas of the timing chain cover and the thermostat housing.
8. Install the thermostat (spring side down) into the recessed machined groove on the timing chain cover.

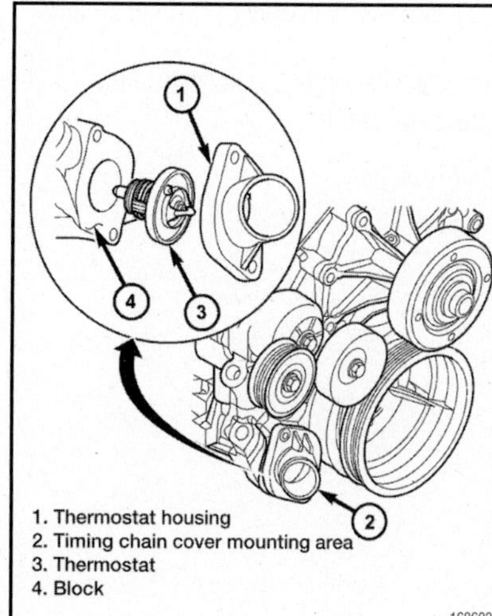

Fig. 26 Showing thermostat mounting

✻✻ CAUTION

The housing must be tightened evenly and the thermostat must be centered into the recessed groove in the timing chain cover. If not, it may result in a cracked housing, damaged timing chain cover threads or coolant leaks.

9. Position the thermostat housing on the timing chain cover.
10. Install the housing-to-timing chain cover bolts. Tighten the bolts to 112 inch lbs. (13 Nm).
11. Install the lower radiator hose on the thermostat housing.
12. Install the splash shield.
13. Lower the vehicle.
14. Fill the cooling system.
15. Connect negative battery cable.
16. Start and warm the engine. Check for leaks.

5.7L

1. Disconnect the negative battery cable.
2. Drain the cooling system.
3. Remove the radiator hose clamp and radiator hose at the thermostat housing.
4. Remove the thermostat housing mounting bolts, thermostat housing and thermostat.
5. Installation is the reverse of the removal procedure.

WATER PUMP

REMOVAL & INSTALLATION

3.7L & 4.7L

See Figure 27.

1. Disconnect the negative battery cable.
2. Drain cooling system.
3. Remove the radiator fan.
4. Remove accessory drive belt.
5. Remove the lower radiator hose clamp and remove the lower hose at the water pump.
6. Remove the water pump mounting bolts.

✻✻ CAUTION

Do not pry on the water pump at the timing chain case/cover. The machined surfaces may be damaged resulting in leaks.

7. Remove the water pump and gasket. Discard gasket.

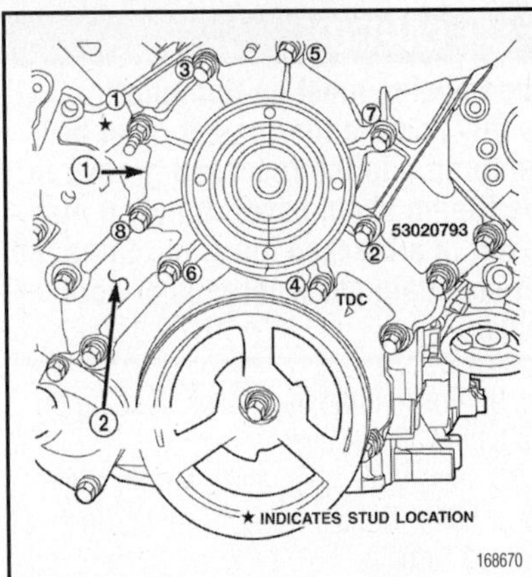

Fig. 27 Showing the water pump (1) location on the timing cover (2) and the water pump bolt tightening sequence

To install:

8. Clean the gasket mating surfaces.
9. Using a new gasket, position water pump and install the mounting bolts. Tighten the water pump mounting bolts to 43 ft. lbs. (58 Nm).
10. Spin the water pump to be sure that the pump impeller does not rub against the timing chain case/cover.
11. Connect the radiator lower hose to the water pump.
12. Install accessory drive belt tensioner.
13. Install the drive belt.
14. Evacuate air and refill the cooling system.
15. Connect the negative battery cable.
16. Check cooling system for leaks.

5.7L

See Figure 28.

1. Disconnect negative battery cable.
2. Remove the air intake assembly.
3. Remove the resonator mounting bracket.
4. Remove cooling fan assembly, as described in this section.
5. Drain coolant into a clean container.
6. Remove the upper radiator hose from the thermostat housing and position aside.
7. Remove serpentine belt. See "Accessory Drive Belt" in "ENGINE MECHANICAL" section.
8. Remove idler pulley.
9. Remove belt tensioner assembly.
10. Remove lower radiator hose from the water pump and position aside.
11. Remove the upper metal heater tube from the cylinder head.
12. Remove water pump mounting bolts and remove pump.

To install:

13. Clean mating surfaces and install water pump. Tighten mounting bolts to 18 ft. lbs. (24 Nm).

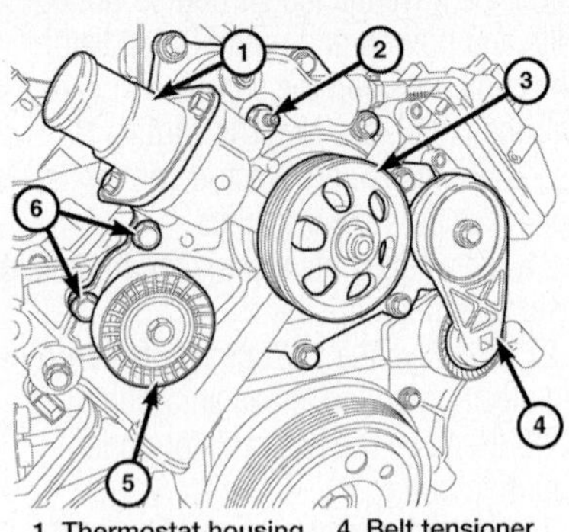

Fig. 28 Showing water pump and related components

14. Install upper metal heater tube.
15. Install belt tensioner assembly.
16. Install idler pulley.
17. Install the lower radiator hose.
18. Install serpentine belt.
19. Install the resonator mounting bracket.
20. Install cooling fan assembly.
21. Install the upper radiator hose to the thermostat housing.
22. Install the air intake assembly.
23. Connect negative battery cable.
24. Evacuate air and refill cooling system, as described in this section.
25. Check cooling system for leaks.

ENGINE ELECTRICAL

BATTERY

REMOVAL & INSTALLATION

1. Turn the ignition switch to the Off position. Be certain that all electrical accessories are turned off.
2. Disconnect the battery negative cable from the battery.
3. Disconnect the battery positive cable from the battery.
4. Remove the battery thermal cover.
5. Remove the battery hold down retaining bolt and battery hold down.
6. Remove the battery from the battery tray.
7. Installation is the reverse of the removal procedure.
8. Apply a thin coating of petroleum jelly or chassis grease to the exposed surfaces of the battery cable terminal clamps and the battery terminal posts.
9. Obtain an appropriate scan tool and check the PCM for any stored battery disconnect trouble codes. Clear codes if required.

GENERATOR

REMOVAL & INSTALLATION

3.7L & 4.7L

✱✱ CAUTION

Disconnect negative cable from battery before removing battery output wire (b+ wire) from generator. Failure to do so can result in injury or damage to electrical system.

1. Disconnect the negative battery cable.
2. Remove the generator drive belt.
3. Unsnap the plastic insulator cap from the B+ output terminal.
4. Remove the B+ terminal mounting nut at the rear of generator. Disconnect the terminal from the generator.
5. Disconnect the field wire connector at the rear of the generator by pushing on the connector tab.
6. Remove the one rear vertical generator mounting bolt.
7. Remove the two front horizontal generator mounting bolts.
8. Remove the generator from vehicle.

To install:

9. Position the generator to the engine and install the two horizontal bolts and the one vertical bolt. Tighten all three bolts to 40 ft. lbs. (55 Nm).
10. Snap the field wire connector into the rear of the generator.
11. Install the B+ terminal eyelet to the generator output stud. Tighten to 9 ft. lbs. (12 Nm).

✱✱ CAUTION

Never force a belt over a pulley rim using a screwdriver. The synthetic fiber of the belt can be damaged.

✱✱ CAUTION

When installing a serpentine accessory drive belt, the belt must be routed correctly. The water pump may be rotating in the wrong direction if the belt is installed incorrectly, causing the engine to overheat.

12. Install the accessory drive belt.
13. Connect the negative battery cable.

5.7L

✱✱ CAUTION

Disconnect the negative battery cable before removing the battery output wire from generator. Failure to do so can result in injury or damage to electrical system.

1. Disconnect the negative battery cable.

✱✱ CAUTION

Do not let the tensioner arm snap back to the freearm position, severe damage may occur to the tensioner.

2. Insert a suitable square drive ratchet into the square hole on the belt tensioner arm.
3. Release the belt tension by rotating the tensioner clockwise until the accessory drive belt can be removed from the generator pulley only.
4. Unsnap the plastic insulator cap from the B+ output terminal.
5. Remove the B+ terminal retaining nut and disconnect the B+ terminal eyelet from the generator output stud.
6. Disconnect the field wire electrical connector by pushing on the connector tab.
7. Remove the generator support bracket nuts and bolt and remove the support bracket.
8. Remove the two generator mounting bolts and the generator.

To install:

9. Position the generator into the mounting bracket and install the two retaining bolts and tighten the bolts to 30 ft. lbs. (41 Nm).
10. Install the support bracket to the front of the generator and install the bolt and nuts and tighten the bolt and nuts to 30 ft. lbs. (41 Nm).
11. Install the field wire electrical connector into the generator.
12. Connect the B+ terminal eyelet onto the generator output stud and install the retaining nut and tighten the nut to 9 ft. lbs. (12 Nm).
13. Snap the plastic insulator cap onto the B+ output terminal.

✱✱ CAUTION

Never force a belt over a pulley rim using a screwdriver. The synthetic fiber of the belt can be damaged.

✱✱ CAUTION

When installing a serpentine accessory drive belt, the belt must be routed correctly. The water pump may be rotating in the wrong direction if the belt is installed incorrectly, causing the engine to overheat. Refer to belt routing label in engine compartment.

✱✱ CAUTION

Do not let the tensioner arm snap back to the freearm position, severe damage may occur to the tensioner.

14. Insert a suitable square drive ratchet into the square hole on the belt tensioner arm. Rotate the tensioner clockwise until the accessory drive belt can be install onto the generator pulley.
15. Connect the negative battery cable.

FIRING ORDER

3.7L

1–6–5–4–3–2

4.7L & 5.7L

1–8–4–3–6–5–7–2

IGNITION COIL

REMOVAL & INSTALLATION

3.7L & 4.7L

See Figure 29.

An ignition coil with a spark plug wire attached is used for two cylinders. Another three coils fit into machined holes in the cylinder head for cylinders 1, 3, and 5. A mounting stud/nut secures each coil to the top of the intake manifold . The bottom of the coil is equipped with a rubber boot to seal the spark plug to the coil. Inside each rubber boot is a spring. The spring is used for a mechanical contact between the coil and the top of the spark plug. These rubber boots and springs are a permanent part of the coil and are not serviced separately. An O-ring is used to seal the coil at the opening into the cylinder head.

1. Depending on which coil is being removed, the throttle body air intake tube or intake box may need to be removed to gain access to coil.
2. Disconnect electrical connector from coil by pushing downward on release lock on top of connector and pull connector from coil.
3. Disconnect spark plug wire from coil.
4. Clean area at base of coil with compressed air before removal.
5. Remove coil mounting bolt.
6. Carefully pull up coil from cylinder head opening with a slight twisting action.
7. Remove coil from vehicle.

To install:

8. Using compressed air, blow out any dirt or contaminants from around top of spark plug.
9. Check the condition of the coil rubber boot. To aid in coil installation, apply silicone based grease such as Mopar Dielectric Grease (J8126688) into the spark plug end of the rubber boot and to the top of the spark plug.
10. Position the ignition coil assembly into the cylinder head opening. Using a twisting action, push the ignition coil assembly onto the spark plug.
11. Install coil mounting bolt. Tighten to 70 inch lbs. (8 Nm).
12. Connect the electrical connector to the ignition coil assembly by snapping into position.
13. Install the spark plug wires.
14. If necessary, install the throttle body air intake tube, or intake air box.

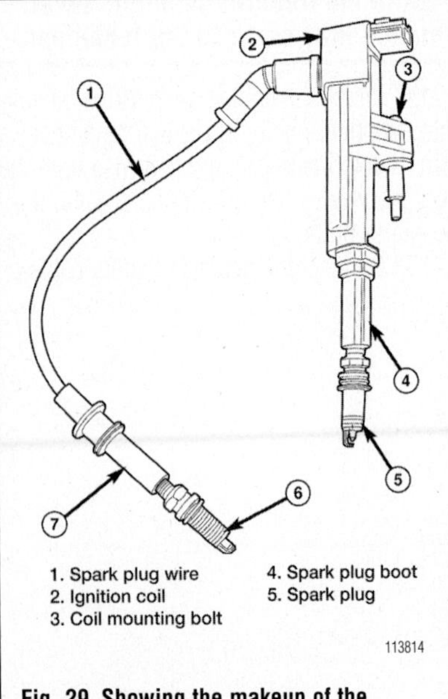

Fig. 29 Showing the makeup of the ignition coil with spark plug

5.7L

See Figure 30.

1. Disconnect the electrical connector from coil.
2. Clean area at base of coil with compressed air before removal.
3. Remove 2 mounting bolts (note that mounting bolts are retained to coil).
4. Carefully pull up coil from valve cover. Remove coil from vehicle.

To install:

5. Using compressed air, blow out any dirt or contaminants from around top of spark plug.
6. Use dielectric grease on each of the spark plug boots before installing the coil.
7. Position ignition coil into valve cover and push onto spark plugs.
8. Install 2 coil mounting bolts and tighten to 62 inch lbs. (7 Nm).
9. Connect electrical connector to coil by snapping into position.

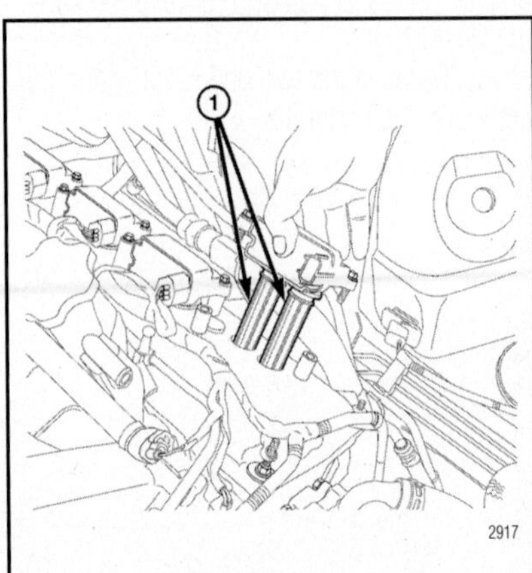

Fig. 30 Carefully pull up coil (1) from valve cover. Remove coil from vehicle.

IGNITION CAPACITOR

REMOVAL & INSTALLATION

The coil capacitor is located in the right-rear section of the engine compartment. It is attached with a mounting stud and nut.

1. Disconnect electrical connector at capacitor.
2. Remove mounting nut and remove ground strap.
3. Remove capacitor.
4. Installation is the reverse of the removal procedure.

IGNITION TIMING

ADJUSTMENT

➡Ignition timing is computer controlled and not manually adjusted.

SPARK PLUGS

REMOVAL & INSTALLATION

3.7L & 4.7L

1. Remove the necessary air filter tubing and air intake components at the top of the engine at the throttle body.

➡The three spark plugs located on the left bank of the engine are under three individual ignition coils. Each individual ignition coil must be removed to gain access to each spark plug located on the left bank of the engine.

2. Prior to removing the ignition coil, spray compressed air around the coil base at the cylinder head.
3. Remove the ignition coil and check the condition of ignition coil O-ring and replace as necessary.
4. Prior to removing the spark plug, spray compressed air into the cylinder head opening. This will help prevent foreign

material from entering combustion chamber.

5. Remove the spark plug from the cylinder head using a quality thin wall socket with a rubber or foam insert.

6. Inspect the spark plug condition.

To install:

7. Check and adjust the spark plug gap with a gap gauging tool. Gap should be 0.043 in. (1.1 mm).

CAUTION

Special care should be taken when installing spark plugs into the cylinder head spark plug wells. Be sure the plugs do not drop into the plug wells as electrodes can be damaged.

8. Start the spark plug into the cylinder head by hand to avoid cross threading.

9. Tighten the spark plugs to 20 ft. lbs. (27 Nm).

10. Before installing the ignition coil, check the condition of the coil O-ring and replace as necessary.

11. Apply silicone based grease such as Mopar Dielectric Grease into the spark plug end of the rubber boot, coil O-rings and to the top of spark plugs.

12. Install the ignition coil.

13. Install all the necessary air filter tubing and air intake components at the top of the engine and at the throttle body.

5.7L

1. Remove all the necessary air filter tubing and air intake components at the top of the engine and at the throttle body.

2. Prior to removing the ignition coil, spray compressed air around the base of the ignition coil at the cylinder head.

3. Remove the ignition coil.

4. Prior to removing the spark plug, spray compressed air into the cylinder head opening.

5. Remove the spark plug from the cylinder head using a quality thin wall socket with a rubber or foam insert.

6. Inspect the spark plug condition.

To install:

➡Do not attempt to clean any of the spark plugs. Replace only.

7. Check and adjust the spark plug gap with a gap gauging tool. Gap should be 0.040 in. (1.0 mm).

CAUTION

Special care should be taken when installing spark plugs into the cylinder head spark plug wells. Be sure the plugs do not drop into the plug wells as electrodes can be damaged.

8. Start the spark plug into the cylinder head by hand to avoid cross threading.

CAUTION

Always tighten spark plugs to the specified torque. Certain engines use torque sensitive spark plugs. Over tightening can cause distortion resulting in a change in the spark plug gap, or a cracked porcelain insulator.

9. Tighten the spark plugs to 13 ft. lbs. (18 Nm). Do not over-torque.

10. To aid in coil installation, apply silicone based grease such as Mopar® Dielectric Grease into spark plug end of ignition coil rubber boots. Also apply this grease to the tops of spark plugs. Install the ignition coils.

11. Install all necessary air filter tubing and air intake components to top of engine and to throttle body.

ENGINE ELECTRICAL

STARTING SYSTEM

STARTER

REMOVAL & INSTALLATION

3.7L & 4.7L

1. Disconnect and isolate the negative battery cable.

2. Raise and support the vehicle.

3. On some applications, a support bracket is used between front axle and side of transmission. Remove two support bracket bolts at the transmission. Pry the support bracket slightly to gain access to the lower starter mounting bolt.

4. Remove the one bolt and one nut if equipped with a manual transmission .

5. Remove the two bolts if equipped with an automatic transmission .

6. Move the starter motor towards the front of vehicle far enough for the nose of the starter pinion housing to clear the housing. Always support the starter motor during this process, do not let the starter motor hang from the wire harness.

7. Tilt the nose downwards and lower the starter motor far enough to access and remove the nut that secures the battery positive cable connector eyelet to the solenoid battery terminal stud. Do not let the starter motor hang from the wire harness.

8. Remove the battery positive cable connector eyelet from the solenoid battery terminal stud.

9. Disconnect the battery positive cable connector from the solenoid terminal connector receptacle.

10. Remove the starter motor.

To install:

11. Connect the solenoid wire to the starter motor (snaps on).

12. Position the battery cable to the solenoid stud. Install and tighten the battery cable eyelet nut to 10 ft. lbs. (13 Nm). Do not allow the starter motor to hang from the wire harness.

13. Position the starter motor to the transmission.

14. Slide the cooler tube bracket into position.

15. Install and tighten both bolts to 50 ft. lbs. (68 Nm).

16. Lower the vehicle.

17. Connect the negative battery cable.

5.7L

1. Disconnect and isolate the negative battery cable.

2. Raise and support the vehicle.

➡If equipped with 4WD and certain transmissions, a support bracket is used between front axle and side of transmission. Remove 2 support bracket bolts at transmission. Pry support bracket slightly to gain access to lower starter mounting bolt.

3. Remove the two starter mounting bolts.

4. Move the starter motor towards front of vehicle far enough for the nose of the starter pinion housing to clear the housing. Always support the starter motor during this process, do not let the starter motor hang from wire harness.

5. Tilt nose the downwards and lower starter motor far enough to access and remove the nut that secures the battery positive cable wire harness connector to the solenoid battery terminal stud . Do not let the starter motor hang from the wire harness.

6. Remove the battery positive cable wire harness connector eyelet from the solenoid battery terminal stud.

7. Disconnect the battery positive cable wire harness connector from the solenoid terminal connector receptacle.
8. Remove the starter motor.

To install:

9. Connect the solenoid wire to starter motor (snaps on).
10. Position the battery cable to the solenoid stud. Install and tighten the battery cable eyelet nut to 10 ft. lbs. (13 Nm). Do not allow the starter motor to hang from the wire harness.
11. Position the starter motor to engine.
12. Slide the transmission cooler tube bracket into position.
13. Install and tighten both mounting bolts. Tighten to 50 ft. lbs. (68 Nm).
14. Lower the vehicle.
15. Connect the negative battery cable.

ENGINE MECHANICAL

➡Disconnecting the negative battery cable may interfere with the functions of the on board computer systems and may require the computer to undergo a relearning process, once the negative battery cable is reconnected.

ACCESSORY DRIVE BELTS

ACCESSORY BELT ROUTING

See Figures 31 and 32.

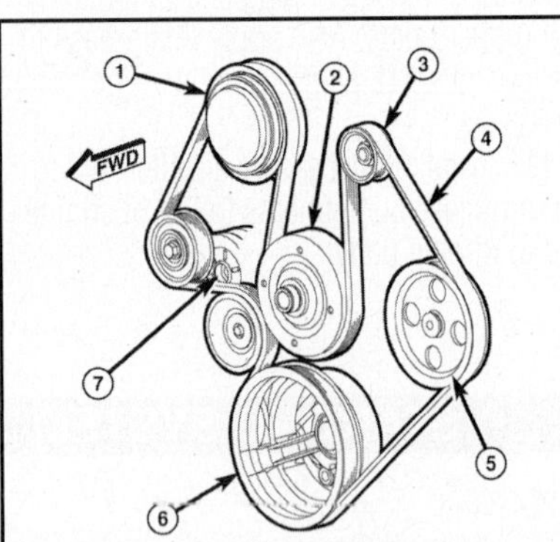

Fig. 31 Showing accessory belt routing—3.7L & 4.7L

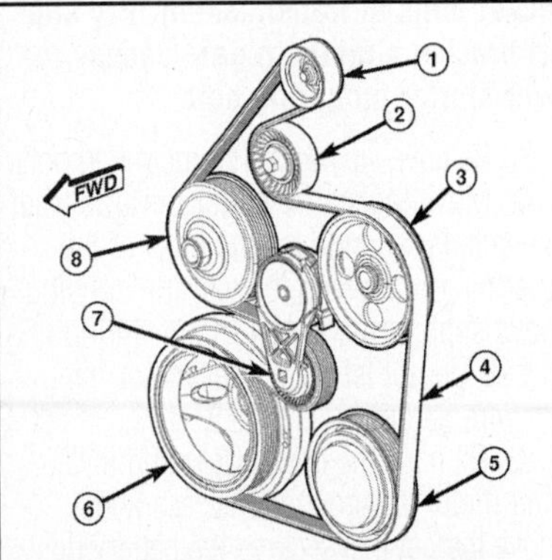

Fig. 32 Showing accessory belt routing—5.7L

INSPECTION

Visual Diagnosis

When diagnosing serpentine accessory drive belts, small cracks that run across the ribbed surface of the belt from rib to rib, are considered normal. These are not a reason to replace the belt. However, cracks running along a rib (not across) are not normal. Any belt with cracks running along a rib must be replaced. Also replace the belt if it has excessive wear, frayed cords or severe glazing.

Noise Diagnosis

Noises generated by the accessory drive belt are most noticeable at idle. Before replacing a belt to resolve a noise condition, inspect all of the accessory drive pulleys for alignment, glazing, or excessive end play.

ADJUSTMENT

Belt tension is automatically maintained by the tensioner; no adjustment is needed.

REMOVAL & INSTALLATION

3.7L & 4.7L

⁂ CAUTION

Do not let tensioner arm snap back to the freearm position, severe damage may occur to the tensioner.

1. Disconnect negative battery cable from battery.
2. Rotate belt tensioner until it contacts it's stop. Remove belt, then slowly rotate the tensioner into the freearm position.
3. Installation is the reverse of the removal procedure.

5.7L

1. Insert a suitable square drive ratchet into the square hole on belt tensioner arm.
2. Release the belt tension by rotating the tensioner clockwise. Rotate the belt tensioner until the accessory belt can be removed from pulleys.

⁂ CAUTION

Do not let the tensioner arm snap back to the freearm position, severe damage may occur to the tensioner.

3. Remove the accessory belt.
4. Gently release the tensioner.
5. Installation is the reverse of the removal procedure.

AIR CLEANER

REMOVAL & INSTALLATION

3.7L & 4.7L

1. Loosen the clamp and disconnect air duct at air cleaner cover.
2. Pry over 4 spring clips from housing cover.
3. Release housing cover from locating tabs on housing and remove cover.
4. Remove air cleaner element (filter) from housing.
5. Clean inside of housing before replacing element.
6. Installation is the reverse of the removal procedure.

5.7L

1. Disengage the retaining clamps that secure the air cleaner body cover to air cleaner body.
2. Lift and push the air cleaner body cover toward the engine to disengage the cover locating tabs from the air cleaner body and position the cover out of the way.
3. Remove the air cleaner element from the inside of the air cleaner body.
4. Clean out the inside of the air cleaner body.
5. Installation is the reverse of the removal procedure.

CAMSHAFT & VALVE LIFTERS

REMOVAL & INSTALLATION

3.7L

See Figures 33 through 35.

➡Left side head shown in illustrations, right side is similar.

⁂ CAUTION

When the timing chain is removed and the cylinder heads are still installed, Do not forcefully rotate the camshafts or crankshaft independently of each other. Severe valve and/or piston damage can occur.

⁂ CAUTION

When removing the cam sprocket, timing chains or camshaft, Failure to use the Wedge Locking Tool (8379 or equivalent) will result in hydraulic tensioner ratchet over extension, requiring timing chain cover removal to reset the tensioner ratchet.

1. Remove cylinder head cover.
2. Set engine cylinder #1 to TDC, camshaft sprocket V6 marks at the 12 o'clock position.
3. Mark one link on the secondary timing chain on both sides of the V6 mark on the camshaft sprocket to aid in installation.

⁂ CAUTION

Do not hold or pry on the camshaft target wheel (located on the right side camshaft sprocket) for any reason, Severe damage will occur to the target wheel resulting in a vehicle no start condition.

4. Loosen but DO NOT remove the camshaft sprocket retaining bolt. Leave the bolt snug against the sprocket.

⁂ CAUTION

The timing chain tensioners must be secured prior to removing the camshaft sprockets. Failure to secure tensioners will allow the tensioners to extend, requiring timing chain cover removal in order to reset tensioners.

5. Position the Wedge Locking Tool (8379 or equivalent) between the timing chain strands, tap the tool to securely wedge the timing chain against the tensioner arm and guide. Do not force past narrowest chain point.
6. Hold the camshaft with the Camshaft Holder (8482A or equivalent), while removing the camshaft sprocket bolt and sprocket.
7. Using the Camshaft Holder, gently allow the camshaft to rotate 5 degrees clockwise until the camshaft is in the neutral position (no valve load).

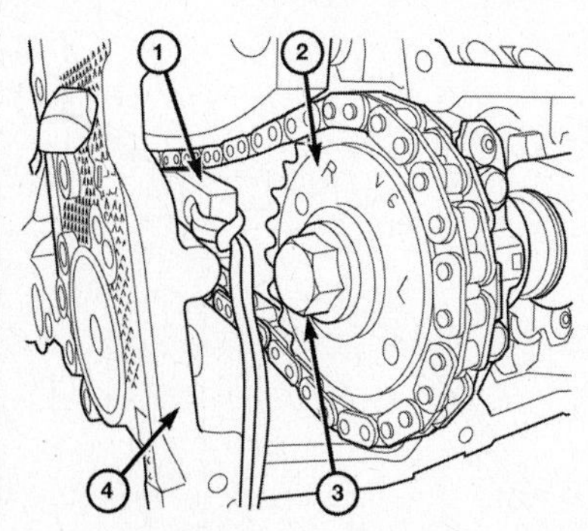

Fig. 33 Position the Wedge Locking Tool (8379 or equivalent) (1) between the timing chain strands, tap the tool to securely wedge the timing chain against the tensioner arm and guide. Do not force past narrowest chain point.

8. Starting at the outside working inward, loosen the camshaft bearing cap retaining bolts 1/2 turn at a time. Repeat until all load is off the bearing caps.

⁂ CAUTION

Do not stamp or strike the camshaft bearing caps. Severe damage will occur to the bearing caps.

➡When the camshaft is removed the rocker arms may slide downward, mark the rocker arms before removing camshaft.

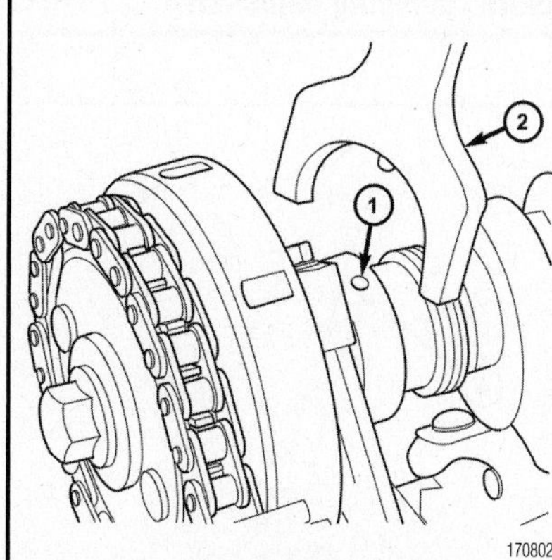

Fig. 34 Hold the camshaft with the Camshaft Holder (8482A or equivalent) (2), while removing the camshaft sprocket bolt and sprocket, and gently allow the camshaft (1) to rotate 5 degrees clockwise until the camshaft is in the neutral position (no valve load).

9. Remove the camshaft bearing caps and the camshaft.

To install:

10. Lubricate camshaft journals with clean engine oil.
11. Position the camshaft into the cylinder head.
12. Position the left side camshaft so that the camshaft sprocket dowel is near the 1 o'clock position, This will place the camshaft at the neutral position easing the installation of the camshaft bearing caps.
13. Install the camshaft bearing caps, hand tighten the retaining bolts.
14. Caps should be installed so that the stamped numbers on the caps are in numerical order, (1 through 4) from the front to the rear of the engine. All caps should be installed so that the stamped arrows on the caps point toward the front of the engine.
15. Working in 1/2 turn increments, tighten the bearing cap retaining bolts in the sequence shown. Tighten the camshaft bearing cap retaining bolts to 100 inch lbs. (11 Nm).
16. Position the camshaft drive gear into the timing chain aligning the V6 mark between the two marked chain links (Two links marked during removal).
17. Using the Camshaft Holder, rotate the camshaft until the camshaft sprocket dowel is aligned with the slot in the camshaft sprocket. Install the sprocket onto the camshaft.
18. Remove excess oil from bolt, then install the camshaft sprocket retaining bolt and hand tighten.
19. Remove Wedge Locking Tool.
20. Using the Spanner Wrench with adapter pins (6958 and 8346, or equivalent tool set), tighten the camshaft sprocket retaining bolt to 90 ft. lbs. (122 Nm).
21. Install the cylinder head cover

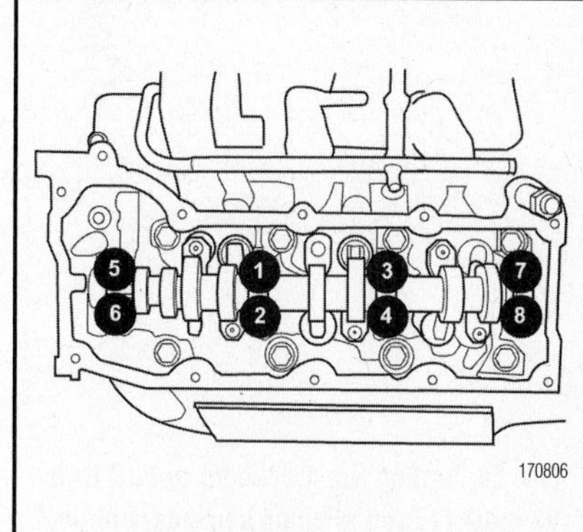

Fig. 35 Camshaft bolt tightening sequence

4.7L

Left Camshaft

See Figures 36 through 39.

1. Remove the cylinder head cover.

CAUTION

When the timing chain is removed and the cylinder heads are still installed, Do not forcefully rotate the camshafts or crankshaft independently of each other. Severe valve and/or piston damage can occur.

2. Set No. 1 cylinder to TDC and align the camshaft sprocket V8 mark to the 12 o'clock position.
3. Mark the link on the secondary timing chain that is aligned with the two dots on the camshaft sprocket as shown to aid in installation.

CAUTION

When removing the camshaft sprocket, timing chains or camshaft, the timing chain tensioner must be secured, failure to use Locking Wedge (9867 or equivalent) will result in hydraulic tensioner ratchet over extension, requiring timing chain cover removal to reset the tensioner ratchet. Do not force Locking Wedge past the narrowest point between the chain strands. Damage to the tensioners may occur.

4. Position Locking Wedge (9867 or equivalent) between the timing chain strands, gently tap the wedge into position and secure the timing chain against the tensioner arm and guide.

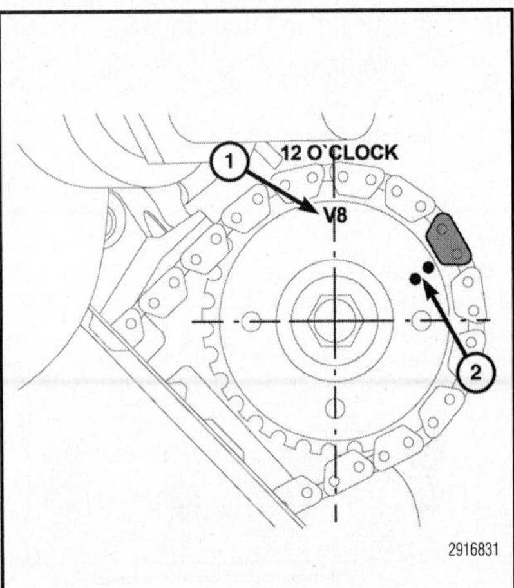

Fig. 36 Setting No. 1 cylinder to TDC with V8 mark (1) and aligning secondary timing chain link (2).

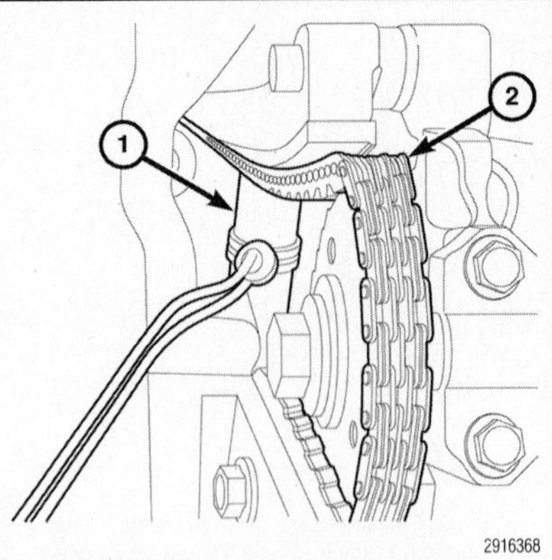

Fig. 37 Position Locking Wedge (9867 or equivalent) (1) between the timing chain strands (2), gently tap the wedge into position and secure the timing chain against the tensioner arm and guide.

5. Using a Spanner Wrench (6958 or equivalent) with Adapter Pins (8346), secure the camshaft sprocket and remove the camshaft sprocket bolt.
6. Position Camshaft Holder (8428A or equivalent) onto the camshaft to lock it from turning. Hold the camshaft while removing the camshaft sprocket.
7. Using the camshaft holder, gently allow the camshaft to rotate 15 degrees clockwise until the camshaft is in the neutral position (no valve load).

CAUTION

Do not stamp or strike the camshaft bearing caps or severe engine damage may result. When the camshaft is removed the rocker arms may slide downward, mark the rocker arms before removing camshaft.

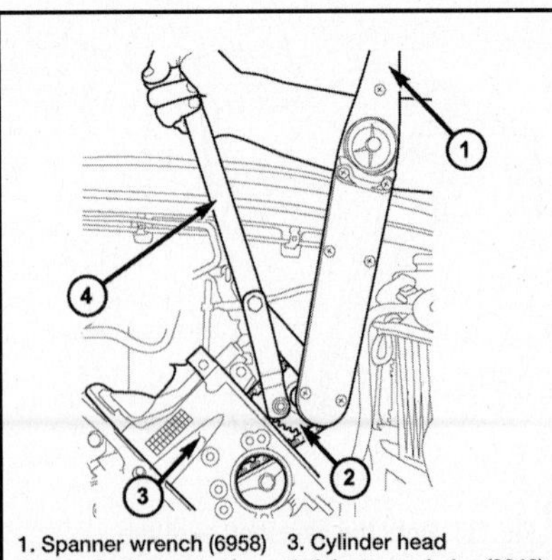

Fig. 38 Using a Spanner Wrench (6958 or equivalent) (4) with Adapter Pins (8346), secure the camshaft sprocket (2) and remove the camshaft sprocket bolt.

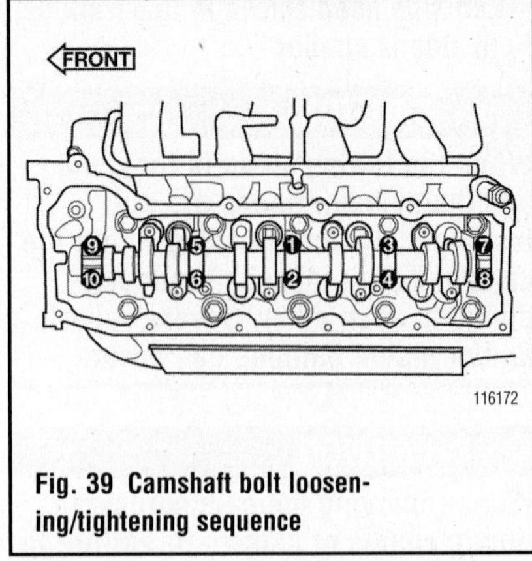

Fig. 39 Camshaft bolt loosening/tightening sequence

8. Using the sequence shown, loosen the camshaft bearing cap retaining bolts 1/2 turn at a time until all load is off the bearing caps and remove bolts.
9. Remove the camshaft bearing caps and the camshaft.

To install:

10. Lubricate the camshaft journals with clean engine oil.
11. Position the left side camshaft so that the camshaft sprocket dowel is near the 1 o'clock position, this will place the camshaft at the neutral position easing the installation of the camshaft bearing caps. Install the camshaft into the cylinder head while aligning the camshaft sprocket dowel.

➡The camshaft caps are marked for location. The arrow must point to the front of the engine.

12. Install the camshaft bearing caps in the same position as noted during removal.
13. Install the camshaft bearing cap retaining bolts hand tight.
14. Using the sequence shown, working in 1/2 turn increments, tighten the bearing cap retaining bolts to 8 ft. lbs. (11 Nm).
15. Check the camshaft end play.
16. Position the camshaft drive gear into the timing chain while aligning the two dots on the camshaft sprocket with the chain link marked during removal.
17. Using camshaft holder, rotate the camshaft until the camshaft sprocket dowel is aligned with the slot in the camshaft sprocket.
18. Position the sprocket onto the camshaft.
19. Remove excess oil from the camshaft sprocket retaining bolt.
20. Install the camshaft sprocket retaining bolt hand tight.
21. Remove the timing chain locking wedge.
22. Using a spanner wrench and adapter pins, secure the camshaft sprocket and

tighten the retaining bolt to 90 ft. lbs. (122 Nm).

23. Install the cylinder head cover

Right Camshaft

See Figures 40 through 43.

1. Remove the cylinder head cover.

**** CAUTION**

When the timing chain is removed and the cylinder heads are still installed, Do not forcefully rotate the camshafts or crankshaft independently of each other. Severe valve and/or piston damage can occur.

2. Set No. 1 cylinder to TDC and align the camshaft sprocket V8 mark to the 12 o'clock position. Mark the link on the secondary timing chain that is aligned with the two dots on the camshaft sprocket to aid in installation.

**** CAUTION**

Do not hold or pry on the camshaft target wheel for any reason, severe damage will occur to the target wheel resulting in a vehicle no start condition. When removing the camshaft sprocket, timing chains or camshaft, the timing chain tensioner must be secured, failure to use Locking Wedge 9867 will result in hydraulic tensioner ratchet over extension, requiring timing chain cover removal to reset the tensioner ratchet.

3. Position Locking Wedge (9867 or equivalent) (2) between the timing chain strands (1), gently tap the wedge into position and secure the timing chain against the tensioner arm and guide.

4. Using a Spanner Wrench (6958 or equivalent) (2) with Adapter Pins (8346 or equivalent), secure the camshaft sprocket (3) and remove the camshaft sprocket bolt.

5. Disconnect the electrical connector to the Camshaft Position Sensor (CMP). Remove the CMP sensor retaining bolt. Using a slight rocking motion, carefully remove the CMP sensor (1). Check the condition of the CMP sensor O-ring, replace as necessary.

6. Position Camshaft Holder (8428A or equivalent wrench) onto the flat of the camshaft. Using the holder, hold the camshaft while removing the camshaft sprocket.

7. Using the holder, gently allow the camshaft to rotate 45 degrees counterclockwise until the camshaft is in the neutral position (no valve load).

**** CAUTION**

Do not stamp or strike the camshaft bearing caps or severe engine damage may result. When the camshaft is removed the rocker arms may slide downward, mark the rocker arms before removing camshaft.

8. Using the sequence shown, loosen the camshaft bearing cap retaining bolts 1/2 turn at a time until all load is off the bearing caps and remove bolts.

9. Remove the camshaft bearing caps and the camshaft.

Fig. 40 Position Locking Wedge (9867 or equivalent) (2) between the timing chain strands (1), gently tap the wedge into position and secure the timing chain against the tensioner arm and guide.

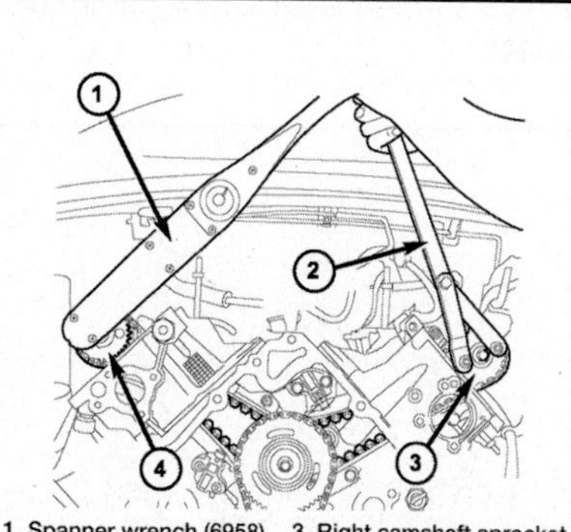

Fig. 41 Using a Spanner Wrench (6958 or equivalent) (2) with Adapter Pins (8346 or equivalent), secure the camshaft sprocket (3) and remove the camshaft sprocket bolt.

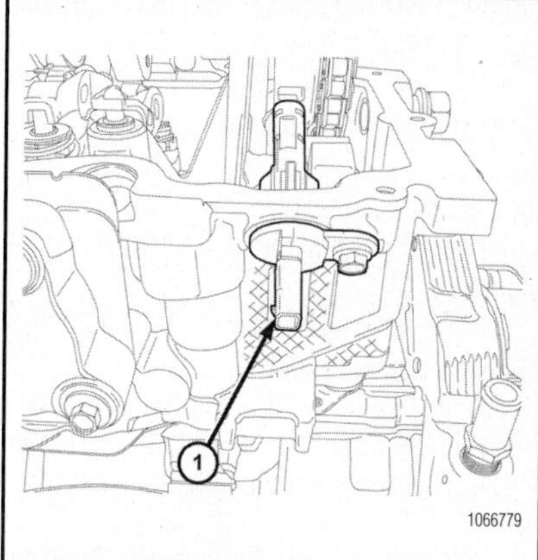

Fig. 42 Disconnect the electrical connector to the Camshaft Position Sensor (CMP). Remove the CMP sensor retaining bolt. Using a slight rocking motion, carefully remove the CMP sensor (1).

To install:

10. Lubricate the camshaft journals with clean engine oil.

11. Position the right side camshaft so that the camshaft sprocket dowel is near the 10 o'clock position, this will place the camshaft at the neutral position easing the installation of the camshaft bearing caps. Install the camshaft into the cylinder head while aligning the camshaft sprocket dowel near the 10 o'clock position.

➡The camshaft caps are marked for location. The arrow must point to the front of the engine.

12. Install the camshaft bearing caps in the same position as noted during removal.

13. Install the camshaft bearing cap retaining bolts hand tight.

14. Using the sequence shown, working in 1/2 turn increments, tighten the bearing cap retaining bolts to 8 ft. lbs. (11 Nm).

15. Check the camshaft end play.

16. Position the camshaft drive gear into the timing chain while aligning the two dots

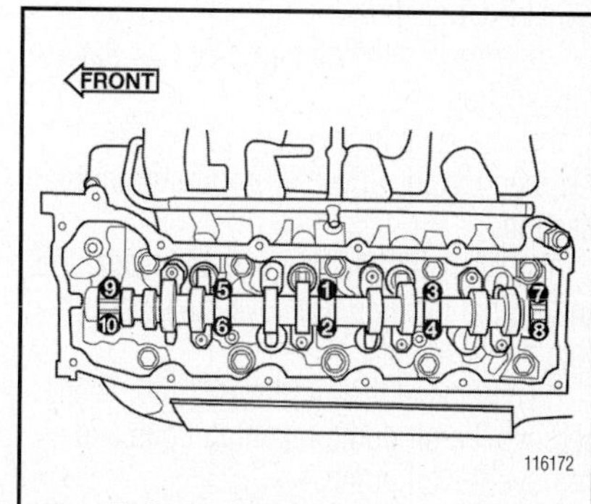

Fig. 43 Camshaft bearing cap loosening/tightening sequence

on the camshaft sprocket with the chain link marked during removal.

17. Using the camshaft holder wrench, rotate the camshaft until the camshaft sprocket dowel is aligned with the slot in the camshaft sprocket.

18. Position the sprocket onto the camshaft.

19. Remove excess oil from the camshaft sprocket retaining bolt.

20. Install the camshaft sprocket retaining bolt hand tight.

21. Remove the timing chain locking wedge.

22. Using Spanner Wrench with Adapter Pins, secure the camshaft sprocket and tighten the retaining bolt to 90 ft. lbs. (122 Nm).

23. Install the cylinder head cover.

24. Clean machined CMP sensor hole in the cylinder head. Apply a small amount of engine oil to CMP sensor O-ring. Install the CMP sensor (2) into the cylinder head with a slight rocking motion. Do not twist sensor into position as damage to O-ring may result.

25. Before tightening sensor mounting bolt, be sure sensor is completely flush to cylinder head. If sensor is not flush, damage to sensor mounting tang may result. Install the retaining bolt and tighten to 9 ft. lbs. (12 Nm).

26. Connect the electrical connector to the CMP sensor.

5.7L

See Figures 44 through 46.

1. Remove the battery negative cable.
2. Remove the air cleaner assembly.
3. Raise and support the vehicle.
4. Drain the engine oil.
5. Drain the coolant.
6. Remove the accessory drive belt.
7. Remove the left and right cylinder heads. See "Cylinder Head" in this section.
8. Remove the radiator. See "ENGINE COOLING" section.
9. Remove the oil pan. See "Oil Pan" in this section.
10. Remove timing case cover. See "Timing Chain, Cover & Sprockets" in this section.
11. Mark all lifters to ensure installation in original location. Remove the tappets and retainer assembly.
12. Remove the oil pick up tube. Then, remove the oil pump retaining bolts and remove the oil pump.
13. Remove timing chain. See "Timing Chain, Cover & Sprockets" in this section.

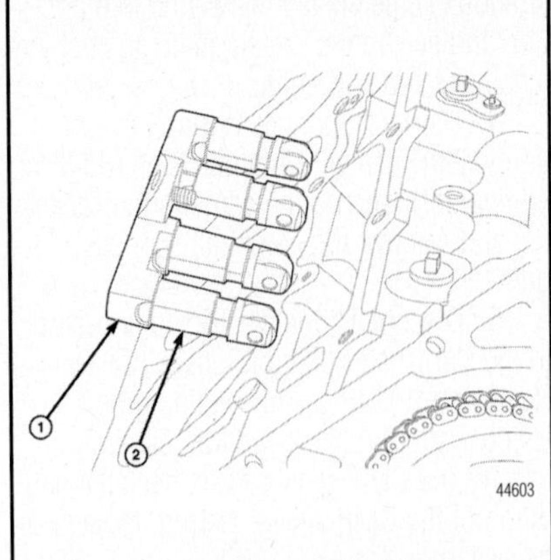

Fig. 44 Mark all lifters to ensure installation in original location. Remove the tappets (2) and retainer (1) assembly.

14. Remove camshaft thrust plate, once the timing chain and sprocket are removed.

15. Install a long bolt into front of camshaft to aid in removal of the camshaft. Remove camshaft, being careful not to damage cam bearings with the cam lobes. Slowly rotate the camshaft while pulling camshaft out.

To install:

16. Lubricate the camshaft lobes and camshaft bearing journals and insert the camshaft.

➡Ensure that the plate is installed on the correct side. The fasteners are flat head fasteners so the top of the head of the fastener should not stick above the front face of the plate after they are torqued. The plate has chamfered fastener holes and the chamfered side should be facing forward to ensure the fasteners are flush or below the front surface.

17. Install the camshaft thrust plate and tighten the bolts, in alternating sequence, to 9 ft. lbs. (12 Nm).

18. Measure camshaft end play. It should be 0.0031–0.0114 in. (0.080—0.290 mm). If not within limits, disassemble, clean, and inspect for burrs or debris. Reassemble and measure end play again. If the end play is still out, then install a new thrust plate.

19. Install the timing chain and sprockets. See "Timing Chain, Cover & Sprockets" in this section.

20. Install the oil pump and tighten bolts to 21 ft. lbs. (28 Nm).

21. Inspect the oil pick up tube O-rings and replace as necessary. Install the oil pick up tube and tighten fasteners to 21 ft. lbs. (28 Nm).

22. Install the timing chain cover. See "Timing Chain, Cover & Sprockets" in this section.

23. Install the oil pan. See "Oil Pan" in this section.

➡Engines equipped with MDS use both standard roller lifters (2) and deactivating roller lifters (1). The deactivating roller lifters must be used in cylinders 1,4,6,7. The deactivating lifters can be identified by the two holes in the side of the lifter body (3), for the latching pins.

⁂ CAUTION

Each tappet reused must be installed in the same position from which it was removed. When camshaft is replaced, all of the tappets must be replaced.

24. Install the rear MDS lifter assembly (2) and tighten bolt (1) to 12 N·m (106 in. lbs.).

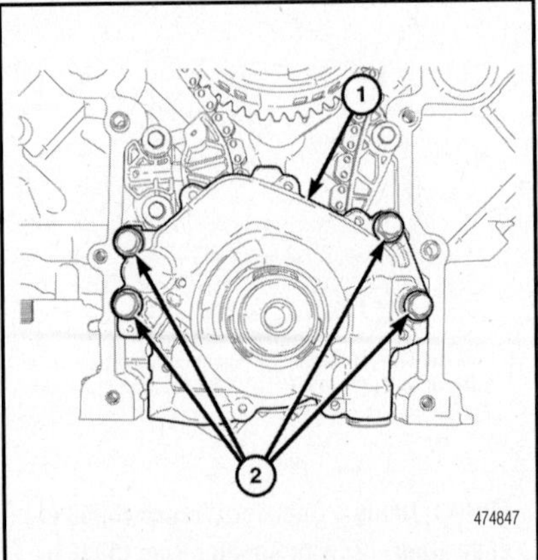

Fig. 45 Remove the oil pick up tube. Then, remove the oil pump retaining bolts (2) and remove the oil pump (1).

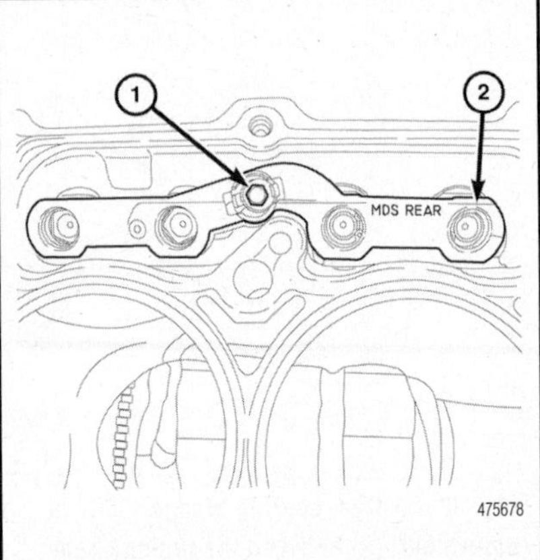

Fig. 46 Install the rear MDS lifter assembly (2) and tighten bolt (1) to 106 inch lbs. (12 Nm).

25. Install the front MDS lifter assembly and tighten bolt to 106 inch lbs. (12 Nm).
26. Install both the left and right cylinder heads. See "Cylinder Head" in this section.
27. Install cylinder head covers.
28. Install the accessory drive belt.
29. Install the radiator. See "ENGINE COOLING" section.
30. Install the air cleaner assembly.
31. Install the negative battery cable.
32. Fill the radiator with coolant.
33. Fill the engine with oil.
34. Start the engine and check for leaks.

CATALYTIC CONVERTER

REMOVAL & INSTALLATION

1. Raise and support vehicle.
2. Saturate the bolts and nuts with heat valve lubricant. Allow 5 minutes for penetration.
3. Disconnect oxygen sensor electrical connectors.
4. Remove clamp.
5. Remove bolts at exhaust to manifold.
6. Remove catalytic converter(s).

To install:

7. Install catalytic converter to exhaust clamp on catalytic converter and position into exhaust pipe.
8. Install and hand-tighten catalytic converter to exhaust manifold bolts.
9. Install C-clip nut and bolt to converter to manifold.
10. Tighten catalytic converter to exhaust manifold bolts to 23 ft. lbs. (31 Nm).
11. Tighten all clamp nuts to 40 ft. lbs. (52 Nm) torque.
12. Check the exhaust system for contact with the body panels. A minimum of 1.0 in. (25 mm) is required between the exhaust system components and body/frame parts, including oil pan. Make the necessary adjustments, if needed.
13. Plug in O2 sensor wiring.
14. Lower the vehicle.
15. Start the engine and inspect for exhaust leaks. Repair exhaust leaks as necessary.

CRANKSHAFT DAMPER & FRONT SEAL

REMOVAL & INSTALLATION

3.7L

1. Disconnect negative cable from battery.
2. Remove accessory drive belt.
3. Remove A/C compressor mounting fasteners and set compressor aside.
4. Drain cooling system.
5. Remove upper radiator hose.
6. Disconnect electrical connector for fan mounted inside radiator shroud.
7. Remove radiator shroud attaching fasteners.

➡Transmission cooler line snaps into shroud lower right hand corner.

8. Remove radiator cooling fan and shroud.
9. Remove crankshaft damper bolt.
10. Remove damper using Crankshaft Insert (8513A, or equivalent) and Three Jaw Puller.
11. Using Crankshaft Front Seal Remover (8511 or equivalent), remove crankshaft front seal.

To install:

➡To prevent severe damage to the Crankshaft, Damper or the Damper Installer Tool (8512A), thoroughly clean the damper bore and the crankshaft nose before installing Damper.

12. Using Seal Installer (8348) and Damper Installer (8512A), install crankshaft front seal.
13. Install vibration damper
14. Install radiator cooling fan and shroud.
15. Install upper radiator hose.
16. Install A/C compressor and tighten fasteners to 40 ft. lbs. (54 Nm).
17. Install accessory drive belt.
18. Refill cooling system.
19. Connect negative cable to battery.

4.7L

See Figure 47.

1. Disconnect and isolate the negative battery cable.

✻✻ CAUTION

Do not let the tensioner arm snap back to the freearm position, severe damage may occur to the tensioner.

2. Rotate the belt tensioner until it contacts its stop and remove the belt, then slowly rotate the tensioner into the freearm position.
3. Raise and support the vehicle.

✻✻ WARNING

Do not remove the radiator pressure cap, cylinder block drain plugs or loosen the radiator draincock with the system hot and under pressure. Serious burns from coolant can occur.

4. Drain the cooling system.
5. Lower the vehicle.
6. Remove the upper radiator hose.

✻✻ CAUTION

The thermal viscous fan drive/fan blade assembly is attached (threaded) to the water pump hub shaft. The transmission cooler line snaps onto the lower right hand corner of the fan shroud. After removing fan blade/viscous fan drive assembly, do not place viscous fan drive in horizontal position. If stored horizontally, silicone fluid in the viscous fan drive could drain into the bearing assembly and contaminate the bearing lubricant.

7. Remove the fan shroud and fan blade/viscous fan drive assembly as a complete unit from the vehicle.
8. Remove the vibration damper retaining bolt.
9. Using the crankshaft insert (8513A or equivalent) and the three jaw puller, remove the crankshaft damper.
10. Using Crankshaft Front Seal Remover (8511 or equivalent), remove crankshaft front seal.

To install:

11. Using Seal Installer (8348 or equivalent) and Damper Installer (8512A or equivalent), install crankshaft front seal.

✻✻ CAUTION

To prevent severe damage to the crankshaft, damper, and damper installer, thoroughly clean the damper bore and the crankshaft nose before installing damper.

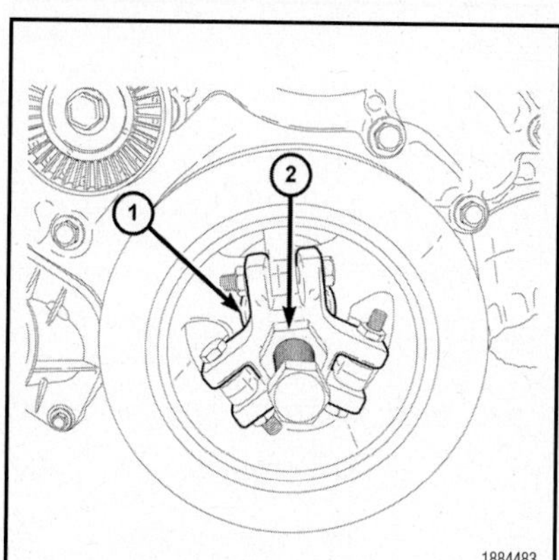

Fig. 47 Using the crankshaft insert (8513A or equivalent) (1) and the three jaw puller (2), remove the crankshaft damper.

12. Position the damper onto the crankshaft. Assemble the damper installer and the A/C hub installer cup (6871 or equivalent). Press the damper onto the crankshaft.

13. Coat the vibration damper bolt threads with Mopar Nickel Anti-Seize or equivalent, install and tighten the bolt to 130 ft. lbs. (175 Nm).

14. Install the cooling fan assembly.

15. Install the radiator upper shroud and tighten fasteners.

16. Install the radiator upper hose.

17. Install the accessory drive belt.

18. Refill the cooling system.

19. Connect the negative battery cable.

5.7L

See Figure 48.

1. Disconnect negative cable from battery.
2. Remove accessory drive belt.
3. Drain cooling system.
4. Remove radiator upper hose.
5. Remove fan shroud.
6. Remove crankshaft damper bolt.
7. Remove damper using Crankshaft Insert and Three Jaw Puller.
8. Using Seal Remover (9071 or equivalent) (1), remove crankshaft front seal (2).

To install:

9. Using Crankshaft Front Oil Seal Installer (9072 or equivalent) and Damper Installer (8512A or equivalent), install crankshaft front seal.

**** CAUTION**

To prevent severe damage to the crankshaft, damper, and damper installer, thoroughly clean the damper bore and the crankshaft nose before installing damper.

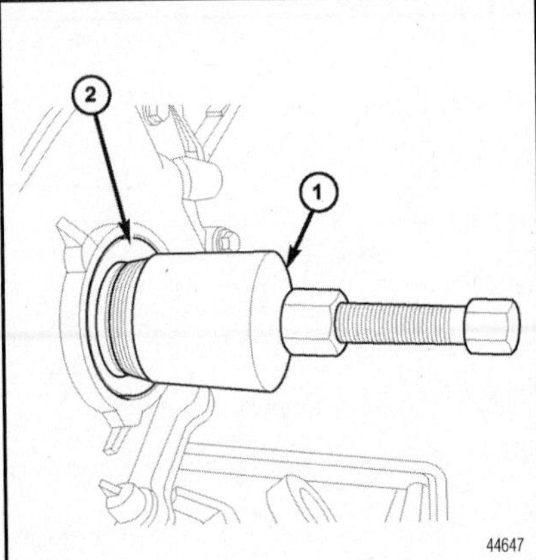

Fig. 48 Using Seal Remover (9071 or equivalent) (1), remove crankshaft front seal (2).

10. Position the damper onto crankshaft. Assemble the damper installer, and the pressing cup from A/C hub installer (6871 or equivalent). Press the damper onto crankshaft.

11. Install the crankshaft damper bolt and tighten to 130 ft. lbs. (176 Nm).

12. Install the cooling fan.

13. Install the radiator upper shroud and tighten the fasteners.

14. Install the radiator upper hose.

15. Install the accessory drive belt.

16. Refill the cooling system.

17. Connect the negative cable to battery.

CYLINDER HEAD

REMOVAL & INSTALLATION

3.7L & 4.7L

See Figures 49 through 55.

➡**Procedure is the same for both cylinder heads. Some illustrations show left cylinder head, but right side head is similar.**

1. Disconnect the negative battery cable.
2. Raise and support the vehicle.
3. Disconnect the exhaust pipe at the left side exhaust manifold.
4. Drain the engine coolant.
5. Lower the vehicle.
6. Remove the intake manifold. See "Intake Manifold" in this section.
7. Remove the master cylinder and booster assembly.
8. As needed, remove power steering pump from mounting and set aside.
9. Remove the cylinder head cover.
10. Remove the fan shroud and fan blade assembly.
11. Remove accessory drive belt. See "Accessory Drive Belt" in this section.
12. Remove the power steering pump and set aside. See "STEERING" section.
13. Rotate the crankshaft until the damper timing mark is aligned with TDC indicator mark.
14. Verify the "V6" or "V8" mark on the camshaft sprocket is at the 12 o'clock position. Rotate the crankshaft one turn if necessary.
15. Remove the crankshaft damper. See "Crankshaft Damper & Seal" in this section.

➡**For timing chain reference, see "Timing Chain, Cover & Seal" in this section.**

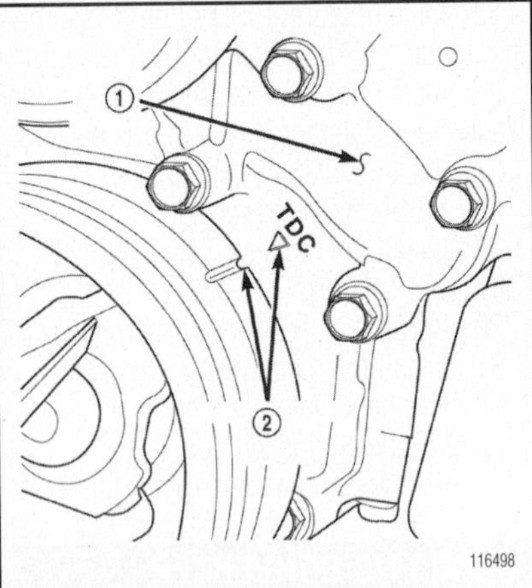

Fig. 49 Rotate the crankshaft until the damper timing mark is aligned with TDC indicator mark (2) on engine block (1).

16. Remove the timing chain cover. Lock the secondary timing chains to the idler sprocket using special tool (8249 or equivalent) timing chain holding fixture.
17. Mark the secondary timing chain, one link on each side of the V6 mark on the camshaft drive gear.
18. Remove the left side secondary chain tensioner.
19. Remove the cylinder head access plug (2).
20. Remove the left side secondary chain guide.
21. Remove the retaining bolt and the camshaft drive gear.

**** CAUTION**

Do not allow the engine to rotate. Severe damage to the valve train can occur.

**** CAUTION**

Do not overlook the four smaller bolts at the front of the cylinder head. Do not attempt to remove the cylinder head without removing these four bolts.

22. Remove the cylinder head retaining bolts.
23. Remove the cylinder head and gasket. Discard the gasket.

**** CAUTION**

Do not lay the cylinder head on its gasket sealing surface, due to the design of the cylinder head gasket any distortion to the cylinder head sealing surface may prevent the gasket from properly sealing resulting in leaks.

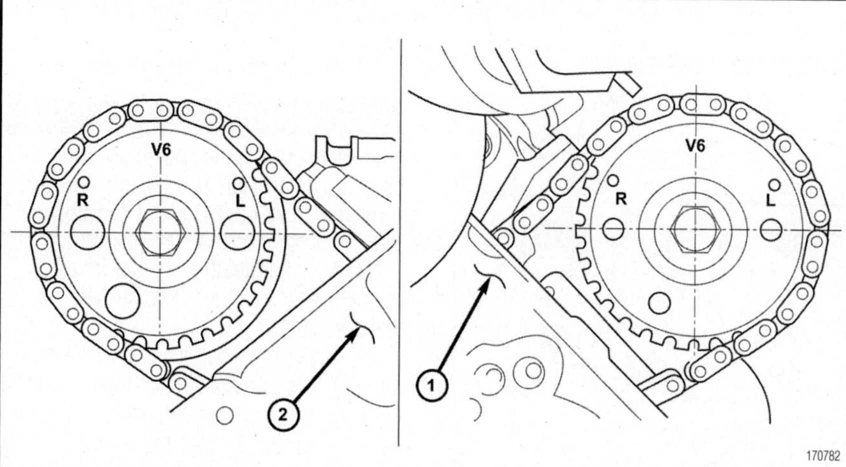

Fig. 50 Verify the "V6" or "V8" mark on the camshaft sprocket is at the 12 o'clock position. Rotate the crankshaft one turn if necessary—V6 shown; V8 same.

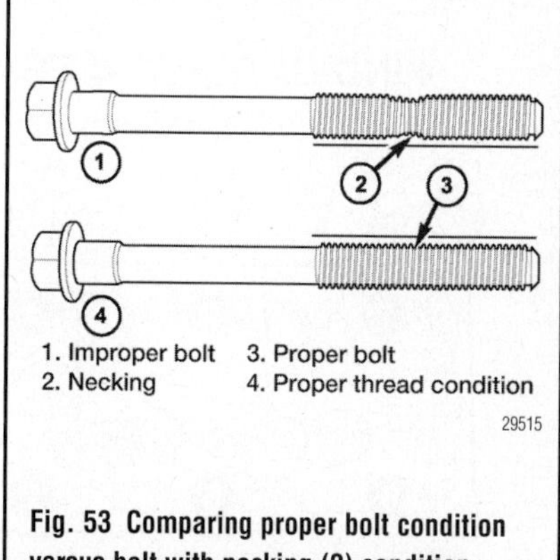

Fig. 53 Comparing proper bolt condition versus bolt with necking (2) condition.

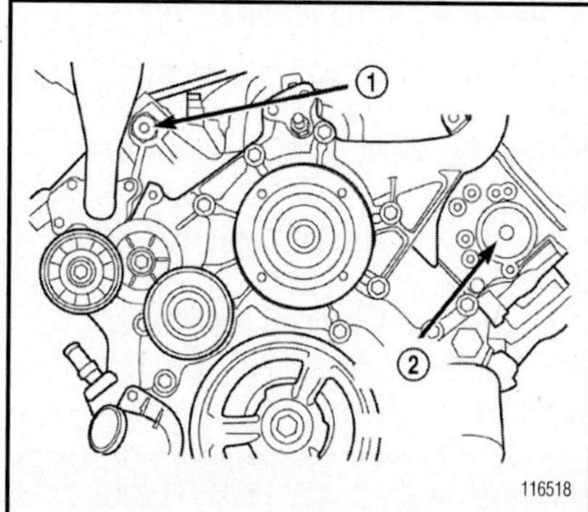

Fig. 51 Remove the cylinder head access plug (2).

To install:

➡The cylinder head bolts are tightened using a torque plus angle procedure. The bolts must be examined BEFORE reuse. If the threads are necked down (2) the bolts should be replaced. Necking can be checked by holding a straight edge against the threads. If all the threads do not contact the scale, the bolt should be replaced.

✲✲ CAUTION

When cleaning cylinder head and cylinder block surfaces, DO NOT use a metal scraper because the surfaces could be cut or ground. Use only a wooden or plastic scraper.

24. Clean the cylinder head and cylinder block mating surfaces .
25. Position the new cylinder head gasket on the locating dowels.
26. When installing cylinder head, use care not damage the tensioner arm or the guide arm. Position the cylinder head onto the cylinder block. Make sure the cylinder head seats fully over the locating dowels.

✲✲ CAUTION

The four smaller cylinder head mounting bolts require sealant to be added to them before installing. Failure to do so may cause leaks.

27. Lubricate the cylinder head bolt threads with clean engine oil and install the eight M11 bolts. Coat the four M8 cylinder head bolts with Mopar Lock and Seal Adhesive, or equivalent, then install the bolts.
28. The cylinder head bolts are tightened using an angle torque procedure, however, the bolts are not a torque-to-yield design.
29. Tighten the bolts in sequence using the following steps and torque values:
    a. Step 1: Tighten bolts 1–8 to 20 ft. lbs. (27 Nm).
    b. Step 2: Verify that bolts 1–8, all reached 20 ft. lbs. (27 Nm), by repeating previous step 1 without loosening the bolts.
    c. Tighten bolts 9–12 to 10 ft. lbs. (14 Nm).

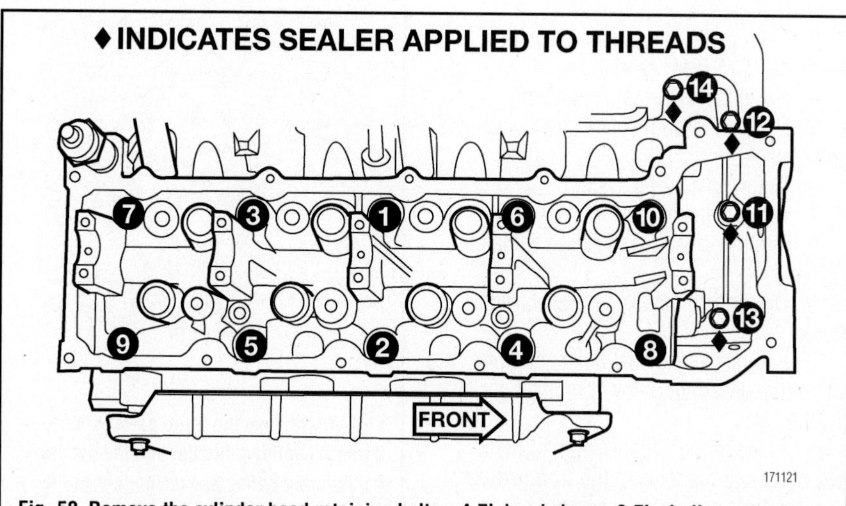

Fig. 52 Remove the cylinder head retaining bolts—4.7L head shown; 3.7L similar sequence

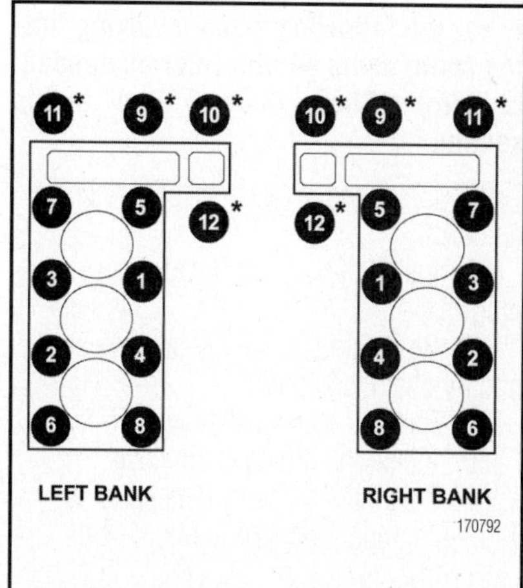

Fig. 54 Cylinder head bolt tightening sequence—3.7L

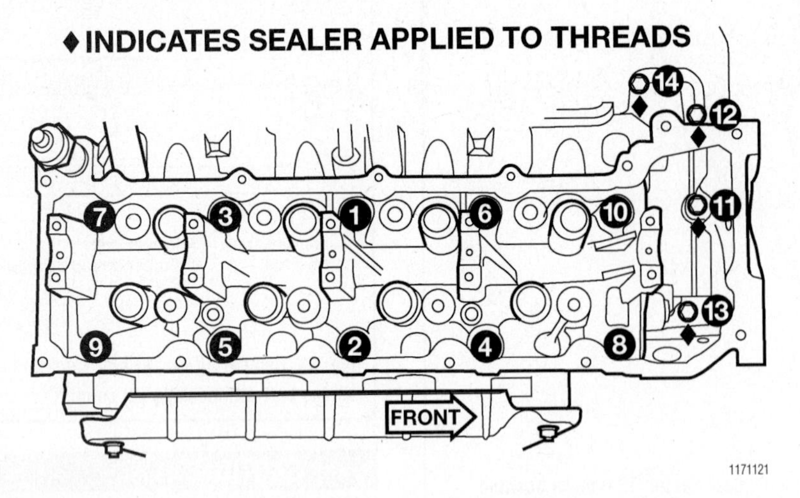

Fig. 55 Cylinder head bolt tightening sequence—4.7L left head shown; right head similar

d. Step 3: Tighten bolts 1–8 an additional 90 degrees.

e. Step 4: Tighten bolts 1–8 an additional 90 degrees, again.

f. Tighten bolts 9–12 to 19 ft. lbs. (26 Nm).

30. Position the secondary chain onto the camshaft drive gear, making sure one marked chain link is on either side of the "V6" or "V8" mark on the gear; then, using Camshaft Wrench (8428A or equivalent), position the gear onto the camshaft.

CAUTION

Remove excess oil from camshaft sprocket retaining bolt before reinstalling bolt. Failure to do so may cause over-torquing of bolt resulting in bolt failure.

31. Install the camshaft drive gear retaining bolt.

➡For the following steps involving timing chain components, refer as needed to "Timing Chain, Cover & Seal" in this section.

32. Install the left side secondary chain guide.

33. Install the cylinder head access plug.

34. Re-set and install the left side secondary chain tensioner.

35. Remove the camshaft wrench.

36. Install the timing chain cover.

37. Install the crankshaft damper. Tighten damper bolt 130 ft. lbs. (175 Nm).

38. Install the power steering pump.

39. If removed, reposition and install power steering pump.

40. Install the fan blade assembly and fan shroud.

41. Install the cylinder head cover.

42. Install the master cylinder and booster assembly.

43. Install the intake manifold. See "Intake Manifold" in this section.

44. Refill the cooling system.

45. Raise the vehicle.

46. Install the exhaust pipe onto the left exhaust manifold.

47. Lower the vehicle.

48. Connect the negative cable to the battery.

49. Start the engine and check for leaks.

5.7L

See Figures 56 through 58.

1. Remove the cowl grille.
2. Remove the engine cover.
3. Release the fuel system pressure. See "FUEL SYSTEM" section.
4. Disconnect the fuel supply line.
5. Disconnect and isolate the negative battery cable.
6. Drain the cooling system.
7. Remove the air cleaner assembly.
8. Remove closed crankcase ventilation system.
9. Disconnect the oxygen sensor connectors.
10. Saturate all exhaust bolts and nuts with a rust penetrant. Allow 5 minutes for penetration.
11. Remove the exhaust pipe to manifold bolts and disconnect the front exhaust pipe/catalytic converter assembly.
12. Disconnect the evaporation control system.
13. Disconnect the heater hoses.

CAUTION

Do not let the tensioner arm snap back to the freearm position, sever damage may occur to the tensioner.

14. Insert a suitable square drive ratchet into the square hole on belt tensioner arm.
15. Release the belt tension by rotating the tensioner arm clockwise. Rotate the belt tensioner arm until the belt can be removed from the pulleys, remove the accessory drive belt, then gently release the tensioner arm.

➡It is not necessary to disconnect the hoses from the power steering pump, for power steering pump removal.

16. Remove the three power steering pump mounting bolts through the access holes in the pulley and secure out of the way.
17. Remove the cylinder head covers and gaskets.
18. Remove the intake manifold and throttle body as an assembly. See "Intake Manifold" in this section.

CAUTION

Rocker arm assemblies and pushrods must be installed in their original locations or engine damage could result.

19. Identify the original locations for assembly, remove rocker arm assemblies and pushrods.

Fig. 56 Remove the three power steering pump mounting bolts through the access holes in the pulley and secure out of the way.

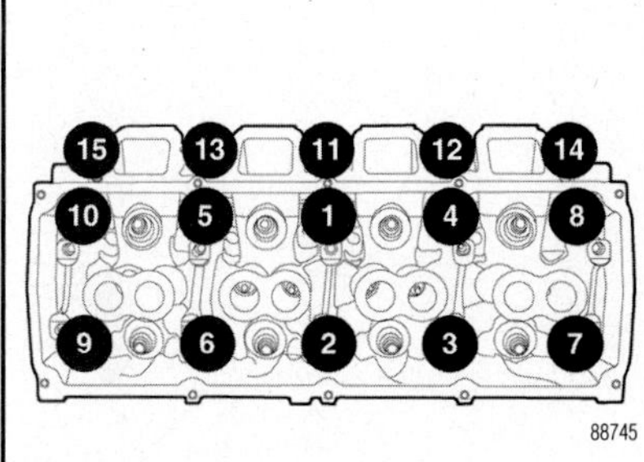

Fig. 57 Cylinder head bolt loosening sequence

20. Using the sequence shown, remove the head bolts from each cylinder head. Remove the cylinder head and discard the cylinder head gasket.

To install:

21. Clean all surfaces of cylinder block and cylinder heads.
22. Clean cylinder block front and rear gasket surfaces using a suitable solvent.

➡The cylinder head gaskets are not interchangeable between the left and right sides. They are marked with an "L" and "R" to indicate the left or right side and they are marked "TOP" to indicate which side goes up.

23. Position the new cylinder head gasket and cylinder head onto the cylinder block.
24. Using the sequence shown, tighten the cylinder head bolts in the following order:
    a. Bolt 1–10 to 25 ft. lbs. (34 Nm).
    b. Bolts 11–15 to 15 ft. lbs. (20 Nm).
    c. Bolts 1–10 to 40 ft. lbs. (54 Nm).
    d. Bolts 11–15 to 15 ft. lbs. (20 Nm).
    e. Rotate the cylinder head bolts 1–10 an additional 90 degrees.
    f. Bolts 11–15 to 25 ft. lbs. (34 Nm).
25. Install the push rods and rocker arm assemblies in their original position, using Pushrod Retainer (9070 or equivalent).
26. Install the intake manifold and throttle body. See "Intake Manifold" in this section.
27. Install the spark plugs.
28. Connect the heater hoses.
29. Connect the fuel supply line.
30. Install the 3 power steering pump mounting bolts through the access holes in the pulley and tighten bolts to 21 ft. lbs. (28 Nm).
31. Install the accessory drive belt. See "Accessory Drive Belt" in this section.
32. Install the cylinder head cover and hand start all fasteners. Verify that all double ended studs are in the correct location.

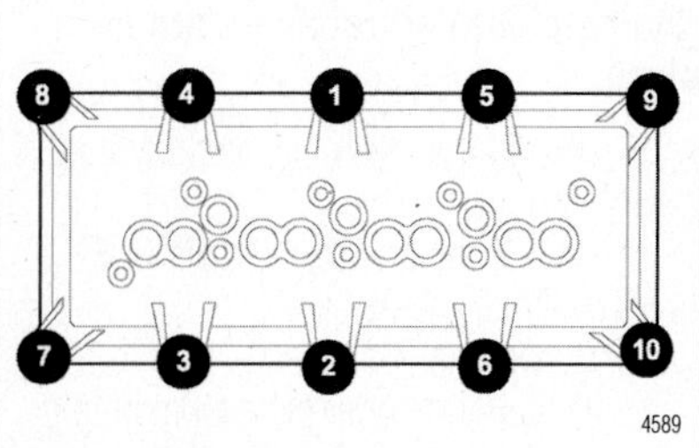

Fig. 58 Using the sequence shown, tighten the cylinder head cover bolts and double ended studs to 70 inch lbs. (8 Nm).

33. Using the sequence shown, tighten the cylinder head cover bolts and double ended studs to 70 inch lbs. (8 Nm).
34. Connect the evaporation control system.
35. Install the air cleaner.
36. Install cowl grille.
37. Install the engine cover.
38. Fill the cooling system.
39. Drain and fill the engine with new oil.
40. Connect the negative battery cable.
41. Start the engine and check for leaks.

ENGINE OIL & FILTER

REPLACEMENT

➡The engine oil level indicator is located at the right rear of the engine on the 3.7L/4.7L engines.

CAUTION

Do not overfill crankcase with engine oil, pressure loss or oil foaming can result.

1. Inspect engine oil level approximately every 500 miles. Unless the engine has exhibited loss of oil pressure, run the engine for about five minutes before checking oil level. Checking engine oil level on a cold engine is not accurate.

➡To ensure proper lubrication of an engine, the engine oil must be maintained at an acceptable level. The acceptable levels are indicated between the ADD and SAFE marks on the engine oil dipstick.

2. Hoist and support vehicle on safety stands.
3. Remove oil fill cap.
4. Place a suitable drain pan under crankcase drain and oil filter.
5. Using a suitable oil filter wrench loosen filter.
6. Rotate the oil filter counterclockwise to remove it from the cylinder block oil filter boss.
7. When filter separates from cylinder block oil filter boss, tip gasket end upward to minimize oil spill.
8. Remove filter from vehicle. Make sure filter gasket was removed with filter.
9. With a wiping cloth, clean the gasket sealing surface of oil and grime.
10. Remove drain plug from crankcase and allow oil to drain into pan. Inspect drain plug threads for stretching or other damage. Replace drain plug if damaged.
11. Install drain plug in crankcase.
12. Lightly lubricate oil filter gasket with engine oil.
13. Thread filter onto adapter nipple. When gasket makes contact with sealing surface, hand tighten filter one full turn, do not over tighten.
14. Lower vehicle and fill crankcase with specified type and amount of engine oil.
15. Install oil fill cap.
16. Start engine and inspect for leaks.
17. Stop engine and inspect oil level.

EXHAUST MANIFOLD

REMOVAL & INSTALLATION

3.7L

1. Disconnect the negative cable from the battery.
2. Raise and support the vehicle.
3. Remove the bolts and nuts attaching the exhaust pipe to the engine exhaust manifold.
4. Lower the vehicle.
5. Remove the exhaust heat shield.
6. Remove bolts, nuts and washers attaching manifold to cylinder head.
7. Remove manifold and gasket from the cylinder head.

To install:

8. Position the engine exhaust manifold and gasket on the two studs located on the cylinder head. Install conical washers and nuts on these studs.
9. Install remaining conical washers. Starting at the center arm and working outward, tighten the bolts and nuts to 18 ft. lbs. (25 Nm).
10. Install the exhaust heat shields.
11. Raise and support the vehicle.

CAUTION

Over tightening heat shield fasteners, may cause shield to distort and/or crack.

12. Assemble exhaust pipe to manifold and secure with bolts, nuts and retainers. Tighten the bolts and nuts to 25 ft. lbs. (34 Nm).

4.7L

✻✻ CAUTION

When servicing or replacing exhaust system components, disconnect the oxygen sensor connector(s). Allowing the exhaust to hang by the oxygen sensor wires will damage the harness and/or sensor.

1. Disconnect the negative battery cable.
2. Remove the air cleaner assembly.
3. On right manifold, perform the following:
   a. Remove the accessory drive belt.
   b. Remove the A/C compressor. See "HEATING & AIR CONDITIONING" section.
   c. Remove A/C accumulator support bracket fastener.
4. Drain the coolant below heater hose level.
5. Remove the heater hoses at the engine.
6. Remove the exhaust manifold heat shield retaining nuts and remove the heat shield.
7. Remove the upper exhaust manifold retaining bolts.
8. Raise and support the vehicle.
9. Saturate the exhaust pipe/catalytic converter assembly flanged nuts at the exhaust manifold with heat valve lubricant, allow 5 minutes for penetration. Disconnect the exhaust pipe/catalytic converter at the exhaust manifold.
10. Remove the starter. See "ENGINE ELECTRICAL" section.
11. Remove the lower exhaust manifold retaining bolts.

➡The exhaust manifold is removed from below the engine compartment.

12. Remove the exhaust manifold and gasket.
13. Clean the mating surfaces.

To install:

14. Prior to installation, make sure all gasket mating surfaces are clean and free of any debris.

➡The exhaust manifold is installed from below the engine compartment.

15. Position the exhaust manifold and gasket.

➡Do not tighten exhaust manifold retainers until all retainers are in place.

16. Install the lower exhaust manifold retaining bolts.
17. Install the starter. See "ENGINE ELECTRICAL" section.
18. Lower the vehicle.
19. Install the upper exhaust manifold retaining bolts and tighten starting at center and working outward, tighten all manifold bolts to 18 ft. lbs. (25 Nm).

✻✻ CAUTION

Over tightening heat shield fasteners, may cause shield to distort and/or crack.

20. Install the exhaust manifold heat shield and tighten retaining nuts to 72 inch lbs. (8 Nm), then loosen 45 degrees.
21. Connect the heater hoses at the engine.
22. On right manifold, perform the following:
   a. Install the A/C accumulator support bracket retainers.
   b. Install the A/C compressor. See "HEATING & AIR CONDITIONING" section.
   c. Install the accessory drive belt.
23. Raise and support the vehicle.
24. Connect the exhaust pipe/catalytic converter to the exhaust manifold.
25. Lower the vehicle.
26. Install air cleaner assembly.
27. Connect the negative battery cable.
28. Fill the cooling system.
29. Start the engine and check for leaks.

5.7L

See Figures 59 through 61.

✻✻ CAUTION

When servicing or replacing exhaust system components, disconnect the oxygen sensor connector(s). Allowing the exhaust to hang by the oxygen sensor wires will damage the harness and/or sensor.

1. Disconnect the intake air temperature (IAT) sensor electrical connector at intake air assembly.
2. Remove the clean air hose, then remove the air cleaner housing.
3. Remove the engine cover.
4. Disconnect the negative battery cable.
5. Install Engine Support Fixture (8534B or equivalent).
6. Raise and support the vehicle.

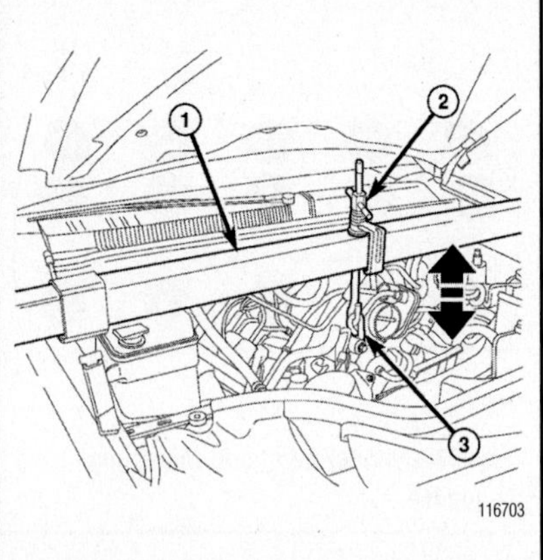

Fig. 59 Showing engine support fixture (1) with clamping device (2) and lifting eye (3)

7. Disconnect the oxygen sensor electrical connectors.
8. Saturate the front exhaust pipe/catalytic converter retaining bolts and nuts with Mopar Rust Penetrant or equivalent and allow 5 minutes for penetration.
9. Remove the right and left exhaust pipe/catalytic converter assembly.
10. Remove the right and left engine mount through bolts.
11. Lower the vehicle.
12. Using the Engine Support Fixture, raise the engine enough to gain access to the exhaust manifold retaining bolts.
13. Remove the exhaust manifold heat shield.
14. Starting with the center bolt and working up and down, alternate bolt removal and remove the exhaust manifold retaining bolts.
15. Remove the exhaust manifold and gasket.
16. Inspect the exhaust manifold for any damage.
17. Clean the mating surfaces.

To install:

18. Prior to installation, make sure all gasket mating surfaces are clean and free of any debris.

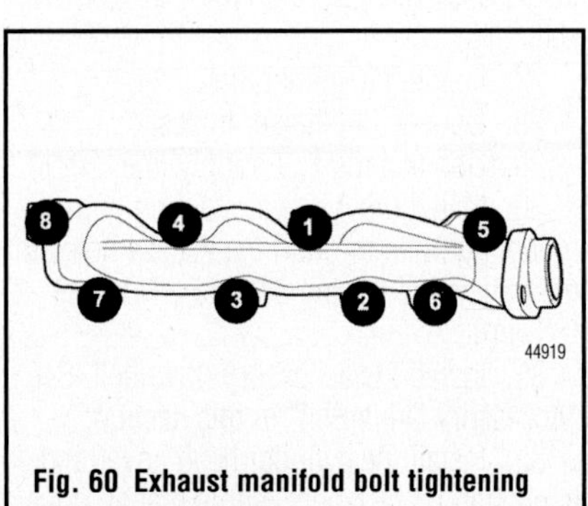

Fig. 60 Exhaust manifold bolt tightening sequence—left side

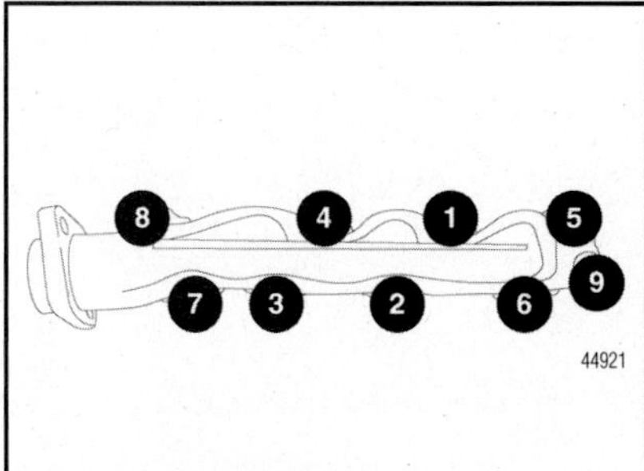

Fig. 61 Exhaust manifold bolt tightening sequence—right side

19. Position the exhaust manifold gasket and manifold.

20. Using the sequence shown, install the exhaust manifold retaining bolts and tighten to 18 ft. lbs. (25 Nm). Use this torque for both exhaust manifolds.

21. Install the heat shield and tighten nuts to 70 inch lbs. (8 Nm).

⁂ CAUTION

Do not damage engine harness while lowering the engine.

22. Using the Engine Support Fixture, lower the engine into position.

23. Raise and support the vehicle.

24. Install the right and left engine mount through bolts and tighten to 74 ft. lbs. (100 Nm).

25. Install the right and left exhaust pipe/catalytic converter assembly.

26. Connect the oxygen sensor electrical connectors.

27. Lower the vehicle.

28. Remove the Engine Support Fixture.

29. Install the air cleaner housing, the clean air hose, and connect the intake air temperature (IAT) sensor electrical connector.

30. Install the engine cover.

31. Connect the negative battery cable.

32. Start the engine and check for leaks.

INTAKE MANIFOLD

REMOVAL & INSTALLATION

3.7L

See Figures 62 and 63.

1. Relieve pressure from the fuel system. See "FUEL SYSTEMS" section.

2. Disconnect the negative cable from battery.

3. Remove the resonator assembly and air inlet hose.

4. Drain the cooling system below coolant temperature sensor level.

5. Disconnect the electronic throttle control (ETC) connector.

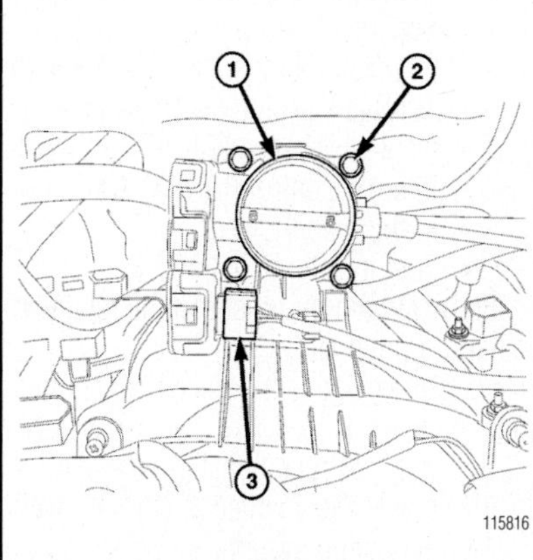

Fig. 62 Disconnect the electronic throttle control (ETC) connector (1).

6. Disconnect electrical connectors for the Engine Coolant Temperature (ECT) sensor and the Manifold Absolute Pressure (MAP) Sensor.

7. Disconnect vapor purge hose, brake booster hose, and positive crankcase ventilation (PCV) hose.

8. Disconnect and remove ignition coil towers.

9. Remove the top oil dipstick tube retaining bolt.

10. Remove the EGR tube.

11. Remove fuel rail and the throttle body assembly. See "FUEL SYSTEM" section.

12. Remove the intake manifold retaining fasteners in reverse order of tightening sequence.

13. Remove the intake manifold.

To install:

14. Install the intake manifold seals.

15. Install the intake manifold.

16. Install the intake manifold retaining bolts and tighten in sequence shown to 105 inch lbs. (12 Nm).

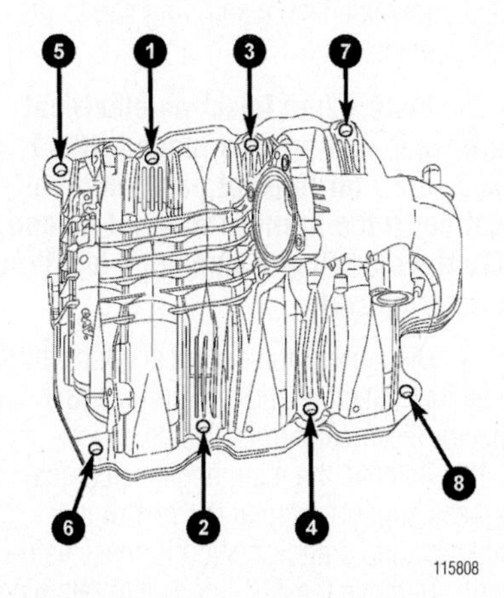

Fig. 63 Intake manifold bolt tightening sequence

⁂ CAUTION

Proper torque of the throttle body is critical to normal operation. If the throttle body is over-torqued, damage to the throttle body can occur resulting in throttle plate malfunction.

17. Install the throttle body-to-intake manifold O-ring. Install the throttle body to intake manifold. Install the four mounting bolts and tighten bolts to 60 inch lbs. (7 Nm).

18. Install ETC electrical connector.

19. Install the fuel rail. See "FUEL SYSTEMS" section.

20. Install the EGR tube.

21. Install ignition coil towers. See "ENGINE ELECTRICAL" section.

22. Connect electrical connectors for the following components:
- Manifold Absolute Pressure (MAP) Sensor
- Coolant Temperature (CTS) Sensor
- Ignition coil towers

23. Install top oil dipstick tube retaining bolt.

24. Connect vapor purge hose, brake booster hose, and PCV hose.

25. Fill the cooling system.

26. Install the resonator assembly and air inlet hose.

27. Connect the negative cable to battery.

28. Using the scan tool, perform the ETC Relearn function.

4.7L

See Figure 64.

1. Disconnect negative cable from battery.

2. Remove resonator assembly and air inlet hose.

3. Disconnect throttle and speed control cables.

4. Disconnect electrical connectors for the following components:
- Manifold Absolute Pressure (MAP) Sensor
- Intake Air Temperature (IAT) Sensor
- Throttle Position (TPS) Sensor
- Coolant Temperature (CTS) Sensor
- Idle Air Control (IAC) Motor

5. Disconnect brake booster hose and positive crankcase ventilation (PCV) hose.

6. Disconnect generator electrical connections.

7. Disconnect air conditioning compressor electrical connections.

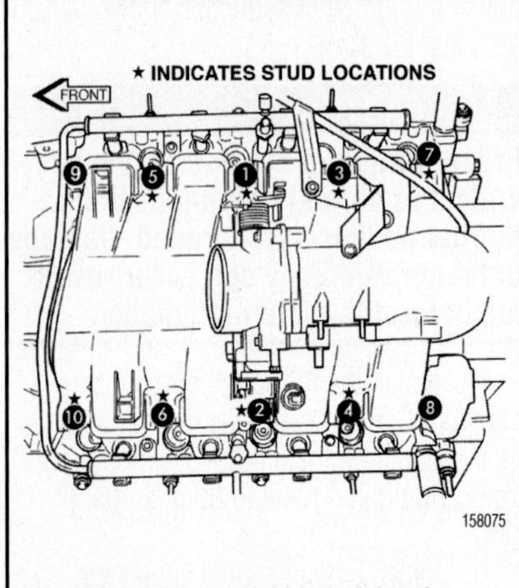

Fig. 64 Intake manifold bolt tightening sequence

8. Disconnect left and right radio suppressor straps.
9. Disconnect and remove ignition coil towers.
10. Remove top oil dipstick tube retaining bolt and ground strap.
11. Release pressure from the fuel system. See "FUEL SYSTEM" section.
12. Remove fuel rail and the throttle body assembly and mounting bracket. See "FUEL SYSTEM" section.
13. Drain cooling system below thermostat level.
14. Remove the heater hoses from the engine front cover and the heater core.
15. Unclip and remove heater hoses and tubes from intake manifold.
16. Remove coolant temperature sensor.
17. Remove intake manifold retaining fasteners in reverse order of tightening sequence.
18. Remove intake manifold.

To install:

19. Install new intake manifold gaskets. Position the intake manifold.
20. Install intake manifold retaining bolts and tighten in sequence shown in to 105 inch lbs. (12 Nm).
21. Install left and right radio suppressor straps.
22. Install throttle body assembly. Install throttle cable bracket. Connect throttle cable and speed control cable to throttle body.
23. Install fuel rail. See "FUEL SYSTEM" section.
24. Install ignition coil towers.
25. Position and install heater hoses and tubes onto intake manifold.
26. Install the heater hoses to the heater core and engine front cover.
27. Connect electrical connectors for the following components:

- Manifold Absolute Pressure (MAP) Sensor
- Intake Air Temperature (IAT) Sensor
- Throttle Position (TPS) Sensor
- Coolant Temperature (CTS) Sensor
- Idle Air Control (IAC) Motor
- Ignition coil towers
- Fuel injectors

28. Install top oil dipstick tube retaining bolt and ground strap.
29. Connect generator electrical connections.
30. Connect Brake booster hose and Positive crankcase ventilation (PCV) hose.
31. Fill cooling system.
32. Install resonator assembly and air inlet hose.
33. Connect negative cable to battery.

5.7L

See Figures 65 and 66.

1. Disconnect the intake air temperature (IAT) sensor electrical connector at the throttle body end of the clean air tube.
2. Remove the clean air tube from the air cleaner housing and the throttle body.
3. Disconnect the makeup air hose.
4. Remove the air cleaner housing.
5. Lift up the front of the engine cover and separate the engine cover front grommets from the ball studs on the intake manifold, then remove the rear engine cover pegs from the grommets on the rear of the intake manifold.
6. Perform the fuel pressure release procedure. See "FUEL SYSTEM" section.
7. Disconnect the negative battery cable.

➡Excessive fuel spillage onto the gaskets can cause gaskets to expand and dislodge from the gasket groove.

8. Disconnect the fuel supply line quick connect fitting at the fuel rail and plug the fuel supply line with a shipping cap to prevent spillage.

➡The factory fuel injection electrical harness is numerically tagged (INJ 1, INJ 2, etc.) for injector position identification. If the harness was not tagged, note the electrical connector's location during removal.

9. Disconnect the electrical connectors to all fuel injectors and position the fuel injector electrical harness aside.
10. Remove the main engine electrical harness support strap at the rear of the intake manifold and position harness aside.
11. Remove the A/C line P-clip retaining bolt from the throttle body bracket and remove the P-clip.

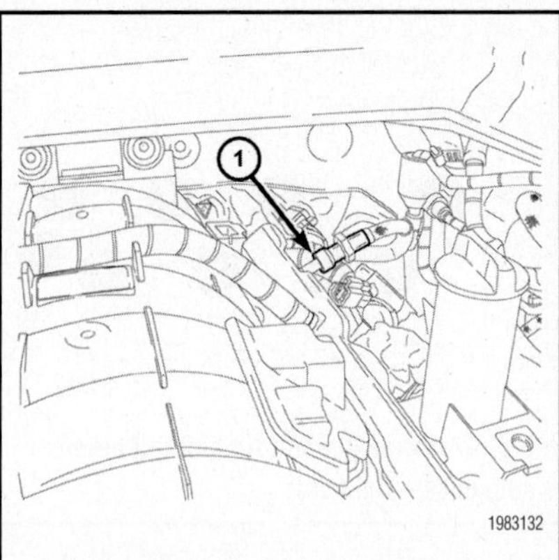

Fig. 65 Disconnect the fuel supply line quick connect fitting (1) at the fuel rail and plug the fuel supply line with a shipping cap to prevent spillage.

12. Secure the A/C line out of the way.
13. Remove the generator. See "ENGINE ELECTRICAL" section.
14. Remove the throttle body bracket retaining bolt from the intake manifold and remove the bracket.
15. Disconnect the electrical connector at the throttle body and reposition the harness.
16. Disconnect the brake booster vacuum hose, and the vacuum lines.
17. Using the sequence shown, remove the intake manifold retaining bolts.
18. Slide the intake manifold forward and disconnect both the manifold air pressure (MAP) sensor and the short runner valve (SRV) connectors located at the rear of the intake manifold.
19. Remove the intake manifold and throttle body as an assembly.

To install:

20. If reinstalling the original manifold apply Mopar Lock & Seal Adhesive to the intake manifold bolts. Not required when installing a new manifold.
21. Install the intake manifold seals and positive crankcase ventilation (PCV) seals.

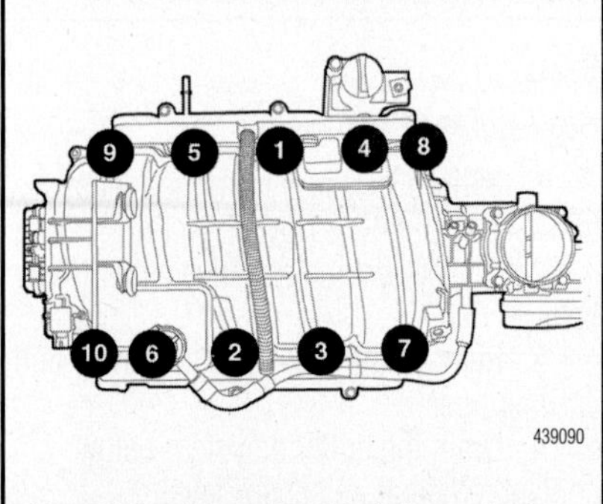

Fig. 66 Intake manifold bolt loosening/tightening sequence

22. Connect both the manifold air pressure (MAP) sensor and the short runner valve (SRV) electrical connectors located at the rear of the intake manifold as you position the intake manifold in place.

23. Using the sequence shown, tighten the intake manifold bolts to 9 ft. lbs. (12 Nm).

24. Position the main engine electrical harness at the rear of the intake manifold and install the support strap.

25. Connect the fuel supply line quick connect fitting at the fuel rail.

➡The factory fuel injection electrical harness is numerically tagged (INJ 1, INJ 2, etc.) for injector position identification. If the harness was not tagged, use the noted the electrical connector's location during removal.

26. Position the fuel injector electrical harness and connect the electrical connectors to all fuel injectors.

27. Connect the brake booster vacuum hose, and the vacuum lines.

28. Install the throttle body bracket and securely tighten the retaining bolt.

29. Install the generator. See "ENGINE ELECTRICAL" section.

30. Position the A/C lines, install the A/C line P-clip and tighten P-clip retaining bolt.

31. Position the wiring harness and connect the electrical connector at the throttle body.

32. Slightly tilt the rear of the engine cover and slide the rear engine cover pegs into the grommets on the rear of the intake manifold until the cover stops.

33. Check to make sure the engine cover is installed properly by reaching behind the cover to verify that the pegs are located in the rear grommets.

➡While installing the engine cover the front ball studs will make a popping or suction sound as the ball studs are inserted into the front grommets.

34. Lower the front of the engine cover and line up the front grommets with the ball studs on the front of the intake manifold and with a downward motion push the engine cover front grommets onto the ball studs.

35. Lightly lift the front of the engine cover to insure the front ball studs are seated into the front grommets correctly.

36. Install the air cleaner assembly. Connect the clean air tube to the air cleaner assembly and the throttle body.

37. Connect the IAT sensor electrical connector.

38. Connect the negative battery cable

OIL PAN

REMOVAL & INSTALLATION

3.7L & 4.7L

See Figures 67 through 70.

1. Disconnect the negative battery cable.

2. Install engine support/lift fixture special tool (8534B or equivalent). Do not raise engine at this time.

3. Loosen both left and right side engine mount through bolts. Do not remove bolts.

4. Remove the structural dust cover, if equipped.

5. Drain engine oil.

6. Disconnect transmission fluid cooler lines at radiator, transmission fittings and clips.

➡When disconnecting the transmission oil cooler lines, it is necessary to replace the line clip that is located on the oil pan stud. The retention force of the clip is severely degraded upon removal.

7. Remove the front crossmember.

8. Only raise the engine enough to provide clearance for oil pan removal. Check for proper clearance at fan shroud to fan and cowl to intake manifold. Raise engine using engine lift fixture to provide clearance to remove oil pan.

9. Remove the oil pan mounting bolts and oil pan.

✲✲ CAUTION

Do not pry on oil pan or oil pan gasket. Gasket is integral to engine windage tray and does not come out with oil pan.

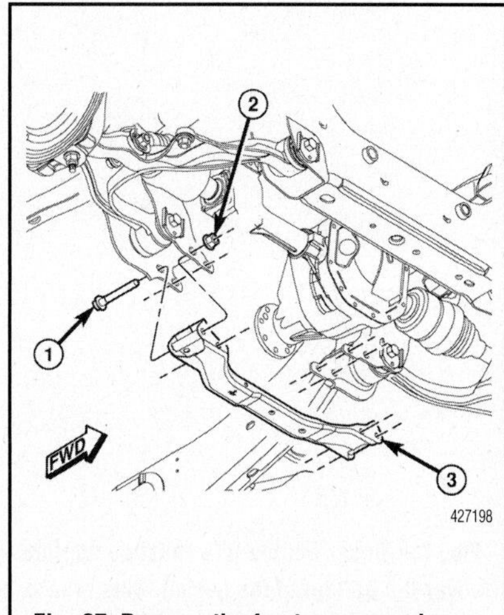

Fig. 67 Remove the front crossmember

10. Unbolt oil pump pickup tube and remove tube.

11. Inspect the integral windage tray and gasket and replace as needed.

To install:

12. Clean the oil pan gasket mating surface of the bedplate and oil pan.

13. Inspect integrated oil pan gasket, and replace as necessary.

14. Position the integrated oil pan gasket/windage tray assembly.

15. Install the oil pickup tube to the engine. Tighten nuts to 20 ft. lbs. (28 Nm).

16. If removed, install stud at position No. 9 (see illustration).

17. Position the oil pan and install the mounting bolts and nut (1–17). Tighten the mounting bolts and nut to 11 ft. lbs. (15 Nm) in the sequence shown.

18. Lower the engine into mounts, using the engine lift fixture.

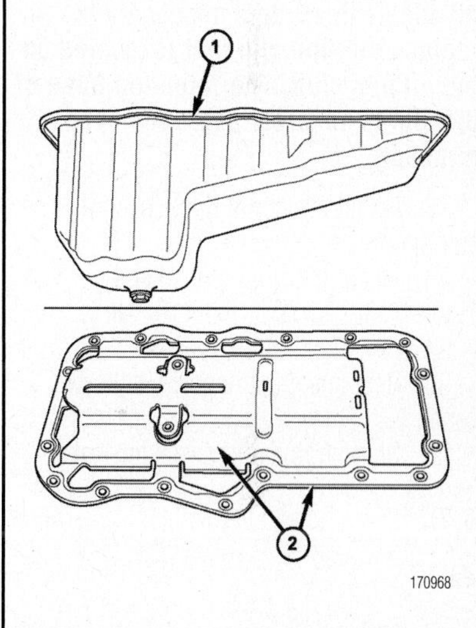

Fig. 68 Showing the oil pan (1) and integrated windage tray and gasket (2)

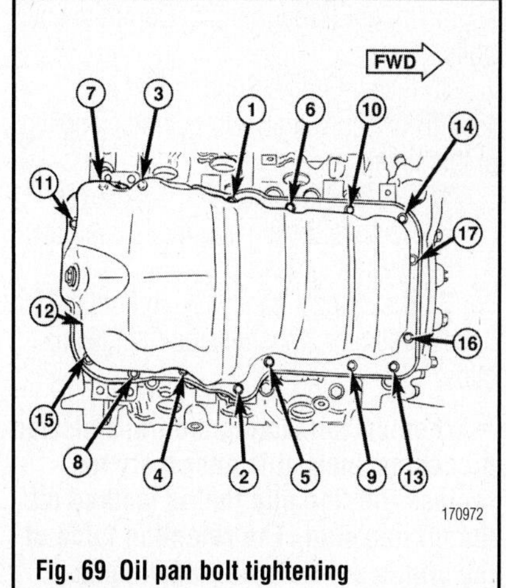

Fig. 69 Oil pan bolt tightening sequence—3.7L

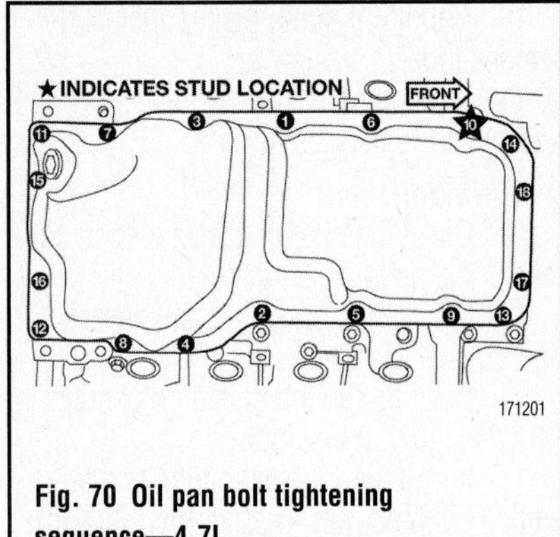

Fig. 70 Oil pan bolt tightening sequence—4.7L

19. Install both the left and right side engine mount through bolts. Tighten the nuts to 50 ft. lbs. (68 Nm).
20. Remove the engine lift fixture tool.
21. Connect cooler lines to radiator, transmission and clips.

➡When connecting the transmission oil cooler lines, it is necessary to replace the line clip that is located on the oil pan stud. The retention force of the clip is severely degraded upon removal.

22. Install structural dust cover, if equipped.
23. Install the front crossmember. Tighten bolts to 75 ft. lbs. (102 Nm).
24. Fill engine oil.
25. Reconnect the negative battery cable.
26. Start engine and check for leaks.

5.7L

4X2

See Figures 71 and 72.

1. Disconnect the negative battery cable.
2. Loosen both the left and right side engine mount through bolts. Do not remove bolts.
3. Install Engine Support Fixture (8534B or equivalent). Do not raise engine at this time.
4. Remove the structural dust cover.
5. Remove the fan and the fan shroud.
6. Drain engine oil.
7. Disconnect transmission fluid cooler lines at radiator, transmission fittings and clips.

➡When disconnecting the transmission oil cooler lines, it is necessary to replace the line clip that is located on the oil pan stud. The retention force of the clip is severely degraded upon removal.

8. Remove the front crossmember.
9. Raise engine using Engine Support Fixture to provide clearance to remove oil pan.

CAUTION

Do not pry on oil pan or oil pan gasket. The gasket is integral to engine windage tray and does not come out with oil pan.

➡If more clearance is needed to remove oil pan the transmission mount can be removed, and the transmission can be raised to gain clearance.

➡The double ended oil pan studs must be installed in the same location that they were removed from.

10. Remove the oil pan mounting bolts using the sequence provided.
11. Unbolt oil pump pickup tube and remove tube.

➡When the oil pan is removed, a new integral windage tray and gasket assembly must be installed. The old gasket cannot be reused.

12. Discard the integral windage tray and gasket and replace.

To install:

13. Clean the oil pan gasket mating surface of the block and oil pan.
14. Mopar Engine RTV must be applied to the four T-joints. The bead of RTV should cover the bottom of the gasket. This area is approximately 4.5 mm x 25 mm in each of the four T-joint locations.

➡When the oil pan is removed, a new integral windage tray and gasket assembly must be installed. The old gasket cannot be reused.

15. Install a new integral windage tray and gasket.
16. Reinstall the oil pump pickup tube with new O-rings. Tighten tube to pump fasteners to 21 ft. lbs. (28 Nm).

➡The double ended oil pan studs must be installed in the same location that they were removed from.

17. Position the oil pan and install the mounting bolts and studs. Tighten the mounting bolts to 105 inch lbs. (12 Nm).
18. Connect cooler lines to radiator, transmission and clips.

➡When connecting the transmission oil cooler lines, it is necessary to replace the line clip that is located on the oil pan stud. The retention force of the clip is severely degraded upon removal.

19. Install the structural dust cover and tighten the bolts as follows:

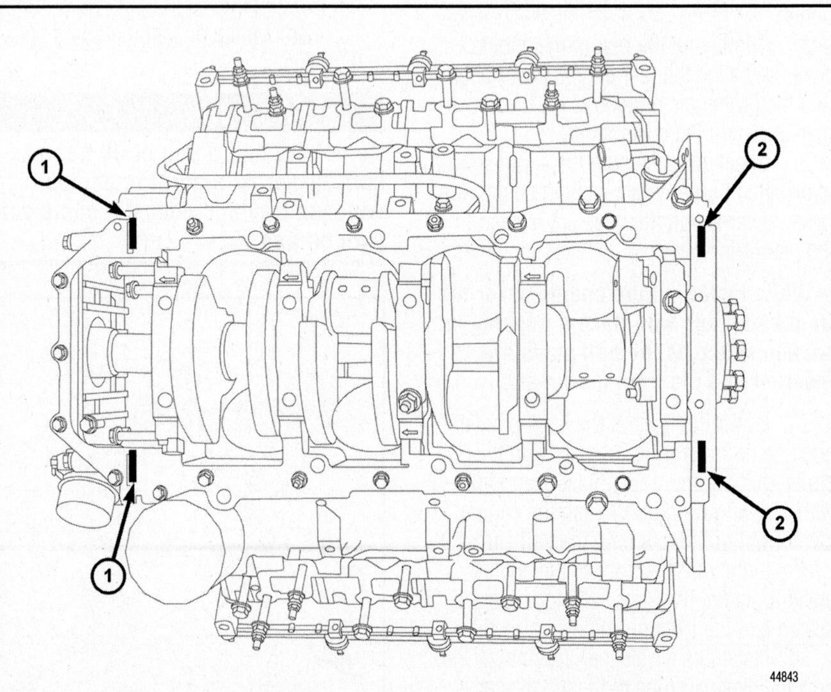

Fig. 71 Mopar Engine RTV must be applied to the four T-joints (1,2). The bead of RTV should cover the bottom of the gasket. This area is approximately 4.5 mm x 25 mm in each of the four T-joint locations.

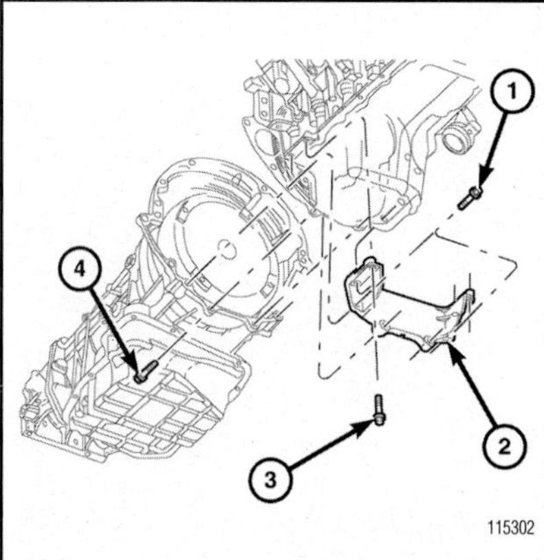

Fig. 72 Structural dust cover bolt locations

a. Tighten the structural dust cover-to-transmission bolts (1, 2 & 4) to 80 inch lbs. (9 Nm).

b. Tighten the structural dust cover-to-engine block bolts (3) to 80 inch lbs. (9 Nm).

c. Retighten the structural dust cover-to-transmission bolts to 40 ft. lbs. (54 Nm).

d. Retighten the structural dust cover-to-engine block bolts to 40 ft. lbs. (54 Nm).

20. Lower the engine into mounts, using the Engine Support Fixture.
21. Install both the left and right side engine mount through bolts. Tighten the nuts to 50 ft. lbs. (68 Nm).
22. Reinstall the front axle, if removed. See "DRIVE TRAIN" section.
23. Install the steering rack, if removed. See "STEERING" section.
24. Install the rear transmission mount, if removed. Tighten bolt/nut to 50 ft. lbs. (68 Nm).
25. Remove Engine Support Fixture.
26. Install the front crossmember. Tighten nuts to 75 ft. lbs. (102 Nm).
27. Install the fan shroud and fan.
28. Fill engine oil.
29. Connect the negative battery cable.
30. Start engine and check for leaks.

4X4

1. Follow all steps for 4X2 removal, plus perform the following:

a. Unbolt and lower the steering rack, without disconnecting the lines.

➡The front axle must be lowered to remove the oil pan on 4X4 vehicles.

b. Remove the front driveshaft at the axle. Mark for reassembly.

c. Support the front axle.

d. Remove the right and left axle to mount bolts.

e. Lower axle.

f. Remove the oil pan mounting bolts and oil pan.

g. Unbolt oil pump pickup tube and remove tube.

➡When the oil pan is removed, a new integral windage tray and gasket assembly must be installed. The old gasket cannot be reused.

h. Discard the integral windage tray and gasket and replace.

To install:

2. Clean the oil pan gasket mating surface of the block and oil pan.
3. Mopar Engine RTV must be applied to the four T-joints. The bead of RTV should cover the bottom of the gasket. This area is approximately 4.5 mm x 25 mm in each of the four T-joint locations.

➡When the oil pan is removed, a new integral windage tray and gasket assembly must be installed. The old gasket cannot be reused.

4. Install a new integral windage tray and gasket.
5. Reinstall the oil pump pickup tube with new O-rings. Tighten tube to pump fasteners to 21 ft. lbs. (28 Nm).

➡The double ended oil pan studs must be installed in the same location that they were removed from.

6. Position the oil pan and install the mounting bolts and studs. Tighten the mounting bolts to 105 inch lbs. (12 Nm).
7. Connect cooler lines to radiator, transmission and clips.

➡When connecting the transmission oil cooler lines, it is necessary to replace the line clip that is located on the oil pan stud. The retention force of the clip is severely degraded upon removal.

8. Install the structural dust cover and tighten the bolts as follows:

a. Tighten the structural dust cover-to-transmission bolts (1, 2 & 4) to 80 inch lbs. (9 Nm).

b. Tighten the structural dust cover-to-engine block bolts (3) to 80 inch lbs. (9 Nm).

c. Retighten the structural dust cover-to-transmission bolts to 40 ft. lbs. (54 Nm).

d. Retighten the structural dust cover-to-engine block bolts to 40 ft. lbs. (54 Nm).

9. Lower the engine into mounts using Engine Support Fixture.
10. Install both the left and right side engine mount through bolts. Tighten the nuts to 50 ft. lbs. (68 Nm).
11. Reinstall the front axle, if removed. See "DRIVE TRAIN" section.
12. Install the steering rack, if removed. See "STEERING" section.
13. Install the rear transmission mount, if removed. Tighten bolt/nut to 50 ft. lbs. (68 Nm).
14. Remove Engine Support Fixture.
15. Install the front crossmember. Tighten nuts to 75 ft. lbs. (102 Nm).
16. Install the fan shroud and fan.
17. Fill engine oil.
18. Connect the negative battery cable.
19. Start engine and check for leaks.

OIL PUMP

REMOVAL & INSTALLATION

3.7L & 4.7L

See Figure 73.

1. Remove the oil pan and pick-up tube.
2. Remove the timing chain cover. See "Timing Chain Front Cover" in this section.
3. Remove the timing chains and tensioners. See "Timing Chain & Sprockets" in this section.
4. Remove the four bolts, primary timing chain tensioner and the oil pump.

To install:

5. Position the oil pump onto the crankshaft and install one oil pump retaining bolt.
6. Position the primary timing chain tensioner and install three retaining bolts.
7. Tighten the oil pump and primary timing chain tensioner retaining bolts to 20 ft. lbs. (28 Nm) in the sequence shown.

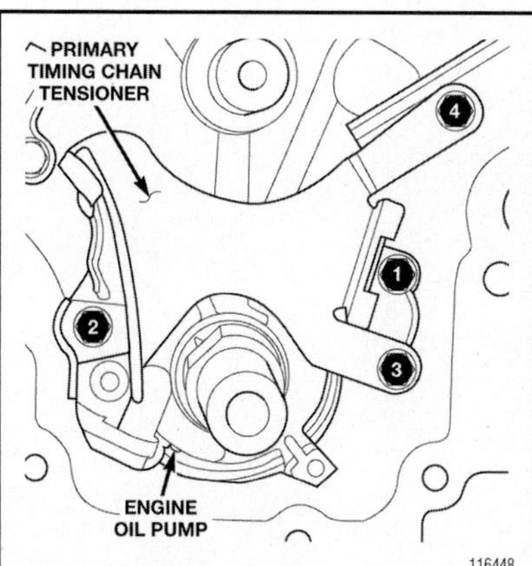

Fig. 73 Tighten the oil pump and primary timing chain tensioner retaining bolts to 20 ft. lbs. (28 Nm) in the sequence shown.

8. Install the secondary timing chain tensioners and timing chains. See "Timing Chain & Sprockets" in his section.

9. Install the timing chain cover See "Timing Chain Front Cover" in this section.

10. Install the pick-up tube and oil pan

5.7L

See Figure 74.

1. Remove the oil pan, as described in this section.
2. Remove the timing cover. See "Timing Chain Front Cover" in this section.
3. Remove the four bolts and the oil pump.

To install:

4. Position the oil pump on the crankshaft and install the oil pump retaining bolts finger tight.
5. Using an alternating sequence, tighten the oil pump retaining bolts to 21 ft. lbs. (28 Nm).
6. Install the timing cover. See "Timing Chain Front Cover" in this section.
7. Install the oil pan.

INSPECTION

➡The oil pump pressure relief valve and spring should not be removed from the oil pump. If these components are disassembled and or removed from the pump the entire oil pump assembly must be replaced.

1. Remove the pump cover.
2. Clean all parts thoroughly. Mating surface of the oil pump housing should be smooth. If the pump cover is scratched or grooved the oil pump assembly should be replaced.
3. Slide outer rotor into the body of the oil pump. Press the outer rotor to one side of the oil pump body and measure clearance between the outer rotor and the body. If the measurement is 0.009 in. (0.235 mm) or more the oil pump assembly must be replaced.
4. Install the inner rotor into the oil pump body. Measure the clearance between the inner and outer rotors. If the clearance between the rotors is 0.006 in. (0.150 mm) or more the oil pump assembly must be replaced.
5. Place a straight edge across the body of the oil pump (between the bolt holes), if a feeler gauge of 0.0038 in. (0.095 mm) or greater can be inserted between the straightedge and the rotors, the pump must be replaced.
6. Reinstall the pump cover. Tighten fasteners to 132 inch lbs. (15 Nm).

➡The oil pump is serviced as an assembly. In the event the oil pump is not functioning or out of specification, it must be replaced as an assembly.

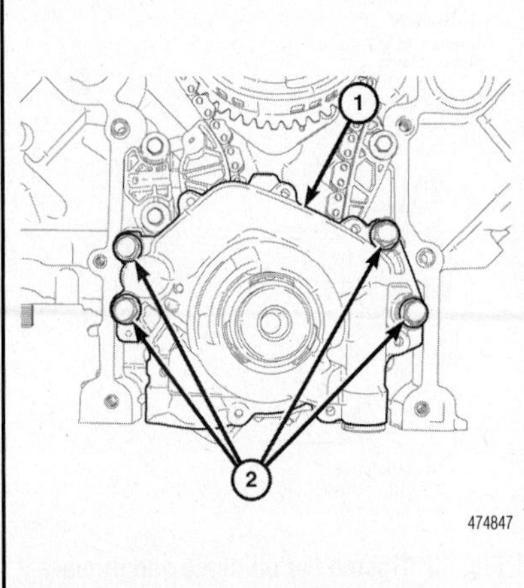

Fig. 74 Showing oil pump (1) and mounting bolts (2)

PISTON & RING

POSITIONING

See Figure 75.

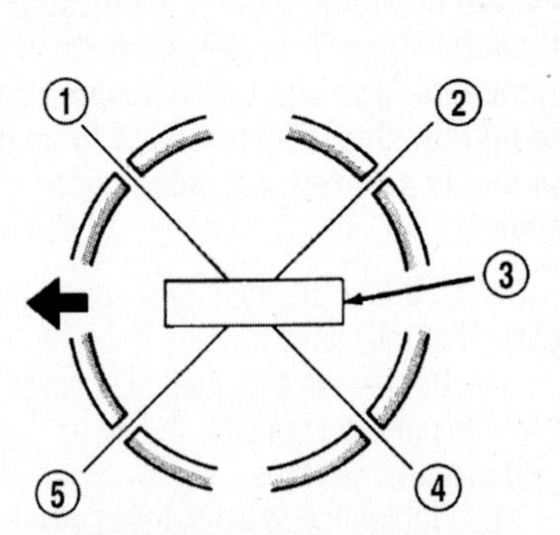

Fig. 75 Showing the piston ring gap positioning

REAR MAIN SEAL

REMOVAL & INSTALLATION

3.7L & 4.7L

See Figure 76.

➡This procedure can be performed in vehicle.

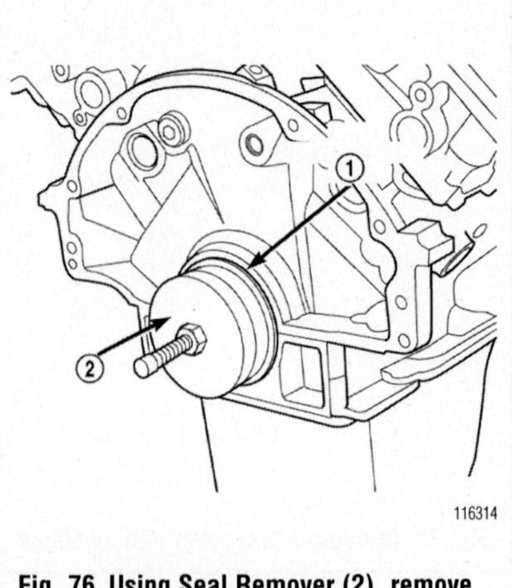

Fig. 76 Using Seal Remover (2), remove the crankshaft rear oil seal (1).

1. If being performed in vehicle, remove the transmission.
2. Remove the flexplate.

➡The crankshaft oil seal cannot be reused after removal.

➡The crankshaft rear oil seal remover (8506) must be installed deeply into the seal. Continue to tighten the removal tool into the seal until the tool can not be turned farther. Failure to install tool correctly the first time will cause tool to pull free of seal without removing seal from engine.

3. Using Seal Remover, remove the crankshaft rear oil seal.

To install:

4. Lubricate the crankshaft flange with engine oil.
5. Position the magnetic seal guide (8349-2 or equivalent) onto the crankshaft rear face. Then position the crankshaft rear oil seal onto the guide.
6. Using Crankshaft Rear Oil Seal Installer and Driver Handle, with a hammer, tap the seal into place. Continue to tap on the driver handle until the seal installer seats against the cylinder block crankshaft bore.
7. Install the flexplate.
8. Install the transmission.

5.7L

➡The crankshaft rear oil seal is integral to the crankshaft rear oil seal retainer and must be replaced as an assembly. The crankshaft rear oil seal retainer can not be reused after removal.

➡This procedure can be performed in vehicle.

1. Disconnect the negative battery cable.
2. Remove the transmission.
3. Remove the flexplate.
4. Remove the oil pan. See "Oil Pan" in this section.
5. Using a criss-cross sequence, remove the rear oil seal retainer mounting bolts.
6. Carefully remove the retainer from the engine block.

To install:

7. Thoroughly clean all gasket residue from the engine block.
8. Position the gasket onto the new crankshaft rear oil seal retainer.
9. Position the crankshaft rear oil seal retainer onto the engine block.
10. Using a criss-cross sequence, install the crankshaft rear oil seal retainer mounting bolts and tighten to 11 ft. lbs. (15 Nm).
11. Install the oil pan. See "Oil Pan" in this section.
12. Install the flexplate.
13. Install the transmission.
14. Fill the engine with oil.
15. Start the engine and check for leaks.

TIMING CHAIN FRONT COVER

REMOVAL & INSTALLATION

3.7L

See Figures 77 and 78.

1. Disconnect the battery negative cable.
2. Drain cooling system.
3. Remove electric cooling fan and fan shroud assembly. See "ENGINE COOLING" section.
4. Remove fan and fan drive assembly. See "ENGINE COOLING" section.
5. Disconnect both heater hoses at timing cover.
6. Disconnect lower radiator hose at engine.
7. Remove accessory drive belt tensioner assembly.
8. Remove crankshaft damper. See "Crankshaft Damper" in this section.
9. Remove the generator. See "ENGINE ELECTRICAL" section.
10. Remove A/C compressor. See "HEATING & AIR CONDITIONING" section.

➡The 3.7L engine uses an anaerobic sealer instead of a gasket to seal the front cover to the engine block, from the factory. For service, Mopar Grey Engine RTV sealant must be substituted.

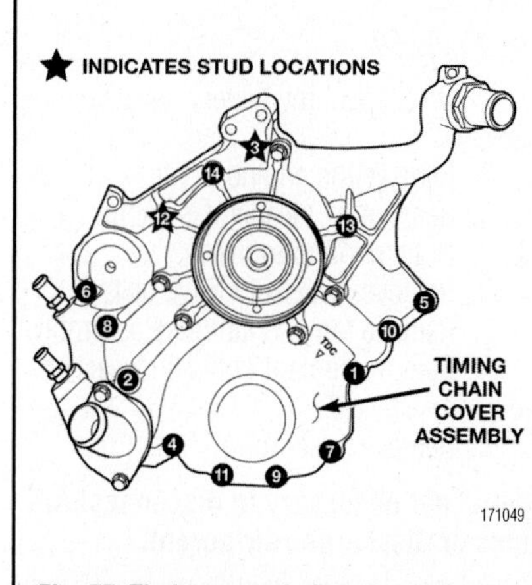

Fig. 77 Timing cover bolt and stud loosening/tightening sequence

➡It is not necessary to remove the water pump for timing cover removal.

11. Remove the bolts holding the timing cover to engine block . Remove the timing cover.

To install:

⁂ CAUTION

Do not use oil based liquids to clean timing cover or block surfaces. Use only rubbing alcohol, along with plastic or wooden scrapers. Use no wire brushes or abrasive wheels or metal scrapers, or damage to surfaces could result.

12. Clean timing chain cover and block surface using rubbing alcohol.

➡The 3.7L uses a special anaerobic sealer instead of a gasket to seal the timing cover to the engine block, from the factory. For service repairs, Mopar Engine Grey RTV must be used as a substitute.

13. Inspect the water passage O-rings for any damage, and replace as necessary.
14. Apply Mopar Grey Engine RTV sealer to front cover following the path provided using a 3 to 4mm thick bead.
15. Install cover. Tighten fasteners in sequence as shown in to 43 ft. lbs. (58 Nm).
16. Install crankshaft damper. See "Crankshaft Damper" in this section.
17. Install the A/C compressor. See "HEATING & AIR CONDITIONING" section.

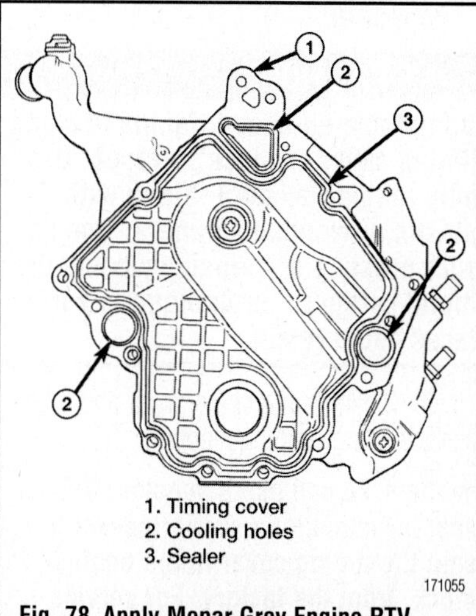

Fig. 78 Apply Mopar Grey Engine RTV sealer to front cover following the path provided using a 3 to 4mm thick bead.

18. Install the generator. See "ENGINE ELECTRICAL" section.
19. Install accessory drive belt tensioner assembly.
20. Install radiator upper and lower hoses.
21. Install both heater hoses.
22. Install electric fan shroud and viscous fan drive assembly. See "ENGINE COOLING" section.
23. Fill cooling system
24. Connect the battery negative cable.

4.7L

See Figure 79.

1. Disconnect the battery negative cable.
2. Drain cooling system.
3. Disconnect both heater hoses at timing cover.
4. Disconnect lower radiator hose at engine.
5. Remove crankshaft damper. See "Crankshaft Damper" in this section.
6. Remove accessory drive belt tensioner assembly.
7. Remove the generator and A/C compressor.

➡The 4.7L engine uses an RTV sealer instead of a gasket to seal the front cover to the engine block, from the factory. For service, Mopar® Grey Engine RTV sealant must be substituted.

➡It is not necessary to remove the water pump for timing cover removal.

8. Remove the bolts holding the timing cover to engine block. Remove cover

To install:

⁂ CAUTION

Do not use oil based liquids to clean timing cover or block surfaces. Use only rubbing alcohol, along with plastic or wooden scrapers. Use no wire brushes or abrasive wheels or metal scrapers, or damage to surfaces could result.

9. Clean timing chain cover and block surface using rubbing alcohol.

➡The 4.7L can use a special RTV sealer instead of a carrier gasket to seal the timing cover to the engine block, from the factory. For service repairs, Mopar® Grey Engine RTV must be used as a substitute, if RTV is present. If the front cover being used has no provisions for the water passage O-rings, then Mopar Grey Engine RTV must be applied around the water passages.

10. Inspect the water passage O-rings, if equipped for any damage, and replace as necessary.
11. Apply Mopar Grey Engine RTV sealer to the front cover following the path above, using a 3 to 4mm thick bead.
12. Install cover. Tighten flange head fasteners in sequence as shown in to 43 ft. lbs. (58 Nm).
13. Install the A/C compressor and generator.
14. Install crankshaft damper.
15. Install accessory drive belt tensioner assembly. Tighten fastener to 40 ft. lbs. (54 Nm).
16. Install lower radiator hose.
17. Install both heater hoses.
18. Fill cooling system.
19. Connect the battery negative cable.

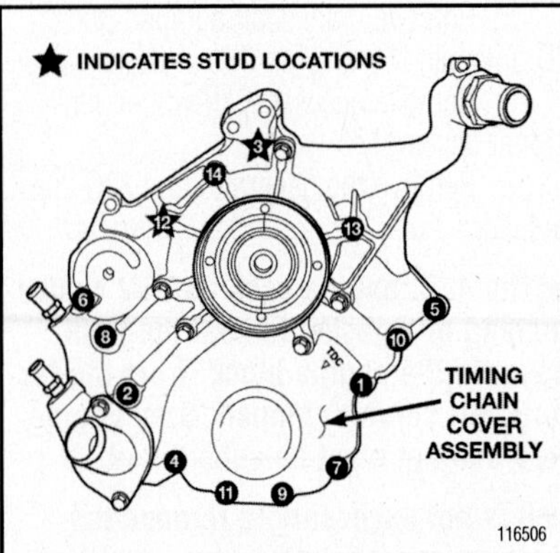

Fig. 79 Tighten flange head fasteners in sequence as shown in to 43 ft. lbs. (58 Nm).

5.7L

See Figure 80.

1. Disconnect the battery negative cable.
2. Remove the engine cover.
3. Remove air cleaner assembly.
4. Drain cooling system.
5. Remove accessory drive belt.
6. Remove fan and fan drive assembly.
7. Remove coolant bottle and washer bottle.
8. Remove fan shroud.

➡It is not necessary to disconnect A/C lines or discharge refrigerant.

9. Remove A/C compressor and set aside. Without disconnecting the hoses.
10. Remove the generator. See "ENGINE ELECTRICAL" section.
11. Remove upper radiator hose.
12. Disconnect both heater hoses at timing cover.
13. Disconnect lower radiator hose at engine.
14. Remove accessory drive belt tensioner and both idler pulleys.
15. Remove crankshaft damper. See "Crankshaft Damper" in this section.

➡Do not remove the hoses from the power steering pump.

16. Remove power steering pump and set aside.
17. Remove the dipstick support bolt.
18. Drain the engine oil.
19. Remove the oil pan and pick up tube.

➡It is not necessary to remove water pump for timing cover removal.

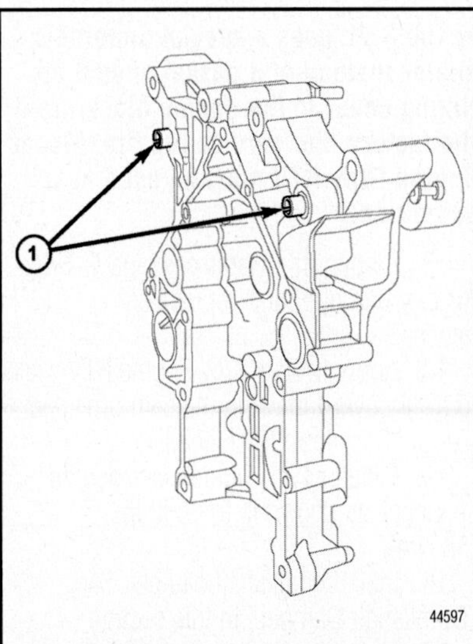

Fig. 80 Verify that timing cover slide bushings (1) are located in timing cover.

20. Remove timing cover bolts and remove cover.
21. Verify that timing cover slide bushings are located in timing cover.

To install:

22. Clean timing chain cover and block surface.

➡Always install a new gasket on timing cover.

23. Verify that the slide bushings are installed in timing cover.
24. Install cover and new gasket. Tighten fasteners to 21 ft. lbs. (28 Nm). The large lifting stud is tightened to 40 ft. lbs. (55 Nm).
25. Install the oil pan and pick up tube. See "Oil Pan" in this section.
26. Install the A/C compressor. See "HEATING & AIR CONDITIONING" section.
27. Install the generator. See "ENGINE ELECTRICAL" section.
28. Install power steering pump. See "STEERING" section.
29. Install the dipstick support bolt.
30. Install the thermostat housing.
31. Install crankshaft damper. See "Crankshaft Damper" in this section.
32. Install accessory drive belt tensioner assembly and both idler pulleys.
33. Install radiator lower hose.
34. Install both heater hoses.
35. Install the cooling module.
36. Install the accessory drive belt.
37. Install the coolant bottle and washer bottle.
38. Install the upper radiator hose.
39. Install the air cleaner assembly.
40. Fill cooling system.
41. Refill engine oil.
42. Connect the battery negative cable.

TIMING CHAIN & SPROCKETS

REMOVAL & INSTALLATION

3.7L

See Figures 81 through 88.

1. Disconnect the negative battery cable.
2. Drain the cooling system.
3. Remove right and left cylinder head covers.
4. Remove the radiator fan shroud. See "ENGINE COOLING" section.
5. Rotate engine until the timing mark on crankshaft damper aligns with TDC mark on timing chain cover and the camshaft sprocket "V6"or "V8" marks are at the 12 o'clock position (No. 1 TDC exhaust stroke).
6. Remove the power steering pump. See "STEERING" section.

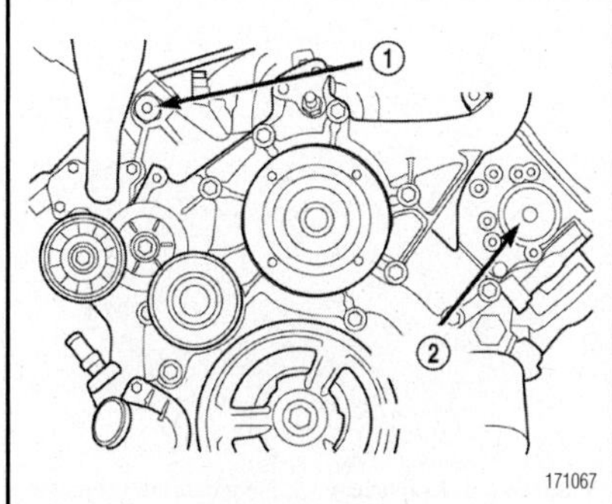

Fig. 81 Remove the access plugs from the left (2) and right (1) cylinder heads for access to the chain guide fasteners.

7. Remove the access plugs from the left and right cylinder heads for access to the chain guide fasteners.

8. Remove the oil fill housing to gain access to the right side tensioner arm fastener.

9. Remove the crankshaft damper. See "Crankshaft Damper" in this section.

10. Remove the timing chain cover. See "Timing Chain Cover" in this section.

11. Collapse and pin primary chain tensioner (1).

➡Plate behind left secondary chain tensioner could fall into oil pan. Therefore, cover pan opening.

12. Remove secondary chain tensioners.

13. Remove camshaft position sensor bolt and remove sensor.

⁂ CAUTION

Care should be taken not to damage the camshaft target wheel. Do not hold the target wheel while loosening or tightening the camshaft sprocket.

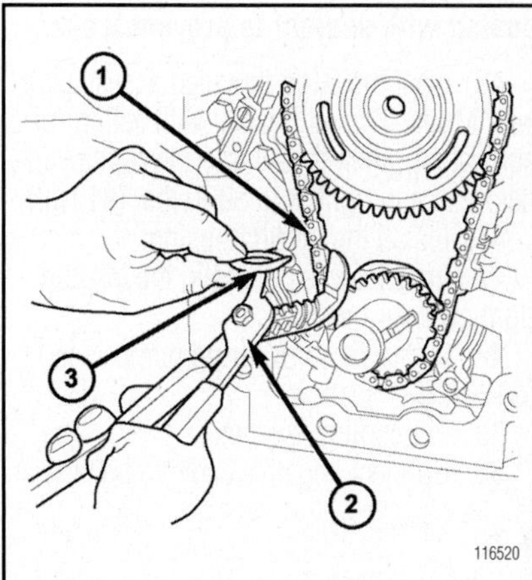

Fig. 82 Collapse and pin primary chain tensioner (1).

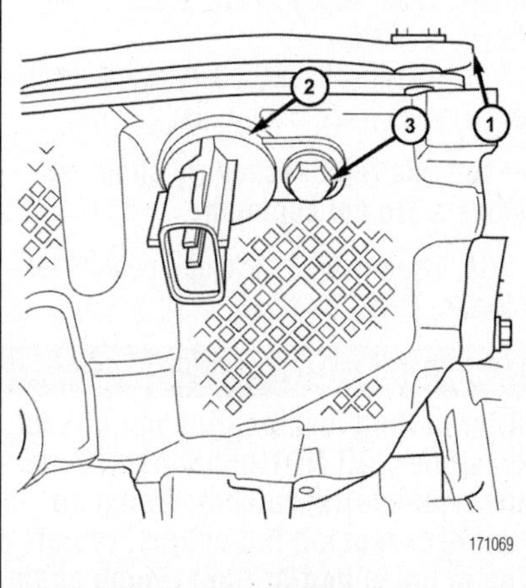

Fig. 83 Remove camshaft position sensor bolt (3) and remove sensor (2).

Do not place the target wheel near a magnetic source of any kind. A damaged or magnetized target wheel could cause a vehicle no start condition.

⁂ CAUTION

Do not forcefully rotate the camshafts or crankshaft independently of each other. Damaging intake valve to piston contact will occur. Ensure the negative battery cable is disconnected and isolated to guard against accidental starter engagement.

14. Remove left and right camshaft sprocket bolts.

15. While holding the left camshaft with a spanner wrench (8428A or equivalent), remove the left camshaft sprocket. Slowly rotate the camshaft approximately 15 degrees clockwise to a neutral position.

16. While holding the right camshaft with a spanner wrench, remove the left camshaft sprocket. Slowly rotate the camshaft approximately 45 degrees counterclockwise to a neutral position.

17. Remove idler sprocket assembly bolt.

18. Slide the idler sprocket assembly and crank sprocket forward simultaneously to remove the primary and secondary chains.

19. Remove both pivoting tensioner arms and chain guides.

20. Remove primary chain tensioner.

To install:

21. Using a vise, lightly compress the secondary chain tensioner piston (5) until the piston step is flush with the tensioner body. Using a pin or suitable tool, release ratchet pawl by pulling pawl back against spring force through access hole on side of tensioner. While continuing to hold pawl back, Push ratchet device to approximately 2 mm from the tensioner body. Install Tensioner pin 8514 (3) into hole on front of tensioner. Slowly open vise (1) to transfer piston spring force to lock pin.

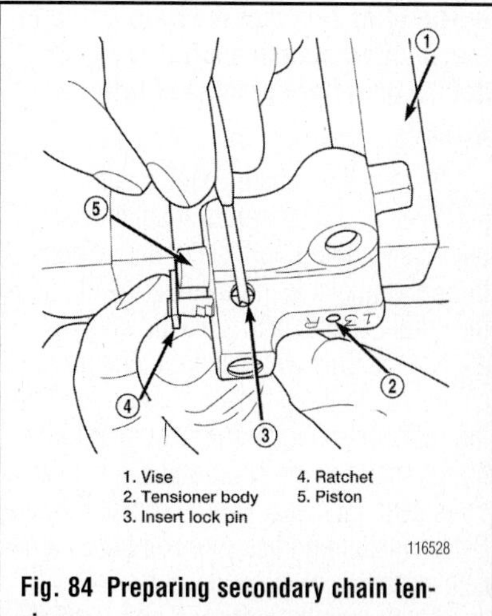

Fig. 84 Preparing secondary chain tensioner

22. Position primary chain tensioner over oil pump and insert bolts into lower two holes on tensioner bracket. Tighten bolts to 21 ft. lbs. (28 Nm).

23. Install right side chain tensioner arm. Install Torx bolt. Tighten Torx bolt to 21 ft. lbs. (28 Nm).

➡The silver bolts retain the guides to the cylinder heads and the black bolts retain the guides to the engine block.

24. Install the left side chain guide. Tighten the bolts to 21 ft. lbs. (28 Nm).

25. Install left side chain tensioner arm, and Torx bolt. Tighten Torx bolt to 21 ft. lbs. (28 Nm).

26. Install the right side chain guide. Tighten the bolts to 21 ft. lbs. (28 Nm).

27. Install both secondary chains onto the idler sprocket. Align two plated links on the secondary chains to be visible through the two lower openings on the idler sprocket (4 o'clock and 8 o'clock). Once the secondary timing chains are installed, position the Secondary Camshaft Chain Holder (8429 or equivalent) to hold chains in place for installation.

28. Align primary chain double plated links with the timing mark at 12 o'clock on the idler sprocket. Align the primary chain single plated link with the timing mark at 6 o'clock on the crankshaft sprocket.

29. Lubricate idler shaft and bushings with clean engine oil.

➡The idler sprocket must be timed to the counterbalance shaft drive gear before the idler sprocket is fully seated.

30. Install all chains, crankshaft sprocket, and idler sprocket as an assembly. After guiding both secondary chains through the block and cylinder head openings, affix chains with a elastic strap or equivalent. This will maintain tension on chains to aid in installation. Align the timing mark on the idler sprocket gear to the timing mark on the counterbalance shaft drive gear, then seat idler sprocket fully. Before installing idler sprocket bolt, lubricate washer with oil, and tighten idler sprocket assembly retaining bolt to 25 ft. lbs. (34 Nm).

➡It will be necessary to slightly rotate camshafts for sprocket installation.

31. Align left camshaft sprocket "L" dot to plated link on chain.
32. Align right camshaft sprocket "R" dot to plated link on chain.

⁂ CAUTION

Remove excess oil from the camshaft sprocket bolt. Failure to do so can result in over-torque of bolt resulting in bolt failure.

33. Remove Secondary Camshaft Chain Holder 8429 , then attach both sprockets to camshafts. Remove excess oil from bolts, then Install sprocket bolts, but do not tighten at this time.
34. Verify that all plated links are aligned with the marks on all sprockets and the "V6" marks on camshaft sprockets are at the 12 o'clock position.
35. Ensure the plate between the left secondary chain tensioner and block is correctly installed.
36. Install both secondary chain tensioners. Tighten bolts to 21 ft. lbs. (28 Nm).

➡Left and right secondary chain tensioners are not common.

37. Remove all 3 locking pins from tensioners.

⁂ CAUTION

After pulling locking pins out of each tensioner, DO NOT manually extend the tensioner(s) ratchet. Doing so will over-tension the chains, resulting in noise and/or high timing chain loads.

38. Using Spanner Wrench (6958) with Adaptor Pins (8346), tighten left and right camshaft sprocket bolts to 90 ft. lbs. (122 Nm).
39. Rotate engine two full revolutions. Verify timing marks are at the follow locations:
- Primary chain idler sprocket dot is at 12 o'clock
- Primary chain crankshaft sprocket dot is at 6 o'clock
- Secondary chain camshaft sprockets "V6" marks are at 12 o'clock
- Counterbalance shaft drive gear dot is aligned to the idler sprocket gear dot

40. Lubricate all three chains with engine oil.
41. After installing all chains, it is recommended that the idler gear end play be checked. The end play must be within 0.004–0.010 in. (0.10–0.25 mm). If not within specification, the idler gear must be replaced.

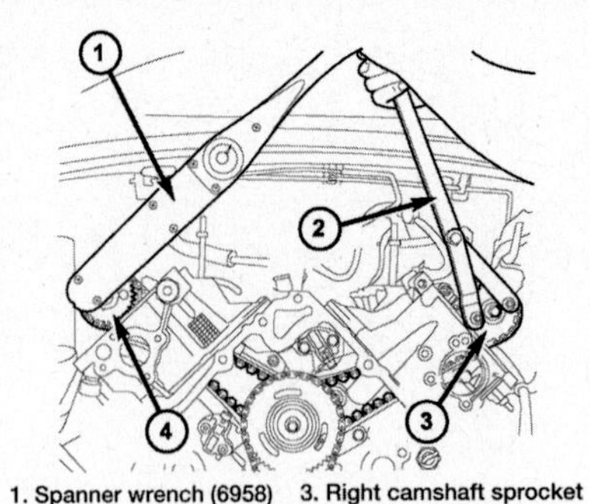

Fig. 87 Using Spanner Wrench (6958) with Adaptor Pins (8346), (4) tighten right camshaft sprocket bolts to 90 ft. lbs. (122 Nm).

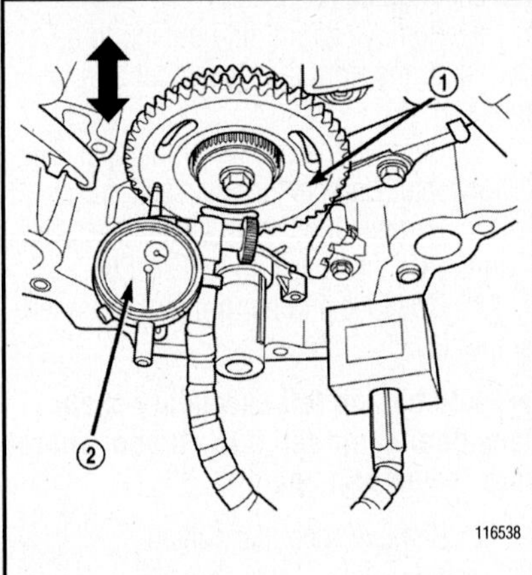

Fig. 88 Checking idle gear (1) end play using dial gauge (2)

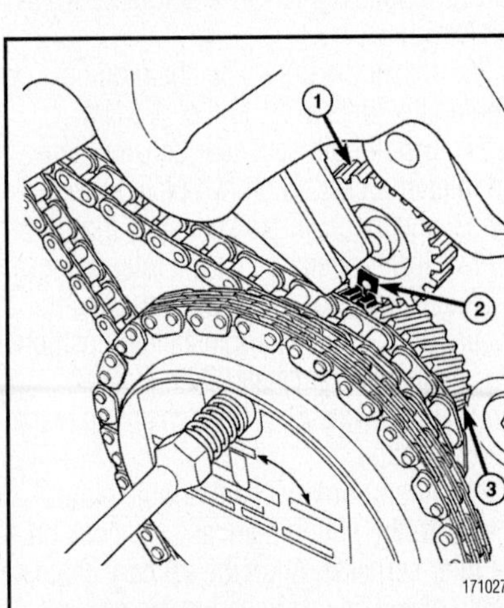

Fig. 85 Timing the idler sprocket gear (3) to counterbalance shaft drive gear (1) by aligning timing mark (2)

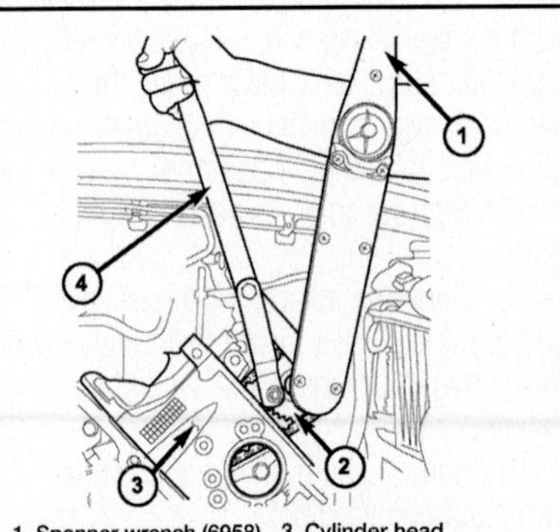

Fig. 86 Using Spanner Wrench (6958) with Adaptor Pins (8346), (4) tighten left camshaft sprocket bolts to 90 ft. lbs. (122 Nm).

42. Install timing chain cover.
43. Install the crankshaft damper. See "Crankshaft Damper" in this section.
44. Install cylinder head covers.

➡Before installing threaded plug in right cylinder head, the plug must be coated with sealant to prevent leaks.

45. Coat the large threaded access plug with Mopar Thread Sealant with Teflon (or equivalent), then install into the right cylinder head and tighten to 60 ft. lbs. (81 Nm).
46. Install the oil fill housing.
47. Install access plugs in the left and right cylinder heads.
48. Install power steering pump. See "STEERING" section.
49. Fill cooling system.
50. Connect negative cable to battery.

4.7L

See Figures 89 through 96.

1. Disconnect the negative battery cable.

2. Drain the cooling system.

3. Remove right and left cylinder head covers.

4. Remove the radiator fan shroud. See "ENGINE COOLING" section.

5. Rotate engine until the timing mark on crankshaft damper aligns with TDC mark on timing chain cover and the camshaft sprocket "V8" marks are at the 12 o'clock position (No. 1 TDC exhaust stroke).

6. Remove the power steering pump, without disconnecting the hoses, and secure aside.

7. Remove the access plugs from the left and right cylinder heads for access to the chain guide fasteners.

8. Remove the oil fill housing to gain access to the right side tensioner arm fastener.

9. Remove the crankshaft damper. See "Crankshaft Damper" in this section.

10. Remove the timing chain cover. See "Timing Chain Cover" in this section.

11. Collapse and pin primary chain tensioner (1).

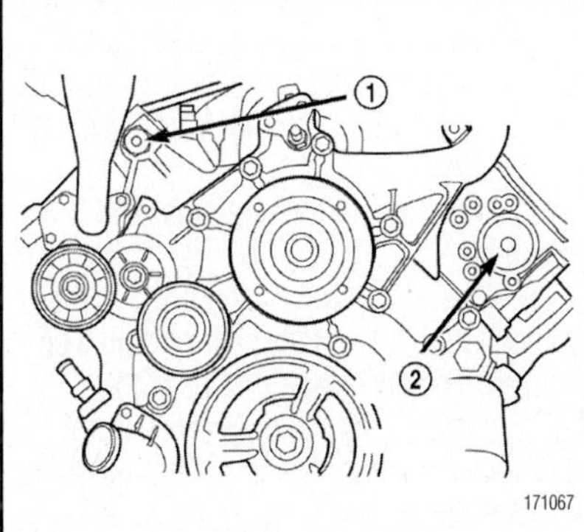

Fig. 89 Remove the access plugs from the left (2) and right (1) cylinder heads for access to the chain guide fasteners.

➡Plate behind left secondary chain tensioner could fall into oil pan. Therefore, cover pan opening.

12. Remove secondary chain tensioners.

13. The Camshaft Position Sensor (CMP) (2) is bolted to the front/top of the right cylinder head (1), remove as follows:

a. Disconnect the electrical connector (4) at the CMP sensor.

b. Remove the sensor mounting bolt (3).

c. Carefully twist the sensor from the cylinder head.

d. Check the condition of the sensor O-ring.

CAUTION

Care should be taken not to damage the camshaft target wheel. Do not hold the target wheel while loosening or tightening the camshaft sprocket. Do not place the target wheel near a magnetic source of any kind. A damaged or magnetized target wheel could cause a vehicle no start condition.

CAUTION

Do not forcefully rotate the camshafts or crankshaft independently of each other. Damaging intake valve to piston contact will occur. Ensure the negative battery cable is disconnected and isolated to guard against accidental starter engagement.

14. Remove left and right camshaft sprocket bolts.

15. While holding the left camshaft with a spanner wrench (8428A or equivalent), remove the left camshaft sprocket. Slowly rotate the camshaft approximately 15 degrees clockwise to a neutral position.

16. While holding the right camshaft with a spanner wrench, remove the left camshaft sprocket. Slowly rotate the camshaft approximately 45 degrees counterclockwise to a neutral position.

17. Remove idler sprocket assembly bolt.

18. Slide the idler sprocket assembly and crank sprocket forward simultaneously to remove the primary and secondary chains.

19. Remove both pivoting tensioner arms and chain guides.

20. Remove primary chain tensioner.

To install:

21. Using a vise, lightly compress the secondary chain tensioner piston (5) until the piston step is flush with the tensioner body. Using a pin or suitable tool, release ratchet pawl by pulling pawl back against spring force through access hole on side of tensioner. While continuing to hold pawl back, Push ratchet device to approximately 2 mm from the tensioner body. Install Tensioner pin 8514 (3) into hole on front of tensioner. Slowly open vise (1) to transfer piston spring force to lock pin.

22. Position primary chain tensioner over oil pump and insert bolts into lower two holes on tensioner bracket. Tighten bolts to 21 ft. lbs. (28 Nm).

23. Install right side chain tensioner arm. Install Torx bolt. Tighten Torx bolt to 21 ft. lbs. (28 Nm).

➡The silver bolts retain the guides to the cylinder heads and the black bolts retain the guides to the engine block.

24. Install the left side chain guide. Tighten the bolts to 21 ft. lbs. (28 Nm).

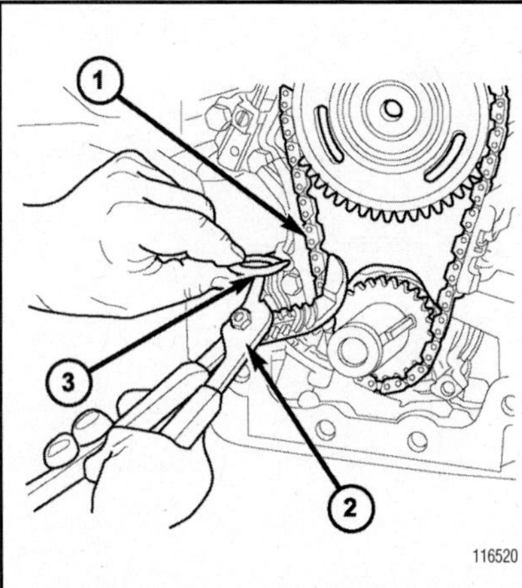

Fig. 90 Collapse and pin primary chain tensioner (1).

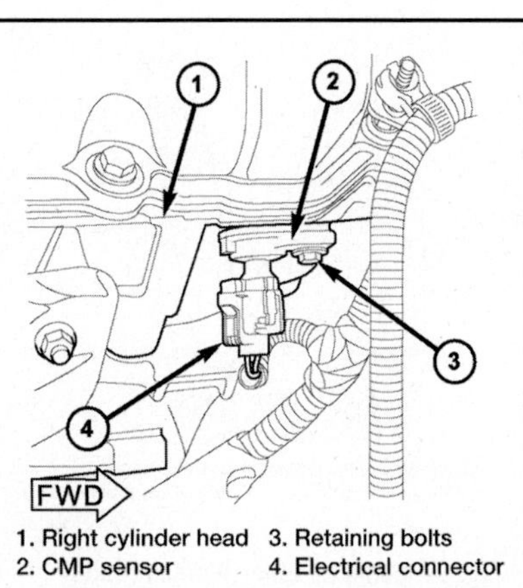

Fig. 91 Remove camshaft position sensor bolt (3) and remove sensor (2).

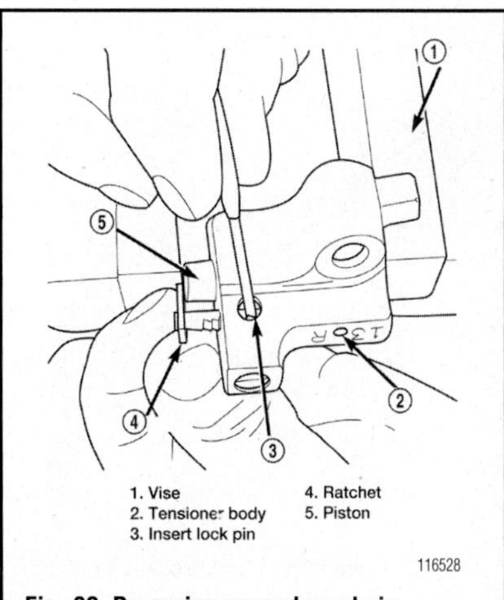

Fig. 92 Preparing secondary chain tensioner

25. Install left side chain tensioner arm, and Torx bolt. Tighten Torx bolt to 21 ft. lbs. (28 Nm).

26. Install the right side chain guide. Tighten the bolts to 21 ft. lbs. (28 Nm).

27. Install both secondary chains onto the idler sprocket. Align two plated links on the secondary chains to be visible through the two lower openings on the idler sprocket (4 o'clock and 8 o'clock). Once the secondary timing chains are installed, position the Secondary Camshaft Chain Holder (8429 or equivalent) to hold chains in place for installation.

28. Align primary chain double plated links with the timing mark at 12 o'clock on the idler sprocket. Align the primary chain single plated link with the timing mark at 6 o'clock on the crankshaft sprocket.

29. Lubricate idler shaft and bushings with clean engine oil.

➡The idler sprocket must be timed to the counterbalance shaft drive gear before the idler sprocket is fully seated.

30. Install all chains, crankshaft sprocket, and idler sprocket as an assembly. After guiding both secondary chains through the block and cylinder head openings, affix chains with a elastic strap or equivalent. This will maintain tension on chains to aid in installation. Align the timing mark on the idler sprocket gear to the timing mark on the counterbalance shaft drive gear, then seat idler sprocket fully. Before installing idler sprocket bolt, lubricate washer with oil, and tighten idler sprocket assembly retaining bolt to 25 ft. lbs. (34 Nm).

➡It will be necessary to slightly rotate camshafts for sprocket installation.

31. Align left camshaft sprocket "L" dot to plated link on chain.

32. Align right camshaft sprocket "R" dot to plated link on chain.

✲✲ CAUTION

Remove excess oil from the camshaft sprocket bolt. Failure to do so can result in over-torque of bolt resulting in bolt failure.

33. Remove Secondary Camshaft Chain Holder 8429 , then attach both sprockets to camshafts. Remove excess oil from bolts, then Install sprocket bolts, but do not tighten at this time.

34. Verify that all plated links are aligned with the marks on all sprockets and the "V6" marks on camshaft sprockets are at the 12 o'clock position.

35. Ensure the plate between the left secondary chain tensioner and block is correctly installed.

36. Install both secondary chain tensioners. Tighten bolts to 21 ft. lbs. (28 Nm).

➡Left and right secondary chain tensioners are not common.

37. Remove all 3 locking pins from tensioners.

✲✲ CAUTION

After pulling locking pins out of each tensioner, DO NOT manually extend the tensioner(s) ratchet. Doing so will over-tension the chains, resulting in noise and/or high timing chain loads.

38. Using Spanner Wrench (6958) with Adaptor Pins (8346), tighten left and right camshaft sprocket bolts to 90 ft. lbs. (122 Nm).

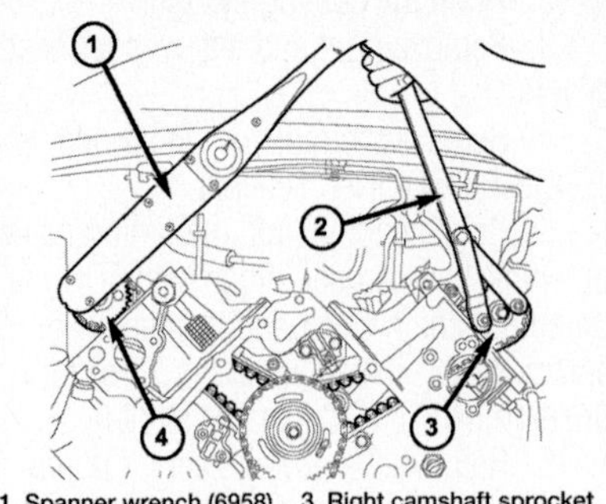

Fig. 95 Using Spanner Wrench (6958) with Adaptor Pins (8346), (4) tighten right camshaft sprocket bolts to 90 ft. lbs. (122 Nm).

39. Rotate engine two full revolutions. Verify timing marks are at the follow locations:

- Primary chain idler sprocket dot is at 12 o'clock
- Primary chain crankshaft sprocket dot is at 6 o'clock
- Secondary chain camshaft sprockets "V8" marks are at 12 o'clock
- Counterbalance shaft drive gear dot is aligned to the idler sprocket gear dot

40. Lubricate all three chains with engine oil.

41. After installing all chains, it is recommended that the idler gear end play be checked. The end play must be within 0.004–0.010 in. (0.10–0.25 mm). If not within specification, the idler gear must be replaced.

42. Install timing chain cover.

43. Install the crankshaft damper. See "Crankshaft Damper" in this section.

44. Install cylinder head covers.

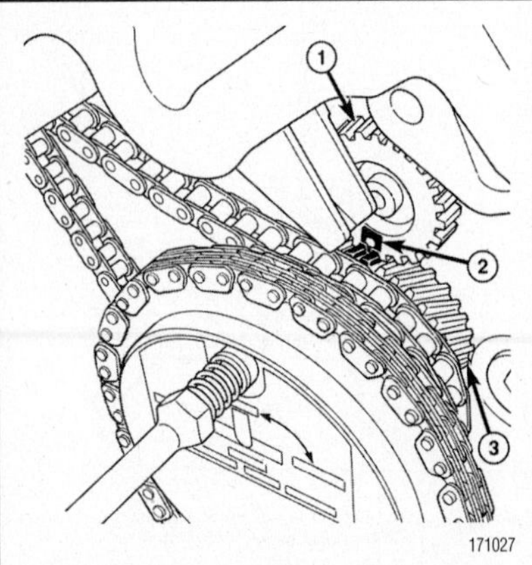

Fig. 93 Timing the idler sprocket gear (3) to counterbalance shaft drive gear (1) by aligning timing mark (2)

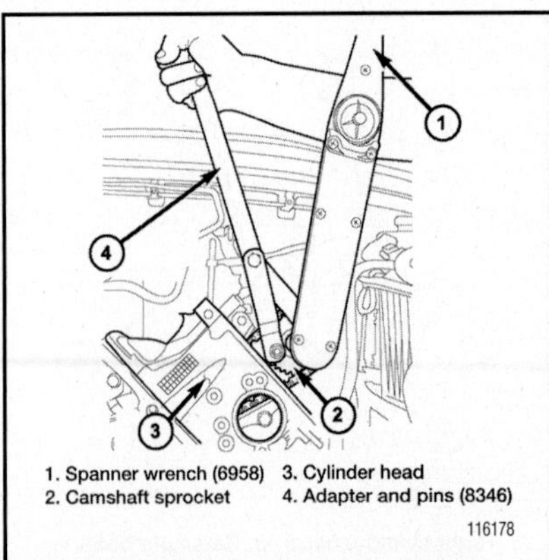

Fig. 94 Using Spanner Wrench (6958) with Adaptor Pins (8346), (4) tighten left camshaft sprocket bolts to 90 ft. lbs. (122 Nm).

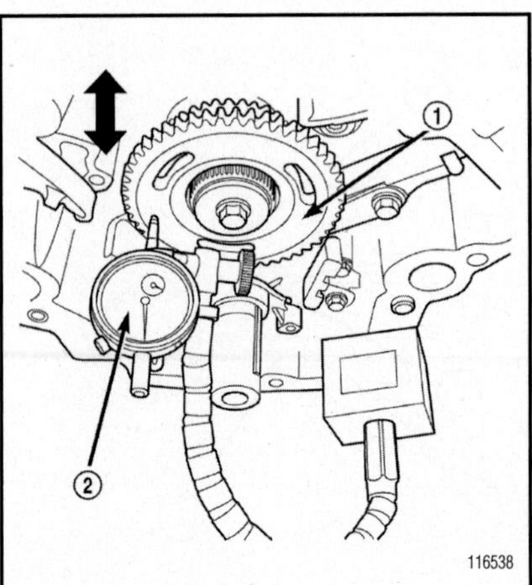

Fig. 96 Checking idle gear (1) end play using dial gauge (2)

➡Before installing threaded plug in right cylinder head, the plug must be coated with sealant to prevent leaks.

45. Coat the large threaded access plug with Mopar Thread Sealant with Teflon (or equivalent), then install into the right cylinder head and tighten to 60 ft. lbs. (81 Nm).
46. Install the oil fill housing.
47. Install access plugs in the left and right cylinder heads.
48. Install power steering pump. See "STEERING" section.
49. Fill cooling system.
50. Connect negative cable to battery.

5.7L

See Figures 97 through 103.

1. Disconnect the negative battery cable.
2. Drain the cooling system.

➡It is not necessary to remove water pump for timing chain cover removal.

3. Remove the timing chain cover. See "Timing Chain Cover" in this section.
4. Verify the slide bushings remain installed in the timing chain cover during removal.
5. Remove the oil pump retaining bolts and remove the oil pump.
6. Install the vibration damper bolt finger tight. Using a suitable socket and breaker bar, rotate the crankshaft to align the timing marks with the timing chain sprockets.

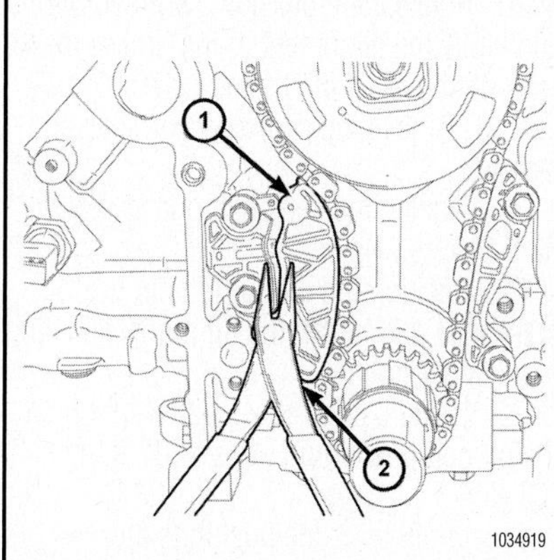

Fig. 98 Retract the chain tensioner arm (1) until the hole in the arm lines up with the hole in the bracket.

7. Retract the chain tensioner arm until the hole in the arm lines up with the hole in the bracket.
8. Install the Tensioner Pin (8514 or equivalent) into the chain tensioner holes.

⁂ CAUTION

Never attempt to disassemble the camshaft phaser, severe engine damage could result.

9. Remove the camshaft sprocket (phaser) retaining bolt and remove the timing chain with the camshaft phaser and crankshaft sprocket.

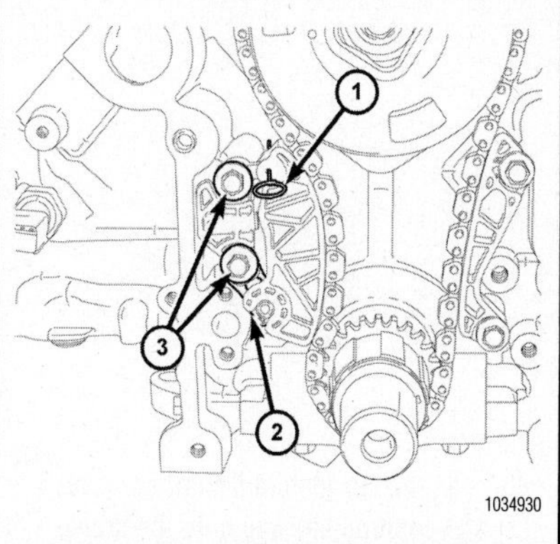

Fig. 99 Install the Tensioner Pin (8514 or equivalent) (1) into the chain tensioner (3) holes—tensioner retaining bolts (2) shown.

10. If the timing chain tensioner is being replaced, remove the retaining bolts and remove the timing chain tensioner.
11. If the timing chain guide is being replaced, remove the retaining bolts and remove the timing chain guide.

To install:

12. Install the crankshaft sprocket and position halfway onto the crankshaft.
13. While holding the camshaft phaser in hand, position the timing chain on the camshaft phaser and align the timing marks as shown.
14. While holding the camshaft phaser and timing chain in hand, position the timing chain on the crankshaft sprocket and align the timing mark as shown.
15. Align the slot in the camshaft phaser with the dowel on the camshaft and position the camshaft phaser on the camshaft while sliding the crankshaft sprocket into position.
16. Install the camshaft phaser retaining bolt finger tight.

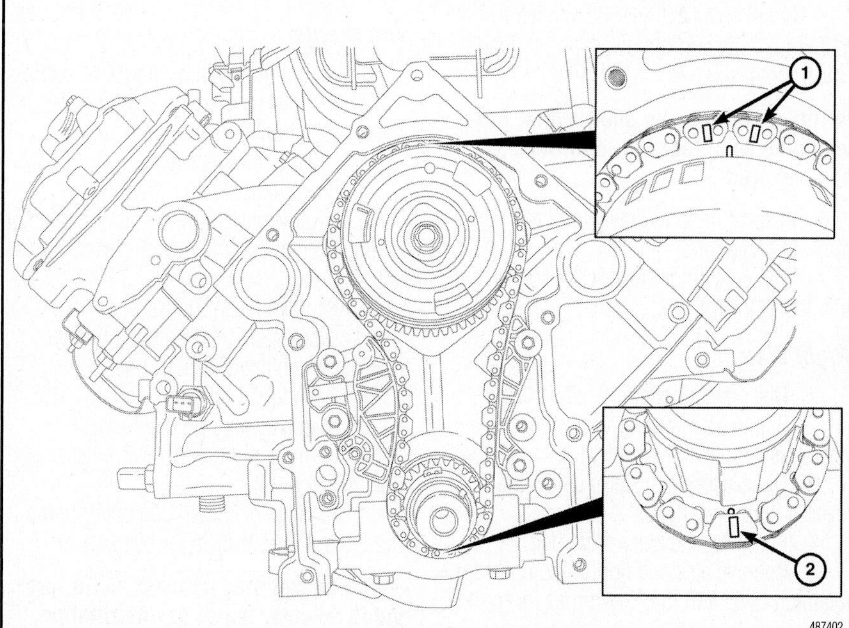

Fig. 97 Install the vibration damper bolt finger tight. Using a suitable socket and breaker bar, rotate the crankshaft to align the timing marks with the timing chain sprockets (1, 2).

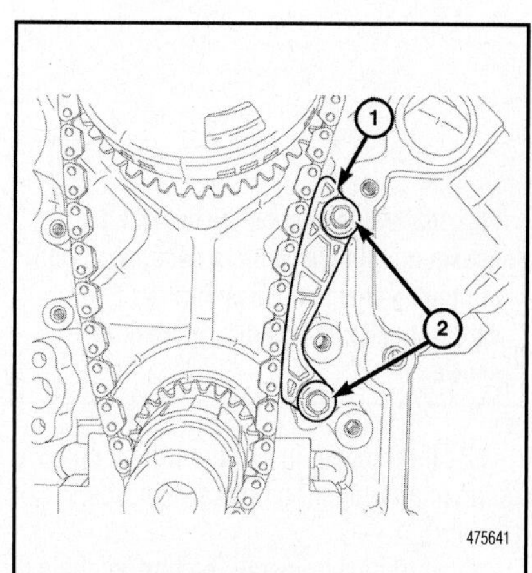

Fig. 100 If the timing chain guide (1) is being replaced, remove the retaining bolts (2) and remove the timing chain guide.

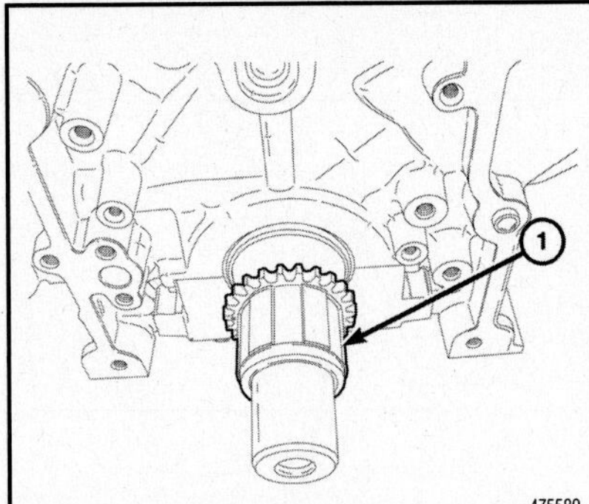

Fig. 101 Install the crankshaft sprocket (1) and position halfway onto the crankshaft.

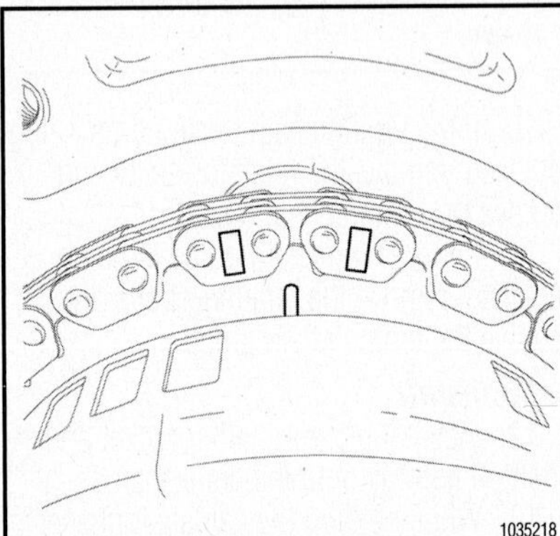

Fig. 102 While holding the camshaft phaser in hand, position the timing chain on the camshaft phaser and align the timing marks as shown.

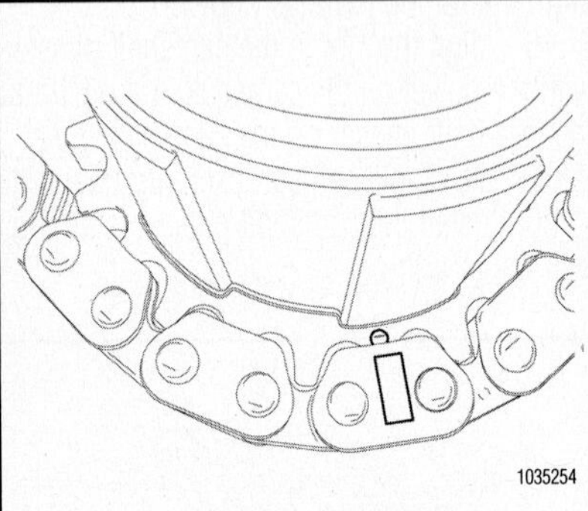

Fig. 103 While holding the camshaft phaser and timing chain in hand, position the timing chain on the crankshaft sprocket and align the timing mark as shown.

17. If removed, install the timing chain guide and tighten the bolts to 8 ft. lbs. (11 Nm).
18. If removed, install the timing chain tensioner and tighten the bolts to 8 ft. lbs. (11 Nm).
19. Remove the tensioner pin (8514).
20. Rotate the crankshaft two revolutions and verify the alignment of the timing marks (shown above). If the timing marks do not line up, remove the camshaft sprocket and realign.
21. Tighten the camshaft phaser bolt to 63 ft. lbs. (85 Nm).
22. Position the oil pump onto the crankshaft and install the oil pump retaining bolts finger tight.
23. Using a criss-cross pattern, tighten the oil pump retaining bolts to 21 ft. lbs. (28 Nm).
24. Verify the slide bushings are installed in the timing chain cover and install the timing chain cover. See "Timing Chain Cover" in this section.
25. Fill the engine with oil.
26. Fill the cooling system.
27. Connect the negative battery cable.
28. Start the engine and check for leaks.

VALVE COVERS

REMOVAL & INSTALLATION

3.7L

Left Side

1. Disconnect negative cable from battery.
2. Remove the resonator assembly and air inlet hose.
3. Disconnect injector connectors and unclip the injector harness. Route injector harness in front of cylinder head cover.
4. Disconnect the left side breather tube and remove the breather tube.
5. Remove the cylinder head cover mounting bolts and remove cylinder head cover and gasket.

➡The gasket may be used again, providing no cuts, tears, or deformation has occurred.

6. Installation is the reverse of the removal procedure.
7. Tighten cylinder head cover bolts to 9 ft. lbs. (12 Nm).

Right Side

1. Disconnect battery negative cable.
2. Remove air cleaner assembly, resonator assembly and air inlet hose.
3. Drain cooling system, below the level of the heater hoses.
4. Remove accessory drive belt.
5. Remove air conditioning compressor retaining bolts and move compressor to the left.
6. Remove heater hoses.
7. Disconnect injector and ignition coil connectors.
8. Disconnect and remove positive crankcase ventilation (PCV) hose.
9. Remove oil fill tube.
10. Un-clip injector and ignition coil harness and move away from cylinder head cover.
11. Remove right rear breather tube and filter assembly.
12. Remove cylinder head cover retaining bolts. Remove cylinder head cover.
13. Installation is the reverse of the removal procedure.
14. Tighten cylinder head cover bolts to 9 ft. lbs. (12 Nm).

4.7L

Left Side

1. Disconnect negative cable from battery.
2. Remove the resonator assembly and air inlet hose.
3. Disconnect injector connectors and unclip the injector harness. Route injector harness in front of cylinder head cover.
4. Disconnect the left side breather tube and remove the breather tube.
5. Remove the cylinder head cover mounting bolts and remove cylinder head cover and gasket.

➡The gasket may be used again, providing no cuts, tears, or deformation has occurred.

6. Installation is the reverse of the removal procedure.
7. Tighten cylinder head cover bolts to 9 ft. lbs. (12 Nm).

Right Side

1. Disconnect battery negative cable.
2. Remove air cleaner assembly, resonator assembly and air inlet hose.
3. Drain cooling system.
4. Remove accessory drive belt.
5. Remove air conditioning compressor retaining bolts and move compressor to the left.
6. Remove heater hoses.
7. Disconnect and remove positive crankcase ventilation (PCV) hose.
8. Remove oil fill tube.
9. Remove spark plug wires.
10. Remove right rear breather tube and filter assembly.
11. Remove cylinder head cover retaining bolts. Remove cylinder head cover.

➡The gasket may be used again, provided no cuts, tears, or deformation has occurred.

12. Installation is the reverse of the removal procedure.

13. Tighten cylinder head cover bolts to 9 ft. lbs. (12 Nm).

5.7L

➡**Both sides similar.**

1. Disconnect and isolate the negative battery cable.
2. Remove the engine cover.
3. Disconnect the ignition coil electrical connectors.
4. Position the electrical harness aside.
5. Remove the ignition coil retaining bolts and remove the ignition coils.
6. Starting from the middle and working across and in alternating sides, remove the cylinder head cover retaining bolts.

⁂ CAUTION

Do not use harsh cleaners to clean the cylinder head covers. Severe damage to covers may occur.

7. Remove the cylinder head cover.
8. Clean the sealing surface of the cylinder head and cover.

➡**The cylinder head cover gasket may be used again, provided no cuts, tears, or deformation have occurred.**

9. Installation is the reverse of the removal procedure.
10. Tighten cylinder head cover bolts, in an alternating criss-cross pattern, to 70 inch lbs. (8 Nm).

VALVE LASH

ADJUSTMENT

➡**Valve lash is maintained automatically by hydraulic valve adjusters. No clearance check or adjustment is needed.**

ENGINE PERFORMANCE & EMISSION CONTROLS

ACCELERATOR PEDAL POSITION (APP) SENSOR

LOCATION

See Figure 104.

The Accelerator Pedal Position Sensor (APPS) (1) is located inside the vehicle. It is attached to the accelerator pedal assembly (3). It is used only with 3.7L V-6 and 5.7L V-8 gas engines.

REMOVAL & INSTALLATION

3.7L & 5.7L

⁂ CAUTION

Do not attempt to separate or remove the Accelerator Pedal Position Sensor (APPS) from the accelerator pedal assembly. The APPS and the accelerator pedal is replaced as an assembly. If the sensor is removed from the pedal, the electronic calibration may be destroyed.

1. Remove the accelerator pedal assembly as follows:
   a. Disconnect the 6-way electrical connector at the APPS.
   b. Remove the upper accelerator pedal mounting bolt.
   c. Remove the lower accelerator pedal mounting bolt.
   d. Remove the accelerator pedal assembly from the vehicle.
2. Installation is the reverse of the removal procedure.

CAMSHAFT POSITION (CMP) SENSOR

LOCATION

3.7L

See Figure 105.

The Camshaft Position Sensor (CMP) is bolted to the right-front side of the right cylinder head.

4.7L

See Figure 106.

The Camshaft Position Sensor (CMP) is bolted to the right-front side of the right cylinder head.

5.7L

See Figure 107.

The Camshaft Position Sensor (CMP) (3) is located on right side of timing gear/chain cover below generator (1).

REMOVAL & INSTALLATION

3.7L

1. Disconnect electrical connector at CMP sensor.
2. Remove sensor mounting bolt.
3. Carefully twist sensor from cylinder head.
4. Check condition of sensor O-ring.

To install:

5. Clean out machined hole in cylinder head.

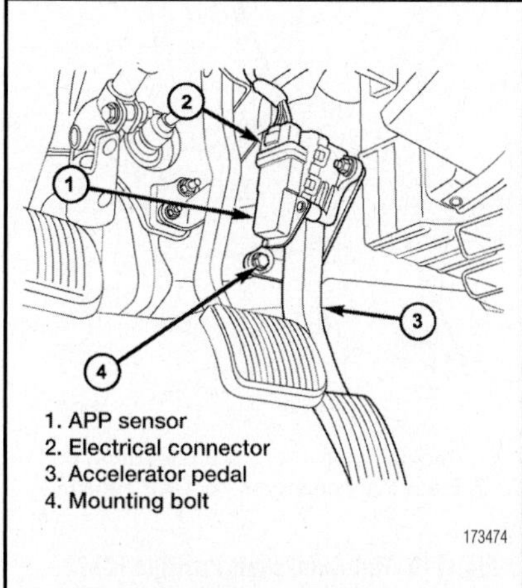

Fig. 104 Showing the Accelerator Pedal Position Sensor—3.7L & 5.7L only

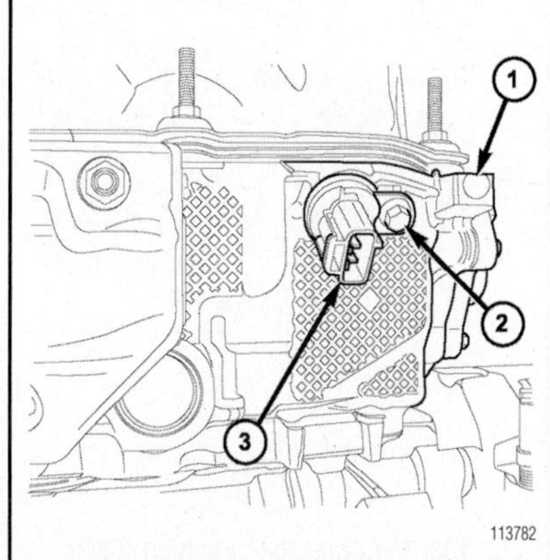

Fig. 105 The Camshaft Position Sensor (CMP) (3) is bolted (2) to the right-front side of the right cylinder head (1).

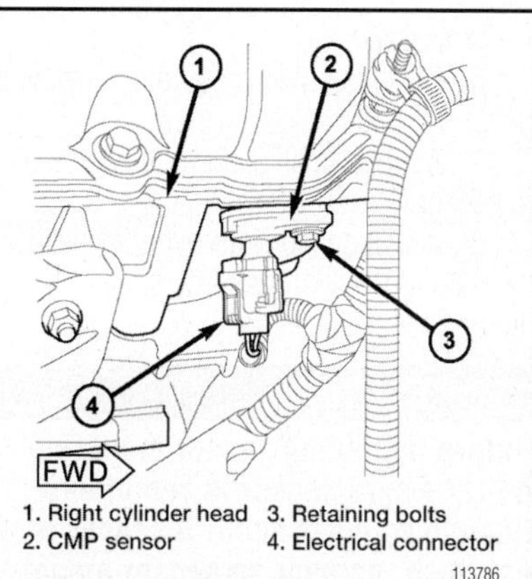

Fig. 106 The Camshaft Position Sensor (CMP) is bolted to the right-front side of the right cylinder head.

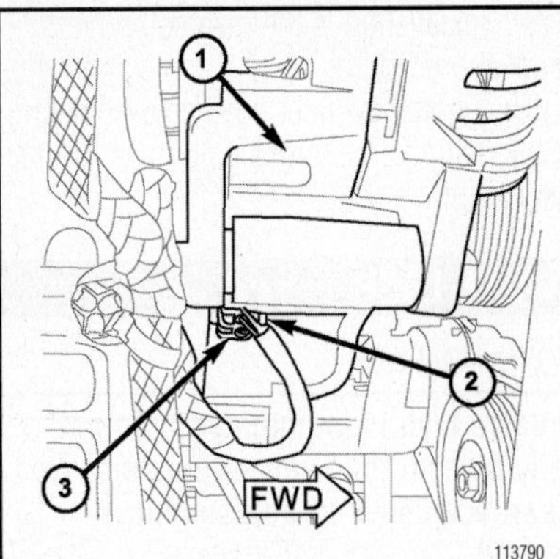

Fig. 107 Camshaft Position Sensor (CMP) (3) and electrical connector (2) are located on right side of timing gear/chain cover below generator (1).

6. Apply a small amount of engine oil to sensor O-ring.
7. Install sensor into cylinder head with a slight rocking and twisting action.

⁂ CAUTION

Before tightening sensor mounting bolt, be sure sensor is completely flush to cylinder head. If sensor is not flush, damage to sensor mounting tang may result.

8. Install mounting bolt and tighten to 9 ft. lbs. (12 Nm).
9. Connect electrical connector to sensor.

4.7L

1. Raise and support vehicle.
2. Disconnect electrical connector at CMP sensor.
3. Remove sensor mounting bolt.
4. Carefully twist sensor from cylinder head.
5. Check condition of sensor O-ring.

To install:

6. Clean out machined hole in cylinder head.
7. Apply a small amount of engine oil to sensor O-ring.
8. Install sensor into cylinder head with a slight rocking and twisting action.

⁂ CAUTION

Before tightening sensor mounting bolt, be sure sensor is completely flush to cylinder head. If sensor is not flush, damage to sensor mounting tang may result.

9. Install mounting bolt and tighten to 9 ft. lbs. (12 Nm).
10. Connect electrical connector to sensor.

5.7L

1. Disconnect electrical connector at CMP sensor.
2. Remove sensor mounting bolt.
3. Carefully twist sensor from cylinder head.
4. Check condition of sensor O-ring.

To install:

5. Clean out machined hole in cylinder head.
6. Apply a small amount of engine oil to sensor O-ring.
7. Install sensor into cylinder head with a slight rocking and twisting action.

⁂ CAUTION

Before tightening sensor mounting bolt, be sure sensor is completely flush to cylinder head. If sensor is not flush, damage to sensor mounting tang may result.

8. Install mounting bolt and tighten to 9 ft. lbs. (12 Nm).
9. Connect electrical connector to sensor.

CRANKSHAFT POSITION (CKP) SENSOR

LOCATION

3.7L

See Figure 108.

The Crankshaft Position (CKP) (2) sensor is mounted into the right rear side of the cylinder block. It is positioned and bolted into a machined hole.

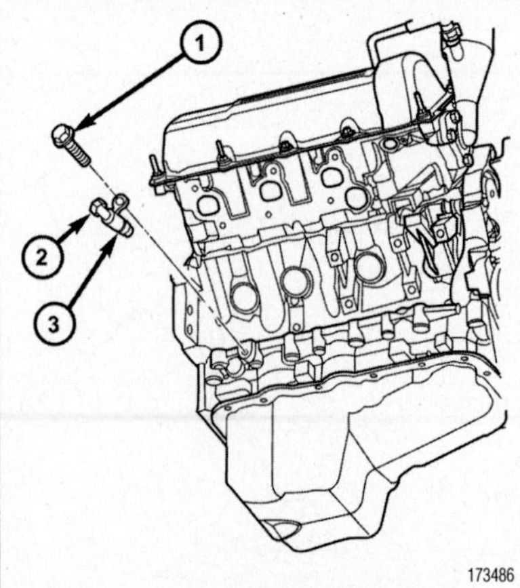

Fig. 108 The Crankshaft Position (CKP) (2) sensor is mounted into the right rear side of the cylinder block. It is positioned and bolted into a machined hole.

4.7L

See Figure 109.

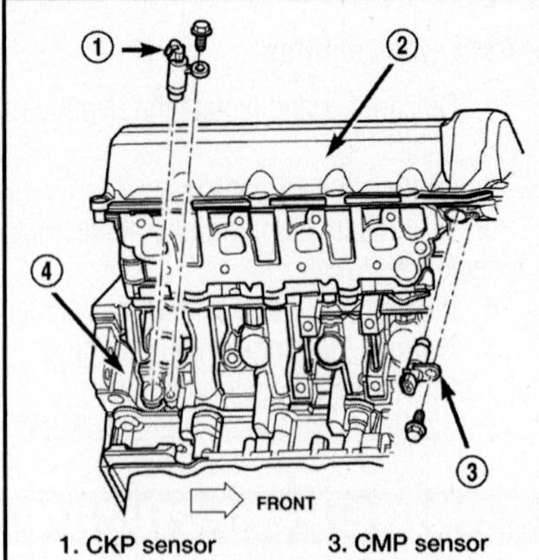

Fig. 109 Crankshaft Position (CKP) sensor is located on the rear lower side of the engine block

5.7L

See Figure 110.

The Crankshaft Position (CKP) sensor is mounted into the right rear side of the cylinder block. It is positioned and bolted into a machined hole and attached via an electrical connector.

REMOVAL & INSTALLATION

1. Raise vehicle (4.7L and 5.7L).
2. Disconnect sensor electrical connector.
3. Remove sensor mounting bolt.
4. Carefully twist sensor from cylinder block.
5. Check condition of sensor O-ring.

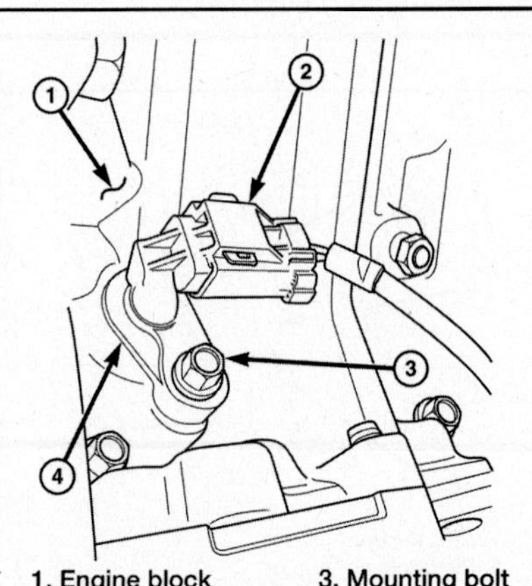

Fig. 110 The Crankshaft Position (CKP) sensor is mounted into the right rear side of the cylinder block.

To install:

6. Clean out machined hole in engine block.
7. Apply a small amount of engine oil to sensor O-ring.
8. Install sensor into engine block with a slight rocking and twisting action.

⁂ CAUTION

Before tightening the CKP sensor mounting bolt, be sure the sensor is completely flush to the cylinder block. If the CKP sensor is not flush, damage to the sensor mounting tang may result.

9. Install mounting bolt and tighten to 21 ft. lbs. (28 Nm) torque.
10. Connect electrical connector to sensor.
11. Lower vehicle.

ENGINE COOLANT TEMPERATURE (ECT) SENSOR

LOCATION

See Figures 111 through 113.

3.7L

The ECT sensor is mounted on top of the intake manifold, near the air intake housing.

4.7L

See Figure 112.

5.7L

REMOVAL & INSTALLATION

1. Partially drain the cooling system.
2. Disconnect the electrical connector from the ECT sensor.

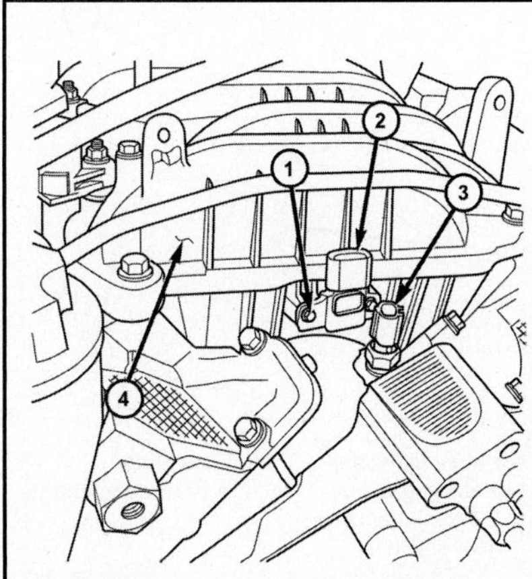

Fig. 111 Showing ECT sensor location—3.7L

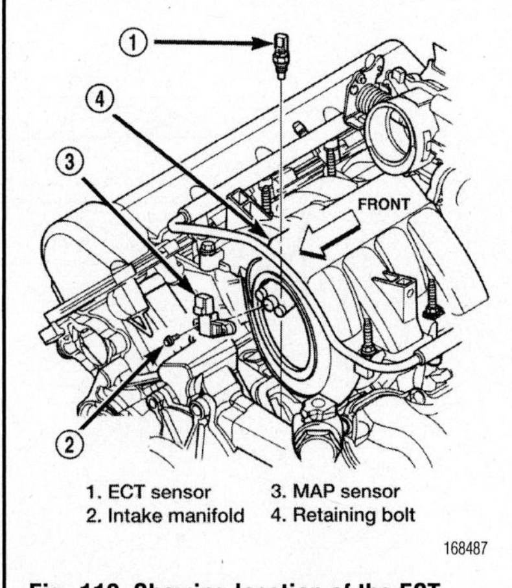

Fig. 112 Showing location of the ECT sensor—4.7L

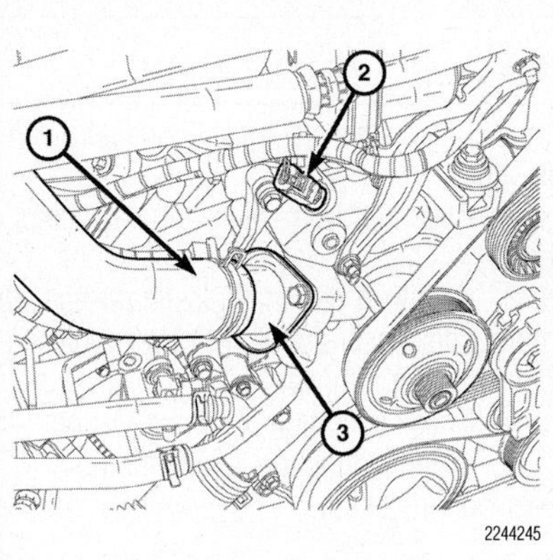

Fig. 113 ECT sensor is located just above the radiator hose connection to the block—5.7L

3. Remove the sensor from the intake manifold

To install:

4. Apply thread sealant to ECT sensor threads.
5. Install ECT sensor to engine.
6. Tighten sensor to 8 ft. lbs. (11 Nm) torque.
7. Connect electrical connector to ECT sensor.
8. Replace any lost engine coolant.

HEATED OXYGEN (HO2S) SENSOR

LOCATION

See Figure 114.

The Oxygen Sensors (O2S) are attached to, and protrude into the vehicle exhaust system. Depending on the engine or emission package, the vehicle may use a total of either 2 or 4 sensors.

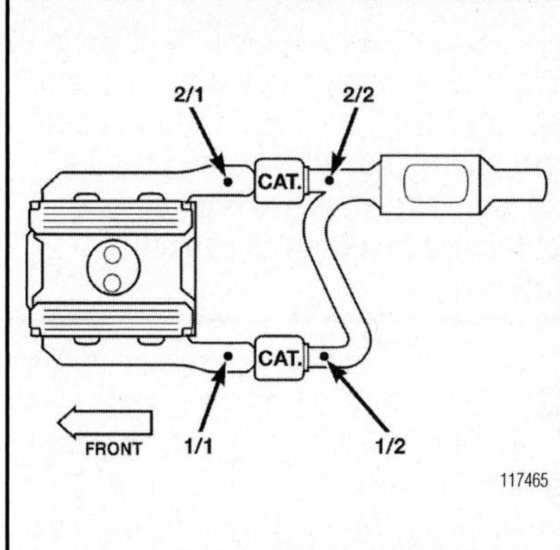

Fig. 114 Typical arrangement of oxygen sensor locations—all engines

Federal Emission Packages: Two sensors are used: upstream (referred to as 1/1) and downstream (referred to as 1/2). With this emission package, the upstream sensor (1/1) is located just before the main catalytic convertor. The downstream sensor (1/2) is located just after the main catalytic convertor.

California Emission Packages: On this emissions package, 4 sensors are used: 2 upstream (referred to as 1/1 and 2/1) and 2 downstream (referred to as 1/2 and 2/2). With this emission package, the right upstream sensor (2/1) is located in the right exhaust downpipe just before the mini-catalytic convertor. The left upstream sensor (1/1) is located in the left exhaust downpipe just before the mini-catalytic convertor. The right downstream sensor (2/2) is located in the right exhaust downpipe just after the mini-catalytic convertor, and before the main catalytic convertor. The left downstream sensor (1/2) is located in the left exhaust downpipe just after the mini-catalytic convertor, and before the main catalytic convertor.

REMOVAL & INSTALLATION

⁂ CAUTION

Never apply any type of grease to the oxygen sensor electrical connector, or attempt any repair of the sensor wiring harness.

⁂ WARNING

The exhaust pipes and catalytic converter become very hot during engine operation. Allow the engine to cool before removing the oxygen sensor.

1. Raise and support vehicle.
2. Disconnect wire connector from O2S sensor.

CAUTION

When disconnecting the oxygen sensor electrical connector, do not pull directly on the wire going into the sensor. The sensor wiring can be damaged resulting in sensor failure.

3. Remove O2S sensor with an oxygen sensor removal and installation tool.
4. Clean threads in exhaust pipe using appropriate tap.

To install:

➡Threads of new oxygen sensors are factory coated with anti-seize compound to aid in removal. DO NOT add any additional anti-seize compound to threads of a new oxygen sensor.

5. Install O2S sensor. Tighten to 30 ft. lbs. (41Nm) torque.
6. Connect O2S sensor wire connector.
7. Lower vehicle.

INTAKE AIR TEMPERATURE (IAT) SENSOR

LOCATION

3.7L & 4.7L

See Figure 115.

The intake manifold air temperature (IAT) sensor is installed into the air intake tube near the throttle body.

5.7L

See Figure 116.

The intake manifold air temperature (IAT) sensor is installed into the front of the intake manifold air box plenum.

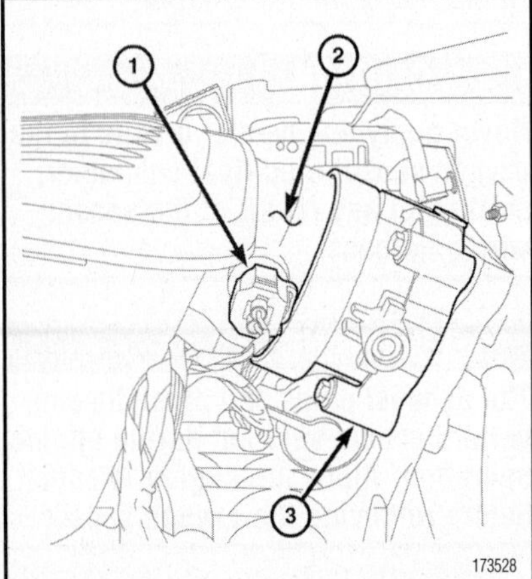

Fig. 115 Showing Intake Air Temperature (IAT) sensor—3.7L shown; 4.7L similar

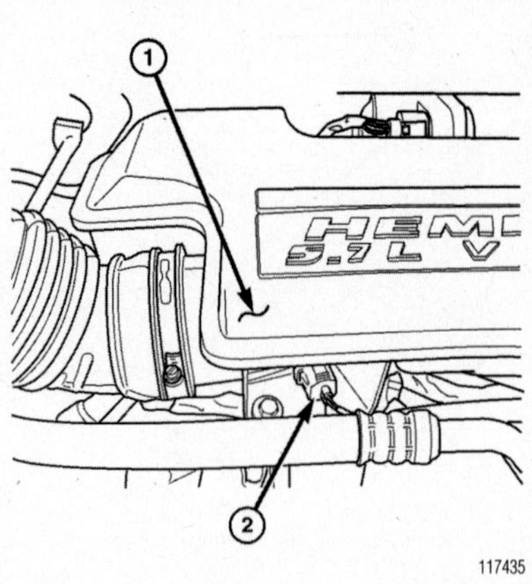

Fig. 116 The intake manifold air temperature (IAT) sensor (2) is installed into the front of the intake manifold air box plenum (1)

REMOVAL & INSTALLATION

1. Disconnect electrical connector from IAT sensor.
2. Clean dirt from intake tube at sensor base.
3. Gently lift on small plastic release tab and rotate sensor about 1/4 turn counterclockwise for removal.
4. Check condition of sensor O-ring.
5. Installation is the reverse of the removal procedure.

KNOCK SENSOR (KS)

LOCATION

3.7L

See Figure 117.

Two knock sensors are bolted into the cylinder block under the intake manifold and share one electrical connector. Knock sensor wiring is held in place by a retaining clip.

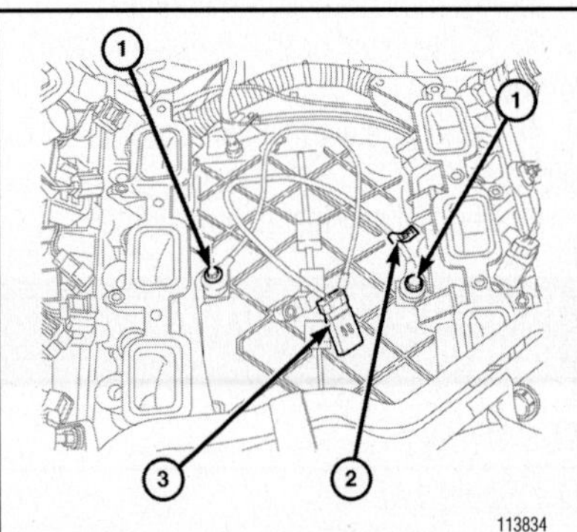

Fig. 117 Two knock sensors (1) are bolted into the cylinder block under the intake manifold and share one electrical connector (3). Knock sensor wiring is held in place by a retaining clip (2)

4.7L

See Figure 118.

The knock sensor is bolted to the cylinder block under the intake manifold.

5.7L

See Figure 119.

Two knock sensors are also used with the 5.7L. These are bolted into each side of the cylinder block (outside) under the exhaust manifold.

REMOVAL & INSTALLATION

3.7L & 4.7L

➡The left sensor is identified by an identification tag (LEFT). It is also identified by a larger bolt head. The

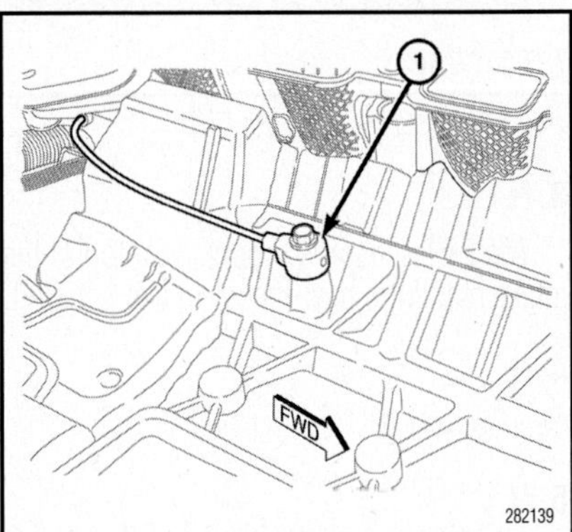

Fig. 118 The knock sensor (1) is bolted to the cylinder block under the intake manifold.

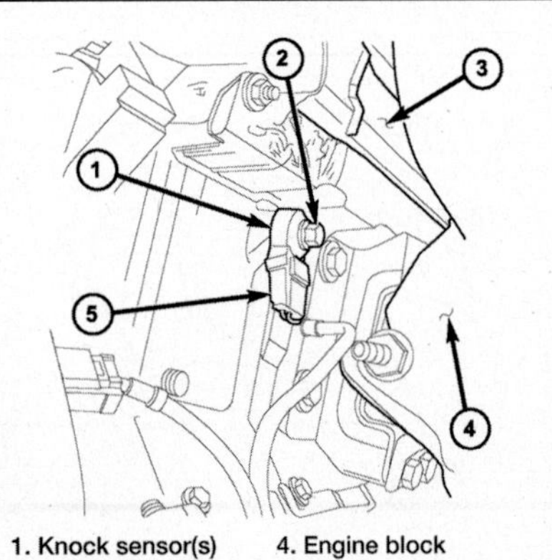

Fig. 119 Two knock sensors are also used with the 5.7L. These are bolted into each side of the cylinder block (outside) under the exhaust manifold.

Powertrain Control Module (PCM) must have and know the correct sensor left/right positions. Do not mix the sensor locations.

1. Remove the intake manifold. See "ENGINE MECHANICAL" section.
2. Disconnect knock sensor dual pigtail harness from engine wiring harness. This connection is made near rear of engine.
3. Remove both sensor mounting bolts. Note foam strip on bolt threads.

➡This foam is used only to retain the bolts to sensors for plant assembly. It is not used as a sealant. Do not apply any adhesive, sealant or thread locking compound to these bolts.

4. Remove sensor(s) from the engine.

To install:

5. Thoroughly clean knock sensor mounting holes.
6. Install sensors into cylinder block, checking that LEFT knock sensor is in the proper location.

⁂ CAUTION

Over or under tightening the sensor mounting bolts will affect knock sensor performance, possibly causing improper spark control. Always use the specified torque when installing the knock sensors. The torque for the knock senor bolt is relatively light for an 8 mm bolt.

➡Note foam strip on bolt threads. This foam is used only to retain the bolts to sensors for plant assembly. It is not used as a sealant. Do not apply any adhesive, sealant or thread locking compound to these bolts.

7. Install and tighten mounting bolts 15 ft.lbs. (20 Nm).
8. Connect knock sensor wiring harness to engine harness at rear of intake manifold.
9. Install intake manifold. See "ENGINE MECHANICAL" section.

5.7L

1. Raise and support the vehicle.
2. Disconnect the knock sensor electrical connector(s).
3. Remove the knock sensor retaining bolt(s).

➡Note the foam strip on bolt threads. This foam strip is used only to retain the bolts to the sensors for plant assembly. It is not used as a sealant. Do not apply any adhesive, sealant or thread locking compound to these bolts.

4. Remove the knock sensor(s) from the cylinder block.

To install:

5. Thoroughly clean knock sensor mounting holes.
6. Install sensors into cylinder block, checking that LEFT knock sensor is in the proper location.

⁂ CAUTION

Over or under tightening the sensor mounting bolts will affect knock sensor performance, possibly causing improper spark control. Always use the specified torque when installing the knock sensors. The torque for the knock senor bolt is relatively light for an 8 mm bolt.

➡Note foam strip on bolt threads. This foam is used only to retain the bolts to sensors for plant assembly. It is not used as a sealant. Do not apply any adhesive, sealant or thread locking compound to these bolts.

7. Install and tighten mounting bolts 15 ft.lbs. (20 Nm).
8. Connect the electrical connector(s).
9. Lower the vehicle.

MANIFOLD ABSOLUTE PRESSURE (MAP) SENSOR

LOCATION

3.7L & 4.7L

See Figure 120.

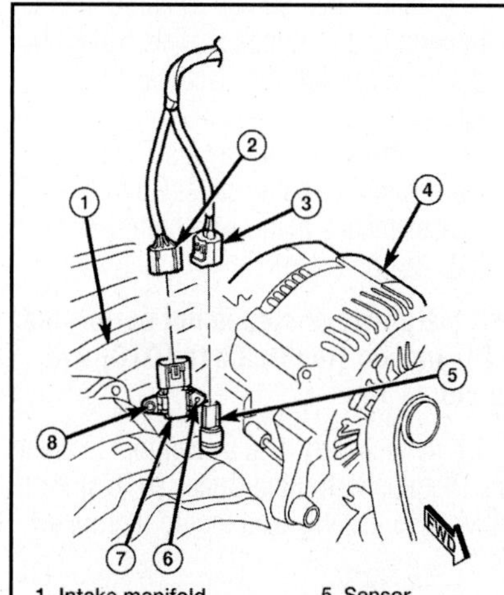

Fig. 120 The Manifold Absolute Pressure (MAP) sensor is mounted into the front of the intake manifold.

The Manifold Absolute Pressure (MAP) sensor is mounted into the front of the intake manifold.

5.7L

See Figure 121.

The Manifold Absolute Pressure (MAP) sensor is mounted to the front of the intake manifold air plenum box.

REMOVAL & INSTALLATION

3.7L & 4.7L

1. Disconnect electrical connector at MAP sensor.
2. Clean area around MAP sensor.
3. Remove one sensor mounting screw.
4. Remove MAP sensor from intake manifold by slipping it from locating pin.
5. Check condition of sensor O-ring.

To install:

6. Clean MAP sensor mounting hole at intake manifold.
7. Position MAP sensor into manifold by sliding sensor over locating pin.
8. Install mounting bolt. Tighten to 25 inch lbs. (3 Nm) torque.
9. Connect electrical connector.

5.7L

1. Disconnect electrical connector at sensor by sliding release lock out . Press down on lock tab for removal.
2. Rotate sensor 1/4 turn counterclockwise for removal.
3. Check condition of sensor O-ring.
4. Installation is the reverse of the removal procedure.

Fig. 121 The Manifold Absolute Pressure (MAP) sensor (2) and electrical connector (1) are mounted to the front of the intake manifold air plenum box.

POWERTRAIN CONTROL MODULE (PCM)

LOCATION

See Figure 122.

The Powertrain Control Module (PCM) is located in the right-rear section of the engine compartment under the cowl.

REMOVAL & INSTALLATION

➡Certain ABS systems rely on having the Powertrain Control Module (PCM) broadcast the Vehicle Identification Number (VIN) over the bus network. To prevent problems of DTCs and other items related to the VIN broadcast, it is recommend that you disconnect the ABS CAB (controller) temporarily when replacing the PCM. Once the PCM is replaced, write the VIN to the PCM using a scan tool. This is done from the engine main menu. Arrow over to the second page to "1. Miscellaneous". Select "Check VIN" from the choices. Make sure it has the correct VIN entered before continuing. When the VIN is complete, turn off the ignition key and reconnect the ABS module connector. This will prevent the setting of DTCs and other items associated with the lack of a VIN detected when you turn the key ON after replacing the PCM.

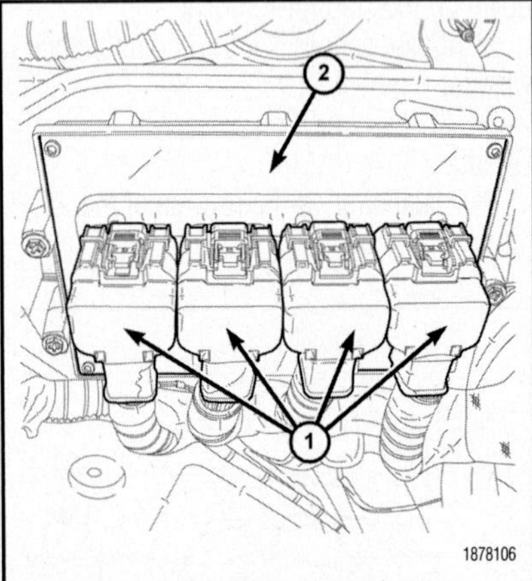

Fig. 122 Location of the PCM (2) and the connectors (1)

1. Use the scan tool to reprogram the new PCM with the vehicles original identification number (VIN) and the vehicles original mileage. If this step is not done, a Diagnostic Trouble Code (DTC) may be set.
2. To avoid possible voltage spike damage to the PCM, ignition key must be off, and negative battery cable must be disconnected before unplugging PCM connectors.
3. Disconnect and isolator the negative battery cable.
4. Carefully unplug the four 38-way connectors from the PCM.
5. Remove the four PCM mounting bolts and remove the PCM from vehicle.

To install:

6. Install the PCM and 4 mounting bolts to vehicle.
7. Check pin connectors in the PCM and the three 32-way connectors (four 38-way connectors if equipped with NGC) for corrosion or damage. Also, the pin heights in connectors should all be same. Repair as necessary before installing connectors.
8. Install the three 32-way connectors (four 38-way connectors if equipped with NGC).
9. The 5.7L V-8 engine is equipped with a fully electronic accelerator pedal position sensor. If equipped with a 5.7L, also perform the following steps:
    a. Connect the negative battery cable.
    b. Turn the ignition switch ON, but do not crank the engine.
    c. Leave the ignition switch ON for a minimum of 10 seconds. This will allow the PCM to learn the electrical parameters.
    d. The scan tool may also be used to learn electrical parameters. Go to the Miscellaneous menu, and then select ETC Learn.

➡If the previous step is not performed, a Diagnostic Trouble Code (DTC) will be set.

10. If necessary, use a scan tool to erase any Diagnostic Trouble Codes (DTC's) from PCM. Also use the scan tool to reprogram new PCM with vehicles original Vehicle Identification Number (VIN) and original vehicle mileage.

VEHICLE SPEED SENSORS (INPUT & OUTPUT SPEED SENSORS)

LOCATION

See Figure 123.

The Input and Output Speed Sensors are two-wire magnetic pickup devices that generate AC signals as rotation occurs. They are mounted in the left side of the transmission case and are considered primary inputs to the Transmission Control Module (TCM).

REMOVAL & INSTALLATION

1. Raise vehicle.
2. Place a suitable fluid catch pan under the transmission.
3. Remove the wiring connector from the input and/or output speed sensor.
4. Remove the bolt holding the input and/or output speed sensor to the transmission case.
5. Remove the input and/or output speed sensor from the transmission case.
6. Installation is the reverse of the removal procedure.
7. Tighten the retaining bolt(s) to 9 ft. lbs. (12 Nm).

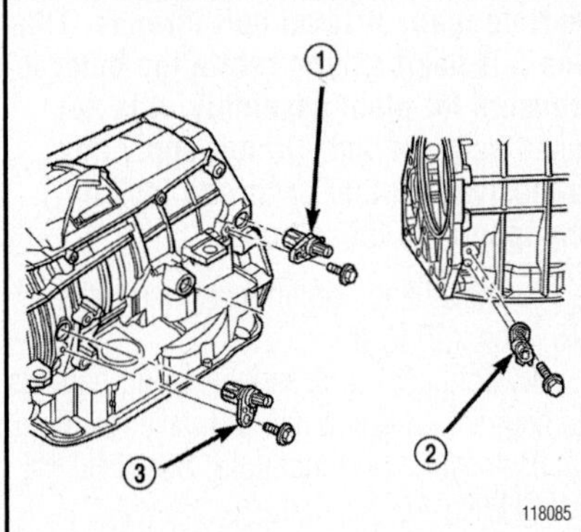

Fig. 123 Showing the location of the output speed sensor (1), transmission line pressure sensor (2), and the input speed sensor (3)

FUEL SYSTEM SERVICE PRECAUTIONS

Safety is the most important factor when performing not only fuel system maintenance but any type of maintenance. Failure to conduct maintenance and repairs in a safe manner may result in serious personal injury or death. Maintenance and testing of the vehicle's fuel system components can be accomplished safely and effectively by adhering to the following rules and guidelines.

- To avoid the possibility of fire and personal injury, always disconnect the negative battery cable unless the repair or test procedure requires that battery voltage be applied.
- Always relieve the fuel system pressure prior to disconnecting any fuel system component (injector, fuel rail, pressure regulator, etc.), fitting or fuel line connection. Exercise extreme caution whenever relieving fuel system pressure to avoid exposing skin, face and eyes to fuel spray. Please be advised that fuel under pressure may penetrate the skin or any part of the body that it contacts.
- Always place a shop towel or cloth around the fitting or connection prior to loosening to absorb any excess fuel due to spillage. Ensure that all fuel spillage (should it occur) is quickly removed from engine surfaces. Ensure that all fuel soaked cloths or towels are deposited into a suitable waste container.
- Always keep a dry chemical (Class B) fire extinguisher near the work area.
- Do not allow fuel spray or fuel vapors to come into contact with a spark or open flame.
- Always use a back-up wrench when loosening and tightening fuel line connection fittings. This will prevent unnecessary stress and torsion to fuel line piping.
- Always replace worn fuel fitting O-rings with new Do not substitute fuel hose or equivalent where fuel pipe is installed.

Before servicing the vehicle, make sure to also refer to the precautions in the beginning of this section as well.

RELIEVING FUEL SYSTEM PRESSURE

See Figures 124 and 125.

➡Use this procedure whether or not the fuel rail is equipped with a fuel pressure test port.

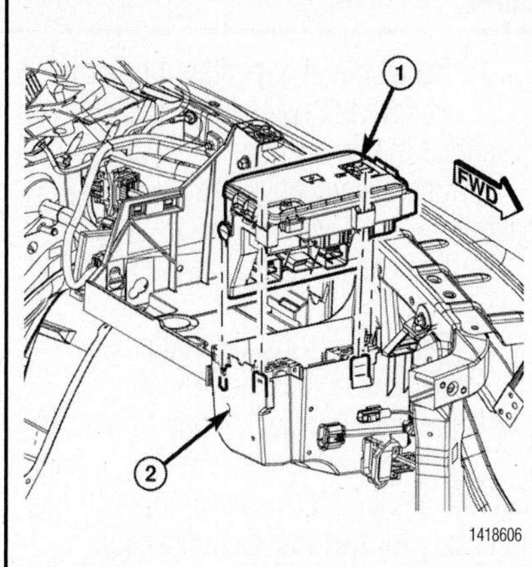

Fig. 124 Showing the TIPM cover (1) and housing (2)

➡A separate fuel pump relay is no longer used. A circuit within the Totally Integrated Power Module (TIPM) is used to control the electric fuel pump located within the fuel pump module. The TIPM is located in the engine compartment in front of the battery.

1. Remove the fuel fill cap.
2. Remove the TIPM cover from the TIPM housing base.
3. Remove fuse M22 from the TIPM.
4. Start and run the engine until it stalls.
5. Attempt restarting the engine until it will no longer start.
6. Turn the ignition key to the OFF position.

➡Excessive fuel spillage onto the gaskets can cause gaskets to expand and dislodge from gasket groove.

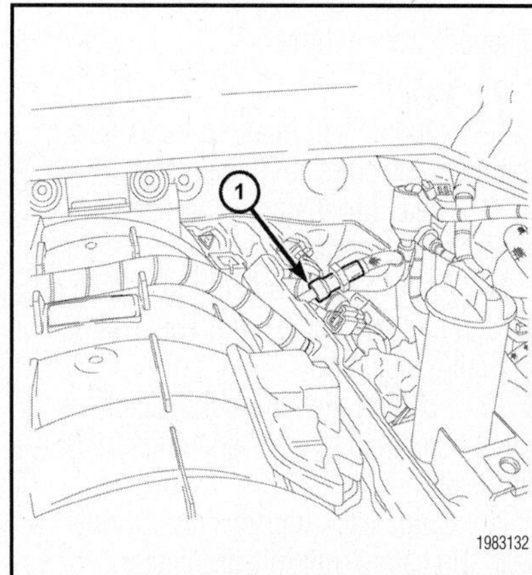

Fig. 125 Disconnect the fuel line quick-connect fitting (1) at the fuel rail and plug with a shipping cap to prevent spillage.

7. Place a rag or towel below the fuel line quick-connect fitting at the fuel rail.
8. Disconnect the fuel line quick-connect fitting at the fuel rail and plug with a shipping cap to prevent spillage.

➡One or more Diagnostic Trouble Codes (DTC's) may have been stored in the PCM memory due to disconnecting fuel pump module circuit. A diagnostic scan tool must be used to erase a DTC.

FUEL INJECTORS

REMOVAL & INSTALLATION

1. Remove the fuel rail assembly. See "Fuel Rail" in this section.
2. Using suitable pliers, remove the fuel injector retaining clip.
3. Remove the fuel injector from the fuel rail, using a side to side motion while pulling the injector out of the fuel rail assembly.
4. Installation is the reverse of the removal procedure.

FUEL PUMP

REMOVAL & INSTALLATION

See Figure 126.

1. Perform the fuel system pressure release procedure.
2. Disconnect and isolate the negative battery cable.
3. Remove the fuel tank. See "Fuel Tank" in this section.
4. Prior to removing the fuel pump module, use compressed air to remove any accumulated dirt and debris from around fuel tank opening.

➡An indexing arrow is located on top of the main fuel pump module to indicate the position into the fuel tank. Note the location for reassembly.

5. Position the lock ring remover/installer (9340 or equivalent) into the notches on the outside edge of the lock ring.
6. Install a 1/2 inch drive breaker bar into the lock ring remover/installer.
7. Rotate the breaker bar counterclockwise and remove the lock ring.
8. Remove the fuel pump module from the fuel tank. Be careful not to bend float arm during removal.
9. Remove and discard the rubber O-ring seal.

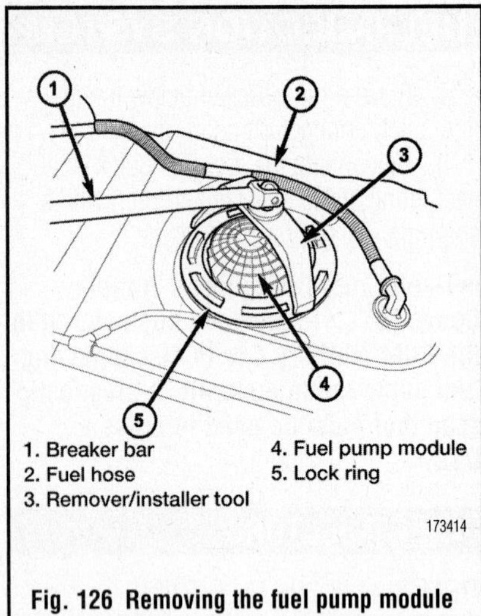

Fig. 126 Removing the fuel pump module

To install:

10. Using a new rubber O-ring seal, position the fuel pump module into the fuel tank opening.
11. Position the lock ring over top of the fuel pump module.
12. Rotate the fuel pump module until the embossed alignment arrow points to the center alignment mark or the same position as noted during removal. This step must be performed to prevent the float from contacting the side of the fuel tank.
13. Install the lock ring remover/installer into the notches on the outside edge of the lock ring.
14. Install a 1/2 inch drive breaker bar into the lock ring remover/installer.
15. Rotate the breaker bar clockwise until all seven notches of the lock ring have engaged.
16. Install the fuel tank. See "Fuel Tank" in this section.
17. Connect the fuel line quick-connect fitting at the fuel rail.
18. Connect the negative battery cable.
19. Fill the fuel tank.
20. Start the engine and check for leaks at all fuel tank connections.

FUEL RAIL

REMOVAL & INSTALLATION

3.7L & 4.7L

CAUTION

The left and right fuel rails are replaced as an assembly. Do not attempt to separate rail halves at connector tubes . Due to design of tubes, it does not use any clamps. Never attempt to install a clamping device of any kind to tubes. When removing fuel rail assembly for any reason, be careful not to bend or kink tubes.

1. Remove fuel tank filler tube cap.
2. Relieve the fuel system pressure, as described in this section.
3. Remove negative battery cable at battery.
4. Remove air duct at throttle body air box.
5. Remove air box at throttle body.
6. Remove air resonator mounting bracket at front of throttle body (2 bolts).
7. Disconnect fuel line latch clip and fuel line at fuel rail. A special tool will be necessary for fuel line disconnection.
8. Remove necessary vacuum lines at throttle body.
9. Disconnect electrical connectors at all 6 fuel injectors.
   a. To remove connector, push red colored slider away from injector.
   b. While pushing slider, depress tab and remove connector from injector.

➡The factory fuel injection wiring harness is numerically tagged (INJ 1, INJ 2, etc.) for injector position identification. If harness is not tagged, note wiring location before removal.

10. Disconnect electrical connectors at all throttle body sensors.
11. Remove 6 ignition coils.
12. Remove 4 fuel rail mounting bolts.
13. Gently rock and pull left side of fuel rail until fuel injectors just start to clear machined holes in cylinder head. Gently rock and pull right side of rail until injectors just start to clear cylinder head holes.
14. Repeat this procedure (left/right) until all injectors have cleared cylinder head holes.
15. Remove fuel rail (with injectors attached) from engine.

To install:

16. If fuel injectors are to be installed, see "Fuel Injectors" in this section.
17. Clean out fuel injector machined bores in intake manifold.
18. Apply a small amount of engine oil to each fuel injector O-ring. This will help in fuel rail installation.
19. Position fuel rail/fuel injector assembly to machined injector openings in cylinder head.
20. Guide each injector into cylinder head. Be careful not to tear injector O-rings.
21. Push right side of fuel rail down until fuel injectors have bottomed on cylinder head shoulder. Push left fuel rail down until injectors have bottomed on cylinder head shoulder.
22. Install 4 fuel rail mounting bolts and tighten to 100 inch lbs. (11 Nm).
23. Install 6 ignition coils. See "ENGINE ELECTRICAL" section.
24. Connect electrical connectors to throttle body.
25. Connect electrical connectors at all fuel injectors. To install connector, refer to . Push connector onto injector and then push and lock red colored slider. Verify connector is locked to injector by lightly tugging on connector.
26. Connect necessary vacuum lines to throttle body.
27. Install air resonator mounting bracket near front of throttle body (2 bolts).
28. Connect fuel line latch clip and fuel line to fuel rail.
29. Install air box to throttle body.
30. Install air duct to air box.
31. Connect battery cable to battery.
32. Start engine and check for leaks.

5.7L

1. Perform the fuel system pressure release procedure.
2. Remove the negative battery cable.
3. Disconnect the IAT sensor electrical connector.
4. Remove the clean air tube from the air cleaner housing and the throttle body.

➡The front grommets are a ball stud type mount and the rear grommets are a sliding peg design.

5. Lift up the front of the engine cover and separate the engine cover front grommets from the ball studs on the intake manifold.
6. Slightly raise the front of the engine cover and slide forward to remove the rear engine cover pegs from the grommets located on the rear of the intake manifold and remove the engine cover.

CAUTION

The left and right fuel rails are replaced as an assembly. Do not attempt to separate the fuel rail halves at the connector tube. Due to the design of the connector tube, it does not use any clamps. Never attempt to install a clamping device of any kind to the connector tube. When removing the fuel rail assembly for any reason, be careful not to bend or kink the connector tube.

➡The factory fuel injection electrical harness is numerically tagged (INJ 1,

INJ 2, etc.) for injector position identification. If the electrical harness is not tagged, note the injector position before electrical harness removal.

7. Disconnect the electrical connectors at all eight fuel injectors. Push the red colored slider away from the injector while pushing slider, depress tab and remove the electrical connector from the injector.
8. Disconnect the PCV hose and position aside to gain access to the fuel rail.
9. Disconnect the fuel line quick connect fitting at the fuel rail.
10. Disconnect the make up air hose and position aside to gain access to the fuel rail.
11. Remove the four fuel rail mounting bolts from both the left and right fuel rails.
12. Using a side to side motion, gently rock the left fuel rail while pulling up until all four left side fuel injectors just start to clear the machined holes in the intake manifold.
13. Using a side to side motion, gently rock the right fuel rail while pulling up until all four right side fuel injectors just start to clear the machined holes in the intake manifold.

➡Make sure the O-rings are still attached to the fuel injectors during removal.

14. Remove the left and right fuel rails (with injectors attached) as an assembly from the engine.

To install:

See Figure 127.

15. If the fuel injectors are to be installed into the fuel rail.
16. Clean out the fuel injector machined holes in the intake manifold.

➡If the same fuel injectors are to be reinstalled, install new O-rings.

17. Apply a small amount of engine oil to each fuel injector O-ring. This will help in the fuel rail installation.
18. Position the fuel rail assembly while aligning the injectors into the machined holes in the intake manifold.
19. Guide each injector into the intake manifold using care not to tear the injector O-rings.
20. Using a side to side motion, gently rock the left fuel rail while pushing down until all four left side fuel injectors have completely seated into the machined holes in the intake manifold.
21. Using a side to side motion, gently rock the right fuel rail while pushing down until all four right side fuel injectors have completely seated into the machined holes in the intake manifold.

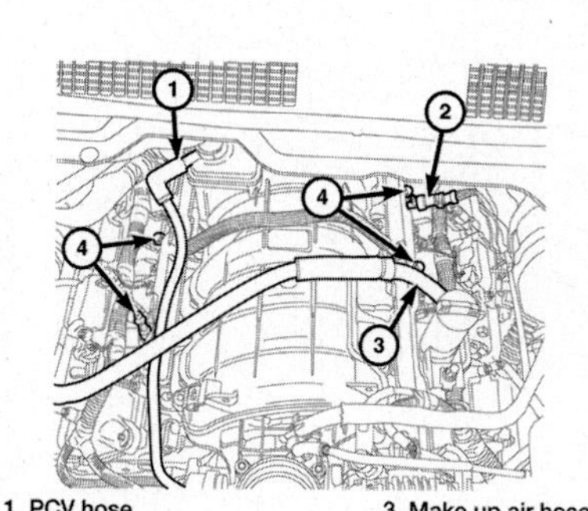

1. PCV hose
2. Quick connect fitting to fuel rail
3. Make up air hose
4. Fuel rail bolts

2256643

Fig. 127 Showing locations of fuel rail mounting bolts, make up air hose, fuel line fitting and PCV hose

22. Install the four fuel rail mounting bolts and tighten to 8 ft. lbs. (11 Nm).
23. Connect the make up air hose.
24. Connect the fuel line quick connect fitting to the fuel rail.
25. Connect the PCV hose.
26. Connect the electrical connectors to all eight fuel injectors. Push the connector onto the injector and then push and lock the red colored slider. Verify the connector is locked to the injector by lightly tugging on the connector.
27. Slightly tilt the rear of the engine cover and slide the rear engine cover pegs into the grommets on the rear of the intake manifold until the cover stops.

➡While installing the engine cover, the front ball studs will make a popping or suction sound as the ball studs are inserted into the front grommets.

28. Lower the front of the engine cover and line up the front ball studs with the grommets on the front of the intake manifold and with a downward motion push the engine cover front grommets onto the ball studs.
29. Lightly lift the front of the engine cover to insure the front the front grommets are seated onto the ball studs correctly.
30. Check to insure the engine cover is installed properly by reaching behind the left side of the cover to verify that the pegs are located in the grommets.
31. Install the clean air tube onto the air cleaner housing and the throttle body.
32. Connect the IAT sensor electrical connector.
33. Connect the negative battery cable.
34. Start the engine and check for leaks.

FUEL TANK

DRAINING

➡Due to a one-way check valve installed into the fuel fill fitting at the tank, the tank cannot be drained at the fuel fill cap.

1. Perform the fuel system pressure release procedure. See "Relieving Fuel System Pressure" in this section.
2. Disconnect the fuel supply line from the fuel rail.

➡Tool number 8978-2 is used on 5/16" fuel lines while tool number 8531-1 is used on 3/8" fuel lines.

3. Install the appropriate fuel line adapter fitting from the Decay Tool, Fuel 8978A (or equivalent) to the fuel supply line. Route the opposite end of this hose to an OSHA approved fuel storage tank such as the John Dow Gas Caddy 320-FC-P30-A or equivalent.
4. Using a diagnostic scan tool, activate the fuel pump until the fuel tank has been evacuated.

Alternative Procedure

➡If the electric fuel pump is not operating, the fuel tank must be removed and drained through the fuel pump module opening of the fuel tank.

1. Perform the fuel system pressure release procedure. See "Relieving Fuel System Pressure" in this section.
2. Disconnect and isolate the negative battery cable.
3. Raise and support the vehicle.
4. Remove the fuel tank. See "Fuel Tank" in this section.
5. Remove the fuel pump module. See "Fuel Pump" in this section.
6. Position a 3/8" hose into the fuel pump module opening of the fuel tank.
7. Attach the opposite end of this hose to the Fuel Chief Gas Caddy 320-FC-P30-A or an OSHA approved gas caddy.
8. Using the gas caddy, evacuate the fuel tank.

REMOVAL & INSTALLATION

See Figure 128.

1. Perform the fuel system pressure release procedure. See "Relieving Fuel System Pressure" in this section.
2. Disconnect and isolate the negative battery cable.

Raise and support vehicle.

3. Perform the fuel tank draining procedure.

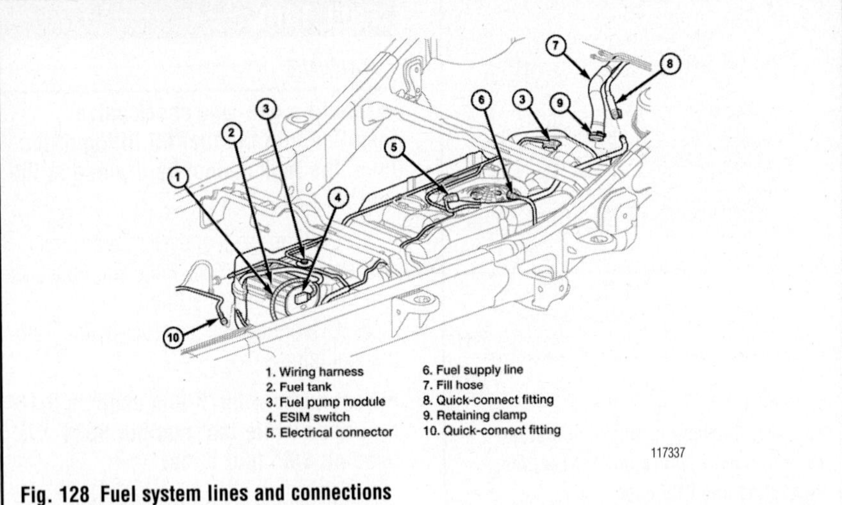

Fig. 128 Fuel system lines and connections

4. Disconnect the electrical connector from ESIM switch.
5. Disconnect the quick-connect fitting at the front of the fuel tank.
6. Disconnect the quick-connect fitting at the rear of the fuel tank.
7. Loosen the fill hose retaining clamp at the rear of the fuel tank and disconnect the fill hose.
8. Using a suitable hydraulic jack with a fuel tank adapter, support the fuel tank.
9. Remove the two fuel tank support strap retaining nuts and remove both fuel tank support straps.
10. Carefully lower the fuel tank a few inches and disconnect the fuel pump module electrical connector.
11. Disconnect the fuel line quick-connect fitting at the fuel pump module.
12. Lower the fuel tank and remove from hydraulic jack.
13. If fuel pump module removal is necessary, see "Fuel Pump" in this section.

To install:

14. If fuel pump module installation is necessary, see "Fuel Pump" in this section.
15. Secure the fuel tank onto a suitable hydraulic jack with a fuel tank adapter.
16. Raise and position the fuel tank leaving room to make the connections at the top of the fuel tank.
17. Connect the fuel supply line to the fuel pump module.
18. Connect the electrical connector to the fuel pump module.
19. Raise the fuel tank until snug to the body.
20. Install the fuel tank straps. Install the strap nuts and tighten to 30 ft. lbs. (41 Nm).
21. Remove the hydraulic jack.
22. Connect the electrical connector to the ESIM switch.
23. Connect the quick connect fitting at the front of the fuel tank.
24. Connect the quick-connect fitting at the rear of the fuel tank.
25. Connect the fill hose at the rear of the fuel tank and securely tighten the fill hose retaining clamp.
26. Connect the fuel line quick-connect fitting at the fuel rail.
27. Connect the negative battery cable.
28. Fill the fuel tank.
29. Start the engine and check for leaks at all fuel tank connections.

IDLE SPEED

ADJUSTMENT

➡Idle speed is computer-controlled and therefore no adjustment is required.

THROTTLE BODY

REMOVAL & INSTALLATION

1. Using a diagnostic scan tool, record any previous DTC's (Diagnostic Trouble Codes).

⁂ CAUTION

Never have the ignition key in the ON position when checking the throttle body shaft for a binding condition. This may set DTC's.

➡A (factory adjusted) set screw is used to mechanically limit the position of the throttle body throttle plate. Never attempt to adjust the engine idle speed using this screw. All idle speed functions are controlled by the Powertrain Control Module (PCM).

2. Disconnect and isolate negative battery cable at battery.
3. Remove air intake tube at throttle body flange.
4. Disconnect throttle body electrical connector.
5. Disconnect necessary vacuum lines at throttle body.
6. Remove four throttle body mounting bolts.
7. Remove throttle body from intake manifold.
8. Check condition of old throttle body-to-intake manifold O-ring.
9. Installation is the reverse of the removal procedure.
10. Using the diagnostic scan tool, erase all previous DTC's and perform the ETC Relearn function.

HEATING & AIR CONDITIONING SYSTEM

BLOWER MOTOR

REMOVAL & INSTALLATION

1. Disconnect and isolate the negative battery cable.
2. Disconnect the HVAC wire harness lead from the blower motor.
3. Remove the three screws that secure the blower motor to the bottom of the HVAC housing and remove the blower motor.
4. Installation is the reverse of the removal procedure.

HEATER CORE

REMOVAL & INSTALLATION

See Figures 129 and 130.

1. Remove the HVAC housing and place it on a workbench. See "HVAC Module" in this section.
2. Remove the foam seal from the flange.
3. Remove the two screws that secure the flange to the front of the HVAC housing.
4. Carefully disengage the retaining tab that secures the flange to the HVAC housing and remove the flange.
5. Carefully pull the heater core out of the front of the HVAC housing.
6. Inspect all foam seals and replace as required.

To install:

7. Inspect the foam seals on the heater core and replace as required.
8. Carefully install the heater core into the front of the HVAC housing.
9. Position the flange onto the front of the HVAC housing. Make sure the retaining tab is fully engaged.

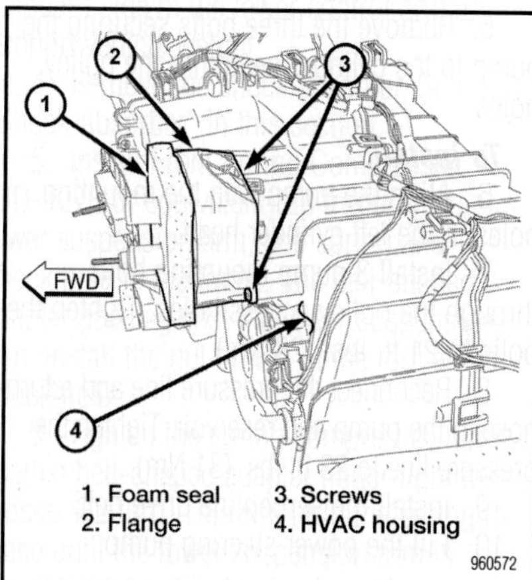

Fig. 129 Removing foam seal and flange from HVAC housing.

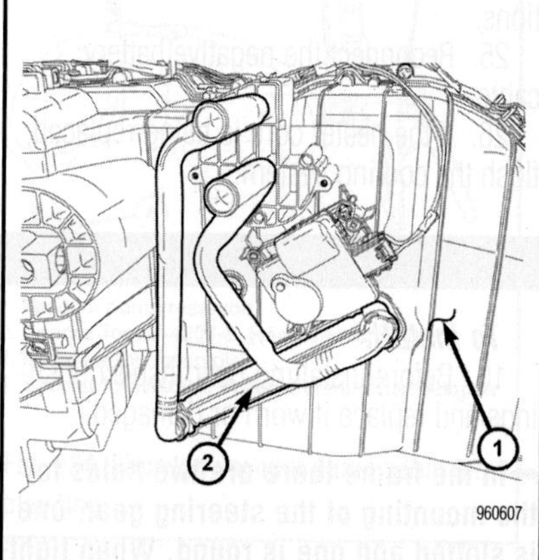

Fig. 130 Removing the heater core (2) from the HVAC housing (1)

10. Install the two screws that secure the flange to the HVAC housing. Tighten the screws snugly.
11. Install the foam seal onto the flange.

➡**If the heater core is being replaced, flush the cooling system.**

12. Install the HVAC housing. See "HVAC Module" in this section.

HVAC MODULE

REMOVAL & INSTALLATION

See Figure 131.

➡**This procedure requires removal of the instrument panel. If not equipped to perform this operation, refer the vehicle to a proper repair facility.**

1. Properly disable the air bag system before beginning work. See "AIR BAG (SUPPLEMENTAL RESTRAINT SYSTEM)" section.
2. Disconnect and isolate the negative battery cable.
3. Recover the refrigerant from the refrigerant system.
4. Drain the engine cooling system.
5. Disconnect the A/C liquid line and the A/C suction line from the A/C expansion valve.
6. Disconnect the heater hoses from the heater core tubes at the firewall.
7. If required, remove the Powertrain Control Module (PCM) to gain access to the two nuts that secure the HVAC housing to the engine compartment side of the dash panel.
8. Remove the two nuts from the studs that secure the HVAC housing to the engine compartment side of the dash panel.
9. If equipped with center floor console, remove the floor console duct.
10. Remove the instrument panel from the passenger compartment.
11. If equipped, remove the rear floor ducts.
12. Remove the bolt that secures the HVAC housing to the floor bracket.
13. Remove the two nuts that secure the HVAC housing to the passenger compartment side of the dash panel.
14. Pull the HVAC housing assembly rearward and remove the housing assembly from the passenger compartment.

To install:

CAUTION

Be certain to adjust the refrigerant oil level when servicing the A/C refrigerant system. Failure to properly adjust the refrigerant oil level will prevent the A/C system from operating as designed and can cause serious A/C compressor damage.

15. Position the HVAC housing assembly into the passenger compartment and over the studs on the dash panel, with the condensate drain tube in its proper location.
16. Install the two nuts that secure the HVAC housing to the passenger compartment side of the dash panel. Tighten the nuts to 60 inch lbs. (7 Nm).
17. Install the bolt that secures the HVAC housing to the floor bracket. Tighten the bolt to 60 inch lbs. (7 Nm).
18. If equipped, install the rear floor ducts.
19. Install the instrument panel assembly.
20. If equipped with center floor console, install the floor console duct.

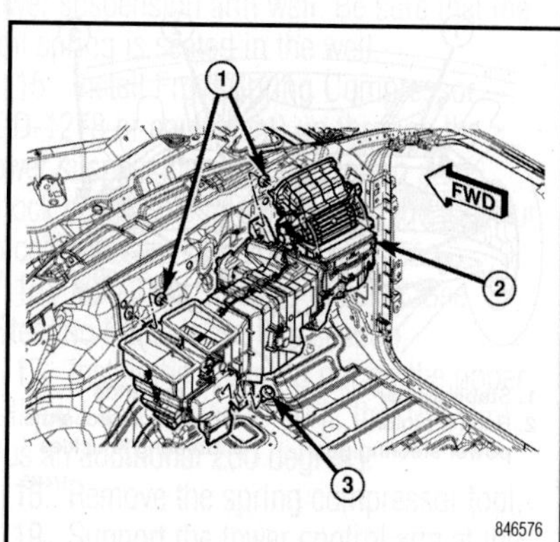

Fig. 131 Removing retaining nuts and bolts (1, 3) to remove HVAC module (2)

21. Install the two nuts onto the two studs that secure the HVAC housing to the engine compartment side of the dash panel. Tighten the nuts to 60 inch lbs. (7 Nm).

22. If removed, install the powertrain control module (PCM).

23. Connect the heater hoses to the heater core tubes.

24. Connect the A/C liquid line and the A/C suction line to the A/C expansion valve, using new O-ring seals at all connections.

25. Reconnect the negative battery cable.

26. If the heater core is being replaced, flush the cooling system.

27. Refill the engine cooling system.

28. Evacuate the refrigerant system.

29. Charge the refrigerant system, including adding refrigerant oil as required.

30. Initiate the "Actuator Calibration" function using a scan tool.

STEERING

POWER STEERING GEAR

REMOVAL & INSTALLATION

See Figure 132.

➡The steering column on vehicles with an automatic transmission may not be equipped with an internal locking shaft that allows the ignition key cylinder to be locked with the key. Alternative methods of locking the steering wheel for service will have to be used.

1. Lock the steering wheel.
2. Drain and siphon the power steering fluid from the reservoir.
3. Raise and support the vehicle.
4. Remove and discard the steering coupler pinch bolt.
5. Disconnect the power steering hoses from the rack and pinion. Plug openings to prevent contamination.
6. Remove the front tires and wheels.
7. Remove the outer tie rod nuts and separate outer tie rods from the knuckles, using Ball Joint Remover (8677 or equivalent).
8. If equipped, remove the skid plate.
9. Remove the rack and pinion mounting bolts and remove the rack from the vehicle.

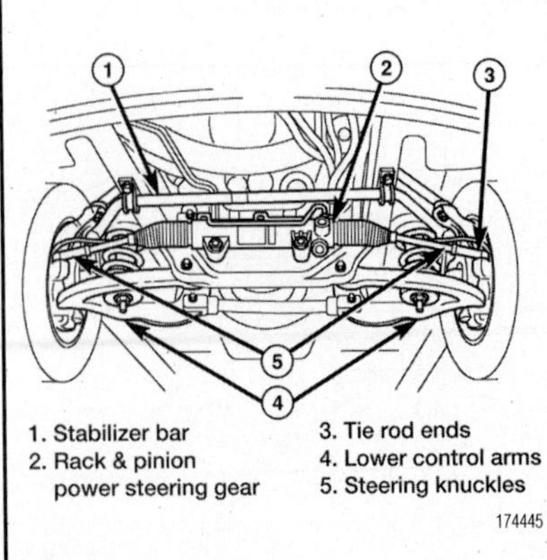

Fig. 132 Showing the steering gear mounting

To install:

10. Before installing gear inspect bushings and replace if worn or damaged.

➡In the frame there are two holes for the mounting of the steering gear, one is slotted and one is round. When tightening the gear to specifications make sure to tighten the mounting bolt with the hole first to avoid movement of the steering gear.

11. Position the rack and pinion to the front crossmember.
12. Install the retaining bolts. Tighten the bolts to 235 ft. lbs. (319 Nm).
13. Slide the shaft coupler onto the gear and install a new pinch bolt. Tighten the pinch bolt to 36 ft. lbs. (49 Nm).
14. Clean and dry the tie rod end studs and the tapers in the knuckles.
15. Install the tie rod ends into the steering knuckles. Install and tighten the retaining nuts to 45 ft. lbs. (61 Nm), then turn an additional 90 degrees.
16. Connect the pressure power steering hose to the steering gear and tighten to 23 ft. lbs. (32 Nm).
17. Connect the return power steering hose to the steering gear and tighten to 37 ft. lbs. (50 Nm).
18. If equipped, install the front skid plate.
19. Install the front tires and wheels.
20. Lower the vehicle.
21. Fill the power steering system with fluid.
22. Adjust the toe alignment.

POWER STEERING PUMP

REMOVAL & INSTALLATION

See Figure 133.

1. Drain and siphon the power steering fluid from the reservoir.
2. Remove the serpentine belt.

⁂ CAUTION

Do not remove the high pressure hose fitting on the pump. The fitting may come loose unless it is backed up using another wrench. If the fitting does come loose, it must be retightened to 40–50 ft. lbs. (57–67 Nm) before continuing. If this fitting comes out of the pump body, the internal spring and valve parts will fall out of the pump and they cannot be reinstalled properly. If this occurs the pump needs to be replaced with a new pump.

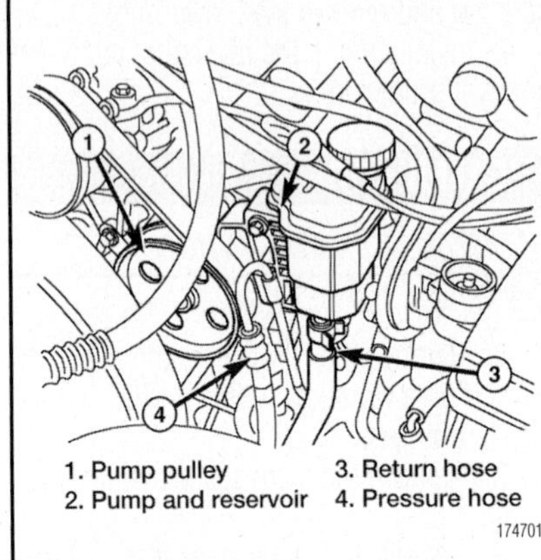

Fig. 133 Locating the power steering pump and components

3. Disconnect the return hose.
4. Disconnect the pressure hose.
5. Remove the three bolts securing the pump to the cylinder head thru the pulley holes.

To install:

6. Align the pump with the mounting holes in the left cylinder head.
7. Install 3 pump mounting bolts through the pulley access holes. Tighten the bolts to 21 ft. lbs. (28 Nm).
8. Reconnect the pressure line and return hose to the pump and reservoir. Tighten the pressure line to 23 ft. lbs. (31 Nm).
9. Install the serpentine drive belt.
10. Fill the power steering pump.

BLEEDING

See Figure 134.

CAUTION

Mopar Power Steering Fluid + 4 or Mopar ATF+4 Automatic Transmission Fluid is to be used in the power steering system. Both Fluids have the same material standard specifications (MS-9602). No other power steering or automatic transmission fluid is to be used in the system. Damage may result to the power steering pump and system if another fluid is used. Do not overfill the system.

CAUTION

If the air is not purged from the power steering system correctly, pump failure could result.

➡Be sure the vacuum tool used in the following procedure is clean and free of any fluids.

1. Check the fluid level. As measured on the side of the reservoir, the level should indicate between MAX and MIN when the fluid is at normal ambient temperature. Adjust the fluid level as necessary.
2. Tightly insert P/S Cap Adapter (9688A or equivalent) into the mouth of the reservoir.

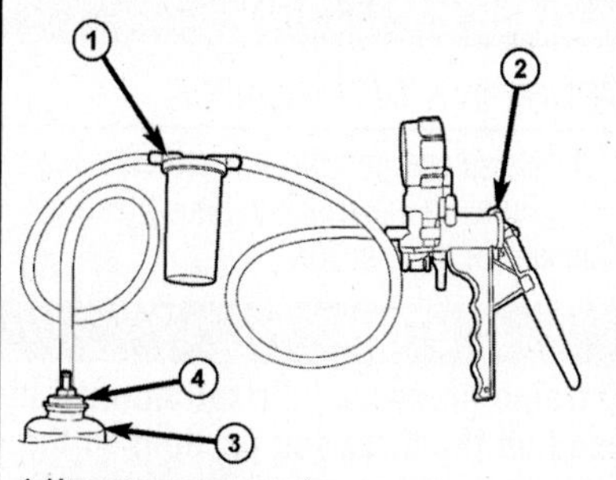

Fig. 134 Showing vacuum pump setup for bleeding

CAUTION

Failure to use a vacuum pump reservoir may allow power steering fluid to be sucked into the hand vacuum pump.

3. Attach Hand Vacuum Pump (C-4207-A or equivalent), with reservoir attached, to the P/S Cap Adapter.

CAUTION

Do not run the vehicle while vacuum is applied to the power steering system. Damage to the power steering pump can occur.

➡When performing the following step make sure the vacuum level is maintained during the entire time period.

4. Using Hand Vacuum Pump, apply 20–25 in. Hg of vacuum to the system for a minimum of three minutes.
5. Slowly release the vacuum and remove the special tools.
6. Adjust the fluid level as necessary.
7. Repeat the previous steps until the fluid no longer drops when vacuum is applied.
8. Start the engine and cycle the steering wheel lock-to-lock three times. Do not hold the steering wheel at the stops.
9. Stop the engine and check for leaks at all connections.
10. Check for any signs of air in the reservoir and check the fluid level. If air is present, repeat the procedure as necessary.

SUSPENSION

FRONT SUSPENSION

COIL SPRING

REMOVAL & INSTALLATION

4X2

See Figure 135.

1. Raise and support vehicle.
2. Remove the front wheel and tire assembly.
3. Support the lower control arm at the outboard side of the lower control arm to support vehicle weight.
4. Remove the shock absorber. See "Shock Absorber" in this section.
5. Install Front Spring Compressor (DD-1278 or equivalent) up through the lower suspension arm, coil spring and shock hole in the frame. The bell-shaped adapter goes against the lower suspension arm. Install the nut on top of the tool at the shock hole.
6. Tighten the spring compressor nut against bell-shaped adapter finger tight then loosen 1/2 turn. This will hold the spring in place until the lower suspension arm is separated from the steering knuckle.
7. Remove the steering knuckle. See "Steering Knuckle" in this section.
8. Remove the stabilizer link. See "Stabilizer Bar Link" in this section.
9. Remove the lower control arm support.
10. Tighten the spring compressor tool to collapse the coil spring.

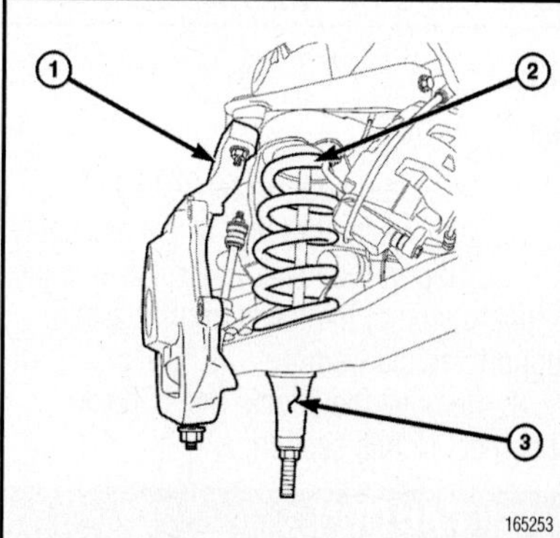

Fig. 135 Install Front Spring Compressor (DD-1278 or equivalent) (3) up through the lower suspension arm, coil spring (2) and shock hole in the frame. The bell-shaped adapter (3) goes against the lower suspension arm. Install the nut on top of the tool at the shock hole. Also showing brake caliper adapter (1).

➡It may necessary to loosen the control arm pivot bolt to allow downward swing.

11. Loosen the tension on the spring compressor tool slowly allowing the lower suspension arm to pivot downward.
12. Remove the spring compressor tool.
13. Remove coil spring and isolator pad from the vehicle.

To install:

14. Tape the isolator pad to the top of the coil spring. Position the spring in the lower suspension arm well. Be sure that the coil spring is seated in the well.
15. Install Front Spring Compressor (DD-1278 or equivalent) up through the lower suspension arm, coil spring and shock hole in the frame. Tighten the tool nut to compress the coil spring.
16. Install the steering knuckle. See "Steering Knuckle" in this section.
17. Install the retaining nut on the upper ball joint and tighten to 40 ft. lbs. (54 Nm), plus an additional 200 degrees.
18. Remove the spring compressor tool.
19. Support the lower control arm at the outboard side of the lower control arm to support vehicle weight.

20. Install the shock absorber. See "Shock Absorber" in this section.
21. Install the stabilizer link. See "Stabilizer Bar Link" in this section.
22. Remove the lower control arm support.
23. Install the wheel and tire assembly.
24. Remove the support and lower the vehicle to the floor with vehicle weight. Tighten the front and rear control arm frame pivot bolts if loosened to:
    - Lower control arm to frame nuts: 155 ft. lbs. (210 Nm)
    - Upper control arm to frame nuts: 130 ft. lbs. (176 Nm)
25. Perform a wheel alignment

4X4

1. Remove the shock. See "Shock Absorber" in this section.
2. Place the spring-over-shock assembly in the Branick 7200 (or equivalent) Spring Removal/Installation tool. Compress the spring.
3. Position Strut Nut Wrench (9362 or equivalent), on shock shaft retaining nut. Next, insert 8 mm socket though Wrench onto hex located on end of shock shaft. While holding shock shaft from turning, remove nut from shock shaft using the wrench.
4. Remove the upper shock nut.
5. Remove the shock upper mounting plate.
6. Remove the dust cover.
7. Remove and inspect the upper spring isolator.
8. Remove the shock absorber from the coil spring.

To install:

9. Position the shock into the coil spring.
10. Install the upper isolator.
11. Install the dust cover.
12. Install the upper shock mounting plate.
13. Install the shock upper mounting nut.
14. Install Strut Nut Wrench (9362 or equivalent) on end of a torque wrench and then on the shock shaft retaining nut. Next, insert 8 mm socket though Wrench onto hex located on end of shock shaft. While holding shock shaft from turning, tighten nut to 45 ft. lbs. (61 Nm).
15. Decompress the spring.
16. Remove the shock assembly from the spring compressor tool.
17. Install the shock assembly. See "Shock Absorber" in this section.

LOWER BALL JOINT

REMOVAL & INSTALLATION

1. Raise and support the vehicle.
2. Remove the knuckle. See "Steering Knuckle" in this section.

CAUTION

Extreme pressure lubrication must be used on the threaded portions of the tool. This will increase the longevity of the tool and insure proper operation during the removal and installation process.

3. Press the ball joint from the lower control arm using Ball Joint Press (C-4212F or equivalent), Remover/Installer Driver (8836-6 or equivalent) and Ball Joint Remover/Installer Receiver (8698-2 or equivalent).
4. Remove ball joint from the lower control arm.

To install:

5. Install the ball joint into the control arm and press in, using Ball Joint Press, Ball Joint Remover/Installer Driver and Ball Joint Remover/Installer Receiver. Remove the tools.
6. Stake the ball joint flange in four evenly spaced places around the ball joint flange, using a punch and hammer.
7. Install the steering knuckle. See "Steering Knuckle" in this section.
8. Check the vehicle ride height.
9. Perform a wheel alignment.

LOWER CONTROL ARM

REMOVAL & INSTALLATION

4X2

See Figure 136.

1. Raise and support the vehicle.
2. Remove the tire and wheel assembly.
3. Support the lower control arm at the outboard side of the lower control arm to support vehicle weight.
4. Remove the shock. See "Shock Absorber" in this section.

CAUTION

Do not allow the caliper to hang freely, support the caliper assembly.

5. Remove the disc brake caliper adapter, then the brake rotor. See "BRAKES" section.
6. Remove the upper ball joint nut.
7. Install Front Spring Compressor (DD-1278 or equivalent) up through the lower control arm, coil spring and shock hole in the frame. The bell-shaped adapter goes against the lower control arm. Install the nut on top of the tool at the shock hole.

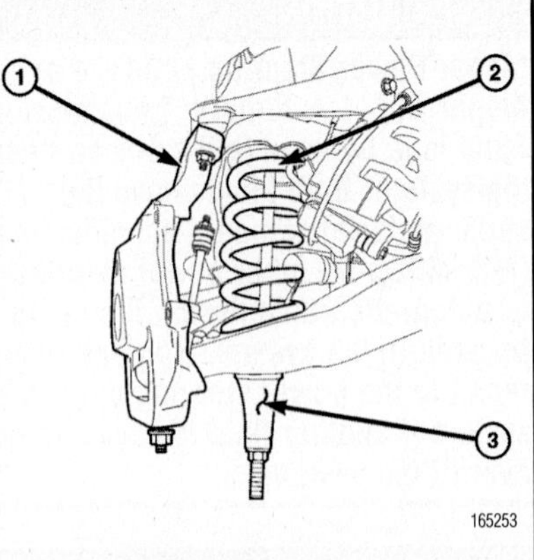

Fig. 136 Installing the front spring compressor (3) into the coil spring (2), next to the steering knuckle (1)

8. Tighten the spring compressor nut against bell-shaped adapter finger tight then loosen 1/2 turn to hold the spring in place.
9. Separate the upper ball joint from the knuckle, using Ball Joint Remover (9360 or equivalent).
10. Remove the knuckle from the vehicle.
11. Remove the lower stabilizer link nut.
12. Remove the lower ball joint nut at the steering knuckle.
13. Separate the ball joint from the knuckle using Ball Joint Remover (8677 or equivalent).

CAUTION

Do not allow the upper control arm to rebound downward, it must be supported.

14. Remove the lower control arm support.
15. Tighten the spring compressor tool to allow clearance for the lower ball joint to be removed out of the knuckle.
16. Loosen the tension on the spring compressor tool slowly allowing the lower control arm to pivot downward.
17. Remove the spring compressor tool.
18. Remove coil spring and isolator pad from the vehicle.
19. Remove the front and rear pivot bolts.
20. Remove the lower control arm.

To install:

21. Install the lower control arm into place on the vehicle.

22. Install the front and rear control arm pivot bolts finger tight.

23. Install the coil spring into the frame pocket.

24. Install the Spring Compressor (DD-1278 or equivalent) up through the lower suspension arm, coil spring and shock hole in the frame.

25. Tighten the tool nut to compress the coil spring.

26. Install the knuckle to the control arms. See "Steering Knuckle" in this section.

27. Position the lower ball joint into the steering knuckle.

28. Install the retaining nut on the lower ball joint and tighten to 38 ft. lbs. (51 Nm), plus an additional 90 degrees.

29. Position the upper ball joint to the knuckle.

30. Install the retaining nut on the upper ball joint and tighten to 40 ft. lbs. (54Nm), plus an additional 200 degrees.

31. Support the lower control arm at the outboard side of the lower control arm to support vehicle weight.

32. Remove the spring compressor tool.

33. Install the shock absorber. See "Shock Absorber" in this section.

34. Install the stabilizer link. See "Stabilizer Link" in this section.

35. Remove the lower control arm support.

36. Install the wheel and tire assembly and lower the vehicle.

37. Lower the vehicle to the floor with vehicle weight and tighten the front and rear control arm to frame nuts to:

- Lower control arm to frame nuts: 155 ft. lbs. (210 Nm)
- Upper control arm to frame nuts: 130 ft. lbs. (176 Nm)

38. Perform a wheel alignment.

4X4

1. Raise and support the vehicle.
2. Remove the wheel and tire assembly.
3. Remove half shaft nut from the shaft.

⁂ CAUTION

Never allow the disc brake caliper to hang from the brake hose. Damage to the brake hose will result. Provide a suitable support to hang the caliper securely.

4. Compress the disc brake caliper. Remove the caliper adapter bolts. Remove the disc brake caliper and the caliper adapter as an assembly. Remove the rotor from the hub/bearing. See "BRAKES" section.

5. Remove the wheel speed sensor wiring clips and disconnect the electrical connector.

6. Remove the upper ball joint nut. Separate the ball joint from the steering knuckle using Ball Joint Remover (9360 or equivalent).

7. Disengage inner C/V joint from axle shaft with two pry bars between the C/V housing and axle housing.

8. Remove the front halfshaft. See "DRIVE TRAIN" section.

9. Remove the shock absorber lower nut/bolt.

10. Remove the stabilizer bar link lower nut.

11. Using a suitable tie strap, support the knuckle. Remove the lower ball joint nut. Separate ball joint from the steering knuckle using Ball Joint Remover (8766 or equivalent).

12. Remove the two control arm pivot bolts and control arm from frame rail brackets.

To install:

13. Position the lower control arm at the frame rail brackets. Install the pivot bolts and nuts, and tighten the nuts finger-tight.

➡The ball joint stud taper must be CLEAN and DRY before installing the knuckle. Clean the stud taper with mineral spirits to remove dirt and grease.

14. Insert the lower ball joint stud into the steering knuckle. Install and tighten the retaining nut to 38 ft. lbs. (51 Nm), plus an additional 90 degrees.

15. Install shock absorber lower bolt/nut and tighten to 155 ft. lbs. (210 Nm).

16. Install the stabilizer bar link lower nut and tighten to 75ft. lbs. (102 Nm).

17. Install the front halfshaft to the axle by pushing the inner CV joint firmly to engage axle shaft snap ring into the inner CV housing.

18. Clean hub bearing bore, hub bearing mating surface and half shaft splines and apply a light coating of grease to the front axle shaft output splines.

19. Install half shaft into the knuckle.

20. Insert the upper ball joint into the steering knuckle.

21. Install and tighten the upper ball joint retaining nut to 40 ft. lbs. (54 Nm), plus an additional 200 degrees.

22. Tighten the lower control arm front pivot nut and rear pivot bolt to 130 ft. lbs. (176 Nm).

23. Install half shaft hub nut and tighten to 185ft. lbs. (251 Nm).

24. Install the wheel and tire assembly.

25. Remove the support and lower the vehicle.

26. Perform a wheel alignment.

SHOCK ABSORBER

REMOVAL & INSTALLATION

4X2

1. Raise and support vehicle.
2. Support the lower control arm outboard end.
3. Remove the upper shock absorber nut by using Strut Nut Wrench (9362 or equivalent), retainer and grommet. If necessary, insert 11/32 socket though Wrench onto hex located on end of shock shaft to prevent shaft from turning.
4. Remove the lower bolts and remove the shock absorber.

To install:

5. Install the lower retainer and grommet on the shock absorber stud. Insert the shock absorber through the frame bracket hole.
6. Install the lower bolts and tighten the bolts to 19 ft. lbs. (26 Nm).
7. Install the upper grommet, retainer and new nut or use Mopar Lock 'N Seal or Loctite 242 on existing nut, on the shock absorber stud. Using Strut Nut Wrench, tighten nut to 40 ft. lbs. (54 Nm).
8. Remove the support from the lower control arm outboard end.
9. Remove the support and lower the vehicle.

4X4

1. Raise and support the vehicle.
2. Remove the tire and wheel assembly.
3. Support the lower control arm outboard end.
4. Remove the three upper shock nuts.
5. Remove the lower shock bolt and nut.
6. Remove the caliper adapter with the caliper, then remove the rotor. See "BRAKES" section.
7. Disconnect the wheel speed sensor wiring from the knuckle and upper control arm.
8. Remove the upper ball joint retaining nut and separate the upper ball joint from the knuckle using Ball Joint Remover (9360 or equivalent).
9. Remove the stabilizer link lower nut.
10. Remove the axle hub nut.
11. Remove the shock assembly.

To install:

12. Install the shock back in place in the vehicle:

   a. Install the upper part of the shock into the frame bracket.

b. Install the upper nuts and tighten to 45 ft. lbs. (61 Nm).

c. Install the lower part of the shock into the lower control arm shock bushing.

d. Install and position bolt so head of bolt is facing rearward of vehicle and hand start nut. Tighten the bolt and nut to 155 ft. lbs. (210 Nm).

13. Install the upper ball joint to the knuckle and install the retaining nut and tighten to 40 ft. lbs. (54 Nm), plus an additional 200 degrees.

14. Install the axle hub nut and tighten to 185 ft. lbs. (251 Nm).

15. Install the stabilizer link lower nut and tighten to 75 ft. lbs. (102 Nm).

16. Reconnect the wheel speed sensor wiring to the knuckle and upper control arm.

17. Install the rotor and the caliper adapter with the caliper. See "BRAKES" section.

18. Remove the support from the lower control arm outboard end.

19. Install the tire and wheel assembly.

20. Remove the support and lower the vehicle.

STABILIZER BAR

REMOVAL & INSTALLATION

1. Remove the stabilizer bar link upper nuts and remove the retainers and grommets.

2. Remove the stabilizer bar mounting bolts and discard the mounting bolts.

3. Remove the retainers from the frame crossmember and remove the bar.

4. If necessary, remove the bushings from the stabilizer bar. Do not cut the old bushings off the stabilizer bar use a mixture of soapy water in order to aid in sliding the bushing off.

To install:

➡To service the stabilizer bar the vehicle must be on a drive on hoist. The vehicle suspension must be at curb height for stabilizer bar installation.

5. If the bushings were removed, Clean the bar and install the bushings on the stabilizer bar using a mixture of soapy water or equivalent in order to slide the bushing over the bar with ease. Do not cut the new bushing for installation.

6. Install new mounting bolts Do not reuse old bolts.

7. Check the alignment of the bar to ensure there is no interference with the either frame rail or chassis component. Spacing should be equal on both sides.

8. Position the stabilizer bar on the frame crossmember brackets and install the bracket bolts finger-tight.

9. Install the stabilizer bar to the stabilizer link and install the grommets and retainers.

10. Install the nuts to the stabilizer link and tighten to 20 ft. lbs. (27 Nm).

11. Tighten the brackets to the frame to 43 ft. lbs. (59 Nm).

STABILIZER BAR LINK

REMOVAL & INSTALLATION

See Figure 137.

➡It may be necessary to remove the other stabilizer link upper nut in order to remove the link being worked on from the vehicle.

1. Raise and support the vehicle.

2. Remove the lower nut.

3. Remove the upper nut, retainers and grommets.

4. Remove the stabilizer link from the vehicle.

To install:

5. Install the stabilizer link to the vehicle.

6. Install the lower nut and tighten to 75 ft. lbs. (102 Nm).

7. Install the retainers, grommets and upper nut and tighten to 20 ft. lbs. (27 Nm).

8. Remove the support and lower the vehicle.

STEERING KNUCKLE

REMOVAL & INSTALLATION

See Figure 138.

1. Raise and support the vehicle.

2. Remove the wheel and tire assembly.

3. Remove the ABS wheel speed sensor, disconnecting the electrical harness as necessary to remove knuckle.

4. Remove the tie rod end nut from the ball stud.

5. Separate the tie rod ball stud from the knuckle with Ball Joint Remover (9360 or equivalent).

6. Remove the halfshaft nut (4X4 only).

7. Remove the upper ball joint nut. Separate the ball joint from the knuckle with the Ball Joint Remover.

8. Support the outboard side of the lower control arm to support vehicle weight.

9. Remove the lower ball joint nut. Separate the ball joint from the knuckle with Ball Joint Remover (8677 or equivalent).

10. Remove the steering knuckle from the vehicle.

11. If required, remove the hub/bearing and dust shield from the knuckle.

12. Remove the three hub/bearing mounting bolts from the steering knuckle.

13. Slide the hub/bearing out of the steering knuckle.

14. Remove the brake dust shield.

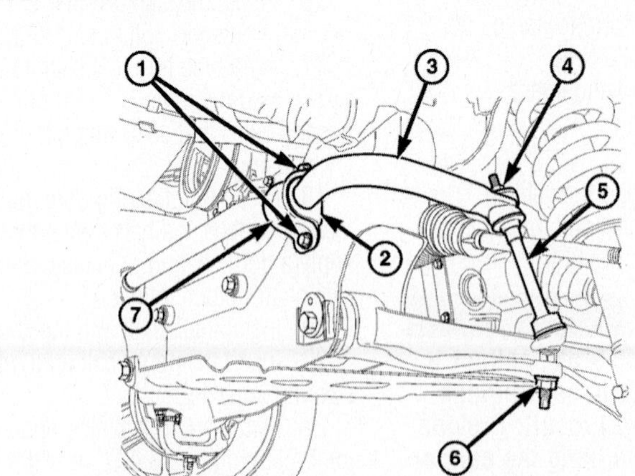

1. Stabilizer bar mounting nuts
2. Grommet
3. Stabilizer bar
4. Stabilizer bar link upper nut
5. Stabilizer bar link
6. Stabilizer bar link lower nut
7. Stabilizer bar retainer

165345

Fig. 137 Showing the stabilizer bar link

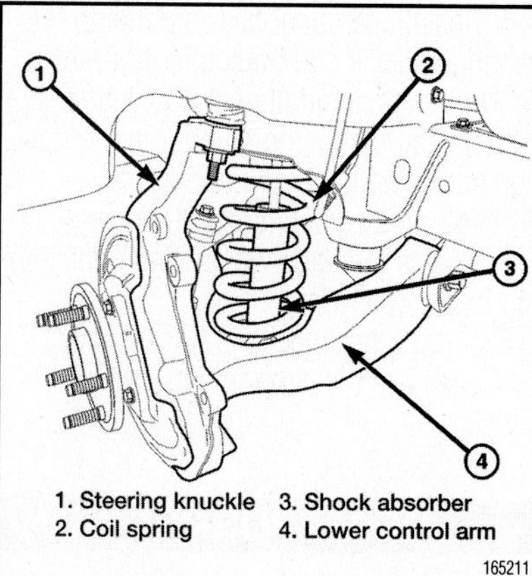

Fig. 138 Showing the steering knuckle installed

To install:

➡The ball joint stud tapers must be CLEAN and DRY before installing the knuckle. Clean the stud tapers with a clean cloth to remove dirt and grease.

15. Install the brake dust shield and hub and bearing to the steering knuckle, position the speed sensor opening towards the front of the vehicle, and tighten the 3 bolts to 120 ft. lbs. (163 Nm).
16. Install the knuckle onto the upper and lower ball joints.
17. Install the upper and lower ball joint nuts and tighten to:
    - Upper control arm ball joint nut: 40 ft. lbs. (54 Nm), plus an additional 200 degrees
    - Lower control arm ball joint nut: 38 ft. lbs. (51 Nm), plus an additional 90 degrees
18. Remove the hydraulic jack from the lower control arm.
19. If a new tie rod end is to be installed, make sure the boot is properly lubricated.
20. Clean all old grease and debris from the boot with a clean cloth.
21. Apply outer tie rod grease (68088623AA or equivalent) to the tie rod end boot.
22. Install the tie rod end and tighten the nut to 45 ft. lbs. (61 Nm), plus an additional 90 degrees.
23. Install the front halfshaft into the hub and bearing. Install the halfshaft nut (if equipped) and tighten to 185 ft. lbs. (251 Nm).
24. Install the ABS wheel speed sensor and the caliper. See "BRAKES" section.
25. Install the wheel and tire assembly.
26. Remove the support and lower the vehicle.
27. Perform a wheel alignment.

UPPER BALL JOINT

REMOVAL & INSTALLATION

1. Raise vehicle and support the vehicle.
2. Remove the tire and wheel.
3. Remove the upper ball joint retaining nut.
4. Separate the upper ball joint from the knuckle using Ball Joint Remover (9360 or equivalent).
5. Remove the wheel speed sensor wire from the upper control arm.
6. Move the knuckle out of the way for access to remove the ball joint.
7. Remove the ball joint boot.

➡It may be necessary to install a block of wood between the control arm and frame bracket to allow clearance for the ball joint press tool.

⁂ CAUTION

Extreme pressure lubrication must be used on the threaded portions of the tool. This will increase the longevity of the tool and insure proper operation during the removal and installation process .

8. Remove the ball joint from the upper control arm using Ball Joint Press (C-4212F or equivalent) and Ball Joint Remover set (9770-1 and 9770-2 or equivalent).

To install:

9. Install the ball joint into the upper control arm and press in using Ball Joint Press and Ball Joint Installer Set.
10. Install the upper ball joint into the knuckle. Install the retaining nut and tighten to 40 ft. lbs. (54 Nm), plus an additional 200 degrees.
11. Install the wheel speed sensor wire to the upper control arm.
12. Install the tire and wheel.
13. Remove the supports and lower the vehicle.
14. Perform a wheel alignment.

UPPER CONTROL ARM

REMOVAL & INSTALLATION

1. Raise and support the vehicle.
2. Remove wheel and tire assembly.
3. Remove the disc brake caliper adapter with the caliper, then remove the rotor. See "BRAKES" section.
4. Remove the wheel speed sensor wire from the upper control arm.
5. Remove the nut from upper ball joint.

➡When installing remover tool to separate the ball joint, be careful not to damage the ball joint seal.

6. Separate upper ball joint from the steering knuckle with Ball Joint Remover (9360 or equivalent).
7. Remove the control arm pivot bolts and flag nuts remove control arm.

To install:

8. Position the control arm into the frame brackets. Install bolt and nut, and tighten to 130 ft. lbs. (176 Nm).
9. Insert the upper control arm ball joint in the steering knuckle and tighten the upper ball joint nut to 40 ft. lbs. (54 Nm), plus an additional 200 degrees.
10. Install the rotor to the hub. Install the disc brake caliper and adapter to the knuckle. See "BRAKES" section.
11. Install the wheel speed sensor wire to the upper control arm.
12. Install the wheel and tire assembly.
13. Remove the support and lower vehicle.
14. Perform a wheel alignment.

WHEEL HUB & BEARING

REMOVAL & INSTALLATION

4X2

See Figure 139.

1. Raise and support the vehicle.
2. Remove the wheel and tire assembly.
3. Remove the brake caliper and rotor. See "BRAKES" section.
4. Remove the ABS wheel speed sensor.
5. Remove the three hub and bearing mounting bolts from the steering knuckle.
6. Slide the hub and bearing out of the steering knuckle.

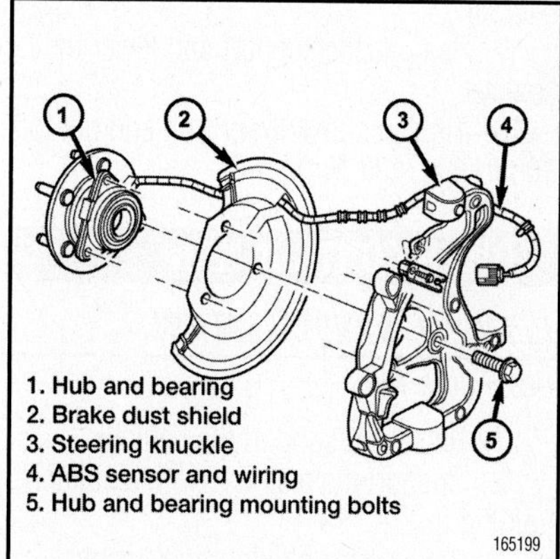

Fig. 139 Separating wheel hub and bearing

7. Remove the brake dust shield.

To install:

8. Install the brake dust shield.
9. Install the hub and bearing into the steering knuckle and tighten the bolts to 120 ft. lbs. (163 Nm).
10. Install the brake rotor and caliper. See "BRAKES" section.
11. Install the ABS wheel speed sensor.
12. Install the wheel and tire assembly.
13. Remove the support and lower vehicle.

4X4

1. Install the brake dust shield.
2. Install the hub/bearing into the steering knuckle and tighten the bolts to 120 ft. lbs. (163 Nm).
3. Install the brake rotor and caliper. See "BRAKES" section.
4. Install the ABS wheel speed sensor.
5. Install the upper ball joint nut to the steering knuckle and tighten to 40 ft. lbs. (54 Nm), plus an additional 200 degrees.
6. Install the tie rod end nut to the steering knuckle and tighten to 45 ft. lbs. (61 Nm), plus an additional 90 degrees.
7. Install the halfshaft nut and tighten to 185 ft. lbs. (251 Nm).
8. Install the wheel and tire assembly.
9. Remove the support and lower vehicle.

SUSPENSION

REAR SUSPENSION

COIL SPRING

REMOVAL & INSTALLATION

1. Raise and support the vehicle.
2. Support the axle with a suitable holding fixture.
3. Remove the shock lower bolt and nut.

⁂ CAUTION

Lower the axle carefully and avoid putting stress on the flexible brake line.

4. Lower the axle support and tilt the axel to remove the spring and isolator from the vehicle.

To install:

➡All torques should be made with the full vehicle weight on the ground being supported by the tires.

5. Position spring and isolator on the axle and align into the spring upper pocket.
6. Carefully raise the rear axle into place.
7. Install the shock lower bolt and nut, and do not tighten.
8. Remove the holding fixture for the rear axle.
9. Remove the support and lower the vehicle.
10. Tighten shock lower bolt and nut to 100 ft. lbs. (136 Nm).

LOWER CONTROL ARM

REMOVAL & INSTALLATION

See Figure 140.

1. Raise and support the vehicle.
2. Support the rear axle with a suitable holding fixture.
3. Remove the parking brake cable guide bolt (left side only).
4. Remove the lower control arm bolt and nut at the axle and discard the nut.

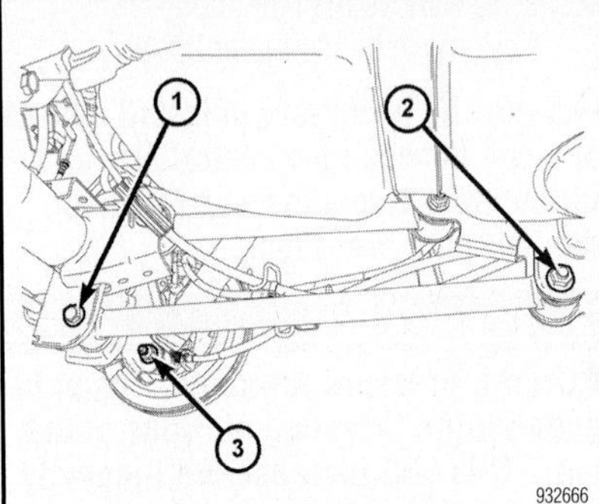

Fig. 140 Remove the lower control arm bolt and nut at the axle (1) and discard the nut. Remove the lower control arm bolt and nut at the frame (2). Parking brake cable bolt (3).

5. Remove the lower control arm bolt and nut at the frame.
6. Remove the lower control arm from the vehicle.

To install:

7. The small bushing attaches to the frame and the large bushing to the axle.
8. Install the lower control arm to the vehicle.
9. Install the lower control arm bolt with a new nut at the axle. Do not tighten.
10. Install the lower control arm bolt and nut at the frame. Do not tighten.
11. Position the parking brake cable guide (left side only), install the guide bolt and tighten to 15 ft. lbs. (20 Nm).
12. Remove the holding fixture supporting the axle.
13. Remove the support and lower the vehicle.
14. Tighten the lower control arm bolts to 225 ft. lbs. (305 Nm).

STABILIZER BAR

REMOVAL & INSTALLATION

1. Raise and support vehicle.
2. Remove both stabilizer bar link lower mounting nuts.
3. Remove stabilizer bar retainer bolts and retainers.
4. Remove stabilizer bar.
5. Remove and transfer the bushings if necessary.

To install:

6. Install stabilizer bar bushings.
7. Install the stabilizer bar and center it with equal spacing on both sides.
8. Install stabilizer bar retainers and bolts. Do not tighten.
9. Install the stabilizer bar links on the stabilizer bar and install link lower mounting nuts. Do not tighten.
10. Remove the support and lower the vehicle.
11. Tighten the stabilizer bar retainers to:
    - Stabilizer bar to axle bolts/nuts: 37 ft. lbs. (50 Nm)
    - Stabilizer bar link to frame bolts/nuts: 56 ft. lbs. (75 Nm)
    - Stabilizer bar link to stabilizer bar nut: 79 ft. lbs. (107 Nm)

STABILIZER BAR LINK

REMOVAL & INSTALLATION

See Figure 141.

1. Raise and support the vehicle.
2. Support the rear axle with a suitable holding fixture.
3. Remove the stabilizer link upper bolt and nut.
4. Remove the stabilizer link lower nut.
5. Remove stabilizer link.

To install:

6. Position the stabilizer link and install the link upper bolt and nut. Do not tighten.
7. Install the stabilizer link lower nut. Do not tighten.
8. Remove the holding fixture supporting the axle.
9. Remove the support and lower the vehicle.

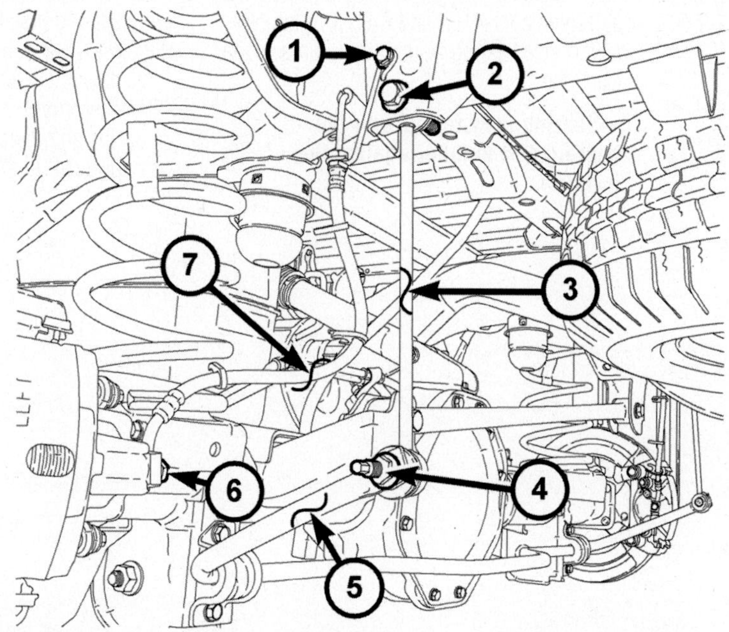

Fig. 141 Showing the stabilizer bar link and related components.

10. Tighten stabilizer link retainers to:
    - Upper bolt and nut: 56 ft. lbs. (75 Nm)
    - Lower nut: 79 ft. lbs. (107 Nm)

SHOCK ABSORBER

REMOVAL & INSTALLATION

1. Raise and support the vehicle.
2. Support the rear axle with a suitable holding fixture.
3. Remove the shock upper bolt and nut.
4. Remove the shock lower bolt and nut.
5. Remove the shock absorber from the vehicle.
6. Installation is the reverse of the removal procedure.
7. Tighten bolts and nuts to 100 ft. lbs. (136 Nm).

TRACK BAR

REMOVAL & INSTALLATION

1. Raise and support the vehicle.
2. Support the rear axle with a suitable holding fixture.
3. Remove the track bar bolt/nut from the frame bracket.
4. Remove the track bar bolt/nut from the axle bracket.
5. Remove the track bar.

To install:

6. Position the track bar onto the vehicle.
7. Install the track bar bolt and nut in the frame bracket. Do not tighten.
8. Install the track bar bolt and nut in the axle bracket. Do not tighten.
9. Remove the holding fixture supporting the axle.
10. Remove the supports and lower the vehicle.
11. Tighten the track bar mounting bolts/nuts to 129 ft. lbs. (175 Nm).

UPPER CONTROL ARM

REMOVAL & INSTALLATION

1. Raise and support the vehicle.
2. Support the rear axle with a suitable holding fixture.
3. Remove the upper control arm bolt and nut at the axle and discard the nut.
4. Remove the upper control arm front bolt and nut at the frame.
5. Remove the upper control arm from the vehicle.

To install:

➡The small bushing attaches to the axel and the large bushing to the frame.

6. Position the upper control arm to the vehicle.
7. Install the upper control arm bolt and nut at the frame. Do not tighten.
8. Install the upper control arm bolt with a new nut at the axle. Do not tighten.
9. Remove the holding fixture supporting the axle.
10. Remove the support and lower the vehicle.
11. Tighten the upper control arm bolts/nuts to 225 ft. lbs. (305 Nm).

WHEEL BEARINGS

REMOVAL & INSTALLATION

1. Remove rear axle shaft. See "DRIVE TRAIN" section.
2. Remove axle shaft seal from axle tube with a small pry bar.

➡The seal and bearing can be removed at the same time with the bearing removal tool.

3. Remove axle shaft bearing with Bearing Remover and Foot (6310 and 6310-9 or equivalent).

To install:

4. Wipe axle tube bore clean and remove any old sealer or burrs from the tube.

5. Install axle shaft bearing with Installer and Handle (C-4198 and C4171 or equivalent). Drive bearing in until tool contacts the axle tube.

➡Bearing is installed with the bearing part number against the installer.

6. Coat lip of the new axle seal with axle lubricant and install with Installer and Handle (C-4076-B and C-4735).

7. Install the axle shaft. See "DRIVE TRAIN" section.

8. Install differential cover and fill with gear lubricant to the bottom of the fill plug hole.

DODGE

Ram 2500/3500

16

SPECIFICATIONS AND MAINTENANCE CHARTS

ENGINE AND VEHICLE IDENTIFICATION

Engine							Model Year	
Code ①	Liters (cc)	Cu. In.	Cyl.	Fuel Sys.	Engine Type	Eng. Mfg.	Code ②	Year
T	5.7 (5700)	348	8	Fuel Inj.	SOHC	Chrysler	A	2010
L	6.7 (6700)	409	8	Turbo Diesel	SOHC	Cummins	B	2011

① 8th position of VIN

② 10th position of VIN

25766_RAM2_C0001

GENERAL ENGINE SPECIFICATIONS

All measurements are given in inches.

Year	Model	Engine Displacement Liters	Engine ID/VIN	Fuel System Type	Net Horsepower @ rpm	Net Torque @ rpm (ft. lbs.)	Bore x Stroke (in.)	Com-pression Ratio	Oil Pressure @ rpm
2010	2500	5.7	T	Fuel Inj.	310@5650	330@3950	3.66x3.40	9.6:1	30-105@3000
	2500	6.7	L	T-Diesel	350@3013	305@3013	4.21x4.88	17.2:1	30@2500
	3500	6.7	L	T-Diesel	350@3013	305@3013	4.21x4.88	17.2:1	30@2500
2011	2500	5.7	T	Fuel Inj.	310@5650	330@3950	3.66x3.40	9.6:1	30-105@3000
	2500	6.7	L	T-Diesel	350@3013	305@3013	4.21x4.88	17.2:1	30@2500
	3500	6.7	L	T-Diesel	350@3013	305@3013	4.21x4.88	17.2:1	30@2500

25766_RAM2_C0002

ENGINE TUNE-UP SPECIFICATIONS

Year	Engine Displacement Liters	Engine ID/VIN	Spark Plug Gap (in.)	Ignition Timing (deg.) MT	Ignition Timing (deg.) AT	Fuel Pump (psi)	Idle Speed (rpm) MT	Idle Speed (rpm) AT	Valve Clearance Intake	Valve Clearance Exhaust
2010	5.7	T	0.04	N/A	①	58 +/- 2	N/A	①	②	②
	6.7	L	N/A	N/A	①	N/A	N/A	①	②	②
2011	5.7	T	0.04	N/A	①	58 +/- 2	N/A	①	②	②
	6.7	L	N/A	N/A	①	N/A	N/A	①	②	②

N/A: Information not available.

① Not adjustable on any engine; computer controlled.

② Valve clearance is maintained by hydraulic lash adjusters.

25766_RAM2_C0003

CAPACITIES

Year	Model	Engine Displacement Liters	Engine ID/VIN	Engine Oil with Filter	Transmission/axle (pts.) Auto.	Transmission/axle (pts.) Manual	Drive Axle (pts.) Front	Drive Axle (pts.) Rear	Transfer Case (pts.)	Fuel Tank (gal.)	Cooling System (qts.)
2010	2500	5.7	T	7.0 qts.	①	②	③	④	⑤	⑥	16.0
	2500	6.7	L	12.0 qts.	①	②	②	③	④	⑤	22.6
	3500	6.7	L	12.0 qts.	①	②	②	③	④	⑤	22.6
2011	2500	5.7	T	7.0 qts.	①	②	③	④	⑤	⑥	16.0
	2500	6.7	L	12.0 qts.	①	②	②	③	④	⑤	22.6
	3500	6.7	L	12.0 qts.	①	②	②	③	④	⑤	22.6

NOTE: All capacities are approximate. Add fluid gradually and ensure a proper fluid level is obtained.

① 68RFE 6-Spd. A/T:
Overhaul/fill: 32.8-35.0 pts.
AS68RC 6-Spd. A/T:
Service fill: 14.4 pts.
Overhaul/fill: 37.48 pts.

② G56 6-Spd. M/T:
Overhaul/fill: 10.0 pts.

③ Corporate Axles:
C200F axle: 3.5 pts.
C205F axle: 3.4 pts.
Dana Axles:
Dana 186 FBI axle: 2.11 pts.
Dana 186 FIA axle: 2.26 pts.
Dana 216 FBI axle: 2.74 pts.
American Axles:
9.25 axle: 4.64 pts.
9.25 axle w/anti-spin: 4.22 pts.

④ Corporate Axles:
8.25 axle: 4.39 pts
8.25 w/anti-spin: 4.43 pts.
9.25 axle: 4.64 pts.
9.25 w/anti-spin: 4.43 pts.
Dana Axles:
226 RBI axle: 4.75 pts
226 RIA w/anti-spin: 2.85 pts.
American Axles:
10.5 axle: 5.28 pts.
10.5 axle w/anti-spin: 5.28 pts.

⑤ NV243: 3.4 pts.
NV271: 4.0 pts.
NV273: 4.0 pts.
BW 44-44: 3.0 pts.

⑥ Standard: 26 gal.
Optional: 32 gal.

25766_RAM2_C0004

FLUID SPECIFICATIONS

Year	Model	Engine Disp. Liters	Engine Oil	Auto. Trans.	Drive Axle Front & Rear	Transfer Case	Power Steering Fluid	Brake Master Cylinder	Cooling System
2010	2500	5.7	5W-20	Mopar® ATF+4	75W-140 ①	Mopar® ATF+4	Mopar® ATF+4	DOT 3	Mopar® Coolant
		6.7	5W-40 ②	③	75W-140 ①	Mopar® ATF+4	Mopar® ATF+4	DOT 3	Mopar® Coolant
	3500	6.7	5W-40 ②	③	75W-140 ①	Mopar® ATF+4	Mopar® ATF+4	DOT 3	Mopar® Coolant
2011	2500	5.7	5W-20	Mopar® ATF+4	75W-140 ①	Mopar® ATF+4	Mopar® ATF+4	DOT 3	Mopar® Coolant
		6.7	5W-40 ②	③	75W-140 ①	Mopar® ATF+4	Mopar® ATF+4	DOT 3	Mopar® Coolant
	3500	6.7	5W-40 ②	③	75W-140 ①	Mopar® ATF+4	Mopar® ATF+4	DOT 3	Mopar® Coolant

① Synthetic gear lubricant for all axles, except C205F which uses 75W-90 synthetic gear oil.

② Synthetic engine oil meeting MS-10902 and API CJ-4 standards.

③ 68RFE: Mopar ATF+4; AS68RC: Mopar AS68RC ATF.

DOT: Department Of Transpotation

25766_RAM2_C0005

VALVE SPECIFICATIONS

Year	Engine Displacement Liters	Engine ID/VIN	Seat Angle (deg.)	Face Angle (deg.)	Spring Test Pressure (lbs. @ in.)	Spring Free-Length (in.)	Spring Installed Height (in.)	Stem-to-Guide Clearance (in.) Intake	Stem-to-Guide Clearance (in.) Exhaust	Stem Diameter (in.) Intake	Stem Diameter (in.) Exhaust
2010	5.7	T	44.5-45.0	44.5-45.0	①	2.189	1.810	0.0008-0.0025	0.0009-0.0025	0.312-0.313	0.312-0.313
	6.7	L	②	N/A	N/A	1.880	N/A	0.0310	0.0310	0.2760-0.2740	0.2760-0.2740
2011	5.7	T	44.5-45.0	44.5-45.0	①	2.189	1.810	0.0008-0.0025	0.0009-0.0025	0.312-0.313	0.312-0.313
	6.7	L	②	N/A	N/A	1.880	N/A	0.0310	0.0310	0.2760-0.2740	0.2760-0.2740

N/A: Information not available.

① Intake & exhaust (valve closed): 92.8-102.8 lbs. @ 1.771 in.
Intake & exhaust (valve open): 231.0-253.0 lbs. @ 1.283 in.

② Intake valve seat angle: 30 degrees.
Exhaust valve seat angle: 45 degrees.

25766_RAM2_C0006

CAMSHAFT SPECIFICATIONS

All measurements in inches unless noted

Year	Engine Displacement Liters	Engine Code/VIN	Journal Diameter	Brg. Oil Clearance	Shaft End-play	Runout	Journal Bore	Lobe Height Intake	Lobe Height Exhaust
2010	5.7	T	①	②	0.0031-0.0114	N/A	N/A	N/A	N/A
	6.7	L	2.0904-2.1278	0.002-0.005	0.005-0.020	N/A	2.1293-2.1318	N/A	N/A
2011	5.7	T	①	②	0.0031-0.0114	N/A	N/A	N/A	N/A
	6.7	L	2.0904-2.1278	0.002-0.005	0.005-0.020	N/A	2.1293-2.1318	N/A	N/A

N/A: Information not available.

① No. 1: 2.29 in.
No. 2 2.28 in.
No. 3: 2.26 in.
No. 4: 2.24 in.
No. 5: 1.72 in.

② No. 1: 0.0015-0.003 in.
No. 2: 0.0019-0.0035 in.
No. 3: 0.0015-0.003 in.
No. 4: 0.0019-0.0035 in.
No. 5: 0.0015-0.003 in.

25766_RAM2_C0007

CRANKSHAFT AND CONNECTING ROD SPECIFICATIONS

All measurements are given in inches.

	Engine		Crankshaft				Connecting Rod		
Year	Engine Displacement Liters	Engine ID/VIN	Main Brg. Journal Dia.	Main Brg. Oi Clearance	Shaft End-play	Thrust on No.	Journal Diameter	Oil Clearance	Side Clearance
2010	5.7	T	2.5585-2.5595	0.0009-0.0020	0.002-0.011	N/A	2.1260	0.0007-0.0023	0.003-0.0137
	6.7	L	3.2662-3.2682	0.002-0.005	0.004-0.017	0.002	2.7150-2.7170	N/A	0.0130
2011	5.7	T	2.5585-2.5595	0.0009-0.0020	0.002-0.011	N/A	2.1260	0.0007-0.0023	0.003-0.0137
	6.7	L	3.2662-3.2682	0.002-0.005	0.004-0.017	0.002	2.7150-2.7170	N/A	0.0130

N/A: Information not available.

25766_RAM2_C0008

PISTON AND RING SPECIFICATIONS

All measurements are given in inches.

	Engine			Ring Gap			Ring Side Clearance		
Year	Engine Displacement Liters	Engine ID/VIN	Piston Clearance	Top Compression	Bottom Compression	Oil Control	Top Compression	Bottom Compression	Oil Control
2010	5.7	T	0.0001-0.0005	0.015-0.021	0.009-0.020	0.0059-0.0259	0.001-0.0035	0.001-0.0031	0.002-0.008
	6.7	L	N/A	0.012-0.018	0.032-0.047	0.010-0.023	①	0.0016-0.0031	0.0016-0.0033
2011	5.7	T	0.0001-0.0005	0.015-0.021	0.009-0.020	0.0059-0.0259	0.001-0.0035	0.001-0.0031	0.002-0.008
	6.7	L	N/A	0.012-0.018	0.032-0.047	0.010-0.023	①	0.0016-0.0031	0.0016-0.0033

N/A: Information not available.

① Clearance for top piston ring groove cannot be measured accurately with a typical feeler gauge.

25766_RAM2_C0009

SCHEDULED MAINTENANCE INTERVALS

2010-2011 Ram 2500/3500 5.7L Engine - Normal & Severe (as noted)

TO BE SERVICED	TYPE OF SERVICE	VEHICLE MILEAGE INTERVAL (x1000)												
		6	12	18	24	30	36	42	48	54	60	66	72	84
Engine oil & filter	Replace	✓	✓	✓	✓	✓	✓	✓	✓	✓	✓	✓	✓	✓
Rotate tires, inspect tread wear, measure tread depth and check pressure	Rotate/Inspect	✓	✓	✓	✓	✓	✓	✓	✓	✓	✓	✓	✓	✓
Brake system components	Inspect/Service		✓		✓		✓		✓		✓		✓	
Exhaust system & heat shields	Inspect		✓		✓		✓		✓		✓		✓	
Inspect the front suspension, tie rod ends and boot seals for cracks or leaks and all parts for damage, wear, improper looseness or end play.	Inspect		✓		✓		✓		✓		✓		✓	
CV Joints	Inspect			✓			✓			✓			✓	
Engine air filter - Normal	Replace				✓				✓				✓	
Engine air filter - Severe	Replace		✓		✓		✓		✓		✓		✓	
Adjust parking brake on vehicles equipped with four-wheel disc brakes	Adjust				✓				✓				✓	
Engine coolant	Flush/Replace										✓			
Spark plugs	Replace				✓				✓				✓	
PCV valve	Inspect/Service												✓	
Automatic transmission fluid and filter - Normal	Inspect	Every 60,000 miles												
Automatic transmission fluid and filter - Severe	Inspect	Every 120,000 miles												
Accessory drive belt	Replace	Every 120,000 miles												
Battery	Inspect/Service	✓	✓	✓	✓	✓	✓	✓	✓	✓	✓	✓	✓	✓
Horn, exterior lamps, turn signals and hazard warning light operation	Inspect	✓	✓	✓	✓	✓	✓	✓	✓	✓	✓	✓	✓	✓
Fluid levels (all)	Inspect/Service	✓	✓	✓	✓	✓	✓	✓	✓	✓	✓	✓	✓	✓
Rear axle fluid	Inspect/Service			✓			✓			✓			✓	
Passenger compartment air filter	Replace		✓		✓		✓		✓		✓		✓	

25766_RAM2_C0014

SCHEDULED MAINTENANCE INTERVALS

2010-2011 Ram 2500/3500 6.7L Engine - Normal & Severe (as noted)

TO BE SERVICED	TYPE OF SERVICE	VEHICLE MILEAGE INTERVAL (x1000)												
		7.5	15	22.5	30	37.5	45	52.5	60	67.5	75	82.5	90	97.5
Engine oil & filter	Replace	✓	✓	✓	✓	✓	✓	✓	✓	✓	✓	✓	✓	✓
Rotate tires, inspect tread wear, measure tread depth and check pressure	Rotate/Inspect	✓	✓	✓	✓	✓	✓	✓	✓	✓	✓	✓	✓	✓
Brake system components	Inspect/Service			✓			✓			✓			✓	
Exhaust system & heat shields	Inspect	✓	✓	✓	✓	✓	✓	✓	✓	✓	✓	✓	✓	✓
Inspect the front suspension, tie rod ends and boot seals for cracks or leaks and all parts for damage, wear, improper looseness or end play.	Inspect	✓	✓	✓	✓	✓	✓	✓	✓	✓	✓	✓	✓	✓
Engine air filter - Normal	Replace				✓				✓				✓	
Engine air filter - Severe	Replace		✓		✓		✓		✓		✓		✓	
Parking brake	Adjust			✓			✓			✓			✓	
Engine coolant	Flush/Replace										✓			
Crankcase Ventilation Filter (CCV)	Replace				✓				✓				✓	
Spark plugs	Replace				✓				✓				✓	
PCV valve	Inspect/Service												✓	
Manual transmission fluid and filter - Normal	Inspect	Every 60,000 miles												
Manual transmission fluid and filter - Severe	Inspect	Every 120,000 miles												
Accessory drive belt	Replace			✓			✓			✓			✓	
Battery	Inspect/Service	✓	✓	✓	✓	✓	✓	✓	✓	✓	✓	✓	✓	✓
Horn, exterior lamps, turn signals and hazard warning light operation	Inspect	✓	✓	✓	✓	✓	✓	✓	✓	✓	✓	✓	✓	✓
Fluid levels (all)	Inspect/Service	✓	✓	✓	✓	✓	✓	✓	✓	✓	✓	✓	✓	✓
EGR valve	Clean									✓				
Fuel filter	Replace		✓		✓		✓		✓		✓		✓	
EGR cooler	Clean									✓				
Rear axle fluid	Inspect/Service				✓				✓				✓	
Valve lash clearance	Adjust		✓		✓		✓		✓		✓		✓	

25766_RAM2_C0015

PRECAUTIONS

Before servicing any vehicle, please be sure to read all of the following precautions, which deal with personal safety, prevention of component damage, and important points to take into consideration when servicing a motor vehicle:

- Never open, service or drain the radiator or cooling system when the engine is hot; serious burns can occur from the steam and hot coolant.
- Observe all applicable safety precautions when working around fuel. Whenever servicing the fuel system, always work in a well-ventilated area. Do not allow fuel spray or vapors to come in contact with a spark, open flame, or excessive heat (a hot drop light, for example). Keep a dry chemical fire extinguisher near the work area. Always keep fuel in a container specifically designed for fuel storage; also, always properly seal fuel containers to avoid the possibility of fire or explosion. Refer to the additional fuel system precautions later in this section.
- Fuel injection systems often remain pressurized, even after the engine has been turned **OFF**. The fuel system pressure must be relieved before disconnecting any fuel lines. Failure to do so may result in fire and/or personal injury.
- Brake fluid often contains polyglycol ethers and polyglycols. Avoid contact with the eyes and wash your hands thoroughly after handling brake fluid. If you do get brake fluid in your eyes, flush your eyes with clean, running water for 15 minutes. If eye irritation persists, or if you have taken brake fluid internally, IMMEDIATELY seek medical assistance.
- The EPA warns that prolonged contact with used engine oil may cause a number of skin disorders, including cancer. You should make every effort to minimize your exposure to used engine oil. Protective gloves should be worn when changing oil. Wash your hands and any other exposed skin areas as soon as possible after exposure to used engine oil. Soap and water, or waterless hand cleaner should be used.
- All new vehicles are now equipped with an air bag system, often referred to as a Supplemental Restraint System (SRS) or Supplemental Inflatable Restraint (SIR) system. The system must be disabled before performing service on or around system components, steering column, instrument panel components, wiring and sensors. Failure to follow safety and disabling procedures could result in accidental air bag deployment, possible personal injury and unnecessary system repairs.
- Always wear safety goggles when working with, or around, the air bag system. When carrying a non-deployed air bag, be sure the bag and trim cover are pointed away from your body. When placing a non-deployed air bag on a work surface, always face the bag and trim cover upward, away from the surface. This will reduce the motion of the module if it is accidentally deployed. Refer to the additional air bag system precautions later in this section.
- Clean, high quality brake fluid from a sealed container is essential to the safe and proper operation of the brake system. You should always buy the correct type of brake fluid for your vehicle. If the brake fluid becomes contaminated, completely flush the system with new fluid. Never reuse any brake fluid. Any brake fluid that is removed from the system should be discarded. Also, do not allow any brake fluid to come in contact with a painted surface; it will damage the paint.
- Never operate the engine without the proper amount and type of engine oil; doing so WILL result in severe engine damage.
- Timing belt maintenance is extremely important. Many models utilize an interference-type, non-freewheeling engine. If the timing belt breaks, the valves in the cylinder head may strike the pistons, causing potentially serious (also time-consuming and expensive) engine damage. Refer to the maintenance interval charts for the recommended replacement interval for the timing belt, and to the timing belt section for belt replacement and inspection.
- Disconnecting the negative battery cable on some vehicles may interfere with the functions of the on-board computer system(s) and may require the computer to undergo a relearning process once the negative battery cable is reconnected.
- When servicing drum brakes, only disassemble and assemble one side at a time, leaving the remaining side intact for reference.
- Only an MVAC-trained, EPA-certified automotive technician should service the air conditioning system or its components.

BRAKES — ANTI-LOCK BRAKE SYSTEM (ABS)

GENERAL INFORMATION

PRECAUTIONS

- Certain components within the ABS system are not intended to be serviced or repaired individually.
- Do not use rubber hoses or other parts not specifically specified for and ABS system. When using repair kits, replace all parts included in the kit. Partial or incorrect repair may lead to functional problems and require the replacement of components.
- Lubricate rubber parts with clean, fresh brake fluid to ease assembly. Do not use shop air to clean parts; damage to rubber components may result.
- Use only DOT 3 brake fluid from an unopened container.
- If any hydraulic component or line is removed or replaced, it may be necessary to bleed the entire system.
- A clean repair area is essential. Always clean the reservoir and cap thoroughly before removing the cap. The slightest amount of dirt in the fluid may plug an orifice and impair the system function. Perform repairs after components have been thoroughly cleaned; use only denatured alcohol to clean components. Do not allow ABS components to come into contact with any substance containing mineral oil; this includes used shop rags.
- The Anti-Lock control unit is a microprocessor similar to other computer units in the vehicle. Ensure that the ignition switch is **OFF** before removing or installing controller harnesses. Avoid static electricity discharge at or near the controller.
- If any arc welding is to be done on the vehicle, the control unit should be unplugged before welding operations begin.

DYNAMICS SENSOR (YAW RATE & LATERAL ACCELERATION SENSORS)

DESCRIPTION & OPERATION

See Figure 1.

The yaw rate, lateral acceleration and longitudinal acceleration sensors are housed into one unit known as the dynamics sensor. The sensor is used to measure vehicle rotational sensing (how fast the vehicle is turning - yaw), side-to-side (lateral) motion and longitudinal acceleration (forward). The dynamics sensor is located

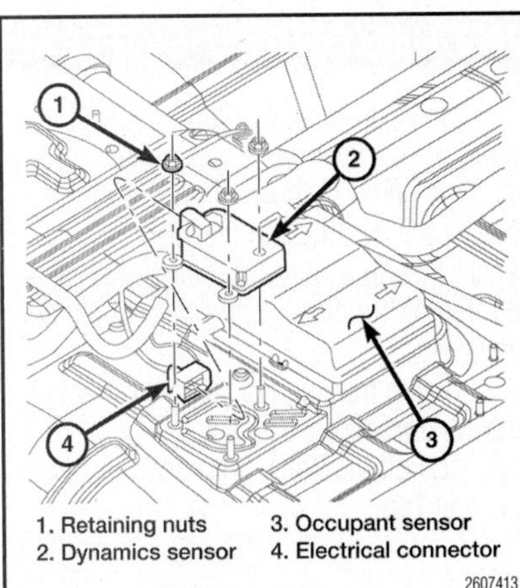

Fig. 1 Showing the location of the dynamics sensor

on the floor panel transmission tunnel under the center floor console (or if equipped with a bench seat, under the front center seat section) next to the Occupant Restraint Controller (ORC).

➡**If the dynamics sensor is replaced, it must be initialized using the scan tool.**

The yaw rate and lateral acceleration sensors cannot be serviced separately. The entire dynamics sensor must be replaced when necessary.

REMOVAL & INSTALLATION

1. Disconnect and isolate the battery negative cable.
2. If equipped with a center floor console, remove the console.
3. If equipped with a 40/20/40 bench seat, remove the passenger seat.
4. Disconnect the electrical connector for the dynamics sensor.
5. Remove the three mounting nuts for the sensor.
6. Remove the sensor from the vehicle.
7. Installation is the reverse of the removal procedure.

ELECTRONIC STABILITY CONTROL (ESC) SWITCH

REMOVAL & INSTALLATION

1. Remove the instrument panel center bezel.
2. Disconnect the Electronic Stability Control (ESC) electrical connector from the radio trim panel.
3. Remove the ESC switch from the switch bank.
4. Installation is the reverse of the removal procedure.

HYDRAULIC CONTROL UNIT

REMOVAL & INSTALLATION

See Figure 2.

1. Disconnect the battery cables from the battery.
2. Remove the battery.
3. Disconnect the electrical harness connectors.
4. Remove the brake lines from the HCU (3).
5. Remove HCU/ABM mounting bolts (1) and remove the HCU/ABM (3) from the battery tray (4).

To install:

6. Installation is the reverse of the removal procedure.
7. Tighten retaining bolts firmly.

SPEED SENSORS

REMOVAL & INSTALLATION

Front

See Figure 3.

1. Remove the front rotor. See "Brake Rotor" in this section.

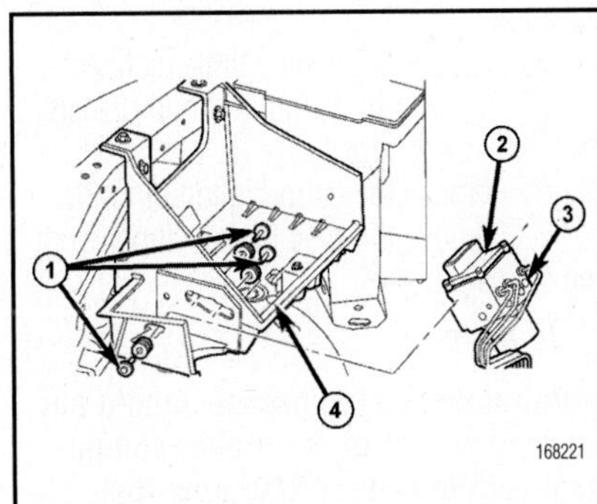

Fig. 2 Showing HCU module mounting

2. Remove the wheel speed sensor mounting bolt from the hub.
3. Remove the wheel speed sensor from the hub.
4. Remove the wiring from the clips and disconnect the electrical connector.

To install:

5. Installation is the reverse of the removal procedure.
6. Tighten sensor retaining bolt to 190 inch lbs. (21 Nm).

Rear

See Figure 4.

1. Raise and support the vehicle.
2. Remove the brake line mounting nut and remove the brake line from the sensor stud.
3. Remove the mounting stud from the sensor and shield.
4. Remove the sensor and shield from the differential housing.
5. Disconnect the sensor wire harness and remove the sensor.

To install:

6. Connect the harness to the sensor. Be sure the seal is securely in place between the sensor and the wiring connector.
7. Install the O-ring on the sensor (if removed).
8. Insert the sensor in the differential housing.
9. Install the sensor shield.
10. Install the sensor mounting stud and tighten to 200 inch lbs. (24 Nm).
11. Install the brake line on the sensor stud and install the nut.
12. Remove the support and lower the vehicle.

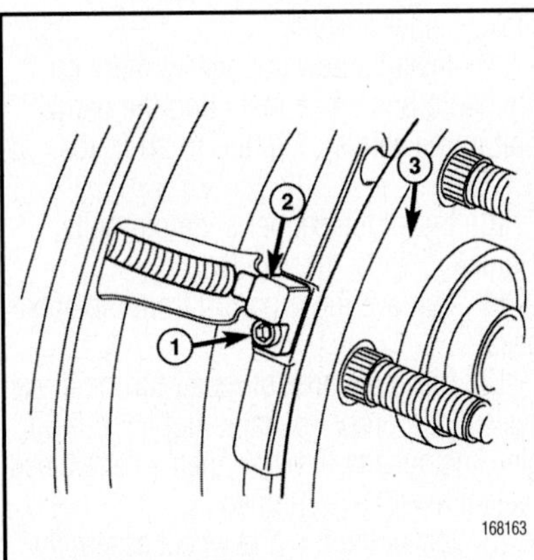

Fig. 3 Remove the mounting bolt (1) and wheel speed sensor (2) from the hub and rotor (3).

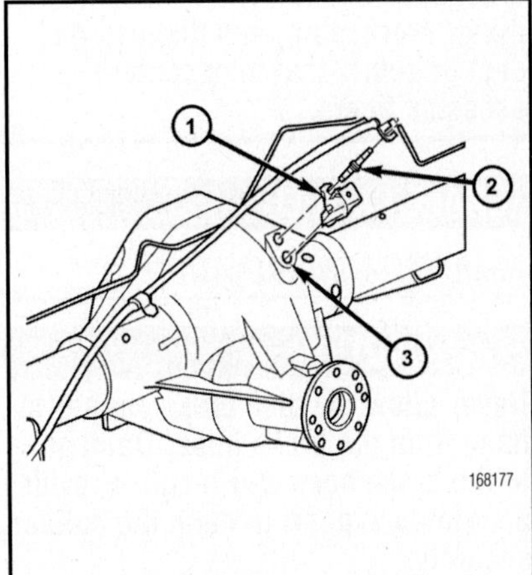

Fig. 4 Remove sensor (1) mounting stud (2) from differential housing (3)

BLEEDING PROCEDURE

BLEEDING PROCEDURE

➡Use Mopar brake fluid, or an equivalent quality fluid meeting SAE J1703-F and DOT 3 standards only. Use fresh, clean fluid from a sealed container at all times.

1. Remove reservoir filler caps and fill reservoir.
2. If calipers were overhauled, open all caliper bleed screws. Then close each bleed screw as fluid starts to drip from it. Top off master cylinder reservoir once more before proceeding.
3. Attach one end of bleed hose to bleed screw and insert opposite end in glass container partially filled with brake fluid. Be sure end of bleed hose is immersed in fluid.

➡Bleed procedure should be in this order: Right rear, Left rear, Right front, Left front.

4. Open up bleeder, then have a helper press down the brake pedal. Once the pedal is down, hold the pedal down while closing the bleeder. Repeat bleeding until fluid stream is clear and free of bubbles. Then move to the next wheel.
5. Before moving the vehicle verify the pedal is firm and not mushy.
6. Top off the brake fluid and install the reservoir cap.

⁂ CAUTION

Dust and dirt accumulating on brake parts during normal use may contain asbestos fibers from production or aftermarket brake linings. Breathing excessive concentrations of asbestos fibers can cause serious bodily harm. Exercise care when servicing brake parts. Do not sand or grind brake lining unless equipment used is designed to contain the dust residue. Do not clean brake parts with compressed air or by dry brushing. Cleaning should be done by dampening the brake components with a fine mist of water, then wiping the brake components clean with a dampened cloth. Dispose of cloth and all residue containing asbestos fibers in an impermeable container with the appropriate label. Follow practices prescribed by the Occupational Safety and Health Administration (OSHA) and the Environmental Protection Agency (EPA) for the handling, processing, and disposing of dust or debris that may contain asbestos fibers.

BRAKE CALIPER

REMOVAL & INSTALLATION

⁂ CAUTION

Never allow the disc brake caliper to hang from the brake hose. Damage to the brake hose will result. Provide a suitable support to hang the caliper securely.

1. Install prop rod on the brake pedal to keep pressure on the brake system, Holding pedal in this position will isolate master cylinder from hydraulic brake system and will not allow brake fluid to drain out of brake fluid reservoir while brake lines are open. This will allow you to bleed out the area of repair instead of the entire system.
2. Raise and support the vehicle.
3. Remove the tire and wheel assembly.
4. Compress the disc brake caliper.
5. Remove the banjo bolt and discard the copper washers.
6. Remove the caliper slide pin bolts.
7. Remove the disc brake caliper from the caliper adapter.

To install:

➡Petroleum based grease should not be used on any of the rubber components of the caliper, Use only Non-Petroleum based grease.

8. Install the disc brake caliper to the brake caliper adapter.
9. Install a new copper washers on the banjo bolt when installing the banjo bolt to the caliper. Tighten to 20 ft. lbs. (27 Nm).
10. Install the caliper slide pin bolts. Tighten to 24 ft. lbs. (32 Nm).
11. Remove the prop rod from the brake pedal.
12. Bleed the area of repair for the brake system. If a proper pedal is not felt during bleeding an area of repair then a base bleed system must be performed.
13. Install the tire and wheel assembly.
14. Remove the supports and lower the vehicle.

DISC BRAKE PADS

REMOVAL & INSTALLATION

1. Raise and support vehicle.
2. Remove the wheel and tire assemblies.
3. Compress the caliper.
4. Remove the caliper slide pin bolts.
5. Remove the caliper from the caliper adapter.

⁂ CAUTION

Do not allow brake hose to support caliper assembly.

6. Support and hang the caliper.
7. Remove the inboard brake pad from the caliper adapter.
8. Remove the outboard brake pad from the caliper adapter.
9. Remove the anti-rattle clips from the pad.

To install:

10. Bottom pistons in caliper bore with C-clamp. Place an old brake shoe between a C-clamp and caliper piston.
11. Clean caliper mounting adapter.
12. Install new anti-rattle clips to the brake pads.
13. Install inboard brake pad in adapter.
14. Install outboard brake pad in adapter.
15. Install the caliper over rotor, Then push the caliper onto the adapter.
16. Install caliper slide pin bolts.
17. Install wheel and tire assemblies and lower vehicle.
18. Apply brakes several times to seat caliper pistons and brake shoes and obtain firm pedal.
19. Top off master cylinder fluid level.

**** CAUTION**

Dust and dirt accumulating on brake parts during normal use may contain asbestos fibers from production or aftermarket brake linings. Breathing excessive concentrations of asbestos fibers can cause serious bodily harm. Exercise care when servicing brake parts. Do not sand or grind brake lining unless equipment used is designed to contain the dust residue. Do not clean brake parts with compressed air or by dry brushing. Cleaning should be done by dampening the brake components with a fine mist of water, then wiping the brake components clean with a dampened cloth. Dispose of cloth and all residue containing asbestos fibers in an impermeable container with the appropriate label. Follow practices prescribed by the Occupational Safety and Health Administration (OSHA) and the Environmental Protection Agency (EPA) for the handling, processing, and disposing of dust or debris that may contain asbestos fibers.

BRAKE CALIPER

REMOVAL & INSTALLATION

**** CAUTION**

Never allow the disc brake caliper to hang from the brake hose. Damage to the brake hose will result. Provide a suitable support to hang the caliper securely.

1. Install prop rod on the brake pedal to keep pressure on the brake system, Holding pedal in this position will isolate master cylinder from hydraulic brake system and will not allow brake fluid to drain out of brake fluid reservoir while brake lines are open. This will allow you to bleed out the area of repair instead of the entire system.
2. Raise and support vehicle.
3. Remove the wheel and tire assembly.
4. Drain small amount of fluid from master cylinder brake reservoir with suction gun.
5. Remove the brake hose banjo bolt and discard the copper washers if replacing caliper.
6. Remove the caliper slide bolts.
7. Remove the caliper from vehicle.

To install:

8. Install caliper to the caliper adapter.
9. Coat the caliper mounting slide pin bolts with silicone grease. Then, install and tighten the bolts to 22 ft. lbs. (30 Nm).
10. Verify that the brake hose is not twisted or kinked before tightening the fitting bolt.
11. Install the brake hose to the caliper with new copper washers and tighten fitting bolt to 20 ft. lbs. (27 Nm).
12. Remove the prop rod from the brake pedal.
13. Bleed the area of repair for the brake system. If a proper pedal is not felt during bleeding an area of repair then a base bleed system must be performed.
14. Install the wheel and tire assemblies.
15. Remove the supports and lower the vehicle.
16. Verify a firm pedal before moving the vehicle.

DISC BRAKE PADS

REMOVAL & INSTALLATION

1. Raise and support the vehicle.
2. Remove the rear wheel and tire assemblies.
3. Compress the caliper.
4. Remove caliper slide bolts.

**** CAUTION**

Do not allow brake hose to support caliper assembly.

5. Remove the caliper by tilting the top out and off the caliper adapter.
6. Remove inboard brake shoe from the caliper adapter.
7. Remove outboard brake shoe from caliper adapter.

**** CAUTION**

Anti-rattle springs are not interchangeable.

8. Remove the top anti-rattle spring from the caliper adapter.
9. Remove the bottom anti-rattle spring from the caliper adapter

To install:

10. Clean caliper mounting adapter and anti-rattle springs.

Lubricate anti-rattle springs with Mopar brake grease.

**** CAUTION**

Anti-rattle springs are not interchangeable.

11. Install new top anti-rattle spring.
12. Install new bottom anti-rattle spring.
13. Install inboard brake shoe in adapter.
14. Install outboard brake shoe in adapter.
15. Tilt the bottom of the caliper over rotor and under adapter. Then push the top of the caliper down onto the adapter.
16. Install caliper.
17. Install wheel and tire assemblies.
18. Remove the supports and lower the vehicle.
19. Apply brakes several times to seat caliper pistons and brake shoes and obtain firm pedal.
20. Top off master cylinder fluid level.

PARKING BRAKE CABLES

ADJUSTMENT

See Figure 5.

➡**Tensioner adjustment is only necessary when the tensioner, or a cable has been replaced or disconnected for service. When adjustment is necessary, perform adjustment only as described in the following procedure. This is necessary to avoid faulty park brake operation.**

1. Raise the vehicle.
2. Back off the cable tensioner adjusting nut to create slack in the cables.
3. Remove the rear wheel/tire assemblies. Then remove the brake rotors.
4. Verify the brakes are in good condition and operating properly.
5. Verify the park brake cables operate freely and are not binding, or seized.
6. Check the rear brake shoe adjustment with standard brake gauge.
7. Install the rotors and verify that the rotors rotate freely without drag.
8. Install the wheel/tire assemblies.
9. Lower the vehicle enough for access to the park brake foot pedal. Then fully apply the park brakes.

➡**Leave park brakes applied until adjustment is complete.**

10. Raise the vehicle again.
11. Mark the tensioner rod 1/4 in. (6.35 mm) from edge of the tensioner.
12. Tighten the adjusting nut on the tensioner rod until the mark is no longer visible.

➡**Do not loosen, or tighten the tensioner adjusting nut for any reason after completing adjustment.**

13. Lower the vehicle until the rear wheels are 6–8 in. (15–20 cm) off the shop floor.
14. Release the park brake foot pedal and verify that rear wheels rotate freely without drag. Then lower the vehicle.

PARKING BRAKE SHOES

REMOVAL & INSTALLATION

See Figures 6 through 8.

1. Raise and support the vehicle.
2. Remove the tire and wheel assembly.
3. Remove the disc brake caliper and rotor, as described in this section.
4. Lockout the parking brake cable.
5. Disengage the park brake cable from behind the rotor assembly to allow easier disassembly of the park brake shoes.
6. Remove the rear axle shaft. See "DRIVE TRAIN" section.
7. Disassemble the rear park brake shoes

To install:

8. Reassemble the rear park brake shoes.
9. Install the axle shaft. See "DRIVE TRAIN" section.
10. Install the park brake cable to the lever behind the support plate.
11. Unlock the park brake cable.
12. Install the disc brake rotor.
13. Install the disc brake caliper.
14. Adjust the rear brake shoes.
15. Install the tire and wheel assembly.
16. Remove the support and lower the vehicle.

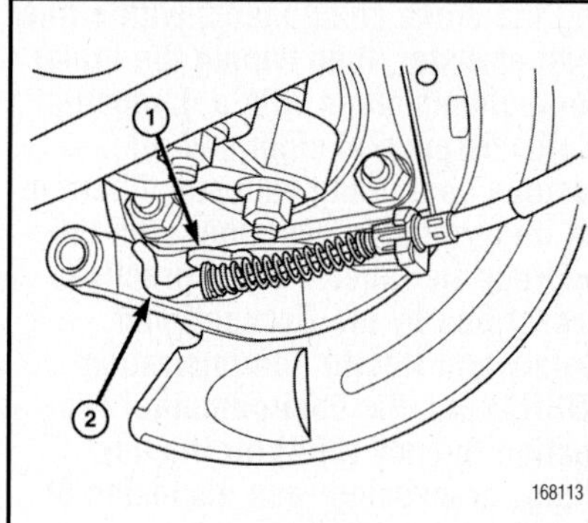

Fig. 7 Disengage the park brake cable (2) from behind the rotor assembly (1) to allow easier disassembly of the park brake shoes.

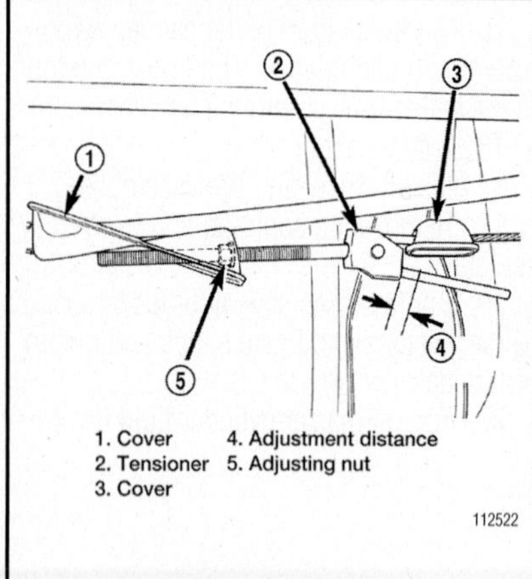

Fig. 5 Showing the parking brake adjustment points

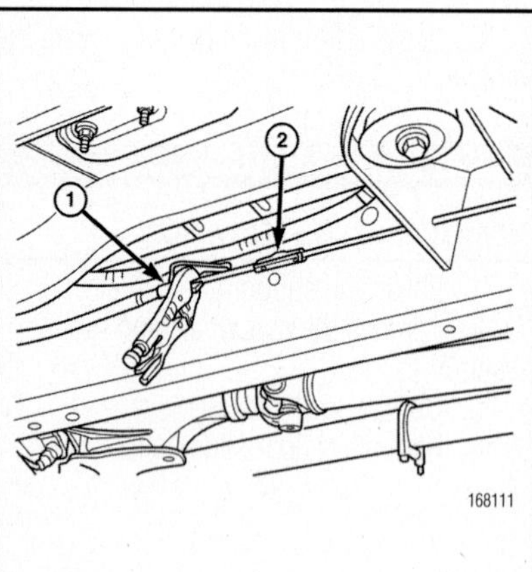

Fig. 6 Lockout the parking brake cable (2), using vice grip pliers (1).

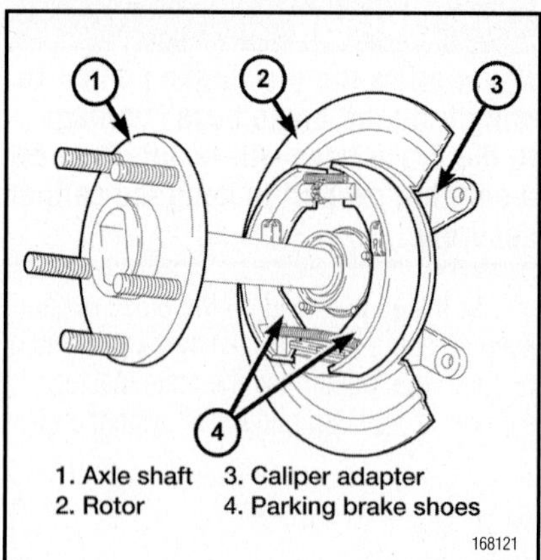

Fig. 8 Showing parking brake shoes and components

GENERAL INFORMATION

**** CAUTION**

These vehicles are equipped with an air bag system. The system must be disarmed before performing service on, or around, system components, the steering column, instrument panel components, wiring and sensors. Failure to follow the safety precautions and the disarming procedure could result in accidental air bag deployment, possible injury and unnecessary system repairs.

SERVICE PRECAUTIONS

Disconnect and isolate the battery negative cable before beginning any airbag system component diagnosis, testing, removal, or installation procedures. Allow system capacitor to discharge for two minutes before beginning any component service. This will disable the airbag system. Failure to disable the airbag system may result in accidental airbag deployment, personal injury, or death.

Do not place an intact undeployed airbag face down on a solid surface. The airbag will propel into the air if accidentally deployed and may result in personal injury or death.

When carrying or handling an undeployed airbag, the trim side (face) of the airbag should be pointing away from the body to minimize possibility of injury if accidental deployment occurs. Failure to do this may result in personal injury or death.

Replace airbag system components with OEM replacement parts. Substitute parts may appear interchangeable, but internal differences may result in inferior occupant protection. Failure to do so may result in occupant personal injury or death.

Wear safety glasses, rubber gloves, and long sleeved clothing when cleaning powder residue from vehicle after an airbag deployment. Powder residue emitted from a deployed airbag can cause skin irritation. Flush affected area with cool water if irritation is experienced. If nasal or throat irritation is experienced, exit the vehicle for fresh air until the irritation ceases. If irritation continues, see a physician.

Do not use a replacement airbag that is not in the original packaging. This may result in improper deployment, personal injury, or death.

The factory installed fasteners, screws and bolts used to fasten airbag components have a special coating and are specifically designed for the airbag system. Do not use substitute fasteners. Use only original equipment fasteners listed in the parts catalog when fastener replacement is required.

During, and following, any child restraint anchor service, due to impact event or vehicle repair, carefully inspect all mounting hardware, tether straps, and anchors for proper installation, operation, or damage. If a child restraint anchor is found damaged in any way, the anchor must be replaced. Failure to do this may result in personal injury or death.

Deployed and non-deployed airbags may or may not have live pyrotechnic material within the airbag inflator.

Do not dispose of driver/passenger/curtain airbags or seat belt tensioners unless you are sure of complete deployment. Refer to the Hazardous Substance Control System for proper disposal.

Dispose of deployed airbags and tensioners consistent with state, provincial, local, and federal regulations.

After any airbag component testing or service, do not connect the battery negative cable. Personal injury or death may result if the system test is not performed first.

If the vehicle is equipped with the Occupant Classification System (OCS), do not connect the battery negative cable before performing the OCS Verification Test using the scan tool and the appropriate diagnostic information. Personal injury or death may result if the system test is not performed properly.

Never replace both the Occupant Restraint Controller (ORC) and the Occupant Classification Module (OCM) at the same time. If both require replacement, replace one, then perform the Airbag System test before replacing the other.

Both the ORC and the OCM store Occupant Classification System (OCS) calibration data, which they transfer to one another when one of them is replaced. If both are replaced at the same time, an irreversible fault will be set in both modules and the OCS may malfunction and cause personal injury or death.

If equipped with OCS, the Seat Weight Sensor is a sensitive, calibrated unit and must be handled carefully. Do not drop or handle roughly. If dropped or damaged, replace with another sensor. Failure to do so may result in occupant injury or death.

If equipped with OCS, the front passenger seat must be handled carefully as well. When removing the seat, be careful when setting on floor not to drop. If dropped, the sensor may be inoperative, could result in occupant injury, or possibly death.

If equipped with OCS, when the passenger front seat is on the floor, no one should sit in the front passenger seat. This uneven force may damage the sensing ability of the seat weight sensors. If sat on and damaged, the sensor may be inoperative, could result in occupant injury, or possibly death.

DISARMING THE SYSTEM

1. Disconnect and isolate the battery negative cable.
2. Wait two minutes for the system capacitor to discharge before further service.

ARMING THE SYSTEM

1. Reconnect battery negative cable.

CLOCKSPRING CENTERING

Like the clockspring in a timepiece, the clockspring tape has travel limits and can be damaged by being wound too tightly during full stop-to-stop steering wheel rotation. To prevent this from occurring, the clockspring is centered when it is installed on the steering column. Centering the clockspring indexes the clockspring tape and the SAS integral to the clockspring to the movable steering components so that the tape can operate within its designed travel limits and the SAS can accurately monitor and communicate steering wheel inputs.

However, if the clockspring is removed from the steering column or if the steering shaft is disconnected from the steering gear, the clockspring spool and the SAS can change position relative to the movable steering components and relative to each other. The clockspring must be replaced if proper centering has been compromised or the tape may be damaged and Diagnostic Trouble Codes (DTC) or faults may be set within the SAS.

Service replacement clocksprings are shipped pre-centered and with a plastic locking pin installed. This locking pin should not be removed until the clockspring has been installed on the steering column. If the locking pin is removed before the clockspring is installed on a steering column, the clockspring must be replaced with a new unit. Proper clockspring installation must also be confirmed by viewing the SAS Menu Item, Data Display function using a diagnostic scan tool.

DRIVE TRAIN

AUTOMATIC TRANSMISSION FLUID

FLUID REFILL

68RFE

1. Remove dipstick and insert clean funnel in transmission fill tube.
2. Add following initial quantity of Mopar ATF +4 to transmission:
   a. If only fluid and filter were changed, add 10 pts. (5 qts.) of ATF +4 to transmission.
   b. If transmission was completely overhauled and the torque converter was replaced or drained, add 24 pts. (12 qts.) of ATF +4 to transmission.
3. Check the transmission fluid and adjust as required.

AS68RC

1. Remove dipstick and insert clean funnel in transmission fill tube.
2. Add following initial quantity of MoparAS68RC ATF to transmission:
   a. If only fluid and filter were changed, add 14.4 pts. (7.2 qts.) of AS68RC to transmission.
   b. If transmission was completely overhauled and the torque converter was replaced or drained, add 27.5 pts. (13.75 qts.) of Mopar AS68RC ATF to transmission.
3. Check the transmission fluid and adjust as required.

FLUID & FILTER REPLACEMENT

68RFE

1. Hoist and support vehicle on safety stands.
2. Place a large diameter shallow drain pan beneath the transmission pan.
3. Remove bolts holding front and sides of pan to transmission.
4. Loosen bolts holding rear of pan to transmission.
5. Slowly separate front of pan away from transmission allowing the fluid to drain into drain pan.
6. Hold up pan and remove remaining bolts holding pan to transmission.
7. While holding pan level, lower pan away from transmission.
8. Pour remaining fluid in pan into drain pan.
9. Remove the screw holding the primary oil filter to valve body.
10. Separate filter from valve body and oil pump and pour fluid in filter into drain pan.
11. Inspect the oil filter seal in the bottom of the oil pump. If the seal is not installed completely in the oil pump, or is otherwise damaged, then remove and discard the oil filter seal from the bottom of the oil pump. If the seal is installed correctly and is in good condition, it can be reused.
12. Remove the cooler return filter.
13. Dispose of used trans fluid and filter(s) properly.
14. Inspect bottom of pan and magnet for excessive amounts of metal. A light coating of clutch material on the bottom of the pan does not indicate a problem unless accompanied by a slipping condition or shift lag. If fluid and pan are contaminated with excessive amounts of debris, refer to the diagnosis section of this group.

To install:

⁂ CAUTION

The primary oil filter seal MUST be fully installed flush against the oil pump body. DO NOT install the seal onto the filter neck and attempt to install the filter and seal as an assembly. Damage to the transmission will result.

15. If necessary, install a new primary oil filter seal in the oil pump inlet bore. Seat the seal in the bore with a suitable tool (appropriately sized drift or socket, the butt end of a hammer etc.).
16. Place replacement filter in position on valve body and into the oil pump.
17. Install screw to hold the primary oil filter to valve body.
18. Install new cooler return filter onto the transmission, if necessary.
19. Place bead of Mopar RTV sealant onto the transmission case sealing surface.
20. Place pan in position on transmission.
21. Install bolts to hold pan to transmission. Tighten bolts to 105 inch lbs. (12 Nm) torque.
22. Lower vehicle and fill transmission with Mopar ATF +4.

AS68RC

1. Raise vehicle.
2. Place a large diameter drain pan beneath the transmission pan.
3. Remove the drain plug bolt and allow the oil to drain from the transmission pan.
4. Remove the drain pan bolts from the transmission case.
5. Remove the drain pan.
6. Remove the transmission oil filter bolts.
7. Remove the transmission oil filter and O-ring seal from the valve body.
8. Inspect bottom of pan, pick-up magnets and magnetic drain plug and fluid filter for excessive amounts of metal. A light coating of clutch material on the bottom of the pan does not indicate a problem unless accompanied by a slipping condition or shift lag. If fluid and pan are contaminated with excessive amounts of debris, refer to the diagnosis section of this group.
9. Using a suitable solvent, clean pan and magnet.
10. Using a suitable gasket scraper, clean original sealing material from surface of transmission case and the transmission pan.

To install:

11. Lubricate the transmission oil filter seal with Mopar AS68RC ATF.
12. Install the new transmission oil filter in position on valve body and into the oil pump.
13. Install the transmission oil filter bolts.
14. Tighten bolts to 88 inch lbs. (10 Nm) torque.
15. Install a new transmission oil pan gasket.
16. Place pan in position on transmission.
17. Install and tighten bolts to hold pan to transmission. Use an alternating tightening sequence.
18. Install transmission drain plug bolt. Tighten oil pan drain plug to 16 ft. lbs. (22 Nm) torque.
19. Lower vehicle and fill transmission with Mopar AS68RC ATF.

FRONT AXLE ASSEMBLY

REMOVAL & INSTALLATION

9 1/4 AA

See Figure 9.

1. With vehicle in neutral, position vehicle on hoist.
2. Remove brake calipers and rotors and disconnect ABS wheel speed sensors. See "BRAKES" section.
3. Disconnect axle vent hose.
4. Remove front propeller shaft.
5. Remove stabilizer bar links from connection at the axle brackets.

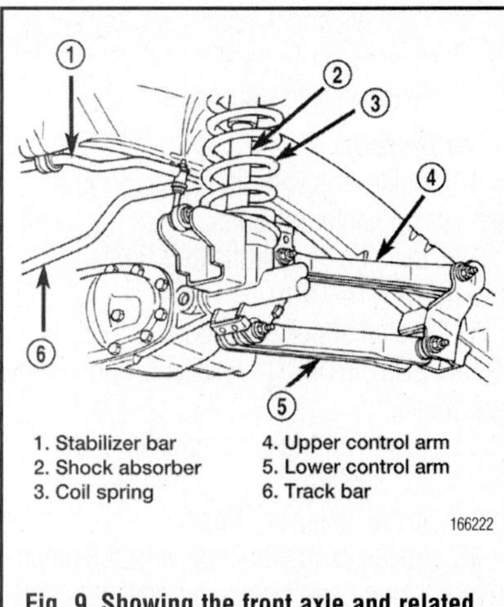

Fig. 9 Showing the front axle and related components

6. Remove lower shock absorber bolts from axle brackets.
7. Remove track bar bolt from the axle bracket.
8. Remove tie rod and drag link from the steering knuckles.
9. Position lift under the axle assembly and secure axle to lift.
10. Mark suspension alignment cams for installation reference.
11. Remove upper control arms and lower control arms from the axle bracket. See "FRONT SUSPENSION" section.
12. Lower the axle. The coil springs will drop with the axle.
13. Remove coil springs from the axle bracket.

To install:

CAUTION

Suspension components with rubber bushings should be tightened with the weight of the vehicle on the suspension. Failure to follow these instructions will result in damage.

14. Support the axle on a suitable lifting device. Secure axle to lifting device.
15. Position the axle under the vehicle.
16. Install coil springs, retainer clip and bolts.
17. Raise axle and align it with the spring pads.
18. Position upper and lower control arms in the axle brackets. Install bolts, nuts and align the suspension alignment cams to the reference marks. Do not tighten at this time.
19. Connect track bar to the axle bracket and install the bolt. Do not tighten at this time.
20. Install shock absorber and stabilizer bar.
21. Install drag link and tie rod to the steering knuckles.
22. Install ABS wheel speed sensors, rotors and brake calipers. See "BRAKES" section.
23. Connect the axle vent hose.
24. Install front propeller shaft.
25. With vehicle on the ground, tighten upper control arm nuts at axle, then at frame, to 110 ft. lbs. (149 Nm).
26. With vehicle on the ground, tighten lower control arm nuts at axle, then at frame, to 140 ft. lbs. (190 Nm).
27. Tighten track bar bolt at the axle bracket to 130 ft. lbs. (176 Nm).
28. Check front wheel alignment.

275FBI

1. With vehicle in neutral, position vehicle on hoist.
2. Position a lift under axle and secure lift to the axle.

➡Mark propeller shaft and companion flange for installation alignment reference.

3. Remove propeller shaft from pinion flange.
4. Remove brake calipers, rotors, ABS wheel speed sensors. Remove brake hose retainer bolts from axle. See "BRAKES" section.
5. Disconnect axle vent hose.
6. Remove stabilizer bar link nuts. Remove stabilizer bar links from axle.
7. Remove lower shock absorbers bolts from axle brackets.
8. Remove track bar bolt from the axle bracket.
9. Remove damper from axle bracket.
10. Remove tie rod and drag link from the steering knuckles.
11. Remove upper control arm nuts and bolts from axle brackets.
12. Remove lower control arm nuts and bolts from the axle brackets.
13. Lower the axle. The coil springs will drop with the axle.
14. Remove coil springs from the axle bracket.

To install:

CAUTION

Suspension components with rubber bushings should be tightened with the weight of the vehicle on the suspension. Failure to follow these instructions will result in damage to the bushings.

15. Secure axle to lifting device.
16. Align axle under the vehicle.
17. Install springs, retainer clip and bolts.
18. Raise axle and align it with the spring pads.
19. Install lower control arms in the axle brackets. Install bolts and nuts and hand tighten nuts.
20. Install upper control arms in the axle brackets. Install bolts and nuts and hand tighten nuts.
21. Install track bar in axle bracket and install bolt and nut hand tighten.
22. Install shock absorbers and install nuts and bolts hand tighten.
23. Install stabilizer bar link in axle bracket and tighten nut to 111 ft. lbs. (150 Nm).
24. Install track bar and tighten bolt to 40 ft. lbs. (54 Nm).
25. Install drag link and tie rod to the steering knuckles.
26. Install steering damper in axle bracket and tighten to 55 ft. lbs. (75 Nm).
27. Install rotors, brake calipers, and ABS wheel speed sensors.
28. Install brake hose retainers and bolts.
29. Install axle vent hose.
30. Install propeller shaft with all reference marks aligned. Install transfer case companion flange bolts and tighten to 65 ft. lbs. (88 Nm).
31. Install new axle companion flange bolts and tighten to 21 ft. lbs. (28 Nm).

➡Companion flange bolts incorporate a Loctite patch, new bolts should be used. If bolts are not available, clean bolts and apply Loctite 242 to the threads.

32. Lower vehicle on the ground and tighten the following components at the axle:
    - Upper control arm nuts: 184 ft. lbs. (250 Nm)
    - Lower control arm nuts: 276 ft. lbs. (375 Nm)
    - Shock absorber nuts: 100 ft. lbs. (136 Nm)
    - Track bar bolt: 273 (370 Nm)
33. Check front wheel alignment.

PROPELLER SHAFT

REMOVAL & INSTALLATION

Front

1. With vehicle in neutral, position vehicle on hoist.
2. Remove exhaust crossover pipe.
3. Mark a line across the axle compan-

ion flange, propeller shaft, flange yoke and transfer case for installation reference.

4. Remove axle/transfer case companion flange bolts. Remove dust boot clamp from the CV joint end of the shaft if equipped.

5. Remove propeller shaft.

To install:

6. Install front propeller shaft with all reference marks aligned.

7. Install with dust boot clamp at transfer case end.

8. Install new axle companion flange bolts and tighten as follows:

- Front flange (DP heavy duty): 55 ft. lbs. (75 Nm)
- Front flange (DJ/D2/DD heavy duty): 21 ft. lbs. (28 Nm)
- Rear flange (DP heavy duty): 55 ft. lbs. (75 Nm)
- Rear flange (DJ/D2/DD heavy duty): 85 ft. lbs. (115 Nm)

➡Companion flange bolts incorporate a Loctite patch and new bolts should be used. If bolts are not available, clean bolts and apply Loctite 242 to the threads.

9. Install exhaust crossover pipe.

10. Install skid plate, if equipped.

Rear

1. With vehicle in neutral, position vehicle on hoist.

2. Mark propeller shaft pinion flange and propeller shaft flange with installation reference marks.

3. If equipped with a center bearing, mark an outline of the center bearing on the center bearing bracket for installation reference. Then support propeller shaft and remove mounting bolts.

4. Remove pinion flange bolts from propeller shaft.

5. Slide rear propeller shaft back off automatic transmission output shaft, then mark propeller shaft and transmission output shaft for installation reference.

6. Remove rear propeller shaft from vehicle.

⁂ CAUTION

Failure to follow these instructions may result in a driveline vibration.

To install:

7. Slide slip yoke onto automatic transmission output shaft with reference marks aligned.

8. If equipped with manual transmission, align reference marks on rear propeller shaft and pinion flange. Install new companion flange bolts and tighten to 85 ft. lbs. (115 Nm).

9. If two-piece propeller shaft, align center bearing with reference marks on center bearing bracket and tighten as follows:

- Bolts: 40 ft. lbs. (50 Nm)
- Center bearing yoke nut: 500 ft. lbs. (678 Nm)

10. Align reference marks on rear of propeller shaft and pinion flange. Install new companion flange bolts and tighten as follows:

- Rear flange (DP heavy duty): 55 ft. lbs. (75 Nm)
- Rear flange (DJ/D2/DD heavy duty): 85 ft. lbs. (115 Nm)

⁂ CAUTION

Failure to follow these instruction may result in a driveline vibration.

REAR AXLE SHAFT, BEARING & SEAL

REMOVAL & INSTALLATION

10 1/2 AA & 11 1/2 AA

See Figure 10.

1. With vehicle in neutral, position vehicle on hoist.

2. Position a lift under axle and secure lift to the axle.

3. Remove all rear brake components. See "BRAKES" section.

4. Remove axle vent hose.

5. Mark propeller shaft and companion flange for installation alignment reference.

6. Remove propeller shaft, as described in this section.

1. Leaf springs
2. Insulators
3. U-bolt nuts
4. Leaf spring front attachments
5. U-bolts
6. Leaf spring rear attachments

166953

Fig. 10 Showing rear axle assembly mounting

7. Remove shock absorbers from axle.

8. Remove U-bolts from axle.

9. Remove axle from the vehicle.

To install:

10. Raise axle with lift and align to the leaf spring centering bolts.

11. Install axle U-bolts and tighten to 110 ft. lbs. (149 Nm).

12. Install shock absorbers to axle. See "REAR SUSPENSION" section for tightening specifications.

13. Install all brake components. See "BRAKES" section.

14. Install axle vent hose.

15. Install propeller shaft with reference marks aligned and tighten all fasteners. See "Propeller Shaft" in this section.

16. Fill differential to specifications.

302RBI

1. With vehicle in neutral, position vehicle on hoist.

2. Position a lift under axle and secure lift to the axle.

3. Mark propeller shaft and companion flange for installation alignment reference.

4. Remove propeller shaft from pinion flange, as described in this section.

5. Remove axle vent hose axle housing.

6. Remove wiring harness from brake sensor.

7. Remove brake calipers, rotors, brake lines and park cables from axle housing. See "BRAKES" section.

8. Remove shock absorbers and stabilizer bar from the axle.

9. Remove U-bolt (1) nuts, then remove U-bolts and lower the axle from the vehicle.

To install:

10. Raise axle with lift and align to the leaf spring centering bolts.

11. Install axle U-bolts and tighten nuts to 336 ft. lbs. (455 Nm).

12. Install shock absorbers to axle and tighten nuts to 118 ft. lbs. (160 Nm).

13. Install stabilizer bar to axle and tighten nuts to 48 ft. lbs. (65 Nm).

14. Install rotors, brake calipers, brake lines and park cables to axle housing.

15. Install wiring harness to brake sensor.

16. Install axle vent hose to axle housing.

17. Install propeller shaft to pinion flange with reference marks aligned and tighten to specification. See "Propeller Shaft" in this section.

18. Fill differential to specifications.

19. Remove lift from axle and lower the vehicle.

REAR PINION SEAL

REMOVAL & INSTALLATION

10 1/2 AA & 11 1/2 AA

See Figure 11.

1. Remove axle shafts. See "Rear Axle Shaft" in this section.
2. Mark propeller shaft and pinion flange for installation reference and remove shaft.
3. Rotate pinion gear three or four times.
4. Record pinion torque to rotate with an inch pound torque wrench.
5. Hold pinion flange with special wrench (8979 or equivalent) and remove pinion flange nut and washer.
6. Mark a line across the pinion shaft and flange for installation reference.
7. Remove pinion flange with a suitable puller (8992 or equivalent).
8. Remove pinion shaft seal with a pry tool or slide hammer mounted screw.

To install:

9. Install new pinion seal, using proper installer and handle (8896 and C-4171 or equivalent).
10. Apply a light coat of Teflon sealant to the pinion flange splines.
11. Install flange on the pinion shaft with the reference marks aligned.
12. Lightly tap the pinion flange onto the pinion until a few threads are showing.
13. Install flange washer and new pinion nut.
14. Hold flange with flange wrench and tighten pinion nut until pinion end play is taken up.
15. Rotate pinion several times to seat bearings.
16. Measure pinion torque to rotate with an inch pound torque wrench. Pinion torque to rotate should be equal to recorded reading plus an additional 3–5 inch lbs. (0.40–0.57 Nm).
17. If torque to rotating is low, tighten the pinion nut in 5 ft. lbs. (6.8 Nm) increments until pinion torque to rotate is achieved.
18. Rotate pinion several times then verify pinion torque to rotate again.
19. Install axle shafts. See "Rear Axle Shaft" in this section.
20. Install propeller shaft with reference marks aligned.
21. Check and fill differential if necessary.

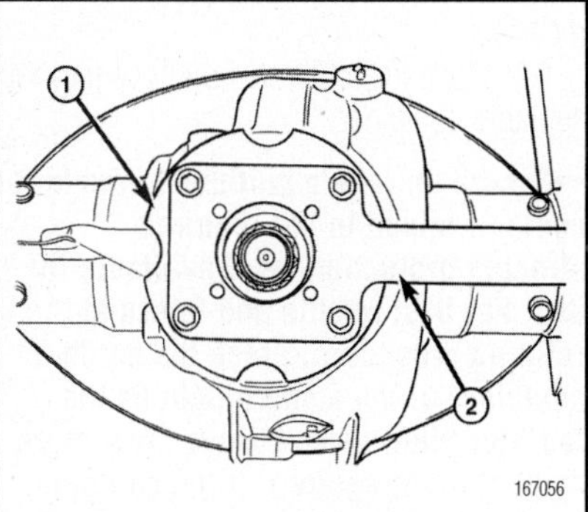

Fig. 11 Hold pinion flange (1) with special wrench (8979 or equivalent) (2) and remove pinion flange nut and washer.

302RBI

See Figures 12 and 13.

1. Remove propeller shaft.
2. Install adapter (10054 or equivalent) on pinion flange and bolt in place.
3. Hold pinion flange with holder and adapter (6971 and 10054 or equivalent).
4. Remove pinion nut with a torque multiplier and ratchet.
5. Bolt puller (8992) to adapter (10054) and remove pinion flange.
6. Remove pinion seal with seal puller.

To install:

7. Install pinion seal in housing with a proper installer (10055 or equivalent).
8. Install pinion flange on pinion.
9. Install new pinion nut.
10. Install adapter (10054 or equivalent) on pinion flange and bolt in place.
11. Hold pinion flange with holder and adapter, as used during removal.
12. Tighten pinion nut to 689 ft. lbs. (937 Nm) with a torque multiplier and torque wrench.

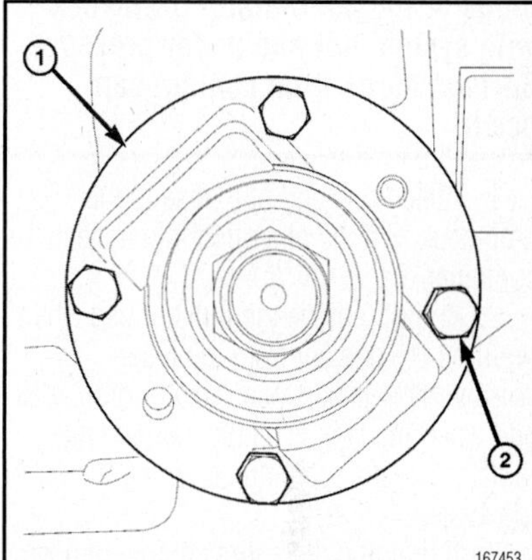

Fig. 12 Install adapter (10054 or equivalent) (1) on pinion flange and bolt (2) in place.

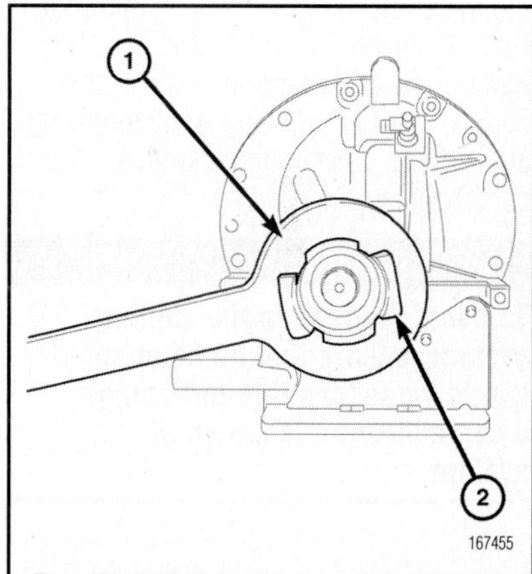

Fig. 13 Hold pinion flange with holder (1) and adapter (2) (6971 and 10054 or equivalent).

ENGINE COOLING

ENGINE COOLANT

DRAINING PROCEDURE

See Figure 14.

✻✻ CAUTION

Do not remove cylinder block drain plugs or loosen radiator draincock with system hot and under pressure. Serious burns from coolant can occur.

1. Attach one end of a hose to the draincock. Put the other end into a clean container.
2. do not remove the radiator cap when draining the coolant from the reservoir/overflow tank. Open radiator draincock and when the tank is empty, remove the radiator cap and continue draining the cooling system.
3. If draining the entire engine, remove the cylinder block drain plugs.

BLEEDING

Evacuating or purging air from the cooling system involves the use of a pressurized air operated vacuum generator. The vacuum created allows for a quick and complete coolant refilling while removing any airlocks present in the system components.

✻✻ CAUTION

To avoid damage to the cooling system, ensure that no component would be susceptible to damage when a vacuum is drawn on the system.

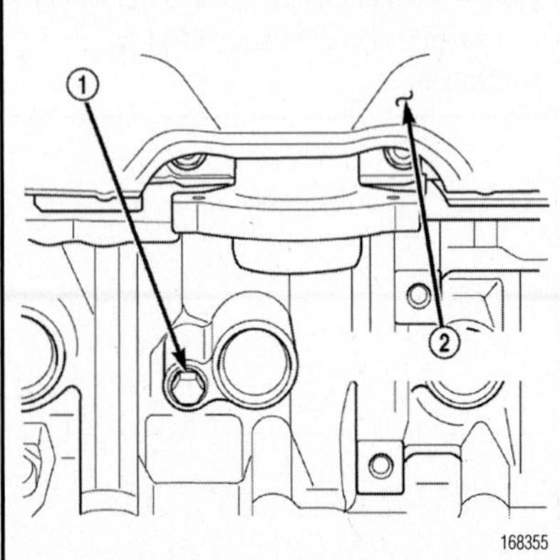

Fig. 14 If draining the entire engine, remove the cylinder block drain plugs (1)—intake manifold noted (2).

✻✻ WARNING

Antifreeze is an ethylene glycol base coolant and is harmful if swallowed or inhaled. If swallowed, drink two glasses of water and induce vomiting. If inhaled, move to fresh air area. Seek medical attention immediately. Do not store in open or unmarked containers. Wash skin and clothing thoroughly after coming in contact with ethylene glycol. Keep out of reach of children. Dispose of glycol based coolant properly. Contact your dealer or government agency for location of collection center in your area. Do not open a cooling system when the engine is at operating temperature or hot under pressure; personal injury can result. Avoid radiator cooling fan when engine compartment related service is performed; personal injury can result.

✻✻ CAUTION

Wear appropriate eye and hand protection when performing this procedure.

➡The service area where this procedure is performed should have a minimum shop air requirement of 80 PSI (5.5 bar) and should be equipped with an air dryer system.

➡For best results, the radiator should be empty. The vehicle's heater control should be set to the heat position (ignition may need to be turned to the on position but do not start the motor).

➡Refer to the Chrysler Pentastar Service Equipment (Chrysler PSE) Coolant Refiller #85-15-0650 or equivalent tool's operating manual for specific assembly steps.

1. Choose an appropriate adapter cone that will fit the vehicle's radiator filler neck or reservoir tank.
2. Attach the adapter cone to the vacuum gauge.
3. Make sure the vacuum generator/venturi ball valve is closed and attach an airline hose (minimum shop air requirement of 80 PSI/5.5 bar) to the vacuum generator/venturi.
4. Position the adaptor cone/vacuum gauge assembly into the radiator filler neck or reservoir tank. Ensure that the adapter cone is sealed properly.
5. Connect the vacuum generator/venturi to the positioned adaptor cone/vacuum gauge assembly.
6. Open the vacuum generator/venturi ball valve.

➡Do not bump or move the assembly as it may result in loss of vacuum. Some radiator overflow hoses may need to be clamped off to obtain vacuum.

7. Let the system run until the vacuum gauge shows a good vacuum through the cooling system. Refer to the tool's operating manual for appropriate pressure readings.

➡If a strong vacuum is being created in the system, it is normal to see the radiator hoses to collapse.

8. Close the vacuum generator/venturi ball valve.
9. Disconnect the vacuum generator/venturi and airline from the adaptor cone/vacuum gauge assembly.
10. Wait approximately 20 seconds, if the pressure readings do not move, the system has no leaks. If the pressure readings move, a leak could be present in the system and the cooling system should be checked for leaks and the procedure should be repeated.
11. Place the tool's suction hose into the coolant's container.

➡Ensure there is a sufficient amount of coolant, mixed to the required strength/protection level available for use. For best results and to assist the refilling procedure, place the coolant container at the same height as the radiator filler neck. Always draw more coolant than required. If the coolant level is too low, it will pull air into the cooling system which could result in airlocks in the system.

12. Connect the tool's suction hose to the adaptor cone/vacuum gauge assembly.
13. Open the suction hose's ball valve to begin refilling the cooling system.
14. When the vacuum gauge reads zero, the system is filled.

➡On some remote pressurized tanks, it is recommended to stop filling when the proper level is reached.

15. Close the suction hose's ball valve and remove the suction hose from the adaptor cone/vacuum gauge assembly.
16. Remove the adaptor cone/vacuum gauge assembly from the radiator filler neck or reservoir tank.

17. With heater control unit in the HEAT position, operate engine with container cap in place.

18. After engine has reached normal operating temperature, shut engine off and allow it to cool. When engine is cooling down, coolant will be drawn into the radiator from the pressure container.

19. Add coolant to the recovery bottle/container as necessary.

➡Only add coolant to the container when the engine is cold. Coolant level in a warm engine will be higher due to thermal expansion.

20. Add necessary coolant to raise container level to the COLD MINIMUM mark after each cool down period.

21. Once the appropriate coolant level is achieved, attach the radiator cap or reservoir tank cap.

ENGINE FAN

REMOVAL & INSTALLATION

Electric Fan

1. Disconnect and isolate the negative battery cable.
2. Remove the upper radiator seal push pins and plastic rivets. Remove the upper radiator seal.
3. If equipped, remove the viscous fan assembly from the water pump hub shaft.(
4. Disconnect the radiator fan electrical connector.
5. Remove the fan shroud to radiator mounting bolts.
6. Disengage the fan shroud's lower retaining clips and position the fan shroud towards the rear of vehicle.
7. Disengage the electric cooling fan to radiator upper retaining clips.
8. Disengage the electric fan to radiator lower retaining clips.
9. Pulling upward remove the viscous fan, radiator fan shroud and the electric cooling fan as an assembly.

➡The lower fan shroud can be removed from the upper fan shroud if needed.

10. If damaged, remove radiator fan resistor from shroud.

To install:

11. If removed, install the electric cooling fan resistor. Tighten the mounting screw securely.
12. If removed, install the lower fan shroud to the upper fan shroud.
13. Position the viscous fan (if equipped), radiator fan shroud and electric cooling fan into the vehicle as an assembly.
14. Install the electric cooling fan by engaging the upper and lower retaining clips to the radiator.
15. Install the fan shroud by engaging the lower retaining clips to the radiator/electric cooling fan.

➡Make sure all retaining clips lock into place.

16. Install the fan shroud mounting bolts. Tighten to 89 inch lbs. (10 Nm).
17. Connect the electric cooling fan electrical connector.
18. Position the upper radiator seal. Install the upper radiator seal plastic rivets. Install the upper radiator push pins.
19. Connect the negative battery cable.

Viscous Fan

5.7L

See Figure 15.

➡Do not attempt to remove the fan/viscous fan drive assembly from the vehicle at this time.

➡If the viscous fan drive is replaced because of mechanical damage, the cooling fan blades should also be inspected. Inspect for fatigue cracks, loose blades, or loose rivets that could have resulted from excessive vibration. Replace fan blade assembly if any of these conditions are found. Also inspect water pump bearing and shaft assembly for any related damage due to a viscous fan drive malfunction.

1. Disconnect negative battery cable from battery.
2. The thermal viscous fan drive/fan blade assembly is attached (threaded) to the water pump hub shaft. Remove the fan blade/viscous fan drive assembly from the water pump by turning the mounting nut clockwise as viewed from the front. Threads on the viscous fan drive are LEFT-HAND. A 36 mm fan wrench should be used to prevent pulley from rotating.

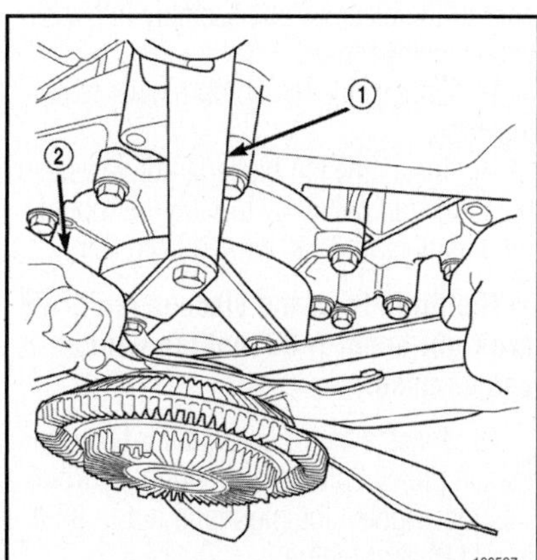

Fig. 15 Showing the fan drive assembly (2) and the fan wrench (1) used to prevent pulley rotation.

3. Do not unbolt the fan blade assembly from viscous fan drive at this time.
4. Remove the fan shroud-to-radiator mounting bolts. Pull the lower shroud mounts out of the radiator tank clips.
5. Remove the fan shroud, electric cooling fan, and fan blade/viscous fan drive assembly as a complete unit from vehicle.
6. After removing the fan blade/viscous fan drive assembly, do not place the viscous fan drive in a horizontal position. If stored horizontally, silicone fluid in the viscous fan drive could drain into its bearing assembly and contaminate lubricant.

✲✲ CAUTION

Do not remove water pump pulley-to-water pump bolts. This pulley is under spring tension.

7. Remove four bolts securing fan blade assembly to viscous fan drive.

✲✲ CAUTION

Some engines equipped with serpentine drive belts have reverse rotating fans and viscous fan drives. They are marked with the word REVERSE to designate their usage. Installation of the wrong fan or viscous fan drive can result in engine overheating.

To install:

➡If the viscous fan drive is replaced because of mechanical damage, the cooling fan blades should also be inspected. Inspect for fatigue cracks, loose blades, or loose rivets that could have resulted from excessive vibration. Replace fan blade assembly if any of these conditions are found. Also inspect water pump bearing and shaft assembly for any related damage due to a viscous fan drive malfunction.

➡Viscous Fan Drive Fluid Pump Out Requirement: After installing a new viscous fan drive, bring the engine speed up to approximately 2000 rpm and hold for approximately two minutes. This will ensure proper fluid distribution within the drive.

8. Install fan blade assembly to the viscous fan drive. Tighten the bolts to 18 ft. lbs. (24 Nm) torque.

9. Position the fan shroud, electric cooling fan and the fan blade/viscous fan drive assembly to the vehicle as a complete unit.

10. Install the fan shroud.

➡The thermal viscous fan drive/fan blade assembly is attached (threaded) to the water pump hub shaft.

11. Install the fan blade/viscous fan drive assembly to the water pump by turning the mounting nut counterclockwise as viewed from the front. Threads on the viscous fan drive are LEFT-HAND. A 36 mm fan wrench should be used to prevent pulley from rotating. Tighten mounting nut to 37 ft. lbs. (50 Nm).

12. Connect the negative battery cable.

6.7L Diesel

➡If the electronically controlled viscous fan drive is replaced because of mechanical damage, the cooling fan blades should also be inspected. Inspect for fatigue cracks, or chipped blades that could have resulted from excessive vibration. Replace fan blade assembly if any of these conditions are found. Also inspect wiring harness and connectors for damage.

1. Remove the upper radiator shroud.
2. Disconnect and isolate the battery negative cable.
3. If equipped, disconnect and isolate the negative battery cable from the auxiliary battery.
4. Disconnect the electronically controlled viscous fan electrical connector at the fan shroud.
5. Remove and re-position the fan drive wire harness support from the fan shroud.
6. Remove the two fan shroud-to-radiator shroud mounting bolts, located on the driver side of the vehicle.
7. Remove the fan shroud-to-radiator shroud mounting bolt, located on the passenger side of the vehicle.
8. Remove the fan shroud-to-lower radiator shroud push pins.

➡Do not remove the fan pulley bolts. This pulley is under spring tension.

➡The electronically controlled viscous fan drive/fan blade assembly is attached (threaded) to the fan pulley shaft. Remove the fan blade/fan drive assembly from fan pulley by turning the mounting nut counterclockwise (as viewed from front). Threads on the viscous fan drive are RIGHT-HAND. A 36 MM Fan Wrench can be used. Place a bar or screwdriver between the fan pulley bolts to prevent pulley from rotating.

9. Disengage the fan shroud lower retaining clips.
10. Collapse fan shroud toward front of vehicle and remove fan drive/fan blade and fan shroud as an assembly.
11. Remove the electrical connector bracket by disengaging the retainer clip and sliding the connector bracket out of the fan shroud.

⁂ CAUTION

The electronically controlled viscous fan drive is vibration and impact sensitive, especially at the electrical connectors. Do not drop the unit.

12. Remove the four fan blade mounting bolts from the viscous fan drive.
13. Inspect the fan for cracked, chipped or damaged fan blades.

To install:

⁂ CAUTION

The electronically controlled viscous fan drive is vibration and impact sensitive, especially at the electrical connectors. Do not drop the unit.

14. Install the fan blade assembly to the electrically controlled viscous fan drive. Tighten the mounting bolts to 18 ft. lbs. (24 Nm) torque.
15. Position the fan/fan drive assembly inside fan shroud.
16. Install the electrical connector bracket by sliding the connector bracket into the fan shroud and engaging the retainer clip.
17. Tilt the fan shroud/fan blade toward front of vehicle and position the fan shroud/fan blade as an assembly into the engine compartment.
18. Engage the fan shroud lower retaining clips.
19. Install the fan blade/fan drive assembly to the fan pulley by turning the mounting nut clockwise (as viewed from front).

➡The threads on the viscous fan drive are right-hand. A 36 mm fan wrench can be used.

20. Place a bar or screwdriver between the fan pulley bolts to prevent pulley from rotating. Tighten the mounting nut to 85 ft. lbs. (115 Nm) torque.
21. Install the fan shroud-to-lower radiator shroud push pins.
22. Install the fan shroud-to-radiator shroud mounting bolt, located on the passenger side of the vehicle. Tighten the bolt to 18 ft. lbs. (24 Nm).
23. Install the two fan shroud-to-radiator shroud mounting bolts, located on the driver side of the vehicle. Tighten the bolts to 18 ft. lbs. (24 Nm).
24. Position and connect the fan drive wire harness support to the fan shroud.
25. Connect the electronically controlled viscous fan electrical connector at the fan shroud.
26. If equipped, connect the negative battery cable to the auxiliary battery.
27. Connect the negative battery cable.
28. Install the upper radiator shroud.
29. Perform the viscous fan drive fluid pump out requirement:
    a. After installing a new viscous fan drive, bring the engine speed up to approximately 2000 rpm and hold for approximately two minutes.
    b. This will ensure proper fluid distribution within the drive.
30. Start the vehicle and check for proper clearance between the fan blade assembly and the fan shroud.

RADIATOR

REMOVAL & INSTALLATION

5.7L

1. Disconnect and isolate the negative battery cable.
2. Raise and secure the vehicle.
3. Drain the cooling system.

⁂ WARNING

Do not remove the cylinder block drain plugs or loosen the radiator draincock with the system hot and under pressure. Serious burns from the coolant can occur.

4. Remove the lower radiator clamp and hose.
5. Remove the lower radiator seal.
6. Remove the lower center electric fan to radiator retaining clip.
7. Lower the vehicle.
8. Remove the upper radiator clamp and hose.
9. Remove the upper radiator seal push pins and plastic rivets. Remove the upper radiator seal.
10. Remove the grille as follows:
    a. Remove the four push pins, remove the two plastic rivets, and remove the upper radiator seal.

b. Remove the four upper grille support bolts.

c. Using a trim stick, separate the two lower spring clips.

d. Release the two lower hooks and remove the grille.

11. Remove the bolt from the transmission cooler line to radiator bracket.
12. Remove the washer reserve tank.
13. Remove the coolant overflow/recovery bottle.
14. Remove the front bolts from the A/C compressor/transmission combination cooler.
15. Remove the upper center electric fan to radiator retaining clip.
16. Disconnect the transmission cooler lines from the transmission cooler, then plug the transmission lines and cooler to prevent leakage.
17. Disengage the two A/C compressor/transmission combination cooler mounting brackets from the left side of the radiator. Do not disconnect the A/C lines.
18. After the A/C compressor/transmission combination cooler is disengaged, secure it to the upper radiator support with a strap, cord or equivalent.
19. Remove the fan shroud mounting bolts and pull up and out of the radiator tank clips. Position the shroud rearward over the fan blades towards engine.
20. Disengage the electric cooling fan to radiator upper retaining clips.
21. Disengage the electric fan to radiator lower retaining clips.
22. Remove the viscous fan, fan shroud and electric cooling fan as an assembly.
23. Remove the two radiator upper mounting bolts.
24. Lift the radiator straight up and out of the engine compartment. Take care not to damage cooling fins or tubes on the radiator and oil coolers when removing.

To install:

25. Position the radiator into the engine compartment. Take care not to damage cooling fins or tubes on the radiator and oil coolers when installing.
26. Install the rubber insulators to the lower radiator mounting features (alignment dowel and support bracket at the lower part of the radiator).
27. Install and tighten the two radiator upper mounting bolts.
28. Install the electric cooling fan.
29. Install the fan shroud by engaging the fan shroud lower retaining clips to the radiator/electric cooling fan.
30. Install the fan shroud to radiator lower center retaining clip.
31. Install the fan shroud mounting bolts. Tighten to 89 inch lbs. (10 Nm).
32. Install the fan shroud to radiator upper center retaining clip.

➡Make sure all retaining clips lock into place.

33. Connect the electric cooling fan electrical connector.
34. Engage the two A/C compressor/transmission combination cooler mounting brackets to the left side of the radiator.
35. Connect the transmission cooler lines to the transmission cooler.
36. Install and tighten the two bolts that secure the A/C condenser to the right side of the radiator.
37. Install the bolt securing the transmission cooler line to radiator bracket. Tighten the bolt securely.
38. Install the coolant overflow/recovery bottle.
39. Install the windshield washer reserve tank.
40. Install the front grille in reverse of the removal sequence.
41. Connect the upper radiator hose and install the clamp in it's proper position.
42. Install the upper radiator seal plastic rivets and push pins.
43. Raise and secure the vehicle.
44. Install the lower center electric fan to radiator retaining clip.
45. Install the lower radiator clamp and hose.
46. Install the lower radiator seal.
47. Install battery negative cable.
48. Fill cooling system.
49. Check the system for any leaks.
50. Operate the engine until it reaches normal operating temperature. Check cooling system fluid levels.

6.7L Diesel

1. Remove the upper radiator shroud.
2. Disconnect and isolate the battery negative cable.
3. If equipped, disconnect and isolate the negative battery cable from the auxiliary battery.

WARNING

Do not remove the cylinder block drain plugs or loosen the radiator draincock with the system hot and under pressure. Serious burns from coolant can occur.

4. Drain the cooling system.
5. Disconnect the ambient air temperature sensor electrical connector and mass airflow sensor electrical connector (if equipped).
6. Remove air box and turbocharger inlet tube.
7. Remove coolant tank hose from the fastening clips located on top of the radiator.
8. Remove the viscous fan and fan shroud.
9. Remove the hose clamps and hoses from radiator.
10. Disconnect the transmission cooler lines at the transmission cooler. The transmission cooler will remain on the radiator and can be removed as an assembly.
11. Remove the two radiator upper mounting bolts.
12. Lift and support the vehicle.
13. Remove the power steering cooler mounting bolts and position the power steering cooler out of the way.
14. Lower the vehicle.
15. Tilt the radiator towards the rear of the vehicle and lift it out of the engine compartment.

CAUTION

The bottom of the radiator is equipped with two alignment dowels that fit into holes in the lower radiator support panel. Rubber biscuits (insulators) are installed to these dowels. Take care not to damage cooling fins or tubes on the radiator and air conditioning condenser or the electronic viscous fan connector when removing.

To install:

16. Install the rubber insulators to the alignment dowels at the lower part of radiator.
17. Lower the radiator into position while guiding the two alignment dowels into the lower radiator support.
18. Raise the vehicle.
19. Position the power steering cooler on the radiator and tighten the nuts to 90 inch lbs. (10 Nm)
20. Lower the vehicle.
21. Install the two upper radiator mounting bolts. Tighten the bolts to 105 inch lbs. (12 Nm) torque.
22. If equipped, connect the transmission cooler lines to the transmission cooler. Inspect quick connect fittings for debris and install until an audible "click" is heard. Tug on lines to verify connection.
23. Connect both radiator hoses and install hose clamps.
24. Install the cooling fan.
25. Position the coolant recovery tank

hose into the clips located on the top of the radiator.

26. Install the air box and the turbocharger inlet hose. Tighten clamps.

27. Connect the mass airflow sensor electrical connector and ambient air temp sensor electrical connector (if equipped).

28. Install the upper radiator shroud.

29. If equipped, connect the negative battery cable to the auxiliary battery.

30. Connect the battery negative cable.

31. Position heater controls to Full Heat position.

32. Fill cooling system with coolant.

33. Operate the engine until it reaches normal operating temperature. Check the cooling system and automatic transmission (if equipped) for leaks.

THERMOSTAT

REMOVAL & INSTALLATION

5.7L

1. Disconnect the negative battery cable.
2. Drain the cooling system.
3. Remove the radiator hose clamp and radiator hose at the thermostat housing.
4. Remove the thermostat housing mounting bolts, thermostat housing and thermostat.
5. Installation is the reverse of the removal procedure.

6.7L Diesel

➡Thermostats for the Cummins diesel, while physically interchangeable, should not be mixed and matched. For model year 2010 and forward, the 6.7L diesel engine uses a 200°F thermostat. Confirm the temperature stamp on the thermostat rim prior to removal or installation.

⁂ CAUTION

Do not loosen the radiator draincock with the system hot and pressurized. Serious burns from the coolant can occur.

1. Disconnect the battery negative cables.
2. Remove the vent plug near EGR cooler.
3. Drain the cooling system until the coolant level is below the thermostat.
4. Disconnect the exhaust gas pressure sensor electrical connector.
5. Remove the exhaust pressure tube from the thermostat housing.
6. Remove the EGR cooler cross over tube.
7. Remove the radiator hose clamp and hose from the thermostat housing.
8. Remove the heat shield.
9. Remove the three water outlet-to-cylinder head bolts and remove the water outlet connector.
10. Clean the mating surfaces of the thermostat housing and clean the thermostat seat groove at the top of the thermostat housing.

To install:

11. Inspect the thermostat seal for cuts or nicks. Replace if damaged.
12. Install the thermostat into the groove in the top of the cylinder head.
13. Install the thermostat housing and bolts. Tighten the bolts to 89 inch lbs. (10 Nm).
14. Install the heat shield. Tighten the bolts to 79 inch lbs. (9 Nm).
15. Install the exhaust pressure tube. Tighten to 89 inch lbs. (10 Nm).
16. Connect exhaust pressure sensor electrical connector.
17. Install the EGR cross over tube.
18. Install the P-clip and bolt and tighten.
19. Install the radiator upper hose and clamp.
20. Fill the cooling system with coolant.
21. Connect the battery negative cables.
22. Start the engine and check for any coolant leaks. Run engine to check for proper thermostat operation.

WATER PUMP

REMOVAL & INSTALLATION

5.7L

See Figure 16.

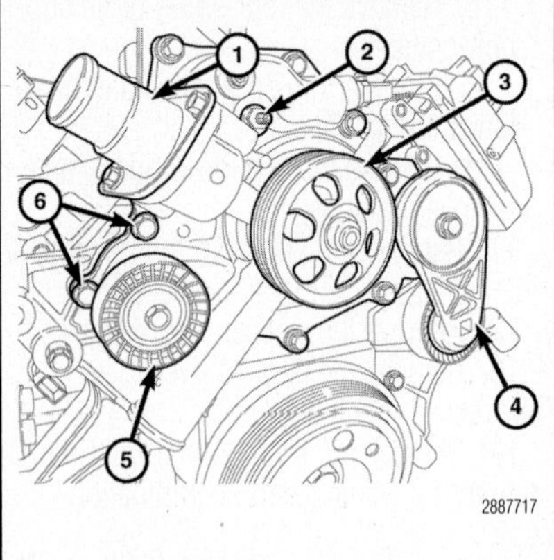

Fig. 16 Showing water pump and related components

1. Disconnect negative battery cable.
2. Remove the air intake assembly.
3. Remove the resonator mounting bracket.
4. Remove cooling fan assembly, as described in this section.
5. Drain coolant into a clean container.
6. Remove the upper radiator hose from the thermostat housing and position aside.
7. Remove serpentine belt. See "Accessory Drive Belt" in "ENGINE MECHANICAL" section.
8. Remove idler pulley.
9. Remove belt tensioner assembly.
10. Remove lower radiator hose from the water pump and position aside.
11. Remove the upper metal heater tube from the cylinder head.
12. Remove water pump mounting bolts and remove pump.

To install:

13. Clean mating surfaces and install water pump. Tighten mounting bolts to 18 ft. lbs. (24 Nm).
14. Install upper metal heater tube.
15. Install belt tensioner assembly.
16. Install idler pulley.
17. Install the lower radiator hose.
18. Install serpentine belt.
19. Install the resonator mounting bracket.
20. Install cooling fan assembly.
21. Install the upper radiator hose to the thermostat housing.
22. Install the air intake assembly.
23. Connect negative battery cable.
24. Evacuate air and refill cooling system, as described in this section.
25. Check cooling system for leaks.

6.7L Diesel

1. Disconnect battery negative cables.
2. Drain cooling system.
3. Disconnect ambient air temp sensor electrical connector and mass airflow sensor electrical connector (if equipped).
4. Remove turbocharger inlet tube and air filter housing.
5. Remove generator assembly. See "ENGINE ELECTRICAL" section.
6. Remove the accessory drive belt. See "ENGINE MECHANICAL" section.
7. Remove water pump mounting bolts.
8. Remove O-ring from water pump.
9. Remove water pump.
10. Clean water pump sealing surface on cylinder block.

To install:

11. Install new O-ring seal in groove on water pump.
12. Install water pump with the weep hole facing downward. Tighten mounting bolts to 18 ft. lbs. (24 Nm) torque.
13. Install generator assembly. See "ENGINE ELECTRICAL" section.
14. Install accessory drive belt. See "ENGINE MECHANICAL" section.
15. Install air box and tube assembly.
16. Install air filter housing.
17. Bleed air and refill cooling system. See "Engine Coolant" heading in this section.
18. Connect both battery cables.
19. Start and warm the engine. Check for leaks.

ENGINE ELECTRICAL — BATTERY SYSTEM

BATTERY

REMOVAL & INSTALLATION

1. Turn the ignition switch to the Off position. Be certain that all electrical accessories are turned off.
2. Disconnect the battery negative cable from the battery.
3. Disconnect the battery positive cable from the battery.
4. Remove the battery thermal cover.
5. Remove the battery hold down retaining bolt and battery hold down.
6. Remove the battery from the battery tray.
7. Installation is the reverse of the removal procedure.
8. Apply a thin coating of petroleum jelly or chassis grease to the exposed surfaces of the battery cable terminal clamps and the battery terminal posts.
9. Obtain an appropriate scan tool and check the PCM for any stored battery disconnect trouble codes. Clear codes if required.

ENGINE ELECTRICAL — CHARGING SYSTEM

GENERATOR

REMOVAL & INSTALLATION

5.7L

**** CAUTION**

Disconnect the negative battery cable before removing the battery output wire from generator. Failure to do so can result in injury or damage to electrical system.

1. Disconnect the negative battery cable.

**** CAUTION**

Do not let the tensioner arm snap back to the freearm position, severe damage may occur to the tensioner.

2. Insert a suitable square drive ratchet into the square hole on the belt tensioner arm.
3. Release the belt tension by rotating the tensioner clockwise until the accessory drive belt can be removed from the generator pulley only.
4. Unsnap the plastic insulator cap from the B+ output terminal.
5. Remove the B+ terminal retaining nut and disconnect the B+ terminal eyelet from the generator output stud.
6. Disconnect the field wire electrical connector by pushing on the connector tab.
7. Remove the generator support bracket nuts and bolt and remove the support bracket.
8. Remove the two generator mounting bolts and the generator.

To install:

9. Position the generator into the mounting bracket and install the two retaining bolts and tighten the bolts to 30 ft. lbs. (41 Nm).
10. Install the support bracket to the front of the generator and install the bolt and nuts and tighten the bolt and nuts to 30 ft. lbs. (41 Nm).
11. Install the field wire electrical connector into the generator.
12. Connect the B+ terminal eyelet onto the generator output stud and install the retaining nut and tighten the nut to 9 ft. lbs. (12 Nm).
13. Snap the plastic insulator cap onto the B+ output terminal.

**** CAUTION**

Never force a belt over a pulley rim using a screwdriver. The synthetic fiber of the belt can be damaged.

**** CAUTION**

When installing a serpentine accessory drive belt, the belt must be routed correctly. The water pump may be rotating in the wrong direction if the belt is installed incorrectly, causing the engine to overheat. Refer to belt routing label in engine compartment.

**** CAUTION**

Do not let the tensioner arm snap back to the freearm position, severe damage may occur to the tensioner.

14. Insert a suitable square drive ratchet into the square hole on the belt tensioner arm. Rotate the tensioner clockwise until the accessory drive belt can be install onto the generator pulley.
15. Connect the negative battery cable.

6.7L Diesel

**** CAUTION**

Disconnect both negative cables from both batteries before removing battery output wire (B+ wire) from generator. Failure to do so can result in injury or damage to electrical system.

1. Disconnect both negative battery cables at both batteries.
2. Remove generator drive belt.
3. Remove upper mounting bracket bolt.
4. Remove lower mounting bracket bolt and nut.
5. Remove generator from engine.
6. Unsnap plastic insulator cap from B+ output terminal.
7. Remove B+ terminal mounting nut at rear of generator. Disconnect terminal from generator.
8. Disconnect field wire connector at rear of generator by pushing on connector tab.

To install:

9. Position generator to upper and lower mounting brackets and install upper bolt and lower bolt and nut.
10. Tighten all bolts and nut to 30 ft. lbs. (41 Nm).

11. Snap field wire connector into rear of generator.
12. Install B+ terminal eyelet to generator output stud. Tighten mounting nut.

**** CAUTION**

Never force a belt over a pulley rim using a screwdriver. The synthetic fiber of the belt can be damaged.

**** CAUTION**

When installing a serpentine accessory drive belt, the belt must be routed correctly. The water pump may be rotating in the wrong direction if the belt is installed incorrectly, causing the engine to overheat. Refer to belt routing label in engine compartment, or to the "ENGINE MECHANICAL" section.

13. Install generator drive belt.
14. Install both negative battery cables to both batteries.

ENGINE ELECTRICAL

IGNITION SYSTEM

FIRING ORDER

5.7L

1–8–4–3–6–5–7–2

6.7L Diesel

1–5–3–6–2–4

IGNITION COIL

REMOVAL & INSTALLATION

5.7L

See Figure 17.

1. Disconnect the electrical connector from coil.
2. Clean area at base of coil with compressed air before removal.
3. Remove 2 mounting bolts (note that mounting bolts are retained to coil).
4. Carefully pull up coil from valve cover. Remove coil from vehicle.

To install:

5. Using compressed air, blow out any dirt or contaminants from around top of spark plug.

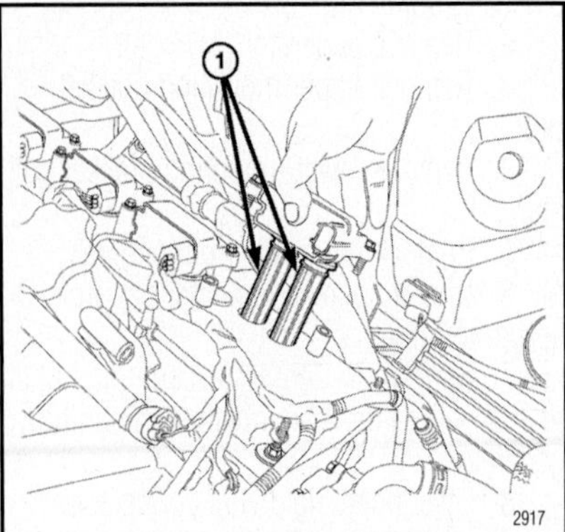

Fig. 17 Carefully pull up coil (1) from valve cover. Remove coil from vehicle.

6. Use dielectric grease on each of the spark plug boots before installing the coil.
7. Position ignition coil into valve cover and push onto spark plugs.
8. Install 2 coil mounting bolts and tighten to 62 inch lbs. (7 Nm).
9. Connect electrical connector to coil by snapping into position.

IGNITION CAPACITOR

REMOVAL & INSTALLATION

The coil capacitor is located in the right-rear section of the engine compartment. It is attached with a mounting stud and nut.

1. Disconnect electrical connector at capacitor.
2. Remove mounting nut and remove ground strap.
3. Remove capacitor.
4. Installation is the reverse of the removal procedure.

IGNITION TIMING

ADJUSTMENT

➡Ignition timing is computer controlled and not manually adjusted.

SPARK PLUGS

REMOVAL & INSTALLATION

5.7L

1. Remove all the necessary air filter tubing and air intake components at the top of the engine and at the throttle body.
2. Prior to removing the ignition coil, spray compressed air around the base of the ignition coil at the cylinder head.
3. Remove the ignition coil.
4. Prior to removing the spark plug, spray compressed air into the cylinder head opening.
5. Remove the spark plug from the cylinder head using a quality thin wall socket with a rubber or foam insert.
6. Inspect the spark plug condition.

To install:

➡Do not attempt to clean any of the spark plugs. Replace only.

7. Check and adjust the spark plug gap with a gap gauging tool. Gap should be 0.040 in. (1.0 mm).

**** CAUTION**

Special care should be taken when installing spark plugs into the cylinder head spark plug wells. Be sure the plugs do not drop into the plug wells as electrodes can be damaged.

8. Start the spark plug into the cylinder head by hand to avoid cross threading.

**** CAUTION**

Always tighten spark plugs to the specified torque. Certain engines use torque sensitive spark plugs. Over tightening can cause distortion resulting in a change in the spark plug gap, or a cracked porcelain insulator.

9. Tighten the spark plugs to 13 ft. lbs. (18 Nm). Do not over-torque.
10. To aid in coil installation, apply silicone based grease such as Mopar® Dielectric Grease into spark plug end of ignition coil rubber boots. Also apply this grease to the tops of spark plugs. Install the ignition coils.
11. Install all necessary air filter tubing and air intake components to top of engine and to throttle body.

ENGINE ELECTRICAL

STARTER

REMOVAL & INSTALLATION

5.7L

1. Disconnect and isolate the negative battery cable.
2. Raise and support the vehicle.

➡If equipped with 4WD and certain transmissions, a support bracket is used between front axle and side of transmission. Remove 2 support bracket bolts at transmission. Pry support bracket slightly to gain access to lower starter mounting bolt.

3. Remove the two starter mounting bolts.
4. Move the starter motor towards front of vehicle far enough for the nose of the starter pinion housing to clear the housing. Always support the starter motor during this process, do not let the starter motor hang from wire harness.
5. Tilt nose the downwards and lower starter motor far enough to access and remove the nut that secures the battery positive cable wire harness connector to the solenoid battery terminal stud . Do not let the starter motor hang from the wire harness.
6. Remove the battery positive cable wire harness connector eyelet from the solenoid battery terminal stud.
7. Disconnect the battery positive cable wire harness connector from the solenoid terminal connector receptacle.
8. Remove the starter motor.

To install:

9. Connect the solenoid wire to starter motor (snaps on).
10. Position the battery cable to the solenoid stud. Install and tighten the battery cable eyelet nut to 10 ft. lbs. (13 Nm). Do not allow the starter motor to hang from the wire harness.
11. Position the starter motor to engine.
12. Slide the transmission cooler tube bracket into position.
13. Install and tighten both mounting bolts. Tighten to 50 ft. lbs. (68 Nm).
14. Lower the vehicle.
15. Connect the negative battery cable.

6.7L Diesel

1. Disconnect and isolate both negative battery cables at both batteries.
2. Raise and support vehicle.
3. Disconnect solenoid electrical connector.
4. Remove battery cable mounting nut.
5. Remove battery cable from stud.
6. Remove three starter mounting bolts.
7. Remove starter motor from engine.

To install:

8. Connect solenoid wire to starter motor and tighten the nut.
9. Position battery cable to starter stud. Install and tighten battery cable nut to 10 ft. lbs. (14 Nm).

⁂ CAUTION

Do not allow starter motor to hang from wire harness.

10. Position starter motor to transmission.
11. Install and tighten 3 starter mounting bolts to 32 ft. lbs. (43 Nm).
12. Lower vehicle.
13. Connect both negative battery cables to both batteries.

ENGINE MECHANICAL

➡Disconnecting the negative battery cable may interfere with the functions of the on board computer systems and may require the computer to undergo a relearning process, once the negative battery cable is reconnected.

ACCESSORY DRIVE BELTS

ACCESSORY BELT ROUTING

See Figure 18.

6.7L Diesel

See Figure 19.

INSPECTION

Visual Diagnosis

When diagnosing serpentine accessory drive belts, small cracks that run across the ribbed surface of the belt from rib to rib, are considered normal. These are not a reason to replace the belt. However, cracks running along a rib (not across) are not normal. Any belt with cracks running along a rib must be replaced. Also replace the belt if it has excessive wear, frayed cords or severe glazing.

Noise Diagnosis

Noises generated by the accessory drive belt are most noticeable at idle. Before replacing a belt to resolve a noise condition, inspect all of the accessory drive pulleys for alignment, glazing, or excessive end play.

ADJUSTMENT

Belt tension is automatically maintained by the tensioner; no adjustment is needed.

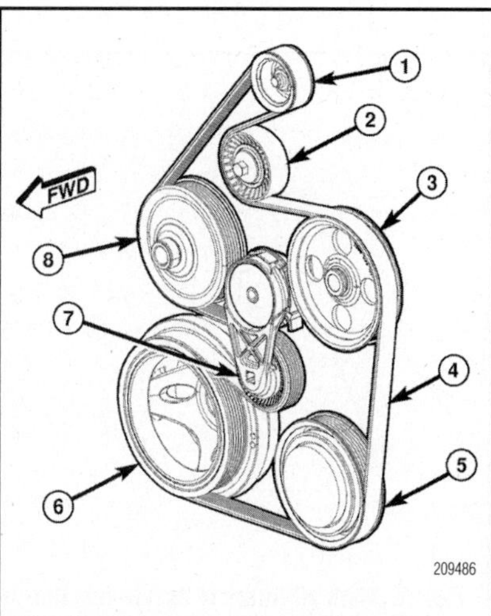

Fig. 18 Showing accessory belt routing—5.7L

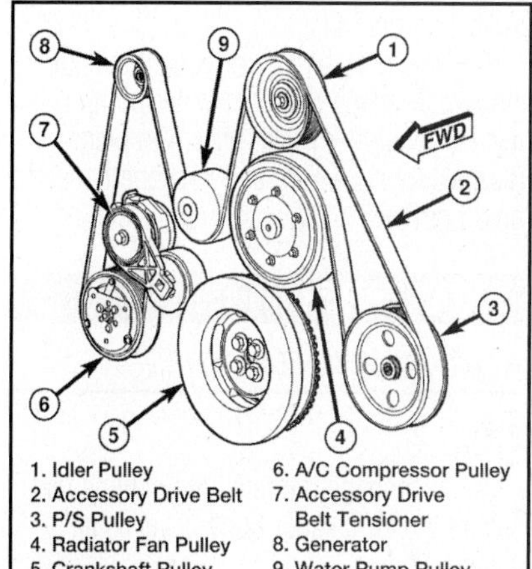

Fig. 19 Showing accessory belt routing—6.7L diesel

REMOVAL & INSTALLATION

5.7L

1. Insert a suitable square drive ratchet into the square hole on belt tensioner arm.
2. Release the belt tension by rotating the tensioner clockwise. Rotate the belt tensioner until the accessory belt can be removed from pulleys.

CAUTION

Do not let the tensioner arm snap back to the freearm position, severe damage may occur to the tensioner.

3. Remove the accessory belt.
4. Gently release the tensioner.
5. Installation is the reverse of the removal procedure.

6.7L Diesel

➡A 1/2 inch square hole is provided in the automatic belt tensioner. Attach a suitable tool into this hole.

1. Rotate tensioner assembly clockwise (as viewed from front) until tension has been relieved from belt.
2. Remove belt from water pump pulley first.
3. Remove belt from vehicle.

To install:

CAUTION

When installing the accessory drive belt, the belt must be routed correctly. If not, engine may overheat due to water pump rotating in wrong direction.

4. Position drive belt over all pulleys except water pump pulley.
5. Attach a suitable tool to the accessory drive belt tensioner.
6. Rotate accessory drive belt tensioner clockwise. Place belt over water pump pulley. Let tensioner rotate back into place. Remove tool. Be sure belt is properly seated on all pulleys.

AIR CLEANER

REMOVAL & INSTALLATION

5.7L

1. Disengage the retaining clamps that secure the air cleaner body cover to air cleaner body.
2. Lift and push the air cleaner body cover toward the engine to disengage the cover locating tabs from the air cleaner body and position the cover out of the way.
3. Remove the air cleaner element from the inside of the air cleaner body.
4. Clean out the inside of the air cleaner body.
5. Installation is the reverse of the removal procedure.

6.7L Diesel

➡There is no filter minder on the air intake for the 6.7L. There will be an EVIC message which will display when the filter restriction reaches it's maximum. The customer will be required to replace it with-in 250 miles (402 KM).

➡The housing cover is equipped with over-center clips and is hinged with plastic tabs.

1. Unlatch clips from top of air cleaner housing and tilt housing cover up for removal.
2. Remove air cleaner filter from air cleaner housing.
3. Installation is the reverse of the removal procedure.

CAMSHAFT & VALVE LIFTERS

REMOVAL & INSTALLATION

5.7L

See Figures 20 through 22.

1. Remove the battery negative cable.
2. Remove the air cleaner assembly.
3. Raise and support the vehicle.
4. Drain the engine oil.
5. Drain the coolant.
6. Remove the accessory drive belt.
7. Remove the left and right cylinder heads. See "Cylinder Head" in this section.
8. Remove the radiator. See "ENGINE COOLING" section.

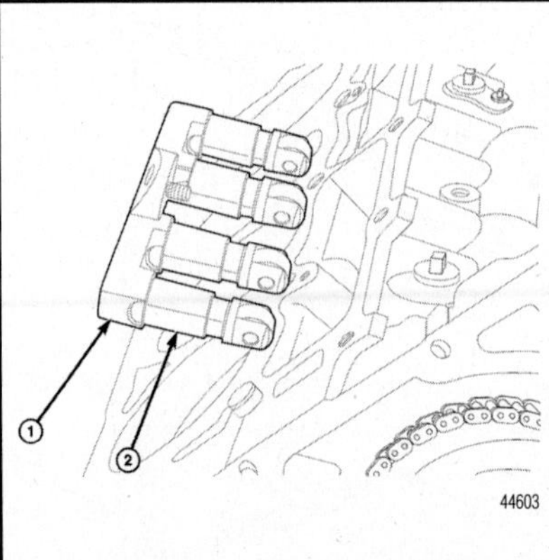

Fig. 20 Mark all lifters to ensure installation in original location. Remove the tappets (2) and retainer (1) assembly.

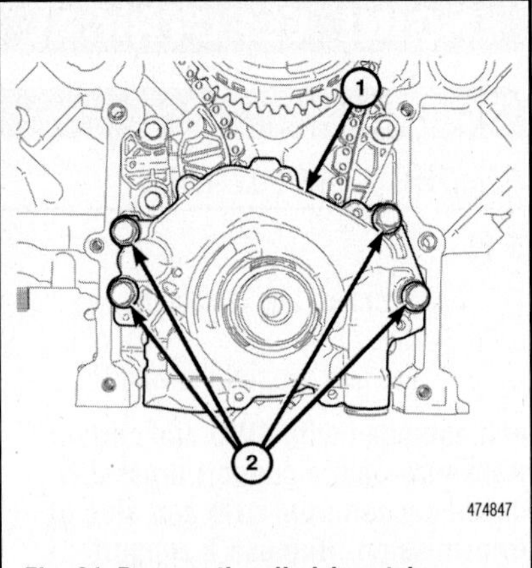

Fig. 21 Remove the oil pick up tube. Then, remove the oil pump retaining bolts (2) and remove the oil pump (1).

9. Remove the oil pan. See "Oil Pan" in this section.
10. Remove timing case cover. See "Timing Chain, Cover & Sprockets" in this section.
11. Mark all lifters to ensure installation in original location. Remove the tappets and retainer assembly.
12. Remove the oil pick up tube. Then, remove the oil pump retaining bolts and remove the oil pump.
13. Remove timing chain. See "Timing Chain, Cover & Sprockets" in this section.
14. Remove camshaft thrust plate, once the timing chain and sprocket are removed.
15. Install a long bolt into front of camshaft to aid in removal of the camshaft. Remove camshaft, being careful not to damage cam bearings with the cam lobes. Slowly rotate the camshaft while pulling camshaft out.

To install:

16. Lubricate the camshaft lobes and camshaft bearing journals and insert the camshaft.

➡Ensure that the plate is installed on the correct side. The fasteners are flat head fasteners so the top of the head of the fastener should not stick above the front face of the plate after they are torqued. The plate has chamfered fastener holes and the chamfered side should be facing forward to ensure the fasteners are flush or below the front surface.

17. Install the camshaft thrust plate and tighten the bolts, in alternating sequence, to 9 ft. lbs. (12 Nm).
18. Measure camshaft end play. It should be 0.0031–0.0114 in. (0.080—0.290 mm). If not within limits, disassemble, clean, and inspect for burrs or debris.

Reassemble and measure end play again. If the end play is still out, then install a new thrust plate.

19. Install the timing chain and sprockets. See "Timing Chain, Cover & Sprockets" in this section.

20. Install the oil pump and tighten bolts to 21 ft. lbs. (28 Nm).

21. Inspect the oil pick up tube O-rings and replace as necessary. Install the oil pick up tube and tighten fasteners to 21 ft. lbs. (28 Nm).

22. Install the timing chain cover. See "Timing Chain, Cover & Sprockets" in this section.

23. Install the oil pan. See "Oil Pan" in this section.

➡Engines equipped with MDS use both standard roller lifters (2) and deactivating roller lifters (1). The deactivating roller lifters must be used in cylinders 1,4,6,7. The deactivating lifters can be identified by the two holes in the side of the lifter body (3), for the latching pins.

⁂ CAUTION

Each tappet reused must be installed in the same position from which it was removed. When camshaft is replaced, all of the tappets must be replaced.

24. Install the rear MDS lifter assembly (2) and tighten bolt (1) to 12 N·m (106 in. lbs.).

25. Install the front MDS lifter assembly and tighten bolt to 106 inch lbs. (12 Nm).

26. Install both the left and right cylinder heads. See "Cylinder Head" in this section.

27. Install cylinder head covers.

28. Install the accessory drive belt.

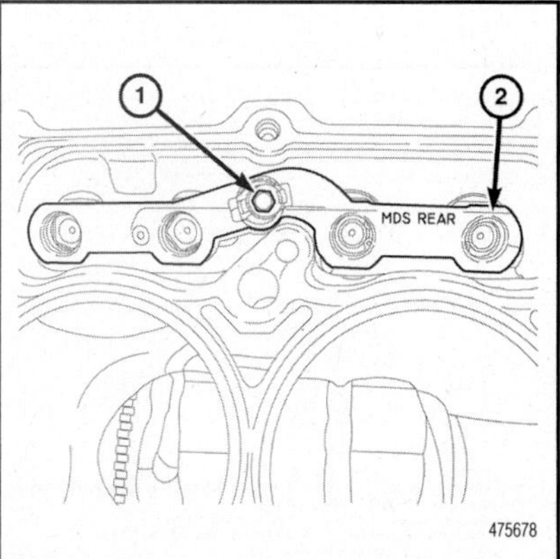

Fig. 22 Install the rear MDS lifter assembly (2) and tighten bolt (1) to 106 inch lbs. (12 Nm).

29. Install the radiator. See "ENGINE COOLING" section.

30. Install the air cleaner assembly.

31. Install the negative battery cable.

32. Fill the radiator with coolant.

33. Fill the engine with oil.

34. Start the engine and check for leaks.

6.7L Diesel

See Figures 23 through 25.

1. Disconnect both negative battery cables.
2. Remove the engine cover.
3. Recover A/C refrigerant.
4. Drain engine coolant.
5. Remove radiator upper hose.
6. Remove viscous fan/drive/shroud assembly. See "ENGINE COOLING" section.
7. Disconnect the coolant recovery bottle hose from the radiator filler neck.
8. Disconnect lower radiator hose from radiator outlet.
9. On automatic transmission equipped models, disconnect transmission oil cooler lines from radiator.
10. Remove radiator mounting screws and lift radiator out of engine compartment.
11. Remove upper radiator support panel.
12. Disconnect A/C condenser refrigerant lines.
13. Disconnect charge air cooler piping from the cooler inlet and outlet.
14. Remove the two charge air cooler mounting bolts. Remove charge air cooler and A/C condenser from vehicle.
15. Remove the power steering pump and position aside.
16. Remove accessory drive belt and accessory drive belt tensioner.
17. Remove the fan support/hub assembly.
18. Remove crankshaft damper, as described in this section.
19. Remove the gear cover-to-housing bolts and gently pry the cover away from the housing, taking care not to mar the sealing surfaces. Remove dust seal with cover.
20. Using Barring Tool (7471B or equivalent), rotate the crankshaft to align the timing marks on the crankshaft and the camshaft gears.
21. Remove the cylinder head cover.

➡The No. 5 cylinder intake and the No. 6 cylinder intake and exhaust pushrods are removed by lifting them up and through the provided cowl panel access holes. Remove the rubber plugs to expose these relief holes.

22. Remove the rocker arms, cross heads and push rods. Mark each component so they can be installed in their original positions.

Fig. 23 Raise the tappets using the wooden dowel rods positioned as shown

23. Raise the tappets as follows, using the wooden dowel rods provided with the Tool Kit (8502):
    a. Insert the slotted end of the dowel rod into the tappet. (The dowel rods for the rear two cylinders will have to be cut for cowl panel clearance.) Press firmly to ensure that it is seated in the tappet.
    b. Raise the dowel rod to bring the tappet to the top of its travel, and wrap a rubber band around the dowel rods to prevent the tappets from dropping into the crankcase.
    c. Repeat this procedure for the remaining cylinders.
24. Verify that the camshaft timing marks are aligned with the crankshaft mark.
25. Remove the bolts from the thrust plate.
26. Remove engine mount through bolts.
27. Install Engine Support Fixture (8534B or equivalent).

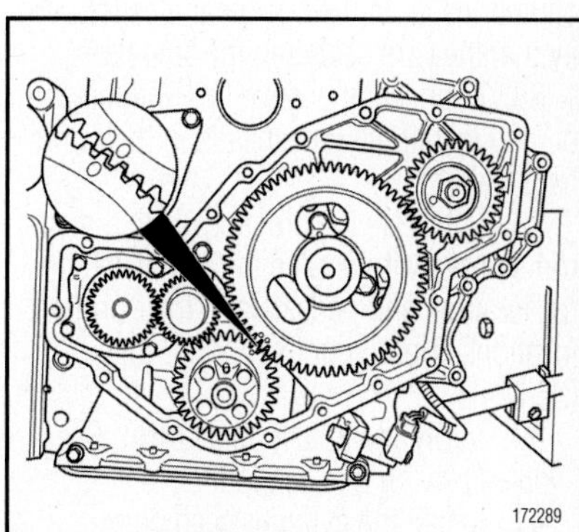

Fig. 24 Verify that the camshaft timing marks are aligned with the crankshaft mark.

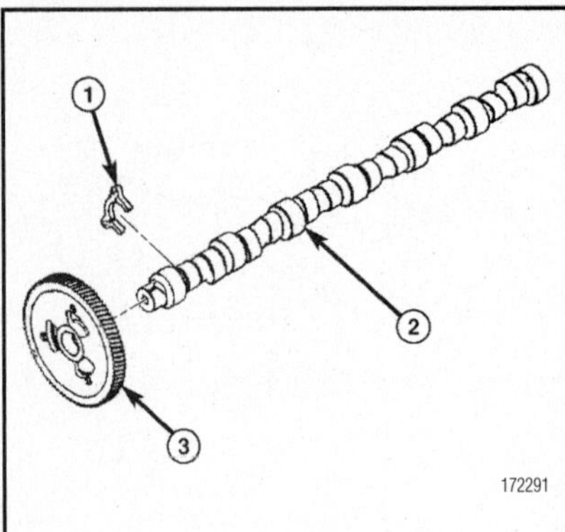

Fig. 25 Removing camshaft (2), gear (3) and thrust plate (1)

28. Raise engine enough to allow camshaft removal.
29. Remove the camshaft, gear, and thrust plate.

To install:

30. Lubricate the camshaft bearings and with fresh engine oil or suitable equivalent.
31. Liberally coat the thrust plate and the lobes and journals of the camshaft with fresh engine oil or suitable equivalent.

➡When installing the camshaft, DO NOT push it in farther than it will go with the thrust plate in place.

32. Install the camshaft and thrust plate. Align the timing marks.
33. Install the thrust plate bolts and tighten to 18 ft. lbs. (24 Nm).
34. Measure camshaft back lash. Backlash should be within 0.003–0.010 in. (0.075–0.250 mm).
35. Measure camshaft end clearance. End clearance should be within 0.001–0.020 in. (0.025–0.500 mm).
36. Remove the wooden dowel rods and rubber bands from the tappets.
37. Lubricate the push rods with engine oil and install in their original location. Verify that they are seated in the tappets.
38. Lubricate the valve tips with engine oil and install the crossheads in their original locations.
39. Lubricate the crossheads and push rod sockets with engine oil and install the rocker arms and pedestals in their original locations. Tighten bolts to 27 ft. lbs. (36 Nm).
40. Verify valve lash adjustment. See "Valve Lash" in this section.
41. Install the cylinder head cover.
42. Install gear housing cover.
43. Install front crankshaft dust seal.
44. Install the crankshaft damper. See "Crankshaft Damper & Front Seal" in this section.
45. Install the fan support/hub assembly.
46. Install the power steering pump. See "STEERING" section.
47. Install the accessory drive belt tensioner. Tighten bolt to 32 ft. lbs. (43 Nm).
48. Install the accessory drive belt.
49. Install the charge air cooler (with a/c condenser and auxiliary transmission oil cooler) and tighten the mounting bolts.
50. Connect charge air cooler inlet and outlet pipes. Tighten clamps to 97 inch lbs. (11 Nm).
51. Install the radiator upper support panel.
52. Close radiator petcock and lower the radiator into the engine compartment. Tighten the mounting bolts to 97 inch lbs. (11 Nm).
53. Raise vehicle on hoist.
54. Connect radiator lower hose and install clamp.
55. Connect transmission auxiliary oil cooler lines (if equipped).
56. Lower vehicle.
57. Install the fan drive/shroud assembly.
58. Install the coolant recovery and windshield washer fluid reservoirs to the fan shroud.
59. Connect the coolant recovery hose to the radiator filler neck.
60. Add engine coolant as needed.
61. Charge A/C system.
62. Connect the negative battery cables.
63. Start engine and check for engine oil and coolant leaks.
64. Install the engine cover.

CATALYTIC CONVERTER

REMOVAL & INSTALLATION

5.7L

1. Raise and support vehicle.
2. Saturate the bolts and nuts with heat valve lubricant. Allow 5 minutes for penetration.
3. Disconnect oxygen sensor electrical connectors.
4. Remove clamp.
5. Remove bolts at exhaust to manifold.
6. Remove catalytic converter(s).

To install:

7. Install catalytic converter to exhaust clamp on catalytic converter and position into exhaust pipe.
8. Install and hand-tighten catalytic converter to exhaust manifold bolts.
9. Install C-clip nut and bolt to converter to manifold.
10. Tighten catalytic converter to exhaust manifold bolts to 23 ft. lbs. (31 Nm).
11. Tighten all clamp nuts to 40 ft. lbs. (52 Nm) torque.
12. Check the exhaust system for contact with the body panels. A minimum of 1.0 in. (25 mm) is required between the exhaust system components and body/frame parts, including oil pan. Make the necessary adjustments, if needed.
13. Plug in 02 sensor wiring.
14. Lower the vehicle.
15. Start the engine and inspect for exhaust leaks. Repair exhaust leaks as necessary.

6.7L Diesel

See Figure 26.

⁂ WARNING

If torches are used when servicing the exhaust system, do not allow any flame near the fuel lines or the fuel tank. Failure to follow these instructions may result in possible serious or fatal injury.

1. Raise and support the vehicle.
2. Saturate the bolts and nuts with heat valve lubricant. Allow 5 minutes for penetration.
3. Disconnect flexible exhaust differential pressure sensor tubing.
4. Remove exhaust pressure differential sensor tubing from NOx Absorber Catalyst (NAC).
5. On 4X4 Vehicles, do the following:
   a. Remove transfer case skid plate.
   b. Remove transmission crossmember.
6. Remove Diesel Particulate Filter (DPF) to NOx Absorber Catalyst (NAC) flange nuts.
7. Remove NAC to Diesel Oxidation Catalyst (DOC) to NAC flange nuts.

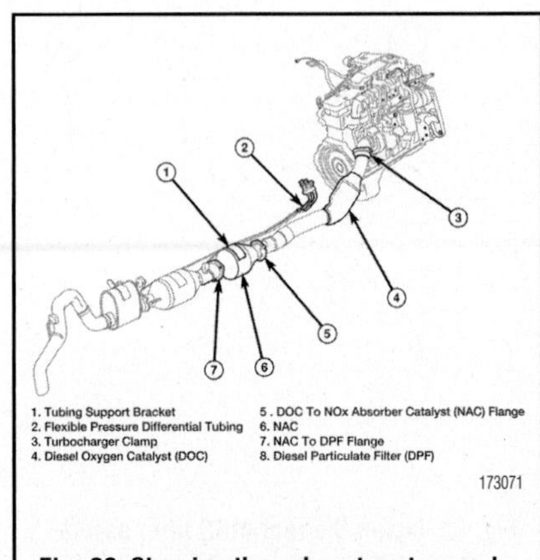

Fig. 26 Showing the exhaust system and catalytic converter—6.7L diesel

8. Remove NAC from isolators.
9. Remove NAC and discard gaskets.
10. Remove DOC to turbocharger clamp at turbocharger.
11. Remove DOC from vehicle and discard gasket.

To install:

12. Position the DOC onto the turbocharger with the clamp facing down. Install the clamp finger tight.
13. Position DOC onto the turbocharger. Install clamp finger tight.
14. Using new gaskets position NAC onto the DOC and Diesel Particulate Filter (DPF).
15. Install DOC to NAC and NAC to PDF flange nuts. Tighten nuts to 40 ft. lbs. (54 Nm).
16. Install and tighten differential pressure tube support nut.
17. Install flexible differential pressure tubing.
18. Tighten the catalytic converter to turbocharger clamp to 13 ft. lbs. (17 Nm). Using a rubber mallet, hit the DOC to turbocharger clamp three times around the perimeter of the clamp and tighten the clamp to 13 ft. lbs. (17 Nm).
19. On 4X4 Vehicles, do the following:
    a. Install transmission crossmember.
    b. Install transfer case skid plate.
20. Check the exhaust system for contact with the body panels. A minimum of 10 in. (25 mm) is required between the exhaust system components and body/frame parts. Make the necessary adjustments, if needed.
21. Lower the vehicle.

CRANKSHAFT DAMPER & FRONT SEAL

REMOVAL & INSTALLATION

5.7L

See Figure 27.

1. Disconnect negative cable from battery.
2. Remove accessory drive belt.
3. Drain cooling system.
4. Remove radiator upper hose.
5. Remove fan shroud.
6. Remove crankshaft damper bolt.
7. Remove damper using Crankshaft Insert and Three Jaw Puller.
8. Using Seal Remover (9071 or equivalent) (1), remove crankshaft front seal (2).

To install:

9. Using Crankshaft Front Oil Seal Installer (9072 or equivalent) and Damper Installer (8512A or equivalent), install crankshaft front seal.

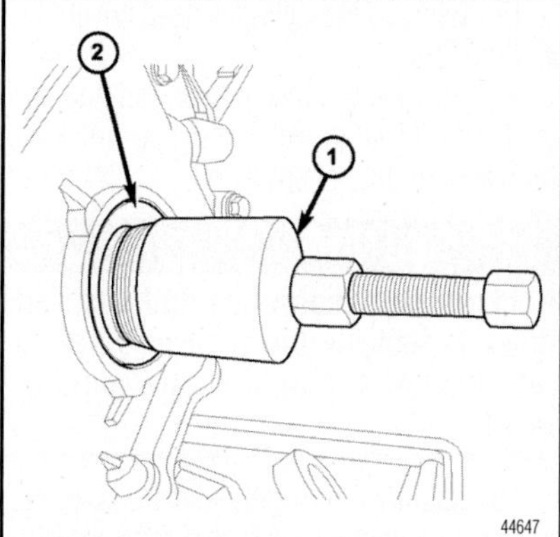

Fig. 27 Using Seal Remover (9071 or equivalent) (1), remove crankshaft front seal (2).

CAUTION

To prevent severe damage to the crankshaft, damper, and damper installer, thoroughly clean the damper bore and the crankshaft nose before installing damper.

10. Position the damper onto crankshaft. Assemble the damper installer, and the pressing cup from A/C hub installer (6871 or equivalent). Press the damper onto crankshaft.
11. Install the crankshaft damper bolt and tighten to 130 ft. lbs. (176 Nm).
12. Install the cooling fan.
13. Install the radiator upper shroud and tighten the fasteners.
14. Install the radiator upper hose.
15. Install the accessory drive belt.
16. Refill the cooling system.
17. Connect the negative cable to battery.

6.7L Diesel

1. Remove the accessory drive belt.

➡Ensure that the friction shim stays with the damper when it is removed. It will need to be reinstalled with the damper.

2. Remove the four bolts, vibration damper, and friction shim.
3. Remove the gear cover-to-housing bolts and gently pry the cover away from the housing, taking care not to mar the gasket surfaces. Remove crank seal dust shield with cover.
4. Support the cover on a flat work surface with wooden blocks, and using a suitable punch and hammer, drive the old seal out of the cover from the back side of the cover to the front side.

To install:

➡The seal lip and the sealing surface on the crankshaft must be free of all oil residue, to prevent leaks. The crankshaft and seal surface must be completely dry when the seal is installed.

5. Clean cover and housing gasket mating surfaces. Use a suitable scraper and be careful not to damage the gear housing surface. Remove any old sealer from the oil seal bore. Thoroughly clean the front seal area of the crankshaft.
6. Inspect the gear housing and cover for cracks and replace if necessary. Carefully straighten any bends or imperfections in the gear cover with a ball-peen hammer on a flat surface. Inspect the crankshaft front journal for any grooves or nicks that would affect the integrity of the new seal.
7. Apply a bead of Mopar Stud and Bearing Mount to the outside diameter of the seal. Do not lubricate the inside diameter of the new seal.
8. With the cover supported by wood blocks, install the seal into the rear of the cover using crankshaft seal installer (10136 or equivalent) and driver handle (C-4171 or equivalent). Strike the driver handle until the installation tool bottoms out on the inside of the cover.

CAUTION

Do not distort or damage seal.

9. Install the plastic seal pilot (provided with seal kit) into the crankshaft seal.
10. Apply a bead of Mopar Silicone Rubber Adhesive Sealant or equivalent to the gear housing cover sealing surface.
11. Install the cover to the gear housing, aligning the seal pilot with the nose of the crankshaft.

CAUTION

Failure to follow the cover installation procedure can result in misalignment of the crankshaft seal to the crankshaft, causing an oil leak.

12. Install the cover bolts and hand snug 2 capscrews at the 3 o'clock and 9 o'clock position, to keep the cover from moving when the first capscrew is torqued. Tighten to 18 ft. lbs. (24 Nm). Remove pilot tool.
13. Install accessory drive belt tensioner. Tighten bolt to 32 ft. lbs. (43 Nm).
14. Install power steering pump. See "STEERING" section.

➡Ensure that the friction shim is installed, and that the damper is installed so the hole is located over the dowel pin.

15. Install the friction shim and vibration damper. Tighten bolts to 30 ft. lbs. (40 Nm), plus an additional 60 degrees in a criss-cross pattern.
16. Install the accessory drive belt

CYLINDER HEAD

REMOVAL & INSTALLATION

5.7L

See Figures 28 through 30.

1. Remove the cowl grille.
2. Remove the engine cover.
3. Release the fuel system pressure. See "FUEL SYSTEM" section.
4. Disconnect the fuel supply line.
5. Disconnect and isolate the negative battery cable.
6. Drain the cooling system.
7. Remove the air cleaner assembly.
8. Remove closed crankcase ventilation system.
9. Disconnect the oxygen sensor connectors.
10. Saturate all exhaust bolts and nuts with a rust penetrant. Allow 5 minutes for penetration.
11. Remove the exhaust pipe to manifold bolts and disconnect the front exhaust pipe/catalytic converter assembly.
12. Disconnect the evaporation control system.
13. Disconnect the heater hoses.

CAUTION

Do not let the tensioner arm snap back to the freearm position, sever damage may occur to the tensioner.

14. Insert a suitable square drive ratchet into the square hole on belt tensioner arm.
15. Release the belt tension by rotating the tensioner arm clockwise. Rotate the belt tensioner arm until the belt can be removed from the pulleys, remove the accessory drive belt, then gently release the tensioner arm.

➡It is not necessary to disconnect the hoses from the power steering pump, for power steering pump removal.

16. Remove the three power steering pump mounting bolts through the access holes in the pulley and secure out of the way.
17. Remove the cylinder head covers and gaskets.
18. Remove the intake manifold and throttle body as an assembly. See "Intake Manifold" in this section.

CAUTION

Rocker arm assemblies and pushrods must be installed in their original locations or engine damage could result.

19. Identify the original locations for assembly, remove rocker arm assemblies and pushrods.
20. Using the sequence shown, remove the head bolts from each cylinder head. Remove the cylinder head and discard the cylinder head gasket.

To install:

21. Clean all surfaces of cylinder block and cylinder heads.
22. Clean cylinder block front and rear gasket surfaces using a suitable solvent.

Fig. 28 Remove the three power steering pump mounting bolts through the access holes in the pulley and secure out of the way.

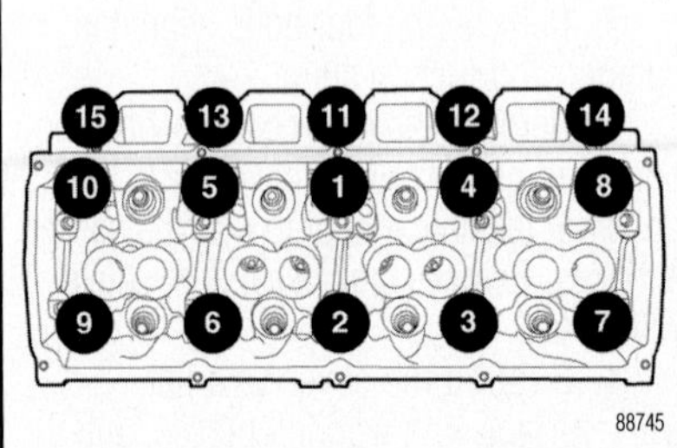

Fig. 29 Cylinder head bolt loosening sequence

➡The cylinder head gaskets are not interchangeable between the left and right sides. They are marked with an "L" and "R" to indicate the left or right side and they are marked "TOP" to indicate which side goes up.

23. Position the new cylinder head gasket and cylinder head onto the cylinder block.
24. Using the sequence shown, tighten the cylinder head bolts in the following order:
    a. Bolt 1–10 to 25 ft. lbs. (34 Nm).
    b. Bolts 11–15 to 15 ft. lbs. (20 Nm).
    c. Bolts 1–10 to 40 ft. lbs. (54 Nm).
    d. Bolts 11–15 to 15 ft. lbs. (20 Nm).
    e. Rotate the cylinder head bolts 1–10 an additional 90 degrees.
    f. Bolts 11–15 to 25 ft. lbs. (34 Nm).
25. Install the push rods and rocker arm assemblies in their original position, using Pushrod Retainer (9070 or equivalent).
26. Install the intake manifold and throttle body. See "Intake Manifold" in this section.
27. Install the spark plugs.
28. Connect the heater hoses.
29. Connect the fuel supply line.
30. Install the 3 power steering pump mounting bolts through the access holes in the pulley and tighten bolts to 21 ft. lbs. (28 Nm).
31. Install the accessory drive belt. See "Accessory Drive Belt" in this section.
32. Install the cylinder head cover and hand start all fasteners. Verify that all double ended studs are in the correct location.
33. Using the sequence shown, tighten the cylinder head cover bolts and double ended studs to 70 inch lbs. (8 Nm).

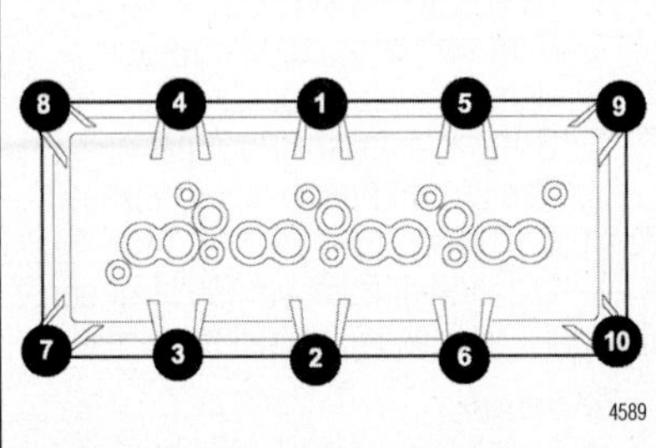

Fig. 30 Using the sequence shown, tighten the cylinder head cover bolts and double ended studs to 70 inch lbs. (8 Nm).

34. Connect the evaporation control system.
35. Install the air cleaner.
36. Install cowl grille.
37. Install the engine cover.
38. Fill the cooling system.
39. Drain and fill the engine with new oil.
40. Connect the negative battery cable.
41. Start the engine and check for leaks.

6.7L Diesel

See Figures 31 and 32.

1. Disconnect both negative battery cables.
2. Drain engine coolant.
3. Disconnect exhaust pipe from turbocharger elbow.
4. Remove the right engine mount.
5. Remove turbocharger drain tube bolts at turbocharger. Cap off ports to prevent dirt or foreign material from en tering.
6. Disconnect air inlet temperature/ pressure sensor.
7. Remove air cleaner housing and snorkel from the vehicle. Cap off turbocharger air inlet to prevent intrusion of dirt or foreign material.
8. Disconnect cab heater core supply and return hoses from the cylinder head and heater pipe.
9. Disconnect turbocharger oil supply line at the turbocharger end. Cap off open ports to prevent intrusion of dirt or foreign material.
10. Remove the turbocharger coolant lines.
11. Remove EGR cooler and associated hardware. See "ENGINE PERFORMANCE & EMISSION CONTROLS" section.
12. Remove exhaust manifold-to-cylinder head bolts, spacers, heat shield, retention straps, and cab heater plumbing. Remove exhaust manifold and turbocharger from the vehicle as an assembly.
13. Remove cooling fan, drive and shroud assembly.
14. Remove accessory drive belt.
15. Remove cooling fan support from cylinder block.
16. Remove upper generator bolt, loosen lower generator bolt, and rotate generator away from cylinder head.
17. Disconnect radiator upper hose from the thermostat housing.
18. Disconnect the Intake Air Temperature/Manifold Air Pressure (IAT/MAP), and Engine Coolant Temperature (ECT) sensor connectors. See "ENGINE PERFORMANCE & EMISSION CONTROLS" section for locations.
19. Remove the engine harness to cylinder head attaching bolts and P-clips at front of head.
20. Remove the intake air grid heater wire from the grid heater.
21. Remove engine oil level indicator tube attaching bolt at fuel filter housing bracket and inlet air connection.
22. Remove the charge air cooler-to-air inlet housing pipe.
23. Remove the engine wire harness attaching bolt and wire harness push-in fastener from air inlet housing.
24. Remove the air inlet housing.
25. Remove the two grid heater harness-to-cylinder head attaching bolts at front of cylinder head.

⁂ CAUTION

Extreme care should be used to keep dirt/debris from entering the fuel lines. Plastic caps should be used on the ends of the fuel lines.

26. Remove the high pressure pump to fuel rail fuel line as follows:
    a. Loosen fuel line nuts at fuel pump and at fuel rail.
    b. Use a back-up wrench on the fitting at the fuel pump to keep it from loosening.
27. Remove the fuel rail to cylinder head fuel lines as follows:
    a. Loosen No. 6 high pressure fuel line shield and position out of way.
    b. Loosen the fuel line nuts at the fuel rail and at the cylinder head. Use a back-up wrench on HPC nut.
28. Remove the engine lift bracket from the rear of the cylinder head.
29. Remove the fuel rail as follows:
    a. Remove fuel rail pressure sensor connector.
    b. Remove banjo fitting at pressure limiting valve.
    c. Remove the banjo fitting at fuel rail.
    d. Remove fuel rail bolts and fuel rail.
30. Remove P-clip from cylinder head.
31. Remove the breather cover and cylinder head cover.
32. Remove injector harness nuts from injectors.
33. Remove the rocker levers, cross heads and push rods. Mark each component so they can be installed in their original positions.

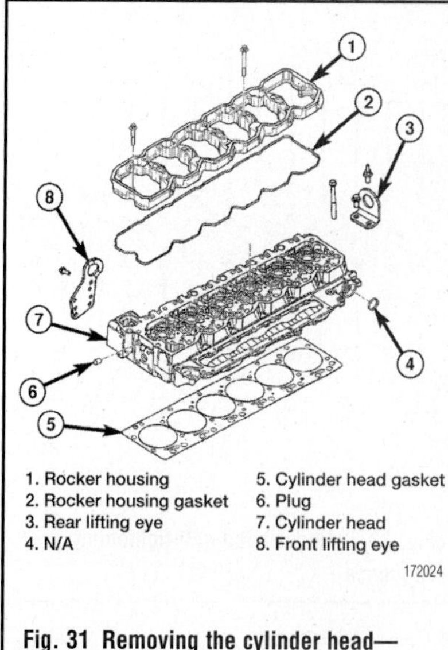

Fig. 31 Removing the cylinder head—6.7L diesel

➡The No. 5 cylinder exhaust and the No. 6 cylinder intake and exhaust push rods are removed by lifting them up and through the provided cowl panel access holes. Remove the rubber plugs to expose these relief holes.

34. Remove the fuel return line and banjo bolt at the rear of the cylinder head. Be careful not to drop the two sealing washers.
35. Remove the fuel injectors.
36. Remove rocker housing bolts and rocker housing and gasket.
37. Reinstall the engine lift bracket at the rear of cylinder head. Tighten to 57 ft. lbs. (77 Nm).
38. Starting on the outside and working towards the center, remove 26 cylinder head bolts.
39. Attach an engine lift crane to engine lift brackets and lift cylinder head off engine and out of vehicle.
40. Remove the head gasket and inspect.

To install:

⁂ WARNING

The outside edge of the head gasket is very sharp. When handling the new head gasket, use care not to injure yourself.

41. Install a new gasket with the part number side up, and locate the gasket over the dowel sleeves.
42. Using an engine lifting crane, lower the cylinder head onto the engine.
43. Lightly lubricate head bolts under bolt head and on threads, with engine oil and install. Using the sequence shown, tighten bolts in the following steps:

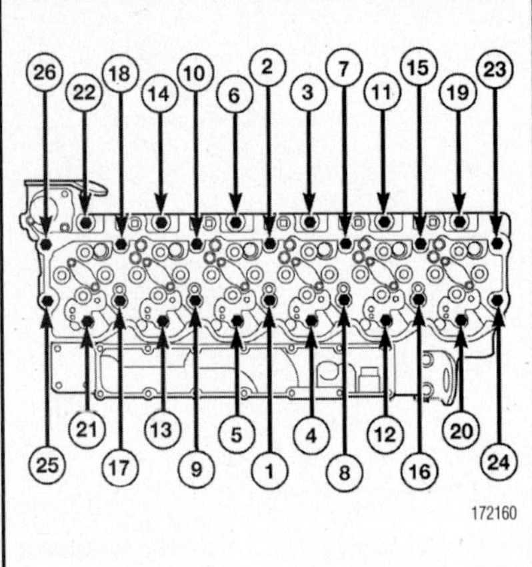

Fig. 32 Cylinder head bolt tightening sequence

a. Tighten bolts to 52 ft. lbs. (70 Nm).
b. Back off 360 degrees, in sequence.
c. Tighten bolts to 77 ft. lbs. (105 Nm).
d. Re-check all bolts, in sequence, to 77 ft. lbs. (105 Nm).
e. Tighten all bolts an additional 90 degrees, in sequence.

44. Install push rods into their original locations. Verify that they are seated in the tappets.
45. Inspect rocker housing gasket for cuts and proper installation into groove. Replace if damaged.
46. Install rocker housing. Tighten bolts to 18 ft. lbs. (24 Nm).
47. Install fuel injector.
48. Lubricate valve stem tips and install the crossheads in their original locations.
49. Lubricate the rocker arms and pedestals and install them in their original locations. Install the bolts and tighten them to 27 ft. lbs. (36 Nm).
50. Verify that the valve lash settings are maintained at 0.010 in. (0.254 mm) for the intake valve and 0.026 in. (0.660 mm) for the exhaust valve. See "Valve Lash" in this section for adjustment procedure.
51. Install cylinder head cover gasket onto rocker housing.
52. Install and tighten injector harness nuts.
53. Connect injector harness connectors at cylinder head cover gasket.
54. Install P-clip to cylinder head and tighten to 18 ft. lbs. (24 Nm).
55. Connect the IAT/MAP sensor connector.

CAUTION

Failure to follow procedure will result in fuel leaks and/or fuel system failure.

56. Install the fuel rail and high pressure fuel lines as follows:
    a. Hand tighten fuel rail bolts.
    b. Hand tighten fuel drain line to pressure limiting valve.
    Hand tighten fuel rail-to-cylinder head high pressure fuel lines.
    Hand tighten fuel pump to fuel rail line.
    Tighten fuel line nuts at cylinder head to 30 ft. lbs. (40 Nm).
    c. Tighten fuel line nuts at fuel rail to 30 ft. lbs. (40 Nm).
    d. Using a back up wrench, tighten fuel pump to fuel rail line to 30 ft. lbs. (40 Nm) at injection pump.
    e. Tighten fuel pump to fuel rail line to 30 ft. lbs. (40 Nm) at fuel rail.
    Tighten banjo bolt at pressure limiting valve and fuel rail to 18 ft. lbs. (24 Nm).
    f. Tighten rail bolts to 18 ft. lbs. (24 Nm).
    g. Connect fuel pressure sensor.
57. Reposition No. 6 fuel line shield and tighten to 32 ft. lbs. (43 Nm).
58. Install the fuel filter to injection pump low pressure line. Inspect and replace sealing washers if necessary.
59. Connect fuel return line at back of cylinder head hand tight.
60. Tighten banjo connections at cylinder head to 18 ft. lbs. (24 Nm).
61. Using new gaskets, install the air inlet housing. Tighten bolts to 18 ft. lbs. (24 Nm).
62. Install wire harness P-clip and push on clip to air inlet housing.
63. Connect engine oil level indicator tube at fuel filter housing and at air inlet housing.
64. Install the charge air cooler-to-air inlet housing duct assembly. Tighten all clamps to 97 inch lbs. (11 Nm).
65. Connect intake grid heater wire.
66. Secure engine harness to front of cylinder head with bolt at four locations.
67. Connect engine coolant temperature sensor connector.
68. Connect radiator upper hose to thermostat housing.
69. Rotate generator into position. Install upper bolt and tighten upper and lower bolts.
70. Install wire harness push-on clip below bracket.
71. Install wire harness P-clip to top of bracket.
72. Install fan support and tighten to 24 ft. lbs. (32 Nm).
73. Install cooling fan and drive. See "ENGINE COOLING" section.
74. Install accessory drive belt. See "Accessory Drive Belt" in this section.
75. Install exhaust manifold/turbocharger assembly, using new gaskets. Start all bolts/spacers by hand. Starting from the center bolts out, Tighten bolts to 32 ft. lbs. (43 Nm), then retighten from the center out again.
76. Install exhaust manifold heat shield to exhaust manifold studs. Install retaining nuts. Tighten to 18 ft. lbs. (24 Nm).
77. Install exhaust bolt retention straps across cylinders No. 5 and No. 6.
78. Using a new gasket, connect the turbocharger oil drain tube. Tighten to 18 ft. lbs. (24 Nm).
79. Install the right motor mount. Tighten fasteners to 70 ft. lbs. (95 Nm).
80. Perform the turbocharger pre-lube procedure. Pre-lube the turbocharger with 1–2 oz. clean engine oil.
81. Connect the turbocharger oil supply line. Tighten to 18 ft. lbs. (24 Nm).
82. Connect the turbocharger coolant lines. Tighten the banjo bolts to 18 ft. lbs. (24 Nm).
83. Install the EGR cooler and associated hardware. See "ENGINE PERFORMANCE & EMISSION CONTROLS" section.
84. Install air cleaner housing and duct.
85. Connect air inlet temperature/pressure sensor.
86. Raise vehicle on hoist.

➡Do not reuse the clamp for the exhaust pipe to turbocharger elbow connection.

87. Install the exhaust pipe to turbocharger elbow using a new clamp. Tighten bolts to 89 inch lbs. (10 Nm).
88. Lower vehicle.
89. Connect both negative battery cables.
90. Fill engine coolant.
91. Start engine and check for leaks.

ENGINE OIL & FILTER

REPLACEMENT

5.7L

➡The engine oil level indicator is located at the right rear of the engine on the 3.7L/4.7L engines.

CAUTION

Do not overfill crankcase with engine oil, pressure loss or oil foaming can result.

1. Inspect engine oil level approximately every 500 miles. Unless the engine

has exhibited loss of oil pressure, run the engine for about five minutes before checking oil level. Checking engine oil level on a cold engine is not accurate.

➡To ensure proper lubrication of an engine, the engine oil must be maintained at an acceptable level. The acceptable levels are indicated between the ADD and SAFE marks on the engine oil dipstick.

2. Hoist and support vehicle on safety stands.
3. Remove oil fill cap.
4. Place a suitable drain pan under crankcase drain and oil filter.
5. Using a suitable oil filter wrench loosen filter.
6. Rotate the oil filter counterclockwise to remove it from the cylinder block oil filter boss.
7. When filter separates from cylinder block oil filter boss, tip gasket end upward to minimize oil spill.
8. Remove filter from vehicle. Make sure filter gasket was removed with filter.
9. With a wiping cloth, clean the gasket sealing surface of oil and grime.
10. Remove drain plug from crankcase and allow oil to drain into pan. Inspect drain plug threads for stretching or other damage. Replace drain plug if damaged.
11. Install drain plug in crankcase.
12. Lightly lubricate oil filter gasket with engine oil.
13. Thread filter onto adapter nipple. When gasket makes contact with sealing surface, hand tighten filter one full turn, do not over tighten.
14. Lower vehicle and fill crankcase with specified type and amount of engine oil.
15. Install oil fill cap.
16. Start engine and inspect for leaks.
17. Stop engine and inspect oil level.

6.7L Diesel

1. Clean the area around the oil filter head.
2. Remove the filter from below using a cap-style filter wrench.
3. Clean the gasket surface of the filter head.

➡The filter canister O-ring seal can stick on the filter head. Make sure it is removed.

To install:

4. Fill the oil filter element with clean oil before installation.

➡Use the same type oil that will be used in the engine.

5. Apply a light film of lubricating oil to the sealing surface before installing the filter.

⁂ CAUTION

Mechanical over-tightening may distort the threads or damage the filter element seal.

6. Install the filter until it contacts the sealing surface of the oil filter adapter. Tighten filter an additional 1/2 turn.

EXHAUST MANIFOLD

REMOVAL & INSTALLATION

5.7L

See Figures 33 through 35.

⁂ CAUTION

When servicing or replacing exhaust system components, disconnect the oxygen sensor connector(s). Allowing the exhaust to hang by the oxygen sensor wires will damage the harness and/or sensor.

1. Disconnect the intake air temperature (IAT) sensor electrical connector at intake air assembly.
2. Remove the clean air hose, then remove the air cleaner housing.
3. Remove the engine cover.
4. Disconnect the negative battery cable.
5. Install Engine Support Fixture (8534B or equivalent).
6. Raise and support the vehicle.
7. Disconnect the oxygen sensor electrical connectors.
8. Saturate the front exhaust pipe/catalytic converter retaining bolts and nuts with Mopar Rust Penetrant or equivalent and allow 5 minutes for penetration.
9. Remove the right and left exhaust pipe/catalytic converter assembly.
10. Remove the right and left engine mount through bolts.
11. Lower the vehicle.
12. Using the Engine Support Fixture, raise the engine enough to gain access to the exhaust manifold retaining bolts.
13. Remove the exhaust manifold heat shield.
14. Starting with the center bolt and working up and down, alternate bolt removal and remove the exhaust manifold retaining bolts.
15. Remove the exhaust manifold and gasket.
16. Inspect the exhaust manifold for any damage.
17. Clean the mating surfaces.

To install:

18. Prior to installation, make sure all gasket mating surfaces are clean and free of any debris.
19. Position the exhaust manifold gasket and manifold.
20. Using the sequence shown, install the exhaust manifold retaining bolts and tighten to 18 ft. lbs. (25 Nm). Use this torque for both exhaust manifolds.
21. Install the heat shield and tighten nuts to 70 inch lbs. (8 Nm).

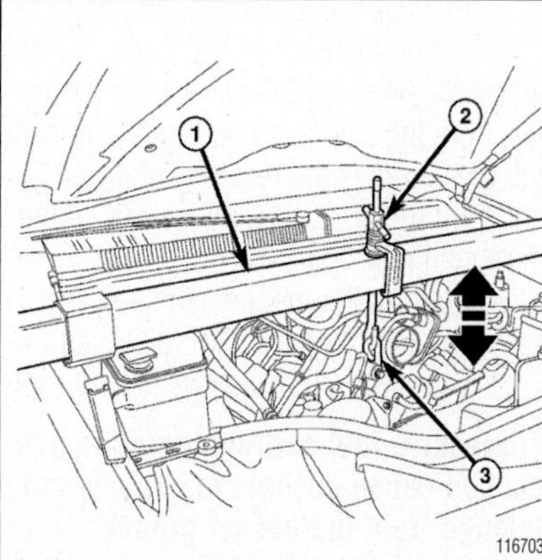

Fig. 33 Showing engine support fixture (1) with clamping device (2) and lifting eye (3)

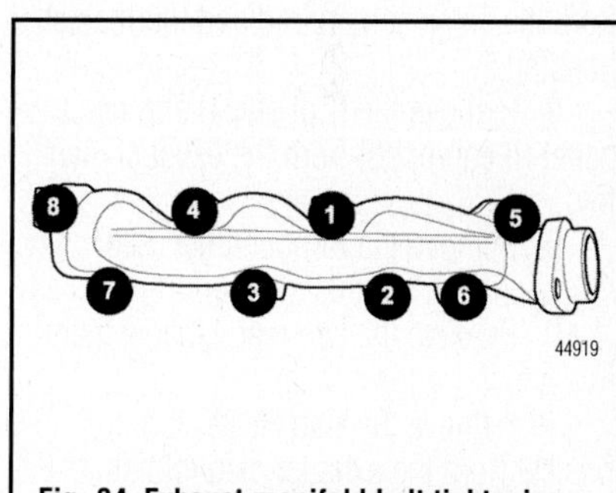

Fig. 34 Exhaust manifold bolt tightening sequence—left side

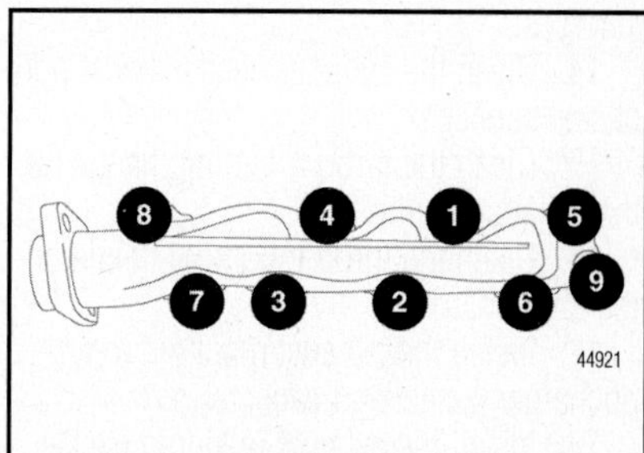

Fig. 35 Exhaust manifold bolt tightening sequence—right side

CAUTION

Do not damage engine harness while lowering the engine.

22. Using the Engine Support Fixture, lower the engine into position.
23. Raise and support the vehicle.
24. Install the right and left engine mount through bolts and tighten to 74 ft. lbs. (100 Nm).
25. Install the right and left exhaust pipe/catalytic converter assembly.
26. Connect the oxygen sensor electrical connectors.
27. Lower the vehicle.
28. Remove the Engine Support Fixture.
29. Install the air cleaner housing, the clean air hose, and connect the intake air temperature (IAT) sensor electrical connector.
30. Install the engine cover.
31. Connect the negative battery cable.
32. Start the engine and check for leaks.

6.7L Diesel

1. Disconnect the battery negative cables.
2. Drain the coolant.
3. Raise vehicle on hoist.
4. Remove the EGR cooler.
5. Remove the air filter housing.
6. Remove the air filter inlet hose from the turbo inlet.
7. Remove the Delta-P line bracket capscrew nuts and remove the Delta-P line from the exhaust manifold and thermostat housing.
8. Remove the heat shield and noise panel (if equipped) from the exhaust manifold.
9. Remove the turbocharger. See "Turbocharger" in this section.
10. Remove the two rear exhaust manifold capscrew lock plates.
11. Remove the Cab Heater tubing/bracket from the exhaust manifold stud.
12. Remove the exhaust manifold.

To install:

13. Clean the exhaust manifold gasket surfaces.
14. Clean the cylinder head exhaust port gasket surfaces.
15. Clean the turbo mounting flange on the exhaust manifold.
16. Clean the turbo mounting flange on the turbocharger.
17. Install the exhaust manifold to turbocharger gasket and capscrews.
18. Install the exhaust manifold gasket.

➡The five exhaust manifold capscrews with studs are used at the No. 1 and No. 2 cylinder locations for the heat shield mounting and one on the rear lower corner of the manifold for the cabin heater tube bracket.

19. Install the exhaust manifold spacers and capscrews.
20. Starting from the center and moving in a pattern outward, tighten the exhaust manifold bolts to 32 ft. lbs. (43 Nm).
21. Install the exhaust manifold capscrew lock plates.
22. Install the exhaust manifold heat shields/noise panels. Tighten the mounting nuts to 18 ft. lbs. (24 Nm).
23. Install the turbocharger. See "Turbocharger" in this section.
24. Attach the mounting tabs and start the Delta-P tube to exhaust manifold and thermostat capscrews.
25. Tighten the Delta-P line bracket nut to 18 ft. lbs. (24 Nm).
26. Tighten the Delta-P line bracket bolt to 89 inch lbs. (10 Nm).
27. Tighten the Delta-P flare nuts to 89 inch lbs. (10 Nm).
28. Install the EGR cooler.
29. Install the air filter housing.
30. Fill the coolant.
31. Connect the battery negative cables.
32. Start the engine to check for leaks.

INTAKE MANIFOLD

REMOVAL & INSTALLATION

5.7L

See Figures 36 and 37.

1. Disconnect the intake air temperature (IAT) sensor electrical connector at the throttle body end of the clean air tube.
2. Remove the clean air tube from the air cleaner housing and the throttle body.
3. Disconnect the makeup air hose.
4. Remove the air cleaner housing.
5. Lift up the front of the engine cover and separate the engine cover front grommets from the ball studs on the intake manifold, then remove the rear engine cover pegs from the grommets on the rear of the intake manifold.
6. Perform the fuel pressure release procedure. See "FUEL SYSTEM" section.
7. Disconnect the negative battery cable.

➡Excessive fuel spillage onto the gaskets can cause gaskets to expand and dislodge from the gasket groove.

8. Disconnect the fuel supply line quick connect fitting at the fuel rail and plug the fuel supply line with a shipping cap to prevent spillage.

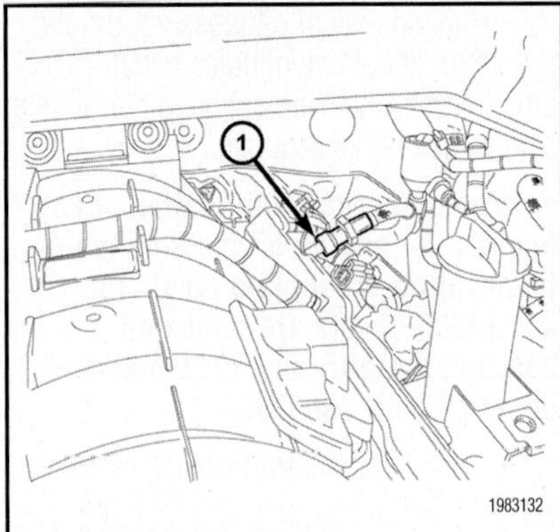

Fig. 36 Disconnect the fuel supply line quick connect fitting (1) at the fuel rail and plug the fuel supply line with a shipping cap to prevent spillage.

➡The factory fuel injection electrical harness is numerically tagged (INJ 1, INJ 2, etc.) for injector position identification. If the harness was not tagged, note the electrical connector's location during removal.

9. Disconnect the electrical connectors to all fuel injectors and position the fuel injector electrical harness aside.
10. Remove the main engine electrical harness support strap at the rear of the intake manifold and position harness aside.
11. Remove the A/C line P-clip retaining bolt from the throttle body bracket and remove the P-clip.
12. Secure the A/C line out of the way.
13. Remove the generator. See "ENGINE ELECTRICAL" section.
14. Remove the throttle body bracket retaining bolt from the intake manifold and remove the bracket.
15. Disconnect the electrical connector at the throttle body and reposition the harness.
16. Disconnect the brake booster vacuum hose, and the vacuum lines.

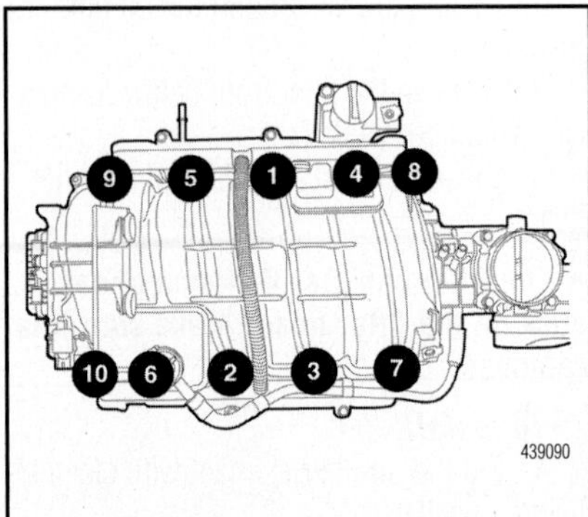

Fig. 37 Intake manifold bolt loosening/tightening sequence

17. Using the sequence shown, remove the intake manifold retaining bolts.

18. Slide the intake manifold forward and disconnect both the manifold air pressure (MAP) sensor and the short runner valve (SRV) connectors located at the rear of the intake manifold.

19. Remove the intake manifold and throttle body as an assembly.

To install:

20. If reinstalling the original manifold apply Mopar Lock & Seal Adhesive to the intake manifold bolts. Not required when installing a new manifold.

21. Install the intake manifold seals and positive crankcase ventilation (PCV) seals.

22. Connect both the manifold air pressure (MAP) sensor and the short runner valve (SRV) electrical connectors located at the rear of the intake manifold as you position the intake manifold in place.

23. Using the sequence shown, tighten the intake manifold bolts to 9 ft. lbs. (12 Nm).

24. Position the main engine electrical harness at the rear of the intake manifold and install the support strap.

25. Connect the fuel supply line quick connect fitting at the fuel rail.

➡The factory fuel injection electrical harness is numerically tagged (INJ 1, INJ 2, etc.) for injector position identification. If the harness was not tagged, use the noted the electrical connector's location during removal.

26. Position the fuel injector electrical harness and connect the electrical connectors to all fuel injectors.

27. Connect the brake booster vacuum hose, and the vacuum lines.

28. Install the throttle body bracket and securely tighten the retaining bolt.

29. Install the generator. See "ENGINE ELECTRICAL" section.

30. Position the A/C lines, install the A/C line P-clip and tighten P-clip retaining bolt.

31. Position the wiring harness and connect the electrical connector at the throttle body.

32. Slightly tilt the rear of the engine cover and slide the rear engine cover pegs into the grommets on the rear of the intake manifold until the cover stops.

33. Check to make sure the engine cover is installed properly by reaching behind the cover to verify that the pegs are located in the rear grommets.

➡While installing the engine cover the front ball studs will make a popping or suction sound as the ball studs are inserted into the front grommets.

34. Lower the front of the engine cover and line up the front grommets with the ball studs on the front of the intake manifold and with a downward motion push the engine cover front grommets onto the ball studs.

35. Lightly lift the front of the engine cover to insure the front ball studs are seated into the front grommets correctly.

36. Install the air cleaner assembly. Connect the clean air tube to the air cleaner assembly and the throttle body.

37. Connect the IAT sensor electrical connector.

38. Connect the negative battery cable

6.7L Diesel

See Figure 38.

1. Disconnect both negative battery cables.

2. Disconnect the Charge Air Cooler (CAC) tube from the EGR air flow control valve.

3. Remove the EGR crossover tube.

4. Disconnect EGR air flow control valve harness connector and the EGR valve harness connector.

5. Disconnect the boost pressure sensor harness connector.

6. Remove bolt and nut securing oil dipstick tube.

7. Remove bolts and the intake manifold. Remove and discard the gasket.

To install:

8. Clean all gasket mating surfaces.

9. Using a new gasket, install the intake manifold. Tighten bolts to 18 ft. lbs. (24 Nm).

10. Install bolt securing the oil dip stick tube-to-intake manifold and tighten to 18 ft. lbs. (24 Nm).

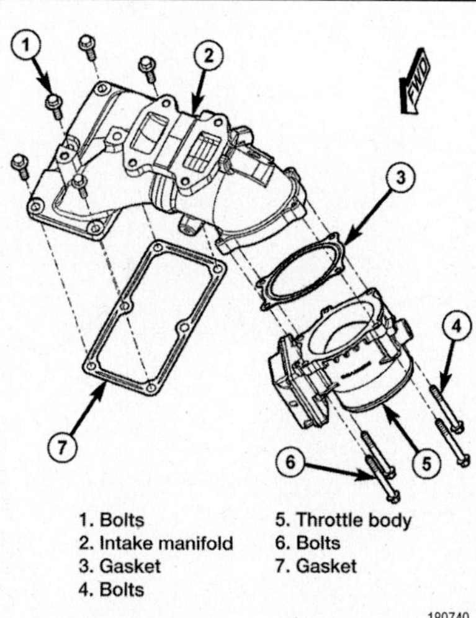

Fig. 38 Exploded view of the intake manifold mounting

11. Connect the boost pressure sensor harness connector, the EGR valve harness connector, and the EGR air flow control valve harness connector.

12. Install the EGR crossover tube.

13. Connect the Charge Air Cooler (CAC) tube to the EGR air flow control valve. Tighten clamp to 97 inch lbs. (11 Nm).

14. Connect both negative battery cables.

OIL PAN

REMOVAL & INSTALLATION

5.7L

4X2

See Figures 39 and 40.

1. Disconnect the negative battery cable.

2. Loosen both the left and right side engine mount through bolts. Do not remove bolts.

3. Install Engine Support Fixture (8534B or equivalent). Do not raise engine at this time.

4. Remove the structural dust cover.

5. Remove the fan and the fan shroud.

6. Drain engine oil.

7. Disconnect transmission fluid cooler lines at radiator, transmission fittings and clips.

➡When disconnecting the transmission oil cooler lines, it is necessary to replace the line clip that is located on the oil pan stud. The retention force of the clip is severely degraded upon removal.

8. Remove the front crossmember.

9. Raise engine using Engine Support Fixture to provide clearance to remove oil pan.

CAUTION

Do not pry on oil pan or oil pan gasket. The gasket is integral to engine windage tray and does not come out with oil pan.

➡If more clearance is needed to remove oil pan the transmission mount can be removed, and the transmission can be raised to gain clearance.

➡The double ended oil pan studs must be installed in the same location that they were removed from.

10. Remove the oil pan mounting bolts using the sequence provided.

11. Unbolt oil pump pickup tube and remove tube.

➡When the oil pan is removed, a new integral windage tray and gasket assembly must be installed. The old gasket cannot be reused.

12. Discard the integral windage tray and gasket and replace.

To install:

13. Clean the oil pan gasket mating surface of the block and oil pan.
14. Mopar Engine RTV must be applied to the four T-joints. The bead of RTV should cover the bottom of the gasket. This area is approximately 4.5 mm x 25 mm in each of the four T-joint locations.

➡When the oil pan is removed, a new integral windage tray and gasket assembly must be installed. The old gasket cannot be reused.

15. Install a new integral windage tray and gasket.
16. Reinstall the oil pump pickup tube with new O-rings. Tighten tube to pump fasteners to 21 ft. lbs. (28 Nm).

➡The double ended oil pan studs must be installed in the same location that they were removed from.

17. Position the oil pan and install the mounting bolts and studs. Tighten the mounting bolts to 105 inch lbs. (12 Nm).
18. Connect cooler lines to radiator, transmission and clips.

➡When connecting the transmission oil cooler lines, it is necessary to replace the line clip that is located on the oil pan stud. The retention force of the clip is severely degraded upon removal.

19. Install the structural dust cover and tighten the bolts as follows:
    a. Tighten the structural dust cover-to-transmission bolts (1, 2 & 4) to 80 inch lbs. (9 Nm).
    b. Tighten the structural dust cover-to-engine block bolts (3) to 80 inch lbs. (9 Nm).
    c. Retighten the structural dust cover-to-transmission bolts to 40 ft. lbs. (54 Nm).
    d. Retighten the structural dust cover-to-engine block bolts to 40 ft. lbs. (54 Nm).
20. Lower the engine into mounts, using the Engine Support Fixture.
21. Install both the left and right side engine mount through bolts. Tighten the nuts to 50 ft. lbs. (68 Nm).
22. Reinstall the front axle, if removed. See "DRIVE TRAIN" section.
23. Install the steering rack, if removed. See "STEERING" section.

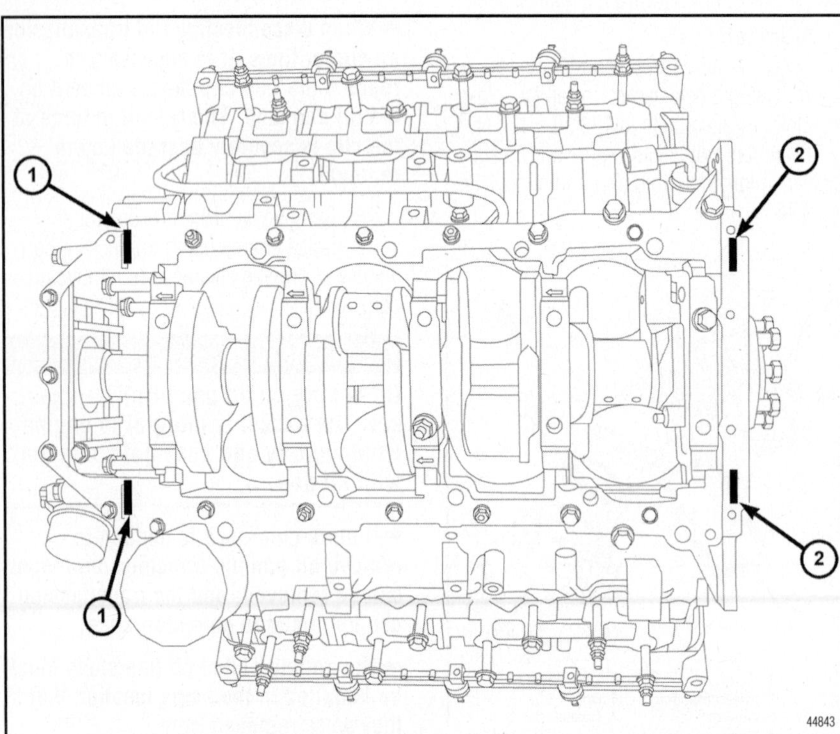

Fig. 39 Mopar Engine RTV must be applied to the four T-joints (1,2). The bead of RTV should cover the bottom of the gasket. This area is approximately 4.5 mm x 25 mm in each of the four T-joint locations.

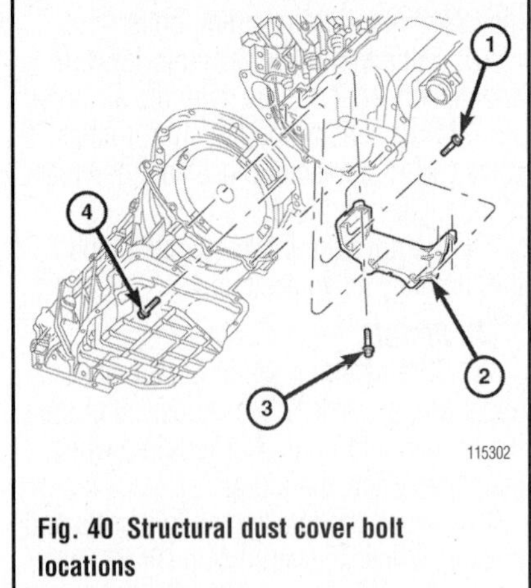

Fig. 40 Structural dust cover bolt locations

24. Install the rear transmission mount, if removed. Tighten bolt/nut to 50 ft. lbs. (68 Nm).
25. Remove Engine Support Fixture.
26. Install the front crossmember. Tighten nuts to 75 ft. lbs. (102 Nm).
27. Install the fan shroud and fan.
28. Fill engine oil.
29. Connect the negative battery cable.
30. Start engine and check for leaks.

4X4

1. Follow all steps for 4X2 removal, plus perform the following:
    a. Unbolt and lower the steering rack, without disconnecting the lines.

➡The front axle must be lowered to remove the oil pan on 4X4 vehicles.

    b. Remove the front driveshaft at the axle. Mark for reassembly.
    c. Support the front axle.
    d. Remove the right and left axle to mount bolts.
    e. Lower axle.
    f. Remove the oil pan mounting bolts and oil pan.
    g. Unbolt oil pump pickup tube and remove tube.

➡When the oil pan is removed, a new integral windage tray and gasket assembly must be installed. The old gasket cannot be reused.

    h. Discard the integral windage tray and gasket and replace.

To install:

2. Clean the oil pan gasket mating surface of the block and oil pan.
3. Mopar Engine RTV must be applied to the four T-joints. The bead of RTV should cover the bottom of the gasket. This area is approximately 4.5 mm x 25 mm in each of the four T-joint locations.

➡When the oil pan is removed, a new integral windage tray and gasket assembly must be installed. The old gasket cannot be reused.

4. Install a new integral windage tray and gasket.
5. Reinstall the oil pump pickup tube with new O-rings. Tighten tube to pump fasteners to 21 ft. lbs. (28 Nm).

➡The double ended oil pan studs must be installed in the same location that they were removed from.

6. Position the oil pan and install the mounting bolts and studs. Tighten the mounting bolts to 105 inch lbs. (12 Nm).
7. Connect cooler lines to radiator, transmission and clips.

➡When connecting the transmission oil cooler lines, it is necessary to replace the line clip that is located on the oil pan stud. The retention force of the clip is severely degraded upon removal.

8. Install the structural dust cover and tighten the bolts as follows:
   a. Tighten the structural dust cover-to-transmission bolts (1, 2 & 4) to 80 inch lbs. (9 Nm).
   b. Tighten the structural dust cover-to-engine block bolts (3) to 80 inch lbs. (9 Nm).
   c. Retighten the structural dust cover-to-transmission bolts to 40 ft. lbs. (54 Nm).
   d. Retighten the structural dust cover-to-engine block bolts to 40 ft. lbs. (54 Nm).
9. Lower the engine into mounts using Engine Support Fixture.
10. Install both the left and right side engine mount through bolts. Tighten the nuts to 50 ft. lbs. (68 Nm).
11. Reinstall the front axle, if removed. See "DRIVE TRAIN" section.
12. Install the steering rack, if removed. See "STEERING" section.
13. Install the rear transmission mount, if removed. Tighten bolt/nut to 50 ft. lbs. (68 Nm).
14. Remove Engine Support Fixture.
15. Install the front crossmember. Tighten nuts to 75 ft. lbs. (102 Nm).
16. Install the fan shroud and fan.
17. Fill engine oil.
18. Connect the negative battery cable.
19. Start engine and check for leaks.

6.7L Diesel

4X2

1. Disconnect both negative battery cables.
2. Raise and support the vehicle.
3. Remove the fan and fan shroud. See "ENGINE COOLING" section.
4. Remove the starter. See "ENGINE ELECTRICAL" section.
5. Remove the transmission.
6. Remove the flywheel housing bolts.
7. Remove the flex plate bolts.
8. Remove the engine oil dip stick.
9. Drain the oil.
10. Remove the steering rack bolts.
11. Remove the oil pan bolts.
12. Remove the oil pickup bolts.
13. Remove the oil pan.

To install:

14. Clean the sealing surfaces of the cylinder block and oil pan with a suitable cleaner.
15. Clean the oil pan.
16. Clean the oil pan T-joints.
17. Fill the T-joint between the pan rail/gear housing and pan rail/rear seal retainer with sealant. Use Mopar Silicone Rubber Adhesive Sealant or equivalent.
18. Position the new oil pan gasket.
19. Place suction tube in oil pan and guide into place. Using a new tube-to-block gasket, install the suction tube bolts. Tighten the bolts to 18 ft. lbs. (24 Nm). Tighten the remaining tube brace bolts to 32 ft. lbs. (43 Nm).
20. Starting in the center and working outward, tighten the oil pan bolts to 21 ft. lbs. (28 Nm).
21. Install the steering rack bolts. Tighten bolts to 185 ft. lbs. (251 Nm).
22. Install the flex plate. Tighten bolts to 101 ft. lbs. (137 Nm).
23. Install the flywheel to crankshaft adapter. Tighten to 101 ft. lbs. (137 Nm).
24. Install the flywheel housing assembly with the starter motor attached and tighten bolts to 57 ft. lbs. (77 Nm).
25. Install transmission.
26. Install the starter. See "ENGINE ELECTRICAL" section.

➡Make sure that the fan shroud seal is properly seated in the radiator fan shroud and that it is not out of position causing excessive contact with the radiator coolant tubes.

27. Install the fan and fan shroud. See "ENGINE COOLING" section.
28. Connect both negative battery cables.

4X4

1. Disconnect the battery negative cables.
2. Remove the intake air assembly.
3. Remove the radiator shroud retaining bolts.
4. Install Engine Support Fixture (8534B or equivalent).
5. Raise and support the vehicle.
6. Drain the engine oil.
7. Loosen the front engine mount bolts.
8. Use the Engine Support Fixture to raise engine out of the front mounts.
9. Remove the engine oil dipstick.
10. Remove oil pan bolts, break the pan to block seal, and lower pan slightly.
11. Remove oil suction tube bolts and lower the suction tube into oil pan.
12. Remove the 2 bolts from the front of the engine block stiffener.
13. Remove the oil pan.

To install:

14. Clean the sealing surfaces of the cylinder block and oil pan with a suitable cleaner.
15. Clean the oil pan and the oil pan T-joints.
16. Fill the T-joint between the pan rail/gear housing and pan rail/rear seal retainer with sealant. Use Mopar Silicone Rubber Adhesive Sealant or equivalent.
17. Position the new oil pan gasket.
18. Place suction tube in oil pan and guide them into place. Using a new tube-to-block gasket, install the suction tube. Tighten the bolts to 18 ft. lbs. (24 Nm).
19. Install the engine block stiffener. Tighten bolts to 32 ft. lbs. (43 Nm).
20. Install the oil pan. Starting from the center and working outward, tighten the oil pan bolts to 21 ft. lbs. (28 Nm).
21. Install the engine oil dipstick.
22. Install the flywheel to crankshaft adapter. Tighten to 101 ft. lbs. (137 Nm).
23. Lower the engine into the motor mounts and tighten the through bolts to 64 ft. lbs. (88 Nm).
24. Remove the Engine Support Fixture.

CAUTION

Make sure that the fan shroud seal is properly seated in the radiator fan shroud and that it is not out of position causing excessive contact with the radiator coolant tubes.

25. Install the fan and fan shroud.
26. Connect both negative battery cables.
27. Fill the crankcase with new engine oil.
28. Start engine and check for leaks. Stop engine, check oil level, and adjust, if necessary.

OIL PUMP

REMOVAL & INSTALLATION

5.7L

See Figure 41.

1. Remove the oil pan, as described in this section.
2. Remove the timing cover. See "Timing Chain Front Cover" in this section.
3. Remove the four bolts and the oil pump.

To install:

4. Position the oil pump on the crankshaft and install the oil pump retaining bolts finger tight.
5. Using an alternating sequence, tighten the oil pump retaining bolts to 21 ft. lbs. (28 Nm).
6. Install the timing cover. See "Timing Chain Front Cover" in this section.
7. Install the oil pan.

6.7L Diesel

See Figures 42 and 43.

1. Disconnect the battery negative cables.
2. Remove cooling fan and drive assembly. See "ENGINE COOLING" section.
3. Remove the accessory drive belt. See "Accessory Drive Belt" in this section.
4. Remove the fan support and hub assembly.
5. Remove crankshaft damper. See "Crankshaft Damper & Front Seal" in this section.
6. Remove power steering pump. See "STEERING" section.
7. Remove accessory drive belt tensioner.
8. Remove the gear housing cover.
9. Remove the four mounting bolts and pull the oil pump from the bore in the cylinder block.

To install:

10. Lubricate the pump with clean engine oil. Filling the pump with clean engine oil during installation will help to prime the pump at engine start up.
11. Install the pump. Verify the idler gear pin is installed in the locating bore in the cylinder block. Tighten the oil pump in 3 steps, in the following sequence:
    a. Step 1: Push the pump firmly against the cylinder block and install the 4 bolts finger tight.
    b. Step 2: Tighten the bolts, in an alternating pattern, to 72 inch lbs. (8 Nm).
    c. Step 3: Tighten the bolts again, in an alternating pattern, to 18 ft. lbs. (24 Nm).

➡The back plate on the pump seats against the bottom of the bore in the cylinder block. When the pump is correctly installed, the flange on the pump will not touch the cylinder block.

12. Measure the idler gear to pump drive gear backlash and the idler gear to crankshaft gear backlash. The backlash should be 0.006–0.010 in. (0.15–0.25 mm). If the backlash is out of limits, replace the oil pump.

➡If the adjoining gear moves when you measure the backlash, the reading will be incorrect.

13. Apply a bead of Mopar Silicone Rubber Adhesive Sealant or equivalent to the gear housing cover sealing surface.
14. Install the gear housing cover.
15. Install the crankshaft damper. See "Crankshaft Damper & Front Seal" in this section.
16. Install the fan support/hub assembly.
17. Install power steering pump. See "STEERING" section.
18. Install accessory drive belt tensioner. Tighten bolt to 32 ft. lbs. (43 Nm).
19. Install the accessory drive belt. See "Accessory Drive Belt" in this section.
20. Install the cooling fan. See "ENGINE COOLING" section.
21. Connect battery negative cables.
22. Start engine and check for oil leaks.

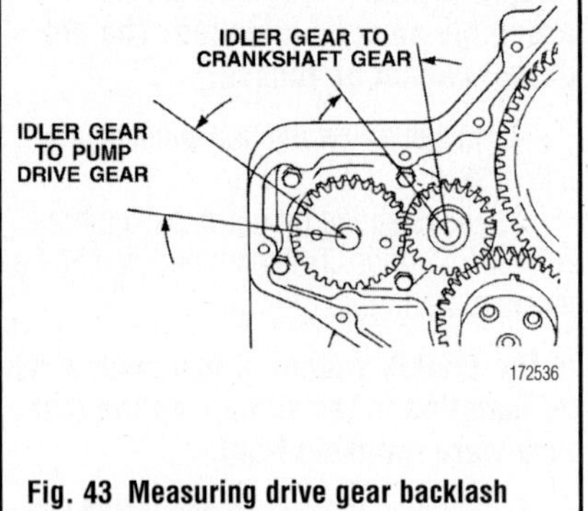

Fig. 43 Measuring drive gear backlash

INSPECTION

5.7L

➡The oil pump pressure relief valve and spring should not be removed from the oil pump. If these components are disassembled and or removed from the pump the entire oil pump assembly must be replaced.

1. Remove the pump cover.
2. Clean all parts thoroughly. Mating surface of the oil pump housing should be smooth. If the pump cover is scratched or grooved the oil pump assembly should be replaced.
3. Slide outer rotor into the body of the oil pump. Press the outer rotor to one side of the oil pump body and measure clearance between the outer rotor and the body. If the measurement is 0.009 in. (0.235 mm) or more the oil pump assembly must be replaced.
4. Install the inner rotor into the oil pump body. Measure the clearance between the inner and outer rotors. If the clearance between the rotors is 0.006 in. (0.150 mm) or more the oil pump assembly must be replaced.
5. Place a straight edge across the body of the oil pump (between the bolt holes), if a feeler gauge of 0.0038 in. (0.095 mm) or greater can be inserted between the straight-

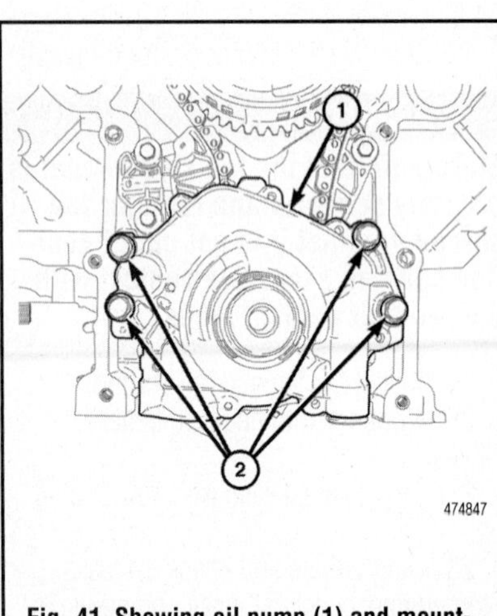

Fig. 41 Showing oil pump (1) and mounting bolts (2)

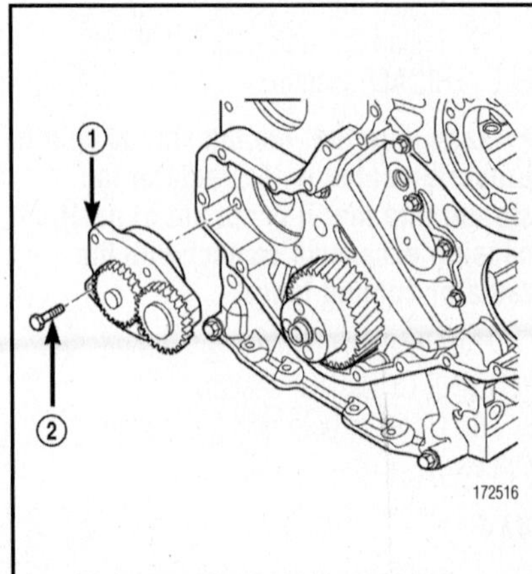

Fig. 42 Removing the oil pump (1) and mounting bolts (2)

edge and the rotors, the pump must be replaced.

6. Reinstall the pump cover. Tighten fasteners to 132 inch lbs. (15 Nm).

➡**The oil pump is serviced as an assembly. In the event the oil pump is not functioning or out of specification, it must be replaced as an assembly.**

6.7L Diesel

See Figures 44 through 47.

1. Visually inspect the lube pump gears for chips, cracks or excessive wear.
2. Remove the oil pump back plate.
3. Mark TOP on the gerotor planetary using a felt tip pen.
4. Remove the gerotor planetary and inspect for excessive wear or damage. Inspect the pump housing and gerotor drive for damaged and excessive wear.
5. Install the gerotor planetary in the original position.
6. With a feeler gauge, measure the tip clearance of the gerotor to the housing. Maximum clearance is 0.007 in. (0.178 mm). If the oil pump is out of limits, replace the pump.
7. Using a straight edge across the face and a feeler gauge, measure the clearance of the gerotor drive/gerotor planetary to port plate. Maximum clearance is 0.005 in. (0.127 mm). If the oil pump is out of limits, replace the pump.
8. Measure the clearance of the gerotor planetary to the body bore. Maximum clearance is 0.015 in. (0.381 mm). If the oil pump is out of limits, replace the pump.
9. Measure the gears backlash. The limits of a used pump is 0.006–0.010 in. (0.15–0.25 mm). If the backlash is out of limits, replace the oil pump.
10. Install the back plate.

PISTON & RING

POSITIONING

5.7L

See Figure 48.

6.7L Diesel

See Figure 49.

REAR MAIN SEAL

REMOVAL & INSTALLATION

5.7L

➡**The crankshaft rear oil seal is integral to the crankshaft rear oil seal retainer and must be replaced as an assembly. The crankshaft rear oil seal retainer can not be reused after removal.**

➡**This procedure can be performed in vehicle.**

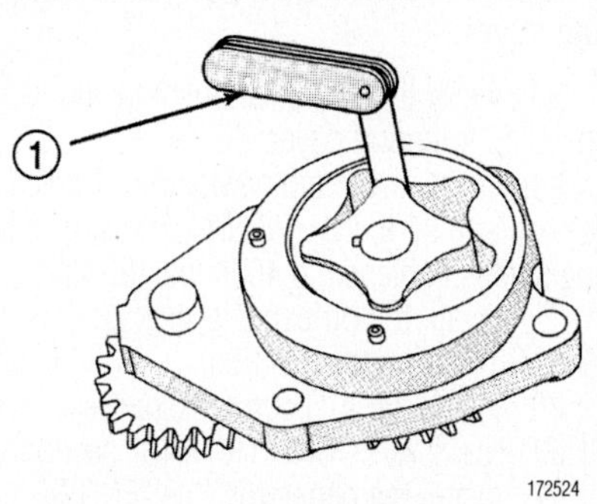

Fig. 44 With a feeler gauge, measure the tip clearance (1) of the gerotor to the housing. Maximum clearance is 0.007 in. (0.178 mm). If the oil pump is out of limits, replace the pump.

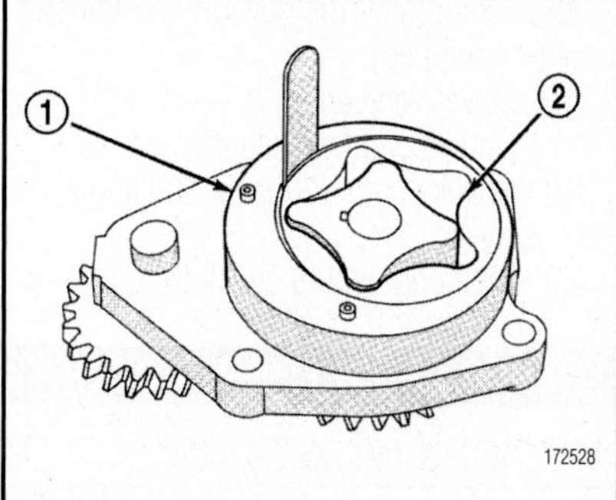

Fig. 46 Measure the clearance of the gerotor planetary to the body bore (1). Maximum clearance is 0.015 in. (0.381 mm). If the oil pump is out of limits, replace the pump.

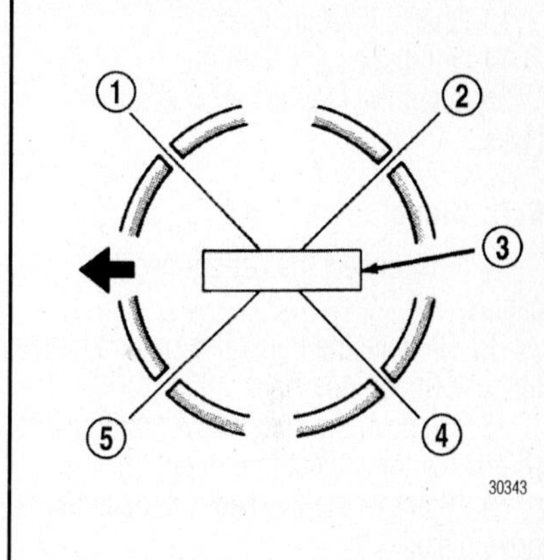

Fig. 48 Showing the piston ring gap positioning—5.7L

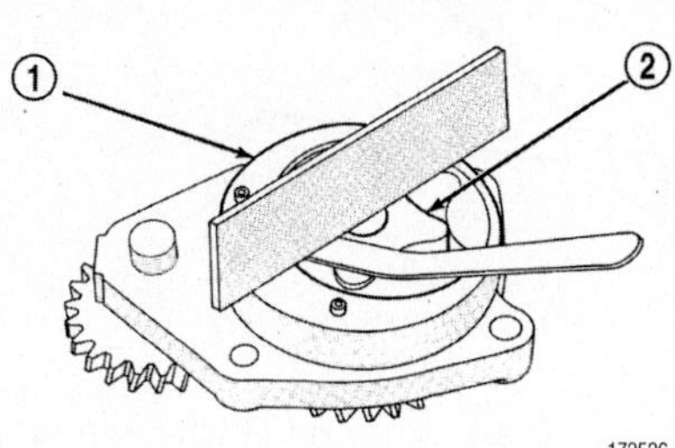

Fig. 45 Using a straight edge across the face and a feeler gauge, measure the clearance of the gerotor drive/gerotor planetary (2) to port plate (1). Maximum clearance is 0.005 in. (0.127 mm). If the oil pump is out of limits, replace the pump.

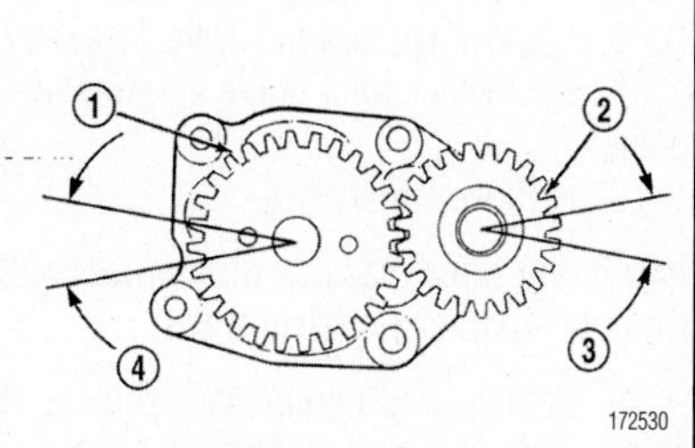

Fig. 47 Measure the gears (1, 2) backlash (3, 4). The limits of a used pump is 0.006–0.010 in. (0.15–0.25 mm). If the backlash is out of limits, replace the oil pump.

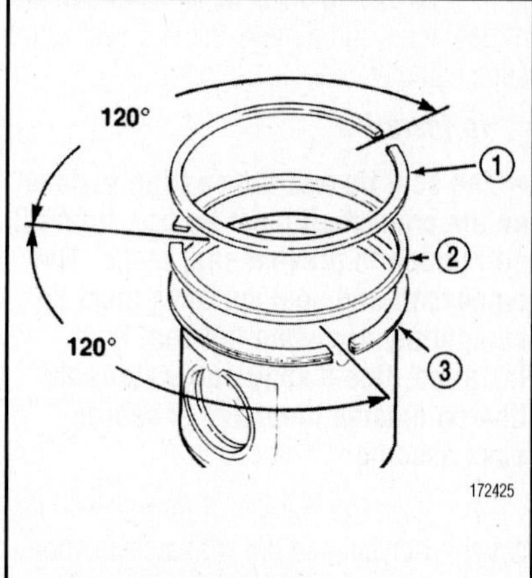

Fig. 49 Showing the piston ring gap positioning—6.7L diesel

1. Disconnect the negative battery cable.
2. Remove the transmission.
3. Remove the flexplate.
4. Remove the oil pan. See "Oil Pan" in this section.
5. Using a criss-cross sequence, remove the rear oil seal retainer mounting bolts.
6. Carefully remove the retainer from the engine block.

To install:

7. Thoroughly clean all gasket residue from the engine block.
8. Position the gasket onto the new crankshaft rear oil seal retainer.
9. Position the crankshaft rear oil seal retainer onto the engine block.
10. Using a criss-cross sequence, install the crankshaft rear oil seal retainer mounting bolts and tighten to 11 ft. lbs. (15 Nm).
11. Install the oil pan. See "Oil Pan" in this section.
12. Install the flexplate.
13. Install the transmission.
14. Fill the engine with oil.
15. Start the engine and check for leaks.

6.7L Diesel

1. Disconnect the battery negative cables.
2. Remove the transmission and transfer case (if equipped).
3. Remove the clutch cover and disc (if manual transmission equipped).
4. Remove the flywheel or converter drive plate.
5. Remove the flywheel adapter plate.
6. Drill holes 180 degrees apart into the seal. Be careful not to contact the drill against the crankshaft.
7. Install #10 sheet metal screws in the drilled holes and remove the rear seal with a slide hammer.

To install:

➡The seal lip and the sealing surface on the crankshaft must be free from all oil residue to prevent seal leaks. The crankshaft and seal surfaces must be completely dry when the seal is installed. Use a soap and water solution on outside diameter of seal to ease assembly.

8. Clean the crankshaft journal with a suitable solvent and dry with a clean shop towel or compressed air. Wipe the inside bore of the crankshaft seal retainer with a clean shop towel.
9. Inspect the crankshaft journal for gouges, nicks, or other imperfections. If the seal groove in the crankshaft is excessively deep, install the new seal 1/8 in. deeper into the retainer bore, or obtain a crankshaft wear sleeve that is available in the aftermarket.
10. Install the seal pilot and new seal, provided in the replacement kit, onto the crankshaft.
11. Remove the seal pilot.
12. Install the installation tool over crankshaft.
13. Using a ball peen hammer, strike the tool at the 12, 3, 6, and 9 o'clock positions until the alignment tool bottoms out on the retainer.

➡Always install a new clamping ring, never reuse the old clamping ring.

14. Install the flywheel or converter drive plate, and clamping ring. Tighten the bolts to 101 ft. lbs. (137 Nm).
15. Install the clutch cover and disc (if equipped).
16. Install the transmission and transfer case (if equipped).
17. Lower vehicle.
18. Connect battery negative cables.
19. Check engine oil level and adjust, if necessary.
20. Start engine and check for oil leaks.

TIMING CHAIN FRONT COVER

REMOVAL & INSTALLATION

5.7L

See Figure 50.

1. Disconnect the battery negative cable.
2. Remove the engine cover.
3. Remove air cleaner assembly.
4. Drain cooling system.
5. Remove accessory drive belt.
6. Remove fan and fan drive assembly.
7. Remove coolant bottle and washer bottle.
8. Remove fan shroud.

➡It is not necessary to disconnect A/C lines or discharge refrigerant.

9. Remove A/C compressor and set aside. Without disconnecting the hoses.
10. Remove the generator. See "ENGINE ELECTRICAL" section.
11. Remove upper radiator hose.
12. Disconnect both heater hoses at timing cover.
13. Disconnect lower radiator hose at engine.
14. Remove accessory drive belt tensioner and both idler pulleys.
15. Remove crankshaft damper. See "Crankshaft Damper & Front Seal" in this section.

➡Do not remove the hoses from the power steering pump.

16. Remove power steering pump and set aside.
17. Remove the dipstick support bolt.
18. Drain the engine oil.
19. Remove the oil pan and pick up tube.

➡It is not necessary to remove water pump for timing cover removal.

20. Remove timing cover bolts and remove cover.
21. Verify that timing cover slide bushings are located in timing cover.

To install:

22. Clean timing chain cover and block surface.

➡Always install a new gasket on timing cover.

23. Verify that the slide bushings are installed in timing cover.
24. Install cover and new gasket. Tighten fasteners to 21 ft. lbs. (28 Nm). The large lifting stud is tightened to 40 ft. lbs. (55 Nm).
25. Install the oil pan and pick up tube. See "Oil Pan" in this section.
26. Install the A/C compressor. See "HEATING & AIR CONDITIONING" section.
27. Install the generator. See "ENGINE ELECTRICAL" section.
28. Install power steering pump. See "STEERING" section.

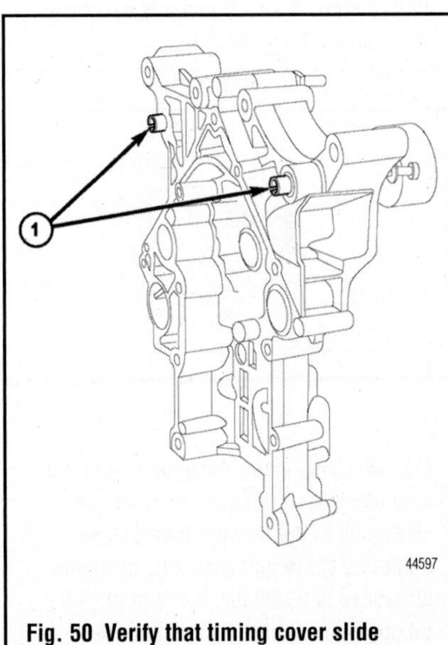

Fig. 50 Verify that timing cover slide bushings (1) are located in timing cover.

29. Install the dipstick support bolt.
30. Install the thermostat housing.
31. Install crankshaft damper. See "Crankshaft Damper & Front Seal" in this section.
32. Install accessory drive belt tensioner assembly and both idler pulleys.
33. Install radiator lower hose.
34. Install both heater hoses.
35. Install the cooling module.
36. Install the accessory drive belt.
37. Install the coolant bottle and washer bottle.
38. Install the upper radiator hose.
39. Install the air cleaner assembly.
40. Fill cooling system.
41. Refill engine oil.
42. Connect the battery negative cable.

6.7L Diesel

1. Disconnect both battery negative cables.
2. Raise vehicle on hoist.
3. Partially drain engine coolant into container suitable for re-use.
4. Lower vehicle.
5. Remove radiator upper hose.
6. Remove viscous fan/drive/shroud assembly. See "ENGINE COOLING" section.
7. Remove the accessory drive belt. See "Accessory Drive Belt" in this section.
8. Remove the cooling fan support/hub from the front of the engine.
9. Raise the vehicle on hoist.
10. Remove power steering pump. See "STEERING" section.
11. Remove accessory drive belt tensioner.
12. Remove the crankshaft damper. See "Crankshaft Damper & Front Seal" in this section.
13. Lower the vehicle.
14. Remove the gear cover-to-housing bolts and gently pry the cover away from the housing, taking care not to mar the gasket surfaces.

To install:

15. Install a new front crankshaft oil seal. See "Crankshaft Damper & Front Seal" in this section.
16. Obtain a seal pilot installation tool from a crankshaft front seal service kit and install the pilot into the seal.
17. Apply a bead of Mopar Silicone Rubber Adhesive Sealant or equivalent to the gear housing cover. Be sure to surround all bolt holes.
18. Using the seal pilot to align the cover , install the cover to the housing and install the bolts. Tighten the bolts at the 3 and 9 o'clock position finger tight, then in a clockwise direction starting at the 3 o'clock position, tighten to 18 ft. lbs. (24 Nm).
19. Snug, but do not torque one bolt at the 3 o'clock and 9 o'clock positions. This centers the seal on the crankshaft.
20. Tighten the bolts to 18 ft. lbs. (24 Nm) in a circular pattern.
21. Remove the seal pilot. Install front seal dust shield.
22. Raise and support vehicle.
23. Install the crankshaft damper. See "Crankshaft Damper & Front Seal" in this section.
24. Install the fan support/hub assembly, and tighten bolts to 24 ft. lbs. (32 Nm).
25. Install power steering pump. See "STEERING" section.
26. Install accessory drive belt tensioner. Tighten bolt to 32 ft. lbs. (43 Nm).
27. Install the accessory drive belt. See "Accessory Drive Belt" in this section.
28. Install the cooling fan/drive/shroud assembly. See "ENGINE COOLING" section.
29. Install the radiator upper hose and clamps.
30. Fill the coolant system.
31. Connect both battery negative cables.
32. Start engine and inspect for leaks.

TIMING CHAIN & SPROCKETS

REMOVAL & INSTALLATION

5.7L

See Figures 51 through 57.

1. Disconnect the negative battery cable.
2. Drain the cooling system.

➡It is not necessary to remove water pump for timing chain cover removal.

3. Remove the timing chain cover. See "Timing Chain Cover" in this section.
4. Verify the slide bushings remain installed in the timing chain cover during removal.
5. Remove the oil pump retaining bolts and remove the oil pump.
6. Install the vibration damper bolt finger tight. Using a suitable socket and breaker bar, rotate the crankshaft to align the timing marks with the timing chain sprockets.
7. Retract the chain tensioner arm until the hole in the arm lines up with the hole in the bracket.
8. Install the Tensioner Pin (8514 or equivalent) into the chain tensioner holes.

⁂ CAUTION

Never attempt to disassemble the camshaft phaser, severe engine damage could result.

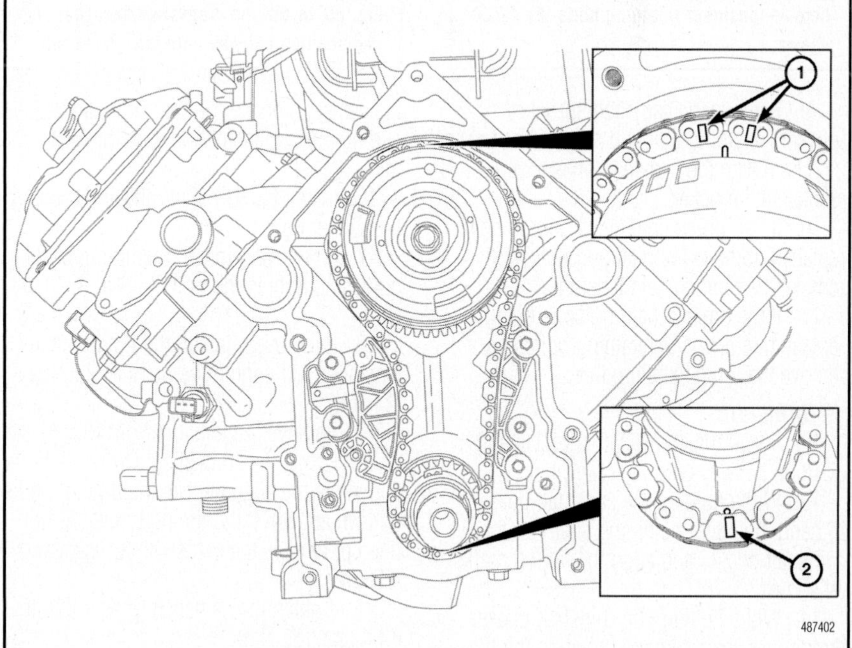

Fig. 51 Install the vibration damper bolt finger tight. Using a suitable socket and breaker bar, rotate the crankshaft to align the timing marks with the timing chain sprockets (1, 2).

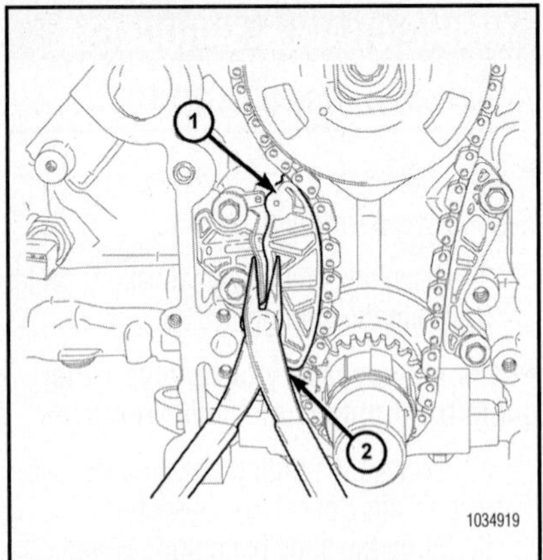

Fig. 52 Retract the chain tensioner arm (1) until the hole in the arm lines up with the hole in the bracket.

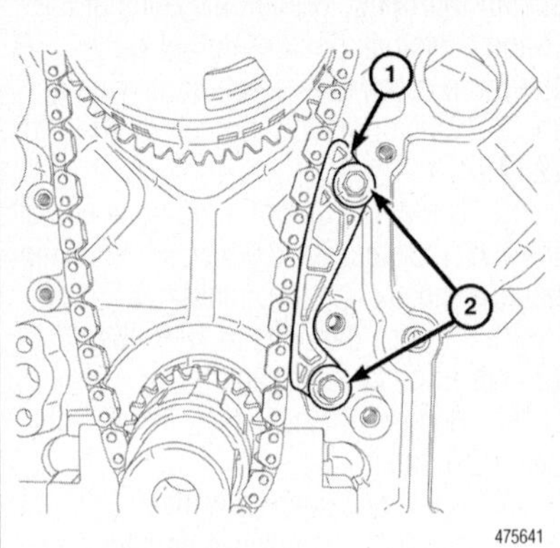

Fig. 54 If the timing chain guide (1) is being replaced, remove the retaining bolts (2) and remove the timing chain guide.

Fig. 56 While holding the camshaft phaser in hand, position the timing chain on the camshaft phaser and align the timing marks as shown.

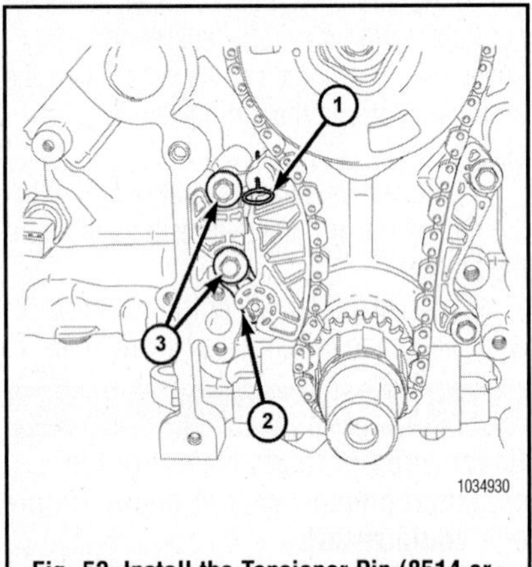

Fig. 53 Install the Tensioner Pin (8514 or equivalent) (1) into the chain tensioner (3) holes—tensioner retaining bolts (2) shown.

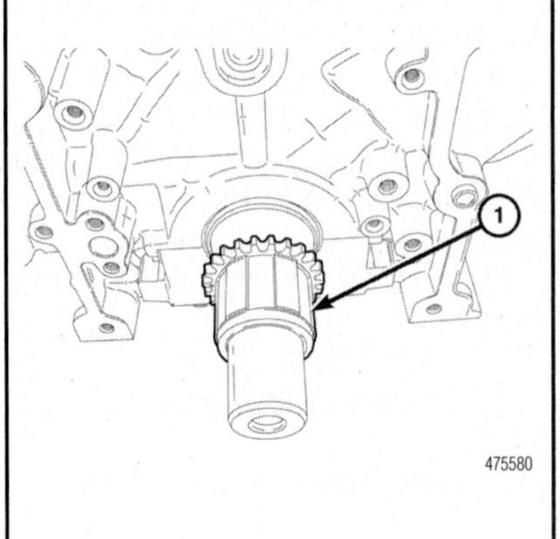

Fig. 55 Install the crankshaft sprocket (1) and position halfway onto the crankshaft.

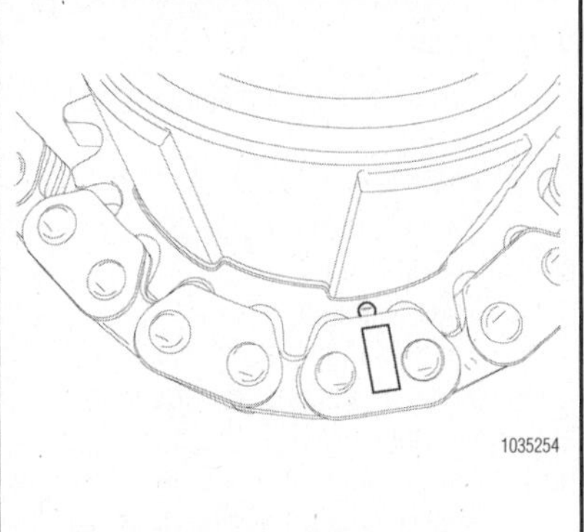

Fig. 57 While holding the camshaft phaser and timing chain in hand, position the timing chain on the crankshaft sprocket and align the timing mark as shown.

9. Remove the camshaft sprocket (phaser) retaining bolt and remove the timing chain with the camshaft phaser and crankshaft sprocket.
10. If the timing chain tensioner is being replaced, remove the retaining bolts and remove the timing chain tensioner.
11. If the timing chain guide is being replaced, remove the retaining bolts and remove the timing chain guide.

To install:

12. Install the crankshaft sprocket and position halfway onto the crankshaft.
13. While holding the camshaft phaser in hand, position the timing chain on the camshaft phaser and align the timing marks as shown.
14. While holding the camshaft phaser and timing chain in hand, position the timing chain on the crankshaft sprocket and align the timing mark as shown.
15. Align the slot in the camshaft phaser with the dowel on the camshaft and position the camshaft phaser on the camshaft while sliding the crankshaft sprocket into position.
16. Install the camshaft phaser retaining bolt finger tight.
17. If removed, install the timing chain guide and tighten the bolts to 8 ft. lbs. (11 Nm).
18. If removed, install the timing chain tensioner and tighten the bolts to 8 ft. lbs. (11 Nm).
19. Remove the tensioner pin (8514).
20. Rotate the crankshaft two revolutions and verify the alignment of the timing marks (shown above). If the timing marks do not line up, remove the camshaft sprocket and realign.
21. Tighten the camshaft phaser bolt to 63 ft. lbs. (85 Nm).
22. Position the oil pump onto the crankshaft and install the oil pump retaining bolts finger tight.
23. Using a criss-cross pattern, tighten the oil pump retaining bolts to 21 ft. lbs. (28 Nm).
24. Verify the slide bushings are installed in the timing chain cover and install the timing chain cover. See "Timing Chain Cover" in this section.
25. Fill the engine with oil.
26. Fill the cooling system.
27. Connect the negative battery cable.
28. Start the engine and check for leaks.

TURBOCHARGER

REMOVAL & INSTALLATION

6.7L Diesel

1. Disconnect the negative battery cable on both batteries.
2. Disconnect and re-position the right hand side positive battery cable.
3. Drain the coolant from the radiator and engine.
4. Remove the air filter housing.

5. Disconnect the crankcase vent hose at the turbocharger air intake.

6. Remove the intake air tube at the turbocharger.

7. Remove the charge air cooler inlet tube at the turbocharger inlet.

8. Disconnect the turbocharger speed sensor electrical connector.

9. Disconnect the turbocharger actuator electrical connector.

10. Remove the turbocharger oil pressure line.

11. Remove the turbocharger coolant lines at the engine block and turbocharger.

12. Remove the right side wheelhouse splash shield.

13. Lower the vehicle.

14. Install the engine support fixture tool (8353B or equivalent).

15. Remove the right hand side engine mount.

16. Raise and support the vehicle.

17. Remove the exhaust steady rest bracket from transmission.

18. Remove the V-clamp from the turbocharger exhaust outlet.

19. Remove the turbocharger drain tube at the turbocharger.

20. Remove the turbocharger drain tube from the cylinder block.

21. Lower the vehicle.

22. Remove and reposition the grid heater relay from the battery tray.

23. Remove the turbocharger to exhaust manifold mounting nuts.

24. Remove the turbocharger from the vehicle by lifting from the top of the engine compartment.

25. Clean the turbocharger mating surfaces.

26. Inspect the turbocharger for damage, if necessary replace the turbocharger.

To install:

27. Ensure that turbocharger and charge air cooler are free of excess oil and debris. Do not allow any water or solvents to enter the turbocharger inlet or outlet. If necessary, clean turbocharger and the charge air cooler.

28. Prior to installation, inspect the turbocharger for any damage.

29. Clean the turbocharger mating surfaces.

30. Replace the banjo fitting seals on the turbocharger coolant lines.

31. Using a new gasket, position the turbocharger onto the exhaust manifold studs by lowering the turbocharger through the engine compartment.

32. If old gasket appeared to be leaking, check the turbocharger/exhaust manifold mounting flanges for warping. Using a straight edge and feeler gauge measure along the two longest sides of the flanges for warpage. Spec is 0.0039 in. (0.1 mm) for the turbocharger flange and 00.002 in. (0.05 mm) maximum.

33. Install the turbocharger mounting nuts. Using a proper tool (9866 or equivalent), using an alternating pattern, tighten the nuts to 32 ft. lbs. (43 Nm).

34. Install the grid heater relay to the battery tray.

35. Inspect the oil drain tube O-rings for nicks or cuts. Replace if necessary. Oil the O-rings with new oil.

36. Raise and support the vehicle.

37. Position the turbocharger drain tube into engine block.

38. Using a new gasket, install the turbocharger drain tube mounting bolts. Tighten the mounting bolts to 18 ft. lbs. (24 Nm).

39. Using a new clamp, connect the exhaust pipe to the turbocharger exhaust outlet with the clamp facing down as shown. Tighten the clamp to 13 ft. lbs. (17 Nm). Using a rubber mallet, hit the exhaust pipe to turbocharger clamp three times around the perimeter of the clamp and tighten the clamp to 13 ft. lbs. (17 Nm).

40. Install the exhaust steady rest bracket to the transmission. Tighten bolts to 32 ft. lbs. (43 Nm).

41. Install the right hand side engine mount:

a. With engine just slightly raised, install mount and tighten bracket bolts to 70 ft. lbs. (95 Nm).

b. After engine is lowered and vehicle rests on ground, tighten mount through bolt nut to 95 ft. lbs. (129 Nm).

42. Install the right side wheelhouse splash shield.

43. Lower the vehicle.

44. Remove the engine support fixture tool.

45. Install the coolant lines at the engine block and turbocharger. Tighten the banjo fittings 18 ft. lbs. (24 Nm).

46. Install the turbocharger oil return line. Tighten the fitting to 27 ft. lbs. (36 Nm).

47. Install the turbocharger oil pressure line. Tighten the fitting to 27 ft. lbs. (36 Nm).

48. Connect the turbocharger actuator electrical connector and the turbocharger speed sensor electrical connector.

49. Install the charge air tube to turbocharger inlet. Tighten the clamp.

50. Pre-lube the turbocharger with 1–2 oz. clean engine oil.

51. Install the intake air tube at the turbocharger. Tighten the clamp.

52. Connect the crankcase vent hose at the turbocharger air intake.

53. Install the air filter housing.

54. Fill the cooling system.

55. Position and connect the right hand side positive battery cable.

56. Connect the negative battery cable on both batteries.

57. Check for any cooling or exhaust leaks and confirm the turbocharger is operating properly.

VALVE COVERS (CYLINDER HEAD COVERS)

REMOVAL & INSTALLATION

5.7L

➡Both sides similar.

1. Disconnect and isolate the negative battery cable.

2. Remove the engine cover.

3. Disconnect the ignition coil electrical connectors.

4. Position the electrical harness aside.

5. Remove the ignition coil retaining bolts and remove the ignition coils.

6. Starting from the middle and working across and in alternating sides, remove the cylinder head cover retaining bolts.

⁂ CAUTION

Do not use harsh cleaners to clean the cylinder head covers. Severe damage to covers may occur.

7. Remove the cylinder head cover.

8. Clean the sealing surface of the cylinder head and cover.

➡The cylinder head cover gasket may be used again, provided no cuts, tears, or deformation have occurred.

9. Installation is the reverse of the removal procedure.

10. Tighten cylinder head cover bolts, in an alternating criss-cross pattern, to 70 inch lbs. (8 Nm).

6.7L Diesel

See Figure 58.

1. Remove the bolts and the engine cover.

2. Disconnect both negative battery cables.

⁂ CAUTION

Pneumatic tools should NOT be used to remove or install the cover.

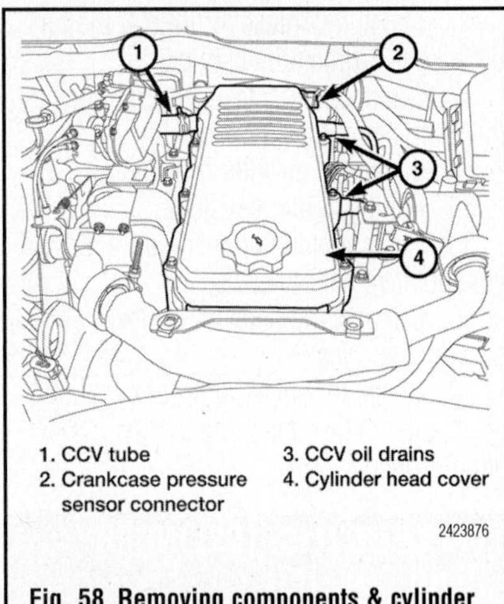

Fig. 58 Removing components & cylinder head cover

3. Remove the oil fill cap.
4. Remove the breather cover capscrews.
5. Remove the Close Crankcase Ventilation (CCV) cover and breather filter.
6. Disconnect the CCV tube at the Crankcase Depression Regular (CDR) valve.
7. Disconnect the crankcase pressure sensor connector.
8. Remove the CCV oil drains from cylinder head cover (2 hoses).
9. Remove the cylinder head cover capscrews.
10. Remove the cylinder head cover.
11. Disconnect both injector harness connectors.
12. Remove the injector wire nuts from the valve cover gasket.
13. Remove the cylinder head cover gasket .

To install:

➡Gasket must be completely dry and free of oil before installation. Pneumatic tools should NOT be used to remove or install the cover.

14. Wipe oil from the cylinder head cover gasket, rocker box, and cylinder head cover.
15. Inspect cylinder head cover gasket for tears, or splits. Replace if necessary.
16. Install the cylinder head cover gasket on the rocker box.
17. Install the injector nuts to injector studs. Tighten nuts.
18. Connect both injector harness connectors.
19. Install cylinder head cover and cylinder head cover capscrews . Tighten from center out. Tighten to 18 ft. lbs. (24 Nm).
20. Install the Close Crankcase Ventilation (CCV) drain hoses to the cylinder head cover.
21. Connect the crankcase pressure sensor connector.
22. Connect the CCV tube at the Crankcase Depression Regular (CDR) valve.
23. Remove any oil from the CCV seal area and install the CCV breather filter.
24. Install the CCV cover and capscrews. Tighten to 89 inch lbs. (10 Nm).
25. Install the oil fill cap.
26. Connect both negative battery cables.
27. Install the engine cover. Tighten the bolts 89 inch lbs. (10 Nm).
28. Start the vehicle and check for leaks.

VALVE LASH

ADJUSTMENT

5.7L

➡Valve lash is maintained automatically by hydraulic valve adjusters. No clearance check or adjustment is needed.

6.7L Diesel

➡To obtain accurate readings, valve lash measurements and adjustments should only be performed when the engine coolant temperature is less than 140°F (60°C).

➡The 24-valve overhead system is a "low-maintenance" design. Routine adjustments are no longer necessary, however, measurement should still take place when troubleshooting performance problems, or upon completion of a repair that includes removal and installation of the valve train components or injectors.

1. Disconnect battery negative cables.
2. Remove cylinder head cover. See "Valve Covers (Cylinder Head Covers)" in this section.
3. Using an appropriate tool (7471B or equivalent), rotate crankshaft to align damper TDC mark to 12 o'clock position.
    a. If both number one cylinder rocker levers are loose, continue to next step.
    b. If both number one cylinder rocker levers are not loose, rotate crankshaft 360 degrees.
4. With the engine in this position, valve lash can be measured at the following rocker arms:
    - Intake 1, 2, 4
    - Exhaust 1, 3, 5.
5. Measure the valve lash by inserting a feeler gauge between the rocker arm socket and crosshead. Refer below for the correct specifications.
    a. If the measurement falls within the limits, adjustment/resetting is not necessary.
    b. If measurement finds the lash outside of the limits, adjustment/resetting is required.
6. Measurements should be as follows:
    - Intake Minimum: 0.006 in. (0.152 mm)
    - Intake Maximum: 0.015 in. (0.381 mm)
    - Exhaust Minimum: 0.021 in. (0.533 mm)
    - Exhaust Maximum: 0.034 in. (0.863 mm)

➡If measured valve lash falls within these specifications, no adjustment/reset is necessary. Engine operation within these ranges has no adverse affect on performance, emissions, fuel economy or level of engine noise.

7. If adjustment/resetting is required, loosen the lock nut on rocker arms and turn the adjusting screw until the desired lash is obtained:
    - Intake: 0.010 in. (0.254 mm)
    - Exhaust: 0.026 in. (0.660 mm)
8. Tighten the lock nut to 18 ft. lbs. (24 Nm) and recheck the valve lash.
9. Using the crankshaft barring tool, rotate the crankshaft one revolution (360 degrees) to align the damper TDC mark to the 12 o'clock position.
10. With the engine in this position, valve lash can be measured at the remaining rocker arms:
    - Intake: 3, 5, 6
    - Exhaust: 2, 4, 6
11. Use the same method as above for determining whether adjustment is necessary, and adjust those that are found to be outside of the limits.
12. Install the cylinder head cover.
13. Connect the battery negative cables.

ENGINE PERFORMANCE & EMISSION CONTROLS

ACCELERATOR PEDAL POSITION (APP) SENSOR

LOCATION

5.7L

See Figure 59.

The Accelerator Pedal Position Sensor (APPS) is located inside the vehicle. It is attached to the accelerator pedal assembly.

6.7L Diesel

See Figure 60.

REMOVAL & INSTALLATION

5.7L

CAUTION

Do not attempt to separate or remove the Accelerator Pedal Position Sensor (APPS) from the accelerator pedal assembly. The APPS and the accelerator pedal is replaced as an assembly. If the sensor is removed from the pedal, the electronic calibration may be destroyed.

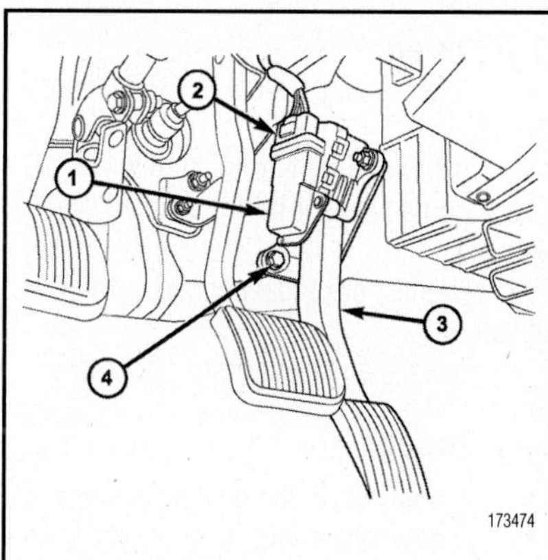

Fig. 59 Showing the Accelerator Pedal Position Sensor—5.7L

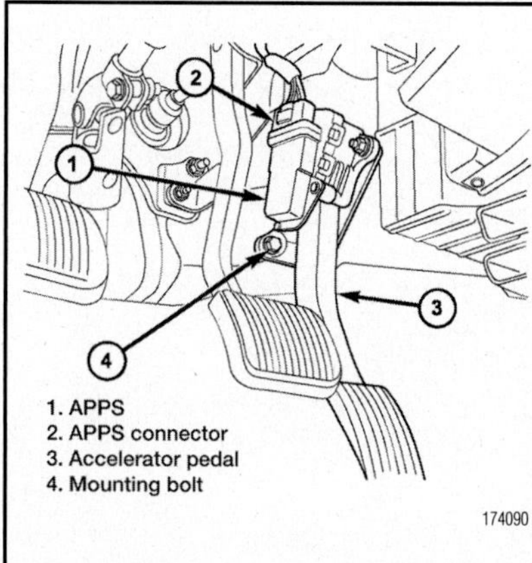

Fig. 60 Showing the Accelerator Pedal Position Sensor—6.7L Diesel

1. Remove the accelerator pedal assembly as follows:
   a. Disconnect the 6-way electrical connector at the APPS.
   b. Remove the upper accelerator pedal mounting bolt.
   c. Remove the lower accelerator pedal mounting bolt.
   d. Remove the accelerator pedal assembly from the vehicle.
2. Installation is the reverse of the removal procedure.

6.7L Diesel

CAUTION

Do not attempt to separate or remove the Accelerator Pedal Position Sensor (APPS) from the accelerator pedal assembly. The APPS and the accelerator pedal is replaced as an assembly. If the sensor is removed from the pedal, the electronic calibration may be destroyed.

1. Disconnect 6-way electrical connector at top of APPS.
2. Remove APPS lower mounting bolt and two mounting nuts.
3. Remove pedal and APPS assembly from vehicle.
4. Installation is the reverse of the removal procedure.

CAMSHAFT POSITION (CMP) SENSOR

LOCATION

5.7L

See Figure 61.

The Camshaft Position Sensor (CMP) is located on right side of timing gear/chain cover below generator.

REMOVAL & INSTALLATION

5.7L

1. Disconnect electrical connector at CMP sensor.
2. Remove sensor mounting bolt.
3. Carefully twist sensor from cylinder head.
4. Check condition of sensor O-ring.

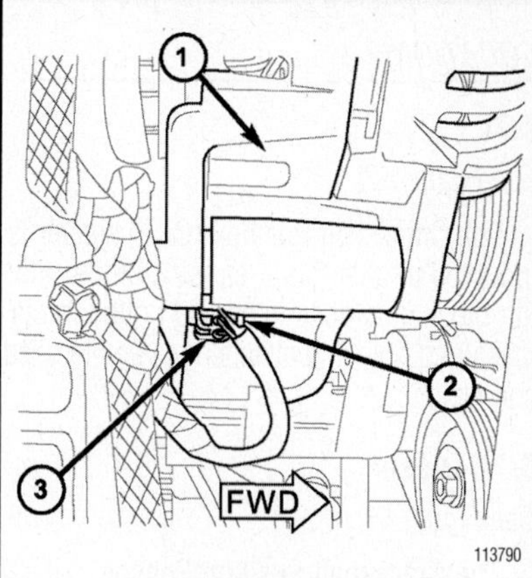

Fig. 61 Camshaft Position Sensor (CMP) (3) and electrical connector (2) are located on right side of timing gear/chain cover below generator (1).

To install:

5. Clean out machined hole in cylinder head.
6. Apply a small amount of engine oil to sensor O-ring.
7. Install sensor into cylinder head with a slight rocking and twisting action.

CAUTION

Before tightening sensor mounting bolt, be sure sensor is completely flush to cylinder head. If sensor is not flush, damage to sensor mounting tang may result.

8. Install mounting bolt and tighten to 9 ft. lbs. (12 Nm).
9. Connect electrical connector to sensor.

CRANKCASE PRESSURE (CP) SENSOR

LOCATION

6.7L Diesel

The Crankcase Pressure Sensor is located on the valve cover.

REMOVAL & INSTALLATION

6.7L Diesel

1. Disconnect both negative battery cables.
2. Disconnect the CP sensor harness connector.
3. Remove bolt and the CP sensor from valve cover.
4. Installation is the reverse of the removal procedure.

CRANKSHAFT POSITION (CKP) SENSOR

LOCATION

5.7L

See Figure 62.

The Crankshaft Position (CKP) sensor is mounted into the right rear side of the cylinder block. It is positioned and bolted into a machined hole and attached via an electrical connector.

6.7L Diesel

See Figure 63.

The Crankshaft Position Sensor (CKP) on the diesel engine is attached at the front left side of the engine next to the engine harmonic balancer (crankshaft damper).

REMOVAL & INSTALLATION

5.7L

1. Raise vehicle.
2. Disconnect sensor electrical connector.
3. Remove sensor mounting bolt.
4. Carefully twist sensor from cylinder block.
5. Check condition of sensor O-ring.

To install:

6. Clean out machined hole in engine block.
7. Apply a small amount of engine oil to sensor O-ring.
8. Install sensor into engine block with a slight rocking and twisting action.

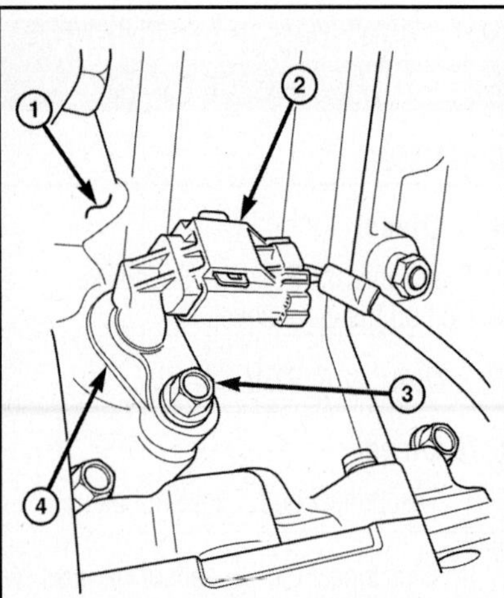

Fig. 62 The Crankshaft Position (CKP) sensor is mounted into the right rear side of the cylinder block.

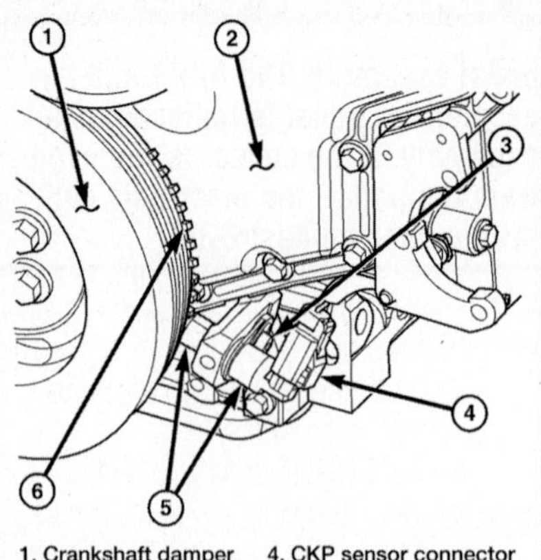

Fig. 63 Showing the Crankshaft Position (CKP) Sensor location—6.7L diesel

CAUTION

Before tightening the CKP sensor mounting bolt, be sure the sensor is completely flush to the cylinder block. If the CKP sensor is not flush, damage to the sensor mounting tang may result.

9. Install mounting bolt and tighten to 21 ft. lbs. (28 Nm) torque.
10. Connect electrical connector to sensor.
11. Lower vehicle.

6.7L Diesel

1. Disconnect both negative battery cables.
2. Disconnect Crankshaft Position (CKP) sensor harness connector.
3. Remove the bolt and the CKP sensor.
4. Installation is the reverse of the removal procedure.
5. Tighten bolt to 89 inch lbs. (10 Nm).

ENGINE COOLANT TEMPERATURE (ECT) SENSOR

LOCATION

5.7L

See Figure 64.

6.7L Diesel

See Figure 65.

The Engine Coolant Temperature (ECT) sensor is used to sense engine coolant temperature. The ECT sensor protrudes into an engine water jacket in the cylinder head.

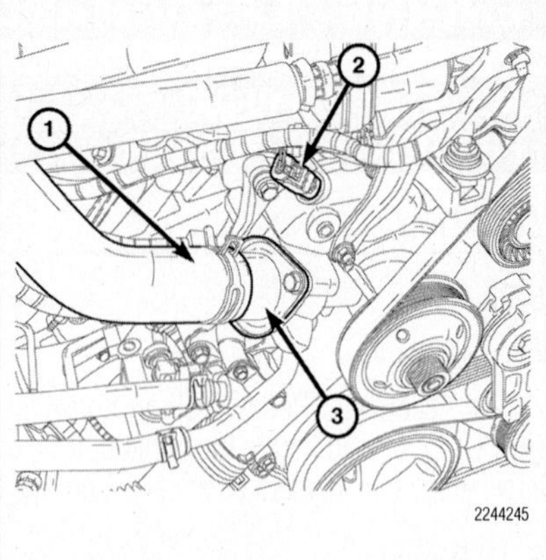

Fig. 64 ECT sensor is located just above the radiator hose connection to the block—5.7L

REMOVAL & INSTALLATION

5.7L

1. Partially drain the cooling system.
2. Disconnect the electrical connector from the ECT sensor.
3. Remove the sensor from the intake manifold

To install:

4. Apply thread sealant to ECT sensor threads.
5. Install ECT sensor to engine.
6. Tighten sensor to 8 ft. lbs. (11 Nm) torque.
7. Connect electrical connector to ECT sensor.
8. Replace any lost engine coolant.

6.7L Diesel

1. Partially drain the cooling system.
2. Remove the engine trim cover.
3. Remove the upper EGR tube.
4. Remove heat shield.

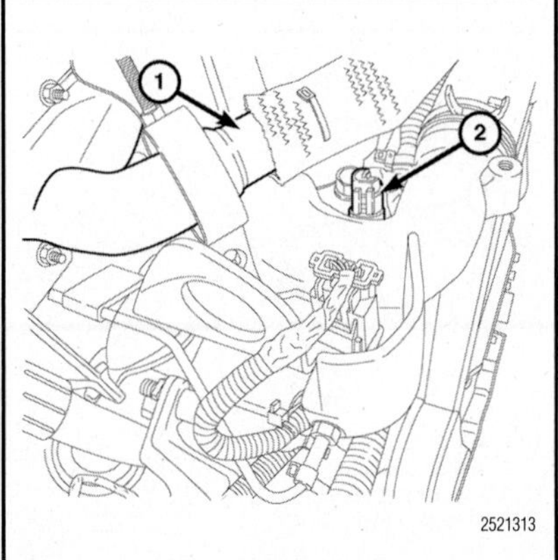

Fig. 65 Showing the ECT sensor (2) location, below the upper radiator hose (1)

5. Disconnect the electrical connector from the ETC sensor.
6. Remove the ETC sensor from the cylinder head.
7. Installation is the reverse of the removal procedure.
8. Tighten the sensor to 13 ft. lbs. (18 Nm).

EVAPORATIVE EMISSIONS (EVAP) CANISTER

LOCATION

See Figure 66.

➡These engines may use different types of canister configurations. Type 1 canister is shown. The mounting location is the same for all types of canisters, but the design and connections may vary.

REMOVAL & INSTALLATION

1. Raise and support vehicle.
2. If equipped, remove necessary skid plates. Certain models, equipped with a certain fuel tank size, may require the removal of the fuel tank skid plate and/or the transfer case skid plate to gain access to the EVAP canister(s).
3. Disconnect electrical wiring connector from Evaporative Emission System Monitor (ESIM) switch.
4. Disconnect vapor line from ESIM switch.
5. Disconnect quick-connect vapor line from canister.
6. Remove canister mounting bracket bolt. This is located below and near the ESIM switch.

TYPE-1

1. EVAP canister
2. ESIM cover
3. ESIM valve
4. Not identified
5. Vapor line
6. Vapor line

180636

Fig. 66 Showing EVAP canister location—Type 1 canister shown; other type canisters are mounted in same location

7. Pull canister from mounting bracket while guiding two canister locating pins from mounting bracket.
8. Installation is the reverse of the removal procedure.

EXHAUST GAS PRESSURE SENSOR

REMOVAL & INSTALLATION

6.7L Diesel

See Figure 67.

1. Disconnect both negative battery cable.
2. Disconnect exhaust gas pressure sensor harness connector and remove the exhaust gas pressure sensor.
3. Installation is the reverse of the removal procedure.

EXHAUST GAS RECIRCULATION (EGR) VALVE

LOCATION

6.7L Diesel

See Figure 68.

REMOVAL & INSTALLATION

6.7L Diesel

1. Disconnect both negative battery cables.
2. Remove bolts and the EGR crossover tube cover.
3. Remove clamp at end of EGR crossover tube.
4. Remove bolt at center bottom of EGR crossover tube.

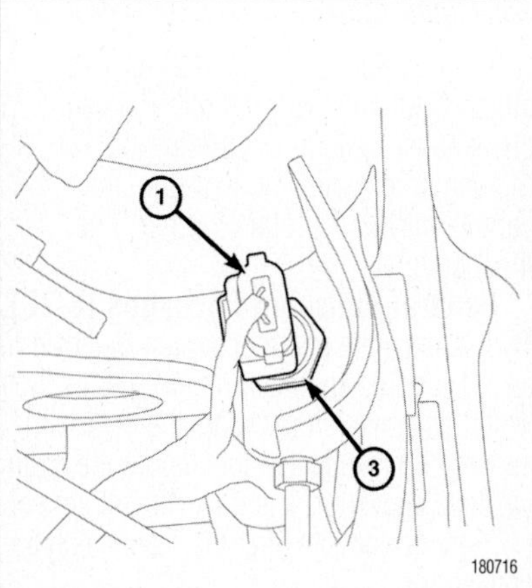

Fig. 67 Disconnect exhaust gas pressure sensor harness connector (1) and remove the exhaust gas pressure sensor (3).

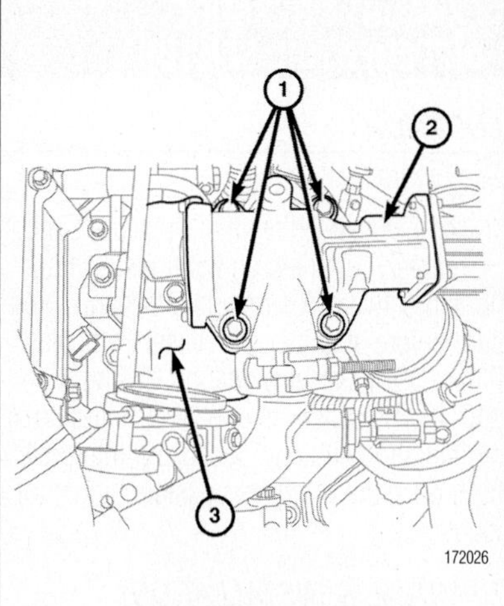

Fig. 68 Showing the mounting bolts (1), EGR valve assembly (2) and intake manifold connector (3)—6.7L diesel

5. Disconnect the EGR valve harness connector.
6. Remove the four EGR valve assembly mounting bolts.
7. Remove EGR valve assembly from intake connector by prying up.
8. Remove crossover tube gasket and clean EGR valve. Also clean end of EGR tube of any old gasket material.
9. Remove two gaskets on bottom EGR valve. Clean bottom of EGR valve and top of its intake connection point of any old gasket material.

To install:

10. Install a new EGR crossover tube gasket.
11. Install a new gasket to bottom of EGR valve.
12. Position EGR valve assembly and install the four EGR valve mounting bolts finger tight.
13. Install clamps at end of EGR crossover tube.
14. Install bolt at center bottom of EGR crossover tube finger tight.
15. Tighten clamps to 89 inch lbs. (10 Nm).
16. Tighten EGR tube bolt to 89 inch lbs. (10 Nm).
17. Tighten the four EGR valve mounting bolts in a criss-cross fashion to 18 ft. lbs. (24 Nm).
18. Connect the EGR valve harness connector.
19. Install EGR crossover tube cover. Tighten bolts to 89 inch lbs. (10 Nm).
20. Connect both negative battery cables.

EXHAUST PRESSURE DIFFERENTIAL SENSOR

LOCATION

See Figure 69.

The Exhaust Differential Pressure Sensor is remotely mounted on the transmission housing. Two pressure tubes measure pressure before and after the Diesel Particulate Filter (DPF)/Diesel Oxidation Catalyst (DOC). The sensor is critical for fail-safe of regeneration strategy, because it interprets high pressure drops as possible high soot loads.

REMOVAL & INSTALLATION

1. Raise and support vehicle.
2. Disconnect electrical connector.
3. Disconnect hoses at pressure differential pressure sensor.
4. Remove mounting bolt and differential pressure sensor.
5. Remove mounting bolts.
6. Remove pressure differential pressure tubing.
7. Installation is the reverse of the removal procedure.
8. Tighten tubing fittings, if removed, to 22 ft. lbs. (30 Nm), and the sensor mounting bolts to 89 inch lbs. (10 Nm).

EXHAUST TEMPERATURE SENSOR

LOCATION

6.7L Diesel

See Figure 70.

The Diesel Exhaust Temperature Sensors are thermistors and change resistance based on the temperature being measured.

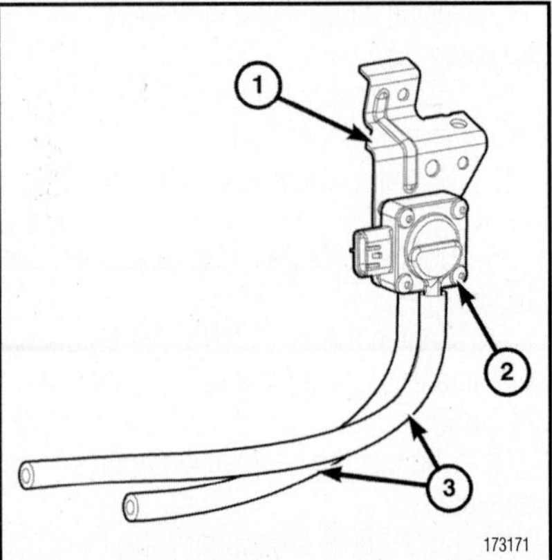

Fig. 69 Showing the bracket (1), Differential Pressure Sensor (2), and connecting tubes (3)

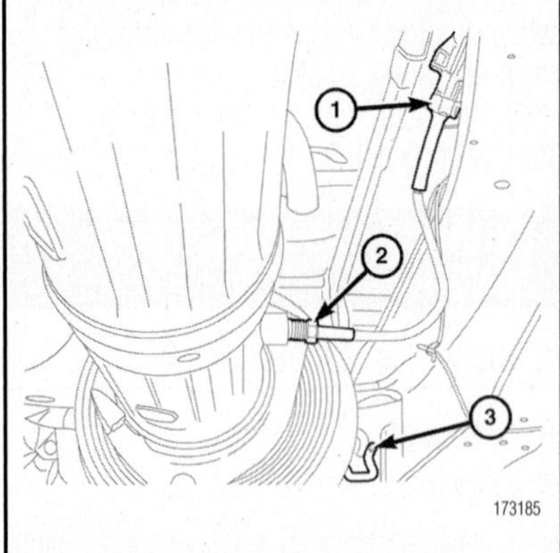

Fig. 70 Showing the location of the diesel exhaust temperature sensor (2) and electrical connector (1)—item (3) not identified

The Engine Control Module (ECM) provides a 5 volt reference voltage to the sensor. The ECM monitors the change in signal voltage and converts this to a temperature value.

REMOVAL & INSTALLATION

1. Raise and support vehicle.
2. Disconnect diesel exhaust temperature sensor electrical connector.
3. Remove diesel exhaust temperature sensor.
4. Installation is the reverse of the removal procedure.
5. Tighten sensor to 22 ft. lbs. (30 Nm).

HEATED OXYGEN (H02S) SENSOR

LOCATION

See Figure 71.

The Oxygen Sensors (02S) are attached to, and protrude into the vehicle exhaust system. Depending on the engine or emission package, the vehicle may use a total of either 2 or 4 sensors.

Federal Emission Packages (5.7L): Two sensors are used: upstream (referred to as 1/1) and downstream (referred to as 1/2). With this emission package, the upstream sensor (1/1) is located just before the main catalytic convertor. The downstream sensor (1/2) is located just after the main catalytic convertor.

California Emission Packages (5.7L): On this emissions package, 4 sensors are used: 2 upstream (referred to as 1/1 and 2/1) and 2 downstream (referred to as 1/2 and 2/2). With this emission package, the right upstream sensor (2/1) is located in the right exhaust downpipe just before the mini-catalytic convertor. The left upstream sensor (1/1) is located in the left exhaust downpipe just before the mini-catalytic convertor. The right downstream sensor (2/2) is located in the right exhaust downpipe just after the mini-catalytic convertor, and before the main catalytic convertor. The left downstream sensor (1/2) is located in the left exhaust downpipe just after the mini-catalytic convertor, and before the main catalytic convertor.

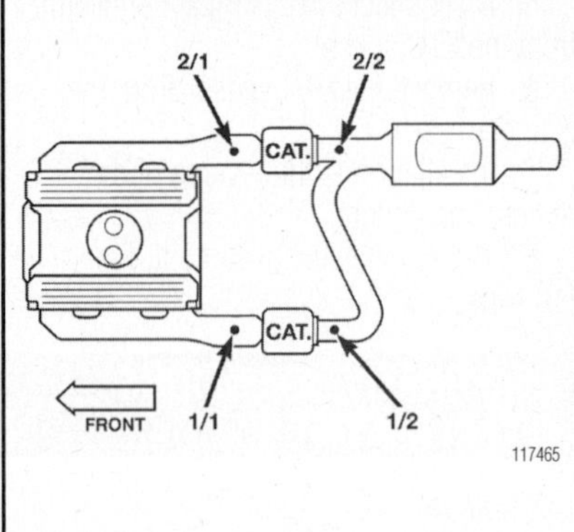

Fig. 71 Typical arrangement of oxygen sensor locations—all engines

REMOVAL & INSTALLATION

CAUTION

Never apply any type of grease to the oxygen sensor electrical connector, or attempt any repair of the sensor wiring harness.

WARNING

The exhaust pipes and catalytic converter become very hot during engine operation. Allow the engine to cool before removing the oxygen sensor.

1. Raise and support vehicle.
2. Disconnect wire connector from 02S sensor.

CAUTION

When disconnecting the oxygen sensor electrical connector, do not pull directly on the wire going into the sensor. The sensor wiring can be damaged resulting in sensor failure.

3. Remove 02S sensor with an oxygen sensor removal and installation tool.

4. Clean threads in exhaust pipe using appropriate tap.

To install:

➡Threads of new oxygen sensors are factory coated with anti-seize compound to aid in removal. DO NOT add any additional anti-seize compound to threads of a new oxygen sensor.

5. Install O2S sensor. Tighten to 30 ft. lbs. (41Nm) torque for 5.7L, or to 37 ft. lbs. (50 Nm) for 6.7L diesel.
6. Connect O2S sensor wire connector.
7. Lower vehicle.

INTAKE AIR TEMPERATURE (IAT) SENSOR

LOCATION

5.7L

See Figure 72.

The intake manifold air temperature (IAT) sensor is installed into the front of the intake manifold air box plenum.

REMOVAL & INSTALLATION

1. Disconnect electrical connector from IAT sensor.
2. Clean dirt from intake tube at sensor base.
3. Gently lift on small plastic release tab and rotate sensor about 1/4 turn counterclockwise for removal.
4. Check condition of sensor O-ring.
5. Installation is the reverse of the removal procedure.

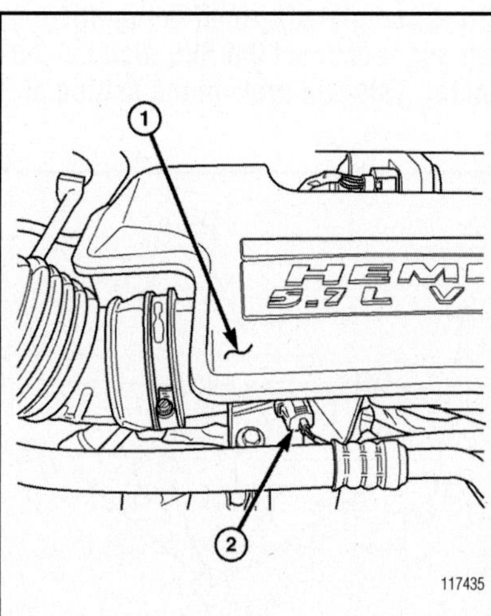

Fig. 72 The intake manifold air temperature (IAT) sensor (2) is installed into the front of the intake manifold air box plenum (1)

INTAKE AIR TEMPERATURE/ MANIFOLD ABSOLUTE PRESSURE (IAT/MAP) SENSOR

LOCATION

6.7L Diesel

The combination, dual function Intake Manifold Air Temperature Sensor/ MAP (IAT/MAP) sensor is installed into the intake air connection manifold, below, and to the rear of the EGR valve.

REMOVAL & INSTALLATION

6.7L Diesel

1. Clean area around sensor.
2. Disconnect electrical connector from IAT/MAP sensor.
3. Remove mounting screw.
4. Remove sensor from manifold.
5. Check condition of sensor O-ring.
6. Installation is the reverse of the removal procedure.

KNOCK SENSOR (KS)

LOCATION

5.7L

See Figure 73.

Two knock sensors are also used with the 5.7L. These are bolted into each side of the cylinder block (outside) under the exhaust manifold.

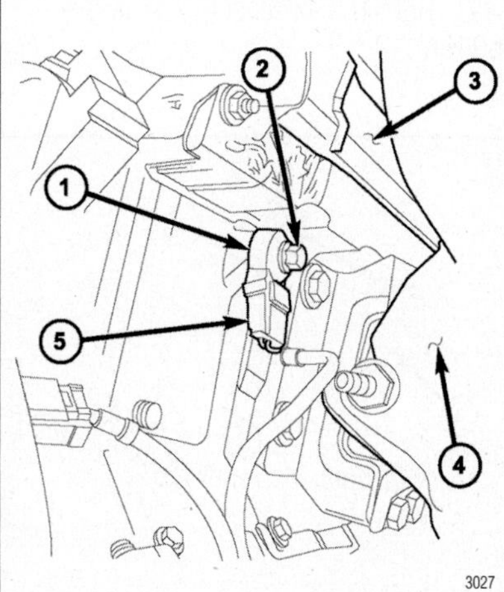

Fig. 73 Two knock sensors are also used with the 5.7L. These are bolted into each side of the cylinder block (outside) under the exhaust manifold.

REMOVAL & INSTALLATION

5.7L

1. Raise and support the vehicle.
2. Disconnect the knock sensor electrical connector(s).
3. Remove the knock sensor retaining bolt(s).

➡Note the foam strip on bolt threads. This foam strip is used only to retain the bolts to the sensors for plant assembly. It is not used as a sealant. Do not apply any adhesive, sealant or thread locking compound to these bolts.

4. Remove the knock sensor(s) from the cylinder block.

To install:

5. Thoroughly clean knock sensor mounting holes.
6. Install sensors into cylinder block, checking that LEFT knock sensor is in the proper location.

⁂ CAUTION

Over or under tightening the sensor mounting bolts will affect knock sensor performance, possibly causing improper spark control. Always use the specified torque when installing the knock sensors. The torque for the knock senor bolt is relatively light for an 8 mm bolt.

➡Note foam strip on bolt threads. This foam is used only to retain the bolts to sensors for plant assembly. It is not used as a sealant. Do not apply any adhesive, sealant or thread locking compound to these bolts.

7. Install and tighten mounting bolts 15 ft.lbs. (20 Nm).
8. Connect the electrical connector(s).
9. Lower the vehicle.

MANIFOLD ABSOLUTE PRESSURE (MAP) SENSOR

LOCATION

5.7L

See Figure 74.

The Manifold Absolute Pressure (MAP) sensor is mounted to the front of the intake manifold air plenum box.

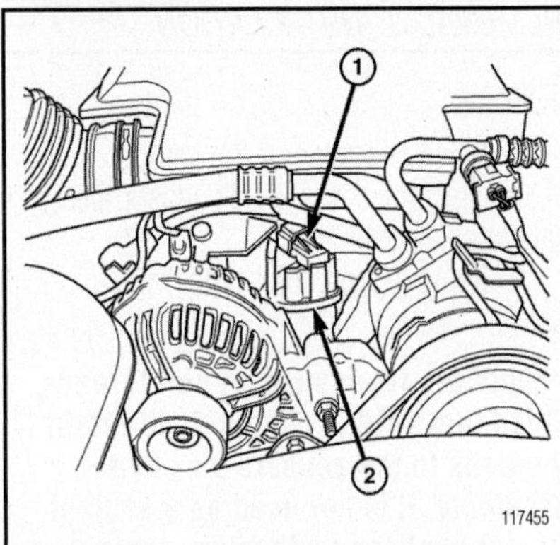

Fig. 74 The Manifold Absolute Pressure (MAP) sensor (2) and electrical connector (1) are mounted to the front of the intake manifold air plenum box.

REMOVAL & INSTALLATION

5.7L

1. Disconnect electrical connector at sensor by sliding release lock out . Press down on lock tab for removal.
2. Rotate sensor 1/4 turn counterclockwise for removal.
3. Check condition of sensor O-ring.
4. Installation is the reverse of the removal procedure.

NOX SENSOR

LOCATION

6.7L Diesel

The Pre-NOx sensor is mounted at the inlet of Selective Catalytic Reduction (SCR) Catalyst and measures incoming NOx gases. The Post-NOx sensor is mounted at the rear outlet of Selective Catalytic Reduction (SCR) Catalyst and measures outgoing NOx gases.

REMOVAL & INSTALLATION

6.7L Diesel

Bank 1 Sensor 1

See Figure 75.

1. Disconnect both negative battery cables.
2. Remove nuts and the NOx sensor module cover.
3. Disconnect the NOx sensor wire harness retainer.
4. Disconnect the NOx sensor harness connector.
5. Remove nuts and the NOx sensor module.
6. Remove the NOx sensor from the

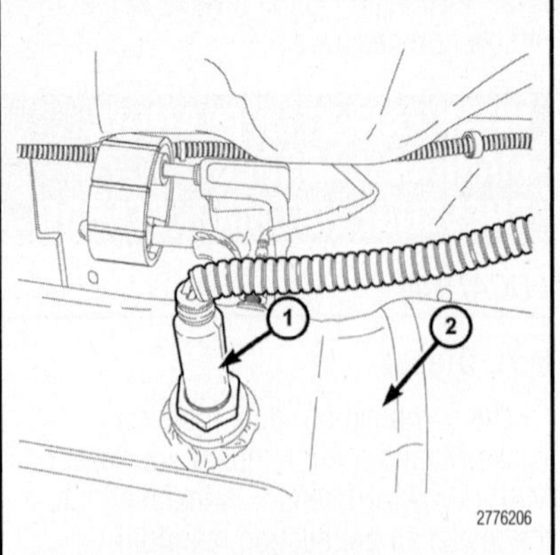

Fig. 75 Remove the NOx sensor (1) from the Diesel Oxidation Catalytic/Diesel Particulate Filter (DOC/DPF) (2).

Diesel Oxidation Catalytic/Diesel Particulate Filter (DOC/DPF).

7. Installation is the reverse of the removal procedure.
8. Tighten NOx sensor to 37 ft. lbs. (50 Nm).

Bank 1 Sensor 2

See Figure 76.

1. Disconnect both negative battery cables.
2. Disconnect the NOx sensor module harness connector.
3. Remove nuts and the NOx module.
4. Disconnect the wire harness retainers.
5. Remove the NOx sensor from the Selective Catalytic Reduction (SCR) catalyst.
6. Installation is the reverse of the removal procedure.
7. Tighten NOx sensor to 37 ft. lbs. (50 Nm).

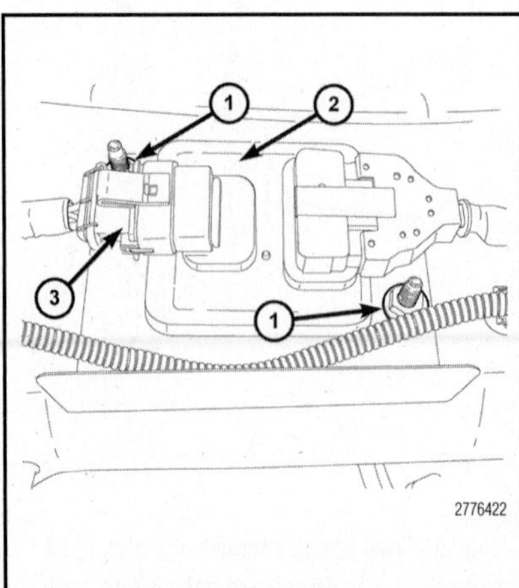

Fig. 76 Showing NOx module (2), connector (3) and mounting nuts (1)

POWERTRAIN CONTROL MODULE (PCM)

LOCATION

5.7L

See Figure 77.

The Powertrain Control Module (PCM) is located in the right-rear section of the engine compartment under the cowl.

6.7L Diesel

See Figure 78.

The Powertrain Control Module (PCM) is used to control the functions of the engine and transmission. The PCM is bolted to the left side of the engine below the intake manifold.

REMOVAL & INSTALLATION

5.7L

➡Certain ABS systems rely on having the Powertrain Control Module (PCM) broadcast the Vehicle Identification Number (VIN) over the bus network. To prevent problems of DTCs and other items related to the VIN broadcast, it is recommend that you disconnect the ABS CAB (controller) temporarily when replacing the PCM. Once the PCM is replaced, write the VIN to the PCM using a scan tool. This is done from the engine main menu. Arrow over to the second page to "1. Miscellaneous". Select "Check VIN" from the choices. Make sure it has the correct VIN entered before continuing. When the VIN is complete, turn off the ignition key and reconnect the ABS module connector. This will prevent the setting of

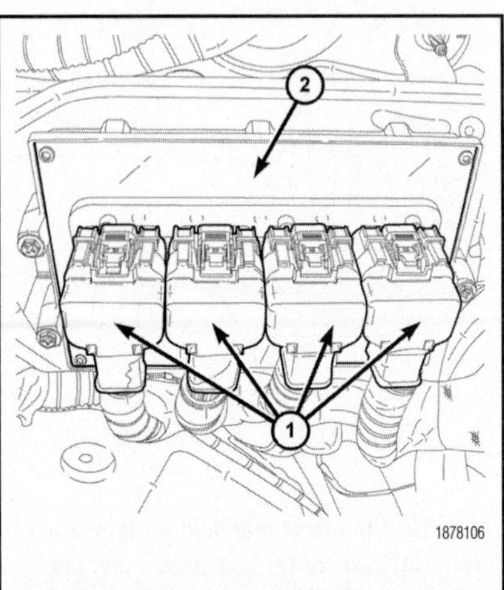

Fig. 77 Location of the PCM (2) and the connectors (1)—5.7L

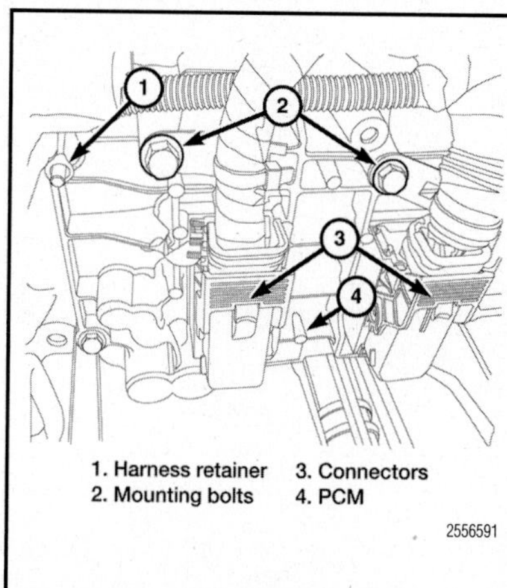

Fig. 78 Showing PCM location—6.7L diesel

DTCs and other items associated with the lack of a VIN detected when you turn the key ON after replacing the PCM.

1. Use the scan tool to reprogram the new PCM with the vehicles original identification number (VIN) and the vehicles original mileage. If this step is not done, a Diagnostic Trouble Code (DTC) may be set.
2. To avoid possible voltage spike damage to the PCM, ignition key must be off, and negative battery cable must be disconnected before unplugging PCM connectors.
3. Disconnect and isolator the negative battery cable.
4. Carefully unplug the four 38-way connectors from the PCM.
5. Remove the four PCM mounting bolts and remove the PCM from vehicle.

To install:

6. Install the PCM and 4 mounting bolts to vehicle.
7. Check pin connectors in the PCM and the three 32-way connectors (four 38-way connectors if equipped with NGC) for corrosion or damage. Also, the pin heights in connectors should all be same. Repair as necessary before installing connectors.
8. Install the three 32-way connectors (four 38-way connectors if equipped with NGC).
9. The 5.7L V-8 engine is equipped with a fully electronic accelerator pedal position sensor. If equipped with a 5.7L, also perform the following steps:
   a. Connect the negative battery cable.
   b. Turn the ignition switch ON, but do not crank the engine.
   c. Leave the ignition switch ON for a minimum of 10 seconds. This will allow the PCM to learn the electrical parameters.
   d. The scan tool may also be used to learn electrical parameters. Go to the Miscellaneous menu, and then select ETC Learn.

➡If the previous step is not performed, a Diagnostic Trouble Code (DTC) will be set.

10. If necessary, use a scan tool to erase any Diagnostic Trouble Codes (DTC's) from PCM. Also use the scan tool to reprogram new PCM with vehicles original Vehicle Identification Number (VIN) and original vehicle mileage.

6.7L Diesel

⁂ CAUTION

To avoid possible voltage spike damage to the Powertrain Control Module (PCM), ignition key must be off, and both negative battery cables must be disconnected before unplugging PCM harness connectors.

1. Record any Diagnostic Trouble Codes (DTC's) found in the (PCM).
2. For automatic transmission vehicles, disconnecting the battery before the 10 minute power down will result in the Fault Code P2509. This fault code will need to be cleared before returning to the customer. Also, same for manual transmissions but the time limit is 75 seconds.
3. Disconnect both negative battery cables.

⁂ CAUTION

If the connector latch is packed with dirt or debris, clean connector latch first with electrical contact cleaner otherwise damage to the connector housing may result when trying to open a dirty connector.

4. Disconnect the PCM harness connectors and harness retainer from PCM.
5. Remove bolts and the PCM from engine.

To install:

⁂ CAUTION

Do not apply paint to Powertrain Control Module (PCM) or a poor ground will result.

6. Install PCM to the engine block. Tighten bolts to 18 ft. lbs. (24 Nm).
7. Check pins in electrical connectors for corrosion, damage or dirt intrusion. Also, check all the PCM pins for being bent. Repair as necessary. Damaged, dirty, bent or corroded pins could result in poor conductivity, causing intermittent electrical issues or DTC's.
8. Clean pins in electrical connectors with an electrical contact cleaner.
9. Install PCM harness connectors and harness retainer to PCM.
10. Connect both negative battery cables.
11. Program the PCM, as described below.
12. After programming the PCM, allow the module to fully power down. This process will require 10 minutes for automatic transmission vehicles, or 75 seconds for manual transmission vehicles.
13. Vehicles having 6.7L diesel engine with automatic transmissions will require a transmission quick learn after programming the PCM.
14. Use a diagnostic scan tool to erase any Diagnostic Trouble Codes (DTC's) from PCM.

Fuel Injector ID Correction Codes

Each fuel injector has a six-digit alphanumeric correction code. The correction code is printed on the intake side of the fuel injector and is used to identify injector calibration. When replacing any fuel injectors, this code must be entered into the vehicles Powertrain Control Module (PCM) using a diagnostic scan tool. In addition, if a new PCM is installed, use a diagnostic scan tool to program all six of the injector codes from the original fuel injectors into the new PCM.

Programming The PCM

➡The secret key is an ID code that is unique to each Wireless Ignition Node (WIN). This code is programmed and stored in the WIN, the PCM, and each ignition key transponder chip. When the PCM or WIN is replaced, it is necessary to program the Secret Key Code into the new module using a diagnostic scan tool.

1. Programming the PCM or WIN is done using a diagnostic scan tool and a PIN to enter secure access mode.
   a. If three attempts are made to enter secure access mode using an incorrect PIN, secure access mode will be locked out for one hour.
   b. To exit this lockout mode, turn the ignition to the RUN position for one hour and then enter the correct PIN. Be certain that all accessories are turned OFF.
   c. Also, monitor the battery state and connect a battery charger if necessary.

2. Read all notes and cautions for programming procedures.
3. Connect a battery charger to the vehicle.
4. Connect the scan tool.
5. Have a unique vehicle PIN readily available before running the routine.
6. Ignition key should be in RUN position.
7. Select "ECU View".
8. Select "WIN Wireless Control".
9. Select "Miscellaneous Functions."
10. Select "PCM Replaced".
11. Enter the PIN when prompted.
12. Verify the correct information.
13. Cycle ignition key after the successful routine completion.

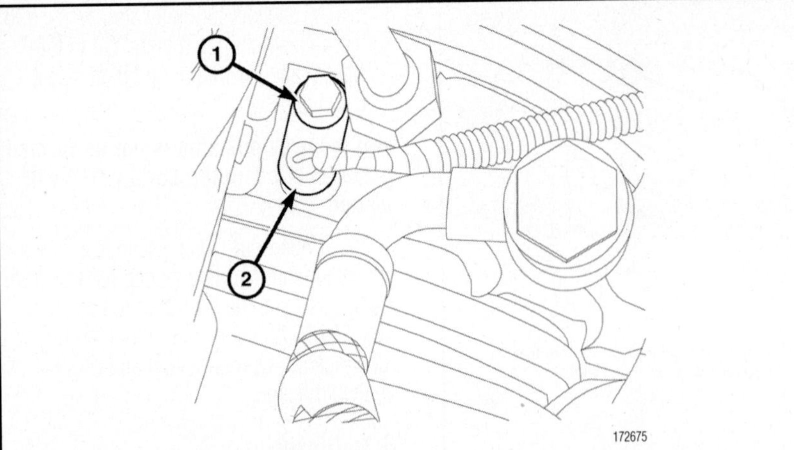

Fig. 79 Remove turbocharger speed sensor mounting bolt (1) and remove turbocharger speed sensor (2).

TURBOCHARGER SPEED SENSOR

LOCATION

➡Refer to illustration under "Removal & Installation" for location.

REMOVAL & INSTALLATION

See Figure 79.

⁂ CAUTION

Do not use a screw driver or tool to pry sensor out of the turbocharger bearing housing. Damage to sensor may result. If sensor is damaged during removal, install a new sensor.

1. Disconnect negative battery cable.
2. Remove turbocharger oil supply line.
3. Disconnect speed sensor electrical connector.
4. Remove turbocharger speed sensor mounting bolt and remove turbocharger speed sensor.

VEHICLE SPEED SENSORS (INPUT & OUTPUT SPEED SENSORS)

LOCATION

See Figure 80.

The Input and Output Speed Sensors are two-wire magnetic pickup devices that generate AC signals as rotation occurs. They are mounted in the left side of the transmission case and are considered primary inputs to the Transmission Control Module (TCM).

REMOVAL & INSTALLATION

1. Raise vehicle.
2. Place a suitable fluid catch pan under the transmission.
3. Remove the wiring connector from the input and/or output speed sensor.
4. Remove the bolt holding the input and/or output speed sensor to the transmission case.
5. Remove the input and/or output speed sensor from the transmission case.

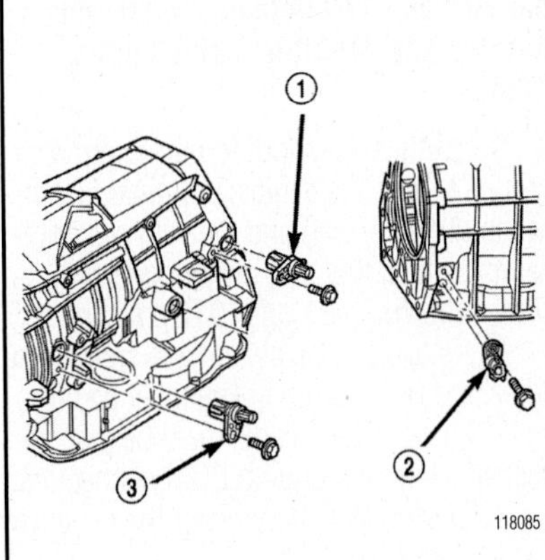

Fig. 80 Showing the location of the output speed sensor (1), transmission line pressure sensor (2), and the input speed sensor (3)

6. Installation is the reverse of the removal procedure.
7. Tighten the retaining bolt(s) to 9 ft. lbs. (12 Nm).

FUEL SYSTEM SERVICE PRECAUTIONS

Safety is the most important factor when performing not only fuel system maintenance but any type of maintenance. Failure to conduct maintenance and repairs in a safe manner may result in serious personal injury or death. Maintenance and testing of the vehicle's fuel system components can be accomplished safely and effectively by adhering to the following rules and guidelines.

- To avoid the possibility of fire and personal injury, always disconnect the negative battery cable unless the repair or test procedure requires that battery voltage be applied.
- Always relieve the fuel system pressure prior to disconnecting any fuel system component (injector, fuel rail, pressure regulator, etc.), fitting or fuel line connection. Exercise extreme caution whenever relieving fuel system pressure to avoid exposing skin, face and eyes to fuel spray. Please be advised that fuel under pressure may penetrate the skin or any part of the body that it contacts.
- Always place a shop towel or cloth around the fitting or connection prior to loosening to absorb any excess fuel due to spillage. Ensure that all fuel spillage (should it occur) is quickly removed from engine surfaces. Ensure that all fuel soaked cloths or towels are deposited into a suitable waste container.
- Always keep a dry chemical (Class B) fire extinguisher near the work area.
- Do not allow fuel spray or fuel vapors to come into contact with a spark or open flame.
- Always use a back-up wrench when loosening and tightening fuel line connection fittings. This will prevent unnecessary stress and torsion to fuel line piping.
- Always replace worn fuel fitting O-rings with new Do not substitute fuel hose or equivalent where fuel pipe is installed.

Before servicing the vehicle, make sure to also refer to the precautions in the beginning of this section as well.

RELIEVING FUEL SYSTEM PRESSURE

5.7L

See Figures 81 and 82.

➡Use this procedure whether or not the fuel rail is equipped with a fuel pressure test port.

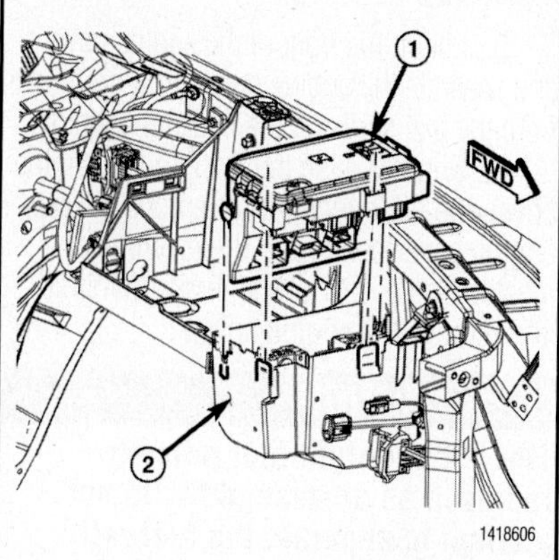

Fig. 81 Showing the TIPM cover (1) and housing (2)

➡A separate fuel pump relay is no longer used. A circuit within the Totally Integrated Power Module (TIPM) is used to control the electric fuel pump located within the fuel pump module. The TIPM is located in the engine compartment in front of the battery.

1. Remove the fuel fill cap.
2. Remove the TIPM cover from the TIPM housing base.
3. Remove fuse M22 from the TIPM.
4. Start and run the engine until it stalls.
5. Attempt restarting the engine until it will no longer start.
6. Turn the ignition key to the OFF position.

➡Excessive fuel spillage onto the gaskets can cause gaskets to expand and dislodge from gasket groove.

7. Place a rag or towel below the fuel line quick-connect fitting at the fuel rail.

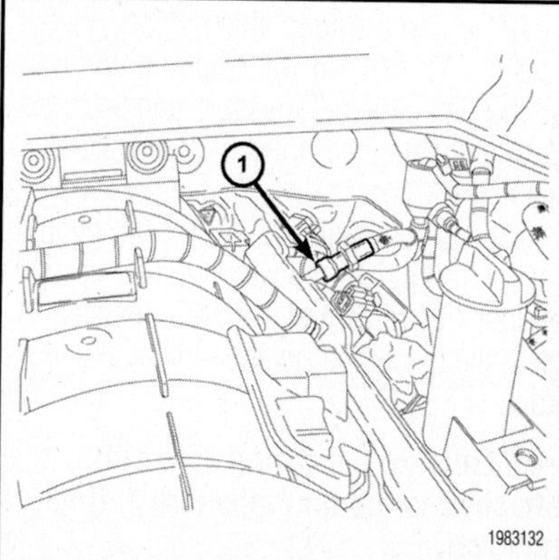

Fig. 82 Disconnect the fuel line quick-connect fitting (1) at the fuel rail and plug with a shipping cap to prevent spillage.

8. Disconnect the fuel line quick-connect fitting at the fuel rail and plug with a shipping cap to prevent spillage.

➡One or more Diagnostic Trouble Codes (DTC's) may have been stored in the PCM memory due to disconnecting fuel pump module circuit. A diagnostic scan tool must be used to erase a DTC.

FUEL INJECTORS

REMOVAL & INSTALLATION

5.7L

1. Remove the fuel rail assembly. See "Fuel Rail" in this section.
2. Using suitable pliers, remove the fuel injector retaining clip.
3. Remove the fuel injector from the fuel rail, using a side to side motion while pulling the injector out of the fuel rail assembly.
4. Installation is the reverse of the removal procedure.

FUEL PUMP

REMOVAL & INSTALLATION

5.7L

See Figure 83.

1. Perform the fuel system pressure release procedure.
2. Disconnect and isolate the negative battery cable.
3. Remove the fuel tank. See "Fuel Tank" in this section.
4. Prior to removing the fuel pump module, use compressed air to remove any accumulated dirt and debris from around fuel tank opening.

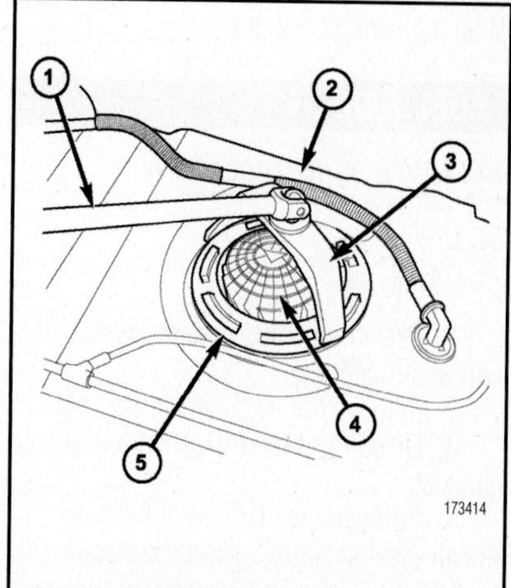

Fig. 83 Removing the fuel pump module

➡An indexing arrow is located on top of the main fuel pump module to indicate the position into the fuel tank. Note the location for reassembly.

5. Position the lock ring remover/installer (9340 or equivalent) into the notches on the outside edge of the lock ring.
6. Install a 1/2 inch drive breaker bar into the lock ring remover/installer.
7. Rotate the breaker bar counterclockwise and remove the lock ring.
8. Remove the fuel pump module from the fuel tank. Be careful not to bend float arm during removal.
9. Remove and discard the rubber O-ring seal.

To install:

10. Using a new rubber O-ring seal, position the fuel pump module into the fuel tank opening.
11. Position the lock ring over top of the fuel pump module.
12. Rotate the fuel pump module until the embossed alignment arrow points to the center alignment mark or the same position as noted during removal. This step must be performed to prevent the float from contacting the side of the fuel tank.
13. Install the lock ring remover/installer into the notches on the outside edge of the lock ring.
14. Install a 1/2 inch drive breaker bar into the lock ring remover/installer.
15. Rotate the breaker bar clockwise until all seven notches of the lock ring have engaged.
16. Install the fuel tank. See "Fuel Tank" in this section.
17. Connect the fuel line quick-connect fitting at the fuel rail.
18. Connect the negative battery cable.
19. Fill the fuel tank.
20. Start the engine and check for leaks at all fuel tank connections.

FUEL RAIL

REMOVAL & INSTALLATION

5.7L

See Figure 84.

1. Perform the fuel system pressure release procedure.
2. Remove the negative battery cable.
3. Disconnect the IAT sensor electrical connector.
4. Remove the clean air tube from the air cleaner housing and the throttle body.

➡The front grommets are a ball stud type mount and the rear grommets are a sliding peg design.

5. Lift up the front of the engine cover and separate the engine cover front grommets from the ball studs on the intake manifold.
6. Slightly raise the front of the engine cover and slide forward to remove the rear engine cover pegs from the grommets located on the rear of the intake manifold and remove the engine cover.

⁂ CAUTION

The left and right fuel rails are replaced as an assembly. Do not attempt to separate the fuel rail halves at the connector tube. Due to the design of the connector tube, it does not use any clamps. Never attempt to install a clamping device of any kind to the connector tube. When removing the fuel rail assembly for any reason, be careful not to bend or kink the connector tube.

➡The factory fuel injection electrical harness is numerically tagged (INJ 1, INJ 2, etc.) for injector position identification. If the electrical harness is not tagged, note the injector position before electrical harness removal.

7. Disconnect the electrical connectors at all eight fuel injectors. Push the red colored slider away from the injector while pushing slider, depress tab and remove the electrical connector from the injector.
8. Disconnect the PCV hose and position aside to gain access to the fuel rail.
9. Disconnect the fuel line quick connect fitting at the fuel rail.
10. Disconnect the make up air hose and position aside to gain access to the fuel rail.
11. Remove the four fuel rail mounting bolts from both the left and right fuel rails.
12. Using a side to side motion, gently rock the left fuel rail while pulling up until all four left side fuel injectors just start to clear the machined holes in the intake manifold.
13. Using a side to side motion, gently rock the right fuel rail while pulling up until all four right side fuel injectors just start to clear the machined holes in the intake manifold.

➡Make sure the O-rings are still attached to the fuel injectors during removal.

14. Remove the left and right fuel rails (with injectors attached) as an assembly from the engine.

To install:

15. If the fuel injectors are to be installed into the fuel rail.
16. Clean out the fuel injector machined holes in the intake manifold.

➡If the same fuel injectors are to be reinstalled, install new O-rings.

17. Apply a small amount of engine oil to each fuel injector O-ring. This will help in the fuel rail installation.
18. Position the fuel rail assembly while aligning the injectors into the machined holes in the intake manifold.
19. Guide each injector into the intake manifold using care not to tear the injector O-rings.
20. Using a side to side motion, gently rock the left fuel rail while pushing down until all four left side fuel injectors have completely seated into the machined holes in the intake manifold.
21. Using a side to side motion, gently rock the right fuel rail while pushing down until all four right side fuel injectors have completely seated into the machined holes in the intake manifold.
22. Install the four fuel rail mounting bolts and tighten to 8 ft. lbs. (11 Nm).
23. Connect the make up air hose.
24. Connect the fuel line quick connect fitting to the fuel rail.
25. Connect the PCV hose.
26. Connect the electrical connectors to all eight fuel injectors. Push the connector onto the injector and then push and lock the red colored slider. Verify the connector is locked to the injector by lightly tugging on the connector.
27. Slightly tilt the rear of the engine cover and slide the rear engine cover pegs into the grommets on the rear of the intake manifold until the cover stops.

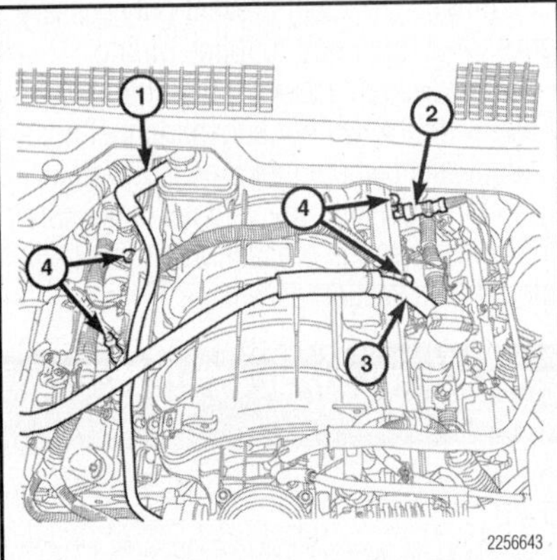

Fig. 84 Showing locations of fuel rail mounting bolts, make up air hose, fuel line fitting and PCV hose

➡While installing the engine cover, the front ball studs will make a popping or suction sound as the ball studs are inserted into the front grommets.

28. Lower the front of the engine cover and line up the front ball studs with the grommets on the front of the intake manifold and with a downward motion push the engine cover front grommets onto the ball studs.
29. Lightly lift the front of the engine cover to insure the front the front grommets are seated onto the ball studs correctly.
30. Check to insure the engine cover is installed properly by reaching behind the left side of the cover to verify that the pegs are located in the grommets.
31. Install the clean air tube onto the air cleaner housing and the throttle body.
32. Connect the IAT sensor electrical connector.
33. Connect the negative battery cable.
34. Start the engine and check for leaks.

FUEL TANK

DRAINING

➡Due to a one-way check valve installed into the fuel fill fitting at the tank, the tank cannot be drained at the fuel fill cap.

1. Perform the fuel system pressure release procedure. See "Relieving Fuel System Pressure" in this section.
2. Disconnect the fuel supply line from the fuel rail.

➡Tool number 8978-2 is used on 5/16" fuel lines while tool number 8531-1 is used on 3/8" fuel lines.

3. Install the appropriate fuel line adapter fitting from the Decay Tool, Fuel 8978A (or equivalent) to the fuel supply line. Route the opposite end of this hose to an OSHA approved fuel storage tank such as the John Dow Gas Caddy 320-FC-P30-A or equivalent.
4. Using a diagnostic scan tool, activate the fuel pump until the fuel tank has been evacuated.

Alternative Procedure

➡If the electric fuel pump is not operating, the fuel tank must be removed and drained through the fuel pump module opening of the fuel tank.

1. Perform the fuel system pressure release procedure. See "Relieving Fuel System Pressure" in this section.
2. Disconnect and isolate the negative battery cable.
3. Raise and support the vehicle.
4. Remove the fuel tank. See "Fuel Tank" in this section.
5. Remove the fuel pump module. See "Fuel Pump" in this section.
6. Position a 3/8" hose into the fuel pump module opening of the fuel tank.
7. Attach the opposite end of this hose to the Fuel Chief Gas Caddy 320-FC-P30-A or an OSHA approved gas caddy.
8. Using the gas caddy, evacuate the fuel tank.

REMOVAL & INSTALLATION

See Figure 85.

1. Perform the fuel system pressure release procedure. See "Relieving Fuel System Pressure" in this section.
2. Disconnect and isolate the negative battery cable.

Raise and support vehicle.

3. Perform the fuel tank draining procedure.
4. Disconnect the electrical connector from ESIM switch.
5. Disconnect the quick-connect fitting at the front of the fuel tank.
6. Disconnect the quick-connect fitting at the rear of the fuel tank.
7. Loosen the fill hose retaining clamp at the rear of the fuel tank and disconnect the fill hose.
8. Using a suitable hydraulic jack with a fuel tank adapter, support the fuel tank.
9. Remove the two fuel tank support strap retaining nuts and remove both fuel tank support straps.
10. Carefully lower the fuel tank a few inches and disconnect the fuel pump module electrical connector.
11. Disconnect the fuel line quick-connect fitting at the fuel pump module.
12. Lower the fuel tank and remove from hydraulic jack.
13. If fuel pump module removal is necessary, see "Fuel Pump" in this section.

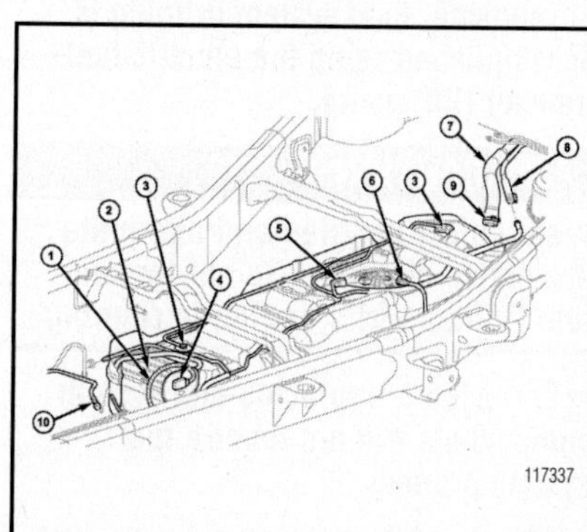

Fig. 85 Fuel system lines and connections

To install:

14. If fuel pump module installation is necessary, see "Fuel Pump" in this section.
15. Secure the fuel tank onto a suitable hydraulic jack with a fuel tank adapter.
16. Raise and position the fuel tank leaving room to make the connections at the top of the fuel tank.
17. Connect the fuel supply line to the fuel pump module.
18. Connect the electrical connector to the fuel pump module.
19. Raise the fuel tank until snug to the body.
20. Install the fuel tank straps. Install the strap nuts and tighten to 30 ft. lbs. (41 Nm).
21. Remove the hydraulic jack.
22. Connect the electrical connector to the ESIM switch.
23. Connect the quick-connect fitting at the front of the fuel tank.
24. Connect the quick-connect fitting at the rear of the fuel tank.
25. Connect the fill hose at the rear of the fuel tank and securely tighten the fill hose retaining clamp.
26. Connect the fuel line quick-connect fitting at the fuel rail.
27. Connect the negative battery cable.
28. Fill the fuel tank.
29. Start the engine and check for leaks at all fuel tank connections.

IDLE SPEED

ADJUSTMENT

➡Idle speed is computer-controlled and therefore no adjustment is required.

THROTTLE BODY

REMOVAL & INSTALLATION

1. Using a diagnostic scan tool, record any previous DTC's (Diagnostic Trouble Codes).

⁂ CAUTION

Never have the ignition key in the ON position when checking the throttle body shaft for a binding condition. This may set DTC's.

➡A (factory adjusted) set screw is used to mechanically limit the position of the throttle body throttle plate. Never attempt to adjust the engine idle

speed using this screw. All idle speed functions are controlled by the Powertrain Control Module (PCM).

2. Disconnect and isolate negative battery cable at battery.
3. Remove air intake tube at throttle body flange.
4. Disconnect throttle body electrical connector.
5. Disconnect necessary vacuum lines at throttle body.
6. Remove four throttle body mounting bolts.
7. Remove throttle body from intake manifold.
8. Check condition of old throttle body-to-intake manifold O-ring.
9. Installation is the reverse of the removal procedure.
10. Using the diagnostic scan tool, erase all previous DTC's and perform the ETC Relearn function.

FUEL SYSTEM SERVICE PRECAUTIONS

Safety is the most important factor when performing not only fuel system maintenance but any type of maintenance. Failure to conduct maintenance and repairs in a safe manner may result in serious personal injury or death. Maintenance and testing of the vehicle's fuel system components can be accomplished safely and effectively by adhering to the following rules and guidelines.

- To avoid the possibility of fire and personal injury, always disconnect the negative battery cable unless the repair or test procedure requires that battery voltage be applied.
- Always relieve the fuel system pressure prior to disconnecting any fuel system component (injector, fuel rail, pressure regulator, etc.), fitting or fuel line connection. Exercise extreme caution whenever relieving fuel system pressure to avoid exposing skin, face and eyes to fuel spray. Please be advised that fuel under pressure may penetrate the skin or any part of the body that it contacts.
- High-pressure fuel lines deliver diesel fuel under extreme pressure from the injection pump to the fuel injectors. This may be as high as 26,107 psi. Use extreme caution when inspecting for high-pressure fuel leaks. Inspect for high-pressure fuel leaks with a sheet of cardboard. High fuel injection pressure can cause personal injury if contact is made with the skin.
- Always place a shop towel or cloth around the fitting or connection prior to loosening to absorb any excess fuel due to spillage. Ensure that all fuel spillage (should it occur) is quickly removed from engine surfaces. Ensure that all fuel soaked cloths or towels are deposited into a suitable waste container.
- Always keep a dry chemical (Class B) fire extinguisher near the work area.
- Do not allow fuel spray or fuel vapors to come into contact with a spark or open flame.
- Always use a back-up wrench when loosening and tightening fuel line connection fittings. This will prevent unnecessary stress and torsion to fuel line piping.
- Always replace worn fuel fitting O-rings with new Do not substitute fuel hose or equivalent where fuel pipe is installed.

Before servicing the vehicle, make sure to also refer to the precautions in the beginning of this section as well.

Cleanliness cannot be overemphasized when handling or replacing diesel fuel system components. This especially includes the fuel injectors, high-pressure fuel lines and fuel injection pump. Very tight tolerances are used with these parts. Dirt contamination could cause rapid part wear and possible plugging of fuel injector nozzle tip holes. This in turn could lead to possible engine misfire. Always wash/clean any fuel system component thoroughly before disassembly and then air dry. Cap or cover any open part after disassembly. Before assembly, examine each part for dirt, grease or other contaminants and clean if necessary. When installing new parts, lubricate them with clean engine oil or clean diesel fuel only.

DIESEL FUEL SYSTEM PRIMING

➡A certain amount of air becomes trapped in the fuel system when fuel system components on the supply and/or high-pressure side are serviced or replaced. Fuel system priming is accomplished using the electric fuel transfer (lift) pump.

CAUTION

Wear safety goggles and adequate protective clothing. Do not loosen fuel fittings while engine is running.

➡Servicing or replacing fuel system components will not require fuel system priming.

➡The fuel transfer (lift) pump is self-priming: When the key is first turned on (without cranking engine), the pump operates for approximately 1 to 2 second and then shuts off (Note: When ambient temperatures are cold enough to cause the intake air heaters to operate, the fuel lift pump will operate during the entire intake air pre-heat cycle). The pump will also operate for up to 25 seconds after the starter is quickly engaged, and then disengaged without allowing the engine to start. The pump shuts off immediately if the key is on and the engine stops running.

1. Turn key to CRANK position and quickly release key to ON position before engine starts. This will operate fuel transfer pump for approximately 25 seconds.
2. Crank engine. If the engine does not start after 25 seconds, turn key to OFF position, and leave it off for at least 5 seconds. Repeat previous step until engine starts.
3. Fuel system priming is now completed.
4. Attempt to start engine. If engine will not start, proceed to following steps. When engine does start, it may run erratically and be noisy for a few minutes. This is a normal condition.
5. Do not engage the starter motor for more than 30 seconds at a time. Allow two minutes between cranking intervals.
6. Perform previous fuel priming procedure steps using fuel transfer pump. Be sure fuel is present at fuel tank.
7. Crank the engine for 30 seconds at a time to allow fuel system to prime.
8. The fuel injection pump supplies extremely high fuel pressure to each individual injector through the high-pressure lines. Fuel under this amount of pressure can penetrate the skin and cause personal injury.

➡Engine may start while cranking starter motor.

RELIEVING FUEL SYSTEM PRESSURE

6.7L Diesel

➡Manufacturer does not provide a specific procedure for this operation. The following procedure is merely a suggested method.

1. Pressure may be relieved by carefully opening the fuel drain valve at the fuel rail (use caution when opening this valve and proceed slowly), or by opening the draincock at the fuel/water separator canister.

FUEL & WATER SEPARATOR & FILTER

REMOVAL & INSTALLATION

6.7L Diesel

1. Remove all low-pressure fuel lines at filter housing.
2. Disconnect the Water In Fuel (WIF) sensor harness connector.
3. Disconnect the fuel heater harness connector.
4. Remove bolts and the fuel filter housing from engine block.
5. Installation is the reverse of the removal procedure.
6. Tighten fuel filter housing to engine block bolts to 24 ft. lbs. (32 Nm).

FUEL INJECTORS

REMOVAL & INSTALLATION

6.7L Diesel

See Figures 86 through 89.

Six individual, solenoid actuated high-pressure fuel injectors are used. The injectors are vertically mounted into a bored hole in the top of the cylinder head. This bored hole is located between the intake/exhaust valves. High-pressure connectors, mounted into the side of the cylinder head, connect each fuel injector to each high-pressure fuel line.

➡Each fuel injector has a six-digit alphanumeric correction code. The correction code is printed on the intake side of the fuel injector and is used to identify injector calibration. When replacing any fuel injectors, this code must be entered into the vehicles Powertrain Control Module (PCM) using a scan tool. In addition, if a new PCM is installed, use a scan tool to program all six of the injector codes from the original fuel injectors into the new PCM.

➡If the fuel injectors are being removed such as for engine teardown or diagnostic purposes, be sure to mark each injector with its corresponding cylinder number. The fuel injectors MUST be reinstalled into the original (same) cylinder due to the fuel injector correction code.

1. Disconnect both negative battery cables.
2. Remove engine cover.
3. Remove breather assembly and tubes.
4. Remove cylinder head cover.
5. Mark each injector with its corresponding cylinder number. If required, make note of each fuel injector six-digit alphanumeric correction code.
6. Remove all 12 fuel injector wire harness nuts securing integrated wiring harness to all 6 fuel injectors.
7. Disconnect both fuel injector harness connectors and remove the integrated gasket.
8. Remove the high pressure fuel tubes.
9. Remove connector retainer nuts.
10. Install the High Pressure Connector Remover (9015 or equivalent) onto high-pressure connector tube located in cylinder head.
11. Using Thread High Pressure Connector Remover, pry and remove the high-pressure connector tube(s) from the cylinder head.
12. Remove fuel injector hold-down clamp bolts.
13. Remove necessary intake and exhaust rocker arm assembly(s).

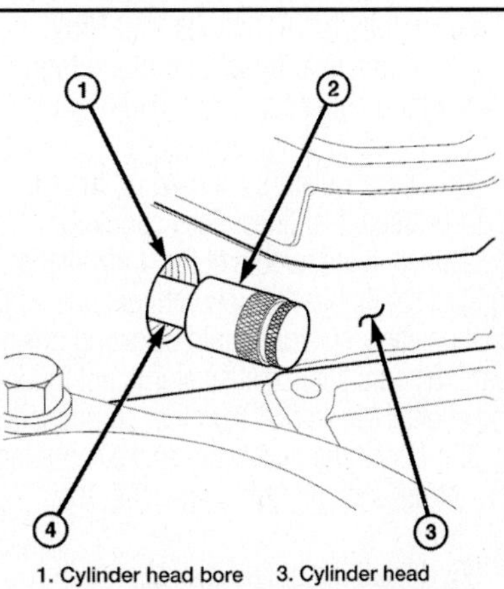

Fig. 86 Using Thread High Pressure Connector Remover, pry and remove the high-pressure connector tube(s) from the cylinder head.

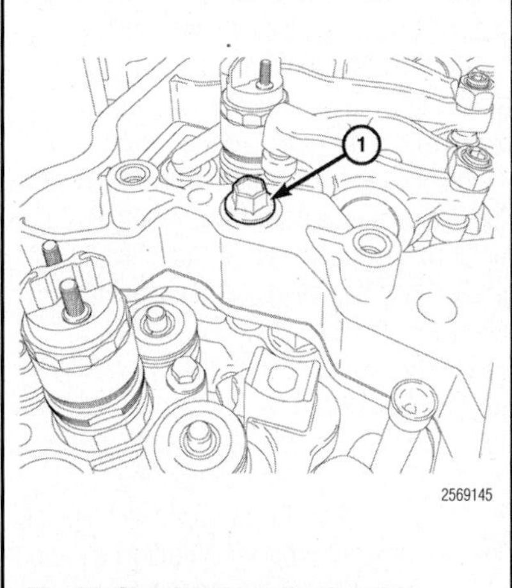

Fig. 87 Showing the rocker housing mounting bolt (1)

14. The rocker housing support bridge is bolted to the top of cylinder head. The mounting stud from Fuel Injector Removal/Installer was meant to temporarily replace a rocker housing mounting bolt.
15. Remove the necessary rocker housing mounting bolt.
16. Fuel Injector Removal/Installer (9010A or equivalent) is equipped with 2 clamshell clamps, a sliding retainer sleeve to retain the clamshell clamps, a 2-piece mounting stud and a pivoting handle. Do not attempt to remove the fuel injectors with any other device. Damage to injector will occur.
17. Install and tighten 2-piece mounting stud of Fuel Injector Removal/Installer, to rocker housing. If removing the No. 6 fuel injector, separate the 2-piece mounting stud. Install lower half of mounting stud to

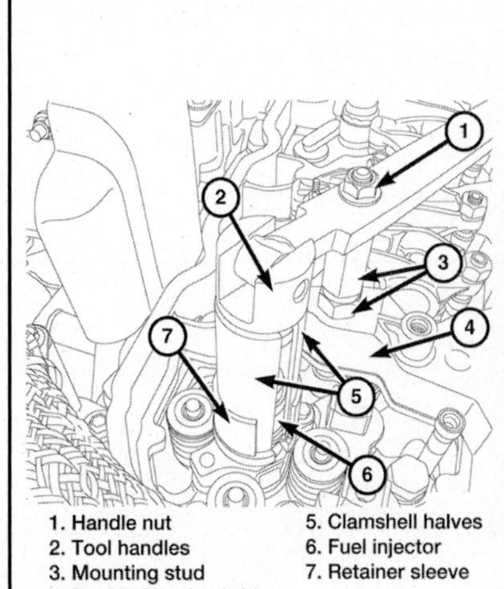

Fig. 88 Using remover/installer tool (9010A) to remove injector(s)

center of rocker housing bridge and upper half of mounting stud to lower half.

18. Position tool handle to mounting stud and install handle nut. Leave handle nut loose to allow a pivoting action.

19. Position lower part of clamshell halves to sides of fuel injector (wider shoulder to bottom). The upper part of clamshell halves should also be positioned into machined shoulder on the handles pivoting head.

20. Slide the retainer sleeve over pivoting handle head to lock clamshell halves together. Be sure handle pivot nut is loose.

21. Depress handle of Fuel Injector Removal/Installer downward to remove fuel injector straight up from cylinder head bore.

22. If the fuel injectors are being removed such as for engine teardown or diagnostic purposes, be sure to mark each injector with its corresponding cylinder number. The fuel injectors MUST be reinstalled into the original (same) cylinder due to the fuel injector correction code.

23. Remove and discard injector sealing washer. This washer should be located on tip of injector, or may have remained in the injector bore.

➡Do not install new fuel injectors unless the alphanumeric codes have been recorded.

24. Measure injector sealing washer.

To install:

25. Inspect fuel injectors as follows:

a. Look for burrs on injector inlet.

b. Check nozzle holes for hole erosion or plugging.

c. Inspect end of nozzle for burrs or rough machine marks.

d. Look for cracks at nozzle end.

e. If any of these conditions occur, replace injector.

26. Record six-digit alphanumeric correction code located on the side of injector.

27. Inspect high-pressure fuel injector connector for the following:

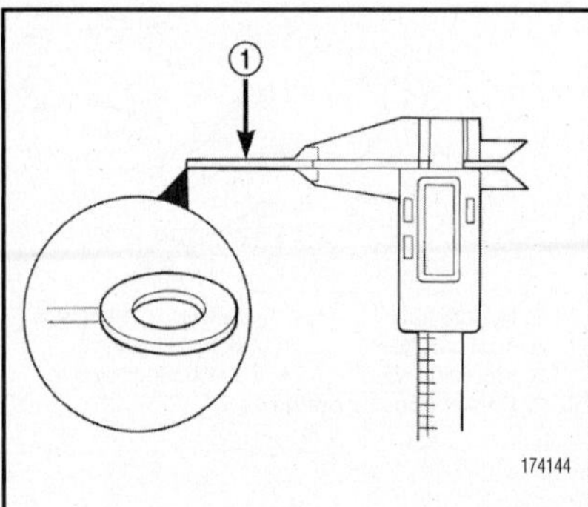

Fig. 89 Measuring injector sealing washer (1)

- Damaged tip
- Loose of missing alignment pin
- Cut or missing O-ring

28. Thoroughly clean fuel injector cylinder head bore. Blow out bore hole with compressed air.

29. The bottom of fuel injector is sealed to cylinder head bore with a copper sealing washer (shim) of a certain thickness. A new shim with correct thickness must always be reinstalled after removing injector. Measure thickness of injector shim. Shim thickness should be 0.60 in. (1.5 mm).

30. Install new shim (washer) to bottom of injector. Apply light coating of clean engine oil to washer. This will keep washer in place during installation.

31. Install new O-ring to fuel injector. Apply small amount of clean engine oil to O-ring and injector bore.

32. Install injector into cylinder head with male (high-pressure) connector port facing the intake manifold. Push down on fuel injector mounting flange to engage O-ring and seat injector.

33. When tightening, use the following sequence:

a. Install fuel injector hold-down clamp (mounting flange) bolts. Be sure the clamp is perpendicular to the injector body. Do a preliminary tightening of these bolts to 44 inch lbs. (5 Nm) torque. This preliminary tightening insures the fuel injector is seated and centered.

b. After tightening, relieve bolt torque, but leave both bolts threaded in place.

c. Install high-pressure connector and retaining nut. Do a preliminary tightening of nut to 133 inch lbs. (15 Nm).

d. Alternately, tighten injector hold-down bolts to 89 inch lbs. (10 Nm).

e. Do a final tightening of the high-pressure connector and retaining nut. Tighten to 37 ft. lbs. (50 Nm).

34. Noise isolators are used on the six high-pressure fuel lines. They should be positioned in the middle of the horizontal or longest straight section of each fuel line. The split on each isolator should be facing downward. Be sure the noise isolator is not touching another isolator or any other components.

35. Install the necessary rocker housing mounting bolt and tighten to 18 ft. lbs. (24 Nm).

36. Install integrated gasket.

37. Connect fuel injector solenoid wires and nuts to top of injectors. Tighten connector nuts to 11 inch lbs. (1.25 Nm). Be very careful not to overtighten these nuts as damage to fuel injector will occur.

38. Install the intake and exhaust rocker arm assembly.

39. Set exhaust valve lash See "ENGINE MECHANICAL" section.

40. Install fuel connector tube nut at cylinder head and tighten to 37 ft. lbs. (50 Nm). Be sure to use a secondary back-up wrench on the connector nut (fitting) while torquing fuel line fitting.

41. Install valve cover.

42. Install breather assembly.

➡Each fuel injector has a six-digit alphanumeric correction code. The correction code is printed on the intake side of the fuel injector and is used to identify injector calibration. When replacing any fuel injectors, this code must be entered into the vehicles Powertrain Control Module (PCM) using a diagnostic scan tool. In addition, if a new PCM is installed, use a diagnostic scan tool to program all six of the injector codes from the original fuel injectors into the new PCM.

43. Connect negative battery cables to both batteries.

44. Programming Fuel Injector Correction Code:

a. Turn ignition switch "ON".

b. Using a diagnostic scan tool, select ECU View, then PCM, then MISCELLANEOUS FUNCTIONS.

c. Select Injector Quantity Adjustments and click Start.

d. Choose appropriate cylinder number and click next.

e. Click on Show Keyboard.

➡A fault code will be set if incorrect serialization codes have been inputted.

f. Select Input Six-Digit Injector Correction Code and click enter.

g. Review code as it was typed, then click Next if correct, or edit if necessary.

h. Repeat the preceding steps for other cylinders if necessary.

i. Once all fuel injector correction codes are entered, cycle the ignition to complete.

FUEL PRESSURE LIMITING VALVE

REMOVAL & INSTALLATION

6.7L Diesel

➡The fuel pressure limiting valve is screwed into the front of the fuel rail. The fuel pressure limiting valve drain port is located on the side of the fuel rail next to the limiting valve. The drain port is not serviceable.

1. Thoroughly clean area at pressure limiting valve.
2. Remove the EGR crossover tube.
3. Remove six bolts and the intake manifold. Discard gasket.
4. Remove pressure limiting valve from fuel rail.
5. Installation is the reverse of the removal procedure.
6. Tighten the pressure limiting valve to 74 ft. lbs. (100 Nm).

FUEL PUMP

REMOVAL & INSTALLATION

6.7L Diesel

Fuel Injection Pump

See Figures 90 and 91.

1. Disconnect both negative battery cables at both batteries. Cover and isolate ends of both cables.
2. Remove intake manifold air intake tube (above injection pump) and its rubber connector hose.
3. Remove accessory drive belt.
4. Thoroughly clean rear of injection pump, and attachment points for its fuel lines. Also clean the opposite ends of these same lines at their attachment points.
5. Disconnect quick-connect fitting by pressing on button.

***** CAUTION**

Whenever a fuel line fitting is connected to a secondary fitting, always use a back-up wrench on the secondary fitting. Do not allow the secondary fitting to rotate.

6. Remove high-pressure fuel line to fuel rail. Remove banjo bolt. Disconnect FCA (Fuel Control Actuator) electrical connector.
7. Remove line clamp.
8. Remove fuel pump drive gear access cover with a 3/8" drive ratchet. Access cover is threaded to timing gear cover.
9. Remove fuel pump drive gear mounting nut and washer.
10. Attach C3428B, L-4407A (or equivalent) gear puller to pump drive gear with 2 bolts, and separate gear from pump (a keyway is not used on this particular injection pump). Leave drive gear hanging loose within timing gear cover.
11. Remove three injection pump mounting nuts, and remove pump from engine.

To install:

12. Inspect pump mounting surfaces at pump and mounting flange and pilot bore for nicks, cuts or damage. Inspect O-ring surfaces for nicks, cuts or damage.
13. Clean injection pump mounting flange and pilot bore at gear housing. Also clean front of injection pump.
14. Install new rubber O-ring (square) into machined groove at pump mounting area.
15. Apply clean engine oil to injection pump O-ring and pilot bore only.

***** CAUTION**

The machined tapers on both injection pump shaft and injection pump gear must be absolutely dry, clean and free of any dirt or oil film. This will ensure proper gear-to-shaft tightening.

16. Clean pump gear and pump shaft at machined tapers with an evaporative type cleaner such as brake cleaner.
17. Perform the following phasing procedure anytime the injection pump has been removed and reinstalled.
    a. Locate the end of the fuel injection pump shaft. Two numbers (750 or 754 and 0) are stamped into the end of the shaft.
    b. Rotate the injection pump shaft until the number 5 (located in the center of number 750 or 754) is positioned at 9 o'clock.
    c. Position injection pump to mounting flange on gear housing while aligning injection pump shaft through back of injection pump gear. Be sure the number 5 is still at the 9 o'clock position.
    d. Bring the engine to TDC position. Do this by rotating the crankshaft until the TDC mark on the crankshaft damper is at 12 o'clock position. It does not matter if cylinder No. 1 or No. 6 is at TDC. Again, check to be sure the number 5 is still at the 9 o'clock position. Rotate pump shaft accordingly.
18. After pump is positioned flat to mounting flange, install three pump mounting nuts and tighten finger tight only. Do not attempt a final tightening at this time.

***** CAUTION**

Do not attempt to tighten (pull) pump to gear housing using mounting nuts. Damage to pump or gear housing may occur. The pump must be positioned flat to its mounting flange before attempting to tighten three mounting nuts.

19. To prevent damage or cracking of components, install and tighten nuts in the following sequence:
    a. Install injection pump shaft washer and nut to pump shaft. Tighten nut finger tight only.
    Do preliminary (light) tightening of injection pump shaft nut.
    Tighten three injection pump mounting nuts to 18 ft. lbs. (24 Nm).
    Do a final tightening of pump shaft nut to 77 ft. lbs. (105 Nm).
20. Install drive gear access cover using a 3/8" drive ratchet. Access cover is threaded to timing gear cover. Tighten to 71 inch lbs. (8 Nm).

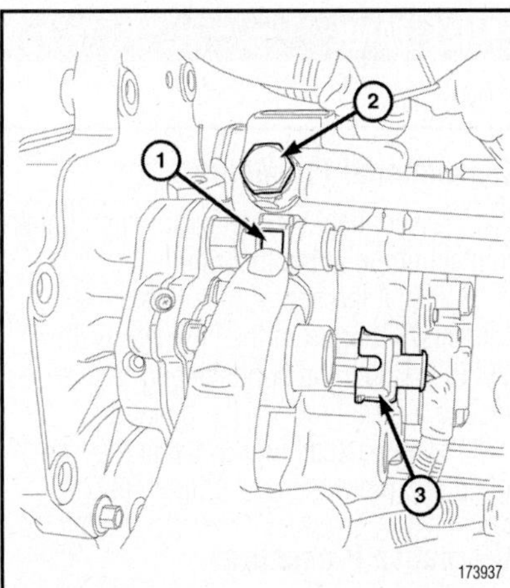

Fig. 90 Remove high-pressure fuel line to fuel rail. Remove banjo bolt (2). Disconnect FCA (Fuel Control Actuator) electrical connector (3). Showing quick-disconnect button (1)

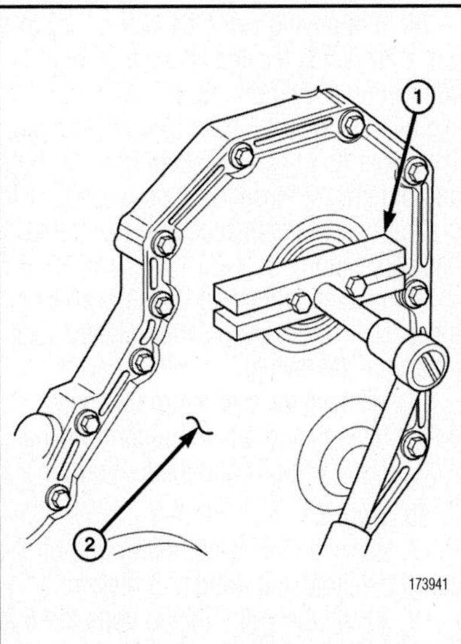

Fig. 91 Using gear puller (1) to separate gear from pump and timing cover (3)

21. Install fuel return line. Tighten banjo bolt to 18 ft. lbs. (24 Nm).
22. Install quick-connect fitting.
23. Install fuel line (injection pump-to-fuel rail). Using a back up wrench, tighten fitting at fuel pump to 30 ft. lbs. (40 Nm). Tighten fitting at fuel rail to 30 ft. lbs. (40 Nm).
24. Install clamp.
25. Connect Fuel Control Actuator (FCA) electrical connector to rear of injection pump.
26. Install rubber intake manifold air intake tube. Tighten clamps.
27. Install accessory drive belt.
28. Connect both negative battery cables.
29. Check system for fuel or engine oil leaks.

Fuel Pump Module With Fuel Transfer Pump

➡The fuel transfer pump (fuel lift pump) is a part of the fuel tank module. It is not serviced separately.

1. Drain and remove the fuel tank, as described in this section.

➡Note rotational position of module before attempting removal. An indexing arrow is located on top of module for this purpose.

2. Position SAE Fuel Pump Lock Ring Wrench (9340 or equivalent) into notches on outside edge of lock ring.
3. Install 1/2 inch drive breaker bar to the wrench. Rotate breaker bar counterclockwise to remove lock ring. Remove lock ring. The module will spring up slightly when lock ring is removed.
4. Remove module from fuel tank. Be careful not to bend float arm while removing.

To install:

➡Whenever the fuel pump module is serviced, the rubber O-ring seal must be replaced.

5. Using a new O-ring seal (gasket), position fuel pump module into opening in fuel tank and align the locator tab with index mark on fuel tank.
6. Position lock ring over top of fuel pump module.
7. Rotate module until embossed alignment arrow points to center alignment mark. This step must be performed to prevent float from contacting side of fuel tank. Also be sure fuel fitting on top of pump module is pointed to drivers side of vehicle.
8. Install SAE Fuel Pump Lock Ring Wrench (9340 or equivalent) to lock ring. Install 1/2 inch drive breaker into wrench and tighten lock ring (clockwise) until all seven notches have engaged.
9. Install fuel tank. See "Fuel Tank" in this section.

FUEL RAIL

REMOVAL & INSTALLATION

6.7L Diesel

1. Disconnect both negative battery cables.
2. Remove the oil dipstick tube.
3. Remove bolts and EGR crossover tube cover.
4. Remove the Closed Crankcase Ventilation (CCV) oil drains hoses from cylinder head cover.
5. Disconnect the crankcase pressure sensor connector.
6. Disconnect both fuel injector harness connectors.
7. Disconnect the fuel pressure sensor harness connector at end of fuel rail.
8. Disconnect necessary wiring harness retention clips from intake manifold.
9. Remove bolt and nut securing the oil dipstick tube.

➡When loosening or tightening high-pressure line fittings attached to a separate fitting, use a back-up wrench on fitting. Do not allow fitting to rotate. Damage to both fuel line and fitting will result.

10. Remove the fuel tubes.
11. Loosen fittings for all fuel tubes at fuel rail.
12. Clean any dirt/debris from around fuel injector area.
13. If removing fuel tube at No. 6 cylinder, a bracket is located above fuel tube connection at cylinder head. Two bolts secure this bracket to rear of cylinder head. The upper bolt hole is slotted. Loosen (but do not remove) these two bracket bolts. Tilt bracket down to gain access to No. 6 fuel line connection.
14. Loosen fittings and remove all fuel tubes. Note and mark position of each fuel tube while removing.
15. Remove the fuel return line banjo bolt at fuel rail and discard sealing washers.
16. Remove bolts and the fuel rail.

To install:

17. Clean any dirt/debris from top of intake manifold and bottom of fuel rail.
18. Install fuel rail. Tighten bolts to 18 ft. lbs. (24 Nm).
19. Install two new sealing washers to fuel line banjo bolt connecting injection pump to fuel rail. Tighten to 18 ft. lbs. (24 Nm).
20. Noise isolators are used on the six high-pressure fuel lines. They should be positioned in the middle of the horizontal or longest straight section of each fuel line. The split on each isolator should be facing downward. Be sure the noise isolator is not touching another isolator or any other components.
21. If fuel tube at No. 6 cylinder has been replaced, tilt metal bracket upward to install the No. 6 fuel tube.
22. Install all high-pressure tubes to rail and fuel injectors. Tighten fittings to 30 ft. lbs. (40 Nm).
23. Position the metal bracket at the rear of cylinder head back and tighten bolts to 32 ft. lbs. (43 Nm).
24. Install the oil dipstick nut and tighten to 80 inch lbs. (9 Nm). Install the oil dipstick bolt and tighten to 18 ft. lbs. (24 Nm).
25. Connect necessary wiring harness retention clips to the intake manifold.
26. Connect the fuel pressure sensor harness connector.
27. Connect both fuel injector harness connectors.
28. Connect the crankcase pressure sensor connector.
29. Install the CCV oil drains hoses to cylinder head cover.
30. Install the EGR crossover tube cover. Tighten bolts to 89 inch lbs. (10 Nm).
31. Install the oil dipstick tube.
32. Connect both negative battery cables.
33. Start engine and check for leaks.

FUEL TANK

DRAINING

Conventional Procedure

1. Disconnect the fuel supply line quick-connect fitting at the fuel filter.
2. Install the appropriate Fuel Line Adapters/Fitting from the Fuel Decay Tool (8978A). Route the opposite end of this hose to a diesel fuel draining station.
3. Using a scan tool, activate the fuel pump and drain the tank until empty.

Alternative Procedure

1. Disconnect the negative battery cable.
2. Remove the fuel pump module. See "Fuel Pump" in this section.
3. After the fuel pump module has been removed, drain fuel tank into an approved diesel fuel draining station.

REMOVAL & INSTALLATION

6.7L Diesel

See Figure 92.

➡Procedure is very similar whether vehicle is equipped with rear-mounted or mid-vehicle mounted tank.

1. Ensure fuel system pressure is released. See "Relieving Fuel System Pressure" in this section.
2. Raise and support vehicle.
3. Drain fuel tank, as described above.
4. Remove fuel hose clamps.
5. Remove ground wire screw and disconnect ground wire.
6. Remove fuel fill hose assembly.
7. Disconnect electrical connector from fuel pump module.
8. Disconnect fuel return and supply line quick-connect fittings.
9. Support tank with a hydraulic jack.
10. Remove retaining bolts (including at skid plate if equipped) and lower the tank assembly from vehicle and lift tank from skid plate.
11. If fuel pump module is being removed, see "Fuel Pump" in this section.

To install:

12. If fuel pump module is being installed, see "Fuel Pump" in this section.
13. Position fuel tank into fuel tank skid plate (if equipped).
14. Place assembly to a hydraulic jack and raise assembly up to frame.
15. Install retaining bolts and tighten to 41 ft. lbs. (55 Nm) for rear mount or to 30 ft. lbs. (40 Nm) for mid-mount tank.

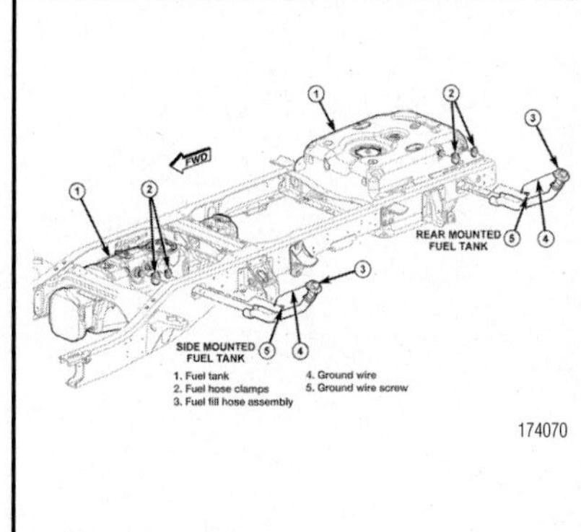

Fig. 92 Showing mid-mount and rear-mount fuel tank components

16. Connect fuel return and supply line quick-connect fittings.
17. Connect harness connector to fuel pump module.

HEATING & AIR CONDITIONING SYSTEM

BLOWER MOTOR

REMOVAL & INSTALLATION

1. Disconnect and isolate the negative battery cable.
2. Disconnect the HVAC wire harness lead from the blower motor.
3. Remove the three screws that secure the blower motor to the bottom of the HVAC housing and remove the blower motor.
4. Installation is the reverse of the removal procedure.

EVAPORATOR CORE

REMOVAL & INSTALLATION

1. Remove the HVAC housing and place it on a workbench. See "HVAC Module" in this section.
2. Disconnect the HVAC wiring harness from the recirculation door actuator, power module or blower resister (depending on application) and the blower motor.
3. Disengage the HVAC wiring harness from the two retaining clips and position the harness out of the way.

➡If any of the foam seals is deformed or damaged, they must be replaced.

4. Remove the foam seal from the front of the HVAC housing.
5. Remove the two bolts that secure the A/C expansion valve to the evaporator tube tapping block and remove the valve.
6. Remove the three screws that secure the blower motor and evaporator housing to the HVAC housing.
7. Carefully disengage the nine retaining tabs that secure the blower motor and evaporator housing the HVAC housing.
8. Carefully separate the blower motor and evaporator housing from the HVAC housing
9. Remove the A/C evaporator from the blower motor and evaporator housing.
10. If the A/C evaporator is going to be reused, remove and discard the O-ring seals from the evaporator fittings and install plugs into, or tape over the evaporator ports.

To install:

➡Replacement of the O-ring seals is required anytime the A/C expansion valve is removed from the A/C evaporator. Failure to replace the rubber O-ring seals may result in a refrigerant system leak.

➡If the foam insulator around the A/C evaporator is deformed or damaged, the insulator must be replaced.

11. Carefully install the A/C evaporator into the blower motor and evaporator housing.
12. Carefully install the blower motor and evaporator housing onto the HVAC housing. Align the dowel pins to the holes in the housing.
13. Carefully engage the nine retaining tabs. Make sure the retaining tabs are fully engaged.
14. Install the three screws that secure the blower motor and evaporator housing to the HVAC housing. Tighten the screws.
15. Remove the tape or plugs from the evaporator tube fittings.
16. Lubricate new O-ring seals with clean refrigerant oil and install them onto the evaporator tube fittings.

➡Use only the specified O-ring seals as they are made of a special material for the R-134a system. Use only refrigerant oil of the type recommended for the A/C compressor in the vehicle.

17. Install the A/C expansion valve onto the evaporator tube tapping block.
18. Install the two bolts that secure the A/C expansion valve to the evaporator tube tapping block. Tighten the bolts to 97 inch lbs. (11 Nm).
19. Install the foam seal onto the HVAC housing.
20. Connect the HVAC wiring harness to the recirculation door actuator, power module or blower resistor (depending on application) and the blower motor.
21. Engage the HVAC wiring harness to the two retaining clips. Make sure the wire harness is fully engaged to the retaining clips.
22. Install the HVAC housing. See "HVAC Module" in this section.
23. If the A/C evaporator is being replaced, add 60 milliliters (2 fluid ounces) of refrigerant oil to the refrigerant system.

HEATER CORE

REMOVAL & INSTALLATION

See Figures 93 and 94.

1. Remove the HVAC housing and place it on a workbench. See "HVAC Module" in this section.

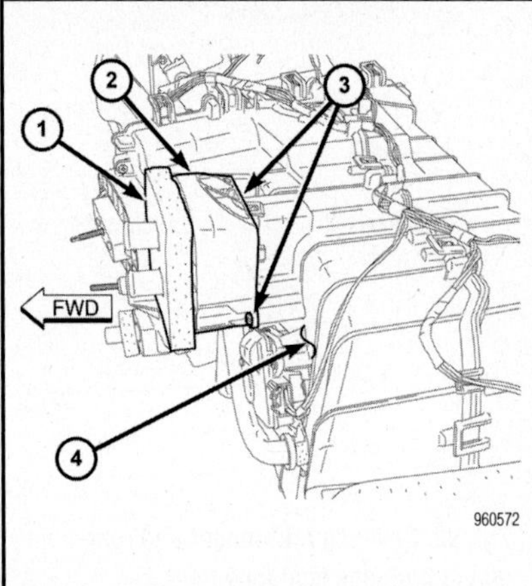

Fig. 93 Removing foam seal and flange from HVAC housing.

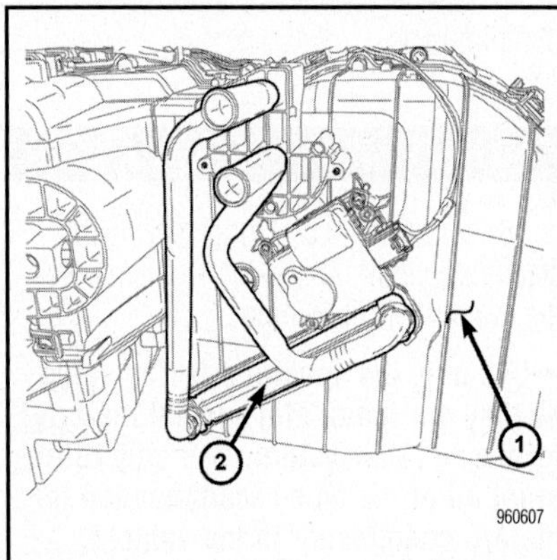

Fig. 94 Removing the heater core (2) from the HVAC housing (1)

2. Remove the foam seal from the flange.
3. Remove the two screws that secure the flange to the front of the HVAC housing.
4. Carefully disengage the retaining tab that secures the flange to the HVAC housing and remove the flange.
5. Carefully pull the heater core out of the front of the HVAC housing.
6. Inspect all foam seals and replace as required.

To install:

7. Inspect the foam seals on the heater core and replace as required.
8. Carefully install the heater core into the front of the HVAC housing.
9. Position the flange onto the front of the HVAC housing. Make sure the retaining tab is fully engaged.
10. Install the two screws that secure the flange to the HVAC housing. Tighten the screws snugly.
11. Install the foam seal onto the flange.

➡If the heater core is being replaced, flush the cooling system.

12. Install the HVAC housing. See "HVAC Module" in this section.

HVAC MODULE

REMOVAL & INSTALLATION

See Figure 95.

➡This procedure requires removal of the instrument panel. If not equipped to perform this operation, refer the vehicle to a proper repair facility.

1. Properly disable the air bag system before beginning work. See "AIR BAG (SUPPLEMENTAL RESTRAINT SYSTEM)" section.
2. Disconnect and isolate the negative battery cable.
3. Recover the refrigerant from the refrigerant system.
4. Drain the engine cooling system.
5. Disconnect the A/C liquid line and the A/C suction line from the A/C expansion valve.
6. Disconnect the heater hoses from the heater core tubes at the firewall.
7. If required, remove the Powertrain Control Module (PCM) to gain access to the two nuts that secure the HVAC housing to the engine compartment side of the dash panel.
8. Remove the two nuts from the studs that secure the HVAC housing to the engine compartment side of the dash panel.
9. If equipped with center floor console, remove the floor console duct.
10. Remove the instrument panel from the passenger compartment.
11. If equipped, remove the rear floor ducts.
12. Remove the bolt that secures the HVAC housing to the floor bracket.
13. Remove the two nuts that secure the HVAC housing to the passenger compartment side of the dash panel.
14. Pull the HVAC housing assembly rearward and remove the housing assembly from the passenger compartment.

To install:

CAUTION

Be certain to adjust the refrigerant oil level when servicing the A/C refrigerant system. Failure to properly adjust the refrigerant oil level will prevent the A/C system from operating as designed and can cause serious A/C compressor damage.

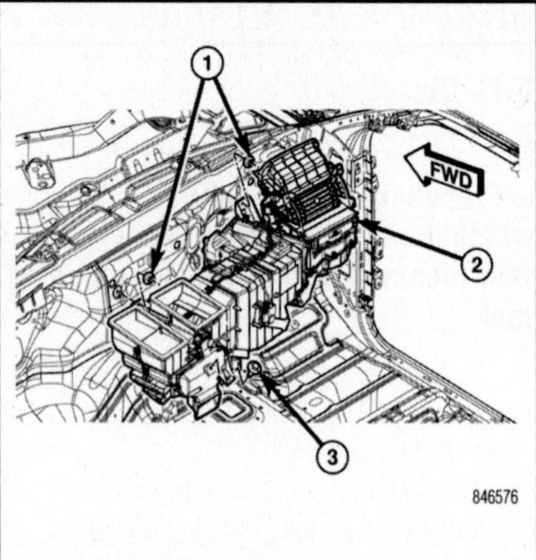

Fig. 95 Removing retaining nuts and bolts (1, 3) to remove HVAC module (2)

15. Position the HVAC housing assembly into the passenger compartment and over the studs on the dash panel, with the condensate drain tube in its proper location.
16. Install the two nuts that secure the HVAC housing to the passenger compartment side of the dash panel. Tighten the nuts to 60 inch lbs. (7 Nm).
17. Install the bolt that secures the HVAC housing to the floor bracket. Tighten the bolt to 60 inch lbs. (7 Nm).
18. If equipped, install the rear floor ducts.
19. Install the instrument panel assembly.
20. If equipped with center floor console, install the floor console duct.
21. Install the two nuts onto the two studs that secure the HVAC housing to the engine compartment side of the dash panel. Tighten the nuts to 60 inch lbs. (7 Nm).
22. If removed, install the powertrain control module (PCM).
23. Connect the heater hoses to the heater core tubes.
24. Connect the A/C liquid line and the A/C suction line to the A/C expansion valve, using new O-ring seals at all connections.
25. Reconnect the negative battery cable.
26. If the heater core is being replaced, flush the cooling system.
27. Refill the engine cooling system.
28. Evacuate the refrigerant system.
29. Charge the refrigerant system, including adding refrigerant oil as required.
30. Initiate the "Actuator Calibration" function using a scan tool.

STEERING

POWER STEERING GEAR

REMOVAL & INSTALLATION

With Independent Front Suspension

See Figure 96.

➡The steering column on vehicles with an automatic transmission may not be equipped with an internal locking shaft that allows the ignition key cylinder to be locked with the key. Alternative methods of locking the steering wheel for service will have to be used.

1. Lock the steering wheel.
2. Drain and siphon the power steering fluid from the reservoir.
3. Raise and support the vehicle.
4. Remove and discard the steering coupler pinch bolt.
5. Disconnect the power steering hoses from the rack and pinion. Plug openings to prevent contamination.
6. Remove the front tires and wheels.
7. Remove the outer tie rod nuts and separate outer tie rods from the knuckles, using Ball Joint Remover (8677 or equivalent).
8. If equipped, remove the skid plate.
9. Remove the rack and pinion mounting bolts and remove the rack from the vehicle.

To install:

10. Before installing gear inspect bushings and replace if worn or damaged.

➡In the frame there are two holes for the mounting of the steering gear, one is slotted and one is round. When tightening the gear to specifications make sure to tighten the mounting bolt with the hole first to avoid movement of the steering gear.

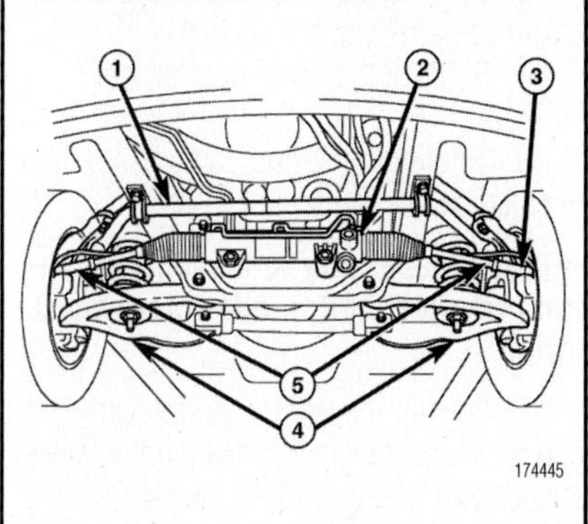

Fig. 96 Showing the steering gear mounting

11. Position the rack and pinion to the front crossmember.
12. Install the retaining bolts. Tighten the bolts to 235 ft. lbs. (319 Nm).
13. Slide the shaft coupler onto the gear and install a new pinch bolt. Tighten the pinch bolt to 36 ft. lbs. (49 Nm).
14. Clean and dry the tie rod end studs and the tapers in the knuckles.
15. Install the tie rod ends into the steering knuckles. Install and tighten the retaining nuts to 45 ft. lbs. (61 Nm), then turn an additional 90 degrees.
16. Connect the pressure power steering hose to the steering gear and tighten to 23 ft. lbs. (32 Nm).
17. Connect the return power steering hose to the steering gear and tighten to 37 ft. lbs. (50 Nm).
18. If equipped, install the front skid plate.
19. Install the front tires and wheels.
20. Lower the vehicle.
21. Fill the power steering system with fluid.
22. Adjust the toe alignment.

With Link & Coil Suspension

➡The steering column on vehicles with an automatic transmission may not be equipped with an internal locking shaft that allows the ignition key cylinder to be locked with the key. Alternative methods of locking the steering wheel for service will have to be used.

1. Place the front wheels in a straight-ahead position.
2. Lock the steering wheel.
3. Siphon out as much power steering fluid as possible.
4. Disconnect and cap the fluid hoses from steering gear.
5. Remove the steering shaft coupler pinch bolt at the steering gear and slide coupler off steering gear.
6. Remove the steering gear shaft to pitman arm retaining nut and washer.
7. Mark the steering gear shaft and pitman arm for installation reference.
8. Using the Pitman Arm Remover (9615A or equivalent), remove the pitman arm from the steering gear shaft.
9. Remove the steering gear 3 retaining bolts and remove the steering gear from the vehicle.

To install:

10. Position the steering gear to the frame rail. Install the three mounting bolts and tighten to 145 ft. lbs. (196 Nm).
11. Align steering coupler on gear shaft. Install pinch bolt and tighten to 36 ft. lbs. (49 Nm) torque.
12. Align and install the pitman arm. Install the washer and retaining nut on the pitman shaft. Tighten the nut to 225 ft. lbs. (305 Nm).
13. Connect fluid hoses to steering gear and tighten to 23 ft. lbs. (32 Nm).
14. Add power steering fluid.
15. Reset the toe and center the steering wheel.

POWER STEERING PUMP

REMOVAL & INSTALLATION

See Figure 97.

1. Drain and siphon the power steering fluid from the reservoir.
2. Remove the serpentine belt.

⁂ CAUTION

Do not remove the high pressure hose fitting on the pump. The fitting may come loose unless it is backed up using another wrench. If the fitting does come loose, it must be retightened to 40–50 ft. lbs. (57–67 Nm) before continuing. If this fitting comes out of the pump body, the internal spring and valve parts will fall out of the pump and they cannot be reinstalled properly. If this occurs the pump needs to be replaced with a new pump.

3. Disconnect the return hose.
4. Disconnect the pressure hose.
5. Remove the three bolts securing the pump to the cylinder head thru the pulley holes.

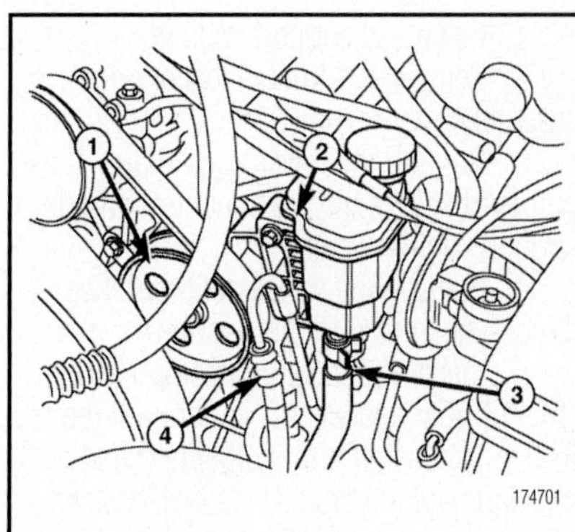

Fig. 97 Locating the power steering pump and components

To install:

6. Align the pump with the mounting holes in the left cylinder head.
7. Install 3 pump mounting bolts through the pulley access holes. Tighten the bolts to 21 ft. lbs. (28 Nm).
8. Reconnect the pressure line and return hose to the pump and reservoir. Tighten the pressure line to 23 ft. lbs. (31 Nm).
9. Install the serpentine drive belt.
10. Fill the power steering pump.

BLEEDING

See Figure 98.

CAUTION

Mopar Power Steering Fluid + 4 or Mopar ATF+4 Automatic Transmission Fluid is to be used in the power steering system. Both Fluids have the same material standard specifications (MS-9602). No other power steering or automatic transmission fluid is to be used in the system. Damage may result to the power steering pump and system if another fluid is used. Do not overfill the system.

CAUTION

If the air is not purged from the power steering system correctly, pump failure could result.

➡Be sure the vacuum tool used in the following procedure is clean and free of any fluids.

1. Check the fluid level. As measured on the side of the reservoir, the level should indicate between MAX and MIN when the fluid is at normal ambient temperature. Adjust the fluid level as necessary.
2. Tightly insert P/S Cap Adapter (9688A or equivalent) into the mouth of the reservoir.

CAUTION

Failure to use a vacuum pump reservoir may allow power steering fluid to be sucked into the hand vacuum pump.

3. Attach Hand Vacuum Pump (C-4207-A or equivalent), with reservoir attached, to the P/S Cap Adapter.

CAUTION

Do not run the vehicle while vacuum is applied to the power steering system. Damage to the power steering pump can occur.

➡When performing the following step make sure the vacuum level is maintained during the entire time period.

4. Using Hand Vacuum Pump, apply 20–25 in. Hg of vacuum to the system for a minimum of three minutes.

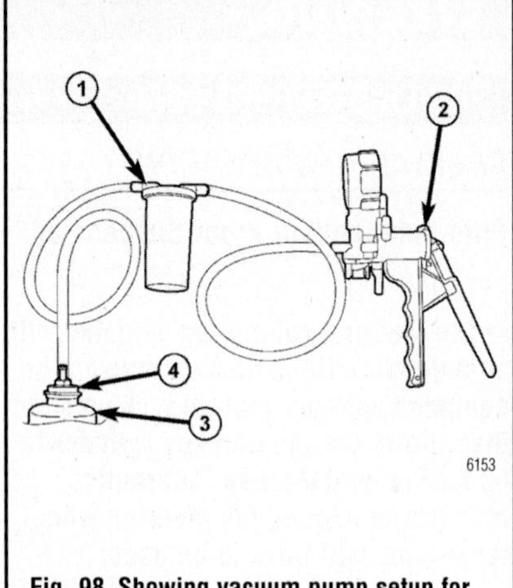

Fig. 98 Showing vacuum pump setup for bleeding

5. Slowly release the vacuum and remove the special tools.
6. Adjust the fluid level as necessary.
7. Repeat the previous steps until the fluid no longer drops when vacuum is applied.
8. Start the engine and cycle the steering wheel lock-to-lock three times. Do not hold the steering wheel at the stops.
9. Stop the engine and check for leaks at all connections.
10. Check for any signs of air in the reservoir and check the fluid level. If air is present, repeat the procedure as necessary.

SUSPENSION

FRONT SUSPENSION

COIL SPRING

REMOVAL & INSTALLATION

With Independent Front Suspension

4X2

See Figure 99.

1. Raise and support vehicle.
2. Remove the front wheel and tire assembly.
3. Support the lower control arm at the outboard side of the lower control arm to support vehicle weight.
4. Remove the shock absorber. See "Shock Absorber" in this section.
5. Install Front Spring Compressor (DD-1278 or equivalent) up through the lower suspension arm, coil spring and shock hole in the frame. The bell-shaped adapter goes against the lower suspension arm. Install the nut on top of the tool at the shock hole.

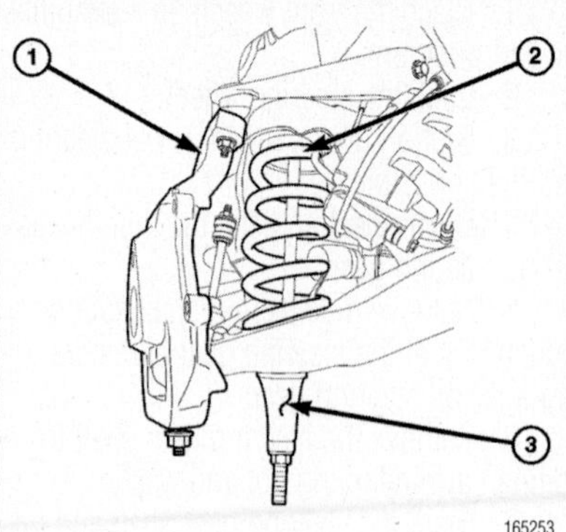

Fig. 99 Install Front Spring Compressor (DD-1278 or equivalent) (3) up through the lower suspension arm, coil spring (2) and shock hole in the frame. The bell-shaped adapter (3) goes against the lower suspension arm. Install the nut on top of the tool at the shock hole. Also showing brake caliper adapter (1).

6. Tighten the spring compressor nut against bell-shaped adapter finger tight then loosen 1/2 turn. This will hold the spring in place until the lower suspension arm is separated from the steering knuckle.
7. Remove the steering knuckle. See "Steering Knuckle" in this section.
8. Remove the stabilizer link. See "Stabilizer Bar Link" in this section.
9. Remove the lower control arm support.
10. Tighten the spring compressor tool to collapse the coil spring.

➡It may necessary to loosen the control arm pivot bolt to allow downward swing.

11. Loosen the tension on the spring compressor tool slowly allowing the lower suspension arm to pivot downward.
12. Remove the spring compressor tool.
13. Remove coil spring and isolator pad from the vehicle.

To install:

14. Tape the isolator pad to the top of the coil spring. Position the spring in the lower suspension arm well. Be sure that the coil spring is seated in the well.

15. Install Front Spring Compressor (DD-1278 or equivalent) up through the lower suspension arm, coil spring and shock hole in the frame. Tighten the tool nut to compress the coil spring.

16. Install the steering knuckle. See "Steering Knuckle" in this section.

17. Install the retaining nut on the upper ball joint and tighten to 40 ft. lbs. (54 Nm), plus an additional 200 degrees.

18. Remove the spring compressor tool.

19. Support the lower control arm at the outboard side of the lower control arm to support vehicle weight.

20. Install the shock absorber. See "Shock Absorber" in this section.

21. Install the stabilizer link. See "Stabilizer Bar Link" in this section.

22. Remove the lower control arm support.

23. Install the wheel and tire assembly.

24. Remove the support and lower the vehicle to the floor with vehicle weight. Tighten the front and rear control arm frame pivot bolts if loosened to:

- Lower control arm to frame nuts: 155 ft. lbs. (210 Nm)
- Upper control arm to frame nuts: 130 ft. lbs. (176 Nm)

25. Perform a wheel alignment

4X4

1. Remove the shock. See "Shock Absorber" in this section.

2. Place the spring-over-shock assembly in the Branick 7200 (or equivalent) Spring Removal/Installation tool. Compress the spring.

3. Position Strut Nut Wrench (9362 or equivalent), on shock shaft retaining nut. Next, insert 8 mm socket though Wrench onto hex located on end of shock shaft. While holding shock shaft from turning, remove nut from shock shaft using the wrench.

4. Remove the upper shock nut.

5. Remove the shock upper mounting plate.

6. Remove the dust cover.

7. Remove and inspect the upper spring isolator.

8. Remove the shock absorber from the coil spring.

To install:

9. Position the shock into the coil spring.

10. Install the upper isolator.

11. Install the dust cover.

12. Install the upper shock mounting plate.

13. Install the shock upper mounting nut.

14. Install Strut Nut Wrench (9362 or equivalent) on end of a torque wrench and then on the shock shaft retaining nut. Next, insert 8 mm socket though Wrench onto hex located on end of shock shaft. While holding shock shaft from turning, tighten nut to 45 ft. lbs. (61 Nm).

15. Decompress the spring.

16. Remove the shock assembly from the spring compressor tool.

17. Install the shock assembly. See "Shock Absorber" in this section.

With Coil & Link Suspension

See Figure 100.

1. Raise and support the vehicle. Position a hydraulic jack under the axle to support it.

2. Paint or scribe alignment marks on lower suspension arm cam adjusters and axle bracket for installation reference.

3. Remove the upper suspension arm and loosen lower suspension arm bolts.

4. Mark and disconnect the front propeller shaft from the axle 4x4 models.

5. Disconnect the track bar from the frame rail bracket.

6. Disconnect the drag link from pitman arm.

7. Disconnect the stabilizer bar link and shock absorber from the axle.

8. Lower the axle until the spring is free from the upper mount. Remove the coil spring.

To install:

9. Position the coil spring on the axle pad.

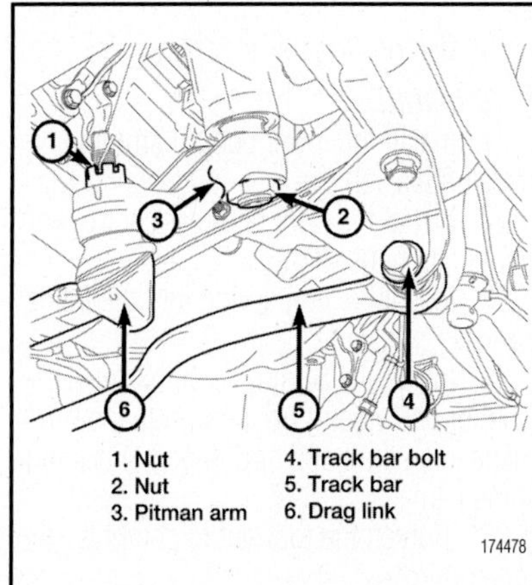

Fig. 100 Showing pitman arm and components

10. Raise the axle into position until the spring seats in the upper mount.

11. Connect the stabilizer bar links and shock absorbers to the axle bracket. Connect the track bar to the frame rail bracket.

12. Install the upper suspension arm.

13. Install the front propeller shaft to the axle, if equipped.

14. Install drag link to pitman arm and tighten nut to 40 ft. lbs. (54 Nm) Install a new cotter pin.

15. Remove the supports and lower the vehicle.

16. Tighten the following suspension components to specifications given:

- Link to stabilizer bar nut: 50 ft. lbs. (68 Nm)
- Lower shock bolt: 100 ft. lbs. (136 Nm)
- Track bar bolt at axle shaft tube bracket: 200 ft. lbs. (271 Nm)
- Upper suspension arm nut at axle bracket: 120 ft. lbs. (163 Nm)
- Upper suspension nut at frame bracket: 120 ft. lbs. (163 Nm)
- Cam nut (align lower suspension arm reference marks): 200 ft. lbs. (271 Nm)
- Lower suspension nut at frame bracket: 200 ft. lbs. (271 Nm)

LOWER BALL JOINT

REMOVAL & INSTALLATION

With Independent Front Suspension

1. Raise and support the vehicle.

2. Remove the knuckle. See "Steering Knuckle" in this section.

CAUTION

Extreme pressure lubrication must be used on the threaded portions of the tool. This will increase the longevity of the tool and insure proper operation during the removal and installation process.

3. Press the ball joint from the lower control arm using Ball Joint Press (C-4212F or equivalent), Remover/Installer Driver (8836-6 or equivalent) and Ball Joint Remover/Installer Receiver (8698-2 or equivalent).

4. Remove ball joint from the lower control arm.

To install:

5. Install the ball joint into the control arm and press in, using Ball Joint Press, Ball Joint Remover/Installer Driver and Ball Joint Remover/Installer Receiver. Remove the tools.

6. Stake the ball joint flange in four evenly spaced places around the ball joint flange, using a punch and hammer.
7. Install the steering knuckle. See "Steering Knuckle" in this section.
8. Check the vehicle ride height.
9. Perform a wheel alignment.

With Coil & Link Suspension

1. Remove the steering knuckle. See "Steering Knuckle" in this section.
2. Remove the axle shaft from the axle. See "DRIVE TRAIN" section.
3. Remove lower snap ring from the lower ball joint.
4. Using special tool, (8975-2, 8975-4 and C4212F), remove lower ball stud.

To install:

5. Position special tool set and install lower ball stud.
6. Install the axle shaft into the axle. See "DRIVE TRAIN" section.
7. Install the steering knuckle. See "Steering Knuckle" in this section.

LOWER CONTROL ARM

REMOVAL & INSTALLATION

With Independent Front Suspension

4X2

See Figure 101.

1. Raise and support the vehicle.
2. Remove the tire and wheel assembly.
3. Support the lower control arm at the outboard side of the lower control arm to support vehicle weight.
4. Remove the shock. See "Shock Absorber" in this section.

⁂ CAUTION

Do not allow the caliper to hang freely, support the caliper assembly.

5. Remove the disc brake caliper adapter, then the brake rotor. See "BRAKES" section.
6. Remove the upper ball joint nut.
7. Install Front Spring Compressor (DD-1278 or equivalent) up through the lower control arm, coil spring and shock hole in the frame. The bell-shaped adapter goes against the lower control arm. Install the nut on top of the tool at the shock hole.
8. Tighten the spring compressor nut against bell-shaped adapter finger tight then loosen 1/2 turn to hold the spring in place.
9. Separate the upper ball joint from the knuckle, using Ball Joint Remover (9360 or equivalent).

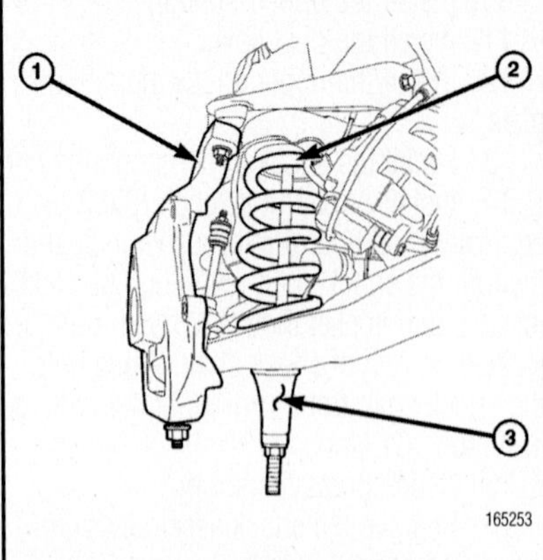

Fig. 101 Installing the front spring compressor (3) into the coil spring (2), next to the steering knuckle (1)

10. Remove the knuckle from the vehicle.
11. Remove the lower stabilizer link nut.
12. Remove the lower ball joint nut at the steering knuckle.
13. Separate the ball joint from the knuckle using Ball Joint Remover (8677 or equivalent).

⁂ CAUTION

Do not allow the upper control arm to rebound downward, it must be supported.

14. Remove the lower control arm support.
15. Tighten the spring compressor tool to allow clearance for the lower ball joint to be removed out of the knuckle.
16. Loosen the tension on the spring compressor tool slowly allowing the lower control arm to pivot downward.
17. Remove the spring compressor tool.
18. Remove coil spring and isolator pad from the vehicle.
19. Remove the front and rear pivot bolts.
20. Remove the lower control arm.

To install:

21. Install the lower control arm into place on the vehicle.
22. Install the front and rear control arm pivot bolts finger tight.
23. Install the coil spring into the frame pocket.
24. Install the Spring Compressor (DD-1278 or equivalent) up through the lower suspension arm, coil spring and shock hole in the frame.
25. Tighten the tool nut to compress the coil spring.
26. Install the knuckle to the control arms. See "Steering Knuckle" in this section.
27. Position the lower ball joint into the steering knuckle.
28. Install the retaining nut on the lower ball joint and tighten to 38 ft. lbs. (51 Nm), plus an additional 90 degrees.
29. Position the upper ball joint to the knuckle.
30. Install the retaining nut on the upper ball joint and tighten to 40 ft. lbs. (54Nm), plus an additional 200 degrees.
31. Support the lower control arm at the outboard side of the lower control arm to support vehicle weight.
32. Remove the spring compressor tool.
33. Install the shock absorber. See "Shock Absorber" in this section.
34. Install the stabilizer link. See "Stabilizer Link" in this section.
35. Remove the lower control arm support.
36. Install the wheel and tire assembly and lower the vehicle.
37. Lower the vehicle to the floor with vehicle weight and tighten the front and rear control arm to frame nuts to:
    - Lower control arm to frame nuts: 155 ft. lbs. (210 Nm)
    - Upper control arm to frame nuts: 130 ft. lbs. (176 Nm)
38. Perform a wheel alignment.

4X4

1. Raise and support the vehicle.
2. Remove the wheel and tire assembly.
3. Remove half shaft nut from the shaft.

⁂ CAUTION

Never allow the disc brake caliper to hang from the brake hose. Damage to the brake hose will result. Provide a suitable support to hang the caliper securely.

4. Compress the disc brake caliper. Remove the caliper adapter bolts. Remove the disc brake caliper and the caliper adapter as an assembly. Remove the rotor from the hub/bearing. See "BRAKES" section.
5. Remove the wheel speed sensor wiring clips and disconnect the electrical connector.
6. Remove the upper ball joint nut. Separate the ball joint from the steering knuckle using Ball Joint Remover (9360 or equivalent).
7. Disengage inner C/V joint from axle shaft with two pry bars between the C/V housing and axle housing.
8. Remove the front halfshaft. See "DRIVE TRAIN" section.
9. Remove the shock absorber lower nut/bolt.

10. Remove the stabilizer bar link lower nut.

11. Using a suitable tie strap, support the knuckle. Remove the lower ball joint nut. Separate ball joint from the steering knuckle using Ball Joint Remover (8766 or equivalent).

12. Remove the two control arm pivot bolts and control arm from frame rail brackets.

To install:

13. Position the lower control arm at the frame rail brackets. Install the pivot bolts and nuts, and tighten the nuts finger-tight.

➡The ball joint stud taper must be CLEAN and DRY before installing the knuckle. Clean the stud taper with mineral spirits to remove dirt and grease.

14. Insert the lower ball joint stud into the steering knuckle. Install and tighten the retaining nut to 38 ft. lbs. (51 Nm), plus an additional 90 degrees.

15. Install shock absorber lower bolt/nut and tighten to 155 ft. lbs. (210 Nm).

16. Install the stabilizer bar link lower nut and tighten to 75ft. lbs. (102 Nm).

17. Install the front halfshaft to the axle by pushing the inner CV joint firmly to engage axle shaft snap ring into the inner CV housing.

18. Clean hub bearing bore, hub bearing mating surface and half shaft splines and apply a light coating of grease to the front axle shaft output splines.

19. Install half shaft into the knuckle.

20. Insert the upper ball joint into the steering knuckle.

21. Install and tighten the upper ball joint retaining nut to 40 ft. lbs. (54 Nm), plus an additional 200 degrees.

22. Tighten the lower control arm front pivot nut and rear pivot bolt to 130 ft. lbs. (176 Nm).

23. Install half shaft hub nut and tighten to 185ft. lbs. (251 Nm).

24. Install the wheel and tire assembly.

25. Remove the support and lower the vehicle.

26. Perform a wheel alignment.

With Coil & Link Suspension

See Figure 102.

1. Raise and support the vehicle.

2. Paint or scribe alignment marks on the cam adjusters and control arm for installation reference.

➡Discard the nuts and bolts and do not reuse, New nuts and bolts should be used when replacing or servicing the control arms.

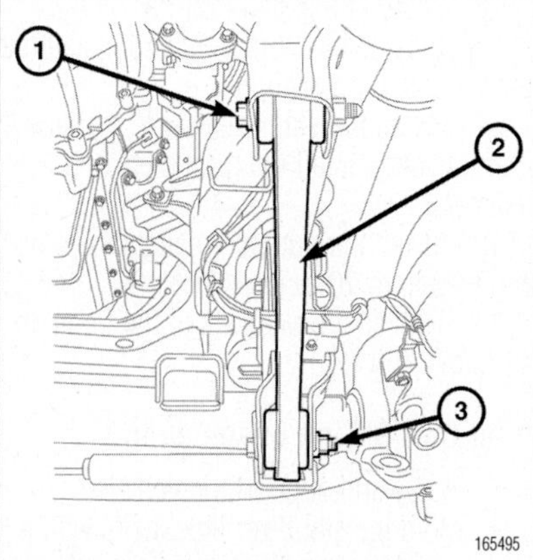

Fig. 102 Showing the lower control arm cam bolt (1), control arm (2) and frame rail bracket (3)

3. Remove the lower control arm nut, cam and cam bolt from the axle.

4. Remove the nut and bolt from the frame rail bracket and remove the lower control arm.

To install:

5. Position the lower control arm at the axle bracket and frame rail bracket.

6. Install the rear bolt and finger tighten the nut.

7. Install the cam bolt, cam and nut in the axle and align the reference marks.

8. Remove support and lower the vehicle.

9. Tighten cam nut at the axle bracket and the rear nut at the frame bracket to 200 ft. lbs. (271 Nm).

SHOCK ABSORBER

REMOVAL & INSTALLATION

With Independent Front Suspension

4X2

1. Raise and support vehicle.

2. Support the lower control arm outboard end.

3. Remove the upper shock absorber nut by using Strut Nut Wrench (9362 or equivalent), retainer and grommet. If necessary, insert 11/32 socket though Wrench onto hex located on end of shock shaft to prevent shaft from turning.

4. Remove the lower bolts and remove the shock absorber.

To install:

5. Install the lower retainer and grommet on the shock absorber stud. Insert the shock absorber through the frame bracket hole.

6. Install the lower bolts and tighten the bolts to 19 ft. lbs. (26 Nm).

7. Install the upper grommet, retainer and new nut or use Mopar Lock 'N Seal or Loctite 242 on existing nut, on the shock absorber stud. Using Strut Nut Wrench, tighten nut to 40 ft. lbs. (54 Nm).

8. Remove the support from the lower control arm outboard end.

9. Remove the support and lower the vehicle.

4X4

1. Raise and support the vehicle.

2. Remove the tire and wheel assembly.

3. Support the lower control arm outboard end.

4. Remove the three upper shock nuts.

5. Remove the lower shock bolt and nut.

6. Remove the caliper adapter with the caliper, then remove the rotor. See "BRAKES" section.

7. Disconnect the wheel speed sensor wiring from the knuckle and upper control arm.

8. Remove the upper ball joint retaining nut and separate the upper ball joint from the knuckle using Ball Joint Remover (9360 or equivalent).

9. Remove the stabilizer link lower nut.

10. Remove the axle hub nut.

11. Remove the shock assembly.

To install:

12. Install the shock back in place in the vehicle:

a. Install the upper part of the shock into the frame bracket.

b. Install the upper nuts and tighten to 45 ft. lbs. (61 Nm).

c. Install the lower part of the shock into the lower control arm shock bushing.

d. Install and position bolt so head of bolt is facing rearward of vehicle and hand start nut. Tighten the bolt and nut to 155 ft. lbs. (210 Nm).

13. Install the upper ball joint to the knuckle and install the retaining nut and tighten to 40 ft. lbs. (54 Nm), plus an additional 200 degrees.

14. Install the axle hub nut and tighten to 185 ft. lbs. (251 Nm).

15. Install the stabilizer link lower nut and tighten to 75 ft. lbs. (102 Nm).

16. Reconnect the wheel speed sensor wiring to the knuckle and upper control arm.

17. Install the rotor and the caliper adapter with the caliper. See "BRAKES" section.

18. Remove the support from the lower control arm outboard end.

19. Install the tire and wheel assembly.

20. Remove the support and lower the vehicle.

With Coil & Link Suspension

1. Remove the nut, retainer and grommet from the upper stud in the engine compartment.
2. Remove three nuts from the upper shock bracket.
3. Remove the lower bolt from the axle bracket . Remove the shock absorber from engine compartment.

To install:

4. Position the lower retainer and grommet on the upper stud. Insert the shock absorber through the spring from engine compartment.
5. Install the lower bolt and tighten to 100 ft. lbs. (136 Nm).
6. Install the upper shock bracket and three nuts and tighten nuts to 55 ft. lbs. (75 Nm).
7. Install upper grommet and retainer. Install upper shock nut and tighten to 40 ft. lbs. (54 Nm).

STABILIZER BAR

REMOVAL & INSTALLATION

With Independent Front Suspension

1. Remove the stabilizer bar link upper nuts and remove the retainers and grommets.
2. Remove the stabilizer bar mounting bolts and discard the mounting bolts.
3. Remove the retainers from the frame crossmember and remove the bar.
4. If necessary, remove the bushings from the stabilizer bar. Do not cut the old bushings off the stabilizer bar use a mixture of soapy water in order to aid in sliding the bushing off.

To install:

➡To service the stabilizer bar the vehicle must be on a drive on hoist. The vehicle suspension must be at curb height for stabilizer bar installation.

5. If the bushings were removed, Clean the bar and install the bushings on the stabilizer bar using a mixture of soapy water or equivalent in order to slide the bushing over the bar with ease. Do not cut the new bushing for installation.
6. Install new mounting bolts Do not reuse old bolts.
7. Check the alignment of the bar to ensure there is no interference with the either frame rail or chassis component. Spacing should be equal on both sides.
8. Position the stabilizer bar on the frame crossmember brackets and install the bracket bolts finger-tight.
9. Install the stabilizer bar to the stabilizer link and install the grommets and retainers.
10. Install the nuts to the stabilizer link and tighten to 20 ft. lbs. (27 Nm).
11. Tighten the brackets to the frame to 43 ft. lbs. (59 Nm).

With Coil & Link Suspension

1. Raise and support the vehicle.
2. Hold the stabilizer link shafts with a wrench and remove the link nuts at the stabilizer bar.
3. Remove the retainers and grommets from the stabilizer bar links.
4. Remove the stabilizer bar clamps from the frame rails and remove the stabilizer bar.

To install:

5. Position the stabilizer bar on the frame rail and install the clamps and bolts. Ensure the bar is centered with equal spacing on both sides.
6. Tighten the clamp bolts to 45 ft. lbs. (61 Nm).
7. Install links, retainers, grommets and nuts to the stabilizer bar. Hold the link shaft with a wrench and tighten the nuts to 27 ft. lbs. (38 Nm).
8. Remove the supports and lower the vehicle.

STABILIZER BAR LINK

REMOVAL & INSTALLATION

With Independent Front Suspension

See Figure 103.

➡It may be necessary to remove the other stabilizer link upper nut in order to remove the link being worked on from the vehicle.

1. Raise and support the vehicle.
2. Remove the lower nut.
3. Remove the upper nut, retainers and grommets.
4. Remove the stabilizer link from the vehicle.

To install:

5. Install the stabilizer link to the vehicle.
6. Install the lower nut and tighten to 75 ft. lbs. (102 Nm).
7. Install the retainers, grommets and upper nut and tighten to 20 ft. lbs. (27 Nm).
8. Remove the support and lower the vehicle.

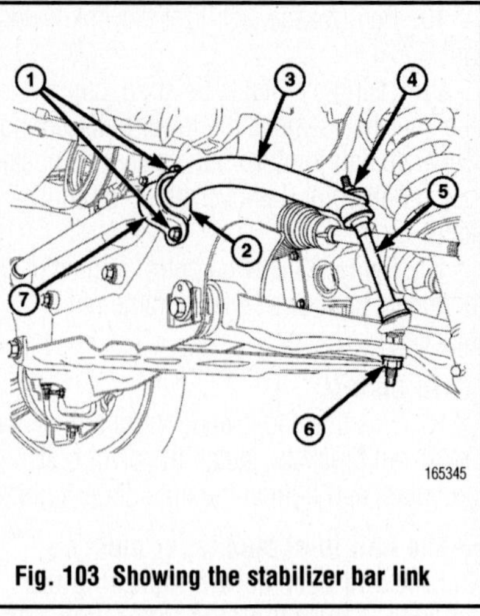

Fig. 103 Showing the stabilizer bar link

With Coil & Link Suspension

1. Raise and support the vehicle.
2. Hold the stabilizer link shafts with a wrench and remove the link nuts at the stabilizer bar.
3. Remove the retainers and grommets from the stabilizer bar links.
4. Remove the stabilizer bar link nuts from the axle brackets.
5. Remove the links from the axle brackets with a suitable puller (C-3894-A or equivalent).

To install:

6. Install links to the axle bracket and tighten nut to specifications. Tighten to 110 ft. lbs. (149 Nm).
7. Install links, retainers, grommets and nuts to the stabilizer bar. Hold the link shaft with a wrench and tighten the nuts to 27 ft. lbs. (38 Nm).
8. Remove the supports and lower the vehicle.

STEERING KNUCKLE

REMOVAL & INSTALLATION

With Independent Front Suspension

See Figure 104.

1. Raise and support the vehicle.
2. Remove the wheel and tire assembly.
3. Remove the ABS wheel speed sensor, disconnecting the electrical harness as necessary to remove knuckle.
4. Remove the tie rod end nut from the ball stud.
5. Separate the tie rod ball stud from the knuckle with Ball Joint Remover (9360 or equivalent).
6. Remove the halfshaft nut (4X4 only).
7. Remove the upper ball joint nut. Separate the ball joint from the knuckle with the Ball Joint Remover.

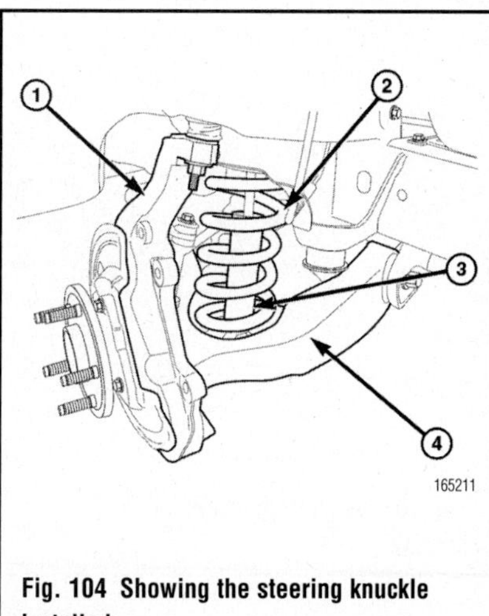

Fig. 104 Showing the steering knuckle installed

8. Support the outboard side of the lower control arm to support vehicle weight.
9. Remove the lower ball joint nut. Separate the ball joint from the knuckle with Ball Joint Remover (8677 or equivalent).
10. Remove the steering knuckle from the vehicle.
11. If required, remove the hub/bearing and dust shield from the knuckle.
12. Remove the three hub/bearing mounting bolts from the steering knuckle.
13. Slide the hub/bearing out of the steering knuckle.
14. Remove the brake dust shield.

To install:

➡The ball joint stud tapers must be CLEAN and DRY before installing the knuckle. Clean the stud tapers with a clean cloth to remove dirt and grease.

15. Install the brake dust shield and hub and bearing to the steering knuckle, position the speed sensor opening towards the front of the vehicle, and tighten the 3 bolts to 120 ft. lbs. (163 Nm).
16. Install the knuckle onto the upper and lower ball joints.
17. Install the upper and lower ball joint nuts and tighten to:
    - Upper control arm ball joint nut: 40 ft. lbs. (54 Nm), plus an additional 200 degrees
    - Lower control arm ball joint nut: 38 ft. lbs. (51 Nm), plus an additional 90 degrees
18. Remove the hydraulic jack from the lower control arm.
19. If a new tie rod end is to be installed, make sure the boot is properly lubricated.
20. Clean all old grease and debris from the boot with a clean cloth.
21. Apply outer tie rod grease (68088623AA or equivalent) to the tie rod end boot.
22. Install the tie rod end and tighten the nut to 45 ft. lbs. (61 Nm), plus an additional 90 degrees.
23. Install the front halfshaft into the hub and bearing. Install the halfshaft nut (if equipped) and tighten to 185 ft. lbs. (251 Nm).
24. Install the ABS wheel speed sensor and the caliper. See "BRAKES" section.
25. Install the wheel and tire assembly.
26. Remove the support and lower the vehicle.
27. Perform a wheel alignment.

With Coil & Link Suspension

1. Remove the hub bearing. See "Wheel Bearing & Hub" in this section.
2. Remove tie-rod or drag link end from the steering knuckle arm.
3. Remove the wheel speed sensor. See "BRAKES" section.
4. Loosen the upper ball stud nut.
5. Remove the lower ball joint nut.
6. Separate the lower ball joint from the control arm.
7. Remove the upper ball joint nut.
8. Remove the steering knuckle.

To install:

9. Position the steering knuckle on the ball studs.
10. Install and tighten lower ball stud nut to initial torque of 35 ft. lbs. (47 Nm).
11. Install and tighten upper ball stud nut to 70 ft. lbs. (94 Nm).
12. Re-torque lower ball stud nut to a final torque of 148 ft. lbs. (200 Nm).
13. Install the hub bearing. See "Wheel Bearing & Hub" in this section.
14. Install tie-rod or drag link end onto the steering knuckle arm and tighten to 200 ft. lbs. (271 Nm).
15. Install the wheel speed sensor See "BRAKES" section.

UPPER BALL JOINT

REMOVAL & INSTALLATION

With Independent Front Suspension

1. Raise vehicle and support the vehicle.
2. Remove the tire and wheel.
3. Remove the upper ball joint retaining nut.
4. Separate the upper ball joint from the knuckle using Ball Joint Remover (9360 or equivalent).
5. Remove the wheel speed sensor wire from the upper control arm.
6. Move the knuckle out of the way for access to remove the ball joint.
7. Remove the ball joint boot.

➡It may be necessary to install a block of wood between the control arm and frame bracket to allow clearance for the ball joint press tool.

⁂ CAUTION

Extreme pressure lubrication must be used on the threaded portions of the tool. This will increase the longevity of the tool and insure proper operation during the removal and installation process .

8. Remove the ball joint from the upper control arm using Ball Joint Press (C-4212F or equivalent) and Ball Joint Remover set (9770-1 and 9770-2 or equivalent).

To install:

9. Install the ball joint into the upper control arm and press in using Ball Joint Press and Ball Joint Installer Set.
10. Install the upper ball joint into the knuckle. Install the retaining nut and tighten to 40 ft. lbs. (54 Nm), plus an additional 200 degrees.
11. Install the wheel speed sensor wire to the upper control arm.
12. Install the tire and wheel.
13. Remove the supports and lower the vehicle.
14. Perform a wheel alignment.

With Coil & Link Suspension

1. Remove the steering knuckle. See "Steering Knuckle" in this section.
2. Remove the axle shaft from the axle. See "DRIVE TRAIN" section.
3. Position a suitable Ball Joint Remover/Installer tool assembly (6761, 8445-3 and C4212F or equivalent) to remove upper ball stud.
4. Installation is the reverse of the removal procedure.

UPPER CONTROL ARM

REMOVAL & INSTALLATION

With Independent Front Suspension

1. Raise and support the vehicle.
2. Remove wheel and tire assembly.
3. Remove the disc brake caliper adapter with the caliper, then remove the rotor. See "BRAKES" section.
4. Remove the wheel speed sensor wire from the upper control arm.
5. Remove the nut from upper ball joint.

➡When installing remover tool to separate the ball joint, be careful not to damage the ball joint seal.

6. Separate upper ball joint from the steering knuckle with Ball Joint Remover (9360 or equivalent).
7. Remove the control arm pivot bolts and flag nuts remove control arm.

To install:

8. Position the control arm into the frame brackets. Install bolt and nut, and tighten to 130 ft. lbs. (176 Nm).
9. Insert the upper control arm ball joint in the steering knuckle and tighten the upper ball joint nut to 40 ft. lbs. (54 Nm), plus an additional 200 degrees.
10. Install the rotor to the hub. Install the disc brake caliper and adapter to the knuckle. See "BRAKES" section.
11. Install the wheel speed sensor wire to the upper control arm.
12. Install the wheel and tire assembly.
13. Remove the support and lower vehicle.
14. Perform a wheel alignment.

With Coil & Link Suspension

Left

See Figure 105.

1. Raise and support the vehicle.

➡Discard the nuts and bolts and do not reuse. New nuts and bolts should be used when replacing or servicing the control arms.

2. Remove the upper control arm nut and bolt at the axle bracket.
3. Remove the nut and bolt at the frame rail and remove the upper control arm.

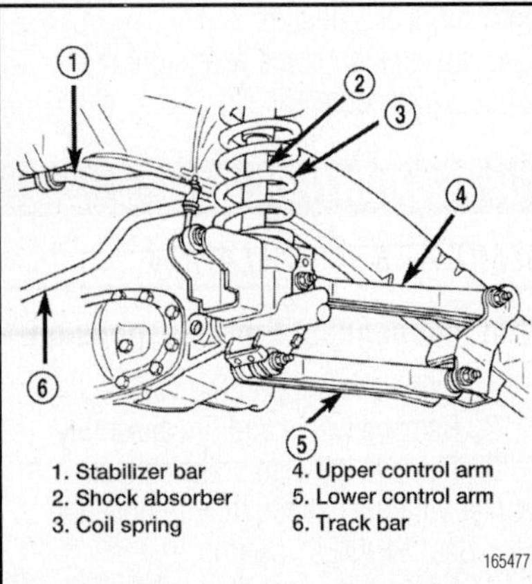

Fig. 105 Showing upper control arm and other suspension components

To install:

4. Position the upper control arm at the axle and frame rail.
5. Install the bolts and finger tighten the nuts.
6. Remove the supports and lower the vehicle.
7. Tighten nut at the axle bracket and frame bracket to 120 ft. lbs. (163 Nm).

Right

1. Raise and support the vehicle.
2. Support the axle.
3. Disconnect the exhaust system at the manifold(s).
4. Disconnect the exhaust bracket at the transmission.
5. Disconnect the rubber exhaust mounts for the exhaust.
6. Raise the exhaust system up and back in order to gain access to the removal of the upper bolt.

➡Discard the nuts and bolts and do not reuse. New nuts and bolts should be used when replacing or servicing the control arms.

7. Remove the nut and bolt at the frame rail and detach the upper control arm.
8. Remove the upper control arm nut and bolt at the axle bracket.
9. Remove the control arm from the vehicle.

To install:

10. Position the upper control arm at the axle and frame rail.
11. Install the bolts, then finger tighten the nuts.
12. Tighten nut at the axle bracket and frame bracket to 120 ft. lbs. (163 Nm).
13. Remove the support for the axle.
14. Install the exhaust system back into place.
15. Reconnect the rubber exhaust mounts.
16. Reconnect the exhaust at the manifold(s).
17. Reconnect the exhaust bracket at the transmission.
18. Remove the supports and lower the vehicle.

WHEEL HUB & BEARING

REMOVAL & INSTALLATION

With Independent Front Suspension

4X2

See Figure 106.

1. Raise and support the vehicle.
2. Remove the wheel and tire assembly.

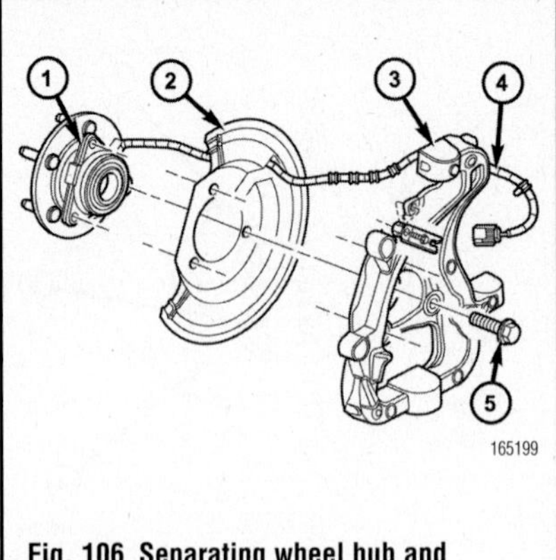

Fig. 106 Separating wheel hub and bearing

3. Remove the brake caliper and rotor. See "BRAKES" section.
4. Remove the ABS wheel speed sensor.
5. Remove the three hub and bearing mounting bolts from the steering knuckle.
6. Slide the hub and bearing out of the steering knuckle.
7. Remove the brake dust shield.

To install:

8. Install the brake dust shield.
9. Install the hub and bearing into the steering knuckle and tighten the bolts to 120 ft. lbs. (163 Nm).
10. Install the brake rotor and caliper. See "BRAKES" section.
11. Install the ABS wheel speed sensor.
12. Install the wheel and tire assembly.
13. Remove the support and lower vehicle.

4X4

1. Install the brake dust shield.
2. Install the hub/bearing into the steering knuckle and tighten the bolts to 120 ft. lbs. (163 Nm).
3. Install the brake rotor and caliper. See "BRAKES" section.
4. Install the ABS wheel speed sensor.
5. Install the upper ball joint nut to the steering knuckle and tighten to 40 ft. lbs. (54 Nm), plus an additional 200 degrees.
6. Install the tie rod end nut to the steering knuckle and tighten to 45 ft. lbs. (61 Nm), plus an additional 90 degrees.
7. Install the halfshaft nut and tighten to 185 ft. lbs. (251 Nm).
8. Install the wheel and tire assembly.
9. Remove the support and lower vehicle.

With Coil & Link Suspension

See Figure 107.

1. Raise and support the vehicle.
2. Remove the wheel and tire assembly.

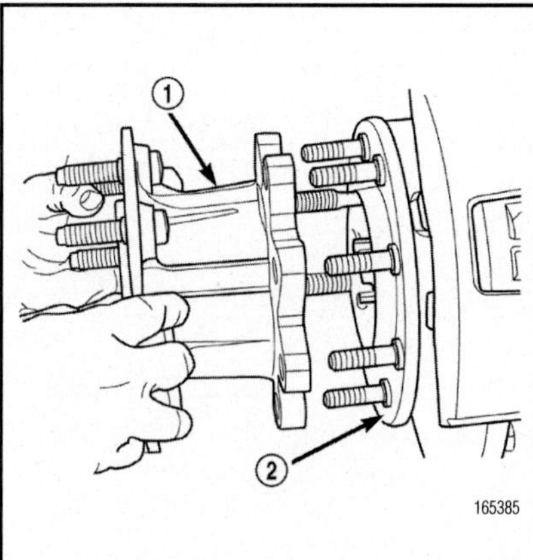

Fig. 107 Removing hub extension (1) from rotor (2)—3500

3. Remove the hub extension mounting nuts and remove the extension from the rotor if equipped.

4. Remove the brake caliper. See "BRAKES" section.

5. Remove the cotter pin and the hub nut from the axle shaft.

6. Remove the caliper adapter and the disc brake rotor. See "BRAKES" section.

7. Disconnect the wheel speed sensor wire.

8. Remove the hub/bearing 4 mounting bolts and remove the hub and bearing.

To install:

9. Install the hub/bearing to the knuckle and tighten the hub/bearing bolts to 149 ft. lbs. (202 Nm).

10. Install the hub nut and tighten to 132 ft. lbs. (179 Nm), rotate hub 5–10 times, then tighten nut to 263 ft. lbs. (256 Nm).

11. Install the wheel speed sensor to the hub.

12. Install the disc brake rotor and caliper adapter with the caliper. See "BRAKES" section.

13. On 3500, install the hub extension and nuts to the front rotor and tighten nuts to 96 ft. lbs. (130 Nm).

14. Install the wheel and tire assemblies.

15. Remove the support and lower the vehicle.

16. Apply the brakes several times to seat the brake shoes and caliper piston. Do not move the vehicle until a firm brake pedal is obtained.

SUSPENSION

REAR SUSPENSION

COIL SPRING

REMOVAL & INSTALLATION

1. Raise and support the vehicle.

2. Support the axle with a suitable holding fixture.

3. Remove the shock lower bolt and nut.

CAUTION

Lower the axle carefully and avoid putting stress on the flexible brake line.

4. Lower the axle support and tilt the axel to remove the spring and isolator from the vehicle.

To install:

➡All torques should be made with the full vehicle weight on the ground being supported by the tires.

5. Position spring and isolator on the axle and align into the spring upper pocket.

6. Carefully raise the rear axle into place.

7. Install the shock lower bolt and nut, and do not tighten.

8. Remove the holding fixture for the rear axle.

9. Remove the support and lower the vehicle.

10. Tighten shock lower bolt and nut to 100 ft. lbs. (136 Nm).

LEAF SPRING

REMOVAL & INSTALLATION

See Figures 108 and 109.

➡Two types of shackles are used for different vehicle applications. There are tension shackles and compression shackles. A tension shackle sits on its frame mounting bracket (spring above), and a compression shackle hangs from its mounting bracket (spring below. The tension type shackle must be removed with the spring.

1. Raise and support the vehicle.

2. Support the axle with a suitable holding fixture.

3. Remove the nuts, spring clamp bolts and the plate that attach the spring to the axle.

4. Remove the nuts and bolts from the spring front eye to frame.

5. For a tension type shackle only, remove the shackle to mounting bracket bolt and flag nut.

6. For a compression type shackle only, remove the spring eye to shackle bolt and nut.

7. Remove the spring from the vehicle.

8. Remove and transfer any necessary components.

To install:

9. Position spring on axle shaft tube so spring center bolt is inserted into the locating hole in the axle tube.

10. Align the front of the spring with the bolt hole in the front bracket. Install the eye pivot bolt and nut

11. Do not tighten.

12. For a compression type shackle only, align the spring to the shackle and install the spring eye to shackle bolt and nut. Do not tighten,

13. For a tension type shackle only, align the shackle to the mounting bracket and install the shackle to mounting bracket bolt and flag nut. Do not tighten.

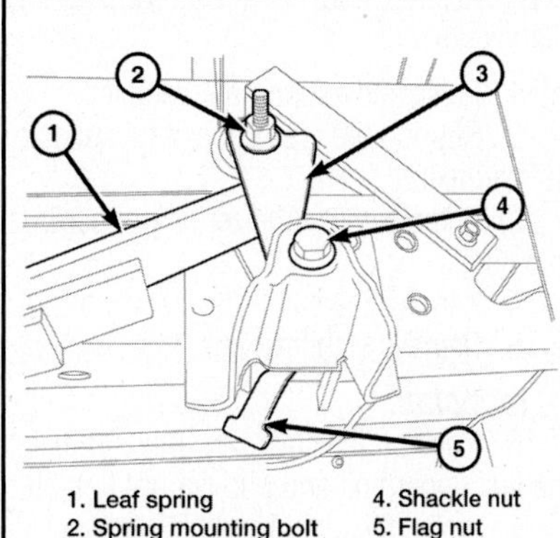

Fig. 108 For a tension type shackle only, remove the shackle to mounting bracket bolt and flag nut.

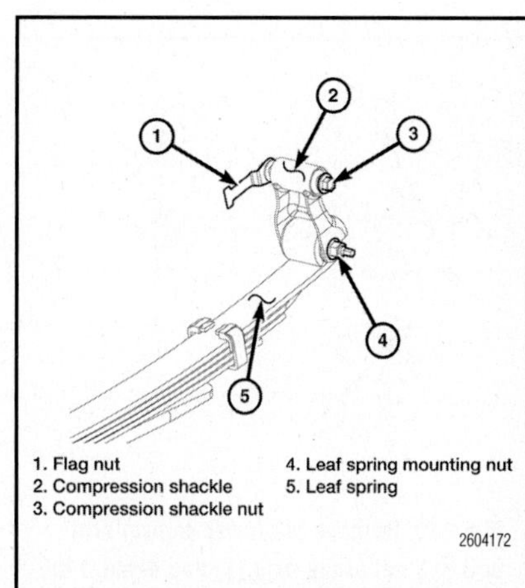

Fig. 109 For a compression type shackle only, remove the spring eye to shackle bolt and nut.

14. Install the spring clamp bolts, plate and the retaining nuts.
15. Remove the holding fixture for the rear axle.
16. Remove the supports and lower the vehicle so that the weight is being supported by the tires.
17. Tighten the spring clamp retaining nuts, spring front and rear pivot nuts, and the shackle nut/bolts as follows:
- Spring clamp U-bolt nuts: 110 ft. lbs. (149 Nm)
- Spring front nut/bolt to frame: 254 ft. lbs. (345 Nm)
- Spring shackle nut/bolt, upper and lower: 160 ft. lbs. (217 Nm)

LOWER CONTROL ARM

REMOVAL & INSTALLATION

See Figure 110.

1. Raise and support the vehicle.
2. Support the rear axle with a suitable holding fixture.
3. Remove the parking brake cable guide bolt (left side only).
4. Remove the lower control arm bolt and nut at the axle and discard the nut.
5. Remove the lower control arm bolt and nut at the frame.
6. Remove the lower control arm from the vehicle.

To install:

7. The small bushing attaches to the frame and the large bushing to the axle.
8. Install the lower control arm to the vehicle.
9. Install the lower control arm bolt with a new nut at the axle. Do not tighten.
10. Install the lower control arm bolt and nut at the frame. Do not tighten.
11. Position the parking brake cable guide (left side only), install the guide bolt and tighten to 15 ft. lbs. (20 Nm).
12. Remove the holding fixture supporting the axle.
13. Remove the support and lower the vehicle.
14. Tighten the lower control arm bolts to 225 ft. lbs. (305 Nm).

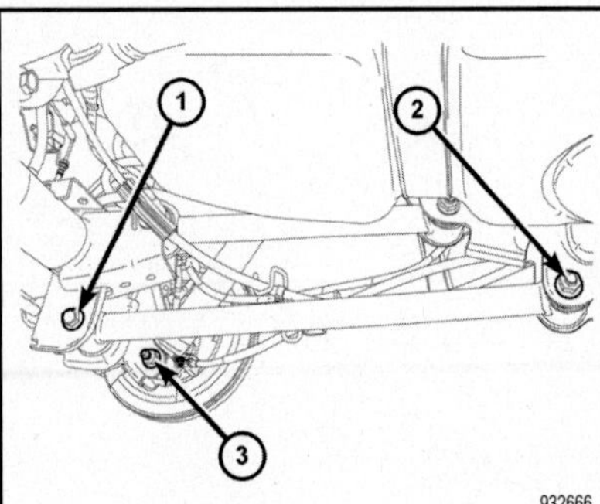

Fig. 110 Remove the lower control arm bolt and nut at the axle (1) and discard the nut. Remove the lower control arm bolt and nut at the frame (2). Parking brake cable bolt (3).

STABILIZER BAR

REMOVAL & INSTALLATION

1. Raise and support vehicle.
2. Remove both stabilizer bar link lower mounting nuts.
3. Remove stabilizer bar retainer bolts and retainers.
4. Remove stabilizer bar.
5. Remove and transfer the bushings if necessary.

To install:

6. Install stabilizer bar bushings.
7. Install the stabilizer bar and center it with equal spacing on both sides.
8. Install stabilizer bar retainers and bolts. Do not tighten.
9. Install the stabilizer bar links on the stabilizer bar and install link lower mounting nuts. Do not tighten.
10. Remove the support and lower the vehicle.
11. Tighten the stabilizer bar retainers to:
- Stabilizer bar to axle bolts/nuts: 37 ft. lbs. (50 Nm)
- Stabilizer bar link to frame bolts/nuts: 56 ft. lbs. (75 Nm)
- Stabilizer bar link to stabilizer bar nut: 79 ft. lbs. (107 Nm)

STABILIZER BAR LINK

REMOVAL & INSTALLATION

See Figure 111.

1. Raise and support the vehicle.
2. Support the rear axle with a suitable holding fixture.
3. Remove the stabilizer link upper bolt and nut.
4. Remove the stabilizer link lower nut.
5. Remove stabilizer link.

To install:

6. Position the stabilizer link and install the link upper bolt and nut. Do not tighten.
7. Install the stabilizer link lower nut. Do not tighten.
8. Remove the holding fixture supporting the axle.
9. Remove the support and lower the vehicle.

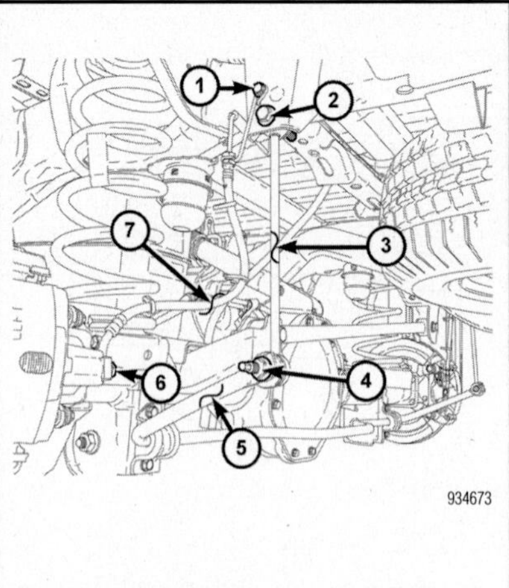

Fig. 111 Showing the stabilizer bar link and related components.

10. Tighten stabilizer link retainers to:
- Upper bolt and nut: 56 ft. lbs. (75 Nm)
- Lower nut: 79 ft. lbs. (107 Nm)

SHOCK ABSORBER

REMOVAL & INSTALLATION

1. Raise and support the vehicle.
2. Support the rear axle with a suitable holding fixture.
3. Remove the shock upper bolt and nut.
4. Remove the shock lower bolt and nut.
5. Remove the shock absorber from the vehicle.
6. Installation is the reverse of the removal procedure.
7. Tighten bolts and nuts to 100 ft. lbs. (136 Nm).

TRACK BAR

REMOVAL & INSTALLATION

1. Raise and support the vehicle.
2. Support the rear axle with a suitable holding fixture.
3. Remove the track bar bolt/nut from the frame bracket.
4. Remove the track bar bolt/nut from the axle bracket.
5. Remove the track bar.

To install:

6. Position the track bar onto the vehicle.
7. Install the track bar bolt and nut in the frame bracket. Do not tighten.
8. Install the track bar bolt and nut in the axle bracket. Do not tighten.
9. Remove the holding fixture supporting the axle.
10. Remove the supports and lower the vehicle.

11. Tighten the track bar mounting bolts/nuts to 129 ft. lbs. (175 Nm).

UPPER CONTROL ARM

REMOVAL & INSTALLATION

1. Raise and support the vehicle.
2. Support the rear axle with a suitable holding fixture.
3. Remove the upper control arm bolt and nut at the axle and discard the nut.
4. Remove the upper control arm front bolt and nut at the frame.
5. Remove the upper control arm from the vehicle.

To install:

➡The small bushing attaches to the axel and the large bushing to the frame.

6. Position the upper control arm to the vehicle.
7. Install the upper control arm bolt and nut at the frame. Do not tighten.
8. Install the upper control arm bolt with a new nut at the axle. Do not tighten.
9. Remove the holding fixture supporting the axle.
10. Remove the support and lower the vehicle.
11. Tighten the upper control arm bolts/nuts to 225 ft. lbs. (305 Nm).

WHEEL BEARINGS

REMOVAL & INSTALLATION

With 10 1/2 AA

1. Remove rear axle shaft. See "DRIVE TRAIN" section.
2. Remove axle shaft seal from axle tube with a small pry bar.

➡The seal and bearing can be removed at the same time with the bearing removal tool.

3. Remove axle shaft bearing with Bearing Remover and Foot (6310 and 6310-9 or equivalent).

To install:

4. Wipe axle tube bore clean and remove any old sealer or burrs from the tube.
5. Install axle shaft bearing with Installer and Handle (C-4198 and C4171 or equivalent). Drive bearing in until tool contacts the axle tube.

➡Bearing is installed with the bearing part number against the installer.

6. Coat lip of the new axle seal with axle lubricant and install with Installer and Handle (C-4076-B and C-4735).
7. Install the axle shaft. See "DRIVE TRAIN" section.
8. Install differential cover and fill with gear lubricant to the bottom of the fill plug hole.

With 11 1/2 AA

1. Remove axle shaft flange bolts and remove shaft. See "DRIVE TRAIN" section.
2. Remove retainer ring from the axle shaft tube.
3. Remove hub bearing nut locking key from the axle tube.
4. Remove hub bearing nut with a proper socket (8954 or equivalent).
5. Remove hub and bearings from the axle.
6. Pry out hub bearing seal from the back of the hub.

➡The inner part of the seal may stay on the axle tube. This part must also be removed with a pry tool.

7. Remove the rear bearing.
8. Remove the hub bearing cups with a hammer and drift.

To install:

9. Install outer hub bearing cup with proper bearing installer set (8961 and C-4171 or equivalent).
10. Install inner hub bearing cup with proper installer (8153 and C-4171 or equivalent).
11. Pack bearings with the appropriate wheel bearing grease.
12. Install rear bearing and install new grease seal with a proper bearing installer (8963 and C-4171 or equivalent).
13. Slide hub on the axle tube and install front bearing into the hub.
14. Install hub bearing nut with and tighten with torque wrench to 22 ft. lbs. (30 Nm) while rotating the hub.
15. Back off the nut about 30 degrees and align next hub nut key slot with axle tube key slot and install locking key.
16. Measure the end-play of the axle shaft. End play should be 0.010 in. (0.025 mm).
17. Install retainer ring with ring end in the key slot.
18. Install new axle shaft gasket and install the axle shaft. See "DRIVE TRAIN" section.

With 302RBI

1. Remove axle bolts from axle flange.
2. Remove axle shaft from axle. See "DRIVE TRAIN" section for more information.
3. With a socket (10051 or equivalent), remove the hub nut with the integrated lock washer from the hub spindle.
4. Install a hub/rotor guide (10064 or equivalent) into the hub spindle. Slide the hub/rotor assembly, with bearings, off the hub spindle and hub/rotor guide.
5. Remove the outer bearing from hub.
6. Remove the hub seal from the back of the hub with a seal puller.
7. Remove the inner bearing from the hub.
8. Remove the outer bearing cup from the hub with a hammer and brass drift.
9. Remove the inner bearing cup from the hub with a hammer and brass drift.

To install:

10. Install outer hub bearing cup with a proper installer (10052 and C-4171 or equivalent).
11. Install inner hub bearing cup with proper installer (10049 and C-4171 or equivalent).
12. Lubricate and install inner hub bearing into hub.
13. Install hub seal with seal installer (10053 and C-4171).
14. Lubricate and install outer hub bearing into hub.
15. Install hub/rotor guide (10064 or equivalent) into the axle spindle.
16. Install the hub/rotor over the guide tool and onto the axle spindle.

⁂ CAUTION

Never support hub with just the inner bearing and seal. Failure to follow these instruction will result in damaging the hub seal.

17. Remove the guide tool from the axle spindle.
18. Install hub bearing nut with integrated lock washer. The integrated lock washer tab must be aligned with the spindle keyway.
19. Tighten the hub nut with a proper socket to 70 ft. lbs. (95 Nm) while rotating the hub. Then back off nut 90 degrees and retighten nut to 30 ft. lbs. (41 Nm).

➡This will set hub to zero end-play.

20. Install new O-ring on axle flange.

21. Install axle shaft into the hub and axle housing.
22. Install axle bolts through the axle flange and tighten to 98 ft. lbs. (133 Nm).
23. Remove the fill plug, from the right side of the carrier.
24. With the axle level, fill the carrier with lubricant to the bottom of the fill plug hole.
25. Install the fill plug and tighten to 50 ft. lbs. (68 Nm).

WHEEL HUB OIL FILL

CAUTION

Wheel hub cavities must be filled with lubricant before using the axle. Failure to follow these instructions will result in hub bearing damage.

1. Raise the right end of axle six inches. Hold in this position for one minute to fill left hub with lubricant. Then, lower the axle.
2. Raise the left end of the axle six inches. Hold in this position for one minute to fill the right hub with lubricant. Lower the axle.
3. Remove the fill plug from the right side of the carrier.
4. With axle level, fill carrier with lubricant to the bottom of the fill plug hole.

➡Axle will require approximately 40 oz, (1.18 L) of additional lubricant.

5. Install the fill plug and tighten to 50 ft. lbs. (68 Nm).

JEEP

Wrangler

17

SPECIFICATIONS AND MAINTENANCE CHARTS

ENGINE AND VEHICLE IDENTIFICATION

Engine							Model Year	
Code ①	Liters (cc)	Cu. In.	Cyl.	Fuel Sys.	Engine Type	Eng. Mfg.	Code ②	Year
1	3.8 (3778)	231	V6	SMPI	OHV	Chrysler LLC	A	2010
							B	2011

① 8th position of VIN

② 10th position of VIN

25766_WRAN_C0001

GENERAL ENGINE SPECIFICATIONS

All measurements are given in inches.

Year	Model	Engine Displacement Liters (cc)	Engine ID/VIN	Fuel System Type	Net Horsepower @ rpm	Net Torque @ rpm (ft. lbs.)	Bore x Stroke (in.)	Com-pression Ratio	Oil Pressure @ rpm
2010	Wrangler	3.8 (3778)	1	SMPI	202 ①	237 ①	3.78x3.43	9.6:1	30-80@3000
2011	Wrangler	3.8 (3778)	1	SMPI	202 ①	237 ①	3.78x3.43	9.6:1	30-80@3000

① No rpm specification given.

25766_WRAN_C0002

ENGINE TUNE-UP SPECIFICATIONS

Year	Engine Displacement Liters	Engine ID/VIN	Spark Plug Gap (in.)	Ignition Timing (deg.)		Fuel Pump (psi)	Idle Speed (rpm)		Valve Clearance	
				MT	AT		MT	AT	Intake	Exhaust
2010	3.8	1	0.048-0.053	①	①	56-60	②	②	0.032-0.038	0.061-0.067
2011	3.8	1	0.048-0.053	①	①	56-60	②	②	0.032-0.038	0.061-0.067

① The 3.8L V-6 engine uses a fixed ignition timing system. Basic ignition timing is not adjustable. All spark advance is determined by the PCM.

② Idle speed is maintained by the Powertrain Control Module. No adjustment is required.

25766_WRAN_C0003

CAPACITIES

Year	Model	Engine Displacement Liters	Engine ID/VIN	Engine Oil with Filter	Transmission/axle (pts.) Auto.	Transmission/axle (pts.) Manual	Drive Axle (pts.) Front	Drive Axle (pts.) Rear	Transfer Case (pts.)	Fuel Tank (gal.)	Cooling System (qts.)
2010	Wrangler	3.8	1	6.0 qts.	①	3.2 ②	③	4.75	4.2 ②	④	13.0
2011	Wrangler	3.8	1	6.0 qts.	①	3.2 ②	③	4.75	4.2 ②	④	13.0

NOTE: All capacities are approximate. Add fluid gradually and ensure a proper fluid level is obtained.

① Service fill: 8.0 pts.
Overhaul fill: 17.6 pts.

② Approximate amount shown; fill to bottom of fill hole.

③ Model 30: 2.1 pts.
Model 40: 2.7 pts.

④ 2-door model: 18.5 gal.
4-door model: 22.5 gal.

25766_WRAN_C0004

FLUID SPECIFICATIONS

Year	Model	Engine Disp. Liters	Engine Oil	Manual Trans.	Auto. Trans.	Drive Axle Front	Drive Axle Rear	Transfer Case	Power Steering Fluid	Brake Master Cylinder	Cooling System
2010	Wrangler	3.8	5W-20	Mopar® M/T Lubricant	ATF+4	80W-90	80W-90	AFT+4	ATF+4	DOT3	①
2011	Wrangler	3.8	5W-20	Mopar® M/T Lubricant	ATF+4	80W-90	80W-90	AFT+4	ATF+4	DOT3	①

DOT: Department Of Transpotation

① Mopar Antifreeze/Coolant 5 Year/100,000 Mile Formula HOAT (Hybrid Organic Additive Technology)

25766_WRAN_C0005

VALVE SPECIFICATIONS

Year	Engine Displacement Liters	Engine ID/VIN	Seat Angle (deg.)	Face Angle (deg.)	Spring Test Pressure (lbs. @ in.)	Spring Free-Length (in.)	Spring Installed Height (in.)	Stem-to-Guide Clearance (in.) Intake	Stem-to-Guide Clearance (in.) Exhaust	Stem Diameter (in.) Intake	Stem Diameter (in.) Exhaust
2010	3.8	1	44.5-45.0	45.0-45.5	①	2.020	1.61-1.68	0.001-0.0025	0.002-0.0037	0.2718-0.2725	0.2718-0.2725
2011	3.8	1	44.5-45.0	45.0-45.5	①	2.020	1.61-1.68	0.001-0.0025	0.002-0.0037	0.2718-0.2725	0.2718-0.2725

① With valve closed: 84.6-95.4 lbs. @ 1.65 in.
With valve open: 199.0-221.0 @ 1.22 in.

25766_WRAN_C0006

CAMSHAFT SPECIFICATIONS

All measurements in inches unless noted

Year	Engine Displacement Liters	Engine Code/VIN	Journal Diameter	Brg. Oil Clearance	Shaft End-play	Runout	Journal Bore	Lobe Height Intake	Lobe Height Exhaust
2010	3.8	1	①	0.001-0.004	0.010-0.020	N/A	N/A	N/A	N/A
2011	3.8	1	①	0.001-0.004	0.010-0.020	N/A	N/A	N/A	N/A

N/A: Information not available.

① Journal #1: 1.997-1.999 in.

Journal #2: 1.9809-1.9829 in.

Journal #3: 1.9659-1.9679 in.

Journal #4: 1.9499-1.9520 in.

25766_WRAN_C0007

CRANKSHAFT AND CONNECTING ROD SPECIFICATIONS

All measurements are given in inches.

Year	Engine Displacement Liters	Engine ID/VIN	Crankshaft Main Brg. Journal Dia.	Crankshaft Main Brg. Oi Clearance	Crankshaft Shaft End-play	Crankshaft Thrust on No.	Connecting Rod Journal Diameter	Connecting Rod Oil Clearance	Connecting Rod Side Clearance
2010	3.8	1	2.5192-2.5202	0.0005-0.0022	0.0036-0.0095	N/A	2.2829-2.2837	0.0007-0.0026	0.005-0.016
2011	3.8	1	2.5192-2.5202	0.0005-0.0022	0.0036-0.0095	N/A	2.2829-2.2837	0.0007-0.0026	0.005-0.016

25766_WRAN_C0008

PISTON & RING SPECIFICATIONS

All measurements are given in inches.

Year	Engine Displacement Liters	Engine ID/VIN	Piston Clearance	Ring Gap Top Compression	Ring Gap Bottom Compression	Ring Gap Oil Control	Ring Side Clearance Top Compression	Ring Side Clearance Bottom Compression	Ring Side Clearance Oil Control
2010	3.8	1	-0.0002 – 0.0015	0.008-0.014	0.012-0.022	0.010-0.030	0.0012-0.0027	0.0016-0.0033	0.0006-0.0089
2011	3.8	1	-0.0002 – 0.0015	0.008-0.014	0.012-0.022	0.010-0.030	0.0012-0.0027	0.0016-0.0033	0.0006-0.0089

25766_WRAN_C0009

TORQUE SPECIFICATIONS

All readings in ft. lbs.

Year	Engine Disp. Liters	Engine ID/VIN	Cylinder Head Bolts	Main Bearing Bolts	Rod Bearing Bolts	Crankshaft Damper Bolts	Flywheel Bolts	Manifold Intake	Manifold Exhaust	Spark Plugs	Oil Pan Drain Plug
2010	3.8	1	①	②	③	40	65	④	17	12	20
2011	3.8	1	①	②	③	40	65	④	17	12	20

① Sequence, bolt identification and torque settings are found in "ENGINE MECHANICAL" section.

② Main bearing bolts: 30 ft. lbs., plus 90 degrees

Main bearing cap cross bolts: 45 ft. lbs.

③ Step 1: 5 ft. lbs.

Step 2: 21 ft. lbs.

Step 3: additional 90 degrees.

② Lower bolts: 200 inch lbs.

Lower gasket retainer bolts: 105 inch lbs.

Upper bolts: 105 inch lbs.

25766_WRAN_C0010

WHEEL ALIGNMENT

Year	Model		Caster Range (+/-Deg.)	Caster Preferred Setting (Deg.)	Camber Range (+/-Deg.)	Camber Preferred Setting (Deg.)	Toe-in (in.)
2010	Wrangler	F	①	①	-0.62 to +0.12	②	③
		R	NA	NA	0.0 to -0.50	-0.25	④
2011	Wrangler	F	①	①	-0.62 to +0.12	②	③
		R	NA	NA	0.0 to -0.50	-0.25	④

NA: Information not available

① Left side preferred setting: +4.2 degrees.

Left side range: +3.2 to +5.2 degrees.

Right side preferred setting: +4.4 degrees.

Right side range: +3.4 to +5.4 degrees.

Cross caster (max. side-to-side difference) preferred: -0.2 degrees

Cross caster (max. side-to-side difference) range: -0.7 to +0.3 degrees

② Preferred setting (fixed angle): -0.25

Cross camber (max. side-to-side difference): +/- 0.5 degrees.

③ Preferred setting: +0.20

Range: +0.17 to +0.23 degrees

④ Preferred setting: +0.25 degrees

Range: 0.0 to -0.50 degrees

25766_WRAN_C0011

TIRE, WHEEL & BALL JOINT SPECIFICATIONS

Year	Model	OEM Tires		Tire Pressures (psi)		Wheel	Ball Joint	Lug Nut
		Standard	Optional	Front	Rear	Size	Inspection	(ft. lbs.)
2010	Wrangler	①	①	②	②	③	N/A	92-132 ④
2011	Wrangler	①	①	②	②	③	N/A	92-132 ④

OEM: Original Equipment Manufacturer

PSI: Pounds Per Square Inch

NA: Information not available

① Available sizes (standard and optional)

P225/75R16

P245/75R16

P255/75R17

P255/70R18

LT255/75R17

② Dependent on tire size; consult Owner's Manual or door jamb plate.

③ Dependent on corresponding tire size.

④ Standard lug nut 1/2 X 20 with 60 degree cone

25766_WRAN_C0012

BRAKE SPECIFICATIONS

All measurements in inches unless noted

Year	Model		Brake Disc			Brake Drum Diameter			Minimum Pad/Lining Thickness		Brake Caliper	
			Original Thickness	Minimum Thickness	Max. Runout	Original Inside Diameter	Max. Wear Limit	Maximum Machine Diamter	Front	Rear	Bracket Bolts (ft. lbs.)	Mounting Bolts (ft. lbs.)
2010	Wrangler	F	N/A	1.049	0.0008	NA	NA	NA	0.040	---	120	26
		R	N/A	0.409	0.0008	NA	N A	NA	---	0.040	77	18
2011	Wrangler	F	N/A	1.049	0.0008	NA	NA	NA	0.040	---	120	26
		R	N/A	0.409	0.0008	NA	N A	NA	---	0.040	77	18

F: Front

R: Rear

NA: Information not available

25766_WRAN_C0013

SCHEDULED MAINTENANCE INTERVALS

2011 Jeep Wrangler - Normal

TO BE SERVICED	TYPE OF SERVICE	VEHICLE MILEAGE INTERVAL (x1000)												
		6	12	18	24	30	36	42	48	54	60	66	72	78
Engine oil & filter	Replace	✓	✓	✓	✓	✓	✓	✓	✓	✓	✓	✓	✓	✓
Rotate tires, inspect tread wear, measure tread depth and check pressure	Rotate/Inspect	✓	✓	✓	✓	✓	✓	✓	✓	✓	✓	✓	✓	✓
Brake system components	Inspect/Service						✓		✓		✓		✓	
Exhaust system & heat shields	Inspect		✓		✓				✓		✓			
Inspect the front suspension, tie rod ends and boot seals for cracks or leaks and all parts for damage, wear, improper looseness or end play.	Inspect		✓		✓		✓		✓		✓		✓	
CV Joints	Inspect		✓		✓		✓		✓		✓		✓	
Front & rear axle fluid	Inspect			✓			✓			✓			✓	
Engine air filter	Replace					✓					✓			
Adjust parking brake on vehicles equipped with four-wheel disc brakes.	Adjust					✓					✓			
Engine coolant	Flush/Replace										✓			
Accessory drive belts	Replace	Every 120,000 miles												
Spark plugs and ignition wires	Replace	Every 102,000 miles												
PVC valve	Replace	Every 90,000 miles												
Automatic transmission fluid & filter	Replace	Every 120,000 miles												
Fluid levels (all)	Top off	✓	✓	✓	✓	✓	✓	✓	✓	✓	✓	✓	✓	✓
Horn, exterior lamps, turn signals and hazard warning light operation	Inspect	✓	✓	✓	✓	✓	✓	✓	✓	✓	✓	✓	✓	✓
Transfer case fluid	Inspect					✓					✓			
Transfer case fluid	Replace	Every 120,000 miles												
Battery	Inspect/Service	✓	✓	✓	✓	✓	✓	✓	✓	✓	✓	✓	✓	✓

25766_WRAN_C0014

SCHEDULED MAINTENANCE INTERVALS

2011 Jeep Wrangler - Severe

		VEHICLE MILEAGE INTERVAL (x1000)												
TO BE SERVICED	TYPE OF SERVICE	6	12	18	24	30	36	42	48	54	60	66	72	78
Engine oil & filter	Replace	✓	✓	✓	✓	✓	✓	✓	✓	✓	✓	✓	✓	✓
Rotate tires, inspect tread wear, measure tread depth and check pressure	Rotate/Inspect	✓	✓	✓	✓	✓	✓	✓	✓	✓	✓	✓	✓	✓
Brake system components	Inspect/Service		✓		✓		✓		✓		✓		✓	
Exhaust system & heat shields	Inspect		✓		✓		✓		✓		✓		✓	
Inspect the front suspension, tie rod ends and boot seals for cracks or leaks and all parts for damage, wear, improper looseness or end play.	Inspect		✓		✓		✓		✓		✓		✓	
CV Joints	Inspect		✓		✓		✓		✓		✓		✓	
Front & rear axle fluid	Inspect			✓			✓			✓			✓	
Engine air filter	Replace		✓		✓		✓		✓		✓		✓	
Adjust parking brake on vehicles equipped with four-wheel disc brakes.	Adjust					✓					✓			
Engine coolant	Flush/Replace										✓			
Accessory drive belts	Replace	Every 120,000 miles												
Spark plugs and ignition wires	Replace	Every 102,000 miles												
PVC valve	Replace	Every 90,000 miles												
Automatic transmission fluid & filter	Replace										✓			
Fluid levels (all)	Top off	✓	✓	✓	✓	✓	✓	✓	✓	✓	✓	✓	✓	✓
Horn, exterior lamps, turn signals and hazard warning light operation	Inspect	✓	✓	✓	✓	✓	✓	✓	✓	✓	✓	✓	✓	✓
Transfer case fluid	Inspect					✓					✓			
Transfer case fluid	Replace										✓			
Battery	Inspect/Service	✓	✓	✓	✓	✓	✓	✓	✓	✓	✓	✓	✓	✓

25766_WRAN_C0015

PRECAUTIONS

Before servicing any vehicle, please be sure to read all of the following precautions, which deal with personal safety, prevention of component damage, and important points to take into consideration when servicing a motor vehicle:

- Never open, service or drain the radiator or cooling system when the engine is hot; serious burns can occur from the steam and hot coolant.
- Observe all applicable safety precautions when working around fuel. Whenever servicing the fuel system, always work in a well-ventilated area. Do not allow fuel spray or vapors to come in contact with a spark, open flame, or excessive heat (a hot drop light, for example). Keep a dry chemical fire extinguisher near the work area. Always keep fuel in a container specifically designed for fuel storage; also, always properly seal fuel containers to avoid the possibility of fire or explosion. Refer to the additional fuel system precautions later in this section.
- Fuel injection systems often remain pressurized, even after the engine has been turned **OFF**. The fuel system pressure must be relieved before disconnecting any fuel lines. Failure to do so may result in fire and/or personal injury.
- Brake fluid often contains polyglycol ethers and polyglycols. Avoid contact with the eyes and wash your hands thoroughly after handling brake fluid. If you do get brake fluid in your eyes, flush your eyes with clean, running water for 15 minutes. If eye irritation persists, or if you have taken brake fluid internally, IMMEDIATELY seek medical assistance.
- The EPA warns that prolonged contact with used engine oil may cause a number of skin disorders, including cancer. You should make every effort to minimize your exposure to used engine oil. Protective gloves should be worn when changing oil. Wash your hands and any other exposed skin areas as soon as possible after exposure to used engine oil. Soap and water, or waterless hand cleaner should be used.
- All new vehicles are now equipped with an air bag system, often referred to as a Supplemental Restraint System (SRS) or Supplemental Inflatable Restraint (SIR) system. The system must be disabled before performing service on or around system components, steering column, instrument panel components, wiring and sensors. Failure to follow safety and disabling procedures could result in accidental air bag deployment, possible personal injury and unnecessary system repairs.
- Always wear safety goggles when working with, or around, the air bag system. When carrying a non-deployed air bag, be sure the bag and trim cover are pointed away from your body. When placing a non-deployed air bag on a work surface, always face the bag and trim cover upward, away from the surface. This will reduce the motion of the module if it is accidentally deployed. Refer to the additional air bag system precautions later in this section.
- Clean, high quality brake fluid from a sealed container is essential to the safe and proper operation of the brake system. You should always buy the correct type of brake fluid for your vehicle. If the brake fluid becomes contaminated, completely flush the system with new fluid. Never reuse any brake fluid. Any brake fluid that is removed from the system should be discarded. Also, do not allow any brake fluid to come in contact with a painted surface; it will damage the paint.
- Never operate the engine without the proper amount and type of engine oil; doing so WILL result in severe engine damage.
- Timing belt maintenance is extremely important. Many models utilize an interference-type, non-freewheeling engine. If the timing belt breaks, the valves in the cylinder head may strike the pistons, causing potentially serious (also time-consuming and expensive) engine damage. Refer to the maintenance interval charts for the recommended replacement interval for the timing belt, and to the timing belt section for belt replacement and inspection.
- Disconnecting the negative battery cable on some vehicles may interfere with the functions of the on-board computer system(s) and may require the computer to undergo a relearning process once the negative battery cable is reconnected.
- When servicing drum brakes, only disassemble and assemble one side at a time, leaving the remaining side intact for reference.
- Only an MVAC-trained, EPA-certified automotive technician should service the air conditioning system or its components.

BRAKES

ANTI-LOCK BRAKE SYSTEM (ABS)

GENERAL INFORMATION

PRECAUTIONS

- Certain components within the ABS system are not intended to be serviced or repaired individually.
- Do not use rubber hoses or other parts not specifically specified for and ABS system. When using repair kits, replace all parts included in the kit. Partial or incorrect repair may lead to functional problems and require the replacement of components.
- Lubricate rubber parts with clean, fresh brake fluid to ease assembly. Do not use shop air to clean parts; damage to rubber components may result.
- Use only DOT 3 brake fluid from an unopened container.
- If any hydraulic component or line is removed or replaced, it may be necessary to bleed the entire system.
- A clean repair area is essential. Always clean the reservoir and cap thoroughly before removing the cap. The slightest amount of dirt in the fluid may plug an orifice and impair the system function. Perform repairs after components have been thoroughly cleaned; use only denatured alcohol to clean components. Do not allow ABS components to come into contact with any substance containing mineral oil; this includes used shop rags.
- The Anti-Lock control unit is a microprocessor similar to other computer units in the vehicle. Ensure that the ignition switch is **OFF** before removing or installing controller harnesses. Avoid static electricity discharge at or near the controller.
- If any arc welding is to be done on the vehicle, the control unit should be unplugged before welding operations begin.

SPEED SENSORS

REMOVAL & INSTALLATION

Front

1. Raise vehicle and support the vehicle.
2. Remove the disc brake caliper and adapter. See "FRONT DISC BRAKES" section.
3. Remove the disc brake rotor. See "FRONT DISC BRAKES" section.

4. Clean sensor and surrounding area with shop towel before removal.

5. Remove bolt attaching sensor to hub/bearing.

6. Remove the sensor through the hole in the brake shield.

7. Remove sensor wire from brake hose.

8. Disconnect sensor wire connector at harness plug.

To install:

9. Install the sensor through the hole in the brake shield.

10. Install the sensor in the hub and bearing and tighten sensor attaching bolt to 50 inch lbs. (6 Nm).

11. Install the disc brake rotor. See "FRONT DISC BRAKES" section.

12. Install the disc brake caliper and adaptor. See "FRONT DISC BRAKES" section.

13. Route the sensor wire and secure to the brake hose.

14. Connect sensor wire to harness.

15. Install the tire and wheel assembly.

16. Remove the support and lower the vehicle.

Rear

1. Raise and support the vehicle.

2. Disconnect the wheel speed sensor electrical connector.

3. Remove the wheel speed sensor mounting bolt from the rear support plate.

4. Remove the wheel speed sensor.

5. Installation is the reverse of the removal procedure.

BRAKES

BLEEDING THE BRAKE SYSTEM

BLEEDING PROCEDURE

STANDARD BLEEDING PROCEDURE

➡Use Mopar brake fluid, or an equivalent quality fluid meeting SAE J1703-F and DOT 3 standards only. Use fresh, clean fluid from a sealed container at all times.

1. Remove reservoir filler caps and fill reservoir.

2. If calipers were overhauled, open all caliper bleed screws. Then close each bleed screw as fluid starts to drip from it. Top off master cylinder reservoir once more before proceeding.

3. Attach one end of bleed hose to bleed screw and insert opposite end in glass container partially filled with brake fluid. Be sure end of bleed hose is immersed in fluid.

4. Bleed procedure should be in this order: Right rear. Left rear, Right front, Left front.

5. Open up bleeder, then have a helper press down the brake pedal. Once the pedal is down, hold the pedal down while closing the bleeder. Repeat bleeding until fluid stream is clear and free of bubbles. Then move to the next wheel.

6. Before moving the vehicle verify the pedal is firm and not mushy.

7. Top off the brake fluid and install the reservoir cap.

ABS BLEEDING PROCEDURE

➡The base brake's hydraulic system must be bled anytime air enters the hydraulic system. The ABS must always be bled anytime it is suspected that the HCU has ingested air.

➡Brake systems with ABS must be bled as two independent braking systems. The non-ABS portion of the brake system with ABS is to be bled the same as any non-ABS system.

➡The ABS portion of the brake system must be bled separately. Use the following procedure to properly bleed the brake hydraulic system including the ABS.

➡During the brake bleeding procedure, be sure the brake fluid level remains close to the FULL level in the master cylinder fluid reservoir. Check the fluid level periodically during the bleeding procedure and add Mopar® DOT 3 brake fluid as required.

➡When bleeding the ABS system, the following bleeding sequence must be followed to insure complete and adequate bleeding.

1. Make sure all hydraulic fluid lines are installed and properly torqued.

2. Connect the scan tool to the diagnostics connector. The diagnostic connector is located under the lower steering column cover to the left of the steering column.

3. Using the scan tool, check to make sure the ABM does not have any fault codes stored. If it does, clear them.

4. When bleeding the brake system wear safety glasses. A clear bleed tube must be attached to the bleeder screws and submerged in a clear container filled part way with clean brake fluid. Direct the flow of brake fluid away from yourself and the painted surfaces of the vehicle. Brake fluid at high pressure may come out of the bleeder screws when opened.

➡Pressure bleeding is recommended to bleed the base brake system to ensure all air is removed from system. Manual bleeding may also be used, but additional time is needed to remove all air from system.

5. Bleed the base brake system, as described above.

6. Using the scan tool, select ECU VIEW, followed by ABS MISCELLANEOUS FUNCTIONS to access bleeding. Follow the instructions displayed. When finished, disconnect the scan tool and proceed.

7. Bleed the base brake system a second time. Check brake fluid level in the reservoir periodically to prevent emptying, causing air to enter the hydraulic system.

8. Fill the master cylinder fluid reservoir to the FULL level.

9. Test drive the vehicle to be sure the brakes are operating correctly and that the brake pedal does not feel spongy.

MASTER CYLINDER BLEEDING

➡A new master cylinder should be bled before installation on the vehicle. Required bleeding tools include bleed tubes and a wood dowel to stroke the pistons. Bleed tubes can be fabricated from brake line.

1. Mount master cylinder in vise.

2. Attach bleed tubes to cylinder outlet ports. Then position each tube end into reservoir.

3. Fill reservoir with fresh brake fluid.

4. Press cylinder pistons inward with wood dowel. Then release pistons and allow them to return under spring pressure. Continue bleeding operations until air bubbles are no longer visible in fluid.

FLUID FILL PROCEDURE

1. Always clean the master cylinder reservoir and caps before checking fluid level. If not cleaned, dirt could enter the fluid.

2. The fluid fill level is indicated on the side of the master cylinder reservoir.

3. The correct fluid level is to the MAX indicator on the side of the reservoir. If necessary, add fluid to the proper level.

BRAKES

FRONT DISC BRAKES

⁂ CAUTION

Dust and dirt accumulating on brake parts during normal use may contain asbestos fibers from production or aftermarket brake linings. Breathing excessive concentrations of asbestos fibers can cause serious bodily harm. Exercise care when servicing brake parts. Do not sand or grind brake lining unless equipment used is designed to contain the dust residue. Do not clean brake parts with compressed air or by dry brushing. Cleaning should be done by dampening the brake components with a fine mist of water, then wiping the brake components clean with a dampened cloth. Dispose of cloth and all residue containing asbestos fibers in an impermeable container with the appropriate label. Follow practices prescribed by the Occupational Safety and Health Administration (OSHA) and the Environmental Protection Agency (EPA) for the handling, processing, and disposing of dust or debris that may contain asbestos fibers.

BRAKE CALIPER

REMOVAL & INSTALLATION

1. Install prop rod on the brake pedal to keep pressure on the brake system, Holding pedal in this position will isolate master cylinder from hydraulic brake system and will not allow brake fluid to drain out of brake fluid reservoir while brake lines are open. This will allow you to bleed out the area of repair instead of the entire system.
2. Raise and support vehicle.
3. Remove front wheel and tire assembly.
4. Drain small amount of fluid from master cylinder brake reservoir with **clean** suction gun.
5. Bottom caliper pistons into the caliper by prying the caliper over.
6. Remove brake hose banjo bolt and gasket washers. Discard gasket washers.
7. Remove the caliper slide bolts.
8. Remove the caliper from the adapter.

To install:

9. Install the caliper on the adapter.
10. Caliper slide pins should be free from debris and lightly lubricated.
11. Install the caliper slide pin bolts and tighten to 26 ft. lbs. (35 Nm).
12. Gently lift one end of the slide pin boot to equalize air pressure, then release the boot and verify that the boot is fully covering the slide pin.

➡Verify brake hose is not twisted or kinked before tightening banjo bolt.

13. Install brake hose to caliper with new copper washers and tighten banjo bolt to 23 ft. lbs. (31 Nm).
14. Verify brake fluid level.
15. Remove the prop rod from the brake pedal.
16. Bleed the area of repair for the brake system, If a proper pedal is not felt during bleeding an area of repair then a base bleed system must be performed. See "Bleeding the Brake System" section.
17. Install wheel and tire assemblies.
18. Remove supports and lower vehicle.

DISC BRAKE PADS

REMOVAL & INSTALLATION

1. Raise and support vehicle.
2. Remove wheel and tire assembly.
3. Drain small amount of fluid from master cylinder brake reservoir with clean suction gun.
4. Remove the 2 caliper mounting bolts.
5. Compress the caliper and remove from the adaptor.
6. Secure caliper to nearby suspension part with wire. Do not allow brake hose to support caliper weight.
7. Remove the inboard and outboard brake pads from the caliper adapter.
8. Remove the anti-rattle clips from the brake caliper adapter.

To install:

9. Remove and clean all rust and debris from the anti-rattle clip mounting surfaces on the brake caliper adapter.
10. Install new anti-rattle clips into the caliper adapter.
11. Install the inboard and outboard brake pads onto the caliper adapter.
12. Install caliper on the caliper adapter.
13. Install the caliper slide pin bolts and tighten to 32 ft. lbs. (44 Nm).
14. Install wheel and tire assembly.
15. Remove support and lower vehicle.
16. Pump brake pedal until caliper pistons and brake pads are seated and a firm brake pedal is obtained.
17. Fill brake fluid.

BRAKES

REAR DISC BRAKES

⁂ CAUTION

Dust and dirt accumulating on brake parts during normal use may contain asbestos fibers from production or aftermarket brake linings. Breathing excessive concentrations of asbestos fibers can cause serious bodily harm. Exercise care when servicing brake parts. Do not sand or grind brake lining unless equipment used is designed to contain the dust residue. Do not clean brake parts with compressed air or by dry brushing. Cleaning should be done by dampening the brake components with a fine mist of water, then wiping the brake components clean with a dampened cloth. Dispose of cloth and all residue containing asbestos fibers in an impermeable container with the appropriate label. Follow practices prescribed by the Occupational Safety and Health Administration (OSHA) and the Environmental Protection Agency (EPA) for the handling, processing, and disposing of dust or debris that may contain asbestos fibers.

BRAKE CALIPER

REMOVAL & INSTALLATION

1. Install prop rod on the brake pedal to keep pressure on the brake system, Holding pedal in this position will isolate master cylinder from hydraulic brake system and will not allow brake fluid to drain out of brake fluid reservoir while brake lines are open. This will allow you to bleed out the area of repair instead of the entire system.
2. Raise and support vehicle.
3. Remove rear wheel and tire assembly.
4. Drain small amount of fluid from master cylinder brake reservoir with a clean suction gun.
5. Bottom caliper pistons into the caliper by prying the caliper over.
6. Remove brake hose banjo bolt and discard gasket washers.
7. Remove the caliper slide pins.
8. Remove caliper from the adapter.

9. Remove the brake pads.

To install:

10. Install the brake pads if removed.
11. Install caliper to the caliper adapter.
12. Coat the caliper mounting slide pin bolts with silicone grease. Then install and tighten the bolts to 26 ft. lbs. (35 Nm).
13. Install the brake hose banjo bolt if removed.
14. Install the brake hose to the caliper with new seal washers and tighten fitting bolt to 23 ft. lbs. (31 Nm).

➡Verify that the brake hose is not twisted or kinked before tightening the fitting bolt.

15. Remove the prop rod from the brake pedal.
16. Bleed the area of repair for the brake system. If a proper pedal is not felt during bleeding an area of repair then a base bleed system must be performed. See "Bleeding the Brake System" section.
17. Install the wheel and tire assemblies.
18. Remove the supports and lower the vehicle.
19. Verify a firm pedal before moving the vehicle.

DISC BRAKE PADS

REMOVAL & INSTALLATION

1. Raise and support vehicle.
2. Remove the wheel and tire assemblies.
3. Compress the caliper.
4. Remove the caliper. See "Brake Caliper".

➡Do not allow brake hose to support caliper assembly.

5. Support and hang the caliper.
6. Remove the inboard brake pad from the caliper adapter.
7. Remove the outboard brake pad from the caliper adapter.

To install:

8. Bottom pistons in caliper bore with C-clamp. Place an old brake shoe between a C-clamp and caliper piston.
9. Clean caliper mounting adapter and anti-rattle springs.
10. Install anti-rattle springs in proper locations. Anti-rattle springs are not interchangeable.
11. Install inboard brake pad in adapter.
12. Install outboard brake pad in adapter.
13. Install caliper. See "Brake Caliper".
14. Install wheel and tire assemblies and lower vehicle.
15. Apply brakes several times to seat caliper pistons and brake pads to obtain firm pedal.
16. Top off master cylinder fluid level.

BRAKES

PARKING BRAKE

PARKING BRAKE CABLES

ADJUSTMENT (LOCK OUT PROCEDURE)

See Figures 1 through 3.

1. Remove the center floor console.
2. Pull up on the equalizer cable and then install a suitable tool to lockout the park brake lever.
3. Remove the rear park brake cables from the equalizer.
4. When repairs are completed install the rear park brake cables to the equalizer, remove the lockout tool, check the operation of the system and then install the center floor console

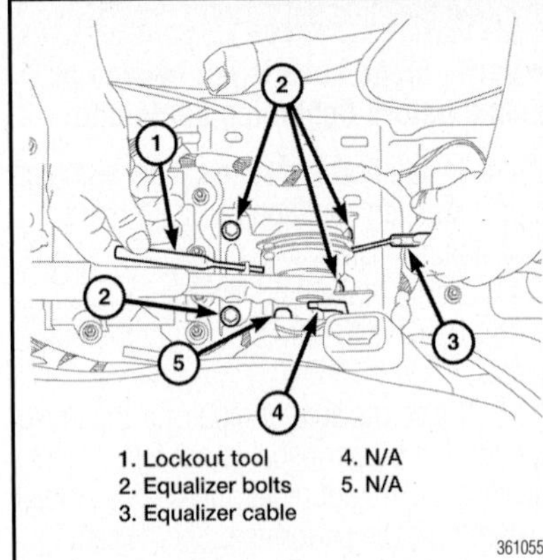

Fig. 2 Pull up on the equalizer cable and then install a suitable tool to lockout the park brake lever.

REMOVAL & INSTALLATION

See Figure 4.

➡Park brake system must be locked out for servicing, as described above.

1. Remove the cables from the equalizer.
2. Remove the cables from the body bracket, using a wrench to fit the end of the cable snug to depress the tangs.
3. Raise and support the vehicle.
4. Remove the cables and grommets from the floor of the vehicle.
5. Remove the cable from the rear axle bracket.
6. Remove the brake cable from the brake lever at the support plate.

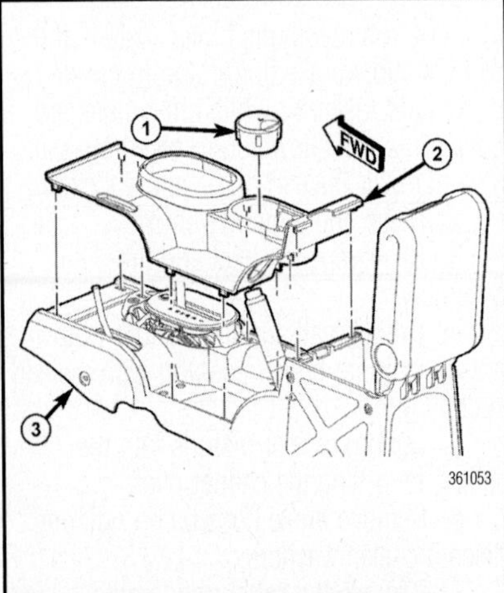

Fig. 1 Remove the center floor console.

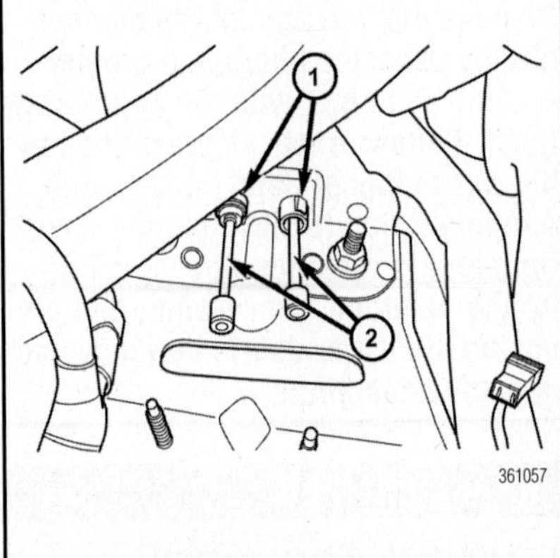

Fig. 3 Remove the rear park brake cables (2) from the equalizer—showing cable retainer tangs (1)

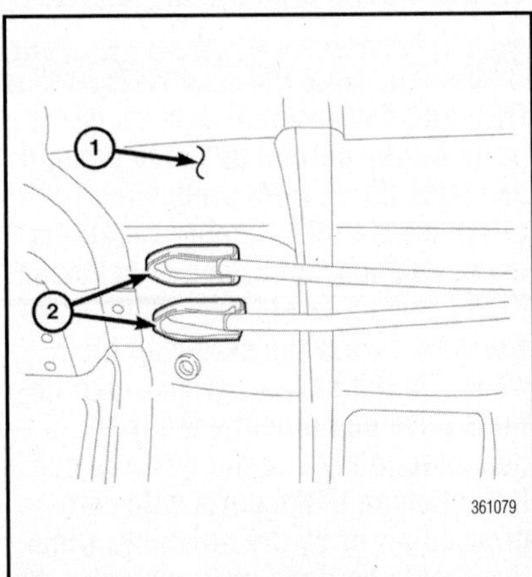

Fig. 4 Remove the cables and grommets (2) from the floor (1) of the vehicle.

To install:

7. Install the cable to the rear axle bracket.
8. Install the cable into the brake lever at the support plate.
9. Install the cables and grommets into the floor of the vehicle.
10. Lower the vehicle.
11. Install the brake cables to the body bracket and install the cables to the equalizer.
12. Remove the lockout tool for the park brake cable.
13. Check the park brake system operation.
14. Install the center floor console.

PARKING BRAKE SHOES

REMOVAL & INSTALLATION

See Figures 5 through 7.

1. Raise and support the vehicle.
2. Remove the tire and wheel assembly.
3. Remove the disc brake caliper adapter.
4. Remove the disc brake rotor.
5. Remove the rear wheel speed sensor. See "ANTI-LOCK BRAKE SYSTEM (ABS)" section.
6. Remove the center floor console.
7. Lock out the park brake system at the lever using a suitable tool and pulling upward on the brake cable. See "Parking Brake Cable".
8. Remove the rear parking brake cables from the equalizer.
9. Remove the parking brake cable from the brake shoe lever at the rear axle.
10. Remove the rear axle shaft. See "DRIVE TRAIN" section.
11. Tap the seal plate from the brake support on the axle shaft.
12. Remove the support plate with the brake shoes from the axle shaft.
13. Disassemble the rear park brake shoes.

➡As a general rule, riveted brake shoes should be replaced when worn to within 1/32 in. (0.78 mm) of the rivet heads. Bonded lining should be replaced when worn to a thickness of 1/16 in. (1.6 mm).

To install:

14. Reassemble the rear park brake shoes.
15. Install the support plate on the axle shaft.
16. Install the axle shaft to the axle housing. See "DRIVE TRAIN" section.
17. Reconnect the brake cable to the park brake shoe lever behind the support plate.
18. Install the rear wheel speed sensor.
19. Adjust the rear brake shoes as follows:

➡When measuring the brake drum diameter, the diameter should be measured in the center of the area in which the park brake shoes contact the surface of the brake drum.

a. Using Brake Shoe Gauge C-3919 or equivalent), accurately measure the inside diameter of the park brake drum portion of the rotor.
b. Using a ruler that reads in 64th of an inch, accurately read the measurement of the inside diameter of the park brake drum from the special tool.
c. Reduce the inside diameter measurement of the brake drum that was taken using the brake shoe gauge tool by 1/64 of an inch. Reset the gauge so that the outside measurement jaws are set to the reduced measurement.
d. Place the gauge over the park brake shoes.

➡The special tool must be located diagonally across at the top of one shoe and bottom of opposite shoe (widest point) of the park brake shoes.

e. Using the star wheel adjuster, adjust the park brake shoes until the lining on the park brake shoes just touches the jaws on the special tool.
f. Repeat the previous steps to measure and adjust shoes in both directions.

20. Install the disc brake rotor.
21. Install the disc brake caliper adapter.
22. Install the tire and wheel assembly.
23. Lower the vehicle.
24. Install the rear park brake cables at the equalizer.
25. Remove the lockout tool on the front park brake lever.
26. Check the operation of the park brake system.
27. Install the center floor console.
28. After parking brake lining replacement, it is recommended that the parking brake system be conditioned prior to use. This is done by making one stop from 25 mph on dry pavement or concrete using light to moderate force on the parking brake lever.

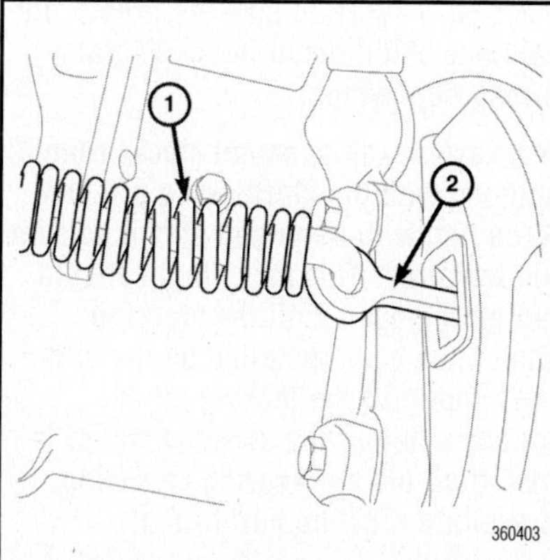

Fig. 5 Remove the parking brake cable (1) from the brake shoe lever (2) at the rear axle.

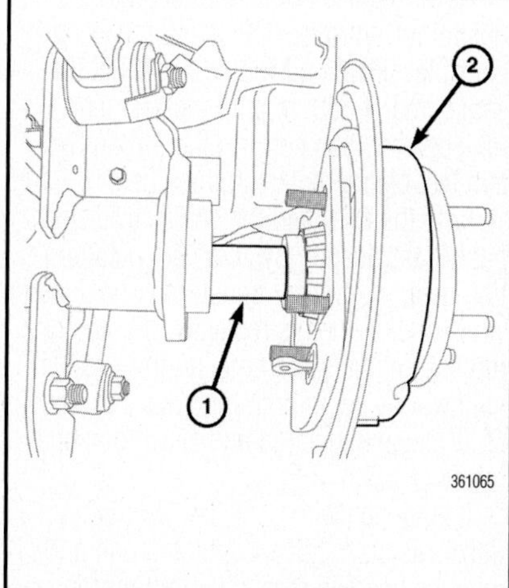

Fig. 6 Remove the rear axle shaft.

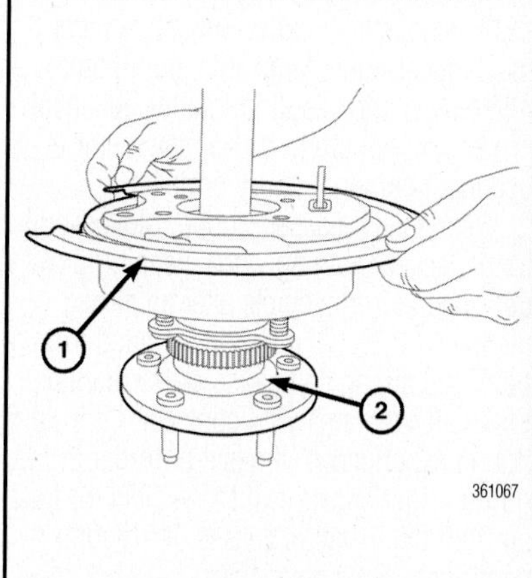

Fig. 7 Tap the seal plate from the brake support (1) on the axle shaft (2).

GENERAL INFORMATION

CAUTION

These vehicles are equipped with an air bag system. The system must be disarmed before performing service on, or around, system components, the steering column, instrument panel components, wiring and sensors. Failure to follow the safety precautions and the disarming procedure could result in accidental air bag deployment, possible injury and unnecessary system repairs.

SERVICE PRECAUTIONS

Disconnect and isolate the battery negative cable before beginning any airbag system component diagnosis, testing, removal, or installation procedures. Allow system capacitor to discharge for two minutes before beginning any component service. This will disable the airbag system. Failure to disable the airbag system may result in accidental airbag deployment, personal injury, or death.

Do not place an intact undeployed airbag face down on a solid surface. The airbag will propel into the air if accidentally deployed and may result in personal injury or death.

When carrying or handling an undeployed airbag, the trim side (face) of the airbag should be pointing away from the body to minimize possibility of injury if accidental deployment occurs. Failure to do this may result in personal injury or death.

Replace airbag system components with OEM replacement parts. Substitute parts may appear interchangeable, but internal differences may result in inferior occupant protection. Failure to do so may result in occupant personal injury or death.

Wear safety glasses, rubber gloves, and long sleeved clothing when cleaning powder residue from vehicle after an airbag deployment. Powder residue emitted from a deployed airbag can cause skin irritation. Flush affected area with cool water if irritation is experienced. If nasal or throat irritation is experienced, exit the vehicle for fresh air until the irritation ceases. If irritation continues, see a physician.

Do not use a replacement airbag that is not in the original packaging. This may result in improper deployment, personal injury, or death.

The factory installed fasteners, screws and bolts used to fasten airbag components have a special coating and are specifically designed for the airbag system. Do not use substitute fasteners. Use only original equipment fasteners listed in the parts catalog when fastener replacement is required.

During, and following, any child restraint anchor service, due to impact event or vehicle repair, carefully inspect all mounting hardware, tether straps, and anchors for proper installation, operation, or damage. If a child restraint anchor is found damaged in any way, the anchor must be replaced. Failure to do this may result in personal injury or death.

Deployed and non-deployed airbags may or may not have live pyrotechnic material within the airbag inflator.

Do not dispose of driver/passenger/curtain airbags or seat belt tensioners unless you are sure of complete deployment. Refer to the Hazardous Substance Control System for proper disposal.

Dispose of deployed airbags and tensioners consistent with state, provincial, local, and federal regulations.

After any airbag component testing or service, do not connect the battery negative cable. Personal injury or death may result if the system test is not performed first.

If the vehicle is equipped with the Occupant Classification System (OCS), do not connect the battery negative cable before performing the OCS Verification Test using the scan tool and the appropriate diagnostic information. Personal injury or death may result if the system test is not performed properly.

Never replace both the Occupant Restraint Controller (ORC) and the Occupant Classification Module (OCM) at the same time. If both require replacement, replace one, then perform the Airbag System test before replacing the other.

Both the ORC and the OCM store Occupant Classification System (OCS) calibration data, which they transfer to one another when one of them is replaced. If both are replaced at the same time, an irreversible fault will be set in both modules and the OCS may malfunction and cause personal injury or death.

If equipped with OCS, the Seat Weight Sensor is a sensitive, calibrated unit and must be handled carefully. Do not drop or handle roughly. If dropped or damaged, replace with another sensor. Failure to do so may result in occupant injury or death.

If equipped with OCS, the front passenger seat must be handled carefully as well. When removing the seat, be careful when setting on floor not to drop. If dropped, the sensor may be inoperative, could result in occupant injury, or possibly death.

If equipped with OCS, when the passenger front seat is on the floor, no one should sit in the front passenger seat. This uneven force may damage the sensing ability of the seat weight sensors. If sat on and damaged, the sensor may be inoperative, could result in occupant injury, or possibly death.

DISARMING THE SYSTEM

1. Disconnect and isolate the battery negative cable.
2. Wait two minutes for the system capacitor to discharge before further service.

ARMING THE SYSTEM

1. Reconnect the battery negative cable.

CLOCKSPRING CENTERING

See Figure 8.

1. To avoid serious or fatal injury on vehicles equipped with airbags, disable the Supplemental Restraint System (SRS) before attempting any steering wheel, steering column, airbag, seat belt tensioner, impact sensor or instrument panel component diagnosis or service. Disconnect and isolate the battery negative (ground) cable, then wait two minutes for the system capacitor to discharge before performing further diagnosis or service.

➡This is the only sure way to disable the SRS. Failure to take the proper precautions could result in accidental airbag deployment.

➡A service replacement clockspring is shipped with the clockspring pre-centered and with a molded plastic locking pin installed. This locking pin should not be removed until the steering wheel has been installed on the steering column. If the locking pin is removed before the steering wheel is installed, the clockspring centering procedure must be performed.

CAUTION

When a clockspring is installed into a vehicle without properly centering and locking the entire steering system, the Steering Angle Sensor (SAS)

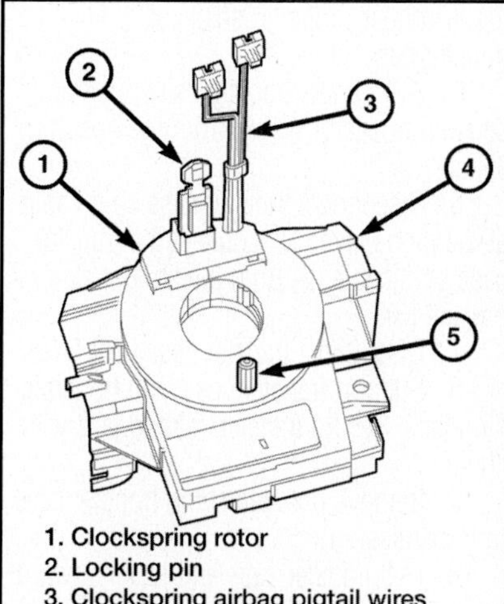

Fig. 8 Showing the clockspring and related parts for centering

data does not agree with the true position of the steering system and causes the Electronic Stability Program (ESP) system to shut down. This may also damage the clockspring without any immediate malfunction. Unlike some other Chrysler vehicles, this SAS never requires calibration. However, upon each new ignition ON cycle, the steering wheel must be rotated slightly to initialize the SAS.

➡Determining if the clockspring/SAS is centered is also possible electrically using the diagnostic scan tool. Steering wheel position is displayed as ANGLE with a range of up to 900 degrees. Refer to the appropriate menu item on the diagnostic scan tool.

2. Place the front wheels in the straight-ahead position and inhibit the steering column shaft from rotation.
3. Remove the steering wheel from the steering shaft.
4. Rotate the clockspring rotor clockwise to the end of its travel. Do not apply excessive torque.
5. From the end of the clockwise travel, rotate the rotor about two and one-half turns counterclockwise. Turn the rotor slightly clockwise or counterclockwise as necessary so that the clockspring airbag pigtail wires and connector receptacle are at the top and the dowel or drive pin is at the bottom.
6. The clockspring is now centered. Secure the clockspring rotor to the clockspring case using a locking pin or some similar device to maintain clockspring centering until the steering wheel is reinstalled on the steering column.

DRIVE TRAIN

AUTOMATIC TRANSMISSION FLUID

DRAIN & REFILL & FILTER SERVICE

➡Only fluids of the type labeled Mopar® ATF+4, Automatic Transmission Fluid, should be used in the transmission sump. A filter change should be made at the time of the transmission oil change. The magnet (on the inside of the oil pan) should also be cleaned with a clean, dry cloth. If the transmission is disassembled for any reason, the fluid and filter should be changed.

1. Raise vehicle on a hoist. Place a drain container with a large opening, under transmission oil pan.

➡One of the oil pan bolts has a sealing patch applied from the factory. Separate this bolt for reuse.

2. Loosen pan bolts and tap the pan at one corner to break it loose allowing fluid to drain, then remove the oil pan.
3. Install a new filter and o-ring on bottom of the valve body and tighten retaining screws.
4. Before installing the oil pan bolt with the sealing patch, in the bolt hole located between the torque converter clutch on and U/D clutch pressure tap circuits, it will be necessary to replenish the sealing patch on the bolt using Mopar Lock & Seal Adhesive.
5. Clean the oil pan and magnet. Reinstall pan using new Mopar® Silicone Adhesive sealant. Tighten oil pan bolts to 15 ft. lbs. (20 Nm).
6. Pour 4 quarts of Mopar ATF+4 through the dipstick opening.
7. Start engine and allow to idle for at least one minute. Then, with parking and service brakes applied, move selector lever momentarily to each position, ending in the park or neutral position.
8. Check the transmission fluid level and add an appropriate amount to bring the transmission fluid level to 1/8 in. below the lowest mark on the dipstick.
9. Recheck the fluid level after the transmission has reached normal operating temperature of 180°F (82°C).
10. To prevent dirt from entering transmission, make certain that dipstick is fully seated into the dipstick opening.

MANUAL TRANSMISSION FLUID

DRAIN & REFILL

1. With vehicle in neutral, position vehicle on hoist.
2. Loosen the exhaust as necessary to gain access to drain plug.
3. Remove drain plug and drain fluid.
4. Install drain plug and remove fill plug.
5. Fill transmission with 3.2 pts. (1.5 L) of Mopar Manual Transmission Lubricant MS-9224 or to the bottom of the fill plug hole.
6. Install the exhaust.

CLUTCH

REMOVAL & INSTALLATION

1. Remove transmission.
2. Mark position of pressure plate on flywheel with paint or a scriber for assembly reference, if clutch is not being replaced.
3. Loosen pressure plate bolts evenly and in rotation to relieve spring tension and avoid warping the plate.
4. Remove pressure plate bolts and pressure plate and disc.

To install:

5. Lightly scuff sand flywheel face with 180 grit emery cloth, then clean with a wax and grease remover.
6. Lubricate pilot bearing with Mopar high temperature bearing grease or equivalent.
7. Check runout and operation of new clutch disc. Disc must slide freely on transmission input shaft splines.
8. With the disc on the input shaft, check face runout with dial indicator. Check runout at disc hub 1/4 in. (6 mm) from outer edge of facing. Obtain another clutch disc if runout exceeds 0.020 in. (0.5 mm).
9. Position clutch disc on flywheel with side marked flywheel against the flywheel.

➡If not marked, the flat side of disc hub goes towards the flywheel.

10. Insert a proper clutch alignment tool through the clutch disc and into the pilot bearing.

11. Position clutch pressure plate over disc and on the flywheel.

12. Install pressure plate bolts finger tight.

➡Use only the factory bolts to mount the pressure plate. The bolts must be the correct size. If bolts are too short, there isn't enough thread engagement, if too long bolts interfere with the Dual Mass Flywheel.

13. Tighten pressure plate bolts evenly and in rotation a few threads at a time.

✲✲ CAUTION

The bolts must be tightened evenly and to specified torque. Failure to follow these instructions will distort the pressure plate.

14. Tighten pressure plate bolts 24 ft. lbs. (33 Nm).

15. Apply light coat of Mopar high temperature bearing grease or equivalent to clutch disc hub and splines of transmission input shaft.

✲✲ CAUTION

Do not over lubricate shaft splines. This will result in grease contamination of disc.

16. Install transmission.

BLEEDING

➡Use Mopar brake fluid, or an equivalent quality fluid meeting SAE J1703-F and DOT 3 standards only. Use fresh, clean fluid from a sealed container at all times.

✲✲ CAUTION

Do not allow the master cylinder to run out of fluid during bleed operations. An empty cylinder will allow additional air to be drawn into the system. Check the cylinder fluid level frequently and add fluid as needed.

Manual Bleed Clutch Hydraulic Circuit

1. Verify fluid level in brake master cylinder, top off brake fluid as necessary.

➡Pre filling a new slave cylinder will reduce bleeding time required.

2. Install a length of clear hose to divert fluid into suitable container.

3. Push and hold clutch pedal down, open bleeder on slave cylinder, allow fluid to bleed out, then close bleeder. Repeat this step several times until no air is observed coming out of the bleeder.

4. Remove drain hose and replace dust cap on bleeder and install slave cylinder on transmission.

5. Actuate clutch pedal 25 times, then start engine and verify clutch operation and pedal feel.

6. If pedal feels spongy or clutch does not fully disengage, air is still trapped in the hydraulic circuit and must be bleed again.

Pressure Bleed Clutch Hydraulic Circuit

1. Follow manufacturers instructions carefully when using pressure equipment. Do not exceed the tank manufacturers pressure recommendations. Generally, a tank pressure of 15-20 psi is sufficient for bleeding.

2. Fill bleeder tank with recommended DOT 3 fluid and purge air from the tank lines before bleeding.

3. Do not pressure bleed without a proper master cylinder adapter. The wrong adapter can lead to leakage, or drawing air back into the system. Use adapter provided with the equipment.

TRANSFER CASE ASSEMBLY

REMOVAL & INSTALLATION

See Figure 9.

1. Shift transfer case into NEUTRAL.
2. Raise vehicle and remove skid plate.
3. Drain transfer case lubricant.
4. Mark front and rear propeller shaft yokes for alignment reference. Remove the front/rear propeller shafts at transfer case.
5. Disconnect transfer case position sensor connector wiring from the position sensor.
6. Disconnect transfer case shift cable at the range lever. Disconnect the transfer case shift cable (2) from the shift cable bracket (5).
7. Disconnect transfer case vent hose.
8. Support transfer case with transmission jack. Secure transfer case to jack with chains.
9. Remove nuts attaching transfer case to transmission.
10. Pull transfer case and jack rearward to disengage transfer case.
11. Remove transfer case from under vehicle.

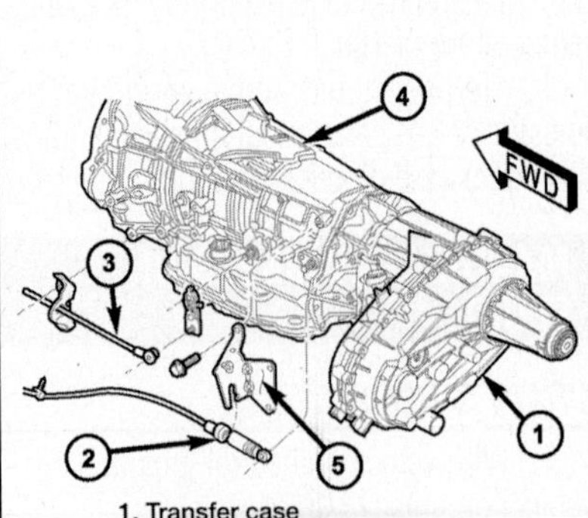

Fig. 9 Disconnect transfer case shift cable at the range lever. Disconnect the transfer case shift cable from the shift cable bracket.

To install:

12. Mount transfer case on a transmission jack. Secure transfer case to jack with chains.
13. Position transfer case under vehicle. Align transfer case and transmission shafts and install transfer case on transmission.
14. Install and tighten transfer case attaching nuts to 26 ft. lbs. (35 Nm) torque.
15. Connect vent hose.
16. Connect transfer case position sensor wiring connector to sensor.
17. Align and connect propeller shafts. See "Propeller Shaft" in this section.
18. Connect shift cable to transfer case bracket (range lever).
19. Fill transfer case with correct fluid. Check transmission fluid level. Correct as necessary.
20. Install skid plate.
21. Remove transmission jack and any support stand.
22. Lower vehicle and verify transfer case shift operation.

FRONT AXLE HUB BEARING & SHAFT

REMOVAL & INSTALLATION

See Figure 10.

1. With transmission in neutral, position vehicle on hoist.
2. Remove brake components. See "BRAKES" section.
3. Remove wheel speed sensor from hub bearing.
4. Remove hub nut from axle shaft.
5. Remove three hub bearing bolts from steering knuckle.
6. Remove hub bearing with axle shaft through steering knuckle.

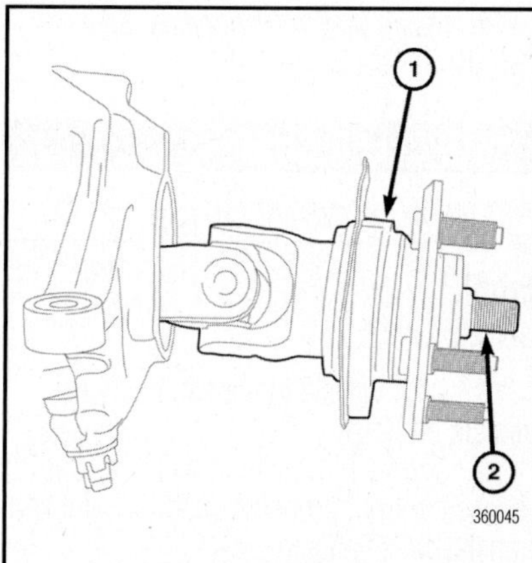

Fig. 10 Remove hub bearing (1) with axle shaft (2) through steering knuckle.

7. Remove brake shield and hub bearing from axle.

To install:

8. Clean axle shaft and apply a thin film of Mopar Wheel Bearing Grease or equivalent to the shaft splines and seal contact surface.
9. Install hub bearing and brake shield on axle shaft.
10. Install axle shaft with hub bearing through steering knuckle and into differential side gears.
11. Install three hub bearing bolts through steering knuckle and tighten to 75 ft. lbs. (102 Nm).
12. Install hub nut on axle shaft and tighten to 100 ft. lbs. (136 Nm).
13. Install wheel speed sensor.
14. Install brake components.

FRONT AXLE SHAFT

REMOVAL & INSTALLATION

With 186FBI or 216FBI Axle

See Figure 11.

➡Procedure is the same for a 4x2 tube axle except for propeller shaft and axle vent removal.

1. With transmission in neutral, position vehicle on hoist. Position and secure lift to axle.
2. Mark an installation reference line across the front propeller shaft flange and the axle flange.
3. With 186FBI axle, remove vent hose from axle housing.
4. With 216FBI axle, disconnect Tru-Lok® wiring connectors (1, 2) and axle vent hose.
5. Remove brake calipers and rotors. Remove wheel speed sensors from hub bearings. See "BRAKES" section.

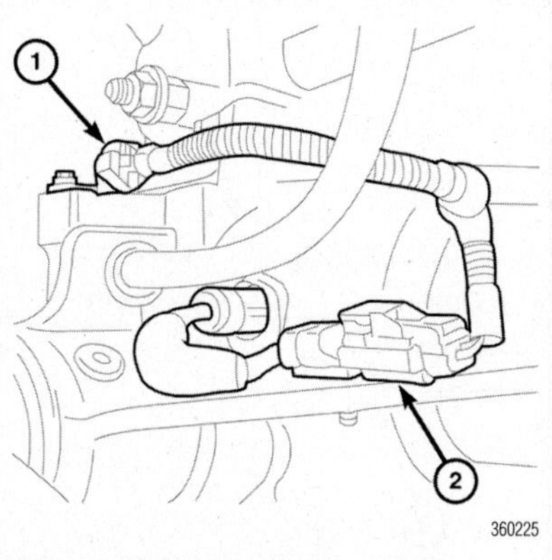

Fig. 11 Disconnect Tru-Lok® wiring connectors (1, 2) and axle vent hose—216FBI axle

6. Remove brake lines and sensor wiring from axle.

➡For suspension component removal, see "FRONT SUSPENSION" section as needed.

7. Remove stabilizer bar links from axle brackets.
8. Remove shock absorbers from axle brackets.
9. Remove track bar bolt and track bar from axle bracket.
10. Remove steering damper from axle bracket.
11. Remove drag link and tie rod ends from steering knuckles.
12. Remove upper control arms from axle brackets.
13. Mark lower control arm cams for installation reference and loosen nuts.
14. Lower axle enough to remove coil springs from axle.
15. Remove lower control arm bolts remove axle from vehicle.

To install:

⁂ CAUTION

The weight of the vehicle must be supported by the springs before suspension arms and track bar fasteners are tightened. Failure to follow these instructions will result in damaging the bushings.

➡Procedure is the same for a 4x2 tube axle except for propeller shaft and axle vent installation.

16. Position axle under vehicle.

➡For assistance with installation of suspension components, refer to "FRONT SUSPENSION" section as needed.

17. Install lower control arms in axle brackets. Install lower control arm bolts, cams and loosely install nuts.
18. Install coil springs on axle and raise axle into position.
19. Install upper control arms on axle brackets and loosely install bolts and nuts.
20. Install track bar in axle bracket and loosely install bolt.
21. Install steering damper on axle bracket and tighten to specification.
22. Install drag link and tie rod ends on steering knuckles and tighten to 63 ft. lbs. (85 Nm).
23. Install shock absorbers on axle brackets and tighten to 56 ft. lbs. (76 Nm).
24. Install stabilizer bar links on axle brackets and tighten to 75 ft. lbs. (102 Nm).
25. Install wheel speed sensors harness on axle and install sensors in hub bearings.
26. Install brake rotors, calipers and brakes lines. See "BRAKES" section.
27. With 186FBI axle, install vent hose on axle housing.
28. With 216FBI axle, connect wiring connectors and axle vent hose.
29. Clean all propeller shaft bolts and apply Mopar® Lock & Seal Adhesive, or equivalent, to the threads before installation.
30. Install propeller shaft with axle flange and propeller shaft marks aligned. Tighten bolts to 81 ft. lbs. (110 Nm).
31. Remove lift from the axle.
32. Install wheel and lower vehicle.
33. Align lower control arm cams to reference marks and tighten control arm nuts to 63 ft. lbs. (85 Nm).
34. Tighten upper control arm nuts to 75 ft. lbs. (102 Nm).
35. Tighten track bar bolt at axle bracket to 125 ft. lbs. (169 Nm).

FRONT PINION SEAL

REMOVAL & INSTALLATION

See Figures 12 through 14.

1. With transmission in neutral, position vehicle on hoist.
2. Remove brake rotors and calipers. See "BRAKES" section.
3. Remove propeller shaft. See "Propeller Shaft" in this section.
4. Rotate pinion gear three or four times.
5. Record pinion torque to rotate with an inch pound torque wrench, for installation reference.
6. Hold pinion flange with Flange Wrench C-3281 (or equivalent) and remove pinion nut.

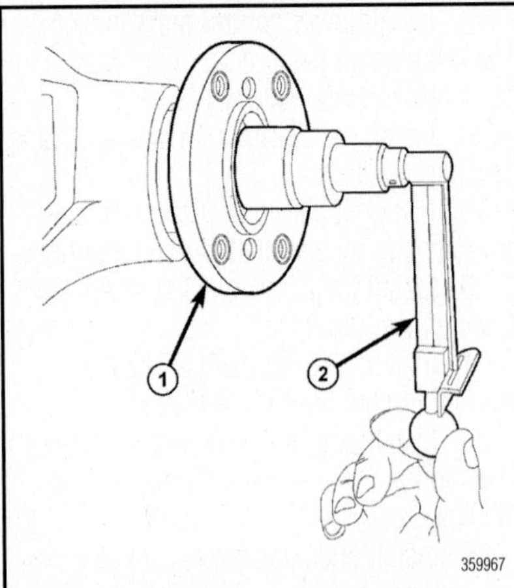

Fig. 12 Record pinion torque to rotate (1) with an inch pound torque wrench (2), for installation reference.

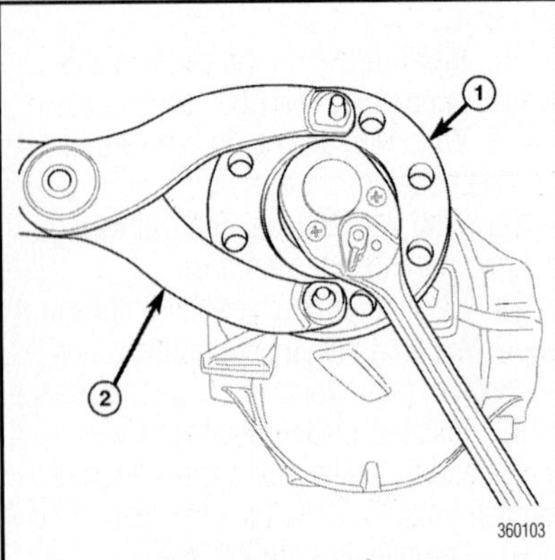

Fig. 13 Hold pinion flange (1) with Flange Wrench C-3281 (or equivalent) and remove pinion nut.

7. Mark a reference line across the pinion shaft and flange for installation reference.
8. Remove pinion flange with a suitable puller (C-452 or equivalent).
9. Remove seal with a seal puller.

To install:

10. Apply a light coating of gear lubricant on the lip of pinion seal. Install seal with a proper installer (8681 and C-4171 or equivalent).
11. Install flange on the pinion shaft with the reference marks aligned.
12. Install flange with Installer 8112 and Cup 8109 (or equivalent).
13. Install new pinion nut.
14. Hold pinion flange with Flange Wrench and tighten pinion nut to 160 ft. lbs. (217 Nm).
15. For 186FBI axle, do the following:
    a. Measure pinion torque to rotating with an inch pound torque wrench. With

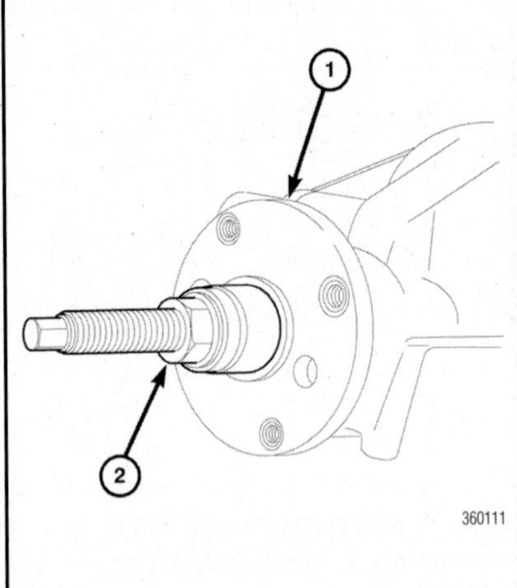

Fig. 14 Install flange (1) with Installer 8112 (2) and Cup 8109 (or equivalent).

a torque wrench set at 400 ft. lbs. (542 Nm), tighten nut in 5 ft. lbs. (6.8 Nm) increments until pinion torque to rotating is achieved. Pinion torque to rotating is the recorded reading plus an additional 5 inch lbs. (0.56 Nm).

⁂ CAUTION

If maximum tightening torque of 400 ft. lbs. (542 Nm) is reached before torque to rotate is achieved, the collapsible spacer may have been damaged. Never loosen pinion gear nut to decrease pinion gear bearing rotating torque and never exceed specified preload torque. Failure to follow these instruction may result in damage.

16. For 216FBI axle, do the following:
    a. Measure pinion torque to rotate with an inch pound torque wrench. Pinion torque to rotate is recorded reading plus 5 inch lbs. (0.56 Nm). If torque to rotate is low, tighten pinion nut in 5ft. lbs. (6.8 Nm) increments until torque to rotate is achieved.

⁂ CAUTION

If maximum tightening torque of 200 ft. lbs. (271 Nm) is reached before torque to rotate is achieved, the collapsible spacer may have been damaged. Never loosen pinion gear nut to decrease pinion gear bearing rotating torque and never exceed specified preload torque. Failure to follow these instruction may result in damage.

17. Install propeller shaft. See "Propeller Shaft" in this section.
18. Install brake components. See "BRAKES" section.

PROPELLER SHAFT

REMOVAL & INSTALLATION

Front

See Figure 15.

1. With vehicle in neutral, position vehicle on hoist.
2. Mark an installation reference line across the front propeller shaft CV joint and transfer case flange.
3. Mark an installation reference line across the front propeller shaft flange and the axle flange.
4. Remove the axle flange bolts.
5. Remove the CV joint bolts and retainers.
6. Compress the propeller shaft enough to remove the shaft from the flanges.

To install:

7. Clean all propeller shaft bolts and apply Mopar Lock & Seal Adhesive or equivalent to the threads before installation.
8. Compress the propeller shaft enough to install the shaft into the axle and transfer case flanges.
9. Align installation reference marks on the transfer case flange front shaft CV joint.
10. Install CV joint retainers and bolts. Tighten bolts to 15 ft. lbs. (20 Nm).
11. Align installation reference marks on the front propeller shaft flange and axle flange.
12. Install the axle flange bolts and tighten to 81 ft. lbs. (110 Nm).

Rear

1. With vehicle in neutral, position vehicle on hoist.

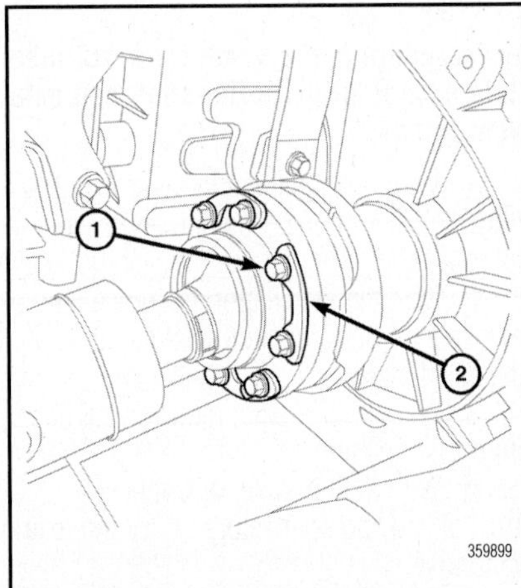

Fig. 15 Remove the CV joint bolts and retainers.

2. Mark installation reference line across the rear propeller shaft CV joint and the axle flange. Also mark to indicate propeller shaft axle end.

➡Propeller shaft can be installed either way.

3. Mark installation reference line across the front propeller shaft CV joint and the transmission/transfer case flange. Also mark to indicate propeller shaft transmission/transfer case flange end.
4. Remove front propeller shaft CV joint bolts and retainers.
5. Remove rear propeller shaft CV joint bolts and retainers.
6. Compress the propeller shaft enough to remove it from the axle flange and transmission/transfer case flange.

To install:

7. Clean all propeller shaft bolts and apply Mopar® Lock AND Seal Adhesive or equivalent to the threads before installation.
8. Compress the propeller shaft enough to install it into the axle flange and transmission/transfer case flange.
9. Align installation reference marks on the transmission/transfer case flange and propeller shaft transmission/transfer end CV joint.
10. Install propeller shaft CV joint retainers and bolts. Tighten bolts to 15 ft. lbs. (20 Nm).
11. Align installation reference marks on the propeller shaft CV joint and axle flange.
12. Install propeller shaft CV joint retainers and bolts. Tighten bolts to 15 ft. lbs. (20 Nm).

REAR AXLE HOUSING

REMOVAL & INSTALLATION

See Figure 16.

1. With vehicle in neutral, position vehicle on hoist.
2. Position and secure a lift under the axle.
3. Mark propeller shaft flange and axle pinion flange for installation reference.
4. Remove propeller shaft and suspend under the vehicle. See "Propeller Shaft" in this section.
5. Remove vent hose from the axle tube.
6. Disconnect wiring connectors from the rear axle.
7. Remove brake calipers and rotors from axle. See "BRAKES" section.
8. Remove park brake cables from axle. See "BRAKES" section for Lock Out procedure and park brake removal.

➡Park brake cables are self adjusting and must be locked out before removal.

9. Remove brake sensors connector from sensors.

➡For assistance with suspension component removal, see "REAR SUSPENSION" section.

10. Remove track bar from axle bracket.
11. Remove stabilizer bar links from axle brackets.
12. Remove shock absorbers from axle brackets.
13. Remove upper control arms from axle brackets.
14. Loosen lower control arm bolts and lower axle enough to remove coil springs and spring insulators. Remove lower control arm from axle brackets.
15. Lower and remove the axle.

To install:

CAUTION

The weight of the vehicle must be supported by the springs before the control arms and track bar are tightened. Failure to follow these instructions will cause premature bushing failure.

16. Raise the axle under the vehicle.

➡For assistance with suspension component removal, see "REAR SUSPENSION" section.

17. Install lower control arms onto axle brackets and loosely install mounting bolts and nuts.
18. Install coil spring isolators and springs. Raise axle up until springs are seated.
19. Install upper control arms onto axle brackets and loosely install mounting bolts and nuts.
20. Install shock absorbers onto axle brackets and tighten nuts to 56 ft. lbs. (76 Nm).
21. Install stabilizer links onto axle brackets and tighten nuts to:
    - Upper nut to the stabilizer bar: 66 ft. lbs. (90 Nm)
    - Lower nut and bolt to axle: 75 ft. lbs. (102 Nm).
22. Install track bar onto axle bracket and loosely install track bar bolt.
23. Install brake sensors connector on sensors.
24. Install park brake cables on axle. See "PARKING BRAKE" section.
25. Install brake rotors and calipers on axle. See "BRAKES" section.
26. Install vent hose on axle tube.
27. Connect wiring connectors to axle.
28. Install propeller shaft with propeller shaft flange and pinion flange reference marks aligned. See "Propeller Shaft" in this section.
29. Clean all propeller shaft bolts and apply Mopar Lock & Seal Adhesive or equivalent to the threads before installation.
30. Install propeller shaft bolts and tighten to specifications.
31. Install wheels and tires.
32. Remove lift from axle and lower vehicle.
33. Tighten lower control arms, upper control arms and track bar nuts and bolts to 125 ft. lbs. (169 Nm).

REAR AXLE SHAFT

REMOVAL & INSTALLATION

See Figure 17.

1. With transmission in neutral, position vehicle on hoist.

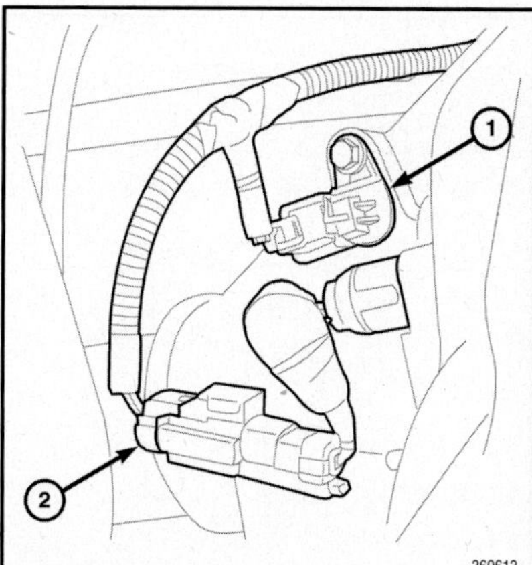

Fig. 16 Disconnect Tru-Lok® wiring connectors (1, 2).

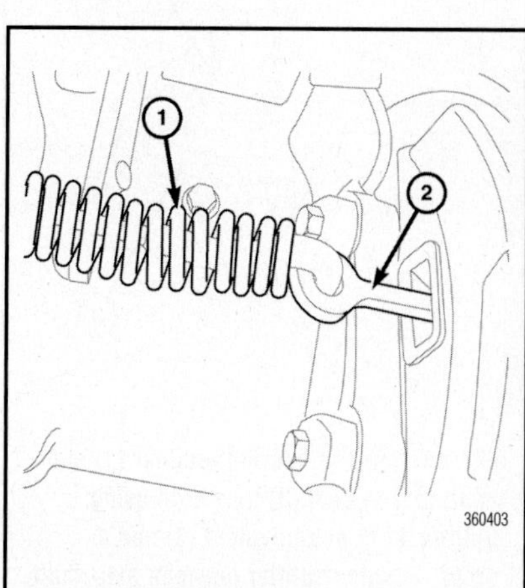

Fig. 17 Remove park brake cable (1) from support plate (2)

2. Remove brake caliper with adapter and rotor. See "BRAKES" section.

3. Remove park brake cable from support plate. See "PARKING BRAKES" section.

➡Park brake cables are self adjusting and must be locked out before removal.

4. Remove brake (wheel speed) sensor harness and remove sensor from support plate.

5. Remove axle retainer plate nuts.

6. Pull axle shaft with support plate, bearing and seal from axle tube.

To install:

7. Install axle assembly into the axle tube.

CAUTION

Never reuse axle retainer nuts. Used torque nuts can loosen up. Failure to follow these instructions may result in personal injury.

8. Install new axle retainer nuts and tighten to 45 ft. lbs. (61 Nm).

9. Install brake (wheel speed) sensor and harness.

10. Install park brake cables. See "PARKING BRAKES" section.

REAR AXLE SHAFT BEARING & SEAL

REMOVAL & INSTALLATION

See Figure 18.

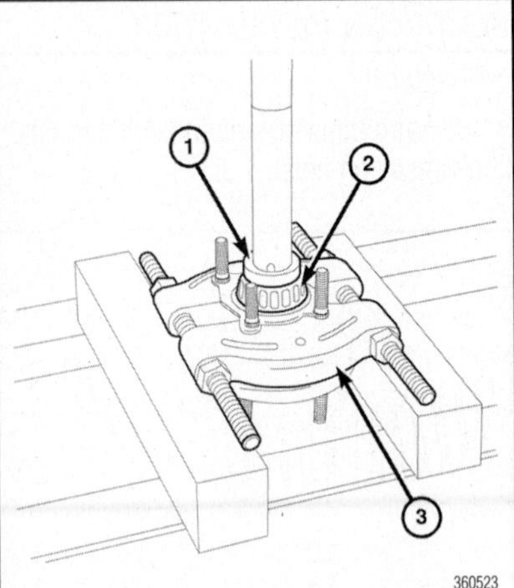

Fig. 18 Remove bearing retainer (1) and bearing with seal (2) from axle using Splitter 1130 or equivalent (3) and a press. Position splitter between axle shaft retainer and tone ring and press assembly off shaft.

1. Remove axle shaft from vehicle. See "Rear Axle Shaft" in this section.

➡Axle bearing race is a slip fit in the axle tube. No tool are required.

2. Remove brake dust shield and support plate from the axle.

➡Bearing retainer, axle bearing, axle shaft seal and axle shaft retainer are removed as an assembly.

3. Remove bearing retainer and bearing with seal from axle using Splitter 1130 or equivalent and a press. Position splitter between axle shaft retainer and tone ring and press assembly off shaft.

To install:

4. Inspect axle shaft retaining plate; if plate is bent or warped replace plate.

5. Install retaining plate on axle shaft.

6. Apply a coat of multi-purpose grease on sealing surface of axle seal.

7. Install seal on axle shaft with cavity away from axle shaft retaining.

8. Press bearing and bearing retaining ring onto axle shaft with press and press blocks.

9. Install dust shield and support plate on axle shaft retainer.

10. Lubricate bearing with Mopar Wheel Bearing Grease or equivalent. Wipe excess grease from outside of bearing.

11. Install axle in vehicle. See "Rear Axle Shaft" in this section.

REAR DRIVE PINION SEAL

REMOVAL & INSTALLATION

See Figure 19.

1. With transmission in neutral, position vehicle on hoist.

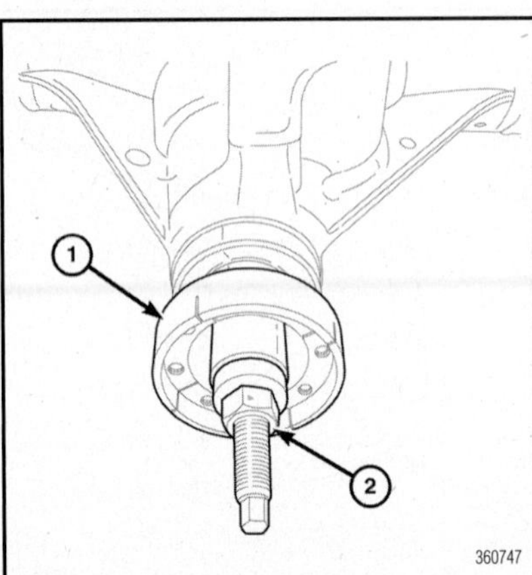

Fig. 19 Install flange (1) and installer (2) on pinion shaft.

2. Remove brake component to eliminate drag. See "BRAKES" section.

3. Remove propeller shaft at pinion flange. See "Propeller Shaft" in this section.

4. Rotate pinion gear three or four times. Record pinion torque to rotate, using an inch pound torque wrench.

5. Hold pinion flange with a Spanner Wrench (6958 or equivalent) and remove pinion nut and washer.

6. Mark a line across the pinion shaft and flange for installation reference.

7. Remove pinion flange with a proper puller.

8. Remove pinion seal with a seal puller.

To install:

9. Apply a light coating of gear lubricant on the lip of pinion seal.

10. Install seal with Installer and Handle (8681 and C-4171 or equivalent).

11. Install flange on the pinion shaft with the reference marks aligned.

12. Install flange and installer on pinion shaft.

13. Hold pinion flange with a spanner wrench and tighten the installer tool nut to remove all end play.

14. Install pinion washer and a new nut on the pinion gear.

15. Hold pinion flange with a spanner wrench and tighten pinion nut to 160 ft. lbs. (217 Nm).

16. Measure pinion torque to rotate with an inch pound torque wrench. Pinion torque to rotate is recorded reading plus 5 inch lbs. (0.56 Nm).

17. If pinion rotating torque is low. Hold pinion flange with spanner wrench and tighten pinion nut in 5 ft. lbs. (6.8 Nm) increments until pinion torque to rotating is achieved.

CAUTION

If maximum tightening torque of 200 ft. lbs. (271 Nm) is reached before torque to rotate is achieved, the collapsible spacer may have been damaged. Never loosen pinion gear nut to decrease pinion gear bearing rotating torque and never exceed specified preload torque. Failure to follow these instructions may result in damage.

18. Install propeller shaft. See "Propeller Shaft" in this section.

19. Install brake components. See "BRAKES" section.

ENGINE COOLING

ENGINE COOLANT

DRAIN & REFILL PROCEDURE

✲✲ CAUTION

Do not remove the cylinder block drain plugs or loosen the radiator draincock with system hot and under pressure. Serious burns from coolant can occur.

➡Radiator draincock is located on the right/lower side of radiator facing to front of vehicle.

1. Remove radiator pressure cap from radiator or coolant recovery container as necessary.
2. Raise and support vehicle.
3. Attach one end of a hose to the draincock. Put the other end into a clean container. Open draincock and drain coolant from radiator.

FLUSHING

✲✲ CAUTION

The cooling system normally operates at 14–16 psi pressure. Exceeding this pressure may damage the radiator or hoses.

Reverse flushing of the cooling system is the forcing of water through the cooling system. This is done using air pressure in the opposite direction of normal coolant flow. It is usually only necessary with very dirty systems with evidence of partial plugging.

Chemical Cleaning

➡If visual inspection indicates the formation of sludge or scaly deposits, use a radiator cleaner, Mopar Radiator Kleen or equivalent, before flushing. This will soften scale and other deposits and aid the flushing operation.

➡Be sure instructions on the container are followed.

Reverse Flushing Radiator

1. Disconnect the radiator hoses from the radiator fittings. Attach a section of radiator hose to the radiator bottom outlet fitting and insert the flushing gun. Connect a water supply hose and air supply hose to the flushing gun.
2. Allow the radiator to fill with water. When radiator is filled, apply air in short blasts allowing radiator to refill between blasts.
3. Continue this reverse flushing until clean water flows out through rear of radiator cooling tube passages.

➡For more information, refer to operating instructions supplied with flushing equipment. Have radiator cleaned more extensively by a radiator repair shop.

Reverse Flushing Engine

1. Drain the cooling system.
2. Remove the thermostat housing and thermostat. Install the thermostat housing.
3. Disconnect the radiator upper hose from the radiator and attach the flushing gun to the hose.
4. Disconnect the radiator lower hose from the water pump. Attach a lead away hose to the water pump inlet fitting.

✲✲ CAUTION

Be sure that the heater control valve is closed (heat off). This is done to prevent coolant flow with scale and other deposits from entering the heater core.

5. Connect the water supply hose and air supply hose to the flushing gun. Allow the engine to fill with water.
6. When the engine is filled, apply air in short blasts, allowing the system to fill between air blasts.
7. Continue until clean water flows through the lead away hose.

➡For more information, refer to operating instructions supplied with flushing equipment.

8. Remove the lead away hose, flushing gun, water supply hose and air supply hose.
9. Remove the thermostat housing, install the thermostat and a replacement gasket. Reinstall the housing.
10. Connect the radiator hoses.
11. Refill the cooling system with the correct antifreeze/water mixture

ENGINE FAN

REMOVAL & INSTALLATION

1. Disconnect the negative battery cable.
2. Remove the overflow bottle supply line.
3. Remove the coolant overflow container by pulling upwards.
4. Remove the air filter lid and position aside.
5. Remove the upper cooling fan mounting bolts.
6. Remove the upper radiator seal.
7. Disconnect the electric fan jumper harness at the fan shroud.
8. Remove the fan shroud by pulling upwards and away from the radiator.

To install:

9. Position fan assembly into the lower support mounts.
10. Install the upper fan mounting bolts. Tighten the bolts to 53 inch lbs. (6 Nm).
11. Install the upper fan seal.
12. Connect the electric fan jumper harness at the fan.
13. Install the coolant recovery bottle and the hose.
14. Install the air filter lid.
15. Connect the negative battery cable.

RADIATOR

REMOVAL & INSTALLATION

See Figures 20 and 21.

✲✲ CAUTION

When removing the radiator or A/C condenser for any reason, note the location of all radiator-to-body and radiator-to-A/C condenser rubber air seals. These are used at the top, bottom and sides of the radiator and A/C condenser. To prevent overheating, these seals must be installed to their original positions.

1. Disconnect negative battery cable at battery.
2. Drain cooling system. Drain coolant into a clean container for reuse, if appropriate.
3. Remove coolant recovery container.
4. Remove radiator upper seal.
5. Remove the electric cooling fan.
6. Remove lower radiator seal.
7. Remove lower radiator hose.
8. Remove front grille.
9. Remove two A/C condenser mounting bolts. Lift A/C condenser out of J-clips.
10. Remove evaporator line tapping block and mounting bolt.

ENGINE ELECTRICAL — IGNITION SYSTEM

FIRING ORDER

1–2–3–4–5–6

IGNITION COIL

REMOVAL & INSTALLATION

➡The ignition coil pack is located above the left valve cover.

1. Disconnect negative battery cable.
2. Remove six spark plug cables.
3. Disconnect electrical connector from ignition coil.
4. Remove two coil mounting nuts.
5. Pull coil pack from mounting studs.
6. Installation is the reverse of the removal procedure.

IGNITION TIMING

ADJUSTMENT

➡Ignition timing is controlled by the engine control module and no manual adjustment is needed.

SPARK PLUGS

REMOVAL & INSTALLATION

CAUTION

When replacing the spark plugs and spark plug cables, route the cables correctly and secure them in the appropriate retainers. Failure to route the cables properly can cause the radio to reproduce ignition noise, cross ignition of the spark plugs or short circuit the cables to ground.

CAUTION

Always remove cables by grasping at the boot, rotating the boot 1/2 turn, and pulling straight back in a steady motion.

1. Prior to removing the spark plug, spray compressed air around the spark plug hole and the area around the spark plug.
2. Remove the spark plug using a quality socket with a foam insert.
3. Inspect the spark plug condition.
4. Installation is the reverse of the removal procedure.
5. Tighten spark plugs to 13 ft. lbs. (17.5 Nm).

ENGINE ELECTRICAL — STARTING SYSTEM

STARTER

REMOVAL & INSTALLATION

1. Disconnect and isolate negative battery cable.
2. Raise and support vehicle.
3. While supporting starter motor, remove two bolts securing starter motor to transmission.
4. Lower starter motor far enough to access and remove nut securing battery cable to starter solenoid B+ terminal stud.

CAUTION

Always support starter motor during this process. Do not let starter motor hang from wire harness.

5. Remove battery cable at starter.
6. Disconnect solenoid terminal wire harness connector from starter solenoid.
7. Remove starter motor.
8. Installation is the reverse of the removal procedure.
9. Tighten starter mounting bolts to 40 ft. lbs. (54 Nm).

ENGINE MECHANICAL

ACCESSORY DRIVE BELTS

ACCESSORY BELT ROUTING

See Figure 23.

INSPECTION

When diagnosing serpentine accessory drive belts, small cracks that run across the ribbed surface of the belt from rib to rib are considered normal. These are not a reason to replace the belt. However, cracks running along a rib (not across) are not normal. Any belt with cracks running along a rib must be replaced. Also replace the belt if it has excessive wear, frayed cords or severe glazing.

REMOVAL & INSTALLATION

1. Disconnect negative battery cable from battery.
2. Rotate accessory belt tensioner clockwise until it contacts its stop. Remove accessory drive belt, then slowly rotate the accessory drive belt tensioner into the freearm position.

To install:

3. Route accessory drive belt around all pulleys except the idler pulley.

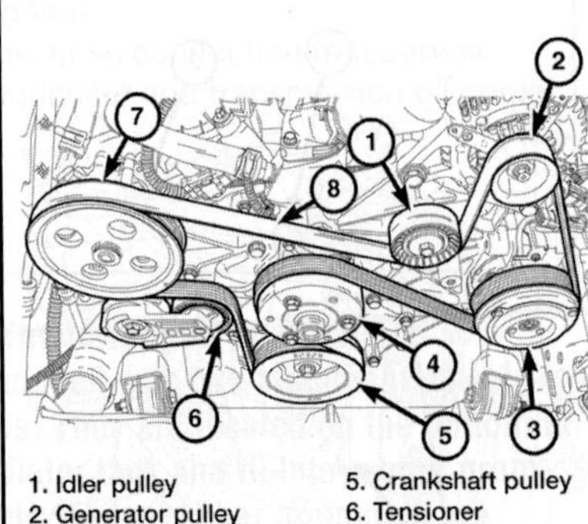

Fig. 23 Serpentine (accessory) drive belt routing

4. Rotate the accessory drive belt tensioner clockwise until it contacts its stop position.
5. Route the accessory drive belt around the idler pulley and slowly let the tensioner rotate into the belt.
6. Make sure the accessory drive belt is properly seated onto all pulleys.

AIR CLEANER

REMOVAL & INSTALLATION

1. Disconnect the negative battery cable.
2. Disconnect the inlet air temperature sensor connector.
3. Disconnect the CCV hose from the air cleaner cover.
4. Remove the air inlet tube from the throttle body.
5. Remove the bolt for air cleaner housing at upper radiator cross member.
6. Pull air box up and off over the single locating pin.
7. Remove air box from vehicle.

8. Installation is the reverse of the removal procedure.

FILTER/ELEMENT REPLACEMENT

1. Disconnect the IAT sensor connector.
2. Disconnect the CCV hose.
3. Separate the air inlet tube from the throttle body.
4. Remove the air cleaner cover bolts.
5. Lift cover and pull toward the engine and remove cover tabs from air cleaner housing.
6. Lift cover and remove the filter.
7. Installation is the reverse of the removal procedure.

CAMSHAFT & HYDRAULIC VALVE LIFTERS

REMOVAL & INSTALLATION

See Figure 24.

1. Remove the radiator and cooling fans from the vehicle. See "ENGINE COOLING" section.
2. Remove the cylinder heads. See "Cylinder Head" in this section.
3. Remove the timing chain and camshaft sprocket. See "Timing Chain & Sprockets" in this section.
4. Remove the yoke retainer bolts, yoke retainer, aligning yokes and hydraulic lifters. Identify each lifter for reinstallation in original location.

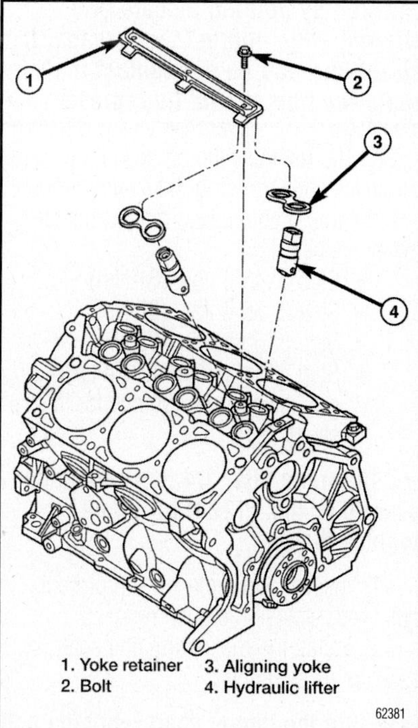

Fig. 24 Showing the hydraulic lifters and related components

5. Remove camshaft thrust plate on the front end of the block.

CAUTION

Slowly remove the camshaft from the engine taking precautions not to damage the camshaft bearings.

6. Install a long bolt into front of camshaft to facilitate removal of the camshaft.
7. Carefully remove the camshaft.

➡The camshaft bearings are serviced with the engine block.

To install:

8. Lubricate camshaft lobes and camshaft bearing journals with engine oil.
9. Install a long bolt into the camshaft to assist in the installation of the camshaft.
10. Carefully install the camshaft in engine block.
11. Install camshaft thrust plate and bolts. Tighten to 105 inch lbs. (12 Nm) torque.
12. Measure camshaft end play. It should be 0.010–0.020 in. (0.254–0.508 mm). If not within specifications, replace thrust plate.
13. Install the timing chain and sprockets. See "Timing Chain & Sprockets" in this section.

➡When camshaft is replaced, all of the hydraulic lifters must be replaced.

14. Install the hydraulic lifters with lubrication hole in the upward position.
15. Install the timing chain cover. See "Timing Chain Cover" in this section.
16. Install the cylinder heads. See "Cylinder Head" in this section.
17. Install the cylinder head covers.
18. Install the lower and upper intake manifolds. See "Intake Manifold" in this section.
19. Install the radiator and cooling fan. See "ENGINE COOLING" section.

CATALYTIC CONVERTER

REMOVAL & INSTALLATION

WARNING

If torches are used when servicing the exhaust system, do not allow any flame near the fuel lines or the fuel tank. Failure to follow these instructions may result in possible serious or fatal injury.

1. Raise and support the vehicle.
2. Saturate the bolts and nuts with heat valve lubricant. Allow 5 minutes for penetration.
3. Disconnect oxygen sensor electrical connectors.
4. Remove the transmission crossmember as follows:
   a. Remove the transmission skid plate
   b. Remove the transfer case skid plate.
   c. Remove the left side bolts.
   d. Remove the fuel tank skid plate bolts.
   e. Remove the right side bolts and remove the crossmember.
5. Remove the nuts from the front exhaust pipe and catalytic converter assembly to muffler flange.
6. Remove bolts and flanged nuts at the manifold.
7. Lower the front exhaust pipe/catalytic converter assembly and slide out of the mount at the transmission (if equipped).
8. Remove the front exhaust pipe/catalytic converter assembly from the vehicle.

To install:

9. Position the front exhaust pipe and catalytic converter assembly into the mount at the transmission (if equipped) and onto the exhaust manifold flange connection.
10. Install the nuts at the front exhaust pipe and catalytic converter assembly to muffler flange. Do not tighten.
11. Position the exhaust pipe for proper clearance with the frame and underbody parts. A minimum clearance of 1.0 in. (25 mm) is required.
12. Tighten the bolt at exhaust manifold to 20 ft. lbs. (27 Nm) torque.
13. Tighten the front exhaust pipe and catalytic converter assembly to muffler flange nuts to 20 ft. lbs. (27 Nm) torque.
14. Position the front pipe onto the exhaust manifold flange connection. Tighten the clamp to 89 inch lbs. (10 Nm) torque.
15. Connect oxygen sensor electrical connectors.
16. Install the transmission crossmember as follows:
   a. Install the crossmember and install the bolts.
   b. Install the right side bolts and tighten all four crossmember bolts to 90 ft. lbs. (122 Nm).
   c. Install the fuel tank skid plate bolts and tighten to 73 ft. lbs. (99 Nm).
   d. Install the transmission skid plate.
   e. Install the transfer case skid plate.
17. Lower the vehicle.

18. Start the vehicle and inspect for exhaust leaks. Repair exhaust leaks as necessary.

19. Check the exhaust system for contact with the body panels. Make adjustments, if necessary.

CRANKSHAFT FRONT SEAL

REMOVAL & INSTALLATION

See Figures 25 and 26.

1. Disconnect negative cable from battery.
2. Remove accessory drive belt. See "Accessory Drive Belt" in this section.
3. Remove crankshaft damper. See "Crankshaft Damper" in this section.
4. Position Seal Removal Tool (6341A or equivalent) on crankshaft nose. Carefully screw the tool into the seal until it engages firmly.

**** CAUTION**

Be careful not to damage that crankshaft seal surface of cover.

5. Remove oil seal by turning the forcing screw until the seal disengages from the cover.

To install:

6. Position Seal Installer Guide Tool (C-4992-2 or equivalent), on the crankshaft nose.
7. Position new seal over the guide with the seal spring in the direction of the engine front cover.
8. Install seal using Seal Installer Tool (C-4992-1 or equivalent) until seal is flush with cover.
9. Install crankshaft damper. See "Crankshaft Damper" in this section.
10. Install accessory drive belt. See "Accessory Drive Belt" in this section.

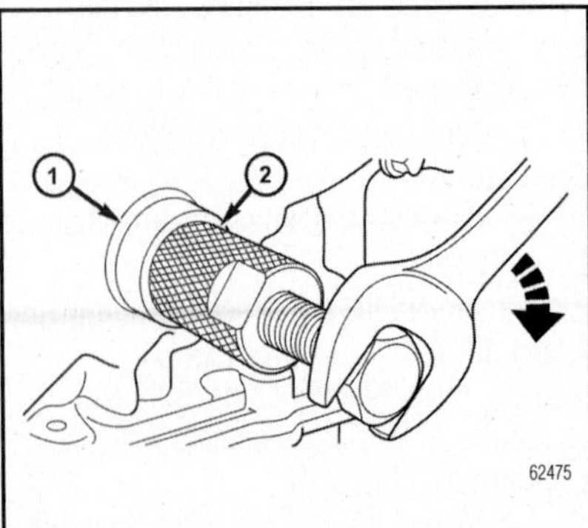

Fig. 25 Remove oil seal (1) by turning the forcing screw of the tool (2) until the seal disengages from the cover.

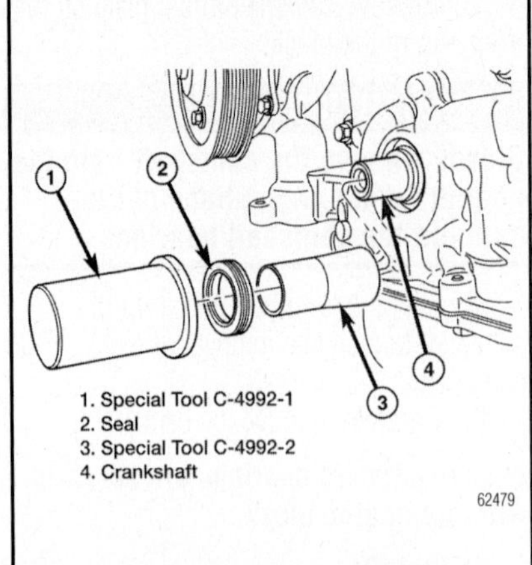

Fig. 26 Installing the crankshaft oil seal

11. Lower vehicle and connect negative cable to battery.

CYLINDER HEAD

REMOVAL & INSTALLATION

See Figure 27.

1. Drain the cooling system. See "ENGINE COOLING" section.
2. Disconnect negative cable from battery.
3. Remove upper and lower intake manifolds. See "Intake Manifold" in this section.

**** CAUTION**

Intake manifold gasket is made of very thin metal and may cause personal injury, handle with care.

4. Remove the cylinder head covers. See "Valve (Cylinder Head) Covers" in this section.
5. Remove the spark plugs from cylinder head.
6. Remove the oil level indicator and tube.
7. Remove exhaust manifold(s). See "Exhaust Manifold" in this section.

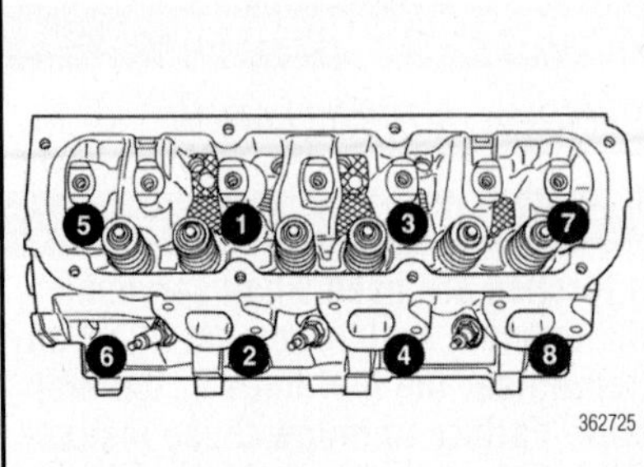

Fig. 27 Cylinder head bolt loosening and tightening sequence

8. Remove rocker arm and shaft assemblies as follows:

➡Rocker arm shaft bolts are captured to the shaft.

a. Loosen the rocker shaft bolts , rotating one turn each, until all valve spring pressure is relieved.
b. Remove the rocker arms and shaft assembly.

9. Remove push rods and mark positions to ensure installation in original locations.
10. Remove the eight head bolts from each cylinder head and remove cylinder heads.

To install:

11. Clean all sealing surfaces of engine block and cylinder heads.
12. Position new gasket(s) on engine block .

➡The left bank gasket is identified with the "L" stamped in the exposed area of the gasket located at front of engine. The right bank gasket is identified with a "R" stamped in the exposed area of the gasket also, but is located at the rear of the engine.

**** CAUTION**

The cylinder head bolts should be examined BEFORE reuse. If the threads are necked down, the bolts must be replaced. Necking can be checked by holding a scale or straight edge against the threads. If all the threads do not contact the scale the bolt should be replaced.

13. Tighten the cylinder head bolts in the sequence shown. Using the 4 step torque turn method, tighten according to the following values:
   - Step 1: 45 ft. lbs. (61 Nm)
   - Step 2: 65 ft. lbs. (88 Nm)
   - Step 3: 65 ft. lbs. (88 Nm)
   - Step 4: an additional 1/4 turn (do not use a torque wrench for this step.)

➡Bolt torque after 1/4 turn should be over 90 ft. lbs. (122 Nm). If not, replace the bolt.

14. Inspect and replace worn or bent push rods. Install the push rods.
15. Install the rocker arm and shaft assemblies as follows:

➡Ensure the longer shaft retaining bolt is installed in the proper location on the rocker shaft.

a. Position the rocker arm and shaft assemblies on the pedestal mounts.

b. Ensure all pushrods are properly located on the lifter and the rocker arm socket.

c. Align each rocker arm socket with each pushrod end.

d. The rocker arm shaft should be tightened down slowly, starting with the center bolts. Allow 20 minutes lifter bleed down time after installation of the rocker shafts before engine operation.

e. Slowly tighten rocker shaft bolts evenly until shaft is seated. Tighten bolts to 200 inch lbs. (23 Nm).

16. Install the cylinder head covers. See "Valve (Cylinder Head) Covers" in this section.

17. Install the exhaust manifolds. See "Exhaust Manifold" in this section.

18. Install new O-ring on oil level indicator tube. Install oil level indicator tube assembly.

19. Install upper and lower intake manifolds. See "Intake Manifold" in this section.

20. Fill the cooling system. See "ENGINE COOLING" section.

21. Connect negative cable to battery.

ENGINE OIL & FILTER

REPLACEMENT

1. Run engine until achieving normal operating temperature.
2. Open hood, remove oil fill cap.
3. Place a suitable drain pan under crankcase drain.
4. Remove drain plug from crankcase and allow oil to drain into pan. Inspect drain plug threads for stretching or other damage. Replace drain plug if damaged.
5. Remove oil filter.
6. Install and tighten drain plug in crankcase.
7. Install new oil filter.
8. Lower vehicle and fill crankcase with specified type and amount of engine oil.
9. Install oil fill cap.
10. Start engine and inspect for leaks.
11. Stop engine and inspect oil level.

EXHAUST MANIFOLD

REMOVAL & INSTALLATION

Left

1. Disconnect battery negative cable.
2. Remove the fresh air hose.
3. Disconnect applicable cylinder bank spark plug wires.
4. For the right side exhaust manifold, remove the IAC,TPS and the EVAP hose to the throttle body
5. Remove heat shield attaching bolts.
6. Remove bolts attaching exhaust to manifold.
7. Disconnect the left side oxygen sensors.
8. Remove bolts attaching exhaust manifold to cylinder head.
9. Remove the exhaust manifold.

To install:

10. Position exhaust manifold on cylinder head. Install bolts to center runner (cylinder #4) and initially tighten to 25 inch lbs. (2.8 Nm).
11. Position heat shield on manifold.
12. Install the remaining manifold attaching bolts. Tighten all bolts to 200 inch lbs. (23 Nm).
13. Install and tighten heat shield attaching nut to 105 inch lbs. (12 Nm).
14. Attach exhaust pipe to exhaust manifold and tighten bolts to 30 ft. lbs. (41 Nm).
15. Connect the left side oxygen sensors.
16. For the right side exhaust manifold, install the IAC,TPS and the EVAP hose to the throttle body
17. Install the spark plug wires.
18. Install the fresh air hose.
19. Connect battery negative cable.

INTAKE MANIFOLD

REMOVAL & INSTALLATION

Upper

See Figure 28.

1. Disconnect and isolate the negative battery cable.
2. Disconnect the Inlet Air Temperature (IAT) sensor electrical connector.
3. Remove air inlet resonator to throttle body hose assembly.
4. Disconnect the throttle body electrical connector.
5. Disconnect the EVAP hose at the throttle body.
6. Remove the EGR tube.
7. Disconnect the Manifold Absolute Pressure (MAP) sensor electrical connector at the rear of the intake manifold.
8. Disconnect the power brake booster hose at the rear of the intake manifold and position aside.
9. Disconnect the PCV hose from the upper intake manifold.
10. Remove the upper intake manifold bolts and remove the manifold.

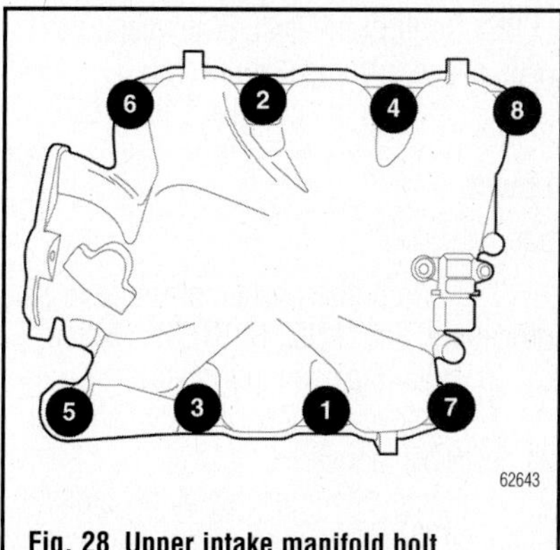

Fig. 28 Upper intake manifold bolt loosening and tightening sequence

11. Cover the lower intake manifold ports with a suitable cover while the upper manifold is removed.
12. Clean and inspect the upper intake manifold.

To install:

13. Clean the gasket surfaces and remove the covering from the lower intake manifold ports.
14. Inspect the intake manifold gasket condition (gaskets can be re-used if not damaged).
15. Position the intake manifold gaskets into the seal channels and press lightly into place.
16. Position the upper intake manifold onto the lower intake manifold.
17. Apply Mopar Lock & Seal Adhesive (medium strength threadlocker) to each upper intake manifold bolt.
18. Install the intake manifold bolts and tighten bolts in the sequence shown to 105 inch lbs. (12 Nm).
19. Connect the PCV hose (1) to the upper intake manifold.
20. Connect the power brake booster hose at the rear of the intake manifold.
21. If removed, install the MAP sensor at the rear of the intake manifold by pushing down on the MAP sensor while rotating clockwise about 1/4 turn. Connect the MAP sensor electrical connector.

➡The special screws used for attaching the EGR tube to the manifold must be installed slowly using hand tools only. This requirement is to prevent the melting of material that causes stripped threads. If threads become stripped, an oversize repair screw is available.

22. Install the EGR tube.
23. Connect the EVAP hose and the electrical connector to the throttle body.
24. Install the air cleaner and air inlet hose assembly.

25. Connect the inlet air temperature (IAT) sensor electrical connector.

26. Connect the negative battery cable.

Lower

See Figure 29.

1. Perform fuel system pressure release procedure. See "FUEL SYSTEM" section.
2. Drain the cooling system.
3. Remove the upper intake manifold, as described above.
4. Remove the fuel line at the connection near the valve cover.
5. Remove ignition coil and bracket.
6. Disconnect heater supply hose and engine coolant temperature sensor.
7. Disconnect the fuel injector wire harness.
8. Remove the fuel injectors and rail assembly.
9. Remove radiator upper hose.
10. Remove the intake manifold bolts and remove lower intake manifold.

⁂ CAUTION

Intake manifold gasket is made of very thin metal and may cause personal injury, handle with care.

11. Remove intake manifold seal retainers screws. Remove intake manifold gasket.

To install:

12. Place a bead (approximately 1/4 in. diameter) of Mopar Engine RTV GEN II (or equivalent) onto each of the four manifold to cylinder head gasket corners.
13. Carefully install the new intake manifold gasket. Tighten end seal retainer screws to 105 inch lbs. (12 Nm).
14. Install lower intake manifold. Install the bolts and hand tighten. Then torque bolts to 200 inch lbs. (22 Nm) in sequence shown. Then, torque again to 200 inch lbs. (22 Nm), in sequence. After intake manifold is in place, inspect to make sure seals are in place.
15. Install the fuel injectors and rail assembly. See "FUEL SYSTEM" section.
16. Connect fuel injector electrical harness.
17. Connect the engine coolant temperature sensor.
18. Connect the heater supply and radiator upper hoses to manifold.
19. Connect the fuel line near the valve cover.
20. Install the upper intake manifold, as described in this section.
21. Connect negative battery cable.
22. Fill the cooling system.
23. Connect the negative battery cable.

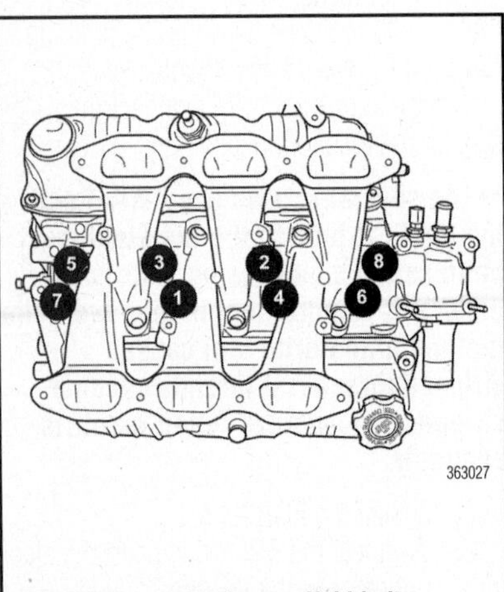

Fig. 29 Lower intake manifold bolt loosening and tightening sequence

OIL PAN

REMOVAL & INSTALLATION

See Figure 30.

1. Disconnect negative cable from battery.
2. Remove engine oil level indicator tube.
3. Raise vehicle on hoist, drain engine oil, and remove the oil filter.
4. Remove the structural cover fasteners and structural cover.

➡Do not remove the lower oil pan bolts. Only remove the upper oil pan-to-engine block bolts.

5. Remove the oil pan fasteners, oil pan and gasket.

To install:

6. Thoroughly clean sealing surfaces of any oil, dirt, or original sealer, and apply a 1/8 inch bead of Mopar Engine RTV GEN II (or equivalent) at the parting line of the chain case cover and the rear seal retainer.
7. Position a new pan gasket on oil pan.
8. Install oil pan and tighten fasteners to 105 inch lbs. (12 Nm).
9. Install the structural cover and tighten fasteners.
10. Lower vehicle and install oil level indicator.
11. Install new oil filter.
12. Fill crankcase with oil to proper level.
13. Connect negative cable to battery.

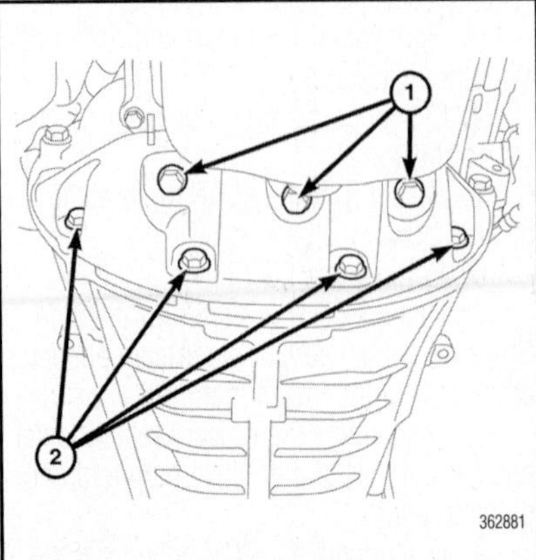

Fig. 30 Remove the structural cover fasteners (1, 2) and structural cover.

OIL PUMP

REMOVAL & INSTALLATION

➡The oil pump is contained within the timing chain cover housing.

1. Remove oil pan, as described above.
2. Remove the timing chain cover. See "Timing Chain Cover" in this section.
3. Disassemble oil pump from timing chain cover.
4. Clean and Inspect oil pump components.
5. Installation is the reverse of the removal procedure.

INSPECTION

1. Inspect mating surface of the chain case cover. Surface should be smooth. Replace cover if scratched or grooved.
2. Lay a straightedge across the pump cover surface . If a 0.001 in. (0.025 mm) feeler gauge can be inserted between cover and straight edge, cover should be replaced.
3. Measure thickness and diameter of outer rotor. If outer rotor thickness measures 0.301 in. (7.64 mm) or less , or if the diameter is 3.148 in. (79.95 mm) or less, replace outer rotor.
4. If inner rotor thickness measures 0.301 in. (0.64 mm) or less, replace inner rotor.
5. Install outer rotor into chain case cover. Press rotor to one side with fingers and measure clearance between rotor and chain case cover. If measurement is -/015 in. (0.39 mm) or more, replace chain case cover, only if outer rotor is in specification.
6. Install inner rotor into chain case cover. If clearance between inner and outer rotors is 0.008 in. (0.203 mm) or more, replace both rotors.
7. Place a straightedge across the face of the chain case cover, between bolt holes. If a feeler gauge of 0.004 in. (0.10 mm) or more can be inserted between rotors and the straightedge, replace pump assembly. ONLY if rotors are in specs.

8. Remove oil pressure relief valve.

a. Inspect oil pressure relief valve and bore. Inspect for scoring, pitting and free valve operation in bore. Small marks may be removed with 400-grit wet or dry sandpaper.

b. The relief valve spring has a free length of approximately 1.95 in. (49.5 mm), it should test between 19.5 and 20.5 pounds when compressed to 1-11/32 in. (34 mm). Replace spring that fails to meet specifications.

9. If oil pressure is low and pump is within specifications, inspect for worn engine bearings or other reasons for oil pressure loss.

PISTON & RING

POSITIONING

See Figure 31.

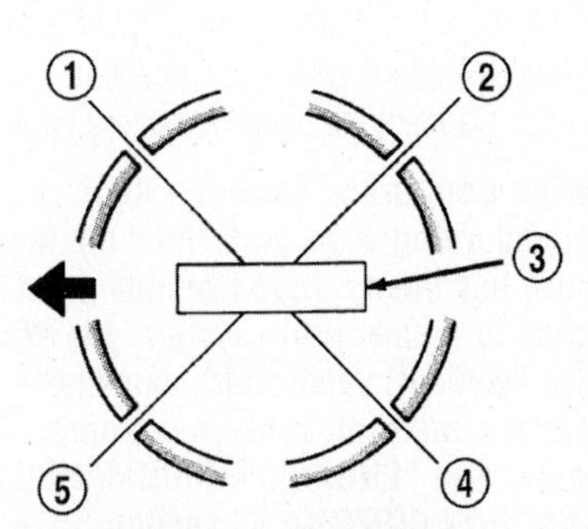

Fig. 31 Showing positioning of piston ring end gaps

REAR MAIN SEAL

REMOVAL & INSTALLATION

➡Any time the rear crank oil seal has been removed from the engine block, a new seal assembly must be installed. Do not re-use a real crank oil seal assembly once it has been removed.

1. Remove the transmission.
2. Remove the flex plate/flywheel.
3. Remove oil seal retainer bolts and remove oil seal retainer.
4. Clean engine block and retainer of oil and gasket material. Make sure surfaces are clean and free of oil.
5. Remove the oil seal.

To install:

⁂ CAUTION

Before installing a new rear oil seal assembly, ensure that the plastic installation sleeve (1) is present in the seal assembly. The new seal cannot be properly installed without the plastic installation sleeve, and if the seal assembly is installed without it, oil leakage will result.

6. Remove any original sealer, oil, or debris from the rear oil seal retainer assembly mounting area.
7. Place a bead (approximately 1/4 in. diameter) of Mopar Engine RTV GEN II (or equivalent) in the lower corners of the rear crankshaft oil seal retainer mounting surface, where the seal retainer meets the oil pan (the T-Joint).
8. Place the rear crankshaft oil seal assembly over the rear crankshaft flange. Do not press the seal assembly over the rear crankshaft flange at this time.
9. Using both hands, one on each side of the rear crankshaft flange, press the rear crankshaft oil seal over the rear crankshaft flange.
10. Ensure that the extruded dowels in the rear of the crankshaft oil seal retainer are seated in the locating holes in the rear of the engine block.
11. Install the five rear crankshaft oil seal retainer fasteners. Do not tighten at this time.
12. Remove and discard the plastic installation sleeve.
13. Tighten the five rear crankshaft oil seal retainer fasteners to 105 inch lbs. (12 Nm).
14. Install the flex plate/flywheel.
15. Install the transmission.

TIMING CHAIN FRONT COVER

REMOVAL & INSTALLATION

See Figures 32 and 33.

1. Disconnect and isolate the negative battery cable.
2. Drain the cooling system. See "ENGINE COOLING" section.
3. Remove the air cleaner hose and housing assembly.
4. Loosen the three mounting bolts at the water pump pulley.
5. Remove the accessory drive belt and belt tensioner.
6. Remove the water pump pulley bolts. Rotate the pulley until the openings in the pulley align with the water pump drive hub spokes and remove the pulley.
7. Remove the generator. See "ENGINE ELECTRICAL" section.
8. Raise and support the vehicle on a hoist.
9. Drain the engine oil and remove the oil filter.
10. Remove the oil level indicator and tube.
11. Remove the structural cover and oil pan. See "Oil Pan" in this section.
12. Disconnect the lower radiator hose, heater hose and the oil pressure switch.
13. Remove the power steering pump fasteners and reposition the power steering pump.
14. Remove the A/C compressor mounting bolts and reposition the A/C compressor.
15. Remove the crankshaft vibration damper. See "Crankshaft Damper" in this section.
16. Remove the camshaft position (CMP) sensor from the timing chain cover.
17. Remove the timing chain cover fasteners and remove the timing chain cover.

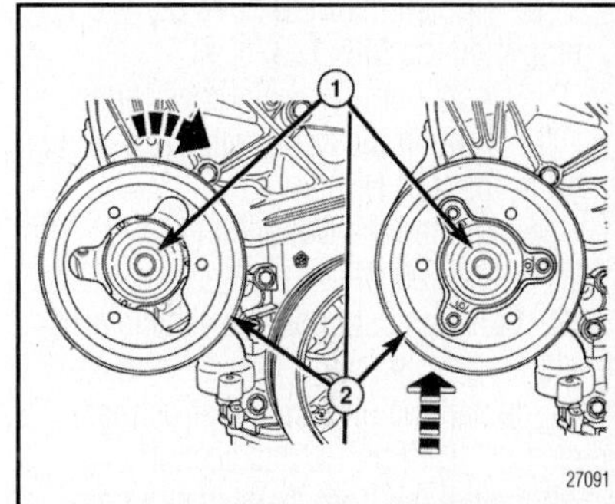

Fig. 32 Remove the water pump pulley bolts. Rotate the pulley (2) until the openings in the pulley align with the water pump drive hub spokes (1) and remove the pulley (2).

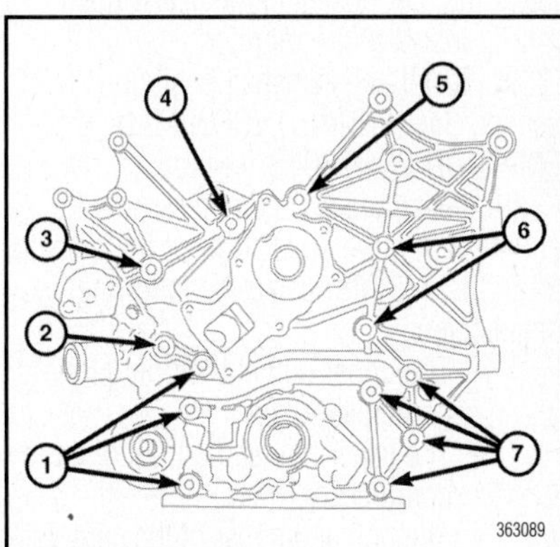

Fig. 33 Timing chain cover fasteners (1 thru 7) shown

To install:

➡Crankshaft oil seal must be removed to insure correct oil pump engagement.

18. Be sure the mating surfaces of the chain case cover and cylinder block are clean and free from burrs.

➡Do not use sealer on the timing cover gasket

19. Position the new timing cover gasket on the timing cover. Adhere the new gasket to the chain case cover, making sure that the lower edge of the gasket is 0.020 in. (0.5 mm) beyond the lower edge of the cover.
20. Rotate the crankshaft so that the oil pump drive flats are in the vertical position.
21. Position the oil pump inner rotor so that the mating flats are in the same position as the crankshaft drive flats.

⁂ CAUTION

Make sure the oil pump is engaged on the crankshaft correctly or severe damage may result.

a. Install the timing cover.
b. Tighten the M10 bolts (2, 4, 6,) first, then the M8 (1, 3, 5, 7).
c. Install timing chain cover bolts.
d. Tighten the M10 bolts (2, 4, 6) to 40 ft. lbs. (54 Nm).
e. Tighten the M8 bolts (1, 3, 5, 7) to 21 ft. lbs. (28 Nm).

22. Raise and support the vehicle on a hoist.
23. Install the oil pan and structural cover. See "Oil Pan" in this section.
24. Install the front crankshaft oil seal. See "Crankshaft Front Seal" in this section.
25. Install the crankshaft vibration damper. See "Crankshaft Damper" in this section. Install the vibration damper bolt. Tighten bolt to 40 ft. lbs. (54 Nm).
26. Connect the oil pressure switch, lower radiator hose and the heater hose.
27. Install a new oil filter.
28. Install the camshaft position (CMP) sensor. See "ENGINE PERFORMANCE & EMISSION CONTROLS" section.
29. Install the A/C compressor to the engine with three bolts. Tighten the bolts to 21 ft. lbs. (28 Nm) using the following sequence:
    - The upper bolt at the front of the compressor.
    - The lower bolt at the front of the compressor.
    - The bolt at the rear of the compressor.
30. Install the oil level indicator tube and indicator. Tighten the bolt to 15 ft. lbs. (20 Nm).
31. Install the generator. See "ENGINE ELECTRICAL" section.
32. Install the power steering pump. Tighten pump mounting bolts to 19 ft. lbs. (26 Nm).
33. Install the water pump pulley on the water pump hub. Install the bolts and tighten to 250 inch lbs. (28 Nm).
34. Install the belt tensioner and accessory drive belt.
35. Install the air cleaner housing assembly and hose.
36. Fill the engine crankcase with the proper oil to the correct level.
37. Fill the cooling system.
38. Connect the negative battery cable

TIMING CHAIN & SPROCKETS

REMOVAL & INSTALLATION

See Figures 34 and 35.

1. Disconnect negative cable from battery.
2. Remove the timing chain cover bolts and timing cover, as described above.
3. Rotate engine by turning crankshaft until the timing marks are aligned as shown.
4. Remove camshaft sprocket attaching bolt. Remove the timing chain with camshaft sprocket.
5. Remove the crankshaft sprocket, if necessary.

To install:

6. Install the crankshaft sprocket, if removed, using the tool set as during removal.
7. Rotate the crankshaft so the timing arrow on the crankshaft sprocket is to the 12 o'clock position.

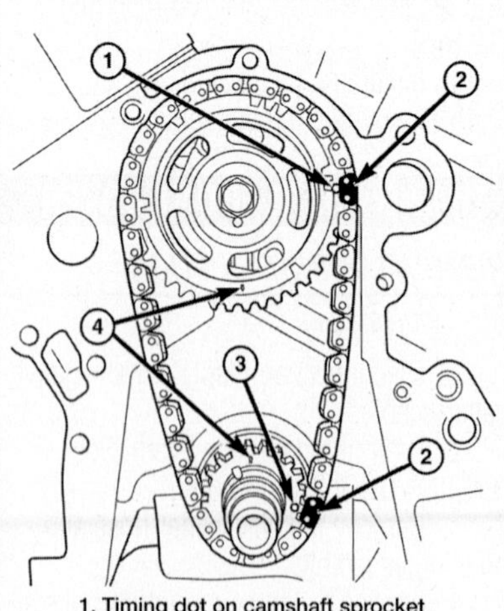

Fig. 34 Rotate engine by turning crankshaft until the timing marks are aligned as shown.

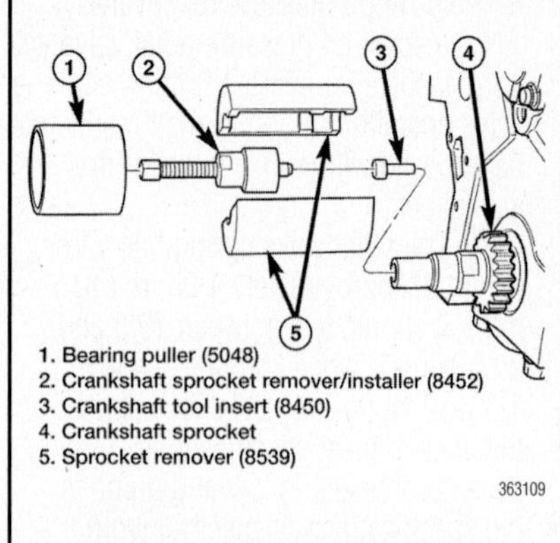

Fig. 35 Remove the crankshaft sprocket, if necessary, with the special tools shown

8. Lubricate the timing chain and sprockets with clean engine oil before installation.
9. While holding the camshaft sprocket and chain in hand, place the timing chain around the camshaft sprocket, aligning the plated link with the dot on the sprocket. Position the timing arrow on the camshaft sprocket to the 6 o'clock position. See illustration above.
10. Place the timing chain around crankshaft sprocket with the plated link lined up with the dot on the crankshaft sprocket. Install the camshaft sprocket into position.
11. Use a straight edge to check alignment of timing marks.
12. Install the camshaft sprocket bolt and washer. Tighten the bolt to 40 ft. lbs. (54 Nm).
13. Rotate the crankshaft two revolutions and check the timing mark alignment. If timing marks do not line up, remove the camshaft sprocket and realign.
14. Install the timing chain cover. See "Timing Chain Cover" in this section.
15. Connect the negative battery cable

➡The Cam/Crank Variation Relearn procedure must be performed anytime there has been a repair/replacement made to a powertrain system, for example: flywheel, valve train, camshaft and/or crankshaft sensors or components. See "ENGINE PERFORMANCE & EMISSION CONTROLS" section.

VALVE (CYLINDER HEAD) COVERS

REMOVAL & INSTALLATION

1. On the left side head, do the following:
    a. Remove the ignition coil pack.
    b. Disconnect PCV hose from cylinder head cover.

c. Remove the generator support bracket.

2. On the right side head, disconnect the CCV hose from the cover.

3. Disconnect spark plug wires from spark plugs.

4. Remove cylinder head cover bolts.

5. Remove cylinder head cover and gasket.

To install:

6. Clean cylinder head and cylinder head cover mating surfaces. Inspect cylinder head cover surface for flatness. Replace gasket as necessary.

7. Assemble gasket to cylinder cover by inserting the fasteners through each bolt hole on cover and gasket.

8. Install the cylinder head cover and bolts. Tighten bolts to 105 inch lbs. (12 Nm).

9. On the left side head, do the following:

a. Connect PCV hose.

b. Install the ignition coil pack.

c. Install the generator support bracket.

10. On the right side head, connect the CCV hose.

11. Connect spark plug wires to spark plugs.

VALVE LASH

ADJUSTMENT

➡Valve lash (clearance) is maintained by hydraulic lifters. No manual adjustment is required.

ENGINE PERFORMANCE & EMISSION CONTROLS

ACCELERATOR PEDAL POSITION (APP) SENSOR

LOCATION

➡The APP sensor is an integral part of the accelerator pedal assembly.

REMOVAL & INSTALLATION

1. Disconnect electrical connector at the APP sensor.

2. Remove two accelerator pedal mounting bracket nuts.

3. Remove accelerator pedal/APP sensor assembly from vehicle.

To install:

4. Position the accelerator pedal/APP sensor assembly over the two mounting studs.

5. Install two accelerator pedal mounting bracket nuts and tighten to 9 ft. lbs. (12 Nm).

6. Connect the accelerator pedal electrical connector to the APP sensor.

7. Use a scan tool to learn electrical parameters. Go to the Miscellaneous menu, and then select ETC Learn.

➡If the previous step is not performed, a Diagnostic Trouble Code (DTC) will be set.

8. If necessary, also use a scan tool to erase any Diagnostic Trouble Codes (DTC's) from the PCM.

9. Before starting the engine, operate the accelerator pedal to check for any binding.

CAMSHAFT POSITION (CMP) SENSOR

LOCATION

See Figure 36.

REMOVAL & INSTALLATION

1. Disconnect and isolate the negative battery cable.

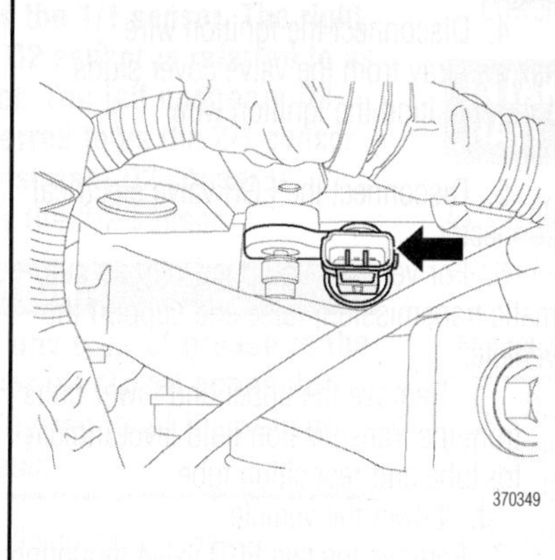

Fig. 36 Showing the CMP sensor location

2. Disconnect the electrical connector from the camshaft position (CMP) sensor.

3. Loosen the CMP sensor retaining bolt.

4. Pull the sensor up and out of the chain case cover. Leave the retaining bolt in place.

To install:

➡If reinstalling the sensor, check the sensor O-ring for damage and replace if necessary. Lubricate the O-ring with clean engine oil before installing the sensor. Clean off the old spacer on the sensor face. A new spacer must be attached to the face before installation. The spacer sets the correct clearance between the sensor and the camshaft gear. An improperly positioned sensor can result in sensor damage, a faulty signal or no signal at all.

5. Install the camshaft position (CMP) sensor in the chain case cover and rotate into position.

6. Push the sensor down until contact is made with the camshaft gear. While holding the sensor in this position, install and tighten the retaining bolt to 125 inch lbs. (14 Nm).

7. Connect and lock the electrical connector to the CMP sensor.

8. Connect the negative battery cable.

➡The Cam/Crank Variation Relearn procedure must be performed anytime there has been a repair/replacement made to a powertrain system, for example: flywheel, valve train, camshaft and/or crankshaft sensors or components.

CAM/CRANK RELEARN PROCEDURE

➡If a repair/replacement was made to a powertrain system, with the scan tool select the "Cam Crank Relearn" procedure under PCM Miscellaneous Menu Option.

CRANKSHAFT POSITION (CKP) SENSOR

LOCATION

The Crankshaft Position (CKP) sensor is mounted into the right side of the transmission bellhousing. It is positioned and bolted into a machined hole.

REMOVAL & INSTALLATION

1. Raise vehicle.

2. Disconnect sensor electrical connector.

3. Remove sensor mounting bolt.

4. Carefully twist sensor from cylinder block.

5. Check condition of sensor O-ring.

To install:

6. If reinstalling the sensor, check the sensor O-ring for damage and replace if necessary. Lubricate the O-ring with clean engine oil before installing the sensor.

7. Push the crankshaft position (CKP) sensor into the transmission case with a twisting motion until fully seated.

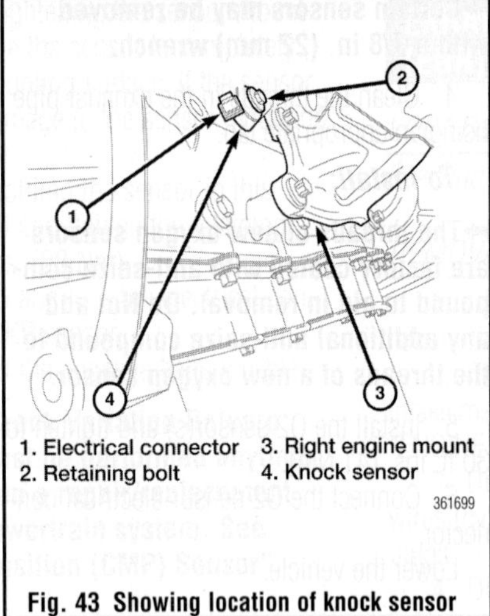

Fig. 43 Showing location of knock sensor

REMOVAL & INSTALLATION

1. Disconnect negative battery cable.
2. Raise vehicle and support.
3. Disconnect electrical connector from knock sensor.
4. Remove mounting bolt.
5. Remove sensor from engine.

To install:

6. Thoroughly clean knock sensor mounting hole.
7. Position sensor to engine.

CAUTION

Over or under tightening the sensor mounting bolts will affect knock sensor performance, possibly causing improper spark control. Always use the specified torque when installing the knock sensors. The torque for the knock sensor bolt is relatively light for an 8 mm bolt (2).

➡Note foam strip on bolt threads. This foam is used only to retain the bolts to sensors for plant assembly. It is not used as a sealant. Do not apply any adhesive, sealant or thread locking compound to these bolts.

8. Install and tighten mounting bolt. Tighten to 15 ft. lbs. (20 Nm).
9. Attach electrical connector to knock sensor.
10. Lower vehicle.

MANIFOLD ABSOLUTE PRESSURE (MAP) SENSOR

LOCATION

See Figure 44.

The MAP sensor is installed into the rear of the upper intake manifold.

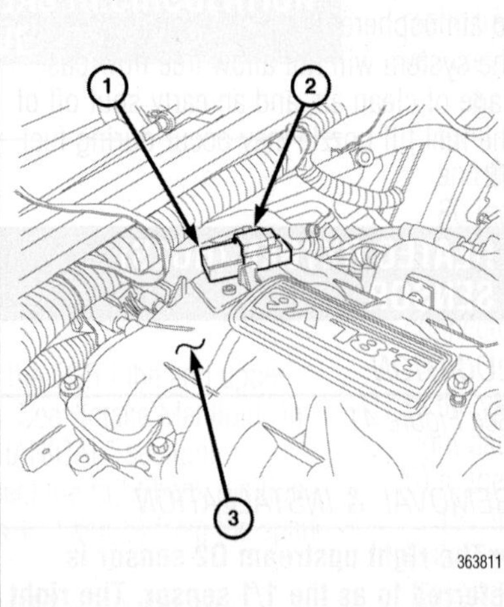

Fig. 44 Showing the MAP sensor (1), electrical connector (2) and upper intake manifold (3)

REMOVAL & INSTALLATION

1. Disconnect the MAP sensor electrical connector.
2. Clean the MAP sensor mounting base.
3. Pull up on MAP sensor while rotating counterclockwise about 1/4 turn for removal.
4. Check the condition of the MAP sensor O-ring and replace if necessary.
5. Installation is the reverse of the removal procedure.

POSITIVE CRANKCASE VENTILATION (PCV) VALVE

LOCATION

The PCV valve is located in the left valve cover near the ignition coil.

REMOVAL & INSTALLATION

1. Remove hose clamp.
2. Remove the hose.
3. Remove the PCV valve.
4. Installation is the reverse of the removal procedure.

POWERTAIN CONTROL MODULE (PCM)

LOCATION

See Figure 45.

REMOVAL & INSTALLATION

➡Use a diagnostic scan tool to reprogram the new Powertrain Control Module (PCM) with the vehicles original identification number (VIN) and the vehicles original mileage. If this step is not done, a Diagnostic Trouble Code (DTC) may be set.

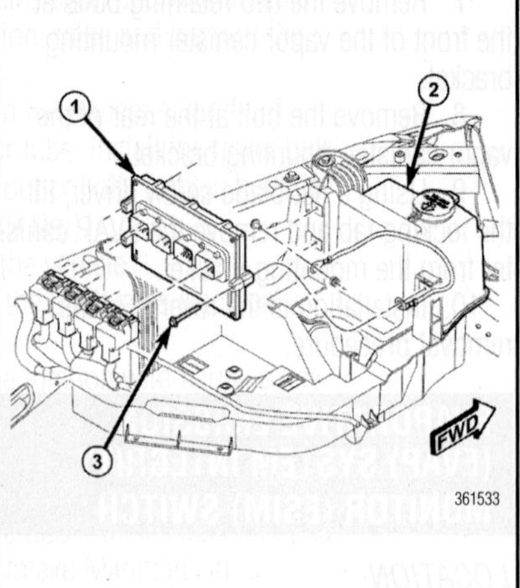

Fig. 45 The PCM (Powertrain Control Module) (1) is located in the engine compartment near the windshield washer reservoir tank (2).

CAUTION

To avoid possible voltage spike damage to the PCM, ignition key must be off, and negative battery cable must be disconnected before unplugging PCM connectors.

1. Disconnect negative battery cable at battery.
2. Remove plastic shields from over four electrical connectors. Shields snap to connectors.
3. Carefully unplug four electrical connectors from PCM.
4. Remove three PCM mounting bolts and remove PCM from vehicle.

To install:

5. Install PCM and three mounting screws to vehicle.
6. Check pin connectors in PCM and four electrical connectors for corrosion or damage. Also check pin heights in connectors. Pin heights should all be the same. Repair as necessary before installing electrical connectors.
7. Install four electrical connectors to PCM.
8. Install plastic shield to electrical connectors. Shields snap to connectors.
9. Install battery cable.
10. Use a diagnostic scan tool to reprogram new PCM with vehicles original Vehicle Identification Number (VIN) and original vehicle mileage.

FUEL SYSTEM SERVICE PRECAUTIONS

Safety is the most important factor when performing not only fuel system maintenance but any type of maintenance. Failure to conduct maintenance and repairs in a safe manner may result in serious personal injury or death. Maintenance and testing of the vehicle's fuel system components can be accomplished safely and effectively by adhering to the following rules and guidelines.

- To avoid the possibility of fire and personal injury, always disconnect the negative battery cable unless the repair or test procedure requires that battery voltage be applied.
- Always relieve the fuel system pressure prior to disconnecting any fuel system component (injector, fuel rail, pressure regulator, etc.), fitting or fuel line connection. Exercise extreme caution whenever relieving fuel system pressure to avoid exposing skin, face and eyes to fuel spray. Please be advised that fuel under pressure may penetrate the skin or any part of the body that it contacts.
- Always place a shop towel or cloth around the fitting or connection prior to loosening to absorb any excess fuel due to spillage. Ensure that all fuel spillage (should it occur) is quickly removed from engine surfaces. Ensure that all fuel soaked cloths or towels are deposited into a suitable waste container.
- Always keep a dry chemical (Class B) fire extinguisher near the work area.
- Do not allow fuel spray or fuel vapors to come into contact with a spark or open flame.
- Always use a back-up wrench when loosening and tightening fuel line connection fittings. This will prevent unnecessary stress and torsion to fuel line piping.
- Always replace worn fuel fitting O-rings with new Do not substitute fuel hose or equivalent where fuel pipe is installed.

Before servicing the vehicle, make sure to also refer to the precautions in the beginning of this section as well.

RELIEVING FUEL SYSTEM PRESSURE

1. Remove fuel fill cap.
2. Disconnect wiring harness leading to fuel pump module at top of fuel tank.
3. Start and run engine until it stalls.
4. Attempt restarting engine until it will no longer run.
5. Turn ignition key to OFF position.
6. Place a rag or towel below fuel line quick-connect fitting at fuel rail.
7. Disconnect quick-connect fitting at fuel rail.
8. After performing service procedure, reconnect fuel pump module.
9. One or more Diagnostic Trouble Codes (DTC's) may have been stored in PCM memory due to the disconnection of fuel pump module. A diagnostic scan tool must be used to erase a DTC.

FUEL FILTER

REMOVAL & INSTALLATION

Two fuel filters are used. One is located at the bottom of the fuel pump module. The other is located inside the module. A separate frame mounted fuel filter is not used with any engine.

➡Both fuel filters are designed for extended service. They do not require normal scheduled maintenance. Filters should only be replaced if a diagnostic procedure indicates to do so.

FUEL INJECTORS

REMOVAL & INSTALLATION

See Figure 46.

1. Remove the fuel rail. See "Fuel Rail" in this section.
2. Disconnect injector wiring connector from each injector.
3. Rotate injector and pull out of fuel rail. The clip will stay on injector.
4. Check injector O-ring for damage. If O-ring is damaged, it must be replaced. If injector is reused, a protective cap must be installed on injector tip to prevent damage. Replace injector clip if it is damaged.
5. Repeat procedures for remaining injectors.
6. Installation is the reverse of the removal procedure.

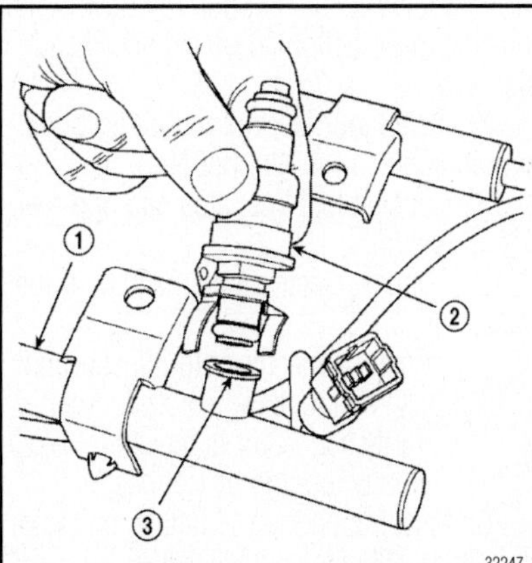

Fig. 46 Rotate and pull the injector (2) out of the fuel rail (1). Check condition of the O-ring (3)

FUEL PUMP MODULE

REMOVAL & INSTALLATION

See Figure 47.

The electric fuel pump is located inside of the fuel pump module. A 12 volt, permanent magnet, electric motor powers the fuel pump. The electric fuel pump is not a separate, serviceable component.

1. Relieve fuel system pressure. See "Relieving Fuel System Pressure" in this section.
2. Drain and remove fuel tank. See "Fuel Tank" in this section.

➡Prior to removing the fuel pump module, use compressed air to remove any accumulated dirt and debris from around fuel tank opening.

3. Position the lock-ring remover/installer (9340 or equivalent) into the notches on the outside edge of the lock-ring.
4. Install a 1/2 inch drive breaker bar into the lock-ring remover/installer. Rotate the breaker bar counterclockwise and remove the lock-ring.

➡The fuel pump module has to be properly located in the fuel tank for the fuel level gauge to work properly.

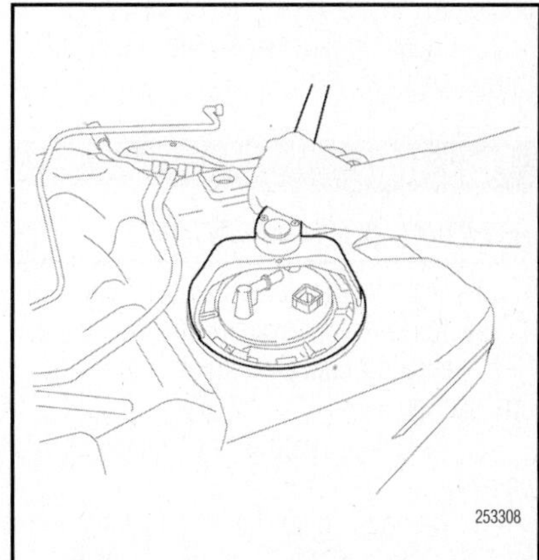

Fig. 47 Using the lock ring remover/installer and breaker bar to remove the fuel pump module lock ring.

5. Mark the fuel pump module orientation.

➡**The fuel pump module reservoir does not empty out when the tank is drained. The fuel in the reservoir will spill out when the module is removed. Do not spill fuel into the interior of the vehicle.**

6. Raise the fuel pump module out of the fuel tank using caution not spill fuel inside the vehicle.
7. Tip the fuel pump module on its side and drain all fuel from the reservoir.
8. Remove the fuel pump module from the fuel tank using caution not to bend the float arm.
9. Remove and discard the rubber O-ring seal.

To install:

10. Clean the rubber O-ring seal area of the fuel tank and install a new rubber O-ring seal.
11. Lower the fuel pump module into the fuel tank using caution not to bend the float arm.

➡**The main fuel pump module must be properly located in the fuel tank for the fuel level gauge to work properly.**

12. Align the rubber O-ring seal and rotate the fuel pump module to the orientation marks noted during removal. This step must be performed for the fuel level gauge to work properly.
13. Position the lock-ring over top of the fuel pump module.
14. Position the lock-ring remover/installer into the notches on the outside edge of the lock-ring. Install a 1/2 inch drive breaker bar into the lock-ring remover/installer.
15. Rotate the breaker bar clockwise until all seven notches of the lock-ring have engaged.
16. Install the fuel tank. See "Fuel Tank" in this section.

FUEL RAIL

REMOVAL & INSTALLATION

1. Remove fuel tank filler tube cap.
2. Perform fuel system pressure release See "Relieving Fuel System Pressure" in this section.
3. Remove negative battery cable at battery.
4. Remove upper half of intake manifold. See "Intake Manifold" in "ENGINE MECHANICAL" section.
5. Disconnect electrical connectors at all six fuel injectors:
    a. Push red colored slider away from injector.
    b. While pushing slider, depress tab and remove connector from injector.

➡**The factory fuel injection wiring harness is numerically tagged (INJ 1, INJ 2, etc.) for injector position identification. If harness is not tagged, note wiring location before removal.**

6. Disconnect fuel line latch clip and fuel line at fuel rail.
7. Remove four fuel rail mounting bolts.
8. Gently rock and pull left side of fuel rail until fuel injectors just start to clear machined holes in cylinder head. Gently rock and pull right side of rail until injectors just start to clear cylinder head holes. Repeat this procedure (left/right) until all injectors have cleared cylinder head holes.
9. Remove fuel rail (with injectors attached) from engine.
10. If fuel injectors are to be removed, see "Fuel Injectors" in this section.

To install:

11. Install fuel injectors to fuel rail, if removed. See "Fuel Injectors" in this section.
12. Clean out fuel injector machined bores in intake manifold.
13. Apply a small amount of engine oil to each fuel injector O-ring. This will help in fuel rail installation.
14. Position fuel rail/fuel injector assembly to machined injector openings in cylinder head.
15. Guide each injector into cylinder head. Be careful not to tear injector O-rings.
16. Push right side of fuel rail down until fuel injectors have bottomed on cylinder head shoulder. Push left fuel rail down until injectors have bottomed on cylinder head shoulder.
17. Install four fuel rail mounting bolts and tighten to 17 ft. lbs. (22 Nm).
18. Connect fuel line latch clip and fuel line to fuel rail.
19. Connect electrical connectors at fuel injectors:
    a. Push connector onto injector and then push and lock red colored slider.
    b. Verify connector is locked to injector by lightly tugging on connector.
20. Install upper half of intake manifold. See "Intake Manifold" in "ENGINE MECHANICAL" section.
21. Connect battery cable to battery.
22. Start engine and check for leaks.

FUEL TANK

DRAINING

1. Disconnect negative battery cable.
2. Remove fuel fill cap.
3. Raise and support vehicle.
4. Remove fuel fill hose clamp at rear of tank.
5. Remove fuel fill hose from fuel tank.
6. Position a drain hose into the fuel fill hose opening. Note that a small flapper valve is installed into the opening.
7. Drain fuel tank using an approved gasoline draining station.

REMOVAL & INSTALLATION

See Figure 48.

1. Remove fuel tank filler tube cap.
2. Perform fuel system pressure release procedure. See "Relieving Fuel System Pressure" in this section.
3. Remove fuel fill cap.
4. Raise and support vehicle.
5. Drain fuel tank, as described above.

➡**The fuel tank skid plate and the fuel tank assembly are removed at the same time. They share common fasteners.**

6. Disconnect quick-connect fittings.
7. Remove hose clamp and disconnect hose at tank.
8. Support tank with a hydraulic jack.
9. Disconnect quick-connect fittings at front of tank.
10. Remove two tank mounting bolts at rear of fuel tank.
11. Remove three tank mounting bolts at right side and three bolts at left side of fuel tank.
12. Partially lower tank to gain access to pump module electrical connector. Disconnect electrical connector at fuel pump module.
13. Continue lowering tank for removal.
14. Lift fuel tank from skid plate.
15. If fuel tank is to be replaced, remove fuel pump module from tank.

To install:

16. If fuel pump module had been removed, install module to tank.
17. Position fuel tank into skid plate.
18. Support tank with a hydraulic jack.
19. Partially raise tank to allow connections at top of tank.
20. Connect electrical connector to fuel pump module.
21. Continue raising tank snugly to body.
22. Connect quick-connect fittings.

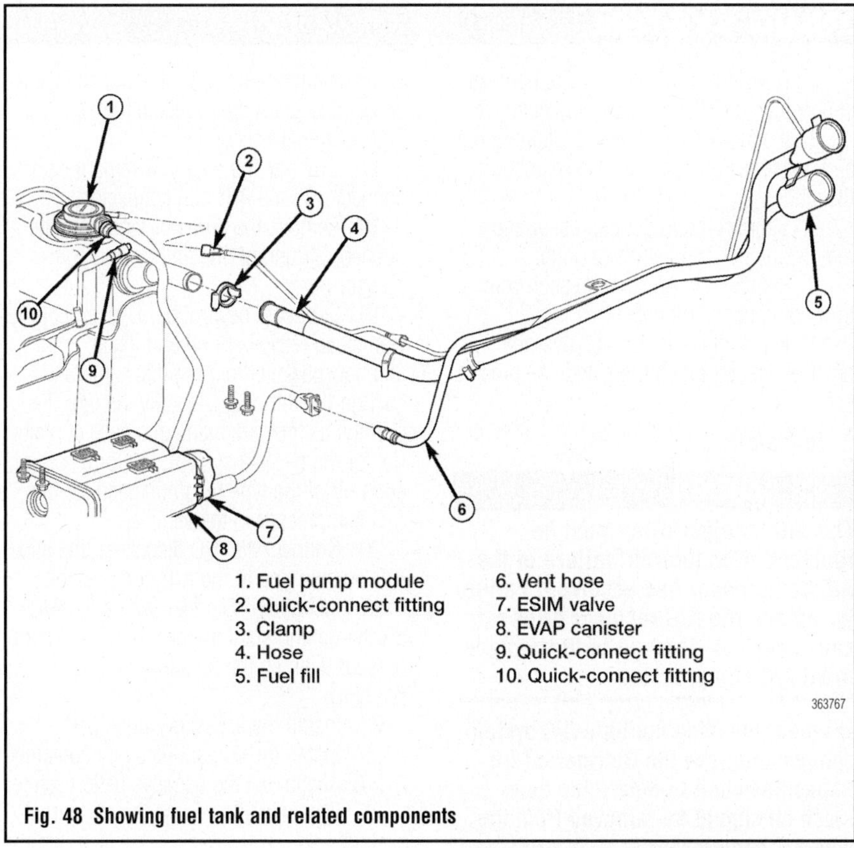

Fig. 48 Showing fuel tank and related components

23. Install hose to tank and install clamp.
24. Connect quick-connect fittings at front of tank.
25. Install two tank mounting bolts at rear of fuel tank.
26. Install three tank mounting bolts at right side of fuel tank.
27. Install three tank mounting bolts at left side of fuel tank.

IDLE SPEED

ADJUSTMENT

➡Idle speed is controlled by the Powertrain Control Module (PCM) and is not adjustable.

THROTTLE BODY

REMOVAL & INSTALLATION

1. Using a diagnostic scan tool, record any previous DTC's (Diagnostic Trouble Codes).

✱✱ CAUTION

Do not have the ignition key in the ON position when checking the throttle body shaft for a binding condition. This may set DTC's.

2. Disconnect and isolate negative battery cable at battery.
3. Remove throttle body air intake hose.
4. Disconnect throttle body electrical connector.
5. Remove four bolts and remove throttle body from intake manifold.
6. Inspect intake manifold to throttle body gasket for damage. Inspect the j-nuts for damage or excessive wear. Replace as necessary.
7. Inspect the four J-nuts for damage or excessive wear, remove if necessary.
8. Inspect intake manifold to throttle body gasket for damage, remove if necessary.

To install:

9. Install a new intake manifold to throttle body gasket, if replacement was necessary.
10. Install four new four J-nuts, if replacement was necessary.

✱✱ CAUTION

The throttle body mounting bolts MUST be tightened to specifications. Over tightening can cause damage to the throttle body or the intake manifold.

11. Install throttle body to intake manifold, with new gasket.
12. Install four bolts and hand tighten.
13. Connect throttle body electrical connector.
14. Tighten mounting bolts in a mandatory criss-cross pattern sequence to 65 inch lbs. (7.5 Nm).
15. Install clean air hose and tighten clamps.
16. Connect negative battery cable.
17. Using the diagnostic scan tool, erase all previous DTC's and perform the ETC Relearn function with scan tool.

HEATING & AIR CONDITIONING SYSTEM

BLOWER MOTOR

REMOVAL & INSTALLATION

The blower motor is located on the bottom of the passenger side of the HVAC housing. The blower motor can be removed from the vehicle without having to remove the HVAC housing.

1. Disconnect and isolate the negative battery cable.
2. From underneath the instrument panel, disconnect the instrument panel wire harness connector from the blower motor.
3. Remove the three screws that secure the blower motor to the bottom of the HVAC housing and remove the blower motor.
4. Installation is the reverse of the removal procedure.

COMPRESSOR

REMOVAL & INSTALLATION

See Figure 49.

1. Disconnect and isolate the negative battery cable.
2. Recover the refrigerant from the refrigerant system.
3. Remove the coolant recovery container.
4. Remove the accessory drive belt. See "ENGINE MECHANICAL" section.
5. Remove the nuts that secure the A/C discharge line and A/C suction line to the A/C compressor.
6. Disconnect the A/C discharge and suction lines from the A/C compressor. Remove and discard the O-ring seals and gaskets.

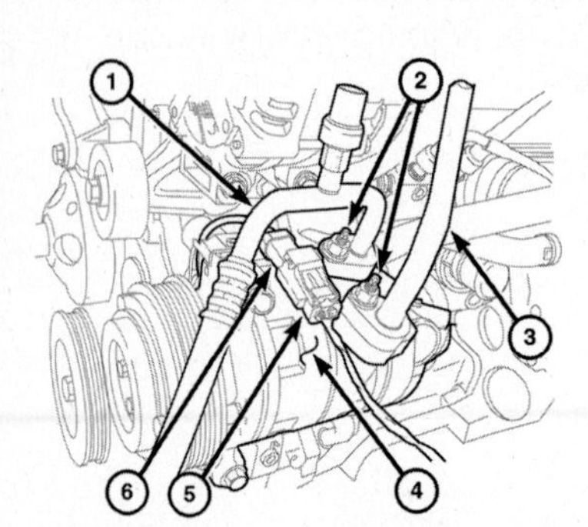

Fig. 49 Showing compressor connections

7. Disconnect the engine wire harness connector from the field coil connector.
8. If equipped, remove the retaining nut and transmission cooler line bracket from the stud.
9. Support the A/C compressor and remove the nut, stud and two bolts.
10. Remove the A/C compressor from the engine compartment.
11. Install plugs in, or tape over the open refrigerant line fittings and compressor ports.

To install:

CAUTION

The A/C receiver/drier must be replaced if an internal failure of the A/C compressor has occurred. Failure to replace the A/C receiver drier can cause serious damage to the replacement A/C compressor.

➡When replacing multiple A/C system components, see the Refrigerant Oil Capacities chart to determine how much oil should be removed from the new A/C compressor.

CAUTION

Replacement of the refrigerant line O-ring seals and gaskets is required anytime a refrigerant line is disconnected. Failure to replace the rubber O-ring seals and metal gaskets may result in a refrigerant system leak.

12. If the A/C compressor is being replaced, the refrigerant oil in the old compressor must be first drained and measured. Then the oil in the new A/C compressor must be drained. Finally, the new compressor must be refilled with the same amount of new refrigerant oil that was drained out of the old compressor. When replacing multiple A/C system components, determine how much oil should be added to the refrigerant system for the components replaced.
13. Position the A/C compressor onto the engine.
14. Loosely install the two bolts, stud and nut that secure the A/C compressor to the engine.
15. Tighten each of the fasteners to 21 ft. lbs. (28 Nm) using the following sequence:
    - The bolt at the front of the compressor.
    - The nut at the front of the compressor.
    - The bolt at the rear of the compressor.
16. If equipped, install the transmission cooler line bracket and retaining nut. Tighten the nut securely.
17. Connect the engine wire harness connector to the A/C coil connector.
18. Remove the plugs or tape from the opened refrigerant line fittings and compressor ports.
19. Lubricate new rubber O-ring seals with clean refrigerant oil and install them and new gaskets onto the discharge and suction line fittings. Use only the specified O-rings as they are made of a special material for the R-134a system. Use only refrigerant oil of the type recommended for the A/C compressor in the vehicle.
20. Connect the A/C discharge line and A/C suction line to the A/C compressor.
21. Install the nuts that secure the A/C discharge and suction lines to the A/C compressor. Tighten the nuts to 17 ft. lbs. (23 Nm).
22. Install the accessory drive belt.
23. Install the coolant recovery container.
24. Reconnect the negative battery cable.
25. Evacuate and charge the refrigerant system.

EVAPORATOR CORE

REMOVAL & INSTALLATION

➡Evaporator core removal requires removal of the HVAC assembly. See "HVAC Module" in this section. After module is removed to workbench, evaporator core can be removed and replaced.

HEATER CORE

REMOVAL & INSTALLATION

➡Heater core removal requires removal of the HVAC assembly. See "HVAC Module" in this section. After module is removed to workbench, heater core can be removed and replaced.

HVAC MODULE

REMOVAL & INSTALLATION

See Figures 50 through 52.

➡The HVAC housing and instrument panel must be removed from the vehicle as an assembly.

➡The HVAC housing must be removed from the instrument panel and disassembled for service of the A/C

evaporator, air intake housing, mode-air and blend-air doors and the heater core.

1. Disconnect and isolate the negative battery cable.
2. Recover the refrigerant from the refrigerant system.
3. Partially drain the engine cooling system.
4. Remove the nut that secures the A/C liquid line and A/C suction line to the A/C expansion valve.
5. Disconnect the A/C liquid and suction lines from the A/C expansion valve and remove and discard the O-ring seals.
6. Install plugs in, or tape over the opened refrigerant line fittings and the expansion valve ports.
7. Remove the upper intake manifold to help gain access to the hose clamps that secure the heater hoses to the heater core. See "Intake Manifold" in "ENGINE MECHANICAL" section.
8. Using cable-type spring clamp pliers or equivalent, release the hose clamps that secure the heater hoses to the heater core tubes at the bulkhead and disconnect the hoses from the tubes. Install plugs in, or tape over the opened heater core tubes to prevent coolant spillage during HVAC housing assembly removal.
9. Remove the instrument panel. Remove or disconnect the following, then place it on a workbench:
    - Electrical connector at the A-pillar cowl area
    - Center console
    - Center I/P wire harness connectors
    - Steering column opening cover
    - Audio amplifier
    - Steering column
    - I/P end caps
    - Shifter (A/T)
    - Transfer case shifter
    - Radio
    - Center support brackets
    - Clutch and brake pedal rods
    - Wiring ground connections at body contacts
    - Remaining I/P electrical connections
    - Antenna connector
    - Glove box
    - Battery positive cable
    - Right side ground (in engine compartment)
    - Power steering reservoir (position aside)
    - Battery and tray
    - EGR tube
    - Harness at brake booster
    - Brake booster bracket nuts
    - Wire harness grommet at bulkhead
    - Wire harness clips
    - I/P trim caps and nuts inside vehicle at windshield
    - I/P side support bolts
    - I/P cover
    - I/P assembly
10. Disconnect the instrument panel wire harness connectors from the evaporator temperature sensor, blower motor resistor, blower motor and the recirculation door actuator.
11. Remove the two bolts that secure the air inlet housing to the passenger side of the instrument panel support. Use caution not to damage the housing alignment pin during removal of the HVAC housing assembly from the support.
12. Remove the instrument panel ducts.
13. Remove the four bolts that secure the HVAC housing assembly to the center of the instrument panel support and remove the housing from the support. Use caution not to damage the housing alignment pin during removal of the housing from the support.

To install:

14. Position the HVAC housing assembly into the instrument panel support. Be certain that the housing alignment pin is correctly located.
15. Install the four bolts that secure the HVAC housing assembly to the center of instrument panel support. Tighten the bolts.

➡If a foam seal on the top of the HVAC housing is deformed or damaged, the seal must be replaced.

16. Install the instrument panel ducts.
17. Verify that the housing alignment pin is correctly located in the passenger side of the instrument panel support.
18. Install the two bolts that secure the air inlet housing to the instrument panel support. Tighten the bolts.
19. Connect the instrument panel wire harness connectors to the evaporator temperature sensor, blower motor resistor, blower motor and the recirculation door actuator.
20. Install the instrument panel cover.
21. Install the instrument panel. (Follow the item list under removal in reverse order).
22. Remove the previously installed plugs or caps and connect the heater hoses to the heater core tubes.
23. Using cable-type spring clamp pliers or equivalent, correctly position the two hose clamps that secure the heater hoses to

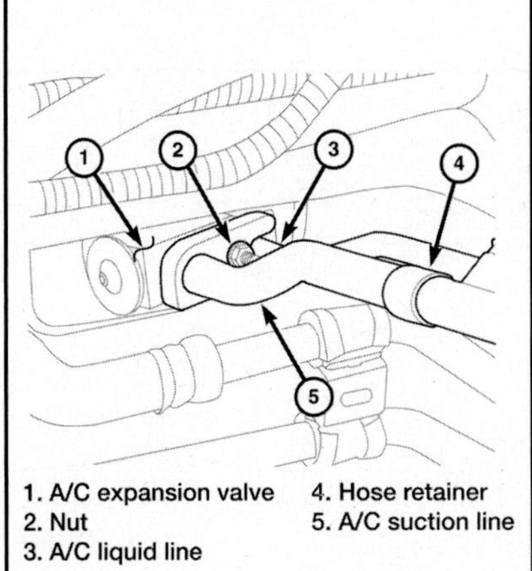

Fig. 50 Removing the A/C lines from the expansion valve

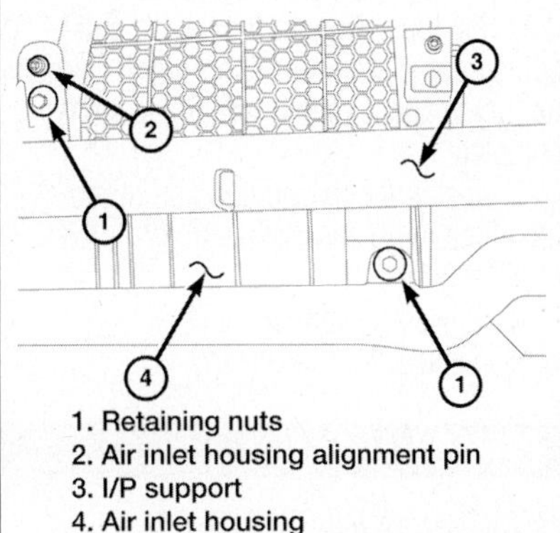

Fig. 51 Remove the two bolts that secure the air inlet housing to the passenger side of the instrument panel support.

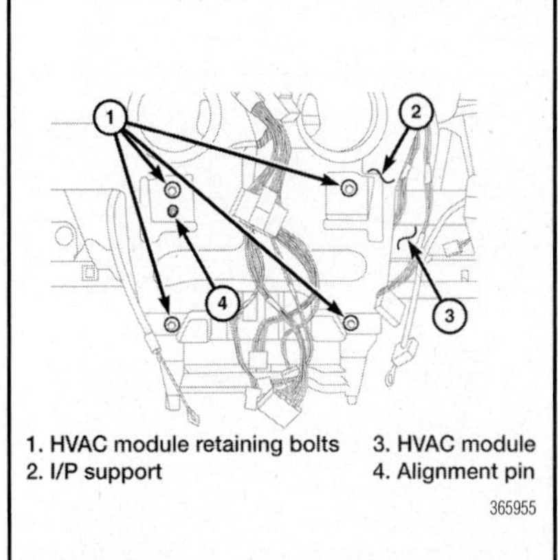

Fig. 52 Remove the four bolts that secure the HVAC housing assembly to the center of the instrument panel support and remove the housing from the support.

the heater core tubes and engage the clamps to the tubes.

24. Install the upper intake manifold. See "Intake Manifold" in "ENGINE MECHANICAL" section.

25. Remove the tape or plugs from the opened refrigerant line fittings and the expansion valve ports.

26. Lubricate new O-ring seals with clean refrigerant oil and install them onto the refrigerant line fittings.

➡Use only the specified O-rings as they are made of special materials compatible to the R-134a system. Use only refrigerant oil of the type recommended for the A/C compressor in the vehicle.

27. Connect the A/C liquid line and A/C suction line onto the A/C expansion valve.

28. Install the nut that secures the A/C liquid and suction lines to the A/C expansion valve. Tighten the nut to 70 inch lbs. (8 Nm).

29. Reconnect the negative battery cable.

30. If the heater core is being replaced, flush the cooling system. See "ENGINE COOLING" section.

31. Refill the engine cooling system.

32. Evacuate and charge the refrigerant system.

33. Initiate the Actuator Calibration function using a scan tool

STEERING

DRAG LINK

REMOVAL & INSTALLATION

Knuckle Side

See Figure 53.

1. Raise and support the vehicle.
2. Remove the right front tire.
3. Remove the right side drag link nut at the knuckle.
4. Separate the drag link using special tool (9360 or equivalent) separator.
5. Remove the tie rod nut at the knuckle.
6. Separate the tie rod using the same separator tool.

➡Count the number of turns when removing the tie rod end, This will give a good starting point when reassembling and toe adjustment.

7. Loosen the nut and bolt for the drag link adjustment sleeve.
8. Unthread the drag link socket from the adjuster.

To install:

9. Thread the drag link socket into the adjuster the same number of turns as during removal.

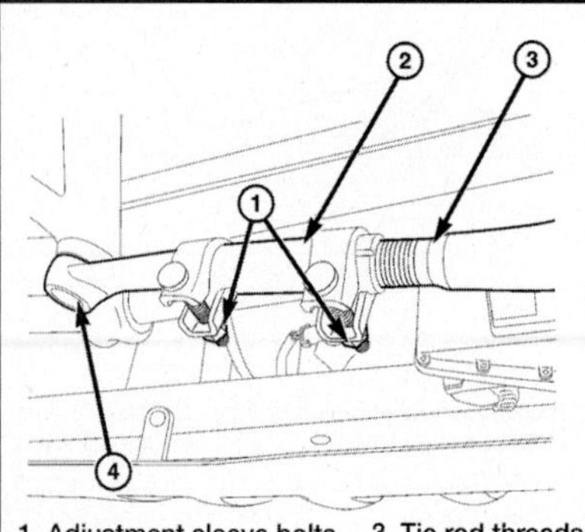

Fig. 53 Showing the knuckle side drag link

10. Tighten the adjustment sleeve bolt finger tight. Do not tighten to specs until after the toe set is complete.
11. Install the drag link to the knuckle and tighten the nut to 63 ft. lbs. (85 Nm).
12. Install the tie rod end to the knuckle and tighten to 63 ft. lbs. (85 Nm).
13. Install the right side tire.
14. Lower the vehicle.
15. Set the toe.

Pitman Arm Side

1. Raise and support the vehicle.
2. Remove the drag link nut at the pitman arm.
3. Separate the drag link from the pitman arm, using a separator tool (9360 or equivalent).

➡Count the number of turns when removing the tie rod end, This will give a good starting point when reassembling and toe adjustment.

4. Loosen the nut and bolt for the drag link adjustment sleeve.
5. Unthread the tie rod end from the tube.

To install:

6. Thread the tie rod end onto the drag link tube. Tighten the tie rod end adjustment sleeve bolt finger tight. Do not tighten to specs until after the toe set is complete.
7. Install the tie rod end and nut to the pitman arm and tighten to 77 ft. lbs. (105 Nm).
8. Lower the vehicle.
9. Set the toe.

PITMAN ARM

REMOVAL & INSTALLATION

See Figure 54.

1. Raise and support the vehicle.
2. Remove the track bar retaining bolt at the frame and lower the track bar.
3. Remove the pitman arm retaining nut at the drag link. Using the Ball Joint Remover (9360 or equivalent), separate the pitman arm from the drag link.
4. Mark the steering gear shaft and pitman arm for installation reference.
5. Remove the pitman arm retaining nut.
6. Using the Ball Joint Press (C-4105A or equivalent), remove the pitman arm from the steering gear

To install:

7. Align and install the pitman arm on steering gear shaft.
8. Install the washer and nut on the shaft and tighten the nut to 185 ft. lbs. (251 Nm).
9. Install drag link ball stud to pitman arm. Install nut and tighten to 77 ft. lbs. (105 Nm).
10. Install the track bar back into position at the frame.
11. It may be necessary to pry the axle assembly over to install the track bar at the frame rail. Install track bar at the frame rail bracket. Install the nut and bolt at the frame rail bracket. Tighten the bolt at the frame bracket to 125 ft. lbs. (169 Nm).

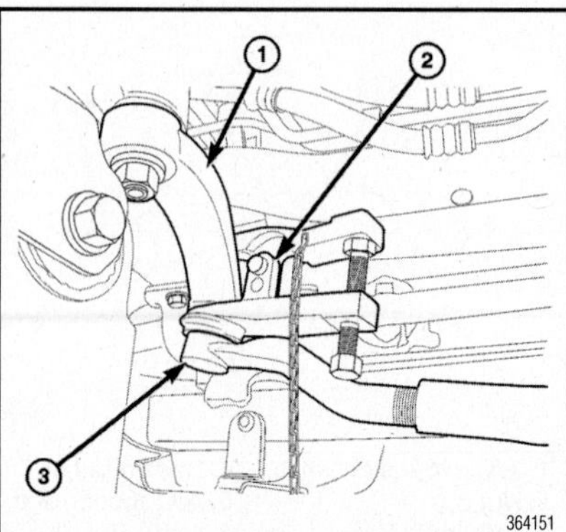

Fig. 54 Remove the pitman arm retaining nut (1) at the drag link (3). Using the Ball Joint Remover (9360 or equivalent) (2), separate the pitman arm from the drag link.

12. Remove the support and lower the vehicle.
13. Fill power steering system to proper level.
14. Check the toe setting.

POWER STEERING GEAR

REMOVAL & INSTALLATION

➡The steering column on vehicles with an automatic transmission may not be equipped with an internal locking shaft that allows the ignition key cylinder to be locked with the key. Alternative methods of locking the steering wheel for service will have to be used.

1. Place the front wheels in the straight ahead position with the steering wheel centered and locked.
2. Siphon out as much power steering fluid as possible.
3. Position the coolant bottle aside.
4. Remove the steering shaft coupler pinch bolt at the steering gear, and remove the steering shaft coupler from the steering gear.
5. Remove the power steering hoses/tubes from the steering gear.
6. Raise and support the vehicle.
7. Remove the track bar retaining bolt at the frame and lower the track bar.
8. Remove the pitman arm retaining nut.
9. Using the Ball Joint Press (C4105A or equivalent), remove the pitman arm from the steering gear.
10. Remove the steering gear retaining bolts and remove the steering gear.

To install:

11. Install the steering gear on the frame rail and tighten the bolts to 87 ft. lbs. (118 Nm).
12. Align and install the pitman arm and tighten the nut to 185 ft. lbs. (251 Nm).
13. It may be necessary to pry the axle assembly over to install the track bar at the frame rail. Install the track bar at the frame rail bracket. Install the nut and bolt at the frame rail bracket and tighten to 125 ft. lbs. (169 Nm).
14. Remove the support and lower the vehicle.
15. Align the column coupler shaft to the steering gear. Install a new coupler pinch bolt and tighten to 36 ft. lbs. (49 Nm).
16. Install the power steering hoses/tubes to the steering gear and tighten fittings to 27 ft. lbs. (36 Nm).
17. Reinstall the coolant bottle back into position.
18. Fill the power steering system to the proper level.
19. Check the toe setting.

POWER STEERING PUMP

REMOVAL & INSTALLATION

1. Remove cap from power steering fluid reservoir.
2. Siphon as much fluid as possible from the power steering fluid reservoir.
3. Remove the air cleaner assembly.
4. Remove the pressure hose at the pump.
5. Remove the supply hose from the pump.
6. Remove the power steering drive belt. See "Accessory Drive Belt" in "ENGINE MECHANICAL" section.
7. Remove the three front mounting bolts through the pulley.
8. Remove the pump (with pulley).

To install:

9. Install pump on the engine.
10. Install 3 pump mounting bolts and tighten to 19 ft. lbs. (26 Nm).
11. Install the pressure line on the pump and tighten to 23 ft. lbs. (31 Nm).
12. Install supply hose on pump.
13. Install accessory drive belt.
14. Fill and bleed the power steering system.
15. Check for leaks.
16. Install the air cleaner box assembly

BLEEDING THE SYSTEM

⁂ CAUTION

Fluid level should be checked with the engine OFF to prevent personal injury from moving parts and to assure an accurate fluid level reading.

⁂ CAUTION

Mopar Power Steering Fluid + 4 or Mopar ATF+4 Automatic Transmission Fluid is to be used in the power steering system. Both Fluids have the same material standard specifications (MS-9602). No other power steering or automatic transmission fluid is to be used in the system. Damage may result to the power steering pump and system if another fluid is used. Do not overfill the system.

➡Be sure the vacuum tool used in the following procedure is clean and free of any fluids.

1. Check the fluid level. The power steering fluid level can be viewed through the side of the power steering fluid reservoir. Compare the fluid level to the markings on the side of the reservoir. When the fluid is at normal ambient temperature, approximately 70–80°C (21–27°C), the fluid level should read between the MAX and MIN markings. When the fluid is hot, fluid level is allowed to read up to the MAX line.

➡Do not fill fluid beyond the MAX mark. Check cap seal for damage and replace if needed.

2. Remove the cap from the fluid reservoir and fill the power steering fluid reservoir up to the MAX marking with Mopar Power Steering Fluid + 4 or Mopar ATF+4 Automatic Transmission Fluid.
3. Tightly insert Power Steering Cap Adapter, Special Tool 9688A or equivalent, into the mouth of the reservoir.

⁂ CAUTION

Failure to use a vacuum pump reservoir may allow power steering fluid to be sucked into the hand vacuum pump.

4. Attach Hand Vacuum Pump, Special Tool C-4207-A or equivalent, with reservoir attached, to the Power Steering Cap Adapter.

⁂ CAUTION

Do not run the vehicle while vacuum is applied to the power steering system. Damage to the power steering pump can occur.

➡When performing the following step make sure the vacuum level is maintained during the entire time period.

5. Using Hand Vacuum Pump, apply 20–25 in. Hg of vacuum to the system for a minimum of three minutes.
6. Slowly release the vacuum and remove the special tools.
7. Adjust the fluid level as necessary.
8. Repeat the previous steps until the fluid no longer drops when vacuum is applied.
9. Start the engine and cycle the steering wheel lock-to-lock three times.
10. Do not hold the steering wheel at the stops.
11. Stop the engine and check for leaks at all connections.
12. Check for any signs of air in the reservoir and check the fluid level. If air is present, repeat the procedure as necessary.

FLUID FILL PROCEDURE

➡**See "Bleeding the System" above.**

STEERING COLUMN

REMOVAL & INSTALLATION

See Figure 55.

➡**This procedure involves removal of the driver's side air bag. If not equipped or trained to perform this procedure, refer the vehicle to a proper repair facility.**

1. Position front wheels straight ahead.
2. Remove and isolate the negative ground cable from the battery.
3. Remove the driver's side airbag as follows:
    a. With battery negative cable disconnected, wait at least two minutes for the system capacitor to discharge before further service.
    b. Working through the access holes in each side of the steering wheel rear trim cover, remove the two screws that secure the floating horn switch and the Driver Air Bag (DAB) unit to the steering wheel armature.
    c. Pull the DAB and floating horn switch unit away from the steering wheel far enough to access the electrical connections at the back of the airbag housing and switch unit.
    d. Disconnect the steering wheel wire harness connector from the floating horn switch connector on the back of the switch.

CAUTION

Do not pull on the clockspring pigtail wires or pry on the connector insulators to disengage them from the Driver Air Bag (DAB) inflator initiator connector receptacles. Improper removal of these pigtail wires and their connector insulators can result in damage to the airbag circuits or the connector insulators.

    e. The clockspring DAB pigtail wire connector insulators are secured by integral latches and a Connector Position Assurance (CPA) lock to the airbag inflator connector receptacles, which are located on the back of the DAB housing. Pull the lock straight out from the connector insulator, then pull the insulators straight out from the airbag inflator to disengage the latches and disconnect them from the connector receptacles.
    f. Remove the driver airbag from the steering wheel.
4. If equipped with cruise control, disconnect clock spring harness from the cruise switch harness on the steering wheel.
5. Remove the steering wheel with puller C-3894-A or equivalent.
6. Remove steering column opening cover.
7. Remove screws from the lower column shroud and remove both the upper and lower shrouds.
8. Turn ignition key to the on position.
9. If vehicle is equipped with automatic transmission, disconnect shifter interlock cable from the column.
10. Remove the steering coupler bolt and column mounting nuts then lower column off the mounting studs.
11. Disconnect and remove the wiring harness from the column.
12. Slide the shifter interlock cable from the tie straps.
13. Remove the column.

To install:

14. Align and install column into the steering coupler.
15. Install column harness and connect harness to switches.
16. Reroute the shifter interlock cable through the tie straps.
17. Install the column onto the mounting studs. Install the two mounting nuts and the two mounting bolts all finger tight.

➡**Lower nuts must be installed and tightened first then the upper nuts in order to prevent damage to the capsules.**

18. Tighten the lower, then the upper, mounting nuts to 150 inch lbs. (17 Nm).
19. Install the steering column coupler bolt and tighten to 36 ft. lbs. (49 Nm).
20. Reconnect the shifter interlock cable.
21. Center the clock spring (if necessary) and install it on the column. See "AIR BAG (SUPPLEMENTAL RESTRAINT SYSTEM)" section.
22. Snap together the column shrouds and install the mounting screws.
23. Install the steering column opening cover.

➡**Be certain that the steering wheel mounting bolt is tightened to the proper torque specification to ensure proper clockspring operation.**

24. Install the steering wheel and tighten the new bolt to 40 ft. lbs. (54 Nm).
25. If equipped with cruise control, connect clock spring harness to cruise switch harness on the steering wheel.
26. Install the air bag as follows:
    a. Position the Driver Air Bag (DAB) and floating horn switch unit close enough to the steering wheel to reconnect the electrical connections to the back of the airbag housing.
    b. Reconnect the steering wheel wire harness connector to the floating horn switch connector on the back of the switch.

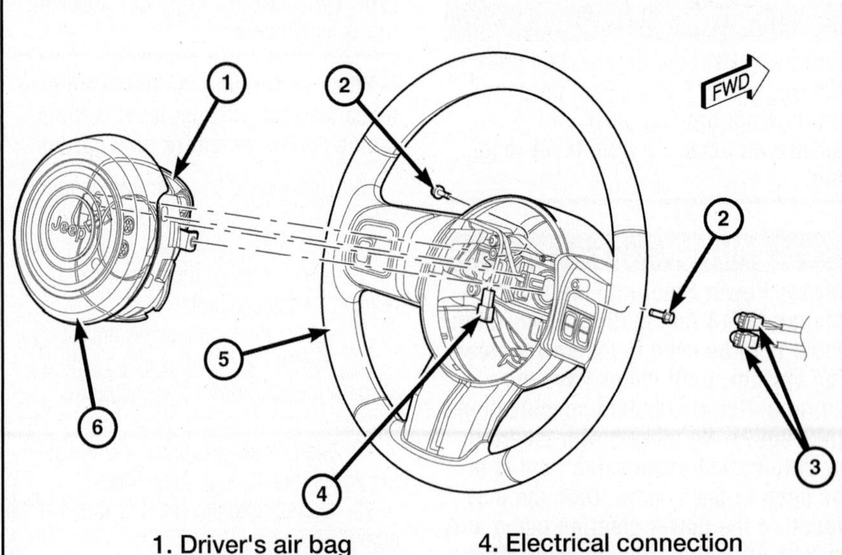

Fig. 55 Showing the driver's air bag, steering wheel and connections

c. Reconnect the wire connectors to the airbag inflator connector receptacles by pressing straight in on the connector insulator. Be certain to engage each keyed and color-coded connector to the matching connector receptacle. You can be certain that each connector is fully engaged in its receptacle by listening carefully for a distinct, audible click as the connector latches snap into place.

d. Push each of the Connector Position Assurance (CPA) locks firmly into the DAB connector insulator until it is flush with the upper surface of the insulator.

e. Carefully position the DAB and floating horn switch unit into the steering wheel hub while tugging lightly upward on the clockspring pigtail wires for the airbag and tucking the wires into the upper hub cavity of the steering wheel. Be certain that none of the steering wheel wiring is pinched between the airbag housing or the horn switch and the steering wheel armature or the steering wheel damper.

f. Working through the access holes in each side of the steering wheel rear trim cover, install and tighten the two screws that secure the floating horn switch and DAB unit to the steering wheel armature. Tighten the screws to 10 ft. lbs. (13 Nm).

g. Do not reconnect the battery negative cable at this time. The Supplemental Restraint System (SRS) Verification Test procedure should be performed following service of any SRS component, using a scan tool.

27. Install the negative battery terminal.

STEERING DAMPER

REMOVAL & INSTALLATION

See Figure 56.

1. Place the front wheels in a straight ahead position.
2. Raise and support the vehicle.
3. Remove the steering damper retaining nut from the link bracket.
4. Remove the steering damper retaining nut and bolt from the axle bracket.
5. Remove the steering damper from the vehicle.

To install:

6. Position the steering damper to the axle bracket and link bracket.

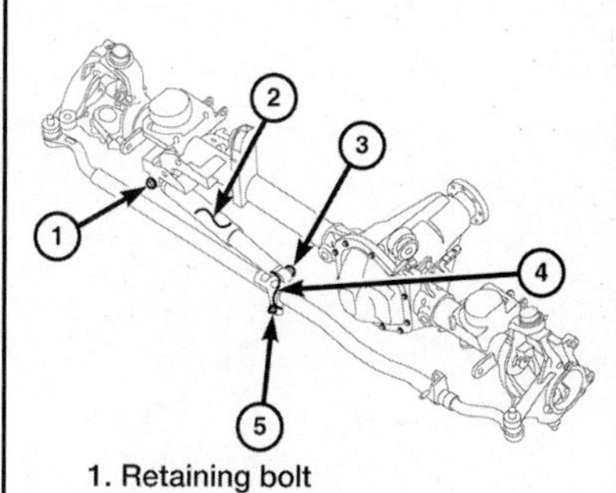

Fig. 56 Showing steering damper and related components

7. Install the steering damper bolt and nut in the axle bracket and tighten to 50 ft. lbs. (68 Nm).
8. Install the steering damper nut on the link bracket and tighten to 50 ft. lbs. (68 Nm).
9. Remove the support and lower the vehicle

SUSPENSION

FRONT SUSPENSION

COIL SPRING

REMOVAL & INSTALLATION

➡For related component removal referenced during this procedure, see applicable component headings in this section.

1. Raise and support the vehicle.
2. Remove the wheel and tire assemblies.
3. Position a hydraulic jack under the axle to support it.
4. Remove the front shocks at the lower mountings.
5. Remove lower suspension arms mounting nuts and bolts from the frame.
6. Remove the track bar from the axle bracket.
7. Remove the right side of the drag link from the right side knuckle.
8. Lower the axle until the spring is free from the upper mount.

➡Rotation of the spring and prying down slightly on the axle will aid in removal.

9. Remove the upper spring isolator. (if needed).
10. Pull jounce bumper out of mount. (if needed).

To install:

➡For related component installation referenced during this procedure, see applicable component headings in this section.

11. Install jounce bumper into mount.
12. Install the spring isolator.

➡Rotation of the spring and prying down slightly on the axle will aid in installation.

13. Position the coil spring on the axle pad. It may be necessary to rotate the spring while installing.
14. Raise the axle into position until the spring seats in the upper mount.
15. Install the shock at the axle.
16. Install the track bar to the axle bracket.
17. Install the lower suspension arms to the frame. Install mounting bolts and nuts finger tight.
18. Install the drag link to the right side knuckle.
19. Remove the hydraulic jack from under the axle.
20. Install the wheel and tire assemblies.
21. Remove the supports and lower the vehicle.
22. Tighten the lower suspension arms nuts to 125 ft. lbs. (169 Nm) at normal ride height with the vehicle weight.

LOWER BALL JOINT

REMOVAL & INSTALLATION

1. Remove the hub/bearing, as described in this section.
2. Remove the axle shaft from the axle. See "DRIVE TRAIN" section.
3. Remove the steering knuckle. See "STEERING" section.
4. Position appropriate ball joint removal tools set (9949, 8975-4 and C-4212F or equivalent) and remove lower ball stud.
5. Installation is the reverse of the removal procedure.

LOWER CONTROL ARM

REMOVAL & INSTALLATION

See Figure 57.

1. Raise and support the vehicle.

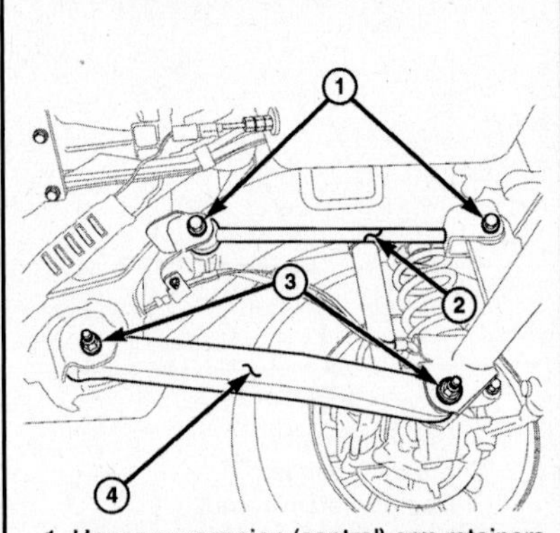

Fig. 57 Showing the lower control arm and related components

2. If the vehicle is equipped with a cam bolt service kit, paint or scribe marks on the cam adjuster and the suspension (control) arm for installation reference.
3. Remove the lower control arm nut and cam/bolt from the axle.
4. Remove the nut and bolt from the frame rail bracket and remove the lower control arm.

To install:

5. Position the lower suspension (control) arm in the axle bracket and frame rail bracket.

➡Position the paint dot located on the control arm toward the axle and facing outboard. If paint dot is not visible, the bend should point inboard, and the short end should attach to the axle side.

➡Frame and axle bolts should be installed outboard to inboard.

6. Install the frame bolt and nut finger tighten.
7. Lower the vehicle.

➡If a castor adjustment kit has been installed, there is a different torque specification.

8. For original equipment bolt/nut, tighten the axle bracket nut to 117 ft. lbs. (159 Nm). For a castor adjustment kit bolt/nut, tighten the axle bracket nut to 63 ft. lbs. (85 Nm).
Tighten frame bracket nut to 125 ft. lbs. (169 Nm).
9. Align vehicle to specifications.

SHOCK ABSORBER

REMOVAL & INSTALLATION

1. Raise and support the vehicle.
2. Remove the inner fender well.
3. Remove the nut, retainer and grommet from the upper stud.
4. Remove the lower nut and bolt from the axle bracket and remove the shock absorber.
5. Installation is the reverse of the removal procedure.
6. Tighten the upper shock absorber nut to 20 ft. lbs. (27 Nm).
7. Tighten the lower shock absorber bolt and nut to 56 ft. lbs. (76 Nm).

STABILIZER BAR ACTUATOR

REMOVAL & INSTALLATION

See Figure 58.

The actuator is a motor driven unit that engages and disengages the disconnecting stabilizer bar.

This system allows greater front suspension travel in off-road situations. It consists of a disconnecting unit, electronic actuator, stabilizer bar.

➡The disconnecting stabilizer bar unit is not serviced separately from the bar. Do not disassemble this unit from the stabilizer bar. The stabilizer links, stabilizer bar retainers/ bushings, stabilizer bar actuator and the stabilizer bar are serviceable. The new bar consists of the disconnecting unit attached as an assembly to the bar.

1. Raise and support the vehicle.
2. Before removing the connector from the actuator clean the outside of the connector with a cleaner and compressed air, to remove any dirt or debris.
3. Disconnect the electronic actuator electrical connector for the disconnecting stabilizer bar.
4. Remove the 3 actuator bolts then remove the actuator.
5. Installation is the reverse of the removal procedure.
6. Tighten the actuator bolts to 37 ft. lbs. (45 Nm).

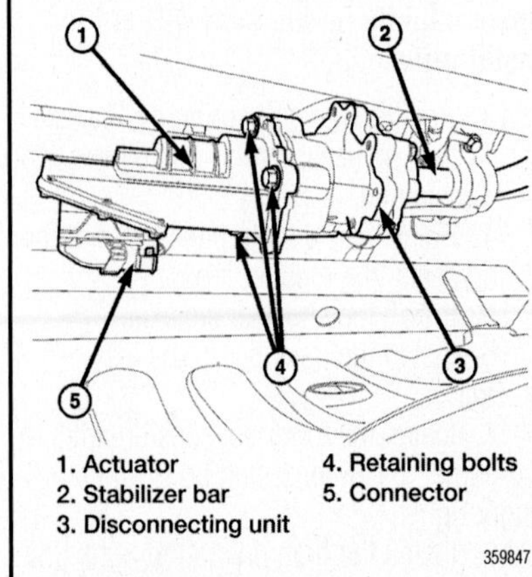

Fig. 58 Showing the disconnecting stabilizer bar actuator

STABILIZER BAR

REMOVAL & INSTALLATION

Stabilizer Bar

1. Raise and support the vehicle.
2. Remove the left upper stabilizer bar link nut from the stabilizer bar.
3. Remove the right upper stabilizer bar link nut from the stabilizer bar.
4. Remove the splash shield.
5. Remove the right side stabilizer bar bracket bolts at the frame.
6. Remove the left side stabilizer bar bracket bolts at the frame.
7. Remove the stabilizer bar to the bench.
8. Installation is the reverse of the removal procedure.
9. Tighten all bolts to 75 ft. lbs. (102 Nm).

Disconnecting Stabilizer Bar

➡See illustration under "Stabilizer Bar Actuator" in this section.

This feature will provide feedback to the driver and be controlled by an electronic module (part of the stabilizer bar) which communicates via CAN C at 500 kbps. The disconnecting stabilizer bar module will read the ignition switch, vehicle speed, transfer case, and stabilizer bar switch messages on the CAN C bus and control the disconnecting stabilizer bar. The module will send a stabilizer bar status message and a lighting message on CAN C.

The stabilizer bar will ENGAGE with the loss of ignition switch, vehicle speed, or stabilizer bar switch signals

The bar will DISENGAGE when ALL the following conditions are met:

- Vehicle speed under 18 MPH
- Automatically at speeds over 14 MPH if the switch is in the ON position
- Transfer case in 4 HI or 4 LO
- Stabilizer bar switch message received for DISENGAGE
- Ignition switch in the RUN or START position

- No stabilizer bar faults detected

The bar will ENGAGE when ANY of the following conditions are met:

- Vehicle speed is greater or equal to 18 MPH
- Stabilizer bar switch message received for ENGAGE
- Transfer case in 2WD or neutral

The disconnecting stabilizer bar system will latch the momentary switch through software for an ignition switch OFF condition if the stabilizer bar was DISENGAGED and the transfer case was in 4LO at ignition switch OFF. Upon ignition switch RUN/START and the transfer case in 4LO, the system checks to verify all conditions to DISENGAGE the stabilizer bar are correct and then DISENGAGE the stabilizer bar without switch input.

➡The disconnecting stabilizer bar unit is not serviced separately from the bar. Do not disassemble this unit from the stabilizer bar. The stabilizer links, stabilizer bar retainers/ bushings, stabilizer bar actuator and the stabilizer bar are serviceable. The new bar consists of the disconnecting unit attached as an assembly to the bar.

1. Raise and support the vehicle.
2. Hold the stabilizer link shafts with a wrench and remove the link nuts at the stabilizer bar.
3. Before removing the connector from the actuator, clean the outside of the connector with a cleaner and compressed air, to remove any dirt or debris.
4. Disconnect the electronic actuator electrical connector for the disconnecting stabilizer bar.
5. Remove the actuator bolts then remove the actuator.
6. Remove the stabilizer bar retainers from the frame rails and remove the stabilizer bar.

To install:

7. Position the stabilizer bar on the frame rail and install the retainers with bushings and bolts. Ensure the bar is centered with equal spacing on both sides.
8. Tighten the retainer bolts to 45 ft. lbs. (61 Nm).

➡The seal must be clean and intact in the electrical connector when reconnecting to the actuator.

9. Install the actuator to the disconnecting unit. If the actuator was removed, see "Stabilizer Bar Actuator" in this section.
10. Reconnect the electronic actuator electrical connector for the disconnecting stabilizer bar.

➡Stabilizer bar link to axle bolt should be tightened with vehicle sitting on its tires

11. Install links and nuts to the stabilizer bar.
12. Remove the supports and lower the vehicle.
13. Hold the stabilizer link shaft with a wrench and tighten the nuts to 75 ft. lbs. (102 Nm).
14. Using a scan tool program the new stabilizer bar to the vehicle.

STABILIZER BAR LINK

REMOVAL & INSTALLATION

See Figure 59.

1. Raise and support the vehicle.
2. Remove the left upper stabilizer bar link nut from the stabilizer bar.
3. Remove the left lower stabilizer bar link bolt to the axle.
4. Remove the right upper stabilizer bar link nut from the stabilizer bar.
5. Remove the right lower stabilizer bar link bolt to the axle.
6. Remove the stabilizer link.

To install:

➡Stabilizer bar link to axle bolt should be tightened with vehicle sitting on its tires

7. Install the stabilizer link to the vehicle.
8. Install the right lower stabilizer bar link bolt to the axle. Tighten to 75 ft. lbs. (102 Nm) after vehicle is lowered to curb weight.
9. Install the right upper stabilizer bar link nut to the stabilizer bar. Tighten to 75 ft. lbs. (102 Nm).
10. Install the left lower stabilizer bar link bolt to the axle. Tighten to 75 ft. lbs. (102 Nm) after vehicle is lowered to curb weight.
11. Install the left upper stabilizer bar link nut to the stabilizer bar. Tighten to 75 ft. lbs. (102 Nm).
12. Remove the support and lower the vehicle.

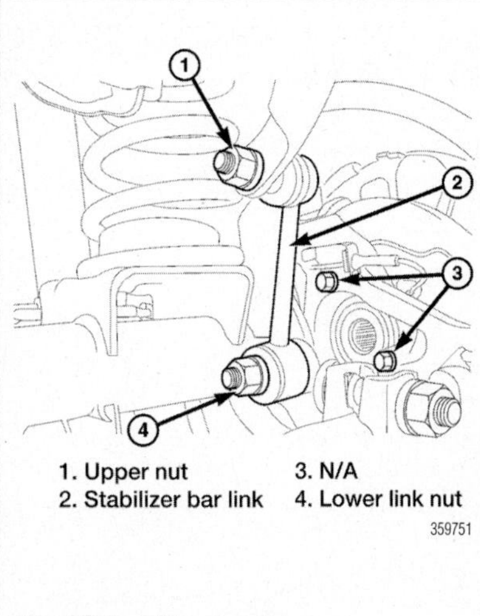

Fig. 59 Stabilizer bar link

STEERING KNUCKLE

REMOVAL & INSTALLATION

See Figure 60.

1. Raise and support the vehicle.
2. Remove the tire and wheel assembly.
3. Remove the outer tie rod end nut.
4. Separate the tie rod from the knuckle using special separator tool (9360 or equivalent).
5. For the right side only, remove the drag link nut. Separate the drag link from the knuckle, using special separator tool.
6. Remove the disc brake caliper adapter bolts and support the caliper so it does not hang by the brake hose. Remove the disc brake rotor. See "BRAKES" section.
7. Remove axle shaft nut (if equipped).
8. Remove the wheel speed sensor.
9. Remove the lower and upper ball joint cotter pins and nuts.
10. Separate the lower, then the upper, ball joints from the knuckle.
11. Remove the knuckle from the vehicle and transfer the hub/bearing with brake shield if needed.

To install:

12. Install the knuckle to the ball joint studs.
13. Install the upper ball joint nut and cotter pin, then the lower ball joint nut

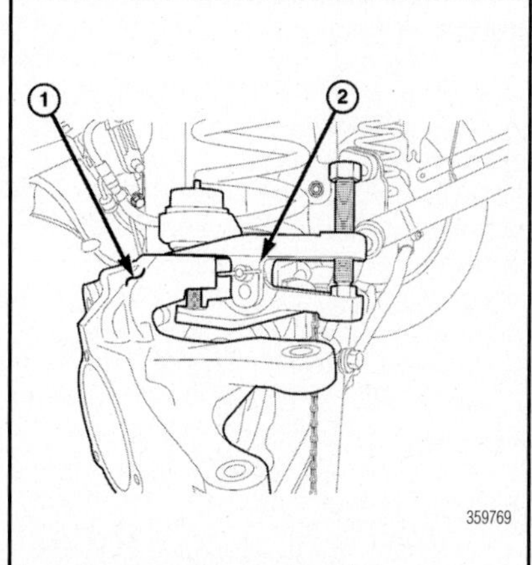

Fig. 60 Separate the upper ball joint from the knuckle (1) using special tool 9360 separator (2).

and cotter pin. Tighten to 70 ft. lbs. (95 Nm).

14. Install the axle shaft nut (if equipped). Tighten to 100 ft. lbs. (136 Nm).

15. Install the wheel speed sensor in the hub/bearing and tighten the bolt.

16. Install the disc brake rotor and caliper. Tighten the caliper adaptor mounting bolts to 120 ft. lbs. (163 Nm).

17. Install the drag link to the knuckle and install the mounting nut. Tighten to 55 ft. lbs. (74 Nm).

18. Install the tire and wheel assembly.

19. Remove the support and lower the vehicle.

TRACK BAR

REMOVAL & INSTALLATION

See Figure 61.

1. Raise and support the vehicle.
2. Remove the track bar nut and bolt from the frame rail bracket.
3. Remove the bolt and flag nut from the axle bracket.
4. Remove the track bar.

To install:

5. Install the track bar at axle tube bracket. Loosely install the retaining bolt and flag nut.

➡Frame bolt must be installed from front to rear.

6. It may be necessary to pry the axle assembly over to install the track bar at the frame rail. Install track bar at the frame rail bracket. Install the nut and bolt at the frame rail bracket.
7. Remove the supports and lower the vehicle.
8. Tighten the bolt at the frame and axle bracket to 125 ft. lbs. (169 Nm).
9. Check toe if a new track bar was installed.

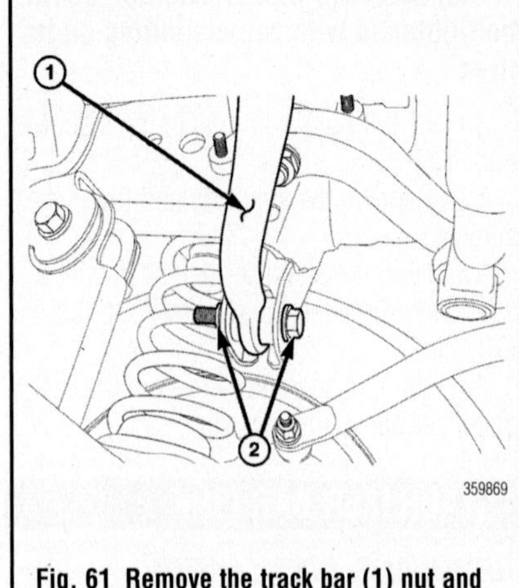

Fig. 61 Remove the track bar (1) nut and bolt (2) from the frame rail bracket.

UPPER BALL JOINT

REMOVAL & INSTALLATION

1. Remove the steering knuckle. See "STEERING" section.
2. Remove the axle shaft from the axle. See "DRIVE TRAIN" section.
3. Position proper ball joint remover tool set (6761, 6289-3 and C-4121F or equivalent), to remove upper ball joint.
4. Installation is the reverse of the removal procedure.

UPPER CONTROL ARM

REMOVAL & INSTALLATION

1. Raise and support the vehicle.
2. Remove electrical clip from the control arm clevis bracket, if equipped.
3. Remove the upper control arm nut and bolt at the axle bracket.
4. Remove the nut and bolt at the frame rail and remove the upper control arm

To install:

5. Position the upper control arm at the axle and frame rail.

➡Axle bolt must be installed from the inboard to outboard.

6. Install the bolts and finger tighten the nuts.
7. Remove the supports and lower the vehicle.
8. Tighten the bolt at the axle and frame brackets to 75 ft. lbs. (102 Nm).

WHEEL HUB & BEARINGS

REMOVAL & INSTALLATION

1. Raise and support the vehicle.
2. Remove the wheel and tire assembly.

➡Support the caliper, Do not let the caliper hang by the hose.

3. Remove the disc brake caliper, adaptor and rotor. Remove wheel speed sensor through the brake shield. See "BRAKES" section.
4. Remove the axle shaft nut if equipped.
5. Remove the 3 hub bearing mounting bolts from the back of the steering knuckle. Remove hub bearing from the steering knuckle.

To install:

6. Install the hub bearing to the knuckle.
7. Install the hub bearing to knuckle and the 3 bolts, then tighten to 75 ft. lbs. (102 Nm).
8. Install the axle nut if equipped. Tighten to 100 ft. lbs. (136 Nm).
9. Install the wheel speed sensor and connector. Install the brake rotor, adapter and caliper. See "BRAKES" section.
10. Install the wheel and tire assembly.
11. Remove the support and lower the vehicle.

COIL SPRING

REMOVAL & INSTALLATION

➡For assistance with related component removal, see appropriate component head in this section.

1. Raise and support the vehicle. Position a hydraulic jack under the axle to support it.
2. Disconnect the stabilizer bar links from the axle brackets.
3. Disconnect the shock absorbers from the axle brackets.
4. Disconnect the track bar from the axle bracket.
5. Lower the axle until the spring is free from the upper mount seat and remove the spring.

To install:

➡For installation and torque values of related components, see appropriate component head in this section.

6. Position the coil spring on the axle pad isolator.
7. Raise the axle into position until the spring seats on the upper isolator.
8. Connect the stabilizer bar links to the axle bracket.
9. Connect the shock absorbers to the axle bracket.
10. Connect the track bar to the frame axle bracket.
11. Remove the supports (2) and lower the vehicle.

LOWER CONTROL ARM

REMOVAL & INSTALLATION

See Figure 62.

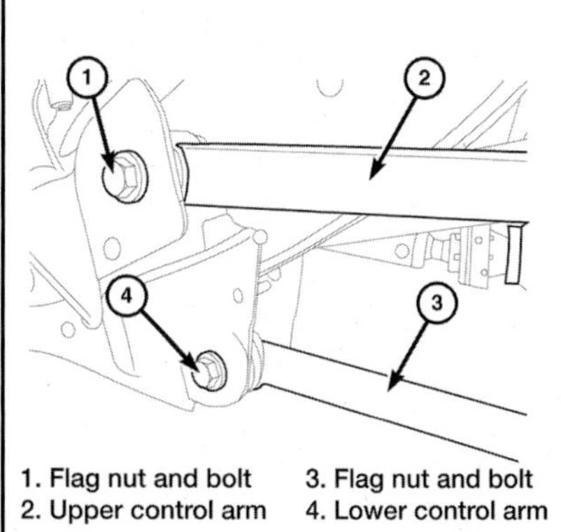

Fig. 62 Showing the lower and upper control arms

1. Raise and support the vehicle.
2. Remove the tire and wheel assembly.
3. Remove the lower suspension (control) arm nut and bolt at the axle bracket.
4. Remove the flag nut and bolt at the frame rail mount and remove the lower control arm.

To install:

5. Position the lower suspension arm in the axle bracket and frame rail mount. Install the frame mounting bolt finger tight.
6. Install the axle mounting bolt and nut at the axle bracket finger tight.
7. Remove the supports and lower the vehicle.
8. Tighten the lower suspension arm bolts to 125 ft. lbs. (169 Nm) with vehicle at curb weight.

SHOCK ABSORBER

REMOVAL & INSTALLATION

1. Raise and support the vehicle and the axle.
2. Remove the upper shock absorber mounting bolts.
3. Remove the lower shock absorber nut and bolt from the axle bracket.
4. Remove the shock absorber.

To install:

5. Install the shock absorber on the upper frame rail and install mounting bolts. Tighten the upper bolts to 37 ft. lbs. (50 Nm).
6. Install lower bolt and nut finger tight.
7. Remove the supports and lower the vehicle.
8. Tighten the lower nut to 56 ft. lbs. (76 Nm).

STABILIZER BAR

REMOVAL & INSTALLATION

1. Raise and support the vehicle.
2. Remove the left upper stabilizer bar link nut from the stabilizer bar.
3. Remove the right upper stabilizer bar link nut from the stabilizer bar.
4. Remove the splash shield.
5. Remove the right side stabilizer bar bracket bolts at the frame.
6. Remove the left side stabilizer bar bracket bolts at the frame.
7. Remove the stabilizer bar to the bench.

To install:

8. Install the stabilizer bar to the frame and install the retainer brackets and bolts. Ensure the bar is centered with equal spacing on both sides.
9. Tighten the retainer bolts to 45 ft. lbs. (61 Nm).
10. Install the stabilizer bar links onto the stabilizer bar. Install the nut finger tight.
11. Support the axle and Tighten the upper link nut to 66 ft. lbs. (90 Nm).

STABILIZER BAR LINK

REMOVAL & INSTALLATION

See Figure 63.

1. Raise and support the vehicle.
2. Remove the rear tire.
3. Support the rear axle with a jack.
4. Remove the upper link nut at the stabilizer bar.
5. Remove the lower link nut and bolt at the axle.
6. Remove stabilizer link.

To install:

➡The stabilizer bar link to axle bracket fastener must be tightened with full vehicle weight.

7. Install the stabilizer link to the vehicle.
8. Install the upper nut for the stabilizer link to the stabilizer bar and tighten to 66 ft. lbs. (90 Nm).
9. Install the nut and bolt to the axle and hand tighten.
10. Remove the jack and lower the vehicle.
11. Tighten the lower bolt and nut at axle connection to 75 ft. lbs. (102 Nm).

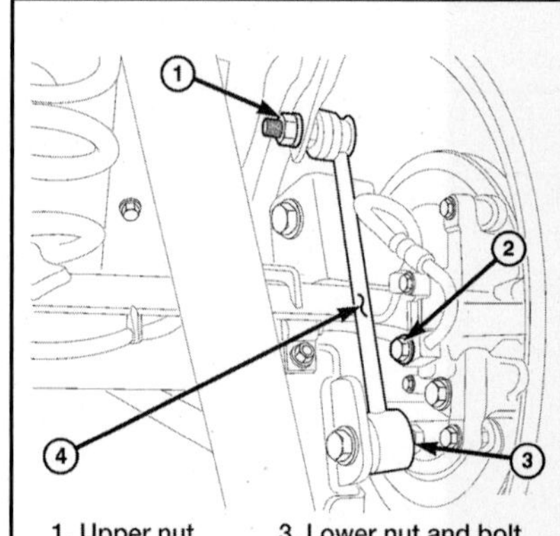

Fig. 63 Showing the stabilizer bar link

OBD II Trouble Code List (P0XXX Codes)

DTC	Trouble Code Title, Conditions, Possible Causes
DTC: P0003	**-FUEL QUANTITY CONTROL CIRCUIT LOW:** With the ignition on and the ECM command of the Fuel Quantity Solenoid off. The ECM detects that the (K365) Fuel Quantity Solenoid Control circuit voltage is shorted to ground for 0. 2 seconds.
DTC: P0004	**-FUEL QUANTITY CONTROL CIRCUIT HIGH:** With the ignition on and the ECM command of the Fuel Quantity Solenoid on. The ECM detects excessive current on the (K365) Fuel Quantity Solenoid Control circuit for 0. 2 of a second.
DTC: P000A	**-BANK 1 CAMSHAFT 1 POSITION SLOW RESPONSE:** Variable Valve Timing (VVT) rationality is monitored under the following conditions:(1) Cam phasing is commanded; (2) Oil temperature is between -12°C to 139° C (10° F to 282° F); (3) Battery voltage is greater than10 volts; (3) Engine speed is at least 650 to 1400 rpm, depending on oil temperature; (4) No CMP sensor, CKP sensor, or OBDI plausibility errors. Before VVT can be enabled, reference adaptation must be completed. The actual camshaft phasing position does not match the desired camshaft phasing position during camshaft phasing position changes.
DTC: P000A	**-BANK 1 CAMSHAFT 1 POSITION SLOW RESPONSE:** Variable Valve Timing (VVT) rationality is monitored under the following conditions:(1) Cam phasing is commanded off of the default (lockpin) position;(2) Oil temperature is between -12°C to 139°C (10°F to 282°F); (3)Battery voltage is greater than 10. 0 Volts; (3) Engine speed is at least 650 to 1400 rpm, depending on oil temperature; (4) No CMP Sensor, CKP Sensor or OBDI plausibility errors. Before VVT can be enabled, reference adaptation must be completed. The actual Camshaft phasing position does not match the desired Camshaft phasing position during Camshaft phasing position changes.
DTC: P000B	**-BANK 1 CAMSHAFT 2 POSITION SLOW RESPONSE:** Variable Valve Timing (VVT) rationality is monitored under the following conditions:(1) Cam phasing is commanded off of the default (lockpin) position;(2) Oil temperature is between -12° C to 139° C (10° F to 282° F);(3) Battery voltage is greater than 10 Volts; (3) Engine speed is at least 650 to 1400 rpm, depending on oil temperature; (4) No CMP sensor, CKP sensor or OBDI plausibility errors. Before VVT can be enabled, reference adaptation must be completed. The actual camshaft phasing position does not match the desired camshaft phasing position during camshaft phasing position changes.
DTC: P000B	**-BANK 1 CAMSHAFT 2 POSITION SLOW RESPONSE:** Variable Cam Timing (VCT) phasing accuracy is monitored under the following conditions: (1) Engine speed is at least 150 rpm; (2) No CMP sensor or CKP sensor plausibility errors. This is performed even when phasing control is not enabled, to verify the actuator is keeping the camshaft at the default (lockpin) phase. The actual measured camshaft phase does not match the desired camshaft phasing set point. Two Trip Fault. Three good trips to turn off the MIL.
DTC: P000B	**-BANK 1 CAMSHAFT 2 POSITION SLOW RESPONSE:** The Variable Cam Timing (VCT) phasing accuracy is monitored under the following conditions: (1) Engine speed is at least 150 rpm. (2) No CMP sensor or CKP sensor plausibility errors. This is performed even when phasing control is not enabled, to verify the actuator is keeping the camshaft at the default (lockpin) phase. The actual measured camshaft phase does not match the desired camshaft phasing set point. Two Trip Fault. Three good trips to turn off the MIL.
DTC: P000B	**-BANK 1 CAMSHAFT 2 POSITION SLOW RESPONSE:** Variable Valve Timing (VVT) rationality is monitored under the following conditions:(1) Cam phasing is commanded; (2) Oil temperature is between -12°C to 139° C (10° F to 282° F); (3) Battery voltage is greater than10 Volts; (3) Engine speed is at least 650 to 1400 rpm, depending on oil temperature; (4) No CMP sensor, CKP sensor, or OBDI plausibility errors. Before VVT can be enabled, reference adaptation must be completed. The actual camshaft phasing position does not match the desired camshaft phasing position during camshaft phasing position changes.
DTC: P000C	**-BANK 2 CAMSHAFT 1 POSITION SLOW RESPONSE :** Variable Valve Timing (VVT) rationality is monitored under the following conditions:(1) Cam phasing is commanded off of the default (lockpin) position;(2) Oil temperature is between -12° C to 139° C (10° F to 282° F);(3) Battery voltage is greater than 10 Volts; (3) Engine speed is at least 650 to 1400 rpm, depending on oil temperature; (4) No CMP sensor, CKP sensor or OBDI plausibility errors. Before VVT can be enabled, reference adaptation must be completed. The actual camshaft phasing position does not match the desired camshaft phasing position during camshaft phasing position changes.
DTC: P000D	**-BANK 2 CAMSHAFT 2 POSITION SLOW RESPONSE:** Variable Valve Timing (VVT) rationality is monitored under the following conditions:(1) Cam phasing is commanded off of the default (lockpin) position;(2) Oil temperature is between -12° C to 139° C (10° F to 282° F);(3) Battery voltage is greater than 10 Volts; (3) Engine speed is at least 650 to 1400 RPM, depending on oil temperature; (4) No CMP sensor, CKP sensor or OBDI plausibility errors. Before VVT can be enabled, reference adaptation must be completed. The actual camshaft phasing position does not match the desired camshaft phasing position during camshaft phasing position changes.
DTC: P0010	**-BANK 1 CAMSHAFT 1 POSITION ACTUATOR CIRCUIT OPEN:** With the engine running and battery voltage greater than 10. 4 Volts. The Powertrain Control Module (PCM) detects that the actual state of the VVT Intake Solenoid does not match the intended state.

DTC	Trouble Code Title, Conditions, Possible Causes
DTC: P0010	**-BANK 1 CAMSHAFT 1 POSITION ACTUATOR CIRCUIT OPEN:** With the engine running and battery voltage greater than 10. 4 volts. The Powertrain Control Module (PCM) detects that the actual state of the Camshaft1/1 Position Solenoid does not match the intended state.
DTC: P0013	**-BANK 1 CAMSHAFT 2 POSITION ACTUATOR CIRCUIT OPEN:** With the engine running and battery voltage greater than 10. 4 volts. The Powertrain Control Module (PCM) detects that the actual state of the Camshaft1/2 Position Solenoid does not match the intended state.
DTC: P0013	**-BANK 1 CAMSHAFT 2 POSITION ACTUATOR CIRCUIT OPEN:** With the battery voltage is between 11 and 18 volts with the engine running. The PCM detects that the actual voltage of the Variable Cam Timing (VCT) Solenoid Control circuit does not match the intended state. Two Trip Fault. Three good trips to turn off the MIL.
DTC: P0014	**-EXHAUST TARGET ERROR BANK 1:** Variable Cam Timing (VCT) rationality is monitored under the following conditions: (1) Cam phasing is commanded off of the default (lockpin) position; (2) Oil temperature is between -12° C to 139° C (10° F to 282° F); (3) Battery voltage is greater than 10 Volts; (3) Engine speed is at least 650 to 1400 rpm, depending on oil temperature; (4) No CMP sensor, CKP sensor or OBDI plausibility errors. Before VCT can be enabled, reference adaptation must be completed. The actual camshaft phasing position is not moving towards the desired camshaft phasing position during steady state operation.
DTC: P0016	**-CRANKSHAFT/CAMSHAFT TIMING MISALIGNMENT:** Engine cranking and Engine running Powertrain Control Module detects an error when the camshaft position is out of phase with the crankshaft position. One Trip Fault. Three good trips to turn off the MIL.
DTC: P0016	**-CRANKSHAFT/CAMSHAFT TIMING MISALIGNMENT:** With the engine speed between 480 and 6816 RPM and no CMP or CKP sensor DTCs detected. Powertrain Control Module detects an error when the camshaft position is out of phase with the crankshaft position. One Trip Fault. Three good trips to turn off the MIL.
DTC: P0017	**-CRANKSHAFT/CAMSHAFT 1/2 TIMING MISALIGNMENT:** Engine cranking and Engine running Powertrain Control Module (PCM) detects an error when the camshaft position is out of phase with the crankshaft position. One Trip Fault. Three good trips to turn off the MIL.
DTC: P0018	**-CRANKSHAFT/CAMSHAFT TIMING MISALIGNMENT:** Engine cranking and Engine running Powertrain Control Module (PCM) detects an error when the camshaft position is out of phase with the crankshaft position. One Trip Fault. Three good trips to turn off the MIL.
DTC: P0019	**-CRANKSHAFT/CAMSHAFT TIMING MISALIGNMENT:** Engine cranking and Engine running Powertrain Control Module (PCM) detects an error when the camshaft position is out of phase with the crankshaft position. One Trip Fault. Three good trips to turn off the MIL.
DTC: P0020	**-BANK 2 CAMSHAFT 1 POSITION ACTUATOR CIRCUIT:** Variable Valve Timing (VVT) rationality is monitored under the following conditions:(1) Cam phasing is commanded off of the default (lockpin) position;(2) Oil temperature is between -12°C to 139°C (10°F to 282°F); (3)Battery voltage is greater than 10 Volts; (3) Engine speed is at least650 to 1400 RPM, depending on oil temperature; (4) No CMP sensor, CKP sensor or OBDI plausibility errors. Before VVT can be enabled, reference adaptation must be completed. The PCM detects that the Camshaft 2/1 Control circuit is open.
DTC: P0023	**-BANK 2 CAMSHAFT 2 POSITION ACTUATOR CIRCUIT OPEN:** Variable Valve Timing (VVT) rationality is monitored under the following conditions:(1) Cam phasing is commanded off of the default (lockpin) position;(2) Oil temperature is between -12°C to 139°C (10°F to 282°F); (3)Battery voltage is greater than 10 Volts; (3) Engine speed is at least650 to 1400 RPM, depending on oil temperature; (4) No CMP sensor, CKP sensor or OBDI plausibility errors. Before VVT can be enabled, reference adaptation must be completed. The PCM detects that the Camshaft 2/2 Control circuit is open.
DTC: P0030	**-O2 SENSOR 1/1 HEATER CIRCUIT:** With the ignition on and the Oxygen Sensor Heater command on. The ECM detects an implausible voltage on the (K99) O2 1/1 Heater Control circuit for 2. 0 seconds.
DTC: P0031	**-O2 SENSOR 1/1 HEATER CIRCUIT LOW:** With the engine running and battery voltage greater than 10. 4 Volts. The Powertrain Control Module (PCM) detects that the Oxygen Sensor 1/1 Heater Control circuit is shorted low.
DTC: P0031	**-O2 SENSOR 1/1 HEATER CIRCUIT LOW:** With the ignition on and the Oxygen Sensor Heater command on. The ECM detects that the (K99) O2 1/1 Heater Control circuit is shorted to ground for 2. 0 seconds.
DTC: P0031	**-O2 SENSOR 1/1 HEATER CIRCUIT LOW:** Continuously during O2 heater operation with battery voltage between 10. 4 and 15. 75 Volts. The PCM detects that the O2 sensor heater element input is below the minimum acceptable voltage. One trip fault. Three good trips to turn off the MIL.
DTC: P0032	**-O2 SENSOR 1/1 HEATER CIRCUIT HIGH:** With the engine running and battery voltage greater than 10. 4 volts. The Powertrain Control Module (PCM) detects that the Oxygen Sensor 1/1 heater control circuit is shorted high.

DTC	Trouble Code Title, Conditions, Possible Causes
DTC: P0032	**-O2 SENSOR 1/1 HEATER CIRCUIT HIGH:** With the ignition on and the Oxygen Sensor Heater command on. The ECM detects that the (K99) O2 1/1 Heater Control circuit is shorted to voltage for 2. 0 seconds.
DTC: P0032	**-O2 SENSOR 1/1 HEATER CIRCUIT HIGH:** Continuously during O2 heater operation with battery voltage between 10. 4 and 15. 75 Volts. The Powertrain Control Module (PCM) detects that the O2 sensor heater element input is above the maximum acceptable voltage. One trip fault. Three good trips to turn off the MIL.
DTC: P0037	**-O2 SENSOR 1/2 HEATER CIRCUIT LOW:** Continuously during O2 heater operation with battery voltage between 10. 4 and 15. 75 Volts. The Powertrain Control Module (PCM) detects that the O2 Sensor 1/2 heater element input is below the minimum acceptable voltage. One trip fault. Three good trips to turn off the MIL.
DTC: P0038	**-O2 SENSOR 1/2 HEATER CIRCUIT HIGH:** Continuously during O2 heater operation with battery voltage between 10. 4 and 15. 75 volts. The Powertrain Control Module (PCM) detects that the O2 sensor heater element input is above the maximum acceptable voltage. One trip fault. Three good trips to turn off the MIL.
DTC: P0045	**TURBOCHARGER BOOST CONTROL CIRCUIT/OPEN:** With the ignition on and the Boost Pressure Servo Motor command off. The ECM detects that the (X635) Boost Pressure Servo Motor Control circuit is open for 2. 0 seconds.
DTC: P0046	**TURBOCHARGER BOOST CONTROL CIRCUIT PERFORMANCE:** With the ignition on and the Boost Pressure Servo Motor command on. The ECM detects that the (X635) Boost Pressure Servo Motor Control circuit voltage is implausible.
DTC: P0047	**TURBOCHARGER BOOST CONTROL CIRCUIT LOW:** With the ignition on and the Boost Pressure Servo Motor command off. The ECM detects that the (X635) Boost Pressure Servo Motor Control circuit is shorted to ground for 5. 3 seconds.
DTC: P0048	**TURBOCHARGER BOOST CONTROL CIRCUIT HIGH:** With the ignition on and the Boost Pressure Servo Motor command on. The ECM detects that the (X635) Boost Pressure Servo Motor Control circuit is shorted to voltage for 2. 0 seconds.
DTC: P0051	**-O2 SENSOR 2/1 HEATER CIRCUIT LOW:** Continuously during O2 heater operation with battery voltage between 10. 4 and 15. 75 Volts. The Powertrain Control Module (PCM) detects that the O2 Sensor 2/1 heater element input is below the minimum acceptable voltage. One trip fault. Three good trips to turn off the MIL.
DTC: P0052	**-O2 SENSOR 2/1 HEATER CIRCUIT HIGH:** Continuously during O2 heater operation with battery voltage between 10. 4 and 15. 75 volts. The PCM detects that the O2 sensor heater element input is above the maximum acceptable voltage. One trip fault. Three good trips to turn off the MIL.
DTC: P0057	**-O2 SENSOR 2/2 HEATER CIRCUIT LOW:** Continuously during O2 heater operation with battery voltage between 10. 4 and 15. 75 volts. The PCM detects that the O2 sensor heater element input is below the minimum acceptable voltage. One trip fault. Three good trips to turn off the MIL.
DTC: P0058	**-O2 SENSOR 2/2 HEATER CIRCUIT HIGH:** Continuously during O2 heater operation with battery voltage between 10. 4 and 15. 75 volts. The PCM detects that the O2 sensor heater element input is above the maximum acceptable voltage. One trip fault. Three good trips to turn off the MIL.
DTC: P0069	**-MANIFOLD PRESSURE/BAROMETRIC PRESSURE CORRELATION:** Engine speed is below 720 RPM. Intake Air Temperature is between 9. 96°C and 84. 9°C. There are no Sensor Reference Voltage DTC's. There are no other Boost Pressure related DTC's. There are no Inlet Pressure Sensor DTC's. The difference between the Boost Pressure Sensor Signal and the Atmospheric/Barometric Pressure Sensor Signal is greater than 150 hpa (2. 175 psi.) for at least 6. 0 seconds.
DTC: P006D	**-BAROMETRIC PRESSURE - INLET AIR PRESSURE CORRELATION:** With the ignition on. No other IAT DTC's present in the ECM. Engine speed below 800 rpm. The difference between the Inlet Pressure Sensor signal and the Atmospheric Pressure Sensor signal is 45 hpa (0. 65 psi) for 5. 0 seconds.
DTC: P0070-11	**-AMBIENT AIR TEMPERATURE SENSOR CIRCUIT - CIRCUIT SHORT TO GROUND:** With the ignition on. Battery voltage greater than 10. 4 volts. The Body Control Module (BCM) detects the Ambient Air Temperature Sensor input voltage is below the minimum acceptable value.
DTC: P0070-15	**-AMBIENT AIR TEMPERATURE SENSOR CIRCUIT - CIRCUIT SHORT TO BATTERY OR OPEN:** With the ignition on. Battery voltage greater than 10. 4 volts. The Body Control Module (BCM) detects the Ambient Air Temperature Sensor input voltage is above the maximum acceptable value.

DTC	Trouble Code Title, Conditions, Possible Causes
DTC: P0071	**-AMBIENT AIR TEMPERATURE SENSOR PERFORMANCE:** With engine off time greater than 480 minutes and ambient temperature greater than - 7° C (19. 4° F). After a calibrated amount of cool down time, the PCM compares the AAT, ECT, and IAT Sensor values. If one sensor value is not within 10° C (18° F) of the other temperature sensors for two consecutive trips, a DTC will set. Three good trips to turn off the MIL.
DTC: P0071	**-AMBIENT AIR TEMPERATURE SENSOR PERFORMANCE:** Engine off time is greater than 480 minutes and the vehicle has been driven for one minute over 35 mph. Ambient temperature is greater than -64° C (-83° F). The PCM compares the ambient, engine coolant, and intake air temperature sensor values. If engine coolant and intake air temperature sensors agree with each other but ambient air temperature does not agree with them, the ambient air temperature sensor is declared as irrational. Two Trip Fault. Three good trips to turn off the MIL.
DTC: P0072	**-AMBIENT AIR TEMPERATURE SENSOR CIRCUIT LOW:** With the ignition on and battery voltage greater than 10. 4 volts. The PCM detects that the Ambient Air Temperature Sensor input voltage is below the minimum acceptable value.
DTC: P0072	**-AMBIENT AIR TEMPERATURE SENSOR CIRCUIT LOW:** With the ignition on and battery voltage greater than 10. 4 volts. The PCM detects that the Ambient Air Temperature Sensor input voltage is below the minimum acceptable value.
DTC: P0073	**-AMBIENT AIR TEMPERATURE SENSOR CIRCUIT HIGH:** With the ignition on. Battery voltage greater than 10 volts. The Ambient Temperature Sensor voltage is greater than maximum acceptable value. One Trip Fault. Three good trips to turn off the MIL.
DTC: P0073	**-AMBIENT AIR TEMPERATURE SENSOR CIRCUIT HIGH:** With the ignition on and battery voltage greater than 10. 4 volts. The Powertrain Control Module (PCM) detects that the Ambient Air Temperature Sensor input voltage is above the maximum acceptable value.
DTC: P0087	**-FUEL RAIL PRESSURE TOO LOW:** With the engine running. The ECM determines that the fuel rail pressure is too low for a given engine speed and load.
DTC: P0088	**-FUEL RAIL PRESSURE TOO HIGH:** With the engine running. The ECM determines that the fuel rail pressure is too high for a given engine speed and load.
DTC: P0089	**-FUEL PRESSURE 1 CONTROL PERFORMANCE:** With the ignition on and the Fuel Pressure Solenoid command on. The ECM detects a fault on the (K370) Fuel Pressure Solenoid Control circuit for 0. 28 of a second.
DTC: P0090	**-FUEL PRESSURE 1 CONTROL CIRCUIT/OPEN:** With the ignition on and the Fuel Pressure Solenoid command off. The ECM detects that the (K370) Fuel Pressure Solenoid Control circuit is open for 0. 28 of a second.
DTC: P0091	**-FUEL PRESSURE 1 CONTROL CIRCUIT LOW:** With the ignition on and the Fuel Pressure Solenoid command off. The ECM detects that the (K370) Fuel Pressure Solenoid Control circuit is shorted to ground for 0. 22 second.
DTC: P0092	**-FUEL PRESSURE 1 CONTROL CIRCUIT HIGH:** With the ignition on and the Fuel Pressure Solenoid command on. The ECM detects excessive current on the (K370) Fuel Pressure Solenoid Control circuit for 0. 28 of a second.
DTC: P0100	**-MASS AIR FLOW SENSOR:** With the ignition on. The ECM detects that the (K157) Mass Air Flow Sensor Signal circuit or the (K362) Inlet Air Temperature Sensor Signal circuit voltage is not within a valid range.
DTC: P0102	**-MASS AIR FLOW SENSOR CIRCUIT LOW:** With the ignition on. The Mass Air Flow Sensor Signal is below the valid operating range.
DTC: P0103	**-MASS AIR FLOW SENSOR CIRCUIT HIGH:** With the ignition on. The Mass Air Flow Sensor Signal is above the valid operating range.
DTC: P0107	**-MANIFOLD ABSOLUTE PRESSURE SENSOR CIRCUIT LOW:** Engine speed between 600 to 3500 RPM. Battery voltage greater than 10 Volts. The MAP sensor signal voltage is below the minimum acceptable value. One Trip Fault. Three good trips to turn off the MIL. MIL will illuminate and the ETC light will flash if equipped.
DTC: P0107	**-MANIFOLD ABSOLUTE PRESSURE SENSOR CIRCUIT LOW:** Engine speed between 600 to 3500 RPM. Battery voltage greater than 10 volts. The PCM detects that the MAP Sensor input voltage is below the minimum acceptable value. One Trip Fault. Three good trips to turn off the MIL. The MIL will illuminate and the ETC light will flash if equipped.
DTC: P0107	**-MANIFOLD ABSOLUTE PRESSURE SENSOR CIRCUIT LOW:** With the ignition on and battery voltage greater than 10. 4 Volts. The Powertrain Control Module (PCM) detects that the MAP Sensor input voltage is below the minimum acceptable value.

DTC	Trouble Code Title, Conditions, Possible Causes
DTC: P0108	**-MANIFOLD ABSOLUTE PRESSURE SENSOR CIRCUIT HIGH:** With the ignition on and battery voltage greater than 10. 4 volts. The Powertrain Control Module (PCM) detects that the Manifold Absolute Pressure (MAP) Sensor input voltage is above the maximum acceptable value.
DTC: P0108	**-MANIFOLD ABSOLUTE PRESSURE SENSOR CIRCUIT HIGH:** Engine speed between 600 to 3500 RPM. Battery voltage greater than 10. 37 volts. The MAP sensor signal voltage is greater than the maximum allowable voltage One trip fault. Three good trips to turn off the MIL. MIL is illuminated and the ETC light is flashing, if equipped.
DTC: P0111	**-INTAKE AIR TEMPERATURE SENSOR PERFORMANCE:** With the engine off time greater than 480 minutes and ambient temperature greater than -7° C (19. 4° F). After a calibrated amount of cool down time, the Powertrain Control Module (PCM) compares the Ambient Air Temperature (AAT), Engine Coolant Temperature (ECT), and Intake Air Temperature (IAT) Sensor values. If one sensor value is not within 10° C (18° F) of the other temperature sensors for two consecutive trips, a DTC will set. Three good trips to turn off the MIL.
DTC: P0111	**-INTAKE AIR TEMPERATURE SENSOR RATIONALITY:** The engine off time is greater than 480 minutes. Ambient Temperature if greater than -64° C (-83° F). Once the vehicle is soaked for a calibrated engine off time and then driven over calibrated speed and load conditions for some calibrated time, the PCM compares the ambient, engine coolant, and intake air temperature sensor values. If engine coolant and ambient air temperature sensors agree with each other but intake air temperature does not agree with them, the intake air temperature sensor is declared as irrational. Two Trip Fault. Three good trips to turn off the MIL.
DTC: P0112	**-INTAKE AIR TEMPERATURE SENSOR CIRCUIT LOW:** With the ignition on and the battery voltage greater than 10. 4 Volts. The Powertrain Control Module (PCM) detects that the Intake Air Temperature (IAT) Sensor input voltage is below the minimum acceptable value.
DTC: P0112	**-INTAKE AIR TEMPERATURE SENSOR CIRCUIT LOW:** With the ignition on and battery voltage greater than 10. 4 Volts. When the Inlet Air Temp Sensor Signal circuit voltage is less than the minimum acceptable value. One trip failure. Three good trips to clear the MIL.
DTC: P0113	**-INTAKE AIR TEMPERATURE SENSOR CIRCUIT HIGH:** With the ignition on. Battery voltage greater than 10. 4 volts. The PCM detects that the Intake Air Temperature Sensor input voltage is above the maximum acceptable value. One Trip Fault. Three good trips to turn off the MIL.
DTC: P0113	**-INTAKE AIR TEMPERATURE SENSOR CIRCUIT HIGH:** With the ignition on and the battery voltage greater than 10. 4 Volts. The Powertrain Control Module (PCM) detects that the Intake Air Temperature (IAT) Sensor input voltage is above the maximum acceptable value.
DTC: P0113	**-INTAKE AIR TEMPERATURE SENSOR CIRCUIT HIGH:** With the ignition on. The (K21) Intake Air Temperature Sensor Signal circuit voltage is above 4. 96 volts for 2. 0 seconds.
DTC: P0116	**-ENGINE COOLANT TEMPERATURE SENSOR CIRCUIT PERFORMANCE:** Engine off time is greater than 480 minutes and the vehicle has been driven for one minute over 35 mph. Ambient temperature is greater than -64° C (-83° F). Once the vehicle is soaked for a calibrated engine off time and then driven over calibrated speed and load conditions for some calibrated time, the PCM compares the ambient, engine coolant, and intake air temperature sensor values. If ambient air and intake air temperature sensors agree with each other but engine coolant temperature does not agree with them, the engine coolant temperature sensor is declared as irrational. Two Trip Fault. Three good trips to turn off the MIL.
DTC: P0116	**-ENGINE COOLANT TEMPERATURE SENSOR PERFORMANCE:** With the ignition on. The Engine Control Module (ECM) detects an implausible voltage on the (K2) Engine Coolant Temperature Sensor Signal circuit.
DTC: P0117	**-ENGINE COOLANT TEMPERATURE SENSOR CIRCUIT LOW:** With the ignition on. The (K2) Engine Coolant Temperature Sensor Signal circuit voltage is below 0. 18 volt for 0. 5 second.
DTC: P0117	**-ENGINE COOLANT TEMPERATURE SENSOR CIRCUIT LOW:** With the ignition on. Battery voltage greater than 10. 4 volts. The PCM detects that the Engine Coolant Temperature Sensor input voltage is below the minimum acceptable value. One Trip Fault. Three good trips to clear the MIL. The MIL and ETC light will illuminate if equipped.
DTC: P0117	**-ENGINE COOLANT TEMPERATURE SENSOR CIRCUIT LOW:** With the ignition on. Battery voltage greater than 10. 4 Volts. The Powertrain Control Module (PCM) detects that the Engine Coolant Temperature Sensor input voltage is below the minimum acceptable value. One Trip Fault. Three good trips to clear the MIL. The MIL and ETC light will illuminate if equipped.
DTC: P0118	**-ENGINE COOLANT TEMPERATURE SENSOR CIRCUIT HIGH:** With the ignition on. Battery voltage greater than 10. 4 volts. The PCM detects that the Engine Coolant Temperature Sensor input voltage is above the maximum acceptable value. One Trip Fault. Three good trips to turn off the MIL. The MIL and ETC light will illuminate if equipped.

DTC	Trouble Code Title, Conditions, Possible Causes
DTC: P0118	**-ENGINE COOLANT TEMPERATURE SENSOR CIRCUIT HIGH:** With the ignition on. The (K2) Engine Coolant Temperature Sensor Signal circuit voltage is above 4. 97 volts for 0. 5 second.
DTC: P0121	**THROTTLE POSITION SENSOR 1 PERFORMANCE:** With the ignition on and battery voltage greater than 10. 4 volts. The Powertrain Control Module (PCM) detects that the Throttle Position Sensor 1 circuit input voltage is implausible.
DTC: P0121	**THROTTLE POSITION SENSOR 1 PERFORMANCE:** With the engine running and no TPS or MAP sensor DTCs present. The Powertrain Control Module (PCM) detects that the sensor input voltage does not fall within a valid range based on engine speed and load. Two Trip Fault. (Electronic Throttle Control) ETC light will illuminate. P2135 should set with this code also.
DTC: P0122	**TPS/APP CIRCUIT LOW:** Continuously with the ignition on and engine running. This DTC will set if the monitored TPS voltage drops below . 078 of a volt for the period of 0. 48 of a second.
DTC: P0122	**THROTTLE POSITION SENSOR 1 CIRCUIT LOW:** With the ignition on and battery voltage greater than 10. 4 volts. The Powertrain Control Module (PCM) detects that the Throttle Body input voltage is below the maximum acceptable value.
DTC: P0122	**THROTTLE POSITION SENSOR 1 CIRCUIT LOW:** With the ignition on. Battery voltage greater than 10 volts. Throttle Position Sensor voltage at the PCM is less than 0. 16 of a volt for 0. 7 of a second. One Trip Fault. Three good trips to turn off the MIL. ETC light will illuminate.
DTC: P0122	**THROTTLE POSITION SENSOR 1 CIRCUIT LOW:** With the ignition on and battery voltage greater than 10. 4 volts. The Powertrain Control Module (PCM) detects that the Throttle Position Sensor 1 input voltage is below the minimum acceptable value.
DTC: P0123	**TPS/APP CIRCUIT HIGH:** Continuously with the ignition on and engine running. This DTC will set if the monitored TPS voltage rises above 4. 94 volts for the period of 0. 48 of a second.
DTC: P0123	**THROTTLE POSITION SENSOR 1 CIRCUIT HIGH:** With the ignition on and battery voltage greater than 10. 4 volts. The Powertrain Control Module (PCM) detects that the Throttle Position Sensor 1 input voltage is above the maximum acceptable value.
DTC: P0123	**THROTTLE POSITION SENSOR 1 CIRCUIT HIGH:** With the ignition on. Battery voltage greater than 10 Volts. Throttle Position Sensor No. 1 voltage is greater than 4. 8 Volts for 25 ms. One Trip Fault. ETC light will illuminate.
DTC: P0124	**TPS/APP INTERMITTENT:** Continuously with the ignition on and engine running. This DTC will set if the monitored TPS throttle angle between the angles of 6° and 120° and the degree change is greater than 5° within a period of less than 7. 0 msec.
DTC: P0125	**-INSUFFICIENT COOLANT TEMP FOR CLOSED-LOOP FUEL CONTROL:** With battery voltage greater than 10. 4 volts and after engine is started. The engine temperature does not go above -10° C (15° F). Failure time depends on start-up coolant temperature and ambient temperature. (i.e. two minutes for a start temp of -10° C (15° F) or up to 10 minutes for a vehicle with a start-up temp of -28° C (5° F). Two Trip Fault. Three good trips to turn off the MIL.
DTC: P0128	**THERMOSTAT RATIONALITY:** With the engine running, start up coolant temperature between –8° C (17. 6° F) and 50° C (122° F), the difference between ambient temperature and coolant temperature less than 10° C (50° F) and average vehicle speed greater than 16 kph (10 mph) for more than 18% of vehicle run time. The Powertrain Control Module (PCM) detects that the actual engine coolant temperature does not reach the predicted engine coolant temperature within a specific time. Two trip fault. Three good trips to turn off the MIL.
DTC: P0128	**THERMOSTAT RATIONALITY:** With the engine running, ambient temperature between -8° C (17. 6° F) and 50° C (122° F), start up coolant temperature less than 50° C (122° F), and average vehicle speed greater than 16 kph (10 mph) until coolant temperature reaches 85° C (185° F). The PCM detects that the actual engine coolant temperature falls too far below the predicted engine coolant temperature and the predicted coolant temperature reaches the predicted target value before the actual coolant temperature reaches the actual coolant temperature target value. Two trip fault. Three good trips to turn off the MIL.
DTC: P0129	**-BAROMETRIC PRESSURE OUT-OF-RANGE LOW:** With the ignition key on. No Cam or Crank signal within 75 ms. Engine speed less than 250 RPM. The PCM senses the voltage from the MAP sensor to be less than 2. 2 volts but above 0. 04 of a volt for 300 milliseconds. One Trip Fault. Three good trips to turn off the MIL. MIL is illuminated and the ETC lamp will flash.

DTC	Trouble Code Title, Conditions, Possible Causes
DTC: P0129	**-BAROMETRIC PRESSURE OUT-OF-RANGE LOW:** With engine speed within 64 RPM of target idle, MAP sensor voltage between . 04 of a volt and 4. 96 volts, no vehicle speed, and the throttle closed. Each time the Powertrain Control Module (PCM) detects that the MAP sensor value is greater than a calibrated value for BARO, a counter is incremented. If the counter reaches a calibrated limit, the test fails. One trip fault. Three good trips to turn off the MIL.
DTC: P012C	**TURBO INLET AIR PRESSURE SENSOR CIRCUIT LOW:** With the ignition on. The (K68) Inlet Air Pressure Sensor Signal circuit voltage is below 0. 35 volt for 2. 0 seconds.
DTC: P012D	**TURBO INLET AIR PRESSURE SENSOR CIRCUIT HIGH:** With the ignition on. The (K68) Inlet Air Pressure Sensor Signal circuit voltage is above 4. 41 volts for 2. 0 seconds.
DTC: P0130	**-O2 SENSOR 1/1 CIRCUIT OPEN:** With the ignition on and the O2 1/1 Sensor at operating temperature. The ECM detects an open on the (Z43) O2 1/1 Negative Current Control circuit for 2. 0 seconds.
DTC: P0131	**-O2 SENSOR 1/1 CIRCUIT LOW:** Engine running for less than 30 seconds and the O2 Sensor Heater Temperature is less than 251° C (484° F) with battery voltage greater 10. 4 volts. The PCM detects that the 1/1 Oxygen Sensor signal voltage is below the minimum acceptable value. The DTC will set as Pending after one trip and Active after two trips. Three good trips to turn off the MIL.
DTC: P0131	**-O2 SENSOR 1/1 CIRCUIT LOW:** With the ignition on and the O2 1/1 Sensor at operating temperature. The ECM detects a short to ground on the (Z43) O2 1/1 Negative Current Control circuit for 2. 0 seconds.
DTC: P0132	**-O2 SENSOR 1/1 CIRCUIT HIGH:** With the Oxygen Sensor 1/1 heater temperature greater than 496° C (925° F) and the battery voltage greater than 10. 4 volts. The Powertrain Control Module (PCM) detects that the Oxygen Sensor 1/1 voltage is greater than 3. 99 volts for 40 seconds. One Trip Fault. Three good trips to turn off the MIL.
DTC: P0132	**-O2 SENSOR 1/1 CIRCUIT HIGH:** Continuously with the engine running, no O2 sensor heater DTCs present, 1/1 Oxygen Sensor heater temperature within a specific range, and battery voltage greater than 10. 4 volts. The Oxygen Sensor voltage is above the maximum acceptable value. The DTC will set as Pending after one trip and Active after two trips. Three good trips to turn off the MIL.
DTC: P0133	**-O2 SENSOR 1/1 SLOW RESPONSE:** With the ECT above 70° C (158° F), engine RPM between 1400 and 2300, vehicle speed between 64 and 96 kph (40 and 60 mph), and engine run time greater than three minutes. The Powertrain Control Module (PCM) detects that the oxygen sensor signal does not switch adequately during monitoring. Two Trip Fault. Three good trips to turn off the MIL.
DTC: P0134	**-O2 SENSOR 1/1 SIGNAL INACTIVE:** With the ignition on and the O2 1/1 Sensor at operating temperature. The ECM detects an implausible voltage on the (Z43) O2 1/1 Negative Current Control circuit for 2. 0 seconds.
DTC: P0135	**-O2 SENSOR 1/1 HEATER PERFORMANCE:** Engine running and heater duty cycle greater than 0%. Battery voltage greater than 11. 0 volts. The PCM detects no temperature change in the O2 sensor heater element when the heater circuit is active. The heater temperature is obtained by measuring the heater resistance and calculating the heater temperature. Two trip fault. Three good trips to turn off the MIL.
DTC: P0135	**-O2 SENSOR 1/1 HEATER PERFORMANCE:** Continuously during O2 sensor heater operation with battery voltage between 10. 4 and 15. 75 volts and no O2 sensor circuit DTCs present. The PCM detects no temperature change in the O2 sensor heater element when the heater circuit is active. The heater temperature is obtained by measuring the heater resistance and calculating the heater temperature. Two trip fault. Three good trips to turn off the MIL.
DTC: P0135	**-O2 SENSOR 1/1 HEATER PERFORMANCE:** With the ignition on and the Oxygen Sensor Heater command on. The ECM detects an implausible voltage on the (K99) O2 1/1 Heater Control circuit for 2. 0 seconds.
DTC: P0137	**-O2 SENSOR 1/2 CIRCUIT LOW:** Engine running for less than 30 seconds and the O2 Sensor Heater Temperature is less than 251° C (484° F) with battery voltage greater 10. 99 Volts. The Powertrain Control Module (PCM) detects that the 1/2 Oxygen Sensor signal voltage is below minimum acceptable value. The DTC will set as Pending after one trip and Active after two trips. Three good trips to turn off the MIL.
DTC: P0138	**-O2 SENSOR 1/2 CIRCUIT HIGH:** Continuously with the engine running, no O2 sensor heater DTCs present, 1/2 Oxygen Sensor heater temperature within a specific range, and battery voltage greater than 10. 4 volts. The PCM detects that the 1/2 Oxygen Sensor voltage is greater than the maximum acceptable value for a specific amount of time, based on O2 sensor heater temperature. The DTC will set as Pending after one trip and Active after two trips. Three good trips to turn off the MIL.

DTC	Trouble Code Title, Conditions, Possible Causes
DTC: P0139	**-O2 SENSOR 1/2 SLOW RESPONSE:** With engine run time greater than five minutes, the coolant temperature greater than 75 C (167 F), vehicle speed greater than 64 kph (40 mph) and the vehicle in decel fuel shut-off (coasting with the accelerator pedal fully released). The O2 signal voltage does not switch quickly enough from rich to lean when the fuel is turned off during a coast with the throttle closed. Two Trip Fault. Three good trips to turn off the MIL.
DTC: P0139	**-O2 SENSOR 1/2 SLOW RESPONSE:** Vehicle is started and driven between 32 and 88. 5 km/h (20 and 55 mph) with the Throttle open for a minimum of 120 seconds. Coolant greater than 70° C (158° F). Catalytic Converter Temp greater than 600° C (1112° F) and Evap Purge is active. The PCM detects that the oxygen sensor signal switches from lean to rich less than 16 times within 20 seconds during monitoring. Two Trip Fault. Three good trips to turn off the MIL.
DTC: P013A	**-O2 SENSOR 1/2 SLOW RESPONSE - RICH TO LEAN:** With the engine running, vehicle speed above 96 kph (60 mph), throttle open for a minimum of 120 seconds, ECT greater than 70° C (158° F), catalytic converter temperature greater than 600° C (1112° F), and downstream oxygen sensor in a rich state. During a decel fuel shutoff event, the downstream oxygen sensor should switch from rich to lean within a specific time. The PCM monitors the downstream O2 sensor. If the PCM does not detect a rich to lean switch within a specific time during a decel fuel shutoff event, the monitor will fail. One trip fault. Three good trips to turn off the MIL.
DTC: P0140	**-O2 SENSOR 1/2 NO ACTIVITY DETECTED:** With the engine running, vehicle speed between 32 and 88 kph (20 and 55 mph), throttle open for a minimum of 120 seconds, ECT greater than 70° C (158° F), Catalytic Converter Temperature greater than 600° C (1112° F) and EVAP Purge active. The Powertrain Control Module (PCM) detects that the oxygen sensor signal switches from lean to rich less than 16 times within 20 seconds during monitoring. Two Trip Fault. Three good trips to turn off the MIL.
DTC: P0140	**-O2 SENSOR 1/2 SIGNAL INACTIVE:** For six minutes after engine start up and the vehicle speed between 20 and 55 MPH. The O2 signal voltage does not switch lean or rich during monitoring for at least2 to 4 minutes. Two Trip Fault. Three good trips to turn off the MIL.
DTC: P0141	**-O2 SENSOR 1/2 HEATER PERFORMANCE:** Continuously during O2 sensor heater operation with battery voltage between 10. 4 and 15. 75 volts and no O2 sensor circuit DTCs present. The PCM detects no temperature change in the O2 sensor heater element when the heater circuit is active. The heater temperature is obtained by measuring the heater resistance and calculating the heater temperature. Two trip fault. Three good trips to turn off the MIL.
DTC: P0151	**-O2 SENSOR 2/1 CIRCUIT LOW:** With the engine running, battery voltage greater than 10. 4 volts, and no O2 sensor heater DTCs present. The PCM detects that the 2/1 Oxygen Sensor signal voltage is below approximately 1. 5 volts for 2. 8 seconds after engine startup. The DTC will set as Pending after one trip and Active after two trips. Three good trips to turn off the MIL.
DTC: P0151	**-O2 SENSOR 2/1 CIRCUIT LOW:** Engine running for less than 30 seconds and the O2 Sensor Heater Temperature is less than 251° C (484° F) with battery voltage greater 10. 99 volts. The PCM detects that the 2/1 Oxygen Sensor signal voltage is below the minimum acceptable value. The DTC will set as Pending after one trip and Active after two trips. Three good trips to turn off the MIL.
DTC: P0152	**-O2 SENSOR 2/1 CIRCUIT HIGH:** Continuously with the engine running, no O2 sensor heater DTCs present, 2/1 Oxygen Sensor heater temperature within a specific range, and battery voltage greater than 10. 4 volts. The PCM detects that the 2/1 Oxygen Sensor voltage is greater than the maximum acceptable value for a specific amount of time, based on O2 sensor heater temperature. The DTC will set as Pending after one trip and Active after two trips. Three good trips to turn off the MIL.
DTC: P0153	**-O2 SENSOR 2/1 SLOW RESPONSE:** With the ECT is above 70 °C (158 °F), engine RPM between 1400 and 2300, vehicle speed between 64 and 96 kph (40 and 60 mph) and engine run time greater than three minutes. The Powertrain Control Module (PCM) detects that the Oxygen Sensor signal does not switch adequately during monitoring. Two Trip Fault. Three good trips to turn off the MIL.
DTC: P0153	**-O2 SENSOR 2/1 SLOW RESPONSE:** Vehicle is started and driven between 32 and 88. 5 km/h (20 and 55 mph) with the Throttle open for a minimum of 120 seconds. Coolant greater than 70° C (158° F). Catalytic Converter Temp greater than 600° C (1112° F) and EVAP Purge is active. The PCM detects that the oxygen sensor signal switches from lean to rich less than 16 times within 20 seconds during monitoring. Two Trip Fault. Three good trips to turn off the MIL.
DTC: P0155	**-O2 SENSOR 2/1 HEATER PERFORMANCE:** Engine running and heater duty cycle greater than 0%. Battery voltage greater than 11. 0 volts. No sensor output is received when the PCM powers up the sensor heater. Two trip fault. Three good trips to turn off the MIL.

DTC	Trouble Code Title, Conditions, Possible Causes
DTC: P0155	**-O2 SENSOR 2/1 HEATER PERFORMANCE:** Continuously during O2 sensor heater operation with battery voltage between 10. 4 and 15. 75 volts and no O2 sensor circuit DTCs present. The PCM detects no temperature change in the O2 sensor heater element when the heater circuit is active. The heater temperature is obtained by measuring the heater resistance and calculating the heater temperature. Two trip fault. Three good trips to turn off the MIL.
DTC: P0157	**-O2 SENSOR 2/2 CIRCUIT LOW:** With the engine running, battery voltage greater than 10. 4 volts, and no O2 sensor heater DTCs present. The PCM detects that the 2/2 Oxygen Sensor signal voltage is below approximately 1. 5 volts for 2. 8 seconds after engine startup. The DTC will set as Pending after one trip and Active after two trips. Three good trips to turn off the MIL.
DTC: P0157	**-O2 SENSOR 2/2 CIRCUIT LOW:** Engine running for less than 30 seconds and the O2 Sensor Heater Temperature is less than 251° C (484° F) with battery voltage greater 10. 99 volts. The PCM detects that the 2/2 Oxygen Sensor signal voltage is below the minimum acceptable value. The DTC will set as Pending after one trip and Active after two trips. Three good trips to turn off the MIL.
DTC: P0158	**-O2 SENSOR 2/2 CIRCUIT HIGH:** Continuously with the engine running, no O2 Sensor Heater DTCs present, Oxygen Sensor 2/2 heater temperature within a specific range and battery voltage greater than 10. 4 Volts. The Powertrain Control Module (PCM) detects that the Oxygen Sensor 2/2 voltage is greater than the maximum acceptable value for a specific amount of time, based on O2 sensor heater temperature. The DTC will set as Pending after one trip and Active after two trips. Three good trips to turn off the MIL.
DTC: P0159	**-O2 SENSOR 2/2 SLOW RESPONSE:** Vehicle is started and driven between 32 and 88. 5 km/h (20 and 55 mph) with the Throttle open for a minimum of 120 seconds. Coolant greater than 70° C (158° F). Catalytic Converter Temp greater than 600° C (1112° F) and Evap Purge is active. The oxygen sensor signal voltage switches less than 16 times from lean to rich within 20 seconds during monitoring. Two Trip Fault. Three good trips to turn off the MIL.
DTC: P0159	**-O2 SENSOR 2/2 SLOW RESPONSE:** With the engine running, vehicle speed above 96 kph (60 mph), throttle open for a minimum of 120 seconds, ECT greater than 70°C (158°F), Catalytic Converter temperature greater than 600°C (1112°F), and downstream oxygen sensor in a rich state. During a decel fuel shutoff event, the downstream oxygen sensor should switch from rich to lean within a specific time. The Powertrain Control Module (PCM) monitors the Downstream O2 Sensor. If the PCM does not detect a rich to lean switch within a specific time during a decel fuel shutoff event, the monitor will fail. One trip fault. Three good trips to turn off the MIL.
DTC: P0160	**-O2 SENSOR 2/2 NO ACTIVITY DETECTED:** Vehicle is started and driven between 32 and 88. 5 km/h (20 and 55 mph) with the Throttle open for a minimum of 120 seconds. Coolant greater than 70° C (158° F). Catalytic Converter Temp greater than 600° C (1112° F) and EVAP Purge is active. The oxygen sensor signal voltage switches less than 16 times from lean to rich within 20 seconds during monitoring. Two Trip Fault. Three good trips to turn off the MIL.
DTC: P0161	**-O2 SENSOR 2/2 HEATER PERFORMANCE:** Continuously during O2 sensor heater operation with battery voltage between 10. 4 and 15. 75 volts and no O2 sensor circuit DTCs present. The PCM detects no temperature change in the O2 sensor heater element when the heater circuit is active. The heater temperature is obtained by measuring the heater resistance and calculating the heater temperature. Two trip fault. Three good trips to turn off the MIL.
DTC: P0161	**-O2 SENSOR 2/2 HEATER PERFORMANCE:** Engine running and heater duty cycle greater than 0%. Battery voltage greater than 11. 0 volts. No sensor output is received when the PCM powers up the sensor heater. Two trip fault. Three good trips to turn off the MIL.
DTC: P0171	**-FUEL SYSTEM 1/1 LEAN:** With the engine running in closed loop mode, the ambient/battery temperature above -6. 7°C (20°F) and altitude below 2590. 8 m (8500 ft). If the PCM multiplies short term compensation by long term adaptive and a certain percentage is exceeded for two trips, a freeze frame is stored, the MIL illuminates and a trouble code is stored. Two Trip Fault. Three good trips to turn off the MIL.
DTC: P0171	**-FUEL SYSTEM 1/1 LEAN:** With the engine running in closed loop, the ambient/battery temperature above -7° C (20° F) and altitude below 8500 ft. The Powertrain Control Module (PCM) monitors the Adaptive Memory factor (a combination of Short Term Adaptive and Long Term Adaptive). If the total fuel addition exceeds a calibrated threshold for an extended period, a fuel system lean fault is stored. If the total fuel subtraction exceeds a calibrated threshold, a fuel system rich fault is stored. Two Trip Fault. Three good trips to turn off the MIL.
DTC: P0174	**-FUEL SYSTEM 2/1 LEAN:** With the engine running in closed loop mode, the ambient/battery temperature above -6. 7°C (20°F) and altitude below 2590. 8 m (8500 ft). If the Powertrain Control Module (PCM) multiplies short term compensation by long term adaptive and a certain percentage is exceeded for two trips, a freeze frame is stored, the MIL illuminates and a trouble code is stored. Two Trip Fault. Three good trips to turn off the MIL.

DTC	Trouble Code Title, Conditions, Possible Causes
DTC: P0174	**-FUEL SYSTEM 2/1 LEAN:** With the engine running in closed loop mode, the ambient/battery temperature above -6. 7°C (20°F) and altitude below 2590. 8 m (8500 ft). If the PCM multiplies short term compensation by long term adaptive and a certain percentage is exceeded for two trips, a freeze frame is stored, the MIL illuminates and a trouble code is stored. Two Trip Fault. Three good trips to turn off the MIL.
DTC: P0175	**-FUEL SYSTEM 2/1 RICH:** With the engine running in closed loop mode, the ambient/battery temperature above -6. 7°C (20°F) and altitude below 2590. 8 m (8500 ft). If the PCM multiplies short term compensation by long term adaptive and a purge fuel multiplier and the result is below a certain value for 30 seconds over two trips, a freeze frame is stored, the MIL illuminates and a trouble code is stored. Two Trip Fault. Three good trips to turn off the MIL.
DTC: P0182	**-FUEL TEMPERATURE SENSOR CIRCUIT LOW:** With the ignition on. The (K156) Fuel Temperature Sensor Signal circuit voltage is below 0. 12 volt for 0. 6 second.
DTC: P0183	**-FUEL TEMPERATURE SENSOR CIRCUIT HIGH:** With the ignition on. The (K156) Fuel Temperature Sensor Signal circuit voltage is above 4. 96 volts for 0. 6 second.
DTC: P0192	**-FUEL RAIL PRESSURE SENSOR LOW:** With the ignition on. The (K181) Fuel Pressure Sensor Signal circuit voltage is below 0. 25 volt for 0. 14 second.
DTC: P0193	**-FUEL RAIL PRESSURE SENSOR HIGH:** With the ignition on. The (K181) Fuel Pressure Sensor Signal circuit voltage is above 4. 75 volts for 0. 14 second.
DTC: P0196	**-ENGINE OIL TEMPERATURE SENSOR CIRCUIT PERFORMANCE:** With engine off time greater than 480 minutes and ambient temperature greater than -7° C (19. 4° F). After a calibrated amount of cool down time, the Powertrain Control Module (PCM) compares the AAT, ECT and IAT Sensor values. If the general temperature rationality passes, the PCM compares the Oil Temperature Sensor value to a threshold based on the other temp sensor values. If the difference is greater than a calibrated value, the diagnostic fails.
DTC: P0197	**-ENGINE OIL TEMPERATURE SENSOR CIRCUIT LOW:** With the ignition on. Battery voltage greater than 10. 4 volts. The Engine Oil Temperature sensor circuit voltage at the PCM is less than the calibrated amount. One Trip Fault. Three good trips to clear the MIL.
DTC: P0197	**-ENGINE OIL TEMPERATURE SENSOR CIRCUIT LOW:** With the ignition on. The (G224) Oil Temperature Sensor Signal circuit voltage is below 0. 18 of a Volt for 0. 5 of a second.
DTC: P0198	**-ENGINE OIL TEMPERATURE SENSOR CIRCUIT HIGH:** With the ignition on. The (G224) Oil Temperature Sensor Signal circuit voltage is above 4. 95 volts for 0. 5 second.
DTC: P0198	**-ENGINE OIL TEMPERATURE SENSOR CIRCUIT HIGH:** With the ignition on. Battery voltage greater than 10. 4 volts. The Engine Oil Temperature sensor circuit voltage at the PCM is greater than the calibrated amount. One Trip Fault. Three good trips to turn off the MIL.
DTC: P0201	**-FUEL INJECTOR 1 CIRCUIT / OPEN:** With the engine running. The ECM detects an open in the Fuel Injector 1 circuit.
DTC: P0201	**-FUEL INJECTOR 1 CIRCUIT/OPEN:** With the engine running, battery voltage greater than 12 volts, and engine RPM less than 3000. The Powertrain Control Module (PCM) monitors the continuity of the injector circuits as well as the voltage spike created by the collapse of the magnetic field in the injector coil. Any condition that reduces the maximum current flow or the magnitude of the voltage spike can cause this DTC to set.
DTC: P0201	**-FUEL INJECTOR 1 CIRCUIT:** With battery voltage greater than 10 volts. Auto Shutdown Relay energized. Engine speed less than 3000 rpm. The PCM monitors the continuity of the injector circuits as well as the voltage spike created by the collapse of the magnetic field in the injector coil. Any condition that reduces the maximum current flow or the magnitude of the voltage spike can cause this DTC to set.
DTC: P0202	**-FUEL INJECTOR 2 CIRCUIT / OPEN:** With the engine running. The ECM detects an open in the Fuel Injector 2 circuit.
DTC: P0202	**-FUEL INJECTOR 2 CIRCUIT:** With battery voltage greater than 10 volts. Auto Shutdown Relay energized. Engine speed less than 3000 rpm. The PCM monitors the continuity of the injector circuits as well as the voltage spike created by the collapse of the magnetic field in the injector coil. Any condition that reduces the maximum current flow or the magnitude of the voltage spike can cause this DTC to set.
DTC: P0202	**-FUEL INJECTOR 2 CIRCUIT/OPEN:** With the engine running, battery voltage greater than 12 volts, and engine RPM less than 3000. The Powertrain Control Module (PCM) monitors the continuity of the injector circuits as well as the voltage spike created by the collapse of the magnetic field in the injector coil. Any condition that reduces the maximum current flow or the magnitude of the voltage spike can cause this DTC to set.

DTC	Trouble Code Title, Conditions, Possible Causes
DTC: P0203	**-FUEL INJECTOR 3 CIRCUIT:** With battery voltage greater than 10 volts. Auto Shutdown Relay energized. Engine speed less than 3000 rpm. The PCM monitors the continuity of the injector circuits as well as the voltage spike created by the collapse of the magnetic field in the injector coil. Any condition that reduces the maximum current flow or the magnitude of the voltage spike can cause this DTC to set.
DTC: P0203	**-FUEL INJECTOR 3 CIRCUIT/OPEN:** With the engine running, battery voltage greater than 12 volts, and engine RPM less than 3000. The Powertrain Control Module (PCM) monitors the continuity of the injector circuits as well as the voltage spike created by the collapse of the magnetic field in the injector coil. Any condition that reduces the maximum current flow or the magnitude of the voltage spike can cause this DTC to set.
DTC: P0204	**-FUEL INJECTOR 4 CIRCUIT/OPEN:** With the engine running, battery voltage greater than 12 volts, and engine RPM less than 3000. The Powertrain Control Module (PCM) monitors the continuity of the injector circuits as well as the voltage spike created by the collapse of the magnetic field in the injector coil. Any condition that reduces the maximum current flow or the magnitude of the voltage spike can cause this DTC to set.
DTC: P0204	**-FUEL INJECTOR 4 CIRCUIT:** With battery voltage greater than 10 volts. Auto Shutdown Relay energized. Engine speed less than 3000 rpm. The PCM monitors the continuity of the injector circuits as well as the voltage spike created by the collapse of the magnetic field in the injector coil. Any condition that reduces the maximum current flow or the magnitude of the voltage spike can cause this DTC to set.
DTC: P0205	**-FUEL INJECTOR 5 CIRCUIT/OPEN:** With the engine running, battery voltage greater than 12 volts, and engine RPM less than 3000. The Powertrain Control Module (PCM) monitors the continuity of the injector circuits as well as the voltage spike created by the collapse of the magnetic field in the injector coil. Any condition that reduces the maximum current flow or the magnitude of the voltage spike can cause this DTC to set.
DTC: P0205	**-FUEL INJECTOR 5 CIRCUIT:** With battery voltage greater than 10 volts. Auto Shutdown Relay energized. Engine speed less than 3000 rpm. The PCM monitors the continuity of the injector circuits as well as the voltage spike created by the collapse of the magnetic field in the injector coil. Any condition that reduces the maximum current flow or the magnitude of the voltage spike can cause this DTC to set.
DTC: P0206	**-FUEL INJECTOR 6 CIRCUIT/OPEN:** With the engine running, battery voltage greater than 12 volts, and engine RPM less than 3000. The Powertrain Control Module (PCM) monitors the continuity of the injector circuits as well as the voltage spike created by the collapse of the magnetic field in the injector coil. Any condition that reduces the maximum current flow or the magnitude of the voltage spike can cause this DTC to set.
DTC: P0206	**-FUEL INJECTOR 6 CIRCUIT:** With battery voltage greater than 10 volts. Auto Shutdown Relay energized. Engine speed less than 3000 rpm. The PCM monitors the continuity of the injector circuits as well as the voltage spike created by the collapse of the magnetic field in the injector coil. Any condition that reduces the maximum current flow or the magnitude of the voltage spike can cause this DTC to set.
DTC: P0207	**-FUEL INJECTOR 7 CIRCUIT/OPEN:** With the engine running, battery voltage greater than 12 volts, and engine RPM less than 3000. The Powertrain Control Module (PCM) monitors the continuity of the injector circuits as well as the voltage spike created by the collapse of the magnetic field in the injector coil. Any condition that reduces the maximum current flow or the magnitude of the voltage spike can cause this DTC to set.
DTC: P0207	**-FUEL INJECTOR 7 CIRCUIT:** With battery voltage greater than 10 volts. Auto Shutdown Relay energized. Engine speed less than 3000 rpm. The PCM monitors the continuity of the injector circuits as well as the voltage spike created by the collapse of the magnetic field in the injector coil. Any condition that reduces the maximum current flow or the magnitude of the voltage spike can cause this DTC to set.
DTC: P0208	**-FUEL INJECTOR 8 CIRCUIT:** With battery voltage greater than 10 volts. Auto Shutdown Relay energized. Engine speed less than 3000 rpm. The PCM monitors the continuity of the injector circuits as well as the voltage spike created by the collapse of the magnetic field in the injector coil. Any condition that reduces the maximum current flow or the magnitude of the voltage spike can cause this DTC to set.
DTC: P0208	**-FUEL INJECTOR 8 CIRCUIT/OPEN:** With the engine running, battery voltage greater than 12 volts, and engine RPM less than 3000. The Powertrain Control Module (PCM) monitors the continuity of the injector circuits as well as the voltage spike created by the collapse of the magnetic field in the injector coil. Any condition that reduces the maximum current flow or the magnitude of the voltage spike can cause this DTC to set.
DTC: P0218	**-HIGH TEMPERATURE OPERATION ACTIVATED:** Whenever the engine is running. Immediately after a Overheat shift schedule is activated when the Transmission temperature exceeds 127° C or 260° F.
DTC: P0219	**-ENGINE OVERSPEED:** Ignition on, engine running with the transmission in a valid forward gear. No active CAN Bus DTCs present. Monitored engine speed over the CAN Bus is greater than 6800 rpm for the period of 100 msecs.

DTC	Trouble Code Title, Conditions, Possible Causes
DTC: P0219	**-ENGINE OVERSPEED:** Continuously with the ignition on, engine running, with the transmission in gear with a valid Engine RPM message received at least once, and the CAN Bus Circuit and Engine CAN Message Missing are not active. Engine speed is greater than a calibrated limit (see table).
DTC: P0221	**THROTTLE POSITION SENSOR 2 CIRCUIT PERFORMANCE:** With the ignition on and battery voltage greater than 10. 4 volts. The Powertrain Control Module (PCM) detects that the Throttle Position Sensor (TPS) 2 circuit input voltage is implausible.
DTC: P0221	**THROTTLE POSITION SENSOR 2 CIRCUIT PERFORMANCE:** With the engine running and no TPS or MAP sensor DTCs present. TP Sensor signals do not correlate to the MAP Sensor signal. Two Trip Fault. ETC light will illuminate. P2135 should set with this code also.
DTC: P0222	**THROTTLE POSITION SENSOR 2 CIRCUIT LOW:** With the ignition on. Battery voltage greater than 10 volts. The PCM detects that the TP Sensor 2 voltage is lower than the acceptable value. One Trip Fault. Three good trips to turn off the MIL. The ETC light will illuminate.
DTC: P0222	**THROTTLE POSITION SENSOR 2 CIRCUIT LOW:** With the ignition on. Battery voltage greater than 10 volts. Throttle Position Sensor voltage at the PCM is less than 0. 16 of a volt for 0. 7 of a second. One Trip Fault. Three good trips to turn off the MIL. ETC light will illuminate.
DTC: P0223	**THROTTLE POSITION SENSOR 2 CIRCUIT HIGH:** With the ignition on. Throttle Position Sensor No. 2 Signal circuit voltage is greater than the maximum acceptable value. One Trip Fault. ETC light will illuminate.
DTC: P0223	**THROTTLE POSITION SENSOR 2 CIRCUIT HIGH:** With the ignition on and battery voltage greater than 10. 4 volts. The Powertrain Control Module (PCM) detects that the Throttle Position Sensor (TPS) 2 input voltage is above the maximum acceptable value.
DTC: P0234	**TURBOCHARGER OVERBOOST CONDITION:** With the engine running and the ECM attempting to govern turbocharger boost pressure. The Boost Pressure Sensor indicates actual turbocharger boost is greater than the ECM setpoint for engine boost.
DTC: P0237	**TURBO BOOST PRESSURE SENSOR CIRCUIT LOW:** With the ignition on. The (K37) Boost Pressure Sensor Signal circuit voltage is below 0. 29 volt for 0. 5 second.
DTC: P0238	**TURBO BOOST PRESSURE SENSOR CIRCUIT HIGH:** With the ignition on. The (K37) Boost Pressure Sensor Signal circuit voltage is above 4. 70 volts for 2. 0 seconds.
DTC: P0261	**-FUEL INJECTOR 1 CIRCUIT LOW:** With the engine cranking or running. The ECM detects a short to ground on a Fuel Injector Control circuit.
DTC: P0262	**-FUEL INJECTOR 1 CIRCUIT HIGH:** With the engine cranking or running. The ECM detects a short to voltage on a Fuel Injector Control circuit.
DTC: P0263	**-CYLINDER 1 CONTRIBUTION/BALANCE:** With the ignition on. The Engine Control Module (ECM) detects an internal failure.
DTC: P0264	**-FUEL INJECTOR 2 CIRCUIT LOW:** With the engine cranking or running. The ECM detects a short to ground on a Fuel Injector Control circuit.
DTC: P0265	**-FUEL INJECTOR 2 CIRCUIT HIGH:** With the engine cranking or running. The ECM detects a short to voltage on a Fuel Injector Control circuit.
DTC: P0266	**-CYLINDER 2 CONTRIBUTION/BALANCE:** With the ignition on. The Engine Control Module (ECM) detects an internal failure.
DTC: P0267	**-FUEL INJECTOR 3 CIRCUIT LOW:** With the engine cranking or running. The ECM detects a short to ground on a Fuel Injector Control circuit.
DTC: P0268	**-FUEL INJECTOR 3 CIRCUIT HIGH:** With the engine cranking or running. The ECM detects a short to voltage on a Fuel Injector Control circuit.
DTC: P0269	**-CYLINDER 3 CONTRIBUTION/BALANCE:** With the ignition on. The Engine Control Module (ECM) detects an internal failure.
DTC: P0270	**-FUEL INJECTOR 4 CIRCUIT LOW:** With the engine cranking or running. The ECM detects a short to ground on a Fuel Injector Control circuit.
DTC: P0271	**-FUEL INJECTOR 4 CIRCUIT HIGH:** With the engine cranking or running. The ECM detects a short to voltage on a Fuel Injector Control circuit.

DTC	Trouble Code Title, Conditions, Possible Causes
DTC: P0272	**-CYLINDER 4 CONTRIBUTION/BALANCE:** With the ignition on. The Engine Control Module (ECM) detects an internal failure.
DTC: P0273	**-FUEL INJECTOR 5 CIRCUIT LOW:** With the engine cranking or running. The ECM detects a short to ground on a Fuel Injector Control circuit.
DTC: P0274	**-FUEL INJECTOR 5 CIRCUIT HIGH:** With the engine cranking or running. The ECM detects a short to voltage on a Fuel Injector Control circuit.
DTC: P0275	**-CYLINDER 5 CONTRIBUTION/BALANCE:** With the ignition on. The Engine Control Module (ECM) detects an internal failure.
DTC: P0276	**-FUEL INJECTOR 6 CIRCUIT LOW:** With the engine cranking or running. The ECM detects a short to ground on a Fuel Injector Control circuit.
DTC: P0277	**-FUEL INJECTOR 6 CIRCUIT HIGH:** With the engine cranking or running. The ECM detects a short to voltage on a Fuel Injector Control circuit.
DTC: P0278	**-CYLINDER 6 CONTRIBUTION/BALANCE:** With the ignition on. The Engine Control Module (ECM) detects an internal failure.
DTC: P0298	**-ENGINE OIL TEMPERATURE TOO HIGH:** The engine oil temperature has dropped below a calibrated value. Engine start up. The Engine Oil temperature rises faster than a calibrated modeled temperature. When the actual oil temperature exceeds the high boundary of the calibrated modeled temperature for three minutes the fault is set. Two trip fault. Three good trips to turn off the MIL.
DTC: P0299	**TURBOCHARGER UNDERBOOST CONDITION:** With the engine running and the ECM attempting to govern turbocharger boost pressure. The Boost Pressure Sensor indicates actual turbocharger boost is less than the ECM setpoint for engine boost.
DTC: P0300	**-MULTIPLE CYLINDER MISFIRE:** Any time the engine is running and the adaptive numerator has been successfully updated. The threshold to set the fault is application specific; it is tied to the level of misfire that will cause emissions to increase to 1. 5 times the standard or in some cases 1%. It is always a two trip fault above the calibrated RPM. It takes one soft fail to set a malfunction and two trips to set the MIL. Three good trips to turn off the MIL.
DTC: P0301	**-CYLINDER 1 MISFIRE:** Any time the engine is running and the adaptive numerator has been successfully updated. The threshold to set the fault is application specific; it is tied to the level of misfire that will cause emissions to increase to 1. 5 times the standard or in some cases 1%. It is always a two trip fault above the calibrated RPM. It takes 1 soft fail to set a malfunction and two trips to set the MIL. Three good trips to turn off the MIL.
DTC: P0302	**-CYLINDER 2 MISFIRE:** Any time the engine is running, and the adaptive numerator has been successfully updated. The threshold to set the fault is application specific; it is tied to the level of misfire that will cause emissions to increase to 1. 5 times the standard or in some cases 1%. It is always a two trip fault above the calibrated RPM. It takes one failure to set a Pending Fault and two trips to set the MIL. Three good trips to turn off the MIL.
DTC: P0303	**-CYLINDER 3 MISFIRE:** Any time the engine is running and the adaptive numerator has been successfully updated. The threshold to set the fault is application specific; it is tied to the level of misfire that will cause emissions to increase to 1. 5 times the standard or in some cases 1%. It is always a two trip fault above the calibrated RPM. It takes one soft fail to set a malfunction and two trips to set the MIL. Three good trips to turn off the MIL.
DTC: P0304	**-CYLINDER 4 MISFIRE:** Any time the engine is running, and the adaptive numerator has been successfully updated. The threshold to set the fault is application specific; it is tied to the level of misfire that will cause emissions to increase to 1. 5 times the standard or in some cases 1%. It is always a two trip fault above the calibrated RPM. It takes one failure to set a Pending Fault and two trips to set the MIL. Three good trips to turn off the MIL.
DTC: P0305	**-CYLINDER 5 MISFIRE:** Any time the engine is running and the adaptive numerator has been successfully updated. The threshold to set the fault is application specific; it is tied to the level of misfire that will cause emissions to increase to 1. 5 times the standard or in some cases 1%. It is always a two trip fault above the calibrated RPM. It takes 1 soft fail to set a malfunction and two trips to set the MIL. Three good trips to turn off the MIL.

DTC	Trouble Code Title, Conditions, Possible Causes
DTC: P0306	**-CYLINDER 6 MISFIRE:** Any time the engine is running, and the adaptive numerator has been successfully updated. The threshold to set the fault is application specific; it is tied to the level of misfire that will cause emissions to increase to 1. 5 times the standard or in some cases 1%. It is always a two trip fault above the calibrated RPM. It takes one fail to set a Pending Fault and two trips to set the MIL. Three good trips to turn off the MIL.
DTC: P0307	**-CYLINDER 7 MISFIRE:** Any time the engine is running and the adaptive numerator has been successfully updated. The threshold to set the fault is application specific; it is tied to the level of misfire that will cause emissions to increase to 1. 5 times the standard or in some cases 1%. It is always a two trip fault above the calibrated RPM. It takes 1 soft fail to set a malfunction and two trips to set the MIL. Three good trips to turn off the MIL.
DTC: P0308	**-CYLINDER 8 MISFIRE:** Any time the engine is running, and the adaptive numerator has been successfully updated. The threshold to set the fault is application specific; it is tied to the level of misfire that will cause emissions to increase to 1. 5 times the standard or in some cases 1%. It is always a two trip fault above the calibrated RPM. It takes 1 soft fail to set a malfunction and two trips to set the MIL. Three good trips to turn off the MIL.
DTC: P0315	**-NO CRANK SENSOR LEARNED:** Under closed throttle decel and A/C off. ECT above 75° C (167° F). Engine start time is greater than 50 seconds. One of the CKP sensor target windows has more than 2% variance from the reference. One Trip Fault. Three good trips to turn off the MIL.
DTC: P0315	**-NO CRANK SENSOR LEARNED:** During deceleration, when fuel is cut off by the Powertrain Control Module (PCM). The Powertrain Control Module (PCM) measures the variation between crankshaft position reference points. The measurements are compared to an ideal reference that is stored in the PCM. If the variation exceeds a calibrated percentage, a fault is stored. One Trip Fault. Three good trips to turn off the MIL.
DTC: P0325	**-KNOCK SENSOR 1 CIRCUIT:** This monitor runs above 2000 RPM, under open throttle conditions. The Knock diagnostic does not run at idle or during decelerations. The high voltage test runs all the times the engine is running. The Powertrain Control Module (PCM) detects that the Knock Sensor input voltage is: Above 4. 0 Volts, less than or equal to 1. 0 Volt with engine RPM at or above 2200 or equal to 0. 0 Volts with engine RPM below 2200. Two Trip Fault. Three good trips to turn off the MIL.
DTC: P0330	**-KNOCK SENSOR 2 CIRCUIT:** This monitor runs above 2000 RPM, under open throttle conditions. The Knock diagnostic does not run at idle or during decelerations. The high voltage test runs all the times the engine is running. The Powertrain Control Module (PCM) detects that the Knock Sensor input voltage is: Above 4. 0 Volts, less than or equal to 1. 0 Volt with engine RPM at or above 2200 or equal to 0. 0 Volts with engine RPM below 2200. Two Trip Fault. Three good trips to turn off the MIL.
DTC: P0335	**-CRANKSHAFT POSITION SENSOR CIRCUIT:** Engine cranking. No CKP signal is present during engine cranking and at least eight Camshaft Position Sensor signals have occurred. One Trip Fault. Three good trips to turn off the MIL.
DTC: P0336	**-CRANKSHAFT POSITION SENSOR PERFORMANCE:** Engine cranking. No CKP signal is present during engine cranking and at least eight Camshaft Position Sensor signals have occurred. One Trip Fault. Three good trips to turn off the MIL.
DTC: P0336	**-CRANKSHAFT POSITION SENSOR PERFORMANCE:** With the engine cranking or running. The Engine Control Module (ECM) does not receive a signal from the Crankshaft Position Sensor when the Camshaft Position Sensor indicates engine rpm.
DTC: P0339	**-CRANKSHAFT POSITION SENSOR INTERMITTENT:** While cranking the engine and with the engine running. When the CKP Sensor failure counter reaches 20. One Trip Fault. Three good trips to turn off the MIL.
DTC: P0339	**-CRANKSHAFT POSITION SENSOR INTERMITTENT:** With the ignition on and battery voltage greater than 10. 4 volts. The Powertrain Control Module (PCM) detects that the Crankshaft Position Sensor input voltage is implausible.
DTC: P0340	**-CAMSHAFT POSITION SENSOR CIRCUIT:** During engine cranking and with the engine running. Battery voltage greater than 10 volts. At least 5 seconds or 2. 5 engine revolutions have elapsed with crankshaft position sensor signals present but no camshaft position sensor signal. One Trip Fault. Three good trips to turn off the MIL.
DTC: P0340	**-CAMSHAFT POSITION SENSOR CIRCUIT - BANK 1 SENSOR 1:** With the ignition on and the battery voltage greater than 10. 4 volts. The Powertrain Control Module (PCM) detects that the Camshaft Position (CMP) Sensor input voltage is implausible. One Trip Fault. Three good trips to turn off the MIL.

DTC	Trouble Code Title, Conditions, Possible Causes
DTC: P0340	**-CAMSHAFT POSITION SENSOR CIRCUIT:** During engine cranking and with the engine running. Battery voltage greater than 10 Volts. At least five seconds or 2. 5 engine revolutions have elapsed with crankshaft position sensor signals present but no camshaft position sensor signal. One Trip Fault. Three good trips to turn off the MIL.
DTC: P0341	**-CAMSHAFT POSITION SENSOR PERFORMANCE:** With the engine cranking or running The Engine Control Module (ECM) does not receive a signal from the Camshaft Position Sensor when the Crankshaft Position Sensor indicates engine rpm.
DTC: P0344	**-CAMSHAFT POSITION SENSOR INTERMITTENT:** With the ignition on and the battery voltage greater than 10. 4 volts. The Powertrain Control Module (PCM) detects that the Camshaft Position (CMP) Sensor input voltage is implausible. One Trip Fault. Three good trips to turn off the MIL.
DTC: P0344	**-CAMSHAFT POSITION SENSOR INTERMITTENT:** While cranking the engine and engine running. When the failure counter reaches 20. One Trip Fault. Three good trips to turn off the MIL.
DTC: P0349	**-CAMSHAFT 1/3 POSITION SENSOR INTERMITTENT:** While cranking the engine and engine running. When the failure counter reaches 20. One Trip Fault. Three good trips to turn off the MIL.
DTC: P0365	**-CAMSHAFT POSITION SENSOR CIRCUIT - BANK 1 SENSOR 2:** With the engine running or cranking. The Powertrain Control Module (PCM) receives either no signal or an incorrect signal from the Camshaft 1/2 Position Sensor.
DTC: P0365	**-CAMSHAFT 1/2 POSITION SENSOR CIRCUIT:** During engine cranking and with the engine running. Battery voltage greater than 10. 0 Volts. At least five seconds or 2. 5 engine revolutions have elapsed with Crankshaft Position Sensor signals present but no camshaft position sensor signal. One Trip Fault. Three good trips to turn off the MIL.
DTC: P0369	**-CAMSHAFT POSITION SENSOR INTERMITTENT - BANK 1 SENSOR 2:** With the engine cranking or running. The Powertrain Control Module (PCM) detects an intermittent signal error from the Camshaft 1/2 Position Sensor. One Trip Fault. Three good trips to turn off the MIL.
DTC: P0369	**-CAMSHAFT 1/2 POSITION SENSOR INTERMITTENT:** While cranking the engine and engine running. When the failure counter reaches 20. One Trip Fault. Three good trips to turn off the MIL.
DTC: P0390	**-CAMSHAFT 1/4 POSITION SENSOR CIRCUIT:** During engine cranking and with the engine running. Battery voltage greater than 10. 0 Volts. At least five seconds or 2. 5 engine revolutions have elapsed with Crankshaft Position Sensor signals present but no camshaft position sensor signal. One Trip Fault. Three good trips to turn off the MIL.
DTC: P0394	**-CAMSHAFT 1/4 POSITION SENSOR INTERMITTENT:** While cranking the engine and engine running. When the failure counter reaches 20. One Trip Fault. Three good trips to turn off the MIL.
DTC: P0401	**- EGR SYSTEM PERFORMANCE:** With the engine running. The Engine Control Module (ECM) detects and EGR flow problem for eight seconds
DTC: P0401	**-EGR SYSTEM PERFORMANCE:** Engine running for greater than two minutes with the Engine Coolant Temp greater than 70° C (158° F). EGR active. Less than 8500 feet. Ambient temperature greater than -6° C (20° F). The PCM closes the EGR valve while monitoring the O2 Sensor signal. Once a closed EGR fueling sample has been established the PCM then ramps in EGR and additional fueling while monitoring the O2 sensor signal in the open state. A fueling sample is again established. The PCM then compares the different O2 Sensor signal readings (fueling samples). If a larger than expected variation is detected, a soft failure is recorded. Three soft failures set a one trip failure. After two failed trips, a DTC is set and the MIL is illuminated.
DTC: P0402	**- EGR EXCESSIVE FLOW DETECTED:** With the engine running. The ECM detects and EGR flow problem for 8. 0 seconds
DTC: P0403	**-EGR SOLENOID CIRCUIT:** Engine running. Battery voltage greater than 10 volts. The EGR solenoid control circuit is not in the expected state when requested to operate by the PCM. One Trip Fault.
DTC: P0404	**-EGR POSITION SENSOR RATIONALITY OPEN:** Engine running. The EGR flow or valve movement is not what is expected. A rationality error has been detected from the EGR Close Position Performance. Two trip fault.

DTC	Trouble Code Title, Conditions, Possible Causes
DTC: P0405	**-EGR POSITION SENSOR CIRCUIT LOW:** With the ignition on. Battery voltage above 10. 0 volts. EGR Position Sensor Signal is less than the minimum acceptable value. One trip Fault.
DTC: P0406	**-EGR POSITION SENSOR CIRCUIT HIGH:** With the ignition on. Battery voltage greater than 10 volts. EGR position sensor signal is greater than the maximum acceptable value. One trip Fault.
DTC: P0406	**-EGR POSITION SENSOR CIRCUIT HIGH:** With the ignition on. Battery voltage greater than 10 Volts. EGR position sensor signal is greater than 4. 5 Volts. One trip Fault.
DTC: P0407	**-EGR AIRFLOW THROTTLE POSITION SENSOR CIRCUIT LOW:** With the ignition on. The (K312) EGR Airflow Control Valve Position Sensor Signal circuit voltage is below 0. 07 volt for 0. 30 second.
DTC: P0408	**-EGR AIRFLOW THROTTLE POSITION SENSOR CIRCUIT HIGH:** With the ignition on. The (K312) EGR Airflow Control Valve Position Sensor Signal circuit voltage is above 4. 7 volts for 0. 30 seconds.
DTC: P0411	**-SECONDARY AIR INJECTION SYSTEM INCORRECT FLOW DETECTED:** The Secondary Air Pump is on. Actual air flow is less than the expected air flow.
DTC: P0418	**-SECONDARY AIR INJECTION SYSTEM CONTROL CIRCUIT:** With the engine running, battery voltage greater than 10. 4 volts, and the control circuit active. The Powertrain Control Module (PCM) detects that the control circuit voltage is not within a specified range based on operating conditions.
DTC: P0420	**-CATALYST EFFICIENCY (BANK 1):** The monitor will run at between 1400 and 2300 RPM and MAP vacuum between 40 to 70 kPa (15. 0 and 21. 0 (Hg)). If the final State of Change index is within the calibrated fail threshold. Two trip fault. Three good trips to turn off the MIL.
DTC: P0420	**-CATALYST EFFICIENCY (BANK 1):** With the ECT above 70 C (158 F), engine RPM between 1400 and 2300, vehicle speed between 64 and 96 kph (40 and 60 mph), and engine run time greater than 3 minutes. If the final state of change index is within the calibrated fail threshold. Two trip fault. Three good trips to turn off the MIL.
DTC: P0420	**-CATALYST EFFICIENCY (BANK 1):** The monitor will run at between 1400 and 2300 RPM. It also runs between 40 and 70 kPa. If the final State of Change index is within the calibrated fail threshold. Two trip fault. Three good trips to turn off the MIL.
DTC: P0426	**-CATALYST TEMPERATURE SENSOR CIRCUIT PERFORMANCE - BANK 1 SENSOR 1:** At ignition on before engine crank. With no Intake Air Temp sensor DTCs The Engine Control Module (ECM) detects that the (K352) Pre-Catalyst Exhaust Temperature Sensor Signal circuit voltage is implausible.
DTC: P0430	**-CATALYST EFFICIENCY (BANK 2):** The monitor will run at between 1400 and 2300 RPM and MAP vacuum between 40 to 70 kPa (15. 0 and 21. 0 (Hg)). . If the final State of Change index is within the calibrated fail threshold. Two trip fault. Three good trips to turn off the MIL.
DTC: P0440	**-GENERAL EVAP SYSTEM FAILURE:** Engine running after a cold start with the difference between ECT and AAT is less than 10° C (19° F). Fuel Level between 12% and 88% full. Manifold vacuum greater than a calculated minimum value. Ambient Temperature between 4° C and 32° C (39° F and 89° F). When the monitor conditions are met, the Powertrain Control Module (PCM) will ramp in purge flow. If the PCM does not sense an ESIM switch closure after a calculated amount of purge flow accumulation, an error is detected. Two Trip Fault. Three good trips to turn off the MIL.
DTC: P0441	**-EVAP PURGE SYSTEM PERFORMANCE:** After the Evaporative System small leak test has passed, with the engine running, ambient temperature between 4° C (39° F) and 35° (95° F), with the engine at idle after a calibrated amount of drive time has accumulated. If the Powertrain Control Module (PCM) detects that the purge vapor ratio and the ESIM switch closed ratio are below a calculated value, the PCM commands the purge solenoid to flow at a specified rate to update the purge vapor ratio. If the ratio remains below a specified value, a one trip failure is recorded. Two Trip Fault. Three good trips to turn off the MIL.
DTC: P0441	**-EVAP PURGE SYSTEM PERFORMANCE:** With the engine running, after the Evap System small leak test has passed. If the PCM detects that the purge vapor ratio and the ESIM switch closed ratio are below a calculated value, the PCM commands the purge solenoid to flow at a specified rate to update the purge vapor ratio. If the ratio remains below a specified value, a one trip failure is recorded. Two Trip Fault. Three good trips to turn off the MIL.
DTC: P0443	**-EVAP PURGE SOLENOID CIRCUIT:** The ignition on or engine running. Battery voltage greater than 10 volts. The Powertrain Control Module (PCM) will set a trouble code if the actual state of the solenoid does not match the intended state. One Trip Fault. Three good trips to turn off the MIL.

DTC	Trouble Code Title, Conditions, Possible Causes
DTC: P0443	**-EVAP PURGE CONTROL CIRCUIT:** With the engine run time above a calibrated value, battery voltage greater than 10. 4 Volts, ECT within a specific range, and the Evap Purge Solenoid control active. This PCM compares the circuit feedback to a calibrated closed range when the circuit is de-energized or to a calibrated open range when the circuit is energized. If the value is determined to be out of the calibrated range in either the de-energized or energized state for more than a calibrated amount of time, this DTC will set.
DTC: P0452	**-EVAP PRESSURE SWITCH STUCK CLOSED:** Immediately after the ignition has been turned off. At key off, the Powertrain Control Module (PCM) energizes the Purge Solenoid for a calibrated amount of time (30 seconds maximum) and stores the state of the ESIM switch. The state is evaluated again at the next key on. If the PCM does not detect that the ESIM switch is open, an error is detected. Two Trip Fault. Three good trips to turn off the MIL.
DTC: P0455	**-EVAP PURGE SYSTEM LARGE LEAK:** With the engine running, during a cold start test with the fuel level above 12%, ambient temperature between 4° C and 32° C (39° F and 89° F) and the fuel system in closed loop. The test runs when the small leak test is maturing. The Powertrain Control Module (PCM) activates the Evap Purge solenoid to pull the Evaporative system into a vacuum to close the ESIM switch. Once the ESIM switch is closed, the PCM turns the Evap Purge solenoid off to seal the Evaporative system. If the ESIM switch reopens before the calibrated amount of time, a large leak error is detected. Two Trip Fault. Three good trips to turn off the MIL.
DTC: P0456	**-EVAP PURGE SYSTEM SMALL LEAK:** With the ignition off, fuel level less than 88%, ambient temperature between 4° C and 43° C (39° F and 109° F) and the fuel system in closed loop. As temperatures change, a vacuum is created in the fuel tank and Evaporative System. With the Evaporative System sealed, the Powertrain Control Module (PCM) monitors the ESIM Switch. If the ESIM Switch does not close within a calibrated time, an error is detected by the PCM. One Trip Fault. Three good trips to turn off the MIL.
DTC: P0457	**-LOOSE FUEL CAP:** Ignition on. Ambient Temperature between 4° C and 32° C (39° F and 89° F). Close Loop fuel system. Test runs after the medium leak test is inconclusive and the PCM has senses a fuel increase. The Powertrain Control Module (PCM) activates the Evap Purge Solenoid to pull the Evap system into a vacuum to close the ESIM switch. Once the ESIM switch is closed, the PCM turns the Evap Purge Solenoid off to seal the Evap system. If the ESIM switch reopens before the calibrated amount of time after a fuel tank fill, an error is detected. Two Trip Fault. Three good trips to turn off the MIL.
DTC: P0460	**-FUEL LEVEL SENSOR 1 CIRCUIT:** With the ignition on. The ECM does not receive a valid fuel level signal message from the Instrument Cluster (CCN) for 2. 0 seconds.
DTC: P0460-11	**-FUEL LEVEL SENSOR 1 - CIRCUIT SHORT TO GROUND:** With the ignition on. Battery voltage greater than 10. 4 volts. The Body Control Module (BCM) detects that the Fuel Level Sensor input voltage is below the minimum acceptable value.
DTC: P0460-15	**-FUEL LEVEL SENSOR 1 - CIRCUIT SHORT TO BATTERY OR OPEN:** With the ignition on. Battery voltage greater than 10. 4 volts. The Body Control Module (BCM) detects that the Fuel Level Sensor input voltage is above the maximum acceptable value.
DTC: P0461	**-FUEL LEVEL SENSOR 1 PERFORMANCE:** TEST No. 1: With the ignition on, the fuel level is compared to the previous key down after a 20 second delay. TEST No. 2: The PCM monitors the fuel level at ignition on. TEST No. 1: If the PCM does not see a difference in fuel level of greater than 0. 1 Volt the test will fail. TEST No. 2: If the PCM does not see a change in the fuel level over a set amount of miles the test will fail. Two trip fault. Three good trips to turn off the MIL.
DTC: P0461	**-FUEL LEVEL SENSOR 1 PERFORMANCE:** TEST No. 1: With the ignition on, the fuel level is compared to the previous key down after a 20 second delay. TEST No. 2: The PCM monitors the fuel level at ignition on. TEST No. 1: If the PCM does not see a difference in fuel level of greater than 0. 1 volt the test will fail. TEST No. 2: If the PCM does not see a change in the fuel level of . 1765 over a set amount of miles the test will fail. Three good trips to turn off the MIL.
DTC: P0462	**-FUEL LEVEL SENSOR 1 CIRCUIT LOW:** Ignition on and battery voltage above 10. 4 Volts. The Fuel Level Sensor signal voltage goes below the minimum acceptable value. One Trip Fault. Three good trips to turn off the MIL.
DTC: P0463	**-FUEL LEVEL SENSOR 1 CIRCUIT HIGH:** With the ignition on. The Cluster detects that the Fuel Level Sensor input voltage is above the maximum acceptable value.
DTC: P0463	**-FUEL LEVEL SENSOR 1 HIGH CIRCUIT:** With the ignition on. The CAN Bus message from the Instrument Cluster indicates Fuel Level Sensor 1 voltage is above 2. 51 Volts.
DTC: P0463	**-FUEL LEVEL SENSOR 1 CIRCUIT HIGH:** Ignition on and battery voltage above 10. 4 volts. The fuel level sensor signal voltage at the PCM goes above the maximum acceptable value. One Trip Fault. Three good trips to turn off the MIL.

DTC	Trouble Code Title, Conditions, Possible Causes
DTC: P0471	**-EXHAUST PRESSURE SENSOR 1 PERFORMANCE:** Engine speed is below 670 rpm. There are no other Exhaust Pressure Sensor DTCs. There are no Atmospheric/Barometric Pressure Sensor DTCs. The difference between the Exhaust Pressure Sensor Signal and the Atmospheric/Barometric Pressure Signal is greater than 400 hpa (5. 8 psi.) for at least 3. 0 seconds.
DTC: P0472	**-EXHAUST PRESSURE SENSOR 1 LOW:** With the ignition on. The Exhaust Gas Pressure Sensor Signal circuit voltage is below 4. 58 volts for 2. 0 seconds.
DTC: P0473	**-EXHAUST PRESSURE SENSOR 1 HIGH:** With the ignition on. The Exhaust Gas Pressure Sensor Signal circuit voltage is below 0. 25 volt for 2. 0 seconds.
DTC: P0480	**-COOLING FAN 1 CONTROL CIRCUIT:** With the ignition on. Battery voltage greater than 10 Volts. The ECM receives a CAN Bus message from the FCM indicating an open or shorted circuit on the Radiator Fan Relay Control circuit.
DTC: P0480	**-COOLING FAN 1 CONTROL CIRCUIT:** With the ignition on. Battery voltage greater than 10 volts. An open or shorted circuit is detected in the Low/High Rad Fan Control circuit. One Trip Fault. Three good trips to turn off the MIL.
DTC: P0480	**-COOLING FAN 1 CONTROL CIRCUIT:** With the ignition on and the battery voltage greater than 10 volts. The Powertrain Control Module (PCM) receives a Controller Area Network (CAN) Bus message from the Totally Integrated Power Module (TIPM) with TIPM indicating an open or shorted circuit on the Radiator Fan Relay Control circuit. One Trip Fault. Three good trips to turn off the Malfunction Indicator Lamp (MIL).
DTC: P0481	**-COOLING FAN 2 CONTROL CIRCUIT:** With the ignition on. Battery voltage greater than 10. 0 Volts. The Powertrain Control Module (PCM) is requesting the Totally Integrated Power Module (TIPM) to turn on the Cooling Fan and it is not operating.
DTC: P0481	**-COOLING FAN 2 CONTROL CIRCUIT:** With the ignition on and the battery voltage greater than 10 volts. The Powertrain Control Module (PCM) receives a Controller Area Network (CAN) Bus message from the Totally Integrated Power Module (TIPM) indicating an open or shorted circuit on the Radiator Fan High Relay Control circuit. One Trip Fault. Three good trips to turn off the Malfunction Indicator Lamp (MIL).
DTC: P0487	**-EGR AIRFLOW THROTTLE CONTROL CIRCUIT A OPEN:** With the engine running and the EGR Airflow Control Valve Motor command off. The Engine Control Module (ECM) detects an open (K314) EGR Airflow Control Valve Motor (+) circuit for 0. 5 second.
DTC: P0488	**-EGR AIRFLOW THROTTLE CONTROL CIRCUIT PERFORMANCE:** With the engine running and the EGR Airflow Control Valve Motor command on. The Engine Control Module (ECM) detects an implausible voltage on the (K314) EGR Airflow Control Valve Motor (+) circuit.
DTC: P0489	**-EGR CONTROL CIRCUIT LOW:** With the ignition on and the EGR Solenoid command off. The ECM detects a short to ground on the (K34) EGR Solenoid Control circuit for 2. 3 seconds.
DTC: P0490	**-EGR CONTROL CIRCUIT HIGH:** With the ignition on and the EGR Solenoid command on. The ECM detects excessive current on the (K34) EGR Solenoid Control circuit for 2. 0 seconds.
DTC: P0491	**-SECONDARY AIR INJECTION SYSTEM INSUFFICIENT FLOW:** After the diagnostics for air injection system stuck closed (P2441) and stuck off (P2445) have passed. ECT above 0° C (32° F), ambient air temperature within approximately 2 degrees of ECT, actual air flow is less than or equal to model air flow, and Secondary Air Flow diagnostic counter above 150 (approximately 4. 5 seconds). Actual air flow is less than model air flow, and the difference between model air flow and actual air flow is greater than 10 kg/h.
DTC: P0501	**-VEHICLE SPEED SENSOR 1 PERFORMANCE:** With the engine running, transmission not in park or neutral, brakes not applied, and engine RPM greater than 1500. This code will set if no vehicle speed signal is received from the ABS Module for more than 11 seconds for two consecutive trips. Two Trip Fault. Three good trips to turn off the MIL.
DTC: P0501	**-VEHICLE SPEED SENSOR 1 PERFORMANCE:** Continuously with the ignition on. The DTC will set if multiple ABS wheel speed signals are invalid.
DTC: P0503	**-VEHICLE SPEED SENSOR 1 ERRATIC (MTX NONABS):** With the ignition on and battery voltage greater than 10. 4 volts. The Powertrain Control Module (PCM) detects an implausible voltage on the Vehicle Speed Sensor circuit.
DTC: P0503	**-VEHICLE SPEED SENSOR 1 ERRATIC (EXC MTX NONABS):** With the engine running, transmission not in park or neutral, brakes not applied, and engine rpm greater than 1500. This code will set if no vehicle speed signal is received from the ABS Module for more than 11 seconds for 2 consecutive trips. Two Trip Fault. Three good trips to turn off the MIL.

DTC	Trouble Code Title, Conditions, Possible Causes
DTC: P0503	**-VEHICLE SPEED SENSOR 1 ERRATIC:** Ignition on and battery voltage greater than 10 volts. Transmission in Drive or Reverse. This code will set if no vehicle speed signal is received from the ABS Module up to 120 seconds for 2 consecutive trips. One Trip Fault. Three good trips to turn off the MIL.
DTC: P0504	**-BRAKE SWITCH SIGNAL CIRCUITS PLAUSIBILITY WITH REDUNDANT CONTACT:** With the ignition on. The Primary Brake Switch Signal and Secondary Brake Switch Signal inputs to the ECM do not agree for 2 minutes.
DTC: P0506	**-IDLE SPEED PERFORMANCE LOWER THAN EXCEPTED:** With the engine idling in drive, the brake applied, engine run time above a minimum calibrated value, and no VSS, MAF/MAP, ECT, TPS, ETC, CKP Sensor, fuel system, or injector DTCs present. Engine speed is 100 RPM or more below target idle speed for 30 seconds. Two Trip Fault. Three good trips to turn off the MIL.
DTC: P0506	**-IDLE SPEED PERFORMANCE LOWER THAN EXPECTED:** With the engine idling in drive, the brake applied, engine run time below a calibrated minimum value, and no VSS, MAF/MAP, ECT, TPS, ETC, CKP Sensor, fuel system, or injector DTCs present. Engine speed is 100 RPM or more below target idle speed for 30 seconds. Two Trip Fault. Three good trips to turn off the MIL.
DTC: P0507	**-IDLE SPEED PERFORMANCE HIGHER THAN EXCEPTED:** With the engine idling in drive, the brake applied, engine run time above a minimum calibrated value, and no VSS, MAF/MAP, ECT, TPS, ETC, CKP Sensor, fuel system, or injector DTCs present. Engine speed is 200 RPM or more above idle speed for 7 seconds. Two Trip Fault. Three good trips to turn off the MIL.
DTC: P050B	**-COLD START IGNITION TIMING PERFORMANCE:** Cold start condition. Ambient Air temperature between -7° C and 50° C (19. 4° F and 122° F). Engine Coolant temperature between -7° C and 50° C (19. 4° F and 122° F). The difference between the Ambient Air temp and ECT temp at Start is equal to or less than 10° C (50° F). Engine running at idle only. Engine RPM is 50 RPM or more (depending on vehicle specifications), below idle speed for at least 3 seconds and the average spark advance is above the threshold, too much spark advance, for a specified time limit. Two trip fault. Three good trips to turn off the MIL.
DTC: P050B	**-COLD START IGNITION TIMING PERFORMANCE:** During a cold start condition, with the difference between the AAT and ECT at startup below 10° C, and the engine running at idle. The PCM detects that engine speed is 50 RPM or more (depending on vehicle specifications) below target idle speed for more than 3 seconds, and the average spark advance is above the failure threshold for more than the specified limit. Two trip fault. Three good trips to turn off the MIL.
DTC: P050D	**-COLD START ROUGH IDLE:** Cold start condition. Ambient Air temperature between -7° C and 50° C (19. 4° F and 122° F). Engine Coolant temperature between -7° C and 50° C (19. 4° F and 122° F). The difference between the Ambient Air temp and ECT temp at Start is equal to or less than 10° C (50° F). Engine running at idle only. If a rough idle is detected and the Dynamic Crankshaft Fuel Control remains or returns to the high limit window for a calibrated time. Two trip fault.
DTC: P0513	**-INVALID SKIM KEY:** Ignition on. The Powertrain Control Module (PCM) detects an invalid SKREEM key. One Trip Fault.
DTC: P0520	**-ENGINE OIL PRESSURE SENSOR CIRCUIT:** Ignition on, engine not running. The Powertrain Control Module (PCM) senses the oil pressure is out of the calibrated range. One Trip fault.
DTC: P0520	**-OIL PRESSURE TOO LOW:** Ignition on, engine not running. The Powertrain Control Module (PCM) senses the oil pressure is out of the calibrated range. One Trip fault.
DTC: P0521	**-ENGINE OIL PRESSURE SENSOR PERFORMANCE:** Engine running. The engine oil pressure never reaches the calibrated specification with the engine RPM at 1250. One trip fault.
DTC: P0522	**-OIL PRESSURE SENSOR CIRCUIT LOW:** With the ignition key on and battery voltage above 10. 4 Volts. The Oil Pressure Sensor voltage at Powertrain Control Module (PCM) goes below the minimum acceptable value. One Trip Fault. Three good trips to turn off the MIL.
DTC: P0522	**-ENGINE OIL PRESSURE SENSOR CIRCUIT LOW:** At engine start-up. The ECM detects that the (G6) Oil Pressure Sensor Signal circuit is below 0. 2 volt for 0. 5 second.
DTC: P0523	**-ENGINE OIL PRESSURE SENSOR CIRCUIT HIGH:** At engine start-up. The ECM detects that the (G6) Oil Pressure Sensor Signal circuit is above 4. 88 volts for 0. 5 second.
DTC: P0523	**-ENGINE OIL PRESSURE SENSOR CIRCUIT HIGH:** With the ignition on. Battery voltage greater than 10 Volts. The Engine Oil pressure signal is greater than the calibrated amount. One Trip Fault.

DTC	Trouble Code Title, Conditions, Possible Causes
DTC: P0524	**- ENGINE OIL PRESSURE IS TOO LOW:** With the engine running. The Oil Pressure Sensor indicates low oil pressure for 5 seconds.
DTC: P0524	**-ENGINE OIL PRESSURE TOO LOW:** Engine running. The engine oil pressure never reaches the calibrated specification to allow the MDS activation. One trip fault.
DTC: P0532	**-A/C PRESSURE SENSOR CIRCUIT LOW:** Engine running, AC is learned, and AC Clutch Relay energized. The A/C pressure transducer signal voltage at the PCM goes below the minimum acceptable value. One Trip Fault. Three good trips to turn off the MIL.
DTC: P0532	**-A/C PRESSURE SENSOR CIRCUIT LOW:** With the ignition on and battery voltage greater than 10. 4 volts. The Powertrain Control Module (PCM) detects that the A/C Pressure Sensor input voltage is below the minimum acceptable value.
DTC: P0533	**-A/C PRESSURE SENSOR CIRCUIT HIGH:** Engine running and the A/C Clutch Relay energized. The A/C pressure transducer signal at the PCM goes above the maximum acceptable value. One trip Fault. Three good trips to turn off the MIL.
DTC: P0533	**-A/C PRESSURE SENSOR CIRCUIT HIGH:** With the ignition on and battery voltage greater than 10. 4 volts. The Powertrain Control Module (PCM) detects that the A/C Pressure Sensor input voltage is above the maximum acceptable value.
DTC: P053A	**-CRANKCASE VENT HEATER CONTROL CIRCUIT OPEN:** With the ignition on and the Crankcase Vent Heater command off. The ECM does not detect voltage on the (N116) Crankcase Vent Heater Control circuit for 2. 0 seconds.
DTC: P053B	**-CRANKCASE VENT HEATER CONTROL CIRCUIT LOW:** With the ignition on and the Crankcase Vent Heater command off. The ECM detects a short to ground on the (N116) Crankcase Vent Heater Control circuit for 2. 0 seconds.
DTC: P053C	**-CRANKCASE VENT HEATER CONTROL CIRCUIT HIGH:** With the ignition on and the Crankcase Vent Heater command on. The ECM detects excessive current on the (N116) Crankcase Vent Heater Control circuit for 2. 0 seconds.
DTC: P0545	**-EXHAUST GAS TEMPERATURE SENSOR CIRCUIT LOW - BANK 1 SENSOR 1:** With the ignition on. The ECM detects that the (K352) Pre-Catalyst Exhaust Temperature Sensor Signal circuit is shorted to ground.
DTC: P0546	**-EXHAUST GAS TEMPERATURE SENSOR CIRCUIT HIGH - BANK 1 SENSOR 1:** With the ignition on. The ECM detects that the (K352) Pre-Catalyst Exhaust Temperature Sensor Signal circuit is open shorted to voltage.
DTC: P054A	**-CAMSHAFT POSITION TIMING OVER - ADVANCED-BANK1:** Engine cranking and engine running If the Camshaft Position Signal (angular variation) is more than 15° of the Crankshaft Position Signal, this DTC is set.
DTC: P054C	**-CAMSHAFT POSITION TIMING OVER - ADVANCED-BANK 2:** Engine cranking and engine running If the Camshaft Position Signal (angular variation) is more than 15° of the Crankshaft Position Signal, this DTC is set.
DTC: P0562	**-ECM VOLTAGE TOO LOW:** With the ignition on or the engine running. The ECM detects battery voltage of 8. 0 volts or less for 5. 0 seconds.
DTC: P0562	**-BATTERY VOLTAGE LOW:** With engine running for more than 30 seconds. Battery voltage at the Powertrain Control Module (PCM) is less than 11. 7 Volts for a set period of time. One Trip Fault.
DTC: P0562	**-BATTERY VOLTAGE LOW:** With the engine running and the PCM has closed the Transmission Control Relay. If the battery voltage of the Transmission Control Output circuit(s) to the PCM is less than 10. 0 volts for the period of 15 seconds. **NOTE: P0562 generally indicates a gradually falling battery voltage or a resistive connection(s) to the PCM. The DTC will also set if the battery voltage sensed at the PCM is less than 6. 5v for 200ms or where Transmission Control Output circuit(s) is less than 7. 2v for 200ms.**
DTC: P0562	**-BATTERY VOLTAGE LOW:** The engine running. The engine speed greater than 1000 RPM. Battery voltage is less than 6. 0 Volts. One Trip Fault.
DTC: P0563	**-BATTERY VOLTAGE HIGH:** Continuously with the ignition on. When the monitored battery voltage rises above 16. 9 volts.
DTC: P0563	**-BATTERY VOLTAGE HIGH:** Continuously with the ignition in the run position. When the monitored battery voltage rises above 16. 0 volts.

DTC	Trouble Code Title, Conditions, Possible Causes
DTC: P0563	**-BATTERY VOLTAGE HIGH:** With the ignition on. Engine RPM greater than 1000 RPM. With no other charging system codes set. Battery voltage is 1 Volt greater than desired voltage for more than 10 seconds. Battery voltage greater than 15. 75 Volts. One Trip Fault. Three good trips to turn off the MIL.
DTC: P0571	**-BRAKE SWITCH 1 PERFORMANCE:** Ignition on. If the output of Brake Switch No. 1 to the PCM looks like it is not applied, while Brake Lamp Switch Output circuit is applied the fault will mature in 60ms. One Trip Fault.
DTC: P0571	**-BRAKE SWITCH 1 PERFORMANCE:** Ignition on and battery voltage above 10. 4 Volts. If the output of Brake Switch to the PCM looks like it is not applied, while Brake Lamp Switch Output circuit is applied. One Trip Fault.
DTC: P0571	**-BRAKE SWITCH 1 PERFORMANCE:** After initial start and any time the shift lever is changed from park to drive. System voltage between 9. 0 and 16 volts. No active CAN Bus DTCs present. Vehicle speed is greater than 30Km/h (18. 5 mph) for at least 10 seconds. The brake switch status does not change during a drive cycle with a vehicle speed greater than 30Km/h (18. 5 mph) for the period of 10 seconds. It takes two consecutive problem identification trips to mature the fault. After two consecutive trips, the MIL is illuminated on the next key on cycle (start of a third trip).
DTC: P0572	**-BRAKE SWITCH 1 STUCK ON:** With the ignition on, battery voltage greater than 10. 4 volts, and ambient temperature above -23 C. The PCM detects that the state of Brake Signal 1 does not change as expected.
DTC: P0572	**-BRAKE SWITCH 1 STUCK ON:** With the gear selector in drive, vehicle speed above a minimum value, and battery voltage greater than 10. 4 volts. The Powertrain Control Module (PCM) detects that the actual state of Brake Signal 1 or Brake Signal 2 does not match the desired state during monitoring. Two trip fault.
DTC: P0573	**-BRAKE SWITCH 1 STUCK OFF:** With the ignition on, battery voltage greater than 10. 4 volts, ambient temperature above -23 C. The PCM detects that the state of Brake Signal 1 does not change as expected.
DTC: P0573	**-BRAKE SWITCH 1 STUCK OFF:** When vehicle speed cycles from 0 kph to 48 kph (30 mph) at least 10 times. When the PCM recognizes Brake Switch No. 1 is stuck in the high/off position. Two Trip Fault. Three good trips to turn off the MIL.
DTC: P0578	**-SPEED CONTROL SWITCH 1 STUCK:** With the ignition on and no other Speed Control Switch DTCs present. The S/C Switch Sense 1 signal indicates that a switch is pressed continuously for 60 seconds.
DTC: P0579	**-SPEED CONTROL SWITCH 1 PERFORMANCE:** With the ignition key on. Speed Control (S/C) switch voltage output is not out of range but it does not equal any of the values for any of the button positions. One trip fault.
DTC: P0579	**-SPEED CONTROL SWITCH 1 PERFORMANCE:** With the ignition on. The S/C Switch Sense 1 signal is invalid for 60 seconds.
DTC: P0579-00	**-SPEED CONTROL SWITCH 1 PERFORMANCE:** Continuously with the ignition on. The Steering Column Control Module (SCCM) has detected that a non-permissible combination has occurred in the Right Steering Wheel Switch (Speed Control Switch).
DTC: P0580	**-SPEED CONTROL SWITCH 1 CIRCUIT LOW:** Continuously with the ignition on. Fault signifies when the switch voltage is shorted low.
DTC: P0580	**-SPEED CONTROL SWITCH 1 CIRCUIT LOW:** With the ignition on and battery voltage greater than 10. 4 Volts. The S/C Signal1 voltage is below a calibrated threshold for 0. 06 second.
DTC: P0580-00	**-SPEED CONTROL SWITCH 1 CIRCUIT LOW:** Continuously with the ignition on. Fault signifies when the switch voltage is shorted low.
DTC: P0581	**-SPEED CONTROL SWITCH 1 CIRCUIT HIGH:** Continuously with the ignition on. Fault signifies when the switch voltage is shorted high.
DTC: P0581	**-SPEED CONTROL SWITCH 1 CIRCUIT HIGH:** With the ignition key on. Speed Control (S/C) switch input above the maximum acceptable voltage at the Powertrain Control Module (PCM). One trip fault.
DTC: P0581-00	**-SPEED CONTROL SWITCH 1 CIRCUIT HIGH:** Continuously with the ignition on. Fault signifies when the switch voltage is shorted high.

DTC	Trouble Code Title, Conditions, Possible Causes
DTC: P0585	**-SPEED CONTROL SWITCH 1/2 CORRELATION:** With the ignition on and no other S/C Switch DTCs present. The (V71) S/C Switch No. 1 Signal and (V72) S/C Switch No. 2 Signal do not indicate the same S/C Switch position.
DTC: P0585	**-SPEED CONTROL SWITCH 1/2 CORRELATION:** Ignition on. Speed Control (S/C) switch inputs are not coherent with each other. Example: Powertrain Control Module (PCM) is reading Switch No. 1 as Accel and Switch No. 2 as Coast at the same time. One trip fault.
DTC: P0585	**-SPEED CONTROL SWITCH 1/2 CORRELATION:** Continuously with the ignition on. The Steering Column Control Module (SCCM) has detected that a non-permissible combination has occurred in the Speed Control Switch.
DTC: P0585-00	**-SPEED CONTROL SWITCH 1/2 CORRELATION:** Continuously with the ignition on. The Steering Column Control Module (SCCM) has detected that a non-permissible combination has occurred in the Speed Control Switch.
DTC: P0590	**-SPEED CONTROL SWITCH 2 STUCK:** With the ignition on and no other Speed Control Switch DTCs present. The S/C Switch Sense 2 signal indicates that a switch is pressed continuously for 60 seconds.
DTC: P0591	**-SPEED CONTROL SWITCH 2 PERFORMANCE:** With the ignition on. The S/C Switch Sense 2 signal is invalid for 60 seconds.
DTC: P0591	**-SPEED CONTROL SWITCH 2 PERFORMANCE:** With the ignition key on. Cruise switch voltage output is not out of range but it does not equal any of the values for any of the button positions. One trip fault.
DTC: P0591	**-SPEED CONTROL SWITCH 2 PERFORMANCE:** With the ignition key on. Speed Control (S/C) switch voltage output is not out of range but it does not equal any of the values for any of the button positions. One trip fault.
DTC: P0591-00	**-SPEED CONTROL SWITCH 2 PERFORMANCE:** Continuously with the ignition on. The Steering Column Control Module (SCCM) has detected that a non-permissible combination has occurred in the Speed Control Switch.
DTC: P0592	**-SPEED CONTROL SWITCH 2 CIRCUIT LOW:** With the ignition on. The S/C Switch Sense 2 voltage is below 0. 39 of a Volt for 0. 06 of a second.
DTC: P0592	**-SPEED CONTROL SWITCH 2 CIRCUIT LOW:** With the ignition key on. Speed Control (S/C) switch input No. 2 is below the minimum acceptable voltage at the Powertrain Control Module (PCM). One trip fault.
DTC: P0592-00	**-SPEED CONTROL SWITCH 2 CIRCUIT LOW:** Continuously with the ignition on. Fault signifies when the switch voltage is shorted low.
DTC: P0593	**-SPEED CONTROL SWITCH 2 CIRCUIT HIGH:** With the ignition key on. Speed Control Switch No. 2 input above the maximum acceptable voltage at the PCM. One trip fault.
DTC: P0593	**-SPEED CONTROL SWITCH 2 CIRCUIT HIGH:** Continuously with the ignition on. Fault signifies when the switch voltage is shorted high.
DTC: P0593-00	**-SPEED CONTROL SWITCH 2 CIRCUIT HIGH:** Continuously with the ignition on. Fault signifies when the switch voltage is shorted high.
DTC: P0600	**-SERIAL COMMUNICATION LINK:** With the ignition on. Internal Bus communication failure between processors. One Trip Fault. Three Global Good Trips to clear.
DTC: P0600	**-SERIAL COMMUNICATION LINK:** With the ignition on. The Powertrain Control Module (PCM) detects an internal failure.
DTC: P0601	**-INTERNAL MEMORY CHECKSUM INVALID:** With the ignition on. Internal checksum for software failed, does not match calculated value. One Trip Fault, Three Good Trips to clear.
DTC: P0601	**-INTERNAL MEMORY CHECKSUM INVALID:** With the ignition on. The Powertrain Control Module (PCM) detects an internal failure.
DTC: P0602	**-CONTROL MODULE PROGRAMING ERROR/NOT PROGRAMMED:** After an initial vehicle start with a system voltage between 9. 0 and 16. 0 volts. Transmission Control Module (TCM) does not receive valid vehicle information from the Front Control Module (FCM) for the period of 5 seconds.

DTC	Trouble Code Title, Conditions, Possible Causes
DTC: P0602	**-CONTROL MODULE PROGRAMMING ERROR/NOT PROGRAMMED:** Check for generic software is made at power-up. If generic software is found , the MIL will light immediately. This DTC is designed to signal the technician that the controller still has generic software installed.
DTC: P0602	**-CONTROL MODULE PROGRAMMING ERROR/NOT PROGRAMMED:** Continuously with the ignition on. If the TCM detects that the variables that dictate the vehicle application are not present.
DTC: P0604	**-INTERNAL CONTROL MODULE RAM:** One time after the controller is reset (ignition turned to the RUN position). Whenever the Powertrain Control Module (PCM) detects an internal controller problem.
DTC: P0604	**-INTERNAL CONTROL MODULE RAM:** Continuously with the ignition on. If the TCM detects an error with the controllers Random Access Memory (RAM).
DTC: P0605	**-INTERNAL CONTROL MODULE ROM:** One time after the ignition switch is turned to the run position. The read value does not match the written value in any ROM location. **Possible causes:** • TRANSMISSION CONTROL MODULE (TCM) - INTERNAL ERROR
DTC: P0605	**-INTERNAL CONTROL MODULE ROM:** One time after the ignition key is turned to the run position. If the ROM checksum does not match a known constant. **Possible causes:** • PCM - INTERNAL ERROR
DTC: P0605	**-INTERNAL CONTROL MODULE ROM:** One time after the controller is reset (ignition turned to the RUN position). Whenever the Powertrain Control Module (PCM) detects an internal controller problem. **Possible causes:** • POWER OR GROUND CIRCUIT • POWERTRAIN CONTROL MODULE (PCM)
DTC: P0606	**-INTERNAL ECM PROCESSOR:** With the ignition on. The Powertrain Control Module (PCM) detects an internal failure. **Possible causes:** • POWERTRAIN CONTROL MODULE (PCM)
DTC: P0606	**-INTERNAL ECM PROCESSOR:** Engine running. When the Powertrain Control Module (PCM) recognizes an internal failure to communicate with the ECM or the CMP and CKP Sensor count periods are too short. One trip fault. ETC light is flashing. **Possible causes:** • POWERTRAIN CONTROL MODULE (PCM)
DTC: P0607	**-ECU INTERNAL PERFORMANCE:** With the ignition on. The Engine Control Module (ECM) detects an internal failure. **Possible causes:** • INTERMITTENT DTC • ENGINE CONTROL MODULE (ECM)
DTC: P0607	**-ECU INTERNAL PERFORMANCE:** Continuously with the ignition in the run position. If the Shift Lever Assembly controller detects an invalid calibration (checksum value). **Possible causes:** • SHIFTER LEVER ASSEMBLY
DTC: P060B	**-ETC A/D GROUND PERFORMANCE:** When the Throttle Motor is powered. When ASD reading does not return to ground within a set period of time of test activation, this fault sets. The test typically runs a couple of times per second, and is the reason why APP2 signal spikes to ground a couple of times per second in normal running. Reprogramming the module may not always fix this fault. One trip fault. ETC lamp will illuminate. **Possible causes:** • PCM NEEDS TO BE PROGRAMMED • POWERTRAIN CONTROL MODULE (PCM)
DTC: P060B	**-ETC A/D GROUND PERFORMANCE:** With the ignition on. When the A/D reading does not return to ground within a set period of time during test activation, this DTC will set. Reprogramming the module may not fix this DTC. ETC lamp will flash. **Possible causes:** • POWERTRAIN CONTROL MODULE (PCM)

DTC	Trouble Code Title, Conditions, Possible Causes
DTC: P060B	**-INTERNAL CONTROL MODULE A/D PROCESSING PERFORMANCE:** One time after the ignition switch is turned to the run position. The TCM has detected an error with the internal processor. **Possible causes:** • TRANSMISSION CONTROL MODULE (TCM) - INTERNAL ERROR
DTC: P060D	**-ETC LEVEL 2 APP PERFORMANCE:** Throttle motor is powered and no matured faults related to APP Sensors. When secondary software determines that APPS 1 and APPS 2 signals do not match for a period of time. One trip fault. ETC lamp will flash. **Possible causes:** • PCM NEEDS TO BE PROGRAMMED • POWERTRAIN CONTROL MODULE (PCM)
DTC: P060D	**-ETC LEVEL 2 APP PERFORMANCE:** With the ignition on. When secondary software determines that the APPS 1 and APPS 2 signals do not match for a period of time. ETC lamp will flash **Possible causes:** • POWERTRAIN CONTROL MODULE (PCM)
DTC: P060E	**-ETC LEVEL 2 TPS PERFORMANCE:** With the ignition on. When secondary software determines that the TPS 1 and TPS 2 signals do not match for a period of time. ETC lamp will flash. **Possible causes:** • POWERTRAIN CONTROL MODULE (PCM)
DTC: P060E	**-ETC LEVEL 2 TPS PERFORMANCE:** Throttle motor is powered and no matured faults related to TP Sensors. When secondary software determines that TPS 1 and TPS 2 signals do not match for a period of time. One trip fault. ETC lamp will flash. **Possible causes:** • PCM NEEDS TO BE PROGRAMMED • POWERTRAIN CONTROL MODULE (PCM)
DTC: P060F	**-ETC LEVEL 2 ECT PERFORMANCE:** Throttle motor is powered and no matured faults related to the Engine Coolant Temp Sensor. When secondary software determines that the Coolant Temperature is implausible for a period of time. One trip fault. ETC lamp will flash. **Possible causes:** • PCM NEEDS TO BE PROGRAMMED • POWERTRAIN CONTROL MODULE (PCM)
DTC: P060F	**-ETC LEVEL 2 ECT PERFORMANCE:** With the ignition on. When secondary software determines that the Coolant Temperature is implausible for a period of time. ETC lamp will flash. **Possible causes:** • POWERTRAIN CONTROL MODULE (PCM)
DTC: P0610	**-ECU VEHICLE OPTIONS MISMATCH:** With the ignition on. The Engine Control Module (ECM) detects an internal failure. **Possible causes:** • INTERMITTENT DTC • ENGINE CONTROL MODULE (ECM)
DTC: P0610	**-ECU VEHICLE OPTIONS MISMATCH:** One time at initial ignition on with system voltage between 9. 0 and 16. 0 volts. FCM/TIPM variant data received more than once over the CAN Bus. FCM/TIPM variant data is in a valid range. Vehicle Configuration Learn Routine not finished. The vehicle option data received over the CAN Bus does not match the data stored in the EEPROM of the TCM. It takes one trip of problem identification to set the MIL. **Possible causes:** • USED CONTROLLER INSTALLED WITH WRONG CONFIGURATION • FCM/TIPM NOT PROPERLY PROGRAMED OR WAS REPLACED AND NOT PROGRAMED • NEW TCM INSTALLED • TRANSMISSION CONTROL MODULE
DTC: P0613	**-INTERNAL TRANSMISSION PROCESSOR:** After the ignition is turned to the run position and every 60 seconds thereafter. Either of the following conditions occur 3 times in less than 590 milliseconds: The watchdog line remains high after the watchdog test The transmission relay coil is detected as energized and remains on after the watchdog delay expires. **Possible causes:** • PCM - INTERNAL ERROR

DTC	Trouble Code Title, Conditions, Possible Causes
DTC: P0613	**-INTERNAL TRANSMISSION PROCESSOR:** Continuously with the ignition on. If the TCM detects an error with the controllers processor. **Possible causes:** • TRANSMISSION CONTROL MODULE
DTC: P0613	**-INTERNAL TRANSMISSION PROCESSOR:** 1) One time after the controller is reset (ignition turned to the RUN position) and every 60 seconds thereafter. The Delay Test is executed after a reset only. 2) Two seconds after an invalid test. If either of the following conditions occur three times:1) The watchdog fault line remains high after the period has elapsed for the too early - too late watchdog test. 2) The Transmission Control Relay remains on after the watchdog delay expired. **Possible causes:** • POWER OR GROUND CIRCUIT • POWERTRAIN CONTROL MODULE (PCM)
DTC: P0615	**-STARTER CONTROL CIRCUIT - OPEN:** With the engine running and battery voltage greater than 10. 4 volts. The Powertrain Control Module (PCM) detects that the actual state of the starter control does not match the intended state. **Possible causes:** • (T752) STARTER CONTROL CIRCUIT SHORTED TO VOLTAGE • (T752) STARTER CONTROL CIRCUIT SHORTED TO GROUND • (T752) STARTER CONTROL CIRCUIT OPEN OR HIGH RESISTANCE • TOTALLY INTEGRATED POWER MODULE (TIPM) • POWERTRAIN CONTROL MODULE (PCM)
DTC: P0615	**-STARTER CONTROL CIRCUIT/OPEN:** With the ignition on and the Starter Relay command off. The ECM does not detect voltage on the (T752) Engine Starter Motor Relay Control circuit for 1. 0 second. **Possible causes:** • INTERMITTENT DTC • (T752) ENGINE STARTER MOTOR RELAY CONTROL CIRCUIT SHORTED TO GROUND • (T752) ENGINE STARTER MOTOR RELAY CONTROL CIRCUIT OPEN OR HIGH RESISTANCE • (T751) FUSED IGNITION SWITCH OUTPUT (START) CIRCUIT OPEN OR HIGH RESISTANCE • STARTER RELAY • ENGINE CONTROL MODULE (ECM)
DTC: P0616	**-STARTER CONTROL CIRCUIT LOW:** With the ignition on and the Starter Relay command off. The ECM detects a short to ground on the (T752) Engine Starter Motor Relay Control circuit for 1. 0 second. **Possible causes:** • INTERMITTENT DTC • (T752) ENGINE STARTER MOTOR RELAY CONTROL CIRCUIT SHORTED TO GROUND • (T752) ENGINE STARTER MOTOR RELAY CONTROL CIRCUIT OPEN OR HIGH RESISTANCE • STARTER RELAY • ENGINE CONTROL MODULE (ECM)
DTC: P0616	**-STARTER CONTROL CIRCUIT LOW :** With the ignition on. Battery voltage greater than 10 volts. A shorted condition is detected in the Starter Control Output circuit. One Trip Fault. Three good trips to turn off the MIL. **Possible causes:** • (T752) STARTER RELAY CONTROL CIRCUIT SHORTED TO GROUND • (T752) STARTER RELAY CONTROL CIRCUIT OPEN • STARTER RELAY • POWERTRAIN CONTROL MODULE (PCM) • TOTALLY INTEGRATED POWER MODULE (TIPM)
DTC: P0617	**-STARTER CONTROL CIRCUIT HIGH:** With the ignition on and the Starter Relay command on. The ECM detects a short circuit on the (T752) Engine Starter Motor Relay Control circuit for at 1. 0 second. **Possible causes:** • INTERMITTENT DTC • (T752) ENGINE STARTER MOTOR RELAY CONTROL CIRCUIT SHORTED TO VOLTAGE • (T752) ENGINE STARTER MOTOR RELAY CONTROL CIRCUIT SHORTED TO THE (T751) FUSED IGNITION SWITCH OUTPUT (START) CIRCUIT • (T752) ENGINE STARTER MOTOR RELAY CONTROL CIRCUIT OPEN OR HIGH RESISTANCE • STARTER RELAY • ENGINE CONTROL MODULE (ECM)

DTC	Trouble Code Title, Conditions, Possible Causes
DTC: P061A	**-ETC LEVEL 2 TORQUE PERFORMANCE:** Throttle motor is powered. When secondary software determines that the customer requested output is not being achieved by the engine for a period of time. One trip fault. ETC lamp will flash. **Possible causes:** • PCM NEEDS TO BE PROGRAMMED • POWERTRAIN CONTROL MODULE (PCM)
DTC: P061A	**-ETC LEVEL 2 TORQUE PERFORMANCE:** With the ignition on. When secondary software determines that the requested output is not being achieved by the engine for a period of time. ETC lamp will flash. **Possible causes:** • POWERTRAIN CONTROL MODULE (PCM)
DTC: P061C	**-ETC LEVEL 2 RPM PERFORMANCE:** With the ignition on. When secondary software determines that the engine speed is implausible for a period of time. ETC lamp will flash. **Possible causes:** • POWERTRAIN CONTROL MODULE (PCM)
DTC: P061C	**-ETC LEVEL 2 RPM PERFORMANCE:** Throttle motor is powered and no camshaft or crankshaft electrical signal related DTCs are set. When secondary software determines that the engine speed is implausible for a period of time. One trip fault. ETC lamp will flash. **Possible causes:** • PCM NEEDS TO BE PROGRAMMED • POWERTRAIN CONTROL MODULE (PCM)
DTC: P0622	**-GENERATOR FIELD CONTROL CIRCUIT:** With the ignition on. Engine running. When the PCM tries to regulate the generator field with no result during monitoring. One Trip Fault. Three good trips to turn off the MIL. **Possible causes:** • (K20) GEN FIELD CONTROL CIRCUIT SHORTED TO VOLTAGE • (K20) GEN FIELD CONTROL CIRCUIT OPEN • (K20) GEN FIELD CONTROL CIRCUIT SHORTED TO GROUND • GENERATOR • POWERTRAIN CONTROL MODULE (PCM)
DTC: P0622	**-GENERATOR FIELD CONTROL CIRCUIT:** With the engine running and battery voltage greater than 10. 4 volts. The Powertrain Control Module (PCM) detects that the actual state of the generator field control does not match the intended state. **Possible causes:** • (K20) GEN FIELD CONTROL CIRCUIT SHORTED TO VOLTAGE • (K20) GEN FIELD CONTROL CIRCUIT SHORTED TO GROUND • (K20) GEN FIELD CONTROL CIRCUIT OPEN OR HIGH RESISTANCE • GENERATOR • POWERTRAIN CONTROL MODULE (PCM)
DTC: P0627	**-FUEL PUMP CONTROL CIRCUIT OPEN:** With the ignition on and the Fuel Pump Relay command off. The ECM does not detect voltage on the (K31) Fuel Pump Relay Control circuit for 2. 0 seconds. **Possible causes:** • (K31) FUEL PUMP RELAY CONTROL CIRCUIT SHORTED TO GROUND • (K31) FUEL PUMP RELAY CONTROL CIRCUIT OPEN OR HIGH RESISTANCE • (A15) FUSED ASD RELAY OUTPUT CIRCUIT OPEN OR HIGH RESISTANCE • FUEL PUMP RELAY • ENGINE CONTROL MODULE (ECM)
DTC: P0627	**-FUEL PUMP RELAY CIRCUIT:** With the ignition on. Battery voltage greater than 10. 4 volts. An open or shorted condition is detected in the fuel pump relay control circuit. One Trip Fault. Three good trips to turn off the MIL. **Possible causes:** • INTERNAL FUSED B+ CIRCUIT • (F202) FUSED IGNITION SWITCH CIRCUIT • (K31) FUEL PUMP RELAY CONTROL CIRCUIT OPEN • (K31) FUEL PUMP RELAY CONTROL CIRCUIT SHORTED TO GROUND • FUEL PUMP RELAY • POWERTRAIN CONTROL MODULE (PCM)

DTC	Trouble Code Title, Conditions, Possible Causes
DTC: P0627	**-FUEL PUMP CONTROL CIRCUIT/OPEN:** With the engine running and the battery voltage greater than 10. 4 Volts. The Powertrain Control Module (PCM) detects that the actual state of the fuel pump control does not match the intended state. **Possible causes:** • (A109) FUSED B(+) CIRCUIT OPEN OR HIGH RESISTANCE • (F950) RUN/START RELAY OUTPUT CIRCUIT OPEN OR HIGH RESISTANCE • (K31) FUEL PUMP RELAY CONTROL CIRCUIT SHORTED TO VOLTAGE • (K31) FUEL PUMP RELAY CONTROL CIRCUIT SHORTED TO GROUND • (K31) FUEL PUMP RELAY CONTROL CIRCUIT OPEN OR HIGH RESISTANCE • FUEL PUMP RELAY • POWERTRAIN CONTROL MODULE (PCM)
DTC: P0628	**-FUEL PUMP CONTROL CIRCUIT LOW:** With the ignition on and the Fuel Pump Relay command off. The ECM detects a short to ground on the (K31) Fuel Pump Relay Control circuit for 2. 0 seconds. **Possible causes:** • (K31) FUEL PUMP RELAY CONTROL CIRCUIT SHORTED TO GROUND • (K31) FUEL PUMP RELAY CONTROL CIRCUIT OPEN OR HIGH RESISTANCE • FUEL PUMP RELAY • ENGINE CONTROL MODULE (ECM)
DTC: P0628	**-FUEL PUMP CONTROL CIRCUIT LOW:** With the engine running and the battery voltage greater than 10. 4 Volts. The Powertrain Control Module (PCM) detects that the fuel pump control circuit is low. **Possible causes:** • (K31) FUEL PUMP CONTROL CIRCUIT SHORTED TO GROUND • (K31) FUEL PUMP CONTROL CIRCUIT OPEN OR HIGH RESISTANCE • TOTALLY INTEGRATED POWER MODULE (TIPM) • POWERTRAIN CONTROL MODULE (PCM)
DTC: P0629	**-FUEL PUMP CONTROL CIRCUIT HIGH:** With the ignition on and the Fuel Pump Relay command on. The ECM detects a short circuit on the (K31) Fuel Pump Relay Control circuit for 2. 0 seconds. **Possible causes:** • (K31) FUEL PUMP RELAY CONTROL CIRCUIT SHORTED TO VOLTAGE • (K31) FUEL PUMP RELAY CONTROL CIRCUIT SHORTED TO THE (A15) FUSED ASD RELAY OUTPUT CIRCUIT • (K31) FUEL PUMP RELAY CONTROL CIRCUIT OPEN OR HIGH RESISTANCE • FUEL PUMP RELAY • ENGINE CONTROL MODULE (ECM)
DTC: P062C	**-ETC LEVEL 2 MPH PERFORMANCE:** Throttle motor is powered and no vehicle speed related DTCs have matured. When secondary software determines that the vehicle speed is implausible for a period of time. One trip fault. ETC lamp will flash. **Possible causes:** • PCM NEEDS TO BE PROGRAMMED • POWERTRAIN CONTROL MODULE (PCM)
DTC: P062C	**-ETC LEVEL 2 MPH PERFORMANCE:** With the ignition on. When secondary software determines that the vehicle speed is implausible for a period of time. ETC lamp will flash. **Possible causes:** • POWERTRAIN CONTROL MODULE (PCM)
DTC: P062F	**-INTERNAL CONTROL MODULE EEPROM ERROR:** One time after the ignition switch is turned to the run position. The TCM has detected an error with the internal processor. **Possible causes:** • TRANSMISSION CONTROL MODULE (TCM) - INTERNAL ERROR
DTC: P0630	**-VIN NOT PROGRAMMED IN PCM:** At initialization. The VIN has not been programmed into the Powertrain Control Module (PCM). One Trip Fault. Three good trips to turn off the MIL. **Possible causes:** • VIN NOT PROGRAMMED IN THE POWERTRAIN CONTROL MODULE (PCM) • POWERTRAIN CONTROL MODULE (PCM)

DTC	Trouble Code Title, Conditions, Possible Causes
DTC: P0632	**-ODOMETER NOT PROGRAMMED IN PCM:** Ignition on. The vehicle mileage is not programmed into the Powertrain Control Module (PCM). One Trip Fault. Three good trips to turn off the MIL. **Possible causes:** • MILEAGE NOT PROGRAMMED IN THE POWERTRAIN CONTROL MODULE (PCM) • POWERTRAIN CONTROL MODULE (PCM)
DTC: P0633	**-SKIM SECRET KEY NOT STORED IN PCM:** Ignition on. The Secret Key information has not been programmed into the Powertrain Control Module (PCM). One Trip Fault. Three good trips to turn off the MIL. **Possible causes:** • SECRET KEY INFORMATION NOT PROGRAMMED IN THE POWERTRAIN CONTROL MODULE (PCM) • POWERTRAIN CONTROL MODULE (PCM)
DTC: P0633	**-SKIM SECRET KEY NOT STORED IN PCM:** Ignition on. The Secret Key information has not been programmed into the Powertrain Control Module (PCM). One Trip Fault. Three good trips to turn off the MIL. **Possible causes:** • PROGRAMMING SECRET KEY INTO THE PCM • POWERTRAIN CONTROL MODULE (PCM)
DTC: P063A	**-GENERATOR VOLTAGE SENSE CIRCUIT:** The engine running. The engine speed greater than 1157 RPM. The Powertrain Control Module (PCM) recognizes the alternator output voltage is less than the Battery feed circuit voltage. One trip failure. The Generator light will illuminate. The fault will be checked again on the next key cycle. **Possible causes:** • EXCESSIVE RESISTANCEIN THE (A804) GENERATOR SENSE CIRCUIT • (A804) GENERATOR SENSECIRCUIT SHORTED TO GROUND • GENERATOR • POWERTRAIN CONTROL MODULE (PCM)
DTC: P063A	**-GENERATOR VOLTAGE SENSE CIRCUIT:** With the engine running and battery voltage greater than 10. 4 volts. The Powertrain Control Module (PCM) detects no change when attempting to regulate the generator output. **Possible causes:** • (A804) GEN SENSE CIRCUIT SHORTED TO VOLTAGE • (A804) GEN SENSE CIRCUIT SHORTED TO GROUND • (A804) GEN SENSE CIRCUIT OPEN OR HIGH RESISTANCE • GENERATOR • POWERTRAIN CONTROL MODULE (PCM)
DTC: P0641	**-SENSOR REFERENCE VOLTAGE 1 CIRCUIT:** Ignition on with system voltage between 9. 0 and 16. 0 volts. When the monitored input voltage from primary pressure sensor and secondary pressure sensor is less than 0. 005 volts for a continuous period of 5. 0 seconds. **Possible causes:** • (T72) 5-VOLT SUPPLY CIRCUIT OPEN • (T72) 5-VOLT SUPPLY CIRCUIT SHORT TO GROUND • INTERNAL TRANSMISSION • TRANSMISSION CONTROL MODULE
DTC: P0642	**-SENSOR REFERENCE VOLTAGE 1 CIRCUIT LOW:** With the ignition on. The Powertrain Control Module (PCM) detects that the 5 volt supply circuit voltage is below the minimum acceptable value. One Trip Fault. ETC light is flashing. **Possible causes:** • 5-VOLT SUPPLY CIRCUIT SHORTED TO GROUND • ACCELERATOR PEDAL POSITION SENSOR • A/C PRESSURE TRANSDUCER • CRANKSHAFT POSITION SENSOR • THROTTLE BODY • POWERTRAIN CONTROL MODULE (PCM)

DTC	Trouble Code Title, Conditions, Possible Causes
DTC: P0642	**-SENSOR REFERENCE VOLTAGE 1 CIRCUIT LOW:** With the ignition on. The ECM detects a low voltage on the Sensor Supply #1 circuit for 0. 10 of a second. **Possible causes:** • 5-VOLT SUPPLY CIRCUIT SHORTED TO GROUND • CRANKSHAFT POSITION SENSOR • BOOST PRESSURE SENSOR • FUEL PRESSURE SENSOR • ENGINE CONTROL MODULE
DTC: P0642	**-SENSOR REFERENCE VOLTAGE 1 CIRCUIT LOW:** Ignition on. When the Powertrain Control Module (PCM) recognizes the Primary 5-Volt Supply circuit voltage is too low. One Trip Fault. ETC light is flashing. **Possible causes:** • (F855) 5-VOLT SUPPLY CIRCUIT SHORTED TO GROUND • (K854) 5-VOLT SUPPLY CIRCUIT SHORTED TO GROUND • CRANKSHAFT POSITION SENSOR • OIL PRESSURE SENSOR • THROTTLE BODY ASSEMBLY • A/C PRESSURE TRANSDUCER • ACCELERATOR PEDAL POSITION (APP) SENSOR • POWERTRAIN CONTROL MODULE (PCM)
DTC: P0643	**-PRIMARY 5-VOLT SUPPLY CIRCUIT HIGH:** Ignition on. When the Powertrain Control Module (PCM) recognizes the Primary 5-Volt Supply circuit voltage is too high. One Trip Fault. ETC light is flashing. **Possible causes:** • (F855) 5-VOLT SUPPLY SHORTED TO VOLTAGE • (K854) 5-VOLT SUPPLY CIRCUIT SHORTED TO VOLTAGE • POWERTRAIN CONTROL MODULE (PCM)
DTC: P0643	**-SENSOR REFERENCE VOLTAGE 1 CIRCUIT HIGH:** Continuously with the ignition on and no overvoltage condition exist. When the monitored sensor voltage is not within specified limits and rises above 7. 2 volts. **Possible causes:** • (T72) SENSOR SUPPLY VOLTAGE CIRCUIT SHORT TO VOLTAGE • (T72) SENSOR SUPPLY VOLTAGE CIRCUIT SHORT TO OTHER CIRCUITS • TRANSMISSION CONTROL MODULE
DTC: P0643	**-SENSOR REFERENCE VOLTAGE 1 CIRCUIT HIGH:** Ignition on. When the Powertrain Control Module (PCM) recognizes the Primary 5-Volt Supply circuit voltage is too high. One Trip Fault. ETC light is flashing. **Possible causes:** • (F855) 5-VOLT SUPPLY SHORTED TO VOLTAGE • (K852) 5-VOLT SUPPLY SHORTED TO VOLTAGE • POWERTRAIN CONTROL MODULE (PCM)
DTC: P0643	**-SENSOR REFERENCE VOLTAGE 1 TOO HIGH:** With the ignition on. The ECM detects a short to voltage on the Sensor Supply #1 circuit for 0. 10 of a second. **Possible causes:** • (K350) FUEL PRESSURE SENSOR 5 VOLT SUPPLY CIRCUIT SHORTED TO VOLTAGE • (K356) BOOST PRESSURE SENSOR 5 VOLT SUPPLY CIRCUIT SHORTED TO VOLTAGE • (K853) CRANKSHAFT POSITION SENSOR 5 VOLT SUPPLY CIRCUIT SHORTED TO VOLTAGE • ENGINE CONTROL MODULE (ECM)
DTC: P0645	**-A/C CLUTCH RELAY CIRCUIT:** With the ignition on. Battery voltage greater than 10. 0 Volts. A/C is being requested. An open or shorted condition is detected in the A/C Clutch Relay control circuit. One Trip Fault. Three good trips to turn off the MIL.
DTC: P0645	**-A/C CONTROL CIRCUIT/OPEN:** With the engine running and battery voltage greater than 10. 4 volts. The Powertrain Control Module (PCM) detects that the A/C Compressor control circuit voltage is not within an acceptable range.
DTC: P0646	**-A/C CLUTCH CONTROL CIRCUIT 2 LOW:** With the ignition on. Battery voltage greater than 10 volts. A/C Switch on. A shorted condition is detected in the A/C clutch control circuit. One Trip Fault. Three good trips to turn off the MIL.

DTC	Trouble Code Title, Conditions, Possible Causes
DTC: P0646	**-A/C CLUTCH CONTROL CIRCUIT LOW:** With the ignition on and the A/C Clutch Relay command off. The ECM detects a short to ground on the (C13) A/C Clutch Relay Control circuit for 1. 0 second.
DTC: P0647	**-A/C CLUTCH CONTROL CIRCUIT HIGH:** With the ignition on and the A/C Clutch Relay command on. The ECM detects a short circuit on the (C13) A/C Clutch Relay Control circuit for 1. 0 second.
DTC: P0647	**-A/C CLUTCH CONTROL CIRCUIT 2 HIGH:** With the ignition on. Battery voltage greater than 10 volts. A/C Switch on. A shorted high or open condition has been detected in the A/C Clutch Control output circuit by the TIPM. One Trip Fault. Three good trips to turn off the MIL.
DTC: P0652	**-SENSOR REFERENCE VOLTAGE 2 CIRCUIT LOW:** Ignition on. When the Powertrain Control Module (PCM) recognizes the Secondary 5-Volt Supply circuit voltage is too low. One Trip Fault. ETC light is flashing.
DTC: P0652	**-SENSOR REFERENCE VOLTAGE 2 CIRCUIT LOW:** With the ignition on. The Powertrain Control Module (PCM) detects that the 5 volt supply circuit voltage is below the minimum acceptable value. One Trip Fault. ETC light is flashing.
DTC: P0653	**-SENSOR REFERENCE VOLTAGE 2 CIRCUIT HIGH:** With the ignition on. The Powertrain Control Module (PCM) detects that the 5 volt supply circuit voltage is above the maximum acceptable value. One Trip Fault. ETC light is flashing.
DTC: P0653	**-SENSOR REFERENCE VOLTAGE 2 TOO HIGH:** With the ignition on. The ECM detects a short to voltage on the Sensor Supply #2 circuit for 0. 10 of a second.
DTC: P0657	**-SOLENOID SUPPLY VOLTAGE CIRCUIT:** With the ignition on. The ECM receives a CAN Bus message indicating the presence of a DTC in the TCM.
DTC: P0657	**-SOLENOID SUPPLY VOLTAGE CIRCUIT:** When the output is active and no under voltage condition exists. When the monitored supply voltage and battery voltage differ by 3. 6 volts.
DTC: P065A	**-GENERATOR PERFORMANCE:** With the engine running. The ECM detects that the Generator output is not within specifications.
DTC: P0671	**-CYLINDER 1 GLOW PLUG CIRCUIT:** With the ignition on and the Glow Plug Module Glow Plug command on. The Cylinder 1 Glow Plug circuit is open or shorted for 0. 5 seconds.
DTC: P0672	**-CYLINDER 2 GLOW PLUG CIRCUIT:** With the ignition on and the Glow Plug Module Glow Plug command on. The Cylinder 2 Glow Plug circuit is open or shorted for 0. 5 seconds.
DTC: P0673	**-CYLINDER 3 GLOW PLUG CIRCUIT:** With the ignition on and the Glow Plug Module Glow Plug command on. The Cylinder 3 Glow Plug circuit is open or shorted for 0. 5 seconds.
DTC: P0674	**-CYLINDER 4 GLOW PLUG CIRCUIT:** With the ignition on and the Glow Plug Module Glow Plug command on. The Cylinder 4 Glow Plug circuit is open or shorted for 0. 5 seconds.
DTC: P0675	**-CYLINDER 5 GLOW PLUG CIRCUIT:** With the ignition on and the Glow Plug Module Glow Plug command on. The Cylinder 5 Glow Plug circuit is open or shorted for 0. 5 seconds.
DTC: P0676	**-CYLINDER 6 GLOW PLUG CIRCUIT:** With the ignition on and the Glow Plug Module Glow Plug command on. The Cylinder 6 Glow Plug circuit is open or shorted for 0. 5 seconds.
DTC: P0685	**-AUTO SHUTDOWN RELAY CONTROL CIRCUIT:** With ignition on. Battery voltage above 10 volts. The actual ASD state is not equal to the desired ASD state. One Trip Fault. Three good trips to turn off the MIL.
DTC: P0685	**-ASD CONTROL CIRCUIT:** When the ignition is turned off, during after-run mode of operation. The Powertrain Control Module (PCM) determines that the ASD Relay has shut off before the AFTER-RUN mode of operation has been completed.

DTC	Trouble Code Title, Conditions, Possible Causes
DTC: P0688	**-AUTO SHUTDOWN RELAY SENSE CIRCUIT LOW:** With ignition key on. Battery voltage greater than 10 volts. No voltage sensed at the PCM when the ASD relay is energized. One Trip Fault. Three good trips to turn off the MIL.
DTC: P0688	**-ASD RELAY CONTROL SENSE:** With ignition key on. Battery voltage greater than 10. 0 Volts. The Powertrain Control Module (PCM) detects an open or short to ground in the (K51) ASD Relay control circuit. One Trip Fault. Three good trips to turn off the MIL.
DTC: P0689	**-AUTO SHUTDOWN RELAY SENSE CIRCUIT LOW:** Ignition on. Battery voltage between 9 and 16 volts and the ASD Relay is powered on. The ASD Output circuit voltage drops below an acceptable value at the FCM. The circuit is continuously monitored.
DTC: P068A	**-ECM RELAY OFF TOO EARLY:** When the ignition is turned off, during after-run mode of operation. The internal ECM timer determines that the ASD Relay has shut off before the AFTER-RUN mode of operation has been completed.
DTC: P068B	**-ECM RELAY OFF TOO LATE:** When the ignition is turned off, during AFTER-RUN mode of operation. The internal ECM timer determines that the ASD Relay remained on for 2. 0 seconds once AFTER-RUN mode of operation has been completed.
DTC: P0690	**-AUTO SHUTDOWN RELAY SENSE CIRCUIT HIGH:** With the ignition on and battery voltage greater than 10 volts. If the FCM detects high voltage on the ASD Relay Sense circuit for more than 3. 5 seconds.
DTC: P0691	**-COOLING FAN 1 CONTROL CIRCUIT LOW:** With the ignition on. Battery voltage greater than 10 volts. The Powertrain Control Module (PCM) is requesting the Totally Integrated Power Module (TIPM) to turn on the Cooling Fan On low speed and it is not operating. The TIPM detects an open in the Low/High Rad Fan Relay Control circuit. One Trip Fault. Three good trips to turn off the MIL.
DTC: P0692	**-COOLING FAN 1 CONTROL CIRCUIT HIGH:** With the ignition on. Battery voltage greater than 10 volts. The Powertrain Control Module (PCM) is requesting the Totally Integrated Power Module (TIPM) to turn on the Cooling Fan On low speed and it is not operating. The TIPM detects a shorted condition in the Low/High Rad Fan Relay Control circuit. One Trip Fault. Three good trips to turn off the MIL.
DTC: P0693	**-COOLING FAN 2 CONTROL CIRCUIT LOW:** With the ignition on. Battery voltage greater than 10 volts. Radiator fan off. The Powertrain Control Module (PCM) requests the Totally Integrated Power Module (TIPM) to turn on the radiator fan and it is not operating. The TIPM detects an open in the coil control circuit of both the radiator fan high relay (20) and radiator fan high/low control relay (19). One trip fault. Three good trips to turn off the Malfunction Indicator Lamp (MIL).
DTC: P0694	**-COOLING FAN 2 CONTROL CIRCUIT HIGH:** With the ignition on. Battery voltage greater than 10 volts. Engine running and above normal temperature. The Powertrain Control Module (PCM) requests the Totally Integrated Power Module (TIPM) to turn on the radiator fan and it is not operating. The TIPM detects a short to voltage in the coil control circuit of either the radiator fan high relay (20) or radiator fan high/low control relay (19). One trip fault. Three good trips to turn off the Malfunction Indicator Lamp (MIL).
DTC: P0698	**-SENSOR REFERENCE VOLTAGE 3 CIRCUIT LOW:** With the ignition on. The ECM detects low voltage on the Sensor Supply #3 circuit for 0. 10 of a second.
DTC: P0699	**-SENSOR REFERENCE VOLTAGE 3 CIRCUIT HIGH:** With the ignition on. The ECM detects a short to voltage on the Sensor Supply #3 circuit for 0. 10 seconds.
DTC: P06DA	**- DUAL STAGE OIL PUMP CIRCUIT:** With the battery voltage is between 11 and 18 Volts with the engine running. The Powertrain Control Module (PCM) detects that the actual voltage of the oil pump solenoid control circuit does not match the intended state. One Trip Fault. Three good trips to turn off the MIL.
DTC: P06DA	**-ENGINE OIL PRESSURE CONTROL CIRCUIT OPEN:** With the engine running. The Powertrain Control Module (PCM) detects and open on the (G62) Variable Oil Pump Control circuit for 1. 5 seconds.
DTC: P06DD	**-DUAL STAGE OIL PUMP STUCK LOW:** Based upon Engine oil temperature, the monitor runs when engine speed (RPM) is over a calibrated value. The cooler the engine oil, the lower is the enable engine speed (Minimum 1000rpm). To evaluate the dual stage oil pump, fully warm up the engine. To run DUAL STAGE OIL PUMP STUCK LOW (P06DD), drive vehicle with engine speed over 3500 rpm. The Powertrain Control Module (PCM) senses the oil pressure is less than a low threshold for 5 seconds. One Trip fault.

DTC	Trouble Code Title, Conditions, Possible Causes
DTC: P06DE	**-DUAL STAGE OIL PUMP STUCK HIGH:** Based upon Engine oil temperature, the monitor runs when engine speed (RPM) is over a calibrated value. The cooler the engine oil, the lower is the enable engine speed (Minimum 1000rpm). To evaluate dual stage oil pump, fully warm up the engine. To run DUAL STAGE OIL PUMP STUCK HIGH (P06DE), drive vehicle over 2500 rpm. The Powertrain Control Module (PCM) senses the oil pressure is more than a high threshold for 50 seconds . One Trip fault.
DTC: P0700	**TRANSMISSION CONTROL SYSTEM (MIL REQUEST):** With the ignition on. The ECM receives a CAN Bus message indicating the presence of a DTC in the TCM.
DTC: P0700	**TRANSMISSION CONTROL SYSTEM (MIL REQUEST):** Ignition on and battery voltage greater than 10 volts. An active DTC is stored in the TCM. One Trip Fault. Three good trips to turn off the MIL.
DTC: P0703	**-BRAKE SWITCH 2 PERFORMANCE:** Ignition on and battery voltage above 10. 4 Volts. When the Powertrain Control Module (PCM) recognizes Brake Switch voltage is not equal to the applied value at the PCM when Brake Switch is applied. This could be a normal condition. If this condition is seen repeatedly by the PCM the fault is set. Cruise will not work for the rest of the key cycle.
DTC: P0703	**-BRAKE SWITCH 2 PERFORMANCE:** Ignition on. When the PCM recognizes Brake Switch No. 2 voltage is not equal to the applied value at the PCM when Brake Switch No. 1 is applied. This could be a normal condition. If this condition is seen repeatedly by the PCM the fault is set. Cruise will not work for the rest of the key cycle.
DTC: P0706	**TRANSMISSION RANGE SENSOR RATIONALITY:** Continuously with the ignition on. The DTC will set if the controller detects an invalid PRNDL code which lasts for more than 0. 042 of a second.
DTC: P0706	**TRANSMISSION RANGE SENSOR RATIONALITY:** Continuously with the ignition on. The DTC will set if the controller detects an invalid PRNDL code which lasts for more than 0. 042 seconds.
DTC: P0706	**TRANSMISSION RANGE SENSOR RATIONALITY:** Continuously with the ignition on in the run position. The DTC will set if an invalid PRNDL code exists for more than 100 milliseconds within one second of power-up or if the PRNDL code error does not correct itself when (or before) the shift lever is moved to a different position (P, R, N, or OD), or if the PCM sees the PRNDL code rapidly (within 7 ms) jump across more than three shift lever detent positions.
DTC: P0706	**TRANSMISSION RANGE SENSOR RATIONALITY:** With the ignition on. The ECM receives a CAN Bus message indicating the presence of a DTC in the TCM.
DTC: P0707	**TRANSMISSION RANGE SENSOR CIRCUIT LOW:** Ignition on with system voltage between 9. 0 and 16. 0 volts. Vehicle speed above 10 Km/h (6 mph). No other Transmission Range Sensor (TRS) DTCs present. If a continuous input signal loss is read by the TCM from the TRS for the period of 5 seconds. It takes two consecutive one trips of problem identification to light the MIL.
DTC: P0708	**TRANSMISSION RANGE SENSOR CIRCUIT HIGH:** Ignition on with system voltage between 9. 0 and 16. 0 volts. No other Transmission Range Sensor (TRS) DTCs present. When the Transmission Control Module (TCM) receives more than one Transmission Range Sensor (TRS) signal from the TRS continuously for the period of 2. 0 seconds.
DTC: P0710	**TRANSMISSION TEMPERATURE SENSOR CIRCUIT:** Continuously with the ignition on. When the TCM detects an open circuit when in Reverse or any forward drive position the DTC will set.
DTC: P0711	**TRANSMISSION TEMPERATURE SENSOR PERFORMANCE:** Condition one : Transmission in a valid forward gear. System voltage between 9. 0 and 16. 0 Volts. Vehicle speed greater than 10 Km/h (6 mph). Accelerator Pedal Position (APP) greater than 12. 5%. Engine rpm greater than 450 rpm. Condition two: Ignition off for greater than 8 hours. Difference between the engine coolant temperature and the intake temperature is less than 3° C (37° F). No other temperature sensor or sensor ground DTCs present. Condition one: No change in the Transmission oil temperature the period of 10 minutes. Condition two: Transmission oil temperature is 40° C (104° F) different than the average temperature which consists of the combined average of the Engine Coolant temperature, Intake Temperature, Oil Temperature, and Ambient Temperature for the period of 5 seconds.

DTC	Trouble Code Title, Conditions, Possible Causes
DTC: P0711	**TRANSMISSION TEMPERATURE SENSOR PERFORMANCE:** Continuously with the ignition on and engine running. DTC will set when the transmission temperature does not reach a normal operating temperature within a given time frame. Time is variable due to ambient temperature. Approximate DTC set time is 10 to 35 minutes. The following are starting temperature to warm up times to set this **DTC:** starting temperature -40° C (-40° F) warm up time 35 minutes, starting temperature -28° C (-20° F) 25 minutes, starting temperature -6. 6° C (20° F) 20 minutes, starting temperature 15. 5 ° C (60° F) 10 minutes. When the fault is set, calculated temperature is substituted for measured temperature, however the DTC is stored only after three consecutive occurrences.
DTC: P0712	**TRANSMISSION TEMPERATURE SENSOR LOW:** Continuously with the ignition on and engine running. The DTC will set when the monitored Temperature Sensor voltage drops below 0. 078 of a volt for the period of 1. 45 seconds. When the fault is set, calculated temperature is substituted for measured temperature, however the fault code is stored only after three consecutive occurrences of the problem identification.
DTC: P0712	**TRANSMISSION TEMPERATURE SENSOR LOW:** Ignition on with battery voltage between 9. 0 and 16. 0 Volts. Vehicle speed greater than 10 Km/h (6 mph). No secondary speed sensor or sensor ground DTCs detected. Indicated temperature is greater than 180° C (356° F) for the continuous period of five seconds.
DTC: P0712	**TRANSMISSION TEMPERATURE SENSOR LOW:** Continuously with the ignition on and engine running. The DTC will set when the monitored Temperature Sensor voltage drops below 0. 078 of a volt for the period of 0. 45 of a second.
DTC: P0712	**TRANSMISSION TEMPERATURE SENSOR LOW:** Continuously with the ignition on and engine running. The DTC will set when the monitored Temperature Sensor voltage drops below 0. 078 volts for the period of 1. 45 seconds. When the fault is set, calculated temperature is substituted for measured temperature, however the fault code is stored only after three consecutive occurrences of the fault.
DTC: P0713	**TRANSMISSION TEMPERATURE SENSOR HIGH:** Continuously with the ignition on and engine running. The DTC will set when the monitored Temperature Sensor voltage rises above 4. 94 volts for the period of 1. 45 seconds. When the fault is set, calculated temperature is substituted for measured temperature, however the fault code is stored only after three consecutive occurrences of the fault.
DTC: P0713	**TRANSMISSION TEMPERATURE SENSOR HIGH:** Ignition on engine running with battery voltage between 9. 0 and 16. 0 Volts. Vehicle speed greater than 10 Km/h (6 mph). No secondary speed sensor or sensor ground DTCs present. Indicated temperature drops below -40° C (-40° F) for the continuous period of 5. 0 seconds.
DTC: P0714	**TRANSMISSION TEMPERATURE SENSOR INTERMITTENT:** Continuously with the ignition on and the Transmission Temperature below 170 °C (338 °F). When the TCM detects the Temperature sensor input changes more than 10 °C (18 °F) between each 20 msec sensor read.
DTC: P0714	**TRANSMISSION TEMPERATURE SENSOR INTERMITTENT:** Continuously with the ignition on and engine running. The DTC will set when the monitored Temperature Sensor voltage fluctuates or changes abruptly within a predetermined period of time.
DTC: P0715	**-INPUT SPEED SENSOR 1 CIRCUIT:** The transmission gear ratio is monitored continuously while the transmission is in gear. If there is an excessive change in the Input rpm in any valid gear (R, 1st, 2nd, 3rd, or 4th).
DTC: P0716	**-INPUT SPEED SENSOR 1 CIRCUIT PERFORMANCE:** The transmission gear ratio is monitored continuously while the transmission is in gear. If there is an excessive change in the Input rpm in any valid gear (R, 1st, 2nd, 3rd, or 4th).
DTC: P0716	**-INPUT SPEED SENSOR 1 CIRCUIT PERFORMANCE:** Ignition on, engine running with the transmission in a valid forward gear. System voltage between 9. 0 and 16. 0 volts Vehicle speed greater than 10 Km/h (6 mph). Accelerator Pedal Position (APP) greater than 12. 5%. Engine rpm greater than 450 rpm with TCC lock-up enabled. No DTCs from the following: TCC Solenoid Lock-up solenoid Step motor Input or Output Speed Sensor No Signal Transmission Range Sensor (TRS)Sensor Ground CAN Engine speed minus the primary speed is greater than 1000 rpm. Secondary speed multiplied by the estimated ratio, minus the Primary speed is greater than 1000 rpm. Engine speed minus the Secondary speed, multiplied by the estimated ratio is less than 1000 rpm.
DTC: P0717	**-INPUT SPEED SENSOR 1 CIRCUIT NO SIGNAL:** Engine speed greater than 450 RPM with none of the following DTCs present: engine speed, TCM under voltage, output speed sensor, and/or rear wheel speed DTCs. Also required are all wheel speeds above 250 RPM and no wheel slip detected (signal from the ABS system). If the Input Speed Sensor 1 (N2) signal is equal to 0 RPM.

DTC	Trouble Code Title, Conditions, Possible Causes
DTC: P0717	**-INPUT SPEED SENSOR 1 CIRCUIT NO SIGNAL:** Ignition on, engine running with system voltage between 9. 0 and 16. 0 volts. No detected Primary Speed Sensor and/or Sensor ground DTCs. Condition one: Input speed rpm is less than 150 rpm with a Output speed rpm greater than 1000 rpm for the period of 5 seconds. Condition two: Input speed rpm last value is greater than 1000 rpm where as the Input speed rpm current value is zero rpm for the period of 500 msec. Condition three: Both the Input and Output Speed sensors are less than 150 rpm with a actual vehicle speed greater than 10 Km/h. **(NOTE: this is an indication of either the power supply to both sensors is open or the C106 connector is disconnected.)**
DTC: P0720	**-OUTPUT SPEED SENSOR CIRCUIT:** The transmission gear ratio is monitored continuously while the transmission is in gear. If there is an excessive change in output RPM in any gear. This DTC can take up to five minutes of problem identification before illuminating the MIL.
DTC: P0721	**-OUTPUT SPEED SENSOR CIRCUIT PERFORMANCE:** The transmission gear ratio is monitored continuously while the transmission is in gear. If there is an excessive change in output RPM in any gear. This DTC can take up to five minutes of problem identification before illuminating the MIL.
DTC: P0721	**-OUTPUT SPEED SENSOR CIRCUIT PERFORMANCE:** The transmission gear ratio is monitored continuously while the transmission is in gear. If there is an excessive change in the Output rpm in any gear.
DTC: P0721	**-OUTPUT SPEED SENSOR CIRCUIT PERFORMANCE:** Ignition on, engine running with the transmission in a valid forward gear. System voltage between 9. 0 and 16+. 0 volts. Vehicle speed greater than 10 Km/h (6 mph). Accelerator Pedal Position (APP) greater than 12. 5%. Engine rpm greater than 450 rpm with TCC lock-up enabled. No active DTCs from the following: Torque Convertor Clutch (TCC)Lock-up Solenoid CAN Bus Step Motor Input or Output Speed Sensor No Signal Transmission Range Sensor (TRS)Sensor Ground
DTC: P0721	**-OUTPUT SPEED SENSOR CIRCUIT PERFORMANCE:** Ignition on, engine running with the transmission in a valid forward gear. System voltage between 9. 0 and 16. 0 volts Vehicle speed greater than 10 Km/h (6 mph). Accelerator Pedal Position (APP) greater than 12. 5%. Engine rpm greater than 450 rpm with TCC lock-up enabled. No DTCs from the following: TCC Solenoid Lock-up solenoid Step motor Input or Output Speed Sensor No Signal Transmission Range Sensor (TRS)Sensor Ground CAN Engine speed minus the primary speed is greater than 1000 rpm. Secondary speed multiplied by the estimated ratio, minus the Primary speed is greater than 1000 rpm. Engine speed minus the Secondary speed, multiplied by the estimated ratio is less than 1000 rpm.
DTC: P0722	**-OUTPUT SPEED SENSOR CIRCUIT NO SIGNAL:** Ignition on, engine running with system voltage between 9. 0 and 16. 0 volts. No detected Primary Speed Sensor DTCs. Condition one: Output speed rpm is less than 150 rpm with a Input speed rpm greater than 1000 rpm for the period of 5 seconds. Condition two: Vehicle speed is greater than 20 Km/h (12. 5 mph) calculated by the last secondary speed with the current Output Speed value equals to 0 rpm for the period of 500 msec. Condition three: Both the Input and Output Speed sensors are less than 150 rpm with a actual vehicle speed greater than 10 Km/h. **(NOTE: this is an indication of either the power supply to both sensors is open or the C106 connector is disconnected.)**
DTC: P0725	**-ENGINE SPEED SENSOR CIRCUIT:** Whenever the engine is running. The Engine RPM is less than 390 or greater than 8000 for more than 2 seconds while the engine is running.
DTC: P0726	**-ENGINE SPEED INPUT CIRCUIT RANGE/PERFORMANCE:** Continuously every 7 msec with the ignition on and engine running. This DTC will set when the calculated engine speed is less than 390 rpm with the engine running, or greater than 8000 rpm, for the period of 2. 0 seconds. The PCM will place the Transmission in Limp-in when this DTC is set. **NOTE: This is not a Transmission Input Speed Sensor DTC.**
DTC: P0726	**-ENGINE SPEED INPUT CIRCUIT RANGE/PERFORMANCE:** Whenever the engine is running. The Engine RPM is less than 390 or greater than 8000 for more than two seconds while the engine is running.
DTC: P0729	**-GEAR RATIO ERROR IN 6TH:** The Transmission gear ratio is monitored continuously while the transmission is in gear. If the ratio of the Input RPM to the Output RPM does not match the current gear ratio when compared to the known gear ratio.
DTC: P0730	**-INCORRECT GEAR RATIO:** If the difference between the transmission estimated pulley speed and the measured primary pulley speed is greater than 1000 rpm (belt slipping)for the continuous period of 5. 0 seconds.
DTC: P0730	**-INCORRECT GEAR RATIO:** With the ignition on. The ECM receives a CAN Bus message indicating the presence of a DTC in the TCM.

DTC	Trouble Code Title, Conditions, Possible Causes
DTC: P0731	**-GEAR RATIO ERROR IN 1ST:** The Transmission gear ratio is monitored continuously while the transmission is in gear. If the ratio of the Input RPM to the Output RPM does not match the current gear ratio when compared to the known gear ratio.
DTC: P0731	**-GEAR RATIO ERROR IN 1ST:** Continuously with the ignition on, engine running, and after the transmission has achieved the proper gear ratio. If the ratio of the Input rpm to the Output rpm does not match the current gear ratio. This DTC can take up to five minutes of problem identification before illuminating the MIL
DTC: P0732	**-GEAR RATIO ERROR IN 2ND:** Continuously with the ignition on, engine running, and after the transmission has achieved the proper gear ratio. If the ratio of the Input rpm to the Output rpm does not match the current gear ratio. This DTC can take up to five minutes of problem identification before illuminating the MIL
DTC: P0732	**-GEAR RATIO ERROR IN 2ND:** The Transmission gear ratio is monitored continuously while the transmission is in gear. If the ratio of the Input RPM to the Output RPM does not match the current gear ratio when compared to the known gear ratio.
DTC: P0733	**-GEAR RATIO ERROR IN 3RD:** The Transmission gear ratio is monitored continuously while the transmission is in gear. If the ratio of the Input RPM to the Output RPM does not match the current gear ratio when compared to the known gear ratio.
DTC: P0733	**-GEAR RATIO ERROR IN 3RD:** Continuously with the ignition on, engine running, and after the transmission has achieved the proper gear ratio. If the ratio of the Input rpm to the Output rpm does not match the current gear ratio. This DTC can take up to five minutes of problem identification before illuminating the MIL
DTC: P0734	**-GEAR RATIO ERROR IN 4TH:** Continuously with the ignition on, engine running, and after the transmission has achieved the proper gear ratio. If the ratio of the Input rpm to the Output rpm does not match the current gear ratio. This DTC can take up to five minutes of problem identification before illuminating the MIL.
DTC: P0734	**-GEAR RATIO ERROR IN 4TH:** The Transmission gear ratio is monitored continuously while the transmission is in gear. If the ratio of the Input RPM to the Output RPM does not match the current gear ratio when compared to the known gear ratio.
DTC: P0735	**-GEAR RATIO ERROR IN 5TH:** The Transmission gear ratio is monitored continuously while the transmission is in gear. If the ratio of the Input RPM to the Output RPM does not match the current gear ratio when compared to the known gear ratio.
DTC: P0735	**-GEAR RATIO ERROR IN 5TH:** Continuously with the ignition on, engine running, and after the transmission has achieved the proper gear ratio. If the ratio of the Input rpm to the Output rpm does not match the current gear ratio. This DTC can take up to five minutes of problem identification before illuminating the MIL.
DTC: P0736	**-GEAR RATIO ERROR IN REVERSE:** The Transmission gear ratio is monitored continuously while the transmission is in gear. If the ratio of the Input RPM to the Output RPM does not match the current gear ratio when compared to the known gear ratio.
DTC: P0736	**-GEAR RATIO ERROR IN REVERSE:** Continuously with the ignition on, engine running, and after the transmission has achieved the proper gear ratio. If the ratio of the Input rpm to the Output rpm does not match the current gear ratio. This DTC can take up to five minutes of problem identification before illuminating the MIL
DTC: P0740	**TCC OUT OF RANGE:** The Torque Converter Clutch (TCC) is in FEMCC or PEMCC, Transmission temperature is hot, Engine temperature is greater than 38° C or 100° F, Transmission Input Speed greater than engine speed, TPS less than 30°, and brake not applied. The TCC is modulated by controlling the duty cycle of the L/R Solenoid until the difference between the Engine RPM and the Transmission Input Speed RPM or duty cycle is within a desired range. The DTC is set after the period of 10 seconds and 3 occurrences of either: FEMCC - with slip greater than 100 RPM or PEMCC - duty cycle greater than 85%.
DTC: P0740	**TCC OUT OF RANGE:** During Electronically Modulated Converter Clutch (EMCC) Operation. Transmission must be in EMCC, with input speed greater than 1750 rpm. L/RTCC Solenoid achieves the maximum duty cycle and cannot pull engine speed within 60 rpm of input speed. Also when the transmission is in FEMCC and the engine slips TCC more than 100 rpm for 10 seconds. This DTC can take up to five minutes of problem identification before illuminating the MIL.

DTC	Trouble Code Title, Conditions, Possible Causes
DTC: P0741	**TORQUE CONVERTER CLUTCH CIRCUIT PERFORMANCE:** Ignition on, engine running with the transmission in a valid forward gear. System voltage between 9. 0 and 16. 0 Volts. Vehicle speed greater than 10 Km/h (6 mph). Accelerator Pedal Position (APP) greater than 12. 5%. Engine rpm greater than 450 rpm with TCC lock-up enabled. TCC Lock up command is ON (True). No active DTCs from the following: Step motor, Line Pressure Solenoid Secondary Solenoid Input or Output Speed Sensor Primary or Secondary Pressure Sensor CAN Bustle DTC is detected If the Torque Convertor Clutch (TCC) slip monitored by the Transmission Control Module (TCM) is greater than a predetermined value for the period of 30 seconds. **NOTE: This is not an electrical fault but a mechanical malfunction such as a control valve sticking in its bore or a TCC Solenoid hydraulic malfunction. It takes two consecutive problem identification trips for the DTC to mature and illuminate the MIL.**
DTC: P0741	**TORQUE CONVERTER CLUTCH CIRCUIT PERFORMANCE:** Ignition on, TCM not in initialization phase, no input speed sensor 1 or 2 (N2-N3) DTCs, no CAN bus or ECM DTCs, no CAN engine speed signal or engine torque signal not implausible DTCs, engine speed greater than 450 rpm, no shift in progress, gear 1, 2, 3, 4 or 5 engaged, and the TCM torque converter status is SLIP While in Slip Mode operation, the TCM detects TCC slippage greater than a calibrated value.
DTC: P0742	**TORQUE CONVERTER CLUTCH STUCK ON:** Ignition on, TCM not in initialization phase, No input speed sensor 1 or 2 (N2-N3) DTCs, No CAN bus or ECM DTCs, No CAN engine speed signal or engine torque signal not implausible DTCs, Engine speed greater than 450 rpm, No shift in progress, Gear 1, 2, 3, 4 or 5 engaged, and the TCM torque converter status is OPEN Engine RPM (Turbine Speed) is greater than 30 RPM when engine torque less than 100 Nm (74. 0 ft. lbs.) for period of 1. 0 second.
DTC: P0743	**TCC SOLENOID CIRCUIT:** Continuously with the ignition on, engine running, with the transmission in gear, the TCC Solenoid is inactive, or when the TCC Solenoid is active and controlled above 25% duty cycle, with the Solenoid Supply voltage active. If the TCM detects on the TCC Solenoid control circuit a open, short to ground, short to voltage, internal short in the TCC Solenoid or open in the TCC Solenoid.
DTC: P0743	**TCC SOLENOID CIRCUIT:** With the ignition on. The ECM receives a CAN Bus message indicating the presence of a DTC in the TCM.
DTC: P0746	**-LINE PRESSURE SOLENOID PERFORMANCE:** Ignition on, engine running with the transmission in a valid forward gear. Vehicle speed greater than 10 Km/h (6 mph). Accelerator Pedal Position (APP) greater than 12. 5%. Engine rpm greater than 450 rpm. Primary Pulley Speed greater than 500 rpm. No active DTCs from the following: Line Pressure Solenoid Temperature Sensor Primary or Secondary Pressure Sensor Transmission Range Sensor Step Motor Secondary Solenoid electrical Input and Output Speed Sensor Torque Convertor Clutch CAN Bus Over Temperature Condition Condition one: Gear ratio is greater than 2. 7 - 2 for the period of 0. 2 seconds (first trip). Condition two: Gear ratio is greater than 3. 5 - 1 for the period of 0. 1 seconds (second trip).
DTC: P0748	**-MODULATOR PRESSURE SOLENOID CIRCUIT:** With the ignition on. The ECM receives a CAN Bus message indicating the presence of a DTC in the TCM.
DTC: P0748	**-MODULATOR PRESSURE SOLENOID CIRCUIT:** Continuously with the ignition on, engine running, the Modulating Pressure Control Solenoid Valve is either off, or active with 25-75% duty cycle, with no Solenoid Supply Voltage DTCs present. When the Modulating Pressure Control Solenoid Valve is turned on and the Solenoid driver detects an error (the measured current is too different then the target current) or when the solenoid is off and a short to ground is detected.
DTC: P0750	**-LR SOLENOID CIRCUIT:** Initially at power-up, then every 10 seconds thereafter. The solenoid circuits will also be tested immediately after a gear ratio or pressure switch error is detected. After three consecutive solenoid continuity test failures, or one failure if test is run in response to a gear ratio or pressure switch error. This DTC is strictly an electrical fault and cannot be caused by any internal transmission failure other than an open in the Transmission Solenoid/TRS Assembly. If the Transmission Solenoid/TRS Assembly is in need of replacement — do not replace the Valve Body.
DTC: P0750	**-LR SOLENOID CIRCUIT:** Initially at ignition on, then every 10 seconds thereafter. The solenoids will also be tested immediately after a gear ratio error or pressure switch error is detected. Three consecutive solenoid continuity test failures, or one failure if test is run in response to a gear ratio or pressure switch error.
DTC: P0752	**-1-2/4-5 SOLENOID:** When both the 1-2/4-5 Solenoid and the Solenoid Supply voltage is active. When 1-2/4-5 Solenoid is turned on and the TCM detects any of the following in the 1-2/4-5 Solenoid or circuit: open, short to ground, short to voltage, or the solenoid driver in the TCM.
DTC: P0753	**-1/2 4/5 SOLENOID CIRCUIT:** With the ignition on. The ECM receives a CAN Bus message indicating the presence of a DTC in the TCM.
DTC: P0753	**-1-2/4-5 SOLENOID CIRCUIT:** When both the 1-2/4-5 Solenoid and the Solenoid Supply voltage is active. When 1-2/4-5 Solenoid is turned on and the TCM detects any of the following in the 1-2/4-5 Solenoid or circuit: open, short to ground, short to voltage, or the solenoid driver in the TCM.

DTC	Trouble Code Title, Conditions, Possible Causes
DTC: P0755	**-2/4 SOLENOID CIRCUIT:** Initially at ignition on, then every 10 seconds thereafter. The solenoids will also be tested immediately after a gear ratio error or pressure switch error is detected. Three consecutive solenoid continuity test failures, or one failure if test is run in response to a gear ratio or pressure switch error.
DTC: P0755-2C	**- SOLENOID CIRCUIT:** Initially at power-up, then every 10 seconds thereafter. The solenoid circuits will also be tested immediately after a gear ratio or pressure switch error is detected. After three consecutive solenoid continuity test failures, or one failure if test is run in response to a gear ratio or pressure switch error. This DTC is strictly an electrical fault and cannot be caused by any internal transmission failure other than an open in the Transmission Solenoid/TRS Assembly. If the Transmission Solenoid/TRS Assembly is in need of replacement — do not replace the Valve Body.
DTC: P0757	**-2-3 SOLENOID:** When both the 2-3 Solenoid and the Solenoid Supply voltage is active. When 2-3 Solenoid is turned on and the TCM detects any of the following in the 2-3 Solenoid or circuit: open, short to ground, short to voltage, or the solenoid driver in the TCM.
DTC: P0758	**-2/3 SOLENOID CIRCUIT:** With the ignition on. The ECM receives a CAN Bus message indicating the presence of a DTC in the TCM.
DTC: P0758	**-2-3 SOLENOID CIRCUIT:** When both the 2-3 Solenoid and the Solenoid Supply voltage is active. When 2-3 Solenoid is turned on and the TCM detects any of the following in the 2-3 Solenoid or circuit: open, short to ground, short to voltage, or the solenoid driver in the TCM.
DTC: P075A	**-LC SOLENOID CIRCUIT:** Initially at ignition on, then every 10 seconds thereafter. The solenoids will also be tested immediately after a gear ratio error or pressure switch error is detected. Three consecutive solenoid continuity test failures, or one failure if test is run in response to a gear ratio or pressure switch error.
DTC: P0760	**-OD SOLENOID CIRCUIT:** Initially at power-up, then every 10 seconds thereafter. The solenoid circuits will also be tested immediately after a gear ratio or pressure switch error is detected. After three consecutive solenoid continuity test failures, or one failure if test is run in response to a gear ratio or pressure switch error. This DTC is strictly an electrical fault and cannot be caused by any internal transmission failure other than an open in the Transmission Solenoid/TRS Assembly. If the Transmission Solenoid/TRS Assembly is in need of replacement — do not replace the Valve Body.
DTC: P0760	**-OD SOLENOID CIRCUIT:** Initially at ignition on, then every 10 seconds thereafter. The solenoids will also be tested immediately after a gear ratio error or pressure switch error is detected. Three consecutive solenoid continuity test failures, or one failure if test is run in response to a gear ratio or pressure switch error.
DTC: P0762	**-3-4 SOLENOID:** When both the 3-4 Solenoid and the Solenoid Supply voltage is active. When 3-4 Solenoid is turned on and the TCM detects any of the following in the 3-4 Solenoid or circuit: open, short to ground, short to voltage, or the solenoid driver in the TCM.
DTC: P0763	**-3/4 SOLENOID CIRCUIT:** With the ignition on. The ECM receives a CAN Bus message indicating the presence of a DTC in the TCM.
DTC: P0763	**-3-4 SOLENOID CIRCUIT:** When both the 3-4 Solenoid and the Solenoid Supply voltage is active. When 3-4 Solenoid is turned on and the TCM detects any of the following in the 3-4 Solenoid or circuit: open, short to ground, short to voltage, or the solenoid driver in the TCM.
DTC: P0765	**-UD SOLENOID CIRCUIT:** Initially at ignition on, then every 10 seconds thereafter. The solenoids will also be tested immediately after a gear ratio error or pressure switch error is detected. Three consecutive solenoid continuity test failures, or one failure if test is run in response to a gear ratio or pressure switch error.
DTC: P0765	**-UD SOLENOID CIRCUIT:** Initially at power-up, then every 10 seconds thereafter. The solenoid circuits will also be tested immediately after a gear ratio or pressure switch error is detected. After three consecutive solenoid continuity test failures, or one failure if test is run in response to a gear ratio or pressure switch error. This DTC is strictly an electrical fault and cannot be caused by any internal transmission failure other than an open in the Transmission Solenoid/TRS Assembly. If the Transmission Solenoid/TRS Assembly is in need of replacement — do not replace the Valve Body.
DTC: P076A-DC	**- SOLENOID CIRCUIT:** Initially at ignition on, then every 10 seconds thereafter. The solenoids will also be tested immediately after a gear ratio error or pressure switch error is detected. Three consecutive solenoid continuity test failures, or one failure if test is run in response to a gear ratio or pressure switch error.

DTC	Trouble Code Title, Conditions, Possible Causes
DTC: P0770-4C	**- SOLENOID CIRCUIT:** Initially at power-up, then every 10 seconds thereafter. The solenoid circuits will also be tested immediately after a gear ratio or pressure switch error is detected. After three consecutive solenoid continuity test failures, or one failure if test is run in response to a gear ratio or pressure switch error. This DTC is strictly an electrical fault and cannot be caused by any internal transmission failure other than an open in the Transmission Solenoid/TRS Assembly. If the Transmission Solenoid/TRS Assembly is in need of replacement — do not replace the Valve Body.
DTC: P0776	**-SECONDARY PRESSURE SOLENOID STUCK OFF (HIGH PRESSURE):** Ignition on, engine running with the transmission in a valid forward gear. Vehicle speed greater than 10 Km/h (6 mph). Accelerator Pedal Position (APP) greater than 12. 5%. Engine rpm greater than 450 rpm with a transmission fluid temperature greater than 20° C (68° F)No active DTCs from the following: Line Pressure Solenoid Lock-up Solenoid Primary or Secondary Pressure Sensor Transmission Range Sensor Step Motor Secondary Solenoid electrical Input and Output Speed Sensor Torque Convertor Clutch CAN Bus Over Temperature Condition When the difference between actual secondary pressure compared to the target (desired) secondary pressure is greater than 1200 Kpa (174 psi) for the period of 30 seconds. It takes two consecutive problem identified trips to set the DTC.
DTC: P0777	**-SECONDARY PRESSURE SOLENOID STUCK ON (LOW PRESSURE):** Ignition on, engine running with the transmission not in neutral or park. Transmission fluid temperature greater than -20° C (-4° F). Brake Switch in the OFF mode. Change rate of vehicle speed greater than 24 Km/h (15 mph). Change rate of accelerator pedal position less than ±6. 25%. Engine rpm greater than 450 rpm with a transmission fluid temperature greater than 20° C (68° F). No active DTCs from the following: Line Pressure Solenoid Primary or Secondary Pressure Sensor Step Motor Secondary Solenoid electrical Input and Output Speed Sensor CAN Bus When the secondary pressure goes down gradually below a predetermined value during a drive cycle. The DTC could be due to the failure of the secondary pressure control system, secondary pressure solenoid performance or line pressure solenoid. There are two possible setting conditions to set this DTC.
DTC: P0778	**-SHIFT PRESSURE SOLENOID CIRCUIT:** With the ignition on. The ECM receives a CAN Bus message indicating the presence of a DTC in the TCM.
DTC: P0778	**-SHIFT PRESSURE SOLENOID CIRCUIT:** When the Shift Pressure Solenoid is: off, or active with 25-75% duty cycle, and the Solenoid Supply voltage is active. When Shift Pressure Solenoid is turned on and the TCM detects any of the following in the Shift Pressure Solenoid or circuit: open, short to ground, short to voltage, or the solenoid driver in the TCM.
DTC: P0791	**TRANSFER SPEED SENSOR CIRCUIT:** The transmission gear ratio is monitored continuously while the transmission is in gear. If there is an excessive change in the Transfer RPM in any gear.
DTC: P0792	**-COMPOUNDER SPEED RATIO ERROR:** The transmission gear ratio is monitored continuously while the transmission is in gear. If there is an excessive change in the Output RPM in any gear.
DTC: P0801	**-REVERSE GEAR LOCKOUT CIRCUIT OPEN OR SHORTED:** Engine running. Battery voltage greater than 10 volts. Reverse Lockout Solenoid Control circuit is not in the expected state when requested to operate by the Powertrain Control Module (PCM). One trip fault.
DTC: P0803	**-SKIP SHIFT CONTROL SOLENOID CIRCUIT:** Engine running. Battery voltage greater than 10 volts. The Skip Shift Solenoid Control Circuit is not in the expected state when requested to operate by the Powertrain Control Module (PCM). One Trip Fault.
DTC: P080B	**-SKIP SHIFT RATIONALITY:** Engine RPM greater than 1300. Transmission in 1st gear. Skip shift requested between 15 - 25 mph. The Skip Shift solenoid control circuit is not in the expected state when requested to operate by the PCM.
DTC: P0815-2A	**-UPSHIFT SWITCH - STUCK:** With the ignition on. The Upshift Switch has been pressed for greater than 20 seconds.
DTC: P0826	**-UP/DOWN SHIFT SWITCH CIRCUIT:** Ignition on with a system voltage between 9. 0 and 16 volts. Upshift and Downshift requested simultaneously while in the Drive position or the Upshift and/or Downshift request during while not in the Drive position for the period of 1. 0 second.
DTC: P0830	**-CLUTCH UPSTOP SWITCH STUCK ON:** Engine running. Battery voltage greater than 10. 4 Volts. The Powertrain Control Module (PCM) receives a signal from the Clutch Interlock Switch indicating that the clutch pedal is depressed while the vehicle is driven.
DTC: P0835	**-CLUTCH UPSTOP SWITCH STUCK OFF:** Engine running. Battery voltage greater than 10. 4 Volts. The Powertrain Control Module (PCM) receives a signal from the Clutch Interlock Switch indicating that the clutch pedal is not depressed when the vehicle is started.

DTC	Trouble Code Title, Conditions, Possible Causes
DTC: P083A	**-LC HYDRAULIC PRESSURE TEST:** In any forward gear with engine speed above 1000 rpm, shortly after a shift and every minute thereafter. After a shift into a forward gear, with engine speed greater than 1000 rpm, the Powertrain Control Module (PCM) momentarily turns on element pressure to the clutch circuits that don't have pressure to verify that the correct pressure switch closes. If the pressure switch does not close 2 times the DTC will set.
DTC: P083B	**-LC PRESSURE SWITCH RATIONALITY:** Whenever the engine is running. The DTC is set if one of the pressure switches are open or closed at the wrong time in a given gear. If the problem is identified for 3 successive key starts, the transmission will go into Limp-in mode and the MIL will turn on after 10 seconds of vehicle operation.
DTC: P0841	**-LR PRESSURE SWITCH RATIONALITY:** Whenever the engine is running. The DTC is set if one of the pressure switches are open or closed at the wrong time in a given gear. If the problem is identified for 3 successive key starts, the transmission will go into Limp-in mode and the MIL will turn on after 10 seconds of vehicle operation.
DTC: P0841	**-LR PRESSURE SWITCH RATIONALITY:** Continuously with the ignition on and engine running. The DTC will set if the L/R Pressure Switch reads open or closed at the wrong time in a given gear.
DTC: P0842	**-PRIMARY OIL PRESSURE SENSOR CIRCUIT LOW:** Ignition on, system voltage between 9. 0 and 16. 0 Volts. Transmission temperature greater than -20° C (-4° F)No active DTCs from the following: Primary Oil Pressure Sensor High Sensor ground When the monitored voltage drops below 0. 09 Volts for the period of five seconds.
DTC: P0843	**-PRIMARY OIL PRESSURE SENSOR CIRCUIT HIGH:** Ignition on, system voltage between 9. 0 and 16. 0 volts. Transmission temperature greater than -20° C (-4° F)No active DTCs from the following: Primary Oil Pressure Sensor Low Sensor ground When the monitored voltage rises above 4. 7 volts for the period of five seconds.
DTC: P0845	**-2/4 HYDRAULIC PRESSURE TEST:** In any forward gear with engine speed above 1000 rpm, shortly after a shift and every minute thereafter. After a shift into a forward gear, with engine speed greater than 1000 rpm, the PCM momentarily turns on element pressure to the clutch circuits that don't have pressure to verify that the correct pressure switch closes. If the pressure switch does not close 2 times the DTC sets
DTC: P0845-2C	**- HYDRAULIC PRESSURE TEST:** In any forward gear with engine speed above 1000 RPM shortly after a shift and every minute thereafter. After a shift into a forward gear, with engine speed above 1000 RPM, the PCM momentarily turns on element pressure to the Clutch circuits that don't have pressure to identify the correct Pressure Switch closes. If the Pressure Switch does not close two times, the DTC sets.
DTC: P0846	**-2/4 PRESSURE SWITCH RATIONALITY:** Whenever the engine is running. The DTC is set if one of the pressure switches are open or closed at the wrong time in a given gear. If the problem is identified for 3 successive key starts, the transmission will go into Limp-in mode and the MIL will turn on after 10 seconds of vehicle operation.
DTC: P0846-2C	**- PRESSURE SWITCH RATIONALITY:** Continuously with the ignition on, engine running, with the transmission in gear. The DTC is set if the 2C Pressure Switch reads open or closed at the wrong time in a given gear.
DTC: P0847	**-SECONDARY OIL PRESSURE SENSOR CIRCUIT LOW:** Ignition on, system voltage between 9. 0 and 16. 0 Volts. Transmission temperature greater than -20° C (-4° F)No active DTCs from the following: Primary Oil Pressure Sensor High Sensor ground When the monitored voltage drops below 0. 09 Volts for the period of five seconds.
DTC: P0848	**-SECONDARY OIL PRESSURE SENSOR CIRCUIT HIGH:** Ignition on, system voltage between 9. 0 and 16. 0 Volts. Transmission temperature greater than -20° C (-4° F). No active DTCs from the following: Secondary Oil Pressure Sensor Low Sensor ground When the monitored voltage rises above 4. 7 Volts for the period of five seconds.
DTC: P084A-DC	**- HYDRAULIC PRESSURE TEST:** In any forward gear with engine speed above 1000 rpm, shortly after a shift and every minute thereafter. After a shift into a forward gear, with engine speed greater than 1000 rpm, the PCM momentarily turns on element pressure to the clutch circuits that don't have pressure to verify that the correct pressure switch closes. If the pressure switch does not close 2 times the DTC sets
DTC: P084B-DC	**- PRESSURE SWITCH RATIONALITY:** Whenever the engine is running. The DTC is set if one of the pressure switches are open or closed at the wrong time in a given gear. If the problem is identified for 3 successive key starts, the transmission will go into Limp-in mode and the MIL will turn on after 10 seconds of vehicle operation.

DTC	Trouble Code Title, Conditions, Possible Causes
DTC: P0850	**-PARK/NEUTRAL SWITCH PERFORMANCE:** Continuously with the transmission in Park, Neutral, or Drive and NOT in Limp-in mode. This code will set if the PCM detects an incorrect Park/Neutral switch state for a given mode of vehicle operation. Two trip fault. Three good trips to turn off the MIL.
DTC: P0850	**-PARK/NEUTRAL SWITCH PERFORMANCE:** Continuously with the transmission in Park, Neutral, or Drive and NOT in Limp-in mode. This code will set if the PCM detects an incorrect Park/Neutral switch state for a given mode of vehicle operation. One trip fault. Three good trips to turn off the MIL.
DTC: P0868	**-LINE PRESSURE LOW:** Continuously while driving in a forward gear. The Powertrain Control Module (PCM) continuously monitors Actual Line Pressure and compares it to Desired Line Pressure. If the Actual Line Pressure is more than 69 kPa (5 psi) below Desired Line Pressure while the PCS duty cycle is at or near its minimum value, this DTC will set.
DTC: P0868	**-LINE PRESSURE LOW:** Continuously while driving in a forward gear. The PCM continuously monitors Actual Line Pressure and compares it to Desired Line Pressure. If the Actual Line Pressure is more than 10 psi below Desired Line Pressure, this DTC will set.
DTC: P0869	**-LINE PRESSURE HIGH:** Continuously while driving in a forward gear. The Powertrain Control Module (PCM) continuously monitors Actual Line Pressure. If the Actual Line Pressure reading is greater than the highest Desired Line Pressure ever used in the current gear, while the Pressure Control Solenoid duty cycle is at or near its maximum value (which should result in minimum line pressure), the DTC will set.
DTC: P0869	**-LINE PRESSURE HIGH:** Continuously while driving in a forward gear. The Powertrain Control Module (PCM) continuously monitors Actual Line Pressure. If the Actual Line Pressure reading is greater than 827 kPa (120 psi), while the Pressure Control Solenoid duty cycle is at or near its maximum value (which should result in minimum line pressure) for 3. 5 seconds continuously, the DTC will set.
DTC: P0870	**-OD HYDRAULIC PRESSURE TEST:** In any forward gear with engine speed above 1000 rpm, shortly after a shift and every minute thereafter. After a shift into a forward gear, with engine speed greater than 1000 rpm, the PCM momentarily turns on element pressure to the clutch circuits that don't have pressure to identify the correct pressure switch closes. If the pressure switch does not close 2 times the DTC sets.
DTC: P0871	**-OD PRESSURE SWITCH RATIONALITY:** Whenever the engine is running. The DTC is set if one of the pressure switches are open or closed at the wrong time in a given gear. If the problem is identified for 3 successive key starts, the transmission will go into Limp-in mode and the MIL will turn on after 10 seconds of vehicle operation.
DTC: P0875	**-UD HYDRAULIC PRESSURE TEST:** In any forward gear with engine speed above 1000 RPM shortly after a shift and every minute thereafter. After a shift into a forward gear, with engine speed above 1000 RPM, the Powertrain Control Module (PCM) momentarily turns on element pressure to the Clutch circuits that don't have pressure to identify the correct Pressure Switch closes. If the Pressure Switch does not close two times, the DTC sets.
DTC: P0876	**-UD PRESSURE SWITCH RATIONALITY:** Continuously with the ignition on and engine running. This DTC is set if the UD pressure switch is in the wrong state for the current gear. For example, this code would be set if the UD pressure switch remained off while the transmission was in second gear.
DTC: P0882	**TCM POWER INPUT LOW:** When the ignition is turned from "OFF" position to "RUN" position and/or the ignition is turned from "START" position to "RUN" position. This DTC is set when there is less than 3. 0 volts present at the transmission control output circuits located in the Powertrain Control Module (PCM) when the Transmission Control System requests the power up of those circuits.
DTC: P0882	**TCM POWER INPUT LOW:** When the ignition is turned from "OFF" position to "RUN" position and/or the ignition is turned from "START" position to "RUN" position. This DTC is set when there is less than 3. 0 volts present at the transmission control output circuits located in the Powertrain Control Module (PCM) when the Transmission Control System request the power up of those circuits. **NOTE: Due to the integration of the Transmission Control Module and the Powertrain Control Module, both systems have their own power and ground circuits. .**
DTC: P0883	**TCM POWER INPUT HIGH:** When the ignition is turned from "OFF" position to "RUN" position and/or the ignition is turned from "START" position to "RUN" position. This DTC is set if the Powertrain Control Module senses greater than 3. 0 volts on the Transmission Control Relay Output circuits prior to a request from the PCM to energize the Transmission Control Relay.
DTC: P0884	**-POWER UP AT SPEED:** One time after each controller reset. **NOTE: the Transmission Control Module is integrated with Powertrain Control Module. The Transmission Control Module has separate powers and grounds specifically to its portion of the PCM.** This DTC will set if the PCM powers up and senses the vehicle in a valid forward gear (no PRNDL DTCs) with an output speed above 800 rpm, approximately 32 km/h or 20 mph.

DTC	Trouble Code Title, Conditions, Possible Causes
DTC: P0884	**-POWER UP AT SPEED:** When Powertrain Control Module initially powers up. Due to the integration of the Powertrain and Transmission Control Modules, the transmission part of the PCM has its own specific power and ground circuits. This DTC will set if the PCM powers up and senses the vehicle in a valid forward gear, with no PRNDL DTCs, and an output speed above 800 rpm, approximately 32Km/h or 20 mph.
DTC: P0888	**TRANSMISSION RELAY ALWAYS OFF:** When the ignition is turned from "OFF" position to "RUN" position and/or the ignition is turned from "START" position to "RUN" position. This DTC is set when there is less than 3. 0 volts present at the transmission control output circuits located in the Powertrain Control Module (PCM) when the Transmission Control System requests the power up of those circuits.
DTC: P0888	**TRANSMISSION RELAY ALWAYS OFF:** When the ignition is turned from "OFF" position to "RUN" position and/or the ignition is turned from "START" position to "RUN" position. This DTC is set when there is less than 3. 0 volts present at the transmission control output circuits located in the Powertrain Control Module (PCM) when the Transmission Control System request the power up of those circuits. **NOTE: Due to the integration of the Transmission Control Module and the Powertrain Control Module, both systems have their own power and ground circuits. .**
DTC: P0890	**-SWITCHED BATTERY:** One time after a reset (ignition key turned to the RUN position or after cranking engine). A fault is set if voltage greater than 4. 5 volts is detected for 7 msec on any of the pressure switch circuits before the relay is energized. The transmission is placed in Limp-In. The MIL is on after 10 seconds. of vehicle operation.
DTC: P0890	**-SWITCHED BATTERY:** One time after a reset (ignition turned to the RUN position or after cranking engine). A fault is set if the sensed voltage on any of the pressure switch circuits is greater than 4. 5 volts for the period of 7 msec before a request by the Transmission Control System requests the Transmission Control Output circuit to be energized. The transmission is placed in Limp-In and the MIL is illuminated after 10 seconds of vehicle operation.
DTC: P0891	**TRANSMISSION RELAY ALWAYS ON:** When the ignition is turned from "OFF" position to "RUN" position and/or the ignition is turned from "START" position to "RUN" position. This DTC is set if the Powertrain Control Module senses greater than 3. 0 volts on the Transmission Control Relay Output circuits prior to a request from the PCM to TIPM to energize the Transmission Output circuits.
DTC: P0897	**TRANSMISSION FLUID DETERIORATED:** Each transition from full EMCC to partial EMCC for A/C bump prevention. DTC set if 20 occurrences of a turbine acceleration sum. Fault Set Time: 20 transitions from full EMCC to partial EMCC. Transmission will not use partial EMCC. Established for A/C bump prevention.
DTC: P0928	**-BTSI CONTROL CIRCUIT:** Continuously with the ignition on. The Diagnostic trouble Code (DTC) will set if the high side driver detects a short to ground for 10 seconds.
DTC: P0928	**-BTSI CONTROL CIRCUIT:** With the ignition on. The Cluster detects a fault on the (K321) Brake Transmission Shift Interlock Solenoid Unlock circuit.
DTC: P0928	**-BTSI CONTROL CIRCUIT:** Continuously with the ignition on. The DTC will set if the high side driver detects a short to ground for 10 seconds.
DTC: P0928-11	**-BTSI CONTROL - CIRCUIT SHORT TO GROUND:** With the ignition on. Brake pedal applied. The BCM detects a short to ground on the (K321) BTSI Control circuit for more than one second.
DTC: P0930	**-BTSI CONTROL CIRCUIT LOW :** Continuously with the ignition on. The DTC will set if the high side driver detects a short to ground for 10 seconds.
DTC: P0930	**-BTSI CONTROL CIRCUIT LOW:** Continuously with the ignition on. The DTC will set if the high side driver detects a short to ground for 10 seconds.
DTC: P0930	**-BTSI CONTROL CIRCUIT LOW:** With the ignition in the Unlock or Run position and the driver's foot applied to the brake pedal. The Instrument Cluster detects a low value on the BTSI Solenoid Control circuit.
DTC: P0931	**-BTSI CONTROL CIRCUIT HIGH :** Continuously with the ignition key on. The DTC will set if the high side driver detects an open load for 10 seconds.
DTC: P0931	**-BTSI CONTROL CIRCUIT HIGH - COLUMN SHIFT:** Continuously with the ignition key on. The DTC will set if the high side driver detects an open load for 10 seconds.
DTC: P0931	**-BTSI CONTROL CIRCUIT HIGH:** With the ignition in the Unlock or Run position and the driver's foot applied to the brake pedal. The Instrument Cluster detects a high value on the BTSI Solenoid Control circuit.

DTC	Trouble Code Title, Conditions, Possible Causes
DTC: P0932	**-LINE PRESSURE SENSOR CIRCUIT:** Continuously with the ignition on, engine running, with the transmission in gear. The Powertrain Control Module (PCM) continuously monitors Actual Line Pressure and compares it to Desired Line Pressure. If the Actual Line Pressure reading is more than 172. 4 kPa (25 psi) higher than the Desired Line Pressure, but is less than the highest Line Pressure ever used in the current gear, the DTC sets.
DTC: P0933	**-HYDRAULIC PRESSURE SENSOR RANGE/PERFORMANCE:** Continuously with the ignition on, engine running, with the transmission in gear. The Powertrain Control Module (PCM) continuously monitors Actual Line Pressure and compares it to Desired Line Pressure. If the Actual Line Pressure reading is more than 172. 4 kPa (25 psi) higher than the Desired Line Pressure, but is less than the highest Line Pressure ever used in the current gear, the DTC sets.
DTC: P0934	**-LINE PRESSURE SENSOR CIRCUIT LOW:** Continuously with the ignition on and engine running. This DTC will set when the monitored Line Pressure Sensor voltage is less than or equal to 0. 35 of a volt for 0. 18 of a second.
DTC: P0935	**-LINE PRESSURE SENSOR CIRCUIT HIGH:** Continuously with ignition on and engine running. This DTC will set if the monitored Line Pressure Sensor voltage is greater than or equal to 4. 75 volts for the period of 0. 18 of a second.
DTC: P0944	**-LOSS OF HYDRAULIC PUMP PRIME:** If the transmission is slipping in any forward gear and all the pressure switches are not indicating pressure, a loss of prime test is run. If the transmission begins to slip in a forward gear and all the pressure switch(s) that should be closed are open a loss of prime test begins. Available elements are turned on by the Powertrain Control Module (PCM) to see if pump prime exists. The DTC sets if no pressure switch(s) respond.
DTC: P0944	**-LOSS OF HYDRAULIC PUMP PRIME:** Every 350 msec the transmission begins to slip in any forward gear, and the pressure switch or switches that should be closed for a given gear are open, a loss of prime test begins. All available elements (in 1st gear LR, 2/4 and OD, in 2nd, 3rd, and 4th gear 2/4 and OD) are turned on by the Powertrain Control Module (PCM) to see if pump prime exists. The code is set if none of the pressure switches respond. The PCM will continue to run the loss of prime test until pump pressure returns. The vehicle will not move or the transmission will slip. Normal operation will continue if pump prime returns.
DTC: P0952	**-AUTOSTICK INPUT CIRCUIT LOW:** Whenever the engine is running. The transmission is not in the AutoStick® position and the upshift or downshift is reporting closed - below 0. 3 of a volt or if both switches are reported closed at the same time.
DTC: P0957	**-AUTOSTICK CIRCUIT LOW:** Whenever the engine is running. The transmission is not in the AutoStick® position and the upshift or downshift is reporting closed - below 0. 71 of a volt or if both switches are reported closed at the same time.
DTC: P0957	**-AUTOSTICK CIRCUIT LOW:** Ignition on and engine running and after 0. 5 seconds. When the monitored AutoStick Up/Down Sense circuit voltage drops below 0. 35 volts.
DTC: P0958	**-AUTOSTICK CIRCUIT HIGH:** Ignition on and engine running and after 0. 5 of a second. When the monitored AutoStick Up/Down Sense circuit voltage rises above 4. 75 volts.
DTC: P0962	**-PRESSURE CONTROL SOLENOID A CONTROL CIRCUIT LOW:** Ignition on with a system voltage between 9. 0 and 16. 0 volts. If the monitored line pressure solenoid voltage is less than 70% of the target line pressure solenoid voltage for the period of 1. 0 second.
DTC: P0963	**-PRESSURE CONTROL SOLENOID A CONTROL CIRCUIT HIGH:** Ignition on with a system voltage between 9. 0 and 16. 0 volts. No Line Pressure Solenoid Circuit Low DTC present. When the target line pressure solenoid current is greater than 0. 75 of an amp while the monitored line pressure solenoid current is less than 0. 4 of an amp for the period of five seconds.
DTC: P0966	**-PRESSURE CONTROL SOLENOID B CONTROL CIRCUIT LOW:** Ignition on with a system voltage between 9. 0 and 16. 0 volts. If the monitored secondary pressure solenoid voltage is less than 70% of the target secondary pressure solenoid voltage for the period of 1. 0second.
DTC: P0967	**-PRESSURE CONTROL SOLENOID B CONTROL CIRCUIT HIGH:** Ignition on with a system voltage between 9. 0 and 16. 0 volts. No Secondary Pressure Solenoid Low DTC present. When the target secondary pressure solenoid current is greater than 0. 75 of an amp while the monitored secondary pressure solenoid current is less than0. 4 of an amp for the period of five seconds.
DTC: P0987-4C	**- HYDRAULIC PRESSURE TEST:** In any forward gear with engine speed above 1000 rpm shortly after a shift and every minute thereafter. After a shift into a forward gear, with engine speed above 1000 rpm, the Powertrain Control Module (PCM) momentarily turns on element pressure to the Clutch circuits that don't have pressure to identify the correct Pressure Switch closes. If the Pressure Switch does not close two times, the DTC sets.

DTC	Trouble Code Title, Conditions, Possible Causes
DTC: P0988-4C	**- PRESSURE SWITCH RATIONALITY:** Continuously with the ignition on, engine running, with the transmission in gear. The DTC is set if the 4C Pressure Switch reads open or closed at the wrong time in a given gear .
DTC: P0992	**-2/4/OD HYDRAULIC PRESSURE TEST:** In any forward gear with engine speed above 1000 rpm, shortly after a shift and every minute thereafter. After a shift into a forward gear, with engine speed greater than 1000 rpm, the PCM momentarily turns on element pressure to the clutch circuits that do not have pressure to identify that the correct pressure switch closes. If the pressure switch does not close 2 times the DTC sets.

OBD II Trouble Code List (P1XXX Codes)

DTC	Trouble Code Title, Conditions, Possible Causes
DTC: P1009-00	**-HUMIDITY SENSOR MODULE:** With the ignition on. The Humidity Sensor detects an internal failure.
DTC: P1103-DC	**- TO AC CONVERTER SWITCH STUCK:** With the ignition on. If the Instrument Cluster/Cabin Compartment Node (CCN) senses the Inverter switch input for more than 10 seconds.
DTC: P1115	**-GENERAL TEMPERATURE RATIONALITY:** With the ignition on and battery voltage greater than 10 volts. AAT, ECT, and IAT sensor inputs are compared during a cold start. After start up, the values are monitored. If one of the readings is not plausible for two consecutive trips, a DTC is stored. Three good trips turns off the MIL.
DTC: P1115	**-GENERAL TEMPERATURE RATIONALITY:** Engine off time is greater than 480 minutes and the vehicle has been driven for one minute over 35 mph. Ambient temperature is greater than -64° C (-83° F). Once the vehicle is soaked for a calibrated engine off time and then driven over calibrated speed and load conditions for some calibrated time, the PCM compares the ambient air, engine coolant, and intake air temperature sensor values. If the values of all the three sensors disagree with one another, a general temperature sensor irrationality is declared. Two Trip Fault. Three good trips to turn off the MIL.
DTC: P1128	**-CLOSED LOOP FUELING NOT ACHIEVED - BANK 1:** Engine running in closed loop mode. Enable conditions are met and the 02 sensor has not been in closed loop control at least once on each of the two consecutive trips, the MIL illuminates and the DTC is set. Two Trip Fault. Three good trips to turn off the MIL
DTC: P1128	**-CLOSED LOOP FUELING NOT ACHIEVED - BANK 1:** With engine run time and coolant temperature above a calibrated value. The Powertrain Control Module (PCM) detects a condition where the vehicle has remained in open loop fuel control, from a start-up condition, longer than a calibrated amount of time, when conditions would have otherwise expected closed loop operation. Two Trip Fault. Three good trips to turn off the MIL.
DTC: P1129	**-CLOSED LOOP FUELING NOT ACHIEVED - BANK 2:** Engine running in closed loop mode. Enable conditions are met and the 02 sensor has not been in closed loop control at least once on each of the two consecutive trips, the MIL illuminates and the DTC is set. Two Trip Fault. Three good trips to turn off the MIL
DTC: P113D	**-02 SENSOR 1/1 SLOW RESPONSE:** With the Engine Coolant Temperature (ECT) at least 60°C (140°F), engine RPM between1000 and 2750, minimum engine run time of 20 seconds and Manifold Absolute Pressure (MAP) reading is between 21 - 96 Kpa (6. 2 - 28. 3in Hg). The Powertrain Control Module (PCM) detects that the Oxygen Sensor signal does not switch adequately at high frequency. Two Trip Fault. Three good trips to turn off the MIL.
DTC: P113D	**-02 SENSOR 1/1 SLOW RESPONSE:** With the Engine Coolant Temperature (ECT) at least 60°C (140°F), engine RPM between 1000 and 2750, minimum engine run time of 20 seconds and Manifold Absolute Pressure (MAP) reading is between 21 - 96 Kpa (6. 2 - 28. 3 in Hg). The Powertrain Control Module (PCM) detects that the Oxygen Sensor signal does not switch adequately at high frequency. Two Trip Fault. Three good trips to turn off the MIL.
DTC: P113E	**-02 SENSOR 2/1 SLOW RESPONSE (HIGH FREQUENCY):** With the ECT at least 60°C (140°F), engine RPM between 1000 and 2750, minimum engine run time of 20 seconds and Manifold Absolute Pressure (MAP) readings between 21 - 96 Kpa (6. 2 - 28. 3 in Hg). The Powertrain Control Module (PCM) detects that the Oxygen Sensor signal does not switch adequately at high frequency. Two Trip Fault. Three good trips to turn off the MIL.
DTC: P1239	**-ENGINE OIL TEMPERATURE TOO LOW:** The engine oil temperature has dropped below a calibrated temperature value. Engine start up. The Engine Oil temperature rises slower than a calibrated modeled temperature. When the actual oil temperature falls below the low boundary of the calibrated modeled temperature for three minutes the fault is set. Two trip fault. Three good trips to turn off the MIL.

DTC	Trouble Code Title, Conditions, Possible Causes
DTC: P1270	**-INTAKE MANIFOLD RUNNER (SWIRL) PERFORMANCE:** With the ignition on and the Intake Swirl Servo Motor command on. The Engine Control Module (ECM) detects that the (N117) Intake Swirl Servo Motor Control circuit voltage is implausible.
DTC: P1272	**-A/C CLUTCH CONTROL CIRCUIT 2 LOW :** With the ignition on. Battery voltage greater than 10 volts. A/C Switch on. A shorted condition is detected in the A/C clutch control circuit. One Trip Fault. Three good trips to turn off the MIL.
DTC: P1273	**-A/C CLUTCH CONTROL CIRCUIT 2 HIGH:** With the ignition on. Battery voltage greater than 10 volts. A/C Switch on. A shorted high condition has been detected in the A/C Clutch Control output circuit by the TIPM. One Trip Fault. Three good trips to turn off the MIL.
DTC: P1274	**-A/C CLUTCH CONTROL CIRCUIT 2 OPEN:** With the ignition on. Battery voltage greater than 10. 4 volts. TIPM requesting A/C Clutch operation. An open condition has been detected in the A/C Clutch Control Output circuit by the TIPM. One Trip Fault. Three good trips to turn off the MIL.
DTC: P1276-11	**-STARTER CONTROL 2 - CIRCUIT SHORT TO GROUND:** Battery voltage greater than 10. 4 volts. Body Control Module (BCM) commanding Starter operation. The BCM detects a lower than expected voltage level on the starter relay control circuit for more than one second.
DTC: P1277	**-STARTER CONTROL CIRCUIT 2 LOW:** With the ignition on. Battery voltage greater than 10. 4 volts and Main Relay is on. Totally Integrated Power Module (TIPM) requesting Starter operation. Actual Starter state is not equal to desired state. One Trip Fault. Three good trips to turn off the Malfunction Indicator Lamp (MIL).
DTC: P1278	**-STARTER CONTROL CIRCUIT 2 HIGH:** With the ignition on. Battery voltage greater than 10. 4 volts and Main Relay is on. Totally Integrated Power Module (TIPM) requesting Starter operation. Actual Starter state is not equal to desired state. One Trip Fault. Three good trips to turn off the MIL.
DTC: P1279	**-STARTER CONTROL CIRCUIT 2 OPEN:** With the ignition on. Battery voltage greater than 10. 4 volts and Main Relay is on. Totally Integrated Power Module (TIPM) requesting Starter operation. Actual Starter state is not equal to desired state. One Trip Fault. Three good trips to turn off the MIL.
DTC: P127A	**-STARTER CONTROL CIRCUIT 2 OVERCURRENT:** With the ignition on. Battery voltage greater than 10. 4 volts and Main Relay is on. Totally Integrated Power Module (TIPM) requesting Starter operation. An overcurrent condition is detected in the Starter control output circuit. One Trip Fault. Three good trips to turn off the MIL.
DTC: P127C	**-FUEL PUMP CONTROL CIRCUIT 2 LOW:** With the ignition on. The battery voltage greater than 10. 4 volts and the Main Relay on. Totally Integrated Power Module (TIPM) requesting Fuel Pump operation. The actual Fuel Pump state is not equal to the desired state. One Trip Fault. Three good trips to turn off the Malfunction Indicator Lamp (MIL).
DTC: P127D	**-FUEL PUMP CONTROL CIRCUIT 2 HIGH:** With the ignition on. The battery voltage greater than 10. 4 volts and the Main Relay on. Totally Integrated Power Module (TIPM) requesting Fuel Pump operation. Actual Fuel Pump state is not equal to the desired state. One Trip Fault. Three good trips to turn off the MIL.
DTC: P127E	**-FUEL PUMP CONTROL CIRCUIT 2 OPEN:** With the ignition on. Battery voltage greater than 10. 4 volts and the Main relay is on. Totally Integrated Power Module (TIPM) requesting Fuel Pump operation. Actual Fuel Pump state is not equal to desired state. One Trip Fault. Three good trips to turn off the MIL.
DTC: P127F	**-FUEL PUMP CONTROL CIRCUIT 2 OVERCURRENT:** With the ignition on. The battery voltage greater than 10. 4 volts. Totally Integrated Power Module (TIPM) requesting fuel pump operation. An overcurrent condition is detected in the Fuel Pump control output circuit. One Trip Fault. Three good trips to turn off the MIL.
DTC: P128B	**TCM POWER CONTROL CIRCUIT 2 LOW:** With the ignition on. Battery voltage greater than 10. 0 volts. A shorted condition is detected in the Transmission Control Output circuit.
DTC: P128B	**TCM POWER CONTROL CIRCUIT 2 LOW:** With the ignition on. Battery voltage greater than 10. 0 volts. The Totally Integrated Power Module (TIPM) has detected a short to ground condition in the Transmission Control Output circuit.
DTC: P128C	**TCM POWER CONTROL CIRCUIT 2 HIGH - 41TE NGC:** With the ignition on with the battery voltage greater than 10. 0 volts. The Totally Integrated Power Module (TIPM) has detected voltage on the Transmission Control Output circuit when none should be present.

DTC	Trouble Code Title, Conditions, Possible Causes
DTC: P128C	**TCM POWER CONTROL CIRCUIT 2 HIGH:** With the ignition on. Battery voltage greater than 10 volts. A shorted condition is detected in the TIPM Transmission Control Output circuit.
DTC: P128D	**TCM POWER CONTROL CIRCUIT 2 OPEN:** With the ignition on. Battery voltage greater than 10 volts. An open condition of the Transmission Control Output circuit is detected by the Totally Integrated Power Module (TIPM).
DTC: P128D	**TCM POWER CONTROL CIRCUIT 2 OPEN:** With the ignition on. Battery voltage greater than 10. 0 volts. The Totally Integrated Power Module (TIPM) has detected an open condition on the Transmission Control Output circuit.
DTC: P128E	**TCM POWER CONTROL CIRCUIT 2 OVERCURRENT:** With the ignition on. Battery voltage greater than 10 volts. An overcurrent condition is detected in the TCM Power Control circuit. One Trip Fault. Three good trips to turn off the MIL.
DTC: P128E	**TCM POWER CONTROL CIRCUIT 2 OVERCURRENT:** With the ignition on. Battery voltage greater than 10. 0 volts. The Totally Integrated Power Module (TIPM) has detected an overcurrent condition in the Transmission Control Output circuit.
DTC: P1404	**-EGR POSITION SENSOR RATIONALITY CLOSED:** Engine running. The EGR flow or valve movement is not what is expected. A rationality error has been detected for the EGR Open Position Performance. Two trip fault.
DTC: P1411	**-CYLINDER 1 REACTIVATION CONTROL PERFORMANCE:** Transition from 8 to 4 cylinder mode. The MDS fails to active and take place for cylinder 1. One trip fault.
DTC: P1411	**-CYLINDER 1 REACTIVATION CONTROL PERFORMANCE:** Transition from 4 to 8 cylinder mode. The MDS fails to disengage for cylinder 1.
DTC: P1414	**-CYLINDER 4 REACTIVATION CONTROL PERFORMANCE:** Transition from 4 to 8 cylinder mode. The MDS fails to disengage for cylinder 4.
DTC: P1414	**-CYLINDER 4 REACTIVATION CONTROL PERFORMANCE:** Transition from 8 to 4 cylinder mode. The MDS fails to active and take place for cylinder 4. One trip fault.
DTC: P1416	**-CYLINDER 6 REACTIVATION CONTROL PERFORMANCE:** Transition from 8 to 4 cylinder mode. The MDS fails to active and take place for cylinder 6. One trip fault.
DTC: P1416	**-CYLINDER 6 REACTIVATION CONTROL PERFORMANCE:** Transition from 4 to 8 cylinder mode. The MDS fails to disengage for cylinder 6.
DTC: P1417	**-CYLINDER 7 REACTIVATION CONTROL PERFORMANCE:** Transition from 8 to 4 cylinder mode. The MDS fails to active and take place for cylinder 7. One trip fault.
DTC: P1417	**-CYLINDER 7 REACTIVATION CONTROL PERFORMANCE:** Transition from 4 to 8 cylinder mode. The MDS fails to disengage for cylinder 7.
DTC: P1452	**-DIFFERENTIAL PRESSURE SENSOR HOSE PERFORMANCE:** With the engine running. Differential Pressure Sensor signal indicates (–)10 hpa for 15. 0 seconds.
DTC: P1453	**-DIFFERENTIAL PRESSURE SENSOR HOSE BLOCKED:** With the engine running. The ECM detects differential pressure that are lower than expected for certain engine operating conditions for 2. 0 seconds.
DTC: P1454	**-DIFFERENTIAL PRESSURE SENSOR FLOW TOO HIGH:** With the engine running. The ECM detects incorrect exhaust flow through the particulate filter during certain engine operating conditions.
DTC: P1462	**-FUEL LEVEL OUTPUT CIRCUIT LOW:** With the ignition switch on. The Vehicle System Integration Module (VSIM) has detected the Fuel Level Status Signal circuit below a calibrated value.
DTC: P1463	**-FUEL LEVEL OUTPUT CIRCUIT HIGH:** With the ignition switch on. The Vehicle System Integration Module (VSIM) has detected the Fuel Level Status Signal circuit above a calibrated value.
DTC: P1501	**-VEHICLE SPEED SENSOR 1/2 CORRELATION - DRIVE WHEELS:** Ignition on and vehicle moving. Cruise is learned and customer is trying to use the Cruise. The PCM recognizes rear wheel speed is greater than front wheel speed. One trip fault.

DTC	Trouble Code Title, Conditions, Possible Causes
DTC: P1501	**-VEHICLE SPEED SENSOR 1/2 CORRELATION - DRIVE WHEELS:** With the ignition on and battery voltage greater than 10. 4 volts. The Powertrain Control Module (PCM) detects an implausible voltage on the Vehicle Speed Sensor circuit.
DTC: P1502	**-VEHICLE SPEED SENSOR 1/2 CORRELATION - NON DRIVE WHEELS:** Ignition on and vehicle moving. Brake pedal must not be applied. The PCM recognizes front axle speed is greater than rear axle speed. One trip fault.
DTC: P1502	**-VEHICLE SPEED SENSOR 1/2 CORRELATION - NON-DRIVE WHEELS:** With the engine running, transmission not neutral, brakes not applied, and engine RPM greater than 1500. This code will set if the Powertrain Control Module (PCM) receives an implausible vehicle speed signal from the Totally Integrated Power Module (TIPM).
DTC: P1504	**-VEHICLE SPEED OUTPUT CIRCUIT LOW:** With the ignition switch on. The Vehicle System Integration Module (VSIM) has detected the Vehicle Speed Signal circuit below a calibrated value.
DTC: P1505	**-VEHICLE SPEED OUTPUT CIRCUIT HIGH:** With the ignition switch on. The Vehicle System Integration Module (VSIM) has detected the Vehicle Speed Signal circuit above a calibrated value.
DTC: P150D	**-COLD START ROUGH IDLE - OPEN THROTTLE START:** Any time the engine is running and the adaptive numerator has been successfully updated. If the PCM detects that the variation in crankshaft speed between each cylinder exceeds a calibrated value, based on engine rpm and load, a fault is set.
DTC: P1513	**-STARTER REQUEST SWITCH STUCK:** With the ignition on and battery voltage greater than 10. 4 volts. The Powertrain Control Module (PCM) detects voltage on the (F963) Start Enable circuit for a specified time after the engine is running.
DTC: P1519	**-CRUISE CONTROL FRONT DISTANCE SENSOR LENS CRACKED MISSING:** Continuously monitored with the ignition in run and the Adaptive Cruise Control(ACC) Module in normal mode. ACC Module detects that the lens is damaged or missing. The ACC module will disable the ACC system and the SERVICE ACC message will display in the Cabin Compartment Node (CCN). Once the Diagnostic Trouble Code (DTC) goes to stored, the ACC system will return to normal operation. The DTC will be cleared after the ACC Module sees 100 consecutive key cycles of the STOREDDTC.
DTC: P1521	**-INCORRECT ENGINE OIL TYPE:** Engine Running. Using the oil pressure, oil temperature and other vital engine inputs the Powertrain Control Module (PCM) can determine the engine oil viscosity. Incorrect viscosity will affect the operation of the MDS by delaying cylinder activation .
DTC: P1524	**-OIL PRESSURE OUT OF RANGE - CAMSHAFT ADVANCE/RETARD DISABLED:** Engine running. RPM greater than or equal to 1100. Oil temperature less than or equal to 100° C (212° F)The engine oil pressure never reaches the calibrated specification to allow the VCT activation. One trip fault.
DTC: P1572	**-BRAKE PEDAL STUCK ON:** With the ignition on and battery voltage greater than 10. 4 Volts. The Powertrain Control Module (PCM) detects that the state of brake switch does not change as expected.
DTC: P1572	**-BRAKE PEDAL STUCK ON:** Ignition on. In plant mode only. PCM recognizes the Brake Pedal could not electrically indicate the applied (On) position with both switch inputs. One trip fault.
DTC: P1572	**-BRAKE PEDAL STUCK ON:** With the gear selector in drive, vehicle speed above a minimum value, and battery voltage greater than 10. 4 volts. The Powertrain Control Module (PCM) recognizes the Brake Pedal could not electrically indicate the applied (On) position with both switch inputs. One trip fault.
DTC: P1573	**-BRAKE PEDAL STUCK OFF:** Ignition on, In plant mode passed the Applied test. PCM recognizes the Brake Pedal could not electronically indicate the released (Off) position with both switches. If P1572 sets, P1573 will also set. One trip fault.
DTC: P1573	**-BRAKE PEDAL STUCK OFF:** Ignition on and battery voltage above 10. 4 Volts. The Powertrain Control Module (PCM) recognizes the Brake Pedal could not electronically indicate the released (Off) position with both switches. If P1572 sets, P1573 will also set. One trip fault.
DTC: P1573	**-BRAKE PEDAL STUCK OFF:** With the ignition on and battery voltage greater than 10. 4 Volts. The Powertrain Control Module (PCM) detects that the state of Brake Signal 2 does not change as expected.
DTC: P1593	**-SPEED CONTROL SWITCH 1/2 STUCK:** With the ignition on and battery voltage greater than 10. 4 Volts. The Powertrain Control Module (PCM) detects that the (V71) S/C Signal 1 voltage does not match the (V72) S/C Signal 2 voltage.

DTC	Trouble Code Title, Conditions, Possible Causes
DTC: P1593	**-SPEED CONTROL SWITCH 1 STUCK:** Ignition on. Cruise Switch inputs are not coherent with each other. Example: The Powertrain Control Module (PCM) is reading Switch No. 1 as Accel and Switch No. 2 as Coast at the same time. One trip fault.
DTC: P1593	**-SPEED CONTROL SWITCH 1/2 STUCK:** Ignition on. One of the S/C Switches is mechanically stuck in the On/Off, Resume/Accel, or Set position for too long. One trip fault.
DTC: P1593	**-SPEED CONTROL SWITCH 1/2 STUCK:** Continuously with the ignition on. Fault signifies when the switch voltage does not register a valid cruise position.
DTC: P1593-2A	**-SPEED CONTROL SWITCH 1/2 STUCK:** Continuously with the ignition on. Fault signifies any Speed Control Switch is held/stuck for greater than 120 seconds.
DTC: P1602	**-PCM NOT PROGRAMMED:** Ignition on and battery voltage greater than 10 volts. The Powertrain Control Module (PCM) has not been programmed.
DTC: P1607	**-PCM INTERNAL SHUTDOWN TIMER SLOW RATIONALITY:** The Powertrain Control Module (PCM) internal timer is continuously monitored. Upon power up, the Powertrain Control Module (PCM) compares the change in engine coolant temp sensor since last engine shut down and compares it to the amount of time the engine was turned off. If not enough time has occurred to account for the difference in engine coolant temperature then the fault will set. Two Trip Fault. Three good trips to turn off the MIL.
DTC: P1607	**-PCM INTERNAL SHUTDOWN TIMER SLOW RATIONALITY:** With the engine running after a cycle when a complete engine warm up was achieved, the difference between engine coolant temperature and ambient air temperature less than or equal to 10° C (50° F), and battery voltage greater than 10 volts. This DTC sets if the engine coolant temp does not drop enough or drops too much during engine off time. This DTC may also set if the controller timer is inaccurate. Two Trip Fault. Three good trips to turn off the MIL.
DTC: P160A	**-ECU OVERTEMPERATURE:** Continuously monitored with the engine running, the Adaptive Cruise Control (ACC)Module voltage at battery voltage, and the ACC Module in normal mode. ACC Module detects ambient temperatures greater than 85°C (185°F). The ACC module will disable the ACC system and the ACC UNAVAILABLE message will displaying the Cabin Compartment Node (CCN). Once the Diagnostic Trouble Code(DTC) goes to stored, the ACC system will return to normal operation. The DTC will be cleared after the ACC Module sees 100 consecutive key cycles of the STORED DTC.
DTC: P1614	**-ECU RESET/RECOVERY OCCURRED:** Continuously monitored with the engine running and the Adaptive Cruise Control (ACC) Module in normal mode. The power supply was interrupted for less than 100ms. The ACC module will disable the ACC system and the ACC UNAVAILABLE message will displaying the Cabin Compartment Node (CCN). Once the Diagnostic Trouble Code (DTC) goes to stored, the ACC system will return to normal operation. The DTC will be cleared after the ACC Module sees 100consecutive key cycles of the STORED DTC.
DTC: P1618	**-SENSOR REFERENCE VOLTAGE 1 ERRATIC:** With the ignition on. The Powertrain Control Module (PCM) detects that the 5 volt supply circuit voltage is below the minimum acceptable value. One Trip Fault. ETC light is flashing.
DTC: P1618	**-SENSOR REFERENCE VOLTAGE 1 CIRCUIT ERRATIC:** With the ignition on. The Powertrain Control Module (PCM) detects an excessive voltage variation on the5-Volt supply circuit.
DTC: P1618	**-SENSOR REFERENCE VOLTAGE 1 CIRCUIT ERRATIC:** Ignition on. When the PCM recognizes the Primary 5-volt Supply circuit voltage is varying too much too quickly. One Trip Fault. ETC light is flashing.
DTC: P1618	**-SENSOR REFERENCE VOLTAGE 1 CIRCUIT ERRATIC:** Ignition on. When the Powertrain Control Module (PCM) recognizes the Primary 5-Volt Supply circuit voltage is varying too much too quickly. One Trip Fault. ETC light is flashing.
DTC: P161A	**-ECU IN-PLANT MODE ACTIVE:** Continuously monitored with the ignition key in run, the Adaptive Cruise Control (ACC) Module voltage at battery voltage, and the ACC Module in normal mode. ACC Module is in the In-Plant mode. The ACC module will disable the ACC system and the ACC PLANT MODE message will display in the Cabin Compartment Node (CCN). Once the Diagnostic Trouble Code (DTC) goes to stored, the ACC system will return to normal operation. After a successful learning process, the active DTC will be cleared automatically.
DTC: P161B	**-BATTERY DISCONNECT / TCM INTERNAL:** One time at every ignition on cycle. When the calculated checksum does not equal the stored checksum configuration or loss of power to the controller. It takes one trip of problem identification to set the MIL.
DTC: P1628	**-SENSOR REFERENCE VOLTAGE 2 ERRATIC:** With the ignition on. The Powertrain Control Module (PCM) detects that the 5 volt supply circuit voltage is below the minimum acceptable value. One Trip Fault. ETC light is flashing.

DTC	Trouble Code Title, Conditions, Possible Causes
DTC: P1628	**-SENSOR REFERENCE VOLTAGE CIRCUIT ERRATIC:** With the ignition on. The Powertrain Control Module (PCM) detects an excessive voltage variation on the 5-Volt supply circuit.
DTC: P1629	**TCM INTERNAL - SOLENOID SUPPLY/ WATCHDOG:** Continuously with the ignition on. If the TCM detects voltage on the Solenoid Supply Voltage circuit when the TCM request the circuit to be off.
DTC: P1631	**TCM INTERNAL- PROCESSOR CLOCK PERFORMANCE:** Continuously with the ignition on. If the TCM detects an error with the controllers internal clock.
DTC: P1632	**TCM INTERNAL - TEST INTERNAL WATCHDOG PERFORMANCE:** Continuously with the ignition on. If the TCM detects an error with the controllers internal watchdog.
DTC: P1633	**TCM INTERNAL - TEST EXTERNAL WATCHDOG PERFORMANCE:** Continuously with the ignition on. If the TCM detects an error with the controllers external watchdog failed the power up test.
DTC: P1634	**TCM INTERNAL- INTERNAL WATCHDOG PERFORMANCE:** Continuously with the ignition on. If the TCM microprocessor internal watchdog detects an error.
DTC: P1636	**TCM INTERNAL- EXTERNAL WATCHDOG PERFORMANCE:** Continuously with the ignition on. If the TCM watch dog circuitry external to the microprocessor detects an error.
DTC: P1637	**TCM INTERNAL-EEPROM PERFORMANCE:** Continuously with the ignition on. If the TCM indicates that there is an internal error with the controllers Random Access Memory.
DTC: P1638	**TCM INTERNAL-CAN 1 RAM PERFORMANCE:** Continuously with the ignition on. If the TCM detects an internal error with the controllers Random Access Memory (RAM) on the CAN controller 1 section of the microprocessor.
DTC: P1639	**TCM INTERNAL-CAN 2 RAM PERFORMANCE:** Continuously with the ignition on. If the TCM detects an internal error with the controllers Random Access Memory (RAM) on the CAN controller 2 section of the microprocessor.
DTC: P1644	**-INCORRECT VARIANT/CONFIGURATION:** Continuously with the ignition on. If the TCM detects that the variables that dictate the vehicle application are not present.
DTC: P1644	**-INCORRECT VARIANT/CONFIGURATION:** Continuously monitored with the engine running, the Adaptive Cruise Control (ACC) Module voltage at battery voltage, and the ACC Module in normal mode. Current and original Vehicle Configuration do not match. The ACC module will disable the ACC system and the SERVICE ACC message will displaying the Cabin Compartment Node (CCN). Once the DTC goes to stored, the ACC system will return to normal operation. After a successful learning process, the active DTC will be cleared automatically.
DTC: P1648	**-GLOW PLUG MODULE INTERNAL:** With the ignition on. The Glow Plug Control Module reports an internal fault to the ECM.
DTC: P1649	**-GLOW PLUG MODULE POWER SUPPLY CIRCUIT:** With the ignition on and the Glow Plugs commanded on. The Glow Plug Control Module reports a power supply circuit fault to the ECM.
DTC: P164A	**-MIL OUTPUT CIRCUIT LOW:** With the ignition switch on. The Vehicle System Integration Module (VSIM) has detected the Malfunction Indicator Signal circuit below a calibrated value.
DTC: P164B	**-MIL OUTPUT CIRCUIT HIGH:** With the ignition switch on. The Vehicle System Integration Module (VSIM) has detected the Malfunction Indicator Signal circuit above a calibrated value.
DTC: P1661	**-SENSOR GROUND REFERENCE CIRCUIT:** With the ignition on and a system voltage between 9. 0 and 16. 0 volts. When all are present for the period of 200 msec:
DTC: P1666	**-CRUISE CONTROL MODULE INTERNAL:** Continuously monitored with the engine running, the Adaptive Cruise Control (ACC) Module voltage at battery voltage, and the ACC Module in normal mode. Internal ACC Module failure detected. The ACC module will disable the ACC system and the SERVICE ACC message will display in the Cabin Compartment Node (CCN). Once the Diagnostic Trouble Code (DTC) goes to stored, the ACC system will return to normal operation. The DTC will be cleared after the ACC Module sees 100 consecutive key cycles of the STORED DTC.

DTC	Trouble Code Title, Conditions, Possible Causes
DTC: P1678	**-ECU SENSOR ADJUSTMENT REQUIRED:** Continuously monitored with the engine running, the Adaptive Cruise Control (ACC) Module voltage at battery voltage, and the ACC Module in normal mode. There is horizontal misalignment between Sensor Axis and the vehicle driving axis that is greater than the performance threshold. The ACC module will disable the ACC system and the SERVICE ACC message will display in the Cabin Compartment Node (CCN). The DTC will be cleared after the ACC Module sees 100 consecutive key cycles of the STOREDDTC.
DTC: P1679	**-CALIBRATION NOT LEARNED:** Ignition on with a system voltage between 9. 0 and 16. 0 volts. The TCM is unable to read the hydraulic calibration data stored in the TCM EEPROM for the period of 5. 0 seconds.
DTC: P167A	**-CALIBRATION MISMATCH:** One time at initial ignition on with a system voltage between 9. 0 and 16. 0 volts. If the TCM stored calibration does not match the EEPROM assembly in the transmission. This DTC requires only one problem identification to set the MIL.
DTC: P1684	**-BATTERY WAS DISCONNECTED:** Whenever the ignition is in the Run/Start position. This DTC will set whenever Powertrain Control Module (PCM) is disconnected from Fused B(+) or ground. It will also be set using the scan tool to perform a Battery Disconnect and/or Quick Learn procedure.
DTC: P1684	**-BATTERY WAS DISCONNECTED:** After a reset (ignition turned to the RUN position). The checksum of the battery backed RAM does not match the stored checksum. Set Time: Less than 7 msec.
DTC: P1685	**-SKIM SYSTEM:** With the ignition on. A communication error occurs between the ECM and SKREEM.
DTC: P1696	**-EEPROM MEMORY WRITE DENIED/INVALID:** Continuously with the ignition on. An attempt to program/write to the internal EEPROM failed, Also checks at power down. One Trip Fault. Three good trips to turn off the MIL.
DTC: P1696	**-EEPROM MEMORY WRITE DENIED/INVALID:** Continuously with the ignition on. An attempt to program/write to the internal EEPROM failed, Also checks at power down. One Trip Fault. Three good trips to turn off the MIL.
DTC: P1697	**-EMR (SRI) MILEAGE NOT STORED:** Ignition on and battery voltage greater than 10 volts. The SRI Mileage has not been programmed into the PCM.
DTC: P1697	**-EMR (SRI) MILEAGE NOT STORED:** Continuously with the ignition on. The Powertrain Control Module (PCM) Odometer mileage has not been programmed into the PCM.
DTC: P1702	**-PRIMARY OIL PRESSURE SENSOR / SECONDARY OIL PRESSURE SENSOR CORRELATION:** Ignition on, system voltage between 9. 0 and 16. 0 volts. Engine running with the transmission in Drive. Vehicle speed greater than 10. 0Km/h (6. 0 mph). Accelerator Pedal Position (APP) greater than 12. 5%. Engine rpm greater than 450rpm. No active DTCs from the following: Primary or Secondary Pressure Sensor Transmission Temperature Sensor TCC Lock Up Solenoid Step Motor Input or Output Speed Sensor Transmission Range Sensor (TRS)Line Pressure Solenoid Secondary Pressure Solenoid Condition one: Reported primary pressure is less than the lower limit of the primary pressure correlated with the reported secondary pressure for more than five seconds. Condition two: Reported primary pressure is greater than the upper limit of the primary pressure correlated with the reported secondary pressure for more than five seconds.
DTC: P1704	**-INPUT SPEED SENSOR 1 OVERSPEED:** Continuously with the ignition on, engine running, transmission in gear, and Input Speed Sensor 1 (N2) greater than 0 RPM. If the RPM of the Input Speed Sensor 1 (N2) is greater than 7700 RPM.
DTC: P1705	**-INPUT SPEED SENSOR 2 OVERSPEED:** Continuously with the ignition on, engine running, transmission in gear, and Input Speed Sensor 2 (N3) greater than 0 RPM If the RPM of the Input Speed Sensor 2 (N3) is greater than 7700 RPM.
DTC: P170A	**-PARK/NEUTRAL OUTPUT CIRCUIT LOW:** With the ignition switch on. The Vehicle System Integration Module (VSIM) has detected the P/N Switch Sense circuit below a calibrated value.
DTC: P170B	**-PARK/NEUTRAL OUTPUT CIRCUIT HIGH:** With the ignition switch on. The Vehicle System Integration Module (VSIM) has detected the P/N Switch Sense circuit above a calibrated value.
DTC: P170C	**-ENGINE RPM OUTPUT CIRCUIT LOW:** With the ignition switch on. The Vehicle System Integration Module (VSIM) has detected the Engine Running Status Signal circuit below a calibrated value.

DTC	Trouble Code Title, Conditions, Possible Causes
DTC: P170D	**-ENGINE RPM OUTPUT CIRCUIT HIGH:** With the ignition switch on. The Vehicle System Integration Module (VSIM) has detected the Engine Running Status Signal above a calibrated value.
DTC: P1713	**-RESTRICTED MANUAL VALVE IN T2 RANGE:** Ignition on, engine running with the gear shift selector in a valid forward gear. This DTC sets whenever Transmission control system detects the manual valve is in the T2 range when it should be in OD. This is mainly an informational DTC.
DTC: P1715	**-RESTRICTED MANUAL VALVE IN T3 RANGE:** Whenever the PRNDL code indicates Temp 3. This DTC sets when conditions for the DTC P1776 are satisfied or three unsuccessful attempts to engage 1st gear while the shifter is in the temp 3 zone. This indicates a restricted port at the manual valve because the shifter is not fully engaged in the drive position.
DTC: P1718	**-EEPROM INTEGRITY FAILURE:** Continuously with the ignition on. An attempt to program/write to the internal EEPROM failed, Also checks at power down. One Trip Fault. Three good trips to turn off the MIL.
DTC: P1723	**-LOCK UP / SELECT CONTROL CIRCUIT:** Ignition on with a system voltage between 9. 0 and 16. 0 volts. If the TCC ON/OFF Solenoid status does not match the TCM requested ON/OFF status for the period of 200 msec the DTC will set. It takes two consecutive problem identification trips to illuminate the MIL.
DTC: P1729	**TRANSMISSION RATIO CONTROL CIRCUIT:** If the Step motor ON/OFF status does not match the TCM requested ON/OFF status for the period of 200 msec the DTC will set. It takes two consecutive problem identification trips to illuminate the MIL.
DTC: P1729	**TRANSMISSION RATIO CONTROL CIRCUIT:** If the Step motor ON/OFF status does not match the TCM requested ON/OFF status for the period of 200 msec the DTC will set. It takes two consecutive problem identification trips to illuminate the MIL.
DTC: P172A-00	**-GEAR SELECTOR SWITCH:** With the ignition on. The Gear Selector Switch has set an internal failure status.
DTC: P1736	**-GEAR RATIO ERROR IN 2ND PRIME:** Continuously with the ignition on, engine running, and after the transmission has achieved the proper gear ratio. If the ratio of the Input rpm to the Output rpm does not match the current gear ratio. This DTC can take up to five minutes of problem identification before illuminating the MIL
DTC: P1741	**-GEAR RATIO ERROR IN 4 PRIME:** The Transmission gear ratio is monitored continuously while the transmission is in gear. If the ratio of the Input RPM to the Output RPM does not match the current gear ratio when compared to the known gear ratio.
DTC: P1744	**TORQUE CONVERTER LOCK-UP CLUTCH HEAT CONTROL:** Ignition on, engine running with the transmission in a valid forward or reverse gear. No inhibitor switch, secondary speed sensor, or engine speed DTCs present. The DTC will set if an Engine stall speed condition is detected for the period of 18 seconds.
DTC: P1745	**TRANSMISSION LINE PRESSURE TOO HIGH FOR TOO LONG:** Continuously with ignition on. If the transmission has been operating in an open-loop line pressure control for 3220 kilometers (2000 miles) or 1000 2-3 upshifts.
DTC: P1771	**-INADEQUATE ELEMENT VOLUME 2/4:** Whenever the engine is running. The 2/4 Clutch Volume Index (CVI) is updated during a 3-1 or 2-1 manual downshift with throttle angle below 5 degrees. Transmission temperature must be at least 43° C (110° F). When the 2/4 Clutch Volume Index (CVI) falls below a calibrated value.
DTC: P1775	**-SOLENOID SWITCH VALVE LATCHED IN TCC POSITION:** During an attempted shift into 1st gear. This DTC is set if three unsuccessful attempts are made to shift the Solenoid Switch Valve (SSV) into the downshifted position in one given ignition start. This DTC can take up to five minutes to mature before illuminating the MIL.
DTC: P1775	**-SOLENOID SWITCH VALVE LATCHED IN TCC POSITION:** Prior to a shift into 1st gear. Transmission temperature must be hot. DTC is set after six unsuccessful attempts to shift into 1st gear.
DTC: P1776	**-SOLENOID SWITCH VALVE LATCHED IN LR POSITION:** Every 7 ms when doing PEMCC or FEMCC. Must be in partial or full EMCC. The DTC is set if L/R pressure is detected high for the fourth time.
DTC: P1776	**-SOLENOID SWITCH VALVE LATCHED IN LR POSITION:** Continuously when performing partial or full EMCC - PEMCC or FEMCC. If the transmission senses the L/R pressure switch closing while performing PEMCC or FEMCC. This DTC will set after two unsuccessful attempts to perform PEMCC or FEMCC. This DTC can take up to five minutes of problem identification before illuminating the MIL.

DTC	Trouble Code Title, Conditions, Possible Causes
DTC: P1790	**-FAULT IMMEDIATELY AFTER SHIFT:** After a Gear Ratio Error code is stored. After a Gear Ratio Error DTC has already been set. The DTC is set if the fault happened within 1. 3 seconds of a shift. The DTC set time will vary from 1. 214 seconds to 15 seconds.
DTC: P1794	**-SPEED SENSOR GROUND ERROR:** Every 7ms after a controller reset with transmission in neutral. After a PCM reset in neutral and Input and Output sensor ratio equals 2. 50 to 1. 0±50. 0rpm.
DTC: P1794	**-SPEED SENSOR GROUND ERROR:** Every 7ms after a controller reset with transmission in neutral. After a PCM reset in neutral and Input and Output sensor ratio equals 2. 50 to 1. 0±50. 0rpm.
DTC: P1794	**-SPEED SENSOR GROUND ERROR:** Every 7 msec after a controller reset with transmission in neutral. After a Powertrain Control Module (PCM) reset in neutral and Input and Output sensor ratio equals 2. 50 to 1. 0 (± 50. 0rpm).
DTC: P1794	**-SPEED SENSOR GROUND ERROR:** The gear ratio is monitored continuously while the Transmission is in gear. After a controller reset in neutral and a ratio of input to output, of 1 to 2. This DTC can take up to five minutes of problem identification before illuminating the MIL.
DTC: P1797	**-MANUAL SHIFT OVERHEAT:** Continuously with engine running. If the Engine Temperature exceeds 123° C (255° F) or the Transmission Temperature exceeds 135° C (275° F) while in AutoStick® mode. **NOTE: Aggressive driving or driving in Low for extended periods of time will set this DTC.**
DTC: P1797	**-MANUAL SHIFT OVERHEAT:** Continuously with engine running. If the Engine Temperature exceeds 123° C (255° F) or the Transmission Temperature exceeds 135° C (275° F). **NOTE: Aggressive driving or driving in low for extended periods of time will set this DTC.**
DTC: P1897	**-LEVEL 1 RPM BUS UNLOCK:** Engine running. When the Powertrain Control Module (PCM) recognizes an internal failure to communicate with the Front Control Module (FCM) or the Camshaft Position (CMP) Sensor and Crankshaft Position (CKP) Sensor count periods are too short. One trip fault. ETC light is flashing.
DTC: P198A	**-AWD SYSTEM PERFORMANCE:** Ignition on, no CAN DTCs from either the AWD control module or the TIPM. Condition One: Received On/Off-road signal pattern but not an existing pattern for the period of 20 seconds. Condition Two: Received On/Off-road signal pattern but not a proper pattern for the period of 60 seconds.
DTC: P1C4E	**-FAULT IN ABS/ESP MODULE:** Ignition on and battery voltage greater than 10. 0 Volts. An active DTC is stored in the ABS/ESP Module. One Trip Fault. Three good trips to turn off the MIL.

OBD II Trouble Code List (P2XXX Codes)

DTC	Trouble Code Title, Conditions, Possible Causes
DTC: P2002	**-DIESEL PARTICULATE FILTER EFFICIENCY BELOW THRESHOLD:** With the engine running. The ECM detects incorrect exhaust flow through the particulate filter during certain engine operating conditions.
DTC: P2004	**-INTAKE MANIFOLD RUNNER CONTROL STUCK OPEN:** With the engine running, when the valve closes, below a calibrated RPM, depending upon pedal position. The Powertrain Control Module (PCM) detects that the position feedback of the Manifold Flow Valve Position Sensor is not within range of the adapted value learned during in-plant initialization or after a non volatile memory reset (adaptive memory clear).
DTC: P2006	**-INTAKE MANIFOLD RUNNER CONTROL STUCK CLOSED:** With the engine running, when the valve opens, above a calibrated RPM depending upon pedal position. The Powertrain Control Module (PCM) detects that the position feedback of the Manifold Flow Valve Position Sensor is not within range of the adapted value learned during in-plant initialization or after a non volatile memory reset (adaptive memory clear).
DTC: P2008	**-SHORT RUNNER VALVE (SRV) CONTROL CIRCUIT:** With the engine run time above a calibrated value, battery voltage greater than 10. 4 Volts, ECT within a specific range and the Short Runner Valve Assembly control active. This Powertrain Control Module (PCM) compares the circuit feedback to a calibrated closed range when the circuit is de-energized or to a calibrated open range when the circuit is energized. If the value is determined to be out of the calibrated range in either the de-energized or energized state for more than a calibrated amount of time, this DTC will set.

DTC	Trouble Code Title, Conditions, Possible Causes
DTC: P2008	**-INTAKE MANIFOLD RUNNER (SWIRL) CONTROL CIRCUIT OPEN:** With the ignition on and the Intake Swirl Servo Motor command off. The ECM does not detect voltage on the (N117) Intake Swirl Servo Motor Control circuit for 2. 0 seconds.
DTC: P2008	**-INTAKE MANIFOLD RUNNER (SWIRL) CONTROL CIRCUIT/OPEN:** With the engine running and battery voltage greater than 10. 4 volts. The Powertrain Control Module (PCM) detects that the Manifold Flow Valve control circuit voltage is not within an acceptable range.
DTC: P2009	**-INTAKE MANIFOLD RUNNER (SWIRL) CONTROL CIRCUIT LOW:** With the ignition on and the Intake Swirl Servo Motor command off. The ECM detects a short to ground on the (N117) Intake Swirl Servo Motor Control circuit for 2. 3 seconds.
DTC: P2010	**-INTAKE MANIFOLD RUNNER (SWIRL) CONTROL CIRCUIT HIGH:** With the ignition on and the Intake Swirl Servo Motor command on. The ECM detects excessive current on the (N117) Intake Swirl Servo Motor Control circuit for 2. 0 seconds.
DTC: P2015	**-INTAKE MANIFOLD RUNNER POSITION SENSOR PERFORMANCE:** With the ignition on and battery voltage greater than 10. 4 volts. The Powertrain Control Module (PCM) detects an implausible voltage on the Manifold Flow Valve circuit.
DTC: P2016	**-INTAKE MANIFOLD RUNNER POSITION SENSOR CIRCUIT LOW:** With the ignition on and battery voltage greater than 10. 4 volts. The Powertrain Control Module (PCM) detects that the Manifold Flow Valve (MFV) Position Sensor input voltage is below the minimum acceptable value.
DTC: P2016	**-SHORT RUNNER VALVE (SRV) POSITION SENSOR CIRCUIT LOW:** With the ignition on and battery voltage greater than 10. 4 Volts. The Powertrain Control Module (PCM) detects that the PWM signal from the Short Runner Valve position sensor circuit is below the minimum acceptable value.
DTC: P2017	**-SHORT RUNNER VALVE (SRV) POSITION SENSOR CIRCUIT HIGH:** With the ignition on and battery voltage greater than 10. 4 Volts. The Powertrain Control Module (PCM) detects that the PWM signal from the Short Runner Valve Position sensor is greater than the maximum acceptable value.
DTC: P2017	**-INTAKE MANIFOLD RUNNER POSITION SENSOR CIRCUIT HIGH:** With the ignition on and battery voltage greater than 10. 4 volts. The Powertrain Control Module (PCM) detects that the MFV Position Sensor input voltage is above the maximum acceptable value.
DTC: P2032	**-EXHAUST GAS TEMPERATURE SENSOR CIRCUIT LOW - BANK 1 SENSOR 2:** With the ignition on. The ECM detects that the (K353) Post-Catalyst Exhaust Temperature Sensor Signal circuit is shorted to ground.
DTC: P2033	**-EXHAUST GAS TEMPERATURE SENSOR CIRCUIT HIGH - BANK 1 SENSOR 2:** With the ignition on. The ECM detects that the (K353) Post-Catalyst Exhaust Temperature Sensor Signal circuit is shorted to voltage.
DTC: P2065-11	**-FUEL LEVEL SENSOR 2 - CIRCUIT SHORT TO GROUND:** With the ignition on. Battery voltage greater than 10. 4 volts. The Body Control Module (BCM) detects that the Fuel Level Sensor 2 input voltage is below the minimum acceptable value.
DTC: P2065-15	**-FUEL LEVEL SENSOR 2 - CIRCUIT SHORT TO BATTERY OR OPEN:** With the ignition on. Battery voltage greater than 10. 4 volts. The Body Control Module (BCM) detects that the Fuel Level Sensor 2 input voltage is above the maximum acceptable value.
DTC: P2066	**-FUEL LEVEL SENSOR 2 PERFORMANCE:** With engine run time greater than three minutes and Fuel Level Sensor 1 reading high. The Powertrain Control Module (PCM) detects no change in Fuel Level Sensor 2 circuit voltage after a significant amount of fuel should have been consumed based on a calculated value and the vehicle operating conditions.
DTC: P2067	**-FUEL LEVEL SENSOR 2 CIRCUIT LOW:** With the ignition on. The Cluster detects that the Fuel Level Sensor input voltage is below the minimum acceptable value.
DTC: P2068	**-FUEL LEVEL SENSOR 2 CIRCUIT HIGH:** With the ignition on. The Cluster detects that the Fuel Level Sensor input voltage is above the maximum acceptable value.
DTC: P2068	**-FUEL LEVEL SENSOR 2 CIRCUIT HIGH:** With the ignition on and battery voltage greater than 10. 4 Volts. The Fuel Level Sensor 2 input voltage is above the maximum acceptable value.

DTC	Trouble Code Title, Conditions, Possible Causes
DTC: P2072	**-ELECTRONIC THROTTLE CONTROL SYSTEM - ICE BLOCKAGE:** With the ignition on and battery voltage greater than 10. 4 volts. The Powertrain Control Module (PCM) detects that the throttle plate is stuck during extremely cold ambient temperature operation. The PCM will initiate a throttle de-icing procedure, and if the throttle blade still doesn't move, this DTC will set. The MIL will not illuminate. The vehicle will be in Limp home condition, limiting rpm and vehicle speed.
DTC: P2072	**-ELECTRONIC THROTTLE CONTROL SYSTEM - ICE BLOCKAGE:** Ignition on. The PCM recognizes the Throttle plate is stuck during extremely cold Ambient Temperature operation. The throttle plate goes through a de-icing procedure. If the throttle blade still doesn't move this fault sets. The MIL will not illuminate. ETC light will illuminate. The vehicle will be in Limp home condition, limiting rpm and vehicle speed.
DTC: P2080	**-EXHAUST GAS TEMPERATURE SENSOR CIRCUIT PERFORMANCE - BANK 1 SENSOR 1:** At ignition on before engine crank. With no Intake Air Temp sensor DTC's The Engine Control Module (ECM) detects that the (K352) Pre-Catalyst Exhaust Temperature Sensor Signal circuit voltage is implausible.
DTC: P2084	**-EXHAUST GAS TEMPERATURE SENSOR CIRCUIT PERFORMANCE - BANK 1 SENSOR 2:** With the ignition on. The Engine Control Module (ECM) detects that the (K353) Post-Catalyst Exhaust Temperature Sensor Signal circuit voltage is implausible.
DTC: P2096	**-DOWNSTREAM FUEL TRIM SYSTEM 1 LEAN:** With the engine running in closed loop, the ambient/battery temperature above -7° C (20° F) and altitude below 8500 ft. The conditions that cause this diagnostic to fail is when the upstream O2 sensor becomes biased from an exhaust leak, O2 sensor contamination, or some other extreme operating condition. The downstream O2 sensor is considered to be protected from extreme environments by the catalyst. The Powertrain Control Module (PCM) monitors the downstream O2 sensor feedback control, called downstream fuel trim, to detect any shift in the upstream O2 sensor target voltage from nominal target voltage. The value of the downstream fuel trim is compared with the lean thresholds. Every time the value exceeds the calibrated threshold, a fail timer is incremented and mass flow through the exhaust is accumulated. If the fail timer and accumulated mass flow exceed the fail thresholds, the test fails and the diagnostic stops running for that trip. If the test fails on consecutive trips, a DTC is set.
DTC: P2097	**-DOWNSTREAM FUEL TRIM SYSTEM 1 RICH:** With the engine running in closed loop, the ambient/battery temperature above -7° C (20° F) and altitude below 8500 ft. The conditions that cause this diagnostic to fail is when the upstream O2 sensor becomes biased from an exhaust leak, O2 sensor contamination, or some other extreme operating condition. The downstream O2 sensor is considered to be protected from extreme environments by the catalyst. The Powertrain Control Module (PCM) monitors the downstream O2 sensor feedback control, called downstream fuel trim, to detect any shift in the upstream O2 sensor target voltage from nominal target voltage. The value of the downstream fuel trim is compared with the rich thresholds. Every time the value exceeds the calibrated threshold, a fail timer is incremented and mass flow through the exhaust is accumulated. If the fail timer and accumulated mass flow exceed the fail thresholds, the test fails and the diagnostic stops running for that trip. If the test fails on consecutive trips, a DTC is set.
DTC: P2097	**-DOWNSTREAM FUEL TRIM SYSTEM 2 RICH:** With the engine running in closed loop, the ambient/battery temperature above -7°C (20°F) and altitude below 8500 ft. The conditions that cause this diagnostic to fail is when the upstream O2 Sensor becomes biased from an exhaust leak, O2 Sensor contamination, or some other extreme operating condition. The downstream O2 Sensor is considered to be protected from extreme environments by the catalyst. The Powertrain Control Module (PCM) monitors the downstream O2 Sensor feedback control, called downstream fuel trim, to detect any shift in the upstream O2 Sensor target voltage from nominal target voltage. The value of the downstream fuel trim is compared with the lean thresholds. Every time the value exceeds the calibrated threshold, a fail timer is incremented and mass flow through the exhaust is accumulated. If the fail timer and accumulated mass flow exceed the fail thresholds, the test fails and the diagnostic stops running for that trip. If the test fails on consecutive trips, a DTC is set.
DTC: P2098	**-DOWNSTREAM FUEL TRIM SYSTEM 2 LEAN:** With the engine running in closed loop mode, the ambient/battery temperature above -6. 7°C (20°F) and altitude below 2590. 8 m (8500 ft) and fuel level greater than 15%. The conditions that cause this diagnostic to fail is when the upstream O2 sensor becomes biased from an exhaust leak, O2 sensor contamination, or some other extreme operating condition. The downstream O2 sensor is considered to be protected from extreme environments by the catalyst. The PCM monitors the downstream O2 sensor feedback control, called downstream fuel trim, to detect any shift in the upstream O2 sensor target voltage from nominal target voltage. The value of the downstream fuel trim is compared with the lean thresholds. Every time the value exceeds the calibrated threshold, a fail timer is incremented and mass flow through the exhaust is accumulated. If the fail timer and accumulated mass flow exceed the fail thresholds, the test fails and the diagnostic stops running for that trip. If the test fails on consecutive trips, a DTC is set.

DTC	Trouble Code Title, Conditions, Possible Causes
DTC: P2099	**-DOWNSTREAM FUEL TRIM SYSTEM 2 RICH:** With the engine running in closed loop mode, the ambient/battery temperature above -6. 7°C (20°F) and altitude below 2590. 8 m (8500 ft). The conditions that cause this diagnostic to fail is when the upstream O2 sensor becomes biased from an exhaust leak, O2 sensor contamination, or some other extreme operating condition. The downstream O2 sensor is considered to be protected from extreme environments by the catalyst. The PCM monitors the downstream O2 sensor feedback control, called downstream fuel trim, to detect any shift in the upstream O2 sensor target voltage from nominal target voltage. The value of the downstream fuel trim is compared with the lean thresholds. Every time the value exceeds the calibrated threshold, a fail timer is incremented and mass flow through the exhaust is accumulated. If the fail timer and accumulated mass flow exceed the fail thresholds, the test fails and the diagnostic stops running for that trip. If the test fails on consecutive trips, a DTC is set.
DTC: P2100	**-ELECTRONIC THROTTLE CONTROL MOTOR CIRCUIT:** With the ignition on and the ETC Motor is not in Limp mode. When the Powertrain Control Module (PCM) detects an internal error or a short between the ETC Motor (+) and ETC Motor (-) circuits in the ETC Motor Driver. One trip fault. ETC light is flashing.
DTC: P2101	**-ELECTRONIC THROTTLE CONTROL MOTOR PERFORMANCE:** With the engine running, ETC motor not in limp home mode, and TPS adaptation complete. The Powertrain Control Module (PCM) detects too large of an error between the actual position of the throttle plate and the desired set point. One trip fault. The DTC will set within 5 seconds. Three good trips to turn off the MIL ETC light is flashing.
DTC: P2106	**-ELECTRONIC THROTTLE CONTROL SYSTEM - FORCED LIMITED POWER:** Ignition on. This DTC sets for OBDII MIL illumination purposes. This DTC will always have associated DTCs indicating a system failure. Engine speed is being limited and/or throttle motor is power free. ETC light is flashing.
DTC: P2107	**-ELECTRONIC THROTTLE CONTROL MODULE PROCESSOR:** With the ignition on. Internal Powertrain Control Module (PCM) failure. Module will attempt to reset, so you will be able to hear the throttle relearning. If the condition is continuous, the vehicle may not be drivable. One trip fault. ETC light is flashing.
DTC: P2107	**-ELECTRONIC THROTTLE CONTROL MODULE PROCESSOR:** With the ignition on and the ETC Motor is not in Limp Home mode. When the Powertrain Control Module (PCM) detects an internal error or a short between the ETC Motor - and ETC Motor + circuits in the ETC Motor Driver. One trip fault. ETC light is flashing.
DTC: P2108	**-ELECTRONIC THROTTLE CONTROL MODULE PERFORMANCE:** Ignition on. Internal PCM failure. Customer may experience an extended cranking condition with limited driving and a rough idle. One trip fault and the code will set within 5 seconds. ETC light is flashing.
DTC: P2110	**-ELECTRONIC THROTTLE CONTROL - FORCED LIMITED RPM:** Ignition on and ETC motor is working. When the Powertrain Control Module (PCM) requests to limit engine speed if PWM is too high for 20. five seconds and before P2118 sets. One trip fault and the code will set within five seconds. ETC light is illuminated.
DTC: P2110	**-ELECTRONIC THROTTLE CONTROL SYSTEM - FORCED LIMITED RPM:** With the ignition on and the ETC Motor not in Limp Home mode. When the Powertrain Control Module (PCM) requests to limit engine speed if PWM is too high for 20. five seconds and before P2118 sets. One trip fault and the code will set within five seconds. ETC light is illuminated.
DTC: P2110	**-ELECTRONIC THROTTLE CONTROL - FORCED LIMITED RPM:** Ignition on and ETC motor is working. When the Powertrain Control Module (PCM) requests to limit engine speed if PWM is too high for 20. five seconds and before P2118 sets. One trip fault and the code will set within five seconds. ETC light is illuminated.
DTC: P2111	**-ELECTRONIC THROTTLE CONTROL - UNABLE TO CLOSE:** Ignition on and battery voltage greater than 10 volts. Just after key on, the throttle is opened and closed to test the system. If the TP Sensor does not return to Limp Home Position at the end of this test, this DTC will set. One trip fault and the code will set within 5 seconds. ETC light is flashing.
DTC: P2112	**-ELECTRONIC THROTTLE CONTROL - UNABLE TO OPEN:** Ignition on and battery voltage greater than 10. 0 Volts. Just after key on, the throttle is opened and closed to test the system. If the TP Sensor does not return to Limp Position at the end of this test, this DTC will set. One trip fault and the code will set within five seconds. ETC light is flashing.
DTC: P2112	**-ELECTRONIC THROTTLE CONTROL SYSTEM - UNABLE TO OPEN:** With the ignition on and the ETC Motor not in Limp Home mode. When the Powertrain Control Module (PCM) detects an error in the ETC Motor Driver or throttle position.
DTC: P2112	**-ELECTRONIC THROTTLE CONTROL - UNABLE TO OPEN:** Ignition on and battery voltage greater than 10 volts. Just after key on, the throttle is opened and closed to test the system. If the Powertrain Control Module (PCM) detects that the TP Sensor does not move from Limp Home Position, this DTC will set. One trip fault. The DTC will set within five seconds. ETC light is flashing.

DTC	Trouble Code Title, Conditions, Possible Causes
DTC: P2115	**-ACCELERATOR PEDAL POSITION SENSOR 1 MINIMUM STOP PERFORMANCE:** With the igniting on. During in-plant testing, the APPS is checked to make sure the minimum and maximum values can be reached. The PCM performs the diagnostic test for this DTC after the diagnostic test for P2166 has passed. APPS 1 has failed to achieve the required minimum value during In-Plant testing. One trip fault and the code will set within 5 seconds. Engine will only idle.
DTC: P2115	**-ACCELERATOR PEDAL POSITION SENSOR 1 MINIMUM STOP PERFORMANCE:** Ignition on. During in plant mode the APP Sensors need to be checked to make sure that idle and full pedal travel can be reached on both sensors. The test for P2115 is only enabled once test for P2166 has passed. APPS No. 1 has failed to achieve the required minimum value during In Plant testing. One trip fault and the code will set within 5 seconds. Engine will only idle. ETC light is illuminated.
DTC: P2116	**-ACCELERATOR PEDAL POSITION SENSOR 2 MINIMUM STOP PERFORMANCE:** Ignition on. During in plant mode the APP Sensors need to be checked to make sure that idle and full pedal travel can be reached on both sensors. The test for P2116 is only enabled once test for P2167 has passed. APPS No. 2 has failed to achieve the required minimum value during In Plant testing. One trip fault and the code will be stored within 5 seconds. Engine will only idle. ETC light is illuminated.
DTC: P2116	**-ACCELERATOR PEDAL POSITION SENSOR 2 MINIMUM STOP PERFORMANCE:** With the igniting on. During in-plant testing, the APPS is checked to make sure the minimum and maximum values can be reached. The PCM performs the diagnostic test for this DTC after the diagnostic test for P2167 has passed. APPS 2 has failed to achieve the required minimum value during In-Plant testing. One trip fault and the code will be stored within 5 seconds. Engine will only idle.
DTC: P2118	**-ELECTRONIC THROTTLE CONTROL MOTOR CIRCUIT:** With the ignition on and the ETC Motor is not in Limp mode. When the Powertrain Control Module (PCM) detects an internal error or a short between the ETC Motor (+) and ETC Motor (-) circuits in the ETC Motor Driver. One trip fault. ETC light is flashing.
DTC: P2121	**-ACCELERATOR PEDAL POSITION SENSOR 1 PERFORMANCE:** With the ignition on. APP Sensor #1 and APP Sensor #2 signals do not agree.
DTC: P2122	**-ACCELERATOR PEDAL POSITION SENSOR 1 CIRCUIT LOW:** With the ignition on and battery voltage greater than 10. 4 volts. The Powertrain Control Module (PCM) detects that the APP Sensor 1 input voltage is below the minimum acceptable value.
DTC: P2122	**-ACCELERATOR PEDAL POSITION SENSOR 1 CIRCUIT LOW:** With the ignition on and no other APPS No. 1 DTCs present. When the APP Sensor No. 1 voltage is too low. Engine will additionally idle if the brake pedal is pressed or has failed. Acceleration rate and Engine output are limited. One trip fault and the code will set within 5 seconds. ETC light is flashing.
DTC: P2123	**-ACCELERATOR PEDAL POSITION SENSOR 1 CIRCUIT HIGH:** With the ignition on and no other APPS No. 1 DTCs present. When APP Sensor No. 1 voltage is too high. Engine will additionally idle if the brake pedal is pressed or has failed. Acceleration rate and Engine output are limited. One trip fault and the code will set within five seconds. ETC light is flashing.
DTC: P2123	**-ACCELERATOR PEDAL POSITION SENSOR 1 CIRCUIT HIGH:** With the ignition on and battery voltage greater than 10. 4 volts. The Powertrain Control Module (PCM) detects that the APP Sensor 1 input voltage is above the maximum acceptable value.
DTC: P2127	**-ACCELERATOR PEDAL POSITION SENSOR 2 CIRCUIT LOW:** With the ignition on and no other APPS No. 2 DTCs present. When the APP Sensor No. 2 voltage is too low. Engine will only idle if the Brake pedal is Pressed or has failed. Acceleration rate and Engine output are limited. One trip fault and the code will set within 5 seconds. ETC light is flashing.
DTC: P2127	**-ACCELERATOR PEDAL POSITION SENSOR 2 CIRCUIT LOW:** With the ignition on. The APP Sensor #2 Signal circuit is below 0. 097 volts for 0. 32 seconds.
DTC: P2128	**-ACCELERATOR PEDAL POSITION SENSOR 2 CIRCUIT HIGH:** With the ignition on and no other APPS No. 2 DTCs present. When APP Sensor No. 2 voltage is too high. Idle is additionally forced any time the brake is applied or failed. Acceleration rate and Engine output are limited. One trip fault and the code will set within five seconds. ETC light is flashing.
DTC: P2135	**THROTTLE POSITION SENSOR 1/2 CORRELATION:** With the ignition on and no other DTCs present for TP Sensor No. 1 or No. 2. The Powertrain Control Module (PCM) recognizes TP Sensors No. 1 and No. 2 are not coherent. One trip fault and the code will set within five seconds. ETC light is illuminated.
DTC: P2135	**THROTTLE POSITION SENSOR 1/2 CORRELATION:** With the engine running and no TPS or MAP sensor DTCs present. The Powertrain Control Module (PCM) recognizes TP Sensors No. 1 and No. 2 are not coherent. One trip fault and the code will set within five seconds. ETC light is illuminated.

DTC	Trouble Code Title, Conditions, Possible Causes
DTC: P2135	**THROTTLE POSITION SENSOR 1/2 CORRELATION:** With the ignition on, battery voltage greater than 10. 4 volts, and no other TP Sensor DTCs present. The Powertrain Control Module (PCM) detects that the TP Sensor voltages are not plausible. One trip fault and the code will set within five seconds. ETC light is illuminated.
DTC: P2138	**-ACCELERATOR PEDAL POSITION SENSOR 1/2 CORRELATION:** With the ignition on and no APPS No. 1 and APPS No. 2 DTC present. APPS values No. 1 and No. 2 are not coherent. Idle is additionally forced when the brake pedal is pressed or failed. Acceleration rate and Engine output are limited. One trip fault and the code will set within 5 seconds. ETC light is flashing.
DTC: P2138	**-ACCELERATOR PEDAL POSITION SENSOR 1/2 CORRELATION:** With the ignition on, battery voltage greater than 10. 4 Volts, and no APPS 1 and APPS 2 DTCs present. The Powertrain Control Module (PCM) detects that the correlation between APPS 1 and APPS 2 is not plausible. Idle may be affected when the brake pedal is pressed or if a brake switch circuit error is present. Acceleration rate and engine output are limited. One trip fault and the code will set within five seconds. ETC light is flashing.
DTC: P213A	**-EGR AIRFLOW THROTTLE CONTROL CIRCUIT B OPEN:** With the engine running and the EGR Airflow Control Valve Motor command off. The ECM does not detect voltage on the (K315) EGR Airflow Control Valve Motor (-) circuit for 0. 5 second.
DTC: P213C	**-EGR AIRFLOW THROTTLE CONTROL CIRCUIT B LOW:** With the engine running and the EGR Airflow Control Valve Motor command off. The (K315) EGR Airflow Control Valve Motor (-) circuit is shorted to ground for 0. 2 second.
DTC: P213D	**-EGR AIRFLOW THROTTLE CONTROL CIRCUIT B HIGH:** With the engine running and the EGR Airflow Control Valve Motor command on. The (K315) EGR Airflow Control Valve Motor (-) circuit is shorted to voltage for 0. 2 seconds.
DTC: P2141	**-EGR AIRFLOW THROTTLE CONTROL CIRCUIT A LOW:** With the engine running and the EGR Airflow Control Valve Motor command off. The (K314) EGR Airflow Control Valve Motor (+) circuit is shorted to ground for 0. 2 second.
DTC: P2142	**-EGR AIRFLOW THROTTLE CONTROL CIRCUIT A HIGH:** With the engine running and the EGR Airflow Control Valve Motor command on. The (K314) EGR Airflow Control Valve Motor (+) circuit is shorted to voltage for 0. 2 second.
DTC: P2146	**-FUEL INJECTOR GROUP 1 SUPPLY VOLTAGE CIRCUIT OPEN:** With the engine running. The ECM detects an open circuit error on a fuel injector high-side control circuit.
DTC: P2147	**-FUEL INJECTOR GROUP 1 SUPPLY VOLTAGE CIRCUIT LOW:** With the engine running. The ECM detects a short to ground error on the injector high-side control circuit.
DTC: P2148	**-FUEL INJECTOR GROUP 1 SUPPLY VOLTAGE CIRCUIT HIGH:** With the engine running. The ECM detects a short to voltage error on one of the injector high-side control circuits.
DTC: P2149	**-FUEL INJECTOR GROUP 2 SUPPLY VOLTAGE CIRCUIT OPEN:** With the engine running. The ECM detects an open circuit error on a fuel injector high-side control circuit.
DTC: P2150	**-FUEL INJECTOR GROUP 2 SUPPLY VOLTAGE CIRCUIT LOW:** With the engine running. The ECM detects a short to ground error on the injector high-side control circuit.
DTC: P2151	**-FUEL INJECTOR GROUP 2 SUPPLY VOLTAGE CIRCUIT HIGH:** With the engine running. The ECM detects a short to voltage error on one of the injector high-side control circuits.
DTC: P2161	**-VEHICLE SPEED SENSOR 2 ERRATIC:** Ignition on. PCM recognizes Vehicle speed input No. 2 erratic or high. VSS No. 2 is based on the average of the Front Wheel Speeds. One trip fault and the code will set within 5 seconds. No MIL and No ETC light. Cruise is disabled.
DTC: P2161	**-VEHICLE SPEED SENSOR 2 ERRATIC (with ABS):** With engine run time greater than 5 seconds, ECT above -8° C (17. 6° F), transmission not in park or neutral, brakes not applied, engine rpm greater than 1500, and no ECT, MAP, TPS, ETC, or brake switch stuck DTCs present. The Powertrain Control (PCM) receives an erratic vehicle speed signal. One Trip Fault. Three good trips to turn off the MIL.
DTC: P2166	**-ACCELERATOR PEDAL POSITION SENSOR 1 MAXIMUM STOP PERFORMANCE:** Ignition on. During in plant mode the APP Sensors need to be checked to make sure that idle and full pedal travel can be reached on both sensors. APPS No. 1 has failed to achieve the required maximum value during In Plant testing. One trip fault and the code will set within five seconds. Engine will only idle. ETC light will illuminate.

DTC	Trouble Code Title, Conditions, Possible Causes
DTC: P2167	**-ACCELERATOR PEDAL POSITION SENSOR 2 MAXIMUM STOP PERFORMANCE:** With the igniting on. During in-plant testing, the APP Sensors need to be checked to make sure the minimum and maximum values can be reached. APPS 2 has failed to achieve the required maximum value during In-Plant testing. One trip fault and the code will be stored within five seconds. Engine will only idle.
DTC: P2167	**-ACCELERATOR PEDAL POSITION SENSOR 2 MAXIMUM STOP PERFORMANCE:** Ignition on. During in plant mode the APP Sensors need to be checked to make sure that idle and full pedal travel can be reached on both sensors. APPS No. 2 has failed to achieve the required maximum value during In Plant testing. One trip fault and the code will set within five seconds. Engine will only idle. ETC light will illuminate.
DTC: P2172	**-HIGH AIRFLOW/VACUUM LEAK DETECTED (INSTANTANEOUS ACCUMULATION):** Ignition on and engine running with no MAP Sensor DTCs. A large vacuum leak has been detected or both of the TP Sensors have failed based on their position being 2. 5 Volts and the calculated MAP value is less than the actual MAP minus an Offset value. One trip fault and the code will set within five seconds. ETC light will flash.
DTC: P2173	**-HIGH AIRFLOW/VACUUM LEAK DETECTED (SLOW ACCUMULATION):** Ignition on and engine running with no MAP Sensor DTCs. A large vacuum leak has been detected or both of the TP Sensors have failed based on their position being 2. 5 Volts and the calculated MAP value is less than the Gas Flow Adaptation value is too high. One trip fault the code will set within 5 seconds. ETC light will flash.
DTC: P2174	**-LOW AIRFLOW/RESTRICTION DETECTED (INSTANTANEOUS ACCUMULATION):** Ignition on and engine running with no MAP Sensor DTCs. The Powertrain Control Module (PCM) calculated MAP value is greater than actual MAP value plus an offset value. One trip fault. Three good trips to turn of the mil. ETC light will flash.
DTC: P2175	**-LOW AIRFLOW/RESTRICTION DETECTED (SLOW ACCUMULATION):** Ignition on and engine running with no MAP Sensor DTCs. PCM calculated MAP value is greater than actual MAP value plus an offset value. One trip fault and the code will set within 5 seconds. Three good trips to turn of the mil. ETC light will flash.
DTC: P2175	**-LOW AIRFLOW/RESTRICTION DETECTED (SLOW ACCUMULATION):** Ignition on and engine running with no MAP Sensor DTCs. The Powertrain Control Module (PCM) calculated MAP value is greater than actual MAP value plus an offset value. One trip fault and the code will set within five seconds. Three good trips to turn of the mil. ETC light will flash.
DTC: P2181	**-COOLING SYSTEM PERFORMANCE:** Ignition on, Engine running, and no ECT DTCs present. PCM recognizes that the ECT has failed its self coherence test. The coolant temp should only change at a certain rate, if this rate is too slow or too fast this fault will set. One trip fault. Three good trips to clear MIL. ETC light will illuminate on first trip failure.
DTC: P219A	**-AIR-FUEL RATIO CYLINDER IMBALANCE BANK 1:** Engine Coolant Temperature (ECT) is greater than 70°C (158°F), Engine run time of 90 seconds, engine RPM 1000 - 2700, engine load 30 - 90% and in flex fuel vehicles the Fuel Adaptive Learned must be completed. DTC P113D is not set and the high frequency content of the O2 sensor exceeds a calibrated amount. Two Trip Fault. Three good trips to turn off the MIL.
DTC: P219B	**-AIR-FUEL RATIO CYLINDER IMBALANCE BANK 2:** Engine Coolant Temperature (ECT) is greater than 70°C (158°F), Engine run time of 90 seconds, engine RPM 1000 - 2700, engine load 30 - 90% and in flex fuel vehicles the Fuel Adaptive Learned must be completed. DTC P113E is not set and the high frequency content of the O2 Sensor exceeds a calibrated amount. Two Trip Fault. Three good trips to turn off the MIL.
DTC: P2231	**-O2 SENSOR 1/1 SIGNAL CIRCUIT SHORTED TO HEATER CIRCUIT:** With the ignition on. The ECM detects a short between the (Z43) O2 1/1 Negative Current Control circuit and the (K99) O2 1/1 Heater Control circuit.
DTC: P2237	**-O2 SENSOR 1/1 PUMP CELL CURRENT CIRCUIT OPEN:** With the ignition on and the O2 1/1 Sensor at operating temperature. The ECM detects an open on the (K43) O2 1/1 Positive Current Control circuit for 2. 0 seconds.
DTC: P2238	**-O2 SENSOR 1/1 PUMP CELL CURRENT CIRCUIT LOW:** With the ignition on and the O2 1/1 Sensor at operating temperature. The ECM detects a short to ground on the (K43) O2 1/1 Positive Current Control circuit for 2. 0 seconds.
DTC: P2239	**-O2 SENSOR 1/1 PUMP CELL CURRENT CIRCUIT HIGH:** With the ignition on and the O2 1/1 Sensor at operating temperature. The ECM detects a short to voltage on the (K43) O2 1/1 Positive Current Control circuit for 2. 0 seconds.
DTC: P2243	**-O2 SENSOR 1/1 REFERENCE VOLTAGE CIRCUIT OPEN:** With the ignition on and the O2 1/1 Sensor at operating temperature. The ECM detects an open on the (K41) O2 1/1 Reference Signal circuit for 2. 0 seconds.

DTC	Trouble Code Title, Conditions, Possible Causes
DTC: P2244	**-02 SENSOR 1/1 REFERENCE VOLTAGE PERFORMANCE:** With the ignition on and the 02 1/1 Sensor at operating temperature. The ECM detects an implausible voltage on the (K41) 02 1/1 Reference Signal.
DTC: P2245	**-02 SENSOR 1/1, 2/1 REFERENCE VOLTAGE CIRCUIT LOW:** Continuously after 15 seconds of engine runtime, no 02 Sensor Heater DTCs present and battery voltage greater than 10. 4 Volts. The Oxygen Sensor reference voltage is below 0. 9 Volt for 60 seconds. The DTC will set as Pending after one trip and Active after two trips. Three good trips to turn off the MIL.
DTC: P2245	**-02 SENSOR 1/1 REFERENCE VOLTAGE CIRCUIT LOW:** With the ignition on and the 02 1/1 Sensor at operating temperature. The Powertrain Control Module (PCM) detects a short to ground on the (K41) 02 Sensor 1/1 Reference Signal circuit for 2. 0 seconds.
DTC: P2246	**-02 SENSOR 1/1 REFERENCE VOLTAGE CIRCUIT HIGH:** With the ignition on and the 02 Sensor 1/1 at operating temperature. The Powertrain Control Module (PCM) detects a short to voltage on the (K41) 02 Sensor 1/1 Reference Signal circuit for 2. 0 seconds.
DTC: P2246	**-02 SENSOR 1/1, 2/1 REFERENCE VOLTAGE CIRCUIT HIGH:** Engine running for 15 seconds, 02 Sensors at operating temperature and battery voltage greater 10. 4 Volts. The PCM detects that the (K902) Reference Signal voltage is greater than 3. 9 Volts for nine seconds.
DTC: P2270	**-02 SENSOR 1/2 SIGNAL BIASED LEAN:** With the engine running, the odometer greater than the minimum mileage allowable for catalyst break-in, and no global or monitor conflicts or disabling conditions present. The test will only run if the monitor has not already run and passed or failed. The Powertrain Control Module (PCM) detects that the sensor does not output a voltage greater than a calibrated high voltage value and less than a calibrated low voltage value within a specific time period. If the voltage pass values are not achieved after the total accumulated test time, a pending fault will be set. An active fault is matured on a second trip failure. Three good trips will turn off the MIL.
DTC: P2271	**-02 SENSOR 1/2 SIGNAL STUCK RICH:** With the engine running, vehicle speed above 96 kph (60 mph), throttle open for a minimum of 120 seconds, ECT greater than 70° C (158° F), catalytic converter temperature greater than 600° C (1112° F) and downstream oxygen sensor in a rich state. During a decel fuel shutoff event, the downstream oxygen sensor should switch from rich to lean within a specific time. The PCM monitors the downstream 02 sensor. If the PCM does not detect a rich to lean switch within a specific time during a decel fuel shutoff event, the monitor will fail. Two trip fault. Three good trips to turn off the MIL.
DTC: P2271	**-02 SENSOR 1/2 SIGNAL BIASED RICH:** With the engine running, the odometer greater than the minimum mileage allowable for catalyst break-in, and no global or monitor conflicts or disabling conditions present. The test will only run if the monitor has not already run and passed or failed. The Powertrain Control Module (PCM) detects that the sensor does not output a voltage greater than a calibrated high voltage value and less than a calibrated low voltage value within a specific time period. If the voltage pass values are not achieved after the total accumulated test time, a pending fault will be set. An active fault is matured on a second trip failure. Three good trips will turn off the MIL.
DTC: P2273	**-02 SENSOR 2/2 SIGNAL STUCK RICH:** With the engine running, vehicle speed above 96 kph (60 mph), throttle open for a minimum of 120 seconds, ECT greater than 70 C (158 F), catalytic converter temperature greater than 600 C (1112 F), and downstream oxygen sensor in a rich state. During a decel fuel shutoff event, the downstream oxygen sensor should switch from rich to lean within a specific time. The PCM monitors the downstream 02 sensor. If the PCM does not detect a rich to lean switch within a specific time during a decel fuel shutoff event, the monitor will fail. Two trip fault. Three good trips to turn off the MIL.
DTC: P2280	**-AIR FILTER RESTRICTION:** With the engine running. The ECM compares mass airflow volume/engine rpm to atmospheric pressure. The ECM detects a 50% or more drop in airflow through the air filter for five minutes.
DTC: P2299	**-BRAKE PEDAL POSITION/ACCELERATOR PEDAL POSITION INCOMPATIBLE:** Ignition on. No Break or APPS faults present. The PCM recognizes a brake application following the APPS showing a fixed pedal opening. Temporary or permanent. Internally the PCM will reduce throttle opening below driver demand. One trip fault and the code will be set within five seconds. ETC light will illuminate, the light will only stay illuminated while DTC is active.
DTC: P2299	**-BRAKE PEDAL POSITION/ACCELERATOR PEDAL POSITION INCOMPATIBLE:** With the engine running (engine speed above 570 rpm). No other APP or Brake Signal DTCs. Vehicle speed above 3 km/h. The ECM detects a brake signal input (brakes applied) and Accelerator Pedal Position above 3% at the same time for 15. 0 seconds.
DTC: P2302	**-IGNITION COIL 1 SECONDARY CIRCUIT - INSUFFICIENT IONIZATION:** With the engine running. The Powertrain Control Module (PCM) detects the secondary ignition burn time is incorrect or not present. One trip fault. Three good trips to turn off the Malfunction Indicator Lamp (MIL).
DTC: P2302	**-IGNITION COIL 1 SECONDARY CIRCUIT - INSUFFICIENT IONIZATION:** Engine running and battery voltage greater than 10. 0 Volts. If the Powertrain Control Module (PCM) detects that the secondary ignition burn time is incorrect, too short, or not present, an error is detected. One Trip Fault. Three good trips to turn off the MIL.

DTC	Trouble Code Title, Conditions, Possible Causes
DTC: P2305	**-IGNITION COIL 2 SECONDARY CIRCUIT - INSUFFICIENT IONIZATION:** Engine running and battery voltage greater than 10. 0 Volts. If Powertrain Control Module (PCM) detects that the secondary ignition burn time is incorrect, too short, or not present, an error is detected. One Trip Fault. Three good trips to turn off the MIL.
DTC: P2308	**-IGNITION COIL 3 SECONDARY CIRCUIT- INSUFFICIENT IONIZATION:** Engine running and battery voltage greater than 10 volts. If PCM detects that the secondary ignition burn time is incorrect, to short, or not present, an error is detected. One Trip Fault. Three good trips to turn off the MIL.
DTC: P2311	**-IGNITION COIL 4 SECONDARY CIRCUIT- INSUFFICIENT IONIZATION:** Engine running and battery voltage greater than 10 volts. If PCM detects that the secondary ignition burn time is incorrect, too short, or not present, an error is detected. One Trip Fault. Three good trips to turn off the MIL.
DTC: P2314	**-IGNITION COIL 5 SECONDARY CIRCUIT- INSUFFICIENT IONIZATION:** Engine running and battery voltage greater than 10 volts. If PCM detects that the secondary ignition burn time is incorrect, to short, or not present, an error is detected. One Trip Fault. Three good trips to turn off the MIL.
DTC: P2317	**-IGNITION COIL 6 SECONDARY CIRCUIT- INSUFFICIENT IONIZATION:** Engine running and battery voltage greater than 10 volts. If PCM detects that the secondary ignition burn time is incorrect, to short, or not present, an error is detected. One Trip Fault. Three good trips to turn off the MIL.
DTC: P2320	**-IGNITION COIL 7 SECONDARY CIRCUIT - INSUFFICIENT IONIZATION:** With the engine running. The Powertrain Control Module (PCM) detects the secondary ignition burn time is incorrect or not present. One trip fault. Three good trips to turn off the Malfunction Indicator Lamp (MIL).
DTC: P2323	**-IGNITION COIL 8 SECONDARY CIRCUIT - INSUFFICIENT IONIZATION:** With the engine running. The Powertrain Control Module (PCM) detects the secondary ignition burn time is incorrect or not present. One trip fault. Three good trips to turn off the Malfunction Indicator Lamp (MIL).
DTC: P242F	**-DIESEL PARTICULATE FILTER RESTRICTION - ASH ACCUMULATION:** With the engine running. The Differential Pressure Sensor signal indicates partial clogging of the particulate filter due to the accumulation of ash or other debris.
DTC: P2431	**-SECONDARY AIR INJECTION SYSTEM AIR FLOW SENSOR CIRCUIT PERFORMANCE:** Engine Coolant Temperature (ECT) above 0° C (32° F), ambient air temperature within approximately two degrees of ECT, actual air flow is less than or equal to model airflow, and Secondary Air Flow diagnostic counter above 100 (approximately three seconds). Secondary Air Pump Control circuit active. The Powertrain Control Module (PCM) detects that the measured air flow is below a calculated minimum value, above a calculated maximum value, or there is no difference between the minimum measured air flow value and the maximum measured air flow value during monitoring.
DTC: P2432	**-SECONDARY AIR INJECTION SYSTEM AIR FLOW SENSOR CIRCUIT LOW:** With the engine running and battery voltage greater than 10 volts. The Powertrain Control Module (PCM) detects that the sensor input voltage is below the minimum acceptable value.
DTC: P2433	**-SECONDARY AIR INJECTION SYSTEM AIR FLOW SENSOR CIRCUIT HIGH:** With the engine running and battery voltage greater than 10 volts. The Powertrain Control Module (PCM) detects that the sensor input voltage is above the maximum acceptable value.
DTC: P2440	**-AIR PUMP SWITCH VALVE STUCK OPEN:** Engine Coolant Temperature (ECT) above 0 C (32 F), intake temperature (IAT) within approximately 2 degrees of ECT. Measured airflow during pump actuation greater than a calibrated value (approximately 45 kg/h). Monitoring begins six seconds after the air injection pump turns off. The Powertrain Control Module (PCM) detects that the difference between minimum and maximum secondary airflow during monitoring (with the pump off) is greater than 6 kg/h.
DTC: P244B	**-DIESEL PARTICULATE FILTER DIFFERENTIAL PRESSURE TOO HIGH:** With the engine running. The ECM detects excessive pressure at the particulate filter.
DTC: P2453	**-DIESEL PARTICULATE FILTER DIFFERENTIAL PRESSURE SENSOR CIRCUIT PERFORMANCE:** At the beginning of engine crank. The Differential Pressure Sensor Signal is below negative 40 hpa or above positive 40 hpa.
DTC: P2454	**-DIESEL PARTICULATE FILTER DIFFERENTIAL PRESSURE SENSOR CIRCUIT LOW:** With the ignition on. The (K355) Exhaust Differential Pressure Sensor signal is below 0. 24 volts for 2. 0 seconds.
DTC: P2455	**-DIESEL PARTICULATE FILTER DIFFERENTIAL PRESSURE SENSOR CIRCUIT HIGH:** With the ignition on. The (K355) Exhaust Differential Pressure Sensor signal is above 4. 96 volts for 2. 0 seconds.
DTC: P2503	**-CHARGING SYSTEM OUTPUT LOW:** The engine running. The engine RPM is high enough to assure sufficient generator current output to satisfy the electrical loads. The battery sensed voltage is less than the target charging voltage, during engine operation, for a calibrated amount of time. One Trip Fault. Generator light will illuminate.

DTC	Trouble Code Title, Conditions, Possible Causes
DTC: P2503	**-CHARGING SYSTEM OUTPUT LOW:** With the engine speed greater than 1157 RPM. The Powertrain Control Module (PCM) detects that battery voltage is 1 volt below charging goal voltage for 13. 47 seconds. The PCM compares sensed battery voltage with the field driver on and off. If the voltages are the same, this code will set. One Trip Fault. Three good trips to turn off the MIL.
DTC: P2504	**-CHARGING SYSTEM OUTPUT HIGH:** The engine running. The engine speed greater than 1157 RPM. The alternator B+ voltage sense circuit voltage reading exceeds the direct Battery B+ sense circuit. The Generator Output terminal is not connected to the Battery B+ post. One trip fault.
DTC: P2504	**-CHARGING SYSTEM OUTPUT HIGH:** With the engine speed greater than 1157 RPM. The Powertrain Control Module (PCM) compares sensed battery voltage with the Generator Sense circuit voltage. If the Generator Sense circuit voltage if greater than sensed battery voltage, this DTC will set. One Trip Fault. Three good trips to turn off the MIL.
DTC: P2533	**-IGNITION SWITCH RUN/START POSITION CIRCUIT:** With the ignition on and the battery voltage greater than 10. 4 Volts. The Powertrain Control Module (PCM) detects and open or shorted condition in the Ignition Switch Run/Start circuit.
DTC: P258A	**-ELECTRIC VACUUM PUMP CIRCUIT:** With ignition on. Battery voltage above 10. 0 Volts. The actual EVP state is not equal to the desired EVP state. One Trip Fault. Three good trips to turn off the MIL.
DTC: P258D	**-ELECTRONIC VACUUM PUMP PERFORMANCE:** With the ignition on and engine running. Minimum Manifold Absolute Pressure (MAP) reading is 15 kpa (4. 4 in Hg). EVP minimum vacuum is -35 kpa (-10 in Hg) and the EVP cannot create 3 kpa (1. 0 inHg) or the system cannot increase the vacuum from -35 kpa (-10 in Hg) to -38 kpa (-11 in Hg). Two trip fault. Three good trips to turn off the MIL.
DTC: P2610	**-PCM INTERNAL SHUTDOWN TIMER FAST RATIONALITY:** With the engine running after a cycle when a complete engine warm up was achieved, the difference between engine coolant temperature and ambient air temperature greater than 10° C (50° F), after a minimum temperature drop of 10° C (50° F) during ignition off, and battery voltage greater than 10 volts. The PCM detects that the engine coolant temperature drops a specified amount during the measured engine off time. Two trip fault. Three good trips to turn off the MIL.
DTC: P2627	**-O2 SENSOR 1/1 PUMP CELL CURRENT TRIM CIRCUIT LOW:** With the ignition on. The ECM detects a short to ground on the (K902) O2 1/1 Pump Cell Current Trim circuit for 2. 0 seconds.
DTC: P2628	**-O2 SENSOR 1/1 PUMP CELL CURRENT TRIM CIRCUIT HIGH:** With the ignition on. The ECM detects a short to voltage on the (K902) O2 1/1 Pump Cell Current Trim circuit for 2. 0 seconds.
DTC: P2638	**TORQUE MANAGEMENT FEEDBACK SIGNAL PERFORMANCE:** Engine intervention active for at least 20 ms, no engine torque errors, engine torque demand is greater than 0. Torque Reduction acknowledge bit - not set, no shift aborts, the error flag Torque Reduction Acknowledge is not set, Powertrain controller not supporting torque requests.
DTC: P2700	**-INADEQUATE ELEMENT VOLUME LR:** Whenever the engine is running. The L/R clutch volume index (CVI) is updated during a 3-1 or 2-1 manual downshift with throttle angle below 5 degrees. Transmission temperature must be at least 43° C (110° F). When the L/R clutch volume index (CVI) falls below 16.
DTC: P2701	**-INADEQUATE ELEMENT VOLUME 2C:** Whenever the engine is running. The 2C clutch volume index (CVI) is updated during a 3-2 kickdown with throttle angle between 10 and 54 degrees. Transmission temperature must be at least 43° C (110° F). When the 2C CVI falls below 5.
DTC: P2702	**-INADEQUATE ELEMENT VOLUME OD:** Whenever the engine is running. The OD clutch volume index (CVI) is updated during a 2-3 upshift with throttle angle between 10 and 54 degrees. Transmission temperature must be at least 43° C (110° F). When the OD CVI falls below 5.
DTC: P2703	**-INADEQUATE ELEMENT VOLUME UD:** Whenever the engine is running. The UD clutch volume index (CVI) is updated during a 4-3 kickdown with throttle angle between 10 and 54 degrees. Transmission temperature must be at least 43° C (110° F). When the UD CVI falls below 11.
DTC: P2704	**-INADEQUATE ELEMENT VOLUME 4C:** Whenever the engine is running. The 4C clutch volume index (CVI) is updated during a 3-4 upshift with throttle angle between 10 and 54 degrees. Transmission temperature must be at least 43° C (110° F). When the 4C CVI falls below 5.

DTC	Trouble Code Title, Conditions, Possible Causes
DTC: P2706	**-MS SOLENOID CIRCUIT:** Initially at power-up, then every 10 seconds thereafter. The solenoid circuits will also be tested immediately after a gear ratio or pressure switch error is detected. After three consecutive solenoid continuity test failures, or one failure if test is run in response to a gear ratio or pressure switch error. **NOTE: This DTC is strictly an electrical fault and does not apply to any internal transmission failures.**
DTC: P2706	**-MS SOLENOID CIRCUIT:** Initially at power-up, then every 10 seconds thereafter. The solenoid circuits will also be tested immediately after a gear ratio or pressure switch error is detected. After three consecutive solenoid continuity test failures, or one failure if test is run in response to a gear ratio or pressure switch error. This DTC is strictly an electrical fault and cannot be caused by any internal transmission failure other than an open in the Transmission Solenoid/TRS Assembly. If the Transmission Solenoid/TRS Assembly is in need of replacement — do not replace the Valve Body.
DTC: P273A	**-INADEQUATE ELEMENT VOLUME LC:** Whenever the engine is running. The LC Clutch Volume Index (CVI) is updated during a 3-1 or 2-1 manual downshift with throttle angle below 5 degrees. Transmission temperature must be at least 43° C (110° F). When the LC CVI falls below a calibrated value.
DTC: P273B	**-INADEQUATE ELEMENT VOLUME DC:** Whenever the engine is running. The DC LC Clutch Volume Index (CVI) is updated during a 3-1 or 2-1 manual downshift with throttle angle below 5 degrees. Transmission temperature must be at least 43° C (110° F). When the DC CVI falls below a calibrated value.
DTC: P2748	**-INPUT SPEED SENSOR 1/2 CORRELATION:** With the ignition on. The ECM receives a CAN Bus message indicating the presence of a DTC in the TCM.
DTC: P2763	**TORQUE CONVERTER CLUTCH PRESSURE CONTROL CIRCUIT HIGH:** Battery voltage is greater than 7. 0 volts. TCC duty cycle is greater than 42%. Torque converter is in Lock Up or Partial Lock Up. The PCM detects the EMCC VFS voltage is above a calibrated threshold for 1. 785 seconds.
DTC: P2764	**TORQUE CONVERTER CLUTCH PRESSURE CONTROL CIRCUIT LOW:** TCC duty cycle is less than 8%. Torque converter is not in Lock Up or Partial Lock Up. The PCM detects the EMCC VFS voltage is below a calibrated threshold for 357 ms.
DTC: P2767	**-INPUT SPEED SENSOR 2 CIRCUIT NO SIGNAL:** Engine speed greater than 450 RPM with none of the following DTCs present: engine speed, TCM under voltage, output speed sensor, and/or rear wheel speed DTCs. Also required are all wheel speeds above 250 RPM and no wheel slip detected (signal from the ABS system). If the Input Speed Sensor 2 (N3) signal is equal to 0 RPM.
DTC: P2769	**TORQUE CONVERTER CLUTCH CIRCUIT LOW:** Ignition on, engine running with the transmission in a valid forward gear. Vehicle speed greater than 10 Km/h (6 mph). Accelerator Pedal Position (APP) greater than 12. 5%. Engine rpm greater than 450 rpm with TCC lock-up enabled. TCC Lock up command is ON (True). No DTCs active from the following: Step motor Line Pressure Solenoid, Secondary Solenoid Input and Output Speed Sensor Primary or Secondary Pressure Sensor CAN Bus If the actual voltage is 70% of the target voltage for the period of 1. 0 second. It takes two consecutive problem identification trips for the DTC to mature and illuminate the MIL.
DTC: P2770	**TORQUE CONVERTER CLUTCH CIRCUIT HIGH:** Ignition on, engine running with the transmission in a valid forward gear. Vehicle speed greater than 10 Km/h (6 mph). Accelerator Pedal Position (APP) greater than 12. 5%. Engine rpm greater than 450 rpm with TCC lock-up enabled. TCC Lock up command is ON (True). No active DTCs from the following: Torque Convertor Clutch Circuit Low, Step motor, Line Pressure Solenoid, Secondary Solenoid, Input and Output Speed Sensor, Primary or Secondary Pressure Sensor, or CAN BUS. If the target current is greater than 0. 75 amps and the monitored current is less than 0. 4 amps for the period of 5 seconds. It takes two consecutive problem identification trips for the DTC to mature and illuminate the MIL.
DTC: P2775	**-AUTOSTICK UPSHIFT SWITCH CIRCUIT PERFORMANCE (COLUMN SHIFT):** When in AutoStick®mode. When the expected AutoStick® switch state is not correctly sensed by the Electronic Shift Module (ESM). If the upshift switch signal is detected as active in a gear position other than drive or when both the upshift and downshift signals are active at the same time.
DTC: P2775	**-AUTOSTICK UPSHIFT SWITCH CIRCUIT PERFORMANCE:** Continuously with the ignition in the run position. When the expected switch state is not correctly sensed by the Shift Lever Assembly. If the upshift switch signal is detected as active in gear position other than drive.
DTC: P2779	**-AUTOSTICK DOWNSHIFT SWITCH CIRCUIT PERFORMANCE:** Continuously when the ignition is in the run position. When the expected switch state is not correctly sensed by the Shifter Lever Assembly (SLA) Electronic Shift Module (ESM). If the Downshift switch signal is detected as active in gear position other than drive.
DTC: P2779	**-AUTOSTICK DOWNSHIFT SWITCH CIRCUIT PERFORMANCE (COLUMN SHIFT):** When in AutoStick®mode. When the expected AutoStick® switch state is not correctly sensed by the Electronic Shift Module (ESM). If the upshift switch signal is detected as active in a gear position other than drive or when both the upshift and downshift signals are active at the same time.

DTC	Trouble Code Title, Conditions, Possible Causes
DTC: P2783	**TORQUE CONVERTER TEMPERATURE TOO HIGH:** When the solenoid supply voltage is active. With no reporting Input Speed Sensor 1 or 2 (N2 - N3), CAN Bus, PCM, CAN Engine, and/or CAN Engine Speed DTCs present. Torque Converter Clutch in slip mode. When the friction loss factor reaches threshold.
DTC: P2784	**-INPUT SPEED SENSOR 1/2 CORRELATION:** Engine speed greater than 450 RPM, no engine speed DTCs, no TCM under voltage system operation, no output speed sensor DTCs (CAN signal from the ABS system), all wheel speeds above 250 RPM (CAN signal from the ABS system), no rear wheel speed DTCs (signal from the ABS system), and no wheel slip detected (CAN signal from the ABS system), no shifting operation, Input Speed Sensor 2 (N3) greater than 800 RPM and Input Speed Sensor 1 (N2) greater than 0 RPM and the TCM not in reset. If the speed difference between the Input Speed Sensors 1 and 2 (N2 - N3) is greater than 150 RPM.
DTC: P2A00	**-O2 SENSOR 1/1 CIRCUIT PERFORMANCE:** With the ignition on. The ECM detects an open or implausible voltage on the (Z43) O2 1/1 Negative Current Control for 2. 0 seconds.

OBD II Trouble Code List (P3XXX Codes)

DTC	Trouble Code Title, Conditions, Possible Causes
DTC: P3400	**-MDS RATIONALITY BANK 1:** Transition from 4 to 8 cylinder mode. O2 sensor readings on Bank 1 side indicate a lean condition while in 4 cylinder mode.
DTC: P3400	**-MDS RATIONALITY BANK 1:** Transition from 8 to 4 cylinder mode. O2 sensor readings on Bank 1 side indicate a lean condition while in 4 cylinder mode. One trip fault.
DTC: P3401	**-MDS SOLENOID 1 CIRCUIT:** Transition from 8 to 4 cylinder mode. When the PCM recognizes a problem with the Solenoid Control circuit. One trip fault.
DTC: P3401	**-MDS SOLENOID 1 CIRCUIT:** Transition from 8 to 4 cylinder mode. When the Powertrain Control Module (PCM) recognizes an open or shorted condition with the Solenoid Control circuit.
DTC: P3402	**-CYLINDER 1 DEACTIVATION CONTROL PERFORMANCE:** Transition from 8 to 4 cylinder mode. The MDS fails to disengage for cylinder 1. One trip fault.
DTC: P3402	**-CYLINDER 1 DEACTIVATION CONTROL PERFORMANCE:** Transition from 8 to 4 cylinder mode. The MDS fails to engage for cylinder 1.
DTC: P3425	**-MDS SOLENOID 4 CIRCUIT:** Transition from 8 to 4 cylinder mode. When the Powertrain Control Module (PCM) recognizes a problem with the Solenoid Control circuit.
DTC: P3425	**-MDS SOLENOID 4 CIRCUIT:** Transition from 8 to 4 cylinder mode. When the PCM recognizes a problem with the Solenoid Control circuit. One trip fault.
DTC: P3426	**-CYLINDER 4 DEACTIVATION CONTROL PERFORMANCE:** Transition from 8 to 4 cylinder mode. The MDS fails to engage for cylinder 4.
DTC: P3426	**-CYLINDER 4 DEACTIVATION CONTROL PERFORMANCE:** Transition from 8 to 4 cylinder mode. The MDS fails to engage for cylinder 4. One trip fault.
DTC: P3426	**-CYLINDER 4 DEACTIVATION CONTROL PERFORMANCE:** Transition from 8 to 4 cylinder mode. The MDS fails to disengage for cylinder 4. One trip fault.
DTC: P3441	**-MDS SOLENOID 6 CIRCUIT:** Transition from 8 to 4 cylinder mode. When the PCM recognizes a problem with the Solenoid Control circuit. One trip fault.
DTC: P3442	**-CYLINDER 6 DEACTIVATION CONTROL PERFORMANCE:** Transition from 8 to 4 cylinder mode. The MDS fails to disengage for cylinder 6. One trip fault.
DTC: P3442	**-CYLINDER 6 DEACTIVATION CONTROL PERFORMANCE:** Transition from 8 to 4 cylinder mode. The MDS fails to engage for cylinder 6.
DTC: P3449	**-MDS SOLENOID 7 CIRCUIT:** Transition from 8 to 4 cylinder mode. When the Powertrain Control Module (PCM) recognizes a problem with the Solenoid Control circuit.
DTC: P3449	**-MDS SOLENOID 7 CIRCUIT:** Transition from 8 to 4 cylinder mode. When the PCM recognizes a problem with the Solenoid Control circuit. One trip fault.

DTC	Trouble Code Title, Conditions, Possible Causes
DTC: P3450	**-CYLINDER 7 DEACTIVATION CONTROL PERFORMANCE:** Transition from 8 to 4 cylinder mode. The MDS fails to disengage for cylinder 7. Two trip fault.
DTC: P3450	**-CYLINDER 7 DEACTIVATION CONTROL PERFORMANCE:** Transition from 8 to 4 cylinder mode. The MDS fails to engage for cylinder 7.
DTC: P3497	**-MDS RATIONALITY BANK 2:** Transition from 4 to 8 cylinder mode. O2 sensor readings on Bank 2 side indicate a lean condition while in 4 cylinder mode.
DTC: P3497	**-MDS RATIONALITY BANK 2:** Transition from 8 to 4 cylinder mode. O2 sensor readings on Bank 2 side indicate a lean condition while in 4 cylinder mode. One trip fault.

Commonly Used Abbreviations

2

2WD Two Wheel Drive

4

4WD Four Wheel Drive

A

A/C Air Conditioning
ABDC After Bottom Dead Center
ABS Anti-lock Brakes
AC Alternating Current
ACL Air cleaner
ACT Air Charge Temperature
AIR Secondary Air Injection
ALCL Assembly Line Communications Link
ALDL Assembly Line Diagnostic Link
AT Automatic Transaxle/Transmission
ATDC After Top Dead Center
ATF Automatic Transmission Fluid
ATS Air Temperature Sensor
AWD All Wheel Drive

B

BAP Barometric Absolute Pressure
BARO Barometric Pressure
BBDC Before Bottom Dead Center
BCM Body Control Module
BDC Bottom Dead Center
BPT Backpressure Transducer
BTDC Before Top Dead Center
BVSV Bimetallic Vacuum Switching Valve

C

CAC Charge Air Cooler
CARB California Air Resources Board
CAT Catalytic Converter
CCC Computer Command Control
CCCC Computer Controlled Catalytic Converter
CCCI Computer Controlled Coil Ignition
CCD Computer Controlled Dwell
CDI Capacitor Discharge Ignition
CEC Computerized Engine Control
CFI Continuous Fuel Injection
CIS Continuous Injection System
CIS-E Continuous Injection System - Electronic
CKP Crankshaft Position
CL Closed Loop
CMP Camshaft Position
CPP Clutch Pedal Position
CTOX Continuous Trap Oxidizer System
CTP Closed Throttle Position
CVC Constant Vacuum Control
CYL Cylinder

D

DBC Dual Bed Catalyst
DC Direct Current
DFI Direct Fuel Injection
DIS Distributorless Ignition System
DLC Data Link Connector
DMM Digital Multimeter
DOHC Double Overhead Camshaft
DRB Diagnostic Readout Box
DTC Diagnostic Trouble Code
DTM Diagnostic Test Mode
DVOM Digital Volt/Ohmmeter

E

EBCM Electronic Brake Control Module
ECM Engine Control Module
ECT Engine Coolant Temperature
ECU Engine Control Unit or Electronic Control Unit
EDIS Electronic Distributorless Ignition System
EEC Electronic Engine Control
EEPROM Electrically Erasable Programmable Read Only Memory
EFE Early Fuel Evaporation
EGR Exhaust Gas Recirculation
EGRT Exhaust Gas Recirculation Temperature
EGRVC EGR Valve Control
EPROM Erasable Programmable Read Only Memory
EVAP Evaporative Emissions
EVP EGR Valve Position

F

FBC Feedback Carburetor
FEEPROM Flash Electrically Erasable Programmable Read Only Memory
FF Flexible Fuel
FI Fuel Injection
FT Fuel Trim
FWD Front Wheel Drive

G

GND Ground

H

HAC High Altitude Compensation
HEGO Heated Exhaust Gas Oxygen sensor
HEI High Energy Ignition
HO2 Sensor Heated Oxygen Sensor

I

IAC Idle Air Control
IAT Intake Air Temperature
ICM Ignition Control Module
IFI Indirect Fuel Injection
IFS Inertia Fuel Shutoff
ISC Idle Speed Control
IVSV Idle Vacuum Switching Valve

Commonly Used Abbreviations

K

KOEO	Key On, Engine Off
KOER	Key ON, Engine Running
KS	Knock Sensor

M

MAF	Mass Air Flow
MAP	Manifold Absolute Pressure
MAT	Manifold Air Temperature
MC	Mixture Control
MDP	Manifold Differential Pressure
MFI	Multiport Fuel Injection
MIL	Malfunction Indicator Lamp or Maintenance
MST	Manifold Surface Temperature
MVZ	Manifold Vacuum Zone

N

NVRAM	Nonvolatile Random Access Memory

O

O2 Sensor	Oxygen Sensor
OBD	On-Board Diagnostic
OC	Oxidation Catalyst
OHC	Overhead Camshaft
OL	Open Loop

P

P/S	Power Steering
PAIR	Pulsed Secondary Air Injection
PCM	Powertrain Control Module
PCS	Purge Control Solenoid
PCV	Positive Crankcase Ventilation
PIP	Profile Ignition Pick-up
PNP	Park/Neutral Position
PROM	Programmable Read Only Memory
PSP	Power Steering Pressure
PTO	Power Take-Off
PTOX	Periodic Trap Oxidizer System

R

RABS	Rear Anti-lock Brake System
RAM	Random Access Memory
ROM	Read Only Memory
RPM	Revolutions Per Minute
RWAL	Rear Wheel Anti-lock Brakes
RWD	Rear Wheel Drive

S

SBC	Single Bed Converter
SBEC	Single Board Engine Controller
SC	Supercharger
SCB	Supercharger Bypass
SFI	Sequential Multiport Fuel Injection
SIR	Supplemental Inflatible Restraint
SOHC	Single Overhead Camshaft
SPL	Smoke Puff Limiter
SPOUT	Spark Output
SRI	Service Reminder Indicator
SRS	Supplemental Restraint System
SRT	System Readiness Test
SSI	Solid State Ignition
ST	Scan Tool
STO	Self-Test Output

T

TAC	Thermostatic Air Cleamer
TBI	Throttle Body Fuel Injection
TC	Turbocharger
TCC	Torque Converter Clutch
TCM	Transmission Control Module
TDC	Top Dead Center
TFI	Thick Film Ignition
TP	Throttle Position
TR Sensor	Transaxle/Transmission Range Sensor
TVV	Thermal Vacuum Valve
TWC	Three-way Catalytic Converter

V

VAF	Volume Air Flow, or Vane Air Flow
VAPS	Variable Assist Power Steering
VRV	Vacuum Regulator Valve
VSS	Vehicle Speed Sensor
VSV	Vacuum Switching Valve

W

WOT	Wide Open Throttle
WU-TWC	Warm Up Three-way Catalytic Converter

CHILTON® LABOR GUIDE

Chilton's labor times are so trusted, even a competing publisher uses them!

The *Chilton 2012 Labor Guide* features new models and new labor operations in order to stay current with new technologies. Labor times have also been refined for normal and severe maintenance schedules, if applicable. The 2012 edition provides repair times for 1981-current import and domestic vehicles. Chilton's editors consider warranty times, component locations, component type, the environment in which technicians work, the training they receive, and the tools they use when calculating a labor time. To allow for vehicle age, operating conditions, and type of service, the *Chilton 2012 Labor Guide* provides standard and severe service times, plus OEM warranty times. Vehicle makes and models conform to current Automotive Aftermarket Industry Association (AAIA) standards.

978-1-4354-6155-0 Chilton 2012 Labor Guide Manual Set (Domestic & Import)
978-1-4354-6154-3 Chilton 2012 Labor Guide CD-ROM (Domestic & Import)

CD-ROM FEATURES

- access labor times for 1981-current models import and domestic vehicle models
- save time with automatically calculated labor charges, taxes, & parts as total job is estimated
- create professional estimates for your customer and worksheets for your technicians, printing them whenever needed
- keep track of customers, prior estimates, and your own parts or package jobs with less paper
- choose part names for estimates from an industry standard database to reduce typing
- estimate and track your work status with improved forms
- communicate easily with customers using re-designed printouts which show all labor and parts in an easy-to-read format.
- simplify adding parts to your estimate or work order with a helpful parts list
- locate information quick with a keyword search engine
- quickly locate work requests by day, week and month using the calendar feature

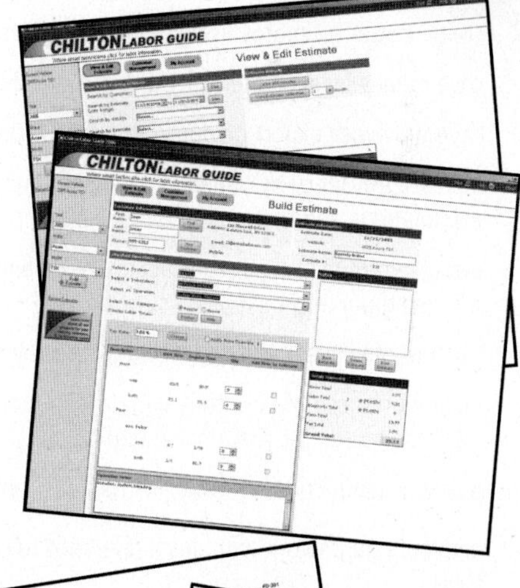

Manual FEATURES

- more than 2,500 pages of updated Chilton labor times split into two volumes includes vehicle information from 1981 to current models
- trusted by more service professionals than any other labor guide
- less flipping though pages with separate domestic and imported vehicle manuals and more specific vehicle groups
- convenient tabs display contents by manufacturer and model
- easy-to-find manufacturers are arranged alphabetically within each volume
- search using two-indexes - labor operations and systems - in each model group
- page numbers include manufacturer code so you know where you are in the book

CHILTONPRO.COM

ChiltonPRO is the alternative for professional technicians who want a cost-effective electronic automotive repair system. It combines Chilton's famous automotive repair information into one solution covering more than 60 years of domestic and imported vehicles. The information is delivered online and is updated regularly throughout the year.

Online Monthly Payment

ISBN: 978-14180-3002-5

Online Annual Payment

ISBN: 978-14180-2876-3

For a free demo visit ChiltonPRO.com

ChiltonPRO FEATURES

- make repairs even easier with videos & animations which explain system operations & contribute to technician knowledge
- create better estimates using labor times developed with real-world factors
- save money by accurately identifying and solving engine performance problems
- save time with expert guidance through OBDII diagnostics
- increase efficiency by understanding system operation through detailed explanations and theory
- increase profits using Technical Service Bulletins (TSBs) to ensure that work is not going unperformed
- execute effective repairs by viewing cutaway diagrams and actual photos
- make better use of your time with information that can be found quicker using AAIA standards for year, make, and model
- increase confidence levels by always being able to print what you need
- eliminate guesswork with quick reference to critical specifications in helpful tables

Coverage Includes:

- OEM recommended maintenance schedules, 1990–current
- trusted Chilton labor times, 1981–current
- step-by-step mechanical procedures, 1940s–current
- diagnostics designed by instructors, 1990–current
- More than 75,000 OEM Technical Service Bulletins issued during the past 20 years

System Requirements:
Web browser

- Internet Explorer 7.0 or above (recommended)
- Firefox 3.6 or 4 or Safari
- High-speed internet connection
- Adobe Flash Player
- Adobe Reader
- Windows XP or above

CHILTON® ESTIMATING

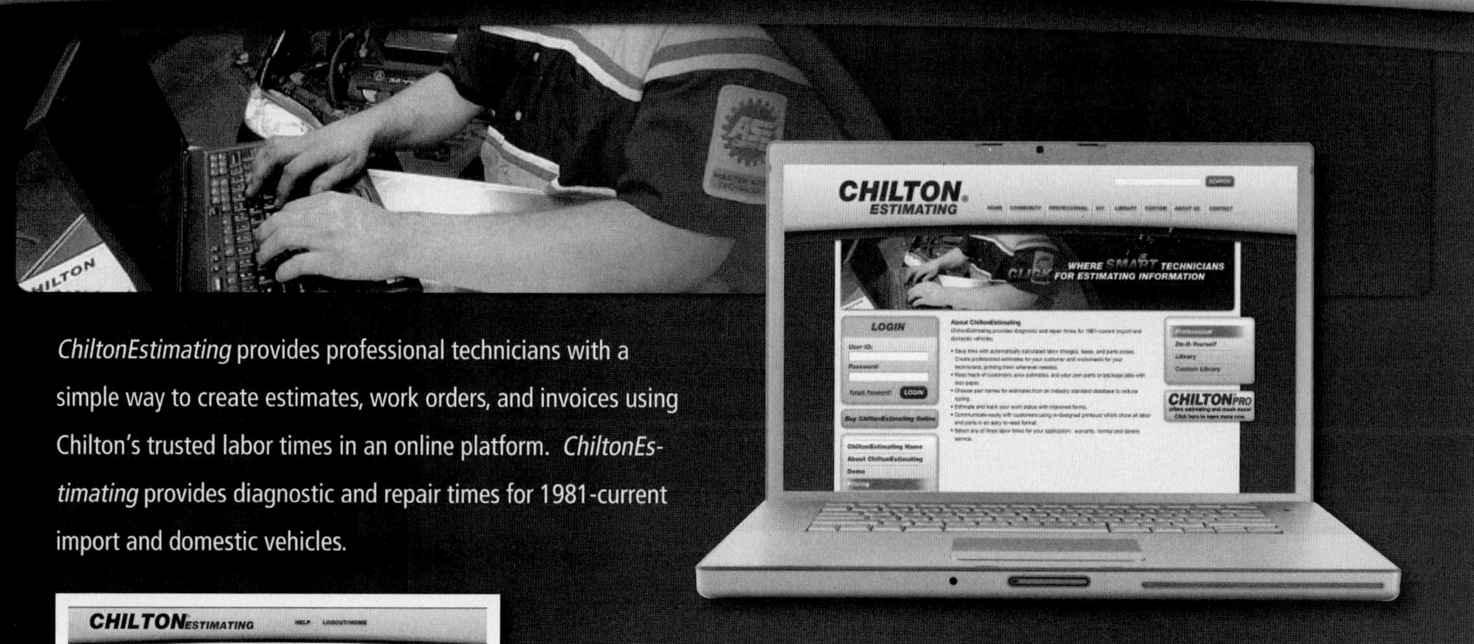

ChiltonEstimating provides professional technicians with a simple way to create estimates, work orders, and invoices using Chilton's trusted labor times in an online platform. *ChiltonEstimating* provides diagnostic and repair times for 1981-current import and domestic vehicles.

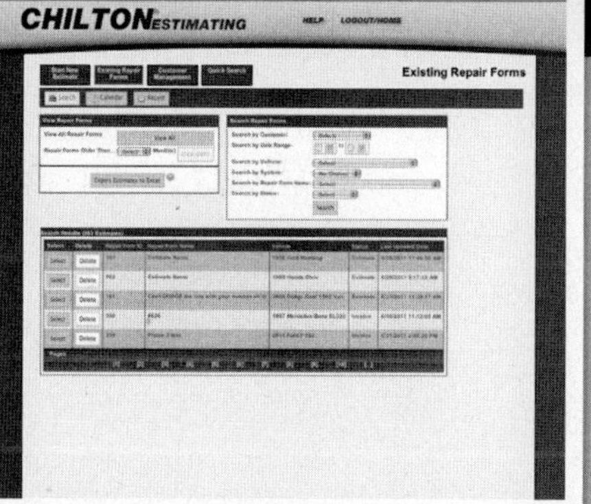

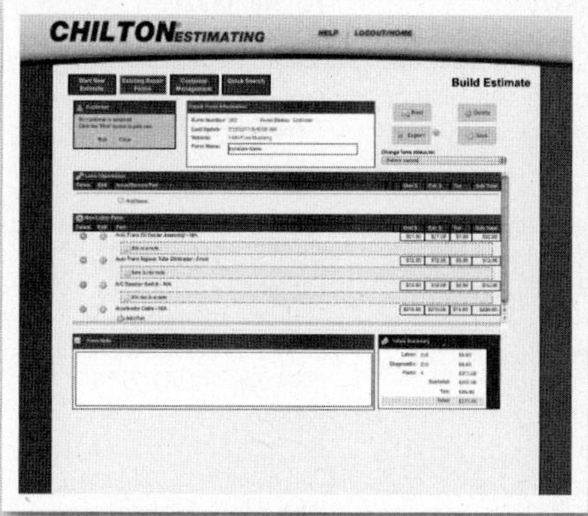

- Access up-to-date information immediately. *ChiltonEstimating* is continuously updated!
- Enjoy a hassle-free product with nothing to download and nothing to install.
- Never fret over lost or damaged software or books again.
- Secure your valuable customer data on our server, which won't be lost if your computer crashes.
- Easily access the program from any web-enabled computer.
- Work on more than one job at a time using *ChiltonEstimating's* two shop-user accounts.
- Download all customer contact information easily for marketing purposes.
- Cancel your subscription at any time by going to the "My Account" tab. No contract or obligation required. Customer data will be available to download for up to six months after a subscription has expired.
- Save time with automatically calculated labor charges, taxes, and parts prices. Create professional estimates for your customer and worksheets for your technicians, printing them whenever needed.
- Keep track of customers, prior estimates, and your own parts or package jobs with less paper.
- Choose part names for estimates from an industry standard database to reduce typing.
- Estimate and track your work status with improved forms.
- Communicate easily with customers using re-designed printouts which show all labor and parts in an easy-to-read format.
- Select any of three labor times for your application: warranty, normal and severe service.

System Requirements:
Web browser

- Internet Explorer 7.0 or above (recommended)
- Firefox 3.6 or 4 or Safari
- High-speed internet connection
- Adobe Flash Player
- Adobe Reader
- Windows XP or above

CHILTON® SERVICE MANUALS

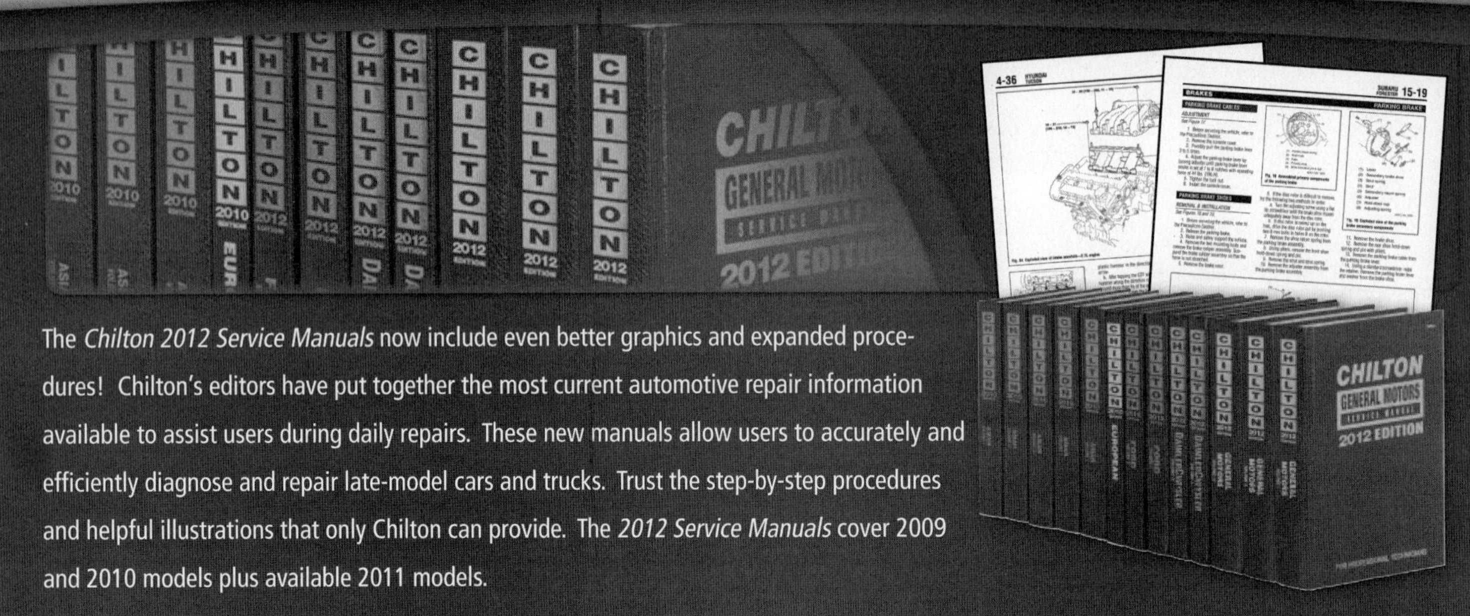

The *Chilton 2012 Service Manuals* now include even better graphics and expanded procedures! Chilton's editors have put together the most current automotive repair information available to assist users during daily repairs. These new manuals allow users to accurately and efficiently diagnose and repair late-model cars and trucks. Trust the step-by-step procedures and helpful illustrations that only Chilton can provide. The *2012 Service Manuals* cover 2009 and 2010 models plus available 2011 models.

KEY FEATURES

- organized by vehicle manufacturer
- provides thousands of pages of expertly written content
- access new year, make, and model information without repeating previous edition's content
- comprehensive, technically detailed content, including exploded view illustrations, diagnostics and specification charts, arranged alphabetically by model group for quick, easy

2012 EDITIONS

Chilton 2012 Chrysler Service Manuals
ISBN: 978-1-1336-2576-6
Part No. 222576

Chilton 2012 Ford Service Manuals
ISBN: 978-1-1336-2575-9
Part No. 222575

Chilton 2012 General Motor Service Manuals
ISBN: 978-1-1336-2574-2
Part No. 222574

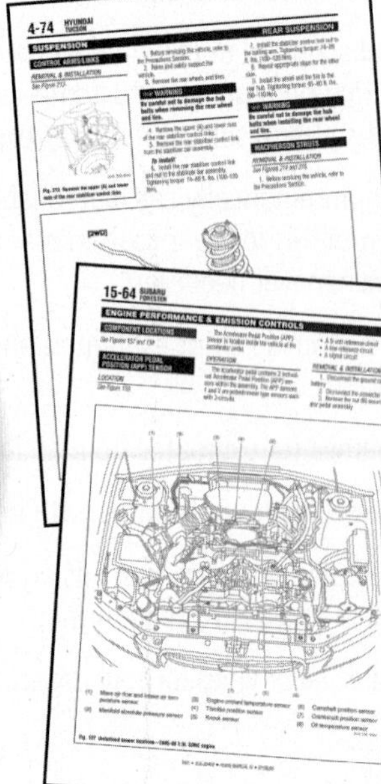

2010 EDITIONS

2010 Asian Service Manual Vol. 1
ISBN 978-1-1110-3764-2
Part No. 163764

2010 Asian Service Manual Vol. 2
ISBN 978-1-1110-3765-9
Part No. 163765

2010 Asian Service Manual Vol. 3
ISBN 978-1-1110-3766-6
Part No. 163766

2010 Asian Service Manual Vol. 4
ISBN 978-1-1110-3767-3
Part No. 163767

2010 Asian Service Manual Vol. 5
ISBN 978-1-1110-3768-0
Part No. 163768

2010 European Service Manual
ISBN 978-1-1110-3769-7
Part No. 163769

2010 Chrysler Service Manual, Volumes 1 & 2
ISBN 978-1-1110-3654-6
Part No. 163654

2010 Ford Service Manual, Vols. 1 & 2
ISBN 978-1-1110-3657-7
Part No. 163657

2010 General Motors Service Manuals, Vols. 1, 2, & 3
ISBN 978-1-111-03661-4
Part No. 163661

2008 EDITIONS

2008 Chrysler Service Manual, Vols. 1 & 2
ISBN 978-1-4283-2204-2
Part No. 142204

2008 Ford Service Manuals, Vols. 1 & 2
ISBN 978-1-4283-2208-0
Part No. 142208

2008 Edition General Motors Service Manuals, Vols. 1 & 2
ISBN 978-1-4283-2211-0
Part No. 142211

2008 Asian Service Manuals, Vols. 1-4
ISBN 978-1-4283-2214-1
Part No. 142214

2008 Asian Service Manual, Vol. 1
ISBN 978-1-4283-2215-8
Part No. 142215

2008 Asian Service Manual, Vol. 2
ISBN 978-1-4283-2216-5
Part No. 142216

2008 Asian Service Manual, Vol. 3
ISBN 978-1-4283-2217-2
Part No. 142217

2008 Asian Service Manual, Vol. 4
ISBN 978-1-4283-2218-9
Part No. 142218

2008 European Service Manual
ISBN 978-1-4283-2220-2
Part No. 142220

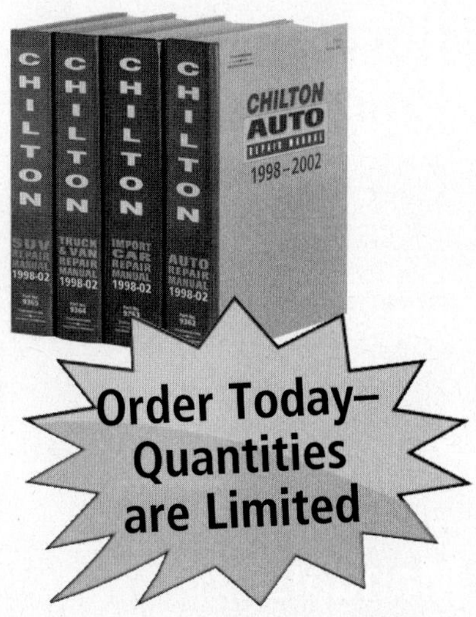

Chilton® Mechanical Service Manuals–Perennial Editions

These manuals contain repair and maintenance information for all major systems. Included are repair and overhaul procedures using thousands of illustrations.

CHILTON AUTO REPAIR MANUALS

1998-2002
ISBN 978-0-8019-9362-6/Part No. 9362
Covers all popular American and Canadian cars. An added feature includes scheduled maintenance interval charts.

1993-97
ISBN 978-0-8019-7919-4/Part No. 7919
Covers all popular American and Canadian cars.

1980-87
ISBN 978-0-8019-7670-4/Part No. 7670
Covers all popular American and Canadian cars.

CHILTON IMPORT AUTO REPAIR MANUALS

1998-2002
ISBN 978-0-8019-9363-3/Part No. 9363
Covers all popular Import cars. An added feature includes scheduled maintenance intervals charts.

1993-97
ISBN 978-0-8019-7920-0/Part No. 7920
Covers all popular Import cars.

1988-92
ISBN 978-0-8019-7907-1/Part No. 7907
Covers all popular Import cars.

1980-87
ISBN 978-0-8019-7672-8/Part No. 7672
Covers all popular Import cars.

CHILTON TRUCK AND VAN REPAIR MANUALS

1998-2002
ISBN 978-0-8019-9364-0/Part No. 9364
Covers popular U.S., Canadian, and Import Pick-Ups, Vans, and 4WDs. An added feature includes scheduled maintenance interval charts.

1993-97
ISBN 978-0-8019-7921-7/Part No. 7921
Covers popular U.S., Canadian, and Import Pick-Ups, Sport-Utilities, Vans, RVs and 4 wheel drives.

1991-95
ISBN 978-0-8019-7911-8/Part No. 7911
Covers popular U.S., Canadian, and Import Pick-Ups, Vans, RVs and 4 wheel drives.

1986-90
ISBN 978-08019-7902-6/Part No. 7902
Covers popular U.S., Canadian, and Import Pick-Us, Vans, RVs and 4 wheel drives.

1979-86
ISBN 978-08019-7655-1/Part No. 7655
Covers popular U.S., Canadian, and Import Pick-Ups, Vans, RVs and 4 wheel drives.

CHILTON SUV REPAIR MANUAL

1998-2002
ISBN 978-08019-9365-7/Part No. 9365
Covers popular U.S., Canadian, and import SUVs. An added feature includes scheduled maintenance intervals charts.

COLLECTOR'S SERIES

CHILTON AUTO REPAIR MANUAL 1964-1971
ISBN 978-08019-5974-5/Part No. 5974

1971-1978
ISBN 978-08019-7012-2/Part No. 7012

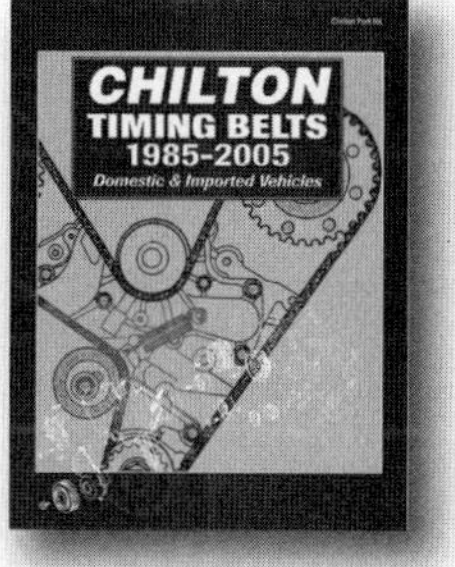

ISBN 978-1-4018-9880-9
Part No. 129880
544 pp, 8" x 11", SC, ©2006

Chilton Timing Belts, 1985-2005

Timing belt procedures can represent increased profits for automotive repair shops and service stations, and this manual contains all the information automotive technicians need to properly service timing belts on domestic and imported cars, vans, and light trucks through 2005 models. Clear, straightforward procedures, illustrations, and specifications help to communicate 20 years of vehicle applications for fast, accurate inspection, replacement, and tensioning of timing belts. Users will learn how to perform key procedures quickly and safely, while learning the correct labor time to charge for the service.

ALSO AVAILABLE:

Quick-Reference Manuals

The Chilton Professional Series offers *Quick-Reference Manuals* for the automotive professional, providing complete coverage on repair and maintenance, adjustments, and diagnostic procedures for specific systems and components.

KEY FEATURES

- step-by-step procedures
- detailed illustrations and exploded views
- easy-to-use manufacturer and model indexing
- handy specifications or data charts

Heater Core Service 1990-2000,
ISBN 978-0-8019-9311-4
Part No. 9311

Brake Specifications and Service 1990-2000
ISBN 978-0-8019-9312-1
Part No. 9312

Electric Cooling Fans, Accessory Drive Belts & Water Pumps, 1995-1999,
ISBN 978-0-8019-9126-4
Part No. 9126

Powertrain Codes & Oxygen Sensors, 1990-1999,
ISBN 978-0-8019-9127-1
Part No. 9127